1

‖‖ ‖ ‖‖‖‖‖‖ ‖‖ ‖‖ ‖‖‖‖‖‖‖‖‖‖‖ ‖ ‖‖
W9-BXX-098

CONTENTS

THE REGIONS

INDEXES

ITALIAN WINES 2010
GAMBERO ROSSO®

EDITOR-IN-CHIEF
DANIELE CERNILLI

SENIOR EDITORS
GIANNI FABRIZIO, ELEONORA GUERINI, MARCO SABELLICO

SPECIAL CONTRIBUTORS
ANTONIO BOCO, DARIO CAPPELLONI, GIUSEPPE CARRUS, PAOLO DE CRISTOFARO,
NICOLA FRASSON, GIORGIO MELANDRI, GIANNI OTTOGALLI,
PIERPAOLO RASTELLI, RICCARDO VISCARDI, PAOLO ZACCARIA.

MAIN CONTRIBUTORS
NINO AJELLO, GILBERTO ARRU, FRANCESCO BEGHI, ALESSANDRO BOCCHETTI,
GOFFREDO D'ANDREA, MASSIMO LANZA, FRANCO PALLINI, NEREO PEDERZOLLI, FABIO PRACCHIA,
CARLO RAVANELLO, LEONARDO ROMANELLI, MORENO ROSSIN, HERBERT TASCHLER.

OTHER CONTRIBUTORS
ENRICO BATTISTELLA, MAURA BERTORELLO, SERGIO BONANNO, MICHELE BRESSAN,
PASQUALE BUFFA, TEODOSIO BUONGIORNO, SERGIO CECCARELLI, GIOVANNI DE VECCHIS,
MARIO DEMATTÈ, ANTONELLO EDONISTA, GIANFRANCO FASSINA, MAURIZIO FAVA, GIOVANNA LAMOLINARA,
CRISTIANA LAURO, LEONARDO MANGANELLI, MARCO MANZOLI, LEONARDO MARCO, NICOLA MASSA,
ENZO MERZ, DANIELE MONTANO, GIACOMO MOJOLI, VANNI MURARO, RENATO ORLANDO, DAVIDE PANZIERI, CIN-
ZIA PESCI, SILVANO PROMPICAI, HELMUT RIEBSCHLÄGER, MAURIZIO ROSSI, ANGELO SARICA, CINZIA TOSETTI,
PAOLO TRIMANI, PAOLO VALDASTRI, VINCENZO VERRASTRO, SIMONE ZOLI, RENZO ZORZI.

EDITORIAL COORDINATOR
GIUSEPPE CARRUS

LAYOUT
GIANNA PETRUCCI

TRANSLATIONS COORDINATED AND EDITED BY
GILES WATSON

TRANSLATORS
ANGELA ARNONE, HELEN DONALD, RACHEL FELL, DAVE HENDERSON, STEPHEN JACKSON,
SARAH PONTING, SIMON TANNER, GILES WATSON, AILSA WOOD

PUBLISHER
GAMBERO ROSSO, INC.
PRESIDENT SERGIO CELLINI
636 BROADWAY – SUITE 111 – NEW YORK, NY 10012
TEL. +1-212-253-5653 FAX +1-212-253-8349 – E-MAIL: GAMBEROUSA@AOL.COM

DISTRIBUTION
USA AND CANADA BY ANTIQUE COLLECTORS' CLUB, EASTWORKS, 116
PLEASANT ST # 18, EASTHAMPTON, MA 010207, USA;
UK AND AUSTRALIA BY ANTIQUE COLLECTORS' CLUB LTD – SANDY LANE, OLD MARTLESHAM, WOODBRIDGE,
SUFFOLK IP12 4SD – UNITED KINGDOM
TEL. +44-1394-389950 – FAX +44-1394-389999

ITALIAN WINES 2010 WAS CLOSED ON 14 SEPTEMBER 2009

ISBN 978-1-890142-15-5

PRINTED IN ITALY FOR G. R. H. SPA IN JANUARY 2010
BY PUNTOWEB SRL – 00040 ARICCIA – ROME

THE GUIDE

Almost 400 Three Glass-winning wines could seem quite a lot of awards. If
you look at it from that angle, it's hard to find a reply but there are other factors
to take into account. To begin with, we received more than 25,000 samples
this year, more than ever before. Not all of them were rated and included in
the Guide – there's only so much space – but all were tasted by our panels.
Obviously, it's the same story with the number of wineries. In several regions,
we also witnessed a sharp rise in the number of cellars sending us good, and in
some cases excellent, wines, which suggests that Italy's producers are reacting
to the impact of the international crisis on the wine sector. Emilia Romagna,
Puglia, Piedmont, Campania and little Liguria all put on performances that were
better than we expected. The final consideration we would like to make regards
a story that involved us directly. The 2010 Guide is the 23rd in the series. The
first was the 1988 edition, which was published at the end of 1987. The 2010
Guide is also the first published by Gambero Rosso alone. Our long-standing
collaboration with Slow Food has come to an end and here we would like to
thank Slow Food for its enormous, invaluable contribution over many years.
It meant we had to reorganize the Guide team and many of the panels in the
regions for which Slow Food had hitherto been responsible. Some of our longest-
serving contributors stayed with us; others are new. Yet almost magically, work
went ahead in an atmosphere of enthusiasm reminiscent of the pioneering spirit
of the early years. The final results and all the assessments were collective as
never before and we all feel we are represented by a job done with consistency
and intellectual honesty. If we have given so many awards, it is because we
believe in them and agreed on the quality of the wines, quite apart from any other
considerations. Once again, we would like to describe how we went about this
vast sensory exploration of Italian wine. This time, we started early. Our panels
were already at work in the regions in early May. In each region, sometimes
in individual provinces, and almost always at official institutions, we began to
taste the wines collected by the consortiums, chambers of commerce and
regional wine cellars that collaborated with us and monitored our operations.
All the bottles were masked and inspected at comparative tastings with others
of the same type and vintage. Panels were formed by at least three tasters.
The venues where we worked, which we thank most sincerely and we hope
without omission, are the consortiums of Chianti Classico, Brunello Rosso di
Montalcino, Vino Nobile di Montepulciano, Vernaccia di San Gimignano, Chianti
Rufina, Morellino di Scansano, Montecucco, Vini di Romagna, Colli Piacentini,
Franciacorta, Oltrepò Pavese, Valtellina, Soave, Valpolicella, Barolo, Barbaresco,
Alba, Langhe e Roero, Gavi and Asti, the Enoteca Regionale del Roero, the
Enoteca Regionale del Monferrato, the Enoteca Regionale di Gattinara e delle
Terre del Nebbiolo del Nord Piemonte, the Enoteca Regionale di Nizza, the
Enoteca Regionale La Serenissima di Gradisca d'Isonzo, the Istituto Agronomico
Mediterraneo di Valenzano, the Bolzano Chamber of Commerce, the Avellino
Chamber of Commerce, the Trento Chamber of Commerce, the Arezzo Chamber
of Commerce, the Genoa Chamber of Commerce, the Perugia Chamber of
Commerce and the Umbrian regional coordination of Wine and Oil Trails, Assivip
at Majolati Spontini, Vinea at Offida and Faenza Fiere. Then there are the Wine

Trails of Carmignano and Costa degli Etruschi, Unioncamere at Matera, the Museo del Vino at Planargia di Magomadas and various privately owned facilities, Réserve at Caramanico in Abruzzo, the Le Due Sorelle restaurant in Moggina and the Cala de' Medici marina at Rosignano. In the first stage of tasting, we used marks out of 100 and selected about 1,500 wines which went through to the Three Glass finals. These wines obtained a score of at least Two Red Glasses. It was a massive effort, followed by meetings of the Three Glass panel made up of leading regional panellists, which evaluated the wines in the final. Again, tasting was blind. This time the verdict was more drastic: yes or no. Each verdict was carefully reasoned because every wine was discussed and analysed by all the panellists before the verdict. For this Guide, panellists at the final tastings, all held at Città del Gusto, Gambero Rosso's headquarters in Rome, were the three senior editors, Marco Sabellico, Eleonora Guerini and Gianni Fabrizio, editor-in-chief Daniele Cernilli, with according to their assigned areas of competence, Nino Aiello, Alessandro Bocchetti, Antonio Boco, Dario Cappelloni, Paolo De Cristofaro, Giuseppe Carrus, Goffredo D'Andrea, Nicola Frasson, Massimo Lanza, Giorgio Melandri, Gianni Ottogalli, Nereo Pederzolli, Pierpaolo Rastelli, Carlo Ravanello, Leonardo Romanelli, Moreno Rossin, Riccardo Viscardi and Paolo Zaccaria. It's an awesome team of tasters, the superstars of the sensory analysis of Italian wine. But what are the criteria for evaluation and assessment? Above all, they are more humanistic, cultural and hedonistic than scientific. This is why we prefer to use a classification by bands instead of by marks out of 100, which may look more precise but are less easy to justify. While it is fairly unlikely that a wine will move from one band to another at different tastings, it is highly probable that its mark out of 100 will change, albeit only slightly. There are also factors that cannot be evaluated in merely sensory terms. Concepts like a wine's conformity with, or representativeness of, its type, or with concepts of oenological correctness, are quite hard to codify. There are wines that appeal to the emotions, rising above any minor oenological defects. Of course, wine should be good but it should also be representative and environmentally friendly. Nor should it bend the knee to fashions in taste or the international market. And it was for this last reason that, alongside our usual Special Awards for the year's best wines, we have included a list of the Three Glass winners that are particularly praiseworthy in terms of eco-sustainability. We have awarded them Three Green Glasses. Finally, editor-in-chief Daniele Cernilli, although no longer contributing profiles, has created his own personal space by adding a "+" next to the Three Glass wines that he particularly enjoyed. These are the Three Glasses Plus. Well, that about wraps it up. Enjoy Italian Wines 2010.

Daniele Cernilli, Gianni Fabrizio, Eleonora Guerini e Marco Sabellico.

THREE GLASSES 2010

VALLE D'AOSTA

Valle d'Aosta Chambave Muscat Flétri Passito '07	La Vrille	22
Valle d'Aosta Chardonnay Cuvée Bois '07	Les Crêtes	21
Valle d'Aosta Chardonnay Élevé en Fût de Chêne '08	Anselmet	18
Valle d'Aosta Fumin Esprit Follet '07	La Crotta di Vegneron	19
Valle d'Aosta Fumin V. Rovettaz '07	F.lli Grosjean	20
Valle d'Aosta Pinot Gris '08	Lo Triolet	21

PIEDMONT

Barbaresco Albesani '05	Cantina del Pino	59
Barbaresco Asili '06	Ca' del Baio	56
Barbaresco Asili '05	Bruno Giacosa	95
Barbaresco Bric Mentina '06	La Ca' Növa	56
Barbaresco Camp Gros '05	Tenute Cisa Asinari dei Marchesi di Grésy	74
Barbaresco Canova '06	Ressia	138
Barbaresco Gallina '05	Piero Busso	54
Barbaresco Rabajà '04	Castello di Verduno	70
Barbaresco Ris. '04	Sottimano	155
Barbaresco Rombone '06	Fiorenzo Nada	123
Barbaresco Serraboella '06	Fontanabianca	90
Barbaresco Vanotu '06	Pelissero	130
Barbaresco Vign. Brich Ronchi Ris. '04	Albino Rocca	141
Barbaresco Vign. in Montestefano Ris. '04	Produttori del Barbaresco	37
Barbera d'Alba Bric du Luv '07	Ca' Viola	58
Barbera d'Asti Bricco della Bigotta '07	Braida	49
Barbera d'Asti Sup. Bionzo '07	La Spinetta	156
Barbera d'Asti Sup. La Mandorla '07	Luigi Spertino	156
Barbera d'Asti Sup. Nizza '06	Tenuta Olim Bauda	126
Barbera d'Asti Sup. Nizza La Court '06	Michele Chiarlo	72
Barbera del M.to Sup. Le Cave '07	Castello di Uviglie	161
Barolo '05	Bartolo Mascarello	115
Barolo Arione '05	Enzo Boglietti	45
Barolo Boscareto '05	Batasiolo	38
Barolo Bricat '05	Giovanni Manzone	110
Barolo Bricco Boschis '05	F.lli Cavallotto – Tenuta Bricco Boschis	71
Barolo Bricco delle Viole '05	G. D. Vajra	162
Barolo Bricco Visette '05	Attilio Ghisolfi	95
Barolo Broglio '05	Schiavenza	151
Barolo Brunate '05	Poderi Marcarini	111
Barolo Brunate '05	Mario Marengo	113
Barolo Cannubi '05	E. Pira & Figli	133
Barolo Cannubi Boschis '05	Luciano Sandrone	148
Barolo Cascina Francia '05	Giacomo Conterno	78
Barolo Cerretta '05	Ettore Germano	94
Barolo Ciabot Mentin Ginestra '05	Domenico Clerico	75
Barolo Costa Grimaldi '05	Einaudi	87
Barolo Ginestra '05	Paolo Conterno	79
Barolo Ginestra V. Casa Maté '05	Elio Grasso	100
Barolo Gramolere '05	F.lli Alessandria	29
Barolo Lazzarito '05	Vietti	164
Barolo Lazzarito V. La Delizia '04	Fontanafredda	91
Barolo Le Coste '05	Pecchenino	129
Barolo Le Rocche del Falletto '05	Bruno Giacosa	95
Barolo Margheria '05	Gabutti - Franco Boasso	92
Barolo Margheria '05	Vigna Rionda - Massolino	165
Barolo Mondoca di Bussia Soprana '04	Oddero	125
Barolo Ornato '05	Pio Cesare	132
Barolo Prapò '05	Bricco Rocche - Bricco Asili	52
Barolo Ravera '04	Flavio Roddolo	143
Barolo Sarmassa '05	Giacomo Brezza & Figli	50
Barolo Sarmassa '05	Marchesi di Barolo	111
Barolo Sorano '05	Claudio Alario	29
Barolo Sotto Castello di Novello '05	Giacomo Grimaldi	102
Barolo V. Elena '04	Elvio Cogno	75
Barolo Vign. Brunate '05	Andrea Oberto	125
Barolo Vign. Gattera '05	Mauro Veglio	163
Boca '05	Le Piane	131
Bramaterra I Porfidi '05	Sella	153
Caluso Passito Sulé '04	Orsolani	126
Colli Tortonesi Timorasso Derthona Grue'07	Pomodolce	135
Colli Tortonesi Timorasso Sterpi'07	Vigneti Massa	166
Diano d'Alba Sup. Sörì Bricco Maiolica'07	Bricco Maiolica	51

THREE GLASSES 2010

Dogliani Papà Celso '07	Abbona	26
Gattinara '05	Torraccia del Piantavigna	160
Gattinara Ris. '04	Giancarlo Travaglini	161
Gattinara Vign. Osso S. Grato '05	Antoniolo	33
Gattinara Vign. S. Francesco '05	Antoniolo	33
Gavi del Comune di Gavi Bruno Broglia '08	Vitivinicola Broglia	53
Gavi del Comune di Gavi Il Nostro Gavi '07	La Giustiniana	99
Gavi del Comune di Gavi Monterotondo '07	Villa Sparina	168
Ghemme '05	Antichi Vigneti di Cantalupo	32
Giuseppe Galliano Brut Ris. '01	Borgo Maragliano	46
Langhe Lariqi '07	Elio Altare - Cascina Nuova	31
Langhe Nebbiolo Sorì S. Lorenzo '06	Gaja	92
Langhe Nebbiolo Sorì Tildin '06	Gaja	92
M.to Rosso Centenario '06	Giulio Accornero e Figli	28
M.to Rosso Sonvico '06	Cascina La Barbatella	37
Piemonte Chardonnay Monteriolo '06	Coppo	81
Roero Audinaggio '07	Cascina Ca' Rossa	57
Roero Bric Valdiana '07	Giovanni Almondo	31
Roero Printi Ris. '06	Monchiero Carbone	118
Roero Renesio Ris. '05	Malvirà	109
Roero Torretta '06	Marco Porello	135

LIGURIA

Colli di Luni Vermentino Lunae Etichetta Nera '08		
	Cantine Lunae Bosoni	187
Colli di Luni Vermentino Sarticola '08	Ottaviano Lambruschi	188
Riviera Ligure di Ponente Pigato Cycnus '08	Poggio dei Gorleri	192
Riviera Ligure di Ponente Pigato U Baccan '07	Bruna	185
Riviera Ligure di Ponente Vermentino Le Serre'07		
	Tommaso Lupi & C.	189
Rossese di Dolceacqua Sup. Vign. Luvaira '07	Maccario Dringenberg	189

LOMBARDY

Brut Rosé	Monsupello	221
Franciacorta Brut '04	Le Marchesine	220
Franciacorta Brut '05	La Montina	223
Franciacorta Brut Collezione Esclusiva Giovanni Cavalleri '01		
	Cavalleri	211
Franciacorta Brut Extrême Palazzo Lana '04	Guido Berlucchi & C.	203
Franciacorta Cuvée Annamaria Clementi '02	Ca' del Bosco	206
Franciacorta Extra Brut '02	Ferghettina	214
Franciacorta Extra Brut Vittorio Moretti '02	Bellavista	201
Franciacorta Satèn '05	Enrico Gatti	217
Franciacorta Satèn '05	Il Mosnel	224
Garda Cabernet Le Zalte '07	Cascina La Pertica	226
Lugana Brolettino '07	Ca' dei Frati	206
OP Barbera Castello di Cigognola '06	Castello di Cigognola	211
OP Pinot Nero Brut Cl. 1870 '05	F.lli Giorgi	217
OP Pinot Nero Noir '06	Tenuta Mazzolino	220
OP Pinot Nero Pernice '06	Conte Carlo Giorgi di Vistarino	218
Valtellina Sfursat 5 Stelle '06	Nino Negri	224
Valtellina Sfursat Fruttaio Ca' Rizzieri '06	Aldo Rainoldi	229

TRENTINO

Olivar '07	Cesconi	257
Ritratto Bianco'07	La Vis/Valle di Cembra	262
San Leonardo '05	Tenuta San Leonardo	267
Teroldego Rotaliano Clesurae '06	Cantina Rotaliana	267
Teroldego Rotaliano Nos Ris. '04	MezzaCorona	264
Trento Altemasi Graal Brut Ris. '02	Cavit	256
Trento Aquila Reale Ris. '02	Cesarini Sforza	256
Trento Brut Cuvée dell'Abate Ris. '04	Abate Nero	254
Trento Giulio Ferrari Riserva del Fondatore Brut '00		
	Ferrari	259
Trento Mach Riserva del Fondatore '04	Istituto Agrario Provinciale	
	San Michele all'Adige	268
Trento Methius Brut Ris. '03	F.lli Dorigati	258

ALTO ADIGE

A. A. Gewürztraminer Kastelaz '08	Elena Walch	281
A. A. Gewürztraminer Nussbaumer '08	Cantina Tramin	302
A. A. Gewürztraminer Terminum V. T. '07	Cantina Tramin	302
A. A. Lagrein Abtei Ris. '06	Cantina Convento Muri-Gries	294
A. A. Lagrein Scuro Mirell'07	Tenuta Waldgries - Christian Plattner	305
A. A. Lagrein Scuro Taber Ris. '07	Cantina Produttori Santa Maddalena/	
	Cantina di Bolzano	300
A. A. Moscato Giallo Passito Serenade '06	Cantina di Caldaro	278

THREE GLASSES 2010

A. A. Pinot Bianco Dellago '08	Cantina Produttori Santa Maddalena/	
	Cantina di Bolzano	300
A. A. Pinot Bianco Sirmian '08	Cantina Nals Margreid	294
A. A. Sauvignon Indra '08	Cantina Produttori Cornaiano	280
A. A. Sauvignon St. Valentin '08	Cantina Produttori San Michele Appiano	299
A. A. Terlano Pinot Bianco Vorberg Ris. '06	Cantina Terlano	301
A. A. Terlano Sauvignon '08	Manincor	292
A. A. Val Venosta Pinot Bianco Sonnenberg '08	Cantina Vini Merano	293
A. A. Valle Isarco Riesling Viel Anders '08	Röckhof - Konrad Augschöll	297
A. A. Valle Isarco Sylvaner '08	Hoandlhof - Manfred Nössing	287
A. A. Valle Isarco Sylvaner '08	Kuenhof - Peter Pliger	290
A. A. Valle Isarco Sylvaner Praepositus '08	Abbazia di Novacella	276
A. A. Valle Isarco Sylvaner R '08	Köfererhof - Günther Kershbaumer	289
A. A. Valle Isarco Veltliner '08	Garlider - Christian Kerchbaumer	283
A. A. Valle Venosta Riesling '08	Falkenstein - Franz Pratzner	283
A. A. Valle Venosta Riesling '08	Tenuta Unterortl - Castel Juval	304
Feldmarschall von Fenner zu Fennberg '08	Tiefenbrunner	303
Manna '07	Franz Haas	286

VENETO

Amarone della Valpolicella Campo dei Gigli '05	Tenuta Sant'Antonio	364
Amarone della Valpolicella Cl. '05	Allegrini	313
Amarone della Valpolicella Cl. '05	Brigaldara	321
Amarone della Valpolicella Cl. '00	Giuseppe Quintarelli	360
Amarone della Valpolicella Cl. '05	Villa Monteleone	376
Amarone della Valpolicella Cl. '05	Zenato	378
Amarone della Valpolicella Cl. Campolongo di Torbe '04		
	Masi	348
Amarone della Valpolicella Cl. Casa dei Bepi '04	Viviani	377
Amarone della Valpolicella Cl. Pergole Vece '05	Le Salette	363
Amarone della Valpolicella Cl. Vign. Monte Ca' Bianca '04		
	Lorenzo Begali	316
Bianco di Custoza Mael '08	Corte Gardoni	333
Breganze Cabernet Vign. Due Santi'07	Vigneto Due Santi	375
Cartizze Brut '08	Silvano Follador	339
Colli Euganei Fior d'Arancio Passito'07	Ca' Lustra	324
Custoza Sup. Amedeo '07	Cavalchina	330
Lugana Sup. Molceo '07	Ottella	358
Montello e Colli Asolani Il Rosso dell'Abazia '06	Serafini & Vidotto	367
Recioto della Valpolicella Cereolo '05	Trabucchi d'Illasi	371
Recioto della Valpolicella Cl. Monte Ca' Paletta 97		
	Giuseppe Quintarelli	360
Recioto della Valpolicella Cl. TB '04	Tommaso Bussola	323
Recioto di Soave La Perlara '07	Ca' Rugate	325
Relógio '07	Ca' Orologio	324
Soave Cl. Calvarino '07	Leonildo Pieropan	358
Soave Cl. Campo Vulcano '08	I Campi	326
Soave Cl. Contrada Salvarenza Vecchie Vigne '07		
	Gini	342
Soave Cl. Monte Carbonare '08	Suavia	368
Soave Cl. Monte Fiorentine '08	Ca' Rugate	325
Soave Cl. Monte Grande '08	Prà	360
Soave Cl. Sup. Monte di Fice '07	I Stefanini	368
Soave Sup. Il Casale '08	Agostino Vicentini	373
Valdobbiadene Grave di Stecca Brut '08	Nino Franco	357
Valpolicella Cl. Sup. Ripasso Poiega '07	Guerrieri Rizzardi	343
Valpolicella Cl. Sup. Vigneto Ognisanti '06	Cav. G. B. Bertani	317
Valpolicella Sup. '05	Marion	347

FRIULI VENEZIA GIULIA

Braide Alte '07	Livon	419
Carso Malvasia '06	Kante	416
COF Merlot V. Cinquant'Anni '06	Le Vigne di Zamò	451
COF Pinot Bianco Zuc di Volpe '08	Volpe Pasini	454
COF Rosazzo Bianco Terre Alte '07	Livio Felluga	411
COF Rosso Montsclapade '06	Girolamo Dorigo	409
COF Rosso Sacrisassi '07	Le Due Terre	410
COF Schioppettino '06	Moschioni	423
COF Schioppettino di Cialla '05	Ronchi di Cialla	434
COF Verduzzo Friulano Cràtis '06	Roberto Scubla	439
Collio Friulano Zegla '05	Renato Keber	417
Collio Bianco '08	Colle Duga	404
Collio Bianco '08	Edi Keber	417
Collio Bianco Broy '08	Eugenio Collavini	404
Collio Bianco Fosarin '08	Ronco dei Tassi	435

THREE GLASSES 2010

Collio Friulano '08	Franco Toros	445
Collio Friulano Fisc '07	Isidoro Polencic	429
Collio Friulano Vigna del Rolat '08	Dario Raccaro	431
Collio Malvasia '08	Doro Princic	430
Collio Pinot Bianco '08	Franco Toros	445
Collio Pinot Grigio '08	Branko	397
Collio Pinot Grigio '07	Matijaz Tercic	444
Collio Ribolla Gialla '05	Franco Terpin	444
Collio Sauvignon de La Tour '00	Villa Russiz	452
Collio Sauvignon Ronco delle Mele '08	Venica & Venica	448
Friuli Grave Merlot Vistorta'07	Conte Brandolini	406
Friuli Isonzo Friulano '07	Borgo San Daniele	395
Friuli Isonzo Malvasia '08	Mauro Drius	409
Friuli Isonzo Rive Alte Sauvignon Piere '07	Vie di Romans	449
Ribolla Anfora '05	Gravner	414
Vintage Tunina '07	Jermann	416

EMILIA ROMAGNA

C. P. Vin Santo Albarola Val di Nure '99	Conte Otto Barattieri di San Pietro	468
Colli di Rimini Cabernet Montepirolo '06	San Patrignano	488
Lambrusco di Sorbara Vecchia Modena Premium '08		
	Chiarli 1860	474
Macchiona '05	La Stoppa	490
Poggio Tura '05	Vigne dei Boschi	494
Reggiano Lambrusco Concerto '08	Ermete Medici & Figli	482
Sangiovese di Romagna Sup. Avi Ris. '06	San Patrignano	488
Sangiovese di Romagna Sup. Corallo Nero Ris. '06		
	Gallegati	479
Sangiovese di Romagna Sup. Il Nespoli Ris. '06	Poderi dal Nespoli	485
Sangiovese di Romagna Sup. Michelangiolo Ris. '06		
	Calonga	470
Sangiovese di Romagna Sup. Ombroso Ris. '06	Giovanna Madonia	481
Sangiovese di Romagna Sup. Petrignone Ris. '06		
	Tre Monti	492
Sangiovese di Romagna Sup. Pietramora Ris. '06		
	Fattoria Zerbina	496
Sangiovese di Romagna Sup. Pruno Ris. '06	Drei Donà Tenuta La Palazza	478

TUSCANY

Acciaiolo '06	Castello d' Albola	505
Baffo Nero'07	Rocca di Frassinello	602
Bolgheri Rosso Sup. Grattamacco '06	Podere Grattamacco	558
Bolgheri Sapaio Sup. '06	Podere Sapaio	612
Bolgheri Sassicaia '06	Tenuta San Guido	609
Bolgheri Sup. Argentiera '06	Argentiera	507
Bolgheri Superiore Arnione '06	Campo alla Sughera	525
Brancaia Il Blu '07	Brancaia	520
Brunello di Montalcino '04	Biondi Santi - Tenuta Il Greppo	516
Brunello di Montalcino '04	Canalicchio - Franco Pacenti	526
Brunello di Montalcino '04	Canalicchio di Sopra	527
Brunello di Montalcino '04	La Cerbaiola	538
Brunello di Montalcino '04	Cerbaiona	538
Brunello di Montalcino '04	Podere La Fortuna	554
Brunello di Montalcino '04	Tenuta La Fuga	556
Brunello di Montalcino '04	Greppone Mazzi - Tenimenti Ruffino	559
Brunello di Montalcino '04	Poggio di Sotto	592
Brunello di Montalcino '04	Talenti	619
Brunello di Montalcino Altero '04	Poggio Antico	590
Brunello di Montalcino Cerretalto '04	Casanova di Neri	533
Brunello di Montalcino Il mio Brunello '04	Il Poggiolo	593
Brunello di Montalcino Rennina '04	Pieve Santa Restituta	587
Brunello di Montalcino Tenuta Friggiali '04	Centolani	537
Brunello di Montalcino Ugolforte '04	San Giorgio	608
Camartina '06	Querciabella	598
Carmignano Sasso'07	Piaggia	586
Cepparello '06	Isole e Olena	562
Chianti Cl.'07	Il Palagio	582
Chianti Cl. Castello di Brolio '06	Barone Ricasoli	512
Chianti Cl. Il Puro Vign. Casanova Ris. '06	Castello di Volpaia	635
Chianti Cl. La Selvanella Ris. '06	Melini	573
Chianti Cl. Poggio ai Frati Ris. '06	Rocca di Castagnoli	601
Chianti Cl. Tenuta di Capraia Ris. '06	Rocca di Castagnoli	601
Coevo '06	Famiglia Cecchi	537
Colline Lucchesi Tenuta di Valgiano '06	Tenuta di Valgiano	629
Cortona Il Bosco '06	Tenimenti Luigi D'Alessandro	620

THREE GLASSES 2010

Do Ut Des '07	Fattoria Carpineta Fontalpino	530
Finisterre '07	Poggio Argentiera	591
Fontalloro '06	Fattoria di Felsina	551
Galatrona '07	Fattoria Petrolo	586
I Sodi di San Niccolò '05	Castellare di Castellina	535
Lupicaia '06	Castello del Terriccio	622
Masseto '06	Tenuta dell' Ornellaia	581
Messorio '06	Le Macchiole	567
Montecucco Sangiovese Lombrone Ris. '05	Colle Massari	544
Montecucco Santa Marta '06	Salustri	605
Nambrot '06	Tenuta di Ghizzano	557
Nobile di Montepulciano '06	Podere Le Berne	515
Nobile di Montepulciano Asinone '06	Poliziano	595
Nobile di Montepulciano Quercetonda '06	Fattoria Le Casalte	532
Orma '06	Podere Orma	580
Pugnitello '07	San Felice	607
Redigaffi '07	Tua Rita	627
Siepi '06	Castello di Fonterutoli	553
Solaia '06	Marchesi Antinori	507
Vernaccia di S. Gimignano Carato '05	Montenidoli	577
Vernaccia di S. Gimignano Isabella Ris. '04	San Quirico	611
Vernaccia di S. Gimignano Ris. '05	Giovanni Panizzi	584
Vignamaggio '06	Villa Vignamaggio	633
Vin Santo Occhio di Pernice '97	Avignonesi	508
MARCHE		
Conero Rossini '06	Piantate Lunghe	681
Kurni '07	Oasi degli Angeli	680
Offida Pecorino Ciprea '08	San Savino - Poderi Capecci	685
Pelago '06	Umani Ronchi	689
Regina del Bosco '06	Fattoria Dezi	670
Rosso Piceno Sup. Roggio del Filare '06	Velenosi	691
Valturio '07	Valturio	690
Verdicchio dei Castelli di Jesi Cl. Misco Ris. '06	Tenuta di Tavignano	688
Verdicchio dei Castelli di Jesi Cl. Plenio Ris. '06	Umani Ronchi	689
Verdicchio dei Castelli di Jesi Cl. Sup. Podium '07	Gioacchino Garofoli	673
Verdicchio dei Castelli di Jesi Cl. Utopia Ris. '07	Montecappone	679
Verdicchio dei Castelli di Jesi Cl. V. Novali Ris. '06	Terre Cortesi Moncaro	689
Verdicchio dei Castelli di Jesi Cl. Villa Bucci Ris.'07	Bucci	661
Verdicchio di Matelica Cambrugiano Ris. '06	Belisario	660
Verdicchio di Matelica Mirum Ris. '07	La Monacesca	678
UMBRIA		
Adarmando '07	Giampaolo Tabarrini	714
Cervaro della Sala '07	Castello della Sala	712
Montefalco Sagrantino '06	Perticaia	710
Montefalco Sagrantino 25 Anni '06	Arnaldo Caprai	700
Montefalco Sagrantino Arquata '05	Adanti	698
Montefalco Sagrantino Chiusa di Pannone '04	Antonelli - San Marco	698
Montefalco Sagrantino Colleallodole '06	Fattoria Colle Allodole	703
Montefalco Sagrantino Gold '05	Còlpetrone	704
Montiano '07	Falesco	726
Torgiano Rosso Vigna Monticchio Ris. '05	Lungarotti	706
LAZIO		
Cesanese del Piglio Romanico '07	Antonello Coletti Conti	724
Grechetto Poggio della Costa '08	Sergio Mottura	728
ABRUZZO		
Montepulciano d'Abruzzo '07	Torre dei Beati	750
Montepulciano d'Abruzzo Cerasuolo '08	Valentini	751
Montepulciano d'Abruzzo Colline Teramane Adrano '06	Villa Medoro	753
Montepulciano d'Abruzzo Colline Teramane Zanna Ris. '06	Dino Illuminati	743
Montepulciano d'Abruzzo Plateo '04	Agriverde	738
Montepulciano d'Abruzzo San Calisto '06	Valle Reale	752
Montepulciano d'Abruzzo Spelt '05	La Valentina	751
Montepulciano d'Abruzzo Tonì '06	Luigi Cataldi Madonna	740
Montepulciano d'Abruzzo Vignafranca '06	F.lli Barba	739
Montepulciano d'Abruzzo Villa Gemma '06	Masciarelli	745
Pecorino '07	Luigi Cataldi Madonna	740
Trebbiano d'Abruzzo '06	F.lli Barba	739
Trebbiano d'Abruzzo Castello di Semivicoli '07	Masciarelli	745

THREE GLASSES 2010

MOLISE

Molise Aglianico Contado Ris. '07	Di Majo Norante	758

CAMPANIA

Centomoggia '07	Terre del Principe	777
Costa d'Amalfi Fiorduva '08	Marisa Cuomo	765
Falerno del Massico Camarato '05	Villa Matilde	780
Fiano di Avellino '08	Colli di Lapio	701
Fiano di Avellino '08	Rocca del Principe	775
Gladius '07	Tenuta Adolfo Spada	776
Greco di Tufo '08	Pietracupa	773
Greco di Tufo Tornante '08	Vadiaperti	779
Montevetrano '07	Montevetrano	772
Pietraincatenata '07	Luigi Maffini	771
Taurasi '05	Di Prisco	766
Taurasi '05	Urciuolo	778
Taurasi Radici '05	Mastroberardino	771
Taurasi Vigna Cinque Querce '05	Salvatore Molettieri	772
Taurasi Vigna Cinque Querce Ris. '04	Salvatore Molettieri	772
Terra di Lavoro '07	Galardi	769

PUGLIA

Amativo'07	Cantele	803
Artas '07	Castello Monaci	810
Castel del Monte Rosso V. Pedale Ris. '06	Torrevento	816
Gioia del Colle Primitivo Ris. '06	Chiaromonte	804
Gioia del Colle Primitivo Ris. '06	Pietraventosa	811
Masseria Maime'07	Tormaresca	815
Nero '06	Conti Zecca	817
Primitivo di Manduria Es '07	Gianfranco Fino	806
Primitivo Old Vines '07	Morella	810
Rasciatano Nero di Troia'07	Rasciatano	813
Salice Salentino Rosso Donna Lisa Ris. '05	Leone de Castris	807
Salice Salentino Rosso Selvarossa Ris. '06	Cantine Due Palme	805

BASILICATA

Aglianico del Vulture Basilisco '06	Basilisco	792
Aglianico del Vulture Don Anselmo Ris. '05	Paternoster	796
Aglianico del Vulture Titolo '07	Elena Fucci	795

CALABRIA

Cirò Rosso Duca Sanfelice Ris.'07	Librandi	827
Moscato Passito '08	Luigi Viola	829

SICILY

Cabernet Sauvignon '07	Tasca d'Almerita	849
Cometa '08	Planeta	847
Contessa Entellina Milleunanotte '06	Donnafugata	839
Don Antonio '07	Morgante	844
Etna Rosso '06	Cottanera	838
Etna Rosso Archineri '07	Pietradolce	846
Etna Rosso Feudo '07	Girolamo Russo	848
Etna Rosso M.I. '07	Vini Biondi	836
Etna Rosso Musmeci '07	Tenuta di Fessina	840
Etna Rosso Prephilloxera La V. di Don Peppino '07		
	Tenuta delle Terre Nere	850
Etna Rosso Serra della Contessa '06	Benanti	835
Faro Palari '07	Palari	845
Harmonium '07	Firriato	842
Lolik '07	Guccione	843
Nero d'Avola Versace '07	Feudi del Pisciotto	841
Rosso del Soprano '07	Palari	845
Sàgana '07	Cusumano	838
Saia '07	Feudo Maccari	841

SARDINIA

Alghero Marchese di Villamarina '04	Tenute Sella & Mosca	873
Angialis '06	Argiolas	862
Cannonau di Sardegna Dule Ris. '06	Giuseppe Gabbas	867
Cannonau di Sardegna Vinìola Ris. '06	Cantina Sociale Dorgali	866
Carignano del Sulcis Is Arenas Ris. '06	Sardus Pater	872
Carignano del Sulcis Sup. Terre Brune '05	Cantina Sociale di Santadi	872
Gerione '06	Feudi della Medusa	866
Perda Pintà '07	Giuseppe Sedilesu	873
Turriga '05	Argiolas	862
Vermentino di Gallura Monteoro '08	Tenute Sella & Mosca	873
Vermentino di Gallura Sup. Genesi '08	Cantina Gallura	867

THE BEST

RED OF THE YEAR
GATTINARA OSSO SAN GRATO '05 - ANTONIOLO

WHITE OF THE YEAR
FIANO DI AVELLINO '08 - COLLI DI LAPIO

SPARKLER OF THE YEAR
TRENTO ALTEMASI GRAAL RIS. '02 - CAVIT

SWEET OF THE YEAR
COLLI PIACENTINI VIN SANTO ALBAROLA VAL DI NURE '99 - CONTE BARATTIERI

WINERY OF THE YEAR

BRUNO GIACOSA

BEST VALUE FOR MONEY

MOLISE AGLIANICO CONTADO RIS. '07 - DI MAJO NORANTE

OENOLOGIST OF THE YEAR

ROBERTO FERRARINI

GROWER OF THE YEAR

GIANFRANCO FINO

UP-AND-COMING WINERY

GALLEGATI

AWARD
FOR SUSTAINABLE VITICULTURE

ELENA PANTALEONI

The publishers wish to thank

RCR
CRISTALLERIA
ITALIANA

THE EDITOR'S "PLUS" WINES

For the past 22 editions, Italian Wines has awarded scores decided on the basis of collective assessment. The same is true in this edition. No Three Glass awards have been made without the agreement of the Guide's editors and regional contributors. This year, however, as the new editor-in-chief of the Guide, I have allowed myself the small privilege of placing a "+" sign next to the names of a few Three Glass winners. These are the wines that most impressed me during tastings, and in most cases my view is shared by the Guide's other editors. Nevertheless, it seemed right that I should take the responsibility personally to avoid creating a new category of superior wines. So here are my own Three Glass Plus selections, including all the wines that won Special Awards in their categories, of course, and one or two others. There are 31 in all, fewer than the number of Three Glass awards made in the Guide's first edition in 1988. I hope you like all of them.

Daniele Cernilli

A. A. Gewurztraminer Kastelaz '08	E. WALCH	ALTO ADIGE
A. A. Valle Isarco Sylvaner R '08	KOFERERHOF	ALTO ADIGE
Aglianico del Vulture Don Anselmo Ris. '05	PATERNOSTER	BASILICATA
Aglianico del Vulture Titolo '07	E. FUCCI	BASILICATA
Barbaresco Asili di Barbaresco '05	B. GIACOSA	PIEDMONT
Barolo Bricco Boschis '05	CAVALLOTTO	PIEDMONT
Barolo Cascina Francia '05	G. CONTERNO	PIEDMONT
Barolo Gramolere '05	FLLI ALESSANDRIA	PIEDMONT
Barolo Lazzarito '05	VIETTI	PIEDMONT
Bolgheri Sassicaia '06	TENUTA SAN GUIDO	TUSCANY
Brunello di Montalcino '04	CERBAIONA	TUSCANY
Brunello di Montalcino Cerretalto '04	CASANOVA DI NERI	TUSCANY
Brunello di Montalcino '04	POGGIO DI SOTTO	TUSCANY
Colli Piacentini Vin Santo Albarola Val di Nure '99	CONTE OTTO BARATTIERI	EMILIA ROMAGNA
Faro Palari '07	PALARI	SICILY
Fiano di Avellino '08	COLLI DI LAPIO	CAMPANIA
Franciacorta Extra Brut Vittorio Moretti '02	BELLAVISTA	LOMBARDY
Gattinara Osso San Grato '05	ANTONIOLO	PIEDMONT
Greco di Tufo '08	PIETRACUPA	CAMPANIA
I Sodi di San Niccolò '05	CASTELLARE	TUSCANY
Langhe Nebbiolo Sorì Tildin '06	GAJA	PIEDMONT
Montepulciano d'Abruzzo San Calisto '06	VALLE REALE	ABRUZZO
Montevetrano '07	MONTEVETRANO	CAMPANIA
Primitivo di Manduria Es '07	FINO	PUGLIA
Recioto della Valpolicella Cl. M. Ca' Paletta '97	QUINTARELLI	VENETO
Taurasi Vigna Cinque Querce '05	MOLETTIERI	CAMPANIA
Tenuta di Valgiano '06	TENUTA DI VALGIANO	TUSCANY
Trebbiano d'Abruzzo Castello di Semivicoli '07	MASCIARELLI	ABRUZZO
Trento Altemasi Graal Ris. '02	CAVIT	TRENTINO
Vin Santo di Montepulciano Occhio di Pernice '97	AVIGNONESI	TUSCANY
Vintage Tunina '07	JERMANN	FRIULI VENEZIA GIULIA

THREE GREEN GLASSES

This year, we are giving a special mention to various wines made using environment-friendly processes and traditional techniques in an eco-sustainable perspective. We are well aware that wine producers alone will never be able to solve the problems arising from pollution and the greenhouse effect but we did think we should let you know which wines are produced with special attention to these issues. The wines below are not the only ones we could have included. They are, however, the one we are sure about because we acquaintance with them is long-standing and first-hand. We have also drawn up a checklist which it is hoped will be a first draft of the criteria we will apply in future when awarding Green Glasses. Here are the ten points we see as fundamental.

1. Elimination of systemic and high chemical-impact products in the vineyard.
2. Only grapes sourced from estate-owned or leased vineyards should be processed; bought-in grapes should be excluded.
3. Guaranteed control of all stages of production by the winery owner.
4. Elimination of winemaking products to alter artificially the basic characteristics of the wines.
5. Respect for the working environment through complete or extensive elimination of invasive practices such as irrigation, the use of non or partially biodegradable materials, or the construction of territory-inappropriate cellars.
6. The use of traditional training systems and prevalently local varieties, vinified in full respect of their most typical characteristics.
7. Elimination of mechanized pruning and harvesting systems
8. Elimination of over-use of sulphur dioxide.
9. Partial or total use of renewable energy sources.
10. Partial or total organic control of vine parasites.

A. A. Lagrein Scuro Mirell '07	TENUTA WALDGRIES CHRISTIAN PLATTNER	ALTO ADIGE
A. A. Terlano Sauvignon '08	MANINCOR	ALTO ADIGE
A. A. Valle Isarco Sylvaner '08	KUENHOF - PETER PLIGER	ALTO ADIGE
A. A. Valle Isarco Veltliner '08	GARLIDER CHRISTIAN KERCHBAUMER	ALTO ADIGE
A. A. Valle Venosta Riesling '08	FALKENSTEIN - FRANZ PRATZNER	ALTO ADIGE
Aglianico del Vulture Don Anselmo Ris. '05	PATERNOSTER	BASILICATA
Aglianico del Vulture Titolo '07	ELENA FUCCI	BASILICATA
Barbaresco Serraboella '06	FONTANABIANCA	PIEMONTE
Barbera d'Asti Bricco della Bigotta '07	BRAIDA	PIEDMONT
Barbera d'Asti Sup. La Mandorla '07	LUIGI SPERTINO	PIEDMONT
Barolo Bricco Boschis '05	F.LLI CAVALLOTTO TENUTA BRICCO BOSCHIS	PIEDMONT
Barolo Bricco delle Viole '05	G. D. VAJRA	PIEDMONT
Barolo Cannubi '05	E. PIRA & FIGLI	PIEDMONT
Barolo Vign. Gattera '05	MAURO VEGLIO	PIEDMONT
Bolgheri Rosso Sup. Grattamacco '06	PODERE GRATTAMACCO	TUSCANY
Brunello di Montalcino '04	BIONDI SANTI - TENUTA IL GREPPO	TUSCANY
Brunello di Montalcino '04	POGGIO DI SOTTO	TUSCANY
Brunello di Montalcino Altero '04	POGGIO ANTICO	TUSCANY
Camartina '06	QUERCIABELLA	TUSCANY
Carso Malvasia '06	KANTE	FRIULI VENEZIA GIULIA
Cartizze Brut '08	SILVANO FOLLADOR	VENETO
Castel del Monte Rosso V. Pedale Ris. '06	TORREVENTO	PUGLIA
Chianti Cl. Il Puro Vign. Casanova Ris. '06	CASTELLO DI VOLPAIA	TUSCANY
COF Rosso Sacrisassi '07	LE DUE TERRE	FRIULI VENEZIA GIULIA
Colli Tortonesi Timorasso Derthona Grue '07	POMODOLCE	PIEDMONT

THREE GREEN GLASSES

Colli Tortonesi Timorasso Sterpi '07		
	VIGNETI MASSA	PIEDMONT
Colline Lucchesi Tenuta di Valgiano '06		
	TENUTA DI VALGIANO	TUSCANY
Collio Bianco '08	EDI KEBER	FRIULI VENEZIA GIULIA
Collio Bianco Broy '08	EUGENIO COLLAVINI	FRIULI VENEZIA GIULIA
Collio Ribolla Gialla '05	FRANCO TERPIN	FRIULI VENEZIA GIULIA
Costa d'Amalfi Fiorduva '08	MARISA CUOMO	CAMPANIA
Do Ut Des '07	FATTORIA CARPINETA FONTALPINO	TUSCANY
Etna Rosso Feudo '07	GIROLAMO RUSSO	SICILY
Etna Rosso M.I. '07	VINI BIONDI	SICILY
Etna Rosso Musmeci '07	TENUTA DI FESSINA	SICILY
Etna Rosso Prephilloxera La V. di Don Peppino '07		
	TENUTA DELLE TERRE NERE	SICILY
Friuli Grave Merlot Vistorta '07	CONTE BRANDOLINI	FRIULI VENEZIA GIULIA
Garda Cabernet Le Zalte '07	CASCINA LA PERTICA	LOMBARDY
Gioia del Colle Primitivo Ris. '06	CHIAROMONTE	PUGLIA
Gioia del Colle Primitivo Ris. '06	PIETRAVENTOSA	PUGLIA
Grechetto Poggio della Costa '08	SERGIO MOTTURA	LAZIO
Kurni '07	OASI DEGLI ANGELI	MARCHE
Langhe Larigi '07	ELIO ALTARE - CASCINA NUOVA	PIEDMONT
Lolik '07	GUCCIONE	SICILY
M.to Rosso Centenario '06	GIULIO ACCORNERO E FIGLI	PIEDMONT
Macchiona '05	LA STOPPA	EMILIA ROMAGNA
Masseria Maime '07	TORMARESCA	PUGLIA
Molise Aglianico Contado Ris. '07		
	DI MAJO NORANTE	MOLISE
Montecucco Sangiovese Lombrone Ris. '05		
	COLLE MASSARI	TUSCANY
Montecucco Santa Marta '06	SALUSTRI	TUSCANY
Montello e Colli Asolani Il Rosso dell'Abazia '06		
	SERAFINI & VIDOTTO	VENETO
Montepulciano d'Abruzzo '07	TORRE DEI BEATI	ABRUZZO
Montepulciano d'Abruzzo Cerasuolo '08		
	VALENTINI	ABRUZZO
Montepulciano d'Abruzzo Plateo '04		
	AGRIVERDE	ABRUZZO
Moscato Passito '08	LUIGI VIOLA	CALABRIA
Nambrot '06	TENUTA DI GHIZZANO	TUSCANY
Nero d'Avola Versace '07	FEUDI DEL PISCIOTTO	SICILY
Offida Pecorino Ciprea '08	SAN SAVINO - PODERI CAPECCI	MARCHE
Perda Pintà '07	GIUSEPPE SEDILESU	SARDINIA
Poggio Tura '05	VIGNE DEI BOSCHI	EMILIA ROMAGNA
Recioto della Valpolicella Cereolo '05		
	TRABUCCHI D'ILLASI	VENETO
Regina del Bosco '06	FATTORIA DEZI	MARCHE
Relógio '07	CA' OROLOGIO	VENETO
Ribolla Anfora '05	GRAVNER	FRIULI VENEZIA GIULIA
Roero Audinaggio '07	CASCINA CA' ROSSA	PIEDMONT
Roero Renesio Ris. '05	MALVIRÀ	PIEDMONT
Saia '07	FEUDO MACCARI	SICILY
Sangiovese di Romagna Sup. Corallo Nero Ris. '06		
	GALLEGATI	EMILIA ROMAGNA
Sangiovese di Romagna Sup. Pruno Ris. '06		
	DREI DONÀ TENUTA LA PALAZZA	EMILIA ROMAGNA
Terra di Lavoro '07	GALARDI	CAMPANIA
Valturio '07	VALTURIO	MARCHE
Verdicchio dei Castelli di Jesi Cl. V. Novali Ris. '06		
	TERRE CORTESI MONCARO	MARCHE
Verdicchio dei Castelli di Jesi Cl. Villa Bucci Ris. '07		BUCCI MARCHE
Verdicchio di Matelica Cambrugiano Ris. '06		
	BELISARIO	MARCHE
Vernaccia di S. Gimignano Carato '05		
	MONTENIDOLI	TUSCANY

STARS

The number of wineries that have been awarded at least one Star, which means they have won at least ten Three Glass prizes, rose to 122. These operations represent the elite of Italian wine. Topping the table with ever more authority is Angelo Gaja, who can look down on the rest from the high ground of 45 Three Glass awards in 23 editions of the Guide, an average of almost two a year. New entries include Sicily's tiny Palari winery from Santo Stefano Briga, near Messina. Others are Benanti and Donnafugata, also from Sicily, Bucci from Marche, Einaudi, Fiorenzo Nada, i Produttori del Barbaresco, Pecchenino, Sottimano, Vietti and Vigna Rionda Massolino in Piedmont, San Patrignano in Emilia Romagna and Volpe Pasini in Friuli Venezia Giulia.

★★★★
45
Gaja (Piedmont)

★★★
35
La Spinetta (Piedmont)
33
Ca' del Bosco (Lombardy)

★★
28
Elio Altare - Cascina Nuova (Piedmont)
25
Allegrini (Veneto)
Castello di Fonterutoli (Tuscany)
24
Fattoria di Felsina (Tuscany)
23
Castello di Ama (Tuscany)
Valentini (Abruzzo)
21
Marchesi Antinori (Tuscany)
C. P. San Michele Appiano (Alto Adige)
Domenico Clerico (Piedmont)
Jermann (Friuli Venezia Giulia)
Masciarelli (Abruzzo)
Poliziano (Tuscany)
Villa Russiz (Friuli Venezia Giulia)
20
Bellavista (Lombardy)
Castello della Sala (Umbria)
Giacomo Conterno (Piedmont)
Girolamo Dorigo (Friuli Venezia Giulia)
Gravner (Friuli Venezia Giulia)
Feudi di San Gregorio (Campania)
Planeta (Sicily)
Tenuta San Guido (Tuscany)

★
19
Cantina Tramin (Alto Adige)
Ferrari (Trentino)
Vie di Romans (Friuli Venezia Giulia)
18
Livio Felluga (Friuli Venezia Giulia)
Tenuta dell'Ornellaia (Tuscany)
Tasca d'Almerita (Sicily)
17
Castello Banfi ((Tuscany)
Isole e Olena (Tuscany)
Cascina La Barbatella (Piedmont)
Tenuta Fontodi ((Tuscany)
Bruno Giacosa (Piedmont)
Leonildo Pieropan (Veneto)
Tenimenti Ruffino ((Tuscany)
Schiopetto (Friuli Venezia Giulia)
16
Argiolas (Sardinia)
Romano Dal Forno (Veneto)
Querciabella (Tuscany)
Paolo Scavino (Piedmont)
15
C. P. Colterenzio (Alto Adige)
C. P. Santa Maddalena/Cantina di Bolzano (Alto Adige)
Arnaldo Caprai (Umbria)
Castello del Terriccio (Tuscany)
Conterno Fantino (Piedmont)
Matteo Correggia (Piedmont)
Miani (Friuli Venezia Giulia)
Nino Negri (Lombardy)
Barone Ricasoli (Tuscany)
Venica & Venica (Friuli Venezia Giulia)

14
Roberto Anselmi (Veneto)
Aldo Conterno (Piedmont)
Montevetrano (Campania)
Tenuta San Leonardo (Trentino)
Le Vigne di Zamò (Friuli Venezia Giulia)
Roberto Voerzio (Piedmont)
Elena Walch (Alto Adige)
13
Ca' Viola (Piedmont)
Cantina di Caldaro (Alto Adige)
Casanova di Neri (Tuscany)
Michele Chiarlo (Piedmont)
Les Crêtes (Valle d'Aosta)
Falesco (Lazio)
Maculan (Veneto)
Mastroberardino (Campania)
Montevertine (Tuscany)
Giuseppe Quintarelli (Veneto)
Ronco del Gelso (Friuli Venezia Giulia)
Luciano Sandrone (Piedmont)
Tenute Sella & Mosca (Sardinia)
Serafini & Vidotto (Veneto)
Uberti (Lombardy)
Fattoria Zerbina (Emilia Romagna)
12
Avignonesi (Tuscany)
Bricco Rocche - Bricco Asili (Piedmont)
Castello dei Rampolla (Tuscany)
Gioacchino Garofoli (Marche)
Elio Grasso (Piedmont)
Franco Toros (Friuli Venezia Giulia)
Tua Rita (Tuscany)
11
Abbazia di Novacella (Alto Adige)
Brancaia (Tuscany)
Cantina Convento Muri-Gries (Alto Adige)
Cantina Sociale di Santadi (Sardinia)
Cantina Terlano (Alto Adige)
Castellare di Castellina (Tuscany)
Còlpetrone (Umbria)
Cusumano (Sicily)
Foradori (Trentino)
Edi Keber (Friuli Venezia Giulia)
Le Macchiole (Tuscany)
La Massa (Tuscany)
Lis Neris (Friuli Venezia Giulia)
Palari (Sicily)
Fattoria Le Pupille (Tuscany)
Bruno Rocca (Piedmont)
Podere Rocche dei Manzoni (Piedmont)
10
Gianfranco Alessandria (Piedmont)
Benanti (Sicily)
Bucci (Marche)
Tenuta Col d'Orcia (Tuscany)
Donnafugata (Sicily)
Einaudi (Piedmont)
Tenute Ambrogio e Giovanni Folonari (Tuscany)
Marchesi de' Frescobaldi (Tuscany)
Tenuta J. Hofstätter (Alto Adige)
Malvirà (Piedmont)
Franco M. Martinetti (Piedmont)
F. Nada (Piedmont)
Pecchenino (Piedmont)
Produttori del Barbaresco (Piedmont)
Prunotto (Piedmont)
A. Rocca (Piedmont)
San Patrignano (Emilia Romagna)
Sottimano (Piedmont)
Vietti (Piedmont)
Vigna Rionda - Massolino (Piedmont)
Volpe Pasini (Friuli Venezia Giulia)

HOW TO USE THE GUIDE

WINERY INFORMATION
ANNUAL PRODUCTION
HECTARES UNDER VINE
VITICULTURE METHOD

SYMBOLS
O WHITE WINE
⊙ ROSÉ WINE
● RED WINE

RATINGS
MENTION WITHOUT GLASSES:
WELL-TYPED WINES OF AVERAGE QUALITY IN THEIR RESPECTIVE CATEGORIES

Ψ
MODERATELY GOOD TO GOOD WINES IN THEIR RESPECTIVE CATEGORIES
ΨΨ
VERY GOOD TO EXCELLENT WINES IN THEIR RESPECTIVE CATEGORIES
ΨΨ
VERY GOOD TO EXCELLENT WINES THAT WENT FORWARD TO THE FINAL TASTINGS
ΨΨΨ
EXCELLENT WINES IN THEIR RESPECTIVE CATEGORIES
ΨΨΨ+
AWARD-WINNING WINES SELECTED BY THE EDITOR

WINES RATED IN PREVIOUS EDITIONS OF THE GUIDE ARE INDICATED BY WHITE GLASSES (Ψ, ΨΨ, ΨΨΨ)),
PROVIDED THEY ARE STILL DRINKING AT THE LEVEL FOR WHICH THE ORIGINAL AWARD WAS MADE.

STAR ★
INDICATES WINERIES THAT HAVE WON TEN THREE GLASS
AWARDS FOR EACH STAR

price ranges (1)
1 up to €3.50
2 from €3.51 to €5
3 from €5.01 to €7.50
4 from €7.51 to €13
5 from €13.01 to €20
6 from €20.01 to €30
7 from €30.01 to €40
8 more than €40
(1) Since prices abroad may vary, the editors have opted to indicate price ranges in euros.

ASTERISK*
INDICATES WINERIES THAT HAVE WON
TEN THREE GLASS AWARDS FOR EACH STAR

N.A.
PRICES INDICATED REFER TO AVERAGE PRICES IN WINE STORES.
PRICE RANGES INDICATED FOR WINES WITH WHITE GLASSES
(RATED IN PREVIOUS EDITIONS OF THE GUIDE)
TAKE INTO ACCOUNT APPRECIATION OVER TIME WHERE APPROPRIATE.

ABBREVIATIONS

A. A.	Alto Adige
C.	Colli
Cl.	Classico
C.S.	Cantina Sociale (Co-operative Winery)
Cant.	Cantina (Cellar)
CEV	Colli Etruschi Viterbesi
Cast.	Castello (Castle)
COF	Colli Orientali del Friuli
Cons.	Consorzio (Consortium)
Coop.Agr.	Cooperativa Agricola (Farm Co-operative)
C. B.	Colli Bolognesi
C. P.	Colli Piacentini
Et.	Etichetta (Label)
M.	Metodo (Method)
M.to	Monferrato
OP	Oltrepò Pavese
P.R.	Peduncolo Rosso (Red Bunchstem
P.	Prosecco
Rif. Agr.	Riforma Agraria (Agrarian Reform)
Ris.	Riserva (Reserve)
Sel.	Selezione (Selection)
Sup.	Superiore
TdF	Terre di Franciacorta
V.	Vigna (Vineyard)
Vign.	Vigneto (Vineyard)
V. T.	Vendemmia Tardiva (Late Harvest)

VALLE D'AOSTA

Want to know how large a part wines from Valle d'Aosta play in the national total? Its 1,500,000 litres make up just 0.03 per cent in an average year. Next to nothing. Yet the following pages show stories of enthusiastic growers, high-altitude vineyards that can withstand the ice and frost of the Alps, native varieties that produce wines with unique aromas and flavours unrepeatable elsewhere, and all this in quantities much lower than production from an average co-operative winery. But these mountain vineyards, as heroic as the growers who work them, have produced six Three Glass wines. No winery can boast as much. If the celebrated Piedmont region had same proportions of quantity produced and prize-winning wines, then it would have 899 Three Glass awards! All joking aside, these numbers give us an idea of the fantastic terroirs and above all the extraordinary commitment of the growers in Valle d'Aosta. Here are the main players. Anselmet with the Chardonnay Élevé en Fût de Chêne '08 and Les Crêtes with the Chardonnay Cuvée Bois '07 prove with stratospheric scores that there is a place in Italy where this much-exploited variety expresses all its finesse and depth: Valle d'Aosta. The Pinot Gris '08 from Lo Triolet also shows how well it has adapted to the territory with an intense, elegant wine. The Fumin Vigne di Rovettaz '07 from Grosjean and Fumin Esprit Follet '07 from La Crotta di Vegneron turn the spotlight on this extraordinary native variety that offers extremely refined, enjoyable wines. In closing, how could we not mention Moscato Passito, a great classic in regional winemaking? The version from Hervé and Luciana Deguillame, Chambave Muscat Flétri '07, comes from a tiny family operation called La Vrille. In other words, these are results to frame and cherish but we feel they are destined to improve even more in future. As the neigbouring French might say, "Chapeau!"

Anselmet

FRAZ. LA CRÊTE, 194
11018 VILLENEUVE [AO]
TEL. 3484127121
www.maisonanselmet.vievini.it

CELLAR SALES
PRE-BOOKED VISITS

ANNUAL PRODUCTION **35,000 bottles**
HECTARES UNDER VINE **5**
VITICULTURE METHOD **Conventional**

Maison Anselmet is now a banker in Valle d'Aosta wine. The owner, Giorgio, works alongside his father Renato to produce a broad range of wines. Almost all their bottles are expressions of the terroir where this small estate operates and are inspired by Valle d'Aosta's heritage. The excellently aspected vineyards are located between Saint Pierre and Villeneuve, one of the historic areas for Torrette, the signature red wine from Valle d'Aosta. Recent completion of the new cellar will help this estate to exploit its full potential.

Anselmet lived up to expectations again this year with the Chardonnay Élevé en Fût de Chêne '08 winning another Three Glasses. It's a white with remarkable elegance and harmony, the complex nose revealing fruity notes run through with touches of spice, mountain herbs and oak, while the satisfying palate is sound and well structured, yet incredibly drinkable and inviting. The '08 Chardonnay is pleasingly fresh. The red Torrette Superiore '07 is quite impressive. This deep, complex wine has delicious red berry fruits aromas, with wafts of wild berries, and a long, balanced palate. The same goes for the '08 Fumin, a well-structured red with slightly rough tannins.

Brégy & Gillioz

VIA VERGNOD, 7
11010 SAINT-PIERRE
TEL. 0041763786668
www.grain-noble.ch

CELLAR SALES
PRE-BOOKED VISITS

ANNUAL PRODUCTION **10,000 bottles**
HECTARES UNDER VINE **3.2**
VITICULTURE METHOD **Conventional**

In the small, scenic village of Saint Pierre, north of Aosta, two friends André Brégy and Pierre-André Gillioz tend one three-hectare vineyard planted to a single variety: petite arvine. For some time, this variety was considered of Swiss origin but recently students, from Switzerland no less, have identified Valle d'Aosta as the origin. This splendid vineyard, which enjoys magnificent sunlight, features a drip-feed irrigation system, essential given Valle d'Aosta's low rainfall, and produces just one, unique wine: Référence.

This dried-grape wine from petite arvine shows a bright, lively gold. Its broad, complex aromas suggest intense candied citrus peel, crème brulée, ripe apricot and pleasing whiffs of botrytis. The palate has a rich, full flavour balanced by enjoyable freshness, and finishes long with refined elegance.

○ Valle d'Aosta Chardonnay Élevé en Fût de Chêne '08	♟♟♟	6
○ Valle d'Aosta Chardonnay '08	♟♟	4*
● Valle d'Aosta Fumin '08	♟♟	6
○ Valle d'Aosta Petite Arvine '08	♟♟	5
○ Valle d'Aosta Pinot Gris '08	♟♟	5
● Valle d'Aosta Torrette Sup. '07	♟♟	6
● Le Prisonnier '07	♟	6
○ Valle d'Aosta Chambave Muscat '08	♟	5
● Valle d'Aosta Pinot Noir V. Toule '07	♟	5
● Valle d'Aosta Syrah Henri '07	♟	6
● Valle d'Aosta Torrette '08	♟	5
○ Valle d'Aosta Chardonnay Élevé en Fût de Chêne '07	♟♟♟	6
○ Valle d'Aosta Chardonnay Élevé en Fût de Chêne '06	♟♟♟	6
○ Valle d'Aosta Chardonnay Élevé en Fût de Chêne '05	♟♟♟	6

○ Référence '07	♟♟	6
○ Référence '06	♟♟♟	6
○ Podium '04	♟♟	6
○ Référence '05	♟♟	6

La Crotta di Vegneron

P.ZZA RONCAS, 2
11023 CHAMBAVE [AO]
TEL. 016646670
www.lacrotta.it

CELLAR SALES
PRE-BOOKED VISITS
FOOD

ANNUAL PRODUCTION **300,000 bottles**
HECTARES UNDER VINE **39**
VITICULTURE METHOD **Conventional**

Started in 1980, Crotta vinified for the first time in 1985. The 120 members still tend their small parcels of vineyards largely by hand with a genuine love for the land. Oenologist Andrea Costa, president Elio Cornaz and all the co-operative's member growers have deserved recognition for some time. Three Glasses went to the Fumin, one of the most typical from Valle d'Aosta and the crowning achievement of a thoroughly committed winery well into its third decade. The historic Chambave Muscat, a dry-vinified Moscato Bianco, is another feather in the cellar's cap.

The Fumin Esprit Follet '07 is very varietal. The intense ruby introduces exuberant, almost aggressive, aromas echoing cinchona over forest floor with shades of black currants, blackberry, blueberry and a touch of juniper. The full palate shows great elegance and extraordinary length. Though blended with other local red varieties, Chambave Supérieur Quatre Vignobles is a splendid interpretation of petit rouge. The Chambave Muscat Passito from this estate is always a sure thing, with a one-of-a-kind bouquet and full palate.

Di Barrò

LOC. CHÂTEAU FEUILLET, 8
11010 SAINT-PIERRE [AO]
TEL. 0165903671
www.vievini.it

CELLAR SALES
PRE-BOOKED VISITS

ANNUAL PRODUCTION **17,000 bottles**
HECTARES UNDER VINE **2.5**
VITICULTURE METHOD **Naturale**

The wine labels feature the "barrò", barrels built to transport grapes crushed directly in the vineyard. Barrò is also a conflation of the surnames Barmaz and Rossan, who began tending the family vineyards in the Conze region during the 1960s. Di Barrò was among the first wineries to produce Torrette, one of the most emblematic wine types from Valle d'Aosta. The estate owner Elvira Rini, assisted by her husband Andrea Barmaz, makes characterful wines rich in personality through meticulous vineyard management that not only provides quality raw material but also respects the environment.

The charming '08 Chardonnay has complex, intense aromas with notes of honey and tropical fruit shading into citrus. The full palate shows excellent balance and closes out long on fruity tones. The '07 Syrah is good, with varietal sensations of white pepper, then plum jam and cocoa powder, elegant, velvety tannins and a long finish. The '07 Fumin is full and rich, redolent of fruitiness and moss. The palate is full, though not adequately supported by tannins. We expected more from the dried-grape Passito Lo Bien Flapì '07, from pinot grigio, and felt the Mayolet '08, which had so pleasantly impressed us last time round, was slightly under par.

● Valle d'Aosta Fumin Esprit Follet '07	▼▼▼ 5*
○ Valle d'Aosta Chambave Moscato Passito Prieuré '07	▼▼ 6
● Valle d'Aosta Chambave Sup. Quatre Vignobles '07	▼▼ 4*
○ Valle d'Aosta Chambave Muscat '08	▼▼ 4*
○ Valle d'Aosta Chambave Muscat Attente '05	▼▼ 6
○ Valle d'Aosta Nus Malvoisie Cuvée Particulière '07	▼▼ 5
○ Valle d'Aosta Müller Thurgau '08	▼ 4
○ Valle d'Aosta Nus Malvoisie Flétri Nonus '07	▼ 6
○ Valle d'Aosta Chambave Moscato Passito Prieuré '06	♈♈ 6
○ Valle d'Aosta Chambave Muscat '07	♈♈ 4
● Valle d'Aosta Chambave Sup. Quatre Vignobles '06	♈♈ 4*
● Valle d'Aosta Fumin Esprit Follet '06	♈♈ 5

○ Valle d'Aosta Chardonnay '08	▼▼ 4*
● Valle d'Aosta Fumin '07	▼▼ 5
● Valle d'Aosta Syrah V. di Conze '07	▼▼ 5
○ Lo Bien Flapì '07	▼ 7
● Valle d'Aosta Mayolet V. de Toule '08	▼ 4
○ Lo Bien Flapì '06	♈♈ 7
● Valle d'Aosta Fumin '06	♈♈ 5
● Valle d'Aosta Mayolet V. de Toule '07	♈♈ 4*
● Valle d'Aosta Torrette '07	♈♈ 4

Feudo di San Maurizio

FRAZ. MAILLOD, 44
11010 SARRE [AO]
TEL. 3383186831
www.feudo.vievini.it

CELLAR SALES
PRE-BOOKED VISITS

ANNUAL PRODUCTION 30,000 bottles
HECTARES UNDER VINE 6
VITICULTURE METHOD Conventional

Sarre is one of the sunniest municipalities in the entire Valle d'Aosta. Here in 1989, Michel Vallet gave shape to his passion for rural traditions and the environment, tenaciously creating Feudo di San Maurizio. Efforts during the early period of activity led to the creation of three white wines and almost all the red grape varieties, which were grown on around three hectares of nearly all new vines. The cellar should be finished in the near future and will finally allow Michel to show off the potential of his vineyards.

His Torrette Superiore was surprising enough to make the finals. Already bright ruby, the intense aromas of red berry fruit elegantly meld delicious notes of cherry with moss and peppery sensations. The dense, well-balanced palate finishes long and intense. The always intriguing Pierrots is an opulent wine from overripe fumin and petit rouge. The interesting Müller Thurgau has delicate floral, fruity aromas shading across citrus notes. The palate shows balanced structure with a long, fresh finish. Saro Djablo, a complex blend of all the local varieties, and Mayolet, are both enjoyable.

F.lli Grosjean

VILLAGGIO OLLIGNAN, 1
11020 QUART [AO]
TEL. 0165775791
www.grosjean.vievini.it

CELLAR SALES
PRE-BOOKED VISITS

ANNUAL PRODUCTION 80,000 bottles
HECTARES UNDER VINE 8
VITICULTURE METHOD Conventional

n 1969, Dauphin Grosjean began bottling his own wine to exhibit at the regional wine show, "Il exposition des vins du Val d'Aoste". It provided the stimulus for expanding the estate from a third of a hectare to the current eight hectares under vine. Dauphin involved his five sons, Eraldo, Piergiorgio, Fernando, Marco and Vincent, in the project. Their wines are products of tradition and territory, and the Fumin confirmed the brilliant results of the previous vintage: Three Glasses.

Vigne di Rovettaz '07 has a deep, bright colour and intense aromas of forest floor with subtle vegetality and tobacco-like spice. The powerful palate has an austere tannic weave and finishes long on notes of cinchona. The excellent '08 Pinot Grigio presents a lovely copper-flecked straw with intense aromas and a rich palate that finishes fresh and long. The varietal '07 Pinot Nero has a classic, pale hue, fruity aromas laced with spicy oak, and a palate that shows freshness and balance. The interesting Torrette Superiore '07 has a rich flavour but lacks a bit of freshness at the back. Finally, the nice Cornalin '07 is worth tasting.

● Valle d'Aosta Torrette Sup. '07	♟♟ 5
● Pierrots '07	♟♟ 6
○ Valle d'Aosta Müller Thurgau '08	♟♟ 4*
● Saro Djablo '07	♟ 4
● Valle d'Aosta Mayolet '08	♟ 5
○ Grapillon '07	♟♟ 4
● Pierrots '06	♟♟ 6
● Valle d'Aosta Fumin '06	♟♟ 5
● Valle d'Aosta Mayolet '07	♟♟ 5
● Valle d'Aosta Torrette '07	♟♟ 4

● Valle d'Aosta Fumin V. Rovettaz '07	♟♟♟ 6
○ Valle d'Aosta Pinot Gris V. Creton '08	♟♟ 5
● Valle d'Aosta Pinot Noir V. Tzeriat '07	♟♟ 5
● Valle d'Aosta Torrette Sup. V. Rovettaz '07	♟♟ 4*
● Valle d'Aosta Cornalin V. Rovettaz '07	♟ 4
● Valle d'Aosta Fumin '06	♟♟♟ 5
○ Blanc de Dauphin '06	♟♟ 4*
● Valle d'Aosta Cornalin V. Rovettaz '06	♟♟ 4
● Valle d'Aosta Fumin '05	♟♟ 5
○ Valle d'Aosta Pinot Gris V. Creton '07	♟♟ 5
● Valle d'Aosta Pinot Noir V. Tzeriat '06	♟♟ 4
● Valle d'Aosta Torrette Sup. V. Rovetta '06	♟♟ 4*

★ Les Crêtes

LOC. VILLETOS, 50
11010 AYMAVILLES [AO]
TEL. 0165902274
www.lescretes.it

CELLAR SALES
PRE-BOOKED VISITS

ANNUAL PRODUCTION **230,000 bottles**
HECTARES UNDER VINE **25**
VITICULTURE METHOD **Conventional**

For the 11th consecutive year, Cuvée Bois from Les Crêtes picked up Three Glasses. Costantino founded the operation with some friends in 1989 but must share credit for its success with his wife Imelda and daughters Eleonora and Elena, who have begun apprenticing at the helm of the estate. The cellar is a genuine icon for Valle d'Aosta as well as a beacon for all those small producers, scattered around the world, who love their land and believe in their work.

Again this year, Chardonnay Cuvée Bois is splendidly harmonious, complex, intense apple-like aromas giving clear notes of Langhe hazelnuts. The fullness and extraordinary balance on the palate translates into a long, satisfying finish. Another great wine is the Fumin, with its pleasing red berry fruit and tobacco leading into good structure and a long, oak-lifted finish. From one of the loveliest vineyards in Valle d'Aosta, Côteau La Tour, Les Crêtes makes an exciting Syrah and the standard Chardonnay Vigne Frissonnière is always pleasing, like the unusual Petite Arvine Vigne Champorette. The Sabla '07 and Passito Les Abeilles '07 are both nice.

Lo Triolet

LOC. JUNOD, 7
11010 INTROD [AO]
TEL. 016595437
www.lotriolet.vievini.it

CELLAR SALES
PRE-BOOKED VISITS

ANNUAL PRODUCTION **30,000 bottles**
HECTARES UNDER VINE **3**
VITICULTURE METHOD **Conventional**

The Martins have always made wine for family consumption. After expanding and replanting his vineyards, Marco, who has the enthusiasm and tenacity characteristic of Valle d'Aosta winemakers, produced his first Pinot Gris in 1993 from a typical, if all too frequently forgotten, Valle d'Aosta variety. Marco's skills at recovering the quality of the variety has won him Three Glasses. Since 2000, with the purchase of new vineyards in the area of Nus, Lo Triolet has expanded its production by planting local red varieties.

Fermented in stainless steel, the '08 Vallée d'Aoste Pinot Gris submitted by Marco is a nice-looking wine with great character. Its bright, deep hue introduces a captivating nose redolent of ripe pear, vanilla and cakes. The satisfyingly tangy, harmonic palate shows full, closing out long on notes of fruit. The equally good '08 Pinot Gris, part-aged in barrique, is pleasing but needs more bottle age. The Nus and Pinot Nero are both from '08 and both pleasant.

○ Valle d'Aosta Chardonnay Cuvée Bois '07	▼▼▼ 7
● Valle d'Aosta Fumin V. La Tour '07	▼▼ 6
● Coteau La Tour Syrah '07	▼▼ 5
○ Valle d'Aosta Chardonnay V. Frissonnière '08	▼▼ 4*
○ Valle d'Aosta Petite Arvine V. Champorette '08	▼▼ 4*
○ Les Abeilles '07	▼ 4
● Valle d'Aosta Pinot Noir V. La Tour '08	▼ 4
● Vin de La Sabla '07	▼ 4
○ Valle d'Aosta Chardonnay Cuvée Bois '06	♀♀♀ 7
○ Valle d'Aosta Chardonnay Cuvée Frissonnière Les Crêtes Cuvée Bois '05	♀♀♀ 7
● La Sabla '06	♀♀ 4
● Valle d'Aosta Fumin V. La Tour '06	♀♀ 6
● Valle d'Aosta Torrette V. Les Toules '07	♀♀ 4

○ Valle d'Aosta Pinot Gris '08	▼▼▼ 4*
○ Valle d'Aosta Pinot Gris Élevé en Barriques '08	▼▼ 5
● Valle d'Aosta Pinot Noir '08	▼ 4
● Valle d'Aosta Rouge Nus '08	▼ 4
○ Valle d'Aosta Pinot Gris '05	♀♀♀ 4*
○ Mistigri '06	♀♀ 6
○ MonAtout '07	♀♀ 4
○ Valle d'Aosta Pinot Gris '07	♀♀ 4
○ Valle d'Aosta Pinot Gris '06	♀♀ 4*
○ Valle d'Aosta Pinot Gris Élevé en Barriques '07	♀♀ 5
● Valle d'Aosta Rouge Coteau Barrage '07	♀♀ 5

Cave du Vin Blanc de Morgex et de La Salle

FRAZ. LA RUINE
CHEMIN DES ÎLES, 19
11017 MORGEX [AO]
TEL. 0165800331
www.caveduvinblanc.com

CELLAR SALES
PRE-BOOKED VISITS

ANNUAL PRODUCTION **170,000 bottles**
HECTARES UNDER VINE **20**
VITICULTURE METHOD **Conventional**

Inspired by Don Bougeat, growers at Morgex and La Salle came together officially. In 1989, Cave du Vin Blanc de Morgex et La Salle began a perfect operation in the only context of its kind in the world. At the foot of Mont Blanc, the highest mountain in Europe, they tend still ungrafted vines of a unique variety: prié blanc. Gianluca Telloli, the Cave's dynamic oenologist, has brought out its potential and made giant steps in the sparkling wines, where the variety works best.

Of the wines submitted this year, we particularly liked the Rayon '08, a fresh, subtle wine with pleasant wafts of wild flowers, as well as a fresh, delicate texture on the palate. From the sparkling versions, we preferred the Brut Cuvée du Prince, a big wine with complex aromas, to the delicious Brut Extreme from last year. Another series of wines from the estate can be found in a separate entry dedicated to the Quatremille Mètres. The Cave also produces a special dessert wine from grapes harvested when frozen in December, Chaudelune.

La Vrille

LOC. GRANGEON, 1
11020 VERRAYES [AO]
TEL. 0166543018
www.lavrille-agritourisme.com

CELLAR SALES
PRE-BOOKED VISITS
OSPITALITÀ
FOOD

ANNUAL PRODUCTION **10,000 bottles**
HECTARES UNDER VINE **1.5**
VITICULTURE METHOD **Conventional**

In 1990, Hervè Deguillame arrived in Valle d'Aosta, purchased what had been the family vineyard and planted the first vines of moscato bianco. Hervè and his wife Luciana chose the name La Vrille, or tendril, for their estate when they started this venture after having been growers for Crotta di Vegneron. Their winery is the realization of a dream driven by consistency and passion for the territory.

Luciana and Hervé came up to all expectations. Their wonderful, intense Chambave Muscat Flétri gives an elegantly expressed range of aromas and a perfectly balanced, sweet, fresh palate. Three Glasses were a formality. It's just a pity there are only 1,500 bottles. But after results like these, we are certain La Vrille may consider increasing production just a bit. The '07 Cornalin is also interesting, offering pleasant fruity sensations in harmony with spicy nuances of tobacco, and a balanced, elegant palate.

Wine		
○ Valle d'Aosta Blanc de Morgex et de La Salle Brut mill. '07	♈	5
○ Valle d'Aosta Blanc de Morgex et de La Salle M. Cl. Brut Cuvée du Prince '04	♈	6
○ Valle d'Aosta Blanc de Morgex et de La Salle Rayon '08	♈	4*
○ Valle d'Aosta Blanc de Morgex et de La Salle Vini Estremi '08	♈	4
○ Valle d'Aosta Blanc de Morgex et de La Salle M. Cl. Brut Extreme '06	♈	5
○ Valle d'Aosta Blanc de Morgex et de La Salle M. Cl. Brut Cuvée du Prince '03	♈	6
○ Valle d'Aosta Blanc de Morgex et de La Salle M. Cl. Extra Brut '06	♈	5
○ Valle d'Aosta Blanc de Morgex et de La Salle Rayon '07	♈	4
○ Valle d'Aosta Blanc de Morgex et de La Salle Rayon '06	♈	4*

Wine		
○ Valle d'Aosta Chambave Muscat Flétri Passito '07	♈	5*
● Valle d'Aosta Cornalin '07	♈	4
○ Valle d'Aosta Chambave Muscat '07	♈	4
○ Valle d'Aosta Chambave Muscat Flétri Passito '06	♈	5
● Valle d'Aosta Fumin '06	♈	5

L'Atoueyo

LOC. URBAINS, 8
11010 AYMAVILLES [AO]
TEL. 0165902550
www.atoueyo.vievini.it

Atoueyo is the term in the local dialect for the small shrines along the mountain paths that inspired Fernanda Saraillon and her son Omar when they decided to start up this estate in 2000. Their Chardonnay is always enjoyable, the Torrette Supérieur never disappoints while the Pinot Nero and Gamay are nice.

○ Valle d'Aosta Chardonnay '08	♀	4
● Valle d'Aosta Gamay '08	♀	4
● Valle d'Aosta Pinot Nero '08	♀	4
● Valle d'Aosta Torrette Sup. '08	♀	4

Le Château Feuillet

LOC. CHÂTEAU FEUILLET
11010 SAINT-PIERRE [AO]
TEL. 0165903905
www.chateaufeuillet.vievini.it

This young estate makes a fine Petite Arvine '08 with vibrant fruity aromas and a rich, powerful palate. The Chardonnay '08 is equally good with elegant aromatics and excellent structure. The whites had a good year but the reds are also very enjoyable. Special mention for the Torrette Supérieur and Fumin.

○ Valle d'Aosta Chardonnay '08	♀♀	4*
○ Valle d'Aosta Petite Arvine '08	♀♀	4*
● Valle d'Aosta Fumin '07	♀	4
● Valle d'Aosta Torrette Sup. '07	♀	4

Diego Curtaz

FRAZ. VISERAN, 61
11020 GRESSAN [AO]
TEL. 0165251079
www.diegocurtazvini.it

The '08 Torrette is a varietal Petit Rouge and Dï Meun, from petit rouge with other native varieties, is also good. This year's nice surprise is Dï Noutro, a pinot grigio-led white blend. It's perhaps a bit too moscato-influenced on the nose but has nice structure on the palate. The Petit Rouge is pleasant.

● Dï Meun '08	♀♀	4*
○ Dï Noutro '08	♀♀	4*
● Valle d'Aosta Torrette '08	♀♀	4*
● Valle d'Aosta Petit Rouge '08	♀	4

Caves Cooperatives de Donnas

VIA ROMA, 97
11020 DONNAS [AO]
TEL. 0125807096
www.donnasvini.it

Tasting the Nebbiolos from the Cave this year was a pleasure that time can only improve. The Donnas Napoléon is intense and stylish, with still developing spicy touches and a soft, elegantly tannic palate. The Donnas Supérieur Vieilles Vignes '05 is intense, spicy powerful on the palate.

● Valle d'Aosta Donnas Napoléon '04	♀♀	5
● Valle d'Aosta Donnas Sup. Vieilles Vignes '05	♀♀	5

Les Granges

FRAZ. LES GRANGES, 8
11020 NUS [AO]
TEL. 0165767229
www.lesgrangesvini.it

This year, we liked the concentrated, clean '07 Fumin. The nose has pleasant notes of red berries shading across spicy tones of tobacco and oak that usher in a balanced, juicy palate. The Pinot Nero is pleasant and the varietal Nus is an easy-drinking treat.

● Valle d'Aosta Fumin '07	♀♀	5
● Valle d'Aosta Nus '08	♀	4
● Valle d'Aosta Pinot Noir '08	♀	4

Institut Agricole Régional

RÉGION LA ROCHÈRE, 1A
11100 AOSTA
TEL. 0165215811
www.iaraosta.it

The '07 Fumin went through to our final tasting. The delicious nose gives forest floor and blackberries before the strong, characterful palate shows extraordinarily full and dense. The nice Pinot Gris is fragrant and elegant. The '08 Petite Arvine and Syrah are pleasant.

● Valle d'Aosta Fumin '07	♀♀	5
○ Valle d'Aosta Pinot Gris '08	♀♀	4*
● Valle d'Aosta Syrah '08	♀♀	4*
○ Valle d'Aosta Petite Arvine '08	♀	4

Cooperativa La Kiuva

FRAZ. PIED DE VILLE, 42
11020 ARNAD [AO]
TEL. 0125966351
lakiuva@libero.it

The Kiuva co-operative works with the variety best suited to this terroir: nebbiolo, also called picoutener. The cellar is introducing a single-variety Nebbiolo. It still has a little way to go but the signs are good. You can bank on the Arnad-Montjovet Superiore and the '08 Chardonnay is very drinkable.

● Valle d'Aosta Arnad-Montjovet Sup. '06	♟♟	4*
○ Valle d'Aosta Chardonnay '08	♟	4

Cave des Onze Communes

LOC. URBAINS, 14
11010 AYMAVILLES [AO]
TEL. 0165902912
www.caveonzecommunes.it

With 220 members operating in 11 towns around Aosta, this is the largest co-operative in the region. The Torrette Superieur is quite sound showing fresh, fruity aromatics and a full, juicy palate. The '08 Torrette has nice structure and fresh aromas while the Pinot Nero and Cornalin are worth a taste.

● Valle d'Aosta Torrette Sup. '07	♟♟	4*
● Valle d'Aosta Cornalin '08	♟	3
● Valle d'Aosta Pinot Noir '08	♟	3
● Valle d'Aosta Torrette '08	♟	3

Quatremillemetres Vins d'Altitude

VIA CORRADO GEX, 52
11010 ARVIER [AO]
TEL. 0165800331
www.4000metres.net

Three co-operative wineries set up this sparkling wine cellar. The elegant, stylish Fripon and Refrain are joined by Ancestrale, a sweet red from gamay that has interesting red berry aromas and a nice balance of sweetness and freshness on the palate. Caronte has a lingering bead and a fresh palate.

● Ancestrale Sec	♟♟	4*
○ Caronte Brut	♟♟	6
○ Fripon	♟	4
○ Refrain	♟	4

Pierre Philippe Quinson

LOC. TORRENT DE MAILLOD, 4
11020 QUART [AO]
TEL. 3485501979
pierreq@libero.it

The structured, concentrated Masarèn is produced from ancient native vines supported by barbera and dolcetto. Beato Emerico, a Vallée d'Aoste Rouge from a vineyard of gamay and mayolet, has a soft, caressing palate with stylish, caressing fruit and spice. The fresh palate has a pleasant mouthfeel.

● Masarèn '08	♟♟	4*
● Valle d'Aosta Beato Emerico '08	♟	3

La Source

LOC. BUSSAN DESSOUS, 1
11010 SAINT-PIERRE [AO]
TEL. 0165904038
info@lasource.it

Stefano Celi showed how well he can make an array of quality wines in two challenging vintages. We liked the Torrette Superiore, its nose dominated by upfront fruit, which a bright, balanced palate with good structure. The base Torrette is a step or two behind and the Syrah is nice.

● Valle d'Aosta Torrette Sup. '07	♟♟	4*
● Valle d'Aosta Syrah '07	♟	4
● Valle d'Aosta Torrette '08	♟	4

Maison Albert Vevey

FRAZ. VILLAIR
S.DA DEL VILLAIR, 67
11017 MORGEX [AO]
TEL. 0165808930
www.vievini.it

Marco and Mirko Vevey produce their Blanc de Morgex et de La Salle at the upper limit of viticulture, some 1,000 to 1,100 metres above sea level. The vineyards are actually the highest in Europe. The Blanc de Morgex has a straw colour leading into an elegant nose with a background of hay and mountain herbs.

○ Valle d'Aosta		
Blanc de Morgex et de La Salle '08	♟	4

PIEDMONT

Yet again, Piedmont is the locomotive region that drives Italian wine. The total of 84 Three Glasses would have been unthinkable only a few years ago. There are many reasons for this success, including increased investment recently in vineyards and cellars, which is bearing fruit. Nor should it be forgotten that despite such investment, the direct link between vines and producers has never been broken in Piedmont. Generation after generation has grown up with an intimate knowledge of the territory and an ability to select the most suitable clones and varieties in full awareness of quality. Finally, there are the pairs that underpin Piedmont wine: nebbiolo-Barolo and nebbiolo-Barbaresco. Not for the first time, these two denominations alone account for more than half of the region's Three Glass awards. If we look at the picture from a slightly different angle, nebbiolo is so crucial that with 52 Three Glass prizes in Langhe, five in Roero and seven reds in the fast-emerging Alto Piemonte zone, it supplies 65 wines either on its own or in blends with small proportions of other native varieties. We would note that 2005 was not such a poor vintage in Piedmont as it was in other regions but quite apart from great years like 2006 and 2007, the winning move by local producers has been to fine-tune their vinification and maturation of nebbiolo-based wines. And apart from nebbiolo and Langhe, we should also stress that all the region's territories merit the same respect. With a little extra effort, they often do the business. Take the Asti area. Barbera d'Asti is superlative – earning five Three Glass awards, two from the fantastic Nizza subzone – and Asti also came up with a wonderful Chardonnay and an aristocratic barbera and cabernet-based red, but above all it produced a superb classic-method sparkling wine. After all, this was the first area in Italy to make classic-method sparklers. Alessandria may look like a red grape province if you glance at the statistics but it is also coming through as a source of great Piedmontese whites. A trio of Three Glasses went to Gavi, currently on a roll, and two to Timorasso, as against only one for an excellent Monferrato Rosso. We will close these notes with some good news and some bad news. The good news is the top prize for a wine with a very ancient tradition, Caluso Passito, the only Three Glass wine from the province of Turin or indeed the dried-grape wine type. The only slightly bad news came from Dolcetto, which lost one or two top awards because of the weather, although we also welcome a first Three Glass prize for a Dolcetto from the Diano d'Alba zone. And the future is looking bright. Ten Piedmont wineries won Three Glasses for the first time.

Abbona

B.TA SAN LUIGI, 40
12063 DOGLIANI [CN]
TEL. 0173721317
www.abbona.com

CELLAR SALES
PRE-BOOKED VISITS

ANNUAL PRODUCTION **255,000 bottles**
HECTARES UNDER VINE **44**
VITICULTURE METHOD **Conventional**

The 40th anniversary of the Abbona family's winery, led by the tireless Marziano, falls in 2010. The new headquarters is thrilling, kitted out for the production of the 250,000 bottles released every year and well worth a visit. Dolcetto may in the doldrums as a wine type but Papà Celso is always exquisite. Soaring over the crisis, it continues to attract fans from all round the world.

Barolo Cerviano '04 is complex, giving dried flowers and liquorice followed by a velvet-smooth mouthfeel thanks to dense, fine-grained tannins. The spicy, fruity Terlo Ravera '05 has superb texture and personality in the mouth. The '05 Pressenda is slightly different. Matured in new barriques, it is currently drinking nicely if you like your Barolo modern. But the whole of the range is a delight, from the lovely Cinerino to the splendid Barbera Rinaldi. That said, it was the Papà Celso that won Three Glasses. Intense in hue with blueberry and cocoa powder fragrances heralding the magnificent palate with assertive extract and a symphonic finish with loads of deliciously chewy fruit.

Anna Maria Abbona

FRAZ. MONCUCCO, 21
12060 FARIGLIANO [CN]
TEL. 0173797228
www.annamariabbona.it

CELLAR SALES
PRE-BOOKED VISITS

ANNUAL PRODUCTION **58,000 bottles**
HECTARES UNDER VINE **10**
VITICULTURE METHOD **Conventional**

The far horizon frames this marvellous and undeservedly little-known corner of Piedmont, which thoroughly deserves further investigation. But apart from the natural beauty, Anna Maria Abbona and Franco Schellino's winery earn our admiration for their unremitting dedication to the promotion of dolcetto, a variety that manages to exhibit originality and character even at these challenging elevations. These appealing wines are superbly drinkable, an important and sometimes neglected feature.

Dogliani Maioli '07 is a little dumb at first but then unfurls nice, subtle red berry fruit and tobacco that quickly give way for cinchona and cocoa powder. Entry on the palate may be a tad rough because of the wine's youth but the close-knit extract takes you slowly through to an elegant long finish Dolcetto di Dogliani Sorì dij But '08 has an admirable powerful palate and upfront aromatics. The nice Cadò '07 is much fresher-tasting and complex. It's from barbera with a dash of dolcetto. And the Langhe Nebbiolo '07 is as complex and stylish as ever while the Langhe Dolcetto '08 is teasingly moreish.

● Dogliani Papà Celso '07	♟♟♟ 5
● Barbera d'Alba Rinaldi '07	♟♟ 4
● Barolo Cerviano '04	♟♟ 8
● Barolo Vign. Terlo Ravera '05	♟♟ 7
● Barolo Pressenda '05	♟♟ 7
● Dolcetto di Dogliani San Luigi '08	♟♟ 4
○ Langhe Bianche Cinerino '08	♟♟ 5
● Nebbiolo d'Alba Bricco Barone '07	♟♟ 4
● Langhe Rosso Zerosolfiti '08	♟ 6
● Dogliani Papà Celso '06	♟♟♟ 5
● Dogliani Papà Celso '05	♟♟♟ 4*
● Barbera d'Alba Rinaldi '06	♟♟ 4
● Barolo Pressenda '04	♟♟ 7

● Dogliani Maioli '07	♟♟ 4*
● Dolcetto di Dogliani Sorì dij But '08	♟♟ 4
● Langhe Nebbiolo '07	♟♟ 4*
● Langhe Rosso Cadò '07	♟♟ 5
● Langhe Dolcetto '08	♟ 3
● Dogliani Maioli '06	♟♟ 4*
● Dogliani San Bernardo '06	♟♟ 5
● Dolcetto di Dogliani Sorì dij But '07	♟♟ 4
● Langhe Nebbiolo '06	♟♟ 4
● Langhe Rosso Cadò '06	♟♟ 5

F.lli Abrigo

VIA MOGLIA GERLOTTO, 2
12055 DIANO D'ALBA [CN]
TEL. 017369104
www.abrigofratelli.com

CELLAR SALES
PRE-BOOKED VISITS

ANNUAL PRODUCTION **60,000 bottles**
HECTARES UNDER VINE **14**
VITICULTURE METHOD **Conventional**

We could sum up this influential Diano d'Alba estate by mentioning its two main guidelines: maximum definition when interpreting the territory of provenance in very expressive, convincingly original Dolcettos; and an absolutely competitive price list. This combination of factors ensures that the list of wines on offer constitutes a very valid reason for discovering Enrico and Mariarita's F.lli Abrigo operation.

The most convincing Dolcetto we tasted is the dense ruby '07 Vigna Pietrìn whose intense, stylish nose proffers superb fruit and a deliciously heady whiff of alcohol. Muscular and characterful in the mouth, it signs of with an impressively long finale. Equally valid is the Barbera La Galúpa '07. Its star-bright ruby frames plum-like aromatics lifted by cocoa powder and toastiness before the beefy palate reveals marked rusticity. Piasusa '07 is simpler and more fruit-themed, embodying the carefree spirit of the entire range.

Orlando Abrigo

VIA CAPPELLETTO, 5
12050 TREISO [CN]
TEL. 0173630232
www.orlandoabrigo.it

CELLAR SALES
PRE-BOOKED VISITS
VISITOR FACILITIES
FOOD

ANNUAL PRODUCTION **80,000 bottles**
HECTARES UNDER VINE **18**
VITICULTURE METHOD **Conventional**

The Abrigo family's lovely estate includes premium vineyards and a cosy farmstay, making it a must-visit stop for anyone seeking good wines with good personality at good prices. The elevation of some of the plots gives the wines their own uniquely personal tones and flavours. Reliability is the keynote of a convincing range that nicely reflects its territory of provenance.

The 2006 growing year was a successful one for the Barbarescos from Rocche Meruzzano. The excellent Vigna Rongalio selection layers subtle greens over tobacco, cocoa powder and red berry fruits, following this with close-knit tannins, compact texture and a reprise of those greens at the back. Rocche mingles ripe fruit with cinchona and cocoa powder before the powerful, clean palate fills the mouth, finishing long. Barbaresco Montersino is distinctly modern, a tad alcoholic and oaky but nonetheless pleasing. Finally, the youthful Barbera Vigna Roreto '07 mixes spiciness with black berry fruit before showing depth on the austere palate, backed up by alcohol and fleshy fruit.

● Barbera d'Alba La Galùpa '07	♙♙ 4*
● Barbera d'Alba Piasusa '07	♙♙ 3*
● Diano d'Alba Sup. V. Pietrìn '08	♙♙ 4
● Dolcetto di Diano d'Alba Intreccio '08	♙ 3
● Dolcetto di Diano d'Alba Rocche dei Berfi '08	♙ 3
○ Langhe Chardonnay Temp dër Fiù '08	♙ 3
● Barbera d'Alba La Galùpa '06	♙♙ 4
● Diano d'Alba Bric Tumlìn '07	♙♙ 3*
● Diano d'Alba Intreccio '07	♙♙ 3*
● Diano d'Alba Sup. V. Pietrìn '07	♙♙ 4*
● Langhe Rosso Tambuss '05	♙♙ 5

● Barbaresco Rocche Meruzzano V. Rongallo '06	♙♙ 7
● Barbaresco Montersino '06	♙♙ 7
● Barbaresco Rocche Meruzzano '06	♙♙ 6
● Barbera d'Alba V. Roreto '07	♙♙ 4*
○ Langhe Bianco D'Amblè '08	♙♙ 4
● Dolcetto d'Alba V. dell'Erto '08	♙ 4
○ Langhe Chardonnay Très '08	♙ 4
● Langhe Nebbiolo Settevie '07	♙ 5
● Barbaresco Montersino '05	♙♙ 6

Giulio Accornero e Figli

CA' CIMA, 1
15049 VIGNALE MONFERRATO [AL]
TEL. 0142933317
www.accornerovini.it

CELLAR SALES
PRE-BOOKED VISITS
VISITOR FACILITIES

ANNUAL PRODUCTION **100,000 bottles**
HECTARES UNDER VINE **22**
VITICULTURE METHOD **Naturale**

The accumulated experience of the Accornero family today totals more than 110 harvests and at least four generations who have succeeded each other in the vineyard, working with all the passion and effort that viticulture demands. Ca' Cima, the winery's headquarters, is a treasure trove of the Accorneros' experience plus the added value of a territory with outstanding wine soils and site climates. Take Girotondo. It's a Nebbiolo sourced from vines planted a few years ago and released in about 1,000 units. All the income from sales goes to the Associazione Massimo Accornero.

Top of this very successful line is the '06 Centenario, to which we awarded Three Glasses. An impenetrably dark ruby discloses balsam and fruitiness that herald a muscular yet beautifully balanced palate. Bricco Battista '06 is a lovely fruit-forward Barbera that gives rich pulpy flesh and plenty of length. Giulìn '07 is as good as ever, in fact its sensory profile as reliable as a Swiss watch. Bricco del Bosco '08 hails from an indifferent vintage for Grignolino but the Malvasia di Casorzo Brigantino and Barbera La Mattacchiona, both '08s, are among the best tasted in their respective categories.

● M.to Rosso Centenario '06	￥￥￥ 6
● Barbera del M.to Sup. Bricco Battista '06	￥￥ 6
● M.to Girotondo '07	￥￥ 6
● Barbera del M.to Giulìn '07	￥￥ 4*
● Barbera del M.to La Mattacchiona '08	￥￥ 4*
● Casorzo Brigantino '08	￥￥ 4
● Grignolino del M.to Casalese Bricco del Bosco '08	￥ 4
● Barbera del M.to Sup. Bricco Battista '04	￥￥￥ 6
● Barbera del M.to Giulìn '05	￥￥ 4*
● Barbera del M.to Sup. Bricco Battista '05	￥￥ 6
● M.to Rosso Centenario '05	￥￥ 6
● Monferrato Rosso Centenario '04	￥￥ 6
● Monferrato Rosso Centenario '03	￥￥ 6

Marco e Vittorio Adriano

FRAZ. SAN ROCCO SENO D'ELVIO, 13A
12051 ALBA [CN]
TEL. 0173362294
www.adrianovini.it

CELLAR SALES
PRE-BOOKED VISITS

ANNUAL PRODUCTION **90,000 bottles**
HECTARES UNDER VINE **20**
VITICULTURE METHOD **Conventional**

The cellar owned by brothers Marco and Vittorio Adriano has traded up to a full profile. It's a new operation run by young wine men. When their father finally hung up his pruning shears in 1994, the two brothers, who were still shy of 30, took over. Today, they and their wives manage an estate that has about 20 hectares under vine. Each year, they bottle an increasingly large proportion of their output and currently they release about 90,000 units. It's a traditional operation that plants most of Langhe's native varieties, which are picked at San Rocco Seno d'Elvio and Basarin di Neive.

The best of wines we tasted were the three Barbarescos. Sanadaive '06 is the most upfront, already offering good breadth of aromatics, full, fleshy pulp and a gratifyingly soft texture, although it stands out for its incredible length on the back palate. Basarin '06 is more reluctant and still needs time to evolve. The tannic weave unfolds slowly but steadily, lending the wine a feeling of austerity. In 2004, the cellar also made a Riserva di Basarin, which is similar to the standard version.

● Barbaresco Basarin '06	￥￥ 5*
● Barbaresco Sanadaive '06	￥￥ 5*
● Barbaresco Basarin Ris. '04	￥￥ 6
● Barbera d'Alba Sup. '07	￥￥ 4*
● Langhe Nebbiolo '07	￥￥ 4*
● Barbera d'Alba '08	￥ 4
● Dolcetto d'Alba '08	￥ 4
○ Langhe Bianco '08	￥ 4
● Barbaresco Basarin '05	￥￥ 6
● Barbaresco Sanadaive '05	￥￥ 6

Claudio Alario

VIA SANTA CROCE, 23
12055 DIANO D'ALBA [CN]
TEL. 0173231808
aziendaalario@tiscali.it

CELLAR SALES
PRE-BOOKED VISITS

ANNUAL PRODUCTION **40,000 bottles**
HECTARES UNDER VINE **10**
VITICULTURE METHOD **Conventional**

Claudio Alario confirms his status as a leading player in his territory and a sure-foodted exponent of the Diana approach to the dolcetto vine, with a profile that combines the characteristics of the Alba and Dogliani zones. Claudio's small plots at Serralunga and Verduno yield two very convincing Barolos, Sorano and Riva, which stand out for their sheer drinkability and innate harmony.

Barolo Sorano '05, from a vineyard about 300 metres above sea level at Diano and Serralunga, has breadth and classic elegance, evoking cinchona, liquorice and dried flowers before the juicy palate unveils its textbook length. All this earned it Three Glasses for the first time. The delicious Riva is a whisper more fruit-led and toastier. There's juicy flesh but oak is still perceptible. Barbera Valletta from the great 2007 vintage is superb, with nicely melded plums and oak in massive body. Best of all the fine Dolcettos is the '08 Costa Fiore, with its lovely dolcetto grape-derived fruit fusing with complex rain-soaked earth as the palate unfolds in a display of juicy power.

F.lli Alessandria

VIA B. VALFRÉ, 59
12060 VERDUNO [CN]
TEL. 0172470113
www.fratellialessandria.it

CELLAR SALES
PRE-BOOKED VISITS

ANNUAL PRODUCTION **60,000 bottles**
HECTARES UNDER VINE **12**
VITICULTURE METHOD **Conventional**

When people are reviewing the subzones of Barolo, they tend to regard the municipality of Verduno as a secondary area where the wines have distinctive aromatics but are less structured than bottles from Monforte or Serralunga. Nowadays, that running order is being challenged by Barolo lovers in search of wines with character, who are increasingly interested in products from this area. Credit for this goes to wineries like the Fratelli Alessandria operation, which has always seen tradition in an authoritative, contemporary perspective.

The line-up for our tasting this year was looking particularly good. On the '05 Barolo front, choose from the cinchona-laced balsam of Movigliero or the earthy sincerity of the San Lorenzo. But we thought that both Verduno selections were outperformed by a stunning Gramolere. Mulberry blossom, roses and medicinal herbs fuse into a classic Monforte aromatic profile before the palate shifts up a gear, bolstered by great thrust and supporting acidity to sign off with an endlessly long salt-veined finale. The performance is matched by the '05 Barolo and the '07 Langhe Nebbiolo Prinsiot.

Wine	Rating
● Barolo Sorano '05	♟♟♟ 8
● Diano d'Alba Costa Fiore '08	♟♟ 4*
● Barbera d'Alba Valletta '07	♟♟ 5
● Barolo Riva '05	♟♟ 7
● Diano d'Alba Montagrillo '08	♟♟ 4
● Diano d'Alba Praderunt Sup. '07	♟♟ 4
● Nebbiolo d'Alba Cascinotto '07	♟♟ 5
● Barolo Riva '01	♟♟ 7
● Barolo Riva '99	♟♟ 7
● Barolo Sorano '04	♟♟ 8

Wine	Rating
● Barolo Gramolere '05	♟♟♟+ 7
● Barolo Monvigliero '05	♟♟ 7
● Barolo S. Lorenzo '05	♟♟ 7
● Barolo '05	♟♟ 6
● Langhe Nebbiolo Prinsiot '07	♟♟ 4
● Barbera d'Alba '08	♟ 4
● Dolcetto d'Alba '08	♟ 4
● Verduno Pelaverga '08	♟ 4
● Barolo S. Lorenzo '04	♟♟ 7
● Barolo S. Lorenzo '01	♟♟ 7
● Barolo Monvigliero '04	♟♟ 7
● Barolo S. Lorenzo '03	♟♟ 7

★ Gianfranco Alessandria

LOC. MANZONI, 13
12065 MONFORTE D'ALBA [CN]
TEL. 017378576
www.gianfrancoalessandria.com

CELLAR SALES
PRE-BOOKED VISITS

ANNUAL PRODUCTION **35,000 bottles**
HECTARES UNDER VINE **7**
VITICULTURE METHOD **Conventional**

Gianfranco Alessandria has been running this influential winery at Monforte d'Alba for more than two decades. Over the years, he has performed with remarkable consistency. His style puts the accent on crisp aromas, whistle-clean flavours and considerable new oak without losing sight of the wine's bond with the territory. These are modern-style bottles that may reveal a certain element of oak in their youth but careful maturation in glass will absorb that.

There are attractive hints of liquorice and spice on the Barolo San Giovanni '05, which gives appealingly intense fine-grained tannins in the mouth. Slightly headier and less structured is the very good standard-label Barolo from the same vintage. Barbera Vittoria has picked up many international prizes and awards, conserving over the years its sensory profile of fruity fullness and mouthfilling texture laced with well-defined oak. The '07 edition adds juicy pulp and a delicious savouriness to the wine's traditional elegance.

● Barbera d'Alba Vittoria '07	TT	6
● Barbera d'Alba '08	TT	4
● Barolo '05	TT	7
● Barolo S. Giovanni '05	TT	8
● Dolcetto d'Alba '08	TT	4
● Langhe Nebbiolo '07	TT	5
● Langhe Rosso L'Insieme '06	TT	6
● Barbera d'Alba Vittoria '98	YYY	6
● Barbera d'Alba Vittoria '97	YYY	6
● Barbera d'Alba Vittoria '96	YYY	5
● Barolo '93	YYY	8
● Barolo S. Giovanni '04	YYY	8
● Barolo S. Giovanni '01	YYY	8
● Barolo S. Giovanni '00	YYY	8
● Barolo S. Giovanni '99	YYY	8
● Barolo S. Giovanni '98	YYY	8
● Barolo S. Giovanni '97	YYY	8

Marchesi Alfieri

P.ZZA ALFIERI, 28
14010 SAN MARTINO ALFIERI [AT]
TEL. 0141976015
www.marchesialfieri.it

CELLAR SALES
PRE-BOOKED VISITS
VISITOR FACILITIES

ANNUAL PRODUCTION **100,000 bottles**
HECTARES UNDER VINE **25**
VITICULTURE METHOD **Conventional**

Here in the municipality of San Martino Alfieri in the part of Monferrato that borders on Langhe, the San Martino di San Germano sisters' winery nestles in the hills that run down to the Tanaro river plain, based in an atmospheric converted baroque castle. Aided by skilled oenologist Mario Oliviero, Emanuela, Antonella and Giovanna have created a range of top-level traditional wines in various barbera-based styles.

The Alfiera was absent from the list, which brought the overall marks for Marchesi Alfieri down but they're still excellent. The very fine Barbera d'Asti La Tota '07 has a swath of incense, tobacco and blueberry aromatics laced with subtle liqueur fruits while the full, dense, velvet-smooth palate takes its leave with class. The nebbiolo-based Monferrato Rosso Costa Quaglia '06 has a wonderful raspberry-themed nose with hints of spices and tobacco, austerity in the mouth but also plenty of pulp and persistence. Piemonte Grignolino Sansoero '08 is vibrantly savoury while the Monferrato Rosso Sostegno '07 from barbera and pinot nero and the pinot nero-only San Germano '07 are well crafted.

● Barbera d'Asti La Tota '07	TT	4
● M.to Rosso Costa Quaglia '06	TT	5
● Piemonte Grignolino Sansoero '08	TT	4*
● M.to Rosso S. Germano '07	T	6
● M.to Rosso Sostegno '07	T	4
● Barbera d'Asti Sup. Alfiera '05	YYY	6
● Barbera d'Asti Sup. Alfiera '01	YYY	6
● Barbera d'Asti Sup. Alfiera '00	YYY	6
● Barbera d'Asti Sup. Alfiera '99	YYY	6
● Barbera d'Asti La Tota '06	YY	4*
● Barbera d'Asti La Tota '05	YY	4*
● Barbera d'Asti La Tota '04	YY	4*
● Barbera d'Asti Sup. Alfiera '06	YY	6

Giovanni Almondo

VIA SAN ROCCO, 26
12046 MONTÀ [CN]
TEL. 0173975256
www.giovannialmondo.com

CELLAR SALES
PRE-BOOKED VISITS

ANNUAL PRODUCTION **80,000 bottles**
HECTARES UNDER VINE **15**
VITICULTURE METHOD **Conventional**

Grower Domenico Almondo has worked hard to develop the potential of this territory. You can tell Domenico is, so to speak, a white man, from the vines in his vineyards, about half of which are planted to arneis, but his output embraces the entire range of Roero wines. The vines stand at elevations of 250 to 380 metres on sandy or limestone-based soil in favourable positions.

Domenico Almondo was back on our Three Glass list with Roero Bric Valdiana '07, confirming that he has earned a place in the exclusive club of world-standard Roero growers. Hugely complex aromatics of tobacco, raspberry and cinchona introduce power and fullness in the mouth. There's lots of juicy pulp but also lovely balance and a vibrantly long finale. We liked the markedly smoky Roero Giovanni Almondo Riserva '06, which follows up with fruit and spice fragrances, intensity, structure and perhaps a touch too much alcohol before signing off with a deep, appealing finish. Finally, an indifferent growing year means Roero Arneis Bricco delle Ciliegie '08 is pleasant enough but lacks grip.

★★ Elio Altare
Cascina Nuova

FRAZ. ANNUNZIATA, 51
12064 LA MORRA [CN]
TEL. 017350835
www.elioaltare.com

PRE-BOOKED VISITS

ANNUAL PRODUCTION **55,000 bottles**
HECTARES UNDER VINE **10**
VITICULTURE METHOD **Naturale**

In recent years, Elio has made clear his intention to start "being a pensioner" as soon as possible. We might even have believed him but then in early August 2008 he presented the fruits of his new wine venture in Cinque Terre. His La Morra cellar is given over exclusively to the production of red wines, crafted by rigorous, natural work in the vineyards and innovative methods in the cellar, where skin contact is particularly brief.

The 2008 wines reflect a growing year that was not great for early-ripening varieties. But the cellar's bankers were in another class. The marvellous Larigi '07 ran away with Three Glasses for its intense mint and spice, dense yet never heavy palate, depth and juicy fruit. Barbera doesn't get any better. Langhe Arborina '07 focuses on tobacco and raspberries, gives serious extract and a touch of savouriness on the finish. Villa '07 is a tad predictable and oaky. The '05 Barolo Vigneto Arborina has distinctly elegant fragrances, with a hint of heavier saddle leather, and shows complex in the mouth. We are waiting for the new '05 Barolo from the Cerretta vineyard at Serralunga.

● Roero Bric Valdiana '07	♟♟♟ 6
● Roero Giovanni Almondo Ris. '06	♟♟ 6
○ Roero Arneis Bricco delle Ciliegie '08	♟♟ 4*
● Barbera d'Alba Valbianchera '07	♟ 5
○ Roero Arneis V. Sparse '08	♟ 4
● Roero Bric Valdiana '03	♟♟♟ 6
● Roero Bric Valdiana '01	♟♟♟ 6
● Roero Bric Valdiana '00	♟♟♟ 6
● Barbera d'Alba Valbianchera '06	♟♟ 5
● Roero '06	♟♟ 5
○ Roero Arneis Bricco delle Ciliegie '07	♟♟ 4*
○ Roero Arneis V. Sparse '07	♟♟ 4
● Roero Bric Valdiana '06	♟♟ 6

● Langhe Larigi '07	♟♟♟ 8
● Barolo Vign. Arborina '05	♟♟ 8
● Langhe Arborina '07	♟♟ 8
● Barolo '05	♟♟ 7
● L'Insieme '07	♟♟ 7
● Langhe La Villa '07	♟♟ 8
● Langhe Nebbiolo '08	♟♟ 5
● Barbera d'Alba '08	♟ 5
● Dolcetto d'Alba '08	♟ 4
● Barolo Vign. Arborina '01	♟♟♟ 8
● Langhe La Villa '06	♟♟♟ 8
● Langhe La Villa '05	♟♟♟ 8
● Langhe Larigi '04	♟♟♟ 8

Antichi Vigneti di Cantalupo

VIA MICHELANGELO BUONARROTI, 5
28074 GHEMME [NO]
TEL. 0163840041
www.cantalupo.net

CELLAR SALES
PRE-BOOKED VISITS

ANNUAL PRODUCTION **200,000 bottles**
HECTARES UNDER VINE **35**
VITICULTURE METHOD **Conventional**

You just have to glance at the wealth of information available on the excellent winery web site to realize that Alberto Arlunno and his family are very much aware of the importance of Novara's history and uniqueness. Breclema, Carella, Livelli and Baraggiola are some of the vineyards around Ghemme where Antichi Vigneti di Cantalupo has plots. Most of the 35-hectare holding is planted to nebbiolo spanna, with a little vespolina, uva rara, greco, arneis and chardonnay.

Tautness, flavour and verticality. Ghemme '05 embodies all the most authentic characteristics of its morainic hills. Florality and iodine nuance barely ripe white-fleshed fruits and progression on the palate is direct, orchestrated by depth-enhancing acidity and stiffish tannins that still manage to expand into a surprisingly harmonious finish. Ghemme Collis Carellae '04 is stylistically similar, showing perhaps too austere and clenched on the nose. Finally, Ghemme Collis Breclemae and Ghemme Signore di Bayard did the best they could with the controversial '03 vintage.

Antico Borgo dei Cavalli

VIA DANTE, 54
28010 CAVALLIRIO [NO]
TEL. 016380115
www.vinibarbaglia.it

CELLAR SALES
PRE-BOOKED VISITS

ANNUAL PRODUCTION **20,000 bottles**
HECTARES UNDER VINE **3**
VITICULTURE METHOD **Conventional**

If the wines of northern Piedmont are making a serious comeback, it's mainly because there are wineries like Antico Borgo dei Cavalli. This small operation was set up in 1946 by Mario Barbaglia and today is run by his son Sergio and granddaughter Silvia. In years when the territory was heading in a very different direction, Antico Borgo dei Cavalli supported viticulture, and we should be grateful for this. That tenacity is now rewarded by the many wine lovers who love the classic range, which features nebbiolo, uva rara, croatina, vespolina and erbaluce.

The absence of a label as significant as Boca '05 is newsworthy but the rest of the line-up goes a long way to making up for it. The '06 Nebbiolo Il Silente is one of the finest versions ever. A little forward on the nose, it has plenty of energy in its depths of citrus peel, cinchona and saddle leather lifted by refreshing acidity. The erbaluce-based Bianco Lucino '08 is subtle yet incisive, revealing remarkably savoury progression. The Curticella Caballi Regis Brut, a classic method sparkler from erbaluce, may not be particularly long but it does have personality.

● Ghemme '05	♟♟♟ 5
● Ghemme Collis Carellae '04	♟♟ 6
○ Carolus '08	♟♟ 4
● Colline Novaresi Agamium '06	♟♟ 4
☉ Colline Novaresi Nebbiolo Il Mimo '08	♟♟ 4
● Ghemme Collis Breclemae '03	♟♟ 7
● Ghemme Signore di Bayard '03	♟♟ 6
● Colline Novaresi Primigenia '07	♟ 3
● Ghemme Collis Breclemae '00	♟♟♟ 7
● Ghemme Signore di Bayard '01	♟♟ 6

● Colline Novaresi Nebbiolo Il Silente '06	♟♟ 5
○ Colline Novaresi Bianco Lucino '08	♟♟ 4
● Colline Novaresi Croatina Gli Otri '08	♟ 4
● Colline Novaresi Vespolina Ledi '08	♟ 4
○ Curticella Caballi Regis Brut	♟ 5
● Boca '04	♟♟ 6
○ Colline Novaresi Bianco Lucino '07	♟♟ 4
● Colline Novaresi Uva Rara Lea '07	♟♟ 3*
● Colline Novaresi Vespolina Ledi '06	♟♟ 4
○ Curticella Caballi Regis Brut M. Cl. '05	♟♟ 5

Antoniolo

C.SO VALSESIA, 277
13045 GATTINARA [VC]
TEL. 0163833612
antoniolovini@bmm.it

CELLAR SALES
PRE-BOOKED VISITS

ANNUAL PRODUCTION **60,000 bottles**
HECTARES UNDER VINE **12**
VITICULTURE METHOD **Conventional**

Antoniolo's bottles contain the best of northern Piedmont's heritage. Hard-boned and only apparently lean, they can survive the decades while making all their greatness immediately obvious. These wines tell the ever-changing story of superb crus like San Francesco, Osso San Grato, Castelle and Borelle, as well as the efforts of a family that always been involved in viticulture and wine. Rosanna is a legend around here; her children Alberto and Lorella are well on the way to acquiring the same status.

This year's offerings are simply fantastic. We'll start with the '05 Gattinara, a standard-label wine with every detail in place and off the scale for drinkability. Next up is San Francesco, which after 12 months in barrique and 18 in large wood raises the bar even higher with its power and spicy length. Just when we thought we had hit the heights, an Osso San Grato left us speechless. It was the '05, a vintage that has established its claim as one of the greatest ever. Medicinal herbs, rust and clear fruit frame a physique as lean and explosive as Bruce Lee, and a killer instinct worthy of Eddy Merckx. Terrifyingly good.

Anzivino

C.SO VALSESIA, 162
13045 GATTINARA [VC]
TEL. 0163827172
www.anzivino.it

CELLAR SALES
PRE-BOOKED VISITS
FOOD

ANNUAL PRODUCTION **90,000 bottles**
HECTARES UNDER VINE **11**
VITICULTURE METHOD **Conventional**

A superb synthesis of historic memory and modern sensitivity has projected Emanuele and Alessandro Anzivino's cellar into northern Piedmont's wine elite. In the late 1990s, they moved from Milan to Gattinara to restructure an old distillery near the town centre. It was the start of an adventure that now embraces innovative wines like Nemesi, a blend of nebbiolo, merlot and syrah, Faticato, from rack-dried nebbiolo, and other more traditional nebbiolo-based wines, some in blends with croatina, vespolina or bonarda.

This year, there was no Gattinara Riserva '04, which we did taste out of the barrel, but the rest of the range performed very well indeed. The very good, very affordable Bramaterra '05 came within an ace of a third Glass, drinking slightly short on the finish after unfurling a swath of Mediterranean scrubland, citrus and iodine. Coste della Sesia Rosso Faticato '05 is a truly elegant example of a dried-grape Nebbiolo, giving rose petals, sour cherry cream, candied peel and a seamless palate that behaves impeccably. The '05 Gattinara is uncomplicated but juicily flavoursome.

● Gattinara Vign. Osso S. Grato '05	♙♙♙+	7
● Gattinara Vign. S. Francesco '05	♙♙♙	7
● Gattinara '05	♙♙	6
☉ Coste della Sesia Rosato Bricco Lorella '08	♙	4
○ Erbaluce di Caluso '08	♙	4
● Gattinara Vign. Castelle '00	♟♟♟	7
● Gattinara Vign. Castelle '99	♟♟♟	7
● Gattinara Vign. Osso S. Grato '04	♟♟♟	7
● Gattinara Vign. Osso S. Grato '01	♟♟♟	7
● Gattinara Vign. S. Francesco '03	♟♟♟	7
● Gattinara Vign. S. Francesco '01	♟♟♟	6

● Bramaterra '05	♙	4
● Coste della Sesia Faticato '05	♙	6
● Gattinara '05	♙♙	5
● Coste della Sesia Il Tarlo '07	♙	4
● Nemesi '08	♙	3
● Bramaterra '03	♟♟	5*
● Gattinara '04	♟♟	5
● Gattinara Ris. '03	♟♟	6

Araldica Vini Piemontesi

V.LE LAUDANO, 2
14040 CASTEL BOGLIONE [AT]
TEL. 014176311
www.araldicavini.com

CELLAR SALES
PRE-BOOKED VISITS

ANNUAL PRODUCTION **6,000,000 bottles**
HECTARES UNDER VINE **900**
VITICULTURE METHOD **Conventional**

The estate's 900 hectares enable it to pick and choose from southern Piedmont's wine types but the heart of the range is Barbera d'Asti among the reds and Gavi for whites. The quality project launched during the 1990s forges ahead. Results are coming through particularly in the product line for the off-trade, as you can see in the table below, which renders due homage to the excellent team of estate agronomists and oenologists.

The most famous product on the list, the Barbera d'Asti D'Annona from the wonderful 2007 vintage, came very close to top honours. Its sophisticated, intense nose has plenty of personality thanks to aromatics that range from tobacco to sour cherries. The seriously good, fresh-tasting palate reveals the true quality of the original grapes. A recent acquisition, the stupendous Battistina estate, produced two absolutely typical '08 Gavis with crisp fragrances and a pleasingly fresh palate. The Roero Arneis '08 is straightforward.

L'Armangia

FRAZ. SAN GIOVANNI, 122
14053 CANELLI [AT]
TEL. 0141824947
www.armangia.it

CELLAR SALES
PRE-BOOKED VISITS

ANNUAL PRODUCTION **78,000 bottles**
HECTARES UNDER VINE **9.35**
VITICULTURE METHOD **Conventional**

Founded in 1988, Armangia has been run since 1993 by the go-ahead, highly competent grower Ignazio Giovine. Over the years, Ignazio has created a wide range of excellent wines. His approach hinges on promoting the territory, with the accent on meticulous vineyard management. The varieties planted are both native, like barbera and moscato, and internationals such as sauvignon and chardonnay, which perform very well here in 30-year-old plantings.

Barbera d'Asti Sopra Berruti '08 is a splendid current release. Its concentrated aromatics range from rain-soaked earth to sour cherry while the vibrantly savoury palate is held up through the finish by delicious acidity. An example to others. The '06 Robi & Robi from overripe chardonnay tempts with dried apricot fragrances and a deep, full palate whose finish is perhaps a whisper too sweet for its acidity but which does have plenty of length. The minerally, slightly spicy Piemonte Chardonnay Pratorotondo '07 tempts with its bitterish finish, the sauvignon Monferrato Bianco EnneEnne '07 is vibrantly complex and the Moscato d'Asti Il Giai '08 is clean and fragrant.

● Barbera d'Asti Sup. D'Annona '07	♥♥ 4*
● Barbera d'Asti Sup. Rive '07	♥♥ 4
○ Gavi Bricco Battistina '08	♥♥ 4
○ Gavi La Battistina '08	♥♥ 4*
○ Roero Arneis Sorilaria '08	♥ 4
● Barbera d'Asti Sup. Rive '06	♡♡ 4*
○ Gavi La Battistina '07	♡♡ 4*

● Barbera d'Asti Sopra Berruti '08	♥♥ 3*
○ Robi & Robi '06	♥♥ 4
○ M.to Bianco EnneEnne '07	♥ 3
○ Moscato d'Asti Il Giai '08	♥ 3
○ Piemonte Chardonnay Pratorotondo '07	♥ 3
● Barbera d'Asti Sopra Berruti '07	♡♡ 3
● Barbera d'Asti Sup. Nizza Titon '06	♡♡ 4
● Barbera d'Asti Sup. Nizza Titon '04	♡♡ 4
○ Mesicaseu '07	♡♡ 4

Ascheri

VIA PIUMATI, 23
12042 BRA [CN]
TEL. 0172412394
www.ascherivini.it

CELLAR SALES
PRE-BOOKED VISITS
VISITOR FACILITIES
FOOD

ANNUAL PRODUCTION **240,000 bottles**
HECTARES UNDER VINE **40**
VITICULTURE METHOD **Conventional**

Wine lovers and other visitors to the Ascheri family winery are greeted by a sort of large sailing vessel. A short distance from the centre of Bra, the estate also embraces the Muri Vecchi eatery and a delightful hotel but the whole enterprise hinges on Langhe wines interpreted with an idiosyncratic mix of tradition and innovation. The 40 hectares are in three districts: the Sorano estate at Serralunga, Rivalta, on the border between La Morra and Verduno, and Montelupa, the hill where the Ascheris grow their syrah and viognier.

This time, the wines presented were perhaps not at their best. The '05 vintage produced no Barolo Sorano Coste & Bricco, Barolo Sorano or Langhe Rosso Montelupa so attention focused on Barolo Vigna dei Pola. We tasted it just after it went into bottle and thought it would benefit from further maturation in glass to bring out the full harmony its considerable power. From the rest of the range, we loved the Nebbiolo d'Alba Bricco San Giacomo '07 but the Dolcetto d'Alba Nirane '08 is a tad lean.

Paolo Avezza

REG. MONFORTE, 62
14053 CANELLI [AT]
TEL. 0141822296
www.paoloavezza.com

CELLAR SALES
PRE-BOOKED VISITS

ANNUAL PRODUCTION **20,000 bottles**
HECTARES UNDER VINE **7**
VITICULTURE METHOD **Conventional**

As is so often the case around here, this is a family winery with a heritage passed down over the years but which has only recently, in the third generation, moved over to quality-driven wines. The estate comprises just seven hectares, planted to barbera, dolcetto, nebbiolo, pinot nero, chardonnay and moscato, that yield traditional wines and one or two more international-style Monferrato.

What earned the Avezzas a profile in the Guide was a series of excellent Barberas. Barbera d'Asti Superiore Nizza Sotto la Muda '06 was one of the best we tasted this year and in fact we sent it on to the national finals. Dark ruby with superbly complex aromatics ranging from red berry fruits to cinchona, tobacco and cinnamon, it satisfies in the mouth with its fullness while maintaining the type's classic controlled austerity. The complex, earthy Barbera d'Asti '07 is also excellent with its well-defined cherry and cocoa powder, and a crisp, nicely weighted finish. Over the next few years, we look forward to seeing the rest of the range performing at the same level.

● Barolo '05	♟♟	6
● Barolo V. dei Pola '05	♟♟	6
● Nebbiolo d'Alba Bricco S. Giacomo '07	♟♟	4
● Barbera d'Alba Fontanelle '08	♟	4
● Dolcetto d'Alba Nirane '08	♟	4
● Dolcetto d'Alba S. Rocco '08	♟	4
○ Langhe Arneis Cristina Ascheri '08	♟	4
○ Langhe Bianco Montalupa '07	♟	5
● Barolo Sorano '00	♟♟♟	6*
● Barolo Sorano '03	♟♟	6*
● Barolo Sorano '01	♟♟	6*
● Barolo Sorano Coste & Bricco '04	♟♟	7

● Barbera d'Asti Nizza Sotto la Muda '06	♟♟	5*
● Barbera d'Asti '07	♟♟	3*

Azelia

FRAZ. GARBELLETTO
VIA ALBA-BAROLO, 53
12060 CASTIGLIONE FALLETTO [CN]
TEL. 017362859
l.scavino@azelia.it

CELLAR SALES
PRE-BOOKED VISITS

ANNUAL PRODUCTION 52,000 bottles
HECTARES UNDER VINE 12
VITICULTURE METHOD Conventional

We think it's safe to say that Luigi Scavino's family winery is well on its way to the front rank of winemaking. The wines have enviable balance, oak is used with increasingly impressive skill and the quality of the fruit is faultless. With 15-year-old Lorenzo already finding his feet in the cellar, Luigi has ensured continuity for the future. We are very pleased to express our admiration for this calm, skilled winemaker.

The '05 Barolos leave you spoilt for choice. Bricco Fiasco is supremely elegant, with an agile, florality-led nose and a beautifully gauged palate. There's power and depth in the youthful, austere and very long San Rocco, with its stunning tobacco and spice-laced damp earth aromatics. And the vibrant-hued Margheria proffers saddle leather and raspberries to introduce a stupendously juicy palate with fireworks on the finish. In other words, a line-up of Barolos like this is every connoisseur's dream. There simply isn't enough space to describe the whole range but everything here is good, balanced and wonderfully drinkable.

Antonio Baldizzone Cascina Lana

c.so ACQUI, 187
14049 NIZZA MONFERRATO [AT]
TEL. 0141726734

CELLAR SALES

ANNUAL PRODUCTION 60,000 bottles
HECTARES UNDER VINE 18
VITICULTURE METHOD Conventional

Antonio Baldizzone and his wife Graziana Rizzoli run an operation that in recent years has become a landmark on the lively Asti wine scene. Cascina Lana has some of the finest vineyards in the area, which enjoy perfect locations on the border of the municipalities of Nizza Monferrato and Acqui Terme. The wines they yield are as good as you would expect from such great sites and faithfully reflect both provenance and variety.

As we wait for the new vintage of Nizza to mature, we very much enjoyed the Barbera d'Asti l'Anniversario '07. Inky dark, it still has hints of oak mingling with the cinchona and incense aromatics that give to plum and cocoa powder, while the palate's power and fruitiness sign off unhurriedly on spiciness. The '08 Barbera d'Asti La Cirimela is a fine example of a current Barbera with its black cherries and plums over earthier notes and a close-knit mouthfeel that takes its leave on lingering tones of dense, ripe fruit. The coffee and cinchona Monferrato Rosso Vën ëd Michen '07 is uncomplicated but attractively fresh-tasting.

Wine	Rating
● Barbera d'Alba Vign. Punta '07	⟐⟐ 5
● Barolo Bricco Fiasco '05	⟐⟐ 8
● Barolo Margheria '05	⟐⟐ 8
● Barolo S. Rocco '05	⟐⟐ 7
● Barolo '05	⟐⟐ 7
● Dolcetto d'Alba Bricco dell'Oriolo '08	⟐⟐ 4
● Langhe Nebbiolo '08	⟐ 4
● Barolo '91	⟐⟐⟐ 8
● Barolo Bricco Fiasco '01	⟐⟐⟐ 8
● Barolo Bricco Fiasco '96	⟐⟐⟐ 8
● Barolo Bricco Fiasco '95	⟐⟐⟐ 8
● Barolo Bricco Fiasco '93	⟐⟐⟐ 8
● Barolo S. Rocco '99	⟐⟐⟐ 8
● Barolo Voghera Brea Ris. '01	⟐⟐⟐ 8

Wine	Rating
● Barbera d'Asti l'Anniversario '07	⟐⟐ 5
● Barbera d'Asti La Cirimela '08	⟐⟐ 3*
● M.to Rosso Vën ëd Michen '07	⟐ 5
● Barbera d'Asti La Cirimela '07	⟐⟐ 3*
● Barbera d'Asti Sup. Nizza '06	⟐⟐ 5
● Barbera d'Asti Sup. Nizza '05	⟐⟐ 5
● Barbera d'Asti Sup. Nizza '04	⟐⟐ 5
● Barbera d'Asti Sup. Nizza '01	⟐⟐ 5
● M.to Rosso Vën ëd Michen '06	⟐⟐ 5
● M.to Rosso Vën ëd Michen '05	⟐⟐ 5

★ Produttori del Barbaresco

VIA TORINO, 54
12050 BARBARESCO [CN]
TEL. 0173635139
www.produttoridelbarbaresco.com

CELLAR SALES
PRE-BOOKED VISITS
VISITOR FACILITIES

ANNUAL PRODUCTION **420,000 bottles**
HECTARES UNDER VINE **110**
VITICULTURE METHOD **Conventional**

Founded in 1958 and inspired by the story of the co-operative set up by Domizio Cavazza in 1894, Produttori del Barbaresco today has more than 100 hectares planted to nebbiolo and tended by its 56 members. Half a century of unremitting success has been driven by the ageing capacity of the various Barbaresco Riservas and a pricing policy that is very much in the consumer's favour. The only wines are Nebbiolo and Barbaresco, from prolonged skin contact and maturation in large wood. This is pure, classic Barbaresco that spurns passing fashions.

Expectations were high for the '04 Riservas for the growing year was excellent. The Produttori made the best of the opportunity, releasing solidly structured wines with pleasing acidity and excellent cellar prospects. We do not have the space to describe all the selections but we feel obliged to point out that the great Asili and Rabajà crus, as well as the superlative Montestefano, perform even better than they have on other occasions. We also suggest you investigate the very fine Riserva wines from Rio Sordo and Pora.

★ Cascina La Barbatella

S.DA ANNUNZIATA, 55
14049 NIZZA MONFERRATO [AT]
TEL. 0141701434
sonvico.barbatella@libero.it

CELLAR SALES
PRE-BOOKED VISITS

ANNUAL PRODUCTION **22,000 bottles**
HECTARES UNDER VINE **4**
VITICULTURE METHOD **Conventional**

Since its foundation in 1982, La Barbatella has become a regular Three Glass winner and a shrine to quality. Angelo Sonvico, with help from Giuliano Noè and Beppe Rattazzo, has been making outstandingly elegant wines that add lustre to the whole of Asti's production. He has done so by focusing unswervingly on quality, keeping production low – he releases about 20,000 bottles a year – and coaxing the best out of the vineyards that stand around his winery in some of the loveliest wine country at Nizza Monferrato.

Three Glasses duly went to the '06 Monferrato Rosso Sonvico, a blend of equal parts of barbera and cabernet sauvignon that year after year confirms Angelo's intuition. Cinchona, pepper and fruit precede a vibrant, juicy palate with a long, elegant finale. Also in our final was the '06 Barbera d'Asti Superiore Nizza Vigna dell'Angelo, still closed on the truffle-led nose and showing power and close-knit tannins on the palate, while the '08 Barbera d'Asti La Barbatella is nicely acidic, flaunting cinchona, tobacco, earthiness and black cherries. We will close with the Monferrato Bianco Noè '08, a 70-30 blend of cortese and sauvignon with plenty of structure and tropical fruit tones.

● Barbaresco Vign. in Montestefano Ris. '04	♟♟♟	6*
● Barbaresco Vigneti in Asili Ris. '04	♟♟	7
● Barbaresco Vigneti in Pora Ris. '04	♟♟	7
● Barbaresco Vigneti in Rabajà Ris. '04	♟♟	7
● Barbaresco Vigneti in Rio Sordo Ris. '04	♟♟	7
● Barbaresco '05	♟♟	6
● Barbaresco Vign. in Moccagatta Ris. '04	♟♟	7
● Barbaresco Vigneti in Montefico Ris. '04	♟♟	7
● Barbaresco Vigneti in Ovello Ris. '04	♟♟	7
● Barbaresco Vigneti in Pajé Ris. '04	♟♟	7
● Langhe Nebbiolo '07	♟♟	4
● Barbaresco Vign. in Montestefano Ris. '01	♕♕♕	6
● Barbaresco Vign. in Pajé Ris. '01	♕♕♕	6*
● Barbaresco Vign. in Rio Sordo Ris. '01	♕♕♕	6*

● M.to Rosso Sonvico '06	♟♟♟	6
● Barbera d'Asti Sup. Nizza V. dell'Angelo '06	♟♟	6
● Barbera d'Asti La Barbatella '08	♟♟	4
○ M.to Bianco Noè '08	♟	4
● Barbera d'Asti Sup. Nizza V. dell'Angelo '01	♕♕♕	7
● Barbera d'Asti Sup. V. dell'Angelo '98	♕♕♕	7
● Barbera d'Asti Sup. V. dell'Angelo '96	♕♕♕	7
● La Vigna di Sonvico '96	♕♕♕	7
● La Vigna di Sonvico '95	♕♕♕	7
● M.to Rosso Mystère '01	♕♕♕	7
● M.to Rosso Sonvico '04	♕♕♕	6
● M.to Rosso Sonvico '03	♕♕♕	7
● M.to Rosso Sonvico '00	♕♕♕	7
● M.to Rosso Sonvico '98	♕♕♕	7
● M.to Rosso Sonvico '97	♕♕♕	7

Cascina Barisél

REG. SAN GIOVANNI, 30
14053 CANELLI [AT]
TEL. 0141824848
www.barisel.it

CELLAR SALES
PRE-BOOKED VISITS

ANNUAL PRODUCTION 35,000 bottles
HECTARES UNDER VINE 4
VITICULTURE METHOD Naturale

Just outside Canelli is the lovely Barisél farmhouse, nestling among a few hectares of vines. Since 1965, it has been run by the Penna family, which opted for nature-friendly viticulture and the typical native wines of the territory, with a particular regard for Moscato. Well-aspected vineyards, limestone-based soil and low cropping levels contribute to the quality of the wines.

This year wasn't a brilliant one for Cascina Barisél but it was still pretty good, as the '06 Barbera d'Asti Superiore La Cappelletta shows with its intense fragrances, distinct spiciness and balanced fruit. The modern palate has lots of power, extract and alcohol, nicely offset by acidity. The fragrant '08 Moscato d'Asti is good, its classic citrus weaving into notes of prickly pear in a very agreeable whole. We also like the low-run L'Avìja '07, an overripe, botrytis-laced Moscato that is not terribly complex but has great fruit, and the '07 Barbera d'Asti for its red berry fruits and cinchona preceding a well-made but smallish.

Batasiolo

FRAZ. ANNUNZIATA, 87
12064 LA MORRA [CN]
TEL. 017350130
www.batasiolo.com

PRE-BOOKED VISITS

ANNUAL PRODUCTION 2.500,000 bottles
HECTARES UNDER VINE 107
VITICULTURE METHOD Conventional

This major, very typical Piedmont operation is run by the Dogliani family. Over the years, they have shown they can maintain quality at production levels that are unusually high for this part of the world, proof that even complex varieties like nebbiolo, when produced on a very large scale, can yield results comparable to those from the best small wineries. Obviously, those results are not restricted to Barolo. The range is wide, from classic method sparklers to Moscato, and caters for all palates in Italy and abroad.

The '05 Barolos brought home the bacon, winning Three Glasses for Batasiolo after 15 years thanks to a Barolo Boscareto from Serralunga that is as well structured as it is refined. A classic, balsamic nose leads into a concentrated palate with balanced extract and great length. The equally elegant Cerequio is only a whisper less pulpy. Although its tannins are less balanced, the Bofani is another winner and the standard Barolo is pleasingly well crafted. Barbera Sovrana '07 is rather rustic and a little hard but the rest of the range isn't as good as usual.

● Barbera d'Asti Sup. La Cappelletta '06	♥♥	5
○ Moscato d'Asti '08	♥♥	4*
● Barbera d'Asti '07	♥	4
○ L'Avìja '07	♥	5
● Barbera d'Asti Barisél '06	♀♀	4
● Barbera d'Asti Sup. La Cappelletta '05	♀♀	5
○ Enrico Penna Brut '04	♀♀	4
○ L'Avìja '06	♀♀	5
○ Moscato d'Asti '07	♀♀	4

● Barolo Boscareto '05	♥♥♥	8
● Barolo Cerequio '05	♥♥	8
● Barolo '05	♥♥	7
● Barolo Bofani '05	♥♥	8
○ Piemonte Moscato Passito Muscatel Tardì '07	♥♥	6
● Barbaresco '06	♥	6
● Barbera d'Alba Sovrana '07	♥	5
● Barbera d'Asti Sabri '07	♥	4
● Dolcetto d'Alba Bricco di Vergne '08	♥	4
○ Gavi del Comune di Gavi Granée '08	♥	4
○ Langhe Chardonnay Serbato '08	♥	4
○ Moscato d'Asti Bosc dla Rei '08	♥	4
○ Spumante Dosage Zéro '05	♥	5
● Barolo Cerequio '04	♀♀	8
● Barolo Cerequio '01	♀♀	8

Fabrizio Battaglino

LOC. BORGONUOVO
VIA MONTALDO ROERO, 44
12040 VEZZA D'ALBA [CN]
TEL. 0173658156
www.battaglino.com

CELLAR SALES
PRE-BOOKED VISITS

ANNUAL PRODUCTION **17,000 bottles**
HECTARES UNDER VINE **4**
VITICULTURE METHOD **Conventional**

This Roero winery's few hectares are in the hills at La Colla and Mombello on south west-facing sandy soils. Nebbiolo, barbera and arneis are the grapes that go into the range of classic wines from the area. Managing Battaglino is Fabrizio, who keeps up the family winemaking tradition with notable passion.

Fabrizio had a very good year and skipped straight into a full Guide profile with a brilliant range of wines. First up is a subtly complex '06 Roero with nice cinchona and dried flowers followed up by a powerful, full-bodied palate whose tannins are a little over-assertive but with plenty of juicy fruit and marvellous length. The rest of the range is admirable. Barbera d'Alba Vigna Munbèl '06 gives tobacco and black cherries, with a well-gauged wash of spice, deep, savoury palate and a well-sustained finish. The '08 Roero Arneis is attractive, showing spring flowers, and the Langhe Rosso Ancreus '06 is complex, muscular and laced with cinchona, liquorice and tobacco.

Luigi Baudana

FRAZ. BAUDANA, 43
12050 SERRALUNGA D'ALBA [CN]
TEL. 0173613354
www.baudanaluigi.com

CELLAR SALES
PRE-BOOKED VISITS

ANNUAL PRODUCTION **25,000 bottles**
HECTARES UNDER VINE **4.5**
VITICULTURE METHOD **Conventional**

This small estate has been in the Guide since 1999. It has been run very successfully by Luigi Baudana and his wife Fiorina, who have had to take a very painful decision. They are giving up wine, selling part of the operation and leasing the cellar and vineyards to Barolo-based G.D. Vajra. It's a decision that saddens us, both because of the very high quality of the wines and because it means one fewer of the small wineries that have represented the Langhe territory so well.

This year, the Baudanas presented three '05 Barolos. The very traditional standard wine discloses earthy fragrances, robust extract, good structure and a long finish. The Cerretta is minerally and powerful, the finish still redolent of oak. Finally, the Baudana is distinctly oaky and still over-assertive on a palate with a sweet vanillaed finish. The florality-themed '08 Chardonnay is fresh on both nose and palate

Wine	Rating
● Roero '06	♈♈ 4*
● Barbera d'Alba V. Munbèl '06	♈♈ 4*
● Langhe Rosso Ancreus '06	♈♈ 4*
● Nebbiolo d'Alba V. Colla '06	♈♈ 4*
○ Roero Arneis '08	♈♈ 3*
● Nebbiolo d'Alba '06	♈ 4

Wine	Rating
● Barolo '05	♈♈ 6
● Barolo Baudana '05	♈♈ 7
● Barolo Cerretta Piani '05	♈♈ 7
○ Langhe Chardonnay '08	♈ 4
● Barbera d'Alba Donatella '06	♈♈ 5
● Barbera d'Alba Donatella '05	♈♈ 5
● Barolo Baudana '04	♈♈ 7
● Barolo Baudana '01	♈♈ 7
● Barolo Cerretta Piani '04	♈♈ 7
● Dolcetto d'Alba Baudana '06	♈♈ 4
● Langhe Rosso Lorenso '05	♈♈ 5

Bava

S.DA MONFERRATO, 2
14023 COCCONATO [AT]
TEL. 0141907083
www.bava.com

CELLAR SALES
PRE-BOOKED VISITS

ANNUAL PRODUCTION **500,000 bottles**
HECTARES UNDER VINE **60**
VITICULTURE METHOD **Conventional**

The new generation of the Bava family forges successfully ahead along the route mapped out by this influential, long-standing Piedmont wine estate. Its dynamic production combines premium still and sparkling wines, all released with great attention to value for money. Carefully targeted events and promotions of undisputed interest to those in the wine sector are very much part of Bava's programme.

Sadly, this edition of the Guide offers little in the way of serious satisfaction for the family as we were unable to taste most of the cellar's flagship bottles, such as the Alta Langa sparklers or the Piano Alto and Stradivario Barbera Superiore wines. It was a context in which the '04 Barolo Scarrone stood out. The ruby already shading into garnet proffers nut-led fragrances accompanied by pleasing sweet spice. A slight mouth-drying palate signs off with a cinnamon-edged finish. Libera '07 plays its part as a ready-to-drink Barbera very well, following elegant red berry fruit with nicely poised progression.

Bel Colle

FRAZ. CASTAGNI, 56
12060 VERDUNO [CN]
TEL. 0172470196
www.belcolle.it

CELLAR SALES
PRE-BOOKED VISITS

ANNUAL PRODUCTION **150,000 bottles**
HECTARES UNDER VINE **10**
VITICULTURE METHOD **Conventional**

Bel Colle is a long-established Piedmont winery that releases Langhe and Roero wines. It has always made reliability and consistency its watchwords. Pelaverga, the distinctive local variety of Verduno, is joined in the very complete, attractively styled range by serious Barolo and Barbaresco reds and whites like Arneis and Favorita that seduce with their smooth, balanced palates. We would also point out that the Bava pricing policy is consumer-friendly. Behind this success are oenologist Paolo Torchio and his team.

We are happy to report that a Bel Colle Barolo went through to the finals. Given the changes of the past few years, it is easy to see why a subtle yet deep wine that whispers rather than cries, came close to a top award this year. The quality of the '05 Monvigliero was confirmed by a retasting of the '04 and we look forward to the release next year of the Riserva. The equally subtle Barbaresco Roncaglie '06 is a swath of dried roses and liquorice, with barely hinted at fruit and pulp taking nothing away from the purity of its tannic weave.

● Barbera d'Asti Libera '07	🍷🍷	4*
● Barolo Scarrone '04	🍷🍷	7
● Malvasia di Castelnuovo Don Bosco Rosetta '08	🍷	4
○ Moscato d'Asti Bass Tuba '08	🍷	4
○ Piemonte Chardonnay Thou Bianc '08	🍷	4
○ Alta Langa Brut Bianc 'd Bianc Giulio Cocchi '04	🏆	6
☉ Alta Langa Brut Rösa Giulio Cocchi '04	🏆	6
☉ Alta Langa Brut Rösa Giulio Cocchi '04	🏆	6
○ Alta Langa Brut Toto Corde Giulio Cocchi '05	🏆	5
● Barbera d'Asti Libera '06	🏆	4*
● Barbera d'Asti Sup. Nizza Piano Alto '03	🏆	6
● Barbera d'Asti Sup. Stradivario '03	🏆	7

● Barbaresco Roncaglie '06	🍷🍷	6
● Barolo Monvigliero '05	🍷🍷	6
● Barbera d'Alba Ape Reale '07	🍷🍷	5
● Dolcetto d'Alba Borgo Castagni '08	🍷	4
○ Roero Arneis '08	🍷	4
● Verduno Pelaverga '08	🍷	4
● Barbaresco Roncaglie '05	🏆	6
● Barbaresco Roncaglie '04	🏆	6
● Barbera d'Alba Le Masche '06	🏆	4*
● Barolo Boscato '04	🏆	6
● Barolo Boscato '03	🏆	6
● Barolo Monvigliero '04	🏆	6
● Barolo Monvigliero '03	🏆	7

Benotto

VIA SAN CARLO, 52
14055 COSTIGLIOLE D'ASTI [AT]
TEL. 0141966406
www.benottovini.it

CELLAR SALES
PRE-BOOKED VISITS

ANNUAL PRODUCTION **50,000 bottles**
HECTARES UNDER VINE **15**
VITICULTURE METHOD **Conventional**

Benotto is a small winery founded in the early 20th century and run today by the third generation of the family. Carlo Benotto focuses on making wines from the Asti tradition, understandably enough paying special attention to Barbera, and has replanted the almost entirely neglected gamba di pernice variety. Nebbiolo, dolcetto, arneis and cortese make up the rest of the vine stock.

This Barberas enabled the Benottos to get back into the main section of the Guide. Barbera d'Asti Rupestris '05 has depth on its traditional nose of liqueur cherries and cinchona, showing intricate complexity, density and length while avoiding any sensation of heaviness. Barbera d'Asti Superiore Vigneto Casot '05 gives cinchona and toasty oak laced with fruit plus power and fullness on a palate that is nevertheless austere with a long, well-orchestrated finish. Finally, Barbera d'Asti Superiore Balau '05 gives fresh red berry fruit over tobacco and cinchona before the three-dimensional palate unveils depth, character and plenty of alcohol.

Bera

VIA CASTELLERO, 12
12050 NEVIGLIE [CN]
TEL. 0173630194
www.bera.it

CELLAR SALES
PRE-BOOKED VISITS

ANNUAL PRODUCTION **120,000 bottles**
HECTARES UNDER VINE **20**
VITICULTURE METHOD **Conventional**

This exciting, versatile winery is confidently run by Walter Bera, who makes everything from reliable Moscatos to seriously good reds like Barbaresco and Barbera without a dip in quality anywhere in the range. Prices are extremely competitive making the whole line-up tempting. Serious skill and reliability in a sector as overcrowded and consistency-attentive as wine are excellent credentials and a guarantee for the consumer.

Langhe Sassisto '06 from barbera, nebbiolo and merlot has character and an intense nose that suggests black berry fruits, cinchona and oak before the full, dense mouthfeel exudes pleasurable sensations even though there's an underlying hint of huskiness. The attractive Barbera d'Alba La Lena '06 is an almost impenetrable ruby framing the intense nose of ripe fruit and sweet spice, assertive power in the mouth and an unhurriedly fresh finish. From the Moscatos, we enjoyed the good, fresh-tasting Su Reimond '08 themed around peaches and mint. The appealing standard label is a shade lighter but equally drinkable.

● Barbera d'Asti Sup. Balau '05	♟♟ 4*
● Barbera d'Asti Sup. Rupestris '05	♟♟ 5
● Barbera d'Asti Sup. Vign. Casot '05	♟♟ 4*
● Monferrato Rosso Nebieul '06	♟ 3
● Barbera d'Asti '06	♟♟ 3*
● Barbera d'Asti Sup. Vign. Casot '04	♟♟ 3*
● Monferrato Rosso Nebieul '04	♟♟ 5

● Barbera d'Alba Sup. La Lena '06	♟♟ 4*
● Langhe Sassisto '06	♟♟ 5
○ Moscato d'Asti '08	♟♟ 4
○ Moscato d'Asti Su Reimond '08	♟♟ 4
○ Asti '08	♟ 4
○ Asti '07	♟♟ 4*
● Barbaresco '04	♟♟ 5
● Barbera d'Alba Sup. La Lena '05	♟♟ 4
● Langhe Sassisto '05	♟♟ 5
○ Moscato d'Asti '07	♟♟ 4
○ Moscato d'Asti Su Reimond '07	♟♟ 4

Cinzia Bergaglio

VIA GAVI, 29
15060 TASSAROLO [AL]
TEL. 0143342203
la.fornace@virgilio.it

CELLAR SALES
PRE-BOOKED VISITS

ANNUAL PRODUCTION **25,000 bottles**
HECTARES UNDER VINE **5**
VITICULTURE METHOD **Conventional**

Bergaglio is one of the most common surnames here on the border of Piedmont and Liguria, especially in Tassarolo, Gavi and Novi Ligure. This is the most recent of the many Gavi-bottling cellars that bear the name. It's a small-scale operation and concentrates on just two cortese-based wines. Grapes come from estate-owned plots in the municipalities of Tassarolo and Gavi, particularly in the Rovereto district, one of the best wine subzones in the area extending over about 1,000 hectares scattered across 11 municipal areas.

The cellar style aims for aromatic purity and finesse on the palate. The first of the wines we tasted, Fornaci '08, is a splendid star-bright straw with a nose of spring flowers and white-fleshed fruits heralding a full, well-structured palate with plenty of length. Grifone delle Roveri '08 is a lovely green-flecked straw yellow. The aromatics recall acacia blossom and very ripe damsons leading into a substantial, harmonious palate with seamless freshness.

Nicola Bergaglio

FRAZ. ROVERETO
LOC. PEDAGGERI, 59
15066 GAVI [AL]
TEL. 0143682195
nicolabergaglio@alice.it

CELLAR SALES
PRE-BOOKED VISITS

ANNUAL PRODUCTION **120,000 bottles**
HECTARES UNDER VINE **15**
VITICULTURE METHOD **Conventional**

This historic Gavi winery, number ten on the provincial register of wine producers and one of the most respected, is in the Rovereto production zone. Its 15 hectares are entirely planted to cortese, including a small, south-facing plot with roughly 40-year-old vines which supply the grapes for Minaia, regarded as the designated zone's first vineyard selection. We can assure wine lovers that uncorking an old vintage of Minaia is a great way to appreciate the incredible allure of an old Gavi's tertiary aromatics. The 2005 vintage that went into the finals a year or two ago would probably have no trouble repeating the exploit today.

This time, another Minaia – '08 – did go through to the taste-offs. Its deep straw is flecked with greenish highlights and gives complex aromatics that range from rosemary to pine resin by way of intriguing minerally hints. Savoury, broad and distinctly persistent in the mouth, it keeps its freshness through to the finish. The base Gavi is youthfully brilliant with elegant spring flowers, almonds and gunflint aromatics and a stylishly well-structured palate.

O Gavi del Comune di Tassarolo Fornaci '08	♟♟ 3*
O Gavi del Comune di Gavi Grifone delle Roveri '08	♟♟ 3*
O Gavi del Comune di Gavi Grifone delle Roveri '07	♟♟ 3*
O Gavi del Comune di Gavi Grifone delle Roveri '06	♟♟ 3*
O Gavi del Comune di Gavi Grifone delle Roveri '05	♟♟ 3*

O Gavi del Comune di Gavi Minaia '08	♟♟ 4*
O Gavi del Comune di Gavi '08	♟♟ 4*
O Gavi del Comune di Gavi '07	♟♟ 3*
O Gavi del Comune di Gavi Minaia '07	♟♟ 4*
O Gavi del Comune di Gavi Minaia '06	♟♟ 4*
O Gavi del Comune di Gavi Minaia '05	♟♟ 4*

Bersano

P.ZZA DANTE, 21
14049 NIZZA MONFERRATO [AT]
TEL. 0141720211
www.bersano.it

CELLAR SALES
PRE-BOOKED VISITS

ANNUAL PRODUCTION **2.600,000 bottles**
HECTARES UNDER VINE **240**
VITICULTURE METHOD **Conventional**

Bersano is a large-scale Nizza Monferrato winery of long standing. It's an extensive operation that manages to combine big numbers with quality products. There are eleven wine estates in the Bersano portfolio in Langhe and the Alessandria area as well as Asti. This gives the range breath and considerable diversity in wine types and price points.

Bersano is back with a full profile thanks to overall production of a very good level, starting with the Barberas. The '07 Superiore Cremosina is in the classic mould with sophisticated cherry, tobacco and spice aromatics, power on the palate and a long finish. The '07 Superiore Generala is a medley of balsam and spice over close-knit tannins and the '06 Superiore Nizza has pulp, texture and savouriness. Check out the balanced '06 Arturosé Brut with its sweet, fresh red berry fruits and the whistle-clean, intense '08 Ruché di Castagnole Monferrato San Pietro, which gives classic strawberries and roses.

Guido Berta

LOC. SALINE, 53
14050 SAN MARZANO OLIVETO [AT]
TEL. 0141856193
www.guidoberta.com

ANNUAL PRODUCTION **30,000 bottles**
HECTARES UNDER VINE **12**
VITICULTURE METHOD **Naturale**

Since Guido Berta rejoined his father Giuseppe on the 12-hectare family winery in 2001, production has risen both in quantity and quality. Most of the output comprises native varieties with barbera getting special attention. Vineyards are mainly in the municipality of San Marzano Oliveto, where the winery is based, and aspected to the south-east and south-west.

Guido spoiled us with another range of excellent wines, first of which was the '06 Barbera d'Asti Superiore Nizza Canto di Luna with its fresh cherries and plums over cinchona, power and density on the palate and remarkably close-knit texture. It's forward but the finish is long. Another wine we liked was the very varietal '08 Moscato d'Asti, which gives a rich, fat nose and brioche-veined palate. The '08 Piemonte Chardonnay is good, its attractive white-fleshed fruit nose slightly veined with smokiness and its palate juicy and delicate. The '06 Barbera d'Asti Superiore is nicely made but already evolved.

⊙ Arturosé Brut '06	♥♥	5
● Barbera d'Asti Sup. Cremosina '07	♥♥	4
● Barbera d'Asti Sup. Generala '07	♥♥	6
● Barbera d'Asti Sup. Nizza '06	♥♥	5
● Ruché di Castagnole Monferrato S. Pietro '08	♥♥	4
○ Arturo Bersano Brut Ris. '06	♥	5
● Barbera d'Asti Sup. Cremosina '06	♀♀	4
● Barbera d'Asti Sup. Cremosina '05	♀♀	6
● Barbera d'Asti Sup. Generala '06	♀♀	6
● Barbera d'Asti Sup. Nizza '04	♀♀	5
● Monferrato Rosso Pomona '04	♀♀	6

● Barbera d'Asti Sup. Nizza Canto di Luna '06	♥♥	5
○ Moscato d'Asti '08	♥♥	4
○ Piemonte Chardonnay '08	♥♥	4
● Barbera d'Asti Sup. '06	♥	4
● Barbera d'Asti Sup. '05	♀♀	4
● Barbera d'Asti Sup. Canto di Luna '05	♀♀	4
● Barbera d'Asti Sup. Canto di Luna '04	♀♀	4

Eugenio Bocchino

FRAZ. SANTA MARIA
LOC. SERRA, 96A
12064 LA MORRA [CN]
TEL. 0173500358
www.eugeniobocchino.it

CELLAR SALES
PRE-BOOKED VISITS

ANNUAL PRODUCTION 30,000 bottles
HECTARES UNDER VINE 5.5
VITICULTURE METHOD Conventional

Bocchino may be a new winery but it has well-focused quality and professional objectives. This compact estate run by Eugenio and Cinzia Bocchino continues along its allotted path, interpreting the noblest Barolo variety in admirable products, which include an ever-successful version of Nebbiolo d'Alba called Perucca. In an area where the major local wineries have been around for some time, it is always exciting to discover new cellars like this one.

Eugenio's only regret is just missing out on our top award. Otherwise, this year has been a triumph from start to finish. It's almost impossible to choose between the two '05 Barolos. Serra has balsam and fruit aromatics and an austere palate graced with very elegant tannins. Lu is juicier and more muscular, suggesting dried flowers, liquorice and rhubarb on the nose. Both embody the finesse of Barolos from La Morra. The '07 Barbera has made the most of its excellent vintage, enhancing its intensity and depth on the nose, which foregrounds cherry and tobacco aromatics while the palate unfolds an exciting mix of extract and savouriness.

Alfiero Boffa

VIA LEISO, 50
14050 SAN MARZANO OLIVETO [AT]
TEL. 0141856115
www.alfieroboffa.com

CELLAR SALES
PRE-BOOKED VISITS

ANNUAL PRODUCTION 100,000 bottles
HECTARES UNDER VINE 25
VITICULTURE METHOD Conventional

In an age when wine people talk increasingly about the importance of terroir and stress how the individual cru – the expression of a single plot – is the quintessence of premium wine, Alfiero Boffa's cellar is very much one of a kind. Finding the essence of individual plots of barbera has been the cellar's stock in trade for the past 20 years or so.

The wines have character and depth, unveiling very distinct sensory nuances in each of the many labels. The exquisitely intense '07 Barbera More '07 gives very ripe black berry fruit that doesn't quite mask a complexity-enhancing note of game and earthiness. The rich, beefy palate unwinds into an intriguingly long, savoury finish. Spices and prunes dominate the aromatics of the Cua Longa '07, which is slightly tannic in the mouth. Muntrivé '07 gives very ripe cocoa powder-like fragrances and a balanced palate with a hint of alcohol peeking through. Finally, the good Collina della Vedova '06 has heady liqueur cherry aromatics with vibrant acidity on the palate.

● Barbera d'Alba '07	♟♟ 4*
● Barolo La Serra '05	♟♟ 8
● Barolo Lu '05	♟♟ 7
● Nebbiolo d'Alba La Perucca '05	♟♟ 6
● Barolo La Serra '03	♟♟ 7
● Barolo Lu '04	♟♟ 7
● Nebbiolo d'Alba La Perucca '04	♟♟ 6

● Barbera d'Asti Sup. V. More '07	♟♟ 5*
● Barbera d'Asti Sup. Collina della Vedova '06	♟♟ 5
● Barbera d'Asti Sup. V. Cua Longa '07	♟♟ 5
● Barbera d'Asti Sup. V. Muntrivé '07	♟♟ 5
○ Asti Moscato V. La Lupa '08	♟ 4
● Barbera d'Asti Sup. Nizza V. La Riva '06	♟ 5
☉ Monferrato Ciaret Gran Buchet '08	♟ 4
● Barbera d'Asti Sup. Collina della Vedova '04	♟♟ 5
● Barbera d'Asti Sup. V. Cua Longa '06	♟♟ 5
● Barbera d'Asti Sup. V. Cua Longa '05	♟♟ 5
● Barbera d'Asti Sup. V. Muntrivé '05	♟♟ 5

Enzo Boglietti

VIA FONTANE, 18A
12064 LA MORRA [CN]
TEL. 017350330
www.enzoboglietti.com

CELLAR SALES
PRE-BOOKED VISITS
VISITOR FACILITIES

ANNUAL PRODUCTION **100,000 bottles**
HECTARES UNDER VINE **23**
VITICULTURE METHOD **Conventional**

Enzo Boglietti's wines are a benchmark for lovers of the modern style, in the sense of forthrightness, elegance, power, maturation in small wood and intense colour. After a few years in glass, it wins even more fans as the nebbiolo grape comes through, winning over sensitive tasters no matter what their stylistic preferences. The new cellar deserves a visit, not least for its owner's friendly, outgoing personality.

Barolo Arione '05 is a sumptuously pervasive Three Glass wine from Serralunga that convinces with its depth, freshness and tobacco and spice fragrances layered over classic red berry fruits. It's utterly drinkable despite its relative youth and powerful structure. Complex, balsamic and fruity, the Fossati '05 is fresh-tasting on a palate with still rather mouth-drying tannins. The subtle Case Nere '05 is rather clenched and muscular, with a slightly closed nose for now. There are no '05 or '06 Barolos from the superb Brunate plot, which has been replanted. Barbera and nebbiolo go into the '07 Buio, which is already drinking beautifully. Both Barberas are amazing.

Bondi

S.DA CAPPELLETTE, 73
15076 OVADA [AL]
TEL. 0143821369
www.bondivini.it

CELLAR SALES
PRE-BOOKED VISITS

ANNUAL PRODUCTION **20,000 bottles**
HECTARES UNDER VINE **7**
VITICULTURE METHOD **Conventional**

When the Bondi family purchased Cascina Banaia in 2000, they focused on the territory, the production zone and the white soil of Dolcetto d'Ovada where the south-facing Colle della Banaia rises to 730 metres. Part of the seven hectares under vine was planted in the 1960s while the rest comprises new plantings managed for carefully controlled quantity and quality. The results speak for themselves. In every Guide, at least one wine goes through to the finals. Average quality is high and as good as any in the zone.

The wine that earned a well-deserved place in the taste-off is Le Guie '07, a barbera and dolcetto Monferrato Rosso of great finesse on its balanced nose, velvety texture and impressive persistence. Ansensò '06 is a single-variety Merlot. Its impenetrable inky colour heralds oak and spice followed by a warm, muscular palate. The '07 Dolcetto d'Ovada d'Uien is deep garnet. The broad nose is fruit-led and still youthfully alcoholic and there's concentration and great persistence in the mouth. Nani '07 is an intensely fragranced Dolcetto d'Ovada with an energetic palate. Finally, the '06 Barbera Superiore Ruvrin offers fruit and balsam while the '07 Banaiotta is slightly more evolved.

Wine		Score
● Barolo Arione '05	▼▼▼	8
● Barbera d'Alba Roscaleto '07	▼▼	6
● Barbera d'Alba V. dei Romani '06	▼▼	7
● Barolo Fossati '05	▼▼	8
● Langhe Rosso Buio '07	▼▼	6
● Barolo Case Nere '05	▼▼	8
● Dolcetto d'Alba Tigli Neri '08	▼▼	4
● Langhe Cabernet V. Talpone '06	▼▼	7
● Langhe Merlot V. Talpone '06	▼▼	7
● Langhe Nebbiolo '08	▼▼	5
● Dolcetto d'Alba '08	▼	4
● Barolo Brunate '01	♈♈♈	8
● Barolo Brunate '97	♈♈♈	8
● Barolo Case Nere '04	♈♈♈	8
● Barolo Case Nere '99	♈♈♈	8

Wine		Score
● M.to Rosso Le Guie '07	▼▼	4
● Dolcetto di Ovada Nani '07	▼▼	3*
● Dolcetto di Ovada Sup. d'Uien '07	▼▼	4
● M.to Barbera Sup. Ruvrin '06	▼▼	4
● M.to Rosso Ansensò '06	▼▼	4
● M.to Barbera Banaiotta '07	▼	3
● Dolcetto di Ovada Nani '06	♈♈	3*
● Dolcetto di Ovada Sup. Du'ien '06	♈♈	4
● Dolcetto di Ovada Sup. Du'ien '05	♈♈	4*
● M.to Barbera Banaiotta '05	♈♈	5
● M.to Barbera Ruvrin '04	♈♈	5
● M.to Barbera Ruvrin Sup. '04	♈♈	5

Borgo Maragliano

REG. SAN SEBASTIANO, 2
14050 LOAZZOLO [AT]
TEL. 014487132
www.borgomaragliano.com

CELLAR SALES
PRE-BOOKED VISITS

ANNUAL PRODUCTION **210,000 bottles**
HECTARES UNDER VINE **21**
VITICULTURE METHOD **Conventional**

Carlo Galliano's vines stand at elevations of 350 to 450 metres on marl and sandstone soil in the Loazzolo area, swept by the marin sea winds that help the grapes to ripen. This special site climate imbues the wine's fragrances with freshness and depth. Moscato, chardonnay and pinot nero are the varieties planted on the estate's 21 hectares and they yield elegant wines of great finesse, particularly the sparklers.

Carlo's efforts have been rewarded this year by Three Glasses. The '01 Giuseppe Galliano Brut Riserva from an 80-20 blend of pinot nero and chardonnay gives yeast and nuts aromas, loads of structure and a long, creamy final backed up by nice acidity. The '06 Francesco Galliano Blac de Blancs went into the final for its citrus and spring flowers over honey and a taut, long palate that unfolds gradually, as did the '08 Moscato d'Asti La Caliera, which gives nicely poised citrus peel and mint followed by depth, length and freshness in the mouth. There was also a good show from the Giovanni Galliano Brut Rosé '06, a complex, understated wine redolent of currants and tangerines.

○ Giuseppe Galliano Brut Ris. '01	♥♥♥	5*
○ Francesco Galliano Blanc de Blancs M. Cl. '06	♥♥	5*
○ Moscato d'Asti La Caliera '08	♥♥	4*
○ El Calié '08	♥♥	3*
⊙ Giovanni Galliano Brut Rosé M. Cl. '06	♥♥	5
○ Loazzolo Borgo Maragliano V. T. '06	♥♥	6
○ Piemonte Chardonnay Crevoglio '08	♥	3
○ Giuseppe Galliano Brut M. Cl. '04	♀♀	5
○ Loazzolo Borgo Maragliano V. T. '04	♀♀	6

Giacomo Borgogno & Figli

VIA GIOBERTI, 1
12060 BAROLO [CN]
TEL. 017356108
www.borgogno-wine.com

CELLAR SALES
PRE-BOOKED VISITS

ANNUAL PRODUCTION **130,000 bottles**
HECTARES UNDER VINE **15**
VITICULTURE METHOD **Conventional**

Borgogno means the authentic, historic roots of Barolo for the cellar's first production dates right back to 1761. The Borgogno winery rose to fame above all thanks to the batches of bottles it matured for decades, often with stunning results. Even today, you can buy well-stored bottles from 1961 on at the cellar. Borgogno's vineyard holding includes a number of prestigious plots around the municipality of Barolo. Recently, the winery was acquired by the Eataly group, which looks determined to follow the same production philosophy but in the meantime has already given the entire winery a makeover, restoring it to its original appearance.

As ever, the Borgogno range is a compact one. And as ever, top of the list is the Barolo Liste, this time the '04, from a vineyard as superb as it is little known. This austere, less than approachable Barolo has little fruitiness on the nose and a very tannic palate that will bring satisfaction over the years. The '04 Barolo is a very different proposition: open, approachable and ready for the corkscrew. Also excellent is the sumptuously rich '07 Barbera d'Alba Superiore.

● Barolo Liste '04	♥♥	8
● Barbera d'Alba Sup. '07	♥♥	5
● Barolo '04	♥♥	8
● Dolcetto d'Alba '08	♥	4
● Barolo Cl. '98	♀♀♀	8
● Barbera d'Alba '07	♀♀	4
● Barbera d'Alba '06	♀♀	4
● Barolo Cl. '03	♀♀	8
● Barolo Cl. '01	♀♀	8
● Barolo Cl. '00	♀♀	8
● Barolo Liste '03	♀♀	8
● Langhe Nebbiolo '05	♀♀	5

Boroli

Loc. Madonna di Como, 34
12051 Alba [CN]
Tel. 0173365477
www.boroli.it

CELLAR SALES
PRE-BOOKED VISITS

ANNUAL PRODUCTION **200,000 bottles**
HECTARES UNDER VINE **32**
VITICULTURE METHOD **Conventional**

The Boroli family's campaign to expand the cellar forges ahead. The family is focusing particular attention on non-domestic markets, where major communications initiatives are in place to raise the visibility of the Boroli brand. Most of the wine production is carried out at Alba, at the Bompé farm, but Brunella at Castiglione Falletto is well worth visiting now it has been restored by the in-house architect, Guido Boroli. This is where Boroli Barolo is made.

The winemaking style is intelligently modern, with the assurance and definition of the aromatics a priority. Villero '05 has great ageing prospects thanks to seriously good raw material and close-knit extract that guarantee longevity. Actually, the standard Barolo is outstandingly successful, showing elegant traditional notes of liquorice and tobacco with an understated palate. The rest of the range is very good indeed. A special mention goes to the Barbera Superiore Fagiani '06 which nicely fuses fruit with oak, and alcohol with acidity. Finally, the juicy, alcohol-rich Barbera Quattro Fratelli with its mouthfilling power is from the hot 2007 growing year.

● Barbera d'Alba Sup. Fagiani '06	TT	6
● Barolo Villero '05	TT	8
● Barbera d'Alba Quattro Fratelli '07	TT	4
● Barolo '05	TT	7
● Barolo Cerequio '05	TT	8
● Langhe Anna '07	TT	4*
○ Moscato d'Asti Aureum '08	T	4
● Dolcetto d'Alba Madonna di Como '08	T	4
○ Langhe Chardonnay Bel Amì '08	T	4
● Barolo Villero '01	YYY	8
● Barolo Villero '00	YYY	8
● Barolo Cerequio '04	YY	8
● Barolo Cerequio '04	YY	8
● Barolo Villero '03	YY	8
● Barolo Villero Ris. '00	YY	8
● Dolcetto d'Alba Madonna di Como '08	YY	4

Francesco Boschis

Fraz. San Martino di Pianezzo, 57
12063 Dogliani [CN]
Tel. 017370574
www.marcdegrazia.com

CELLAR SALES
PRE-BOOKED VISITS

ANNUAL PRODUCTION **40,000 bottles**
HECTARES UNDER VINE **11**
VITICULTURE METHOD **Conventional**

"A winery with a vocation for Dolcetto" would be a reasonable way to describe Boschis. Over the years, though, we have seen a number of welcome newcomers, such as Freisa and Barbera, join the area's main variety to fill out a range that is genuinely exciting. What sets the wines from this lovely farm estate apart is their consistency, and on occasion rusticity, with intense, vigorously flavoursome fruit.

The latest releases are all better than good, starting with the magnificent Dogliani Vigna dei Prey '07. Star-bright, almost impenetrable ruby introduces an intense, textbook nose with elegantly classy complexity in its blueberry, tobacco and liquorice aromatics before the still youthful palate unfolds harmonious and full bodied through to a long, juicy finale. Equally valid is the other '07 Dogliani. Initially a little closed on the nose, it opens into spice and cinchona with fruitiness in the background and then a stiffish, austere palate with unresolved tannins but the unhurried finish offers hope for the future. Plaudits also go to the '06 Barbera and Dogliani, both in excellent form.

● Dogliani V. dei Prey '07	TT	4*
● Barbera d'Alba Le Masserie '06	TT	5
● Dolcetto di Dogliani Pianezzo '08	TT	4*
● Dolcetto di Dogliani Sup. V. del Ciliegio '06	TT	4
● Dolcetto di Dogliani V. Sorì San Martino '07	TT	4
● Langhe Freisa Bosco delle Cicale '08	T	4
● Barbera d'Alba Le Masserie '05	YY	5
● Dogliani V. dei Prey '06	YY	4
● Dolcetto di Dogliani Pianezzo '07	YY	4

Luigi Boveri

LOC. MONTALE CELLI
VIA XX SETTEMBRE, 6
15050 COSTA VESCOVATO [AL]
TEL. 0131838165
www.boveriluigi.com

CELLAR SALES
PRE-BOOKED VISITS

ANNUAL PRODUCTION **60,000 bottles**
HECTARES UNDER VINE **15**
VITICULTURE METHOD **Conventional**

For the past few years, Luigi Boveri has been able to take advantage of the new cellar that gives him the space required for a winery that may be family run but has earned a reputation for itself beyond the bounds of the region. If you want to visit, ring beforehand because Luigi will show you round himself but is often busy working in the vineyards, driving his tractor or even out making deliveries.

This year, we noted another great vintage of the Barbera Poggio delle Amarene (which we flagged up in last year's Guide) with headily fruity fragrances and lovely structure that took it through to our finals. Vignalunga, a historic Colli Tortonesi label, is still a little oaky on the nose. Croatina Sensazioni is on its second release and gives greens on the nose followed by attractive structure. As we wait for release of the '07 Filari di Timorasso, the standard Derthona is also good. Meanwhile, Cortese Vigna del Prete and Barbera Boccanera are bankers when you're looking for great value for money. For those who like the style, the Barbera is also available in a semi-sparkling version.

● Colli Tortonesi Barbera Poggio delle Amarene '06	TT	4*
● Colli Tortonesi Barbera Boccanera '08	TT	3*
● Colli Tortonesi Barbera Vignalunga '06	TT	6
○ Colli Tortonesi Timorasso Derthona '07	TT	4
○ Colli Tortonesi Cortese V. del Prete '08	T	3
● Colli Tortonesi Croatina Sensazioni '07	T	4
● Colli Tortonesi Barbera Boccanera '06	YY	3*
● Colli Tortonesi Barbera Poggio delle Amarene '06	YY	4
● Colli Tortonesi Barbera Poggio delle Amarene '05	YY	6
● Colli Tortonesi Barbera Vignalunga '05	YY	6
● Colli Tortonesi Barbera Vignalunga '04	YY	6
○ Colli Tortonesi Bianco Filari di Timorasso '05	YY	5
○ Colli Tortonesi Timorasso Filari di Timorasso '06	YY	5

Gianfranco Bovio

FRAZ. ANNUNZIATA
B.TA CIOTTO, 63
12064 LA MORRA [CN]
TEL. 017350667
www.boviogianfranco.com

CELLAR SALES
PRE-BOOKED VISITS

ANNUAL PRODUCTION **55,000 bottles**
HECTARES UNDER VINE **10**
VITICULTURE METHOD **Conventional**

Work goes on apace at the cellar of the well-matched team formed by Gianfranco Bovio and Walter Porasso, with winemaking consultancy input from Beppe Caviola. Again, there was no Barolo Bricco Parussi – the '03 this time – which will only be released to market next year. The big new development is that after the 2008 harvest, much of the dolcetto was grubbed up to make way for nebbiolo. We will of course have to wait several years for the results. The wines we did taste are beautifully clean and very territory-focused: classic products intelligently interpreted.

As usual, the '05 Barolos impressed, the Gattera in particular. Dried roses and violets usher in solid, sweet extract and plenty of length. The Aroborino is reminiscent of wild strawberries and the elegantly juicy palate is savoury. Rocchettevino comes from further up the hillslopes. It's a classic La Morra Barolo, showing vigorous yet subtle with tannins with no hint of roughness. The half sauvignon, half chardonnay Langhe Bianco '08 is as good as ever while the enjoyable Nebbiolo '06 and Dolcetto '08 delight the nose.

● Barolo V. Arborina '05	TT	7
● Barolo V. Gattera '05	TT	7
● Barolo Rocchettevino '05	TT	6
○ Langhe Bianco V. La Villa '08	TT	3*
● Dolcetto d'Alba Dabbene '08	T	4
● Langhe Nebbiolo '06	T	5
● Barolo Bricco Parussi Ris. '01	YYY	7
● Barbera d'Alba Regiaveja '04	YY	5
● Barolo V. Arborina '04	YY	7
● Barolo V. Arborina '03	YY	7
● Barolo V. Gattera '04	YY	7
● Dolcetto d'Alba Dabbene '07	YY	3*

Braida

S.DA PROVINCIALE, 9
14030 ROCCHETTA TANARO [AT]
TEL. 0141644113
www.braida.it

CELLAR SALES
PRE-BOOKED VISITS

ANNUAL PRODUCTION **600,000 bottles**
HECTARES UNDER VINE **53**
VITICULTURE METHOD **Naturale**

Over almost half a century of activity, the winery founded by Giacomo Bologna, whose nickname was Braida, has made its name on the world wine scene by unremittingly promoting Barbera. Today, the job of living up to the man and his heritage of super wines is carried forward by Giacomo's wife Anna, their children Beppe and Raffaella, and son-in-law Norbert. Although they have expanded the business by acquiring new vineyards, they have remained true to Giacomo's production philosophy.

This year, not for the first time, our favourite Barbera d'Asti was the '07 version of Bricco della Bigotta with its well-defined cinnamon aromatics segueing into cherries and tobacco. Finesse and harmony in the mouth are underpinned by perfectly matched acidity and alcohol and the finish is all class and character. The tobacco, spice and red berry fruits Ai Suma '07, its subtle, complex palate braced by extract, is good, as is the poised '07 Bricco dell'Uccellone, which has a rich ripe fruit palate. Barbera d'Asti Montebruna '07 has lots of fruit but tends to be a little too oaky. Also interesting are the Serra dei Fiori whites, which put the accent on structure and generous aromatics.

● Barbera d'Asti Bricco della Bigotta '07	ŸŸŸ	7
● Barbera d'Asti Ai Suma '07	ŸŸ	8
● Barbera d'Asti Bricco dell'Uccellone '07	ŸŸ	7
● Barbera d'Asti Montebruna '07	ŸŸ	4*
○ Langhe Bianco Riesling Re di Fiori '08	ŸŸ	5
● Brachetto d'Acqui '08	Ÿ	4
● Grignolino d'Asti '08	Ÿ	4
○ Langhe Bianco Il Fiore '08	Ÿ	4
○ Langhe Chardonnay Asso di Fiori '07	Ÿ	5
● M.to Barbera La Monella '08	Ÿ	4
● M.to Rosso Il Bacialé '07	Ÿ	4
○ Moscato d'Asti V. Senza Nome '08	Ÿ	4
● Barbera d'Asti Ai Suma '04	ŸŸŸ	7
● Barbera d'Asti Bricco dell'Uccellone '05	ŸŸŸ	7
● Barbera d'Asti Bricco della Bigotta '06	ŸŸŸ	7

Brema

VIA POZZOMAGNA, 9
14045 INCISA SCAPACCINO [AT]
TEL. 014174019
vinibrema@inwind.it

CELLAR SALES
PRE-BOOKED VISITS

ANNUAL PRODUCTION **140,000 bottles**
HECTARES UNDER VINE **20**
VITICULTURE METHOD **Conventional**

This historic farm estate, founded in the 19th century, is run today by Alessandra and Ermanno Brema. Their name has strong links with local territory and in particular with Barbera d'Asti, a wine they have always interpreted with great passion and vinify in several styles. But the range includes various other wines, almost all of them from native varieties. The Brema vineyards are at Incisa Scarpaccino, Nizza Monferrato, Mombaruzzo and Fontamile d'Asti.

The line-up of Barbera d'Astis is good but lacks the brilliance of other years. The '08 Ai Cruss is unusually mature, giving hints of liqueur fruit and lots of oak, while the rich, rounded palate is rather forward. Tre Gelsi '07 has subtle red fruits and tobacco as well as decent complexity with savouriness on a palate that finishes long. The richly structured '07 Volpettona tempts with wafts of cocoa powder and cherries. Monferrato Rosso Il Fulvo '07 is from barbera and cabernet sauvignon offers greens, sweet oaky notes and spiciness. Both Dolcetto d'Astis are well crafted. Montera '08 proffers classic dried herbs and tea while Vigna Impaginato '07 is rich and powerful but still oaky.

● Barbera d'Asti Ai Cruss '08	ŸŸ	4*
● Barbera d'Asti Sup. Tre Gelsi '07	ŸŸ	6
● Barbera d'Asti Sup. Volpettona '07	Ÿ	6
● Dolcetto d'Asti Montera '08	Ÿ	4
● Dolcetto d'Asti V. Impagnato '07	Ÿ	4
● M.to Rosso Il Fulvo '07	Ÿ	5
● Barbera d'Asti Sup. Nizza A Luigi Veronelli '06	ŸŸŸ	5
● Barbera d'Asti Ai Cruss '07	ŸŸ	4*
● Barbera d'Asti Sup. Bricco della Volpettona '06	ŸŸ	6
● Barbera d'Asti Sup. Bricco della Volpettona '03	ŸŸ	6
● Barbera d'Asti Sup. Bricco della Volpettona '01	ŸŸ	6
● M.to Rosso Il Fulvo '06	ŸŸ	5
○ Piemonte Moscato Mariasole '07	ŸŸ	4

Giacomo Brezza & Figli

VIA LOMONDO, 4
12060 BAROLO [CN]
TEL. 0173560921
www.brezza.it

CELLAR SALES
PRE-BOOKED VISITS
VISITOR FACILITIES
FOOD

ANNUAL PRODUCTION 80,000 bottles
HECTARES UNDER VINE 16.5
VITICULTURE METHOD Conventional

In its more than 130 years of history, the winery now led by Enzo Brezza is something of an institution in Barolo. The family eatery and hotel continue to welcome lovers of classic Nebbiolos, in the noblest sense of the word. Obtained by extended skin contact in medium and large casks, the Barolo selections are sourced from the east-facing part of Cannubi, Castellero and Sarmassa, the upper part of which also provides the Bricco Sarmassa in the best vintages.

The 2005 growing year was not considered good enough for Bricco Sarmassa but its near twin leaves us wondering if this was the right decision. Barolo Sarmassa '05 blew our panel away to win Three Glasses with a sensory profile of sheer class. Iron and iodine mingle with damp earth aromas, complementing nebbiolo's signature acidic fruit and hints of balsam. The minerally breadth of the aromatics may not be backed up by an explosive palate but there is plenty of support from ripe, fine-grained tannins. The '05 Barolo Cannubi is meatier but has less depth or complexity, although it does flaunt a long cocoa powder and liquorice finale.

Bric Cenciurio

VIA ROMA, 24
12060 BAROLO [CN]
TEL. 017356317
www.briccenciurio.com

CELLAR SALES
PRE-BOOKED VISITS

ANNUAL PRODUCTION 45,000 bottles
HECTARES UNDER VINE 13
VITICULTURE METHOD Conventional

The felicitous fusion of ideas between Langhe and Roero makes this a very original winemaking concern both in its organization and in the range of wines on offer. The Pittatore and Sacchetto manage with an estate split between the municipalities of Castellinaldo and Barolo, vinifying white and red grapes with equal skill to craft a range that runs from Roero Arneis to Barolo. Distinguishing features are styles that are never ordinary, well-gauged use of oak in the serious reds and lashings of freshness and drinkability in the whites.

The '05 Barolo Costa di Rose may not be terribly subtle but it has great personality. There's power and depth, although it is a tad severe and cropped. The cabernet sauvignon-only Rosso di Caialupo '06 is successful, showing slightly vegetal, austere and long. The very moreish Barbera '07 has warmth and power. But we particularly like the '07 version of Arneis Sito dei Fossili, an outstandingly vibrant, complex wine with a honey and incense nose and serious structure in the mouth.

● Barolo Sarmassa '05	♟♟♟ 7
● Barolo Cannubi '05	♟♟ 7
● Barbera d'Alba Cannubi Muscatel '07	♟♟ 5
● Nebbiolo d'Alba Santa Rosalia '07	♟♟ 4
● Barbera d'Alba Santa Rosalia '08	♟ 4
● Dolcetto d'Alba S. Lorenzo '08	♟ 4
● Langhe Freisa Santa Rosalia '08	♟ 4
● Barolo Cannubi '01	♟♟♟ 7
● Barolo Sarmassa '04	♟♟♟ 7
● Barolo Sarmassa '03	♟♟♟ 7
● Barbera d'Alba Santa Rosalia '07	♟♟ 4
● Barolo Bricco Sarmassa '04	♟♟ 8
● Dolcetto d'Alba S. Lorenzo '07	♟♟ 4

○ Roero Arneis Sito dei Fossili '07	♟♟ 4*
● Barbera d'Alba '07	♟♟ 4*
● Barolo '05	♟♟ 6
● Barolo Costa di Rose '05	♟♟ 7
● Langhe Rosso Rosso di Caialupo '06	♟♟ 5
● Birbét '08	♟ 4
○ Roero Arneis '08	♟ 4
● Barbera d'Alba Sup. Naunda '06	♟♟ 5
● Barolo Costa di Rose '04	♟♟ 7
● Barolo Costa di Rose '02	♟♟ 6
● Barolo Costa di Rose '01	♟♟ 8*
● Langhe Rosso Rosso di Caialupo '05	♟♟ 5
○ Sito dei Fossili V. T. '06	♟♟ 6

Bricco del Cucù

LOC. BRICCO, 10
12060 BASTIA MONDOVÌ [CN]
TEL. 017460153
www.briccocucu.com

CELLAR SALES
PRE-BOOKED VISITS

ANNUAL PRODUCTION 50,000 bottles
HECTARES UNDER VINE 10
VITICULTURE METHOD Conventional

Dario Sciolla is the sort of farmer we hope will not die out. He runs this small estate, located in a particularly atmospheric spot, where the vines reflect the robust temperament of their natural environment. Don't miss a visit to this winery, which is sure to delight you and where you will be able to discover new or forgotten taste sensations.

Outstanding among this year's Dolcettos is the '08 Dogliani. Impenetrable ruby red, its delicious cinchona, cocoa powder and ripe blackberries introduce a palate with few equals for power this year. Also very uncorkable is the Langhe Rosso Diavolisanti '07. Its classic merlot aromas foreground currants against clear vegetality before acidity unfolds on the palate into a satisfying finish. The flagship '07 Dogliani Bricco San Bernardo could do with further ageing in bottle to remove one or two remaining rough edges. From experience, we know that at its peak of maturation this powerfully structured Dogliani reaches enviable fullness of flavour and aromatic complexity.

Bricco Maiolica

FRAZ. RICCA
VIA BOLANGINO, 7
12055 DIANO D'ALBA [CN]
TEL. 0173612049
www.briccomaiolica.it

CELLAR SALES
PRE-BOOKED VISITS

ANNUAL PRODUCTION 90,000 bottles
HECTARES UNDER VINE 20
VITICULTURE METHOD Conventional

Consistency is the common thread that runs through Beppe Accomo's life and work. It's a quality that can also be found in the crystal-clear definition of his wines. Beppe's bottles quietly express themselves in superbly drinkable aromatic and varietal qualities that showcase the features of the territory. Dolcetto is at the forefront, but there are also Barberas and Nebbiolos, with a few whites, all extremely reliable.

The Diano d'Alba Superiore Sörì Bricco Maiolica '07 is a stand-out: Accomo has skilfully harnessed the power of the vintage, adding elegance, clear fragrances and a caressing mouthfeel. The pleasant Dolcetto di Diano '08 is classic, with a blackberry bouquet and good tannins on the palate. The Barbera '06 is estery and full of bottled fruit, softened in the mouth by a little residual oak. Lorié '05, from pinot nero, lacks freshness and gives gamey notes and spice on the nose while in the mouth the delicate Burgundy grapes is overpowered by the Langhe soil and its tannins. Check out the debut of Pensiero Infinito, a Chardonnay in magnums that spent three years on the lees.

● Dogliani Bricco S. Bernardo '07	♀♀ 4
● Dolcetto di Dogliani '08	♀♀ 4*
● Langhe Rosso Diavolisanti '07	♀♀ 4*
○ Langhe Bianco Livor '08	♀ 3
● Langhe Dolcetto '08	♀ 4
● Langhe Rosso Superboum '06	♀ 5
● Dolcetto di Dogliani '07	♀♀ 4*
● Dolcetto di Dogliani '05	♀♀ 3*
● Dolcetto di Dogliani Sup. Bricco S. Bernardo '06	♀♀ 4*
● Dolcetto di Dogliani Sup. Bricco S. Bernardo '01	♀♀ 4
● Langhe Rosso Diavolisanti '05	♀♀ 4*

● Diano d'Alba Sup. Sörì Bricco Maiolica '07	♀♀♀ 4*
● Barbera d'Alba Sup. V. Vigia '06	♀♀ 5
○ Langhe Bianco Pensiero Infinito '05	♀♀ 6
● Dolcetto di Diano d'Alba '08	♀♀ 4
● Langhe Rosso Filius '05	♀♀ 6
● Langhe Rosso Lorié '05	♀♀ 6
● Nebbiolo d'Alba Cumot '06	♀♀ 5
○ Langhe Bianco Rolando '08	♀ 4
● Barbera d'Alba Sup. V. Vigia '05	♀♀ 5
● Barbera d'Alba V. Vigia '04	♀♀ 5
● Diano d'Alba Sörì Bricco Maiolica '06	♀♀ 4
● Diano d'Alba Sörì Bricco Maiolica '05	♀♀ 4
● Diano d'Alba Sup. Sörì Bricco Maiolica '06	♀♀ 4

Bricco Mondalino

REG. MONDALINO, 5
15049 VIGNALE MONFERRATO [AL]
TEL. 0142933204
www.briccomondalino.it

CELLAR SALES
PRE-BOOKED VISITS

ANNUAL PRODUCTION 80,000 bottles
HECTARES UNDER VINE 13
VITICULTURE METHOD Conventional

A historic Vignale Monferrato estate and a standard-bearer for the classic local varieties sum up Mauro Gaudio's winery. Barbera and Grignolino are the pillars on which the history and future of the estate rest. On the subject of the future, it is worth mentioning the new driving forces, as Mauro's daughters are now working in the winery: Valentina and, since this year, Beatrice, who is at university studying agriculture, specializing in viticulture and oenology.

Il Bergantino '06 is on admirable form, with intense aromas of plum and cinchona, good acidity on the palate and a long finish. Zerolegno '07 gives concentrated balsam-veined red fruits over a full, juicy palate. In the less successful '08 growing year for Grignolino, Bricco Mondalino has more marked varietal characteristics and slightly more concentration than the basic version. The Monferrina is a pleasant, drinkable semi-sparkling Freisa. The Cortese '08 is nicely made, with intense, stylish aromas, and Malvasia di Casorzo d'Asti Molignano '08 finds an excellent balance of acidity and residual sugar.

★ Bricco Rocche - Bricco Asili

VIA MONFORTE, 63
12060 CASTIGLIONE FALLETTO [CN]
TEL. 0173282582
www.ceretto.com

CELLAR SALES
PRE-BOOKED VISITS

ANNUAL PRODUCTION 45,000 bottles
HECTARES UNDER VINE 18.5
VITICULTURE METHOD Conventional

This profile reviews wines from the two estates that the Ceretto family created in 1978 at Castiglione Falletto and Barbaresco. These are two Piedmont châteaux dedicated to the two Langhe wines and set atop two splendid hills. Bricco Rocche vinifies the selection of the same name as well as the Brunate cru from La Morra, Prapò from Serralunga and soon also a Cannubi selection from Barolo. Bricco Asili is flanked by Bernardot from Treiso. Brief macerations and barrique ageing are the features that link these world-renowned wines.

After a gap of a few years, Three Glasses returned to Ceretto for a vigorous Barolo Prapò '05 that holds together beautifully. Despite its dense, modern hue, it has penetrating sensations of forest floor and aromatic herbs, good momentum on the palate and generous, well-integrated tannins. The Barbaresco Asili '06 is outgoing and opulent, with an almost grassy finish. Barolo Bricco Rocche '05 is decidedly backward, though still recognizable in its richness and style. The Barbaresco Bernardot '06 is somewhat simple and the linear Barolo Brunate '05 is austere.

● Barbera d'Asti Il Bergantino '06	♛♛ 4
● Barbera del M.to Zerolegno '07	♛♛ 4*
● Grignolino del M.to Casalese Bricco Mondalino '08	♛♛ 4
● Grignolino del M.to Casalese '08	♛ 4
● M.to Freisa La Monferrina '08	♛ 3
● Malvasia di Casorzo d'Asti Molignano '08	♛ 4
○ Monferrato Casalese Cortese '08	♛ 3
● Barbera del M.to Zerolegno '06	♛♛ 4*
● Barbera del M.to Zerolegno '05	♛♛ 4
● Grignolino del M.to Casalese Bricco Mondalino '07	♛♛ 4*
● Grignolino del M.to Casalese Bricco Mondalino '06	♛♛ 4
● Malvasia di Casorzo d'Asti Molignano '07	♛♛ 4*

● Barolo Prapò '05	♛♛♛ 8
● Barbaresco Bricco Asili '06	♛♛ 8
● Barbaresco Bernardot '06	♛♛ 8
● Barolo Bricco Rocche '05	♛♛ 8
● Barolo Brunate '05	♛♛ 8
● Barbaresco Bricco Asili '99	♛♛♛ 8
● Barbaresco Bricco Asili '97	♛♛♛ 8
● Barbaresco Bricco Asili '96	♛♛♛ 8
● Barolo Bricco Rocche '00	♛♛♛ 8
● Barolo Brunate '90	♛♛♛ 8

Vitivinicola Broglia

LOC. LOMELLINA, 22
15066 GAVI [AL]
TEL. 0143642998
www.broglia.eu

CELLAR SALES
PRE-BOOKED VISITS

ANNUAL PRODUCTION **N.D.**
HECTARES UNDER VINE **57**
VITICULTURE METHOD **Conventional**

This is one of the most beautiful estates in southern Piedmont, historically committed to the cortese grape and the principal wine of these enchanting hills: Gavi. The style is firmly classic, without so much as a hint of intervention in the vineyard or cellar that could compromise the purity of a white wine that has seen demand stay buoyant and continues to be appreciated in the best restaurants round the world.

The '08 Bruno Broglia is at its finest, easily winning the Three Glasses. Straw with greenish tinges, it is very intense on the minerally nose with gunflint and white-fleshed fruits. The palate is substantial, with an austerely rigid, very clean finish. Meirana '08 is fruity and slightly simpler, foregrounding attractive florality before the rounded palate finds refreshing acidity again on the finish. The '08 Roverello is uncomplicated, fruit-driven and even a little too soft, though pleasantly drinkable. We will write about the excellent estate red, still to be released when we tasted, in the next Guide.

Brovia

VIA ALBA-BAROLO, 54
12060 CASTIGLIONE FALLETTO [CN]
TEL. 017362852
www.brovia.net

CELLAR SALES
PRE-BOOKED VISITS

ANNUAL PRODUCTION **60,000 bottles**
HECTARES UNDER VINE **18**
VITICULTURE METHOD **Conventional**

Brovia is not only the name of one of the oldest estates in the Langhe: it is also a style. The range produced from the property's 18 hectares or so seems to want to take the gracefulness and elegance so insistently sought by its fans to the limits. This impression is particularly evident in the Barolos, all traditionally fermented in cement vats for 15 to 20 days, often with ambient yeasts, and aged in large barrels for about three years. Besides the current version, selections are released from Rocche, Villero and Garblèt Sué at Castiglione and Ca' Mia at Serralunga.

A super performance overall does nothing to eliminate disappointment at the failure to wine a ninth Three Glass award by a whisker. The candidate was Barolo Villero '04, an excellent interpretation of an austere, fine-boned selection with a penetrating fruity aroma of watermelon and root-like notes of liquorice and ginseng before the palate reveals stiffish, edgy texture. It will probably improve, though. Ca' Mia '05 is less in the Brovia style, giving fat, chewy fruit checked only by a touch of dryness in the finish. The Barolo '05 and the Barbera d'Alba Sorì del Drago '07 are quite simply delicious.

○ Gavi del Comune di Gavi Bruno Broglia '08	▼▼▼	6
○ Gavi del Comune di Gavi La Meirana '08	▼▼	4
○ Gavi del Comune di Gavi Roverello '08	▼	4
○ Gavi del Comune di Gavi Bruno Broglia '07	♀♀♀	6
○ Gavi del Comune di Gavi Bruno Broglia '06	♀♀	5
○ Gavi del Comune di Gavi Bruno Broglia '05	♀♀	5

● Barolo Ca' Mia '05	▼▼	8
● Barolo Villero '04	▼▼	8
● Barbera d'Alba Sorì del Drago '07	▼▼	4
● Barolo '05	▼▼	7
● Barolo Rocche dei Brovia '05	▼▼	8
● Dolcetto d'Alba Solatìo '07	▼▼	7
● Dolcetto d'Alba Vignavillej '07	▼▼	4
● Barolo Ca' Mia '00	♀♀♀	8
● Barbera d'Alba Sorì del Drago '04	♀♀	4*
● Barolo Ca' Mia '04	♀♀	8
● Barolo Garblèt Sué '04	♀♀	7
● Barolo Rocche dei Brovia '04	♀♀	8
● Barolo Rocche dei Brovia '03	♀♀	8

G. B. Burlotto

VIA VITTORIO EMANUELE, 28
12060 VERDUNO [CN]
TEL. 0172470122
www.burlotto.com

CELLAR SALES
PRE-BOOKED VISITS

ANNUAL PRODUCTION 60,000 bottles
HECTARES UNDER VINE 12
VITICULTURE METHOD Conventional

As a traditional fine wine-producing region, Piedmont numbers some influential grower-producers, for whom historical authenticity is a mark of distinction. One such, quite rightly, is Marina Burlotto at the property she runs with her son Fabio Alessandria, offering delightful farm holidays as well as wine. The exquisitely interpreted range has always been dependable over the years, and the range includes some of the most important designated areas in Langhe, with special attention for certain white-skinned varieties, which are always interesting.

Much can be understood from the table below. First, the winery has been taking off for some years now. Second, the house specialities are clear: Barolo and Langhe Bianco from sauvignon grapes. Of the Barolo '05s, we prefer the fresher-tasting, elegant Acclivi al Cannubi. Among the Sauvignons, the stainless steel-aged Viridis '08 gives refined varietal notes while Dives '07, expertly aged in wood, confirms its standing as one of the finest in the region, if not the country. Assertive aromas of peach and mint come together with beautifully balanced acid and alcohol. Finally, we give the usual approval for the Pelaverga, which is one of the best two again this year.

● Barolo Acclivi '05	♀♀	7
○ Langhe Bianco Dives '07	♀♀	4*
● Barbera d'Alba Aves '07	♀♀	5
● Barolo Vign. Cannubi '05	♀♀	7
○ Langhe Bianco Viridis '08	♀♀	4*
● Langhe Mores '06	♀♀	5
● Langhe Nebbiolo '07	♀♀	4*
● Verduno Pelaverga '08	♀♀	4*
● Barbera d'Alba Aves '04	♀♀	5
● Barolo Acclivi '04	♀♀	7
● Barolo Vign. Cannubi '03	♀♀	7
● Barolo Vign. Cannubi '00	♀♀	7
● Barolo Vign. Monvigliero '04	♀♀	7
● Barolo Vign. Monvigliero '00	♀♀	7

Piero Busso

VIA ALBESANI, 8
12052 NEIVE [CN]
TEL. 017367156
www.bussopiero.com

CELLAR SALES
PRE-BOOKED VISITS

ANNUAL PRODUCTION 30,000 bottles
HECTARES UNDER VINE 8
VITICULTURE METHOD Conventional

What makes the work of this family of Neive producers stand out is Barbaresco in its various versions, all interesting in their distinctive aromatics and personalities. The complexity of Barbaresco comes through best after a period of ageing in bottle. Indeed, the wines produced by Piero Busso often need a certain period of time after release to market to allow them to assert their character and varietal depth to the full.

This is the way to craft a perfect Barbaresco Gallina '05, a further year of ageing having lent it the harmony to earn our Three Glasses. Cinchona and liquorice are followed by a full, long, tight-knit palate, with wonderful fruity flesh and a hint of wood. Barbaresco Santo Stefanetto '06 – written "San Stunet" in Piedmontese on the label – puts the accent on power, spices and a punchy personality emerging from tightish aromas. Borgese '06 is elegant, with sweet tobacco and raspberries leading to a powerful, long palate marked by nice oak in the finish. The woody Barbera Santo Stefanetto '06 is dense and spicy while the harmonious Langhe Bianco '08 is a stunning success.

● Barbaresco Gallina '05	♀♀♀	8
● Barbaresco Borgese '06	♀♀	7
● Barbaresco S. Stefanetto '06	♀♀	8
● Barbera d'Alba S. Stefanetto '06	♀♀	4
● Barbera d'Alba V. Majano '07	♀♀	4
● Dolcetto d'Alba V. Majano '08	♀♀	4
○ Langhe Bianco '08	♀♀	4
● Langhe Nebbiolo '07	♀♀	5
● Barbaresco S. Stefanetto '04	♀♀♀	8
● Barbaresco S. Stefanetto '03	♀♀♀	8
● Barbaresco Borgese '05	♀♀	7
● Barbaresco Borgese '04	♀♀	7
● Barbaresco S. Stunet S. Stefanetto '05	♀♀	8

Ca' Bianca

REG. SPAGNA, 58
15010 ALICE BEL COLLE [AL]
TEL. 0144745420
www.cantinacabianca.it

CELLAR SALES
PRE-BOOKED VISITS

ANNUAL PRODUCTION **550,000 bottles**
HECTARES UNDER VINE **39**
VITICULTURE METHOD **Conventional**

Although not so well known among Piedmont's wine zones, the Alessandria area of Monferrato offers striking views and an enchanting rural feel rarely matched by other wine areas. This important estate, owned by Gruppo Italiano Vini, offers a steady, dependable range that has justly won market share and great loyalty on the part of discriminating in Italy and abroad.

All the main southern Piedmont designations are here, from Gavi to Barbera and Barolo. The '05 Barolo is absolutely stunning. Deep ruby, it proffers spice and fruit aromatics and then a meltingly soft, temptingly easy palate. The most characteristic wines are still the two Barbera Superiore '07s, Chersì and Antè. The first is powerful and exuberant at each stage of tasting: impenetrably dark, with oak and black cherry jam introducing in an opulent, well-extracted palate. Antè is more measured though equally pleasant. The rest of the range reflects the winery's philosophy of easy-drinking wines at sensible prices.

Ca' d' Gal

FRAZ. VALDIVILLA
S.DA VECCHIA DI VALDIVILLA, 1
12058 SANTO STEFANO BELBO [CN]
TEL. 0141847103
www.cadgal.it

CELLAR SALES
PRE-BOOKED VISITS
VISITOR FACILITIES
FOOD

ANNUAL PRODUCTION **60,000 bottles**
HECTARES UNDER VINE **8**
VITICULTURE METHOD **Conventional**

In just a few years, Alessandro Boido has managed to create one of the most important cellars in the Moscato area at Valdivilla, Santo Stefano Belbo. From vines dating up to 50 years in age, mostly planted on light, whitish, sandy soils, all south-facing, he produces a range of high quality Moscatos that can stand the test of time. For some years, he has also been running a farm holiday centre and restaurant in a gorgeous location with views over the vineyards of the estate.

Although 2008 was not a great year for Moscato, Alessandro Boido managed to produce a couple of deliciously successful wines. We particularly liked the Moscato d'Asti Lumine '08, which is all delicately clean freshness and fragrance, and the Asti, a long-finishing spumante with lingering bead and mousse, scents of citrus and mint, a stylish palate and good body. The Moscato d'Asti Vigna Vecchia '08 is less successful than other versions, having suffered more from the difficult year. It is flowery on the nose and the palate is rather unexciting and light, but it is fragrant and pleasant enough.

● Barbera d'Asti Sup. Chersì '07	♀♀ 5
● Barbera d'Asti Sup. Antè '07	♀♀ 4
● Barolo '05	♀♀ 6
● Barbera d'Asti Teis '08	♀ 4
● Dolcetto d'Acqui '08	♀ 4
○ Gavi '08	♀ 4
● Barbera d'Asti Antè '06	♀♀ 4
● Barbera d'Asti Sup. Chersì '06	♀♀ 5
● Barbera d'Asti Sup. Chersì '05	♀♀ 5
● Barbera d'Asti Sup. Chersì '04	♀♀ 5
● Barbera d'Asti Teis '07	♀♀ 4
● Barolo '04	♀♀ 6

○ Asti	♀♀ 4
○ Moscato d'Asti Lumine '08	♀♀ 4
○ Moscato d'Asti V. Vecchia '08	♀ 5
○ Moscato d'Asti Lumine '07	♀♀ 4
○ Moscato d'Asti V. Vecchia '07	♀♀ 5
○ Moscato d'Asti V. Vecchia '06	♀♀ 5
○ Moscato d'Asti V. Vecchia '05	♀♀ 5

Ca' del Baio

VIA FERRERE, 33
12050 TREISO [CN]
TEL. 0173638219
www.cadelbaio.com

CELLAR SALES
PRE-BOOKED VISITS

ANNUAL PRODUCTION **100,000 bottles**
HECTARES UNDER VINE **25**
VITICULTURE METHOD **Conventional**

Let's begin with some important news. Soon, another of Giulio Grasso's daughters, Valentina, who has just turned 20, will shortly start working alongside her father and Paola, his elder daughter who is now an established part of the family winery. The performance again achieved by Giulio with the help of the ineffable Beppe Caviola is not news, though. All the wines have bags of character, impeccable cleanness, depth, pure, clear expression of their territory and show beautifully gauged balance. Hard to imagine that anyone could do better!

Eleven wines were presented. The two whites and the Moscato, all '08s, are precise, made as they should be and great to drink. The Nebbiolo '07 is good, the Dolcetto '08 almost as excellent as the fabulous '07, the Barbera Giardin '07 is lovely and the Barbera Paolina '07 exquisite. Now for the '06 Barbarescos. As ever, the caressing Valgrande is more approachable while the Marcarini is one of the best ever, presenting succulent and long with a finish nuanced by damp earth. The Asili is less open but wonderfully deep, its exceptional grace winning it Three Glasses. The Barbaresco Pora '05 is stylish, flowery and perfectly gauged. All in all, a showing to remember.

La Ca' Növa

S.DA OVELLO, 4
12050 BARBARESCO [CN]
TEL. 0173635123
lacanova@libero.it

CELLAR SALES
PRE-BOOKED VISITS

ANNUAL PRODUCTION **50,000 bottles**
HECTARES UNDER VINE **13.5**
VITICULTURE METHOD **Conventional**

This is an estate with historic roots. The vine stock stands entirely within the prestigious municipality of Barbaresco, with around 15 hectares of red grapes. Nebbiolo dominates and reflects the characteristics of this major territory in the contrasting vineyards of Montestefano and Bric Mentina. The winery style is as natural as possible, with ageing in large wooden barrels and the exclusion of any treatment that could alter the essence of the nebbiolo grape. Importantly, the Roccas have always been noted for their very fair pricing.

In classic style, the '06 Bric Mentina offers tobacco and dried flowers on the nose and a perfectly balanced palate, ensuring that it came away with Three Glasses. The Barbaresco Montestefano from the same vintage is a little more closed but still stylish, with a well balanced palate. The fruity Barbera d'Alba Loreto, here in the '07 version, is consistently good drinking, as is the Dolcetto d'Alba '08.

● Barbaresco Asili '06	♟♟♟ 6
● Barbaresco Marcarini '06	♟♟ 6
● Barbaresco Pora '05	♟♟ 7
● Barbaresco Valgrande '06	♟♟ 6
● Barbera d'Alba Paolina '07	♟♟ 4*
● Barbera d'Alba Giardin '07	♟♟ 4
○ Langhe Chardonnay Luna d'Agosto '08	♟♟ 4*
○ Langhe Chardonnay Sermine '08	♟♟ 5
● Langhe Nebbiolo Bric del Baio '07	♟♟ 4
○ Moscato d'Asti '08	♟♟ 4*
● Dolcetto d'Alba Lodoli '08	♟ 4
● Barbaresco Pora '04	♟♟♟ 7
● Barbaresco Valgrande '04	♟♟♟ 6
● Barbaresco Asili '04	♟♟ 6

● Barbaresco Bric Mentina '06	♟♟♟ 5*
● Barbaresco Montestefano '06	♟♟ 5
● Barbaresco '06	♟♟ 5
● Barbera d'Alba Loreto '07	♟♟ 4*
● Dolcetto d'Alba '08	♟ 3
● Barbaresco Bric Mentina '01	♟♟♟ 6*
● Barbaresco '05	♟♟ 5*
● Barbaresco Bric Mentina '05	♟♟ 5*
● Barbaresco Montestefano '05	♟♟ 5*
● Barbera d'Alba Loreto '06	♟♟ 4*

Ca' Rome' - Romano Marengo

S.DA RABAJÀ, 86/88
12050 BARBARESCO [CN]
TEL. 0173635126
www.carome.com

CELLAR SALES
PRE-BOOKED VISITS

ANNUAL PRODUCTION **30,000 bottles**
HECTARES UNDER VINE **5**
VITICULTURE METHOD **Conventional**

Romano Marengo began his career as an oenologist in 1980, when he took over a small, very well maintained cellar and began fermenting only classic Langhe red wines. In view of the exciting results, he then acquired small plots in some of the prestigious vineyards in the Barolo and Barbaresco areas. The flagship wine of the cellar, where his son Giuseppe also works nowadays as an oenologist and his daughter Paola in public relations, is without doubt the Barbaresco Maria di Brun, a selection of the best nebbiolo grapes that is only bottled in great years.

Excellent results came from the '06 Barbarescos. The very decent Rio Sordo has a complex nose of spice and raspberry, with dense, developing tannins helped by pleasing acidity. The Maria di Brun is particularly stylish, with violets on the nose and delicate harmony on the palate. In a similar vein but slightly less structured is the equally good Chiaramanti. The intense Barolo Cerretta '05, from Serralunga d'Alba, has a powerful palate and a weighty texture of tannins that reflect the cellar's refined production techniques. The Barbera La Gamberaja is always beautifully classic, the '07 vintage being especially successful.

● Barbaresco Chiaramanti '06	♙♙ 7
● Barbaresco Maria di Brun '06	♙♙ 8
● Barbaresco Sorì Rio Sordo '06	♙♙ 7
● Barolo V. Cerretta '05	♙♙ 8
● Barbera d'Alba La Gamberaja '07	♙♙ 5
● Barolo Rapet '05	♙♙ 8
● Barbaresco '05	♟♟ 7
● Barbaresco Maria di Brun '05	♟♟ 8
● Barbaresco Maria di Brun '04	♟♟ 8
● Barbaresco Sorì Rio Sordo '05	♟♟ 7
● Barolo Rapet '04	♟♟ 7
● Barolo Rapet '03	♟♟ 7
● Barolo V. Cerretta '04	♟♟ 7

Cascina Ca' Rossa

LOC. CASCINA CA' ROSSA, 56
12043 CANALE [CN]
TEL. 017398348
www.cascinacarossa.com

CELLAR SALES
PRE-BOOKED VISITS

ANNUAL PRODUCTION **60,000 bottles**
HECTARES UNDER VINE **15**
VITICULTURE METHOD **Naturale**

Angelo Ferrio is the creative force of this lovely winery at Canale. Thanks to total commitment, relentless work in the vineyards, strict attention to quality and the development of organic techniques in recent years, Angelo now produces of some of the best wines in Roero. The farm has several vineyard selections, such as Mompissano and Audinaggio, where a hectare of more than 40-year-old vines on sandy soil yield fruit for the estate's top wine.

Roero Audinaggio won the Three Glasses again this year, showing that it is one of the finest expressions of a Nebbiolo grown on Roero's trademark sandy soil. The 2007 version offers aromas of dried flowers and liquorice in an aristocratic nose while the palate is stylish, with body, fruit, an elegant weave of tannins and a long, characterful finish. Roero Mompissano Riserva '06 is also superb, presenting complex, harmonious, with a refined tannic weave and great length. The two Barbera d'Albas are excellent. Mulassa '07 is fruity, well-balanced, and has nicely-gauged acid and tannins while the basic '08 has tones of berry fruit and tobacco. Roero Arneis Merica '08 is agreeable.

● Roero Audinaggio '07	♙♙♙ 6
● Roero Mompissano Ris. '06	♙♙ 6
● Barbera d'Alba '08	♙♙ 4*
● Barbera d'Alba Mulassa '07	♙♙ 6
○ Roero Arneis Merica '08	♙ 4
● Barbera d'Alba Mulassa '04	♟♟♟ 6
● Barbera d'Alba Mulassa '99	♟♟♟ 6
● Roero Audinaggio '06	♟♟♟ 6
● Roero Audinaggio '01	♟♟♟ 6
● Roero Vigna Audinaggio '96	♟♟♟ 6
● Barbera d'Alba Mulassa '06	♟♟ 6
● Langhe Nebbiolo '07	♟♟ 4*
○ Roero Arneis Merica '07	♟♟ 4*
● Roero Mompissano Ris. '05	♟♟ 6

★ Ca' Viola

B.TA SAN LUIGI, 11
12063 DOGLIANI [CN]
TEL. 017370547
www.caviola.com

Marco Canato

FRAZ. FONS SALERA
LOC. CA' BALDEA, 18/2
15049 VIGNALE MONFERRATO [AL]
TEL. 0142933653
www.canatovini.it

CELLAR SALES
PRE-BOOKED VISITS

CELLAR SALES
PRE-BOOKED VISITS

ANNUAL PRODUCTION 50,000 bottles
HECTARES UNDER VINE 11
VITICULTURE METHOD Conventional

ANNUAL PRODUCTION 30,000 bottles
HECTARES UNDER VINE 11
VITICULTURE METHOD Conventional

Beppe Caviola is one of the most respected oenologists in Italy. Involved with many of Italy's leading estates as a consultant, he continues to preside over his own small operation with unwavering passion. Each year, with his wife Simonetta and the aid of their trusty helpers, especially Simone Dodi, Beppe produces around 50,000 bottles, busying himself with Dolcetto, his long time love, and seeking to impart a sense of place into all his wines, including the Barbera and the Nebbiolo.

Bric du Luv '07, a Barbera d'Alba DOC since this year, is superlative and earned Three very stylish and Three Glasses. The nose is intense, refined, complex and fresh-tasting while the palate is long and subtly stylish. The Langhe Nebbiolo '07 encored last year's great performance. It's one of the very best in this category with its raspberry and sweet tobacco on the nose, a powerful palate with a juicy finish and perfectly balanced tannins. The Dolcetto d'Alba Barturot '08, from vines at Montelupo, is just as exciting. Fabulous caressing aromas put it at the peak of its category. An elegant and harmonious rather than powerful palate makes it already delicious.

Ca' Baldea, the home of the Canato farm estate, lies in the hills of Vignale Monferrato, above the historic village of Fons Salera. Ca' Baldea has been making news since 1740, when Bishop Caravadossi purchased the farmstead known as Baldea, in Vignale. The Canato family has run it since the 1950s, first as tenant farmers then as owners. In 2006, to celebrate half a century of work, they made a wine from native Monferrato barbera, freisa and grignolino grapes, released this year in 600 magnums.

The name of the wine is 50 Anni. The ruby tends to garnet red ushering in scents of spice and walnutskin. The Barbera Superiore Rapet '06 presents an intense garnet, with tobacco, blackberry and spice aromas and a harmonious, lingering palate. Gambaloita '08 is an uncomplicated, well-made Barbera. Anyone who loves a semi-sparkling Barbera should not miss La Birbona, an excellent example of a classic Monferrato wine. We will end with one of the best Grignolinos tasted this year, Celio '08. It's in fine form, highlighting the characteristic aromatics of the grapes.

● Barbera d'Alba Bric du Luv '07	♀♀♀ 6
● Dolcetto d'Alba Barturot '08	♀♀ 5
● Langhe Nebbiolo '07	♀♀ 5*
● Barbera d'Alba Brichet '08	♀♀ 5
● Dolcetto d'Alba Vilot '08	♀♀ 4*
● Dolcetto d'Alba Barturot '07	♀♀♀ 5
● Dolcetto d'Alba Barturot '05	♀♀♀ 5
● Dolcetto d'Alba Barturot '01	♀♀♀ 5
● Langhe Rosso Bric du Luv '05	♀♀♀ 6
● Langhe Rosso Bric du Luv '03	♀♀♀ 6
● Langhe Rosso Bric du Luv '01	♀♀♀ 6
● Langhe Rosso Bric du Luv '99	♀♀♀ 6
● Langhe Rosso Bric du Luv '98	♀♀♀ 6
● Langhe Rosso Bric du Luv '96	♀♀♀ 6

● 50 Anni '06	♀♀ 4
● Barbera del M.to La Birbona '08	♀♀ 3*
● Barbera del M.to Sup. Rapet '06	♀♀ 4
● Grignolino del M.to Casalese Celio '08	♀♀ 4*
● Barbera del M.to Gambaloita '08	♀ 3
● Barbera del M.to Gambaloita '07	♀♀ 3*
● Barbera del M.to Sup. La Baldea '06	♀♀ 4*
● Barbera del M.to Sup. Rapet '05	♀♀ 4*
● Grignolino del M.to Casalese Celio '07	♀♀ 4*
○ Piemonte Chardonnay Bric di Bric '05	♀♀ 4*

Cantina del Pino

S.DA OVELLO, 31
12050 BARBARESCO [CN]
TEL. 0173635147
www.cantinadelpino.com

ANNUAL PRODUCTION 35,000 bottles
HECTARES UNDER VINE 7
VITICULTURE METHOD Conventional

Renato Vacca's beautiful, efficient winery was only established in 1997 but it is on course towards consistent, reliable quality. Well-organized production and an intelligent, personal style characterize all the wines offered. The cellar aims to be a benchmark for the Barbaresco designation and has for some time been at the top of the DOCG's production with the ever successful Ovello vineyard selection. The overall style of the winery is basically modern but Renato pays meticulous attention to the longevity and classic nature of his wines.

The complex Barbaresco Albesani '05 comes from a lovely vineyard at Neive, near the famous Gallina cru, facing west and south-west). Three Glasses for its first appearance. Dried roses and liquorice on the nose precede a flavoursome palate with great concentration and perfect balance. The extremely successful Ovello '05 is similar, though with some sweeter notes, and its thrust on the palate is somewhat more contained. A lovely fruit component makes the Barbaresco '06 very appealing

● Barbaresco Albesani '05	▼▼▼	7
● Barbaresco Ovello '05	▼▼	7
● Barbaresco '06	▼▼	6
● Barbera d'Alba '07	▼▼	5
● Langhe Nebbiolo '07	▼▼	4*
● Dolcetto d'Alba '08	▼	4
● Langhe Freisa '08	▼	4
● Barbaresco '04	▽▽▽	6*
● Barbaresco '03	▽▽▽	5*
● Barbaresco '05	▽▽	6*
● Barbaresco Ovello '04	▽▽	7
● Barbaresco Ovello '03	▽▽	7

La Caplana

VIA CIRCONVALLAZIONE, 4
15060 BOSIO [AL]
TEL. 0143684182
lacaplana@libero.it

CELLAR SALES
PRE-BOOKED VISITS

ANNUAL PRODUCTION 100,000 bottles
HECTARES UNDER VINE 1.5
VITICULTURE METHOD Conventional

Guido Natalino has moved up to a full profile after a few years of waiting. His work over the period has improved the quality of his products exponentially. So hats off to this small winery at Bosio which, like other great competitors, has managed to carve out a space for itself. The range is impressive. Four wines were presented, of which two reached the final, with special praise for the Narciso, the finest Dolcetto di Ovada we tasted this year.

The Gavi di Gavi '08 entices on the nose for its complex aromas and on the palate for its savoury, slowly unfolding chewy fruit. The Narciso '07 is ruby verging on garnet red in hue, with fruity aromas that show its youth, and a phenomenally intense, long, alcohol-rich palate. The Barbera Rubis '06 has cinchona and tobacco on the nose with a concentrated, pervasive mouthfeel. Our review of the range ends with one of La Caplana's fortes, the Gavi Vigna Vecchia '08, a well-co-ordinated white that is as intense on the nose as it is elegant and lingering on the palate.

● Dolcetto di Ovada Narciso '07	▼▼	3*
○ Gavi del Comune di Gavi '08	▼▼	4
● Barbera d'Asti Rubis '06	▼▼	3*
○ Gavi V. Vecchia '08	▼▼	3*
● Barbera d'Asti Rubis '05	▽▽	3*
● Dolcetto di Ovada Narciso '06	▽▽	3*
○ Gavi del Comune di Gavi '07	▽▽	4*
○ Gavi del Comune di Gavi V. Vecchia '07	▽▽	3*
○ Gavi Vigna Vecchia '05	▽▽	3*

La Casaccia

VIA BARBANO DANTE, 10
15034 CELLA MONTE [AL]
TEL. 0142489986
www.lacasaccia.biz

CELLAR SALES

ANNUAL PRODUCTION **25,000 bottles**
HECTARES UNDER VINE **7.5**
VITICULTURE METHOD **Conventional**

Having taken up the viticultural heritage of their grandparents in Monferrato, Elena and Giovanni Rava, both agriculture graduates, are making a name for themselves. In the space of a few years, technical knowledge and enthusiasm have transformed this winery into one of the benchmarks of the Casale Monferrato area. Great attention is paid to product quality, both on the vine and in the cellar, and since 2000 vineyard management has been organic. The range of wines presented is fine evidence of the work carried out at La Casaccia.

The Barbera Superiore Calichè '06 is complex on the nose and offers exciting sensations on the palate, where it picks up the fruit from the bouquet, together with exceptional density. The Poggetto '08 is tip-top. One of the best Grignolinos tasted this year, its spice and fruit notes on the nose are the prelude to a savoury, well-structured and balanced palate. The Piemonte Chardonnay Charnò '08 is worth uncorking for its flowery aromas and lovely intense palate.

Casalone

VIA MARCONI, 100
15040 LU [AL]
TEL. 0131741280
www.casalone.it

CELLAR SALES
PRE-BOOKED VISITS

ANNUAL PRODUCTION **50,000 bottles**
HECTARES UNDER VINE **10**
VITICULTURE METHOD **Conventional**

Casale Monferrat is showing its potential year after year. The varied composition of its soil contributes to the uniqueness of this area, and the patient work of the growers is fundamental to a territory that continues to produce new talent. The Casalone family winery has proved its worth for some time now and every year turns in a notable performance. The range is admirably uniform, with a peak of excellence in the Monferrato Rosso Rus, which performed well enough to get to the final tastings.

Rus '07, from barbera, merlot and pinot nero, is deep garnet red. A nose of plum jam and tertiary notes converges into a masterfully firm, lingering palate. Rubermillo '07 is a Barbera d'Asti with a headily elegant nose and a warm, intense palate. Fandamat '07, from pinot nero grapes only, has spicy notes let the fruit shine through and a harmonious, firm palate. The Monemvasia '08, from malvasia greca, is aromatic and intense on nose and palate. Finally, the Vendemmia Tardiva Monemvasia '06 is complex on the nose while the palate find a beautiful balance of sweetness and acidity.

● Barbera d'Asti Sup. Calichè '06	▼▼	5
● Grignolino del M.to Casalese Poggeto '08	▼▼	4*
○ Piemonte Chardonnay Charnò '08	▼	4
● Barbera d'Asti Sup. Calichè '04	♈♈	5
● Barbera d'Asti V. Sant'Anna '07	♈♈	4*
● Barbera d'Asti V. Sant'Anna '06	♈♈	4*
● Barbera del M.to Sup. Bricco del Bosco '06	♈♈	5
● Grignolino del M.to Casalese Poggeto '07	♈♈	4*
● Grignolino del M.to Casalese Poggeto '06	♈♈	4*

● M.to Rosso Rus '07	▼▼	4*
● Barbera d'Asti Rubermillo '07	▼▼	4
○ Monemvasia '08	▼▼	4
○ Monemvasia V. T. '06	▼▼	5
● Monferrato Rosso Fandamat '07	▼▼	4
● Barbera d'Asti Rubermillo '05	♈♈	4*
● Barbera del M.to Bricco Morlantino Sup. '06	♈♈	4*
● M.to Rosso Rus '06	♈♈	4
● M.to Rosso Rus '05	♈♈	4*
○ Monemvasia '06	♈♈	3*

Cascina Adelaide

VIA AIE SOTTANE, 14
12060 BAROLO [CN]
TEL. 0173560503
www.cascinaadelaide.com

CELLAR SALES
PRE-BOOKED VISITS

ANNUAL PRODUCTION 50,000 bottles
HECTARES UNDER VINE 9
VITICULTURE METHOD Conventional

This winery operating in the Barolo area is a good example of synergy between significant investment by a non-agricultural entrepreneur and the will to set out on the hard road of quality in winemaking. The winery, futuristic and functional, blends well into its rural landscape. From the various wines, which are increasingly interesting, it seems appropriate to highlight Preda, a little known selection from a vineyard of tufa and calcareous marl, which imparts totally unique, intriguing qualities to the flavour.

The product of a difficult year, the Barolo Riserva '03 is a little rustic, tannic and ready for drinking. The Preda '05 is complex and not yet fully focused on the nose, but soft and generous on the palate. The modern Barolo Cannubi '05 evokes raspberries, and the palate is already velvety. The Barolo 4 Vigne '05 is slightly less stylish in the tasting due to its rigid tannins. The Barbera Superiore Preda '07 is still faintly woody, but it has very sound texture. Made from the extremely rare nascetta grapes, the unusual Langhe Bianco Le Pernici '08 is worth noting.

● Barbera d'Alba Sup. V. Preda '07	♙♙	5
● Barolo 4 Vigne '05	♙♙	7
● Barolo Cannubi '05	♙♙	8
● Barolo Preda '05	♙♙	8
● Barolo Per Elen Ris. '03	♙	8
○ Langhe Bianco Le Pernici '08	♙	4
● Barbera d'Alba Sup. Amabilin '06	♙♙	6
● Barbera d'Alba Sup. V. Preda '06	♙♙	5
● Barolo Cannubi '04	♙♙	8
● Barolo Fossati '04	♙♙	8
● Barolo Per Elen Ris. '01	♙♙	8
● Barolo Preda '04	♙♙	8
● Dolcetto di Diano d'Alba Costa Fiore '07	♙♙	4

Cascina Ballarin

FRAZ. ANNUNZIATA, 115
12064 LA MORRA [CN]
TEL. 017350365
www.cascinaballarin.it

CELLAR SALES
PRE-BOOKED VISITS
VISITOR FACILITIES

ANNUAL PRODUCTION 40,000 bottles
HECTARES UNDER VINE 7
VITICULTURE METHOD Conventional

The wines of the Viberti family are very representative of Langhe. Year after year, they reveal the Vibertis' skills in sensory profiles that are sure to appeal. Combine wine with farm holidays and you have a marriage of professionalism and hospitality that caters for the increasing numbers of visitors from Italy and abroad who are attracted by the prospect. The wines are balanced and produced from top varieties. Sourced from the territories of Monforte and La Morra, they reveal different angles and nuances as only nebbiolo knows how.

The Barolo Bricco Rocca '05 has notes of fruit in liqueur and a rugged palate, despite prominent alcohol. Another alcohol-rich Barolo, the Bussia '05, is softer. Although less expensive, Barolo Tre Ciabot '05 is very decent, showing slightly more evolved and short on the palate. Over the years, Barbera Giuli has become a benchmark for pleasant drinking, not so much because of its power as for its well-orchestrated taste. The '07 vintage is no exception and has a bit more attack on the palate.

● Barolo Bussia '05	♙♙	8
● Barbera d'Alba Giuli '07	♙♙	6
● Barbera d'Alba Pilade '07	♙♙	4*
● Barolo Bricco Rocca '05	♙♙	8
● Barolo Tre Ciabot '05	♙♙	6
● Langhe Nebbiolo '07	♙♙	5
● Langhe Rosso Ballarin '06	♙♙	5
● Dolcetto d'Alba Bussia '08	♙	4
● Dolcetto d'Alba Pilade '08	♙	4
○ Langhe Bianco Ballarin '08	♙	4
● Langhe Rosso Cino '08	♙	3
● Barolo Bricco Rocca Tistot Ris. '00	♙♙	8
● Barolo Bussia '04	♙♙	8
● Barolo Bussia '03	♙♙	8

Cascina Bongiovanni

FRAZ. UCCELLACCIO
VIA ALBA BAROLO, 4
12060 CASTIGLIONE FALLETTO [CN]
TEL. 0173262184
www.cascinabongiovanni.com

CELLAR SALES
PRE-BOOKED VISITS

ANNUAL PRODUCTION 35,000 bottles
HECTARES UNDER VINE 6.2
VITICULTURE METHOD Conventional

This tiny estate seldom harvests more than 400 quintals of grapes, with which it produces no more than 30,000 bottles each year. But it is the right size to offer a serene lifestyle for the lively, passionate Davide Mozzone, a man who is apparently tireless in the effort he lavishes on vineyard and cellar.

The Barolo Pernanno '05 presents a rich, still distinctly ruby red. The nose is initially marked by oak, which gives way to red berries and liquorice, before the powerful palate reprises sweet wood on the finish. The long, characterful Barolo '05 is fresher-tasting and more balsamic but less structured. From the now classic blend of cabernet, barbera and nebbiolo comes an enjoyable, not too complex Langhe Faletto '07, which has lovely thrust on the palate. Of the two Dolcetto '08s, the Diano d'Alba is deeper, with more harmony on the palate. The Arneis '08 is not a big wine but it has a nice hint of aniseed, showing uncomplicated, not too intense, refreshing and vegetal.

Cascina Bruciata

S.DA RIO SORDO, 46
12050 BARBARESCO [CN]
TEL. 0173638826
cascina.bruciata@tiscali.it

CELLAR SALES
PRE-BOOKED VISITS

ANNUAL PRODUCTION 35,000 bottles
HECTARES UNDER VINE 7
VITICULTURE METHOD Conventional

Rio Sordo, a major Barbaresco vineyard with superb exposure to the south and south-west, forms the enchanting natural setting for this producer's small, young estate. The Balbo family has been committed to quality-oriented farming and winemaking with no short cuts ever since they started out in 2001.

Barbaresco and Dolcetto, the two cornerstones of the estate, are both complex. The Riserva '04 is a success, with lovely ripe fruit and sweet spices on the nose preceding a full-flavoured, soft, caressing palate. The Barbaresco Rio Sordo '06 has breadth on the nose, with tannins that still bite a little on the back palate. Nebbiolo Usignolo '07 is well structured and very clean on the nose. The charming Dolcetto Rio Sordo '08, which spent a brief period in casks, has a particularly rich, palate for it comes from the oldest vines on the estate. The Dolcetto Rian '08 is less complex and decidedly rustic.

● Barolo Pernanno '05	▼▼ 7
● Barbera d'Alba '07	▼▼ 5
● Barolo '05	▼▼ 6
● Dolcetto di Diano d'Alba '08	▼▼ 4
● Langhe Rosso Faletto '07	▼▼ 6
● Dolcetto d'Alba '08	▼ 4
○ Langhe Arneis '08	▼ 4
● Barolo Pernanno '01	♈♈♈ 7
● Barolo '03	♈♈ 6
● Barolo Pernanno '04	♈♈ 7
● Barolo Pernanno '00	♈♈ 7
● Langhe Rosso Faletto '05	♈♈ 5
● Langhe Rosso Faletto '03	♈♈ 5

● Barbaresco Rio Sordo Ris. '04	▼▼ 7
● Barbaresco Rio Sordo '06	▼▼ 6
● Dolcetto d'Alba Vign. Rio Sordo '08	▼▼ 4*
● Langhe Nebbiolo Vign. dell'Usignolo '07	▼▼ 4
● Dolcetto d'Alba Rian '08	▼ 4
● Barbaresco '05	♈♈ 6
● Barbaresco '04	♈♈ 6
● Barbaresco Rio Sordo '05	♈♈ 6
● Barbaresco Rio Sordo '03	♈♈ 6
● Dolcetto d'Alba Rian '07	♈♈ 4
● Dolcetto d'Alba Vign. Rio Sordo '07	♈♈ 4
● Dolcetto d'Alba Vign. Rio Sordo '06	♈♈ 4*

Cascina Castlet

S.DA CASTELLETTO, 6
14055 COSTIGLIOLE D'ASTI [AT]
TEL. 0141966651
www.cascinacastlet.com

CELLAR SALES
PRE-BOOKED VISITS

ANNUAL PRODUCTION **200,000 bottles**
HECTARES UNDER VINE **20**
VITICULTURE METHOD **Naturale**

Situated at Costigliole d'Asti, Cascina Castlet has belonged to the Borio family for generations. Currently, it is run by the dynamic Mariuccia, an indefatigable winemaker. Over the last few years, she has been working to create a winery with a low environmental impact – producing organic wines – and to recover varieties that are almost extinct, such as uvalino. The 20 hectares of the estate are principally devoted to the typical grapes of this area, moscato and barbera.

Cascina Castlet presented one of the best Moscato Passitos we tasted this year. Avié '07 has fresh, refined lemon cream and candied citrus peel, a beautifully elegant palate and a zesty, vibrant, leisurely finish. The Barbera d'Asti Superiore Passum '06 is subtly intense, with cherry notes and cinchona on the nose, marked acidity on the classic palate and a vibrant finish lacking only a little more flesh. The rest of the wines are well made, in particular the Barbera del Monferrato Casalese Vivace Goj '08, a fruity easy drinker, and the Barbera d'Asti Superiore Litina '06, which shows intense, rustic and alcohol-rich.

Cascina Chicco

VIA VALENTINO, 144
12043 CANALE [CN]
TEL. 0173979411
www.cascinachicco.com

CELLAR SALES
PRE-BOOKED VISITS

ANNUAL PRODUCTION **230,000 bottles**
HECTARES UNDER VINE **28**
VITICULTURE METHOD **Conventional**

The winery of brothers Enrico and Marco Faccenda, founded halfway through the last century, has got much larger in recent years, with modernization of the cellar and purchases of new land. They have added plots at Monforte d'Alba to the vineyards at Canale, Anterisio and Mompissano, and the plots at Vezza d'Alba, Castellinaldo and Castagnito. Production concentrates on vines traditional to the area.

There was a good showing overall from the Faccendas. The Roero Valmaggiore Riserva '06 stands out for its wild strawberry, raspberry, dried flowers and liquorice, followed by a powerful, well-structured palate. Arcass '06 is very distinguished. A characterful late harvest of arneis with aromas of white truffle and caramel, it has a powerful, refreshing palate while Barbera d'Alba Granera Alta '08 has notes of ripe dark berries, spice and tar leading to a long palate. Langhe Nebbiolo '07 is tangy and fruity, with subtle, juicy tannins, and Nebbiolo d'Alba Mompissano '07 has lovely wild raspberry, tobacco, spice and liquorice, with a soft, full palate.

○ Piemonte Moscato Passito Avié '07	♟♟	5
● Barbera d'Asti Sup. Passum '06	♟♟	6
● Barbera d'Asti '08	♟	4
● Barbera d'Asti Sup. Litina '06	♟	4
● Barbera del M.to Casalese Vivace Goj '08	♟	4
○ Moscato d'Asti '08	♟	4
○ Piemonte Chardonnay A Taj '08	♟	4
● Barbera d'Asti Sup. Litina '05	♟♟	5
● Barbera d'Asti Sup. Passum '05	♟♟	5
● Barbera d'Asti Sup. Passum '05	♟♟	5
● Barbera d'Asti Sup. Passum '04	♟♟	5
● Barbera d'Asti Sup. Passum '01	♟♟	5

● Roero Valmaggiore Ris. '06	♟♟	5
○ Arcass V. T. '06	♟♟	5
● Barbera d'Alba Granera Alta '08	♟♟	4*
● Langhe Nebbiolo '07	♟♟	4*
● Nebbiolo d'Alba Mompissano '07	♟♟	5
● Barbera d'Alba Bric Loira '07	♟	5
○ Langhe Favorita '08	♟	4
● Langhe Nebbiolo '08	♟	4
○ Arcàss Passito '04	♟♟♟	5
● Barbera d'Alba Bric Loira '98	♟♟♟	5
● Barbera d'Alba Bric Loira '97	♟♟♟	5
● Nebbiolo d'Alba Mompissano '99	♟♟♟	5
○ Arcàss Passito '06	♟♟	5
● Barbera d'Alba Bric Loira '06	♟♟	5
● Nebbiolo d'Alba Mompissano '06	♟♟	5
○ Roero Arneis Anterisio '07	♟♟	4*
● Roero Montespinato '06	♟♟	4*
● Roero Valmaggiore '05	♟♟	5

Cascina Corte

FRAZ. SAN LUIGI
B.TA VALDIBERTI, 33
12063 DOGLIANI [CN]
TEL. 0173743539
www.cascinacorte.it

CELLAR SALES
PRE-BOOKED VISITS
VISITOR FACILITIES

ANNUAL PRODUCTION 30,000 bottles
HECTARES UNDER VINE 5
VITICULTURE METHOD Organic certified

It's impossible to ignore the enthusiasm and friendliness shown by the two proprietors, Amalia Battaglia and Sandro Barosi. Having fallen in love with this small abandoned farm at Dogliani, the pair now devote themselves to the production of a few thousand bottles a year of mainly Dolcetto, with small batches of Nebbiolo and Barbera.

Vigna Pirochetta '07 has an intense, vibrant nose with wonderfully fruity spiced notes that expand the usual complexity of the grape. It is rich and powerful on a palate backed by elegant tannins and a long warm finish. The Dolcetto di Dogliani '08 rises to its role as archetype of the variety, with its heady, almondy sensations, followed by exuberant red berries with a refreshing, soft palate not short of pulp. The Nebbiolo '07 offers aromas of moderate intensity, characterized by perceptions of raspberries and liquorice. The palate is harmonious, with power, alcohol and tannins. Note that all the wines are organically farmed and very reasonably priced.

● Dogliani V. Pirochetta '07	♀♀	4*
● Dolcetto di Dogliani '08	♀♀	3*
● Langhe Nebbiolo '07	♀♀	5
☉ Matilde '08	♀	4
● Dogliani V. Pirochetta '06	♀♀	4
● Dolcetto di Dogliani '07	♀♀	3*
● Langhe Nebbiolo '06	♀♀	5

Cascina Cucco

LOC. CUCCO
VIA MAZZINI, 10
12050 SERRALUNGA D'ALBA [CN]
TEL. 0173613003
www.cascinacucco.com

CELLAR SALES
PRE-BOOKED VISITS

ANNUAL PRODUCTION 60,000 bottles
HECTARES UNDER VINE 12
VITICULTURE METHOD Conventional

The winery of the Stroppiana family, Piedmontese entrepreneurs known throughout the world, is on the edge of the municipality of Serralunga and the headquarters is located in a site of great charm and elegance. All the investment undertaken by this young estate comes under the heading of research into winemaking excellence. The range of wines is convincing and moving towards a precise definition of style, in search of the personality necessary to earn a suitable place in the pantheon of Langhe wines.

From the Barolo '05 series, the Cerrati, sourced from the celebrated vineyard at Serralunga, is outstanding. Vivid, intense garnet-tinged ruby ushers in a modern-style nose with an agreeable, well-balanced medley of red fruit and prominent oak before sensations of cinchona and dried flowers come through. The performance on the palate is similar. Oak again plays an important role while supporting dense fruity pulp.

● Barbera d'Alba Sup. '07	♀♀	5
● Barolo Cerrati '05	♀♀	6
● Langhe Rosso Mondo '07	♀♀	5
● Barbera d'Alba '08	♀	4
● Dolcetto d'Alba Vughera '08	♀	4
○ Langhe Chardonnay '08	♀	4
● Barbera d'Alba Sup. '05	♀♀	5
● Barolo Cerrati '04	♀♀	6
● Barolo V. Cerrati '01	♀♀	7
● Barolo V. Cerrati '00	♀♀	7
● Barolo V. Cucco '03	♀♀	7
● Barolo V. Cucco '01	♀♀	7

Cascina Fonda

VIA SPESSA, 27
12057 NEIVE [CN]
TEL. 0173677156
www.cascinafonda.com

CELLAR SALES
PRE-BOOKED VISITS
VISITOR FACILITIES

ANNUAL PRODUCTION **120,000 bottles**
HECTARES UNDER VINE **12**
VITICULTURE METHOD **Conventional**

The Barbero brothers' winery has been full of dynamism and personality for years. Commitment to improving the moscato grape has led them to take on the role as a benchmark for quality, which consumers have learnt to recognize and appreciate. The bottles presented also feature a distinctive design on the interesting and original labels.

The style of the estate tends towards subtle, stylish Moscato d'Astis with aromatic freshness and flavour, so perfectly in tune with the overall style of the '08. In the Moscato Del Piano, the general freshness is obvious and the nose brims with candied lemon fragrances and nice vegetal notes, moving on to a lively, tasty finale. On a similar note, the Asti '08 is essentially delicate, in line with its wine type. Erroneously rated in the last edition of the Guide, the Asti Metodo Classico '05 was disgorged at the end of 2008 and will reward investigation.

○ Asti Driveri M. Cl. '05	♥♥	6
○ Asti Spumante Bel Paisì '08	♥♥	4*
○ Moscato d'Asti Del Piano '08	♥♥	4*
● Dolcetto d'Alba Brusalino '08	♥	4
● Piemonte Brachetto '08	♥	4

Cascina Garitina

VIA GIANOLA, 20
14040 CASTEL BOGLIONE [AT]
TEL. 0141762162
www.cascinagaritina.it

CELLAR SALES
PRE-BOOKED VISITS

ANNUAL PRODUCTION **180,000 bottles**
HECTARES UNDER VINE **26**
VITICULTURE METHOD **Conventional**

Cascina Garitina, a working estate that has been family run since the 20th century, is now managed by Gianluca Morino, a capable, passionate wine man. Gianluca's main objective is to improve the main Asti variety, barbera. He has planted 70 per cent of the estate, in various municipalities in upper Monferrato, to the grape and works in the vineyard with care, respecting the territory and producing wines with lashings of personality, also inventing new products. As well as his barbera, Gianluca harvests dolcetto, pinot nero, cabernet sauvignon, merlot and brachetto.

Morino loves to experiment and so we have the Rugiada '04, the first year for a sweet wine from dried barbera grapes. It has great complexity on the nose of olives, baked plums and chocolate, and a rich, sweet palate with huge structure that lacks a little balance. Monferrato Rosso Amis '05, from half merlot, 35 per cent cabernet sauvignon and barbera, is classy, with green notes and a powerful, juicily long palate. Barbera d'Asti Superiore Nizza Neuvsent '06 is fruity, minerally and long but not quite as complex or deep as earlier versions. Brachetto d'Acqui Niades '08 has roses and forest fruits on the nose and a pleasant palate with a nice encore of fruit.

● Barbera d'Asti Sup. Nizza Neuvsent '06	♥♥	5
● Brachetto d'Acqui Niades '08	♥♥	4
● M.to Rosso Amis '05	♥♥	5
● Rugiada '04	♥♥	6
● Barbera del M.to Vivace Il Morinaccio '08	♥	4
● M.to Rosso Alfero '06	♥	5
● Barbera d'Asti Sup. Caranti '06	♥♥	4*
● Barbera d'Asti Sup. Nizza Neuvsent '05	♥♥	5
● Barbera d'Asti Sup. Nizza Neuvsent '04	♥♥	5
● M.to Rosso Alfero '04	♥♥	5

Cascina Gilli

VIA NEVISSANO, 36
14022 CASTELNUOVO DON BOSCO [AT]
TEL. 0119876984
www.cascinagilli.it

CELLAR SALES
PRE-BOOKED VISITS

ANNUAL PRODUCTION **140,000 bottles**
HECTARES UNDER VINE **23**
VITICULTURE METHOD **Conventional**

Lying in lower Monferrato, Cascina Gilli is the love child of Gianni Vergnano and his well-trained staff, Bruno Tamagnone, Giovanni Matteis and Marco Piovano. The team has put everything into improving the typical varieties of the area – freisa in particular but also barbera, bonarda and malvasia – grown in the hills in the municipalities of Castelnuovo Don Bosco and Passerano Marmorito, where the soil is clay marl and produces fragrant wines with body.

Cascina Gilli offers fruit-forward wines from varieties many consider to be second string. Dlicà, from late-harvested malvasia, is charming. Intense, with nice strawberries and dried roses, it shows round in the mouth, where tidy tannins accompany a lovely balance of sweetness and bitter notes. The Malvasia di Castelnuovo Don Bosco '08 is fresh, giving roses and liquorice over a mid-structured palate with a lingering finish. Freisa d'Asti Vigna del Forno '07 has classic forest floor notes, then tobacco and cinchona. It's a tad rustic on the palate but it does have personality. Finally, the uncomplicated but pleasant Freisa d'Asti Vivace '08 is long and easy drinking.

Cascina La Maddalena

FRAZ. SAN GIACOMO
LOC. PIANI DEL PADRONE, 257
15078 ROCCA GRIMALDA [AL]
TEL. 0143876074
www.cascina-maddalena.com

CELLAR SALES
PRE-BOOKED VISITS
VISITOR FACILITIES

ANNUAL PRODUCTION **30,000 bottles**
HECTARES UNDER VINE **4.27**
VITICULTURE METHOD **Conventional**

The range presented by Cascina La Maddalena was missing various wines: Bricco del Bagatto, Migulle, Rossa d'Ocra and Barbera del Monferrato '08. They were not presented because they are still maturing and will be tasted for the 2011 Guide. New this year is Pian Del Merlo, a Monferrato Rosso from merlot grapes grown in a new vineyard that came into production in 2006. The yield is around 60 quintals per hectare. Ageing is special, as the wine is divided into three lots: one third matures in American oak, another in French oak and the last in stainless steel.

This new Pian Del Merlo is very deep ruby while the nose is generous and fragrant with spice-laced cherry. In the mouth, it impresses with its fine body, velvet-soft tannins and a nicely lingering flavour. The Dolcetta d'Ovada '08 is very deep ruby red and has an intense, lingering nose with clear fruitiness and a palate marked by plenty of extract made more caressing by excellent length on the rich fleshy fruit. Bricco della Maddalena is a Barbera del Monferrato characterized by the oakiness on the nose and appeal on the solid palate.

Wine	Rating
● Dlicà	⟡⟡ 5
● Freisa d'Asti V. del Forno '07	⟡⟡ 4*
● Freisa d'Asti Vivace '08	⟡⟡ 3*
● Malvasia di Castelnuovo Don Bosco '08	⟡⟡ 4*
● Barbera d'Asti V. delle More '07	⟡ 4
● Freisa d'Asti Vivace Luna di Maggio '08	⟡ 3
● Piemonte Bonarda Sernù '06	⟡ 4
● Barbera d'Asti V. delle More '06	♀♀ 4*
● Barbera d'Asti V. delle More '05	♀♀ 4*
● Barbera d'Asti V. delle More '04	♀♀ 4*
● Piemonte Bonarda Sernù '05	♀♀ 4

Wine	Rating
● Dolcetto di Ovada '08	⟡⟡ 3*
● M.to Rosso Pian del Merlo '07	⟡⟡ 4
● Barbera del M.to Bricco della Maddalena '07	⟡ 5
● Dolcetto di Ovada '07	♀♀ 3
● Dolcetto di Ovada Bricco del Bagatto '06	♀♀ 4
● Dolcetto di Ovada Bricco del Bagatto '05	♀♀ 4*
● M.to Rosso Bricco della Maddalena '04	♀♀ 5
● M.to Rosso La Decima Vendemmia '06	♀♀ 6

Cascina Roera

FRAZ. BIONZO
VIA BIONZO, 32
14055 COSTIGLIOLE D'ASTI [AT]
TEL. 0141968437
www.cascinaroera.com

CELLAR SALES
PRE-BOOKED VISITS

ANNUAL PRODUCTION **20,000 bottles**
HECTARES UNDER VINE **4**
VITICULTURE METHOD **Naturale**

The joint intentions of Carlo Rosso and Piero Nebiolo led to the creation in 2002 of this small, lively wine estate. The vineyards are located partly around the cellar in Bionzo and partly close to the castle at Costigliole. The two partners show a real interest in safeguarding the territory and decided to move into organic farming. In recent years, production has been turning increasingly to the typical vines of Asti, particularly barbera.

Carlo and Piero continue to release a range of well-made wines, such as the Barbera d'Asti Superiore San Martino '05, which has somewhat evolved scents of berry fruit in alcohol and a full palate with a long finish. Barbera d'Asti Superiore Cardin '05, again slightly evolved on the nose, gives spice and dried flowers over a fresh and agreeable palate, full of fruit and with good structure. The single-variety nebbiolo Monferrato Rosso Vigna Piva '05 is also well made. Cinchona and balsam on the nose are still marked by wood and the rather fine palate has a long finish despite the somewhat rugged tannins.

● Barbera d'Asti Sup. Cardin '05	▼▼ 4
● Barbera d'Asti Sup. S. Martino '05	▼▼ 4
● M.to Rosso V. Piva '05	▼▼ 4
● Barbera d'Asti La Roera '06	♀♀ 3*
● Barbera d'Asti Sup. Cardin '04	♀♀ 4*
● Barbera d'Asti Sup. Cardin Sel. '04	♀♀ 5
● Barbera d'Asti Sup. S. Martino '04	♀♀ 4*

Renzo Castella

VIA ALBA, 15
12055 DIANO D'ALBA [CN]
TEL. 017369203
renzocastella@virgilio.it

CELLAR SALES
PRE-BOOKED VISITS

ANNUAL PRODUCTION **25,000 bottles**
HECTARES UNDER VINE **10**
VITICULTURE METHOD **Conventional**

The Diano d'Alba area brims with character and potential, still partly undeveloped, and it deserves more attention. As it is squeezed, geographically speaking, between more famous municipalities, Diano risks not receiving the appreciation it merits. All the more reason, then, to include small estates such as that of Renzo Castella, a dynamic young Diano winemaker whose wines, with their great temperament and very competitive pricing, are object lessons in quality.

The two Dolcettos presented this year show us that Renzo has fine grape-growing plots but also that he is particularly skilful at turning them into wine. The classic Rivolta '08 is outstanding. The nose is a brilliant marriage of dark-skinned berries and youthful alcohol while the palate is full and velvety as only Dolcetto di Dianos can be. Compared to the more exclusive selection, the Dolcetto di Diano d'Alba '08 shows the same roundness but cannot compete in sheer elegance. It is a nice red with earthier connotations. Though they should be worthwhile reds, for now the Barbera Sarcat and Nebbiolo Madonnina are not quite up to it.

● Dolcetto di Diano d'Alba V. della Rivolia '08	▼▼ 3
● Dolcetto di Diano d'Alba '08	▼▼ 3*
● Barbera d'Alba V. Sarcat '07	▼ 3
● Nebbiolo d'Alba V. Madonnina '07	▼ 4
● Dolcetto di Diano d'Alba Rivolia '07	♀♀ 3*
● Dolcetto di Diano d'Alba V. della Piadvenza '07	♀♀ 3*
● Nebbiolo d'Alba V. Madonnina '06	♀♀ 4

Castellari Bergaglio

FRAZ. ROVERETO, 136
15066 GAVI [AL]
TEL. 0143644000
www.castellaribergaglio.it

CELLAR SALES
PRE-BOOKED VISITS

ANNUAL PRODUCTION **70,000 bottles**
HECTARES UNDER VINE **12**
VITICULTURE METHOD **Conventional**

Running this most famous Gavi name nowadays is Marco Bergaglio with his parents. After years of experimentation to find a new Gavi typology, he seems to have returned to the strictest classic principles, albeit in wines with a strong personality. On first tasting, these Gavis may seem simple but with ageing they become complex and flavoursome, expressing crystal-clear minerality. The vine stock is glorious, with the Fornaci and Rovereto vineyards – including some 80-year-old plants – to guarantee superb raw materials.

The Fornaci '08 has fresh herbs and damson on a minerally background. The palate is powerful, with a long finish marked by vibrant acidity and the faintest hint of bitterness. Vignavecchia '08 seems uncomplicated at first but this is contradicted by the particularly long, complex back palate, which is delightful. The Rolona '08 is the simplest of the range, although it has its own aromatics on the nose, which extend to gamey perceptions.

○ Gavi del Comune di Gavi Rovereto Vignavecchia '08	TT	4
○ Gavi del Comune di Tassarolo Fornaci '08	TT	4
○ Gavi del Comune di Gavi Rolona '08	T	4
○ Gavi del Comune di Gavi Rolona '07	YY	4
○ Gavi del Comune di Gavi Rovereto Vignavecchia '07	YY	4
○ Gavi del Comune di Tassarolo Fornaci '07	YY	4

Castello di Neive

VIA CASTELBORGO, 1
12052 NEIVE [CN]
TEL. 017367171
www.castellodineive.it

PRE-BOOKED VISITS

ANNUAL PRODUCTION **150,000 bottles**
HECTARES UNDER VINE **28**
VITICULTURE METHOD **Conventional**

If an official classification of the territories of the Barbaresco area existed, Santo Stefano di Neive would be in right up there. The expressiveness of this selection is obvious particularly after long ageing, and it contributes, together with rigorous selection in the vineyard and a winery that makes for an unforgettable visit, to making Castello di Neive one of the pinnacles of Piedmontese winemaking excellence. The style of the wines is genuine, respectful of tradition and never bows the knee to fashion or passing trends.

The Barbaresco Santo Stefano '06 is very elegant, a little light on structure, perhaps, but well balanced and harmonious. The Riserva '04 is engaging on the nose, with an incisive, varied palate, a little thin as the flavour develops but with great, convincing elegance. The muscular, fruit-packed Barbera Mattarello '07 is a good example of an excellent vintage. In line with the general interest that is developing in this area about the albarossa grape, we have the Castello '07 version, which gives lots of black berry fruit, sweet oakiness and great concentration in a slightly unruly Langhe Rosso.

● Barbaresco S. Stefano '06	TT	7
● Barbaresco S. Stefano Ris. '04	TT	8
● Barbera d'Alba Mattarello '07	TT	5
● Barbaresco '06	TT	6
● Barbera d'Alba S. Stefano '08	TT	4
○ Piemonte Pinot Nero Extra Brut '05	TT	6
○ Castello di Neive Passito '07	T	6
● Dolcetto d'Alba Basarin '08	T	4
● Dolcetto d'Alba Messoirano '08	T	4
○ Langhe Arneis Montebertotto '08	T	4
● Langhe Rosso '07	T	5
● Barbaresco S. Stefano Ris. '01	YYY	8
● Barbaresco S. Stefano Ris. '99	YYY	8
● Barbaresco S. Stefano '05	YY	6

Tenuta Castello di Razzano

FRAZ. CASARELLO
LOC. RAZZANO, 2
15021 ALFIANO NATTA [AL]
TEL. 0141922124
www.castellodirazzano.it

CELLAR SALES
PRE-BOOKED VISITS

ANNUAL PRODUCTION 200,000 bottles
HECTARES UNDER VINE 38
VITICULTURE METHOD Conventional

Tenuta Castello di Razzano lies on the border of the provinces of Alessandria and Asti. The heart of the estate is a noble dwelling with an enclosed courtyard dating from the late 17th century, renovated a few years ago and transformed into a stylish facility for wine tourists. The cellar, also part of the complex, is used for ageing important wines. Barriques and casks store the fruits of the Olearo family's labours. The flagship wines are the Barbera d'Astis, which have been appearing at our final tastings for years.

Leading the range is the Barbera Superiore Eugenea '06, which is the main player in a splendid performance for the second year running. Deep ruby introduces cherry and spices on the nose, leading to a velvety palate rich in pulp. Campasso '06 is layered on the nose, just as it is full and enveloping on the palate and very long on the finish. The Superiore Vigna del Beneficio '07 is impenetrable in colour, with toasty, estery aromatics while the Valentino Caligaris '06 gives cinchona and cherry. Completing the range are the intense, youthful Barbera Munfrà '08 and the Piemonte Chardonnay Costa al Sole '08.

Castello di Tassarolo

CASCINA ALBORINA, 1
15060 TASSAROLO [AL]
TEL. 0143342248
www.castelloditassarolo.it

CELLAR SALES
PRE-BOOKED VISITS

ANNUAL PRODUCTION 130,000 bottles
HECTARES UNDER VINE 20
VITICULTURE METHOD Organic certified

This history-soaked winery is run these days by Massimiliana Spinola, who is undertaking a total makeover of the winery, starting with conversion of the vineyards to biodynamic cultivation. The style of the wines is also moving towards natural principles, and important experiments are being carried out to avoid any type of winemaking additive, as can be seen from the message on the labels: No Sulphites.

The Gavi Alborina '07 is delightfully delicate on the nose, which has soft notes of spice and apple that follow through nicely on the not too assertive but agreeably balanced palate. Castello di Tassarolo '8 is fresh-tasting, with lovely balsam and vegetality slightly obscured by hints of gaminess. On the palate there's good body leading to a slightly bitterish long finish. The Gavi S '08 has distinctive green aromas on the nose while on the palate it is approachable, not long but pleasing and plush. The Monferrato Rosso No Sulphites '08 is pleasing, full of fruit, clean, juicy and enfolding, though a little predictable.

● Barbera d'Asti Sup. Campasso '06	♥♥ 4*
● Barbera d'Asti Sup. Eugenea '06	♥♥ 5
● Barbera d'Asti Sup. V. del Beneficio '07	♥♥ 5
● Barbera d'Asti Sup. V. Valentino Caligaris '06	♥♥ 5
● Barbera del M.to Munfrà '08	♥ 3
○ Piemonte Chardonnay Costa al Sole '08	♥ 3
● Barbera d'Asti Sup. Beneficio '06	♀♀ 5
● Barbera d'Asti Sup. Eugenea '05	♀♀ 4*
● Barbera d'Asti Sup. V. del Beneficio '03	♀♀ 4*
● Barbera d'Asti Sup. V. Valentino Caligaris '05	♀♀ 5
● Barbera d'Asti Sup. V. Valentino Caligaris '04	♀♀ 5
● Barbera d'Asti Sup. V. Valentino Caligaris '03	♀♀ 6
● Barbera del M.to Munfrà '07	♀♀ 3*

○ Gavi Vign. Alborina '07	♥♥ 5*
○ Gavi Castello di Tassarolo '08	♥♥ 4*
○ Gavi Tassarolo S '08	♥♥ 3*
● M.to Rosso No Sulphites '08	♥♥ 4*
○ Gavi Castello di Tassarolo '07	♀♀ 4
○ Gavi Castello di Tassarolo '05	♀♀ 4*
○ Gavi Tassarolo S '07	♀♀ 3
○ Gavi Vign. Alborina '06	♀♀ 5
○ Gavi Vign. Alborina '05	♀♀ 5

Castello di Verduno

VIA UMBERTO I, 9
12060 VERDUNO [CN]
TEL. 0172470284
www.castellodiverduno.com

CELLAR SALES
PRE-BOOKED VISITS
VISITOR FACILITIES
FOOD

ANNUAL PRODUCTION **50,000 bottles**
HECTARES UNDER VINE **7.4**
VITICULTURE METHOD **Conventional**

Not many estates are able to perform at the highest levels with both Barolo and Barbaresco. And even fewer can do so with the authority that oozes from the wines of Gabriella Burlotto and Franco Bianco. Pelaverga, dolcetto and barbera are important at this cellar but it is the nebbiolos that make the difference these days. There are the Massara and Monvigliero Barolos from Verduno, and the Faset and Rabajà Barbarescos, as well as the basic version. Often also released in Riserva versions, they all age in large barrels.

From a range that is wonderful to say the least, we chose the Barbaresco Rabajà '04 as this year's king. Its almost tertiary impact actually masks a youthful energy that unfolds with tannic progression and density that put it in a class of its own. But there's not much space between the king and the other royalty, starting with a tasty, stylish Barolo Massara '04 and moving on to a Barbaresco '05 that has subtle complexity available at the price of a basic wine. As if that were not enough, the Barbera d'Alba Bricco del Cuculo '07 is triumphant and the Barolo Monvigliero Riserva is successful, despite a fraught vintage year like 2003.

La Caudrina

S.DA BROSIA, 21
12053 CASTIGLIONE TINELLA [CN]
TEL. 0141855126
www.caudrina.it

CELLAR SALES
PRE-BOOKED VISITS

ANNUAL PRODUCTION **200,000 bottles**
HECTARES UNDER VINE **30**
VITICULTURE METHOD **Conventional**

La Caudrina is an important winery in the world of quality Piedmont wines. Surely and steadily, the cellar pursues the improvement of the moscato grape and more. Within such a highly fragmented and contrasting context as that of Asti and Moscato, La Caudrina has succeeded year after year in consolidating a brand synonymous with reliability and visibility. There are always characterful versions of Moscato and an Asti La Selvatica that is a benchmark for originality and complexity.

As so often at this historic estate, the Dogliotti family has achieved a good overall result. The standard bearer for the winery in this edition is the less well-known Redento '04, a Moscato Passito full of brioche and crystallized fruit aromas, with hints of sultana and vanilla, leading to a beautifully orchestrated palate where bitterness and acidity balance out the richness of the sugar. The Moscatos are also fresher tasting in the '07 vintage, proffering chlorophyll and sage against a background of peach with a precisely gauged balance that makes them so quaffable. On balance, La Galeisa '08 offers only a little extra richness.

● Barbaresco Rabajà '04	♟♟♟ 7
● Barbaresco '05	♟♟ 6
● Barbera d'Alba Bricco del Cuculo '07	♟♟ 7
● Barolo Massara '04	♟♟ 7
● Barolo Monvigliero Ris. '03	♟♟ 8
● Langhe Nebbiolo '07	♟♟ 4
● Dolcetto d'Alba Campot '08	♟ 4
● Verduno Basadone '08	♟ 4
● Barolo Massara '01	♟♟♟ 7
● Barolo Massara Ris. '99	♟♟ 7

○ Piemonte Moscato Passito Redento '04	♟♟ 5
● Barbera d'Asti La Solista '07	♟♟ 4
○ Moscato d'Asti La Caudrina '08	♟♟ 4
○ Moscato d'Asti La Galeisa '08	♟♟ 4
○ Asti La Selvatica '08	♟ 4
● Barbera d'Asti Sup. Montevenere '06	♟ 5
○ Piemonte Chardonnay Mej '07	♟ 4
○ Asti La Selvatica '07	♟♟ 4*
● Barbera d'Asti La Solista '06	♟♟ 4*
● Barbera d'Asti Sup. Montevenere '05	♟♟ 5
○ Moscato d'Asti La Caudrina '07	♟♟ 4*
○ Moscato d'Asti La Galeisa '07	♟♟ 3*

F.lli Cavallotto
Tenuta Bricco Boschis

LOC. BRICCO BOSCHIS
S.DA ALBA-MONFORTE
12060 CASTIGLIONE FALLETTO [CN]
TEL. 017362814
www.cavallotto.com

CELLAR SALES
PRE-BOOKED VISITS

ANNUAL PRODUCTION 100,000 bottles
HECTARES UNDER VINE 24
VITICULTURE METHOD Naturale

When we saw the winery of Alfio, Giuseppe and Laura Cavallotto, we thought it was an estate that turns out millions of bottles. But, by their own admission, the young siblings like to feel comfortable and the ample space is used more than anything else to hold the large barrels they use for ageing their most important wines. These are classic bottles to the core, the result of rigorous management in the vineyard and long maceration in the cellar. The Barolos are sourced from Bricco Boschis and from Vignolo di Castiglione Falletto, the latter only in the Riserva version.

It was another year to remember for the wines of Cavallotto and for the Barolo Bricco Boschis, which is spectacular again in the '05 version. The nose is a special marriage of typicity and originality. Alongside the raspberry and spices, there are marine and wood resin-like nuances integrating into a generous structure, Mediterranean touches and impressively dense tannins. The cellar had a more challenging job with the Barolo Riserva, which bears the scars of the scorching summer of 2003. It was a good tasting for the two Dolcetto d'Albas. Vigna Scot '08 is tangy and crisp while Vigna Melera '07 is more complex.

Ceretto

LOC. SAN CASSIANO, 34
12051 ALBA [CN]
TEL. 0173282582
www.ceretto.com

CELLAR SALES
PRE-BOOKED VISITS

ANNUAL PRODUCTION 900,000 bottles
HECTARES UNDER VINE 87
VITICULTURE METHOD Conventional

This is the headquarters of the Ceretto organization, a constellation of estates that have helped shape the history of Piedmontese wine and of which Bricco Rocche-Bricco Asili and Vignaioli di Santo Stefano form a part, each one with its own entry. With more than 87 hectares of vineyards and nearly a million bottles released annually, the Alba-based winery has a wide and varied range on its hands, with traditional varieties such as arneis, nebbiolo, and barbera together with riesling, merlot and syrah.

Again this year, we found a good, solid range that showed the Barolo Zonchera '05 in all its finery. It is a soft, relaxed interpretation, combining spicy, delicately oaky sensations with an expansive, graceful profile. The Langhe Arbarei '07 is also lovely, from riesling grapes. The varietal aromas are accentuated by the intense impact on the nose and the almondy finish modulates the finish without cramping it. Langhe Rosso Monsordo '06 is more introverted but solid in profile from a blend of cabernet, merlot, syrah and nebbiolo. The Barbaresco Asij '06 is less gutsy, held back by a rather dry tannins.

Wine	Rating	Score
● Barolo Bricco Boschis '05	ŢŢŢ+	7
● Barolo Bricco Boschis V. S. Giuseppe Ris. '03	ŢŢ	8
● Dolcetto d'Alba V. Melera '07	ŢŢ	4
● Dolcetto d'Alba V. Scot '08	ŢŢ	4
● Langhe Nebbiolo '07	ŢŢ	5
● Barolo Vignolo Ris. '03	Ţ	8
● Barolo Bricco Boschis '04	ҰҰҰ	8
● Barolo Bricco Boschis V. S. Giuseppe Ris. '01	ҰҰҰ	8
● Barolo Bricco Boschis V. S. Giuseppe Ris. '00	ҰҰҰ	8
● Barbera d'Alba V. del Cuculo '05	ҰҰ	5
● Barolo Vignolo Ris. '01	ҰҰ	8
● Barolo Vignolo Ris. '00	ҰҰ	8

Wine	Rating	Score
● Barolo Zonchera '05	ŢŢ	8
○ Langhe Arbarei '07	ŢŢ	5
● Langhe Rosso Monsordo '06	ŢŢ	6
● Barbaresco Asij '06	Ţ	8
● Barbera d'Alba Piana '08	Ţ	6
● Dolcetto d'Alba Rossana '08	Ţ	5
○ Langhe Arneis Blangé '08	Ţ	6
● Nebbiolo d'Alba Bernardina '07	Ţ	6
● Barolo Zonchera '04	ҰҰ	6
○ Langhe Bianco Arbarei '06	ҰҰ	5
● Langhe Rosso Monsordo '05	ҰҰ	5
● Langhe Rosso Monsordo '04	ҰҰ	5
● Nebbiolo d'Alba Bernardina '05	ҰҰ	5

Erede di Armando Chiappone

S.DA SAN MICHELE, 51
14049 NIZZA MONFERRATO [AT]
TEL. 0141721424
www.eredechiappone.com

CELLAR SALES
PRE-BOOKED VISITS
5000

ANNUAL PRODUCTION 35,000 bottles
HECTARES UNDER VINE 10
VITICULTURE METHOD Conventional

The vineyards of the Chiappone family grow around the hill of San Michele, at an altitude of 250 to 300 metres, on calcareous clay and marl soils. The family has been in the area for generations and aims to get the most out of the native vines. Nowadays, it is mainly Daniele who looks after the running of the estate, applying himself unstintingly to quality-oriented experiments. Production is small and concentrates mainly on barbera, alongside freisa, dolcetto, cortese and favorita.

Daniele Chiappone has decided to bring his Nizza out a year later than the others, convinced that the structure and complexity of his Barbera will benefit from a further year's ageing in bottle. In the absence of the Ru, we liked the Barbera d'Asti Brentura '07 very much for its aromas of ripe yet fresh cherry and blackberry fruit. The palate is fine and layered, with nice harmony, remarkable structure and a lingering, savoury finish. The Freisa d'Asti Sanpedra '05 is convincing and in fact one of the most interesting on the market. Angel, a rather fine Chardonnay with notes of camomile and wild flowers, is well executed but not terribly exciting.

★ Michele Chiarlo

S.DA NIZZA-CANELLI, 99
14042 CALAMANDRANA [AT]
TEL. 0141769030
www.chiarlo.it

CELLAR SALES
PRE-BOOKED VISITS

ANNUAL PRODUCTION 950,000 bottles
HECTARES UNDER VINE 100
VITICULTURE METHOD Conventional

A visit to the cellar gives a good idea of the size of this estate's production, made possible by the acquisition of vineyards in splendid locations in southern Piedmont, from Barolo to Gavi, Barbaresco and Castelnuovo Calcea. In just a few years, Michele Chiarlo has been able to obtain particularly satisfying results in all types of Piedmontese wine, thanks in no small part to his sons Alberto and Stefano. Michele's fame is based above all on his extraordinary Barolos and rich Barberas but actually any bottle with the Chiarlo signature on the label, from Moscato to Gavi, is a safe choice.

After a few years' wait, the Barbera La Court is back with Three Glasses and in the best possible way with one of the finest versions ever. La Court '06 is a wonderful wine with a striking colour. On the nose its complexity and strong personality come through in hints of cinchona, juniper berries and tobacco over an all-pervading backdrop of cherry. In the mouth it is just as impressive with rich savoury, velvety sensations that linger on the flavour. Among the Langhe wines, it was the Cannubi that, unusually, continued to outperform the Cerequio. Again this time, the Cannubi is more layered and expansive than the Cerequio, which is still very austere.

● Barbera d'Asti Brentura '07	♥♥ 4*
● Freisa d'Asti Sanpedra '05	♥♥ 3*
○ Angel '08	♥ 3
● Barbera d'Asti Brentura '06	♀♀ 4*
● Barbera d'Asti Brentura '05	♀♀ 4
● Barbera d'Asti Sup. Nizza Ru '05	♀♀ 5
● Barbera d'Asti Sup. Nizza Ru '04	♀♀ 5
● Barbera d'Asti Sup. Nizza Ru '03	♀♀ 5
● Freisa d'Asti Sanpedra '04	♀♀ 3*

● Barbera d'Asti Sup. Nizza La Court '06	♥♥♥ 6
● Barolo Cannubi '05	♥♥ 8
● Barolo Cerequio '05	♥♥ 8
● Barbaresco Asili '06	♥♥ 7
● Barbera d'Asti Sup. Cipressi della Court '07	♥♥ 4*
● Barolo Tortoniano '05	♥♥ 6
○ Gavi del Comune di Gavi Rovereto '08	♥♥ 4*
● M.to Rosso Montald '07	♥♥ 5
● M.to Rosso Montemareto Countacc! '06	♥♥ 6
○ Moscato d'Asti Nivole '08	♥ 3
● Barbera d'Asti Sup. Nizza La Court '03	♀♀♀ 6
● Barbera d'Asti Sup. Nizza La Court '01	♀♀♀ 6
● Barbera d'Asti Sup. Nizza La Court '00	♀♀♀ 6
● Barolo Cannubi '04	♀♀♀ 8

Quinto Chionetti & Figlio

B.TA VALDIBERTI, 44
12063 DOGLIANI [CN]
TEL. 017371179
www.chionettiquinto.com

CELLAR SALES
PRE-BOOKED VISITS

ANNUAL PRODUCTION **84,000 bottles**
HECTARES UNDER VINE **15**
VITICULTURE METHOD **Conventional**

A historic name in quality Piedmontese wine and a man of influence, Quinto Chionetti continues tirelessly on the path of improving a variety, dolcetto, unfairly considered a minor player in the region's wine heritage. The term indigenous is often highlighted as a distinguishing characteristic but the intrinsic qualities of Dolcetto are hardly mentioned. Yet it is an excellent easy-drinking wine that can reveal unexpected surprises after a few years in bottle. Quinto's wines are emblematic expressions of the true essence of Dogliano's territory.

Briccolero '08 is a beautiful purplish ruby red then lively and vibrant on a nose full of fruity, warm sensations against a lovely almondy backdrop. On the palate there are plenty of youthful, still slightly edgy, tannins but the sweet, velvety pulp softens the initial hardness at once, making way for a lingering, chewy finish. The San Luigi '08 has a deep, enfolding nose with clean notes of blackberry and cocoa powder. The fabulous richness and roundness of the palate are expressed with harmony and balance, and lead to an elegant, long finish.

Cieck

FRAZ. SAN GRATO
VIA BARDESONO
10011 AGLIÈ [TO]
TEL. 0124330522
www.cieck.it

CELLAR SALES
PRE-BOOKED VISITS

ANNUAL PRODUCTION **100,000 bottles**
HECTARES UNDER VINE **20**
VITICULTURE METHOD **Conventional**

Few wineries know how to get the most out of such varied soils as Cieck has been doing since 1985. It's an adaptability that enhances Erbaluce di Caluso especially, made in still, sparkling and dried-grape versions, using maturation in stainless steel for the basic wine and the Misobolo, and large barrels for the T selection. Calliope and San Giorgio spend 36 months on the lees and have been joined in the last few years by a Brut Rosé produced using neretto di San Giorgio. Nebbiolo, freisa and barbera complete the palette of vines in an estate that is always in the lead, except on price.

The show this time just missed being labelled outstanding, but it was a great team performance by the Cieck range. The first finalist was the Erbaluce di Caluso Misobolo '08. Reduced in style, it has a crisp almost chalky nose, unfolding acidity, moderate volume and great progression. Erbaluce di Caluso T '07 is rounder and more layered. It hasn't yet integrated but does already possess lots of personality from the interplay of toastiness, grapeskin, ripe citrus and malt. One of Piedmont's best sweet wines, Erbaluce di Caluso Passito Alladium Riserva '01, completes the group.

● Dolcetto di Dogliani Briccolero '08	♟♟ 4*
● Dolcetto di Dogliani S. Luigi '08	♟♟ 4
● Dolcetto di Dogliani Briccolero '07	♟♟♟ 4*
● Dolcetto di Dogliani Briccolero '04	♟♟♟ 4*
● Dolcetto di Dogliani Briccolero '06	♟♟ 4*
● Dolcetto di Dogliani Briccolero '05	♟♟ 4*
● Dolcetto di Dogliani S. Luigi '07	♟♟ 4*
● Dolcetto di Dogliani S. Luigi '06	♟♟ 4*
● Dolcetto di Dogliani S. Luigi '05	♟♟ 4*

○ Erbaluce di Caluso Misobolo '08	♟♟ 4*
○ Erbaluce di Caluso Passito Alladium Ris. '01	♟♟ 6
○ Erbaluce di Caluso T '07	♟♟ 4
● Canavese Nebbiolo '06	♟♟ 4*
● Canavese Rosso Cieck '05	♟♟ 3*
● Canavese Rosso Neretto '06	♟♟ 4*
○ Erbaluce di Caluso Calliope Brut '05	♟♟ 5
○ Erbaluce di Caluso Cieck '08	♟♟ 3*
○ Erbaluce di Caluso Spumante Brut S. Giorgio '05	♟♟ 5
○ Caluso Brut Calliope '01	♟♟ 5*
○ Erbaluce di Caluso Misobolo '07	♟♟ 4
○ Erbaluce di Caluso Spumante Brut S. Giorgio '04	♟♟ 5*
○ Erbaluce di Caluso Spumante Brut S. Giorgio '02	♟♟ 4*
○ Erbaluce di Caluso T '05	♟♟ 4

F.lli Cigliuti

VIA SERRABOELLA, 17
12052 NEIVE [CN]
TEL. 0173677185
www.cigliuti.it

CELLAR SALES
PRE-BOOKED VISITS

ANNUAL PRODUCTION **30,000 bottles**
HECTARES UNDER VINE **6.5**
VITICULTURE METHOD **Conventional**

A dependable, long-established label from the Barbaresco area, this small winery produces bottles of character and personality. In youth, they tend to lack continuity but with time, they open out to reveal class and depth, as only great wines based on nebbiolo can. Not long ago over a Barbaresco Serraboella '97, from a controversial vintage that has given us wines that are sometimes too mature, but not in this case. It is a stupendous wine, of which the Cigliuti family can be proud.

We have not yet been able to taste the traditional forte of the estate, the '06 Barbaresco Serraboella, which will be released at a later date. But the Vigne Erte '06 is more than decent, and like all the wines here, it is not for drinking immediately. The structure needs to find balance in the bottle but it is already well up to Three Glass standard, thanks to its intense, deep aromas of red berries and spices and a long, powerful palate that is firm but without too much tannin. In a range that is well up to snuff all round, we recommend the juicy, spicy and tangy Barbera Campass '07.

Tenute Cisa Asinari dei Marchesi di Grésy

S.DA DELLA STAZIONE, 21
12050 BARBARESCO [CN]
TEL. 0173635222
www.marchesidigresy.com

CELLAR SALES
PRE-BOOKED VISITS

ANNUAL PRODUCTION **200,000 bottles**
HECTARES UNDER VINE **35**
VITICULTURE METHOD **Conventional**

Alberto de Grésy has been in charge of this winery since, in 1973, he began to label the wines originating from a prestigious estate founded at the start of the century. Since then, quality has been consistently top-notch, with a seriously good Barbaresco. It's totally classic and natural, not deep in colour, and with aromas that only open fully after a few years.

All the '05 Barbarescos are first rate. Camp Gros is a textbook wine, emblematic, highly characteristic and very good indeed. It's austere, with dried flowers and faint hints of leather while the palate is rich but not excessive, with elegant tannins. The Gaiun is slightly softer and rather more sumptuous. The basic wine is spicy and readier to drink, yet still delicate. From the whites, we like the attractive Sauvignon '08 with its pennyroyal and tomato leaf leading to a palate that is acidic at first but finds more harmony in the finish. The Barbera d'Asti Monte Colombo '06 is not as well-behaved as usual. Too much oak overpowers the nice fruit on the palate.

● Barbaresco V. Erte '06	♆♆ 6
● Barbera d'Alba Campass '07	♆♆ 5
● Barbera d'Alba Serraboella '07	♆♆ 5
● Langhe Rosso Briccoserra '06	♆♆ 6
● Barbaresco V. Erte '04	♆♆♆ 7
● Barbaresco '02	♆♆ 6*
● Barbaresco Serraboella '04	♆♆ 7
● Barbaresco Serraboella '03	♆♆ 7
● Barbaresco V. Erte '05	♆♆ 7
● Barbaresco V. Erte '03	♆♆ 6
● Barbera d'Alba Campass '03	♆♆ 5
● Barbera d'Alba Serraboella '05	♆♆ 5

● Barbaresco Camp Gros '05	♆♆♆ 8
● Barbaresco Gaiun '05	♆♆ 8
● Barbaresco Martinenga '06	♆♆ 8
● Barbera d'Asti Monte Colombo '06	♆♆ 6
● Langhe Rosso Villa Martis '06	♆♆ 5
● Langhe Rosso Virtus '05	♆♆ 7
○ Langhe Sauvignon '08	♆♆ 5
● M.to Rosso Merlot da Solo '05	♆♆ 6
○ Langhe Bianco Villa Giulia '08	♆ 4
○ Langhe Chardonnay '08	♆ 4
○ Langhe Chardonnay Grésy '05	♆ 6
● Langhe Nebbiolo Martinenga '08	♆ 5
○ Moscato d'Asti La Serra '08	♆ 4
● Barbaresco Camp Gros '01	♆♆♆ 8
● Barbaresco Gaiun '04	♆♆♆ 8

★★ Domenico Clerico

LOC. MANZONI, 67
12065 MONFORTE D'ALBA [CN]
TEL. 017378171
domenicoclerico@libero.it

PRE-BOOKED VISITS

ANNUAL PRODUCTION **30,000 bottles**
HECTARES UNDER VINE **21**
VITICULTURE METHOD **Conventional**

Domenico Clerico has been one of the finest exponents innovative Barolo making for over 30 years. From his plots in the Ginestra vineyard at Monforte, he has made some of the best modern-style wines, bottles that have shaped the recent history of Barolo and the wines of the Langhe in general. These are powerful Barolos, tannic in youth and sometimes showing new wood from the barriques, but always wines of great personality.

Once again, Barolo Ciabot Mentin Ginestra '05, which comes from the long-standing Clerico plot, shows itself to be truly outstanding. It has complex, caressing aromas of flowers and peach. It's still a little tight on the palate because of its extreme youth. It needs a few more years but it promises great things. The most modern wine in the range, the '05 Pajana, is oakier. Percristina '03 comes from an unexceptional growing year but still passes muster, showing somewhat evolved on the nose. The '07 Arte, from nebbiolo with a splash of barbera, is as good as ever. The Barbera d'Alba Trevigne '07 and the fragrant, moreish Dolcetto d'Alba Visadì '08 are delicious.

Elvio Cogno

VIA RAVERA, 2
12060 NOVELLO [CN]
TEL. 0173744006
www.elviocogno.com

CELLAR SALES
PRE-BOOKED VISITS

ANNUAL PRODUCTION **70,000 bottles**
HECTARES UNDER VINE **13**
VITICULTURE METHOD **Conventional**

What a splendid sight the two hectares of Bricco Pernice is perched high above the Ravera vineyard in Novello beneath the glorious 18th-century winery. The vines were thriving when we saw them and you can bet that Nadia Cogno and Walter Fissore will obtain the most delicious Barolo from them. It will be dedicated to Elvio Cogno. In the meantime, they continue to expand their hospitality space while observing strict respect for the environment and the view. Nadia and Walter are an exuberant couple, their minds always focused on the future and full of contagious optimism.

Each wine is better than the last. The sumptuous Vigna Elena '04, produced exclusively from the very fragrant nebbiolo rosé clone, is brilliant in colour, with exquisite aromas and bags of grip on the palate. The '05 Ravera is equally fragrant, zippy, juicy and minty. Cascina Nuova '05, produced from the youngest vines, is succulent and never mouth-drying, if somewhat simpler. The white Anas-cëtta '08 is wonderfully fresh-tasting and savoury, ending on a pleasant note of apricots. Then there's the enjoyable Rosso Montegrilli '07, from nebbiolo and barbera grapes in equal parts, and the Dolcetto, the Barbera, and so it goes on. Our congratulations.

● Barolo Ciabot Mentin Ginestra '05	♆♆♆ 8
● Barolo Pajana '05	♆♆ 8
● Barolo Percristina '03	♆♆ 8
● Barbera d'Alba Trevigne '07	♆♆ 5
● Langhe Arte '07	♆♆ 6
● Langhe Dolcetto Visadì '08	♆♆ 4*
● Barolo Ciabot Mentin Ginestra '04	♆♆♆ 8
● Barolo Ciabot Mentin Ginestra '01	♆♆♆ 8
● Barolo Ciabot Mentin Ginestra '99	♆♆♆ 8
● Barolo Ciabot Mentin Ginestra '89	♆♆♆ 8
● Barolo Pajana '95	♆♆♆ 8
● Barolo Percristina '01	♆♆♆ 8
● Barolo Percristina '99	♆♆♆ 8
● Barolo Percristina '98	♆♆♆ 8
● Barolo Percristina '97	♆♆♆ 8
● Barolo Percristina '96	♆♆♆ 8
● Barolo Percristina '95	♆♆♆ 8

● Barolo V. Elena '04	♆♆♆ 8
● Barbera d'Alba Bricco dei Merli '07	♆♆ 5
● Barolo Ravera '05	♆♆ 8
● Barolo Cascina Nuova '05	♆♆ 7
● Dolcetto d'Alba V. del Mandorlo '08	♆♆ 4
O Langhe Bianco Anas-cëtta '08	♆♆ 4
● Langhe Rosso Montegrilli '07	♆♆ 5
● Barolo Ravera '04	♆♆♆ 7
● Barolo Ravera '01	♆♆♆ 7
● Barolo V. Elena '01	♆♆♆ 8
● Barolo V. Elena '99	♆♆♆ 8

Colle Manora

S.DA BOZZOLE, 5
15044 QUARGNENTO [AL]
TEL. 0131219252
www.collemanora.it

CELLAR SALES
PRE-BOOKED VISITS

ANNUAL PRODUCTION **70,000 bottles**
HECTARES UNDER VINE **20**
VITICULTURE METHOD **Conventional**

In the 2006 edition of the Guide, we reported that Colle Manora had planted a vineyard to the albarosssa grape and that in a few years we would be able to get a good idea of the variety's quality potential. Our curiosity, and any doubts anyone had at that time, have now been fully resolved. After years of study and experimentation, wine lovers can now uncork an Albarossa, and the results are more than surprising. On its very first release, Ray went through to the final taste-offs..

Ray '07 appears dense ruby before impressions of animal fur and crisp mineral foreground light nuances of fruit but the palate truly impresses, everything in majestic balance. Palo Alto '05, a ruby-hued mosaic of pinot nero, cabernet and merlot, shows raspberry and smooth spices, developing fine power in the mouth but keeps it in balance and the finish is lengthy. Cabernet, merlot and barbera compose Rosso Barchetta, which still shows some imbalance. Manora '06, now a Barbera d'Asti Superiore, exhibits a somewhat countryish appeal but rich, pulpy fruit still breaks through. The remaining wines are soundly made and impressively varietal.

● M.to Rosso Palo Alto '05	2 glasses (black)	6
● M.to Rosso Ray '07	2 glasses (black)	5
● Barbera d'Asti Sup. Manora '06	2 glasses (black)	5
● Barbera del M.to Pais '07	1 glass (black)	4
○ M.to Bianco Mila '07	1 glass (black)	6
○ M.to Bianco Mimosa '08	1 glass (black)	4
● M.to Rosso Barchetta '06	1 glass (black)	6
● Barbera del M.to Manora '05	2 glasses (outline)	5
● Barbera del M.to Manora '04	2 glasses (outline)	5
● Barbera del M.to Pais '06	2 glasses (outline)	4*
○ M.to Bianco Mimosa '06	2 glasses (outline)	4*
● M.to Rosso Palo Alto '04	2 glasses (outline)	6

Collina Serragrilli

VIA SERRAGRILLI, 30
12057 NEIVE [CN]
TEL. 0173677010
www.serragrilli.it

CELLAR SALES
PRE-BOOKED VISITS

ANNUAL PRODUCTION **100,000 bottles**
HECTARES UNDER VINE **15**
VITICULTURE METHOD **Conventional**

We applaud Collina Serragrilli for being a women-at-the-top operation, a laudable exception to a lamentable contrary phenomenon among Italy's wine producers. The Lequio sisters are the confident, competent trio steering this mid-sized operation located on the Serragrilli hill. Every new season witnesses its share of growth and innovation here and the result is a line of high-quality bottlings at reasonable prices.

The Basarin subzone yields Barbaresco '06 of middling complexity but clean-edged and nicely balanced. Not huge by any means, it drives well, ending with a well-sculpted, aromatic finish for a pleasurable wine overall. Serragrilli, from the vineyards that surround the attractive cellar, is cut from the same cloth, but ramps up the power a bit more. Barbera Grillaia '07 is an interesting bottling. Despite lingering cask influence, pleasurable fruit and mineral impressions enrich both nose and finish. Dolcetto '08 is perhaps a bit too ambitious, although it still has plenty of appeal, including a note of bitterish almond at the finish.

● Barbaresco Basarin '06	2 glasses (black)	6
● Barbaresco Serragrilli '06	2 glasses (black)	6
● Barbera d'Alba Grillaia '07	2 glasses (black)	4
● Langhe Grillorosso '06	2 glasses (black)	4
● Dolcetto d'Alba '08	1 glass (black)	4
● Barbaresco Basarin '04	2 glasses (outline)	6
● Barbaresco Serragrilli '05	2 glasses (outline)	6
● Barbaresco Serragrilli '04	2 glasses (outline)	6
● Barbera d'Alba '06	2 glasses (outline)	4
● Barbera d'Alba Grillaia '05	2 glasses (outline)	4*
● Langhe Grillorosso '05	2 glasses (outline)	4*

La Colombera

S.C. VHO, 7
15057 TORTONA [AL]
TEL. 0131867795
www.lacolomberavini.it

CELLAR SALES
PRE-BOOKED VISITS

ANNUAL PRODUCTION **50,000 bottles**
HECTARES UNDER VINE **22**
VITICULTURE METHOD **Conventional**

The chick is now a swan, with last year's top award to Timorasso Il Montino ample proof that a well-run family operation can reach the top rung. Piercarlo manages the vines and the cellar while daughter Elisa, with her degree in winemaking, both assists with production and does a fine job with marketing and sales. Add to that team a few expert helpers who give a hand when needed and the gears run very smoothly. This year's performances clearly demonstrate that continuity.

Timorasso Il Montino shows the character that propelled it into the final round with a splendid duet of fruit and slaty mineral on the nose and a palate that is all finesse. High marks went to the other Timorasso, Derthona '07, with its lovely, pungent citrus and exemplary balance. Kudos to the all-cortese Bricco Bartolomeo '08 for its best performance ever. Elisa '07, one of the most impressive Barberas in the Colli Tortonesi, had the right stuff to get into the national taste-offs. The 2007 growing year was great both for Suciaja, made from nibiò, a clone of dolcetto, and for the croatina Arché '07. Finally, Vegia Rampana '07, a steel-aged Barbera, is terrific.

● Colli Tortonesi Rosso Elisa '07	YY	5
○ Colli Tortonesi Timorasso Il Montino '07	YY	6
○ Colli Tortonesi Bricco Bartolomeo '08	YY	3*
○ Colli Tortonesi Timorasso Derthona '07	YY	5
● Colli Tortonesi Rosso Suciaja '07	YY	5
● Colli Tortonesi Rosso Vegia Rampana '07	YY	4
● Colli Tortonesi Colle del Grillo '08	Y	4
● Colli Tortonesi Croatina Arché '07	Y	3
○ Colli Tortonesi Timorasso Il Montino '06	YYY	5
○ Colli Tortonesi Timorasso Derthona '06	YY	5
● Piemonte Barbera Elisa '05	YY	4
● Piemonte Barbera Elisa '04	YY	4

Il Colombo - Barone Riccati

VIA DEI SENT, 2
12084 MONDOVÌ [CN]
TEL. 017441607
www.ilcolombo.com

CELLAR SALES
PRE-BOOKED VISITS

ANNUAL PRODUCTION **14,000 bottles**
HECTARES UNDER VINE **3.3**
VITICULTURE METHOD **Organic certified**

When people express regret, with good reason, for the loss to vineyards of precious woodlands in certain areas of Piedmont, there are no complaints about this part of Langhe around Mondovì. Here, you can admire a splendidly judicious equilibrium with the wilder areas of nature. This beautiful landscape is the setting for the winery owned by the Holms, a family with Norwegian origins. Meticulous attention to detail by winemaking consultant Bruno Chionetti helps Colombo-Barone Ricatti to produce a line of wines that admirably reflect their territory.

Performances this year mirror past triumphs. Colombo '07 is astonishing, a stunningly deep, broad wine that opens to gamey notes that then make way for alluring nuances of tobacco, cinchona and black liquorice, all supported by a splendid foundation of dark fruit. A huge-volumed, smooth mouthfeel and a sharp-edged finish crown this fine bottling. La Chiesetta '08, which is almost equally superb, shows more dark berry on the nose and an ultra-tasty savouriness. Completing this terrific trilogy is the dolcetto and merlot Monteregale '06, with pungent hints of truffle and sweet tobacco leaf adding considerably to its compelling complexity.

● Dolcetto delle Langhe Monregalesi Sup. Il Colombo '07	YY	4*
● Langhe Rosso Monteregale '06	YY	4
● Dolcetto delle Langhe Monregalesi La Chiesetta '08	YY	3*
● Dolcetto delle Langhe Monregalesi Il Colombo '98	YYY	4
● Dolcetto delle Langhe Monregalesi Il Colombo '97	YYY	4
● Dolcetto delle Langhe Monregalesi La Chiesetta '07	YY	3*
● Dolcetto delle Langhe Monregalesi Sup. Il Colombo '06	YY	4*
● Dolcetto delle Langhe Monregalesi Sup. Il Colombo '05	YY	4*

★ Aldo Conterno

LOC. BUSSIA, 48
12065 MONFORTE D'ALBA [CN]
TEL. 017378150
www.poderialdoconterno.com

ANNUAL PRODUCTION **120,000 bottles**
HECTARES UNDER VINE **25**
VITICULTURE METHOD **Conventional**

Aldo Conterno is one of the founders of the modernist style of Barolo but that is not to say that he exaggerated in any way his vinifications or practised extremes in the vineyards. Rather, when Aldo left his father's operation, 40 years ago, he began to put out Barolos of great elegance, ageing them still in large casks but replacing the oak more often so that he took advantage of the best of tradition and of more modern practices. Assisted by sons Franco and Stefano, he continues down his self-appointed path and the results are great wines from his vineyards at Bussia in Monforte.

We were unable to taste the noble Barolo Gran Bussia Riserva since the '04 will be out in 2010. The three Bussia crus, Romirasco, Colonnello and Cicala, earned very high marks. The growing year granted them finesse but withheld great structure, and some new wood is still hovering about on the nose, so they remain a hair's breadth shy of the top award. Barolo '05 is a pleasure, though not one for the ages, while Barbera d'Alba Conca Tre Pile '06 is truly first-rate. Il Favot '06, an impressively structured Nebbiolo, has a modernist bent. Bussiador '06 is still the tropical fruit-and-vanilla Chardonnay that it prides itself on being.

★★ Giacomo Conterno

LOC. ORNATI, 2
12065 MONFORTE D'ALBA [CN]
TEL. 017378221

PRE-BOOKED VISITS

ANNUAL PRODUCTION **50,000 bottles**
HECTARES UNDER VINE **14**
VITICULTURE METHOD **Conventional**

This venerable Serralunga operation has been directed for some years now by Roberto Conterno, a serious-minded and thoroughgoing traditionalist. In this, he is the worthy heir of his father Giovanni, who passed away several years ago, and of his grandfather Giacomo, founder of Giacomo Conterno. The vineyards are located in Serralunga and Monforte, one of the best areas for producing long-lived Barolos of great class. Which is precisely what Roberto Conterno's wines are: exemplars of richness and tradition.

This year did not see a release of the mythic Barolo Monfortino Riserva so Cascina Francia '05 in one of its finest versions ever was our consolation. This stupendous wine is a paean to this classic style and perhaps the best of its vintage we tasted this year. Exhilarating fragrances of dark liquorice, sweet violets and yellow peach are followed by an assertive palate studded with dense yet supple tannins. Its nervy, muscular progression is that of a true long-distance runner. Highly recommended are the superb Barbera d'Alba Cascina Francia '07 and the large cask-aged Barolo, which shows acid-etched and typical as few others out there.

Wine	Rating
● Barolo Colonnello '05	▼▼ 8
● Barolo Romirasco '05	▼▼ 8
● Barbera d'Alba Conca Tre Pile '06	▼▼ 6
● Barolo '05	▼▼ 8
○ Langhe Bianco Bussiador '06	▼▼ 6
● Langhe Nebbiolo Il Favot '06	▼▼ 7
● Langhe Dolcetto Il Masante '08	▼ 4
● Barolo Gran Bussia Ris. '01	♀♀♀ 8
● Barolo Gran Bussia Ris. '95	♀♀♀ 8
● Barolo Gran Bussia Ris. '90	♀♀♀ 8
● Barolo Gran Bussia Ris. '89	♀♀♀ 8
● Barolo Gran Bussia Ris. '88	♀♀♀ 8
● Barolo Gran Bussia Ris. '82	♀♀♀ 8
● Barolo Romirasco '04	♀♀♀ 8
● Barolo Cicala '00	♀♀ 8

Wine	Rating
● Barolo Cascina Francia '05	▼▼▼+ 8
● Barbera d'Alba Cascina Francia '07	▼▼ 6
● Barolo Cascina Francia '04	♀♀♀ 8
● Barolo Cascina Francia '01	♀♀♀ 8
● Barolo Cascina Francia '97	♀♀♀ 8
● Barolo Cascina Francia '90	♀♀♀ 8
● Barolo Cascina Francia '89	♀♀♀ 8
● Barolo Cascina Francia '87	♀♀♀ 8
● Barolo Cascina Francia '85	♀♀♀ 8
● Barolo Monfortino Ris. '01	♀♀♀ 8
● Barolo Monfortino Ris. '00	♀♀♀ 8
● Barolo Monfortino Ris. '99	♀♀♀ 8
● Barolo Monfortino Ris. '97	♀♀♀ 8
● Barolo Monfortino Ris. '96	♀♀♀ 8
● Barolo Monfortino Ris. '90	♀♀♀ 8
● Barolo Monfortino Ris. '88	♀♀♀ 8
● Barolo Monfortino Ris. '87	♀♀♀ 8
● Barolo Monfortino Ris. '85	♀♀♀ 8

Paolo Conterno

VIA GINESTRA, 34
12065 MONFORTE D'ALBA [CN]
TEL. 017378415
www.paoloconterno.com

PRE-BOOKED VISITS

ANNUAL PRODUCTION **55,000 bottles**
HECTARES UNDER VINE **11**
VITICULTURE METHOD **Conventional**

The Ginestra di Monforte vineyard is the iconic focus of this small family-run winery. It's an utterly unique terroir, with as much prestige as a piece of land can boast, and one of the most highly respected in all of Langhe. Wines from Paolo Conterno are not made for immediate enjoyment, since during their first years in the bottle they remain closed and even rebarbative. Time, however, inevitably endows them with compelling sensations, and a depth and complexity that are not easily forgotten.

Barolo Ginestra '05 casts off its usual rigidity and aggressiveness to show so rich, clean-edged and crisp that it won Three Glasses. The nose is still taut and austere, with dark fruit foregrounding subtle balsam followed by a crisp, tannin-rich palate that is quite seductive. The classically styled Barolo '05 flaunts fine definition, with a pleasurable but medium-weight mid-palate. Fresh greens and ripe fruit infuse Barolo Ginestra Riserva '03 but the tannins are slightly drying. Barbera Ginestra '07, which nearly picked up Three Glasses, imposes itself as a powerful exemplar of both its terroir and an exceptional vintage for barbera.

● Barolo Ginestra '05	♟♟♟ 8
● Barbera d'Alba Ginestra '07	♟♟ 5
● Barolo '05	♟♟ 7
● Barolo Ginestra Ris. '03	♟♟ 8
● Langhe Nebbiolo '07	♟♟ 5
● Barbera d'Alba Bricco Sant'Ambrogio '08	♟ 4
● Dolcetto d'Alba Ginestra '08	♟ 4
● Barolo Ginestra Ris. '01	♟♟♟ 8
● Barbera d'Alba Ginestra '06	♟♟ 5
● Barolo '04	♟♟ 7
● Barolo Ginestra '04	♟♟ 8
● Barolo Ginestra Ris. '00	♟♟ 8

★ Conterno Fantino

VIA GINESTRA, 1
12065 MONFORTE D'ALBA [CN]
TEL. 017378204
www.conternofantino.it

PRE-BOOKED VISITS

ANNUAL PRODUCTION **140,000 bottles**
HECTARES UNDER VINE **25**
VITICULTURE METHOD **Conventional**

From Conterno Fantino's strikingly modern headquarters, there is a fabulous view over the treasure-filled slopes of the Langhe hills. It is an appropriate icon for the operation that Claudio Conterno and Guido Fantino direct with such a clear-eyed style. Their wines, both on release and after years in the cellar, exhibit an overall consistency and a territorial character that elevates them to benchmark status. One cannot help but admire their clean, sculpted lines from first to last, as well as their perfectly calibrated extractive weight.

Sorì Ginestra '05 is already a delight, with impressions of fruit, spice, cocoa and tobacco preceding pulpy fruit with emphatic tannins. Oak and gorgeous, ripe fruit entwine in Mosconi '05 and although the massive palate is still heavily tannic, the next few years should gift it fine balance. Vigna del Gris '05 is still closed, with generous oak, and its tannin-rich palate dries somewhat towards the end. The modern-styled Monprà '06 is one of the best Langhe Rossos. Appealing and well balanced, it is a true pleasure as always. Chardonnay Bastia '07 boasts a medley of toasty oak, spice and butter, and lively acidity cuts nicely through its oak.

● Barolo Mosconi '05	♟ 8
● Barolo Sorì Ginestra '05	♟♟ 8
● Langhe Rosso Monprà '06	♟♟ 6
● Barolo V. del Gris '05	♟♟ 8
○ Langhe Chardonnay Bastia '07	♟♟ 6
● Barbera d'Alba Vignota '08	♟ 5
● Dolcetto d'Alba Bricco Bastia '08	♟ 4
● Langhe Nebbiolo Ginestrino '08	♟ 5
● Barolo V. del Gris '04	♟♟♟ 8
● Barolo V. del Gris '01	♟♟♟ 8
● Barolo Mosconi '04	♟♟ 8
● Barolo Sorì Ginestra '04	♟♟ 8
● Barolo Sorì Ginestra '03	♟♟ 8
● Langhe Rosso Monprà '05	♟♟ 6

Contratto

VIA G. B. GIULIANI, 56
14053 CANELLI [AT]
TEL. 0141823349
www.contratto.it

CELLAR SALES
PRE-BOOKED VISITS

ANNUAL PRODUCTION **290,000 bottles**
HECTARES UNDER VINE **55**
VITICULTURE METHOD **Conventional**

The Contratto name conjures up both venerable market presence and romantic allure. Visitors to the headquarters in the heart of Canelli come for the wine of course but also for the unforgettable atmosphere it exudes. Before Franciacorta launched its sparkling wine and classic method adventure, the name Contratto was widely known and respected as a byword for quality sparklers at reasonable prices. Contratto's illustrious past is matched its current standing and top-quality production on a par with its ambitious goals.

It was another fine year for Contratto, since their team of wines continues to perform impressively overall. The front runner again is De Miranda and the '06 came close to capturing Three Glasses. What is immediately striking is its cornucopia of luscious fragrances, including white chocolate, brioche, candied fruit and peaches in syrup, which perform a delicious duet with a palate of well-measured richness and splendid proportions. Barolo Cerequio '05 is powerful, lean and austere, still betraying some youthful roughness and oak overlay on the nose.

Vigne Marina Coppi

VIA SANT'ANDREA, 5
15051 CASTELLANIA [AL]
TEL. 3385360111
www.vignemarinacoppi.com

CELLAR SALES
PRE-BOOKED VISITS

ANNUAL PRODUCTION **20,000 bottles**
HECTARES UNDER VINE **4**
VITICULTURE METHOD **Conventional**

The Castellania hills, once the paradise of cycling legend Fausto Coppi, have become, 60 years on, the land that sustains the winemaking of his grandson, Francesco Bellocchio, son of Marina Coppi, whose name the winery bears. Bellocchio, now one of the Tortona area's most modern, market-savvy producers, has a favourite mount in Barbera and he goes through all the gears, from the unoaked, fresh and drinkable, style to the fuller-bodied, more cellarable versions. This year, a Timorasso dedicated to Francesco's grandfather beefs up the limited production of whites.

And on its first appearance, Timorasso went into the national finals. A white of terrific finesse and complexity, it releases intriguing apricot along with the expected petrol and gunflint. Refreshing, very elegant acidity beautifully complements its appreciable richness in the mouth. From the Barberas, we preferred the velvet, fruity Sant'Andrea '08 to the more complex Castellania '07, which seems still in search of a definitive balance. Less impressive at this stage are Favorita Marine '08 and Monferrato Lindin '07, which needs more richness.

○ Asti De Miranda M. Cl. '06	♀♀ 6
● Barolo Cerequio '05	♀♀ 8
● Barbera d'Asti Solus Ad '07	♀♀ 7
☉ For England Rosé '06	♀♀ 6
○ Giuseppe Contratto Brut Ris. '05	♀♀ 6
○ For England Pas Dosé '06	♀ 6
○ Asti De Miranda M. Cl. '00	♀♀♀ 6
● Barolo Cerequio '99	♀♀♀ 8
● Barolo Cerequio Tenuta Secolo '97	♀♀♀ 8
○ Spumante M. Cl. Brut Ris. Giuseppe Contratto '96	♀♀♀ 6

○ Colli Tortonesi Timorasso Fausto '07	♀♀ 7
● Colli Tortonesi Barbera Castellania '07	♀♀ 5
● Colli Tortonesi Barbera Sant'Andrea '08	♀♀ 4
○ Colli Tortonesi Favorita Marine '08	♀ 6
● Colli Tortonesi Rosso Lindin '07	♀ 6
● Colli Tortonesi Barbera I Grop '06	♀♀ 5
● Colli Tortonesi Barbera I Grop '05	♀♀ 5
● Colli Tortonesi Barbera Sant'Andrea '07	♀♀ 4*

Coppo

VIA ALBA, 68
14053 CANELLI [AT]
TEL. 0141823146
www.coppo.it

CELLAR SALES
PRE-BOOKED VISITS

ANNUAL PRODUCTION **420,000 bottles**
HECTARES UNDER VINE **56**
VITICULTURE METHOD **Conventional**

Founded as far back as 1892, this operation is an integral part of Asti's wine history. The third and fourth generations of the Coppo family are currently at the helm and family management has succeeded in crafting a line of wines in a broad range of styles at eminently reasonable prices. Moreover, the Coppos also manage to produce examples of all of southern Piedmont's classic wine styles.

The Coppo Monteriolo received our top award for the second year running. The '06, in our opinion Piedmont's finest 2006 white, is a rich, multi-layered Chardonnay, with a Meursault-like structure and enchanting minerally impressions. The distinctive Mondaccione is a good reason to re-assess the oft-underrated or poorly vinified freisa variety. Barolo has returned to the line and both versions are excellent. The Barbera d'Astis are fine, with Camp du Rouss '07 in the front rank, holding for Pomorosso '07, which returns next year. High marks went to Alterego '06. Made of cabernet sauvignon and barbera, it is the line's only non-traditional offering.

Giovanni Corino

FRAZ. ANNUNZIATA, 24B
12064 LA MORRA [CN]
TEL. 0173509452

CELLAR SALES
PRE-BOOKED VISITS

ANNUAL PRODUCTION **40,000 bottles**
HECTARES UNDER VINE **8**
VITICULTURE METHOD **Conventional**

Corino continues its superb performances. Giuliano Corino, who knows this area like the back of his hand, again presented a line-up of wines which, from his Barolo crus down, display unfaltering consistency of style. These are wines of great fullness that show succulent and delectable even in their youth. But they are at the same time fully capable of standing up to the years and offering the noble impressions that only the great can. One Barolo, Vecchie Vigne, is from particularly old plantings.

Barolo Vecchie Vigne '04 is profound and full-fruited, developing an elegant, finely structured palate of rare harmony. Three Glasses went to a wine destined to mature for many years. Vigna Giachini '05 is as fine as ever but slightly stiffened by assertive tannins. The smoother Vigna Arborina '05 offers more spice, as well as better elegance and structure. The standard Barolo '05 is fairly simple, though without defects. The 2008 vintage brought a pleasing, very drinkable Barbera and Dolcetto, and Barbera Ciabot du Re '07 debuts in thrilling style.

○ Piemonte Chardonnay Monteriolo '06	▼▼▼ 6
● Langhe Rosso Mondaccione '05	▼▼ 7
● Barbera d'Asti Camp du Rouss '07	▼▼ 4*
● Barbera d'Asti L'Avvocata '08	▼▼ 4
● Barolo '05	▼▼ 8
● Barolo '04	▼▼ 8
○ Luigi Coppo Brut '06	▼▼ 5
● M.to Rosso Alterego '06	▼▼ 6
○ Moscato d'Asti Moncalvina '08	▼ 4
○ Piemonte Chardonnay Costebianche '08	▼ 4
● Barbera d'Asti Pomorosso '05	▼▼▼ 7
● Barbera d'Asti Pomorosso '04	▼▼▼ 7
● Barbera d'Asti Pomorosso '03	▼▼▼ 7
● Barbera d'Asti Pomorosso '01	▼▼▼ 7
● Barbera d'Asti Pomorosso '99	▼▼▼ 7
● Barbera d'Asti Pomorosso '90	▼▼▼ 5
○ Piemonte Chardonnay Monteriolo '05	▼▼▼ 6

● Barbera d'Alba Ciabot du Re '07	▼▼ 6
● Barolo V. Arborina '05	▼▼ 8
● Barolo V. Giachini '05	▼▼ 8
● Barolo Vecchie Vigne '04	▼▼ 8
● Barbera d'Alba '08	▼▼ 4
● Barolo '05	▼▼ 7
● Langhe Nebbiolo '08	▼▼ 4
● Dolcetto d'Alba '08	▼ 4
● Barbera d'Alba V. Pozzo '97	▼▼▼ 8
● Barbera d'Alba V. Pozzo '96	▼▼▼ 8
● Barolo Rocche '01	▼▼▼ 8
● Barolo Rocche '90	▼▼▼ 8
● Barolo V. Giachini '89	▼▼▼ 8
● Barolo Vecchie Vigne '99	▼▼▼ 8
● Barolo Vecchie Vigne '98	▼▼▼ 8

Renato Corino

FRAZ. ANNUNZIATA - B.TA POZZO, 49A
12064 LA MORRA [CN]
TEL. 0173500349
renatocorino@alice.it

CELLAR SALES
PRE-BOOKED VISITS

ANNUAL PRODUCTION **40,000 bottles**
HECTARES UNDER VINE **7**
VITICULTURE METHOD **Conventional**

A good reason for searching out this modest but first-rate Langhe winery is its stunning facility, set among the vines, which offers a breathtaking view over much of the Barolo-producing area. A landscape such as this is excellent preparation for the superb quality of the wines that Renato Corino makes here. This affable, open winegrower continues to produce, in an ever-rising trajectory of quality, unfailingly excellent Barolos and Barberas, bottlings that are cleanly delineated and modernist, rich yet refined, with considerable power but well-calibrated proportions.

After sweet tobacco leaf and bright, sun-ripened herbs, Barolo '05 Vigneto Rocche develops a compelling, full-volumed palate of impressive power pushing through to a finish that reveals even richer flavours. The massive Barolo Vecchie Vigne '04 flaunts rich tar and Peruvian bark, with still a trace of oak at this youthful stage. Vigneto Arborina '05 boasts a multi-faceted, balsam-edged bouquet as well as admirably self-confident structure, only a whisper less elegant than that of Rocche. The superb Pozzo vineyard yields an equally superlative Barbera '06.

● Barolo Vign. Rocche '05	TT	8
● Barbera d'Alba V. Pozzo '06	TT	6
● Barolo Vecchie Vigne '04	TT	8
● Barolo Vign. Arborina '05	TT	7
● Barolo '05	TT	6
● Nebbiolo d'Alba '07	TT	5
● Barbera d'Alba '08	T	4
● Dolcetto d'Alba '08	T	4
● Barolo Vign. Rocche '04	YYY	8
● Barolo Vign. Rocche '03	YYY	8
● Barbera d'Alba V. Pozzo '05	YY	6
● Barolo '04	YY	6
● Barolo Vecchie Vigne '03	YY	8
● Barolo Vign. Arborina '04	YY	8

Cornarea

VIA VALENTINO, 150
12043 CANALE [CN]
TEL. 017365636

CELLAR SALES
PRE-BOOKED VISITS
VISITOR FACILITIES

ANNUAL PRODUCTION **80,000 bottles**
HECTARES UNDER VINE **15**
VITICULTURE METHOD **Conventional**

The Bovone family winery, now with almost 30 years of wine production, continues to thrive in the Roero area. In spite of substantial growth, the family has never lost sight of its original mission to develop the potential of arneis, which they fashion in numerous styles. In fact, they can boast of the oldest vineyard exclusively planted to the variety. On the Cornarea hill, which gives the winery its name, is the lovely estate villa, which serves as both the winemaking facility and an agriturismo hospitality centre.

All of the wines performed well. Impressive Peruvian bark and black liquorice enrich Roero '06 and it sports a fine, beautifully-proportioned body. Emphatic oak accompanies sweet tobacco and dark raspberry on Nebbiolo d'Alba '06. Its massive, expansive body concludes with a finale showing unyielding, somewhat drying tannins. Roero Arneis '08 expresses superb varietal fidelity, almond and blossoms preceding a palate that is uncomplicated but delicious and pleasurable. The much more complex and refined Tarasco Passito '05 presents delicious fragrances of dried figs and chestnut honey plus an ultra-rich, dense palate that may be a trifle too sweet.

● Nebbiolo d'Alba '06	TT	4*
● Roero '06	TT	6
○ Roero Arneis '08	TT	4*
○ Tarasco Passito '05	TT	6
○ Andrè '05	YY	5
● Nebbiolo d'Alba '05	YY	4
● Roero '05	YY	4
○ Roero Arneis '07	YY	4*
○ Tarasco Passito '04	YY	6
○ Tarasco Passito '03	YY	6
○ Tarasco Passito '01	YY	6

★ Matteo Correggia

LOC. GARBINETTO
VIA SANTO STEFANO ROERO, 124
12043 CANALE [CN]
TEL. 0173978009
www.matteocorreggia.com

CELLAR SALES
PRE-BOOKED VISITS

ANNUAL PRODUCTION **120,000 bottles**
HECTARES UNDER VINE **20**
VITICULTURE METHOD **Naturale**

Mention of the name Correggia inevitably brings to mind Matteo, the winery's founder, who tragically passed away in 2001. Currently directing operations with spirited dedication is his wife Ornella, who in these last few years has put in place a programme to raise quality levels even higher, and has begun the changeover to organic production. Assisted by winemaker Luca Rostagno, she has succeeded in reburnishing some of the area's classics, such as Roero Ròche d'Ampsèj and Barbera Marun. Correggia continues to feature in the Roero dream team thanks to a number of superbly crafted wines.

Three wines from the range went into the finals. The historic Barbera d'Alba Marun came up with a '07 that is thrillingly varietal, refreshing and splendidly fruited. The equally renowned Roero Ròche d'Ampsèj Riserva '05 gives wafts of spice, hazelnut, cinchona and raspberry before building a palate of great volume, energy and length but the oak too easily outpaces the fruit. The third of the trio, Langhe Rosso Le Marne Grigie '05, is a rich blend of cabernet, petit verdot, merlot and syrah. The result is a wine of enormous depth and breadth, with fresh greens on the nose animating elegant, lithe notes of pencil lead and redcurrant.

Giuseppe Cortese

S.DA RABAJÀ, 80
12050 BARBARESCO [CN]
TEL. 0173635131
www.cortesegiuseppe.it

CELLAR SALES
PRE-BOOKED VISITS

ANNUAL PRODUCTION **50,000 bottles**
HECTARES UNDER VINE **8**
VITICULTURE METHOD **Conventional**

Cortese is a small operation but eight full hectares of estate vineyards in Rabajà, one of Barbaresco's most celebrated crus, has assured it an outsize reputation among wine lovers. Winemaking here follows the canons of tradition with large and medium-capacity oak casks, and lengthy ageing, which can exceed five years in a combination of cask and bottle, as is the case with the renowned Barbaresco Riserva Rabajà.

Barbaresco Rabajà '06 is very solidly built, with assertive tannins and loads of pulpy fruit. After a few moments in the glass, youthful fruit appears, followed by more complexity, with cinchona and liquorice. Barbera d'Alba Morassina '06 received two full years' maturation, which brought its basically austere profile a fine, polished harmony. The much-awaited Riserva '04 will be released only at the seventh year from harvest. The standard wines are, as usual, well up to snuff with a nod to Barbera d'Alba '07 for its exceptionally reasonable price tag.

● Barbera d'Alba Marun '07	♀♀	6
● Langhe Rosso Le Marne Grigie '05	♀♀	7
● Roero Ròche d'Ampsèj Ris. '05	♀♀	7
● Anthos Passito '08	♀♀	5
● Barbera d'Alba '07	♀♀	4*
○ Langhe Bianco Matteo Correggia '07	♀♀	6
● Nebbiolo d'Alba La Val dei Preti '07	♀♀	6
● Roero '07	♀♀	4*
● Anthos '08	♀	4
○ Roero Arneis '08	♀	4
● Barbera d'Alba Marun '04	♀♀♀	6
● Roero Ròche d'Ampsèj '04	♀♀♀	7
● Roero Ròche d'Ampsèj '01	♀♀♀	8
● Roero Ròche d'Ampsèj '00	♀♀♀	8

● Barbaresco Rabajà '06	♀♀	6
● Barbera d'Alba '07	♀♀	4*
● Barbera d'Alba Morassina '06	♀♀	5
● Langhe Nebbiolo '07	♀♀	5
● Dolcetto d'Alba Trifolera '08	♀	4
● Barbaresco Rabajà Ris. '96	♀♀♀	8
● Barbaresco Rabajà '05	♀♀	6
● Barbaresco Rabajà '01	♀♀	6*
● Barbaresco Rabajà Ris. '01	♀♀	8

Costa Olmo

VIA SAN MICHELE, 18
14040 VINCHIO [AT]
TEL. 0141950423
www.costaolmo.com

PRE-BOOKED VISITS

ANNUAL PRODUCTION 50,000 bottles
HECTARES UNDER VINE 5
VITICULTURE METHOD Conventional

The year 2010 marks the 20th birthday for Paola and Vittorio Limone's modest wine operation. Since Costa Olmo's vineyards are almost all located in Vinchio and Vaglio Serra, an area particularly noted for growing fine barbera, the Limones naturally focus on coaxing out the best qualities of that terroir, and their wines are indeed distinctive for their typicity. The sole international "foreigner" is their Chardonnay.

This year, Costa Olmo submitted only Barbera, and a fine, reliable lot they are. Barbera d'Asti Superiore Costa Olmo '06 offers a nose of finely sculpted complexity, with dense balsam preceding Peruvian bark and black berry fruit. Although the finish is perhaps a tad too hot and less broad than one would wish, the palate shows excellent drive and volume. Barbera d'Asti La Madrina '07, on the other hand, offers a beautiful, classic array of aromas, which include moist earth, tobacco leaf and dark cherry. There's an abundance of superb fruit on the palate, which exhibits appreciable volume and proportion, as well as on a lengthy, smooth finish.

● Barbera d'Asti La Madrina '07	♟♟ 4
● Barbera d'Asti Sup. Costa Olmo '06	♟♟ 5
● Barbera d'Asti La Madrina '06	♟♟ 4
● Barbera d'Asti Sup. '04	♟♟ 5
● Barbera d'Asti Sup. Costa Olmo '05	♟♟ 5
○ Piemonte Chardonnay A Paola '07	♟♟ 4

Dacapo

S.DA ASTI MARE, 4
14040 AGLIANO TERME [AT]
TEL. 0141964921
www.dacapo.it

CELLAR SALES
PRE-BOOKED VISITS

ANNUAL PRODUCTION 43,000 bottles
HECTARES UNDER VINE 7.5
VITICULTURE METHOD Naturale

In 1997, Paolo Dania and Dino Riccomagno decided to purchase an old farmhouse complex with eight hectares of vines, wanting to restructure it and produce top-flight wines that would be eloquent expressions of the local terroir. They have succeeded admirably, focusing on organic viticulture and native grape varieties, with pride of place to barbera. Dacapo has seen growth but the Riccomagnos have kept its size down, in accord with their determination to keep the emphasis on quality and not quantity.

Cantacucco '07, from pinot nero and nebbiolo, is an elegant wine of notable complexity, with black pepper and dark berry fruit, and a lengthy finish of great heft. If Sanbastiàn '07 shows a bit high in alcohol, it is still a fine wine overall, with tobacco, dark berry and cinchona preceding a lively, spacious palate with supple tannins. Equally fine is the full-bodied Monferrato Rosso Tre '06, an equal blend of barbera, merlot and nebbiolo, which gives red fruits. Good marks went to Ruché di Castagnole Monferrato Bric Majoli '08, with appealing aromas and a long, smooth finish, and to the tasty but somewhat straightforward Vigna Dacapo '06.

● Barbera d'Asti Sanbastiàn '07	♟♟ 4*
● Cantacucco '07	♟♟ 6
● M.to Rosso Tre '06	♟♟ 6
● Barbera d'Asti Sup. Nizza V. Dacapo '06	♟ 5
● Ruché di Castagnole M.to Bric Majoli '08	♟ 4
● Barbera d'Asti Sanbastiàn '06	♟♟ 4
● Barbera d'Asti Sanbastiàn '05	♟♟ 4*
● Barbera d'Asti Sup. Nizza V. Dacapo '05	♟♟ 5
● Barbera d'Asti Sup. Nizza V. Dacapo '03	♟♟ 5
● Barbera d'Asti Sup. Nizza V. Dacapo '01	♟♟ 5
● M.to Rosso Tre '05	♟♟ 6
● M.to Rosso Tre '04	♟♟ 6

Damilano

VIA ROMA, 31
12060 BAROLO [CN]
TEL. 017356105
www.cantinedamilano.it

CELLAR SALES
PRE-BOOKED VISITS

ANNUAL PRODUCTION **360,000 bottles**
HECTARES UNDER VINE **48**
VITICULTURE METHOD **Conventional**

The operation owned by Guido and Margherita Damilano, and cousins Paolo and Mario, has seen significant developments this past year. They rented a number of hectares in Barolo's famed Cannubi cru, purchased a little over half a hectare in the great Brunate vineyard at La Morra and Barolo and eight hectares of barbera in Casorzo, near Asti. That represents quite a challenge at a time of global economic difficulties. But their first results are promising, and we're sure that finer showings will follow from this modern, forward-looking winery with deep roots in the Langhe culture.

New this year is Barolo Brunate Cannubi '05, made in 4,500 bottles sourced 70 per cent from the first cru and the rest from the second. It shows a deliciously decadent nose of dusty earth and dried rose petals, a sturdily built palate and stunning depth. It's still a bit closed but Barolo fans will treasure it. Cannubi '05 flaunts a nose of remarkable finesse and a still finer palate: pulpy, leisurely and already delicious. Liste is more restrained, gradually developing energy with tasty fruit throughout. Lecinquevigne '05 is sharp-edged, juicy and very good. Barbera d'Asti '08 debuts with a mineral-edged finish after lengthy, savoury development.

Sergio Degiorgis

VIA CIRCONVALLAZIONE, 3
12056 MANGO [CN]
TEL. 014189107
www.degiorgis-sergio.com

CELLAR SALES
PRE-BOOKED VISITS

ANNUAL PRODUCTION **70,000 bottles**
HECTARES UNDER VINE **11**
VITICULTURE METHOD **Conventional**

Sergio and Patrizia Degiorgis are tucked away in a little-known but fascinating corner of Piedmont. Year after year, they determinedly indulge their unusually fortunate fascination with moscato. The grape is too often undervalued, in terms of both its quality potential and of the distinctive appeal of its various styles. The rich variety of the Degiorgis versions, including a Passito when the weather god smiles, raises the estate into the upper ranks of Moscato producers. The Degiorgis also produce other wines classic to their area.

These two versions attest to Sergio's sapient hand in working with moscato, whether the year be favourable or recalcitrant. Sorì del Re '08 is a soberly styled Moscato with terrific balance, releasing lovely sage and ripe peach while showing just the right acidity. Its younger brother exemplifies the same qualities and elegance. Sadly, it is not generally known that Mango is also a great terroir for Dolcetto d'Alba and Degiorgis has been turning out fine versions for quite a time now. The Barberas need some more improvement time in the bottle.

● Barolo Brunate Cannubi '05	♊ 8
● Barolo Cannubi '05	♊ 8
● Barolo Liste '05	♊ 8
● Barbera d'Alba La Blu '07	♊ 5
● Barbera d'Asti '08	♊ 4*
● Barolo Lecinquevigne '05	♊ 7
● Nebbiolo d'Alba '07	♊ 5
● Dolcetto d'Alba '08	♉ 4
○ Langhe Arneis '08	♉ 4
● Barolo Cannubi '04	♈ 8
● Barolo Cannubi '01	♈ 8
● Barolo Cannubi '00	♈ 8

● Dolcetto d'Alba Bricco Peso '08	♊ 4
○ Moscato d'Asti '08	♊ 4
○ Moscato d'Asti Sorì del Re '08	♊ 4
● Barbera d'Alba '07	♉ 5
● Barbera d'Alba Luna Nuova '08	♉ 4
○ Moscato d'Asti '07	♈ 4*
○ Moscato d'Asti Sorì del Re '07	♈ 4*
○ Moscato d'Asti Sorì del Re '06	♈ 4*
○ Moscato d'Asti Sorì del Re '05	♈ 4

Deltetto

C.SO ALBA, 43
12043 CANALE [CN]
TEL. 0173979383
www.deltetto.com

CELLAR SALES
PRE-BOOKED VISITS

ANNUAL PRODUCTION **170,000 bottles**
HECTARES UNDER VINE **21**
VITICULTURE METHOD **Conventional**

Carlo Deltetto planted the winery's estate vineyards almost 60 years ago. Located in the municipalities of Canale, Santo Stefano Roero and Castellinaldo, they are now tended by his son Antonio. Deltetto's wines run a wide gamut, ranging from classic method sparklers and traditional Roero-area still whites to barbera and nebbiolo-based bottlings, Langhe varietals and dessert wines.

In a year that was a struggle for arneis, Roero San Michele '08 is a standout. Opening to intriguing citrus, plum and wild flowers, it develops a full-body with minerally sapidity and a compelling, lengthy finish. Barbera d'Alba Superiore Rocca delle Marasche '07, another finalist, exhibits well-integrated aromas of fruit, tobacco and Peruvian bark. Despite still unsettled tannins, the palate shows impressive power and a fresh tang. We liked the smooth, fruity Roero Riserva Braja '06, with its tobacco, cinnamon and raspberry, and Barbera d'Alba Superiore Bramé '07. Although somewhat simple, it is silky, well-fruited and pleasurable.

Luigi Dessilani e Figlio

VIA CESARE BATTISTI, 21
28073 FARA NOVARESE [NO]
TEL. 0321829252
www.dessilani.it

CELLAR SALES
PRE-BOOKED VISITS

ANNUAL PRODUCTION **250,000 bottles**
HECTARES UNDER VINE **50**
VITICULTURE METHOD **Conventional**

Novara generously displays its rich variety across the entire line of wines produced by Dessilani e Figlio. Enzio Lucca and his son Nicola are now in charge of this historic family wine operation, assisted in winemaking by Dante Scaglione. Located in the area of Fara, their wines represent the diverse characters of the lesser-known denominations spread through these morainic hills, from Ghemme and Sizzano to fully three selections from Fara: Lochera, Caramino and, since 2004, Vecchie Vigne. Soon to join their company is a Gattinara sourced from the renovated Galizia vineyard.

No doubt about it, this year brings the finest showings ever for Dessilani. Enzio and Nicola leave their artistic imprint on the denominations, all of which display those common traits of impressive volume and lifting linearity that make them distinctive and at the same time full of potential for future development. Fara Vecchie Vigne '05 is an austere, powerful champion, exuding red berry and candied orange shot through with elegant hints of fresh greens. Its volume and acidic grip are unfailingly impressive, and a youthful finish is likewise spacious. Ghemme '05, Sizzano '05 and Fara Caramino '05 are almost its twins in style and performance.

Wine	Rating
● Barbera d'Alba Sup. Rocca delle Marasche '07	♟♟ 6
○ Roero Arneis S. Michele '08	♟♟ 4*
● Barbera d'Alba Sup. Bramé '07	♟♟ 4*
● Roero Braja Ris. '06	♟♟ 6
○ Deltetto Extra Brut Ris. '06	♟ 5
○ Langhe Favorita Sarvai '08	♟ 4
● Langhe Nebbiolo '07	♟ 4
● Barbera d'Alba Sup. Rocca delle Marasche '04	♟♟♟ 6
● Barbera d'Alba Sup. Bramé '06	♟♟ 4*
● Barbera d'Alba Sup. Rocca delle Marasche '06	♟♟ 6
● Barbera d'Alba Sup. Rocca delle Marasche '05	♟♟ 6
○ Deltetto M. Cl. Brut	♟♟ 6
○ Deltetto M. Cl. Extra Brut Ris. '05	♟♟ 5
○ Roero Arneis S. Michele '07	♟♟ 4*
● Roero Braja '05	♟♟ 5

Wine	Rating
● Fara Vecchie Vigne '05	♟♟ 8
● Fara Caramino '05	♟♟ 7
● Ghemme '05	♟♟ 6
● Sizzano '05	♟♟ 5
● Colline Novaresi Nebbiolo '06	♟♟ 4
● Fara Lochera '06	♟♟ 6
● Fara Caramino '99	♟♟♟ 6
● Fara Caramino '04	♟♟ 6
● Fara Caramino '01	♟♟ 5
● Fara Lochera '05	♟♟ 6
● Fara Lochera '04	♟♟ 6
● Fara Lochera '03	♟♟ 5
● Fara Vecchie Vigne '04	♟♟ 7

Destefanis

VIA MORTIZZO, 8
12050 MONTELUPO ALBESE [CN]
TEL. 0173617189
www.marcodestefanis.it

CELLAR SALES
PRE-BOOKED VISITS

ANNUAL PRODUCTION **60,000 bottles**
HECTARES UNDER VINE **12**
VITICULTURE METHOD **Conventional**

We always take pleasure in drawing attention to any winery that effectively combines a high-quality line of wines with a reasonable price list, and that felicitous marriage is absolutely true of Marco Destefanis' small operation. His production focuses on dolcetto, and his always impressive Vigna Monia Bassa, sourced from exceptionally fine old vines, has become a benchmark over the years. But Marco works with barbera, nebbiolo and chardonnay as well, which round out a line of extraordinary reliability.

A hailstorm kept Monia Bassa out of the lists this year so running in its place was the new Langhe Rosso '07, in a very limited production. A magisterial assemblage of nebbiolo, barbera and cabernet, it is a powerful red brimming with personality, compellingly rich and complex from first to last. We tasted the always enjoyable Dolcetto d'Alba Galluccio '08, with emphatic black liquorice and dried blossoms standing up enticingly to a mass of red berry fruit. Barbera '08 is delicate, pleasingly tart and delicious right now while Chardonnay '08, also leaning to the light side, offers clean impressions of green apple and fresh-picked herbs.

★ Einaudi

B.TA GOMBE, 31/32
12063 DOGLIANI [CN]
TEL. 017370191
www.poderieinaudi.com

CELLAR SALES
PRE-BOOKED VISITS
VISITOR FACILITIES

ANNUAL PRODUCTION **220,000 bottles**
HECTARES UNDER VINE **50**
VITICULTURE METHOD **Conventional**

Einaudi's history began in 1897, when the future president of the Italian Republic purchased a lovely farming estate and began production and sale of Dolcetto. A string of successes followed, as well as a strong commercial presence even beyond Italy, thanks in particular to the committed efforts of the heirs over the past 15 years. Those have included the purchase of prestigious vineyards, the enlargement and modernization of the cellars and the building of an elegant Relais hotel.

The '05 Barolos display superb finesse, particularly Costa Grimaldi, with intensely aromatic dried rose petals, cinchona and raspberry, followed by a palate of rich fascination whose clean profile, velvety mouthfeel and impressive length stand out. After cinchona and forest floor, Terlo offers an austere dryness that promises fine ageing. Cannubi shows vibrant, youthful and quite long but still oak-laden. Barbera '07 is fruit-driven, with rich, ripe plum and notes of toasty oak. Both '07 Doglianis are superbly elegant, rounded and lengthy. Luigi Einaudi '06 is simply magnificent. Vigna Meira '08, Einaudi's only white, is worth uncorking.

● Dolcetto d'Alba Bricco Galluccio '08	♟♟	3*
● Langhe Rosso '07	♟♟	4*
● Barbera d'Alba '08	♟	3
○ Langhe Chardonnay '08	♟	2
● Dolcetto d'Alba Bricco Galluccio '07	♟♟	3*
● Dolcetto d'Alba V. Monia Bassa '07	♟♟	4*

● Barolo Costa Grimaldi '05	♟♟♟	8
● Barolo nei Cannubi '05	♟♟	8
● Barolo Terlo '05	♟♟	8
● Dogliani I Filari '07	♟♟	6
● Dogliani V. Tecc '07	♟♟	5
● Langhe Rosso Luigi Einaudi '06	♟♟	8
● Barolo '05	♟♟	8
● Dolcetto di Dogliani '08	♟♟	5
● Langhe Nebbiolo '07	♟♟	5
○ Langhe V. Meira '08	♟♟	5
● Piemonte Barbera '07	♟♟	6
● Dogliani V. Tecc '06	♟♟♟	5
● Langhe Rosso Luigi Einaudi '04	♟♟♟	6
● Dogliani I Filari '06	♟♟	6

Tenuta Il Falchetto

FRAZ. CIOMBI
VIA VALLE TINELLA, 16
12058 SANTO STEFANO BELBO [CN]
TEL. 0141840344
www.ilfalchetto.com

CELLAR SALES
PRE-BOOKED VISITS

ANNUAL PRODUCTION **190,000 bottles**
HECTARES UNDER VINE **33.5**
VITICULTURE METHOD **Conventional**

The Forno brothers, Giorgio, Roberto, Adriano and Fabrizio, operate their winery at Santo Stefano Belbo but for some years now they have also been able to exploit two properties in the Asti area, in the municipality of Agliano Terme. These marl and sandstone soils largely grow the local native varieties, with moscato the leader, and that wine has been Tenuta Il Falchetto's standard-bearer over the past few years. But their other wines, for example, Barbera, are increasingly widely praised.

Falchetto again sent two wines to the finals. A tobacco and spice-rich Barbera d'Asti Superiore Bricco Paradiso '06 has lots of fruit to balance its oak, plus enviable power and good tannins. Moscato d'Asti Tenuta del Fant '08 is deliciously rich, offering mint, peach and citrus zest, then an admirably lengthy, balanced finale. The other wines are fine. Moscato d'Asti Ciombi '08 is well crafted and luscious while Barbera d'Asti Superiore Lurëi '07 is redolent of spice, with subtle red berry and cinchona. The barbera and cabernet Monferrato Rosso La Mora '07 shows balsam and tobacco while Solo '07, from pinot nero, is all elegant berry fruit.

Alessandro e Gian Natale Fantino

VIA G. SILVANO, 18
12065 MONFORTE D'ALBA [CN]
TEL. 017378253

CELLAR SALES

ANNUAL PRODUCTION **40,000 bottles**
HECTARES UNDER VINE **10**
VITICULTURE METHOD **Conventional**

The municipality of Monforte, the home of some of the finest Langhe producers, includes Fantino with its historically fascinating premises. The Fantinos are on the traditionalist side of the street, custom-tailoring their vinifications to the characteristics of each separate variety. Almost obsequious to the quality of the fruit that comes in, they employ small-lot fermentations and absolutely minimal use of technology. That naturally follows the meticulous, respectful attention they lavish on their vineyards, which enjoy splendid exposures.

Dense, complex and already fairly full-volumed, Barolo Vigna dei Dardi '05 sports tempting impressions of dried rose petals and black liquorice. True, there are few tannic burrs on the palate but it possesses all of the rich stuffing and promise of a traditional-styled Barolo destined for a long life. Only next year will we be able to discuss Barbera Vigna dei Dardi '07, which had not yet been bottled by the time of our tastings, and the extravagant, hedonistic Nepas '01, produced from semi-dried nebbiolo grapes.

● Barbera d'Asti Sup. Bricco Paradiso '06	♟♟	6
○ Moscato d'Asti Tenuta del Fant '08	♟♟	4*
● Barbera d'Asti Sup. Lurëi '07	♟♟	4*
● M.to Rosso La Mora '07	♟♟	4*
● M.to Rosso Solo '07	♟♟	5
○ Moscato d'Asti Ciombi '08	♟♟	4*
● Barbera d'Asti Sup. Bricco Paradiso '05	♟♟	6
● Barbera d'Asti Sup. Bricco Paradiso '03	♟♟	4
● M.to Rosso La Mora '05	♟♟	5
● M.to Rosso Solo '06	♟♟	6
○ Moscato d'Asti Ciombi '07	♟♟	4
○ Moscato d'Asti Tenuta del Fant '07	♟♟	4*
○ Moscato d'Asti Tenuta del Fant '06	♟♟	3*

● Barolo V. dei Dardi '05	♟♟	7
● Barolo V. dei Dardi Ris. '00	♟♟♟	7
● Barbera d'Alba V. dei Dardi '06	♟♟	4
● Barolo V. dei Dardi '04	♟♟	6
● Barolo V. dei Dardi Ris. '01	♟♟	7
● Nepas Rosso '00	♟♟	6

Favaro

S.DA CHIUSURE, 1BIS
10010 PIVERONE [TO]
TEL. 012572606
www.cantinafavaro.it

CELLAR SALES
PRE-BOOKED VISITS

ANNUAL PRODUCTION **18,000 bottles**
HECTARES UNDER VINE **3**
VITICULTURE METHOD **Conventional**

It took Benito and Camillo Favaro only a few vintages to turn Favaro into one of the most exciting winemaking trendsetters in the Canavese hill country. Their three hectares yield barely 18,000 bottles, but their innovative image is the result of a series of compelling wines, which also feature outside grape varieties including syrah. But Favaro's finest results have come with bottlings more traditional to the area, beginning with two Erbaluce di Calusos. Le Chiusure is produced in steel and released the same year, while 13 Mesi is given about a year in barrique.

We are convinced that Erbaluce di Caluso has shown thus far only a sliver of its great potential as a wine, in rich evidence in Favaro's Le Chiusure '08. Far from being an uncomplicated wine, it vaunts a multi-layered nose composed of wet stone, kiwi, sea salt and basil, and develops further complexity through a succulent palate marked by mineral salts. Erbaluce di Caluso 13 Mesi '07 is velvet-smooth and ample, leaning more to fruit than mineral. The reds hew to more expected grooves. Syrah Rossomeraviglia '07 explores the variety but doesn't quite connect while the freisa F2 '07 is solid.

○ Erbaluce di Caluso 13 Mesi '07	🍷🍷	4
○ Erbaluce di Caluso Le Chiusure '08	🍷🍷	4*
● Rossomeraviglia '07	🍷🍷	6
● Basy '07	🍷	4
● F2 '07	🍷	4
● Basy '06	🍸🍸	4
● Basy '03	🍸🍸	4
○ Caluso Passito Sole d'Inverno '03	🍸🍸	6
○ Caluso Passito Sole d'Inverno '00	🍸🍸	7
○ Erbaluce di Caluso '06	🍸🍸	4*
○ Sole d'Inverno '00	🍸🍸	6

Ferrando

VIA TORINO, 599
10015 IVREA [TO]
TEL. 0125633550
www.ferrandovini.it

CELLAR SALES
PRE-BOOKED VISITS

ANNUAL PRODUCTION **50,000 bottles**
HECTARES UNDER VINE **7**
VITICULTURE METHOD **Conventional**

The Carema area is an ideal stylistic intermediary between Valle d'Aosta and Piedmont. Its climate and geography are similar to the tiny Alpine region but it cultivates the grape varieties typical of Piedmont. One could call Roberto Ferrando's historic operation in Ivrea the kingdom of mountain-grown nebbiolo, since his are much loved and respected benchmark versions. Ferrando's approximately seven hectares of vineyards produce a classically styled line of wines that offers not only Nebbiolo but also Barbera and Erbaluce di Caluso across a wide range of styles.

Carema wines are creatures of the frontier, not only geographically but in particular stylistically. The best versions exhibit a purity and superb elegance but there is always the risk of too-slender structure to bear up to the hard, earthy tannins that mark high-elevation nebbiolo. That is the sole drawback in Carema Etichetta Nera '04, an otherwise ultra-alluring and complex wine that releases intriguing peat, camphor and fruit preserves. Carema Etichetta Bianca '05 is all verve, driven by juicy, tangy acidity. Caluso Passito Vigneto Cariola '04 makes it almost, but not quite, to the peak.

○ Caluso Passito Vign. Cariola '04	🍷🍷	6
● Carema Et. Bianca '05	🍷🍷	5
● Carema Et. Nera '04	🍷🍷	7
○ Erbaluce di Caluso Cariola '08	🍷🍷	4
○ Solativo '06	🍷	5
● Carema Et. Nera '01	🍸🍸🍸	6
○ Caluso Passito Vign. Cariola '03	🍸🍸	6
○ Caluso Passito Vign. Cariola '02	🍸🍸	6
● Canavese Rosso La Torrazza '06	🍸🍸	4*
● Carema Et. Nera '03	🍸🍸	7
○ Solativo V. T. '05	🍸🍸	5
○ Solativo V. T. '04	🍸🍸	5

Roberto Ferraris

FRAZ. DOGLIANO, 33
14041 AGLIANO TERME [AT]
TEL. 0141954234
www.robertoferraris.it

CELLAR SALES
PRE-BOOKED VISITS

ANNUAL PRODUCTION 35,000 bottles
HECTARES UNDER VINE 9
VITICULTURE METHOD Conventional

Roberto Ferraris' small wine estate in Agliano devotes its attention almost exclusively to barbera. This municipality is known in fact for the high quality that the variety is able to achieve here. Ferraris can rely on a splendid terroir, vines that are up to 70 years old and low crop levels per hectare. But it is the indefatigable efforts of Ferraris himself, who has ceaselessly made improvements to his vineyards and winery, which are largely responsible for keeping this operation in the front rank of producers in the Asti area.

This year's surprise is Barbera d'Asti Superiore La Cricca '07, which went to the finals. A lovely vein of tobacco lifts fragrant dark cherry and spices, then the palate turns powerful and perhaps a tad too alcoholic but the leisurely finish delights with its rich fruit and tasty acidity. Barbera d'Asti '07 is as sure as ever, with subtle tobacco-laden spiciness and red berry fruit preceding a generous, savoury mid-palate. The same goes for the multi-layered Barbera d'Asti Superiore Riserva del Bisavolo '07, with its mosaic of tobacco leaf, spice and dark berry. Barbera d'Asti Nobbio '07 disappointed with a version not up to past vintages.

Fontanabianca

VIA BORDINI, 15
12057 NEIVE [CN]
TEL. 017367195
www.fontanabianca.it

CELLAR SALES
PRE-BOOKED VISITS

ANNUAL PRODUCTION 50,000 bottles
HECTARES UNDER VINE 14
VITICULTURE METHOD Naturale

Meticulous vineyard management and painstaking attention to winemaking practices ensure bottles of superb composition, always exhibiting multi-faceted varietal fidelity and rich, succulent fruit. Savvy wine lovers have always zeroed in on Fontanabianca but it deserves a much broader market penetration, since not only is the quality level of its line-up often flawless but its price tags are also very consumer-friendly and absolutely in line with the quality the wines deliver.

The new Barbaresco Serraboella '06 is a terrific surprise and its sheer harmony won Three Glasses. Gorgeous red fruit mingles with spice and tobacco on the nose followed by absolutely classic volume and length, without any distortion of oak. Sorì Burdin '06 serves up espresso and toasty oak over red berry while massive development suffers some dryness from assertive tannins but they will tamp down nicely in time. Raspberry and spice give Langhe Nebbiolo '07 rich but refined aromatics while the palate, with its nicely understated structure, shows rounded and well proportioned. We'll see the promising Barbera Brunet '07 next year.

Wine	Rating
● Barbera d'Asti Sup. La Cricca '07	♟ 4*
● Barbera d'Asti '07	♟ 3*
● Barbera d'Asti Sup. Riserva del Bisavolo '07	♟ 5
● Barbera d'Asti Nobbio '07	♟ 4
● Barbera d'Asti '06	♟♟ 3*
● Barbera d'Asti Nobbio '06	♟♟ 4*
● Barbera d'Asti Nobbio '04	♟♟ 4*
● Barbera d'Asti Sup. La Cricca '06	♟♟ 4
● Barbera d'Asti Sup. La Cricca '05	♟♟ 4
● Barbera d'Asti Sup. La Cricca '03	♟♟ 5*
● Barbera d'Asti Sup. La Cricca '01	♟♟ 5*
● Barbera d'Asti Sup. Riserva del Bisavolo '06	♟♟ 5

Wine	Rating
● Barbaresco Serraboella '06	♟♟♟ 7
● Barbaresco Sorì Burdin '06	♟♟ 7
● Langhe Nebbiolo '07	♟♟ 4
● Dolcetto d'Alba '08	♟ 4
○ Langhe Arneis '08	♟ 4
● Barbaresco Sorì Burdin '05	♟♟♟ 7
● Barbaresco Sorì Burdin '04	♟♟♟ 7
● Barbaresco Sorì Burdin '01	♟♟♟ 7
● Barbaresco Sorì Burdin '98	♟♟♟ 7

Fontanafredda

VIA ALBA, 15
12050 SERRALUNGA D'ALBA [CN]
TEL. 0173626111
www.fontanafredda.it

CELLAR SALES
PRE-BOOKED VISITS
VISITOR FACILITIES
FOOD

ANNUAL PRODUCTION **6,000,000 bottles**
HECTARES UNDER VINE **85**
VITICULTURE METHOD **Conventional**

The history-laden Fontanafredda winery, directed by Giovanni Minetti, is owned by the Monte Paschi Siena foundation and by Oscar Farinetti and Luca Baffigo Filangieri. This giant producing 6,000,000 bottles annually appeals both to the public at large and to discriminating wine lovers, thanks largely to a line of Langhe-grown wines with great personality and steadiness. Barolo crus Vigna La Rosa, Lazzarito and Vigna La Villa are the fruit of a no-nonsense approach focused on the fundamentals and on a sapient combination of medium-size wood and barriques, some new.

The line-up is rich in stand-outs but the crown this year goes to Barolo Lazzarito Vigna La Delizia '04, and not for the first time. A wine of admirable consistency and typicity, it sports a rich aromatic panoply that ranges through impressions of fruit, sea salt, nutmeg and liquorice before gliding along the track of a supple, relaxed progression. Barolo Fontanafredda Vigna La Rosa '05 is similar in expression, both taut and ductile but with a less sustained finale. Barolo Serralunga '05 performs as expected all the way through while Barbera d'Alba Superiore Papagena '07 shows surprising intensity and verve. Kudos to Asti Galarej '08.

Forteto della Luja

REG. CANDELETTE, 4
14051 LOAZZOLO [AT]
TEL. 014487197
www.fortetodellaluja.it

CELLAR SALES
PRE-BOOKED VISITS

ANNUAL PRODUCTION **60,000 bottles**
HECTARES UNDER VINE **8.5**
VITICULTURE METHOD **Organic certified**

Silvia and Gianni Scaglione run an attractive wine estate that is eco-compatible to boot. They have installed solar panels for their energy needs, set aside numerous hectares of woods as a WWF oasis, and practise organic farming, thus creating an operation that is highly respectful of its local environment. And that local terroir is mirrored in Forteto della Luja's wines. Their individual bottlings are few, and made largely from local traditional grape varieties, grown in vineyards planted to a density of 8,000 vines per hectare.

We immediately liked the refined, complex Loazzolo Piasa Rischei '06 made from late-picked moscato bianco. A subtle oxidative note suggests roasted nuts, further enriching its varietal charms. The multi-faceted palate achieves a fine-tuned balance and approachability, thanks to a sensational acidity. Rich notes of strawberry and cherry help Piemonte Brachetto Pian dei Sogni '07 to stand out, as does its long, dynamic progression. Monferrato Rosso Le Grive '07 has 20 per cent pinot nero but its barbera gives it lovely red berry fruit. Powerful and complex in the mouth, it gives just a trace of oak over tasty fruit and crisp acidity.

● Barolo Lazzarito V. La Delizia '04	♥♥♥	8
● Barolo Fontanafredda V. La Rosa '05	♥♥	8
⊙ Alta Langa Brut Contessa Rosa '06	♥♥	5
○ Asti Galarej '08	♥♥	4
● Barbera d'Alba Sup. Papagena '07	♥♥	5
● Barolo Paiagallo V. La Villa '05	♥♥	7
● Barolo Serralunga '05	♥♥	6
● Diano d'Alba La Lepre '08	♥♥	4
○ Moscato d'Asti Moncucco '08	♥	4
○ Roero Arneis Pradalupo '08	♥	4
● Barolo Lazzarito V. La Delizia '01	♀♀♀	8
● Barolo V. La Rosa '04	♀♀♀	8
● Barolo V. La Rosa '00	♀♀♀	8
● Barolo Paiagallo V. La Villa '04	♀♀	7

○ Loazzolo Piasa Rischei V.T. '06	♥	7
● M.to Rosso Le Grive '07	♥♥	5
● Piemonte Brachetto Pian dei Sogni '07	♥♥	6
○ Loazzolo Piasa Rischei '05	♀♀	7
● M.to Rosso Le Grive '06	♀♀	5
● M.to Rosso Le Grive '04	♀♀	5
● Piemonte Brachetto Forteto Pian dei Sogni '05	♀♀	6
● Piemonte Brachetto Forteto Pian dei Sogni '04	♀♀	6
● Piemonte Brachetto Pian dei Sogni '06	♀♀	6

Gabutti - Franco Boasso

B.TA GABUTTI, 3A
12050 SERRALUNGA D'ALBA [CN]
TEL. 0173613165
www.gabuttiboasso.com

★★★★ Gaja

VIA TORINO, 18
12050 BARBARESCO [CN]
TEL. 0173635158
info@gajawines.com

CELLAR SALES
PRE-BOOKED VISITS
VISITOR FACILITIES

ANNUAL PRODUCTION 30,000 bottles
HECTARES UNDER VINE 6
VITICULTURE METHOD Conventional

The Serralunga hills are the alluring setting for the combined winemaking and farm hospitality activities of this small family-run operation. We have often written of the notable progress that Gabutti-Franco Boasso have made along the path to even higher quality. Their exceptional terroir certainly provides the stylistic framework for the wines we tasted, which are both vigorous and elegant at the same time, but so does a generous dose of sensitive expertise in the cellar.

Barolo Margheria '05 exudes rich, evolved impressions of cinchona, tobacco and gentian wafting over dense berry fruit, then opens huge and succulent. It displays only a touch of dryness from superbly crafted tannins, and faultless progression fuels a long finish, truly worthy of Three Glasses. Gabutti '05 privileges aromatic complexity and refinement over intensity, expressed through subtle gentian, dried flowers, tobacco and earthiness. Vibrant pulp and a tannin-driven, linear progression create a terrific finale in the most classic tradition. The less complex Barolo Serralunga '05 is fine while Barbera '07 shows power but a slender nose.

ANNUAL PRODUCTION 300,000 bottles
HECTARES UNDER VINE 92
VITICULTURE METHOD Conventional

It may be taken for granted but it remains true that when you get to grips with Angelo Gaja's wines, all you can say is that their technical perfection and stylistic register are truly remarkable, right across the entire line. We are in the realm of international greatness here, where Langhe-area wines are crafted with an eye to faultless balance and staying power over time. All of this is in a modernist key but at the same time with a marked respect for terroir. These are wines capable of being understood by everyone, even if you couldn't call them farm-style bottles.

The '06 Langhe Nebbiolos, Sorì Tildin and Sorì San Lorenzo from the Barbaresco zone are masterpieces of balance and finesse. The first combines a measure of terroir character with a rich, silky mouthfeel that communicates both sensuality and power. The second, toastier and more complex on the nose, shows a palate whose sapidity is a tad more rustic and assertive. Costa Russi '06, from the same zone, is terrific in its elegance, showing only a shade less personality. Sperss '05, sourced from the Barolo area, is as big-hitting and self-confident as ever. Barbaresco '06 is wonderfully delicious but the other superstars put it somewhat in the shade.

● Barolo Margheria '05	♟♟♟	6*
● Barolo Gabutti '05	♟♟	6
● Barbera d'Alba '07	♟♟	4*
● Barolo Serralunga '05	♟♟	6
● Dolcetto d'Alba Meriame '08	♟♟	4*
○ Moscato d'Asti Grappoli '08	♟	4
● Primi Grappoli '07	♟	4
● Barolo Serralunga '04	♟♟	6
● Barolo Serralunga '99	♟♟	7

● Langhe Nebbiolo Sorì S. Lorenzo '06	♟♟♟	8
● Langhe Nebbiolo Sorì Tildin '06	♟♟♟+	8
● Barbaresco '06	♟♟	8
● Langhe Nebbiolo Costa Russi '06	♟♟	8
● Langhe Nebbiolo Sperss '05	♟♟	8
● Barbaresco '04	♟♟♟	8
● Barbaresco '01	♟♟♟	8
● Langhe Nebbiolo Costa Russi '05	♟♟♟	8
● Langhe Nebbiolo Costa Russi '05	♟♟♟	8
● Langhe Nebbiolo Costa Russi '04	♟♟♟	8
● Langhe Nebbiolo Sorì S. Lorenzo '03	♟♟♟	8
● Langhe Nebbiolo Sorì S. Lorenzo '01	♟♟♟	8
● Langhe Nebbiolo Sorì S. Lorenzo '99	♟♟♟	8
● Langhe Nebbiolo Sorì S. Lorenzo '98	♟♟♟	8
● Langhe Nebbiolo Sorì Tildin '00	♟♟♟	8
● Langhe Nebbiolo Sorì Tildin '98	♟♟♟	8
● Langhe Nebbiolo Sorì Tildin '97	♟♟♟	8
● Langhe Nebbiolo Sperss '04	♟♟♟	8

Filippo Gallino

FRAZ. MADONNA LORETO
VALLE DEL POZZO, 63
12043 CANALE [CN]
TEL. 017398112
www.filippogallino.com

CELLAR SALES
PRE-BOOKED VISITS

ANNUAL PRODUCTION **82,000 bottles**
HECTARES UNDER VINE **14**
VITICULTURE METHOD **Conventional**

The Gallinos, Filippo and his son Gianni, are the engine of this modest but highly respected Roero wine operation, founded in 1961. Their production focuses on a handful of wines and styles traditional to the area, created by a viticulture that still reflects the world of the small farmer. The local grape varieties – arneis, barbera, nebbiolo – are planted around Canale in sandy-clay soils. Gallino wines are always genuine, expressions of the land and hands that yield them, whether they win Three Glasses or not.

Roero '07 shows dense fruit, with earth and dried flowers on the nose. It is certainly a bit countryish but also supple, refreshing and approachable, with a fine, long finish. The excellent Barbera d'Alba Elaine '07 presents a notable, typically floral nose, with its hints of Peruvian bark and forest floor while the palate is rich and dense. It concludes long but still lacks suppleness. Barbera d'Alba Superiore '07 is equally impressive, with a spacious aromatic richness, followed by a lean-profiled palate with dense fruit and good length. The rest of the line is also soundly made.

Gancia

C.SO LIBERTÀ, 66
14053 CANELLI [AT]
TEL. 01418301
www.gancia.it

CELLAR SALES
PRE-BOOKED VISITS

ANNUAL PRODUCTION **30,000,000 bottles**
HECTARES UNDER VINE **N.D.**
VITICULTURE METHOD **Conventional**

Nine years have gone by since Edoardo, Lamberto and Max Gancia decided to focus efforts on the Monferrato area, in order to add still wines to their long-standing sparkling portfolio. They launched Tenuta Vallarino, centred on the Bricco di Asinari vineyards, in the municipality of San Marzano Oliveto and then in 2003 added another 20 hectares near Casorzio, also in the province of Asti. In spite of its plethora of labels, Gancia evidences a high standard of quality for both styles of wines, sparkling and still.

All of the sparklers have new names and they are impressive products. The Cuvée 36 Brut '06 and Cuvée 60 Brut Riserva '03 are outstanding. The former is fragrant, giving apple and pear with yeast and fresh bread to conclude with a classy, leisurely finish. The second is complex, with spice and tea biscuits. We liked the varietal sage and ripe peach on Asti Metodo Classico Cuvée 24 '07, and the finesse and balance of its palate. Turning to the still wines, Castello di Canelli '08 impressed with its richness and masterful length, after fragrant brioche and candied fruit. The harmonious, easy-drinking Barbera d'Asti Filvoia '08, though a bit oaky, gives tasty dark berry fruit.

● Roero '07	♈	5
● Barbera d'Alba Elaine '07	♈	5
● Barbera d'Alba Sup. '07	♈	5
● Barbera d'Alba '08	♈	4
● Langhe Nebbiolo Licin '07	♈	5
○ Roero Arneis '08	♈	4
● Barbera d'Alba Sup. '05	♈♈♈	5
● Barbera d'Alba Sup. '04	♈♈♈	5
● Barbera d'Alba Sup. '97	♈♈♈	5
● Roero '06	♈♈♈	6
● Roero Sup. '03	♈♈♈	6
● Roero Sup. '01	♈♈♈	6
● Roero Sup. '99	♈♈♈	6
● Roero Sup. '98	♈♈♈	6
● Barbera d'Alba '07	♈♈	4*
● Barbera d'Alba Sup. '06	♈♈	5
● Roero '05	♈♈	6

○ Alta Langa Cuvée 36 Brut '06	♈	6
○ Alta Langa Cuvée 60 Brut Ris. '03	♈	6
○ Asti M. Cl. Cuvée 24 '07	♈	6
● Barbera d'Asti Filovia '08	♈	4
○ Moscato d'Asti Castello di Canelli '08	♈	4
○ Cuvée 18 M. Cl. Brut	♈	5
☉ Cuvée 18 M. Cl. Brut Rosé	♈	5
○ Alta Langa Vintage Integral M. Cl. Riserva del Fondatore '04	♈	6
○ Asti Camillo Gancia '04	♈	6
○ Asti Camillo Gancia M. Cl. '06	♈	6
○ Asti Camillo Gancia M. Cl. '05	♈	6

Tenuta Garetto

S.DA ASTI MARE, 30
14041 AGLIANO TERME [AT]
TEL. 0141954068
www.garetto.it

CELLAR SALES
PRE-BOOKED VISITS

ANNUAL PRODUCTION **100,000 bottles**
HECTARES UNDER VINE **20**
VITICULTURE METHOD **Conventional**

Tenuta Garetto, from its origins in the first decades of the 20th century, has grown to become one of the most impressive producers in the entire Asti area. Youthful Alessandro Garetto directs it today with dedicated expertise and oenologist Enzo Quinterno is at his side. The vineyards are located near the winery in the hills around Agliano, planted on limestone marl soils and facing south and southwest. There are two new plantings but the bulk of the vineyards are 50 to 60 years old.

Two of the Barberas competed in our finals. Barbera d'Asti Superiore Nizza Favà '06 is exceptional for its finesse and richness, with aromas as diverse as cherry, cinchona, black pepper and earthy mineral. Stunning progression fuels its dense, juicy palate and ringing acidity and dense, succulent fruit ennoble a lengthy finale. In contrast, Barbera d'Asti Superiore In Pectore '07 starts with clean-edged, intense fruit. If its palate lacks some length, it does build massive presence in the mouth, showing pulpy and well framed with a delicious, well-proportioned finish. Barbera d'Asti Tra Neuit e Dì '08 is crisp, spicy and powerful.

● Barbera d'Asti Sup. In Pectore '07	🍷🍷 4*
● Barbera d'Asti Sup. Nizza Favà '06	🍷🍷 5
● Barbera d'Asti Tra Neuit e Dì '08	🍷🍷 3*
● Grignolino d'Asti 'L Giget '08	🍷 3
● Barbera d'Asti Sup. Nizza Favà '04	🍷🍷🍷 5
● Barbera d'Asti Sup. Favà '01	🍷🍷 5
● Barbera d'Asti Sup. In Pectore '06	🍷🍷 4*
● Barbera d'Asti Sup. Nizza Favà '05	🍷🍷 5

Ettore Germano

LOC. CERRETTA, 1
12050 SERRALUNGA D'ALBA [CN]
TEL. 0173613528
www.germanoettore.com

CELLAR SALES
PRE-BOOKED VISITS
VISITOR FACILITIES

ANNUAL PRODUCTION **70,000 bottles**
HECTARES UNDER VINE **13.5**
VITICULTURE METHOD **Conventional**

The Cerretta area of Serralunga hosts Sergio Germano's cellar, the headquarters, as it were, of a wine operation that has made a quantum leap forward in the last few years. Now superb whites stand alongside the traditional Langhe reds, soon to be joined by distinctive sparkling wines. Yet the broad wine-consuming public has yet to discover the vineyards of Cigliè, 30 kilometres farther down in upper Langhe, dedicated to riesling and chardonnay. The oft-hymned cru vineyards of Prapò, Cerretta and Lazzarito yield Barolos which Sergio vinifies according to the growing year.

We tasted a spectacular group of wines this year. Barolo Cerretta returns to the podium, of course. It is usually the most extrovert and strapping of crus but in a vintage such as the controversial 2005 it surpasses in overall balance and harmony Prapò, which as always is austere and earthy. If Barolo Lazzarito Riserva presents so many fine points in the 2003 growing year, it is hard to imagine what it will do in more classic years. We do however cherish the strong points of Langhe Bianco Hérzu '07, a rich wine flaunting the classic florality of a great German Riesling and which lays out a magnificently structured palate of beautiful proportions.

● Barolo Cerretta '05	🍷🍷🍷 8
● Barolo Prapò '05	🍷🍷 8
○ Langhe Bianco Hérzu '07	🍷🍷 6
● Barolo Lazzarito Ris. '03	🍷🍷 8
● Barolo Serralunga '05	🍷🍷 7
● Dolcetto d'Alba Vign. Lorenzino '08	🍷🍷 4
● Dolcetto d'Alba Vign. Pra di Pò '08	🍷🍷 4
○ Langhe Bianco Binel '07	🍷🍷 5
○ Langhe Chardonnay '08	🍷🍷 4
● Langhe Nebbiolo '07	🍷🍷 5
● Barolo Cerretta '01	🍷🍷🍷 7
● Barolo Prapò '04	🍷🍷🍷 7
● Barolo Cerretta '04	🍷🍷 7
○ Langhe Bianco Hérzu '06	🍷🍷 5*

Attilio Ghisolfi

LOC. BUSSIA, 27
12065 MONFORTE D'ALBA [CN]
TEL. 017378345
www.ghisolfi.com

CELLAR SALES
PRE-BOOKED VISITS

ANNUAL PRODUCTION **45,000 bottles**
HECTARES UNDER VINE **6.5**
VITICULTURE METHOD **Conventional**

This family winery concentrates its efforts on coaxing the maximum quality possible out of traditional local grapes, above all nebbiolo for Barolo, and for quite a few years now Gianmarco Ghisolfi has achieved the highest levels of quality. He is a man of stubborn perseverance and consistency, virtues that make a fine producer. Ghisolfi's approach refuses to play to the crowd or rely on technology for popularity. The watchwords are winemaking perfection and clarity, qualities that endure even through lengthy cellaring.

Three Glasses went to Barolo Bricco Visette '05, a wine of tremendous character aromas that range through cinchona, spices and forest floor. A monumental palate exhibits stunning density without worrying too much about near-term harmony. The standard Barolo is less dynamic and doesn't completely dominate the barrique. Barbera Vigna Lisi '06 appears impenetrable, exuberant and even too rich perhaps. It delivers pleasure but not gracefully. Alta Bussia is a fortunate conjunction of innovation and tradition and even the '06 is particularly felicitous. The pinot nero Pinay '07 is pleasant but the early 2007 year did it no favours.

★ Bruno Giacosa

VIA XX SETTEMBRE, 52
12057 NEIVE [CN]
TEL. 017367027
www.brunogiacosa.it

ANNUAL PRODUCTION **400,000 bottles**
HECTARES UNDER VINE **20**
VITICULTURE METHOD **Conventional**

Giving the Winery of the Year award to Bruno Giacosa means recognizing the extraordinary long-standing efforts that Giacosa, one of the fathers of Italy's wine industry, has exerted over more than half a century of activity. His wines, including those presented this year, are always outstanding, and in some cases astonishing, whether they are produced from his own grapes or from fruit brought in from long-time grower suppliers.

We thought that the monumental Barbaresco Asili '05 merited Giacosa's red label, which he gives to the wines highest in quality. Traditional in style, it is elegant, self-confident and endless, showing clean berry fruit, liquorice and yellow peach over dense, silken tannins. Hardly less fine is Barolo Le Rocche del Falletto '05, a great, energy-laden Serralunga whose only drawback is its youth, which maturity will soon take care of. The utterly classic Barbaresco Santo Stefano di Neive '05 has less power but more nerve and agility. A delicious Roero Arneis '08 is not to be missed nor is the all-pinot nero Bruno Giacosa Extra Brut '05.

● Barolo Bricco Visette '05	♟♟♟ 7
● Barbera d'Alba V. Lisi '06	♟♟ 5
● Barolo '05	♟♟ 6
● Langhe Rosso Alta Bussia '06	♟♟ 6
● Langhe Rosso Pinay '07	♟ 4
● Barolo Bricco Visette '01	♟♟♟ 7
● Langhe Rosso Alta Bussia '01	♟♟♟ 6
● Langhe Rosso Alta Bussia '00	♟♟♟ 6
● Langhe Rosso Alta Bussia '99	♟♟♟ 6

● Barbaresco Asili '05	♟♟♟+ 8
● Barolo Le Rocche del Falletto '05	♟♟♟ 8
● Barbaresco Santo Stefano '05	♟♟ 8
● Barbera d'Alba Falletto '07	♟♟ 7
O Bruno Giacosa Extra Brut '05	♟♟ 6
● Dolcetto d'Alba Falletto '08	♟♟ 5
O Roero Arneis '08	♟♟ 6
● Barbaresco Asili '99	♟♟♟ 8
● Barbaresco Asili Ris. '04	♟♟♟ 8
● Barbaresco Asili Ris. '96	♟♟♟ 8
● Barbaresco Rabajà Ris. '01	♟♟♟ 8
● Barbaresco Santo Stefano '01	♟♟♟ 8
● Barbaresco Santo Stefano '00	♟♟♟ 8
● Barolo Falletto '04	♟♟♟ 8
● Barolo Falletto '01	♟♟♟ 8
● Barolo Le Rocche del Falletto Ris. '01	♟♟♟ 8

Carlo Giacosa

S.DA OVELLO, 9
12050 BARBARESCO [CN]
TEL. 0173635116
www.carlogiacosa.it

CELLAR SALES
PRE-BOOKED VISITS

ANNUAL PRODUCTION 45,000 bottles
HECTARES UNDER VINE 5
VITICULTURE METHOD Conventional

Reasonable prices, terrific quality and respect for provenance are three good reasons for knowing this Barbaresco winery. Carlo Giacosa's facility is modest in size, containing only what is needed for vinification, but it is a warm and welcoming spot with a functional tasting room. The determined approach by Maria Grazia Giacosa, assisted by the entire family, results in a well thought-out style that finds substance in a very consistent line of Barberas. They differ in the facets of their personalities but are all easily recognizable ambassadors of their terroir.

Barbaresco Narin '06 is very appealing, with rich, deep fruit and supple, clean linearity. Some might find it too simple but most will find it utterly alluring. Equally great is Barbera Lina '07, more succulent and balanced than ever. Barbaresco Montefico '06 will be out next year, since it needs some more time to buff up. Barbera Mucin '08 is soundly made but doesn't offer too much else while Dolcetto''08 is a real classic, a heady, youthful, utterly delicious quaffer.

F.lli Giacosa

VIA XX SETTEMBRE, 64
12057 NEIVE [CN]
TEL. 017367013
www.giacosa.it

CELLAR SALES
PRE-BOOKED VISITS

ANNUAL PRODUCTION 500,000 bottles
HECTARES UNDER VINE 40
VITICULTURE METHOD Conventional

Founded in 1895, Fratelli Giacosa boasts ancient roots but today it enjoys larger dimensions than most Langhe wine operations. In fact, its 40 hectares of vineyards allow it to effectively exploit various terroirs and wine types, so that it can offer a very broad range of Piedmont's vinous classics. The house style has grown and sharpened in focus over the years, as the cellar has coaxed the best from a varied array of winemaking equipment, both oak and lined concrete. The pricing policy has always been well-calibrated and reasonable.

Barbaresco Vigna Gian Maté '06 lacks a sturdy framework but its refinement and equilibrium make it a stand-out. Even finer is Basarin '06, with spice everywhere, while slightly burred tannins do not detract from its overall savouriness and fine length. Barolo Bussia '05 shows just a bit much oak but lots of raspberry-led wild berries on the nose while dense tannins lead into a long finish. Dolcetto Madonna di Como '08 is self-confident, offering fragrant, dark-fleshed fruit and bitter almond. The venerable Barbera Maria Gioana is now flanked by Madonna di Como, in '06 editions. They are juicy, rich, well-balanced easy drinkers.

● Barbaresco Narin '06	♀♀ 6*
● Barbera d'Alba Lina '07	♀♀ 4*
● Dolcetto d'Alba Cuchet '08	♀♀ 4
● Barbera d'Alba Mucin '08	♀ 4
● Barbaresco Montefico '05	♀♀ 6
● Barbaresco Montefico '04	♀♀ 6
● Barbaresco Narin '05	♀♀ 6*
● Barbaresco Narin '04	♀♀ 6
● Barbaresco Narin '01	♀♀ 6
● Barbera d'Alba Lina '06	♀♀ 4
● Barbera d'Alba Mucin '07	♀♀ 4*
● Dolcetto d'Alba Cuchet '07	♀♀ 4*

● Barbaresco Basarin '06	♀♀ 6
● Barbera d'Alba Madonna di Como '06	♀♀ 4*
● Barbaresco Basarin V. Gian Matè '06	♀♀ 6
● Barbera d'Alba Maria Gioana '06	♀♀ 5
● Barolo Bussia '05	♀♀ 6
● Dolcetto d'Alba Madonna di Como '08	♀♀ 4*
○ Langhe Chardonnay Ca' Lunga '07	♀ 5
○ Langhe Chardonnay Rorea '08	♀ 4
○ Roero Arneis '08	♀ 4
● Barbaresco Basarin '03	♀♀ 6
● Barbaresco Basarin V. Gian Matè '05	♀♀ 6
● Barbaresco Gian Matè '04	♀♀ 6
● Barbera d'Alba Maria Gioana '05	♀♀ 5
● Barolo V. Mandorlo '01	♀♀ 6

Raffaele Gili

LOC. PAUTASSO, 7
12050 CASTELLINALDO [CN]
TEL. 0173639011

PRE-BOOKED VISITS

ANNUAL PRODUCTION 55,000 bottles
HECTARES UNDER VINE 8
VITICULTURE METHOD Conventional

This attractive wine estate lies at the entrance to Castellinaldo, one of Roero's most robust wine centres. Raffaele Gili and his wife Laura, who direct this operation with skill and commitment, produce only a handful of bottlings, but they pay close attention to the traditional varieties of the area, in their case barbera, nebbiolo, cabernet sauvignon, arneis and favorita. The overall performance is solid enough but they seem not to reach those true high notes.

We liked Barbera d'Alba Pautasso '07. It gives clean aromatic fruit and then a palate that offers more pleasure and balanced complexity than heft and power. Nebbiolo d'Alba Sansivé '06 is winning, proffering a complex array of raspberry and dried flowers, despite some spicy oak intrusiveness. Here, there is considerable power in the mouth, along with rich, pulpy fruit and a finish with stunning length, although it loses some complexity at the tail end. The remaining wines are soundly crafted, in particular the straightforward, fruity Roero Bric Angelino '06.

Giovanni Battista Gillardi

CASCINA CORSALETTO, 69
12060 FARIGLIANO [CN]
TEL. 017376306
www.gillardi.it

CELLAR SALES
PRE-BOOKED VISITS

ANNUAL PRODUCTION 35,000 bottles
HECTARES UNDER VINE 7
VITICULTURE METHOD Conventional

A long-time, successful Dolcetto producer in Langhe, Gillardi has developed a reputation for reliable, high-quality wines. His new, architecturally handsome cellar is the perfect operational complement to the meticulous work he lavishes on the estate vineyards, particularly on Cursalet, one of the area's most sublime crus. Gillardi's ever-consistent Dolcettos are joined by an intriguingly diverse array of other wines.

Cursalet, even in the difficult '08 vintage, attests to the viticultural value of Dogliani. It's a wine with great spirit that opens impetuously with dark aromas and taut tannins, only to soften after a few moments of air, mutating into great elegance and roundedness on the nose, with dark berry and cocoa powder, as well as on the palate. Harys '07 is a great wine, and one more quickly understood, given its vinification in a well-calibrated international style. But Gillardi's passion for the great French wines should lead him to implant in this Syrah a heart that has more of Dogliani. The hard-to-find Granaccio '06 remains impressive.

● Barbera d'Alba Pautasso '07	🍷🍷 4*
● Nebbiolo d'Alba Sansivé '06	🍷🍷 4*
● Barbera d'Alba Castellinaldo '06	🍷 4
○ Langhe Favorita '08	🍷 3
● Langhe Rosso L'Assemblato '06	🍷 4
○ Roero Arneis '08	🍷 4
● Roero Bric Angelino '06	🍷 4
● Barbera d'Alba Pautasso '05	🍷🍷 4*
● Castellinaldo Barbera d'Alba '05	🍷🍷 4
● Langhe Rosso L'Assemblato '04	🍷🍷 5
● Nebbiolo d'Alba Sansivé '05	🍷🍷 4
● Roero Bric Angelino '05	🍷🍷 4
● Roero Bric Angelino '04	🍷🍷 5

● Dolcetto di Dogliani Cursalet '08	🍷🍷 4
● Langhe Rosso Harys '07	🍷🍷 7
● Dolcetto di Dogliani Vign. Maestra '08	🍷🍷 4*
● Granaccio '06	🍷🍷 8
● Langhe Rosso Yeta '07	🍷🍷 5
● Harys '00	🍷🍷🍷 7
● Dolcetto di Dogliani Cursalet '07	🍷🍷 4*
● Dolcetto di Dogliani Cursalet '06	🍷🍷 4*
● Dolcetto di Dogliani Cursalet '05	🍷🍷 4*
● Dolcetto di Dogliani Cursalet '04	🍷🍷 4*
● Harys '04	🍷🍷 7
● Langhe Rosso Harys '06	🍷🍷 7
● Langhe Rosso Harys '05	🍷🍷 7

Cascina Giovinale

S.DA SAN NICOLAO, 102
14049 NIZZA MONFERRATO [AT]
TEL. 0141793005
www.cascinagiovinale.com

CELLAR SALES
PRE-BOOKED VISITS

ANNUAL PRODUCTION **25,000 bottles**
HECTARES UNDER VINE **7**
VITICULTURE METHOD **Conventional**

The lovely San Nicolao hill, rising 260 metres, has been the site since 1980 of Bruno Ciocca and his wife Anna Solaini's wine estate. Giovinale is a small operation with big plans. Bruno and Anna, assisted by oenologist Giuliano Noè and agronomist Piero Roseo, have invested mightily in quality, lavishing attention on their vineyards and winemaking facility. The south and southwest-facing vineyards are largely planted to barbera and moscato, along with some dolcetto and cabernet sauvignon.

Year after year, Barbera d'Asti Superiore Nizza Anssèma '06 emerges as one of the finest Barberas in Asti. A slightly alcohol-rich nose vaunts intense, richly faceted aromas, of earth, cinchona and more while the massive palate truly commands, with energy and enthralling savouriness. It only lacks that extra length to be a true champion. Barbera d'Asti Superiore '07 is not far behind. Some residual oak toast fails to dent the pleasure provided by bright, fragrant cherry and the palate displays firm structure alongside a vibrant, magisterial freshness, plus an enviable equilibrium of forces and a long finish of fine breed.

● Barbera d'Asti Sup. Nizza Anssèma '06	🍷🍷 5*
● Barbera d'Asti Sup. '07	🍷🍷 4*
● Barbera d'Asti '05	ΥΥ 4
● Barbera d'Asti Sup. '06	ΥΥ 4*
● Barbera d'Asti Sup. Nizza Anssèma '05	ΥΥ 5
● Barbera d'Asti Sup. Nizza Anssèma '04	ΥΥ 5
● M.to Trinum '04	ΥΥ 5

La Giribaldina

REG. SAN VITO, 39
14042 CALAMANDRANA [AT]
TEL. 0141718043
www.giribaldina.com

CELLAR SALES
PRE-BOOKED VISITS

ANNUAL PRODUCTION **60,000 bottles**
HECTARES UNDER VINE **10**
VITICULTURE METHOD **Conventional**

The Colombo family launched their wine operation in the mid 1990s and adopted the ancient Giribaldi farm as their estate. With the help of oenologist Beppe Caviola and agronomist Piero Roseo, the Colombos have been able to concentrate on the area's most typical grapes and on teasing the best qualities from their terroir. For this reason, La Giribaldina is best represented by barbera, from the Bricco Castellaro and Monte del Mare vineyards at Vinchio and Vaglio Serra, and by moscato, grown in the municipality of Calamandrana, although there is some cabernet sauvignon, also from Calamandrana.

Wine lovers have come to trust Giribaldina's Barbera d'Astis. The standard Monte del Mare '08 is its usual refreshing, well sculpted and fruit filled self. Nizza Cala della Mandrie '06 shows a more complex nose of pungent balsam and ripe red berry fruit. Its volume impresses, as does the finish, although there could have been a bit more liveliness throughout. Vigneti della Val Sarmassa '07 centres on ripe fruit and tobacco leaf but has room for improvement. Piemonte Moscato Passito '07 is a pleasure, brimming with honey and candied fruit. Equally attractive is Monferrato Bianco Ferro di Cavallo '08, a nicely varietal Sauvignon that unleashes a complex, alcohol-rich finish.

● Barbera d'Asti Monte del Mare '08	🍷🍷 3*
● Barbera d'Asti Sup. Nizza Cala delle Mandrie '06	🍷🍷 5
● Barbera d'Asti Sup. Vign. della Val Sarmassa '07	🍷 4
○ M.to Bianco Ferro di Cavallo '08	🍷 4
○ Piemonte Moscato Passito '07	🍷 5
● Barbera d'Asti Monte del Mare '07	ΥΥ 3*
● Barbera d'Asti Sup. Cala delle Mandrie '04	ΥΥ 5
● Barbera d'Asti Sup. Cala delle Mandrie '03	ΥΥ 5
● Barbera d'Asti Sup. Nizza Cala delle Mandrie '05	ΥΥ 5
● Barbera d'Asti Sup. Sarmassa '01	ΥΥ 5
● Barbera d'Asti Sup. Vign. della Val Sarmassa '06	ΥΥ 4*
○ M.to Bianco Ferro di Cavallo '07	ΥΥ 4*

La Gironda

S.DA BRICCO, 12
14049 NIZZA MONFERRATO [AT]
TEL. 0141701013
www.lagironda.com

CELLAR SALES
PRE-BOOKED VISITS

ANNUAL PRODUCTION **40,000 bottles**
HECTARES UNDER VINE **8**
VITICULTURE METHOD **Conventional**

After over 30 years in the winemaking equipment business, Agostino Galandrino and his family decided ten years ago to devote all of their time to producing wines. Their operation is located in the Bricco della Cremosina vineyard in Nizza Monferrato, one of the most prestigious areas for growing barbera, and good results came almost immediately. Gironda rapidly gained a reputation as one of the zone's benchmark producers with wines that uniquely express the qualities of the local terroir.

Barbera d'Asti Superiore Nizza Le Nicchie '06 competed in our final round. We liked the cleanness of its fruit and its smooth spice while its full-volumed, massive body is awesome, with a fine-handed balance between acidity and alcohol. It concludes on an almost endless finish. Monferrato Rosso Chiesavecchia '06 is a multi-layered assemblage of cabernet franc, merlot, nebbiolo and barbera that presents lean, austere notes of cinchona, spice and red berry. But it then opens up a spacious palate with fine intensity and its vibrant acidity powers into a long, aristocratic finish. All of the other wines we taste were well crafted.

La Giustiniana

FRAZ. ROVERETO, 5
15066 GAVI [AL]
TEL. 0143682132
www.lagiustiniana.it

CELLAR SALES
PRE-BOOKED VISITS

ANNUAL PRODUCTION **200,000 bottles**
HECTARES UNDER VINE **39**
VITICULTURE METHOD **Conventional**

One the most magnificent residences of the Genovese nobility now houses this splendid winery. Not one for resting long on its laurels, La Giustiniana is continuously carrying out research and experimentation, under the expert direction of Enrico Tomalino. The estate comprises 120 hectares, of which some 40 are under vine, with cortese the leading variety by far.

Three Glasses went to Il Nostro Gavi '07 for demonstrating in an utterly classic manner what the cortese grape is capable of achieving. Its hallmark minerally aromas are shot through with appealing pear and apple while the palate is stunning and ultra-savoury, and the finish lengthy and vibrant. Emphatic acidity renders Montessora '08 a bit less ample but good fruit makes for a fine, multi-layered palate. Lugarara '08 is simpler and very easy drinking. Just '06 is also based on cortese. It labours slightly under its oak but still displays good flashes of personality.

● Barbera d'Asti Sup. Nizza Le Nicchie '06	♥♥	5
● M.to Rosso Chiesavecchia '06	♥♥	4*
● Barbera d'Asti La Gena '07	♥	4
● Barbera d'Asti La Lippa '08	♥	3
● Brachetto d'Acqui '08	♥	4
○ Moscato d'Asti '08	♥	4
● Barbera d'Asti La Gena '06	♀♀	4*
● Barbera d'Asti La Gena '05	♀♀	4*
● Barbera d'Asti La Lippa '07	♀♀	3
● Barbera d'Asti La Lippa '06	♀♀	3*
● Barbera d'Asti Sup. Nizza Le Nicchie '05	♀♀	5
● Barbera d'Asti Sup. Nizza Le Nicchie '04	♀♀	5
● Barbera d'Asti Sup. Nizza Le Nicchie '03	♀♀	5

○ Gavi del Comune di Gavi Il Nostro Gavi '07	♥♥♥	5
○ Gavi del Comune di Gavi Lugarara '08	♥♥	4
○ Gavi del Comune di Gavi Montessora '08	♥♥	5
● M.to Rosso Just '05	♥♥	6
● Piemonte Barbera Grangiarossa '07	♥♥	4*
○ Just Bianco '06	♥	6
○ Gavi del Comune di Gavi Il Nostro Gavi '06	♀♀	5
○ Gavi del Comune di Gavi Il Nostro Gavi '04	♀♀	5
○ Gavi del Comune di Gavi Lugarara '07	♀♀	4

Cantina del Glicine

VIA GIULIO CESARE, 1
12052 NEIVE [CN]
TEL. 017367215
www.cantinadelglicine.it

CELLAR SALES
PRE-BOOKED VISITS

ANNUAL PRODUCTION 45,000 bottles
HECTARES UNDER VINE 4
VITICULTURE METHOD Naturale

There are many good reasons for visiting Cantina del Glicine in the venerable heart of Neive. One of course is the magnificent 17th-century building itself, constructed with steep surfaces to convey rainwater and condensation into an underground cistern, located at the end of a narrow corridor, into whose walls are carved niches containing bottles, casks and what not. Adriana Mazzi and Roberto Bruno have succeeded in utilizing this enchanting complex to produce flawless bottlings of the wines classic to this Bacchus-blessed corner of Piedmont.

Barbaresco Marcorino '06 takes this vintage skywards, with a glorious nose, clean-edged and kaleidoscopic in its florality, followed by a palate of electric vibrancy and an extravagantly succulent finish. Barbaresco Currà '06 – now with a second "r" – flaunts a shimmering purple and an ultra-varietal nose. The palate is assertive but not harsh while the finish is laden with tempting black liquorice. Both Barberas are fine. La Sconsolata '07 displays noble fruit and enrapturing acidity while La Dormiosa '06 shows clean, dense fruit and a more structured, fruit-based palate with good length. The rest are soundly made, particularly Dolcetto '08.

★ Elio Grasso

LOC. GINESTRA, 40
12065 MONFORTE D'ALBA [CN]
TEL. 017378491
www.eliograsso.it

CELLAR SALES
PRE-BOOKED VISITS

ANNUAL PRODUCTION 75,000 bottles
HECTARES UNDER VINE 14
VITICULTURE METHOD Conventional

The operation owned by Elio Grasso and his wife Marina, now assisted full time by their son Gianluca, is a model winery in every sense of the term. They have some 14 hectares of vineyards, plus a modern, efficient cellar, which is largely hewn into the rock face behind their house, minimalizing environmental impact. Their estate is in Monforte, one of the areas most prized for growing nebbiolo and for the production of powerful, long-lived Barolos.

From the 2005s, we preferred Ginestra Vigna Casa Maté, its classic nose veined with subtle minerality and the palate showing supple and full. In comparison, Gavarini Vigna Chiniera is a tad rough, its tannins still undigested. The '06 is one the best versions of Barbera Vigna Martina, a fragrant, very typical wine, although its tannic mass and alcohol tamp down the marked acidity. Langhe Nebbiolo Gavarini and Dolcetto d'Alba dei Grassi are fine, with the youthful excesses expected of '08s. Barolo Runcot '04 is not out yet but our advance tastings convince us that is the best version ever. We'll review it next year but in the meantime, grab any bottles you see.

● Barbaresco Currà '06	♟♟ 6
● Barbaresco Marcorino '06	♟♟ 6
● Barbera d'Alba La Sconsolata '07	♟♟ 4
● Barbera d'Alba Sup. La Dormiosa '06	♟♟ 5
● Dolcetto d'Alba Olmiolo '08	♟ 4
○ Moscato d'Asti '08	♟ 4
● Nebbiolo d'Alba Calcabrume '07	♟ 4
○ Roero Arneis Il Mandolo '08	♟ 4
● Barbaresco Curà '05	♟♟ 6
● Barbaresco Marcorino '05	♟♟ 6*
● Barbaresco Marcorino '04	♟♟ 6
● Barbera d'Alba La Sconsolata '06	♟♟ 4*
● Barbera d'Alba Sup. La Dormiosa '05	♟♟ 5
● Barbera d'Alba Sup. La Sconsolata Maturata in Barrique '05	♟♟ 5

● Barolo Ginestra V. Casa Maté '05	♟♟♟ 8
● Barbera d'Alba V. Martina '06	♟♟ 5*
● Barolo Gavarini V. Chiniera '05	♟♟ 8
● Dolcetto d'Alba dei Grassi '08	♟♟ 4*
● Langhe Nebbiolo Gavarini '08	♟♟ 5
● Barolo Gavarini V. Chiniera '01	♟♟♟ 8
● Barolo Gavarini V. Chiniera '00	♟♟♟ 8
● Barolo Gavarini V. Chiniera '99	♟♟♟ 8
● Barolo Gavarini V. Chiniera '98	♟♟♟ 8
● Barolo Ginestra V. Casa Maté '04	♟♟♟ 8
● Barolo Ginestra V. Casa Maté '03	♟♟♟ 8
● Barolo Rüncot '01	♟♟♟ 8
● Barolo Rüncot '00	♟♟♟ 8
● Barolo Rüncot '99	♟♟♟ 8
● Barolo Rüncot '98	♟♟♟ 8
● Barolo Rüncot '96	♟♟♟ 8

Silvio Grasso

FRAZ. ANNUNZIATA
CASCINA LUCIANI, 112
12064 LA MORRA [CN]
TEL. 017350322

CELLAR SALES

ANNUAL PRODUCTION **70,000 bottles**
HECTARES UNDER VINE **11**
VITICULTURE METHOD **Conventional**

A close-knit family and shared goals are the essence of the Grasso family, which runs this trim, ten-hectare estate in the Barolo zone with a sure hand. The results they have obtained over the years show exemplary consistency of quality. The extensive range of Barolo selections caters for a variety of tastes and demands but we would point out Bricco Luciani, the leading wine, whose remarkable ageing potential places it firmly alongside the absolute greats of the zone.

The Barolo Turné '05, replacing the André, has dried herbs and tobacco on the nose followed by a confidently austere and still rather stiff palate, partly due to ageing in large barrels. The very enjoyable Bricco Luciani '05 is spot on. The other Barolos from the same growing year are not very vibrant and lack harmony but will certainly express themselves better after more bottle ageing. The Barbera Fontanile '05 was released after a lengthy maturation, a shrewd decision. This ageworthy wine, somewhat sharp-edged when young, has found balance today.

Bruna Grimaldi

VIA PAREA, 7
12060 GRINZANE CAVOUR [CN]
TEL. 0173262094
www.grimaldibruna.it

CELLAR SALES

ANNUAL PRODUCTION **60,000 bottles**
HECTARES UNDER VINE **10**
VITICULTURE METHOD **Conventional**

Good quality at interesting prices. That could be a simple, concise description of this versatile estate run by Bruna Grimaldi and Franco Fiorino for the last 20 years or so with plots in several municipalities including Serralunga and Grinzane Cavour. The wines presented proved to be nicely interpreted, showing clear definition, balance and varietal expression. This winery is still too little-known but we are watching, and showcasing, its relentless progress.

The solid Barolo Badarina Vigna Regnola '05 from Serralunga already shows garnet tones. Pungent sensations on the nose are reminiscent of rhubarb over a good fruity base. There is considerable tannic weight on the palate, which is confidently compact and requires further softening from bottle ageing. The well-typed Barbera d'Alba Superiore Scassa '07 has a lovely intense, full ruby red colour and a fairly intense nose redolent of very ripe red berry fruit. The palate is quite delicious thanks to the harmonious and very weighty, if only moderately elegant, body. The Nebbiolo '07 has fantastic fruit.

● Barolo Bricco Luciani '05	▼▼	8
● Barolo Turné '05	▼▼	7
● Barbera d'Alba Fontanile '05	▼▼	5
● Barolo Ciabot Manzoni '05	▼▼	8
● Barolo Giachini '05	▼▼	7
● Barolo Pì Vigne '05	▼▼	6
● Langhe Nebbiolo Peirass '05	▼▼	6
● Dolcetto d'Alba '08	▼	4
● Barolo Bricco Luciani '04	♗♗♗	8
● Barolo Bricco Luciani '01	♗♗♗	8
● Barolo Bricco Luciani '96	♗♗♗	8
● Barolo Bricco Luciani '95	♗♗♗	8
● Barolo Bricco Luciani '90	♗♗♗	8
● Barolo Ciabot Manzoni '04	♗♗	8
● Barolo L'André '04	♗♗	7

● Barolo Badarina V. Regnola '05	▼▼	7
● Barbera d'Alba Sup. Scassa '07	▼▼	4
● Nebbiolo d'Alba Briccola '07	▼▼	4
○ Langhe Chardonnay Valscura '08	▼	4
● Barolo Badarina V. Regnola '03	♗♗	6*
● Nebbiolo d'Alba Briccola '06	♗♗	4*

Giacomo Grimaldi

VIA LUIGI EINAUDI, 8
12060 BAROLO [CN]
TEL. 0173560536
ferruccio.grimaldi@libero.it

CELLAR SALES
PRE-BOOKED VISITS

ANNUAL PRODUCTION **50,000 bottles**
HECTARES UNDER VINE **10**
VITICULTURE METHOD **Conventional**

Year after year, Ferruccio Grimaldi is establishing himself as a producer who can offer reliable quality at very competitive prices, two extremely important virtues in an increasingly overcrowded market with ever stricter selection criteria. The municipalities of Barolo and Novello give Ferruccio unquestionably classy Barolos, complemented by Barbera and Dolcetto d'Alba, which always live up to expectations. The general style is confident and uncompromising, in confirmation of the steady growth of this winery.

The powerful Barolo Sotto Castello '05 – earning its first well-deserved Three Glasses – has traditional aromas with the classic hints of dried roses and red berries. The palate shows the slightly rough edges typical of young Barolos but already expresses magnificent character. The Le Coste of the same vintage year is harmonious and while it still shows slightly prominent oak on the palate, it is particularly flavoursome. The Barbera Fornaci is a consistently sound wine and has coaxed warmth, pervasiveness and also savouriness from the lovely summer of '07.

● Barolo Sotto Castello di Novello '05	▼▼▼ 7
● Barbera d'Alba Fornaci '07	▼▼ 5
● Barolo Le Coste '05	▼▼ 7
● Barolo '05	▼▼ 6
● Nebbiolo d'Alba Valmaggiore '07	▼▼ 5
● Barbera d'Alba Pistin '08	▼ 4
● Dolcetto d'Alba '08	▼ 4
● Barbera d'Alba Fornaci '06	♈♈ 5
● Barbera d'Alba Fornaci '05	♈♈ 5
● Barbera d'Alba Fornaci '04	♈♈ 5
● Barolo Le Coste '04	♈♈ 7
● Barolo Le Coste '03	♈♈ 7

Sergio Grimaldi - Ca' du Sindic

LOC. SAN GRATO, 15
12058 SANTO STEFANO BELBO [CN]
TEL. 0141840341
grimaldi.sergio@virgilio.it

CELLAR SALES
PRE-BOOKED VISITS

ANNUAL PRODUCTION **45,000 bottles**
HECTARES UNDER VINE **10**
VITICULTURE METHOD **Conventional**

Sergio Grimaldi, with the help of his wife Angela and son Paolo, is firmly at the helm of this small but influential estate in the San Grato area of Santo Stefano Belbo, a very suitable growing zone for moscato, a noble and sometimes underrated Piedmontese grape. The wines presented are consistently among the best in their category, standing out for their depth and clear-cut varietal qualities. Alongside the captivating sweet wines there is also a nicely textured Barbera and a sound Brachetto.

From the 2008 vintage, the house flagship, and indeed one of the best in its category, is the Moscato Capsula Oro. Vibrant and sophisticated as ever with candied lemon peel and peppermint on the nose and a full, buttery palate supported by gratifyingly refreshing acidity through to the long, characterful finish. A great Moscato from a difficult year. The Capsula Argento is not so intense but still absolutely traditional, with ripe grape and peach fruit and a hint of aniseed on the nose. The rounded, fleshy palate has a balanced, generous finish. The enjoyable Barbera d'Asti San Grato '06 is beautifully balanced with moderate structure.

○ Moscato d'Asti Ca' du Sindic Capsula Oro '08	▼▼ 4*
● Barbera d'Asti San Grato '06	▼▼ 4*
○ Moscato d'Asti Ca' du Sindic Capsula Argento '08	▼▼ 3*
○ Piemonte Moscato Passito Montaldi '06	▼▼ 6
● Piemonte Barbera Vivace Rossodisera '08	▼ 3*
● Piemonte Brachetto '08	▼ 3
○ Moscato d'Asti Ca' du Sindic Capsula Argento '07	♈♈ 3*
○ Moscato d'Asti Ca' du Sindic Capsula Oro '07	♈♈ 4*
○ Moscato d'Asti Ca' du Sindic Capsula Oro '06	♈♈ 4*

La Guardia

POD. LA GUARDIA, 74
15010 MORSASCO [AL]
TEL. 014473076
www.laguardiavini.it

CELLAR SALES
PRE-BOOKED VISITS

ANNUAL PRODUCTION **150,000 bottles**
HECTARES UNDER VINE **40**
VITICULTURE METHOD **Conventional**

The winery is situated at Morsasco, about 13 kilometres from Ovada, in a lovely setting where the vineyards are grouped together on a hillside that forms a natural amphitheatre. The varieties grown here were selected to suit the soil and location so we find native barbera, dolcetto and brachetto vines alongside the internationals cabernet sauvignon, pinot nero and merlot. The wines age in the cellars of the 17th-century Villa Delfini, whose chapel was consecrated in 1746 by papal bull under Benedict XIV and is still used today for weddings.

L'Innominato '06, a blend of dolcetto and cabernet sauvignon, shows a ruby, almost garnet, red and a heady, fruity nose followed by a well-balanced, lingering palate. The '05 Sacro e Profano has prevalently jammy, ripe fruit aromas with a warm, persistent palate. The '06 Bricco Riccardo proffers subtle, fragrant aromas over a powerful, harmonious palate. Lastly, the Chardonnay Villa Delfini '07 is stylish with good varietal features.

Clemente Guasti

C.SO IV NOVEMBRE, 80
14049 NIZZA MONFERRATO [AT]
TEL. 0141721350
www.guasti.it

CELLAR SALES
PRE-BOOKED VISITS

ANNUAL PRODUCTION **200,000 bottles**
HECTARES UNDER VINE **35**
VITICULTURE METHOD **Conventional**

La bella azienda fondata da Clemente Guasti, che ha superato i sessant'anni di attività, si è imposta fin dall'inizio come una realtà molto importante per l'astigiano, segnalandosi come una delle prime aziende a selezionare i migliori cru nicesi per dare vita a produzioni di qualità. Oggi la tenuta è condotta dai figli Andrea e Alessandro che continuano a produrre vini dallo stile tradizionale e austero. La produzione, piuttosto ampia, ha un occhio di riguardo per i classici dell'Astigiano.

The cellar postponed release of some leading wines but those presented lived up to its reputation. The Barbera d'Asti Desideria '08 shows all the typical Guasti features: vibrant, austere aromas with hints of damp earth, undergrowth and black cherries, the tannin and acidity complemented by subtle, nicely evident fruit on a very balanced palate. The Barbera del Monferrato Frizzante Clementina '08, probably the best from its vintage, has classic earth and ripe cherry aromas and a powerful, lingering, but rather too serious palate for the type. The Moscato d'Asti Santa Teresa '08 and Barbera d'Asti Superiore Classica '06 are both good.

● Dolcetto di Ovada Sup. Bricco Riccardo '06	♥♥ 4
● M.to Rosso Innominato '06	♥♥ 5
● M.to Rosso Sacro e Profano '05	♥♥ 5
○ Piemonte Chardonnay Villa Delfini '07	♥♥ 4
● Barbera del M.to Ornovo '06	♀♀ 4
● Barbera del M.to V. di Dante '05	♀♀ 5
● Dolcetto di Ovada Sup. Bricco Riccardo '05	♀♀ 4*
● Dolcetto di Ovada Sup. Villa Delfini '03	♀♀ 4*
● M.to Rosso Innominato '05	♀♀ 5
● M.to Rosso Sacroeprofano '01	♀♀ 5

● Barbera d'Asti Desideria '08	♥♥ 4*
● Barbera del M.to Frizzante Clementina '08	♥♥ 4*
● Barbera d'Asti Sup. Classica '06	♥ 4
○ Moscato d'Asti Santa Teresa '08	♥ 4
● Barbera d'Asti Desideria '07	♀♀ 4*
● Barbera d'Asti Sup. Barcarato '04	♀♀ 6
● Barbera d'Asti Sup. Cascina Boschetto Vecchio '05	♀♀ 5
● Barbera d'Asti Sup. Cascina Fonda San Nicolao '05	♀♀ 5
● Barbera d'Asti Sup. Nizza Barcarato '05	♀♀ 6
● Barbera d'Asti Sup. Nizza Barcarato '04	♀♀ 6

Hilberg - Pasquero

VIA BRICCO GATTI, 16
12040 PRIOCCA [CN]
TEL. 0173616197
www.hilberg-pasquero.com

CELLAR SALES
PRE-BOOKED VISITS

ANNUAL PRODUCTION **23,000 bottles**
HECTARES UNDER VINE **5.5**
VITICULTURE METHOD **Naturale**

The winery owned by Michelangelo Pasquero and his wife Annette Hilberg, at the top of Bricco Gatti just outside Priocca, is one of the loveliest wine estates in Roero. Driven by their great passion, they have pursued excellence in a range of wines that are faithful to their terroir. The vineyards are organically farmed on prevalently marly soil and produce exclusively red wines from nebbiolo, barbera and brachetto grapes.

The winery's products are now among the best in Roero, whether or not they bear the designation's name. The deep, powerful Nebbiolo d'Alba '07 gives black berry fruit and liquorice. The Barbera d'Alba Superiore '07 has balsamic aromas, toastiness and with alluring damson before the vibrant palate's densely woven, elegant tannins take you into a long smoky finish. Both reached our finals. Also beautifully made are the lingering Langhe Nebbiolo '07, with its raspberries and fresh flowers, the simpler but clear-cut and enjoyable Barbera d'Alba '08 and the '08 Vareij Rosso, from brachetto and barbera, with its vibrant aromatic nose and nice full palate.

Icardi

LOC. SAN LAZZARO
VIA BALBI, 30
12053 CASTIGLIONE TINELLA [CN]
TEL. 0141855159
icardivini@libero.it

CELLAR SALES
PRE-BOOKED VISITS

ANNUAL PRODUCTION **351,000 bottles**
HECTARES UNDER VINE **75**
VITICULTURE METHOD **Biodynamic certified**

Starting from the assumption that "the focal point is healthy land, as it was 100 years ago, and the grapes will grow well" ,Claudio Icardi decided to farm all his vineyards organically or biodynamically, and use non-invasive techniques in the cellar to guarantee that the characteristics of each variety and vineyard are fully preserved. The vast range of wines presented includes 18 from the main Langa and Monferrato types.

Leading the huge battery of wines this year are the Barolo and Barbaresco, as well as the two '07 Barberas. The first two go hand-in-hand, buoyed up by substantial fresh fruit aromas and densely woven tannic structure that is never too edgy. We liked the Barolo but only by a short head. The Barbera Nuj Suj presents an explosion of red berry fruit on the nose and lovely harmonious flavour on a palate with fresh, well-balanced acidity and weighty extract. Just slightly less characterful, but in the same style, is the Sorì di Mù '07.

● Barbera d'Alba Sup. '07	🍷🍷	6
● Nebbiolo d'Alba '07	🍷🍷	6
● Barbera d'Alba '08	🍷	4
● Langhe Nebbiolo '07	🍷	5
● Vareij Rosso '08	🍷	4
● Barbera d'Alba Sup. '98	🍷🍷🍷	6
● Barbera d'Alba Sup. '97	🍷🍷🍷	6
● Nebbiolo d'Alba '06	🍷🍷🍷	6
● Nebbiolo d'Alba '05	🍷🍷🍷	6
● Nebbiolo d'Alba '04	🍷🍷🍷	6
● Nebbiolo d'Alba '03	🍷🍷🍷	6
● Nebbiolo d'Alba '01	🍷🍷🍷	6
● Nebbiolo d'Alba '00	🍷🍷🍷	6
● Nebbiolo d'Alba '99	🍷🍷🍷	6

● Barbera d'Asti Nuj Suj '07	🍷🍷	6
● Barbaresco Montubert '06	🍷🍷	8
● Barbera d'Alba Surì di Mù '07	🍷🍷	6
● Barolo Parej '05	🍷🍷	8
● Dolcetto d'Alba Rousori '08	🍷🍷	4
● Langhe Rosso Nej '07	🍷🍷	6
○ M.to Bianco Pafoj '08	🍷🍷	6
○ Moscato d'Asti La Rosa Selvatica '08	🍷🍷	5
● Barbaresco Montubert '04	🍷🍷	6
● Barolo Parej '04	🍷🍷	8

Isabella

FRAZ. CORTERANZO
VIA GIANOLI, 64
15020 MURISENGO [AL]
TEL. 0141693000
info@isabellavini.com

CELLAR SALES
PRE-BOOKED VISITS
VISITSOR FACILITIES FOOD

ANNUAL PRODUCTION **120,000 bottles**
HECTARES UNDER VINE **25.5**
VITICULTURE METHOD **Conventional**

The Tenuta Isabella estate embraces the whole Corteranzo hillside. The Calvo family, growers here for three generations, lived on this spot back in the 17th century. The Canonica dates from the same period. Once an aristocratic hunting lodge, it was later donated to the diocese of Casale and was the parish rectory for Corteranzo. Today, it is an elegant hotel with a scenic view, owned since 2003 by the Calvos, who have made over its architectural features. Naturally, the principal activity is wine production, mainly from native grape varieties..

Leading the field is the Barbera d'Asti Bric Stupui '05. Deep ruby red in colour, it gives aromas of oak and fruit that enhance the generous, lingering flavour. Barbera Truccone '06 is intense ruby red with a fruity and vegetal nose before marked acidity comes through on the back palate. The Barbera del Monferrato Bricco Montemà Tardivo '07 flaunts ripe, jammy fruit on the nose while the '08 Grignolino Montecastello has strongly varietal features. The Piemonte Chardonnay Carpe Diem '06 has a nicely balanced nose and palate and a long finish.

Isolabella della Croce

REG. CAFFI, 3
14051 LOAZZOLO [AT]
TEL. 014487166
www.isolabelladellacroce.it

CELLAR SALES
PRE-BOOKED VISITS

ANNUAL PRODUCTION **50,000 bottles**
HECTARES UNDER VINE **15**
VITICULTURE METHOD **Conventional**

This estate, owned by Maria Teresa Isolabella and her husband Lodovico, is situated in the small municipality of Loazzolo and includes vineyards over 50 years old at altitudes of up to 500 metres. The small winery is developing nicely in quality, thanks also to the help of consultant winemaker Giuliano Noè, and produces very typical wines with remarkably rich extract. A series of very respectable wines brings another Loazzolo estate into the main section of the Guide.

The Loazzolo Solio '05 reached the finals with sophisticated aromas of pear jam and candied fruit, and a rounded and weighty yet nicely harmonious and never cloying palate. The very lingering finish is more harmonious than powerful or sweet. The excellent Monferrato Rosso Superlodo '06, a 50-20-15-15 blend of barbera, cabernet franc, merlot and pinot nero, is vibrant, subtle, veined with red berries and powerful on the generous palate. The velvety, substantially structured Barbera d'Asti Superiore Nizza Augusta '06 is also very good.

● Barbera d'Asti Sup. Bric Stupui '05	▼▼	5
● Barbera d'Asti Truccone '06	▼▼	4*
● Barbera del M.to Bricco Montemà Tardivo '07	▼	4
● Grignolino del M.to Casalese Montecastello '08	▼	4
○ Piemonte Chardonnay Carpe Diem '06	▼	4
● Barbera d'Asti Bric Stupui '04	♈♈	5
● Barbera d'Asti Truccone '04	♈♈	4*
● Barbera del M.to Bricco Montemà Tardivo '05	♈♈	4
● Grignolino del M.to Casalese Montecastello '06	♈♈	4*
● Grignolino del M.to Casalese Montecastello '04	♈♈	4*
● Monferrato Freisa Bioc '05	♈♈	4*
● Monferrato Freisa Bioc '03	♈♈	4*

○ Loazzolo Solio '05	▼▼	6
● Barbera d'Asti Sup. Nizza Augusta '06	▼▼	5
● M.to Rosso Superlodo '06	▼▼	6
● M.to Le Marne '07	▼	4
● M.to Le Marne '06	♈♈	4*
● M.to Le Marne '05	♈♈	4

Iuli

FRAZ. MONTALDO
VIA CENTRALE, 27
15020 CERRINA MONFERRATO [AL]
TEL. 0142946657
www.iuli.it

CELLAR SALES
PRE-BOOKED VISITS

ANNUAL PRODUCTION **35,000 bottles**
HECTARES UNDER VINE **9**
VITICULTURE METHOD **Naturale**

The home of this winery, founded 11 years ago at Montaldo di Cerrina, is a traditional Piedmontese farmhouse. The vineyards, located in the municipal areas of Cerrina Monferrato, Odalengo, Sala Monferrato and Quarti di Pontestura, are part of a detailed project to produce fine quality wines by making the best use of the soils and aspects of vineyards in different zones. The results obtained over the years speak for themselves and the battery of wines presented for this Guide is further confirmation.

The splendid Barbera Barabba '06 is an inky ruby with aromas of cinchona and tobacco leading to an unusually rounded and substantial palate backed up by strong acidity. The '06 Barbera Rossore is on great form. Complex, incense-like ripe cherry and plum aromatics accompany huge elegance and finesse on nose and palate. Also good is the Umberta '07 Barbera, with hints of cherries developing into toasted sensations of cocoa powder and tar, with full body and beautiful balance on the palate. Of the Monferrato Rossos, we preferred the pinot nero-based Nino '07 to the Malidea '06.

● Barbera del M.to Sup. Barabba '06	♥♥ 6
● Barbera del M.to Sup. Rossore '06	♥♥ 4*
● Barbera del M.to Umberta '07	♥♥ 4*
● M.to Rosso Nino '07	♥♥ 5
● M.to Rosso Malidea '06	♥ 5
● Barbera del M.to Sup. Barabba '04	♀♀♀ 6
● Barbera del M.to Sup. Barabba '03	♀♀ 6
● Barbera del M.to Sup. Rossore '05	♀♀ 5
● Barbera del M.to Sup. Umberta '07	♀♀ 4*
● Barbera del M.to Sup. Umberta '06	♀♀ 4*
● M.to Rosso Nino '05	♀♀ 5

Tenuta La Volta - Cabutto

VIA SAN PIETRO, 13
12060 BAROLO [CN]
TEL. 017356168
www.cabuttolavolta.com

PRE-BOOKED VISITS

ANNUAL PRODUCTION **100,000 bottles**
HECTARES UNDER VINE **10**
VITICULTURE METHOD **Conventional**

This is a long-established Langhe winery in a pleasant setting where brothers Osvaldo and Bruno Cabutto continue a long tradition of quality and faithfulness to the territory. These are terroir-driven wines that combine the strong character of Piedmontese grapes with a structure that will satisfy the palates of those who love traditional wines, both Italian and international. We approve the decision to limit production to focus exclusively on nebbiolo and barbera. These classic wines mature in large barrels and are very cellarable.

The Barolo Riserva del Fondatore '03 originates in the splendid Sarmassa vineyard. Warm aromas back up a palate slightly dried by tannin but satisfyingly drinkable overall. The Barolo '05 has a simpler nose with huskier tannin on a very compact, not excessively mouthfilling, palate to create an enjoyable sensory profile. The Barbera Superiore '07 is very sound and bright with plum and pencil lead aromas and a savoury, complex palate of character.

● Barolo La Volta '05	♥♥ 7
● Barbera d'Alba Sup. '07	♥♥ 5
● Barolo Ris. del Fondatore V. Sarmassa '03	♥♥ 8
● Barbera d'Alba Sup. '06	♀♀ 5
● Barbera d'Alba Sup. '04	♀♀ 5
● Barolo La Volta '04	♀♀ 7
● Barolo La Volta '03	♀♀ 7
● Barolo Ris. del Fondatore '99	♀♀ 8
● Barolo Ris. del Fondatore V. Sarmassa '01	♀♀ 8
● Barolo Ris. del Fondatore V. Sarmassa '00	♀♀ 8

Gianluigi Lano

FRAZ. SAN ROCCO SENO D'ELVIO
S.DA BASSO, 38
12051 ALBA [CN]
TEL. 0173286958
lano.vini@tiscali.it

CELLAR SALES
PRE-BOOKED VISITS

ANNUAL PRODUCTION **40,000 bottles**
HECTARES UNDER VINE **6**
VITICULTURE METHOD **Conventional**

This small estate stands out for consistently reliable quality and excellent value for money throughout the range of wines presented. Gianluigi Lano, helped by skilled winemaker Gianfranco Cordero, gives the best interpretation possible of this terroir on the fringes of the Barbaresco zone, but no less interesting for that. The overall style is extremely drinkable wines at very affordable prices.

Release of the Barbaresco '06 has been postponed for a year so we only tasted the five wines already released to market. The no-nonsense Dolcetto Ronchella '07 has generous aromas of black berry fruit and cocoa powder on an earthy base while the tannin never disturbs the powerful palate. The outstanding Barbera Altavilla '07 is made from grapes grown on the hillsides above Alba, the main town in Langhe. Quite elegant, intense spice and fruit aromas precede a powerful, deliciously tangy palate. The basic Dolcetto and Barbera are slightly less vibrant and full bodied but hew to the winery's philosophy of approachability over complexity.

● Barbera d'Alba Altavilla '07	♟♟ 4
● Dolcetto d'Alba Ronchella '07	♟♟ 4*
● Barbera d'Alba '07	♟ 3
● Dolcetto d'Alba '08	♟ 3
○ Langhe Favorita '08	♟ 3
● Barbaresco '05	♟♟ 6
● Barbaresco '04	♟♟ 6
● Barbera d'Alba Altavilla '06	♟♟ 4*
● Barbera d'Alba Altavilla '05	♟♟ 4
● Barbera d'Alba Fondo Prà '06	♟♟ 4
● Barbera d'Alba Fondo Prà '04	♟♟ 4
● Langhe Rosso Samuele '06	♟♟ 4

Ugo Lequio

VIA DEL MOLINO, 10
12057 NEIVE [CN]
TEL. 0173677224
www.ugolequio.it

CELLAR SALES
PRE-BOOKED VISITS

ANNUAL PRODUCTION **25,000 bottles**
HECTARES UNDER VINE **N.D.**
VITICULTURE METHOD **Conventional**

Affable producer Ugo Lequio certainly doesn't suffer from performance anxiety. He may not own his own vineyards but this does not prevent him from making some of the most intriguing, long-lived Barbarescos around. With his extraordinary knowledge of the area and good relationship with some local growers, there are no surprises from one year to the next. This is further highlighted by the opportunity to vinify grapes from the very special Gallina vineyard at Neive. These are wines in a classic style, aged in medium-sized wood.

The classic top note is missing to reward the umpteenth admirable performance by Ugo Lequio's wines. His Barbaresco Gallina '06 has all it takes to get to the top: integrity, texture, vigour and good quality tannic extract. However the wine is a little held back and slightly static on the nose. Time will tell whether this is just a passing phase and for now it stops at Two Glasses. The excellent Barbera d'Alba Superiore Gallina '06 is enjoyably weighty and dynamic while the Langhe Nebbiolo '08 is subtle and appetizing.

● Barbaresco Gallina '06	♟♟ 6
● Barbera d'Alba Sup. Gallina '06	♟♟ 5
● Langhe Nebbiolo '08	♟♟ 5
○ Langhe Arneis '08	♟ 4
● Barbaresco Gallina '05	♟♟ 6
● Barbaresco Gallina '04	♟♟ 6
● Barbaresco Gallina Ris. '01	♟♟ 7
● Barbera d'Alba Sup. Gallina '05	♟♟ 4*

Cascina Luisin

S.DA RABAJÀ, 34
12050 BARBARESCO [CN]
TEL. 0173635154
cascinaluisin@tiscali.it

PRE-BOOKED VISITS

ANNUAL PRODUCTION 30,000 bottles
HECTARES UNDER VINE 7
VITICULTURE METHOD Conventional

History and tradition link the Minuto family, Luigi and his son Roberto, to a prestigious area from which they create very typical wines with plenty of character. Because they age well, time in glass enhances their increasingly satisfying drinking quality. The Barbaresco is beautifully textured, and the Barbera Asili, from vineyards over 50 years old, often stands out as one of the zone's ultimate benchmark wines.

The '07 version of this Barbera is almost too powerful and concentrated. Its palate is still in need of harmony despite the pleasant fruity, oaky sensations. The delicious Barbaresco Sorì Paolin '05 has a vibrant, very characterful nose with a generous, still slightly down-to-earth palate, while the Rabajà from the same year is rather weary and very marked by ageing in oak. The Barolo Leon '05 is distinctly well made and nicely balanced with good ageing potential. Also well put-together, especially on the nose, are the Barberas and the Dolcetto d'Alba Bric Trifüla '08.

Malabaila di Canale

FRAZ. MADONNA DEI CAVALLI, 19
12043 CANALE [CN]
TEL. 017398381
www.malabaila.com

CELLAR SALES
PRE-BOOKED VISITS

ANNUAL PRODUCTION 80,000 bottles
HECTARES UNDER VINE 22
VITICULTURE METHOD Conventional

This beautiful estate is situated inside a large, traditional farm property owned by the Conti Malabaila di Canale. The typical grape varieties of this area – arneis, favorita, barbera and nebbiolo – are planted on marl and sand soil at an average altitude of 300 metres. Malabaila wines are produced with the help of winemaker Valerio Falletti.

Malabaila di Canale maintains its position in the main section of the Guide thanks to a couple of very well-typed wines. The Barbera d'Alba Mezzavilla '08 has very varietal earthy, cinchona and red berry aromas and a powerful, generous palate with a heady yet long, savoury finish. Although the palate is not too broad, the Roero Arneis Pradvaj '08 opens slowly into apple and pear fruit and almonds with a light hint of peel. The generous, full-bodied, well-rounded palate is coherent and unquestionably classy with lots of personality. The fresh, fruity Roero '08 is simple but well styled.

● Barbaresco Sorì Paolin '05	▼▼ 7
● Barbera d'Alba Asili '07	▼▼ 5
● Barolo Leon '05	▼▼ 7
● Barbaresco Rabajà '05	▼ 7
● Barbera d'Alba Maggiur '08	▼ 4
● Dolcetto d'Alba Bric Trifüla '08	▼ 4
● Barbaresco Rabajà '04	♈♈ 7
● Barbaresco Sorì Paolin '04	♈♈ 7
● Barbera d'Alba Asili '06	♈♈ 5
● Barolo Leon '01	♈♈ 8

● Barbera d'Alba Mezzavilla '08	▼▼ 4*
○ Roero Arneis Pradvaj '08	▼▼ 4*
● Dolcetto d'Alba '08	▼ 4
○ Roero '08	▼ 4
● Barbera d'Alba Mezzavilla '05	♈♈ 4*
● Barbera d'Alba Mezzavilla Barrique '06	♈♈ 4
● Roero Bric Volta '05	♈♈ 5
● Roero Castelletto Ris. '05	♈♈ 5
● Roero Sup. Castelletto '04	♈♈ 5

Malgrà

LOC. BAZZANA
VIA NIZZA, 8
14046 MOMBARUZZO [AT]
TEL. 0141725055
www.malgra.it

CELLAR SALES
PRE-BOOKED VISITS

ANNUAL PRODUCTION 800,000 bottles
HECTARES UNDER VINE 110
VITICULTURE METHOD Conventional

Nine years after it was founded, Malgrà is well-established as a leading Monferrato estate which combines large quantities with a good standard of quality and affordable prices. The winery is managed with passion and skill by Nico Conta, Massimiliano Diotto, Ezio and Giorgio Chiarle. The vineyards are located in all the leading areas of Piedmont: Langhe, Gavi and upper Piedmont in the Coste della Sesia zone.

Again this year, Malgrà got its best results from the Barberas. The Barbera d'Asti Superiore Nizza Mora di Sassi '06 has complex, characterful aromas with hints of balsam and cinchona, and a full, rounded palate, although the finish is a little sweet with a slight hint of overripe fruit. Equally good is the Barbera d'Asti Superiore Fornace di Cerreto '07 has marked spice on the nose, as well as lovely cherry-led fruit, while the palate is fruity, supple and fluid. The Monferrato Rosso Treviri '06, a monovarietal Cabernet Sauvignon, the Gavi Poggio Basco '08 and the Barbera d'Asti Briga della Mora '08 are all well made.

★ Malvirà

LOC. CANOVA
VIA CASE SPARSE, 144
12043 CANALE [CN]
TEL. 0173978145
www.malvira.com

CELLAR SALES
PRE-BOOKED VISITS
VISITOR FACILITIES
FOOD

ANNUAL PRODUCTION 350,000 bottles
HECTARES UNDER VINE 40
VITICULTURE METHOD Naturale

If anyone has invested in Roero, it is brothers Massimo and Roberto Damonte. Back when it was founded in 1974, the Malvirà estate was designed to pursue quality. Because they believe so strongly in the specific characteristics of the vineyards, the Damontes decided to ferment the grapes separately to enhance the features of each site. Their investment in the land is not limited to the wines for they have also set up one of Piedmont's most charming hotels, Villa Tiboldi.

There was another great performance from the Damonte brothers' wines. Three Glasses went to the Roero Renesio Riserva '05 for its aromas of raspberries, dried flowers, tobacco and white truffles and a subtle, complex, austere palate that lingers with silky tannins and superb fruit. Into the finals went: the Roero Trinità Riserva '06 with generous dried flowers, liquorice and raspberry aromas and a very dynamic palate with fine-grained, mouthwatering extract; the clear-cut, fresh Roero Mombeltramo Riserva '06, its palate slightly marked by hard tannins; and the Roero Arneis Trinità '08 with classic fruit and spring flowers on the nose and a long, minerally palate.

● Barbera d'Asti Sup. Fornace di Cerreto '07	♟♟ 4*
● Barbera d'Asti Sup. Nizza Mora di Sassi '06	♟♟ 6
● Barbera d'Asti Briga della Mora '08	♟ 3
○ Gavi del Comune di Gavi Poggio Basco '08	♟ 4
● M.to Rosso Treviri '06	♟ 4
● Barbera d'Asti Sup. Fornace di Cerreto '06	♟♟ 4*
● Barbera d'Asti Sup. Gaiana '05	♟♟ 4*
● Barbera d'Asti Sup. Nizza Mora di Sassi '05	♟ 6

● Roero Renesio Ris. '05	♟♟♟ 6
○ Roero Arneis Trinità '08	♟♟ 4*
● Roero Mombeltramo Ris. '06	♟♟ 6
● Roero Trinità Ris. '06	♟♟ 6
● Langhe Rosso S. Guglielmo '06	♟♟ 5
○ Langhe Bianco Tre Uve '07	♟ 4
○ Roero Arneis '08	♟ 4
○ Roero Arneis Renesio '08	♟ 4
● Roero Mombeltramo Ris. '05	♟♟♟ 6
● Roero Sup. '97	♟♟♟ 6
● Roero Sup. '93	♟♟♟ 6
● Roero Sup. '90	♟♟♟ 6
● Roero Sup. Mombeltramo '04	♟♟♟ 6
● Roero Sup. Mombeltramo '00	♟♟♟ 6
● Roero Sup. Trinità '03	♟♟♟ 6
● Roero Sup. Trinità '01	♟♟♟ 6
● Roero Sup. Trinità '99	♟♟♟ 6

Giovanni Manzone

VIA CASTELLETTO, 9
12065 MONFORTE D'ALBA [CN]
TEL. 017378114
www.manzonegiovanni.com

CELLAR SALES
PRE-BOOKED VISITS

ANNUAL PRODUCTION **40,000 bottles**
HECTARES UNDER VINE **7.5**
VITICULTURE METHOD **Conventional**

If nothing else, the Manzone family deserves praise for helping to highlight the superlative qualities of one of Monforte's lesser known crus, Gramolere, once part of the now-abolished municipality of Castelletto. Promoting a fine growing area is one of a wine man's noblest tasks. That said, all the strongly characterful wines produced are coherent and absolutely respectful of nature and grape. This is not one of the best-known wineries in the area but it deserves attention.

Giovanni Manzone shows skill with his '05 Barolo. The Bricat '05's overall harmony earns it Three impressive Glasses for herbs, red berries and liquorice on the nose and an outstandingly balanced palate, not too full with a clear-cut, very long finish. The Castelletto '05 is nicely layered with dried flowers, cinchona and raspberries on the nose. The palate is powerful, dynamic and still a little ruggedly stiff. Le Gramolere '05 has fresher, balsamic aromas and a slightly edgy palate that will certainly age well. Do try the characterful Rosserto '07, from rossese bianco. The other products were not yet ready when we tasted.

Paolo Manzone

LOC. MERIAME, 1
12050 SERRALUNGA D'ALBA [CN]
TEL. 0173613113
www.barolomeriame.com

CELLAR SALES
PRE-BOOKED VISITS
VISITOR FACILITIES

ANNUAL PRODUCTION **80,000 bottles**
HECTARES UNDER VINE **10**
VITICULTURE METHOD **Conventional**

A natural, breathtakingly beautiful setting creates the perfect backdrop for this recently founded winery, which includes a charming and very welcoming holiday centre. Paolo Manzone relies on the lengthy winemaking experience he has accumulated at a large local winery to get the very best out of all the grape varieties he has available to ensure consistently dependable quality.

The Meriame '05 is a little austere but rich in personality with hints of balsam, cinchona and rhubarb on the nose and considerable tannic extract on the palate, which finishes long. The Serralunga '05 is even better typed with generous aromas of spices, flowers and red berry fruit over a hint of oak. The palate is not too powerful but beautifully balanced with mouthwatering liquorice in the finish. The Barbera Fiorenza '08 has lovely black cherries and earth on the nose and a slightly acidulous palate. The Dolcetto '08 is deep ruby in colour with clear ripe fruit aromas and a well-balanced, drinkable palate. A very respectable range all round.

● Barolo Bricat '05	♟♟♟	7
● Barolo Castelletto '05	♟♟	6
● Barolo Le Gramolere '05	♟♟	7
○ Langhe Bianco Rosserto '07	♟♟	4
● Barolo Le Gramolere '04	♟♟♟	7
● Barolo Le Gramolere Ris. '01	♟♟♟	8
● Barolo Le Gramolere Ris. '00	♟♟♟	8
● Barolo Le Gramolere Ris. '99	♟♟♟	8
● Barolo Bricat '04	♟♟	7
● Barolo Castelletto '04	♟♟	6
○ Langhe Bianco Rosserto '06	♟♟	4

● Barolo Serralunga '05	♟♟	6
● Barbera d'Alba Fiorenza '08	♟♟	4*
● Barolo Meriame '05	♟♟	7
● Dolcetto d'Alba Magna '08	♟♟	4*
● Nebbiolo d'Alba Mirinè '07	♟♟	5
● Barbera d'Alba Fiorenza '07	♟♟	4*
● Nebbiolo d'Alba Mirinè '06	♟♟	5

Poderi Marcarini

P.ZZA MARTIRI, 2
12064 LA MORRA [CN]
TEL. 017350222
www.marcarini.it

CELLAR SALES
PRE-BOOKED VISITS
VISITOR FACILITIES

ANNUAL PRODUCTION **125,000 bottles**
HECTARES UNDER VINE **20**
VITICULTURE METHOD **Conventional**

Traditional or modern? That is always the question in the winemaking world, although it may well find an answer in well-defined interpretations such as those from the long-established, attractive winery owned by Luisa Marcarini and Manuel Marchetti. The wines they have presented over the years are now a benchmark for the ancient spirit of the king of all wines, Barolo. Long maceration, large barrels and mellow tones characterize these long-lived bottles with the extraordinary ageing potential that only the world's greatest wines possess.

The Barolo La Serra '05 is sophisticated and harmonious with hints of gentian and tobacco on the nose and elegance rather than strength on the palate. The Brunate '05 is even more generous and complex, the palate slightly stiffened by close-knit, but not rugged, tannins. Three beautifully elegant Glasses. While we wait for the imminent release of the very traditional Dolcetto Boschi di Berri, we tasted the simpler, heady Fontanazza '08. The '07 Barbera Ciabot Camerano is nicely fruity with medium structure. The Nebbiolo Lasarin '08 is simpler and a little tannic but enjoyable.

Marchesi di Barolo

VIA ROMA, 1
12060 BAROLO [CN]
TEL. 0173564400
www.marchesibarolo.com

CELLAR SALES
PRE-BOOKED VISITS

ANNUAL PRODUCTION **1.350,000 bottles**
HECTARES UNDER VINE **117**
VITICULTURE METHOD **Conventional**

This may be the oldest Barolo winery, founded in the mid 19th century by the Marchesi Faletti and owned today by the Abbona family. The range of wines is huge and varied but reliable in quality and excellent value for money. The products, exported to many countries around the world, are a lodestar in the vast constellation of Langhe reds.

The '05 version of Barolo Sarmassa again won Three Glasses for an impressive performance. Typical aromas precede a supple, stylish palate with not too harsh tannins and the signature savouriness of this leading Barolo cru. Hot on its heels is the stylish Barolo Cannubi '05, its best features being finesse and balance. Also good are the simpler Barolo Costa di Rose '05, the winery workhorse, and the more ambitious Barolo Vigneti di Proprietà in Barolo '05. The rest of the range is nice, from the '06 Barbaresco Serragrilli through to the Nebbiolo, Barbera, Dolcetto, all from single vineyards in Alba, and the white Roero Arneis '08 with its fragrant nose and good palate.

● Barolo Brunate '05	▼▼▼ 7
● Barolo La Serra '05	▼ 7
● Barbera d'Alba Ciabot Camerano '07	▼▼ 4
● Dolcetto d'Alba Fontanazza '08	▼ 4
● Langhe Nebbiolo Lasarin '08	▼ 4
● Barolo Brunate '03	♀♀♀ 8
● Barolo Brunate '01	♀♀♀ 7
● Barolo Brunate '99	♀♀♀ 7
● Barolo Brunate '96	♀♀♀ 7
● Barolo Brunate Ris. '85	♀♀♀ 7
● Dolcetto d'Alba Boschi di Berri '96	♀♀♀ 5
● Barbera d'Alba Ciabot Camerano '06	♀♀ 4*
● Barolo Brunate '04	♀♀ 7
● Barolo La Serra '04	♀♀ 7

● Barolo Sarmassa '05	▼▼▼ 8
● Barbaresco Serragrilli '06	▼▼ 6
● Barolo Cannubi '05	▼▼ 8
● Barolo Coste di Rose '05	▼▼ 7
● Barolo Vign. di Proprietà in Barolo '05	▼▼ 7
● Barbera d'Alba Ruvei '07	▼▼ 4*
● Dolcetto d'Alba Madonna di Como '08	▼▼ 4*
● Nebbiolo d'Alba Michet '07	▼▼ 5
○ Roero Arneis '08	▼▼ 4*
● Barolo Estate Vineyard '97	♀♀♀ 8
● Barolo Ris. Grande Annata '99	♀♀♀ 7
● Barolo Cannubi '04	♀♀ 7
● Barolo Sarmassa '04	♀♀ 7
● Barolo Vign. di Proprietà in Barolo '99	♀♀ 8

Marchesi Incisa della Rocchetta

VIA ROMA, 66
14030 ROCCHETTA TANARO [AT]
TEL. 0141644647
www.lacortechiusa.it

CELLAR SALES
PRE-BOOKED VISITS
VISITOR FACILITIES
FOOD

ANNUAL PRODUCTION 40,000 bottles
HECTARES UNDER VINE 27
VITICULTURE METHOD Conventional

The Marchesi Incisa della Rocchetta, who boast a fine old tradition in the wine sector, have revived this estate, which has come on well in quality in recent years and is now one of the best around Asti. The Guyot-pruned vineyards in the hills at Rocchetta Tanaro, and the natural park of the same name, produce excellent wines, especially from the barbera and pinot nero, which are made with the help of consultant winemaker Donato Lanati.

The Barbera d'Asti Superiore Sant'Emiliano '06 is a classic wine with hints of tobacco, cinchona and bottled cherries, and shows powerful and subtle on the palate. The Monferrato Rosso Rollone '07, a blend of barbera and pinot nero, has varietal pinot aromas alongside huskier, but also more expressive, sensations from the barbera. The palate is harmonious, enjoyable and lingering, with well-gauged extract. Also well-typed is the Monferrato Rosso Marchese Leopoldo '08, a Pinot Nero with citrus peel and red berries on the nose and a taut, pepper spice palate with good fruit and a long, dynamic finish.

Marenco

P.ZZA VITTORIO EMANUELE, 10
15019 STREVI [AL]
TEL. 0144363133
www.marencovini.com

CELLAR SALES
PRE-BOOKED VISITS

ANNUAL PRODUCTION 300,000 bottles
HECTARES UNDER VINE 80
VITICULTURE METHOD Conventional

The Marenco family once just grew and sold grapes but for about 60 years now they have fermented their own grapes for wine. It all began in Valle Bagnario, a very suitable part of Acqui for the production of Moscato di Strevi. Over the years, the family has purchased other farms in Strevi and the surrounding areas, enabling them to expand with new, modern systems to reach production levels that place them among Alessandria's leading wineries today.

Leading the range is Ciresa '06, a pale garnet Barbera d'Asti Superiore with red berries and greens aromatics and a full-bodied, lingering palate. Red Sunrise '07, from albarossa, has an inky, purple-red hue, an exuberantly fruity nose and a powerful, balanced palate. The youthfulness of the '08 La Marchesa comes through in heady aromatics while the Moscato Scrapona '08 gives vibrant perceptions on the nose. The dried grape Moscato, Passrì Scrapona '06, has hints of acacia honey and dried fruit. The '08 Brachetto Pineto is enjoyably drinkable, as is the lively Cortese Valtignosa '08.

● Barbera d'Asti Sup. Sant'Emiliano '06	♥♥ 5
● M.to Rosso Marchese Leopoldo '08	♥♥ 5
● M.to Rosso Rollone '07	♥♥ 4*
● Barbera d'Asti Valmorena '07	♥ 4
● Grignolino d'Asti '08	♥ 4
● Barbera d'Asti Sup. Sant'Emiliano '05	♀♀ 5
● Barbera d'Asti Sup. Sant'Emiliano '04	♀♀ 5
● Barbera d'Asti Sup. Sant'Emiliano '03	♀♀ 5
● Barbera d'Asti Valmorena '06	♀♀ 4
● M.to Rosso Angelus Novus '06	♀♀ 7
● M.to Rosso Marchese Leopoldo '07	♀♀ 5
● M.to Rosso Rollone '06	♀♀ 4

● Barbera d'Asti Sup. Ciresa '06	♥♥ 6
● Dolcetto d'Acqui Marchesa '08	♥♥ 4*
● M.to Albarossa Red Sunrise '07	♥♥ 5
O Moscato d'Asti Scrapona '08	♥♥ 4
O Strevi Passrì di Scrapona '06	♥♥ 6
● Brachetto d'Acqui Pineto '08	♥ 5
O Cortese dell'Alto M.to Valtignosa '08	♥ 4
● Barbera d'Asti Bassina '06	♀♀ 4*
● Brachetto d'Acqui Pineto '07	♀♀ 4
● Dolcetto d'Acqui Marchesa '07	♀♀ 4
O MaMu '07	♀♀ 6
O Moscato d'Asti Scrapona '07	♀♀ 4

Mario Marengo

VIA XX SETTEMBRE, 34
12064 LA MORRA [CN]
TEL. 017350115
marengo1964@libero.it

CELLAR SALES
PRE-BOOKED VISITS

ANNUAL PRODUCTION **22,000 bottles**
HECTARES UNDER VINE **4**
VITICULTURE METHOD **Conventional**

Marco Marengo's family-run winery may be small but its ambitions are big. Apart from one plot in the Valmaggiore subzone of Roero, well-known as a growing area for quality nebbiolo grapes, and small batches of classic Langhe reds, the range focuses on Barolo, with the prestigious Brunate cru at the top of the limited list. The style is nicely balanced between structure, depth and elegant flavour. Small quantities of each wine are produced, mainly destined for export.

The Barolo Brunate '05 is broad, charming, fruity and liquorice-veined with a mouthfilling, very satisfying palate and we awarded Three Glasses to this wine from one of the DOCG zone's most important vineyards. Also splendid is the Bricco Viole '05 with its engaging aromas of dried flowers, tobacco and liquorice followed by a subtle, very stylish palate with close-knit tannins and a nice vein of acidity. The Barbera Pugnane is one of the best typed from '07, thanks to a fruity nose with strong plum-like aromas and a powerfully dense, delightfully drinkable palate with wonderful personality. A memorable vintage.

Claudio Mariotto

S.DA PER SAREZZANO, 29
15057 TORTONA [AL]
TEL. 0131868500
www.claudiomariotto.it

CELLAR SALES
PRE-BOOKED VISITS

ANNUAL PRODUCTION **100,000 bottles**
HECTARES UNDER VINE **32**
VITICULTURE METHOD **Conventional**

The results Claudio has recently obtained have not changed him one iota. He is the same wine man he was a few years ago and enjoys the company of anyone who ventures into the Tortona hills to buy his wines. A glass of wine and maybe a couple of slices of the very good local salami are the starting point for a chat about the difficult days when Tortona wines were only sold in demijohns. Now things are different, thanks to wineries like Claudio's which have contributed to the development of this area through their Timorasso and Barbera wines.

Judging by the interminable list of wines presented this year, we wonder whether Claudio ought just to focus on the varieties best acclimatized to his area and his most successful wines. Make no mistake, all his products are affordable and drinkable but the stand-outs are still the Timorasso and Barbera. Of the '07 Timorassos, the Derthona is the most subtle and minerally while the Pitasso is the fullest and deepest. The two Barberas are again up to snuff. Poggio del Rosso '06 is harmonious and lingering while the '07 Vho is warmer and more pervasive.

● Barolo Brunate '05	▼▼▼ 7
● Barbera d'Alba Pugnane '07	▼▼ 4*
● Barolo Bricco Viole '05	▼▼ 7
● Nebbiolo d'Alba Valmaggiore '07	▼▼ 4*
● Dolcetto d'Alba '08	▼▼ 4
● Barolo Brunate '04	♀♀♀ 7
● Barolo Bricco Viole '04	♀♀ 7
● Barolo Brunate '03	♀♀ 7
● Barolo Brunate '01	♀♀ 7*

○ Colli Tortonesi Timorasso Derthona '07	▼▼ 5
○ Colli Tortonesi Timorasso Pitasso '07	▼▼ 6
○ Colli Tortonesi Cortese Profilo '08	▼▼ 4
● Colli Tortonesi Rosso Montemirano '07	▼▼ 6
● Colli Tortonesi Rosso Poggio del Rosso '06	▼▼ 6
● Colli Tortonesi Rosso Vho '07	▼▼ 5
○ Colli Tortonesi Bianco Coccalina '08	▼ 4
● Colli Tortonesi Rosso Braghè '08	▼ 4
● Colli Tortonesi Rosso Campo del Gatto '08	▼ 4
● Colli Tortonesi Rosso Martirella '08	▼ 4
● Colli Tortonesi Rosso Territorio '08	▼ 4
○ Colli Tortonesi Bianco Pitasso '06	♀♀♀ 6
○ Colli Tortonesi Bianco Pitasso '05	♀♀♀ 5
○ Colli Tortonesi Bianco Pitasso '04	♀♀♀ 5

Marsaglia

VIA MADAMA MUSSONE, 2
12050 CASTELLINALDO [CN]
TEL. 0173213048
www.cantinamarsaglia.it

CELLAR SALES
PRE-BOOKED VISITS

ANNUAL PRODUCTION 70,000 bottles
HECTARES UNDER VINE 15
VITICULTURE METHOD Conventional

This traditional winery is located at Castellinaldo, in the Roero hills and run enthusiastically by the entire Marsaglia family. Marina and her husband Emilio have been the driving force for growth over the years. The fairly broad range of wines, all focusing on native varieties, manages to guarantee an impeccable standard of quality. The vineyards, all in the Castellinaldo area, face south.

It was another good performance from the Marsaglia family's varietal, nicely made wines. The Barbera d'Alba Castellinaldo '06 has pleasantly evolved aromas with hints of undergrowth and a powerful, heady palate supported by fresh, dynamic acidity. The Roero Brich d'America '06 is vibrant and intense with aromas of tobacco and raspberries and a dense, savoury palate that lingers. The Roero Arneis Serramiana '08 is one of the best of the year, with fresh greens aromatics on an understated but lively nose and a leanish, citrussy yet attractively drinkable palate. The other products are well made or better.

★ Franco M. Martinetti

VIA SAN FRANCESCO DA PAOLA, 18
10123 TORINO
TEL. 0118395937
www.francomartinetti.it

PRE-BOOKED VISITS

ANNUAL PRODUCTION 150,000 bottles
HECTARES UNDER VINE 4
VITICULTURE METHOD Conventional

Franco Martinetti is not a typical figure in the Italian winemaking world: he is what the French call an "éleveur". He has no winery of his own but selects wines from the best producers in the various zones of Piedmont to cellar and mature, which he does with great skill. So much so that often Franco's wines are better in tasting than those of his suppliers. It is thanks to his knowledge and skill as a taster that Franco achieves these small miracles.

The '05 Barolo Marasco is good as ever, showing soft and generous, and the very good Barbera d'Asti Montruc '07 leads with hints of cocoa powder and black cherries on the nose into a gutsy, savoury palate. The surprising Colli Tortonesi Bianco Timorasso Biancofranco '08 gives white truffle aromas as well as complex fruit and powerful structure. The '07 Martin, from timorasso grapes, is much better than the oakier, less layered barrique-aged version. The '07 Monferrato Rosso Sul Bric from barbera and cabernet sauvignon is less interesting than usual and the Gavi Minaia '08 is merely well typed.

● Barbera d'Alba Castellinaldo '06	♙♙ 5
○ Roero Arneis Serramiana '08	♙♙ 4*
● Roero Brich d'America '06	♙♙ 5
● Barbera d'Alba S. Cristoforo '08	♙ 4
● Nebbiolo d'Alba S. Pietro '07	♙ 4
● Barbera d'Alba S. Cristoforo '07	♙♙ 4*
● Castellinaldo Barbera d'Alba '05	♙♙ 5
● Nebbiolo d'Alba S. Pietro '06	♙♙ 4*
○ Roero Arneis Serramiana '07	♙♙ 4*
● Roero Brich d'America '05	♙♙ 5

● Barbera d'Asti Sup. Montruc '07	♙♙ 6
● Barolo Marasco '05	♙♙ 8
○ Colli Tortonesi Timorasso Biancofranco '08	♙♙ 4*
○ Colli Tortonesi Bianco Martin '07	♙♙ 7
● M.to Rosso Sul Bric '07	♙♙ 7
○ Gavi Minaia '08	♙ 6
● Barbera d'Asti Sup. Montruc '06	♙♙♙ 6
● Barbera d'Asti Sup. Montruc '01	♙♙♙ 6
● Barbera d'Asti Sup. Montruc '97	♙♙♙ 6
● Barbera d'Asti Sup. Montruc '96	♙♙♙ 6
● Barolo Marasco '01	♙♙♙ 8
● Barolo Marasco '00	♙♙♙ 8
● M.to Rosso Sul Bric '00	♙♙♙ 6
○ Minaia '98	♙♙♙ 6
● Sul Bric '95	♙♙♙ 6
● Sul Bric '94	♙♙♙ 6

Bartolo Mascarello

VIA ROMA, 15
12060 BAROLO [CN]
TEL. 017356125

CELLAR SALES
PRE-BOOKED VISITS

ANNUAL PRODUCTION **30,000 bottles**
HECTARES UNDER VINE **5**
VITICULTURE METHOD **Conventional**

Many have knocked at this door in Via Roma, a stone's throw from the centre of Barolo. And even more have spent entire afternoons talking – not just about wine – to one of the best-loved figures in Langhe. Now that Bartolo Mascarello has left us, his daughter Maria Teresa has taken up his legacy not only in production but also, and especially, with that special Mascarello way of crafting truly authentic bottles from traditional, unhurried maceration and ageing in large barrels. Wines that will endure for decades.

Cannubi, San Lorenzo and Rué at Barolo. Rocche at La Morra. For almost a century, this has been the Bartolo Mascarello recipe for the leading house wine, a Barolo that managed to put on one of its best ever performances in the difficult 2005 vintage. Magnificent, almost oriental, in its intensely spice and citrus aromas, with a smoky touch bringing depth and linking in to the taut, sharp and flavoursome but never needlessly green or dry palate. Further bottle ageing will bring more depth but it is beautifully drinkable now, along with the Barbera d'Alba and Langhe Freisa '07.

Giuseppe Mascarello e Figlio

VIA BORGONUOVO, 108
12060 MONCHIERO [CN]
TEL. 0173792126
www.mascarello1881.com

CELLAR SALES
PRE-BOOKED VISITS

ANNUAL PRODUCTION **60,000 bottles**
HECTARES UNDER VINE **12**
VITICULTURE METHOD **Conventional**

Mauro and Giuseppe Mascarello's wines are utterly distinctive. Their lustrous, near-translucent hue heralds interpretations of the most prestigious Langhe vineyards that are subtle, austere and initially perplexing, often needing time to be fully understood. The Barolo crus mature in large barrels for at least 40 months and bear awesome names like Villero, Santo Stefano di Perno and Monprivato, the Castiglione vineyard which in great years produces Cà d'Morissio, a selection made exclusively with the michet clone.

We were looking forward to tasting Mauro Mascarello's '04 Barolos but the test proved harder than expected. Perhaps the classic, austere growing year was especially hard to interpret but for the time being, we have to report aromas that are not particularly precise and still rather slender structure. The wines are unquestionably appealing but we expected more backbone from the Villero and more integrity of aromas and tannins from the Monprivato. The Santo Stefano di Perno impressed us most with a distinctive, almost anchovy-like sensation and a lean, dry sensory profile.

● Barolo '05	♟♟♟ 8
● Barbera d'Alba '07	♟♟ 5
● Langhe Freisa '07	♟♟ 5
● Dolcetto d'Alba '08	♟ 4
● Barolo '01	♟♟♟ 8
● Barolo '04	♟♟ 8
● Barolo '03	♟♟ 8

● Barolo Monprivato '04	♟♟ 8
● Barolo Monprivato Ca' d' Morissio '01	♟♟ 6
● Barolo S. Stefano di Perno '04	♟♟ 8
● Barolo Villero '04	♟♟ 8
● Langhe Nebbiolo '06	♟♟ 6
● Barolo Monprivato '01	♟♟♟ 8
● Barolo S. Stefano di Perno '98	♟♟♟ 8
● Barbera d'Alba Sup. Codana '04	♟♟ 7
● Barolo S. Stefano di Perno '03	♟♟ 8
● Langhe Freisa Toetto '04	♟♟ 5

Tenuta La Meridiana

VIA TANA BASSA, 5
14048 MONTEGROSSO D'ASTI [AT]
TEL. 0141956172
www.tenutalameridiana.com

CELLAR SALES
PRE-BOOKED VISITS

ANNUAL PRODUCTION **90,000 bottles**
HECTARES UNDER VINE **12**
VITICULTURE METHOD **Naturale**

Members of the Bianco family have been growers at Montegrosso d'Asti since 1890. Today the fourth generation, Gianpiero and Grazia, run the winery, assisted by winemaker Lorenzo Quinterno. Although they also work with international grape varieties, the Biancos focus almost exclusively on the main Asti variety, barbera, and in recent years have managed to work their way into the exclusive club of top-level producers of this wine.

The Bianco family presented several good Barberas. The Barbera d'Asti Superiore Nizza Tra La Terra e Il Cielo '06 is still oak-dominated but has varietal earthy aromas, plenty of texture, fruit, spice and a very long finish. The Barbera d'Asti Vitis '07 has intense, balsamic aromas of tobacco and bottled fruit and a crisp, pleasant that is less generous than the nose would suggest. Lastly, the Barbera d'Asti Le Gagie '07 has earthy, cinchona-laced aromas and an enjoyably rounded palate. The Passito Sol '06, a monovarietal Chardonnay, is full and concentrated with hints of confectioner's cream and crème brulée. The other wines are well made.

Noceto Michelotti

S.DA BOGLIONA, 15/17
14040 CASTEL BOGLIONE [AT]
TEL. 0141762170
www.nocetomichelotti.com

CELLAR SALES
PRE-BOOKED VISITS

ANNUAL PRODUCTION **120,000 bottles**
HECTARES UNDER VINE **32**
VITICULTURE METHOD **Conventional**

This modern winery in the upper Monferrato hills has become one of the most interesting in the Asti area. Owners Graham Kresfelder and Margret Schratt-Kresfelder have put together a great team of professionals, including winemaker Giuseppe Caviola and agronomist Federico Curtaz. Over the years, they have created wines with bags of personality that reflect the features of a particularly good growing area for barbera. The vineyards are planted on limestone-based soil facing south and west in an area that tends to have a wide range of temperatures.

We like the Barbera d'Asti Superiore Nizza Montecanta and the 2006 version made the finals with aromas of spice and black berries and an austere, balanced palate with good acidity and texture and a persistent, fruit-forward finish. A step behind is the Barbera d'Asti Superiore Montecanta '06, which shows vibrant, classic aromas of tobacco and ripe red berries and then distinctive earthiness and cherry hints on the hefty, traditional and very long palate. The Monferrato Rosso '07 and the fresh, fruity Barbera d'Asti '07 are both well typed.

● Barbera d'Asti Le Gagie '07	▼▼ 4*
● Barbera d'Asti Sup. Nizza Tra La Terra e Il Cielo '06	▼▼ 5
● Barbera d'Asti Vitis '07	▼▼ 3*
○ Passito Sol '06	▼▼ 6
● Barbera d'Asti Sup. Bricco Sereno '07	▼ 4
● M.to Rosso Rivaia '06	▼ 5
● Barbera d'Asti Le Gagie '06	♀♀ 4*
● Barbera d'Asti Sup. Bricco Sereno '06	♀♀ 4*
● Barbera d'Asti Sup. Nizza Tra La Terra e Il Cielo '05	♀♀ 5
● Barbera d'Asti Sup. Nizza Tra La Terra e Il Cielo '04	♀♀ 5
● Barbera d'Asti Sup. Nizza Tra La Terra e Il Cielo '03	♀♀ 5
● Barbera d'Asti Vitis '06	♀♀ 3*
● M.to Rosso Rivaia '05	♀♀ 5

● Barbera d'Asti Sup. Nizza Montecanta '06	▼▼ 5
● Barbera d'Asti Sup. Montecanta '06	▼▼ 5
● Barbera d'Asti '07	▼ 4
● M.to Rosso '07	▼ 4
● Barbera d'Asti '06	♀♀ 4*
● Barbera d'Asti '05	♀♀ 4*
● Barbera d'Asti Strada del Sole '06	♀♀ 4*
● Barbera d'Asti Sup. Montecanta '05	♀♀ 5
● M.to Rosso Oro '04	♀♀ 6

Moccagatta

S.DA RABAJÀ, 46
12050 BARBARESCO [CN]
TEL. 0173635228

CELLAR SALES
PRE-BOOKED VISITS

ANNUAL PRODUCTION **65,000 bottles**
HECTARES UNDER VINE **12**
VITICULTURE METHOD **Conventional**

This leading Barbaresco label, managed with a sure hand by brothers Franco and Sergio Minuto, astonished the winemaking world with its prestigious, fine wines back in the late 1980s. Careful vineyard management and a tried and tested winemaking style help to coax all the potential out of the estate's 12 or so hectares. A combination of the traditional and the modern underpins this wide range of well-designed and well-defined wines, released mainly under the Barbaresco DOCG.

The enjoyable Cole '06 has a fairly evolved nose and a mature palate with slightly drying tannins while the soft Basarin has coffee aromas and quite a buttery palate. The winery's deepest, most complex Barbaresco is once again the Bric Balin, this time the '06, which gives sophisticated toastiness and a soft, mouthfilling tannic texture. The Buschet '07 is marked by oak and shows a little New World in style, maintaining its buttery, caressing style over time. The Chardonnay '08 presents the winery style in a much more youthful key, with a fresh, acidulous flavour and lovely tropical fruit on the nose.

F.lli Molino

LOC. AUSARIO
VIA AUSARIO, 5
12050 TREISO [CN]
TEL. 0173638384
www.molinovini.com

CELLAR SALES
PRE-BOOKED VISITS
VISITOR FACILITIES

ANNUAL PRODUCTION **80,000 bottles**
HECTARES UNDER VINE **11.5**
VITICULTURE METHOD **Conventional**

The Molino brothers, Dario, Franco and Tommaso, have run this winery for several years with an increasingly confident touch. The estate is situated on a hillside with an extraordinary view of the Treiso area: a succession of vineyards spread like waves across a sea of beautifully aspected slopes. This is a typical small Langhe winery whose products are inextricably linked to the terroir. New this year is the Barbera d'Asti originating from a one-hectare vineyard.

Clean, well-made wines this year. There are two '08 Dolcettos: Ausario, still closed but very promising, and Le Querce with a beautiful palate and juicy fruit. The Barbera d'Asti Loreto '08 is heady, fruity, breezy and savoury. The '07 Barbera d'Alba Ausario, aged in used barriques, is vibrant, powerful, lively and lingering while the Barbaresco Teorema '06, from the Montersino cru at San Rocco Seno d'Elvio near Alba, is floral and elegant with sweet tannins and a mouthwatering, very long-lingering finish. The Barbaresco Ausario '06 has vibrant fruit aromas and a savoury, long palate with nice fruit, powerful tannic structure and nebbiolo's classic florality in the finish.

● Barbaresco Bric Balin '06	♀♀	7
● Barbaresco Basarin '06	♀♀	7
● Barbaresco Cole '06	♀♀	7
○ Langhe Chardonnay '08	♀♀	4
○ Langhe Chardonnay Buschet '07	♀	6
● Barbaresco Bric Balin '05	♀♀♀	7
● Barbaresco Bric Balin '04	♀♀♀	7
● Barbaresco '02	♀♀	6*
● Barbaresco Basarin '05	♀♀	7
● Barbaresco Cole '05	♀♀	7
● Barbaresco Cole '04	♀♀	7
● Barbaresco Cole '03	♀♀	7

● Barbaresco Teorema '06	♀♀	6
● Barbaresco Ausario '06	♀♀	6
● Barbera d'Alba Ausario '07	♀♀	5
● Dolcetto d'Alba Ausario '08	♀♀	4*
● Barbera d'Asti Loreto '08	♀	4
● Dolcetto d'Alba Le Querce '08	♀	3
○ Langhe Arneis '08	♀	4
● Barbaresco Ausario '05	♀♀	6
● Barbaresco Ausario '04	♀♀	6
● Barbaresco Teorema '05	♀♀	6
● Barbaresco Teorema '04	♀♀	6
● Barbera d'Alba Ausario '06	♀♀	5
● Dolcetto d'Alba Ausario '07	♀♀	4*
● Dolcetto d'Alba Ausario '06	♀♀	4*

Mauro Molino

FRAZ. ANNUNZIATA
B.TA GANCIA, 111
12064 LA MORRA [CN]
TEL. 017350814
www.mauromolino.com

CELLAR SALES
PRE-BOOKED VISITS

ANNUAL PRODUCTION **50,000 bottles**
HECTARES UNDER VINE **10**
VITICULTURE METHOD **Conventional**

The baton of management is passing increasingly to the new generation of the Molino family at this winery which has succeeded over the years in maintaining an absolutely impeccable standard of quality. The estate is tended with the greatest care and the cellar is fully equipped to guarantee the best possible quality for the quantities of excellent fruit processed. The wines are mainly Barolos, from several different, complementary vineyards, with one Barbera which is among the best in the DOCG zone.

The five '05 Barolos are all very sound. Vigna Gancia is more elegant than powerful, with an impressively fruity, mouthfilling palate. The Vigna Conca is similar in style but slightly more tannic and less harmonious. The new Barolo Rocche dell'Annunziata demonstrates the potential of this splendid La Morra cru with aromas of roses, sweet spice and raspberries and a powerful palate whose tannins are slightly drying. In this consistently good range, we recommend the impressive Barbera Vigna Gattere '07, with its awesomely dense fruit and a rounded flavour.

Monchiero Carbone

VIA SANTO STEFANO ROERO, 2
12043 CANALE [CN]
TEL. 017395568
www.monchierocarbone.com

CELLAR SALES
PRE-BOOKED VISITS

ANNUAL PRODUCTION **90,000 bottles**
HECTARES UNDER VINE **11**
VITICULTURE METHOD **Conventional**

This winery, founded in 1990 by renowned winemaker Marco Monchiero and Lucetta Carbone, is now run by son Francesco, a clear-headed young wine man. In the last 15 years, Francesco has worked hard to boost the image of Roero as a wine area and to give his own wines a distinctively unique stamp. The estate has a series of crus from Monbirone to the Frailin hills, where the Printi comes from, and has recently purchased a vineyard on the Renesio hill, which is the origin of the name Arneis.

Monchiero Carbone is still at the peak of Roero production. Three Glasses went to the Roero Printi Riserva '06 for its splendid spices, undergrowth and liquorice preceding a deep palate still slightly cropped by oak but with good texture, fruit and silky tannins. Wait to taste it at its best. Into the finals went Barbera d'Alba MonBirone '07 with its dense aromas of cocoa powder and cherries, velvety texture, fresh, fruity palate and a long acidity-braced finish. It was accompanied by Roero Arneis Cecu d'la Biunda '08, which is slightly less minerally than before but has lovely plums, hazelnuts and wild flowers and a subtle, rounded palate with bags of fruit and character.

● Barbera d'Alba V. Gattere '07	♥♥ 6
● Barolo Rocche dell'Annunziata '05	♥♥ 8
● Barolo V. Gallinotto '05	♥♥ 7
● Barolo V. Gancia '05	♥♥ 8
● Barolo '05	♥♥ 6
● Barolo V. Conca '05	♥♥ 8
● Dolcetto d'Alba '08	♥♥ 4
● Langhe Nebbiolo '08	♥♥ 4
○ Langhe Chardonnay Livrot '08	♥ 4
● Barbera d'Alba V. Gattere '00	♥♥♥ 6
● Barbera d'Alba V. Gattere '97	♥♥♥ 6
● Barolo V. Conca '00	♥♥♥ 8
● Barolo V. Conca '97	♥♥♥ 8
● Barolo V. Gallinotto '03	♥♥♥ 8
● Barolo V. Gallinotto '01	♥♥♥ 8

● Roero Printi Ris. '06	♥♥♥ 6
● Barbera d'Alba MonBirone '07	♥♥ 5
○ Roero Arneis Cecu d'la Biunda '08	♥♥ 4*
● Barbera d'Alba Pelisa '07	♥♥ 4*
○ Langhe Bianco Tamardì '08	♥♥ 4*
○ Roero Arneis Recit '08	♥♥ 4*
● Roero Srü '07	♥♥ 5
○ Piemonte Moscato Passito Sorì di Ruchin '06	♥ 5
● Roero Printi '04	♥♥♥ 6
● Roero Printi '00	♥♥♥ 6
● Roero Printi '99	♥♥♥ 7
● Roero Srü '06	♥♥♥ 5
● Barbera d'Alba MonBirone '05	♥♥ 5
○ Roero Arneis Cecu d'la Biunda '07	♥♥ 4*
● Roero Printi Ris. '05	♥♥ 6
● Roero Srü '05	♥♥ 5

Monfalletto
Cordero di Montezemolo

FRAZ. ANNUNZIATA, 67
12064 LA MORRA [CN]
TEL. 017350344
www.corderodimontezemolo.com

CELLAR SALES
PRE-BOOKED VISITS

ANNUAL PRODUCTION **220,000 bottles**
HECTARES UNDER VINE **35**
VITICULTURE METHOD **Naturale**

Many images of the extraordinary Langhe landscape show the iconic cedar of Lebanon which can be seen from this historical winery. The estate is a leading brand in Piedmontese and Italian winemaking, fully committed to releasing wines that live up to a name that is also well-known abroad. There are several Barolos in a distinctive, ageworthy style that is never commonplace, combining tradition and innovation to embody the spirit of this respected winery.

From the very sound range of '05 Barolos, we recommend the Monfalletto, the winery's workhorse. The aromatics are complex if restrained and the generous palate is only slightly less persistent than those of its stablemates. The famous Villero vineyard at Castiglione Falletto yields the Enrico VI, with its distinctive beautifully balanced palate and classic aromas of dried herbs and leather. The Bricco Gattera, from the scenic vineyard next to the cellar, blends meaty aromas with red berries and a particularly soft, velvety palate.

Montaribaldi

FRAZ. TRE STELLE
S.DA NICOLINI ALTO, 12
12050 BARBARESCO [CN]
TEL. 0173638220
www.montaribaldi.com

CELLAR SALES
PRE-BOOKED VISITS

ANNUAL PRODUCTION **70,000 bottles**
HECTARES UNDER VINE **21**
VITICULTURE METHOD **Conventional**

The estate run by the Taliano family is a good size for Langhe with its 20-odd hectares scattered across leading terroirs mainly located in the Barbaresco, Barolo and Barbera designations. There are also white varieties, specifically arneis, moscato and chardonnay. The list offers a full selection, all consistently dependable.

After lengthy ageing, the '04 Barbaresco Ricü beautifully reflects its excellent vintage. A subtle, complex and slightly heady nose is followed by a distinctly soft palate rich in fruity texture. The enjoyable Palazzina '06 has hints of raspberries and sweet tobacco, a powerful palate and a finish slightly dried by the tannins. The Sörì Montaribaldi '06 is fresh and balsamic on the nose while the palate is held back by nonetheless elegant oakiness. In its '07 incarnation, the very appealing Barbera dü Gir is even fruitier and more impetuous than usual. La Consolina '08 is calmer but quite enjoyably drinkable. But the entire affordable range is delicious.

● Barolo Enrico VI '05	▼▼ 8
● Barolo Monfalletto '05	▼▼ 7
● Barolo V. Bricco Gattera '05	▼▼ 8
○ Langhe Chardonnay Elioro '07	▼▼ 5
● Dolcetto d'Alba '08	▼ 4
○ Langhe Arneis '08	▼ 4
● Langhe Nebbiolo '08	▼ 5
● Barolo Enrico VI '04	▼▼▼ 8
● Barolo Enrico VI '03	▼▼▼ 8
● Barolo V. Bricco Gattera '99	▼▼▼ 8
● Barolo V. Enrico VI '00	▼▼▼ 8
● Barolo V. Enrico VI '97	▼▼▼ 8
● Barolo V. Enrico VI '96	▼▼▼ 8
● Barolo Monfalletto '04	▼▼ 7
● Barolo V. Bricco Gattera '04	▼▼ 8

● Barbaresco Ricü '04	▼▼ 7
● Barbera d'Alba dü Gir '07	▼▼ 5
● Barbaresco Palazzina '06	▼▼ 5*
● Barbaresco Sörì Montaribaldi '06	▼▼ 6
● Barbera d'Asti La Consolina '08	▼▼ 3*
○ Langhe Chardonnay Stissa d'le Favole '08	▼▼ 3*
● Dolcetto d'Alba Vagnona '08	▼ 3
● Langhe Rosso Nicolini '08	▼ 4
○ Moscato d'Asti Righey '08	▼ 4
○ Roero Arneis Capural '08	▼ 4
● Barbaresco Sörì Montaribaldi '04	▼▼ 6
● Barbaresco Sörì Montaribaldi '03	▼▼ 6*
● Barbera d'Alba dü Gir '06	▼▼ 5

Monti

LOC. SAN SEBASTIANO
FRAZ. CAMIE, 39
12065 MONFORTE D'ALBA [CN]
TEL. 017378391
www.paolomonti.com

CELLAR SALES
PRE-BOOKED VISITS

ANNUAL PRODUCTION 50,000 bottles
HECTARES UNDER VINE 11
VITICULTURE METHOD Naturale

Paolo Monti's winery, founded in 1996, strides on towards quality and the promotion of Langhe's noble varieties. A short while ago, we re-tasted the 1997 Barbera, from the early days, and were very gratified to find it on good form, still showing varietal with intriguing complexity. The style of these wines reflects a precise temperament and the desire to create a distinctive personal space. The grapes for the Barolo selection come from the Bussia Sottana vineyard included by Renato Ratti on his list of especially favourable locations for nebbiolo.

The appealing Barolo Bussia '05 has a spicy nose and a palate still swathed in oak despite raw material that will surely assert itself in the coming years. The basic Barolo is still notable for alcohol and oak so it should be tasted after further bottle ageing. The complex, enjoyable Barbera '06 presents a nice ruby with aromas of cinchona, liquorice and emphatic oak complementing a balanced tannic element. The Langhe Bianco L'Aura '07, from an unusual blend of chardonnay and riesling renano, has complex aromas and a rounded palate.

● Barbera d'Alba '06	♟♟	6
● Barolo '05	♟♟	8
● Barolo Bussia '05	♟♟	8
○ Langhe Bianco L'Aura '07	♟♟	5
● Barolo '04	♟♟	7
● Barolo Bussia '04	♟♟	8
● Barolo Bussia '01	♟♟	8
● Barolo Bussia '00	♟♟	8
● Nebbiolo d'Alba '06	♟♟	5

La Morandina

LOC. MORANDINI, 11
12053 CASTIGLIONE TINELLA [CN]
TEL. 0141855261
www.lamorandina.com

CELLAR SALES
PRE-BOOKED VISITS

ANNUAL PRODUCTION 100,000 bottles
HECTARES UNDER VINE 20
VITICULTURE METHOD Conventional

Giulio and Paolo Morando run this well-established winery with confidence, presenting a well-stocked series of wines from the estate's favourably aspected vineyards. The products range from Moscato, for which La Morandina has long been a leading label, to Barbera and Barbaresco, showing striking temperament and definition. In an increasingly overcrowded market, the intelligently organized selection of distinctive products underpins the winery's position, catering to its wide range of enthusiastic consumers.

The two most impressive wines are L'Insieme '06 and the '07 Barbera Varmat. The former shows an inky deep ruby red with juicy fruit on a fresh nose alongside hints of spice and chocolate over faint damp earth. The full, powerful palate has beautiful freshness to brighten the long finish. The Varmat '07 is inky dark and viscous with marked oak as well as complexity from the huge fruit and lashings of chocolate. The powerful, rounded palate has a concentrated but nicely harmonious finish. This wine will evolve wonderfully for several years.

● Barbera d'Asti Sup. Varmat '07	♟♟	6
● Langhe Rosso L'Insieme '06	♟♟	7
● Barbaresco Bricco Spessa '06	♟♟	7
● Barbera d'Asti Zucchetto '08	♟♟	4
○ Moscato d'Asti '08	♟♟	4
○ Langhe Chardonnay '08	♟	5
● Barbera d'Asti Cinque Vigne '07	♟♟	4
● Barbera d'Asti Varmat '06	♟♟	5
● Barbera d'Asti Zucchetto '07	♟♟	4*
● L'Insieme '05	♟♟	8

Cascina Morassino

S.DA BERNINO, 10
12050 BARBARESCO [CN]
TEL. 0173635149

CELLAR SALES
PRE-BOOKED VISITS

ANNUAL PRODUCTION **20,000 bottles**
HECTARES UNDER VINE **4.5**
VITICULTURE METHOD **Conventional**

For years, this small-scale grower has produced consistent quality from just over four hectares of beautifully positioned vineyards. Small does not mean backward, though. The newly constructed cellar came onstream a short while ago, technologically equipped to manage a production range which, in the Barbaresco DOCG, finds its greatest expression in wines from two cru vineyards, Ovello and Morassino, both in the municipal area of Barbaresco.

The '06 version of the appealing Morassino is simple, direct and clean with marked alcohol on the palate. The engaging Ovello, from the excellent Ovello vineyard, is vibrant, heady and harmonious, showing beautifully complex thanks to fruit and spice, with a generous, mouthfilling and already quite balanced palate. The contemporary Barbera Vignot '07 is very complex thanks to a wonderful growing year and delicate acidity that gives it an especially enjoyable palate. The fresh, fruity Dolcetto d'Alba '08 has mellow tannins while the well-typed Langhe Rosso Vigna del Merlo '07 is almost austerely characterful. The Langhe Nebbiolo '07 is well typed and enjoyable.

Stefanino Morra

VIA CASTAGNITO, 50
12050 CASTELLINALDO [CN]
TEL. 0173213489
www.morravini.it

CELLAR SALES
PRE-BOOKED VISITS

ANNUAL PRODUCTION **65,000 bottles**
HECTARES UNDER VINE **10**
VITICULTURE METHOD **Conventional**

The historic Morra family winery is at Castellinaldo, one of Roero's leading winemaking centres. Owner Stefanino is assisted by his parents Antonio and Margherita, wife Edda and brother-in-law Gianni. In recent years, the Morras have made significant investments to improve the vineyards and cellar, and are now beginning to reap the results.

Some of Stefanino Morra's best wines are back with the 2006 vintage and the results reflect this. Two wines went into the finals. The vibrant, heady Roero '06 has light aromas of dried flowers, liquorice and tobacco and an impressively textured palate with close-knit tannin and fruit, and a long, rounded finish. the other finalist, the '06 Barbera d'Alba Castlè, has the cinchona aromatics typical of Roero-grown Barbera, tobacco and sweet spice followed by an austere palate with a long, fruity finish and lingering freshness. The other wines are good, with a special mention for the '06 Barbera d'Alba Castellinaldo's earthy, cinchona aromas and tangy, characterful palate.

● Barbaresco Ovello '06	♟ 7
● Barbera d'Alba Vignot '07	♟ 5*
● Barbaresco Morassino '06	♟ 7
● Dolcetto d'Alba '08	♟ 4
● Langhe Nebbiolo '07	♟ 5
● Langhe Rosso V. del Merlo '07	♟ 5
● Barbaresco Morassino '05	♟♟ 7
● Barbaresco Ovello '05	♟♟ 7
● Barbaresco Ovello '04	♟♟ 7
● Barbaresco Ovello '03	♟♟ 7
● Barbaresco Ovello '02	♟♟ 7

● Barbera d'Alba Castlè '06	♟ 5
● Roero '06	♟ 5
● Barbera d'Alba '07	♟♟ 4*
● Castellinaldo Barbera d'Alba '06	♟♟ 5
○ Roero Arneis '08	♟♟ 4
○ Roero Arneis Vign. S. Pietro '07	♟♟ 4
● Barbera d'Alba '06	♟♟ 4*
● Roero '05	♟♟ 5
● Roero Srai '04	♟♟ 6

F.lli Mossio

FRAZ. CASCINA CARAMELLI
VIA MONTÀ, 12
12050 RODELLO [CN]
TEL. 0173617149
www.mossio.com

CELLAR SALES
PRE-BOOKED VISITS

ANNUAL PRODUCTION **5.500 bottles**
HECTARES UNDER VINE **10**
VITICULTURE METHOD **Conventional**

Rodello stands in a lovely position just outside Alba. Although the town is just a few kilometres away, the everyday pace of life is very different. This is where the Mossio family works, year after year asserting their place among the benchmark wineries for premium Dolcetto. This original, native Piedmontese variety is the key to the range of very drinkable wines presented, wines that will age with ease.

The Bricco Caramelli '08 opens with extraordinarily memorable blackberry and blackcurrant fruit that continues onto the harmonious palate with its long-lingering finish. The Piano delli Perdoni '08 is equally enjoyable with fresh fruit on the nose and a palate showing a beautiful balance of acidity, alcohol and tannin. The well-typed Langhe Rosso '06 is a polished and not excessively tannic blend of mainly nebbiolo with dolcetto and barbera.

Mutti

LOC. SAN RUFFINO, 49
15050 SAREZZANO [AL]
TEL. 0131884119

ANNUAL PRODUCTION **55,000 bottles**
HECTARES UNDER VINE **15**
VITICULTURE METHOD **Conventional**

Andrea is now firmly in charge of the Mutti winery, replacing his father Dino, who was a pioneer of wine quality in the difficult borderland territory of Colli Tortonesi. Dino was one of the first to understand the importance of bottling the best selections from the estate's vineyards and Andrea, who has degrees in both agriculture and oenology, has followed in his foodtsteps, establishing Mutti as one of the leading wineries in the DOC zone.

We liked the Timorasso Castagnoli '07, one of the best versions made from this native grape and always an extremely good wine that goes through to our finals every year. From the whites, the Sauvignon Sull'Aia '08 deserves a mention for its fresh, fruity aromas and nice acidity, as does one of the best Corteses in the province, the '08 Noceto. There are also some interesting reds, like the Barbera San Ruffino '07 and Boscobarona '08. The former, aged in small wood, is engaging, concentrated and powerful while the steel-fermented Boscobarona is fruity with lovely heady sensations. The Rivadestra '05, from cabernet sauvignon, is sound.

● Dolcetto d'Alba Bricco Caramelli '08	♟♟	4
● Dolcetto d'Alba Piano delli Perdoni '08	♟♟	4*
● Barbera d'Alba '06	♟♟	5
● Langhe Rosso '06	♟♟	5
● Dolcetto d'Alba Bricco Caramelli '06	♟♟	4*
● Dolcetto d'Alba Bricco Caramelli '05	♟♟	4*
● Langhe Rosso '05	♟♟	5

● Colli Tortonesi Rosso S. Ruffino '07	♟♟	5
○ Colli Tortonesi Timorasso Derthona Castagnoli '07	♟♟	5
○ Colli Tortonesi Bianco Noceto '08	♟♟	3*
○ Colli Tortonesi Bianco Sull'Aia '08	♟♟	4
● Colli Tortonesi Rosso Rivadestra '05	♟♟	5
● Colli Tortonesi Rosso Boscobarona '08	♟	3
○ Colli Tortonesi Bianco Castagnoli '06	♟♟	5
○ Colli Tortonesi Bianco Castagnoli '05	♟♟	5
○ Colli Tortonesi Bianco Castagnoli '04	♟♟	5
○ Colli Tortonesi Bianco Castagnoli '03	♟♟	5
○ Colli Tortonesi Bianco Noceto '07	♟♟	3*
○ Colli Tortonesi Bianco Noceto '06	♟♟	3*
○ Colli Tortonesi Bianco Sull'Aia '06	♟♟	4
● Colli Tortonesi Rosso S. Ruffino '05	♟♟	5
● Colli Tortonesi Rosso S. Ruffino '04	♟♟	5

★ Fiorenzo Nada

LOC. ROMBONE
VIA AUSARIO, 12C
12050 TREISO [CN]
TEL. 0173638254
www.nada.it

CELLAR SALES
PRE-BOOKED VISITS

ANNUAL PRODUCTION **40,000 bottles**
HECTARES UNDER VINE **7**
VITICULTURE METHOD **Conventional**

He may be Treiso's city councillor for the arts, committed to promoting the area by for example proposing Langhe as a UNESCO world heritage site, but Bruno Nada keeps an eye on the wine estate that has brought him, and us, such satisfaction. Today, we await the arrival of his son Danilo, who will join the business and ensure the continuity of a Nada presence in Treiso. It's a family saga that deserves to be told elsewhere.

Standing out among this year's wines is the elegant, sophisticated Barbaresco Rombone '06, which earned Three Glasses for perfectly balanced fruit, extract and acidity on a very clean, powerful, and long-lingering palate. Flanking it is the Barbaresco Manzola '06, still closed on the nose with confident tannins and strong alcohol on the palate. It's a wine needing further bottle time. The barbera and nebbiolo Seifile '06 is sweet and very fruity on the nose with a juicy palate supported by wonderful acidity. The Barbera '07 and the new Nebbiolo '07 from the younger vineyards are both very good and the Dolcetto '08 hits the spot as ever.

Cantina dei Produttori Nebbiolo di Carema

VIA NAZIONALE, 32
10010 CAREMA [TO]
TEL. 0125811160
www.saporipiemontesi.it

CELLAR SALES
PRE-BOOKED VISITS

ANNUAL PRODUCTION **65,000 bottles**
HECTARES UNDER VINE **17**
VITICULTURE METHOD **Conventional**

This is the smallest and most extreme DOC zone in northern Piedmont, a hunting ground for sophisticated wine mavens. If Carema is a spiritual home for those in search of wines that shun the usual sweet, fruity style, it is thanks especially to Cantina Produttori Nebbiolo di Carema and others like them who have kept alive a challenging – to put it mildly – wine tradition in less fortunate times. The co-operative has 79 member growers and about 17 hectares under overhead trellis-trained vines on tiny plots of land stolen from the mountainside.

The '05 Carema, aged for 36 months in large casks, does not entirely succeed in smoothing out the rough tannic edges typical of the DOC but does show its trademark aromatics of dried flowers and herbal infusions. These features are emphasized with greater complexity and length in the Riserva '04. Traditional to the hilt, it proffers of antique wood and citrus peel with an almost chalky texture perked up by lean acidity that extends the aromatic persistence but requires a touch more backbone to scale the heights of quality.

● Barbaresco Rombone '06	▼▼▼ 8
● Barbaresco V. Manzola '06	▼▼ 7
● Langhe Rosso Seifile '06	▼▼ 8
● Barbera d'Alba '07	▼▼ 5
● Dolcetto d'Alba '08	▼▼ 4*
● Langhe Nebbiolo '07	▼▼ 4
● Barbaresco '01	♈♈♈ 7
● Barbaresco Rombone '05	♈♈♈ 8
● Barbaresco Rombone '04	♈♈♈ 8
● Barbaresco Rombone '99	♈♈♈ 8
● Langhe Rosso Seifile '01	♈♈♈ 8
● Barbaresco V. Manzola '04	♈♈ 7
● Langhe Rosso Seifile '05	♈♈ 8

● Carema Ris. '04	▼▼ 4*
● Carema '05	▼▼ 4
● Carema '04	♈♈ 4
● Carema Barricato '01	♈♈ 5
● Carema Et. Nera '01	♈♈ 4*
● Carema Ris. '02	♈♈ 4

Angelo Negro & Figli

FRAZ. SANT'ANNA, 1
12040 MONTEU ROERO [CN]
TEL. 017390252
www.negroangelo.it

CELLAR SALES
PRE-BOOKED VISITS

ANNUAL PRODUCTION **250,000 bottles**
HECTARES UNDER VINE **54**
VITICULTURE METHOD **Conventional**

The Negro family has been growing grapes since 1670 and theirs is one of the leading estates in Roero, both in quality and size. Giovanni and Marisa, along with their children Angelo, Emanuela, Gabriele and Giuseppe, have created a dynamic, forward-looking winery that aims to expand beyond its home territory. Witness their purchase of a vineyard at Neive to produce Barbaresco. But Roero remains the family's most representative wine.

There were gratifying results from the local wines and the Barbaresco with two finalists. The Roero Sudisfà Riserva '06, with hints of cinchona, dried flowers and raspberries on the nose and a generous, very deep palate with close-knit, nicely integrated tannins, and the Barbaresco Basarin '06, which has bottled fruit, tobacco and spices and a classy, powerful, austere palate. The unusual but engaging Roero Arneis Sette Anni '01, released this year in limited numbers, is generous and complex, unveiling camomile and apricots that lead into a long finish supported more by savouriness than acidity. The other products are all beautifully made.

Nervi

C.SO VERCELLI, 117
13045 GATTINARA [VC]
TEL. 0163833228
www.gattinara-nervi.it

CELLAR SALES
PRE-BOOKED VISITS

ANNUAL PRODUCTION **100,000 bottles**
HECTARES UNDER VINE **33**
VITICULTURE METHOD **Conventional**

This long-established Gattinara winery, founded in the early 20th century by Luigi Nervi, was purchased by Gruppo Sitindustrie in 1991 and became a new wine holding, with Malgrà, in 2005 under the name Tenute & Case Vinicole Italiane. Leaving aside its commercial history, Nervi owns almost a third of all the area under vine in Gattinara and has always maintained its stylistic tradition, producing a basic wine and two selections that age unhurriedly in Slavonian oak before release, Vigneto Molsino and Podere dei Ginepri.

At last, Coste della Sesia Spanna is back. The '05 is slightly vegetal on the nose with rather austere extract but the palate is bright and convincing. When we came to the Gattinaras, we were a little surprised to find the lean but slightly alcoholic 2003 presented after the release of its two elder brothers. These have always alternated in recent editions and this time it's the turn of the Vigneto Molsino '04. It was a shoo-in for our finals with its classic profile of tobacco and medicinal herbs, sophisticated tannins but also some tertiary aromatics that make it seem a tad over-evolved.

Wine	Rating
● Barbaresco Basarin '06	♟♟ 6
● Roero Sudisfà Ris. '06	♟♟ 6
● Barbera d'Alba Nicolon '07	♟♟ 4*
● Langhe Rosso Million '06	♟♟ 5
O Roero Arneis Giovanni Negro Extra Brut '05	♟♟ 5
O Roero Arneis Sette Anni '01	♟♟ 8
● Roero Prachiosso '06	♟♟ 5
O Roero Arneis Perdaudin '08	♟ 4
● Roero Sudisfà '04	♟♟♟ 6
● Roero Sudisfà '03	♟♟♟ 6
● Barbera d'Alba Bertu '06	♟♟ 5
● Barbera d'Alba Nicolon '06	♟♟ 4
O Roero Arneis '07	♟♟ 4
O Roero Arneis Perdaudin '07	♟♟ 4
● Roero Prachiosso '05	♟♟ 5
● Roero Sudisfà Ris. '05	♟♟ 6

Wine	Rating
● Gattinara Vign. Molsino '04	♟♟ 6
● Coste della Sesia Spanna '05	♟♟ 4
● Gattinara '03	♟♟ 5
● Gattinara Podere dei Ginepri '01	♟♟♟ 6
● Gattinara Vign. Molsino '00	♟♟♟ 6
● Gattinara '00	♟♟ 5*
● Gattinara Podere dei Ginepri '03	♟♟ 6
● Gattinara Vign. Molsino '03	♟♟ 6
● Gattinara Vign. Molsino '01	♟♟ 6

Andrea Oberto

B.TA SIMANE, 11
12064 LA MORRA [CN]
TEL. 017350104
obertoandrea@libero.it

CELLAR SALES
PRE-BOOKED VISITS

ANNUAL PRODUCTION 100,000 bottles
HECTARES UNDER VINE 16
VITICULTURE METHOD Conventional

Andrea and Fabio Oberto's wines are distinctive, especially when young, for their remarkable exuberance. Vigorous, fruity and structured, they come from well cared-for grapes harvested for excellence. This sums up the profile of this range, along with a certain assertive note of oak. Particular feathers in the winery's cap are the impressive Barolo selections and the innovative Barbera Giada. The beautifully positioned winery enjoys a very attractive view.

The Three Glass '05 Barolo from the prestigious Brunate cru has a broad, well-defined nose with very subtle, complex aromas of dried flowers and red berries, backed up by a compact, seductively full palate. Only slightly less stylish is the Vigneto Albarella '05 with meaty aromas of cinchona, tobacco and dried flowers and a powerful palate refreshed by enjoyable acidity. The Rocche dell'Annunziata '05 is quite subtle but marked by oak which, although elegant, is always evident. The rest of the range is excellent, especially the complex Barbera Giada '06, while we'll have to taste the '06 Langhe Fabio next year.

Oddero

FRAZ. SANTA MARIA
VIA TETTI, 28
12064 LA MORRA [CN]
TEL. 017350618
www.oddero.it

CELLAR SALES
PRE-BOOKED VISITS

ANNUAL PRODUCTION 110,000 bottles
HECTARES UNDER VINE 35
VITICULTURE METHOD Conventional

With over 35 hectares of vineyards, just under half planted to nebbiolo for Barolo, Oddero is one of Langhe's largest wineries. But it's not just about numbers. The estate's vineyards portfolio includes plots in Villero and Rocche in Castiglione Falletto, Brunate in La Morra, Mondoca di Bussia Soprana in Monforte and Vigna Rionda in Serralunga, all grands crus interpreted in a dry, sophisticated idiom achieved by skilful use of large and small oak barrels. This is the signature style created by Mariacristina and Mariavittoria Oddero, who run the business today.

The extraordinary results obtained by Oddero this year can be described in a few words. The Three Glasses awarded are simply the tip of the large iceberg carrying all the Barolo selections to success. The Bussia Soprana Vigna Mondoca '04 has an almost enigmatic charm with its hint of sweetness and generous mineral-driven energy. Tobacco, pencil lead, coffee powder usher in a very youthful palate of great depth. Rocche di Castiglione '05 is hews to the almost Burgundyesque features of the vineyard and the '05 Villero does nothing to conceal its customary brooding power.

● Barolo Vign. Brunate '05	♟♟♟ 8
● Barolo Vign. Albarella '05	♟♟ 8
● Barbera d'Alba Bricco San Giuseppe '08	♟♟ 4
● Barbera d'Alba Giada '06	♟♟ 6
● Barolo '05	♟♟ 7
● Barolo Vign. Rocche dell'Annunziata '05	♟♟ 8
● Dolcetto d'Alba Vign. Vantrino Albarella '08	♟♟ 4
● Langhe Nebbiolo '08	♟♟ 4
● Barbera d'Alba '08	♟ 4
● Dolcetto d'Alba '08	♟ 4
● Barbera d'Alba Giada '00	♟♟♟ 6
● Barbera d'Alba Giada '97	♟♟♟ 6
● Barbera d'Alba Giada '96	♟♟♟ 6
● Barolo Vign. Albarella '01	♟♟♟ 8
● Barolo Vign. Rocche dell'Annunziata '96	♟♟♟ 8

● Barolo Mondoca di Bussia Soprana '04	♟♟♟ 8
● Barolo Brunate '05	♟♟ 8
● Barolo Mondoca di Bussia Soprana '05	♟♟ 8
● Barolo Rocche di Castiglione '05	♟♟ 8
● Barolo Villero '05	♟♟ 7
● Barbera d'Asti Vinchio '07	♟♟ 4
● Barolo '05	♟♟ 6
● Langhe Nebbiolo '07	♟♟ 4
○ Moscato d'Asti '08	♟♟ 4
● Barbera d'Alba '07	♟ 4
● Dolcetto d'Alba '08	♟ 4
○ Langhe Bianco '08	♟ 4
● Langhe Furesté '08	♟ 4

Tenuta Olim Bauda

VIA PRATA, 50
14045 INCISA SCAPACCINO [AT]
TEL. 0141702171
www.tenutaolimbauda.it

CELLAR SALES
PRE-BOOKED VISITS

ANNUAL PRODUCTION 150,000 bottles
HECTARES UNDER VINE 27
VITICULTURE METHOD Conventional

The winery, established in the 1960s, is run today by the latest generation of the Bertolino family, siblings Diana, Dino and Gianni, and in recent years has achieved heights of excellence, becoming a benchmark for the Nizza wine scene. The vineyards, some planted back in the 1950s, are situated in Nizza Monferrato, Isola d'Asti, Fontanile and Castelnuovo Calcea. The Bertolino family is helped in vineyard and winery by agronomist Federico Curtaz and oenologist Giuseppe Caviola.

The Bertolinos' passion has paid off with Three Glasses for Barbera d'Asti Superiore Nizza '06 and its balsam, tobacco, quinine and cherry aromas. Rich yet fresh on the palate, it finishes deep, long and consistent. Barbera d'Asti Superiore Le Rocchette '07 has earthy aromas and dark berry fruit, leading to a dynamic, mineral, full-bodied, fruity palate. It also made the finals. We loved the rounded, elegant Piemonte Chardonnay I Boschi '07, which has nicely gauged power, and the supple, fresh Moscato d'Asti Centive '08. The spicy Barbera d'Asti La Villa '08, with ripe red berry fruit, quinine and rain-soaked earth, is first-rate.

Orsolani

VIA MICHELE CHIESA, 12
10090 SAN GIORGIO CANAVESE [TO]
TEL. 012432386
www.orsolani.it

CELLAR SALES
PRE-BOOKED VISITS

ANNUAL PRODUCTION 150,000 bottles
HECTARES UNDER VINE 20
VITICULTURE METHOD Conventional

The story of the Orsolani family could be summed up as a glorious erbaluce-inspired quest. Gian Luigi is heir to a tradition going back to the 1800s, which over the last 40 years has dictated developments for the main Canavese variety: early experiments with sparkling winemaking in the 1960s, the idea of a dry vineyard selection for ageing, and limiting the oxidative tendency of wines made with sun-dried grapes. Today, the company focuses its efforts on 20 hectares of morainic hillslopes with sandy, clayey and pebbly soils.

It's good to see Caluso Passito Sulé back with Three Glasses. The vibrant, old gold '04 has an intense nose, beautifully playing the freshness of dried fruit off against walnut and espresso coffee notes from oxidation. It packs a punch on the palate but retains an enviable sweetness-acidity balance. We also liked Erbaluce di Caluso La Rustia '08, aged in stainless steel, which gives a timid bouquet offset by a stylish, flavoursome palate. Just a touch too much butteriness holds back the Caluso Vignot Sant'Antonio '07 while the Caluso Spumante Brut Cuvée Tradizione Gran Riserva '04 is as reliable as ever.

● Barbera d'Asti Sup. Nizza '06	🍷🍷🍷 6
● Barbera d'Asti Sup. Le Rocchette '07	🍷🍷 5
● Barbera d'Asti La Villa '08	🍷🍷 4*
○ Moscato d'Asti Centive '08	🍷🍷 4*
○ Piemonte Chardonnay I Boschi '07	🍷🍷 4*
○ Gavi del Comune di Gavi '08	🍷 4
● Barbera d'Asti La Villa '07	🍷🍷 4
● Barbera d'Asti Sup. Le Rocchette '06	🍷🍷 5
● Barbera d'Asti Sup. Nizza '05	🍷🍷 5
○ Moscato d'Asti Centive '07	🍷🍷 4
○ Piemonte Chardonnay I Boschi '06	🍷🍷 4
○ Piemonte Moscato Passito S. Giovanni '03	🍷🍷 6

○ Caluso Passito Sulé '04	🍷🍷🍷 6
○ Erbaluce di Caluso La Rustia '08	🍷🍷 4*
○ Caluso Bianco Vignot S. Antonio '07	🍷🍷 5
○ Caluso Spumante Brut Cuvée Tradizione Gran Ris. '04	🍷🍷 6
● Canavese Rosso Acini Sparsi '07	🍷 4
○ Caluso Passito Sulé '98	🍷🍷🍷 6
○ Caluso Bianco Vignot S. Antonio '06	🍷🍷 5
○ Caluso Passito Sulé '02	🍷🍷 6
○ Caluso Spumante Brut Cuvée Tradizione Gran Ris. '03	🍷🍷 6
○ Caluso Spumante Brut Gran Ris. '99	🍷🍷 6
○ Erbaluce di Caluso Passito Sulé '01	🍷🍷 8
○ Erbaluce di Caluso Vignot S. Antonio '04	🍷🍷 5

Pace

FRAZ. MADONNA DI LORETO
CASCINA PACE, 52
12043 CANALE [CN]
TEL. 0173979544
aziendapace@infinito.it

CELLAR SALES
PRE-BOOKED VISITS

ANNUAL PRODUCTION 40,000 bottles
HECTARES UNDER VINE 20
VITICULTURE METHOD Organic certified

The winery of brothers Dino and Pietro Negri is a solid Roero family business, and also a fairly large one. It started out some generations back by selling grapes and then producing unbottled wine. The business then changed direction, as it started to bottle wine and focus on quality, with evident success. The wines, based on arneis, barbera and nebbiolo, are typical of Roero and are produced with the help of the oenologist Lorenzo Quinterno.

It was a good year for Dino and Pietro, even if in we expected more progress with quality. The elegant, complex nose of the Roero Arneis '08 shows damson and apple-led white-fleshed fruit leading to a weighty, structured palate and a satisfyingly long, fresh finish. The Barbera d'Alba '07, with cocoa powder and plum notes, is still a touch too woody, but has good structure on a generous, tannin-rich, nicely acidic palate. Barbera d'Alba Superiore Carolina '06 is juicy and refreshing but rustic, and shows slightly blurred tannins. It merely passed muster, as did the Langhe Nebbiolo '07, which has complex structure but is a little too alcoholic for its type.

Paitin

LOC. BRICCO
VIA SERRA BOELLA, 20
12052 NEIVE [CN]
TEL. 017367343
www.paitin.it

CELLAR SALES
PRE-BOOKED VISITS

ANNUAL PRODUCTION 60,000 bottles
HECTARES UNDER VINE 17
VITICULTURE METHOD Naturale

The attractive, reliable winery of the Pasquero Elia family is even better known abroad than in Italy. It's a consistent performer, and has rightly earned admiration and respect in Barbaresco. Going back to taste a Sorì Paitin Vecchie Vigne '99, you sense all the cellar's dedication to quality over the years. Already appealing in their youth, the estate's wines express remarkable complexity and depth after a period of bottle ageing..

Barbaresco Sorì Paitin '06 gives concentrated aromas, with quinine and dry herbs enveloped in refreshing balsamic oak. On the highly seductive palate the marked tannins are pleasant, not too dry, and promise excellent development. Even better was the impenetrably dark Langhe Paitin '07, with tobacco and black berry fruit. The confident, spicy, full flavoured palate shows excellent length. We found pleasant cherry and vegetal notes on Barbera Campolive '07, which was intense, alcoholic and potent. Nebbiolo Ca Veja '07 opens on complex eucalyptus and tobacco nuances, followed by a stiff palate built on solid tannins.

● Barbera d'Alba '07	♟♟ 3*
○ Roero Arneis '08	♟♟ 4*
● Barbera d'Alba Sup. Carolina '06	♟ 5
● Langhe Nebbiolo '07	♟ 3
● Roero Ris. '06	♟ 5
● Barbera d'Alba Sup. '06	♟♟ 5
○ Roero Arneis '07	♟♟ 4*
● Roero Ris. '05	♟♟ 5

● Barbaresco Sorì Paitin '06	♟♟ 6
● Langhe Paitin '07	♟♟ 4
● Barbera d'Alba Campolive '07	♟♟ 5
● Dolcetto d'Alba Sorì Paitin '08	♟♟ 4
● Nebbiolo d'Alba Ca Veja '07	♟♟ 5
● Barbera d'Alba Serra Boella '08	♟ 4
○ Langhe Arneis Elisa '08	♟ 4
● Barbaresco Sorì Paitin '04	♟♟♟ 6
● Barbaresco Sorì Paitin Vecchie Vigne '04	♟♟♟ 8
● Barbaresco Sorì Paitin Vecchie Vigne '01	♟♟♟ 8
● Barbaresco Sorì Paitin '05	♟♟ 6
● Barbaresco Sorì Paitin Vecchie Vigne '03	♟♟ 8
● Barbera d'Alba Campolive '06	♟♟ 5*

Armando Parusso

LOC. BUSSIA, 55
12065 MONFORTE D'ALBA [CN]
TEL. 017378257
www.parusso.com

CELLAR SALES
PRE-BOOKED VISITS

ANNUAL PRODUCTION **120,000 bottles**
HECTARES UNDER VINE **23**
VITICULTURE METHOD **Naturale**

Marco Parusso runs this important winery in the Langhe region with his sister Tiziana. The winery is particularly well equipped and functional, and serves an estate which boasts some of the best terroirs in the entire zone. As usual, the range of wines presented is wide enough to satisfy all tastes. Until recently, the wines tended to be a little too modern but now seem to have achieved fine stylistic harmony and balance.

The magnificent Barolo Vigna Rocche Riserva '99 is exuberant and intense, with prominent coffee cream, tobacco and raspberry. The palate shows good body, with subtle tannins, pronounced pulp and pleasing overall softness. To celebrate the winery's 35th anniversary, in 2005 the Parusso family decided to blend the various Barolo selections and produce a single wine. Trentacinquesima Annata is well styled, with dried flowers, smoke and red fruit. The tannins are slightly rugged but the palate is impressively long. The straightforward Dolcetto '08 is lively and acidulous. The '08 Barbera is a slightly more complex easy drinker.

Massimo Pastura
Cascina Ghersa

VIA SAN GIUSEPPE, 19
14050 MOASCA [AT]
TEL. 0141856012
www.laghersa.it

CELLAR SALES
PRE-BOOKED VISITS

ANNUAL PRODUCTION **185,000 bottles**
HECTARES UNDER VINE **22**
VITICULTURE METHOD **Conventional**

Established in 1935, Cascina Ghersa has in recent years undergone a complete change and now focuses solely on the production of quality wines, in particular barbera, which occupies most of the estate's vineyards. Over the last two years, development has stepped up with the creation of a new line named after the young owner Massimo Pastura, which includes wines representing some of the region's most interesting DOC zones.

Massimo Pastura gave us some fine Barberas, plus an interesting Timorasso. The elegant Barbera d'Asti Superiore Muascae '06 shows balance and nice fruit. As ever, Barbera d'Asti Superiore Camparò '07 is solid, lingering and well structured while Barbera d'Asti Superiore Nizza Vignassa '06 brims with spice and quinine over a rich, fruity palate. Colli Tortonesi Timorasso Timian '07 gives petrol and grapefruit, a generous palate and good character on the finish. The fruity, spicy Barbera d'Asti Superiore Le Cave '06 is well made as is Piemonte Barbera Piagé '08, with sweetish but appealing fruit, and the pleasant, damson-themed Monferrato Bianco Sivoy '08.

● Barolo Bussia V. Rocche Ris. '99	▼▼ 8
● Barolo Trentacinquesima Annata '05	▼▼ 7
○ Langhe Bianco '08	▼▼ 4
● Langhe Nebbiolo '07	▼▼ 5
● Barbera d'Alba Ornati '08	▼ 5
● Dolcetto d'Alba Piani Noci '08	▼ 4
● Barbera d'Alba Sup. '00	▼▼▼ 6
● Barolo Bussia V. Munie '99	▼▼▼ 8
● Barolo Bussia V. Munie '97	▼▼▼ 8
● Barolo Bussia V. Munie '96	▼▼▼ 8
● Barolo Le Coste Mosconi '03	▼▼▼ 8
● Barolo Vecchie Vigne in Mariondino Ris. '99	▼▼▼ 8
● Langhe Rosso Bricco Rovella '96	▼▼▼ 6
● Barolo Le Coste Mosconi '04	▼▼ 8
● Barolo Mariondino '04	▼▼ 7

● Barbera d'Asti Sup. Camparò '07	▼▼ 4*
● Barbera d'Asti Sup. Muascae Massimo Pastura '06	▼▼ 7
● Barbera d'Asti Sup. Nizza Vignassa '06	▼▼ 5
○ Colli Tortonesi Timorasso Timian Massimo Pastura '07	▼▼ 5
● Barbera d'Asti Sup. Le Cave Massimo Pastura '06	▼ 4
○ Gavi Il Poggio Massimo Pastura '08	▼ 4
○ M.to Bianco Piagé '08	▼ 4
○ M.to Bianco Sivoy '08	▼ 4
● Piemonte Barbera Piagé '08	▼ 3
● Barbera d'Asti Sup. Camparò '06	▼▼ 4*
● Barbera d'Asti Sup. Muascae Massimo Pastura '04	▼▼ 7
● Barbera d'Asti Sup. Nizza Vignassa '05	▼▼ 5

Agostino Pavia e Figli

FRAZ. BOLOGNA, 33
14041 AGLIANO TERME [AT]
TEL. 0141954125
www.agostinopavia.it

CELLAR SALES
PRE-BOOKED VISITS
VISITOR FACILITIES

ANNUAL PRODUCTION **75,000 bottles**
HECTARES UNDER VINE **9**
VITICULTURE METHOD **Conventional**

The winery run by Agostino Pavia and his sons, Mauro and Giuseppe, has witnessed constant improvement over recent years and what it lacks in size, it makes up for in dedication. In a particularly good area for barbera, the Pavia family has vineyards over 50 years old, extending all around the farmhouse. The soil is mostly sand and clay, with some marly-clayey sections. The vines are Guyot-trained with a planting density of around 4,000 to 4,500 plants per hectare.

The 2006 is one of the best versions ever of Barbera d'Asti Superiore La Marescialla, with a vibrant, complex nose of tobacco, cherry, spices and dark berry fruit. The palate shows harmony and fullness, with a long, characterful finish where acidity and pulp dominate. Also good were the rounded, succulent Barbera d'Asti Superiore Moliss '06; the Grignolino d'Asti '08, with a rugged personality typical of the variety; and the elegant, dynamic Monferrato Rosso Talin '06, with spice and tobacco layered over a fruit backdrop. The cherry and plum Barbera d'Asti Blina '07 is well typed but overly alcoholic.

● Barbera d'Asti Sup. La Marescialla '06	▼▼	5
● Barbera d'Asti Sup. Moliss '06	▼▼	4
● Grignolino d'Asti '08	▼▼	3*
● M.to Rosso Talin '06	▼▼	4
● Barbera d'Asti Bricco Blina '07	▼	4
● Barbera d'Asti Sup. La Marescialla '05	♀♀	5
● Barbera d'Asti Sup. La Marescialla '04	♀♀	4

★ Pecchenino

B.TA VALDIBERTI, 59
12063 DOGLIANI [CN]
TEL. 017370686
www.pecchenino.com

CELLAR SALES
PRE-BOOKED VISITS
VISITOR FACILITIES

ANNUAL PRODUCTION **90,000 bottles**
HECTARES UNDER VINE **25**
VITICULTURE METHOD **Conventional**

Not content with having made a name for themselves internationally as the stars of Dolcetto di Dogliani, the Pecchenino brothers, Attilio and Orlando, have recently begun to apply their skills to Barolo. The results have already received important accolades in the American press. The 30,000 bottles of Dogliani Sirì d'Jermu nevertheless remain the winery's forte, thanks to its polish and elegance, qualities which are rarely achieved with this difficult variety.

The exceptional Barolo Le Coste '05 rightly took home Three Glasses. This elegant, balsamic, flowery Barolo shows an austere, powerful palate underpinned by textbook acidity and tannins. The more modern, less concentrated San Giuseppe '05 is still hemmed in by oak. Nebbiolo Vigna Botti '07 also performed well. The Sirì d'Jermu '07 was, as always, the epitome of elegance. The blackcurrant, cocoa powder and bitter almond nose leads to a complex, well-orchestrated palate for a Dogliani of great class. We also loved Dogliani Bricco Botti, kept back for three years after the harvest, which exude charm and velvet smoothness. Overall, the results were excellent.

● Barolo Le Coste '05	▼▼▼	7
● Dogliani Bricco Botti '06	▼▼	5*
● Dogliani Sirì d'Jermu '07	▼▼	5*
● Langhe Nebbiolo V. Botti '07	▼▼	5
● Barbera d'Alba Quass '07	▼▼	5
● Barolo S. Giuseppe '05	▼▼	7
● Dolcetto di Dogliani S. Luigi '08	▼▼	4
○ Langhe V. Maestro '08	▼▼	5
● Dogliani Sirì d'Jermu '06	♀♀♀	5
● Dolcetto di Dogliani Sup. Bricco Botti '04	♀♀♀	5
● Barbera d'Alba Quass '05	♀♀	5
● Barolo Le Coste '04	♀♀	7
● Dogliani Bricco Botti '05	♀♀	5
● Dogliani Sirì d'Jermu '05	♀♀	5

Pelissero

VIA FERRERE, 10
12050 TREISO [CN]
TEL. 0173638430
www.pelissero.com

CELLAR SALES
PRE-BOOKED VISITS

ANNUAL PRODUCTION **250,000 bottles**
HECTARES UNDER VINE **35**
VITICULTURE METHOD **Conventional**

This dynamic, well established Langhe cellar, well known in Italy and abroad, continues to pursue quality with determination and clear ideas. The large estate lets the cellar select and make the most of the splendid local grapes. The wines presented often impress with their temperament and interpretative originality, demonstrating character as well as great ageing potential.

Barbaresco Vanotu '06 earned Three Glasses, with intense coffee cream aromas from toasted wood over raspberries, tobacco and spice. The rich, succulent, highly supple palate boasts a long, focused finish. The appealing Nubiola '06 brims with red berry fruit against cocoa powder and tobacco. The convincing palate is lively, with well-sustained, well-behaved tannins. The modern Long Now '07, a 50-50 blend of nebbiolo and barbera, impresses with black and red berry fruit powering through on the nose, offset by cocoa powder and sweet spice. It lacks some personality on the palate but is still highly enjoyable.

● Barbaresco Vanotu '06	￦￦￦	8
● Barbaresco Nubiola '06	￦	6
● Barbaresco Tulin '06	￦￦	7
● Barbera d'Alba Piani '08	￦￦	4
● Dolcetto d'Alba Augenta '08	￦￦	4
● Langhe Nebbiolo '08	￦￦	5
● Langhe Rosso Long Now '07	￦￦	6
● Dolcetto d'Alba Munfrina '08	￦	4
○ Langhe Favorita Le Nature '08	￦	3
● Langhe Freisa Le Nature '08	￦	3
● Barbaresco Vanotu '01	￦￦￦	8
● Barbaresco Vanotu '99	￦￦￦	8
● Langhe Rosso Long Now '06	￦￦	6

Cascina Pellerino

LOC. SANT'ANNA, 93
12040 MONTEU ROERO [CN]
TEL. 0173978171
www.cascinapellerino.com

CELLAR SALES
PRE-BOOKED VISITS

ANNUAL PRODUCTION **85,000 bottles**
HECTARES UNDER VINE **10**
VITICULTURE METHOD **Conventional**

Cascina Pellerino is currently in the hands of Cristiano Bono and Roberto Ghione. While Cristiano takes care of the vineyard and winery, Roberto deals with the business side of things. Over the years, the two partners have worked hard to expand and diversify their range, without losing sight of their fundamental goal of producing quality wines. Cascina Pellerino's vineyards are situated in the municipalities of Canale, Monteu Roero, Santo Stefano Roero and Vezza d'Alba.

Look no further for a fine Roero than the vibrant, intense Vicot '06, with bags of red berry fruit and subtle quinine, although still muffled by oak. Lovely fruit and a long finish wind up a stylish palate that lacks just a little character. But the whole range is solid. The leisurely Roero Arneis Desiré '08 has damson and spring flowers while Barbera d'Alba Diletta '07 shows tobacco, quinine and cherry while Barbera d'Alba Gran Madre '07 vaunts cinnamon and vanilla spice, and although a touch oaky, has gorgeous fruit. Nebbiolo d'Alba Denise '06 gives aromas of liquorice and dried flowers, and somewhat rugged tannins, but good acid freshness.

● Roero Vicot '06	￦￦	6
● Barbera d'Alba Diletta '07	￦￦	4*
● Barbera d'Alba Sup. Gran Madre '07	￦￦	6
● Nebbiolo d'Alba Denise '06	￦￦	5
○ Roero Arneis Desiré '08	￦￦	4*
○ Felizia Brut	￦	5
○ Langhe Favorita Lorena '08	￦	4
○ Roero Arneis Boneur '08	￦	4
● Barbera d'Alba Diletta '06	￦￦	4*
● Barbera d'Alba Sup. Gran Madre '06	￦￦	5
● Barbera d'Alba Sup. Gran Madre '05	￦￦	5
● Langhe Rosso René '06	￦￦	6
● Roero André '06	￦￦	4*
○ Roero Arneis Boneur '07	￦￦	4*
● Roero Leoni '04	￦￦	6
● Roero Vicot '05	￦￦	5

Elio Perrone

S.DA SAN MARTINO, 3BIS
12053 CASTIGLIONE TINELLA [CN]
TEL. 0141855803
www.elioperrone.it

PRE-BOOKED VISITS

ANNUAL PRODUCTION **150,000 bottles**
HECTARES UNDER VINE **12**
VITICULTURE METHOD **Conventional**

This interesting family winery in the Asti area of Langhe could be summed up in a few words: unfaltering quality, a distinctive, highly personal estate style and fair prices. The cellar's vocation for Moscato extends to a consistently first-rate selection of Barberas, and the range intelligently focuses on a limited number of wines. In passing, we should also mention the extremely attractive labels, an extra point in the cellar's favour in a market where the plethora of products can lead to consumer confusion.

The wine that most impressed us was Mongovone, from the fine '07 harvest, which shows off the qualities of the barbera grape like few others. This version combines depth and a complex nose of plum and bitter chocolate with harmony on the palate. Richness of flavour, alternating with acidity and sustained by generous pulp make for a stimulating tipple. The confident, approachable Sourgal '08 cuts a fine figure, embodying the essence of Moscato. On the one hand, it's refined and aristocratic, with aromas of candied lemon peel and pineapple, and on the other, vivacious and well-orchestrated, with refreshing acidity.

Le Piane

LOC. LE PIANE
VIA CERRI, 10
28010 BOCA [NO]
TEL. 3483354185
www.bocapiane.com

CELLAR SALES
PRE-BOOKED VISITS

ANNUAL PRODUCTION **25,000 bottles**
HECTARES UNDER VINE **7**
VITICULTURE METHOD **Conventional**

The story of Cristoph Künzli is one of the most heart-wrenching in the Piedmont wine world. Originally a wine importer in Switzerland, in the early 1990s he fell in love with the landscape of the Monte Fenere Natural Park, and dreamed of setting up a winery here with his friend, the oenologist Alexander Trolf. This led to a meeting with Antonio Cerri, an elderly grower from Boca, and the purchase of his old vineyards in Montalbano and Campo Le Piane. Sadly, Alexander then died. But this small winery is now a fully-fledged member of the Italy's wine elite.

The meaty, hot and spicy Boca '05 Le Piane, from 85 per cent nebbiolo, is simply breathtaking. With three years' ageing in large barrels, it masterfully marries power and sharpness in a kaleidoscope of oriental spices. In some ways, it's reminiscent of the great Rhône wines. This is no coincidence, since the geological makeup of its hillside home includes porphyry with a gravelly topsoil, very similar to the conditions found in the Côte-Rôtie. Colline Novaresi Le Piane '07 is being kept back until next year but we were very impressed with the Colline Novaresi La Maggiorina '08, from nebbiolo, croatina, vespolina and uva rara.

● Barbera d'Asti Sup. Mongovone '07	♟♟	6
● Barbera d'Asti Tasmorcan '08	♟♟	4
○ Clartè '08	♟♟	4
○ Moscato d'Asti Sourgal '08	♟♟	4
● Bigarò '08	♟	4
● Barbera d'Asti Grivò '06	♟♟	4*
● Barbera d'Asti Sup. Mongovone '06	♟♟	6
● Barbera d'Asti Sup. Mongovone '04	♟♟	6
● Barbera d'Asti Tasmorcan '07	♟♟	4*
○ Moscato d'Asti Clarté '06	♟♟	4*
○ Moscato d'Asti Sourgal '07	♟♟	4*

● Boca '05	♟♟♟	7
● Colline Novaresi La Maggiorina '08	♟♟	4*
● Boca '04	♟♟♟	7
● Boca '03	♟♟♟	7
● Boca '01	♟♟	7
● Colline Novaresi Le Piane '06	♟♟	6

Pio Cesare

VIA CESARE BALBO, 6
12051 ALBA [CN]
TEL. 0173440386
www.piocesare.it

PRE-BOOKED VISITS

ANNUAL PRODUCTION 400,000 bottles
HECTARES UNDER VINE 52
VITICULTURE METHOD Conventional

This historic, prestigious Alba winery, established way back in 1881, invariably offers technically impeccable, traditionally styled wines, whose ageing potential can be surprising but which are also sometimes difficult to gauge when young. Their forte is great reds, above all Barolo and Barbaresco, which perfectly embody their terroir. The bottles are widely exported and are great ambassadors for Langhe wine.

Barolo Ornato '05, produced using grapes from the Ornato vineyard in Serralunga, was on fine form this year. This solid, concentrated red has tight-knit tannins and good ageing prospects. The '05 is one of the best versions ever, and has recovered the varietal character missing in other years. We also liked Barbaresco Il Bricco '05, which has more finesse than past versions, and the textbook Barolo '05, which will hit top form after another few years in bottle. Barbaresco '05 was supple and uncomplicated, and the rest of the wines are all well-made, particularly the spot-on Barbera d'Alba '07 and the fragrant white Arneis '08.

● Barolo Ornato '05	♥♥♥	8
● Barbaresco Il Bricco '05	♥♥	8
● Barolo '05	♥♥	8
● Barbaresco '05	♥♥	8
● Barbera d'Alba '07	♥♥	6
○ Langhe Arneis '08	♥♥	4*
● Nebbiolo d'Alba '06	♥	5
● Barbaresco Il Bricco '97	♈♈♈	8
● Barolo Ornato '89	♈♈♈	8
● Barolo Ornato '85	♈♈♈	8
● Barbaresco Il Bricco '04	♈♈	8
● Barbaresco Il Bricco '01	♈♈	8
● Barolo Ornato '04	♈♈	8
● Barolo Ornato '01	♈♈	8
● Barolo Ornato '00	♈♈	8

Pioiero

CASCINA PIOIERO, 1
12040 VEZZA D'ALBA [CN]
TEL. 017365492
www.pioiero.com

CELLAR SALES
PRE-BOOKED VISITS

ANNUAL PRODUCTION 30,000 bottles
HECTARES UNDER VINE 5.4
VITICULTURE METHOD Conventional

The rows of Rabino family vines stand around an attractive farmhouse. This small yet busy winery has invested in quality over the years and the varieties are local classics: arneis, favorita, barbera and nebbiolo. The Rabino family champions a traditional approach, aimed at pinpointing and exploiting the distinctive traits of local varieties and making the most of their expressive potential.

The range of wines presented this year was somewhat limited but still good and well crafted. The Nebbiolo d'Alba '07 shows intense, refined aromas with raspberry, tobacco and quinine to the fore. Vibrant, elegant and fairly complex on the palate, it gives generous flesh and backbone but overly rough tannins in the finish. The flowery Roero Arneis '08 is stylishly elegant, with white-fleshed fruit on the nose and a slightly mineral palate showing good freshness despite evident residual sugar. Last off, the Barbera d'Alba '08 is enjoyable and fruity.

● Nebbiolo d'Alba '07	♥♥	4*
○ Roero Arneis '08	♥♥	3*
● Barbera d'Alba '08	♥	3
○ Langhe Favorita '08	♥	3
● Barbera d'Alba '06	♈♈	3*
● Barbera d'Alba Sup. '05	♈♈	4*
● Roero '06	♈♈	4*
○ Roero Arneis '07	♈♈	3*

Luigi Pira

VIA XX SETTEMBRE, 9
12050 SERRALUNGA D'ALBA [CN]
TEL. 0173613106

CELLAR SALES
PRE-BOOKED VISITS

ANNUAL PRODUCTION **50,000 bottles**
HECTARES UNDER VINE **10**
VITICULTURE METHOD **Conventional**

This small, prestigious winery, run by Gianpaolo and Romolo Pira, became famous in the USA before it did in Italy, thanks to the extremely good reviews received by the brothers' Barolo. Credit goes not only to the splendid positions of the vineyards at Serralunga but also to the winemaking techniques, which play their part in producing highly polished, full-bodied wines. Remarkably self-assured on the nose, they display marked hints of oak, which fade after a few years' ageing.

Barolo Vigna Margheria '05 gave a superb performance, with spice layered over quinine and tobacco leading to a complex palate, still overpowered by roughish tannins. The Barolo Vigna Rionda '05 also performs well, with its elegant aromas of coffee cream and raspberry introducing a powerful fruit-laced palate with plenty of extract that ensures excellent ageing potential. The '05 Vigna Marenca is not on its usual outstanding form, and is still stifled by oak. The fruity, alcoholic Barbera '07 is well made. Nebbiolo '07 has graceful aromas of raspberry, dried herbs and tobacco, and shows soft and lingering in the mouth.

● Barolo V. Margheria '05	♟♟	7
● Barolo V. Rionda '05	♟♟	8
● Barbera d'Alba '07	♟♟	5
● Barolo '05	♟♟	7
● Barolo V. Marenca '05	♟♟	8
● Dolcetto d'Alba '08	♟♟	4
● Langhe Nebbiolo '07	♟♟	5
● Barolo V. Marenca '01	♟♟♟	8
● Barolo V. Marenca '97	♟♟♟	8
● Barolo V. Rionda '04	♟♟♟	8
● Barolo V. Rionda '00	♟♟♟	8

E. Pira & Figli

VIA VITTORIO VENETO, 1
12060 BAROLO [CN]
TEL. 017356247
www.pira-chiaraboschis.com

CELLAR SALES
PRE-BOOKED VISITS

ANNUAL PRODUCTION **20,000 bottles**
HECTARES UNDER VINE **3.5**
VITICULTURE METHOD **Organic certified**

We will need to be patient to taste the new wine from Chiara Boschis, a Barolo from a small plot in the Conterni subzone of Monforte d'Alba, not far from the Ginestra vineyard. But wine is not the only string to Chiara's bow. She is part of a group of enthusiasts who have decided to relaunch production of one of Piedmont's most famous cheeses, Castelmagno. This intelligent, able woman is clearly not short of energy or entrepreneurial spirit. She is even thinking of including larger barrels in her cellar stock.

The bad news is that hail wiped out the '08 Dolcetto so only three wines were presented. The Barbera '07, from an excellent year for the variety, shows a fragrant morello cherry nose, followed by a juicy, fleshy, potent and lingering palate with good typing. The Barolo Via Nuova '05 still has a hint of oak on the nose and elegant, close-woven tannins, with superb juice, length and energy. The Cannubi '05 aged mainly in new oak and proffers the earthy, liquorice aromatics that are typical of the vineyard. The lingering, well-orchestrated palate shows that this is an incredibly traditional yet modern Three Glass wine.

● Barolo Cannubi '05	♟♟♟	8
● Barbera d'Alba '07	♟♟	6
● Barolo Via Nuova '05	♟♟	8
● Barolo Cannubi '00	♟♟♟	8
● Barbera d'Alba '06	♟♟	6
● Barolo Cannubi '04	♟♟	8
● Barolo Cannubi '03	♟♟	8
● Barolo Via Nuova '03	♟♟	8
● Barolo Via Nuova '01	♟♟	8

Poderi Colla

LOC. SAN ROCCO SENO D'ELVIO, 82
12051 ALBA [CN]
TEL. 0173290148
www.podericolla.it

PRE-BOOKED VISITS

ANNUAL PRODUCTION 150,000 bottles
HECTARES UNDER VINE 27
VITICULTURE METHOD Conventional

Poderi Colla's strict style policy is based on a classic, traditional approach, not so much in terms of the types of wines, since they have just brought out an attractive, characterful rosé, as in the working methods. Here, you will find only large barrels and long maceration, and wines with excellent flesh but not too heavy on extract, and with textbook varietal aromas.

The fine Bussia vineyard provides Barolo Dardi Le Rose '05, with dried rose-petal aromas over a thrusting palate that will unfold over the coming years. The sound, bright-hued Barbaresco Roncaglie '06, from a vineyard worth visiting for its spectacular views, shows raspberries and good flesh. Thanks to a good '06, the fine, drinkable Bricco del Drago, from 85 per cent dolcetto and 15 per cent nebbiolo, cuts an austere figure with juniper on the nose. Good fruit and alcohol mark out the simple, appealing Barbera '07. From the whites, look out for the well-managed Sanrocco '08, from pinot nero, chardonnay and riesling renano, and the focused Riesling '08.

Paolo Poggio

VIA ROMA, 67
15050 BRIGNANO FRASCATA [AL]
TEL. 0131784929
cantinapoggio@tiscali.it

CELLAR SALES
PRE-BOOKED VISITS

ANNUAL PRODUCTION 17,000 bottles
HECTARES UNDER VINE 3.1
VITICULTURE METHOD Conventional

In the world of wine, it is increasingly difficult to find small wineries such as Paolo Poggio's achieving prestigious results. But professionalism and passion bear dependable, high-quality fruit and Paolo possesses both of these qualities. Although beset by a host of difficulties, he has always managed to produce excellently made wines that offer fantastic value for money.

Good examples are Barbera Campo La Bà '07 and Croatina Prosone '07, definitely one of the best selections from this variety. Both are on sale at the winery at yesterday's prices. The range of reds is rounded off again by an excellent selection of cask-conditioned Barbera Derio '06. It opens on tobacco and spice, followed by a full-bodied, powerful palate with a lingering, complex finish. The Timorasso Ronchetto '07 was a little below its usual standard and the attractive palate fails to compensate for some oxidation. The Cortese Campogallo '08 is simple and fresh.

Poderi Colla		
● Barbaresco Roncaglie '06	♀♀	7
● Barolo Bussia Dardi Le Rose '05	♀♀	7
● Langhe Bricco del Drago '06	♀♀	5
● Barbera d'Alba Costa Bruna '07	♀♀	4
○ Langhe Bianco Riesling '08	♀♀	4
○ Langhe Bianco Sanrocco '08	♀♀	4
● Nebbiolo d'Alba '07	♀♀	5
○ Pietro Colla Extra Brut	♀♀	5
● Dolcetto d'Alba Pian Balbo '08	♀	4
● Barolo Bussia Dardi Le Rose '99	♀♀♀	7
● Barolo Bussia Dardi Le Rose '04	♀♀	7
● Barolo Bussia Dardi Le Rose '01	♀♀	7

Paolo Poggio		
● Colli Tortonesi Rosso Prosone '07	♀♀	2*
● Colli Tortonesi Barbera Campo La Bà '07	♀♀	2*
● Colli Tortonesi Barbera Derio '06	♀♀	4
○ Colli Tortonesi Cortese Campogallo '08	♀	2
○ Colli Tortonesi Ronchetto '07	♀	3
● Colli Tortonesi Barbera Derio '04	♀♀	4*
● Colli Tortonesi Barbera Derio '04	♀♀	4*
○ Colli Tortonesi Ronchetto '06	♀♀	3
○ Colli Tortonesi Ronchetto '05	♀♀	3*
○ Colli Tortonesi Ronchetto '04	♀♀	3
● Colli Tortonesi Rosso Prosone '06	♀♀	2
● Colli Tortonesi Rosso Prosone '05	♀♀	2*
● Colli Tortonesi Rosso Prosone '04	♀♀	4

Pomodolce

VIA IV NOVEMBRE, 7
15050 MONTEMARZINO [AL]
TEL. 0131878135
www.pomodolce.it

CELLAR SALES
PRE-BOOKED VISITS
FOOD

ANNUAL PRODUCTION **15,000 bottles**
HECTARES UNDER VINE **4**
VITICULTURE METHOD **Organic certified**

The excellent results achieved by Silvio Davico's organic winery may seem surprising but the family has farming in the blood. Their fruit and vegetables have for years supplied the family restaurant and the vineyards yield the house wine. A turning point came a few years ago, when they had the chance to buy a better equipped winery and larger plots, allowing them to expand their range. As a result, the Croatina Fontanino, the Pomodolce flagship wine which has yet to be bottled, was joined by Barbera and Timorasso Diletto, which immediately achieved impressive scores.

This year, for the first time, Silvio brought out a selection of Timorasso, Grue '07, which earned Three Glasses at the first shot. Hydrocarbons and pear aromas usher in a complex, faintly almondy nose, paving the way for extraordinary concentration on a complex, minerally, well balanced palate. Diletto '07 is fruity with good acidity. The range is completed by the deep ruby Barbera Marsén '06 that gives forthright spiciness but still a little too much oak.

○ Colli Tortonesi Timorasso Derthona Grue '07	♈♈♈ 5
● Colli Tortonesi Barbera Marsén '06	♈♈ 5
○ Colli Tortonesi Timorasso Derthona Diletto '07	♈♈ 5
● Colli Tortonesi Barbera '05	♉♉ 4*
○ Colli Tortonesi Bianco Diletto '06	♉♉ 4
○ Colli Tortonesi Bianco Diletto '05	♉♉ 5
● Colli Tortonesi Rosso '04	♉♉ 5

Marco Porello

C.SO ALBA, 71
12043 CANALE [CN]
TEL. 0173979324
www.porellovini.it

CELLAR SALES
PRE-BOOKED VISITS

ANNUAL PRODUCTION **70,000 bottles**
HECTARES UNDER VINE **15**
VITICULTURE METHOD **Conventional**

The Porellos and wine go back a long way. Today, the company is run by Marco, a dedicated believer in hard work in the vineyard to obtain strongly terroir-led wines. The estate boasts two winemaking facilities: a modern winery at Canale, which also houses the offices, and an ageing cellar near Guarene. There are various Porello wines, all from native varieties.

The decision to give Roero Torretta an extra year's ageing was providential and the '06 deservedly notched up another Three Glasses. Balsam, red berry fruit and dried flowers make for a subtle, well-developed nose, while the juicy, savoury palate has tightly woven extract and a lingeringly fresh, fleshy finish. We also liked the varietal fruit aromas of the Barbera d'Alba Filatura '07 and its intensely sweet, seductive tobacco and spice. The powerful, palate showed juicy, dynamic tannins and a fresh, lively finish. The succulent, fruity Nebbiolo d'Alba '07, and Roero Arneis Camestrì '08, with beautifully ripe apple-like fruit, are also well made.

● Roero Torretta '06	♈♈♈ 5*
● Barbera d'Alba Filatura '07	♈♈ 5
● Nebbiolo d'Alba '07	♈♈ 4*
○ Roero Arneis Camestrì '08	♈♈ 4*
● Barbera d'Alba Mommiano '08	♈ 4
○ Langhe Favorita '08	♈ 4
● Roero Torretta '04	♉♉♉ 5
● Barbera d'Alba Filatura '06	♉♉ 5
● Barbera d'Alba Filatura '05	♉♉ 5
● Barbera d'Alba Filatura '04	♉♉ 5
● Barbera d'Alba Mommiano '07	♉♉ 4
● Nebbiolo d'Alba '06	♉♉ 4
○ Roero Arneis Camestrì '07	♉♉ 4*
● Roero Torretta '05	♉♉ 5

Ferdinando Principiano

VIA ALBA, 19
12065 MONFORTE D'ALBA [CN]
TEL. 0173787158
www.ferdinandoprincipiano.it

★ Prunotto

REG. SAN CASSIANO, 4G
12051 ALBA [CN]
TEL. 0173280017
www.prunotto.it

CELLAR SALES
PRE-BOOKED VISITS

PRE-BOOKED VISITS

ANNUAL PRODUCTION 50,000 bottles
HECTARES UNDER VINE 8.5
VITICULTURE METHOD Conventional

ANNUAL PRODUCTION 600,000 bottles
HECTARES UNDER VINE 55
VITICULTURE METHOD Conventional

The youngest generation of Langhe growers, to which Ferdinando Principiano belongs, is the future of Piedmont winemaking. Focused, uncompromising farm management and respect for the environment are the cornerstones of policy at this small yet successful winery. The style of the wines, which always require some ageing to reveal their potential, reflects the typicity and natural expression of the varieties. The rows of nebbiolo are at Serralunga, which explains their hefty tannins. Depending on the growing year, they can take some time to mellow out.

The heady, spicy Barolo Boscareto '05 shows tight-knit, well-defined tannins, offset but not overwhelmed by lovely fruity pulp, elegant oak coming in to temper the finish. The Barolo Serralunga shows elegant, pervasive aromas and, although lacking in intensity of flavour, is succulent on the palate, with appealingly well-sustained, unobtrusive tannins. Although slightly over-evolved, warm and alcoholic, Barbera La Romualda '07 has a highly appealing palate. The simpler wines in the range are well made, fruity and not without charm or appeal.

This historic Alba winery was established in 1923. Just over a decade ago, it was purchased by Marchesi Antinori, who revamped the style and range. Today, it is one of the most famous estates in Piedmont and the wines reach dozens of foreign countries, as well as major outlets in Italy. Alongside the classic wines of Langhe, Prunotto also offers a sound series of top-notch, reliable Asti reds.

The champion, however, is still Barolo Bussia, this year the '05, which comes from estate plots in the famous Monforte vineyard. This technically well made, firm, potent red offers varietal violet and liquorice aromas, concentrated flavour and good length. The '05 Barbera d'Asti Costamiòle, now considered a classic, was very good. It's a complex, full-bodied red, nicely underpinned by evident but not overpowering acidity. The rest of the range is well executed, and an excellent '06 version of the austere Nebbiolo Occhetti deserves a special mention, as does the Dolcetto Mosesco '07, a minor masterpiece of its type.

● Barolo Boscareto '05	♟♟	7
● Barolo Serralunga '05	♟♟	6
● Barbera d'Alba La Romualda '07	♟♟	6
● Dolcetto d'Alba S. Anna '08	♟♟	4*
● Langhe Nebbiolo Coste '08	♟♟	4
● Barbera d'Alba Laura '08	♟	4
● Barolo Boscareto '93	♟♟♟	8
● Barbera d'Alba La Romualda '06	♟♟	6
● Barolo Boscareto '04	♟♟	8
● Barolo Boscareto '01	♟♟	8
● Barolo Boscareto '99	♟♟	8

● Barbera d'Asti Costamiòle '05	♟♟	7
● Barolo Bussia '05	♟♟	8
● Barbaresco '06	♟♟	7
● Barbaresco Bric Turot '05	♟♟	8
● Barbera d'Alba Pian Romualdo '06	♟♟	6
● Barolo '05	♟♟	7
● Dolcetto d'Alba Mosesco '07	♟♟	5
● Nebbiolo d'Alba Occhetti '06	♟♟	5
● Barbera d'Alba '07	♟	4
● Barbera d'Asti Fiulòt '08	♟	4
● Dolcetto d'Alba '08	♟	4
● Barolo Bussia '01	♟♟♟	8
● Barolo Bussia '99	♟♟♟	8
● Barolo Bussia '98	♟♟♟	8
● Barolo Bussia '96	♟♟♟	8

Carlo Quarello

VIA MARCONI, 3
14020 COSSOMBRATO [AT]
TEL. 0141905204
valerio.quarello@libero.it

ANNUAL PRODUCTION **20,000 bottles**
HECTARES UNDER VINE **5.5**
VITICULTURE METHOD **Conventional**

Carlo Quarello's winery is, above all, a Grignolino winery. Back in the 1960s, Carlo decided to invest everything in this grape, which is often considered less interesting than other Piedmont varieties. Over the years, Carlo has racked up a long line of successes, proving that his intuition was spot-on. The vineyard supplying the grapes for his signature wine is Cré, situated in the municipality of Alfiano Natta. Today, the business is run by the tireless Carlo and his son Valerio.

The maestro of Grignolino lives up to his name. Yet again this year, he has brought us a wine that is nothing less than archetypal, albeit to some extent in a category of its own. Grignolino del Monferrato Casalese Cré Marcaleone '08 again combines drinkability with finesse, wrapping its depth and complexity in a fine tannic weave. We were also very satisfied with the Monferrato Rosso Pionda '07, a Nebbiolo whose aromas of medicinal herbs and gentian are reminiscent of Nebbiolos from northern Piedmont. Generous and complex, it shows dynamic tannins and a classy, well-orchestrated, lingering finish.

● Grignolino del M.to Casalese Cré Marcaleone '08	♟♟ 4*
● M.to Rosso Pionda '07	♟♟ 4*
● Grignolino del M.to Casalese Cré Marcaleone '07	♟♟ 4
● Grignolino del M.to Casalese Cré Marcaleone '06	♟♟ 4
● Grignolino del M.to Casalese Cré Marcaleone '05	♟♟ 4

La Querciola

LOC. PIANCERRETO, 85TER
12060 FARIGLIANO [CN]
TEL. 0713737026
www.laquerciola.com

CELLAR SALES
PRE-BOOKED VISITS

ANNUAL PRODUCTION **90,000 bottles**
HECTARES UNDER VINE **25**
VITICULTURE METHOD **Conventional**

La Querciola gets its name from a beautiful copse nestling in the midst of Barolo's famous vineyards. This newish, well-organized winery, run by the highly respected Bruno Chionetti who used to manage San Romano, owns good grape-growing land in areas between Barolo and Farigliano. This allows the cellar to work on various fronts and varieties, and means it can produce a highly representative range of Piedmont wines. There is no lack of character here. All the wines presented are well-typed and characterful.

The results of the latest wines presented were particularly impressive, starting with the Dolcettos. The Cornole '07 opens on intense notes of quinine and spice, nicely sustained by the depth of fruit and followed up on the palate with close-woven tannic thrust. It displays a certain aristocratic austerity, balanced by velvety soft, fleshy fruit. The intense, alcoholic Carpeneta '08 shows full ripe fruit on the nose, paving the way for a powerful, succulent palate with elegant tannins and a lingering, triumphantly characterful finish.

● Dogliani Cornole '07	♟♟ 4
● Barolo Donna Bianca '05	♟♟ 6
● Barolo Donna Bianca '04	♟♟ 6
● Dolcetto di Dogliani Carpeneta '08	♟♟ 4
● Langhe Rosso Chicchivello '08	♟♟ 4
● Piemonte Barbera Barilin '07	♟ 5

Renato Ratti

FRAZ. ANNUNZIATA, 7
12064 LA MORRA [CN]
TEL. 017350185
www.renatoratti.com

CELLAR SALES
PRE-BOOKED VISITS

ANNUAL PRODUCTION **300,000 bottles**
HECTARES UNDER VINE **40**
VITICULTURE METHOD **Conventional**

Sensitive architectural design has enabled this imposing winery to avoid ruining the surrounding landscape of the Annunziata hill, into which it is unobtrusively set, in the municipality of La Morra. A highly respected name in Italy, and even more so abroad, Pietro Ratti's winery continues in the prestigious family tradition, presenting reliable, well-typed, classic wines in fairly large quantities for the area.

Barolo Marcenasco '05 gave a textbook performance, with elegant fruit and incense over a well-orchestrated palate that puts balance before power. The well-made Rocche '05 is toasty on the nose, with generous pulp and an elegant oaky finish. The pungent, spicy Barolo Conca is mouthfilling and full of character, with tannins still prominent. The classic Nebbiolo Ochetti '07, from the Ochetti vineyard at Roero, tempts with caressing aromas. The lip-smacking, focused fruit of the Barbera Torriglione '08 is deliciously drinkable. The Dolcetto '08 from Mango d'Alba is enjoyable and the Bianco del Monferrato Sauvignon is well up to scratch.

Ressia

VIA CANOVA, 28
12052 NEIVE [CN]
TEL. 0173677305
www.ressia.com

CELLAR SALES
PRE-BOOKED VISITS

ANNUAL PRODUCTION **30,000 bottles**
HECTARES UNDER VINE **4.6**
VITICULTURE METHOD **Conventional**

What it lacks in size, this winery makes up in commitment and passion. In just a few years, the progress Fabrizio Ressia has made, together with his clear vision, have focused on bringing the best out of nebbiolo, a variety whose praises we never tires of singing for its finesse and unique varietal character. The results are particularly impressive in the Barbaresco Canova, the most easterly vineyard in the Neive district. All the wines presented are invitingly priced.

Ressia took home Three Glasses for his outstanding Barbaresco Canova '06. Its well-orchestrated quinine, tobacco, liquorice and dried flowers on the nose pave the way for powerful, austere development in the mouth. Although beefy, the tannins are never mouth-drying or over-assertive. We were particularly impressed with the successful use of ten to 15-hectolitre French and Austrian oak barrels. The delightfully drinkable Barbera Superiore '07 brims with rich fruit and turns out to be the best of a good bunch. We also like Evien, a dry wine from moscato.

● Barolo Marcenasco '05	♟♟	7
● Barolo Rocche '05	♟♟	8
● Barolo Conca '05	♟♟	8
○ M.to Bianco I Cedri di Villa Pattono '07	♟♟	4
● Nebbiolo d'Alba Ochetti '07	♟♟	5
● Barbera d'Alba Torriglione '08	♟	4
● Dolcetto d'Alba Colombè '08	♟	4
● Barolo Rocche Marcenasco '84	♟♟♟	8
● Barolo Rocche Marcenasco '83	♟♟♟	8
● Barbera d'Alba Torriglione '07	♟♟	4
● Barolo Conca Marcenasco '04	♟♟	8
● Barolo Marcenasco '04	♟♟	7
● Barolo Rocche Marcenasco '04	♟♟	8
● Nebbiolo d'Alba Ochetti '06	♟♟	5

● Barbaresco Canova '06	♟♟♟	6*
● Barbera d'Alba Sup. Canova '07	♟♟	4*
● Barbera d'Alba Canova '07	♟♟	4
○ Evien '08	♟♟	4*
○ Evien Oro '07	♟♟	4
● Dolcetto d'Alba Canova '08	♟	4
● Barbaresco Canova '05	♟♟	6
● Barbaresco Canova '04	♟♟	6
● Barbera d'Alba Sup. Canova '06	♟♟	4
● Dolcetto d'Alba Sup. Canova '06	♟♟	3
● Langhe Nebbiolo Gepù '06	♟♟	5
● Langhe Rosso Resiot '04	♟♟	5

F.lli Revello

FRAZ. ANNUNZIATA, 103
12064 LA MORRA [CN]
TEL. 017350276
www.revellofratelli.it

CELLAR SALES
PRE-BOOKED VISITS

ANNUAL PRODUCTION **65,000 bottles**
HECTARES UNDER VINE **12**
VITICULTURE METHOD **Naturale**

This delightful estate, half farm holiday centre and half winery, has its own attractively furnished tasting room where great care has been lavished on even the smallest details. The use of new oak can penalize the palate of the young wines but with time, especially in the case of Barolos, precision and careful management will shine through in the end.

The '05 Barolos are deep in hue, starting with the simple, approachable basic version. The attractive Vigna Gattera displays rain-soaked earth and floral aromatics, a complex palate and some dryness on the finish. The concentrated, tidy Vigna Conca shows red berry fruit and sweet spice, followed by a rounded, smooth, supple and enjoyably mouthfilling palate. The dense, almost impenetrable Giachini has elegant oak. Straightforward and uncomplicated on the palate, it is already drinking beautifully. The distinctly modern, vibrant Rocche gives exuberant fruit over oak, mirrored on an appealing palate with no rough tannins.

Michele Reverdito

FRAZ. RIVALTA
B.TA GARASSINI, 74B
12064 LA MORRA [CN]
TEL. 017350336
www.reverdito.it

CELLAR SALES
PRE-BOOKED VISITS

ANNUAL PRODUCTION **70,000 bottles**
HECTARES UNDER VINE **18**
VITICULTURE METHOD **Conventional**

There is no stopping the young Reverdito winery in its quest for professional development. Once again, we cannot stress too much the great commitment shown by all the members of the family in cellar and vineyard. Various plots in some of the best wine areas in Langhe enable them to offer a range of products from Barolo to Barbera and Dolcetto, not forgetting Pelaverga, the historic variety from Verduno. Reverdito wines offer character and substance at very reasonable prices.

The stylish Badarina '05 has elegant aromas of spice and quinine, and a fresh palate, nicely rounded off by a meaty finish. It's great for drinking now and great for laying down. The deep ruby Barolo Moncucco '04 has quinine and tobacco while the powerful palate's incisive tannins precede a focused finish. Codane '05 is the most traditional of the wines, with dried flowers and liquorice, surefoodted tannic grip and a very long finish. Although very powerful, the Barbera '07 pays the price in aromatic elegance. Tastings of the Barolo Bricco Cogni '04 and the Barberas Delia '06 and Butti '07 will have to wait until next year.

Wine	Rating
● Barbera d'Alba Ciabot du Re '07	♛♛ 6
● Barolo Rocche dell'Annunziata '05	♛♛ 8
● Barolo V. Conca '05	♛♛ 8
● Barolo V. Gattera '05	♛♛ 7
● Barolo '05	♛♛ 6
● Barolo V. Giachini '05	♛♛ 8
● Langhe Nebbiolo '08	♛♛ 5
● Langhe Rosso L'Insieme '06	♛♛ 7
● Barbera d'Alba '08	♛ 4
● Dolcetto d'Alba '08	♛ 4
● Barbera d'Alba Ciabot du Re '05	♛♛♛ 6
● Barbera d'Alba Ciabot du Re '00	♛♛♛ 7
● Barolo '93	♛♛♛ 8
● Barolo Rocche dell'Annunziata '01	♛♛♛ 8
● Barolo Rocche dell'Annunziata '00	♛♛♛ 8
● Barolo Rocche dell'Annunziata '97	♛♛♛ 8
● Barolo V. Conca '99	♛♛♛ 8

Wine	Rating
● Barolo Badarina '05	♛♛ 6
● Barolo Moncucco '04	♛♛ 6
● Barbera d'Alba '07	♛♛ 4
● Barolo Codane '05	♛♛ 6
● Dolcetto d'Alba Sup. Formica '07	♛♛ 4
● Langhe Nebbiolo Simane '07	♛♛ 4
● Verduno Pelaverga '08	♛ 4
● Barbera d'Alba Butti '06	♛♛ 4
● Barbera d'Alba Delia '05	♛♛ 5
● Barolo Bricco Cogni '03	♛♛ 7
● Barolo Codane '04	♛♛ 6
● Barolo Serralunga '04	♛♛ 6
● Verduno Pelaverga '07	♛♛ 4

Carlo Daniele Ricci

VIA MONTALE CELLI, 9
15050 COSTA VESCOVATO [AL]
TEL. 0131838115
www.aziendaagricolaricci.com

CELLAR SALES
PRE-BOOKED VISITS
VISITOR FACILITIES
FOOD

ANNUAL PRODUCTION **30,000 bottles**
HECTARES UNDER VINE **8**
VITICULTURE METHOD **Conventional**

Daniele Ricci could hardly be accused of being a slave to the latest winemaking fashions. Although he listens to everyone, he then goes on to make the wines that he feels are right. This approach has often proved him right, and has produced some excellent wines. And when they are less convincing, at least Daniele knows it is his own fault and not because he has followed bad advice.

For example, we still prefer the simpler Terre del Timorasso to the Timorasso San Leto, thanks to fruit and mineral aromas, underpinned by powerful yet well-modulated alcohol. Daniele came up with an interesting range of reds this year, starting with the ruby-hued San Martino, from barbera and nebbiolo, whose full-bodied, fleshy palate is framed by cherry-like notes. Bonarda El Matt '07 is another excellent example of its type. Fresh, fruit-fuelled and graced with tobacco and liquorice aromas, it shows how a semi-sparkling wine can also be an interesting one.

Giuseppe Rinaldi

VIA MONFORTE, 3
12060 BAROLO [CN]
TEL. 017356156

ANNUAL PRODUCTION **30,000 bottles**
HECTARES UNDER VINE **6.5**
VITICULTURE METHOD **Naturale**

If you are enthusiasts, but in a hurry, you had best steer clear of Beppe Rinaldi. The inimitable "Citrico" is one of a kind, and it would be a pity to listen only to this extraordinary man's reflections on the world of wine. The last time we met he was in the guise of a Futurist poet, in perfect contrast to his range of wines, which are the very essence of the classic style. As always, Beppe paired off his four Barolo vineyards, to bring us Brunate Le Coste and Cannubi San Lorenzo Ravera.

This time, the in-house contest was won by Barolo Cannubi San Lorenzo Ravera '05. From the very first sip, we found it better focused in terms of elegance, aromatic range, integrity and measured style. On the nose, it is expansive, thanks to floral and delicately grassy hints. Quinine notes come back on the delightful palate, which finishes stiffer and more austere, although absolutely seamless. The Barolo Brunate Le Coste '05 is a tad less confident on the nose, with hints of fermentation and also of reduction, which hold back the fruit. The tannins are also less fine-grained than the other Barolo's but this is still an impressive wine.

● Colli Tortonesi Rosso S. Martino '06	🍷🍷 5
○ Colli Tortonesi Terre del Timorasso '07	🍷🍷 4
● Piemonte Bonarda El Matt '07	🍷🍷 4*
● Colli Tortonesi Rosso Agapè '03	🍷 5
● Colli Tortonesi Rosso Elso '06	🍷 4
○ Colli Tortonesi Timorasso S. Leto '07	🍷 5
● Colli Tortonesi Barbera Castellania '06	🍷🍷 5
● Colli Tortonesi Barbera Castellania '05	🍷🍷 5
○ Colli Tortonesi Bianco S. Leto '03	🍷🍷 5
● Colli Tortonesi Rosso Elso '05	🍷🍷 4
● Colli Tortonesi Rosso S. Martino '05	🍷🍷 5
○ Colli Tortonesi Terre del Timorasso '06	🍷🍷 4
○ Colli Tortonesi Terre del Timorasso '05	🍷🍷 4
○ Colli Tortonesi Terre del Timorasso '04	🍷🍷 4

● Barolo Brunate-Le Coste '05	🍷🍷 7
● Barolo Cannubi S. Lorenzo-Ravera '05	🍷🍷 7
● Langhe Nebbiolo '07	🍷🍷 5
● Barbera d'Alba '07	🍷🍷 4
⊙ Rosae '07	🍷 4
● Barolo Brunate-Le Coste '01	🍷🍷🍷 7
● Barolo Brunate-Le Coste '00	🍷🍷🍷 7
● Barolo Cannubi S. Lorenzo-Ravera '04	🍷🍷🍷 7
● Barolo Brunate-Le Coste '04	🍷🍷 7
● Barolo Brunate-Le Coste '03	🍷🍷 7
● Barolo Brunate-Le Coste '02	🍷🍷 7
● Barolo Cannubi S. Lorenzo-Ravera '04	🍷🍷 7
● Barolo Cannubi S. Lorenzo-Ravera '03	🍷🍷 7

Rizzi

VIA RIZZI, 15
12050 TREISO [CN]
TEL. 0173638161
www.cantinarizzi.it

CELLAR SALES
PRE-BOOKED VISITS
VISITOR FACILITIES

ANNUAL PRODUCTION **50,000 bottles**
HECTARES UNDER VINE **35**
VITICULTURE METHOD **Conventional**

The charming winery of the Dellapiana family is anything but an outsider. With 35 hectares in a single plot on the Rizzi hill, they have one of the best sites in Treiso and the whole of the Barbaresco area. The extremely classic style of the wines involves almost exclusive use of large Slavonian oak and separate vinification for the various vineyard selections of Boito, Nervo Fondetta and Pajorè. Nor should we forget the Dolcetto, which acquires personality on this terroir.

Top honours may have eluded the Dellapianas but they have little to be unhappy about. Two Barbarescos out of three went to our finals: the Pajorè and the Nervo Fondetta '06. The former has the typical sumptuous fibre and spice of the Treiso cru but seems to thin out in the finish, leaving only lean acidity. Progression is similar in the Nervo Fondetta, which shows tarter aromas of herbs, apples and pears, and mellower, more delicately woven tannins. Close on its heels is Barbaresco Rizzi Boito '06, as always more broader and more austere but this time lacking depth.

★ Albino Rocca

S.DA RONCHI, 18
12050 BARBARESCO [CN]
TEL. 0173635145
www.roccaalbino.com

CELLAR SALES
PRE-BOOKED VISITS

ANNUAL PRODUCTION **130,000 bottles**
HECTARES UNDER VINE **23**
VITICULTURE METHOD **Conventional**

Year after year, Angelo Rocca continues, with help from his daughter Paola, to consolidate his reputation, both in Italy and abroad, as one of the most reliable names in Langhe. The cellar's sound production philosophy, evident in the precise winemaking style, produces fantastic results in its distinctive, characterful Barbarescos and indeed in the rest of the range. The winery itself is very attractive and well worth a visit.

The '06 Barbarescos are stunning, led by a shining Vigneto Loreto from the little-known but excellent Casotto Loreto vineyard that regales the nose with upfront tobacco and spice before giving a classic performance on the confident, powerful, pervasive palate. Brich Ronchi, from a vineyard facing east-south-east, is also complex, if slightly less potent and fruitier than the Loreto. The basic Barbaresco is good, presenting fresher and more approachable than the selections. The first 2,500 bottles of the new Riserva Brich Ronchi '04, emerging after 46 months in oak, are fantastic and easily took Three Glasses.

● Barbaresco Nervo Fondetta '06	♟♟ 6
● Barbaresco Pajorè '06	♟♟ 6
● Barbaresco Rizzi Boito '06	♟♟ 6
● Barbera d'Alba '07	♟ 4
● Dolcetto d'Alba '08	♟ 4
○ Langhe Chardonnay '08	♟ 4
● Barbaresco '05	♟♟ 6
● Barbaresco Boito '04	♟♟ 6
● Barbaresco Nervo Fondetta '05	♟♟ 6
● Barbaresco Pajorè '05	♟♟ 6
● Barbaresco Rizzi Boito '05	♟♟ 6
● Barbera d'Alba '06	♟♟ 4*

● Barbaresco Vign. Brich Ronchi Ris. '04	♟♟♟ 8
● Barbaresco '06	♟♟ 6
● Barbaresco Vign. Brich Ronchi '06	♟♟ 7
● Barbaresco Vign. Loreto '06	♟♟ 7
● Barbera d'Alba Gepin '07	♟♟ 5
● Dolcetto d'Alba Vignalunga '08	♟♟ 4
○ Langhe Bianco La Rocca '08	♟♟ 5
○ Langhe Chardonnay da Bertü '08	♟♟ 4
● Barbera d'Alba '08	♟ 4
● Barbaresco Vign. Brich Ronchi '05	♟♟♟ 7
● Barbaresco Vign. Brich Ronchi '03	♟♟♟ 7
● Barbaresco Vign. Loreto '04	♟♟♟ 7
● Barbaresco Vign. Brich Ronchi '04	♟♟ 7
● Barbaresco Vign. Loreto '05	♟♟ 7
● Barbera d'Alba Gepin '06	♟♟ 5
● Barbera d'Alba Gepin '05	♟♟ 5

★ Bruno Rocca

VIA RABAJÀ, 60
12050 BARBARESCO [CN]
TEL. 0173635112
www.brunorocca.it

CELLAR SALES
PRE-BOOKED VISITS

ANNUAL PRODUCTION **60,000 bottles**
HECTARES UNDER VINE **15**
VITICULTURE METHOD **Conventional**

Bruno Rocca has been consistently at the top of the Barbaresco DOCG since the 1980s, thanks to magnificent vine stock, especially rows in the celebrated Rabajà vineyard, good vineyard management and non-invasive winemaking techniques, in which small oak barrels enhance the nebbiolo grapes without overwhelming them.

The '06 Rabajà is still fairly closed on the nose but offers a velvety, mouthfilling palate. The more open Coparossa '06, although oaky on the nose, has dense fruit leading to a complex palate with a long, clean, finish. Although it's simpler than its big brothers, we liked the '06 Barbaresco. The impenetrable Barbera d'Asti '07 bursts with plums and spice, showing smooth on the palate. Even more convincing is the ultra-modern Barbera d'Alba, with its perky acidity. The only white is Chardonnay Cadet and the '08 shows spices, hazelnuts and vanilla leading into a sturdy, balanced palate. The modern, alcohol-rich Rabajolo '07 is impenetrable and woody.

Rocche Costamagna

VIA VITTORIO EMANUELE, 8
12064 LA MORRA [CN]
TEL. 0173509225
www.rocchecostamagna.it

CELLAR SALES
PRE-BOOKED VISITS
VISITOR FACILITIES

ANNUAL PRODUCTION **85,000 bottles**
HECTARES UNDER VINE **14**
VITICULTURE METHOD **Conventional**

The Locatelli family winery deserves a visit for its delightful location, with a breathtaking terrace and a handful of pretty rooms for paying guests. It is the ideal setting to appreciate the wines produced here, not least the Barolo selections whose distinctive style is never over-the-top and respects the finest traditions of nebbiolo.

We preferred the '05 Barolo dell'Annunziata to the Bricco Francesco selection from the same year, thanks to classic, focused aromas of dried flowers, liquorice, rain-soaked earth and autumn leaves. The Bricco Francesco still needs time to unfold its grace and aromatic complexity, although the palate already displays nice structure, if less than perfect balance. Of the two '07 Barberas, Rocche delle Rocche is more international, with lovely fruit over oak. The more classic Annunziata shows upfront plum and cherry. The rest of the range passes muster, particularly the Dolcetto d'Alba Rùbis '08, which is as flavoursome as ever.

● Barbaresco Coparossa '06	♟♟ 8
● Barbaresco Rabajà '06	♟♟ 8
● Barbera d'Alba '07	♟♟ 6
● Barbaresco '06	♟♟ 7
● Barbera d'Asti '07	♟♟ 5
○ Langhe Chardonnay Cadet '08	♟♟ 5
● Langhe Rosso Rabajolo '07	♟♟ 6
● Dolcetto d'Alba V. Trifole '08	♟ 4
● Barbaresco Coparossa '04	♟♟♟ 8
● Barbaresco Maria Adelaide '04	♟♟♟ 8
● Barbaresco Maria Adelaide '01	♟♟♟ 8
● Barbaresco Rabajà '01	♟♟♟ 8
● Barbaresco Rabajà '93	♟♟♟ 8

● Barolo Rocche dell'Annunziata '05	♟♟ 6
● Barbera d'Alba Annunziata '07	♟♟ 4
● Barbera d'Alba Sup. Rocche delle Rocche '07	♟♟ 5
● Barolo Bricco Francesco Rocche dell'Annunziata '05	♟♟ 7
● Dolcetto d'Alba Rùbis '08	♟♟ 4
● Dolcetto d'Alba Murrae '08	♟ 4
○ Langhe Arneis '08	♟ 4
● Langhe Nebbiolo Roccardo '08	♟ 4
☉ Osé '08	♟ 4
● Barolo Rocche dell'Annunziata '04	♟♟♟ 6
● Barbera d'Alba Annunziata '06	♟♟ 4
● Barbera d'Alba Sup. Rocche delle Rocche '06	♟♟ 5
● Barolo Bricco Francesco Rocche dell'Annunziata '04	♟♟ 7
● Dolcetto d'Alba Murrae '07	♟♟ 4

★ Podere Rocche dei Manzoni

LOC. MANZONI SOPRANI, 3
12065 MONFORTE D'ALBA [CN]
TEL. 017378421
www.rocchedeimanzoni.it

CELLAR SALES
PRE-BOOKED VISITS

ANNUAL PRODUCTION **250,000 bottles**
HECTARES UNDER VINE **40**
VITICULTURE METHOD **Conventional**

Rodolfo Migliorini has courageously taken over the reins of this prestigious winery, and with it a challenging job. The winery has always worked on various fronts, from the big reds of Langhe to Metodo Classico sparklers, precursors of a world in which quality Italian fizz, even from the lesser-known subzones, is now universally popular. The wines are generous, successful examples of a modern approach which has received widespread acclaim, especially outside Italy.

The Barolo Cappella di Santo Stefano '05, from one of the best vineyards in Langhe, offers sweet oak on the nose, slightly overpowering the rich, fresh fruit. The palate gives mouthfilling, silky power, and finishes with an elegant reprise of oak. The Barolo Big 'd Big '05 brims with balsam but also with pleasing aromas of ripe fruit. On the palate it is mouthfilling, but slightly dried by the oak. The tasty, complex Vigna d'la Roul '05 shows aromas ranging from dried herbs to liquorice, leading to a full-bodied palate with slightly rugged tannins. It signs off stylishly with faint oak. The rest of the range will be tasted for next year's Guide.

Flavio Roddolo

FRAZ. BRICCO APPIANI
LOC. SANT'ANNA, 5
12065 MONFORTE D'ALBA [CN]
TEL. 017378535

ANNUAL PRODUCTION **22.500 bottles**
HECTARES UNDER VINE **6**
VITICULTURE METHOD **Conventional**

Flavio Roddolo is living proof that you don't need to say much to earn admiration and respect. Shy and taciturn, Flavio lets his splendid wines do the talking. They are made at his farm at Bricco Appiani, geographically outside the DOCG zone and the first outpost of upper Langhe. A firm supporter of natural winemaking, both in vineyard and winery, he only produces one Barolo, from the Ravera vineyard, and two Dolcetto d'Albas, one of which is a Superiore. The range is completed by a Barbera, the Nebbiolo, and the singe-variety Cabernet, Bricco Appiani.

We only tasted one of Roddolo's wines this year but it is the one that is most representative of his style. The Barolo Ravera '04 has an almost gutsy core, of rain-soaked earth, topsoil and cloves. The first impact is in some ways harsh but sweetens in the glass with flowery hints and balsamic talc notes. The vibrant, gutsy palate is full of stuffing and fine-grained tannins, with a youthful finish of bitter chocolate and freshly turned earth.

● Barolo V. Cappella di S. Stefano '05	♥♥ 8
● Barolo V. d'la Roul '05	♥♥ 8
● Barolo V. Big 'd Big '05	♥♥ 8
● Barolo V. Big 'd Big '99	♥♥♥ 8
● Barolo V. Cappella di S. Stefano '01	♥♥♥ 8
● Barolo V. Cappella di S. Stefano '96	♥♥♥ 8
● Langhe Rosso Quatr Nas '99	♥♥♥ 7
● Langhe Rosso Quatr Nas '96	♥♥♥ 8
○ Valentino Brut Zero Ris. '98	♥♥♥ 6
● Barolo V. Big 'd Big '04	♥♥ 8
● Barolo V. Cappella di S. Stefano '04	♥♥ 8
● Barolo V. d'la Roul '04	♥♥ 8
● Langhe Bricco Manzoni '04	♥♥ 7

● Barolo Ravera '04	♥♥♥ 6
● Barolo Ravera '01	♥♥♥ 6
● Barolo Ravera '97	♥♥♥ 6
● Bricco Appiani '99	♥♥♥ 6
● Langhe Rosso Bricco Appiani '04	♥♥ 6

Ronchi

STR. RONCHI, 23
12050 BARBARESCO [CN]
TEL. 0173635156
az.ronchi@libero.it

CELLAR SALES
PRE-BOOKED VISITS

ANNUAL PRODUCTION **25,000 bottles**
HECTARES UNDER VINE **6**
VITICULTURE METHOD **Conventional**

Meticulous care and vineyard management are what makes this small Barbaresco estate so interesting. In his functional, technically well-equipped winery, Giancarlo Rocca produces wines with vigorous structure, such as his signature wine, the Barbaresco Ronchi, from the east-south-east facing nebbiolo plot of the same name, one of the largest in the DOCG zone. These are wines of substance, which make no overtures to fashion and eschew approachable drinkability in favour of character.

When we were tasting, the basic Barbaresco, which spends more than 30 months in medium and large oak barrels, had not yet been bottled, so we'll talk about it next year. The lively ruby Barbaresco Ronchi '06 offers a complex nose of tobacco, spice and above all fruit. The characterful palate shows impressive backbone, lovely tannins and fine harmony. We were won over by the deep ruby, modern Barbera Terlé '07, showing toastiness on the nose against a fruit backdrop and a fleshy palate nicely balanced by acidity. The no-nonsense Dolcetto '07 is potent and tannic.

Giovanni Rosso

LOC. BAUDANA, 6
12050 SERRALUNGA D'ALBA [CN]
TEL. 0173613340
www.giovannirosso.com

CELLAR SALES
PRE-BOOKED VISITS

ANNUAL PRODUCTION **55,000 bottles**
HECTARES UNDER VINE **10**
VITICULTURE METHOD **Naturale**

The dynamic Davide Rosso, a man people remember, runs this important, growing winery at Serralunga with a steady hand. The estate's own excellent vineyards form the basis for wines of temperament, produced without excessive technical intervention, to which traditional winemaking methods confer a recognizable style. A good period of bottle ageing will allow their hidden nuances to come to the fore.

There are no surprises this year in the range of wines presented by this estate's exuberant owner, who promises to stick to Barolo in the future. The two equally good crus come from different site climates and unveil different aromatic profiles. While both epitomize the Serralunga style, the Cerretta '05, with liquorice and tobacco aromas, shows more generous fruit to offset the tannins. The uncompromisingly pure Serra '05, however, is almost aristocratically austere and stiff. In line with the winery's philosophy, all the other wines, starting with the Barbera '07, express the character of their terroir without any recourse to artifice.

● Barbaresco Ronchi '06	▼▼ 6*
● Barbera d'Alba Terlé '07	▼▼ 4
● Dolcetto d'Alba Rosario '07	▼ 4
● Barbaresco Ronchi '04	▼▼▼ 7
● Barbaresco '05	▼▼ 6
● Barbaresco Ronchi '05	▼▼ 6
● Barbaresco Ronchi '03	▼▼ 6
● Barbera d'Alba Terlé '06	▼▼ 4
● Dolcetto d'Alba '07	▼▼ 5
○ Langhe Chardonnay '05	▼▼ 4

● Barolo Cerretta '05	▼▼ 8
● Barolo La Serra '05	▼▼ 8
● Barbera d'Alba Donna Margherita '07	▼▼ 4
● Barolo Serralunga '05	▼▼ 6
● Dolcetto d'Alba Le Quattro Vigne '08	▼▼ 4*
● Barbera d'Alba Donna Margherita '06	▼▼ 4
● Barolo Cerretta '04	▼▼ 8
● Barolo Cerretta '03	▼▼ 8
● Barolo La Serra '04	▼▼ 8
● Barolo Serralunga '04	▼▼ 6
● Barolo Serralunga '03	▼▼ 6

Rovellotti

INTERNO CASTELLO, 22
28074 GHEMME [NO]
TEL. 0163841781
www.rovellotti.it

CELLAR SALES
FOOD

ANNUAL PRODUCTION 70,000 bottles
HECTARES UNDER VINE 16
VITICULTURE METHOD Naturale

Half a day spent in the company of Antonello Rovellotti is like a journey into a parallel dimension. In his splendid winery, situated in the heart of the historic Ricetto, Ghemme's citadel, you can forget the passing hours and delight in his eccentric ways. The same idiosyncrasies are found in his wines, which are unpredictable to say the least, bringing together traditional grapes such as nebbiolo and vespolina, and international varieties such as cabernet, merlot and pinot nero. The results are classic interpretations, sold in bottles sporting newly made-over labels.

While appreciating the variations on a theme, we felt that Rovellotti continues to show his best in traditional designations. Both the Ghemme '04s tasted this year show an uncommon capacity to embody the rugged, yet deep-rooted soul of these southwest-facing morainic hills. Chiuso dei Pomi came in just a whisker ahead of the Costa del Salmino Riserva, thanks to a tidier, earthy profile of tar and ripe cherry, with a touch of dryness on the finish. The other is headier on the nose, and has more extract on the palate. The Valdenrico '06, from sun-dried erbaluce grapes, performed superbly.

● Ghemme Chioso dei Pomi '04	♟♟	6
☉ Colline Novaresi Nebbiolo Valplazza '08	♟♟	4
● Ghemme Costa del Salmino Ris. '04	♟♟	6
● Sciatò Muloeta '05	♟♟	5
○ Valdenrico Passito '06	♟♟	7
● Colline Novaresi Nebbiolo Valplazza '07	♟♟	4
● Colline Novaresi Vespolina Ronco al Maso '07	♟♟	3*
● Ghemme Chioso dei Pomi '03	♟♟	6

Podere Ruggeri Corsini

LOC. BUSSIA CORSINI, 106
12065 MONFORTE D'ALBA [CN]
TEL. 017378625
www.ruggericorsini.com

CELLAR SALES
PRE-BOOKED VISITS

ANNUAL PRODUCTION 58,000 bottles
HECTARES UNDER VINE 7
VITICULTURE METHOD Conventional

In the winemaking community of Monforte, well-known wineries are flanked by small estates which, as in this case, are more successful abroad than at home. The great wines of Langhe are in fact world-beaters, but in Italy they can tend to get lost in the sea of labels from the most aggressive zones in a very tough market. Loredana Addari and Nicola Argamante continue to produce accomplished, expressive wines and you only have to taste them to see the progress they have made in recent years.

The best indication of this coming of age is Barolo San Pietro '05. Intense aromas of quinine, mint, dried flowers and spice give complexity before the beautifully orchestrated palate signs off long and juicy. The Barolo Corsini '05 has a rather more rustic character with drying tannins. The Dolcetto '08 pleases the palate and plays on drinkability rather than finesse. The Langhe Bianco '08, from chardonnay, sauvignon and arneis, releases peach and apricot aromas, backed up by an uncomplicated palate with a bitterish finish.

● Barolo S. Pietro '05	♟♟	6
● Barbera d'Alba Armujan '07	♟♟	4
● Barolo Corsini '05	♟♟	6
● Dolcetto d'Alba '08	♟♟	4
● Langhe Nebbiolo '07	♟♟	4
○ Langhe Bianco '08	♟	4
● Barbera d'Alba Sup. Armujan '06	♟♟	5
● Barolo Corsini '04	♟♟	6
● Barolo S. Pietro '04	♟♟	6
● Langhe Nebbiolo '06	♟♟	4

Josetta Saffirio

LOC. CASTELLETTO, 39
12065 MONFORTE D'ALBA [CN]
TEL. 0173787278
www.josettasaffirio.com

CELLAR SALES
PRE-BOOKED VISITS

ANNUAL PRODUCTION **20,000 bottles**
HECTARES UNDER VINE **5**
VITICULTURE METHOD **Conventional**

Wineries run by women have particular appeal. Sara Vezza, with the help of her family, continues the splendid tradition of this small, successful Langhe estate that two decades ago astounded the world with its first spectacular wines. All the labels are dependable, showing marked temperament and good ageing potential.

The Barolo Riserva '03 is from a difficult year. Already lacking bite, it opens with dried flowers, but the palate lacks acidity, and the stiff tannins dry the mouth. The concentrated Persiera '05 shows quinine, spice and forthright fruit, a vibrant palate and a lingering finish with great personality. The attractive mid-structured Barolo '05 has a tad too much alcohol. The Barbera opens with oak, offering black berry fruit and spices and a velvety palate, with oak coming back in the finish. The Langhe Alna Rosso '07, from merlot with a splash of nebbiolo, has only been in production for a few years and is still a touch tart. We preferred the more complex Nebbiolo '07.

Cascina Salicetti

VIA CASCINA SALICETTI, 2
15050 MONTEGIOCO [AL]
TEL. 0131875192
www.cascinasalicetti.it

CELLAR SALES
PRE-BOOKED VISITS

ANNUAL PRODUCTION **25,000 bottles**
HECTARES UNDER VINE **16**
VITICULTURE METHOD **Conventional**

It is rare in the Colli Tortonesi to find an estate where all the vineyards are situated around the farmhouse, so when you arrive at Cascina Salicetti and find yourself in a natural amphitheatre, in the midst of the winery's own vineyards, the sensation is memorable. Anselmo, the estate oenologist and manager, gained experience in other wineries before taking over the reins of the operation, which the whole family helps manage.

The two selections of Timorasso '07 scored extremely well. For the first year, in fact, our old friend Ombra di Luna was joined by the Derthona, whose mineral notes and fruity apricot aromas took it into our finals. The same holds true for the Barberas. We preferred the Morganti '07, with its vibrant fruit aromas and fresh fleshiness, to its elder brother, the Punta del Sole '06, which was more concentrated and potent but requires time for its oak to mellow. The excellent, ruby-coloured Dolcetto Di Marzi '07 shows ripe fruit and cocoa on the nose. We should also mention the good debut of the red Il Seguito '07.

● Barbera d'Alba '07	⛾⛾	4
● Barolo '05	⛾⛾	6
● Barolo Persiera '05	⛾⛾	8
● Langhe Nebbiolo '07	⛾⛾	5
● Barolo Persiera Ris. '03	⛾	8
● Langhe Rosso Alna Rosso '07	⛾	5
● Barolo '89	⛾⛾⛾	8
● Barolo '88	⛾⛾⛾	8
● Barbera d'Alba '06	⛾⛾	4
● Barolo '04	⛾⛾	6
● Barolo Persiera '04	⛾⛾	8
● Langhe Rosso Alna Rosso '06	⛾⛾	5

○ Colli Tortonesi Timorasso Derthona '07	⛾⛾	4*
● Colli Tortonesi Barbera Morganti '07	⛾⛾	4
● Colli Tortonesi Rosso Il Seguito '07	⛾⛾	4
○ Colli Tortonesi Timorasso Ombra di Luna '07	⛾⛾	5
● Colli Tortonesi Barbera Punta del Sole '06	⛾	5
● Colli Tortonesi Dolcetto Di Marzi '07	⛾	3
● Colli Tortonesi Barbera Morganti '06	⛾⛾	4
○ Colli Tortonesi Cortese Montarlino '07	⛾⛾	4
○ Colli Tortonesi Cortese Montarlino '06	⛾⛾	4
● Colli Tortonesi Dolcetto Rugras '05	⛾⛾	3
● Colli Tortonesi Rosso Morganti '05	⛾⛾	4
○ Colli Tortonesi Timorasso Ombra di Luna '06	⛾⛾	5
○ Colli Tortonesi Timorasso Ombra di Luna '05	⛾⛾	3

San Fereolo

LOC. SAN FEREOLO
B.TA VALDIBÀ, 59
12063 DOGLIANI [CN]
TEL. 0173742075
www.sanfereolo.com

PRE-BOOKED VISITS

ANNUAL PRODUCTION **46,000 bottles**
HECTARES UNDER VINE **12**
VITICULTURE METHOD **Conventional**

Nicoletta Bocca, who is charm and professionalism personified, lives and works on the pretty hill of Valdibà, in the municipality of Dogliani. This enthusiastic believer in promoting and safeguarding the region has a genuine love for nature, and manages her vineyards according to environmental principles. It is hard to categorize her wines into rigid, pre-established aromatic profiles, since they are often hard to interpret, especially when young, because of their captivating character and original style originality.

The Dogliani, in this case from the favourable '07 growing year, again leads a faultless selection. This powerful, edgy wine goes far beyond what we normally expect from Dolcetto di Dogliani, showing its strong personality in aromas of blackberry, quinine and autumn leaves. On the palate, the measured yet powerful tannins, together with the length of a great wine, put this wine in a superior class. We were extremely impressed with Il Provinciale '07, from nebbiolo, which marries the finesse of this variety with the wild harshness of the Dogliani terroir. The other wines lived up to their reputation.

● Dogliani '07	🍷🍷	4*
● Langhe Rosso Il Provinciale '07	🍷🍷	5
○ Coste di Riavolo '07	🍷🍷	4
● Dolcetto di Dogliani Valdibà '08	🍷🍷	4*
● Dolcetto di Dogliani S. Fereolo '99	🍷🍷🍷 (white)	4
● Langhe Rosso Austri '03	🍷🍷🍷 (white)	5
● Dogliani '06	🍷🍷 (white)	4*
● Dogliani '05	🍷🍷 (white)	4*

Tenuta San Sebastiano

CASCINA SAN SEBASTIANO, 41
15040 LU [AL]
TEL. 0131741353
www.dealessi.it

CELLAR SALES
PRE-BOOKED VISITS

ANNUAL PRODUCTION **80,000 bottles**
HECTARES UNDER VINE **10**
VITICULTURE METHOD **Conventional**

The hills of Lu Monferrato have for some time been attracting the attention of wine lovers. Among the most popular wineries is the operation run by Roberto De Alessi and his wife Noemi, who, with young Fabio, are the keystones of Tenuta San Sebastiano, which for years has shown great continuity and above all quality. A recent retasting of Mepari '01 found it still magnificently youthful and fruity, with excellent ageing prospects. This is a fine example of how much Barbera can give when low yields in the vineyard and careful work in the winery come together in the bottle.

The impenetrable Mepari '06 opens with balsam, followed by fruit and spice leading into a well-orchestrated palate with generous, fleshy fruit. The basic Barbera is intense, alcoholic and lingering. Ripe fruit and spices characterize the Monferrato Rosso Dalera '05, from cabernet sauvignon and merlot, while the fragrant Piemonte Grignolino '07 shows evident varietal characteristics. We ended with LV '07, one of the best dried-grape wines in Monferrato.

● Barbera del M.to Sup. Mepari '06	🍷🍷	5
● Barbera del M.to '08	🍷🍷	3*
○ LV Passito '07	🍷🍷	4
● M.to Rosso Dalera '05	🍷🍷	6
● Piemonte Grignolino '07	🍷	3
● Barbera del M.to Sup. Mepari '06	🍷🍷 (white)	4*
● Barbera del M.to Sup. Mepari '05	🍷🍷 (white)	4*
● Grignolino del M.to Casalese '07	🍷🍷 (white)	3*
● M.to Rosso Dalera '04	🍷🍷 (white)	4
● M.to Rosso Sol-Do '06	🍷🍷 (white)	4*

★ Luciano Sandrone

VIA PUGNANE, 4
12060 BAROLO [CN]
TEL. 0173560023
www.sandroneluciano.com

PRE-BOOKED VISITS

ANNUAL PRODUCTION **95,000 bottles**
HECTARES UNDER VINE **25**
VITICULTURE METHOD **Conventional**

The winery where Luciano Sandrone, his daughter Barbara and brother Luca have been producing wine for a decade is an example of how to combine elegance, efficiency and respect for the environment. They offer an object lesson to those who have littered the beautiful local landscape with horrendous concrete sheds. Here, gravity is exploited to the full to move the wines from one container to another and much of the necessary electricity is provided by solar panels covering part of the roof. The grapes from the various vineyards or plots are vinified separately and then assembled.

The Barolo Cannubi Boschis '05 presents a lovely floral nose with classic earthy notes. The palate is equally true to type, proffering firm tannins and appealing sweetness, with excellent pulp mid palate and a long, juicy finish. Three Glasses for an elegant classic with plenty of zip. Le Vigne '05, made using grapes from various zones, offers balsamic aromas over floral background notes, leading to a stylish, well-balanced palate, with just a touch less energy than its sibling. As usual, the '07 Nebbiolo Valmaggiore, a genuine Roero vineyard selection, is a success and the splendid Barbera '07 shows rich fruit aromas backed up by a lively, juicy palate.

Cantine Sant'Agata

REG. MEZZENA, 19
14030 SCURZOLENGO [AT]
TEL. 0141203186
www.santagata.com

CELLAR SALES
PRE-BOOKED VISITS

ANNUAL PRODUCTION **150,000 bottlo**
HECTARES UNDER VINE **11**
VITICULTURE METHOD **Conventional**

This is a winery with a long history, named after the votive column standing outside the estate. Brothers Claudio and Franco Cavallero, who have been in charge for ten years, have worked hard to promote ruché, an aromatic native variety used in many of their wines. In addition to ruché, the other typical varieties of Monferrato – barbera, grignolino and cortese – are at the heart of this successful estate's range.

Ruché di Castagnole Monferrato 'Na Vota '08 performed well again this year, releasing intriguing rose and liquorice aromas over earthy notes, backed up by decent structure on the palate, and a long, well-orchestrated finish. The Barbera d'Asti Superiore Cavalé '07 shows power and backbone, as well as marked toastiness, which somewhat subdues its finesse and harmony. The vibrant, fruit-fuelled Barbera d'Asti Baby '08, the ultra-classic Grignolino d'Asti Miravalle '08, with its red berry fruit and pepper, and the supple, spicy, easy-drinking Ruché di Castagnole Monferrato Il Cavaliere '08 are all well styled.

● Barolo Cannubi Boschis '05	♙♙♙ 8
● Barolo Le Vigne '05	♙♙ 5
● Barbera d'Alba '07	♙♙ 6
● Dolcetto d'Alba '08	♙♙ 4
● Nebbiolo d'Alba Valmaggiore '07	♙♙ 6
● Barolo Cannubi Boschis '04	♟♟♟ 8
● Barolo Cannubi Boschis '03	♟♟♟ 8
● Barolo Cannubi Boschis '01	♟♟♟ 8
● Barolo Cannubi Boschis '00	♟♟♟ 8
● Barolo Le Vigne '99	♟♟♟ 8

● Barbera d'Asti Sup. Cavalé '07	♙♙ 5
● Ruché di Castagnole M.to 'Na Vota '08	♙♙ 4
● Barbera d'Asti Baby '08	♙ 3
● Grignolino d'Asti Miravalle '08	♙ 4
● Ruché di Castagnole M.to Il Cavaliere '08	♙ 4
● Barbera d'Asti Sup. Altea '06	♟♟ 4*
● Barbera d'Asti Sup. Cavalé '06	♟♟ 5
● Grignolino d'Asti Miravalle '07	♟♟ 4
● Ruché di Castagnole M.to 'Na Vota '07	♟♟ 4*
● Ruché di Castagnole M.to 'Na Vota '06	♟♟ 4

Paolo Saracco

VIA CIRCONVALLAZIONE, 6
12053 CASTIGLIONE TINELLA [CN]
TEL. 0141855113
info@paolosaracco.it

CELLAR SALES
PRE-BOOKED VISITS

ANNUAL PRODUCTION **400,000 bottles**
HECTARES UNDER VINE **40**
VITICULTURE METHOD **Conventional**

Established a century ago, this winery has witnessed a period of intense development since being taken over by Paolo Saracco, who is set on proving that Moscato may, and indeed must, achieve international recognition for its unique aromatic qualities. Evidently, Paolo has succeeded, if we consider that at least half of the 400,000 bottles of Moscato he produces every year, of which the Autunno selection is the special hit, make their way abroad.

These impressive quantities are accompanied by small experimental selections of Riesling and Chardonnay, which give less uniform results. The attractive Pinot Nero '06 is a touch tannic but extremely well typed. Despite the difficult growing year for early harvest varieties, Paolo has proved to be a skilled interpreter of the area's main variety, producing a textbook Moscato d'Autunno '08. Beautifully rich and unctuous on the palate, with marvellous aromatic verve, it again finishes top of its class. We also liked the basic version but the Riesling was a little disappointing.

○ Piemonte Moscato d'Autunno '08	ŸŸ (black)	4*
● M.to Rosso Pinot Nero '06	ŸŸ (black)	5
○ Moscato d'Asti '08	ŸŸ (black)	4
○ M.to Bianco Riesling '08	Ÿ (black)	4
○ Langhe Chardonnay Prasuè '07	ŸŸ	4
○ M.to Bianco Riesling '06	ŸŸ	4
● M.to Rosso Pinot Nero '05	ŸŸ	5
○ Moscato d'Asti '07	ŸŸ	4
○ Moscato d'Asti '06	ŸŸ	4
○ Piemonte Moscato d'Autunno '07	ŸŸ	4*
○ Piemonte Moscato d'Autunno '06	ŸŸ	4*
○ Piemonte Moscato d'Autunno '05	ŸŸ	4*
○ Piemonte Moscato d'Autunno '04	ŸŸ	4*

Roberto Sarotto

VIA RONCONUOVO, 13
12050 NEVIGLIE [CN]
TEL. 0173630228
www.robertosarotto.com

CELLAR SALES
PRE-BOOKED VISITS

ANNUAL PRODUCTION **150,000 bottles**
HECTARES UNDER VINE **50**
VITICULTURE METHOD **Conventional**

This large, dynamic winery has many strings to its bow. Running it with bright confidence is the brilliant Roberto Sarotto. His job is made particularly challenging by the fact that he has to manage a range of company facilities, with differing characteristics and needs. The level of quality achieved reflects Roberto's dedicated care and hard work. It is also worth mentioning that the wines are on the whole attractively priced.

This year, the winery's pride and joy is Barbaresco Gaia Principe Riserva '04, which gives a superb, complex, elegant nose leading to a powerful, delightfully-orchestrated palate. The Barolo Audace '05 is darker, with a stylish, variegated nose hinging on seductive notes of quinine, incense and liquorice. The palate shows all the hallmarks of youth. Particular mention should be made of the Barbera Elena '07, a demo perhaps, but one with undoubted character. The Gavi '08 is a real success. Despite lacking intensity, the nose is attractively complex, with lovely mineral notes, and the fresh, characterful palate signs off zestily.

● Barbaresco Gaia Principe Ris. '04	ŸŸ (black)	7
● Barbera d'Alba Briccomacchia '07	ŸŸ (black)	4*
● Barbera d'Alba Elena '07	ŸŸ (black)	4
● Barolo Audace '05	ŸŸ (black)	6
○ Gavi del Comune di Gavi Bric Sassi '08	ŸŸ (black)	4*
○ Langhe Chardonnay Briccomoro '08	ŸŸ (black)	4*
○ Moscato d'Asti Solatio '08	ŸŸ (black)	4
○ Langhe Arneis Runcneuv '08	Ÿ (black)	4
● Barolo Audace Ris. '00	ŸŸ	7

Scagliola

VIA SAN SIRO, 42
14052 CALOSSO [AT]
TEL. 0141853183
scagliola@libero.it

CELLAR SALES
PRE-BOOKED VISITS

ANNUAL PRODUCTION **140,000 bottles**
HECTARES UNDER VINE **23**
VITICULTURE METHOD **Conventional**

In recent years, the Scagliola family winery, established in 1930, has shown clear dedication to improving production. The aim is to produce a range of quality wines and at the same time safeguard the territory. Considering the position of the estate, in the Calosso hills, the Scagliolas have rightly focused on exploiting local varieties, above all moscato and barbera, and created some of the best wines produced with these grapes.

We were impressed with this year's Barbera d'Asti Superiore SanSì '07. Harmonious and subtle on the nose, with fruity, spicy aromas, it follows up with a full, rounded palate whose awesome length is underpinned by acidity. The attractive Barbera d'Asti Superiore Sansì Selezione '06 shows real finesse but is still overshadowed by oak. Nevertheless, it has enough flesh to sustain the impact of the marked toastiness and cherry notes. We enjoyed the Barbera d'Asti Frem '08. Apart from a tad too much alcohol, this is an archetypal young Barbera. The subtle, spicy Moscato d'Asti Volo di Farfalle '08 is also very good, showing stylish, leisurely and drinkable.

Giorgio Scarzello e Figli

VIA ALBA, 29
12060 BAROLO [CN]
TEL. 017356170
www.barolodibarolo.com

CELLAR SALES
PRE-BOOKED VISITS

ANNUAL PRODUCTION **25,000 bottles**
HECTARES UNDER VINE **5.5**
VITICULTURE METHOD **Conventional**

The standard bearer of this interesting family winery is the Barolo Vigna Merenda, whose grapes come from the Sarmassa vineyard, Barolo's heartland of absolute excellence. The estate has other quality plots in Paiagallo, which lies within in the municipality of Barolo, and Terlo, on the way to Novello. These provide the raw materials for a small series of excellently priced wines that beautifully reflect Langhe, offering traditional taste profiles, fantastic drinkability and outstanding ageworthiness.

Vigna Merenda '05 is the epitome of classic Barolo, in other words a wine whose flavours and aromas derive exclusively from the grape, showing austere, slightly astringent tannins. The colour lacks intensity and although the nose is not yet fully expressive, the aromas are forthright, with upfront dried flowers and tobacco. The somewhat stiff palate is a little held back by the tannins but is nevertheless appealing and lively. The basic wine is no slacker either, thanks to more developed aromas and a slightly softer palate. An austere style distinguishes the pleasing, nicely fruit-driven Barbera '06, aged in large oak barrels.

● Barbera d'Asti Sup. SanSì '07	♀♀ 7
● Barbera d'Asti Frem '08	♀♀ 5
● Barbera d'Asti Sup. SanSì Sel. '06	♀♀ 8
○ Moscato d'Asti Volo di Farfalle '08	♀♀ 5
○ Piemonte Chardonnay Casot dan Vian '08	♀ 4
● Barbera d'Asti Sup. SanSì Sel. '01	♀♀♀ 7
● Barbera d'Asti Sup. SanSì Sel. '00	♀♀♀ 7
● Barbera d'Asti Sup. SanSì Sel. '99	♀♀♀ 7
● Barbera d'Asti Sup. SanSì '06	♀♀ 7
● Barbera d'Asti Sup. SanSì Sel. '05	♀♀ 8
● Barbera d'Asti Sup. SanSì Sel. '04	♀♀ 7

● Barolo '05	♀♀ 6
● Barolo V. Merenda '05	♀♀ 7
● Barbera d'Alba Sup. '06	♀♀ 5
● Langhe Nebbiolo '07	♀♀ 4*
● Barolo V. Merenda '99	♀♀♀ 6
● Barolo V. Merenda '04	♀♀ 7
● Barolo V. Merenda '01	♀♀ 7

★ Paolo Scavino

FRAZ. GARBELLETTO
VIA ALBA-BAROLO, 59
12060 CASTIGLIONE FALLETTO [CN]
TEL. 017362850
e.scavino@libero.it

CELLAR SALES
PRE-BOOKED VISITS

ANNUAL PRODUCTION **100,000 bottles**
HECTARES UNDER VINE **20**
VITICULTURE METHOD **Conventional**

Noted Castiglione Falletto grower Enrico Scavino owns plots in various parts of the Barolo DOCG zone, at Cannubi in Barolo, Monvigliero in Verduno, Rocche dell'Annunziata, La Morra and Bricco Ambrogio, the last of which actually falls within the municipality of Roddi. These prestigious vineyards produce stunning Barolos but also Dolcettos, Barberas, Nebbiolo d'Albas and other excellent Langhe reds, all of which contribute to boost the winery's reputation.

This year, we were only able to taste some of Scavino's lesser wines. The '05 Barolos weren't ready so we decided to wait until next year. We consoled ourselves with a good, reasonably priced Barbera d'Alba '07, which focuses on drinkability and typicity. Next up was a stiffish Langhe Nebbiolo '06, with an austere, complex sensory profile. We finished off with a fragrant, smooth Dolcetto d'Alba '07, which has surprising staying power and an appealing palate shot through with an attractively savoury, almost salty, vein.

Schiavenza

VIA MAZZINI, 4
12050 SERRALUNGA D'ALBA [CN]
TEL. 0173613115
www.schiavenza.com

CELLAR SALES
PRE-BOOKED VISITS
FOOD

ANNUAL PRODUCTION **35,000 bottles**
HECTARES UNDER VINE **8**
VITICULTURE METHOD **Conventional**

Don't be foodled by the magical atmosphere of peace on the terrace of the family-run eatery. Go downstairs to the cellar and you will find yourself in the trenches, beset on all sides by a series of wines that take no prisoners. Metaphors aside, however, the Schiavenza Barolos really are the absolute benchmark for anyone looking for the pure, hard soul of nebbiolo. For Luciano Pira, the key to getting the most out of Broglio, Cerretta, Prapò and Perno is time. Slow development requires long barrel ageing and a healthy dose of patience.

Schiavenza wines have acquired almost legendary status in Langhe. Despite the difficult 2005 harvest, especially for vineyards on the east side of Serralunga, the two Barolos came through in impeccable shape. As can be imagined, they are still extremely hard, and make no concessions to appeal for its own sake, but they have the structure of superlative wines, especially Broglio '05, which relies on minerality and extraordinarily complex, throbbing acidity. The Prapò shows a slightly more estery edge on the nose, and above all unyielding tannins that lack sufficient support from the structure.

● Barbera d'Alba '07	♀♀ 4*
● Dolcetto d'Alba '07	♀♀ 4*
● Langhe Nebbiolo '06	♀♀ 6
● Barolo Bric dël Fiasc '96	♀♀♀ 8
● Barolo Bric dël Fiasc '95	♀♀♀ 8
● Barolo Bric dël Fiasc '93	♀♀♀ 8
● Barolo Bric dël Fiasc '90	♀♀♀ 6
● Barolo Rocche dell'Annunziata '93	♀♀♀ 6
● Barolo Rocche dell'Annunziata Ris. '01	♀♀♀ 8
● Barolo Rocche dell'Annunziata Ris. '97	♀♀♀ 8
● Barolo Rocche dell'Annunziata Ris. '96	♀♀♀ 8
● Barolo Rocche dell'Annunziata Ris. '90	♀♀♀ 8

● Barolo Broglio '05	♀♀♀ 6
● Barolo Prapò '05	♀♀ 6
● Barbera d'Alba Perno '06	♀♀ 4
● Dolcetto d'Alba Sorì '08	♀♀ 4*
● Dolcetto d'Alba Vughera '08	♀♀ 4*
● Barolo Broglio '04	♀♀♀ 6
● Barbera d'Alba Perno '05	♀♀ 4
● Barolo '04	♀♀ 6
● Barolo Bricco Cerretta '04	♀♀ 6
● Barolo Bricco Cerretta '03	♀♀ 6
● Barolo Broglio Ris. '01	♀♀ 6
● Barolo Prapò '04	♀♀ 6

Franco e Mario Scrimaglio

S.DA ALESSANDRIA, 67
14049 NIZZA MONFERRATO [AT]
TEL. 0141721385
www.scrimaglio.it

CELLAR SALES
PRE-BOOKED VISITS

ANNUAL PRODUCTION **700,000 bottles**
HECTARES UNDER VINE **20**
VITICULTURE METHOD **Organic certified**

In operation since 1921, the Scrimaglio brothers' estate produces a vast range of wines in various price bands organized into two lines: "classic wines" and "fashion wines". Many of the Piemonte DOC wines are available but the cellar's pride and joy is still the Barbera. A few years back, the winery gained ISO 14001 environmental management system certification, showing how committed the owners are to environmental issues. They are also experimenting with crown caps in the now famous Barbera No Cork.

Scrimaglio is back in the finals with a complex Barbera d'Asti Superiore Crôutin '07, whose tobacco and cherry aromas usher in a long palate with good structure, and Barbera d'Asti Superiore Nizza Acsé '06, which gives balsam, quinine, tobacco and plums, followed by a potent, austere palate with a lingering, tannic finish. We liked the fresh, well-orchestrated Barbera d'Asti Superiore Rocca Nivo '07 for its cocoa powder, spice and red berry fruit, and the Monferrato Rosso Tantra '07, from barbera with 20 per cent cabernet, which shows oak and sweet spice with red berry fruit and a close-knit, rounded palate. The other wines are very good, especially the Barberas.

Mauro Sebaste

FRAZ. GALLO
VIA GARIBALDI, 222BIS
12051 ALBA [CN]
TEL. 0173262148
www.maurosebaste.it

CELLAR SALES
PRE-BOOKED VISITS

ANNUAL PRODUCTION **150,000 bottles**
HECTARES UNDER VINE **25**
VITICULTURE METHOD **Conventional**

Mauro Sebaste's passion is a family legacy from the volcanic personality of his mother, Sylla. In 1991, Mauro started work on a project which is now very close to completion, and will see him vinifying the classic Langhe wines himself: Barolos from various crus, Barbera, Nebbiolo and Dolcetto as well as the Freisa named after his mother. He leaves Langhe only for his three whites: Roero Arneis, Moscato and Gavi.

Prapò, from the Serralunga vineyard of the same name, rises above the other good '05 Barolos, showing long, balsamic, and nicely acidic. The Brunate shows clearer signs of barrel ageing, with oak still slightly muffling the terroir's innate elegance. The simpler Monvigliero, from the historic Verduno vineyard, is beautifully fruited, with appealing spice on the nose and suppleness in the mouth. The Nebbiolo Parigi '07 is elegant but it's not in the same league as the big boys. The semi-sparkling, quaffable '08 Freisa is sound while the '08 Roero Arneis is delicate and fragrant. Hail in the Diano d'Alba vineyard meant there was no Centobricchi Bianco in 2008.

● Barbera d'Asti Sup. Crôutin '07	♀♀ 6
● Barbera d'Asti Sup. Nizza Acsé '06	♀♀ 6
● Barbera d'Asti Sup. Vign. Rocca Nivo '07	♀♀ 4*
● M.to Rosso Tantra '07	♀♀ 6
● Barbera d'Asti NoCork '08	♀ 4
● Barbera d'Asti NoWood '08	♀ 4
● Barbera d'Asti Sup. Crôutin '06	♀♀ 6
● Barbera d'Asti Sup. Nizza Acsé '05	♀♀ 6
● Barbera d'Asti Sup. Nizza Acsé '01	♀♀ 6

● Barolo Prapò '05	♀♀ 8
● Barolo Brunate '05	♀♀ 8
● Barolo Monvigliero '05	♀♀ 7
● Dolcetto d'Alba S. Rosalia '08	♀♀ 4
● Langhe Freisa Sylla '08	♀♀ 4
● Nebbiolo d'Alba Parigi '07	♀♀ 5
○ Gavi '08	♀ 4
○ Roero Arneis '08	♀ 4
● Barolo Brunate '04	♀♀ 8
● Barolo Monvigliero '04	♀♀ 7
● Barolo Prapò '04	♀♀ 8
○ Langhe Bianco Centobricchi '07	♀♀ 4
● Langhe Rosso Centobricchi '06	♀♀ 6
● Nebbiolo d'Alba Parigi '06	♀♀ 5

F.lli Seghesio

LOC. CASTELLETTO, 19
12065 MONFORTE D'ALBA [CN]
TEL. 017378108
az.agricolaseghesio@libero.it

CELLAR SALES
PRE-BOOKED VISITS

ANNUAL PRODUCTION **60,000 bottles**
HECTARES UNDER VINE **10**
VITICULTURE METHOD **Conventional**

The winery run by brothers Aldo and Riccardo Seghesio is situated in at Monforte in a small patch of hillside with views over a stupendous panorama of vineyards. The winery's style is reasonably modern, involving small and medium oak. But what really distinguishes the Seghesios is their capacity to retain plenty of fruit in their wines, even in long-ageing Barolos. We recently retasted a Barolo La Villa '99, which was still extremely fresh, spot-on in terms of complexity and charm, and living proof of a job well done. All the wines presented are temptingly priced.

The only wine ready for the corkscrew this year was the '05 Barolo La Villa, a real must-taste among the Monforte selections. As often happens when these wines are tasted too young, the nose failed to open up, only partially expressing its usual aromatic complexity, which hinges on deep, heady balsam and fruit aromas. These are mirrored by the follow-through on the palate, where the close-knit, and still somewhat austere, tannic weave gets in the way of harmonious progression.

●	Barolo Vign. La Villa '05	TT	7
●	Barbera d'Alba Vign. della Chiesa '00	YYY	6
●	Barbera d'Alba Vign. della Chiesa '97	YYY	6
●	Barolo Vign. La Villa '04	YYY	7
●	Barolo Vign. La Villa '99	YYY	7
●	Barolo Vign. La Villa '91	YYY	7
●	Barbera d'Alba '07	YY	4
●	Barbera d'Alba Vign. della Chiesa '06	YY	5
●	Dolcetto d'Alba Vign. della Chiesa '07	YY	4
●	Langhe Rosso Bouquet '06	YY	6
●	Langhe Rosso Bouquet '06	YY	6
●	Langhe Rosso Bouquet '06	YY	6

Sella

VIA IV NOVEMBRE
13060 LESSONA [BI]
TEL. 01599455
aziendeagricolesella@virgilio.it

CELLAR SALES
PRE-BOOKED VISITS

ANNUAL PRODUCTION **80,000 bottles**
HECTARES UNDER VINE **20**
VITICULTURE METHOD **Conventional**

You can't say you know northern Piedmont if you haven't tried wines from Sella, which dates back to the 17th century. Bright and sophisticated, these are wines with a pure, deep style that perfectly reflects the differences of the various zones. The sandy soil of Lessona is interpreted in one basic wine and two selections while the Bramaterra I Porfidi selection's name pays tribute to its very different, porphyry soil. Vespolina, croatina and uva rara flank the predominant nebbiolo in the vineyards and in the winery large barrels rub shoulders with barriques of various ages.

Again, it was a magical year for Gioacchino Sella's wines. This was clear as soon as we took our first sip of the Lessona '06, which shows precision and nose-palate balance, with flowers and medicinal herbs to the fore. The two big hitters tied. San Sebastiano allo Zoppo '05 is archetypal, with its ferrous, linear, but also somewhat grassy aromas and the Omaggio a Quintino Sella '04 is big on flavour but also develops with less complexity than expected. Top honours for Bramaterra I Porfidi '05, which marries a tight weave and power with sprightly acidity and a seemingly endless liquorice finish.

●	Bramaterra I Porfidi '05	TTT	6
●	Lessona '06	TT	5
●	Lessona Omaggio a Quintino Sella '04	TT	7
●	Lessona S. Sebastiano allo Zoppo '05	TT	6
●	Coste della Sesia Casteltorto '07	TT	5
⊙	Coste della Sesia Rosato Majoli '08	TT	4
●	Bramaterra I Porfidi '03	YYY	6
●	Lessona S. Sebastiano allo Zoppo '04	YYY	6
●	Bramaterra I Porfidi '04	YY	6
●	Coste della Sesia Rosso Casteltorto '06	YY	5

Enrico Serafino

c.so Asti, 5
12043 Canale [CN]
tel. 0173979485
www.enricoserafino.it

CELLAR SALES
PRE-BOOKED VISITS

ANNUAL PRODUCTION **450,000 bottles**
HECTARES UNDER VINE **13**
VITICULTURE METHOD **Conventional**

Enrico Serafino, now owned by Campari, is a long-established winery set up in the 19th century, which boasts vineyards planted more than 30 years ago in Roero and in other zones, such as Langhe. Restructuring and hard work over recent years have brought the wines back on a par with the best products from Roero. In 2008, the drive for improvement saw the presentation of the Cantina Maestra line, which aims to be a selection of the highest quality.

The new-look Serafino winery did well with the classic line and Cantina Maestra wines, sending two to the finals. The spicy Roero Pasiunà Cantina Maestra '06 shows dried flower aromas that confer a certain aristocratic finesse while the medium-bodied palate gives good fruit, leading to an alcoholic but well-orchestrated finish. The fresh Alta Langa Metodo Classico '05 is also excellent, with flowers and apples on the nose and a long, creamy finish. The rest of the range is well executed, with a special mention for the '06 Roero, its dried herb and red berry fruit slightly veiled by oak, and the deep Barbera d'Alba '07, with spice and tobacco.

Poderi Sinaglio

fraz. Ricca
via Sinaglio, 5
12055 Diano d'Alba [CN]
tel. 0173612209
www.poderisinaglio.it

CELLAR SALES
PRE-BOOKED VISITS
VISITOR FACILITIES
FOOD

ANNUAL PRODUCTION **44,000 bottles**
HECTARES UNDER VINE **13**
VITICULTURE METHOD **Conventional**

The winery of the brothers Bruno and Silvano Accomo is based on a happy combination of farm holidays and quality wines. The enviable location of this fine farmhouse is the ideal setting for attracting wine tourists from Italy and abroad in search of new discoveries and old friends. The range of wines available, which covers the classic Langhe types, is dependable and far from uninteresting on the palate, offering very drinkable bottles, above all in the Dolcettos. Interesting work is also being done with moscato.

Dolcetto di Diano Sorì Bric Maiolica '08 is a great success, with intense blackberry and chocolate aromas over a delicately vegetal backdrop, backed up by full body and a fine tannic weave that bodes well for ageing prospects. The Barbera d'Alba Vigna Erta '07 may be still a touch too oaky but it has full fruit flesh and a lingering, fresh finish. The fruity, no-nonsense Dolcetto di Diano '08 also performed well. Its sound, spontaneous approachability makes it an excellent foodd wine. The appealing Langhe Nebbiolo '08 proffers subtle, appetizing notes of flowers and spice.

○ Alta Langa M. Cl. '05	♟♟ 5
● Roero Pasiunà Cantina Maestra '06	♟♟ 5
● Barbera d'Alba '07	♟♟ 4
● Barbera d'Alba Bacajé Cantina Maestra '08	♟♟ 4*
● Barbera d'Alba Sup. Parduné Cantina Maestra '06	♟♟ 4*
● Nebbiolo d'Alba Diauleri Cantina Maestra '07	♟♟ 4*
● Roero '06	♟♟ 4*
○ Roero Arneis '08	♟ 4
○ Roero Arneis Canteiò Cantina Maestra '08	♟ 4
○ Alta Langa M. Cl. '04	♟♟ 5
● Barbera d'Alba Bacajé Cantina Maestra '07	♟♟ 4
● Barbera d'Alba Sup. Parduné Cantina Maestra '05	♟♟ 5
● Roero '05	♟♟ 4
○ Roero Arneis '07	♟♟ 4
○ Roero Arneis Canteiò Cantina Maestra '07	♟♟ 4
● Roero Pasiunà Cantina Maestra '05	♟♟ 5

● Barbera d'Alba V. Erta '07	♟♟ 4*
● Dolcetto di Diano d'Alba Sorì Bric Maiolica '08	♟♟ 4*
● Langhe Nebbiolo '08	♟♟ 4
● Langhe Rosso Sinaij '06	♟♟ 5
● Barbera d'Alba '08	♟ 3
● Dolcetto di Diano d'Alba '08	♟ 3
○ Langhe Chardonnay '08	♟ 4
● Nebbiolo d'Alba Giachét '07	♟ 5
● Barbera d'Alba V. Erta '06	♟♟ 4
● Diano d'Alba Sörì Bric Maiolica '07	♟♟ 4
● Dolcetto di Diano d'Alba '07	♟♟ 3
● Langhe Rosso Sinaij '05	♟♟ 5
○ Piemonte Moscato Passito Le Monache '06	♟♟ 5

La Smilla

VIA GARIBALDI, 7
15060 BOSIO [AL]
TEL. 0143684245
www.lasmilla.it

CELLAR SALES

ANNUAL PRODUCTION **100,000 bottles**
HECTARES UNDER VINE **6**
VITICULTURE METHOD **Conventional**

La Smilla earns a full-length profile this time, thanks to impressive results over the years, the excellent range presented for this Giude clinching promotion. The Bosio-based cellar owns vineyards in Gavi and Ovada, where respectively cortese and dolcetto are planted, and which provide grapes for the top wines in the range. The winery is still located in the centre of the town, and uses the old cement vats alongside modern, temperature-controlled stainless steel tanks and barriques for ageing the front-rank wines.

Dolcetto Nsè Pesa '07 made the finals with rich fruit aromas lent complexity by wafts of tobacco and spice, nicely offset by a muscular palate with a satisfyingly long finish. The '08 Gavi di Gavi boasts excellent overall harmony, intense aromatics and a rounded palate. The Bergi '07 is more austere but balanced and well sustained. The excellent basic Gavi '08 shows freshness at every stage of tasting. There are fruit aromas and estery notes on the '07 Dolcetto while the two Barbera del Monferratos are varietal and faithful to their territory.

★ Sottimano

LOC. COTTÀ, 21
12052 NEIVE [CN]
TEL. 0173635186
www.sottimano.it

CELLAR SALES
PRE-BOOKED VISITS

ANNUAL PRODUCTION **65,000 bottles**
HECTARES UNDER VINE **14**
VITICULTURE METHOD **Conventional**

It's always a pleasure to see the owners of one of the most successful wineries in the Langhe, Rino Sottimano and his son Andrea, at work together. The former's seraphic wisdom and the letter's shrewd curiosity seem to meld in a range of increasingly high-quality wines, in which four Barbaresco selections, and since 2004 a Riserva, stand out. With moderately long skin contact, malolactic and ageing in part-new barriques, the winery's approach is modern but the substance remains extremely classic.

For some years, there were rumours going round about a fantastic Barbaresco Riserva that the Sottimano family intended to unveil in the memorable Langhe vintage of 2004. Our high expectations were not disappointed in the glass. There are no concessions, no corners cut, in this impressively compact wine with an austere, spicy nose and a palate with still very boisterous extract. From the 2006 selections, we just preferred the juicy, very smoky Cottà, followed by the Pajoré, more balsamic than spicy this year. The Currà is more closed and still needs to absorb its oak. It came in a step below the Fausoni.

● Dolcetto di Ovada Nsè Pesa '07	♟♟ 4*
● Dolcetto di Ovada '07	♟♟ 3*
○ Gavi '08	♟♟ 3*
○ Gavi del Comune di Gavi '08	♟♟ 3*
○ Gavi I Bergi '07	♟♟ 4
● Barbera del M.to '07	♟ 3
● Barbera del M.to Scarlatta '07	♟ 3
● Dolcetto di Ovada Nsè Pesa '06	♟♟ 4*
○ Gavi del Comune di Gavi '07	♟♟ 3*
○ Gavi del Comune di Gavi I Bergi '05	♟♟ 4
○ Gavi del Comune di Gavi I Bergi '04	♟♟ 4*
○ Gavi I Bergi '06	♟♟ 4

● Barbaresco Ris. '04	♟♟♟ 8
● Barbaresco Cottà '06	♟♟ 8
● Barbaresco Currà '06	♟♟ 8
● Barbaresco Pajoré '06	♟♟ 8
● Barbaresco Fausoni '06	♟♟ 8
● Barbera d'Alba Pairolero '07	♟♟ 5
● Langhe Nebbiolo '07	♟♟ 5
● Maté '08	♟♟ 4*
● Dolcetto d'Alba Bric del Salto '08	♟ 4
● Barbaresco Cottà '05	♟♟♟ 8
● Barbaresco Cottà '99	♟♟♟ 7
● Barbaresco Cottà '98	♟♟♟ 7
● Barbaresco Currà '04	♟♟♟ 7
● Barbaresco Pajoré '01	♟♟♟ 7
● Barbaresco Pajoré '00	♟♟♟ 7
● Barbaresco Pajoré '98	♟♟♟ 7

Luigi Spertino

VIA LEA, 505
14047 MOMBERCELLI [AT]
TEL. 0141959098
www.luigispertino.it

CELLAR SALES
PRE-BOOKED VISITS

ANNUAL PRODUCTION 40,000 bottles
HECTARES UNDER VINE 9
VITICULTURE METHOD Naturale

This winery gets its name from its founder, Luigi Spertino, who in the late 1970s decided to start bottling his wine. It's come a long way since then. Mauro, who now manages the estate with his father Luigi, works dedicatedly in the vineyard to create wines that are a faithful expression of their terroir. The Barbera is the finest product of their untiring commitment.

We are particularly happy to award Three Glasses to the Spertinos for their passion, willingness to experiment and constant quest for improvement. Barbera d'Asti Superiore La Mandorla '07 comes from part-dried grapes, rather like a barbera-based Amarone, and shows intense, focused aromas of spice, quinine, tobacco and plum. The deep, layered palate somehow manages to give great density while remaining fresh and harmonious. The finish is also fantastically long. We very much liked the Barbera d'Asti '07 with its classic earthy and quinine notes veering towards black berry fruit and leather, and the subtle, well-typed Grignolino d'Asti '08.

★★★ La Spinetta

VIA ANNUNZIATA, 17
14054 CASTAGNOLE DELLE LANZE [AT]
TEL. 0141877396
www.la-spinetta.com

PRE-BOOKED VISITS

ANNUAL PRODUCTION 600,000 bottles
HECTARES UNDER VINE 100
VITICULTURE METHOD Conventional

This winery straddles the Asti area, where the owners, the Rivetti family, come from, and Langhe, with vineyards in Barbaresco and Grinzane Cavour in the Barolo production area. The innovative house style hinges on a search for easy-drinking, yet still satisfying, wines with fruity, cohesive aromas. The Spinetta approach, and their modern, highly individual wines, makes this one of the most controversial, but also most internationally appreciated, wineries.

The solid, complex Barbera d'Asti Superiore Bionzo '07 is the most representative wine this year, made with textbook vineyard and cellar technique. The excellent Piemonte Moscato Passito Oro '04 is sweet but not cloying. The '06 Barbarescos are a little less convincing than usual, with the beefy Starderi ahead of the Gallina and the Valeirano, which put the accent on fruit. The tidier, more austere Barolo Campè '05 is better. The reds wound up with a fair '07 version of Monferrato Pin, from nebbiolo and barbera, and the always delicious Moscato d'Asti Bricco Quaglia '08, Barbera d'Alba Gallina '07 and Barbera d'Asti Ca' di Pian '07, all classics of their genre.

● Barbera d'Asti Sup. La Mandorla '07	♟♟♟	8
● Barbera d'Asti '07	♟♟	5
● Grignolino d'Asti '08	♟♟	5
● Barbera d'Asti '06	♟♟	4*
● Barbera d'Asti '05	♟♟	4*
● Barbera d'Asti '04	♟♟	4*
● Barbera d'Asti Sup. La Mandorla '06	♟♟	6

● Barbera d'Asti Sup. Bionzo '07	♟♟♟	7
● Barbaresco Vign. Starderi '06	♟♟	8
● Barolo Campè '05	♟♟	8
○ Piemonte Moscato Passito Oro '04	♟♟	7
● Barbaresco Vign. Gallina '06	♟♟	8
● Barbaresco Vign. Valeirano '06	♟♟	8
● Barbera d'Alba Vign. Gallina '07	♟♟	7
● Barbera d'Asti Ca' di Pian '07	♟♟	5*
● M.to Rosso Pin '07	♟♟	7
○ Moscato d'Asti Bricco Quaglia '08	♟♟	4*
● Barbaresco Vign. Starderi '05	♟♟♟	8
● Barbaresco Vign. Starderi '04	♟♟♟	8
● Barbaresco Vign. Starderi '01	♟♟♟	8
● Barbaresco Vign. Valeirano '04	♟♟♟	8
● Barolo Campè '01	♟♟♟	8
● M.to Rosso Pin '06	♟♟♟	7

Luigi Tacchino

VIA MARTIRI DELLA BENEDICTA, 26
15060 CASTELLETTO D'ORBA [AL]
TEL. 0143830115
www.luigitacchino.it

CELLAR SALES
PRE-BOOKED VISITS

ANNUAL PRODUCTION 120,000 bottles
HECTARES UNDER VINE 10
VITICULTURE METHOD Conventional

The Tacchino family has been in wine for at least three generations. Today, the exuberant Romina and her brother Alessio deal with production, from vineyard to distribution. The estate today covers 25 hectares, of which nearly half is under vine and beautifully aspected, mainly south-southeast. Guyot pruning is used and the average yield is around 60-70 quintals per hectare. The vineyards that supply the grapes are 20 to 50 years old. And it all comes together in a range of wines whose excellence never varies from year to year.

In particular, the purplish ruby Albarola '07 flaunts a fruity, spicy nose, paving the way for a powerful, well-orchestrated palate with a lingering finish. The young but characterful Barbera '08 is well-balanced throughout. Cabernet sauvignon, barbera and dolcetto join forces in Di Fatto, with its fruit aromas and weighty, well-balanced palate. The almost impenetrably dark Du Riva '06 shows heady, evolved notes on nose and palate while the Dolcetto '08 is very drinkable. Finally, there are two whites: the complex, minerally Gavi and the fruit-fuelled, nicely acidic Cortese, both '08s.

Michele Taliano

C.SO A. MANZONI, 24
12046 MONTÀ [CN]
TEL. 0173976512
www.talianomichele.com

CELLAR SALES
PRE-BOOKED VISITS

ANNUAL PRODUCTION 60,000 bottles
HECTARES UNDER VINE 12
VITICULTURE METHOD Conventional

Michele Taliano's estate, run today by his sons Alberto and Ezio, the latter also the winery's oenologist, is situated in Montà, but the vineyards are located on either side of the river Tanaro, in Roero and Barbaresco. The range of wines produced is fairly diversified, despite low production levels. Most of the labels are based on native varieties, accompanied by the internationals, sauvignon and cabernet.

Roero Roche dra Bòssora Riserva '06 lived up to its reputation as one of the best Roeros around, once more reaching our finals. Dry herb and citrus zest aromas deliver complexity and finesse while the rounded, full-bodied palate shows a long, stylish finish, slightly thinned by the underlying alcohol. We also liked the rich Barbera d'Alba Laboriosa '06, with its marked acidity, and the floral, tannic Nebbiolo d'Alba Blagheur '07. From the vineyards on the other side of the Tanaro, we liked Barbaresco Ad Altiora '06, with its pervasive strawberry, dried flowers and liquorice, leading to good pulp and a long finish.

● Barbera del M.to Albarola '07	♥♥ 4*
● Barbera del M.to '08	♥♥ 4
● Dolcetto di Ovada Du Riva '06	♥♥ 4*
○ Gavi del Comune di Gavi '08	♥♥ 4
● M.to Rosso Di Fatto '06	♥♥ 5
○ Cortese dell'Alto M.to Marsenca '08	♥ 3
● Dolcetto di Ovada '08	♥ 4
● Barbera del M.to '07	♀♀ 4
● Barbera del M.to Albarola '06	♀♀ 4
● Dolcetto di Ovada '07	♀♀ 4
● Dolcetto di Ovada Du Riva '04	♀♀ 4
○ Gavi del Comune di Gavi '07	♀♀ 4

● Roero Ròche dra Bòssora Ris. '06	♥♥ 5
● Barbaresco Ad Altiora '06	♥♥ 6
● Barbera d'Alba Laboriosa '06	♥♥ 4*
● Nebbiolo d'Alba Blagheur '07	♥♥ 4*
● Barbera d'Alba A Bon Rendre '08	♥ 4
● Langhe Rosso '06	♥ 4
○ Roero Arneis Sernì '08	♥ 4
● Barbaresco Ad Altiora '05	♀♀ 6
● Barbera d'Alba A Bon Rendre '07	♀♀ 4*
● Barbera d'Alba Laboriosa '05	♀♀ 4
● Langhe Nebbiolo Blagheur '07	♀♀ 4*
● Roero Ròche dra Bòssora '05	♀♀ 5
● Roero Ròche dra Bòssora '04	♀♀ 5
● Roero Ròche dra Bòssora '03	♀♀ 5*

Tenuta La Tenaglia

S.DA SANTUARIO DI CREA, 5C
15020 SERRALUNGA DI CREA [AL]
TEL. 0142940252
www.latenaglia.com

CELLAR SALES
PRE-BOOKED VISITS

ANNUAL PRODUCTION 100,000 bottles
HECTARES UNDER VINE 30
VITICULTURE METHOD Conventional

The hills around Serralunga di Crea boast an important winemaking history, dating back to the 17th century, when the governor of Moncalvo, Giorgio Tenaglia, established the estate. Lying at 450 metres above sea level, it offers beautiful views over woodland and vineyards. Behind the estate stands a much-visited 16th-century sanctuary. Wine has always been important here and excellent results have been achieved over the years, especially with native Monferrato varieties.

The Barbera d'Asti Giorgio Tenaglia '07 opens with estery green aromas, leading to a balanced, lingering palate. Emozioni '07 shows ruby tending to garnet, with good nose-palate balance and an attractive finish. Bricco Crea '08, a simple, approachable Barbera, offers a beefy palate and nice acidity. The Monferrato Rosso Olivieri '07 takes its name from the Neapolitan painter whose work features on the label. Impenetrably dark, it shows evolved, balsamic notes over a slightly rustic but lingering palate. The well-typed Grignolino '08 shows spice on the nose and succulent tannins on the finish.

Tenuta dei Fiori

FRAZ. RODOTIGLIA
VIA VALCALOSSO, 3
14052 CALOSSO [AT]
TEL. 0141853819
www.tenutadeifiori.com

CELLAR SALES
PRE-BOOKED VISITS
VISITOR FACILITIES

ANNUAL PRODUCTION 20,000 bottles
HECTARES UNDER VINE 4.5
VITICULTURE METHOD Conventional

Valter Bosticardo's small winery, established in 1985, is in the beautiful natural setting of Valcalosso. Here, amidst hill vineyards, is the lovingly renovated family farmhouse, now transformed into an attractive farm holiday centre. Valter is focused on promoting and getting the most out of the area's typical varieties, in particular gamba di pernice. The estate also has barbera vineyards dating back over 70 years and other plots planted to moscato, dolcetto, freisa and some non-local varieties.

This year, Valter presented his signature wine, the dry Gamba di Pernice '06. Elegant and well-developed on the nose, with slightly smoky notes and juniper berries, it has a lean palate with austere tannins and a long, vibrant finish. The outstanding Moscato d'Asti Rairì '08 is one of the best from a difficult year, and throws a characterful nose of peppermint and gingerbread over a fresh, impressively long palate. Valter's distinctive style is also evident in the Asti Metodo Classico 12 Anni Pensiero, with evolved eucalyptus and dried fruit ushering in an extraordinarily full-bodied, long palate that signs off with honey and more eucalyptus.

● Barbera d'Asti Emozioni '07	⅌⅌	6
● Barbera d'Asti Giorgio Tenaglia '07	⅌⅌	5
● Grignolino del M.to Casalese '08	⅌⅌	4*
● M.to Rosso Olivieri '07	⅌⅌	6
● Barbera d'Asti Bricco Crea '08	⅌	4
● Barbera d'Asti Emozioni '04	♀♀	6
● Barbera d'Asti Emozioni '03	♀♀	6
● Barbera d'Asti Giorgio Tenaglia '03	♀♀	5
● Barbera del M.to Sup. Tenaglia è... '04	♀♀	4
● Grignolino del M.to Casalese '07	♀♀	4
● Grignolino del M.to Casalese '05	♀♀	3
○ Piemonte Chardonnay '05	♀♀	3*

○ Asti M. Cl. 12 Anni Pensiero	⅌⅌	5
● Gamba di Pernice '06	⅌⅌	4
○ Moscato d'Asti Rairì '08	⅌⅌	3
● Barbera d'Asti Sup. Rusticardi 1933 Castello di Calosso '05	♀♀	6
● Barbera d'Asti Sup. Rusticardi 1933 Castello di Calosso '04	♀♀	6
● M.to Rosso Cinque File '04	♀♀	5
● M.to Rosso Cinque File '03	♀♀	5

Terralba

FRAZ. INSELMINA
15050 BERZANO DI TORTONA [AL]
TEL. 013180403
www.terralbavini.com

CELLAR SALES
PRE-BOOKED VISITS

ANNUAL PRODUCTION **40,000 bottles**
HECTARES UNDER VINE **15**
VITICULTURE METHOD **Conventional**

The hills of Volpeglino and Berzano extending from Valcurone form a natural backdrop for the vineyards owned by the Terralba estate. In this marvellous natural setting, we find Stefano Daffonchio's recently finished winery. His wines are not easy, because Tortona area often yields muscular, concentrated wines that only give their best with time, in the sense of cellar ageing and aeration in the glass. But experience teaches us that those who are prepared to wait will not be disappointed.

This is also why in recent years, the Croatina Montegrande has been left to age for a few months longer. The '06 is now back at the best levels of past years. Barbera Identità '07 is superb. One of the best in the area, it exhibits perfect harmony of fruit and structure, signing off with impressive length and great character. The first-rate Timorasso Derthona '07 is fresh, fruit-driven and nicely mineral. Vigna di Mezzo '06, from barbera and croatina, and Moradella '07, from the native variety of the same name, are also well made. We will wait to assess the two major wines, Barbera Terralba and Timorasso Stato, which need more time to open up.

● Piemonte Barbera Identità '07	♟♟	5
● Colli Tortonesi Rosso Montegrande '06	♟♟	5
● Colli Tortonesi Rosso Terralba '06	♟♟	6
● Colli Tortonesi Rosso V. di Mezzo '06	♟♟	5
○ Colli Tortonesi Timorasso Derthona '07	♟♟	5
○ Colli Tortonesi Bianco Stato '07	♟	6
● Moradella '07	♟	4
○ Colli Tortonesi Bianco Stato '05	♟♟	6
○ Colli Tortonesi Bianco Stato '04	♟♟	6
○ Colli Tortonesi Bianco Stato '03	♟♟	5
● Colli Tortonesi Rosso Terralba '01	♟♟	6
○ Colli Tortonesi Timorasso Derthona '06	♟♟	5

Terre da Vino

VIA BERGESIA, 6
12060 BAROLO [CN]
TEL. 0173564611
www.terredavino.it

CELLAR SALES
PRE-BOOKED VISITS

ANNUAL PRODUCTION **5.500,000 bottles**
HECTARES UNDER VINE **4500**
VITICULTURE METHOD **Conventional**

In 2010 this winery, which has invested heavily in Barbera, celebrates its 30th birthday. The achievement is down to the success of the Superbarbera project, embodied by the brilliant La Luna e i Falò released in hundreds of thousands of bottles each year, all first-rate. The impressive, new winery is based in Barolo, straddling Cannubi and Brunate.

In the wide range presented for our tastings this year, three wines stand out: Barolo Poderi Scarrone '04, Barbera Croere and La Luna e i Falò, both '07s. The first opens with evident alcohol supporting attractive spice and dried flowers. Oak is still evident on the palate but supple, well-honed tannins ensure an extremely pleasing drink. As always, the Barbera d'Alba is fruit-driven while the Barbera d'Asti is darker, with aromas of rain-soaked earth and a significantly tastier, acidic palate. The rest of the range comprises complex wines, such as Barolo Essenze '05, Nebbiolo La Malora '07 or Passito La Bella Estate '07, and more approachable labels.

● Barbera d'Alba Sup. Croere '07	♟	5
● Barbera d'Asti Sup. La Luna e i Falò '07	♟♟	4
● Barolo Essenze '05	♟♟	7
● Barolo Poderi Scarrone '04	♟♟	7
● Langhe Nebbiolo La Malora '07	♟♟	5
○ M.to Bianco Tra Donne Sole '08	♟♟	4*
○ Piemonte Moscato Passito La Bella Estate '07	♟♟	5
● Barbaresco La Casa in Collina '06	♟	6
● Barolo Paesi Tuoi '05	♟	6
○ Gavi del Comune di Gavi Masseria dei Carmelitani '08	♟	4
○ Roero Arneis La Villa '08	♟	4
● Barbera d'Alba Sup. Croere '06	♟♟	5
● Barbera d'Asti Sup. Nizza Martlet '06	♟♟	5
● Barolo Essenze '04	♟♟	7

Terre del Barolo

VIA ALBA-BAROLO, 5
12060 CASTIGLIONE FALLETTO [CN]
TEL. 0173262053
www.terredelbarolo.com

CELLAR SALES
PRE-BOOKED VISITS

ANNUAL PRODUCTION 2.500,000 bottles
HECTARES UNDER VINE 610
VITICULTURE METHOD Conventional

The Terre del Barolo co-operative was established in 1959 by Arnaldo Rivera and a group of growers who wanted to create a point of reference for Barolo. Over the years, the winery, today managed by Matteo Bosco, has become a giant, especially if we take into consideration the scale of production in an area made up mainly of small, family-run concerns. The wines in the range represent the various local types.

Terre di Barolo did well, above all thanks to the 2004 Barolos. The gutsy Cannubi shows fresh fruit and a full-flavoured, crunchy, fruit-rich palate with impressive length. The Monvigliero has less thrust but is stylish, with well-typed dried flowers over a focused, attractive palate where the floral notes re-emerge. We were less taken with Rocche Riserva '01, which is well made and nicely concentrated but also a touch stiff. As always, we had no complaints about the earthy, fruit-fuelled Barbera Valdisera '07 or the structured Dogliani '07, with black berry fruit followed by a rounded, fresh palate. The rest of the wines are well up to snuff.

Torraccia del Piantavigna

VIA ROMAGNANO, 69A
28074 GHEMME [NO]
TEL. 0163840040
www.torracciadelpiantavigna.it

CELLAR SALES
PRE-BOOKED VISITS

ANNUAL PRODUCTION 120,000 bottles
HECTARES UNDER VINE 40
VITICULTURE METHOD Conventional

When your name explicitly refers to planting vineyards, your destiny is clear. Actually, Piantavigna was the surname of the Francoli brothers' maternal grandmother. In 1990, they established this operation with over 40 hectares spread over six distinct zones in the provinces of Novara and Vercelli, entirely planted to nebbiolo, vespolina and erbaluce. In the cellar, the collaboration with Beppe Caviola has led to the creation of a wide, varied range of wines, the most serious of which repay careful cellaring and patience.

After winning their first Three Glasses with the '04 Ghemme, Torraccia del Piantavigna scored again this year with the Gattinara '05. This monovarietal Nebbiolo aged for three years in 23 to 28-hectolitre oak casks. The first impression is of a dark, austere wine, with thrust and close-knit stuffing particularly on the palate, which will fuel its development for a long time to come. The Ghemme '05 is on the same lines but more clenched and woody. The Colline Novaresi Vespolina Maretta '07 is extremely spicy but we were less impressed by the Colline Novaresi Nebbiolo Ramale '06.

● Barolo Cannubi '04	♟♟	7
● Barbera d'Alba Valdisera '07	♟♟	3*
● Barolo Monvigliero '04	♟♟	6
● Barolo Rocche Ris. '01	♟♟	6
● Dogliani '07	♟♟	4
● Dolcetto d'Alba '08	♟	3
● Nebbiolo d'Alba '07	♟	4
● Verduno Pelaverga '08	♟	4
● Barolo '04	♟♟	6
● Barolo Castello Ris. '01	♟♟	7

● Gattinara '05	♟♟♟	6
● Ghemme '05	♟♟	6
● Colline Novaresi Vespolina Maretta '07	♟♟	5
○ Colline Novaresi Bianco Erbavoglio '08	♟	4
● Colline Novaresi Nebbiolo Ramale '06	♟	5
⊙ Colline Novaresi Nebbiolo Rosato Barlan '08	♟	4
● Colline Novaresi Nebbiolo Tre Confini '07	♟	4
● Ghemme '04	♟♟♟	6
● Gattinara '04	♟♟	6
● Gattinara '03	♟♟	6

Giancarlo Travaglini

VIA DELLE VIGNE, 36
13045 GATTINARA [VC]
TEL. 0163833588
www.travaglinigattinara.it

CELLAR SALES
PRE-BOOKED VISITS

ANNUAL PRODUCTION **250,000 bottles**
HECTARES UNDER VINE **42**
VITICULTURE METHOD **Conventional**

Even without their unusual asymmetrical, convex bottles, there is no mistaking Travaglini wines for their trademark limpid purity and the natural ease with which they evoke some of the best terroirs of Gattinara. We are at an altitude of around 350 metres, in a zone characterized by acid soil rich in iron-bearing minerals, which enjoys a dry, windy climate, thanks to the nearby Alps. The winery is run today by Cinzia Travaglini, who continues on a path strongly anchored to tradition, starting with her winemaking style.

Travaglini's Gattinara Riserva '04 fully lives up to expectations. We had been waiting for an austere, classic debut vintage and here we have a wine that is all this and much more. Earthy to the core, spicy and generous, it never relinquishes its acid, crunchy fruit with lingering flavour and caressing tannic weave. Equally thrilling is Il Sogno '05, a Nebbiolo from part-dried grapes, which brings together sweetness and austerity with a lingering liquorice finish. The meaty Coste della Sesia Nebbiolo '07 is well focused.

● Gattinara Ris. '04	♟♟♟	6
● Coste della Sesia Nebbiolo '07	♟♟	4
● Il Sogno '05	♟♟	8
● Gattinara Ris. '01	♟♟♟	6
● Gattinara Tre Vigne '04	♟♟♟	6
● Gattinara '04	♟♟	5*
● Gattinara '01	♟♟	5*
● Gattinara Ris. '00	♟♟	6
● Gattinara Ris. '99	♟♟	6
● Gattinara Tre Vigne '01	♟♟	6

Castello di Uviglie

VIA CASTELLO DI UVIGLIE, 73
15030 ROSIGNANO MONFERRATO [AL]
TEL. 0142488132
www.castellodiuviglie.com

CELLAR SALES
PRE-BOOKED VISITS

ANNUAL PRODUCTION **70,000 bottles**
HECTARES UNDER VINE **25**
VITICULTURE METHOD **Conventional**

Castello di Uviglie is situated to the east of Rosignano Monferrato, eight kilometres from Casale Monferrato, and extends over 150 hectares, 25 of which are under vine. Guyot pruning is used and vine density ranges from 4,500 to 4,700 plants per hectare. The vineyards provide barbera, grignolino and freisa, as well as small amounts of sauvignon and chardonnay, for the Monferrato Bianco and the Piemonte Chardonnay Ninfea. In the Ferdinanda vineyard, situated just below the castle, albarossa was planted a few years ago and we can see the first separately vinified results in the '06 1491.

The range of wines kicks off with a fantastic Three Glasses for the deep ruby Barbera Superiore Le Cave '07, which opens on quinine and tobacco, leading into a palate with great structure and interminable length. The almost impenetrably deep ruby Pico Gonzaga '06 shows toasty, spicy oak. The 1491, produced in only 3,500 bottles, astounded us with its imposing structure and tarry, tertiary notes which never overpower the fruit. The other wines presented are also well made with a special mention for the Grignolino San Bastiano, which performed well, despite a difficult year for the variety.

● Barbera del M.to Sup. Le Cave '07	♟♟♟	5
● Barbera del M.to Sup. Pico Gonzaga '06	♟♟	5
● M.to Rosso 1491 '06	♟♟	5
● Barbera del M.to Bricco del Conte '08	♟	4
● Grignolino del M.to Casalese San Bastiano '08	♟	4
○ M.to Bianco San Martino '08	♟	4
● M.to Freisa La Costa '08	♟	4
● Barbera del M.to Sup. Le Cave '05	♟♟	4*
● Barbera del M.to Sup. Le Cave '04	♟♟	4
● Barbera del M.to Sup. Pico Gonzaga '04	♟♟	5
● Barbera del M.to Sup. Pico Gonzaga '03	♟♟	5
● Grignolino del M.to Casalese San Bastiano '06	♟♟	3*

G. D. Vajra

LOC. VERGNE
VIA DELLE VIOLE, 25
12060 BAROLO [CN]
TEL. 017356257
www.gdvajra.it

CELLAR SALES
PRE-BOOKED VISITS

ANNUAL PRODUCTION **220,000 bottles**
HECTARES UNDER VINE **50**
VITICULTURE METHOD **Naturale**

It's always a pleasure to visit the attractive winery of Aldo and Milena Vaira, who are now helped out full-time by their children Giuseppe and Francesca. The family's kindness and hospitality play a decisive role in their success but their winery is highly functional, and fully exploits the excellent fruit from the perfect terroir of their vineyards, mainly located in Barolo. The big news this year is the takeover of Luigi Baudana's winery at Serralunga d'Alba, whose wines in coming years will be made by the Vairas. This major change is bound to bring interesting results.

Great reds and great whites. That pretty much sums up this year's selection. The Moscato '08 is good and the Langhe Bianco '08 from riesling magnificent. In future, it may be released later. Breathing in the overwhelming aromas of the Barolo Bricco delle Viole '05 is like lying in a meadow of flowers. The stylish, fleshy, lingering palate is swathed in sweet tannins. Barolo Albe '05, too, foregrounds finesse and elegance and shows long, with measured tannins. The Kyè '06, a dry, Freisa with exceptional fruit pulp, is particularly good and the Dolcetto Coste & Fossati '08 is as captivating as usual. We also liked the other wines.

● Barolo Bricco delle Viole '05	🍷🍷🍷	8
● Barolo Albe '05	🍷🍷	7
● Dolcetto d'Alba Coste & Fossati '08	🍷🍷	5
○ Langhe Bianco '08	🍷🍷	5
● Barbera d'Alba '07	🍷🍷	5
● Langhe Freisa Kyè '06	🍷🍷	6
● Langhe Nebbiolo '07	🍷🍷	5
○ Moscato d'Asti '08	🍷🍷	5
● Dolcetto d'Alba '08	🍷	4
● Barbera d'Alba Sup. '01	ΨΨΨ	5
● Barolo Bricco delle Viole '01	ΨΨΨ	8
● Barolo Bricco delle Viole '00	ΨΨΨ	8
● Barolo Bricco delle Viole '99	ΨΨΨ	8
○ Langhe Bianco '02	ΨΨΨ	5

Cascina Val del Prete

S.DA SANTUARIO, 2
12040 PRIOCCA [CN]
TEL. 0173616534
valdelprete@tiscali.it

CELLAR SALES
PRE-BOOKED VISITS

ANNUAL PRODUCTION **40,000 bottles**
HECTARES UNDER VINE **13**
VITICULTURE METHOD **Naturale**

Mario Roagna is the current owner of this winery in the middle of a splendid natural amphitheatre. It was purchased over 30 years ago by his parents, who until then had been tenant farmers. The winery, whose name probably derives from a priest who lived there in the 18th century, focuses entirely on native varieties: arneis, barbera and nebbiolo. Mario's aim is to produce wines that reflect their terroir and this is why he opted for biodynamic viticulture, although the estate is not yet certified.

Val del Prete performed well with two wines in the finals. The vibrant Roero Bricco Medica '06 has beautifully spiced oak that never overpowers the fruit, accompanied by quinine and liquorice. The potent, full-flavoured palate has good structure and a long finish. Barbera d'Alba Superiore Carolina '07 releases sweet spice and cherry jam on the nose, underpinned by lovely acidity and close-knit tannins in the mouth. Toasty oak is too evident in the Roero '06 but it brims with fruit. Nebbiolo d'Alba Vigna di Lino '07 is also good, showing liquorice, tobacco and raspberry, but a touch rustic on the palate.

● Barbera d'Alba Sup. Carolina '07	🍷🍷	6
● Roero Bricco Medica '06	🍷🍷	6
● Nebbiolo d'Alba V. di Lino '07	🍷🍷	5
● Roero '06	🍷🍷	7
● Barbera d'Alba Serra de' Gatti '08	🍷	4
○ Roero Arneis Luet '08	🍷	4
● Nebbiolo d'Alba V. di Lino '00	ΨΨΨ	5
● Roero '04	ΨΨΨ	7
● Roero '03	ΨΨΨ	7
● Roero '01	ΨΨΨ	7
● Roero '00	ΨΨΨ	6
● Barbera d'Alba Serra de' Gatti '07	ΨΨ	4*
● Barbera d'Alba Sup. Carolina '06	ΨΨ	6
● Nebbiolo d'Alba V. di Lino '06	ΨΨ	6
● Roero '05	ΨΨ	7

Mauro Veglio

FRAZ. ANNUNZIATA
CASCINA NUOVA, 50
12064 LA MORRA [CN]
TEL. 0173509212
www.mauroveglio.com

CELLAR SALES
PRE-BOOKED VISITS

ANNUAL PRODUCTION **60,000 bottles**
HECTARES UNDER VINE **12**
VITICULTURE METHOD **Naturale**

Mauro and Daniela, inseparable in life and at work, ply their trade in the delightful setting of Annunziata, where they are neighbours of the legendary Elio Altare. Their steady progress is due to the intelligent decision to constantly put themselves to the test. Rather than blindly pursuing their ideas, they consciously measure themselves against their competitors. As a result, nearly all the wines have achieved an unprecedented degree of balance and perfection.

The superb Barolo Vigneto Gattera '05 gives aristocratic, almost austere, quinine and rhubarb followed by finesse on the full-flavoured, powerful palate, with tight-knit tannins. This concentrated, already enjoyable Barolo was a natural for Three Glasses. The stylish Rocche dell'Annunziata '05 shows forthright fruit and oak on the nose, leading to a lingering palate. Vigneto Arborina '05 is also still a tad too oaky but the fruit pulp is remarkable. The fruit-forward, sweetly alcoholic Castelletto '05, from Monforte, has slightly stiffer tannins. But the whole range is good, starting with the charming '07 version of the ageworthy, fruit-led Barbera d'Alba Cascina Nuova.

Eraldo Viberti

FRAZ. SANTA MARIA
B.TA TETTI, 53
12064 LA MORRA [CN]
TEL. 017350308
www.eraldoviberti.com

CELLAR SALES
PRE-BOOKED VISITS

ANNUAL PRODUCTION **27,000 bottles**
HECTARES UNDER VINE **5**
VITICULTURE METHOD **Conventional**

This small estate releases very few wines and attention to detail is the guiding principle, both in the rows and at the winery. Here we find Barolo, Barbera and Dolcetto, the three great classics of the area, interpreted with consummate self-assurance. The house style will not disappoint even the most demanding palates, and the consistent quality across the range is a guarantee that makes this able grower a benchmark. Eraldo Viberti is nothing less than a wine craftsman with a great love of the land and little time for public relations.

Eraldo's appealing Barolo '05 has fresh, somewhat citrussy notes in a profile that is not overly complex but very well managed, with still somewhat prominent tannins. The oak is well gauged and does not compromise the fruit. The Barbera Vigna Clara '06 is as ever distinctive for its elegant modernity, based on the use of oak but above all on the ever-present, crunchy fruit. The style is up to date, with forthright ripe cherries against a backdrop of rain-soaked earth.

● Barolo Vign. Gattera '05	♟♟♟ 7
● Barbera d'Alba Cascina Nuova '07	♟♟ 6
● Barolo Vign. Rocche dell'Annunziata '05	♟♟ 8
● Barolo Castelletto '05	♟♟ 7
● Barolo Vign. Arborina '05	♟♟ 7
● Langhe Nebbiolo Angelo '07	♟♟ 5
● Langhe Rosso L'Insieme '06	♟♟ 7
● Barbera d'Alba '08	♟ 4
● Dolcetto d'Alba '08	♟ 4
● Barbera d'Alba Cascina Nuova '99	♟♟♟ 5
● Barbera d'Alba Cascina Nuova '96	♟♟♟ 5
● Barolo V. Rocche '96	♟♟♟ 7
● Barolo Vign. Arborina '01	♟♟♟ 7
● Barolo Vign. Arborina '00	♟♟♟ 7
● Barbera d'Alba Cascina Nuova '06	♟♟ 6
● Barolo Vign. Arborina '04	♟♟ 7
● Barolo Vign. Arborina '03	♟♟ 7
● Barolo Vign. Rocche dell'Annunziata '04	♟♟ 7

● Barolo '05	♟♟ 7
● Barbera d'Alba V. Clara '06	♟♟ 5
● Barolo '93	♟♟♟ 8
● Barbera d'Alba V. Clara '05	♟♟ 6
● Barbera d'Alba V. Clara '04	♟♟ 6
● Barbera d'Alba V. Clara '03	♟♟ 6
● Barolo '04	♟♟ 7
● Barolo '01	♟♟ 7*
● Barolo '00	♟♟ 7*

Vicara

CASCINA MADONNA DELLE GRAZIE, 5
15030 ROSIGNANO MONFERRATO [AL]
TEL. 0142488054
www.vicara.it

CELLAR SALES
PRE-BOOKED VISITS

ANNUAL PRODUCTION 180,000 bottles
HECTARES UNDER VINE 40
VITICULTURE METHOD Biodynamic certified

The three estates forming Vicara are located at Ozzano, Salabue and Rosignano Monferrato, and have around 40 hectares under vine in five municipalities: Salabue, Serralunga di Crea, Ozzano, Treville and Rosignano Monferrato. The areas are geologically different, a fact that has been exploited to the full by selecting the most suitable varieties for each block. The vineyards, where Guyot pruning is the norm, are aged from seven to 60 years. Great care is dedicated to vineyard management, with eco-friendly farming methods.

The first thing you notice in Vicara's wines is their great balance. Excellence is achieved in the impenetrably hued Cantico della Crosia '06, where blackberries and spices open onto a well-structured palate which nicely handles the weight of the alcohol. Superiore Vadmò '05 shows tertiary aromas from barrel ageing. The highly drinkable Volpuva '08 has concentrated aromas. The Barbera Vivace '08 is a fine example of this typical Monferrato wine. Despite the difficult growing year, the Grignolino '08 does very well. Last up is the Rubello '06, from barbera, nebbiolo and cabernet sauvignon, which is ready for drinking.

★ Vietti

P.ZZA VITTORIO VENETO, 8
12060 CASTIGLIONE FALLETTO [CN]
TEL. 017362825
www.vietti.com

CELLAR SALES
PRE-BOOKED VISITS

ANNUAL PRODUCTION 250,000 bottles
HECTARES UNDER VINE 35
VITICULTURE METHOD Conventional

Few wineries manage to please both enthusiasts and professionals like this historic Castiglione Falletto operation, brilliantly managed by Luca Currado. In many ways, Vietti's wines are on the cusp where modern sensibilities meet tradition. There is no cast-iron policy behind their style, just a deep knowledge of the characteristics of each of the marvellous vineyards, such as Rocche, Brunate, Lazzarito and Villero, as well as an ability to bring out the best from other varieties like barbera, dolcetto, arneis and moscato.

This year's show from Vietti wines is almost embarrassing, with no fewer than six finalists, all clamouring for Three Glasses. In the end, it was the Barolo Lazzarito '05 that won the day, with splendidly vibrant density introduced by a meaty nose of roots and spices, and backed up by a deep, thrusting palate. The less graceful Barolo Rocche '05 has more bite than usual. The Barolo Brunate '05 is faintly evolved and the Barbaresco Masseria '06 stylish and streamlined. The Barbera d'Alba Scarrone Vigna Vecchia '07 and the Barbera d'Asti Superiore Nizza La Crena '07 are also just short of perfection.

● Barbera del M.to Sup. Cantico della Crosia '06	♟♟ 5
● Barbera del M.to Sup. Vadmò '05	♟♟ 4*
● Barbera del M.to Vivace '08	♟♟ 4
● Barbera del M.to Volpuva '08	♟♟ 4
● Grignolino del M.to Casalese '08	♟♟ 4
● M.to Rosso Rubello '06	♟ 5
● Barbera del M.to Sup. Cantico della Crosia '05	♟♟ 5
● Barbera del M.to Sup. Cantico della Crosia '03	♟♟ 5
● Barbera del M.to Sup. Vadmò '04	♟♟ 4
● Grignolino del M.to Casalese '07	♟♟ 4
● Grignolino del M.to Casalese '06	♟♟ 4*
○ Monferrato Bianco Airales '06	♟♟ 4*

● Barolo Lazzarito '05	♟♟♟+ 8
● Barbaresco Masseria '06	♟♟ 8
● Barbera d'Alba Scarrone V. Vecchia '07	♟♟ 7
● Barbera d'Asti Sup. Nizza La Crena '07	♟♟ 6
● Barolo Brunate '05	♟♟ 8
● Barolo Rocche '05	♟♟ 8
● Barbera d'Alba Scarrone '07	♟♟ 6
● Barbera d'Alba Tre Vigne '07	♟♟ 5
● Barbera d'Asti Tre Vigne '07	♟♟ 5
● Barolo Castiglione '05	♟♟ 7
● Langhe Nebbiolo Perbacco '06	♟♟ 4
● Dolcetto d'Alba Tre Vigne '08	♟ 4
○ Roero Arneis '08	♟ 4
● Barbera d'Asti Sup. Nizza La Crena '03	♟♟♟ 6
● Barolo Lazzarito '04	♟♟♟ 8
● Barolo Villero Ris. '01	♟♟♟ 8

★ Vigna Rionda - Massolino

P.ZZA CAPPELLANO, 8
12050 SERRALUNGA D'ALBA [CN]
TEL. 0173613138
www.massolino.it

CELLAR SALES
PRE-BOOKED VISITS

ANNUAL PRODUCTION **100,000 bottles**
HECTARES UNDER VINE **19**
VITICULTURE METHOD **Conventional**

Franco and Roberto Massolino's Barolos embody the very soul of the Serralunga hills. Far from being subtle or rigid, these wines exude roundness and power, showing closer-knit tannins with more bite than wines from elsewhere, and they have what it takes to age unhurriedly. Barbera, Dolcetto, Chardonnay and Moscato complete a range that includes some of the best-known crus on the west side: Parafada, the only wine part-aged in barrique, Margheria and of course Vigna Rionda.

After achieving top marks in the last two editions with Parafada and Vigna Rionda, the Massolino brothers complete a fantastic hat-trick this year with Three Glasses for Margheria '05. This is a Serralunga Barolo to the core, with nuances of talc and herbs swathing classic earthy, ripe dark fruit. The juicy, vibrant palate makes the difference, with impressively well-integrated alcohol and tannins. More compressed, but equally good, is the Barolo Parafada '05. There was no 2003 vintage of the Vigna Rionda Riserva but we retasted the Dieci Anni '99.

● Barolo Margheria '05	🍷🍷🍷	8
● Barbera d'Alba Gisep '07	🍷🍷	6
● Barolo Parafada '05	🍷🍷	8
● Barolo '05	🍷🍷	6
● Langhe Nebbiolo '06	🍷🍷	5
○ Moscato d'Asti di Serralunga '08	🍷🍷	4*
● Barbera d'Alba '08	🍷	4
● Dolcetto d'Alba '08	🍷	4
● Barolo Parafada '04	🍸🍸🍸	8
● Barolo V. Rionda Ris. '01	🍸🍸🍸	8
● Barolo V. Rionda Ris. '99	🍸🍸🍸	8
● Barolo V. Rionda Ris. '98	🍸🍸🍸	8
● Barolo V. Rionda Ris. '97	🍸🍸🍸	8
● Barolo V. Rionda Ris. '96	🍸🍸🍸	8

I Vignaioli di Santo Stefano

LOC. MARINI, 26
12058 SANTO STEFANO BELBO [CN]
TEL. 0141840419
www.ceretto.com

CELLAR SALES
PRE-BOOKED VISITS

ANNUAL PRODUCTION **325,000 bottles**
HECTARES UNDER VINE **40**
VITICULTURE METHOD **Conventional**

This famous winery opened for business in 1976. Its forte is getting the best out of moscato, which serves as the basis for a complete line of single-variety wines. In times when talk of Asti was limited almost exclusively to industrial production, Vignaioli di Santo Stefano chose the arduous path of quality, beginning with meticulous vineyard management. The shape of the bottles and their style has set a fashion and are still today a benchmark for many Italian and international wine lovers.

The straw yellow-pale green Asti '08 combines an intense nose of sage and lemon with a fairly closed palate, offering lovely, refreshing acidity. The pleasing Moscato d'Asti '08 displays faint but persistent fizziness, and a well-rounded, classic varietal nose. The stylish, fresh palate signs off on a bright note and is not too sweet. We are looking forward to tasting the new edition of the ever charming Passito.

○ Moscato d'Asti '08	🍷🍷	5
○ Asti '08	🍷	6
○ Asti '07	🍸🍸	4
○ Moscato d'Asti '07	🍸🍸	4
○ Piemonte Moscato Passito IL '04	🍸🍸	5
○ Piemonte Moscato Passito IL '03	🍸🍸	5

Vigne Regali

VIA VITTORIO VENETO, 76
15019 STREVI [AL]
TEL. 0144362600
www.castellobanfi.it

PRE-BOOKED VISITS

ANNUAL PRODUCTION **2,000,000 bottles**
HECTARES UNDER VINE **75**
VITICULTURE METHOD **Conventional**

Vigne Regali, with 75 hectares under vine, is one of the most important estates in the province of Alessandria. The wide range of DOC and DOCG wines produced covers most of the varieties native to Alessandria. The estate's standard-bearer is LaLus, from the native Piedmont variety albarossa. Vinified for the first time in 2006, we finally had a chance to taste it and see if the investment made in 2001, when rooted cutting of the variety were planted, had borne the expected fruit.

The dense ruby Monferrato Rosso LaLus '06 gives concentrated, complex aromas, backed up by a potent, lingering palate with good structure. Barbera d'Asti Superiore Vigneto Banin '06 is always up to scratch, showing poised with good nose-palate balance. L'Ardì '08 is a fine, varietal Dolcetto, intense on the nose and in the mouth. Brachetto performed extremely well in the Vigneto La Rosa, as did moscato in the Strevi, both '08s, which bring out the aromatic qualities to the full.

Vigneti Massa

P.ZZA G. CAPSONI, 10
15059 MONLEALE [AL]
TEL. 013180302
vignetimassa@libero.it

CELLAR SALES
PRE-BOOKED VISITS

ANNUAL PRODUCTION **80,000 bottles**
HECTARES UNDER VINE **19.5**
VITICULTURE METHOD **Naturale**

Trying to describe Walter Massa is as hard as assessing his wines. You need to know his eclectic, exuberant character. He's always up for a new challenge yet also pragmatic. And always ready to lend a helping hand. His wines may seem difficult to an experienced taster, but they are simply the result of vinification methods that tend to exalt all the aromatic qualities of the varieties used, whether in a complex wine such as Timorasso, or the simple Freisa.

And if the Timorasso turns out like Sterpi '07, then Three well-deserved Glasses are in the offing. Great minerality, pear and fruit syrup on the nose and a beautifully long finish confirm this as one of Piedmont's best whites. Hot on its heels is Costa del Vento '07 with the same basic traits, but a touch less finesse. Derthona '07 is consciously simpler but equally forthright on the palate. From the reds, we again preferred the more appealing, fruit-heavy Monleale '06 to the weighty, concentrated Bigolla '06. The Pertichetta, from croatina, is also reliable, as is the ever excellent Muscatè.

○ Banfi Brut Talento	♟♟	4
● Barbera d'Asti Sup. Vign. Banin '06	♟♟	6
● Brachetto d'Acqui Vign. La Rosa '08	♟♟	5
● Dolcetto d'Acqui L'Ardì '08	♟♟	4
● M.to Rosso LaLus '06	♟♟	6
○ Moscato d'Asti Strevi '08	♟♟	4
○ Gavi Principessa Gavia '08	♟	4
○ Pinot Brut	♟	4
○ Tener Brut	♟	4
○ Alta Langa Cuvée Aurora '03	♟♟	6
● Barbera d'Asti Vign. Banin '05	♟♟	6
● Dolcetto d'Acqui L'Ardì '07	♟♟	4
○ Moscato d'Asti Strevi '07	♟♟	4

○ Colli Tortonesi Timorasso Sterpi '07	♟♟♟	7
● Colli Tortonesi Monleale '06	♟♟	6
○ Colli Tortonesi Timorasso Derthona '07	♟♟	6
○ Colli Tortonesi Bianco Costa del Vento '07	♟♟	6
● Colli Tortonesi Bigolla '06	♟♟	7
● Colli Tortonesi Barbera Sentieri '08	♟	5
○ Colli Tortonesi Moscato Muscatè '08	♟	3
● Colli Tortonesi Rosso Pertichetta '06	♟	5
● Colli Tortonesi Rosso Pietra del Gallo '08	♟	4
○ Colli Tortonesi Bianco Costa del Vento '05	♟♟♟	8
○ Colli Tortonesi Bianco Sterpi '04	♟♟♟	7
○ Colli Tortonesi Timorasso Derthona '06	♟♟♟	6
○ Colli Tortonesi Bianco Sterpi '05	♟♟	7
● Colli Tortonesi Monleale Bigolla '05	♟♟	7
● Colli Tortonesi Rosso Bigolla '04	♟♟	7
○ Colli Tortonesi Timorasso Sterpi '06	♟♟	7

Villa Fiorita

VIA CASE SPARSE, 2
14034 CASTELLO DI ANNONE [AT]
TEL. 0141401231
www.villafiorita-wines.com

CELLAR SALES
PRE-BOOKED VISITS
VISITOR FACILITIES

ANNUAL PRODUCTION **80,000 bottles**
HECTARES UNDER VINE **12**
VITICULTURE METHOD **Conventional**

In the hills overlooking the Tanaro valley, a few kilometres from Asti, we find Francesco Rondolino's estate. Francesco has focused on producing quality wines from native varieties, such as barbera and grignolino, and from internationals like chardonnay, sauvignon and pinot nero. He is assisted by vineyard manager Sergio Carpignano and oenologist Piero Ballario. For some years now, the winery has been flanked by a farm holiday centre.

Francesco Rondolino's winery did very well. Even with a reduced range of wines, it manages to offer labels of quality and charm, such as Barbera d'Asti Superiore Il Giorgione '07, which again this year made our finals. Bright ruby in colour, it shows complex and elegant on the nose, with coffee cream, cherry and liquorice aromas to the fore. The impressively dynamic palate offers great softness perked up by decent acidity and classy roundness. The Barbera d'Asti Superiore '07 is also good, with rich fruit and hints of spice over a long, well-sustained palate. The Piemonte Chardonnay Le Tavole '08 is well made.

Villa Giada

REG. CEIROLE, 4
14053 CANELLI [AT]
TEL. 0141831100
www.andreafaccio.it

CELLAR SALES
PRE-BOOKED VISITS
VISITOR FACILITIES
FOOD

ANNUAL PRODUCTION **198,000 bottles**
HECTARES UNDER VINE **25**
VITICULTURE METHOD **Conventional**

Andrea Faccio's adventure in the world of wine began in the early 1990s, and it soon became clear that he knew what he was doing. The winery owns three estates: Ceirole, the headquarters, at Canelli; Cascina del Parroco at Calosso; and Cascina Dani at Agliano Terme, where the farm holiday centre is also located. The fairly wide range of products reflects the different shades of wine at Asti.

Andrea Faccio's two flagship Nizza wines did well. Barbera d'Asti Superiore Nizza Dedicato A Federico '05 shows toasty wood on the nose, and ripe fruit laced with spice, while the beautifully long palate is nicely rounded. The Barbera d'Asti Superiore Nizza Bricco Dani '06 shows sweet spice and tobacco with blackberry fruit, followed by a close-knit palate, and a long finish that opens sweet and closes tannic. PrimoVolo '06, from barbera, merlot and sangiovese, is equally good. A little over-evolved, but complex, with spice, dried flowers and tobacco, it has a long, weighty finish. We liked Barbera d'Asti Superiore La Quercia '07 with its ripe fruit, cocoa powder and tobacco.

● Barbera d'Asti Sup. Il Giorgione '07	▼▼	5
● Barbera d'Asti Sup. '07	▼▼	4
○ Piemonte Chardonnay Le Tavole '08	▼	4
● Barbera d'Asti Sup. '06	♉♉	4*
● Barbera d'Asti Sup. '05	♉♉	4*
● Barbera d'Asti Sup. Il Giorgione '06	♉♉	5
● Barbera d'Asti Sup. Il Giorgione '03	♉♉	5
● Grignolino d'Asti Pian delle Querce '07	♉♉	3*
● M.to Rosso Abaco '06	♉♉	3*

● Barbera d'Asti Sup. Nizza Bricco Dani '06	▼▼	5
● Barbera d'Asti Sup. Nizza Dedicato a Federico '05	▼▼	6
● PrimoVolo '06	▼▼	6
● Barbera d'Asti I Surì '08	▼	3*
● Barbera d'Asti Sup. Vign. La Quercia '07	▼	4
● Barbera d'Asti Sup. Bricco Dani '05	♉♉	5
● Barbera d'Asti Sup. Nizza Bricco Dani '05	♉♉	5
● Barbera d'Asti Sup. Nizza Bricco Dani '04	♉♉	5

Villa Sparina

FRAZ. MONTEROTONDO, 56
15066 GAVI [AL]
TEL. 0143633835
www.villasparina.it

PRE-BOOKED VISITS
VISITOR FACILITIES
FOOD

ANNUAL PRODUCTION **480,000 bottles**
HECTARES UNDER VINE **56**
VITICULTURE METHOD **Conventional**

It's hard to believe that this oasis of peace is so close to the chaotic industrial centre of Novi Ligure. The Moccagattas renovated one of the many splendid Genovese stately homes in the hills of southern Piedmont – the 17th-century Villa Sparina – to create one of the region's finest resorts. After established the winery here in the late 1970s, it grew bringing the entire area to life. Over the years, styles and fashions have changed, but today the Moccagattas are convinced that the way forward is respect for the territory. Today, they produce fresh, minerally Gavis and deep, beefy reds.

After a long wait, we finally have Three Glasses for Monterotondo, a frills-free Gavi, mineral on the nose and austere on the palate, with fabulous ageing potential. The basic Gavi is simpler, but still good, showing fresh and long. The stand-out red is Rivalta, from barbera and a splash of merlot. Although still a touch conditioned by toastiness on the nose, its class is evident in the rounded, lingering palate, set against a deep, full-flavoured back palate. The rest of the range is well executed.

Cantina Sociale di Vinchio Vaglio Serra

REG. SAN PANCRAZIO, 1
14040 VINCHIO [AT]
TEL. 0141950903
www.vinchio.com

CELLAR SALES
PRE-BOOKED VISITS

ANNUAL PRODUCTION **1,000,000 bottles**
HECTARES UNDER VINE **320**
VITICULTURE METHOD **Conventional**

This co-operative winery, established in 1959, now brings together over 220 growers, whose vineyards are mainly located in Vinchio and Vaglio Serra, and in the bordering municipalities of Incisa Scapaccino, Cortiglione and Nizza Monferrato. For many years, the co-operative has been working to produce quality wines with genuine personality. It has also made a significant contribution to relaunching Barbera d'Asti, becoming a benchmark for the entire Asti winemaking community.

The attractive 2006 edition of the Barbera d'Asti Superiore Sei Vigne Insynthesis has an intense spicy tobacco nose, followed by a potent, beefy palate. The extremely well-typed Barbera d'Asti Superiore Vigne Vecchie '06 is also excellent, showing fruit, quinine, tobacco and spice on the nose. The palate has great structure, with acidity and fullness offsetting each other and sustaining the finish. Also good are the Barbera d'Asti Superiore I Tre Vescovi '07, with fruit and flavour on the over-alcoholic palate, and the fresh, drinkable Barbera d'Asti Sorì dei Mori '08.

O Gavi del Comune di Gavi Monterotondo '07	🍷🍷🍷	6
● M.to Rosso Rivalta '06	🍷🍷	6
● Barbera del M.to '06	🍷🍷	4
O Brut M. Cl.	🍷🍷	5
O M.to Bianco Montej '08	🍷🍷	4
● Barbera del M.to Montej '07	🍷	4
O Gavi del Comune di Gavi Monterotondo '08	🍷🍷	4
● Barbera del M.to Rivalta '97	🍷🍷🍷	6
O Gavi del Comune di Gavi Monterotondo '99	🍷🍷🍷	5
● M.to Rosso Rivalta '04	🍷🍷🍷	6
● M.to Rosso Rivalta '00	🍷🍷🍷	6
● M.to Rosso Rivalta '99	🍷🍷🍷	6
O Gavi del Comune di Gavi Monterotondo '06	🍷🍷	6
● M.to Rosso Rivalta '05	🍷🍷	6

● Barbera d'Asti Sup. Sei Vigne Insynthesis '06	🍷🍷	7
● Barbera d'Asti Sup. Vigne Vecchie '06	🍷🍷	5
● Barbera d'Asti Sorì dei Mori '08	🍷	3
● Barbera d'Asti Sup. I Tre Vescovi '07	🍷	4
● Barbera d'Asti Sup. Sei Vigne Insynthesis '01	🍷🍷🍷	7
● Barbera d'Asti Sup. Nizza Bricco Laudana '05	🍷🍷	5
● Barbera d'Asti Sup. Nizza Bricco Laudana '04	🍷🍷	4
● Barbera d'Asti Sup. Sei Vigne Insynthesis '04	🍷🍷	7
● Barbera d'Asti Sup. Sei Vigne Insynthesis '03	🍷🍷	7

Gianni Voerzio

S.DA LORETO, 1
12064 LA MORRA [CN]
TEL. 0173509194
voerzio.gianni@tiscali.it

CELLAR SALES
PRE-BOOKED VISITS

ANNUAL PRODUCTION **60.300 bottles**
HECTARES UNDER VINE **12**
VITICULTURE METHOD **Naturale**

Barolos and other wines: Barbera, Dolcetto, Freisa, Arneis and Moscato complete a range that reflects all the excellence of Langhe from this successful winery at La Morra. Retasting the Barolo La Serra '96 early this year, we noted the great capacity for ageing and complexity of expression we have often found in the estate's wines. The style is modern without being extreme and careful selection of the grapes completes a picture of all-round quality.

The deeply hued Barolo La Serra '05 proffers intense blackberries, with generous, tight-knit tannins. This is a Barolo with a very special personality that defies traditional classifications. The highly concentrated, already highly drinkable Barbera '07 is extreme. Impenetrable ruby in colour, it gives cocoa powder and red berry fruit on the nose, backed up by somewhat assertive tannins in the pleasing finish. Langhe Nebbiolo Ciabot della Luna '07 is up to its usual standards of aromatic complexity and harmony on the palate. But the difficult '08 harvest did no favours for early-ripening varieties so the Moscato d'Astis and Dolcetto d'Albas are uncomplicated easy drinkers.

★ Roberto Voerzio

LOC. CERRETO, 1
12064 LA MORRA [CN]
TEL. 0173509196

ANNUAL PRODUCTION **35,000 bottles**
HECTARES UNDER VINE **17**
VITICULTURE METHOD **Conventional**

Roberto Voerzio and his wife Pinuccia passionately manage their 17 hectares of vineyard, five of which are leased, in the best crus of La Morra: Brunate, Rocche, Torriglione, i Capalot; and Barolo: Cerequio, La Serra and Sarmassa. Roberto aims to obtain great wines from extremely low yields, at 30 quintals of grapes, meaning around 2,000 bottles, per hectare. The wines have great character and concentration, and are notable for their skilful use of oak. The limited quantities released have cult status among enthusiasts.

This year, we tasted three '05 Barolos that flaunt Roberto's signature overripe aromas. Our favourite was the Cerequio, whose full structure is accompanied by the delicate balsamic nuances typical of the cru. Appealing liquorice enhances the bouquet of the La Serra, which shows a firm, compact body, but slightly drying oak, while the Brunate seems more relaxed, with berries and violets on the nose and finesse in the mouth. Langhe Nebbiolo Vigneti San Francesco e Fontanazza '06 shows opulent fruit, and signs off astringent and leisurely. The juicy Dolcetto Priavino '07 offers juicy pulp. The other labels are as usual excellent.

● Barbera d'Alba Ciabot della Luna '07	♟♟ 5
● Barolo La Serra '05	♟♟ 8
○ Langhe Arneis Bricco Cappellina '08	♟♟ 5
● Langhe Nebbiolo Ciabot della Luna '07	♟♟ 6
● Dolcetto d'Alba Rocchettevino '08	♟ 4
● Langhe Freisa Sotto I Bastioni '08	♟ 4
○ Moscato d'Asti Vignasergente '08	♟ 5
● Barolo La Serra '98	♟♟♟ 8
● Barolo La Serra '97	♟♟♟ 8
● Barolo La Serra '96	♟♟♟ 8
● Barbera d'Alba Ciabot della Luna '06	♟♟ 5
● Barolo La Serra '04	♟♟ 8
● Langhe Nebbiolo Ciabot della Luna '06	♟♟ 6

● Barolo Brunate '05	♟♟ 8
● Barolo Cerequio '05	♟♟ 8
● Barolo La Serra '05	♟♟ 8
● Barbera d'Alba Vign. Cerreto '06	♟♟ 5
● Dolcetto d'Alba Priavino '07	♟♟ 6
● Langhe Nebbiolo Vign. San Francesco Fontanazza '06	♟♟ 7
● Barolo Brunate '99	♟♟♟ 8
● Barolo Brunate '98	♟♟♟ 8
● Barolo Rocche dell'Annunziata Torriglione '00	♟♟♟ 8

Valerio Aloi

VIA PIETRO FISSORE, 6
12046 MONTÀ [CN]
TEL. 0173975604
nico.bono@libero.it

Nicoletta Aloi's winery continues on track. This year, we tasted a well-crafted Roero Arneis '08 that gives subtle wafts of spring flowers and almonds, a taut, balanced palate and a long, savoury finish. Roero Bricco Morinaldo '07 is spicy and long.

O Roero Arneis '08	🍷🍷 4*
● Roero Bricco Morinaldo '07	🍷 5

Tenuta dell' Arbiola

LOC. ARBIOLA
REG. SALINE, 67
14050 SAN MARZANO OLIVETO [AT]
TEL. 0141856194
www.arbiola.it

This long-established Asti winery was acquired by the Saiagricola group in early 2009. We were offered only two wines this time. Barbera d'Asti Carlotta '08 is restrained with a hint of sweet fruit, nice acidity and good extract and Moscato d'Asti Ferlingot '08 i s peach-themed with a deep, creamy mouthfeel.

● Barbera d'Asti Carlotta '08	🍷🍷 4*
O Moscato d'Asti Ferlingot '08	🍷🍷 4

Barni

VIA FORTE, 63
13862 BRUSNENGO [BI]
TEL. 015985977
filippo.barni@alice.it

Filippo Barni is one of the most original figures in Biella. His six hectares in the Mesola amphitheatre yield barely 25,000 bottles with nebbiolo and erbaluce prominent. We thought the best wine this year was Canatagal '06, a powerful, sweet Erbaluce from dried grapes with good length.

O Cantagal '06	🍷🍷 7
● Bramaterra Vigna Belvedere '04	🍷🍷 5
● Coste della Sesia Rosso Mesolone '05	🍷 5

Beccaria

VIA GIOVANNI BIANCO, 3
15039 OZZANO MONFERRATO [AL]
TEL. 0142487321
www.beccaria-vini.it

Another fine performance from Beccaria, which this time had its flagship Barbera Convivium '06 on parade. Fruit, oak and tobacco combine in a pleasing sensory experience. The ruby-hued Evoè '07 unfolds fruit aromas and a muscular, alcoholic palate.

● Barbera del M.to Sup. Convivium '06	🍷🍷 4
● Barbera del M.to Evoè '07	🍷 3

Bianchi

VIA ROMA, 37
28070 SIZZANO [NO]
TEL. 0321810004
www.bianchibiowine.it

Bianchi presses on, ever faithful to the tenets of organic grape farming. The wide range of excellent wines includes an almost Burgundy-like Ghemme '05 with grassy notes and red berry fruits introducing a youthful, earthy tannic weave. Sizzano '04 is spicy and caressing.

● Ghemme '05	🍷🍷 5
● Gattinara '05	🍷🍷 5
● Sizzano '04	🍷🍷 4
O Colline Novaresi Bianco Luminae '08	🍷 3

Massimo Bo

FRAZ. SANT'ANNA
VIA SANT'ANNA, 19
14055 COSTIGLIOLE D'ASTI [AT]
TEL. 0141961891
bo.massimo@hotmail.com

The Bo family has been tending vines at Costigliole d'Asti for generations. Barbera reigns supreme here. With the assistance of oenologist Luca Caramellino, Massimo is pulling out all the stops to bring us two fine wines, the beefy, complex Costiliolae '07 and the fruitily drinkable Arbuc '08.

● Barbera d'Asti Arbuc '08	🍷🍷 4*
● Barbera d'Asti Sup. Costiliolae '07	🍷🍷 4*

OTHER WINERIES

Francesco Brigatti
via Olmi, 31
28019 Suno [NO]
tel. 032285037
www.vinibrigatti.it

Francesco Brigatti is a one-man band, combining the roles of owner, oenologist and agronomist. Every year, he amazes us with a compact, very personal range topped by Colline Novaresi Rosso MötZiflon, the '06 this time. It's a lean, dynamic blend of nebbiolo, uva rara and vespolina.

● Colline Novaresi Barbera V. Campazzi '07	♥♥	4
● Colline Novaresi Nebbiolo V. Mötfrei '06	♥♥	4
● Colline Novaresi Rosso MötZiflon '06	♥♥	4*
● Colline Novaresi Vespolina '08	♥	4

Renato Buganza
loc. Cascina Garbinotto, 4
12040 Piobesi d'Alba [CN]
tel. 0173619370
www.renatobuganza.it

This small Roero winery encored previous years' fine performances. Particularly good are the '06 Barbera d'Alba Vigna Veja, giving cinchona and tobacco over fruit and a juicily savoury palate, and the intense, minerally Langhe Rosso '04, which finishes long. Roero Arneis dla Trifula '08 is nicely made.

● Barbera d'Alba V. Veja '06	♥♥	4*
● Langhe Rosso '04	♥♥	4*
○ Roero Arneis dla Trifula '08	♥	4

Ca' dei Mandorli
via IV Novembre, 15
14010 Castel Rocchero [AT]
tel. 0141760131
www.cadeimandorli.com

The candied citrus-themed Moscato d'Asti dei Giari '08 is exciting and the fresh, flowery Asti Spumante '08 is delicious. The uncomplicated, fruity '07 Barbera d'Asti La Bellalda '07 is an easy drinker with good weight and the delicate Barbera d'Asti Superiore La Bellalda Oro '06 is fresh-tasting.

○ Moscato d'Asti dei Giari '08	♥♥	4
○ Asti Spumante '08	♥	4
● Barbera d'Asti La Bellalda '07	♥	4
● Barbera d'Asti Sup. La Bellalda Oro '06	♥	5

Ca' Nova
via San Isidoro, 1
28010 Bogogno [NO]
tel. 0322863406
www.cascinacanova.it

In less than a decade, Giada Codecasa's small operation has reached the front rank of north Piedmontese winemaking. It's all down to a very laid-back style embodied to perfection in the intriguing Colline Novaresi Nebbiolo Vigna San Quirico '05.

● Colline Novaresi Nebbiolo Bocciòlo '07	♥♥	4
● Colline Novaresi Nebbiolo Melchiòr '05	♥♥	4
● Colline Novaresi Nebbiolo V. San Quirico '05	♥♥	5
● Ghemme '04	♡♡	5

Carussin
reg. Mariano, 27
14050 San Marzano Oliveto [AT]
tel. 0141831358
www.carussin.it

The Ferro family farms its 13 hectares biodynamically. The estate, one of the most intriguing around Asti, releases a long, complex '06 Barbera La Tranquilla that hangs together well. The unusual Respiro di Vigna is an intense, if rather alcoholic, late-harvest Barbera.

● Barbera d'Asti La Tranquilla '06	♥♥	5
● Respiro di Vigna V.T.	♥♥	5
● Barbera d'Asti Asinoi '08	♥	3
○ Carica l'Asino '08	♥	3

Cascina Christiana
s.da San Michele, 24
14049 Nizza Monferrato [AT]
tel. 0141725100

Aldino Bellazini's winery has earned a Guide profile with some splendid Barbera d'Astis. Mòta '07 is in the classic mould with its cocoa powder, red berry fruit and cinchona ushering in a long, savoury palate with great texture. The approachable Reiss '08 gives ripe fruit and restrained spice.

● Barbera d'Asti Reiss '08	♥♥	3*
● Barbera d'Asti Sup. La Mòta '07	♥♥	5
● M.to Rosso Balôss '07	♥	5

Cascina Flino

VIA ABELLONI, 7
12055 DIANO D'ALBA [CN]
TEL. 017369231
flino@flino.com

Cascina Flino is a great place to come for premium wines at competitive prices. The house style puts muscle before elegance but the wines are still characterful, from the Diano d'Alba Vigna Vecchia to the Nebbiolo d'Alba and Barbera Flin.

● Barbera d'Alba Flin '07	♀♀	4
● Barolo San Lorenzo '05	♀♀	6
● Nebbiolo d'Alba '07	♀♀	4
● Diano d'Alba V. Vecchia '08	♀	4

Cascina Montagnola

S.DA MONTAGNOLA, 1
15058 VIGUZZOLO [AL]
TEL. 0131898558
www.cascinamontagnola.com

Yet again, it was the '08 Chardonnay Risveglio we liked. This white is still a bit oaky but there's depth in the spring flowers aromatics and freshness in the mouth. Just behind is the second release of Timorasso Morasso, the '07, which is also still oak-dominated, and the husky Barbera Amaranto '07.

○ Colli Tortonesi Bianco Risveglio '08	♀♀	5
● Colli Tortonesi Barbera Amaranto '07	♀	4
○ Colli Tortonesi Timorasso Morasso '07	♀	5

Castello di Gabiano

VIA DEFENDENTE, 2
15020 GABIANO [AL]
TEL. 0142945004
www.castellodigabiano.com

This cellar makes Gabiano and Rubino di Cantavenna from the same grapes in different proportions. Gabiano is 90 per cent barbera with freisa and grignolino nel Gabiano while Rubino di Cantavenna has only 75 per cent barbera plus the other two. The range includes Barbera d'Asti, Grignolino and a Monferrato Rosso.

● Barbera d'Asti Sup. Adornes '06	♀♀	4
● Gabiano Matilde Giustiniani Ris. '06	♀♀	5
● M.to Rosso Gavius '06	♀♀	5
● Grignolino del M.to Casalese II Ruvo '08	♀	3

Castello di Tagliolo

VIA CASTELLO, 1
15070 TAGLIOLO MONFERRATO [AL]
TEL. 014389195
www.castelloditagliolo.com

We were impressed by this year's wines from Castello di Tagliolo. The Dolcetto '06 has a complex nose and a fragrant, long palate. The '04 Rosso Nobile presents tertiary aromas introducing good structure and a lingering finish. Both whites are very exciting.

○ Cortese dell'Alto Monferrato '08	♀♀	3*
● Dolcetto di Ovada Sup. '06	♀♀	4
○ M.to Bianco Nobile '07	♀♀	4
● Rosso Nobile '04	♀♀	4

Cave di Moleto

REG. MOLETO, 4
15038 OTTIGLIO [AL]
TEL. 0142921468
www.moleto.it

Cave di Moleto trotted out a series of excellent '06 Barberas. Procchio has deep aromatics and a lively, lingering palate. The fruity Bricco alla Prera is well structured. There's great nose-palate balance on the standard Barbera and we round off with Mulej, an intense, mouthfilling Monferrato Rosso.

● Barbera del M.to '06	♀♀	3*
● Barbera del M.to Bricco della Prera '06	♀♀	5
● Barbera del M.to Procchio '06	♀♀	4
● M.to Rosso Mulej '06	♀	5

Le Cecche

VIA MOGLIA GERLOTTO, 10
12055 DIANO D'ALBA [CN]
TEL. 017369323
www.lececche.com

Belgian doctor Jan De Bruyne set up this farm estate in the hills of Diano for fun and started making great wines out of passion. The excellent range has this year acquired a muscular '05 Barolo from a half-hectare plot at Serralunga.

● Barolo '05	♀♀	7
● Diano d'Alba Sörì Le Cecche '08	♀♀	4*
● Langhe Rosso '07	♀♀	4*
● Diano d'Alba '08	♀	3

OTHER WINERIES

La Chiara

LOC. VALLEGGE, 24
15066 GAVI [AL]
TEL. 0143642293
www.lachiara.it

Chiara again presented two excellent wines. The cabernet sauvignon, barbera and dolcetto Monferrato Rosso Nabarì '07 has intense fruit and balance in the mouth. The '08 Gavi gives florality-laced fruitiness and marked acidity.

○ Gavi del Comune di Gavi '08	♟♟ 3*
● M.to Rosso Nabarì '07	♟♟ 4

Clemente Cossetti

VIA GUARDIE, 1
14043 CASTELNUOVO BELBO [AT]
TEL. 0141799803
www.cossetti.it

The Cossetti winery turns out 600,000 bottles keeping average quality fairly high. Stand-outs are the intense, generously spicy Barbera Venti di Marzo '08 and the beefy, balanced Barbera Vigna Vecchia '07 with its long, bright finish.

● Barbera d'Asti La Vigna Vecchia '07	♟♟ 3*
● Barbera d'Asti Venti di Marzo '08	♟♟ 4*
● Ruchè di Castagnole Monferrato '08	♟ 4

Stefanino Costa

B.TA BENNA, 5
12046 MONTÀ [CN]
TEL. 0173976336
www.ninocosta.eu

Nino Costa's seven-hectare estate is in the Guide. Roero Bric del Medic '06 is a little closed but offers liquorice and wild strawberries, nice acidity, a tight tannic weave and a long, expansive finish. The austere, savoury Barbera d'Alba Superiore Bric Cichin '06 has a distinct hint of oak.

● Barbera d'Alba Sup. Bric Cichin '06	♟♟ 4
● Roero Bric del Medic '06	♟♟ 4

Costa dei Platani

S.DA MAGGIORA, 89
15011 ACQUI TERME [AL]
TEL. 014456253
www.costadeiplatani.it

A Guide debut for the winery Laura and Carlo Ricagni set up at Acqui Terme in 2000. Thanks to input from Beppe Caviola and Nicola Argamante, the range has plenty of depth. Madrigale '05, from merlot, cabernet sauvignon and barbera, the two '05 Barbera Superiores and Albarossa Faetta '06 are all excellent.

● Albarossa Faetta '06	♟♟ 6
● Barbera del M.to Sup. Maggiora '05	♟♟ 5
● Barbera del M.to Sup. Piandendice '05	♟♟ 5
● M.to Rosso Madrigale '05	♟♟ 6

Daniele Coutandin

B.TA CIABOT, 12
10063 PEROSA ARGENTINA [TO]
TEL. 0121803473
ramie.countadin@alpimedia.it

We are sorry to see Coutandin drop into the Other Wineries but red tape has tied up the cellar's – and Pinerolo's – emblematic wine, Ramìe. The family deserves a special prize for its commitment to the ancient signature varieties of a genuinely heroic mountain viticulture.

● Barbichè '05	♟♟ 4*

Giovanni Daglio

VIA MONTALE CELLI, 10
15050 COSTA VESCOVATO [AL]
TEL. 0131838262
giovanni.daglio@tiscali.it

Last year, Timorasso Cantico went through to the finals and this time skilful wine man Giovanni Daglio did it again with Dolcetto Nibiò '07. Intense fragrances and well-meshed tannins bolster the massive structure of what is one of the territory's finest reds.

● Colli Tortonesi Barbera Basinas '06	♟♟ 4*
○ Colli Tortonesi Cortese V. del Re '08	♟♟ 3*
● Colli Tortonesi Dolcetto Nibiò '07	♟♟ 4
○ Colli Tortonesi Timorasso Cantico '07	♟♟ 5

Gianni Doglia

VIA ANNUNZIATA, 56
14054 CASTAGNOLE DELLE LANZE [AT]
TEL. 0141878359
wine-doglia@libero.it

Gianni Doglia's dedication to winemaking is truly commendable. His first love is moscato, which repays him with unfailingly high quality, but his reds are coming on. The Barbera Superiore '07 is a miracle of concentration and balance. Also powerful is the slightly less characterful Monferrato.

● Barbera d'Asti Sup. '07	♀♀	5
● M.to Rosso "!" '06	♀♀	6
○ Moscato d'Asti '08	♀♀	4*
● Barbera d'Asti Boscodonne '08	♀	4

Cascina Ferro

VIA NOSSERIO, 14
14055 COSTIGLIOLE D'ASTI [AT]
TEL. 0141966693

Brothers Piero and Maggiorino Ferro turn out 25,000 bottles a year from roughly seven hectares under vine at their Cascina Ferro. Monferrato Cin '07 is vibrantly intense right from the first sniff, following up with a muscular, attractively long palate. The other wines we tasted are all decent.

● M.to Rosso Cin '07	♀♀	5
● Barbera d'Asti Bric '07	♀	5
○ Piemonte Chardonnay Realtà '07	♀	5

Fabio Fidanza

VIA RODOTIGLIA, 55
14052 CALOSSO [AT]
TEL. 0141826921
www.castellodicalosso.it

Three noteworthy wines from the competent Fabio Fidanza. The classy Barbera d'Asti Sterlino '06 has lots of structure and good balance. The Barbera d'Asti '07 is nice if a tad oaky while the nebbiolo and cabernet sauvignon Monferrato Rosso Que Duàn '07 has intriguing spice and good length.

● Barbera d'Asti Sup. Sterlino '06	♀♀	5
● M.to Rosso Que Duàn '07	♀♀	4*
● Barbera d'Asti '07	♀	3

Funtanin

VIA TORINO, 191
12043 CANALE [CN]
TEL. 0173979488
www.funtanin.com

Brothers Bruno and Piercarlo Sperone run a cellar that is part of Roero's wine history. The bottle we liked this year was the Roero Bricco Barbisa '06, its intense aromatics showing good breadth of dried flowers and the finish plenty of character. Roero Arneis Pierin di Soc '08 is uncomplicated but nice.

● Roero Bricco Barbisa '06	♀♀	5
○ Roero Arneis Pierin di Soc '08	♀	4

Gaggino

S.DA SANT'EVASIO, 29
15076 OVADA [AL]
TEL. 0143822345
vinigaggino@libero.it

Even with the economy in the doldrums, Gabriele Gaggino is courageously implementing new wine projects. From his range, we like the outstandingly balanced fruit and spice Convivio '08. The other bottles are good, especially the Chardonnay La Pagliuzza '08.

● Dolcetto di Ovada Il Convivio '08	♀♀	3
○ Piemonte Chardonnay La Pagliuzza '08	♀♀	3
● Barbera del M.to La Lazzarina '08	♀	3
● Dolcetto di Ovada Sup. S. Evasio '07	♀	4

Gianni Gagliardo

B.TA SERRA DEI TURCHI, 88
12064 LA MORRA [CN]
TEL. 017350829
www.gagliardo.it

No need for introductions here. Gianni Gagliardo, a Piedmont wine veteran with deep ties to Monticello d'Alba, rediscovered the favorita variety in the 1970s and continues to vinify it better than anyone else. With the arrival of his children at the winery, the focus has shifted towards Langhe.

● Barolo Cannubi '05	♀♀	8
● Barolo Serre '05	♀♀	8
● Langhe Nebbiolo Batié '06	♀♀	6

Piero Gatti

LOC. MONCUCCO, 28
12058 SANTO STEFANO BELBO [CN]
TEL. 0141840918
www.vinigatti.it

Moncucco is one of the finest places there are to grow moscato. Needless to say, Rita and her daughter Barbara make excellent examples of the type in a range completed by a fragrant Brachetto and two freisa-based reds.

○ Piemonte Moscato '08	♟♟ 4*
● Verbeia '07	♟♟ 4*
○ Vignot V. T. '07	♟♟ 5
● Langhe Freisa La Violetta '08	♟ 4

Pierfrancesco Gatto

VIA VITTORIO EMANUELE, 13
14030 CASTAGNOLE MONFERRATO [AT]
TEL. 0141292149

Gatto has eight hectares in the hills of Castagnole Monferrato, Montemagno and Refrancore planted to ruché, grignolino and barbera. This year's results were excellent, starting with the long Barbera Vigna Serra '07 and the fragrant, varietal '08 Ruché Caresana. The '08 Grignolino is deliciously authentic.

● Barbera d'Asti Vigna Serra '07	♟♟ 4*
● Grignolino d'Asti '08	♟♟ 3*
● Ruché di Castagnole M.to Caresana '08	♟♟ 4*
● M.to Rosso Percento '07	♟ 4

La Ghibellina

FRAZ. MONTEROTONDO, 61
15066 GAVI [AL]
TEL. 0143686257
www.laghibellina.it

Alberto and Marina Ghibellini presented us with some excellent Gavis this year. The most convincing seems to be Mainìn '08, which has a varietal sensory profile and an easy-drinking nature. Altius '07 is more straightforward but well defined and nicely made. Monferrato Chiaretto Sandrino '08 is interesting.

○ Gavi del Comune di Gavi Mainìn '08	♟♟ 4
○ Gavi del Comune di Gavi Altius '07	♟ 5
◉ M.to Chiaretto Sandrino '08	♟ 4

Incisiana

VIA SANT'AGATA, 10/12
14045 INCISA SCAPACCINO [AT]
TEL. 0141747113
www.incisiana.com

Florian Oelssner and Eckhard Fischer's winery confirmed how good it is with a fresh-tasting, complex Barbera d'Asti '07 that gives spice, earthiness and cherries with savouriness and length. The sauvignon Monferrato Bianco Serafino Bianco '08 has peaches and chlorophyll, showing length and character.

● Barbera d'Asti '07	♟♟ 4
○ M.to Bianco Serafino Bianco '08	♟♟ 4
● Barbera d'Asti Sup. Zerosso '04	♟ 6

Ioppa

VIA DELLE PALLOTTE 10
28078 ROMAGNANO SESIA [NO]
TEL. 0163833079
www.viniioppa.it

Giampiero and Giorgio Ioppa's small operation has a big tradition, interpreting the main types in the Novara area in a modern style. Ghemme '05 has great stuffing but the cask conditioning hasn't been completely absorbed while the dried-grape vespolina-based Stransì '05 is very original.

● Ghemme '05	♟♟ 5
● Stransì Rosso '05	♟♟ 4
● Colline Novaresi Uva Rara '08	♟ 3
● Colline Novaresi Vespolina '06	♟ 5

Tenuta Langasco

FRAZ. MADONNA DI COMO, 10
12051 ALBA [CN]
TEL. 0173286972
www.tenutalangasco.it

Just outside Alba, Claudio Sacco runs his operation with a steady hand. This year's results are fantastic, with a powerful succulent '07 Barbera that still manages to be stylishly balanced. It went on to the finals. The Nebbiolo '07 is complex and cellarable while the Dolcetto '08 has pulpy fruit.

● Barbera d'Alba Madonna di Como '07	♟♟ 4
● Dolcetto d'Alba Madonna di Como V. Miclet '08	♟♟ 3*
● Nebbiolo d'Alba Sorì Coppa '07	♟♟ 5

Marchese Luca Spinola
LOC. CASCINA MASSIMILIANA
15066 GAVI [AL]
TEL. 0143682514
www.marcheselucaspinola.it

This estate is at Rovereto, one of the finest wine zones in Gavi. A fine range of wines earned it a Guide profile. Tenuta Massimiliana '08 has volume and drive on the palate. The '08 Gavi is fragrantly fruity with superb balance in the mouth and the intense Gavi di Tassarolo '08 shows concentration.

O Gavi di Gavi '08	🍷🍷 4
O Gavi di Tassarolo '08	🍷🍷 3
O Gavi Tenuta Massimiliana '08	🍷🍷 4

Le Marie
VIA CARDÉ, 5
12032 BARGE [CN]
TEL. 0175345159
raviolobeltramo@tiscali.it

Valerio Raviolo grows a wide range of Piedmontese varieties – barbera, nebbiolo, bonarda, freisa and dolcetto – near Barge in the province of Turin and Cuneo. As we wait for release of the top labels, Blanc de Lissart '04, from old local white varieties, and the lesser wines are coming on.

O Blanc de Lissart '04	🍷🍷 3*
O Blançonnay	🍷🍷 3*
● Pinerolese Dolcetto '08	🍷 3

Franco Mondo
REG. MARIANO, 33
14050 SAN MARZANO OLIVETO [AT]
TEL. 0141834096
www.francomondo.net

The Mondo family farms 13 hectares at San Marzano Oliveto near Asti, turning out about 60,000 bottles a year. We liked the elegant Barbera d'Asti Vigna del Salice '06, which has great structure and fine-grained tannins. Monferrato Rosso Di.Vino '08 is simpler and a little roughish.

● Barbera d'Asti V. del Salice '07	🍷🍷 4*
O M.to Bianco Di. Vino '08	🍷 4

Morgassi Superiore
CASE SPARSE SERMORIA, 7
15066 GAVI [AL]
TEL. 0143642007
www.morgassisuperiore.it

Morgassi Superiore is run by the Piacitelli family, who presented us with two well-made, well-typed wines. Gavi del Comune di Gavi Etichetta Oro '08 is delightfully drinkable and the Cortesia di Morgassi '05 from part-dried overripe grapes has flowers and an alcohol-rich finish.

O Cortesia di Morgassi '05	🍷 5
O Gavi del Comune di Gavi Et. Oro '08	🍷 4

Giuseppe Negro
VIA GALLINA, 22
12052 NEIVE [CN]
TEL. 0173677468
www.negrogiuseppe.com

The first Guide profile for this winery whose cellar is located in one of Neive's most celebrated vineyards, Gallina. Two wines contributed to this exploit. The first was a stunning Barbaresco Pian Cavallo '06, with its refined aromatics and superb harmony, while the second was the fine Barbera Pulin '07.

● Barbaresco Pian Cavallo '06	🍷🍷 6
● Barbera d'Alba Pulin '07	🍷🍷 4*

Fabrizio Pinsoglio
FRAZ. MADONNA DEI CAVALLI, 31BIS
12050 CANALE [CN]
TEL. 0173968401
fabriziopinsoglio@libero.it

It wasn't a great year for Pinsoglio. Still, we liked the fruit and balsam Barbera d'Alba Bric La Rondolina '07 for its depth and length. Roero Arneis Vigneto Malinat '08 is stylish and fresh-tasting with subtle florality. Barbera d'Alba Vigna Giaconi '08 give liqueur fruit and tobacco sensations.

● Barbera d'Alba Bric La Rondolina '07	🍷🍷 5
● Barbera d'Alba V. Giaconi '08	🍷 4
O Roero Arneis Vign. Malinat '08	🍷 3

OTHER WINERIES

Podere Macellio

VIA ROMA, 18
10014 CALUSO [TO]
TEL. 0119833511
www.erbaluce-bianco.it

Renato and Daniele Bianco's little cellar seems to have an inborn ability to get the very best out of the multi-faceted erbaluce variety. The reliable Erbaluce di Caluso '08 and Caluso Passito '05 are excellent, and don't forget the Spumante Metodo Classico.

○ Caluso Passito '05	♥♥	6
○ Erbaluce di Caluso '08	♥♥	3*
○ Erbaluce di Caluso Spumante M. Cl.	♥♥	4

Giovanni Prandi

FRAZ. CASCINA COLOMBÈ
VIA FARINETTI, 5
12055 DIANO D'ALBA [CN]
TEL. 017369248
www.prandigiovanni.it

A first Guide entry for this traditional Diano d'Alba operation. Since the arrival of the new generation, Cascina Colombè has been making and bottling good wines. Top of the range is a muscular Nebbiolo d'Alba '07, followed by two drinkable '08 Dolcetto di Dianos and a nice '07 Barbera d'Alba.

● Dolcetto di Diano Sorì Cristina '08	♥♥	4*
● Nebbiolo d'Alba Colombè '07	♥♥	4*
● Barbera d'Alba '07	♥	4
● Dolcetto di Diano Sorì Colombè '08	♥	3

Prinsi

VIA GAIA, 5
12052 NEIVE [CN]
TEL. 017367192
www.prinsi.it

Prinsi is owned by Ottavio Lequio. It may not be shining as of old but it still releases excellent Langhe wines. The style is modern, and the use of oak is sometimes over-liberal, yet these are wines that have shown they can age. Apart from the Barbaresco selections, there is a nice Barbera.

● Barbaresco Gallina '05	♥♥	6
● Barbera d'Alba Sup. Vign. Much '07	♥♥	5
● Barbaresco Fausoni '04	♥	6

Produttori del Gavi

VIA CAVALIERI DI VITTORIO VENETO, 45
15066 GAVI [AL]
TEL. 0143642786
cantina.prodgavi@libero.it

This co-operative keeps up its excellent quality standards. Primi Grappoli '08 gives fruit and flowers preceding a balanced, long-lingering palate. The '08 GG combines fruit with intense minerality and a well-orchestrated, beautifully balanced palate. The '08 Gavi G is nicely typed and well crafted.

○ Gavi del Comune di Gavi GG '08	♥♥	4
○ Gavi Primi Grappoli '08	♥♥	4
○ Gavi G '08	♥	4

La Raia

S.DA MONTEROTONDO, 79
15067 NOVI LIGURE [AL]
TEL. 0143743685
www.la-raia.it

La Raia is a Demeter-certified biodynamic operation that is emblematic of a positive trend in winemaking. The '07 Barbera Largé impresses with its intense fruit aromatics and pulpy palate. The other wines are well typed.

● Piemonte Barbera Largé '07	♥♥	6
○ Gavi '08	♥	4
● Piemonte Barbera '08	♥	4

Franco Roero

VIA ZUCCHETTO, 8
14048 MONTEGROSSO D'ASTI [AT]
TEL. 0141956160
franco.roero@gmail.com

Franco Roero's compact winery, in the hill country to the south of Asti, continues a generations-long tradition of making the area's classic red wines at very affordable prices. Barbera d'Asti Cellarino '07 has balance and power while the Barbera d'Asti Superiore '07 is a tad woody but still juicy.

● Barbera d'Asti Cellarino '07	♥♥	4*
● Barbera d'Asti Sup. '07	♥♥	5

OTHER WINERIES

Poderi Giovanni Rosso

P.ZZA ROMA, 1
14041 AGLIANO TERME [AT]
TEL. 0141954006
www.poderirossogiovanni.it

The ten lovely hectares of the Rosso estate are planted exclusively to barbera. The wines have a modern feel but still have lots of character. Cascina Perno '07 is dense and very long while the elegantly oaked Vigna del Carlinet '07 is similar in style. Monferrato Infinito '07 is complex and refined.

● Barbera d'Asti Sup. Cascina Perno '07	♥♥	5
● Barbera d'Asti Sup. V. del Carlinet '07	♥♥	5
● M.to Rosso Infinito '07	♥♥	4
● Barbera d'Asti '07	♥	4

Daniele Saccoletto

S.S. CASALE-ASTI, 82
15020 SAN GIORGIO MONFERRATO [AL]
TEL. 0142806509
www.saccolettovini.com

Daniele Saccoletto continues to make excellent wines. The Barbera d'Asti Superiore '07 has an elegant profile and lingering persistence. Barbera del Monferrato Aurum '07 is a heady easy drinker.

● Barbera d'Asti Sup. '07	♥♥	5
● Barbera del M.to Aurum '07	♥♥	5
● Barbera del M.to Vigna Minerva '07	♥	4
● Monferrato Freisa V. Fiordaliso '08	♥	4

Cascina Salerio

S.DA SALERIO, 16
14055 COSTIGLIOLE D'ASTI [AT]
TEL. 0141966294
casalerio@alice.it

Giuliana Bianco and Claudio Pia joined forces and holdings, five hectares at Montegrosso d'Asti and three or so at Costigliole d'Asti, to create Cascina Salerio. For now, production is restricted to a few premium-quality labels, including a full, fruity Barbera Superiore, released at irresistible prices.

● Barbera d'Asti Sup. Terra '07	♥♥	4*
☉ M.to Chiaretto Aria '08	♥♥	3*
● Barbera d'Asti Terra '08	♥	3

San Pietro

LOC. SAN PIETRO, 2
15067 TASSAROLO [AL]
TEL. 0143342422
www.tenutasanpietro.it

Nero San Pietro '07 from albarossa, cabernet and barbera hints at red berry fruit and tobacco before the palate shows breadth and substance. Orma Romea '07 from nibiô is a Dolcetto dal graspo rosso from a pre-phylloxera ungrafted vineyard more than a century old.

○ Gavi del Comune di Tassarolo Il Mandorlo '08	♥♥	5
● M.to Nero San Pietro '07	♥♥	6
● M.to Orma Romea '07	♥♥	6
○ Gavi del Comune di Tassarolo Gorrina '07	♥	6

San Romano

B.TA GIACHELLI, 8
12063 DOGLIANI [CN]
TEL. 017376289
www.sanromano.com

A visit to the Other Wineries for this exciting Dogliano winery is not so much relegation as a temporary move as we wait for the promising Vigna del Pilone '08. The Bricco delle Lepri '08 presented for this Guide is very successful and absolutely true to its designation.

● Dolcetto di Dogliani Bricco delle Lepri '08	♥♥	3*

Giacomo Scagliola

REG. SANTA LIBERA, 20
14053 CANELLI [AT]
TEL. 0141831146
www.scagliolagiacomo.it

A long-established 15-hectare estate mainly given over to moscato but with space for local red varieties like barbera. Interest focuses on the complex, varietal Barbera d'Asti with its earthy aromas and fresh, vibrant palate. Moscato d'Asti Santa Libera '08 is very nice.

● Barbera d'Asti '07	♥♥	3*
● Barbera d'Asti La Faia '06	♥♥	*
○ Moscato d'Asti Santa Libera '08	♥♥	*

Simone Scaletta

LOC. MANZONI, 61
12065 MONFORTE D'ALBA [CN]
TEL. 3484912733
www.viniscaletta.com

It's not often a new winery comes on the scene at Barolo so we're standing by Simone Scaletta, even though this wasn't one of his better years. The fewer than 20,000 bottles of classic Langhe wines are excellent, except when oak is too much in evidence.

● Barolo Chirlet '05	♟♟ 7
● Langhe Nebbiolo Autin 'd Madama '07	♟♟ 5
● Barbera d'Alba Sarsera '07	♟ 5
● Barolo Chirlet '04	♟♟ 7

La Scamuzza

CASCINA POMINA, 17
15049 VIGNALE MONFERRATO [AL]
TEL. 0142926214
www.lascamuzza.it

Bricco San Tomaso is back with a bang in an almost impenetrable 2007 edition that gives intriguing tobacco and blueberries followed by a dense, balanced palate. Barbera Vigneto della Amorosa '06 is as subtly complex on the nose as it is pulpy and harmonious on the palate, and finishes long.

● M.to Rosso Bricco S. Tomaso '07	♟♟ 5
● Barbera del M.to Sup. Vign. della Amorosa '06	♟♟ 5

Antica Casa Vinicola Scarpa

VIA MONTEGRAPPA, 6
14049 NIZZA MONFERRATO [AT]
TEL. 0141721331
www.scarpavini.it

The tradition nature of the 40 hectares here is perfectly reflected in the wines. To start with, there's a Barbera d'Asti La Bogliona '06 with intense cinchona aromatics and a powerful, attractively complex palate. The Dolcetto d'Acqui La Selva di Moirano '06 is also surprisingly complex.

● Barbera d'Asti La Bogliona '06	♟♟ 6
● Dolcetto d'Acqui La Selva di Moirano '06	♟♟ 4
● La Selva di Moirano '05	♟ 6

La Spinosa Alta

CIRC.NE SPINOSA ALTA 6
15038 OTTIGLIO [AL]
TEL. 0142921372
lanzani.vini@tin.it

The first Guide profile for the family-run winery founded by Paolo Lanzani in 1992. The complex Barbera Superiore gives incense and tobacco introducing a superb palate. Tenebroso '06, from a 90-10 mix of nebbiolo and barbera, has toasty aromas and a balanced palate. The arneis Bianco '08 is nice.

● Barbera del M.to Sup. La Punta '06	♟♟ 4*
● M.to Rosso Tenebroso '06	♟♟ 4
○ Bianco '08	♟ 3

Giuseppe Stella

S.DA BOSSOLA, 8
14055 COSTIGLIOLE D'ASTI [AT]
TEL. 0141966142
stellavini@libero.it

Beppe Stella is in charge of this lovely Costigliole d'Asti operation. Meticulous vineyard management, with 12.5 hectares yielding about 50,000 bottles, and impeccable cellar work are the strong suits. The best bottle is the Barbera d'Asti Starvisan '08, which is somewhat husky but has loads of character.

● Barbera d'Asti Vign. Stravisan '08	♟♟ 3*
● Barbera d'Asti Sup. Bricco Fubine Il Vino del Maestro '07	♟ 5
● Barbera d'Asti Sup. Giaiet '07	♟ 5

Traversa - Cascina Bertolotto

REG. ROCCHETTA 1
15018 SPIGNO MONFERRATO [AL]
TEL. 014491223

The moscato-based dried-grape Surì di Bertolotto '05 from the Traversa family is subtly complex, proffering dried fruits and apricots. Dolcetto d'Acqui La Muïette '07 is an almost impenetrable ruby, giving black berry fruit and warmth on the powerful palate.

● Dolcetto d'Acqui La Muïette '07	♟♟ 4
○ Surì di Bertolotto '05	♟♟ 5
● Barbera del M.to I Cheini '07	♟ 4

Laura Valditerra

S.DA MONTEROTONDO, 75
15067 NOVI LIGURE [AL]
TEL. 0143321451
laura@valditerra.it

Laura Valditerra put in another excellent performance with two very good '08 Gavis. Vigna del Lago has fruit and minerals on the nose preceding structure, nice acidity and great persistence. Tenuta Merlassino offers varietal perceptions at every stage of tasting.

O Gavi Tenuta Merlassino '08	🍷🍷	4
O Gavi V. del Lago '08	🍷🍷	4

La Vecchia Posta

VIA MONTEBELLO, 2
15050 AVOLASCA [AL]
TEL. 0131876254
lavecchiaposta@virgilio.it

Vecchia Posta is farmed organically by Roberto Semino, who makes excellent wines. This year, we loved the depth of the complex, long-lingering Barbera Languia '07. Nobolot '07 did well but Timorasso Il Selvaggio '07 is still trying to find its feet.

● Colli Tortonesi Barbera Languia '07	🍷🍷	4
● Colli Tortonesi Rosso Rebelot '07	🍷🍷	4
O Colli Tortonesi Timorasso Il Selvaggio '07	🍷	4

Vignaioli Elvio Pertinace

LOC. PERTINACE, 2
12050 TREISO [CN]
TEL. 0173442238
www.pertinace.it

After many years of full Guide profiles, Vignaioli Elvio Pertinace has slipped back to the Other Wineries. It's not really so much a quality issue as a prolonged loss of focus. The range of honest wines never quite reaches the heights, and perhaps was never aiming for them.

● Barbaresco Vign. Marcarini '06	🍷🍷	6
● Barbaresco Vign. Nervo '06	🍷🍷	6
● Barbaresco '06	🍷	6
● Barbaresco Vign. Castellizzano '06	🍷	6

Il Vignale

LOC. LOMELLINA
VIA GAVI, 130
15067 NOVI LIGURE [AL]
TEL. 014372715
www.ilvignale.it

The estate acquired by the husband and wife Cappelletti team in 1984 achieved serious quality and recognition was not slow in coming. We were unable to taste the full range of Vignale wines for this edition but keep a space in the Guide for the cellar, which is sure to bounce back in style.

O Gavi Vigne Alte '08	🍷	4
O Gavi Vilma Cappelletti Et. Nera '06	🍷🍷	4
O Gavi Vilma Cappelletti Et. Verde '07	🍷🍷	4

Virna

VIA ALBA, 73
12060 BAROLO [CN]
TEL. 017356120
www.virnabarolo.it

This small Langhe winery is in superb wine country. Both versions of '05 Barolo presented were extremely convincing and very true to their variety. Cannubi Boschis has depth and good definition while Preda Sarmassa is slightly fuzzier, although otherwise satisfying.

● Barolo Cannubi Boschis '05	🍷🍷	6
● Barolo Preda Sarmassa '05	🍷🍷	6

La Zerba

S.DA PER FRANCAVILLA, 1
15060 TASSAROLO [AL]
TEL. 0143342259
www.la-zerba.it

The Lorenzi family's range is thoroughly reliable. The '08 Gavi Terrarossa is subtle on the nose showing savoury, broad and lingering on the palate. Gavi La Zerba '08 combines fruit aromas, minerality and a vibrant, harmonious palate with great length.

O Gavi La Zerba '08	🍷🍷	3*
O Gavi Terrarossa '08	🍷🍷	3*

LIGURIA

In a good year, Liguria produces something like 200,000 hectolitres of wine, accounting for 0.4 per cent of Italy's total output. A trifling amount, compared to the figures for Piedmont, Emilia Romagna or Tuscany, which it borders. The reasons are evident. Apart from its size, the region has 1,650,000 inhabitants, and woodland covers 70 per cent of its territory, in other words twice the average for Italy. The steep, mountainous terrain does nothing to help matters, either. Liguria's wine production is not enough even for the Ligurians themselves. Historically, they have always brought in wines from outside, which further compromises the region's sense of identity. For these reasons, there is no way of extending the vineyards or rationalizing farming methods. That would mean mechanization, unthinkable in Liguria's vineyards, which are terraced and supported by dry stone walls. The only option remaining for the region's growers is to focus on high quality and native varieties. And there is a certain amount of Ligurian pride in defending these vines planted on narrow cliff ledges overlooking the sea, the so-called "fasce" evoked by the poet Montale, and in keeping them under vine without turning to international varieties from Bordeaux or Burgundy. At most, and even then only rarely, you might find grenache or syrah from the Rhône. These rare non-native grapes – if the variously named grenache, cannonau, or guarnaccia actually is such – have in some cases brought a breath of fresh air. In fact, Liguria, restricted for millennia to its sphere of exclusively Mediterranean relations, is urgently in need of a more European outlook. The majority of the native varieties, such as rossese, pigato and ormeasco in the west, and bianchetta genovese, ciliegiolo, rollo, albarola and pollera nera in the east, probably appeared over the centuries as a result of adaptation to the soil and climate, subsequently producing what amount to genetic shifts. Others, such as vermentino, granaccia, moscato, sangiovese and canaiolo, may have lost some of their varietal characteristics but even today betray their origins in the northern Tyrrhenian and central Italy. We have tried to give you an idea of this complex, fascinating, unique picture through the 259 wines tasted, produced by 50 wineries. Twenty-one of those wines made our final tastings, and six – two Pigatos, a Vermentino from the western Liguria, and a Rossese di Dolceacqua and two Vermentinos from the east – took top honours. This sudden surge triples the number of Ligurian wines that made the list of Italy's greats and shows that certain decisions, such as focusing on native varieties and shunning small oak barrels, have reaped dividends.

Massimo Alessandri

VIA COSTA PARROCCHIA
18028 RANZO [IM]
TEL. 018253458
www.massimoalessandri.it

CELLAR SALES
PRE-BOOKED VISITS
FOOD

ANNUAL PRODUCTION **30,000 bottles**
HECTARES UNDER VINE **5**
VITICULTURE METHOD **Conventional**

Massimo Alessandri's estate has five hectares of vineyards at altitudes ranging from 280 to 400 metres. The plots are painstakingly managed and supervised personally by Massimo, who keeps an eye on them through every phase of the grapes' development and ripening. How this young owner also finds time to run his excellent restaurant in Albenga is a mystery, as was his decision to introduce two varieties almost unknown in this area: viognier and roussanne. The results, however, have proved him right.

This year, the wine from the new grapes, Viorus, was absent but Massimo more than made up for this with his Pigato Vigne Vegie '07, which is more complex and intense than the more delicate basic '08 Pigato and Vermentino, and with the two reds for which the young producer nurtures a deep love. In the Ligustico '07, attractive oak nicely takes the edge off the vegetal tones of the two Rhône valley varieties, grenache and syrah, while we were very impressed with the full aroma and palate of A' Seiana '07, an elegant Bordeaux blend.

Laura Aschero

P.ZZA V. EMANUELE, 7
18027 PONTEDASSIO [IM]
TEL. 0183710307
lauraaschero@uno.it

CELLAR SALES
PRE-BOOKED VISITS

ANNUAL PRODUCTION **60,000 bottles**
HECTARES UNDER VINE **2.8**
VITICULTURE METHOD **Conventional**

The winery was established in 1980, when Laura converted the family estate back to vineyards and started to produce wine, shyly at first. The winery has now become important, both in terms of quantity, with around 60,000 bottles per year, and quality, winning awards and receiving rave reviews. Her son, Marco Rizzo, has followed in her footsteps, skilfully managing to maintain a healthy balance between modern and traditional production methods. The estate's extremely well-tended terraced vineyards are situated outside Imperia at an altitude of 150 metres.

Judging by the three wines presented, '08 was a much better year for whites than reds, at least in the Pontedassio valley. In fact, both the Pigato and the Vermentino show impressive nose-palate consistency and admirable savouriness, swathed in generous aromas of ripe peach and damson. The Rossese '08 is full flavoured and firm on the palate but veiled on the nose by herbaceous notes. Although not unpleasant in themselves, they tend to compromise the wine's pleasant roundness.

○ Riviera Ligure di Ponente Pigato Vigne Vegie '07	🍷 5
● A' Seiana '07	🍷🍷 6
● Ligustico '07	🍷🍷 6
○ Riviera Ligure di Ponente Pigato Costa de Vigne '08	🍷 4
○ Riviera Ligure di Ponente Vermentino Costa de Vigne '08	🍷 4
● A' Seiana '06	🍷🍷 6
● A' Seiana '05	🍷🍷 5
● Ligustico '06	🍷🍷 6
● Ligustico '05	🍷🍷 6
● Ligustico '04	🍷🍷 6
○ Riviera Ligure di Ponente Pigato Vigne Vegie '06	🍷🍷 5
○ Riviera Ligure di Ponente Pigato Vigne Vegie '05	🍷🍷 5
○ Riviera Ligure di Ponente Vermentino Costa de Vigne '06	🍷🍷 4*
○ Riviera Ligure di Ponente Vermentino Costa de Vigne '05	🍷🍷 4*

○ Riviera Ligure di Ponente Pigato '08	🍷🍷 4*
○ Riviera Ligure di Ponente Vermentino '08	🍷🍷 4*
● Riviera Ligure di Ponente Rossese '08	🍷 4
○ Riviera Ligure di Ponente Pigato '06	🍷🍷 4
○ Riviera Ligure di Ponente Pigato '03	🍷🍷 4*
○ Riviera Ligure di Ponente Pigato '02	🍷🍷 4
○ Riviera Ligure di Ponente Pigato '01	🍷🍷 4*
● Riviera Ligure di Ponente Rossese '07	🍷🍷 4
○ Riviera Ligure di Ponente Vermentino '07	🍷🍷 4
○ Riviera Ligure di Ponente Vermentino '06	🍷🍷 4
○ Riviera Ligure di Ponente Vermentino '05	🍷🍷 4*
○ Riviera Ligure di Ponente Vermentino '04	🍷🍷 4*
○ Riviera Ligure di Ponente Vermentino '02	🍷🍷 4
○ Riviera Ligure di Ponente Vermentino '01	🍷🍷 4*

La Baia del Sole

FRAZ. LUNI ANTICA
VIA FORLINO, 3
19034 ORTONOVO [SP]
TEL. 0187661821
www.cantinefederici.com

CELLAR SALES
PRE-BOOKED VISITS

ANNUAL PRODUCTION **140,000 bottles**
HECTARES UNDER VINE **11**
VITICULTURE METHOD **Conventional**

Giulio Federici could not have chosen a more appropriate name for his "Bay of the Sun" winery, situated in the archaeological site of ancient Luni, near the amphitheatre built by the Romans after their centuries-long struggle with the Apuan Ligurians. The vineyards are in the hills of Ortonovo and Castelnuovo Magra overlooking the ruins, in a sunny, well-ventilated position. Giulio and his wife Isa started out by renovating an old country farmhouse in 1985 and over the last 20-odd years have achieved great results, thanks to meticulous care in vineyard and cellar.

Our tasters enjoyed a series of quality bottlings, starting with the Vermentino '08 from the Sarticola vineyard. It gives citrus and flower-like aromatic complexity, good structure, and an enchanting, long finish swathed in aromatic herbs and iodine. Mediterranean fragrances are to the fore in the tangy, expansive Muri Grandi '08, also from vermentino. The beautifully deep, brilliant ruby Terre d'Oriente proffers red and black berry fruit, white pepper and spice, followed by elegant tannins on a full-bodied, velvety palate. The other wines were all very well made, especially the '08 Vermentinos.

Maria Donata Bianchi

LOC. VAL CROSA
18013 DIANO ARENTINO [IM]
TEL. 0183498233
www.aziendagricolabianchi.com

CELLAR SALES
PRE-BOOKED VISITS
OSPITALITÀ

ANNUAL PRODUCTION **30,000 bottles**
HECTARES UNDER VINE **4**
VITICULTURE METHOD **Naturale**

Maria Donata Bianchi and Emanuele Trevia are a lively couple, always busy doing something. After giving a new lease of life in 1977 to the family winery, situated in the heart of Diano Castello, they decided to expand by buying a single ten-hectare plot in Diano Aretino, which is also home to the new winery. Their new facilities were designed to produce international wines but for the moment we will have to make do, so to speak, with their textbook Ligurian products: Vermentino, Pigato and a Rosso from grenache, one of the most typical varieties of Liguria's mid-west coast.

Two '08 whites were presented, a Vermentino and a Pigato. Again this year, the former clearly reflected its pride of place in the winery's affections. As in the previous vintage, the Vermentino is beautifully aromatic, with powerful acidity and a close-focused nose, regaling aromatic herbs, spring flowers, peaches and apricots. Exceptional minerality, which is perhaps its most distinctive trait, makes this an approachable, easy drinker. The Pigato is well made but unexciting.

● Colli di Luni Terre D'Oriente '06	♔♔ 5
○ Colli di Luni Vermentino Sarticola '08	♔♔ 5
○ Muri Grandi Golfo dei Poeti '08	♔♔ 3*
○ Colli di Luni Gladius '08	♔ 3
○ Colli di Luni Vermentino Oro d'Isée '08	♔ 4
○ Colli di Luni Vermentino Solaris '08	♔ 4
● Forlino Golfo dei Poeti '06	♔ 5

○ Riviera Ligure di Ponente Vermentino '08	♔♔ 5
○ Riviera Ligure di Ponente Pigato '08	♔ 5
○ Riviera Ligure di Ponente Vermentino '07	♔♔♔ 4*
○ Antico Sfizio '05	♔♔ 4*
○ Antico Sfizio '04	♔♔ 4*
● Bormano '07	♔♔ 5
● La Mattana '06	♔♔ 6
● La Mattana '04	♔♔ 6
○ Riviera Ligure di Ponente Pigato '07	♔♔ 5*
○ Riviera Ligure di Ponente Pigato '06	♔♔ 5
○ Riviera Ligure di Ponente Pigato '05	♔♔ 6*
○ Riviera Ligure di Ponente Vermentino '06	♔♔ 4*
○ Riviera Ligure di Ponente Vermentino '05	♔♔ 4*

Luigi Bianchi Carenzo

Via I. Lantero, 19
18013 Diano San Pietro [IM]
tel. 0183429072

CELLAR SALES
PRE-BOOKED VISITS

ANNUAL PRODUCTION **N.D.**
HECTARES UNDER VINE **0.7**
VITICULTURE METHOD **Conventional**

Luigi is one of those people who leaves a mark. We first met him as the proprietor of a busy bar in the centre of Diano Marina. He realized that by leaving the running of the bar to his children, he could dedicate himself in the hours of sunlight to his passion of growing grapes and making wine, and then take over the bar in the evening. This very driven wine man has introduced a highly technological approach, both in the rows and at the winery. Nothing is left to chance, as the results in the glass clearly show.

His Vermentino, as always, deserves a special mention for its bright, sunny colour, its fresh, fragrant aromas – albeit with a faintly herbaceous note – and impressive length on nose and palate. All in all, it's extremely enjoyable drinking and a fine expression of the Diano terroir from which it hails. We were also pleased to see another good performance from the bright, pale straw yellow Pigato, which opens on aromatic herbs and follows up with a nice zesty palate. The varietal Riviera Ligure di Ponente Rossese '08 is well made but lacks zip.

○ Riviera Ligure di Ponente Vermentino '08	♟♟	4*
○ Riviera Ligure di Ponente Pigato '08	♟♟	4*
● Riviera Ligure di Ponente Rossese '08	♟	4
○ Riviera Ligure di Ponente Pigato '07	♟♟	4
○ Riviera Ligure di Ponente Pigato '06	♟♟	4
● Riviera Ligure di Ponente Vermentino '07	♟♟	4*
○ Riviera Ligure di Ponente Vermentino '06	♟♟	4

BioVio

Fraz. Bastia
via Crociata, 24
17031 Albenga [SV]
tel. 018220776
www.biovio.it

CELLAR SALES
PRE-BOOKED VISITS

ANNUAL PRODUCTION **40,000 bottles**
HECTARES UNDER VINE **4.5**
VITICULTURE METHOD **Organic certified**

BioVio started out growing organically certified vegetables and herbs with astounding success. But some years ago, Aimone Vio, driven by determination and supported by his wife Clara, restored the family's old two-hectare vineyard and added another two hectares higher up on the slopes. This, however, may only be the beginning since Caterina, the eldest of Aimone and Clara's three daughters, has started to study oenology and we are sure that before long she too will be making a name for herself.

The first harvest was in 2000 and since then the wines have gradually acquired surprising character, albeit in keeping with the traditional Ligurian style. Of the five wines tasted, we were particularly taken with the Vermentino Aimone '08, whose rich, highly distinctive bouquet of aromatic and medicinal herbs accompanies an almost perfect taste profile. The two '08 Pigatos – the Bon in da Bon and the Marixe – are very well made but not quite as good. There is still work to be done on the two reds, the Rossese Bastiò '08 and the grenache-based Bacilò from the same vintage, perhaps more in the vineyard than in the winery.

○ Riviera Ligure di Ponente Vermentino Aimone '08	♟♟	4*
○ Riviera Ligure di Ponente Pigato Bon in da Bon '08	♟♟	4
○ Riviera Ligure di Ponente Pigato Marixe '08	♟♟	4*
● Bacilò '08	♟	4
● Riviera Ligure di Ponente Rossese Bastiò '08	♟	4
○ Riviera Ligure di Ponente Pigato '03	♟♟	4*
○ Riviera Ligure di Ponente Pigato Bon in da Bon '06	♟♟	4*
● Riviera Ligure di Ponente Rossese Bastiò '07	♟♟	4
○ Riviera Ligure di Ponente Vermentino '07	♟♟	4
○ Riviera Ligure di Ponente Vermentino Aimone '06	♟♟	4*

Enoteca Bisson

c.so Gianelli, 28
16043 Chiavari [GE]
tel. 0185314462
www.bissonvini.it

CELLAR SALES
PRE-BOOKED VISITS

ANNUAL PRODUCTION **80,000 bottles**
HECTARES UNDER VINE **N.D.**
VITICULTURE METHOD **Naturale**

Piero Lugano, a respected wine merchant from Chiavari, has managed to transfer the experience acquired in other fields into viticulture and oenology. In just over 30 years, he has gone from selling wines to producing his own, after acquiring with great difficulty some fine vineyards overlooking the Gulf of Paradiso and the cliffs of Cinque Terre. He has replanted many native varieties, in particular bianchetta genovese and ciliegiolo, giving them a new lease of life and keeping the use of plant protection products to a minimum. Care in the winery has done the rest.

Of the many wines presented from a large collection covering all the native Ligurian varieties, we appreciated the '08 Vermentino Vigna Erta and the '07 Cinque Terre Costa du Campu. Both offer great freshness, accompanied by mineral notes in the former and savouriness in the latter. The Bianchetta Genovese hews to tradition and we also liked Il Granaccio, from granaccia, aka grenache, grapes. This variety has always been widely planted in the west of the region but has shown it can also acclimatize well to conditions in the east.

Bruna

fraz. Borgo
via Umberto I, 81
18020 Ranzo [IM]
tel. 0183318082
www.brunapigato.it

CELLAR SALES
PRE-BOOKED VISITS

ANNUAL PRODUCTION **42,000 bottles**
HECTARES UNDER VINE **6.5**
VITICULTURE METHOD **Conventional**

To reach the Bruna winery, you need to leave the main road that runs along the river Arroscia, head inland into the provinces of Savona and Imperia, and then make for Borgo di Ranzo. Just before crossing the small bridge that leads into the historic town, you will come to a grocery shop on the right. Go in, and you're bound to find some member or other of the Bruna family at work: Riccardo nicknamed U Baccàn, or head of the house, his wife, or one of their two daughters. Each has his or her own duties for this is an estate whose development hinges on the organized division of labour.

U Baccan, the estate's flagship Pigato, has already won Three Glasses on four occasions, as testimony to its great, consistent quality. The '07 also hit the top spot, showing complex aromatics ranging from citrus fruits to aromatic herbs, as well as weighty structure and great length. Close on its heels are the '06 and '07 versions of Rosso Pulin, a well-judged blend of grenache, syrah, cinsault and barbera. Of the two, the better-orchestrated '06 is slightly superior but both offer nose and palate rich, complex aromas with beautifully intact fruit, balanced structure and a full body.

○ Cinque Terre Marea Costa du Campu '07	♀♀	5
○ Golfo del Tigullio Vermentino V. Erta '08	♀♀	4
○ Cinque Terre Costa da Posa '07	♀	4
○ Cinque Terre Marea '08	♀	4
○ Golfo del Tigullio Bianchetta Genovese Ü Pastine '08	♀	4
● Il Granaccio '07	♀	6
● Braccorosso Granaccia Barrique '07	♀♀	5
○ Cinque Terre Sciacchetrà '04	♀♀	6
● Colline del Genovesato Rosso Makallé Il Granaccio '05	♀♀	5
○ Golfo del Tigullio Vermentino V. Intrigoso '07	♀♀	4
● Il Granaccio '06	♀♀	5
● Makallé Il Granaccia '06	♀♀	5
○ Marea Tardiva '06	♀♀	5

○ Riviera Ligure di Ponente Pigato U Baccan '07	♀♀♀	6
● Rosso Pulin '06	♀♀	5
● Rosso Pulin '07	♀♀	5
○ Riviera Ligure di Ponente Pigato Le Russeghine '08	♀	4
○ Riviera Ligure di Ponente Pigato Villa Torrachetta '08	♀	4
● Riviera Ligure di Ponente Rossese '08	♀	4
● Rosso Bansigu '08	♀	4
○ Riviera Ligure di Ponente Pigato U Baccan '06	♀♀♀	5
○ Riviera Ligure di Ponente Pigato U Baccan '05	♀♀♀	5
○ Riviera Ligure di Ponente Pigato U Baccan '04	♀♀♀	5
○ Riviera Ligure di Ponente Pigato U Baccan '03	♀♀♀	5
○ Riviera Ligure di Ponente Pigato U Baccan '00	♀♀	5
● Rosso Pulin '05	♀♀	5
● Rosso Pulin '04	♀♀	5

Buranco

VIA BURANCO, 72
19016 MONTEROSSO AL MARE [SP]
TEL. 0187817677
www.burancocinqueterre.it

CELLAR SALES
PRE-BOOKED VISITS
OSPITALITÀ

ANNUAL PRODUCTION 15,000 bottles
HECTARES UNDER VINE 2
VITICULTURE METHOD Conventional

A hectare in the Cinque Terre can look enormous plot you're used to measuring plots in square metres. For three years, the Grillo family has been working in this environment of precariously balanced dry stone walls, heart-stopping climbs and terraces carved from the mountainside, with sheer drops down to the sea. On their two hectares, the Grillos grow the traditional bosco, vermentino and albarola varieties, renowned for their aromatic notes of Mediterranean herbs and citrus fruit, alongside the less traditional, but perfectly adapted, syrah and cabernet sauvignon.

In this year's tastings, we liked the fresh, zesty, lingering Cinque Terre Bianco '08 and were even more impressed with its sibling, the Rosso '08, which won us over with its intact fruit and rich Mediterranean aromas. Better yet is the Sciacchetrà '07, which unveils extraordinary aromatic complexity in a bouquet of nuts and Mediterranean scrub. In the mouth, there's an extremely appealing off-dryness that is not even slightly cloying. The palate is underpinned by extraordinary acidity, which makes for a fresh and delightfully drinkable experience, despite the concentration. It's a shame that so few bottles are produced.

○ Cinque Terre Sciacchetrà '07	▼▼	8
● Cinque Terre '08	▼▼	5
○ Cinque Terre '08	▼	5
○ Mojou	▼	5
● Buranco '06	♈♈	6
● Buranco '05	♈♈	6
● Buranco '04	♈♈	6
○ Cinque Terre Sciacchetrà '04	♈♈	8
○ Cinque Terre Sciacchetrà '03	♈♈	8

Calleri

LOC. SALEA
REG. FRATTI, 2
17031 ALBENGA [SV]
TEL. 018220085
postmaster@cantinecalleri.com

ANNUAL PRODUCTION 90,000 bottles
HECTARES UNDER VINE N.D.
VITICULTURE METHOD Conventional

Aldo Calleri's winery has been in business for over 40 years and he earned his spurs on the first slopes of the foothills bordering the great Albenga plain to the north. Here, the three native varieties of pigato, vermentino and rossese – the Campochiesa version naturally – have always thrived, seemingly without encouragement, and for years Marcello Calleri has personally selected the best grapes in the vineyard and overseen their vinification.

All of the five wines tasted deserve more than a mere mention but while the Pigato '08 and the Pornassio '07 are attractively well typed, the brace of '08 Vermentinos – a basic version and the I Murazzi selection – are clearly in a different league. These too, however, are in turn eclipsed by the '08 Pigato Saleasco, named after its place of origin, Sàlea. It impressed us with its fresh acidity, rich aromas, well-managed structure and complex minerality, the result of concentration achieved through strict selection in the vineyard.

○ Riviera Ligure di Ponente Pigato Saleasco '08	▼▼	4*
○ Riviera Ligure di Ponente Vermentino '08	▼▼	4*
○ Riviera Ligure di Ponente Vermentino I Muzazzi '08	▼▼	4
● Ormeasco di Pornassio '07	▼	4
○ Riviera Ligure di Ponente Pigato '08	▼	4
○ Riviera Ligure di Ponente Pigato '07	♈♈	4*
○ Riviera Ligure di Ponente Vermentino I Muzazzi '07	♈♈	4

Cantine Lunae Bosoni

FRAZ. ISOLA DI ORTONOVO
VIA BOZZI, 63
19034 ORTONOVO [SP]
TEL. 0187669222
www.cantinelunae.com

CELLAR SALES
PRE-BOOKED VISITS

ANNUAL PRODUCTION **450,000 bottles**
HECTARES UNDER VINE **55**
VITICULTURE METHOD **Conventional**

Paolo Bosoni's vineyards and his extremely modern, bustling winery are situated close to what was once the Roman city of Lunae, where a Roman legion was stationed from the third century BC. It is thanks to legionaries from the "castrum" that viticulture organized according to near-modern standards arrived here at least 200 years before Christ. Centuries later, Paolo Bosoni has inherited their legacy, and together with his large family is committed to producing wines of the highest quality.

Three of the seven wines tasted made our finals and the others scored extremely well. This fine performance saw the '08 Vermentino Lunae Etichetta Nera take Three effortless Glasses. Extraordinarily fresh, it gives florality and aromatic herbs followed by well-rounded softness and an long, gratifying finish of minerality and fruit. Almost equally seductive is the '08 Vermentino from the Cavagino vineyard, with delicate oaky notes, generous citrus on nose and palate, and a long, zesty finish. Finally, the Niccolò V '05 gives a lively nose with intense red berries and spice over complex structure and a soft, appealing body.

○ Colli di Luni Vermentino Lunae Etichetta Nera '08	♟♟♟	4
● Colli di Luni Niccolò V '05	♟♟	5
○ Colli di Luni Onda di Luna '08	♟♟	5
○ Colli di Luni Vermentino Cavagino '08	♟♟	6*
○ Colli di Luni Vermentino Lunae Etichetta Grigia '08	♟♟	4
● Horae '06	♟	6

Walter De Batté

VIA TRARCANTU, 25
19017 RIOMAGGIORE [SP]
TEL. 0187920127

CELLAR SALES

ANNUAL PRODUCTION **15,000 bottles**
HECTARES UNDER VINE **5**
VITICULTURE METHOD **Naturale**

Walter De Batté is one of Liguria's most active growers. He has fought his toughest battles on the inhospitable cliffs of Cinque Terre, where in five years he has carved out a few hectares of vineyards for his winery on these dizzily steep slopes, and built terraces supported by the famous dry stone walls for which the Cinque Terre was made a UNESCO World Heritage Site. Now Walter is one of the partners in the Prima Terra project, which he set up with Riccardo Canesi and Pierfrancesco Donati, to produce white and red wines from new vineyards in Val di Vara and Val di Magra.

Cinque Terre and Sciacchetrà are still maturing but Walter had other great wines for us. The excellent Harmoge '06, from vermentino, bosco and albarola, is tangy, well-focused, complex and almost tannic after macerating on the skins, and finishes long on iodine and mineral notes. The characterful Vermentino Carlaz '07 shows density and grip. From the reds, we liked the Bozòlo '07, an elegant Mediterranean mix of merlot and dolcetto, and the dense, long Tonos '07, a complex blend of sangiovese, canaiolo, ciliegiolo and other red varieties. The Viasso '07, from vermentino, albarola, chardonnay and traminer, and the grenache and syrah Çerico '06, are also good.

● Bozòlo '07	♟♟	5
○ Carlaz '07	♟♟	5
○ Harmoge '06	♟♟	5
● Tonos '07	♟♟	5
● Çerico '06	♟	5
○ Viasso '07	♟	5
● Çerico '05	♟♟	5
○ Cinque Terre '07	♟♟	5
○ Cinque Terre Sciacchetrà '04	♟♟	8
○ Viasso '06	♟♟	5

Durin

via Roma, 202
17037 Ortovero [SV]
tel. 0182547007
www.durin.it

CELLAR SALES
PRE-BOOKED VISITS

ANNUAL PRODUCTION **140,000 bottles**
HECTARES UNDER VINE **15**
VITICULTURE METHOD **Conventional**

The Durin winery owes its name to grandfather Isidoro, whose nickname Doro becomes Durìn in local dialect. It achieved its current size in the 1980s, thanks first of all to Antonio Basso, and then, from the late 1990s, with the help of his young wife Laura. After doing away with the mixed farming methods typical of Valle dell'Arroscia, they purchased new vineyards, and recovered the old ones. Durin today presents a wide range of products, all at the highest level.

The '08 Pigato I S-cianchi made our finals with its great aromatic complexity, iodine salinity and rich fruit, thanks to maceration on the skins and late harvesting. Character and sense of terroir are qualities it shares with another finalist, the well-focused, savoury and elegantly rounded Vermentino '08. We loved the two reds, the characterful I Matti '07, from old vines of dolcetto, grenache and barbera, and the original '07 Ormeasco di Pornassio Passito, from old bush-trained vines, an unusual product for this area and also wonderfully drinkable. The Vermentino Lunghèra '08 and A' Matetta '08, from pigato and vermentino, are both nice.

○ Riviera Ligure di Ponente Pigato I S-cianchi '08	🍷🍷	4*
○ Riviera Ligure di Ponente Vermentino '08	🍷🍷	4*
○ A' Matetta '08	🍷🍷	5
● I Matti '07	🍷🍷	5
● Ormeasco di Pornassio Passito '07	🍷🍷	6
○ Riviera Ligure di Ponente Vermentino Lunghèra '08	🍷🍷	4*
● Ormeasco di Pornassio Sciac-Trà '08	🍷	4
○ Riviera Ligure di Ponente Pigato '08	🍷	4
● Riviera Ligure di Ponente Rossese '08	🍷	4
● I Matti '04	🍸🍸	5
● Ormeasco di Pornassio Sup. '06	🍸🍸	4
○ Riviera Ligure di Ponente Pigato I S-cianchi '06	🍸🍸	4*
● Riviera Ligure di Ponente Rossese '07	🍸🍸	4
○ Riviera Ligure di Ponente Vermentino '07	🍸🍸	4

Ottaviano Lambruschi

via Olmarello, 28
19030 Castelnuovo Magra [SP]
tel. 0187674261
ottavianolambruschi@libero.it

ANNUAL PRODUCTION **30,000 bottles**
HECTARES UNDER VINE **5**
VITICULTURE METHOD **Conventional**

Ottaviano once told us that he didn't know which was more exhausting – his previous job as a marble quarrier in Carrara or doing reclamation work on the estate in Sarticola. Either way, tackling the two hectares of the Costa Marina wood is definitely much more enjoyable. In all, the winery boasts five hectares of excellent vineyards, which this obstinate local has managed to carve out of an inhospitable yet beautiful environment, perfect for wine. With the help of his son Fabio, Ottaviano has achieved results unthinkable only 35 years ago, when his winery first opened.

We tasted two Colli di Luni Vermentino '08s and the Colli di Luni Rosso Maniero '07, which displays intriguing aromas and structure, but has a somewhat sharp-edged finish. We loved the two whites, named after the Sarticola and Costa Marina estates. This year, the former was the better of the two, and took top honours. An excellent nose with generous tropical fruit aromas and a balsamic, mineral vein leads into a confident, well-developed palate where fleshy fruit is sustained by good acidity, which delivers thrust and extraordinary length, and accompanied by complex, mineral roundness. The Costa Marina '08 was slightly softer but less appealing.

○ Colli di Luni Vermentino Sarticola '08	🍷🍷🍷	4*
○ Colli di Luni Vermentino Costa Marina '08	🍷🍷	4*
● Colli di Luni Rosso Maniero '07	🍷	4
○ Colli di Luni Vermentino '03	🍸🍸	4*
○ Colli di Luni Vermentino Alessandro '05	🍸🍸	4*
○ Colli di Luni Vermentino Costa Marina '07	🍸🍸	4*
○ Colli di Luni Vermentino Costa Marina '06	🍸🍸	4*
○ Colli di Luni Vermentino Costa Marina '05	🍸🍸	4*
○ Colli di Luni Vermentino Sarticola '03	🍸🍸	4*
○ Colli di Luni Vermentino Sarticola '01	🍸🍸	4*

Tommaso Lupi & C.

VIA MAZZINI, 9
18026 PIEVE DI TECO [IM]
TEL. 018336161
www.vinilupi.it

CELLAR SALES
PRE-BOOKED VISITS
OSPITALITÀ

ANNUAL PRODUCTION **160,000 bottles**
HECTARES UNDER VINE **10**
VITICULTURE METHOD **Conventional**

Tommaso Lupi set up his winery in Pieve di Teco almost 50 years ago, when the need to provide the many customers of his bar at Oneglia – now a wine shop – with his own wines had become pressing. With Donato Lanati's consultancy and the help of his children, Tiziana, Massimo and Fabio, Tommaso has achieved growth that would probably have been impossible had he relied only on his own efforts. One thing is sure: in this corner of Liguria, hemmed in by the sea and the foothills of the Ligurian Alps, Tommaso realized that he had a terroir with great wine potential.

The winery, with Tommaso's son Massimo at the helm, lays great store by its Vignamare, an elegant blend of vermentino and pigato matured in new oak, which has brought them so much satisfaction. This year, though, we preferred the Vermentino Le Serre '07, with its warm pervasiveness and complex, lingering flower and fruit aromas. A savoury mineral attack opens onto a vibrant, well-rounded palate brimming with fruit and a long, gratifying finish: Three thoroughly deserved Glasses. The rest of the wines are good with the '08 Pigato and Vermentino dei Colli di Luni deserving a special mention.

Maccario Dringenberg

VIA TORRE, 3
18030 SAN BIAGIO DELLA CIMA [IM]
TEL. 0184289947

ANNUAL PRODUCTION **N.D.**
HECTARES UNDER VINE **N.D.**
VITICULTURE METHOD **Conventional**

To reach San Biagio della Cima, you need to drive through Vallecrosia. The valley leads to Perinaldo and Apricale, known to astronomers as the home of mathematician Giovanni Domenico Cassini, to whom we owe much of our knowledge of the solar system. We don't know whether Goetz Dringenberg was seduced more by this fact, the beautiful landscape or the lovely Giovanna but he has never left. He and Giovanna have focused their efforts on Rossese di Dolceacqua, which finds perfect conditions here, especially in the historic Luvaira vineyard.

The Superiore '07 surprised our tasters with its irrepressible freshness, rich red forest fruits and subtle fragrance, flaunting elegant spice and smoky notes on the nose followed by fleshy plum and cherry on complex, well-orchestrated palate of considerable length. Three Glasses were never in doubt. While the Luvaira vineyard is 70 years old, Posaù, also with bush-trained vines, has been cultivated for over a century. Its generous, characterful wine is bursting with fruit but displays a touch of huskiness, which never gets in the way of drinkability and typicity.

○ Riviera Ligure di Ponente Vermentino Le Serre '07	♆♆♆ 5
○ Colli di Luni Pigato '08	♆♆ 4*
○ Colli di Luni Vermentino '08	♆♆ 4*
○ Vignamare '05	♆♆ 5
☉ Ormeasco di Pornassio Sciac-trà '08	♆ 4
● Ormeasco di Pornassio Sup. '08	♆ 5
● Rossese di Dolceacqua '08	♆ 5
○ Riviera Ligure di Ponente Pigato '04	♉♉ 4*
○ Riviera Ligure di Ponente Pigato Le Petraie '05	♉♉ 5
○ Riviera Ligure di Ponente Pigato Le Petraie '04	♉♉ 5
○ Riviera Ligure di Ponente Pigato Le Petraie '03	♉♉ 5
○ Riviera Ligure di Ponente Vermentino '05	♉♉ 4*
○ Riviera Ligure di Ponente Vermentino Le Serre '02	♉♉ 5
○ Vignamare '02	♉♉ 5

● Rossese di Dolceacqua Sup. Vign. Luvaira '07	♆♆♆ 5
● Rossese di Dolceacqua Sup. Vigneto Posaù '07	♆♆ 3

Il Monticello

VIA GROPPOLO, 7
19038 SARZANA [SP]
TEL. 0187621432
www.ilmonticello.vai.li

CELLAR SALES
PRE-BOOKED VISITS
OSPITALITÀ

ANNUAL PRODUCTION **55,000 bottles**
HECTARES UNDER VINE **10**
VITICULTURE METHOD **Naturale**

Back in the early 1980s, when Pierluigi Neri, an electronic engineer, inherited an estate in the hills to the north of the ancient city of Luni, today's Sarzana, and indulged his long-standing passion of winemaking, he could never have imagined it would become his sons' main activity. Davide and Alessandro, with the support of their mother Maria Antonietta Bacciarelli and consultant oenologist Claudio Icardi, have made this one of Luni's leading wineries. With the passion inherited from their father, the Neris produce a limited range of products, all of excellent quality.

The '07 edition of Poggio Paterno, a Vermentino that has already received rave reviews in the past, displays a generosity and stylistic cleanness which took it through to our finals. Lashings of fruit are underpinned by well-dosed oak, with a fresh acid vein providing youthful vigour and great vitality. Close on its heels is the Vermentino '08, boasting elegant mineral notes and Mediterranean scrub over a fleshy, savoury palate. The rosé Serasuolo '08 and the Rosso Rupestro '08 are well crafted.

Cascina Nirasca

FRAZ. NIRASCA
VIA ALPI, 3
18026 PIEVE DI TECO [IM]
TEL. 0183368067
www.cascinanirasca.com

CELLAR SALES
PRE-BOOKED VISITS

ANNUAL PRODUCTION **22,000 bottles**
HECTARES UNDER VINE **3**
VITICULTURE METHOD **Conventional**

If you take the road that climbs up towards Col di Nava, on its way towards the first spurs of the Ligurian Alps, you will come to Pieve di Teco, an ancient town built on one of the many trade routes that still link Piedmont to the sea today. Here, Marco Temesio and Gabriele Maglio have managed to establish a fine, albeit rather small, winery, with three hectares of vineyards – some estate-owned, some rented – at altitudes between 400 and 500 metres, and a well-equipped production facility.

Of the various wines tasted this year, the Pigato '08 was the most interesting, standing out for its beautifully complex structure. Although lacking intensity on the nose, it is utterly self-assured and boasts attractive floral notes. Almost as good is the '08 Vermentino, redolent of cedar, sage and rosemary, but a little insubstantial on the palate. The well-balanced, fruit-driven Pornassio Superiore '07 is savoury and excellent. The Pornassio '08 and the red Senso '06, a blend of syrah and sangiovese grosso, are attractive and well made.

○ Colli di Luni Vermentino Poggio Paterno '07	🍷🍷	4*
○ Colli di Luni Vermentino '08	🍷🍷	4*
● Colli di Luni Rosso Rupestro '08	🍷	4
☉ Serasuolo '08	🍷	4
● Colli di Luni Rosso Poggio dei Magni '05	🍷🍷	4
● Colli di Luni Rosso Poggio dei Magni '01	🍷🍷	4
○ Colli di Luni Vermentino Poggio Paterno '06	🍷🍷	4

● Ormeasco di Pornassio Sup. '07	🍷🍷	4*
○ Riviera Ligure di Ponente Pigato '08	🍷🍷	4*
● Ormeasco di Pornassio '08	🍷	4
○ Riviera Ligure di Ponente Vermentino '08	🍷	4
● Senso '06	🍷	5
● Ormeasco di Pornassio '05	🍷🍷	4*
● Ormeasco di Pornassio Sup. '06	🍷🍷	4
● Ormeasco di Pornassio Sup. '05	🍷🍷	4*
○ Riviera Ligure di Ponente Vermentino '07	🍷🍷	4
● Senso '05	🍷🍷	5
● Senso '04	🍷🍷	5
● Senso '03	🍷🍷	5

Conte Picedi Benettini

VIA MAZZINI, 57
19038 SARZANA [SP]
TEL. 0187625147
www.picedibenettini.it

CELLAR SALES
PRE-BOOKED VISITS
OSPITALITÀ

ANNUAL PRODUCTION **30,000 bottles**
HECTARES UNDER VINE **N.D.**
VITICULTURE METHOD **Conventional**

The aristocratic Picedi family, who can trace their roots back to 1056, have lived for centuries in "il Palà", their ancestral home built in Arcola in the early 1500s. According to land registry records, it was surrounded by an estate of "vineyards, olive groves, chestnut woods and woodland". A subsequent acquisition took the Picedis to Baccano di Arcola, where Il Chioso stands, a classic example of a post-Renaissance villa surrounded by a vast hillside estate of around 150 hectares, partly under vine. The family owns other vineyards at Fattoria di Ceserano in Fivizzano.

Nino Papirio Picedi, known to locals simply as "il Conte", presented a fine selection of wines. The Vermentino Stemma '08 shows elegant, well-focused ripe apple aromas with hints of damask rose and citron zest, over a savoury, supple palate. The Gran Baccano '08 is equally excellent, with red and black berry fruits, nuances of vanilla and spice, followed by good body and delicate tannins on the palate. The sweet Passito del Chioso is an elegant blend of vermentino, albarola and ruzzese. The fine Vermentino Il Chioso '08, the fragrant Ciliegiolo '08 and the Ruzzese '08, from the white variety of the same name, complete the range.

La Pietra del Focolare

FRAZ. ISOLA
VIA DOGANA, 209
19034 ORTONOVO [SP]
TEL. 0187662129
www.lapietradelfocolare.it

CELLAR SALES
PRE-BOOKED VISITS

ANNUAL PRODUCTION **30,000 bottles**
HECTARES UNDER VINE **8**
VITICULTURE METHOD **Naturale**

In 1997, Stefano Salvetti and Laura Angelini decided to drop everything and open a winery, buying what they could and renting the rest. They leased their headquarters from Francesca, owner of an old house and the Bacchiano estate, with a hectare of land planted to vines and olive trees, in a veritable corner of paradise. Today, the Salvettis directly manage eight hectares under vine, four and a half planted to vermentino – spread over three different municipalities, Sarzana, Ortonovo and Castelnuovo Magra – and the rest to sangiovese, canaiolo and their latest planting, merlot.

We tasted the three '08 Vermentinos from three different estates, after which they are respectively named. The vitally fresh Solarancio was the most minerally and complex, showing fragrant fruit and Mediterranean scrub over a tangy, mineral palate while the Augusto impressed us with intense, citrus notes on the nose, mirrored on the palate, where it shows good grip, rich fruit, and an attractive almondy finish. Villa Linda came in just behind these two this time round. This well-typed white shows a complex nose, with floral notes and medicinal herbs, leading to a fresh palate but lacks length.

● Colli di Luni Rosso Gran Baccano '08	♟♟	4*
○ Colli di Luni Vermentino Stemma '08	♟♟	4*
○ Passito del Chioso '08	♟♟	5
☉ Ciliegiolo '08	♟	4
○ Colli di Luni Vermentino Il Chioso '08	♟	4
○ Ruzzese '08	♟	4
● Colli di Luni Rosso Gran Baccano '07	♟♟	4
○ Colli di Luni Vermentino Stemma '07	♟♟	4
○ Colli di Luni Vermentino Stemma '03	♟♟	4*

○ Colli di Luni Vermentino Augusto '08	♟♟	4*
○ Colli di Luni Vermentino Solarancio '08	♟♟	5
○ Colli di Luni Vermentino Villa Linda '08	♟	4
○ Colli di Luni Vermentino Augusto '06	♟♟	4
○ Colli di Luni Vermentino Solarancio '07	♟♟	5
○ Colli di Luni Vermentino Solarancio '06	♟♟	5
○ Colli di Luni Vermentino Solarancio '04	♟♟	4*
○ Colli di Luni Vermentino Solarancio '03	♟♟	4*
○ Colli di Luni Vermentino Villa Linda '05	♟♟	4*
○ Colli di Luni Vermentino Viva Luce '05	♟♟	4*

Poggio dei Gorleri

FRAZ. GORLERI
VIA SAN LEONARDO
18013 DIANO MARINA [IM]
TEL. 0183495207
www.poggiodeigorleri.com

CELLAR SALES
PRE-BOOKED VISITS
OSPITALITÀ

ANNUAL PRODUCTION **60,000 bottles**
HECTARES UNDER VINE **9**
VITICULTURE METHOD **Conventional**

Of all Diano's outlying districts, Gorleri is one of the most panoramic and offers marvellous views of the coast and the Ligurian Alps. Giampiero Merano, the estate owner, has managed to exploit its position to the full, building a fine farm holiday centre to accompany his winemaking activities. The cellar, where his sons Matteo and Davide also work, is equipped with the latest facilities and uses modern techniques such as low temperature skin contact.

The Meranos are interested not only in production but also in the effective marketing of their wines. This year, they presented us with five of their most interesting products from the '08 vintage: three Vermentinos and two Pigatos, each from a different vineyard on their estate. As usual, all the wines impressed us with their typicity, intensity and whistle-clean style. The Pigato Cycnus '08 took home top honours thanks to a rich, complex bouquet, regaling focused Mediterranean notes, followed by a deep, close-knit, nicely coordinated palate with astounding length.

Cascina Praié

S.DA CASTELLO, 20
17051 ANDORA [SV]
TEL. 019602377
m_viglietti@tin.it

CELLAR SALES
PRE-BOOKED VISITS

ANNUAL PRODUCTION **35,000 bottles**
HECTARES UNDER VINE **8**
VITICULTURE METHOD **Conventional**

The nautical skills of Thor Heyerdahl, the great Norwegian anthropologist who lived for many years in Colla Micheri next door to Cascina Praiè, was clearly an inspiration for Massimo Viglietti and Anna Maria Corrent, a guiding star as it were in the rough seas of Ligurian viticulture. Cultivating eight hectares of "fasce", the narrow terraces supported by dry stone walls on the hillside overlooking Andora and Laigueglia is anything but simple, and it is even more difficult to make good wines which respect tradition, while also experimenting with new varieties and production techniques.

The red wines were absent this year, including the Ardesia, which is still resting in the cellars. To compensate, we tasted an excellent Vermentino Le Cicale '07, from overripe grapes, brimming with fruit and freshness and laced with mineral subtlety. This is a significant improvement on the '06. The Vermentino Colla Micheri '08 is savoury and supple, and the Pigato Il Canneto '08 offers delicate tones of aromatic herbs. The Lumassina Zefiro '08, with its citrussy aromas and lovely freshness on the palate, is also well made.

Wine	Rating
○ Riviera Ligure di Ponente Pigato Cycnus '08	♆♆♆ 4*
○ Riviera Ligure di Ponente Vermentino V. Sorì '08	♆♆ 4*
○ Riviera Ligure di Ponente Pigato Albium '08	♆♆ 5
○ Riviera Ligure di Ponente Vermentino '08	♆♆ 4*
○ Riviera Ligure di Ponente Vermentino Apricus '08	♆♆ 5
○ Riviera Ligure di Ponente Pigato Albium '07	♉♉ 5
○ Riviera Ligure di Ponente Pigato Albium '06	♉♉ 5
○ Riviera Ligure di Ponente Pigato Cycnus '07	♉♉ 4
○ Riviera Ligure di Ponente Pigato Cycnus '06	♉♉ 4
○ Riviera Ligure di Ponente Vermentino Apricus '07	♉♉ 5
○ Riviera Ligure di Ponente Vermentino Apricus '06	♉♉ 5
○ Riviera Ligure di Ponente Vermentino V. Sorì '07	♉♉ 4
○ Riviera Ligure di Ponente Vermentino V. Sorì '05	♉♉ 4*

Wine	Rating
○ Riviera Ligure di Ponente Vermentino Le Cicale '07	♆♆ 4*
○ Lumassina Zefiro '08	♆ 4
○ Riviera Ligure di Ponente Pigato Il Canneto '08	♆ 4
○ Riviera Ligure di Ponente Vermentino Colla Micheri '08	♆ 4
● Ardesia '06	♉♉ 4
● Ardesia '05	♉♉ 5
○ Riviera Ligure di Ponente Vermentino Colla Micheri '07	♉♉ 5
○ Riviera Ligure di Ponente Vermentino Le Cicale '05	♉♉ 4*
● Sciurbì '05	♉♉ 4*

Sancio

VIA LAIOLO, 73
17028 SPOTORNO [SV]
TEL. 019743255
cantinasancio@libero.it

CELLAR SALES
PRE-BOOKED VISITS
OSPITALITÀ
FOOD

ANNUAL PRODUCTION **60,000 bottles**
HECTARES UNDER VINE **4.3**
VITICULTURE METHOD **Conventional**

Driving up to the Sancio winery, situated in a dominant position on high ground overlooking Spotorno, is in itself a wonderful experience. The small farm holiday centre has a traditional restaurant where you can try local specialities from the Ligurian hills. Riccardo Sancio seems to be omnipresent in the vineyard and the winery, but also in the kitchens and dining room. His constant, attentive involvement gives a highly personal style to both his wines and his food.

We liked the Baciocco Passito, with its harmonious, balanced elegance, beautifully rich citrus notes, marked hints of honey and self-assured roundness, evidently the product of carefully dried grapes. With just a touch more effort, we are sure this wine will soon bring Riccardo the top award. In contrast, the '08 Pigato struck us as a tad below par compared to previous years. Although fresh, drinkable, deliciously savoury and brimming with fruit, it lacks complexity. We didn't taste the Cappellania selection, which is still maturing. This year's Vermentino and Rossese are good, as always.

Luigi Sartori

FRAZ. LECA
REGIONE TORRE PERNICE, 3
17031 ALBENGA [SV]
TEL. 018220042
sartoripigato@libero.it

ANNUAL PRODUCTION **N.D.**
HECTARES UNDER VINE **N.D.**
VITICULTURE METHOD **Conventional**

Torre Pernice still stands on the outskirts of Albenga. This imposing tower was built in the Middle Ages to fend off the Saracens, whose raids had already led to the city's destruction in the late tenth century. All around the tower, the rows of vines are neatly laid out on what is the largest plain in the whole of Liguria, the Piana di Albenga, formed by the confluence of the Arroscia and Neva rivers. Old, still ungrafted pigato vines are said to thrive in this loose sedimentary soil, and have never been affected by phylloxera, which finds it hard to take hold in the stony soil here.

Roberto Sartori and his wife Bianca Dulbecco produce western Ligurian classics as well as more original wines, such as the Passito Rosa d'Aleramo, from rossese grapes, with rich wild berry jam and cakes over a sweet, fresh, well-balanced palate. The elegant golden Oro di Aleramo, from part-dried pigato grapes, shows focused aromas of overripe fruit and honey swathed in intense balsam over a delicately sweet palate with a vanilla finish. We also liked the soft, full-bodied Antico Rubino, a fruit-forward blend of rossese, barbera and cabernet, the last two aged in small oak barrels. The Vermentino and the Pigato '08 are well typed and enjoyable.

○ Il Baciocco Passito	▼▼ 6
○ Riviera Ligure di Ponente Pigato '08	▼ 4
● Riviera Ligure di Ponente Rossese '08	▼ 4
○ Riviera Ligure di Ponente Vermentino '08	▼ 4
○ Riviera Ligure di Ponente Pigato '07	♀♀ 4
○ Riviera Ligure di Ponente Pigato '06	♀♀ 4*
○ Riviera Ligure di Ponente Pigato Cappellania '07	♀♀ 4
○ Riviera Ligure di Ponente Pigato Cappellania '06	♀♀ 5
○ Riviera Ligure di Ponente Pigato Cappellania '05	♀♀ 5
● Riviera Ligure di Ponente Rossese '06	♀♀ 4

● Antico Rubino di Aleramo	▼▼ 5
○ Oro di Aleramo	▼▼ 7
☉ Passito Rosa di Aleramo	▼▼ 5
○ Riviera Ligure di Ponente Pigato Torre Pernice '08	▼ 4
○ Riviera Ligure di Ponente Vermentino Torre Pernice '08	▼ 4

Terre Bianche

LOC. ARCAGNA
18035 DOLCEACQUA [IM]
TEL. 018431426
www.terrebianche.com

CELLAR SALES
PRE-BOOKED VISITS
OSPITALITÀ

ANNUAL PRODUCTION **61,000 bottles**
HECTARES UNDER VINE **8.5**
VITICULTURE METHOD **Conventional**

When, many years ago, the Rondelli brothers bravely opened the Terre Bianche estate, people thought they were on to a loser, not least because their crops – grapes and olives – grow along a ridge so steep that survival here seems impossible, for plants or people. Moreover, the strict quality criteria introduced by the two brothers to regulate growing and winemaking were, back then, simply unthinkable. But dedication paid off and Filippo Rondelli, together with Franco Laconi, is successfully continuing the work begun by his father and uncle.

The Rossese di Dolceacqua '08 stole the show this year, gracing the finals with its attractively deep, bright ruby and a rich nose of red berry fruit and spice over intense balsam. The firm, full-flavoured palate develops nicely and signs off with finesse on gentle tannins. The Bricco Arcagna '07 gives rich Mediterranean aromas, good backbone and flavour but is let down by a slightly rustic note on the palate. The Arcana Rosso '06, from cabernet sauvignon and rossese, charmed us with its structure and depth, and we liked the Bianco '07, from pigato and vermentino, for its intact fruit and fresh, well-focused minerality. The Pigato and the Vermentino '08 are up to snuff.

Cascina delle Terre Rosse

VIA MANIE, 3
17024 FINALE LIGURE [SV]
TEL. 019698782

CELLAR SALES
PRE-BOOKED VISITS

ANNUAL PRODUCTION **30,000 bottles**
HECTARES UNDER VINE **4.5**
VITICULTURE METHOD **Naturale**

Reaching the Manie plateau, behind Finale Ligure, is an unforgettable experience, whether you drive up from the town on the coast or leave the Autostrada dei Fiori at the Spotorno junction. In 1985, Vladimiro Galluzzo relaunched the family business here by investing in facilities and above all in quality. He has had success but also some bitter disappointments, mainly due to his eclectic, innovative approach. Today, Vladimiro's troubles are behind him. What he discovered years ago has become common knowledge, thanks in part to the masterly hand of Giuliano Noè, his long-time oenologist.

This year's tastings were dominated by the red Solitario '07, from grenache, rossese and barbera. Rich, aristocratic aromas and well-coordinated, complex structure, underpinned by a sumptuous body, make this a truly distinctive wine that is gratifying to drink. The excellent Pigato '08 is fresh and Mediterranean, with an intriguing mineral finish. Le Banche '08, also from pigato but oak-matured, is equally attractive. The fresh, spirited L'Acerbina '08 comes from the rare lumassina variety. The range is completed by a well-made Vermentino '08 and the Pigato Apogeo, also '08.

● Rossese di Dolceacqua '08	♀♀ 4*
○ Arcana Bianco '07	♀♀ 5
● Arcana Rosso '06	♀♀ 6
● Rossese di Dolceacqua Bricco Arcagna '07	♀♀ 5
○ Riviera Ligure di Ponente Pigato '08	♀ 4
○ Riviera Ligure di Ponente Vermentino '08	♀ 4
○ Arcana Bianco '06	♀♀ 5
● Arcana Rosso '05	♀♀ 6
● Arcana Rosso '03	♀♀ 5
○ Riviera Ligure di Ponente Pigato '06	♀♀ 4*
○ Riviera Ligure di Ponente Vermentino '07	♀♀ 4*
○ Riviera Ligure di Ponente Vermentino '06	♀♀ 4*
● Rossese di Dolceacqua '07	♀♀ 4*
● Rossese di Dolceacqua '06	♀♀ 4*
● Rossese di Dolceacqua Bricco Arcagna '06	♀♀ 5
● Rossese di Dolceacqua Bricco Arcagna '01	♀♀ 5

● Solitario '07	♀♀ 8
○ L'Acerbina '08	♀♀ 4*
○ Le Banche '08	♀♀ 8
○ Riviera Ligure di Ponente Pigato '08	♀♀ 5
○ Apogeo '08	♀ 5
○ Riviera Ligure di Ponente Vermentino '08	♀ 5
○ Apogeo '07	♀♀ 5
○ Apogeo '06	♀♀ 5
○ Le Banche '05	♀♀ 5
○ Riviera Ligure di Ponente Pigato '07	♀♀ 5
○ Riviera Ligure di Ponente Pigato '06	♀♀ 5
● Solitario '05	♀♀ 6
● Solitario '04	♀♀ 6
● Solitario '03	♀♀ 6

A Maccia

FRAZ. BORGO
VIA UMBERTO I, 54
18020 RANZO [IM]
TEL. 0183318003
www.amaccia.it

Established in 1850, Loredana Faraldi's winery has 12 hectares of vineyards and olive groves. Her daughter, Carlotta, will be glad to show you round and let you taste the wines, of which the savoury, well-focused Pigato '08 is without doubt the best.

○ Riviera Ligure di Ponente Pigato '08	▼ 4*
○ Riviera Ligure di Ponente Pigato '07	▼▼ 4*

Cooperativa Agricoltori della Vallata di Levanto

LOC. GHIARE - VIA SAN MATTEO, 20
19015 LEVANTO [SP]
TEL. 0187800867
www.levanto.com/cooperativa

This co-operative's presence in the Guide is more than justified, since Costa di Mattelun is again a richly fruited, well-typed white. The other wines are also interesting, such as the dry, generous Monterosso '08, and the soft, fruity Canuet '08. They could do more, however.

○ Cinque Terre Monterosso '08	▼ 4
● Colline di Levanto Canuet '08	▼ 4
○ Colline di Levanto Costa di Mattelun '08	▼ 4
○ Colline di Levanto Lievàntu '08	▼ 3

Carlo Alessandri

VIA UMBERTO I, 15
18020 RANZO [IM]
TEL. 0183318114
az.alessandricarlo@libero.it

If you cross Ranzo's main square and continue along the narrow street running through the centre of the town, you come to Carlo Alessandri's small winery, which makes traditional west Ligurian bottles. The Pigato '08 is territory-focused with seductive absinthe-like aromas.

○ Riviera Ligure di Ponente Pigato '08	▼ 4

Riccardo Arrigoni

LOC. MIGLIARINI
VIA SARZANA, 224
19126 LA SPEZIA
TEL. 0187504060
www.awf2000.com

The Arrigoni family has been producing and selling wine for four generations and has estates in Liguria and San Gimignano in Tuscany. The Sciacchetrà '95 is traditional and we liked the Albarola '08, from the classic Cinque Terre variety, as well as the Vermentino Vigna del Prefetto '08.

○ Cinque Terre Sciacchetrà '95	▼▼ 8
○ Albarola '08	▼ 4
○ Colli di Luni Vermentino Vigna del Prefetto '08	▼ 4

Samuele Heydi Bonanini

VIA SIGNORINI, 91
19017 RIOMAGGIORE [SP]
TEL. 0187920959
www.possa.it

Although this small grower, who struggles every day with the difficult terroir of the Cinque Terre, releases very few bottles, quality is good. While his Sciacchetrà '07 is not on a par with the '06, we enjoyed the standard Cinque Terre '08, which has its usual appealing freshness and floral aromas.

○ Cinque Terre '08	▼▼ 7
○ Cinque Terre Sciacchetrà '07	▼ 8
● Passito la Rinascita '07	▼ 6

Cantina Bregante

VIA UNITÀ D'ITALIA, 47
16039 SESTRI LEVANTE [GE]
TEL. 018541388
www.cantinebregante.it

Cantina Bregante has been in business since the late 1800s and is currently expanding with the purchase of new vineyards. The nice Vermentino Golfo del Tigullio ì08 has fresh aromas of fruit and Mediterranean scrub while Ca' du Diau '08 has good structure and fruit aromas. The Moscato '08 is good.

○ Golfo del Tigullio Vermentino '08	▼▼ 4*
● Golfo del Tigullio Ca' du Diau '08	▼ 4
○ Golfo del Tigullio Moscato '08	▼ 4

Enoteca Andrea Bruzzone

VIA BOLZANETO, 94/96
16162 GENOVA
TTEL. 0107455157
www.andreabruzzonevini.it

Andrea is a determined man. He not only saved the Valpolcevera designation but inspired the recent recovery in the whole area. The zone embraces the famous three towns referred to in the dialect name of his flagship Treipaexi '00, a youthful, yet full-bodied, nicely structured red.

O Val Polcèvera Bianchetta Genovese '08	♀	3
● Val Polcèvera Rosso Treipaexi '08	♀	3

Luigi Calvini

VIA SOLARO, 76-78A
18038 SAN REMO [IM]
TEL. 0184660242
www.luigicalini.com

Luigi Calvini lovingly tends vineyards we are all familiar with, having seen them dozens of times on TV as we watch the closing stages of the Milan-San Remo cycle race. His Vermentino and Pigato in the '08 editions are characterful, well-typed wines, reflecting a territory of charm and beauty.

O Riviera Ligure di Ponente Pigato '08	♀	4
O Riviera Ligure di Ponente Vermentino '08	♀	4

La Colombiera

LOC. MONTECCHIO, 92
19030 CASTELNUOVO MAGRA [SP]
TEL. 0187674265

The Colli di Luni '08 is a perfect ambassador for the Castelnuovo terroir, just as Piero Ferro, the experienced wine man in charge of La Colombiera, intended. This savoury, fleshy Vermentino flaunts delicate citrussy, aromatics and signs off long and clean.

O Colli di Luni Vermentino '08	♀♀	4*

Cooperativa Vitivinicola Coronata Valpolcevera

VIA MONTE GUANO, 1A
16100 GENOVA
TTEL. 0106516534

Domenico Barisone has been running the Coronata Valpolcevera co-operative for years. Today, the Opera Pia De Ferrari, which owns the vineyards, seems to have other priorities. Let's hope not, because the Bianco from this famous hill has an unusual "sulphury" note loved by generations of Genoese.

O Val Polcèvera Coronata '07	♀	2

Fontanacota

VIA DON ABBO, 12
18100 IMPERIA
TEL. 0183293456
viniberta@tiscali.it

Maria Antonietta Berta never fails to amaze us with her wide range of wines, offering high quality across the board. Her Vermentino, Pigato and Rossese '08 have character and typicity, although the flagship Ormeasco is less self-assured than in previous years, as is the Sciac-Trà.

● Ormeasco di Pornassio '08	♀	4
⊙ Ormeasco di Pornassio Sciac- Trà '08	♀	4
O Riviera Ligure di Ponente Pigato '08	♀	4
● Riviera Ligure di Ponente Rossese '08	♀	4
O Riviera Ligure di Ponente Vermentino '08	♀	4

Foresti

VIA BRAIE, 223
18033 CAMPOROSSO [IM]
TEL. 0184292377
www.forestiwine.it

The winery was established in 1979 and has over 20 hectares under vine, all in the Riviera Ligure di Ponente and Rossese di Dolceacqua DOC zones. The speciality of, Marco, the young owner, is the latter, particularly the version using grapes from the famous Luvaira vineyard, Rossese's grand cru.

● Rossese di Dolceacqua Sup. '07	♀	4
● Rossese di Dolceacqua Vign. Luvaira '06	♀	5

OTHER WINERIES

Forlini Cappellini

LOC. MANAROLA
VIA RICCOBALDI, 45
19010 RIOMAGGIORE [SP]
TEL. 0187920496
forlinicappellini@libero.it

Manarola is a district of Riomaggiore in the Cinque Terre. Winemaking here requires nothing short of heroism, and Forlini Cappellini is a legendary name. The elegantly sweet Sciacchetrà Riserva '03 has extraordinary complexity and brims with Mediterranean aromas. The Cinque Terre '08 is fresh and savoury.

O Cinque Terre Sciacchetrà Ris. '03	♟♟	8
O Cinque Terre '08	♟	5
O Cinque Terre Sciacchetrà Ris. '01	♟♟	8

Gajaudo

LOC. BUNDA
S.DA PROVINCIALE, 7
18030 IMPERIA
TEL. 0184208095
www.cantinagajaudo.com

La Gajaudo is situated in Isolabona, not far from historic Dolceacqua, famous for Monet's painting and Rossese, the Gajaudo family's speciality. They gave us two vineyard selections to try: Arcagna and Luvaira. Both are interesting, as are the basic Vermentino and Rossese, but they could do more

● Dolceacqua Rossese '08	♟	4
● Dolceacqua Rossese Arcagna '06	♟	5
● Dolceacqua Rossese Luvaira '06	♟	5
O Riviera Ligure di Ponente Vermentino '08	♟	5

Ka Manciné

FRAZ. SAN MARTINO
P.ZZA OTTO LUOGHI, 36
18036 SOLDANO [IM]
TEL. 0184289089
www.kamancine.it

Maurizio Anfosso established his winery in 1998 in a historic rossese zone. A specialist in this red variety, he offered us two selections, of which we preferred the Beragna for its aromas of balsam-swathed blackberries, raspberries and blueberries leading to a firm, supple palate.

● Rossese di Dolceacqua Beragna '08	♟♟	4*
● Rossese di Dolceacqua Galeae '08	♟	4
● Rossese di Dolceacqua Beragna '07	♟♟	4

Paganini

LOC. CHIAZZARI, 15
17024 FINALE LIGURE [SV]
TEL. 335211931
www.cantinapaganini.it

This young grower's well-ordered vines, squeezed against the sheer rock faces overlooking Finale, are a fine sight for those driving along the Autostrada dei Fiori towards the east. Both the Vermentino and the Pigato surprised us with their typing and wafts of close-focused Mediterranean scrub.

O Riviera Ligure di Ponente Pigato '08	♟	4
O Riviera Ligure di Ponente Vermentino '08	♟	4

Gino Pino

FRAZ. MISSANO
VIA PODESTÀ, 31
16030 CASTIGLIONE CHIAVARESE [GE]
TEL. 0185408036
pinogino.az.agricola@tin.it

Antonella Pino has followed in her father's footsteps, and named the winery after him. She has focused on the area's two most typical varieties, bianchetta genovese and ciliegiolo, but her real tour de force is Moscato, from a local clone that gives the wine sensual aromatic softness and astonishing length.

O Golfo del Tigullio Moscato '08	♟♟	5
O Golfo del Tigullio Bianchetta Genovese '08	♟	4
● Golfo del Tigullio Ciliegiolo '08	♟	4

Danila Pisano

VIA SAN MARTINO, 20
18036 SOLDANO [IM]
TEL. 0184208551
danila.pisano@alice.it

The Pisano winery is one of the oldest in the area and its Savoia vineyard, of less than a hectare, is one of the best known. The owner supervises production, never more than 60 quintals, or in other words 5,000 bottles. Her organically produced wine is a tad rugged but has great character.

● Rossese di Dolceacqua V. Savoia '07	♟	4

Le Rocche del Gatto

FRAZ. SALEA
REG. RUATO, 4
17031 ALBENGA [SV]
TEL. 3355223547
www.lerocchedelgatto.it

Luigi and Chiara Crosa di Vergagni perhaps decided to settle here after meeting Fausto De Andreis, a legendary grower and skilled craftsman of pigato and vermentino. Spigau Crociata is their flagship wine, with lashings of almost crunchy fruit, great vigour and appealing balsamic and aromatic notes.

○ Spigau Crociata '07   ♥♥ 4*

Agostino Sommariva

VIA MAMELI, 1
17031 ALBENGA [SV]
TEL. 0182559222
info@oliosommariva.it

Sommariva has around six hectares of vineyards, and an attractive wine shop in the historic walled town, as well as the old oil mill and winery. The Vermentino '08 has a spectacular nose of aromatic herbs. Its marked minerality makes it an ideal accompaniment for even the richest food.

○ Vermentino '08   ♥♥ 4*

Innocenzo Turco

VIA BERTONE, 7A
17040 QUILIANO [SV]
TEL. 0192000026
www.innocenzoturco.it

If there is a name that embodies Granaccia di Quiliano, it is Turco. Innocenzo's interpretation of the variety, grown here since time immemorial, is released in excellent wines with exceptional ageing potential. The Vigneto dei Cappuccini '05's youthful freshness bodes well for the future.

● Granaccia '06   ♥♥ 5
● Granaccia di Quiliano Vign. dei Cappuccini '05   ♥♥ 5

La Vecchia Cantina

FRAZ. SALEA
VIA CORTA, 3
17031 ALBENGA [SV]
TEL. 0182559881

With his courteous, thoughtful manner, Umberto Calleri looks more like a vigneron from Côtes du Rhône than an Italian grower used to the difficult growing conditions of the Riviera. His '08s have their usual rich, balsam-laced peach and apricot aromas but are perhaps less expressive than last year's.

○ Riviera Ligure di Ponente Pigato '08   ♥ 4
○ Riviera Ligure di Ponente Vermentino '08   ♥ 4

Claudio Vio

FRAZ. CROSA, 16
17032 VENDONE [SV]
TEL. 018276338
claudio.vio@libero.it

After the success of his '07, this Vendone hills grower is back with his Runcu Brujau '08, from rossese, grenache and dolcetto, although he did not present his white U Grottu. We liked the drinkable, no-nonsense, clean Runcu, offering rich, fragrant fruit and floral tones, and nice length.

● Runcu Brujau '08   ♥ 4

Vis Amoris

LOC. CARAMAGNA
S.DA MOLINO JAVÈ, 23
18100 IMPERIA
TEL. 3483959569
visamoris@libero.it

Roberto Tozzi and Rossana Zappa, with long experience in food management, don't rest on their laurels. Here they are again with their Pigato Vigna Domè '08, once again a cornucopia of Mediterranean fragrances and aromatic herbs over a solid, well-rounded palate of great length.

○ Riviera Ligure di Ponente Pigato V. Domè '08   ♥♥ 5
○ Riviera Ligure di Ponente Pigato V. Domè '07   ♥♥ 5*
○ Riviera Ligure di Ponente Pigato V. Domè '06   ♥♥ 5*
○ Riviera Ligure di Ponente Pigato V. Domè '05   ♥♥ 4*

LOMBARDY

This year Lombardy earned 18 Three Glass awards, reflecting an enthusiastic region in perfect health with a desire to experiment and the will to grow. Regardless of the economic crisis, Lombardy's producers are working with a greater passion than ever. Franciacorta is home to half of the award-winning wines – an impressive nine – confirming for the umpteenth time that a good product alone is not sufficient for success. It also takes strategy, market knowledge, investment and the constant drive for top quality. Local growers are well aware of this and put these factors into practice on a daily basis. Ca' del Bosco's Cuvée Annamaria Clementi '02, Cavalleri's Selezione Esclusiva Giovanni Cavalleri '01, Bellavista's Riserva Vittorio Moretti '02, Ferghettina's Extra Brut '02 and Gatti's Satèn '05 are flanked this year by four other wines that picked up our top accolade for the first time. The newcomers are Le Marchesine's Brut '04, Il Mosnel's Satèn '05, La Montina's Brut '05 and Palazzo Lana Extra Brut Extrême '04 from Franco Ziliani's Guido Berlucchi & C. This is a milestone, because Ziliani can justly be considered the father of the DOCG, having been the first to perceive its potential and place a few thousand bottles in pupitres. Only just behind is Oltrepò Pavese, which finally seems to have shaken off the lethargy that had characterized it for years. There are important projects involving Pinot Nero and Metodo Classico, which have recently obtained DOCG status. In fact, alongside Castello di Cignola's Barbera '06, our top award went to four Pinot Neros: the still Pernice '06 by Conte di Vistarino, Mazzolino's classic Noir '06, Fratelli Giorgi's Brut Giorgi 1870 '05 and Monsupello's Rosé. The Garda area put up a good show, with Lugana proving itself one of the leading DOC zones of the region. This year, it took two Three Glass awards, one going to Lombardy, with the return of Ca' dei Frati, and the other to Veneto with Peschiera-based winery Otella. Longstanding biodynamic winery Cascina La Pertica has continued its progress, winning Three Green Glasses for its Garda Cabernet Le Zalte '07. It is business as usual in Valtellina, where the situation is good even though the area took only two Three Glasses this year, for Negri's Sfursat '06 and Rainoldi's Fruttaio Ca' Rizzieri '06. However, 13 Valtellina wines reached our finals and the way things are going, we are sure that the designated zone can only improve. On the whole Lombardy has achieved impressive results and, while it was mainly sparklers that stood out until a few years ago, today we are pleased to say that the region is able to point to excellence in all wine types and growing districts. Lombard wines exert a constantly growing influence on the Italian wine scene, far in excess of the two per cent of total national production they represent.

Agnes

VIA CAMPO DEL MONTE, 1
27040 ROVESCALA [PV]
TEL. 038575206
www.fratelliagnes.it

CELLAR SALES
PRE-BOOKED VISITS

ANNUAL PRODUCTION **70,00 bottles**
HECTARES UNDER VINE **16**
VITICULTURE METHOD **Conventional**

The secret of the winery run by Sergio and Cristiano Agnes is actually anything but clandestine. They have wonderfully aspected vineyards in the eastern area of Rovescala, near the border with Emilia, where they grow the small-clustered pignola variety of croatina that can give excellent results in both still and sparkling versions. Extensive knowledge of Bonarda in all its forms, burning passion and a ceaseless quest for improvement, particularly following the construction of the new winery, do the rest.

Poculum '07 very nearly made it into our finals. A monovarietal Croatina aged in small oak casks, it boasts spice and fruit, prominent yet silky tannins and a pleasant almondy finish. In contrast, Millennium '06 is barrel aged and has backbone, candour, sound fruit and good ageing prospects. The main difference between the two sparkling Bonardas, Cresta del Ghiffi and Campo del Monte '08, is the higher sugar content of the former, while the quality of both is excellent, with the first flaunting elegant, fleshy fruit and the second floral hints. The other wines are decent.

● OP Bonarda Frizzante Campo del Monte '08	♥♥	3*
● OP Bonarda Frizzante Cresta del Ghiffi '08	♥♥	3*
● OP Bonarda Millenium '06	♥♥	5
● Poculum '07	♥♥	5
● OP Bonarda Possessione del Console '08	♥	3
● OP Bonarda Campo del Monte '07	♀♀	3*
● OP Bonarda Cresta del Ghiffi '07	♀♀	3*
● OP Bonarda Cresta del Ghiffi '06	♀♀	3*
● OP Bonarda Millenium '05	♀♀	5
● OP Bonarda Possessione del Console '07	♀♀	3*
● Rosso Poculum '06	♀♀	5
● Rosso Vignazzo '04	♀♀	4

Anteo

LOC. CHIESA
27040 ROCCA DE' GIORGI [PV]
TEL. 038599073
www.anteovini.it

CELLAR SALES
PRE-BOOKED VISITS

ANNUAL PRODUCTION **240,000 bottles**
HECTARES UNDER VINE **26**
VITICULTURE METHOD **Conventional**

Trento Cribellati passed his great passion for Metodo Classico, and pinot nero grapes in particular, to his children Piero and Antonella when, at a ripe old age, he crafted this gem of Oltrepò sparklers on his Rocca de' Giorgi estate. We are in the heart of the finest growing country for this noble Burgundian grape. Don't miss a tour of the ageing cellar, with stacks of bottles and pupitres arranged in rows beneath the cross vaults.

Last year, the estate's Nature '03 took our top award and this year two of its sparklers reached the finals. Riserva del Poeta '02, dedicated to Trento himself, has an excellent balance of complexity, medicinal herbal notes, backbone, structure and lingering finish. The golden Nature Ecrù '04 has strikingly elegant floral hints and characteristic cake notes, while the Rosé offers impressive fullness and depth resulting from more than 36 months on the lees. The basic Brut is also attractive. Bonarda Staffolo '08 is good, with crisp fruit, and the two cuve close method sparklers are scented, zesty and pleasant.

○ OP Pinot Nero Brut Cl. Nature Écru '04	♥♥	5*
○ OP Pinot Nero Brut Cl. Riserva del Poeta '02	♥♥	6
● OP Bonarda Frizzante Staffolo '08	♥♥	4*
○ OP Pinot Nero Brut Cl.	♥♥	5
⊙ OP Pinot Nero Brut Cl. Rosé	♥♥	5
○ OP Pinot Nero Brut Martinotti	♥	4
⊙ OP Pinot Nero Brut Martinotti Rosé	♥	4
○ OP Pinot Nero Brut Cl. Nature Écru '03	♀♀♀	5
○ OP Pinot Nero Brut Cl. Anteo Riserva Del Poeta '98	♀♀	6
○ OP Pinot Nero Brut Cl. Nature Écru '02	♀♀	5
○ OP Pinot Nero Brut Cl. Nature Ecru '00	♀♀	5
○ OP Pinot Nero Brut Cl. Riserva del Poeta '99	♀♀	6
⊙ OP Pinot Nero Extra Dry Cl. Rosé	♀♀	5
○ OP Spumante Brut Riserva del Poeta '01	♀♀	6

Barone Pizzini

LOC. TIMOLINE
VIA BRESCIA, 3A
25050 CORTE FRANCA [BS]
TEL. 0309848311
www.baronepizzini.it

CELLAR SALES
PRE-BOOKED VISITS
OSPITALITÀ

ANNUAL PRODUCTION **340,000 bottles**
HECTARES UNDER VINE **47**
VITICULTURE METHOD **Certified Organic**

Barone Pizzini, founded in 1870, is owned by a group of Brescia businessmen, who appointed the talented Silvano Brescianini as manager. Brescianini transformed Barone Pizzini into a model winery and a paragon of bioarchitecture, converting to organic farming. The estate also generates its own energy, purifies its water and recycles waste. This has led to other ventures at Tenuta del Barco in Puglia, Podere Ghiaccioforte in the Tuscan Maremma and Pievalta in Marche, all run using natural methods to bring out the best of the local varieties.

The estate's flagship is Franciacorta Bagnadore Nature, whose '04 vintage is nice but hard to pin down. Cosseting and completely natural, it has rich aromas of smouldering logs and medicinal herbs and a deep mineral palate. The Satèn '05 has juicy fruit with pleasant hints of vanilla and ripe apples. Franciacorta Extra Dry is very interesting, with good ripe pears and white peaches and soft, controlled sweetness. The Rosé and the Brut are clean, typical and well made. San Carlo is the best of the still wines, a juicy, full-flavoured red with fresh vegetal hints and soft tannins. The rest of the list is good.

★★ Bellavista

VIA BELLAVISTA, 5
25030 ERBUSCO [BS]
TEL. 0307762000
www.bellavistawine.it

PRE-BOOKED VISITS

ANNUAL PRODUCTION **1.300,000 bottles**
HECTARES UNDER VINE **184**
VITICULTURE METHOD **Conventional**

During the 1970s, successful businessman Vittorio Moretti laid the cornerstone of what has become Terra Moretti Holding with prestigious estates in Lombardy and Tuscany. Bellavista now has almost 190 hectares of splendid vineyards and is the jewel in the crown of the group, one of the most respected names in Italian wine worldwide. Oenologist and general manager Mattia Vezzola skilfully interprets the terroir, creating a unique style for Moretti that focuses on elegance and inspires the wineries founded subsequently.

Franciacorta Extra Brut Vittorio Moretti '02 is a very elegant, territory-rooted blend. It gives deep, complex aromas of fresh white fruit with minerality, oak and toast. Its outstanding finesse, fine balance, harmony and length earned it Three Glasses. Pas Operé '03 charms with hints of yeast, antique wood and honey. Bianco dell'Annunciata '06 is elegant, piquant, fresh and juicy while Terre di Franciacorta Uccellanda '06 offers sound fruit, zestiness and attractive vanilla. Gran Cuvée Satèn is succulent and balsamic while the basic Brut won us over with its fresh taste. The other wines are good.

O Franciacorta Brut Nature Bagnadore '04	⟡⟡ 6
O Franciacorta Brut	⟡⟡ 5
O Franciacorta Extra Dry	⟡⟡ 6
⊙ Franciacorta Rosé Brut	⟡⟡ 6
O Franciacorta Satèn '05	⟡⟡ 6
O Polzina Bianco '08	⟡⟡ 4*
● San Carlo '07	⟡⟡ 6
O Franciacorta Brut Nature	⟡ 6
● TdF Rosso Curtefranca '07	⟡ 4
O Franciacorta Bagnadore I '99	⟡⟡ 6
O Franciacorta Extra Brut Bagnadore '03	⟡⟡ 6
O Franciacorta Extra Brut Bagnadore '02	⟡⟡ 6
O Franciacorta Satèn '01	⟡⟡ 6
O Franciacorta Satèn '00	⟡⟡ 6

O Franciacorta Extra Brut Vittorio Moretti '02	⟡⟡⟡+ 8
O Franciacorta Gran Cuvée Pas Operé '03	⟡⟡ 8
O TdF Bianco Convento dell'Annunciata '06	⟡⟡ 6
O Franciacorta Brut	⟡⟡ 6
O Franciacorta Gran Cuvée Brut '05	⟡⟡ 7
O Franciacorta Gran Cuvée Satèn	⟡⟡ 7
O TdF Bianco Uccellanda '06	⟡⟡ 6
⊙ Franciacorta Gran Cuvée Brut Rosé '05	⟡ 7
O TdF Curtefranca Bianco '08	⟡ 4
O Franciacorta Extra Brut Vittorio Moretti '01	⟡⟡⟡ 8
O Franciacorta Gran Cuvée Brut '04	⟡⟡⟡ 7
O Franciacorta Gran Cuvée Brut '02	⟡⟡⟡ 7
O Franciacorta Gran Cuvée Pas Operé '00	⟡⟡⟡ 7
O Franciacorta Gran Cuvée Pas Operé '99	⟡⟡⟡ 7

Cantina Sociale Bergamasca

VIA BERGAMO, 10
24060 SAN PAOLO D'ARGON [BG]
TEL. 035951098
www.cantinabergamasca.it

CELLAR SALES
PRE-BOOKED VISITS

ANNUAL PRODUCTION **650,000 bottles**
HECTARES UNDER VINE **90**
VITICULTURE METHOD **Conventional**

Valcalepio is an atypical designated zone for it actually comprises two completely different territories. The first lies east of Bergamo towards Lake Iseo while the second, much smaller, growing area is further west, in the direction of Lake Como with Bergamo at its centre. Cantina Sociale Bergamasca is the focus of winegrowing activities in the main area. Headed by Sergio Cantoni, it regularly turns in good results at our tastings with a long list of interesting wines.

The second vintage of Sogno '08, from monovarietal incrocio Manzoni, confirms that it is a dynamic, close-focused wine, packed with aromatics ranging from ripe white fruit to medicinal herbs. Valcalepio Rosso Riserva Akros '05 is good, showing spiciness with hay and bell pepper, nice balance, firm structure and a rising finish. The easy-drinking Valcalepio Rosso Orologio '07 is also great value for money with a nose of cherries and medicinal herbs. The mint-veined Moscato Giallo Suite '08 stands out in an array of well-made wines, which also includes the fragrant, floral classic method Sottosopra.

F.lli Berlucchi

LOC. BORGONATO
VIA BROLETTO, 2
25040 CORTE FRANCA [BS]
TEL. 030984451
www.berlucchifranciacorta.it

CELLAR SALES
PRE-BOOKED VISITS

ANNUAL PRODUCTION **400,000 bottles**
HECTARES UNDER VINE **70**
VITICULTURE METHOD **Conventional**

Berlucchi is one of the legendary names of Franciacorta, where the family has always owned farmland and vineyards. Pia Donata Berlucchi, aided by her daughter Tilli Rizzo and oenologist Cesare Ferrari, passionately runs the estate that she owns jointly with her siblings Francesco, Gabriella, Marcello and Roberto. Berlucchi boasts 70 hectares of vineyards in the best wine areas of the DOCG zone, such as Torbiato di Adro and Borgonato di Corte Franca. The cellar is situated next to the family home, a beautiful 16th century-style building.

The particularly good Satèn '05 shows attractive bright straw-yellow with focused aromas of white peach and medicinal herbs and a zesty palate with juicy fruit and a long vanillaed finish. The Pas Dosé '05, which reached our finals, is equally complex but more austere in style, with a charming aftertaste of star anise. Brut '05 is firm and soft, with tangy citrus, good balance and nice freshness. The Rosé '05 has character, but is perhaps a little too soft, while the new Brut 25 cuvée is less challenging although highly drinkable. Terre Rosso Dossi delle Querce '05 is great and the other wines are interesting.

Wine	Rating
○ Manzoni Bianco Sogno '08	❦❦ 4*
○ Moscato Giallo Suite '08	❦❦ 3*
● Valcalepio Rosso Akros Ris. '05	❦❦ 4*
● Valcalepio Rosso Orologio '07	❦❦ 3*
○ Bianco della Bergamasca '08	❦ 2*
● Rosso della Bergamasca '08	❦ 2*
⊙ Schiava '08	❦ 3
○ Sottosopra Brut Cl.	❦ 4
⊙ Schiava '07	♈♈ 3*
● Valcalepio Moscato Passito Perseo '03	♈♈ 6
● Valcalepio Moscato Passito Perseo '02	♈♈ 6
● Valcalepio Rosso Akros Ris. '04	♈♈ 4
● Valcalepio Rosso Orologio '06	♈♈ 3*
● Valcalepio Rosso V. del Conte Ris. '04	♈♈ 5

Wine	Rating
○ Franciacorta Pas Dosé '05	❦❦ 6
○ Franciacorta Brut '05	❦❦ 5
⊙ Franciacorta Rosé '05	❦❦ 5
○ Franciacorta Satèn '05	❦❦ 6
● TdF Rosso Dossi delle Querce '05	❦❦ 4*
○ Franciacorta Brut 25	❦ 4
○ TdF Bianco '08	❦ 3
● TdF Rosso '07	❦ 3
● Casa delle Colonne	♈♈ 8
○ Franciacorta Brut '04	♈♈ 5
○ Franciacorta Casa delle Colonne '01	♈♈ 7
○ Franciacorta Satèn '04	♈♈ 6
○ Franciacorta Satèn '03	♈♈ 6
○ TdF Bianco Dossi delle Querce '05	♈♈ 4

Guido Berlucchi & C.

LOC. BORGONATO
P.ZZA DURANTI, 4
25040 CORTE FRANCA [BS]
TEL. 030984381
www.berlucchi.it

CELLAR SALES
PRE-BOOKED VISITS

ANNUAL PRODUCTION **5,000,000 bottles**
HECTARES UNDER VINE **590**
VITICULTURE METHOD **Conventional**

In 1961 Guido Berlucchi, Franco Ziliani and Giorgio Lanciani fermented the first 3,000 bottles of Pinot di Franciacorta "en tirage", marking the birth of this new wine zone. Over the years, it has been a runaway success and today Berlucchi & C. is one of Italy's leading wineries. However, after a while the growing demand for grapes led the winery to rely on fruit from regions outside its native area. A few years ago Franciacorta made its return in grand style to the Berlucchi list.

Franciacorta Brut Extrême Palazzo Lana '04 is a monovarietal Pinot Nero. Pale straw with copper highlights, it has a complex nose of mineral-veined yeast, toast and red and black berry fruit. Spirited with firm structure, the palate gives elegant fruit and creamy sparkle, although still young and very taut, driving though to a long citrus and mineral finish. Our response was Three Glasses. The same range includes a plush, vanillaed Satèn and a lively Brut with good grip and a palate of good fruit, backbone and impressive balance. Franciacorta Cuvée Storica 61 is juicy, zesty and close-focused, while Cellarius Brut, Rosé '06 and the classic Imperiale Brut are also excellent.

Bersi Serlini

LOC. CERETO
VIA CERETO, 7
25050 PROVAGLIO D'ISEO [BS]
TEL. 0309823338
www.bersiserlini.it

CELLAR SALES
PRE-BOOKED VISITS

ANNUAL PRODUCTION **220,000 bottles**
HECTARES UNDER VINE **32**
VITICULTURE METHOD **Conventional**

Bersi Serlini of Provaglio is one of the legendary names of the designated zone. It was founded in 1886 when the family purchased an old ecclesiastical property. Today, the winery is one of the loveliest and most modern in the district, even though it is laid out around a medieval building that once belonged to the monastery of San Pietro in Lamosa, a reminder of the estate's ancient wine heritage. The family business is run by Maddalena, a keen wine woman, with her sister Chiara.

We were most impressed by the two '02 vintages: Riserva Extra Brut with its soft, complex nose of fruit, elegant oak and spice, and subtle juicy palate, and Riserva Vintage Brut, which offers evolved notes of butter and croissants underpinned by fresh acidity and creamy effervescence. Franciacorta Rosa Rosae shows an attractive deep pink with heady aromas of black and red berry fruit laced with hazelnut before unfolding soft, fresh and juicy in the mouth. Brut Cuvée n. 4 has good balance and freshness and the Satèn, Brut and Demi Sec Nuvola are also pleasing.

○ Franciacorta Brut Extrême Palazzo Lana '04	▼▼▼ 7
○ Franciacorta Satèn Palazzo Lana '04	▼▼ 7
○ Cellarius Brut '06	▼▼ 6
⊙ Cellarius Rosé '06	▼▼ 6
○ Cuvée Imperiale Brut	▼▼ 5
○ Franciacorta Brut Palazzo Lana '04	▼▼ 7
○ Franciacorta Cuvée Storica 61	▼▼ 5
⊙ Cuvée Imperiale Max Rosé	▼ 5
○ Franciacorta Satèn Brut '04	♈♈ 6

○ Franciacorta Brut Cuvée n. 4	▼▼ 6
⊙ Franciacorta Brut Rosa Rosae	▼▼ 6
○ Franciacorta Brut Vintage Ris. '02	▼▼ 6
○ Franciacorta Extra Brut Ris. '02	▼▼ 6
○ Franciacorta Brut	▼ 6
○ Demi Sec Nuvola	▼ 6
○ Franciacorta Satèn	▼ 6
○ Franciacorta Brut Cuvée n. 4	♈♈ 6
○ Franciacorta Brut Vintage '02	♈♈ 8
○ Franciacorta Brut Vintage '01	♈♈ 6
○ Franciacorta Extra Brut '02	♈♈ 6
○ Franciacorta Satèn	♈♈ 6

F.lli Bettini

LOC. SAN GIACOMO
VIA NAZIONALE, 4A
23036 TEGLIO [SO]
TEL. 0342786068
bettvini@tin.it

CELLAR SALES
PRE-BOOKED VISITS

ANNUAL PRODUCTION 200,000 bottles
HECTARES UNDER VINE 15
VITICULTURE METHOD Conventional

The estate brilliantly managed by Pietro Bettini has earned a full profile. Founded in 1881, it is one of the oldest wineries in Valtellina, located near Teglio, in the Valgella subzone. The estate owns approximately 15 hectares of vineyards, all situated in the classic Valtellina Superiore zone. After years of constant improvement, Bettini now consistently offers superior, carefully crafted wines with plenty of character.

Sforzato '06 is promising, displaying an impressively complex nose with notes of overripe fruit and medicinal herbs with mineral hints. Full in the mouth, it has elegant tannins and good acid balance. Sant'Andrea '06 is exceptionally good, with a concentrated elegant nose and a bright, juicy, balanced palate. Inferno Prodigio '05 has warm aromas with hints of cocoa powder and a caressing, dense, spicy palate while Valgella Vigna La Cornella '05 gives an austere, well-typed nose and a full-bodied, smooth palate with well-honed tannins and nice length.

Bisi

LOC. CASCINA SAN MICHELE
FRAZ. VILLA MARONE, 70
27040 SAN DAMIANO AL COLLE [PV]
TEL. 038575037
www.aziendagricolabisi.it

CELLAR SALES
PRE-BOOKED VISITS

ANNUAL PRODUCTION 100,000 bottles
HECTARES UNDER VINE 30
VITICULTURE METHOD Conventional

The enthusiasm and skill with which Claudio Bisi manages this winery on the eastern fringe of Oltrepò deserve our respect and recognition. Although it was founded in 1926, it was the arrival of Claudio, with the invaluable support of his wife Sandra, which marked a turning point in quality thanks to the winning combination of old plots, newly planted vineyards, and crucially particularly low yields per hectare.

Barbera Roncolongo '06 reached our finals yet again, showing concentrated, deep cherry-led berry fruit and spice followed by weight that never compromises elegance. Cabernet Sauvignon Primm '06 has depth of colour and fruit aromas with upfront green notes. Ultrapadum is a new, slightly sparkling blend of half barbera and half croatina that is part-aged in oak and bottle refermented. The traditional dry Bonarda '08 has full body. Pinot Nero Calonga '06 is even better than previous vintages, with less emphasis on power and more on finesse. Riesling '08 and Barbera Pezzabianca '07 are typical, varietal and fragrant.

● Valtellina Sfursat '06	🍷🍷 7
● Valtellina Sup. Inferno Prodigio '05	🍷🍷 5
● Valtellina Sup. Sant'Andrea '06	🍷🍷 5
● Valtellina Sup. Valgella V. La Cornella '05	🍷🍷 5
● Valtellina Sfursat '05	🍷🍷 7
● Valtellina Sfursat '04	🍷🍷 7
● Valtellina Sup. Inferno Prodigio '04	🍷🍷 5
● Valtellina Sup. Sant'Andrea '03	🍷🍷 5
● Valtellina Sup. Sassella Reale '04	🍷🍷 5
● Valtellina Sup. Sforzato Vigneti di Spina '03	🍷🍷 7

● OP Barbera Roncolongo '06	🍷🍷 5
● OP Barbera Pezzabianca '07	🍷🍷 5
● OP Bonarda Frizzante '08	🍷🍷 3*
● OP Cabernet Sauvignon Primm '06	🍷🍷 5
● OP Pinot Nero Calonga '06	🍷🍷 5
○ OP Riesling '08	🍷🍷 3*
● Ultrapadum '07	🍷🍷 4
○ Bianco Passito Villa Marone '05	🍷🍷 5
● OP Barbera Roncolongo '05	🍷🍷 5
● OP Barbera Roncolongo '04	🍷🍷 5
● OP Barbera Roncolongo '03	🍷🍷 5
● OP Barbera Roncolongo '01	🍷🍷 5
● OP Bonarda La Peccatrice '07	🍷🍷 3
● OP Cabernet Sauvignon Primm '01	🍷🍷 5

Bonomi - Tenuta Castellino

VIA SAN PIETRO, 46
25030 COCCAGLIO [BS]
TEL. 0307721015
www.tenutabonomi.it

CELLAR SALES
PRE-BOOKED VISITS

ANNUAL PRODUCTION **148,000 bottles**
HECTARES UNDER VINE **17**
VITICULTURE METHOD **Conventional**

The fine estate once owned by the Bonomi family is at the famous Art Nouveau villa in Coccaglio. This small château in the southern reaches of Franciacorta has a well-aspected site in the natural amphitheatre of Monte Orfano. Many of the high-density, low-yield vineyards are planted on terraces that rise in woodland to almost 300 metres above sea level. It is ideal terrain for vines, which yield excellent base wines for Franciacortas. Recently purchased by the Paladin family, a leading name in the Veneto wine world, the estate is currently being reorganized and relaunched.

Franciacorta Brut Cru Perdu '05 illustrates the new direction. Sourced from an old Pinot Nero vineyard, it won a place in our finals with its exceptionally delicate bead and an elegant, complex fruity nose that shows stylish medicinal herbs and oak. Dense and round on the palate, it has sound fruit, attractive creaminess and a long finish. Rosso Cordelio '06 is full-bodied with alluring notes of blackberry and cherry, while Bianco Solicano '07 bursts with fruit and attractive oak, confirming the quality of the territory. The Satèn is interesting, with a buttery nose, good backbone and freshness on the palate.

Bosio

LOC. TIMOLINE
VIA MARIO GATTI
25040 CORTE FRANCA [BS]
TEL. 030984398
www.bosiofranciacorta.it

CELLAR SALES
PRE-BOOKED VISITS

ANNUAL PRODUCTION **100,000 bottles**
HECTARES UNDER VINE **23**
VITICULTURE METHOD **Conventional**

Cesare and Laura Bosio commenced their adventure about a decade ago, when they purchased 23 hectares of vines for their small family estate and built a welcoming cellar, kitting it out with the latest equipment. Cesare is an agronomist with a deep knowledge of the terroir while Laura, an economics graduate, is responsible for sales and marketing. Despite their youth, the brother-and-sister team are turning out superior products after just a few years and their success continues.

While awaiting the new vintage of Boschedòr Extra Brut, we tasted an excellent, deep pink Rosé, with a delicate bead and an appealing nose of berries, hazelnuts and cakes. The palate is juicy, creamy and dense, with plenty of fruit and good length. The Brut has an attractive, complex nose with hints of yeast, hazelnut, antique wood and honey, accompanied by a solid, balanced palate displaying freshness and mineral notes. We also liked the smooth, vanillaed Satèn and the full-bodied, caressing Terre di Franciacorta Rosso Zenighe '05 with its blueberry aromas.

○ Franciacorta Brut Cru Perdu '05	♈♈ 8
○ Franciacorta Satèn	♈♈ 6
○ TdF Bianco Curtefranca Solicano '07	♈♈ 4*
● TdF Rosso Curtefranca Cordelio '06	♈♈ 5
○ Franciacorta Brut	♈ 6
○ Franciacorta Extra Brut '05	♈ 6
⊙ Franciacorta Rosé	♈ 6
○ Franciacorta Brut	♈♈ 5
○ Franciacorta Extra Brut Lucrezia '01	♈♈ 8
○ TdF Bianco Curtefranca Solicano '06	♈♈ 4
● TdF Rosso Curtefranca Cordelio '05	♈♈ 5
● TdF Rosso Curtefranca Cordelio '04	♈♈ 5

○ Franciacorta Brut	♈♈ 5
⊙ Franciacorta Rosé	♈♈ 5
○ Franciacorta Satèn	♈♈ 5
● TdF Rosso Zenighe '05	♈♈ 4*
○ TdF Bianco '08	♈ 4
○ Franciacorta Extra Brut Boschedòr '04	♈♈ 5

Cà dei Frati

FRAZ. LUGANA
VIA FRATI, 22
25019 SIRMIONE [BS]
TEL. 030919468
www.cadeifrati.it

CELLAR SALES
PRE-BOOKED VISITS

ANNUAL PRODUCTION 700,000 bottles
HECTARES UNDER VINE 110
VITICULTURE METHOD Conventional

Lugana owes much of its recent renown to the commitment with which the Dal Cero family has promoted it over the past 20 years. Ca' dei Frati is now a large estate, with 100 hectares of vineyards in the wine zone, and its bottles are exported all over the world. However, Igino Dal Cero never tires of exploring new directions to express the potential of the wines and the land where he works, demonstrating that Lugana has no fear of ageing. Quite the reverse.

After a break of several years, this historic winery has won Three Glasses with Brolettino '07, a Lugana with charming fullness and harmony. It is a creamy, complex, full-flavoured wine with a lingering finish of ripe fruit, supported by vibrant acidity that tells you the new oak was well gauged. But the most interesting wine is perhaps the basic Lugana, I Frati, whose '08 vintage won us over with its freshness and rich flavour. It shows it can acquire depth and complexity in the Vecchie Annate selection, in this case the '04, released four years after harvest. The rest of the list is excellent.

★★★ Ca' del Bosco

VIA ALBANO ZANELLA, 13
25030 ERBUSCO [BS]
TEL. 0307766111
www.cadelbosco.it

CELLAR SALES
PRE-BOOKED VISITS

ANNUAL PRODUCTION 1.100,000 bottles
HECTARES UNDER VINE 154
VITICULTURE METHOD Conventional

Ca' del Bosco is one of the most prestigious names in Italian wine. Founded in the early 1970s, it now boasts 150 hectares of vineyards and produces just under a million excellent bottles of Franciacortas and still wines. The winery's cellar increasingly resembles an art gallery, which is its talented president Maurizio Zanella's intention. Maurizio, who has created a personal style with his wines, is one of the pioneers of modern Franciacorta and is now also president of the Franciacorta protection consortium.

Cuvée Annamaria Clementi '02 again took Three Glasses. Deep and very elegant, with a tiny persistent bead and aromas ranging from fresh fruit to tropical notes, it ends on with cakes and vanilla. The palate shows deep, firm structure and incredible harmony that makes it exceptionally pleasant and enjoyable. The very long finish is characterized by fruit and mineral notes. Satèn '05 has a nose of stone fruits and medicinal herbs introducing a fresh, opulently creamy palate, while Terre di Franciacorta Chardonnay '06 is elegant with still very young fruit, citrus and perfectly calibrated oak. The other wines are excellent.

O Lugana Brolettino '07	▼▼▼ 4*
O Lugana I Frati Sel. Vecchie Annate '04	▼▼ 5
● Ronchedone Grande Annata '04	▼▼ 6
O Lugana I Frati '08	▼▼ 4*
O Pratto '07	▼▼ 5
O Tre Filer '06	▼▼ 5
⊙ Riviera del Garda Bresciano I Frati Chiaretto '08	▼ 4
O Lugana Brolettino '06	♀♀ 4
O Lugana Brolettino Grande Annata '02	♀♀ 5
O Lugana I Frati '06	♀♀ 4*
O Lugana I Frati Sel. Vecchie Annate '03	♀♀ 5

O Franciacorta Cuvée Annamaria Clementi '02	▼▼▼ 8
O Franciacorta Dosage Zéro '05	▼▼ 7
O Franciacorta Satèn '05	▼▼ 7
O TdF Chardonnay '06	▼▼ 8
O Franciacorta Brut '05	▼▼ 7
O Franciacorta Brut Cuvée Prestige	▼▼ 6
⊙ Franciacorta Cuvée Prestige Rosé	▼▼ 7
● Pinèro '06	▼▼ 8
O TdF Bianco Curtefranca '08	▼▼ 5
● TdF Rosso Curtefranca '06	▼▼ 5
O Franciacorta Cuvée Annamaria Clementi '01	♀♀♀ 8
O Franciacorta Cuvée Annamaria Clementi '99	♀♀♀ 8
O Franciacorta Dosage Zéro '04	♀♀♀ 7
O Franciacorta Dosage Zéro '03	♀♀♀ 7
O Franciacorta Satèn '02	♀♀♀ 7
O TdF Chardonnay '05	♀♀ 8

Ca' del Gè

FRAZ. CA' DEL GÈ, 3
27040 MONTALTO PAVESE [PV]
TEL. 0383870179
www.cadelge.it

CELLAR SALES
PRE-BOOKED VISITS

ANNUAL PRODUCTION **180,000 bottles**
HECTARES UNDER VINE **45**
VITICULTURE METHOD **Conventional**

It is with great pleasure that we dedicate a full profile to the Padroggi family's winery for the first time, after having attentively monitored its constant growth over the years and the passion that Enzo has passed on to his daughters Sara and Stefania. As revealed by the wines tasted, Ca' del Gè is located in an area particularly well suited to growing white grapes, especially riesling, of which Montalto is the capital within this great wine zone.

This year, the Metodo Classico '05, from pinot nero, made the biggest impression. It is more elegant and structured than ever, with aromas of roasted hazelnuts and cinnamon, accompanied by depth and excellent supporting acidity, which carried it through to our finals. We tasted three Rieslings. Marinoni '05, from renano, gives classic evolved minerally notes of benzene. The other two are from riesling italico: Filagn Long '08 has a more complex, intensely floral nose and fruit pulp but the basic version also has pleasant fragrances of melon and medicinal herbs. The rest of the list is well made.

○ OP Pinot Nero Brut Cl. '05	🍷🍷	4
○ OP Moscato Passito Sabiò Pasì	🍷🍷	4
○ OP Riesling '08	🍷🍷	2*
○ OP Riesling Italico Filagn Long '08	🍷🍷	3*
○ OP Riesling Renano V. Marinoni '05	🍷🍷	5
○ Chardonnay '08	🍷	3
● O. P. Bonarda Frizzante '08	🍷	2
○ OP Moscato Frizzante '08	🍷	3
○ OP Pinot Nero '08	🍷	3
● OP Barbera '06	🍷🍷 (previous edition)	2*
○ OP Riesling '06	🍷🍷 (previous edition)	2*
○ OP Riesling Italico Filagn Long '07	🍷🍷 (previous edition)	3*
○ OP Riesling Renano V. Marinoni '04	🍷🍷 (previous edition)	5

Ca' di Frara

VIA CASA FERRARI, 1
27040 MORNICO LOSANA [PV]
TEL. 0383892299
www.cadifrara.it

ANNUAL PRODUCTION **260,000 bottles**
HECTARES UNDER VINE **48**
VITICULTURE METHOD **Conventional**

In just a few years, the work carried out by Luca Bellani and his family, particularly his enterprising mother Daniela, has allowed Ca' di Frara to make a name for itself as one of the most dynamic and interesting wineries in the entire Oltrepò area. After having concentrated on weight, Luca decided to give his wines a touch more finesse. The advent of the Oltre il Classico project has further enhanced the range and overall quality.

Pinot Nero Oltre il Classico Rosé reached our finals with attractive aromas of liquorice, coffee and wild berries and great stylistic coherence, its concentrated finish supported by good acidity. Frater Riserva '06, the estate's top red, also made the finals. Obtained from croatina, it is fruity, full, spicy and balsamic. Two Glasses went to Pinot Grigio and Riesling Apogeo '08, traditional late-harvest whites with exemplary close-focused noses and elegant progression. We also liked Raro Nero '06, a varietal Pinot Nero with stylish tannins, and the smooth, fragrant Rosso '06, from mainly barbera and pinot nero.

⊙ OP Pinot Nero Brut Oltre il Classico Rosé	🍷🍷	5
● OP Rosso Il Frater Ris. '06	🍷🍷	6
● Io Rosso '06	🍷🍷	5
○ Oltre il Classico	🍷🍷	5
○ OP Pinot Grigio Raccolta Tardiva '08	🍷🍷	4
● OP Pinot Nero Il Raro Nero '06	🍷🍷	5
○ OP Riesling Renano Apogeo Raccolta Tardiva '08	🍷🍷	4*
● OP Pinot Nero Pinot '08	🍷	5
○ Io Bianco '02	🍷🍷 (previous edition)	5
● Io Rosso '03	🍷🍷 (previous edition)	5
○ OP Pinot Grigio Raccolta Tardiva '04	🍷🍷 (previous edition)	4
○ OP Riesling Renano Apogeo Raccolta Tardiva '07	🍷🍷 (previous edition)	4*
○ OP Riesling Renano Apogeo Raccolta Tardiva '06	🍷🍷 (previous edition)	4*
● OP Rosso Il Frater Ris. '03	🍷🍷 (previous edition)	6

Ca' Lojera

LOC. ROVIZZA
VIA 1886, 19
25019 SIRMIONE [BS]
TEL. 0457551901
www.calojera.com

CELLAR SALES
PRE-BOOKED VISITS

ANNUAL PRODUCTION 160,000 bottles
HECTARES UNDER VINE 18
VITICULTURE METHOD Conventional

Husband-and-wife team Ambra and Franco Tiraboschi are keen enthusiasts of country living and Lugana wine, to which they dedicate all their energy. Several years ago, they purchased a handsome farmhouse at Sirmione, where they built a state-of-the-art cellar and gradually added 18 hectares of vineyards. Their mission is to bring out the best in the wine and its terroir. Their attentive, unhurriedly released selections once again reveal the potential for ageing of this excellent white.

Evidence comes from Lugana Riserva del Lupo, which did well in our finals, showing that an extra year enhances elegance. The '07 has nicely expressed aromas of ripe fruit, flowers and mineral notes. Its varietal, almost saline, savouriness on the palate is accompanied by good fruity flesh and a very long finish. Lugana Superiore '06 has delicately evolved notes, rich aromatics and aristocratic finesse. The easy-drinking Lugana '08 is among the best of its kind, with dynamic freshness, juicy fruit and nice backbone. Ravel '06, from partially dried grapes, and Rosato Monte della Guardia '08 are both good.

Cabanon

LOC. CABANON, 1
27052 GODIASCO [PV]
TEL. 0383940912
www.cabanon.it

PRE-BOOKED VISITS

ANNUAL PRODUCTION 200,000 bottles
HECTARES UNDER VINE 35
VITICULTURE METHOD Conventional

Following a long absence, we are pleased to see the return to the Guide of Cabanon, one of Oltrepò's legendary wineries. Run by Elena Mercandelli, Cabanon is in the far west of the zone, almost on the border with Piedmont. The estate produces numerous – possibly too many – wines but is well worth a visit, not least because of its splendid grappa distillery, chapel, wild pig farm and all-round obsessive attention to detail.

We started with a Riesling aged for a year in bottle, gives minerality as well as floral aromas and offers a deep, concentrated palate. Pinot Grigio '08 has aromas of medicinal herbs and peaches while Cabanon Blanc, from sauvignon grapes, is also well typed and varietal. Despite long barrique ageing, Barbera Piccolo Principe shows great acidity and fruit that is in no way overpowered by the oak. Prunello '04, the other Barbera, is very different, characterized by spice and a well-defined liquorice finish. Infernot '05 is made from late-harvest grapes, as its soft structure reveals, and has a nice cinnamon finish.

○ Lugana Riserva del Lupo '07	▼▼ 5
○ Lugana '08	▼▼ 4*
○ Lugana Sup. '06	▼▼ 5
⊙ Monte della Guardia Rosato '08	▼ 3
○ Ravel '06	▼ 5
○ Lugana Riserva del Lupo '06	♀♀ 5
○ Lugana Sup. '04	♀♀ 5
○ Lugana Sup. Riserva del Lupo '03	♀♀ 5

● OP Barbera Piccolo Principe '03	▼▼ 6
● OP Barbera Prunello '04	▼▼ 4
○ OP Pinot Grigio '08	▼▼ 4
○ OP Riesling '07	▼▼ 4*
● OP Rosso Infernot '05	▼▼ 6
○ Sauvignon Cabanon Blanc '07	▼▼ 4
○ Chardonnay '08	▼ 4
● OP Bonarda Boisée '05	▼ 4

Il Calepino

VIA SURRIPE, 1
24060 CASTELLI CALEPIO [BG]
TEL. 035847178
www.ilcalepino.it

CELLAR SALES
PRE-BOOKED VISITS

ANNUAL PRODUCTION **200,000 bottles**
HECTARES UNDER VINE **15**
VITICULTURE METHOD **Conventional**

Il Calepino is unusual among Bergamo wineries, for it specializes in classic method sparklers in an area where the DOC does not include this wine type. Consequently, they are all labelled Vino Spumante di Qualità, and there's certainly plenty of quality. However, we should not forget that the estate also produces traditional local wines, like its consistently high-scoring Valcalepios.

Four sparklers were presented this year, all of which achieved good results. Riserva Fra' Ambrogio '03, one of the estate's leading wines, is slightly over-evolved after a torrid growing year but it also has firm structure and a nice complex nose. Trentesima Cuvée '04 offers notes of cakes and candied fruit with an attractive palate. The basic Brut also has nice notes of overripe tropical fruit. But the Rosé shows the biggest improvement over last year, showing fragrant with good body. The rest of the list is good, particularly the sweet Chardonnay Epias.

Cantrina

FRAZ. CANTRINA
VIA COLOMBERA, 7
25081 BEDIZZOLE [BS]
TEL. 0306871052
www.cantrina.it

CELLAR SALES
PRE-BOOKED VISITS

ANNUAL PRODUCTION **25,000 bottles**
HECTARES UNDER VINE **5.8**
VITICULTURE METHOD **Conventional**

Cantrina is a small estate of just under six hectares at Bedizzole in Valtènensi, in the Lombard hinterland of Lake Garda. It is enthusiastically and creatively managed by Cristina Inganni and Diego Lavo, with the aid of consultant oenologist Celestino Gaspari. Named after the hamlet in which it is located, the winery was set up with vineyards planted mainly to international varieties but over the years an increasing proportion of local vines have been added.

Nepomuceno is a full-bodied red, from merlot with some rebo and marzemino aged in new oak. The '05 vintage went to the finals for its impressive concentration. It's a juicy, deep wine with a complex nose of spice-laced, cherry-led red fruits jam followed by a long, well-balanced palate. Groppello '08 has the colour and consistency of a good Burgundy, showing elegant and harmonious. The dried-grape Sole di Dario offers hints of dried figs, apricots and dates, and is sweet and dense on the palate. Rinè '07, from sauvignon, semillon and riesling, has sound fruit, zestiness and elegance. Zerdì '06, from rebo grapes, is also good.

○ Brut Cl. Il Calepino '05	♥♥	5
○ Brut Cl. Ris. Fra' Ambrogio '03	♥♥	5
⊙ Brut Cl. Rosé Il Calepino '05	♥♥	5
○ Chardonnay Epias	♥♥	6
○ Trentesima Cuvée Non Dosato '04	♥♥	6
○ Valcalepio Bianco '08	♥♥	3*
● Kalòs '05	♥	6
○ Brut Magnum Cuvée M. Cl.	♀♀	8
○ Brut Cl. Fra' Ambrogio Ris. '02	♀♀	5
○ Brut Cl. Il Calepino '04	♀♀	5
○ Brut Cl. Ris. Fra Ambrogio '01	♀♀	6
○ Extra Brut Cl. Il Calepino '01	♀♀	5
● Kalòs '04	♀♀	7
○ Trentesima Cuvée Non Dosato '03	♀♀	5

● Nepomuceno Esercizio 5 '05	♥♥	6
● Garda Cl. Groppello '08	♥♥	4
○ Rinè '07	♥♥	4
○ Sole di Dario	♥♥	6
● Zerdì '06	♥	4
● Nepomuceno '04	♀♀	6
● Nepomuceno '03	♀♀	6
● Nepomuceno '01	♀♀	5

Cantina di Casteggio

VIA TORINO, 96
27045 CASTEGGIO [PV]
TEL. 0383806311
www.cantinacasteggio.it

CELLAR SALES
PRE-BOOKED VISITS

ANNUAL PRODUCTION **2.500,000 bottles**
HECTARES UNDER VINE **950**
VITICULTURE METHOD **Conventional**

As mentioned in the last Guide, the winery merged last year with Cantina Sociale di Broni, under the management of Livio Cagnoni, but the top ranges of both establishments remain separate. Consequently, Cantina di Casteggio's Progetto Qualità has maintained its dynamism, with the selection of the finest grapes from individual member growers ensuring the best results for the top-end wines, along the lines of the model adopted in Alto Adige.

As in past years, Barbera Console Marcello stood out from the rest, showing full, complex and balanced in the '07 vintage. Barbera Autari '07 is simpler but very drinkable. Malvasia '08 is noteworthy, with a particularly intense nose of flowers and medicinal herbs. Sauvignon '08 is also good, with a concentrated, varietal nose and a very pleasant palate. Among the three classic method sparklers presented, we were particularly impressed by Postumio Rosé, which like all the other rosé sparklers of the zone, will benefit from the collective Cruasé brand from the autumn.

CastelFaglia

FRAZ. CALINO
LOC. BOSCHI, 3
25046 CAZZAGO SAN MARTINO [BS]
TEL. 059812411
www.cavicchioli.it

CELLAR SALES
PRE-BOOKED VISITS

ANNUAL PRODUCTION **250,000 bottles**
HECTARES UNDER VINE **20**
VITICULTURE METHOD **Conventional**

It has been 20 years since the sparkler-loving Cavicchioli family of Modena – they also own Bellei Spumanti – renowned for their Lambruscos, founded this estate in Franciacorta. The Cavicchiolis purchased the historic property, at the foot of the Faglia castle at Calino with around 20 hectares of vineyards in a well-aspected position on the hillside, approximately 300 metres above sea level. Output is high, in terms of both quantity and quality, and the wine is made entirely from estate-grown grapes.

This year an impressive five cuvées scored high. Brut Blanc de Blancs reached our finals with its sound fruit, refreshing balsamic nose and overall cleanliness. We were impressed by the Extra Brut's crisp notes of flowers and white peach on both nose and palate, where it shows plush and full. The Brut proffers a nose of citrus fruit and white flowers and displays fresh grip on the palate, with a caressing finish. Satèn Blanc de Blancs is juicy and vanillaed while the Rosé has an attractive nose of red fruit and a soft, lingering, oak-veined finish.

● OP Barbera Autari '07	♥♥	4*
● OP Barbera Console Marcello '07	♥♥	4*
○ OP Malvasia '08	♥♥	4*
⊙ OP Pinot Nero Brut Postumio Rosé	♥♥	4
○ OP Sauvignon '08	♥♥	4*
○ Chardonnay Brut Cl. 100 Vendemmie '04	♥	4
○ OP Pinot Grigio '08	♥	4
○ OP Pinot Nero Brut Cl. Postumio	♥	4
● OP Barbera Autari '05	♥♥	4
● OP Barbera Console Marcello '05	♥♥	4*
● OP Barbera Console Marcello '04	♥♥	4*
● OP Barbera Console Marcello '03	♥♥	4

○ Franciacorta Blanc de Blancs Monogram	♥♥	5
○ Franciacorta Brut	♥♥	5
○ Franciacorta Extra Brut	♥♥	5
⊙ Franciacorta Rosé Brut	♥♥	6
○ Franciacorta Satèn Blanc de Blancs	♥♥	6
○ Franciacorta Brut Monogram '03	♥	6
⊙ Franciacorta Rosé Monogram	♥	6
○ Franciacorta Satèn	♥	6
● TdF Rosso Prestigio '07	♥	4
○ Franciacorta Monogram Brut Cuvée Giunone	♥♥	6
○ Franciacorta Satèn Monogram	♥♥	6
○ TdF Bianco '06	♥	4
○ TdF Bianco Prestigio '07	♥	4
● TdF Campo Lungo '04	♥	6
● TdF Rosso Prestigio '06	♥	4

Castello di Cigognola

P.ZZA CASTELLO, 1
27040 CIGOGNOLA [PV]
TEL. 0385284828
www.castellodicigognola

Cavalleri

VIA PROVINCIALE, 96
25030 ERBUSCO [BS]
TEL. 0307760217
www.cavalleri.it

CELLAR SALES
PRE-BOOKED VISITS

CELLAR SALES
PRE-BOOKED VISITS

ANNUAL PRODUCTION **40,000 bottles**
HECTARES UNDER VINE **17**
VITICULTURE METHOD **Conventional**

ANNUAL PRODUCTION **250,000 bottles**
HECTARES UNDER VINE **43**
VITICULTURE METHOD **Conventional**

The Morattis have made major investments at Castello di Cigonola, a splendid estate in the foothills overlooking the plain that stretches towards Milan. At the moment, production is limited to two Barberas, one aged and the other younger, but future projects, guided by Emilio De Filippi with the supervision of Riccardo Cotarella, include the planting of pinot nero vines, which we presume will yield at least one red and a Metodo Classico, which we eagerly await.

Barbera Castello di Cigognola '06, formerly known as Poggio della Maga, shows a deep bright ruby, with top-quality oak that gives spicy, balsamic undertones to a concentrated, typically Barbera nose of impressively sound, well-defined fruit. Awesomely surefooted balance on the palate easily earned it our highest accolade. Barbera Dodicidodici '07 is more purplish and shares its big sister's sound fruit, with top notes of morello cherry, and good supporting acidity, balance and elegance, despite being younger and simpler.

Cavalleri was already an important name in Franciacorta in the mid 15th century. The family has always been landowners and grape growers, although the actual winery was founded in the late 1960s with the establishment of the designated zone. Giovanni Cavalleri was the driving force behind this winery and one of Franciacorta's emblematic figures from its foundation until recently. This family-run estate's flagship wine is named in his memory. Today, the winery is headed by his daughter Giulia, aided by a skilled team that works in a handsome state-of-the-art cellar.

The Erbusco estate repeats the success of its '01 Au Contraire with the spectacular Collezione Esclusiva Giovanni Cavalleri '01, which won Three Glasses. This monovarietal Chardonnay spent six years on the lees before disgorgement and now shows firm, structured, very deep, complex and caressing, reconfirming the winery as a leader in the DOCG zone. Brut Collezione '04 is almost as impressive, with notes of yeast and toast, sound fruit and impressive length. The Rosé Collezione '04 is excellent, while Pas Dosé '05 is invigorating and lively. The other wines are superb.

● OP Barbera Castello di Cigognola '06	▼▼▼ 7	
● OP Barbera Dodicidodici '07	▼▼ 5	
● OP Barbera Poggio Della Maga '05	♀♀♀ 8	
● OP Barbera '04	♀♀ 6	
● OP Barbera '03	♀♀ 6	
● OP Barbera Dodicidodici '06	♀♀ 5	

○ Franciacorta Brut Collezione Esclusiva Giovanni Cavalleri '01	▼▼▼ 8	
○ Franciacorta Collezione Brut '04	▼▼ 7	
⊙ Franciacorta Collezione Rosé '04	▼▼ 7	
○ Franciacorta Pas Dosé '05	▼▼ 6	
○ Franciacorta Satèn	▼▼ 6	
○ TdF Bianco Rampaneto '07	▼▼ 5	
● TdF Curtefranca Rosso '07	▼▼ 4	
● TdF Rosso Tajardino '06	▼▼ 5	
○ Franciacorta Brut	▼ 5	
○ TdF Curtefranca Bianco '08	▼ 4	
○ Franciacorta Au Contraire Pas Dosé '01	♀♀♀ 8	
○ Franciacorta Brut Blanc de Blancs	♀♀ 6	
○ Franciacorta Collezione Brut '02	♀♀ 6	
○ Franciacorta Pas Dosé '04	♀♀ 6	
○ TdF Bianco '07	♀♀ 4	

Battista Cola

VIA INDIPENDENZA, 3
25030 ADRO [BS]
TEL. 0307356195
www.colabattista.it

CELLAR SALES
PRE-BOOKED VISITS

ANNUAL PRODUCTION 60,000 bottles
HECTARES UNDER VINE 10
VITICULTURE METHOD Conventional

Stefano Cola meticulously tends the vineyards of the family estate, which was founded by his father Battista in the mid 1980s and has since acquired modern equipment and new vines for the production of Franciacortas. The Colas' strength lies in their ten hectares of beautiful vineyards in perfect sites on the slopes of Monte Alto, between Adro and Cortefranca. With the aid of consultant oenologist Alberto Musatti, each year Cola presents an array of first-rate cuvées and excellent red and white Curtefrancas.

This year Dosage Zéro Etichetta Storica '05 went to our finals with an elegant bouquet of ripe fruit, yeast, hazelnuts and delicate toast. The palate unfurls elegantly with plenty of fruit, zestiness and impressive length. The Brut, also '05, has notes of spring flowers, overripe apricots and oak introducing a palate so opulent, plush and full that it resembles a Satèn. Notes of coffee and toast on the nose of the Extra Brut usher in a convincingly fresh, deep palate. The non-vintage Brut and Satèn are pleasant and well typed. Chardonnay '08 is good, with floral and vanilla notes, while the Curtefranca Bianco and Rosso are both decent.

Contadi Castaldi

LOC. FORNACE BIASCA
VIA COLZANO, 32
25030 ADRO [BS]
TEL. 0307450126
www.contadicastaldi.it

CELLAR SALES
PRE-BOOKED VISITS

ANNUAL PRODUCTION 750,000 bottles
HECTARES UNDER VINE 120
VITICULTURE METHOD Conventional

Contadi Castaldi was the Moretti family's second estate in Franciacorta. Based on the négociant-manipulant concept, it was established to extend the group's range of Franciacortas without involving Bellavista and over the years it has developed into a formula whereby the Contadi Castaldi team oversees the vineyards of its suppliers, in this sense operating like a large agricultural business. Today, the contracted 120 hectares yield an impressive 750,000 bottles, with Satèn accounting for the lion's share.

This is confirmed by Satèn Soul '01, which strolled into our finals with a complex nose of soft apricots, a caressing velvety palate and a long vanillaed finish. The non-vintage Satèn also did well, making it through to the finals on the strength of its harmony and delicate toast and medicinal herbs. We also liked the excellent Rosés, commencing with the '05, which is full, juicy and tangy while the basic version has a dry, assertive character with attractive close-knit texture and hints of wild berries. Dosage Zéro '05 is firm, complex, creamy and tangy, making it the best edition yet. The other wines are nice.

○ Franciacorta Dosage Zéro Etichetta Storica '05	🍷🍷 5
○ Chardonnay '08	🍷🍷 4*
○ Franciacorta Brut '05	🍷🍷 5
○ Franciacorta Extra Brut	🍷🍷 5
○ Franciacorta Brut	🍷 5
○ Franciacorta Satèn	🍷 5
○ TdF Bianco '08	🍷 3
● TdF Rosso Curtefranca '06	🍷 4
○ Franciacorta Brut '04	🏆🏆 6
○ Franciacorta Brut '02	🏆🏆 6

○ Franciacorta Satèn	🍷🍷 6
○ Franciacorta Soul Satèn '01	🍷🍷 7
⊙ Franciacorta Brut Rosé '05	🍷🍷 6
⊙ Franciacorta Brut Rosé	🍷🍷 5
○ Franciacorta Zéro '05	🍷🍷 6
○ Franciacorta Brut	🍷 5
⊙ Pinodisé	🍷 6
○ TdF Bianco Curtefranca '08	🍷 4
● TdF Rosso Curtefranca '06	🍷 4
⊙ Franciacorta Brut Rosé '04	🏆🏆 6
○ Franciacorta Satèn '03	🏆🏆 6
○ Franciacorta Soul Satèn '00	🏆🏆 7
⊙ Pinodisé '01	🏆🏆 6
○ TdF Bianco Curtefranca '07	🏆🏆 4

Costaripa

VIA COSTA, 1A
25080 MONIGA DEL GARDA [BS]
TEL. 0365502010
www.costaripa.it

CELLAR SALES
PRE-BOOKED VISITS

ANNUAL PRODUCTION **330,000 bottles**
HECTARES UNDER VINE **36**
VITICULTURE METHOD **Conventional**

Renowned as one of the most talented Italian oenologists – and sparkling winemakers – Mattia Vezzola also finds time for the estate founded by his grandfather, after whom he is named. It is located in Moniga, on Lake Garda, where the land and site climate are ideal for wine. This is the northern edge of Mediterranean vegetation, where vineyards alternate with citrus trees and olive groves. Over the years, Costaripa has expanded, now covering an impressive 36 hectares under vine, from which Mattia makes a rich range of local wines.

Groppello is considered by some to be the local alternative to Pinot Nero. Anyone not convinced should try Groppello Maim '07. It's dense and stylish, with a crisp nose of red and black berries, then a harmonious, juicily lingering palate with perfectly calibrated new oak. Marzemino Le Mazane '08 is also excellent, with rich fruit and flowers, as is Cabernet Sauvignon Pradamonte '07, bursting with varietal aromas. Costaripa Brut '02 is very good, with juicy fruit and elegant vanilla notes. We also liked Chiaretto Molmenti '08, with its attractive hints of oak, and the cherry and currants Le Castelline '08.

Doria

LOC. CASA TACCONI, 3
27040 MONTALTO PAVESE [PV]
TEL. 0383870143
www.vinidoria.com

CELLAR SALES
PRE-BOOKED VISITS

ANNUAL PRODUCTION **140,000 bottles**
HECTARES UNDER VINE **30**
VITICULTURE METHOD **Conventional**

The winery run by Giuseppina Doria and her children, with the aid of cellarman Daniele Manini, is unusual. Some wines are unorthodox for the Oltrepò area but the estate also follows ancient traditions, which it implements in two main ways: making wines from nebbiolo grapes and using chestnut barrels. Daniele obsesses about harvesting and vinification, making it his mission to use the soundest possible grapes for his wines.

A.D. Memorial '07 is a monovarietal Nebbiolo, which reveals its potential in its structure, elegance and young, still very lively tannins. Barbera A.D. '06 aged in chestnut barrels. While opinion may be divided over its unusual style, we loved the distinctive notes imparted by the wood, combined with juicy fruit and nice acidity. Riesling Roncobianco '06 offers pleasant piquant, mineral notes and Pinot Nero Querciolo '06 has great potential but is still a little young. The two cuve close method sparklers, one based on pinot nero and the other – Contessa – from riesling renano, are both pleasant and varietal.

● Garda Cl. Groppello Maim '07	♥♥ 5
○ Costaripa Brut '02	♥♥ 6
● Garda Cabernet Sauvignon Pradamonte '07	♥♥ 5
☉ Garda Cl. Chiaretto Molmenti '08	♥♥ 5
● Garda Cl. Groppello Vign. Le Castelline '08	♥♥ 4*
● Marzemino Le Mazane '08	♥♥ 4
☉ Garda Cl. Chiaretto Rosamara '08	♥ 4
● Garda Cl. Rosso Campostarne '07	♥ 4
○ Lugana Pievecroce '08	♥ 4
● Garda Cl. Groppello Maim '05	♀♀ 5
● Garda Cl. Groppello Vign. Le Castelline '07	♀♀ 4

○ Contessa Brut Martinotti	♥♥ 4
● OP Barbera A.D. '06	♥♥ 5
● OP Bonarda Frizzante '08	♥♥ 4*
○ OP Pinot Nero Brut Martinotti Querciolo	♥♥ 4
● OP Pinot Nero Querciolo '06	♥♥ 6
○ OP Riesling Renano Roncobianco '06	♥♥ 4
● Rosso A.D. Memorial '07	♥♥ 6
● OP Rosso Roncorosso Ris. '06	♥ 4
● OP Pinot Nero Querciolo '05	♀♀ 6
○ OP Riesling Renano Roncobianco '05	♀♀ 4
● OP Rosso Roncorosso '03	♀♀ 4
● Rosso A.D. '99	♀♀ 6
● Rosso A.D. Memorial '05	♀♀ 6
● Rosso A.D. Memorial '04	♀♀ 6

Sandro Fay

LOC. SAN GIACOMO DI TEGLIO
VIA PILA CASELLI, 1
23030 TEGLIO [SO]
TEL. 0342786071
elefay@tin.it

CELLAR SALES
PRE-BOOKED VISITS

ANNUAL PRODUCTION **38,000 bottles**
HECTARES UNDER VINE **13**
VITICULTURE METHOD **Conventional**

The Fay family has long formed a great winemaking team. Today, father Sandro can afford to sit back and pass the reins to his children Marco and Elena, who now head the winery. Work aimed at improving the estate's vineyards was completed some time ago and the project was carried out with impressive enthusiasm and clarity of vision. The Fays make wines from Valtellina's finest crus and their Casa Morelli vineyard in Valgella is a fine example of high-quality planting.

This is confirmed by the excellent Valgella Ca' Morèi '06, which gives concentrated autumn leaves with subtle hints of red fruits and a firm, full-flavoured palate, with an impressive yet elegant texture. The unusual, modern Carterìa '06 has spicy aromas and a juicy palate with a deep finish. La Faya '06 displays a complex, fruity nose and a dry, richly flavoured palate while Sassella Il Glicine '06 is well made with fresh aromas. Sforzato Ronco del Picchio '06 is unmistakable, showing concentrated aromatics of ripe fruit and well-calibrated spice before the rounded, juicily full palate hints at cloves.

Ferghettina

VIA SALINE, 11
25030 ADRO [BS]
TEL. 0307451212
www.ferghettina.it

CELLAR SALES
PRE-BOOKED VISITS

ANNUAL PRODUCTION **350,000 bottles**
HECTARES UNDER VINE **120**
VITICULTURE METHOD **Conventional**

Roberto Gatti and his wife Andreina, with their children Laura, an oenologist, and oenology student Matteo, now manage 120 hectares of fine vineyards located in six different municipalities of the DOCG zone, whose grapes are used to make wine in their new, well-equipped cellar in Adro. Their adventure commenced in 1990, when Roberto, who had previously worked as a cellarman in other Franciacorta wineries, decided to purchase his first four hectares in Erbusco. The family's cellar is a monument to enterprise, tenacity and spirit of sacrifice, and one of the finest in Franciacorta.

This year, we awarded Three Glasses to the Extra Brut '02 for its elegant, bright yellowish-green hue and very fine bead, leading into a concentrated, complex nose, whose prominent ripe fruit and flowers mingle with sensations of wholemeal and hazelnut before the firm, fleshy palate signs off triumphantly long. The Satèn is also exemplary, the '05 offering juicy softness, firm structure and an elegant vanillaed finish. The Brut '05 is clean, unfolding fresh fruit with hints of balsam, while the '05 Rosé is full bodied and impressively balanced, with a nose of berries and toast and a tangy, fresh, lingering palate. The other wines are good.

● Valtellina Sforzato Ronco del Picchio '06	♟♟	7
● Valtellina Sup. Valgella Ca' Morèi '06	♟♟	5
● La Faya '06	♟♟	5
● Valtellina Sup. Sassella Il Glicine '06	♟♟	5
● Valtellina Sup. Valgella Carterìa '06	♟♟	5
● Valtellina Sforzato Ronco del Picchio '02	♟♟♟	7
● Valtellina Sforzato Ronco del Picchio '05	♟♟	7
● Valtellina Sforzato Ronco del Picchio '04	♟♟	7
● Valtellina Sforzato Ronco del Picchio '03	♟♟	7
● Valtellina Sup. Valgella Ca' Morèi '02	♟♟	5
● Valtellina Sup. Valgella Carterìa '04	♟♟	5
● Valtellina Sup. Valgella Carteria '03	♟♟	5

○ Franciacorta Extra Brut '02	♟♟♟	6
○ Franciacorta Satèn '05	♟♟	6
○ Franciacorta Brut '05	♟♟	6
⊙ Franciacorta Rosé '05	♟♟	6
○ Franciacorta Brut	♟	5
○ TdF Curtefranca Bianco '08	♟	4
● TdF Curtefranca Rosso '07	♟	4
○ Franciacorta Extra Brut '98	♟♟♟	6
○ Franciacorta Satèn '04	♟♟♟	6
○ Franciacorta Extra Brut '00	♟♟	6
⊙ Franciacorta Rosé '04	♟♟	6
○ TdF Curtefranca Bianco '07	♟♟	4*

Le Fracce

FRAZ. MAIRANO
VIA CASTEL DEL LUPO, 5
27045 CASTEGGIO [PV]
TEL. 038382526
info@le-fracce.it

CELLAR SALES
PRE-BOOKED VISITS

ANNUAL PRODUCTION **200,000 bottles**
HECTARES UNDER VINE **40**
VITICULTURE METHOD **Conventional**

We are talking about one of Oltrepò's legendary estates, with a villa overlooking splendid grounds and two collections of rare vintage cars and carriages. Owned by the Bussolera Branca foundation, the cellar makes reliably good and sometimes excellent wines but each year we find ourselves looking for some outstanding product that has so far struggled to emerge. We will see if oenologist Roberto Gerbino is able to fill this gap with the upcoming production of white and rosé classic method sparklers.

This year, the best wine is one of the estate's oldest. Riesling Landò '08, with a nose of spring flowers and tropical fruit, shows full, refreshing and long on the palate. Pinot Grigio Levriere '08, another of the winery's classics, also scored well. It is less firmly structured than the Riesling but clean and varietal. While we await release of the promising Bohemi '04, the best red is Cirgà '04, with a nose of wild berries and ripe plums and a full, chewy, tasty palate. Bonarda Frizzante La Rubiosa '08 is as good as ever, with a creamy mousse, rich aromas of raspberry and strawberry, and poised fine-grained tannins.

Antica Fratta

VIA FONTANA, 11
25040 MONTICELLI BRUSATI [BS]
TEL. 030652068
www.anticafratta.it

CELLAR SALES
PRE-BOOKED VISITS

ANNUAL PRODUCTION **360,000 bottles**
HECTARES UNDER VINE **N.D.**
VITICULTURE METHOD **Conventional**

While Guido Berlucchi & C., the flagship winery of the Ziliani family, made its roundabout journey from Franciacorta into other top sparkler-producing areas before recently returning to its original terroir, Antica Fratta, part of Berlucchi since 1979, has never abandoned Franciacortas. The winery has been run by Cristina Ziliani for several years now, with a separate staff and vineyards from the parent company, and produces around 360,000 bottles of Franciacorta and Curtefranca each year.

The four cuvées that we tasted this year were very good, starting with a Brut '04 whose scented fruit and flower nose precedes a zestily generous palate. Rosé Essence '05 is also excellent, with a handsome bright pink hue and red and black berry aromas veined with vanilla. In the mouth, it is complex and weighty, faithfully echoing the fruit of the nose with a fresh currant finish. The Satèn is charming, with aromas of tropical fruit and flowers, cakes and medicinal herbs. It is caressing and plush on the palate, supported by good acidity. The Franciacorta Brut is also good, resembling a Satèn in style.

● Barbera Garboso '07	♀♀	4
● OP Bonarda Frizzante La Rubiosa '08	♀♀	4
○ OP Pinot Grigio Levriere '08	♀♀	4
○ OP Pinot Nero Cuvée Bussolera Extra Brut '07	♀♀	4
○ OP Riesling Landò '08	♀♀	4
● OP Rosso Cirgà '04	♀♀	5
● OP Pinot Nero '05	♀	6
● Barbera Garboso '06	♀♀	4*
● OP Bonarda La Rubiosa '07	♀♀	4*
● OP Bonarda La Rubiosa '06	♀♀	4*
○ OP Pinot Nero Cuvée Bussolera Extra Brut '06	♀♀	4
○ OP Riesling Landò '07	♀♀	4
● OP Rosso Bohemi '01	♀♀	6

○ Franciacorta Brut '04	♀♀	6
☉ Franciacorta Essence Rosé '05	♀♀	6
○ Franciacorta Satèn	♀♀	6
○ Franciacorta Brut	♀	5
○ Franciacorta Brut '03	♀♀	5
☉ Franciacorta Rosé	♀♀	6
● TdF Rosso Ragnoli '06	♀♀	4*
● TdF Rosso Ragnoli '05	♀♀	5

Frecciarossa

VIA VIGORELLI, 141
27045 CASTEGGIO [PV]
TEL. 0383804465
www.frecciarossa.com

CELLAR SALES
PRE-BOOKED VISITS

ANNUAL PRODUCTION **150,000 bottles**
HECTARES UNDER VINE **20**
VITICULTURE METHOD **Conventional**

This stunning estate, with villa overlooking the valley and a model cellar, is located precisely on the 45th parallel, which unites some of the world's greatest wine areas. Claudio Giorgi has made impressive changes within the winery, including a recently built tasting room. The estate owned by the Odero family confirms itself as an Oltrepò leader, particularly for Pinot Nero fermented on the skins.

Giorgio Odero '06 almost took our top accolade, which the '05 won last year. It is varietal and fragrant, with notes of berries and Mediterranean scrubland, extremely well defined and elegant, with great verve and integrity. Francigeno '05, from mainly merlot, also scored very highly. It is well made, velvety and harmonious with firm structure. Riesling Gli Orti '08 is captivating, with pronounced floral notes, good acidity, backbone and subtle mineral nuances that will emerge in time, as revealed by tastings of earlier vintages. Le Praielle '06 is a Barbera with fresh notes of cherry and good acid backbone.

Gatta

VIA SAN ROCCO, 33
25064 GUSSAGO [BS]
TEL. 0302772950
www.agricolagatta.com

CELLAR SALES
PRE-BOOKED VISITS

ANNUAL PRODUCTION **150,000 bottles**
HECTARES UNDER VINE **N.D.**
VITICULTURE METHOD **Conventional**

Mario Gatta's estate is situated in the east of Franciacorta, and more precisely on the Stella hill, which rises 270 metres above sea level over Cellatica and Gussago. Wine has been made at Cellatica since the 15th century. Indeed, this small area is not only part of the larger Franciacorta zone; it also has its very own DOC zone. Mario pays tribute with his Cellatica Superiore Negus, which has nothing to do with the Ethiopian ruler but refers to Mario's grandfather, who began the family's wine adventure. In the 1960s, Angelo Gatta, known as Negus, planted the first vineyard that continues to produce this intriguing wine.

Extra Brut Molener '03 is generously characterful, with a fine nose of medicinal herbs and fruit and a tangy, lingering palate. Rosé Extra Brut gives aromas of wild strawberries, shows an attractive pale pink with a very fine bead preceding a juicy, chamois soft palate. The Satèn '04, with nice honey notes, is a rung below, along with the slightly over-evolved Zéro and the Brut. Unusually for this zone, Mario also produces two excellent reds: the solid, well-defined Febo '05 and Cellatica Negus '03, with aromas of spice, ripe blackberries and blueberries, which unfolds complex and soft on the palate.

● OP Pinot Nero Giorgio Odero '06	♟♟ 6
● Francigeno '05	♟♟ 6
● Le Praielle '06	♟♟ 4
○ OP Riesling Renano Gli Orti '08	♟♟ 4*
○ Nai '08	♟ 4
● OP Bonarda Vivace Dardo '08	♟ 4
● Uva Rara '08	♟ 4
● OP Pinot Nero Giorgio Odero '05	♟♟♟ 6
● Francigeno '04	♟♟ 5
● OP Bonarda Vivace Dardo '06	♟♟ 4*
● OP Pinot Nero Giorgio Odero '04	♟♟ 5
● OP Pinot Nero Giorgio Odero '03	♟♟ 5
● OP Pinot Nero Giorgio Odero '00	♟♟ 5
○ OP Riesling Renano Gli Orti '07	♟♟ 4*

● Cellatica Sup. Negus '03	♟♟ 4
○ Franciacorta Extra Brut Molener '03	♟♟ 6
☉ Franciacorta Extra Brut Rosé	♟♟ 5
● TdF Curtefranca Febo '05	♟♟ 4*
○ Franciacorta Brut	♟ 4
○ Franciacorta Brut Satèn '04	♟ 6
○ Franciacorta Dosage Zéro	♟ 5
○ Franciacorta Brut Arcano '94	♟♟ 7
○ Franciacorta Brut Satèn '03	♟♟ 5
○ Franciacorta Extra Brut Molener '00	♟♟ 5

Enrico Gatti

VIA METELLI, 9
25030 ERBUSCO [BS]
TEL. 0307267999
www.enricogatti.it

CELLAR SALES
PRE-BOOKED VISITS

ANNUAL PRODUCTION **120,000 bottles**
HECTARES UNDER VINE **17**
VITICULTURE METHOD **Conventional**

In spite of its relatively small production, the Erbusco-based Gatti winery has shone in recent years with several top-notch Franciacorta cuvées. Well done Lorenzo Gatti, his sister Paola and her husband Enzo Balzarini, who have carried on the tradition of the siblings' father Enrico and created an authentic boutique winery. Their exceptionally well-equipped cellar makes wine exclusively from grapes grown on their 17 hectares under vine. The Franciacortas have made firm structure and elegant mineral notes the estate's hallmark.

The Satèn '05 took our top award for the fifth time in six years, indicative of the winery's consistency and extraordinary stylistic continuity. Gatti's interpretation of this wine is almost extreme, taking chardonnay grapes only and transforming them into a deep, firmly structured cuvée that is softly articulated but always full of character thanks to fermentation of half the base wine in old barriques and long ageing on the lees. The Nature is good, showing supple, fresh and dry, and the Brut is also pleasant, with an elegantly layered, creamily close-knit palate.

F.lli Giorgi

FRAZ. CAMPONOCE, 39A
27044 CANNETO PAVESE [PV]
TEL. 0385262151
www.giorgi-wines.it

CELLAR SALES
PRE-BOOKED VISITS

ANNUAL PRODUCTION **1.600,000 bottles**
HECTARES UNDER VINE **30**
VITICULTURE METHOD **Conventional**

With an annual production of over one and a million bottles, this is one of the largest Valle Versa wineries for quantity and quality. The resourcefulness of Fabiano Giorgi, the en talented consultant oenologist Alberto Musatti ensure that the standard continues to rise, year after year, while maintaining a high-quality commercial base that allows production of exciting top-end wines of all types.

Giorgi's flagship wine is its 1870, whose '05 vintage won Three Glasses for its complex nose, creamy bead and attractively lingering fruitiness. We were also impressed by the other two sparklers dedicated to Gianfranco Giorgi, who was the winery's oenologist for many years, our preference just going to the scented Rosé. Casa del Corno '05 is the best Buttafuoco Storico we tasted this year while the interesting Riesling Bandito is piquant and minerally, and Rosso Cilele is fruity and complex. The rest of the list also did well, including the novel Fusion, a cuvée made using both classic and cuve close methods.

○ Franciacorta Satèn '05	♟♟♟	6
○ Franciacorta Brut	♟♟	5
○ Franciacorta Nature	♟♟	6
○ Franciacorta Satèn '03	♀♀♀	6
○ Franciacorta Satèn '02	♀♀♀	6
○ Franciacorta Satèn '01	♀♀♀	5
○ Franciacorta Brut '02	♀♀	7
○ Franciacorta Satèn '04	♀♀	6

○ OP Pinot Nero Brut Cl. 1870 '05	♟♟♟	6
● OP Bonarda Frizzante La Brughera '08	♟♟	4
● OP Buttafuoco Storico Casa del Corno '05	♟♟	4
○ OP Pinot Nero Brut Cl. Gianfranco Giorgi '06	♟♟	6
○ OP Pinot Nero Brut Cl. Rosé Gianfranco Giorgi	♟♟	6
○ OP Riesling Il Bandito '08	♟♟	5
● OP Rosso Clilele '07	♟♟	6
● OP Sangue di Giuda '08	♟♟	4
○ Zimmolo	♟♟	5
○ Fusion	♟	4
○ OP Pinot Nero Extra Dry Cuvée Eleonor Martinotti	♟	4
⊙ OP Pinot Nero Extra Dry Cuvée Eleonor Rosé Martinotti	♟	4
● OP Pinot Nero Giorginero '08	♟	4
● Vigalòn '08	♟	3*

Conte Carlo Giorgi di Vistarino

FRAZ. SCORZOLETTA, 82/84
27040 PIETRA DE' GIORGI [PV]
TEL. 038585117
www.contevistarino.it

CELLAR SALES
PRE-BOOKED VISITS

ANNUAL PRODUCTION **550,000 bottles**
HECTARES UNDER VINE **180**
VITICULTURE METHOD **Conventional**

At long last the largest and oldest winery in Valle Scuropasso, where pinot nero was introduced from France in the mid 19th century, has started to reap big rewards under the management of Ottavia Giorgi di Vistarino. Given the almost 200 hectares of vineyards in the finest pinot nero growing areas for both base wines for sparklers and for reds, these results are long overdue.

So let's enjoy the elegant, well-typed Pernice, from pinot nero fermented on the skins, whose '06 vintage earned Three Glasses for its balance, well-gauged oak and sound, well-defined wild berries, accompanied by a very well-sustained finish. And of course Pinot Nero also means Metodo Classico. The 1865 scored very well, displaying evolved notes with hints of toast, hay and candied peel, as did Rosé Saignée della Rocca, with varietal wild berry aromas and notes of wild strawberry, vanilla and roasted hazelnut preceding a nice firm palate. The rest of the list is well executed.

Cantina Sociale La Versa

VIA F. CRISPI, 15
27047 SANTA MARIA DELLA VERSA [PV]
TEL. 0385798411
www.laversa.it

CELLAR SALES

ANNUAL PRODUCTION **6,000,000 bottles**
HECTARES UNDER VINE **1300**
VITICULTURE METHOD **Conventional**

We will never tire of praising the extraordinary job that Francesco Cervetti has done in bringing this legendary winery back into fashion, particularly with the production of sparklers. Who can forget the classic white label that made its appearance on official occasions and sporting events like the Giro d'Italia in the 1970s? Over the space of a decade Cervetti has reorganized the winery, rewarding the suppliers of the best grapes and creating an excellent top-end range.

Testarossa Principio '03 echoes the style and quality of its forerunners, showing elegant, flavoursome, balanced and scented with plenty of character and depth. Testarossa Rosé '05 has beautifully sound red fruit that is perfectly echoed on the palate, accompanied by impressive finesse. We also liked Testarossa Brut '04, and Carta Oro, a Metodo Classico that offers surprisingly good value for money. The two Cuvée Storica sparklers, white and rosé, both achieved high scores and the rest of the wines presented also performed well, commencing with Bonarda Ca' Bella.

● OP Pinot Nero Pernice '06	♟♟♟ 4*
● OP Buttafuoco Monte Selva '07	♟♟ 3*
○ OP Pinot Nero Brut Cl. 1865	♟♟ 6
☉ OP Pinot Nero Brut Cl. Saignée della Rocca	♟♟ 4
● OP Pinot Nero Costa del Nero '07	♟♟ 3*
○ Cascina San Silvestro '08	♟ 3
● OP Bonarda L'Alcova '08	♟ 3
○ OP Pinot Nero Brut Martinotti Cuvée della Rocca	♟ 3
● OP Pinot Nero Costa del Nero '06	♟♟ 3*
● OP Pinot Nero Pernice '05	♟♟ 5
○ Riesling Passito '04	♟♟ 6
● Sorbe '06	♟♟ 4

○ Cuvée Testarossa Brut Principio '03	♟♟ 8
☉ OP Pinot Nero Rosé Cuvée Testarossa Brut '05	♟♟ 6
○ Brut Cl. Cuvée Storica	♟♟ 4
● OP Bonarda Frizzante Ca' Bella '08	♟♟ 4
○ OP Pinot Nero Brut Carta Oro Blanc de Noir	♟♟ 4*
○ OP Pinot Nero Cuvée Testarossa Brut '04	♟♟ 8
○ OP Riesling Roccolo delle Fate '08	♟♟ 4
● OP Roccolo Sangue di Giuda '08	♟♟ 3*
● Casale Del Re '05	♟ 5
● OP Bonarda Donelasco '07	♟ 4
● OP Bonarda Frizzante Terre d'Alteni '08	♟ 3
○ OP Moscato di Volpara Frizzante I Roccoli '08	♟ 4
☉ OP Pinot Nero Brut Cuvée Storica Rosé	♟ 4
○ Cuvée Testarossa Principio '01	♟♟ 8
☉ OP Pinot Nero Rosé Cuvée Testarossa Brut '04	♟♟ 6
○ OP Pinot Nero Testarossa Principio '00	♟♟ 8

Lantieri de Paratico

LOC. COLZANO
VIA SIMEONE PARATICO, 50
25031 CAPRIOLO [BS]
TEL. 030736151
www.lantierideparatico.it

CELLAR SALES
PRE-BOOKED VISITS

ANNUAL PRODUCTION **150,000 bottles**
HECTARES UNDER VINE **17**
VITICULTURE METHOD **Conventional**

Today, this Capriolo winery, owned by the same family for centuries, is competently run by the enthusiastic Fabio Lantieri, who in recent years has considerably upped the quality of its sparkling and still wines. The cellar, housed in a 15th-century villa, boasts all the latest equipment and makes wines from the grapes of the estate's 17 hectares of vineyards, almost all adjoining the winery.

Franciacorta Brut Arcadia is the estate's flagship wine. The '05 vintage gives a fresh, complex nose with plenty of fruit, but also notes of coffee and vanilla, and the crisp, fresh palate is enlivened by citrus notes and a caressing prickle. It only just missed our top accolade. The Brut is also good, with a pleasant nose of toast and yeast and a tangy palate, while the very lean-bodied Extra Brut has biscuit-like aromas, followed by a dry, spirited palate with wafts of hazelnut. While the rest of the list is well made, there is still plenty of room for improvement.

Majolini

LOC. VALLE
VIA MANZONI, 3
25050 OME [BS]
TEL. 0306527378
www.majolini.it

CELLAR SALES
PRE-BOOKED VISITS

ANNUAL PRODUCTION **160,000 bottles**
HECTARES UNDER VINE **20**
VITICULTURE METHOD **Conventional**

The Majolinis have created an industrial group of international stature, but in the mid 1980s they felt the need to return to their farming roots and renovated the beautiful cascina in Ome and its holdings. This marked the beginning of the Majolini adventure and, headed by Ezio who is now flanked by his grandson Simone, the winery soon became one of the most important in the designated zone. There are 20 hectares of wonderful vineyards, mainly around Ome, and a handsome, state-of-the art winery adorned with the latest sculpture by Aligi Sassu, a family friend.

With some of the estate's most important cuvées still ageing in the cellar, we tasted an excellent Pas Dosé Aligi Sassu, which reached our finals with concentrated, apricot-led stone fruit and attractive oak and minerality. Dry, spirited and full in the mouth, it closes unhurriedly on minerality and citrus. The Brut has a complex, pleasantly evolved nose, with hints of antique wood, beeswax and vanilla introducing a full palate with creamy effervescence. Rosé Altera is good, with floral and wild berry notes, and the juicy Satèn Ante Omnia '04 is as satisfying and velvety as ever, closing on oak and toast.

○ Franciacorta Brut Arcadia '05	♈♈	6
○ Franciacorta Brut	♈♈	5
○ Franciacorta Extra Brut	♈	5
○ Franciacorta Satèn	♈	5
○ TdF Bianco Curtefranca '08	♈	4
● TdF Rosso Curtefranca '07	♈	4
○ Franciacorta Brut Arcadia '04	♈♈	6
○ Franciacorta Brut Arcadia '02	♈♈	6
○ Franciacorta Brut Arcadia '01	♈♈	6
○ TdF Bianco Colzano '06	♈♈	5
● TdF Rosso Colzano '05	♈♈	5

○ Franciacorta Aligi Sassu Pas Dosé '05	♈♈	8
○ Franciacorta Ante Omnia Satèn '04	♈♈	8
○ Franciacorta Brut	♈♈	7
☉ Franciacorta Rosé Altera	♈♈	6
○ Franciacorta Brut Electo '00	♈♈♈	7
○ Franciacorta Aligi Sassu Pas Dosé '04	♈♈	8
○ Franciacorta Aligi Sassu Pas Dosé '03	♈♈	8
○ Franciacorta Brut Electo '04	♈♈	8
○ Franciacorta Pas Dosé Aligi Sassu '00	♈♈	7
○ Franciacorta Satèn Ante Omnia '03	♈♈	8

Le Marchesine

VIA VALLOSA, 31
25050 PASSIRANO [BS]
TEL. 030657005
www.lemarchesine.it

CELLAR SALES
PRE-BOOKED VISITS

ANNUAL PRODUCTION 320,000 bottles
HECTARES UNDER VINE 40
VITICULTURE METHOD Conventional

Giovanni Biatta and his son Loris have founded one of Franciacorta's most interesting wineries. Their family is documented in the Brescia area since the 12th century and has been making wine for four generations. During the mid 1980s, they started to replant the vineyards and purchase new ones, building a well-equipped modern cellar where they make their wines exclusively from the grapes of the 40 hectares that they manage. Cellar operations are overseen by Jean-Pierre Valade, an oenologist with extensive experience in Champagne.

The Biattas' cuvées have been excellent for several years and this time the fantastic Franciacorta Brut '04 won Three Glasses. Showing bright straw with tiny bubbles, it gives floral and fruity sensations, with top notes of apricot and lavender followed by citrus and vanilla. A firm, tidy palate shows elegant supporting acidity and good length. Franciacorta Rosé '05 is excellent, with a nose of currants and wild strawberries and a rich, zesty palate, while the intriguing Novo Riserva '00 Dosage Zero is complex and floral. The elegantly orchestrated, hazelnut and coffee Secolo Novo Brut '04 is also nicely executed.

Tenuta Mazzolino

VIA MAZZOLINO, 26
27050 CORVINO SAN QUIRICO [PV]
TEL. 0383876122
www.tenuta-mazzolino.com

CELLAR SALES
PRE-BOOKED VISITS

ANNUAL PRODUCTION 100,000 bottles
HECTARES UNDER VINE 25
VITICULTURE METHOD Conventional

The stunning Tenuta Mazzolino, owned by the Braggiotti family, is one of the most charming estates in Oltrepò, with the family villa set in glorious grounds with superb views. Its wines are the work of talented Burgundian oenologist Jean-François Coquard aided by Kiryakos Kynigopulos, who is also French but with evident Greek ancestry. The list is interesting but short, making it somewhat something of a rarity in an area noted for its overabundance of wine types.

Noir, a monovarietal Pinot Nero, is spectacular as ever and won Three Glasses for the '06 vintage. The excellent spicy oak melds with exuberant sound berry fruit and the fine-grained tannins, well-balanced structure and elegance culminate in a long finish. The well-typed, forthright Cabernet Sauvignon Corvino '06 is very good, with a rounded, chewy palate. Blanc '07, a young monovarietal Chardonnay, also took Two Glasses for its top notes of vanilla and excellent ageing potential. The Metodo Classico from white grapes is well executed while the well-crafted still Bonarda, Pinot Nero Terrazze and Chardonnay Camarà are all varietal.

O Franciacorta Brut '04	🍷🍷🍷	6
● Cabernet Sauvignon Alice '04	🍷🍷	6
O Franciacorta Brut	🍷🍷	5
⊙ Franciacorta Brut Rosé '05	🍷🍷	6
O Franciacorta Brut Secolo Novo '04	🍷🍷	8
O Franciacorta Extra Brut	🍷🍷	6
O Franciacorta Satèn	🍷🍷	6
O Franciacorta Secolo Novo Dosage Zero Ris. '00	🍷🍷	8
● Il Podere Pinot Nero	🍷	6
O TdF Bianco Curtefranca '08	🍷	4
● TdF Rosso Curtefranca	🍷	4
O Franciacorta Brut '01	♀♀	6
O Franciacorta Brut Secolo Novo '00	♀♀	7
O Franciacorta Satèn '02	♀♀	6

● OP Pinot Nero Noir '06	🍷🍷🍷	6
O Mazzolino Brut Blanc de Blancs	🍷🍷	4
● OP Cabernet Sauvignon Corvino '06	🍷🍷	5
O OP Chardonnay Blanc '07	🍷🍷	4
O Camarà '08	🍷	3
● OP Bonarda Mazzolino '08	🍷	4
● Terrazze '08	🍷	4
● OP Bonarda Mazzolino '07	♀♀	4*
O OP Chardonnay Blanc '06	♀♀	4*
O OP Mazzolino Brut	♀♀	5
O OP Mazzolino Brut	♀♀	5
● OP Pinot Nero Noir '05	♀♀	6
● OP Pinot Nero Noir '04	♀♀	6

Monsupello

VIA SAN LAZZARO, 5
27050 TORRICELLA VERZATE [PV]
TEL. 0383896043
www.monsupello.it

CELLAR SALES
PRE-BOOKED VISITS

ANNUAL PRODUCTION 280,000 bottles
HECTARES UNDER VINE 48
VITICULTURE METHOD Conventional

The Boatti family's long years of toil consistently yield excellent results. Carlo, who runs the estate, was one of the first to believe in the potential of an area that has often been scorned and, in some cases, insufficiently promoted by the growers themselves. Monsupello is a heritage to be cherished. It is hard to find flaws in the long list of wines, all from estate vineyards, for this Torricella Verzate winery is highly competent.

Now that Italians are finally discovering rosé sparklers, and the Consorzio Oltrepò is staking much on this type of wine, the Boattis have come up with one that earned Three Glasses for its depth and minerality, accompanied by a nose of red fruit and rose petals and an elegant, taut palate. Almost as good are the other two sparklers that have already won our top accolade in the past. The Nature is fresh, close-focused and zesty, while Ca' del Tava's usual opulent fullness and complexity are now accompanied by greater finesse thanks to better use of oak. The rest of the list is, without exception, exemplary.

Monte Rossa

FRAZ. BORNATO
VIA MONTE ROSSA, 1
25040 CAZZAGO SAN MARTINO [BS]
TEL. 030725066
www.monterossa.com

CELLAR SALES
PRE-BOOKED VISITS

ANNUAL PRODUCTION 500,000 bottles
HECTARES UNDER VINE 70
VITICULTURE METHOD Conventional

The Rabotti family estate, founded by Paolo and Paola Rovetta in the 1970s and now skilfully managed by their son Emanuele, is one of the leading names in the history of this prestigious young DOCG. The location is on the hill at Bornato and the modern cellars stand beside the handsome 17th-century family home. The Rabottis manage 70 hectares of vineyards, both estate-owned and leased, and have concentrated production exclusively on Franciacortas for several years now. Their cuvées are as good as it gets.

As we wait for the new vintage of Cabochon, Monte Rossa's prestige cuvée, the Brut P.R. reached our finals. Its complex ripe fruit, oak and vanilla aromatics precede a tangy palate with firm structure and supporting acidity before the long vanillaed finish. The Rosé is excellent, showing pale pink with currants, raspberries and wild strawberries and a velvety palate. This year, the Satèn was below par. It's nice and soft but lacks body and finishes slightly astringent. However, Brut Prima Cuvée is excellent, with an opulent nose of fruit echoed on the elegant, fresh-tasting palate with its attractive creamy finish.

Wine	Rating
⊙ Brut Rosé	♟♟♟ 5*
○ OP Brut Cl. Cuvée Ca' del Tava	♟♟ 7
○ OP Pinot Nero Cl. Nature	♟♟ 5*
○ Chardonnay '08	♟♟ 4
○ Chardonnay Senso '06	♟♟ 6
● OP Cabernet Sauvignon Aplomb '05	♟♟ 6
○ OP Pinot Nero Brut Cl.	♟♟ 5
○ Pinot Grigio '08	♟♟ 4*
○ Riesling Renano '08	♟♟ 4
● OP Bonarda Calcababio '08	♟ 4
● OP Bonarda Vivace Vaiolet '08	♟ 4
● OP Rosso Podere La Borla '06	♟ 4
○ OP Brut Cl. Cuvée Ca' del Tava	♟♟♟ 7
○ OP Pinot Nero Cl. Nature	♟♟♟ 5*

Wine	Rating
○ Franciacorta Brut P. R.	♟♟ 6
○ Franciacorta Prima Cuvée Brut	♟♟ 5
⊙ Franciacorta Rosé	♟♟ 6
○ Franciacorta Satèn	♟ 6
○ Franciacorta Brut Cabochon '04	♟♟♟ 7
○ Franciacorta Brut Cabochon '03	♟♟♟ 7
⊙ Franciacorta Brut Cabochon Rosé '01	♟♟ 8
○ Franciacorta Extra Brut '01	♟♟ 6

Montelio

VIA D. MAZZA, 1
27050 CODEVILLA [PV]
TEL. 0383373090
montelio.gio@alice.it

CELLAR SALES
PRE-BOOKED VISITS
VISITOR FACILITIES FOOD

ANNUAL PRODUCTION **130,000 bottles**
HECTARES UNDER VINE **27**
VITICULTURE METHOD **Conventional**

The Brazzola family estate has long been managed by Mario Maffi, one of the most important, charismatic figures in the entire Oltrepò. Their handsome 18th-century colonnaded courtyard has guest facilities and a fine tasting room in rustic style. Don't miss a tour of the cellars, and particularly the "infernot", an underground room that was once used to store ice and now houses the dusty bottles of vintage wines.

Pinot Nero Costarsa was among the first of its kind in Franciacorta to be red-fermented. The '04 version has pepper-led spice conferred by the nice oak, lets the wild berries shine through. Silky, fine-grained tannins meld with good fruit, body and a long finish. Barbera '07 has balsamic notes and sound, clean fruit while Cortese '08 is well executed with a fragrant floral nose. Bonarda Frizzante '08 gives wild berry aromas and pleasant weight while Rosso Riserva Solarolo '05 is not as exuberant as in the past but still scored well for its nicely balanced fruit and spices.

Montenisa

FRAZ. CALINO
VIA PAOLO VI, 62
25046 CAZZAGO SAN MARTINO [BS]
TEL. 0307750838
www.antinori.it

PRE-BOOKED VISITS

ANNUAL PRODUCTION **220,000 bottles**
HECTARES UNDER VINE **60**
VITICULTURE METHOD **Conventional**

Several years ago, Marchesi Antinori started producing Franciacortas and bought this fine estate from the aristocratic Maggi family. It now has 60 hectares of completely replanted vineyards overlooking Lake Iseo from the hamlet of Calino, where the lovely house and cellar stand. The winery is run by Allegra, Alessia and Albiera Antinori and is named after Mount Nysa, which Greek mythology identifies as the birthplace of the god Bacchus.

A retasting of the '01 cuvée named after Contessa Camilla Maggi, confirmed its excellence. Awaiting the new vintage, we tasted three fabulous Franciacortas. We liked the Satèn '03, which has elegant aromas of ripe apricot-led stone fruit giving way to vanilla, and a firm, well-profiled palate with good fruit and a long caressing finish. The attractive bright straw Brut has tiny bubbles and a fresh, alluring nose of fruit with delicate oak preceding a harmonious, balanced palate with a complex mineral finish. The Rosé is elegant, although we'd have liked a little more structure.

● OP Barbera '07	♀♀	3*
● OP Bonarda Frizzante '08	♀♀	3*
○ OP Cortese '08	♀♀	3*
● OP Pinot Nero Costarsa '04	♀♀	5
● OP Rosso Solarolo Ris. '05	♀♀	5
○ Brut Martinotti La Stroppa	♀	4
● Comprino Rosso '07	♀	3
○ Noblerot '06	♀	5
○ OP Riesling Italic '08	♀	3
⊙ OP Rosato Frizzante '08	♀	3
○ Müller Thurgau La Giostra '06	♀♀	3*
● OP Bonarda Frizzante '07	♀♀	3*
● OP Pinot Nero Costarsa '03	♀♀	5
● OP Rosso Solarolo Ris. '04	♀♀	5

○ Franciacorta Brut	♀♀	6
○ Franciacorta Satèn '03	♀♀	7
⊙ Franciacorta Rosé	♀	6
○ Franciacorta Brut Contessa Camilla Maggi '01	♀♀	7
○ Franciacorta Satèn '02	♀♀	7

La Montina

VIA BAIANA, 17
25040 MONTICELLI BRUSATI [BS]
TEL. 030653278
www.lamontina.it

CELLAR SALES
PRE-BOOKED VISITS

ANNUAL PRODUCTION **500,000 bottles**
HECTARES UNDER VINE **62**
VITICULTURE METHOD **Conventional**

The Bozza brothers' winery, purchased in the early 1980s, is a historic estate named after the Montini family, from which Pope Paul VI hailed. It is run by the close-knit team of oenologist Cesare Ferrari, agronomists Alceo Totò and Rocco Marino, and Michele Bozza, who co-ordinates sales, who have boosted the quantity and quality of production in recent years. Over 60 hectares of vines in prime wine country and a well-equipped cellar have enabled the winery to achieve excellent results.

After coming closer over the past few years, La Montina has finally picked up Three Glasses. Our top accolade went to the excellent, invigorating Brut '05. Its succulent palate is well orchestrated and full flavoured, with a long fruity finish. But the entire list is impressive, for example the Brut, which has a complex nose of yeast and medicinal herbs and a well-defined, weighty palate. The subtly sweet Rosé Demi Sec is interesting while the Satèn is soft and vanillaed. From the still wines, we liked Rubinia, a characterful Chardonnay aged in small oak casks.

○ Franciacorta Brut '05	▼▼▼	6
○ Franciacorta Brut	▼▼	5
⊙ Franciacorta Rosé Demi Sec	▼▼	5
○ Franciacorta Satèn	▼▼	6
○ Rubinia	▼▼	5
○ Franciacorta Extra Brut	▼	5
○ TdF Curtefranca Bianco '08	▼	3
○ Franciacorta Brut '04	♀♀	5
○ Franciacorta Brut '02	♀♀	6
○ TdF Bianco Palanca '07	♀♀	3*

Monzio Compagnoni

VIA NIGOLINE, 18
25030 ADRO [BS]
TEL. 0307457803
www.monziocompagnoni.com

CELLAR SALES
PRE-BOOKED VISITS

ANNUAL PRODUCTION **250,000 bottles**
HECTARES UNDER VINE **30**
VITICULTURE METHOD **Conventional**

Marcello Monzio Compagnoni arrived in Franciacorta a few years ago from Valcalepio, where his original operation continues to thrive. In a few years, he has purchased 30 hectares of fine vineyards, which he tends personally, and a sophisticated cellar at Adro. Painstaking selection of the grapes and care lavished on every stage of fermentation and refermentation has allowed him to create some very fine cuvées, which rank among the designation's best.

Two Franciacortas reached our finals this year. Extra Brut '05 is an attractive bright straw tinged with pale green and has a continuous bead of tiny bubbles. The deep Brut '05 focuses on harmony and elegance, offering fruity pulp and a long, caressing finish. Satèn '05 is as good as ever, with a classic nose of apricot and vanilla and a plush, supple palate. Rosé '05 has rich aromas of red fruit and a juicy palate, while the impressive Bianco della Seta '07 gives medicinal herbs, white-fleshed fruit and charred oak. The other wines are very decent.

○ Franciacorta Brut '05	▼▼	5
○ Franciacorta Extra Brut '05	▼▼	6
⊙ Franciacorta Rosé '05	▼▼	6
○ Franciacorta Satèn '05	▼▼	6
○ TdF Curtefranca Bianco della Seta '07	▼▼	5
● Valcalepio Rosso di Luna '06	▼▼	5
○ TdF Curtefranca Bianco Ronco della Seta '08	▼	4
○ Valcalepio Bianco Colle della Luna '08	▼	3
○ Franciacorta Extra Brut '04	♀♀♀	6
○ Franciacorta Extra Brut '03	♀♀♀	6
○ Franciacorta Brut '02	♀♀	6
○ Franciacorta Satèn '03	♀♀	6
○ Franciacorta Satèn Brut '04	♀♀	6

Il Mosnel

LOC. CAMIGNONE
VIA BARBOGLIO, 14
25040 PASSIRANO [BS]
TEL. 030653117
www.ilmosnel.com

CELLAR SALES
PRE-BOOKED VISITS

ANNUAL PRODUCTION 250,000 bottles
HECTARES UNDER VINE 39
VITICULTURE METHOD Conventional

Giulio and Lucia Barzanò have taken over the reins of the family estate, a producer of excellent wines and Franciacortas since the late 1960s, from their mother Emanuela Barboglio. The winery is housed in a tastefully restored 16th-century building with the very latest cellar equipment. It is situated in Passirano di Camignone, surrounded by vineyards on a single 40-hectare plot, which is unusual in this area. These vineyards yield the top-quality grapes that go into a wide range of still wines and Franciacortas.

Il Mosnel has been crafting excellent products for years and constantly driving up quality. Three Glasses went to the Satèn '05, whose irresistible nose of ripe white fruit, cakes and vanilla is enlivened by elegant citrus notes. The fresh palate is invigorating and well orchestrated with a long mineral finish. Parosé '05 is pale pink but in the mouth there is surprising structure, full flavour and good acid backbone We were also very impressed by the Rosé, the very clean Brut and the Pas Dosé, which delivers spirited freshness, The rest of the scores ranged from good to excellent. Great stuff!

★ Nino Negri

VIA GHIBELLINI
23030 CHIURO [SO]
TEL. 0342485211
www.ninonegri.it

CELLAR SALES
PRE-BOOKED VISITS
RISTORAZIONE

ANNUAL PRODUCTION 000,000 bottles
HECTARES UNDER VINE 36
VITICULTURE METHOD Conventional

Founded in 1897 by Nino Negri, excellence has always been part of the furniture here but the cellar's period of greatest glory commenced during the second half of the 1980s when it joined Gruppo Italiano Vini, Italy's largest producer of quality wines, as the group's standard bearer. The old cellars are home to both tradition and the latest technologies, and the vineyards are in the zone's finest sites. The talented Casimiro Maule runs the estate with great sensitivity and has made it a leading name.

Sfursat 5 Stelle won Three Glasses again for its ability to express the austerity of the nebbiolo grape. The '06 has a complex nose with hints of dried flowers, leather and berry fruit, and a full, sharply defined palate with a deep, concentrated finish. Almost as good is the basic Sfursat, which shows a tad less complexity, while Mazer '06 offers a nose of quinine and plum and a deep, full-flavoured palate. Grumello Sassorosso '06 is gutsy, showing dry and well behaved on the palate, and the '06 Sassella Le Tense is a classic, with a nose of raspberry jam and a generous, balanced palate. The other wines are good.

Wine	Rating
O Franciacorta Satèn '05	♟♟♟ 6
⊙ Franciacorta Pas Dosé Parosé '05	♟♟ 6
O Franciacorta Brut	♟♟ 5
O Franciacorta Pas Dosé	♟♟ 5
⊙ Franciacorta Rosé	♟♟ 6
O Sebino Passito Sulif '06	♟♟ 6
O TdF Bianco Campolarga '08	♟♟ 4
O Franciacorta Brut Emanuela Barboglio '05	♟ 6
● TdF Curtefranca Rosso '06	♟ 4
O Franciacorta Brut '01	♟♟ 6
O Franciacorta Brut '00	♟♟ 6
O Franciacorta Brut Emanuela Barboglio '04	♟♟ 6
⊙ Franciacorta Pas Dosé Parosé '04	♟♟ 6

Wine	Rating
● Valtellina Sfursat 5 Stelle '06	♟♟♟ 8
● Valtellina Sfursat '06	♟♟ 7
● Valtellina Sup. Mazer '06	♟♟ 5
O Ca' Brione '08	♟♟ 6
● Valtellina Sup. Fracia '06	♟♟ 8
● Valtellina Sup. Grumello V. Sassorosso '06	♟♟ 5
● Valtellina Sup. Sassella Le Tense '06	♟♟ 5
● Valtellina Sfursat '05	♟♟♟ 8
● Valtellina Sfursat '04	♟♟♟ 7
● Valtellina Sfursat '03	♟♟♟ 7
● Valtellina Sfursat '02	♟♟♟ 6
● Valtellina Sfursat 5 Stelle '03	♟♟♟ 8
● Valtellina Sfursat 5 Stelle '02	♟♟♟ 7
● Valtellina Sfursat 5 Stelle '01	♟♟♟ 7

Olivini

LOC. DEMESSE VECCHIE, 2
25015 DESENZANO DEL GARDA [BS]
TEL. 0309910268
www.olivini.net

CELLAR SALES
PRE-BOOKED VISITS

ANNUAL PRODUCTION **130,000 bottles**
HECTARES UNDER VINE **26**
VITICULTURE METHOD **Conventional**

Giovanni, Giorgio and Giordana Olivini belong to a dynasty with other business interests but decided to convert the family land into a modern winery. In the space of a few years, the operation made the transition from hobby to quality production, with the help of oenologist Antonio Crescini. Today, Olivini boasts 26 hectares of fine vineyards and a thoroughly decent list, topped by the Lugana Brut.

Merlot Notte a San Martino, from grapes slightly dried before pressing, was the best of this year's wines. It shows dark ruby, with a nose of berry fruit and attractive oak. The palate is compact and pleasantly velvety, with good continuity, balance and length. Condolcezza, an opulent sweet wine made from part-dried turbiana grapes, is also very convincing. Lugana Brut performed well, showing fresh and fruity with mineral notes, and we expect the good basic Lugana and the Demesse Vecchie selection to improve yet further. The Chiaretto '08 is pleasant.

○ Condolcezza	♀♀	5
○ Lugana Brut	♀♀	5
● Notte a San Martino '05	♀♀	5
⊙ Garda Chiaretto Cl. '08	♀	4
○ Lugana '08	♀	4
○ Lugana Sup. Demesse Vecchie '06	♀	4
● Notte a San Martino '04	♀♀	5

Pasini - San Giovanni

FRAZ. RAFFA
VIA VIDELLE, 2
25080 PUEGNAGO SUL GARDA [BS]
TEL. 0365651419
www.pasiniproduttori.it

CELLAR SALES
PRE-BOOKED VISITS

ANNUAL PRODUCTION **300,000 bottles**
HECTARES UNDER VINE **36**
VITICULTURE METHOD **Conventional**

Founded 50 years ago, this fine family estate is now run by the third generation, with Luca and Paolo juggling work in vineyard and cellar with other commitments. Today, La Pasini is a leading estate, with land from Lugana to Valtènesi, and offers the typical wines of the Garda area, made with grapes from its 36 hectares of vineyards in various zones. Groppello is the leading wine in this area, and Pasini pays tribute to it with its excellent interpretations. However, the estate also offers new wines that explore the potential of all the local territory's grapes.

The excellent San Gioan I Carati '05 made it to our finals. An elegant blend of 70 per cent Cabernet Sauvignon aged in new oak and 30 per cent steel-aged Groppello, it is deep and flavoursome with prominent but well gauged spice and oak, and a fresh palate showing plush tannins and a juicy fruit finish. Groppello '08 offers crisp, sound fruit, a crisp aromas and pleasant drinkability. An elegant, balanced Riserva Arzane '06 completes the classy trio. Ceppo 326 Rosé is a well-made classic method sparkler but the white version is rather insubstantial and not quite so good. The Lugana '08 is nice, with plenty of backbone.

● San Gioan Rosso I Carati '05	♀♀	4*
⊙ Ceppo Rosé 326 M. Cl.	♀♀	5
● Garda Cl. Groppello Il Groppello '08	♀♀	4*
● Garda Cl. Groppello Vign. Arzane Ris. '06	♀♀	4*
○ Lugana Il Lugana '08	♀♀	4*
○ Ceppo Brut 326 M. Cl.	♀	5
⊙ Garda Cl. Chiaretto Il Chiaretto '08	♀	4
○ Lugana Brut	♀	4
○ San Gioan Brinat Bianco Dolce	♀	5
● San Gioan Rosso I Carati '04	♀♀	4*

Cascina La Pertica

LOC. PICEDO
VIA ROSARIO, 44
25080 POLPENAZZE DEL GARDA [BS]
TEL. 0365651471
www.cascinalapertica.it

CELLAR SALES
PRE-BOOKED VISITS

ANNUAL PRODUCTION **60,000 bottles**
HECTARES UNDER VINE **14**
VITICULTURE METHOD **Naturale**

Several years ago, successful businessman Ruggero Brunori founded an estate to make wine his way, using natural systems with low environmental impact. Over the years, winery manager Andrea Salvetti has helped him to ingrain this tendency and today the estate's 14 hectares in the morainic hills overlooking Lake Garda are farmed using biodynamic methods. The mainly clay soils give the wines structure and freshness.

Now a classic of Lombard winemaking, Cabernet Le Zalte '07 once again took Three Glasses. This full, flavoursome red has thrust and firm texture, boasting a complex nose of fruit and spice with vegetal hints. Its rich, deep palate reveals mellow tannins and a lingering fruit and oak finish. The chardonnay-based Le Sincette Bianco '08 is deep straw yellow with a complex nose of ripe white fruit and mineral notes leading into a firm, supple, well-orchestrated palate. Groppello '08 gives elegant berry fruit and the Pinot Nero has balance. Marzemino Papüc '08 is also good.

Andrea Picchioni

FRAZ. CAMPONOCE, 8
27044 CANNETO PAVESE [PV]
TEL. 0385262139
www.picchioniandrea.it

CELLAR SALES
PRE-BOOKED VISITS

ANNUAL PRODUCTION **60,000 bottles**
HECTARES UNDER VINE **10**
VITICULTURE METHOD **Naturale**

Year after year, Andrea Picchioni continues his steady winemaking and professional growth. His winery is small but this young grower is has plenty of enthusiasm and the validity of his work is confirmed by the results achieved with the aid of talented Oltrepò oenologist Beppe Zatti. The only "flaw", if we can call it that, is that Picchioni's big reds require many years to express themselves fully and often reach our tasting table when they are still too young.

While last year Picchioni made it to our finals with Profilo '97, a classic method sparkler aged ten years on the lees, this year it was the turn of Profilo '98 flanked by one of Andrea's beloved reds, Rosso d'Asia '05, from 90 per cent croatina and ten per cent ughetta di Canneto, It's fruity, balsamic and mineral, already perfectly drinkable but with great potential for ageing. The elegant Profilo '98 echoes the '97 in style, with cake-like notes, firm structure and good length. Buttafuoco Riva Bianca '05 has sound fruit, liquorice and characteristic balsam integrated in a wine that promises to age well.

● Garda Cabernet Le Zalte '07	♔♔♔	7
● Garda Cl. Groppello Il Colombaio '08	♔♔	4
○ Le Sincette Bianco '08	♔♔	4
● Il Marzemino Papüc '08	♔	4
● Garda Cabernet Le Zalte '05	♔♔♔	7
● Garda Cabernet Le Zalte '04	♔♔♔	7
● Garda Cabernet Le Zalte '03	♔♔♔	7
● Garda Cabernet Le Zalte '01	♔♔♔	7
● Garda Cabernet Le Zalte '00	♔♔♔	7
● Garda Cabernet Le Zalte '99	♔♔♔	5

○ OP Profilo Brut Nature M. Cl. '98	♔♔	6
● Rosso d'Asia '05	♔♔	5
● OP Bonarda Vivace '08	♔♔	4
● OP Buttafuoco Bricco Riva Bianca '05	♔♔	5
● OP Pinot Nero Arfena '07	♔♔	5
● OP Buttafuoco Luogo della Cerasa '07	♔	4
● OP Sangue di Giuda '08	♔	3
● Monnalisa '04	♔♔	5
● OP Bonarda '07	♔♔	3*
● OP Buttafuoco Bricco Riva Bianca '04	♔♔	5
○ OP Profilo Brut Nature M. Cl. '97	♔♔	6
● Pinot Nero Bricco Arfena '06	♔♔	5
● Rosso d'Asia '04	♔♔	5

Plozza

VIA SAN GIACOMO, 22
23037 TIRANO [SO]
TEL. 0342701297
www.plozza.com

CELLAR SALES
PRE-BOOKED VISITS

ANNUAL PRODUCTION **450,000 bottles**
HECTARES UNDER VINE **28**
VITICULTURE METHOD **Conventional**

Plozza has been a name in winemaking for over 80 years but its history as a grower started in 1973. Headed by oenologist Marco Zanolari and his son Andrea, Plozza offers various product ranges, some aimed at the international market and others inspired by tradition. The winery's quest for quality and its extreme attention to packaging give it a well-defined identity, which has been boosted by large investments to purchase the finest vineyards and for the recent renovation of the cellar and the barrel stock.

Numero Uno '05, from part-dried nebbiolo, has elegant fruit that mingles with sweet notes from the judicious use of oak, while Sfursat Vin da Ca' 05 unfolds a fresh, juicy palate with elegant aromas and big varietal body. The unusual Passione '04 is a Nebbiolo with an international flavour that throws a complex, spicy nose with hints of dried flowers and a harmonious palate. Sassella La Scala Riserva '05 is good, with a fruity nose, soft tannins and a long finish, and Grumello Riserva '05 has admirable structure, with dry, floral aromas. Inferno Riserva '05 has an elegant nose, succulent palate and good ageing prospects.

Mamete Prevostini

VIA LUCCHINETTI, 63
23020 MESE [SO]
TEL. 034341522
www.mameteprevostini.com

CELLAR SALES
PRE-BOOKED VISITS

ANNUAL PRODUCTION **160,000 bottles**
HECTARES UNDER VINE **18**
VITICULTURE METHOD **Conventional**

Mamete Prevostini did exceptionally well this year, despite failing to take its usual Three Glasses. Impressively, three wines came very close to achieving the feat. This winery has taken giant steps over the past few years and its success is due in particular to Mamete, whose professional growth and competence have recently earned him the chairmanship the Consorzio Vini di Valtellina.

The Sforzatos Albareda '07 and Corte di Cama '07 jostle for the limelight. The first has an elegant nose of dried flowers and minerality, and a rounded palate with a long, full-flavoured finish. The second is more traditional, showing nice black fruits, complexity, a generous palate and a lingering finish. Sassella San Lorenzo '06 has a subtle tobacco-themed nose and a full-flavoured palate with well-distributed tannins and Sommarovina '07 shows fruity and floral on the nose and balanced on the palate, Grumello '07 and '08 are easy-drinkers and the modern Botonero '08 is fragrant and very drinkable. Opera'08 is fruity and floral.

Plozza		
● Valtellina Numero Uno '05	♈♈	8
● Valtellina Sforzato Vin da Ca' '05	♈♈	6
● Passione Barrique '04	♈♈	7
● Valtellina Sup. Grumello Ris. '05	♈♈	4
● Valtellina Sup. Inferno Ris. '05	♈♈	5
● Valtellina Sup. Sassella La Scala Ris. '05	♈♈	4
● Valtellina Numero Uno '01	♈♈♈	8
● Passione Barrique '03	♈♈	7
● Valtellina Numero Uno '04	♈♈	8
● Valtellina Numero Uno '03	♈♈	8
● Valtellina Sforzato Vin da Ca' '04	♈♈	6
● Valtellina Sforzato Vin da Ca' '03	♈♈	6
● Valtellina Sup. Inferno Ris. '04	♈♈	5
● Valtellina Sup. Sassella La Scala Ris. '04	♈♈	4*
● Valtellina Sup. Sassella La Scala Ris. '03	♈♈	4

Mamete Prevostini		
● Valtellina Sforzato Albareda '07	♈♈	7
● Valtellina Sup. Corte di Cama '07	♈♈	6
● Valtellina Sup. Sassella San Lorenzo '06	♈♈	6
● Valtellina Sup. Sassella '07	♈♈	4
● Valtellina Sup. Sassella Sommarovina '07	♈♈	5
● Botonero '08	♈	3
○ Opera Bianco '08	♈	5
● Valtellina Santarita '08	♈	4
● Valtellina Sup. Grumello '07	♈	4
● Valtellina Sforzato Albareda '06	♈♈♈	7
● Valtellina Sforzato Albareda '05	♈♈♈	7
● Valtellina Sforzato Albareda '04	♈♈♈	7
● Valtellina Sforzato Albareda '03	♈♈♈	7
● Valtellina Sup. Corte di Cama '06	♈♈	6
● Valtellina Sup. Corte di Cama '05	♈♈	6

Provenza

VIA DEI COLLI STORICI
25015 DESENZANO DEL GARDA [BS]
TEL. 0309910006
www.provenzacantine.it

CELLAR SALES
PRE-BOOKED VISITS

ANNUAL PRODUCTION 1.500,000 bottles
HECTARES UNDER VINE 120
VITICULTURE METHOD Conventional

This winery founded by Walter Contato during the 1960s is currently experiencing rapid growth in size – with 120 hectares of fine vineyards located between Valtènesi and Lugana – and quality. In recent years, Walter's children Fabio and Patrizia have further improved the already successful production, which now occupies a leading position in the area, with some of the most representative wines of the DOC zones in question. The wines have gained greater varietal definition and intensity, as attested by many awards.

While Lugana Fabio Contato '08 did not repeat the previous vintage's success, it is a charmer with an elegant nose of citrus-veined fruit and yeast followed by an opulent, buttery palate with nice length. Lugana Molin '08 impressed with its clean style and fresh acidity supporting full-flavoured, generous structure. The Bordeaux-style Giomè '08 has backbone, flesh and soft tannins while Garda Classico Fabio Contato '06 is satisfyingly assertive. Lugana Brut Metodo Classico Ca' Maiol has refreshing florality and white-fleshed fruit on nose and palate. Garda Negresco '07, Tenuta Maiolo '08 and Chiaretto Tenuta Maiolo '08 are captivating, as are the other wines.

Quaquarini

LOC. MONTEVENEROSO
VIA CASA ZAMBIANCHI, 26
27044 CANNETO PAVESE [PV]
TEL. 038560152
www.quaquarinifrancesco.it

CELLAR SALES
PRE-BOOKED VISITS

ANNUAL PRODUCTION 650,000 bottles
HECTARES UNDER VINE 60
VITICULTURE METHOD Biologico certificato

Francesco Quaquarini founded the winery that he runs together with his wife Liliana and his children Umberto, oenologist, and Maria Teresa, sales manager. It is situated in Monteveneroso in the municipality of Canneto Pavese. The wines are produced using organic farming methods and are always interesting. Following a few small hiccups in past years, quality has risen consistently across the list, with several peaks of excellence starting to emerge.

This year, we liked the classic method Classese with its good fruit, pleasing continuity on the palate, backbone and nice development into a long finish. Buttafuoco Storico Vigna Pregana '03 suffered from the hot growing year and has over-evolved, overripe fruit. The young version of Buttafuoco, Vigna La Guasca '07, offers spicy notes with attractive aromas of chocolate and wild berries. We were also impressed by the '08 vintage of the two Sangue di Giudas. Vigna Acqua Calda is firmer, with aromas of cakes, while the basic version is simpler but equally pleasant, giving wild berries.

O Lugana Sup. Sel. Fabio Contato '08	⬥⬥	6
● Garda Cl. Rosso Negresco '07	⬥⬥	5
● Garda Cl. Rosso Sel. Fabio Contato '06	⬥⬥	6
● Garda Cl. Rosso Tenuta Maiolo '08	⬥⬥	4
● Giomè '08	⬥⬥	5
O Lugana Brut Cl. Ca' Maiol	⬥⬥	5
O Lugana Sup. Molin '08	⬥⬥	5
☉ Garda Cl. Chiaretto Roseri '08	⬥	4
☉ Garda Cl. Chiaretto Tenuta Maiolo '08	⬥	4
● Garda Cl. Groppello Tenuta Maiolo '08	⬥	4
O Sol Doré '07	⬥	5
O Lugana Sup. Sel. Fabio Contato '07	⬥⬥⬥	6

● OP Bonarda Frizzante '08	⬥⬥	3
● OP Buttafuoco Storico V. Pregana '03	⬥⬥	6
● OP Buttafuoco V. La Guasca '07	⬥⬥	4
O OP Pinot Nero Brut Classese	⬥⬥	4*
● OP Sangue di Giuda '08	⬥⬥	3*
● OP Sangue di Giuda Acqua Calda '08	⬥⬥	4
● OP Pinot Nero Blau '06	⬥	4
● OP Rosso Magister '08	⬥	4
● OP Bonarda Frizzante '07	⬥⬥	3*
● OP Bonarda Frizzante '06	⬥⬥	3*
O OP Classese Brut	⬥⬥	4*
● OP Pinot Nero Blau '05	⬥⬥	4*
● OP Sangue di Giuda '07	⬥⬥	3*
● OP Sangue di Giuda V. Acqua Calda '06	⬥⬥	4*

Aldo Rainoldi

VIA STELVIO, 128
23030 CHIURO [SO]
TEL. 0342482225
www.rainoldi.com

CELLAR SALES
PRE-BOOKED VISITS

ANNUAL PRODUCTION 220,000 bottles
HECTARES UNDER VINE 9.8
VITICULTURE METHOD Conventional

Peppino Rainoldi and his nephew Aldo make wines with strong personalities. Although the Rainoldis' estate is small, over the years they have established a two-way relationship with their growers based on agronomic competence and the quest for quality. Furthermore, they have not concentrated just on the evident qualities of their Sforzatos but have also sought excellence in their Riservas, bringing out the best of the various terroirs where nebbiolo rules supreme.

Sforzato Ca' Rizzieri '06 has a complex, spice-laced balsamic nose, an elegant palate with balanced structure, and soft tannins that make it highly drinkable. Inferno Riserva '05 is elegant with a warm, concentrated nose featuring hints of quinine. On the palate it's juicy, with a long, silky finish. Tar can be discerned among the intense aromatics of Sassella Riserva '05, which has a complex palate with a long, dry finish. The well-typed Grumello '05 delivers deep fruity aromas while the Crespino has warm, spicy notes. Brut Rosé '05, from nebbiolo, is also good, showing deep pink with a concentrated nose and a lively palate of wild berry pulp.

Ricci Curbastro

VIA ADRO, 37
25031 CAPRIOLO [BS]
TEL. 030736094
www.riccicurbastro.it

CELLAR SALES
PRE-BOOKED VISITS

ANNUAL PRODUCTION 240,000 bottles
HECTARES UNDER VINE 27.5
VITICULTURE METHOD Conventional

Agronomist and keen oenologist Riccardo Ricci Curbastro took over the family estate in the mid 1980s and patiently commenced renovating the cellar and vineyards, enabling the winery to become one of the best in the designated zone in just a few years. Today Ricci Curbastro, housed in the handsome family villa in Capriolo, has almost 30 hectares of vineyards in the finest positions and produces a complete range of Franciacortas and local wines. The interesting agricultural museum adjoining the villa is well worth a visit.

Franciacorta Extra Brut '05 made it into our finals on the strength of its generous complexity. Its concentrated nose of fruit offers mineral and citrus aromas and sweet yeasty hints. The coherent palate is complex and distinctly dry but with succulent fruit. We were also impressed by the Satèn, with medlar and white peaches on the nose and a velvety, supple palate. The non-vintage Brut is exemplary, showing firm and rounded on the full-flavoured, citrussy palate, and the well-balanced, apricot-themed Demi Sec is also very good. We loved the Rosé while our favourite from the still wines was the excellent Pinot Nero '06.

● Valtellina Sfursat Fruttaio Ca' Rizzieri '06	♚♚♚	7
● Valtellina Sup. Inferno Ris. '05	♚♚	6
☉ Brut Rosé '05	♚♚	5
● Valtellina Sup. Crespino '05	♚♚	6
● Valtellina Sup. Grumello '05	♚♚	4
● Valtellina Sup. Sassella Ris. '05	♚♚	5
● Valtellina Sfursat Fruttaio Ca' Rizzieri '02	♚♚♚	7
● Valtellina Sfursat Fruttaio Ca' Rizzieri '00	♚♚♚	7
● Valtellina Sfursat '03	♚♚	6
● Valtellina Sfursat '02	♚♚	6
● Valtellina Sfursat Fruttaio Ca' Rizzieri '04	♚♚	7
● Valtellina Sfursat Fruttaio Ca' Rizzieri '01	♚♚	7
● Valtellina Sup. Inferno Ris. '02	♚♚	5
● Valtellina Sup. Sassella Ris. '01	♚♚	5

○ Franciacorta Extra Brut '05	♚♚	5
○ Brolo dei Passoni	♚♚	5
○ Franciacorta Brut	♚♚	5
☉ Franciacorta Brut Rosé	♚♚	6
○ Franciacorta Demi Sec	♚♚	5
○ Franciacorta Satèn	♚♚	5
● Pinot Nero '06	♚♚	5
○ TdF Curtefranca V. Bosco Alto '06	♚♚	4
○ Sebino Bianco '08	♚	5
● Sebino Rosso '07	♚	2
○ TdF Bianco Curtefranca '08	♚	3
○ Franciacorta Extra Brut '03	♚♚	5*
○ Franciacorta Extra Brut '02	♚♚	6
○ Franciacorta Extra Brut '01	♚♚	6
○ Franciacorta Satèn Brut '03	♚♚	6
○ Franciacorta Extra Brut '05	♚	5

Ronco Calino

FRAZ. TORBIATO
LOC. QUATTRO CAMINI
VIA FENICE, 45
25030 ADRO [BS]
TEL. 0307451073
www.roncocalino.it

PRE-BOOKED VISITS

ANNUAL PRODUCTION **50,000 bottles**
HECTARES UNDER VINE **10**
VITICULTURE METHOD **Conventional**

In 1996, successful businessman Paolo Radici decided to purchase and move into the handsome villa in Calino that had belonged to pianist Arturo Benedetti Michelangeli. Radici soon replanted the surrounding vineyards and built a state-of-the-art cellar for the production of Franciacortas. Today the estate, comprising around ten hectares of vineyards, offers a complete range of wines made with the advice of Professor Leonardo Valenti from the University of Milan.

This year, we tasted an excellent Brut '05 with elegant aromas of fruit and vanilla, which unfolds fresh and savoury on the palate, with sound fruit and caressing fizz. We were also very impressed by the rich, buttery Satèn, which is pleasantly plush and buoyed by a fresh vein of acidity. Rosé Radijan is as good as ever, showing spirited with a mineral finish, while the Franciacorta Brut is very decent, although we found it slightly less complex than in past vintages.

○ Franciacorta Brut '05	♟♟ 6
⊙ Franciacorta Brut Rosé Radijan	♟♟ 6
○ Franciacorta Satèn	♟♟ 5
○ Franciacorta Brut	♟ 5
○ Franciacorta Brut '01	♟♟ 6
○ Franciacorta Brut	♟♟ 5
○ TdF Bianco '06	♟♟ 4*
● TdF Rosso '04	♟♟ 5

Tenuta Roveglia

LOC. ROVEGLIA, 1
25010 POZZOLENGO [BS]
TEL. 030918663
www.tenutaroveglia.it

CELLAR SALES
PRE-BOOKED VISITS

ANNUAL PRODUCTION **250,000 bottles**
HECTARES UNDER VINE **61**
VITICULTURE METHOD **Conventional**

Tenuta Roveglia is a fine estate with approximately 60 hectares of vineyards in the Lugana district, almost all of them planted to turbiana. In these clay soils, this cultivar yields elegant, deep wines, encouraging winery manager Paolo Fabiani and oenologist Flavio Prà to press on. In recent years, the estate's wines, particularly the Luganas, have found their place among the best in the designated area thanks to scrupulous selection in the vineyard and sophisticated cellar techniques.

This year, the richly structured Lugana Superiore Vigne di Catullo '08 made it to our finals. It boasts a complex nose of white fruit with floral, citrus and mineral notes, and a fresh, rounded palate supported by a refreshing vein of acidity that perks up the long finish. Lugana Filo di Arianna '06, made with late-harvest grapes from the oldest vineyards, displays complexity on the nose and depth on the palate, with rich fruit. The refreshing, supple Lugana '08 is very decent while Garda Cabernet Sauvignon Ca' d'Oro '06 is rounded and pleasant.

○ Lugana Sup. Vigne di Catullo '07	♟♟ 4*
● Garda Cabernet Sauvignon Ca' d'Oro '06	♟♟ 5
○ Lugana '08	♟♟ 4*
○ Lugana Sup. Filo di Arianna '06	♟♟ 5
⊙ Garda Cl. Chiaretto '08	♟ 4
○ Lugana Brut	♟ 4
○ Lugana '07	♟♟ 4*
○ Lugana Sup. Filo di Arianna '05	♟♟ 5
○ Lugana Sup. Vigne di Catullo '05	♟♟ 4

San Cristoforo

VIA VILLANUOVA, 2
25030 ERBUSCO [BS]
TEL. 0307760482
www.sancristoforo.eu

CELLAR SALES
PRE-BOOKED VISITS

ANNUAL PRODUCTION **80,000 bottles**
HECTARES UNDER VINE **12**
VITICULTURE METHOD **Conventional**

Bruno Dotti and his wife Claudia Cavalleri invest great enthusiasm and competence in this Erbusco winery, purchased in 1992 and successively extended and improved in terms of quality. Today, the Dottis own 12 hectares of vineyards and a modern cellar that, together with the commitment and passion they lavish on their work, explain the estate's impressive progress in the quality stakes.

Franciacorta Pas Dosé '05 strolled into our finals with its attractive rich structure, succulent fruit, refreshing acidity and a pleasant floral bouquet with hints of white peaches, apricots and delicate citrus notes. The Brut from the same vintage is softer but equally well orchestrated, with a long mineral finish, caressing effervescence and impressive harmony. As usual, the non-vintage Franciacorta Brut is very decent, making it one of the DOCG's most reliable wines. The Franciacorta Rosé is elegant and refined, although a little more structure wouldn't have gone amiss. San Cristoforo Uno '05, a structured Bordeaux blend, is also very good.

Pietro Torti

FRAZ. CASTELROTTO, 9
27047 MONTECALVO VERSIGGIA [PV]
TEL. 038599763
www.pietrotorti.it

CELLAR SALES
PRE-BOOKED VISITS

ANNUAL PRODUCTION **30,000 bottles**
HECTARES UNDER VINE **10**
VITICULTURE METHOD **Conventional**

Passion and misfortune. The very same year that Sandro Torti earned a full profile for the estate that bears his father's name, a landslide wiped away the vineyard from which he used to make one of the zone's most interesting Riesling Italicos. We hope that the excellent results achieved in the tastings of this edition of the Guide will encourage Sandro to persevere and continue the work commenced by his late father, without losing heart.

We'd like to start with the Riesling '08 and its floral notes accompanied by intriguing hydrocarbons, its close-focused, well-defined palate and its long finish. Metodo Classico '06 has nice bubbles and subtly caressing aromas of medicinal herbs, peach tea and cakes. As always, Bonarda Vivace '08 is one of Oltrepò's best, showing compact, taut and deep with a nose of hay and raspberries. The spicy, fruity Barbera Campo Rivera '05 is well typed and the '06 Pinot Nero may well be the best ever with firm structure, nice tannins and more elegance than in previous vintages. The still Bonarda Verzello '08 is pleasant and harmonious.

○ Franciacorta Pas Dosé '05	♈♈ 6
○ Franciacorta Brut '05	♈♈ 6
○ Franciacorta Brut	♈♈ 5
● San Cristoforo Uno '05	♈♈ 5
☉ Franciacorta Rosé	♈ 5
● Re Probus '05	♈ 7
○ TdF Curtefranca Bianco '08	♈ 4
● TdF Curtefranca Rosso '06	♈ 4
○ Franciacorta Brut '04	♈♈ 6
○ Franciacorta Pas Dosé '04	♈♈ 6
○ TdF Bianco '05	♈♈ 3*

● OP Barbera Campo Rivera '05	♈♈ 4
● OP Bonarda Verzello '08	♈♈ 4*
● OP Bonarda Vivace '08	♈♈ 3*
● OP Pinot Nero '06	♈♈ 5
○ OP Pinot Nero Brut M. Cl. Torti '06	♈♈ 5
○ OP Riesling Italico '08	♈♈ 3
○ Fagù '06	♈♈ 4*
○ Fagù '05	♈♈ 3
● OP Bonarda Vivace '07	♈♈ 3*
● OP Bonarda Vivace '06	♈♈ 3*
● OP Bonarda Vivace '05	♈♈ 3
● OP Pinot Nero '03	♈♈ 5

Travaglino

Loc. Travaglino, 6a
27040 Calvignano [PV]
tel. 0383872222
www.travaglino.it

CELLAR SALES
PRE-BOOKED VISITS

ANNUAL PRODUCTION 220,000 bottles
HECTARES UNDER VINE 80
VITICULTURE METHOD Conventional

The winery managed by Fabrizio Marzi is notable for its classic method sparklers and whites. Indeed, its excellent position and white chalk soils make it especially well suited for growing pinot nero and white grapes. While the estate's wines have always displayed good structure, we are pleased to note that elegance has increased considerably over the years. Travaglino is a member of the Valle del Riesling association.

Riesling Campo della Fojada '08 very nearly made it into our finals, with its firm structure, well-defined acid backbone, long finish and characteristic aromas of spring flowers that mingle with an intriguing mixture of sage and mint medicinal herbs. The new sparkling Cuvée 59 '06 scored well for its cleanliness and drinkability, as did Rosé Monteceresino, which brims with wild berries with hints of coffee and toast. Chardonnay Campo della Mojetta '05 is well executed and structured, although slightly overpowered by vanilla from the oak.

Triacca

Via Nazionale, 121
23030 Villa di Tirano [SO]
tel. 0342701352
www.triacca.com

CELLAR SALES
PRE-BOOKED VISITS

ANNUAL PRODUCTION 700,000 bottles
HECTARES UNDER VINE 47
VITICULTURE METHOD Conventional

This prestigious historic estate, owned by a family of Swiss growers for over 100 years, has recently undergone a shake-up. The talented Domenico Triacca has resigned, leaving leadership to his cousins Giovanni and Luca Triacca. They have a veritable agricultural heritage, comprising numerous vineyards replanted with selected clones and vinification and harvesting techniques that have gone down in Valtellina's wine history. The Triaccas own other estates in Tuscany in the Chianti Classico, Morellino di Scansano and Vino Nobile di Montepulciano zones.

Casa La Gatta '06 surprised us with an unusual, very elegant nose of dried flowers and mineral notes, with harmonious fruit and a juicy, flavoursome palate with a long finish. The well-typed Riserva La Gatta '04 is a true Nebbiolo, with complex aromas of tobacco, firm structure and a good tannic weave. Inferno '06 has a warm nose and an elegant palate while Grumello '06 has fruity aromas and a velvety attack with a pleasant encore of fruit. Prestigio '05 is excellent, with a plush, caressing palate, while the white Del Frate '07, from sauvignon, and La Contea '08, from mainly rossola, are also very nice.

○ OP Pinot Nero Brut Cl. Cuvée 59 '06	♟♟	5
⊙ OP Pinot Nero Brut Rosé Monteceresino	♟♟	5
○ OP Riesling Campo della Fojada '08	♟♟	4
○ OP Chardonnay Campo della Mojetta '05	♟	4
○ OP Gran Cuvée Brut	♟	5
● OP Pinot Nero Pernero '08	♟	4
● OP Pinot Nero Poggio della Buttinera '04	♟	5
○ OP Pinot Nero Brut Classese '04	♟♟	5
○ OP Pinot Nero Brut Classese '03	♟♟	5
○ OP Pinot Nero Brut Classese '01	♟♟	5
○ OP Riesling Campo della Fojada '07	♟♟	4
○ OP Riesling Campo della Fojada '06	♟♟	4

● Valtellina Sup. Prestigio '05	♟♟	7
● Valtellina Sup. Casa La Gatta '06	♟♟	5
● Valtellina Sup. Grumello '06	♟♟	5
● Valtellina Sup. Inferno '06	♟♟	5
● Valtellina Sup. La Gatta Ris. '04	♟♟	6
○ La Contea Bianco '08	♟	5
○ Sauvignon Del Frate '07	♟	6
● Valtellina Sforzato San Domenico '03	♟♟♟	7
● Valtellina Sforzato San Domenico '01	♟♟♟	7
● Valtellina Sforzato San Domenico '02	♟♟	7
● Valtellina Sup. Prestigio '04	♟♟	7

★ Uberti

LOC. SALEM
VIA E. FERMI, 2
25030 ERBUSCO [BS]
TEL. 0307267476
www.ubertivini.it

PRE-BOOKED VISITS

ANNUAL PRODUCTION 180,000 bottles
HECTARES UNDER VINE 24
VITICULTURE METHOD Conventional

Agostino and Eleonora Uberti are récoltants-manipulants, or grower-producers. They have expanded the family winery – the Ubertis have been growers since the 18th century – from an annual production of a few thousand bottles 30 years ago to 180,000 today, increasing the holding to 24 hectares and promoting several gems, like the Comari del Salem vineyard in Erbusco, an authentic Franciacorta grand cru. Their daughters are involved in the work and oenologist Silvia now flanks her father in the cellar while her sister Francesca deals with the hospitality side of the business.

Extra Brut Comarì del Salem '04 came within an ace of Three Glasses. Its attractive bright golden straw introduces a complex nose of honey and ripe fruit, with hints of tobacco, hazelnut, coffee and white-fleshed fruit. The elegant, complex palate offers sound, citrus-veined fruit and vanilla. The Non Dosato Sublimis '03 is intriguing and evolved, with aromas of antique wood, beeswax and mineral notes that are nicely echoed on the acidity-braced palate. Franciacorta Brut Francesco I is refreshing and elegant, with enough harmony to make it the DOCG's best non-vintage Brut. The rest of the list is of the usual excellent standard.

Vanzini

FRAZ. BARBALEONE, 7
27040 SAN DAMIANO AL COLLE [PV]
TEL. 038575019
www.vanzini-wine.com

CELLAR SALES
PRE-BOOKED VISITS

ANNUAL PRODUCTION 800,000 bottles
HECTARES UNDER VINE 17
VITICULTURE METHOD Conventional

The Vanzini brothers' estate has earned a full profile with its convincing range of wines and, no less importantly at a time like this, its excellent value for money. It has few rivals in Oltrepò when it comes to wines refermented in pressure tanks, whether they be semi-sparkling or Charmat method sparklers. We confidently await the development of the more important wines and, perhaps, the addition of a Classic Method sparkler, because the potential is certainly there.

Bonarda Frizzante '08 again turned out to be one of the best in the zone, presenting an impenetrable ruby with aromas of violets and wild berries, a complex scented palate and balanced tannins. Much the same can be said for Sangue di Giuda '08, with its fine mousse, crisp fruit, balanced tannins and residual sugar. Excellent scores also went to the two pleasant '08 Barberas, in still and semi-sparkling versions, which have particularly sound fruit. Both the traditional Extra Dry Charmat method sparklers from pinot nero offer very satisfactory freshness, softness and drinkability, although we slightly preferred the Rosé.

O Franciacorta Extra Brut Comarì del Salem '04	♟♟ 7
O Franciacorta Non Dosato Sublimis '03	♟♟ 7
O Franciacorta Brut Francesco I	♟♟ 6
O Franciacorta Satèn Magnificentia	♟♟ 6
● Rosso dei Frati Priori	♟♟ 6
O TdF Bianco Maria Medici '07	♟♟ 5
⊙ Franciacorta Brut Rosé Francesco I	♟ 5
O Franciacorta Extra Brut Francesco I	♟ 6
O TdF Bianco Curtefranca '08	♟ 4
O Franciacorta Extra Brut Comarì del Salem '03	♟♟♟ 7
O Franciacorta Extra Brut Comarì del Salem '02	♟♟♟ 7
O Franciacorta Non Dosato Sublimis '02	♟♟ 7
O Franciacorta Non Dosato Sublimis '01	♟♟ 7
O Franciacorta Non Dosato Sublimis '00	♟♟ 7

● OP Barbera '08	♟♟ 4*
● OP Barbera Frizzante '08	♟♟ 4*
● OP Bonarda Frizzante '08	♟♟ 3*
● OP Pinot Nero '06	♟♟ 5
⊙ OP Pinot Nero Rosé Extra Dry	♟♟ 4
● OP Sangue di Giuda '08	♟♟ 4*
O OP Moscato Spumante	♟ 3
O OP Pinot Nero Extra Dry	♟ 4
● OP Barbera '06	♟♟ 3*
● OP Bonarda Frizzante '07	♟♟ 3*
● OP Bonarda Frizzante '06	♟♟ 3*
● OP Sangue di Giuda '07	♟♟ 4*
● OP Sangue di Giuda '06	♟♟ 4*
● OP Sangue di Giuda '05	♟♟ 4*

Vercesi del Castellazzo

VIA AURELIANO, 36
27040 MONTÙ BECCARIA [PV]
TEL. 038560067
vercesidelcastellazzo@libero.it

CELLAR SALES
PRE-BOOKED VISITS

ANNUAL PRODUCTION **80,000 bottles**
HECTARES UNDER VINE **15**
VITICULTURE METHOD **Conventional**

The Vercesi family's winery, with the handsome 16th-century Castellazzo that dominates the municipality of Montù Beccaria, is a legendary name on the eastern slopes of the Valle Versa. The soil here gives wines plenty of tannins and a consequent hardness in their youth. These bottles need time to express themselves fully, as shown by the excellent Pinot Nero '98 that we tasted last year. However, the wines presented are always more than good.

Fatila, a still Bonarda that reached last year's finals, was absent but we tasted the elegant, beefy, barbera and cabernet sauvignon Rosso del Castellazzo '04, which gives balsam and bottled cherries. Barbera Clà '07 is very good, with sound fruit, chocolate and liquorice. Pinot Nero Luogo dei Monti '06 is well defined and varietal, although still with a way to go. Bonarda Frizzante Luogo della Milla '08 is well made, with fragrant fruit and elegant floral notes. The two basic reds, Pezzalunga and Bacca Rossa '08, are fresh and uncomplicated while Gugiarolo '08, a fragrant still Pinot Nero fermented off the skins, is nice.

Bruno Verdi

VIA VERGOMBERRA, 5
27044 CANNETO PAVESE [PV]
TEL. 038588023
www.verdibruno.it

CELLAR SALES
PRE-BOOKED VISITS

ANNUAL PRODUCTION **100,000 bottles**
HECTARES UNDER VINE **9**
VITICULTURE METHOD **Conventional**

Paolo Verdi is a tough nut. Last spring, he was hit particularly hard by the landslides in Oltrepò which swept away a piece of his historic Cavariola vineyard, including almost all of a highly promising pinot nero vineyard at Casa Zoppini. However, he did not lose heart and has continued the hard work that has allowed him to reach our finals for the ninth time with the estate's flagship wine, which is one of Oltrepò's classics.

Cavariola '06 is a classic Rosso Oltrepò di Canneto Pavese, with prominent balsamic notes associated with unusually sound fruit, depth and balance. Pinot Nero '07 is very varietal and spicy, improving year after year but unfortunately wiped out by the landslide that will preclude vintages from 2009 onwards. Riesling Vigna Costa and Pinot Grigio '08 are also well made and varietal while Moscato Volpara '08 is excellent. Bonarda Possessione di Vergombera '08 is very nice, with prominent raspberry and blueberry, and the classic method Vergomberra Brut '05 is sumptuous and refreshing, with a heady nose of cakes.

● OP Barbera Clà '07	♟♟	4
● OP Bonarda Frizzante Luogo della Milla '08	♟♟	3*
● OP Pinot Nero Luogo dei Monti '06	♟♟	4
● Rosso del Castellazzo '04	♟♟	5
● Bacca Rossa '08	♟	2*
○ OP Pinot Nero in Bianco Gugiarolo '08	♟	3
● OP Rosso Pezzalunga '08	♟	3
● OP Barbera Clà '06	♟♟	4*
● OP Bonarda Fatila '03	♟♟	5
● OP Bonarda Luogo della Milla '07	♟♟	3*
● OP Pinot Nero Luogo dei Monti '98	♟♟	7*
● OP Rosso Pezzalunga '07	♟♟	3*
● Rosso del Castellazzo '03	♟♟	5

● OP Rosso Cavariola Ris. '06	♟♟	5
● OP Bonarda Vivace Possessione di Vergombera '08	♟♟	4*
○ OP Moscato Volpara '08	♟♟	3*
○ OP Pinot Grigio '08	♟♟	4*
● OP Pinot Nero '07	♟♟	4
○ OP Riesling Renano V. Costa '08	♟♟	4*
○ OP Vergomberra Brut '05	♟♟	5
● OP Buttafuoco '07	♟	4
● OP Barbera Campo del Marrone '06	♟♟	4*
● OP Pinot Nero '06	♟♟	4*
● OP Rosso Cavariola Ris. '05	♟♟	5
● OP Rosso Cavariola Ris. '04	♟♟	5
● OP Rosso Cavariola Ris. '03	♟♟	5
● OP Rosso Cavariola Ris. '02	♟♟	5

Giuseppe Vezzoli

VIA COSTA SOPRA, 22
25030 ERBUSCO [BS]
TEL. 0307267579
eveniogv@libero.it

CELLAR SALES
PRE-BOOKED VISITS

ANNUAL PRODUCTION **130,000 bottles**
HECTARES UNDER VINE **40**
VITICULTURE METHOD **Conventional**

Several years ago, Giuseppe Vezzoli took over from his father Attilio, leaving his job in an unrelated sector to tend the small family vineyard and giving the estate an amazing boost. He swiftly expanded the original five hectares to approximately 40, estate-owned and leased, and built a modern, well-equipped cellar that enables the production of high-quality wines, with input from oenologist Cesare Ferrari. The estate's cuvées are now among the most reliable in the DOCG.

Extra Brut Nefertiti Dizeta '03 made it through to our finals with an elegant nose, whose hints of toast and hazelnut never mask the fruit, and a juicy, tangy palate that ends unhurriedly on peach, hazelnut and medicinal herbs. The non-vintage Brut is very similar, just a little less complex and exuberant, but shows equally impressive balance, while the outstanding Satèn has a fruity nose and a zesty palate. Although the rather smoky Brut '05 is less alluring, it is still pleasant. The highly drinkable slim-bodied Rosé is also good.

Villa

VIA VILLA, 12
25040 MONTICELLI BRUSATI [BS]
TEL. 030652329
www.villafranciacorta.it

OSPITALITÀ
RISTORAZIONE

ANNUAL PRODUCTION **300,000 bottles**
HECTARES UNDER VINE **37**
VITICULTURE METHOD **Conventional**

The Bianchi family purchased the ancient settlement of Villa, at Monticelli Brusati, along with 100 hectares of surrounding land in the 1960s, and over the years have restored it to its original splendour. Today, the winery is surrounded by 37 hectares of vines, including the Gradoni vineyard planted on the dry-stone terraces of the Madonna della Rosa hill. The well-equipped cellar and first-rate technical staff make it possible to release a complete range of Franciacortas and local wines. Sandro Bianchi's winery has long been one of the best in Franciacorta.

The top scorer was Franciacorta Brut '05, which exemplifies the house style with its fresh floral nose and clear white peach and ripe pear, accompanied by a juicy palate. Excellent bottle fermentation gives it creamy prickle and a long finish. Rosé Demi Sec is elegant and delicate, with rich texture, enchanting violet aromas and a long, harmonious finish. The silky, slim-bodied Brut Rosé '05 is very attractive and highly drinkable with a wild berry theme. We also liked the Satèn '05, which has a complex nose of fruit, flowers and vanilla and a balanced palate. Curtefranca Bianco '07 is flavoursome, and the other wines are good.

○ Franciacorta Extra Brut Nefertiti Dizeta '03	♙♙ 7
○ Franciacorta Brut	♙♙ 6
○ Franciacorta Brut Nefertiti '05	♙♙ 7
○ Franciacorta Satèn	♙♙ 6
○ Franciacorta Brut '05	♙ 6
⊙ Franciacorta Rosé	♙ 6
○ Franciacorta Brut '04	♟♟ 6
○ Franciacorta Brut '03	♟♟ 6
○ Franciacorta Brut '01	♟♟ 6
○ Franciacorta Brut Nefertiti '01	♟♟ 7
○ Franciacorta Extra Brut Nefertiti Dizeta '02	♟♟ 7

○ Franciacorta Brut '05	♙♙ 5
⊙ Franciacorta Rosé '05	♙♙ 6
⊙ Franciacorta Rosé Demi Sec	♙♙ 5
○ Franciacorta Satèn '05	♙♙ 6
○ TdF Bianco Curtefranca '07	♙♙ 4
○ Franciacorta Brut Cuvette '04	♙ 6
○ Franciacorta Dosage Zero Diamant '04	♙ 6
● TdF Rosso Curtefranca '05	♙ 4
○ Franciacorta Brut '04	♟♟ 5
○ Franciacorta Brut '02	♟♟ 5*
○ Franciacorta Brut '01	♟♟ 5*
⊙ Franciacorta Rosé Demi Sec '03	♟♟ 6

Villa Crespia - Muratori

VIA VALLI, 11
25030 ADRO [BS]
TEL. 0307451051
www.fratellimuratori.com

CELLAR SALES
PRE-BOOKED VISITS

ANNUAL PRODUCTION **400,000 bottles**
HECTARES UNDER VINE **60**
VITICULTURE METHOD **Conventional**

The Muratori brothers – Giuliano, Giorgio, Diego and Bruno – are entrepreneurs from Brescia with a passion for wine. They have turned this passion into a business by entrusting Professor Francesco Iacono with an ambitious project to create a chain of top-quality estates in Lombardy, Tuscany and Campania. Faithful to the principle of "one terroir, one wine", Iacono has dedicated Villa Crespia in Franciacorta exclusively to sparklers, making numerous versions from vineyards planted according to in-depth zoning studies.

Dosage Zero '04, from the Cisiolo di Adro vineyard, again represented the estate in our finals. Somewhat unusually in this land of chardonnay, it is a Blanc de Noirs from pure pinot nero, which shows an elegant gold with tiny bubbles and a complex nose of red berries, liquorice, vanilla and roasted coffee. The palate is harmonious with firm structure and impressive backbone. The Satèn from the Cesonato vineyard gives fresh citrus and white fruits, then a caressing, yet not flabby, palate. Dosaggio Zero Numerozero, from chardonnay, is also interesting, with a pleasant, fresh grip and Miolo offers good full, sound fruit.

Chiara Ziliani

VIA FRANCIACORTA, 7
25050 PROVAGLIO D'ISEO [BS]
TEL. 030981661
www.cantinazilianichiara.it

PRE-BOOKED VISITS

ANNUAL PRODUCTION **200,000 bottles**
HECTARES UNDER VINE **15**
VITICULTURE METHOD **Conventional**

Chiara Ziliani runs this smallish estate with great passion. The cellar at Provaglio d'Iseo is modern and surrounded by 15 hectares of well-aspected vineyards on a morainic hill about 250 metres above sea level. They are modern, high-density plantings, farmed using low environmental impact methods. The estate produces a wide range of wines in three product lines. Ziliani's workhorse is undoubtedly Franciacorta Satèn, of which there are four interpretations.

Satèn Ziliani C '05, the winery's only vintage wine, has charming soft, creamy aromas of white chocolate, coffee and vanilla. The balanced palate has soft vanilla notes and a lingering finish. Rosé Ziliani C is very well executed, displaying complex notes of wild berries on the nose and palate, which is dense and lively. It is echoed to a lesser extent by Rosé Conte di Provaglio, which is still a very pleasant and highly drinkable wine. Satèn Duca d'Iseo offers charming notes of vanilla, pear and apricot and a well-profiled palate, and we also liked C'est la Vie, a blend of white grapes. The rest of the list is good.

○ Franciacorta Dosaggio Zero Cisiolo '04	♍♍	6
○ Franciacorta Dosaggio Zero Numerozero	♍♍	6
○ Franciacorta Miolo	♍♍	6
○ Franciacorta Satèn Brut Cesonato	♍♍	6
☉ Franciacorta Brolese Rosé Extra Brut	♍	6
○ Franciacorta Brut Novalia	♍	6
☉ Franciacorta Brolese Rosé Extra Brut '02	♕♕	8
○ Franciacorta Dosaggio Zero Cisiolo '03	♕♕	6
○ Franciacorta Dosaggio Zero Cisiolo '02	♕♕	5
☉ Franciacorta Rosé Extra Brut Brolese '03	♕♕	8

☉ Franciacorta Brut Rosé Ziliani C	♍♍	5
○ Franciacorta Satèn Duca d'Iseo	♍♍	5
○ Franciacorta Satèn Ziliani C '05	♍♍	5
○ C'est la Vie	♍	4
○ Franciacorta Brut Conte di Provaglio	♍	5
○ Franciacorta Brut Duca d'Iseo	♍	4
☉ Franciacorta Brut Rosé Conte di Provaglio	♍	5
○ Franciacorta Brut Ziliani C	♍	5
○ TdF Bianco Conte di Provaglio '08	♍	3
● TdF Rosso Conte di Provaglio '06	♍	3
○ Franciacorta Satèn Ziliani C mill. '04	♕♕	5

Marchese Adorno

VIA CORIASSA, 4
27050 RETORBIDO [PV]
TEL. 0383374404
www.marcheseadorno-wines.it

This winery has earned a short profile and looks set to become a benchmark for the zone. In the absence of almost all the most important wines, we liked the clean Pinot Grigio and the forthrightness of the Bonarda. Rile Nero '05 is a Pinot Nero that offers only a glimpse of its great potential.

○ OP Pinot Grigio Dama D'Oro '08	🍷🍷 4*
● OP Bonarda Frizzante '08	🍷 4
● OP Pinot Nero Rile Nero '05	🍷 6

Al Rocol

VIA PROVINCIALE, 79
25050 OME [BS]
TEL. 0306852542
www.alrocol.com

Gianluigi Vimercati looks after nine hectares at Ome, which yield a well-crafted range of Franciacortas. Ca' del Luf '05 is very good again this year, with a nose of toast and attractive oak and an invigorating, fruity palate. The minerally Satèn Martignac hangs together well and Rosé Le Rive is good.

○ Franciacorta Brut Ca' del Luf '05	🍷🍷 5
○ Franciacorta Satèn Martignac	🍷🍷 5
○ Franciacorta Castellini '05	🍷 6
☉ Franciacorta Rosé Le Rive	🍷 6

Riccardo Albani

LOC. CASONA
S.DA SAN BIAGIO, 46
27045 CASTEGGIO [PV]
TEL. 038383622
www.vinialbani.it

Albani's Riesling is an extreme" but very interesting wine, showing golden yellow with prominent minerality, firm structure and evolved notes, although it elicits differing reactions. Bonarda Vivace '07 is bright ruby, with good structure and aromas of plum.

○ OP Riesling Renano '07	🍷🍷 4*
● OP Bonarda Vivace '07	🍷 4

Tenuta degli Angeli

FRAZ. SANTO STEFANO
VIA FARA, 2
24060 CAROBBIO DEGLI ANGELI [BG]
TEL. 035687130
www.tenutadegliangeli.it

Oro degli Angeli, a dried-grape wine from late-harvest rack-dried moscato giallo fruit, is very pleasant. It has an amber hue, lavender and acacia honey aromatics and excellent acidity. Brut Degli Angeli is quite good but a little weighed down by oak.

○ Oro degli Angeli Passito '05	🍷🍷 5
○ Spumante Brut Cl. degli Angeli	🍷 5

Antica Tesa

LOC. MATTINA
VIA MERANO, 28
25080 BOTTICINO [BS]
TEL. 0302691500

The Noventa family continues to uphold the honour of this small designated zone. Vigna del Gobbio '05, from old vineyards, is one of the best reds in the Brescia area, showing full bodied with blackberry and spicy aromas. Pià della Tesa '06 is fresh, lively and tannic, and Vigna degli Ulivi '06 is decent.

● Botticino Pià della Tesa '06	🍷🍷 5
● Botticino V. del Gobbio '05	🍷🍷 6
● Botticino V. degli Ulivi '06	🍷 4

Avanzi

VIA TREVISAGO, 19
25080 MANERBA DEL GARDA [BS]
TEL. 0365551013
www.avanzi.net

Avanzi is a legendary name in Garda winemaking and the handsome estate in Sirmione produces numerous wines. We liked the excellent Sirmione '08, a Lugana with tropical and oak notes and a fresh, tangy, mineral palate. Garda Rosso Superiore Giovanni Avanzi is very good and the other wines are well made.

● Garda Rosso Sup. Giovanni Avanzi '07	🍷🍷 4*
○ Lugana Sirmione '08	🍷🍷 4*
☉ Garda Cl. Chiaretto '08	🍷 3

Barbacarlo

S.DA BRONESE, 3
27043 BRONI [PV]
TEL. 038551212
barbacarlodimaga@libero.it

Barbacarlo never ceases to amaze, like its legendary producer Lino Maga. It is an extreme wine, different every year, with the minimum human intervention and capable of surprising decades after the harvest. The '07 is soft, with notes of black berry fruit and a long finish.

● Barbacarlo '07	♥♥	6

Luciano Barberini

VIA EMILIA, 93
27050 REDAVALLE [PV]
TEL. 038574164
www.barberinilucianovini.it

The captivating Montecastello '07, a blend of barbera and cabernet sauvignon, is velvety and very pleasant. Castlà '07, mainly croatina with a little pinot nero, has aromas of wild berries and is uncomplicated and easy drinking while Bonarda Vivace Poggio della Monsella '08 has a fine almondy finish.

● Montecastello '07	♥♥	4*
● Castlà '07	♥	3
● OP Bonarda Vivace Poggio della Monsella '08	♥	3

Barboglio De Gaioncelli

FRAZ. COLOMBARO
VIA NAZARIO SAURO
25040 CORTE FRANCA [BS]
TEL. 0309826831
www.barbogliodegaioncelli.it

The Costa family owns 15 hectares of fine vineyards at Corte Franca that yield grapes for their cuvées. Franciacorta Dosage Zero Claro '04 is elegant with a complex nose and a firmly structured mineral palate. The harmonious, juicy Extra Dry is very pleasant while the Brut is forward and nicely styled.

○ Franciacorta Dosage Zero Claro '04	♥♥	6
○ Franciacorta Brut	♥	5
○ Franciacorta Extra Dry	♥	4

La Basia

LOC. LA BASIA
VIA PREDEFITTE, 31
25080 PUEGNAGO SUL GARDA [BS]
TEL. 0365555958
www.labasia.it

Elena Parona's estate was founded in the hills of Valtènesi in 1975 and now has 20 hectares of vineyards and consistently high-quality wines. This is confirmed by Predefitte '05, which has juicy, sound fruit, complexity and smooth tannins. Martì '04 is decent with lots of red fruit, balance and plush tannins.

● Garda Cl. Sup. Martì '04	♥♥	4*
● Garda Cl. Sup. Predefitte '05	♥♥	4*
⊙ Garda Cl. Chiaretto La Moglie Ubriaca '08	♥	4

Conti Bettoni Cazzago

VIA MARCONI, 6
25046 CAZZAGO SAN MARTINO [BS]
TEL. 0307750875
www.contibettonicazzago.it

Our tastings confirmed that the estate's best wine is Satèn di Vincenzo Bettoni Cazzago. It shows a deep straw yellow, with a fine bead and a nose of ripe fruit and mint-laced flowers. The palate is lean but soft and truly delightful.

○ Franciacorta Satèn	♥♥	5
○ Franciacorta Brut Tetellus '04	♥♥	7

Bonaldi - Cascina del Bosco

LOC. PETOSINO
VIA GASPAROTTO, 96
24010 SORISOLE [BG]
TEL. 035571701
www.cascinadelbosco.it

Cantoalto '05 is a complex, deep Riserva that gives printer's ink and dark berry fruit opening into a long, balanced palate. The Brut Metodo Classico has nice supporting acidity and clean aromatics. Its golden hue frames cake-like aromatics. Valcalepio Bianco '08 has a nice nose of tropical fruit.

● Valcalepio Rosso Cantoalto Ris. '05	♥♥	5
○ Bonaldi Brut M. Cl.	♥	5
○ Valcalepio Bianco '08	♥	3

Borgo La Gallinaccia

VIA IV NOVEMBRE, 15
25050 RODENGO SAIANO [BS]
TEL. 030611314
www.borgolagallinaccia.it

This small estate at Rodengo Saiano continues to stand out for the high quality of its wines. In addition to the classy Franciacorta Brut '05, with its attractive oak nose, full, tangy body and slightly smoky finish, we liked the firmly structured, blueberry-veined Rosso Sebino '06.

○ Franciacorta Brut '05	♟♟ 5
● Rosso Sebino '06	♟♟ 4
○ Franciacorta Brut	♟ 5

La Boscaiola

VIA RICCAFANA, 19
25033 COLOGNE [BS]
TEL. 0307156386
www.laboscaiola.com

Giuliana Cenci crafts fine still wines and Franciacortas on her lovely family estate at Cologne. We liked the Franciacorta Brut '04's complex mineral notes and supple, zesty palate. Curtefranca Giuliana C. '07 is also nice, with pleasant peach aromas, while the red Il Ritorno '05 is balanced and full.

○ Franciacorta Brut '04	♟♟ 5
○ TdF Curtefraqnca Bianco Giuliana C. '07	♟♟ 4
● Il Ritorno '05	♟ 4

Boschi

VIA ISEO, 76
25030 ERBUSCO [BS]
TEL. 03077245
www.agricolaboschi.it

Franco Timoteo Metelli, the owner and visible face of this noted Franciacorta estate, has an extensive list, which includes local wines. We liked the Franciacorta Brut Vela '00, which gives refreshing fruit and citrus aromas, and a firm, juicy, zesty palate with a toast finish.

○ Franciacorta Brut Vela '00	♟♟ 7
○ Franciacorta Brut '00	♟♟ 7

Tenuta Il Bosco

LOC. IL BOSCO
27049 ZENEVREDO [PV]
TEL. 0385245326
www.ilbosco.com

Tenuta Il Bosco's excellent Bonarda Vivace is fragrant, soft and balanced. Il Bosco Brut, a classic method sparkler, has firm structure, full, evolved aromas, vanilla notes and a racy finish. The two Philèo cuve close method sparklers are pleasant, fresh and scented, and the rosé has nice wild berries.

● OP Bonarda Vivace '08	♟♟ 4*
○ OP Brut Cl. Il Bosco	♟♟ 5
○ OP Pinot Nero Brut Martinotti Philèo	♟ 4
☉ Philèo Rosè Martinotti Extra Dry	♟ 4

Bredasole

LOC. BREDASOLE
VIA SAN PIETRO, 44
25030 PARATICO [BS]
TEL. 035910407
www.bredasole.it

The Ferrari brothers and consultant oenologist Corrado Cugnasco produce still wines and Franciacortas. We enjoyed the Brut, with an elegant nose featuring notes of fruit and vanilla and a plush, close-knit palate. The Demi Sec Demi, Nature and Satèn are all interesting and well made.

○ Franciacorta Brut	♟♟ 4
○ Franciacorta Demi Sec Demi	♟ 6
○ Franciacorta Nature	♟ 5
○ Franciacorta Satèn	♟ 5

Luciano Brega

FRAZ. BERGAMASCO, 7
27040 MONTÙ BECCARIA [PV]
TEL. 038560237
www.lucianobrega.it

The Brega family has a talent for classic method wines and this year's Gran Montù Rosé achieved its highest score ever with an intriguing, complex nose and sound fruit. Bonarda Vivace '08 is concentrated, velvety and pleasant.

☉ Gran Montù Brut Rosé	♟♟ 4*
● OP Bonarda Vivace '08	♟♟ 3*

Cantina Sociale di Broni

via Sansaluto, 81
27043 Broni [PV]
tel. 038551505
www.bronis.it

Bonarda Frizzante Bronis Selezione '08 is well made, fragrant and balanced. The two classic method sparklers from pinot nero are nice. The Brut is subtle and caressing while the Rosé has an elegant nose of wild berries. Pinot Nero '06 is uncomplicated and varietal.

● OP Bonarda Frizzante Bronis Sel. '08	🍷🍷 3*
⊙ OP Pinot Nero Brut Cl. Rosé	🍷🍷 4*
○ OP Pinot Nero Brut Cl.	🍷🍷 4*
● OP Pinot Nero Bronis Sel. '06	🍷 3

La Brugherata

fraz. Rosciate
via G. Medolago, 47
24020 Scanzorosciate [BG]
tel. 035655202
www.labrugherata.it

Valcalepio Rosso Doglio Riserva '05 is rounded and harmonious, with firm structure and length. Moscato di Scanzo Doge '06 is upfront, with good acidity and a bitterish finish. Valcalepio Bianco Vescovado del Feudo '08 has aromas of peach and chamomile while Vescovado '07 has varietal bell peppers.

● Moscato di Scanzo Passito Doge '06	🍷🍷 8
● Valcalepio Rosso Doglio Ris. '05	🍷🍷 5
○ Valcalepio Bianco Vescovado del Feudo '08	🍷 4
● Valcalepio Rosso Vescovado '07	🍷 4

Ca' del Santo

loc. Campolungo, 4
27040 Montalto Pavese [PV]
tel. 0383870545
www.cadelsanto.it

Riesling Rivalunga '07 is minerally and varietal, with good fruity texture supported by well-gauged acidity. Bonarda Frizzante '08 and Pinot Nero '06 are both pleasant and varietal, and the latter unveils fine-grained tannins.

○ OP Riesling Italico Rivalunga '07	🍷🍷 3*
● OP Bonarda Frizzante Grand Cuvée '08	🍷 3
● Pinot Nero Il Nero '06	🍷 3

Ca' Tessitori

via Matteotti, 15
27043 Broni [PV]
tel. 038551495
www.catessitori.it

Barbera Marona is always interesting. The '07 has the usual well-defined cherry and oak that need time to mellow. Bonarda Frizzante '08 is admirably fragrant and balanced. The Metodo Classico is pleasant, if a little less concentrated than in past vintages, while the varietal Chardonnay '08 is well made.

● OP Barbera Marona '07	🍷🍷 4*
● OP Bonarda Frizzante '08	🍷🍷 3*
○ Chardonnay '08	🍷 3
○ OP Pinot Nero Cl. Brut	🍷 5

Calvi

fraz. Vigalone, 13
27044 Canneto Pavese [PV]
tel. 038560034
www.andreacalvi.it

Andrea Calvi's Bonarda Vivace '08 is very pleasant, with silky tannins, perceptible residual sugar and attractive aromas of black berry fruit. Barbera Tre '05 has a fine nose of spice and cherries and a powerful palate that needs more time to settle down.

● OP Bonarda Vivace '08	🍷🍷 3*
● OP Barbera Tre '05	🍷 4

Caminella

via Dante Alighieri, 13
24069 Cenate Sotto [BG]
tel. 035941828
www.caminella.it

Verde Luna is a white table wine from chardonnay, sauvignon blanc and pinot bianco. It shows a lustrous gold and vaunts good oak, which still tends to overpower the tropical fruit. Brut Ripa di Luna has notes of lychees and limes and could aspire to greater things if only it had a little more length.

○ Ripa di Luna Brut '05	🍷 5
○ Verde Luna Bianco	🍷 4

Camossi

via Metelli, 5
25030 Erbusco [BS]
tel. 0307268022
azvitcamossi@yahoo.it

In its second year in our Guide, Camossi's quality leap is clear to see. Franciacorta Brut is excellent, with complex, attractive notes of oak and an elegant, juicy palate. The Satèn is equally good, with charming apricot and vanilla echoed on the zesty, supple palate. The Rosé is pleasant.

○ Franciacorta Brut	🍷🍷 5
○ Franciacorta Satèn	🍷🍷 4
⊙ Franciacorta Rosé	🍷 5

Le Cantorìe

fraz. Casaglio
via Castello di Casaglio, 24/25
25064 Gussago [BS]
tel. 0302523723
www.lecantorie.it

The Bontempi family owns vineyards on the hillsides at Gussago, where they produce excellent wines in their well-equipped cellar. We particularly liked the Satèn, which offers fresh fruit with citrus and floral hints and a plush, juicy palate with a vanillaed finish. The two reds are also interesting.

○ Franciacorta Satèn '05	🍷🍷 6
● Cellatica Rosso Sup. Giulia '06	🍷 4
● Rosso Baleno	🍷 4

Cascina Gnocco

fraz. Losana, 20
27040 Mornico Losana [PV]
tel. 0383892280
www.cascinagnocco.it

The refreshing Orione Rosso, from uva di Mornico only, has distinct spice and balsam, ripe wild berries and exceptionally fragrant pulp. Riesling Ambrogina '08 is well made, showing varietal, scented and perfectly balanced.

○ OP Riesling Italico Ambrogina '08	🍷🍷 3*
● Orione '07	🍷🍷 7

Caseo

fraz. Caseo, 9
27040 Canevino [PV]
tel. 038599937
www.caseowines.com

Gioiacaseo Cuvée, a gold classic method sparkler, has structure and acid backbone. The slightly evolved sparkling Rosé is interesting and the two '08 whites from the Naro range are good. The IGT is an unusual blend of chardonnay, sauvignon blanc, riesling and moscato while the Riesling refreshes.

○ Gioia Cuvée Brut Cl.	🍷🍷 5
○ Naro Bianco '08	🍷🍷 3*
⊙ OP Pinot Nero Spumante Cl. Rosé	🍷 5
○ OP Riesling Naro '08	🍷 4

Tenimenti Castelrotto - Torti

fraz. Castelrotto, 6
27047 Montecalvo Versiggia [PV]
tel. 0385951000
www.tortiwinepinotnero.com

This year, the Torti family's top scorers were the two Casaleggio Charmat method sparklers, both of which are very pleasant, offering fruit, balance and attractive aromas. Bonarda Frizzante Brioso '07 is an unusual wine, with evolved aromas of carob and elderflower and silky tannins.

⊙ OP Pinot Nero Brut Martinotti Casaleggio Rosé	🍷🍷 4*
○ OP Pinot Nero Brut Casaleggio	🍷🍷 4*
● OP Bonarda Frizzante Brioso '07	🍷 4

Castelveder

via Belvedere, 4
25040 Monticelli Brusati [BS]
tel. 030652308
www.castelveder.it

Renato and Elena Alberti's 12 hectares of vineyards yield around 100,000 bottles of excellent still wines and Franciacortas. The Brut confirmed its quality with deep aromas of toast, fruit and minerals and a palate of fleshy, well-defined fruit. Curtefranca Monte della Rosa and the Extra Brut are decent.

○ Franciacorta Brut	🍷🍷 5
○ Franciacorta Extra Brut	🍷 5
● TdF Curtefranca Monte della Rosa '05	🍷 4

Il Cipresso

VIA CERRI, 2
24020 SCANZOROSCIATE [BG]
TEL. 0354597005
www.ilcipresso.info

Serafino, a Moscato di Scanzo with evolved notes and good balance, is as classy as ever and Valcalepio Bianco Melardo is also fairly evolved, with a concentrated tropical nose. Valcalepio Rosso Dionisio '07 has hay and fine-grained tannins while Valcalepio Rosso Bartolomeo Riserva '05 needs longer to develop.

● Moscato di Scanzo Serafino '06	¶¶	7
○ Valcalepio Bianco Melardo '08	¶¶	4*
● Valcalepio Rosso Bartolomeo Ris. '05	¶	5
● Valcalepio Rosso Dionisio '07	¶	4

Clastidio Ballabio

VIA SAN BIAGIO, 32
27045 CASTEGGIO [PV]
TEL. 0383805728
nivelli@oltrenet.it

Andrea Ballabio's Clastidio is one of Oltrepò's oldest wineries. This year, it presented a convincing Barbera Vivace, which shows scented and concentrated with lots of residual sugar. Pinot Nero '07 has notes of cocoa with good fruit and fine-grained tannins that will mollow with age.

● Clastidium di Pinot Nero '07	¶¶	4*
● OP Bonarda Vivace Delle Cento Pertiche '08	¶¶	4*

Comincioli

LOC. CASTELLO
VIA ROMA, 10
25080 PUEGNAGO SUL GARDA [BS]
TEL. 0365651141
www.comincioli.it

Gianfranco Comincioli's nine-hectare estate specializes in Groppello. As we await the new vintages of the top selections, we tasted a scented Chiaretto '08 and the white Perlì '08, from the rare local erbamat and trebbiano della Valtènesi varieties, which has rich fruit and citrus notes.

○ Perlì '08	¶	4
⊙ Riviera del Garda Bresciano Chiaretto '08	¶	4

Cornaleto

VIA CORNALETTO, 2
25030 ADRO [BS]
TEL. 0307450507
www.cornaleto.it

Luigi Lancini is Franciacorta's antiquarian, presenting recent disgorgements of old vintages each year. This time, we liked his Dosage Zero Riserva '98, with its alluring velvety nose of jam and antique wood, and an elegant, complex palate. The Satèn '03 is also good, its nose dominated by medicinal herbs.

○ Franciacorta Brut Satèn '03	¶¶	6
○ Franciacorta Dosage Zero Ris. '98	¶¶	6
⊙ Franciacorta Rosé '05	¶	6

La Costa

FRAZ. COSTA
VIA CURONE, 15
23888 PEREGO [LC]
TEL. 0395312218
www.la-costa.it

This winery is moving increasingly towards natural viticulture. San Giobbe '06, from pinot nero, has a balsamic nose with currants and a dense, juicy palate that finishes long. The fragrant, well-integrated Serìz '06, from merlot, cabernet and syrah, has a full-flavoured palate with balanced fruit and acidity.

● San Giobbe '06	¶¶	5
● Serìz '06	¶¶	5

Tenuta La Costaiola

VIA COSTAIOLA, 25
27054 MONTEBELLO DELLA BATTAGLIA [PV]
TEL. 038383169
www.lacostaiola.it

Following support from the consortium, La Costaiola presented two classic method Pinot Nero sparklers for the first time. The fragrant, easy-drinking Rosé is slightly better than the more predictable white version. Bonarda Frizzante Giada '08 is scented and the Charmat method Haris is as well made as ever.

⊙ OP Pinot Nero Brut Cl. Rosé Rossetti & Scrivani	¶¶	5
● OP Bonarda Frizzante Giada '08	¶	3
○ OP Pinot Nero Brut Cl. Rossetti & Scrivani	¶	5
○ OP Pinot Nero Brut Haris	¶	4

Delai

VIA MORO, 1
25080 PUEGNAGO SUL GARDA [BS]
TEL. 0365555527

Sergio Delai presented a fragrant Garda Classico Chiaretto with a deep, bright hue and aromas of ripe currants and cherries laced with greens. The full flavoured palate is refreshing and dynamic with good length. Although generously dosed, the raspberry-scented Delai Rosé is also good.

⊙ Garda Cl. Chiaretto '08	♟♟	4*
⊙ Delai Rosé '08	♟	4

Dirupi

LOC. MADONNA DI CAMPAGNA
VIA GRUMELLO, 1
23020 MONTAGNA IN VALTELLINA [SO]
TEL. 3472909779
www.dirupi.com

This promising estate, enthusiastically run by Pierpaolo Di Franco and Davide Fasolini, produces around 10,000 bottles. While awaiting the release of Valtellina Superiore Dirupi '07, we tasted the excellent Nebbiolo Olè '07. It's a characterful wine with a clean nose, a long, juicy palate and good acidity.

● Nebbiolo Olè '07	♟♟	5

Lorenzo Faccoli & Figli

VIA CAVA, 7
25030 COCCAGLIO [BS]
TEL. 0307722761
az.faccoli@libero.it

The Faccoli brothers lovingly tend their Coccaglio vineyards, which yield well-crafted Franciacortas. Extra Brut Riserva '99 is elegant and austere, giving yeast, smoke and minerals on both nose and palate, where it shows plush and dynamic. Dosage Zero '04 is very good and the Extra Brut is pleasant.

○ Franciacorta Extra Brut Ris. '99	♟♟	5
○ Franciacorta Dosage Zero '04	♟	6
○ Franciacorta Extra Brut	♟	5

Fiamberti

VIA CHIESA, 17
27044 CANNETO PAVESE [PV]
TEL. 038588019
www.fiambertivini.it

Buttafuoco Poderi Fiamberti '05 is impressively consistent and racy at the back while the Pinot Nero Nero '07 is varietal and well sustained. We also tasted the two classic method sparklers, preferring the balanced Rosé with its sharply defined red berry fruit. The white lacks a little backbone.

● OP Buttafuoco Poderi Fiamberti '05	♟♟	4*
⊙ OP Pinot Nero Brut Cl. Fiamberti Rosé	♟♟	5
● OP Pinot Nero Nero '07	♟♟	4*
○ OP Pinot Nero Brut Cl. Fiamberti	♟	5

La Fiòca

FRAZ. NIGOLINE
VIA VILLA, 13B
25040 CORTE FRANCA [BS]
TEL. 0309826313
www.lafioca.com

La Fiòca is owned by the Gatti family and offers a range of interesting wines from estate-owned vineyards. We liked the Franciacorta Brut, with its fruity, floral nose and invigoratingly supple palate with its vanillaed finish. One rung below is the pleasant Satèn, with charming fruity pulp and softness.

○ Franciacorta Brut	♟♟	5
○ Franciacorta Satèn	♟	5

Fattoria Gambero

FRAZ. CASE NUOVE
27045 SANTA MARIA DELLA VERSA [PV]
TEL. 038579268
www.fattoriailgambero.it

The elegant, exemplary Bonarda Frizzante Alborada '08 is one of the best from the vintage. Vittorio Ferrario has also crafted an impressive classic method Principe d'Onore, whose '05 version has greater complexity and finer aromas. The balanced Bacuco '06 is very good, with aromas of medicinal herbs.

● OP Bonarda Frizzante Alborada '08	♟♟	4*
○ OP Pinot Nero Brut Cl. Principe d'Onore '05	♟♟	5
● OP Rosso Bacuco Ris. '06	♟♟	4*

Castello di Grumello

VIA FOSSE, 11
24064 GRUMELLO DEL MONTE [BG]
TEL. 0354420817
www.castellodigrumello.it

Valcalepio Bianco '08 has notes of peach and pear fruit, good pulp, nice supporting acidity and attractive depth. The Riserva '04 offers notes of coffee, chocolate and spices. It shows good structure and is marred only by a slightly short finish.

○ Valcalepio Bianco '08	♟♟	3*
● Valcalepio Rosso Ris. '04	♟	4

Isimbarda

LOC. CASTELLO
CASCINA ISIMBARDA
27046 SANTA GIULETTA [PV]
TEL. 0383899256
www.tenutaisimbarda.it

As always, Riesling Vigna Martina '08 is concentrated, varietal and characterful. It requires several years of bottle ageing to reach its peak. Rosso Montezavo Riserva '06 is well made, with sound fruit, while Bonarda Vivace Vigna delle More '08 has a raspberry theme and a nice tannic weave.

○ OP Riesling Renano Vigna Martina '08	♟♟	4*
● OP Rosso Montezavo Ris. '06	♟♟	5
● OP Bonarda Vivace V. delle More '08	♟	4

La Fiorita

VIA MAGLIO, 14
25020 OME [BS]
TEL. 030652279
www.lafiorita.bs.it

The Bono family has expanded from livestock farming into the production of Franciacorta from the estate's five hectares of vineyards. Guest facilities have also been added. This year we liked the Satèn, which has an attractive fruit and vanilla nose and a fresh, juicy, velvety palate. The Dosaggio Zero is also good.

○ Franciacorta Satèn	♟♟	5
○ Franciacorta Dosaggio Zero	♟	5

La Valle

VIA SANT'ANTONIO, 4
25050 RODENGO SAIANO [BS]
TEL. 0307722045
www.vinilavalle.it

Housed in a lovely 19th-century farmhouse at Rodengo Saiano, La Valle is one of Franciacorta's up-and-coming wineries. This year our favourites were the fresh, complex Dosage Zéro Zerum Riserva '00 and the firm, invigorating, supple Riserva Regium '03. The Satèn is also very good. Keep it up!

○ Franciacorta Brut Regium '03	♟♟	6
○ Franciacorta Dosage Zero Zerum Ris. '00	♟♟	7
○ Franciacorta Satèn	♟♟	6
○ Franciacorta Brut	♟	5

Lazzari

VIA MELLA, 49
25020 CAPRIANO DEL COLLE [BS]
TEL. 0309747387
darilazz@hotmail.com

Giovanni Lazzari and his family are dedicated to the wines of this small Brescian DOC zone and produce around 40,000 bottles a year. The excellent Capriano del Colle Riserva degli Angeli '06 is plush and subtly tannic with notes of cherries. Marzemino '08 and Vulcano '06 are both classy.

● Capriano del Colle Riserva degli Angeli '06	♟♟	4*
● Capriano del Colle Vulcano '06	♟♟	4*
● Capriano del Colle '06	♟	3
● Marzemino '08	♟	3

Leali di Monteacuto

FRAZ. MONTEACUTO
VIA DOSSO, 5
25080 PUEGNAGO SUL GARDA [BS]
TEL. 0365651291
antonio.leali@genie.it

The Lealis make a meticulously crafted range of Garda wines that performed well again this year, particularly the fragrant Chiaretto '08, which is fresh, fruity and full flavoured. The slightly evolved Groppello '07 has clean vegetal hints. Rebo Montagü '07 is nice, showing uncomplicated, fruity and enjoyable.

⊙ Garda Bresciano Chiaretto '08	♟♟	4*
● Garda Bresciano Groppello '07	♟	4
● Rebo Montagü '07	♟	4

Locatelli Caffi

VIA A. MORO, 6
24060 CHIUDUNO [BG]
TEL. 035838308
www.locatellicaffi.it

Valcalepio Rosso Riserva '05 is clean and elegant, with lively crisp fruit, a consistent aromatic profile and good drive. The other Valcalepio Rosso, I Pilendrì '07, also scored highly with fragrant notes of morello cherry. Valcalepio Rosso '07 is very fresh and youthful.

● Valcalepio Rosso '07	🍷🍷	3
● Valcalepio Rosso I Pilendrì '07	🍷🍷	3*
● Valcalepio Rosso Ris. '05	🍷🍷	4*

Longhi de Carli

VIA VERDI, 6
25030 ERBUSCO [BS]
TEL. 0307760280
www.longhi-decarli.com

Alessandro Longhi's estate extends over 13 hectares of vineyards at Erbusco, in the heart of the DOCG zone. We liked the very good Brut, with its aromas of rosemary and vanilla and just the right amount of flesh and softness on the palate. The Satèn is velvety and almost sweet, with a pleasant vanillaed finish.

○ Franciacorta Brut	🍷🍷	6
○ Franciacorta Satèn	🍷	6

Castello di Luzzano

LOC. LUZZANO, 5
27040 ROVESCALA [PV]
TEL. 0523863277
www.castelloluzzano.it

Giovannella Fugazza's Bonarda Frizzante '08 is highly drinkable, with a charming purplish mousse and notes of strawberry and raspberry accompanied by intriguing chocolate. Pinot Nero Umore Nero '08, fermented in steel, is scented and refreshing, with a very clean palate and a good finish.

● OP Bonarda Frizzante '08	🍷🍷	3*
● OP Pinot Nero Umore Nero '08	🍷	4

Eligio Magri

VIA COLLE DEI PASTA, 8A
24060 TORRE DE' ROVERI [BG]
TEL. 0354528868
www.eligiomagri.it

Although Patrizio Riserva is no longer a DOC, the '05 vintage echoes the quality of the previous one, showing dark ruby with sound, ripe fruit, pleasant overtones of hay and very well-calibrated oak. Valcalepio Rosso Lyr '06 gives balsamic aromas and is fresh and pleasant.

● Valcalepio Rosso Patrizio Ris. '05	🍷🍷	6
● Valcalepio Rosso Lyr '06	🍷	4

Marangona

LOC. ANTICA CORTE IALIDY
25010 POZZOLENGO [BS]
TEL. 030919379
www.marangona.com

The Marangona estate at Pozzolengo has 25 hectares under vine in the Lugana DOC zone farmed using low environmental impact techniques. Lugana Trecampane '08 has fresh plums and apricots, and a zesty, supple palate. Lugana Superiore '07 is full and balanced. Garda Rosso '06 is nice, with soft tannins.

○ Lugana Trecampane '08	🍷🍷	4
● Garda Cl. Rosso '06	🍷	4
○ Lugana Sup. '07	🍷	4

Martilde

FRAZ. CROCE, 4A
27040 ROVESCALA [PV]
TEL. 0385756280
www.martilde.it

Malvasia Dedica is again impressive. The '07 vintage is highly evolved and over-extracted but nonetheless stylish with good acid backbone. Bonarda Ghiro Rosso d'Inverno '06 is potentially interesting but requires much more time in bottle to find its balance.

○ OP Malvasia Dedica '07	🍷🍷	5
● OP Bonarda Ghiro Rosso d'Inverno '06	🍷	5

Medolago Albani
via Redona, 12
24069 Trescore Balneario [BG]
tel. 035942022
www.medolagoalbani.it

Valcalepio Bianco '08 has clean hints of pineapple and lime tropical fruit, good flesh, acid backbone and a nice finish while the attractive deep ruby Valcalepio Rosso '07 gives greens and spiciness that hold together well.

○ Valcalepio Bianco '08	🍷🍷 4*
● Valcalepio Rosso '07	🍷🍷 4*
● Villa Redona '05	🍷 4

Cantine di Mezzaluna
loc. Casa Tacconi, 13
27040 Montalto Pavese [PV]
tel. 0383870282
www.cantinedimezzaluna.it

A Pinot Nero '06 with distinct pepper, varietal aromas and good balance tied for the highest score with a mineral, full-flavoured Riesling '05. The Pinot Grigio '08 is also good, showing well typed with good fruity body. Barbera Vigna Massone '05 is well made and highly drinkable.

○ OP Pinot Grigio '08	🍷🍷 4*
● OP Pinot Nero '06	🍷🍷 4*
○ OP Riesling '05	🍷🍷 4*
● Vigna Massone '05	🍷 4

Mirabella
via Cantarane, 2
25050 Rodengo Saiano [BS]
tel. 030611197
www.mirabellavini.it

Mirabella of Rodengo Saiano is one of the legendary names of Franciacorta winemaking. This year, we liked the well-made Brut Cuvée Demetra, with its attractive nose of hawthorn, pears and cakes, and invigorating, lively palate. The rest of the list is good.

○ Franciacorta Brut Cuvée Demetra	🍷🍷 5
⊙ Franciacorta Brut Rosé Cuvée Demetra	🍷 5
⊙ Franciacorta Rosé Brut	🍷 5

Montagna
via Cairoli, 67
27043 Broni [PV]
tel. 038551028
www.cantinemontagna.it

This Broni-based winery made its debut with classic method sparklers, notably an alluring, velvety Rosé and an interesting, characterful Extra Brut with evolved, almost sulphurous, notes. Pinot Nero Viti di Luna '06 is great, with well-typed aromas, nicely calibrated oak and an attractive almondy finish.

○ OP Pinot Nero Extra Brut Cl.	🍷🍷 4*
⊙ OP Pinot Nero Rosé Brut Cl.	🍷🍷 4*
● OP Pinot Nero Viti di Luna '06	🍷🍷 3*

Marchesi di Montalto
loc. Costa Gallotti, 5
27040 Montalto Pavese [PV]
tel. 3394982856
www.marchesidimontalto.it

Monsaltus '06, from botrytized riesling italico grapes, confirmed its appeal. The fragrant classic method Rosé '05 is much improved while the riesling-based Charmat method sparkler is ripe and intense with honey aromas and a long finish. Bonarda Frizzante Cascina Francone '08 is smooth, frank and well defined.

● OP Bonarda Frizzante Cascina Francone '08	🍷🍷 5
⊙ OP Pinot Nero Rosé Brut Cl. '05	🍷🍷 5
○ OP Riesling Brut Martinotti	🍷🍷 4*
○ OP Riesling Italico Monsaltus V. T. '06	🍷🍷 5

Monte Cicogna
via delle Vigne, 6
25080 Moniga del Garda [BS]
tel. 0365503200
www.montecicogna.it

The Materossi family's winery is housed in an old farmstead on a hilltop overlooking Lake Garda. Agronomist Alessandro and his brother Cesare presented a very good, fresh, juicy Lugana Santa Caterina '08, a Chiaretto Siclì '08 with alluring raspberry notes, a decent Brut Classico and other interesting wines.

⊙ Garda Cl. Chiaretto Siclì '08	🍷 4
● Garda Cl. Rosso Groppello Beana '07	🍷 4
○ Lugana S. Caterina '08	🍷 4
○ Spumante Brut M. Cl. '02	🍷 5

Tenuta Montedelma

VIA VALENZANO, 23
25050 PASSIRANO [BS]
TEL. 0306546161
www.montedelma.it

Pietro Berardi invests great passion in the family estate and releases an array of interesting wines. We liked the smooth, well-calibrated Franciacorta Brut, which has a floral nose and full palate, and the very nice Satèn, with classic notes of ripe apricot and vanilla on both nose and palate.

O Franciacorta Brut	♈♈	6
O Franciacorta Satèn	♈♈	6

Monterucco

VALLE CIMA, 38
27040 CIGOGNOLA [PV]
TEL. 038585151
www.monterucco.it

This year, the Classese combines its usual firm structure with attractive finesse while Malvasia Valentina '08 is temptingly varietal. Both the Buttafuoco Sanluigi '07 and the Bonarda Frizzante Vigna Il Modello '08 are well executed, with prominent wild berry aromatics.

O Malvasia Valentina '08	♈♈	4*
O OP Pinot Nero Brut Classese	♈♈	4*
● OP Bonarda Frizzante V. Il Modello '08	♈	3
● OP Buttafuoco Sanluigi '07	♈	4

Il Montù

VIA MARCONI, 10
27040 MONTÙ BECCARIA [PV]
TEL. 0385262252
www.ilmontu.com

Once again, the old Montù Beccaria winery's sparklers really shone. The Blanc Da Noir is elegant and full-flavoured, with minerally notes, and the fragrant, well-made Rosé Da Noir would have scored higher if it had had a little more supporting acidity. Il Millesimato '06 is pleasant and evolved.

O Pinot Blanc Da Noir	♈♈	5
O OP Pinot Nero Brut Cl. Il Millesimato '06	♈	5
☉ Pinot Rosé Da Noir	♈	5

Nettare dei Santi

VIA CAPRA, 17
20078 SAN COLOMBANO AL LAMBRO [MI]
TEL. 0371200523
www.nettaredeisanti.it

The new wine this year is a Charmat method Rosé from barbera and malvasia. It's fairly uncomplicated but pleasant, particularly on the nose. Mombrione '06 offers sound vegetal and fruity notes, while Roverone '07, a Bordeaux blend with croatina and barbera, has an attractive nose and decent texture.

☉ Brut Martinotti Rosé	♈	4
● Roverone Rosso '07	♈	4
● San Colombano Mombrione '06	♈	4

Olmo Antico

VIA MARCONI, 8
27040 BORGO PRIOLO [PV]
TEL. 0383872672
www.olmoantico.it

Paolo Baggini continues his viticultural adventure using natural techniques to make wines from his organically grown grapes. We liked Giorgio Quinto '06, a full-bodied Merlot with soft tannins, the tangy, mineral Riesling '08, and Olmo Bianco '08, with aromas of lavender, tropical fruit and a rounded palate.

● Giorgio Quinto '06	♈♈	6
O Olmo Bianco '08	♈♈	4*
● Croatina 14 Ottobre '08	♈	4
O Riesling '08	♈	4

Panigada - Banino

VIA DELLA VITTORIA, 13
20078 SAN COLOMBANO AL LAMBRO [MI]
TEL. 037189103
vinobanino@hotmail.com

Vigna La Merla Riserva continues to be San Colombano's best red and the '05 vintage associates its trademark huskiness with rather elegant tannins, making it easier to drink. The other two younger reds are pleasant and uncomplicated, with the '08 a shade readier for the corkscrew.

● San Colombano V. La Merla Ris. '05	♈♈	5
● San Colombano Banino Rosso Giovane '08	♈	3
● San Colombano Banino Tranquillo '07	♈	3

Perla del Garda

FRAZ. ESENTA
LOC. BELLINO
25017 LONATO [BS]
TEL. 0309102021
ettore.prandini@libero.it

This young winery has 25 hectares of fine vineyards on the hillsides in Lonato, a modern cellar and plenty of enthusiasm. Lugana Madreperla '07 is excellent, showing zesty and juicy, and Perla '08 is good. Rosa delle Siepi '08 is alluringly refreshing while the Bordeaux blend Terre Lunari '07 is charming.

○ Lugana Madreperla '07	▼▼ 4*
○ Lugana Perla '08	▼ 4
⊙ Rosa delle Siepi '08	▼ 4
● Terre Lunari '07	▼ 5

Piccolo Bacco dei Quaroni

FRAZ. COSTAMONTEFEDELE
27040 MONTÙ BECCARIA [PV]
TEL. 038560521
www.piccolobaccodeiquaroni.it

PBQ, Mario Cavalli and Laura Brazzola's latest wine, is a classic method rosé with an unusual style of citrus fruit aromas and fairly full body. Both the Buttafuoco '05 and the Pino Nero '06 reds have good potential but require further bottle ageing to express themselves to the full.

⊙ OP Pinot Nero Brut Cl. PBQ Rosé	▼▼ 4*
● OP Pinot Nero Vign. La Fiocca '06	▼ 3
● OP Buttafuoco Vign. Ca' Padroni '05	▼ 3

Pilandro

FRAZ. SAN MARTINO DELLA BATTAGLIA
LOC. PILANDRO, 1
25010 DESENZANO DEL GARDA [BS]
TEL. 0309910363
www.pilandro.it

The Lavelli family farms 16 hectares of vineyards in San Martino, following an age-old tradition. They specialize in Lugana and presented an excellent '08 with aromas of mineral-shaded ripe fruit and medicinal herbs, and a full-flavoured, buttery palate with refreshing acidity. The Lugana Brut is good.

○ Lugana '08	▼▼ 4*
○ Lugana Brut	▼ 4

Le Preseglie

FRAZ. SAN MARTINO DELLA BATTAGLIA
25015 DESENZANO DEL GARDA [BS]
TEL. 0309108195
www.agriturismolepreseglie.it

Le Preseglie is a handsome estate with 18 hectares under vine and guest accommodation in San Martino della Battaglia. This year, we liked the fresh, tangy, supple white San Martino Kaivalya '08, the dried-grape Suria with notes of honey and tropical fruit, and Lugana Hamsa '08.

○ Lugana Hamsa '08	▼ 5
○ Passito Suria	▼ 5
○ San Martino della Battaglia Kaivalya '08	▼ 4

Quadra

VIA SANT'EUSEBIO, 1
25033 COLOGNE [BS]
TEL. 0307157314
www.quadrafranciacorta.it

The Ghezzi family has business interests in Italy and Argentina. Founded in 2003, the winery run by Mario Falcetti makes an excellent Satèn '05, with elegant notes of vanilla and coffee and a tangy, juicy palate. Dosso Oriane '04 is also very good, with blueberries and soft tannins.

○ Franciacorta Satèn '05	▼▼ 6
● TdF Curtefranca Rosso Dosso Oriane '04	▼▼ 5

Redaelli de Zinis

VIA N.H. UGO DE ZINIS, 10 (VIA BASSE SOTTO)
25080 CALVAGESE DELLA RIVIERA [BS]
TEL. 030601001
www.dezinis.it

This old estate's meticulously tended vineyards extend around the 18th-century house. Groppello Riserva '03 is interesting, with sound fruit and silky tannins. The Chiaretto is very easy drinking and Groppello '07 is good. Rosse Emozioni '06 is excellent.

● Garda Cl. Groppello Poggio dei Sassi Ris. '03	▼▼ 4
● Garda Cl. Sup. Rosse Emozioni '06	▼▼ 5
⊙ Garda Cl. Chiaretto '08	▼ 4
● Garda Cl. Groppello '07	▼ 4

Riccafana

VIA FACCHETTI, 91
25033 COLOGNE [BS]
TEL. 0307156797
www.riccafana.com

The Fratus family's estate offers a range of Franciacortas and clean, well-crafted local wines. Its Rosés have been impressive of late, as is testified by the '05 vintage, which shows elegant, complex, harmonious hints of berry fruit and a long, satisfying finish. It's one of the best in the designated zone.

⊙ Franciacorta Rosé '05	♟♟ 5
○ Franciacorta Satèn	♟ 4
● Horta '05	♟ 4

Ricchi

FRAZ. RICCHI
VIA FESTONI, 13D
46040 MONZAMBANO [MN]
TEL. 0376800238
www.cantinaricchi.it

Chardonnay Meridiano '08, part-aged in oak, offers alluring honey and tropical fruit while the soft, well-typed Merlot Carpino '05 has good impact. Cabernet Ribò '06 is forthright and firmly structured. Le Cime, a dried-grape wine from moscato and garganega, is golden with distinct honey aromas.

○ Garda Chardonnay Meridiano '08	♟♟ 4
● Garda Cabernet Ribò '06	♟ 4
● Garda Merlot Carpino '05	♟ 4
○ Passito Le Cime	♟ 5

Riva di Franciacorta

LOC. FANTECOLO
VIA CARLO ALBERTO, 19
25040 PROVAGLIO D'ISEO [BS]
TEL. 0309823701
www.rivadifranciacorta.it

The Riva family have purchased over 30 hectares of fine vineyards and renovated an old house, fitting it out with the latest winemaking equipment. We singled out a very good Satèn, with soft, subtle citrus aromas, a Rosé with clean notes of currants and cherries, and a nicely complex Brut.

⊙ Franciacorta Rosé	♟♟ 6
○ Franciacorta Satèn	♟♟ 6
○ Franciacorta Brut	♟ 5
● Terre di Franciacorta Longobardo '06	♟ 3

Ronco della Fola

VIA MONTE BASTIA, 36
24020 SCANZOROSCIATE [BG]
TEL. 035656036
www.roncodellafola.it

At its Guide debut, Ronco della Fola presented three impressively consistent vintages of Moscato di Scanzo. As you might expect, the '03 is more evolved, with dominant notes of India rubber, but all three are intense and balsamic with good supporting acidity.

● Moscato di Scanzo Passito '05	♟♟ 6
● Moscato di Scanzo Passito '04	♟♟ 6
● Moscato di Scanzo Passito '03	♟♟ 6

Tenuta San Francesco

VIA SCAZZOLINO, 55
27040 ROVESCALA [PV]
TEL. 029085141
www.alziati.it

Bonarda di Rovescala and traditional vinification are Annibale Alziati's ingredients for a range of interesting wines. Gaggiarone '07 reveals fruit, printer's ink and liquorice, and a substantial palate with nice length. Vitigni Giovani '06 is balsamic and spicy while the Bonarda '08 is beefy and traditional.

● Gaggiarone '07	♟♟ 5
● Gaggiarone Vitigni Giovani '06	♟♟ 3*
● OP Bonarda '08	♟ 3

Podere San Giorgio

LOC. CASTELLO, 1
27046 SANTA GIULETTA [PV]
TEL. 0383899168
www.poderesangiorgio.it

We are pleased to welcome back the Perdomini family's estate, and its classic method Rosé, at last back to its old standard. Pinot Nero Re Nero '06 is typical and interesting, despite its youth, Pinot Grigio Argento Vivo '08 is varietal and pleasant and Bonarda Frizzante Rebecca '08 has nice body.

⊙ OP Castel San Giorgio Brut Rosé	♟♟ 5
○ OP Pinot Grigio Argento Vivo '08	♟♟ 4*
● OP Pinot Nero Re Nero '06	♟♟ 4*
● OP Bonarda Frizzante Rebecca '08	♟ 3

Poderi di San Pietro

VIA MONTI, 35
20078 SAN COLOMBANO AL LAMBRO [MI]
TEL. 0371208050
www.poderidisanpietro.it

Following a few ups and downs, this large San Colombano winery is back in the Guide. Monastero di Valbissera '01 is very convincing, with good depth and balance. Although less representative of the territory, the Bordeaux blend Trianon '03 is very well executed. Collada '07 is pleasant and refreshing.

● San Colombano Monastero di Valbissera '01	♟♟	6
● Trianon '03	♟♟	7
● Collada '07	♟	4

Tenuta Scarpa Colombi

VIA GROPPALLO, 26
27049 BOSNASCO [PV]
TEL. 0385272081
www.colombiwines.com

The full-bodied white-grape Metodo Classico made a good debut with its tropical fruit aromas. The Charmat method Cuvée di Famiglia is nice, showing complex and scented with an exuberant bead and nose. Pinot Nero Ariolo and Bonarda Marubbio del '07 are varietal and need cellar time to acquire balance.

● OP Pinot Nero Ariolo '07	♟♟	4*
○ OP Pinot Nero Brut Martinotti Cuvée di Famiglia	♟♟	3*
○ Spumante Brut Cl. Blanc de Blancs	♟♟	5
● OP Bonarda Marubbio '07	♟	4

Scuropasso

FRAZ. SCORZOLETTA, 40/42
27043 PIETRA DE' GIORGI [PV]
TEL. 038585143
www.scuropasso.it

This year, the spirited classic method Roccapietra is joined by a rosé, which is potentially interesting but requires more tweaking. Bonarda Frizzante Palatinus '08 is very good while the youthful Pinot Nero Roccapietra '07 is interesting with good ageing potential.

● OP Bonarda Frizzante Palatinus '08	♟♟	3*
○ OP Pinot Nero Brut Cl. Roccapietra	♟♟	5
☉ Brut Cl. Rosé Roccapietra	♟	5
● OP Pinot Nero Roccapietra '07	♟	4

Cantine Selva Capuzza

FRAZ. SAN MARTINO DELLA BATTAGLIA
LOC. SELVA CAPUZZA
25010 DESENZANO DEL GARDA [BS]
TEL. 0309910381
www.selvacapuzza.it

The Formentini family's estate has two good ranges the Riviera del Garda Bresciano: Colli a Lago and Selva Capuzza. Lugana Selva Capuzza '08 is great, showing juicy and clean with mineral notes, and the red Dunant '07 is also very elegant. The best of the Colli a Lago range is the complex Lugana San Vigilio '08.

● Garda Cl. Dunant '07	♟♟	4*
○ Lugana San Vigilio '08	♟♟	4*
○ Lugana Selva Capuzza '08	♟♟	4*

Lo Sparviere

VIA COSTA, 2
25040 MONTICELLI BRUSATI [BS]
TEL. 030652382
www.losparviere.com

The Gussalli Berretta family owns this fine, 30-hectare Gussago estate. The Brut '05 reached the finals with an elegant, harmonious nose of ripe fruit and vanilla and a fresh, invigorating palate with a long finish. The other wines are well made.

○ Franciacorta Brut '05	♟♟	6
○ Franciacorta Extra Brut	♟♟	5
○ Franciacorta Satèn	♟♟	5
☉ Franciacorta Rosé Brut	♟	6

Le Strie

VIA SAN GERVASIO, 13/A
23036 TEGLIO [SO]
TEL. 03422780566
www.lestrie.it

This estate has approximately 10,000 square metres planted to nebbiolo and an annual production of just over 5,000 bottles. Valtellina Le Strie '05 is the result of "rinforzo" with 30 per cent part-dried grapes. An ambitious wine, it has a generous nose, rounded palate, long finish and fine-grained tannins.

● Valtellina Sup. Le Strie '05	♟♟	5

OTHER WINERIES

Vincenzo Tallarini

VIA FONTANILE, 7/9
24060 GANDOSSO [BG]
TEL. 035834003
www.tallarini.com

Many top wines are missing because the new vintages are still ageing in the cellar. The harmonious Valcalepio Bianco Arlecchino '08 scored well for its heady peach aromas, good acid backbone and fruity pulp but the Brut Metodo Classico is better on the nose than on the palate.

○ Valcalepio Bianco Arlecchino '08	♣♣	3*
○ Brut Cl. Cuvée Angelo Tallarini '06	♣	5

Benedetto Tognazzi

FRAZ. CAIONVICO
VIA SANT'ORSOLA, 155
25135 BRESCIA
TEL. 0302692695

Winemakers for three generations, the Tognazzi family about ten years ago purchased new vineyards in the Lugana zone and built a new cellar. This year, they presented an excellent Lugana '08, which has definition, savouriness, rich fruit and a long finish. The soft, fruity Botticino '06 is very good.

○ Lugana Cascina Ardea '08	♣♣	3
● Botticino Cobio '06	♣	4

Togni Rebaioli

FRAZ. ERBANNO
VIA ROSSINI, 19
25047 DARFO BOARIO TERME [BS]
TEL. 0364529706

This little winery keeps interest alive in Valcamonica as a wine area. The wines themselves are the offspring of the mountains and difficult growing condition but they have character, structure and plenty of fruit.

● Lambrù '07	♣	4
● Millesettecentotre '07	♣	5

La Tordela

VIA TORRICELLA, 1
24060 TORRE DE' ROVERI [BG]
TEL. 035580172
www.latordela.it

Riserva Campo Roccoli Vecchi is always one of the best of its kind and the '04 vintage displays ripe berry fruit, elegant spices, firm structure, balance and considerable length. Valcalepio Rosso '06 has fragrant aromatics. The Cabernet Sauvignon '05 has pulp but lacks a bit of acid backbone.

● Valcalepio Rosso '06	♣♣	4
● Valcalepio Rosso		
Campo Roccoli Vecchi Ris. '04	♣♣	5
● Cabernet Sauvignon Bergamasca '05	♣	3

Torrevilla

VIA EMILIA, 4
27050 TORRAZZA COSTE [PV]
TEL. 038377003
www.torrevilla.it

This co-operative winery, run by Guerrino Saviotti, has improved. The minerally Classese is well made and the other classic method sparkler, La Genisia Brut '06, is elegant. The clean, upfront Pinot Nero La Genisia '07 is nice the same line features the pleasant Novemesi, a melon-scented Charmat method sparkler.

○ La Genisia Brut Cl. '06	♣♣	4*
○ OP Pinot Nero Brut Classese	♣♣	4*
● OP Pinot Nero La Genisia '07	♣♣	4*
○ O. P. Pinot Nero Brut		
Martinotti Novemesi La Genisia	♣	3

Cantina Sociale Val San Martino

VIA BERGAMO, 1195
24030 PONTIDA [BG]
TEL. 035795035
www.cantinavalsanmartino.com

The fine dried-grape Moscato Giallo '08 is balanced, with refreshing citrus. Valcalepio Moscato Passito '07 has frank aromas and good attack on the palate, but falls down a little on the finish, while Valcalepio Rosso '07 shows good structure. The rosé Schiava della Bergamasca '08 is attractively spicy.

○ Moscato Giallo Passito della Bergamasca '08	♣♣	4*
⊙ Schiava della Bergamasca '08	♣	2*
● Valcalepio Moscato Passito '07	♣	6
● Valcalepio Rosso '07	♣	4

Cantine Valtenesi - Lugana

VIA PERGOLA, 21
25080 MONIGA DEL GARDA [BS]
TEL. 0365502002
www.civielle.com

Founded in 1979, this co-operative winery vinifies the grapes of 45 small growers. Its comprehensive range includes the deep, elegant Groppello Elianto '07, a taut, fruity Lugana Biocòra '08 with a hint of minerality, and a supple '07 Groppello Pergola with rich fruit and silky-smooth tannins.

● Garda Cl. Groppello Elianto '07	♟♟	4*
○ Lugana Biocòra '08	♟♟	4*
● Garda Cl. Groppello Pergola '07	♟	4

Ugo Vezzoli

LOC. SAN PANCRAZIO
VIA G. B. VEZZOLI, 20
25030 PALAZZOLO SULL'OGLIO [BS]
TEL. 030738018
www.vezzolifranciacorta.com

The Vezzoli family has lived in Franciacorta for centuries and today the old palazzo of San Pancrazio, near Palazzolo, houses the cellars, where the grapes from the vineyards are fermented. This year we picked out the elegant Franciacorta Brut with its fresh fruitiness. The Satèn is also good.

○ Franciacorta Brut	♟♟	5
○ Franciacorta Satèn	♟	5

Vigna Dorata

FRAZ. CALINO
VIA SALA, 80
25046 CAZZAGO SAN MARTINO [BS]
TEL. 0307254275
www.vignadorata.it

Luciana Mingotti's cellar in Calino makes fine still wines and Franciacortas, as a series of excellent cuvées amply confirmed. The fresh, complex Brut has flesh and character, the Satèn has well-defined notes of apple and refreshing tanginess, and the Rosé shows structure and finesse.

○ Franciacorta Brut	♟♟	5
⊙ Franciacorta Rosé	♟♟	5
○ Franciacorta Satèn	♟♟	5

Visconti

VIA C. BATTISTI, 139
25015 DESENZANO DEL GARDA [BS]
TEL. 0309120681
www.luganavisconti.it

Franco Visconti continues the family tradition as the legendary name celebrates its centenary. Lugana Santa Onorata '08 is excellent, showing firm, fruity and mineral, and the Superiore '07 is interesting. The classic Etichetta Nera '08 is very drinkable and the other wines are decent.

○ Lugana S. Onorata '08	♟♟	4*
○ Lugana Brut M. Cl.	♟	5
○ Lugana Collo Lungo Et. Nera '08	♟	4
○ Lugana Sup. S. Onorata '07	♟	5

Zamichele

VIA ROVEGLIA PALAZZINA, 2
25010 POZZOLENGO [BS]
TEL. 030918631
cantinazamichele@libero.it

This Pozzolengo estate presented two excellent wines: the satisfying, fruity, full-flavoured Lugana Gardè '07, aged in new oak, and the edgy, supple Lugana '07.

○ Lugana Gardè '07	♟♟	4*
○ Lugana '07	♟	4

Emilio Zuliani

VIA TITO SPERI, 28
25080 PADENGHE SUL GARDA [BS]
TEL. 0309907026
www.vinizuliani.it

Zuliani is a legendary name in Garda winemaking. Production is carefully crafted from estate-grown grapes. Chiaretto Pink Dream '08 is excellent, giving blueberry, raspberry and a full-flavoured, satisfyingly compact palate. The sparkling Garda Rosé is well made and Groppello Balosse '06 is decent.

⊙ Garda Cl. Chiaretto Pink Dream '08	♟♟	4
● Garda Cl. Groppello Balosse '06	♟	5
⊙ Garda Cl. Rosé '08	♟	3

TRENTINO

 An old advertisement by the Trento provincial authority used a slogan that is very true: "Trentino rhymes with vino". Wine is one of most typical features of this small Italian region, along with apples and winter tourism. But wine really means something around here, especially in the collective imagination of the population. Much winemaking is in the hands of large co-operatives like Cavit, Mezzocorona, La Vis, Cantina Rotaliana and others which always produce well-made wines with excellent value for money. These enterprises are more than just the backbone of the area's entire wine sector for they provide an agricultural income for thousands of families who manage to live, and live well, from their activities. Then there is sparkling winemaking with the return in grand style of the Trento DOC, one of the most prestigious Metodo Classicos in the world. The Lunellis from Ferrari are in the lead, followed by smaller producers like Dorigati, Abate Nero, and once again the co-operative wineries. Finally there are many small private producers led by Carlo and Anselmo Guerrieri Gonzaga from San Leonardo, along with Cesconi, Rosi, Foradori, and many others. But this year we would like to point out our Three Glasses have been awarded to a sparkler from the agricultural college at San Michele all'Adige. This top wine school has over the years trained ranks of young winemakers who today, in addition to being essential to regional wine production, work across Italy and abroad. Most of all, this edition of Italian Wines confirms that "Trentino rhymes with vino" with 11 Three Glass awards, a regional record, and we noted across-the-board quality in the best Trento DOC sparklers as never before. Furthermore, these major results were achieved without the wines from Elisabetta Foradori, one of the best interpreters of local wines and varieties, who decided to allow all of her wines to age for a further year in the cellar. This courageous, very responsible decision deserves a mention to show just how much the "Trentini" love their "vini", and that rhymes as well.

Abate Nero

FRAZ. GARDOLO
SPONDA TRENTINA, 45
38014 TRENTO
TEL. 0461246566
www.abatenero.it

CELLAR SALES
PRE-BOOKED VISITS

ANNUAL PRODUCTION 70,000 bottles
HECTARES UNDER VINE 65
VITICULTURE METHOD Conventional

Dedicated to the legendary father of sparkling wine, this winery for 40 years has been among the undisputed leaders in sparklers in Trentino and beyond. The cellar is located along the banks of the Avisio, right on the edge of Trento at the entrance to the village of Lavis. Luciano Lunelli directs winemaking, and Eugenio de Castel Terlago is managing partner. This harmonious duo is committed to promoting this highly distinctive Trento DOC label.

Domini was born here. This classy vintage sparkling wine came from long, slow planning and now enters the scene with all the grace and charm of its name, showing subtle sensations of peach and apricot, lovely consistency and a silky softness. You could say this sparkler helps to spotlight the house jewel, the Riserva, Cuvée dell'Abate, which won Three Glasses again this year with marvellous finesse, unfailing elegance, great development and smooth finish. The other wines are all sound and represent the best in Trento.

Nicola Balter

VIA VALLUNGA II, 24
38068 ROVERETO [TN]
TEL. 0464430101
www.balter.it

CELLAR SALES
PRE-BOOKED VISITS

ANNUAL PRODUCTION 80,000 bottles
HECTARES UNDER VINE 10
VITICULTURE METHOD Conventional

This year, Nicola Balter has managed to combine his aspirations as a producer of both red wines and sparklers. He submitted wines emblematic of his commitment to vineyards and winemaking, ambassadors for the splendid estate where they are created. The vines stand on the only plateau overlooking the high hill of Rovereto with excellent locations in carefully tended plots among forests of black pine and mountain oak. The rows spread out from the country house and underground cellar that represent a model for environmentally sustainable farming.

Nicola managed to land two wines in our finals, the classic vintage spumante and extraordinary Barbanico '07 from lagrein, cabernet sauvignon and merlot. The wines are brilliantly made, especially the sparklers, which show soft and fragrant, braced by backbone contributed by the admirable winemaking. Yet something keeps them from hitting the heights, perhaps the uncompromising artisanship in production or their development in bottle. But Balter always means good drinking. Barbanico is among the best blends and all the other wines are great value for money.

○ Trento Brut Cuvée dell'Abate Ris. '04	♟♟♟ 7
○ Trento Brut Domini '04	♟♟ 6
○ Trento Abate Nero Brut '06	♟♟ 5
○ Trento Abate Nero Extra Brut '06	♟♟ 5
○ Trento Abate Nero Extra Dry '06	♟ 5
○ Trento Brut Cuvée dell'Abate Ris. '03	♟♟♟ 6
○ Trento Brut Cuvée dell'Abate Ris. '02	♟♟♟ 6
○ Trento Brut Cuvée dell'Abate Ris. '01	♟♟♟ 6

● Barbanico '07	♟♟ 5
○ Trento Balter Ris. '03	♟♟ 6
○ Balter Brut	♟♟♟ 4
● Cabernet Sauvignon '07	♟ 4
● Lagrein-Merlot '08	♟ 4
○ Trento Balter Ris. '01	♟♟♟ 6
● Barbanico '04	♟♟ 5
● Barbanico '03	♟♟ 5
○ Trento Balter Ris. '02	♟♟ 6

Bolognani

VIA STAZIONE, 19
38015 LAVIS [TN]
TEL. 0461246354
www.bolognani.com

CELLAR SALES
PRE-BOOKED VISITS

ANNUAL PRODUCTION **70,000 bottles**
HECTARES UNDER VINE **4.4**
VITICULTURE METHOD **Conventional**

For some time, we have been predicting it. The Bolognanis are showing all their skill and have established themselves at the top of the Trento winemaking pyramid. The entire range of wines shows character and type that go beyond the Dolomites. Merit goes to the technology applied in the cellar and the equally fundamental attention to the vineyards, expertly tended by the Bolognanis, who started out as cellarmen. The synergy of cellar and vineyard has helped this Lavis estate produce wines that are as appealing as they are personal.

Let's start with the Armilo '07, a Teroldego from out of the box since the grapes are sourced from outside the DOC zone. This elegant, juicy wine, with its austere mineral finesse, has a young, satisfying attack and a finish as sound as it is full-flavoured. Growing skill is also evident the Traminer Aromatico sourced from the hillside vineyards above Trento, towards the Vigolana massif, to take advantage of temperature changes and create spirited structure, great minerality and pleasant aromatics. The other wines are correct and convincing, though we expected more from the cabernet sauvignon and merlot Gabàn '06.

Borgo dei Posseri

LOC. POZZO BASSO, 1
38061 ALA [TN]
TEL. 0464671899
www.borgodeiposseri.com

CELLAR SALES
PRE-BOOKED VISITS

ANNUAL PRODUCTION **60,000 bottles**
HECTARES UNDER VINE **18**
VITICULTURE METHOD **Organic certified**

Margherita de Pilati and her husband Martin Mainenti are involving their winery in new developments and synergies, still aimed at sparkling wine production. All these projects are near completion, and we will discuss them at a later date. Meanwhile, this estate continues to be one of the most unusual in Trentino winemaking: on tableland jutting towards Vallagarina, with steep slopes in an isolated, unspoiled area that enables the estate to experiment with sustainable farming and natural growing methods.

As we wait for future developments on the estate and harvests from new plantings, it was again the Merlot Rocol '06 that stood out at our tastings. Only moderately intense in hue, it is pleasantly drinkable with typical notes of berry fruit, like the berries you can pick along the vineyard rows. Pinot Nero Paradis '06 also has stylish form and an easy yet elegant drinkability, with classic, varietal notes of wild strawberries on the nose. The Müller Thurgau Quaron '08 is less interesting than usual.

● Teroldego Armilo '07	♟♟	4*
● Gabàn '06	♟♟	6
○ Trentino Traminer Aromatico Sanròc '07	♟♟	4
○ Trentino Moscato Giallo '08	♟	4
○ Trentino Müller Thurgau '08	♟	4
○ Trentino Nosiola '08	♟	4
● Teroldego Armilo '06	♟♟♟	4*
● Gabàn '04	♟♟	6
● Gabàn '03	♟♟	6
○ Trentino Traminer Aromatico Sanròc '06	♟♟	4

● Merlot Rocol '06	♟♟	4
● Pinot Nero Paradis '06	♟♟	4
○ Müller Thurgau Quaron '08	♟	4
● Merlot Rocol '05	♟♟	4*
● Pinot Nero Paradis '05	♟♟	5

Cavit

VIA DEL PONTE DI RAVINA, 31
38040 TRENTO
TEL. 0461381711
www.cavit.it

CELLAR SALES
PRE-BOOKED VISITS

ANNUAL PRODUCTION 65,000,000 bottles
HECTARES UNDER VINE 5700
VITICULTURE METHOD Conventional

Cavit is an example of how a co-operative-style, winemaking colossus can modify its product offer with wines that show unbeatable value for money yet at the same time reflect the area where they were made. In an ever more competitive market, with the economic crisis reaching even into the cellar, this winemaking bastion defends the hard work of its myriad members, the thousands of growers from the 11 co-operative wineries that form a consortium selling millions of bottles worldwide from China to Brazil, the US and India.

The wines represent a synthesis of this philosophy. The sparkling Altemasi Graal Riserva '02 is not just spectacular. It's also our Sparkler of the Year thanks to a soaring performance. Rich, full, and intense in every facet of tasting, it lives up to its name as a Holy Grail of sparkling wines. But the 20 or so other wines tasted from this broad range are just as praiseworthy. The sparklers were sound and a nice performance came from the classic Teroldego Maso Cervara '06, the mostly chardonnay Maso Toresella '08, an oak-aged white, and the resounding Vino Santo Arièle '98, capping off these truly remarkable results.

Cesarini Sforza

FRAZ. RAVINA
VIA STELLA, 9
38040 TRENTO
TEL. 0461382200
www.cesarinisforza.com

CELLAR SALES
PRE-BOOKED VISITS

ANNUAL PRODUCTION 1.500,000 bottles
HECTARES UNDER VINE N.D.
VITICULTURE METHOD Conventional

This brand goes back to 1974 and was one of the first wineries in Trentino to focus exclusively on sparklers. Changes in the ownership and sales network subsequently led to acquisition by the La Vis group in 2008. More than half of the million and a half bottles are Trento DOC Metodo Classico and the proportion is destined to rise. Oenological management is entrusted to Giorgia Brugnara, who oversees projects to expand this historic brand of sparklers. Early results are more than convincing.

Proof comes from an amazing spumante, Aquila Reale, from all chardonnay harvested from the same vineyard in Sette Fontane at Giovo, in Alta Val di Cembra. A Trento DOC cru, dedicated to the city's emblem the eagle, Aquila Reale Riserva '02 is at its second release, but immediately swooped to snatch Three Glasses from our table. This regally assertive wine can develop further over time. The good Trento Tridentum Rosé shows a nice copper colour and aromatic wild berry tones while the easy drinking Tridentum '05 and the Spumante Charmat are supple and extremely clean.

O Trento Altemasi Graal Brut Ris. '02	♥♥♥+ 7
O Cuvée Maso Toresella '08	♥♥ 5
● Teroldego Rotaliano Maso Cervara '06	♥♥ 5
O Trentino Vino Santo Arèle '98	♥♥ 8
● Teroldego Rotaliano Bottega Vinai '07	♥♥ 4*
O Trentino Chardonnay Maso Toresella Sup. '07	♥♥ 5
O Trentino Müller Thurgau Bottega Vinai '08	♥♥ 4*
O Trentino Müller Thurgau Zeveri Sup. '08	♥♥ 4
O Trentino Pinot Grigio Bottega Vinai '08	♥♥ 4
● Trentino Cabernet Sauvignon Bottega Vinai '06	♥ 4
O Trentino Nosiola Bottega Vinai '08	♥ 3
O Trento Altemasi Graal Brut '01	♀♀♀ 7
O Trento Altemasi Graal Brut Ris. '00	♀♀♀ 6
O Trento Altemasi Graal Brut Ris. '97	♀♀♀ 6
O Trento Altemasi Graal Brut Ris. '96	♀♀♀ 7
O Trento Altemasi Graal Brut Ris. '95	♀♀♀ 6

O Trento Aquila Reale Ris. '02	♥♥♥ 8
O Trento Tridentum '05	♥♥ 5
⊙ Trento Tridentum Rosé	♥♥ 5
O Spumante Charmant	♥ 4
O Trento Tridentum '04	♀♀ 5
O Trento Tridentum '02	♀♀ 5

Cesconi

FRAZ. PRESSANO
VIA MARCONI, 39
38015 LAVIS [TN]
TEL. 0461240355
www.cesconi.it

CELLAR SALES
PRE-BOOKED VISITS

ANNUAL PRODUCTION **130,000 bottles**
HECTARES UNDER VINE **21**
VITICULTURE METHOD **Conventional**

Before entering the modern cellar at Cesconi, do visit the surrounding vineyards where olive trees and vines grow together on the hillside of Lavis and winds gust benevolently off the Dolomites. This relaxing environment is a paragon of viticulture. The Cesconis have been making wine for generations and for a few decades now have been influential makers of good wine, known well beyond Trentino. They look after their vineyards like new others, experiment with innovative cellar techniques and continue to amaze us with increasingly appealing and distinctive wines.

The ten wines tasted showed immediate proof of the utterly Cesconian identity of their signature white, the Olivar '07 from pinot bianco, pinot grigio and chardonnay. It's tangy and full, even opulent, yet never heavy, and fairly lively with a finish that satisfies and stimulates on retasting. Three well-deserved Glasses. Pivier from practically pure Merlot also came close, showing invigorating and racy, although slightly penalized by an odd '06 growing season with uneven results. Outstanding other wines include the Pinot Grigio, perhaps one of the best from Trentino, and a classic Chardonnay with spirited character.

O Olivar '07	♟♟♟	5
● Rosso del Pivier '06	♟♟	6
O Chardonnay '07	♟♟	5
O Pinot Grigio '07	♟♟	5
O Nosiola '07	♟	4
O Prabi Bianco '07	♟	4
O Trentino Traminer Aromatico '07	♟	5
O Olivar '05	♟♟♟	5
O Olivar '01	♟♟♟	5
O Chardonnay '06	♟♟	5
● Rosso del Pivier '04	♟♟	6
● Rosso del Pivier '03	♟♟	6

Cantina d'Isera

VIA AL PONTE, 1
38060 ISERA [TN]
TEL. 0464433795
www.cantinaisera.it

CELLAR SALES
PRE-BOOKED VISITS

ANNUAL PRODUCTION **600,000 bottles**
HECTARES UNDER VINE **N.D.**
VITICULTURE METHOD **Conventional**

Where does Marzemino come from? This issue is at the centre of a full calendar of events promoted by the municipality of Isera and this co-operative winery. The tracks of Marzemino have been traced back to Greece where identical vines, confirmed by DNA testing, were grown on the Ionian island of Lefkada. A scientific expedition also found evidence in the Caucasus. With Marzemino, this co-operative winery has guaranteed progress and prosperity to generations of growers, and continues to do so under the management of Fausto Campostrini, a skilled oenologist as well as effective organizer.

The wines presented showed uneven progress, except for the brand new Trento '05, a spumante named after 1907, the year this co-operative was founded. This important sparkler is an excellently dosed wine, light in structure and long in perlage and taste sensations. But let's get on to the Marzemino. A substantial number of bottles of the classic '08 are released, as well as of the Chardonnay and Pinot Grigio, to satisfy an increasingly demanding market looking for honesty and good value for money.

O Trento Brut 907 '05	♟♟	5
O Trentino Chardonnay '08	♟	4
● Trentino Marzemino '08	♟	4
O Trentino Müller Thurgau '08	♟	4
O Trentino Pinot Grigio '08	♟	4

F.lli Dorigati

VIA DANTE, 5
38016 MEZZOCORONA [TN]
TEL. 0461605313
www.dorigati.it

CELLAR SALES
PRE-BOOKED VISITS

ANNUAL PRODUCTION 100,000 bottles
HECTARES UNDER VINE 13
VITICULTURE METHOD Conventional

A century and a half of growing and winemaking experience does not pass unnoticed. Reflect on this as you pause for a few minutes in the austere cellar, located in the heart of the town of Mezzocorona. It's not a show cellar but it is built with farming country logic. There are no concessions to architectural fads or fashion. Yet this is to be the beating heart of production and the Dorigatis are a guarantee. They have maintained the high quality of their Teroldego, this area's trademark wine, while tackling the challenge of sparkling wine with the same skill and perseverance.

Methius '03, from chardonnay and pinot nero, a paragon for Trento, needs no further praise from us and again proves a winner among classic Trentino sparklers. This wine's impressive aromatic energy gives characteristic resiny tones and intriguing minerality. The Dorigatis also make two textbook versions of Teroldego. The '07 shows structure and class not unlike what we found in the Diedri Riserva '06, which has greater concentration and body. The other, standard quality wines include the unusual Kretzer, a rosé Lagrein.

Endrizzi

LOC. MASETTO, 2
38010 SAN MICHELE ALL'ADIGE [TN]
TEL. 0461650129
www.endrizzi.it

CELLAR SALES
PRE-BOOKED VISITS

ANNUAL PRODUCTION 500,000 bottles
HECTARES UNDER VINE 40
VITICULTURE METHOD Conventional

Friendliness, hospitality and lots of good wines summarize the wine and grape production philosophy of Paolo Endrici's family. Paolo is a manager with a farmer's style and a true interpreter of good Trentino wines. This historic estate still has ancient barrels on display in its eatery-cum-museum, where hospitality is attentive. The vines are managed to environmentally sustainable standards and the rows, which run in the direction of Castel Monreale and the hill at Faedo, are planted with aromatic plants and inhabited by nesting birds.

The top wine this time is Gran Masetto '06. It's designed to amaze and fermented with the addition of grapes left to dry on rush mats, to render the wine even more opulent, mellow and powerful. Winemaking skill is also obvious in the Trento Riserva '04, a well-dosed spumante fragrant with yeasty tones and light yet lingering hints of vanilla. The rest of these wines are well typed and made for immediate drinking.

○ Trento Methius Brut Ris. '03	♟♟♟ 7
● Teroldego Rotaliano '07	♟♟ 4
● Teroldego Rotaliano Diedri Ris. '06	♟♟ 6
● Trentino Cabernet Grener '06	♟ 6
☉ Trentino Lagrein Kretzer '08	♟ 4
○ Trentino Pinot Grigio '08	♟ 4
○ Trento Methius Brut Ris. '02	♟♟♟ 7
○ Trento Methius Brut Ris. '00	♟♟♟ 7
○ Trento Methius Brut. Ris. '98	♟♟♟ 7
● Teroldego Rotaliano Diedri Ris. '05	♟♟ 6
● Teroldego Rotaliano Diedri Ris. '04	♟♟ 6
● Teroldego Rotaliano Diedri Ris. '03	♟♟ 6

● Gran Masetto '06	♟♟ 7
○ Masetto Bianco '07	♟♟ 4*
○ Masetto Dulcis '07	♟♟ 5
● Teroldego Rotaliano '07	♟♟ 4*
● Teroldego Rotaliano Maso Camorz Ris. '06	♟♟ 4
○ Trentino Chardonnay Tradizione '08	♟♟ 4
○ Trento Endrizzi Brut Ris. '04	♟♟ 5
● Trentino Moscato Rosa '07	♟ 5
● Gran Masetto '05	♟♟ 7

Vignaiolo Giuseppe Fanti

FRAZ. PRESSANO
P.ZZA DELLA CROCE, 3
38015 LAVIS [TN]
TEL. 0461240809
vignaiolo@virglilio.it

PRE-BOOKED VISITS

ANNUAL PRODUCTION **20,000 bottles**
HECTARES UNDER VINE **3.5**
VITICULTURE METHOD **Natural**

Alessandro Fanti was born to the trade into a family of winemakers who have always worked behind the scenes, tending their small plots on Lavis hill as if they were gardens. For some time now, Alessandro has been experimenting with organic agriculture, applying biodynamic methods, and in other words making wine as naturally as possible. His vineyards show total environmental sustainability and balance. The same varieties are selected with criteria that assign each established plant to a well-identified plot. These growing systems have become a way of life for this winemaker

The wines already reflect Alessandro's intentions. They have a unique, natural quality with interesting imperfections and identity. The quality of whites as well as reds has benefited from this careful attention. In the Pritianum '07, from a blend of chardonnay, nosiola and incrocio Manzoni, dynamism and minerality meld with zesty length before the clean nose's immediate aromas conjure up hidden taste sensations, inviting yet still to be discovered. Portico '06, a red from cabernet, teroldego and merlot, is just as good. The Incrocio Manzoni '08 is much simpler.

★ Ferrari

VIA PONTE DI RAVINA, 15
38100 TRENTO
TEL. 0461972311
www.ferrarispumante.it

CELLAR SALES
PRE-BOOKED VISITS

ANNUAL PRODUCTION **5.200,000 bottles**
HECTARES UNDER VINE **120**
VITICULTURE METHOD **Conventional**

This winery makes way for the next generation and new major goals, all aimed at a specific Trentino identity, and at more ambitious objectives, some yet to be achieved. Bolstered by widespread acknowledgement of their wines' quality and proud of the family's renowned commercial reliability, cousins Matteo, Marcello and Camilla Lunelli are the new custodians of this famous sparkling wine brand created by the dedication of their parents and uncles. Meanwhile, Gino, Franco and Mauro are still at Ravina to give support to these three young managers.

There is no point repeating that their various spumantes, all Trento DOCs, are must-taste wines that symbolize the marriage of Trentino's terrain and good management of the grape, especially chardonnay. As good as any locally and indeed in Italy, the chardonnay-only Giulio Ferrari '00 is as round as its vintage year, showing austere in its versatility, distinctive and intriguing, as only the greatest wines can. The Perlé was not released this year, leaving centre stage to the new Perlé Nero '03, exclusively from pinot nero. This Blanc de Noirs is a worthy second-in-command to the top-ranking Giulio. The other sparkers are all very sound.

● Portico Rosso '06	♟♟ 4*
○ Pritianum '07	♟♟ 5
○ Incrocio Manzoni '08	♟ 4

○ Trento Giulio Ferrari	
Riserva del Fondatore Brut '00	♟♟♟ 8
○ Trento Extra Brut Perlé Nero '03	♟♟ 8
○ Trento Brut	♟♟ 6
○ Trento Brut Maximum	♟♟ 6
⊙ Trento Brut Perlé Rosé '05	♟♟ 8
○ Trento Maximum Démi Sec	♟♟ 6
○ Trento Giulio Ferrari '97	♟♟♟ 8
○ Trento Giulio Ferrari '96	♟♟♟ 8
○ Trento Giulio Ferrari '95	♟♟♟ 8
○ Trento Giulio Ferrari	
Riserva del Fondatore Brut '99	♟♟♟ 8

Graziano Fontana

VIA CASE SPARSE, 9
38010 FAEDO [TN]
TEL. 0461650400

★ Foradori

VIA DAMIANO CHIESA, 1
38017 MEZZOLOMBARDO [TN]
TEL. 0461601046
www.elisabettaforadori.com

CELLAR SALES
PRE-BOOKED VISITS

ANNUAL PRODUCTION **35,000 bottles**
HECTARES UNDER VINE **7**
VITICULTURE METHOD **Conventional**

The alluvial fan created by ancient glaciers subsequent to volcanic explosions, what geologists call Werfenian siltstone, can be reached by following the road signs marked by the staves of unused barrels and vats. This is the how winemakers in this small town above San Michele all'Adige show advertise work, and the attention they reserve for their vineyards and wine. Just before the town, among vineyards marked by red roses, is the winery of this expert grower, for some years now also a skilled oenologist.

All Graziano's wines are clearly well crafted, as only a confident winemaker knows how. The Müller Thurgau, like others from this hillside where the variety of the same name was first grown and vinified, has less marked features compared to other vintages and shows a simple, clean, light aromatic tone. Another of this winemaker's signature wines, the Lagrein, is also a bit under par, yet still has a lovely ruby red colour and is ready for immediate drinking. The same can be said of the other wines.

ANNUAL PRODUCTION **150,000 bottles**
HECTARES UNDER VINE **24**
VITICULTURE METHOD **Natural**

Few producers can claim to have had an entry in the Guide without any mention of their wines. Elisabetta Foradori deserves this and more, because she is such an honest winemaker, totally committed and completely involved, who never gives in to compromise. She is even more committed since, several harvests ago, she implemented the biodynamic growing principles she had been testing for some time in a life choice as well as a way of making wine. Elisabetta is not one to be moved by passing fashion trends. She has never bowed uncritically to modern winemaking and growing techniques. Invariably, she has aimed to be in the front rank of winemakers, with results that are more than just exciting. This exceptional woman winemaker has now undertaken an even more difficult and absorbing challenge. She waits patiently to offer wines that focus on the recovery of ancient values and experiences buried in the memory of winemakers who still wish to produce wine in natural, ancestral harmony with their local environment.

○ Müller Thurgau '08	♟♟	4
○ Trentino Chardonnay di Faedo '08	♟	4
● Trentino Lagrein di Faedo '07	♟	4
○ Trentino Sauvignon di Faedo '08	♟	4
○ Trentino Traminer Aromatico di Faedo '08	♟	4
● Trentino Lagrein di Faedo '06	♟♟	5
○ Trentino Sauvignon di Faedo '07	♟♟	4

● Granato '04	♟♟♟	7
● Granato '03	♟♟♟	7
● Granato '02	♟♟♟	7
● Granato '01	♟♟♟	7
● Granato '00	♟♟♟	7
● Granato '99	♟♟♟	5
● Granato '06	♟♟	8
○ Myrto '06	♟♟	5
● Teroldego Rotaliano Foradori '06	♟♟	5

Gaierhof

VIA IV NOVEMBRE, 51
38030 ROVERÈ DELLA LUNA [TN]
TEL. 0461658514
www.gaierhof.com

CELLAR SALES
PRE-BOOKED VISITS

ANNUAL PRODUCTION 550,000 bottles
HECTARES UNDER VINE 130
VITICULTURE METHOD Conventional

Either two in one or vice versa, since Gaierhof actually comprises two separate entities, one purely winemaking, the other growing. Both are owned and operated by the same family, the Togns, a dynasty linked with wine for many harvests now. Their main cellar is in Roverè della Luna on the border between Trentino and Alto Adige. But Maso Poli is on the high hill of Lavis, where well-ordered vineyards surround a lovely structure equipped for a whole range of activities connected to wine culture. This enchanting place is on the promontory between Val di Cembra and Val d'Adige.

Around 15 wines were submitted, all aimed at pleasant drinking and an international market. We start with the selection of Teroldego Rotaliano, a balanced, elegant red capable of competing in any position. The Pinot Grigio '08 from Maso Poli shows off pear aromas and a minerally touch. While we were not completely convinced by Marmoran '06, a Bordeaux-style red, this might have been because it had been bottled only recently before tasting. Special mention goes to the rare and always enjoyable Moscato Rosa, this year in the '08 version.

Grigoletti

VIA GARIBALDI, 12
38060 NOMI [TN]
TEL. 0464834215
www.grigoletti.com

CELLAR SALES
PRE-BOOKED VISITS

ANNUAL PRODUCTION 60,000 bottles
HECTARES UNDER VINE 7
VITICULTURE METHOD Conventional

Every sector of this cellar has been expanded and remodelled, transforming the structure of this rustic house into a sort of temple to country wine. The Grigolettis are committed winemakers who focus on lots of hard work in the vineyards and just as much careful work in the cellar, now performed in spaces that are very good to look at. Some of the plots are on alluvial soil in the bend created by flooding from the nearby river Adige, and some run along the hilly ridge of the river's right bank, following the shifting sunshine.

The latest vintage bottled was not one of the best. Scores were inconsistent for white wines and for Marzemino. The only comforting confirmations come from Gonzalier, a classic Bordeaux blend, and the Merlot. Not coincidentally, the latter is the trademark wine from this estate and Vallagarina in general, the area bounded by Rovereto, Nomi and Aldeno. For the past ten years, Aldeno has hosted an exhibition and national wine competition dedicated to Merlot, at which the Grigolettis' Merlot Antica Vigna has always distinguished itself.

● Marmoran Maso Poli '06	¶ 6
● Teroldego Rotaliano Superiore '07	¶ 4
● Trentino Moscato Rosa '08	¶ 6
O Trentino Müller Thurgau dei Settecento '08	¶ 4
O Trentino Pinot Grigio '08	¶ 4
O Trentino Traminer Aromatico '08	¶ 4
● Marmoran Maso Poli '05	¶¶ 6
● Trentino Moscato Rosa '07	¶¶ 6

● Gonzalier '06	¶¶ 5
● Trentino Merlot Antica Vigna di Nomi '07	¶¶ 5
● Maso Federico Passito Rosso '05	¶ 5
● Trentino Cabernet '07	¶ 4
● Trentino Marzemino '08	¶ 4
● Trentino Merlot Antica Vigna di Nomi '05	¶¶ 5
● Trentino Merlot Antica Vigna di Nomi '04	¶¶ 5

La Vis/Valle di Cembra

via Carmine, 7
38034 Lavis [TN]
tel. 0461440111
www.la-vis.com

CELLAR SALES
PRE-BOOKED VISITS

ANNUAL PRODUCTION **5,500.000 bottles**
HECTARES UNDER VINE **1,35**
VITICULTURE METHOD **Conventional**

The idea of combining similar experiences to start new winemaking operations gave rise to the management strategy of the La Vis co-operative, a winemaking power that grew even stronger after linking up with Cantina Sociale di Cembra, control of Cesarini Sforza Spumanti and viticultural projects in Tuscany. These activities involve thousands of member growers and mobilize ranks of agricultural technicians, oenologists and marketing experts, all under the supervision of chairman Roberto Giacomoni and general manager Fausto Peratoner.

The power of wines from this winery is contained in a portrait, the wine called Ritratto, or Portrait, in honour of the famous divisionist painter Giovanni Segantini, whose work appears on most of the winery labels. Our Three Glasses go to the Ritratto '07, from chardonnay, pinot grigio and riesling, a tangy and minerally wine, mature, yet ready for further development. These qualities are also found in most of the 15 or so other wines. Among these we should mention the classic Müller Thurgau '08, real house speciality.

○ Ritratto Bianco '07	▼▼▼	5
○ Trentino Chardonnay Ritratti '08	▼▼	4
● Trentino Merlot Ritratti '07	▼▼	4
○ Trentino Müller Thurgau Dos Caslir '08	▼▼	4*
○ Trentino Müller Thurgau Ritratti '08	▼▼	3*
○ Trentino Sauvignon Maso Tratta '08	▼▼	4
○ Mandolaia '08	▼	5
● Ritratto Rosso '07	▼	5
⊙ Schiava Valvalè Valle di Cembra '08	▼	3
○ Trentino Müller Thurgau Maso Roncador '08	▼	4
○ Trentino Pinot Grigio Ritratti '08	▼	4
● Trentino Pinot Nero Dos Caslir '07	▼	5
● Ritratto Rosso '03	▽▽▽	5
○ Ritratto Bianco '06	▽▽	5
○ Ritratto Bianco '05	▽▽	5

Letrari

via Monte Baldo, 13/15
38068 Rovereto [TN]
tel. 0464480200
www.letrari.it

CELLAR SALES
PRE-BOOKED VISITS

ANNUAL PRODUCTION **150,000 bottles**
HECTARES UNDER VINE **23**
VITICULTURE METHOD **Natural**

No one commands the weather. In viticulture, this old saw refers mainly to the progress of the growing season, which for the Letraris has never been as quirky or unpredictable as during recent harvests. But Nello, the family patriarch, is accustomed to dealing with whatever the weather sends. His children, Lucia and Paolo, currently manage this estate, but he still hands out advice, suggests solutions and even takes on new challenges, especially if they are connected with the sparkling wine he has loved since his youth.

This time, those sparklers made a good showing, starting with the Letrari Brut Rosé '06, the first disgorgement of a wine with lots of allure. But the Riserva '04 del Trento is even more satisfying. Its lovely, stylish nose has a fruity, fragrant texture, and the palate is slightly citrus, zesty and elegant. The still wines are a slightly different matter. The range is too broad with at least a dozen wines. But the elder Letrari has already announced radical change and drastic reduction in the range to improve the sparklers. It will soon be time to raise those glasses.

⊙ Brut Rosé '06	▼▼	6
○ Trento Brut Letrari Ris. '04	▼▼	6
● La Civetta Rosso '07	▼	4
○ Traminer Aromatico '08	▼	4
● Trentino Cabernet Franc Ris. '05	▼	5
○ Trentino Chardonnay '08	▼	4
● Trentino Maso Lodron '05	▼	4
○ Trento Brut Letrari '06	▼	5
● Trentino Cabernet Sauvignon '04	▽▽	5
○ Trento Brut Ris. '99	▽▽	6

Longariva

FRAZ. BORGO SACCO
VIA R. ZANDONAI, 6
38068 ROVERETO [TN]
TEL. 0464437200
www.longariva.it

CELLAR SALES
PRE-BOOKED VISITS
RISTORAZIONE

ANNUAL PRODUCTION 100,000 bottles
HECTARES UNDER VINE 22
VITICULTURE METHOD Natural

The winery is near the family plant that processes sulphur and copper into Bordeaux mixture, an indispensable product for viticulture, and the vineyards are scattered around the Rovereto hills. Rosanna and Marco Manica are level-headed winemakers with great experience who do not like forcing things. They tend their plots like gardens, where orchards, aromatic herbs and trees all co-exist with the vines to beautify the landscape, their way of honouring agricultural biodiversity and the symbolic value of wine.

Although we were sold on the red Quartella last year, this time we felt Chardonnay Praistel Selezione '06 best expressed the Manica style with its extreme simplicity. Nothing spectacular, this honest wine introduces the other wines from Longariva, some penalized by unreliable weather, others by haste, especially the Pinot Grigio '08, and yet others by a lack of haste. This is the case with the Pinot Nero Zinzele, presented five years after vinification. Too long. The same goes for the precious Migoléta '04 from white grapes left to partially dry and released five years after the crush.

Maso Furli

LOC. FURLI
VIA FURLI, 32
38015 LAVIS [TN]
TEL. 0461240667
masofurli@alice.it

CELLAR SALES
PRE-BOOKED VISITS

ANNUAL PRODUCTION 18,000 bottles
HECTARES UNDER VINE 4
VITICULTURE METHOD Natural

That wines from this excellent estate are not listed among the best from Trentino is strange and even hard to believe. But that's the way it is. Marco Zanoni diligently manages this mini-estate, a tiny swath of vines in the Lavis hills with a home-style cellar, so to speak. It's still kitted out with top winemaking technology because the machines were designed and built part by Marco and part with the help of other winemaking friends. Who knows? Perhaps the price of technical perfection is a loss of local identity, to the detriment of the character of the variety itself.

In any case, all the wines tasted were good, although there is still a "but" in that we hoped for something better, The most intriguing is the Rosso Furli '06, from cabernet sauvignon with small amounts of merlot, with a nice minerally imprint on the nose, and a full-flavoured, complex palate with a stylish, velvety tannic weave. The Traminer and Sauvignon from '07 stand out for backbone, intact aromas and excellent technique. The same goes for the Chardonnay '07. But the Incrocio Manzoni has a bit too much acidity.

○ Trentino Chardonnay Praistel Sel. '06	♟♟	5
⊙ Graminè '08	♟	4
● Migoléta Sel. Moresca '04	♟	6
○ Trentino Chardonnay Perer '08	♟	4
○ Trentino Pinot Bianco Pergole '08	♟	5
○ Trentino Pinot Grigio Perer '08	♟	4
○ Migoléta '98	♟♟	6
● Trentino Cabernet Quartella Ris. '04	♟♟	5*
○ Trentino Pinot Bianco Pergole '05	♟♟	5

● Maso Furli Rosso '06	♟♟	5
○ Trentino Sauvignon '07	♟♟	5
○ Trentino Traminer Aromatico '07	♟♟	5
○ Incrocio Manzoni '07	♟	5
○ Trentino Chardonnay '07	♟	5
● Maso Furli Rosso '05	♟♟	5
● Maso Furli Rosso '04	♟♟	5
○ Trentino Sauvignon '04	♟♟	5
○ Trentino Traminer Aromatico '05	♟♟	5

Maso Martis

LOC. MARTIGNANO
VIA DELL'ALBERA, 52
38121 TRENTO
TEL. 0461821057
www.masomartis.it

CELLAR SALES
PRE-BOOKED VISITS

ANNUAL PRODUCTION **65,000 bottles**
HECTARES UNDER VINE **12**
VITICULTURE METHOD **Conventional**

The property is named after the god Mars for the temple built in his honour on the sunniest plateau on Mount Calisio above Trento. On the same site now is Roberta and Antonio Stelzer's winery, founded roughly 30 years ago to produce above all sparkling wines. They planted suitable varieties and transformed this corner of the hill that has avoided development into an admirable winemaking estate with small terraces, dry walls and plots set one against the other to optimize farming and harvests.

Let's start with the still wines. Both the Cabernet Sauvignon Indaco '05 and Chardonnay L'incanto '07 have an immediate impact on tasting, showing elegant and full of character. The house specialty sparklers show very clear, creamy notes in the flavour. This style has been well received by ranks of fans in a constantly evolving range of spumante wines. The Riserva '03 beautifully interprets both Trento and this estate. It's well orchestrated, with buttery tones, vanilla and nice length on the palate. The same goes for the Brut and the Rosé. The Démi Sec is nicely creamy.

MezzaCorona

VIA DEL TEROLDEGO, 1
38016 MEZZOCORONA [TN]
TEL. 0461616399
www.mezzacorona.it

CELLAR SALES
PRE-BOOKED VISITS

ANNUAL PRODUCTION **30,000,000 bottloc**
HECTARES UNDER VINE **3500**
VITICULTURE METHOD **Conventional**

This group, or rather this constantly expanding winemaking colossus, makes almost 30 million bottles distributed worldwide. Production is based in Trentino but it owns wine estates as far afield as Sicily and is involved in commercial relationships with other wineries, especially in Tuscany. MezzaCorona submitted around a dozen still wines and sparklers from Trento for tasting. Each variety is connected to a specific territorial area. Red varieties planted in the Campo Rotaliano go primarily for Teroldego and hillside vineyards supply traditional aromatic wine types.

Teroldego, in different versions, remains the most important estate wine. For the first time, a marvellous selection of this type, the Nos '04, mentioned by mistake in last year's Guide, won Three Glasses. The wine emerges from a long production process and is treated with care in tribute to the area's principal variety. But MezzaCorona also makes fine sparkling wines. Trento Riserva '03, named after Flavio, a medieval nobleman, is interesting and palate-caressing. The other wines are well crafted, from the Teroldego Riserva '06 to the Pinot Grigio Riserva '07, as well as the other three sparklers, the Rosé included.

● Trentino Cabernet Sauvignon L'Indaco '05	♈♈ 5
○ Trentino Chardonnay L'Incanto '07	♈♈ 5
○ Trento Brut Ris. '03	♈♈ 6
☉ Trento Brut Rosé	♈♈ 6
● Moscato Rosa '08	♈ 6
○ Trento Brut	♈ 6
○ Trento Démi Sec	♈ 6
○ Trento Brut Ris. '02	♈♈ 6

● Teroldego Rotaliano Nos Ris. '04	♈♈♈ 6
○ Trento Rotari Flavio Ris. '03	♈♈ 7
● Teroldego Rotaliano Ris. '06	♈♈ 5
○ Trentino Chardonnay Castel Firmian '08	♈ 4
○ Trentino Müller Thurgau Castel Firmian '08	♈ 4
○ Trentino Pinot Grigio Ris. '07	♈ 5
○ Trentino Traminer Castel Firmian '08	♈ 4
☉ Trento Rosé Rotari Brut	♈ 5
○ Trento Rotari Brut Ris. '05	♈ 5
○ Trento Rotari Cuvée 28	♈ 5
● Teroldego Rotaliano Ris. '05	♈♈ 5
○ Trento Rotari Flavio Ris. '02	♈♈ 7

Casata Monfort

VIA CARLO SETTE, 21
38015 LAVIS [TN]
TEL. 0461246353
www.cantinemonfort.it

CELLAR SALES
PRE-BOOKED VISITS

ANNUAL PRODUCTION **140,000 bottles**
HECTARES UNDER VINE **40**
VITICULTURE METHOD **Conventional**

The Simonis, owners of this solid estate, are ubiquitous winemakers and seem to be simultaneously active at Lavis as well as Maso Cantanghel at Forte di Civezzano. The two operations have the same production philosophy, although the Simonis experiment with new cellar techniques and age their most valuable wines here in the austere wartime stronghold between Trento and Valsugana. In the vineyards, you'll find old, endangered grape varieties for microvinifications that confirm the Simonis commitment to defending biodiversity.

Outstanding in the vast range of wines is the Trento '05 sparkler. It has lovely vitality, intriguing aromatics and nice length. Always convincing, the traditional Chardonnay shows clear touches of apple and a tangy, persistent flavour. As unusual as it is interesting, Blanc de Sers '07 blends many local varieties for a wine with an ancient flavour. The other wines are reliable. The always-sound Pinot Nero from Maso Cantanghel, a real classic, takes centre stage this year in the '06 version.

Pojer & Sandri

LOC. MOLINI, 4
38010 FAEDO [TN]
TEL. 0461650342
www.pojeresandri.it

CELLAR SALES
PRE-BOOKED VISITS

ANNUAL PRODUCTION **250,000 bottles**
HECTARES UNDER VINE **25**
VITICULTURE METHOD **Conventional**

This duo has written the history of Trentino wine. Mario Pojer and Fiorentino Sandri love difficult challenges. In the mid 1970s, they created their estate from nothing, and then expanded and improved it with the latest technology, they diversified the vineyard sites and strengthened ties between wine and territory. Now they are recovering old plots intended for vines in the upper Valle di Cembra, above Grumes, exploiting marginal areas to complete a winemaking adventure that has already involved rebuilding Maso Besler on steep terraces in Cembra in the direction of the Avisio.

The wines reflect all this activity. We start with the Faye Bianco '06, from chardonnay and pinot bianco. The wine is splendid from the golden colour and the only, almost imperceptible, criticism is a taste profile that may still show some oak. The other wines are superbly made, although the technology in some vintages has not done proper justice to this estate's proven potential. The sparkler shows well-sustained but less exciting, progression. However, the Rosé is still enjoyable, as are the Nosiola, Müller Thurgau and Pinot Nero.

○ Trentino Chardonnay '08	♥♥ 4
● Trentino Pinot Nero Maso Cantanghel '06	♥♥ 5
○ Trento Brut '05	♥♥ 5
○ Blanc de Sers '07	♥ 4
○ Trentino Müller Thurgau '08	♥ 4
○ Blanc de Sers '06	♀♀ 4
○ Trento Brut '05	♀ 5

○ Bianco Faye '06	♥♥ 5
○ Chardonnay '08	♥♥ 4
☉ Cuvée Rosé	♥♥ 5
○ Müller Thurgau Palai '08	♥♥ 4
● Rosso Faye '06	♥♥ 6
○ Nosiola '08	♥ 4
● Pinot Nero Rodel Pianezzi Ris. '05	♥ 5
○ Sauvignon '08	♥ 5
○ Trentino Traminer Aromatico '08	♥ 5
○ Bianco Faye '01	♀♀♀ 5
● Rosso Faye '05	♀♀♀ 6
● Rosso Faye '00	♀♀♀ 6
○ Besler Biank '04	♀♀ 5

Pravis

LOC. LE BIOLCHE, 1
38076 LASINO [TN]
TEL. 0461564305
www.pravis.it

CELLAR SALES
PRE-BOOKED VISITS

ANNUAL PRODUCTION **200,000 bottles**
HECTARES UNDER VINE **32**
VITICULTURE METHOD **Conventional**

The three partners at Pravis believe in the winemaking philosophy of perfect imperfection. The production style starts in the field, where the vineyards follow the contours of the hills in Valle dei Laghi, with ordered rows obviously not designed merely for large yields. They also plant figs, olive trees, and even mulberries in these fields, one way of saving the identity of the landscape in a splendid valley with castles and eight small lakes. Old grape varieties have been recovered along these steep sloping plots, which would challenge even a mountain goat.

Wines usually come from late harvests, at times lengthened to allow the grapes to dry on rush mats in airy lofts ventilated by the Ora, the wind from Lake Garda. The breeze helps ripen the goldtraminer, a new variety recovered during the 1940s and used to make the new Soliva '06, a white sipping wine with deep colour, juicy fullness and profound softness. The Stravino di Stravino '06, a blend of mostly chardonnay and riesling, and Ora '07, from overripe nosiola fermented in acacia barrels, both show similar profiles. Juiciness and unhurried ripening also mark out the other wines, including the newly created Traminer.

Eugenio Rosi

VIA TAVERNELLE, 3B
38060 VOLANO [TN]
TEL. 0464461375
www.vignaioli.trentino.it

CELLAR SALES
PRE-BOOKED VISITS

ANNUAL PRODUCTION **10,000 bottles**
HECTARES UNDER VINE **5.5**
VITICULTURE METHOD **Organic certified**

Eugenio Rosi's wines deserve special attention because each bottle has its own little story. This winemaker's honest charm and dedication to his vineyards makes up the rest. Eugenio was among the first in Trentino to gamble on the importance of a return to origins, in other words cultivating the land without modern chemicals and respecting the progress of seasons, harvests and spontaneous fermentation. Eugenio Rosi never offers solutions. He flies in the face of convention and encourages people to understand wine.

Anisos '07, from the Greek for unequal, is the synthesis of this vision. This wine undergoes no winemaking intervention, except bottling with a touch of sulphur, and comes from the fermentation of three similar yet unequal varieties: pinot bianco, nosiola and chardonnay. The wine is macerated on the skins and aged in barrels with no filtration. The even more radical Cabernet Franc is an almost incredible wine. Eugenio's classic wines are completely sound, both the cabernet and merlot Esegesi '05 and the marzemino Poiema '07.

O Soliva '06	♟♟	6
O Kerner '08	♟	4
O L'Ora '07	♟	5
O Nosiola Le Frate '08	♟	5
O Stravino di Stravino '06	♟	5
O Trentino Traminer Aromatico Cros del Mont '08	♟	5
O Stravino di Stravino '99	♟♟♟	6
O L'Ora '05	♟♟	5
O Soliva '03	♟♟	5
O Stravino di Stravino '04	♟♟	5

● Trentino Rosso Esegesi '05	♟♟	5
● Cabernet Franc '07	♟♟	6
● Trentino Marzemino Poiema '07	♟♟	5
O Anisos '07	♟	5
● Dòron '05	♟♟	6
● Trentino Marzemino Poiema '04	♟♟	5
● Trentino Rosso Esegesi '04	♟♟	5
● Trentino Rosso Esegesi '03	♟♟	5
● Trentino Rosso Esegesi '02	♟♟	5

Cantina Rotaliana

VIA TRENTO, 65B
38017 MEZZOLOMBARDO [TN]
TEL. 0461601010
www.cantinarotaliana.it

CELLAR SALES
PRE-BOOKED VISITS

ANNUAL PRODUCTION **1,000,000 bottles**
HECTARES UNDER VINE **330**
VITICULTURE METHOD **Conventional**

Teroldego goes inseparably with Rotaliano. This ancient connection evokes Lombard history and medieval times, for the variety was first mentioned in 1360, studies from the early 19th century by Italian patriot Cesare Battisti, and the harvests of generations of hardworking growers. This co-operative winery is always ready to stand up for the special nature of Mezzolombardo and Teroldego Rotaliano. There are a few hundred member growers, united by Teroldego Rotaliano, although other varieties are also farmed.

The broad range – a record 17 wines were submitted – forces this co-operative, managed by Leonardo Pilati, to manage its available forces. The Clesurae '06 proved a prizewinner and again picked up a well-deserved Three Glasses for complexity that starts with deep purple highlights, echoes through balsamic tones on the nose and ends on a practically interminable palate. The '06 version of the always outstanding Teroldego Riserva is ready and easy to drink with its one-of-a-kind backbone and vigour. The Müller Thugau and Pinot Grigio are satisfying.

★ Tenuta San Leonardo

FRAZ. BORGHETTO ALL'ADIGE
LOC. SAN LEONARDO
38060 AVIO [TN]
TEL. 0464689004
www.sanleonardo.it

CELLAR SALES
PRE-BOOKED VISITS

ANNUAL PRODUCTION **145,000 bottles**
HECTARES UNDER VINE **21**
VITICULTURE METHOD **Conventional**

More than just grapes, these rows of vines contain part of Trentino history. Marchesi Carlo and Anselmo Guerrieri Gonzaga own Tenuta San Leonardo, a stronghold of growing traditions on the banks of the river Adige. Vines were grown on this site centuries before the year 100 and for at least 300 years, the Campi Sarni borderlands between the plains of Veneto and the Lagarina hills have been the stage for winemaking's development in the Dolomites.

Both wines presented were impressive. Absolute first place goes to the San Leonardo '05, a classic Bordeaux blend of cabernet sauvignon, cabernet franc and merlot. Once again, this influential red wine was even more powerful, important, and unforgettable than ever, set apart by another unique vintage profile. The 2005 harvest has brought us a San Leonardo that is deep in colour and more immediate than many other vintages, with pencil lead on the nose, and evolved tannins in the mouth. The imposing, nearly all merlot Villa Gresti '05 is a worthy partner for its magnificent fellow.

● Teroldego Rotaliano Clesurae '06	♆♆♆ 6
● Teroldego Rotaliano Ris. '06	♆♆ 5
● Trentino Merlot '08	♆♆ 4*
● Teroldego Rotaliano Et. Rossa '08	♆ 4
○ Trentino Chardonnay '08	♆ 4
○ Trentino Müller Thurgau '08	♆ 4
○ Trentino Pinot Grigio '08	♆ 4
● Teroldego Rotaliano Clesurae '02	♀♀♀ 6
● Teroldego Rotaliano Ris. '04	♀♀♀ 4
● Teroldego Rotaliano Clesurae '05	♀♀ 6
● Teroldego Rotaliano Clesurae '04	♀♀ 6

● San Leonardo '05	♆♆♆ 8
● Villa Gresti '05	♆♆ 6
● San Leonardo '04	♀♀♀ 8
● San Leonardo '03	♀♀♀ 8
● San Leonardo '01	♀♀♀ 8
● San Leonardo '00	♀♀♀ 8
● San Leonardo '99	♀♀♀ 8
● San Leonardo '97	♀♀♀ 5
● San Leonardo '96	♀♀♀ 5
● San Leonardo '95	♀♀♀ 5
● Villa Gresti '03	♀♀♀ 7

Istituto Agrario Provinciale San Michele all'Adige

VIA EDMONDO MACH, 1
38010 SAN MICHELE ALL'ADIGE [TN]
TEL. 0461615252
www.ismaa.it

CELLAR SALES
PRE-BOOKED VISITS

ANNUAL PRODUCTION 250,000 bottles
HECTARES UNDER VINE 60
VITICULTURE METHOD Conventional

Founded as a Hapsburg agricultural school nearly 140 years ago, and later turned into a major viticultural research foundation – it was the first to genetically map grapevines – San Michele is being converted into a university institute for agronomists and crop science engineers. Its history has always hinged on wine research using grapes harvested from the vineyards for teaching agricultural students, and wine made in a cellar that is also a laboratory for aspiring oenologists. The relatively independent cellar is managed by former student and renowned winemaker Enrico Paternoster.

For some years, the wines have been growing in overall quality. A Trento '04 spumante dedicated to the founder, Edmondo Mach, is in great shape, showing big, full, and developed, with the grace and assertiveness of a thoroughbred. We gave it Three Glasses. But more pleasures are in store. Two of the winemaking school's many other products deserve mention. The Merlot '07 and Pinot Bianco Vigneto San Donà '08 are among the best in Trentino. Then comes the Monastero '07, a powerful red, varied in its well-defined tasting profile where carmenère is to the fore.

Toblino

FRAZ. SARCHE
VIA LONGA, 1
38070 CALAVINO [TN]
TEL. 0461564168
www.toblino.it

CELLAR SALES
PRE-BOOKED VISITS
RISTORAZIONE

ANNUAL PRODUCTION 400,000 bottles
HECTARES UNDER VINE 700
VITICULTURE METHOD Conventional

This co-operative winery is constantly adjusting production and management strategies. In the past few months, top management has had a radical makeover, with the chair most of the staff replaced. But the desire to pursue high quality is unchanged. Member-growers continue to be encouraged to do even better in their many small vineyards scattered mainly across the hilly slopes of Valle dei Laghi. This area between Lake Garda and the Trento Dolomites is symbolized by Castel Toblino and splendid lake, icons of grape growing and winemaking in Trentino.

Again this year, we were most convinced by a Teroldego sourced far from the excellent zone of Campo Rotaliano. Yet the wine is powerful, intense and fruity. Superbly drinkable, it is also sold at a very favourable price. Also outstanding, the Goldtraminer is a new variety being trialled in Valle dei Laghi. The other wines, including the excellent Nosiola and Kerner '08, are made in the usual typically Toblinoesque style and are far from expensive.

○ Trento Mach Riserva del Fondatore '04	♈♈♈	6
● Trentino Merlot '07	♈♈	5
● Trentino Moscato Rosa '06	♈♈	5
○ Trentino Pinot Bianco Vign. San Donà '08	♈♈	4*
● Trentino Rosso Monastero '07	♈♈	6
○ Trentino Pinot Bianco '06	♈♈	4
○ Trento Mach Riserva del Fondatore '02	♈♈	5
○ Trento Mach Riserva del Fondatore '01	♈♈	5

○ Goldtraminer '08	♈	4
● Teroldego '07	♈♈	3*
○ Kerner '08	♈	4
○ Trentino Müller Thurgau '08	♈	3
○ Trentino Nosiola '08	♈	3
○ Trentino Pinot Grigio '08	♈	4
○ Trentino Traminer Aromatico '08	♈	4
○ Kerner '07	♈♈	4*
● Teroldego '06	♈♈	3*

Vallarom

FRAZ. MASI, 21
38063 AVIO [TN]
TEL. 0464684297
www.vallarom.it

CELLAR SALES
PRE-BOOKED VISITS

ANNUAL PRODUCTION **40,000 bottles**
HECTARES UNDER VINE **7**
VITICULTURE METHOD **Organic certified**

More as a natural consequence of their personalities and production philosophy than as a strategic decision, Barbara and Filippo Scienza are converting their entire estate, located in the sunniest spot in Campi Sarni, to organic-biodynamic methods. They have already made several wines using absolutely natural growing techniques. Other wines, but above all the vineyards, patiently await biodynamic projects. The rest is as usual: targeted growing techniques, diversified varieties and a functional cellar designed in an unfussy, country style.

The wines are unique in every way. From the elegantly mature, intriguing Chardonnay Riserva '07, with its zesty length and intense colour, to the Campi Sarni '06, a traditional, slightly grassy, blend of cabernet and merlot with good acidity, great mouthfeel and a fine tannic weave. While waiting for the Pinot Neros to mature, the Scienzas served us up a sincere Vadum Caesaris '08, a blend of several white varieties, and an '07 Syrah that is still closed and almost immature, as well as other honest wines.

Vilàr

VIA CAVOLAVILLA, 35
38060 VILLA LAGARINA [TN]
TEL. 0464409028
www.vilar.it

CELLAR SALES
PRE-BOOKED VISITS

ANNUAL PRODUCTION **22,000 bottles**
HECTARES UNDER VINE **4.5**
VITICULTURE METHOD **Natural**

This small estate shows great commitment. Luigi Spagnolli is one of the most experienced, conscientious oenologists in Trentino but he has chosen to be first of all a winemaker. Aided by his partner Ivana, he looks after every phase of the vines' vegetation cycle and creates personal wines that need to be understood. Though vineyard techniques are nature-friendly and biodynamic in approach, this is never flaunted or expressly declared. These few hectares on the Villalagarina slope stand out among the other plots precisely for the way they are farmed and their naturally vigorous plants.

The white wines still seem a tad impenetrable and closed. Yes, they are skilfully made, but they need long ageing, especially the Traminer. It has pulp and hints of citrus and marjoram-like aromatic herbs but still needs to age for a long while, perhaps because it was made with unforced techniques. The simple, quaffable, straw yellow Müller Thurgau is more acidulous than other versions. In line with the type, the Marzemino has a purplish colour and a bitterish finish. The estate's main wine, the Morèla '06, was not submitted because it was still maturing in wood.

● Campi Sarni Rosso '06	￥￥	5
○ Chardonnay Ris. '07	￥￥	5
● Lambrusco a Foglia Frastagliata Enantio '08	￥	4
● Syrah '07	￥	6
○ Vadum Caesaris '08	￥	4
● Campi Sarni Rosso '05	￥￥	5
○ Vadum Caesaris '07	￥￥	4*

○ Müller Thurgau '08	￥	4
○ Traminer Aromatico '08	￥	5
● Trentino Marzemino '08	￥	4
● Cabernet Sauvignon '05	￥￥	4*
● Morela '03	￥￥	6

Vivallis

VIA PER BRANCOLINO, 4
38068 NOGAREDO [TN]
TEL. 0464834113
www.vivallis.it

CELLAR SALES
PRE-BOOKED VISITS

ANNUAL PRODUCTION 1,000,000 bottles
HECTARES UNDER VINE 730
VITICULTURE METHOD Organic certified

All Rovereto growers deal with the SAV, the Vallagarina agricultural association. It's a co-operative structure that manages agricultural stockpiles, produces feed, operates a dairy and runs two co-operative wineries. One of these is Vivallis, created to market the broad range of wines produced from grapes contributed by thousands of member-growers. The strategy begins in the field. Each member must observe precise production regulations and every vineyard is scientifically tested so the most suitable varieties are planted for the soil, site climate and production requirements.

A quick consideration about the best wines, the Cabernet Sauvignon Vigna Carbonera '07 and the white Ultreya '08 blend from chardonnay and pinot bianco. They are characterful, perhaps a bit too rustic, but they also have personality and will probably mature positively. The other whites are pleasant. The three selections of Marzemino, the best-known wines from the range, are less absorbing on tasting, and not just because of the vintage. As the winemakers themselves admit, vineyard management and vinification parameters need to be rethought to restore identity to this emblematic Trentino wine.

Roberto Zeni

FRAZ. GRUMO
VIA STRETTA, 2
38010 SAN MICHELE ALL'ADIGE [TN]
TEL. 0461650456
www.zeni.tn.it

CELLAR SALES
PRE-BOOKED VISITS

ANNUAL PRODUCTION 190,000 bottles
HECTARES UNDER VINE 20
VITICULTURE METHOD Conventional

The Zenis from Grumo have an impressive-sounding surname. There is some nobility here, not because of any dynasty, but in the way the Zenis, from the small village of Grumo outside San Michele all'Adige, have spread the culture of wine. For more than 40 years, brothers Andrea and Roberto Zeni have been among the most active winemakers in Trentino. They have diversified their production, focusing not just on wine, but also spirits, primarily grappa, and reserve each of their plots for specific vinification.

Shrewd vineyard management produces a whole series of wines, from classic sparklers to skilfully made Teroldegos and persuasive sweet wines, while recovering neglected varieties such as rossara. This admirable range shows great attention to the environment and offers wines with good value for money. The Tedroldego Rotaliano Le Albere '07 stands out over all the dozen wines submitted because of its varietal aromas and fresh yet deep flavour in the long finish. Another round of applause goes to the Trento DOC Maso Nero '04, a charming, monovarietal chardonnay sparkler that promises to mature well. The white wines are always reliable.

● Trentino Cabernet Sauvignon V. Carbonera '07	♟♟	4
○ Trentino Bianco Ultreya '08	♟	4
● Trentino Marzemino dei Ziresi Sup. '07	♟	5
● Trentino Merlot V. Borgosacco '07	♟	4
● Trentino Marzemino dei Ziresi Sup. '06	♟♟	5
● Trentino Merlot V. Borgosacco '06	♟♟	4*

● Teroldego Rotaliano Vign. Le Albere '07	♟♟	4
○ Trento Maso Nero '04	♟♟	6
⊙ Rossara '08	♟	4
○ Sortì '08	♟	5
○ Trentino Chardonnay Vigneto Zaraosti '08	♟	4
○ Trentino Nosiola Maso Nero '08	♟	4
● Teroldego Rotaliano Vign. Le Albere '06	♟♟	4*

Agririva

VIA SAN NAZZARO, 4
38066 RIVA DEL GARDA [TN]
TEL. 0464552133
www.agririva.it

This co-operative winery with brand new facilities is also famous for its production of Garda extra virgin olive oil and is active in promoting everything food and agriculture-related in Trentino. From the Nosiola to Marzemino, the honest, uncomplicated wines are sold at great-value prices.

● Trentino Marzemino Sel. Apponale '08	♀ 3
● Trentino Merlot Sel. Crea '07	♀ 3
○ Trentino Müller Thurgau '08	♀ 3
○ Trentino Nosiola '08	♀ 3

Riccardo Battistotti

VIA 3 NOVEMBRE, 21
38060 NOMI [TN]
TEL. 0464834145
www.battistotti.com

The Battistotti family's skilfully made wines are becoming ever more reliable and territorial. This time, the Nosiola was the most convincing, alongside the fascinating Moscato Rosa. The other products are as sound as usual.

● Trentino Moscato Rosa '07	♀♀ 6
○ Trentino Nosiola '08	♀♀ 4*
○ Trentino Chardonnay '08	♀ 3

Bellaveder

LOC. MASO BELVEDERE
38010 FAEDO [TN]
TEL. 0461650171
www.bellaveder.it

Tranquillo Lucchetta set up his small, promising estate in the alluvial fan of Faedo to vinify expertly and make sparkling wines in the future. Meanwhile, Teroldego Mas Picol, from still young vines, is full, fruity, harmonious and on the way up.

● Teroldego Mas Picol '08	♀ 4
○ Trentino Chardonnay '08	♀ 4
⊙ Trentino Lagrein Kretzer '08	♀ 4
○ Trentino Traminer '08	♀ 4

Conti Bossi Fedrigotti

VIA UNIONE, 43
38068 ROVERETO [TN]
TEL. 0464439250
www.bossifedrigotti.com

Since the 2007 harvest, vineyards, cellar and marketing here have all been managed by the Verona-based Masi Agricola company. The Bossi Fedrigottis made this choice to revive the fame of their wines. Scores were good for the Marzemino and Fojaneghe, the two house specialities.

● Fojaneghe Rosso '06	♀♀ 6
● Teroldego '07	♀ 5
● Trentino Marzemino '08	♀ 4
○ Valdadige Pinot Grigio '08	♀ 4

Concilio

ZONA INDUSTRIALE, 2
38060 VOLANO [TN]
TEL. 0464411000
www.concilio.it

The well-known Concilio company distributes products from several co-operative wineries in Trentino, especially the one from Trento – Le Meridiane – as well as the most characteristic selections from its subsidiary winery, Vigneti delle Meridiane. In any case, the wines are always very reliable.

● Trentino Mori Vecio Ris. '05	♀♀ 4*
● Teroldego Rotaliano Braide '07	♀♀ 4*
○ Trentino Müller Thurgau '08	♀♀ 4*
● Trentino Pinot Nero Ris. '06	♀♀ 4

De Tarczal

FRAZ. MARANO D'ISERA
VIA G. B. MIORI, 4
38060 ISERA [TN]
TEL. 0464409134
www.detarczal.com

Ruggero De Tarczal is a wine fancier, an agricultural entrepreneur and a winemaker. He vinifies grapes from vineyards adjacent to his estate in Isera, focusing recently on Marzemino, the area's cult wine. But he also makes a Cabernet Sauvignon, built more for aroma than structure.

● Trentino Cabernet Sauvignon '05	♀ 4
● Trentino Marzemino d'Isera Sup. Husar '06	♀ 5

Marco Donati

VIA CESARE BATTISTI, 41
38016 MEZZOCORONA [TN]
TEL. 0461604141
donatimarcovini@libero.it

Marco Donati avoids distorting or forcing what he harvests. His wines are in the Other Wineries section this year because of uneven progress due only to the growing year. But his Teroldego Rotaliano Bagolari is enjoyable, full of things and developing well, like his distinctive Riesling.

● Teroldego Rotaliano Bagolari '08	🍷🍷	5
○ Trentino Riesling Stellato '08	🍷	4
○ Trentino Traminer AromaticoTramonti '08	🍷	4

Cipriano Fedrizzi

VIA 4 NOVEMBRE, 1
38017 MEZZOLOMBARDO [TN]
TEL. 0461602328
fedrizzicipriano@alice.it

Winemakers for generations, the Fedrizzis tend small plots and vinify their grapes in their small town centre cellar. The wines have an old-time homemade feel and are very well made. There are only a few thousand bottles of their two, absolutely sound, Teroldegos.

● Teroldego Rotaliano '07	🍷🍷	4*
● Teroldego Rotaliano Due Vigneti '07	🍷	6
● Trentino Lagrein '07	🍷	4

Francesco Moser

FRAZ. MEANO
VIA CASTEL DI GARDOLO, 5
38040 TRENTO
TEL. 0461990786
www.cantinemoser.com

Il Checco, as cycling tourists call him, has metaphorically hung up his bike, but has never stopped tending his vineyards. He is still in the process replanting the large plots in his native Valle di Cembra and makes wines as pleasantly individual as they are typically Trentino.

○ Chardonnay '08	🍷	4
○ Müller Thurgau '08	🍷	4
○ Riesling '08	🍷	4

Furlani

LOC. POVO
VIA GABBIOLO, 2
38100 TRENTO
TEL. 3471474234
www.cantinafurlani.it

Matteo Furlani's tiny estate with high altitude vineyards on Vigolana above the city of Trento makes its first appearance on the Trentino winemaking scene. Matteo makes a classic, substantial sparkler and two blends: a Bordeaux-style red and an interesting chardonnay-heavy white.

○ Furlani Brut '06	🍷🍷	5
● Alteo '07	🍷	4
○ Annly '08	🍷	4

Madonna delle Vittorie

VIA LINFANO, 81
38062 ARCO [TN]
TEL. 0464505432
www.madonnadellevittorie.it

The Trentino shore of Lake Garda is better known for yachting than wine production. Yet in just a few years, this estate has gained visibility with fragrant wines and world famous olive oil. The Nosiola and the white blend Summolaco are the best from a nice range of approachable, affordable wines.

● Teroldego Rotaliano '07	🍷🍷	3*
○ Trentino Nosiola '08	🍷🍷	3*
○ Bianco Summolaco '07	🍷	4

Maso Bastie

LOC. BASTIE, 1
38060 VOLANO [TN]
TEL. 0464412747
www.masobastie.it

Giuseppe and Patrizia Torelli tend these scenic estate vineyards in a sunny hollow in the mountains between Rovereto, Volano and Vallagarina. Their wines have character but production is limited. The range includes a robust Bordeaux blend and several delicious sweet wines, above all the Moscato Rosa.

● Moscato Rosa '08	🍷🍷	6
● Pra' dei Fanti '08	🍷🍷	5

Maso Bergamini

FRAZ. COGNOLA
LOC. BERGAMINI, 3
38050 TRENTO
TEL. 0461983079
www.masobergamini.com

Remo Tomasi, a winemaker and enthusiastic experimenter, has for years managed this beautiful estate on the hill above the city towards Calisio. He has converted traditional farming to organic methods and continues to focus on vinifying the small – in quantity – parcels of grapes from his splendid vineyards.

● Teroldego '06	♙♙ 4
○ Trentino Riesling '04	♙ 4
○ Trentino Traminer Aromatico '08	♙ 4

Mori - Colli Zugna

VIA DEL GARDA, 35
38065 MORI [TN]
TEL. 0464918154
www.cantinamoricollizugna.it

Like other Cavit co-operatives, this winery operates on the slope between Rovereto and Lake Garda and promotes estate-bottled wines to showcase the labours of its members. All these wines are competitive in quality and price, from the Marzemino to the excellently crafted Bordeaux blend.

○ Trentino Chardonnay V. del Gelso '08	♙ 3
● Trentino Marzemino Terra di San Mauro '07	♙ 4
● Trentino Merlot V. del Gelso Formigher '06	♙ 3
○ Trentino Müller Thurgau Pendici del Baldo '08	♙ 4

Pisoni

FRAZ. PERGOLESE DI LASINO
LOC. SARCHE
VIA SAN SIRO, 7A
38070 LASINO [TN]
TEL. 0461564106
www.pisoni.net

The Pisoni winemaking dynasty also makes sparklers and distils grappa, but above all they are determined experimenters. They are converting their vineyards to biodynamic methods. Early results are interesting and further major surprises will be forthcoming.

○ Trentino Vino Santo '98	♙♙ 7
● Sarica Rosso '06	♙ 5
○ Trentino Nosiola '08	♙ 4
○ Trento Brut '06	♙ 4

Arcangelo Sandri

VIA VANEGGE, 4
38010 FAEDO [TN]
TEL. 0461650935
www.arcangelosandri.it

Arcangelo's young daughters, Nadia and Sonia, are replanting their tiny vineyards in the hills of Faedo and vinify with dedication. Recent harvests have seen ups and downs from weather issues but the wines are still worthy of attention because of their sheer authenticity.

● Trentino Lagrein Capòr Ris. '06	♙♙ 5
○ Trentino Müller Thurgau Cosler '08	♙ 4

Armando Simoncelli

VIA NAVICELLO, 7
38068 ROVERETO [TN]
TEL. 0464432373
www.simoncelli.it

One again, Navesèl '06 maintains the prestige of wines from this energetic, friendly and experienced winemaker. The family is committed to Marzemino but also produces an eminently drinkable, creamy classic spumante with lovely aromas. The other wines are juicy and undemanding.

● Trentino Rosso Navesèl '06	♙♙ 4
○ Trento Brut	♙♙ 5
● Trentino Marzemino '08	♙ 4

Spagnolli

VIA G. B. ROSINA, 4A
38060 ISERA [TN]
TEL. 0464409054
www.vinispagnolli.it

Wines are reliable and prices honest at this Vallagarina winery. It has been managed by the same family for generations with a commitment to selecting grapes for vinification. Once again, outstanding wines from the convincing range are the Nosiola and Tebro, a traditional blend of cabernet and merlot.

● Rosso Tebro '05	♙♙ 5
○ Nosiola Vallagarina '08	♙ 4

De Vescovi Ulzbach

P.ZZA GARIBALDI, 12
38016 MEZZOCORONA [TN]
TEL. 0461605648
www.devescoviulzbach.it

The De Vescovis have more than a century of winemaking experience but they only recently started vinifying Teroldego, the signature wine of Mezzocorona and Mezzolombardo in Campo Rotaliano. This year, only the '07 was submitted. It has balsamic tones, minerality, powerful colour and a complex profile.

● Teroldego Rotaliano '07	𝟶𝟶 4

Villa Corniole

FRAZ. VERLA
VIA AL GREC', 23
38030 GIOVO [TN]
TEL. 0461695067
www.villacorniole.com

The cellar is carved out of porphyry, the red rock that characterizes the landscape of Valle di Cembra. The Pellegrinis harvest white grapes from their high-altitude vineyards while reds like teroldego are grown in plots along the valley floor.

● Teroldego Rotaliano '07	𝟶𝟶 4
○ Trentino Chardonnay '08	𝟶 4
○ Trentino Pinot Grigio '08	𝟶 4
○ Trentino Traminer Aromatico '08	𝟶 4

Villa Imperiale

LOC. BORGHETTO ALL'ADIGE
38060 AVIO [TN]
TEL. 0464689003

This new joint venture involving Marchesi Guerrieri Gonzaga and Cavit makes vineyard selections of cabernet sauvignon, teroldego, merlot and lagrein, and vinifies at the co-operative winery in Trento. This wine is above all good, showing frank, flavourful and felicitously priced.

● Villa Imperiale '06	𝟶𝟶 3*

Villa Piccola

LOC. VILLA PICCOLA, 4
38010 FAEDO [TN]
TEL. 0461650420

The name of the estate reflects its modest size, with excellently aspected vineyards in the alluvial fan of Faedo. Few varieties are grown and the wines local types, above all Müller Thurgau, but the spicy Traminer and always flavourful, elegant Pinot Nero are just as good.

○ Müller Thurgau Argentarie '08	𝟶𝟶 4
○ Traminer Silbrarii '08	𝟶𝟶 4
● Pinot Nero Silbrarii '07	𝟶 5

Vinicola Aldeno

VIA ROMA, 76
38060 ALDENO [TN]
TEL. 0461842511
www.cantina-aldeno.it

This small co-operative winery is known for its Merlot, a wine that has long been made here between Trento and Rovereto. Vineyards are along the Adige and in the hills of Bondone, where aromatic varieties are grown. The wines are varietal, various and well priced. The high points are in the table below.

● Trentino Merlot Enopere '05	𝟶𝟶 4*
○ Trentino Mueller Thurgau Enopere '08	𝟶𝟶 3*
● Trentino Rosso San Zeno '04	𝟶𝟶 4*
● Madòi '08	𝟶 3

Conti Wallenburg

LOC. MARTIGNANO
VIA BASSANO, 3
38040 TRENTO
TEL. 045913399
www.masowallenburg.it

New owners, the Montresor wine family from Verona, have managed this historic winemaking estate on the hill of Trento for the last few harvests. The newcomers have radically remodelled the estate. Many vineyards have yet to enter production and sparkling winemaking projects are under way.

○ Trentino Traminer Maria Adelaide '08	𝟶𝟶 6
○ Trento Corte Imperiale Brut	𝟶𝟶 5
○ Sauvignon '08	𝟶 4
● Trentino Marquardo '07	𝟶 6

ALTO ADIGE

The 2008 vintage will not be remembered in the province of Bolzano as extraordinary. On the contrary, the cold weather, abundant rain and a devastating hailstorm around Gries forced winemakers, technicians and oenologists to focus on counter-measures. Our compliments go to all the operators in the sector for doing better than just riding out this situation. The number of Three Glass awards, 24, confirms their success. The 2008 whites inevitably turned out leaner, at times even a bit stringy, but this involved mostly the base lines since thorough selection achieved remarkable results. More discreet use of sulphur might not have hurt, though. Pinot Bianco, as well as Sauvignon and the ever-reliable Gewürztraminer, showed high quality in the province of Bolzano. On the red front, while the 2006 Lagreins are still a bit clenched, the average quality achieved with extract, oak and overall balance is truly impressive. The same goes for Pinot Nero. There were no Three Glass awards for the type but there is growth in the quality and variety of products on offer. Above all, there now seems to be a mature awareness of an identity and typicity that should not be compromised in the pursuit of unreachable goals. Schiava confirms everything good we have said lately and this fresher, lighter vintage has returned to the old methods and character. There are new items among the prize-winners, starting with two historic co-operative wineries, Cornaiano and Merano, which won Three Glasses for a splendid Sauvignon Indra '08 and the Pinot Bianco Sonnenberg '08. Outstanding among the small – in this case, tiny – producers is Konrad Augschöll's Röckhof estate, with its Riesling '08 from Valle Isarco, a zone that with Valle Isarco is proving to be a goldmine for quality. Conte Michael Goëss-Enzenberg's Manincor estate makes a welcome return with an elegant Terlano Sauvignon '08. Co-operative wineries have done their part, showing once again that when the going gets tough, they can react flexibly and earn their share of Three Glasses. All this has unfolded in a situation it would be optimistic to call challenging. Still, thanks to tourism, traditionally intelligent pricing policies and quality now almost universally recognized, Alto Adige seems to suffer less than most from the crisis. We also note the range of wine styles from traditional varieties, all aiming to bring out the finest characteristics. On balance, these results are positive and highlight the ability of actors on the Alto Adige wine scene to adapt to a constantly changing situation.

★ Abbazia di Novacella

FRAZ. NOVACELLA
VIA DELL'ABBAZIA, 1
39040 VARNA/VAHRN [BZ]
TEL. 0472836189
www.abbazianovacella.it

CELLAR SALES
PRE-BOOKED VISITS
FOOD

ANNUAL PRODUCTION **650,000 bottles**
HECTARES UNDER VINE **20**
VITICULTURE METHOD **Conventional**

Cantina Abbazia di Novacella is a legend thanks to its long history, starting in 1142, and stunning architectural beauty. In the past few years, Urban von Kleblesberg, manager of this splendid estate owned by the Augustinians, and oenologist Celestino Lucin, have helped make it even more famous with great wines from Valle Isarco and elsewhere: Sylvaner, Veltliner and Kerner, and then Riesling and the reds, Lagrein and Pinot Nero..

When an estate submits 14 wines for tasting and sends seven to the finals, we feel triumphant tones are superfluous and words unnecessary. Abbazia di Novacella is simply one of the most important and reliable estates nationwide. All the wines tasted show stylistic precision, typicity and character. This year our preference was for the Sylvaner Praepositus '08 – but even the base wine is simply delicious – which marries rich extract and aromatic complexity with substantial yet effortless drinkability.

Cantina Produttori Andriano

VIA SILBERLEITEN, 7
39018 TERLANO/TERLAN [BZ]
TEL. 0471257156
www.cantina-andriano.com

CELLAR SALES
PRE-BOOKED VISITS

ANNUAL PRODUCTION **300,000 bottles**
HECTARES UNDER VINE **105**
VITICULTURE METHOD **Conventional**

The die is cast. The merger between the historic co-operatives of Andriano and Terlano is now operational. Production lines remain the same, with an effective label makeover, and the combined experience dates back to 1893, but technical management is with Rudi Kofler, oenologist from Cantina di Terlano. The winery has 102 member growers, from Andriano and neighbouring towns, who farm a total area of 105 hectares for a range that puts the accent on reds.

This year has seen much change so these rather uncertain results are understandable and were not helped by the challenging 2008 growing year. Having said this, signs of improvement are clearly visible, such as the splendid Pinot Bianco '08, a tangy, almost salty wine with dynamic, continuous progression. The balanced, elegant Sauvignon Andrius '08 combines a rather dense palate with a bright palate and an absolutely commendable price. The progress of the reds is less certain but we look forward to next year to gauge the full effect of the "Terlano treatment".

○ A. A. Valle Isarco Sylvaner Praepositus '08	♟♟♟ 5
● A. A. Lagrein Praepositus Ris. '06	♟♟ 6
⊙ A. A. Moscato Rosa Praepositus '08	♟♟ 6
○ A. A. Valle Isarco Gewürztraminer Praepositus '08	♟♟ 5
○ A. A. Valle Isarco Kerner '08	♟♟ 4
○ A. A. Valle Isarco Kerner Praepositus '08	♟♟ 5
○ A. A. Valle Isarco Riesling Praepositus '07	♟♟ 6
○ A. A. Valle Isarco Veltliner Praepositus '08	♟♟ 5*
○ A. A. Sauvignon Praepositus '08	♟♟ 5
○ A. A. Valle Isarco Sylvaner '08	♟♟ 4*
○ Omne Dies '08	♟♟ 4*
● A. A. Pinot Nero Praepositus Ris. '06	♟ 6
○ A. A. Valle Isarco Kerner Praepositus Passito '07	♟ 6
○ A. A. Valle Isarco Müller Thurgau '08	♟ 4
○ A. A. Valle Isarco Riesling Praepositus '06	♟♟♟ 5
○ A. A. Valle Isarco Sylvaner Praepositus '07	♟♟♟ 5

○ A. A. Pinot Bianco '08	♟♟ 4*
● A. A. Merlot Gant Ris. '06	♟♟ 6
○ A. A. Sauvignon Blanc Andrius '08	♟♟ 6
○ A. A. Chardonnay Semereto '08	♟ 4
○ A. A. Gewürztraminer '08	♟ 4
○ A. A. Gewürztraminer Movado '08	♟ 6
● A. A. Lagrein Rubeno '07	♟ 4
○ A. A. Pinot Grigio '08	♟ 4
● A. A. Santa Maddalena '08	♟ 4
● A. A. Schiava '08	♟ 3
● A. A. Cabernet Tor di Lupo '00	♟♟♟ 5
● A. A. Lagrein Scuro Tor di Lupo '00	♟♟♟ 5
● A. A. Lagrein Scuro Tor di Lupo '05	♟♟ 6

Baron Widmann

ENDERGASSE, 3
39040 CORTACCIA/KURTATSCH [BZ]
TEL. 0471880092
www.baron-widmann.it

CELLAR SALES
PRE-BOOKED VISITS

ANNUAL PRODUCTION **35,000 bottles**
HECTARES UNDER VINE **15**
VITICULTURE METHOD **Conventional**

The cellar has been producing wine since 1824. It is worth taking a trip to the lovely village of Cortaccia to see it, enjoy the simple hospitality and taste the wines, which flaunt elegance, drinkability and character. Andreas Widmann's wines are neither demonstrative nor caricatures, but they are made up of tones of dark and light. Apparently reticent, they need to be explored and discovered. Production of both whites and reds is technically impeccable and very reliable.

This year has been a bit tentative for Baron Widmann. Only four wines were submitted for tasting. Having said this, the talented Andreas still manages to produce an absolutely flawless version of the Weiss '08 from a 70-30 blend of pinot bianco and chardonnay, which presents fresh and dynamic with fragrant minerality. The other showcase wine is also interesting. Rot '07 from cabernet sauvignon, franc and merlot overcomes initial reduction to develop an aromatic range and palate with good stylistic precision. The fresh, elegant Sauvignon '08 is well crafted, but the Gewürztraminer '08 is a bit on the lean side.

○ A. A. Gewürztraminer '08	🍷🍷 5*
○ A. A. Sauvignon '08	🍷🍷 4
○ A. A. Weiss '08	🍷🍷 4*
● Rot '07	🍷 5
○ A. A. Gewürztraminer '05	ΥΥ 4
○ A. A. Sauvignon '07	ΥΥ 4*
○ A. A. Weiss '07	ΥΥ 4*
● Rot '06	ΥΥ 5

Josef Brigl

LOC. SAN MICHELE
VIA MADONNA DEL RIPOSO, 3
39057 APPIANO/EPPAN [BZ]
TEL. 0471662419
www.brigl.com

CELLAR SALES
PRE-BOOKED VISITS

ANNUAL PRODUCTION **2,000,000 bottles**
HECTARES UNDER VINE **50**
VITICULTURE METHOD **Conventional**

Ignaz and Josef Brigl own one of the largest and oldest winemaking estates in Alto Adige, with 50 hectares across the best areas in the region. Their interesting wines represent the most typical wine types such as Lagrein, Santa Maddalena, Pinot Nero and Pinot Bianco. The entire range shows excellent average quality that has clearly been on the rise over the past few years, though still missing that high point. Considering the potential of the estate and vineyards, everything is in place for absolute excellence.

Results from Brigl are a bit uneven this year. Alongside well-made, pleasant wines like the classic Lagrein Briglhof Riserva '06, the typical, refined Pinot Nero Kreuzbichler Riserva '06, and the ever delicious Santa Maddalena Rielerhof '08, are simpler products that lack some structure and personality, especially those from the 2008 vintage. These wines are well made, with no defects, but this is no longer enough to stand out on the Alto Adige landscape. But the potential is there.

● A. A. Lagrein Briglhof Ris. '06	🍷🍷 5
● A. A. Pinot Nero Kreuzbichler Ris. '06	🍷🍷 5
● A. A. Santa Maddalena Rielerhof '08	🍷🍷 4*
○ A. A. Sauvignon '08	🍷🍷 4
● A. A. Cabernet Windegg '06	🍷 4
○ A. A. Gewürztraminer Windegg '08	🍷 4
● A. A. Lago di Caldaro Scelto Windegg Cl. Sup. '08	🍷 4
○ A. A. Pinot Bianco Haselhof '08	🍷 4
● A. A. Pinot Nero Briglhof Ris. '06	🍷 6
● A. A. Riesling Kreuzbichler '08	🍷 5
● A. A. Lagrein Briglhof Ris. '03	ΥΥ 5
○ A. A. Pinot Bianco Haselhof '07	ΥΥ 4*
● A. A. Pinot Nero Briglhof Ris. '04	ΥΥ 5
● A. A. Pinot Nero Kreuzbichler Ris. '05	ΥΥ 5
○ A. A. Sauvignon '07	ΥΥ 4*

Cantina Produttori Burggräfler

VIA PALADE, 64
39020 MARLENGO/MARLING [BZ]
TEL. 0473447137
www.burggraefler.it

CELLAR SALES
PRE-BOOKED VISITS
OSPITALITÀ
FOOD

ANNUAL PRODUCTION **1.220,000 bottles**
HECTARES UNDER VINE **140**
VITICULTURE METHOD **Conventional**

Grapes for this co-operative winery near Merano come from 208 member growers. For years now, you could swear by the quality of products from Cantina Produttori Burggräfler and the admirable value they offered. Cellarmaster Hansjörg Donà has been managing cellar operations since 1980 and his experience and skills are obvious in wines that lately have achieved a stylistic definition that makes this winery one of the best in the province of Bolzano.

Burggräfler gave its usual flattering performance. The Sauvignon '08 is especially successful, showing tangy, lean and representative of the vintage. The equally good Cuvée Wais '08 from a 60-20-20 blend of pinot bianco, pinot grigio and sauvignon, is full and flavourful with lovely notes of aromatic herbs and well-balanced acidity. A complex nose of apricot and alpine herbs on the Bianco MerVin V.T. '08 leads to a full, creamy palate and long finish. Among the reds, we mention the Pinot Nero Privat '07, the well-made Merlot-Lagrein Privat '07 and the reliably delicious Meranese Schickenburg '08.

★ Cantina di Caldaro

VIA CANTINE, 12
39052 CALDARO/KALTERN [BZ]
TEL. 0471963149
www.kellereikaltern.com

CELLAR SALES
PRE-BOOKED VISITS

ANNUAL PRODUCTION **1.700,000 bottles**
HECTARES UNDER VINE **295**
VITICULTURE METHOD **Conventional**

Cantina di Caldaro is one of the most important estates in Alto Adige and, among other things, has a taste for forward-looking initiatives such as the conversion to biodynamic methods begun some years ago. Outstanding in their production is a sweet wine regularly among the best in Italy. But the entire range, which includes all the most typical wines from the area, from Lago di Caldaro to Cabernet Sauvignon, Pinot Bianco and Gewürztraminer, is excellent. Then again, only the best was to be expected from chair Armin Dissertori and cellarmaster Andreas Praest.

The stemware harvest was good again this year. Six wines reached our finals and the Moscato Giallo Passito Serenade '06 again won Three Glasses. This year saw two interesting surprises in the Gewürztraminer and Weis from the biodynamic Solos line. The latter, from 40-30-30 pinot bianco, chardonnay and pinot grigio, won us over with its finesse and expressivity. But the jewel in this year's crown Serenade, which in the 2006 version shows sumptuous aromatic richness and complexity.

○ A. A. Bianco V. T. MerVin '08	♟♟	6
● A. A. Lagrein-Cabernet MerVin '07	♟♟	6
● A. A. Meranese Schickenburg '08	♟♟	4*
● A. A. Merlot-Lagrein Privat '07	♟♟	5
● A. A. Pinot Nero Privat '07	♟♟	4
○ A. A. Sauvignon MerVin '08	♟♟	5
○ Cuvée Wais '08	♟♟	4*
○ A. A. Chardonnay Privat '08	♟	4
○ A. A. Pinot Bianco Privat '08	♟	4
● A. A. Bianco V. T. MerVin '07	♟♟	6
● A. A. Meranese Schickenburg '07	♟♟	4*
● A. A. Merlot MerVin '05	♟♟	6
○ A. A. Pinot Bianco Privat '07	♟♟	4*

○ A. A. Moscato Giallo Passito Serenade '06	♟♟♟	6
○ A. A. Gewürztraminer Solos '08	♟♟	4*
● A. A. Lago di Caldaro Scelto Pfarrhof '08	♟♟	4*
● A. A. Lagrein Spigel '07	♟♟	5*
○ A. A. Sauvignon Premstaler '08	♟♟	5*
○ Weiss Solos '08	♟♟	4*
○ A. A. Chardonnay Castel Giovanelli '07	♟♟	6
○ A. A. Gewürztraminer Campaner '08	♟♟	5
○ A. A. Kerner Carned '08	♟♟	4
○ A. A. Pinot Bianco Vial '08	♟♟	4*
● A. A. Santa Maddalena Cardan '08	♟♟	4*
○ A. A. Moscato Giallo Passito Serenade '05	♟♟♟	6
○ A. A. Moscato Giallo Passito Serenade '04	♟♟♟	6
○ A. A. Moscato Giallo Passito Serenade '03	♟♟♟	6
○ A. A. Sauvignon Castel Giovanelli '02	♟♟♟	6
● A. A. Lago di Caldaro Scelto Pfarrhof '07	♟♟	4*

Castelfeder

VIA FRANZ HARPF, 15
39040 CORTINA/KURTINIG [BZ]
TEL. 0471820420
www.castelfeder.it

CELLAR SALES
PRE-BOOKED VISITS

ANNUAL PRODUCTION **400,000 bottles**
HECTARES UNDER VINE **20**
VITICULTURE METHOD **Conventional**

After a few years in the wings, Castelfeder deservedly won a full Guide profile for its reliably good quality. This family-run estate has been managed since 1989 by Günther Giovanett, who moved the cellar to Cortina Sulla Strada del Vino, a village with ancient vineyard traditions, growing mainly white varieties such as chardonnay, pinot grigio, sauvignon and gewürztraminer. Over the past few years, Günther Giovanett has been joined by his two children, who are just as passionate about wine and vineyards.

The quality of the large range of wines presented this year reliable across the range, starting with the Gewürztraminer Fom Lem '08, which is opulent but with acidity that tempers the richness, and a near salty, spicy finish with great complexity. The dried-grape passito version of the same variety, Endiade '07, shows finesse and minerality that gives rare freshness to the mouthfeel. Among the reds, special mention goes to the Lagrein Burgum Novum Riserva '06, which is a bit rustic but has outstanding personality. The rest of the range has good quality and great potential.

★ Cantina Produttori Colterenzio

LOC. CORNAIANO/GIRLAN
S.DA DEL VINO, 8
39057 APPIANO/EPPAN [BZ]
TEL. 0471664246
www.colterenzio.it

CELLAR SALES
PRE-BOOKED VISITS

ANNUAL PRODUCTION **1.600,000 bottles**
HECTARES UNDER VINE **315**
VITICULTURE METHOD **Conventional**

Luis Raifer, long-standing head of this formidable co-operative winery, is a man of few words and many deeds. He has taken the Colterenzio brand to the top in image and quality in Italy and later internationally, as well as here in Alto Adige. What is impressive is the overall quality from this winery and extreme reliability of each of the nearly one and a half million bottles produced annually. This remarkable result is combined with honest value for money.

Even in a difficult year like 2008, Colterenzio produced a range of high quality wines starting with one of the best versions of Sauvignon Lafòa from the past few years. Complex with elegant notes of aromatic herbs and flint, this wine finds rhythm on the palate, where it shows unique depth. Its sibling Cabernet Sauvignon '05 is still too young and, in spite of its inborn class, is still a bit tight and austere. The Pinot Bianco Weisshaus Praedium '08, making the most of the vintage's freshness, and the Pinot Nero St. Daniel '06 are both particularly successful wines.

○ A. A. Gewürztraminer Endidae Passito '07	ΨΨ	6
○ A. A. Gewürztraminer Fom Lem '08	ΨΨ	4*
○ A. A. Chardonnay Burgum Novum Ris. '05	ΨΨ	5
○ A. A. Chardonnay Villa Karneid '08	ΨΨ	4*
● A. A. Lagrein Burgum Novum Ris. '06	ΨΨ	5
○ Kerner '08	ΨΨ	4
○ Sauvignon '08	Ψ	4
● A. A. Lagrein Burgum Novum Ris. '05	ΨΨ	5
○ A. A. Pinot Bianco '07	ΨΨ	4*

● A. A. Cabernet Sauvignon Lafòa '05	ΨΨ	8
○ A. A. Pinot Bianco Weisshaus Praedium '08	ΨΨ	4*
○ A. A. Sauvignon Lafòa '08	ΨΨ	6
○ A. A. Chardonnay Altkirch '08	ΨΨ	4*
● A. A. Lagrein Cornell Sigis Mundus '06	ΨΨ	6
● A. A. Merlot-Cabernet Sauvignon Cornelius Cornell '06	ΨΨ	6
● A. A. Pinot Nero St. Daniel '06	ΨΨ	5
○ A. A. Moscato Giallo Sand Praedium '08	Ψ	4
○ A. A. Pinot Grigio Puiten Praedium '08	Ψ	4
● A. A. Cabernet Sauvignon Lafòa '04	ΨΨΨ	7
● A. A. Cabernet Sauvignon Lafòa '03	ΨΨΨ	8
● A. A. Cabernet Sauvignon Lafòa '01	ΨΨΨ	8
● A. A. Cabernet Sauvignon Lafoa '00	ΨΨΨ	8
○ A. A. Gewürztraminer Cornell '05	ΨΨΨ	5

Cantina Produttori Cornaiano

LOC. CORNAIANO/GIRLAN
VIA SAN MARTINO, 24
39050 APPIANO/EPPAN [BZ]
TEL. 0471662403
www.girlan.it

CELLAR SALES
PRE-BOOKED VISITS

ANNUAL PRODUCTION 1.200,000 bottles
HECTARES UNDER VINE 230
VITICULTURE METHOD Conventional

Innovation and a pioneering spirit have driven this historic Oltradige winery since its beginnings in 1923. This was one of the earliest co-operative winemaking operations to pay growers not just for quantity but also the quality of the grapes. The winery and cellarmaster Gerhard Kofler play a significant role in the Alto Adige winemaking and vineyard scenario. These are all major wines with great technique and personality. Famous for the Schiava Gschleier, the cellar offers a reliable range of high quality wines.

This year's was the greatest all-round performance from this historic estate in memory, and not just because of five wines in the finals and the Three Glasses finally won by the splendid, stylish Sauvignon Indra '08. We applauded a solid show of stylistic maturity. What can we say about the delicious Moscato Rosa Pasithea Rosa '07 or the racy Bianco Riserva '07, from 40-30-30 chardonnay, pinot bianco and sauvignon? Just that these are great Alto Adige wines. Add the Gewürztraminer Flora '08, the Pinot Bianco Plattenriegl and the two Schiavas, also '08s, the Gschleier and the Fass N° 9, and you have a near complete picture of Alto Adige wines.

Cantina Produttori Cortaccia

S.DA DEL VINO, 23
39040 CORTACCIA/KURTATSCH [BZ]
TEL. 0471880115
www.kellerei-kurtatsch.it

CELLAR SALES
PRE-BOOKED VISITS

ANNUAL PRODUCTION 1,000,000 bottles
HECTARES UNDER VINE 200
VITICULTURE METHOD Conventional

Cantina Produttori di Cortaccia has one of the most solid traditions in Alto Adige co-operative winemaking. With a vineyard holding of more than 200 hectares, the operation boasts some plots in gran cru locations such as the Freienfeld vineyard near Cortaccia. The result is a series of well-made wines typical of the lower Adige valley that show full, rich and at times a bit heavy, but always with great character and an excellent range of standard wines.

Cortaccia produced uneven results this year. Alongside clearly worthy wines such as the classic Gewürztraminer Brenntal Riserva '07, the Sauvignon Kofl or the Pinot Bianco Hofstatt, both from 2008, we noticed a series of less certain wines. We got the impression of an estate searching for new directions, but still struggling to find the right path. The technical and human potential are there, as well as the vineyards, which are some of the best in the province of Bolzano. So we continue to wait patiently.

○ A. A. Sauvignon Indra '08	♛♛♛ 4*
○ A. A. Bianco Riserva '07	♛ 5
○ A. A. Gewürztraminer SelectArt Flora '08	♛♛ 5
● A. A. Moscato Rosa Passito Pasithea Rosa '07	♛♛ 6
● A. A. Schiava Gschleier '08	♛♛ 5*
○ A. A. Chardonnay SelectArt Flora '07	♛♛ 5
○ A. A. Gewürztraminer V.T. Pasithea Oro '07	♛♛ 7
● A. A. Lagrein Ris. '06	♛♛ 6
○ A. A. Pinot Bianco Plattenriegl '08	♛♛ 4*
○ A. A. Sauvignon SelectArt Flora '08	♛♛ 5
● A. A. Schiava Fass N° 9 '08	♛♛ 4*
○ 448 slm '08	♛ 3*
○ A. A. Pinot Bianco Plattenriegl '07	♕♕ 4*
○ A. A. Sauvignon Indra '07	♕♕ 4*
○ A. A. Sauvignon SelectArt Flora '07	♕♕ 5

○ A. A. Gewürztraminer Brenntal Ris. '07	♛♛ 6
● A. A. Cabernet Freienfeld '06	♛♛ 6
○ A. A. Chardonnay Pichl '08	♛♛ 4
● A. A. Merlot Cabernet Soma '06	♛♛ 5
○ A. A. Pinot Bianco Hofstatt '08	♛♛ 4
○ A. A. Sauvignon Kofl '08	♛♛ 4*
● A. A. Schiava Grigia Sonntaler '08	♛♛ 4*
○ Bianco Amrita V.T. '07	♛♛ 6
● A. A. Lagrein Freienfeld '06	♛ 5
● A. A. Moscato Rosa Rayas '07	♛ 6
○ A. A. Müller Thurgau Graun '08	♛ 4
○ A. A. Gewürztraminer Brenntal '00	♕♕♕ 5
● A. A. Lagrein Scuro Fohrhof '00	♕♕♕ 5

Egger-Ramer

VIA GUNCINA, 5
39100 BOLZANO/BOZEN
TEL. 0471280541
www.egger-ramer.com

CELLAR SALES
PRE-BOOKED VISITS

ANNUAL PRODUCTION **100,000 bottles**
HECTARES UNDER VINE **14**
VITICULTURE METHOD **Conventional**

Toni and Peter Egger, skilled growers in the Bolzano area, manage this long-established estate with a sure hand. They produce around 100,000 bottles that include all the most typical wines from the zone, which means Lagrein and Santa Maddalena. Over the past few years, they have shown impressive growth in quality, while prices have fortunately remained at truly commendable levels, which is something not to be sniffed at in these times of economic tribulation.

The growing year was so-so for Egger-Ramer. Partial justifications for this are the decisions not to release the estate's flagship wine, the Lagrein Kristan Riserva for years been among the best in its type, or to submit the Santa Maddalena Reiseggerhof. Having said this, we found the typical, fruity Valle Isarco Müller Thurgau Sabbiolino '08 very good, and the Lagrein Kristan '07 well made. We are more than convinced of this is a Bolzano estate to watch and await its swift, certain return to form.

★ Elena Walch

VIA A. HOFER, 1
39040 TERMENO/TRAMIN [BZ]
TEL. 0471860172
www.elenawalch.com

CELLAR SALES
PRE-BOOKED VISITS

ANNUAL PRODUCTION **350,000 bottles**
HECTARES UNDER VINE **30**
VITICULTURE METHOD **Conventional**

For years at the absolute top of Alto Adige wine and grape production, this estate is dynamically managed by Elena Walch, though some credit should also go to Gianfranco Faustin, estate oenologist since 1998. The magnificent Castel Ringberg dominates Lake Caldero from above and Kastelaz hill is the perfect place to produce great white and red wines in the area's most classic types. This estate's trademark is great technical precision and constant quality.

We have always loved the Gewürztraminer Kastelaz because it represents a unique model of elegance and expression for this difficult variety. Kastelaz hill stands there as proof that this minor miracle is possible. Add a finesse-favouring vintage year like 2008 and that's that: Three Glasses. Again from the magical hill of Kastelaz is another excellent wine, the Pinot Bianco '08, which shows juicy and full but with a slightly salty vein that gives the palate suppleness and depth. Finally, we should also mention the Lago di Caldaro '08 for its pleasing, forthright drinkability.

○ A. A. Valle Isarco Müller Thurgau Sabbiolino '08	♀	4
○ A. A. Gewürztraminer '08	♀	4
● A. A. Lagrein Gries Tenuta Kristan '07	♀	5
⊙ A. A. Lagrein Rosato '08	♀	4
● A. A. Lagrein Gries Tenuta Kristan Ris. '05	♀♀	5
● A. A. Lagrein Gries Tenuta Kristan Ris. '04	♀♀	5
● A. A. Lagrein Scuro Gries Tenuta Kristan '06	♀♀	4*

○ A. A. Gewürztraminer Kastelaz '08	♀♀♀+	6
○ A. A. Pinot Bianco Kastelaz '08	♀♀	5
● A. A. Lago di Caldaro Cl. Sup. '08	♀♀	4
○ A. A. Chardonnay Cardellino '08	♀	5
○ A. A. Bianco Beyond the Clouds '06	♀♀♀	7
○ A. A. Gewürztraminer Kastelaz '07	♀♀♀	6
○ A. A. Gewürztraminer Kastelaz '06	♀♀♀	6
○ A. A. Gewürztraminer Kastelaz '05	♀♀♀	6
○ A. A. Gewürztraminer Kastelaz '04	♀♀♀	6
● A. A. Lagrein Castel Ringberg Ris. '04	♀♀♀	6
● A. A. Lagrein Castel Ringberg Ris. '03	♀♀♀	6

Erbhof Unterganzner Josephus Mayr

FRAZ. CARDANO
VIA CAMPIGLIO, 15
39053 BOLZANO/BOZEN
TEL. 0471365582
mayr.unterganzner@dnet.it

CELLAR SALES
PRE-BOOKED VISITS

ANNUAL PRODUCTION **65,000 bottles**
HECTARES UNDER VINE **8.5**
VITICULTURE METHOD **Conventional**

The apparent ease with which Josephus Mayr, a man whose passion and skill are unique, turns out simply spectacular wines every year is disconcerting. Regardless of the vintage, he always manages to get the best from his vineyards even though they are not located in the classic Gries area. In fact, they are situated on the northern slope of the hollow of Bolzano, adjacent to those in Santa Maddalena. Naturally, red wines come first but for some years now Josephus has also delighted us with excellent whites.

For good or ill, character has never been missing in wines from Josephus Mayr. This year his Lagreins, the Riserva '06 and the Lamarein '07, are as usual concentrated, dense, earthy and austere but are perhaps paying the price of their youth. This goes above all for Lamarein. Juicy, quite concentrated and fresh, with acidity that goes well with its powerful structure, the palate never quite manages to unfold completely. In an especially successful '07 version, the Santa Maddalena is as wonderful as ever.

Cantina Sociale Erste & Neue

VIA DELLE CANTINE, 5/10
39052 CALDARO/KALTERN [BZ]
TEL. 0471963122
www.erste-neue.it

CELLAR SALES
PRE-BOOKED VISITS

ANNUAL PRODUCTION **1,000,000 bottles**
HECTARES UNDER VINE **320**
VITICULTURE METHOD **Conventional**

Prima & Nuova/Erste & Neue in Caldaro is one of the best co-operative operations in the region. Production runs to more than a million bottles in three lines of wines, Puntay being the most important. Almost all come from varieties grown in Alto Adige, although special emphasis is placed on Lake Caldaro that somewhat represents the estate's trademark wine. The young, dynamic management, led by the chair, Manfred Schullian, flanked by the cellarmaster, Gerhard Sanin, guarantees a bright future for this long-standing co-operative winery.

The estate seems to have found the right direction for quality. This goes not just for the four wines that reached our finals but also for the overall results of the range presented. Schiava remains the estate's strategic variety with excellent products such as the Santa Maddalena Gröbnerhof and the two Lago di Caldaros, Leuchtenburg and Puntay, all from '08 and all simply delicious, but the whites are significant as well. The Pinot Bianco Prunar '08 is one of the best from the vintage and the Gewürztraminer Puntay shows finesse and class.

Wine	Rating
● A. A. Lagrein Scuro Ris. '06	♖♖ 5
● Lamarein '07	♖ 7
● A. A. Santa Maddalena '07	♖♖ 3*
○ A. A. Chardonnay Platt&Pignat '08	♖ 4
⊙ A. A. Lagrein Rosato '08	♖ 4
● A. A. Lagrein Scuro Ris. '05	♕♕♕ 5
● A. A. Lagrein Scuro Ris. '01	♕♕♕ 5
● A. A. Lagrein Scuro Ris. '00	♕♕♕ 5
● A. A. Lagrein Scuro Ris. '99	♕♕♕ 5

Wine	Rating
○ A. A. Anthos Bianco Passito '05	♖♖ 6
● A. A. Lago di Caldaro Scelto Puntay '08	♖♖ 4*
○ A. A. Pinot Bianco Prunar '08	♖♖ 4*
● A. A. Santa Maddalena Gröbnerhof '08	♖♖ 4*
○ A. A. Chardonnay Puntay '07	♖♖ 5
○ A. A. Gewürztraminer Puntay '08	♖♖ 5
● A. A. Lago di Caldaro Scelto Leuchtenburg '08	♖♖ 4*
● A. A. Merlot Puntay '06	♖♖ 6
○ A. A. Sauvignon Puntay '08	♖♖ 5
○ A. A. Sauvignon Stern '08	♖♖ 5*
○ A. A. Chardonnay Salt '08	♖ 4
○ A. A. Moscato Giallo Secco Barleit '08	♖ 4
○ A. A. Sauvignon Puntay '06	♕♕♕ 5
○ A. A. Pinot Bianco Puntay '07	♕♕ 4*
○ A. A. Sauvignon Puntay '07	♕♕ 5

Falkenstein - Franz Pratzner
VIA CASTELLO, 15
39025 NATURNO/NATURNS [BZ]
TEL. 0473666054
www.falkenstein.bz

CELLAR SALES
PRE-BOOKED VISITS

ANNUAL PRODUCTION **45,000 bottles**
HECTARES UNDER VINE **7**
VITICULTURE METHOD **Natural**

We always recommend making a visit to Falkenstein for several reasons. The first is to enjoy the magnificent view over the valley; second for a chance to see these vineyards that show what the term "heroic viticulture" actually means; third for Franz Pratzner himself, a grower of few words yet many ideas he always puts into practice; and last but not least for really good wines with great personality, an unusual Germanic style and superior elegance. All estate wines are stoppered with screw caps.

This year, Franz Pratzner submitted only three wines for tasting from the 2008 vintage. But what wines they are! There was some embarrassment choosing which one should win Three Glasses: the Pinot Bianco that cuts sharp and deep as a razor; the spicy, vibrant Sauvignon; or the sharp, racy Riesling, full of energy, backbone and character with a long finish. The choice fell to the last wine but was never intended to diminish the other two wines, which are superb in their respective types.

Garlider
Christian Kerchbaumer
VIA UNTRUM, 20
39040 VELTURNO/FELDTHURNS [BZ]
TEL. 0472847296
www.garlider.it

CELLAR SALES
PRE-BOOKED VISITS

ANNUAL PRODUCTION **16,000 bottles**
HECTARES UNDER VINE **3.5**
VITICULTURE METHOD **Natural**

Christian Kerchbaumer is young and determined with new vineyards, projects and experiments in the cellar. Garlider mostly produces the typical white wines from Valle Isarco, and just a few hundred bottles of reds including the only Pinot Nero produced in the area. These natural, expressive wines show great personality with slightly more southern shades with respect to characteristics from the valley, but this is Velturno in the extreme south. This small estate now represents something more than a mere promise.

More than a skilled winemaker, Christian is also a real wine enthusiast, travelling, tasting and meeting other producers, never convinced wine begins and ends in the province of Bolzano. His efforts produce wines that are rich in personality, once and a while with some defects, but never boring. Let's start with the Veltliner '08, Garlider's most representative wine. Intense floral aromas accompany clear mineral notes that return on a palate that unfolds fragrantly with a powerful, tangy progression. The '08 Sylvaner is one of the best, showing sharper and more vibrant than usual. The rest of the range is as interesting as ever.

○ A. A. Valle Venosta Riesling '08	♟♟♟ 6
○ A. A. Valle Venosta Pinot Bianco '08	♟♟ 5
○ A. A. Valle Venosta Sauvignon '08	♟♟ 5
○ A. A. Valle Venosta Pinot Bianco '07	♟♟♟ 5
○ A. A. Valle Venosta Riesling '07	♟♟♟ 6
○ A. A. Valle Venosta Riesling '06	♟♟♟ 6
○ A. A. Valle Venosta Riesling '05	♟♟♟ 6
○ A. A. Valle Venosta Pinot Bianco '06	♟♟ 5
○ A. A. Valle Venosta Sauvignon '07	♟♟ 5

○ A. A. Valle Isarco Veltliner '08	♟♟♟ 5*
○ A. A. Valle Isarco Sylvaner '08	♟♟ 4*
○ A. A. Valle Isarco Gewürztraminer '08	♟♟ 5
○ A. A. Valle Isarco Müller Thurgau '08	♟♟ 4
○ A. A. Valle Isarco Pinot Grigio '08	♟♟ 5
○ A. A. Valle Isarco Veltliner '07	♟♟♟ 5
○ A. A. Valle Isarco Veltliner '05	♟♟♟ 4*
○ A. A. Valle Isarco Pinot Grigio '07	♟♟ 5
○ A. A. Valle Isarco Sylvaner '07	♟♟ 4*
○ A. A. Valle Isarco Sylvaner '06	♟♟ 4*

Glögglhof - Franz Gojer

FRAZ. SANTA MADDALENA
VIA RIVELLONE, 1
39100 BOLZANO/BOZEN
TEL. 0471978775
www.gojer.it

CELLAR SALES
PRE-BOOKED VISITS

ANNUAL PRODUCTION **40,000 bottles**
HECTARES UNDER VINE **6**
VITICULTURE METHOD **Conventional**

Franz Gojer is pleasant, likeable and witty, and also a great winemaker. Since 1982, the year he inherited this estate, Franz has produced some of the finest, most classic wines from the Bolzano area. Glögglhof is actually located on the prominent hill of Santa Maddalena, north of Bolzano, and always produces typical wines, starting with the one named after the area. Franz is a real master of Santa Maddalena. His base version and the Rondell selection are always among the best.

Glögglhof submitted some truly satisfying wines this year, starting with a current version of Lagrein that should be a benchmark for this wine. The nose is spicy and fruity, and the palate fresh, supple, juicy and minerally with a full-flavoured, intriguing mouthfeel. Also top quality is the other estate warhorse, the Santa Maddalena Rondell '08, has crisp fruit and delicate spice. In other words, this is the quintessence of typical Bolzano production, of which Franz Gojer is clearly high priest.

Cantina Gries/ Cantina di Bolzano

FRAZ. GRIES
P.ZZA GRIES, 2
39100 BOLZANO/BOZEN
TEL. 0471270909
www.cantinabolzano.com

CELLAR SALES
PRE-BOOKED VISITS

ANNUAL PRODUCTION **1.500,000 bottles**
HECTARES UNDER VINE **170**
VITICULTURE METHOD **Conventional**

This is one of the most important wineries producing Lagrein Scuro. Gries, immediately south of Bolzano, is the heart of production for this ancient, traditional Alto Adige red. Since 2001, this old, co-operative winery has merged with Santa Maddalena into Cantina di Bolzano under the management of Stephan Filippi. These wines have style, character and excellent technique in the production of the most typical wines from the province of Bolzano.

Lagrein is the most important wine historically for this co-operative operation, which produces various reliable versions with a sound, well-defined style. We start with the Lagrein Prestige Line Riserva '07, which has a distinctive nose of spice and ripe blackberry followed by a creamy fruit and cinchona palate. Moscato Rosa Rosis '08 is impeccably well typed, as is the other major red, the Cabernet Otto Graf Huyn Riserva '07. The Moscato Giallo Passito Vinalia '07 is always one of the best.

● A. A. Lagrein '08	♥♥ 4*
● A. A. Lagrein Scuro Ris. '06	♥♥ 5
● A. A. Santa Maddalena Rondell '08	♥♥ 4*
● A. A. Santa Maddalena Cl. '08	♥ 4
● A. A. Lagrein Scuro Ris. '04	♀♀ 5
● A. A. Lagrein Scuro Ris. '03	♀♀ 5
● A. A. Santa Maddalena Rondell '07	♀♀ 4*

● A. A. Lagrein Scuro Prestige Line Ris. '07	♥ 6
● A. A. Cabernet Collection Otto Graf Huyn Ris. '07	♥♥ 5
● A. A. Lagrein Grieser '08	♥♥ 4
○ A. A. Moscato Giallo Vinalia '07	♥♥ 8
● A. A. Moscato Rosa Rosis '08	♥♥ 6
● A. A. Lagrein Grieser Baron Carl Eyrl '07	♥ 5
☉ A. A. Lagrein Rosé Pischl '08	♥ 4
● A. A. Pinot Nero '08	♥ 4
● A. A. Lagrein Scuro Prestige Line Ris. '06	♀♀♀ 6
● A. A. Lagrein Scuro Prestige Line Ris. '00	♀♀♀ 6
● A. A. Lagrein Scuro Prestige Line Ris. '99	♀♀♀ 6
○ A. A. Moscato Giallo Vinalia '03	♀♀♀ 6
● A. A. Lagrein Grieser Baron Carl Eyrl '06	♀♀ 5
○ A. A. Moscato Giallo Vinalia '06	♀♀ 8

Griesbauerhof
Georg Mumelter
VIA RENCIO, 66
39100 BOLZANO/BOZEN
TEL. 0471973090
www.tirolensisarsvini.it

CELLAR SALES
PRE-BOOKED VISITS

ANNUAL PRODUCTION 25,000 bottles
HECTARES UNDER VINE 3.3
VITICULTURE METHOD Conventional

Appearance is clearly not one of the main aspirations of Georg Mumelter, and his wines represent this philosophy. For him, only his vineyards and cellar near Rencio exist and he produces austere, well-made wines with lots of charm and personality. All the typical types from Bolzano are well represented here, starting with Lagrein and moving on to Santa Maddalena, Cabernet Sauvignon and Pinot Grigio, the only estate white.

There are some ups and downs in the range presented this year by Griesbauerhof. A Lagrein '07, with a dense, minerally palate that expands nicely, corresponds to a clenched, less convincing Riserva '06. In contrast with a deliciously fruity, spicy Santa Maddalena Classico '08, we were less convinced by the Cabernet Sauvignon Riserva '06. We are sure this is a momentary lapse since the estate usually pampers us with very reliable, constant quality.

Gummerhof - Malojer
VIA WEGGESTEIN, 36
39100 BOLZANO/BOZEN
TEL. 0471972885
www.malojer.it

CELLAR SALES
PRE-BOOKED VISITS

ANNUAL PRODUCTION 100,000 bottles
HECTARES UNDER VINE 6
VITICULTURE METHOD Conventional

The earliest references to Gummerhof go back to 1480. Once isolated in a sea of vineyards north of Bolzano, today this winery, managed by Elisabeth, Urban and Alfred Malojer, concentrates above all on producing typical reds from the Bolzano area, though there is no lack of excellent white wines. These typical wines have a significant touch of elegance, the result of great effort in the vineyards and confident technique in the cellar. As always, prices show rare honesty.

The Malojer family turned in a good overall performance, though we expected something more from the whites. The 2008 growing season certainly did not help. So praise goes to a great winery classic, the trusted Lagrein Gummerhof zu Gries '07, a dense, succulent red with seriously good, ripe tannins well supported by lively acidity and all held together by elegance and freshness. The Santa Maddalena Classico '08 is simple and easy drinking. As we mentioned earlier, the whites are well managed but are not of the same calibre as the 2007s. The positive note is that prices remain commendably consumer-friendly.

● A. A. Lagrein '07	▼▼ 4*
● A. A. Santa Maddalena Cl. '08	▼▼ 3*
● A. A. Cabernet Sauvignon Ris. '06	▼ 5
● A. A. Lagrein Scuro Ris. '06	▼ 5
● A. A. Lagrein Scuro Ris. '99	▼▼▼ 5
● A. A. Cabernet Sauvignon '04	▼▼ 5*
● A. A. Lagrein Scuro Ris. '04	▼▼ 5
○ A. A. Pinot Grigio '07	▼▼ 4*
● A. A. Santa Maddalena Cl. '07	▼▼ 3*

● A. A. Lagrein Scuro Gummerhof zu Gries '07	▼▼ 4*
● A. A. Lagrein Scuro Ris. '06	▼ 5
○ A. A. Müller Thurgau '08	▼ 3*
○ A. A. Pinot Bianco '08	▼ 4
● A. A. Santa Maddalena Cl. '08	▼ 3*
○ A. A. Sauvignon Gur zur Sand '08	▼ 4
● A. A. Lagrein Scuro Gummerhof zu Gries '06	▼▼ 4*
● A. A. Lagrein Scuro Gummerhof zu Gries '05	▼▼ 4*
● A. A. Lagrein Scuro Ris. '05	▼▼ 5
● A. A. Lagrein Scuro Ris. '04	▼▼ 5

Gumphof - Markus Prackwieser

NOVALE DI PRESULE, 8
39050 FIÈ ALLO SCILIAR/
VÖLS AM SCHLERN [BZ]
TEL. 0471601190
www.gumphof.it

CELLAR SALES
PRE-BOOKED VISITS

ANNUAL PRODUCTION **4,000 bottles**
HECTARES UNDER VINE **5**
VITICULTURE METHOD **Conventional**

Pleasant, young winemaker Markus Prack-wieser owns a small estate with vineyards along a sheer crag on the slopes of the Sciliar, just a few hundred metres from Valle Isarco. Gumphof wines seem slightly affected by the style of the valley. Markus also gives rare complexity and personality to these fresh, dynamic, minerally whites thanks to his painstaking labours in the vineyard. For some years now, a Pinot Nero has also been produced and Gumphof expects great things from it.

The talented Markus just missed again winning Three Glasses with his '08 Sauvignon Praesulis. The wine is introduced by sage and citrus aromas already accompanied by deep, elegant minerally shades. The palate is balsamic and expressive, though still too young to fully expand. The salty, minerally Pinot Bianco Praesulis '08 has vibrant acid backbone with a finish that is a bit too soft. The rest of the range is its usual quality, in other words, high, with special mention for the delicious Schiava '08.

Franz Haas

VIA VILLA, 6
39040 MONTAGNA/MONTAN [BZ]
TEL. 0471812280
www.franz-haas.it

CELLAR SALES
PRE-BOOKED VISITS

ANNUAL PRODUCTION **290,000 bottles**
HECTARES UNDER VINE **50**
VITICULTURE METHOD **Conventional**

While still waiting for the official inauguration of the new cellar, a wait that has gone on a little long, we recall for those who don't know that Franz Haas is one of the greatest, most scrupulous Pinot Nero experts ever on the face of the earth. His selections of this variety are regularly among the best in the country. But Haas and Luisa Manna, Franz's pleasant, energetic wife, have for years produced a series of top high quality wines with impeccable style.

Franz has accustomed us to high-quality wines but rarely has he released a range like this. It could be that his cellar is now finished, or his new vineyards are planted, or simply that his hard work has been rewarded but this year we were awed. The new wine, a Sauvignon '08, is one of the finest in its category on its first release. And what can we say about Pinot Nero Schweizer '07 or Moscato Rosa '07? In passing, we might mention Three Glasses went to Manna '07, a blend of half riesling, one fifth gewürztraminer and chardonnay, and the rest sauvignon, which has complex tropical fruit and aromatic herbs, a full, taut palate and great balance.

Wine	Rating
○ A. A. Pinot Bianco Praesulis '08	♀♀ 4*
○ A. A. Sauvignon Praesulis '08	♀♀ 5
○ A. A. Gewürztraminer Praesulis '08	♀♀ 5
● A. A. Pinot Nero '07	♀♀ 5
● A. A. Schiava '08	♀♀ 4*
○ A. A. Pinot Bianco '08	♀ 4
○ A. A. Pinot Bianco Praesulis '06	♀♀♀ 4*
○ A. A. Sauvignon Praesulis '07	♀♀♀ 5*
○ A. A. Sauvignon Praesulis '04	♀♀♀ 5*
○ A. A. Gewürztraminer Praesulis '07	♀♀ 5
○ A. A. Pinot Bianco Praesulis '07	♀♀ 4*

Wine	Rating
○ Manna '07	♀♀♀ 5
● A. A. Moscato Rosa '07	♀♀ 6
○ A. A. Pinot Grigio '08	♀♀ 4*
● A. A. Pinot Nero Schweizer '07	♀♀ 7
○ A. A. Sauvignon '08	♀♀ 6
○ A. A. Gewürztraminer '08	♀♀ 5
○ A. A. Müller Thurgau '08	♀♀ 4
○ A. A. Pinot Bianco '08	♀♀ 5
● A. A. Lagrein '07	♀ 5
● A. A. Pinot Nero Schweizer '02	♀♀♀ 6
● A. A. Pinot Nero Schweizer '01	♀♀♀ 6
○ Manna '05	♀♀♀ 5
○ Manna '04	♀♀♀ 5

Haderburg

FRAZ. BUCHOLZ
LOC. POCHI, 30
39040 SALORNO/SALURN [BZ]
TEL. 0471889097
www.haderburg.it

CELLAR SALES
PRE-BOOKED VISITS

ANNUAL PRODUCTION **80,000 bottles**
HECTARES UNDER VINE **12**
VITICULTURE METHOD **Biodinamico certificato**

Alois Ochsenreiter, oenologist and owner of the Haderburg estate, cultivates his vineyards to biodynamic standards, releasing sparklers and other wines. The fruit for Haderburg's cuvée comes from the hill above Salorno in the idyllic location of I Pochi, or Buchholz, one of the great crus of Alto Adige winemaking. As well as the sparklers, there are some still wines with a decisive, austere style in the spotlight, like those sourced from the small Obermairlhof estate in Valle Isarco.

Only a Three Glass award was lacking to complete one of the best performances from Haderburg in the past few years. The zesty Spumante Hausmannhof Riserva '99 shows the usual ripe notes but progression on the palate has great energy and expansion. The Sauvignon Hausmannhof '08 is also excellent with elegant gunflint aromas and an almost cutting, yet deep palate. The Pinot Nero Hausmannhof Riserva '06 and Sylvaner Obermairl '08 stand out for complexity, character and great continuity.

Hoandlhof - Manfred Nössing

FRAZ. KRANEBIH
VIA DEI VIGNETI, 66
39042 BRESSANONE/BRIXEN [BZ]
TEL. 0472832672
www.manninoessing.com

CELLAR SALES
PRE-BOOKED VISITS

ANNUAL PRODUCTION **17,000 bottles**
HECTARES UNDER VINE **4.3**
VITICULTURE METHOD **Conventional**

Manni Nössing is no longer the affable young Alto Adige winemaker he was some while ago. He has now become a star who makes use of the technical collaboration of the talented Vincenzo Bambina. Over the years, Manni's wines have come on in technical precision and, impressively, in stylistic definition. Although clearly Valle Isarco in style, the added touch of grit and mischief makes whites from Hoandlhof easy to identify and much sought after. The valley's typical wines reach some of their highest peaks at this cellar.

It is impressive to observe how wines from Manni Nössing have changed style in the space of a couple of harvests. We have gone from products with great concentration and ripe fruit to sharp, incisive wines with strong acidity. Having said this, it was difficult to choose the best of the four wines submitted. Our vote went to a Sylvaner '08 with an impressive attack but it could have been the Kerner, more elegant than ever, or the Veltliner, achieving new stylistic maturity, but don't overlook Manni's almost unequalled Müller Thurgau.

O A. A. Sauvignon Hausmannhof '08	♈♈ 5
O A. A. Spumante Hausmannhof Ris. '99	♈♈ 7
O A. A. Valle Isarco Sylvaner Obermairl '08	♈♈ 4*
● A. A. Erah '05	♈♈ 6
O A. A. Gewürztraminer Blaspichl '08	♈♈ 5
● A. A. Pinot Nero Hausmannhof Ris. '06	♈♈ 6
O A. A. Spumante Brut	♈♈ 5*
O A. A. Spumante Pas Dosé '04	♈ 6
O A. A. Spumante Hausmannhof Ris. '97	♈♈♈ 7
O A. A. Valle Isarco Sylvaner Obermairlhof '05	♈♈♈ 4*
● A. A. Pinot Nero Hausmannhof Ris. '04	♈♈ 6
● A. A. Pinot Nero Hausmannhof Ris. '03	♈♈ 6
O A. A. Spumante Hausmannhof Ris. '93	♈♈ 7

O A. A. Valle Isarco Sylvaner '08	♈♈♈ 5*
O A. A. Valle Isarco Kerner '08	♈♈ 5*
O A. A. Valle Isarco Müller Thurgau '08	♈♈ 5
O A. A. Valle Isarco Veltliner '08	♈♈ 5*
O A. A. Valle Isarco Kerner '06	♈♈♈ 4*
O A. A. Valle Isarco Kerner '05	♈♈♈ 4*
O A. A. Valle Isarco Kerner '03	♈♈♈ 4*
O A. A. Valle Isarco Kerner '02	♈♈♈ 4
O A. A. Valle Isarco Sylvaner '04	♈♈♈ 4*
O A. A. Valle Isarco Veltliner '07	♈♈♈ 5

★ Tenuta J. Hofstätter

P.ZZA MUNICIPIO, 7
39040 TERMENO/TRAMIN [BZ]
TEL. 0471860161
www.hofstatter.com

CELLAR SALES
PRE-BOOKED VISITS

ANNUAL PRODUCTION **720,000 bottles**
HECTARES UNDER VINE 53.5
VITICULTURE METHOD **Conventional**

Martin Foradori manages one of the most modern, dynamic estates in the country with great attention to vineyards and cellar, special focus on traditional varieties without losing sight of changing market requirements, and aggressive, wide-ranging marketing strategies. It all adds up to a complete range of wines with two outstanding classics: the Gewürztraminer and Pinot Nero.

This is one of the best editions of Gewürztraminer Kolbenhof from the past few years. Aristocratic, elegant and complex with great balance and a good mouthfeel, it is buoyed by a freshness that had been lost somewhat over the years. Moving on to the two estate flagship Pinot Neros, the Barthenau Vigna Sant'Urbano and the Riserva, both from the 2006 vintage, are excellent wines, showing elegant with fine-grained tannins but we encountered some riper notes that slightly weaken the progression.

Tenuta Klosterhof Oskar Andergassen

LOC. CLAVENZ, 40
39052 CALDARO/KALTERN [BZ]
TEL. 0471961046
www.garni-klosterhof.com

CELLAR SALES
PRE-BOOKED VISITS
OSPITALITÀ
FOOD

ANNUAL PRODUCTION **20,000 bottles**
HECTARES UNDER VINE 2.5
VITICULTURE METHOD **Conventional**

The Klosterhof estate deservedly won a full profile thanks to the range of great-quality wines submitted to our tastings over the years. This small, family-run winery, managed by Oskar Andergassen, is located in a sunny position just five minutes from the town centre of Caldaro, deep in the green countryside, surrounded by vineyards. The wines are distinguished by a lean style that aims for elegance with balanced extract, designed to create products that respect the wine types. Pinot Nero is the flagship estate wine.

Scores this year from Oskar Andergassen and Klosterhof are a relative surprise. We have been watching this winemaker for some time now and must admit his wines become more exciting and better defined every year. We'll start with the Pinot Bianco Trifall '08, one of the best from the vintage. Austere and tangy, it unfurls great progression that expands minerally and caressing to a near salty finish with great complexity. Pinot Nero Panigl '06 is even more austere but shows great energy and character. The rest of the range is better than just well made.

Wine		Score
○ A. A. Gewürztraminer Kolbenhof '08	♀♀	6
● A. A. Pinot Nero Barthenau V. S. Urbano '06	♀♀	8
● A. A. Pinot Nero Ris. '06	♀♀	6
○ A. A. Gewürztraminer Kolbenhof '04	♀♀♀	5
○ A. A. Gewürztraminer Kolbenhof '03	♀♀♀	5
○ A. A. Gewürztraminer Kolbenhof '01	♀♀♀	6
● Yngram '00	♀♀♀	7
● A. A. Lagrein Scuro Steinraffler '05	♀♀	6
● A. A. Pinot Nero Barthenau V. S. Urbano '05	♀♀	8
● A. A. Pinot Nero Barthenau V. S. Urbano '04	♀♀	8
● A. A. Pinot Nero Ris. '05	♀♀	6

Wine		Score
○ A. A. Pinot Bianco Trifall '08	♀♀	4*
○ A. A. Gewürztraminer '08	♀♀	4*
● A. A. Lago di Caldaro Plantaditsch '08	♀♀	3*
○ A. A. Moscato Giallo '08	♀♀	4*
● A. A. Pinot Nero Panigl '06	♀♀	6
● A. A. Merlot Ris. '06	♀	5
○ A. A. Gewürztraminer '07	♀♀	4*
○ A. A. Moscato Giallo '07	♀♀	4*
● A. A. Pinot Nero Panigl '04	♀♀	6

Köfererhof
Günther Kershbaumer

FRAZ. NOVACELLA
VIA PUSTERIA, 3
39040 VARNA/VAHRN [BZ]
TEL. 0472836649
info@koefererhof.it

CELLAR SALES
PRE-BOOKED VISITS

ANNUAL PRODUCTION **48,000 bottles**
HECTARES UNDER VINE **5.5**
VITICULTURE METHOD **Conventional**

A man of few words, Günter Kershbaumer has clear ideas on how to make his wines: no barriques, just stainless steel and some large oak, like the containers many producers now use in Valle Isarco. The wines are characterful, like all wines from this area, but with that touch more personality that makes Köfererhof wines one-of-a-kind. These austere, vibrantly rich bottles have over the years achieved surprising heights of expression. The estate has experienced the strongest growth in Valle Isarco over the past few years.

This is a picture-perfect vintage from Kofererhof. Tastings over the past few months foreshadowed great things but the main point here is these exciting results. Five wines landed in the finals and the Sylvaner R '08, a selection of the best fruit, confirmed its Three Glasses in the past two years. But we could have chosen the same vintage's Riesling, more juicy and elegant than ever before, the finish showing touches of the sea and peat. But the Pinot Grigio '08, with its taut, sharp palate, the usual great Müller Thurgau, or the Kerner, more harmonious and incisive than ever, are all excellent.

Tenuta Kornell

FRAZ. SETTEQUERCE
VIA BOLZANO, 23
39018 TERLANO/TERLAN [BZ]
TEL. 0471917507
www.kornell.it

CELLAR SALES
PRE-BOOKED VISITS

ANNUAL PRODUCTION **60,000 bottles**
HECTARES UNDER VINE **14.5**
VITICULTURE METHOD **Conventional**

Ten hectares of family property around this splendid estate, scattered clayey, sandy plots rich in porphyry, a Mediterranean climate, vines planted between 1985 and 2005, the enthusiasm of owner Florian Brigl, and an intense relationship with nature are all elements to be found in these characterful wines, in part because they come from one of the best terroirs in the region. Add to this their great value for money.

Florian Brigl has one of the most dynamic new winemaking estates in the province of Bolzano. Overall scores were good this year, though we have the impression that Kornell's potential has yet to be completely expressed. We felt one of the most convincing wines was the red Zeder '07, a blend of equal parts of merlot and cabernet sauvignon that presents creamy yet elegant with careful, never intrusive use of oak, good crunchy fruit and fine-grained tannins. The two varietal Lagreins, the Greif '07 and Riserva '06, are well made.

O A. A. Valle Isarco Sylvaner R '08	♟♟♟+ 5
O A. A. Valle Isarco Kerner '08	♟♟ 5
O A. A. Valle Isarco Pinot Grigio '08	♟♟ 4*
O A. A. Valle Isarco Riesling '08	♟♟ 5
O A. A. Valle Isarco Veltliner '08	♟♟ 4*
O A. A. Valle Isarco Gewürztraminer '08	♟♟ 5
O A. A. Valle Isarco Müller Thurgau '08	♟♟ 4*
O A. A. Valle Isarco Sylvaner '08	♟♟ 4*
O A. A. Valle Isarco Sylvaner R '07	♟♟♟ 5
O A. A. Valle Isarco Sylvaner R '06	♟♟♟ 5
O A. A. Valle Isarco Pinot Grigio '06	♟♟ 4*
O A. A. Valle Isarco Riesling '07	♟♟ 5
O A. A. Valle Isarco Veltliner '07	♟♟ 4*

● A. A. Zeder '07	♟♟ 4*
● A. A. Lagrein Greif '07	♟♟ 4
● A. A. Lagrein Staves Ris. '06	♟♟ 4*
O A. A. Sauvignon Cosmas '08	♟♟ 4
● A. A. Merlot Staves Ris. '06	♟ 6
● A. A. Cabernet Sauvignon Staves '04	♟♟ 6
● A. A. Cabernet Sauvignon Staves '03	♟♟ 6
O A. A. Sauvignon Cosmas '07	♟♟ 4*
● A. A. Zeder '05	♟♟ 4*

Tenuta Kränzl - Graf Franz Pfeil

VIA PALADE, 1
39010 CERMES/TSCHERMS [BZ]
TEL. 0473564549
www.labyrinth.bz

CELLAR SALES
PRE-BOOKED VISITS

ANNUAL PRODUCTION **35,000 bottles**
HECTARES UNDER VINE **6**
VITICULTURE METHOD **Organic certified**

Wine from this estate perfectly reflects the manager's character. The aristocratic owner Franz Pfeil is slightly distant yet gracious and makes his wines according to his own, very personal ideas, thumbing his nose at market trends and fashions. Strictly organic since 1985, he makes the wines he likes best at his splendid estate in Tscherms. These decent wines may show some ups and downs but they have lashings of character.

Kränzl wines have always divided opinions. Perhaps this is the clearest proof these are never boring. We are among those who appreciate the cellar's vision of wines that are not necessarily perfect technically, yet manage to transmit a feeling, an idea. One taste of the Pinot Bianco Helios '08 will leave you speechless in awe at the ripe fruit notes accompanied by an absolutely unique aromatic vein. The palate is concentrated and alcoholic, yet has well-balanced richness and great depth of flavour. Schiava Baslan '08 is always aristocratic and spicy.

Kuenhof - Peter Pliger

LOC. MARA, 110
29042 BRESSANONE/BRIXEN [BZ]
TEL. 0472850546
pliger.kuenhof@rolmail.net

CELLAR SALES
PRE-BOOKED VISITS

ANNUAL PRODUCTION **27,000 bottles**
HECTARES UNDER VINE **6**
VITICULTURE METHOD **Natural**

Now that Peter and Brigitte Pliger and their Kuenhof estate have become famous and received many awards, they could easily rest on their laurels. But they will have none of this. The duo are constantly redoubling their effort, passion and determination, not least in their absolute respect for nature and faith in non-invasive techniques. The results are expressive, elegant, natural whites with great purity. We wonder what Kuenhof could produce if yields were lowered even further.

The 2008 vintage enhanced, even exaggerated, the characteristics of the Kuenhof style, a style of epic tides and changes. Peter Pliger's wines, always a model of lightness and elegance, have become even more minimalist, stripping away the last baroque residues. A good example of this is the Riesling Kaiton. The nose shows apples, pepper and smoky shades while the sharp palate is almost intangible yet very long. But Three Glasses went to the Sylvaner '08, which is less rich than other versions but with a naturally incisive development.

O A. A. Pinot Bianco Helios '08	♀♀	5
● A. A. Pinot Nero '06	♀♀	5
● Schiava Baslan '08	♀♀	4*
● A. A. Cabernet Sauvignon-Merlot Sagittarius '06	♀	6
O A. A. Gewürztraminer Passito Dorado '04	♀♀	6
● A. A. Meranese Hügel Baslan Ris. '05	♀♀	4*
O A. A. Pinot Bianco Helios '06	♀♀	5
● Schiava Baslan '07	♀♀	4*

O A. A. Valle Isarco Sylvaner '08	♀♀♀	5
O A. A. Valle Isarco Riesling Kaiton '08	♀♀	5
O A. A. Valle Isarco Veltliner '08	♀♀	5*
O A. A. Valle Isarco Gewürztraminer '08	♀♀	5
O A. A. Valle Isarco Riesling Kaiton '07	♀♀♀	5*
O A. A. Valle Isarco Riesling Kaiton '05	♀♀♀	4*
O A. A. Valle Isarco Sylvaner '06	♀♀♀	4*
O A. A. Valle Isarco Sylvaner '03	♀♀♀	4*
O A. A. Valle Isarco Sylvaner '02	♀♀♀	4*
O A. A. Valle Isarco Sylvaner V.T. '04	♀♀♀	4*
O Kaiton '01	♀♀♀	4
O Kaiton '99	♀♀♀	4

Cantina Laimburg

LOC. LAIMBURG, 6
39040 VADENA/PFATTEN [BZ]
TEL. 0471969700
www.laimburg.bz.it

PRE-BOOKED VISITS

ANNUAL PRODUCTION **180,000 bottles**
HECTARES UNDER VINE **45**
VITICULTURE METHOD **Conventional**

Since its founding in 1975, the experimental agricultural institute at Laimburg has been a guarantee for wine lovers. Part of this professional training school is an efficient, working winery that vinifies grapes from several vineyards on different type soils and at different altitudes in the best zones in Alto Adige. Two lines are produced: Vini del Podere, traditional vintage wines; and Selezione Maniero, wines with special characteristics named after the Ladino legends of the Dolomites.

The strength of the winery lies in constant quality and this year is no exception. Wines submitted for tasting – only six this year – are good and well made, perhaps too well made, though they sometimes lack that final zip needed to achieve total success. The particularly well-crafted 2006 version of Pinot Nero Selyèt Riserva has a spicy, shifting nose and an elegant, substantial, progressive palate. The Gewürztraminer Elyònd '08 is quite stylish and balanced, and the always varietal Lagrein Barbagòl '06 has a full-flavoured, minerally palate with a slightly clenched finish.

Loacker Schwarhof

LOC. SANTA GIUSTINA, 3
39100 BOLZANO/BOZEN
TEL. 0471365125
www.loacker.net

CELLAR SALES
PRE-BOOKED VISITS

ANNUAL PRODUCTION **60,000 bottles**
HECTARES UNDER VINE **7**
VITICULTURE METHOD **Biodinamico certificato**

Located in the Santa Maddalena production zone, this historic estate is managed by Rainer and Hayo Loacker to biodynamic standards, and also has outposts in Maremma and Montalcino. The Loackers are artists and philosophers of viticulture, very much pioneers in the winemaking world of Alto Adige. The wines, white and reds from the local wine types, are proud, reliable ambassadors for Alto Adige, the fruit of hard work in the vineyards and great technique in the cellar.

Rainer and Hayo Loacker's unswervingly biodynamic policy may entail some risk of uneven quality. But when everything works the way it should, and this happens more than not in their case, the results are like Lagrein Gran Lareyn '07, a sumptuous red with deep aromas of spice and cinchona followed by a dense, minerally palate. Equally well crafted is the Pinot Nero Norital '07 with its precise nose and full, dynamic, balanced palate with nicely smooth tannins and well-gauged acidity. From the whites, we would mention a lovely '08 version of the Sylvaner.

● A. A. Pinot Nero Selyèt Ris. '06	♉♉ 5
○ A. A. Gewürztraminer Elyònd '08	♉♉ 5
● A. A. Lagrein Scuro Barbagòl Ris. '06	♉♉ 6
○ A. A. Riesling '07	♉♉ 5
● A. A. Cabernet Sauvignon Sass Roà Ris. '05	♉ 6
● A. A. Lagrein Scuro Barbagòl Ris. '00	♉♉♉ 6
○ A. A. Gewürztraminer Elyònd '07	♉♉ 5
● A. A. Pinot Nero Selyèt Ris. '04	♉♉ 5

● A. A. Lagrein Gran Lareyn '07	♉♉ 5
● A. A. Pinot Nero Norital '07	♉♉ 5*
● A. A. Merlot Ywain '07	♉♉ 5
○ A. A. Valle Isarco Sylvaner Ysac '08	♉♉ 4*
○ A. A. Valle Isarco Gewürztraminer Atagis '08	♉ 5
● A. A. Merlot Ywain '04	♉♉♉ 5*
○ A. A. Chardonnay Ateyon '06	♉♉ 5
● A. A. Lagrein Gran Lareyn '06	♉♉ 5
● A. A. Pinot Nero Norital '06	♉♉ 5
○ A. A. Valle Isarco Gewürztraminer Atagis '07	♉♉ 5
○ A. A. Valle Isarco Sylvaner Ysac '07	♉♉ 4*

H. Lun

VIA VILLA, 22/24
39044 EGNA/NEUMARKT [BZ]
TEL. 0471813256
www.lun.it

CELLAR SALES
PRE-BOOKED VISITS

ANNUAL PRODUCTION **300,000 bottles**
HECTARES UNDER VINE **35**
VITICULTURE METHOD **Conventional**

Founded in 1840, Lun is the oldest private winery in Alto Adige. Today headquartered at Plattenhof in Egna, it has for some years now been part of Cantina di Cornaiano under the technical management of cellarmaster Gherard Kofler. His wines – above all the famous Sandbichler line, bottled only in the best vintages – have been high quality for years and equally excellent value for money.

Wines from Lun are a guarantee, even after a difficult growing season like 2008. The range is well made and well typed, perhaps a bit tighter than last year but this was really inevitable. We were consoled by this lovely Pinot Bianco '08, fresh, linear and excellent value for money, and a more complex Sandbichler, from 40 per cent each pinot bianco and chardonnay, 15 per cent sauvignon and a splash of riesling, with a supple, characterful palate. Top red is an elegant, juicy '06 version of the Pinot Nero Sandbichler Riserva.

○ A. A. Bianco Sandbichler '08	♥♥	4*
● A. A. Cabernet Sauvignon Ris. '06	♥♥	4
● A. A. Lagrein Sandbichler Ris. '06	♥♥	6
○ A. A. Pinot Bianco '08	♥♥	4*
● A. A. Pinot Nero Sandbichler Ris. '06	♥♥	4*
○ A. A. Sauvignon '08	♥♥	4
○ A. A. Chardonnay '08	♥	4
○ A. A. Bianco Sandbichler '07	♀♀	4*
● A. A. Lagrein Scuro Albertus Ris. '04	♀♀	5
○ A. A. Moscato Giallo Sandbichler Passito '06	♀♀	6

Manincor

SAN GIUSEPPE AL LAGO, 4
39052 CALDARO/KALTERN [BZ]
TEL. 0471960230
www.manincor.com

CELLAR SALES
PRE-BOOKED VISITS

ANNUAL PRODUCTION **200,000 bottles**
HECTARES UNDER VINE **50**
VITICULTURE METHOD **Biodinamico certificato**

A property with a centuries-old tradition going back to 1608, and a young winery started in 1996, are at the base of the noble Enzenberg family's Manincor estate, located in one of the most beautiful areas in Alto Adige among vineyards just above Lake Caldaro. The owner Count Michael Goëss-Enzenberg and cellarmaster Helmuth Zozin feel the same about wine and agriculture: absolute respect for nature and consistent application of biodynamic principles, with no ifs or buts.

One of the most beautiful estates in Alto Adige is back among the Three Glasses thanks to a splendid Sauvignon '08. It's a wine in the house style, more focused on finesse and elegance than power, and in the style of cellarmaster Elmuth Zozin, who looks for purity of expression. Actually, this is a Sauvignon made somewhat in a Loire style, without those vegetal excesses that characterize many wines of this type. The delicate bouquet shows aromatic herbs and the lean palate has great dynamism and a tangy, even salty finish. Special mention goes to the Moscato Giallo '08, one of the best tasted in the past few years.

○ A. A. Terlano Sauvignon '08	♥♥♥	5
● Castel Campan '05	♥	8
● A. A. Lago di Caldaro Cl. Sup. '08	♥♥	4*
● A. A. Lagrein '07	♥♥	5
○ A. A. Moscato Giallo '08	♥♥	4
● A. A. Pinot Nero Mason di Mason '07	♥♥	8
○ A. A. Sophie '08	♥♥	5
⊙ La Rose de Manincor '08	♥♥	4
● Reserve del Conte '07	♥♥	4
● A. A. Pinot Nero Mason '07	♥	6
● Cassiano '05	♀♀	6
● Cassiano '04	♀♀	6

K. Martini & Sohn

LOC. CORNAIANO/GIRLAN
VIA LAMM, 28
39057 APPIANO/EPPAN [BZ]
TEL. 0471663156
www.martini-sohn.it

CELLAR SALES
PRE-BOOKED VISITS

ANNUAL PRODUCTION **250,000 bottles**
HECTARES UNDER VINE **30**
VITICULTURE METHOD **Conventional**

K. Martini & Sohn has always been one of the most solid, reliable estates in the province of Bolzano. Started in 1976 by Karl Martini and his son Gabriel, this mid-sized operation has successfully combined technological innovation and tradition, and shows better than good quality across the entire range. Gabriel Martini is proud of his wines from the Maturum and Palladium lines but the entire production offers superb quality at honest prices.

The '08 whites from this lovely Cornaiano estate are excellent, though the wines we liked most were the two Lagreins: the full, dense Maturum '07 with its complex nose of spice and ripe fruit, and a mineral vein well-supported by clear, fresh acidity; and the Rueslhof Gurnzan, also '07, which is dense yet supple with great length. Returning to the whites, we felt the Pinot Bianco Palladium '08 was especially successful, presenting fruity and full yet with a racy, spirited structure. The Chardonnay Maturum '07 is one of the best of its type.

● A. A. Lagrein Scuro Maturum '07	🍷🍷	6
○ A. A. Chardonnay Maturum '07	🍷🍷	6
● A. A. Lago di Caldaro Cl. Felton '08	🍷🍷	4
● A. A. Lagrein Cabernet Coldirus Palladium '07	🍷🍷	4
● A. A. Lagrein Scuro Rueslhof Gurnzan '07	🍷🍷	4*
○ A. A. Pinot Bianco Palladium '08	🍷🍷	4*
○ A. A. Valle Isarco Müller Thurgau '08	🍷🍷	4*
○ A. A. Chardonnay Palladium '08	🍷	4
⊙ A. A. Lagrein Rosè Grieser '08	🍷	4
● A. A. Pinot Nero Gurnzan '07	🍷	4
○ A. A. Sauvignon Palladium '08	🍷	4
○ A. A. Sauvignon Palladium '04	🍷🍷🍷 (white)	4*
○ A. A. Chardonnay Maturum '05	🍷🍷 (white)	4
● A. A. Lagrein Scuro Maturum '01	🍷🍷 (white)	5
○ A. A. Sauvignon Palladium '05	🍷🍷 (white)	4

Cantina Vini Merano

LOC. MAIA BASSA
VIA SAN MARCO, 11
39012 MERANO/MERAN [BZ]
TEL. 0473235544
www.meranerkellerei.com

CELLAR SALES
PRE-BOOKED VISITS

ANNUAL PRODUCTION **450,000 bottles**
HECTARES UNDER VINE **140**
VITICULTURE METHOD **Conventional**

Cantina Produttori di Merano is a small, co-operative operation for Alto Adige but one that, under the management of cellarmaster Stefan Kapfinger, releases wines with significantly improving quality, greater stylistic definition, lovely personality and in some cases a fabulous sense of place. Add to this an extremely honest price policy, from the superior Graf Von Meran line to the fantastic Schiavas.

For years, Cantina Produttori di Merano has landed various wines in our finals without ever winning our top prize. This gap has finally been filled this year thanks to a splendid '08 version of the Pinot Bianco Sonnenberg. This is a very Valle Venosta white, in other words subtle, somewhat smoky yet salty, vibrant, with incisive progression and a complex, slightly spicy finish. We also liked the great version of Moscato Giallo Passito Sissi, which hit dizzying heights with the '07 vintage. But the whole range is excellent this year and prices are very affordable.

○ A. A. Val Venosta Pinot Bianco Sonnenberg '08	🍷🍷🍷	4*
○ A. A. Passito Sissi '07	🍷🍷	7
● A. A. Pinot Nero Zeno Ris. '06	🍷🍷	5
● A. A. Val Venosta Schiava Sonnenberg '08	🍷🍷	3*
○ A. A. Gewürztraminer Graf Von Meran '08	🍷🍷	5
● A. A. Meraner Eines Fürsten Traum '08	🍷🍷	4*
● A. A. Meraner St. Valentin '08	🍷🍷	3*
○ A. A. Pinot Bianco Graf von Meran '08	🍷🍷	4
○ A. A. Riesling Graf von Meran '08	🍷🍷	5
○ A. A. Sauvignon '08	🍷🍷	4*
○ A. A. Sauvignon Graf Von Meran '08	🍷🍷	5
● A. A. Val Venosta Pinot Nero Sonnenberg '07	🍷🍷	4*
○ A. A. Muller Thurgau '08	🍷	4
○ A. A. Gewürztraminer Graf Von Meran '07	🍷🍷 (white)	5
○ A. A. Val Venosta Pinot Bianco Sonnenberg '07	🍷🍷 (white)	4*

★ Cantina Convento Muri-Gries

FRAZ. GRIES
P.ZZA GRIES, 21
39100 BOLZANO/BOZEN
TEL. 0471282287
www.muri-gries.com

CELLAR SALES
PRE-BOOKED VISITS

ANNUAL PRODUCTION 450,000 bottles
HECTARES UNDER VINE 30
VITICULTURE METHOD Conventional

History, tradition and research could be the motto of the ancient estate-cum-monastery Muri-Gries. In 1470, Archduke Leopold of Tyrol gave a group of monks the castle in Gries which they later turned into a monastery. The old chapel was transformed into a cellar, where Lagreins are still aged today. Christian Werth took his father's place at the winery in 1988 and was one of the first to focus on this variety and replant the old vineyards by selecting clones best suited to quality. The result is unrivalled, consistent quality.

The distinctive Lagrein Abtei Riserva has intense fruit and a juicy, fragrant palate. But there is more to this wine of stark austerity, elegance that has increased over the last few harvests, fine-grained tannic weave and progression that is simultaneously deep and caressing. In addition, the 2006 vintage seems to have been specially designed to bring out these features so another Three Glass award was a foregone conclusion. But since man cannot live by Lagrein alone, there is an '06 Pinot Nero that drinks fresh and pleasant as it should be here in Alto Adige, and the usual amazing Moscato Rosa '07.

Cantina Nals Margreid

VIA HEILIGENBERG, 2
39010 NALLES/NALS [BZ]
TEL. 0471678626
www.kellerei.it

CELLAR SALES
PRE-BOOKED VISITS

ANNUAL PRODUCTION 900,000 bottles
HECTARES UNDER VINE 150
VITICULTURE METHOD Conventional

Nals Margreid is one of those wineries that never has any nasty surprises. On the contrary, significant growth in quality over the past few years has now made it one of the best in the province of Bolzano, no easy task. It's all down to the extraordinary efforts of the management of this small, co-operative winery, led by the dynamic executive and refined gourmet Gottfried Pollinger and the young yet determined cellarmaster Harald Schraffl, whose bright future is easy to predict.

Nals Margreid is more than Pinot Bianco Sirmian. All the Alto Adige types are represented and all are on their best behaviour. Take Sauvignon Mantele '08, sourced from the first vineyard of this variety in Alto Adige. It's a fine-grained white, delicate yet spirited at the same time, or the Gewürztraminer Baron Salvadori '08, a fresh, elegant wine with a supple mouthfeel. The equally good Pinot Grigio Punggl '08 is zesty and complex with a spicy finish. But this takes nothing away from Sirmian '08, which again won Three Glasses with a full, concentrated version that combines great harmony and freshness with a tangy, balsamic finish.

● A. A. Lagrein Abtei Ris. '06	♟♟♟	5
● A. A. Moscato Rosa Abtei '07	♟♟	6
○ A. A. Bianco Abtei Muri '07	♟♟	5
● A. A. Lagrein '08	♟♟	4*
● A. A. Pinot Nero Abtei Muri Ris. '06	♟♟	5
○ A. A. Terlano Pinot Bianco '08	♟♟	4*
☉ A. A. Lagrein Rosato '08	♟	4*
● A. A. Santa Maddalena '08	♟	3
● A. A. Lagrein Abtei Ris. '05	♟♟♟	5
● A. A. Lagrein Abtei Ris. '04	♟♟♟	5
● A. A. Lagrein Abtei Ris. '03	♟♟♟	5
● A. A. Lagrein Abtei Ris. '02	♟♟♟	5
● A. A. Lagrein Abtei Ris. '01	♟♟♟	5
● A. A. Lagrein Abtei Ris. '00	♟♟♟	5
● A. A. Lagrein Abtei Ris. '99	♟♟♟	5

○ A. A. Pinot Bianco Sirmian '08	♟♟♟	4*
○ A. A. Gewürztraminer Baron Salvadori '08	♟♟	6
○ A. A. Pinot Grigio Punggl '08	♟♟	4*
○ A. A. Sauvignon Mantele '08	♟♟	5
● A. A. Schiava Galea '08	♟♟	4*
● A. A. Cabernet Sauvignon Baron Salvadori Ris. '06	♟♟	6
○ A. A. Chardonnay Baron Salvadori '07	♟♟	6
● A. A. Merlot Levad '06	♟♟	5
○ A. A. Pinot Bianco Penon '08	♟♟	4*
○ A. A. Pinot Grigio '08	♟♟	4*
● A. A. Pinot Nero Mazzon '07	♟♟	5
● A. A. Santa Maddalena Cl. Rieserhof '08	♟♟	4*
○ A. A. Pinot Bianco Sirmian '07	♟♟♟	4*
○ A. A. Pinot Bianco Sirmian '06	♟♟♟	4*

Josef Niedermayr

LOC. CORNAIANO/GIRLAN
VIA CASA DI GESÙ, 15
39050 APPIANO/EPPAN [BZ]
TEL. 0471662451
www.niedermayr.it

CELLAR SALES
PRE-BOOKED VISITS

ANNUAL PRODUCTION **150,000 bottles**
HECTARES UNDER VINE **22**
VITICULTURE METHOD **Conventional**

Josef Niedermayr is one of the main players on the winemaking scene in Alto Adige. He professionally manages his reliable estate with consultancy from Lorenz Martini. Among the various products, the Aureus, a white passito from mostly sauvignon and chardonnay with a dash of gewürztraminer, is one of the best sweet wines in Italy. But Niedermayr offers the best in all the Alto Adige wine types.

This lovely Cornaiano estate is back in the Guide with a series of better than decent wines, starting with its warhorse, Aureus '07, a white passito, or dried-grape wine, from mostly sauvignon and chardonnay, with a dash of gewürztraminer, represents one of the country's best sweet wines. The stylishly floral, elegant Pinot Nero Riserva '07 shows silky tannins and fresh acidity. Lagrein Blacedelle '08 is flavourful, fruity and very typical, and finally the subtle, spirited Gewürztraminer Doss '08 shows a delicate, slightly salty vein.

Niklaserhof - Josef Sölva

LOC. SAN NICOLÒ
VIA DELLE FONTANE, 31A
39052 CALDARO/KALTERN [BZ]
TEL. 0471963432
www.niklaserhof.it

CELLAR SALES
PRE-BOOKED VISITS

ANNUAL PRODUCTION **45,000 bottles**
HECTARES UNDER VINE **5.5**
VITICULTURE METHOD **Conventional**

Josef and Dieter Sölva from the Niklas estate in Caldaro make great white wines and have always believed in pinot bianco, a frequently underrated variety that has attracted growing attention over the past few years. The estate is located in the small village of San Nicolò above Caldaro, and owns vineyards on the highest terrains in the surrounding area. These wines offer character, typicity and decent value for money.

Again this year, Niklaserhof is one of the most reliable estates in the Caldaro area. First place goes to the estate warhorse, the Pinot Bianco Klaser, which has been one of the best in its type for years. The 2007 vintage expresses its characteristic elegance, freshness and minerality, in conjunction with a full-bodied, almost meaty, structure. The particularly interesting Sauvignon, a good representative of the '08 vintage, is salty and tangy with good suppleness in the mouth. The especially lively, fruity '08 version of Lago di Caldaro is as delicious as ever.

○ A. A. Aureus '07	▼▼ 7
○ A. A. Gewürztraminer Lage Doss '08	▼▼ 6
● A. A. Lagrein Aus Gries Ris. '07	▼▼ 6
● A. A. Lagrein Gries Blacedelle '08	▼▼ 5
● A. A. Pinot Nero Ris. '07	▼▼ 6
● A. A. Santa Maddalena Cl. '08	▼ 3
○ A. A. Aureus '99	▼▼▼ 6
○ A. A. Aureus '98	▼▼▼ 6

○ A. A. Pinot Bianco Klaser '07	▼▼ 4
● A. A. Lago di Caldaro Scelto Cl. '08	▼▼ 3*
● A. A. Merlot Klaser '07	▼▼ 5
○ A. A. Sauvignon '08	▼▼ 4*
○ A. A. Kerner '08	▼ 4
● A. A. Lagrein-Cabernet Klaser Ris. '06	▼ 5
○ A. A. Pinot Bianco '08	▼ 4*
○ A. A. Bianco Mondevinum '05	▼▼ 5
● A. A. Lago di Caldaro Scelto Cl. '07	▼▼ 3*
○ A. A. Pinot Bianco Klaser R '05	▼▼ 4*
○ A. A. Sauvignon '06	▼▼ 4*

Pacherhof - Andreas Huber

FRAZ. NOVACELLA
V.LO PACHER, 1
39040 VARNA/VAHRN [BZ]
TEL. 0472835717
www.pacherhof.com

CELLAR SALES
PRE-BOOKED VISITS
OSPITALITÀ
FOOD

ANNUAL PRODUCTION **90,000 bottles**
HECTARES UNDER VINE **11**
VITICULTURE METHOD **Natural**

Pacherhof vineyards are among the oldest and most northerly in Valle Isarco. The estate is situated on land that enjoys splendid southern and south-western exposure at around 700 metres above sea level. The wines, fermented in stainless steel and large barrels, are lively and fragrant with plenty of elegance and backbone. Add to these characteristics the clear imprint of Andreas Huber, with a hand from his father Josef.

Andreas has again this year proved one of the most interesting winemakers in Valle Isarco, even though some of his wines show some slightly overripe notes. Our approval went to the two Sylvaner '08s, with a slight preference for the Alte Reben because of its complexity through the tasting and a spirited, salty grip. The interesting Riesling '08 is still quite young, yet fresh and expressive. The special Pinot Grigio '08 is tangy and minerally with clear depth.

Pfannenstielhof
Johannes Pfeifer

VIA PFANNESTIEL, 9
39100 BOLZANO/BOZEN
TEL. 0471970884
www.pfannenstielhof.it

CELLAR SALES
PRE-BOOKED VISITS

ANNUAL PRODUCTION **38,000 bottles**
HECTARES UNDER VINE **4**
VITICULTURE METHOD **Conventional**

Johannes Pfeifer is a true winemaker: thorough, hard working, enthusiastic about wine, friendly, honest and affable. We must say his wines are rather like him. They are authentic, sincere and technically well made, nicely combining tradition and modernity. Johannes skilfully manages this small estate, which dates back to the mid 16th century, in the heart of the Lagrein production zone. The range represents the best in typical wine types from the area of Bolzano.

When a Santa Maddalena finally wins Three Glasses, Pfannenstielhof will be in pole position for the prize. For years among the best, in the 2008 vintage it maintains this tradition with caressing aromas of spice and cinchona that introduce a supple, supporting palate with a balsamic vein in the finish. The elegant, distinctly moreish Lagrein '08 shows stylish tannins. We found the Lagrein Riserva '06 somewhat closed. It could probably do with a bit more time in bottle.

○ A. A. Valle Isarco Riesling '08	♀♀ 5
○ A. A. Valle Isarco Sylvaner Alte Reben '08	♀♀ 6
○ A. A. Valle Isarco Gewürztraminer '08	♀♀ 5
○ A. A. Valle Isarco Pinot Grigio '08	♀♀ 5
○ A. A. Valle Isarco Sylvaner '08	♀♀ 5
○ A. A. Valle Isarco Veltliner '08	♀♀ 5
○ A. A. Valle Isarco Kerner '08	♀ 5
○ A. A. Valle Isarco Müller Thurgau '08	♀ 4
○ A. A. Valle Isarco Riesling '04	♀♀♀ 5
○ A. A. Valle Isarco Sylvaner Alte Reben '05	♀♀♀ 5
○ A. A. Valle Isarco Riesling '07	♀♀ 5
○ A. A. Valle Isarco Riesling '06	♀♀ 5
○ A. A. Valle Isarco Sylvaner Alte Reben '06	♀♀ 5

● A. A. Santa Maddalena Cl. '08	♀♀ 3*
● A. A. Lagrein Scuro '08	♀♀ 4*
● A. A. Lagrein Scuro Ris. '06	♀ 5
● A. A. Pinot Nero '06	♀ 5
● A. A. Lagrein Scuro '07	♀♀ 4*
● A. A. Lagrein Scuro Ris. '05	♀♀ 5
● A. A. Santa Maddalena Cl. '06	♀♀ 3*

Tenuta Ritterhof

S.DA DEL VINO, 1
39052 CALDARO/KALTERN [BZ]
TEL. 0471963298
www.ritterhof.it

CELLAR SALES
PRE-BOOKED VISITS

ANNUAL PRODUCTION **290,000 bottles**
HECTARES UNDER VINE **7.5**
VITICULTURE METHOD **Conventional**

The history of Ritterhof, owned by the Roner family of distillers, is typical of many winemaking estates in Alto Adige. In the beginning, they made pleasant, competently made wines sold at reasonable prices, then little by little strove for even more reliable quality under the direction of the manager Ludwig Kaneppele and the skilled oenologist Bernard Hannes. The vineyards are scattered around the best areas in Caldaro and Termeno. Grapes from 40 or so tried and trusted growers are vinified with fruit from the seven hectares of estate-owned and rented vineyards.

Ritterhof reds are outstanding this year, starting with the Cabernet-Merlot Crescendo Riserva '06, which shows stuffing and character with a dense palate, fine-grained tannins and fresh acidity that provides dynamic development. Though still showing some oak, the Pinot Nero Crescendo '06 has intense tobacco aromas and a palate that gradually acquires rhythm and expansion. We found the meaty, complex Lagrein Manus '06 dynamic and complex with a delicious liquorice finish. The Pinot Bianco and Sauvignon stood out from the other '08 whites.

Röckhof - Konrad Augschöll

VIA SAN VALENTINO, 9
39040 VILLANDRO/VILLANDERS [BZ]
TEL. 0472847130
roeck@rolmail.net

CELLAR SALES
PRE-BOOKED VISITS
FOOD

ANNUAL PRODUCTION **10,000 bottles**
HECTARES UNDER VINE **3.5**
VITICULTURE METHOD **Conventional**

Born in 1961, Konrad Augschöll was one of the first growers around Chiusa to begin bottling his own wine. He tends around three hectares under vine on the 15th-century Röckhof estate on the road that runs from Chiusa to Villandro. These vineyards grow along steep slopes between 600 and 700 metres above sea level. White grape varieties represent half the vineyards, the other half being pinot nero and zweigelt, an old Austrian variety that is resistant to cold and well suited for areas at the limits of viticulture. The reds are mostly intended for the family-run agriturismo on the estate.

For a couple of years now, Röckhof has been aiming for Three Glasses with its Riesling. The '08 Viel Anders hit the bull's-eye with one of the highest scores in Alto Adige this year. The broad, complex aromatic spectrum gives aromatic herbs and tropical fruit with a final twist of citrus. A fragrant, dynamic palate unveils clear medicinal herbs and pears, and a deep, salty, elegant finish. As usual, the Bianco Caruess '08, from 40-30-30 gewürtztraminer, sylvaner and pinot grigio, is powerful and concentrated. Finally, the delicious Müller Thurgau '08 is always one of the best.

Wine	Rating
● A. A. Cabernet Merlot Crescendo Ris. '06	♟♟ 5
○ A. A. Pinot Nero Crescendo '06	♟♟ 6
● A. A. Lago di Caldaro Scelto '08	♟♟ 3*
● A. A. Lagrein Manus Ris. '06	♟♟ 6
○ A. A. Pinot Bianco '08	♟♟ 4*
○ A. A. Sauvignon '08	♟♟ 4*
○ A. A. Gewürztraminer '08	♟ 4
○ A. A. Muller Thurgau '08	♟ 4
○ A. A. Pinot Grigio '08	♟ 4
○ A. A. Pinot Grigio Crescendo '08	♟ 5
○ A. A. Gewürztraminer Crescendo '07	♟♟ 5
● A. A. Lagrein Manus Ris. '04	♟♟ 6
○ A. A. Pinot Nero Crescendo '05	♟♟ 6

Wine	Rating
○ A. A. Valle Isarco Riesling Viel Anders '08	♟♟♟ 4*
○ A. A. Valle Isarco Müller Thurgau '08	♟♟ 4*
○ Caruess '08	♟♟ 4
○ A. A. Valle Isarco Müller Thurgau '07	♟♟ 4*
○ A. A. Valle Isarco Riesling '07	♟♟ 4*
○ A. A. Valle Isarco Riesling '06	♟♟ 4*
○ Caruess '07	♟♟ 4*

Hans Rottensteiner

FRAZ. GRIES
VIA SARENTINO, 1A
39100 BOLZANO/BOZEN
TEL. 0471282015
www.rottensteiner-weine.com

CELLAR SALES
PRE-BOOKED VISITS

ANNUAL PRODUCTION **450,000 bottles**
HECTARES UNDER VINE **10**
VITICULTURE METHOD **Conventional**

Northwest of Bolzano, at the entrance to Val Sarentino, lies the historic estate managed by Toni Rottensteiner, a major player in Alto Adige winemaking, with his son Hannes. This is without a doubt one of the most reliable wineries in the entire province of Bolzano. Wines with the Rottensteiner label feature excellent technique and great personality, and priority naturally goes to the classic wines from the zone, Lagrein and the always excellent Santa Maddalena.

This vintage was a bit so-so for Rottensteiner, which lacks any point of excellence that might have impressed us. Among the best wines was an estate classic. The Lagrein Riserva '06 stands out with dense structure that shows off lovely ripe fruit supported by well-gauged acidity. From the whites, we mention a balanced, fragrant Pinot Grigio '08. The rest of the range is well made but we expected much more from an estate with this kind of potential.

Castel Sallegg

V.LO DI SOTTO, 15
39052 CALDARO/KALTERN [BZ]
TEL. 0471963132
www.castelsallegg.it

CELLAR SALES
PRE-BOOKED VISITS

ANNUAL PRODUCTION **120,000 bottles**
HECTARES UNDER VINE **31**
VITICULTURE METHOD **Conventional**

Georg von Kuenburg owns one of the most traditional and historic estates in the province of Bolzano. For years, this winery has been mentioned almost exclusively for its famous Moscato Rosas. Things are changing now and the estate offers a range of excellent quality products with outstanding personality. A great connoisseur of wine, Georg has found his ideal partner in the inspired oenologist Matthias Hauser, which augurs well for the future of his estate.

This range of the wines presented by Castel Sallegg could be called "Beyond Moscato Rosa". True enough, the '03 version of this estate's trademark wine reached our finals thanks to its fascinating, almost decadent but irresistible charm. But it came with a solid array of good quality products, starting with an elegant, subtle Lagrein '06 of amazing depth and dynamism. The whites confirm the search for fresh, typical wines without exaggeratedly high alcohol levels. Georg's favourite wine, Lago di Caldaro Bischofsleiten '08, could be quaffed by the bucket.

Wine	Rating
O A. A. Gewürztraminer Passito Cresta '07	♟♟ 6
● A. A. Lagrein Grieser Select Ris. '06	♟♟ 5
O A. A. Pinot Grigio '08	♟♟ 4*
● A. A. Cabernet Select Ris. '06	♟ 5
O A. A. Gewürztraminer Cancenai '08	♟ 5
O A. A. Pinot Bianco Carnol '08	♟ 4
● A. A. Santa Maddalena Cl. Premstallerhof '08	♟ 4
O A. A. Sauvignon '08	♟ 4
● Prem '07	♟ 4
● A. A. Lagrein Ris. '02	♟♟♟ 4*
O A. A. Gewürztraminer Cancenai '07	♟♟ 4
O A. A. Gewürztraminer Passito Cresta '06	♟♟ 6
● A. A. Lagrein Grieser Select Ris. '05	♟♟ 5
● A. A. Lagrein Grieser Select Ris. '04	♟♟ 5
● Prem '06	♟♟ 4

Wine	Rating
● A. A. Moscato Rosa '03	♟♟ 7
O A. A. Chardonnay '08	♟♟ 4*
● A. A. Lago di Caldaro Scelto Bischofsleiten '08	♟♟ 4*
● A. A. Lagrein Ris. '06	♟♟ 5*
O A. A. Pinot Bianco '08	♟♟ 4*
O A. A. Pinot Grigio '08	♟♟ 4
● A. A. Pinot Nero Ris. '05	♟♟ 5
O A. A. Gewürztraminer '08	♟ 4
● A. A. Moscato Rosa '01	♟♟ 7
O A. A. Pinot Grigio '07	♟♟ 4*

★★ Cantina Produttori San Michele Appiano

VIA CIRCONVALLAZIONE, 17/19
39057 APPIANO/EPPAN [BZ]
TEL. 0471664466
www.stmichael.it

CELLAR SALES
PRE-BOOKED VISITS

ANNUAL PRODUCTION **2.300,000 bottles**
HECTARES UNDER VINE **370**
VITICULTURE METHOD **Conventional**

The Sanct Valentin line continues to be the warhorse from this lively co-operative winery, expertly managed by the talented Hans Terzer. More than 300 member growers, mostly scattered around the grape-growing parts of Alto Adige, help produce a broad range, apart from the prestige line, characterized by impeccable wines that offer exemplary value for money. The Sauvignon Sanct Valentin has now become a legend among fans of the wine type.

True, news of Three Glasses for the Sauvignon Sanct Valentin '08 is not really … news. But you would be wrong to think this goes without saying. No wine wins Three Glasses 15 times because it had a lucky streak. We should also point out that this stunner is released in 150,000 bottles each year. The rest of the range features the usual series of top-quality wines, crafted with skills in the vineyard and cellar that have few equals. A final mention goes to one of the best passito dried-grape wines in Italy, Comtess '07 from a gewürztraminer-heavy blend.

Cantina Produttori San Paolo

LOC. SAN PAOLO
VIA CASTEL GUARDIA, 21
39050 APPIANO/EPPAN [BZ]
TEL. 0471662183
www.kellereistpauls.com

CELLAR SALES
PRE-BOOKED VISITS

ANNUAL PRODUCTION **1,000,000 bottles**
HECTARES UNDER VINE **170**
VITICULTURE METHOD **Conventional**

Cantina Sociale di San Paolo is a trim, mid-sized operation in the delightful San Paolo district of Appiano, set in a frame of splendid vineyards in the heart of Oltradige. In such a scenic landscape, the local co-operative winery feels almost obliged to carry on a centuries-old winemaking tradition. Wines made here have a solid profile with lovely definition and immaculate technique, along with decent, constantly improving average quality.

The treatment administered by Wolfgang Tratter, the new estate oenologist, seems to have changed the course of this estate's sluggish progress. This year, it unveiled a series of above average wines with a few absolutely excellent high points. Chairman Leopold Keger should be proud of the Gewürztraminer Exclusiv St. Justina '08, which proffers rare finesse, lively rhythm and minerality with great length. The Pinot Bianco Passion '07 is one of the best of its class. It comes from a selection of old high-altitude vines and shows unique grip and fullness. The rest of the wines are well worth uncorking.

○ A. A. Sauvignon St. Valentin '08	♟♟♟	6
○ A. A. Bianco Passito Comtess '07	♟♟	6
○ A. A. Chardonnay St. Valentin '07	♟♟	6
○ A. A. Pinot Bianco St. Valentin '07	♟♟	6
○ A. A. Chardonnay Merol '08	♟♟	4
○ A. A. Gewürztraminer St. Valentin '08	♟♟	6
○ A. A. Pinot Bianco Schulthauser '08	♟♟	4
○ A. A. Pinot Grigio Anger '08	♟♟	4*
● A. A. Pinot Nero St. Valentin '06	♟♟	6
○ A. A. Sauvignon Lahn '08	♟	4
○ A. A. Bianco Passito Comtess '05	♟♟♟	6
○ A. A. Sauvignon St. Valentin '07	♟♟♟	6
○ A. A. Sauvignon St. Valentin '06	♟♟♟	5
○ A. A. Sauvignon St. Valentin '05	♟♟♟	5

○ A. A. Gewürztraminer St. Justina Exclusiv '08	♟♟	5*
○ A. A. Pinot Bianco Passion '07	♟♟	5
● A. A. Lagrein Passion Ris. '06	♟♟	6
○ A. A. Pinot Bianco Exclusiv Plötzner '08	♟♟	4*
● A. A. Pinot Nero Luziafeld Exclusiv '07	♟♟	5
● A. A. Pinot Passion Ris. '06	♟♟	6
○ A. A. Riesling '08	♟♟	3*
● A. A. Schiava Sarnerhof Exclusiv '08	♟♟	4
○ A. A. Pinot Grigio Exclusiv Egg Leiten '08	♟	4
○ A. A. Pinot Bianco Passion '06	♟♟	5

★ Cantina Produttori Santa Maddalena/ Cantina di Bolzano

VIA BRENNERO, 15
39100 BOLZANO/BOZEN
TEL. 0471270909
www.cantinabolzano.com

CELLAR SALES
PRE-BOOKED VISITS

ANNUAL PRODUCTION 1,000,000 bottles
HECTARES UNDER VINE 130
VITICULTURE METHOD Conventional

Cantina Produttori Santa Maddalena/Cantina di Bolzano never rests on its laurels. No praise, awards or commercial success interrupts its constant search for improvement. The latest news regards the design for a new cellar that should centralize production with Cantina Gries. The wines are fine examples of types from the area around Bolzano, with the Lagrein Taber rising over the years to become an icon of the wine, although most of the cellar's production goes into splendid Santa Maddalenas.

After a year's interval, the 2007 vintage of the Lagrein Taber made a comeback and effortlessly picked up Three Glasses with an iconic version of this wine type. Explosive ripe fruit accompanies intense spice and then the meaty, dense palate shows firm yet sweet tannins and acidity that refreshes the imposing structure. Another powerful, palate-caressing white, which is superbly drinkable with a spicy, complex finish, convinced us to award a second Three Glass prize to the Pinot Bianco Dellago '08, a benchmark for its type. The rest of the wines show astonishingly high quality.

Stroblhof

LOC. SAN MICHELE
VIA PIGANÒ, 25
39057 APPIANO/EPPAN [BZ]
TEL. 0471662250
www.stroblhof.it

CELLAR SALES
PRE-BOOKED VISITS

ANNUAL PRODUCTION 30,000 bottles
HECTARES UNDER VINE 3.7
VITICULTURE METHOD Conventional

Located in the heart of the classic zone for great whites from Appiano, the Stroblhof estate has a long wine tradition. Andreas Nicolussi-Leck has managed the estate and cellar since 1995 and for some years now has show the quality of his mature style. His white wines show great character. They're a bit edgy when young but fresh with good energy and good ageing ability. Having said this, Stroblhof also produces some of the best Italian Pinot Neros.

The 2008 vintage really brought out the characteristics of whites from Andreas Nicolussi-Leck who aims for a taut, vibrant style with acidity near the limits of austerity. We like this sort of wine very much because of the nice surprises in store as it ages, and believe the '08 whites from this small estate will not disappoint. That said, the Pinot Bianco Strahler '08 cuts like a knife garnished with white-fleshed fruit and hawthorn. The surprise is a uniquely sharp Sauvignon Nico '08. The two Pinot Neros, Pigeno '07 and Riserva '06, are elegantly gutsy and the Gewürztraminer Pigeno '08 is subtler than ever.

Wine	Rating	Score
● A. A. Lagrein Scuro Taber Ris. '07	♟♟♟	7
○ A. A. Pinot Bianco Dellago '08	♟♟♟	5
● A. A. Cabernet Mumelter Ris. '07	♟♟	7
○ A. A. Gewürztraminer Kleinstein '08	♟♟	5
○ A. A. Chardonnay Ris. '05	♟♟	6
○ A. A. Gewürztraminer '08	♟♟	5
● A. A. Lagrein Scuro Perl '07	♟♟	5
● A. A. Merlot Siebeneich Ris. '07	♟♟	6
● A. A. Pinot Nero Ris. '07	♟♟	6
● A. A. Santa Maddalena Cl. '08	♟♟	4*
● A. A. Santa Maddalena Cl. Huck am Bach '08	♟♟	4
○ A. A. Sauvignon Mock '08	♟♟	5
○ A. A. Valle Isarco Müller Thurgau '08	♟♟	4
○ A. A. Valle Isarco Silvaner '08	♟♟	4
● A. A. Lagrein Scuro Taber Ris. '05	♟♟♟	6
○ A. A. Pinot Bianco Dellago '07	♟♟♟	5

Wine	Rating	Score
○ A. A. Pinot Bianco Strahler '08	♟♟	4*
● A. A. Pinot Nero Ris. '06	♟♟	6
○ A. A. Chardonnay Schwarzhaus '08	♟♟	4
○ A. A. Gewürztraminer Pigeno '08	♟♟	5
● A. A. Pinot Nero Pigeno '07	♟♟	5
○ A. A. Sauvignon Nico '08	♟♟	5
● A. A. Pinot Nero Ris. '05	♟♟♟	6
○ A. A. Gewürztraminer Pigeno '07	♟♟	5
○ A. A. Pinot Bianco Strahler '07	♟♟	4*
○ A. A. Pinot Bianco Strahler '06	♟♟	4*
● A. A. Pinot Nero Ris. '04	♟♟	6
○ A. A. Sauvignon Nico '07	♟♟	5

Taschlerhof - Peter Wachtler

LOC. MARA, 107
39042 BRESSANONE/BRIXEN [BZ]
TEL. 0472851091
www.taschlerhof.com

CELLAR SALES
PRE-BOOKED VISITS

ANNUAL PRODUCTION 25,000 bottles
HECTARES UNDER VINE 4
VITICULTURE METHOD Conventional

Taschlerhof is a small estate located in Mara, a tiny village south of Bressanone with splendid vineyards arranged on steep terraces. The owner is Peter Wachtler, one of the young lions from Valle Isarco who have driven winemaking in Alto Adige over the past few years. The five wines, all white, are typical and characterful, and show slightly less extreme acidity with respect to other producers in the area, but still with the classic minerality of whites from this zone.

We were especially convinced by Peter Wachtler's wines this year. Perhaps aided by the growing season, they seemed more linear, sharp and progressive. Sylvaner Lahner '08 is particularly austere and complex with notes of smoke and aromatic herbs. The supple, expansive palate shows clear minerality. The base Sylvaner is a bit simple, yet still fragrant and agreeable. On its first release, the Riesling '08 seems to have found the right direction, showing floral, salty and deep. All that holds it back is the slightly soft finish.

★ Cantina Terlano

VIA SILBERLEITEN, 7
39018 TERLANO/TERLAN [BZ]
TEL. 0471257135
www.cantina-terlano.com

CELLAR SALES
PRE-BOOKED VISITS

ANNUAL PRODUCTION 1,000,000 bottles
HECTARES UNDER VINE 140
VITICULTURE METHOD Conventional

A beautiful new cellar, and the merger with their next-door neighbour in the valley, Cantina di Andriano, are the big news items from this estate, now a designer label in Italian wine. Land and longevity should be the motto above the door to this winery, which is pretty much unique in the Terlano area. Wines produced here have one-of-a-kind complexity and character few wineries in Italy or abroad are able to put on the market.

Despite the distraction of the new cellar, Terlano's firepower has not been affected. With seven wines in the finals, the embarrassing question is: which gets the Three Glasses? The prize went to Terlano Pinot Bianco Vorberg Riserva in an especially austere '06 edition. It's almost austere and still a bit closed but this is a Ferrari with the engine idling, ready to race. The two Sauvignons are great: Winkl '08 is smooth and the '07 Quarz is more powerful and zesty. The real surprise is a super-elegant Pinot Grigio '08. In conclusion, the Terlano Chardonnay '97 manages to marry maturity and elegance, framed in mineral freshness.

○ A. A. Valle Isarco Sylvaner Lahner '08	♀♀	6
○ A. A. Valle Isarco Gewürztraminer '08	♀♀	5
○ A. A. Valle Isarco Kerner '08	♀♀	5
○ A. A. Valle Isarco Riesling '08	♀♀	6
○ A. A. Valle Isarco Sylvaner '08	♀♀	5
○ A. A. Valle Isarco Kerner '07	♀♀	5
○ A. A. Valle Isarco Sylvaner Lahner '05	♀♀	5*

○ A. A. Terlano Pinot Bianco Vorberg Ris. '06	♀♀♀	5*
● A. A. Lagrein Porphyr Ris. '06	♀♀	6
○ A. A. Pinot Grigio '08	♀♀	4*
○ A. A. Terlano Chardonnay '97	♀♀	8
○ A. A. Terlano Nova Domus Ris. '06	♀♀	6
○ A. A. Terlano Sauvignon Quarz '07	♀♀	6
○ A. A. Terlano Sauvignon Winkl '08	♀♀	4*
○ A. A. Gewürztraminer Lunare '07	♀♀	6
● A. A. Lagrein Gries Ris. '06	♀♀	5
○ A. A. Müller Thurgau '08	♀♀	4*
○ A. A. Terlano Chardonnay Kreuth '07	♀♀	4
○ A. A. Terlano Pinot Bianco Cl. '08	♀♀	4*
○ A. A. Chardonnay Cl. '08	♀	4*
○ A. A. Terlano Cl. '08	♀	4*
○ A. A. Terlano Pinot Bianco Vorberg Ris. '05	♀♀♀	4*
○ A. A. Terlano Sauvignon Quarz '05	♀♀♀	6

Thurnhof - Andreas Berger

LOC. ASLAGO
VIA CASTEL FLAVON, 7
39100 BOLZANO/BOZEN
TEL. 0471288460
www.thurnhof.com

CELLAR SALES
PRE-BOOKED VISITS

ANNUAL PRODUCTION 25,000 bottles
HECTARES UNDER VINE 3.5
VITICULTURE METHOD Natural

A careful, reserved winemaker with a small estate just outside Bolzano, Andreas Berger makes mostly wine from red grape varieties. But he also makes one of the best Moscato Giallos in Alto Adige. His modern-style wines, austere when young, always need a few years in bottle to show their best and never lack personality. All the most typical wine types from the Bolzano area are on display.

The 2006 growing year was far from being one of the most favourable for Alto Adige reds, which are generally a bit closed and slightly cropped. This Thurnhof is no exception. The concentrated Lagrein Riserva shows cinchona and black pepper aromas but the palate is somewhat low-key and unresolved. The same goes for the '06 Cabernet Sauvignon Riserva, which is dark and rich, yet seemingly unable to expand. The splendid Moscato Giallo '08 is better, with caressing fresh fruit aromas and a flavourful, linear palate. The fresh, sharpish Sauvignon '08 nicely reflects its vintage.

○ A. A. Moscato Giallo '08	♀♀ 4*
○ A. A. Sauvignon '08	♀♀ 4
● A. A. Cabernet Sauvignon Ris. '06	♀ 5
● A. A. Lagrein Scuro Ris. '06	♀ 5
● A. A. Cabernet Sauvignon Ris. '04	♀♀ 5
● A. A. Lagrein Scuro Merlau '07	♀♀ 4*
● A. A. Lagrein Scuro Ris. '04	♀♀ 5
● A. A. Santa Maddalena '07	♀♀ 4*
○ A. A. Sauvignon '07	♀♀ 4*

Tiefenbrunner

FRAZ. NICLARA
VIA CASTELLO, 4
39040 CORTACCIA/KURTATSCH [BZ]
TEL. 0471880122
www.tiefenbrunner.com

CELLAR SALES
PRE-BOOKED VISITS
FOOD

ANNUAL PRODUCTION 800,000 bottles
HECTARES UNDER VINE 23
VITICULTURE METHOD Conventional

Tiefenbrunner is famous because it was one of the first estates to earn Alto Adige wines recognition outside the province of Bolzano. Credit goes to a charismatic character, Herbert Tiefenbrunner, and his most famous wine, Feldmarschall von Fenner, a Müller Thurgau sourced from a vineyard more than 1,000 metres above sea level. Herbert's son Christof has been discreetly, as is his character, taking the reins of this winery over the past few years. Now he makes wines that are elegant, subtle and never overstated.

A dazzling, courageous wine. Dazzling for its bouquet of spring flowers, black pepper, aromatic herbs and peaches, and its subtle, thyme-veined iodine palate; and courageous because it comes from a vineyard over 1,000 metres above sea level, planted before anyone spoke about global warming. If we add the fact that the bottle has a screw cap, we could only be talking about one wine. Naturally we are describing the Müller Thurgau Feldmarschall von Fenner '08, which again won Three Glasses. The rest of the wines are all first-rate, from the Pinot Nero Riserva Linticlarus '06, to the Lagrein '07 and Sauvignon Kirchleiten '08.

○ Feldmarschall von Fenner zu Fennberg '08	♀♀♀ 6
○ A. A. Chardonnay Linticlarus '07	♀♀ 6
● A. A. Lagrein Castel Turmhof '07	♀♀ 4*
● A. A. Pinot Nero Linticlarus Ris. '06	♀♀ 5
○ A. A. Chardonnay Castel Turmhof '08	♀♀ 4*
● A. A. Cuvée Linticlarus '05	♀♀ 6
○ A. A. Gewürztraminer Castel Turmhof '08	♀♀ 6
○ A. A. Gewürztraminer Linticlarus V.T. '07	♀♀ 7
● A. A. Lagrein Linticlarus Ris. '06	♀♀ 6
○ A. A. Sauvignon Kirchleiten '08	♀♀ 4*
● A. A. Cabernet Castel Turmhof '07	♀ 4
○ Feldmarschall von Fenner zu Fennberg '05	♀♀♀ 5
○ A. A. Chardonnay Linticlarus '06	♀♀ 5
○ Feldmarschall von Fenner zu Fennberg '07	♀♀ 5

★ Cantina Tramin

S.DA DEL VINO, 144
39040 TERMENO/TRAMIN [BZ]
TEL. 0471860126
www.tramin-wine.it

CELLAR SALES
PRE-BOOKED VISITS

ANNUAL PRODUCTION **1.500,000 bottles**
HECTARES UNDER VINE **230**
VITICULTURE METHOD **Conventional**

The history of Gewürztraminer in Alto Adige runs through Termeno, thanks to the Cantina Produttori and its long-serving oenologist Willi Stürz. For years the absolute leader in the wine type, the Cantina continues its quest for ever more elegantly territorial, natural wines. But the whole estate range is such high quality it has little competition nationally. White, red and sweet wines – who can forget the cult Gewürztraminer V.T. Terminum? – all show rare quality.

Gewürztraminer is great and Willi Stürz is its prophet. Words fail when faced with wines that continue to amaze us year after year. Depending on the vintage, Willi's Gewürztraminers will be different yet they are always extraordinary. We begin with a version of the Vendemmia Tardiva. The 2007 recalls the excitement of the '98. This extraordinarily complex wine shows thyme and flint aromatics and a concentrated palate with a balance of sugar and acidity that can only be defined as perfect. The Nussbaumer '08 is less imposing than usual yet takes full advantage of the vintage to unfold on the palate with style and elegance.

Untermoserhof
Georg Ramoser

VIA SANTA MADDALENA, 36
39100 BOLZANO/BOZEN
TEL. 0471975481
untermoserhof@rolmail.net

CELLAR SALES
PRE-BOOKED VISITS

ANNUAL PRODUCTION **40,000 bottles**
HECTARES UNDER VINE **4.5**
VITICULTURE METHOD **Conventional**

Georg Ramoser is a serious, passionate winemaker whose efforts in the vineyard are all aimed at drastically reducing yields and safeguarding his wines' typicity, while maintaining a substantially modern profile. The cellar is located in the Santa Maddalena Classico zone just outside Bolzano, famous for red wines that are slightly closed and difficult when young, yet show great potential for ageing and improvement over time.

The range submitted by Untermoserhof was as impressive as ever, though we always expect the best from Georg and so were a bit disappointed when the usual high point was missing. The Lagrein Riserva '06 reached our finals thanks to its clear character. It's perhaps still a bit austere but offers charm as well as complexity and typicity. The '08 Santa Maddalena is as delicious as ever and is one of the most sincere expressions of this wine type. The current Lagrein is pleasant.

O A. A. Gewürztraminer Nussbaumer '08	♀♀♀ 6
O A. A. Gewürztraminer Terminum V. T. '07	♀♀♀ 6
● A. A. Lagrein Urban '08	♀♀ 6
● A. A. Cabernet Merlot Loam '06	♀♀ 6
O A. A. Gewürztraminer '08	♀♀ 4
O A. A. Pinot Bianco '08	♀♀ 4*
O A. A. Pinot Bianco Tauris '07	♀♀ 5
O A. A. Pinot Grigio '08	♀♀ 4*
O A. A. Pinot Grigio Unterebner '08	♀♀ 5
● A. A. Pinot Nero Ris. '06	♀♀ 6
O A. A. Sauvignon Montan '08	♀♀ 5
● A. A. Schiava Freisinger '08	♀♀ 4*
O A. A. Stoan '08	♀♀ 5
O T Bianco '08	♀♀ 3*
● A. A. Pinot Nero '08	♀ 4
O A. A. Gewürztraminer Nussbaumer '07	♀♀♀ 5
O A. A. Gewürztraminer Terminum V. T. '06	♀♀♀ 8

● A. A. Lagrein Scuro Ris. '07	♀♀ 5
● A. A. Santa Maddalena Cl. '08	♀♀ 4
● A. A. Lagrein Scuro '08	♀ 4
● A. A. Lagrein Scuro Ris. '03	♀♀♀ 5*
● A. A. Lagrein Scuro Ris. '97	♀♀♀ 5
● A. A. Santa Maddalena Cl. '07	♀♀ 4*

Tenuta Unterortl - Castel Juval

FRAZ. JUVAL, 1B
39020 CASTELBELLO CIARDES/
KASTELBELL TSCHARS [BZ]
TEL. 0473667580
www.unterortl.it

CELLAR SALES
PRE-BOOKED VISITS

ANNUAL PRODUCTION 30,000 bottles
HECTARES UNDER VINE 4.5
VITICULTURE METHOD Conventional

The dizzyingly beautiful Unterortl estate is owned by Reinhold Messner but has been managed for years by Martin and Gisela Aurich. Martin is also a professor of oenology at the winemaking school in San Michele all'Adige and one of the best wine technicians in the region. This small winery has for years been one of the top wine producers in Alto Adige. Despite this secure position, it manages to surprise us every year. But the Aurichs' passion, modesty and commitment are such that their products always improve from one vintage to the next. And don't miss their marvellous range of spirits.

With the 2008 vintage, Martin and Gisela Aurich introduced a new product, the first Alto Adige Riesling Spätlese, called Spelerei or "Plaything". Despite the name, it is a serious wine, elegant from start to finish with sugar perfectly offset by clear acidity. The Riesling '08 easily won Three Glasses for the customary minerally, slightly smoky aromas accompanied by a sharpish yet nicely solid palate with incisively bright acidity. Just behind is the '07 Pinot Nero, perhaps the best ever produced in Valle Venosta, which proffers evident smoky notes and a delicately mineral palate with stylish extract. The rest of the wines run from good to very good.

O A. A. Valle Venosta Riesling '08	♆♆♆	5
O A. A. Valle Venosta Pinot Bianco '08	♆♆	4
● A. A. Valle Venosta Pinot Nero '07	♆♆	5
O A. A. Valle Venosta Riesling Spielerei V.T. '08	♆♆	6
O A. A. Valle Venosta Riesling Windbichel '07	♆♆	6
● Juval Gneis '08	♆♆	4
O A. A. Valle Venosta Pinot Bianco '07	♆♆♆	4*
O A. A. Valle Venosta Riesling '07	♆♆♆	5*
O A. A. Valle Venosta Riesling '04	♆♆♆	5*
O A. A. Valle Venosta Riesling '03	♆♆♆	5*
O A. A. Valle Venosta Riesling '00	♆♆♆	4
O A. A. Valle Venosta Riesling Windbichel '05	♆♆♆	5

Cantina Produttori Valle Isarco

VIA COSTE, 50
39043 CHIUSA/KLAUSEN [BZ]
TEL. 0472847553
www.cantinavalleisarco.it

CELLAR SALES
PRE-BOOKED VISITS

ANNUAL PRODUCTION 750,000 bottles
HECTARES UNDER VINE 130
VITICULTURE METHOD Conventional

Founded in 1961, Cantina Valle Isarco di Chiusa is the youngest co-operative winery in Alto Adige. The skilled cellarmaster Thomas Dorfmann ensures the quality of this winery's products is constantly improving. Wines from the base line are typical, aromatic, fresh, honest and great value for money. Wines from the showcase line, Aristos, have lots of character, structure and longevity. Both include the entire range of great whites from Valle Isarco: Sylvaner, Müller Thurgau, Kerner, Veltliner, Gewürztraminer, Riesling and Pinot Grigio.

We tasted many wines this year from Cantina di Chiusa and we must say average quality was high. Three wines landed in the finals with excellent scores. Part because it represents a challenging type like Pinot Grigio, we were most impressed by the Aristos '08. Intense but well-defined fruit leads into a palate with sumptuous extract yet great balance, tension and minerality, signing off with a vibrant, headstrong finish. The Müller Thurgau Aristos '08 revealed surprising complexity while the fresh, balanced Kerner Passito Nectaris '07 is an interesting curiosity. We should underline the usual, extremely honest pricing policy.

O A. A. Valle Isarco Kerner Passito Nectaris '07	♆♆	7
O A. A. Valle Isarco Müller Thurgau Aristos '08	♆♆	5*
O A. A. Valle Isarco Riesling Aristos '08	♆♆	5*
O A. A. Valle Isarco Pinot Grigio Aristos '08	♆♆	5
O A. A. Valle Isarco Gewürztraminer Aristos '08	♆♆	5
O A. A. Valle Isarco Gewürztraminer Passito Nectaris '07	♆♆	7
● A. A. Valle Isarco Klausener Laitacher '08	♆♆	4*
O A. A. Valle Isarco Sylvaner Aristos '08	♆♆	5
O A. A. Valle Isarco Veltliner Aristos '08	♆♆	5
O A. A. Valle Isarco Kerner Aristos '08	♆	5
O A. A. Valle Isarco Kerner Aristos '05	♆♆♆	4*
O A. A. Valle Isarco Veltliner Aristos '03	♆♆♆	4*
O A. A. Valle Isarco Riesling Aristos '07	♆♆	5
O A. A. Valle Isarco Riesling Aristos '06	♆♆	4*
O A. A. Valle Isarco Veltliner Aristos '04	♆♆	4*

Vivaldi - Arunda

VIA PAESE, 53
39010 MELTINA/MÖLTEN [BZ]
TEL. 0471668033
www.arundavivaldi.it

CELLAR SALES
PRE-BOOKED VISITS

ANNUAL PRODUCTION **95,000 bottles**
HECTARES UNDER VINE **N.D.**
VITICULTURE METHOD **Conventional**

Joseph Reiterer is the dean of sparkling winemaking in Alto Adige. A skilled, passionate technician, Joseph has always been a reference point for sparklers in an area where this wine type has only recently begun to gather a following. He and his wife Marianna work in their lovely, well-equipped winery at Meltina, at 1,200 metres above sea level, the highest in Europe. Joseph and Marianna have no vineyards. Grapes for their cuvées are selected from the best plots in the province. The broad range is sold under two labels: Vivaldi for the Italian market, Arunda for export.

This year we did not taste the new vintage Arunda, which was still stacked in bottle. Not to worry, we were consoled by an excellent Extra Brut with a delicate, fruity bouquet of Alpine herbs, vanilla and mint, and a subtly effervescent, tangily fresh, supple palate. Another charming label that did well in our finals was the Rosé Brut Excellor, a monovarietal Pinot Nero with great structure and elegant aromas of fruit and cakes. Also excellent is the Arunda Rosé, with its delicate balsamic touches. The Blanc de Blancs is exemplary.

Tenuta Waldgries Christian Plattner

LOC. SANTA GIUSTINA, 2
39100 BOLZANO/BOZEN
TEL. 0471323603
www.waldgries.it

CELLAR SALES
PRE-BOOKED VISITS

ANNUAL PRODUCTION **50,000 bottles**
HECTARES UNDER VINE **5.1**
VITICULTURE METHOD **Natural**

The wines show almost unparalleled character, stylistic definition and above all territoriality. But Christian Plattner is one of the finest interpreters of the most famous and important Alto Adige red, Lagrein. This splendid, old estate – a visit is highly recommended – is situated on five hectares of the Santa Maddalena hill, all being converted to organic farming and all managed with rare skill. Waldgries wines are always elegant and balanced throughout, with great personality.

This year, Christian submitted two '07 Lagreins of impressive style and character. The Riserva is very austere yet concentrated and fresh, with crunchy fruit and robust, nicely textured tannins. Three Glasses went Mirell for its pervasive aromatics ranging from spice to wild berries, with a hint of cinchona at the back, and a sumptuous, multifaceted palate with perfectly gauged acidity and dense, elegant tannins. Progression is fantastic and estimates of the maturation curve should be shifted much further ahead. The only note for Christian is that he released his wonderful Moscato Rosa '07 too early, although it is already good.

⊙ A.A. Spumante Excellor Rosé Brut	♟♟ 6
○ A. A. Spumante Blanc de Blancs	♟♟ 6
○ A. A. Spumante Brut	♟♟ 5
○ A. A. Spumante Extra Brut	♟♟ 5
○ A. A. Spumante Extra Brut Cuvée Marianna	♟♟ 6
⊙ A. A. Spumante Rosé Brut	♟♟ 6
○ A. A. Spumante Brut Vivaldi '99	♟♟ 4
○ A. A. Spumante Extra Brut Arunda Ris. '98	♟♟ 6
○ A. A. Spumante Vivaldi Ris. '97	♟♟ 5

● A. A. Lagrein Scuro Mirell '07	♟♟♟ 7
● A. A. Moscato Rosa Passito '07	♟♟ 6
● A. A. Santa Maddalena Cl. '07	♟♟ 4*
● A. A. Lagrein '08	♟♟ 4
● A. A. Lagrein Scuro Ris. '07	♟♟ 6
● A. A. Cabernet Sauvignon '99	♟♟♟ 6
● A. A. Lagrein Scuro Mirell '01	♟♟♟ 7
● A. A. Lagrein Scuro Mirell '06	♟♟ 7
● A. A. Lagrein Scuro Ris. '05	♟♟ 6
● A. A. Moscato Rosa '05	♟♟ 6
○ A. A. Sauvignon '06	♟♟ 4*

Tenuta Baron Di Pauli

VIA CANTINE, 12
39052 CALDARO/KALTERN [BZ]
TEL. 0471963696
www.barondipauli.com

The Enosi '08, from 55 per cent riesling, 35 per cent sauvignon and the rest pinot bianco, is one of the best whites tasted this year. Vibrant and aromatic, it shows dynamic in the mouth. The rest of the wines are good with the Gewürztraminer Exilissi '07 the top scorer.

○ A. A. Gewürztraminer Exilissi '07	▼▼	7
○ Enosi '08	▼▼	5*
● A. A. Carano Lagrein '07	▼▼	6
○ A. A. Gewürztraminer Exilissi V.T. '07	▼▼	7

Bessererhof - Otmar Mair

NOVALE DI PRESULE, 10
39050 FIÈ ALLO SCILIAR/
VÖLS AM SCHLERN [BZ]
TEL. 0471601011
www.bessererhof.it

Otmar Mair's estate near Novale di Presule did well. Production runs to 30,000 well-made bottles with some interesting peaks, like the tangy, minerally Pinot Bianco '08, and a pleasant Chardonnay, also '08. The Schiava is fresh and delicious.

○ A. A. Chardonnay '08	▼▼	4
○ A. A. Gewürztraminer '08	▼▼	5
○ A. A. Pinot Bianco '08	▼▼	4*
● A. A. Schiava '08	▼▼	3*

Bidermannhof
Johann Innerhofer

VIA MONTE LEONE, 1
39010 CERMES/TSCHERMS [BZ]
TEL. 0473563097
www.biedermannhof.it

Johann Innerhofer's tiny estate only turns out 6,000 bottles but made a good debut. Only two wines were submitted: a well-crafted, elegantly minerally Lagrein '07 and a simpler yet still pleasant Pinot Bianco '08.

● A. A. Lagrein '07	▼	4
○ A. A. Pinot Bianco '08	▼	4

Braunbach

LOC. SETTEQUERCE
VIA PADRE ROMEDIUS, 5
39018 TERLANO/TERLAN [BZ]
TEL. 0471910184
www.braunbach.it

Braunbach always submits a reliable range of wines. We might have expected something better this year but these are still well made, starting with the austere, juicy Cabernet Lagrein Prestige Calldiv '06 and the pleasant, fragrant Spumante Brut.

● A. A. Cabernet Lagrein Prestige Calldiv '06	▼▼	5
○ A. A. Spumante Von Braunbach Brut	▼▼	5
○ A. A. Sauvignon Calldiv '08	▼	4

Brunnenhof - Kurt Rottensteiner

LOC. MAZZON
VIA DEGLI ALPINI, 5
39044 EGNA/NEUMARKT [BZ]
TEL. 0471820687
www.brunnenhof-mazzon.it

Kurt Rottensteiner, a scrupulous winemaker, produces 20,000 bottles at his five-hectare estate near Mazzon. His Pinot Nero Riserva – the '07 has yet to be released – is always one of the best. But man cannot live by Pinot Nero alone, so there is a surprisingly stylish Gewürztraminer '08.

○ A. A. Gewürztraminer '08	▼▼	5

Peter Dipoli

LOC. EGNA/NEUMARKT
VIA VILLA, 5
39055 EGNA/NEUMARKT [BZ]
TEL. 0471813400
www.peterdipoli.com

It is always interesting to comment on wines from Peter Dipoli, a great wine enthusiast and connoisseur. For his followers, his most famous wine is Sauvignon Voglar, which we found in fine fettle in the '08 edition. Elegant and stylish, it lacks just a bit of substance to become truly great.

○ A. A. Sauvignon Voglar '08	▼▼	5

OTHER WINERIES

Ebnerhof - Johannes Plattner

FRAZ. CARDANO
LOC. RENON
LASTE BASSE, 21
39053 BOLZANO/BOZEN
TEL. 0471365120
www.ebnerhof.it

The Plattner family's small, organic estate, with two and a half hectares, presented three wines. Johannes' bottles are well-typed, well made and straightforward. Special mention goes to the usual Sauvignon '08 and a sound Pinot Nero '07.

○ A. A. Sauvignon '08	🍷🍷	4
● A. A. Pinot Nero '07	🍷	5

Happacherhof
Istituto Tecnico Agrario Ora

VIA DEL CASTELLO, 10
39040 ORA/AUER [BZ]
TEL. 0471810538
www.ofl-auer.it

Associated with the agricultural institute at Ora/Auer, this small organic estate produces around 20,000 bottles a year. The range of wines is convincingly well typed and individual. The Lagrein Riserva '07, Chardonnay Passito Aurum '07 and Merlot- Cabernet Aurum '07 are all outstanding this year.

○ A. A. Chardonnay Passito Aurum '07	🍷🍷	6
● A. A. Lagrein Bioland Ris. '07	🍷🍷	5
● A. A. Merlot-Cabernet Sauvignon '07	🍷	4

Kettmeir

VIA DELLE CANTINE, 4
39052 CALDARO/KALTERN [BZ]
TEL. 0471963135
www.kettmeir.com

Founded in 1919 by Giuseppe Kettmeir, the estate is located among vineyards in the hills above Caldaro. For some years now, Kettmeir has been part of the Marzotto family's Santa Margherita group, which has given development a substantial push. The Sauvignon '08 is excellent and very reasonably priced.

○ A. A. Sauvignon '08	🍷🍷	4*
○ A. A. Müller Thurgau Athesis '08	🍷	5
○ A. A. Pinot Bianco '08	🍷	4
● A. A. Pinot Nero Maso Reiner '06	🍷	5

Kössler

VIA CASTEL GUARDIA, 21
39050 APPIANO/EPPAN [BZ]
TEL. 0471662183
www.koessler.it

Kössler produces around 200,000 bottles and has been owned for some years by Cantina Sociale di San Paolo. Kudos goes to the Spumante Brut, Pinot Nero Herr von Zobel '07, Pinot Grigio Glockleiten '08 and the varietal Schiava '08.

○ A. A. Pinot Grigio Glockleiten '08	🍷🍷	4
● A. A. Pinot Nero Herr von Zobel '07	🍷🍷	4*
● A. A. Schiava Nobile Glockleiten '08	🍷🍷	3*
○ A. A. Spumante Praeclarus Brut	🍷🍷	5

Lieselehof - Werner Morandell

VIA KARDATSCH, 6
39052 CALDARO/KALTERN [BZ]
TEL. 0471965060
www.lieselehof.com

Werner Morandell and the small Liesele estate bounce back this year. These two organically managed hectares in Caldaro yield about 10,000 bottles. The splendid Passito Sweet Clair from bronner reached the finals. The other wines are well made with a special mention for the sharpish Pinot Bianco '08.

○ Sweet Claire '07	🍷🍷	6
● Amadeus '08	🍷🍷	4*
○ Julian '08	🍷🍷	5
○ Pinot Bianco '08	🍷🍷	4*

Marinushof - Heinrich Pohl

S.DA VECCHIA 9B
39020 CASTELBELLO CIARDES/
KASTELBELL TSCHARS [BZ]
TEL. 0473624717
www.marinushof.it

Great wines from Marinushof, a tiny estate in Valle Venosta owned by Sabrina and Heiner Pohl, who produce 5,000 bottles from less than a hectare. It's hard to choose between the Pinot Grigio and Pinot Bianco, both from '08. The Pinot Nero '07 and Zweigelt '08 are very Val Venosta in style.

○ A.A. Valle Venosta Pinot Bianco '08	🍷🍷	4*
○ A.A. Valle Venosta Pinot Grigio '08	🍷🍷	4*
● A.A. Valle Venosta Pinot Nero '07	🍷🍷	5
● Zweigelt '08	🍷🍷	4*

Messnerhof - Bernhard Pichler

LOC. SAN PIETRO, 7
39100 BOLZANO/BOZEN
TEL. 0471977162
www.messnerhof.net

Since 1993, the talented Bernhard Pichler
has managed his small estate, which
produces around 10,000 bottles a year of
classic wines from the area of Bolzano. The
Lagrein Riserva '07 has intense aromas
and a creamy palate with ineffably elegant
extract. Santa Maddalena '08 is deliciously
floral.

● A. A. Lagrein Ris. '07	▼▼ 5
● A. A. Santa Maddalena Cl. '08	▼▼ 4*

Obermoser
H. & T. Rottensteiner

FRAZ. RENCIO
VIA SANTA MADDALENA, 35
39100 BOLZANO/BOZEN
TEL. 0471973549
www.obermoser.it

Wines from this small Rencio estate in the
heart of Santa Maddalena are reliable.
Heinrich Rottensteiner and his son Thomas
make fewer than 30,000 bottles from three
hectares under vine. The accent is on
classic local wines: the base '08 and
Riserva '06 Lagreins, and the excellent
Santa Maddalena '08.

● A. A. Santa Maddalena Cl. '08	▼▼ 4*
● A. A. Lagrein '08	▼▼ 4*
● A. A. Lagrein Scuro Grafenleiten Ris. '06	▼ 5

Oberrautner - Anton Schmid

FRAZ. GRIES
VIA M. PACHER, 3
39100 BOLZANO/BOZEN
TEL. 0471281440
www.schmid.bz

Schmid Oberrautner is a typical, family-run
Alto Adige estate in Gries, in the heart of
Lagrein country. Andreas Schmid works
with his son Florian at every stage of
production. We liked the particularly juicy
Lagrein '07 and the fresh, minerally Santa
Maddalena '08.

● A. A. Lagrein Scuro Grieser '07	▼▼ 4*
● A. A. Santa Maddalena Steinbauer '08	▼▼ 4*

Tenuta Pfitscherhof
Klaus Pfitscher

VIA GLENO, 9
39040 MONTAGNA/MONTAN [BZ]
TEL. 0471819773
www.pfitscher.it

Ansiz Pfitscher at Montagna is a small,
family estate managed by Klaus Pfitscher.
The Lagrein Kotznloater '07 and Pinot Nero
Matan '06 were outstanding from the three
wines presented.

● A. A. Lagrein Kotznloater '07	▼▼ 5
● A. A. Pinot Nero Matan '06	▼ 6

Thomas Pichler

VIA DELLE VIGNE, 4
39052 CALDARO/KALTERN [BZ]
TEL. 0471963094
pichler.thomas@dnet.it

This tiny estate in the Caldaro area
produces roughly 7,000 bottles from less
than one hectare under vine. Wines
submitted this year were less exciting than
in the past. The best was the Lagrein
Riserva Sond '07.

● A. A. Lagrein Sond Ris. '07	▼▼ 5
○ A. A. Sauvignon Puiten '08	▼ 4

Pralatenhof - Roland Rohregger

PIANIZZA DI SOTTO, 15A
39052 CALDARO/KALTERN [BZ]
TEL. 0471962541
www.paelatenhof.it

This small but above average estate,
managed by Roland Rohregger, with two
and a half hectares near Pianizza di Sotto,
a village near Caldaro, produces 15,000
bottles sold at attractive prices. The best
wines are a sound Pinot Grigio '08 and the
delicate Lago di Caldaro from the same
vintage.

● A. A. Lago Di Caldaro Sup. '08	▼▼ 4
○ A. A. Pinot Grigio '08	▼▼ 5

OTHER WINERIES

Castello Rametz
LOC. MAIA ALTA
VIA LABERS, 4
39012 MERANO/MERAN [BZ]
TEL. 0473211011
www.rametz.com

Good scores went this year to the historic estate owned by Stanislaus Schmid, which produces around 400,000 bottles annually. Major wines include the slightly faded but charming Pinot Nero '06 and the stylish, elegant Sauvignon '08.

● A. A. Pinot Nero '06		▼▼ 5
○ A. A. Sauvignon '08		▼▼ 4
● A. A. Gaiolo '07		▼ 4

Peter Sölva & Söhne
VIA DELL'ORO, 33
39052 CALDARO/KALTERN [BZ]
TEL. 0471964650
www.soelva.com

Peter Sölva & Söhne is one of the oldest wineries in Caldaro. The estate's wine activities are documented as long ago as 1731. Roughly 60,000 bottles a year go out under two labels, Desilvas and Amistar. Top wines are the De Silva '08 Sauvignon and the Amistar '06 Cabernet Franc.

● A. A. Cabernet Franc Amistar '06		▼▼ 6
○ A. A. Sauvignon Desilvas '08		▼▼ 5

Stachlburg - Baron von Kripp
VIA MITTERHOFER, 2
39020 PARCINES/PARTSCHINS [BZ]
TEL. 0473968014
www.stachlburg.com

Our endorsement goes to wines from Barone Von Kripp's Stachlburg estate in Valle Venosta. The reduced range submitted showcases a smoky, delicately mineral Pinot Nero '07.

● A. A. Valle Venosta Pinot Nero '07		▼▼ 5

Strasserhof
Hannes Baumgartner
FRAZ. NOVACELLA
UNTERRAIN, 8
39040 VARNA/VAHRN [BZ]
TEL. 0472830804
www.strasserhof.info

One of the oldest estates in Valle Isarco, with the northernmost vineyards in the province of Bolzano, Strasserhof guarantees good wine. Hannes Baumgartner tends three hectares under vine. The improving wines are sharper and more linear than usual, starting with the Kerner '08.

○ A. A. Valle Isarco Kerner '08		▼▼ 4*
○ A. A. Valle Isarco Gewürztraminer '08		▼▼ 5
○ A. A. Valle Isarco Sylvaner '08		▼▼ 4
○ A. A. Valle Isarco Müller Thurgau '08		▼ 4

Wilhelm Walch
VIA A. HOFER, 1
39040 TERMENO/TRAMIN [BZ]
TEL. 0471860103
www.walch.it

Progress this year has been a bit uneven for this historic estate in Termeno. There are 35 hectares of vineyards and an output of 400,000 competitively priced bottles. The Schiava Grigia Plattensteig '08 is special and the other products decent.

● A. A. Schiava Plattensteig '08		▼▼ 4*
○ A. A. Pinot Bianco '08		▼ 4

Josef Weger
LOC. CORNAIANO
VIA CASA DEL GESÙ, 17
39050 APPIANO/EPPAN [BZ]
TEL. 0471662416
www.wegerhof.it

A historic Cornaiano estate, Weger produces 80,000 bottles of a broad range of wines with the Maso le Rose line reserved for the top-rank selections. Lagrein Maso le Rose '07 is well typed and elegant, and the Pinot Bianco '08 from the same line is decent. The other wines are a bit uncertain.

○ A. A. Lagrein Maso le Rose '07		▼▼
○ A. A. Pinot Bianco Maso le Rose '06		▼

Peter Zemmer
S.DA DEL VINO, 24
39040 CORTINA/KURTINIG [BZ]
TEL. 0471817143
www.zemmer.com

Quality from this estate, enthusiastically managed by Peter Zemmer and producing around 650,000 bottles a year, has remained better than good for several years now. This season had some ups and downs with first place going to an excellent Pinot Nero '07 and a juicy Gewürztraminer Reserve '08.

● A. A. Pinot Nero '07	�♈♈	5
○ A. A. Gewürztraminer Reserve '08	♈♈	5
○ Cortinie Bianco '08	♈♈	5
● A. A. Lagrein Scuro '07	♈	5

Zohlhof
Josef Michael Unterfrauner
ZOHLHOF, 60
39040 VELTURNO/FELDTHURNS [BZ]
TEL. 0472847400
www.zoehlhof.it

Josef Michael Unterfrauner's tiny organic estate of less than two hectares in Valle Isarco continues to improve with ever more sharply defined wines. Gewürztraminer '08 and the gewürztraminer, müller thurgau and sylvaner Aurum '08 landed in the finals while the Sylvaner '08 was one of the best.

○ A.A. Gewürztraminer '08	♈♈	4*
○ Aurum '08	♈♈	4
○ A.A. Sylvaner '08	♈♈	4*

VENETO

The general trend for growth in Italian wine over the past 25 years has of course affected Veneto, too. Perhaps not as swiftly as other areas but this apparently slow progress is due less to sluggish attitudes than to a long-established wine tradition focused on competitive pricing, a style that works better at table than in the tasting room, and strong adherence to local varieties and classic production zones. Today these aspects, apparently neglected by market and critics alike, have been energetically reappraised and the region has gained in credibility and image. Regional wine geography has traditionally been dominated by the three main centres of Valpolicella, Soave and Valdobbiadenese, and while the big areas remain big, the whole region is emerging with increasing influence, from Colli Euganei to Lison, Berici and Breganze, each with its unqiue grapes and traditions to celebrate. Valpolicella is still the region's driving force with leading wines and estates that are winemakings designer labels. Amarone is the local champion following two excellent years, 2004 and 2005, but we are pleased to note the buoyancy of another even more iconically representative wine, Recioto, from a tradition that deserves greater attention. At last, things are moving on the Valpolicella front, where more than one estate is starting to establish an elegance and appeal-driven oenological identity distinct from the more massive Amarone. Turning to whites, we note an excellent performance from Soave, an ideal mix of significant new and old faces, sealed by the success of local dried-grape wines many years on from the last venture in this direction. Custoza is developing nicely, with an increasing number of estates exploiting the potential offered by the zone and range of grapes available. The Colli Euganei zone failed to repeat last year's results but maintained its status as an emerging force and the nearby Colli Berici demonstrates that great results can be obtained from the local tai rosso grape. In the province of Venice, the clay-based Lison zone offers characterful wines while Treviso, always in the lead with merlot and cabernet especially on the slopes of Montello, is again successful with its traditional Proseccos as the new extended designated area makes its appearance.

Stefano Accordini

LOC. PEDEMONTE
VIA ALBERTO BOLLA, 9
37020 SAN PIETRO IN CARIANO [VR]
TEL. 0457701733
www.accordinistefano.it

CELLAR SALES
PRE-BOOKED VISITS

ANNUAL PRODUCTION **40,000 bottles**
HECTARES UNDER VINE **11**
VITICULTURE METHOD **Conventional**

In recent years, the focus of Tiziano Accordini's estate has moved higher, first with the increased number of vineyards on the higher hills and now with the cellar, which leaves its traditional location in Pedemonte for Mazzurega and Cavalo. The meticulously tended vineyards are in an area where viticulture has ancient roots, a fact which large-scale production has tended to overshadow. The wines presented are the classics of this zone, interpreted with one eye on tradition in a quest for clearer definition and intensity of fruit.

Improved definition of the fruit is evident in the Recioto, which succeeds in contrasting explosive sweetness with the traditional grapes' inherent acidity, giving the palate solidity and grip. The Amarone is very good. We enjoyed its considerable power on the palate but it requires further ageing to achieve proper harmony. The Passo '07, made from a part-dried blend of mainly corvina with rondinella, cabernet sauvignon and merlot, while from the Valpolicellas we particularly liked the standard-label version.

Adami

FRAZ. COLBERTALDO
VIA ROVEDE, 27
31020 VIDOR [TV]
TEL. 0423982110
www.adamispumanti.it

CELLAR SALES
PRE-BOOKED VISITS

ANNUAL PRODUCTION **550,000 bottles**
HECTARES UNDER VINE **10**
VITICULTURE METHOD **Conventional**

Even in complicated times like these, with a review of the production protocol and extension of the DOC, which will soon represent 60,000,000 bottles, consortium chair Franco Adami honours his commitment to the winery founded by his far-seeing grandfather, where Franco works with his brother Armando. The now consolidated range of wines reveals the differing sides of Prosecco's character, aiming to highlight the personalities of wines from various vineyards from the lively Cartizze to Giardino, the family's historic vineyard.

The Giardino vineyard endows the alluring Dry with an extremely generous aromatic profile where ripe fruit plays hide-and-seek with subtler floral notes. The palate shows sweetness but is perfectly balanced. Bosco di Gica is a real thoroughbred, showing taut and assertive, the acidity making its presence felt without becoming aggressive for a sophisticated, savoury palate. The well-defined, juicy Extra Dry dei Casel and pleasantly simple and approachable Prosecco Tranquillo are both well made. The Waldaz is huskier and more compact.

● Recioto della Valpolicella Cl. Acinatico '06	♥♥ 7
● Amarone della Valpolicella Cl. Acinatico '05	♥♥ 8
● Passo Rosso '07	♥♥ 6
● Valpolicella Cl. '08	♥ 4
● Valpolicella Cl. Sup. Ripasso Acinatico '07	♥ 5
● Amarone della Valpolicella Cl. Vign. Il Fornetto '95	♥♥♥ 8
● Amarone della Valpolicella Cl. Vign. Il Fornetto '93	♥♥♥ 8
● Recioto della Valpolicella Cl. Acinatico '04	♥♥♥ 7
● Recioto della Valpolicella Cl. Acinatico '00	♥♥♥ 7
● Recioto della Valpolicella Cl. Acinatico '01	♥♥ 7

○ P. di Valdobbiadene Dry Vign. Giardino '08	♥♥ 4*
○ Cartizze Dry	♥♥ 5
○ P. di Valdobbiadene Bosco di Gica Brut '08	♥♥ 4
○ P. di Valdobbiadene Extra Dry dei Casel '08	♥♥ 4
○ P. di Valdobbiadene Vigneto Giardino Dry '07	♥♥ 4
○ P. di Valdobbiadene Tranquillo Giardino '08	♥ 4
○ Waldaz Brut Ris. '06	♥ 4

Ida Agnoletti

LOC. SELVA DEL MONTELLO
VIA SACCARDO, 55
31040 VOLPAGO DEL MONTELLO [TV]
TEL. 0423620947
ettore.agnoletti@virgilio.it

CELLAR SALES
PRE-BOOKED VISITS

ANNUAL PRODUCTION **50,000 bottles**
HECTARES UNDER VINE **6.5**
VITICULTURE METHOD **Conventional**

This estate's vineyards extend over the foothills of the southern slope of Mount Montello, which shelters them from the cold northern winds, and gaze across the Po valley to the sea. This is one of Italy's leading wine areas and has traditionally grown Bordeaux varieties like merlot and cabernet, ahead of the fashion that took hold in recent decades. Ida Agnoletti's versions are among the most interesting wines here with a land-rootedness that enables them to express themselves in a fresh, elegant style that stands apart from international models.

Seneca '06 is a fine example, thanks to a light flavour, nice savoury texture and mature, evolved notes on the nose. The '06 Ludwy is even more impressive than usual with approachable red berries on the ripe nose and pleasant hints of chocolate. The palate is broad, silky and savoury. The Merlot '07 seems austere and rather intriguing with nicely modulated flavours. The Merlot La Ida '07 is more approachable with its fruity, dense profile. The other wines are well typed.

★★ Allegrini

VIA GIARE, 5
37022 FUMANE [VR]
TEL. 0456832011
www.allegrini.it

ANNUAL PRODUCTION **800,000 bottles**
HECTARES UNDER VINE **70**
VITICULTURE METHOD **Conventional**

Time passes but Marilisa and Franco Allegrini's winery remains an anchor for Valpolicella. This traditional estate began its gearing up to quality before wine became fashionable and today it offers traditional wines in a modern idiom. Its strongpoint is the hills, where it owns vineyards on the best slopes. The older vineyards are still trained to the traditional pergola system while the newer plantings have been converted to Guyot pruning.

There is incredible quality throughout the range as every year, starting with the flagship Amarone '05. It's well defined and fruity with a huge flavoursome entry but then opens out mouthwateringly with excellent grip. La Poja '05 also did well and is on more impressive form than we've seen in several years. This solid red is fresh and very long-lingering with silky tannins, a worthy companion for La Grola '06, from mainly corvina with small quantities of rondinella and syrah, which has a subtler, but equally impressive, profile. Lastly, there were great performances from the Soave '08 and the Valpolicella Classico '08.

● Ludwy '06	🍷🍷 4*
● Montello e Colli Asolani Merlot '07	🍷🍷 3*
● Seneca '06	🍷🍷 4*
○ Manzoni Bianco '07	🍷 3
● Montello e Colli Asolani Cabernet Sauvignon '07	🍷 3
● Montello e Colli Asolani Merlot La Ida '07	🍷 3
○ Prosecco Frizzante P.S.L.	🍷 3
● Ludwy '05	🍷🍷 4
● Ludwy '02	🍷🍷 4
● Seneca '05	🍷🍷 4
● Seneca '04	🍷🍷 4*
● Seneca '03	🍷🍷 4*

● Amarone della Valpolicella Cl. '05	🍷🍷🍷 8
● La Poja '05	🍷🍷 8
● Recioto della Valpolicella Cl. Giovanni Allegrini '06	🍷🍷 7
● La Grola '06	🍷🍷 5
● Palazzo della Torre '06	🍷🍷 5
○ Soave '08	🍷🍷 4*
● Valpolicella Cl. '08	🍷🍷 4*
● Amarone della Valpolicella Cl. '04	🍷🍷🍷 8
● Amarone della Valpolicella Cl. '03	🍷🍷🍷 8
● Amarone della Valpolicella Cl. '01	🍷🍷🍷 8
● Amarone della Valpolicella Cl. '00	🍷🍷🍷 8
● Amarone della Valpolicella Cl. '98	🍷🍷🍷 8
● Amarone della Valpolicella Cl. '97	🍷🍷🍷 8
● Amarone della Valpolicella Cl. '95	🍷🍷🍷 8

Andreola Orsola

loc. Col San Martino
via Cal Longa, 52
31010 Farra di Soligo [TV]
tel. 0438989379
www.andreolaorsola.it

CELLAR SALES
PRE-BOOKED VISITS

ANNUAL PRODUCTION **400,000 bottles**
HECTARES UNDER VINE **20**
VITICULTURE METHOD **Conventional**

Although it is part of the large Prosecco designated zone, this Farra di Soligo winery has never restricted its production to Valdobbiadene fizz. There has always been an extensive range of traditional, less widely distributed wines. As well as the classic red Bordeaux wines, in light, approachable versions, there are semi-sparkling wines in clear and typically hazy sur lie versions with second fermentation in bottle, souvenirs of a drinking style no longer fashionable.

But it is these styles of Prosecco and Verdiso that reveal fascinating savouriness and drinkability that make them delightfully satisfying. Among the well-made sparkling wines, Brut Dirupo and the designation's grand cru, Cartizze, stand out for their generous aromas and tautness on the palate. The reds are uncomplicated, expressing the varietal features of their grapes with simple fresh fruit and vegetality, and a bright palate with prominent acidity. Note that all the wines are very fairly priced.

O Cartizze	🍷🍷	6
O P. di Valdobbiadene Brut Vign. Dirupo	🍷🍷	4
O P. di Valdobbiadene Dry Mill. '08	🍷	4
O P. di Valdobbiadene Extra Dry Vign. Dirupo	🍷	4
O Prosecco Passito Pensieri '06	🍷	6
O Verdiso Frizzante Spago '08	🍷	3
O Verdiso Tranquillo '08	🍷	3

★ Roberto Anselmi

via San Carlo, 46
37032 Monteforte d'Alpone [VR]
tel. 0457611488
www.anselmi.eu

CELLAR SALES
PRE-BOOKED VISITS

ANNUAL PRODUCTION **700,000 bottles**
HECTARES UNDER VINE **70**
VITICULTURE METHOD **Conventional**

Roberto Anselmi's winery needs no introduction after riding the crest of the wave for decades. It has shaped the fortunes of this excellent territory around the production of eclectic whites with exceptional ageing potential, as is clear from tastings of the older vintages. The grapes are grown in the estate's own vineyards in leading areas like Monte Foscarino to produce a smallish range of significant wines that perfectly represent the various facets of the area's character. There's also a red and, in propitious years, a great dried-grape wine.

Capitel Croce is always a sound white and the '07 won us over with its slow, subtle development. The aromas are elegant and layered rather than explosive, with florality and minerally hints criss-crossing the fruit. The palate is striking for its apparent lightness, which conceals laudable grip, firmness and length. Just a step behind it is the Capitel Foscarino '08, its youth enhancing fruit cosseted by juicy, tangy acidity. The San Vincenzo '08, a white for all seasons, is remarkable, especially considering the affordable price.

O Capitel Croce '07	🍷🍷	5
O Capitel Foscarino '08	🍷🍷	4*
● Realda Cabernet Sauvignon '06	🍷🍷	4*
O San Vincenzo '08	🍷🍷	4*
O Capitel Croce '06	🍷🍷🍷	5
O Capitel Croce '05	🍷🍷🍷	5
O Capitel Croce '04	🍷🍷🍷	5
O Capitel Croce '03	🍷🍷🍷	5
O Capitel Croce '02	🍷🍷🍷	5
O Capitel Croce '01	🍷🍷🍷	5
O Capitel Croce '00	🍷🍷🍷	5
O Capitel Croce '99	🍷🍷🍷	5
O Capitel Foscarino '07	🍷🍷	4*
O I Capitelli '04	🍷🍷	6
O I Capitelli '03	🍷🍷	7

Balestri Valda

VIA MONTI, 44
37038 SOAVE [VR]
TEL. 0457675393
www.vinibalestrivalda.com

CELLAR SALES
PRE-BOOKED VISITS

ANNUAL PRODUCTION **45,000 bottles**
HECTARES UNDER VINE **13**
VITICULTURE METHOD **Conventional**

In just a few years, Guido Risotto has created a new winery, buying and planting vineyards in prestigious hillside areas and at the same time building a beautiful, functional cellar that blends perfectly with the surrounding landscape. For a couple of years now, the winery has benefited from the input of Guido's daughter Laura, who has brought a breath of fresh air and revived the sense of challenge. The well-established range of wines presented is based almost entirely on Soave, and a little Recioto.

Rizzotto's Soave has a clearly defined profile with three labels expressing various aspects of the wine's character. The Classico '08 is uncomplicated but not banal, with approachable aromas and a dry, gutsy palate, while the Lunalonga '07 is more generous and fruity, if a little lacking in grip. The most successful of the wines is Sengialta '08, aged in large oak casks, with fresh florality and fruit, a dry, solid palate and impressive length and harmony. The Recioto '06 is simple and alluring while Rosso Scaligio '05 is generously fruity.

○ Soave Cl. Sengialta '08	🍷🍷	4*
○ Soave Cl. '08	🍷🍷	4*
○ Recioto di Soave Cl. '06	🍷	6
● Scaligio '05	🍷	5
○ Soave Cl. Lunalonga '07	🍷	4
○ Soave Cl. '07	ΥΥ	4
○ Soave Cl. '06	ΥΥ	4
○ Soave Cl. '05	ΥΥ	3*
○ Soave Cl. Sengialta '07	ΥΥ	4

Cantina Beato Bartolomeo da Breganze

VIA ROMA, 100
36042 BREGANZE [VI]
TEL. 0445873112
www.cantinabreganze.it

CELLAR SALES
PRE-BOOKED VISITS

ANNUAL PRODUCTION **3.500,000 bottles**
HECTARES UNDER VINE **850**
VITICULTURE METHOD **Conventional**

Cantina Sociale Beato Bartolomeo da Breganze has always promoted the wines of this DOC zone, which extends from the foot of the Asiago plateau along the hills from Thiene to Bassano. Having achieved a high standard of quality, the winery is now committed to fine-tuning the production process. The 800 grower members are supervised by agronomists, who guide them in the management of their vineyards, and encouraged to reduce yields by financial incentives.

Reassuring results emerged again this year, with an excellent performance from the '06 Torcolato, which combines very rich aromas and flavour with a nicely drinkable palate. The intensely ripe, fruity Cabernet Kilò Riserva '06 shows firm, taut progression with good texture. From the Bosco Grande line, we particularly liked the Torcolato and Cabernet, both '06. The former is generous and balanced while the Cabernet is harmonious and very fruity. Lastly, an honourable mention goes to a rigorously characterful Vespaiolo Superiore Savardo '08.

○ Breganze Torcolato '06	🍷🍷	6
● Breganze Cabernet Kilò Ris. '06	🍷🍷	5
● Breganze Cabernet Sup. Bosco Grande '06	🍷🍷	5
○ Breganze Torcolato Bosco Grande Ris. '06	🍷🍷	5
○ Breganze Vespaiolo Sup. Savardo '08	🍷🍷	4
○ Breganze Bianco Sup. Savardo '08	🍷	4
● Breganze Cabernet Sup. Savardo '07	🍷	4
○ Dolce San Giorgio	🍷	4
● Merlot Bosco Grande '06	🍷	5
● Breganze Cabernet Kilò Ris. '04	ΥΥ	5
● Breganze Cabernet Kilò Ris. '03	ΥΥ	5
● Breganze Cabernet Kilò Ris. '01	ΥΥ	5
● Breganze Cabernet Sup. Bosco Grande '04	ΥΥ	4
○ Breganze Torcolato '05	ΥΥ	6
○ Breganze Torcolato '02	ΥΥ	6
○ Breganze Torcolato Bosco Grande '05	ΥΥ	5
○ Breganze Vespaiolo Sup. Savardo '06	ΥΥ	4*
● Merlot Bosco Grande '05	ΥΥ	5

Lorenzo Begali

VIA CENGIA, 10
37020 SAN PIETRO IN CARIANO [VR]
TEL. 0457725148
www.begaliwine.it

CELLAR SALES
PRE-BOOKED VISITS

ANNUAL PRODUCTION **60,000 bottles**
HECTARES UNDER VINE **8**
VITICULTURE METHOD **Conventional**

The Begali family winery perfectly reflects how this area dotted with quality-oriented wineries has evolved over the last 20 years. The estate is now pretty emblematic, and the results have been among the most interesting in the last ten years. Just a few hectares of vineyards, on the flatlands and hillslopes, provide the grapes for a balanced range of very high quality products, particularly the wines obtained from part-drying, Amarone and Recioto, which are much sought-after by those in the know.

Dried-grape wines are again the most successful. Recioto '06 opens intense and juicy on the nose with perfect handling of extraordinarily rich sugars on the palate while the even more impressive Amarones have developed a very clear-cut character over the years. Ca' Bianca '04 is generous, powerful and dry, showing strength and grip. The juicy, extraordinarily drinkable Classico '05 has a leaner but equally impressive profile. We also liked the taut, gutsy Ripasso '07 and the soft, powerful Tigiolo '06, from equal parts of corvina and cabernet sauvignon.

Wine	Rating
● Amarone della Valpolicella Cl. Vign. Monte Ca' Bianca '04	♀♀♀ 8
● Amarone della Valpolicella Cl. '05	♀♀ 7
● Recioto della Valpolicella Cl. '06	♀♀ 7
● Tigiolo '06	♀♀ 6
● Valpolicella Cl. Sup. Ripasso Vign. La Cengia '07	♀♀ 4*
● Valpolicella Cl. '08	♀ 3
● Amarone della Valpolicella Cl. '03	♀♀♀ 7
● Amarone della Valpolicella Cl. Vign. Monte Ca' Bianca '03	♀♀♀ 8
● Amarone della Valpolicella Cl. Vign. Monte Ca' Bianca '01	♀♀♀ 7
● Amarone della Valpolicella Cl. Vign. Monte Ca' Bianca '00	♀♀♀ 8
● Amarone della Valpolicella Cl. Vign. Monte Ca' Bianca '99	♀♀♀ 8
● Amarone della Valpolicella Cl. Vign. Monte Ca' Bianca '97	♀♀♀ 8

Cecilia Beretta - Pasqua

LOC. SAN FELICE EXTRA
VIA BELVEDERE, 135
37131 VERONA
TEL. 0458432111
www.ceciliaberetta.it

CELLAR SALES
PRE-BOOKED VISITS

ANNUAL PRODUCTION **18.200,000 bottles**
HECTARES UNDER VINE **1080**
VITICULTURE METHOD **Conventional**

At a difficult time when the market seems hard to penetrate, it is a pleasure to discover a challenging quest for quality throughout the range, especially in a large estate like Cecilia Beretta, the Pasqua family's emblematic winery. The almost 100 hectares of vineyards make rigorous selection possible so that the cellar staff can work with raw material of the highest quality. Add to this the absolute focus of the range on traditional Veronese wines, and there you are.

As every year, the top wine is the Amarone Terre di Cariano. The '05 is a balance between the wine type's fullness and the cellar's typically drinkable style. The result is very successful, showing ripe but sound fruit and a full-bodied palate supported by acidity with a long, alluring finish. The intriguing Valpolicella Mizzole '06 blends ripe fruit and fresh aromas of flowers and aromatic herbs with a mouthwatering, lustily rustic palate. The Picàie '06, from corvina, cabernet and merlot, has an overripe, mouthfilling profile.

Wine	Rating
● Amarone della Valpolicella Cl. Terre di Cariano '05	♀♀ 8
● Amarone della Valpolicella Cl. Villa Borghetti Pasqua '05	♀♀ 7
● Valpolicella Sup. Ripasso '07	♀♀ 5
● Valpolicella Sup. Ripasso Villa Borghetti Pasqua '07	♀♀ 5
● Valpolicella Sup. Roccolo di Mizzole '06	♀♀ 4
● Picàie '06	♀ 6
● Amarone della Valpolicella Cl. Terre di Cariano '04	♀♀♀ 8
● Amarone della Valpolicella Cl. Terre di Cariano '99	♀♀♀ 7
● Amarone della Valpolicella Cl. Terre di Cariano '03	♀♀ 8
● Valpolicella Sup. Roccolo di Mizzole '05	♀♀ 3*

Cav. G. B. Bertani

VIA ASIAGO, 1
37023 GREZZANA [VR]
TEL. 0458658444
www.bertani.net

CELLAR SALES
PRE-BOOKED VISITS

ANNUAL PRODUCTION **2,000,000 bottles**
HECTARES UNDER VINE **220**
VITICULTURE METHOD **Conventional**

Bertani represents a slice of Italian winemaking history, especially for the Verona area, with more than 150 years of sustained activity. Over 200 hectares of vineyards sprawling across the most prestigious designated areas and a well-matched team, led by Cristian Ridolfi, produce wines ranging from Valpolicella to Soave, Bardolino and Amarone, all excellent and all representative of the well-defined character and style for which the estate is renowned.

In the absence of the Amarone Classico, which often tops our score sheet, attention focused on an excellent line-up led by the sumptuous Valpolicella Ognisanti '06. A fresh, generous nose with fruit-led aromatics accompanied by fines herbes precedes deftly handled but substantial flesh on the palate. Just a step behind is the richer, juicier Ripasso '06 while the impressive Soave Sereole '08 is an understated and very harmonious white. The Secco Bertani '06 didn't quite make it to the final tastings. Amarone Villa Arvedi '06 is charming and dependable.

La Biancara

FRAZ. SORIO
C.DA BIANCARA, 14
36053 GAMBELLARA [VI]
TEL. 0444444244
www.biancaravini.it

CELLAR SALES
PRE-BOOKED VISITS

ANNUAL PRODUCTION **50,000 bottles**
HECTARES UNDER VINE **12**
VITICULTURE METHOD **Natural**

Few estates have influenced Italian winemaking in the last 20 years as much as Angiolino Maule's. It's a model not just for the quality of the wine, but also for its healthfulness and that of the land it grows on. This sea change affects most of the wine production sector, moving towards more environmentally friendly winemaking, is mapped out by La Biancara, one of the first estates to rediscover respectful growing techniques without sacrificing absolute quality.

There are three wines made from garganega, two of which show outstanding character and quality: Pico '07, wrongly included in last year's Guide, and Sassaia '08. The former is rich in colour and gives aromas of Mediterranean undergrowth and iodine. The powerful palate shows excellent savouriness and tension. The even more impressive Sassaia has similar but fresher aromas, with captivating peach fruit and an enviably gutsy palate. We like the performance from the simpler Masieri Bianco '08 while the Merlot '07 and Canà '07 are both well typed. Lastly, we should note that sulphites are now only used in a few of the wines.

● Valpolicella Cl. Sup. Vigneto Ognisanti '06	▼▼▼ 4*
○ Soave Sereole '08	▼▼ 4*
● Valpolicella Cl. Sup. Ripasso Villa Novare '06	▼▼ 4
● Albion Cabernet Sauvignon Villa Novare '06	▼▼ 6
● Amarone della Valpolicella Valpantena Villa Arvedi '06	▼▼ 7
○ Le Lave '07	▼▼ 4
○ Lugana Le Quaiare '08	▼▼ 4
● Valpolicella Valpantena Secco Bertani '06	▼▼ 5*
● Amarone della Valpolicella Cl. '01	♀♀♀ 8
● Amarone della Valpolicella Cl. '00	♀♀♀ 8
● Amarone della Valpolicella Cl. '99	♀♀♀ 8
● Amarone della Valpolicella Cl. '98	♀♀♀ 8
● Amarone della Valpolicella Cl. '97	♀♀♀ 8

○ Pico '07	▼▼ 5
○ Sassaia '08	▼▼ 4*
● Canà Rosso '07	▼▼ 4
○ Masieri Bianco '08	▼▼ 3*
● Merlot '07	▼▼ 5
● Masieri Rosso '08	▼ 4
○ Pico '02	♀♀♀ 4
○ Pico '06	♀♀ 5
○ Pico '04	♀♀ 5
○ Pico '03	♀♀ 4*
○ Recioto di Gambellara '02	♀♀ 7
○ Recioto di Gambellara '00	♀♀ 7
○ Sassaia '07	♀♀ 4*
○ Sassaia '06	♀♀ 4*
○ Sassaia '04	♀♀ 4*
○ Sassaia '03	♀♀ 4*

Desiderio Bisol & Figli

FRAZ. SANTO STEFANO
VIA FOLLO, 33
31049 VALDOBBIADENE [TV]
TEL. 0423900138
www.bisol.it

CELLAR SALES
PRE-BOOKED VISITS

ANNUAL PRODUCTION **1,300,000 bottles**
HECTARES UNDER VINE **100**
VITICULTURE METHOD **Natural**

In just a few years, the Bisol family's winery has expanded its vineyards and output, to the extent that it now represents one of the most highly developed family-run estates in the designation, producing well over a million bottles every year. The vineyards have moved out from the traditional heart of the estate in Valdobbiadene into the beautiful, secluded hillside enclave of Rolle, gradually reaching as far as Conegliano, the DOC zone's natural eastern boundary.

Today's well-stocked range is based principally on sparkling wines, Prosecco above all, although there are also some Metodo Classico products, released after a long period of lees contact. The Bisol line is the winery's diamond head with the simpler, more approachable Jeio hard on its heels. Vigneti del Fol '08 is the most striking wine with its generous aromas of apple and pear fruit and flowers, and a juicy palate with sophisticated sparkle. A step below is the drier, gutsier Crede '08 while the '08 Cartizze is sunny and mouthfilling.

○ Cartizze '08	TT	6
○ Duca di Dolle Prosecco Passito	TT	7
○ P. di Valdobbiadene Brut Crede '08	TT	5
○ P. di Valdobbiadene Extra Dry Vigneti del Fol '08	TT	5
○ Cartizze Jeio	T	5
○ P. di Valdobbiadene Colmei Jeio Extra Dry	T	4
○ P. di Valdobbiadene Extra Dry Jeio	T	4
○ Talento Eliseo Bisol Cuvée del Fondatore Brut '01	T	6
⊙ Talento Rosé Brut '01	T	6

F.lli Bolla

FRAZ. PEDEMONTE
VIA ALBERTO BOLLA, 3
37029 SAN PIETRO IN CARIANO [VR]
TEL. 0458090911
www.bolla.it

CELLAR SALES
PRE-BOOKED VISITS

ANNUAL PRODUCTION **15,000,000 bottles**
HECTARES UNDER VINE **350**
VITICULTURE METHOD **Conventional**

We report further changes at Bolla, and not only in the control room. The Gruppo Italiano Vini has now completed its purchase, including the brand, and there have been changes in the cellar, too, for Giampaolo Vaona retired and was officially replaced by Cristian Scrinzi, who has contributed greatly to boosting GIV's fortunes in recent years. Although the range of wines is large, we are only reviewing the products from the Valpolicella and Soave zones in the province of Verona, which again show the most consistently dependable quality.

Two Amarones were presented. Le Origini '06 is in a classic style and Capo di Torbe '05, from vineyards at Torbe in the upper Valpolicella area, has more modern feel. The former is strikingly mature in its expression and the mouthfilling fruit is nicely reflected on the mouthwatering, husky palate. The Capo di Torbe is slower to open out, with close-knit tannins on the palate. It's very promising but needs time. The same applies, with less concentration, to the traditional Valpolicella Le Pojane '06 and Superiore Capo di Torbe '05.

● Amarone della Valpolicella Cl. Capo di Torbe '05	TT	8
● Amarone della Valpolicella Cl. Le Origini '06	TT	8
● Valpolicella Cl. Sup. Capo di Torbe '05	TT	5
● Valpolicella Cl. Sup. Le Pojane Ripasso '06	TT	4
○ Soave Cl. Tufaie '08	T	4
● Amarone della Valpolicella Cl. '05	YY	7
● Amarone della Valpolicella Cl. '04	YY	7
● Amarone della Valpolicella Cl. '03	YY	7
● Amarone della Valpolicella Cl. Capo di Torbe '04	YY	8
● Amarone della Valpolicella Cl. Capo di Torbe '03	YY	8
● Amarone della Valpolicella Cl. Capo di Torbe '01	YY	8
● Amarone della Valpolicella Cl. Le Origini '04	YY	8
● Amarone della Valpolicella Cl. Le Origini '03	YY	7
● Amarone della Valpolicella Cl. Le Origini '01	YY	8
● Valpolicella Cl. Sup. Capo di Torbe '04	YY	5
● Valpolicella Cl. Sup. Capo di Torbe '03	YY	5
● Valpolicella Cl. Sup. Capo di Torbe '01	YY	5

Bonotto delle Tezze

FRAZ. TEZZE DI PIAVE
VIA DUCA D'AOSTA, 16
31020 VAZZOLA [TV]
TEL. 0438488323
www.bonottodelletezze.it

CELLAR SALES
PRE-BOOKED VISITS

ANNUAL PRODUCTION **40,000 bottles**
HECTARES UNDER VINE **50**
VITICULTURE METHOD **Conventional**

Antonio Bonotto is a determined producer with close links to tradition. Piave is not an easy area. It extends from the Pre-Alps down to the sea, with a typical clayey component in the most suitable growing areas, which produce generous wines that are not always too supple on the palate. Antonio has gradually found his direction and in just a few years the wines have gained the finesse that was lacking. Restricting yields from the estate's 50 hectares of prestigious vineyards is reaping increasingly impressive results.

Quality is dependable throughout the range, which is produced with the help of Marina Polencic. The Raboso Potestà '05 finally gives us a glimpse of this variety's potential for generous aromas and gutsy acidity on an austere rather than edgy palate. The traditional Treviso red Merlot '07 is also very good with ripe aromas of red berries and flowers, and supple, lingering palate. The Raboso Passito '07 is rich and succulent while the two '08 whites are weighty and extremely pleasant.

● Piave Merlot Spezza '07	🍷🍷	4*
● Piave Raboso Potestà '05	🍷🍷	4
● Raboso Passito '07	🍷🍷	6
○ Chardonnay Oseada '08	🍷	4
○ Manzoni Bianco Novalis '08	🍷	4
○ Manzoni Bianco Novalis '02	🍸🍸	4*
○ Manzoni Bianco Novalis '01	🍸🍸	4*
● Piave Merlot Spezza '06	🍸🍸	4*
● Piave Merlot Spezza '03	🍸🍸	4

Borin Vini & Vigne

FRAZ. MONTICELLI
VIA DEI COLLI, 5
35043 MONSELICE [PD]
TEL. 042974384
www.viniborin.it

CELLAR SALES
PRE-BOOKED VISITS

ANNUAL PRODUCTION **140,000 bottles**
HECTARES UNDER VINE **28**
VITICULTURE METHOD **Conventional**

In addition to the traditional meticulous care taken at Borin, Francesco and Giampaolo have brought a breath of fresh air, particularly in the way they face new challenges. Giampaolo brings back his impressions of the market while Francesco and father Gianni explore the potential of the various grape varieties and the great territory that is the Colli Euganei. The aim is to make wines that showcase the spirit of this DOC zone.

A vast range of wines were presented, among which Zuan '07 stands out for its depth and class. It's a red mainly from cabernet sauvignon with intense aromas of berries that offer glimpses of flowers, pencil lead and spices. The palate is nicely solid, sophisticated and very lingering. There are interesting developments in the two Riservas. Cabernet '06 is more austere while the Merlot '07 has gained in freshness and acidic pressure. The classic Fiore di Gaia '08 is a Moscato Secco with clear-cut aromas and a gutsy palate while Chardonnay Vigna Bianca '07 put on a fine show.

● Zuan '07	🍷🍷	6
● Colli Euganei Cabernet Sauvignon Mons Silicis Ris. '06	🍷🍷	5
● Colli Euganei Cabernet Sauvignon V. Costa '07	🍷🍷	4*
○ Colli Euganei Chardonnay Vigna Bianca '07	🍷🍷	4
○ Colli Euganei Fior d'Arancio Passito Sette Chiesette '06	🍷🍷	6
● Colli Euganei Merlot Rocca Chiara Ris. '07	🍷🍷	5
○ Fiore di Gaia '08	🍷🍷	4*
○ Bianco dei Mandorli '08	🍷	3
○ Colli Euganei Fior d'Arancio '08	🍷	4
○ Colli Euganei Pinot Bianco Monte Archino '08	🍷	4

F.lli Bortolin Spumanti

FRAZ. SANTO STEFANO
VIA MENEGAZZI, 5
31049 VALDOBBIADENE [TV]
TEL. 0423900135
www.bortolin.com

CELLAR SALES
PRE-BOOKED VISITS

ANNUAL PRODUCTION 300,000 bottles
HECTARES UNDER VINE 20
VITICULTURE METHOD Conventional

The Bortolins are one of the families that have shaped the fortunes of Prosecco, not perhaps by travelling the world as others have done, but by offering a benchmark for the DOC zone and beyond for anyone interested in discovering Treviso's sparklers. Valeriano is still the mainstay of the winery today, although his children are gradually moving in. Most of the grapes required for production are grown on the estate's 20 hectares while the remainder comes from local growers, many of whom have worked with the estate for decades.

The Extra Dry Rù performed well, embodying a successful expression of the light, breezy spirit of Prosecco that manages to combine it with precision and grip. Enjoy the way fresh flowers mingle with white-fleshed fruits and discreet sweetness contrasts nicely with mouthwatering acidity. Just slightly behind it comes the Dry, with distinctive golden delicious apple and pear aromas on the nose and an explosion of sweetness on the enjoyably rounded palate. The other products are good. We particularly liked the Cartizze.

○ P. di Valdobbiadene Dry	ΨΨ	4*
○ P. di Valdobbiadene Extra Dry Rù	ΨΨ	4*
○ Cartizze '08	Ψ	5
○ P. di Valdobbiadene Brut	Ψ	4
○ P. di Valdobbiadene Extra Dry	Ψ	4
○ Vigneto del Convento Extra Brut	Ψ	4
○ Cartizze '07	ΨΨ	5
○ Cartizze Dry	ΨΨ	5
○ P. di Valdobbiadene Brut '06	ΨΨ	4
○ P. di Valdobbiadene Extra Dry '06	ΨΨ	4
○ P. di Valdobbiadene Extra Dry Rù '06	ΨΨ	4

Bortolomiol

VIA GARIBALDI, 142
31049 VALDOBBIADENE [TV]
TEL. 0423974911
www.bortolomiol.com

CELLAR SALES
PRE-BOOKED VISITS

ANNUAL PRODUCTION 2,000,000 bottles
HECTARES UNDER VINE 5
VITICULTURE METHOD Conventional

Bortolomiol is a female-led winery nowadays. The baton of founder Giuliano Bortolomiol, the first producer of Prosecco Brut in the 1960s, was taken up by his wife Ottavia and subsequently by their four daughters, who play an increasingly important role in the cellar. They show the same grit and determination as their illustrious predecessor, and his same determination in promoting the Valdobbiadene area in Italy and abroad. The Bortolomiol products and image make an important contribution to achieving this noble aim.

The Prosecco Extra Dry Senior shows a broad, elegant range of aromas, particularly apple and pear fruit, and flowers. The harmonious, mouthwatering flavour is framed by creamy prickle. We particularly liked the Prosecco Dry Maior for its pleasant ripe fruit sensations and generous, juicy palate with nicely controlled sweetness. The Extra Brut Riserva Del Governatore '07, a blend of prosecco, pinot nero and chardonnay, shows a more complex nose with hints of almonds and a taut palate. The rest of the range is well up to the usual dependable standard.

○ P. di Valdobbiadene Dry Maior	ΨΨ	4
○ P. di Valdobbiadene Extra Dry Senior	ΨΨ	4
○ Ris. del Governatore Extra Brut '07	ΨΨ	4
○ Cartizze	Ψ	6
⊙ Filanda Rosé Brut Ris.	Ψ	4
○ P. di Valdobbiadene Brut Motus Vitae '07	Ψ	5
○ P. di Valdobbiadene Brut Prior	Ψ	4
○ P. di Valdobbiadene Demi Sec Suavis	Ψ	4
○ P. di Valdobbiadene Extra Dry Sel. Banda Rossa '08	Ψ	4
○ P. di Valdobbiadene Tranquillo Canto Fermo '08	Ψ	4
● Piave Cabernet Sauvignon Mormorò '06	Ψ	4

Bosco del Merlo

VIA POSTUMIA, 14
30020 ANNONE VENETO [VE]
TEL. 0422768167
www.boscodelmerlo.it

CELLAR SALES
PRE-BOOKED VISITS

ANNUAL PRODUCTION **430,000 bottles**
HECTARES UNDER VINE **128**
VITICULTURE METHOD **Natural**

The Lison Pramaggiore zone is dotted with wineries, many of which share the objective of producing uncomplicatedly moreish, very drinkable wines. The Paladin family estate is a pleasant exception. The well-stocked range includes both quaffable wines and more ambitious types. Bosco del Merlo's extensive vineyards are cared for with respect for the environment to yield grapes that express both generous fruitiness and the features of this terroir between the flatlands and the sea.

There are two emblematic grape varieties around here, refosco and tocai, interpreted by the Paladin family in an elegant and characterful style with two taut, leanish wines. Red grapes from Bordeaux found a home in this area over a century ago and the results are more than satisfactory today, as we can see in the subtle, fragrant 360 '06 and especially the increasingly exciting Vineargenti '05. Aromas are generous and well defined while the savoury palate has a silky texture. We also loved the headily vibrant, harmonious Sauvignon Turranio.

○ Lison-Pramaggiore Sauvignon Turranio '08	▼▼	4*
● Vineargenti Rosso '05	▼▼	6
● 360 Ruber Capitae Rosso '06	▼▼	5
○ Lison-Pramaggiore Lison Cl. Juti '07	▼▼	4*
● Lison-Pramaggiore Refosco P. R. Roggio dei Roveri '06	▼▼	6
● Lison-Pramaggiore Merlot Campo Camino '07	▼	4
○ Lison-Pramaggiore Pinot Grigio '08	▼	4
○ Priné '07	▼	5
○ Verduzzo Soandre '07	▼	4
○ Lison-Pramaggiore Lison Cl. Juti '06	YY	4
● Lison-Pramaggiore Merlot Campo Camino '04	YY	4
● Lison-Pramaggiore Refosco P. R. Roggio dei Roveri '05	YY	6
● Lison-Pramaggiore Refosco P. R. Roggio dei Roveri '04	YY	6
○ Lison-Pramaggiore Sauvignon Turranio '07	YY	4*
○ Priné '06	YY	5

Brigaldara

FRAZ. SAN FLORIANO
VIA BRIGALDARA, 20
37020 SAN PIETRO IN CARIANO [VR]
TEL. 0457701055
www.valpolicella.it/brigaldara

CELLAR SALES
PRE-BOOKED VISITS

ANNUAL PRODUCTION **200,000 bottles**
HECTARES UNDER VINE **45**
VITICULTURE METHOD **Conventional**

Success struck Valpolicella area like lightning out of a clear blue sky, sometimes surprising the producers themselves, who were suddenly thrust into a new and complex world. Stefano Cesari has been able to handle the situation with calmly and with lucidity. In fact, his operation is one of the most interesting local estates today with excellent vineyards, a range of wines strongly rooted in tradition and, very importantly, fine quality that represents really good value for money.

The wines presented this year come close to perfection, with three Amarones in the finals, each with its own character. The Case Vecie '04 is complex and multifaceted on the nose with mellow tannins on a palate that shows both power and finesse. The same wine in the '05 version is fresher and livelier. Its aromas are still finding definition but the texture is all there. Lastly, the powerful, lingering Classico '05 shows exemplary integrity and pressure, with vibrant, rich aromas and an enthralling overall drinking experience. The other products are all excellent.

● Amarone della Valpolicella Cl. '05	▼▼▼	7
● Amarone della Valpolicella Case Vecie '05	▼▼	8
● Amarone della Valpolicella Case Vecie '04	▼▼	8
○ Passito Bianco '06	▼▼	5
● Recioto della Valpolicella Cl. '07	▼▼	7
● Valpolicella Cl. Sup. Ripasso Il Vegro '06	▼▼	5
⊙ Dindarella '08	▼	4
● Valpolicella Cl. '08	▼	4
● Amarone della Valpolicella Case Vecie '03	YYY	8
● Amarone della Valpolicella Case Vecie '00	YYY	7
● Amarone della Valpolicella Cl. '99	YYY	7
● Amarone della Valpolicella Cl. '98	YYY	7
● Amarone della Valpolicella Cl. '97	YYY	7

Sorelle Bronca

FRAZ. COLBERTALDO
VIA MARTIRI, 20
31020 VIDOR [TV]
TEL. 0423987201
www.sorellebronca.com

CELLAR SALES
PRE-BOOKED VISITS

ANNUAL PRODUCTION **250,000 bottles**
HECTARES UNDER VINE **20**
VITICULTURE METHOD **Organic certified**

In the world of Prosecco, it is unusual to find wineries that venture beyond the production of sparkling wines, but Antonella and Ersiliana Bronca's estate releases high-profile still wines as well as excellent spumantes. The 20 or so hectares of vineyards extend over the Treviso hills, in the heart of the DOC zone and beyond to the east, the home of the red and white grapes that make Colli di Conegliano wines. For Prosecco, Sorelle Bronca adopts new, more wine-friendly vinification techniques such as direct fermentation of the must.

The technique is used for the Particella 68, an extraordinarily fruity, tangy, and mouthwateringly drinkable Prosecco. The two cuvées produced in larger numbers, Extra Dry and Brut, both '08, are no less impressive or harmonious in the mouth. The more ambitious wines come from nearby Fellettano, with a fragrant red showing red berries, spice, flowers and medicinal herbs on the nose and a savoury, well-textured palate with a long, mouthwatering finish. The interesting Colli di Conegliano Bianco Delico '07 has a subtle, mature nose and a taut, gutsy palate.

Luigi Brunelli

VIA CARIANO, 10
37029 SAN PIETRO IN CARIANO [VR]
TEL. 0457701118
www.brunelliwine.com

CELLAR SALES
PRE-BOOKED VISITS
VISITOR FACILITIES

ANNUAL PRODUCTION **90,000 bottles**
HECTARES UNDER VINE **11**
VITICULTURE METHOD **Conventional**

Luigi Brunelli's winery has been riding the crest of the wave for over ten years. It offers a snapshot of Valpolicella with a smallish but excellent vineyard holding, family management, a simple, functional cellar at Corte Cariano, scrupulous care at all stages of production and welcoming guest accommodation. The cellars hold both barriques and the traditional larger barrels for a vast but dependably good quality range of products embracing all the local grape varieties.

The top quality and results come from the two Riserva di Amarone wines, both from the excellent 2004 growing year. Inferi has vibrant aromas of fruit and crushed flowers on the nose, though the strength of the palate is cropped by the extremely high alcohol content and a slightly bitter sensation. The Titari is more interesting, giving a wide range of aromas that open out deep and slow on the nose, while the palate impresses with its beautifully handled rich texture. The youthful, approachable interpretation of the Recioto succeeds in reining in its exuberant sweetness. The Valpolicellas are reliably good.

● Colli di Conegliano Rosso Ser Bele '06	♛♛	6
○ P. di Valdobbiadene Extra Dry Particella 68 '08	♛♛	5
○ Colli di Conegliano Bianco Delico '07	♛♛	5
○ P. di Valdobbiadene Brut '08	♛♛	4*
○ P. di Valdobbiadene Extra Dry '08	♛♛	4*
○ Difetto Perfetto '06	♛	5
● Colli di Conegliano Rosso Ser Bele '05	♛♛♛	6
○ Colli di Conegliano Bianco Delico '06	♛♛	5
● Colli di Conegliano Rosso Ser Bele '04	♛♛	6
● Colli di Conegliano Rosso Ser Bele '03	♛♛	6
● Colli di Conegliano Rosso Ser Bele '02	♛♛	6
○ Manzoni Bianco '04	♛♛	8
○ P. di Valdobbiadene Brut '07	♛♛	4*
○ P. di Valdobbiadene Brut '06	♛♛	4*
○ P. di Valdobbiadene Extra Dry '07	♛♛	4*
○ P. di Valdobbiadene Extra Dry '06	♛♛	4*
○ P. di Valdobbiadene Extra Dry Particella 68 '07	♛♛	5
○ P. di Valdobbiadene Extra Dry Particella 68 '06	♛♛	4
○ P. di Valdobbiadene Extra Dry Particella 68	♛♛	4*

● Amarone della Valpolicella Cl. Campo del Titari Ris. '04	♛♛	8
● Amarone della Valpolicella Cl. Campo Inferi Ris. '04	♛♛	8
● Recioto della Valpolicella Cl. '07	♛♛	6
● Valpolicella Cl. Sup. Campo Praesel '07	♛♛	4
● Amarone della Valpolicella Cl. '05	♛	8
● Corte Cariano Rosso '07	♛	4
● Valpolicella Cl. Sup. Ripasso Pa' Riondo '07	♛	4
● Amarone della Valpolicella Cl. Campo del Titari '97	♛♛♛	8
● Amarone della Valpolicella Cl. Campo del Titari '96	♛♛♛	8
● Amarone della Valpolicella Cl. Campo del Titari Ris. '03	♛♛	8
● Amarone della Valpolicella Cl. Campo Inferi Ris. '03	♛♛	8

Tommaso Bussola

LOC. SAN PERETTO
VIA MOLINO TURRI, 30
37024 NEGRAR [VR]
TEL. 0457501740
www.bussolavini.com

CELLAR SALES
PRE-BOOKED VISITS

ANNUAL PRODUCTION **80,000 bottles**
HECTARES UNDER VINE **9.5**
VITICULTURE METHOD **Conventional**

The Valpolicella area's emblematic wine is Recioto, both in terms of tradition and of growing conditions, and Tommaso Bussola has an extremely prestigious role among the producers of this generous, very alluring wine. Over the years, the Bussola vineyard has expanded from around the winery at San Peretto up to the border with Negrar and its extended zone, where the grapes gain a finesse that would otherwise be hard to find. The cellar has been renovated, enabling Tommaso to age the wines thoroughly in bottle before releasing them.

The style of the wines is inspired, from all points of view, by an ideal of richness and maturity, as is often underlined by the cellar's reluctance to release the finished product. The Reciotos are very skilfully made, especially the TB '04, an unusually concentrated, fruity, rounded and mature wine with an extremely sweet palate where extract has to rein in the exuberance. The Amarone is also very interesting and despite the difficulties of the 2003 vintage, has impressively solid structure. Of the two Valpolicellas, we preferred the Classico.

Ca' La Bionda

FRAZ. VALGATARA
LOC. BIONDA, 4
37020 MARANO DI VALPOLICELLA [VR]
TEL. 0456801198
www.calabionda.it

CELLAR SALES
PRE-BOOKED VISITS

ANNUAL PRODUCTION **110,000 bottles**
HECTARES UNDER VINE **29**
VITICULTURE METHOD **Natural**

The Marano valley is renowned for grapes whose most interesting features are finesse and generous aromas, although a little power may be lacking as a result. In Valpolicella, where grapes are often dried, power is obviously a ubiquitous quality so Marano's elegance becomes a trump card. The Castellani family makes the most of these qualities with growing techniques that respect the environment and non-invasive cellar procedures. The few wines produced are all territory-focused and obtained from grapes grown on the estate's vineyards.

The two best vineyards, Casal Vegri and Ravazzol, produce the most ambitious wines, the ones that lead the selection we taste each year. Amarone Ravazzol '05 is the most interesting, opening out slowly, gradually revealing its bouquet and winning us over with its juicy strength. The Valpolicella Casal Vegri '07, on the other hand, is too young and further bottle ageing will make it more harmonious. The Recioto '06 is particularly well typed, with youthful aromas and a delicately sweet palate.

● Recioto della Valpolicella Cl. TB '04	♀♀♀ 8
● Amarone della Valpolicella Cl. '03	♀♀ 8
● Recioto della Valpolicella Cl. '06	♀♀ 7
● Valpolicella Sup. Cà del Laito '04	♀♀ 5
● Valpolicella Cl. Sup. TB '05	♀♀ 6
● L'Errante '04	♀ 7
● Recioto della Valpolicella Cl. BG '03	♀♀♀ 7
● Recioto della Valpolicella Cl. TB '99	♀♀♀ 8
● Recioto della Valpolicella Cl. TB '98	♀♀♀ 8
● Recioto della Valpolicella Cl. TB '97	♀♀♀ 8
● Recioto della Valpolicella Cl. TB '95	♀♀♀ 8
● Amarone della Valpolicella Cl. '04	♀♀ 8
● Amarone della Valpolicella Cl. TB '04	♀♀ 8
● Amarone della Valpolicella Cl. TB Vign. Alto '04	♀♀ 8

● Amarone della Valpolicella Cl. Vign. di Ravazzol '05	♀♀ 7
● Recioto della Valpolicella Cl. Vign. Le Tordare '06	♀♀ 6
● Valpolicella Cl. Sup. Campo Casal Vegri '07	♀♀ 5
● Amarone della Valpolicella Cl. '05	♀ 6
● Amarone della Valpolicella Cl. Vign. di Ravazzol '04	♀♀ 7
● Amarone della Valpolicella Cl. Vign. di Ravazzol '03	♀♀ 7
● Amarone della Valpolicella Cl. Vign. di Ravazzol '00	♀♀ 7
● Valpolicella Cl. Sup. Campo Casal Vegri '06	♀♀ 5
● Valpolicella Cl. Sup. Campo Casal Vegri '04	♀♀ 5
● Valpolicella Cl. Sup. Campo Casal Vegri '03	♀♀ 5

Ca' Lustra

LOC. FAEDO
VIA SAN PIETRO, 50
35030 CINTO EUGANEO [PD]
TEL. 042994128
www.calustra.it

CELLAR SALES
PRE-BOOKED VISITS

ANNUAL PRODUCTION 200,000 bottles
HECTARES UNDER VINE 38
VITICULTURE METHOD Conventional

Franco Zanovello is a leading figure in the Colli Euganei. For over two decades, the quality of his products has helped raise the image of the zone and he has been a model for an increasing number of young producers following the same path. Ca' Lustra stands out for its dependable quality and the remarkable value for money of both the simpler wines and the selections, thanks to masterly interpretation of the terroir and a profound knowledge of its marvellous complexity.

Merlot Sassonero '07 and Cabernet Girapoggio '06 did well again. The former shows good, complex aromas with fruitiness and vegetal sensations on the nose, and a solid, juicily taut palate, while the nose of the Cabernet is slightly closed, with light minerally sensations, followed by a fruity, dynamic palate. The Fior d'Arancio Passito '07 has a Mediterranean profile with rich aromas and explosive sweetness, supported by tangy acidity, more than enough to bring home Three Glasses. The Manzoni Bianco '08 and Moscato Secco 'A Cengia '08 are both very good.

Ca' Orologio

VIA CA' OROLOGIO, 7A
35030 BAONE [PD]
TEL. 042950099
www.caorologio.com

CELLAR SALES
PRE-BOOKED VISITS
VISITOR FACILITIES

ANNUAL PRODUCTION 27,000 bottles
HECTARES UNDER VINE 12
VITICULTURE METHOD Organic certified

Ca' Orologio is situated at Baone, in the extreme south of the Colli Euganei, and is managed with great enthusiasm by Maria Gioia Rosellini with the assistance of Roberto Cipresso. The vineyards are organically farmed and the warm, Mediterranean climate in this area ripens the grapes well, guaranteeing generous, mouthwatering wines with fragrant fruit. Although Ca' Orologio is quite a young operation, it is establishing itself year after year as a benchmark for the area.

The Relógio '07, from carmenère with a dash of cabernet sauvignon, is generous and very richly extracted. The well-rounded nose ranges from red berries to fines herbes and dried flowers, without forgetting minerally and spicy hints. Creamy, savoury and well-textured on the palate, it gains harmony from it well-honed tannins. The Calaòne '07, a merlot-heavy Bordeaux blend, has complex minerally aromas that open out slowly and a youthful, solid, densely textured palate. The Salaròla '08, a blend of moscato and tocai, is very good while the Lunisòle '07 is fruity and approachable.

O Colli Euganei Fior d'Arancio Passito '07	♔♔♔ 5	
● Colli Euganei Cabernet Girapoggio '06	♔♔ 5	
● Colli Euganei Merlot Sassonero '07	♔♔ 5	
● Colli Euganei Cabernet '07	♔♔ 4*	
O Colli Euganei Chardonnay Roverello '07	♔♔ 4	
O Manzoni Bianco Pedevenda '08	♔♔ 4*	
O Moscato Secco 'A Cengia '08	♔♔ 4*	
O Colli Euganei Bianco '08	♔ 3	
● Colli Euganei Merlot '07	♔ 3	
O Colli Euganei Pinot Bianco '08	♔ 4	
O Sauvignon Olivetani '08	♔ 4	
● Colli Euganei Cabernet Girapoggio '05	♔♔♔ 5	
● Colli Euganei Merlot Sassonero Villa Alessi '05	♔♔♔ 5	
● Colli Euganei Cabernet Girapoggio Villa Alessi '04	♔♔ 5	
● Colli Euganei Cabernet Girapoggio Villa Alessi '03	♔♔ 5	
O Colli Euganei Fior d'Arancio Passito Villa Alessi '05	♔♔ 4	

● Relógio '07	♔♔♔ 5	
● Colli Euganei Rosso Calaóne '07	♔♔ 5	
O Salaróla '08	♔♔ 4*	
● Lunisóle '07	♔ 5	
● Colli Euganei Rosso Calaóne '05	♔♔♔ 5*	
● Relógio '06	♔♔♔ 5	
● Relógio '04	♔♔♔ 5*	
● Colli Euganei Rosso Calaóne '06	♔♔ 5	
● Colli Euganei Rosso Calaóne '04	♔♔ 4*	
● Colli Euganei Rosso Calaóne '03	♔♔ 5	
● Lunisóle '05	♔♔ 5	
● Relógio '03	♔♔ 5	
O Salaróla '07	♔♔ 4*	
O Salaróla '06	♔♔ 4	
O Salarola '04	♔♔ 4*	

Ca' Rugate

VIA PERGOLA, 36
37030 MONTECCHIA DI CROSARA [VR]
TEL. 0456176328
www.carugate.it

CELLAR SALES
PRE-BOOKED VISITS

ANNUAL PRODUCTION 450,000 bottles
HECTARES UNDER VINE 50
VITICULTURE METHOD Conventional

Soave is undoubtedly one of Italy's leading zones. Every year, it produces some of the country's most impressive wines. For ten years now, Ca' Rugate has been deeply committed to promoting this DOC, thanks to the Tessaris' ability to identify precisely what is needed in the vineyard and cellar. For the Tessaris, external consultancy is not a short-cut. It's a way to acquire greater awareness of the winery's development potential. The results, as they do every year, speak for themselves.

Starting with the whites, obviously, there are two memorable versions of Monte Alto and Monte Fiorentine, the former aged in oak and the other in stainless steel. The '08 Monte Fiorentine has clear-cut, fresh aromas reflected nicely on the palate with confidently vibrant acidity. The same weight on the palate is there in the Monte Alto '07, although the profile is slightly broader and more delicate. Recioto di Soave La Perlara '07 gives a very classy performance with deep aromas and harmony, while the Soave San Michele '08 is fresh and mouthwatering. The reds are also excellent, especially the Campo Lavei '07 and Amarone '05.

Cambrago

FRAZ. SAN ZENO
VIA CAMBRAGO, 7
37030 COLOGNOLA AI COLLI [VR]
TEL. 0457650745
www.cambrago.it

CELLAR SALES
PRE-BOOKED VISITS

ANNUAL PRODUCTION 120,000 bottles
HECTARES UNDER VINE 14
VITICULTURE METHOD Conventional

Cambrago is a lovely estate at Colognola ai Colli, in the extreme west of the designated zone. Most of the vineyards are in the Classico zone, again in the western area, where basalt-based soil gradually gives way to limestone and tufaceous rock. Bruno Fasoli runs the vineyards and cellar, aided by winemaker Flavio Prà, while partner Cesare Sambugaro is in charge of marketing. Over 100,000 bottles are produced annually, all made from estate-grown grapes.

The Soave Vigne Maiores '08 comes from vineyards in the countryside, on gravelly, alluvial soil. This white wine is the jauntiest, most approachable expression of the type but manages to avoid appearing banal. The more ambitious and well typed Soave Classico I Cerceni '08 originates from hillside vineyards near Costeggiola. Deep aromas ranging from fruit to minerally sensations are the prelude to a dry, medium-bodied and very flavoursome wine. I Cerceni '05, from corvina and merlot, is interesting and the Recioto '05 has generous, Mediterranean aromas.

O Recioto di Soave La Perlara '07	♟♟♟	6
O Soave Cl. Monte Fiorentine '08	♟♟♟	4*
● Amarone della Valpolicella '05	♟♟	8
O Soave Cl. Sup. Monte Alto '07	♟♟	4*
● Valpolicella Sup. Campo Lavei '07	♟♟	5
● Recioto della Valpolicella L'Eremita '07	♟♟	6
O Soave Cl. San Michele '08	♟♟	3*
● Valpolicella Rio Albo '08	♟♟	3*
O Soave Cl. Monte Fiorentine '07	♟♟♟	4*
O Soave Cl. Monte Fiorentine '06	♟♟♟	4*
O Soave Cl. Monte Fiorentine '05	♟♟♟	4*
O Soave Cl. Monte Fiorentine '04	♟♟♟	4*
O Soave Cl. Sup. Bucciato '99	♟♟♟	4
O Soave Cl. Sup. Monte Alto '00	♟♟♟	4
O Soave Cl. Sup. Monte Alto '96	♟♟♟	4

● I Cerceni '05	♟♟	5
O Recioto di Soave I Cerceni '05	♟♟	6
O Soave Cl. I Cerceni '08	♟♟	4*
O Soave Vigne Maiores '08	♟	3*
O Recioto di Soave I Cerceni '04	♟♟	6
O Recioto di Soave I Cerceni '03	♟♟	6
O Soave Cl. Sup. I Cerceni Alti '03	♟♟	4
O Soave Cl. I Cerceni '07	♟♟	4*
O Soave Cl. I Cerceni '06	♟♟	3*
O Soave Cl. I Cerceni '05	♟♟	4
O Soave Vigne Maiores '07	♟♟	3*

Giuseppe Campagnola

FRAZ. VALGATARA
VIA AGNELLA, 9
37020 MARANO DI VALPOLICELLA [VR]
TEL. 0457703900
www.campagnola.com

CELLAR SALES
PRE-BOOKED VISITS

ANNUAL PRODUCTION **4.800,000 bottles**
HECTARES UNDER VINE **110**
VITICULTURE METHOD **Conventional**

Judging by the numbers above this profile, you might imagine a typical huge estate bottling wines that follow the market demands. But Giuseppe Campagnola has close links to the territory and focuses on high quality traditional bottles, especially from the valley where the winery is situated. His interests extend from Valpolicella to Lake Garda, where he has taken over an estate with plans to promote the traditional Bardolino DOC zone in the province of Verona.

The most interesting wines come from Valpolicella, with the Caterina Zardini line consisting of an Amarone and a Valpolicella. The former is generous, with intense wild berry and spice aromas, and a solid, dry palate. The other is subtle and succulent rather than powerful, showcasing the characteristics of the Marano valley. The wines from the Le Bine line are also well typed, with a fruity, well-rounded Valpolicella '07 and a Soave '08 with a strikingly tropical, fruity profile. We would also point out the nicely typed Recioto '07 and a beautifully made sweet fortified red wine.

I Campi

VIA, SARMAZZA, 29 A
37032 MONTEFORTE D'ALPONE [VR]
TEL. 0456175915
www.icampi.it

ANNUAL PRODUCTION **20,000 bottles**
HECTARES UNDER VINE **12**
VITICULTURE METHOD **Conventional**

In just two years, Flavio Prà has established I Campi as one of the most interesting new wineries in the Soave DOC zone, where the number of good quality producers is growing. Although Flavio works in nearby Valpolicella, with excellent results, his most significant results come from the volcanic hills of Soave thanks to meticulous viticulture supervised personally by his father Sergio, and a sensitivity in the cellar, where technology aids rather than overpowers nature.

The three wines produced are named after their vineyards of origin in great hillside locations. The excellent Soave Classico Campo Vulcano '08 shows sophisticated aromas and mouthwatering progression that has good body and grip. Extraordinary today, this wine will still improve with further bottle ageing. The reds, Valpolicella Superiore Campo Prognare '05 and Amarone Campo Marna '04, are more imposing with rich fruity sensations, each highlighting powerful body nicely supported by tannins and acidity. These are poised, very drinkable wines.

● Amarone della Valpolicella Cl. Caterina Zardini '05	♟♟ 7
● Valpolicella Cl. Sup. Caterina Zardini '07	♟♟ 5
● Amarone della Valpolicella Cl. '06	♟♟ 6
● Il Fortificato di Giuseppe Campagnola	♟♟ 7
● Recioto della Valpolicella Cl. Casotto del Merlo '07	♟♟ 6
○ Soave Cl. Vign. Monte Foscarino Le Bine '08	♟♟ 4
● Valpolicella Cl. Sup. Ripasso Vign. di Purano Le Bine '07	♟♟ 4*
⊙ Bardolino Cl. Chiaretto Roccolo del Lago '08	♟ 4
● Bardolino Cl. Roccolo del Lago '08	♟ 4
● Amarone della Valpolicella Cl. Caterina Zardini '04	♟♟♟ 7
● Valpolicella Cl. Sup. Caterina Zardini '06	♟♟ 5

○ Soave Cl. Campo Vulcano '08	♟♟♟ 5
● Amarone della Valpolicella Campo Marna '04	♟♟ 8
● Valpolicella Cl. Campo Prognare '05	♟♟ 8
● Amarone della Valpolicella Campo Marna '03	♟♟ 8
○ Soave Cl. Campo Vulcano '07	♟♟ 5
● Valpolicella Cl. Campo Prognare '04	♟♟ 8

Canevel Spumanti

LOC. SACCOL
VIA ROCCAT E FERRARI, 17
31049 VALDOBBIADENE [TV]
TEL. 0423975940
www.canevel.it

CELLAR SALES
PRE-BOOKED VISITS

ANNUAL PRODUCTION **600,000 bottles**
HECTARES UNDER VINE **12**
VITICULTURE METHOD **Conventional**

For years, Canevel has been one of the benchmark wineries for sparkler in this large Treviso DOC and around the world. Over half a million bottles a year are obtained from grapes grown on the estate's dozen or so hectares, or bought in from local growers, a widespread practice in this area. The grapes are vinified in the beautiful cellar at Saccol, which releases mainly sparkling wines under various labels according to their sugar content.

Il Millesimato was one of the first selections from this area and has always been one of the most intriguing wines in the whole DOC zone. Clear-cut, fruity aromas are the prelude to harmonious and very tangy experience of the impressive, engaging palate. Also very good is the Vigneto del Faé, another Extra Dry, which shows more delicate expression on the nose but a gutsier palate. The Cartizze is different again, thanks to more residual sugar and tropical fruit. The remaining wines are dependable and beautifully made, particularly the third Extra Dry.

La Cappuccina

FRAZ. COSTALUNGA
VIA SAN BRIZIO, 125
37032 MONTEFORTE D'ALPONE [VR]
TEL. 0456175036
www.lacappuccina.it

CELLAR SALES
PRE-BOOKED VISITS
FOOD

ANNUAL PRODUCTION **260,000 bottles**
HECTARES UNDER VINE **33**
VITICULTURE METHOD **Organic certified**

The Tessari family, consisting of Elena, Pietro and Sisto – in strict alphabetical order – run the family estate in the eastern part of the Soave DOC zone with considerable skill. Since the earliest years of activity, they have demonstrated great sensitivity in the production of their wines and in the management of their organically farmed vineyards. These are mainly located on the plains but the care and attention with which they are groomed results in very sound products.

Having missed the mark a few times, the Soave Fontégo '08 is back on impressive form and nearly went to our final tastings. Subtle, fascinating aromas of flowers and apple and pear fruit precede a well-rounded palate that stays supple and taut. The lean, juicy and very enjoyable Soave '08 is even more impressive, considering its price and the numbers released. Arzìmo Passito '07 shows its usual class while the reds include a generous, taut Campo Buri '06, made from cabernet franc and oseleta, and an increasingly subtle, harmonious Madégo '08, a Bordeaux blend that is very easy to like.

○ Cartizze	ΨΨ 6
○ P. di Valdobbiadene Extra Dry Il Millesimato '08	ΨΨ 5
○ P. di Valdobbiadene Extra Dry Vign. del Faé	ΨΨ 4*
○ P. di Valdobbiadene Brut	Ψ 4
○ P. di Valdobbiadene Extra Dry	Ψ 4
○ P. di Valdobbiadene Frizzante Vign. S. Biagio	Ψ 4

○ Arzìmo Passito '07	ΨΨ 5
● Campo Buri '06	ΨΨ 5
● Carmenos Passito '07	ΨΨ 5
○ Soave '08	ΨΨ 3*
○ Soave Fontégo '08	ΨΨ 4
● Madégo '08	Ψ 4
○ Sauvignon '08	Ψ 4
○ Soave San Brizio '07	Ψ 4
○ Arzìmo Passito '02	ΨΨ 5
● Campo Buri '05	ΨΨ 5
● Campo Buri '02	ΨΨ 5
○ Soave Fontégo '04	ΨΨ 4
○ Soave Fontégo '03	ΨΨ 4*
○ Soave San Brizio '04	ΨΨ 4*
○ Soave San Brizio '03	ΨΨ 4
○ Soave San Brizio '02	ΨΨ 4
○ Soave San Brizio '06	ΨΨ 4

Casa Cecchin

VIA AGUGLIANA, 11
36054 MONTEBELLO VICENTINO [VI]
TEL. 0444649610
www.casacecchin.it

ANNUAL PRODUCTION **25,000 bottles**
HECTARES UNDER VINE **6**
VITICULTURE METHOD **Conventional**

The Gambellara DOC in Veneto is less well known than nearby Soave and has lower production figures. However, the premises for progress are all present: good volcanic soil, excellent temperature variations, well-ventilated conditions to promote healthy grapes, and the versatile garganega variety, which faithfully reflects its terroir. Casa Cecchin, where Roberta and her father Renato work with garganega and durella from nearby Lessinia, is feeling its way forward. This small winery has good potential for development and is one of the most interesting new estates in this area today.

The few hectares of vineyards around the winery at an altitude of 250 to 300 metres produce an excellent Durello Metodo Classico '04. It has interesting floral and biscuity aromas and a palate which reflects the dry, incisive character of the grape. The still version further emphasizes this personality with vegetal and white-fleshed fruits aromatics following through on the solid, mouthwateringly husky palate. Turning to Gambellara, the La Guarda '07, released after one year's ageing, gives a good performance with its generous, invigorating character.

O Gambellara Cl. La Guarda '07	♟♟	3*
O Lessini Durello Brut M. Cl. '04	♟♟	4*
O Lessini Durello Sup. '08	♟♟	3*
O Gambellara Cl. '08	♟	3
O Lessini Durello Brut M. Cl. '03	♟♟	4*

Casa Roma

VIA ORMELLE, 19
31020 SAN POLO DI PIAVE [TV]
TEL. 0422855339
www.casaroma.com

CELLAR SALES
PRE-BOOKED VISITS

ANNUAL PRODUCTION **200,000 bottles**
HECTARES UNDER VINE **28.15**
VITICULTURE METHOD **Conventional**

It is not easy to work in an area like the Piave DOC zone, with its small and large estates producing wines that are often all standard labels from merlot and cabernet, the most widely planted and over-produced varieties in the country. In Piave, however, they have been grown for over a century. Skilled grape farmers like Adriano and Luigi Peruzzetto have been able to work with them alongside the traditional raboso grape. While the simpler products put the accent on easy approachability, the Raboso is a more serious proposition, revealing the estate's authentic and much more intriguing side.

he 2005 Raboso has a reserved character with red berry and medicinal herb aromas slow to emerge. The palate is bolder, giving assertive acidity and austere extract on the gutsy, long-lingering palate. The two most ambitious whites are very interesting. San Dordi '08 is a Manzoni Bianco which ages slowly on the fine lees to emerge vibrant and citrussy with floral aromas and a solid, racy palate. The Marzemina Bianca '08 is even more unusual, with original aromas of olives and Mediterranean scrubland, and a rounded, harmonious palate.

O Marzemina Bianca '08	♟♟	3*
● Piave Raboso '05	♟♟	5
O San Dordi '08	♟♟	4*
O Manzoni Bianco '08	♟	3*
● Piave Cabernet Sauvignon '08	♟	3
● Piave Carmenère '08	♟	3
● Piave Merlot '08	♟	3
O Piave Pinot Grigio '08	♟	3
● Piave Raboso '04	♟♟	5
● Piave Raboso '03	♟♟	5
● Piave Raboso '02	♟♟	5
● Piave Raboso '01	♟♟	5
● Raboso Passito Callarghe '03	♟♟	6
O San Dordi '07	♟♟	4
O San Dordi '06	♟♟	4
O San Dordi '04	♟♟	4
O Vinegia '07	♟♟	3*

Michele Castellani

FRAZ. VALGATARA
VIA GRANDA, 1
37020 MARANO DI VALPOLICELLA [VR]
TEL. 0457701253
www.castellanimichele.it

CELLAR SALES
PRE-BOOKED VISITS

ANNUAL PRODUCTION **300,000 bottles**
HECTARES UNDER VINE **48**
VITICULTURE METHOD **Conventional**

Sergio Castellani's winery, where his children have also worked for a number of years now, is a reliable operation that impresses us at every tasting. The range presented was quite limited and included only the more important types, notably Amarone and Recioto, interpreted in a style that reflects the estate's trademark pursuit of power. Over the years, the vineyards have expanded so Sergio is able to carry out rigorous selection of the grapes used in these wines, which are from the Ca' del Pipa and I Castei lines.

Recioto Monte Fasenara '07, from the I Castei line, is a red with vibrant wild berry and cherry aromas, and oak which is still not fully absorbed. The palate is explosively sweet but the tannins and acidity keep it firmly on track. The same wine from the Ca' del Pipa line is only slightly inferior, showing equally generous but a little less exciting on the nose. Of the two Amarones, the Campo Casalin '05 stands out for its decadent style and the Ca' del Pipa '05 for its solid but still oak-marked body. The Valpolicella '07 is compact and mature.

Cantina del Castello

CORTE PITTORA, 5
37038 SOAVE [VR]
TEL. 0457680093
www.cantinacastello.it

CELLAR SALES
PRE-BOOKED VISITS

ANNUAL PRODUCTION **130,000 bottles**
HECTARES UNDER VINE **12**
VITICULTURE METHOD **Conventional**

Despite the wine sector's fast-paced progress in the last 30 years, some estates have managed not to lose their bearings, modernizing without losing sight of their origins and staying faithful to the territory. One such operation is Cantina del Castello, owned by Arturo Stocchetti, a winery that has stayed true to a subtle, restrained interpretation of Soave. While the bottled wine remains strongly classic in style, the vineyards have undergone profound transformation to improve the quality of the vine stock and the grapes it produces.

Soave Classico Castello '08 is emblematic of the house style, with subtle aromatics and an unpretentious, enjoyable palate. It is no coincidence that this may be the most popular Soave in town. The Soave Classico Pressoni '08 is a logical stylistic evolution of its younger brother, with slow-to-emerge, layered aromas that show new facets instead of the usual fruit and flowers, supported on the palate by elegance and succulence. The Soave Classico Carniga '07 has been aged for longer and reveals appreciable complexity and austerity.

● Recioto della Valpolicella Cl. Monte Fasenara I Castei '07	♟	7
● Amarone della Valpolicella Cl. Campo Casalin I Castei '05	♟	7
● Amarone della Valpolicella Cl. Le Vigne Ca' del Pipa '05	♟	8
● Recioto della Valpolicella Cl. Le Vigne Ca' del Pipa '06	♟	7
● Valpolicella Cl. Sup. Ripasso Costamaran I Castei '07	♟	5
● Amarone della Valpolicella Cl. Campo Casalin I Castei '04	♟♟	7
● Amarone della Valpolicella Cl. Le Vigne Ca' del Pipa '04	♟♟	7
● Recioto della Valpolicella Cl. Le Vigne Ca' del Pipa '05	♟♟	7
● Recioto della Valpolicella Cl. Monte Fasenara I Castei '06	♟♟	7

○ Soave Cl. Pressoni '08	♟♟	4*
○ Soave Cl. Carniga '07	♟♟	5
○ Soave Cl. Castello '08	♟♟	4
○ Soave Cl. Sup. Monte Pressoni '01	♟♟♟	4
○ Soave Cl. Carniga '04	♟♟	4*
○ Soave Cl. Pressoni '07	♟♟	4
○ Soave Cl. Pressoni '06	♟♟	4*
○ Soave Cl. Pressoni '05	♟♟	4*
○ Soave Cl. Pressoni '04	♟♟	4*

Cavalchina

FRAZ. CUSTOZA
LOC. CAVALCHINA
VIA SOMMACAMPAGNA, 7
37066 SOMMACAMPAGNA [VR]
TEL. 045516002
www.cavalchina.com

CELLAR SALES
PRE-BOOKED VISITS

ANNUAL PRODUCTION **240,000 bottles**
HECTARES UNDER VINE **26**
VITICULTURE METHOD **Conventional**

The work of Franco and Luciano Piona is increasingly challenging as they focus on three fronts: the traditional family winery at Custoza, producing the DOC's classic wines; the Prendina estate near Modena, where the more modern, structured wines are sourced; and the new venture in Valpolicella, which is still being fine-tuned but looks set for excellence. Franco and Luciano also continue to experiment every year striving to produce wines that are ever closer to their ideals of quality and land-rootedness.

The Amedeo '07 is on its customary fine form. This fantastic wine has changed the reputation of Custoza, once known only for its undemanding, moreish wines. But the Pionas' have achieved complex aromas and a mouthwatering palate that is anything but commonplace. The Garda Garganega Paroni '07 is very good, with vibrant aromas and an edgy palate despite its full body. The two Valpolicella wines are also improving, with generous fruity hints and a solid body supported by succulent acidity. From the rest of the long list, we recommend the wonderful sweet rosé, La Rosa '08 and the gutsy Sauvignon Valbruna '07.

Domenico Cavazza & F.lli

C.DA SELVA, 22
36054 MONTEBELLO VICENTINO [VI]
TEL. 0444649166
www.cavazzawine.com

CELLAR SALES
PRE-BOOKED VISITS

ANNUAL PRODUCTION **1,000,000 bottles**
HECTARES UNDER VINE **150**
VITICULTURE METHOD **Conventional**

For years now, the Cavazza family's winery has been dedicated to developing two areas with great potential that has rather failed to find expression, both in the province of Vicenza. Gambellara, with its volcanic soil and garganega grape, is one and the other is Colli Berici, a zone highly suited to red grapes, especially Bordeaux varieties. The range presented is quite extensive and includes both quaffable and more ambitious wines that keep the natural drinkability that characterizes bottles from Veneto.

At a time of worldwide economic crisis, it is a pleasure to discover a wine like the Gambellara Classico La Bocara '08, perhaps the best ever from the Cavazza family. The aromas are vibrant and clearly defined in a mouthwatering wine that combines rounded body with simplicity at an excellent price. The Recioto '07 is very good, with more intense, mature aromas although it too is very drinkable despite its considerable sugar content. The Gambellara Classico Creari '07 has depth while the Colli Berici reds are very sound and poised on the palate.

○ Custoza Sup. Amedeo '07	♀♀♀ 4*
○ Garda Garganega Paroni La Prendina '07	♀♀ 4*
○ Bianco di Custoza '08	♀♀ 4*
● Garda Cabernet Sauvignon Vign. Il Falcone La Prendina '06	♀♀ 5
○ Garda Sauvignon Valbruna La Prendina '07	♀♀ 4*
☉ La Rosa Passito '08	♀♀ 4
● Valpolicella Sup. Morari Terre d'Orti '07	♀♀ 5
● Valpolicella Sup. Terre d'Orti '07	♀♀ 5
● Bardolino '08	♀ 4
☉ Bardolino Chiaretto '08	♀ 4
● Bardolino Sup. S. Lucia '08	♀ 4
☉ Feniletto La Prendina '07	♀ 4
● Garda Merlot Faial La Prendina '06	♀ 6
○ Custoza Sup. Amedeo '06	♀♀♀ 4*

● Colli Berici Cabernet Cicogna '07	♀♀ 5
● Colli Berici Merlot Cicogna '07	♀♀ 5
○ Gambellara Cl. Creari '07	♀♀ 4
○ Gambellara Cl. La Bocara '08	♀♀ 4*
○ Recioto di Gambellara Cl. Capitel S. Libera '07	♀♀ 6
● Syrhae Cicogna '07	♀♀ 5
● Colli Berici Cabernet Cicogna '06	♀♀ 5
● Colli Berici Cabernet Cicogna '03	♀♀ 5
● Colli Berici Merlot Cicogna '06	♀♀ 5
● Colli Berici Merlot Cicogna '05	♀♀ 5
● Colli Berici Merlot Cicogna '04	♀♀ 5
○ Recioto di Gambellara Cl. Capitel S. Libera '06	♀♀ 6

Giorgio Cecchetto

FRAZ. TEZZE DI PIAVE
VIA PIAVE, 67
31020 VAZZOLA [TV]
TEL. 043828598
www.rabosopiave.com

CELLAR SALES
PRE-BOOKED VISITS

ANNUAL PRODUCTION **220,000 bottles**
HECTARES UNDER VINE **60**
VITICULTURE METHOD **Conventional**

For some years now, Giorgio Cecchetto's winery has been committed to promoting the Piave DOC zone, which extends from the Treviso foothills to the plains that reach down to the upper Adriatic coast. This extensive zone has one variety at its heart: raboso, a tricky and troublesome grape which seems to be flourishing today thanks to the efforts of growers like Giorgio. The estate's vineyard holding has increased considerably in recent years with new plantings of international varieties, which have been present in the area for over a century, as well as raboso.

The most impressive wines in the range are the Raboso '05, with vibrant wild berry and aromatic herb aromas and a mouthwatering palate with nicely integrated varietal acidity, and Sante '07, a Merlot with impressively generous aromas that follow through on a palate that opens out with substance and agility. Making its debut is the Carmenère '08, a new addition to the DOC. It's a red that gives fresher, more relaxed sensations, just like the Cabernet Sauvignon and Pinot Grigio, both from '08, while the Manzoni, also '08, is fragrant and very drinkable.

Coffele

VIA ROMA, 5
37038 SOAVE [VR]
TEL. 0457680007
www.coffele.it

CELLAR SALES
PRE-BOOKED VISITS

ANNUAL PRODUCTION **110,000 bottles**
HECTARES UNDER VINE **25**
VITICULTURE METHOD **Conventional**

The Soave DOC allows for different interpretations since the soil ranges from limestone to basalt, tufaceous rock and clay in the space of a few metres, and the local garganega grape is able to capture these subtleties. Alberto and Chiara Coffele's skill in interpreting Castelcerino, with its 25 hectares of vineyards, comes out in the way they coax nature along rather than contrast it. Their efforts focus on the production of subtle wines with very elegantly expressed aromas that showcase the differences and variations from vintage to vintage.

Tasting Soave Classico Ca' Visco '08 tells you what this area is about. Its subtle, sophisticated aromas are dominated by marked florality with apple and pear fruit peeking through in the background, framed by fines herbes and minerally hints. The delicate palate is supported by mouthwatering acidity. The Recioto di Soave Classico Le Sponde '07, a type on which the Coffeles lavish special attention, is livelier with an explosion of fruit and spices, bringing acidity to bear to contrast the mouthfilling sweetness. Soave Classico Alzari '07 is excellent while the Soave Classico '08 is mouthwatering and satisfying.

● Piave Merlot Sante '07	♈♈ 4
● Piave Raboso '05	♈♈ 5
○ Manzoni Bianco '08	♈ 3
● Piave Cabernet Sauvignon '08	♈ 3
● Piave Carmenère '08	♈ 3
○ Piave Pinot Grigio '08	♈ 3
● Piave Merlot Sante '05	♈♈ 4
● Piave Merlot Sante '03	♈♈ 5
● Piave Raboso '04	♈♈ 5
● Piave Raboso '03	♈♈ 5
● Piave Raboso Gelsaia '05	♈♈ 6

○ Recioto di Soave Cl. Le Sponde '07	♈♈ 6
○ Soave Cl. Alzari '07	♈♈ 5
○ Soave Cl. Ca' Visco '08	♈♈ 4*
○ Soave Cl. '08	♈♈ 4*
○ Soave Cl. Ca' Visco '05	♈♈♈ 4*
○ Soave Cl. Ca' Visco '04	♈♈♈ 4
○ Soave Cl. Ca' Visco '03	♈♈♈ 4
○ Recioto di Soave Cl. Le Sponde '06	♈♈ 6
○ Recioto di Soave Cl. Le Sponde '05	♈♈ 6
○ Recioto di Soave Cl. Le Sponde '04	♈♈ 6
○ Soave Cl. Ca' Visco '07	♈♈ 4*
○ Soave Cl. Ca' Visco '06	♈♈ 4*

Col Vetoraz

FRAZ. SANTO STEFANO
S.DA DELLE TRESIESE, 1
31040 VALDOBBIADENE [TV]
TEL. 0423975291
www.colvetoraz.it

CELLAR SALES
PRE-BOOKED VISITS

ANNUAL PRODUCTION **800,000 bottles**
HECTARES UNDER VINE **12**
VITICULTURE METHOD **Conventional**

Col Vetoraz, an estate able to maintain an extraordinary high level of quality in its wines vintage after vintage, never misses the mark. There are only a dozen or so hectares under vine, which is still above the average for this DOC, but it is the working relationship with local growers that makes the difference, enabling the cellar to vinify quantities far superior to what eventually goes into bottle as Col Vetoraz. Loris Dall'Acqua, the cellar manager, is able to make rigorous selections from the base wines, using only the best batches for the house label.

Obviously, the range focuses on prosecco-based sparkling wines, and outstanding among these every year is the Dry Millesimato. The '08 is a strikingly fruity and floral wine, which shows succulent and supple on the palate. The Brut is one of the most interesting of its type in the DOC, especially for its palate which mirrors the apple and pear fruit on the nose with good body and tangy, biting acidity. The Cartizze is heady and Moraio '02 is a good Bordeaux blend that is not produced every year.

Conte Collalto

VIA 24 MAGGIO, 1
31058 SUSEGANA [TV]
TEL. 0438738241
www.cantine-collalto.it

CELLAR SALES
PRE-BOOKED VISITS
VISITOR FACILITIES

ANNUAL PRODUCTION **800,000 bottles**
HECTARES UNDER VINE **135**
VITICULTURE METHOD **Conventional**

After crossing the Piave river at Ponte della Priula and continuing northwards, you'll glimpse the Conti Collalto castle on top of one of the many hills surrounded by olive groves and, here and there, vineyards. On this extensive property, the vines occupy only the best-suited slopes, with the remaining land left for fields and woodlands. Prosecco is the warhorse of the estate's list, as often happens around here, but there are plenty of red varieties to extend a range that is considerable range, if somewhat reduced in comparison to previous years.

Only one red wine was presented, Piave Cabernet Torrai Riserva '05, which is strikingly classic with generous aromas in which fruit is just one component along with flowers, medicinal herbs and spices. The palate is not particularly powerful but tempts the drinker almost on tiptoe with subtly savouriness and smooth tannins. The two Proseccos are both good, although our tasters preferred the Dry, which has more generous aromas and a succulent palate. The other whites are undemanding and very enjoyable.

○ Cartizze	♟♟ 6
● Moraio Rosso '02	♟♟ 5
○ P. di Valdobbiadene Brut	♟♟ 4*
○ P. di Valdobbiadene Dry Millesimato '08	♟♟ 4
○ Brut Longo	♟ 5
○ P. di Valdobbiadene Extra Dry	♟ 4

● Piave Cabernet Torrai Ris. '05	♟♟ 5
○ Chardonnay '08	♟ 3
○ Colli di Conegliano Bianco Schenella I '08	♟ 4
○ Manzoni Bianco '08	♟ 3
○ P. di Conegliano Brut	♟ 4
○ P. di Conegliano Dry Millesimato '08	♟ 4
○ Pinot Grigio '08	♟ 3
○ Colli di Conegliano Bianco Schenella I '06	♟♟ 3
● Incrocio Manzoni 2.15 '06	♟♟ 4
● Piave Cabernet Torrai Ris. '03	♟♟ 5
● Piave Cabernet Torrai Ris. '00	♟♟ 5
● Rambaldo VIII '03	♟♟ 5
● Wildbacher '05	♟♟ 3

Le Colture

FRAZ. SANTO STEFANO
VIA FOLLO, 5
31049 VALDOBBIADENE [TV]
TEL. 0423900192
www.lecolture.it

CELLAR SALES
PRE-BOOKED VISITS

ANNUAL PRODUCTION 520,000 bottles
HECTARES UNDER VINE 50
VITICULTURE METHOD Conventional

The Ruggeri family's estate is untypical, with an unusually extensive vineyard for the Valdobbiadene area. For this reason, near-total control of the production process is necessary and the results show improvement in quality, obviously, and in dependability. Despite the fact that in recent years nearby Montello has attracted more interest, red wine production has not yet really caught on here. This beautiful estate is situated in great wine country so the results will surely begin to arrive.

The range of products focuses on sparkling Prosecco, with four different labels according to area of origin and sugar content. The most impressive of these is the Cartizze, with a fruity nose and confidently mouthwatering, savoury palate showing convincingly creamy fizz and nicely balanced sweetness and acidity. Just a step behind is the Pianer, an Extra Dry with more explosive aromas and a gutsy, racy palate. Cruner and Faghèr are pleasant wines which express the subtly fruity aromas of Treviso's prosecco grape.

Corte Gardoni

LOC. GARDONI, 5
37067 VALEGGIO SUL MINCIO [VR]
TEL. 0457950382
www.cortegardoni.it

CELLAR SALES

ANNUAL PRODUCTION 200,000 bottles
HECTARES UNDER VINE 25
VITICULTURE METHOD Conventional

The Piccoli family's winery is classic, both in terms of the wine types produced – especially Bardolino and Custoza – and the house style, which is elegant and very approachably drinkable. The range is quite extensive but its mainstays are these two classic wines from the west of the province of Verona, with very respectable quantities and results. This is thanks to Gianni and his family, who have developed the winery without being swayed by passing trends and have tried instead to promote typicity and elegance.

The very sound Custoza Mael '08, in its third vintage, so impressed our tasters board that they gave it our highest accolade. The nose proffers the typical subtly elegant aromas of this lakeside DOC while the palate is solid, gutsy and lingering. As usual, the Bardolino Superiore Pradicà '07 is very good. It shows fruity and spicy, with a supple, nicely structured palate while Le Fontane '08 is simpler and more approachable, but just as good. Custoza Passito Fenili '07 fills the mouth, the Bardolino Chiaretto '08 is racy and the Becco Rosso '07, made from corvina, is savoury and graceful.

○ Cartizze	♟♟ 5
○ P. di Valdobbiadene Extra Dry Pianer	♟♟ 4
○ P. di Valdobbiadene Brut Faghèr	♟ 4
○ P. di Valdobbiadene Dry Cruner	♟ 4
○ Cartizze	♟♟ 5
○ Cartizze Dry	♟♟ 6
○ P. di Valdobbiadene Brut	♟♟ 2
○ P. di Valdobbiadene Dry cru di Funèr	♟♟ 3
○ P. di Valdobbiadene Dry Funer	♟♟ 3*
○ P. di Valdobbiadene Extra Dry	♟♟ 2
○ P. di Valdobbiadene Extra Dry	♟♟ 3*

○ Bianco di Custoza Mael '08	♟♟♟ 4*
● Bardolino Sup. Pradicà '07	♟♟ 5*
◉ Bardolino Chiaretto '08	♟♟ 3*
● Bardolino Le Fontane '08	♟♟ 3*
● Becco Rosso '07	♟♟ 4*
○ Bianco di Custoza Passito Fenili '07	♟♟ 6
○ Custoza '08	♟ 3
○ Nichesole Vallidium '07	♟ 4
● Rosso di Corte '06	♟ 5
◉ Bardolino Chiaretto '06	♟♟ 3*
● Bardolino Le Fontane '07	♟♟ 3*
● Bardolino Sup. '06	♟♟ 4
● Becco Rosso '06	♟♟ 4
○ Bianco di Custoza Mael '07	♟♟ 4
○ Bianco di Custoza Passito Fenili '06	♟♟ 6
● Rosso di Corte '05	♟♟ 5

Corte Rugolin

FRAZ. VALGATARA
LOC. RUGOLIN, 1
37020 MARANO DI VALPOLICELLA [VR]
TEL. 0457702153
www.corterugolin.it

CELLAR SALES
PRE-BOOKED VISITS

ANNUAL PRODUCTION **75,000 bottles**
HECTARES UNDER VINE **11**
VITICULTURE METHOD **Conventional**

In the last ten years, many Valpolicella wineries underwent cultural revolutions even before they revolutionized production, and Corte Rugolin is certainly one of these. Elena and Federico took up the reins of the winery founded by their father and re-invented it, following the trend for extensive renewal but without losing sight of their origins. Just over ten hectares of vineyards yield a well-groomed, nicely varied range with Valpolicella Superiore and two Amarones as its strong suits.

In the absence of Amarone Monte Danieli, the flagship of Corte Rugolin's range, we focused our attention on the Crosara de le Strie '05, an Amarone which deliberately seeks a more accessible profile with intensely fruity aromas and softness but good grip on the palate. The Ripasso '06 is an excellent red emphasizing the special features of the traditional varieties – generous aromas and spice – with a palate whose strongest component is acidity, and which manages to combine concentration and suppleness.

Corte Sant'Alda

LOC. FIOI
VIA CAPOVILLA, 28
37030 MEZZANE DI SOTTO [VR]
TEL. 0458880006
www.cortesantalda.it

CELLAR SALES
PRE-BOOKED VISITS

ANNUAL PRODUCTION **82,000 bottles**
HECTARES UNDER VINE **16.8**
VITICULTURE METHOD **Organic certified**

The success of Corte Sant'Alda wines originates from Marinella Camerani's firm belief that absolutely top quality can only be achieved through profound knowledge of the area, the site climate and the vineyards. Driven on by this idea, Marinella decided to carry out zoning studies on her 15 hectares of vineyards in order to focus on the relationship between environment and wines produced, thus enabling her to make better choices.

This year, the Valpolicella Superiore Mithas '06 was presented ahead of release since the 2005 vintage was skipped because of hail damage. The oak is still perceptible on the nose but sweet fruit and flower aromas slowly make their way through. The palate is powerful and shows texture despite the still-roughish tannins, suggesting good ageing potential. The Valpolicella Ca' Fiui '08 is nicely made and shows youthful headiness alongside charming aromas of spice and flowers. With its taut, mouthwatering palate, it is a lovely interpretation of a simple but characterful wine.

Corte Rugolin		
● Amarone della Valpolicella Cl. Crosara de le Strie '05	♀♀	7
● Valpolicella Cl. Sup. Ripasso '06	♀♀	5
● Valpolicella Cl. '08	♀	3
● Amarone della Valpolicella Cl. Crosara de le Strie '04	♀♀	6
● Amarone della Valpolicella Cl. Monte Danieli '03	♀♀	7
● Amarone della Valpolicella Cl. Monte Danieli '01	♀♀	7
● Amarone della Valpolicella Cl. Monte Danieli '00	♀♀	7
● Amarone della Valpolicella Cl. Monte Danieli '99	♀♀	7
● Valpolicella Cl. Sup. Ripasso '05	♀♀	5
● Valpolicella Cl. Sup. Ripasso '04	♀♀	5

Corte Sant'Alda		
● Valpolicella Sup. Mithas '06	♀♀	7
● Valpolicella Ca' Fiui '08	♀♀	4*
○ Soave V. di Mezzane '08	♀	4
● Amarone della Valpolicella '00	♀♀♀	8
● Amarone della Valpolicella '98	♀♀♀	8
● Amarone della Valpolicella '95	♀♀♀	8
● Amarone della Valpolicella '90	♀♀♀	8
● Amarone della Valpolicella Mithas '95	♀♀♀	8
● Valpolicella Sup. '03	♀♀♀	6
● Valpolicella Sup. Mithas '04	♀♀♀	7
● Amarone della Valpolicella '04	♀♀	8
● Amarone della Valpolicella '03	♀♀	8
● Amarone della Valpolicella Mithas '04	♀♀	8
● Amarone della Valpolicella Mithas '00	♀♀	8
● Recioto della Valpolicella '03	♀♀	6
● Valpolicella Sup. Mithas '03	♀♀	7

Casa Coste Piane

FRAZ. SANTO STEFANO
VIA COSTE PIANE, 2
31040 VALDOBBIADENE [TV]
TEL. 0423900219
casacostepiane@libero.it

ANNUAL PRODUCTION **50,000 bottles**
HECTARES UNDER VINE **6**
VITICULTURE METHOD **Conventional**

Loris Follador is a charismatic wine man with many interests. His curiosity has given him a thorough knowledge of the sector, beyond the confines of Valdobbiadene, and to deeper exploration of other, apparently far-removed, sectors like art. His winery has become a meeting point for many painters, sculptors, and poets who exchange ideas and opinions over glasses of wine. This independent, strong-willed man is behind the drive to relaunch the traditional Prosecco Sur Lie, which is the estate's war-horse today.

For those who don't know, Prosecco Sur Lie is a Prosecco which undergoes second fermentation in the spring and summer after the harvest, like a classic method wine. But the Sur Lie (French for on the yeasts), on the other hand, is never separated from the fine lees and never dosed, so that it remains completely dry. We like this wine's approachable, quaffable quality, and especially its simplicity, which is far from banal, a quality shared by very few wines. Tranquillo '08 is very solid and authentic while the San Venanzio is enjoyable.

○ P. di Valdobbiadene Frizzante Sur Lie	🍷🍷	4*
○ P. di Valdobbiadene Extra Dry San Venanzio	🍷	4
○ P. di Valdobbiadene Tranquillo '08	🍷	4

Costozza

FRAZ. COSTOZZA
P.ZZA DA SCHIO, 4
36023 LONGARE [VI]
TEL. 0444555099
www.costozza-villadaschio.it

CELLAR SALES
PRE-BOOKED VISITS
VISITOR FACILITIES

ANNUAL PRODUCTION **10,000 bottles**
HECTARES UNDER VINE **10**
VITICULTURE METHOD **Conventional**

The Colli Berici zone is the sleeping beauty of Veneto. It has extraordinary beauty and potential but unfortunately seems unable to live up to this and fulfil the possibilities of its image and products. The wineries which believe in this area and have established themselves as quality producers certainly include Giulio da Schio's estate, with its just over ten hectares in an enviable location. The cellar releases small quantities of absolutely sound wines, mainly reds.

This year, only two wines were presented but the results are extremely positive. The Cabernet Sauvignon '07 still shows very youthful, and sometimes heady, aromas that give way to ripe red berry fruit and pencil lead, which are nicely picked up on the taut, mouthwatering and full-bodied palate. The Colli Berici Cabernet '07 is of the same high standard, with the cabernet franc making its presence felt in a fresh peppery aroma that mingles with clear, crisp fruit. The palate opens out elegantly, making this a simple but extremely pleasant, long-lingering wine.

● Cabernet Sauvignon '07	🍷🍷	4
● Colli Berici Cabernet '07	🍷🍷	4
● Colli Berici Cabernet '06	YY	4
● Colli Berici Cabernet '04	YY	4
● Colli Berici Cabernet '03	YY	5
● Colli Berici Cabernet '02	YY	5
● Colli Berici Cabernet '01	YY	5
● Colli Berici Cabernet '00	YY	4
● Rosso Costozza '04	YY	5
● Rosso Costozza '03	YY	5
● Rosso Costozza '01	YY	5

★ Romano Dal Forno

FRAZ. CELLORE
LOC. LODOLETTA, 1
37030 ILLASI [VR]
TEL. 0457834923
www.dalforno.net

CELLAR SALES
PRE-BOOKED VISITS

ANNUAL PRODUCTION **45,000 bottles**
HECTARES UNDER VINE **25**
VITICULTURE METHOD **Conventional**

A wine producer's greatness can be judged from the wines he produces and the courageous choices he makes. This year, Romano Dal Forno has made one such brave choice. He had two superb wines available, the Amarone '04 and the Valpolicella '05, the only bottle from that vintage, but realized haste might lead to inferior results. Despite the challenging times, Romano decided to hold back release of these two wines and allow them further time to age in the bottles. Over the years, we have been able to observe how these wines develop and how interpretations and tastes have changed looking back over the releases of recent vintages. The wines evolve very slowly and we need to go back many growing years to find tertiary aromas, which shows how astonishingly long-lived they are. The same wines tasted last year seemed practically unchanged, as if no time had passed at all. The '90 is wonderful though, an alluring, still wonderfully sound proposition almost 20 years from the harvest.

Luigino Dal Maso

C.DA SELVA, 62
36054 MONTEBELLO VICENTINO [VI]
TEL. 0444649104
www.dalmasovini.com

CELLAR SALES
PRE-BOOKED VISITS

ANNUAL PRODUCTION **500,000 bottles**
HECTARES UNDER VINE **30**
VITICULTURE METHOD **Conventional**

Receiving the Guide's highest accolade last year has not changed Nicola, Anna and Silvia Dal Maso's way of working. Indeed, they have tackled the new vintage with even more care and energy. Although the market is struggling to recover, their commitment and investments aim to improve the whole range, starting with the estate's vineyards. This means Gambellara, moving onto the Colli Berici, where their red wine production is concentrated. The stand-out is the classy, elegant Colpizzarda.

Gambellara remains the winery's strong suit with two wines that embody the greatest expression of this area. Riva del Molino '08 highlights its mature, solid nature in a firm, gutsily dry wine with excellent presence. The subtler, more assertive Ca' Fischele '08 has delicate aromas and a confidently succulent palate. The excellent Colpizzarda '07 from the Colli Berici DOC is a spicy Tocai Rosso with a very harmonious flavour, savouriness and medium texture. Merlot and cabernet are the most widespread varieties in this area, and they give wines of huge structure. Terra dei Rovi '07 and the two '06 Casara Roveris stand out in particular.

● Amarone della Valpolicella Vign. di Monte Lodoletta '01	♟♟♟	8
● Amarone della Valpolicella Vign. di Monte Lodoletta '00	♟♟♟	8
● Amarone della Valpolicella Vign. di Monte Lodoletta '99	♟♟♟	8
● Amarone della Valpolicella Vign. di Monte Lodoletta '98	♟♟♟	8
● Amarone della Valpolicella Vign. di Monte Lodoletta '97	♟♟♟	8
● Amarone della Valpolicella Vign. di Monte Lodoletta '96	♟♟♟	8
● Amarone della Valpolicella Vign. di Monte Lodoletta '95	♟♟♟	8
● Amarone della Valpolicella Vigneto di Monte Lodoletta '90	♟♟♟	8
● Valpolicella Sup. Vign. di Monte Lodoletta '04	♟♟♟	8

● Colli Berici Tocai Rosso Colpizzarda '07	♟♟	5
○ Gambellara Cl. Ca' Fischele '08	♟♟	3*
○ Gambellara Cl. Riva del Molino '08	♟♟	4*
● Colli Berici Cabernet Casara Roveri '06	♟♟	5
● Colli Berici Cabernet Montebelvedere '07	♟♟	4*
● Colli Berici Merlot Casara Roveri '06	♟♟	5
○ Recioto di Gambellara Cl. Riva dei Perari '07	♟♟	6
● Terra dei Rovi Rosso '07	♟♟	6
○ Gambellara Cl. '08	♟	2*
● Rosso Montemitorio '07	♟	3
○ Gambellara Cl. Riva del Molino '07	♟♟♟	4*
● Colli Berici Tocai Rosso Colpizzarda '06	♟♟	5

De Stefani
VIA CADORNA, 92
30020 FOSSALTA DI PIAVE [VE]
TEL. 042167502
www.de-stefani.it

CELLAR SALES
PRE-BOOKED VISITS

ANNUAL PRODUCTION **300,000 bottles**
HECTARES UNDER VINE **40**
VITICULTURE METHOD **Natural**

The De Stefani family's winery, which has been active for many years by the Piave, returns to a full profile. The estate is divided into three zones: one at the winery at Fossalta di Piave; a second on the plain slightly to the west at Monastier di Treviso; and the old estate on the Refrontolo hills. The products are organized into a wide variety of labels ranging from very drinkable wines to more ambitious bottles, as well as some from dried grapes.

The whites are very impressive, especially the original Olmera '08, a blend of tocai and sauvignon with a generous, juicy palate. Vitalys '08 is a fruity Chardonnay with plenty of tanginess and good body, while the Tai '08 has typical salty and almondy aromas and a buttery, confidently gutsy palate. Turning to the reds, the interesting Soler '07 is a Bordeaux blend with some part-dried marzemino and refosco. Fruity, spicy aromas on the nose precede a nicely supple palate. The other reds are all approachable with ripe fruit.

F.lli Degani
FRAZ. VALGATARA
VIA TOBELE, 3A
37020 MARANO DI VALPOLICELLA [VR]
TEL. 0457701850
info@deganivini.it

CELLAR SALES
PRE-BOOKED VISITS

ANNUAL PRODUCTION **40,000 bottles**
HECTARES UNDER VINE **6**
VITICULTURE METHOD **Conventional**

For years, the Degani brothers' winery has been a true exponent of Valpolicella, with a reliable range of products emphasizing the huskier, and somehow more authentic, side of this DOC. Today, things have changed. While this remains a small, family-run estate, the wines are more crisply defined and generous, to the detriment of the character we have so much admired in recent years. Nevertheless, the bottles are firmly anchored in tradition, both in grape selection and the types of wine produced, all of which are included in the DOC zone.

In the absence of the leading wine, Amarone La Rosta, we enjoyed the basic '06 version with its generous fruity and vegetal sensations and supple, gutsy palate that shows beautifully tangy with excellent grip. On the quest for soft, fruity, richness, the Valpolicella Cicilio '06, showing ripe, healthy fruit with a juicy, mouthfilling palate. The curious Passito Bianco '07 is a type which has almost entirely disappeared in Valpolicella, while we preferred the fresher La Rosta '07 of the two Reciotos. The Valpolicella '08 and Superiore '06 are enjoyable and harmonious.

O Olmera '08	5
O Passito Passut '06	7
● Soler '07	5
O Tai '08	5
O Vitalys '08	4*
● Carmerosso '07	5
● Colli di Conegliano Refrontolo Passito '05	7
● Merlot '07	4
O Pinot Grigio '08	4
● Refosco P. R. Kreda '07	6
● Stefen 1624 '05	8
● Terre Nobili Rosso '07	6
O Tombola di Pin M. Cl. Brut '02	6
● Stefen 1624 '03	8

● Amarone della Valpolicella Cl. '06	6
● Valpolicella Cl. Sup. Cicilio Ripasso '06	4*
O Passito Bianco '07	5
● Recioto della Valpolicella Cl. '07	5
● Recioto della Valpolicella Cl. La Rosta '07	5
● Valpolicella Cl. '08	3
● Valpolicella Cl. Sup. '06	4
● Amarone della Valpolicella Cl. '05	6
● Amarone della Valpolicella Cl. '04	5
● Amarone della Valpolicella Cl. '03	5
● Amarone della Valpolicella Cl. '01	6
● Amarone della Valpolicella Cl. La Rosta '05	6
● Amarone della Valpolicella Cl. La Rosta '04	6

Conte Emo Capodilista

via Montecchia, 16
35030 Selvazzano Dentro [PD]
tel. 049637294
www.lamontecchia.it

CELLAR SALES
PRE-BOOKED VISITS
VISITOR FACILITIES

ANNUAL PRODUCTION **110,000 bottles**
HECTARES UNDER VINE **23**
VITICULTURE METHOD **Natural**

A few years ago, Giordano Emo Capodilista, who formerly ran the La Montecchia family estate, threw himself into a new venture, purchasing and managing his own estate in the extreme south of the Colli Euganei. We are in the municipality of Baone, with vineyards situated along Mount Castello, one of the southernmost hillsides in Veneto. The mild climate and Mediterranean vegetation prompts Giordano to call the area the "south of the north", and the good breezy weather enables the grapes to ripen healthily. The estate has recently gone organic.

This year, there's a new wine. The '06 Baon is a 60-40 Bordeaux blend of cabernet sauvignon and merlot which shows impressively elegant, sophisticated aromas of ripe fruit with hints of flowers and fines herbes, as well as minerally sensations. The palate is supple and slender despite considerable texture and oak that has still to be completely absorbed. The Colli Euganei Fior d'Arancio Passito Donna Daria '07 is slightly closed on the nose but opens out into fruity, minerally aromas with a hint of botrytis. The palate expands gradually into an elegant finish.

● Baon '06	🍷🍷	6
○ Colli Euganei Fior d'Arancio Passito Donna Daria '07	🍷🍷	6
○ Colli Euganei Fior d'Arancio Passito Donna Daria '06	🍷🍷🍷	6
● Colli Euganei Cabernet Sauvignon Ireneo '06	🍷🍷	6
● Colli Euganei Cabernet Sauvignon Ireneo '05	🍷🍷	6
● Colli Euganei Cabernet Sauvignon Ireneo '04	🍷🍷	6
● Colli Euganei Cabernet Sauvignon Ireneo '03	🍷🍷	6
● Colli Euganei Cabernet Sauvignon Ireneo '02	🍷🍷	6
● Colli Euganei Cabernet Sauvignon Ireneo '01	🍷🍷	6
○ Colli Euganei Fior d'Arancio Passito Donna Daria '05	🍷🍷	6
○ Colli Euganei Fior d'Arancio Passito Donna Daria '04	🍷🍷	6
○ Colli Euganei Fior d'Arancio Passito Donna Daria '02	🍷🍷	6
○ Colli Euganei Fior d'Arancio Passito Donna Daria '01	🍷🍷	6

Fasoli

fraz. San Zeno
via C. Battisti, 47
37030 Colognola ai Colli [VR]
tel. 0457650741
www.fasoligino.com

CELLAR SALES
PRE-BOOKED VISITS

ANNUAL PRODUCTION **300,000 bottles**
HECTARES UNDER VINE **40**
VITICULTURE METHOD **Organic certified**

The Fasoli brothers' winery is situated at Colognola ai Colli, where Amadio and Natalino split their range across whites and reds since this area falls into both the Soave and Valpolicella DOCs. They also produce some IGT wines, which demonstrates a willingness to experiment. The Fasolis' respect for the environment translates into organically farmed vineyards while their passion for well-textured wines is enhanced by the use of dried grapes, for dry wines as well as sweet, a practice borrowed from nearby Valpolicella.

Several of the wines impressed us this year, starting with the excellent Recioto San Zeno '06, a white with fragrant aromas of candied citrus and dried apricots with a nicely handled, explosive sweetness. The very good Soave Borgoletto '08 has a fresh nose of flowers and apple and pear-like fruit while the palate is impressively tangy and lingering. Among the well-structured reds, we liked Calle '07, a fruity Merlot with fresh hints of medicinal herbs and a dry, powerful palate. The interesting garganega-based Liber '07 has an elegant, relaxed palate.

○ Liber Bianco '07	🍷🍷	4
● Merlot Calle '07	🍷🍷	7
○ Recioto di Soave S. Zeno '06	🍷🍷	6
○ Soave Borgoletto '08	🍷🍷	4*
● Amarone della Valpolicella Alteo '04	🍷	8
● Merlot Orgno '07	🍷	7
○ Soave Pieve Vecchia '07	🍷	5
○ Liber Bianco '04	🍷🍷	4
● Merlot Calle '06	🍷🍷	6
● Merlot Calle '05	🍷🍷	7
● Merlot Orgno '05	🍷🍷	7
○ Recioto di Soave S. Zeno '05	🍷🍷	6
○ Recioto di Soave S. Zeno '03	🍷🍷	6
○ Soave Borgoletto '06	🍷🍷	4*
○ Soave Borgoletto '05	🍷🍷	4*

Il Filò delle Vigne

VIA TERRALBA, 14
35030 BAONE [PD]
TEL. 042956243
www.ilfilodellevigne.it

CELLAR SALES
PRE-BOOKED VISITS

ANNUAL PRODUCTION **40,000 bottles**
HECTARES UNDER VINE **18**
VITICULTURE METHOD **Conventional**

Carlo Giordani and Nicolò Voltan are slowly, quietly conquering the Colli Euganei winemaking scene thanks to products prepared meticulously, to say the very least. Their brilliant idea was to involve two high-calibre professionals in this venture, Filippo Giannone and Andrea Boaretti, who have found great operational support in Matteo Zanaica. The 20 or so hectares are tended like a garden, despite the risk of increasingly frequent incursions by wild boar, and the well-organized cellar turns out a seriously good range.

We were used to top-level performances from Cabernet Borgo delle Casette but the magnificent Il Calto delle Fate '07 is a lovely surprise. It's an unusually harmonious white made from non-aromatic grapes aged in oak that combines ripe fruit, suppleness and strength. The excellent Colli Euganei Pinot Bianco Vigna delle Acacie '08 is subtly floral and tangy while the sparkling wine is mouthwatering and delightfully drinkable. The reds are different again. Cecilia di Baone Riserva '04, aged in cement, is firm and juicy, while Borgo delle Casette Riserva '05 emphasizes the sunny, powerful personality of this side of the Colli.

Silvano Follador

FRAZ. SANTO STEFANO
LOC. FOLLO
VIA CALLONGA, 11
31040 VALDOBBIADENE [TV]
TEL. 0423900295
www.silvanofollador.it

CELLAR SALES
PRE-BOOKED VISITS

ANNUAL PRODUCTION **30,000 bottles**
HECTARES UNDER VINE **4**
VITICULTURE METHOD **Natural**

When we think about Prosecco, our minds recall enchanting landscapes, light, fragrant wines and another inevitable image: technology. The wine is produced using the cuve close, or Charmat, method. But Alberta and Silvano make it clear that the vineyards play the most important role, and the cellar is simply a way to give their wines full expression. The grapes grow on the most famous hills in the DOC zone, starting of course with Cartizze. It is no coincidence that the small-scale Follador production is limited to just two wines.

The Brut is a banker. Every year, it is one of the best with its sophisticated apple and pear fruit and flowers on the nose preceding a gutsy palate with tangy grip. The Cartizze '08 is even more interesting, in fact it won Three Glasses. In a courageous move that runs contrary to local practices it has very low residual sugar residue, which focuses on the contribution of the vineyards without extra intervention. This is the winery's way forward as it seeks sublimation in the Metodo Classico, which is still at the experimental stage.

● Colli Euganei Cabernet Borgo delle Casette Ris. '05	♟♟ 6
● Colli Euganei Cabernet Vigna Cecilia di Baone Ris. '04	♟♟ 5
○ Colli Euganei Pinot Bianco Vigna delle Acacie '08	♟♟ 5
○ Il Calto delle Fate '07	♟♟ 6
○ Colli Euganei Fior d'Arancio Spumante '08	♟ 6
● Colli Euganei Cabernet Borgo delle Casette Ris. '04	♟♟ 6
● Colli Euganei Cabernet Borgo delle Casette Ris. '02	♟♟ 5
○ Colli Euganei Fior d'Arancio Luna del Parco '06	♟♟ 6
○ Colli Euganei Fior d'Arancio Luna del Parco '04	♟♟ 6

○ Cartizze Brut '08	♟♟♟ 5
○ P. di Valdobbiadene Brut '08	♟♟ 4*
○ Bianco Passito '03	♟♟ 7
○ Cartizze	♟♟ 5
○ Cartizze	♟♟ 5
○ Cartizze	♟♟ 5
○ Cartizze Dry	♟♟ 6
○ P. di Valdobbiadene Brut	♟♟ 4
○ P. di Valdobbiadene Brut	♟♟ 4
○ P. di Valdobbiadene Extra Dry	♟♟ 4

VENETO

Le Fraghe

Loc. Colombara, 3
37010 Cavaion Veronese [VR]
tel. 0457236832
www.fraghe.it

CELLAR SALES
PRE-BOOKED VISITS

ANNUAL PRODUCTION 90,000 bottles
HECTARES UNDER VINE 28
VITICULTURE METHOD Conventional

Although this estate is now a Guide fixture, because we have always enjoyed the wines and admired the effort expended in the vineyards, in the last couple of years Matilde Poggi has managed to ratchet up quality across the range. From just under 30 hectares of vineyards, she produces a shortish list of wines, focusing mainly on Bardolino, with a little garganega and even less pinot grigio and cabernet, the legacy of a recent past that never really took hold hereabouts.

The winery's two most representative wines, the '08 Bardolino and Garganega Camporengo, are on top form. The former shows convincingly intense aromas of black berry fruit and pepper, typical of the corvina grape which is the backbone of this DOC. These are nicely reflected on the savoury palate which is both concentrated and very light. The Camporengo has riper, sometimes tropical, fruit with a mouthwatering and very enjoyable palate. The Chiaretto and Pinot Grigio, both '08 and both closed with Stelvin screwcaps, are light and succulent, while the Quaiare Cabernet '06 is solid and sophisticated.

Marchesi Fumanelli

Fraz. San Floriano
via Squarano, 1
37029 San Pietro in Cariano [VR]
tel. 0457704875
www.squarano.com

CELLAR SALES
PRE-BOOKED VISITS
FOOD

ANNUAL PRODUCTION 50,000 bottles
HECTARES UNDER VINE 20
VITICULTURE METHOD Conventional

Marchesi Fumanelli is a lovely estate, mainly located around the owner's villa just outside San Pietro in Cariano on a sort of small hillside looking over the surrounding plains. The 20 or so vineyards are only partly used for the estate's own production of mainly classic Valpolicella wines, plus a white and – soon – another red. Flavio Peroni, who knows a thing or two about the area, makes a valid contribution to management of the estate, which only releases its wines after lengthy ageing.

The '04 Amarone performed superbly. It is a wine of depth that unveils its jealously guarded aromatics only slowly. The palate is firm and powerful without being static, indeed it drives on supple and taut into a long, dry finish. The Amarone Octavius Riserva '03 is richer and more mouthfilling while the delicious Valpolicella Classico '08 is approachably fresh while showing concentration and personality. The Terso '05, designed for long ageing, is generous and harmonious with slightly evident oak.

● Bardolino '08	♈♈ 3*
○ Garganega Camporengo '08	♈♈ 4*
☉ Bardolino Chiaretto Ròdon '08	♈♈ 3*
● Quaiare Cabernet '06	♈♈ 5
○ Sover Pinot Grigio '08	♈ 3
● Bardolino '07	♈♈ 3*
● Bardolino '06	♈♈ 3*
● Bardolino '03	♈♈ 3
○ Camporengo Garganega Vendemmia a San Goffredo '04	♈♈ 4
○ Garganega Camporengo '07	♈♈ 4*
○ Garganega Camporengo '04	♈♈ 3*
○ Garganega Camporengo '02	♈♈ 3*
● Quaiare Cabernet '03	♈♈ 4
● Quaiare Cabernet '01	♈♈ 5
● Quaiare Cabernet '00	♈♈ 5
● Quaiare Cabernet '98	♈♈ 5
● Quaiare Cabernet '97	♈♈ 5
● Valdadige Quaiare '98	♈♈ 5

● Amarone della Valpolicella Cl. '04	♈♈ 6
● Amarone della Valpolicella Cl. Octavius Ris. '03	♈♈ 8
● Valpolicella Cl. '08	♈♈ 3*
○ Terso '05	♈ 6
● Amarone della Valpolicella Cl. Pralongo '03	♈♈ 6
● Amarone della Valpolicella Cl. Pralongo '01	♈♈ 6
● Amarone della Valpolicella Ris. '03	♈♈ 8
● Valpolicella Cl. Sup. Squarano '03	♈♈ 6
● Valpolicella Cl. Sup. Squarano '01	♈♈ 5
● Valpolicella Cl. Sup. Squarano '00	♈♈ 5

Tenute Galtarossa

VIA ANDREA MONGA, 9
37029 SAN PIETRO IN CARIANO [VR]
TEL. 0456838307
www.tenutegaltarossa.com

PRE-BOOKED VISITS
FOOD

ANNUAL PRODUCTION **36,000 bottles**
HECTARES UNDER VINE **80**
VITICULTURE METHOD **Conventional**

Giacomo Galtarossa's winery is situated south of San Pietro in Cariano on a sort of small plateau that descends slowly towards the Adige river. Only a small part of the 80-hectare estate is used for the winery's own products, based on Amarone and Valpolicella Superiore. The partnership with GIV has brought excellent results since the first year, demonstrated once again in this year's tastings during which the wines revealed good quality and varietal characteristics.

The Valpolicella Classico Superiore Corte Colombara '07 gives well-defined fruit, the cherries beautifully melding with hints of dried flowers and medicinal herbs, and a soft, well-rounded palate, almost as if it wanted to be an Amarone. The Amarone itself unfurls deep and distinctly raisiny, jammy aromas enhanced with hints of undergrowth and spice. The palate is more powerful but still a little ruffled, with good potential that will find its feet after further bottle ageing.

Fattoria Garbole

LOC. GARBOLE
VIA FRACANZANA, 6
37039 TREGNAGO [VR]
TEL. 0457809020
www.fattoriagarbole.it

CELLAR SALES
PRE-BOOKED VISITS

ANNUAL PRODUCTION **15,000 bottles**
HECTARES UNDER VINE **6**
VITICULTURE METHOD **Conventional**

Fattoria Garbole was created in the wake of the huge success enjoyed in recent years by Valpolicella and, even more so, by Amarone. Ettore and Filippo Finetto are not without experience and a visit to their vineyards is enough to reveal this new winery's skill and ambition. The densely planted vineyards are planted exclusively on hillsides and are trained to the more quality-friendly Guyot system instead of the traditional, high-yield overhead pergolas. Small oak barrels are used in the cellar to achieve solid, nicely defined products.

The Amarone '05 has a nose rich in fruity sensations with the spices and hints of medicinal herbs only peeking through in the background. The palate is remarkably concentrated but maintains a supple, dry profile thanks to mouthwatering acidity. The '06 Valpolicella is a little less impressive and struggles to find harmony. Juicy dried fruit tempts the nose alongside vegetal hints and crushed flowers, while the palate remains fresh, expanding with poise and balance.

● Amarone della Valpolicella Cl. '06	♟♟ 8
● Valpolicella Cl. Sup. Corte Colombara '07	♟♟ 5
● Amarone della Valpolicella Cl. '05	♟♟ 8
● Amarone della Valpolicella Cl. '04	♟♟ 7
● Amarone della Valpolicella Cl. '03	♟♟ 7
● Amarone della Valpolicella Cl. '01	♟♟ 7
● Amarone della Valpolicella Cl. '00	♟♟ 7
● Valpolicella Cl. Sup. Corte Colombara '06	♟♟ 6
● Valpolicella Cl. Sup. Corte Colombara '04	♟♟ 5
● Valpolicella Cl. Sup. Corte Colombara '03	♟♟ 5
● Valpolicella Cl. Sup. Corte Colombara '02	♟♟ 5
● Valpolicella Cl. Sup. Corte Colombara '01	♟♟ 5

● Amarone della Valpolicella '05	♟♟ 8
● Valpolicella Sup. '06	♟ 6
● Amarone della Valpolicella '04	♟♟ 8
● Amarone della Valpolicella '03	♟♟ 7
● Valpolicella Sup. '05	♟♟ 6

Gini

VIA MATTEOTTI, 42
37032 MONTEFORTE D'ALPONE [VR]
TEL. 0457611908
www.ginivini.com

CELLAR SALES
PRE-BOOKED VISITS

ANNUAL PRODUCTION **200,000 bottles**
HECTARES UNDER VINE **30**
VITICULTURE METHOD **Conventional**

Few wineries have contributed to relaunching a DOC zone the way Olinto Gini's has. Olinto's sons Claudio and Sandro have been running it for years with skill and enthusiasm. Their obsessive care in the vineyards not only ensures low yields and ripe fruit but also aims to safeguard traditional varieties by conserving old vineyards, some with pre-phylloxera vines. The results are always impressive and this year was no exception. One increasingly large non-designated vineyard is used for experimentation.

That vineyard is the source of the non-DOC wines: a mouthwatering Maciete Fumé Sauvignon '07, a stylish, mature Sorai Chardonnay '07 and a Pinot Nero, Campo alle More '06, with generous aromas and a very sophisticated palate. But the most impressive wines are the Soaves. The sumptuous Salvarenza '07 has fragrant ripe fruit and dried flowers on the nose and a harmonious palate with an overwhelming finish. La Froscà '08 is more approachable and appetizing, highlighting the accessible, satisfying personality of the garganega grape. The excellent Soave Classico '08 is very fairly priced.

Gregoletto

FRAZ. PREMAOR
VIA SAN MARTINO, 83
31050 MIANE [TV]
TEL. 0438970463
www.gregoletto.com

CELLAR SALES
PRE-BOOKED VISITS

ANNUAL PRODUCTION **N.D.**
HECTARES UNDER VINE **15**
VITICULTURE METHOD **Conventional**

Treviso's iconic wine producer Luigi Gregoletto has maintained a well-defined, personal style of wine over the years, shunning market-influenced trends. All his wines share common characteristics, with marked austerity and a desire to avoid too much technology, using instead the resources nature has made available. "Why use refrigerator units for stabilization when the winter is plenty cold enough?" And so on. We like this down-to-earth, nature-friendly way of thinking.

The wines again reflect Luigi's philosophy. The one we found most fascinating was the Prosecco Tranquillo '08, a wonderful version which turns what are usually weak points into positive qualities. Its lightness comes across as subtlety and finesse, supported by generous aromas and grip. But all the cellar's whites are well-made and savoury. We liked the husky, minerally Manzoni Bianco '08 and the poised body of the Chardonnay '08. The Prosecco Extra Dry is profound and authentic while our favourite from the reds is the '07 Cabernet.

○ Soave Cl. Contrada Salvarenza Vecchie Vigne '07	ㄱㄱㄱ 5
○ Soave Cl. La Froscà '08	ㄱㄱ 5
● Campo alle More Pinot Nero '06	ㄱㄱ 6
○ Chardonnay Sorai '07	ㄱㄱ 5
○ Soave Cl. '08	ㄱㄱ 4*
○ Sauvignon Maciete Fumé '07	ㄱ 5
○ Soave Cl. La Froscà '06	ㅗㅗㅗ 5
○ Soave Cl. La Froscà '05	ㅗㅗㅗ 5
○ Soave Cl. Sup. Contrada Salvarenza Vecchie Vigne '00	ㅗㅗㅗ 6
○ Soave Cl. Sup. Contrada Salvarenza Vecchie Vigne '98	ㅗㅗㅗ 5
○ Soave Cl. Sup. La Froscà '99	ㅗㅗㅗ 5
○ Soave Cl. Sup. La Froscà '97	ㅗㅗㅗ 4
○ Soave Cl. Contrada Salvarenza Vecchie Vigne '06	ㅗㅗ 5
○ Soave Cl. La Froscà '07	ㅗㅗ 5

● Cabernet '07	ㄱㄱ 4
○ Chardonnay '08	ㄱㄱ 4
○ Manzoni Bianco '08	ㄱㄱ 4
○ P. di Conegliano Valdobbiadene Extra Dry	ㄱㄱ 4
○ P. di Conegliano Valdobbiadene Tranquillo '08	ㄱㄱ 4
○ Colli di Conegliano Bianco Albio '08	ㄱ 4
● Merlot '07	ㄱ 4
○ P. di Conegliano Valdobbiadene Extra Dry Monte Corbino	ㄱ 4
○ Pinot Bianco '08	ㄱ 4
○ Prosecco Frizzante '08	ㄱ 4
○ Verdiso Frizzante '08	ㄱ 4
● Cabernet '06	ㅗㅗ 4
○ Chardonnay '07	ㅗㅗ 4
○ Colli di Conegliano Bianco Albio '07	ㅗㅗ 4
○ Colli di Conegliano Bianco Albio '06	ㅗㅗ 4*
● Colli di Conegliano Rosso '04	ㅗㅗ 6
○ Manzoni Bianco '07	ㅗㅗ 4*
● Merlot '06	ㅗㅗ 4
● Merlot '05	ㅗㅗ 3*
○ Pinot Bianco '07	ㅗㅗ 4

Guerrieri Rizzardi

VIA VERDI, 4
37011 BARDOLINO [VR]
TEL. 0457210028
www.guerrieri-rizzardi.it

CELLAR SALES
PRE-BOOKED VISITS

ANNUAL PRODUCTION **600,000 bottles**
HECTARES UNDER VINE **100**
VITICULTURE METHOD **Conventional**

In just a few years, the Rizzardi family's winery has shown a leap in quality throughout the range, putting the estate's huge potential firmly in the limelight. The 100 or so hectares are split across Verona's leading DOC zones, from Valdadige to Soave, via Bardolino and Valpolicella, and while their Amarone has received much recognition, it is the family's Bardolino which has asserted itself as signature Rizzardi wine.

Although we tasted them close to bottling, the two '05 Amarones showed their class, especially the Villa Rizzardi, while the Calcarole has the more complex aromas. We are hoping to see some refocusing in Valpolicella as it is too reliant on the Amarone, and the Pojega '07 is going the right direction. Its generous aromas from the traditional grape varieties are accompanied by a slender, sophisticated body. The excellent Bardolino Tacchetto '08 is intensely fragrant with a gutsy palate, like the Costeggiola '08, a mouthwatering, lingering Soave Classico.

Inama

LOC. BIACCHE, 50
37047 SAN BONIFACIO [VR]
TEL. 0456104343
www.inamaaziendaagricola.it

PRE-BOOKED VISITS

ANNUAL PRODUCTION **300,000 bottles**
HECTARES UNDER VINE **45**
VITICULTURE METHOD **Conventional**

Stefano Inama's winery created something of a fracture within the Soave tradition by presenting rich, structured whites with oak-derived characteristics. It has been over a decade since the first, dazzling appearance of these wines: the tempo has changed but the music hasn't. Stefano's wines remain a benchmark for the whole DOC zone. His Soaves have been joined by reds from nearby Colli Berici, an area this winery believes in. First, there was a classic Bordeaux blend and now there's a Carmenère.

The range is very well-stocked as usual and our favourites are the Soaves, especially the Vigneto Du Lot. The '07 has crisp peach and apricot fruit with florality and a tangy, nicely textured palate which is more sophisticated than any we've seen for several vintages. Just behind it are the very approachable Foscarino '07 and Vin Soave '08, always one of the best buys in the local area. Turning to the reds, we were impressed by the generous and fruity but also dry and lingering Bradisismo '05 while the Oratorio di San Lorenzo '06 has a typically intense note of balsam.

● Valpolicella Cl. Sup. Ripasso Poiega '07	♦♦♦ 4*
● Amarone della Valpolicella Cl. Calcarole '05	♦♦ 8
● Amarone della Valpolicella Cl. Villa Rizzardi '05	♦♦ 7
● Bardolino Cl. Tacchetto '08	♦♦ 4*
○ Recioto di Soave '06	♦♦ 5
○ Soave Cl. Costeggiola '08	♦♦ 4
⊙ Bardolino Chiaretto Cl. '08	♦ 3
⊙ Rosa Rosae '08	♦ 4
● Amarone della Valpolicella Cl. Villa Rizzardi '04	♦♦♦ 7
● Amarone della Valpolicella Cl. Villa Rizzardi '01	♦♦♦ 7

● Bradisismo '05	♦♦ 6
○ Soave Cl. Vign. di Foscarino '07	♦♦ 5
○ Soave Cl. Vign. Du Lot '07	♦♦ 5
● Oratorio di San Lorenzo '06	♦♦ 7
○ Soave Cl. Vin Soave '08	♦♦ 4*
○ Vulcaia Fumé '07	♦♦ 6
○ Chardonnay '08	♦ 4
○ Vulcaia '08	♦ 4
○ Soave Cl. Vign. Du Lot '05	♦♦♦ 5
○ Soave Cl. Vign. Du Lot '01	♦♦♦ 5
○ Soave Cl. Vign. Du Lot '00	♦♦♦ 5
○ Soave Cl. Vign. Du Lot '99	♦♦♦ 5
○ Soave Cl. Vign. Du Lot '96	♦♦♦ 5
○ Soave Cl. Vign. di Foscarino '06	♦♦ 5
○ Soave Cl. Vign. Du Lot '06	♦♦ 5

Castello di Lispida

VIA IV NOVEMBRE, 4
35043 MONSELICE [PD]
TEL. 0429780530
www.lispida.com

CELLAR SALES
PRE-BOOKED VISITS

ANNUAL PRODUCTION 18,000 bottles
HECTARES UNDER VINE 8
VITICULTURE METHOD Natural

Colli Euganei is a superb area in which to make wine, its strong suits being the volcanic soil and a beautifully sunny climate with the variations in temperature and light breezes needed to guarantee healthy grapes. So much the better, then, if Alessandro Sgaravatti cultivates his vineyards with utmost respect for the environment, and for the health of the consumers who will drink his wines. Less than ten hectares under vine stand around the castle and their fruit goes into absolutely natural products made with ancient materials like terracotta for ageing as well as wood.

The most impressive wine is Amphora '06, a monovarietal Tocai aged underground in terracotta amphora. At first sight, it is distinctly cloudy, the first evidence of a personal approach to winemaking. Green tea, Mediterranean undergrowth and iodine on the nose are faithfully reflected on a solid, extraordinarily savoury palate that is attractively balanced. We had a few misgivings about the other wines. Terraforte '03 is very warm and evolved on nose and palate while the Brut is uncomplicated but enjoyable.

Conte Loredan Gasparini

FRAZ. VENEGAZZÙ
VIA MARTIGNAGO ALTO, 23
31040 VOLPAGO DEL MONTELLO [TV]
TEL. 0438870024
www.venegazzu.com

CELLAR SALES
PRE-BOOKED VISITS
VISITOR FACILITIES

ANNUAL PRODUCTION 312,000 bottles
HECTARES UNDER VINE 80
VITICULTURE METHOD Natural

The Palla family's traditional winery has single-handedly raised the profile of Treviso's wines. Despite a dimmer period in the last decade, the estate has now returned to its rightful position over the last few vintages. Supervised by Lorenzo, the extensive vineyards close to the winery have gradually been replanted in a renovation process that maintains the quality and age of the vine stock. In the cellar, renovation involved the oak used, with a return to favour of larger wooden barrels.

The emblematic Capo di Stato '06 remains the most impressive wine, with sophisticated red berries and aromatic herbs on the nose and a solid palate whose slightly forward tannin is bound to find greater harmony with bottle age. The Venegazzù della Casa '06, mainly cabernet sauvignon, is more accessible today with less pronounced body while the rather austere dry profile remains unchanged. The interesting Manzoni Bianco '08 shows peach and apricot fruit on the nose and tangy grip on the palate. The Falconera '07, a single-variety Merlot, is generous and pleasantly husky, like the '07 Cabernet Sauvignon.

Wine		Rating
○ Amphora '06	♀♀	7
○ H Brut '08	♀	5
● Terraforte '03	♀	6
○ Amphora '04	♀♀	7
○ Amphora '02	♀♀	7
○ Amphora '01	♀♀	7
● Montelispida '02	♀♀	6
● Montelispida '01	♀♀	6
● Terraforte '01	♀♀	6
● Terraforte '99	♀♀	6
○ Terralba '04	♀♀	6
○ Terralba '03	♀♀	6
○ Terralba '02	♀♀	6
○ Terralba '01	♀♀	7
○ Terralba '00	♀♀	7
○ Terralba '99	♀♀	7

Wine		Rating
● Capo di Stato '06	♀♀	7
○ Manzoni Bianco '08	♀♀	4*
● Venegazzù della Casa '06	♀♀	5
● Falconera Rosso '07	♀	4
● Montello e Colli Asolani Cabernet Sauvignon '07	♀	4
○ Montello e Colli Asolani Prosecco Brut	♀	4
● Capo di Stato '05	♀♀	6
● Capo di Stato '04	♀♀	6
● Capo di Stato '03	♀♀	6
● Capo di Stato '02	♀♀	6
● Capo di Stato '00	♀♀	6
● Venegazzù della Casa '05	♀♀	5
● Venegazzù della Casa '04	♀♀	5
● Venegazzù della Casa '03	♀♀	5

★ Maculan

VIA CASTELLETTO, 3
36042 BREGANZE [VI]
TEL. 0445873733
www.maculan.net

CELLAR SALES
PRE-BOOKED VISITS

ANNUAL PRODUCTION **850,000 bottles**
HECTARES UNDER VINE **39**
VITICULTURE METHOD **Conventional**

If Veneto is a bright star in Italy's winemaking firmament today, it is thanks to winery owners like Fausto Maculan. Fausto is a true pioneer of fine quality who has made a huge contribution to the visibility of Italian wines better known abroad, and his estate has been an example for many others. This year, too, Breganze is one of the most reliable names in Italy thanks to careful work in the vineyards and impressively efficient cellar procedures that have achieved the superb results in the table below.

Especially good this year are the white dried grape wines and Bordeaux blend reds. Among the former is a Breganze Torcolato '06 on great form with generous fruit and perfectly handled sugar on the palate. Fratta '07 leads the red field with vibrant aromas and very skilful use of oak that produce a wonderfully alluring wine. The merlot-only Breganze Rosso Crosara '07 has a powerful, harmonious body while the Breganze Cabernet Sauvignon Palazzotto '07 has acquired greater concentration over the years. The Chardonnay Ferrata '07 put on a good performance, as did the racy Brentino '07.

Manara

FRAZ. SAN FLORIANO
VIA DON CESARE BIASI, 53
37029 SAN PIETRO IN CARIANO [VR]
TEL. 0457701086
www.manaravini.it

CELLAR SALES
PRE-BOOKED VISITS

ANNUAL PRODUCTION **75,000 bottles**
HECTARES UNDER VINE **11**
VITICULTURE METHOD **Conventional**

Ground-drying in Valpolicella has brought modernization and commercial success thanks to rich wines with endless strength. But there are still wineries today who seek this concentration with caution. They represent a world where wine is for drinking, not just for tasting, wines that tell the story of a local area more completely than any sales push abroad. The Manaras are just like that: authentic producers of subtle, supple wines, never too dense in hue, that come from traditional viticulture on the slopes near the cellar.

The Amarone Classico '05 is a paragon of this approach and very nearly picked up Three Glasses thanks to generous yet subtle aromas in which the fruit is restrained and enhanced by dried flowers and spices that usher in a supple, broad and very savoury palate. The Amarone Postera '05 is richer, fruitier and more modern in style. From the two Valpolicellas, we preferred the solid Ripasso Le Morete '06 with typical pepper aromas while the Recioto '06 follows the winery style, its sweetness held in check and supported by vibrant, succulent acidity.

Maculan	Rating
○ Breganze Torcolato '06	♈♈ 7
● Fratta '07	♈♈ 8
● Breganze Cabernet Sauvignon Palazzotto '07	♈♈ 5
● Breganze Pinot Nero Altura '07	♈♈ 6
● Breganze Rosso Crosara '07	♈♈ 8
● Brentino '07	♈♈ 4
○ Ferrata Chardonnay '07	♈♈ 5
○ Bidibi '08	♈ 4
● Breganze Cabernet '07	♈ 4
○ Breganze Vespaiolo '08	♈ 4
☉ Costadolio '08	♈ 4
○ Dindarello '08	♈ 5
○ Ferrata '08	♈ 5
● Madoro Passito '07	♈ 6
○ Pino & Toi '08	♈ 3
● Speaia '07	♈ 4
● Fratta '01	♈♈♈ 8
● Fratta '00	♈♈♈ 8

Manara	Rating
● Amarone della Valpolicella Cl. '05	♈♈ 6*
● Amarone della Valpolicella Cl. Postera '05	♈♈ 6
● Guido Manara '05	♈♈ 6
● Recioto della Valpolicella Cl. El Rocolo '06	♈♈ 5
● Valpolicella Cl. Sup. '06	♈♈ 3*
● Valpolicella Cl. Sup. Le Morete Ripasso '06	♈♈ 4
○ Strinà Passito '06	♈ 5
● Amarone della Valpolicella Cl. '00	♈♈♈ 6
● Amarone della Valpolicella Cl. '03	♈♈ 6
● Amarone della Valpolicella Cl. '01	♈♈ 6*
● Amarone della Valpolicella Cl. Postera '04	♈♈ 6
● Amarone della Valpolicella Cl. Postera '03	♈♈ 6
● Recioto della Valpolicella Cl. El Rocolo '05	♈♈ 5
● Recioto della Valpolicella Cl. El Rocolo '04	♈♈ 5
● Recioto della Valpolicella Cl. Moronalto '05	♈♈ 5

Le Mandolare

LOC. BROGNOLIGO
VIA SAMBUCO, 180
37032 MONTEFORTE D'ALPONE [VR]
TEL. 0456175083
www.cantinalemandolare.com

CELLAR SALES
PRE-BOOKED VISITS

ANNUAL PRODUCTION 60,000 bottles
HECTARES UNDER VINE 20
VITICULTURE METHOD Conventional

A few hundred metres down the road to Le Rugate, you'll glimpse among the vineyards on the right the functional new winery owned by Renzo Rodighiero and his wife Germana. The estate's own holding extends over about 20 hectares and only some of the grapes are used for the range after careful selection of the best batches. Production focuses on the DOC's classic wines, which are always impressively interpreted with a style that explores the various versions of the garganega grape.

The most striking wine this time was the Soave Classico Monte Sella, from the hillside of the same name where the vineyard is located. Mature aromas dominated by rich, juicy peach and apricot fruit, opening out elegantly on the palate to reveal good harmony and length. The Recioto Le Schiavette '06 is sunny and Mediterranean with aromas of dried apricots and liquorice while the pronounced sweetness on the palate is held in check by fresh acidity. Of the two simpler Soave Classicos, we preferred the racy Corte Menini '08 with its bright palate.

Marcato

VIA PRANDI, 10
37030 RONCÀ [VR]
TEL. 0457460070
www.marcatovini.it

CELLAR SALES
PRE-BOOKED VISITS

ANNUAL PRODUCTION 400,000 bottles
HECTARES UNDER VINE 50
VITICULTURE METHOD Conventional

The Marcato family works in three Veneto DOC zones: Soave, Colli Berici and Lessinia. For Lessinia, the family is an avid promoter of the sadly neglected durello grape, whose high levels of acidity make it very suitable for Metodo Classico and dried grape wines, both of which are close to the Marcatos' collective heart. The extensive vineyards produce less than half a million bottles annually, in a range that tries to cater for all areas of the market, from simple drinkable wines to more challenging products.

Metodo Classico 36 is a good durello-based sparkling wine. The nose shows the usual ripe fruit and croissant aromas but the palate reveals a more restless soul, lingering confidently with assertive acidity. The tropical, mouthwatering Durello Passito '04 and Col Creo '07, an original blend of garganega, sauvignon and pinot bianco aged in oak, are both interesting. In this case, too, the wine performs best on the solid, succulent palate. The reds are a little less impressive, being rather simple or in the case of the Pian Alto, showing concentrated dried grapes.

O Recioto di Soave Le Schiavette '06	♟♟ 5
O Soave Cl. Corte Menini '08	♟♟ 3*
O Soave Cl. Sup. Monte Sella '07	♟♟ 4*
O Soave Cl. Il Roccolo '08	♟ 3
O Recioto di Soave Cl. Le Schiavette '05	♟♟ 5
O Recioto di Soave Cl. Le Schiavette '04	♟♟ 5
O Recioto di Soave Cl. Le Schiavette '03	♟♟ 5
O Recioto di Soave Etichetta Nera '01	♟♟ 5
O Soave Cl. Il Roccolo '07	♟♟ 3*
O Soave Cl. Il Roccolo '06	♟♟ 3*
O Soave Cl. Il Roccolo '05	♟♟ 3*
O Soave Cl. Il Roccolo '02	♟♟ 3*
O Soave Cl. Sup. Monte Sella '06	♟♟ 4
O Soave Cl. Sup. Monte Sella '05	♟♟ 4*
O Soave Cl. Sup. Monte Sella '04	♟♟ 4*
O Soave Cl. Sup. Monte Sella '02	♟♟ 4

O Col Creo '07	♟♟ 4*
O Lessini Durello Brut M. Cl. 36	♟♟ 5
O Lessini Durello Passito '04	♟♟ 5
● Barattaro '07	♟ 5
● Colli Berici Cabernet La Giareta '07	♟ 3
● Colli Berici Cabernet Pianalto Ris. '04	♟ 7
● Colli Berici Merlot Vign. Asinara '04	♟ 4
O Colli Berici Sauvignon '07	♟ 4
O Lessini Durello Brut I Prandi	♟ 3
● Palladiano '07	♟ 4
O Recioto di Soave Il Duello '06	♟ 6
O Soave Cl. Sup. Il Tirso '07	♟ 4
O Soave Cl. Tenute Barche '08	♟ 4
O Soave Colli Scaligeri I Prandi '08	♟ 4
O Lessini Durello Passito '03	♟♟ 5
O Recioto di Soave Il Duello '04	♟♟ 5
O Soave Cl. Sup. Il Tirso '06	♟♟ 4

Marion

FRAZ. MARCELLISE
VIA BORGO MARCELLISE, 2
37036 SAN MARTINO BUON ALBERGO [VR]
TEL. 0458740021
www.marionvini.it

PRE-BOOKED VISITS

ANNUAL PRODUCTION **40,000 bottles**
HECTARES UNDER VINE **14**
VITICULTURE METHOD **Conventional**

In order to understand the objectives pursued by Stefano Campedelli and his wife Nicoletta, just read the numbers above very carefully and do your sums. You'll see that the yield is fewer than 2,500 bottles per hectare. Even using dried grapes and severe selection, that isn't very many but the results are exciting. Alongside traditional products from the DOC zone are a couple of wines that use the presence of non-local grapes like cabernet sauvignon and teroldego, but with a quintessentially Veronese touch.

Since its first harvests not so long ago, Marion has stood out for its style, which performs best on the palate, where allure melds with suppleness despite very firm structure. This year, our highest accolade went to the Valpolicella Superiore '05, which offers enthralling progression in the mouth after red berry and spice aromas. The champion is powerful but savoury with smooth tannins and acid backbone that pleasantly lengthens the finish. The '04 Amarone is generous and mouthfilling while the '05 Teroldego and '04 Cabernet Sauvignon are solid and mature.

Masari

LOC. MAGLIO DI SOPRA
VIA BEVILACQUA, 2A
36078 VALDAGNO [VI]
TEL. 0445410780
www.masari.it

CELLAR SALES
PRE-BOOKED VISITS

ANNUAL PRODUCTION **25,000 bottles**
HECTARES UNDER VINE **4**
VITICULTURE METHOD **Natural**

The Dal Lago estate possesses a modest vineyard holding and consequently produces very few bottles but there is plenty of news, showing just how passionate Massimo and his wife Arianna are. Last year, we reported a delay in release of the San Martino and this year the house flagship, Masari, is absent. The decision was difficult but necessary to allow the wines sufficient bottle ageing. Rigorous vineyard procedures and shrewd cellar management are the trademarks of this dependable Vicenzo winery.

Doro '06 is an interesting dried grape wine made from garganega and durella. Its intense aromas of crisply defined fruit and a striking palate, tautened by the durello grape's acidity, endowing it with suppleness and length. The same blend goes into the refreshing Agnobianco '08 while the Vicenza San Martino '07, cabernet sauvignon and merlot in equal quantities, has fruity, subtly balsamic aromas and a textured, harmonious palate. For the lucky few, we recommend the Antico Pasquale, an oxidized dried grape wine we do review because of the limited quantities produced.

Wine	Rating
● Valpolicella Sup. '05	♔♔♔ 5
● Amarone della Valpolicella '04	♔♔ 8
● Cabernet Sauvignon '04	♔♔ 5
● Teroldego '05	♔♔ 6
● Amarone della Valpolicella '03	♔♔♔ 8
● Amarone della Valpolicella '01	♔♔♔ 8
● Amarone della Valpolicella '00	♔♔ 8
● Amarone della Valpolicella '99	♔♔ 8
● Cabernet Sauvignon '03	♔♔ 5
● Cabernet Sauvignon '01	♔♔ 6
● Teroldego '04	♔♔ 6
● Teroldego '02	♔♔ 6
● Valpolicella Sup. '04	♔♔ 5
● Valpolicella Sup. '03	♔♔ 6
● Valpolicella Sup. '02	♔♔ 6

Wine	Rating
○ Doro Passito Bianco '06	♔♔ 6
● Vicenza Rosso San Martino '07	♔♔ 4
○ Agnobianco '08	♔ 4
○ Agnobianco '07	♔♔ 4*
○ Agnobianco '06	♔♔ 4*
○ Doro Passito Bianco '05	♔♔ 5
○ Doro Passito Bianco '04	♔♔ 5
○ Doro Passito Bianco '03	♔♔ 5
● Masari '06	♔♔ 6
● Masari '05	♔♔ 6
● Masari '04	♔♔ 6

Masi

FRAZ. GARGAGNAGO
VIA MONTELEONE, 26
37015 SANT'AMBROGIO DI VALPOLICELLA [VR]
TEL. 0456832511
www.masi.it

CELLAR SALES
PRE-BOOKED VISITS

ANNUAL PRODUCTION 6.800,000 bottles
HECTARES UNDER VINE 520
VITICULTURE METHOD Conventional

Sandro Boscaini's estate is like a battleship moving through the sea of Valpolicella, with over 500 hectares of vineyards and production close to 7,000,000 bottles. It also owns an estate at Latisana and another in Argentina, which attempt to stamp traditional local wines and grapes with the Veronese style. In Valpolicella, the winery's efforts to recover traditional varieties, especially oseleta, demonstrate its links to the local terroir.

The Amarone is on top form in five different wines: two territorial interpretations, which are our favourites, a powerful, weighty Riserva and two others produced with grapes from different areas. Campolongo di Torbe '04 is a deep Amarone, slow to yield its aromas, with a solid but taut and textured palate that earned it Three Glasses. Mazzano '04 missed out on the highest accolade only because it still seems rather clenched while the '05 Vaio Armaron is generous and approachable. Veronese grapes are also used for the dependable Brolo di Campofiorin '06.

Masottina

LOC. CASTELLO ROGANZUOLO
VIA BRADOLINI, 54
31020 SAN FIOR [TV]
TEL. 0438400775
www.masottina.it

CELLAR SALES
PRE-BOOKED VISITS

ANNUAL PRODUCTION 2,000,000 bottles
HECTARES UNDER VINE 44
VITICULTURE METHOD Conventional

The Dal Bianco family's estate is located at Castello di Roganzuolo, an outlying area of San Fior, on the lower hills leading from the Po valley to the Pre-Alps. The vineyards cover over 40 hectares but are not sufficient to guarantee annual production so the estate also uses grapes from various small wineries, which it supervises during the year. Alongside the prosecco-based sparkling wines, which are the driving force of the Treviso area, Masottina also produces some good local non-sparkling wines.

From the well-stocked range, the '06 Merlot Vigneto ai Palazzi Riserva stood out with its rich aromas and well-handled texture. This wine has always impressed our panels in previous years. Just a step behind it is the Montesco '06, with generous hints of fruit and a softer, pleasantly husky palate. The Cabernet Vigneto ai Palazzi Riserva '06 gave a very elegant performance with flowers and undergrowth on the nose and a winningly lean, lingering palate. The whites are also good overall, especially the '07 Rizzardo.

Wine	Rating
● Amarone della Valpolicella Cl. Campolongo di Torbe '04	♥♥♥ 8
● Amarone della Valpolicella Cl. Mazzano '04	♥♥ 8
● Amarone della Valpolicella Cl. Costasera Ris. '04	♥♥ 8
● Amarone della Valpolicella Cl. Vaio Armaron '05	♥♥ 8
● Campofiorin '06	♥♥ 5
● Il Brolo di Campofiorin '06	♥♥ 5
● Amarone della Valpolicella Cl. Costasera '06	♥ 7
● Possessioni Rosso Serègo Alighieri '08	♥ 4
● Valpolicella Cl. Sup. Anniversario 650 anni Serego Alighieri '06	♥ 6
● Amarone della Valpolicella Cl. Campolongo di Torbe '00	♥♥♥ 8
● Amarone della Valpolicella Cl. Mazzano '01	♥♥♥ 8
● Amarone della Valpolicella Cl. Campolongo di Torbe '03	♥♥ 8
● Amarone della Valpolicella Cl. Costasera Ris. '03	♥♥ 8

Wine	Rating
● Colli di Conegliano Rosso Montesco '06	♥♥ 6
● Piave Cabernet Sauvignon Vign. ai Palazzi Ris. '06	♥♥ 5
● Piave Merlot Vign. ai Palazzi Ris. '06	♥♥ 5
○ Cartizze	♥ 6
○ Colli di Conegliano Bianco Rizzardo '07	♥ 5
○ Incrocio Manzoni 6.0.13 '08	♥ 4
○ Piave Chardonnay '08	♥ 3
○ Piave Chardonnay Vign. ai Palazzi '08	♥ 4
● Piave Merlot '08	♥ 3
○ Piave Pinot Bianco '08	♥ 3
● Colli di Conegliano Rosso Montesco '05	♥♥ 6
○ P. di Conegliano Valdobbiadene Extra Dry	♥♥ 4
● Piave Merlot Vign. ai Palazzi Ris. '05	♥♥ 5

Roberto Mazzi

LOC. SAN PERETTO
VIA CROSETTA, 8
37024 NEGRAR [VR]
TEL. 0457502072
www.robertomazzi.it

CELLAR SALES
PRE-BOOKED VISITS

ANNUAL PRODUCTION 50,000 bottles
HECTARES UNDER VINE 8
VITICULTURE METHOD Conventional

The worldwide success enjoyed by Valpolicella producers in recent years has not gone to Antonio and Stefano Mazzis' heads. They remain firmly focused on tradition and their winery is still family run. There have been changes, first in the now beautifully managed vineyards and then in the cellar, which has been modernized and made more efficient. As ever, attention continues to focus on a classic style, interpreted in a more modern key today, with typically clean, elegantly drinkable products.

The '05 Amarone Castel shows explosive ripe red fruit on the nose with hints of medicinal herbs and spices in the background. The soft, approachable palate reflects this exuberant profile, acquiring a rigorous quality with bottle ageing, as we noted from tasting of previous years. The Valpolicella Poiega '06 is very good, with clear juicy fruit supported by nice acidity and smooth tannins on the palate. Somewhat light but equally impressive, the Sanperetto '07 is a savoury Valpolicella with a dry, lingering palate.

Merotto

LOC. COL SAN MARTINO
VIA SCANDOLERA, 21
31010 FARRA DI SOLIGO [TV]
TEL. 0438989000
www.merotto.it

CELLAR SALES
PRE-BOOKED VISITS

ANNUAL PRODUCTION 400,000 bottles
HECTARES UNDER VINE 25
VITICULTURE METHOD Conventional

Col San Martino may be one of the most interesting Prosecco production zones but it lacks the charm of Valdobbiadene and the traditions of Conegliano. However, when you admire the vineyards stretching over the south-facing, cliff-like ridge above the plain, you have a clear sensation of being in a particularly well-suited growing area. Our tastings of the wines produced with passion and skill by Graziano Merotto and his staff only confirmed this impression.

The vast range focuses on the classic Treviso grape variety and is divided into various, extremely sound labels. The slightly sweeter sparkling wines are the most interesting, starting with the La Primavera di Barbara, which is intensely fragrant and striking for sweetness nicely contrasted by savouriness and acidity that expand and lengthen the palate. The Cartizze and the Colmolina '08 are both very good, the former showing subtle and generous while the latter is drier and subtler. The Colbelo is an Extra Dry with excellent fruit.

● Amarone della Valpolicella Cl. Castel '05	♥♥ 8
● Valpolicella Cl. Sup. Vign. Poiega '06	♥♥ 5
● Valpolicella Cl. Sup. Sanperetto '07	♥♥ 4
● Amarone della Valpolicella Cl. Castel '03	♀♀ 8
● Amarone della Valpolicella Cl. Punta di Villa '04	♀♀ 8
● Amarone della Valpolicella Cl. Punta di Villa '03	♀♀ 8
● Amarone della Valpolicella Cl. Punta di Villa '01	♀♀ 7
● Amarone della Valpolicella Cl. Punta di Villa '00	♀♀ 7
● Recioto della Valpolicella Cl. Le Calcarole '05	♀♀ 6
● Recioto della Valpolicella Cl. Le Calcarole '03	♀♀ 6
● Valpolicella Cl. Sup. '06	♀♀ 4*
● Valpolicella Cl. Sup. Vign. Poiega '05	♀♀ 5
● Valpolicella Cl. Sup. Vign. Poiega '04	♀♀ 5
● Valpolicella Cl. Sup. Vign. Poiega '03	♀♀ 5

○ Cartizze	♥♥ 6
○ P. di Valdobbiadene Dry Colmolina '08	♥♥ 4
○ P. di Valdobbiadene Dry La Primavera di Barbara	♥♥ 4*
○ P. di Valdobbiadene Extra Dry Colbelo	♥♥ 4
⊙ Grani Rosa di Nero	♥ 4
○ P. di Valdobbiadene Brut Barreta	♥ 4
○ P. di Valdobbiadene Tranquillo Olchera '08	♥ 4
○ Prosecco Passito Royam '08	♥ 6
○ Cartizze Dry	♀♀ 6
○ P. di Valdobbiadene Dry Colle Molina '02	♀♀ 3*
○ P. di Valdobbiadene Dry La Primavera di Barbara	♀♀ 4

Ornella Molon Traverso

FRAZ. CAMPO DI PIETRA
VIA RISORGIMENTO, 40
31040 SALGAREDA [TV]
TEL. 0422804807
www.ornellamolon.it

CELLAR SALES
PRE-BOOKED VISITS

ANNUAL PRODUCTION **350,000 bottles**
HECTARES UNDER VINE **42**
VITICULTURE METHOD **Conventional**

A few decades ago, Ornella Molon's winery launched the renaissance of this large DOC zone extending along the river Piave. When everyone locally was selling wine in demijohns, Molon renovated her estate and launched a line of products that were revolutionary for the time. Today, the cellar maintains its role as an icon for this area. The range is increasingly impressive and dependable, both the basic products and those from the Ornella selection, as we confirm every year in this Guide.

The well-stocked range is based on single-varietal wines plus a blended white and red. The most representative is Rosso di Villa '06, a monovarietal Merlot with clearly defined fruit and a solid, well-textured palate, which came within a hair's breadth of the finals. While Merlot is traditionally Molon's most successful wine, this year the Cabernet has overtaken it thanks to crisp aromas and a dry, gutsy, quite light palate. The dependably good Vite Rossa '05 is a classic Bordeaux blend while on the white side of the tracks, we enjoyed the excellent performance of the Chardonnay '08.

Monte dall'Ora

LOC. CASTELROTTO
VIA MONTE DALL'ORA, 5
37029 SAN PIETRO IN CARIANO [VR]
TEL. 0457704462
www.montedallora.com

CELLAR SALES
PRE-BOOKED VISITS

ANNUAL PRODUCTION **35,000 bottles**
HECTARES UNDER VINE **5**
VITICULTURE METHOD **Natural**

Just when you think you have discovered all Valpolicella has to offer, something pops out of the top hat. This year's rabbit is Monte dall'Ora, a small estate nestling on the western slope of the hill leading to Castelrotto, which has always yielded excellent grapes for Valpolicella and Recioto. Respect for the vines and their growing environment is a given for Carlo Venturini, who farms these few hectares with care and limits cellar intervention to a minimum to produce wines rich in quality and character.

The range focuses on carefully interpreted DOC wines. The Amarone Classico '05 is closed on the nose with a powerful, gutsy palate while the Stropa '03 is more evolved and mouthfilling. The two Valpolicellas are interesting. Saustò '06 is a Ripasso of depth in a clearly traditional style while the '06 Superiore has fresher aromas and an extraordinarily supple palate. The Recioto '04 is also very good, showing subtle aromas of dried flowers and pepper followed by balanced sweetness and fresh acidity on the palate to lengthen the flavour. The standard-label Valpolicella is very pleasant.

● Piave Cabernet Ornella '06	♀♀ 5
○ Piave Chardonnay Ornella '08	♀♀ 4*
● Piave Merlot Ornella '06	♀♀ 5
● Piave Merlot Rosso di Villa '06	♀♀ 6
● Vite Rossa Ornella '05	♀♀ 5
○ Bianco di Ornella '06	♀ 5
● Piave Raboso Ornella '05	♀ 5
○ Sauvignon Ornella '08	♀ 4
○ Traminer Ornella '08	♀ 4
○ Vite Bianca Ornella '07	♀ 4
● Piave Merlot Rosso di Villa '05	♀♀ 6
● Piave Raboso Ornella '04	♀♀ 5

● Amarone della Valpolicella Cl. '05	♀♀ 7
● Amarone della Valpolicella Cl. Stropa '03	♀♀ 8
● Recioto della Valpolicella Cl. Sant' Ulderico '04	♀♀ 7
● Valpolicella Cl. Sup. '06	♀♀ 5*
● Valpolicella Cl. Sup. Ripasso Saustò '06	♀♀ 5
● Valpolicella Cl. Saseti '08	♀ 3
● Amarone della Valpolicella Cl. '04	♀♀ 7
● Valpolicella Cl. Sup. Ripasso Saustò '04	♀♀ 5

Monte del Frà

S.DA PER CUSTOZA, 35
37066 SOMMACAMPAGNA [VR]
TEL. 045510490
www.montedelfra.it

CELLAR SALES
PRE-BOOKED VISITS

ANNUAL PRODUCTION **1,000,000 bottles**
HECTARES UNDER VINE **178**
VITICULTURE METHOD **Conventional**

Without turning their backs on their Custoza roots, the Bonomo family has extended their vineyards with purchases in Valpolicella at Tenuta Lena di Mezzo, bringing their total up to about 180 hectares for an output of 1,000,000 bottles. Marica's discerning work has brought about a reduction in the range, with efforts now focusing on a more balanced list of increasingly impressive quality. Well done to her, Eligio and Claudio, her father and uncle, who saw the virtues in this little revolution.

Results have not been slow in coming. The '07 Custoza Ca' del Magro only missed our finals by a whisker. The aromas are still simple and youthful but it is on the palate that the wine shows what it is made of: dry and gutsy, with a staggering finish. The Amarone '05, from the new estate at Fumane, is very good, showing approachable and appetizing with fruity aromas that precede a simple, nicely light palate. Of the two Valpolicellas, we preferred the Superiore '07, which is fresher and tauter. Finally, word of praise for the Bardolino and the Custoza, both from '08.

Monte Fasolo

LOC. FAEDO
VIA MONTE FASOLO, 2
35030 CINTO EUGANEO [PD]
TEL. 0429634030
www.montefasolo.com

CELLAR SALES
PRE-BOOKED VISITS

ANNUAL PRODUCTION **200,000 bottles**
HECTARES UNDER VINE **72**
VITICULTURE METHOD **Conventional**

Production at this large Faedo estate has now weak points. Following a renewal in its spirit and management a few years back, the winery is today one of the most interesting in the Colli Euganei. The vast area under vine and the collaboration of professionals like Andrea Boaretti and Filippo Giannone were always going to yield high profile products and excellent value for money. The Mazzuccato family has also come up with an excellent Metodo Classico.

The Metodo Classico, included but often ignored in the DOC zone, demonstrates the area's huge potential for sparkling wines, as long as producers concentrate on cooler, higher growing areas as Monte Fasolo has done. The aromas are still strongly varietal, heralding a savoury, beautifully harmonious wine with perfectly harmonious effervescence. The Milante Serie Oro '04 is also interesting. It's a white made from aromatic grapes which undergoes lengthy bottle ageing. Smoky and intensely citrus-like on the nose, it unveils a slender, very savoury palate. The uncomplicated, flavoursome Colli Euganei Rusta '07 is excellent.

O Custoza Sup. Ca' del Magro '07	♥♥ 4*
● Amarone della Valpolicella Cl. Tenuta Lena di Mezzo '05	♥♥ 7
● Valpolicella Cl. Sup. Ripasso Tenuta Lena di Mezzo '07	♥♥ 6
● Valpolicella Cl. Sup. Tenuta Lena di Mezzo '07	♥♥ 5
● Bardolino '08	♥ 3
O Custoza '08	♥ 4*
● Valpolicella Cl. Tenuta Lena di Mezzo '08	♥ 4
● Amarone della Valpolicella Cl. Tenuta Lena di Mezzo '04	♥♥ 7
● Bardolino '05	♥♥ 3*
O Bianco di Custoza '07	♥♥ 3*
O Bianco di Custoza '05	♥♥ 3*
O Bianco di Custoza Sup. Ca' del Magro '06	♥♥ 3*
● Valpolicella Cl. Sup. Ripasso '03	♥♥ 5
● Valpolicella Cl. Sup. Ripasso Tenuta Lena di Mezzo '06	♥♥ 6

O Colli Euganei Dosaggio Zero M. Cl. '05	♥♥ 6
O Colli Euganei Fior d'Arancio Spumante '08	♥♥ 4
● Colli Euganei Rosso Rusta '07	♥♥ 4*
O Milante Serie Oro '04	♥♥ 4*
O Milante '08	♥ 4
☉ Rosato '08	♥ 3
● Colli Euganei Cabernet Podere Le Tavole '06	♥♥ 4*
● Colli Euganei Cabernet Podere Le Tavole '05	♥♥ 4*
● Colli Euganei Cabernet Podere Le Tavole '04	♥♥ 4*
O Colli Euganei Fior d'Arancio Passito Solone '05	♥♥ 5

Monte Tondo

LOC. MONTE TONDO
VIA SAN LORENZO, 89
37038 SOAVE [VR]
TEL. 0457680347
www.montetondo.it

CELLAR SALES
PRE-BOOKED VISITS

ANNUAL PRODUCTION **160,000 bottles**
HECTARES UNDER VINE **28**
VITICULTURE METHOD **Conventional**

Chatting with Gino Magnabosco, it immediately becomes clear that he is a distillation of the country soul with his frankness and ability to go straight to the heart of the matter, and the simplicity with which he talks about his life as a wine producer. Today, Monte Tondo is an emerging area in the important Soave DOC, producing a limited number of absolutely sound wines from vineyards on the plains and mid-slope hillsides whose grapes are vinified according to the style of the wine being made.

It is hard to say which wine is best. The types are very different but all have plenty of interest to offer. The Soave Classico Montetondo '08 emphasizes this terroir's brightest, gutsiest side with vibrant varietal aromas and a deliciously juicy, engaging palate. The Superiore Foscarin Slavinus '07 shows a more mature, solid profile enhanced by volcanic mineral sensations, and the '07 Casette Foscarin, aged in small oak barrels, is mouthfilling. The cellar also has a growing production of well-typed, well-priced reds from nearby Valpolicella.

La Montecchia

VIA MONTECCHIA, 16
35030 SELVAZZANO DENTRO [PD]
TEL. 049637294
www.lamontecchia.it

CELLAR SALES
PRE-BOOKED VISITS

ANNUAL PRODUCTION **110,000 bottles**
HECTARES UNDER VINE **23**
VITICULTURE METHOD **Conventional**

La Montecchia, on the northernmost edge of the Colli Euganei, is an unusual estate for the area. While others pursue concentrated, powerful wines, the cooler climate at Selvazzano helps imbue finesse and grip into the wines, which range from reds, obviously, to less frequently found types using grapes like raboso, moscato secco or the newly rediscovered turca, an almost forgotten variety. Production quantities from the quite extensive vineyards are modest, indicating a vineyard management philosophy that aims for quality and selects even more severely the cellar.

The house flagship is always the Colli Euganei Rosso Villa Capodilista, a Bordeaux blend of mainly merlot. The '06 gives very ripe fruit and sweet spice on the nose, reflected on the palate with grip and quite a lingering flavour. The Fior d'Arancio Spumante '08 is always one of the best in the DOC, showing free, easy and remarkably fresh. The two less challenging reds are dependably good. Ca' Emo '07 is a fitting younger brother for the Villa Capodilista and the Godimondo '08, a Cabernet Franc, is youthful, fruity and simple in style.

○ Soave Cl. Monte Tondo '08	♀♀ 4*
○ Soave Cl. Sup. Foscarin Slavinus '07	♀♀ 5
○ Soave Cl. Casette Foscarin '07	♀♀ 4
● Amarone della Valpolicella '03	♀ 6
● Giunone Rosso '06	♀ 4
● Valpolicella San Pietro '06	♀ 4
○ Soave Cl. Monte Tondo '06	♀♀♀ 4*
○ Soave Cl. Casette Foscarin '05	♀♀ 4*
○ Soave Cl. Casette Foscarin '04	♀♀ 4*
○ Soave Cl. Monte Tondo '07	♀♀ 4*
○ Soave Cl. Sup. Foscarin Slavinus '04	♀♀ 5
○ Soave Cl. Sup. Foscarin Slavinus '03	♀♀ 5

○ Colli Euganei Moscato Fior d'Arancio Spumante '08	♀♀ 4*
● Colli Euganei Rosso Ca' Emo '07	♀♀ 3*
● Colli Euganei Rosso Villa Capodilista '06	♀♀ 6
● Godimondo Cabernet Franc '08	♀♀ 4*
○ Colli Euganei Pinot Bianco '08	♀ 3
● Forzatè Raboso '06	♀ 4
○ Piùchebello '08	♀ 4
● Turca	♀ 4
● Colli Euganei Rosso Ca' Emo '06	♀♀ 3
● Godimondo Cabernet Franc '07	♀♀ 4

Cantina Sociale di Monteforte d'Alpone

VIA XX SETTEMBRE, 24
37032 MONTEFORTE D'ALPONE [VR]
TEL. 0457610110
www.cantinadimonteforte.it

CELLAR SALES
PRE-BOOKED VISITS

ANNUAL PRODUCTION 2,000,000 bottles
HECTARES UNDER VINE 1300
VITICULTURE METHOD Conventional

At difficult times like these, wineries react in different ways. Some close up like a clam, some dumb down their products in order to obtain a lower price, some venture into new territory while others, like Cantina di Monteforte, raise the quality of their wines by selecting from huge vineyard holdings and applying consolidated skill in the cellar. The wines focus here on the Soave DOC, with forays into Lessinia and nearby Valpolicella. All are of a good standard and excellent value for money.

As they have for several years now, the Soave Classico Clivus '08 and Il Vicario '08 both made an excellent impression. The former has a very vibrantly tropical, approachable style which is all about simplicity. The second wine is more reserved, showing subtle and floral, with a convincing gutsy palate that has good grip. The Soave Classico Superiore Vigneto di Castellaro '07 is more mature with profound aromas which fail to translate fully on the palate. The interesting Lessini Durello Brut '06 is from a vintage year that managed to tame the grape's rebellious nature.

○ Soave Cl. Clivus '08	♈♈	3*
○ Soave Cl. Il Vicario '08	♈♈	3*
○ Lessini Durello Brut M. Cl. '06	♈	4
● Recioto della Valpolicella		
I Vini del Chiostro '06	♈	5
○ Soave Cl. Sup. Vign. di Castellaro '07	♈	4
● Amarone della Valpolicella Re Teodorico '04	♈♈	6
○ Soave Cl. Clivus '07	♈♈	3*
○ Soave Cl. Clivus '06	♈♈	3*
○ Soave Cl. Clivus '05	♈♈	3*
○ Soave Cl. Il Vicario '07	♈♈	3*
○ Soave Cl. Sup. Vign. di Castellaro '05	♈♈	4*
○ Soave Cl. Sup. Vign. di Castellaro '04	♈♈	4

Montegrande

VIA TORRE, 2
35030 ROVOLON [PD]
TEL. 0495226276
www.vinimontegrande.it

CELLAR SALES
PRE-BOOKED VISITS

ANNUAL PRODUCTION 250,000 bottles
HECTARES UNDER VINE 23
VITICULTURE METHOD Conventional

In the face of a slow revolution in the relationship between wine and consumer, which has been greatly felt in Veneto, the Cristofanon family's estate has reiterated its profound commitment to abandoning previously secure strategies to pursue the goal of greater quality. The transition has been tricky but managed skilfully as new wines were introduced before the door was closed definitively on the past. Today, we reckon the winery is more than halfway to its goal and results are very encouraging.

In the absence of the Rosso Vigna delle Roche, it was up to the Cabernet Sereo '06 to fully express the winery's style, which it did with considerable success. Ripe fruit and florality on the nose precede a mid-bodied, succulent palate. Also very good is the Fior d'Arancio Passito '06, which gives strikingly generous aromas ranging from candied citrus peel to camomile, while the palate remains supple thanks to the nicely controlled sweetness. The Casteāro '08 is a dry, bright and intensely fragrant Moscato. The basic red wines are uncomplicated but enjoyable and reasonably priced.

○ Casteāro '08	♈♈	3*
● Colli Euganei Cabernet Sereo '06	♈♈	4*
○ Colli Euganei Fior d'Arancio Passito '06	♈♈	5
○ Colli Euganei Bianco '08	♈	3
● Colli Euganei Cabernet '08	♈	3
○ Colli Euganei Fior d'Arancio Spumante '08	♈	3
● Colli Euganei Merlot '08	♈	3
○ Colli Euganei Pinot Bianco '08	♈	2
● Colli Euganei Rosso '08	♈	2*
● Colli Euganei Cabernet Sereo '05	♈♈	4*
● Colli Euganei Cabernet Sereo '04	♈♈	4*
● Colli Euganei Rosso V. delle Roche '06	♈♈	4*

Giacomo Montresor

VIA CA' DI COZZI, 16
37124 VERONA
TEL. 045913399
www.vinimontresor.it

PRE-BOOKED VISITS

ANNUAL PRODUCTION **3,000,000 bottles**
HECTARES UNDER VINE **152**
VITICULTURE METHOD **Conventional**

The Montresor family's winery has always proceeded with caution in its pricing policies and reactions to trends, remaining faithful to a consolidated model that aims for enjoyable, recognizable wines. The estate's 150-plus hectares of vineyards make selective production management possible and the whims of the market are less important here than at other estates. The range is fairly wide but the wines presented are mostly from Valpolicella, with three versions of Amarone.

Castelliere delle Guaite '05 is the leading wine both in ambition and in price. Its traditional profile offers aromas of undergrowth and cherry jam followed by a dry, savoury palate for an absolutely sound overall result. The Capitel della Crosara '05 is more agile with rich fruit and hints of chocolate, while the palate is softer and more approachable. The third Amarone is even more geared towards simplicity, and the price is an excessively soft palate. The more impressive Valpolicella Castelliere delle Guaite '06 has generous, sophisticated aromas

Mosole

LOC. CORBOLONE
VIA ANNONE VENETO, 60
30029 SANTO STINO DI LIVENZA [VE]
TEL. 0421310404
www.mosole.com

CELLAR SALES
PRE-BOOKED VISITS

ANNUAL PRODUCTION **220,000 bottles**
HECTARES UNDER VINE **29.5**
VITICULTURE METHOD **Conventional**

The arrival of a consultant oenologist of the stature of Gianni Menotti from neighbouring Friuli has given a new drive to the products of Lucio Mosole, and today this is one of the most interesting wineries in the large Lison-Pramaggiore DOC with its characteristic flat, clayey land. The range is quite well organized with a line of standard-label wines in new packaging, which best represent the cellar's new direction, a more structured Bianco and Rosso Eleo and finally three more ambitious wines.

While we wait for the more ambitious wines to appear, we tasted an excellent version of Hora Sexta '07, a Chardonnay aged in oak which becomes more impressive every year. Vibrant, ripe fruit aromas and discreetly but never excessively evident oak on the palate make this a dry, solid white. The very good Lison Eleo '08 is a salty Tai from the nose on, with a buttery, gutsy palate. The red Eleo simpler but nicely rounded while the basic line has gained in definition and aromatic expression on the nose and palate.

● Amarone della Valpolicella Cl. Capitel della Crosara '05	♟♟ 8
● Amarone della Valpolicella Cl. Castelliere delle Guaite '05	♟♟ 8
● Valpolicella Cl. Primo Ripasso Castelliere delle Guaite '06	♟♟ 6
● Amarone della Valpolicella Cl. Cantina Privata del Fondatore '05	♟ 7
● Recioto della Valpolicella Re Teodorico '06	♟ 7
○ Soave Cl. Capitel Alto '08	♟ 4
● Amarone della Valpolicella Cl. Cantina Privata del Fondatore '02	♟♟ 7
● Amarone della Valpolicella Cl. Capitel della Crosara '04	♟♟ 8
● Amarone della Valpolicella Cl. Castelliere delle Guaite '04	♟♟ 8
● Amarone della Valpolicella Cl. Castelliere delle Guaite '98	♟♟ 8
○ Lugana Gran Guardia '07	♟♟ 5
● Valpolicella Cl. Primo Ripasso Castelliere delle Guaite '05	♟♟ 6

○ Hora Sexta '07	♟♟ 4*
○ Lison-Pramaggiore Eleo Bianco '08	♟♟ 4*
● Lison-Pramaggiore Rosso Eleo '08	♟♟ 4
● Lison-Pramaggiore Cabernet Franc '08	♟ 4
○ Lison-Pramaggiore Chardonnay '08	♟ 4
● Lison-Pramaggiore Merlot '08	♟ 4
● Lison-Pramaggiore Refosco P. R. '08	♟ 4
○ Lison-Pramaggiore Sauvignon '08	♟ 4
○ Pinot Grigio '08	♟ 4
● Lison-Pramaggiore Cabernet Hora Sexta '06	♟♟ 4
● Lison-Pramaggiore Merlot Ad Nonam '06	♟♟ 5
● Lison-Pramaggiore Merlot Ad Nonam '04	♟♟ 5

Il Mottolo

LOC. LE CONTARINE
VIA COMEZZARE
35030 BAONE [PD]
TEL. 049632185

ANNUAL PRODUCTION **15,000 bottles**
HECTARES UNDER VINE **6**
VITICULTURE METHOD **Conventional**

Sergio Fortin and Roberto Dalla Libera made an emphatic appearance on the winemaking scene from entirely different professional contexts. The former is a dentist and the latter a businessman. Their small estate produces about 15,000 bottles per year from grapes grown on the six hectares around the winery. The vineyards at the foot of the hills produce the basic wines while the more coastal vineyards are used for the winery's selection, Serro. They are all nicely aspected and ventilated, so vineyard intervention is kept to a minimum.

The '06 Colli Euganei Rosso Serro took a significant step forward compared to previous versions, proffering aromatics that opening out slowly into delicious minerally and balsamic sensations. The palate is still youthful but generous and as nicely savoury as the wine's development in the glass is interesting. The basic wines are also good. Merlot Comezzara '07 is impressively solid and harmonious on the palate while the '07 Cabernet Vigna Marè has a hard nose, countered by a succulent, balanced flavour. Le Contarine is fresh and engagingly aromatic.

Musella

LOC. FERRAZZE
VIA FERRAZZETTE, 2
37036 SAN MARTINO BUON ALBERGO [VR]
TEL. 045973385
www.musella.it

CELLAR SALES
PRE-BOOKED VISITS
VISITOR FACILITIES

ANNUAL PRODUCTION **120,000 bottles**
HECTARES UNDER VINE **34**
VITICULTURE METHOD **Conventional**

The strength of a winery like this one owned by Maddalena Pasqua and her father Emilio lies in the vineyards, a vast green island emerging from the plains behind Verona. In this unspoilt area with few vineyards, biodiversity is a reality. The few bottles produced from so many hectares provide an idea of the meticulous care taken in both the vineyards and the cellar, where a limited range of wines are produced, mainly in the traditional Veronese style. Alongside these, there is some experimentation with classic grapes and wines.

Amarone and the Recioto remain the diamond-head of the range, especially Amarone. The '05 Riserva missed our highest accolade by a hair's breadth. Its aromas range from ripe fruit to spices, via fines herbes and dried flowers, introducing a mouthfilling wine whose texture is held in check by densely woven tannins. The '06 Recioto is more explosive and approachable, showing restrained, nicely integrated sweetness. The excellent Valpolicella Vigne Nuove '07 has freshness and grip. Monte del Drago '05, from cabernet and corvina, is good as ever.

● Colli Euganei Rosso Serro '06	♈♈ 4*
● Colli Euganei Cabernet V. Marè '07	♈♈ 3*
● Colli Euganei Merlot Comezzara '07	♈♈ 3*
○ Le Contarine '08	♈♈ 3*
● Colli Euganei Cabernet V. Marè '06	♈♈ 3*
○ Colli Euganei Fior d'Arancio Passito Vigna del Pozzo '06	♈♈ 5
● Colli Euganei Merlot Comezzara '06	♈♈ 3*
● Colli Euganei Rosso Serro '05	♈♈ 4*

● Amarone della Valpolicella Ris. '05	♈♈ 7
● Recioto della Valpolicella '06	♈♈ 6
● Monte del Drago Rosso '05	♈♈ 6
● Valpolicella Sup. Ripasso '06	♈♈ 4
● Valpolicella Sup. Vigne Nuove di Musella '07	♈♈ 4
○ Bianco del Drago '06	♈ 4
● Amarone della Valpolicella '03	♈♈ 6
● Amarone della Valpolicella '01	♈♈ 7
● Amarone della Valpolicella '00	♈♈ 7
● Amarone della Valpolicella Senza Titolo '00	♈♈ 8
● Monte del Drago Rosso '03	♈♈ 6
● Recioto della Valpolicella '04	♈♈ 6
● Valpolicella Sup. Ripasso '05	♈♈ 4*
● Valpolicella Sup. Ripasso '04	♈♈ 4*
● Valpolicella Sup. Vigne Nuove '05	♈♈ 4*

Daniele Nardello

VIA IV NOVEMBRE, 56
37032 MONTEFORTE D'ALPONE [VR]
TEL. 0457612116
www.nardellovini.it

CELLAR SALES
PRE-BOOKED VISITS

ANNUAL PRODUCTION **30,000 bottles**
HECTARES UNDER VINE **15**
VITICULTURE METHOD **Conventional**

Daniele and Federica Nardello have finally hit the bull's eye of a full profile in the Guide, thanks to some very exciting wines. The vineyards cover several areas of the DOC zone, although the largest and most interesting part is on Mount Zoppega, halfway between Soave and Monteforte, where they make sunny, mouthfillingly soft wines from the all south-facing rows. The products are strongly traditional including the Recioto, to which Daniele is absolutely devoted.

Daniele's Soave Classico Vigna Turbian uses the maximum percentage of trebbiano allowed in the regulations. The '08 has subtle aromas and a definitely dry, slender palate. Monte Zoppega '07 is softer and more mature, using the local characteristics to give rounded sensations on the palate and generous aromas with fruit playing a leading role. The '06 Recioto Soavissimus shuns explosively sugary aromas in favour of rather elegant, subtle sensations and a supple palate with nicely controlled sweetness. The '08 Soave Classico Meridies is approachable and enjoyable.

Angelo Nicolis e Figli

VIA VILLA GIRARDI, 29
37029 SAN PIETRO IN CARIANO [VR]
TEL. 0457701261
www.vininicolis.com

CELLAR SALES
PRE-BOOKED VISITS

ANNUAL PRODUCTION **200,000 bottles**
HECTARES UNDER VINE **42**
VITICULTURE METHOD **Conventional**

The Nicolis brothers' winery covers over 40 hectares of vineyards in various parts of Valpolicella, both on foothills and at higher altitudes. This makes rigorous selection of the grapes possible, since the various sites have different characteristics. Cellar procedures are limited to treating the raw material as well as possible, with vinification and ageing processes that respect the profile of the classic Veronese types. These are well represented by Nicolis wines, which are firmly founded on tradition.

The two Amarones are always impressive. Ambrosan '04 is generous, powerful and very mature with wonderful, generous fruit while the '05 Classico shows more elegance and varied aromas, supported on the palate by supple suppleness despite the weighty structure. The '06 Seccal is a Valpolicella with generous aromas and a dry, savoury palate while Testal '05, again made from traditional grapes, has very warm, mature aromas reflected on a taut, mouthwatering palate. Lastly, there was an excellent performance from the youthful, explosive Recioto '06.

○ Recioto di Soave Suavissimus '06	♟♟	6
○ Soave Cl. Monte Zoppega '07	♟♟	4*
○ Soave Cl. V. Turbian '08	♟♟	4*
○ Soave Cl. Meridies '08	♟	3*
○ Recioto di Soave Suavissimus '05	♟♟	7
○ Soave Cl. V. Turbian '07	♟♟	4*

● Amarone della Valpolicella Cl. '05	♟	7
● Amarone della Valpolicella Cl. Ambrosan '04	♟♟	8
● Recioto della Valpolicella Cl. '06	♟♟	6
● Testal '05	♟♟	5
● Valpolicella Cl. Sup. Seccal '06	♟♟	5
● Valpolicella Cl. '08	♟	4
● Valpolicella Cl. Sup. '07	♟	4
● Amarone della Valpolicella Cl. Ambrosan '98	♟♟♟	8
● Amarone della Valpolicella Cl. Ambrosan '93	♟♟♟	8
● Amarone della Valpolicella Cl. '01	♟♟	7
● Amarone della Valpolicella Cl. '00	♟♟	7
● Amarone della Valpolicella Cl. Ambrosan '03	♟♟	8
● Amarone della Valpolicella Cl. Ambrosan '01	♟♟	8
● Amarone della Valpolicella Cl. Ambrosan '00	♟♟	8
● Valpolicella Cl. Sup. Seccal '05	♟♟	5

Nino Franco

VIA GARIBALDI, 147
31049 VALDOBBIADENE [TV]
TEL. 0423972051
www.ninofranco.it

CELLAR SALES
PRE-BOOKED VISITS
VISITOR FACILITIES

ANNUAL PRODUCTION 1.200,000 bottles
HECTARES UNDER VINE 2.5
VITICULTURE METHOD Conventional

The fact that Prosecco is one of the world's best-known and loved Italian wines is also thanks to Primo Franco, one of the first to travel around publicizing Treviso's sparkling wines. But don't look for echoes of any tradition chez Franco. Primo's wines are his own, first and foremost, in a style that exalts the terroir and the grape without masking the producer's own hand, which is evident in the vibrant, ripe fruit aromas of every single bottle.

What a great performance from the '08 Grave di Stecca, a Prosecco Brut with rare finesse and grip, at its best a year after bottling as emerged from our tasting of the vintage. Three Glasses. The Primo Franco '08 is a more vibrant, fruity Dry that uses its sugar to enhance the intensity of its aromas while the Cartizze is its usual thoroughbred self. Turning to the Bruts, we note an excellent performance from Rive di San Floriano, with delicate floral and apple fruit aromas, caressing fizz and a savoury flavour. The basic Brut is more approachable and racy.

Novaia

VIA NOVAIA, 1
37020 MARANO DI VALPOLICELLA [VR]
TEL. 0457755129
www.novaia.it

CELLAR SALES
PRE-BOOKED VISITS

ANNUAL PRODUCTION 32,000 bottles
HECTARES UNDER VINE 7
VITICULTURE METHOD Conventional

From on high at Marano, the Vaona family's winery never misses the mark thanks to a shrewd, unhurried process of renewal. First came the vineyards, which have gradually been converted to vertical-trellis training, and then in the cellar, where interpretation of the wines puts the accent on finesse rather than structure. The range presented is divided into two lines, one simpler and more traditional, linked to the DOC, and the other more innovative and ambitious, in which references to the DOC zone are flanked by mentions of the individual vineyard.

The Amarone Corte Vaona '05 is traditional in style with approachable stewed fruit and aniseed on the nose slowly giving way to dried flowers and fines herbes. The palate is dry and nicely balanced. The more interesting Valpolicella I Cantoni '06 has well-defined florality countered by a dry, mouthwatering, gutsy palate. The Ripasso '06 is richer but less expressive, showing rounded and fruity with lovely soft flavours. Lastly, there was an excellent performance from the standard-label Valpolicella.

○ Valdobbiadene Grave di Stecca Brut '08	♀♀♀ 6
○ Cartizze	♀♀ 5
○ P. di Valdobbiadene Brut	♀♀ 4*
○ P. di Valdobbiadene Brut Rive di S. Floriano	♀♀ 4*
○ P. di Valdobbiadene Dry Primo Franco '08	♀♀ 4
⊙ Brut Rosé Faive '08	♀ 4
○ Prosecco Brut Rustico	♀ 4
○ P. di Valdobbiadene Brut Rustico	♀♀ 4
○ P. di Valdobbiadene Dry Primo Franco '07	♀♀ 4
○ P. di Valdobbiadene Dry Primo Franco '06	♀♀ 4
○ Valdobbiadene Grave di Stecca Brut '07	♀♀ 6

● Amarone della Valpolicella Cl. Corte Vaona '05	♀♀ 6
● Valpolicella Cl. Sup. I Cantoni '06	♀♀ 5
● Valpolicella Cl. Sup. Ripasso '06	♀♀ 4
● Recioto della Valpolicella Cl. Le Novaje '06	♀ 5
● Valpolicella Cl. '08	♀ 3*
● Amarone della Valpolicella Cl. Corte Vaona '04	♀♀ 6
● Amarone della Valpolicella Cl. Corte Vaona '03	♀♀ 6*
● Amarone della Valpolicella Cl. Le Balze '01	♀♀ 8
● Valpolicella Cl. '06	♀♀ 3
● Valpolicella Cl. Sup. I Cantoni '05	♀♀ 5
● Valpolicella Cl. Sup. I Cantoni '04	♀♀ 4

Ottella

FRAZ. SAN BENEDETTO DI LUGANA
LOC. OTTELLA
37019 PESCHIERA DEL GARDA [VR]
TEL. 0457551950
www.ottella.it

CELLAR SALES
PRE-BOOKED VISITS

ANNUAL PRODUCTION **200,000 bottles**
HECTARES UNDER VINE **30**
VITICULTURE METHOD **Conventional**

Lugana, which is shared with Lombardy, is one of the smallest Veneto DOC zones, with well under 1,000 hectares of vineyards. But given the fortunate combination of climate, grape varieties and soil, the results are often very good indeed, as is demonstrated by the Montresor products which have for years been our favourites from this corner of Lake Garda. Apart from a few bottles of red wine, the products focus on Lugana, interpreted in a generous style with vigorous acidity. These wines are at their best after a few years' ageing.

There was an extraordinary performance from the '07 Molceo, a Lugana Superiore with strikingly sophisticated aromas perfectly reflected on a mouthwatering, savoury palate with a lingering finish. The '08 Le Creete on the other hand has vibrant, sometimes almost intoxicating aromas with fresh hints of flowers and citrus fruit and a firm, nicely fruity palate. The exemplary Lugana '08 is a wine for all seasons, fruity on the nose and harmonious on the palate. Turning to the reds, once again we liked the '07 Campo Sireso, a Bordeaux blend enhanced by a splash of peppery corvina.

★ Leonildo Pieropan

VIA CAMUZZONI, 3
37038 SOAVE [VR]
TEL. 0456190171
www.pieropan.it

CELLAR SALES
PRE-BOOKED VISITS

ANNUAL PRODUCTION **400,000 bottles**
HECTARES UNDER VINE **45**
VITICULTURE METHOD **Conventional**

It's hard to find anything new to say about Nino and Teresita Pieropan's estate, which has been at the top of Italian winemaking for over four decades. The vineyards, managed in exemplary fashion, cover almost 50 hectares, a small part planted to the classic red varieties of Valpolicella. We finally tasted the first of these products, a goal strongly pursued by the entire winery and particularly by the Pieropan sons, Andrea and Dario, who play an important and increasingly independent role alongside their parents.

The new wine is Ruberpan '04, a red made from grapes belonging to the Valpolicella heritage. It proffers intense wild berries and pepper, with flowers and medicinal herbs peeking out from behind. Elegance is the keynote of the austere palate, which is well supported by incisive acidity. Turning to the whites, the Calvarino '07 gave its usual masterly performance in a memorable version. Its intensity, generosity and class are simply staggering. Just a step behind it are the rich, complex La Rocca '07 and the sophisticated, mouthwateringly drinkable Soave Classico '08.

○ Lugana Sup. Molceo '07	♔♔♔	5
● Campo Sireso '07	♔♔	5
○ Lugana '08	♔♔	4*
○ Lugana Le Creete '08	♔♔	4*
● Gemei Rosso '08	♔	4
☉ Roses Roses '08	♔	4
● Campo Sireso '06	♕♕	5
● Campo Sireso '05	♕♕	5
● Campo Sireso '04	♕♕	5
○ Lugana Le Creete '07	♕♕	4*
○ Lugana Sup. Molceo '06	♕♕	5

○ Soave Cl. Calvarino '07	♔♔♔	5
○ Soave Cl. La Rocca '07	♔♔	6
● Ruberpan '04	♔♔	5
○ Soave Cl. '08	♔♔	4*
○ Soave Cl. Calvarino '06	♕♕♕	5
○ Soave Cl. Calvarino '05	♕♕♕	5
○ Soave Cl. Calvarino '04	♕♕♕	5
○ Soave Cl. Calvarino '03	♕♕♕	5
○ Soave Cl. Calvarino '02	♕♕♕	5
○ Soave Cl. La Rocca '02	♕♕♕	6
○ Soave Cl. Sup. Calvarino '98	♕♕♕	5
○ Soave Cl. Sup. La Rocca '00	♕♕♕	6
○ Soave Cl. Sup. La Rocca '99	♕♕♕	6
○ Soave Cl. Sup. La Rocca '98	♕♕♕	6
○ Soave Cl. Sup. La Rocca '96	♕♕♕	6
○ Soave Cl. Sup. La Rocca '95	♕♕♕	6

Piovene Porto Godi

FRAZ. TOARA
VIA VILLA, 14
36020 VILLAGA [VI]
TEL. 0444885142
www.piovene.com

CELLAR SALES
PRE-BOOKED VISITS

ANNUAL PRODUCTION **80,000 bottles**
HECTARES UNDER VINE **32**
VITICULTURE METHOD **Conventional**

Tommaso Piovene's winery is among those that uphold the name of Colli Berici, an area whose huge winemaking potential is still largely untapped. This is certainly not true for Piovene, where growing practices were converted some time ago to focus on high quality, as shown by tastings in recent years. The 30-plus hectares of vineyards produce fewer than 100,000 bottles with various varieties grown on the best-aspected slopes in the quest for the perfect combination of grapes and terroir.

Two wines came close to the highest accolade this year, the '07 Merlot Fra i Broli and Thovara '07, a Tai Rosso that tips its hat to the Rhône valley. Generous, mature aromas distinguish the mouthfilling, very flavoursome palate with its sweet, smooth tannin. The Merlot '07 gives explosive aromas of ripe, healthy fruit to enhance the soft, rounded palate, nicely offset by succulent acidity. The excellent lighter version of Tai Rosso, Riveselle '08, is bright and savoury while the '07 Passito Thovara from garganega has rich, Mediterranean aromas and a very harmonious palate.

Umberto Portinari

LOC. BROGNOLIGO
VIA SANTO STEFANO, 2
37032 MONTEFORTE D'ALPONE [VR]
TEL. 0456175087
portinarivini@libero.it

CELLAR SALES
PRE-BOOKED VISITS

ANNUAL PRODUCTION **30,000 bottles**
HECTARES UNDER VINE **4**
VITICULTURE METHOD **Conventional**

We are by now used to the fact that Umberto Portinari only presents his wines if he feels they are ready and worthy of their label, which is the case this year. Although the winery is strongly rooted in an old-style country concept of wine, there is an air of constant evolution here and nothing is taken for granted or considered perfect. Every stage in the vineyard and the cellar is called into question should problems arise. The products are traditional in wine type and style, which is strongly influenced by the soul of the garganega grape.

The '07 Albare is the most impressive Soave in the range with its fresh floral and fruity aromas and a light minerally sensation that slowly emerge. It opens out elegantly on the palate into a nicely rounded, savoury progression and lingering finale. The '04 Santo Stefano, on the other hand, seems slightly too mature with generous hints of peach and apricot fruit and a broad, mouthfilling palate. The Ronchetto and Recioto Oro are still ageing in the cellar and were not presented.

● Colli Berici Merlot Fra i Broli '07	♥♥ 5
● Colli Berici Tai Rosso Thovara '07	♥♥ 6
● Colli Berici Tai Rosso Vign. Riveselle '08	♥♥ 3
○ Thovara Passito Bianco '07	♥♥ 5
○ Colli Berici Garganega Vign. Riveselle '08	♥ 4*
○ Colli Berici Sauvignon Vigneto Fostine '08	♥ 4
● Polveriera Rosso '08	♥ 4
○ Sauvignon Campigie '07	♥ 5
● Colli Berici Cabernet Vign. Pozzare '06	♥♥ 5
● Colli Berici Merlot Fra i Broli '06	♥♥ 5
● Colli Berici Tocai Rosso Thovara '04	♥♥ 6

○ Soave Albare Doppia Maturazione Ragionata '07	♥♥ 4
○ Soave Santo Stefano '04	♥ 5
○ Soave Sup. V. Albare Doppia Maturazione Ragionata '97	♥♥♥ 4
○ Recioto di Soave Oro '02	♥♥ 6
○ Recioto di Soave Oro '01	♥♥ 6
○ Recioto di Soave Oro '00	♥♥ 5
○ Soave Albare Doppia Maturazione Ragionata '05	♥♥ 4*
○ Soave Albare Doppia Maturazione Ragionata '04	♥♥ 4*
○ Soave Cl. Ronchetto '07	♥♥ 4*
○ Soave Cl. Ronchetto '06	♥♥ 4*
○ Soave Cl. Ronchetto '05	♥♥ 4*
○ Soave Cl. Sup. V. Ronchetto '01	♥♥ 3

Prà

VIA DELLA FONTANA, 31
37032 MONTEFORTE D'ALPONE [VR]
TEL. 0457612125
grazianopra@libero.it

CELLAR SALES
PRE-BOOKED VISITS

ANNUAL PRODUCTION 220,000 bottles
HECTARES UNDER VINE 20
VITICULTURE METHOD Conventional

Like several colleagues in the Soave area, Graziano Prà decided to try his luck with wines from nearby Valpolicella, purchasing and planting a prestigious plot straddling both DOCs. This year, we tasted the new products, though the estate's heart remains firmly in Soave, its emblematic wine, which has won over a large number of admirers. The vineyards, especially in Valpolicella, are farmed with diminishing use of chemicals and we are of course happy about this. Wines and environment will reap the benefits.

Three reds were presented. The '06 Amarone gives generous aromas and a very elegant, almost light profile. Floral and peppery, the '06 Valpolicella Superiore pervades the palate almost imperceptibly and the '07 Valpolicella is also peppery. The Soaves turned in an excellent performance. The rich, tropical '07 Staforte hands back its crown this year to the '08 Monte Grande, a wonderfully sophisticated Three Glass wine with superb harmony throughout. The very good Colle Sant'Antonio '07 is ripe and mouthfilling while special praise goes to the very fine '08 Classico. It's generous, succulent and racy on the palate.

★ Giuseppe Quintarelli

VIA CERÈ, 1
37024 NEGRAR [VR]
TEL. 0457500016
giuseppe.quintarelli@tin.it

CELLAR SALES
PRE-BOOKED VISITS

ANNUAL PRODUCTION 60,000 bottles
HECTARES UNDER VINE 12
VITICULTURE METHOD Conventional

Quintarelli means history in Valpolicella. Despite a shorter history than some others, the estate has always stood for high quality and, particularly, the identity of the terroir. Quintarelli alone has continued to produce a Recioto only once or twice in a decade, never using grapes for the principal wine unless they were of the highest quality. This is true of the Amarone, released after long ageing, and not every harvest is considered worthy. The products adhere to the designation styles with a couple of forays into international wines, which remain faithful to the Quintarelli style.

This year, we were lucky enough to taste all the wines from the designation, which is a rare thing for Quintarelli. The engaging Amarone '00 is closed on the nose and slow to yield up its aromas of fruit and earth, spices and dried flowers. The palate shows a powerful body, while remaining light and savoury. The monumental Recioto '97 is a hymn to tradition with alluring aromas and an enthralling palate, to say the least. It's a perfect match of sweetness and austerity with an endless finish. Both were runaway Three Glass winners. Lastly, the Valpolicella Superiore '01 is mature and mouthfilling.

O Soave Cl. Monte Grande '08	♟♟♟	5
O Soave Cl. Staforte '07	♟	5
● Amarone della Valpolicella '06	♟♟	8
O Soave Cl. '08	♟♟	4*
O Soave Cl. Colle S. Antonio '07	♟♟	5
● Valpolicella Sup. Morandina '06	♟♟	8
● Valpolicella Morandina '07	♟	4
O Soave Cl. Monte Grande '06	♟♟♟	5
O Soave Cl. Monte Grande '05	♟♟♟	5
O Soave Cl. Monte Grande '04	♟♟♟	5
O Soave Cl. Monte Grande '03	♟♟♟	5
O Soave Cl. Monte Grande '02	♟♟♟	5
O Soave Cl. Staforte '06	♟♟♟	5*
O Soave Cl. Sup. Monte Grande '00	♟♟♟	5

● Amarone della Valpolicella Cl. '00	♟♟♟	8
● Recioto della Valpolicella Cl. Monte Ca' Paletta '97	♟♟♟+	8
● Valpolicella Cl. Sup. '01	♟♟	8
● Alzero Cabernet Franc '90	♟♟♟	8
● Amarone della Valpolicella Cl. '98	♟♟♟	8
● Amarone della Valpolicella Cl. '97	♟♟♟	8
● Amarone della Valpolicella Cl. '86	♟♟♟	8
● Amarone della Valpolicella Cl. '84	♟♟♟	8
● Amarone della Valpolicella Cl. Ris. '83	♟♟♟	8
● Amarone della Valpolicella Cl. Sup. Monte Cà Paletta '93	♟♟♟	8
● Amarone della Valpolicella Cl. Sup. Ris. '85	♟♟♟	6
● Recioto della Valpolicella Cl. '95	♟♟♟	8
● Rosso del Bepi '96	♟♟♟	8
● Valpolicella Cl. Sup. '99	♟♟♟	8

Le Ragose

FRAZ. ARBIZZANO
VIA LE RAGOSE, 1
37020 NEGRAR [VR]
TEL. 0457513241
www.leragose.com

CELLAR SALES
PRE-BOOKED VISITS

ANNUAL PRODUCTION **150,000 bottles**
HECTARES UNDER VINE **19**
VITICULTURE METHOD **Conventional**

The Galli brothers' estate is situated in the upper Negrar valley where homes increasingly make room for vineyards that yield grapes of unusual finesse and freshness at these altitudes. The winery style has always aimed to enhance these features and even when the market demanded robust, concentrated wines, the Gallis maintained their classic nature. Production focuses on DOC wines, which we appreciate every year for their stylistic continuity.

The '05 Valpolicella Classico Superiore Le Sassine embodies the Ragose style more than any other. Its vibrant fruit-led aromas include medicinal herbs, dried flowers, hints of forest floor and Mediterranean scrubland. The astonishingly light palate masks its concentration through to a long, impressive finish. Obviously enough, the Amarone '04 is the most rounded wine, and the fruit is more defined and evident, but the palate is in the same style with plenty of flavour and grip. The very good Valpolicella Classico '08 has a mouthwatering, gutsy palate.

Roccolo Grassi

VIA SAN GIOVANNI DI DIO, 19
37030 MEZZANE DI SOTTO [VR]
TEL. 0458880089
roccolograssi@libero.it

PRE-BOOKED VISITS

ANNUAL PRODUCTION **38,000 bottles**
HECTARES UNDER VINE **14**
VITICULTURE METHOD **Conventional**

The area east of Valpolicella Classica is usually described as "extended", as if it were only included in the DOC for administrative reasons. But in fact this area contains a remarkable concentration of high quality estates, as is shown every year by Marco and Francesca Sartori. The winery's strength is found firstly in the vineyards, which are tended like a garden, and then in the clear-headed cellar strategies aiming at products that are modern in style yet still linked to tradition in their flavour.

In the absence of the Amarone, owing to a problematic 2005 vintage year for this area, we focused our attention on the excellent '06 Valpolicella, which just missed our highest accolade by a hair's breadth. The aromas are profound, slow to unfold, and include overripe fruit and aromatic herbs, while the palate is very solid and harmonious, showing powerful yet supple. The '07 is an interesting interpretation of the Soave Superiore La Broia which plays on structure and strength while the Recioto '05 shows vibrant aromas of nuts and chocolate with a sweet palate supported by densely woven tannin.

Le Ragose		
● Valpolicella Cl. Sup. Le Sassine '05	♟♟	4
● Amarone della Valpolicella Cl. '04	♟♟	8*
● Recioto della Valpolicella Cl. '06	♟♟	6
● Valpolicella Cl. '08	♟♟	4*
● Amarone della Valpolicella Cl. '88	♟♟♟	8
● Amarone della Valpolicella Cl. '86	♟♟♟	8
● Valpolicella Amarone '88	♟♟♟	4
● Valpolicella Amarone '86	♟♟♟	5
● Amarone della Valpolicella Marta Galli '01	♟♟	8
● Valpolicella Cl. Sup. Le Sassine '03	♟♟	4
● Valpolicella Cl. Sup. Le Sassine Ripasso '04	♟♟	4*

Roccolo Grassi		
● Recioto della Valpolicella Roccolo Grassi '05	♟♟	6
○ Soave Sup. La Broia '07	♟♟	4*
● Valpolicella Sup. Roccolo Grassi '06	♟♟	6
● Amarone della Valpolicella Roccolo Grassi '00	♟♟♟	8
● Amarone della Valpolicella Roccolo Grassi '99	♟♟♟	8
● Valpolicella Sup. Roccolo Grassi '04	♟♟♟	6
● Amarone della Valpolicella Roccolo Grassi '04	♟♟	8
● Amarone della Valpolicella Roccolo Grassi '03	♟♟	8
● Recioto della Valpolicella Roccolo Grassi '03	♟♟	6
● Recioto della Valpolicella Roccolo Grassi '02	♟♟	6
○ Soave Sup. La Broia '06	♟♟	4
● Valpolicella Sup. Roccolo Grassi '05	♟♟	6

Vigna Roda

LOC. CORTELÀ
VIA MONTE VERSA, 1569
35030 VÒ [PD]
TEL. 0499940228
www.vignaroda.com

CELLAR SALES
PRE-BOOKED VISITS

ANNUAL PRODUCTION **52,000 bottles**
HECTARES UNDER VINE **17**
VITICULTURE METHOD **Conventional**

The Colli Euganei area's rapid ascent to the heights of Veneto, and consequently Italian, wine owes much to well-known wineries that have established themselves with determination. However there is no lack of wineries like Gianni Strazzacappa's which contribute further strength to the DOC zone. Gianni has less than 20 hectares of vines producing small quantities of significant wines, all in the rich, solid style which is the trademark of these wonderful hills. Two varietal reds, the Scarlatto and a mouthwatering Passito, form the heart of the range.

The Scarlatto '06 is the spearhead. A classic merlot-led Bordeaux blend, it gives clear, vibrant aromas of fruit and spice with a lovely vegetal hint in the background. The palate manages to be both complex and supple with good grip. The encouragingly priced '08 Merlot is huskier but very enjoyable. In fact, it's a weighty wine which should age nicely for a few years. Alluring sweetness is the keynote of the Fior d'Arancio Passito '06, with intoxicating aromas of flowers and citrus fruit, liquorice and minerally hints.

Roeno

VIA MAMA, 5
37020 BRENTINO BELLUNO [VR]
TEL. 0457230110
www.cantinaroeno.com

CELLAR SALES
PRE-BOOKED VISITS
VISITOR FACILITIES
FOOD

ANNUAL PRODUCTION **80,000 bottles**
HECTARES UNDER VINE **25**
VITICULTURE METHOD **Conventional**

Valdadige may be the least known of the Veneto DOCs but it has remarkable potential thanks to a good range of soil types and an even more impressive climate – sunny but with cool breezes – which combine to create good temperature variation and healthy grapes. The Fugatti brothers' winery seems to be the most interesting today. The extensive vineyards are cared for with great passion and attentive work in the cellar, with plenty of experimentation, do much to promote the area.

All the most important wines are in some sense a challenge, starting with the Roeno '06, an original blend of cabernet franc and marzemino that shows fragrant and powerful on the palate, while the Enantio '06, from lambrusco a foglia frastagliata, is rounded with solid structure. Even more intriguing is the Cristina '06, from late-harvested trebbiano, sauvignon, pinot grigio and chardonnay. No two versions are ever the same and this year it is complex, Mediterranean and weighty on the palate. All the basic products are interesting, especially the gutsy Pinot Grigio Terra dei Forti '08.

○ Colli Euganei Fior d'Arancio Passito '06	▼▼ 5
● Colli Euganei Merlot '08	▼▼ 4*
● Colli Euganei Rosso Scarlatto '06	▼▼ 4*
○ Colli Euganei Chardonnay Ca' Zamira '08	▼ 4
● Colli Euganei Rosso Scarlatto '05	♀♀ 4*
● Colli Euganei Rosso Scarlatto '04	♀♀ 4*
● Colli Euganei Rosso Scarlatto '03	♀♀ 4*

○ Cristina V. T. '06	▼▼ 6
● Rosso Roeno '06	▼▼ 5
● Valdadige Terra dei Forti Enantio '06	▼▼ 5
○ Valdadige Terra dei Forti Pinot Grigio '08	▼▼ 4*
☉ Bardolino Chiaretto Brut Matì Curvée Rosé '08	▼ 4
● La Rua Marzemino '08	▼ 4
○ Müller Thurgau Le Giarre '08	▼ 4
○ Valdadige Chardonnay Le Fratte '08	▼ 4
○ Valdadige Pinot Grigio Tera Alta '08	▼ 4
○ Cristina V. T. '05	♀♀ 6
○ Cristina V. T. '04	♀♀ 6
○ Passito Cristina Roeno '03	♀♀ 5
● Valdadige Terra dei Forti Enantio '06	♀♀ 4

Ruggeri & C.

VIA PRÀ FONTANA
31049 VALDOBBIADENE [TV]
TEL. 04239092
www.ruggeri.it

PRE-BOOKED VISITS

ANNUAL PRODUCTION **1,000,000 bottles**
HECTARES UNDER VINE **14**
VITICULTURE METHOD **Conventional**

It often seems as if only those who supervise the whole production process from vineyard to bottle can produce great wines. But there is a small group of producers who do not possess much in the way of vineyards yet still manage to turn out really sound wines thanks to a close collaboration with their growers. This is true of Paolo Bisol and his Ruggeri winery, which relies on the work of over 100 growers in order to craft wines that are excellent after many years.

There are two house flagships, wine that remain superb even when tasted years after the harvest. The '08 Vecchie Viti is a Brut made, as its name suggests, entirely from vines that are close to a century old from all over the Valdobbiadene zone. The aromatics are well defined and profound while the palate shows solid structure and grip. Giustino B. '08 is the summation of Ruggeri's productive skills. A Prosecco of rare finesse and harmony, it has always been one of the best since its first release over ten years ago. The rest of the range is ever-dependable and impressive.

Le Salette

VIA PIO BRUGNOLI, 11C
37022 FUMANE [VR]
TEL. 0457701027
www.lesalette.it

CELLAR SALES
PRE-BOOKED VISITS

ANNUAL PRODUCTION **130,000 bottles**
HECTARES UNDER VINE **18**
VITICULTURE METHOD **Conventional**

Valpolicella is an area in which a number of wineries work in different ways while pursuing the same results. Co-operative wineries farm alongside large-scale bottlers and grape-growers mirror the efforts of the best family-run farming estates. Le Salette, a lovely winery owned by Franco Scamperle and situated in the village of Fumane, falls into the last category. The cellar is small and well equipped but it is the vineyard that best highlights the qualities of an estate dedicated to a balanced range of products focusing on local varieties.

Ten years on, the Amarone Pergole Vece '05 is back on mid-season form with a superb performance. It opens slowly with profound, spicy aromas and a huge impact on the palate which is taut yet harmonious, dry and full of verve. The other wines are all excellent, starting with the Ripasso I Progni '06, which is complex on the nose with a savoury palate. The '05 La Marega is an Amarone with a lighter, more approachable style. Finally, there's a special mention for the '08 Valpolicella, which is fragrant and very enjoyable.

O P. di Valdobbiadene Brut Vecchie Viti '08	♈♈ 5
O P. di Valdobbiadene Extra Dry Giustino B. '08	♈♈ 5
O Cartizze	♈♈ 5
O L'Extra Brut '08	♈♈ 4
O P. di Valdobbiadene Dry S. Stefano	♈♈ 4*
O P. di Valdobbiadene Extra Dry Giall'Oro	♈♈ 4*
O P. di Valdobbiadene Brut Quartese	♈ 4
O Pinot Grigio Vign. Cornuda '08	♈ 4
O P. di Valdobbiadene Brut Vecchie Viti '07	♈♈ 5
O P. di Valdobbiadene Extra Dry Giustino B. '07	♈♈ 5

● Amarone della Valpolicella Cl. Pergole Vece '05	♈♈♈ 8
● Valpolicella Cl. Sup. Ripasso I Progni '06	♈♈ 5
● Amarone della Valpolicella Cl. La Marega '05	♈♈ 6
● Ca' Carnocchio '06	♈♈ 5
● Recioto della Valpolicella Cl. Pergole Vece '06	♈♈ 6
● Valpolicella Cl. '08	♈♈ 4
O Cesare Passito Bianco '06	♈ 6
● Recioto della Valpolicella Cl. Le Traversagne '06	♈ 6
● Amarone della Valpolicella Cl. Pergole Vece '95	♈♈♈ 8
● Amarone della Valpolicella Cl. Pergole Vece '04	♈♈ 8

La Sansonina

LOC. SANSONINA
37019 PESCHIERA DEL GARDA [VR]
TEL. 0457551905
www.sansonina.it

CELLAR SALES
PRE-BOOKED VISITS

ANNUAL PRODUCTION **13,000 bottles**
HECTARES UNDER VINE **12**
VITICULTURE METHOD **Conventional**

Carla Prospero, with the invaluable help of her daughter Nadia, is the woman behind La Sansonina, a young winery operating in the Lugana area. Production is focused on merlot, a variety traditionally grown in the lake area and which reveals unexpected personality when cultivated on clayey soil. About a dozen hectares of vineyards produce limited quantities of Merlot, presented as a single-variety wine for the last ten or so years, and, since the 2008 vintage, a Lugana that shows how perfectly this operation understands its territory.

The '06 Sansonina gave its usual classy performance with intensely ripe aromas in a cavalcade of fruit, spice and medicinal herbs. Acidity and tannin on the generous palate hold the exuberant body in check. In its first edition, the very interesting Lugana '08 almost went forward to our final tastings. It's a characterful white with vibrant floral and apple fruit aromas that open out classily to reveal a savoury, nicely lingering palate.

Tenuta Sant'Antonio

LOC. SAN ZENO
VIA CERIANI, 23
37030 COLOGNOLA AI COLLI [VR]
TEL. 0457650383
www.tenutasantantonio.it

CELLAR SALES
PRE-BOOKED VISITS

ANNUAL PRODUCTION **600,000 bottles**
HECTARES UNDER VINE **80**
VITICULTURE METHOD **Conventional**

In just over ten vintages, the Castagnedi brothers' winery has become one of the most admired and sought after estates in the DOC. The great wine tradition inherited from their father and uncle is clear from the extensive vineyards in a prestigious location, farmed with near obsessive care. One example is Monti Garbi, with densely planted, breeze-wafted vines that produce extraordinary fruit. Cellar procedures aim to preserving the quality of the fruit and allow the wines sufficient time to mature in containers and bottle.

A very sound range this year starts with the '05 Amarone Campo dei Gigli, which led the field and ran away with Three Glasses. Deep aromas with marked red berries and spices precede a striking palate, with a captivating finish, which stays taut and vibrant despite powerful body. The '06 La Bandina is a concentrated, powerful interpretation of Valpolicella while the Soave Monte Ceriani '07 shows distinctly more elegance and subtlety. Finally, the '06 Amarone Selezione Antonio Castagnedi and Valpolicella Monti Garbi '07 are both solid and dependable.

Wine	Rating
● Sansonina '06	♟♟ 7
○ Lugana Sansonina '08	♟♟ 4*
● Sansonina '05	♟♟ 7
● Sansonina '04	♟♟ 7
● Sansonina '03	♟♟ 7
● Sansonina '01	♟♟ 7
● Sansonina '00	♟♟ 7
● Sansonina '98	♟♟ 7
● Sansonina '97	♟♟ 7

Wine	Rating
● Amarone della Valpolicella Campo dei Gigli '05	♟♟♟ 8
○ Soave Monte Ceriani '07	♟♟ 4*
● Valpolicella Sup. La Bandina '06	♟♟ 6
● Amarone della Valpolicella Sel. Antonio Castagnedi '06	♟♟ 7
● Valpolicella Sup. Ripasso Monti Garbi '07	♟♟ 4
● Amarone della Valpolicella Campo dei Gigli '04	♟♟♟ 8
● Amarone della Valpolicella Campo dei Gigli '99	♟♟♟ 8
● Amarone della Valpolicella Campo dei Gigli '98	♟♟♟ 8
● Amarone della Valpolicella Campo dei Gigli '97	♟♟♟ 8
● Cabernet Sauvignon Capitello '97	♟♟♟ 7
○ Soave Monte Ceriani '05	♟♟♟ 4*
● Valpolicella Sup. La Bandina '01	♟♟♟ 6
○ Soave Monte Ceriani '06	♟♟ 4*
● Valpolicella Sup. La Bandina '05	♟♟ 6
● Valpolicella Sup. La Bandina '04	♟♟ 5

Santa Margherita

via Ita Marzotto, 8
30025 Fossalta di Portogruaro [VE]
tel. 0421246111
www.santamargherita.com

CELLAR SALES
PRE-BOOKED VISITS

ANNUAL PRODUCTION **12.500,000 bottles**
HECTARES UNDER VINE **35**
VITICULTURE METHOD **Conventional**

Having underlined for years that Santa Margherita is a reliable estate for the production of simple, fairly priced wines, this year we note a sharp quality spike that promises well for the future.The estate has always used outside growers who provide most of the grapes but is also gradually increasing its own vineyard holding. Estate vines on the Veneto plain and in Alto Adige are currently used for the more ambitious wines. The basic products have also improved in quality and varietal typicity.

At last the Pinot Grigio Impronta del Fondatore '08 truly impresses with a smoky nose that releases fresher hints of flowers, and apple and pear fruit. A restrained impact on the palate gradually reveals classy, uncompromising progression and a dry, gutsy finish. The Merlot and Refosco, both from '07 and both good, provide an elegant, rather than weighty, interpretation of the Veneto plain territory, especially the Merlot with its generous hints of fruit and agile, sleek body. The rest of the range is increasingly impressive, clearly reflecting the grape varieties.

○ A. A. Pinot Grigio Impronta del Fondatore '08	🍷🍷 4*
● Merlot '07	🍷🍷 4*
● Refosco P.R. '07	🍷🍷 4
○ Lison-Pramaggiore Verduzzo Dolce Dulcedo '06	🍷 4
○ Luna dei Feldi '08	🍷 4
● Malbech '07	🍷 4
○ Valdadige Pinot Grigio '08	🍷 4
● Malbech '06	🍷🍷 4
● Malbech '05	🍷🍷 4*
● Refosco '05	🍷🍷 4*

Santa Sofia

fraz. Pedemonte
via Ca' Dedé, 61
37020 San Pietro in Cariano [VR]
tel. 0457701074
www.santasofia.com

PRE-BOOKED VISITS

ANNUAL PRODUCTION **550,000 bottles**
HECTARES UNDER VINE **N.D.**
VITICULTURE METHOD **Conventional**

Santa Sofia is a classic Valpolicella estate. For years, it has produced wines from the DOC but also from the other leading zones in the province of Verona. Production numbers are substantial and the winery relies on small local growers who bring their grapes to Via Ca' Dedé, where Giancarlo Begnoni is still in charge of the cellar. The winery's trademark style is fairly evident throughout the range, typically enhancing traditional features in good quality wines that are also very easy to drink.

From the vast range of wines presented this year, it was the Amarone that stood out. It comes from a cool growing year, 2005, and so gives floral and wild berry aromas with an elegant, light rather than powerful, character in tune with the winery's style. The Recioto '06 is also very impressive, showing youthful and exuberant. Generous sweetness plays a leading role here, nicely held in check by densely woven tannins. The rest of the products reflect DOC zones that put the accent on approachability and agility.

● Amarone della Valpolicella Cl. '05	🍷🍷 7
● Recioto della Valpolicella Cl. '06	🍷🍷 6
● Arleo Rosso '03	🍷 5
⊙ Bardolino Chiaretto Cl. '08	🍷 3
○ Garda Pinot Grigio Le Calderare '08	🍷 3
○ Lugana '08	🍷 3
● Merlot Corvina '07	🍷 3*
● Amarone della Valpolicella Cl. '04	🍷🍷 7
● Amarone della Valpolicella Cl. '01	🍷🍷 7
● Amarone della Valpolicella Cl. '00	🍷🍷 7
● Amarone della Valpolicella Cl. Gioé '03	🍷🍷 8
● Recioto della Valpolicella Cl. '03	🍷🍷 6

Santi

VIA UNGHERIA, 33
37031 ILLASI [VR]
TEL. 0456520077
www.carlosanti.it

CELLAR SALES
PRE-BOOKED VISITS

ANNUAL PRODUCTION 2,000,000 bottles
HECTARES UNDER VINE 70
VITICULTURE METHOD Conventional

This large winery comes under the Gruppo Italiano Vini umbrella and shows it knows about quality in the Valpolicella area with products that offer great value, as well as interpreting its wines in a modern idiom without abandoning traditional features. Over the years, Cristian Scrinzi, with the far-sighted support of Emilio Pedron, has overhauled the range and even more significantly the spirit of the winery itself, with significant results.

The style of the Valpolicella reds highlights generous aromas and taut palates rather than power, often with excellent results. These can be seen this year in our tasting of the Solane '07, a Valpolicella Ripasso, which offers a broad, captivating range of aromas where fruit leaves room for varietal hints of pepper and fines herbes, reflected on the dry, gutsy palate. The '06 Amarone Proemio is penalized by a too-early release but shows considerable potential and simply requires further time in bottle.

Casa Vinicola Sartori

FRAZ. SANTA MARIA
VIA CASETTE, 2
37024 NEGRAR [VR]
TEL. 0456028011
www.sartorinet.com

PRE-BOOKED VISITS

ANNUAL PRODUCTION 15,000,000 bottles
HECTARES UNDER VINE 40
VITICULTURE METHOD Conventional

The numbers look daunting at a time when the market seems intent on clinging to the characteristic caution of the last two years. But the Sartori family is sticking to its guns, and continues to scale the heights of quality in Valpolicella with increasingly impressive products, thanks to input from consultant Franco Bernabei. Starting with the family estate, I Saltari, and today also with the main winery, this operation is one of the best in terms of value for money.

Many of the wines impressed our tasting panel this year, especially an amazingly broad Amarone I Saltari '04 with distinctive slow, multi-layered aromatics followed by a generous yet dry, perfectly austere palate. In a contrasting style, the Valpolicella Montegradella '06 gives subtle, sophisticated aromas especially dried flowers and pepper, with a racy palate. The other two Amarones, the Corte Brà '04 and the fresher Reius '05, are on good form. And there was a fine performance from the rounded, punchy Valpolicella Regolo '05.

Wine	Rating
● Amarone della Valpolicella Proemio '06	♛♛ 7
● Valpolicella Cl. Sup. Solane Ripasso '07	♛♛ 4*
● Bardolino Cl. Vigneto Ca' Bordenis '08	♛♛ 4
○ Soave Cl. Monteforte '08	♛♛ 4
● Amarone della Valpolicella '06	♛ 6
○ Lugana Melibeo '08	♛ 4
● Amarone della Valpolicella Proemio '05	♛♛♛ 7
● Amarone della Valpolicella Proemio '03	♛♛♛ 7*
● Amarone della Valpolicella Proemio '00	♛♛♛ 7
● Amarone della Valpolicella Proemio '04	♛♛ 7
● Amarone della Valpolicella Proemio '01	♛♛ 7
● Valpolicella Cl. Sup. Solane Ripasso '06	♛♛ 4*
● Valpolicella Cl. Sup. Solane Ripasso '05	♛♛ 4
● Valpolicella Cl. Sup. Solane Ripasso '04	♛♛ 4*

Wine	Rating
● Amarone della Valpolicella Le Vigne di Turano I Saltari '04	♛♛ 8
● Amarone della Valpolicella Cl. Corte Brà '04	♛♛ 8
● Amarone della Valpolicella Cl. Reius '05	♛♛ 7
● Valpolicella Cl. Sup. Vign. di Montegradella '06	♛♛ 4*
● Valpolicella Sup. Ripasso Regolo '05	♛♛ 4
● Bardolino Cl. '08	♛ 3
● Bardolino Cl. Ca' Nova '07	♛ 3*
○ Marani '07	♛ 4
○ Recioto di Soave Vernus '07	♛ 6
○ Soave Cl. '08	♛ 3
○ Soave Cl. Sella '08	♛ 4
● Valpolicella Cl. '07	♛ 4
● Amarone della Valpolicella Le Vigne di Turano I Saltari '03	♛♛ 8
● Amarone della Valpolicella Le Vigne di Turano I Saltari '01	♛♛ 8
● Amarone della Valpolicella Le Vigne di Turano I Saltari '00	♛♛ 8

★ Serafini & Vidotto

VIA CARRER, 8/12
31040 NERVESA DELLA BATTAGLIA [TV]
TEL. 0422773281
serafinievidotto@serafinievidotto.com

CELLAR SALES
PRE-BOOKED VISITS

ANNUAL PRODUCTION **100,000 bottles**
HECTARES UNDER VINE **21**
VITICULTURE METHOD **Natural**

Over the last 30 years, the province of Treviso has been associated with Prosecco but it also conceals some red gems, like those produced by Francesco Serafini and Antonello Vidotto. This Bordeaux-style estate produces two main wines, as well as a couple of others either just for the challenge or to fulfil clients' requests and reflect the terroir even more accurately. Along with absolutely sound running of the vineyards and cellar, we were impressed by the wines' splendid ageing potential. These are bottles that acquire class and precision with the years.

The '06 Rosso dell'Abazia is on great form and walks off with Three Glasses. Well-defined aromas, less explosive than usual, slowly reveal their finesse while the flavoursome palate shows its class with smooth tannin and a very lingering finish. Only a step behind, the similarly styled Phigaia '06 has a racier body, mouthwatering and elegant today and well able to age for another ten years at least. We like the good performance from the rounded, juicy sparkling wines that show guts and grip. The sauvignon Il Bianco '08 is well typed.

F.lli Speri

LOC. PEDEMONTE
VIA FONTANA, 14
37020 SAN PIETRO IN CARIANO [VR]
TEL. 0457701154
www.speri.com

CELLAR SALES
PRE-BOOKED VISITS

ANNUAL PRODUCTION **350,000 bottles**
HECTARES UNDER VINE **50**
VITICULTURE METHOD **Conventional**

Valpolicella is dotted with many fairly small wineries that have sprung up like toadstools as the popularity of Amarone has grown. Speri, however, is rooted in three generations of history with a very extensive vineyard holding and a natural affinity with the dynamics of this territory. The products are backed up by a solid tradition, making this one of very few wineries that do not produce non-DOC wines, proof of its strong connection with the land, amply justifying its reputation.

Three wines breezed through to our finals, starting with a lovely Amarone Vignato Monte Sant'Urbano. In recent years, this wine has become richer and more concentrated, as the '05 vintage demonstrates. Intensely fruity aromas are nicely reflected on the rounded, austere palate. The '06 Valpolicella Superiore of the same name is brighter and more youthful, an example of finesse and grip rather than powerful strength. The heady La Roggia '06 is a Recioto with seductive aromas and nicely measured sweetness. The Ripasso '07 is generous and silky.

● Montello e Colli Asolani Il Rosso dell'Abazia '06	🍷🍷🍷 6
● Montello e Colli Asolani Phigaia '06	🍷🍷 5*
○ Il Bianco '08	🍷🍷 4*
○ Montello e Colli Asolani Extra Dry Bollicine di Prosecco	🍷🍷 4
☉ Bollicine Rosé	🍷 4
● Il Rosso dell'Abazia '02	🍷🍷🍷 7
● Il Rosso dell'Abazia '01	🍷🍷🍷 7
● Il Rosso dell'Abazia '00	🍷🍷🍷 7
● Il Rosso dell'Abazia '98	🍷🍷🍷 7
● Il Rosso dell'Abazia '97	🍷🍷🍷 7
● Montello e Colli Asolani Il Rosso dell'Abazia '05	🍷🍷🍷 6
● Montello e Colli Asolani Il Rosso dell'Abazia '04	🍷🍷🍷 6
● Montello e Colli Asolani Il Rosso dell'Abazia '03	🍷🍷🍷 6

● Amarone della Valpolicella Cl. Vign. Monte Sant'Urbano '05	🍷🍷 8
● Recioto della Valpolicella Cl. La Roggia '06	🍷🍷 7
● Valpolicella Cl. Sup. Sant'Urbano '06	🍷🍷 5
● Valpolicella Cl. Sup. Ripasso '07	🍷🍷 5
● Valpolicella Cl. '08	🍷 4*
● Amarone della Valpolicella Cl. Vign. Monte Sant'Urbano '04	🍷🍷🍷 8
● Amarone della Valpolicella Cl. Vign. Monte Sant'Urbano '01	🍷🍷🍷 8
● Amarone della Valpolicella Cl. Vign. Monte Sant'Urbano '00	🍷🍷🍷 8
● Amarone della Valpolicella Cl. Vign. Monte Sant'Urbano '97	🍷🍷🍷 8
● Amarone della Valpolicella Cl. Vign. Monte Sant'Urbano '95	🍷🍷🍷 8
● Amarone della Valpolicella Cl. Vign. Monte Sant'Urbano '93	🍷🍷🍷 8
● Amarone della Valpolicella Cl. Vign. Monte Sant'Urbano '90	🍷🍷🍷 6
● Recioto della Valpolicella Cl. La Roggia '94	🍷🍷🍷 6

I Stefanini

VIA CROSARA, 21
37032 MONTEFORTE D'ALPONE [VR]
TEL. 0456175249
tessari.francesco@genie.it

CELLAR SALES
PRE-BOOKED VISITS

ANNUAL PRODUCTION **40,000 bottles**
HECTARES UNDER VINE **20**
VITICULTURE METHOD **Conventional**

Francesco Tessari's best vineyards, which produce his two most prestigious wines, are located right in the volcanic area on Mount Tenda, where the dark earth changes colour according to its aspect and the conditions under which the lava poured down millions of years ago. While knowledge of vineyards has ancient roots here, this young winery's own history is comparatively recent, with only ten or so vintages under its belt. But in just a few years it has achieved very sound results, confirmed in the tastings this year.

The estate's two crus are both on Mount Tenda. From the higher area comes the Soave Classico Superiore Monte di Fice '07, a very well-textured wine whose aromatic roots lie deep in the volcanic soil. Smoky sulphur aromas on the nose with generous, juicy fruit in the background and a rich, tangy palate lead to an endless, clear finish that fully deserves its Three Glasses. Only slightly inferior in quality, the Monte de Toni '07 comes from a lower altitude while the Il Selese is a Soave with approachable aromatics and a distinctive relaxed, simple palate.

Suavia

FRAZ. FITTÀ DI SOAVE
VIA CENTRO, 14
37038 SOAVE [VR]
TEL. 0457675089
www.suavia.it

CELLAR SALES
PRE-BOOKED VISITS

ANNUAL PRODUCTION **100,000 bottles**
HECTARES UNDER VINE **12**
VITICULTURE METHOD **Conventional**

In just a few years, Suavia has become one of the leading estates in this area, producing a limited number of wines which are all sound. Its strength lies in the vineyards, which are often very old and located in very prestigious zones while cellar work aims to foreground the garganega grape, which is capable of very distinctive results in the dark Fittà hills. Today, the Tessari sisters focus considerable efforts on bottle ageing their wines, which are only released after maturing sufficiently.

The Recioto Acinatium and the Soave Le Rive were both absent for this reason, and will only be available next year. In the meantime, the Soave Monte Carbonare '08 leads the field, as it has done for several years. The aromas are complex with fruit embracing intense mineral and sulphur sensations, a superb link to the soil on which the grapes are grown, and those aromatics are reflected on the dry, extraordinarily savoury palate, closing with an exciting finish and our Three Glasses. The outstanding Soave Classico '08 offers almost equally thrilling sensations at an even more accessible price.

Wine	Rating
○ Soave Cl. Sup. Monte di Fice '07	♛♛♛ 3*
○ Soave Cl. Monte de Toni '07	♛♛ 3*
○ Soave Il Selese '08	♛♛ 2*
○ Soave Cl. Monte de Toni '06	♛♛ 3*
○ Soave Cl. Sup. Monte di Fice '06	♛♛ 3*
○ Soave Il Selese '07	♛♛ 2*
○ Soave Il Selese '06	♛♛ 3*
○ Soave Il Selese '05	♛♛ 3

Wine	Rating
○ Soave Cl. Monte Carbonare '08	♛♛♛ 4*
○ Soave Cl. '08	♛♛ 4*
○ Soave Cl. Le Rive '02	♛♛♛ 5
○ Soave Cl. Monte Carbonare '07	♛♛♛ 4*
○ Soave Cl. Monte Carbonare '06	♛♛♛ 4*
○ Soave Cl. Monte Carbonare '05	♛♛♛ 4*
○ Soave Cl. Monte Carbonare '04	♛♛♛ 4
○ Soave Cl. Monte Carbonare '02	♛♛♛ 4
○ Soave Cl. Sup. Le Rive '00	♛♛♛ 5
○ Soave Cl. Sup. Le Rive '98	♛♛♛ 5
○ Recioto di Soave Acinatium '05	♛♛ 6
○ Soave Cl. Le Rive '06	♛♛ 5

Tamellini

VIA TAMELLINI, 4
37038 SOAVE [VR]
TEL. 0457675328
piofrancesco.tamellini@tin.it

CELLAR SALES
PRE-BOOKED VISITS

ANNUAL PRODUCTION **160,000 bottles**
HECTARES UNDER VINE **17**
VITICULTURE METHOD **Conventional**

In a single decade, the estate belonging to brothers Gaetano and Piofrancesco Tamellini, located to the extreme west of the DOC zone where basalt gives way to limestone and tufaceous rock, has won recognition from market and critics alike. The high standard of viticulture, with special attention paid to the ripeness of the grapes, leads to products showing the typically generous fruit that is the winery's trademark, both in the premium wines and the basic Soave.

Only two Soaves were presented this year, but with excellent results. While we are now used to a superb performance from the Le Bine de Costjola, this time the '07, we were also impressed by the Classico '08, which is sold at an attractive price but behaves like a genuinely great white with well-defined fruit-led aromas mingling with floral and citrus sensations that return on the palate, where the wine shows complexity as well as agility and grip. Le Bine performed with its usual class offering complex, varied aromas and solid body on the mouthwateringly savoury palate.

Giovanna Tantini

LOC. OLIOSI
VIA GOITO, 10
37014 CASTELNUOVO DEL GARDA [VR]
TEL. 0457575070
www.giovannatantini.it

CELLAR SALES
PRE-BOOKED VISITS

ANNUAL PRODUCTION **25,000 bottles**
HECTARES UNDER VINE **11.5**
VITICULTURE METHOD **Conventional**

After a decade of popularity for muscular, hyper-concentrated wines, the fashion now tends towards lighter, more elegant products with generous aromas. Bardolino is one DOC with plenty to offer in this style, especially at Tantini, a winery that has managed to bring a new, interesting identity to lakeside reds in just a few years. Over 11 hectares of vineyards and even more limited production are the calling cards that Giovanna offers, with help from Federico Curtaz, Laura Zuddas and Attilio Pagli.

The most difficult task for a Bardolino producer is to endow the wine with complexity and concentration without compromising the proverbial lightness that makes it so captivating and satisfyingly drinkable. At Tantini, this problem was identified and solved from the very first vintage, as we confirmed in the '08 tastings. The intense aromas reveal distinctive red berry fruit, which gradually gives way to peppery and floral sensations. The palate is light-bodied and supple but never lean. The pleasant Bardolino Chiaretto '08 has fragrant floral and berry aromas.

○ Soave Cl. Le Bine de Costjola '07	♟♟	4*
○ Soave Cl. '08	♟♟	4*
○ Soave Cl. Le Bine '04	♟♟♟	4*
○ Soave Cl. Le Bine de Costjola '06	♟♟♟	4*
○ Soave Cl. Le Bine de Costjola '05	♟♟♟	4*
○ Recioto di Soave V. Marogne '04	♟♟	6
○ Recioto di Soave V. Marogne '03	♟♟	6
○ Recioto di Soave V. Marogne '02	♟♟	6
○ Recioto di Soave V. Marogne '01	♟♟	5
○ Soave '06	♟♟	4*

● Bardolino '08	♟♟	4*
⊙ Bardolino Chiaretto '08	♟	4
● Bardolino '07	♟♟	4*
● Ettore '06	♟♟	5
● Ettore '05	♟♟	7

F.lli Tedeschi

LOC. PEDEMONTE
VIA G. VERDI, 4
37029 SAN PIETRO IN CARIANO [VR]
TEL. 0457701487
www.tedeschiwines.com

CELLAR SALES
PRF-ROOKED VISITS

ANNUAL PRODUCTION **500,000 bottles**
HECTARES UNDER VINE **38**
VITICULTURE METHOD **Conventional**

The Tedeschi family's winery proceeds with caution, aware that it is a mistake to lose sight of balance: in the choice of vineyards to be purchased, or the new wines to be released, or changes in the vineyards or cellar. Every decision is taken with family tradition firmly in mind, reinterpreting the past to enhance territorial expression. The well-stocked range of wines is representative of this philosophy and the most important selections are only presented in the best years.

In recent times, Amarone Capitel Monte Olmi has become more concentrated and the '05 is now among the DOC's weightiest wines with rich fruit-led aromas opening out into hints of pepper and fines herbes. The palate also shows exuberant fullness and needs time to find its best expression. A similar style in a lower key for the Valpolicella Ripasso San Rocco '07, which is intensely fragrant with a solid palate. The Valpolicella Capitel dei Nicalò '07 unfolds with more agility and elegance. Finally, the '05 Amarone Classico is mouthwateringly modern.

Viticoltori Tommasi

LOC. PEDEMONTE
VIA RONCHETTO, 2
37020 SAN PIETRO IN CARIANO [VR]
TEL. 0457701266
www.tommasiwine.it

CELLAR SALES
PRE-BOOKED VISITS

ANNUAL PRODUCTION **900,000 bottles**
HECTARES UNDER VINE **165**
VITICULTURE METHOD **Conventional**

The large Tommasi family has, over the years, been able to diversify its activities, although wine remains the beating heart of the estate. The vineyards have increased in size with time and production quantities too, albeit at a necessarily slower rhythm when the objective is to boost quality. Despite the output statistics – close to 1,000,000 bottles – products are strongly rooted in tradition and even when international grape varieties, are used they are interpreted in the Veronese style.

A fine example is the '07 Crearo della Conca d'Oro, from part-dried cabernet franc, corvina and oseleta. The result is a red with intense wild berry and spice aromas and a generous palate, to which the drying process has added roundedness without losing grip and juice. Both the '05 Amarones presented have taken a leap forward, their aromas appearing sounder and more defined. The Ca' Florian is fruity and mouthfilling on the palate while the Classico is racier and more harmonious. Finally, there was a good performance from the Valpolicellas, though we slightly preferred the Vigneto Rafael '07.

Wine	Rating
● Amarone della Valpolicella Cl. Capitel Monte Olmi '05	♟ 8
● Amarone della Valpolicella Cl. '05	♟♟ 6
● Valpolicella Cl. Sup. Capitel dei Nicalò '07	♟♟ 4*
● Valpolicella Sup. Capitel San Rocco Ripasso '07	♟♟ 5
● Valpolicella Cl. Lucchine '08	♟ 3
● Amarone della Valpolicella Cl. Capitel Monte Olmi '01	♟♟♟ 8
● Amarone della Valpolicella Cl. Capitel Monte Olmi '99	♟♟♟ 8
● Amarone della Valpolicella Cl. Capitel Monte Olmi '97	♟♟♟ 8
● Amarone della Valpolicella Cl. Capitel Monte Olmi '95	♟♟♟ 8
● Rosso della Fabriseria '97	♟♟♟ 6
● Amarone della Valpolicella Cl. Capitel Monte Olmi '04	♟♟ 8

Wine	Rating
● Crearo della Conca d'Oro '07	♟♟ 5*
● Amarone della Valpolicella Cl. '05	♟♟ 7
● Amarone della Valpolicella Cl. Ca' Florian '05	♟♟ 7
● Valpolicella Cl. Sup. Ripasso '07	♟♟ 5
● Valpolicella Cl. Sup. Vign. Rafael '07	♟♟ 5
● Recioto della Valpolicella Cl. Fiorato '06	♟ 6
● Amarone della Valpolicella Cl. '04	♟♟ 7
● Amarone della Valpolicella Cl. Ca' Florian '04	♟♟ 7
● Amarone della Valpolicella Cl. Monte Masua Il Sestante '03	♟♟ 8
● Amarone della Valpolicella Cl. Monte Masua Il Sestante '01	♟♟ 8
● Crearo della Conca d'Oro '06	♟♟ 5
● Crearo della Conca d'Oro '04	♟♟ 5*

Trabucchi d'Illasi

LOC. MONTE TENDA
37031 ILLASI [VR]
TEL. 0457833233
www.trabucchidillasi.it

CELLAR SALES
PRE-BOOKED VISITS

ANNUAL PRODUCTION 70,000 bottles
HECTARES UNDER VINE 15
VITICULTURE METHOD Organic certified

Since their earliest years of production, Raffaella and Giuseppe Trabucchi's pursuit of quality has been clear in their wines, not as an end in itself but as a way to interpret the terroir where they work. The results are increasingly impressive and with the first vintages of the millennium, the wines have acquired more confidence. The winery and most of the vineyards are located on the hill separating Val d'Illasi from Val Tramigna, in a zone which enjoys excellent ventilation and temperature variation.

With the passing harvests, the range of products has broadened as we can see from this year's tasting. An excellent performance from the Recioto '05, which is explosive to say the least, rich in fruity, spicy sensations and bursts onto the palate with sweetness that is only held in check by solid tannic structure through to a long finish. Three classy, powerful Glasses. Also very good is the Valpolicella San Colombano '05, slightly racier and juicier than the Cereolo. Finally, there was a good debut performance from the extraordinarily flavoursome Amarone Alberto Trabucchi '03.

Cantina Sociale della Valpantena

FRAZ. QUINTO
VIA COLONIA ORFANI DI GUERRA, 5B
37034 VERONA
TEL. 045550032
www.cantinavalpantena.it

CELLAR SALES
PRE-BOOKED VISITS

ANNUAL PRODUCTION 7.500,000 bottles
HECTARES UNDER VINE N.D.
VITICULTURE METHOD Conventional

This Quinto cooperative is a purveyor of simple, very enjoyable wines with approachable palates thanks to rounded structure and fruity aromas. The vast area of vineyards is situated in the so-called extended Valpolicella zone, in the eastern part of the DOC, with a significant quota in the Valpantena subzone, which is where many of these wines come from. As well as the DOC wines, there is a small selection of single-varietal Veronese products.

Valpolicella takes the lion's share, starting with the mouthwatering Ripasso Torre del Falasco '07, which proffers overripe fruit and spicy sensations followed by a rounded, soft palate. The ever-interesting Recioto Tesauro '06 is not a showy wine but won us over with style thanks to a prestigious balance of sweetness, savouriness and acid grip. Of the two Amarones presented, we preferred the Torre del Falasco '05 with its robust huskiness full of vibrant tannin and acidity. The selection of simpler wines is good, and the Corvina '08 stands out for its clarity, simplicity and fragrant aromas.

Wine	Rating
● Recioto della Valpolicella Terre del Cereolo '05	♟♟♟ 8
● Valpolicella Sup. Terre di S. Colombano '05	♟♟ 7
● Amarone della Valpolicella Alberto Trabucchi '03	♟♟ 8
● Dandarin '05	♟♟ 6
● Valpolicella Sup. Terre del Cereolo '05	♟♟ 6
○ Margherita '08	♟ 4
● Amarone della Valpolicella '04	♟♟♟ 8
● Valpolicella Sup. Terre di S. Colombano '03	♟♟♟ 5*
● Amarone della Valpolicella '03	♟♟ 8
● Recioto della Valpolicella '04	♟♟ 8
● Valpolicella Sup. Dandarin '04	♟♟ 5
● Valpolicella Sup. Terre del Cereolo '04	♟♟ 6

Wine	Rating
● Amarone della Valpolicella Torre del Falasco '05	♟♟ 7
● Recioto della Valpolicella Tesauro '06	♟♟ 6
● Valpolicella Sup. Ripasso Torre del Falasco '07	♟♟ 4*
● Amarone della Valpolicella Valpantena '06	♟ 6
○ Chardonnay Baroncino '08	♟ 3
● Corvina Torre del Falasco '08	♟ 2
○ Lugana Torre del Falasco '08	♟ 4
● Valpolicella Sup. Torre del Falasco '07	♟ 4
● Valpolicella Valpantena Ritocco '07	♟ 4
● Amarone della Valpolicella Torre del Falasco '04	♟♟ 7

Cantina Sociale Valpolicella

VIA CA' SALGARI, 2
37024 NEGRAR [VR]
TEL. 0456014300
www.cantinanegrar.it

CELLAR SALES
PRE-BOOKED VISITS

ANNUAL PRODUCTION **7.500,000 bottles**
HECTARES UNDER VINE **500**
VITICULTURE METHOD **Conventional**

Co-operative wineries are widespread and well-rooted in Veneto but their prominent role in the rural economy does not always go hand-in-hand with quality in the wines on offer. The brightest exception to this rule comes from Negrar, the largest co-operative. A turning point in quality took place many years ago and today this is one of the leading wineries in Valpolicella with 500 hectares scattered along all the valleys and a range released under several lines. Domini Veneti is the most ambitious of these, showing thoroughly impressive results.

Manara is the leading Amarone, only produced in really impressive years, as 2003 was in this area. The nose is closed and almost reluctant to yield its aromas, which open out slowly, generous and complex, dominated by drying sensations. The palate is full-bodied but also austere and perfectly evolved. Fruit is the protagonist in the explosive Recioto Vigneti di Moron '06, with its exuberant, nicely integrated sweetness. Of the two good Valpolicellas presented, we preferred the Vigneto di Torbe '07 for its greater finesse on the nose and agile palate.

Massimino Venturini

FRAZ. SAN FLORIANO
VIA SEMONTE, 20
37020 SAN PIETRO IN CARIANO [VR]
TEL. 0457701331
www.viniventurini.com

CELLAR SALES
PRE-BOOKED VISITS

ANNUAL PRODUCTION **90,000 bottles**
HECTARES UNDER VINE **12**
VITICULTURE METHOD **Conventional**

In the last 15 years, Valpolicella, and to a greater extent Amarone, has experienced a quantum leap in quality, prices and media attention but there are still some small, family-run wineries, like the one owned by the Venturini brothers, which have not lost their way. These wineries know their strength lies in their vineyards and their equally ancient skills. The Venturinis' dozen or so hectares yield fewer than 100,000 bottles a year in a style halfway between the traditional and the contemporary.

Modern is certainly the style of the '05 Amarone Classico, with its generous sensations of delicately dried grapes and refreshing hints of flowers and fines herbes. The palate opens out with suppleness and grip in a framework of never excessive complexity. The '04 Campomasua is more generous and mature, in part thanks to longer ageing, with more input from dried grapes and a powerful, juicy palate. The Recioto Le Brugnine '04, always very good, has lost a pinch of its usual lightness and become sweeter and more structured, with a long, pleasantly dry finish.

● Amarone della Valpolicella Cl. Manara Domini Veneti '03	¶¶ 8
● Recioto della Valpolicella Cl. Vign. di Moron Domini Veneti '06	¶¶ 6
● Valpolicella Cl. Sup. La Casetta di Ettore Righetti Domini Veneti '05	¶¶ 5
● Valpolicella Cl. Sup. Ripasso Vign. di Torbe Domini Veneti '07	¶¶ 4*
● Amarone della Valpolicella Cl. Domini Veneti '05	¶ 6
● Recioto della Valpolicella Cl. Domini Veneti '07	¶ 5
○ Soave Cl. Vign. di Ca' de Napa Domini Veneti '08	¶ 4
● Recioto della Valpolicella Cl. Vigneti di Moron Domini Veneti '01	¶¶¶ 6
● Amarone della Valpolicella Cl. Manara '97	¶¶ 8

● Amarone della Valpolicella Cl. '05	¶¶ 6*
● Recioto della Valpolicella Cl. Le Brugnine '04	¶¶ 6
● Amarone della Valpolicella Cl. Campomasua '04	¶¶ 7
● Valpolicella Cl. '08	¶ 3
● Valpolicella Cl. Sup. '06	¶ 4
● Valpolicella Cl. Sup. Ripasso Semonte Alto '05	¶ 4
● Recioto della Valpolicella Cl. Le Brugnine '97	¶¶¶ 6
● Amarone della Valpolicella Cl. '04	¶¶ 6
● Amarone della Valpolicella Cl. '03	¶¶ 6*
● Amarone della Valpolicella Cl. Campomasua '03	¶¶ 7
● Amarone della Valpolicella Cl. Campomasua '01	¶¶ 7

Agostino Vicentini

FRAZ. SAN ZENO
VIA C. BATTISTI, 62C
37030 COLOGNOLA AI COLLI [VR]
TEL. 0457650539
vicentini@vinivicentini.com

CELLAR SALES
PRE-BOOKED VISITS

ANNUAL PRODUCTION **60,000 bottles**
HECTARES UNDER VINE **14**
VITICULTURE METHOD **Conventional**

The Vicentini family works in that narrow strip of land contested by the Soave and Valpolicella DOCs, making wines that are getting more and more impressive. The estate is rustic in style, in the noblest sense of the word, with all the family involved in its running in various ways, although Agostino is the driving force of the winery. Alongside him Teresa keeps tabs on communications and sales while son Manuel carving out a role for himself, ready to strike out in new directions in a range of products focused on Soave.

Following last year's success, the Soave Superiore Il Casale swept through our tastings to win another Three Glasses. With the '08 vintage, the aromas have gained in depth and freshness and the palate has become lighter and more sinuous over a solid, dry body leading into a long, engaging finish. Just behind it, the '08 Terre Lunghe has a supler, more slender profile and shows savoury and convincingly approachable. In contrast, the '07 Recioto di Soave is a hymn to explosive, slightly dried, fruit, with mouthfilling, well-balanced sweetness on the palate.

Vignale di Cecilia

LOC. FORNACI
VIA CROCI, 14
35030 BAONE [PD]
TEL. 042951420
www.vignaledicecilia.it

CELLAR SALES
PRE-BOOKED VISITS

ANNUAL PRODUCTION **25,000 bottles**
HECTARES UNDER VINE **8**
VITICULTURE METHOD **Conventional**

A few years ago, Paolo Brunello tiptoed into his new wine business and is now extending his horizons with the construction of a new cellar and experimentation in new directions. His thoughtful approach consists of environment-friendly winemaking and non-invasive cellar techniques, in the quest for a wine that is both good to drink and representative of the Baone terroir. A leading red, a second wine and a white form the basic range, although there are one or two surprises lurking in the cellar.

The Passacaglia '06 is the most ambitious wine in the range, a classic merlot-heavy Bordeaux blend with very pervasive aromas of red berries, flowers and fines herbes, while the palate is nicely solid with a mouthwatering, savoury flavour. Its younger brother, the '07 Covolo, is a similar blend aged exclusively in cement vats, which shows healthy, fresher fruit on the nose and an approachable palate. This is a lean wine, nicely rounded as we would expect from this area. The fragrant, delicious Benavides '08 is from aromatic grape varieties.

O Soave Sup. Il Casale '08	♟♟♟ 5
O Soave Vign. Terre Lunghe '08	♟♟ 3*
O Recioto di Soave '07	♟♟ 6
● Valpolicella Vign. Boccascalucce '07	♟ 3
O Soave Sup. Il Casale '07	♟♟♟ 5
O Soave Vign. Terre Lunghe '07	♟♟ 3*
O Soave Vign. Terre Lunghe '06	♟♟ 3*
O Soave Vign. Terre Lunghe '05	♟♟ 3*

O Benavides '08	♟♟ 4*
● Colli Euganei Rosso Covolo '07	♟♟ 4*
● Colli Euganei Rosso Passacaglia '06	♟♟ 5
O Benavides '07	♟♟ 4*
O Benavides '06	♟♟ 3
O Colli Euganei Folia '06	♟♟ 5
● Colli Euganei Rosso Covolo '06	♟♟ 4*
● Colli Euganei Rosso Covolo '05	♟♟ 4
● Colli Euganei Rosso Passacaglia '04	♟♟ 5
● Colli Euganei Rosso Passacaglia '02	♟♟ 5

Vignalta

VIA SCALETTE, 23
35032 ARQUÀ PETRARCA [PD]
TEL. 0429777305
www.vignalta.it

CELLAR SALES
PRE-BOOKED VISITS

ANNUAL PRODUCTION **250,000 bottles**
HECTARES UNDER VINE **55**
VITICULTURE METHOD **Conventional**

If the Colli Euganei zone is known outside the immediate area today, it is thanks to wineries like Vignalta, which believed in the potential of this great volcanic terroir back in the day when most of the products were for local consumption or at best sold to the park's network of thermal spa hotels. Over 20 years later, nothing has changed. At Vignalta, the vineyards are cared for meticulously while the cellar work aims to highlight the various features of the local terroir, as shown by the Gemola and Arquà.

Gemola '06 is sophisticated, almost stiff, with finely expressed aromas and a dry, taut palate. The Arquà '05 is more approachably fruity with a juicy palate nicely supported by acidity. The excellent Fior d'Arancio Passito Alpianae '07 has vibrant aromas of candied citrus and ginger, and perfectly integrated sweetness on a soft, alluring palate. Excellent performances from the Agno Tinto '07 a full, fruity blend of syrah with local grapes, and the firm, savoury and succulent Colli Euganei Pinot Bianco Agno Casto '08. The other products are all dependably good.

Le Vigne di San Pietro

VIA SAN PIETRO, 23
37066 SOMMACAMPAGNA [VR]
TEL. 045510016
www.levignedisanpietro.it

CELLAR SALES
PRE-BOOKED VISITS

ANNUAL PRODUCTION **80,000 bottles**
HECTARES UNDER VINE **20**
VITICULTURE METHOD **Conventional**

As well as in the DOC itself, the strength of this absolutely sound range is to be found in Carlo Nerozzi and Giovanni Boscaini themselves. After a journey which led this estate to doubt its core values, Le Vigne di San Pietro makes a confident comeback as one of the most interesting operations in the area, and one able to capture the hidden appeal of all its various terroirs. Rigorous viticulture techniques and non-invasive cellar procedures which respect the fruit yield a limited production of wines including Bardolino, Custoza and Valpolicella.

The '08 Bardolino, back in production this year, is one of the most impressive, with an explosion of wild berries and pepper on the nose and a juicy, nicely rounded palate with good structure and the distinctive suppleness of the DOC. The fresh, citrus and flowers Due Cuori Passito from moscato gives well-gauged sweetness. The very good '08 Valpolicella is floral and nicely savoury while the '08 CorDeRosa '08 may well be the best rosé in Veneto with its generous aromas and satisfying palate. There was an excellent performance from the Custoza '08.

○ Colli Euganei Fior d'Arancio Passito Alpianae '07	♀♀ 5	
● Colli Euganei Rosso Arquà '05	♀♀ 6	
● Colli Euganei Rosso Gemola '06	♀♀ 6	
● Agno Tinto '07	♀♀ 6	
○ Colli Euganei Pinot Bianco Agno Casto '08	♀♀ 5	
● Colli Euganei Rosso Ris. '06	♀♀ 4	
○ Colli Euganei Chardonnay '07	♀ 5	
○ Sirio '08	♀ 4	
● Colli Euganei Cabernet Ris. '90	♀♀♀ 6	
● Colli Euganei Rosso Arquà '04	♀♀♀ 6	
● Colli Euganei Rosso Gemola '01	♀♀♀ 6	
● Colli Euganei Rosso Gemola '00	♀♀♀ 6	
● Colli Euganei Rosso Gemola '99	♀♀♀ 6	
● Colli Euganei Rosso Gemola '98	♀♀♀ 6	
● Colli Euganei Rosso Gemola '97	♀♀♀ 7	
● Colli Euganei Rosso Gemola '95	♀♀♀ 6	

● Bardolino '08	♀♀ 4*
⊙ CorDeRosa '08	♀♀ 4*
○ Custoza '08	♀♀ 4*
○ Due Cuori Passito '07	♀♀ 6
● Valpolicella '08	♀♀ 4
● Refolà Cabernet Sauvignon '04	♀♀♀ 7
○ Sud '95	♀♀♀ 7
○ Due Cuori Passito '06	♀♀ 6
● I Balconi Rossi '04	♀♀ 6
● I Balconi Rossi '03	♀♀ 6
● Solocorvina '06	♀♀ 3*
● Valpolicella '07	♀♀ 4

Vigneto Due Santi

V.LE ASIAGO, 174
36061 BASSANO DEL GRAPPA [VI]
TEL. 0424502074
vignetoduesanti@virgilio.it

CELLAR SALES
PRE-BOOKED VISITS

ANNUAL PRODUCTION **100,000 bottles**
HECTARES UNDER VINE **18**
VITICULTURE METHOD **Conventional**

Around 20 vintages have passed since Stefano and Adriano Zonta's winery opened its doors and in the meantime the two cousins have extended their vineyards, rebuilt the cellar and discovered new markets. But the pervading spirit has not changed, remaining simple, uncompromising and able to go to the heart of the matter. No idle speculation here, in the management style or in the wines. Although the vineyards cover just under 20 hectares, production has remained for years at 100,000 bottles, as much as can be obtained without compromising on quality.

The '07 Cabernet Vigneto Due Santi put on a really exciting performance with its strikingly pervasive aromas. Fruit first is followed by mint, hints of pencil lead and spice in continual evolution. The palate succeeds in the difficult task of expressing fullness and structure without losing agility or suppleness. The inevitable result was Three Glasses. The basic wines are developing nicely, like the full-bodied, succulent Cabernet '07 and the subtler, taut '07 Rosso. From the white list, we liked the '08 Rivana, a monovarietal Tocai, and the Malvasia Campo di Fiori '08. Both are enjoyable and substantial.

Villa Bellini

LOC. CASTELROTTO DI NEGARINE
VIA DEI FRACCAROLI, 6
37020 SAN PIETRO IN CARIANO [VR]
TEL. 0457725630
www.villabellini.com

CELLAR SALES
PRE-BOOKED VISITS

ANNUAL PRODUCTION **10,000 bottles**
HECTARES UNDER VINE **3**
VITICULTURE METHOD **Organic certified**

Four harvests ago, Cecilia Trucchi decided to stop producing Amarone and the route she has taken is yielding increasingly impressive results. Cecilia's decision was based on her reading of the terroir, Castelrotto, which offers qualities like sophisticated and complex aromas so that its wines expresses finesse rather than opulent features. The whole wine operation has gradually been made over in order to obtain better grapes in a better environment, in the full respect of tradition.

The '06 Valpolicella Classico Superiore Il Taso is a step away from squaring the circle with its lavish aromas dominated by red berries and pepper-led spice, typical of both the corvina and corvinone grapes. The slightly dried grapes make the palate a tad more rounded and full without distorting grip, lightness or savouriness and the creamy finish is absolutely lovely. Oak is still perceptible today but will be absorbed over time, as we noted from a second tasting of older versions.

● Breganze Cabernet Vign. Due Santi '07	♟♟♟ 5	
○ Breganze Bianco Rivana '08	♟♟ 4*	
● Breganze Cabernet '07	♟♟ 4*	
● Breganze Rosso '07	♟♟ 4*	
○ Breganze Sauvignon '08	♟♟ 4*	
○ Breganze Torcolato '06	♟♟ 6	
○ Malvasia Campo di Fiori '08	♟♟ 4*	
○ Prosecco Extra Dry	♟ 4	
● Breganze Cabernet Vign. Due Santi '05	♟♟♟ 5	
● Breganze Cabernet Vign. Due Santi '04	♟♟♟ 5	
● Breganze Cabernet Vign. Due Santi '03	♟♟♟ 5	
● Breganze Cabernet Vign. Due Santi '00	♟♟♟ 5	
● Breganze Cabernet Vign. Due Santi '06	♟♟ 5	
● Breganze Rosso '03	♟♟ 4*	

● Valpolicella Cl. Sup. Il Taso '06	♟♟ 6
● Recioto della Valpolicella Cl. Uva Passa '06	♟♟ 7
● Recioto della Valpolicella Cl. Uva Passa '04	♟♟ 7
● Valpolicella Cl. Sup. Il Taso '05	♟♟ 6
● Valpolicella Cl. Sup. Il Taso '04	♟♟ 6
● Valpolicella Cl. Sup. Il Taso '03	♟♟ 5
● Valpolicella Cl. Sup. Il Taso '02	♟♟ 4
● Valpolicella Cl. Sup. Il Taso '01	♟♟ 4

Villa Monteleone

FRAZ. GARGAGNAGO
VIA MONTELEONE, 12
37020 SANT'AMBROGIO DI VALPOLICELLA [VR]
TEL. 0457704974
www.villamonteleone.com

CELLAR SALES
PRE-BOOKED VISITS

ANNUAL PRODUCTION **40,000 bottles**
HECTARES UNDER VINE **7**
VITICULTURE METHOD **Conventional**

Lucia Duran's winery is located at Gargagnago, one of the Valpolicella villages that resisted the onslaught of building development and faces onto vines rising up to the summit of the hills. This is not a particularly large operation but it produces prestigious wines exclusively from this DOC, demonstrating the strong links to the territory felt by Lucia and previously by her partner Professor Raimondi, the founder and soul of this estate. Work in the cellar reflects care and respect for the grapes, which yield characterful wines.

After years one step away from the highest accolade, the '05 Amarone Classico walks away with our Three Glasses in a memorable performance. Heady aromas dominated by well-defined, fleshy fruit stand out over hints of spice and crushed flowers, reflected on the palate in a marvellous cavalcade of sweetness and austerity supported by acidity and a mouthwateringly savoury sensation. The interesting Valpolicella Ripasso Campo San Vito '07 has power and lingers but is still very young and a little ruffled. Lastly, the Valpolicella Campo Santa Lena '08 is uncomplicated and satisfyingly drinkable.

Villa Sandi

VIA ERIZZO, 112
31035 CROCETTA DEL MONTELLO [TV]
TEL. 0423665033
www.villasandi.it

CELLAR SALES
PRE-BOOKED VISITS
VISITOR FACILITIES
FOOD

ANNUAL PRODUCTION **2.800,000 bottles**
HECTARES UNDER VINE **301.5**
VITICULTURE METHOD **Conventional**

The Polegato family's estate has earned a full profile thanks to products that are increasingly dependable and attractive. Alongside the many sparkling wines, mostly Prosecco di Valdobbiadene DOC although they include metodo classico wines from the Opere Trevigiane line, there is a now-established range of still wines using the classic Bordeaux varieties that have been grown locally for over a century. One example of this is the Marinali Rosso, which has been very well received at home and abroad.

The top of the line Corpore '06 is a blend of merlot and cabernet franc in equal quantities. Mature, juicy red berry and cocoa powder on the nose lead into a very well-rounded, concentrated palate. Cartizze Brut del Vigneto La Rivetta shows exemplary concentration and full body. The interesting '07 Marinali Rosso, from cabernet franc and sauvignon, has a supple profile with lots of thrust. And there was an excellent performance from the '08 Avitus, a Manzoni Bianco with pervasive aromas and a sophisticated palate. Among the sparkling wines, we especially liked the Opere Riserva. The other products are all good.

● Amarone della Valpolicella Cl. '05	▼▼▼ 8
● Valpolicella Cl. Sup. Campo S. Vito Ripasso '07	▼▼ 5
● Valpolicella Cl. Campo S. Lena '08	▼ 4
● Amarone della Valpolicella Cl. '04	♈♈ 8
● Amarone della Valpolicella Cl. '03	♈♈ 8
● Amarone della Valpolicella Cl. '00	♈♈ 8
● Amarone della Valpolicella Cl. Campo S. Paolo '01	♈♈ 8
● Amarone della Valpolicella Cl. Campo S. Paolo '98	♈♈ 8
● Valpolicella Cl. Campo S. Lena '03	♈♈ 4
● Valpolicella Cl. Sup. Campo S. Vito '01	♈♈ 5
● Valpolicella Cl. Sup. Campo S. Vito Ripasso '06	♈♈ 5

○ Cartizze Brut V. La Rivetta '08	▼▼ 5
● Corpore '06	▼▼ 6
○ Avitus '08	▼▼ 5
● Marinali Rosso '07	▼▼ 5
○ Opere Trevigiane Brut Ris. '04	▼▼ 5
○ Cartizze	▼ 6
○ Marinali Bianco '08	▼ 5
○ Opere Trevigiane Brut	▼ 5
○ P. di Valdobbiadene Brut	▼ 4
○ P. di Valdobbiadene Dry Cuvée Oris	▼ 4
○ P. di Valdobbiadene Extra Dry	▼ 4
● Piave Raboso '05	▼ 4
● Corpore '05	♈♈ 6
● Corpore '04	♈♈ 6
● Corpore '02	♈♈ 6

Villa Spinosa

LOC. JAGO
37024 NEGRAR [VR]
TEL. 0457500093
www.villaspinosa.it

CELLAR SALES
PRE-BOOKED VISITS
VISITOR FACILITIES

ANNUAL PRODUCTION **35,000 bottles**
HECTARES UNDER VINE **18**
VITICULTURE METHOD **Conventional**

Enrico Cascella's winery moves at a different pace from others in this extensive DOC zone. While most producers opt for contemporary, full wines to sell quickly, Villa Spinosa eases up and offers wines that have been properly aged, enabling clients to rediscover qualities that other Valpolicella wines have forgotten, like finesse and lightness. This is why the estate's 20 or so hectares of vineyards produce very few bottles, which do however represent distinctively interpret the winery's ideal of finesse and classic features in a taut-flavoured profile.

Over the years, the range of wines has been rethought. There are two new products, an Amarone in a more youthful key and a Valpolicella which highlights the finesse this DOC can offer. The Amarone, an '04 aptly named Anteprima, expresses nice sweet fruit on the nose with a solid, approachable palate. The more imposing Valpolicella Figari '06 is fresh, vibrant and confidently spicy, with a lithe, vibrant flavour that caresses rather than attacks the palate. The Valpolicella Classico '07 is excellent.

Viviani

LOC. MAZZANO
VIA MAZZANO, 8
37020 NEGRAR [VR]
TEL. 0457500286
www.cantinaviviani.com

CELLAR SALES
PRE-BOOKED VISITS

ANNUAL PRODUCTION **70,000 bottles**
HECTARES UNDER VINE **10**
VITICULTURE METHOD **Conventional**

Claudio Viviani's winery has been courageous enough to turn the estate on its head with a well-judged review of an outdated vineyard management system. Over the years, the vineyards have been renovated, abandoning the traditional overhead trellis pergola in favour of the more suitable vertical-trained system while preserving the best plantings of older vines. The success of the last ten years has not gone to the cellar's head and the style is strongly traditional, as is shown by the absence of specialty wines.

It is difficult to say which is the better wine between the Amarone Casa dei Bepi '04 and the Valpolicella Campo Morar '06. The former expresses the sunny, generous qualities of the DOC while the other highlights its hidden, subtler side, with complex aromas and a savoury flavour. We preferred the Amarone, which impressed us all with its class, silky tannins and practically perfect handling of the considerable texture. There were also excellent performances from the bright, juicy '08 Valpolicella and the '06 Recioto, which is still too young to show its full potential.

Wine	Rating
● Valpolicella Cl. Sup. Figari '06	▼▼ 4*
● Amarone della Valpolicella Cl. Anteprima '04	▼▼ 6
● Valpolicella Cl. '07	▼▼ 3*
● Amarone della Valpolicella Cl. '01	♀♀ 7
● Amarone della Valpolicella Cl. '00	♀♀ 7
● Amarone della Valpolicella Cl. '99	♀♀ 7
● Amarone della Valpolicella Cl. Guglielmi di Jago '98	♀♀ 8
● Valpolicella Cl. Sup. Ripasso Jago '05	♀♀ 4

Wine	Rating
● Amarone della Valpolicella Cl. Casa dei Bepi '04	▼▼▼ 8
● Valpolicella Cl. Sup. Campo Morar '06	▼▼ 6
● Recioto della Valpolicella Cl. '06	▼▼ 7
● Valpolicella Cl. '08	▼▼ 4*
● Amarone della Valpolicella Cl. Casa dei Bepi '01	♀♀♀ 8
● Amarone della Valpolicella Cl. Casa dei Bepi '00	♀♀♀ 8
● Amarone della Valpolicella Cl. Casa dei Bepi '98	♀♀♀ 8
● Amarone della Valpolicella Cl. Casa dei Bepi '97	♀♀♀ 8
● Amarone della Valpolicella Cl. Casa dei Bepi '95	♀♀♀ 8
● Amarone della Valpolicella Cl. Tulipano Nero '97	♀♀♀ 8
● Valpolicella Cl. Sup. Campo Morar '05	♀♀♀ 6
● Valpolicella Cl. Sup. Campo Morar '01	♀♀♀ 6
● Recioto della Valpolicella Cl. '05	♀♀ 7

Zenato

FRAZ. SAN BENEDETTO DI LUGANA
VIA SAN BENEDETTO, 8
37019 PESCHIERA DEL GARDA [VR]
TEL. 0457550300
www.zenato.it

CELLAR SALES
PRE-BOOKED VISITS

ANNUAL PRODUCTION **1.500,000 bottles**
HECTARES UNDER VINE **70**
VITICULTURE METHOD **Conventional**

If there were any doubts about the future of the Zenato estate after the demise of owner Sergio, these have quickly dispersed. Alberto and Nadia's skill and tenacity have compensated for the absence of their father and they have also shown an ability to bounce straight back with wonderfully prestigious wines. Lugana and Valpolicella are the two reference DOCs and the grapes derive partly from the estate's own farms and partly from long-established growers who are supervised throughout the year. The new Valpolicella vineyard is slowly maturing and the early results seem interesting.

We had no doubts about which Amarone we preferred. Three Glasses went to the Classico '05. An explosively rich fruity wine with a full, juicy palate, it reveals a sweetness nicely held in check by densely woven tannins. The Sergio Zenato Riserva '04 shows more complex aromas and a powerful, harmonious body. The interesting '05 Cresasso is quietly, and very nicely, coming along. It's a monovarietal Corvina with strikingly clear aromas and grip. The Lugana wines are all good, starting with the San Benedetto '08.

F.lli Zeni

VIA COSTABELLA, 9
37011 BARDOLINO [VR]
TEL. 0457210022
www.zeni.it

CELLAR SALES
PRE-BOOKED VISITS

ANNUAL PRODUCTION **800,000 bottles**
HECTARES UNDER VINE **25**
VITICULTURE METHOD **Conventional**

The Veneto bank of Lake Garda has always been wine country, with three DOCs vying for space: Lugana, Custoza and, of course, Bardolino. The Zeni brothers' winery, situated here at Bardolino, is committed to a very extensive range released under various lines, including to some extent all the Veronese DOCs as well as a couple of IGT wines. Only some of the grapes are grown on the estate and a large proportion comes from growers supervised by the cellar through the year.

We tasted many wines and the one we enjoyed most was the '06 Amarone Vigne Alte, with intensely sun-ripe, well-defined fruit. The palate is firm-bodied with distinctive, pleasantly husky tannins. From the same line, and just as good, is the lighter '07 Recioto, which is more discreet on the nose and palate. The rest of the products hew to a well-defined, recognizable style that in the various wine types, putting the accent on approachability rather than structure or complexity.

● Amarone della Valpolicella Cl. '05	♟♟♟ 7
● Amarone della Valpolicella Cl. Sergio Zenato Ris. '04	♟♟ 8
● Cresasso '05	♟♟ 6
○ Lugana S. Benedetto '08	♟♟ 4*
○ Lugana Sergio Zenato '07	♟♟ 5
○ Lugana Vign. Massoni Santa Cristina '08	♟♟ 4
● Valpolicella Sup. Ripassa '06	♟♟ 5
● Valpolicella Cl. Sup. '06	♟ 4
● Amarone della Valpolicella Cl. '97	♟♟♟ 6
● Amarone della Valpolicella Cl. Sergio Zenato '03	♟♟♟ 8
● Amarone della Valpolicella Cl. Sergio Zenato '00	♟♟♟ 8
● Amarone della Valpolicella Cl. Sergio Zenato '95	♟♟♟ 8
● Amarone della Valpolicella Cl. Sergio Zenato Ris. '98	♟♟♟ 8

● Amarone della Valpolicella Cl. Vigne Alte '06	♟♟ 7
● Recioto della Valpolicella Cl. Vigne Alte '07	♟♟ 6
● Amarone della Valpolicella Cl. Barrique '05	♟ 7
⊙ Bardolino Chiaretto Cl. Vigne Alte '08	♟ 3
● Bardolino Cl. Vigne Alte '08	♟ 3
● Costalago '07	♟ 3
○ Lugana Marogne '08	♟ 4
○ Lugana Vigne Alte '08	♟ 3
● Merlar Rosso '06	♟ 6
○ Soave Cl. Vigne Alte '08	♟ 3
● Valpolicella Cl. Vigne Alte '08	♟ 4
● Valpolicella Sup. Ripasso Marogne '07	♟ 4
● Amarone della Valpolicella Cl. Barrique '04	♟♟ 7

Zonin

via Borgolecco, 9
36053 Gambellara [VI]
tel. 0444640111
www.zonin.it

CELLAR SALES
PRE-BOOKED VISITS

ANNUAL PRODUCTION **23,000,000 bottles**
HECTARES UNDER VINE **1800**
VITICULTURE METHOD **Conventional**

Although Gianni Zonin's estates are now scattered across the whole of Italy, the business originated in Gambellara, a small town near Vicenza, which remains the focal point of the Zonin galaxy. Production is obviously centred on whites from garganega, alongside a small number of significant Amarone and Ripasso products from nearby Valpolicella. The inevitable Prosecco completes the picture of a balanced range of wines with value for money as one of its kingpins.

The most impressive wine of them all was the '06 Amarone, with red berries and medicinal herbs on the nose and a palate that won us over with its handling of the massive body, held in check by tight-knit tannins. The Valpolicella Ripasso '07 emphasizes the more discreet, hidden side of Valpolicella, with pervasive aromas and a dry, savoury, nicely supple palate. The Gambellara Classico Il Giangio '08 is fresh and approachably fruity. The two Proseccos, both Brut, are also both dependably good.

● Amarone della Valpolicella '06	🍷🍷 6
● Valpolicella Sup. Ripasso '07	🍷🍷 4
O Gambellara Cl. Podere Il Giangio '08	🍷 4
O Prosecco Brut Special Cuvée	🍷 3
O Prosecco Cuvée Brut	🍷 3
● Amarone della Valpolicella '05	🍷🍷 6
● Amarone della Valpolicella '04	🍷🍷 6
● Amarone della Valpolicella '03	🍷🍷 6
● Amarone della Valpolicella Cl. Maso Laito '99	🍷🍷 7
● Valpolicella Sup. Ripasso '04	🍷🍷 4*
● Valpolicella Sup. Ripasso '03	🍷🍷 4*

Zymè

via Ca' del Pipa, 1
37029 San Pietro in Cariano [VR]
tel. 0457701108
www.zyme.it

CELLAR SALES
PRE-BOOKED VISITS

ANNUAL PRODUCTION **30,000 bottles**
HECTARES UNDER VINE **16**
VITICULTURE METHOD **Conventional**

Zymè is one of the most interesting new estates in Valpolicella. It began as a consultancy but quickly changed course and abandoned external collaborations to focus its efforts on its own products. The results are increasingly impressive. The range of wines reflects the originality of the two partners, Celestino Gaspari and Francesco Parisi, with a sumptuous Amarone alongside other wines which all draw on tradition in different ways, using classic varieties or blends of different grapes.

The range of products has been extended as shown by the addition of the I Vigneti '06, a blend of various local grapes. This first version has a generous, fruity nose and a solid, austere body. Even more impressive is the Oseleta Oz '06, which shows more finesse with every vintage. The '03 Harlequin may be the most original wine. It's from a blend of 15 different grapes and presents with power and lots of promise for the future. But the Amarone Classico '03 is the big hitter with its deep, sophisticated aromas and a palate that is even more enticing.

● Amarone della Valpolicella Cl. '03	🍷🍷 8
● Harlequin '03	🍷🍷 8
● Oseleta Oz '06	🍷🍷 7
● I Vigneti '06	🍷 6
O Il Bianco From Black to White '08	🍷 4
● Amarone della Valpolicella Cl. '01	🍷🍷 8
● Harlequin '01	🍷🍷 8
● Kairos '05	🍷🍷 8
● Kairos '04	🍷🍷 8
● Kairos '03	🍷🍷 8
● Oseleta Oz '05	🍷🍷 6
● Oseleta Oz '04	🍷🍷 6
● Oseleta Oz '03	🍷🍷 6

Barollo

VIA RIO SERVA, 4B
35123 PREGANZIOL [TV]
TEL. 0422633014
www.barollo.com

In a few short years, Marco and Nicola Barollo's winery nestling in the Po valley has achieved excellent quality. In the absence of the more ambitious wines, our attention was caught by nice versions of the Pinot Bianco and Pinot Grigio, both enjoyably upfront and solid.

○ Pinot Bianco '08	♟♟	4
○ Pinot Grigio '08	♟♟	4
● Frater Rosso '08	♟	4
○ Incrocio Manzoni '08	♟	5

La Bertolà

VIA SAN NICOLÒ, 84
36070 TRISSINO [VI]
TEL. 0445410780
www.tenutalabertola.it

La Bertolà is a classic Agno valley estate. Thanks to Massimo Dal Lago's efforts, this year red wines are starting to take their place next to the fresh, succulent whites. We noted a good showing from the '08 Riesling with its distinctive aromas and juicy, incisive palate. The other wines are all good.

○ Vicenza Riesling '08	♟♟	4*
○ Pinot Grigio '08	♟	4
● Vicenza Cabernet Sauvignon '07	♟	4
○ Vicenza Chardonnay '08	♟	4

Antonio Bigai

FRAZ. LISON
VIA CADUTI PER LA PATRIA, 29
30026 PORTOGRUARO [VE]
TEL. 336592660
www.amimanera.com

Producer Antonio "Toni" Bigai has reinterpreted tradition and today his few, but dependable, wines have striking personality. The excellent Lison '08 is a salty Tocai with a buttery, punchy palate. The A Mi Manera Bianco '08 is subtly floral and more elegant in style.

○ A Mi Manera Bianco '08	♟♟	4
● A Mi Manera Rosso '08	♟♟	4
○ Lison-Pramaggiore Lison '08	♟♟	3*
● Lison-Pramaggiore Merlot '08	♟	4

Borgoluce

LOC. MUSILE, 2
31058 SUSEGANA [TV]
TEL. 0438435287
www.borgoluce.it

In just two years, Borgoluce has earned recognition for its reliable products, especially the prosecco-based sparkling wines. There was a good performance from the Brut with its lovely pervasive aromas and creamy fizz. Among the Extra Drys, we liked the succulent Millesimato '08.

○ Prosecco di Valdobbiadene Brut	♟♟	4
○ Prosecco di Valdobbiadene Extra Dry Millesimato '08	♟♟	5
○ Prosecco di Valdobbiadene Extra Dry	♟	4

Carlo Boscaini

VIA SENGIA, 15
37010 SANT'AMBROGIO DI VALPOLICELLA [VR]
TEL. 0457731412
www.boscainicarlo.it

Carlo and Mario Boscaini have brought a breath of fresh air to Valpolicella with extensive vineyard renovation but the cellar is traditional in the choice of barrels and wine style. The Amarone '04 has complex aromas and a full, silky palate. The savoury Valpolicella Zane '06 has depth.

● Amarone della Valpolicella Cl. San Giorgio '04	♟♟	7
● Valpolicella Cl. Sup. Ripasso Zane '06	♟♟	4

Buglioni

FRAZ. CORRUBIO
VIA CAMPAGNOLE, 55
37029 SAN PIETRO IN CARIANO [VR]
TEL. 0456760681
www.buglioni.it

Mariano Buglioni's wines are always dependably good. The wide range adheres to Veronese DOCs or grapes, like the flavoursome, succulent Valpolicella Il Bugiardo '05 and the peppery Lo Zingaro '08, made from corvinone.

● Valpolicella Cl. Sup. Ripasso Il Bugiardo '05	♟♟	5
● Lo Zingaro '08	♟	4
● Valpolicella Cl. Il Valpolicella '08	♟	4

Le Carline

VIA CARLINE, 24
30020 PRAMAGGIORE [VE]
TEL. 0421799741
www.lecarline.com

Daniele Piccinin's wines are always impressive. He manages to produce a broad, well-balanced range in the challenging Lison Pramaggiore DOC. The Lison '08, a savoury, gutsy Tocai, stands out for its character and solid flavour. The husky Pinot Grigio '08 is also good, showing nice weight.

○ Lison-Pramaggiore Lison '08	♟♟ 3*
○ Lison-Pramaggiore Pinot Grigio '08	♟♟ 3*
● Lison-Pramaggiore Cabernet Sauvignon '07	♟ 4

Italo Cescon

FRAZ. RONCADELLE
P.ZZA DEI CADUTI, 3
31024 ORMELLE [TV]
TEL. 0422851033
www.cesconitalo.it

In the last year, Cescon has made over the range while maintaining the basic Tralcetto line and a more ambitious selection. We liked the '07 Bordeaux blend Chieto, which gives generous fruit and a very harmonious palate. The even more impressive Manzoni Bianco '08 is vibrantly fruity.

● Chieto '07	♟♟ 4
○ Manzoni Bianco '08	♟♟ 6
● Piave Raboso Rabià '05	♟ 4
○ Sauvignon Mejo '08	♟ 4

Contrà Soarda

LOC. CONTRÀ SOARDA, 26
36061 BASSANO DEL GRAPPA [VI]
TEL. 0424566785
www.contrasoarda.it

Situated just outside Bassano, Mirco Gottardi's lovely estate has a new cellar that blends perfectly with the environment and surrounding vineyards. The cool climate has led to well-established crops of pinot nero, which are yielding promising results. All the products are dependably good.

● Breganze Rosso Terre di Lava Ris. '06	♟♟ 5
● Il Saggio '05	♟♟ 8
● Vigna Correjo '06	♟♟ 8

Corte Adami

VIA CIRCONVALLAZIONE ALDO MORO, 32
37038 SOAVE [VR]
TEL. 0457680423
www.corteadami.it

In a few years, Corte Adami has reached a good level both for the Soave whites and the Valpolicella reds. The nice '08 Soave is a lean, mouthwatering white while the '07 Vigna della Corte is richer and more mature without sacrificing suppleness. The Recioto di Soave '05 is bright and rather rustic.

○ Soave '08	♟♟ 3*
○ Soave Vigna della Corte '07	♟♟ 4
● Amarone della Valpolicella '06	♟ 7
○ Recioto di Soave '05	♟ 6

Crodi

LOC. COMBAI
VIA CAPOVILLA, 19
31030 MIANE [TV]
TEL. 0438960064

The Crodi winery is situated in Combai, a village nestling in the hills where the grapes always yield excellent results. From the wines presented, we liked the 500 '06, a fresh, elegant, Bordeaux blend from a vineyard at 500 metres above sea level. The Prosecco is good and creamy with rather elegant fizz.

● 500 '06	♟♟ 4
○ P. di Conegliano Valdobbiadene Extra Dry	♟♟ 4

De Faveri

FRAZ. BOSCO
VIA SARTORI, 21
31020 VIDOR [TV]
TEL. 0423987673
www.defaverispumanti.it

The Valdobbiadene zone is dotted with different-sized wineries, all producing the classic Treviso sparkling wines. The De Faveri family stands out for its balanced, dependable range, especially the Prosecco Brut Selezione Nera, with subtly expressed aromas and a dry lingering palate.

○ P. di Valdobbiadene Brut Sel. Nera	♟♟ 4
○ P. di Valdobbiadene Extra Dry	♟♟ 4
○ Cartizze	♟ 5
○ P. di Valdobbiadene Brut	♟ 4

Fattori Giovanni

FRAZ. TERROSSA
VIA OLMO, 6
37030 RONCÀ [VR]
TEL. 0457460041
www.fattorigiovanni.it

In the last year, Antonio Fattori's winery, situated slightly outside the heart of Soave, has undergone a restyling of the wines and the cellar organization. The 30-hectare estate produces exclusively white wines in a fruity, approachable style.

O Soave Motto Piane '08	♟♟	4
O Soave Cl. '08	♟	3
O Soave Cl. Danieli '08	♟	3
O Vecchie Scuole Sauvignon '08	♟	4

Fraccaroli

FRAZ. SAN BENEDETTO
LOC. BERRA VECCHIA, 1
37019 PESCHIERA DEL GARDA [VR]
TEL. 0457550949
www.fraccarolivini.it

Products from the Fraccarolis on the banks of Lake Garda are good. The family works with Lugana, the classic white from the provinces of Verona and Brescia. The very good Vigneto Pansere '08 shows faint aromas and a very elegant, savoury palate. The richer, more structured Campo Serà '07 is also good.

O Lugana Sup. V. Campo Serà '07	♟♟	4
O Lugana Vign. Pansere '08	♟♟	4*
O Lugana I Rondinelli '08	♟	3
O Lugana Podere Bazzola '08	♟	4

La Giaretta

FRAZ. VALGATARA
VIA DEL PLATANO, 12
37020 MARANO DI VALPOLICELLA [VR]
TEL. 0457701791
www.cantinalagiaretta.com

At Valgatara, on the lower hills near Marano, Francesco Vaona produces intensely fruity wine with huge extract. A perfect example of this style is the Valpolicella I Quadretti '06, rich in fruit and toasty sensations with a strikingly powerful, lingering palate. The Recioto '04 is also good.

● Recioto della Valpolicella Cl. '04	♟♟	6
● Valpolicella Cl. Sup. I Quadretti '06	♟♟	5
● Amarone della Valpolicella Cl. I Quadretti '03	♟	8

Latium

VIA GIARA, 34
37031 ILLASI [VR]
TEL. 3929048995
www.latiummorini.it

The strength of the Morini family's estate is surely in the vineyards, planted at up to 14,000 vines per hectare, which tells you a lot about their priorities. The Valpolicella Campo Prognai '06 embodies this quest for concentration in a fruity nose and structured palate. The '04 Amarone is solid and powerful.

● Amarone della Valpolicella Campo Leon '04	♟♟	7
● Valpolicella Sup. Campo Prognai '06	♟♟	5

Lenotti

VIA SANTA CRISTINA, 1
37011 BARDOLINO [VR]
TEL. 0457210484
www.lenotti.com

The Lenotti family's wines are always reliably good and the broad range is able to fulfil all possible demands. The very interesting Bardolino Le Olle '07 manages to deliver good structure without sacrificing grip. The Capomastro '07 is a mouthwateringly fresh blend of corvina and rebo.

● Amarone della Valpolicella Cl. Di Carlo '03	♟♟	8
● Bardolino Cl. Sup. Le Olle '07	♟♟	4*
● Capomastro '07	♟♟	4*

Giuseppe Lonardi

VIA DELLE POSTE, 2
37020 MARANO DI VALPOLICELLA [VR]
TEL. 0457755154
www.lonardivini.it

Giuseppe "Bepi" Lonardi's winery is in the upper Marano valley, an area that produces wines with pervasive aromas and juicy lightness. The well-typed Amarone '05 has vibrant fruits and fines herbes aromas and a healthily husky palate with dry body. The floral, spicy Valpolicella '08 is also good.

● Amarone della Valpolicella Cl. '05	♟♟	7
● Privilegia Rosso '06	♟	6
● Valpolicella Cl. '08	♟	4
● Valpolicella Cl. Sup. Ripasso '07	♟	6

OTHER WINERIES

Marsuret

LOC. GUIA
VIA SPINADE, 41
31040 VALDOBBIADENE [TV]
TEL. 0423900139
www.marsuret.it

This winery was founded between the wars by grandpa Agostino, who bought the first vineyard at Guia, east of Valdobbiadene. The current generation of the Marsura family now runs the operation. The Cartizze is the most interesting wine, giving fragrant apple fruit and florality with fine, lingering fizz.

O P. di Valdobbiadene Brut	🍷🍷	4
O P. di Valdobbiadene Sup. Cartizze	🍷🍷	5
O P. di Valdobbiadene Extra Dry	🍷	4

Firmino Miotti

VIA BROGLIATI CONTRO, 53
36042 BREGANZE [VI]
TEL. 0445873006
www.firminomiotti.it

Franca Miotti has managed her father Firmino's winery near Breganze for several years. The range is interesting. Without the Torcolato, still ageing in the cellar, the most interesting wine is Rosso Valletta '06, a Bordeaux blend with jammy, cocoa powder aromas and a powerful palate.

● Rosso Valletta '06	🍷🍷	6
O Breganze Bianco Le Colombare '08	🍷	3

Monte Zovo

LOC. ZOVO, 23
37013 CAPRINO VERONESE [VR]
TEL. 0457281301
www.montezovo.com

In recent years, businessman Diego Cottini, the founder of Monte Zovo, has extended the family vineyards to over 70 hectares in both Valpolicella and the surrounding area. There was a good performance from the Amarone '04, with approachable fruit and a full, rounded palate.

● Amarone della Valpolicella '04	🍷🍷	7
● Ca' Linverno '04	🍷	5
● Valpolicella Sup. Ripasso '06	🍷	5

Monteforche

LOC. ZOVON
VIA ROVAROLLA, 2005
35030 VÒ [PD]
TEL. 3332376035

Alfonso Soranzo is either a musician who has turned to winemaking or vice versa. He farms just under five hectares of environment-friendly hillside vineyards with very promising results. Cellar procedures are kept to a minimum in tribute to the ideal of processing wine as little as possible.

● Cabernet Franc '07	🍷🍷	4
O Cassiara '08	🍷🍷	4
O Vigneto Carantina '08	🍷🍷	4

Marco Mosconi

VIA PARADISO, 5
37031 ILLASI [VR]
TEL. 0457834080
www.marcomosconi.it

Marco Mosconi's wines are getting more exciting, as this year's tasting shows. The Soave Corte Paradiso '08 has generous aromatics and a dry, taut palate. The exuberant Recioto di Soave '06 shows assertive aromas of candied citrus and liquorice followed by nicely balanced sweetness.

O Recioto di Soave '06	🍷🍷	6
O Soave Corte Paradiso '08	🍷🍷	4
O Soave Rosetta '07	🍷	5
● Valpolicella Sup. '06	🍷	6

Paladin

VIA POSTUMIA, 12
30020 ANNONE VENETO [VE]
TEL. 0422768167
www.paladin.it

The Paladin family presents quite a well-stocked range of wines focusing on the Lison Pramaggiore DOC. The interesting Malbech Gli Aceri '06 has fragrant red berry fruit and flowers on the nose and a juicy, supple palate. The Refosco is fresh and juicy and the Cabernet is solid and pleasantly husky.

● Malbech Gli Aceri '06	🍷🍷	5
● Lison-Pramaggiore Cabernet '08	🍷	3
● Lison-Pramaggiore Refosco P.R. '08	🍷	3
O Traminer '08	🍷	4

Albino Piona

FRAZ. CUSTOZA
VIA BELLAVISTA, 48
37060 SOMMACAMPAGNA [VR]
TEL. 045516055
www.albinopiona.it

The Piona family's winery is one of the best known and respected in this part of Veneto south of Lake Garda, where the Custoza and Bardolino DOCs meet. The Campo Massimo '07 is a very interesting single-variety Corvina with a vibrant, spicy palate. The other wines are fresh and enjoyable.

● Campo Massimo Corvina Veronese '07	🍷🍷 4*
● Bardolino '08	🍷 3
⊙ Bardolino Chiaretto '08	🍷 3
○ Bianco di Custoza '08	🍷 3

Urbano Salvan

LOC. PIGOZZO
VIA MINCANA, 143
35020 DUE CARRARE [PD]
TEL. 049525841
giorgio.salvan@libero.it

Giorgio Salvan's winery is at Due Carrare, close to the Colli Euganei hills, where the soil gives the wines roundness and maturity. We loved the Merlot Riserva '05 for its fruitiness and full, nicely savoury palate. The other reds are impressive, especially the Cabernet Franc '07.

● Colli Euganei Cabernet Franc '07	🍷🍷 3*
● Colli Euganei Merlot Ris. '05	🍷🍷 4*
● Colli Euganei Cabernet Sauvignon San Marco '06	🍷 4

Tenuta Sant'Anna

LOC. LONCON
VIA MONS. P. L. ZOVATTO, 71
30020 ANNONE VENETO [VE]
TEL. 0422864511
www.tenutasantanna.it

Sant'Anna wines continue to grow in quality with increasingly promising results. The most interesting this year is the Cabernet Sauvignon Riserva '06, with pervasive aromas of wild berries and medicinal herbs. The palate is medium-bodied and beautifully balanced. The Lison is savoury and nicely salty.

● Lison-Pramaggiore Cabernet Sauvignon Ris. '06	🍷🍷 4*
○ Lison-Pramaggiore Chardonnay '08	🍷 4
○ Lison-Pramaggiore Lison Cl. '08	🍷 4

Santa Eurosia

FRAZ. SAN PIETRO DI BARBOZZA
VIA DELLA CIMA, 8
31040 VALDOBBIADENE [TV]
TEL. 0423973236
www.santaeurosia.it

Santa Eurosia exclusively produces prosecco-based sparkling wines. The skill of Giuseppe Geronazzo, the man behind this estate, translates into remarkably elegant and harmonious wines with discreet, silky effervescence. The Brut and Cartizze are both excellent.

○ Cartizze	🍷🍷 6
○ P. di Valdobbiadene Brut	🍷🍷 4*
○ P. di Valdobbiadene Dry Mill. '08	🍷 5
○ P. di Valdobbiadene Extra Dry	🍷 4

Cantina di Soave

FRAZ. SOAVE
V.LE VITTORIA, 100
37038 SOAVE [VR]
TEL. 0456139811
www.cantinasoave.it

This large Soave co-operative produces wines from all the main Veronese DOCs in a broad range headed by the Rocca Sveva line. The Amarone '05 is rich in hints of fruit and spices, showing power but also suppleness. The Soave Castelcerino '07 is fresh-tasting with lovely grip.

● Amarone della Valpolicella Rocca Sveva '05	🍷🍷 7
○ Soave Cl. Sup. Castelcerino Rocca Sveva '07	🍷🍷 4

David Sterza

LOC. CASTERNA
VIA CASTERNA, 37
37022 FUMANE [VR]
TEL. 0457704201
www.davidsterza.it

Sterza interprets a type of wine that remains faithful to tradition in a contemporary idiom that foregrounds crisply defined aromas. The good performance from the Amarone '05, which is generous and clearly fruity on the nose with a solid, dry palate, is matched by an elegant, supple Corvina '07.

● Amarone della Valpolicella Cl. '05	🍷🍷 6*
● Corvina Veronese '07	🍷🍷 5
● Valpolicella Cl. Sup. Ripasso '07	🍷 4

OTHER WINERIES

Sutto

VIA SAN LORENZETTO, 9
31040 SALGAREDA [TV]
TEL. 0422744063
www.sutto.it

Piave is a generous land but this is not always an advantage for the wine sector. Producers need to be shrewd and sensitive enough to offset its richness with the finesse it so jealously guards. But it's all there in the Sutto siblings' fast-emerging wines, especially the Bordeaux blend Dogma.

● Dogma Rosso '07	▼▼	5
● Piave Cabernet Ris. '07	▼▼	5
● Piave Raboso '06	▼▼	6
○ Manzoni Bianco '08	▼	5

T.E.S.S.A.R.I.

LOC. BROGNOLIGO
VIA FONTANA NUOVA, 86
37032 MONTEFORTE D'ALPONE [VR]
TEL. 0456175169
www.cantinatessari.com

Tessari is a big name in Soave and Antonio deserves respect. In recent years, his wines have gained in definition and quality. We confirmed this when we tasted Grisela, a varietal and nicely husky single-variety Soave from garganega. The Recioto and Soave Le Bine Longhe are both full and mature.

○ Soave Cl. Grisela '08	▼▼	3*
○ Recioto di Soave Tre Colli '06	▼	6
○ Soace Cl. Le Bine Longhe '07	▼	4

Le Tende

FRAZ. COLÀ DI LAZISE
VIA TENDE, 35
37017 LAZISE [VR]
TEL. 0457590748
www.letende.it

Le Tende, at Lazise, is the successful result of a partnership between the Fortuna and Lucillini families. In recent years, the wines have gained continuity and several wines are interesting. The Cicisbeo '07 is full and well structured while the nicely savoury '08 Bardolino has nice pervasive aromas.

● Bardolino Cl. '08	▼▼	3*
● Garda Cabernet Sauvignon Cicisbeo '07	▼▼	4
● Bardolino Cl. Sup. '07	▼	3
○ Bianco di Custoza '08	▼	3*

Terre di Leone

LOC. PORTA
37020 MARANO DI VALPOLICELLA [VR]
TEL. 0456895040
www.terredileone.it

Federico and Chiara Pellizzari's Terre di Leone is one of the most interesting new wineries in Valpolicella. The small vineyard is planted at a high density and managed with skill. The most impressive wine is the Amarone '05, giving fruit and fines herbes on the nose and mouthwatering acidity on the palate.

● Amarone della Valpolicella Cl. '05	▼▼	8
● Valpolicella Cl. Sup. '06	▼▼	6
● Dedicatum '06	▼	6
● Valpolicella Cl. Sup. Ripasso '06	▼	7

Terre di San Venanzio Fortunato

VIA CAPITELLO FERRARI, 1
31049 VALDOBBIADENE [TV]
TEL. 0423974083
www.terredisanvenanzio.it

Terre di San Venanzio operates within what will be the new DOCG of Prosecco, Valdobbiadene. The grapes used for the production of fewer than 200,000 bottles are all grown on the estate. The Prosecco Brut is very good, with floral and apple fruit aromas, and a harmonious palate with silky effervescence.

○ P. di Valdobbiadene Brut	▼▼	4
○ Cartizze	▼	5
○ P. di Valdobbiadene Extra Dry	▼	4

Tessere

LOC. SANTA TERESINA
VIA BASSETTE, 51
30020 NOVENTA DI PIAVE [VE]
TEL. 0421320438
www.tessereonline.it

Emanuela Bincoletto works with passionate determination on the Piave river near the Adriatic, not far from the Pre-Alps. In recent years, the winery has come on nicely, as we see from the '05 Raboso Barbarigo, which tames this very rustic variety, endowing it with taut elegance.

○ Dimmi Chi Sono Passito '07	▼▼	5
● Piave Raboso Barbarigo '05	▼▼	5
● Piave Merlot Galiòn '07	▼	3
○ Piave Pinot Bianco '08	▼	3

Val del Lovo

LOC. COLLALTO
VIA CUCCO, 29
31058 SUSEGANA [TV]
TEL. 0438981232
www.valdellovo.it

Collalto is a small village nestling in the hills behind Castello di San Salvatore, in Susegana. The estate's ten or so hectares of vineyards produce two interesting reds, the Bausk '04 and the Salariato '05. The former is a rich, silky Merlot and the other a sophisticated Bordeaux blend.

● Bausk '04	♙♙ 6
● Salariato '05	♙♙ 6

Villa Canestrari

VIA DANTE BROGLIO, 2
37030 COLOGNOLA AI COLLI [VR]
TEL. 0457650074
www.villacanestrari.com

Villa Canestrari is situated at Colognola ai Colli, an area split between the Valpolicella and Soave DOCs. The winery style emphasizes the more mature and mouthfilling qualities of reds and whites alike, as we discovered when we tasted the Amarone Plenum '04 and the Soave Auge '06.

● Amarone della Valpolicella Plenum '04	♙♙ 7
○ Soave Sup. Auge '06	♙ 4
● Valpolicella Terre di Lanolì '08	♙ 3

Villa di Maser

VIA CORNUDA, 1
31010 MASER [TV]
TEL. 0423923003
www.villadimaser.it

The Colli Asolani are north of Treviso, below the Pre-Alps, in a sunny area with excellent temperature ranges. This is the home of Villa di Maser, a winery that takes care to respect the environment. We noted good performances from the Cabernet '05, and the fresh, harmonious Bordeaux blend Maserino '05.

● Il Maserino '05	♙♙ 6
● Montello e Colli Asolani Cabernet '05	♙♙ 4
○ Verduzzo '07	♙ 4

Villa Medici

VIA CAMPAGNOL, 11
37066 SOMMACAMPAGNA [VR]
TEL. 045515147

Villa Medici is a lovely winery working in the Bardolino and Custoza DOCs with increasingly satisfactory results. The wines are very reasonably priced, which is always nice. The very good Bardolino Superiore '07 succeeds in the difficult task of showing nicely rounded body as well as suppleness and grip.

● Bardolino Sup. '07	♙♙ 4*
⊙ Bardolino Chiaretto '08	♙ 3
○ Custoza '08	♙ 3
○ Custoza Sup. '07	♙ 4

Vigneti Villabella

FRAZ. CALMASINO
LOC. CANOVA, 2
37011 BARDOLINO [VR]
TEL. 0457236448
www.vignetivillabella.com

The Delibori and Cristoforetti families own the Villabella estate of about 300 hectares producing classic Verona wines. The rich, fruity Villa Cordevigo '05 is a good Bordeaux blend with a sprinkling of corvina. The Amarone Fracastoro '03 is generous; the Lugana Ca' del Lago '08 simple and enjoyable.

● Villa Cordevigo Rosso '05	♙♙ 6
● Amarone della Valpolicella Cl. Fracastoro '03	♙ 7
○ Lugana Ca' del Lago '08	♙ 4

Valerio Zenato-Le Morette

V.LE INDIPENDENZA
37019 PESCHIERA DEL GARDA [VR]
TEL. 0457552724
www.valeriozenato.it

Fabio and Paolo Zenato run the winery their grandfather founded at San Benedetto, a great area for Lugana wines. Lugana Benedictus '07 is one of the most interesting in the DOC with vibrant fruit and solid body nicely supported by acidity. The Vigna Mandolara '08 is less complex and very drinkable.

○ Lugana Benedictus '07	♙♙ 4*
○ Lugana Vigna La Mandolara '08	♙♙ 4*
● Bardolino Cl. '08	♙ 4
● Perseo '05	♙ 4

FRIULI VENEZIA GIULIA

Friuli Venezia Giulia in the extreme north east of Italy is a region of great white wines and quite a number of serious reds. Since the inception of Italian Wines, the region has always been a leader in our classifications but the limited extent of its wine territory means that concentration of winning bottles is impressive. The Collio Goriziano, right on the border with Slovenia, with the Colli Orientali del Friuli to the north and the Carso to the south east, as well as part of the flatter Isonzo and Grave DOCs, form Friuli's wine heartland. Equally stunning is the range of varieties, some native and some, as it were, naturalized. It's a waste of time trying to tell Friulians that pinot bianco and merlot – pronounced with the final "t" – are not native to the region. Both have been grown here for more than a century and a half, so the locals have some justification. As always, this edition of the Guide notes the superb average level of quality among Friulian whites, with Friulano, formerly known as Tocai, leading the field. But blends of different varieties are also yielding seriously good results, as you would expect from a region where blending has deep and noble roots. Then we come to the tour de force of various Malvasia Istrianas, most from 2008, and two rather special 2005 Ribolla Giallas from Josko Gravner and Franco Terpin. Yet perhaps the most significant development is the fact that six Friulian reds won our top award, against only one last time. Two Merlots, two Schioppettinos, one schioppettino and refosco blend and a cabernet and merlot mix stood out. And so on to the producers. The only one to bag a brace of Three Glass prizes was that outstanding wine man, Franco Toròs, from Plessiva near Cormòns. Meanwhile the Editor's Three Glasses went to a dazzling edition of Vintage Tunina '07 from the masterly winemaking hand of Silvio Jermann. The vintages on parade, 2008 and 2007 for the most part, were clearly reflected in the wines. The 2008 growing year was cooler and better suited to whites while the 2007s are warmer and richer, especially in areas near the coast. The 2006 vintage produced sumptuous reds while the 2005 versions tend to be slimmer.

Tenuta di Angoris

LOC. ANGORIS, 7
34071 CORMÒNS [GO]
TEL. 048160923
www.angoris.com

CELLAR SALES
PRE-BOOKED VISITS

ANNUAL PRODUCTION 850,000 bottles
HECTARES UNDER VINE 130
VITICULTURE METHOD Conventional

In 1648, Emperor Ferdinand III of Austria gave 300 "campi" of fertile land to his officer, Locatello Locatelli, for bravery on the field of battle during the Thirty Years' War. In the past three centuries and more, the estate has had a number of owners but in 1968, it once again became the property of another Locatelli, Luciano, a far-sighted, dynamic businessman. For the past few years, it has been managed by Luciano's daughter Claudia, who focuses particularly on viticulture and wine.

The vineyards in the Isonzo, Collio and Colli Orientali del Friuli DOC zones are looked after by the expert Marco Simonit while oenologist Alessandro Del Zovo has run the cellar for some time. Recently, Angoris has been turning out excellent wines and yet again sent a bottle to our final taste-offs. Ribolla Gialla Vôs da Vigne '08 stands out for its finesse, the definition of its fruit-rich aromas, its freshness and tangy drinkability. Equally appealing is the coherent, caressing Pinot Bianco Villa Angoris '08. Sauvignon Villa Angoris '08 is minerally and true to type while Chardonnay Vôs da Vigne '08 is very attractive indeed.

Antonutti

FRAZ. COLLOREDO DI PRATO
VIA D'ANTONI, 21
33037 PASIAN DI PRATO [UD]
TEL. 0432662001
www.antonuttivini.it

CELLAR SALES
PRE-BOOKED VISITS

ANNUAL PRODUCTION 600,000 bottles
HECTARES UNDER VINE 17
VITICULTURE METHOD Conventional

Adriana Antonutti, her husband Lino and children Caterina and Nicola continue to plough the furrow first cut by their grandfather Ignazio in 1921, competently managing one of the best-known estates in the Grave del Friuli DOC at Colloredo di Prato, not far from Udine. Ever on the look-out for promising innovations, the Antonuttis are already reaping the rewards of the new Vis Terrae line, created for wines crafted with special care to ensure superior quality.

The fine star-bright Traminer Aromatico '07 proffers yellow rose, honey, candied peel and tropical fruits aromas. Soft-textured and pervasive on the palate, it hits just the right aromatic note. Both Pinot Grigios are excellently made. The current release has headily fruity fragrances and a deep, dynamic palate whereas the Vis Terrae '07 is more concentrated and mouthfilling but very drinkable. The Sauvignon '08 is pale in the glass and very coherent on the nose with varietal notes of well-defined greens and fruit, easy drinkability and a tangy palate. All the other wines we tasted are very well made.

O COF Ribolla Gialla Vôs da Vigne '08	♥♥ 4*
O COF Bianco Spiule '07	♥♥ 5
O Collio Chardonnay Vôs da Vigne '08	♥♥ 5
O Friuli Isonzo Pinot Bianco Villa Angoris '08	♥♥ 4*
O Friuli Isonzo Sauvignon Villa Angoris '08	♥♥ 4*
O COF Friulano Vôs da Vigne '08	♥ 5
O COF Sauvignon Vôs da Vigne '08	♥ 5
O Collio Pinot Grigio Vôs da Vigne '08	♥ 5
O COF Bianco Spiule '06	♀♀ 5
O COF Friulano Vôs da Vigne '07	♀♀ 5
O COF Ribolla Gialla Vôs da Vigne '07	♀♀ 4
O COF Sauvignon Vôs da Vigne '07	♀♀ 5
O COF Sauvignon Vôs da Vigne '06	♀♀ 4*
O Collio Pinot Grigio Vôs da Vigne '06	♀♀ 4
O Collio Tocai Friulano Vôs da Vigne '06	♀♀ 4*

O Friuli Grave Pinot Grigio '08	♥♥ 4*
O Friuli Grave Pinot Grigio Vis Terrae '07	♥♥ 4*
O Friuli Grave Sauvignon '08	♥♥ 4*
O Friuli Grave Traminer Aromatico Vis Terrae '07	♥♥ 4*
● Friuli Grave Cabernet '07	♥ 4
● Friuli Grave Cabernet Sauvignon Vis. Terrae '03	♥ 4
O Friuli Grave Chardonnay Vis Terrae '07	♥ 4
O Friuli Grave Friulano '08	♥ 4
● Friuli Grave Merlot '07	♥ 4
● Friuli Grave Merlot Vis Terrae '04	♥ 4
O Friuli Grave Chardonnay Vis Terrae '06	♀♀ 4
O Friuli Grave Pinot Grigio '07	♀♀ 4
O Friuli Grave Pinot Grigio '06	♀♀ 3*
O Friuli Grave Pinot Grigio Vis Terrae '06	♀♀ 4
O Friuli Grave Sauvignon Blanc Poggio Alto '06	♀♀ 4*

Aquila del Torre

FRAZ. SAVORGNANO DEL TORRE
VIA ATTIMIS, 25
33040 POVOLETTO [UD]
TEL. 0432666428
www.aquiladeltorre.it

CELLAR SALES
PRE-BOOKED VISITS

ANNUAL PRODUCTION 50,000 bottles
HECTARES UNDER VINE 20
VITICULTURE METHOD Conventional

Aquila del Torre is near the country village of Savorgnano del Torre in the northerly, cooler, part of the Colli Orientali del Friuli. Since 1996, the Ciani family has been at the helm. Michele runs the winemaking, with a little advice from his father, Claudia, while sister Francesca looks after public relations and cellar hospitality. Some years ago, the Cianis launched the OasiPicolit project to promote the territory with a wine of excellence.

Grapes are picked by hand and taken to the multi-storey cellar tucked away in the woods. Selections are also made to bring out the potential of individual plots by separate vinification. Picolit is still the Cianis' signature wine, a pale amber nectar whose '06 vintage is redolent of dates and almonds, crisp and pervasive on the palate and juicily long. Refosco SolSiRe '07 hints at morello cherry, liquorice and dark chocolate before the soft, powerful palate unfolds its pulpy fruit. Friulano '08 gives apple, banana and white melon fruit in an outstandingly varietal experience. Lemon verbena fragrances and freshness are the calling cards of the attractively upfront Sauvignon Vit Dai Maz '07.

Ascevi - Luwa

LOC. UCLANZI, 24
34070 SAN FLORIANO DEL COLLIO [GO]
TEL. 0481884140
www.asceviluwa.it

CELLAR SALES
PRE-BOOKED VISITS

ANNUAL PRODUCTION 180,000 bottles
HECTARES UNDER VINE 30
VITICULTURE METHOD Conventional

The wonderful hillslopes of San Floriano del Collio offer perfect site climates for growing grapes as well as a stunning panoramic view. For some time, the Ascevi hill has been home to most of the vineyards owned by the Pintar family, Mariano, his wife Loredana and their children Luana and Walter. The hill, followed by the first syllables of Luana and Walter's names, has also christened the estate. There are other vineyards at Farra in the Isonzo DOC zone.

In earlier editions of the Guide, we have praised the cellar's knack with Sauvignon, attributing the well-structured, varietal wines to the rich mineral content of the subsoil, but this year is was a Pinot Grigio '08 that stood out. Its luscious golden hue heralds warm, penetrating perceptions of overripe fruit, acacia honey and medicinal herbs, before the creamy, concentrated palate unveils its seamless integrity and minerally savouriness. Ribolla Gialla Ronco de Vigna Vecia '08 is very varietal, showing appealing citrus on the nose and freshness on the palate. The juicily mouthfilling Luwa Sauvignon '08 and Chardonnay '08 have plenty of character.

O COF Friulano '08	♟♟	5
O COF Picolit '06	♟♟	8
● COF Refosco P. R. '07	♟♟	5
● COF Refosco P. R. SolSiRe '07	♟♟	5
O COF Sauvignon Vit Dai Maz '07	♟♟	5
● COF Merlot '07	♟	5
O COF Riesling '08	♟	5
O COF Sauvignon '08	♟	5
O COF Picolit '03	♟♟	8
O COF Picolit Oasipicolit '02	♟♟	8

O Collio Pinot Grigio Ascevi '08	♟♟	4*
O Ribolla Gialla Ronco de Vigna Vecia Ascevi '08	♟♟	4*
O Collio Chardonnay Luwa '08	♟	4
O Collio Sauvignon Luwa '08	♟	4
O Collio Sauvignon Ronco dei Sassi Ascevi '07	♟♟	5
O Collio Sauvignon Ronco dei Sassi Ascevi '06	♟♟	5

Attems

FRAZ. LUCINICO
VIA GIULIO CESARE, 36A
34170 GORIZIA
TEL. 0481393619
www.attems.it

CELLAR SALES
PRE-BOOKED VISITS

ANNUAL PRODUCTION **450,000 bottles**
HECTARES UNDER VINE **72**
VITICULTURE METHOD **Conventional**

True to a family tradition with roots deep in the past, Conte Douglas Attems has been making wine since 1935. In 1964, he founded the Collio wine consortium and chaired it all his life. Even today, the severe production protocol he insisted was put in place safeguards the Collio and encourages the production of superior wines. Attems is now part of the Florence-based Marchesi de' Frescobaldi group and Virginia Attems, who works on the estate, keeps up the family tradition.

Thanks to a particularly favourable growing year, the 2008 Pinot Grigio is the leader of a pack of white wines deliciously embodying the unique Collio territory. Spring flowers and tropical fruits introduce a soft-textured, tangy palate that wins you over with its faultless balance. Sauvignon, friulano and pinot bianco are the grapes that go into the Collio Bianco Cicinis '07. Cask conditioning contributes to the ·complexity of the aromatics, which range from yellow peach and pineapple fruit through to spice and toastiness. Finally, the juicy, varietal '08 Friulano is excellent.

Bastianich

LOC. GAGLIANO
VIA DARNAZZACCO, 44/2
33043 CIVIDALE DEL FRIULI [UD]
TEL. 0432700943
www.bastianich.com

CELLAR SALES
PRE-BOOKED VISITS

ANNUAL PRODUCTION **180,000 bottles**
HECTARES UNDER VINE **40**
VITICULTURE METHOD **Conventional**

Joe Bastianich and his mother Lidia have exported Italian style across the pond with their chain of influential restaurants in Manhattan, Kansas City, Las Vegas and New Jersey. At his estate in Friuli, Joe has put together a winning team that he runs himself on his frequent returns to the cellar at Gagliano, near Cividale. Claudio Rizzi is general manager, Wayne Young looks after marketing and PR while Denis Lepore is in charge of sales and distribution.

For production, Joe has turned to experienced oenologist Emilio Del Medico, who is supported by expert input from Maurizio Castelli, the man Joe put in charge of his La Mozza estate in the Tuscan Maremma. The cellar also has a drying room, where winemakers are experimenting with a number of varieties. We're keen to see the results. For now, we'll enjoy this year's new product, a sound, savoury '07 Malvasia Istriana of breath-taking elegance that impresses with the sheer complexity of its aniseed-lifted aromatics. Equally good is the chardonnay, sauvignon and picolit-based Vespa Bianco '07, a taut, agile wine that fills the mouth.

○ Collio Bianco Cicinis '07	▼▼ 5
○ Collio Friulano '08	▼▼ 4*
○ Collio Pinot Grigio '08	▼▼ 4*
○ Chardonnay '08	▼ 4
○ Collio Sauvignon '08	▼ 4
○ Cupra Ramato Pinot Grigio '07	▼ 4
○ Ribolla Gialla '08	▼ 4
○ Collio Bianco Cicinis '06	▼▼ 5
● Collio Merlot '06	▼▼ 4
○ Collio Sauvignon '07	▼▼ 4

○ Malvasia Istriana '07	▼▼ 5
○ Vespa Bianco '07	▼▼ 6
○ COF Tocai Friulano Plus '02	▼▼▼ 5
○ Vespa Bianco '04	▼▼▼ 5
○ Vespa Bianco '03	▼▼▼ 5
○ Vespa Bianco '01	▼▼▼ 5
○ Vespa Bianco '00	▼▼▼ 5
○ Vespa Bianco '99	▼▼▼ 5
○ COF Tocai Plus '06	▼▼ 4
○ Sauvignon "B" '07	▼▼ 4
○ Vespa Bianco '06	▼▼ 6
○ Vespa Bianco '05	▼▼ 5
● Vespa Rosso '05	▼▼ 6
● Vespa Rosso '04	▼▼ 6

Tenuta Beltrame

FRAZ. PRIVANO
LOC. ANTONINI, 4
33050 BAGNARIA ARSA [UD]
TEL. 0432923670
www.tenutabeltrame.it

CELLAR SALES
PRE-BOOKED VISITS

ANNUAL PRODUCTION **100,000 bottles**
HECTARES UNDER VINE **25**
VITICULTURE METHOD **Conventional**

This estate was set up in the 15th century and once belonged to the noble Antonini family. In 1991, it was acquired by the Beltrame family, who restored it to its former glory by carefully restructuring the main building and cellar. Cristian Beltrame manages the business, aided by long-serving oenologist Bepi Gollino. Following a courageous initial replanting programme, the pair are now reaping the rewards of their hard work.

The soil is mainly clay on a layer of gravel one metre under the surface. It has proved particularly suitable for growing top-quality red grapes, such as the ones that went into the full-flavoured Merlot Riserva '05, a subtly balanced wine with a deep colour and intense, complex black berry fruits and tobacco aromatics. We also liked the structured, appealing soft-textured Cabernet Sauvignon Riserva '05, which hints at red berry jam, moss and damp earth. The prune-themed Tazzelenghe '05 is an original wine with pepper and clove spice and a muscular flavour. Headily alcoholic, the Refosco '07 is more straightforward and the whites are nicely crafted.

Anna Berra

VIA RAMANDOLO, 29
33045 NIMIS [UD]
TEL. 0432790296
www.annaberra.it

CELLAR SALES
PRE-BOOKED VISITS

ANNUAL PRODUCTION **25,000 bottles**
HECTARES UNDER VINE **6.5**
VITICULTURE METHOD **Conventional**

The Anna Berra winery is at Ramandalo, a small district of the municipality of Nimis in the province of Udine, in the extreme north of Colli Orientali del Friuli. As you might have guessed, it bears the name of its founder but today it is her son, Ivan Monai, who manages the vineyards in compliance with best agronomic practice using training systems that keep yields per vine naturally low. Ivan also supervises winemaking.

Vini di Casa Berra is the line for steel-fermented red wines while Selezione Anna Berra includes Ramandolo, Refosco Riserva and Picolit. This year, Ivan showed us his new La Bernadia line and sent two of the wines straight into our finals. The splendid '08 Sauvignon has mango and gooseberry fragrances and a full, caressing flavour that holds up beautifully and the Friulano from the same vintage is impeccably varietal, hinting at almonds and spring flowers. The flavoursome, sophisticated '05 Ramandolo is old gold in hue with fragrances of dried apricots and beeswax. Rounding off this review is the clean, upfront '06 Refosco, which gives red berry fruit and pepper.

● Friuli Aquileia Merlot Ris. '05	♟♟	4*
● Friuli Aquileia Cabernet Sauvignon Ris. '05	♟♟	4*
● Friuli Aquileia Refosco P. R. '07	♟♟	4*
● Tazzelenghe '05	♟♟	4*
○ Friuli Aquileia Chardonnay '08	♟	4
○ Friuli Aquileia Friulano '08	♟	4
● Friuli Aquileia Cabernet Franc '05	♟♟	4*
○ Friuli Aquileia Chardonnay Pribus '06	♟♟	4
● Friuli Aquileia Merlot '05	♟♟	4
● Friuli Aquileia Refosco P. R. '06	♟♟	4

○ COF Friulano La Bernadia '08	♟♟	4*
○ COF Sauvignon La Bernadia '08	♟♟	4*
○ Ramandolo '05	♟♟	5
● COF Refosco P. R. La Bernadia '06	♟	4
○ COF Picolit Ris. '03	♟♟	6
○ COF Picolit Ris. '02	♟♟	6
● COF Refosco P. R. Ris. '03	♟♟	5
○ Ramandolo Anno Domini '04	♟♟	6
○ Ramandolo Anno Domini '03	♟♟	6
○ Ramandolo Anno Domini '02	♟♟	6
○ Ramandolo Anno Domini '01	♟♟	4

Tenuta di Blasig

VIA ROMA, 63
34077 RONCHI DEI LEGIONARI [GO]
TEL. 0481475480
www.tenutadiblasig.it

CELLAR SALES
PRE-BOOKED VISITS

ANNUAL PRODUCTION **70,000 bottles**
HECTARES UNDER VINE **16.5**
VITICULTURE METHOD **Conventional**

Founded in 1788 by Domenico Blasig, this is one of the longest-established cellars in Friuli Venezia Giulia. It has stayed in the same family for more than two centuries and today the business is run by the seventh generation, in the person of the capable Elisabetta Bortolotto Sarcinelli and her all-women team. In 2008, the new cellar came onstream with its modern production spaces, joining the older facilities dating from the 18th century and the 19th-century tasting room.

The vineyard holding is in the Rive di Giare subzone of the Isonzo DOC, where the vines benefit from the influence of the nearby river and Adriatic Sea. Commercial affairs are in the hands of Valentina Casula while the outstanding Erica Orlandino supervises vineyard and cellar. This year, Erica presented us with a superb '08 Malvasia that we sent on to the finals. Intriguing aromas laced with salt and balsam greet the nose before the power and varietal character of the palate impress your taste buds. The reds did equally well. The slightly smoky, savoury Merlot '06 has plenty of momentum and the subtle Cabernet '06 is complex on the nose and holds together well on the palate.

○ Friuli Isonzo Malvasia '08	♟♟	4*
● Friuli Isonzo Cabernet '06	♟♟	4*
● Friuli Isonzo Merlot '06	♟♟	4*
○ Friuli Isonzo Friulano '08	♟	4
○ Friuli Isonzo Pinot Grigio '08	♟	4
● Friuli Isonzo Refosco P. R. '06	♟	4
○ Le Lule '07	♟	5
○ Friuli Isonzo Malvasia '05	♟♟	4*
● Friuli Isonzo Rive di Giare Refosco P. R. '05	♟♟	4*
● Friuli Isonzo Rive di Giare Refosco P. R. '04	♟♟	4*
● Rosso Gli Affreschi '03	♟♟	5

La Boatina

VIA CORONA, 62
34071 CORMÒNS [GO]
TEL. 048160445
www.paliwines.com

CELLAR SALES
PRE-BOOKED VISITS

ANNUAL PRODUCTION **120,000 bottles**
HECTARES UNDER VINE **62**
VITICULTURE METHOD **Conventional**

La Boatina's vineyard holding is in the Isonzo DOC at Cormòns and Gorizia, right on the Slovenian border. Its owner is Loretto Pali, who has incorporated the estate into his Pali Wines group so that he can distribute all his output under a single brand. La Boatina's well-respected quality perfectly reflects the philosophy Pali Wines implements here and in all the other group enterprises: high-profile wines for discriminating palates.

Reliable quality across the range is guaranteed by the experience and acknowledged ability of the estate winemaker, Domenico Lovat, who can also call on consultant Gianni Menotti. This year, the '08 Friulano went through to our taste-offs. We liked its headily intense fruit aromas and absolutely loved the crisp definition of the full-bodied, pervasive palate with its varietal twist of bitterness. The coherent Sauvignon '08 was another pleaser, showing varietal on the nose and true to type on the minerally palate. The '08 Chardonnay may not be overly complex but it is enjoyable and has plenty of thrust. Finally, the varietal '08 Ribolla Gialla impressed.

○ Friuli Isonzo Friulano '08	♟♟	4*
○ Friuli Isonzo Chardonnay '08	♟♟	4*
○ Friuli Isonzo Sauvignon '08	♟♟	4*
○ Ribolla Gialla '08	♟♟	4*
● Friuli Isonzo Cabernet Franc '08	♟	4
○ Friuli Isonzo Pinot Bianco '08	♟	4
○ Friuli Isonzo Pinot Grigio '08	♟	4
○ Verduzzo Pèrle '06	♟	4
○ Friuli Isonzo Chardonnay '07	♟♟	4
● Friuli Isonzo Merlot '06	♟♟	4
○ Friuli Isonzo Pinot Bianco '07	♟♟	4*
○ Friuli Isonzo Pinot Grigio '07	♟♟	4
○ Friuli Isonzo Sauvignon '07	♟♟	4

Borgo Conventi

S.DA DELLA COLOMBARA, 13
24070 FARRA D'ISONZO [GO]
TEL. 0481888004
www.ruffino.it

CELLAR SALES

ANNUAL PRODUCTION **350,000 bottles**
HECTARES UNDER VINE **30**
VITICULTURE METHOD **Conventional**

Borgo Conventi is in the Collio Goriziano on the road that takes you from Gradisca to Farra d'Isonzo. A long-standing label on the Friulian wine scene, it joined the Tuscany-based Ruffino group in 2001. Opposite the cellar is a picturesque, pale pink farmhouse with an imposing dining room and a tasting room. Oenologist Paolo Corso is the technical director who manages vineyards and cellars with passion and skill.

Grapes from the estate-owned vineyards come from the Collio and Isonzo DOC zones and are vinified in an underground cellar, which includes a lovely barrel cellar connected to the villa. Naturally enough, Paolo looks after winemaking but for some of the selections he is advised by consultant Gianni Menotti. This year, the '08 Collio Sauvignon went on to our final taste-offs. It's fruit-forward, subtle and complex with a full-bodied, tangy palate. The DOC Isonzo Refosco '08 impressed with its headily pervasive nose and concentration on the palate. Finally, the Sauvignon Colle Blanchis '08 is distinctly promising.

Borgo del Tiglio

FRAZ. BRAZZANO
VIA SAN GIORGIO, 71
34070 CORMÒNS [GO]
TEL. 048162166

CELLAR SALES
PRE-BOOKED VISITS

ANNUAL PRODUCTION **35,000 bottles**
HECTARES UNDER VINE **8.5**
VITICULTURE METHOD **Conventional**

Wines by Nicola Manferrari, the owner of Borgo del Tiglio, reflect the character of the man. Rigorously precise, Nicola leaves nothing to chance in vineyard or cellar. He strives to make wines that will age effortlessly. You may have to wait several years to appreciate them to the full and sometimes, as this year, they may seem closed or still a tad oaky.

In the end, the wine that we liked best was the '07 Malvasia, which is perhaps readier for the corkscrew than the others we tasted. Delicately aromatic on the nose, it still flaunts impressive structure nicely backed up by acidity and the variety's signature hint of bitterness on the finish. As ever, the tocai friulano-heavy '07 Ronco della Chiesa blend is good but distinctly on the young side. Equally young is the Collio Bianco '07, from tocai friulano, sauvignon, riesling and malvasia, which has yet to unbend and is still oaky. It will be a few years before it is able to reveal its full potential.

O Collio Sauvignon '08	♟♟ 5
O Collio Sauvignon Colle Blanchis '08	♟♟ 5
O Friuli Isonzo Friulano '08	♟♟ 4*
● Friuli Isonzo Refosco P. R. '08	♟♟ 4*
● Braida Nuova '06	♟ 5
O Collio Friulano '08	♟ 4
O Collio Pinot Grigio '08	♟ 4
O Friuli Isonzo Sauvignon '08	♟ 4
O Collio Bianco Colle Russian '06	♟♟ 5
O Collio Chardonnay '06	♟♟ 4
O Collio Friulano '07	♟♟ 4
● Collio Merlot '04	♟♟ 4
O Collio Sauvignon Colle Blanchis '07	♟♟ 5
O Collio Sauvignon Colle Blanchis '06	♟♟ 5
O Friuli Isonzo Chardonnay '07	♟♟ 4
O Friuli Isonzo Pinot Grigio '07	♟♟ 4
● Friuli Isonzo Refosco P. R. '07	♟♟ 4

O Collio Malvasia '07	♟♟ 7
O Collio Bianco '07	♟♟ 6
O Collio Bianco Ronco della Chiesa '07	♟♟ 7
O Collio Bianco Ronco della Chiesa '06	♟♟♟ 7
O Collio Bianco Ronco della Chiesa '02	♟♟♟ 7
O Collio Bianco Ronco della Chiesa '01	♟♟♟ 7
O Collio Tocai Friulano Ronco della Chiesa '90	♟♟♟ 6
O Collio Chardonnay '06	♟♟ 6
O Collio Chardonnay Sel. '06	♟♟ 7
O Collio Malvasia '06	♟♟ 7
O Collio Studio di Bianco '06	♟♟ 7
O Collio Tocai Friulano '06	♟♟ 6

Borgo delle Oche

VIA BORGO ALPI, 5
33098 VALVASONE [PN]
TEL. 0434899398
www.borgodelleoche.it

CELLAR SALES
PRE-BOOKED VISITS

ANNUAL PRODUCTION 25,000 bottles
HECTARES UNDER VINE 7
VITICULTURE METHOD Conventional

The winery nestles in the medieval heart of a charming village near Valvasone, in the Grave del Friuli DOC, also called Borgo delle Oche. It was set up in 2004 by Luisa Menini and her partner in life and at work, Nicola Pittini. Reasonably enough, they divide duties between them. Luisa, who has a degree in food technology, loves the open air so she spends most of her time taking care of the vineyards while Nicola, an agronomist and oenologist, looks after the cellar.

In a very short space of time, their unflagging joint efforts have produced great results in a territory that is often wrongly regarded as not being quality-friendly. The grapes Luisa brings to Nicola are perfect and it is Nicola's job to conserve their sensory characteristics, a task he has mastered well. Not for the first time, two of the wines – Lupi Terrae '07 and Alba '08 – went into our finals. The former is a blend of steel-fermented friulano and verduzzo friulano vinified in wood. The wine that emerges is complex, ripe, rich and powerful. In contrast, Alba is an intriguingly aromatic part-dried Traminer that beautifully combines freshness and creaminess.

Borgo Judrio

VIA AQUILEIA, 793
33040 CORNO DI ROSAZZO [UD]
TEL. 3407166240

ANNUAL PRODUCTION 20,000 bottles
HECTARES UNDER VINE N.D.
VITICULTURE METHOD Conventional

Alberto Gigante's winery was founded as recently as 2007. At Corno di Rosazzo, the Gigantes have long been noted as a wine family and Alberto is very much in that tradition. Ferruccio Gigante left his vineyards to his three sons, Arturo, Silvano and Luciano. Each went his own way, setting up separate operations, and now Luciano's sons Alberto and Ariedo have decided to strike out on their own. Alberto set the winery up and Ariedo contributes his winemaking skills.

Ariedo has a few hectares under vine in the Colli Orientali del Friuli and as a skilled oenologist, consults for several other estates in the area. Alberto and Ariedo were raised in the world of wine and share the same passions. The results are there for all to see. Excellent is the adjective that springs to mind when you savour the balance and finesse of their '06 Refosco, an elegantly evolved, fruit and spice-led wine with just a hint of tobacco and liquorice. Mouthfillingly flavoursome. We also loved the very varietal Sauvignon '08 for its subtle nettle-like tones, gutsy character, and tangily refreshing palate.

O Bianco Alba '08	♟♟	6
O Bianco Lupi Terrae '07	♟♟	5
● Merlot '07	♟♟	5
● Refosco P. R. '07	♟♟	5
O Traminer Aromatico '08	♟♟	5
O Pinot Grigio '08	♟	5
● Rosso Svual '06	♟	5
O Bianco Alba '07	♟♟	5
O Bianco Alba '06	♟♟	5
O Bianco Lupi Terrae '06	♟♟	4
O Pinot Grigio '07	♟♟	4
O Pinot Grigio '06	♟♟	4
● Refosco P. R. '06	♟♟	4
● Rosso Svual '04	♟♟	5
O Traminer Aromatico '07	♟♟	4
O Traminer Aromatico '06	♟♟	4*

● COF Refosco P. R. '06	♟♟	4*
O COF Sauvignon '08	♟♟	4*
O COF Friulano '08	♟♟	4*
● COF Cabernet Sauvignon '08	♟	4
O COF Verduzzo Friulano '07	♟	4

Borgo San Daniele

VIA SAN DANIELE, 16
34071 CORMÒNS [GO]
TEL. 048160552
www.borgosandaniele.it

CELLAR SALES
PRE-BOOKED VISITS

ANNUAL PRODUCTION **60,000 bottles**
HECTARES UNDER VINE **18**
VITICULTURE METHOD **Conventional**

A few years ago, when brother and sister Mauro and Alessandra Mauri were still very young, their grandfather left them some plots of vines. They decided to try and make a go of them. The Mauris called the winery they set up after the small village they lived in. Mauro and Alessandra are two special, very sensitive people of good taste and exquisite manners. There are only four Borgo San Daniele wines, two of them monovarietals and two blends, which are joined by Gortmarin but only in outstanding vintages.

Meticulous hard work has found its reward in the Three Glasses won this year by the splendidly varietal, mouthfilling Friulano, a slightly smoky white with lots of freshness and mineral savour. Both blends, Arbis Blanc '07 from friulano, pinot bianco, chardonnay and sauvignon, and Arbis Ros '06 from pignolo and cabernet sauvignon are outstanding territorial wines that find a wonderful point of equilibrium between native and international grapes.

Borgo Savaian

VIA SAVAIAN, 36
34071 CORMÒNS [GO]
TEL. 048160725
stefanobastiani@libero.it

CELLAR SALES
PRE-BOOKED VISITS

ANNUAL PRODUCTION **40,000 bottles**
HECTARES UNDER VINE **12**
VITICULTURE METHOD **Conventional**

First Bruno, then his son Mario, and now Mario's son Stefano Bastiani have managed this estate at the foot of Mount Quarin in the small "borgo", or village, from which it takes its name. Stefano has been putting his recent studies to good use but he relies most of all on his father's experience while his mother, Marinella, makes sure the paperwork is in order and welcomes visitors to the cellar. Grandfather Bruno was an innovator and Stefano is set to follow his example.

There is plenty of space in the recently made-over cellar so Stefano can supervise all stages of production without distraction. Improving quality is obvious throughout the range, which are impeccably made and a delight to drink. This year, there were Red Glasses for a wonderfully aroma-rich elderflower and white peach '08 Sauvignon with a vigorous palate. We also liked the lip-smacking Friulano '08 for its caramel-sweet fragrances and a palate with an attractive twist of almondiness. The '07 Merlot is a tad closed on the nose but agile and full-bodied in the mouth while wisteria and yellow roses are the themes of the '08 Traminer's bouquet.

O Friuli Isonzo Friulano '07	♈♈♈	5*
O Arbis Blanc '07	♈♈	5
● Arbis Ros '06	♈♈	6
O Arbis Blanc '06	♈♈♈	5
O Arbis Blanc '05	♈♈♈	5
O Friuli Isonzo Arbis Blanc '02	♈♈♈	5
O Friuli Isonzo Pinot Grigio '04	♈♈♈	5
O Friuli Isonzo Pinot Grigio '99	♈♈♈	5
O Friuli Isonzo Tocai Friulano '03	♈♈♈	5
O Friuli Isonzo Tocai Friulano '97	♈♈♈	5
● Gortmarin '03	♈♈♈	5
● Arbis Ros '05	♈♈	6
● Arbis Ros '04	♈♈	6
O Friuli Isonzo Pinot Grigio '07	♈♈	5
O Friuli Isonzo Pinot Grigio '06	♈♈	5
O Friuli Isonzo Tocai Friulano '06	♈♈	5

O Collio Sauvignon '08	♈♈	4*
O Collio Friulano '08	♈♈	4*
● Collio Merlot '07	♈♈	4*
O Collio Pinot Grigio '08	♈♈	4*
O Friuli Isonzo Traminer Aromatico '08	♈♈	4*
O Collio Pinot Bianco '08	♈	4
O Friuli Isonzo Verduzzo Friulano '07	♈	4
O Collio Chardonnay '07	♈♈	4
O Collio Friulano '07	♈♈	4
● Collio Merlot Tolrem '04	♈♈	5
O Collio Pinot Grigio '07	♈♈	4
O Collio Sauvignon '07	♈♈	4
● Friuli Isonzo Cabernet Franc '06	♈♈	4
O Friuli Isonzo Traminer Aromatico '07	♈♈	4

Cav. Emiro Bortolusso

VIA OLTREGORGO, 10
33050 CARLINO [UD]
TEL. 043167596
www.bortolusso.it

CELLAR SALES
PRE-BOOKED VISITS

ANNUAL PRODUCTION **120,000 bottles**
HECTARES UNDER VINE **35**
VITICULTURE METHOD **Conventional**

Bortolusso is emblematic of the Annia DOC zone. Siblings Sergio and Clara have spent many years working to promote the territory, taking it from anonymity to results that can justifiably be regarded as excellent. The wines are top-notch and the price-tags are very much in the consumer's favour. A further five hectares have just been planted and not long ago the Bortolussos also opened wine tourism facilities with rooms and a kitchen run by Clara's son, Matteo, at San Gervasio near Carlino.

The '08 Malvasia is a thoroughbred. Star-bright in colour, it unfolds a pervasive, complex bouquet that combines intense fruit with a tempting hint of star anise while the gutsy, minerally palate that is as varietal as they come. The Pinot Bianco, Sauvignon and Pinot Grigio, all '08, more than deserve their Two Glasses for their coherent style: deliciously easy-drinking with great fruit support and considerable minerality. However, the '08 Friulano is every bit as moreish, teasing the nose with dried spring flowers and ripe fruit before the palate unfolds with vibrancy and depth. Closing the range in style is an '07 Refosco that may be a little green but shows plenty of promise.

○ Friuli Annia Malvasia '08	TT	3*
○ Friuli Annia Pinot Bianco '08	TT	3*
○ Friuli Annia Pinot Grigio '08	TT	3*
○ Friuli Annia Sauvignon '08	TT	3*
○ Friuli Annia Friulano '08	T	3
● Friuli Annia Refosco P. R. '07	T	3
○ Friuli Annia Malvasia '07	YY	3*
○ Friuli Annia Pinot Bianco '07	YY	3*
○ Friuli Annia Pinot Bianco '06	YY	3*
○ Friuli Annia Sauvignon '07	YY	3*
○ Friuli Annia Sauvignon '06	YY	3*

Rosa Bosco

VIA ROMA, 5
33040 MOIMACCO [UD]
TEL. 0432722461
www.rosabosco.it

CELLAR SALES
PRE-BOOKED VISITS

ANNUAL PRODUCTION **14,000 bottles**
HECTARES UNDER VINE **N.D.**
VITICULTURE METHOD **Conventional**

Rosetta doesn't actually own any vineyards but with her signature tenacity, she keeps a watchful eye on the ripening grapes that will go into her wines, obtained from a fanatically meticulous selection of the bunches. She also enjoys supervising winemaking, in which she is abetted by the Terra&Vino group. Heading up Terra&Vino is Rosetta's son, Alessio Dorigo, who may not be particularly advanced in years but already has remarkable experience. He is very much in demand as a winemaker and consults for a number of cellars elsewhere in Friuli and Italy.

In the last edition of the Guide, we announced the forthcoming release of a Metodo Classico sparkling wine that we knew had been in the pipeline for years. In the event, we were doubly surprised because an '08 Ribolla Gialla has also been added to the range. The spumante is a chardonnay-only wine called Blanc de Blancs. Golden in hue, it flaunts a seamless perlage of tiny bubbles and proffers ripe fruit, cakes and roasted hazelnuts on the nose, followed up by a satisfyingly powerful, mineral-rich palate. The merlot-only Boscorosso '06 is redolent of liquorice, red roses and gardenias. Finally, Rosetta's Sauvignon Blanc '08 is as creamy and mouthfilling as ever. Utterly distinctive.

○ Blanc de Blancs Brut	TT	6
● Il Boscorosso '06	TT	7
○ Sauvignon Blanc '08	TT	6
○ Ribolla Gialla '08	T	5
○ COF Sauvignon Blanc '02	YYY	6
● COF Rosso Il Boscorosso '04	YY	7
● COF Rosso Il Boscorosso '03	YY	7
● COF Rosso Il Boscorosso '02	YY	7
● COF Rosso Il Boscorosso '01	YY	7
○ COF Sauvignon Blanc '06	YY	6
○ COF Sauvignon Blanc '05	YY	6
○ COF Sauvignon Blanc '04	YY	6
● Il Boscorosso '05	YY	7
○ Sauvignon Blanc '07	YY	6

Branko

LOC. ZEGLA, 20
34071 CORMÒNS [GO]
TEL. 0481639826

CELLAR SALES
PRE-BOOKED VISITS

ANNUAL PRODUCTION 45,000 bottles
HECTARES UNDER VINE 7
VITICULTURE METHOD Conventional

We are at Zegla in the heart of the Collio. It is here that Igor Erzetic runs his small, but highly functional, winery with characteristic meticulousness. Branko is not a brand name, or even a place name. It's simply the name of Igor's father, who still helps out in the vineyard. Igor is young but he already has a lot of experience from collaborating with other local estates.

For the fourth time in a row, Igor's Pinot Grigio picked up Three Glasses. The '08 edition breezed past the almost 200 other contenders and came out on top of its category. Extremely elegant with its star-bright straw hue, it throws a nose of elderflower and ripe fruit. The palate is sumptuous yet supple and agile, signing off with pear-like fruit. Another excellent wine is Igor's complex, extraordinarily varietal '08 Friulano, which delights the nose before impressing even more with its heft on the palate. The Chardonnay '08 is fantastic and the Sauvignon '08 and the Bordeaux blend Red '07 are well worth uncorking.

O Collio Pinot Grigio '08	▼▼▼	5*
O Collio Chardonnay '08	▼▼	5
O Collio Friulano '08	▼▼	5
O Collio Sauvignon '08	▼▼	5
● Red '07	▼▼	5
O Collio Pinot Grigio '07	♀♀♀	5
O Collio Pinot Grigio '06	♀♀♀	5
O Collio Pinot Grigio '05	♀♀♀	5
O Collio Chardonnay '07	♀♀	5
O Collio Friulano '07	♀♀	5
O Collio Pinot Grigio '04	♀♀	5
O Collio Sauvignon '07	♀♀	5

Livio e Claudio Buiatti

VIA LIPPE, 25
33042 BUTTRIO [UD]
TEL. 0432674317
www.buiattivini.it

CELLAR SALES
PRE-BOOKED VISITS

ANNUAL PRODUCTION 35,000 bottles
HECTARES UNDER VINE 8
VITICULTURE METHOD Conventional

The Buiatti vineyards sprawl over the gentle slopes that extend from Buttrio to Premariacco, in a picture-postcard location called in Mont 'e Poanis. A century ago, Buiattis were already growing grapes here and today it is the turn of Claudio to look after the estate, a task he has been performing with a will for some time. His wife Viviana takes care of administration and accounts, as well as offering a smiling welcome to visitors to the estate headquarters at Buttrio.

It's always gratifying when a small winery's efforts are rewarded with outstanding results but all too often it is a hit and miss affair that depends on the conditions of the growing year. But you can't say that about Claudio, who has repeated last year's exploit with a superb '08 Sauvignon that presents well defined, extremely varietal and unusually elegant on the nose and intensely flavoursome on the long, well-sustained palate. The impenetrable ruby of the excellent '07 Refosco heralds a concentrated, complex bouquet of briary fruit and liquorice layered over minerality and pipe tobacco. Markedly tannic, the palate is deep and very enjoyable. The rest of the range is up to snuff.

O COF Sauvignon '08	▼▼	4*
● COF Refosco P. R. '07	▼▼	4*
O COF Friulano '08	▼	4
O COF Pinot Bianco '08	▼	4
O COF Pinot Grigio '08	▼	4
● COF Rosso Momon Ros Ris. '06	▼	5
O COF Friulano '07	♀♀	4
● COF Merlot '06	♀♀	4
● COF Rosso Momon Ros Ris. '05	♀♀	5
● COF Rosso Momon Ros Ris. '05	♀♀	5
● COF Rosso Momon Ros Ris. '04	♀♀	5
O COF Sauvignon '07	♀♀	4*
O COF Sauvignon '06	♀♀	4*
O COF Tocai Friulano '06	♀♀	4*
O COF Verduzzo Friulano '06	♀♀	4

Valentino Butussi

VIA PRÀ DI CORTE, 1
33040 CORNO DI ROSAZZO [UD]
TEL. 0432759194
www.butussi.it

Maurizio Buzzinelli

LOC. PRADIS, 20
34071 CORMÒNS [GO]
TEL. 048160902
www.buzzinelli.com

CELLAR SALES
PRE-BOOKED VISITS
VISITOR FACILITIES

CELLAR SALES
PRE-BOOKED VISITS
VISITOR FACILITIES
FOOD

ANNUAL PRODUCTION **95,000 bottles**
HECTARES UNDER VINE **16**
VITICULTURE METHOD **Natural**

ANNUAL PRODUCTION **100,000 bottles**
HECTARES UNDER VINE **24**
VITICULTURE METHOD **Conventional**

This year's news is that Angelo Butussi, who inherited the winery founded by his father Valentino in the early part of the last century, has handed management responsibilities over to his four children. The transfer formalizes the existing situation, in which each sibling had a clear role. Vineyard management is Tobia's job, Filippo takes care of winemaking and Mattia and Erika look after marketing and distribution. Obviously, Angelo is still on hand with help and advice.

Production continues to climb up the quality curve mapped out by previous vintages but this time two wines went forward to the final taste-offs. One is the superb and very varietal Sauvignon '08 with its tempting kiwi fruit and elderflower aromas and a tangy palate with loads of oomph. Equally gutsy and varietal is the '08 Friulano, an outstandingly elegant wine with white peach-led fresh fruit aromatics. The Pinot Grigio '08 impresses with its sheer drinkability but the Bianco di Corte '08 needs more time. Finally, the mouthfilling '07 Cabernet Sauvignon is beautifully poised but the current reds hadn't gone into bottle when we were tasting.

Maurizio Buzzinelli and his wife Marzia put the winemaking experience of three generations of Maurizio's family to good use and chose Pradis, near Cormòns, in the Collio DOC zone as the place to nurture their children and their dreams. The couple still work with Maurizio's family, co-managing with his father Gigi and mother Luisa holiday apartments high on the hill that offer spectacular views over the peace and quiet of the countryside.

The wines Maurizio presented for tasting are all labelled Collio DOC but we ought to remember that the estate includes several flatlands hectares in the equally good Isonzo DOC wine country, where most of the red grapes are grown. Some selections, released as Ronc de Luis, go into oak-aged wines, most of which were not ready for tasting, with the exception of a stunning '08 Malvasia. It went only briefly into barrique and emerged a luscious golden yellow, flaunting rose fragrances and a juicily full-bodied, aroma-rich palate. We also like the '08 Pinot Grigio's subtle onionskin hue and whiffs of wild strawberries.

○ COF Friulano '08	♈♈ 4*
○ COF Sauvignon '08	♈♈ 4*
○ COF Bianco di Corte '08	♈♈ 4*
● COF Cabernet Sauvignon '07	♈♈ 4*
○ COF Pinot Grigio '08	♈♈ 4*
○ COF Chardonnay '08	♈ 4
○ COF Ribolla Gialla '08	♈ 4
○ COF Verduzzo Friulano '07	♈ 4
○ Friuli Grave Pinot Bianco '08	♈ 4
○ COF Bianco di Corte '07	♈♈ 4
● COF Cabernet Franc '07	♈♈ 4
○ COF Friulano '07	♈♈ 4
○ COF Picolit '06	♈♈ 7
○ COF Pinot Grigio '07	♈♈ 4
○ COF Ribolla Gialla '07	♈♈ 4
● COF Rosso di Corte '06	♈♈ 5
○ COF Sauvignon '07	♈♈ 4
○ COF Verduzzo Friulano '06	♈♈ 4

○ Collio Malvasia Ronc dal Luis '08	♈♈ 4*
○ Collio Pinot Grigio '08	♈♈ 4*
○ Collio Chardonnay '08	♈ 4
○ Collio Friulano '08	♈ 4
○ Collio Sauvignon '08	♈ 4
○ Collio Friulano '07	♈♈ 4
○ Collio Tocai Friulano '06	♈♈ 4
○ Collio Tocai Friulano '05	♈♈ 4
○ Collio Tocai Friulano '04	♈♈ 4
○ Collio Tocai Friulano Ronc dal Luis '06	♈♈ 4

Ca' Bolani

VIA CA' BOLANI, 2
33052 CERVIGNANO DEL FRIULI [UD]
TEL. 043132670
www.cabolani.it

CELLAR SALES
PRE-BOOKED VISITS

ANNUAL PRODUCTION 2.500,000 bottles
HECTARES UNDER VINE 550
VITICULTURE METHOD Conventional

Ca' Bolani, located in the heart of the Friuli Aquileia DOC, has 550 hectares under vine, giving it the region's most extensive vineyard holding. In 1970, the Zonins purchased the property from the Bolani family, whose most eminent scion was Conte Domenico Bolani, the Venetian republic's procurator in Friuli in the early 16th century. The estate is managed by oenologist Marco Rabino, who is helped out in the cellar by Roberto Marcolini under the watchful eye of Franco Giacosa.

The standard wines are labelled simply Ca' Bolani and the selections are released as Gianni Zonin Vineyards. Two of those selections stood out at our tasting. Sauvignon Tamànis '08 gives very varietal white peach-led aromatics laced with lychees and passion fruit. It's a perkily refreshing wine with appealing suppleness and savour on the palate. Its stablemate, Refosco Alturio '05, is wonderful on the nose, showing red berry fruits, forest fruits and rain-soaked earth, and even better on the poised, dynamically drinkable palate. From the base line, the '08 Sauvignon and '08 Friulano stand out for their alluringly varietal character.

Ca' Tullio
& Sdricca di Manzano

VIA BELIGNA, 41
33051 AQUILEIA [UD]
TEL. 0431919700
www.catulllo.lt

CELLAR SALES
PRE-BOOKED VISITS

ANNUAL PRODUCTION 450,000 bottles
HECTARES UNDER VINE 78
VITICULTURE METHOD Conventional

The Ca' Tullio winery is based at Aquileia in a large, early 20th-century edifice once used for drying tobacco but sensitively restructured in 1994. Today, one wing is given over to the cellar, which vinifies fruit grown both locally and in the Colli Orientali del Friul, while the other wing houses a generously proportioned dining and reception room as well as the tasting room where Patrizia Sepulcri entertains visitors.

Current owner Paolo Calligaris releases wines produced in the Aquileia DOC zone under the Ca' Tullio label, reserving the Sdricca di Manzano label for Colli Orientali del Friuli products. Oenologist Francesco Visintin keeps up the cellar's excellent level of quality. Proof is there in the three wines that went forward to the national taste-offs this year. Pignolo Sdricca '06 won friends for its complex, fragrant bouquet and thrusting, subtly elegant development in the mouth. Friulano Sdricca '08 gives a pervasive nose, power and depth on the palate and lashings of varietal character. Finally, the '08 Traminer Aromatico Viola's nice citrus and dried roses are very typical of the variety.

● Friuli Aquileia Refosco P. R. Alturio Gianni Zonin Vineyards '05	♟♟ 4*
○ Friuli Aquileia Sauvignon Tamànis Gianni Zonin Vineyards '08	♟♟ 5*
○ Friuli Aquileia Friulano '08	♟♟ 4*
○ Friuli Aquileia Sauvignon '08	♟♟ 4*
● Friuli Aquileia Refosco P. R. '07	♟ 4
○ Friuli Aquileia Traminer Aromatico '08	♟ 4
○ Prosecco Brut	♟ 3
○ Friuli Aquileia Chardonnay '06	♟♟ 4
○ Friuli Aquileia Traminer Aromatico '07	♟♟ 4
○ Opimio Gianni Zonin Vineyards '07	♟♟ 4

○ COF Friulano Sdricca '08	♟♟ 4*
● COF Pignolo Sdricca '06	♟♟ 5
○ Friuli Aquileia Traminer Viola '08	♟♟ 4*
○ Belladonna Sdricca	♟♟ 6
○ COF Pinot Grigio Sdricca '08	♟♟ 4*
○ COF Verduzzo Friulano Sdricca '07	♟♟ 6
○ COF Ribolla Gialla Sdricca '08	♟ 4
○ Muller Thurgau '08	♟ 4
○ COF Pinot Grigio Sdricca '07	♟♟ 4
○ COF Verduzzo Friulano Sdricca '06	♟♟ 6
○ COF Verduzzo Friulano Sdricca '05	♟♟ 6
○ Friuli Aquileia Traminer Aromatico '07	♟♟ 4
○ Traminer Viola '06	♟♟ 5

Paolo Caccese

LOC. PRADIS, 6
34071 CORMÒNS [GO]
TEL. 048161062
www.paolocaccese.com

CELLAR SALES
PRE-BOOKED VISITS

ANNUAL PRODUCTION **40,000 bottles**
HECTARES UNDER VINE **6**
VITICULTURE METHOD **Conventional**

Paolo Caccese is a prominent figure among winemakers in the Collio Goriziano. A man in love with his land and what he calls his "strange job", Paolo leaves the law degree he earned in his youth to gather dust in the drawer as he throws himself into his work. The vineyards provide him with the gratification he could not find in his studies. He has also chaired the Collio wine protection consortium, albeit briefly..

We have always been fans of Paolo's whites, especially the Traminer Aromatico and Müller Thurgau, which he continues to make with excellent results, but this time he took us by surprise with a marvellous Merlot Riserva '06. The very deep, concentrated ruby red is superb, ushering in crisp varietal fruit over green notes and a savoury, fruit-forward palate with a mouthfilling texture. It's wonderfully long and appealing. On the white front, look out particularly for the supremely drinkable, yellow peach-themed Pinot Bianco '08 and the yellow rose, lychee and grapefruit fragrances of the attractive '08 Traminer Aromatico.

Canus

VIA GRAMOGLIANO, 21
33040 CORNO DI ROSAZZO [UD]
TEL. 0432759427
www.canus.it

CELLAR SALES

ANNUAL PRODUCTION **35,000 bottles**
HECTARES UNDER VINE **12**
VITICULTURE METHOD **Conventional**

The Canus winery is at Gramogliano, on the banks of the Judrio river in the municipality of Corno di Rosazzo. In 2004, it was acquired by Pordenone-based businessman Ugo Rossetto, who put his enterprising children Dario and Lara in charge. Dario now looks after production and has put his design experience to good use by creating a series of extremely elegant, eye-catching labels. Lara is responsible for accounts, marketing and public relations.

Winemaking is now in the capable hands of Renato Cozzarolo, who has had an immediate impact on quality. Previously, the cellar has earned Red Glasses and this year the honour goes to a lovely, rich-hued '06 Refosco redolent of ripe sour cherries and briary fruit, backed by a savoury, well-balanced palate with a caressing mouthfeel. The whites are very varietal and territorial. The '08 Chardonnay is a riot of tropical fruits and the Friulano '08, although a tad rustic, has a very full flavour and the variety's signature twist of bitterness on the finish. The '08 Sauvignon is attractively tangy and the Pignolo '06 looks set to improve, although the tannins are still a little incisive.

● Collio Merlot Ris. '06	♟♟ 6
○ Collio Pinot Bianco '08	♟♟ 4*
○ Collio Traminer Aromatico '08	♟♟ 4*
○ Collio Friulano '08	♟ 4
○ Collio Müller Thurgau '08	♟ 4
○ Collio Sauvignon '08	♟ 4
○ La Veronica	♟ 6
○ Collio Friulano '07	♟♟ 4*
○ Collio Müller Thurgau '07	♟♟ 4
○ Collio Pinot Bianco '07	♟♟ 4
○ Collio Pinot Grigio '07	♟♟ 4*
○ Collio Traminer Aromatico '07	♟♟ 4*

● COF Refosco P. R. '06	♟♟ 5
○ COF Chardonnay '08	♟♟ 4*
● COF Cabernet Franc '08	♟ 5
○ COF Friulano '08	♟ 4
● COF Pignolo '06	♟ 6
○ COF Ribolla Gialla '08	♟ 4
○ COF Sauvignon '08	♟ 4
○ COF Bianco Jasmine '07	♟♟ 5
○ COF Bianco Jasmine '06	♟♟ 4
○ COF Ribolla Gialla '07	♟♟ 4
○ COF Ribolla Gialla Ribuele Blancie '07	♟♟ 5
○ COF Sauvignon '06	♟♟ 4
○ COF Tocai Friulano '06	♟♟ 4*

Il Carpino

LOC. SOVENZA, 14A
34070 SAN FLORIANO DEL COLLIO [GO]
TEL. 0481884097
www.ilcarpino.com

CELLAR SALES
PRE-BOOKED VISITS

ANNUAL PRODUCTION 60,000 bottles
HECTARES UNDER VINE 16
VITICULTURE METHOD Conventional

Anna and Franco Sosol have celebrated their children Manuel and Naike joining them on the estate by releasing a new wine, Exordium. It's a selection of tocai friulano from an old vineyard that Franco was reluctant to replant. And the watchword seems to be "back to the past", albeit adjusted slightly to take account of recent technical progress. Witness the project to expand the cellar and make room for 15 and 20-hectolitre Slavonian oak maturation barrels.

Top of the list is the elegant, complex Bianco Carpino '06, a tried and tested blend of sauvignon, chardonnay and ribolla gialla whose seamlessly fused aromatics are lifted by a well-gauged dose of new oak. Equally attractive is the Chardonnay '06, notable for its confectioner's cream and ripe tropical fruits aromatics and soft, caressingly full-bodied palate. The '06 may be the first edition of Exordium but it has plenty of gutsy personality. Also on its first release is Vis Uvae, an intriguingly copper-hued '06 Pinot Grigio with a delicious flavour. The bouquet of the '08 Malvasia Vigna Runc is stunningly reminiscent of roses while the forward '06 Sauvignon shows great concentration.

Casa Zuliani

VIA GRADISCA, 23
34070 FARRA D'ISONZO [GO]
TEL. 0481888506
www.casazuliani.com

CELLAR SALES
PRE-BOOKED VISITS

ANNUAL PRODUCTION 120,000 bottles
HECTARES UNDER VINE 21
VITICULTURE METHOD Conventional

When Zuliano Zuliani, the great-grandfather of the current owner, decided back in 1923 to buy a home and a few hectares in the Farra d'Isonzo countryside, he probably didn't realize that only a few years later, the land would prove suitable for the production of outstandingly fine wines. His descendant Federico Frumento, recently married to Benedetta, saw the territory's potential and has moved swiftly to exploit it, making the most of his ancestor's hard work and garnering its fruits.

In the cellar, the skilful Omar Caffar, with consultancy from the great Gianni Menotti, crafts a range of outstanding wines. Top of the list is the '08 Friulano, which went into our finals for its varietal typicity and coherence on nose and palate, juicily soft-textured through to the finish. The '05 Merlot Winter Rosso '05 is a tad less exciting than the previous release but it's still a fantastic wine, irresistibly good-looking with perhaps a little too much toastiness but savoury on a palate that hangs together well. We thought the tangy Chardonnay '08 was remarkably elegant on the nose and the heady, fresh-tasting '07 Winter Sauvignon is very varietal with a great palette of aromatics.

○ Bianco Carpino '06	♟♟	5
○ Chardonnay '06	♟♟	5
○ Exordium '06	♟♟	6
⊙ Pinot Grigio Vis Uvae '06	♟♟	6
○ Collio Malvasia V. Runc '08	♟	4
○ Collio Ribolla Gialla V. Runc '08	♟	4
○ Malvasia '06	♟	6
○ Ribolla Gialla '06	♟	5
○ Sauvignon '06	♟	5
● Rubrum '99	♟♟♟	8
○ Bianco Carpino '05	♟♟	5
○ Bianco Carpino '04	♟♟	5
○ Collio Chardonnay '05	♟♟	5
○ Collio Malvasia '05	♟♟	6
○ Collio Malvasia Carpino '04	♟♟	6
○ Collio Ribolla Gialla V. Runc '07	♟♟	4
○ Collio Sauvignon '05	♟♟	5
● Rubrum Carpino '03	♟♟	8

○ Collio Friulano '08	♟♟	4*
○ Collio Chardonnay '08	♟♟	4*
● Collio Merlot '06	♟♟	5
● Winter Rosso '05	♟♟	6
○ Winter Sauvignon '07	♟♟	5
○ Collio Malvasia '08	♟	4
○ Collio Pinot Bianco '08	♟	4
○ Collio Pinot Grigio '08	♟	4
○ Collio Sauvignon Blanc '08	♟	4
● Winter Rosso '04	♟♟♟	6
○ Collio Chardonnay '07	♟♟	4*
○ Collio Friulano '07	♟♟	4*
○ Collio Pinot Bianco '07	♟♟	4*
● Winter Rosso '03	♟♟	5

Lino Casella

VIA ALBANA, 55
33040 PREPOTTO [UD]
TEL. 0432713429
info.casella@libero.it

ANNUAL PRODUCTION **16,000 bottles**
HECTARES UNDER VINE **3.5**
VITICULTURE METHOD **Conventional**

Casella is something of a new development in Friulian wine but the estate was in fact set up in the latter half of the 19th century by the Rieppi family, making it one of the oldest operations in the Albana district of Prepotto. The farm and cellar make up an interesting courtyard-focused complex that faithfully reflects the characteristics of the agriculture of yesteryear in this area. In 2006, the property was acquired by Lino Casella, a dynamic young wine man.

Having spent time working at a number of farms and wine estates in the area, Lino finally made his dream come true and now manages a wine estate of his own, making wines that reflect his deep love of the land. When we came to taste, we found a stunning Bianco Selezione dei Roseti '07, a monovarietal Chardonnay vinified in steel after brief skin contact. The lovely gold-flecked straw yellow heralds intense damson and medlar fruit, following this up with a full-bodied, savoury palate that exudes class. The Schioppettino '07 is soft, fruity and caressingly well balanced while the astonishing '07 Franconia is one of the few appealing examples of the variety from the region.

○ COF Bianco Sel. dei Roseti '07	ΨΨ	4*
● COF Schioppettino '07	ΨΨ	5
● Franconia '07	ΨΨ	4*
○ COF Friulano '08	Ψ	4
● COF Tazzelenghe '07	Ψ	5
○ COF Pinot Bianco '07	ΨΨ	4*
○ COF Tocai Friulano '06	ΨΨ	4*
● Franconia '06	ΨΨ	4*

La Castellada

FRAZ. OSLAVIA, 1
34170 GORIZIA
TEL. 048133670

CELLAR SALES
PRE-BOOKED VISITS

ANNUAL PRODUCTION **23,000 bottles**
HECTARES UNDER VINE **9**
VITICULTURE METHOD **Conventional**

We are in Oslavia, a unique wine laboratory with soil types, aspects and site climates to die for. It was 1978 when Giorgio and Nicolò Bensa shut up their eatery and devoted themselves to their vineyards full time. They set themselves some rules: cover-cropping, organic fertilizers and copper and sulphur only as pesticides. Now Nicolò's sons Stefano and Matteo have joined their father and uncle full time on the estate and his wife Valentina takes care of administration.

Giorgio likes to spend his time among the rows looking after the grapes, leaving his brother to make the wine, but Nicolò has help from Stefano, who has followed his father's example and gained sufficient experience to be self-sufficient, meaning that he can now take responsibility in the cellar. Oslavia has always been the home of Ribolla Gialla and in these parts, people traditionally like to ferment it in oak after extended skin contact. The '05 edition is an amber-flecked old gold redolent of dried herbs, peach and citrus peel, showing structure and savouriness on the palate. We also liked the pinot grigio, chardonnay and sauvignon-based Bianco della Castellada '05.

○ Collio Ribolla Gialla '05	ΨΨ	6
○ Collio Bianco della Castellada '05	ΨΨ	6
○ Bianco della Castellada '95	ΨΨΨ	6
○ Bianco della Castellada '94	ΨΨΨ	6
○ Bianco della Castellada '92	ΨΨΨ	6
○ Collio Bianco della Castellada '99	ΨΨΨ	6
○ Collio Bianco della Castellada '98	ΨΨΨ	6
○ Collio Chardonnay '94	ΨΨΨ	6
● Collio Rosso della Castellada '99	ΨΨΨ	8
○ Collio Sauvignon '93	ΨΨΨ	6
○ Collio Tocai Friulano '03	ΨΨΨ	6
○ Collio Ribolla Gialla '03	ΨΨ	6
● Collio Rosso della Castellada '02	ΨΨ	8
○ Collio Tocai Friulano '04	ΨΨ	6

Castelvecchio

VIA CASTELNUOVO, 2
34078 SAGRADO [GO]
TEL. 048199742
www.castelvecchio.com

CELLAR SALES
PRE-BOOKED VISITS

ANNUAL PRODUCTION **210,000 bottles**
HECTARES UNDER VINE **40**
VITICULTURE METHOD **Conventional**

The Castelvecchio winery is owned by the Terraneo family. For many years, it has benefited from the winemaking skills of Giovanni Bignucolo, who has always sensitively interpreted the Carso terroir and tradition. Located in the northern part of the Carso, on the edge of the Isonzo river plain, Castelvecchio has iron and limestone-rich soil that preserves the varietal characteristics of red and aromatic wines, and the special site climates enhance them.

Reds generally spend four months in steel to complete malolactic fermentation and tartrate precipitation before maturing for a year in small casks of different sizes and ages, and then for a further year in larger casks. The '04 Merlot is superb. Austere and brooding on the complex, spicy nose, it shows juicy, full-bodied and long-lingering on the palate. The Malvasia Istriana '08 is a rare example of varietal typicity, unveiling the signature fragrance of wisteria and saltiness contributed by the nearby Adriatic Sea. The rich-hued Refosco '06 presents fruitiness and minerality. All the other wines are well-made and varietal.

Marco Cecchini

LOC. CASALI DE LUCA
VIA COLOMBANI
33040 FAEDIS [UD]
TEL. 0432720563
www.cecchinimarco.com

CELLAR SALES
PRE-BOOKED VISITS

ANNUAL PRODUCTION **40,000 bottles**
HECTARES UNDER VINE **10**
VITICULTURE METHOD **Conventional**

Marco Cecchini has a degree in economics but loves the countryside. He had to make a life choice and plumped for running his own winery at Faedis, on the northern edge of the Colli Orientali del Friuli. The accompanying notes he sends with his wines are always heart-felt. Here's one: "The satisfaction I experience for my wines is equalled only by the passion and sacrifice they demand from me".

On the winemaking side, Marco has outside consultancy from Sonia Dell'Oste and the Terra&Vino group. This year's table is just reward for Marco's efforts. He sent two wines to the final taste-offs. The '08 Pinot Grigio Vigneto Bellagioia is complex and pervasive on a nose brimming with ripe pear fragrances. Equally fine is the '08 Tovè, from tocai friulano grapes with a splash of verduzzo, which rolls out yellow damsons and almonds that lead into a flavoursome, deliciously bitterish palate. The fresh-tasting '07 Riesling puts the accent on lime-themed citrus while the sweet '07 Verlit hints at apricot jam. To round off, the '07 Refosco is soft-textured and appealing.

● Carso Merlot '04	♈♈ 6
○ Carso Malvasia Istriana '08	♈♈ 4*
● Carso Refosco P. R. '06	♈♈ 5
● Carso Cabernet Franc '06	♈ 5
● Carso Cabernet Sauvignon '06	♈ 5
○ Carso Traminer Aromatico '08	♈ 4
● Terrano '08	♈ 4
● Carso Cabernet Sauvignon '05	♔♔ 5
○ Carso Malvasia Istriana '07	♔♔ 4
○ Carso Malvasia Istriana '06	♔♔ 4
● Carso Merlot '03	♔♔ 6
● Sagrado Rosso '03	♔♔ 6

○ COF Bianco Tovè '08	♈♈ 4*
○ Pinot Grigio Vigneto Bellagioia '08	♈♈ 4*
● COF Refosco P. R. '07	♈♈ 4*
○ COF Verduzzo Friulano Verlit '07	♈♈ 5
○ Riesling '07	♈♈ 4*
○ COF Bianco Tovè '06	♔♔ 4*
○ COF Bianco Tovè '05	♔♔ 4
○ COF Pinot Grigio Vign. Bellagioia '04	♔♔ 4*
○ COF Verduzzo Friulano Verlit '06	♔♔ 5
○ COF Verduzzo Friulano Verlit '03	♔♔ 6
○ Pinot Grigio Bellagioia '06	♔♔ 4*
○ Pinot Grigio Vigneto Bellagioia '07	♔♔ 4*

Eugenio Collavini

LOC. GRAMOGLIANO
VIA DELLA RIBOLLA GIALLA, 2
33040 CORNO DI ROSAZZO [UD]
TEL. 0432753222
www.collavini.it

CELLAR SALES
PRE-BOOKED VISITS

ANNUAL PRODUCTION 1.500,000 bottles
HECTARES UNDER VINE 173
VITICULTURE METHOD Natural

The Collavini family's winemaking story began in 1896, with Eugenio, but if the estate name is now known internationally, it is thanks to Manlio. He is backed up by his wife, Anna, their sons Luigi and Giovanni and an estate staff that runs like clockwork. It was back in 1970 that Manlio launched his project to referment Ribolla Gialla, now a vintage product of outstanding calibre, using an innovative technique called the Collavini method.

This is a winery that turns out big numbers but also one that focuses on image-building niche products to catch the consumer's eye. That goal has been achieved with the crucial input of the estate oenologist, Walter Bergnach. Five Collavini wines went on to the finals but again it was Collio Bianco Broy, the '08 edition this time, which picked up Three Glasses. This magical medley of chardonnay, friulano and sauvignon is unfailingly elegant in the glass and on the nose, showing generous power on the palate. As its name suggests, the Sauvignon Blanc Fumât '08 is edged with subtle smokiness while the estate thoroughbred is Ribolla Gialla Brut '05, a wine to uncork on very special occasions.

Colle Duga

LOC. ZEGLA, 10
34071 CORMÒNS [GO]
TEL. 048161177
info@colleduga.com

CELLAR SALES
PRE-BOOKED VISITS

ANNUAL PRODUCTION 35,000 bottles
HECTARES UNDER VINE 7.5
VITICULTURE METHOD Conventional

The Colle Duga vineyard is at Zegla in the heart of the Collio, right on the border with Slovenia. Grandfather Giuseppe farmed here, as did his father Luciano, but Damian Princic is the man who created the success that the cellar has enjoyed in recent years. Damian has active help from his wife Monica, who looks after administration and public relations, and from their children Karin and Patrik. Despite their youth, both take an enthusiastic part in the estate's activities when necessary.

In the vineyard, Damian has his father Luciano to help him while in the cellar, he takes full responsibility for every decision, albeit with a little pertinent advice from consultant winemaker Giorgio Bertossi. The single-variety wines are magnificent but we liked the Collio Bianco '08, a fine mix of friulano, sauvignon and chardonnay with a dash of malvasia. In an encore of last year's result, it swept up Three Glasses. This wonderful interpretation of the territory's minerality translates into a savoury, muscular palate that progresses seamlessly. A quick glance at the table below will confirm that no bottle earned fewer than two Glasses, proof that you can always count on Damian.

○ Collio Bianco Broy '08	♛♛♛ 5*
● COF Rosso Forresco '05	♛♛ 6
● Collio Merlot dal Pic '05	♛♛ 6
○ Collio Sauvignon Blanc Fumât '08	♛♛ 4*
○ Ribolla Gialla Brut '05	♛♛ 6
● COF Refosco P. R. Pucino '08	♛ 4
○ COF Ribolla Gialla Turian '08	♛ 6
○ Collio Bianco Broy '07	♛♛♛ 5
○ Collio Bianco Broy '06	♛♛♛ 5
○ Collio Bianco Broy '04	♛♛♛ 5
○ COF Ribolla Gialla Turian '07	♛♛ 6
● COF Rosso Forresco '04	♛♛ 6
● COF Rosso Forresco '03	♛♛ 6
● COF Schioppettino Turian '03	♛♛ 6
○ Collio Bianco Broy '05	♛♛ 5
○ Collio Pinot Grigio Black Label '07	♛♛ 4*
○ Collio Sauvignon Blanc Fumât '07	♛♛ 4*

○ Collio Bianco '08	♛♛♛ 5*
○ Collio Chardonnay '08	♛♛ 5
○ Collio Friulano '08	♛♛ 4*
● Collio Merlot '07	♛♛ 5
○ Collio Pinot Grigio '08	♛♛ 5
○ Collio Sauvignon '08	♛♛ 5
○ Collio Bianco '07	♛♛♛ 5
○ Collio Tocai Friulano '06	♛♛♛ 4*
○ Collio Tocai Friulano '05	♛♛♛ 4*
○ Collio Chardonnay '07	♛♛ 5
○ Collio Friulano '07	♛♛ 4
○ Collio Pinot Grigio '07	♛♛ 5
○ Collio Sauvignon '07	♛♛ 5

Colmello di Grotta

LOC. VILLANOVA
VIA GORIZIA, 133
34070 FARRA D'ISONZO [GO]
TEL. 0481888445
www.colmello.it

CELLAR SALES
PRE-BOOKED VISITS

ANNUAL PRODUCTION **100,000 bottles**
HECTARES UNDER VINE **17**
VITICULTURE METHOD **Conventional**

Francesca Bortolotto Possati inherited this winery from her mother, Luciana Bennati. Half of the vine stock is in the Collio DOC and half in the Isonzo zone. The limestone and gravel Isonzo soil produces wines of elegant structure and generous fragrances while the marl and sandstone Collio territory favours aromatic complexity and muscular structure. With consultancy input from oenologist Fabio Coser, Francesca releases an elegant, meticulously groomed range that nicely reflects the nature of the two terrains.

All the current whites in this year's vast line-up impressed us but in the end we preferred the impeccably appealing territoriality of the '08 Sauvignon. Its deep straw yellow is shot through with flecks of green and the nose delights with tropical lychee and passion fruit before the full flavour, freshness and exciting minerality unfold. The attractively uncomplicated '08 Pinot Grigio is also very good, its buttery nose laced with elderflowers and dried roses. The '08 Ribolla Gialla is clear and fragrant, the '08 Friulano is an outstandingly easy drinker while the '07 Cabernet Sauvignon and Merlot share plenty of structure and a lovely hint of balsam.

Paolino Comelli

CASE COLLOREDO, 8
33040 FAEDIS [UD]
TEL. 0432711226
www.comelli.it

CELLAR SALES
PRE-BOOKED VISITS
VISITOR FACILITIES
FOOD

ANNUAL PRODUCTION **50,000 bottles**
HECTARES UNDER VINE **12.5**
VITICULTURE METHOD **Conventional**

Paolino Comelli made a shrewd move back in 1946 when he purchased what was a run-down estate in the hills of Colloredo di Soffumbergo, in the municipality of Faedis. Today, the ancient village, now carefully restored, is a stunningly beautiful hospitality facility, furnished in traditional Friulian fashion and kitted out with every comfort. At the helm is Paolino's heir, Pierluigi, known to his friends as Pigi, helped out by his wife Daniela and their sons Nicola and Filippo.

For winemaking consultancy, Pigi has brought in Emilio Del Medico, who has made a major contribution to improving the standards of the wines. We would particularly like to point out this year's reds, which all our panellists loved. Leading the pack is the refosco, pignolo, merlot and cabernet Rosso Soffumbergo '06, which conjures up bramble and blueberry tart, dark chocolate and coffee beans that accompany a soft, fresh-tasting palate. The Merlot Jacò '06 stands out for varietal character and an appealingly consistent palate. The still youngish Pignolo '05 is encouragingly juicy and the golden-hued '07 Verduzzo Eoos offers well-gauged sweetness.

○ Collio Pinot Grigio '08	▼▼ 4*
○ Collio Sauvignon '08	▼▼ 4*
○ Collio Chardonnay '08	▼ 4
○ Collio Friulano '08	▼ 4
○ Collio Ribolla Gialla '08	▼ 4
● Friuli Isonzo Cabernet Sauvignon '07	▼ 4
● Friuli Isonzo Merlot '07	▼ 4
○ Collio Bianco Sanfilip '07	▼▼ 5
○ Collio Tocai Friulano '06	▼▼ 4
● Friuli Isonzo Cabernet Sauvignon '04	▼▼ 4
● Friuli Isonzo Cabernet Sauvignon '03	▼▼ 4
● Friuli Isonzo Merlot '04	▼ 4

● Rosso Soffumbergo '06	▼▼ 5
● COF Merlot Jacò '06	▼▼ 5
● COF Pignolo '05	▼▼ 5
○ Verduzzo Friulano Eoos '07	▼▼ 5
● COF Cabernet Sauvignon '06	▼ 5
○ COF Sauvignon '08	▼ 4
● COF Cabernet Sauvignon '05	▼▼ 5
○ COF Friulano '07	▼▼ 4*
● COF Rosso Soffumbergo '04	▼▼ 5
○ COF Sauvignon '07	▼▼ 4
○ COF Tocai Friulano '06	▼▼ 4

Conte Brandolini

VIA VISTORTA, 82
33077 SACILE [PN]
TEL. 0434782490
www.vistorta.it

CELLAR SALES
PRE-BOOKED VISITS

ANNUAL PRODUCTION **250,000 bottles**
HECTARES UNDER VINE **36**
VITICULTURE METHOD **Organic certified**

Brandino Brandolini owns what was until recently Villa Ronche and now bears his name. Separately, he also manages another operation under the Vistorta label, turning out serious numbers of a single wine he releases at a very reasonable price. Merlot Vistorta is now emblematic of how the Grave DOC zone can achieve and maintain excellence through meticulous vineyard management and rigorous grape selection.

Brandino has a solid scientific background, having studied in the United States and France, where he met George Pauli and Samuel Tinon, who support the competent Alec Ongaro in the cellar. The '07 Merlot is the fifth edition in a row of Vistorta to earn Three Glasses and a source of pride for the entire region. Fragrant red and black berry fruits, printer's ink and spices usher in a juicily pervasive palate that gratifies the senses. The appealingly well-made whites in the Conte Brandolini range respect the profiles of their respective varieties and Treanni, from the same line, is an unusual blend of refosco, cabernet franc and merlot from three different vintages.

Dario Coos

LOC. RAMANDOLO
VIA RAMANDOLO, 5
33045 NIMIS [UD]
TEL. 0432790320
www.dariocoos.it

CELLAR SALES
PRE-BOOKED VISITS

ANNUAL PRODUCTION **45,000 bottles**
HECTARES UNDER VINE **7**
VITICULTURE METHOD **Conventional**

The name Dario Coos is synonymous with Ramandolo, where he lives and makes his excellent version of the wine that bears the town's name, This year, Dario also presented us with a range of tip-top dry wines that make up a fine range of products. Dario looks after all cellar operations himself. The winemaking facilities are modern but the grapes are still harvested by hand. Actually, there is no other way to pick them because they grow on steep terraced slopes. Everything is done in the unhurried fashion of the past and only estate-grown grapes are vinified.

The splendid '06 Picolit is the colour of fine gold and tempts the nostrils with jammy notes of stone fruits, sponge cake fresh out of the oven and crème caramel sweetness. The soft, creamy sweetness of the palate lingers forever. A hint of extract tempers the sweetness of the slightly amber-hued '05 Ramandolo, whose luscious nose gives baked pears and dried apricots. The full-bodied, dense '08 Friulano Sdricca '08 gives a pervasive nose, power and depth on the palate, and lashings of varietal character. Dario's '08 Ribolla Gialla has a perky, well-meshed body while the satisfyingly fat Romandus '05 and leaner, very drinkable Longhino '06 stand comparison with the best.

● Friuli Grave Merlot Vistorta '07	♟♟♟ 5
○ Friuli Grave Friulano '08	♟♟ 4*
○ Friuli Grave Sauvignon '08	♟♟ 4*
○ Friuli Grave Chardonnay '08	♟ 3
○ Friuli Grave Pinot Grigio '08	♟ 4
○ Friuli Grave Traminer Aromatico '08	♟ 4
● Treanni Rosso	♟ 4
● Friuli Grave Merlot Vistorta '06	♟♟♟ 5
● Friuli Grave Merlot Vistorta '05	♟♟♟ 5
○ Friuli Grave Chardonnay '07	♟♟ 3*
○ Friuli Grave Sauvignon '07	♟♟ 4*

○ COF Picolit '06	♟ 7
○ COF Friulano '08	♟♟ 4*
○ Ramandolo V. T. '05	♟♟ 5
○ Ribolla Gialla '08	♟♟ 4*
○ Ramandolo Il Longhino '06	♟ 5
○ Ramandolo Romandus '05	♟ 6
○ Sauvignon Blanc '08	♟ 4
○ Ramandolo Il Longhino '05	♟♟ 5
○ Ramandolo Il Longhino '04	♟♟ 5
○ Ramandolo Il Longhino '03	♟♟ 5
○ Ramandolo Romandus '04	♟♟ 6
○ Ramandolo Romandus '02	♟♟ 6
○ Ramandolo V. T. '04	♟♟ 5
○ Sauvignon Blanc '07	♟♟ 4

Conte D'Attimis-Maniago

VIA SOTTOMONTE, 21
33042 BUTTRIO [UD]
TEL. 0432674027
www.contedattimismaniago.it

CELLAR SALES
PRE-BOOKED VISITS

ANNUAL PRODUCTION **400,000 bottles**
HECTARES UNDER VINE **85**
VITICULTURE METHOD **Conventional**

Tenuta Sottomonte has belonged to the D'Attimis family for almost 500 years. Today, Alberto manages the estate. Almost the entire holding of 110 hectares is under vine and we would like to stress that more than 70 per cent of the vine stock comprises local biotypes, in other words vineyard selections of the vines that over the years have adapted best to local site climates. It's an unfashionable policy that lengthens production times but it does enhance the varietal characteristics of the vines.

This year, we thought that the '05 Rosso Vignaricco was the best on the list. The sheer depth and concentration of the colour draws your attention and the nose unfurls a swath of red berry fruit preserves and liquorice layered over roasted coffee beans. That opulence fades into a relaxed, even palate bolstered by balanced extract that has already mellowed out. In contrast, the tannins of the Pignolo '05 have still to unbend but augur well for the future. Bianco Ronco Broilo '05, a blend of chardonnay and pinot bianco matured in Slavonian oak casks and Allier oak barriques, is streaked with gold and proffers a complex, subtly spicy bouquet. Serious alcohol and savouriness add to the appeal.

di Lenardo

FRAZ. ONTAGNANO
P.ZZA BATTISTI, 1
33050 GONARS [UD]
TEL. 0432928633
www.dilenardo.it

CELLAR SALES
PRE-BOOKED VISITS

ANNUAL PRODUCTION **600,000 bottles**
HECTARES UNDER VINE **50**
VITICULTURE METHOD **Conventional**

Out on the Friulian flatlands, a few kilometres from the star-shaped town of Palmanova, you'll find the village of Ontagnano, in the middle of which are the cellars of Lenardo Vineyards. A long-established operation but young at heart, it is run by Massimo Di Lenardo, a textbook example of an intelligent wine man who makes seriously good wines sourced from vineyards on the plains. Massimo knows all about markets, particularly in America and elsewhere abroad. In fact, 80 per cent of his output goes for export.

Di Lenardo's flatland vineyards are mainly in the Grave del Friuli DOC zone, although some are located around Aquileia. Massimo avoids unnecessary confusion by releasing all his wines as IGTs. Always in the front line in the cellar, Massimo has for many years been assisted in winemaking by Giuliano Cattinelli. The wine names are original, reflecting Massimo's very original personality. One of the cellar's most emblematic wines is Father's Eyes '08, from chardonnay mosqué matured in American oak. Very successful abroad, it leads off an extremely fine list of wines.

○ COF Bianco Ronco Broilo '05	♟♟ 5
● COF Pignolo '05	♟♟ 6
● COF Rosso Vignaricco '05	♟♟ 6
○ COF Chardonnay '08	♟ 5
○ COF Friulano '08	♟ 4
○ COF Malvasia '08	♟ 4
● COF Tazzelenghe '05	♟ 6
○ COF Verduzzo Friulano Tore delle Signore '07	♟ 5
○ COF Chardonnay '07	♟♟ 5
○ COF Malvasia '07	♟♟ 4
○ COF Malvasia '06	♟♟ 4*
○ COF Pinot Grigio '07	♟♟ 4
○ COF Ribolla Gialla '07	♟♟ 4
● COF Schioppettino '06	♟♟ 6
● COF Tazzelenghe '04	♟♟ 6
● COF Tazzelenghe '03	♟♟ 6

○ Father's Eyes '08	♟♟ 4*
○ Chardonnay '08	♟♟ 4*
○ Pinot Bianco '08	♟♟ 3*
○ Pinot Grigio '08	♟♟ 3*
○ Verduzzo Pass the Cookies '08	♟♟ 4*
○ Friuli Grave Friulano Toh! '08	♟ 4
● Merlot Just Me '07	♟ 5
● Ronco Nolè Rosso '07	♟ 4
○ Sarà Brut	♟ 5
○ Sauvignon '08	♟ 3
○ Friuli Grave Sauvignon '07	♟♟ 3
● Merlot Just Me '05	♟♟ 5
● Merlot Just Me '04	♟♟ 5
○ Pinot Bianco '07	♟♟ 3

Carlo Di Pradis

LOC. PRADIS, 22BIS
34071 CORMÒNS [GO]
TEL. 048162272
www.carlodipradis.it

CELLAR SALES
PRE-BOOKED VISITS

ANNUAL PRODUCTION **80,000 bottles**
HECTARES UNDER VINE **14**
VITICULTURE METHOD **Conventional**

Carlo Buzzinelli inherited his father's fantastic vineyard holding at Pradis, near Cormòns, as well as his passion for grape growing. Today, Carlo has sons of his own, Boris and David, who offer prospects of continuity in the estate management policy that Carlo laid down some 20 years ago. Wines from the Collio vineyards bear his name while those sourced from the eight hectares in the Isonzo DOC are released as BorDavi, underlining the shared sense of purpose that unites the brothers.

This year, we were most impressed by the three different versions of Friulano '08. The Collio version is a deep straw with very varietal aromatics of almonds and gentian, leading into a savoury palate with plenty of thrust, great minerality and considerable personality. The BorDavi edition is slightly paler, more alcoholic and shows florality on the nose but the same power is evident on the palate with its elegantly typical almondiness on the finish. Scusse was fermented with 17 day's skin contact and has emerged flecked with gold, redolent of candied peel, confectioner's cream and biscuit. It's powerfully well-structured on the rich, fleshy palate. The Pinot Grigio '08 is also excellent.

Giovanni Donda

VIA MANLIO ACIDINIO, 4
33051 AQUILEIA [UD]
TEL. 043191185
www.vinidonda.it

CELLAR SALES
PRE-BOOKED VISITS

ANNUAL PRODUCTION **30,000 bottles**
HECTARES UNDER VINE **6**
VITICULTURE METHOD **Conventional**

In 1924, Giovanni Battista Donda settled at Aquileia and purchased a few hectares of land in the countryside. When his son Bruno took over, he started growing vines and making excellent wine. Now the third generation is in the saddle in the shape of Giovanni Battista's grandson Giovanni. There is treasure buried in the soil at Aquileia, as everyone knows, but you have to dig carefully to find it and this is particularly true of wine. But Giovanni has flair and determination.

Consultancy input from oenologist Giorgio Bertossi has helped the cellar to achieve great things this year. We can imagine how happy Gianni will be when he sees some colour in his Guide Glasses. The honour went to a superbly crafted '08 Sauvignon that regales the nose with fresh white peach and elderflower aromatics, a wealth of flavour in the mouth and plenty of length. The '08 Pinot Grigio has an onionskin hue, intense, varietal fragrances and a deliciously easy-drinking character. In contrast, the '08 Pinot Bianco is lustrous, flecked with green and tangily juicy in the mouth. There is also confirmation from the '06 edition that this is great Refosco country.

○ Collio Friulano '08	♥♥ 4*
○ Collio Friulano Scusse '07	♥♥ 5
○ Collio Pinot Grigio '08	♥♥ 4*
○ Friuli Isonzo Friulano BorDavi '08	♥♥ 4*
● Friuli Isonzo Cabernet BorDavi '08	♥ 4
○ Friuli Isonzo Pinot Grigio BorDavi '08	♥ 4
○ Friuli Isonzo Sauvignon BorDavi '08	♥ 4
○ Collio Pinot Grigio '06	♥♥ 4
○ Collio Tocai Friulano '06	♥♥ 4
○ Collio Tocai Friulano '05	♥♥ 4
○ Friuli Isonzo Friulano BorDavi '07	♥♥ 4*
○ Friuli Isonzo Pinot Grigio BorDavi '04	♥♥ 4

○ Friuli Aquileia Sauvignon '08	♥♥ 4*
○ Friuli Aquileia Pinot Bianco '08	♥♥ 3*
○ Friuli Aquileia Pinot Grigio '08	♥♥ 4*
● Friuli Aquileia Refosco P. R. '06	♥♥ 4*
● Friuli Aquileia Merlot '07	♥ 4
● Friuli Aquileia Refosco P. R. '05	♥♥ 4
○ Friuli Aquileia Sauvignon '07	♥♥ 4
○ Friuli Aquileia Sauvignon '05	♥♥ 4

★★ Girolamo Dorigo

LOC. VICINALE
VIA DEL POZZO, 5
33042 BUTTRIO [UD]
TEL. 0432674268
www.montsclapade.com

CELLAR SALES
PRE-BOOKED VISITS
VISITOR FACILITIES

ANNUAL PRODUCTION **180,000 bottles**
HECTARES UNDER VINE **40**
VITICULTURE METHOD **Conventional**

Recent restyling of the winery headquarters has changed the face of Girolamo Dorigo's operation. It's now more welcoming and, crucially, much more functional. His children, Alessio in the cellar and Alessandra in the office, now have plenty of space to work in and visitors to the estate can be catered for in style. Some time age, Alessio took over the whole of the production cycle, in addition to which he also heads a team of wine consultants that advises a number of leading estates.

Partly because of the growing year, and not for the first time, the quality of the Dorigo reds outshone the whites. Three great wines went through to the finals and the Bordeaux blend '06 Monsclapade duly picked up Three Glasses. Its broodingly dark ruby precedes austere aromatics that hint at prunes, coffee and bitter chocolate followed by a soft-textured, flavoursome palate with lovely body. Ripe briary fruit, liquorice and rhubarb on the nose precede the Refosco's structured, varietal palate. The '06 Pignolo is massive yet elegant. Let's not forget that it was Girolamo who saved the variety from extinction. Best of the whites is the '08 Sauvignon.

● COF Rosso Montsclapade '06	🍷🍷🍷	7
● COF Pignolo di Buttrio '06	🍷🍷	8
● COF Refosco P. R. '06	🍷🍷	6
○ COF Sauvignon '08	🍷🍷	4*
○ COF Chardonnay '08	🍷	4
○ COF Pinot Grigio '08	🍷	4
○ COF Sauvignon Vign. Ronc di Juri '08	🍷	4
○ COF Traminer '08	🍷	4
● COF Pignolo di Buttrio '03	YYY	8
● COF Pignolo di Buttrio '02	YYY	8
● COF Pignolo di Buttrio '01	YYY	8
● COF Rosso Montsclapade '04	YYY	7
● COF Rosso Montsclapade '01	YYY	7
● COF Pignolo di Buttrio '05	YY	8
● COF Rosso Montsclapade '05	YY	7

Mauro Drius

VIA FILANDA, 100
34071 CORMÒNS [GO]
TEL. 048160998
info@driusmauro.it

CELLAR SALES
PRE-BOOKED VISITS

ANNUAL PRODUCTION **70,000 bottles**
HECTARES UNDER VINE **14.5**
VITICULTURE METHOD **Conventional**

Drius is one of the Cormòns area's historic estates. For many generations, the family has handed down a love of the land and some marvellous vineyards on the upper Isonzo plain and the slopes of Mount Quarin in the Collio. The current incumbent is Mauro Drius. Still helped out by his father Sergio, Mauro runs the estate in an impeccable manner. Mauro's wife Valentina is in charge of administration and sales while the future is ensured by Denis, who is studying oenology, Erika and Valentina.

It is not exactly news that Mauro has a flair for making premium wine but very few cellars manage to send five bottles to our taste-offs. Mauro has always been a Friulano specialist however this year it is his '08 Malvasia that stands out. Faint aromatic nuances interweave with the apple and yellow peach fruit, the palate is weighty, soft-texture and pervasive, closing on a salty note with a hint of almondiness. The crisply defined, freshly varietal fragrances of the refreshing, nicely structured '08 Chardonnay are also excellent. The '08 Friulano and '08 Sauvignon embody all the energy of the Collio and the Pinot Bianco from the same vintage is impressively varietal.

○ Friuli Isonzo Malvasia '08	🍷🍷🍷	4*
○ Collio Friulano '08	🍷🍷	4*
○ Collio Sauvignon '08	🍷🍷	4*
○ Friuli Isonzo Chardonnay '08	🍷🍷	4*
○ Friuli Isonzo Pinot Bianco '08	🍷🍷	4*
○ Friuli Isonzo Friulano '08	🍷🍷	4*
● Friuli Isonzo Merlot '06	🍷🍷	4*
○ Friuli Isonzo Pinot Grigio '08	🍷	4
○ Collio Tocai Friulano '05	YYY	4*
○ Collio Tocai Friulano '02	YYY	4*
○ Friuli Isonzo Bianco Vìgnis di Sìris '02	YYY	4*
○ Friuli Isonzo Friulano '07	YYY	4
○ Collio Friulano '07	YY	4
○ Friuli Isonzo Bianco Vìgnis di Sìris '06	YY	5
○ Friuli Isonzo Chardonnay '07	YY	4
○ Friuli Isonzo Malvasia '07	YY	4
○ Friuli Isonzo Pinot Grigio '07	YY	4

Le Due Terre

via Roma, 68b
33040 Prepotto [UD]
tel. 0432713189

CELLAR SALES
PRE-BOOKED VISITS

ANNUAL PRODUCTION **20,000 bottles**
HECTARES UNDER VINE **5**
VITICULTURE METHOD **Natural**

Due Terre, a genuine jewel of Prepotto and the Colli Orientali del Friuli, is run by the splendidly matched couple of Flavio Basilicata and Silvana Forte. There is no arguing with the table below, with three out of four labels going to the finals. Flavio loves a challenge so in the homeland of white wines he puts most of his effort into native and international red varieties, while still finding enough energy to make a superb white that delights critics and wine-drinking public alike.

Vinification at Due Terre has always meant ambient yeasts, spontaneous fermentation and prolonged barrique maturation without racking to avoid any alteration of varietal characteristics. Sacrisassi Rosso '07, a superb territorial 50-50 blend of refosco and schioppettino, is back on the Three Glass podium. Dark red, concentrated and redolent of ripe briary fruit, liquorice, pepper, coffee and cocoa powder, it gives soft texture, juiciness and powerful but velvet-smooth tannins. The Merlot '07 is intensely fruity, full and satisfying. The Scarisassi Bianco '07's friulano and ribolla gialla mix is savoury and aristocratic while the uncomplicated '07 Pinot Nero is a pleaser.

● COF Rosso Sacrisassi '07	🍷🍷🍷	7
○ COF Bianco Sacrisassi '07	🍷🍷	5
● COF Merlot '07	🍷🍷	7
● COF Pinot Nero '07	🍷🍷	5
○ COF Bianco Sacrisassi '05	🍷🍷🍷	6
● COF Merlot '03	🍷🍷🍷	6
● COF Merlot '02	🍷🍷🍷	7
● COF Merlot '00	🍷🍷🍷	7
● COF Rosso Sacrisassi '98	🍷🍷🍷	7
● COF Rosso Sacrisassi '97	🍷🍷🍷	7
○ COF Bianco Sacrisassi '06	🍷🍷	5
○ COF Bianco Sacrisassi '04	🍷🍷	6
● COF Merlot '06	🍷🍷	5
● COF Rosso Sacrisassi '06	🍷🍷	5

Ermacora

fraz. Ipplis
via Solzaredo, 9
33040 Premariacco [UD]
tel. 0432716250
www.ermacora.com

CELLAR SALES
PRE-BOOKED VISITS

ANNUAL PRODUCTION **165,000 bottles**
HECTARES UNDER VINE **25**
VITICULTURE METHOD **Conventional**

Brothers Antonio and Giuseppe Ermacora began to make wine in the hills of Ipplis, in the Colli Orientali del Friuli, as long ago as 1922. Family management has become a tradition and two other brothers, Dario and Luciano, now run this forward-looking operation. Luciano spends all his time in the vineyards and cellar while Dario takes care of the office work, in addition duties connected with his important roles in various farming-sector organisations.

It's always a pleasure to see native varieties at the top of a winery's score sheet. We picked out two very fine wines, the '07 Picolit and the '05 Pignolo, both of which are great ambassadors for Friuli. The Picolit is all elegance, the star-bright gold heralding ripe yellow peaches, lime blossom honey and confectioner's cream followed up by a deliciously sophisticated and very long palate. Dark ruby introduces the Pignolo's liqueur fruit, cocoa powder and cigar tobacco nose, full flavour and persuasively soft texture. The Friulano '08 and '07 Refosco are paragons of varietal appeal. There's also a new Ribolla Gialla, first made in '08 with fruit from a newly acquired 50-year-old vineyard.

○ COF Picolit '07	🍷🍷	7
● COF Pignolo '05	🍷🍷	6
○ COF Friulano '08	🍷🍷	4*
○ COF Pinot Grigio '08	🍷🍷	4*
● COF Refosco P. R. '07	🍷🍷	4*
○ COF Ribolla Gialla '08	🍷🍷	4*
○ COF Pinot Bianco '08	🍷	4
○ COF Sauvignon '08	🍷	4
● COF Pignolo '00	🍷🍷🍷	5
○ COF Friulano '07	🍷🍷	4
○ COF Picolit '06	🍷🍷	7
● COF Pignolo '04	🍷🍷	6
● COF Pignolo '03	🍷🍷	6
● COF Pignolo '02	🍷🍷	6
● COF Pignolo '01	🍷🍷	6
○ COF Pinot Bianco '07	🍷🍷	4
○ COF Pinot Grigio '07	🍷🍷	4

Fantinel

FRAZ. TAURIANO
VIA TESIS, 8
33097 SPILIMBERGO [PN]
TEL. 0427591511
www.fantinel.com

CELLAR SALES
PRE-BOOKED VISITS

ANNUAL PRODUCTION **4,000,000 bottles**
HECTARES UNDER VINE **N.D.**
VITICULTURE METHOD **Conventional**

The Fantinel story began in 1969 when Mario, a hotelier and restaurateur from Carnia, purchased some vines to make wine for his customers. Soon afterwards, in 1973, his sons Luciano, Gianfranco and Loris expanded the family holding and acquired more vineyards in the Collio, Grave and Colli Orientali del Friuli DOC zones. Those 16 hectares are now 300 and it is the third generation, Marco, Stefano and Mariaelena, who keep up what is now the family tradition.

The Fantinel group has three separate wineries: Sant'Helena at Vencò, La Roncaia at Nimis and Borgo Tesis at Tauriano near Spilimbergo, in an elegant complex where the offices and cellar nestle among the verdant vineyards. This is where the group's oenologists, Gianni Campo Dall'Orto and Adriano Copetti, work. The wine we liked best this year comes from the Grave DOC and did very well at our taste-offs. It is the consistent, aromatically complex '06 Refosco, a deliciously well-orchestrated drinking experience. The '08 Collio Pinot Grigio is a wonderfully varietal easy-drinker. Equally attractive is the merlot, cabernet franc and pinot nero Collio Rosso '05.

● Friuli Grave Refosco P. R. Sant'Helena '06	♟♟	5
○ Collio Bianco Sant'Helena '08	♟♟	5
○ Collio Pinot Grigio Sant'Helena '08	♟♟	5
● Collio Rosso Sant'Helena '05	♟♟	5
○ Collio Friulano Sant'Helena '08	♟	5
○ Collio Sauvignon Sant'Helena '08	♟	5
○ Collio Pinot Grigio Sant'Helena '05	♟♟	5
○ Collio Sauvignon Sant'Helena '06	♟♟	5
○ Collio Tocai Friulano Sant'Helena '06	♟♟	5
● Friuli Grave Merlot Borgo Tesis '04	♟♟	4
● Friuli Grave Merlot Borgo Tesis '03	♟♟	4*
● Friuli Grave Merlot Borgo Tesis '02	♟♟	4

★ Livio Felluga

FRAZ. BRAZZANO
VIA RISORGIMENTO, 1
34071 CORMÒNS [GO]
TEL. 048160203
www.liviofelluga.it

PRE-BOOKED VISITS

ANNUAL PRODUCTION **800,000 bottles**
HECTARES UNDER VINE **155**
VITICULTURE METHOD **Conventional**

This is the story of a family that lived first in the Austro-Hungarian empire and then in the recently formed kingdom of Italy, on the rocky coast of the Istrian peninsula and then the lagoon at Grado, before settling in the rolling hills of Friuli. The "Patriarch", Livio Felluga, is more than 90 years old and has passed on to his children Maurizio, Elda, Andrea and Filippo a heritage of tradition, love of the land and the day by day challenge of defending the family label's prestige.

The '07 version of the flagship Rosazzo Bianco Terre Alte does just that. This well-tried blend of pinot bianco, sauvignon and friulano is elegant, fragrant and faintly aromatic, showing poised and slightly veined with white pepper spice. Just as elegant and pervasive is the '07 Illivio, a wine that the four younger Fellugas created as a birthday present for their father a while back. It tempts the nostrils with rich white peaches, almonds and yellow damsons and fills the palate with flavour. Dark, deep and very good, the '06 Refosco delivers crushed black berry fruit and liquorice. Finally, the pale gold '06 Picolit is aristocratically refined on the nose and unforgettable in the mouth.

○ COF Rosazzo Bianco Terre Alte '07	♟♟♟	8
○ COF Bianco Illivio '07	♟♟	6
● COF Refosco P. R. '06	♟♟	6
○ Picolit '06	♟♟	8
○ COF Pinot Grigio '08	♟♟	5
○ COF Friulano '08	♟	5
○ COF Sauvignon '08	♟	5
○ Collio Bianco Rosenplatz '07	♟	5
● COF Refosco P. R. '99	♟♟♟	7
○ COF Rosazzo Bianco Terre Alte '06	♟♟♟	7
○ COF Rosazzo Bianco Terre Alte '04	♟♟♟	7
○ COF Rosazzo Bianco Terre Alte '02	♟♟♟	6
○ COF Rosazzo Bianco Terre Alte '01	♟♟♟	6
○ COF Rosazzo Bianco Terre Alte '99	♟♟♟	6
○ COF Rosazzo Bianco Terre Alte '97	♟♟♟	6
COF Rosazzo Bianco Terre Alte '96	♟♟♟	5

Marco Felluga

VIA GORIZIA, 121
34070 GRADISCA D'ISONZO [GO]
TEL. 048199164
www.marcofelluga.it

CELLAR SALES
PRE-BOOKED VISITS

ANNUAL PRODUCTION 600,000 bottles
HECTARES UNDER VINE 100
VITICULTURE METHOD Conventional

Roberto Felluga, who runs the winery now, is the fifth generation of a wine dynasty that began in Istria in the latter half of the 19th century. But it was Roberto's father, Marco, who took winemaking to another level and turned the operation into a benchmark for the entire territory. After completing his wine education at the prestigious school of oenology in Conegliano, Marco proved a great innovator and for years chaired the protection consortium.

At the estate headquarters in Gradisca d'Isonzo, winemaking is entrusted to the oenological skills of Raffaela Bruno, who has unexpectedly wide experience for one so young and whom Roberto trusts unquestioningly. He is right to do so. This year, we gave our top award to a classy, uncompromisingly gutsy '06 Merlot with a wealth of pervasive, well-defined fruit. We enjoyed the '05 Carantan, a classic, inky dark Bordeaux blend with austere charred wood and forest fruits aromatics, good structure and softness. The Cabernet Sauvignon '06 is nice and juicy while the stand-outs among the fragrant, faultlessly typed whites are the Molamatta '08, the Friulano '08 and the Chardonnay '08.

Fiegl

FRAZ. OSLAVIA
LOC. LENZUOLO BIANCO, 1
34070 GORIZIA
TEL. 0481547103
www.fieglvini.com

CELLAR SALES
PRE-BOOKED VISITS

ANNUAL PRODUCTION 140,000 bottles
HECTARES UNDER VINE 30
VITICULTURE METHOD Conventional

Fiegls have been growing grapes on the steep hills of Oslavia, north of Gorizia, since 1782. Every year, we come back to sing the praises of brothers Alessio, Giuseppe and Rinaldo, who have made giant strides towards excellence. Today, they have the enthusiasm and energy of the younger generation, Martin, Robert and Matej, who have completed their oenology studies and work full-time on the estate, combining passion with innovation.

The '04 Merlot from the Leopold line spends a long time maturing to emerge a splendid, intensely concentrated shade of garnet-ruby red. Its red fruits preserve fragrances are laced with balsamic hints and star anise, balance in the mouth is impressive and there is a lovely twist of bitterness at the back. Cuvée Blanc Leopold '07 is from pinot bianco, ribolla gialla, friulano and sauvignon, and its upfront, mouthfilling flavour is still headily alcoholic. The very well-made current wines have good nose-palate consistency, remain faithful to their variety and drink beautifully while the Cuvée Rouge Leopold '03 is a touch closed and still needs to absorb its long sojourn in wood.

● Collio Merlot Varneri '06	♈♈	4*
○ Collio Bianco Molamatta '08	♈♈	5
● Collio Cabernet Sauvignon '06	♈♈	4*
● Collio Carantan '05	♈♈	6
○ Collio Chardonnay '08	♈♈	4*
○ Collio Friulano '08	♈♈	4*
○ Collio Pinot Grigio Mongris '08	♈	4
○ Collio Pinot Grigio Mongris Ris. '06	♈	5
○ Collio Ribolla Gialla '08	♈	5
⊙ Moscato Rosa '06	♈	5
○ Collio Bianco Molamatta '07	♈♈	5
● Collio Carantan '04	♈♈	6
○ Collio Chardonnay '07	♈♈	4
○ Collio Pinot Grigio Mongris '07	♈♈	4
○ Collio Pinot Grigio Mongris Ris. '05	♈♈	5
○ Collio Ribolla Gialla '07	♈♈	5
⊙ Moscato Rosa '05	♈♈	5
● Refosco P. R. Ronco dei Moreri '06	♈♈	5

● Collio Merlot Leopold '04	♈♈	5
○ Collio Chardonnay '08	♈♈	4*
○ Collio Cuvée Blanc Leopold '07	♈♈	5
○ Collio Friulano '08	♈♈	4*
● Collio Cuvée Rouge Leopold '03	♈	6
○ Collio Malvasia '08	♈	4
○ Collio Pinot Grigio '08	♈	4
○ Collio Sauvignon '08	♈	4
○ Collio Pinot Grigio '04	♈♈♈	4*
○ Collio Cuvée Blanc Leopold '06	♈♈	5
○ Collio Malvasia '07	♈♈	4
● Collio Merlot Leopold '03	♈♈	5
● Collio Merlot Leopold '02	♈♈	4
● Collio Merlot Leopold '00	♈♈	4*
○ Collio Sauvignon '07	♈♈	4

Foffani

FRAZ. CLAUIANO
P.ZZA GIULIA, 13
33050 TRIVIGNANO UDINESE [UD]
TEL. 0432999584
www.foffani.it

CELLAR SALES
PRE-BOOKED VISITS
VISITOR FACILITIES
FOOD

ANNUAL PRODUCTION **100,000 bottles**
HECTARES UNDER VINE **10**
VITICULTURE METHOD **Conventional**

In the centre of Clauiano, one of Italy's loveliest medieval villages, Giovanni and Elisabetta Foffani work away steadily to improve the estate they have already enhanced with an original permanent exhibition dedicated to the colours of wine, bed and breakfast facilities and an inviting farm restaurant they open at weekends. The farm itself dates back to the 16th century and actually looks onto the square at Clauiano while the estate sprawls across the busy Friulian plain.

Quality here is rising steadily and this year the '08 Sauvignon Superiore actually went through to the finals. This lovely wine has distinct notes of sage, pennyroyal and tomato leaf before the subtle palate unfolds with admirable dynamism. Ripe pear is the keynote of the complex fragrances proffered by the slightly rustic but very full and juicy '08 Pinot Grigio. The '08 Chardonnay is all elegance, giving subtle spring flowers and fragrant fruit followed by a fresh, savoury palate. And the '08 Friulano is equally successful, confirming that whites do better than reds here.

Adriano Gigante

VIA ROCCA BERNARDA, 3
33040 CORNO DI ROSAZZO [UD]
TEL. 0432755835
www.adrianogigante.it

CELLAR SALES
PRE-BOOKED VISITS

ANNUAL PRODUCTION **60,000 bottles**
HECTARES UNDER VINE **13**
VITICULTURE METHOD **Conventional**

This operation started in 1957 when Ferruccio Gigante noted that an already existing Tocai Friulano vineyard, known as Storico, produced exceptional wine. He gave up his job as a miller, which he had been doing for 40 years, and concentrated on grape growing with his sons Arturo, Silvano and Luciano. Today, Adriano Gigante and his wife Giuliana keep up that family tradition on the slopes of Rocca Bernarda.

Everyone in the family contributes but Adriano's successes are mainly due to the wine experience of his cousin, Ariedo, who ensures that the cellar's standards are impeccable. It is true to say that over the years, the most exciting Gigante wines have been the ones from the Vigneto Storico planted by grandfather Ferruccio. That Friulano is extremely varietal, complex in its aromatics and slightly smoky while the palate is mouthfilling, subtle and well-poised. The '05 Picolit is soft and creamy, attractively sweet and very long-lingering. "Broodingly dark, attractively tannic and complex" sums up the '06 Refosco. Finally, the '08 Sauvignon is well-defined, juicy and flows across the palate.

Foffani		
○ Friuli Aquileia Sauvignon Sup. '08	♟♟	4*
○ Friuli Aquileia Chardonnay Sup. '08	♟♟	4*
○ Friuli Aquileia Friulano Sup. '08	♟♟	4*
○ Friuli Aquileia Pinot Grigio Sup. '08	♟♟	4*
● Friuli Aquileia Cabernet Franc '07	♟	4
● Friuli Aquileia Refosco P. R. '06	♟	4
● Friuli Aquileia Cabernet Sauvignon '05	♟♟	4
○ Friuli Aquileia Friulano Sup. '07	♟♟	4
○ Friuli Aquileia Pinot Grigio Sup. '06	♟♟	4

Adriano Gigante		
○ COF Friulano Vign. Storico '08	♟♟	5
○ COF Picolit '05	♟♟	7
● COF Refosco P. R. '06	♟♟	4*
○ COF Sauvignon '08	♟♟	4*
○ COF Friulano '08	♟♟	4*
● COF Merlot '06	♟♟	4*
● COF Rosso Giudizio '06	♟♟	5
○ COF Chardonnay '08	♟	4
○ COF Pinot Grigio '08	♟	4
○ COF Ribolla Gialla '08	♟	4
○ COF Verduzzo Friulano '06	♟	5
⊙ Ribolla Nera Brut Rosè	♟	5
○ COF Tocai Friulano Storico '00	♟♟♟	5
○ COF Tocai Friulano Vign. Storico '06	♟♟♟	5
○ COF Tocai Friulano Vign. Storico '05	♟♟♟	5
○ COF Tocai Friulano Vign. Storico '03	♟♟♟	5

Gradis'ciutta

LOC. GIASBANA, 10
34070 SAN FLORIANO DEL COLLIO [GO]
TEL. 0481390237
robigradis@libero.it

CELLAR SALES
PRE-BOOKED VISITS

ANNUAL PRODUCTION **60,000 bottles**
HECTARES UNDER VINE **17**
VITICULTURE METHOD **Conventional**

A small village near San Floriano del Collio has lent its name to the winery that Robert Princic runs with an authority that belies his years. For some time, Roberto has been one of the supporters of the move to make Collio the name of a territory-identifying wine. As Roberto knows, it will take time and he has already renewed some of his vineyards. Soon, they will come onstream, enabling him to make the wines he has in mind.

The varieties that go into Collio Bianco Bratinis '07 aren't important – if you're really interested, they are chardonnay, sauvignon and ribolla gialla – for the main thing is that this is a great wine. Vinified exclusively in steel, it has complex aromatics that meld the profiles of the three varieties into an invitingly original bouquet. Pineapple on the palate takes you through to a pleasingly mineral-veined finish. Collio Bianco Bratinis went through to the finals with Roberto's '08 Pinot Grigio, a varietal, ripe pear-led wine with well-defined flavours. Also excellent and true to their varieties are the Ribolla Gialla '08, Friulano '08 Cabernet Franc '07.

○ Collio Bianco Bratinis '07	TT	4*
○ Collio Pinot Grigio '08	TT	4*
● Collio Cabernet Franc '07	TT	4*
○ Collio Friulano '08	TT	4*
○ Collio Ribolla Gialla '08	TT	4*
○ Collio Sauvignon '08	T	4
○ Collio Bianco Bratinis '06	YY	4*
○ Collio Bianco del Tùzz '05	YY	4*
● Collio Cabernet Franc '05	YY	4
○ Collio Chardonnay '07	YY	4
○ Collio Chardonnay '06	YY	4
○ Collio Friulano '07	YY	4
○ Collio Pinot Grigio '07	YY	4
○ Collio Pinot Grigio '06	YY	4
○ Collio Ribolla Gialla '07	YY	4*
○ Collio Ribolla Gialla '06	YY	4
○ Collio Sauvignon '07	YY	4

★★ Gravner

FRAZ. OSLAVIA
LOC. LENZUOLO BIANCO, 9
34070 GORIZIA
TEL. 048130882
www.gravner.it

ANNUAL PRODUCTION **39,000 bottles**
HECTARES UNDER VINE **18**
VITICULTURE METHOD **Natural**

It's especially difficult to write about Josko Gravner's wines this year. His young son Miha, who was also Josko's righthand man on the estate, died in a motorbike accident. We offer our condolences here to Josko and respectfully urge him to carry on his extraordinary winemaking adventure, which is taking him along paths hitherto untrodden. Josko's amphora-fermented wines will always be controversial. Some love them, some loathe them. We remain in the first category.

The '05 Ribolla Anfora is a very exciting wine and one of the most successful editions of recent years. It is almost amber in colour and veined with smokiness, giving beeswax and nuts on the nose. The assertively savoury flavour verges on the briny. It goes without saying that this is light years away from a standard Friulian Ribolla. The skins were left in the amphora in contact with the wine for months. Breg '05, from sauvignon, pinot grigio, riesling and chardonnay, is deeper in colour and perhaps a shade less elegant on the nose, where hints of oxidation tend to emerge. But there's plenty of power on the tannin-edged palate before the finish signs off with almondiness.

○ Ribolla Anfora '05	TTT	8
○ Breg Anfora '05	TT	8
○ Breg '00	YYY	8
○ Breg '99	YYY	8
○ Breg '98	YYY	8
○ Breg Anfora '03	YYY	8
○ Breg Anfora '02	YYY	8
○ Ribolla Anfora '04	YYY	8
○ Ribolla Anfora '02	YYY	8
○ Ribolla Anfora '01	YYY	8
○ Breg Anfora '04	YY	8
○ Ribolla Anfora '03	YY	8
● Rosso Gravner '02	YY	8
● Rosso Gravner '01	YY	8

Iole Grillo

VIA ALBANA, 60
33040 PREPOTTO [UD]
TEL. 0432713201
www.vinigrillo.it

CELLAR SALES
PRE-BOOKED VISITS
VISITOR FACILITIES

ANNUAL PRODUCTION **40,000 bottles**
HECTARES UNDER VINE **8.5**
VITICULTURE METHOD **Conventional**

If you are heading into Albana, near Prepotto, in the Colli Orientali del Friuli, you can't miss the spot where the road widens at the votive chapel of Santa Justina and the impressive gateway of an 18th-century villa. This is the home of the Grillo estate, now run by Anna Muzzolini with help from her husband, Andrea, and mother, Iole Grillo. Careful restructuring has recovered the charming spaces now used for ageing wine in barrels of various sizes and for the winery's delightful farmstay accommodation.

For the past few years, Giuseppe Tosoratti has been lending a capable hand in the vineyards and cellar but Anna herself makes all the strategic decisions. Often, these require courage but Anna never puts a foot wrong. One winning move was to discontinue the long-established white Santa Justina blend and vinify the Ribolla Gialla as a monovarietal. It was an instant success. The '07 edition is a lovely gold colour with a headily pervasive bouquet. Structure is excellent and vibrant minerality perks up the delicious palate. Flecks of garnet vein the intense ruby of Anna's characterful, very varietal Merlot Riserva '05, a rare example of excellence from a challenging growing year.

Jacùss

FRAZ. MONTINA
V.LE KENNEDY, 35A
33040 TORREANO [UD]
TEL. 0432715147
www.jacuss.com

PRE-BOOKED VISITS

ANNUAL PRODUCTION **50,000 bottles**
HECTARES UNDER VINE **10**
VITICULTURE METHOD **Conventional**

Sandro and Andrea Jacuzzi have made a solid name for themselves in Friulian wine. Their compact estate is a classic family-run affair and the two work amazingly well together managing plots scattered across the hills at Montina, a small district of the municipality of Torreano di Cividale, and keeping up with tasks in the cellar. The wines are as uncomplicatedly sincere, controlled and true to their territory as the brothers are themselves.

In earlier Guides, we have noted that the quality of the cellar's whites and reds alternated, a clear sign that both are extremely well made, but this year the whites were distinctly superior. Top of our list was the green-flecked Friulano '08 with its intense acacia blossom and fragrant fruit aromas leading into an invitingly clean, consistent palate. Also excellent is the appealingly fragranced '08 Sauvignon, which unveils a juicy palate with plenty of heft. High marks also went to the impeccably varietal Pinot Bianco '08 while the Schioppettino '07, Tazzelenghe '05 and Merlot '06 are well enough executed but lack a little structure and personality.

○ COF Ribolla Gialla '07	♟♟	4*
● COF Merlot Ris. '05	♟♟	5
○ COF Chardonnay '08	♟	4
● COF Refosco P. R. '07	♟	4
○ COF Sauvignon '08	♟	4
● COF Schioppettino '07	♟	5
● COF Refosco P. R. '06	♟♟	4
● COF Refosco P. R. '05	♟♟	4
● COF Rosso Guardafuoco '04	♟♟	5
● COF Rosso Guardafuoco '03	♟♟	5
○ COF Sauvignon '07	♟♟	4*
○ COF Sauvignon '06	♟♟	4

○ COF Friulano '08	♟♟	4*
○ COF Pinot Bianco '08	♟♟	4*
○ COF Sauvignon '08	♟♟	4*
● COF Merlot '06	♟	4
● COF Schioppettino Fucs e Flamis '07	♟	4
● COF Tazzelenghe '05	♟	5
○ COF Picolit '05	♟♟	7
○ COF Picolit '04	♟♟	7
○ COF Pinot Bianco '07	♟♟	4*
○ COF Pinot Bianco '06	♟♟	4*
● COF Refosco P. R. '05	♟♟	4
○ COF Tocai Friulano '06	♟♟	4

★★ Jermann

FRAZ. RUTTARS
LOC. TRUSSIO, 11
34070 DOLEGNA DEL COLLIO [GO]
TEL. 0481888080
www.jermann.it

ANNUAL PRODUCTION **750,000 bottles**
HECTARES UNDER VINE **110**
VITICULTURE METHOD **Conventional**

We have already told you about Silvio Jermann's magnificent new cellar at Trussio, near Ruttars. This is where the estate's flagship wines are made, among the vineyards that supply Capo Martino and Pignolo Vigna Truss. The new facility complements, but does not replace the original base at Villanova di Farra, which is still operational and where the offices are located. Silvio is very proud of his family's roots and is constantly sending out central European signals, for example on his labels.

Three very well-earned Glasses went to the stunning '07 Vintage Tunina, the cellar's emblematic wine and created more than three decades ago from what Silvio calls a "folly of youth". Folly it may have been but this lip-smacking white is the wine that made the winery's fortune. It's a regal blend of sauvignon and chardonnay with dashes of ribolla gialla, malvasia istriana and picolit. The star-bright gold-flecked straw heralds complex, elegant honey and wild flower aromatics, fullness, luscious fruit and interminable length. W... Dreams '07, a butter-rich, caressing Chardonnay is also superb and the appealingly varietal concentration of Pignolo Vigna Truss'04 finishes triumphantly.

Kante

FRAZ. SAN PELAGIO
LOC. PREPOTTO, 1A
34011 DUINO AURISINA [TS]
TEL. 040200255
kante.edi@libero.it

ANNUAL PRODUCTION **40,000 bottles**
HECTARES UNDER VINE **13**
VITICULTURE METHOD **Natural**

Edi Kante's cellar is a monument to winemaking. Carved out of the living Carso rock, it perfectly reflects the personality of its creator. Edi is a volcano of ideas, a poet, a painter, a man of sensitivity and tenaciously inquisitive. A child of his land, he has experienced the harsh side of life and knows that you need imagination and pluck to overcome its difficulties. Never one to conform, Edi trod his own path, one that others are now following, to raise the profile of Carso wines.

Orderly semi-circular rows of barriques trace the cellar's elliptical configuration, its rugged, glittering walls ensuring constant temperature and humidity. Here in the silent bowels of the Carso, Edi's wines continue to breathe the salty breezes that arrive from mysterious underground bays. Such slow rhythms impress upon the wines unique characteristics. Take the marvellous minerally '06 Malvasia, a mouthfilling varietal wine with freshness, softness and balance. A Three Glass wine. But the dry, firm-bodied '06 Vitovska is equally amazing with its candied peel and gunflint aromatics, as is the alluring minerality of the '06 Chardonnay..

○ Vintage Tunina '07	♟♟♟+	8
● Pignolo Vigna Truss '04	♟♟	7
○ Vinnae '08	♟♟	5
○ W.... Dreams... .... '07	♟♟	7
● Blau&Blau '07	♟♟	5
○ Capo Martino '07	♟♟	7
○ Chardonnay '08	♟♟	5
○ Sauvignon '08	♟♟	5
○ Traminer Aromatico '08	♟	5
○ Capo Martino '05	♟♟♟	7
○ Vintage Tunina '01	♟♟♟	8
○ Vintage Tunina '00	♟♟♟	7
○ Vintage Tunina '99	♟♟♟	7
○ Vintage Tunina '97	♟♟♟	6
○ W.... Dreams... .... '06	♟♟♟	7

○ Carso Malvasia '06	♟♟♟	6
○ Carso Chardonnay '06	♟♟	6
○ Carso Vitovska '06	♟♟	6
○ Carso Chardonnay Sel. '01	♟♟	7
○ Carso Sauvignon '06	♟♟	6
○ Carso Malvasia '05	♟♟♟	6
○ Carso Malvasia '98	♟♟♟	6
○ Carso Sauvignon '92	♟♟♟	6
○ Carso Sauvignon '91	♟♟♟	6
○ Chardonnay '94	♟♟♟	6
○ Chardonnay '90	♟♟♟	6
○ Carso Chardonnay '05	♟♟	6
○ Carso Chardonnay Sel. '00	♟♟	7

★ Edi Keber

LOC. ZEGLA, 17
34071 CORMÒNS [GO]
TEL. 048161184
edi.keber@virgilio.it

CELLAR SALES
PRE-BOOKED VISITS

ANNUAL PRODUCTION **70,000 bottles**
HECTARES UNDER VINE **10**
VITICULTURE METHOD **Natural**

This has been a great year for Edi Keber. At last, he has managed to implement the project he has been pursuing for nearly 20 years. He has made just one white and called it simply Collio. We think others will follow. It could be that Collio, no longer with any mention of the variety, will become the territory's signature white. Helping Edi on the estate is his son Kristian, who finished his oenology studies a few years ago.

Edi first gained attention for his superb Tocai Friulano, which of course he continues to release, but it is also an integral part of his Collio – 70 per cent, in fact – while the remaining 30 per cent is ribolla gialla and malvasia istriana. The Collio Riserva is from the same varieties but in equal parts. It's fermented in wood and bottled in a limited number of magnums. There were Three Glasses straight away for the Collio '08. This fantastic wine gives complex aromatics layered over an intriguing benzene-like backdrop and a close-knit, savoury palate. The Riserva '06 has depth and structure in which to show off its lovely oak and exciting minerality.

Renato Keber

LOC. ZEGLA, 15
34071 CORMÒNS [GO]
TEL. 0481639844
www.renatokeber.it

CELLAR SALES
PRE-BOOKED VISITS
VISITOR FACILITIES

ANNUAL PRODUCTION **70,000 bottles**
HECTARES UNDER VINE **15**
VITICULTURE METHOD **Conventional**

It all started when great-grandfather Franz Keber put down roots at Zegla, in the Collio, back in the late 19th century. His son, also called Franz, took over and then came Mirko, whose son Renato now farms an estate with excellent sites and great aspects. Renato is well aware of the potential of his property and makes every effort to promote it. That's why he has called his very successful Friulano Zegla, also the name of the farmstay facilities run by his wife Savina.

Renato's winemaking style is crisp and modern but he respects tradition, the rhythms of nature and the varietal characteristics of each vine type he vinifies. The reward for all this hard work comes in the shape of the Three Glasses earned by Renato's wonderful '05 Friulano Zegla. After maturing slowly in large wood and then steel, it spent another two years in glass. Now that it is on the shelves, it gives a complex swath of balsam-laced fragrances preceding a rich, long-lingering palate. The attractively oaky '05 Grici Sauvignon is also lovely while the '06 Ribolla Gialla and '03 Merlot are worthy companions.

O Collio Bianco '08	♥♥♥	5*
O Collio Bianco Ris. '06	♥♥	7
O Collio Bianco '04	♀♀♀	5
O Collio Bianco '02	♀♀♀	4
O Collio Tocai Friulano '07	♀♀♀	5
O Collio Tocai Friulano '06	♀♀♀	5
O Collio Tocai Friulano '05	♀♀♀	5
O Collio Tocai Friulano '03	♀♀♀	4*
O Collio Tocai Friulano '01	♀♀♀	4
O Collio Tocai Friulano '99	♀♀♀	4
O Collio Tocai Friulano '97	♀♀♀	4
O Collio Tocai Friulano '95	♀♀♀	4

O Collio Friulano Zegla '05	♥♥♥	5*
O Collio Sauvignon Grici '05	♥♥	6
● Collio Merlot Grici Ris. '03	♥♥	6
O Collio Ribolla Gialla Extreme '06	♥♥	5
O Collio Bianco Beli Grici '05	♀♀	4
O Collio Pinot Grigio '06	♀♀	4*
O Collio Ribolla Gialla Extreme '05	♀♀	5
O Collio Sauvignon '06	♀♀	4
O Collio Tocai Friulano '06	♀♀	4

Thomas Kitzmüller

FRAZ. BRAZZANO
VIA XXIV MAGGIO, 56
34070 CORMÒNS [GO]
TEL. 048160853
www.kitzmueller.it

CELLAR SALES
PRE-BOOKED VISITS
VISITOR FACILITIES
FOOD

ANNUAL PRODUCTION 23,000 bottles
HECTARES UNDER VINE 4
VITICULTURE METHOD Conventional

This charming little winery has only four hectares under vine. The location is Brazzano, in the municipality of Cormòns, and the owner is Thomas Kitzmüller, a committed producer who manages his vines using low environmental impact techniques and integrated pest control. The cellar is a restructured 18th-century farm complex which includes the Mummelhaus, a picturesque farmstay that immerses visitors in an atmosphere from another age.

We were particularly impressed by Thomas's wines this year. His '08 version of a notoriously difficult grape like traminer has a wealth of appeal. The elegantly refined bouquet precedes a palate that shows nicely subtle on entry but then unveils great personality and length. The Ribolla Gialla '08 is gutsily assertive on nose and palate while the green-flecked '08 Sauvignon is utterly varietal in its vegetal notes and fragrant fruitiness. Both versions of the '08 Friulano are distinctive, the mouthfilling Collio giving plenty of juicy pulp and the refreshing Isonzo being more upfront.

Albino Kurtin

LOC. NOVALI, 9
34071 CORMÒNS [GO]
TEL. 048160685

CELLAR SALES
PRE-BOOKED VISITS

ANNUAL PRODUCTION 70,000 bottles
HECTARES UNDER VINE 11.00
VITICULTURE METHOD Conventional

Kurtin was founded in 1906 and has been in the family for three generations. It's at Novali, the famously good premium wine territory near Cormòns that produces such superb whites. The operation is now run by Albino, who has inherited the family's knack with the vine. His new cellar has modern technology and he skilfully combines steel with large Slavonian oak casks to get the best out of his wines in full respect of tradition.

This year, the quality of the wines we tasted was very impressive, just reward for Albino's passion and commitment. Malvasia '08 is stunning and went through to the finals thanks to the elegance of its aromas, the exuberance of its fruit and the appeal of the savoury, well-sustained palate. But the muscular '08 Friulano was in the same class, layering citrus and pears over varietal aromas. Another great wine is Diamante Nero, a Bordeaux blend created in 2006 to celebrate Kurtin's centenary, as was the pinot bianco, ribolla and chardonnay Opera Prima Bianco, obtained from slightly overripe grapes.

○ Collio Ribolla Gialla '08	♀♀ 4*
○ Collio Traminer Aromatico '08	♀♀ 4*
○ Collio Friulano '08	♀♀ 4*
○ Collio Sauvignon '08	♀♀ 4*
○ Friuli Isonzo Friulano Corte Marie '08	♀♀ 3*
○ Collio Sauvignon '07	♀♀ 4
○ Collio Tocai Friulano '06	♀♀ 4
○ Collio Traminer Aromatico '07	♀♀ 4
○ Friuli Isonzo Tocai Friulano Corte Marie '06	♀♀ 3*

○ Collio Malvasia '08	♀♀ 4*
○ Collio Friulano '08	♀♀ 4*
○ Collio Pinot Grigio '08	♀♀ 4*
● Diamante Nero '07	♀♀ 4*
● Collio Cabernet Franc '07	♀ 4
● Collio Merlot '07	♀ 4
○ Collio Pinot Grigio '06	♀♀ 3
○ Collio Sauvignon '07	♀♀ 4
○ Collio Sauvignon '06	♀♀ 3
○ Opera Prima Bianco '07	♀♀ 4

★ Lis Neris

VIA GAVINANA, 5
34070 SAN LORENZO ISONTINO [GO]
TEL. 048180105
www.lisneris.it

CELLAR SALES
PRE-BOOKED VISITS

ANNUAL PRODUCTION 350,000 bottles
HECTARES UNDER VINE 54
VITICULTURE METHOD Conventional

Alvaro Pecorari is the fourth generation of a family that settled at San Lorenzo Isontino at the end of the 19th century. In the 1990s, Alvaro gave the estate a thorough makeover that led to the success of the Lis Neris style. Helping our hero are his wife Loredana and daughter Federica but we should not forget the family's commitment to the Francesca Pecorari foundation, a not-for-profit enterprise for underprivileged children in south east Asia.

The Lis Neris vineyards are on tableland between the Slovenian border and the right bank of Isonzo river. There are four sites: Gris, Picol, Jurosa and Neris. Alvaro takes care of winemaking personally, giving the wines their distinctive style, which marries softness with complexity. He always has us expecting excellence and while this year he may not have won our top award, his '07 Chardonnay Jurosa came very close indeed. Its ripe tropical fruits are lifted by perfectly gauged oak and it displays full body and faultless balance. Another stunner is the friulano-only Fiore di Campo '08, an elegantly well-defined wine of depth and power with a refreshing almondy touch in the finale.

Livon

FRAZ. DOLEGNANO
VIA MONTAREZZA, 33
33048 SAN GIOVANNI AL NATISONE [UD]
TEL. 0432757173
www.livon.it

CELLAR SALES

ANNUAL PRODUCTION 700,000 bottles
HECTARES UNDER VINE 105
VITICULTURE METHOD Conventional

The story here is a relatively new one. It began with Dorina Livon and is carried on by his sons Valneo and Tonino, who have expanded amazingly in a just a few years. Now the Livon group has five labels. The original Livon winery is at Dolegnano. RoncAlto is the label reserved for a wonderful vineyard in the Collio Goriziano. Another 110 hectares on the Friulian flatlands supply Villa Chiopris. Outside Friuli, the brothers have purchased Borgo Salcetino at Radda in Chianti and Colsanto in Umbria.

The expert Rinaldo Stocco has been looking after winemaking in Friuli for some time. Valneo and Tonino, now fighting their battles on five fronts, are always on the lookout for new challenges. New developments are the order of the day and this year there are two fantastic new wines. Malvasia Soluna '08 went forward to the taste-offs and the other newcomer is Collio Bianco Solarco '08, from friulano and ribolla gialla. But the biggest satisfaction this year, and not for the first time, comes from Braide Alte, the Livons' unique medley of chardonnay, sauvignon, picolit and moscato giallo, which was back among the Three Glasses after a few years' absence. Just reward for the Livons' tenacity.

○ Fiore di Campo '08	�troph�troph	5
○ Friuli Isonzo Chardonnay Jurosa '07	�troph�troph	5
○ Confini '07	�troph�troph	6
○ Friuli Isonzo Sauvignon '08	�troph�troph	4*
● Lis Neris '05	�troph�troph	6
○ Friuli Isonzo Pinot Grigio Gris '07	�troph	5
○ Fiore di Campo '06	�troph�troph�troph	4
○ Friuli Isonzo Chardonnay Jurosa '00	�troph�troph�troph	5
○ Friuli Isonzo Pinot Grigio Gris '01	�troph�troph�troph	6
○ Friuli Isonzo Pinot Grigio Gris '98	�troph�troph�troph	5
○ Friuli Isonzo Sauvignon Dom Picòl '96	�troph�troph�troph	5
○ Lis '03	�troph�troph�troph	6
○ Lis '99	�troph�troph�troph	6
○ Pinot Grigio Gris '04	�troph�troph�troph	5
○ Sauvignon Picol '06	�troph�troph�troph	4
○ Tal Lùc '02	�troph�troph�troph	7
○ Tal Lûc '99	�troph�troph�troph	6

○ Braide Alte '07	�troph�troph�troph	6
○ Malvasia Soluna '08	�troph�troph	5
● COF Pignolo ElDoro '06	�troph�troph	6
○ Collio Bianco Solarco '08	�troph�troph	5
○ Collio Friulano Ronc di Zorz '08	�troph�troph	5
○ Collio Friulano '08	�troph	5
○ Collio Pinot Bianco '08	�troph	4
○ Collio Ribolla Gialla RoncAlto '08	�troph	5
● Scioppettino Picotis '06	�troph	5
○ Braide Alte '00	�troph�troph�troph	6
○ Braide Alte Grand Cru '98	�troph�troph�troph	6
○ Braide Alte Grand Cru '97	�troph�troph�troph	6
○ Braide Alte Grand Cru '96	�troph�troph�troph	6
● COF Refosco P. R. Riul '02	�troph�troph�troph	5
● TiareBlù '00	�troph�troph�troph	6

Tenuta Luisa

FRAZ. CORONA
VIA CORMÒNS, 19
34070 MARIANO DEL FRIULI [GO]
TEL. 048169680
www.viniluisa.com

CELLAR SALES
PRE-BOOKED VISITS

ANNUAL PRODUCTION **300,000 bottles**
HECTARES UNDER VINE **79**
VITICULTURE METHOD **Conventional**

It was back in 1937 that Francesco Luisa, a 37-year-old widower with six children to raise, had the opportunity to buy a few hectares at Corona, a village near Mariano del Friuli. Francesco handed over to Delciso and then Eddi, who was only 13 when he joined his father to work on the estate. Eddi and his wife Nella patiently and courageously built up the business, which today is run by their sons, Michele and Davide, the former an oenologist and the latter a qualified agricultural technician.

The brothers are still helped out by Eddi, who is ever willing to turn his hand to any necessary task. Working with such modern cellar equipment means that Luisa wines get plenty of attention and the results speak for themselves. In earlier Guides, we have noted that the base wines tended to outperform the selections but this year it was a splendid '07 from the I Ferretti line that topped our score sheet. Wafts of tropical fruits and confectioner's cream set up a tangily assertive palate. The attractively green-flecked '08 Friulano is juicy and varietal. Complex is the adjective for the alluring '08 Chardonnay and the '08 Pinot Grigio is excellent.

Magnàs

LOC. BOATINA
VIA CORONA, 47
34071 CORMÒNS [GO]
TEL. 048160991
www.magnas.it

CELLAR SALES
PRE-BOOKED VISITS
VISITOR FACILITIES
FOOD

ANNUAL PRODUCTION **25,000 bottles**
HECTARES UNDER VINE **10**
VITICULTURE METHOD **Conventional**

The location is Boatina at Cormòns. The estate is a classic family-run winery where love of land and heritage passes seamlessly from one generation to the next. Among grandfather Giovanni's heritage to Luciano was Magnàs, the nickname by which the entire family continues to be known. Luciano's wife Sonia looks after the delightful farmstay accommodation while son Andrea is in charge of making and distributing the estate's wines.

And the '08 Malvasia, Sauvignon and Friulano are tangible proof of the progress Andrea has been making in the past few years. The Malvasia in particular is admirably varietal, its crisp, pervasive nose introducing an alluringly flavoursome palate. Intense, wisteria-like florality and a tangy, thrusting palate are the Sauvignon's calling cards while the Friulano stands out for its depth on the nose and textbook varietal character. Andrea's '07 Merlot is an entrancingly dark ruby, with flowers on the nose and a savoury palate that needs a little more time to absorb its new oak. Finally, the fruit-forward '08 Pinot Grigio and Chardonnay are wonderfully easy to drink.

O Chardonnay I Ferretti '07	♙♙ 5
O Friuli Isonzo Chardonnay '08	♙♙ 4*
O Friuli Isonzo Friulano '08	♙♙ 4*
O Friuli Isonzo Pinot Grigio '08	♙♙ 4*
● Friuli Isonzo Cabernet Franc I Ferretti '05	♙ 5
O Friuli Isonzo Pinot Bianco '08	♙ 4
O Friuli Isonzo Sauvignon '08	♙ 4
O Spumante Brut Ribolla Gialla '08	♙ 4
O Friuli Isonzo Tocai Friulano '03	♙♙♙ 4*
O Friuli Isonzo Chardonnay '07	♟♟ 4
O Friuli Isonzo Pinot Bianco '07	♟♟ 4
O Friuli Isonzo Pinot Bianco '06	♟♟ 4*
O Friuli Isonzo Pinot Grigio '06	♟♟ 4
O Friuli Isonzo Sauvignon '07	♟♟ 4
O Friuli Isonzo Sauvignon '06	♟♟ 4*

O Friuli Isonzo Friulano '08	♙♙ 4*
O Friuli Isonzo Malvasia '08	♙♙ 5*
O Friuli Isonzo Sauvignon '08	♙♙ 4*
O Friuli Isonzo Chardonnay '08	♙ 4
● Friuli Isonzo Merlot '07	♙ 5
O Friuli Isonzo Pinot Grigio '08	♙ 4
O Friuli Isonzo Chardonnay '07	♟♟ 4
O Friuli Isonzo Pinot Grigio '07	♟♟ 4
O Friuli Isonzo Pinot Grigio '06	♟♟ 5
O Friuli Isonzo Sauvignon '07	♟♟ 4
O Friuli Isonzo Sauvignon '06	♟♟ 5

Valerio Marinig

VIA BROLO, 41
33040 PREPOTTO [UD]
TEL. 0432713012
www.marinig.it

CELLAR SALES
PRE-BOOKED VISITS

ANNUAL PRODUCTION **25,000 bottles**
HECTARES UNDER VINE **8**
VITICULTURE METHOD **Conventional**

Valerio Marinig's winery has always been a family affair since great-grandfather Luigi set it up in 1921. It passed to his father Sergio, who still takes an active part in proceedings, but when Valerio completed his education, he took over responsibility for estate management and winemaking. Valerio's mother, Marisa, is a sommelière and looks after visitors while his young wife Michela takes care of distribution and keeps on top of administration.

Progress in the cellar is obvious with every new vintage and this year, a superb '08 Friulano came within an ace of a top award. The lovely straw yellow is flecked with greenish highlights and the impeccably varietal aromatics are reminiscent of spring flowers, lime blossom honey, medlar, golden delicious apple and almonds. But it's the palate that impresses. We also loved the '07 Merlot. It's a little closed on the nose but the deliciously juicy, full-bodied palate is wonderfully well defined. The Cabernet Franc '07 is a worthy stablemate with its varietal greens and delicious drinkability. People round here love Schioppettino and the '07 has plenty of thrust and a nice hint of balsam.

Masut da Rive

VIA MANZONI, 82
34070 MARIANO DEL FRIULI [GO]
TEL. 048169200
www.masutdarive.com

CELLAR SALES
PRE-BOOKED VISITS

ANNUAL PRODUCTION **100,000 bottles**
HECTARES UNDER VINE **20**
VITICULTURE METHOD **Conventional**

Masut da Rive used to be the nickname of the Gallo family at Mariano del Friuli, in the Isonzo zone. In order to export to the United States, Silvano Gallo had to change his winery's name a few years ago after a legal tussle with an American producer of the same name. Silvano handed over to his sons Fabrizio and Marco some time ago but he is still active, particularly out in the vineyard.

It's a well-known fact that the geology of the Isonzo river plain is highly suitable for viticulture. The soil is gravelly and rich in minerals, especially iron, which makes it ideal for white and red wines. The Gallos' '08 Pinot Grigio is a case in point. Elegantly onionskin in hue and varietal in its pear and yeast fragrances, it's a delightfully dynamic wine. Bramble jam aromas and a soft, juicy palate are the keynotes of the Cabernet Sauvignon Riserva '05, which closes with a touch of greens. The purplish Refosco '07 offers young tannins and a violets, black berry fruits and spice nose. Finally, the almond-laced '08 Pinot Bianco and Chardonnay are true to type and savoury.

○ COF Friulano '08	♀♀	4*
● COF Cabernet Franc '07	♀♀	4*
● COF Merlot '07	♀♀	4*
● Biel Cûr Rosso '06	♀	5
○ COF Pinot Bianco '08	♀	4
● COF Refosco P. R. '07	♀	4
○ COF Sauvignon '08	♀	4
● COF Schioppettino '07	♀	4
○ COF Pinot Bianco '07	♀♀	4
○ COF Pinot Bianco '06	♀♀	4
○ COF Sauvignon '07	♀♀	4
○ COF Sauvignon '06	♀♀	4

○ Friuli Isonzo Pinot Grigio '08	♀♀	4*
● Friuli Isonzo Cabernet Sauvignon '07	♀♀	4*
○ Friuli Isonzo Chardonnay '08	♀♀	4*
○ Friuli Isonzo Pinot Bianco '08	♀♀	4*
● Friuli Isonzo Refosco P. R. '07	♀♀	4*
○ Friuli Isonzo Friulano '08	♀	4
● Friuli Isonzo Merlot '07	♀	4
● Friuli Isonzo Rosso Semidis '06	♀	4
○ Friuli Isonzo Sauvignon '08	♀	4
○ Friuli Isonzo Tocai Friulano '04	♀♀♀	4*
● Friuli Isonzo Cabernet Sauvignon '06	♀♀	4
● Friuli Isonzo Cabernet Sauvignon '05	♀♀	4*
● Friuli Isonzo Merlot '06	♀♀	4
○ Friuli Isonzo Pinot Bianco '07	♀♀	4
○ Friuli Isonzo Pinot Bianco '06	♀♀	4
○ Friuli Isonzo Pinot Grigio '07	♀♀	4
● Friuli Isonzo Refosco P. R. '06	♀♀	4
○ Friuli Isonzo Sauvignon '07	♀♀	4

Davino Meroi

VIA STRETTA, 7B
33042 BUTTRIO [UD]
TEL. 0432674025
parco.meroi@virgilio.it

★ Miani

VIA PERUZZI, 10
33042 BUTTRIO [UD]
TEL. 0432674327
aletulissi@libero.it

CELLAR SALES
PRE-BOOKED VISITS

CELLAR SALES
PRE-BOOKED VISITS

ANNUAL PRODUCTION **20,000 bottles**
HECTARES UNDER VINE **12**
VITICULTURE METHOD **Conventional**

ANNUAL PRODUCTION **8,000 bottles**
HECTARES UNDER VINE **16**
VITICULTURE METHOD **Natural**

In the superb hill country at Buttrio, a grand cru of the Colli Orientali del Friuli, Paolo Meroi continues to tend the vineyards planted by his grandfather Domenico. He also manages the Trattoria al Parco, which has been open for more than a century and where Paolo's wines partner traditional Friulian cooking and lovely grilled meat. In the cellar, Enzo Pontoni (well known as the owner of the Miani cellar) helps out and the range is a fixture in the front rank of the region's wine scene.

Everyone knows Paolo matures his wines in wood and his fragrant, mouthfilling '07 Sauvignon is a fine example, having acquired enviable complexity and breadth of aromatics from its stay in oak. The '07 Verduzzo is very good indeed. Its amber hue introduces honey, almond crisp and soft toffee aromas, and sweet, lingeringly concentrated length. Austerity is the keynote of the wonderfully deep '06 Rosso Dominin with its spice and briary fruit. All the other bottles scored well, confirming that the entire Meroi line is up there with the very best.

This tiny cellar in the Colli Orientali is owned by Enzo Pontoni, a seriously committed wine man who has turned it into an emblem of Italy's garage wineries. Output is only a few thousand bottles a year, and there are many wine types, so Enzo's bottles tend to become cult objects with many wine lovers. This year, the best of the range had not gone into bottle when we were tasting so the Guide review is inevitably lower key.

We only tasted and assessed three wines, all of them white. We thought the best was the '07 Sauvignon Saurint, a wine whose very varietal aromatics are free of the oakiness that in the past had led us to raise an eyebrow on more than one occasion. The '07 Chardonnay was also firing on all four cylinders. Although less varietal than some versions, its technical excellence and barely hinted-at oak are irresistible. Wood tends to mask the fruit of the second Sauvignon, Banel '07, rather more, with lactic notes and oak in evidence.

● COF Rosso Dominin '06	♟♟ 8
○ COF Sauvignon '07	♟♟ 5
○ COF Verduzzo Friulano '07	♟♟ 6
○ COF Chardonnay '08	♟♟ 6
● COF Merlot Ros di Buri '08	♟♟ 6
○ COF Picolit '07	♟♟ 7
○ COF Ribolla Gialla '08	♟♟ 6
● COF Rosso Nestri '06	♟♟ 4*
○ COF Friulano '07	♟♟ 6
○ COF Picolit '06	♟♟ 7
○ COF Pinot Grigio '07	♟♟ 6
● COF Rosso Ros di Buri '06	♟♟ 6
○ COF Tocai Friulano '06	♟♟ 6

○ COF Chardonnay '07	♟♟ 7
○ COF Sauvignon Saurint '07	♟♟ 7
○ COF Sauvignon Banel '07	♟ 7
● Calvari '02	♟♟♟ 8
● COF Bianco '97	♟♟♟ 7
● COF Bianco '96	♟♟♟ 7
● COF Merlot '02	♟♟♟ 8
● COF Merlot '99	♟♟♟ 8
● COF Merlot '98	♟♟♟ 8
● COF Merlot '94	♟♟♟ 6
● COF Merlot Filip '04	♟♟♟ 8
● COF Rosso '97	♟♟♟ 8
● COF Rosso '96	♟♟♟ 8
○ COF Sauvignon '96	♟♟♟ 6
○ COF Tocai Friulano '00	♟♟♟ 7
○ COF Tocai Friulano '99	♟♟♟ 7
○ COF Tocai Friulano '98	♟♟♟ 7
○ COF Tocai Friulano '96	♟♟♟ 6

Moschioni

LOC. GAGLIANO
VIA DORIA, 3
33043 CIVIDALE DEL FRIULI [UD]
TEL. 0432730210
info@moschioni.eu

PRE-BOOKED VISITS

ANNUAL PRODUCTION **40,000 bottles**
HECTARES UNDER VINE **14**
VITICULTURE METHOD **Conventional**

Michele Moschioni is one of the region's finest producers. He supervises every stage of winemaking personally, even though his main love is the vineyard. His son Davide is there to help with the heavy jobs while Michele's wife, Sabrina, looks after the paperwork and distribution. Michele and Sabrina hope their children will soon be following in their footsteps. Alessia and Valentina are still students but started gaining experience during the holidays at cellars abroad, in Argentina and Australia respectively.

When you talk about Michele, you have to mention the fact that he makes exclusively red wines, apart from his Picolit, in a territory that is much better-known for its whites. Michele looks after his vines with meticulous care and the results are awesome, especially where native varieties are concerned. It's always a thrill to win Three Glasses and to win them for a Schioppettino adds extra spice. Michele's '06 is deep in colour, entices with its stylishly spice-veined red and black berry fruit, and shows both power and elegance on the dynamic palate. The same goes for the black berry fruit and liquorice '06 Refosco. Finally, the heady '06 Rosso Celtico Bordeaux blend caresses the palate.

Mulino delle Tolle

FRAZ. SEVEGLIANO
VIA MULINO DELLE TOLLE, 15
33050 BAGNARIA ARSA [UD]
TEL. 0432928113
www.mulinodelletolle.it

VISITOR FACILITIES

ANNUAL PRODUCTION **100,000 bottles**
HECTARES UNDER VINE **22**
VITICULTURE METHOD **Conventional**

On the road that takes you to Grado, between the star-shaped town of Palmanova and the Roman remains of Aquileia, stands the Casa Bianca, a farm complex that served as a lazar house in the 17th century and a customs post under the Habsburgs. This is where oenologist Giorgio Bertossi and his cousin Eliseo have set up their new cellar and a delightful farmstay nestling among the verdant vineyards of the lower Friulian flatlands.

Mulino delle Tolle wines have been coming along nicely and scored higher than last time. In fact, two went on to the national finals. One finalist was the Bianco Palmade '08, an intriguing mix of sauvignon, chardonnay and malvasia with a bouquet of yellow peaches set in a delicious swath of aromatics. In the mouth, it manages to combine power and concentration with great finesse. White peaches dominate the nose of the excellent '08 Friulano, an uncompromisingly varietal wine with lashings of gutsy minerality. All the other wines are attractive and well crafted.

● COF Schioppettino '06	♟♟♟	7
● COF Refosco P. R. '06	♟	5
● COF Rosso Celtico '06	♟♟	6
● COF Rosso Reâl '06	♟♟	6
● COF Pignolo '06	♟	8
● COF Rosso Celtico '04	♟♟♟	6
● COF Pignolo '04	♟♟	8
● COF Refosco P. R. '05	♟♟	5
● COF Refosco P. R. '04	♟♟	5
● COF Rosso Bisest '05	♟♟	6
● COF Rosso Reâl '05	♟♟	6
● COF Rosso Reâl '04	♟♟	6

○ Friuli Aquileia Bianco Palmade '08	♟♟	4*
○ Friuli Aquileia Friulano '08	♟♟	4*
○ Friuli Aquileia Malvasia '08	♟	3
○ Friuli Aquileia Traminer Aromatico '08	♟	4
● Friuli Isonzo Merlot '08	♟	4
● Friuli Isonzo Rosso Sabellius '07	♟	4
○ Friuli Aquileia Bianco Palmade '06	♟♟	4
○ Friuli Aquileia Malvasia '06	♟♟	3*
○ Friuli Aquileia Tocai Friulano '06	♟♟	3*
● Pignolo '06	♟♟	6

Muzic

LOC. BIVIO, 4
34070 SAN FLORIANO DEL COLLIO [GO]
TEL. 0481884201
www.cantinamuzic.it

CELLAR SALES
PRE-BOOKED VISITS

ANNUAL PRODUCTION **90,000 bottles**
HECTARES UNDER VINE **15**
VITICULTURE METHOD **Conventional**

The Muzic winery is situated on the wine and cherry trail that winds up from Gorizia to San Floriano del Collio like a jewel set into the hillslopes. Giovanni, known to one and all as Ivan, and his wife Orietta welcome visitors to their charming underground cellar. Dating from the 16th century, it has bare stone walls and vaulted ceilings that house the small oak barrels where the red wines mature. Tastefully connected to the barrel room is a modern vinification cellar.

Ivan personally supervises all operations in vineyard and cellar, with shrewd advice from consultant oenologist Giorgio Bertossi. Leading the list of excellent Collio whites is an '07 Merlot from the flatlands of the Isonzo DOC. We loved its superb, broodingly dark ruby and above all its elegantly varietal aromas and assertive progression on the palate. Collio Bianco Bric '08 scored well again. This mix of friulano, malvasia istriana and ribolla gialla hints at roses and golden delicious apples. The '08 versions of Pinot Grigio, Sauvignon and Friulano are all appealing and very varietal.

Alessandro Pascolo

LOC. RUTTARS, 1
34070 DOLEGNA DEL COLLIO [GO]
TEL. 048161144
www.vinipascolo.it

CELLAR SALES
PRE-BOOKED VISITS

ANNUAL PRODUCTION **25,000 bottles**
HECTARES UNDER VINE **7**
VITICULTURE METHOD **Conventional**

Angelo Pascolo founded this winery in the 1970s. A successful businessman, he wanted to devote more time to his real passion, the countryside. His son Giuseppe then made the transition from the furniture sector to agriculture and now it is the turn of Alessandro, the first member of the Pascolo family to have spent all his working life in the vineyard. An agronomist, oenologist and sommelier, Alessandro loves to be out among the rows and is always more than willing to show visitors around and chat as they taste the wines.

The vines are on the superb hillslopes of Ruttars, in the municipality of Dolegna del Collio, and they have always yielded wonderful wines. Alessandro earned this Guide debut with a fine range, particularly the stunning Merlot Selezione '06, which went straight into the finals. Despite its youth, it is a very dark ruby while the palate is delightfully well-poised. Another impressive wine is Bianco Agnul '07, a blend of pinot bianco, friulano, malvasia and sauvignon that pervades the nostrils and thrills the palate. The other whites are very good, especially the Pinot Grigio '08.

● Friuli Isonzo Merlot '07	♛♛ 4*
○ Collio Bianco Bric '08	♛♛ 4*
○ Collio Friulano V. Valeris '08	♛♛ 4*
○ Collio Pinot Grigio '08	♛♛ 4*
○ Collio Sauvignon V. Pàjze '08	♛♛ 4*
○ Collio Chardonnay '08	♛ 4
○ Collio Ribolla Gialla '08	♛ 4
● Friuli Isonzo Cabernet Franc '07	♛ 4
○ Collio Bianco Bric '07	♛♛ 4*
● Collio Cabernet Sauvignon '06	♛♛ 4
○ Collio Pinot Grigio '07	♛♛ 4
○ Collio Pinot Grigio '05	♛♛ 4*
○ Collio Ribolla Gialla '06	♛♛ 4
● Friuli Isonzo Cabernet Franc '06	♛♛ 4
● Friuli Isonzo Merlot '04	♛♛ 4*

● Collio Merlot Sel. '06	♛♛ 5
○ Collio Bianco Agnul '07	♛♛ 4*
○ Collio Pinot Grigio '08	♛♛ 4*
○ Collio Friulano '08	♛ 4
○ Collio Pinot Bianco '08	♛ 4

Pierpaolo Pecorari

via Tommaseo, 36c
34070 San Lorenzo Isontino [GO]
tel. 0481808775
www.pierpaolopecorari.it

CELLAR SALES
PRE-BOOKED VISITS

ANNUAL PRODUCTION **160,000 bottles**
HECTARES UNDER VINE **32**
VITICULTURE METHOD **Organic certified**

Pierpaolo Pecorari's winery is at San Lorenzo Isontino and his vineyards are in the superb wine country of Cormòns and Gradisca. The wines are all IGTs. We do not know why Pierpaolo opted out of the DOC but it has not changed the very high standards of his range in the slightest. For some time, Pierpaolo's son Alessandro has been helping him at the winery and his wife Alba has shouldered the burden of administration.

When you see Altis on a Pecorari label, you know it is a steel-fermented wine vinified with skin contact. The barrique-aged products are identified by the name of the vineyard from which they were sourced. Olivers is a beautifully crafted, golden-hued '07 Pinot Grigio that meshes ripe fruit aromas with peanut butter and biscuit sensations. There's plenty of freshness and vibrant minerality to perk up the palate. The star-bright Sauvignon Kolaus '07 unveils complex aromatics that shift from flowers to fruit against a backdrop of appealing aromatic herbs. The Altis version of Sauvignon is an attractive pale-straw '07 whose characteristically varietal fragrances are lifted by grapefruit peel.

○ Pinot Grigio Olivers '07	🍷🍷 6
○ Sauvignon Altis '07	🍷🍷 5
○ Sauvignon Kolaus '07	🍷🍷 6
○ Chardonnay '08	🍷 4
○ Pinot Grigio '08	🍷 4
○ Sauvignon Kolàus '96	YYY 5
○ Chardonnay Soris '05	YY 6
○ Malvasia '06	YY 4
○ Pinot Bianco Altis '06	YY 5
○ Pinot Grigio '06	YY 4
○ Sauvignon '06	YY 4
○ Sauvignon Altis '06	YY 5
○ Sauvignon Kolaus '05	YY 6

Perusini

loc. Gramogliano
via Torrione, 13
33040 Corno di Rosazzo [UD]
tel. 0432675018
www.perusini.com

CELLAR SALES
PRE-BOOKED VISITS
VISITOR FACILITIES

ANNUAL PRODUCTION **50,000 bottles**
HECTARES UNDER VINE **12**
VITICULTURE METHOD **Conventional**

The Perusini winery has very intimate links with Picolit. Giacomo, the grandfather of the current owner, rediscovered the noble variety in the 19th century. Today, the estate is run by Teresa Perusini, an expert on history of art and an enthusiastic farmer, in which she is assisted by her husband, Giacomo De Pace. The vineyards are in the hills of Gramogliano, Rosazzo and Rocca Bernarda, superb wine country, where they are supervised by the Preparatori d'Uva consultant agronomists, while winemaking is in the hands of the Terra&Vino group.

Their combined impact and constant striving for quality are producing the hoped-for results. Our tastings revealed a lovely '08 Sauvignon that made a good impression at the final taste-offs. Generosity is its keynote. The colour is deep, the varietal white peach and sage aromas are pervasive and the full palate lingers. Rosso del Postiglione '07 is poised, caressing and balsamic. A classic Bordeaux blend of merlot, cabernet sauvignon and cabernet franc, it bears on the label Vernet's painting, The Postillion. The elegant, stylish '08 Chardonnay is fragrant and tangy.

○ COF Sauvignon '08	🍷🍷 4*
○ COF Chardonnay '08	🍷🍷 4*
● COF Rosso del Postiglione '07	🍷🍷 5
● COF Cabernet Sauvignon '07	🍷 5
● COF Merlot '07	🍷 5
○ COF Pinot Grigio '08	🍷 4
○ COF Ribolla Gialla '08	🍷 4
○ COF Chardonnay '07	YY 4
○ COF Picolit '06	YY 8
○ COF Pinot Grigio '06	YY 4
○ COF Pinot Grigio '05	YY 4
○ COF Pinot Grigio '04	YY 4*
○ COF Sauvignon '07	YY 4

Petrucco

VIA MORPURGO, 12
33042 BUTTRIO [UD]
TEL. 0432674387
www.vinipetrucco.it

CELLAR SALES
PRE-BOOKED VISITS

ANNUAL PRODUCTION 100,000 bottles
HECTARES UNDER VINE 25
VITICULTURE METHOD Conventional

This splendid estate sprawls on the sunny slopes of the hills at Buttrio. Paolo Petrucco, an engineer, and his wife Lina have for some years been running their winery in full respect of tradition while remaining open to innovation. In their constant effort to raise the quality bar, they decided to call in the expert Marco Simonit to consult in the vineyards and flanked their very competent winemaker, Flavio Cabas, with consultant Gianni Menotti.

Changes notoriously require time to mature but results at Petrucco soon started coming through. Not for the first time, Pignolo Ronco del Balbo – the '05 – received the praise of our tasters. Pignolo is proverbially tricky but Paolo has set aside the best-aspected hillslope on the estate for the variety. Assertive in the glass, it gives plums and wild cherries nuanced with elegant balsam. Merlot Ronco del Balbo '06 is mouthfilling and consistent, if a little one-dimensional, but still very appealing. The '08 growing year was as favourable for Friulano as it was for Chardonnay. Merlot Ronco del Balbo '06 is mouthfilling and consistent, if a little one-dimensional, but nonetheless appealing.

Petrussa

VIA ALBANA, 49
33040 PREPOTTO [UD]
TEL. 0432713192
www.petrussa.it

CELLAR SALES
PRE-BOOKED VISITS

ANNUAL PRODUCTION 60,000 bottles
HECTARES UNDER VINE 10
VITICULTURE METHOD Conventional

From the '08 vintage, Schippettino di Prepotto was recognized as a subzone of the Colli Orientali del Friuli DOC. The 30 wineries that produce it have given themselves a strict protocol to promote the wine. Paolo and Gianni Petrussa took an active part in the project, well aware of the potential of the variety – not many know that it is actually ribolla nera – and of the territory. We are confident that success will soon follow.

When a cellar obtains high marks across the board for all wine types, it is ready to take the great leap forward into excellence. And the Petrussas very nearly hit the bull's eye with their '07 Chardonnay. It's oaked with a skilled hand, intriguing on the nose with its soft, tropical perceptions and delicious on the palate, which shows fullness, balance and thrust. His majesty king Schioppettino regales us with red berry fruits preserve, sweet spices and tobacco followed up by a delicious palate. The verduzzo-only sweet Pensiero '06 is fatty, balanced and persistent, suggesting macaroons and pears. Finally, the varietal, upfront Pinot Bianco '08 is reminiscent of fresh almonds.

○ COF Chardonnay '08	⟐⟐	4*
○ COF Friulano '08	⟐⟐	4*
● COF Merlot Ronco del Balbo '06	⟐⟐	5
○ COF Picolit '07	⟐⟐	7
● COF Pignolo Ronco del Balbo '05	⟐⟐	6
● COF Refosco P. R. Ronco del Belbo '06	⟐⟐	5
○ COF Pinot Bianco '08	⟐	4
○ COF Sauvignon '08	⟐	4
● COF Merlot '06	♀♀	4
○ COF Picolit '06	♀♀	7
○ COF Picolit '05	♀♀	7
● COF Pignolo Ronco del Balbo '04	♀♀	6
● COF Pignolo Ronco del Balbo '03	♀♀	6
● COF Refosco P. R. '06	♀♀	4

○ COF Chardonnay '07	⟐⟐	5
○ COF Pinot Bianco '08	⟐⟐	4*
● COF Schioppettino '06	⟐⟐	6
○ Pensiero '06	⟐⟐	6
● COF Cabernet '07	⟐	4
○ COF Friulano '08	⟐	4
● COF Merlot '07	⟐	4
○ COF Sauvignon '08	⟐	4
○ COF Chardonnay '06	♀♀	5
○ COF Friulano '07	♀♀	4
○ COF Pinot Bianco '07	♀♀	4
○ COF Sauvignon '06	♀♀	4*
● COF Schioppettino '04	♀♀	6
○ COF Tocai Friulano '06	♀♀	4*

Roberto Picéch

LOC. PRADIS, 11
34071 CORMÒNS [GO]
TEL. 048160347
www.picech.it

CELLAR SALES
PRE-BOOKED VISITS

ANNUAL PRODUCTION **28,000 bottles**
HECTARES UNDER VINE **7**
VITICULTURE METHOD **Conventional**

In 1963, Roberto's father Egidio acquired ownership of the vineyards the Picèchs had been working for some time. Egidio was known as "Il Ribel", a nickname that doesn't need to be translated and says it all about his boisterous personality. Luckily, his wife Jelka Sirk was on hand to keep the peace in the family home. Roberto has inherited his father's determination and the affably even temper of his mother.

A determined winemaker produces equally assertive wines that are not always easy to interpret. Depending on the growing year and vine type, the grapes are given skin contact, sometimes for several days, which lends them a fatty richness and complexity. Collio Rosso '07, is a blend of cabernet franc, cabernet sauvignon and merlot. Maceration on the skins went on for 25 days with several pump-overs every day before the wine aged unhurriedly in large wood. Intense ruby red, it unveils complex aromas of fruit and spice that precede firm, sumptuous palate with lots of thrust. The current wines still have a little way to go but look very promising.

● Collio Rosso '07	♟♟	5
○ Collio Bianco Athena '06	♟♟	6
○ Collio Friulano '08	♟♟	5
○ Collio Malvasia '08	♟♟	5
○ Collio Pinot Bianco '08	♟♟	5
● Collio Rosso Ris. '06	♟♟	6
○ Collio Bianco Jelka '07	♟	5
○ Collio Bianco Athena '05	♟♟♟	8
○ Collio Bianco Jelka '99	♟♟♟	4
○ Collio Bianco Jelka '06	♟♟	5
○ Collio Malvasia '07	♟♟	5
○ Collio Pinot Bianco '07	♟♟	5
● Collio Rosso '06	♟♟	5

Vigneti Pittaro

VIA UDINE, 67
33033 CODROIPO [UD]
TEL. 0432904726
www.vignetipittaro.com

CELLAR SALES
PRE-BOOKED VISITS

ANNUAL PRODUCTION **500,000 bottles**
HECTARES UNDER VINE **90**
VITICULTURE METHOD **Conventional**

Piero Pittaro's cellar is one of the most modern and best-equipped in the region. It receives hordes of visitors who come not just for the excellent wines but also for its intriguing museum with its reconstructions of farming life in the past and marvellous collection of wine-related glass. Most of the vineyards are around the headquarters at Codroipo, in the heart of the sun-drenched Friulian flatlands, but there are also five hectares in on the lovely slopes at Ramandolo.

A second winemaking unit is dedicated entirely to the production of classic method sparkling wines, which cellar manager Stefano Trinca has taken to admirably high levels of quality. In fact, it was a sparkler, the Pittaro Brut Etichetta Oro, that most intrigued our tasters. The tiny bubbles accompany elegant aromas of ripe tropical fruits, nuts and biscuits. Then comes a deep palate brimming with aromas and minerality. We also liked the Manzoni Bianco '08, a variety from a cross of pinot bianco and riesling renano. It's uncomplicatedly fruity on the nose and shows power and flavour in the mouth. Finally, the Ronco Vieri vineyard at Tarcento brings us a deliciously juicy '06 Ramandolo.

○ Pittaro Brut Et. Oro '01	♟♟	7
○ Manzoni '08	♟♟	4*
○ Ramandolo Ronco Vieri '06	♟♟	5
● COF Refosco Ronco Vieri '06	♟	4
○ Friuli Grave Chardonnay Mousqué '08	♟	4
● Moscato Rosa Valzer in Rosa '08	♟	4
○ Pittaro Brut Et. Argento	♟	5
⊙ Pittaro Brut Pink	♟	5
○ Apicio '06	♟♟	5
● COF Picolit Ronco Vieri '05	♟♟	7
○ Friuli Grave Chardonnay Mousqué '07	♟♟	4
● Moscato Rosa Valzer in Rosa '07	♟♟	4

Plozner

VIA DELLE PRESE, 19
33097 SPILIMBERGO [PN]
TEL. 04272902
www.plozner.it

CELLAR SALES
PRE-BOOKED VISITS

ANNUAL PRODUCTION **500,000 bottles**
HECTARES UNDER VINE **60**
VITICULTURE METHOD **Conventional**

This estate on the flatlands at Spilimbergo was set up by Lisio Plozner in 1967. Today, it is managed with determination by his niece Sabina Maffei, who until recently was helped out by her mother, Valeria. The name Plozner has always been synonymous with modern, meticulously made Friulian whites released at attractive, value-for-money prices. True to that tradition, Sabina offers a range of wines that nicely embody the Magredi terroir.

The recently modernized cellar is hidden away among the vineyards and for more than 20 years, it has been the domain of oenologist and agronomist Francesco Visentin, who advises Sabina on the selections, the cellar's premium line. We were impressed to see that the selections were being held back so only the base wines were presented for tasting. They scored well and two even reached the national finals. The splendid '08 Pinot Bianco convinced our tasters with its crisp definition, the integrity of its aromatics, its finesse and its typicity. Equally good was the complex, subtly almondy '08 Friulano with its rich, well-sustained palate.

Damijan Podversic

VIA BRIGATA PAVIA, 61
34170 GORIZIA
TEL. 048178217
www.damijangodversic.com

CELLAR SALES
PRE-BOOKED VISITS

ANNUAL PRODUCTION **16.500 bottles**
HECTARES UNDER VINE **10**
VITICULTURE METHOD **Organic certified**

Damijan's father, a popular local innkeeper, purchased a few hectares to make wine for customers at his establishment. When Damijan returned from military service, he was fired by a love of the land and the teachings of Josko Gravner, with whom he has a long-standing friendship. He turned his hand to the vines and started the process of transforming them, knowing that he would be learning by doing but determined to achieve his aims.

Courageously, Damijan opted for extended skin contact and shunned selected yeasts, clarification, filtration or temperature control. His intensely hued wines are serious to the point of challenging at times, reflecting Damijan's own personality. Kaplja '06, from malvasia, friulano and chardonnay, is superb. Redolent of barley sugar, apricot preserve and gentian, it shows savoury and slightly tannic in the mouth and came within an ace of a top award. Rosso Prelit '06, from merlot and cabernet sauvignon, has a penetrating fragrance of violets and black figs before the rounded palate reveals its promise. The amber-shaded '06 Ribolla Gialla is alcoholic, complex, minerally and well sustained.

○ Friuli Grave Friulano '08	♈♈ 4*
○ Friuli Grave Pinot Bianco '08	♈♈ 4*
○ Friuli Grave Chardonnay '08	♈♈ 4*
● Friuli Grave Merlot '06	♈♈ 4*
○ Friuli Grave Pinot Grigio '08	♈♈ 4*
● Friuli Grave Cabernet Sauvignon '06	♈ 4
○ Friuli Grave Sauvignon '08	♈ 4
○ Friuli Grave Traminer Aromatico '08	♈ 4
○ Bianco Moscabianca '07	♈♈ 4
○ Friuli Grave Pinot Grigio '07	♈♈ 4
○ Friuli Grave Sauvignon '07	♈♈ 4
○ Friuli Grave Traminer Aromatico '07	♈♈ 4
○ Pinot Grigio Malpelo '07	♈♈ 4
○ Sauvignon Quattroperuno Uno '07	♈♈ 4

○ Kaplja '06	♈♈ 6
● Rosso Prelit '06	♈♈ 6
○ Ribolla Gialla '06	♈♈ 6
○ Kaplja '05	♈♈ 6
○ Kaplja '04	♈♈ 6
○ Kaplja '03	♈♈ 6
○ Ribolla Gialla '03	♈♈ 6
● Rosso Prelit '04	♈♈ 6
● Rosso Prelit '03	♈♈ 6

Aldo Polencic

LOC. PLESSIVA, 13
34071 CORMÒNS [GO]
TEL. 048161027
aldopolencic@virgilio.it

CELLAR SALES
PRE-BOOKED VISITS

ANNUAL PRODUCTION **20,000 bottles**
HECTARES UNDER VINE **7**
VITICULTURE METHOD **Conventional**

Aldo Polencic has a typical family-run Collio winery. The location is Plessiva, in the municipality of Cormòns, a superb place to grow grapes and make wine. The estate is tiny but its modest dimensions allow Aldo, with the help of his father Francesco, to tend his vines with scrupulous care. The recently extended cellar holds neat rows of large oak casks, which are vital to Aldo's winemaking approach.

Aldo is a self-taught winemaker, but a very skilled one, and can call on his mainly Tuscany-based oenologist sister Marinka for consultancy. Our hero likes to ferment in wood and only a skilled hand like his can gauge how much tannin to extract without compromising varietal characteristics. The wines are opulently fatty, concentrated and far from easy to drink, but they are very gratifying. The '08 Pinot Bianco is citron yellow, redolent of lily of the valley, talcum powder and white chocolate with a caressingly soft mouthfeel and a sensation almost of sweetness. The Friulano '08 gives golden delicious apple, banana and honey before the agile, flavoursome palate impresses with its balance.

Isidoro Polencic

LOC. PLESSIVA, 12
34071 CORMÒNS [GO]
TEL. 048160655
www.polencic.com

CELLAR SALES
PRE-BOOKED VISITS

ANNUAL PRODUCTION **120,000 bottles**
HECTARES UNDER VINE **25**
VITICULTURE METHOD **Conventional**

Plessiva is the place in the Collio where Isidoro laid out his rows and meticulously, determinedly tended his vines. Isidoro is no longer with us but his three children, Michele, Elisabetta and Alex, are and they have been working enthusiastically on the estate for some time. The plots are in various locations – Cormòns, Ruttars, Plessiva, Novali, Mossa and Castelletto – with different site climates that enable the family to offer a complete panorama of the Collio's wine potential.

For quite a few years, the entire range of Isidoro Polencic wines has been consistently excellent and has won Three Glasses on many occasions. This year, our top award went to the wonderful '07 version of Friulano Fisc. The grapes are sourced from a particularly fine vineyard, a cru if ever there was one, and the wine matures in large wood. Fresh fragrances intertwine with creaminess on the palate, shading away into a subtly bitterish finish. Friulano's success continues with the current release, the '08, which is less complex but every bit as appealing.

Wine		
○ Collio Friulano Bianco degli Ulivi '08	♀♀	6
○ Collio Pinot Bianco Bianco degli Ulivi '08	♀♀	6
○ Collio Pinot Grigio '08	♀♀	5
○ Collio Tocai Friulano '00	♀♀♀	4
● Collio Merlot Rosso degli Ulivi '06	♀♀	6
○ Collio Pinot Bianco Bianco degli Ulivi '07	♀♀	6
○ Collio Pinot Bianco degli Ulivi '06	♀♀	6
○ Collio Pinot Grigio '07	♀♀	5
○ Collio Pinot Grigio '06	♀♀	5
○ Collio Tocai Friulano Bianco degli Ulivi '07	♀♀	6
○ Collio Tocai Friulano Bianco degli Ulivi '06	♀♀	6

Wine		
○ Collio Friulano Fisc '07	♀♀♀	5
○ Collio Friulano '08	♀♀	4*
○ Collio Bianco Oblin Blanc '07	♀♀	4
○ Collio Pinot Grigio '08	♀♀	5
○ Collio Chardonnay '08	♀	4
○ Collio Ribolla Gialla '08	♀	4
○ Collio Sauvignon '08	♀	4
○ Collio Pinot Bianco '07	♀♀♀	5
○ Collio Pinot Grigio '98	♀♀♀	4
○ Collio Tocai Friulano '04	♀♀♀	4*
○ Collio Bianco '07	♀♀	4
○ Collio Chardonnay '07	♀♀	4
○ Collio Friulano '07	♀♀	4
○ Collio Ribolla Gialla '07	♀♀	4*
○ Collio Sauvignon '07	♀♀	4*

Primosic

FRAZ. OSLAVIA
LOC. MADONNINA DI OSLAVIA, 3
34070 GORIZIA
TEL. 0481535153
www.primosic.com

CELLAR SALES
PRE-BOOKED VISITS

ANNUAL PRODUCTION 200,000 bottles
HECTARES UNDER VINE 31
VITICULTURE METHOD Conventional

The hill at Oslavia, on the border with Slovenia, bristles with wineries that have written the history of the Collio. Silvestro Primosic was ahead of the game in seeing how important it was to set up a Collio DOC protection consortium and proudly shows off "bottle number one", which bears his label. Today, Silvestro has his two sons working with him at the cellar. Marko takes care of sales and marketing while Boris looks after finance and the cellar.

Marko has also completed a major zoning project, matching varieties to the most suitable vineyards that can bring out their full potential. This has led to the Selezionata line, identified by the vineyard name on the label. Not for the first time, the most impressive wine was Klin, from sauvignon blanc, chardonnay, ribolla gialla and picolit. In the '06 edition, it gives fragrant citrus and tropical fruit with a delightfully minerally palate. The Ribolla Gialla Think Yellow! '08, a very characteristic local wine, is fresh and pervasive on both nose and palate. Finally, the Friulano Belvedere '08 is impressively subtle on the nose and very easy drinking.

Doro Princic

LOC. PRADIS, 5
34071 CORMÒNS [GO]
TEL. 048160723
doroprincic@virgilio.it

CELLAR SALES
PRE-BOOKED VISITS

ANNUAL PRODUCTION 60,000 bottles
HECTARES UNDER VINE 10
VITICULTURE METHOD Conventional

This compact estate is one of the jewels in Friuli's oenological crown. Doro Princic is at Pradis, in the Collio, on the superb slopes of the hill country at Cormòns. It bears its founder's name but today is run by his son Alessandro, whom everyone calls Sandro, and his wife Grazia. Doro Princic was a mentor for Collio winemakers and Sandro hews to the same philosophy. His own son Carlo, an oenology student, already helps out so the future is assured.

Oenological consultancy is provided by Luigino De Giuseppe and the Doro Princic label is now an absolute guarantee of quality. The cellar's signature Pinot Bianco is a multiple Three Glass winner, two years ago Sandro's '06 Tocai Friulano won our top prize and this time a splendid Malvasia '08 stepped up for the award. Its aromatics are redolent of the nearby sea mingling with resinous notes, wisteria and passion fruit. Soft and mouthfilling, it closes on the palate with a twist of bitterness. The '08 Pinot Bianco is as good as ever, standing out for finesse and varietal typicity. Finally, the '08 Friulano is remarkable for its fresh almond aromatics and gutsy savouriness in the mouth.

○ Collio Bianco Klin Ris. '06	♀♀	6
○ Collio Friulano Belvedere '08	♀♀	4*
○ Ribolla Gialla Think Yellow! '08	♀♀	5
○ Collio Pinot Grigio Murno '08	♀	4
● Collio Rosso Metamorfosis Ris. '05	♀	6
○ Collio Sauvignon Blanc Gmajne '08	♀	5
○ Collio Pinot Grigio Murno '07	♀♀	4
○ Collio Ribolla di Oslavia Ris. '05	♀♀	5
○ Collio Ribolla Gialla di Oslavia Ris. '06	♀♀	5
○ Collio Sauvignon Blanc Gmajne '07	♀♀	5
○ Collio Sauvignon Gmajne '06	♀♀	5
○ Collio Tocai Friulano Belvedere '06	♀♀	4
○ Ribolla Gialla '06	♀♀	4

○ Collio Malvasia '08	♀♀♀	5
○ Collio Friulano '08	♀♀	5
○ Collio Pinot Bianco '08	♀♀	5
○ Collio Pinot Grigio '08	♀♀	5
○ Collio Sauvignon '08	♀♀	5
○ Collio Pinot Bianco '07	♀♀♀	5
○ Collio Pinot Bianco '05	♀♀♀	5
○ Collio Pinot Bianco '04	♀♀♀	5
○ Collio Pinot Bianco '02	♀♀♀	5
○ Collio Pinot Bianco '95	♀♀♀	5
○ Collio Tocai Friulano '06	♀♀♀	5
○ Collio Tocai Friulano '93	♀♀♀	5
○ Collio Friulano '07	♀♀	5
○ Collio Malvasia '07	♀♀	5
○ Collio Pinot Grigio '07	♀♀	5
○ Collio Sauvignon '07	♀♀	5

Giovanni Puiatti

LOC. ZUCCOLE
VIA AQUILEIA, 30
34070 CAPRIVA DEL FRIULI [GO]
TEL. 0481809922
www.puiatti.com

PRE-BOOKED VISITS

ANNUAL PRODUCTION **600,000 bottles**
HECTARES UNDER VINE **50**
VITICULTURE METHOD **Conventional**

Everyone in Friuli remembers Vittorio Puiatti. An aesthete and a man of vast culture, Vittorio expressed his personal philosophy in prolonged studies and experiments that made him a pioneer and a charismatic figure in new Friulian, and indeed Italian, winemaking. The second generation is now at the helm. Giovanni, the winemaker, and Elisabetta, who is in charge of communication, take the winery forward under the slogan: "An original, distinctive style will leave its mark".

The Puiatti cellar is both traditionalist and innovative. Oak has always been shunned here to let the raw material shine through. Glass stoppers are used for the top products as this pure, neutral seal guarantees the quality and cellar shelf life of the wine. The '04 Chardonnay from the Archetipi collection went through to the finals for its elegantly fruity, complex and beautifully evolved nose and attractively full, savoury palate. The lean, easy-drinking '08 Ribolla Gialla is very varietal, mingling alluring citrus with a whiff of aniseed. Finally, the '08 Pinot Nero Ruttars is soft and sincere, threading a faint hint of spice through its red berry fragrances.

○ Collio Chardonnay Archetipi '04	TT	5
● Collio Pinot Nero Ruttars '08	TT	5
○ Collio Ribolla Gialla '08	TT	5
● Collio Friuliano Zuccole '08	T	4
⊙ Rosé Extra Brut	T	6
● Friuli Isonzo Cabernet Franc Le Zuccole '04	YY	4*
○ Friuli Isonzo Chardonnay '02	YY	4
○ Friuli Isonzo Chardonnay Le Zuccole '03	YY	4
○ Friuli Isonzo Pinot Grigio '00	YY	3*

Dario Raccaro

FRAZ. RÒLAT
VIA SAN GIOVANNI, 87
34071 CORMÒNS [GO]
TEL. 048161425
az.agr.raccaro@alice.it

CELLAR SALES
PRE-BOOKED VISITS

ANNUAL PRODUCTION **25,000 bottles**
HECTARES UNDER VINE **2**
VITICULTURE METHOD **Conventional**

Raccaros have been making wine at Cormòns for nearly a century. It was 1928 when Giuseppe Raccaro moved into an old farmhouse at the foot of Mount Quarin. Giuseppe came from the dry, difficult Natisone river valleys and found fertile land at Cormòns that would enable him to raise a family. His son Mario had the foresight to specialize in viticulture and today Dario has wasted no time in taking the cellar's limited range of ultra-reliable products to the peak of excellence.

Vigna del Rolat continues to draw attention. We have often listened to Dario singing the praises of his Malvasia, which is in fact stunning, but it is always his Friulano from that long-established vineyard that thrills us most of all. The '08 edition swept up Three well-deserved Glasses for its elegantly crisp, complex citrus aromas and assertively full-bodied, long-lingering palate. Thrilling. We also thought the '08 Malvasia was amazing. Its understated wisteria and capers usher in a generous flavour brushed with faint brininess. Dario's friulano, sauvignon and pinot grigio Collio Bianco '08 gives pervasive ripe peaches and pears before showing soft-textured and fruit-led in the mouth.

○ Collio Friulano Vigna del Rolat '08	TTT	5
○ Collio Bianco '08	TT	5
○ Collio Malvasia '08	TT	5
● Collio Merlot '07	TT	6
● Friuli Isonzo Rosso '07	TT	5
○ Collio Bianco '03	YYY	5
○ Collio Bianco '02	YYY	4
○ Collio Friulano Vigna del Rolat '07	YYY	5
○ Collio Tocai Friulano '05	YYY	5
○ Collio Tocai Friulano '04	YYY	5
○ Collio Tocai Friulano '01	YYY	4*
○ Collio Tocai Friulano '00	YYY	4
○ Collio Tocai Friulano Vigna del Rolat '06	YYY	5

La Rajade

LOC. RESTOCINA, 12
34070 DOLEGNA DEL COLLIO [GO]
TEL. 0481639897
rajade@virgilio.it

CELLAR SALES
PRE-BOOKED VISITS

ANNUAL PRODUCTION 40,000 bottles
HECTARES UNDER VINE 7
VITICULTURE METHOD Conventional

La Rajade, which means "sunbeam" in Friulian, is the name of this winery in the Judrio river valley in the northern part of the Collio. In 2005, the property was purchased by Giuseppe Faurlin and Sergio Campeotto, who put wine technician Diego Zanin in charge. The vineyards clamber down the hills downstream of Ronco Petrus and the recently modernized cellar means that there is plenty of space to work in, as well as a comfortable tasting room.

Diego looks after everything, welcoming visitors, tending the vines and working in the cellar, where he has input from oenologist Andrea Romano Rossi. Luckily, the valley's site climates offer the great aspects and good temperature fluctuations that encourage the formation of aroma compounds, as you can tell from the '08 Sauvignon. It went straight through to our finals. Almost Bordeauxesque in style, such is the complexity of its pervasive aromas, it impressed us with its savoury minerality and vibrant fruit. The '08 Malvasia is lovely. Although perhaps a tad rustic, it too is mouthfilling and brims with deliciously aromatic fruit. All the other wines are well made and well typed.

Rocca Bernarda

FRAZ. IPPLIS
VIA ROCCA BERNARDA, 27
33040 PREMARIACCO [UD]
TEL. 0432716914
www.roccabernarda.com

CELLAR SALES
PRE-BOOKED VISITS

ANNUAL PRODUCTION 180,000 bottles
HECTARES UNDER VINE 42.86
VITICULTURE METHOD Conventional

Rocca Bernarda is dominated by an imposing edifice known as a "castle", perhaps because of its four round towers, one at each corner. In reality, it was the former country residence built by the noble Valvason Maniago family in 1567. A plaque reminds visitors that the cellars were constructed even earlier and the winemaking heritage was maintained over the centuries by another noble family, the Perusini-Antoninis. In 1977, ownership passed to the Sovereign Military Order of Malta.

The estate is managed on a day-to-day basis by a locally appointed specialist, a position that for the past several years has been held by Paolo Dolce. In the cellar, Paolo has consultancy input from Piedmont-based winemaker, Marco Monchiero. The most gratifying results have almost always come from the cellar's flagship Picolit, but sadly this year it wasn't ready for our tasting. The highest score went to the '08 Friulano, which impressed us with its sumptuous extract, balance and pervasive aromatics, followed by a muscular palate. Bianco Vineis '08, from chardonnay, sauvignon, friulano and picolit, is also very good, showing intriguingly complex fragrances and lashings of character.

○ Collio Sauvignon '08	♟♟ 5*
○ Collio Malvasia '08	♟♟ 5
● Collio Cabernet Sauvignon '06	♟ 5
○ Collio Friulano '08	♟ 5

○ COF Friulano '08	♟♟ 4*
○ COF Bianco Vineis '08	♟♟ 4*
○ COF Chardonnay '08	♟ 4
○ COF Sauvignon '08	♟ 4
○ COF Friulano '07	♟♟ 4
● COF Merlot Centis '04	♟♟ 5
● COF Merlot Centis '03	♟♟ 5
○ COF Picolit '05	♟♟ 8
○ COF Pinot Grigio '06	♟♟ 4
○ COF Tocai Friulano '06	♟♟ 4

Paolo Rodaro

LOC. SPESSA
VIA CORMÒNS, 60
33040 CIVIDALE DEL FRIULI [UD]
TEL. 0432716066
paolorodaro@yahoo.it

CELLAR SALES
PRE-BOOKED VISITS

ANNUAL PRODUCTION **250,000 bottles**
HECTARES UNDER VINE **45**
VITICULTURE METHOD **Conventional**

Paolo Rodaro's operation is one of the largest and most important in the Colli Orientali del Friuli. Paolo prefers to call himself a farmer, not a grower, and he uses the term in its noblest sense, proud to come from a family that has always farmed everything from livestock to vines with dignity, simplicity and discretion. Paolo's wife Nadia takes care of administration and welcomes visitors to the cellar. Daughter Giulia, now 15, designed the label for Romain when she was only five.

The Romain line features wines from grapes that dry in small cases for about a month after the harvest. It's not so much part-drying as an overripening that the fruit could not have achieved on the plant. We tasted the '06 Merlot from the Romain range, which went on to the final taste-offs. Intense on the eye and nose, it gives headily pervasive fragrances of forest floor and mushrooms before the powerfully full palate satisfies the senses. Verduzzo Friulano Pra Zenâr '07 is extraordinary, showing elegance and honey-laced fruit with delicious sweetness. The very varietal, buttery Picolit '07 is redolent of white chocolate while the '08 Friulano and Sauvignon are excellent.

● COF Merlot Romain '06	¶¶	6
○ COF Verduzzo Passito Pra Zenâr '07	¶¶	6
○ COF Friulano '08	¶¶	4
○ COF Picolit '07	¶¶	7
○ COF Pinot Grigio '08	¶	4
○ COF Ribolla Gialla '08	¶	4
● COF Refosco P. R. Romain '03	¶¶¶	7
○ COF Sauvignon Bosc Romain '96	¶¶¶	5
● COF Merlot Romain '02	¶¶	7
○ COF Picolit '06	¶¶	7
○ COF Picolit '04	¶¶	7
○ COF Picolit '02	¶¶	7
● COF Schioppettino Romain '02	¶¶	6

La Roncaia

FRAZ. CERGNEU
VIA VERDI, 26
33045 NIMIS [UD]
TEL. 0432790280
www.fantinel.com

CELLAR SALES
PRE-BOOKED VISITS

ANNUAL PRODUCTION **60,000 bottles**
HECTARES UNDER VINE **N.D.**
VITICULTURE METHOD **Conventional**

The Fantinels have been making wine for three generations. The group already included the Sant'Helena estate at Vencò in the Collio, and Borgo Tesis at Tauriano near Spilimbergo in the Grave del Friuli, but the constant search for excellence prompted the Fantinels to acquire another property at Cergneu, near Nimis in the northernmost part of the Colli Orientali del Friuli. Group chairman Marco Fantinel says: "La Roncaia strives to express the very best in Friuli's wine heritage by creating original wines of great quality that remain true to type".

Consultant oenologists Marco Pecchiari and Alessio Dorigo of the Terra&Vino team make up a very successful team with Fantinel group wine technicians, Gianni Campo Dall'Orto and Adriano Copetti. Results have been outstanding. The wines presented were genuinely good and the '06 Merlot came within an ace of winning Three Glasses. It's an utterly Friulian wine with tempting hints of balsam pervading nose and palate, where it flaunts its considerable personality to good effect. The Friulano '08 may be rustic but shows complex on the nose and muscular on the palate. The Ramandolo and Picolit from '06 are simply superb. Creamily sweet and dense on the palate, they never threaten to cloy.

● COF Merlot '06	¶¶	5*
○ COF Bianco Eclisse '08	¶¶	5
○ COF Friulano '08	¶¶	5
○ COF Picolit '06	¶¶	6
○ COF Ramandolo '06	¶¶	6
● COF Cabernet Sauvignon '06	¶	5
● COF Refosco '05	¶	6
● COF Rosso Il Fusco '05	¶	6
○ COF Bianco Eclisse '06	¶¶	5
● COF Merlot '02	¶¶	4
○ COF Picolit '01	¶¶	8

Il Roncat - Giovanni Dri

LOC. RAMANDOLO
VIA PESCIA, 7
33045 NIMIS [UD]
TEL. 0432790260
www.drironcat.com

CELLAR SALES
PRE-BOOKED VISITS

ANNUAL PRODUCTION **50,000 bottles**
HECTARES UNDER VINE **10**
VITICULTURE METHOD **Conventional**

Giovanni Dri is the man who years ago introduced the world to Ramandolo, a wine he loves so much that he refuses to waste even the pressings. Giovanni has in fact rented an old distillery and obtained a licence to distil his own spirits. For quite a while now, he has been making his craft Grappa di Ramandolo as well as a range of grape spirits. Giovanni also makes a top-quality extra virgin olive called Uèli, the Friulian for oil, which is yet another reason to visit his marvellous cellar.

The most seductive of Giovanni's wines are always the sweet types that in these parts take the form of Ramandolo. The Uve Dicembrine '05 is a very elegant version. Attractive baked apple juice, beeswax and dried figs tempt the nostrils. Equally alluring is the creamy textured, consistent Ramandolo Il Roncat '06 with its aromas of fruit in syrup, honey and white chocolate. The pleasingly savoury Schioppettino Monte dei Carpini '06 flaunts a very deep ruby red and signs off with a long varietal balsam finish. The pale '07 Picolit makes friends easily with its subtle confectioner's cream and nougat bouquet. Finally, the '07 Cabernet and Merlot stand out for their deep, pervasive aromatics.

Ronchi di Cialla

FRAZ. CIALLA
VIA CIALLA, 47
33040 PREPOTTO [UD]
TEL. 0432731679
www.ronchidicialla.it

PRE-BOOKED VISITS

ANNUAL PRODUCTION **100,000 bottles**
HECTARES UNDER VINE **21**
VITICULTURE METHOD **Conventional**

Cialla is a small valley shrouded in chestnut, oak and wild cherry woods. It is also officially recognized as a subzone for the cultivation of native Friulian varieties. Ronchi di Cialla was set up in 1970 at the initiative of Paolo and Dina Rapuzzi and today, the future is assured by their sons Pierpaolo and Ivan. Despite their success, the estate is still family run and strives to promote native Friulian varieties with a very simple approach: making wines of very high quality.

The results of our tastings speak for themselves: two wines sauntered into our finals, where one picked up Three Glasses. The wine that won our top prize for the Rapuzzis was Schioppettino di Cialla, which has received other awards for rescuing this endangered variety. The ruby of the '05 edition shades into garnet while the pervasive, very varietal nose conjures up plum jam and spices before the full-bodied palate gratifies with its depth and caressing texture. Cialla Picolit '06 is golden in hue, very elegant and redolent of dried flowers, honey and nougat.

○ COF Picolit Il Roncat '07	♟♟	8
● COF Schioppettino Monte dei Carpini '06	♟♟	5
○ Ramandolo Il Roncat '06	♟♟	6
○ Ramandolo Uve Decembrine '05	♟♟	6
● COF Cabernet '07	♟	4
● COF Merlot '07	♟	4
○ COF Sauvignon '08	♟	5
○ COF Picolit '05	♟♟	8
○ COF Picolit Il Roncat '06	♟♟	8
○ Ramandolo '06	♟♟	5
○ Ramandolo Il Roncat '07	♟♟	6
○ Ramandolo Il Roncat '05	♟♟	6

● COF Schioppettino di Cialla '05	♟♟♟	7
○ COF Picolit di Cialla '06	♟♟	8
○ COF Cialla Bianco '07	♟♟	5
● COF Refosco P.R. di Cialla '05	♟♟	7
○ COF Verduzzo di Cialla '06	♟♟	6

Ronchi di Manzano

VIA ORSARIA, 42
33044 MANZANO [UD]
TEL. 0432740718
www.ronchidimanzano.com

CELLAR SALES
PRE-BOOKED VISITS

ANNUAL PRODUCTION **300,000 bottles**
HECTARES UNDER VINE **55**
VITICULTURE METHOD **Conventional**

The counts of Trento chose these "ronchi", or hillslope vineyards, to make wine for the aristocrats of the Austro-Hungarian empire. In 1984, the Borghese family took over and Roberta, a businesswoman with a craftswoman's heart and an instinct for elegance, now runs an estate comprising three separate holdings. Ronc di Scossai and Ronc di Subule are at the cellar while Ronc di Rosazzo is further to the east. These are enchanted locations where time follows the rhythms of the seasons and the clock seems to have stopped hundreds of years ago.

Roberta has put in place an ambitious programme to obtain top-quality wines. She looks after the entire production process herself from vineyard to cellar, where Ivan looks after winemaking with the help of Aldo. We are happy to report that quality is improving and the Merlot Ronc di Subule '06 went through to our finals. What impressed our experts was the intriguingly varietal, balsam-veined bouquet backed up by a good follow-through on the savoury palate. The '07 Cabernet Sauvignon is still very young but already flaunts an upfront flavour and a nice palette of aromatics. Both the elegant Friulano and Sauvignon from '08 have plenty of power and concentration on nose and palate.

● COF Merlot Ronc di Subule '06	♟♟	5
● COF Cabernet Sauvignon '07	♟♟	4
○ COF Friulano '08	♟♟	4
○ COF Sauvignon '08	♟♟	4
○ COF Chardonnay '08	♟	4
● COF Merlot '07	♟	4
● COF Refosco P. R. '07	♟	4
○ COF Rosazzo Bianco Ellègri '08	♟	4
● COF Merlot Ronc di Subule '99	♟♟♟	5
● COF Merlot Ronc di Subule '05	♟♟	5
● COF Merlot Ronc di Subule '05	♟♟	5
○ COF Sauvignon '07	♟♟	4
○ COF Tocai Friulano Sup. '06	♟♟	4

Ronco dei Tassi

LOC. MONTE, 38
34071 CORMÒNS [GO]
TEL. 048160155
www.roncodeitassi.it

CELLAR SALES
PRE-BOOKED VISITS

ANNUAL PRODUCTION **76,000 bottles**
HECTARES UNDER VINE **12**
VITICULTURE METHOD **Conventional**

Ronco dei Tassi was set up in 1989 by Fabio Coser and his wife Daniela, who purchased a farm on the slopes of Mount Quarin at Cormòns. The woods around the vineyards swarm with badgers, which love to guzzle the sweetest bunches when the grapes are ripening. Hence the estate name, which means "badger vineyard". The Cosers have two sons, Matteo and Enrico, who have finished their education and contribute to the family business with a will.

The table below shows how high the overall level of quality is but the flagship wine is Collio Bianco Fosarin, a product that has already garnered five Three Glass triumphs, the last three consecutively. The '08 edition is again a blend of pinot bianco, friulano and malvasia, whose varietal aromatics meld into a unique bouquet of quite remarkable complexity. Fresh and tropical fruit frame vanilla-like perceptions and the deep, powerful palate is an object lesson in balance. But the Malvasia '08 also came close to top honours for its wonderful varietal typing and sheer allure. Finally, the Sauvignon and Friulano '08 both stand out for the depth of their varietal aromas.

○ Collio Bianco Fosarin '08	♟♟♟	4*
○ Collio Friulano '08	♟♟	4*
○ Collio Malvasia '08	♟♟	4*
○ Collio Sauvignon '08	♟♟	4*
○ Collio Pinot Grigio '08	♟♟	4
○ Collio Ribolla Gialla '08	♟♟	4
● Collio Rosso Cjarandon '06	♟♟	5
○ Collio Picolit '07	♟	6
○ Collio Bianco Fosarin '07	♟♟♟	4
○ Collio Bianco Fosarin '06	♟♟♟	4
○ Collio Bianco Fosarin '04	♟♟♟	4*
● Collio Rosso Cjarandon '01	♟♟♟	5
● Collio Rosso Cjarandon '00	♟♟♟	5
○ Collio Sauvignon '05	♟♟♟	4*
○ Collio Friulano '07	♟♟	4
○ Collio Pinot Grigio '07	♟♟	4

★ Ronco del Gelso

VIA ISONZO, 117
34071 CORMÒNS [GO]
TEL. 048161310
www.roncodelgelso.com

CELLAR SALES
PRE-BOOKED VISITS

ANNUAL PRODUCTION **150,000 bottles**
HECTARES UNDER VINE **24**
VITICULTURE METHOD **Conventional**

When Giorgio Badin completed his studies in 1987, he founded a winery that had only two hectares under vine. Growth has been unremitting and today his vine stock extends over 22 hectares. As production rose, the work space also had to expand so Giorgio built a new, modern cellar with a photovoltaic installation and a boiler that utilizes cuttings to ensure self-sufficiency in energy.

Ronco del Gelso wines have always been paragons of style and have won Giorgio a clutch of awards. This year, he sent five wines to our finals. He didn't quite manage a top prize but the sheer quality of the range is undeniable. Giorgio's elegant, savoury Merlot '06 is a stunner, showing off just how well he handles new oak. Pinot Grigio Sot lis Rivis '08 with its pears and sweet almonds is the embodiment of varietal typicity. The friulano, riesling and pinot bianco Bianco Latimis '08 has lots of character and subtly restrained aromas. Finally, Chardonnay Rive Alte '07 is reminiscent of butter and vanilla and the '08 Friulano is as well typed as they come.

Ronco delle Betulle

LOC. ROSAZZO
VIA ABATE COLONNA, 24
33044 MANZANO [UD]
TEL. 0432740547
www.roncodellebetulle.it

CELLAR SALES
PRE-BOOKED VISITS

ANNUAL PRODUCTION **70,000 bottles**
HECTARES UNDER VINE **13.75**
VITICULTURE METHOD **Conventional**

Ronco delle Betulle was set up in 1967 by Gianbattista Adami. It lies in the Rosazzo subzone of the Colli Orientali del Friuli DOC, where the famous abbey is also situated. Since 1990, Gianbattista's daughter Ivana has been managing the estate with her son Simone Sechi. After graduating in economics and working elsewhere as a marketing manager, Simone has brought his accumulated experience into the family winery.

In recent Guides, we have praised the exploits of Rosazzo Rosso Narciso but this year the best wine presented was the Rosazzo Bianco Vanessa '07 with its crisp fragrances of ripe fruit, biscuits and vanilla followed by a dynamic progression of power and savouriness. Power is there again in the dark ruby '05 Pignolo, which gives plum jam and stick liquorice fragrances. Its massive power and structure accompany assertive but very well-gauged tannins. The very nice Refosco '07 is juicy and pervasive, revealing ripe cherry and cinchona sensations. The intriguingly spicy, soft-textured Franconia '07 is one of a kind while the Friulano and Sauvignon '08 are delightfully savoury and varietal.

O Friuli Isonzo Bianco Latimis '08	♟♟ 4
O Friuli Isonzo Friulano '08	♟♟ 4*
● Friuli Isonzo Merlot '06	♟♟ 5
O Friuli Isonzo Pinot Grigio Sot lis Rivis '08	♟♟ 4*
O Friuli Isonzo Rive Alte Chardonnay '07	♟♟ 4*
● Friuli Isonzo Cabernet Franc '08	♟♟ 4
O Friuli Isonzo Malvasia '08	♟♟ 4
O Friuli Isonzo Pinot Bianco '08	♟♟ 4
O Friuli Isonzo Riesling '08	♟ 4
O Friuli Isonzo Tocai Friulano '06	♟♟♟ 4*
O Friuli Isonzo Tocai Friulano '05	♟♟♟ 4
O Friuli Isonzo Tocai Friulano '04	♟♟♟ 4*

O COF Rosazzo Bianco Vanessa '07	♟♟ 5
● COF Rosazzo Pignolo '05	♟♟ 7
O COF Friulano V. Bocois '08	♟♟ 4
● COF Refosco P. R. '07	♟♟ 5
O COF Sauvignon '08	♟♟ 4
● Franconia '07	♟♟ 5
● COF Cabernet Sauvignon '07	♟ 5
O COF Pinot Grigio '08	♟ 4
O COF Ribolla Gialla V. Cedronella '08	♟ 4
● Narciso Rosso '94	♟♟♟ 6
● COF Rosazzo Rosso Narciso '04	♟♟ 6
● COF Rosazzo Rosso Narciso '03	♟♟ 6
● COF Rosazzo Rosso Narciso '01	♟♟ 6
● COF Rosazzo Rosso Narciso '00	♟♟ 6
O COF Tocai Friulano '06	♟♟ 4

Ronco Severo

VIA RONCHI, 93
33040 PREPOTTO [UD]
TEL. 0432713144

CELLAR SALES
PRE-BOOKED VISITS

ANNUAL PRODUCTION **32,000 bottles**
HECTARES UNDER VINE **6**
VITICULTURE METHOD **Conventional**

In 1965, Stefano Novello's father Severo and two of his uncles had the chance to buy a few hectares at Prepotto, in the Colli Orientali del Friuli. Stefano graduated as an oenologist and went off to gain experience in California and New Mexico before setting up the winery he named after his father. At almost 90 years of age, Severo still helps out among the rows. Meanwhile Stefano's wife Laura looks after administration.

Extended skin contact of 22-45 days for whites and up to 120 days for the reds imbues Ronco Severo wines with deep, concentrated colour, excitingly pervasive aromatics and gratifyingly varietal aromatics. Years ago, Stefano did away with selected yeasts, enzymes and sulphur dioxide. These are genuine wines that go into bottle when the moon is on the wane without filtration or fining. They are exciting, like the complex, impeccably poised Severo Bianco '07, from friulano and chardonnay with a dash of picolit. The Friulano '07 gives dried spring flowers and a fruit-led flavour while the Pinot Grigio '08 has a deep coppery hue and a subtly varietal bitterish note reminiscent of absinthe.

○ COF Friulano '07	🍷🍷	5
○ COF Pinot Grigio '08	🍷🍷	4*
○ Severo Bianco '07	🍷🍷	6
○ COF Chardonnay '07	🍷🍷	5
● COF Merlot Artiûl '05	🍷🍷	5

Roncùs

VIA MAZZINI, 26
34076 CAPRIVA DEL FRIULI [GO]
TEL. 0481809349
www.roncus.it

CELLAR SALES
PRE-BOOKED VISITS
VISITOR FACILITIES

ANNUAL PRODUCTION **35,000 bottles**
HECTARES UNDER VINE **12**
VITICULTURE METHOD **Conventional**

Roncùs at Capriva del Friuli, in the heart of the Collio, belongs to Marco Perco. He's one of those wine men who never seem to be in a hurry. His new cellar, which will soon be finished, incorporates farmstay accommodation, La Casa Griunit, which is already open for business and where Marco's mother, Giuseppina, offers visitors a delightful welcome. Everyone in the family lends a hand, including daughter Elisa, who is often to be found in the vineyard tending the meticulously groomed vines.

Marco hired the Colugnatti and Catarossi studio to carry out a zoning study of the vine stock, paying special attention to the older plants, in the conviction that the research could substantially improve the standard of production. And in fact it was a wine from those older vines, the Bianco Vecchie Vigne '06 blend of native malvasia istriana, friulano and ribolla gialla grapes, that really impressed for the complexity of its aromas and the power of its palate. But Val di Miez '06, from merlot and cabernet franc, is every bit as deep, savoury and delicious with its plums, sweet spice and tobacco. To round off, the '07 Sauvignon is a tangy, palate-caressing proposition.

○ Collio Bianco Vecchie Vigne '06	🍷🍷	6
○ Sauvignon '07	🍷🍷	5
● Val di Miez '06	🍷🍷	6
○ Collio Friulano '07	🍷🍷	5
○ Roncùs Bianco '07	🍷🍷	4
○ Pinot Bianco '07	🍷	5
○ Roncùs Bianco Vecchie Vigne '01	YYY	6
○ Collio Bianco Vecchie Vigne '05	YY	6
○ Collio Bianco Vecchie Vigne '04	YY	6
○ Pinot Bianco '06	YY	5

Russiz Superiore

VIA RUSSIZ, 7
34070 CAPRIVA DEL FRIULI [GO]
TEL. 048199164
www.marcofelluga.it

CELLAR SALES
PRE-BOOKED VISITS

ANNUAL PRODUCTION 200,000 bottles
HECTARES UNDER VINE 50
VITICULTURE METHOD Conventional

The hills of Capriva del Friuli where the vineyard are located have lent their name to Russiz Superiore and the eagle that features prominently on the label is its emblem. This well-established winery is synonymous with the family of legendary innovator Marco Felluga, and is now expertly run by his son Roberto, who is supervising the successful consolidation of the project to make cellarable whites. That has always been one of the Fellugas' primary aims.

Russiz Superiore bottles are classics of new-style Friulian winemaking and over they years they have picked up many awards in Italy and abroad. The wine that stood out this time was Pinot Bianco, in both versions. The current '08 release wins friends for its enticing notes of thyme and gentian while the Pinot Bianco Riserva '05 came close to a top award for its pervasive, complex aromatics and muscular poise in the mouth. Top reds on the list are the very varietal '06 Merlot and the soft-textured, nicely structured Rosso Riserva degli Orzoni '05.

Sant'Elena

VIA GASPARINI, 1
34072 GRADISCA D'ISONZO [GO]
TEL. 048192388
www.sant-elena.com

CELLAR SALES
PRE-BOOKED VISITS

ANNUAL PRODUCTION 130,000 bottles
HECTARES UNDER VINE 30
VITICULTURE METHOD Conventional

Sant'Elena was founded in the late 19th century by the Klodic family. In the mid 1990s, the property was purchased by Dominic Nocerino, a prominent importer of Italian wines into the United States. Dominic immediately set about making over the winery with the aim of exploit the full potential of the Isonzo DOC territory. Vineyard management and restructuring of the cellar were entrusted to the capable hands of oenologist Maurizio Drascek and the results were not slow in coming.

This year's table shows a fine range of wines, of which three achieved outstanding scores. The '08 Sauvignon is a pleaser, giving complex aromas of intense white peach-led fruit followed by a taut, linger palate with a tangy flavour and caressing mouthfeel. We also like the Bianco Mil Rosis '07, from a chardonnay-heavy blend with traminer and riesling renano. It's an unusual mix that produces a bouquet ranging from tropical fruits to quince-like fruit with some exciting aromatic grace notes. The '06 Merlot is a good wine if still very young, as are the Cabernet Sauvignon, Pignolo and Tato. Their time will come.

Wine	Rating	Price
● Collio Merlot '06	♟♟	5
○ Collio Pinot Bianco '08	♟♟	5
○ Collio Pinot Bianco Ris. '05	♟♟	6
○ Collio Bianco Col Disôre '07	♟♟	6
● Collio Cabernet Franc '06	♟♟	5
○ Collio Friulano '08	♟♟	5
● Collio Rosso Ris. degli Orzoni '05	♟♟	7
○ Collio Sauvignon '08	♟	5
○ Collio Bianco Russiz Disôre '01	♟♟♟	6
○ Collio Bianco Russiz Disôre '00	♟♟♟	5
○ Collio Pinot Bianco '07	♟♟♟	5
● Collio Rosso Ris. degli Orzoni '93	♟♟♟	6
● Collio Rosso Riserva degli Orzoni '94	♟♟♟	7
○ Collio Sauvignon '05	♟♟♟	5
○ Collio Sauvignon '04	♟♟♟	6
○ Collio Tocai Friulano '06	♟♟	5

Wine	Rating	Price
○ Bianco Mil Rosis '07	♟♟	6
● Merlot '06	♟♟	5
○ Sauvignon '08	♟♟	5
● Cabernet Sauvignon '06	♟	5
● Pignolo '06	♟	6
● Ròs di Rôl Merlot '06	♟	7
● Tato '06	♟	6
○ Bianco JN '04	♟♟	5
○ Bianco Mil Rosis '06	♟♟	6
● Merlot '03	♟♟	5
○ Pinot Grigio '07	♟♟	5
○ Pinot Grigio '06	♟♟	5

★ Schiopetto

VIA PALAZZO ARCIVESCOVILE, 1
34070 CAPRIVA DEL FRIULI [GO]
TEL. 048180332
www.schiopetto.it

CELLAR SALES
PRE-BOOKED VISITS

ANNUAL PRODUCTION **177.050 bottles**
HECTARES UNDER VINE **30**
VITICULTURE METHOD **Conventional**

Mario Schiopetto inherited his passion for wine from his father Giorgio, a popular Udine innkeeper in the early 20th century. Mario was a great traveller and visited Europe's finest cellars as he patiently adapted German technology and French finesse to the Collio territory. He started out in 1965 by leasing an old winery and proceeded to trace the path that his children, Maria Angela, Carlo and Giorgio are now following themselves with the same passion.

The vineyards are in the Collio, at Capriva del Friuli, but the estate later acquired Podere del Blumeri at Rosazzo, in the Colli Orientali del Friuli. The three siblings have been courageous. They have cut the number of labels and this year delayed bottling. In fact, we will be reviewing the Mario Schiopetto Bianco next year. Nonetheless, the range is still excellent. The ever elegant Blanc des Rosis '08, from friulano, pinot grigio, sauvignon, malvasia and ribolla, triumphed again. There was also confirmation of excellence among the reds for the Bordeaux blend Rivarossa '07 and the merlot, cabernet sauvignon and refosco Blumeri '06, while the '08 Friulano and Sauvignon are also good.

○ Blanc des Rosis '08	TT	5
○ Collio Friulano '08	TT	5
○ Collio Sauvignon '08	TT	5
● Poderi dei Blumeri Rosso '06	TT	6
● Rivarossa '07	TT	5
○ Collio Pinot Bianco '08	TT	5
○ Collio Pinot Grigio '08	TT	5
○ Blanc des Rosis '07	YYY	5
○ Blanc des Rosis '06	YYY	5
○ Collio Tocai Friulano '00	YYY	5
○ Mario Schiopetto Bianco '02	YYY	6

Roberto Scubla

FRAZ. IPPLIS
VIA ROCCA BERNARDA, 22
33040 PREMARIACCO [UD]
TEL. 0432716258
www.scubla.com

CELLAR SALES
PRE-BOOKED VISITS

ANNUAL PRODUCTION **60,000 bottles**
HECTARES UNDER VINE **12**
VITICULTURE METHOD **Conventional**

The story of how Roberto Scubla threw up his job at the bank to work the land is well known. He purchased a few hectares of vines with a tumbledown farmhouse on the slopes of Rocca Bernarda back in 1991 and success was easy to predict. He transformed the estate and turned the abandoned farmhouse into a superb piece of rural architecture with tasting rooms, modern cellar and, recently, a barrel cellar completely underground.

Meticulous care of the vines yields low-quantity, high-quality wines and Roberto's friendship with Gianni Menotti has influenced work in the cellar. Remember that Bianco Pomedès is named after the Alpine refuge where the two dreamed up the wine while they were snowed in. But this year, Cràtis is back. It's an extraordinarily well-made '06 Verduzzo Friulano from grapes part-dried on racks exposed to the bora winds. The star-bright old gold ushers in fragrances of baked apples and caramel. Bianco Pomèdes '07 also impresses with the complexity of its aromatics and the softness of the mouthfeel. Finally, the morello cherry-themed Merlot '07 enchants as it unfolds elegantly in the mouth.

○ COF Verduzzo Friulano Cràtis '06	TTT	6
○ COF Bianco Pomèdes '07	TT	6
● COF Merlot '07	TT	5
○ COF Friulano '08	TT	4
● COF Rosso Scuro '06	TT	5
○ COF Pinot Bianco '08	T	4
○ COF Sauvignon '08	T	4
○ COF Bianco Pomèdes '04	YYY	5
○ COF Verduzzo Friulano Cràtis '04	YYY	6
○ COF Verduzzo Friulano Graticcio '99	YYY	6
○ COF Bianco Pomèdes '06	YY	6

Renzo Sgubin

via Faet, 15
34071 Cormòns [GO]
tel. 0481630297
renzo.sgubin@tiscali.it

CELLAR SALES
PRE-BOOKED VISITS

ANNUAL PRODUCTION **30,000 bottles**
HECTARES UNDER VINE **11**
VITICULTURE METHOD **Conventional**

The Sgubin cellar was set up by Eugenio, who passed it on to his son Bruno, who in turn handed over to Renzo. Next up will be Leonardo. In other words, this is a textbook example of a family winery where love of the land is handed down from father to son and drives everyone to do their very best all the time. There is no such thing as a perfect wine, of course, but that doesn't stop people trying to make one. With the help of his partner Michela, Renzo strives for perfection at every harvest. His latest label is the white 3,4,3 blend, dedicated to Leonardo who was born on 3 April 2003.

Quality continues to improve and this time two wines went through to the finals. The '08 Pinot Grigio is a deep, green-flecked straw with an appealingly fruity nose and a complex, savoury palate that satisfies the senses. But the '08 Sauvignon has just as much stuffing, as well as tropical fruit, medicinal herbs and a caressingly soft-textured, full-bodied palate. The '08 Friulano offers an abundance of aromatics and structure while the Chardonnay '08 tempts with its wisteria-laced aromatics. The '07 3,4,3 is a full-bodied white from friulano, malvasia, chardonnay and sauvignon that unfurls good complexity.

○ Friuli Isonzo Pinot Grigio '08	TT 4*
○ Friuli Isonzo Sauvignon '08	TT 4*
○ 3, 4, 3 '07	TT 4
○ Friuli Isonzo Friulano '08	TT 4*
○ Friuli Isonzo Chardonnay '08	TT 4*
● Plagnis '05	T 4
○ 3, 4, 3 '06	YY 4
○ Friuli Isonzo Chardonnay '07	YY 4
○ Friuli Isonzo Tocai Friulano Rive Alte '05	YY 4

Giordano Sirch

via Fornalis, 277
33043 Cividale del Friuli [UD]
tel. 0432709835
www.sirchwine.com

ANNUAL PRODUCTION **50,000 bottles**
HECTARES UNDER VINE **11**
VITICULTURE METHOD **Conventional**

It was a genuine pleasure last year to give Luca Sirch's '07 Friulano Three Glasses and our prize for Best Priced Wine in tribute to its astonishing value for money. Luca embarked on his campaign in 2002 when he took over the family vineyards with the modest ambition of making classic single-variety wines in a clean, modern style that transcends fashion and market trends.

Luca is lucky enough to have help with vineyard management from his brother Pierpaolo, co-creator and founder of Preparatori d'Uva, a studio that provides consultancy services to many wineries. In the cellar, he has assistance from the Terra&Vino group led by Alessio Dorigo and Marco Pecchiari. This year, we enjoyed the savoury, crisply defined Sauvignon '08, which is utterly varietal. Luca's Friulano Mis Mas '08 is equally outstanding, again flaunting intense peach-like fruit and a thoroughly appealing palate. All the other wines are simpler but well made, reflecting their variety and territory.

○ COF Friulano Mis Mas '08	TT 3*
○ COF Sauvignon '08	TT 4*
○ COF Pinot Grigio '08	TT 4*
○ COF Friulano '08	T 4
○ COF Malvasia '08	T 4
○ COF Ribolla Gialla '08	T 4
○ COF Friulano '07	YYY 4*
○ COF Friulano Mis Mas '07	YY 3*
○ COF Pinot Grigio '06	YY 4*
○ COF Sauvignon '06	YY 4*
○ COF Tocai Friulano '05	YY 4*

Skerk

FRAZ. SAN PELAGIO
LOC. PREPOTTO, 20
34011 DUINO AURISINA [TS]
TEL. 040200156
www.skerk.com

CELLAR SALES
PRE-BOOKED VISITS
FOOD

ANNUAL PRODUCTION **20,000 bottles**
HECTARES UNDER VINE **6**
VITICULTURE METHOD **Organic certified**

Sandi Skerk is a qualified engineer. A few years ago, he gave up the idea of pursuing the profession to follow in his father Boris's footsteps, working full-time in the family's Carso vineyards. The area's harsh geography failed to intimidate him. Sandi accepted the challenge of the terrain, carving a stunning yet functional cellar out of the rock where the smooth walls provide a constant temperature and natural ventilation mysteriously finds its way into the work spaces.

In the cellar, the wines are vinified naturally without fining or filtration, undergoing lengthy skin contact and racking when the moon is on the wane. The wine may be less than limpid but it preserves the varietal characteristics of the fruit. The thrilling '07 Malvasia and Vitovska are the reward for Sandi's hard work. Both are gold in colour and their aromas come straight from the grapeskin, with notes of resin on the Malvasia and thyme on the Vitovska, vibrantly taut palates and plenty of savouriness, power and appeal. The newcomer is Ograde '07, from vitovska, malvasia, sauvignon and other varieties. It's an antique rose-coloured wine that expresses the essence of its territory.

Edi Skok

LOC. GIASBANA, 15
34070 SAN FLORIANO DEL COLLIO [GO]
TEL. 0481390280
www.skok.it

CELLAR SALES
PRE-BOOKED VISITS

ANNUAL PRODUCTION **35,000 bottles**
HECTARES UNDER VINE **11**
VITICULTURE METHOD **Conventional**

The Skok winery is at Giasbana, near San Floriano del Collio, on the border with Slovenia. Its main tasting room is in a stately home built for the counts of Salzburg in the 16th century. The property had several noble owners until Edi and his sister Orietta bought it from the Teuffenbachs. The natural beauty of the setting, the quality of the wines and Edi and Orietta's hospitality all make a visit well worthwhile.

Several Guides ago, we noted improvement and this year the '08 Sauvignon made it into our finals. Its elegant aromatics recall a medley of tropical fruits, with lychees and passion fruit prominent before the fatty fullness of the mouthfilling palate confirms that this is a great wine. Bianco Pe Ar '07 takes its name from the cellar's founders, Edi and Orietta's father Giuseppe, known as Pepi, and their uncle Armando. The wine gives medlar and yellow damsons with savouriness and good thrust on the palate. The tropically-themed '08 Chardonnay is characterful and intriguing. Finally, there is a varietal '08 Friulano, now identified by a Z for Zabura, the old name of the vineyard it comes from.

○ Carso Malvasia Non Filtrato '07	♟♟ 5
○ Carso Vitovska Non Filtrato '07	♟♟ 5
○ Carso Sauvignon Non Filtrato '07	♟ 5
● Carso Terrano Non Filtrato '07	♟ 5
○ Ograde Bianco Non Filtrato '07	♟ 5
○ Carso Malvasia Non Filtrato '06	♟♟ 5
○ Carso Malvasia Non Filtrato '05	♟♟ 4
○ Carso Sauvignon Non Filtrato '06	♟♟ 5
○ Carso Sauvignon Non Filtrato '05	♟♟ 4
○ Carso Vitovska Non Filtrato '06	♟♟ 5
○ Carso Vitovska Non Filtrato '05	♟♟ 4

○ Collio Sauvignon '08	♟♟ 4*
○ Collio Bianco Pe Ar '07	♟♟ 5
○ Collio Chardonnay '08	♟♟ 4*
○ Collio Friulano Zabura '08	♟♟ 4*
● Collio Merlot '07	♟ 4
○ Collio Pinot Grigio '08	♟ 4
○ Collio Bianco Pe Ar '05	♟♟ 5*
○ Collio Pinot Grigio '07	♟♟ 4
○ Collio Pinot Grigio '06	♟♟ 4
○ Collio Sauvignon '06	♟♟ 4
○ Collio Sauvignon '05	♟♟ 4*
○ Collio Tocai Friulano Zabura '06	♟♟ 4

Leonardo Specogna

VIA ROCCA BERNARDA, 4
33040 CORNO DI ROSAZZO [UD]
TEL. 0432755840
www.specogna.it

CELLAR SALES
PRE-BOOKED VISITS

ANNUAL PRODUCTION **100,000 bottles**
HECTARES UNDER VINE **19**
VITICULTURE METHOD **Conventional**

Having fallen in love with the rolling hillslopes at Rocca Bernarda, skilfully terraced by generations of growers, Leonardo Specogna invested the hard-earned savings he had tucked away while working in Switzerland. In 1963, he bought some land and set up his winery. His passion was inherited by his sons Graziano and Gianni, who built up the business and are now assisted by the creative energy of Michele and Cristian, Graziano's oenology graduate sons.

One of the most impressive wines this time is the green-flecked '07 Chardonnay, which thrills the nostrils with vanilla-veined citrus showing lots of finesse on the fragrant palate. Merlot Oltre '05 is a very different wine. Dense, concentrated and still very fruity, it is appealingly consistent yet heady on the palate, which also revels in soft tannins. The current releases are very good. The Sauvignon '08 is very varietal, the Friulano '08 is savoury and well sustained, and the onionskin '08 Pinot Grigio gives fresh-baked bread. Next year, there will be new developments as soon as Michele and Cristian's trials with part-dried red grapes are successfully completed.

O COF Chardonnay '07	♟♟	4*
O COF Friulano '08	♟♟	4*
● COF Merlot Oltre '05	♟♟	6
O COF Sauvignon '08	♟♟	4*
O COF Pinot Grigio '08	♟	4
O COF Friulano '07	♟♟	4
O COF Chardonnay '06	♟♟	4
● COF Merlot Oltre '04	♟♟	6
● COF Merlot Oltre '03	♟♟	6
● COF Pignolo '05	♟♟	5
O COF Sauvignon '07	♟♟	4*
O COF Tocai Friulano '06	♟♟	4
O Pinot Grigio '07	♟♟	4

Castello di Spessa

VIA SPESSA, 1
34070 CAPRIVA DEL FRIULI [GO]
TEL. 0481639914
www.paliwines.com

CELLAR SALES
PRE-BOOKED VISITS

ANNUAL PRODUCTION **80,000 bottles**
HECTARES UNDER VINE **28**
VITICULTURE METHOD **Conventional**

The Castello di Spessa estate is part of Pali Wines, set up by Loretto Pali as an umbrella brand for his entire production of wines and spirits. The castle itself is a magnificent building in the heart of the Collio, perched on a lovely hilltop in the midst of a superb Italianate garden. It origins date from the 13th century but there is plenty of evidence that the Romans were here in the third century AD.

Wines rest in the castle's cellars in naturally constant temperature and humidity conditions as they mature and increase in value but only the bottles from the last vintage were presented for the Guide. They performed very well indeed. Credit must go to long-serving estate oenologist Domenico Lovat and to the invaluable consultancy input of Gianni Menotti. The Ribolla Gialla '08 went into the taste-offs thanks to its pervasive aromas, opening on intense fruit and signing off with a lovely touch of liquorice, but above all for its full body and sheer appeal. The '08 Sauvignon stood out for its finesse on the nose and juicy soft texture.

O Collio Ribolla Gialla '08	♟♟	5
O Collio Sauvignon '08	♟♟	5
O Collio Pinot Bianco '08	♟♟	5
O Collio Sauvignon Segrè '08	♟♟	6
O Collio Friulano '08	♟	5
O Collio Pinot Grigio '08	♟	5
O Collio Pinot Bianco '06	♟♟♟	6
O Collio Sauvignon Segrè '03	♟♟♟	6
O Collio Sauvignon Segrè '02	♟♟♟	6
O Collio Friulano '07	♟♟	5
O Collio Pinot Bianco '07	♟♟	5
O Collio Pinot Bianco di Santarosa '05	♟♟	5
O Collio Pinot Grigio '07	♟♟	5
O Collio Ribolla Gialla '07	♟♟	5
O Collio Sauvignon Segrè '07	♟♟	6
O Collio Sauvignon Segrè '06	♟♟	6
O Collio Sauvignon Segrè '05	♟♟	6

Oscar Sturm

LOC. ZEGLA, 1
34071 CORMÒNS [GO]
TEL. 048160720
www.sturm.it

CELLAR SALES
PRE-BOOKED VISITS

ANNUAL PRODUCTION **80,000 bottles**
HECTARES UNDER VINE **10**
VITICULTURE METHOD **Conventional**

The Sturm family came from the Austrian village of Andritz to settle at Zegla in 1850. Oscar, founder and owner of the winery, is Pepi and Lojza's descendant but now his own sons, Denis and Patrick, run the operation smoothly together. Patrick, the younger son, is a quick learner and is now in charge of production. Denis, an economics graduate from the Bocconi university, looks after administration and if necessary helps out his father on the estate.

The scores show that Sturm means quality. All the wines earned at least two Glasses and two of them went on to the finals. We already knew how well the Sturms make white wines but we were especially impressed by the elegance of their stunning '06 Merlot, a mouthfilling delight with loads of flavour and beautiful balance. Another wine we liked was the '08 Pinot Grigio for its williams pears aromas and powerful, soft-textured palate. Sauvignon '08 is flavoursome and very varietal, hinting at elderflowers and tomato leaf. Finally, the '08 Ribolla Gialla is fresh and tangy, the '08 Friulano is heady and firm-textured and the Chardonnay Andritz, also from '08, is delightfully consistent.

Subida di Monte

LOC. MONTE, 9
34071 CORMÒNS [GO]
TEL. 048161011
www.subidadimonte.it

CELLAR SALES
PRE-BOOKED VISITS

ANNUAL PRODUCTION **60,000 bottles**
HECTARES UNDER VINE **10**
VITICULTURE METHOD **Natural**

For some time, Subida di Monte has been run by brothers Cristian and Andrea Antonutti but the man who tied his name to the property is their father Luigi, the dean of Friulian wine, who believed in what his sons were doing and backed up their modernization of the estate. It was a courageous decision to use only natural organic fertilizers, and only sulphur and copper for pesticide treatments but their aim, amply achieved, is to obtain sound, healthful, fascinatingly fragrant wines.

The Collio is superb white wine country and the 2008 bottles respect the territory to the full in a textbook range of wines with distinct varietal aromatics and delicious drinkability. The soft, mouthfilling Pinot Grigio is redolent of citrus-led fruit and the subtly fragranced Friulano is tangy, closing on an attractive note of bitterness, while the Sauvignon adds a nice touch of aniseed to its understated classic varietal aromatics. Unfortunately, we were unable to taste the Malvasia, which impressed so much last time, as it was still maturing. Finally, the reds are also good and improving all the time.

● Collio Merlot '06	♟♟	5
○ Collio Pinot Grigio '08	♟♟	4*
○ Chardonnay Andritz '08	♟♟	4
○ Collio Friulano '08	♟♟	4
○ Collio Ribolla Gialla '08	♟♟	4
○ Collio Sauvignon '08	♟♟	4
○ Collio Sauvignon '06	♟♟♟	4
○ Collio Tocai Friulano '05	♟♟♟	4*
○ Collio Bianco Andritz '07	♟♟	5*
○ Collio Bianco Andritz '06	♟♟	5
○ Collio Pinot Grigio '07	♟♟	4*
○ Collio Sauvignon '05	♟♟	4
○ Collio Tocai Friulano '06	♟♟	4

○ Collio Friulano '08	♟♟	4*
○ Collio Pinot Grigio '08	♟♟	4*
○ Collio Sauvignon '08	♟♟	4*
● Collio Cabernet Franc '07	♟	4
● Collio Merlot '07	♟	4
● Collio Rosso Poncaia '06	♟	5
○ Collio Pinot Grigio '07	♟♟	4
○ Collio Tocai Friulano '06	♟♟	4
○ Collio Tocai Friulano '05	♟♟	4*

Matijaz Tercic

LOC. BUKUJE, 9
34070 SAN FLORIANO DEL COLLIO [GO]
TEL. 0481884193
tercic@tiscalinet.it

CELLAR SALES
PRE-BOOKED VISITS

ANNUAL PRODUCTION **30,000 bottles**
HECTARES UNDER VINE **11.5**
VITICULTURE METHOD **Conventional**

Viticulture and winemaking have long been part of the Tercic family's life. The first wine man was Alojz, followed by his son Zdenko and now Matijaz carries on the tradition. As you can guess from the names, were are right on the border with Slovenia, at San Floriano del Collio. This is one of the finest subzones for wine, partly because of the soil and partly because of the dual impact of the bora winds blowing down the Vipacco valley and the sea breezes from the south. One by one, all the local farms have switched to viticulture.

In 1990, Matijaz began a process that brought him slowly but surely to the wine public's attention with frank, fragrant wines that have conquered the most discriminating palates and wine stores. This year saw the first Tercic triumph with a Three Glass prize for the '07 Pinot Grigio, a wine that thrilled our experts with its full fragrances and pervasive, minerally palate. The complex, forward Merlot '06 very nearly joined it for its elegant expansion on a distinctly pleasurable palate. All the other wines confirm the cellar's overall excellence.

Franco Terpin

LOC. VALERISCE, 6A
34070 SAN FLORIANO DEL COLLIO [GO]
TEL. 0481884215
francoterpin@virgilio.it

CELLAR SALES
PRE-BOOKED VISITS

ANNUAL PRODUCTION **15,000 bottles**
HECTARES UNDER VINE **10**
VITICULTURE METHOD **Natural**

Franco Terpin's winery is at San Floriano del Collio, next door to Slovenia. "This land is damnably beautiful, lethargic, empathetic and quixotic. People here are conspiratorial, determined and on occasion brusque, often instinctively arrogant, but infinitely real". We quote this from the winery web site because it is a perfect portrait of Franco, a man of few words and great wines, a tireless worker and a determined defender of the farming heritage.

Ask anyone in these parts what the best variety is and they will tell you "ribolla gialla". Ribolla has found an ideal habitat here, people have always planted it and love it above all other grapes. Imagine, then, how gratifying it was for Franco to pick up Three Glasses for his '05 Ribolla Gialla, released only now after years of patient maturation. Its lovely yellow is flecked with amber that introduces a complex, smoke and mineral nose layered over candied peel and pine resin, followed by a seamless, almost saltily savoury flavour. Equally exciting are the headily alcoholic Bianco Jakot '06 and Franco's Bordeaux blend, the elegant, aristocratically structured Rosso Stamas '05.

O Collio Pinot Grigio '07	♟♟♟	4*
● Collio Merlot '06	♟♟	5
O Collio Chardonnay '07	♟♟	4*
O Collio Sauvignon '07	♟♟	4*
O Vino degli Orti '07	♟♟	5
O Collio Bianco Planta '05	♟♟	5
O Collio Ribolla Gialla '07	♟♟	4
O Pinot Bianco '07	♟♟	4*

O Collio Ribolla Gialla '05	♟♟♟	5*
● Collio Rosso Stamas '05	♟♟	5
O Jakot Bianco '06	♟♟	5
O Collio Chardonnay '06	♟♟	5
O Collio Sauvignon '06	♟♟	5
O Collio Pinot Grigio Sialis '06	♟	6
O Collio Bianco Stamas '04	♟♟	5
O Collio Ribolla Gialla '04	♟♟	5
● Collio Rosso Stamas '04	♟♟	5
O Pinot Grigio Sialis '05	♟♟	6

Terre di Ger

FRAZ. FRATTINA
S.DA DELLA MEDUNA
33076 PRAVISDOMINI [PN]
TEL. 0434644452
www.terrediger.it

CELLAR SALES
PRE-BOOKED VISITS

ANNUAL PRODUCTION **120,000 bottles**
HECTARES UNDER VINE **48**
VITICULTURE METHOD **Conventional**

Gianni, Edda and Robert are the members of the Spinazzè family who started up Terre di Ger, with almost 80 hectares stretching across the Grave del Friuli between the Lemene and Livenza rivers. Having discarded the idea of producing bulk wine, the estate is now aiming to promote the territory by releasing fuller-bodied, longer-lived wines with more substance. Since the 2008 harvest, the cellar has been advised by oenological consultant Mario Ercolino and the initial results are truly exciting.

This year's range of wines earned very good marks, particularly for the reds. Best of the bunch was the '07 Cabernet Franc, which is still young but very rounded and savoury with promising depth. The upfront, extract-rich Merlot '07 is impeccably varietal while the Refosco from the same vintage is fruity and pervasive. El Masut '05, from merlot, cabernet franc, cabernet sauvignon and refosco, is equally fruity with nice minerality. The best whites were the lingeringly aromatic Pinot Grigio and Sauvignon Blanc '08. Limine '06, an unusual blend of verduzzo and chardonnay, has a creamily soft texture. Finally, the '08 Traminer and Chardonnay round the list off in style.

★ Franco Toros

LOC. NOVALI, 12
34071 CORMÒNS [GO]
TEL. 048161327
www.vinitoros.com

CELLAR SALES
PRE-BOOKED VISITS

ANNUAL PRODUCTION **70,000 bottles**
HECTARES UNDER VINE **10**
VITICULTURE METHOD **Conventional**

Edoardo Toros was the man who in the early 20th century found a perfect place to grow grapes at Novali, near Cormòns, and promptly settled there. It was a winning move and today Franco, with a little help from the many members of his extended family, takes full advantage to produce some of the finest wines in Friuli. Franco - it says Francesco on his birth certificate – has reached such heights of quality that his label on a bottle is a guarantee of supreme excellence.

A Three Glass award repays a producer for a year's hard work and provides stimulus for the year to come. Winning two Three Glass prizes in the same year is a rare achievement reserved only for winemakers who present a range that is performing at its peak. We join Franco in celebrating a marvellous '08 Friulano with overwhelming, utterly varietal and deliciously pervasive aromatics followed by a reassuringly powerful palate. The same goes for the '08 Pinot Bianco, which thrills the nose with the elegance of its bouquet. Also excellent are the delightfully rustic '06 Merlot with its hint of liquorice, and the '08 Chardonnay and Sauvignon, both of which are better than good.

● Friuli Grave Cabernet Franc '07	♟	4*
● El Masut '05	♟♟	5
● Friuli Grave Merlot '07	♟♟	4*
○ Friuli Grave Pinot Grigio '08	♟♟	4*
○ Limine '06	♟♟	5
● Refosco '07	♟♟	4*
○ Sauvignon Blanc '08	♟♟	4
○ Friuli Grave Chardonnay '08	♟	4
○ Friuli Grave Traminer '08	♟	4
● Friuli Grave Cabernet Franc '06	♟♟	4
○ Friuli Grave Chardonnay '07	♟♟	4*
○ Friuli Grave Pinot Grigio '07	♟♟	4*
○ Sauvignon Blanc '07	♟♟	4*
○ Sauvignon Blanc '06	♟♟	3

○ Collio Friulano '08	♟♟♟	5*
○ Collio Pinot Bianco '08	♟♟♟	5*
○ Collio Chardonnay '08	♟♟	5
● Collio Merlot '06	♟♟	5
○ Collio Sauvignon '08	♟♟	5
○ Collio Pinot Grigio '08	♟♟	5
● Collio Merlot Sel. '97	♟♟♟	6
○ Collio Pinot Bianco '07	♟♟♟	5
○ Collio Pinot Bianco '05	♟♟♟	5
○ Collio Pinot Bianco '03	♟♟♟	5
○ Collio Pinot Bianco '01	♟♟♟	4
○ Collio Pinot Bianco '00	♟♟♟	4
○ Collio Tocai Friulano '06	♟♟♟	5
○ Collio Tocai Friulano '04	♟♟♟	5
○ Collio Tocai Friulano '03	♟♟♟	5
○ Collio Tocai Friulano '02	♟♟♟	5

Torre Rosazza

FRAZ. OLEIS
LOC. POGGIOBELLO, 12
33044 MANZANO [UD]
TEL. 0422864511
www.torrerosazza.com

CELLAR SALES
PRE-BOOKED VISITS

ANNUAL PRODUCTION 350,000 bottles
HECTARES UNDER VINE 95
VITICULTURE METHOD Conventional

Torre Rosazza is the premium estate of Le Tenute di Genagricola, a group that in Friuli also includes Poggiobello, Borgo Magredo and Tenuta Sant'Anna, with other holdings in Veneto, Piedmont, Romagna and Lazio. Torre Rosazza was acquired in 1974 and is managed by Enrico Raddi, who is the administrative director. When Mario Zuliani arrived to look after sales and external relations, he brought with him a new stimulus in the direction of excellence.

The 18th-century Palazzo De Marchi houses the offices and cellar among vineyards on two superb terraced natural amphitheatres, tended by agronomist Ennio Venuto. The cellar is in the charge of the experienced group oenologist Luca Zuccarello. Both men can call on Mario Zuliani's vineyard management and winemaking skills, and the results are evident. The Pignolo '07 is a stand-out for its pervasive, balsam-veined aromatics and thrust on the savoury palate, even though it is still very young. The '08 Sauvignon has depth and power on both nose and palate while the tangy, fresh-tasting Pinot Grigio '08 is redolent of pears. Finally, the honey and caramel '06 Picolit is harmoniously sweet.

La Tunella

FRAZ. IPPLIS
VIA DEL COLLIO, 14
33040 PREMARIACCO [UD]
TEL. 0432716030
www.latunella.it

CELLAR SALES
PRE-BOOKED VISITS

ANNUAL PRODUCTION 450,000 bottles
HECTARES UNDER VINE 80
VITICULTURE METHOD Conventional

The La Tunella story spans three generations. First, there was Min, the founder; then came his son, Livio; and now Massimo and Marco Zorzettig, who with their mother Gabriella run an operation that is one of the jewels of the Colli Orientali del Friuli. This is a model estate. Modern and forward-looking, it turns out serious numbers with a young, well-coordinated team bursting with enthusiasm. The new cellar deserves a visit both for its imaginative architecture and for the state-of-the-art technology inside.

Massimo is a tireless promoter of the estate and Marco is equally busy in the vineyards while their wives Romina and Barbara join forces with Gabriella on the hospitality front. Luigino Zamparo is the long-serving oenologist with experience rare in one so young. Yet again, BiancoSesto – the '08 this time – impressed out tasters. We remind readers that BiancoSesto is a 50-50 mix of friulano and ribolla gialla matured in large wood and then steel, which gives it a fruity, subtly aromatic character and a gutsy freshness in the mouth. Friulano Selènze '08 is stylish and savoury, closing unhurriedly on very youthful fruit-led aromas.

● COF Pignolo '07	♟♟	6
○ COF Bianco Ronco del Masiero '08	♟♟	5
○ COF Friulano '08	♟♟	4*
○ COF Pinot Grigio '08	♟♟	4*
○ COF Ribolla Gialla '08	♟♟	4*
○ COF Sauvignon '08	♟♟	4*
○ Picolit '06	♟♟	6
● COF Merlot '08	♟	5
○ COF Picolit '04	♟♟	6
○ COF Sauvignon Poggiobello '05	♟♟	4

○ COF BiancoSesto '08	♟♟	5
○ COF Friulano Selènze '08	♟♟	4*
○ COF Ribolla Gialla Rjgialla '08	♟♟	4*
● COF Rosso L'Arcione '05	♟♟	6
● COF Schioppettino Selènze '06	♟♟	5
○ COF Pinot Grigio '08	♟	4
○ Noans '07	♟	6
○ COF BiancoSesto '07	♟♟♟	5
○ COF BiancoSesto '06	♟♟♟	4*
○ COF Chardonnay '07	♟♟	4
○ COF Friulano Selènze '07	♟♟	4
○ COF Pinot Grigio '07	♟♟	4
● COF Rosso L'Arcione '04	♟♟	6
● COF Schioppettino Selènze '05	♟♟	5
○ Noans '06	♟♟	6

Valchiarò

FRAZ. TOGLIANO
VIA DEI LAGHI, 4C
33040 TORREANO [UD]
TEL. 0432715502
www.valchiaro.it

CELLAR SALES
PRE-BOOKED VISITS

ANNUAL PRODUCTION **40,000 bottles**
HECTARES UNDER VINE **15**
VITICULTURE METHOD **Conventional**

"Love and passion" is the watchword of the five friends who in 1991 decided to pool their efforts and set up Valchiarò. Love of the vine and passion for winemaking are still their driving forces, embodied in Lauro Devincenti who manages the cellar and keeps the enthusiasm very much alive. The modern, spacious cellar at Torreano was inaugurated in 2006 in superb natural surroundings and Gianni Menotti continues to contribute his top-notch winemaking consultancy skills.

The reliable quality of recent vintages, and flattering reports in the various wine guides, have enabled the range to find space in the market, first in Italy and then abroad. We have always had a preference for the Verduzzo Friulano, which again in the '07 edition proved excellent and went on to the national taste-offs. The old gold ushers in fragrances of apricot tart, dried figs, candied peel and almonds before the concentrate depth of the palate reveals its balance and persistence. The fruit and flowers '08 Friulano Nexus is very gratifying in the mouth while the very varietal, no-nonsense '08 Sauvignon wins friends for its tangy energy.

Valpanera

VIA TRIESTE, 5A
33059 VILLA VICENTINA [UD]
TEL. 0431970395
www.valpanera.it

PRE-BOOKED VISITS

ANNUAL PRODUCTION **450,000 bottles**
HECTARES UNDER VINE **55**
VITICULTURE METHOD **Conventional**

The sign at the winery entrance with "Casa del Refosco" (Home of Refosco) in big letters tells you that this is a cellar that has always believed in the variety's potential on the local clay and sand soil, and with the benefit of local site climates. This bold project is proving very successful for Giampietro Dal Vecchio, co-owner of the estate with his son, Giovanni, and their enterprising winemaker, Luca Marcolini.

But Valpanera means more than just Refosco. Last year, we were liberal with our praise for a white Chardonnay Carato. This time, the top scorer was Refosco Riserva '05, despite a far from easy growing year for reds. But that is one of the reasons we were so impressed. The splendid ruby red is flecked with garnet and red berry fruit jam, tobacco, coffee and cocoa powder clamour to please the nose. Soft and mouthfilling, the palate also has plenty of balance. We also liked the refosco, cabernet sauvignon and merlot Rosso Alma '05, which is more evolved, giving blueberry and spice sensations. Finally, there is a special word of praise for the aromatics and appeal of the Refosco Superiore '06.

O COF Verduzzo Friulano '07	♟♟	4*
O COF Friulano Nexus '08	♟♟	4*
O COF Sauvignon '08	♟♟	4*
O COF Friulano '08	♟	4
O COF Pinot Grigio '08	♟	4
● COF Rosso Torre Qual '04	♟	4
● COF Refosco P. R. '04	♟♟	4
O COF Tocai Friulano '07	♟♟	4
O COF Verduzzo Friulano '06	♟♟	4*
O COF Verduzzo Friulano '05	♟♟	4*

● Friuli Aquileia Refosco P. R. Ris. '05	♟♟	5
● Friuli Aquileia Refosco P. R. Sup. '06	♟♟	4*
● Friuli Aquileia Rosso Alma '05	♟♟	5
● Friuli Aquileia Cabernet Sauvignon '08	♟	4
● Friuli Aquileia Refosco P. R. '07	♟	3
O Friuli Aquileia Chardonnay '04	♟♟	4*
O Friuli Aquileia Chardonnay Carato '06	♟♟	5
● Friuli Aquileia Refosco P. R. Ris. '03	♟♟	5
● Friuli Aquileia Refosco P. R. Sup. '05	♟♟	4
● Friuli Aquileia Rosso Alma '03	♟♟	5
O Friuli Aquileia Sauvignon '05	♟♟	4
● Rosso di Valpanera '03	♟♟	3*

★ Venica & Venica

LOC. CERÒ, 8
34070 DOLEGNA DEL COLLIO [GO]
TEL. 048161264
www.venica.it

CELLAR SALES
PRE-BOOKED VISITS
VISITOR FACILITIES

ANNUAL PRODUCTION 240,000 bottles
HECTARES UNDER VINE N.D.
VITICULTURE METHOD Conventional

Venica & Venica is a love story that started 80 years ago on 6 February 1930, when Daniele Venica purchased a farmhouse with vineyards at Cerò, near Dolegna del Collio. His son Adelchi was equally enamoured of the spot and now Gianni and Giorgio, the current owners, have turned the estate into one of Friuli's most influential thanks to an ongoing programme of shrewd expansion. The future is assured since Gianni's son Gianpaolo has been part of the operation for some time, helping out his father and uncle on the production side.

Venica & Venica was one of the first estates to hire fruitmakers Sirch and Simonit, of Preparatori d'Uva, who still watch over the vine stock. Market relations are the charge of Gianni's wife, Ornella, a former chair of the Collio protection consortium, who also manages a beautiful farmstay. But what about the wines? Just look at the table. The '08 edition of Ronco delle Mele picked up Three Glasses again. This magnificent wine is a benchmark for Friulian Sauvignon, showing rich fruit and minerality as it explodes onto the palate. The rich, powerful '08 Pinot Bianco is supremely elegant while the '06 Refosco Bottaz teases the palate with hints of liquorice and rhubarb.

○ Collio Sauvignon Ronco delle Mele '08	▽▽▽	6
○ Collio Bianco Tre Vignis '08	▽▽	6
○ Collio Pinot Bianco '08	▽▽	5
● Collio Refosco P. R. Bottaz '06	▽▽	6
○ Collio Friulano Ronco delle Cime '08	▽▽	5
○ Collio Malvasia '08	▽▽	5
○ Collio Sauvignon Ronco del Cerò '08	▽▽	5
● Collio Merlot Perilla '06	▽	6
○ Collio Pinot Grigio Jesera '08	▽	5
○ Collio Ribolla Gialla L'Adelchi '08	▽	5
○ Collio Sauvignon Ronco delle Mele '07	▽▽▽	6
○ Collio Sauvignon Ronco delle Mele '05	▽▽▽	6
○ Collio Sauvignon Ronco delle Mele '02	▽▽▽	6
○ Collio Tocai Friulano Ronco delle Cime '06	▽▽▽	5
○ Collio Tocai Friulano Ronco delle Cime '02	▽▽▽	6

La Viarte

VIA NOVACUZZO, 51
33040 PREPOTTO [UD]
TEL. 0432759458
www.laviarte.it

CELLAR SALES
PRE-BOOKED VISITS

ANNUAL PRODUCTION 100,000 bottles
HECTARES UNDER VINE 26
VITICULTURE METHOD Conventional

La Viarte – the name means springtime in Friulian – is a splendid estate in the Colli Orientali del Friuli. And not just for the splendour of its beautiful setting but also for its splendid wines and the people who make them. Giulio Ceschin, son of the founders Giuseppe and Carla, has now taken on full management responsibility, flanked by his wife Federica, who looks after administration and public relations.

The La Viarte Schioppettino went on to our finals together with Siùm. Giulio Ceschin is a firm believer in Schioppettino and leads the producers' association that won subzone status for Prepotto's Schoppettino dei Colli Orientali. The '06 is a vibrantly elegant wine in the glass and on the complex, pervasive nose, which is a paragon of varietal typicity. The '06 Siùm – it means dream – is a splendid mix of verduzzo and picolit that gives candied peel, raisins and marron glacé. It's sweet but not cloying, with loads of balance and persistence. All the other whites and reds are well up to snuff. A splendid range, in fact.

● COF Schioppettino '06	▽	5
○ Siùm '06	▽	6
○ COF Friulano '08	▽▽	4*
● COF Merlot '06	▽▽	5
○ COF Pinot Bianco '08	▽▽	4*
○ COF Sauvignon '08	▽▽	4*
● COF Tazzelenghe '05	▽▽	6
○ COF Pinot Grigio '08	▽	4
○ COF Ribolla Gialla '08	▽	4
○ COF Friulano '07	♟♟	4
○ COF Pinot Grigio '07	♟♟	4
● COF Refosco P. R. '05	♟♟	5
● COF Tazzelenghe '04	♟♟	6
○ Siùm '05	♟♟	6

Gestioni Agricole Vidussi

VIA SPESSA, 18
34071 CAPRIVA DEL FRIULI [GO]
TEL. 048180072
www.vinimontresor.it

CELLAR SALES
PRE-BOOKED VISITS

ANNUAL PRODUCTION **400,000 bottles**
HECTARES UNDER VINE **30**
VITICULTURE METHOD **Conventional**

The Vidussi vineyards sprawl over most of the hills that go from Capriva del Friuli to Cormòns, in the heart of the Collio, while the Borgo dai Fradis vineyard is at Rocca Bernarda in the Colli Orientali del Friuli. Management of the estate is in the hands of the Verona-based Montresor family. They are assisted locally by Luigino De Giuseppe, who looks after the entire production process.

Again this year, the overall quality is distinctly gratifying. Score across the board were impressive and the careful attention to varietal typicity is clear. Wines from native grapes did best of all, and in particular the '08 Friulano, which has always been the everyday wine in these parts. The Vidussi version is juicy, savoury, fruit-led and faintly herbaceous over a superb background note of gentian. We also like the rose and wisteria aromatics of the '08 Malvasia. Finally, the '08 Ribolla Gialla is fresh and so tangy it is almost salty while the '08 Ribolla Nera, aka Schioppettino, is very youthful but already nicely balanced.

★ Vie di Romans

LOC. VIE DI ROMANS, 1
34070 MARIANO DEL FRIULI [GO]
TEL. 048169600
www.viediromans.it

CELLAR SALES
PRE-BOOKED VISITS

ANNUAL PRODUCTION **230,000 bottles**
HECTARES UNDER VINE **44**
VITICULTURE METHOD **Conventional**

The uncommonly beautiful yet very functional cellar at Mariano del Friuli, run by Gianfranco Gallo for almost 25 years, never ceases to amaze. The wines are very territorial, with impressive structure and skilful use of oak, even for the whites, which is not yet common practice in Italy. We are in the Isonzo DOC, a few kilometres from the Gulf of Trieste, and the climate imbues the wines with a Mediterranean feel, pervasive fragrances and soft savours.

Not many wineries send six bottles to our finals. Three Glasses went to the varietal, elegant Sauvignon Piere '07, a wine of depth and allure that unveils a hint of vanilla. Chardonnay Vie di Romans '07, an exceptionally subtle, minerally wine, has great character. The '07 Malvasia Istriana Dis Cumieris is a lovely exercise in aromas, power and harmony. The Sauvignon Vieris '07 is very varietal, giving sage and tomato leaf before unfurling a juicily rich palate. Friulano Dolée '07 is complex and fills the mouth, opening softly and signing off with a faint hint of bitterness. Last on our list is the '07 Chardonnay Ciampagnis Vieris, and elegant wine fragrant with aniseed and spice.

○ Collio Friulano '08	♟♟	4*
○ Collio Malvasia '08	♟♟	4*
○ Collio Pinot Bianco '08	♟	4
○ Collio Ribolla Gialla '08	♟	4
● Collio Rosso Are di Miute '08	♟	5
○ Collio Traminer Aromatico '08	♟	4
● Ribolla Nera o Schioppettino '08	♟	4
○ Collio Malvasia '07	♟♟	4
○ Collio Malvasia '06	♟♟	4
○ Collio Pinot Bianco '06	♟♟	4
○ Collio Sauvignon '06	♟♟	4

○ Friuli Isonzo Rive Alte Sauvignon Piere '07	♟♟♟	5*
○ Friuli Isonzo Chardonnay Ciampagnis Vieris '07	♟♟	5
○ Friuli Isonzo Chardonnay Vie di Romans '07	♟♟	6
○ Friuli Isonzo Friulano Dolée '07	♟♟	6
○ Friuli Isonzo Malvasia Istriana Dis Cumieris '07	♟♟	5
○ Friuli Isonzo Rive Alte Sauvignon Vieris '07	♟♟	6
○ Dut'Un '06	♟♟	7
○ Friuli Isonzo Bianco Flors di Uis '07	♟♟	5
○ Friuli Isonzo Pinot Grigio Dessimis '07	♟♟	5
○ Dut'Un '02	♟♟♟	7
○ Friuli Isonzo Malvasia Istriana Dis Cumieris '06	♟♟♟	5
○ Friuli Isonzo Pinot Grigio Dessimis '99	♟♟♟	5
○ Friuli Isonzo Sauvignon Piere '01	♟♟♟	5
○ Friuli Isonzo Sauvignon Vieris '04	♟♟♟	5
○ Friuli Isonzo Sauvignon Vieris '02	♟♟♟	5
○ Friuli Isonzo Sauvignon Vieris '00	♟♟♟	5

Vigna del Lauro

LOC. MONTE, 38
34071 CORMÒNS [GO]
TEL. 048160155
www.roncodeitassi.it

CELLAR SALES
PRE-BOOKED VISITS

ANNUAL PRODUCTION 42,000 bottles
HECTARES UNDER VINE 6
VITICULTURE METHOD Conventional

Vigna del Lauro is named after an old vineyard of tocai friulano, almost completely surrounded by well-established sweet laurels that fill the air with their characteristic fragrance. The enterprise started in 1994 with a project dreamed up by Fabio Coser and the German importer of Italian wines, Eberhard Spangenberg. It's still run as a family business by Fabio, his wife Daniela and their sons Matteo and Enrico in superb wine country in the Collio and Isonzo DOC zones, all within the municipality of Cormòns.

Winemaking at Vigna del Lauro is driven by attention to the raw materials, a necessary condition for bringing out varietal and territorial character. The wines are uncompromisingly sound and genuinely delicious. The Sauvignon '08 proffers fragrant, fruit-laced aromas lifted by an elegant hint of aniseed. Appealingly full in the mouth, it closes on a faint twist of bitterness. Typicity is the keynote of the beautifully drinkable cherry and raspberry '06 Merlot. The Friulano '08 stands out for assertive varietal character while the Chardonnay, Ribolla Gialla and Pinot Grigio, all from '08, also remain true to their respective grapes.

Vigna Petrussa

VIA ALBANA, 47
33040 PREPOTTO [UD]
TEL. 0432713021
www.vignapetrussa.it

CELLAR SALES
PRE-BOOKED VISITS

ANNUAL PRODUCTION 30,000 bottles
HECTARES UNDER VINE 6.5
VITICULTURE METHOD Conventional

Albana near Prepotto lies in a valley coursed by the river Judrio, an area that has always been synonymous with the native ribolla nera, a native variety also known as schioppettino. Its wine is associated indissolubly with Hilde Petrussa, who for years has chaired a committee of local producers to promote Schioppettino di Prepotto, eventually obtaining recognition of a specific subzone of Colli Orientali del Friuli.

But this time, it was the '06 Picolit that went through to the finals. Its old gold hue heralds delicious fragrances of ripe banana, marron glacé and chestnut honey. Creamily soft-textured in the mouth, it leaves an indelible gustatory memory. Selected grapes left to dry until late autumn went into the purple-flecked ruby red Schioppettino '06 with its red berry fruit and cyclamen. Slightly austere but fresh-tasting and savoury in the mouth, it signs off with balsamic notes and smokiness. There's similar character in the '06 Cabernet Franc and the complex Richenza '07 blend but the '08 Friulano and Sauvignon were not ready when we were tasting.

O Collio Friulano '08	♟♟ 4*
O Collio Sauvignon '08	♟♟ 4*
● Friuli Isonzo Merlot '06	♟♟ 4*
O Collio Pinot Grigio '08	♟ 4
O Collio Ribolla Gialla '08	♟ 4
O Friuli Isonzo Chardonnay '08	♟ 4
O Collio Sauvignon '99	♟♟♟ 4
O Collio Friulano '07	♟♟ 4
O Collio Pinot Grigio '07	♟♟ 4
O Collio Ribolla Gialla '06	♟♟ 4*
O Collio Ribolla Gialla '05	♟♟ 4*
O Collio Sauvignon '07	♟♟ 4*

O COF Picolit '06	♟♟ 6
● COF Schioppettino '06	♟♟ 5
● COF Cabernet Franc '06	♟ 4
O Richenza '07	♟ 5
O COF Picolit '05	♟♟ 6
O COF Picolit '04	♟♟ 6
● COF Schioppettino '05	♟♟ 5
● COF Schioppettino '05	♟♟ 5
● COF Schioppettino '04	♟♟ 5
O COF Tocai Friulano '06	♟♟ 4*
O COF Tocai Friulano '05	♟♟ 4*

Vigna Traverso

VIA RONCHI, 73
33040 PREPOTTO [UD]
TEL. 0422804807
www.vignatraverso.it

CELLAR SALES
PRE-BOOKED VISITS

ANNUAL PRODUCTION **60,000 bottles**
HECTARES UNDER VINE **45**
VITICULTURE METHOD **Conventional**

The first stage of the new cellar is finished. Stefano Traverso, the young winemaker who was already in charge of the family winery in 1998, will soon have adequate working space for changing needs. Recovery of the old vineyards has been carried out with input from vine physiologist Stefano Zaninotti and for the past few years, Stefano has had very useful assistance from Alessio Dorigo and Marco Pecchiari's Terra&Vino consultancy group.

The Cabernet Franc '07 comes from a special French clone. It presents an impenetrably dark ruby giving black berry fruits, coffee and toasted wood on the nose, followed by a pervasive, aroma-rich palate. The whites are utterly true to type. The '08 Friulano has citron and grapefruit citrus, the '08 Ribolla Gialla is refreshingly upfront and the '08 Sauvignon '08 has depth, energy and excellent typicity. The '07 Refosco's vibrant hue frames ripe morello cherry and liquorice while the palate is every bit as juicily soft-textured as the '07 Schioppettino, which is a tad more alcohol-led.

★ Le Vigne di Zamò

LOC. ROSAZZO
VIA ABATE CORRADO, 4
33044 MANZANO [UD]
TEL. 0432759693
www.levignedizamo.com

CELLAR SALES
PRE-BOOKED VISITS

ANNUAL PRODUCTION **250,000 bottles**
HECTARES UNDER VINE **67**
VITICULTURE METHOD **Conventional**

The Zamò family has been involved with wine since 1924, when Tullio's father Luigi opened an unpretentious eatery in Manzano. In time, Tullio set up first the Vigne dal Leon winery and then Abbazia di Rosazzo. Today, his sons Pierluigi and Silvano run Le Vigne di Zamò, based on a hilltop that dominates eastern Friuli with views that stretch as far as the coast. It's not easy to spot the splendid, very practical new cellars, which have been artfully concealed beneath the hill.

The wines did fantastically well. Five went through to the finals, where Merlot Vigne Cinquant'Anni earned Three Glasses. Its superb, broodingly dark ruby ushers in intense jammy red fruit and the sweet spice that tells you the new oak was gauged to perfection before stunning balance and finesse gratify the palate. The '07 Tullio Zamò, a Pinot Bianco named after the cellar's founder, is still young but already brims with personality and will acquire complexity with the passage of time. Re Fosco '06 has depth, pervasiveness and plenty of heft. Finally, the deliciously drinkable '07 Friulano Vigne Cinquant'Anni is its usual firm, fruit-led, fresh-tasting self.

Wine		Rating
● COF Cabernet Franc '07	▼▼	4*
○ COF Friulano '08	▼▼	4*
● COF Refosco P. R. '07	▼▼	4*
○ COF Ribolla Gialla '08	▼▼	4*
○ COF Sauvignon '08	▼▼	4*
● COF Schioppettino '07	▼▼	5
● COF Merlot Sottocastello '06	▼	6
● COF Cabernet Franc '05	♀♀	4
○ COF Chardonnay '07	♀♀	4
○ COF Friulano '07	♀♀	4
● COF Merlot Sottocastello '05	♀♀	6
● COF Schioppettino '06	♀♀	5
○ COF Tocai Friulano '06	♀♀	4
○ COF Tocai Friulano '05	♀♀	4*

Wine		Rating
● COF Merlot V. Cinquant'Anni '06	▼▼▼	6
○ COF Friulano V. Cinquant'Anni '07	▼▼	6
○ COF Pinot Bianco Tullio Zamò '07	▼▼	5
● COF Refosco P. R. Re Fosco '06	▼▼	6
● COF Schioppettino '05	▼▼	6
○ COF Malvasia '07	▼▼	5
○ COF Rosazzo Bianco Ronco delle Acacie '07	▼▼	6
○ COF Sauvignon '08	▼▼	5
● COF Rosazzo Pignolo '04	▼	8
○ COF Malvasia '00	♀♀♀	4
● COF Merlot V. Cinquant'Anni '99	♀♀♀	6
○ COF Rosazzo Bianco Ronco delle Acacie '01	♀♀♀	5
● COF Rosazzo Pignolo '01	♀♀♀	8
○ COF Tocai Friulano V. Cinquant'Anni '06	♀♀♀	6
○ COF Tocai Friulano V. Cinquant'Anni '00	♀♀♀	5
○ COF Tocai Friulano V. Cinquant'Anni '99	♀♀♀	5

Villa de Puppi

VIA ROMA, 5
33040 MOIMACCO [UD]
TEL. 0432722461
www.depuppi.it

CELLAR SALES
PRE-BOOKED VISITS

ANNUAL PRODUCTION 40,000 bottles
HECTARES UNDER VINE 35
VITICULTURE METHOD Conventional

The winery has belonged to the noble De Puppi family for many generations. Originally from Tuscany, the family descends from the celebrated house of Guidi, lords of Poppi in the Casentino area. The current owner is Conte Luigi De Puppi but management is in the hands of his two children. Caterina, soon to graduate in biology, looks after the estate, including work on the land. Her brother Valfredo, who has just earned a degree in economics and business, is in charge of external relations.

Most of the vines are at the estate's country house at Moimacco, where the cellar is also located, but the holding includes ten more hectares in the hills of Rosazzo in the Colli Orientali del Friuli. Our two heroes are flanked in the cellar by Marco Pecchiari and in the vineyard by Pierpaolo Sirch. They are in safe hands, as you can see from the wines. Taj Blanc '08, from friulano, is as good as ever, its wealth of fragrant aromas preceding a juicy, easy-drinking palate. Oak-derived aromas characterize the '07 Chardonnay Cate, which signs off with tropical fruits and coffee.

★★ Villa Russiz

VIA RUSSIZ, 6
34070 CAPRIVA DEL FRIULI [GO]
TEL. 048180047
www.villarussiz.it

CELLAR SALES
PRE-BOOKED VISITS

ANNUAL PRODUCTION 220,000 bottles
HECTARES UNDER VINE 35
VITICULTURE METHOD Conventional

Villa Russiz owes its origin to the foresight of the French count, Théodore de La Tour, who settled in the Collio hills with is Austrian wife, Elvine Ritter. A passion for viticulture prompted him to import new varieties and the modern oenological techniques used in France at that time. Since they had no heirs, they decided their estate should be used to create a charitable institute for children in need, which became the Casa Famiglia Adele Cerruti.

It is satisfying to see how well a publicly owned institution can work, without any need for support. The estate pays for itself and the charity. Credit for this must go to the dynamic director, Silvano Stefanutti, and the estate manager, Gianni Menotti, universally admired for his professional skills. The leading selections bear the names of the two benefactors and this year it was the Sauvignon de La tour '08 that picked up Three Glasses for its tempting elderflowers and astonishing power on the palate, lifted by freshness and complex varietal character. Merlot Gräf de La Tour '06, Chardonnay Gräfin de La Tour '07 and the '08 Pinot Bianco are all outstanding.

O Chardonnay Cate '07	♟♟	5
O Taj Blanc '08	♟♟	4*
O Chardonnay '08	♟♟	4*
● Merlot '08	♟♟	4*
● Cabernet '07	♟	4
● Refosco P. R. '07	♟	4
● Refosco P.R. Cate '07	♟	5
O Sauvignon '08	♟	4
O Chardonnay '06	♟♟	4*
● Refosco P.R. Cate '06	♟♟	6
O Sauvignon '07	♟♟	4
O Sauvignon '06	♟♟	4*
O Taj Blanc '07	♟♟	4
O Taj Blanc '06	♟♟	4*

O Collio Sauvignon de La Tour '08	♟♟♟	6
O Collio Chardonnay Gräfin de La Tour '07	♟♟	7
● Collio Merlot Graf de La Tour '06	♟♟	7
O Collio Pinot Bianco '08	♟♟	5
● Collio Cabernet Sauvignon '07	♟♟	5
O Collio Friulano '08	♟♟	5
O Collio Malvasia '08	♟♟	5
O Collio Pinot Grigio '08	♟♟	5
● Collio Merlot '07	♟	5
O Collio Ribolla Gialla '08	♟	5
O Collio Chardonnay Gräfin de La Tour '02	♟♟♟	6
● Collio Merlot Graf de La Tour '02	♟♟♟	7
● Collio Merlot Graf de La Tour '99	♟♟♟	7
O Collio Pinot Bianco '07	♟♟♟	5
O Collio Sauvignon de La Tour '05	♟♟♟	6
O Collio Sauvignon de La Tour '02	♟♟♟	6
O Collio Tocai Friulano '04	♟♟♟	5

Tenuta Villanova

LOC. VILLANOVA
VIA CONTESSA BERETTA, 29
34072 FARRA D'ISONZO [GO]
TEL. 0481889311
www.tenutavillanova.com

CELLAR SALES
PRE-BOOKED VISITS

ANNUAL PRODUCTION 800,000 bottles
HECTARES UNDER VINE 130
VITICULTURE METHOD Conventional

Villanova has a long history dating back to 1499. In 1932, the estate was purchased by businessman Arnaldo Bennati, who saw its potential, and it is still managed today by his wife Giuseppina Grossi Bennati. She is helped out by the dynamic general manager, Renato Romanzin, who has given the operation a seriously quality-oriented direction in recent years.

Today, the "mansi", literally hides of land, of Tenuta Villanova are in the Collio and Isonzo DOC zones and care has been taken to match varieties to the local terrain. Agronomist Alfieri Chiappo looks after the vines and in the cellar is long-serving estate oenologist Massimiliano Cattarin, who sent two wines to our finals this year. Malvasia Saccoline '08 is an Isonzo DOC wine that stands out for the aroma-lifted definition and finesse of its bouquet, and its elegant savouriness. The other finalist, Chardonnay del Collio Ronco Cucco '07, is oak-veined, well-balanced and graced with an elegant, minerally finale.

Andrea Visintini

VIA GRAMOGLIANO, 27
33040 CORNO DI ROSAZZO [UD]
TEL. 0432755813
www.vinivisintini.com

CELLAR SALES
PRE-BOOKED VISITS

ANNUAL PRODUCTION 140,000 bottles
HECTARES UNDER VINE 28
VITICULTURE METHOD Conventional

A listed 16th-century tower dominated the entrance to this winery, as well as being its symbol. Domenico Visintini, his grandfather Umberto and father Andrea have left this wonderful heritage to Oliviero and twins Cinzia e Palmira, currently engaged in modernizing the cellar's underground spaces and the vineyards. Their approach is simple: bring great raw material into the cellar and do as little to it as possible.

A marvellous '08 Ribolla Gialla opens a list of wines with many peaks of excellence. Its varietal, slightly lemony fruit follow-through nicely on the crisp, energetically savoury palate. There are two Merlots, both worth uncorking. The sound '07 version gives varietal morello cherry before unfolding nicely with bright acid grip. Merlot Riserva Torion '06 is a nobler proposition, its deep ruby accompanying pervasive aromas of fruit and spice. It's still young but very savoury and well structured. Pinot Grigio '08 is pinkish in the glass and soft on the concentrated palate. Rounding off the list are two expertly made '08s, a Verduzzo and a Friulano.

○ Collio Chardonnay Ronco Cucco '07	♀♀ 5
○ Friuli Isonzo Malvasia Saccoline '08	♀♀ 4*
○ Collio Friulano '08	♀♀ 4*
○ Collio Friulano Ronco Cucco '08	♀ 5
○ Collio Ribolla Gialla '08	♀ 4
○ Collio Sauvignon Ronco Cucco '08	♀ 5
○ Friuli Isonzo Pinot Grigio '08	♀ 4
● Friuli Isonzo Refosco P. R. '08	♀ 4
○ Collio Chardonnay Monte Cucco '97	♀♀♀ 4
○ Collio Friulano Ronco Cucco '07	♀♀ 5
○ Collio Picolit Ronco Cucco '06	♀♀ 6
○ Collio Sauvignon Ronco Cucco '07	♀♀ 5
○ Friuli Isonzo Chardonnay '07	♀♀ 4
○ Friuli Isonzo Malvasia Saccoline '07	♀♀ 4

○ COF Ribolla Gialla '08	♀♀ 3*
● COF Merlot '07	♀♀ 3*
● COF Merlot Torion Ris. '06	♀♀ 4
○ COF Pinot Grigio '08	♀♀ 3*
○ COF Friulano '08	♀ 3
○ COF Verduzzo Friulano '08	♀ 3
○ COF Bianco '06	♀♀ 4
○ COF Pinot Bianco '07	♀♀ 3
○ Collio Malvasia '06	♀♀ 4

★ Volpe Pasini

FRAZ. TOGLIANO
VIA CIVIDALE, 16
33040 TORREANO [UD]
TEL. 0432715151
www.volpepasini.it

CELLAR SALES
PRE-BOOKED VISITS
VISITOR FACILITIES

ANNUAL PRODUCTION **400,000 bottles**
HECTARES UNDER VINE **52**
VITICULTURE METHOD **Conventional**

Chronicles tell of how in the days of the Venetian doges, the Volpe family of Friulian farmers in 1596 joined with Venice-based merchants, the Pasinis, to found Volpe Pasini. This is a winery with serious history, which the current owner, Emilio Rotolo, Calabrian-born but now Friulian by adoption, has restored to its former splendour, expanding the vine stock with new acquisitions and impressively restoring a 17th-century villa that is now called Villa Rosa in honour of his wife.

Over the past few years, Volpe Pasini has earned a place in the elite front rank of Friulian cellars. Kudos to Emilio for this, of course, but also Francesco Torresin, who runs the cellar with advice from Alessio Dorigo of the Terra&Vino consultancy. Pinot Bianco Zuc di Volpe '08 repeated the success of the '07 with its varietal typicity and crisply defined, deliciously complex aromas followed by a palate that brims with allure. Sauvignon Zuc di Volpe '08 is excellent, teasing the nose with elegant varietal tones and satisfying the taste buds with its energy, intense fruit and vegetality. There simply isn't enough space to describe all the wines. You're going to have to try them.

○ COF Pinot Bianco Zuc di Volpe '08	🍷🍷🍷	5
○ COF Chardonnay Zuc di Volpe '07	🍷🍷	5
● COF Merlot Focus Zuc di Volpe '06	🍷🍷	6
○ COF Pinot Grigio Zuc di Volpe '08	🍷🍷	5
● COF Refosco P. R. Zuc di Volpe '06	🍷🍷	5
○ COF Sauvignon Zuc di Volpe '08	🍷🍷	5
○ COF Friulano Zuc di Volpe '08	🍷🍷	5
○ COF Pinot Grigio Ipso '07	🍷🍷	6
○ COF Ribolla Gialla Zuc di Volpe '08	🍷🍷	5
○ COF Sauvignon Volpe Pasini '08	🍷🍷	4
○ COF Pinot Bianco Zuc di Volpe '07	YYY	5
○ COF Pinot Bianco Zuc di Volpe '01	YYY	4
● COF Refosco P. R. Zuc di Volpe '01	YYY	5
○ COF Sauvignon Zuc di Volpe '05	YYY	5
○ COF Tocai Friulano Zuc di Volpe '06	YYY	5
● Merlot Focus Zuc di Volpe '02	YYY	6

Zidarich

LOC. PREPOTTO, 23
34011 DUINO AURISINA [TS]
TEL. 040201223
www.zidarich.it

CELLAR SALES
PRE-BOOKED VISITS

ANNUAL PRODUCTION **18,000 bottles**
HECTARES UNDER VINE **6**
VITICULTURE METHOD **Natural**

Benjamin Zidarich's winery is at Prepotto in the municipality of Duino Aurisina, in the Carso DOC zone. Last July, there was a memorable party for the inauguration of the new cellar, which is stunning. Carved out of the rock they way you see only in the Carso, it recycles the stone to create enchanting tunnels and enjoys a wonderful view of the Adriatic. It's well worth visiting but you might need to ask the way. There aren't any street signs yet.

The winery's successes are just reward for Benjamin's hard work and courageous winemaking decisions: skin contact, native yeasts only, no filtration and no stabilization. It takes time, of course. You have to wait for these wines, like the merlot and terrano Ruje '03, which spent three years in Slavonian oak casks before maturing unhurriedly in glass. But what awesome structure, what freshness, what fine-grained tannins and what sheer drinkability have resulted. Two well-earned Glasses went to the other wines. Prulke '07 is a blend of sauvignon, vitovska and malvasia, the single-variety '07 Vitovska is agreeably agile and the '07 Malvasia has loads of muscle.

● Ruje '03	🍷🍷	7
○ Carso Malvasia '07	🍷🍷	6
○ Carso Vitovska '07	🍷🍷	6
○ Prulke '07	🍷🍷	6
○ Carso Malvasia '06	YYY	6
○ Carso Vitovska '06	YY	6
○ Prulke '06	YY	6
○ Prulke '04	YY	6
○ Prulke '02	YY	6

Zof

FRAZ. SANT'ANDRAT DEL JUDRIO
VIA GIOVANNI XXIII, 32A
33040 CORNO DI ROSAZZO [UD]
TEL. 0432759673
www.zof.it

CELLAR SALES
PRE-BOOKED VISITS
VISITOR FACILITIES

ANNUAL PRODUCTION 90,000 bottles
HECTARES UNDER VINE 15
VITICULTURE METHOD Conventional

The Zof winery is at Sant'Andrat del Judrio, a small district of the municipality of Corno di Rosazzo in the Colli Orientali del Friuli. It's run by Daniele, the latest generation of a family with roots in Austria and Prussia that settled here more than a century ago. Daniele took over from his father, Alberto, and now works with his mother, Angela, who looks after the estate's comfortable farmstay in the converted guest wing of an 18th-century country home.

Daniele took his crucial first steps in the cellar under the authoritative eye of Donato Lanati. Now, Daniele manages operations independently and his year-on-year progress is steady. This year's list-topper is the '08 Pinot Grigio, a marvellous wine that went on to the finals for its varietal typicity and appeal. What characterizes the nose is the mix of elderflowers and pears but the aroma-rich, minerally palate is even more impressive. Daniele's '08 Sauvignon stands out for its assertive personality and the subtle whiff of smokiness that tempts the nose. Finally, the Picolit '06 is an elegantly sweet exercise in honey, confectioner's cream and biscuity aromatics.

Zuani

LOC. GIASBANA, 12
34070 SAN FLORIANO DEL COLLIO [GO]
TEL. 0481391432
www.zuanivini.it

PRE-BOOKED VISITS

ANNUAL PRODUCTION 45,000 bottles
HECTARES UNDER VINE 10
VITICULTURE METHOD Conventional

The winery set up by Patrizia Felluga is a gem. It's at Giasbana on the splendid slopes of San Floriano del Collio. Born into a leading wine family, Patrizia chaired the Collio wine protection consortium, a position held for many years by her father Marco, and she has passed on her love of the land and viticulture to her own children, Antonio and Caterina. Antonio is already a part of the winery and the family is waiting for Caterina to finish her studies so that she, too, can work on the estate full time.

Patrizia has taken the bold decision to release just one wine, Collio Bianco, in two versions. Zuani Vigne is steel matured and Zuani is aged in oak. Both are blends of equal parts of friulano, chardonnay, sauvignon and pinot grigio. Last year, Zuani Vigne secured Three Glasses and this time, too, it duly went through to the final taste-offs. The varietal aromas of the various grapes have fused into an original flower and fruit bouquet that precedes a deep, mouthfilling palate. It's the sauvignon that tends to dominate in the '07 Zuani but the drinking experience is all softness.

○ COF Pinot Grigio '08	♀♀ 4*
○ COF Picolit '06	♀♀ 6
○ COF Sauvignon '08	♀♀ 4*
● COF Cabernet Franc '07	♀ 4
○ COF Ribolla Gialla '08	♀ 4
● Refosco P. R. '07	♀ 4
○ COF Ribolla Gialla '06	♀♀ 4*
○ COF Sauvignon '07	♀♀ 4

○ Collio Bianco Zuani Vigne '08	♀♀ 4*
○ Collio Bianco Zuani '07	♀♀ 6
○ Collio Bianco Zuani Vigne '07	♀♀♀ 5
○ Collio Bianco Zuani '06	♀♀ 6
○ Collio Bianco Zuani '05	♀♀ 6
○ Collio Bianco Zuani Vigne '06	♀♀ 5

Alberice

VIA BOSCO ROMAGNO, 4
33040 CORNO DI ROSAZZO [UD]
TEL. 0422765571
www.tenutealeandri.it

Alberice is part of the Veneto-based Tenute Aleandri group, which immediately realized and exploited the estate's potential. This year's stand-out is the '08 Pinot Grigio, with subtly varietal aromas that heralds a soft-textured, attractively savoury palate.

○ COF Pinot Grigio '08	♥♥	4*
○ COF Chardonnay '08	♥♥	4*
○ COF Friulano '08	♥	4
○ COF Sauvignon '08	♥	4

Blason

VIA ROMA, 32
34072 GRADISCA D'ISONZO [GO]
TEL. 048192414
www.blasonwines.com

Giovanni Blason's modern operation stands on the red earth of the Isonzo DOC, where he is helped by family and competent collaborators. Quality continues to rise and the wines are all elegant, juiciness and varietal typicity. The reds are easy drinkers and the refreshing whites pack a punch.

● Friuli Isonzo Cabernet Franc '08	♥♥	4
● Friuli Isonzo Merlot '08	♥♥	4*
○ Friuli Isonzo Friulano '08	♥	4
○ Friuli Isonzo Pinot Grigio '08	♥	4

Borgo Magredo

LOC. TAURIANO
VIA BASALDELLA, 5
33090 SPILIMBERGO [PN]
TEL. 0422864511
www.borgomagredo.it

Borgo Magredo is part of the Le Tenute di Genagricola group. The estate has 87 hectares under vine in the Grave del Friuli and capacity for about 1,000,000 bottles. The pervasive, varietal '08 Friulano has energy and personality. The savoury Pinot Grigio '08 is complex and the other wines are good.

○ Friuli Grave Friulano '08	♥♥	3*
○ Friuli Grave Pinot Grigio '08	♥♥	4*
● Friuli Grave Merlot '08	♥	3
○ Friuli Grave Sauvignon '08	♥	3

Ca' Madresca

VIA LOMBARDIA, 5
33080 FIUME VENETO [PN]
TEL. 0434560013
adriano_test@libero.it

Since 2004, Adriano Teston has chaired the regional oenologists' association and with 20 years' experience, has started distributing wines made by farmers for whom he consults. Bianco Ninfa '08 is full, elegant and refreshingly complex while the crisp '08 Elfo, a Collio Chardonnay, is pervasively aromatic.

○ Collio Chardonnay Elfo '08	♥♥	4
○ Ninfa '08	♥♥	4
● Collio Cabernet Sauvignon '06	♥	4
○ Collio Sauvignon Reys '08	♥	4

Ca' Ronesca

LOC. LONZANO
CASALI ZORUTTI, 2
34070 DOLEGNA DEL COLLIO [GO]
TEL. 048160034
www.caronesca.it

Set up in 1972 by Sergio Comunello and extending over more than 100 hectares, 52 currently under vine, Ca' Ronesca is in the Colli Orientali del Friuli. We retasted the pinot bianco and malvasia Collio Bianco Marnà '05, which gives lip-smacking almonds and liqueur fruit, and a whistle-clean palate.

● COF Sariz '01	♥♥	5
○ COF Sauvignon '07	♥	5
○ Collio Friulano '08	♥	5
○ Collio Bianco Marnà '05	♥♥	5

Cadibon

VIA CASALI GALLO, 1
33040 CORNO DI ROSAZZO [UD]
TEL. 0432759316
www.cadibon.com

Luca and Francesca Bon run the estate set up by their father, Gianni, at Corno di Rosazzo and a traditional eatery on the main Udine-Trieste road. Quality has come on a treat and four wines earned Two Glasses: Pinot Grigio, Ronco del Nonno, Ribolla Gialla and Sauvignon.

○ COF Pinot Grigio '08	♥♥	4*
○ COF Ribolla Gialla '08	♥♥	4*
○ COF Sauvignon '08	♥♥	4*
○ Ronco del Nonno '08	♥♥	4*

OTHER WINERIES

Castello di Buttrio

VIA MORPURGO, 9
33042 BUTTRIO [UD]
TEL. 0432673015
www.castellodibuttrio.it

Castello di Buttrio is a winery with a long tradition in the Colli Orientali del Friuli. Today, it is run by Alessandra Felluga, daughter of the great Marco. Bianco Mon Blanc '08 is the subtle, aroma-rich blend of friulano, malvasia and ribolla gialla that tops a list of attractive, well-made wines.

○ COF Bianco Mon Blanc '08	♈ 4
○ COF Friulano '08	♈ 5
● COF Merlot '07	♈ 5
○ COF Sauvignon '08	♈ 5

Castello di Rubbia

FRAZ. SAN MICHELE DEL CARSO
GORNJI VRH, 40
34070 SAVOGNA D'ISONZO [GO]
TEL. 0481882681
www.castellodirubbia.it

This marvellous Carso winery is run by Nataša Cernic, who is assisted by Marco Simonit in the vineyard and Marco Pecchiari in the cellar, which focuses on native wines: Terrano, Vitovska and Malvasia. The '07 Trubar is a single-variety, oak-fermented Vitovska.

○ Trubar '07	♈♈ 6
○ Malvasia '08	♈ 5
● Terrano '07	♈ 5
○ Vitovska '08	♈ 5

Gianpaolo Colutta

VIA ORSARIA, 32A
33044 MANZANO [UD]
TEL. 0432510654
www.coluttagianpaolo.com

Gianpaolo Colutta is helped on the estate by his daughter Elisabetta, who wrote her degree thesis on sparkling winemaking. The wines are great, especially the reds. The nicely evolved Tazzelenghe '05 has structure and stylish extract. The '04 Pignolo is soft, fruity and delicious.

● COF Pignolo '04	♈♈ 8
● COF Tazzelenghe '05	♈♈ 7
○ COF Pinot Bianco '08	♈ 4
● COF Schioppettino '08	♈ 6

Giorgio Colutta

VIA ORSARIA, 32
33044 MANZANO [UD]
TEL. 0432740315
www.colutta.it

Giorgio Colutta is the current owner of this property, also known as Bandut, from the ancient name of one of the plots. The vineyards lie in the prestigious vine and wine park. Schioppettino '07 was the wine that earned most approval for its complex aromatics but the '06 Picolit is also excellent.

○ COF Picolit '06	♈♈ 8
● COF Schioppettino '07	♈♈ 5
○ COF Friulano '08	♈ 4
● COF Refosco P. R. '06	♈ 5

Crastin

LOC. RUTTARS, 33
34070 DOLEGNA DEL COLLIO [GO]
TEL. 0481630310

Crastin is a farmstay estate at Ruttars a few metres from Slovenia. Sergio Collarig has been making and bottling his own wine in this breathtaking setting since 1991. His '08 Friulano is simple, attractive and redolent of flowers. All the other wines are well made.

○ Collio Friulano '08	♈♈ 4*
● Collio Cabernet Franc '08	♈ 4
○ Collio Pinot Bianco '08	♈ 4
○ Collio Pinot Grigio '08	♈ 3

Draga

LOC. SCEDINA, 8
34070 SAN FLORIANO DEL COLLIO [GO]
TEL. 0481884182
www.draga.it

This winery at Draga on the slopes of San Floriano del Collio is run by Milan Miklus, the third generation of the family. A new line, Miklus, has been created for premium wines. It joins the Draga range. Ribolla Gialla Miklus picked up Two Glasses for its intense aromas and nicely balanced palate.

○ Collio Ribolla Gialla Miklus '06	♈♈ 5
○ Collio Friulano '08	♈ 4
○ Collio Malvasia Miklus '07	♈ 4
○ Collio Ribolla Gialla '08	♈ 5

Le Due Torri

LOC. VICINALE DEL JUDRIO
VIA SAN MARTINO, 19
33040 CORNO DI ROSAZZO [UD]
TEL. 0432759150
www.le2torri.com

Antonino Volpe's care for his vineyards near the Parco del Torre has brought the cellar into the limelight with sincere, utterly delicious wines. The '08 Chardonnay is attractively varietal. The '07 Friulano fills the mouth. The powerful Pinot Grigio '08 has depth and the '07 Malvasia is juicy.

○ Friuli Grave Chardonnay '08	🍷🍷	3
○ Friuli Grave Friulano '07	🍷🍷	3
○ Friuli Grave Pinot Grigio '08	🍷🍷	3
○ Malvasia '07	🍷🍷	4

I Feudi di Romans

LOC. PIERIS
VIA CÀ DEL BOSCO, 16
34075 SAN CANZIAN D'ISONZO [GO]
TEL. 048176445
www.ifeudi.it

Enzo Lorenzon and sons Davide and Nicola run one of the loveliest estates in the region. Today, I Feudi di Romans has 50 hectares under vine. The '08 Sauvignon is complex and varietal, drinking full, savoury and juicy. Merlot Alfiere Rosso '06 is fruit-forward, balsamic, generous and balanced.

● Friuli Isonzo Merlot Alfiere Rosso '06	🍷🍷	5
○ Friuli Isonzo Sauvignon '08	🍷🍷	5
○ Friuli Isonzo Pinot Grigio '08	🍷	4
○ Friuli Isonzo Traminer Aromatico '08	🍷	4

Flaibani

VIA CASALI COSTA, 7
33043 CIVIDALE DEL FRIULI [UD]
TEL. 0432730943
www.flaibani.it

Pino Flaibani was in publishing in Milan but the call of the land and a passion for winemaking brought him back to Friuli, where he set up Riviere Flaibani with his wife Dorina and their sons, Maurizio and Michele. This year, the '07 Schioppettino and the '05 Merlot Riserva Seduzione picked up Two Glasses.

● COF Schioppettino '07	🍷🍷	5
● Merlot Seduzione Ris. '05	🍷🍷	5
● COF Cabernet Franc '07	🍷	4
○ Riviere Bianco '08	🍷	4

Forchir

FRAZ. FELETTIS
VIA CODROIPO, 18
33050 BICINICCO [UD]
TEL. 042796037
www.forchir.it

Gianfranco Bianchini and Enzo Deana run a winery with a long history. Founded at Felettis near Bicinicco, it expanded into the gravel plains at Camino al Tagliamento and Spilimbergo. The '07 Refoscone impresses in the glass with its rich hue, impenetrable aromas and complex, balsamic palate.

● Refoscone '07	🍷🍷	5
○ Friuli Grave Sauvignon L'Altro '08	🍷🍷	4*
○ Friuli Grave Pinot Bianco Campo dei Gelsi '08	🍷	4
○ Ribolla Gialla '08	🍷	4

Conti Formentini

VIA OSLAVIA, 5
34070 SAN FLORIANO DEL COLLIO [GO]
TEL. 0481884131
www.contiformentini.it

Founded in 1520 by the noble Formentini family, this estate is now part of Gruppo Italiano Vini. The cellars, opposite the 16th-century castle, are the charge of oenologist Marco Del Piccolo. The '07 Chardonnay Torre di Tramontana is subtle and pervasive but the whole range is good.

○ Collio Chardonnay Torre di Tramontana '07	🍷🍷	5
○ Collio Chardonnay '08	🍷	4
○ Collio Friulano '08	🍷	4
○ Collio Sauvignon '08	🍷	4

Grandi & Gabana

VIA CROSARIS, 14
33050 POCENIA [UD]
TEL. 0432777448
www.grandiegabana.it

Marcello Gabana and Daniela Grandi own this modern operation. The agronomist is Francesco Crivellaro and the oenologist is Alessio Rossetto. The mouthfilling, complex Merlot Borgo Crosaris '08 gives wafts of violets and a full flavour while the friulano and pinot bianco '07 Bianco Villa Rem is very good.

○ Friuli Latisana Friulano Sel. Grandi & Gabana '07	🍷🍷	4*
● Friuli Latisana Merlot Borgo Crosaris '08	🍷🍷	2*
● Friuli Latisana Refosco P. R. '06	🍷🍷	4*
○ Villa Rem '07	🍷🍷	4*

Albano Guerra

LOC. MONTINA
V.LE KENNEDY, 39A
33040 TORREANO [UD]
TEL. 0432715077
www.guerraalbano.it

Since 1997, Dario Guerra has been running the cellar named after his father Albano with very good results. The '06 Refosco has structure, momentum and minerality. Dario's sauvignon, picolit, friulano, pinot grigio and verduzzo Bianco Passiòn '07 is fragrantly fruity with a full-bodied, minerally palate.

O COF Bianco Passiòn '07	♈♈	5
● COF Refosco P. R. '06	♈♈	5
O COF Friulano '08	♈	4
O COF Pinot Grigio '08	♈	4

Vigna Lenuzza

VIA BROLO, 51
33040 PREPOTTO [UD]
TEL. 0432713236
www.vignalenuzza.it

Gianpaolo Lenuzza and his wife Emanuela manage the cellar with input from Luigino De Giuseppe as they wait for their son Daniele to finish his oenology studies. The subtle '07 Friulano Sottocastello '07 is pervasive on the nose and lively in the mouth. The other wines are appealing and well typed.

O COF Friulano Sottocastello '07	♈♈	4*
● COF Cabernet Franc '06	♈	4
● COF Refosco P. R. '06	♈	4
O COF Sauvignon '08	♈	4

Lupinc

FRAZ. PREPOTTO, 11B
34011 DUINO AURISINA [TS]
TEL. 040200848

Matej Lupinc's estate is at Prepotto near Duino Aurisina, on the Carso tableland. It aims to promote local varieties and the balanced '07 Vitovska '07 is a revelation, brimming with iodine and Mediterranean scrubland aromatics. The aromatic Dulcis in Fundo '06 is from part-dried malvasia istriana.

O Carso Vitovska '07	♈♈	4*
O Dulcis in Fundo '06	♈♈	6
O Carso Malvasia '07	♈	4
O Stara Brajda '07	♈	4

Marega

VIA VALERISCE, 4
34070 SAN FLORIANO DEL COLLIO [GO]
TEL. 0481 884058
www.maregacollio.com

Livio and Giorgio Marega's cellar recovered the holbar, a two to five-hectolitre acaciawood cask. The standard wines are excellent, particularly the '08 Pinot Grigio, the '05 Malvasia and the '08 Sauvignon. The nicely evolved '03 Holbar Rosso, from merlot, cabernet franc and gamay, comes together well.

● Collio Holbar Rosso '03	♈♈	6
O Collio Malvasia Istriana '05	♈♈	5
O Collio Pinot Grigio '08	♈♈	4
O Collio Sauvignon '08	♈♈	4

Piera Martellozzo

VIA PORDENONE, 33
33080 SAN QUIRINO [PN]
TEL. 0434963100
www.martellozzo.com

"There's a wine man who still tells it like it is. And she's a woman" is the slogan that put Piera Martellozzo into the inner circle of wine. The estate's oenologists are Gianpietro Poveglian and Damiano Canali. The attractively structured Bianco Milo '06 is salty with fruit tones over elegant dried flowers.

O Friuli Grave Bianco Milo '06	♈♈	4*
● Friuli Grave Cabernet Franc '08	♈	3
O Friuli Grave Friulano '08	♈	3
☉ Spumante Dry Cuvée Rosé	♈	3

Midolini

VIA DELLE FORNACI, 1
33044 MANZANO [UD]
TEL. 0432754555
www.midolini.com

Gloria Midolini's 70 hectares of vineyard continue to provide gratification in the Rosacroce-label wines. The '08 Bianco tempers sauvignon's exuberance with friulano and chardonnay. The juicy '08 Pinot Grigio '08 has structure and a nice twist of bitterness while the '08 Ronco dell'Angelica is all friulano.

O COF Bianco Rosacroce '08	♈♈	5
O COF Pinot Grigio Rosacroce '08	♈♈	5
O COF Bianco Rosacroce Ronco dell'Angelica '08	♈	5
O COF Chardonnay Rosacroce '08	♈	5

Ilvo Nadali

LOC. CORONA
VIA CORMÒNS, 41
34070 MARIANO DEL FRIULI [GO]
TEL. 048169169

When Ilvo Nadali hung up his professional football boots, he started a new career on the farm he now runs with his sons Massimo and Alberto at Corona in the Isonzo DOC. His Cabernet Franc '07 is good with nice definition and pervasive aromas followed by power and depth in the mouth.

● Cabernet Franc '07	♟♟	4
○ Chardonnay '07	♟	4
○ Friuli Isonzo Friulano '07	♟	4

Evangelos Paraschos

LOC. BUCUJE, 13A
34070 SAN FLORIANO DEL COLLIO [GO]
TEL. 0481884154
www.paraschos.it

This winery was set up in 1998 at San Floriano in the heart of the Collio. Evangelos Paraschos farms his ten hectares biodynamically. Kaj '06 is from friulano grapes. Skala '04 is a blend of merlot, refosco and barbera. Ponka '06 is a sauvignon and chardonnay-heavy white with other varieties in the blend.

○ Kaj '06	♟♟	6
○ Ribolla Gialla '06	♟♟	5
○ Ponka '06	♟	5
● Skala '04	♟	5

Parovel

LOC. CARESANA, 81
34018 SAN DORLIGO DELLA VALLE [TS]
TEL. 040227050
www.parovel.com

Euro Parovel's estate is on the cutting edge of Carso wine and extra virgin olive oil production. Vinja Barde is his premium-quality line supervised by the Terra&Vino group. His '08 Vitovska is fresh and citrussy. The Terrano '07 and Refosco '07 are fine ambassadors for their territory.

○ Carso Vitovska Vinja Barde '08	♟♟	4
● Refosco P. R. Vinja Barde '07	♟	4
● Terrano Vinja Barde '07	♟	4
○ Carso Malvasia Istriana Vinja Barde '07	♟♟	4*

Tenuta Pinni

VIA SANT'OSVALDO, 3
33096 SAN MARTINO AL TAGLIAMENTO [PN]
TEL. 0434899464
www.tenutapinni.com

Art, passion and commitment drive brothers Francesco and Roberto Pinni, who combine innovative winemaking with a strong family tradition. Rosso della Tenuta went through to our finals this year for its headily pervasive fragrances and fruity palate.

● Rosso della Tenuta '05	♟♟	5
○ Sauvignon '08	♟♟	3*
● Cabernet Franc '07	♟	3
○ Friuli Grave Friulano '08	♟	3

Flavio Pontoni

VIA PERUZZI, 8
33042 BUTTRIO [UD]
TEL. 0432674352
www.pontoni.it

Flavio Pontoni has taken a big step forward in quality. We loved his '08 Friulano, very nearly a finalist, for its varietal fragrances and stylish palate. The fruit-forward, aroma-rich '08 is laced with wisteria. The '08 Pinot Grigio and Chardonnay are complex and savoury.

○ COF Chardonnay '08	♟♟	3*
○ COF Friulano '08	♟♟	3*
○ COF Malvasia '08	♟♟	3*
○ COF Pinot Grigio '08	♟♟	3*

Pradio

LOC. FELETTIS
VIA UDINE, 17
33050 BICINICCO [UD]
TEL. 0432990123
www.pradio.it

Prado was founded in the Grave del Friuli DOC in the 1970s by the Cielo brothers. Today, Luca Cielo runs the estate while Pierpaolo Cielo is export manager and Beppe Bassi is the winemaker. Chardonnay Teraje '08 stood out for its pervasive aromas and drinkability. It leads a list of excellent wines.

○ Friuli Grave Chardonnay Teraje '08	♟♟	4*
○ Friuli Grave Friulano Gaiare '08	♟	4
○ Friuli Grave Pinot Grigio Priara '08	♟	4
● Friuli Grave Rosso Rok '06	♟	5

OTHER WINERIES

Teresa Raiz

LOC. MARSURE DI SOTTO
VIA DELLA ROGGIA, 22
33040 POVOLETTO [UD]
TEL. 0432679556
www.teresaraiz.it

Paolo Tosolini comes from a family of distillers. He set up the cellar in 1971, naming it after his grandmother, Teresa Raiz, from whom he inherited his love of wine. The Ribolla Gialla '08 is crisp and pervasive, showing subtle on the palate. Pinot Grigio Le Marsure '08 is a no-nonsense easy drinker.

O COF Ribolla Gialla '08	🍷🍷 4
O Pinot Grigio Le Marsure '08	🍷🍷 4*
O Chardonnay Le Marsure '08	🍷 4
O COF Pinot Grigio '08	🍷 4

Roman Rizzi

LOC. PIEDIMONTE
VIA MONTE CALVARIO, 30
34170 GORIZIA
TEL. 0481391338
www.piedimont.it

Roman Rizzi made a fine debut with a classic method sparkler that impresses on its first release. Roman's kitchen garden-tidy vineyard sticks to the same numbers: 60-20-20 proportions of chardonnay, pinot nero and ribolla gialla and 10,000 bottles. Winning numbers that are not going to change.

O Piè di Mont Brut '06	🍷🍷 7

Il Roncal

VIA FORNALIS, 148
33043 CIVIDALE DEL FRIULI [UD]
TEL. 0432730138
www.ilroncal.it

This new winery in the Colli Orientali del Friuli at Montebello was designed by Roberto Zorzettig, who passed away in 2006. His wife Martina continues to aim for excellence. The '05 Rosso Civon from schioppettino, refosco and cabernet franc is full, complex and structured. The other wines are good.

● COF Rosso Civon '05	🍷🍷 5
● COF Refosco P.R. '07	🍷 5
O COF Sauvignon '08	🍷 5
● COF Schioppettino '07	🍷 5

Ronchi Rò delle Fragole

LOC. CIME DI DOLEGNA, 12
34070 DOLEGNA DEL COLLIO [GO]
TEL. 0481639897
ronchiro.vini@tiscali.it

Founded in 2005 by Romeo Rossi. The original intention was to concentrate on Sauvignon but you don't grub up 50-year-old vineyards so there are two labels. The '08 Sauvignon is very varietal, giving mango tropical fruit and a savoury, pervasive palate. The '08 Friulano also has Sauvignon's green notes.

O Collio Friulano '08	🍷🍷 5
O Collio Sauvignon '08	🍷🍷 5

Ronco Blanchis

VIA BLANCHIS, 70
34070 MOSSA [GO]
TEL. 0438492250
www.venegazzu.com

A few years ago, Lorenzo and Giancarlo Palla took over a cellar active Austro-Hungarian times. With Sirch and Simonit in the vineyards, and Gianni Menotti overseeing the cellar, they got off to a cracking start. Only whites are made but they are excellent, especially the '08 Pinot Bianco and Pinot Grigio.

O Collio Pinot Bianco '08	🍷🍷 3*
O Collio Pinot Grigio '08	🍷🍷 4*
O Collio Chardonnay '08	🍷 4
O Collio Sauvignon '08	🍷 4

Ronco dei Pini

VIA RONCHI, 94
33040 PREPOTTO [UD]
TEL. 0432713239
www.roncodeipini.it

Since 1997, Giuseppe and Claudio Novello have run the winery set up by their father Vito. They look after winemaking with technicians De Noni and Stramare. This year, the lovely '08 Pinot Bianco scored high for its attractive spring flowers and yellow peaches followed by an elegant palate.

O COF Pinot Bianco '08	🍷🍷 4*
● COF Cabernet '08	🍷 5
O COF Friulano '08	🍷 4
O COF Pinot Grigio '08	🍷 4

Ronco di Prepotto

VIA BROLO, 45
33040 PREPOTTO [UD]
TEL. 0432281118
www.roncodiprepotto.com

Owner Giampaolo Macorig is the son of
Annibale, who still works with successful
oenologist Emilio Del Medico in the cellar,
turning out excellent wines. Rosso Zeus '06
from schioppettino, refosco and merlot,
Schioppettino '07 and the friulano,
malvasia and riesling Bianco Anatema '06
are all good.

● COF Rosso Zeus '06	♟♟ 6
● COF Schioppettino '07	♟♟ 4
○ COF Bianco Anatema '06	♟ 5
○ COF Bianco Lavinia '04	♟♟ 6

Rubini

LOC. SPESSA
VIA CASE RUBINI, 1
33043 CIVIDALE DEL FRIULI [UD]
TEL. 0432716141
www.villarubini.eu

Back in 1814, Conte Domenico Rubini
purchased a property at Praduccello near
Spessa, still the winery headquarters.
Winemaking is in the hands of oenologist
Dimitri Pintar. The Friulano '08 is a stand-
out for its complexity and varietal character.
The '08 Schioppettino is savoury and
mouthfilling.

○ COF Friulano '08	♟♟ 4*
● COF Schioppettino '08	♟♟ 4*
○ COF Sauvignon '08	♟ 4
○ Pinot Grigio '08	♟ 3

San Simone

LOC. RONDOVER
VIA PRATA, 30
33080 PORCIA [PN]
TEL. 0434578633
www.sansimone.it

Winemaking here dates from 1915 and
Liviana Brisotto has passed on the tradition
to Chiara, Anna and Antonio. Their whites
did very well this year. The characterful '08
Pinot Grigio is redolent of ripe fruit and
honey while the '08 Friulano gives florality
and understated smokiness.

○ Friuli Grave Friulano '08	♟♟ 3*
○ Friuli Grave Pinot Grigio '08	♟♟ 3*
● Friuli Grave Cabernet Franc Sugano '07	♟ 4
○ Friuli Grave Sauvignon '08	♟ 3

Scarbolo

FRAZ. LAUZACCO
V.LE GRADO, 4
33050 PAVIA DI UDINE [UD]
TEL. 0432675612
www.scarbolo.com

Valter Scarbolo inherited a farm at Lauzacco
from his father Gino. Today, he has 25
hectares. Most of his 140,000-bottle annual
production goes to the United States. The
base and Campo del Viotto '06 Merlots
appealingly soft and fruity and My Time,
from chardonnay, friulano and pinot grigio, is
good.

● Campo del Viotto Merlot '06	♟♟ 5*
● Friuli Grave Merlot '06	♟♟ 4*
○ My Time '06	♟♟ 5*
○ Friuli Grave Pinot Grigio '08	♟ 4

La Sclusa

LOC. SPESSA
VIA STRADA DI SANT'ANNA, 7/2
33043 CIVIDALE DEL FRIULI [UD]
TEL. 0432716259
www.lasclusa.it

Germano, Maurizio and Luciano Zorzettig
keep up the family tradition, still helped out
in the vineyard by their hard-working father
Gino. This time, the excellent Picolit wasn't
ready for us. The best La Sclusa product
was the varietal '08 Friulano with its
pervasive, almond-veined aromatics.

○ COF Friulano '08	♟♟ 4
○ COF Chardonnay '08	♟ 4
○ COF Pinot Grigio '08	♟ 4
○ COF Picolit '06	♟♟ 7

Agriturismo Skerlj

VIA SALES, 44
34010 SGONICO [TS]
TEL. 040229253
www.agriturismoskerlj.com

Matej and Kristina Skerlj with their parents
Just and Danila run a farmstay on the Carso
Triestino, producing about 2,400 bottles
from native varieties on their two hectares.
The '06 Malvasia is stunningly complex on
the nose and powerful in the mouth. Also
delightful is the pine resin-veined '06
Vitovska.

○ Malvasia '06	♟♟ 5
○ Vitovska '06	♟♟ 5
● Terrano '06	♟ 5

OTHER WINERIES

F.lli Stanig

VIA ALBANA, 44
33040 PREPOTTO [UD]
TEL. 0432713234
www.stanig.it

Federico and Francesco run the farmstay and winery founded in 1920 by their grandfather Giuseppe Stanig at Albana. The wines are great. The smoky Friulano '08 caresses the nose with varietal almonds. The '08 Pinot Bianco gives gentian and the spicy '07 Schioppettino has good structure.

○ COF Friulano '08	♥♥	4*
○ COF Pinot Bianco '08	♥♥	4*
● COF Schioppettino '07	♥♥	5
○ COF Sauvignon '08	♥	4

Tiare - Roberto Snidarcig

VIA MONTE, 58A
34071 CORMÒNS [GO]
TEL. 048160064
www.tiaredoc.com

Roberto Snidarig farms nine hectares in the Collio and Isonzo DOC zones and, with his wife Sandra, also runs a farmstay by the former Vencò border crossing. The restrained '07 Cabernet Sauvignon is varietal and deliciously drinkable. The equally varietal Pinot Bianco '08 is headily alcoholic.

○ Collio Pinot Bianco '08	♥♥	4
● Friuli Isonzo Cabernet Sauvignon '07	♥♥	4
○ Collio Sauvignon '08	♥	4
○ Malvasia '08	♥	4

Toblâr

LOC. RAMANDOLO, 17
33045 NIMIS [UD]
TEL. 0432755840
www.specogna.it

Michele and Cristian Specogna, "winemakers in Ramandolo" as they like to call themselves, vinify fruit from trusted growers at their very modern cellar. The all pinot grigio '08 Grîs gives golden delicious apples and a succulent palate. The '08 Sauvignonas is a rather rustic Sauvignon.

○ Gris '08	♥♥	4*
○ Ribolla Gialla Vino Spumante	♥	4
○ Sauvignonas '08	♥	4
● Uve Rosse '04	♥♥	5

Vendrame Vignis del Doge

FRAZ. PASSARIANO
VIA CARTIERA, 14B
33033 CODROIPO [UD]
TEL. 0432906642
www.vendrame-vignis.it

In 1968, Elia Vendrame set up an arable farm in the Grave del Friuli but in 1996 he went over to viticulture. Today, Elia and his family run Vignis del Doge. The whites impressed more than the reds with the '08 Friulano, Pinot Grigio and Chardonnay outstanding.

○ Friuli Grave Chardonnay '08	♥♥	3*
○ Friuli Grave Friulano '08	♥♥	4*
○ Friuli Grave Pinot Grigio '08	♥♥	3*
● Friuli Grave Merlot '08	♥	4

Paolo Venturini

VIA ISONZO, 135
34071 CORMÒNS [GO]
TEL. 048160446
www.venturinivini.it

Set up in the 1960s by Bruno Venturini, the 15-hectare estate is run by his son Paolo, who tends the Pradis and Bosc di Sot vineyards in the Collio and Isonzo DOCs. There's an excellent aniseed-themed '08 Sauvignon, which shows savoury and coherent, and a varietal, faintly aromatic '08 Malvasia.

○ Collio Malvasia '08	♥♥	4*
○ Collio Sauvignon '08	♥♥	4*
○ Collio Friulano '08	♥	4
○ Collio Pinot Bianco '08	♥	4

Vignai da Duline

LOC. VILLANOVA DEL JUDRIO
VIA IV NOVEMBRE, 136
33048 SAN GIOVANNI AL NATISONE [UD]
TEL. 0432758115
www.vignaidaduline.com

In 1997, Lorenzo Mocchiutti and Federica Magrini set up this estate with two hectares, which today have become six. The stand-outs this year are the malvasia and sauvignon '07 Morus Alba with its wealth of aromatics and an attractive Pinot Grigio Ronco Pitotti '08.

○ COF Bianco Morus Alba '07	♥♥	6
○ COF Pinot Grigio Ronco Pitotti '08	♥♥	5
● Refosco P. R. Morus Nigra '07	♥	6
● Refosco P. R. Morus Nigra '05	♥♥♥	6

Vigne del Malina

FRAZ. ORZANO
VIA PASINI VIANELLI, 9
33047 REMANZACCO [UD]
TEL. 0432649258
www.vignedelmalina.com

Vigne del Malina was set up in 2007 at Orzano in the Grave del Friuli. The owners are Roberto Bacchetti and Maria Luisa Trevisan but vineyards and cellar are in the care of the versatile Omar Pantarotto. There were excellent scores for the juicily varietal '08 Sauvignon and the fresh-tasting '07 Chardonnay.

○ Friuli Grave Chardonnay '07	♀♀	5
○ Friuli Grave Sauvignon '08	♀♀	4*
○ Friuli Grave Chardonnay '08	♀	4
○ Friuli Grave Pinot Grigio '08	♀	4

Vinài dell'Abbàte

LOC. ROSAZZO
P.ZZA ABBAZIA, 15
33044 MANZANO [UD]
TEL. 0432759429
www.abbaziadirosazzo.it

Vinài dell'Abbàte is part of the Aleandri group and manages the historic vineyards at the abbey of Rosazzo, owned by the archdiocese of Udine. The '04 Cabernet Sauvignon Ronco dei Domenicani is complex, savoury and pervasive. The '06 Cabernet Sauvignon is fruitier, soft-textured and juicy.

● COF Cabernet Sauvignon '06	♀♀	4
● COF Cabernet Sauvignon Ronco dei Domenicani '04	♀♀	5
● Broili Ros '07	♀	4
○ COF Bianco Ronco degli Agostiniani '05	♀	4

Franco Visintin

VIA ROMA, 37
34072 GRADISCA D'ISONZO [GO]
TEL. 048199974

Franco and Iselma Visintin's estate is near Gradisca and extends over four hectares on the flatlands of the Isonzo DOC. Annual output is 50-60,000 bottles. The '06 Merlot has a brooding but complex nose and a concentrated, savoury palate. The '08 Chardonnay is juicy, lusciously textured and faintly bitterish.

○ Friuli Isonzo Chardonnay '08	♀♀	3*
● Friuli Isonzo Merlot '06	♀♀	4
● Friuli Isonzo Cabernet Franc '06	♀	4
○ Friuli Isonzo Friulano '08	♀	3

Vodopivec

VIA COLLUDROZZA, 4
34010 SGONICO [TS]
TEL. 040229181
www.vodopivec.it

Paolo Vodopivec is emblematic of the Carso. Boldly, in 1994, he opted to produce only his Vitovska Classica, in 30-hectolitre Slavonian oak casks and Georgian amphorae buried in the earth. Not for the first time, we loved this year's Vitovska Classica, the '06. It's dry, refreshing, tangy and lingers.

○ Vitovska '06	♀♀	8
○ Vitovska Classica '06	♀♀	7
○ Vitovska '05	♀♀	8
○ Vitovska Classica '05	♀♀	7

Francesco Vosca

FRAZ. BRAZZANO
VIA SOTTOMONTE, 19
34070 CORMÒNS [GO]
TEL. 048162135
voscafrancesco@libero.it

Francesco Vosca farms about eight hectares in the Collio and Isonzo DOCs with the help of his wife Anita and their children Gabriele and Elisabetta. This year, three wines scored high. The faintly coppery Pinot Grigio '08 has character, the '08 Friulano is nicely varietal and the '08 Chardonnay is sound.

○ Collio Friulano '08	♀♀	4*
○ Collio Pinot Grigio '08	♀♀	4*
○ Friuli Isonzo Chardonnay '08	♀♀	4*
○ Collio Malvasia '08	♀	4

Zaglia

VIA CRESCENZA, 10
33050 PRECENICCO [UD]
TEL. 0431510320
www.zaglia.com

Giorgio Zaglia's estate was founded by Aldo in the late 1960s. It extends over 30 hectares near the coast in the Friuli Latisana DOC zone and also features a farm restaurant. The '07 Friulano is complex, fresh and appealing. The faintly onionskin-hued savoury Pinot Grigio '08 is tangy and mouthfilling.

○ Friuli Latisana Pinot Grigio '08	♀♀	4
○ Latisana Friulano '07	♀♀	4
○ Friuli Latisana Chardonnay '08	♀	4
● Friuli Latisana Merlot '07	♀	4

EMILIA ROMAGNA

There's quite a lot of news from Emilia Romagna and all of it is significant. We saw the first Three Glass prize for Gutturnio, a wine that pays increasingly dearly for its uncomfortable bracketing of still and sparkling wines in the same DOC. Piacenza's Three Glasses went to one of the most authentic products in the whole area, the razor-sharp, whistle-clean La Macchiona '05 from La Stoppa. The result should prompt those who continue to dilute the considerable character potential of this zone to think again and, we hope, encourage Piacenza's producers to work on courageously authentic, original wines. The zone's proud tradition of sweet winemaking was duly acknowledged in Barattieri's Vin Santo Albarola Val di Nure '99, obtained from the oldest mother-wine in Italy, dating back to 1823. The Emilia area, from Parma to Modena via Reggio-Emilia, made an amazing leap forward in quality, with twice as many profiles and a first-ever Three Glass award for two Lambruscos, a Sorbara and a Reggiano. This extraordinary success rewards continuing investment by larger wineries in the quality and hard work of small growers, who have started producing well-defined, reliably focused wines. At last, we can admire beautifully run vineyards in these three provinces, the most tangible sign of a renaissance in Lambrusco, a new culture that stands proudly alongside the area's tradition of fine bottlers and retailers. The Colli Bolognesi zone struggles more than ever and the wines from this area are increasingly disappointing and standardized. The ongoing decline has lasted for several years now but in this Guide it has become glaringly obvious, relegating the designated zone to the bottom of the region's classification. Romagna won an all-time record number of Three Glass prizes with nine Sangioveses – ten, if we count Valturio '07, a Romagna wine that bureaucracy has deemed to be in Marche region – thanks to wines of character that now speak a common language and reflect their terroirs: the clayey lowlands, the limestone soil of Bertinoro or the elegance of the marl and sandstone uplands. We should also mention the battery of basic Sangioveses which show increasingly impressive quality and an ability to express a strong identity. Romagna's tenth Three Glass award deserves a separate comment: the Montepirolo '06, a Bordeaux blend produced at the rehabilitation community of San Patrignano, originates in the excellent Colli Riminesi, where the climate is special and temperature fluctuations are regulated by the sea. There are still too few seekers after top quality but we are starting to see an interesting situation in what could become something of a little Bolgheri on the Adriatic coast.

Altavita - Fattoria dei Gessi

VIA TRANZANO, 820
47023 CESENA [FC]
TEL. 0547645996
www.altavita-wine.com

CELLAR SALES

ANNUAL PRODUCTION 20,000 bottles
HECTARES UNDER VINE 20
VITICULTURE METHOD Conventional

The Altavita project brings together three experienced Cesena growers, Enrico Giunchi, Maurizio Fuzzi and Stefania Migani, all keen to promote the area. Also involved is Enrico's brother, agronomist Alessandro Giunchi. The grapes from Altavita's own vineyards are selected for quality and terroir-related characteristics – clayey soils, looser soils higher up and chalky terrain, all between Cesena and Saiano – to produce two Sangioveses and a white. Enrico and Maurizio are expert farmers who have taken up a complex challenge.

The Altavita project gained ground quickly thanks to the excellent quality of the wines. Evoca '07 reached the finals with its clean character and taut, vibrant palate, showing uncomplicated but never commonplace. This stylish wine has a subtle personality. Tempora Riserva '06 is warm on the nose and too sweet to fulfil the producers' ambitions but it is still a well-made, very clean wine. The Diapente '08 from sauvignon blanc, albana and trebbiano was fermented in oak and aged in stainless steel after a period on the fine lees. The interesting but the rather weary style lacks energy.

● Sangiovese di Romagna Sup. Evoca '07	♟♟	4*
● Sangiovese di Romagna Sup. Tempora Ris. '06	♟♟	5
○ Diapente '08	♟	4

Ancarani

VIA SAN BIAGIO ANTICO, 14
48018 FAENZA [RA]
TEL. 0546642162
www.viniancarani.it

CELLAR SALES
PRE-BOOKED VISITS
FOOD

ANNUAL PRODUCTION 30,000 bottles
HECTARES UNDER VINE 14
VITICULTURE METHOD Conventional

This small family-run winery is doing valuable work with two native grapes: albana, which combines a high sugar content with acidity and tannins, and centesimino, found only around Faenza. Claudio Ancarani, who has inherited his grandfather's passion for the countryside and vineyards, implements the project with authenticity and coherence, always aware of the value of promoting and land and culture. His evident pride in his country origins is his best calling-card.

The quality for this edition of the Guide was exciting but Claudio has been giving us reliable, original wines for several years. Uvappesa '07, made from dried red centesimino grapes, went into the final with its well-defined varietal aromas of roses, petunias, elderflower and candied fruit laced with white pepper. The palate is taut and the sugar never cloys. There are two good Albanas, the late-harvested Santa Lusa '07 and the Perlagioia '07. The former is slightly warm, complex and minerally while Perlagioia is fresh-tasting and supremely varietal with its hint of honey, husky tannins and nice acidity.

● Uvappesa '07	♟♟	4
○ Albana di Romagna Perlagioia '07	♟♟	4
○ Albana di Romagna Santa Lusa '07	♟♟	4
● Sangiovese di Romagna Biagio Antico Sup. '08	♟♟	4
● Sâvignon Rosso '08	♟♟	4
○ Albana di Romagna Santa Lusa '06	♟♟	4*
● Sâvignon Rosso '06	♟♟	4*
● Uvappesa Vino da Uve Stramature	♟♟	5

Ariola 1956

FRAZ. PILASTRO
LOC. CALICELLA DI PILASTRO
S.DA DELLA BUCA 5A
43010 LANGHIRANO [PR]
TEL. 0521637678
www.viniariola.it

CELLAR SALES
PRE-BOOKED VISITS
FOOD

ANNUAL PRODUCTION **600,000 bottles**
HECTARES UNDER VINE **70**
VITICULTURE METHOD **Conventional**

Marcello Ceci, who has a longstanding working relationship with his brothers, who own the operation, gave up retailing wine and started making it from estate-grown grapes. In 2003, he bought Forte Rigoni Ariola, a traditional property in the hills above Parma, simplified the name and began serious work in the vineyards and cellar. Ariola sells estate wines plus a selection of local quality products, mainly cheeses and cured meats, sold under the Casale del Groppone label.

The archetypal Lambrusco Marcello '08, made entirely from maestri grapes, went to the finals for its definition and a rounded palate with a supple, fruity texture. Grasponero '08, from maestri and marani, is classic, rustic in style and fruity. The Forte Rigoni Malvasia Frizzante '08 has a fragrant, elegantly varietal nose and a fresh-tasting palate. The fresh Rosa Nera '08, from barbera and bonarda with a little cabernet sauvignon, has a slightly husky palate. The maestri only Angiol d'Or '08 is fruity and perhaps too keen to please while the Malvasia Frizzante '08 is subtle and floral.

Balìa di Zola

VIA CASALE, 11
47015 MODIGLIANA [FC]
TEL. 0546940577
bzolav@libero.it

CELLAR SALES
PRE-BOOKED VISITS

ANNUAL PRODUCTION **25,000 bottles**
HECTARES UNDER VINE **5**
VITICULTURE METHOD **Conventional**

Renovations of the farmhouse purchased by Veruska Eluci in 2003 are now complete and the building includes a modern cellar. The estate's most extensive vineyard is south to south-west facing. It was partly planted with ungrafted vines in 2004, using genetic material from old vines, at a density of 6,500 per hectare. The property also includes old plots, one of which below the Modigliana monastery covers about a hectare. The soil is largely marl and sandstone, loose in texture and rich in limestone.

Redinoce '06, from sangiovese grapes, has a spicy nose alongside fresh, taut fruit. The acidity on the palate opens out to express good character nicely underlined by the tannins. This is a balanced, stylish wine rich in flavour. Balitore '08 is dry and fresh-tasting with a vibrant palate where the abundant stylish tannins play a leading role. The lively, fragrant Rosé Zolarosa is made from sangiovese grapes.

● Lambrusco Marcello '08	▼▼ 4*
○ Forte Rigoni Malvasia Frizzante '08	▼▼ 4
● Lambrusco Gaspronero '08	▼▼ 3
● Angiol d'Or Maestri in Purezza	▼ 3
○ Colli di Parma Malvasia Frizzante '08	▼ 4
● Fortanina Marcello Frizzante Dolce	▼ 4
● Forte Rigone Rosa Nera '08	▼ 4

● Redinoce '06	▼▼ 5
● Sangiovese di Romagna Balitore '08	▼▼ 4
☉ Zolarosa '08	▼ 4
● Redinoce '05	♈ 5
● Redinoce '04	♈ 5

Baraccone

LOC. CA' DEI MORTI, 1
29028 PONTE DELL'OLIO [PC]
TEL. 0523877147
www.baraccone.it

CELLAR SALES
PRE-BOOKED VISITS

ANNUAL PRODUCTION 22,000 bottles
HECTARES UNDER VINE 7.5
VITICULTURE METHOD Conventional

Since 1995, Andreana Burgazzi has run the Baraccone estate in Val Nure, situated 400 metres above the town of Ponte dell'Olio. This was once a site for travelling fairs and circuses, known in the Piacenza dialect as "baracconi". Andreana manages about eight hectares of reddish iron-rich land which endows the wines with powerful structure. Particularly interesting are the grapes grown in barbera vineyards more than 50 years old set in wild, unspoilt woodlands.

Andreana's wines are reliably good today and there is every indication that there is significant potential, which can only be brought out by a courageous, strongly territory-based approach. Colombaia '07 is the most impressive of those presented, showing compact and fruity with a deep, dynamic palate. The Gutturnio Frizzante '08 also impressed. This is supple and characterful, with good acidity punctuating the developing rhythm and underlining the territorial features. The Zagaia '08 from ortrugo, malvasia, trebbiano and chardonnay is fresh and approachable but far from ordinary.

Conte Otto Barattieri di San Pietro

VIA DEI TIGLI, 100
29020 VIGOLZONE [PC]
TEL. 0523875111
ottobarattieri@libero.it

CELLAR SALES
PRE-BOOKED VISITS

ANNUAL PRODUCTION 120,000 bottles
HECTARES UNDER VINE 34
VITICULTURE METHOD Conventional

The Barattieri estate was among the first to take Piacenza's wines outside the territory in the days of the legendary semi-sparkling Sauvignon and long-serving cellar manager Francesco Rossi. Unfortunately, the winery is currently in the doldrums and the only outstanding wine is the Vin Santo from grapes grown in oldest, most prestigious vineyard, Mercati. Strong links to the local terroir remain along with the classic, rustic winemaking touch. That could be a good starting point for the recovery of one of Piacenza's historic cellars.

Vin Santo Albarola Val di Nure towers over the rest of the range, most of which is fairly disappointing and lacks personality. This Vin Santo from malvasia di Candia grapes is dried naturally using traditional techniques. Nothing has been changed in the mother wine's almost two centuries of history. A galaxy of aromas, from zabaglione, orange, apricot and candied citrus fruit to chamomile and tea, comes through on a fresh, firm nose. The endless palate is dynamic and dry, unfolding a new kaleidoscope of fragrances in the finish. It's our Sweet Wine of the Year.

Baraccone		
● C. P. Gutturnio Frizzante '08	♟♟	3*
● C. P. Gutturnio Sup. Colombaia '07	♟♟	4*
● C. P. Gutturnio Ronco Alto Ris. '06	♟	4
○ Zagaia Frizzante '08	♟	3
● C. P. Gutturnio Frizzante '07	♟♟	3*
● C. P. Gutturnio Frizzante '06	♟♟	3*
● C. P. Gutturnio Ronco Alto Ris. '04	♟♟	4*
● C. P. Gutturnio Sup. Colombaia '06	♟♟	4*

Conte Otto Barattieri di San Pietro		
○ C. P. Vin Santo Albarola Val di Nure '99	♟♟♟+	8
● C. P. Gutturnio Frizzante '08	♟	3
○ C. P. Ortrugo Frizzante '08	♟	3
○ C. P. Vin Santo Albarola Val di Nure '97	♟♟♟	6
○ C. P. Vin Santo Albarola Val di Nure '96	♟♟♟	6

Stefano Berti

LOC. RAVALDINO IN MONTE
VIA LA SCAGNA, 18
47100 FORLÌ
TEL. 0543488074
www.stefanoberti.com

CELLAR SALES
PRE-BOOKED VISITS

ANNUAL PRODUCTION 30,000 bottles
HECTARES UNDER VINE 8
VITICULTURE METHOD Conventional

Stefano Berti cares passionately about his vineyards, partly on clay-based soil and partly on a fluvial terrace in the Ravaldino in Monte hills, between Predappio and Forlì. After a first vintage characterized by ripe, concentrated fruit, Stefano replaced the barriques in 2008 with 400-litre tonneaux and has progressively decreased the percentage of other grapes in the blends with his sangiovese. This has opened a new phase of less power and more balance for this skilled winemaker. The new direction has more freshness and speaks the language of the terroir.

The Calisto '06 is mature, fruity and quite fresh, albeit penalized by distinct alcohol and a slightly dry palate. Sangiovese di Romagna Superiore Ravaldo is always dependable, showing continuing quality while respecting the profile of individual vintages. The '08 shows guts and firm structure with a slightly dry finish. A pleasant surprise this year came from the winery's least ambitious product, Bartimeo '08. It's austere on the nose and approachable on the lingering palate with its moreish elegance.

● Sangiovese di Romagna Sup. Calisto Ris. '06	♀♀	5
● Sangiovese di Romagna Sup. Ravaldo '08	♀♀	4*
● Sangiovese di Romagna Sup. Bartimeo '08	♀	3
● Sangiovese di Romagna Sup. Calisto '01	♀♀♀	5
● Sangiovese di Romagna Sup. Calisto '04	♀♀	5
● Sangiovese di Romagna Sup. Calisto '03	♀♀	5
● Sangiovese di Romagna Sup. Ravaldo '07	♀♀	4*

Raffaella Alessandra Bissoni

LOC. CASTICCIANO
VIA COLECCHIO, 280
47032 BERTINORO [FC]
TEL. 0543460382
www.vinibissoni.com

CELLAR SALES
PRE-BOOKED VISITS

ANNUAL PRODUCTION 20,000 bottles
HECTARES UNDER VINE 5
VITICULTURE METHOD Conventional

Raffaella Bissoni is determined and emotionally connected to her vineyards as only someone who spends her days working among the rows can be. This small estate's wines are important ambassadors for Bertinoro and their value goes beyond objective quality. For many years, Raffaella has vinified extraordinary grapes, gradually honing an impressive touch. Her slow, reflective progress has been complex, nourished more by doubt than by certainty, and ever ready to acknowledge subtleties. Today, the estate is close to concluding this long period of research.

Raffaella's very authentic wines are finding definition, expressing themselves naturally in a benchmark style for the zone. The Sangiovese Riserva '06 has a very expressive nose with a hint of oak-derived spice alongside stylish, white peach-led fruit, and a dry, almost challenging, palate with pleasant acidity. The Albana Passito '06 is also good, perhaps a touch too varietally husky, but impressive and minerally.

○ Albana di Romagna Passito '06	♀♀	4*
● Sangiovese di Romagna Sup. Ris. '06	♀♀	5
● Sangiovese di Romagna Sup. '08	♀	4
● Sangiovese di Romagna Sup. Ris. '05	♀♀	4
● Sangiovese di Romagna Sup. Ris. '03	♀♀	4

Tenuta Bonzara

VIA SAN CHIERLO, 37A
40050 MONTE SAN PIETRO [BO]
TEL. 0516768324
www.bonzara.it

CELLAR SALES
PRE-BOOKED VISITS

ANNUAL PRODUCTION **70,000 bottles**
HECTARES UNDER VINE **16**
VITICULTURE METHOD **Conventional**

Back in 1963, Angelo Lambertini purchased a 100-hectare property in the excellent San Chierlo di Monte San Pietro area, aiming to establish high production standards. The objective was achieved in 1975, when the unforgettable maestro Luigi Veronelli recognized the very characterful sensory profile of the estate's leading wine and suggested its name: Bonzarone. Since 1986, respected university lecturer Francesco has been at the winery's helm, supported by oenologist Lorenzo Landi and cellar manager Mario Carboni.

The estate enjoys one of the highest locations in the Colli Bolognesi and this terroir's calling card is elegance. The vibrant, austere wines are always interesting and complex. In recent years, these features have intensified and the range of products is reliable overall. The '06 Bonzarone is impressive, despite excessive maturity on the nose and a palate that should be deeper. The crisp, varietal Le Carrate '08 has nice pressure and intriguing hints of sage. The Vigna Antica '08 is fresh, tangy, lean and racy.

Calonga

LOC. CASTIGLIONE
VIA CASTEL LEONE, 8
47100 FORLÌ
TEL. 0543753044
www.calonga.it

CELLAR SALES
PRE-BOOKED VISITS

ANNUAL PRODUCTION **30,000 bottles**
HECTARES UNDER VINE **8**
VITICULTURE METHOD **Conventional**

Maurizio Baravelli runs this small estate with his wife Monica and three sons, Lorenzo, Matteo and Francesco, exploiting the sensitivity that makes him as rare a winemaker for Romagna as it is rare to find sandy soil like this in the region. The property covers about 12 hectares on the lower Forlì hills at an elevation of about 100 metres. The land is sandy and clayey, in the centre of a sandy lens pure in some areas and mixed with clayey soil in others. The leading wines are remarkably ageworthy.

The grapes from the estate's oldest vineyards, some planted 40 years ago, are used for the flagship wine, Michelangiolo, which won Three Glasses for the fourth year running. The nose is already deep with sound, velvety fruit and a sumptuously generous but very fresh palate with close-knit, stylish tannins. Michelangiolo proves that sangiovese di Romagna can express the diversity of soil and climate, and interpret terroir, when treated with due respect. Castellione '06 is good, showing slightly mature on the nose and more impressive on the flavoursome, characterful palate.

● C. B. Cabernet Sauvignon Bonzarone '06	♀♀ 5
○ Colli Bolognesi Sauvignon Le Carrate '08	♀♀ 3*
● C. B. Merlot Rocca di Bonacciara '06	♀ 5
○ C. B. Pignoletto Vigna Antica '08	♀ 4
○ Monte Severo '07	♀ 4
○ U Pàsa	♀ 4
● C. B. Cabernet Sauvignon Bonzarone '05	♀♀♀ 5
● C. B. Merlot Rocca di Bonacciara '05	♀♀ 5
○ C. B. Pignoletto Cl. Vigna Antica '07	♀♀ 4*
○ C. B. Sauvignon Sup. Le Carrate '07	♀♀ 4*

● Sangiovese di Romagna Sup. Michelangiolo Ris. '06	♀♀♀ 5
● Castellione Cabernet Sauvignon '06	♀♀ 6
● Ordelaffo '07	♀ 4
● Sangiovese di Romagna Sup. Il Bruno '08	♀ 3
● Sangiovese di Romagna Sup. Michelangiolo Ris. '05	♀♀♀ 5
● Sangiovese di Romagna Sup. Michelangiolo Ris. '04	♀♀♀ 5
● Sangiovese di Romagna Sup. Michelangiolo Ris. '03	♀♀♀ 5

Cardinali

POD. MONTEPASCOLO
29014 CASTELL'ARQUATO [PC]
TEL. 0523803502
www.cardinalidoc.it

CELLAR SALES
PRE-BOOKED VISITS

ANNUAL PRODUCTION 30,000 bottles
HECTARES UNDER VINE 8
VITICULTURE METHOD Conventional

Laura Cardinali and her brother Alberto have worked full-time at this little winery since 1996, Alberto in the vineyard and cellar, and Laura in the sales and PR department. They are excellent example of the back-to-the-countryside revolution, well-educated youngsters who spotted untapped potential in a place in the country and launched themselves on an interesting, courageous venture. Castell'Arquato is situated in the southernmost part of the Colli Piacentini, in a historic wine zone with a beautiful landscape densely planted with vineyards.

The Cardinalis did not present any wines for the Guide this year, a decision which has been postponed several times and of which we wholeheartedly approve. The wines are not yet ready and although they are as reliable as usual, they are still youthfully alcoholic and the structure needs to find the harmony that comes with maturity. But we must stress how impressive the whole of the range is, from the simplest wines to the most ambitious. We look forward to the next edition when the whole range will be tasted again.

La Casetta dei Frati

VIA DEI FRATI, 8
47015 MODIGLIANA [FC]
TEL. 0546940628
www.casettadeifrati.com

CELLAR SALES
PRE-BOOKED VISITS
VISITOR FACILITIES
FOOD

ANNUAL PRODUCTION 12,000 bottles
HECTARES UNDER VINE 8
VITICULTURE METHOD Conventional

Casetta dei Frati was purchased in 2003 by Renzo Maria Morresi and his wife Maria Adele Ubaldi, who stole as much time as possible from their legal office in Bologna to plant new vineyards and build 24 rooms for guests. The vineyards are planted on unusual marl and sandstone soil which is quite shallow but never suffers from drought, at an average altitude of 300-400 metres. Francesco Bordini, who manages the vineyards and cellar, is becoming an expert on high-altitude sites.

The interesting Framonte '06 is subtle and stylish with appealing tannins and edgy acidity. Chardonnay Fracielo '06 is sharp, taut, fragrant and expressive. Frasòle '06, a blend of sangiovese and cabernet sauvignon, is dry and elegant with crisply defined fruit and a juicy, flavoursome palate. The pleasant, clean Fravento '07 is obtained from trebbiano.

● C. P. Gutturnio Cl. Nicchio '07	⟡⟡ 4*
● C. P. Gutturnio Cl. Nicchio '06	⟡⟡ 4*
● C. P. Gutturnio Cl. Nicchio '05	⟡⟡ 4*
● C. P. Gutturnio Cl. Torquato Ris. '05	⟡⟡ 5
● C. P. Gutturnio Cl. Torquato Ris. '04	⟡⟡ 5
● C. P. Gutturnio Cl. Torquato Ris. '03	⟡⟡ 5
○ C. P. Monterosso Val d'Arda Solata '07	⟡⟡ 4*
○ Dolce Montepascolo '05	⟡⟡ 5

○ Fracielo '06	⟡⟡ 4
● Frasòle '06	⟡⟡ 4*
● Sangiovese di Romagna Framonte '06	⟡⟡ 3
○ Fravento '07	⟡ 3

Casetto dei Mandorli

LOC. PREDAPPIO ALTA
VIA UMBERTO I, 21
47010 PREDAPPIO [FC]
TEL. 0543922361
www.vini-nicolucci.it

CELLAR SALES
PRE-BOOKED VISITS

ANNUAL PRODUCTION **90,000 bottles**
HECTARES UNDER VINE **15**
VITICULTURE METHOD **Conventional**

Alessandro Nicolucci deserves praise for applying three generations' worth of growing experience to safeguarding a very classic interpretation of the sangiovese grape that trims away excess hardness and imperfections. He is aided by exceptionally good terroir for this variety at Predappio Alta, which was well-known in Romagna in the 19th century for its densely planted bush-trained vineyards and the quality of its wines. Casetto dei Mandorli is a benchmark of style for Sangiovese aged in large barrels and an asset for the whole of Romagna.

Vigna del Generale reached the finals thanks to its distinctive austere, elegant style. With a palate that is dynamic, expressive and minerally, it confirms its position as one of the most consistently reliable bottles in Romagna. Tre Rocche '08 has flavour, character and an impressively keen palate. We also liked Nero di Predappio '06, from sangiovese and refosco dal peduncolo rosso. Fragrant cherry-led fruit introduces a long, taut, racy palate.

● Sangiovese di Romagna V. del Generale Ris. '06	♟♟	5
● Nero di Predappio '06	♟♟	5
● Sangiovese di Romagna Sup. Tre Rocche '08	♟♟	4
● Sangiovese di Romagna V. del Generale Ris. '05	♟♟♟	5
● Nero di Predappio '05	♟♟	5
● Sangiovese di Romagna V. del Generale Ris. '04	♟♟	5

Castelluccio

LOC. POGGIOLO DI SOTTO
VIA TRAMONTO, 15
47015 MODIGLIANA [FC]
TEL. 0546942486
www.ronchidicastelluccio.it

CELLAR SALES

ANNUAL PRODUCTION **90,000 bottles**
HECTARES UNDER VINE **14**
VITICULTURE METHOD **Conventional**

Castelluccio is a traditional Romagna winery, run since 1999 by Claudio Fiore in continuation of the work of his father Vittorio, who as a young man saw the first harvests here. Claudio has reinterpreted the style of the legendarily lean, hard Ronchi wines to create products that are more generous and accessible, with far less austerity. This is also due to a makeover in the vineyards that started in the year when he took up the reins, a project that is now reaching maturity. The result is a more international style focused on spicy, mouthfilling wines.

The stylish Massicone '06, from cabernet sauvignon and sangiovese, explodes on the senses, opening out in a sustained, flavoursome progression. It's the most impressive and characterful of the cellar's reds. Ronco delle Ginestre '06, from sangiovese, has an excessively sweet nose but finds more personality on the palate, where it recovers a degree of elegance. The sauvignon blanc Lunaria '08 is an uncomplicated, tangily fresh-tasting white. Ronco Ciliegi '06 falls short of expectations, overwhelmed by toasty, unwieldy oak.

● Massicone '06	♟♟	5
○ Lunaria '08	♟♟	4
● Ronco delle Ginestre '06	♟♟	6
● Ronco dei Ciliegi '06	♟	5
● Sangiovese di Romagna Le More '08	♟	4
● Massicone '01	♟♟♟	6
● Ronco dei Ciliegi '02	♟♟♟	6
● Ronco dei Ciliegi '00	♟♟♟	6

Cavicchioli U. & Figli

VIA CANALETTO, 52
41030 SAN PROSPERO [MO]
TEL. 059812411
www.cavicchioli.it

CELLAR SALES
PRE-BOOKED VISITS

ANNUAL PRODUCTION 18,000,000 bottles
HECTARES UNDER VINE 150
VITICULTURE METHOD Conventional

This traditional, benchmark Emilia winery is run by Sandro Cavacchioli, who now also presents wines from another big name, Francesco Bellei, the region's leading Metodo Classico maker. Ownership of Bellei may have changed but not the location at Bomporto near Modena, and technical management of the cellar is still firmly in the hands of Christian Bellei. In recent years, Cavicchioli's production has returned to its excellent standards and some of the benchmark wines are regular participants at the finals.

There were three finalists this year. Vigna del Cristo '08 is stylish, teasing the nose with roses and wild strawberries before progressing confidently across the palate, spurred on by acidity and the sweetest of tannins. The subtlety of Rosé del Cristo '05 on the nose shifts up a gear on the brashly dynamic palate. Ancestrale '08 is from sorbara grapes refermented in bottle without disgorgement. Straight as a dart, it gradually builds up a rhythm of little thrills on a palate that complements freshness with complexity. The Grasparossa Amabile Tre Medaglie '08 is a champion in its category, showing fresh, fruity and balanced with a pleasant hint of sweetness.

Cantine Ceci

VIA PROVINCIALE, 99
43030 TORRILE [PR]
TEL. 0521810252
www.lambrusco.it

ANNUAL PRODUCTION 800,000 bottles
HECTARES UNDER VINE 20
VITICULTURE METHOD Conventional

This beautiful winery in the lower part of the province of Parma has purchased wines since 1938, selling them under its own brand with a commercial and communicative ability practically unparalleled in the region. The Ceci family, now in its third generation, is proficient, enthusiastic and as committed as ever to seizing every opportunity that offers visibility, backed up by meticulously designed original packaging.

The wines are generous and mouthfilling, a style that has traditionally met with great success in Parma, and Alessandro Ceci's interpretation emphasizes this. The Otello range, dedicated to founder Otello Ceci, is very reliable. Otello NerodiLambrusco '08, from 100 per cent maestri grapes selected on the hillslopes, is creamy and well rounded. The version presented this year of Otello, the '08 from flatlands-grown marani and maestri fruit, is particularly stylish. The Otello Rosé '08 also impressed, with pinot noir grapes adding a touch of elegance to the lambrusco. Its slightly oxidative nose accompanies a lean palate.

Wine		Score
● Lambrusco di Sorbara Rifermentazione Ancestrale Francesco Bellei '08	♈♈	5
● Lambrusco di Sorbara V. del Cristo '08	♈♈	4*
⊙ Rosé del Cristo Spumante '05	♈♈	6
○ Brut Extra Cuvée Francesco Bellei	♈♈	5
● Lambrusco Grasparossa di Castelvetro Amabile Tre Medaglie '08	♈♈	2
● Lambrusco di Sorbara Tre Medaglie '08	♈	2
● Lambrusco di Sorbara Contessa Matilde '07	♈♈	3
● Lambrusco di Sorbara V. del Cristo '07	♈♈	4*
⊙ Rosé del Cristo Spumante '04	♈♈	6
⊙ Rosé del Cristo Spumante '03	♈♈	6

Wine		Score
⊙ Extra Dry Rosé Otello '08	♈♈	4*
● Otello Lambrusco Et. Nera '08	♈♈	3*
● Otello NerodiLambrusco '08	♈♈	4
● 13 di Terre VerdianeFortana '08	♈	4
○ Colli di Parma Malvasia Frizzante Corti della Duchessa '08	♈	4
● Lambrusco Terre Verdiane	♈	3
● Otello NerodiLambrusco '07	♈♈	4*

Umberto Cesari

VIA STANZANO, 1120
40050 CASTEL SAN PIETRO TERME [BO]
TEL. 051941896
www.umbertocesari.it

CELLAR SALES
PRE-BOOKED VISITS

ANNUAL PRODUCTION **2,000,000 bottles**
HECTARES UNDER VINE **128**
VITICULTURE METHOD **Conventional**

In the early 1960s, it was hard to buy into Umberto Cesari's dream of selling quality Romagna wines worldwide. But in 1965, the dream finally came true and the first Umberto Cesari wine was released. It was the beginning of a wonderful story that would grow and develop to become one of the most important in Romagna by the 1980s. Umberto began to travel the world, to the US, Canada and the United Kingdom, creating a unique international market for Romagna, with clients in 54 countries today.

Umberto's wines do not strive for excessively terroir-based features. Instead, they interpret the identity of Romagna in a way the international market understands. The most traditional wine is the Riserva di Sangiovese '06, aged in large barrels, which has a lean, elegant feel. Moma Rosso, from sangiovese, merlot and cabernet sauvignon, is enjoyably agile with very lively expression. The sangiovese-based Tauleto '04 and the Liano '06, a sangiovese and cabernet sauvignon mix, are reliably good and the most international in style, showing caressingly generous in the mouth.

Chiarli 1860

VIA DANIELE MANIN, 15
41100 MODENA
TEL. 0593163311
www.chiarli.it

CELLAR SALES

ANNUAL PRODUCTION **24,000,000 bottles**
HECTARES UNDER VINE **110**
VITICULTURE METHOD **Conventional**

Large-scale production of Lambrusco from bought-in grapes is flanked nowadays by commercially significant businesses like this, making ambitiously well-crafted wines sourced from the estate's own vineyards. The results have been excellent for a number of years and the experience acquired with these grapes has a knock-on effect on large-scale production, as Anselmo Chiarli and Roberto Saletta, who run this major winery, can testify.

There was a milestone result for the winery and Lambrusco in general: Three Glasses went to Sorbara Vecchia Modena Premium '08 for its fragrant floral aromas, marked minerality, lean, incisive palate and bags of complexity and length. The similarly styled Sorbara del Fondatore '08 complexity, not least because of its bottle refermentation without disgorgement. The Villa Cialdini '08 is also nicely compact, well made and vibrant. Grasparossa's character is different, nicely embodied in the austere Pruno Nero '08 with its cherries and white peaches, and dynamic, dry palate. The Nivola '08 from grasparossa and salamino is dense and juicy.

● Sangiovese di Romagna Ris. '06	♥♥ 4*
● Tauleto Sangiovese '04	♥♥ 6
● Liano '06	♥♥ 5
● Moma Rosso '07	♥♥ 4*
● Sangiovese di Romagna Laurento Ris. '06	♥♥ 4
● Yemula '06	♥♥ 4
○ Albana di Romagna Secco Colle del Re '08	♥ 3
○ Moma Bianco '08	♥ 4
● Sangiovese di Romagna Sup. Ca' Grande '08	♥ 3
● Liano '05	♀♀ 5
● Moma '04	♀♀ 4*
● Tauleto Sangiovese '04	♀♀ 6
● Tauleto Sangiovese '01	♀♀ 6

● Lambrusco di Sorbara Vecchia Modena Premium '08	♥♥♥ 3*
● Lambrusco di Sorbara del Fondatore '08	♥♥ 4*
● Lambrusco Grasparossa di Castelvetro Pruno Nero '08	♥♥ 3*
● Lambrusco Grasparossa di Castelvetro Villa Cialdini '08	♥♥ 4*
● Nivola Lambrusco Scuro '08	♥♥ 3*
● Lambrusco di Sorbara '08	♥ 3
● Lambrusco Grasparossa di Castelvetro Frizzante Amabile '08	♥ 3

Floriano Cinti

FRAZ. SAN LORENZO
VIA GAMBERI, 48
40037 SASSO MARCONI [BO]
TEL. 0516751646
www.collibolognesi.com

CELLAR SALES
PRE-BOOKED VISITS

ANNUAL PRODUCTION **95,000 bottles**
HECTARES UNDER VINE **24**
VITICULTURE METHOD **Conventional**

While he waits to inaugurate his new cellar, currently under construction, with the 2010 vintage, Floriano Cinti continues his exploration of Bologna's terroir. He has been a small independent farmer since 1992 and has a rational, composed approach, two qualities which are increasingly rare in the hectic winegrowing world. This enables him to tackle difficult years like 2008 in a positive way. The result is dependably high quality throughout his vast range of traditional local wines.

The most impressive wine in this round of tastings was Pignoletto Frizzante '08, which gives clear-cut, nicely expressed fruit and broom-led floral aromas, and a fresh, balanced palate. We also liked the buttery, weighty Chardonnay '08, with confident oaky hints contributing to the complexity provided by fragrant citrus and minerally sensations, and the typical, sharp Barbera '07, scored high for the second year running. Overall, the simpler wines are more impressive but the Sassobacco winery selections are below par.

La Collina

VIA PAGLIA, 19
48013 BRISIGHELLA [RA]
TEL. 054683110
www.lacollina-vinicola.com

CELLAR SALES
PRE-BOOKED VISITS

ANNUAL PRODUCTION **10,000 bottles**
HECTARES UNDER VINE **5.2**
VITICULTURE METHOD **Conventional**

Located in one of the most beautiful hillside terroirs around Brisighella, Collina has been run since 2002 by André Eggli, a German-speaking Swiss, who has travelled extensively in Italy and Spain in search of a place to welcome his winemaking project. The winery produces only one wine, Cupola, but the long-term objective is to make a monovarietal Sangiovese for a pure expression of the hard, subtle nature of this area, and also a more international wine. Collina also makes a fine, wonderfully characterful extra virgin Brisighella olive oil.

Cupola '06 has a spicy nose that perhaps lacks varietal qualities but shows complex with very ripe but taut, well-defined fruit emerging. The palate is a balance of acidity and exuberant flavour with a long, iridescent, complex finish. In order to hit the heights, it needs the austerity of fruit and the taut, vibrant tone that monovarietal Sangioveses from this terroir are capable of producing.

● C. B. Barbera '07	♥♥	4*
○ C. B. Chardonnay '08	♥♥	4*
○ C. B. Pignoletto Frizzante '08	♥♥	3*
● C. B. Merlot Sassobacco '07	♥	4
○ C. B. Pignoletto Cl. Sassobacco '08	♥	4
○ C. B. Pinot Bianco '08	♥	4
○ C. B. Sauvignon '08	♥	4
● C. B. Barbera '06	♀♀	4
○ C. B. Pignoletto Cl. Sassobacco '07	♀♀	4

● Colli di Faenza Sangiovese Cupola '06	♥♥	5
● Colli di Faenza Sangiovese Cupola '05	♀♀	5
● Colli di Faenza Sangiovese Cupola '04	♀♀	5
● Sangiovese di Romagna Sup. Cupola '03	♀♀	5

Leone Conti

LOC. SANTA LUCIA
VIA POZZO, 1
48018 FAENZA [RA]
TEL. 0546642149
www.leoneconti.it

CELLAR SALES
PRE-BOOKED VISITS

ANNUAL PRODUCTION **70,000 bottles**
HECTARES UNDER VINE **17**
VITICULTURE METHOD **Conventional**

This traditional Romagna estate's products are improving every year. While Leone Conti interprets his chosen profession of winemaking as an opportunity to exercise his sensitivity rather than seek absolute quality, he gets excellent results with some wines every year. The winery is also a benchmark for Albana, which Leone always brings to exciting levels, and whose ageing potential is always nicely expressed.

Contiriserva '06 is very well-balanced with a dry, supple tangy palate. Albana Progetto 1 '08 combines identity and quality in the honey of the albana grape, extraordinary freshness, a salty streak and a very stylish finish with lingering mineral acidity. Le Betulle '07 did well, showing slightly limp on the nose but the mellow racy palate finds the right direction. The native ruggine grape, in An Ghin Gà, and famoso di Cesena, in LeOne, impressed. We liked the newest addition, the tangy, incisive Earth Heart '08. The two sweet wines are also good. Oro et Laboro is from sauvignon blanc and albana, and Tu Chiamale se Vuoi Emozioni Lato B '07 is centesimino based.

Corte Manzini

LOC. CÀ DI SOLA DI CASTELVETRO
VIA PER MODENA, 131/3
41014 CASTELVETRO DI MODENA [MO]
TEL. 059702658
www.cortemanzini.it

CELLAR SALES
PRE-BOOKED VISITS
VISITOR FACILITIES
FOOD

ANNUAL PRODUCTION **80,000 bottles**
HECTARES UNDER VINE **10**
VITICULTURE METHOD **Natural**

This small family-run winery is in the lower Colli Modenesi hills in lambrusco grasparossa territory. This is the least hardy of the lambrusco varieties, preferring the poorer hillside soil, and has its own character with well-structured tannins and an alcoholic impact. The Manzinis have perfected their own crisp, fruity winemaking style, which needs a full rounded palate to find its best expression and suffers in more complicated years. However the Manzinis' work in the vineyards is so thorough that results are always interesting.

Acino '08, which has been the winery's most impressive wine on other occasions, is sharp and vibrant with a blend of fruity character and a gutsy, dry, lingering palate that shifts register in the finish, recovering some austerity. The Amabile '08 is well-defined and elegant, with marked fragrant cherry fruit aromas, and a fresh palate with perfectly balanced sweetness.

○ Albana di Romagna Progetto 1 '08	⟡	4*
● Sangiovese di Romagna Sup. Contiriserva Ris. '06	⟡	5
○ An Ghin Gà '08	⟡	4
○ Earth Heart '08	⟡	4
○ LeOne '08	⟡	4
○ Oro et Laboro	⟡	5
● Sangiovese di Romagna Sup. Le Betulle '07	⟡	4
○ Tu Chiamale se Vuoi Emozioni Lato B '07	⟡	7
● Arcolaio '06	⟣	5
● Sangiovese di Romagna Sup. Le Betulle '06	⟣	4*
○ Tu Chiamale se Vuoi Emozioni Lato B '03	⟣	6
○ Tu Chiamale se Vuoi Emozioni Lato B '06	⟣	7

● Lambrusco Grasparossa di Castelvetro Amabile '08	⟡	3*
● Lambrusco Grasparossa di Castelvetro L'Acino '08	⟡	4*
○ Dolce Incanto Malvasia '08	⟡	3
● Lambrusco Grasparossa di Castelvetro '08	⟡	4
● Lambrusco Grasparossa di Castelvetro L'Acino '07	⟣	4*
● Lambrusco Grasparossa di Castelvetro Secco '06	⟣	4*
● Lambrusco Grasparossa di Castelvetro Secco Bolla Rossa '06	⟣	3*
● Lambrusco Grasparossa di Castelvetro Secco L'Acino '06	⟣	4*

Il Cortile - Dall'Asta

LOC. CASATICO DI LANGHIRANO
S.DA DELLA NAVE, 14
43010 PARMA
TEL. 0521863576
cantinedallasta@libero.it

CELLAR SALES
PRE-BOOKED VISITS

ANNUAL PRODUCTION 270,000 bottles
HECTARES UNDER VINE 15
VITICULTURE METHOD Conventional

Founded in 1910 by Luigi Dall'Asta, the oldest label in Parma began as by selling wines produced in the family's flatlands vineyards and small selected lots. In the 1960s, the estate took over the Il Cortile farm, where it is based today, and began to experiment with the classic method. Emilio Dall'Asta passed on this passion to his son Giovanni, the current owner and manager. The estate makes wines exclusively with grapes grown on the 15-hectare property.

The dry, windy climate in the area is similar to the famous nearby Langhirano zone, making it possible for the winery to ferment healthy, sound grapes. The Metodo Classico Dama Bianca '07 went to the final, showing fragrant, minerally and suave with a flavoursome palate that unfolds with some complexity. The Torrechiara '08 is subtle and vibrant, enlivened by acidity that brings out its subtle tone with personality. The Mefistofele '08, from maestri grapes grown in the estate's oldest vineyards, is stylish and taut with austere aromas. The impressive Torchiara '08 is from a barbera-heavy mix with bonarda.

Camillo Donati

LOC. AROLA, 32
43013 LANGHIRANO [PR]
TEL. 0521637204
camdona@tin.it

CELLAR SALES
PRE-BOOKED VISITS

ANNUAL PRODUCTION 70,000 bottles
HECTARES UNDER VINE 14
VITICULTURE METHOD Organic certified

In the early 1990s, Camillo Donati took over his father's vineyards at Arola, 20 kilometres from Parma on the road to Langhirano, at an altitude of 250 metres. Helped by his niece Monia, he personally runs the 14-hectare estate which produces very personal, exciting wines. He uses skin contact, fermentation without controls, no chemicals, no selected yeasts and no enzymes, just great sensitivity.

Through to the final was Il Mio Sauvignon '07, a complex, ever-changing, mineral and saltiness-tinged wine. Sauvignon blanc arrived here from France before phylloxera took hold and is traditionally grown in the area. Also impressive are the Groppone d'Orlando '04, a subtle, stylish sparkling Barbera, and the Lambrusco '06, made from maestri, a wine for the mind with an astoundingly flavoursome, balanced palate braced by closely woven tannins.

○ Colli di Parma Malvasia Dama Bianca '08	♥♥	4*
○ Colli di Parma Malvasia Torrechiara '08	♥♥	2*
● Colli di Parma Pinot Nero '08	♥♥	4*
● Colli di Parma Rosso Torchiara '08	♥♥	4*
● Lambrusco dell'Emilia Mefistofele '08	♥♥	2*
○ Colli di Parma Sauvignon Frizzante Gatao '08	♥	3
☉ La Corona Ferrea Brut Rosé '06	♥	4
● Lambrusco Brut Parmigianino '07	♥	3
● Lambrusco dell'Emilia Le Viole '08	♥	2

○ Il Mio Sauvignon '07	♥♥	4*
● Il Groppone d'Orlando '04	♥♥	4*
○ Il Mio Malvasia Dolce '07	♥♥	4*
● Lambrusco '06	♥♥	4*

Drei Donà Tenuta La Palazza

LOC. MASSA DI VECCHIAZZANO
VIA DEL TESORO, 23
47100 FORLÌ
TEL. 0543769371
www.dreidona.it

CELLAR SALES
PRE-BOOKED VISITS

ANNUAL PRODUCTION **130,000 bottles**
HECTARES UNDER VINE **30**
VITICULTURE METHOD **Natural**

Claudio and Enrico Drei Donà are among Romagna's longest-standing producers and their Sangioveses are among the area's few benchmark wines, both for their coherent style and their respect for the nature of the grape. The vineyards are starting to mature and the products are dependable and interesting. The first modern vineyards were planted in 1981, when Claudio Drei Donà decided to give up his day job as a lawyer and work on the family estate full-time, setting out to build up a serious business inspired by the model of a small Bordeaux château.

The Drei Donàs' Sangioveses have always been reliable communicators of their terroir and the cellar's best products. Pruno '06 picked up Three Glasses for its austere nose and a wonderful palate that unfolds fresh, precise and nicely thrown into focus by acidity that lightens and lengthens the finish. Notturno '07, made from sangiovese, is also good with gutsy tannins making way for a fragrant, fruity finish. We always like the Cabernet Sauvignon Magnificat '06 and the Chardonnay Il Tornese '08.

Stefano Ferrucci

VIA CASOLANA, 3045/2
48014 CASTEL BOLOGNESE [RA]
TEL. 0546651068
www.stefanoferrucci.it

CELLAR SALES
PRE-BOOKED VISITS

ANNUAL PRODUCTION **95,000 bottles**
HECTARES UNDER VINE **15**
VITICULTURE METHOD **Conventional**

In 2007, Ilaria Ferrucci took over her father's winery and immediately revolutionized approaches and running methods. The results are beginning to show, although Ilaria's project to overhaul the quality of the vineyards is long term. Winemaker Federico Giotto is now in charge of the oenological side. The results are taking shape and the wines are settling into the style Ilaria is looking for.

Domus Caia is a project that began many years ago with Stefano Ferrucci's experiments as the first Romagna producer to use the drying technique. Without betraying the wine's original spirit, Ilaria has gradually reduced the drying, given the delicate nature of sangiovese. Her wine is still original but now more balanced. The '06 combines raisiny notes with nice freshness and fragrant cherry fruit while the palate is clear and rugged, finishing fresh. Albana Passita Domus Aurea '07 is citrussy with varietal hints of honey, and generous fruit. Centurione '08 has a slightly forced nose but shows an impressively dynamic, tannic palate with character in the finish.

● Sangiovese di Romagna Sup. Pruno Ris. '06	▼▼▼ 6
○ Il Tornese Chardonnay '07	▼▼ 4*
● Magnificat Cabernet Sauvignon '06	▼▼ 6
● Notturno Sangiovese '07	▼▼ 4*
● Sangiovese di Romagna Sup. Pruno Ris. '01	♈♈♈ 5
● Sangiovese di Romagna Sup. Pruno Ris. '00	♈♈♈ 5
● Graf Noir '01	♈♈ 8
○ Il Tornese Chardonnay '06	♈♈ 5
● Magnificat Cabernet Sauvignon '03	♈♈ 5

○ Albana di Romagna Passito Domus Aurea '07	▼▼ 6
● Sangiovese di Romagna Sup. Domus Caia Ris. '06	▼▼ 6
● Sangiovese di Romagna Sup. Centurione '08	▼ 4
○ Albana di Romagna Passito Domus Aurea '06	♈♈ 6
● Sangiovese di Romagna Sup. Centurione '07	♈♈ 4*
● Sangiovese di Romagna Sup. Domus Caia Ris. '04	♈♈ 6
● Sangiovese di Romagna Sup. Domus Caia Ris. '03	♈♈ 6
● Sangiovese di Romagna Sup. Domus Caia Ris. '05	♈♈ 6

Paolo Francesconi

LOC. SARNA
VIA TULIERO, 154
48018 FAENZA [RA]
TEL. 054643213
pfrancesconi@racine.ra.it

CELLAR SALES
PRE-BOOKED VISITS

ANNUAL PRODUCTION **15,000 bottles**
HECTARES UNDER VINE **14**
VITICULTURE METHOD **Organic certified**

For several years, Paolo Francesconi has been committed to a long-term project for biodynamic farming and naturally made wines. The red clay lands where the vines stand can yield quality, but at a price. After a few years' experience, the wines today are generally dependable in quality and are beginning to show a precise character that Paolo has always respected and tried to support. The winery also produces an excellent extra virgin olive oil from the nostrana di Brisighella cultivar.

The basic Sangiovese Limbecca '08 went to the finals. Territory-based, fresh and precise, it has very clear-cut youthful character and plenty of vibrancy without sacrificing elegance. The long, richly flavoursome finish gradually emerges as the driving acidity fades away. We liked the Miniato '07, from cabernet sauvignon, sangiovese and ancellotta, with its very expressive fruity nose and generous but not excessively weighty palate. The interesting centesimino Passito D'Incanto is almost peppery in places, with prominent varietal hints of roses and elderflower.

Gallegati

VIA ISONZO, 4
48018 FAENZA [RA]
TEL. 0546621149
www.aziendaagricolagallegati.it

CELLAR SALES
PRE-BOOKED VISITS

ANNUAL PRODUCTION **15,000 bottles**
HECTARES UNDER VINE **6**
VITICULTURE METHOD **Natural**

Cesare and Antonio Gallegati's small winery has in recent years become a benchmark for the Faenza area for its courageous decisions and impeccable vineyard management. Both brothers are well prepared with degrees in agricultural science – Cesare is also an oenology graduate – and unusual sensitivity. The estate is in the lower Faenza hills in Senio and Lamone valleys, at the heart of a typically clayey area. Gallegati wines are perfect interpretations of this terroir.

Corallo Nero '06, a pure Sangiovese in blend and execution, won Three Glasses for a personality that combines dense texture with stylish, fresh expression. The nose is complex and fragrant while the palate is characterful with nice acidity and fleshing out the flavour. Regina di Cuori Riserva '06 is extraordinary, with figs, apricots, candied citrus peel and the albana grape's character flanking a salty palate with well-gauged sweetness. Corallo Blu '06, from merlot and cabernet sauvignon with a splash of sangiovese, did well, showing fresh, fast-paced, stylish and tight, with spicy complex fruit.

● Sangiovese di Romagna Sup. Limbecca '08	▼▼ 4*
● Colli di Faenza Rosso Miniato '07	▼▼ 4
● D'Incanto	▼▼ 5
● Impavido Merlot '07	▼ 5
● Impavido Merlot '06	♀♀ 5
● Sangiovese di Romagna Sup. Limbecca '07	♀♀ 4*

● Sangiovese di Romagna Sup. Corallo Nero Ris. '06	▼▼▼ 5
○ Albana di Romagna Passito Regina di Cuori Ris. '06	▼▼ 6
● Colli di Faenza Rosso Corallo Blu Ris. '06	▼▼ 5
○ Albana di Romagna Passito Regina di Cuori '04	♀♀ 5
○ Albana di Romagna Passito Regina di Cuori '03	♀♀ 5
● Sangiovese di Romagna Sup. Corallo Nero Ris. '05	♀♀ 5

Lini 910

LOC. CANOLO DI CORREGGIO
VIA VECCHIA CANOLO, 7
42015 CORREGGIO [RE]
TEL. 0522690162
www.lini910.it

CELLAR SALES
PRE-BOOKED VISITS

ANNUAL PRODUCTION **300,000 bottles**
HECTARES UNDER VINE **25**
VITICULTURE METHOD **Organic certified**

Lini is a prestigious traditional Lambrusco label, well-known for the production of Metodo Classico with which the Lini family began experimenting in the early 1960s. The new generation, Alicia and her cousin Alberto, has taken over the business with enthusiasm and pride in carrying forward a tradition that has trends come and go for a century. The brief range of fine-quality products includes traditional Reggio Emilia vinegar made with 100 sets of containers in the new vinegar house designed by Paolo Rizzato.

This small estate's products are always good and it continues to present bottles of quality and character with surprising results, especially in the Metodo Classico wines. Into the finals went In Correggio Brut '04, from pinot nero fermented off the skins, which presents complex, subtle, intense and full of personality. The Rosé '03, from pinot nero that spent 36 months on the lees, has alluring aromas and a generous dry palate. In Correggio Rosso '05, from 100 per cent salamino, is nice and austere with subtle complex fruit and good depth.

○ In Correggio Brut M. Cl. '04	🍷🍷	5
● In Correggio Brut Rosso M. Cl. '05	🍷🍷	5
⊙ In Correggio Brut Rosé M. Cl. '03	🍷🍷	5
○ In Correggio Brut Pinot '08	🍷	4
⊙ In Correggio Lambrusco Rosato '08	🍷	3
● In Correggio Lambrusco scuro '08	🍷	4
○ In Correggio Moscato Spumante '08	🍷	4
● In Correggio Brut Rosso M. Cl. '04	🍷🍷	5
● In Correggio Brut Rosso M. Cl. '03	🍷🍷	5

Luretta

LOC. CASTELLO DI MOMELIANO
29010 GAZZOLA [PC]
TEL. 0523971070
www.luretta.com

CELLAR SALES
PRE-BOOKED VISITS

ANNUAL PRODUCTION **250,000 bottles**
HECTARES UNDER VINE **43**
VITICULTURE METHOD **Organic certified**

To reiterate what we wrote a few years ago, Felice Salamini is the kind of man who can come up with a perspective-changing insight at any moment. His original explorations of winemaking suffer from the very severe limitations of Piacenza's local varieties and wines. So Felice moves in new directions, freely challenging tradition, and the result are always interesting. Felice started out in 1992 and his son Lucio is also involved today. The winery uses grapes grown on its 43 hectares situated in Val Luretta and in Val Nure.

Selin D'Armari '07 is a very stylish wine that opens on sensations of gunflint, clearly expressing minerality, and follows with a suave palate underpinned by enduring acidity. On Attend les Invités '04 is fair, showing complex with aromas ranging from florality to hazelnuts. I Nani e Le Ballerine '08 did well with its fragrant aromas and a racy, supple palate. The '08 version of Boccadirosa is a successful demonstration of the elegant style the Salaminis have perfected for this wine, presenting subtle varietal aromas with a hint of lavender and pace on the upfront palate.

⊙ C. P. Brut Rosé On Attend les Invités '04	🍷🍷	5
○ C. P. Chardonnay Selin Dl'Armari '07	🍷🍷	5
○ C. P. Malvasia Boccadirosa '08	🍷🍷	4
○ C. P. Sauvignon I Nani e Le Ballerine '08	🍷🍷	4
● C. P. Gutturnio Sup. L'Ala del Drago '06	🍷	4
● C. P. Cabernet Sauvignon Corbeau '00	🍷🍷🍷	6
○ C. P. Malvasia Boccadirosa '07	🍷🍷	4*

Gaetano Lusenti

LOC. CASE PICCIONI, 57
29010 ZIANO PIACENTINO [PC]
TEL. 0523868479
www.lusentivini.it

CELLAR SALES
PRE-BOOKED VISITS

ANNUAL PRODUCTION 100,000 bottles
HECTARES UNDER VINE 17
VITICULTURE METHOD Conventional

Ludovica Lusenti's winery is in one of the most spectacular locations in Val Tidone, a short distance from Oltrepò Pavese, in a landscape of rolling hills covered with vineyards as far as the eye can see. The Lusenti family has a longstanding relationship with the land and almost unparalleled experience in winemaking for this area. Ludovica comes from a modest country family and combines the farming tradition with winemaking modernity to safeguard an identity shaped by tradition.

The winery's Gutturnio Frizzante '08 is always a dependable classic. The nose has clean, vibrant, cherry-led fruit and a tidy, racy palate marked out by freshness. The Bianca Regina '07, from malvasia lightly macerated on the skins, is both husky and stylish, its aromas developing nicely into an edgy, lively palate. Vigna Martin IV '08, a four-square Gutturnio, has a fruity nose and a well-paced, generous palate.

● C. P. Gutturnio Frizzante '08	▼▼ 3*
○ C. P. Malvasia Bianca Regina '07	▼▼ 4
● Vigna Martin IV '08	▼▼ 4
● C. P. Cabernet Sauvignon Villante '06	▼ 4
○ C. P. Malvasia Passito Il Piriolo '07	▼ 6
○ C. P. Pinot Grigio Fiocco di Rose '08	▼ 4
○ C. P. Malvasia V. T. Bianca Regina '06	♀♀ 4*
○ C. P. Malvasia V. T. Bianca Regina '05	♀♀ 4*
● Vigna Martin '07	♀♀ 4*

Giovanna Madonia

LOC. VILLA MADONIA
VIA DE' CAPPUCCINI, 130
47032 BERTINORO [FC]
TEL. 0543444361
www.giovannamadonia.it

CELLAR SALES
PRE-BOOKED VISITS
FOOD

ANNUAL PRODUCTION 45,000 bottles
HECTARES UNDER VINE 12
VITICULTURE METHOD Conventional

Giovanna Madonia has her own style, which may seem confused but shows extraordinary overall coherence. She avoids blueprints, which she dislikes, and prefers to work freely without clichés. An example of this is her labels, by Altan, which she drew herself in pencil when she got tired of the proposals of graphic designers. This is a well-established Romagna winery, and a leading player in the emerging Bertinoro area, where the soil is rich in active limestone and spungone, the tufaceous marine rock found everywhere.

Ombroso '06 walked away with Three Glasses for its extraordinarily genuine character. It throws an austere, deep nose and then erupts onto the palate with an impressive array of flavours showing almost ruggedly dry and dynamic with a fresh, stylish finish. Fermavento '07 is slightly forced on the nose but more impressive on the palate, where it avoids the excessively weighty tannin to find elegant expression in its acidity.

● Sangiovese di Romagna Sup. Ombroso Ris. '06	▼▼▼ 5
● Sangiovese di Romagna Sup. Fermavento '07	▼▼ 4
● Sterpigno Merlot '05	▼ 6
● Sangiovese di Romagna Sup. Ombroso Ris. '01	♀♀♀ 5
● Sangiovese di Romagna Sup. Fermavento '05	♀♀ 4*
● Sangiovese di Romagna Sup. Ombroso Ris. '05	♀♀ 5
● Sangiovese di Romagna Sup. Ombroso Ris. '03	♀♀ 5

Ermete Medici & Figli

LOC. GAIDA
VIA NEWTON, 13A
42040 REGGIO EMILIA
TEL. 0522942135
www.medici.it

CELLAR SALES
PRE-BOOKED VISITS

ANNUAL PRODUCTION **800,000 bottles**
HECTARES UNDER VINE **60**
VITICULTURE METHOD **Conventional**

The Medici family traditionally produces wines from grapes bought in from other growers, as well as fine quality wines from the estate's own grapes, harvested in well-managed vineyards and crafted to achieve ambitious results. Giorgio Medici has carried out significant research into fermentation and today's products are the increasingly impressive culmination of a process conducted with great passion and skill. This successful example of a cru-oriented philosophy is rare in Lambrusco but shows astonishing results.

Three Glasses went to the wine that best represents the estate, the 100 per cent salamino Concerto '08. This perfectly centred wine is elegant and traditional in style, combining a down-to-earthness on the nose with very crisp cherry fruit and a perfect balance of weight, tannin and acidity on the palate. Assolo '08, from ancellotta and salamino, also made the finals, where is showed alluringly creamy, fruity and generous, with lots of juicy flavour. The Metodo Classico Gran Concerto '07, disgorged in 2009, is a 100 per cent salamino bottle with perfectly ripe fruit.

Monte delle Vigne

LOC. OZZANO TARO
VIA MONTICELLO, 13
43046 COLLECCHIO [PR]
TEL. 0521309704
www.montedellevigne.it

CELLAR SALES
PRE-BOOKED VISITS

ANNUAL PRODUCTION **250,000 bottles**
HECTARES UNDER VINE **45**
VITICULTURE METHOD **Conventional**

Andrea Ferrari and Paolo Pizzarotti's operation is one of the most interesting in the Parma hills. The partners have not stinted on resources to plant fine quality vineyards, which are fully productive today, and equip the winery with a modern, functional underground cellar. Their goal is to produce excellent quality still wines, which are not traditional for this area, in a different interpretation of traditional grape varieties like barbera, bonarda and aromatic malvasia di Candia.

Lambrusco '08, from 100 per cent maestri, made the finals for its very stylish nose of fragrant cherries and white peaches, and a subtle, well-poised palate with nicely measured acidity. The impressive Callas Malvasia '08 from malvasia di Candia is complex and combines citrus sensations with aromatic herbs and mint. The biting palate is leaner than previous versions but still unfolds with generous breadth. The barbera-heavy Nabucco '07 is clean and elegant but slightly too oaky. Colli di Parma Rosso '07 from barbera and bonarda is crisp and fruity with a stylish palate.

● Reggiano Lambrusco Concerto '08	♟♟♟	3*
● Reggiano Assolo '08	♟♟	3*
☉ Granconcerto Brut Metodo Cl. '07	♟♟	4
● Reggiano Lambrusco Secco I Quercioli '08	♟♟	2*
● Reggiano Lambrusco Secco Libesco '08	♟♟	3*
● Reggiano Assolo '07	♟♟	3*
● Reggiano Lambrusco Secco Concerto '07	♟♟	3*
● Reggiano Lambrusco Secco I Quercioli '06	♟♟	2*

● Lambrusco '08	♟♟	3*
○ Callas Malvasia '08	♟♟	5
● Colli di Parma Rosso '07	♟	4
● Nabucco '07	♟	5
○ Callas Malvasia '07	♟♟	5
● Lambrusco '07	♟♟	3*
● Nabucco '06	♟♟	5

Roberto Monti

VIA MONTECCHIO, 54
48013 BRISIGHELLA [RA]
TEL. 054681701
robertomonti5@virgilio.it

ANNUAL PRODUCTION **4,000 bottles**
HECTARES UNDER VINE **12**
VITICULTURE METHOD **Conventional**

Paolo Monti, who runs the estate's 12 hectares under vine with his father, decided a few years ago to begin fermenting and bottling some of the grapes he usually passed on to the local co-operative winery. His sensitivity and commitment bring us some very good wines that beautifully reflect their terroir. Even more credit is due if we consider the challenging, almost exclusively clay, soil on which the vineyards are planted in Faenza and the village of Brisighella in an attractive, ravine-scarred landscape.

Millo '07 is a Sangiovese with all the generous, edgy character shown by the variety when grown on clayey terrain. Millo is fresh and characterful with a lively fragrant flavour that combines elegance with the crucial contribution of acidity and cool, deep fruit. Colli di Faenza Iaia Riserva '07 is richer and more rounded but the nose and palate are both built on freshness. The generous texture of the palate is masterfully handled and the weight is never excessive. Oak is used nicely in both wines.

Fattoria Monticino Rosso

VIA MONTECATONE, 7
40026 IMOLA [BO]
TEL. 054240577
www.fattoriadelmonticinorosso.it

CELLAR SALES
PRE-BOOKED VISITS

ANNUAL PRODUCTION **70,000 bottles**
HECTARES UNDER VINE **18**
VITICULTURE METHOD **Conventional**

Monticino Rosso is one of the northernmost estates in Romagna, with a site climate so special that Mussolini built a sanatorium here in the 1930s. The Zeolis are painstaking growers with strong links to the terroir, as is demonstrated by their extensive and devoted clientele for their excellent unbottled wines. The trade is important for this winery as it enables thorough selection of the wines to go into bottle. Consultant winemaker Giancarlo Soverchia also works with the cellar.

The winery's reds struggle to find a length and generally appear rather weary but the whites put on a more impressive performance, particularly the Albana. Codronchio '07 is a nicely complex, multi-faceted wine with a floral nose of chamomile, broom, lime blossom and acacia heralding a salty, minerally palate. We also liked the Albana Passito '06, with citrus and candied fruit aromas and a fresh palate with its classic hint of honey. Albana Secco '08 is supple.

● Colli di Faenza Rosso Iaia Ris. '07	♟♟ 4*
● Sangiovese di Romagna Sup. Millo '07	♟♟ 4*

○ Albana di Romagna Secco '08	♟♟ 3*
○ Albana di Romagna Passito '06	♟♟ 5
○ Albana di Romagna Secco Codronchio '07	♟♟ 4
○ Colli d'Imola Pignoletto '08	♟♟ 3*
● Sangiovese di Romagna Sup. '07	♟ 3
○ Albana di Romagna Secco Codronchio '06	♟♟ 4*
○ Albana di Romagna Secco Codronchio '04	♟♟ 4*
● Colli d'Imola Cabernet Sauvignon Pradello Ris. '04	♟♟ 4
○ Malvasia Passito '03	♟♟ 5
● Sangiovese di Romagna Sup. '06	♟♟ 3*

Il Negrese

LOC. IL NEGRESE
29010 ZIANO PIACENTINO [PC]
TEL. 0523864804

Gianfranco Paltrinieri

FRAZ. SORBARA
VIA CRISTO,49
41030 BOMPORTO [MO]
TEL. 059902047
www.cantinapaltrinieri.it

CELLAR SALES

ANNUAL PRODUCTION **30,000 bottles**
HECTARES UNDER VINE **8**
VITICULTURE METHOD **Conventional**

Matteo Braga has run this small estate since 2001, after a long apprenticeship with Elena Pantaleoni and Giulio Armani of La Stoppa, which profoundly affected his winemaking style. Matteo ferments the grapes from small plots at Ziano under the Montepo hill, locally considered the best cru for barbera. The holding is planted exclusively to malvasia and the two varieties used in Gutturnio, barbera and bonarda. Rigorous work in the vineyards and Matteo's application in the cellar are geared to conveying the fruits of the growing year and the terrain.

The Malvasia Passito '07 is remarkable. A complex wine with hints of figs, apricots, citrus, candied fruit and white peaches, it reveals a fresh, barely sweet palate with plenty of weight and a long, aroma-rich finish. The Gutturnio '07 aged in large oak barrels, which is not to be confused with the steel-aged wine reviewed in last year's Guide under a different label, is authentic, dry and lively with a sharp, biting palate. Gutturnio Frizzante '08 is dense, alcoholic, fast-paced and rustic yet sophisticated, with a still taut fruity finish.

ANNUAL PRODUCTION **60,000 bottles**
HECTARES UNDER VINE **15**
VITICULTURE METHOD **Conventional**

This family-run winery, founded in the 1920s, is located at Cristo in the heart of Sorbara. Alberto Paltrinieri and his wife Barbara Galassi run the 15-hectare estate and cellar personally, helped by the whole family, using grapes grown exclusively on the property. The Paltrinieris belong to a group of producers who have determinedly protected the subtly varietal, minerally style of Sorbara, an identity which is much appreciated today and represents one of the most original styles on the varied Lambrusco panorama.

It was a trying year for Sorbara because of hailstorms so congratulations to the Paltrinieris on the quality achieved. The finals beckoned Leclisse '08, a selection of 100 per cent sorbara made at Cristo di Sorbara, which proffers a delicate, minerally nose and very stylish, biting palate with a whistle-sharp, minerally finish. Sant'Agata '08 is complex, with apple fruit and violet-led florality. The palate is linear, taut and supple. The La Piria '08, sorbara fermented with a dash of salamino in the traditional manner, has a vibrantly edgy palate.

○ C. P. Malvasia Passito '07	♀	5
● C. P. Gutturnio '07	♀♀	4*
● C. P. Gutturnio Frizzante '08	♀♀	4
○ C. P. Malvasia Passito '06	♀♀♀	5
● C. P. Gutturnio '07	♀♀	4
○ C. P. Malvasia Passito '05	♀♀	5
○ C. P. Malvasia Passito '04	♀♀	5

● Lambrusco di Sorbara Leclisse '08	♀♀	4*
● Lambrusco di Sorbara La Piria '08	♀♀	2*
● Lambrusco di Sorbara Sant'Agata '08	♀♀	3*

Tenuta Pertinello

S.DA ARPINETO PERTINELLO, 2
47010 GALEATA [FC]
TEL. 0543983156
www.tenutapertinello.altervista.org

CELLAR SALES

ANNUAL PRODUCTION 30,000 bottles
HECTARES UNDER VINE 9
VITICULTURE METHOD Conventional

Tenuta Pertinello is high up in Valle del Bidente and the vineyards stand on marl and sandstone soil at an altitude of 350 metres, peaking at 430 metres in places. Moreno Mancini, the current owner, bought the winery in 2006, having spotted the evident potential for quality. The winery had always produced just one wine, Pertinello, but since 2008 when Fabrizio Moltard joined the business, it has made three. Pertinello is now joined by Sasso, a Riserva di Sangiovese made from grapes grown in the oldest vineyard, and a simpler wine, Il Bosco.

Luigi Martini, who looks after vineyards and cellar with passion and skill, is a link with the previous owners and never fails to bring astonishingly healthy grapes to the cellar. The '05 Pertinello is very austere and complex, drinking dry in the traditional style before finding more expression on the finish. The steel-fermented Bosco '08, from sangiovese with a dash of merlot, is fragrant and fruity with a piquant nose and taut, fresh palate that is surprisingly flavoursome and drinkable.

Poderi dal Nespoli

LOC. NESPOLI
VILLA ROSSI, 50
47012 CIVITELLA DI ROMAGNA [FC]
TEL. 0543989637
www.poderidalnespoli.com

CELLAR SALES
PRE-BOOKED VISITS

ANNUAL PRODUCTION 300,000 bottles
HECTARES UNDER VINE 41
VITICULTURE METHOD Conventional

Poderi dal Nespoli is a well-established traditional Romagna estate, vinifying grapes from over 40 hectares around the village of Cusercoli in the upper Bidente valley. The soil is clayey and marly-arenaceous, and all the winery's products foreground elegance rather than strength, a difficult route but an interesting one for the future. Fabio Ravaioli remains at the winery's helm following a reshuffle that brought in new partners and capital.

Three Glasses went to Nespoli Riserva '06, one of Romagna's most elegant Sangioveses. The grapes come from the higher vineyards on mainly marly soil. Austere and precise on the nose, with a knife-sharp palate, it has pace, focus and bags of character. Perfectly gauged extract frames its lean physique. Also in the finals was Prugneto Riserva '08, from sangiovese grown in the clayey Prugneto vineyard, which has good temperature fluctuations. It's floral, fragrant and vibrantly juicy in the mouth. Santodeno '08 is lean and racy while the sangiovese, cabernet sauvignon and raboso del Piave Borgo dei Guidi has a warm, overripe nose and an agile, well-balanced palate.

● Colli della Romagna
  Centrale Sangiovese Pertinello '05 ▼▼ 4
● Sangiovese di Romagna Il Bosco '08 ▼▼ 4

● Sangiovese di Romagna Sup.
  Il Nespoli Ris. '06 ▼▼▼ 5
● Sangiovese di Romagna Sup.
  Prugneto Ris. '08 ▼▼
● Borgo dei Guidi '06 ▼▼ 6
● Sangiovese di Romagna Sup. Santodeno '08 ▼▼ 3
○ Da Maggio '08 ▼ 3
○ Da Maggio Chardonnay '07 ♀♀ 3*
○ Damaggio Chardonnay '06 ♀♀ 3*
● Sangiovese di Romagna Prugneto '07 ♀♀ 4*
● Sangiovese di Romagna Prugneto '06 ♀♀ 4*
● Sangiovese di Romagna Sup.
  Il Nespoli Ris. '05 ♀♀ 5

Il Poggiarello

LOC. SCRIVELLANO DI STATTO
29020 TRAVO [PC]
TEL. 0523957241
www.ilpoggiarellovini.it

CELLAR SALES
PRE-BOOKED VISITS

ANNUAL PRODUCTION **100,000 bottles**
HECTARES UNDER VINE **18**
VITICULTURE METHOD **Conventional**

Stefano, Massimo and Paolo Perini are heirs to a great family tradition at the Quattro Valli winery and Il Poggiarello embodies their dream of setting up a winery, alongside the family business, to work with new ideas, important objectives and the stimulus of an ambitious challenge. Il Poggiarello was set up in the 1980s when Franco Illari of Antica Osteria del Teatro awoke in trio's interest in wine. Today, the dream is a solid operation which has established itself as a benchmark for the whole Piacenza territory.

La Barbona Riserva '07 went to the final with its nose of redcurrant fruit spiced with cocoa powder and coffee, and fresh, slightly dry palate. This wine has always shown much more quality than typicity but this version seems to have taken a big step towards finding territorial identity. Perticato Valandrea '08 is also impressive, with a fresh, rounded palate and austere character. The Perticato La Piana '07 is interesting with its stylish, minerally nose and intriguingly taut, sharp palate.

Il Pratello

VIA MORANA, 14
47015 MODIGLIANA [FC]
TEL. 0546942038
www.ilpratello.net

CELLAR SALES
PRE-BOOKED VISITS

ANNUAL PRODUCTION **20,000 bottles**
HECTARES UNDER VINE **5.5**
VITICULTURE METHOD **Conventional**

The road to Pratello climbs gradually from Modigliana along the Ibola river to reach a wild area where bracken and chestnuts grow among the broom. This altitude of 600 metres is at the limit for growing vines and the climate and often shallow sandy soil mean the struggle with nature is constant. Up here Emilio Placci planted sangiovese back in 1991, cultivating and fermenting his grapes without consultants or chemicals and clinging to a concept of wine as a way of life in harmony with the local territory.

Pratello wines are hard and authentic and need time. Mantignano '04 perfectly reflects the considerable temperature variations in these hills and their ability to calibrate the sangiovese grape in a subtle register that brought it to the finals for the first time. Mantignano is austere, compact and stylish with wonderful acidity that carries the palate on to a characterful, delicately fruity finish. The sauvignon blanc Campore is one of the most interesting whites in Romagna, showing salty, minerally and very fresh. Badia Raustignolo '03 has thrust and rhythm.

● C. P. Gutturnio La Barbona Ris. '07	♟♟ 5
● C. P. Barbera 'L Piston '08	♟♟ 4
● C. P. Gutturnio Perticato Valandrea '08	♟♟ 4
○ C. P. Malvasia Perticato Beatrice Quadri '08	♟♟ 5
● Colli Piacentini Cabernet Sauvignon Perticato del Novarei '07	♟♟ 6
○ Colli Piacentini Chardonnay Perticato La Piana '07	♟♟ 5
○ C. P. Sauvignon Perticato Il Quadri '08	♟ 5
● Colli Piacentini Pinot Nero Perticato Le Giastre '08	♟ 5
● C. P. Barbera 'L Piston '07	♟♟ 4*
● C. P. Gutturnio La Barbona Ris. '06	♟♟ 5
● C. P. Gutturnio La Barbona Ris. '04	♟♟ 5
● C. P. Gutturnio Perticato Valandrea '07	♟♟ 4*

○ Campore '05	♟♟ 4*
● Colli di Faenza Sangiovese Mantignano Ris. '04	♟♟ 4*
● Colli di Faenza Sangiovese Badia Raustignolo Ris. '03	♟♟ 6
● Sangiovese di Romagna Morana '06	♟♟ 3*
● Colli di Faenza Sangiovese Badia Raustignolo Ris. '01	♟♟ 4*
● Colli di Faenza Sangiovese Mantignano Ris. '03	♟♟ 4*

Rocca Le Caminate

S.DA MELDOLA ROCCA DELLE CAMINATE 15A
47014 MELDOLA [FC]
TEL. 0543493482
www.roccalecaminate.it

CELLAR SALES
PRE-BOOKED VISITS

ANNUAL PRODUCTION **10,000 bottles**
HECTARES UNDER VINE **6**
VITICULTURE METHOD **Conventional**

The Fabbri family winery near Rocca delle Caminate, in the Rabbi and Bidente valleys, is on clay-based land, potentially one of the most interesting types in the Forlì hills. Antonio Fabbri is a true Romagnolo man, communicative, rugged and affable, and involves his sons Michele and Luca in the venture. Oenologist Francesco Naldi consults. There is great potential for quality although the wines have not always obtained consistent results, alternating exciting Sangioveses with more ordinary wines. At last the family's work is bearing fruit with impressive versions of both types.

The quality of the Sbargoleto shows that Antonio's intuition was right in producing a monovarietal Sangiovese. The '07 Sbargoleto reached the final with generous, clean aromas of complex flowers before the tannins snap into action on a sharp palate with a very flavoursome finish. Vitignano '06, sangiovese with a small proportion of merlot, is well-made, tangy and tidy, albeit slightly trivialized by the merlot fruit which tickles the nose and slackens the palate a tad.

Vigne di San Lorenzo

VIA CAMPIUME, 6
48013 BRISIGHELLA [RA]
TEL. 3391137070
www.campiume.it

CELLAR SALES
PRE-BOOKED VISITS
VISITOR FACILITIES
FOOD

ANNUAL PRODUCTION **10,000 bottles**
HECTARES UNDER VINE **3**
VITICULTURE METHOD **Organic certified**

In Valle del Lamone just north of Brisighella, Filippo Manetti has renovated the beautiful settlement of Campiume to make a home, a small cellar and five guest bedrooms. Filippo's philosophy is to live in harmony with nature, drawing sustenance from intellectual challenges, as his wines demonstrate to perfection. The vineyards are organic and the wines are made without chemicals or undue haste. The products released are characterful, and sometimes less than formally precise, but always exciting.

Campiume '06 needs time in the glass before it slowly opens to illustrate superbly the nature of sangiovese grown at this elevation. The nose hints at leanness in its fruit and upfront, complex minerality. The palate is bolstered by nice acidity and very stylish tannins. We also liked the San Lorenzo '06, a Bordeaux blend which is excellent despite a slightly fuzzy nose with blackberry and cherry aromas and a lean palate, with fine-grained tannins melding into a structure that finds rhythm with good supporting acidity.

● Sangiovese di Romagna Sbargoleto '07	♥♥	3*
● Vitignano '06	♥♥	5
● Sangiovese di Romagna Sup. Sbargoleto '05	♡♡	3*
● Sangiovese di Romagna Sup. Sbargoleto '04	♡♡	3*
● Sangiovese di Romagna Sup. Vitignano '05	♡♡	4*
● Sangiovese di Romagna Sup. Vitignano '04	♡♡	4
● Vitignano '03	♡♡	4*

● Sangiovese di Romagna Sup. Campiume Ris. '06	♥♥	5
● Fieni '06	♥♥	6
● San Lorenzo '06	♥♥	5

Tenimenti San Martino in Monte

via San Martino in Monte
47015 Modigliana [FC]
tel. 3292984507
www.sanmartinoinmonte.com

ANNUAL PRODUCTION 4,000 bottles
HECTARES UNDER VINE 5.6
VITICULTURE METHOD Conventional

At the age of 12, successful architect Maurizio Costa left Romagna for Rome with his family. He is back now with a fascinating, deeply felt project which involves several of his friends. His estate is high up above Modigliana and the grapes are fermented in another winery's cellar. The operation is overseen by Francesco Bordini, who rightly suggested that Costa should invest primarily in the vineyards. The results are already good and the construction of the underground cellar will enable a big leap in the direction of quality.

Vigna alle Querce '06, from sangiovese, merlot, syrah and cabernet franc, is deep, slightly vegetal and minerally on the nose with a weighty palate that opens out into an endearingly pronounced echo of the fruit at the back. The Vigna 1922 Riserva '06 is taut, vibrant and extraordinarily elegant. Unfortunately, it lacks the purity of previous versions. Vigna della Signora '07, from chardonnay musquet, sauvignon blanc and riesling, is less focused because of an ill-proportioned palate. The estate also makes excellent Brisighella olive oil.

● Sangiovese di Romagna Sup. V. 1922 Ris. '06	🍷🍷	7
● Vigna alle Querce '06	🍷🍷	5
○ V. della Signora '07	🍷	6
● Sangiovese di Romagna V. 1922 '04	YY	7
● Vigna alle Querce '05	YY	5
● Vigna alle Querce '03	YY	6

★ San Patrignano

via San Patrignano, 53
47853 Coriano [RN]
tel. 0541362111
www.sanpatrignano.org

PRE-BOOKED VISITS

ANNUAL PRODUCTION 500,000 bottles
HECTARES UNDER VINE 110
VITICULTURE METHOD Conventional

San Patrignano, founded by Vincenzo Muccioli in 1978, is now Europe's leading community for recovering drug addicts. Since Vincenzo's death in 1995, his son Andrea run the complex and his passion for wine has transformed one of the community's rehabilitation activities into an ambitious project. The San Patrignano vineyards cover 110 hectares of limestone and clay soil in the Coriano hills overlooking the Rimini coast. This is an excellent place to grow for sangiovese and Bordeaux varieties.

A best-ever score sheet saw Three Glass awards for the two leading wines. Avi '06 is a single-variety Sangiovese with an elegantly lean, fresh palate poised between minerality and lively extract. The exciting Montepirolo '06, from cabernet sauvignon, merlot and cabernet franc, is spicy, deep and ever-changing. The palate puts elegance before volume and brims with flavour from start to finish. It's a great, perfectly made wine. And there was a good performance from the winery's basic red, Aulente Rosso '08, a sangiovese-heavy blend with other varieties that has never been drinking so dry and crisply territorial.

● Colli di Rimini Cabernet Montepirolo '06	🍷🍷🍷	6
● Sangiovese di Romagna Sup. Avi Ris. '06	🍷🍷🍷	6
○ Aulente Bianco '08	🍷🍷	4
● Aulente Rosso '08	🍷🍷	4
● Colli di Rimini Rosso Noi '07	🍷🍷	5
○ Vie '08	🍷🍷	5
● Colli di Rimini Cabernet Montepirolo '04	YYY	6
● Colli di Rimini Cabernet Montepirolo '01	YYY	6
● Colli di Rimini Rosso Noi '04	YYY	6
● Sangiovese di Romagna Sup. Avi Ris. '05	YYY	6
● Colli di Rimini Cabernet Montepirolo '05	YY	6
● Sangiovese di Romagna Sup. Avi Ris. '04	YY	6

San Valentino

FRAZ. SAN MARTINO IN VENTI
VIA TOMASETTA, 13
47900 RIMINI
TEL. 0541752231
www.vinisanvalentino.com

CELLAR SALES
PRE-BOOKED VISITS
VISITOR FACILITIES

ANNUAL PRODUCTION **140,000 bottles**
HECTARES UNDER VINE **28**
VITICULTURE METHOD **Conventional**

Roberto Mascarin's winery on the well-ventilated gently rolling lower Colli Riminesi enjoys the influence of the nearby sea, which tempers summer heat and winter cold. It was a memorable 2009 with important developments in administration, where Roberto's wife replaced his sister Maria Cristina, and production, with winemaking entrusted to former export manager Benoit Coster. San Valentino also offers four elegant holiday rooms at its farmstay, Ai 4 Acini.

Roberto Mascarin and Benoit Coster share an international idea of wine: clearly defined, powerful and enjoyable. The results are interesting but tend to lack territoriality, even at the cost of producing rather hard wines. Terra di Covignano '06 suffers from intrusive oak and excessive ripeness on the nose but the palate is more agile, although it tends to dryness. We preferred Luna Nuova '06, a vivacious Bordeaux blend that unveils a ripe nose and taut palate, with clean fruit returning in the long finish. The Superiore Scabi '08 is good, showing rounded, supple and tannic.

● Luna Nuova '06	🍷🍷 6
● Sangiovese di Romagna Sup. Scabi '08	🍷🍷 4
● Sangiovese di Romagna Sup. Terra di Covignano Ris. '06	🍷🍷 6
○ Alta Marea '08	🍷 3
● Eclissi di Sole '07	🍷 5
● Sangiovese di Romagna Sup. Terra di Covignano Ris. '06	YYY 6
● Sangiovese di Romagna Sup. Terra di Covignano Ris. '05	YYY 6
● Luna Nuova '04	YY 6
● Montepulciano '04	YY 8
● Sangiovese di Romagna Sup. Scabi '07	YY 4*

Tenuta Santini

FRAZ. PASSANO
VIA CAMPO, 33
47853 CORIANO [RN]
TEL. 0541656527
www.tenutasantini.com

CELLAR SALES
PRE-BOOKED VISITS

ANNUAL PRODUCTION **30,000 bottles**
HECTARES UNDER VINE **22**
VITICULTURE METHOD **Conventional**

The rolling, open, warm lower Rimini hills between the Valmarecchia valley and Marche border are covered in fields of wheat alternating with olives and vineyards. The climate is influenced by the blue strip of sea visible even from the hilltop forts, villages and roads. Nestling in this fairy-tale landscape with its rich culture, dialect and customs, is Tenuta Santini at Passano di Coriano, near the sea but away from the swarming coastal resorts. In 2001 Sandro Santini, who runs the estate, refocused the family business on quality with his uncle Enrico.

Following initial quality improvements, Tenuta Santini wines remain dependably good but are having difficulty expressing that quality in the right language. This is probably a matter of time, given the estate's potential. Cornelianum '06 has a spicy nose with prevalent aromas of cocoa powder and slight oaky sweetness but lacks the character to achieve depth remains rudderless. The Bordeaux blend Battarreo '06 is slightly warm on the nose and its rounded, juicy palate reveals lovely freshness. We liked Beato Enrico '08, which has a taut palate and a lovely fruit finish.

● Battarreo '06	🍷🍷 4
● Sangiovese di Romagna Sup. Beato Enrico '08	🍷🍷 4*
● Sangiovese di Romagna Sup. Cornelianum Ris. '06	🍷🍷 5
● Battarreo '04	YY 4*
● Battarreo '03	YY 4*
● Sangiovese di Romagna Sup. Cornelianum Ris. '05	YY 5

La Stoppa

LOC. ANCARANO
29029 RIVERGARO [PC]
TEL. 0523958159
www.lastoppa.it

CELLAR SALES
PRE-BOOKED VISITS
FOOD

ANNUAL PRODUCTION 160,000 bottles
HECTARES UNDER VINE 32
VITICULTURE METHOD Organic certified

La Stoppa is a long-standing Colli
Piacentini winery, acquired by the
Pantaleoni family in 1973. Over a century
ago, a Genoese lawyer called Ageno saw
the potential in this lean soil and began
experimenting with quality viticulture using
local and French varieties. Today, owner
Elena Pantaleoni and Giulio Armani, who
manages the vineyards and cellar, get their
best results with native grapes and the
vines planted when Elena first took over are
beginning to find balance as they mature.
Work at La Stoppa is based on respect for
nature in the vineyard, in winemaking and
in maturation times.

Macchiona '05 from barbera and bonarda
won the first ever Three Glass prize for the
type with a fresh, minerally nose that
gradually proffers clean, precise fruit and a
pure, sharp palate where tannins and
acidity blend into one distinctive
personality. The excellent performance
from the '07 Gutturnio is first discreet and
then explosive. Dry, lingering and fresh
from start to finish, it is a benchmark for the
type. We also liked the complex, elegant
Vigna del Volta '07.

Tenuta Tenuta La Viola

VIA COLOMBARONE, 888
47032 BERTINORO [FC]
TEL. 0543445496
www.tenutalaviola.it

CELLAR SALES
PRE-BOOKED VISITS

ANNUAL PRODUCTION 36,000 bottles
HECTARES UNDER VINE 5
VITICULTURE METHOD Organic certified

The modern era for Tenuta La Viola began
in 1998 when Stefano Gabellini, born in
1969, took up the reins of the family
business after his father's untimely death.
Motivated by his awareness of the
Bertinoro area's potential – the estate's
vineyards are planted on the eastern slopes
– and supported by invaluable work in the
vineyards by his mother Lidia, in just a few
years Stefano has managed to put his
winery in the forefront of local winemaking.

Tenuta La Viola wines have been getting
increasingly dependable in recent years
and are now some of the best-quality
products in the Bertinoro area. One last
push is needed to achieve the quality that
comes through in character and purity.
Petra Honorii '06 is a wine with two
speeds, untypical on the nose and gutsily
agile on the palate. We also liked the
Particella 25 '06, a blend of cabernet and
merlot with ten per cent sangiovese, which
has a powerful entry and plenty of lively
texture that have yet to open out fully.

● Macchiona '05	♟♟♟	5
● C. P. Gutturnio '07	♟♟	4*
● C. P. Cabernet Sauvignon Stoppa '06	♟♟	5
○ C. P. Malvasia Passito V. del Volta '07	♟♟	6
● C. P. Gutturnio Frizzante '08	♟	3
○ C. P. Malvasia Passito V. del Volta '06	♟♟♟	6
○ C. P. Malvasia Passito V. del Volta '04	♟♟♟	6
○ C. P. Malvasia Passito V. del Volta '03	♟♟♟	5
● C. P. Gutturnio '06	♟♟	3*

● Particella 25 '06	♟♟	6
● Sangiovese di Romagna Sup. Petra Honorii Ris. '06	♟♟	5
● Sangiovese di Romagna Sup. Il Colombarone '07	♟	4
● Sangiovese di Romagna Sup. Oddone '08	♟	3
● Particella 25 '05	♟♟	6
● Sangiovese di Romagna Sup. Petra Honorii Ris. '04	♟♟	5

Tizzano

VIA MARESCALCHI, 13
40033 CASALECCHIO DI RENO [BO]
TEL. 051571208
visconti@tizzano.191.it

CELLAR SALES
PRE-BOOKED VISITS

ANNUAL PRODUCTION **140,000 bottles**
HECTARES UNDER VINE **35**
VITICULTURE METHOD **Conventional**

The Tizzano farm is unique and incredibly attractive. At the heart of the 230 hectares over Casalecchio di Reno is the sumptuous mid-18th century Villa Marescalchi, built by the noble Bolognese family of the same name and owned since 1961 by Luca Visconti di Modrone. Farming duties have long been performed by Gabriele Forni, whose vast baggage of wine culture enables him to keep tabs on all aspects of this spectacular Colli Bolognesi estate.

This year, the best wine in the range is the Merlot '07, which combines nicely varietal character with an assertive but not intrusive hint of oak and clear-cut red berry fruit. The palate is dense, juicy and unfolds with balanced elegance and sweetness. The successful Pignoletto Frizzante '08 is simple, citrus-fresh and fragrantly clean. Also good are the dependable Cabernet Sauvignon '07 and Pignoletto Superiore '08, uncomplicated but very well crafted.

La Tosa

LOC. LA TOSA
29020 VIGOLZONE [PC]
TEL. 0523870727
www.latosa.it

CELLAR SALES
PRE-BOOKED VISITS

ANNUAL PRODUCTION **120,000 bottles**
HECTARES UNDER VINE **13**
VITICULTURE METHOD **Natural**

In 1984, the Pizzamiglio family from Milan brought about a minor revolution in Colli Piacentini with the production of non-sparkling wines and, especially, by concentrating on quality in the vineyards. The methodical but imaginative Stefano has pursued this idea and knows each of his vines' individual history. This legacy will one day be an important legacy for the whole of Val Nure. Stefano has studied tradition and then moved away from it to form his own extreme, original vision of the territory in a style that aims for clearly defined, well-rounded wines.

The distinctive style of La Tosa wines yields good all-round results but paradoxically the excessive sweetness and maniacal quest for formal precision prevent the wines from achieving the usual standards. Vignamorello '08 is as spicy and dense as usual, although it lacks the area's signature incisive palate. Gutturnio '08 is mellower and more dynamic. Sorriso di Cielo '08 has a good profile but suffers from excessive residual sweetness in the finish. Rio del Tordo '08 is a nice surprise, showing citrussy and clean with an acidity-tautened palate.

● C. B. Merlot '07	♟♟ 5
● C. B. Cabernet Sauvignon '07	♟ 4
○ C. B. Pignoletto Frizzante '08	♟ 3
○ C. B. Pignoletto Sup. '08	♟ 4
● C. B. Cabernet Sauvignon Ris. '03	♟♟ 5
● C. B. Merlot '06	♟♟ 4*
● C. B. Merlot '05	♟♟ 5
○ C. B. Pignoletto Spumante Brut	♟♟ 4*

● C. P. Cabernet Sauvignon Luna Selvatica '07	♟♟ 6
● C. P. Gutturnio '08	♟♟ 4
● C. P. Gutturnio Vignamorello '08	♟♟ 5
○ C. P. Malvasia Sorriso di Cielo '08	♟♟ 4
○ C. P. Sauvignon '08	♟♟ 4
○ C. P. Valnure Rio del Tordo '08	♟♟ 3*
○ C. P. Malvasia Passito L'Ora Felice '08	♟ 5
○ C. P. Valnure Frizzante '08	♟ 3
● C. P. Cabernet Sauvignon Luna Selvatica '06	♟♟♟ 6
● C. P. Cabernet Sauvignon Luna Selvatica '04	♟♟♟ 6
○ C. P. Malvasia Sorriso di Cielo '07	♟♟ 4*
○ C. P. Sauvignon '07	♟♟ 4*

Tre Monti

LOC. BERGULLO
VIA LOLA, 3
40026 IMOLA [BO]
TEL. 0542657116
www.tremonti.it

CELLAR SALES
PRE-BOOKED VISITS

ANNUAL PRODUCTION 180,000 bottles
HECTARES UNDER VINE 50
VITICULTURE METHOD Conventional

The Tre Monti estate's two main holdings are at Serra in the Colli Imolesi, with the winemaking cellar, and Petrignone in the Colli Forlivesi, where the historic Thea vineyard is located. The soil at Serra is mainly light clay with some silt and active limestone areas that bring out the very best in the albana grape. At Petrignone, the clay contains up to 20 per cent sand and a stony fluvial terrace emerges here and there all over the sangiovese vineyards.

Unusually for Romagna, the winery traditionally specializes in whites but this year there is an exciting range of reds. Three Glasses went to the austere yet supple Petrignone Riserva '06, which is almost stiff on the nose and lavished bags of energy on the generous palate, where the ripe, close-knit tannins are highlighted by acidity that lends character without affecting the overall balance. Thea Riserva '07 is oaky and overripe on the nose while the palate is impressive, fresh and weighty yet supple. The surprisingly good value for money Campo di Mezzo '08 is laudable, apart from superfluous oakiness, for its varietal character and lean, vibrant palate.

Vallona

FRAZ. FAGNANO
VIA SANT'ANDREA, 203
40050 CASTELLO DI SERRAVALLE [BO]
TEL. 0516703333
fattorie.vallona@serravallewifi.net

CELLAR SALES
PRE-BOOKED VISITS

ANNUAL PRODUCTION 90,000 bottles
HECTARES UNDER VINE 29
VITICULTURE METHOD Conventional

The ultra-experienced Maurizio Vallona is typical of wine men from the Colli Bolognesi and with a character to match: comfortable in vineyard and cellar; limelight-shunning and taciturn in public. He loves flawlessly made, clean wines and although average quality is good, his passion does slightly compromise the wines' personality. They suffer from excessive technical input, residual sugars that limit their drive on the palate and a lack of originality.

Diggioanni '06, from cabernet sauvignon, is the best wine presented. The dynamic palate has good texture but fails to open out fully, reprising the ripeness of the nose in the finish. Bottle age should bring greater balance and harmonize the distinct oakiness. We again liked the Essè Brut Spumante, produced with the Isola winery, which combines a fragrant tropical nose with a deliciously enjoyable palate. The Cabernet Sauvignon '08 is good, showing elegant, rounded and ever-shifting with hints of spice and cocoa powder. The Merlot Affederico '06 is less well-made. Good texture is overshadowed by weighty oak, it's sweet on the nose and the palate is bitter.

Wine	Rating
● Sangiovese di Romagna Sup. Petrignone Ris. '06	▼▼▼ 4
● Sangiovese di Romagna Sup. Thea Ris. '07	▼▼ 5
○ Albana di Romagna Passito Casa Lola '07	▼▼ 5
○ Albana di Romagna Secco V. della Rocca '08	▼▼ 4
● Colli d'Imola Boldo '07	▼▼ 4
● Sangiovese di Romagna Sup. Campo di Mezzo '08	▼▼ 4
○ Colli d'Imola Chardonnay Ciardo '08	▼ 4
○ Colli di Imola Salcerella '07	▼ 4
○ Colli d'Imola Bianco Thea Bianco '06	♍♍ 5
● Sangiovese di Romagna Sup. Petrignone Ris. '05	♍♍ 4*
● Sangiovese di Romagna Sup. Ris. '03	♍♍ 4*
● Sangiovese di Romagna Sup. Thea Ris. '05	♍♍ 5

Wine	Rating
● C. B. Cabernet Sauvignon '08	▼▼ 4*
● Diggioanni Cabernet Sauvignon '06	▼▼ 5
○ Essè Brut Spumante	▼▼ 4
● Affederico Merlot '06	▼ 5
○ Permartina '06	▼ 4
○ Pignoletto Vivace '08	▼ 3
● Diggioanni Cabernet Sauvignon '04	♍♍♍ 5
● Affederico Merlot '05	♍♍ 5
● Affederico Merlot '04	♍♍ 5
○ Pignoletto Vivace '07	♍♍ 3*

Podere Vecciano

VIA VECCIANO, 23
47852 CORIANO [RN]
TEL. 0541658388
www.poderevecciano.it

CELLAR SALES
PRE-BOOKED VISITS

ANNUAL PRODUCTION **70,000 bottles**
HECTARES UNDER VINE **10**
VITICULTURE METHOD **Organic certified**

Davide Bigucci's winery has grown steadily to become an important part of the Colli Riminesi, a DOC with potential needing a group of skilled, passionate winemakers to become established. Davide's timely and accurate work in the vineyards intelligently avoids aiming for a robust result at any cost. He makes minimal use of chemical products and the vinification process aims to respect the grapes and interfere as little as possible with natural processes. This estate has strong links to the territory and its clients.

For years, we've seen Davide Bigucci's wines at the top of the area's quality table. Today, they show potential for clearer, more territorial expression, the last small step to excellence. D'Enio '06 is good with a very fresh, crisp nose led by fragrant, slightly showy cherries in a wine with an excellent profile. The nicely balanced VignalMonte '06 has white peaches on the nose and a lean palate, elegantly marked out by acidity. The simplest Sangiovese, Montetauro '08, is peppery, alcoholic and fun.

Francesco Vezzelli

CANALETTO NORD, 878A
41122 MODENA
TEL. 059318695
aavezzelli@gmail.com

CELLAR SALES

ANNUAL PRODUCTION **110,000 bottles**
HECTARES UNDER VINE **15**
VITICULTURE METHOD **Conventional**

Founded in 1958 by Delmo Vezzelli and run today by Francesco Vezzelli, who looks after the vineyards and vinification, with his son Roberto, the sales manager. The vinification cellar is in the San Matteo district of Modena and the vineyards are in Sozzigalli on flood plains that lie between the lower and upper banks of the Secchia river. This loose, poor soil is superb territory for lambrusco sorbara, enhancing its florality and mineral features.

The Sorbara Enrico Vezzelli '08 selection miraculously reached the finals, despite a summer hailstorm that halved production. Roses, spring flowers and the classic fragrant apple aromas on the nose are followed by a strongly mineral palate with a pleasantly husky character. Also in the finals was the Il Bricco di Checco '08, from salamino and ancellotta, gives white peaches and cherries, and a stylish, well-defined lingering palate. It's a truly elegant interpretation of lambrusco salamino. Also nice is the Rive dei Ciliegi '08, made from grasparossa purchased from two local growers, which shows tannic, fragrant and long-lingering.

● Sangiovese di Romagna Sup. D'Enio V.V. Ris. '06	♟♟ 5
● Montetauro '08	♟♟ 2*
● Sangiovese di Romagna Sup. VignalMonte '06	♟♟ 4*
● Vignalavolta '06	♟♟ 4*
○ Pagadebit di Romagna Vigna delle Rose '08	♟ 3
● Sangiovese di Romagna Sup. D'Enio Ris. '04	♟♟ 5
● Sangiovese di Romagna Sup. D'Enio Ris. '03	♟♟ 5
● Sangiovese di Romagna Sup. VignalMonte '05	♟♟ 4*

● Lambrusco Il Bricco di Checco '08	♟♟ 2*
● Lambrusco di Sorbara Enrico Vezzelli '08	♟♟ 4*
● Lambrusco Grasparossa di Castelvetro Rive dei Ciliegi '08	♟♟ 4*

Vigne dei Boschi

VIA TURA, 7A
48013 BRISIGHELLA [RA]
TEL. 054651648
paolobabini@brisighella.net

CELLAR SALES

ANNUAL PRODUCTION **19,000 bottles**
HECTARES UNDER VINE **11**
VITICULTURE METHOD **Natural**

Paolo Babini's few hectares of organic vineyards in the upper Valle del Lamone stand on marl and sandstone almost at the limits of the vine's growing conditions, besieged by woodlands and steep cliffs exposed by the river. The estate is like a laboratory and the most exciting results come from sangiovese while a research has led to significant experience of the territory. This is underlined by the University of Milan's zoning work in the valley, supervised personally by Paolo.

Vinification without technological or chemical support means the wines reflect the vintage year clearly and are eloquent in the glass. Patience is rewarded by subtle sensations that expand with every sip. Three Glasses went to Poggio Tura '05, a stylish, minerally wine driven by an extraordinary project. The sangiovese vineyard consists of scions taken from old sangiovese vines in the valley, a population of rare and valuable biodiversity. Sedici Anime '07 from riesling is an original wine combining a rich nose of mint, apples, gunflint, peach and apricot fruit with a blade-sharp palate.

● Poggio Tura '05	♟♟♟	6
● Rosso per Te '06	♟♟	5
○ Sedici Anime '07	♟♟	5
● Nero Selva '05	♟	5
● Borgo Stignani '02	♟♟	4*
● Sette Pievi '03	♟♟	5

Villa Bagnolo

LOC. BAGNOLO
VIA BAGNOLO, 160
47011 CASTROCARO TERME [FC]
TEL. 0543769047
www.villabagnolo.it

CELLAR SALES

ANNUAL PRODUCTION **80,000 bottles**
HECTARES UNDER VINE **15**
VITICULTURE METHOD **Conventional**

Villa Bagnolo, in the lower Colli Forlivesi above Castrocaro Terme, enjoys breezes from the plains and sea, and stands on the unusual salty clay earth also used by the local spa. Lombard businessman Vito Ballarati retired here with his family, transferring all the energy, creativity and curiosity of his professional life into this project. The initial results are highly positive. Villa Bagnolo has become known as a promising winery, applying itself to the difficult challenge of forming a precise identity to reflect this clayey terrain.

The wines are dependable this year. However, a common theme is lacking and character is lost among the various warm and non-territorial perceptions. An obvious example is the hint of strawberries in the Sorgara. We liked the Alloro '07, from sangiovese, cabernet sauvignon and cabernet franc, a wine with presence and expressive fruit, not to mention an alluringly taut palate. Untypical nose aside, the '07 Sorgara, aged in large barrels, is flavoursome and dry. The simple, enjoyable Sassetto '08 is fruity and fun, showing balance and a hint of greens.

● Alloro '07	♟♟	5
● Sangiovese di Romagna Sup. Sorgara '07	♟♟	4
● Sangiovese di Romagna Sup. Sassetto '08	♟	4
● Alloro '06	♟♟	5
● Sangiovese di Romagna Sup. Bagnolo Ris. '06	♟♟	5
● Sangiovese di Romagna Sup. Sassetto '06	♟♟	3*
● Sangiovese di Romagna Sup. Sorgara '06	♟♟	4*

Villa Liverzano

FRAZ. RONTANA
VIA VALLONI, 47
48013 BRISIGHELLA [RA]
TEL. 054680461
www.liverzano.it

CELLAR SALES
PRE-BOOKED VISITS
VISITOR FACILITIES

ANNUAL PRODUCTION **10,000 bottles**
HECTARES UNDER VINE **3.2**
VITICULTURE METHOD **Conventional**

Following his success as a grower in Tuscany, Romagna-born Swiss citizen Marco Montanari came to Brisighella a few years ago to try his luck with a region far removed from the wine sector spotlight. Instead of producing wines that speak the language of the terroir, Marco pursues an elegant, original style, aided by special sandy, chalky soil which contributes stylishly idiosyncratic expression even to sangiovese.

Don '07 is a very original wine that successfully blends spicy hints of ripe peppery fruit with alluring, never intrusive oak. The result is Mediterranean and stylish with a vibrant, focused and fragrant palate. The cabernet franc grape and special merlot clones used by Montanari come through in tones previously unexplored in the area. The Rebello '07, made from merlot and sangiovese, is more discreet and austere with a complex nose ranging from cocoa powder to redcurrants and a very elegant palate that unfolds effortlessly into a reprise of austerity in the finish. The flavour lingers unobtrusively from attack to back palate.

Villa Papiano

VIA IBOLA, 24
47015 MODIGLIANA [FC]
TEL. 0546941790
www.villapapiano.it

CELLAR SALES
PRE-BOOKED VISITS

ANNUAL PRODUCTION **25,000 bottles**
HECTARES UNDER VINE **10**
VITICULTURE METHOD **Conventional**

The ten-year-old Villa Papiano project is now established as an interesting winery, the flagship of a new phenomenon in Romagna: high-altitude estates growing sangiovese on marl and sandstone soil. The vineyards are situated on the wooded southern slope of Monte Chioda at 500 metres above sea level and the wines are elegant, becoming clearer and more vertical every year, benefiting from the personality imbued by these challenging lands, provided they are treated with respect.

I Probi '06 has a distinctive rounded, if not terribly varietal, nose with nice ripe fruit melding into oak and a mouthwatering palate that expands over close-knit tannins and lovely mineral sensations. It's elegant and fresh-tasting. The merlot and centesimino '06 Papiano di Papiano presented this year is held back by an excessively ripe nose but the palate is convincing. The dependable Le Papesse '07 is a dry, slightly stiff Sangiovese with good flavour and freshness. We liked the Le Tresche di Papiano '08, made from sauvignon grapes, with its stylish tropical feel and dense but supple texture.

● Don '07	♈♈ 6
● Rebello '07	♈♈ 6
● Don '06	♈♈ 6
● Rebello '06	♈♈ 6
● Rebello '05	♈♈ 6
● Rebello '04	♈♈ 6

● Sangiovese di Romagna I Probi di Papiano Ris. '06	♈♈ 4*
○ Le Tresche di Papiano '08	♈♈ 4
● Papiano di Papiano '06	♈♈ 5
● Sangiovese di Romagna Le Papesse di Papiano '07	♈♈ 4*
○ Tregenda '07	♈ 5
● Papiano di Papiano '04	♈♈♈ 5
● Papiano di Papiano '05	♈♈ 5
● Sangiovese di Romagna I Probi di Papiano Ris. '03	♈♈ 4*

Villa Trentola

LOC. CAPOCOLLE DI BERTINORO
VIA MOLINO BRATTI, 1305
47032 BERTINORO [FC]
TEL. 0543741389
www.villatrentola.it

CELLAR SALES
PRE-BOOKED VISITS

ANNUAL PRODUCTION 30,000 bottles
HECTARES UNDER VINE 20
VITICULTURE METHOD Conventional

This estate, purchased in 1890 by Enrico Prugnoli, was a union of three distinct smaller farms, Valle, Colombaia and Molino. This is classic Bertinoro territory, with limestone clay and spungone soil, and the spurred cordon-trained Villa Trentola vineyards are managed with precision. Owner and agronomist Enrico Prugnoli manages the vineyards while his daughter Federica supervises the cellar with consultant Fabrizio Moltard, who is a constant presence in the winery.

For about three years, Villa Trentola has focused on Sangiovese, aiming for an elegant, austere style. The wines, including the impressive Riserva of which we enjoyed an advance tasting, typify this new direction with good results. The three sangiovese clones, and each vineyard selection, are fermented separately. The Prugnolo '07 is an incisive, mouthwatering wine with mature, close-knit tannins while the Ultimo Atto '08 appears simple but combines clarity and elegance with silky tannins and characterful acidity through to the reprise of austere, clean fruit in the finish.

★ Fattoria Zerbina

FRAZ. MARZENO
VIA VICCHIO, 11
48018 FAENZA [RA]
TEL. 054640022
www.zerbina.com

CELLAR SALES
PRE-BOOKED VISITS

ANNUAL PRODUCTION 220,000 bottles
HECTARES UNDER VINE 33
VITICULTURE METHOD Conventional

For 20 years, Fattoria Zerbina has been one of Romagna's most dependable wineries, turning out consistent quality in a linear, coherent style that reflects the local area, especially for sangiovese. Obsessive care in the vineyards underpins Zerbina's management policies. Now that the vineyards have reached maturity, there are high levels of quality and territorial identity in all the wines, from the simplest to the most ambitious Riserva, because the grapes are tended with care, knowledge and absolute respect.

Pietramora '06, a monovarietal Sangiovese, has a distinctive character and a sumptuously deep, flavoursome palate braced by bold acidity and plenty of mature tannins. Pietramora originated from the traditional bush-trained vineyards of Romagna clones, now 20 years old, using microbatch selection on clay and limestone soil. The excellent Marzieno, from sangiovese with international varieties, is elegant and austere. The 2005 vintage has now been released after a long stay in bottle. And there was a great performance by the winery's basic product, Ceregio, which went through to the finals for the first time.

● Sangiovese di Romagna Sup. Il Prugnolo di Villa Trentola '07	♟♟ 4
● Sangiovese di Romagna Ultimo Atto Sup. '08	♟♟ 5
● Sangiovese di Romagna Sup. Il Moro di Villa Trentola '05	♟♟ 5
● Sangiovese di Romagna Sup. Il Moro di Villa Trentola '04	♟♟ 6
● Sangiovese di Romagna Sup. Il Prugnolo di Villa Trentola '06	♟♟ 4*
● Sangiovese di Romagna Sup. Placidio '04	♟♟ 8

● Sangiovese di Romagna Sup. Pietramora Ris. '06	♟♟♟ 7
● Marzieno '05	♟♟ 6
● Sangiovese di Romagna Sup. Ceregio '08	♟♟ 3*
○ Albana di Romagna Passito Arrocco '07	♟♟ 6
● Sangiovese di Romagna Sup. Torre di Ceparano '06	♟♟ 4
○ Trebbiano di Romagna Dalbiere '08	♟ 3
● Marzieno '04	♟♟♟ 6
● Marzieno '03	♟♟♟ 6
● Sangiovese di Romagna Sup. Pietramora Ris. '04	♟♟♟ 7
○ Albana di Romagna Passito Scacco Matto '06	♟♟ 7

OTHER WINERIES

Aldrovandi

VIA MARZATORE, 36
40050 MONTEVEGLIO [BO]
TEL. 0516810296

Federico Aldrovandi cares passionately about his merlot vineyard, vinification and selection of oak for maturing. His wines are always intriguing. Alto Vanto '07 is more elegant than previous editions, with nice acidity and fine-grained tannins.

● C. B. Merlot Alto Vanto '07	TT 5
● C. B. Merlot Alto Vanto '06	YY 5
● C. B. Merlot Alto Vanto '05	YY 5

Cantina di Arceto

VIA PAGLIANI, 27
42019 SCANDIANO [RE]
TEL. 0522989107

This leading 70-year-old Colli Reggiani co-operative has about 400 members in the foothills of Reggio Emilia. There was a place in the finals for Migliolungo '08, a Lambrusco made from the 21 varieties in the local agricultural college's experimental vineyards. It gives a warm nose and robust palate.

● Migliolungo Lambrusco '08	TT 3*
● Reggiano Niveo '08	T 3

Barbolini

LOC. CASINALBO
VIA FIORI, 40
41043 FORMIGINE [MO]
TEL. 059550154
www.barbolinicantina.it

This small family-run estate in the Modena foothills uses grapes from its 35 hectares of vineyards. The wines are good, especially the simpler versions as the more ambitious products are a tad heavy and overripe. Lancillotto '08 is dry and incisive.

● Lambrusco Grasparossa di Castelvetro Lancillotto '08	TT 3*
● Lambrusco Grasparossa di Castelvetro Trimalcione '08	T 3

Andrea Bragagni

FRAZ. FOGNANO
VIA DEL SUFFRAGIO, 52
48013 BRISIGHELLA [RA]
TEL. 3394700143
www.bragagni.com

Andrea Bragagni is a small producer in Valle del Lamone who ferments his grapes naturally. Rigogolo '06 from albana shows a gunflint and salt nose and a round vibrant palate. The cabernet Monte Canneto '06 is muzzy on the nose but unfurls an excitingly complex palate.

● Monte Canneto '06	TT 4
○ Rigogolo '06	TT 4

Branchini

FRAZ. TOSCANELLA DI DOZZA
VIA MARSIGLIA, 3
40060 DOZZA [BO]
TEL. 054253778
branchini1858@libero.it

Branchini, below the Via Emilia valley, has lean soil thanks to the junction of three rivers depicted on the winery's logo. The Branchini brothers are heirs to a family tradition dating back to 1958. The two Sangioveses are sound, clean, modern and fundamentally well-made.

● Sangiovese di Romagna '07	TT 4*
● Sangiovese di Romagna Sup. Ris. '05	TT 4
○ Albana di Romagna Secco D'or Luce '06	T 4
○ Pignoletto '08	T 3

Ca' de' Medici

LOC. CADÈ
VIA DELLA STAZIONE, 34
42040 REGGIO EMILIA
TEL. 0522942141
www.cademedici.it

The Medicis, experienced in the selection of locally sourced Lambrusco, release wines under their own and the Caprari brands, having done so since the 19th century. Terra Calda '08 stands out for an austere nose and a gutsy palate. Caprari-La Foieta '08 is creamy and fragrant.

● Caprari-La Foieta Lambrusco '08	TT 3*
● Terra Calda Lambrusco '08	TT 3*
● Reggiano Lambrusco Piazza San Prospero '08	T 2
● Rubigallia Malvasia Dolce Frizzante '08	T 3

Ca' di Sopra

LOC. MARZENO
VIA FELIGARA, 15
48013 BRISIGHELLA [RA]
TEL. 0544521209
www.cadisopra.com

The winery owned by brothers Camillo and
Giacomo Montanari is coming on. Crepe
'08 from sangiovese is expressive with a
fresh, dry palate. Remel '07 from
sangiovese, cabernet sauvignon and merlot
has excellent pulp but is held back by
heavy sweet oak.

● Crepe '08	♟♟	4*
● Remel '07	♟♟	3*

Ca' Montanari

FRAZ. LEVIZZANO DI CASTELVETRO
VIA MEDUSIA, 32
41014 MODENA
TEL. 059741019
www.opera02.it

Ca' Montanari is a lovely winery that sells
traditional local products – hazelnut liqueur,
preserves, grape juice, Modena balsamic
vinegar, vinegars and syrups – including
Lambruscos from the 21 hectares of
organic vineyards. The wines are attractively
austere and husky.

● Opera 02 Lambrusco di Modena '08	♟♟	4*
● Opera Pura Lambrusco di Modena '08	♟♟	4*

Carra di Casatico

LOC. CASATICO
VIA LA NAVE, 10B
43013 LANGHIRANO [PR]
TEL. 0521863510
www.carradicasatico.com

This interesting Colli di Parma winery has
invested heavily in 20 hectares of vineyards
and the cellar to work with local varieties.
We sent Torcularia Lambrusco '08 from
maestri to the finals for a deep rustic nose
that expands over discreetly austere fruit
and gives a vibrant, lingering palate.

● Torcularia Lambrusco '08	♟♟	3*
○ Colli di Parma Malvasia Acuto Extra Dry '08	♟♟	4*
○ Eden Passito '07	♟♟	5
○ Colli di Parma Malvasia Frizzante '08	♟	3*

Casa Benna

LOC. CASA BENNA
29010 CASTELL'ARQUATO [PC]
TEL. 0523803356
casabenna@alice.it

This traditional co-operative winery,
well-known for selling unbottled wines to
Romagna's trattorias, now presents a
range of bottled wines combining well-
typed quality with affordable prices. The
Riserva Serrafelina is very varietal and
classically fresh.

● C.P. Gutturnio Cl. Ris '06	♟♟	3*
● C.P. Gutturnio Sup. '06	♟	2

Cavim
Cantina Viticoltori Imolesi

FRAZ. SASSO MORELLI
VIA CORRECCHIO, 54
40026 IMOLA [BO]
TEL. 054255003
www.cavimimola.it

This traditional co-operative winery,
well-known for selling unbottled wines to
Romagna's trattorias, now presents a
range of bottled wines combining well-
typed quality with affordable prices. The
Riserva Serrafelina is very varietal and
classically fresh.

● Sangiovese di Romagna Sup.		
Moro di Serrafelina Ris. '06	♟♟	3*
● Colli d'Imola Cabernet Sauvignon		
Moro di Serrafelina '08	♟	2
○ Colli d'Imola Chardonnay Blumanne '08	♟	2

Celli

VIA CARDUCCI, 5
47032 BERTINORO [FC]
TEL. 0543445183
www.celli-vini.com

Mauro Sirri runs this traditional Romagna
winery whose wines have been weary,
overripe and over-evolved of late. The
characterful I Croppi '08 confidently brings
out the best in the tricky albana grape. The
Le Grillaie '08 is well typed.

○ Albana di Romagna Secco I Croppi '08	♟♟	3*
● Bron & Rusèval Sangiovese-Cabernet '07	♟	5
● Sangiovese di Romagna Sup. Le Grillaie '08	♟	3

Cantine Cooperative Riunite

VIA G. BRODOLINI, 24
42040 CAMPEGINE [RE]
TEL. 0522905711
www.riunite.it

This large co-operative winery releases wine under two brands, Cantine Riunite and Albinea Canali, a carefully managed 110-hectare hillside estate. The wines are generally dependable but sometimes show excessive residual sugar. L'Olma '08 and Ottocentonero '08 are well focused..

● Albinea Canali - Chiaro della Falconaia Lambrusco '08	♟♟ 3*
● Albinea Canali - Ottocentonero Lambrusco '08	♟♟ 3*
● Reggiano Lambrusco Ronchi dell'Olma '08	♟♟ 3*

Costa Archi

LOC. SERRA
VIA RINFOSCO, 1690
48014 CASTEL BOLOGNESE [RA]
TEL. 3384818346

Gabriele Succi loves powerful wines and oak-derived spice and his wines reflect this. Given that he usually harvests perfectly ripe grapes, the wines are exciting when overall balance is maintained. The Prima Luce '07 from cabernet sauvignon has nice fruit, a fresh palate and well-judged tannins.

● Colli di Faenza Prima Luce '07	♟♟ 4*
● Sangiovese di Romagna Sup. Assiolo '08	♟ 3
● Sangiovese di Romagna Sup. Monte Brullo Ris. '06	♟ 4

Denavolo

FRAZ. DENAVOLO
LOC. GATTAVERA
29020 TRAVO [PC]
TEL. 3356480766
giulio.armani@gmail.it

The wines made by the man behind the La Stoppa winery, Giulio Armani, are the result of the many years' research that enables him to operate with even greater freedom. The whites enjoy long skin contact and show complex salt and mint-like aromas, and deep, incisive palates.

○ Denavolo '06	♟♟ 6
○ Denavolo '05	♟♟ 6

Cantina Sociale Formigine Pedemontana

VIA PASCOLI, 4
41043 FORMIGINE [MO]
TEL. 059558122
info@lambruscodoc.it

This co-operative was formed by the merger of the Formigine winery, founded in 1920, and Cantina Pedemontana, which vinifies grapes from the foothills of Modena. Rosso Fosco '08 went to the finals with a fresh, elegant nose and sharp palate with vibrant cherry and white peach fruit.

● Lambrusco Grasparossa di Castelvetro Rosso Fosco '08	♟♟ 3*
● Lambrusco Grasparossa di Castelvetro Semisecco '08	♟♟ 3*
● Lambrusco Grasparossa di Castelvetro Amabile '08	♟ 3

Maria Galassi

LOC. PADERNO DI CESENA
VIA CASETTE, 688
47023 CESENA [FC]
TEL. 054721177
www.galassimaria.it

This estate is at San Vittore di Cesena and Bertinoro and has an utterly typical Bertinoro terrain of clay soil rich in active limestone and spungone, a local marine tufaceous rock. The 18 hectares are organically farmed. Paternus '07 is authentic and typical with a vibrant palate.

● Sangiovese di Romagna Paternus '07	♟♟ 4*
● Sangiovese di Romagna Sup. NatoRe '07	♟♟ 4

La Grotta

LOC. SAIANO
VIA CIMADORI, 621
47023 CESENA [FC]
TEL. 0547326368
lagrottavini@libero.it

This small winery run by Giovanni Amadori in the hills above Cesena has made confident progress in quality since Lorenzo Landi joined the business. The impressive Mazzapegul '08 has an austere nose and a gutsily taut, fresh palate. The chardonnay and trebbiano Duca dell'Olmo '08 is fragrant and tangy.

○ Duca dell'Olmo '08	♟♟ 3*
● Sangiovese di Romagna Mazzapegul '08	♟♟ 3*
○ Albana di Romagna Damodora '08	♟ 3

Lamoretti

LOC. CASATICO
S.DA DELLA NAVE, 6
43013 LANGHIRANO [PR]
TEL. 0521863590
www.lamorettivini.com

Isidoro Lamoretti and his son Giovanni vinify fruit from their 20 hectares under vine, following a family tradition dating back to the 1930s. The impressive maestri-based Lambrusco '08 is well rounded. The Serbato '07 from barbera is slightly grassy on the nose with a relaxed, vibrant palate.

● Colli di Parma Lambrusco '08	ΨΨ	3*
● Serbato '07	ΨΨ	4
○ Colli di Parma Malvasia Frizzante '08	Ψ	3

Tenuta Masselina

LOC. SERRÀ
VIA POZZE, 1030
48014 CASTEL BOLOGNESE [RA]
TEL. 0545284711
www.masselina.it

La Masselina is a small estate owned by a large co-operative, CEVICO. Set up by Ruenza Santandrea, it is a quality laboratory providing experience for the whole range. Results were good. The 158 slm '08 from sangiovese and cabernet is vibrant and clean while the Chardonnay 147 slm '08 is fresh and fragrant.

○ 147 slm '08	ΨΨ	4*
● 158 slm '08	ΨΨ	4*

Francesco Montesissa

FRAZ. REZZANO
LOC. BUFFALORA, 91
29013 CARPANETO PIACENTINO [PC]
TEL. 0523850123
www.vinimontesissa.it

Nicola Montesissa is a champion of Gutturnio Frizzante. He runs a family winery he has transformed from a humble supplier of the Montesissa eatery in Piacenza into an influential producer. Ronco Stagnino '08 is attractively clean and the Gutturnio Classico '07 is bright and savoury.

● C. P. Gutturnio Cl. Sup. '07	ΨΨ	3*
● C. P. Gutturnio Frizzante Ronco Stagnino '08	ΨΨ	3*
○ C. P. Sel. Rio Magreto Ortrugo Frizzante '08	Ψ	3

Perinelli

LOC. I PERINELLI
29028 PONTE DELL'OLIO [PC]
TEL. 0523877185
www.perinelli.it

Giorgia Sguazzi is enthusiastic about the Val Nure winery her family acquired about two decades ago. Costa dei Salina '08 is a characterful wine with a crisply defined nose and plenty of extract on the palate. Torre della Ghiacciaia '08 is opulent and closes brightly.

● C. P. Gutturnio Costa dei Salina '08	ΨΨ	4
○ C. P. Malvasia Torre della Ghiacciaia '08	ΨΨ	4
● C. P. Gutturnio Vivace '08	Ψ	4
○ C. P. Ortrugo Vivace '08	Ψ	4

Tenuta la Piccola

VIA CASONI, 3
42027 MONTECCHIO EMILIA [RE]
TEL. 0522864712

This small Val d'Enza estate has 25 hectares of organically farmed vine. Nero di Cio '08 went to the finals. It's a Lambrusco made from gentile, salamino, maestri, ancellotta and malbo gentile grapes with pure fruit and lovely acidity. The Picol Ross '08 is also bright and tasty.

● Lambrusco Nero di Cio '08	ΨΨ	4*
● Lambrusco Picol Ross '08	ΨΨ	4*
○ Malvasia Frizzante '08	Ψ	4

Cantina Sociale Santa Croce

S.S. 468 DI CORREGGIO, 35
41012 CARPI [MO]
TEL. 059664007
www.cantinasantacroce.it

This small 100-year-old co-operative produces a great monovarietal Lambrusco Salamino every year from the grapes grown at Santa Croce. This is one of the simplest wines on the list and fantastic value for money. The '08 is clean, harmonious and relaxed.

⊙ Brut Rosé 100 Vendemmie '08	ΨΨ	4
● Lambrusco Salamino di S. Croce '08	ΨΨ	2*
⊙ Il Castello Lambrusco di Modena Rosato '08	Ψ	2
● Lambrusco Salamino di S. Croce Tradizione '08	Ψ	2*

Spalletti Colonna di Paliano

LOC. CASTELLO DI RIBANO
VIA SOGLIANO, 104
47039 SAVIGNANO SUL RUBICONE [FC]
TEL. 0541945111
www.spalletticolonnadipaliano.com

Principe Giovanni Colonna di Paliano's estate is in the lowest hills behind Savignano sul Rubicone, about ten kilometres from the sea. The land is clay-based and the vineyards have mostly been renovated in the last ten years. The Principe di Ribano '08 has a taut, tasty palate.

● Sangiovese di Romagna Sup. Principe di Ribano '08	♥♥ 3*
○ Albana di Romagna Duchessa di Montemar '08	♥ 3
● Monaco di Ribano Cabernet '06	♥ 5
● Sangiovese di Romagna Sup. Villa Rasponi Ris. '06	♥ 4

Tenuta Volpe

LOC. MONTELEONE DI RONCOFREDDO
P.ZZA BYRON, 19
47020 CESENA [FC]
TEL. 0541949183
www.tenutavolpe.it

This beautiful castle near Cesena is the home of Andrea Volpe and Cecilia Fanfani, who moved here a few years ago. Castello di Monteleone '06 has overripe tones on the nose and a lovely palate. The well-managed Fedro '06 has untypical aromas but the palate has thrust with a warm style.

● Sangiovese di Romagna Sup. Castello di Monteleone Ris. '06	♥♥ 4
○ Albana di Romagna Ladoro '08	♥ 4
● Sangiovese di Romagna Sup. Fedro '06	♥ 4

Torre Fornello

LOC. FORNELLO
29010 ZIANO PIACENTINO [PC]
TEL. 0523861001
www.torrefornello.it

Enrico Sgorbati has run this Val Tidone winery since 1998. The Pratobianco '08, a blend of malvasia and other varieties, has tension and depth while the Colli Piacentini Malvasia Donna Luigia '08 is complex and fresh-tasting.

○ C. P. Malvasia Donna Luigia '08	♥♥ 4
○ Pratobianco '08	♥♥ 4*
● C. P. Gutturnio Sup. Sinsäl '07	♥ 4
○ Olubra Extra Dry '07	♥ 4

Trerè

LOC. MONTICORALLI
VIA CASALE, 19
48018 FAENZA [RA]
TEL. 054647034
www.trere.com

Gutsy, determined Morena Treré runs this traditional estate with flair. The Renero '07 is an untypical but well-managed Sangiovese with a savoury palate. The Vigna del Monte '08 has slightly unripe fruit and a tasty palate with nice freshness. The Sperone '08 is well typed but less convincing.

● Colli di Faenza Sangiovese Renero '07	♥♥ 4*
● Sangiovese di Romagna Sup. Sperone '08	♥ 3
● Sangiovese di Romagna V. del Monte '08	♥ 2

Uve delle Mura

VIA CÀ GNANO, 231
47032 BERTINORO [FC]
TEL. 0543743700
uvedellemura@virgilio.it

Massimo Rocchi's vineyards are in one of Bertinoro's most promising terrains. The wines are excellent when they put elegance first. Selva d'Olmo '06 made the final with white peach aromas and a deep, elegantly lean palate. The '06 Riserva Tre Pastori was not released.

● Sangiovese di Romagna Sup. Selva d'Olmo '06	♥♥ 4*

Cantina Valtidone

VIA MORETTA, 58
29011 BORGONOVO VAL TIDONE [PC]
TEL. 0523862168
www.cantinavaltidone.it

This leading co-operative winery is coming on steadily and will certainly take a further step forward in quality with the arrival of Marcello Galetti to work alongside his father Sergio. The Aurora '08 is rounded, open and flavoursome while the Caesar Augustus '08 is well defined and nicely poised.

● C. P. Gutturnio Cl. Caesar Augustus '08	♥♥ 3*
○ C. P. Malvasia Frizzante Aurora '08	♥♥ 3*
○ C. P. Ortrugo Armonia Frizzante '08	♥ 3

Vicobarone

FRAZ. VICOBARONE
VIA CRETA, 60
29010 ZIANO PIACENTINO [PC]
TEL. 0523868522
www.cantinavicobarone.com

A young, motivated management team has brought a breath of freshness, innovation and quality to the products of this traditional winery. In the dependable range of wines, the stand-out is Gutturnio Frizzante '08 with clear fruit and a lively palate. The fresh, complex Malvasia Passito Astrea '07 is also nice.

● C. P. Gutturnio Frizzante '08	ΨΨ	2*
● C. P. Gutturnio Pleitone Cl. Ris. '05	ΨΨ	4*
○ C. P. Malvasia '08	ΨΨ	2*
○ C. P. Malvasia Passito Astrea '07	ΨΨ	5

Vigne di Ciso

FRAZ. CARPINETA DI CESENA
VIA MAGNI, 700
47023 FORLÌ
TEL. 0307450488
info@spilellisrl.eu

Giampiero Spinelli has sunk money and energy into the family vineyards in the Colli Cesenati. Ciso '06 has a great palate but suffers from a marked sweetness due to excessive vanilla from the oak. Gianto '07 has crisp fruit contrasting with a sweet nose and a relaxed, rounded palate.

● Sangiovese di Romagna Sup. Ciso Ris. '06	ΨΨ	4
☉ Sangiovese di Romagna Sup. Gianto '07	ΨΨ	3*

Villa di Corlo

LOC. BAGGIOVARA
S.DA CAVEZZO, 200
41100 MODENA
TEL. 059510736
www.villadicorlo.com

This winery owned by Maria Antonietta Munari embraces two estates. The lambrusco vineyards are at Villa di Corlo, in Modena and Sassuolo, and the cellar at Cà del Vento in the Reggio hills, where international varieties are grown. The lovely Grasparossa '08 is dry and fruity.

● Corleto Lambrusco '08	ΨΨ	3*
● Lambrusco Grasparossa di Castelvetro '08	ΨΨ	3*

Villa Venti

LOC. VILLAVENTI DI RONCOFREDDO
VIA DOCCIA, 1442
47020 FORLÌ
TEL. 0541949532
www.villaventi.it

Passion, a desire to grow and improving results characterize the exciting winery run by Mauro Giardini and Davide Castellucci. The Primo Segno '07 starts from excellent raw material. The palate is fresh and the nose warm and sweet.

● Sangiovese di Romagna Sup. Primo Segno '07	ΨΨ	4*
● Felis Leo '07	Ψ	4

TUSCANY

Tuscany's haul of 60 Three Glass awards is an important accomplishment in itself. That total is fully 11 more than last year and the second best showing ever for a region considered one of the world's very finest wine-producing areas. But for the second year in a row, in Italian Wines, Tuscany is Italy's second-ranked wine region, and that fact must irritate many Tuscan producers. There is more than one reason for this situation. The first is the logical result of the region's production capacity. Its wineries are not huge in size, although they are certainly larger on average than those in many other parts of Italy. Tuscany therefore puts out numerically fewer wines. Add to that a vintage such as 2006. Initially greeted almost universally with genuflections, it is now turning out to be not quite so exceptional, at least in our opinion. There is no gainsaying that it is a fine vintage overall, but a few too many overripe wines are cropping up. That is to be expected, given weather that brought some scorchers that hit a few local areas here and there fairly hard. The 2004 vintage, on the other hand, is turning out to be good, even very good, for Brunello di Montalcino. Brunello is finally showing renewed expressiveness, following some skipped releases and some rather bumpy rides, to put the matter delicately. Some remaining 2005s and some 2007s are showing well, all things considered, but for diametrically opposite reasons. The former was a cool growing season while the latter was hot everywhere, although with fewer torrid peaks than 2006.The final point that should be made is that we are seeing more rational viticultural placement of grape varieties. Under this rubric, sangiovese now seems less "assisted" by the internationals, and these latter varieties are now grown in. They now typify areas where they yield their best, in Bolgheri, and around Pisa, and in some interior areas such as Cortona. But the main point is that Tuscany seems to have taken a step or two backwards compared to the headlong rush forward witnessed in some places in the recent past. Such retrenchment can only be beneficial for the more prestigious wines' faithfulness to terroir. We number ourselves among those who prize this quality, provided of course it respects the particular winemaking styles that various producers wish to adopt. But we will always strive, within the limits to which are constrained, to encourage all those who produce wines that are more natural and more faithful to their specific corner of this earth. It is a winning combination for the future.

Abbadia Ardenga

FRAZ. TORRENIERI
VIA ROMANA, 139
53028 MONTALCINO [SI]
TEL. 0577834150
www.abbadiardengapoggio.it

CELLAR SALES
PRE-BOOKED VISITS

ANNUAL PRODUCTION **35,000 bottles**
HECTARES UNDER VINE **10**
VITICULTURE METHOD **Conventional**

Abbadia Ardenga, an example of a well-managed state-owned operation, offers more than decent wines at truly reasonable prices. Located on the northern slope of Montalcino, its ten hectares are planted in largely chalk-rich galestro soils, at about 300 metres' elevation. The more recent vineyards have been put in at high density. Fabio Ciacci, who directs the winery, has steadily improved wine quality over the years, producing classic-style wines aged in large, Slavonian oak casks.

The classically styled Brunello Vigna Piaggia '04 captures the attention effectively. A medium ruby is followed by a clean, nicely varietal nose, with dark cherry supporting evolved notes of sweet tobacco and subtle leather. The palate is all balance, showing judicious depth, a fine complement of acidity and flawlessly sculpted tannins, expanding out into a tasty finish. Rosso di Montalcino '07 is delicious, its acidity vivacious and bouquet laden with cherry. Brunello di Montalcino '04 displays interesting complexity, releasing an amalgam of red berry, herbs and a subtle gaminess, followed by succulent fruit and tannins just a tad burred.

Agricoltori del Chianti Geografico

LOC. MULINACCIO, 10
53013 GAIOLE IN CHIANTI [SI]
TEL. 0577749489
www.chiantigeografico.it

CELLAR SALES
PRE-BOOKED VISITS
VISITOR FACILITIES

ANNUAL PRODUCTION **1,600,000 bottles**
HECTARES UNDER VINE **580**
VITICULTURE METHOD **Organic certified**

In 1961, a group of 18 growers in Gaiole launched the Agricoltori del Chianti Geografico co-operative, determined to preserve the distinctive qualities of Chianti, whose identity was under assault by imitators. Their contribution was crucial to safeguarding the integrity of Chianti Classico. Today, the co-operative numbers more than 200 members and is one of Tuscany's most impressive operations, with a geographical range that extends from Chianti to Montalcino by way of Scansano and San Gimignano.

This year's offerings testify to the high quality and reliability that distinguish the entire line. Chianti Classico Contessa di Radda '07 opens to notes of dark cherry and sweet violets and then develops significant depth in the mouth. We were impressed by its overall balance. Not far behind is the elegantly floral Chianti Classico '07, which expands nicely in the mouth. Riserva '06 Montegiachi, from the vineyard of that name at Castelnuovo Berardenga, came in a step behind. The nose still shows a tad awkward but the other components are in decent balance, and everything is in place for a fine performance after more time in the bottle.

● Brunello di Montalcino V. Piaggia '04	♟♟	6
● Brunello di Montalcino '04	♟	6
● Rosso di Montalcino '07	♟	4
● Brunello di Montalcino '03	♟♟	6
● Brunello di Montalcino V. Piaggia '03	♟♟	6

● Chianti Cl. Contessa di Radda '07	♟♟	5
● Brunello di Montalcino Castello Tricerchi '04	♟	8
● Chianti Cl. '07	♟	4
● Chianti Cl. Montegiachi Ris. '06	♟	5
● Rosso di Montalcino Castello Tricerchi '07	♟	5
● Chianti Cl. Montegiachi Ris. '05	♟♟♟	5
● Brunello di Montalcino Castello Tricerchi '03	♟♟	8
● Chianti Cl. Contessa di Radda '04	♟♟	4
● Ferraiolo '05	♟♟	6
● Ferraiolo '04	♟♟	6
● Pulleraia '03	♟♟	5
● Rosso di Montalcino Castello Tricerchi '06	♟♟	5

Podere l'Aione

LOC. AIONE, 12
56040 MONTECATINI VAL DI CECINA [PI]
TEL. 058830339
stefano-baldacci@libero.it

CELLAR SALES
PRE-BOOKED VISITS

ANNUAL PRODUCTION 25,000 bottles
HECTARES UNDER VINE 6
VITICULTURE METHOD Conventional

The surrounding landscape is stunning, and Robert Walti and Doris Portner's Podere l'Aione gleams out like a jewel, set just beneath the venerable village of Montecatini Val di Cecina. The performance of their wines is equally outstanding, as usual, but they struck us this year as more effortlessly expressive. The reason may lie, we believe, in more modern and expert vineyard management, as well as in the six hectares of variously aged vineyards, ranging from l'Aione, which is some 80 years of life, to more recent plantings designed to yield lower crop levels.

The sangiovese-merlot L'Aione '06 displays a nose still in search of its identity, with near-clumsy tones of oak somewhat offset by red berry fruit preserves and spice. Fine-grained tannins smooth fine progression in the mouth, with lovely lilt of zesty acidity, while a leisurely finale portends a promising future in the cellar. Despite its obvious youth, we liked the merlot-heavy Etico '06, in particular its varietally clean grassy notes and a spacious, succulent mouth. Its depth is equally impressive but the finish unfortunately suffers from distinctly obstreperous tannins.

Castello d'Albola

LOC. PIAN D'ALBOLA, 31
53017 RADDA IN CHIANTI [SI]
TEL. 0577738019
www.albola.it

CELLAR SALES
PRE-BOOKED VISITS

ANNUAL PRODUCTION 800,000 bottles
HECTARES UNDER VINE 157
VITICULTURE METHOD Conventional

The Zonin family's Castello d'Albola, in Pian d'Albola in the municipality of Radda in Chianti, is one of Chianti Classico's most extensive properties. The vineyards, planted on alberese and galestro soil types at elevations of 250 to 500 metres, are located on individual farm parcels that stud the pages of history of the Radda area, such as Ellere, Montevertine and Acciaiolo. Thanks to these impressive viticultural resources and to heavy investment, Castello d'Albola wines are effective showcases of what this area can do.

Chianti Classico Riserva '05 is fantastic. Orange pulp, sweet violets and smooth spices pack the nose, while the linear, ultra-succulent progression enfolds dense-packed tannins. Acciaolo '06 is opulent on all levels. This sangiovese-cabernet blend starts with a near-black red, then offers sour cherry and strawberry-tree fruit veined with crisp vegetal notes while terrific acidic grip powers the progression. Three Glasses right from the starting gate. Chianti Classico Le Ellere '06, with its floral notes, juicy fruit and natural expressiveness, could easily stand in for the Riserva. Solatio '06 shows taut, wired and balanced.

● Etico '06	♈♈	6
● Aione '06	♈	6
● Aione '03	♈♈	6
● Aione '01	♈♈	6
● Etico '05	♈♈	6
● Etico '04	♈♈	6
● Etico '03	♈♈	6
● Salve '05	♈♈	6

● Acciaiolo '06	♈♈♈	7
● Chianti Cl. Ris. '05	♈♈	5
● Chianti Cl. Le Ellere '06	♈♈	5
● Il Solatio '06	♈♈	6
● Acciaiolo '04	♈♈♈	7
● Acciaiolo '01	♈♈♈	7
● Acciaiolo '95	♈♈♈	6
● Chianti Cl. Ris. '04	♈♈	5

★★ Castello di Ama

LOC. AMA
53013 GAIOLE IN CHIANTI [SI]
TEL. 0577746031
www.castellodiama.com

PRE-BOOKED VISITS

ANNUAL PRODUCTION **350,000 bottles**
HECTARES UNDER VINE **90**
VITICULTURE METHOD **Conventional**

Castello di Ama has made enormous contributions to the rebirth of Chianti Classico , winning global recognition as one of Italy's star producers. The renewal of the winery began in the 1970s but Lorenza Sebasti and Marco Pallanti, who took over in the 1980s, brought it to its current heights. Singling out the parcels best suited for sangiovese and adopting some innovative vineyard practices were just two of the initiatives that coaxed truly exceptional results from some of Tuscany's finest vineyards.

Chianti Classico Castello di Ama '06 initially conjures up impressions of iron filings and blood-rich meat but less fierce notes of ripe blackberry arrive a few moments later. Drying tannins brake the progression somewhat but time in the bottle will bring everything into fine balance. Chianti Classico Bellavista is one of Ama's iconic crus. The '06 version is still callow and its tannins stiffish but its depth shows great promise, while the nose is rich with red berry, spices, and old leather. Casuccia '06 is a Chianti Classico defined by its density and the ripeness of its fruit, but above all by the fleshy volume of its finale.

Ampeleia

LOC. MELETA
58028 ROCCASTRADA [GR]
TEL. 0564567155
www.ampeleia.it

CELLAR SALES
PRE-BOOKED VISITS

ANNUAL PRODUCTION **120,000 bottles**
HECTARES UNDER VINE **40**
VITICULTURE METHOD **Conventional**

Ampeleia, located in Roccastrada, is one of the Maremma's rising stars. Dating back only to 2002, it rose phoenix-like from the ashes of Fattoria di Meleta, which in the 1980s was one of the coastal area's few success stories. Now, under Elisabetta Foradori, Thomas Widmann and Giovanni Podini, the operation seems to have found its stride, and the results are consistent and good. The wines already evince a clear house style of luscious elegance.

The strong suit of Ampeleia '06, a blend of cabernet franc and sangiovese, is its impressively complex bouquet. The nose is a fitting prelude to equally kaleidoscopic impressions on the palate, which rounds out an elegant wine displaying fine balance. Clean-edged aromas pour out from Kepos '07, an intriguing mélange of five Mediterranean varieties, grenache, mourvèdre, marselan, carignan and alicante. Its ductile, almost electric agility in the mouth makes it a splendid quaffer.

● Chianti Cl. Bellavista '06	♟♟ 8
● Chianti Cl. Castello di Ama '06	♟♟ 7
● Chianti Cl. La Casuccia '06	♟♟ 8
● l'Apparita Merlot '06	♟♟ 8
○ Al Poggio Chardonnay '08	♟ 5
⊙ Rosato '08	♟ 4
○ Vin Santo del Chianti Cl. '03	♟ 6
● Chianti Cl. Bellavista '01	♟♟♟ 8
● Chianti Cl. Bellavista '99	♟♟♟ 8
● Chianti Cl. Castello di Ama '05	♟♟♟ 6
● Chianti Cl. Castello di Ama '03	♟♟♟ 6
● Chianti Cl. Castello di Ama '01	♟♟♟ 6
● Chianti Cl. Castello di Ama '00	♟♟♟ 6
● Chianti Cl. La Casuccia '04	♟♟♟ 8
● Chianti Cl. La Casuccia '01	♟♟♟ 8
● l'Apparita Merlot '01	♟♟♟ 8
● l'Apparita Merlot '00	♟♟♟ 8

● Ampeleia '06	♟♟ 6
● Kepos '07	♟♟ 4
● Kepos '06	♟♟♟ 6
● Ampeleia '05	♟♟ 6
● Ampeleia '04	♟♟ 6

★★ Marchesi Antinori

P.ZZA DEGLI ANTINORI, 3
50123 FIRENZE
TEL. 05523595
www.antinori.it

PRE-BOOKED VISITS
VISITOR FACILITIES

ANNUAL PRODUCTION 20,000,000 bottles
HECTARES UNDER VINE 2,200
VITICULTURE METHOD Conventional

The name Antinori summons up 26 generations of involvement in wine going back more than 600 years to 1385, when Giovanni di Piero Antinori was admitted to the Arte dei Maestri Vinattieri , Florence's wine guild. Whenever people talk about Italian wine, due attention must be paid to the impressive dynasty that has so deeply influenced our approach to wine drinking. One example can suffice: Tignanello, the first Chianti-area Supertuscan.

Tignanello '06, largely sangiovese with some cabernet and cabernet franc, offers a nose of dark berry fruit, blackcurrant and prune, nicely lifted by hints of balsam and evolved notes of leather. The entry is immediately compelling while the body shows a glorious complement of silky, dense tannins and grippy acidity. Equally extraordinary is Solaia '06, a mix of cabernet, sangiovese and some cabernet franc. It won Three Glasses, thanks to a thrilling combination of juicy redcurrant that segues into pungent greens and damp earth, followed by dynamic progression sculpted by velvety tannins and nervy acidity. Villa Antinori '06 impresses.

Argentiera

LOC. DONORATICO
VIA AURELIA, 410
57024 CASTAGNETO CARDUCCI [LI]
TEL. 0565773176
www.argentiera.eu

CELLAR SALES
PRE-BOOKED VISITS

ANNUAL PRODUCTION 400,000 bottles
HECTARES UNDER VINE 60
VITICULTURE METHOD Conventional

Thanks to wines of indisputable elegance, Argentiera, owned jointly by the Fratini and Antinori families, has in just a few years earned prominence on the Bolgheri scene. Located in the southern reaches of the coastal district, its vineyard boasts near-perfect siting on diverse soils ranging from clay to rock and enjoying magnificent exposure to sunlight. Add to that meticulous cellar work programmed to extract the most from precious fruit and it is clear why the wines here are so elegant and supple.

Bolgheri Superiore Argentiera '06 again won our highest award. A blend of cabernet sauvignon, merlot and cabernet franc, it matures some14 months in barriques and a year in glass before release. A Bordeaux-style nose offers fine blackcurrant, fresh-mown grass and sweet tobacco leaf. A long charge of racy acidity contributes to an energy-laden palate bursting with succulent fruit, and fine-grained tannins complete a wine of stunning refinement. We liked Bolgheri Villa Donoratico '07, Argentiera's other cru. Though well balanced, an overcharge of oak slows it down a shade. The standard Poggio ai Ginepri '07 is, as always, reliably good.

● Solaia '06	♟♟♟	8
● Tignanello '06	♟♟	8
● Villa Antinori Rosso '06	♟♟	5
● Chianti Cl. Pèppoli '07	♟	5
● Chianti Cl. Badia a Passignano Ris. '01	♟♟♟	6
● Chianti Cl. Badia a Passignano Ris. '97	♟♟♟	5
● Solaia '03	♟♟♟	8
● Solaia '01	♟♟♟	8
● Solaia '00	♟♟♟	8
● Solaia '99	♟♟♟	8
● Solaia '98	♟♟♟	8
● Solaia '97	♟♟♟	8
● Tignanello '05	♟♟♟	8
● Tignanello '04	♟♟♟	8

● Bolgheri Sup. Argentiera '06	♟♟♟	8
● Bolgheri Villa Donoratico '07	♟♟	5
● Bolgheri Poggio ai Ginepri '07	♟	4
● Bolgheri Sup. Argentiera '05	♟♟♟	8
● Bolgheri Sup. Argentiera '04	♟♟♟	8

Artimino

FRAZ. ARTIMINO
V.LE PAPA GIOVANNI XXIII, 1
59015 CARMIGNANO [PO]
TEL. 0558751423
www.artimino.com

CELLAR SALES
PRE-BOOKED VISITS
VISITOR FACILITIES
FOOD

ANNUAL PRODUCTION 350,000 bottles
HECTARES UNDER VINE 86
VITICULTURE METHOD Conventional

A duet of finely crafted Vin Santos won Artimino a full profile this year. In addition to its locally well-known villa of the "hundred chimneys", the estate comprises over 730 hectares, with 86 of those in vine. Alongside classics such as cabernet sauvignon and sangiovese grow less frequently encountered varieties, for instance mammolo and san colombano, which are invaluable for giving the Artimino wines their distinctive personalities.

The best wine at our tastings turned out to be Santo Occhio di Pernice '01, a mix of sangiovese and malvasia nera that exudes rich Peruvian bark and tamarind, followed by a fine balance and complex flavours that linger impressively through a lengthy finale. Trebbiano, malvasia and san colombano make up Vin Santo '05, composing an aromatic mosaic of citrus, honey and dried fruit and nuts, plus a full-bodied, velvet-smooth fabric in the mouth. The rest of the line is soundly made with a special mention going to Riserva Vigna Grumarello '05, which sports fragrant fresh greens and an admirable palate, but rather peremptory tannins.

★ Avignonesi

FRAZ. VALIANO DI MONTEPULCIANO
VIA COLONICA, 1
53040 MONTEPULCIANO [SI]
TEL. 0578724304
www.avignonesi.it

CELLAR SALES
PRE-BOOKED VISITS

ANNUAL PRODUCTION 700,000 bottles
HECTARES UNDER VINE 119
VITICULTURE METHOD Conventional

Avignonesi is one of Tuscany's most respected producers, with wines that consistently win kudos worldwide. Responsible for its success are fully 30 years of activity at its facility in Valiano, spent both in research, exemplified in its "vigna tonda" (round vineyard) experiment and in tenacious pursuit of its local traditions. Witness the superb quality of its Vin Santos, a wine type whose Platonically ideal location may indeed be in Montepulciano.

Vin Santo and Vin Santo Occhio di Pernice, both '97 vintages, remain Avignonesi's standard-bearers, the first true to its legendary refinement, the second showcasing its always intriguing personality. Nobile '06 is probably one of the finest recent versions while consumers will find the delicious merlot and cabernet sauvignon Rosso Avignonesi '07a stand-out for its price tag. Rosso di Montepulciano '08 is a super-tasty quaffer, and ditto for the chardonnay Cortona Il Marzocco '07. 50 & 50, produced in collaboration with nearby Cappannelle, is a powerhouse red made from sangiovese and merlot but it drags a bit from over-much oak.

● Vin Santo di Carmignano Occhio di Pernice '01	♈♈	6
○ Vin Santo di Carmignano Villa Artimino '05	♈♈	5
● Barco Reale '08	♈	3
● Carmignano Ris. '06	♈	4
● Carmignano V. Grumarello Ris. '05	♈	5
⊙ Carmignano Vin Ruspo Rosato '08	♈	3
● Carmignano Villa Medicea Ris. '04	♈♈	5
● Carmignano Villa Medicea Ris. '01	♈♈	5
● Carmignano Villa Medicea Ris. '00	♈♈	5
○ Vin Santo di Carmignano Villa Artimino '04	♈♈	5

● Vin Santo Occhio di Pernice '97	♈♈♈+	8
○ Vin Santo '97	♈♈	8
● Nobile di Montepulciano '06	♈♈	5
● Rosso Avignonesi '07	♈♈	4
● 50 & 50 Avignonesi e Cappannelle '05	♈	8
○ Cortona Il Marzocco '07	♈	4
● Rosso di Montepulciano '08	♈	4
● 50 & 50 Avignonesi e Cappannelle '99	♈♈♈	8
○ Vin Santo '96	♈♈♈	8
○ Vin Santo '95	♈♈♈	8
○ Vin Santo '93	♈♈♈	8
● Vin Santo Occhio di Pernice '93	♈♈♈	8
○ Vin Santo Occhio di Pernice '90	♈♈♈	8
○ Vin Santo Occhio di Pernice '89	♈♈♈	8

Badia a Coltibuono

LOC. BADIA A COLTIBUONO
53013 GAIOLE IN CHIANTI [SI]
TEL. 0577746110
www.coltibuono.com

CELLAR SALES
PRE-BOOKED VISITS
VISITOR FACILITIES
FOOD

ANNUAL PRODUCTION 950,000 bottles
HECTARES UNDER VINE 72
VITICULTURE METHOD Organic certified

Set in the magnificent countryside of Gaiole in Chianti, Badia a Coltibuono is literally rooted in an ancient medieval monastery complex. Owner Emanuela Stucchi Prinetti committed several years ago to a certified totally organic operation, with the aim of instilling in her wines the innermost essence of their Gaiole terroir. The courageous conversion could be the source of a pervasive quality rise over the winery's entire line, a leap very obvious over the past few years.

In Chianti Classico Riserva '06, liqueur berry fruit, cassis and chocolate are eloquent on the nose, and the palate is remarkably supple and expressive, with notable depth, juicy, rich fruit and a near limitless finish. It turned in a terrific performance, successfully fusing harmony and complexity. Coltibuono strives for wines with a certain level of delicacy and Chianti Classico RS '07 is a fine example. Tangerine, raspberry and wild red berry fruit make up a fresh, live nose, with more crisp fruit in the mouth and on a toothsome finish. Chianti Classico '07 is easy drinking but a bit of a lightweight, with bitterish extract.

Badia di Morrona

VIA DEL CHIANTI, 6
56030 TERRICCIOLA [PI]
TEL. 0587656013
www.badiadimorrona.it

CELLAR SALES
PRE-BOOKED VISITS
VISITOR FACILITIES

ANNUAL PRODUCTION 220,000 bottles
HECTARES UNDER VINE 85,0
VITICULTURE METHOD Conventional

Badia di Morrona, with almost 90 hectares under vine in the centre of the extensive territory that makes up the Colline Pisane district, is one of the largest operations in this part of Tuscany. The vineyards are planted in clay-rich soils from the Pliocene. Over the years, the Gaslini Alberti family has made reliability the hallmark of their winery, with a line that shows impressive winemaking expertise. Granted, the wines may lack a whisper of personality but they have acquired many satisfied aficionados.

We were struck this year by Antia '06, a predominantly cabernet Bordeaux blend with generous draughts of crisp-edged dark berry fruit and smooth spice. The tannins show still a tad clenched but it is remarkably tasty overall, with a fruit-filled, appealing development. The 2005 growing year wasn't great for sangiovese, as can be seen from Vignalta '05. Although the nose offers nice florality and rich, blood-like impressions, over-extracted tannins tend to dry out the palate and skew the balance. We recommend Chianti Sodi del Paretaio '08 to discriminating consumers, who will find it dependable and reasonably priced.

● Chianti Cl. Ris. '06	ΨΨ 6
● Chianti Cl. '07	Ψ 5
● Chianti Cl. RS '07	Ψ 4
● Chianti Cl. '06	ΨΨΨ 5*
● Chianti Cl. Ris. '04	ΨΨΨ 6
● Sangioveto '95	ΨΨΨ 6
● Chianti Cl. Cultus Boni '03	ΨΨ 5
● Chianti Cl. Cultus Boni '01	ΨΨ 5
● Chianti Cl. Ris. '05	ΨΨ 6
● Sangioveto '04	ΨΨ 7
● Sangioveto '01	ΨΨ 7
O Trappoline '06	ΨΨ 4
O Vin Santo del Chianti Cl. '02	ΨΨ 6

● N'Antia '06	ΨΨ 5
● Chianti I Sodi del Paretaio '08	Ψ 3
● Colli dell'Etruria Centrale Vignalta '05	Ψ 6
● Taneto '07	Ψ 4
● Chianti I Sodi del Paretaio '07	ΨΨ 3*
● N'Antia '05	ΨΨ 5
● N'Antia '04	ΨΨ 5
● Taneto '06	ΨΨ 4*
● Vigna Alta '04	ΨΨ 6
● Vigna Alta '99	ΨΨ 6
O Vin Santo '03	ΨΨ 6

Fattoria di Bagnolo

LOC. BAGNOLO-CANTAGALLO
VIA IMPRUNETANA PER TAVARNUZZE, 48
50023 IMPRUNETA [FI]
TEL. 0552313403
www.bartolinibaldelli.it

CELLAR SALES
PRE-BOOKED VISITS

ANNUAL PRODUCTION 27,000 bottles
HECTARES UNDER VINE 10
VITICULTURE METHOD Conventional

Marco Bartolini Baldelli continues to drive forward the growth of his wines, and not just in quantity. His operation is a quite a handful to manage, since Fattoria di Bagnolo's properties lie in three different provinces. Wine and oil production is centred at Impruneta, the extra virgin olive oil comes from Pergine Valdarno while grain is grown at San Miniato, near Siena. But none of these multiple activities can distract him from his real passion, wine, and little now separates the winery from truly splendid results.

The performances of all three wines were impressive. Chianti Colli Fiorentini '07 shone with fresh vegetal notes and bright florality, vibrant energy and a zippy acidity on the palate, and a deliciously flavourful finale. La Riserva '06 brings more layers on the nose, with an intriguing mélange of spice, followed by a rich, mouthfilling palate which carries on forever. Capro Rosso '06, from sangiovese, colorino and cabernet sauvignon, is a stand-out for minerally essences on the nose and very appealing menthol notes on the finish, plus its full-volumed palate.

I Balzini

LOC. PASTINE, 19
50021 BARBERINO VAL D'ELSA [FI]
TEL. 0558075503
www.ibalzini.it

PRE-BOOKED VISITS

ANNUAL PRODUCTION 50,000 bottles
HECTARES UNDER VINE 5.4
VITICULTURE METHOD Conventional

I Balzini returns to the full profiles this year, a fitting marker for the D'Isantos, its husband and wife owners, who just this year celebrate the silver anniversary of their professional activities in wine. They own some ten hectares, part in olives and over five hectares of vineyard. The novelty of this year's offerings is that they gave us two vintages of the same two wines to taste, probably a sign that in the future they intend to bring forward their release dates. We were unable to taste the Green Label, their steel-aged wine made from local varieties.

The two versions of I Balzini White Label, a 50-50 blend of sangiovese and cabernet sauvignon, are quite similar on the nose, with the younger showing more fruit. Tannins that remain fairly tight hamper the progression of the '05 while the '06 powers impressively into a lengthy finish. Black Label is an assemblage of cabernet sauvignon, sangiovese and merlot. Once again, the younger version has a more complex nose, with refreshing spice and pungent balsam, but the palate is somewhat one-dimensional whereas the '06 exhibits sturdy structure, robust body and a full-flavoured finale.

● Capro Rosso '06	6
● Chianti Colli Fiorentini '07	4*
● Chianti Colli Fiorentini Ris. '06	5
● Capro Rosso '05	6
● Capro Rosso '04	5
● Capro Rosso '03	5
● Chianti Colli Fiorentini '06	4*
● Chianti Colli Fiorentini '05	3*
● Chianti Colli Fiorentini '04	3*
● Chianti Colli Fiorentini Ris. '05	5
● Chianti Colli Fiorentini Ris. '04	5
● Chianti Colli Fiorentini Ris. '03	5

● I Balzini Black Label '06	6
● I Balzini Black Label '05	6
● I Balzini White Label '06	6
● I Balzini White Label '05	6
● I Balzini Black Label '03	6
● I Balzini White Label '04	5
● I Balzini White Label '03	5

★ Castello Banfi

LOC. SANT'ANGELO SCALO
CASTELLO DI POGGIO ALLE MURA
53024 MONTALCINO [SI]
TEL. 0577840111
www.castellobanfi.com

CELLAR SALES
PRE-BOOKED VISITS
VISITOR FACILITIES
FOOD

ANNUAL PRODUCTION **10,000,000 bottles**
HECTARES UNDER VINE **850**
VITICULTURE METHOD **Conventional**

Owned by the Italo-American Mariani family, Banfi possesses the expertise and physical capacity to produce well-made wines at all price levels, which puts it in the company of Italy's best wine operations. The estate vineyards, some 850 hectares, are all in the Montalcino district, and 150 go exclusively to producing DOC and DOCG wines. Banfi is able to control every step of production, from barrel-making to the manual selection of incoming fruit destined for the top wines.

Brunello di Montalcino Poggio alle Mura '04 is as fine as we've come to expect, offering fragrant dried plum preserves and a silky, caressing palate. Summus '06, an equal partnership of cabernet sauvignon and sangiovese with a kiss of syrah, is strikingly complex from first to last, exuding red and black berry fruit and lingering into the sunset on the finish. Cum Laude '06, an amalgam of cabernet sauvignon, merlot, syrah and sangiovese, presents lovely fresh greens followed by plenty of crisp, succulent fruit in the mouth. We also tasted Banfi's latest wine, Belnero '05, a sangiovese and merlot blend of international stamp.

Riccardo Baracchi

LOC. SAN MARTINO
VIA CEGLIOLO, 21
52044 CORTONA [AR]
TEL. 0575612679
www.baracchiwinery.com

CELLAR SALES
PRE-BOOKED VISITS
VISITOR FACILITIES
FOOD

ANNUAL PRODUCTION **75,000 bottles**
HECTARES UNDER VINE **22**
VITICULTURE METHOD **Naturale**

Riccardo Baracchi had the satisfaction of seeing his most representative wine, Ardito '06, go to our national finals. That should also serve as a confirmation of his efforts to relaunch a family tradition in the wine business that dates back to the mid 19th century. He planted his 20 hectares of vineyard to tried and tested local varieties, such as sangiovese and malvasia, but added internationals as well. Riccardo himself carries out the vineyard and winemaking duties, with consultant Stefano Chioccioli, and his son Benedetto is following in his footsteps.

Ardito '06, a blend of syrah and cabernet sauvignon, lays out a satisfying aromatic medley featuring mixed spices and assorted berry fruit, then slides caressingly into an impressively volumed palate that is both smooth and mouthfilling. Syrah '07 is a charmer, with an intriguing, spicy nose, ductile progression and a leisurely, winning finish. Merlot '07 pays faithful homage to its variety on the nose, then expands to considerable pleasure in the mouth with fine acidic grip. Astore '08 is straightforward, refreshing and inviting.

Wine	Rating
● Summus '06	♟♟ 8
● Brunello di Montalcino Poggio alle Mura '04	♟♟ 8
● Cum Laude '06	♟♟ 6
○ Moscadello di Montalcino Florus '07	♟♟ 6
● Belnero '05	♟ 6
● Brunello di Montalcino '04	♟ 8
○ Chardonnay Fontanelle '08	♟ 6
● Rosso di Montalcino '07	♟ 6
○ Serena '08	♟ 6
● Brunello di Montalcino Poggio all'Oro Ris. '99	♟♟♟ 8
● Brunello di Montalcino Poggio all'Oro Ris. '95	♟♟♟ 8
● Brunello di Montalcino Poggio alle Mura '99	♟♟♟ 8
● Brunello di Montalcino Poggio alle Mura '98	♟♟♟ 8
● Sant'Antimo Excelsus '03	♟♟♟ 7
● Sant'Antimo Excelsus '99	♟♟♟ 8
● Sant'Antimo Mandrielle '04	♟♟♟ 5
● Sant'Antimo Summus '97	♟♟♟ 6

Wine	Rating
● Ardito '06	♟♟ 7
● Cortona Smeriglio Merlot '07	♟♟ 5
● Cortona Smeriglio Syrah '07	♟♟ 5
○ Astore '08	♟ 4
● Cortona Smeriglio Sangiovese '07	♟ 5
● Ardito '05	♟♟ 7
● Ardito '04	♟♟ 6
● Cortona Smeriglio Merlot '06	♟♟ 5
● Cortona Smeriglio Merlot '05	♟♟ 5

Fattoria dei Barbi

LOC. PODERNOVI, 170
53024 MONTALCINO [SI]
TEL. 0577841111
www.fattoriadeibarbi.it

CELLAR SALES
PRE-BOOKED VISITS
VISITOR FACILITIES
FOOD

ANNUAL PRODUCTION 800,000 bottles
HECTARES UNDER VINE 90
VITICULTURE METHOD Conventional

Fattorie dei Barbi, which has been in the hands of the Colombini family since the 18th century, is one of the oldest farm estates in Montalcino and has been producing wine since the end of the 19th century. As documented in the Brunello museum in Montalcino, fundamental to this history are its 70 hectares dedicated to Brunello production, planted in loose, galestro-type soils rich in silt and sand, and located predominantly in the area between Montalcino and Castelnuovo dell'Abate. The wines are unabashedly classic in style, and their quality is on the upswing, thanks to increased attention to vineyards and winemaking.

All of the wines performed well in our tastings, with Brunello di Montalcino Vigna del Fiore the team leader. It is particularly fine on the nose, where fragrant bright cherry, blackberry and blueberry are in glorious evidence. Although the tannins are a trifle obvious and lend a slight edginess to the palate, the mouth shows a vivacious acidity and fine heft on the finish. All signs point to good cellarability. Brunello di Montalcino '04 is equally impressive. Despite some reductive notes of gaminess on opening, it shows dynamic progression and perfectly extracted tannins.

★ Barone Ricasoli

LOC. CASTELLO DI BROLIO
53013 GAIOLE IN CHIANTI [SI]
TEL. 05777301
www.ricasoli.it

CELLAR SALES
PRE-BOOKED VISITS
FOOD

ANNUAL PRODUCTION 2,000,000 bottles
HECTARES UNDER VINE 249
VITICULTURE METHOD Conventional

Barone Ricasoli, with1,200 hectares in the southern part of Chianti Classico, is one of the denomination's key players. The vineyards lie around the medieval Castello di Brolio, at elevations of 200 to 490 metres. They have always been managed to ensure high-quality fruit, and the entire vineyard was replanted in the mid 1990s in order to implement the latest viticultural methods and at the same time to improve the terroir expression of the Brolio wines.

The sangiovese and merlot Casalferro '06 has gradually drawn closer to reflecting its terroir. Modernist in its approach, it shows smooth fruit and notes of earth while dense but elegant tannin complements its supple fabric. As a lean, austere Chianti Classico, the '06 Castello di Brolio effortlessly picked up Three Glasses. Floral notes, luscious dark berry jam and smooth spice precede incredible depth in the mouth, all contributing to fine overall balance. It's a great example of a terroir-driven bottle in a modern key. The more traditional Riserva Rocca Guicciarda is as good as always, as is the eminently drinkable Chianti Classico '07.

● Brunello di Montalcino '04	♥♥ 6
● Brunello di Montalcino V. del Fiore '04	♥♥ 8
● Brusco dei Barbi '08	♥♥ 3*
● Brunello di Montalcino Ris. '03	♥ 8
● Rosso di Montalcino '07	♥ 4
● Brunello di Montalcino '01	♀♀ 6
● Brunello di Montalcino '00	♀♀ 6
● Brunello di Montalcino Ris. '01	♀♀ 8
● Brunello di Montalcino Ris. '00	♀♀ 8
● Brunello di Montalcino V. del Fiore '03	♀♀ 8
● Brunello di Montalcino V. del Fiore '01	♀♀ 7
● Morellino di Scansano Sole '07	♀♀ 5

● Chianti Cl. Castello di Brolio '06	♥♥♥ 8
● Casalferro '06	♥♥ 8
● Chianti Cl. Rocca Guicciarda Ris. '06	♥♥ 6
● Chianti Cl. Brolio '07	♥ 6
○ Granello '08	♥ 6
○ Vin Santo del Chianti Cl. Castello di Brolio '04	♥ 7
● Casalferro '05	♀♀♀ 8
● Casalferro '03	♀♀♀ 6
● Casalferro '99	♀♀♀ 6
● Chianti Cl. Castello di Brolio '04	♀♀♀ 8
● Chianti Cl. Castello di Brolio '03	♀♀♀ 7
● Chianti Cl. Castello di Brolio '01	♀♀♀ 7
● Chianti Cl. Castello di Brolio '00	♀♀♀ 7
● Chianti Cl. Castello di Brolio '99	♀♀♀ 7
● Chianti Cl. Castello di Brolio '98	♀♀♀ 6

Mattia Barzaghi

LOC. SAN DONATO, 13
53037 SAN GIMIGNANO [SI]
TEL. 0577941501
www.mattiabarzaghi.com

CELLAR SALES

ANNUAL PRODUCTION **45,000 bottles**
HECTARES UNDER VINE **7.5**
VITICULTURE METHOD **Naturale**

After his debut last year with a small profile, Mattia Barzaghi merits the full treatment this year. He boasts a generous line of top-notch offerings, with distinctive character traits that somehow mirror those of Barzaghi himself. After many years as a cellar worker, Barzaghi struck out on his own, with very precise personal ideas and directions, so much so that his entrance onto the wine stage brought a true of fresh air.

His Vernaccia di San Gimignano Riserva Cassandra '07, which matures a year in oak, displays an intriguing suite of aromas, quite firm structure and a tasty, leisurely finale. Zeta '08 is put into large wood, and emerges with a refreshingly crisp, floral bouquet and a powerful palate with a come-hither acidity. The finish is delicious. The all-sangiovese Sciamano '07 marches to a different drummer, exuding pungent wild herbs, Mediterranean scrub and wild berries. The mouth is well balanced, full volumed and supple. We found the easy-drinking Sorriso '08 is very interesting while Vernaccia Impronta '08 shows camomile and a well-sculpted palate.

Fattoria di Basciano

V.LE DUCA DELLA VITTORIA, 159
50068 RUFINA [FI]
TEL. 0558397034
www.renzomasibasciano.it

CELLAR SALES
PRE-BOOKED VISITS

ANNUAL PRODUCTION **200,000 bottles**
HECTARES UNDER VINE **35**
VITICULTURE METHOD **Conventional**

The Masi family's operation is as steady as ever and although there were no bull's-eyes, the wines are in fine form as always. If we had to find fault, we would note a slight drop in attentiveness to their flagship wine, Chianti Rufina, which betrays a lack of clarity on the nose. But this reservation detracts nothing from the fine job that Paolo, Renzo's son, is doing. Fattoria di Basciano continues to merit praise for combining high wine quality with laudably competitive prices, something that cannot be taken for granted in today's market.

The sangiovese and cabernet sauvignon Erta e China '07 emerged a high scorer again, with berry fruit smoothing out peppery balsam and a palate that is generous, rich and succulent. I Pini '07, from syrah, cabernet sauvignon and merlot, is fine. Briny notes appear on a somewhat reticent nose but the palate is warm and appealing with good nervy acidity. Not quite so successful is the '07 edition of Il Corto, from sangiovese with a dollop of cabernet, since over-obvious tannins stiffen the palate. Vin Santo is as good as ever, with the '03 showing refined aromas plus unctuous, fat weight. The two Chianti Rufinas lack expressiveness.

● Sciamano '07	♥♥ 5
○ Vernaccia di S. Gimignano Cassandra Ris. '07	♥♥ 5
○ Vernaccia di S. Gimignano Zeta '08	♥♥ 4*
● Sorriso '08	♥ 4
○ Vernaccia di S. Gimignano Impronta '08	♥ 4
○ Vernaccia di S. Gimignano Zeta '07	♥♥ 5

● Erta e China '07	♥♥ 3*
● I Pini '07	♥♥ 5
○ Vin Santo Rufina '03	♥♥ 5
● Chianti Rufina '07	♥ 3
● Chianti Rufina Ris. '06	♥ 5
● Il Corto '07	♥ 4
● Chianti Rufina '05	♥♥ 3*
● Erta e China '06	♥♥ 3*
● Erta e China '05	♥♥ 3*
● I Pini '06	♥♥ 5
● Il Corto '06	♥♥ 5
○ Vin Santo Rufina '02	♥♥ 4
○ Vin Santo Rufina '01	♥♥ 4

Cantine Bellini

VIA PIAVE, 1
50068 RUFINA [FI]
TEL. 0558399102
www.bellinicantine.it

CELLAR SALES

ANNUAL PRODUCTION **12,600 bottles**
HECTARES UNDER VINE **7**
VITICULTURE METHOD **Conventional**

Although the Bellini family has always graced these pages with wines from Podere Il Pozzo, the siblings' Cantine Fratelli Bellini now makes its first appearance in the Guide. What was once a bottling operation gradually shifted in recent years to winemaking as well, based on the family-owned farm in the municipality of Pontassieve. The seven hectares of vineyard there have been carefully brought up to modern standards.

The garnet-hued Riserva '06 del Chianti Rufina, aptly named Vigna Vecchia, or Old Vineyard, displays pleasurably evolved impressions of game, wet fur and tanned leather. The fruit remains juicy and tasty in the mouth, the palate impressively complex. We also liked the velvety, mouthfilling character of Canto del Lupo '06, a mix of sangiovese, cabernet sauvignon and merlot. The remaining wines are soundly made.

Belpoggio

FRAZ. CASTELNUOVO DELL'ABATE
LOC. BELLARIA
53024 MONTALCINO [SI]
TEL. 0423982147
www.belpoggio.it

ANNUAL PRODUCTION **25,000 bottles**
HECTARES UNDER VINE **5**
VITICULTURE METHOD **Conventional**

The modest-sized Belpoggio winery lies just a few metres away from the abbey of Sant'Antimo, on a small rise at an elevation of 400 metres. The Martellozzo family, growers for many generation in Veneto, have only a few hectares dedicated to Brunello production but they have shown such a terrific quality leap that a Belpoggio wine went to our final tasting round for the second year in a row. The vines are planted in pebble-rich galestro with a favourable exposure, and vine density doesn't exceed 4,500 per hectare. The wines, modern in style, age fairly long in 30-hectolitre casks.

Brunello di Montalcino '04 is a champion on all levels. A fetching deep ruby precedes an ultra-rich, fruit-filled nose brimming with yellow peach, wild cherry and ripe blackberry, plus an intriguing edge of toasted almond. A rich weft of tannins and a delicious vein of acidity are masterfully integrated into the fabric, and the wine concludes with a remarkably long, aromatic finish. We found Rosso di Montalcino '07 lacking in balance. The tannins, though well crafted, are in excess and crop the finish.

● Canto del Lupo Il Pozzo '06	♟♟ 5
● Chianti Rufina V. Vecchia Il Pozzo Ris. '06	♟♟ 5
● Chianti '08	♟ 2*
● Chianti Rufina Il Pozzo '07	♟ 4
● Chianti Rufina Ris. '05	♟♟ 4*
● Chianti Rufina Ris. '04	♟♟ 4
● Chianti Rufina Ris. '03	♟♟ 5

● Brunello di Montalcino '04	♟♟ 7
● Rosso di Montalcino '07	♟ 5
● Brunello di Montalcino '03	♟♟ 7

Podere Le Berne

LOC. CERVOGNANO
VIA POGGIO GOLO, 7
53040 MONTEPULCIANO [SI]
TEL. 0578767328
www.leberne.it

CELLAR SALES

ANNUAL PRODUCTION **25,000 bottles**
HECTARES UNDER VINE **6**
VITICULTURE METHOD **Conventional**

Podere Le Berne could very well symbolize the quality potential of so many of Italy's small producers. It's a family operation, run by the talented Andrea Natalini, whose father Giuseppe founded it in 1960 and who continues to lend a hand. The vineyards lie at Cervognano, which can be considered one of Montepulciano's historic subzones, and the grapes produce sturdily structured wines that live fine, long lives.

We were mightily impressed by Nobile di Montepulciano '06. With sharply focused aromas, enormous breadth and energy-laden development, it is a fine example of what the type should be and possibly the best Le Berne has produced. Close behind is Nobile di Montepulciano Riserva '05, though of more austere character. The nose is softer but the structure is solid enough, with some oak still to be absorbed. Rosso di Montepulciano '08 is an easy-drinking, super-delicious quaffer.

Tenuta di Bibbiano

VIA BIBBIANO, 76
53011 CASTELLINA IN CHIANTI [SI]
TEL. 0577743065
www.tenutadibibbiano.com

CELLAR SALES
PRE-BOOKED VISITS

ANNUAL PRODUCTION **90,000 bottles**
HECTARES UNDER VINE **25**
VITICULTURE METHOD **Conventional**

Bibbiano, one of Chianti Classico's most traditional operations, has been in the hands of the current owners, the Marrocchesi Marzi family, since 1865. The most important modernization programme took place between 1950 and 1970, when the family, assisted by Giulio Gambelli, built the winemaking facility and replanted the vineyards. Today, their various Chianti Classicos are made and bottled separately by source vineyard but they all exhibit a traditionalist approach and reflect their individual terroir.

The Capannino vineyard yields full-bodied, long-lived wines and its Riserva Vigna is justly renowned. The '06 lives up to that billing, displaying ripe red berry fruit and lovely nuances of fruit jam and balsam, while fleshy depth is the theme in the mouth, which unfurls a mass of dense, toothsome tannins. Chianti Classico '07 is impressive even while still young. It's supple, very flavourful and eminently enjoyable right now. Chianti Classico Montornello '07, on the other hand, does show some complexity and good flavours but the nose is muddled, uncertain and still in search of some definition.

● Nobile di Montepulciano '06	▼▼▼ 4
● Nobile di Montepulciano Ris. '05	▼▼ 6
● Rosso di Montepulciano '08	▼▼ 4
● Nobile di Montepulciano '05	♀♀ 4*
● Nobile di Montepulciano '04	♀♀ 4
● Nobile di Montepulciano '03	♀♀ 4
● Nobile di Montepulciano Ris. '04	♀♀ 6
● Nobile di Montepulciano Ris. '03	♀♀ 6
● Nobile di Montepulciano Ris. '01	♀♀ 6
● Nobile di Montepulciano Ris. '00	♀♀ 6

● Chianti Cl. '07	▼▼ 4*
● Chianti Cl. V. del Capannino Ris. '06	▼▼ 6
● Chianti Cl. Montornello '07	▼ 5
● Chianti Cl. '06	♀♀ 4*
● Chianti Cl. Montornello '07	♀♀ 5*
● Chianti Cl. Montornello '06	♀♀ 4*
● Chianti Cl. V. del Capannino Ris. '05	♀♀ 5
● Chianti Cl. V. del Capannino Ris. '04	♀♀ 5

Bindella

FRAZ. ACQUAVIVA
VIA DELLE TRE BERTE, 10A
53045 MONTEPULCIANO [SI]
TEL. 0578767777
www.bindella.it

CELLAR SALES
PRE-BOOKED VISITS

ANNUAL PRODUCTION **120,000 bottles**
HECTARES UNDER VINE **31**
VITICULTURE METHOD **Conventional**

Rudi Bindella, Swiss by birth but Tuscan by love, started his wine operation in 1984. Over 25 years, he has shown himself to be a serious winemaker. Not one to run after the latest fad, he produces consistently fine wines that have been steadily acquiring refinement. His facility is located in Vallocaia and most of his vineyards are planted in the Argiano area, one of Montepulciano's finest growing zones.

Nobile di Montepulciano I Quadri remains Bindella's standard-bearer and the '06 version unsurprisingly reached our final round. As always, it is solidly built and perhaps on the austere side but very complex. A blend of sangiovese, cabernet sauvignon and syrah gives the impressive Vallocaia '06 rich fragrances and pulpy fruit in the mouth. Nobile '06 shows more delicate aromas, plus a robust palate with some still rough edges, but it is fine overall. Bindella debuted two new additions to the line. Gemella '08 is a pleasurable, rich-flavoured sauvignon while the all-merlot Antenata '07 sports well-focused aromas and a multi-layered, generous palate.

Biondi Santi - Tenuta Il Greppo

LOC. VILLA GREPPO, 183
53024 MONTALCINO [SI]
TEL. 0577848087
www.biondisanti.it

CELLAR SALES
PRE-BOOKED VISITS

ANNUAL PRODUCTION **80,000 bottles**
HECTARES UNDER VINE **25**
VITICULTURE METHOD **Naturale**

The Biondi Santi profile carries a double-barrelled review, one for Il Greppo and the other for the Poggio Salvi wines, which Biondi Santi distributes. It is by now well known that Brunello was first created at Il Greppo, thanks to a brilliant winemaking initiative by Ferruccio Biondi Santi. Even after more than a century, Biondi Santi's passionate commitment to the wine remains undiminished. All of the vineyards lie around the winery, apart from a small parcel a bit to the east, and the planting material is the fruit of viticultural research on the property.

Brunello di Montalcino '04 has its own inimitable characteristics, requiring some oxygenation to be at its best, but it soon pours out its classic sweet tobacco leaf and floral notes of oleander. That expected vein of acidity is prominent on the palate and a glossy tannic weave does nothing to impede the crescendo of a spacious, rich finish. Rosso di Montalcino '06 shows somewhat less balanced. Redolent of ripe cherry and blossoms, it has greenish tannins that clench the progression. Although its nose is a tad hesitant, Poggio Salvi's '04 Brunello is very well put together, with a well-delineated palate of admirable depth and juicy succulence.

● Nobile di Montepulciano I Quadri '06	♀♀	5
● Antenata '07	♀♀	6
● Vallocaia '06	♀♀	6
○ Gemella '08	♀	4
● Nobile di Montepulciano '06	♀	5
● Nobile di Montepulciano '05	♀♀	6
● Nobile di Montepulciano '03	♀♀	5
● Nobile di Montepulciano I Quadri '05	♀♀	5
● Nobile di Montepulciano I Quadri '04	♀♀	5
● Nobile di Montepulciano I Quadri '03	♀♀	5
● Nobile di Montepulciano I Quadri '01	♀♀	5
● Nobile di Montepulciano I Quadri '00	♀♀	5
● Nobile di Montepulciano Ris. '04	♀♀	6
● Vallocaia '04	♀♀	6
● Vallocaia '03	♀♀	6
○ Vin Santo Dolce Sinfonia '99	♀♀	6

● Brunello di Montalcino '04	♀♀♀	8
● Brunello di Montalcino Poggio Salvi '04	♀♀	7
● Rosso di Montalcino '06	♀	6
● Rosso di Montalcino Poggio Salvi '07	♀	5
● Brunello di Montalcino '03	♀♀♀	8
● Brunello di Montalcino '01	♀♀♀	8
● Brunello di Montalcino Ris. '01	♀♀♀	8
● Brunello di Montalcino Ris. '99	♀♀♀	8
● Brunello di Montalcino Ris. '95	♀♀♀	6

Castello di Bolgheri

LOC. BOLGHERI
57020 CASTAGNETO CARDUCCI [LI]
TEL. 0565762110
www.castellodibolgheri.eu

CELLAR SALES
PRE-BOOKED VISITS
VISITOR FACILITIES

ANNUAL PRODUCTION **120,000 bottles**
HECTARES UNDER VINE **50**
VITICULTURE METHOD **Conventional**

Another in a string of outstanding performances reinforces the position of Castello di Bolgheri as one of the best emerging producers on the Tuscan coast. The cellars are built into the magnificent medieval castle that dominates the ancient town while the vineyards are in the far northern corner of the Bolgheri zone. Planted in 1997 on gravel-rich, sandy clay soils, the vines make a significant contribution to the finesse and aromatic breadth of the cellar's wines.

Bolgheri Superiore Castello di Bolgheri '06 is a distinctive wine that competed in our finals. This blend of cabernet sauvignon, cabernet franc and merlot undergoes lengthy maceration on the skins under quasi-reductive conditions, which imbues the wine with pent-up energy, an unusual characteristic, at least for this area. Crisp vegetal notes on the nose are a foil to impressions of iron filings and blood-rich meat, while its youthful, clean-edged acidity drives taut, dynamic progression. Varvàra '07 releases lovely fresh greens and balsam, followed by a palate with impressive balance. Its considerable charms are ready to be enjoyed now.

Il Borghetto

LOC. MONTEFIRIDOLFI
VIA COLLINA SANT'ANGELO, 21
50026 SAN CASCIANO IN VAL DI PESA [FI]
TEL. 0558244491
www.borghetto.org

CELLAR SALES
PRE-BOOKED VISITS

ANNUAL PRODUCTION **16,000 bottles**
HECTARES UNDER VINE **6**
VITICULTURE METHOD **Conventional**

Borghetto boasts little more than six hectares in vineyards, lying along the hills overlooking the Val di Pesa. Though a fairly new operation, it has developed a distinctive style of its own which has brought in into the top ranks of Chianti Classico. The owner is Antonio Cavallini while Tim Manning is responsible for winemaking. Their modus operandi focuses on meticulous work in the vineyard and on winemaking techniques that are innovative, at least for this area. Ageing is in barriques, with a mix of new and used oak.

We were again impressed by Chianti Classico Bilaccio. After some initial reductive notes, the '06 opens up to a full spate of delicious earthy minerality, layered over morello cherry and floral blossoms, plus a generous whiff of spice. This is a wine of generous flavour and good weight, although jacketed at the moment by excessive wood. Chianti Classico Riserva '05 is fine, showing notes of toasted wood and some evolution. Collina 21 '06, a mix of sangiovese, cabernet and merlot is every bit as good..

● Bolgheri Sup. Castello di Bolgheri '06	♀♀ 8
● Bolgheri Varvàra '07	♀♀ 5
● Bolgheri Sup. '05	♀♀ 8
● Bolgheri Varvàra '06	♀♀ 5

● Chianti Cl. Bilaccio '06	♀♀ 4*
● Chianti Cl. Ris. '05	♀♀ 7
● Collina 21 '06	♀♀ 4*
● Chianti Cl. Bilaccio '05	♀♀ 4*
● Collina 21 '05	♀♀ 4*

Borgo Salcetino

LOC. LUCARELLI
53017 RADDA IN CHIANTI [SI]
TEL. 0577733541
www.livon.it

CELLAR SALES
PRE-BOOKED VISITS

ANNUAL PRODUCTION **126,000 bottles**
HECTARES UNDER VINE **15**
VITICULTURE METHOD **Conventional**

Borgo Salcetino, part of the Livon group, is a strikingly attractive wine estate in the municipality of Radda in Chianti. About half of its 30 or so hectares is in vineyard, planted to sangiovese of course, but also to canaiolo, merlot and cabernet sauvignon. The barrel room is exclusively dedicated to large oak casks, a very visible sign of the new approach adopted by all of Livon's various wineries. Our tastings this year revealed that the wines show better balance and focus than in the past, a sign of a significant jump in quality.

Chianti Classico Riserva Lucarello '06 is a truly terrific bottling. After initial hesitation, the wine delivers an impressive, no-nonsense draught of well-ripened fruit and delicate spice, then builds a self-confident progression that features a tasty acidity, to finish in grand style. Chianti Classico '07 is in the same class, showing ample and spacious, needing only a few more months for a splendid maturity.

Il Borro

FRAZ. SAN GIUSTINO VALDARNO
LOC. IL BORRO, 1
52020 LORO CIUFFENNA [AR]
TEL. 0559772921
www.ilborro.it

CELLAR SALES
PRE-BOOKED VISITS

ANNUAL PRODUCTION **150,000 bottles**
HECTARES UNDER VINE **40**
VITICULTURE METHOD **Conventional**

A spot of hunting did it. Ferruccio Ferragamo enjoyed the Borro estate for sport, then purchased it in 1993, launching wine operations and even renovating the original settlement itself. The labour was Herculean, involving rebuilding ruined farmhouses, planting new vineyards and building a brand-new wine cellar, but the results have been0 stellar. Ferruccio's son Salvatore, who manages the complex, also directs operations in the vineyards, which cover 40 of the estate's more than 700 hectares.

Borro '07, mostly merlot and cabernet sauvignon with some help from petit verdot and syrah, went on to the national finals. After a refined bouquet redolent of elegant spice and ripe berry, the entry is majestic, with an ultra-creamy mouthfeel, and the long-lingering finale is spot on. We found Polissena '07 very pleasurable. All sangiovese in a modern key, it boasts a fruity nose, well-balanced body and a refreshing, zingy acidity before finishing with generous flavours.

● Chianti Cl. Lucarello Ris. '06	♟♟	5
● Chianti Cl. '07	♟♟	4*
● Chianti Cl. '03	♟♟	4
● Chianti Cl. '01	♟♟	4
● Rossole '06	♟♟	4
● Rossole '04	♟♟	5
● Rossole '00	♟♟	5

● Il Borro '07	♟♟	7
● Polissena '07	♟♟	4*
● Il Borro '06	♟♟	7
● Il Borro '05	♟♟	7
● Il Borro '04	♟♟	7
● Il Borro '03	♟♟	7
● Pian di Nova '06	♟♟	4*
● Polissena '06	♟♟	6

Poderi Boscarelli

FRAZ. CERVOGNANO
VIA DI MONTENERO, 28
53045 MONTEPULCIANO [SI]
TEL. 0578767277
www.poderiboscarelli.com

CELLAR SALES
PRE-BOOKED VISITS

ANNUAL PRODUCTION **80,000 bottles**
HECTARES UNDER VINE **14**
VITICULTURE METHOD **Conventional**

Boscarelli has been one of the most highly respected producers in the Nobile di Montepulciano zone for quite some time now. The De Ferraris, who arrived in this corner of Tuscany as far back as 1962, have never wavered in focusing on their local Cervognano terroir, convinced of its centrality to the character of their Nobiles. They pay little attention to the vagaries of oenological fads and the Boscarelli wines have thus enjoyed consistency in both style and quality.

Nobile Nocio dei Boscarelli is perhaps most representative of their philosophy. The '06 vintage is as uncompromising as it is elegant, making it once again one of the finest of the denomination. Boscarelli dei Boscarelli '06, an assemblage of sangiovese, merlot and carmenère, is just as impressive, with a fine, full body, good balance and plenty of verve. Nobile '06 and Nobile di Montepulciano Riserva '05 are supple and approachable, though the latter has a few rough edges that need sanding. Rosso di Montepulciano Prugnolo '07 is fragrant and delicious.

Castello di Bossi

LOC. BOSSI IN CHIANTI
53019 CASTELNUOVO BERARDENGA [SI]
TEL. 0577359330
www.castellodibossi.it

CELLAR SALES
PRE-BOOKED VISITS

ANNUAL PRODUCTION **600,000 bottles**
HECTARES UNDER VINE **124**
VITICULTURE METHOD **Conventional**

You could call Castello di Bossi, owned by Marco and Maurizio Bacci, a far-flung empire, with its headquarters in the Chianti area's Castelnuovo Berardenga and its various other properties located in some of Tuscany's other iconic areas, Montalcino and Maremma. It comprises more than 600 hectares and concentrates on growing sangiovese but some of its cabernet sauvignon and merlot vineyards now number over 40 harvests.

Chianti Classico Riserva Berardo '06 is outstanding. After a slightly sluggish opening, the nose opens very confidently, laying out appealing, ripe fruit, such as blackcurrant, edged with hints of fresh grass and lavender. On a par is Chianti Classico '07, richly layered and with admirable contrasts, though perhaps a tad bitter on the finish. Just mid-range marks for Corbaia '06 and Girolamo '06, the former lacking interest, the latter overly ripe. The Maremma-area wines are as fine as ever. Tempo '08 is fresh and fruity, and zesty acidity gives Vermentino Vento '08 impressive length. The Montalcino bottlings seem down a notch this year.

● Boscarelli dei Boscarelli '06	♟♟	8
● Nobile di Montepulciano Nocio dei Boscarelli '06	♟♟	8
● Nobile di Montepulciano '06	♟♟	6
● Nobile di Montepulciano Ris. '05	♟♟	6
● Rosso di Montepulciano Prugnolo '07	♟♟	4
● Nobile di Montepulciano Nocio dei Boscarelli '04	♟♟♟	7
● Nobile di Montepulciano Nocio dei Boscarelli '03	♟♟♟	7
● Nobile di Montepulciano Nocio dei Boscarelli '01	♟♟♟	7
● Nobile di Montepulciano V. del Nocio Ris. '91	♟♟♟	7
● Boscarelli dei Boscarelli '05	♟♟	8
● Nobile di Montepulciano Nocio dei Boscarelli '05	♟♟	7

● Chianti Cl. Berardo Ris. '06	♟♟	6
● Morellino di Scansano Tempo Terra di Talamo '08	♟♟	4
○ Vento Vermentino '08	♟♟	4
● Brunello di Montalcino Renieri '04	♟	8
● Chianti Cl. '07	♟	5
● Corbaia '06	♟	7
● Girolamo '06	♟	8
☉ Piano...Piano '08	♟	4
● Re di Renieri '06	♟	7
● Regina di Renieri '06	♟	7
● Rosso di Montalcino Renieri '07	♟	5
● Corbaia '03	♟♟♟	7
● Corbaia '99	♟♟♟	8
● Chianti Cl. Berardo Ris. '04	♟♟	6
● Girolamo '05	♟♟	8
● Girolamo '04	♟♟	7
● Morellino di Scansano Tempo Terra di Talamo '07	♟♟	4

★ Brancaia

LOC. POPPI, 42
53017 RADDA IN CHIANTI [SI]
TEL. 0577742007
www.brancaia.com

CELLAR SALES
PRE-BOOKED VISITS
VISITOR FACILITIES

ANNUAL PRODUCTION 400,000 bottles
HECTARES UNDER VINE 26.00 + 20
VITICULTURE METHOD Conventional

After last year's Star for its tenth Three Glass award, Brancaia shows no let-up in quality. It enjoys a presence in two historic Chianti Classico zones, with vineyards on the Podere Brancaia in Castellina in Chianti and on the Poppi estate near Radda. Add to those considerable viticultural resources an up-to-date, efficient cellar and it is no wonder that the Widmers are able to achieve the lofty goals they set for their winery.

Blu '07, a blend of sangiovese, merlot and cabernet, is Brancaia's iconic wine, and won another Three Glasses. Polished, ripe fruit fairly glides over liquorice, pepper and vanilla, segueing into a luscious, concentrated palate with a silky weft of tannins and refreshing acidity. Tre '07, from sangiovese, merlot and cabernet, is hardly less, with subtle white chocolate lifting rich berry fruit jam on the nose, and a palate and lengthy finish characterized by glossy smoothness. The delicious Ilatraia '07 is a cabernet, sangiovese and petit verdot blend from the Maremma, with bright red fruit, expansive succulence and a leisurely conclusion.

Tenute Toscane di Bruna Baroncini

LOC. SOVESTRO, 62
53037 SAN GIMIGNANO [SI]
TEL. 0577 1912053
www.tenutetoscane.com

ANNUAL PRODUCTION 250,000 bottles
HECTARES UNDER VINE 55
VITICULTURE METHOD Conventional

Bruna Baroncini, scion of a family long-rooted in Tuscan viticulture, first gave a crucial hand to her family's San Gimignano-based wine operation, then, with the meticulous attention of a true wine woman, she set up four new wineries in the region, each with its own dedicated staff. Tenuta il Faggeto is located in Montepulciano, Poggio del Castellare in Montalcino and Querciarossa in the Maremma. Casuccio Tarletti, which is just about to release its first bottlings, is in Chianti Classico.

We liked Brunello di Montalcino '04. The nose is an elegant amalgam of red and dark berry, floral notes and subtle oak tones, while the palate shows fine construction, solid fruit and polished tannins. The '07 shows that the Rosso di Montalcino is as good as always. From Querciarossa comes a succulent Morellino Poggio della Paura '07, whose clean-edged fragrances are matched by a rich, well-cadenced progression. Morellino Rinaldone dell'Osa '08 is full-fruited and spacious. Last, and delightful, is Nobile Pietra del Diavolo '06, infused with dark berry fruit and pungent underbrush, which shows luscious fruit and solid structure in the mouth.

● Brancaia Il Blu '07	♢♢♢	8
● Ilatraia '07	♢♢	7
● Brancaia Tre '07	♢♢	5
● Chianti Cl. Brancaia '07	♢	6
● Brancaia '99	♀♀♀	8
● Brancaia '98	♀♀♀	6
● Brancaia '97	♀♀♀	6
● Brancaia '94	♀♀♀	6
● Brancaia Il Blu '06	♀♀♀	7
● Brancaia Il Blu '05	♀♀♀	7
● Brancaia Il Blu '04	♀♀♀	7
● Brancaia Il Blu '03	♀♀♀	7
● Brancaia Il Blu '01	♀♀♀	7
● Brancaia Il Blu '00	♀♀♀	7

● Brunello di Montalcino Poggio del Castellare '04	♢♢	6
● Morellino di Scansano Poggio della Paura Fatt. Querciarossa '07	♢♢	4
● Nobile di Montepulciano Pietra del Diavolo Ten. Il Faggeto '06	♢♢	6
● Morellino di Scansano Rinaldone dell'Osa '08	♢	3
● Rosso di Montalcino Poggio del Castellare '07	♢	4

Brunelli - Le Chiuse di Sotto

LOC. PODERNOVONE, 157
53024 MONTALCINO [SI]
TEL. 0577849337
www.giannibrunelli.it

CELLAR SALES
PRE-BOOKED VISITS
VISITOR FACILITIES

ANNUAL PRODUCTION **35,000 bottles**
HECTARES UNDER VINE **6.3**
VITICULTURE METHOD **Conventional**

Gianni Brunelli, an impassioned lover of art and of life, passed away prematurely last year and he is still much in our thoughts. Laura, his muse and partner in life, carries on his work. The winery's vineyards are both in Montalcino but in two different locations. The original property is at Le Chiuse in the northern portion of the zone while Podernuovi lies on the southeast slope. Vinification and maturation are traditional in style, carried out in 30-hectolitre casks.

The '04 Brunello di Montalcino is impressive. The cleanly delineated nose is rich and classically varietal while spot-on, self-confident tannins power the dynamic progression and an appetizing finish. We found Rosso di Montalcino '07 somewhat disappointing. Crisp vegetal notes and floral impressions compose a fine nose, and the palate shows good, pulpy fruit, but both the palate and particularly the finale seem lacklustre. Amor Costante '05, from sangiovese and a dollop of merlot, is a constant beauty. We liked it last year and it was back on duty this year.

● Brunello di Montalcino '04	♟♟	7
● Rosso di Montalcino '07	♟	5
● Amor Costante '05	♟♟♟	6
● Amor Costante '03	♟♟	6
● Amor Costante	♟♟	5
● Brunello di Montalcino '01	♟♟	7
● Brunello di Montalcino '00	♟♟	7
● Brunello di Montalcino '99	♟♟	8
● Brunello di Montalcino '97	♟♟	7
● Brunello di Montalcino Ris. '01	♟♟	8

Bruni

FRAZ. FONTEBLANDA
LOC. LA MARTA, 6
58010 ORBETELLO [GR]
TEL. 0564885445
www.aziendabruni.it

CELLAR SALES
PRE-BOOKED VISITS

ANNUAL PRODUCTION **400,000 bottles**
HECTARES UNDER VINE **36**
VITICULTURE METHOD **Conventional**

Bruni, located in Fonteblanda on Tuscany's Maremma coast, was founded in 1974. Under the direction of brothers Marco and Moreno Bruni, it has become one of that area's most notable producers. The cellar has solved some past inconsistencies and achieved a reliable level of admirable quality, putting out well-crafted wines in a distinctive style. They have shown steady improvement and will probably continue to do so.

Morellino di Scansano Laire Riserva '07 attests to that progress. If the nose is still a trifle muffled, its development is expansive and its fruit as luscious as one would want. Perlaia '08 boasts well-developed aromas faithful to its vermentino and viognier component grapes, and it continues in the mouth firm and richly flavoured. Morellino Marteto '08 is notably supple and approachable, standing out for the refined elegance of its bouquet. Vermentino and viognier again characterize Plinio '08, while Polare '08 is a rosé from sangiovese and alicante. Both are uncomplicated but absolutely delicious.

● Morellino di Scansano Laire Ris. '07	♟♟	5
○ Vermentino Perlaia '08	♟♟	4
● Morellino di Scansano Marteto '08	♟	4
○ Plinio '08	♟	4
⊙ Polare '08	♟	4
● Morellino di Scansano Laire '04	♟♟	5
● Morellino di Scansano Laire '03	♟♟	5
● Morellino di Scansano Laire Ris. '05	♟♟	5
● Morellino di Scansano Marteto '07	♟♟	4*
● Morellino di Scansano Marteto '04	♟♟	4

Le Buche - Cantine Olivi

LOC. LE BUCHE
VIA CASELFAVA, 25
53047 SARTEANO [SI]
TEL. 0578274066
www,lebuche.eu

CELLAR SALES
PRE-BOOKED VISITS
VISITOR FACILITIES
FOOD

ANNUAL PRODUCTION 41,000 bottles
HECTARES UNDER VINE 30
VITICULTURE METHOD Conventional

Making its first appearance in our Guide is
Le Buche, owned by Giuseppe Olivi. After
restructuring the Sovana farm property into
an agriturismo, Olivi was bitten by the
winemaking bug in 1996 and purchased
the Le Buche farm, located in an area of
the Siena hills that was still little known. He
chose not to work with local grape
varieties, believing that their use was simply
customary and not indicated by any serious
study of local conditions. He preferred
instead to experiment with international
varieties, and obtained more than decent
results almost immediately.

Memento '06, a partnership of sangiovese
and syrah, offers an elegant mix of fragrant
spice and subtle oak notes, followed by a
palate with impressive volume and
complexity, concluding with a finish that is
all smooth plush. Le Buche '07, largely
sangiovese, may be fairly simple, but its
crisp nose and supple body make it an
easy-drinking pleasure. Tempore '06 is not
quite as fluid. This cabernet and merlot
blend impresses at the outset with a
refreshing nose of crisp mineral
impressions, and there is pulpy fruit aplenty
on the mid palate, but the progression
never seems to engage beyond first gear.

● Le Buche '07	♟	6
● Memento '06	♟♟	7
● Tempore '06	♟	7

Tenuta del Buonamico

LOC. CERCATOIA
VIA PROVINCIALE DI MONTECARLO, 43
55015 MONTECARLO [LU]
TEL. 058322038
www.buonamico.it

CELLAR SALES
PRE-BOOKED VISITS
VISITOR FACILITIES

ANNUAL PRODUCTION 130,000 bottles
HECTARES UNDER VINE 29
VITICULTURE METHOD Conventional

After passing last year into the hands of the
Fontanas, Tenuta del Buonamico
underwent changes in its name and in its
technical staff, but the Montecarlo-based
operation continues its role as a
benchmark quality producer in the Lucca
area. The fact that the vineyards have been
partly replanted and that a modern,
spacious tasting room-cum-kitchen has
been opened seems to presage a
strengthened presence in the market at
large, which we hope can engage the entire
Montecarlo area.

We have always considered Cercatoja a
particularly felicitous partnership of
sangiovese, cabernet and merlot. The '06
confirms the view, parading captivating
impressions of fresh greens and smooth
spices, then displaying a delicately
sculpted, linear palate of rare succulence.
The all-syrah Il Fortino '06 is also
impressive, redolent of pungent spices and
well-ripened fruit, with a well-balanced mid
palate and lengthy conclusion. Buonamico's
star, Montecarlo Rosso '08, is its usual
splendid self and demonstrates productive
continuity between the old and new
regimes. Vermentino '08 is an impeccably
crafted varietal.

● Cercatoja Rosso '06	♟♟	6
● Il Fortino Syrah '06	♟♟	6
● Montecarlo Rosso '08	♟♟	3
○ Montecarlo Bianco '08	♟	3
○ Vermentino '08	♟	4
● Cercatoja Rosso '04	♟♟	5
● Cercatoja Rosso '03	♟♟	5
● Il Fortino Syrah '03	♟♟	7
● Montecarlo Rosso '07	♟♟	3*
● Villa Lombardi '07	♟♟	4

Ca' Marcanda

LOC. SANTA TERESA, 272
57022 CASTAGNETO CARDUCCI [LI]
TEL. 0173635158
info@gajawines.com

ANNUAL PRODUCTION 390,000 bottles
HECTARES UNDER VINE 100
VITICULTURE METHOD Conventional

Angelo Gaja's winery at Castagneto Carducci is simply a marvel. Some 100 hectares are in vineyard, many surrounding the gorgeous cellar, a futuristic and graceful complex that is almost totally underground and perfectly integrated into its environment. Ca' Marcanda spreads a production of almost 400,000 bottles over three separate Bordeaux blends, all of them well able to interpret their terroir in Gaja's inimitable style, at once refined and contemporary.

Camarcanda is the winery star, a blend of merlot and cabernet sauvignon with a hand from cabernet franc. The '06 is outstanding, giving dark draughts of rich blackberry-led fruit preserve lifted by a lovely note of balsam. Imposing structure is well served by densely woven tannins and judicious acidity, although a tad more might have helped. Magari '07 is half merlot and the rest equal parts cabernet sauvignon and cabernet franc. The nose leans towards fresh garden greens, the palate fresh and juicy. Mouthwatering acidity makes this a winner. Promis '07, from merlot, syrah and sangiovese, is simpler but equally successful.

● Bolgheri Camarcanda '06	🍷🍷	8
● Magari '07	🍷🍷	7
● Promis '07	🍷🍷	6
● Bolgheri Camarcanda '01	🍷🍷🍷	8
● Bolgheri Camarcanda '05	🍷🍷	8
● Bolgheri Camarcanda '04	🍷🍷	8
● Magari '06	🍷🍷	8
● Magari '05	🍷🍷	8
● Magari '04	🍷🍷	8
● Promis '06	🍷🍷	8

Castello di Cacchiano

FRAZ. MONTI IN CHIANTI
LOC. CACCHIANO
53010 GAIOLE IN CHIANTI [SI]
TEL. 0577747018
cacchiano@chianticlassico.com

CELLAR SALES
PRE-BOOKED VISITS
VISITOR FACILITIES

ANNUAL PRODUCTION 120,000 bottles
HECTARES UNDER VINE 31
VITICULTURE METHOD Conventional

Castello di Cacchiano, owned by Giovanni Ricasoli Firidolfi, is perched on top of a promontory in Monti in Chianti that offers limitless panoramas of heart-stopping beauty, perfect for anyone wishing to taste deep the primal allure of the Chianti countryside. Of which the wines seem the perfect mirror. Delicate, whispered rather than eloquent, they cleave to a tradition and to a finesse that only sangiovese on these hills can impart. Inside, the castle's historically evocative spaces enfold imposing large and small Slavonian oak casks. A visit is worth the journey.

We were enchanted by Chianti Classico '06, a wine whose veil of simplicity opens to reveal pent-up energy and complexity. It is the Platonic idea of a Chianti Classico, offering up delicate florality and fruitiness, with hovering impressions of stony earth, and then a palate of surpassing finesse and vibrant acidity. Riserva '05 suffers from its poor year and Merlot Fontemerlano '06 also steps down a few rungs. Vin Santo del Chianti Classico '01 is stunning, fairly exploding in herbs, dried fruit and nuts and a riot of spices. The palate shows a magisterial balance between sweetness and acidity, and a rising, expansive finish.

● Chianti Cl. '06	🍷🍷	5
○ Vin Santo del Chianti Cl. '01	🍷🍷	7
● Chianti Cl. Ris. '05	🍷	6
● Fontemerlano '06	🍷	6
● Chianti Cl. '05	🍷🍷	5
● Chianti Cl. '03	🍷🍷	5
● Chianti Cl. '02	🍷🍷	4

Tenuta Le Calcinaie

LOC. SANTA LUCIA, 36
53037 SAN GIMIGNANO [SI]
TEL. 0577943007
www.tenutalecalcinaie.it

CELLAR SALES
PRE-BOOKED VISITS

ANNUAL PRODUCTION 60,000 bottles
HECTARES UNDER VINE 10
VITICULTURE METHOD Organic certified

This year brought good showings for Le Calcinaie, owned by Simone Santini, a passionate producer who succeeds in crafting wines with fascinating personalities. We believe however that there is still room for improvement in the wines, in particular as regards the nose, which at times fails to achieve the potential of which Le Calcinaie is well capable. We were unable to taste Vernaccia Riserva, one of the winery standard-bearers.

Vernaccia '08 won high marks for its medley of apple, peach and blossoms, matched by a vibrant palate of luscious fruit and a dynamic finish. Teodoro '06, from sangiovese, merlot and cabernet sauvignon in equal parts, stands out among the reds. Delectable spice introduces a velvety, well-rounded mid palate, and fine-grained tannins taper into a tasty conclusion. The new all-merlot Gabriele '06 debuts with fresh greens and overripe impressions that fail to convince, and though the palate is rich, the progression is sluggish. Chianti Colli Senesi '08 shows crisp and delicious while Santa Maria Riserva '06 has more heft and a longer finish.

La Calonica

FRAZ. VALIANO DI MONTEPULCIANO
VIA DELLA STELLA, 27
53045 MONTEPULCIANO [SI]
TEL. 0578724119
www.lacalonica.com

CELLAR SALES
PRE-BOOKED VISITS

ANNUAL PRODUCTION 120,000 bottles
HECTARES UNDER VINE 38
VITICULTURE METHOD Conventional

La Calonica can almost be said to be venerable, considering that its winemaking production dates back to 1972. You could also say that its activities are somewhat divergent, since some of its vineyards are located in the Nobile di Montepulciano denomination and the remainder in the zone of Cortona. The wine style is distinctive, leaning more in the direction of elegance than of power. The wines demonstrate a solid level of quality and at times there are real stand-outs.

Nobile di Montepulciano Riserva '05 is very appealing, with still youthful aromas and a solid, well-delineated palate. We found Cortona Sangiovese Girifalco '06 quite a good performer, its bouquet elegant and crisp-edged, and with fine fruit on a nicely multi-layered palate. Nobile di Montepulciano '06 is spirited enough but the effects of barrique-ageing are still too marked. A debut for Cortona Sangiovese Calcinaio '08 reveals a supple, crisp pleaser, ready to enjoy now, as is Rosso di Montepulciano '08. Cortona Sauvignon '08 is uncomplicated but with tasty fruit.

● Teodoro '06	▼▼	5
○ Vernaccia di S. Gimignano '08	▼▼	4*
● Chianti Colli Senesi '08	▼	4
● Chianti Colli Senesi Santa Maria Ris. '06	▼	5
● Gabriele '06	▼	4
○ Vernaccia di S. Gimignano '07	♀♀	4*
○ Vernaccia di S. Gimignano '06	♀♀	4*
○ Vernaccia di S. Gimignano V. ai Sassi '06	♀♀	4
○ Vernaccia di S. Gimignano V. ai Sassi '05	♀♀	4
○ Vernaccia di S. Gimignano V. ai Sassi '04	♀♀	4
○ Vernaccia di S. Gimignano V. ai Sassi '03	♀♀	4

● Cortona Girifalco '06	▼▼	5
● Nobile di Montepulciano Ris. '05	▼▼	6
● Cortona Sangiovese Calcinaio '08	▼	4
○ Cortona Sauvignon '08	▼	5
● Nobile di Montepulciano '06	▼	5
● Rosso di Montepulciano '08	▼	4
● Nobile di Montepulciano Ris. '04	♀♀♀	6
● Cortona Girifalco '05	♀♀	6
● Cortona Girifalco '04	♀♀	6
● Nobile di Montepulciano '03	♀♀	5

Camigliano

LOC. CAMIGLIANO
VIA D'INGRESSO, 2
53024 MONTALCINO [SI]
TEL. 0577816061
www.camigliano.it

CELLAR SALES
PRE-BOOKED VISITS
VISITOR FACILITIES

ANNUAL PRODUCTION 300,000 bottles
HECTARES UNDER VINE 92
VITICULTURE METHOD Naturale

This lovely wine estate, lying on the Maremma-facing slope of the Montalcino hill, owes its revival to the wine passion of Gualtiero and Laura Ghezzi. Their comprehensive and detailed restructuring project, which included the entire settlement, resulted in a cellar brought totally up-to-date, with modern equipment for the best possible handling of the fruit. The vineyards, some 60 hectares on silt-clay soils rich in marl and marine fossils, have also been completely replanted. Camigliano's style reflects a classical approach, utilizing 30- and 60-hectolitre casks.

The '04 is the new regime's first Brunello di Montalcino, and it's a terrific effort. We especially liked its vivacious nose, brimming with appealing impressions of cherry and black mulberry, enriched with sweet tobacco leaf. In the mouth, juicy acidity and fine tannins serve as a good foil to the power you expect from the Maremma terroir, and the finale is luscious. The international wines showed well, too. The cabernet Sant'Antimo Campo ai Mori '06 offers well-defined bell pepper, well-tensioned progression and judicious tannins. Poderuccio '07, from cabernet sauvignon, merlot and sangiovese, is spacious and long-lived.

● Brunello di Montalcino '04	TT	6
● Poderuccio '07	TT	4*
● Sant'Antimo Cabernet Sauvignon Campo ai Mori '06	TT	5
● Rosso di Montalcino '07	T	4
● Brunello di Montalcino '03	YY	6
● Brunello di Montalcino '99	YY	6
● Brunello di Montalcino '98	YY	6
● Brunello di Montalcino Gualto '99	YY	8
● Poderuccio '02	YY	4
● Sant'Antimo Cabernet Sauvignon '02	YY	5
● Sant'Antimo Cabernet Sauvignon '01	YY	4

Campo alla Sughera

LOC. CACCIA AL PIANO, 280
57020 BOLGHERI [LI]
TEL. 0565766936
www.campoallasughera.com

CELLAR SALES
PRE-BOOKED VISITS

ANNUAL PRODUCTION 90,000 bottles
HECTARES UNDER VINE 16.25
VITICULTURE METHOD Conventional

Campo alla Sughera, having now completed a decade of history, has strengthened its role as one of the most consistently high-quality producers in the Bolgheri area. The Knauf firm has poured considerable investment into this operation, and the winery is still growing vigorously in terms of staff, technicians and marketing. You can always rely on the high quality of the wines, year in year out. The bottlings are characterized by good, full body and dynamic progression, qualities they derive from their local terroir.

Bolgheri Superiore Arnione '06, the winery's iconic label, won its first Three Glass award. The senses revel in a complex, multi-faceted array of red berry fruit and spice, teased with pungent balsam, followed by enthralling opulence in the mouth and a near-endless finale. The outstanding Adeo '07 demonstrates the quality of the line in general. After refreshing notes of fresh greens, it lays out taut progression and a refined tannic weave. The whites are as good as usual, and Achenio '08 finally gains the tangy acidic grip that stands up to its juicy heft.

● Bolgheri Superiore Arnione '06	TTT	7
● Bolgheri Rosso Adeo '07	TT	5
○ Bolgheri Bianco Achenio '08	T	5
● Bolgheri Rosso Adeo '06	YY	5
● Bolgheri Superiore Arnione '05	YY	7
● Bolgheri Superiore Arnione '04	YY	7

Campogiovanni

FRAZ. SANT'ANGELO IN COLLE
LOC. CAMPOGIOVANNI
53020 MONTALCINO [SI]
TEL. 0577844001
www.agricolasanfelice.it

CELLAR SALES
PRE-BOOKED VISITS

ANNUAL PRODUCTION **80,000 bottles**
HECTARES UNDER VINE **20**
VITICULTURE METHOD **Conventional**

Campogiovanni, a subsidiary of the Chianti zone's well-known Agricola San Felice, has completed over the past few years the replanting of its vineyards at a very high density of 7,500 vines per hectare. This figure was dictated by the soils prevalent in the southwest sector of the Montalcino hill, largely silt-sand with a high proportion of clay, which makes them quite cool, despite the vineyard's aspect and its elevation of about 300 metre. Fermentations are in steel, with macerations lasting about 20 days, and the wines are aged in various-sized Slavonian oak casks.

Brunello di Montalcino Il Quercione Riserva '03 was most impressive, not least because it is a selection from a vineyard block that seemed to shrug off the tremendous heat of 2003. Delicious fruit and morello cherry, both fresh and in preserve, meld temptingly with classic sweet tobacco leaf while alcohol, acidity and tannins are equally well intertwined, and launch an expansive finish. Brunello di Montalcino '04 is also impressive. Rich, well-ripened fruit is a pleasure on the nose, as is the taut energy in the mouth, although the tannins still need to unwind somewhat.

● Brunello di Montalcino '04	♟♟	7
● Brunello di Montalcino Il Quercione Ris. '03	♟♟	8
● Rosso di Montalcino '07	♟	4
● Brunello di Montalcino '01	♟♟	7
● Brunello di Montalcino '99	♟♟	7
● Brunello di Montalcino '97	♟♟	7

Canalicchio - Franco Pacenti

LOC. CANALICCHIO DI SOPRA, 6
53024 MONTALCINO [SI]
TEL. 0577849277
www.canalicchiofrancopacenti.it

CELLAR SALES
PRE-BOOKED VISITS

ANNUAL PRODUCTION **30,000 bottles**
HECTARES UNDER VINE **10**
VITICULTURE METHOD **Conventional**

his winery is as classic as they come, located in the equally classic Canalicchi subzone north of the town of Montalcino, on the road to Buonconvento. It lies in a changeover zone between clay-rich soils and medium-textured schist and sandstone. Some ten hectares of vineyard, dedicated to Brunello, are planted at a density of about 4,000 vines per hectare near the winery, at about 300 metres' elevation. Macerations on the skin last more than 15 days, and the wines age in medium-size Slavonian oak casks.

Brunello di Montalcino '04 is a stand-out, classic in style and very reflective of this northern area of Montalcino. A medium-dense ruby introduces well-edged aromas of strawberry-tree fruit, Virginia tobacco and crisp, bright cherry. The palate is elegantly crafted, showing supple tannins and a magisterial, focused development, concluding with absolutely fabulous length. Less impressive is Rosso di Montalcino '07 but the price is certainly right. Varietally faithful aromas alternate tobacco, peach and cherry while the tannins, though not bitter, are a tad exuberant.

● Brunello di Montalcino '04	♟♟♟	6
● Rosso di Montalcino '07	♟	5
● Brunello di Montalcino '01	♟♟	6
● Brunello di Montalcino '00	♟♟	6*
● Brunello di Montalcino '99	♟♟	6*
● Brunello di Montalcino Ris. '93	♟♟	5

Canalicchio di Sopra

LOC. CASACCIA, 73
53024 MONTALCINO [SI]
TEL. 0577848316
www.canalicchiodisopra.com

CELLAR SALES
PRE-BOOKED VISITS
VISITOR FACILITIES

ANNUAL PRODUCTION **55,000 bottles**
HECTARES UNDER VINE **15**
VITICULTURE METHOD **Conventional**

The family-run Canalicchio di Sopra winery exhibits the classic stamp of a Montalcino-area producer. A closely focused philosophy is based on uncompromising quality in the vineyard and cellar practices fine-tuned to bring out the best from the fruit. The style can best be described as lean and austere, utilizing fairly lengthy macerations and 30 to 50-hectolitre casks. Some five hectares are dedicated to Brunello, planted on largely clay soils lightened by a substantial proportion of galestro. This is typical of the Canalicchi subzone on the northern Montalcino hillslope, a very distinctive area.

A finely turned-out Brunello di Montalcino '04 needs a few moments' rest, but then flaunts gorgeous morello, crisp blackberry and pungent hints of medicinal herbs. A tangy acidity enlivens already supple tannins and the finish commands full respect for its sharp definition and impressive length. Rosso di Montalcino '07 begins with compelling floral and fruit impressions but ultimately falls victim to drying tannins. Brunello di Montalcino Riserva '03 shows bitterish tannins and a lack of balance.

Capanna

LOC. CAPANNA, 333
53024 MONTALCINO [SI]
TEL. 0577848298
www.capannamontalcino.com

CELLAR SALES
PRE-BOOKED VISITS

ANNUAL PRODUCTION **70,000 bottles**
HECTARES UNDER VINE **19**
VITICULTURE METHOD **Conventional**

Capanna certainly figures as one of Montalcino's historic producers, since Giuseppe Cencioni was one of the founding members of the Consorzio del Brunello and Capanna's first bottlings go back to the 1960s. Another Cencioni, consortium president Patrizio, has been at the helm for quite some time now. The winery is located in the northern sector of the Montalcino zone, near Montesoli, and the cellar has recently been updated and enlarged. Winemaking practices hew closely to tradition, with fermentations in wood vats and ageing in large-size Slavonian oak casks.

Brunello di Montalcino '04 is superlative, a step forward from the somewhat muddled noses that bedevilled the wines in the past. Here instead we have rich draughts of morello cherry and blueberry fruit, with a nice, ripe note of blackberry as well. Improved delineation is observable in the mouth too, with a smooth weave of fine-grained tannins that eschew obstreperousness. The finish is spacious and long-lingering. Rosso di Montalcino '07 is tasty, showing lovely florality with hints of fresh grass, then succulent fruit, which however does get nipped off a bit at the end by some drying tannins.

● Brunello di Montalcino '04	♟♟♟ 7
● Brunello di Montalcino Ris. '03	♟ 8
● Rosso di Montalcino '07	♟ 5
● Brunello di Montalcino Ris. '01	♟♟♟ 8
● Brunello di Montalcino '01	♟♟ 6
● Brunello di Montalcino '00	♟♟ 6
● Brunello di Montalcino '99	♟♟ 8
● Brunello di Montalcino Ris. '99	♟♟ 7
● Rosso di Montalcino '06	♟♟ 5

● Brunello di Montalcino '04	♟♟ 6
● Rosso di Montalcino '07	♟ 4
● Brunello di Montalcino Ris. '90	♟♟♟ 6
● Brunello di Montalcino Ris. '01	♟♟ 8
● Brunello di Montalcino Ris. '99	♟♟ 8
● Sant'Antimo Rosso Capanna '01	♟♟ 5

Tenuta Caparzo

LOC. CAPARZO
S.P. DEL BRUNELLO
53024 MONTALCINO [SI]
TEL. 0577848390
www.caparzo.it

CELLAR SALES
PRE-BOOKED VISITS
VISITOR FACILITIES

ANNUAL PRODUCTION **455,000 bottles**
HECTARES UNDER VINE **80**
VITICULTURE METHOD **Conventional**

It is truly a wonder to behold the enthusiasm with which Elisabetta Gnudi is rationalizing and updating Caparzo, which has always enjoyed a position of prestige in the market and been a fine ambassador of Montalcino. There have been new purchases in the Sesta area, where a new vineyard has just been planted, and older vineyards in the areas of Montosoli and Castelgiocondo have been replanted. Structural improvements have been made in the cellar too, and in the barrel room, all in the name of even better wine quality.

Brunello di Montalcino La Casa '04 returns as best of team again this year. It displays intriguing white cherry notes, backgrounded by subtle balsam and spring blossoms. Not a huge wine, it is characterized by judicious breadth in the mouth, animated by vibrant acidity, plus fine length. With impeccable elegance, it is clearly terroir-driven, attesting to its source in the vineyards on the Montosoli hill in northern Montalcino. Rosso di Montalcino La Caduta '06 is as dependable as always. Despite an overbearing presence of oak notes on the nose and palate, progression flows along unimpeded, supple and succulent.

Tenuta di Capezzana

LOC. SEANO
VIA CAPEZZANA, 100
59015 CARMIGNANO [PO]
TEL. 0558706005
www.capezzana.it

CELLAR SALES
PRE-BOOKED VISITS

ANNUAL PRODUCTION **600,000 bottles**
HECTARES UNDER VINE **106**
VITICULTURE METHOD **Conventional**

Capezzana is an illustrious example of how effective family management can be. Conte Ugo Contini Bonacossi, one of the moving spirits behind the denomination, provides overall guidance while daughter Beatrice, who is current head of the consortium, directs sales and marketing, assisted by niece Serena. Finally, Filippo tends the vines and Benedetta the cellar. The result is outstanding quality in all areas, plus a synergistic enthusiasm poured into myriad special events and activities on a wine estate that certainly doesn't show its age of more than 1,200 years.

Carmignano Villa di Capezzana '06 never disappoints, nor did it this year. The gorgeous ruby announces a multi-faceted bouquet of wild blackberry preserves interwoven with a delicate vein of spice and evolved notes. That complexity is displayed as well on the entry, throughout the progression and into a well-rounded finish. No less admirable are the other labels, in particular Ghiaie della Furba '05, from cabernet sauvignon, merlot and syrah, and that sweet siren, Vin Santo '03. Trebbiano '06 shows rich and appealing, with perhaps just a shade too much oak.

● Brunello di Montalcino La Casa '04	♟♟	8
● Rosso di Montalcino La Caduta '06	♟♟	5
● Brunello di Montalcino '04	♟	7
● Rosso di Montalcino '07	♟	5
● Brunello di Montalcino La Casa '93	♟♟♟	7
● Brunello di Montalcino La Casa '88	♟♟♟	7
● Brunello di Montalcino '03	♟♟	7
● Brunello di Montalcino Ris. '99	♟♟	8
● Rosso Caparzo '07	♟♟	4*

● Carmignano Villa di Capezzana '06	♟♟	5
● Carmignano Villa di Trefiano '05	♟♟	6
● Ghiaie della Furba '05	♟♟	6
○ Trebbiano '06	♟♟	5
○ Vin Santo di Carmignano Ris. '03	♟♟	6
● Barco Reale '07	♟	4
● Carmignano Villa di Capezzana '05	♟♟♟	5
● Carmignano Villa di Capezzana '99	♟♟♟	6
● Ghiaie della Furba '01	♟♟♟	6
● Ghiaie della Furba '98	♟♟♟	5
● Ghiaie della Furba '04	♟♟	6
● Ghiaie della Furba '03	♟♟	6
○ Trebbiano '05	♟♟	5
○ Trebbiano '04	♟♟	5
○ Vin Santo di Carmignano Ris. '02	♟♟	6
○ Vin Santo di Carmignano Ris. '01	♟♟	6

Capua Winery

LOC. PIAN D'ARTINO 21
58014 MANCIANO [GR]
TEL. 0564601032
www.capuawinery.net

PRE-BOOKED VISITS

ANNUAL PRODUCTION **13,000 bottles**
HECTARES UNDER VINE **6**
VITICULTURE METHOD **Conventional**

The Capua Winery is owned by a young Milanese lawyer who gave up his practice to focus completely on wine. Riccardo Capua founded his business in 2002 and it has become one of the most ambitious winemaking projects to be found in Maremma. The winery near Saturnia is uncompromising in conception so that means high-density vineyards and state-of-the-art cellars. The result is a range of decidedly well-made wines with their own personal style.

We were impressed by the cabernet franc Fiammante '07, with its spot-on aromas and smooth, expansive palate. Just as good is Miosogno '07, a pure Alicante, with intense spice aromas and striking acidic verve that enhances the wine's freshness and depth. The sangiovese Tutto Cuore '07 is appealing, with plenty of character on the palate but a few nose issues to be resolved. The Chardonnay Dolcemore '08 is simple but well made.

Podere Il Carnasciale

LOC. PODERE IL CARNASCIALE
52020 MERCATALE VALDARNO [AR]
TEL. 0559911142

ANNUAL PRODUCTION **7,000 bottles**
HECTARES UNDER VINE **2.5**
VITICULTURE METHOD **Conventional**

This unique wine is in a class of its own and that may be why it's so popular with aficionados looking for out-of-the-ordinary products. Caberlot produced by Bettina Rogosky is feels the effects of its growing year, of course, but its personality never wavers. Over the last few years, the two-hectare estate has also been producing Carnasciale, a sort of second label that enables stricter bunch selection of the caberlot, the name given to the grape by Bettina's husband, Wolf Rogosky.

The '06 Caberlot made the finals – it always does – thanks to a heady, very complex aromatic profile. There are hints of exotic curry and ginger spice, strong aromatic herbs like tarragon and thyme, underpinned by delicate fruit, and pleasing chocolate nuances to close. The well-sustained body is powerful on the palate but without excess, the finesse of the tannins and the positive freshness of the acidity holding everything in place. The finish is layered and lingering.

● Fiammante '07	♟♟ 6
● Miosogno '07	♟♟ 6
○ Dolcemore '08	♟ 6
● Tutto Cuore '07	♟ 5

● Caberlot '06	♟♟ 8
● Caberlot '05	♟♟♟ 8
● Caberlot '04	♟♟♟ 8
● Caberlot '00	♟♟♟ 8

Fattoria Carpineta Fontalpino

FRAZ. MONTAPERTI
LOC. CARPINETA
53019 CASTELNUOVO BERARDENGA [SI]
TEL. 0577369219
www.carpinotafontalpino.it

CELLAR SALES
PRE-BOOKED VISITS
VISITOR FACILITIES

ANNUAL PRODUCTION **100,000 bottles**
HECTARES UNDER VINE **19**
VITICULTURE METHOD **Organic certified**

Capineta Fontalpino is owned by Filippo and Gioia Cresti, the latter an established oenologist with experience as a consultant for producers all over Italy. The winery is in the municipality Montaperti in the province of Siena, bordering on the southern edge of Chianti Classico. The terrain, located at an elevation of 230 to 380 metres, comprises mixed clayey sands with lots of gravel. The wines have a modern character that emphasizes the intense fruit found here, combined with the traits derived from the use of small casks.

Do Ut Des won its first Three Glasses for the '07 vintage of this cabernet sauvignon, merlot and sangiovese blend. The bouquet is a concentration of red and black berries with explicit oaky notes leading into a succulent, compact and nicely tannic palate. The excellent Chianti Classico Fontalpino '07 is fleshy and enfolding with ripe, warm hints, but never loses momentum. The firm, well-structured Riserva di Chianti Classico '06 has plenty of lingering oak.

Casa al Vento

LOC. CASA AL VENTO
53013 GAIOLE IN CHIANTI [SI]
TEL. 0577749485
www.borgocasaalvento.com

CELLAR SALES
PRE-BOOKED VISITS

ANNUAL PRODUCTION **30,000 bottles**
HECTARES UNDER VINE **4**
VITICULTURE METHOD **Organic certified**

The Casa al Vento winery is named after the village where it is located, a quaint, charming nook in the municipality of Gaiole. The estate is the brainchild of its resolute owners Ria and Pino Gioffreda, whose operation includes accommodation, a spa, restaurant and, of course, wine. They are in close contact with nature, made closer by their organic farming policy. The reds age in barrique, retaining a convincing style without going over the top.

The top-notch Chianti Classico Aria '07 is a pure sangiovese nuanced with citrus and spice that weave into an easy-going palate, rich in contrast and with great depth, supported by nice acid backbone. Two other success stories are the Chianti Classico Riserva Foho '06, a sangiovese topped up with merlot, which has lots of ripe berry fruits, great consistency and a pleasant, refined palate, and a Gaiolè '06, with notes of black berry fruit and greens on the nose leading into an elegant, nicely dynamic palate with confident progression.

Wine		
● Do Ut Des '07	♟♟♟	6
● Chianti Cl. Ris. '06	♟♟	6
● Chianti Cl. Fontalpino '07	♟♟	4
● Do Ut Des '06	♟♟	6
● Do Ut Des '05	♟♟	6
● Do Ut Des '04	♟♟	6
● Dofana '06	♟♟	8
● Dofana '04	♟♟	8

Wine		
● Chianti Cl. Aria '07	♟♟	4*
● Chianti Cl. Foho Ris. '06	♟♟	5
● Gaiolè '06	♟♟	5
○ Vin Santo del Chianti Classico '01	♟	6

Casa alle Vacche

FRAZ. PANCOLE
LOC. LUCIGNANO, 73A
53037 SAN GIMIGNANO [SI]
TEL. 0577955103
www.casaallevacche.it

CELLAR SALES
PRE-BOOKED VISITS

ANNUAL PRODUCTION **120,000 bottles**
HECTARES UNDER VINE **21.5**
VITICULTURE METHOD **Conventional**

The Ciappi family's wines made a good impression. They are quality products, a fine expression of their territory, and offer good value for money, which naturally makes them popular with consumers. Over 20 hectares of vines are mainly given over to vernaccia, which is the key wine, released in various versions to keep all aficionados of the grape happy.

The Vernaccia Riserva '07 Crocus has an enjoyable nose, with notes of citrus and aromatic herbs, with excellent continuity and an intriguing finish. The less austere Vernaccia '08 is a gem, with lively, fruit-rich aromas and a fresh palate with that finishes on florality. We thought the best red was an Aglieno '07 sangiovese and merlot blend, with a nose profile of black berry fruit and solid, poised body with a well-balanced, savoury finish. The Colli Senesi Riserva Cinabro '06 is rather craggy and clenched but delicious nonetheless, and the tasty Merlot '08 is fresh and enjoyable.

Casa Emma

LOC. CORTINE
S.P. DI CASTELLINA IN CHIANTI, 3
50021 BARBERINO VAL D'ELSA [FI]
TEL. 0558072239
www.casaemma.com

CELLAR SALES
PRE-BOOKED VISITS

ANNUAL PRODUCTION **85,000 bottles**
HECTARES UNDER VINE **21**
VITICULTURE METHOD **Conventional**

Casa Emma, on the San Donato in Poggio hillside at over 400 metres in altitude, was acquired by the Bucalossi family in the 1970s from the Florentine noblewoman Emma Bizzarri. There are 21 hectares of vines and olives, as well as a botanical garden that surrounds the family's farmhouse and cellars. The wines have a modern feel and are aged in small French oak barrels, achieving a very distinctive style.

The Chianti Classico '07 is excellent, despite a slight aromatic haziness that settles quickly, and unfolds lovely red and black berry nuances, hints of blossom and a touch of almond. The palate is still very young, with a tannic weave that is seeking greater precision, but overall we think it will evolve nicely in bottle, given the body and richness of the fruit. The pure merlot Soloìo '06 is sound, the clenched, mouth-drying Riserva '06 less so.

● Aglieno '07	¶¶ 4*
○ Vernaccia di S. Gimignano '08	¶¶ 2*
○ Vernaccia di S. Gimignano Crocus Ris. '07	¶¶ 4*
● Chianti Colli Senesi Cinabro Ris. '06	¶ 4
● Merlot '08	¶ 4
○ Vernaccia di S. Gimignano I Macchioni '08	¶ 4
● Aglieno '06	¶¶ 4*
● Chianti Colli Senesi Cinabro Ris. '05	¶¶ 4*
○ Vernaccia di S. Gimignano '07	¶¶ 2*
○ Vernaccia di S. Gimignano Crocus Ris. '06	¶¶ 4*
○ Vernaccia di S. Gimignano I Macchioni '07	¶¶ 4*

● Chianti Cl. '07	¶¶ 4
● Soloìo '06	¶¶ 7
● Chianti Cl. Ris. '06	¶ 6
● Chianti Cl. '06	¶¶ 4*
● Chianti Cl. Ris. '05	¶¶ 6
● Chianti Cl. Ris. '04	¶¶ 6
● Chianti Cl. Ris. '03	¶¶ 6
● Soloìo '05	¶¶ 7
● Soloìo '04	¶¶ 7
● Soloìo '01	¶¶ 8
● Soloìo '00	¶¶ 6

Casale - Falchini

VIA DI CASALE, 40
53037 SAN GIMIGNANO [SI]
TEL. 0577941305
www.falchini.com

CELLAR SALES
PRE-BOOKED VISITS

ANNUAL PRODUCTION 350,000 bottles
HECTARES UNDER VINE 35
VITICULTURE METHOD Conventional

Riccardo Falchini, a Florentine entrepreneur who decided a while back to make his wine at San Gimignano, brought his cellar back into the Guide with a great performance. Riccardo was one of the first to see the potential of the local reds and has an ongoing love story with the signature vernaccia grape. Riccardo even began working on vineyard selections some time ago and also uses vernaccia to make a classic method sparkler.

We received several labels and noted a first-class Vernaccia Ab Vinea Doni '07. Elegant aromas of spring flowers, fruit and almonds accompany a full, solid body with a lingering finish. The soft-textured, smooth Riserva Vigna Solatio '07 differs in style, with vanilla and spice nuances on the nose and a refreshing acidic backbone. The Vin Santo '02 has a traditional nose followed by with a fleshy, velvet-smooth front palate and a sweet finish. Paretaio '05, from sangiovese with a hint of merlot, is also intriguing. The rest are well typed, with the cabernet sauvignon-heavy Campora '04 revealing notable opulence.

Fattoria Le Casalte

FRAZ. SANT'ALBINO
VIA DEL TERMINE, 2
53045 MONTEPULCIANO [SI]
TEL. 0578798246
www.lecasalte.com

CELLAR SALES
PRE-BOOKED VISITS

ANNUAL PRODUCTION 50,000 bottles
HECTARES UNDER VINE 13
VITICULTURE METHOD Conventional

Fattoria Le Casalte, currently managed by Chiara Barioffi, was purchased by her father as a country home in 1975. It was only years later, in the mid 1990s, that the estate began operating as a winery. The quality route was preferred right from the start, although we noticed that results didn't really start appearing until recently. The production philosophy aims to express the most typical traits of the local territory.

Le Casalte's most iconic wine is undoubtedly the Nobile Quercetonda selection. We tasted an '06 with austere aromas of red berries, blossom and wet earth, following through compact and very long, with tannins that are already smooth. The subtle, well-balanced Nobile di Montepulciano '06 has more immediate impact. Rosso di Montepulciano '07 is smooth and quaffable, with a delicate, alluring nose. We enjoyed the Rosso Toscano '07, a sangiovese and canaiolo blend and the white Celius '08, a trebbiano, malvasia and grechetto blend, is also agreeable.

● Paretaio '05	ŶŶ 6
○ Vernaccia di S. Gimignano Ab Vinea Doni '07	ŶŶ 5
○ Vernaccia di S. Gimignano V. a Solatio Ris. '07	ŶŶ 5
○ Vin Santo del Chianti '02	ŶŶ 5
● Campora '04	Ŷ 7
● Chianti Colli Senesi Titolato '08	Ŷ 4
○ Falchini Brut '05	Ŷ 5
○ Vernaccia di S. Gimignano V. a Solatio '08	Ŷ 4

● Nobile di Montepulciano Quercetonda '06	ŶŶŶ 6
● Nobile di Montepulciano '06	ŶŶ 5
○ Celius '08	Ŷ 3
○ Rosso di Montepulciano '07	Ŷ 4
● Rosso Toscano '07	Ŷ 3
● Nobile di Montepulciano Quercetonda '04	♀♀ 6
● Nobile di Montepulciano Quercetonda '03	♀♀ 5
● Rosso Toscano '06	♀♀ 2*
○ Vin Santo '97	♀♀ 5

Casanova della Spinetta

LOC. CASANOVA
56030 TERRICCIOLA [PI]
TEL. 0587690508
www.la-spinetta.com

PRE-BOOKED VISITS

ANNUAL PRODUCTION 150,000 bottles
HECTARES UNDER VINE 65
VITICULTURE METHOD Conventional

The Rivetti family's Tuscan venture is starting to yield significant results. After a lifetime of dealing with moscato, nebbiolo and barbera, it can't have been easy to tackle sangiovese, but characteristic Rivetti determination and temperament ensured their mission was successful. There are 65 hectares under vine and they produce 150,000 bottles a year.

We tasted three wines this year. A Gentile di Casanova '05, from sangiovese, known here as prugnolo gentile, which gives a good, medium-intense garnet. There are crisp, pervasive notes of red berries on the nose and a savoury, juicy, long-lingering palate. It's not a huge wine but very drinkable. In the all-colorino Colorino di Casanova '05, spice prevails over the fruit on the nose, and a solid, round, richly-extracted palate is only slightly clenched by oak-derived tannins. Nero di Casanova '07, a sangiovese with five per cent colorino, has a pervasive nose of balsamic and black fruit followed by a feisty palate that sets acidity off against extract.

★ Casanova di Neri

POD. FIESOLE
53024 MONTALCINO [SI]
TEL. 0577834455
www.casanovadineri.com

CELLAR SALES
PRE-BOOKED VISITS

ANNUAL PRODUCTION 225,000 bottles
HECTARES UNDER VINE 55
VITICULTURE METHOD Conventional

Giacomo Neri's Montalcino winery is one of the most famous in the world. A first-rate, efficient cellar, completely underground, with a view that ranges from Montalcino to Siena, vineyards on various slopes in the district, and an estate philosophy whose mission is to obtain the best possible grapes. The cellars have an assortment of different-sized casks from various kinds of wood. The wines have a modern style, seeking the most extreme style perfection. Colours are intense and nose profiles impeccable, thanks to significant extract.

Another great selection from Casanova di Neri includes a flawless Brunello di Montalcino Cerretalto '04, with a layered, expansive nose of red berries and spicy, balsamic notes. The lengthy, compact palate is tannic yet restrained and more refined than ever. There's the '04 Brunello di Montalcino Tenuta Nuova, the most persuasive so far, with intense, compelling cherry and blackberry perceptions on the nose that keep the oak in place. Relaxed tannins accompany well-sustained acidity, assuring an intense, well-rounded finish. We liked the Brunello di Montalcino '04. It's a little more classic in style, with sweet tobacco and wild cherry jam.

● Il Colorino di Casanova '05	♥♥ 5
● Il Gentile di Casanova '05	♥♥ 6
● Il Nero di Casanova '07	♥♥ 5

● Brunello di Montalcino Cerretalto '04	♥♥♥+ 8
● Brunello di Montalcino Tenuta Nuova '04	♥♥ 8
● Brunello di Montalcino '04	♥♥ 7
● Pietradonice '06	♥♥ 8
● Rosso di Montalcino '07	♥ 5
● Brunello di Montalcino '00	♥♥♥ 6
● Brunello di Montalcino Cerretalto '01	♥♥♥ 8
● Brunello di Montalcino Cerretalto '99	♥♥♥ 8
● Brunello di Montalcino Cerretalto '95	♥♥♥ 8
● Brunello di Montalcino Tenuta Nuova '01	♥♥♥ 7
● Brunello di Montalcino Tenuta Nuova '99	♥♥♥ 7
● Brunello di Montalcino Tenuta Nuova '97	♥♥♥ 7
● Pietradonice '05	♥♥♥ 8
● Sant'Antimo Pietradonice '01	♥♥♥ 8
● Sant'Antimo Pietradonice '00	♥♥♥ 8

Casavyc

POD. CAMPOROMANO, 43
58054 SCANSANO [GR]
TEL. 3356880673
www.casavyc.it

CELLAR SALES

ANNUAL PRODUCTION **30,000 bottles**
HECTARES UNDER VINE **8**
VITICULTURE METHOD **Naturale**

Viviana Filocamo's Casavyc winery, which opened in 2004, is located in the Poggioferro area of Scansano, making it yet another newcomer to the hectic Maremma winemaking scenario. The Casavyc viticulture mission focuses not only on modern, high-density vineyards but also on recovering and cultivating very old vines to ensure that wines acquire the right level of complexity and are able to express the territory's most deep-rooted, unique traits.

We're keen on the SY unocinquantasei '07. This pure Syrah, cask-aged for 12 months, has very complex aromas, nicely offset by the palate, where the wine is juicy and well-rounded. The '07 Morellino di Scansano 070707 is another winner, with rich, distinctive aromas and a lively, well-sustained palate. The Morellino di Scansano '08 has one or two aromatic hiccoughs. We think its best features are on the tasty, fresh palate.

● SY unocinquantasei '07	▼▼ 8
● Morellino di Scansano 070707 '07	▼▼ 7
● Morellino di Scansano '08	▼ 5

Castell'in Villa

LOC. CASTELL'IN VILLA
53019 CASTELNUOVO BERARDENGA [SI]
TEL. 0577359074
www.castellinvilla.com

CELLAR SALES
PRE-BOOKED VISITS

ANNUAL PRODUCTION **100,000 bottles**
HECTARES UNDER VINE **54**
VITICULTURE METHOD **Conventional**

This is one of the most fascinating, enigmatic wineries in Castelnuovo Berardenga and indeed all Chianti Classico. Each wine is imbued with the territory's traits. The owner Coralia Pignatelli is a self-taught grower, a lady who can be as engagingly solicitous as she can be retiring and elusive when the mood takes her. There's no doubt about her love for sangiovese, the authentic wines it yields and her estate at Castell'in Villa, which she bought in the late 1960s. Actually, Coralia's wines are a mirror of her character. They are obtained by low-key, minimum intervention methods, including the use of native yeasts, casks of different sizes and lengthy bottle ageing.

Coralia Pugnatelli doesn't stick to timetables when presenting her wines so they arrive only when she thinks they are ready to express themselves to the full, not when the trade says they should be. This year, we have a Chianti Classico '05 and a Riserva '04. The former has fresh aromas of red berries, medicinal herbs and dried flowers. The taut, honed palate has acidity to the fore driving the flavour, and spiky but well-extracted tannins. The Riserva has more forward notes on the nose, with the fruit ripening into jam, and herbs making way for pipe tobacco and freshly cut hay. The open, mouth-caressing palate is in the same style.

● Chianti Cl. Castell'in Villa '05	▼▼ 6
● Chianti Cl. Ris. '04	▼▼ 7
● Chianti Cl. Ris. '85	▼▼▼ 4
● Chianti Cl. Ris. '95	▼▼ 5

Castellani

FRAZ. SANTA LUCIA
56025 PONTEDERA [PI]
TEL. 0587292900
www.castelwine.com

CELLAR SALES
PRE-BOOKED VISITS

ANNUAL PRODUCTION **626.800 bottles**
HECTARES UNDER VINE **250**
VITICULTURE METHOD **Conventional**

Over the years, the Castellani family built up a veritable collection of estates in the Pisa hills, skirting Maremma and on into Chianti Classico. The operation has four properties for a total vineyard holding of 250 hectares but there are also almost 800 hectares farmed by growers who deliver fruit. Each branch has its own winemaking and ageing cellar so that the freshness of the grapes and quality of the end products are guaranteed.

We liked them all. The Burchino Rosso '06, a sangiovese, cabernet sauvignon and merlot mix from the Terricciola cellars, is an intense, well-balanced wine, with brisk fruit on a nose nuanced with oak, followed up by the lingering aromatics on the palate. The pervasive, savoury Poggio al Casone '06 is a sangiovese and syrah blend from the Crespina cellars and shows excellent progression in the mouth. The same goes for Travalda '06, from cabernet sauvignon, cabernet franc and petit verdot, which has fragrant vegetality and spicy hints partnering a round, harmonious structure. The Chianti '08, from the Antica Cantina di Ceppaiano, is good.

★ Castellare di Castellina

LOC. CASTELLARE
53011 CASTELLINA IN CHIANTI [SI]
TEL. 0577742903
www.castellare.it

CELLAR SALES
PRE-BOOKED VISITS

ANNUAL PRODUCTION **180,000 bottles**
HECTARES UNDER VINE **24**
VITICULTURE METHOD **Conventional**

Publisher Paolo Panerai's magnificent estate in the heart of Chianti Classico is set in a sort of natural amphitheatre facing south east. The location, in the municipality of Castellina, is at an average elevation of over 350 metres, where the plots have excellent exposure and are characterized by soil that the terrain mix of porous galestro and marl with a little clay. The winery and its cellars, with the barriques used to age the wines, are expertly managed by Alessandro Cellai.

The flagship wine is I Sodi di San Niccolò, from sangioveto – as sangiovese is called here – with a dash of malvasia. Even the 2005 vintage has exceptional class and elegance, with a blaze of berry fruits nuanced with violets on a nose delicately interwoven with spice. The immediately pervasive palate has great depth and a long, lingering finish. Another impressive wine is the complex, refined Riserva di Chianti Classico Vigna il Poggiale '06, with its lovely extract. The crisp, tasty Chianti Classico '07 is also excellent, giving sour cherry and sweet almonds.

● Chianti L'Antico di Burchino '07	♟♟ 4
● Chianti Sup. Poggio al Casone '06	♟♟ 3*
● Il Burchino '06	♟♟ 4
● Poggio al Casone '06	♟♟ 4*
● Travalda '06	♟♟ 4
● Chianti Antica Cantina di Ceppaiano '08	♟ 4

● I Sodi di San Niccolò '05	♟♟♟+ 8
● Chianti Cl. V. il Poggiale Ris. '06	♟♟ 6
● Chianti Cl. '07	♟♟ 4*
● Chianti Cl. Ris. '06	♟ 5
● Coniale '05	♟ 7
● Chianti Cl. V. il Poggiale Ris. '01	♟♟♟ 6
● Chianti Cl. V. il Poggiale Ris. '00	♟♟♟ 6
● Chianti Cl. V. il Poggiale Ris. '97	♟♟♟ 6
● I Sodi di San Niccolò '04	♟♟♟ 8
● I Sodi di San Niccolò '03	♟♟♟ 8
● I Sodi di San Niccolò '02	♟♟♟ 8
● I Sodi di San Niccolò '01	♟♟♟ 8
● I Sodi di San Niccolò '98	♟♟♟ 8
● I Sodi di San Niccolò '97	♟♟♟ 8
● I Sodi di San Niccolò '95	♟♟♟ 8

La Castellina

LOC. FERROZZOLA, 1
53011 CASTELLINA IN CHIANTI [SI]
TEL. 0577740454
www.lacastellina.it

CELLAR SALES
PRE-BOOKED VISITS
VISITOR FACILITIES

ANNUAL PRODUCTION 175,000 bottles
HECTARES UNDER VINE 36
VITICULTURE METHOD Organic certified

The winery, in the medieval village of Castellina in Chianti, is owned by Monica Targioni and Tommaso Bojola, who produce large numbers of bottles and a range of labels. One of the latter is dedicated to the Squarcialupi family, the first proprietors of the estate when was founded in the 11th century and who also gave their name to the palazzo where the winery is located. Down in the cellars, the wines age in large casks of Slavonian oak barrels and in some cases in medium-sized French barrels. The vineyards are very close to the village.

Our favourite was the Chianti Classico '07 and even if its aromatics aren't quick off the mark, they develop positively and follow through very well. The fruit is sweet and quite fleshy as the flavours combine nicely with a pinprick of acidity that rolls into a tasty finish. We also like the Chianti Classico Riserva Squarcialupi '06, which has quite a rounded, velvety style, and minerally balsamic nuances. We'd also recommend the Vin Santo del Chianti Classico '05, which has just the right amount of acidity, and the Vin Santo l'Occhio di Pernice '04, with its succulent, generous palate and rising finish.

● Chianti Cl. '07	♟♟	4*
● Chianti Cl. Squarcialupi Ris. '06	♟♟	5
○ Vin Santo del Chianti Cl. '05	♟♟	5
○ Vin Santo del Chianti Cl. Occhio di Pernice '04	♟♟	6
● Chianti Cl. Squarcialupi Ris. '05	♟♟	5
○ Vin Santo del Chianti Cl. Occhio di Pernice '03	♟♟	6

Castelvecchio

LOC. SAN PANCRAZIO
VIA CERTALDESE, 30
50026 SAN CASCIANO IN VAL DI PESA [FI]
TEL. 0558248032
www.castelvecchio.it

CELLAR SALES
PRE-BOOKED VISITS
VISITOR FACILITIES

ANNUAL PRODUCTION 100,000 bottles
HECTARES UNDER VINE 27
VITICULTURE METHOD Conventional

The Rocchi family winery has reached full maturity, having completed its range of wines. The available choice goes from the simplest, tailored to the concept of an everyday wine, to the more ambitious that make use of both local and international vines. The operation is managed and carried forward mainly by Filippo, who applies his enthusiasm and passion above all to the vineyard and the cellar, while his sister Stefania works in the sales sector.

The excellent all-canaiolo Numero Otto '07 got to our finals thanks to its serene fragrances of aromatic herbs and berry fruits preceding a supple body perfectly balanced by acidity. The rising finish is sweet and lingering. The first-timer Vin Santo '03 is also delicious, showing an intense nose of hazelnuts and figs, a velvety body and a sweet but not cloying palate. The Brecciolino '06, a sangiovese with merlot and petit verdot, and the fresh, agreeable '07 Chianti Colli Fiorentini, are both excellent. We also liked the newcomer, Orme in Rosso '07, from the same blend as the Brecciolino with a splash of cabernet sauvignon.

● Numero Otto '07	♟♟	5
● Vin Santo del Chianti Chiacchierata Notturna '03	♟♟	7
● Chianti Colli Fiorentini '07	♟♟	4*
● Il Brecciolino '06	♟♟	6
● Chianti Colli Fiorentini V. La Quercia '06	♟	4
● Chianti Santa Caterina '07	♟	3
● Orme in Rosso '07	♟	4
○ San Lorenzo '08	♟	3
● Chianti Colli Fiorentini Il Castelvecchio '06	♟♟	4*
● Chianti Colli Fiorentini V. La Quercia Ris. '05	♟♟	5
● Il Brecciolino '05	♟♟	6
● Il Brecciolino '04	♟♟	6

Famiglia Cecchi

LOC. CASINA DEI PONTI, 56
53011 CASTELLINA IN CHIANTI [SI]
TEL. 057754311
www.cecchi.net

PRE-BOOKED VISITS

ANNUAL PRODUCTION **7.200,000 bottles**
HECTARES UNDER VINE **292**
VITICULTURE METHOD **Conventional**

The Cecchi family has shown in recent years that it knows how to bring together enormous production and great quality. However deep their roots may be, it hasn't stopped Cesare and Andrea Cecchi making some brave decisions to define a winery style that despite the vast territory covered, is as faithful as possible a reflection of its place of origin. All this, combined with ongoing research and improvements, makes this winery one of the front-runners in Italian viticulture, hence its first Three Glasses.

The Chianti Classico Riserva di Famiglia '06 is a wine with a fine sense of provenance. The nose opens with violet blossom followed by red berry fruit and mint notes, offset by a palate whose extract finds balance in the succulent, pervasive pulp. The stunning Coevo '06, a new concept blending Chianti sangiovese with Maremma cabernet, has impressive progression. It's a modern wine with intense flavours. Three Glasses. The Chianti Classico Villa Cerna '07 confirms the great work being done across the range, with its spicy, floral nose and smooth, savoury palate. Satisfaction guaranteed.

Centolani

LOC. FRIGGIALI
S.DA MAREMMANA
53024 MONTALCINO [SI]
TEL. 0577849454
www.tenulafriggialiepietranera.it

CELLAR SALES
PRE-BOOKED VISITS
VISITOR FACILITIES

ANNUAL PRODUCTION **260,000 bottles**
HECTARES UNDER VINE **43**
VITICULTURE METHOD **Conventional**

An impeccable 40-hectare Brunello estate, split into two very different areas. The first is Friggiali, in the western part of Montalcino, at about 450 metres above sea level, which produces a very elegant Brunello. The other property is called Pietranera, located on the south-east slope, has quite unique volcanic terrain producing a fuller Brunello. The winery style is classic although it does use some small casks, especially at the Pietranera estate. The business is run by Olga Peluso, who elected to make Montalcino her home.

The '04 Brunello di Montalcino Friggiali is flawless, its pervasive bouquet showing slightly smoky and intense, with cherry and blackberry notes. We thought it had a great sense of place with excellent texture from well-coordinated acidity and tannins, the latter still young but nicely honed. The lingering finish mirrors the aromas on the nose. Just a step behind is Brunello Pietranera '04, with plenty of alcohol and jammy notes on the nose, before the balanced palate shows moderately complex and not too deep on the finish. The Rosso di Montalcino '07 is long, juicy and taut. It's a well-made wine and one of the best this year.

● Coevo '06	▼▼▼	6
● Chianti Cl. Riserva di Famiglia '06	▼▼	6
● Chianti Cl. Villa Cerna '07	▼▼	5
● Morellino di Scansano Val delle Rose Ris. '06	▼▼	5
● Morellino di Scansano Val delle Rose '08	▼	3
● Chianti Cl. '00	♀♀	4*
● Chianti Cl. Riserva di Famiglia '02	♀♀	5
● Chianti Cl. Villa Cerna Ris. '05	♀♀	5
● Chianti Cl. Villa Cerna Ris. '04	♀♀	5
● Morellino di Scansano Ris. '05	♀♀	5
● Spargolo '04	♀♀	7
● Spargolo '01	♀♀	7

● Brunello di Montalcino Tenuta Friggiali '04	▼▼▼	6
● Brunello di Montalcino Donna Olga '04	▼▼	8
● Rosso di Montalcino Pietranera '07	▼▼	4*
● Brunello di Montalcino Pietranera '04	▼	7
● Brunello di Montalcino Donna Olga '01	♀♀♀	7
● Brunello di Montalcino Ris. '01	♀♀♀	8
● Brunello di Montalcino Tenuta Friggiali Ris. '99	♀♀♀	8
● Brunello di Montalcino Donna Olga '03	♀♀	7
● Brunello di Montalcino Pietranera '01	♀♀	7
● Brunello di Montalcino Tenuta Friggiali '03	♀♀	6
● Brunello di Montalcino Tenuta Friggiali Ris. '01	♀♀	7

La Cerbaiola

P.ZZA CAVOUR, 19
53024 MONTALCINO [SI]
TEL. 0577848499

Cerbaiona

LOC. CERBAIONA
53024 MONTALCINO [SI]
TEL. 0577848660

CELLAR SALES
PRE-BOOKED VISITS

CELLAR SALES

ANNUAL PRODUCTION 15,000 bottles
HECTARES UNDER VINE 4
VITICULTURE METHOD Conventional

ANNUAL PRODUCTION 15,000 bottles
HECTARES UNDER VINE 3.2
VITICULTURE METHOD Conventional

The Salvioni family's Cerbaiola winery is in the eastern Cerbaie hills at about 400 metres. The terrain is a mix of sandstones and clays, enjoying good temperatures that endow the estate's wines with their well-developed, complex aromatic profiles. The fermentation cellars are near the vineyards while most of the wines are aged in cellars in the centre of Montalcino. Since the 1980s, Giulio Salvioni's wines have shown an elegant style deriving from mellow tannins and polished acidity.

The Brunello di Montalcino '04 is an absolute thoroughbred, one of the best presented this year. The initially reduced nose has enticing notes of red berry, peach, rain-soaked earth and medicinal herbs, before an austere, integrated palate gives assertive but fine-grained tannin, while the acidity doesn't miss a beat through to the massive, lingering finish. Three Glasses with a great future. The Rosso di Montalcino is in the same style; it's just a little simpler.

Diego Molinari, Nora and their feline friends are the heart and soul of La Cerbaiona, a small but truly outstanding winery in the eastern area of Montalcino. The Molinaris produce a monumental classic Brunello. They began their wine venture in the early 1980s and their first Brunello came out in 1982, since when nothing has changed, including the use of 30-hectolitre casks, which was cutting-edge at the time but has since become a symbol of tradition. Utmost attention goes to management of the vine stock to ensure results that are excellent expressions of their territory.

After two consecutive let-downs with the 2002 and 2003 harvests, outstanding winemaker Diego finally had a good year to work with and brought us this very classy Brunello di Montalcino, which had no trouble at all in securing Three Glasses. After admiring the gleaming colour, we find a classic, highly complex ripe cherry nose with hints of sweet tobacco, liquorice and violet. The palate has a refined, compact tannic weave, with impeccable acidity assuring a lingering finish of quite awesome finesse and length. We also made the acquaintance of the Diego Molinari Sangiovese '06, a small-scale Brunello.

● Brunello di Montalcino '04	♡♡♡	8
● Rosso di Montalcino '07	♡♡	6
● Brunello di Montalcino '00	♡♡♡	8
● Brunello di Montalcino '99	♡♡♡	8
● Brunello di Montalcino '97	♡♡♡	8
● Brunello di Montalcino '90	♡♡♡	8
● Brunello di Montalcino '89	♡♡♡	8
● Brunello di Montalcino '88	♡♡♡	8
● Brunello di Montalcino '87	♡♡♡	8
● Brunello di Montalcino '85	♡♡♡	8

● Brunello di Montalcino '04	♡♡♡+	8
● Diego Molinari '06	♡♡	5
● Cerbaiona '06	♡	6
● Brunello di Montalcino '01	♡♡♡	8
● Brunello di Montalcino '99	♡♡♡	8
● Brunello di Montalcino '97	♡♡♡	8
● Brunello di Montalcino '90	♡♡♡	8
● Brunello di Montalcino '88	♡♡♡	8
Brunello di Montalcino '85	♡♡♡	8

Fattoria del Cerro

FRAZ. ACQUAVIVA
VIA GRAZIANELLA, 5
53040 MONTEPULCIANO [SI]
TEL. 0578767722
www.saiagricola.it

CELLAR SALES
PRE-BOOKED VISITS
VISITOR FACILITIES
FOOD

ANNUAL PRODUCTION **800,000 bottles**
HECTARES UNDER VINE **170**
VITICULTURE METHOD **Conventional**

There are few Montepulciano producers who can boast the sheer number of vineyards owned by Fattoria del Cerro, a Gruppo Saiagricola estate founded in 1978. The main distinction of the winery, located in the Acquaviva district, is its ability to exploit its vineyard assets to achieve consolidated, very dependable quality, which often soars to total excellence with flawlessly made wines.

Our outright favourite is the totally elegant, poised Nobile di Montepulciano Riserva '05. We were curious about the Caggio al Vescovo '06, a pure Colorino, and we were not disappointed by this new wine in the cellar's extensive product portfolio. It was no surprise to find the quality of the delicious Nobile di Montepulciano '06 and the Vendemmia Tardiva Corte d'Oro '07 was as impressive as always. We found the rest of the range reliable, with the trebbiano-only white Braviolo '08 also offering a very competitive price tag. The Fattoria del Cerro flagship wine, Nobile Antica Chiusina, was absent as the '06 is having another year of bottle ageing.

Vincenzo Cesani

FRAZ. PANCOLE
VIA PIAZZETTA, 82D
53037 SAN GIMIGNANO [SI]
TEL. 0577955084
www.agriturismo-cesani.com

CELLAR SALES
PRE-BOOKED VISITS

ANNUAL PRODUCTION **100,000 bottles**
HECTARES UNDER VINE **19**
VITICULTURE METHOD **Conventional**

Letizia Cesani, a passionate winemaker with years of experience, has been elected president of the Consorzio della Vernaccia for the next three years, and she's already at work with the enthusiasm she is famous for. In recent years, her winery's focus has been on the historic San Gimignano vine, with increasingly exciting results.

We enjoyed the Sanice '07 selection for its minerally aromas and savoury, succulent body. The Vernaccia '08 unveils a nose of floral and white-fleshed peach-like fruit, distinct acidic verve in the mouth and a polished texture leading into a rising finish. Nor were we disappointed by the mostly sangiovese Cellori '05 with its complex nose of cinnamon and cloves, sturdy body and decent finish. Not quite so persuasive is the Luenzo '06, a sangiovese with a touch of colorino, which has evolved aromas but lacks backbone on the palate. The Colli Senesi '08 is well typed.

Wine	Rating
● Caggio al Vescovo '06	♀♀ 5
○ Corte d'Oro V.T. '07	♀♀ 6
● Nobile di Montepulciano '06	♀♀ 5
● Nobile di Montepulciano Ris. '05	♀♀ 5
○ Braviolo '08	♀ 2
● Chianti Colli Senesi '08	♀ 3
○ Poggio a Tramontana '08	♀ 4
● Rosso di Montepulciano '08	♀ 4
○ Vin Santo di Montepulciano Sangallo '03	♀ 6
● Nobile di Montepulciano Vign. Antica Chiusina '00	♀♀♀ 7
● Nobile di Montepulciano Vign. Antica Chiusina '99	♀♀♀ 7
● Nobile di Montepulciano Vign. Antica Chiusina '98	♀♀♀ 7
● Nobile di Montepulciano Ris. '04	♀♀ 5
● Nobile di Montepulciano Vign. Antica Chiusina '05	♀♀ 7

Wine	Rating
● San Gimignano Rosso Cellori '05	♀♀ 5
○ Vernaccia di S. Gimignano '08	♀♀ 3*
○ Vernaccia di S. Gimignano Sanice '07	♀♀ 4*
● Chianti Colli Senesi '08	♀ 3
● Luenzo '06	♀ 5
● Luenzo '99	♀♀♀ 5
● Luenzo '97	♀♀♀ 5
● Chianti Colli Senesi '07	♀♀ 3*
● San Gimignano Rosso Cellori '04	♀♀ 5
○ Vernaccia di S. Gimignano '07	♀♀ 3*
○ Vernaccia di S. Gimignano Sanice '06	♀♀ 4*

Ciacci Piccolomini D'Aragona

FRAZ. CASTELNUOVO DELL'ABATE
LOC. MOLINELLO
53024 MONTALCINO [SI]
TEL. 0577835616
www.ciaccipiccolomini.com

CELLAR SALES
PRE-BOOKED VISITS
VISITOR FACILITIES

ANNUAL PRODUCTION 200,000 bottles
HECTARES UNDER VINE 40
VITICULTURE METHOD Conventional

This winery has stunning vineyards along the track leading from Castelnuovo to Sant'Angelo in Colle, where the rows face south-east and the Eocene soil is rich in marl. Its headquarters is Palazzo Piccolomini at Castelnuovo dell'Abate, where the ancient cellars can still be visited. Paolo and Lucia Bianchini manage this family winery, recently enlarged by acquisitions in the Montecucco area, opposite the southern side of Montalcino. The cellars are outside the town near the vineyards. Wine styles are dictated by type and the approach to Brunello di Montalcino is very traditional.

The wines we tasted were all good on the whole. Sant'Antimo Ateo '06 from cabernet sauvignon and merlot has improved and is now well-defined on the nose, with pencil lead and black berries introducing a taut body and a good tannic weave. The Brunello di Montalcino Pianrosso is open on the nose, with rather too much fruit, and a round, sustained palate. The Brunello di Montalcino '04 is a classic, with a fresh nose where fruit mingles with medicinal herbs. The succulent palate isn't assertive but it is well balanced. The syrah-only Sant'Antimo Fabius '06 is held back by sweetish oak.

● Brunello di Montalcino '04	TT 6
● Brunello di Montalcino V. di Pianrosso '04	TT 7
● Montecucco Sangiovese '07	TT 5
● Sant'Antimo Ateo '06	TT 5
● Sant'Antimo Fabius '06	TT 6
● Rosso di Montalcino '07	T 5
● Brunello di Montalcino V. di Pianrosso '98	YYY 7
● Brunello di Montalcino V. di Pianrosso '90	YYY 8
● Brunello di Montalcino V. di Pianrosso '88	YYY 8
● Brunello di Montalcino V. di Pianrosso Ris. '01	YYY 8
● Brunello di Montalcino V. di Pianrosso Ris. '99	YYY 8
● Brunello di Montalcino V. di Pianrosso Ris. '95	YYY 6
● Brunello di Montalcino V. di Pianrosso '03	YY 7
● Montecucco Sangiovese '06	YY 5

Fattoria di Cinciano

LOC. CINCIANO, 2
53036 POGGIBONSI [SI]
TEL. 0577936588
www.cinciano.it

ANNUAL PRODUCTION 70,000 bottles
HECTARES UNDER VINE 25
VITICULTURE METHOD Conventional

Fattoria di Cinciano has very ancient origins, dating back to the Middle Ages. It is located on the border of the municipalities of Siena and Florence, so it's easy to imagine how its history was shaped by the rivalry between the two cities. Today, the winery belongs to the Garrè family. The vineyards cover hillsides at over 300 metres and the wines are aged in medium-size oak barrels and barriques. The traditional designation wines are made exclusively from appropriate grapes like sangiovese and canaiolo.

We liked the pure sangiovese Chianti Classico Riserva '06 for its close-knit intensity, with notes of black cherry and other dark berries, while the palate is still dominated by tannins but should be able to unfold if given some time in a bottle. The sangiovese and merlot Pietraforte '07 is a plush wine, ready to drink now and nuanced with jam both on the nose and on the palate. Not bad, but only not bad, is the warm, quite open, Chianti Classico '07, with its vigorous dose of tannins.

● Chianti Cl. Ris. '06	TT 5
● Pietraforte '07	TT 5
● Chianti Cl. '07	T 4
● Chianti Cl. '06	YY 4*
● Chianti Cl. Ris. '05	YY 5

Le Cinciole

via Case Sparse, 83
50020 Panzano [FI]
tel. 055852636
www.lecinciole.it

CELLAR SALES
PRE-BOOKED VISITS

ANNUAL PRODUCTION **45,000 bottles**
HECTARES UNDER VINE **11**
VITICULTURE METHOD **Organic certified**

Podere Le Cinciole, owned by Luca Orsini and Valeria Viganò Orsini, covers about 30 hectares, of which 11 are given over to vines. The winery's terrain comprises surface galestro limestone and marl over a massive substrate of rock, with the vineyards set at quite a high altitude of about 500 metres. These soil and weather conditions, combined with vineyard management that respects the environment, are the foundation for authentic, original wines that genuinely express of their territory.

It may seem odd that a wine which isn't from sangiovese can reflect the Panzano terroir, but Camalaione '06, a cabernet sauvignon, syrah and merlot blend, does just that with its boisterous aromas and tannins weaving subtly into the body to create vibrant, balanced layering. The Chianti Classico '07 has a delightful, supple palate after sweet fruit on the nose. Succulence in the mouth just lacks a little complexity to back it up. The deep nose of the Chianti Classico Riserva Petresco '05 combines hints of florality with earthy and mineral notes. The palate has continuity and length but the finish is flawed by lack of balance because the tannins are out of kilter.

● Camalaione '06	**YY**	8
● Chianti Cl. '07	**YY**	5
● Chianti Cl. Petresco Ris. '05	**YY**	6
● Camalaione '04	YYY	8
● Chianti Cl. Petresco Ris. '01	YYY	6
● Camalaione '05	YY	8
● Camalaione '03	YY	7
● Chianti Cl. '04	YY	5
● Chianti Cl. '01	YY	4
● Chianti Cl. Petresco Ris. '04	YY	6

Donatella Cinelli Colombini

loc. Casato Prime Donne
53024 Montalcino [SI]
tel. 0577849421
www.cinellicolombini.it

CELLAR SALES
PRE-BOOKED VISITS

ANNUAL PRODUCTION **180,000 bottles**
HECTARES UNDER VINE **37**
VITICULTURE METHOD **Conventional**

Donatella Cinelli Colombini is one of the busiest bodies in the Montalcino district. Despite her many commitments, she's still able to manage her women-only business with great skill. The winery is located in the north of Montalcino and makes quite modern wines, with plenty of oak and a specific emphasis on fruitiness, a characteristic that is abetted by substantial day to night temperature differences in the vineyards as well as by the pebble-rich composition of the terrain.

The brightest star in this year's firmament was the Brunello di Montalcino '04, with its intensely fruit-rich bouquet of distinct currants, blackberries and cherries. The palate has plenty of structure, with a refined, poised continuity, thanks to excellent tannins, while acidity is well proportioned and leads into a deep finish. The Brunello di Montalcino Prime Donne '04 isn't so interesting or well typed, with its distinct greens on the nose, together with hints of fruit and candied orange. The palate is still quite raw and needs some maturing. The Riserva '03 is typical of the vintage with rather dusty tannins.

● Brunello di Montalcino '04	**YY**	6
● Brunello di Montalcino Prime Donne '04	**Y**	7
● Brunello di Montalcino Ris. '03	**Y**	7
● Brunello di Montalcino Prime Donne '01	YYY	7
● Brunello di Montalcino '03	YY	6
● Brunello di Montalcino '00	YY	6
● Brunello di Montalcino Prime Donne '03	YY	7
● Brunello di Montalcino Prime Donne '00	YY	7
● Brunello di Montalcino Ris. '01	YY	7
● Brunello di Montalcino Ris. '00	YY	7

La Cipriana

LOC. CAMPASTRELLO, 176B
57022 CASTAGNETO CARDUCCI [LI]
TEL. 0565775568
www.lacipriana.it

PRE-BOOKED VISITS
VISITOR FACILITIES

ANNUAL PRODUCTION **30,000 bottles**
HECTARES UNDER VINE **8.5**
VITICULTURE METHOD **Conventional**

La Cipriana is a piece of Bolgheri wine history. The Fabiani family took over this estate, beneath the delightful village of Castagneto Carducci, in 1975. The vineyards are partly next to the cellars, in the Campastrello area, and partly below the provincial road that runs parallel to the sea towards Bolgheri itself. Thanks to some of the territory's most deeply rooted vines, La Cipriana's wines have a natural feel and expressive appeal.

Bolgheri Superiore San Martino '06 is a paragon of balance. The depth on the nose is underpinned by blackberry jam, hints of strawberry-tree and whispers of sweet spice, especially cinnamon. The mouth is dynamic and full bodied, with well-extracted tannin for a very persuasive experience overall in the mouth. Bolgheri Rosso Scopaio '06, from the vineyard of the same name, has well-focused bottled black cherries and vanilla while the palate is well developed and lingering. The only off note is a tad too much alcohol that dulls the overall pleasing flavour. We thought the Bolgheri Vermentino Paguro '08 was pleasant and well made.

● Bolgheri Rosso Sup. San Martino '06	♟♟ 7
● Bolgheri Rosso Scopaio '06	♟ 5
○ Bolgheri Vermentino Paguro '08	♟ 4
● Bolgheri Rosso Scopaio '02	♟♟ 5
● Bolgheri Rosso Sup. San Martino '05	♟♟ 6
● Bolgheri Rosso Sup. San Martino '04	♟♟ 6
● Bolgheri Rosso Sup. San Martino '03	♟♟ 6

Citille di Sopra

FRAZ. TORRENIERI
LOC. CITILLE DI SOPRA, 46
53024 MONTALCINO [SI]
TEL. 0577832749
www.citille.com

CELLAR SALES

ANNUAL PRODUCTION **35,000 bottles**
HECTARES UNDER VINE **5.5**
VITICULTURE METHOD **Conventional**

This winery is on the lesser-known, but recently much more highly quoted for Brunello, Torrenieri slope. It's on the hillside, after the railway line, at an elevation of 300 metres. The vineyards are on medium-packed clay terrain with silt outcrops and a fair amount of gravel. The impeccable cellars have a split personality because ageing is very traditional but there are some small casks and winemaking installations are state of the art. The results are very interesting and the quality continues to improve.

The results of constant evolution can be seen in the Brunello di Montalcino '04, which strolled into our finals. It shows a lovely dense ruby red with a full, fruit-rich and very clean nose of wild cherries and blackberries, as well as some alluring smoky notes rounding out the profile with tobacco. Continuity on the palate is special, with evident but excellent tannins and decent acidity in the background. The Brunello di Montalcino Riserva '03 is less together on the nose, with distinctly clenched tannins. The Rosso di Montalcino '07 is well made but held back by oak that dry out the tannin.

● Brunello di Montalcino '04	♟♟ 6
● Brunello di Montalcino Ris. '03	♟ 7
● Rosso di Montalcino '07	♟ 4

★ Tenuta Col d'Orcia

LOC. SANT'ANGELO IN COLLE
53020 MONTALCINO [SI]
TEL. 057780891
www.coldorcia.it

CELLAR SALES
PRE-BOOKED VISITS

ANNUAL PRODUCTION 800,000 bottles
HECTARES UNDER VINE 142
VITICULTURE METHOD Conventional

This large estate is at an elevation of about 450 metres on the southern slope of Montalcino towards Sant'Angelo in Colle. It covers 540 hectares, of which 142 are under vine. These figures sum up an operation whose wines have written the history of Brunello di Montalcino, Col d'Orcia. News from the winery includes the departure of oenologist Pablo Harri and the full-time return of Marone Cinzano, after his time out as president of the Consorzio del Brunello.

This year, a wine of personality, Brunello di Montalcino Poggio al Vento Riserva '01, led the pack, despite a below-par vintage. The nose is slow to bring on its intense tobacco and leather with hints of medicinal herbs that veil the fruit. Dense, tight tannins tend to rein in continuity so we don't get the wine's expected depth. The Brunello di Montalcino '04 is better, its slightly flawed bouquet offset by a focused palate with good length. There were good showings from both the '04 and '05 Sant'Antimo Olmaias, from cabernet sauvignon only with a vegetal nose and succulent palate, and from Sant'Antimo Nearco, a merlot, cabernet sauvignon and syrah blend mellowed by oak.

Col di Bacche

S.DA DI CUPI
58010 MAGLIANO IN TOSCANA [GR]
TEL. 0577738526
www.coldibacche.com

PRE-BOOKED VISITS

ANNUAL PRODUCTION 70,000 bottles
HECTARES UNDER VINE 11
VITICULTURE METHOD Conventional

Alberto Carnasciali, born a Chianti man, prefers Maremma to Radda in Chianti for his winemaking and viticulture project, which he initiated with his first plantings in 1998. His first wines hit the market in 2004 and were an immediate hit for their harmony and impeccable style. Today, this winery is a major player in the vibrant Maremma oenological arena, standing as a very successful fusion of the winemaker's craft and modern entrepreneurial planning.

The Morellino di Scansano Rovente '07 is again the winery's flagship label, with its layered, refined nose profile, matched nicely by a quite round, but equally nuanced, progression. The Cupinero '07, from merlot with a dash of cabernet sauvignon, is also good stuff, with subtly spiced aromas, first-rate structure and an affable, balanced follow-through. In many respects, the Morellino di Scansano '08, with its surprisingly satisfying drinkability, is a model of its type.

Wine	Rating
● Brunello di Montalcino '04	♟♟ 8
● Brunello di Montalcino Poggio al Vento Ris. '01	♟♟ 8
● Sant'Antimo Cabernet Olmaia '05	♟♟ 7
● Sant'Antimo Cabernet Olmaia '04	♟♟ 7
● Sant'Antimo Nearco '05	♟♟ 6
● Rosso di Montalcino '07	♟ 5
● Rosso di Montalcino Banditella '06	♟ 6
● Brunello di Montalcino Poggio al Vento Ris. '99	♟♟♟ 8
● Brunello di Montalcino Poggio al Vento Ris. '97	♟♟♟ 8
● Brunello di Montalcino Poggio al Vento Ris. '95	♟♟♟ 8
● Olmaia '01	♟♟♟ 7
● Olmaia '00	♟♟♟ 7
● Olmaia '94	♟♟♟ 7

Wine	Rating
● Cupinero '07	♟♟ 6
● Morellino di Scansano Rovente '07	♟♟ 6
● Morellino di Scansano '08	♟♟ 4
● Morellino di Scansano Rovente '05	♟♟♟ 5
● Cupinero '05	♟♟ 6
● Cupinero '04	♟♟ 6
● Cupinero '03	♟♟ 6
● Cupinero '02	♟♟ 6
● Morellino di Scansano '06	♟♟ 4
● Morellino di Scansano '05	♟♟ 4
● Morellino di Scansano Rovente '06	♟♟ 5
● Morellino di Scansano Rovente '04	♟♟ 5
● Morellino di Scansano Rovente '03	♟♟ 5

Colle Bereto

LOC. COLLE BERETO
53017 RADDA IN CHIANTI [SI]
TEL. 0554299330
www.collebereto.com

CELLAR SALES
PRE-BOOKED VISITS

ANNUAL PRODUCTION **50,000 bottles**
HECTARES UNDER VINE **15**
VITICULTURE METHOD **Conventional**

The first documents that mention Colle Bereto date back as far as the 11th century, when a wealthy landowner in Radda, the municipality where the estate is located, donated it to the church of San Lorenzo a Coltibuono. This gem is now owned by the Pinzauti family, who bought it as a country home and gradually developed its winemaking potential. The vineyards face south west and the terrain is rich in marl and limestone on a rock substrate. The Chianti Classico wines are aged in Slavonian oak barrels and the IGT labels in barrique.

Last year, we sang the praises of the IGT wines but this year we prefer the recent tastings of Chianti Classico. The Riserva '06 seems to be evolving, so we have high hopes for the future, but the wine is already perfectly drinkable and has a pleasingly succulent, relaxed palate, with lots of flavour and easy progression. The Chianti Classico '07 is also a fine label, with a few extra toasty and vegetal hints, possibly a slight excess of alcohol in the finish and an enjoyably rounded, fleshy palate.

● Chianti Cl. '07	♟♟	4*
● Chianti Cl. Ris. '06	♟♟	5
● Chianti Cl. '06	♟♟	4*
● Chianti Cl. Ris. '04	♟♟	5
● Il Cenno '06	♟♟	6
● Il Cenno '03	♟♟	5
● Il Tocco '06	♟♟	6

Colle Massari

LOC. POGGI DEL SASSO
58044 CINIGIANO [GR]
TEL. 0564990496
www.collemassari.it

CELLAR SALES
PRE-BOOKED VISITS

ANNUAL PRODUCTION **250,000 bottles**
HECTARES UNDER VINE **83**
VITICULTURE METHOD **Organic certified**

The Colle Massari winemaking project began in 1999, when entrepreneur Claudio Tipa and his sister Iris identified an area of Maremma that was still relatively unknown. It was just the place for them to make their old dream come true. In ten years, Colle Massari has become a leader not just in the Montecucco area but also in Italian winemaking as a whole, thanks to a range of wines that are beautifully made and have tons of personality. The vineyards are organically farmed.

Colle Massari's flagship Montecucco Sangiovese Lombrone Riserva won Three Glasses to consolidate its status as top bottle. This '05 has superb layered aromas with surefooted, vibrantly dynamic flavours. The Montecucco Rosso Colle Massari Riserva '06 is also exciting, with an enticing bouquet and velvety, structured palate. The Montecucco Rosso Rigoleto '07 is especially drinkable. The Montecucco Vermentino Le Melacce '08 and the more layered Montecucco Vermentino Irisse '07 are both reliable. We enjoyed the rosé Grottolo '08 from sangiovese, ciliegiolo and montepulciano vinified with brief skin contact.

● Montecucco Sangiovese Lombrone Ris. '05	♟♟♟	7
● Montecucco Rosso Colle Massari Ris. '06	♟♟	5
⊙ Grottolo '08	♟	4
● Montecucco Rosso Rigoleto '07	♟	4
○ Montecucco Vermentino Irisse '07	♟	5
○ Montecucco Vermentino Le Melacce '08	♟	4
● Montecucco Sangiovese Lombrone Ris. '04	♟♟♟	7
● Montecucco Rosso Colle Massari Ris. '05	♟♟	5
● Montecucco Rosso Colle Massari Ris. '04	♟♟	6
● Montecucco Rosso Colle Massari Ris. '03	♟♟	6
● Montecucco Rosso Rigoleto '06	♟♟	4*
○ Montecucco Vermentino Le Melacce '07	♟♟	4*

Collemattoni

LOC. SANT'ANGELO IN COLLE
POD. COLLEMATTONI, 100
53020 MONTALCINO [SI]
TEL. 0577844127
www.collemattoni.it

CELLAR SALES
PRE-BOOKED VISITS

ANNUAL PRODUCTION **35,000 bottles**
HECTARES UNDER VINE **6.7**
VITICULTURE METHOD **Conventional**

A glance at a photo of Marcello Bucci and his father carrying an ox yoke tells you all you need to know about the philosophy behind this small winery on the outskirts of Sant'Angelo in Colle. The underlying concepts are humility and hard work, two qualities that have assured the success of the business. The wines have a classic style, with long maceration in Slavonian oak barrels of about 35 hectolitres. The vineyards are on the southern Montalcino slope, at about 350 metres, on mainly marly terrain with some clays. A new vineyard was purchased recently in the Castelnuovo dell'Abate area.

Collemattoni wines are classic in style. The Brunello di Montalcino '04 has a mature nose laced with red berries and jammy hints, medicinal herbs and roots. The compact, tannic palate is resolute and possibly still a little raw but will certainly improve over time thanks to polished underlying acidity. The Rosso di Montalcino '07 is in the same style as the Brunello but not quite so structured.

● Brunello di Montalcino '04	🍷🍷 7
● Rosso di Montalcino '07	🍷🍷 4
● Brunello di Montalcino '01	🍷🍷🍷 (white) 6
● Brunello di Montalcino '00	🍷🍷 (white) 6
● Brunello di Montalcino '99	🍷🍷 (white) 6
● Rosso di Montalcino '06	🍷🍷 (white) 4*

Villa la Colombaia

LOC. BAGNOLO
VIA IMPRUNETANA PER TAVARNUZZE, 50
50023 IMPRUNETA [FI]
TEL. 0552025041
www.villabagnolo.it

ANNUAL PRODUCTION **50,000 bottles**
HECTARES UNDER VINE **14**
VITICULTURE METHOD **Conventional**

After the Guide debut last year, the Beltrami family has now progressed to a long profile. The winery was founded in the 19th century by a family of Florentine musicians who fell in love with the area mainly for its famous terracotta, which they immediately started making. The estate was later used by the Beltramis as a country home but it is only recently that farming has been developed, first with olive groves and later with vineyards and fruit orchards.

The Beltramis presented three wines. The very good Chianti Colli Fiorentini Terre delle Fornaci '07 has a pleasant, intriguing nose and a round, inviting palate with a rising finish. The sangiovese-only Terre del Cotto '07 is also excellent with a complex aroma profile ranging from aromatic herbs to spices and berry fruits. Its supple body is balanced and very drinkable, with a lingering flavour. Lastly, the Passito Duca Alessandro '06, from malvasia and trebbiano grapes, is still working on its aromas but has a generous palate.

● Chianti Colli Fiorentini Terre delle Fornaci '07	🍷🍷 4*
● Terre del Cotto '07	🍷🍷 5
○ Duca Alessandro Passito '06	🍷 6
● Chianti Colli Fiorentini Terre delle Fornaci '06	🍷🍷 (white) 4*
● Terre del Cotto '06	🍷🍷 (white) 5

Il Colombaio di Cencio

LOC. CORNIA
53013 GAIOLE IN CHIANTI [SI]
TEL. 0577747178
www.ilcolombaiodicencio.com

CELLAR SALES
PRE-BOOKED VISITS
VISITOR FACILITIES
FOOD

ANNUAL PRODUCTION 80,000 bottles
HECTARES UNDER VINE 25
VITICULTURE METHOD Naturale

Werner Wilhelm, a Bavarian businessman, owns this Chianti estate where he makes wine in one of Tuscany's lovelier corners. He uses organic methods, the hallmark of a winery whose philosophy focuses on respect for nature and achieving the best possible quality, thanks to a modern style of vineyard management, with high-density plantings. The most recently planted rows are at Cornia, Monticello and Montelodoli while the new cellars are home to the many barriques used to age the wines.

We are fans of the Chianti Classico Riserva I Massi '06. Despite the perceptible oak, the wine has great fruit and is well on its way to achieving overall balance, not least of all because the mouth is full-bodied, generous, warm and deep. Equally interesting is Futuro '06, a cabernet sauvignon and merlot blend with a dash of sangiovese, where toasty and smoky notes accompany black berries with a whisper of mint. The palate is crisp, with rich body and perhaps a tad too much alcohol. Hot on its heels is the Monticello '06, a sangiovese, cabernet and merlot mix with grassy hints and sprightly tannins.

Il Colombaio di Santa Chiara

LOC. SAN DONATO, 1
53037 SAN GIMIGNANO [SI]
TEL. 0577942004
www.colombaiosantachiara.it

CELLAR SALES
PRE-BOOKED VISITS
VISITOR FACILITIES

ANNUAL PRODUCTION 47,000 bottles
HECTARES UNDER VINE 7
VITICULTURE METHOD Conventional

The Guide confirms its profile for the Logi siblings, who are increasingly involved in the winemaking venture they started a few years ago. There are only a few hectares under vine, managed with great care and with input from oenologists Paolo Caciorna and Nicola Berti. The cellar turns out two versions of the Vernaccia, one aged in steel and the other in wood.

The most polished wines, however, are the reds, as well as a faultless Vin Santo with notes of incense and nuts on the nose, fat, velvety, rounded body and good length. Also confirmed is last year's score for the sangiovese-heavy '06 Colombaio with its clean aromas of aromatic herbs and lively whole red berry fruit. The even palate has balance and a satisfactory finish. The best of the Vernaccias is the full-flavoured Selvabianca '08, with vegetal aromatics, while the Albereta seems to lack some balance on the nose although the palate has substance. The Priore '07, a sangiovese and canaiolo blend, has too much vanilla.

● Chianti Cl. I Massi Ris. '06	♟♟ 6
● Il Futuro '06	♟♟ 7
● Monticello '06	♟ 4
● Chianti Cl. I Massi Ris. '03	♟♟♟ 6
● Il Futuro '99	♟♟♟ 7
● Il Futuro '97	♟♟♟ 7
● Il Futuro '95	♟♟♟ 7
● Chianti Cl. I Massi '04	♟♟ 5
● Chianti Cl. I Massi Ris. '05	♟♟ 6
● Chianti Cl. I Massi Ris. '04	♟♟ 6
● Guglielmo '03	♟♟ 8
● Il Futuro '05	♟♟ 7
● Il Futuro '04	♟♟ 7
● Monticello '05	♟♟ 4*

● S. Gimignano Rosso Colombaio '06	♟♟ 5
○ Vin Santo di San Gimignano ...... di Mario '04	♟♟ 6
● Il Priore '07	♟ 4
○ Vernaccia di S. Gimignano Albereta '08	♟ 4
○ Vernaccia di San Gimignano Selvabianca '08	♟ 4
● Il Priore '06	♟♟ 4
● S. Gimignano Rosso Colombaio '05	♟♟ 5
● S. Gimignano Rosso Colombaio '04	♟♟ 5

Conti Toggenburg

LOC. LA ROMITA
S.DA ROMITA, 29
50028 TAVARNELLE VAL DI PESA [FI]
TEL. 0558070012
www.toggenburg.it

CELLAR SALES
PRE-BOOKED VISITS
VISITOR FACILITIES

ANNUAL PRODUCTION **25,000 bottles**
HECTARES UNDER VINE **8**
VITICULTURE METHOD **Conventional**

There's a Guide debut for the Tuscan estate of the Toggenburgs, who already operate in Alto Adige as fruit growers and distillers of various kinds of fruit brandy. In Tuscany, they have about 20 hectares on the border of Chianti Classico, where they have a farmstay business as well as producing wine and extra virgin olive oil. Farming and winemaking are managed directly by the owner, Eberhard Toggenburg, who uses only traditional grapes, mainly sangiovese.

Ulrico '06, a pure sangiovese, has restrained but clean, fresh, green aromas and shows slim-bodied but persuasive, with a satisfactory if not ultra-long finish. The pleasing, quirky Eccellenza '07, also from sangiovese grapes but part-dried, has mature jammy perceptions and aromatic herbs on the nose, with a broad, plush entry on the palate. The Chianti L'Alano '07 has fresh, floral aromas and a lithe, dynamic body.

Fattoria Le Corti

LOC. LE CORTI
VIA SAN PIERO DI SOTTO, 1
50026 SAN CASCIANO IN VAL DI PESA [FI]
TEL. 055829301
www.principecorsini.com

CELLAR SALES
PRE-BOOKED VISITS
VISITOR FACILITIES
FOOD

ANNUAL PRODUCTION **240,000 bottles**
HECTARES UNDER VINE **50**
VITICULTURE METHOD **Conventional**

Fattoria Le Corti is an icon of viticulture in Tuscany. Apart from winemaking, this splendid typical Tuscan Renaissance villa is the venue for events to promote wine appreciation and responsible drinking. The vineyards cover 50 or so hectares on the gentle slopes leading down to the Terzona torrential stream, a tributary of the Pesa. Culture, art and agriculture are the passions of Duccio Corsini, the enthusiastic owner who focuses on maintaining the high quality of the estate's products.

Again it was the character of the Chianti Classico Cortevecchia Riserva '06 that had the panel nodding in approval. Earthy notes on the nose open into clean, spicy fruit before entry on the palate is reined in by tannins but progression is linear and succulent. It's a wine with stuffing and will soon be great. Don Tommaso '06 is a Chianti Classico with a more modern slant. The aromatics hinge on the sweetness of brisk, intense black berries and the palate thrills with well-rounded body and acidity. Perfect balance for a wine that is acquiring alluring spontaneity.

● Eccellenza '07	▼▼ 6
● Ulrico '06	▼▼ 4*
● Chianti L'Alano '07	▼ 3

● Chianti Cl. Cortevecchia Ris. '06	▼▼ 5
● Chianti Cl. Don Tommaso '06	▼▼ 6
● Chianti Cl. Le Corti '07	▼ 4
● Chianti Cl. Cortevecchia Ris. '05	▼▼▼ 5
● Chianti Cl. Don Tommaso '99	▼▼▼ 5
● Chianti Cl. Don Tommaso '05	▼▼ 6
● Chianti Cl. Don Tommaso '04	▼▼ 6
● Marsiliana '05	▼▼ 6
● Marsiliana '04	▼▼ 6
● Marsiliana '03	▼▼ 6

Fattoria Corzano e Paterno

FRAZ. SAN PRANCAZIO
VIA PATERNO, 8
50020 SAN CASCIANO IN VAL DI PESA [FI]
TEL. 0558248179
www.corzanoepaterno.it

CELLAR SALES
PRE-BOOKED VISITS

ANNUAL PRODUCTION **75,000 bottles**
HECTARES UNDER VINE **16**
VITICULTURE METHOD **Conventional**

Aljoscha Goldschmidt didn't manage to repeat his Corzano '06 coup of last year, but he got two wines into the finals, one of them the Passito '99, in a very respectable overall performance. The estate was acquired by the family of today's owners about 40 years ago. Initially there were six hectares of vineyard but over the years these have increased to 16. It an all-round farm, known not just for its wine and oil but also for cheese and farmstay accommodation.

The Corzano '06, a mix of sangiovese, cabernet sauvignon and merlot, has a fascinatingly rich, velvety, balsamic nose, a succulent palate and an elegantly savoury, thrusting finish. Passito '99, from trebbiano and malvasia, has an intriguing nose of jam and aromatic herbs followed by a sweet, silky, concentrated palate with a long, well-coordinated progression. Chianti Riserva I Tre Borri '06 is well made but hard while Corzanello '08, a trebbiano, chardonnay and sémillon blend, is relaxed and enjoyable.

● Il Corzano '06	▼▼	6
○ Passito di Corzano '99	▼▼	7
● Chianti I Tre Borri Ris. '06	▼	6
○ Il Corzanello '08	▼	4
● Il Corzano '05	▼▼▼	6
● Il Corzano '97	▼▼▼	5
● Chianti I Tre Borri Ris. '04	▼▼	6
● Il Corzano '04	▼▼	6

Maria Caterina Dei

VIA DI MARTIENA, 35
53045 MONTEPULCIANO [SI]
TEL. 0578716878
www.cantinedei.com

CELLAR SALES
PRE-BOOKED VISITS
VISITOR FACILITIES

ANNUAL PRODUCTION **200,000 bottles**
HECTARES UNDER VINE **55**
VITICULTURE METHOD **Conventional**

Maria Caterina Dei runs her winery in person and has done since 1991. The estate was set up in 1964 by her grandfather Alibrando when he acquired the Bossona vineyard. In 1973, another important addition was made with the purchase of the Martiena property, where the winery is now based. The first bottled releases date back to 1985 and from that moment on, Dei label wines have gradually worked their way up the rankings of the Nobile di Montepulciano designation.

The flawless Nobile di Montepulciano '06 has an alluring aromatic composition, with a full, assertive flavour. We're also keen on the Sancta Catherina '07 sangiovese, cabernet sauvignon, syrah and petit verdot blend, a weighty, complex wine. The Rosso di Montepulciano '08 is easy to like with its lively aromas and savoury, relaxed palate. This year, we missed Nobile Riserva Bossona, the Villa Martiena-based winery's top-end product, since the '05 edition wasn't considered up to scratch by the producer's technical team.

● Nobile di Montepulciano '06	▼▼	5
● Rosso di Montepulciano '08	▼▼	4
● Sancta Catharina '07	▼▼	6
● Nobile di Montepulciano Bossona Ris. '04	▼▼▼	6
● Nobile di Montepulciano '01	▼▼	5
● Nobile di Montepulciano '99	▼▼	5
● Nobile di Montepulciano Bossona Ris. '03	▼▼	6
● Nobile di Montepulciano Bossona Ris. '01	▼▼	6
● Nobile di Montepulciano Bossona Ris. '99	▼▼	6
● Rosso di Montepulciano '07	▼▼	4
● Rosso di Montepulciano '06	▼▼	4
● Sancta Catharina '06	▼▼	6
● Sancta Catharina '04	▼▼	6

Tenuta di Sesta

FRAZ. CASTELNUOVO DELL'ABATE
LOC. SESTA
53020 MONTALCINO [SI]
TEL. 0577835612
www.tenutadisesta.it

CELLAR SALES
PRE-BOOKED VISITS

ANNUAL PRODUCTION 150,000 bottles
HECTARES UNDER VINE 30
VITICULTURE METHOD Conventional

Tenuta di Sesta is in the southern part of Montalcino, at 200 to 400 metres, at Sant'Angelo in Colle and Castelnuovo dell'Abate, near the famous Romanesque abbey of Sant'Antimo. The soil tends to be poor, generally clayey, rich in limestone, and interspersed with large tufaceous areas. The estate covers 200 hectares with 30 under vine, of which 13.5 are registered Brunello di Montalcino, shielded from cold winds by nearby Mount Amiata, which fosters a mild site climate ideal for the healthy, complete ripening of the grapes.

The Tenuta di Sesta wines are solid, concentrated and very cellarable. The Brunello di Montalcino '04 has a generous, even jammy, morello cherry nose and substantial palate with ripe tannins and crisp acidity. The '07 Rosso di Montalcino is full-bodied, pleasing and well made, although it's not a muscular wine and is a good example of the type. The Riserva '03 is a little too alcoholic but it was a torrid growing year.

Fattoria di Dievole

VIA DIEVOLE, 6
53010 CASTELNUOVO BERARDENGA [SI]
TEL. 0577322613
www.dievole.it

CELLAR SALES
PRE-BOOKED VISITS

ANNUAL PRODUCTION 550,000 bottles
HECTARES UNDER VINE 89
VITICULTURE METHOD Conventional

The Schwenn family winery is just 12 kilometres from Siena, in the Vagliagli district. Over recent years, it has increased the number of wine project irons it has in the fire and the overall quality of the range. The Dievole philosophy is to view the past from a modern perspective and the winery has also achieved great things in the study and recovery of ancient local varieties. The top wines are aged in French and American barriques.

The superb Chianti Classico La Vendemmia '07 shows lovely, tight, fresh red berries accompanied by elegant smoky and spicy nuances. The wine has finesse, balancing its acid backbone with savoury notes before finishing long and intense. The Chianti Classico Novecento Riserva '06 is also worth uncorking for its aromas of ripe cherries and blossom ushering in a tight, fleshy palate with lots of flavour. The same can be said for the surprising plum and aromatic herb-laced Chianti Classico Dieulele Riserva '06. The sangiovese, merlot and petit verdot Broccato '06 is fair, with sweetish, predictable tones.

● Brunello di Montalcino '04	▼▼ 6
● Poggio d'Arna '07	▼▼ 4
● Rosso di Montalcino '07	▼▼ 4
● Brunello di Montalcino Ris. '03	▼ 8
● Brunello di Montalcino '02	♀♀ 6
● Brunello di Montalcino '01	♀♀ 7
● Brunello di Montalcino '00	♀♀ 6
● Brunello di Montalcino '99	♀♀ 7
● Brunello di Montalcino Ris. '01	♀♀ 8
● Brunello di Montalcino Ris. '99	♀♀ 8

● Chianti Cl. Dieulele Ris. '06	▼▼ 8
● Chianti Cl. La Vendemmia '07	▼▼ 5
● Chianti Cl. Novecento Ris. '06	▼▼ 6
● Broccato '06	▼ 6
● Broccato '05	♀♀ 6
● Broccato '01	♀♀ 5
● Chianti Cl. Dieulele Ris. '01	♀♀ 5
● Chianti Cl. La Vendemmia '06	♀♀ 5
● Chianti Cl. Novecento Ris. '04	♀♀ 6

Fanti - San Filippo

FRAZ. CASTELNUOVO DELL'ABATE
POD. PALAZZO
53020 MONTALCINO [SI]
TEL. 0577835795
balfanti@tin.it

CELLAR SALES
PRE-BOOKED VISITS

ANNUAL PRODUCTION **150,000 bottles**
HECTARES UNDER VINE **50**
VITICULTURE METHOD **Conventional**

The winery has taken off in the last 15 years thanks to the dynamic Fanti Baldassarre, known as Sarrino, who has just finished work on his new underground cellars on the hillside opposite the abbey of Sant'Antimo. Traditional barrels, casks and barriques are kept separately in the cellars and all are used for Brunello di Montalcino production. Lately the winery's philosophy has become more restrained, with less oak and ageing impact, which allows the territory to emerge. The vineyards are mainly on marly soil, with light clay in areas lower down.

The new tack brings us this striking Brunello di Montalcino '04, with fresh leaf tobacco and leather on the nose, plumping out the ripe spice-laced cherries. The supple, succulent structure reveals slightly mouth-drying tannin that tends to hold back the finish. The Rosso di Montalcino '07 is well made, with a brisk nose of wild cherry notes and a pleasingly fresh palate. The fresh Sant'Antimo Rosso '07 unfolds nicely and is very drinkable while the persuasive Vin Santo '04 is one of Montalcino's best.

● Brunello di Montalcino '04	🍷🍷	7
● Rosso di Montalcino '07	🍷🍷	5
● Sant'Antimo Rosso '07	🍷🍷	4*
○ Vin Santo '04	🍷🍷	5
● Brunello di Montalcino '00	🍷🍷🍷	7
● Brunello di Montalcino '97	🍷🍷🍷	7
● Brunello di Montalcino Ris. '95	🍷🍷🍷	7
● Brunello di Montalcino '03	🍷🍷	7
● Brunello di Montalcino '01	🍷🍷	7
● Sant'Antimo Rosso '06	🍷🍷	4

Tenuta Farnete

FRAZ. COMEANA
VIA MACIA
59100 CARMIGNANO [PO]
TEL. 0571910078
www.enricopierazzuoli.com

CELLAR SALES
PRE-BOOKED VISITS

ANNUAL PRODUCTION **31.500 bottles**
HECTARES UNDER VINE **8.5**
VITICULTURE METHOD **Conventional**

There's a return to the Guide for Enrico Pierazzuoli, the dynamic winemaker who works in a number of territories but whose best wines come from Carmignano. His property is in the Montalbano area, where the Cantagallo estate extends over 180 hectares, with 18 under vine and 30 used for olive groves. Enrico has a plot of just two hectares in Chianti Classico, near Greve, while the main estate of 45 hectares has eight under vine and ten of olive groves.

The Carmignano Riserva '06 is very persuasive with its refreshing spice and aromatic herbs on the nose, a solid but well-distributed body and a satisfying finish. The basic version of the '07 is also convincing, with various fruit notes on the nose, a rich but not excessive structure and an appetizingly long finish. The other wines are nicely crafted with an intriguing Barco Reale '07 and the Gioveto '06, a Supertuscan from sangiovese, merlot and syrah that is a little too concentrated.

● Carmignano '07	🍷🍷	4*
● Carmignano Ris. '06	🍷🍷	5
● Barco Reale '07	🍷	3
● Chianti Montalbano Tenuta Cantagallo '08	🍷	3
● Chianti Montalbano Tenuta Cantagallo Ris. '06	🍷	4
● Gioveto '06	🍷	5

Fassati

FRAZ. GRACCIANO
VIA DI GRACCIANELLO, 3A
53040 MONTEPULCIANO [SI]
TEL. 0578708708
www.fazibattaglia.it

CELLAR SALES
PRE-BOOKED VISITS

ANNUAL PRODUCTION 800,000 bottles
HECTARES UNDER VINE 70
VITICULTURE METHOD Conventional

The time-honoured Montepulciano winery of Fassati was founded in 1913 and acquired in 1969 by Spartaco Sparaco, who was already the owner of Fazi Battaglia, in Marche, and one of Italy's foremost wine producers. Luca, Barbara and Chiara, the children of Maria Luisa and Sparaco Giannotti, took over this Tuscan winery in 1990. Early in the new millennium, they added the Greto delle Fate property, located at Magliano in Tuscany, in the heart of the Morellino di Scansano production area.

Stand-outs in the extensive line-up of wines are the Nobile Salarco Riserva '05 and the Gersemi '06 selection. The former has pleasant, mild-toned aromas perfectly echoed on the palate while the Gersemi has spicy aromas and considerable structure. The Morellino '08 is delightful, with a fresh, brisk nose and dynamic, savoury flavour continuity. Rosso Selciaia '08 is simple and straightforward while Spigo '08, a sangiovese rosé, is even-textured and deliciously drinkable.

★★ Fattoria di Felsina

VIA DEL CHIANTI, 101
53019 CASTELNUOVO BERARDENGA [SI]
TEL. 0577355117
www.felsina.it

CELLAR SALES
PRE-BOOKED VISITS

ANNUAL PRODUCTION 400,000 bottles
HECTARES UNDER VINE 62
VITICULTURE METHOD Conventional

Felsina can be found on the southern edge of the Chianti Classico designation zone, at the point where Chianti rock gives way to Siena clay. The soil mixture and the varied, changing landscape give Felsina sangiovese, and Castelnuovo Berardenga in general, the nuances and complexity that constitute the true essence of the wine, first of all, and also of its territory. The winery's range is the epitome of class and elegance, uniquely and unambiguously reflecting its territorial provenance.

Chianti Classico Riserva Rancia '06 embodies the winery philosophy. After aeration, the vigorous aromatics suggest deep cassis and blood oranges. The palate is dominated by acidity and tannins in structure that is more concentrated than usual. Blame the vintage. But savoury, succulent comfort is to hand. Fontalloro '06, from sangiovese picked mostly in Chianti, with some from the Siena hills, reveals the variety's wild nature, which calms as it evolves. Leather, earth and minerals tempt the nose, then the body unveils austere tannins and vigorous alcohol. We are in the adolescence of a great territory wine. Three Glasses. The lovely Chianti Classico Riserva '06 is more immediate

● Morellino di Scansano Greto delle Fate '08	♟♟	4
● Nobile di Montepulciano Gersemi '06	♟♟	6
● Nobile di Montepulciano Salarco Ris. '05	♟♟	7
● Nobile di Montepulciano Pasiteo '06	♟	5
● Rosso di Montepulciano Selciaia '08	♟	4
☉ Spigo '08	♟	4
● Nobile di Montepulciano Gersemi '03	♟♟	6
● Nobile di Montepulciano Gersemi '01	♟♟	6
● Nobile di Montepulciano Gersemi '00	♟♟	6
● Nobile di Montepulciano Pasiteo '04	♟♟	5
● Nobile di Montepulciano Pasiteo '03	♟♟	5
● Nobile di Montepulciano Pasiteo '02	♟♟	5
● Nobile di Montepulciano Salarco Ris. '04	♟♟	6
● Nobile di Montepulciano Salarco Ris. '01	♟♟	6

● Fontalloro '06	♟♟♟	7
● Chianti Cl. Rancia Ris. '06	♟♟♟	7
● Poggio Granoni Castello della Farnetella '06	♟♟	7
● Chianti Cl. Ris. '06	♟♟	5
● Chianti Cl. Rancia Ris. '05	♟♟♟	6
● Chianti Cl. Rancia Ris. '04	♟♟♟	6
● Chianti Cl. Rancia Ris. '03	♟♟♟	6
● Chianti Cl. Rancia Ris. '00	♟♟♟	6
● Fontalloro '05	♟♟♟	7
● Fontalloro '01	♟♟♟	6
● Fontalloro '99	♟♟♟	6
● Fontalloro '98	♟♟♟	6
● Fontalloro '97	♟♟♟	6
● Fontalloro '95	♟♟♟	6
● Maestro Raro '01	♟♟♟	6

Ferrero

FRAZ. SANT'ANGELO IN COLLE
LOC. PASCENA
53024 MONTALCINO [SI]
TEL. 0577844170
claudia.forroro@gmail.com

CELLAR SALES
PRE-BOOKED VISITS

ANNUAL PRODUCTION **20,000 bottles**
HECTARES UNDER VINE **5.5**
VITICULTURE METHOD **Conventional**

This small Sant'Angelo in Colle winery has recently shown considerable, constant improvement in its designation wines and in some labels from international varieties. Paola Ferrero went to the Alba school of oenology, one of the most important in Italy. He runs the company with his three daughters, assisted by Pablo Harri, a consultant oenologist known throughout Montalcino. The vineyards are generally on clay and limestone at about 300 metres above sea level, on the southern slope. The grapes ripen well and the wines are quite muscular.

The Brunello di Montalcino '04 is very good, its intense nose weaving morello cherry, sweet tobacco and hints of balsam. Subtle and elegant, it offers progression and considerable length, thanks to vigorous, refreshing acidity, before the lovely intense finish lingers on perceptions of leather. The good Maremma Alicante '06 has a brooding nose, sensations of currants and blueberries, lots of spice and some fiery pepper, even if the finish is held back by the slightly boisterous extract. The Cabernet, also '06 and also from Maremma, is persuasive with its fresh bell pepper nose and full, balanced palate.

★ Tenute Ambrogio e Giovanni Folonari

LOC. PASSO DEI PECORAI
VIA DI NOZZOLE, 12
50022 GREVE IN CHIANTI [FI]
TEL. 055859811
www.tenutefolonari.com

CELLAR SALES
PRE-BOOKED VISITS

ANNUAL PRODUCTION **1,500,000 bottles**
HECTARES UNDER VINE **300**
VITICULTURE METHOD **Conventional**

The Folonaris' affair with wine began back in the 1700s. There have been many ups and downs, many different owners and far-sighted projects that soon became successful strategies and today this is still one of Tuscany's most representative operations, with interests in Chianti Classico, Montalcino, Maremma and Montepulciano. The wines have a modern style but always reflect their terroir and always make a major mark on the international scene.

The Cabreo Il Borgo sangiovese and cabernet sauvignon blend is a legendary house Supertuscan that sprang from a forward-looking project in the 1980s. The '07 vintage is ripe overall, with a nose underpinned by intense, jammy, red berry fruit and a hint of greens. The palate is rich, creamy, meaty and quite long, although the aromatics are less complex and nuanced. The varietal Chardonnay Cabreo La Pietra '07 is fair. The '07 edition of Bolgheri Campo al Mare is attractive for its pervasive nose of blueberries and bell peppers, and a tight palate with close-knit tannins.

● Alicante '06	ŶŶ 6
● Brunello di Montalcino '04	ŶŶŶ 7
● Cabernet '06	ŶŶ 6
● Mo '06	ŶŶ 6
● Rosso di Montalcino '07	ŶŶ 5
● Merlot '06	Ŷ 6
● Brunello di Montalcino '02	♔♔ 7
● Brunello di Montalcino '00	♔♔ 7

● Cabreo Il Borgo '07	ŶŶ 6
● Bolgheri Campo al Mare '07	ŶŶ 5
○ Cabreo La Pietra '07	Ŷ 6
● Cabreo Il Borgo '06	♔♔♔ 6
● Chianti Cl. La Forra Ris. '90	♔♔♔ 5
● Il Pareto '04	♔♔♔ 8
● Il Pareto '01	♔♔♔ 8
● Il Pareto '00	♔♔♔ 8
● Il Pareto '98	♔♔♔ 7
● Il Pareto '97	♔♔♔ 7
● Il Pareto '93	♔♔♔ 7
● Il Pareto '90	♔♔♔ 7
● Il Pareto '88	♔♔♔ 7

Fontaleoni

LOC. SANTA MARIA, 39A
53037 SAN GIMIGNANO [SI]
TEL. 0577950193
www.fontaleoni.com

CELLAR SALES
PRE-BOOKED VISITS

ANNUAL PRODUCTION **100,000 bottles**
HECTARES UNDER VINE **23.5**
VITICULTURE METHOD **Conventional**

Franco Troiani's winery repeated last year's positive performance and again earned a full profile that acknowledges the continuity of Franco's meticulous work tending over 20 hectares under vine. It was no coincidence that he decided to present four Vernaccia labels. That's Franco's his way of showing the importance he places on the various, quite diverse terrains that make up his estate.

The most convincing is Vernaccia Notte di Luna '08, aged only in steel. The nose is nuanced with camomile and honey, the body is rich, velvety and enfolding, and the finish is a delight. We also liked the Riserva '07, a first-timer that struggles at first but then unveils traditional sensations of white-fleshed fruit and a palate with lovely progression. The other two 2008s are simpler but still very drinkable. The most persuasive red is the Chianti '07 for its instant pleasure and the acidity-driven freshness. Cerreta '05 has plenty of stuffing but just can't express itself to the full, although it is basically well crafted.

★★ Castello di Fonterutoli

LOC. FONTERUTOLI
VIA OTTONE III DI SASSONIA, 5
53011 CASTELLINA IN CHIANTI [SI]
TEL. 057773571
www.fonterutoli.it

CELLAR SALES
PRE-BOOKED VISITS
VISITOR FACILITIES
FOOD

ANNUAL PRODUCTION **710,000 bottles**
HECTARES UNDER VINE **117**
VITICULTURE METHOD **Conventional**

Fonterutoli is a must for anyone wishing to expand their Chianti Classico experience. This is where the 1202 and 1208 treaties were signed, assigning Chianti to the republic of Florence. The owners are the Mazzei family, whose history has evolved in parallel with the celebrated district where they live. Today, Fonterutoli is a modern-style winery where cutting-edge technology vinifies fruit from long-established vineyards in magnificent wine country.

Siepi '06 is the summation of all this. The wine, from a six-hectare vineyard selection, is a half sangiovese-half merlot blend. The nose tempts with black berry fruit enriched with chocolate and vanilla notes before the palate unveils its essential concentration in dense flavours that can only improve with the passage of time. Three Glasses. Chianti Classico Castello di Fonterutoli '06 reflects its vintage perfectly in palpable perceptions of ripe fruit and flowers. On the palate, the body shows all its muscle with prominent tannins that give harmony and balance to the overall drinking experience. The full-bodied, well-made Chianti Classico '07 is very pleasant.

○ Vernaccia di S. Gimignano Notte di Luna '08	♀♀ 3*
○ Vernaccia di S. Gimignano Ris. '07	♀♀ 5
● Chianti Colli Senesi '07	♀ 3
● S. Gimignano Rosso La Cerreta '05	♀ 4
○ Vernaccia di S. Gimignano '08	♀ 3
○ Vernaccia di S. Gimignano V. Casanuova '08	♀ 4
● Chianti Colli Senesi '06	♀♀ 4*
○ Vernaccia di S. Gimignano Notte di Luna '07	♀♀ 3*
○ Vernaccia di S. Gimignano Notte di Luna '06	♀♀ 3*
○ Vernaccia di S. Gimignano V. Casanuova '07	♀♀ 4*
○ Vernaccia di S. Gimignano V. Casanuova '06	♀♀ 4*

● Siepi '06	♀♀♀ 8
● Chianti Cl. Castello di Fonterutoli '06	♀♀ 8
● Chianti Cl. '07	♀ 6
● Chianti Cl. Castello di Fonterutoli '04	♀♀♀ 7
● Chianti Cl. Castello di Fonterutoli '03	♀♀♀ 7
● Chianti Cl. Castello di Fonterutoli '01	♀♀♀ 7
● Chianti Cl. Castello di Fonterutoli '00	♀♀♀ 8
● Chianti Cl. Castello di Fonterutoli '99	♀♀♀ 8
● Siepi '05	♀♀♀ 8
● Siepi '03	♀♀♀ 8
● Siepi '01	♀♀♀ 8
● Siepi '00	♀♀♀ 8
● Siepi '99	♀♀♀ 8

★ Tenuta Fontodi

FRAZ. GREVE IN CHIANTI
VIA SAN LEOLINO, 89
50020 PANZANO [FI]
TEL. 055852005
www.fontodi.com

CELLAR SALES
PRE-BOOKED VISITS

ANNUAL PRODUCTION 300,000 bottles
HECTARES UNDER VINE 70
VITICULTURE METHOD Naturale

Fontodi's vineyards lie in the Conca d'Oro at Panzano in Chianti in a location that is ideal for cultivating vines. The Manetti family went organic several years ago and their aim is to bring out all the characteristics of this wonderful territory in their wines. They combine this approach with the most up-to-date techniques in their functional, cutting-edge cellar, built in 1998.

Flaccianello della Pieve is a classic Supertuscan and was one of the first based solely on sangiovese. The '06 version has enormous aromatic impact, offering earthy, almost iron sensations that meld into black berry fruit and coffee with a vegetal undertone. On the palate, the wine shows rather over-stated extraction whose tannins – at least at this young juncture – are a tad rough. The Chianti Classico '07 is still dominated by oak that compromises the nose, where toasty notes obscure the fruit. But the palate is pleasant with dynamic body that bodes well for future tastings and for bottle ageing. Case Via Syrah '06 is spicy and full-bodied but not overly complex.

Podere La Fortuna

LOC. LA FORTUNA, 83
53024 MONTALCINO [SI]
TEL. 0577848308
www.tenutalafortuna.it

CELLAR SALES
PRE-BOOKED VISITS

ANNUAL PRODUCTION 60,000 bottles
HECTARES UNDER VINE 13
VITICULTURE METHOD Conventional

Situated on the stunning north-west slope of Montalcino, this estate belonging to Gioberto Zannoni, one of the founding members of the Brunello consortium, presented a series of wines that reflect their terroir of origin. Their style is distinctive. Barrels of varying sizes are used for maturation of the Brunello di Montalcino while the Riserva version is aged in barriques and medium-sized casks. The cellar and body of the La Fortuna estate, completely renovated in recent years, form a small village that merges into the territory and makes a perfect setting for winemaking.

The Brunello di Montalcino '04 is superb and we awarded it Three Glasses. The classic nose offers clear notes of morello cherry and cherry blending to perfection with light spicy notes of cinnamon and vanilla. The palate owes its good balance to sharp acidity and tannins of superb quality and the finish is deep. We were less impressed by the Rosso di Montalcino '07, largely because of its over-assertive tannins.

● Flaccianello della Pieve '06	♟♟ 7
○ Vin Santo del Chianti Cl. '01	♟♟ 6
● Chianti Cl. '07	♟ 5
● Syrah Case Via '06	♟ 7
● Chianti Cl. V. del Sorbo Ris. '01	♟♟♟ 7
● Chianti Cl. V. del Sorbo Ris. '94	♟♟♟ 7
● Flaccianello della Pieve '05	♟♟♟ 7
● Flaccianello della Pieve '03	♟♟♟ 7
● Flaccianello della Pieve '01	♟♟♟ 7
● Flaccianello della Pieve '00	♟♟♟ 7
● Flaccianello della Pieve '97	♟♟♟ 7
● Flaccianello della Pieve '91	♟♟♟ 7
● Syrah Case Via '98	♟♟♟ 7

● Brunello di Montalcino '04	♟♟♟ 7
● Rosso di Montalcino '07	♟ 5
● Brunello di Montalcino '01	♟♟♟ 7
● Brunello di Montalcino '03	♟♟ 7
● Brunello di Montalcino '00	♟♟ 6
● Brunello di Montalcino Ris. '01	♟♟ 7
● Brunello di Montalcino Ris. '99	♟♟ 7
● Rosso di Montalcino '06	♟♟ 5
● Rosso di Montalcino '03	♟♟ 4
● Sant'Antimo La Fortuna '04	♟♟ 6
● Sant'Antimo La Fortuna '01	♟♟ 6

Frascole

LOC. FRASCOLE, 27A
50062 DICOMANO [FI]
TEL. 0558386340
www.frascole.it

CELLAR SALES
PRE-BOOKED VISITS

ANNUAL PRODUCTION **55,000 bottles**
HECTARES UNDER VINE **15**
VITICULTURE METHOD **Organic certified**

The big news from the Lippi family estate is that the Vin Santo has not been released. It remains in the cellar post-bottling where it will stay until it is deemed perfect for the market. This allowed us to concentrate our tastings on the rest of the estate's production, which is often over-shadowed by the very popular sweet wine. The other wines have character but tend to lack clarity on the nose before going on to express themselves fully.

The cream of this year's crop is Venìa '06, an equal blend of sangiovese and merlot. Faintly toasty notes emerge in the nose with very agreeable nuances of mint. Entry on the palate is warm and fruity with a rising finish. The two versions of the Chianti Rufina Discrete are decent. The '07 is simpler with fruity aromas, and a lean body, while the Riserva '06 has a more complex nose showing clear tertiary notes. It is full and succulent but the palate is rather low-key at the back.

★ Marchesi de' Frescobaldi

VIA SANTO SPIRITO, 11
50125 FIRENZE
TEL. 05527141
www.frescobaldi.it

CELLAR SALES
PRE-BOOKED VISITS

ANNUAL PRODUCTION **9,000,000 bottles**
HECTARES UNDER VINE **1200**
VITICULTURE METHOD **Conventional**

Marchesi Frescobaldi wines never disappoint. Production spans several territories but Nipozzano remains the heart of operations, although Castello di Pomino is carrying out the most interesting experiments. The cold climate is perfect for the cultivation of varieties that are not typically Tuscan. After the versions of pure Pinot Nero, and the blends based on white grape types such as pinot bianco, pinot grigio and traminer aromatico, we are very excited about the new Pomino Spumante, which we expect to be very good.

Yet again, it is Mormoreto that reigns supreme in the '06 edition. This blend of cabernet sauvignon, merlot, cabernet franc and petit verdot possesses estery sensations of blackberry and blueberry jam, a solid, full body with measured tannins and a finish that powers through nicely. We also liked the Riserva Montesodi '06's rich nose and generous substance, the Pomino Rosso '06's elegance, the agreeable cabernet, merlot and sangiovese blend Tenuta di Castiglioni '07 and the Pomino Vin Santo '04's seductive sweetness. As ever, the Riserva '06 Nipozzano is good.

● Venìa '06	♀♀ 5
● Chianti Rufina '07	♀ 4
● Chianti Rufina Ris. '06	♀ 5
● Chianti Rufina '06	♀♀ 4*
● Chianti Rufina Ris. '03	♀♀ 5
● Venìa '04	♀♀ 5
○ Vin Santo del Chianti Rufina '99	♀♀ 8
○ Vin Santo del Chianti Rufina '97	♀♀ 8

● Mormoreto '06	♀♀ 7
● Casafonte Pinot Nero '06	♀♀ 7
○ Castello di Pomino Vin Santo '04	♀♀ 6
● Chianti Rufina Montesodi Ris. '06	♀♀ 7
● Chianti Rufina Nipozzano Ris. '06	♀♀ 4
● Lucente '07	♀♀ 5
○ Pomino Il Benefizio Ris. '07	♀♀ 6
● Pomino Rosso '06	♀♀ 5
● Tenuta di Castiglioni '07	♀♀ 5
○ Albizzia '08	♀ 3
○ Pomino Bianco '08	♀ 4
○ Pomino V.T. '07	♀ 5
● Rèmole '07	♀ 3
☉ Tenuta di Castiglioni Saltagrilli '08	♀ 4
● Mormoreto '05	♀♀♀ 7
● Mormoreto '01	♀♀♀ 7

Tenuta La Fuga

LOC. CAMIGLIANO
53024 MONTALCINO [SI]
TEL. 055859811
www.tenutefolonari.com

PRE-BOOKED VISITS
VISITOR FACILITIES

ANNUAL PRODUCTION **50,000 bottles**
HECTARES UNDER VINE **10**
VITICULTURE METHOD **Conventional**

La Fuga belongs to Ambrogio and Giovanni Folonari, who in the space of just a few short years have turned it into a point of reference for the territory. The estate lies on the south-west slope of Montalcino near the village of Camigliano. This is the DOCG's warmest zone thanks to the airstreams that arrive from the Maremma. Here the grapes are harvested early and the risk of overripening of the fruit is very high. The soil is largely clay-based and with plenty of pebbles, which lighten the texture and allow the right level of oxygenation. Wines are modern in style.

The wines on offer this year are interesting and the Brunello di Montalcino '04 won Three Glasses. What really impressed us is the capacity of this wine to wed the grapes' natural density with a good measure of acidity and clear tannic maturity. The generous nose offers aromas of black cherry and blackberry jam, typical of the zone. The finish is ample and lingering. The well-made Rosso di Montalcino '07 shows ripe fruit notes and nice weight.

Castello di Gabbiano

FRAZ. MERCATALE VAL DI PESA
VIA GABBIANO, 22
50020 SAN CASCIANO IN VAL DI PESA [FI]
TEL. 055821053
www.castellogabbiano.it

CELLAR SALES
PRE-BOOKED VISITS
VISITOR FACILITIES
FOOD

ANNUAL PRODUCTION **360,000 bottles**
HECTARES UNDER VINE **127**
VITICULTURE METHOD **Conventional**

Gabbiano in San Casciano Val di Pesa is one of the oldest and noblest of Tuscany's castles. It was sold several years ago and today it in is the firm hands of American Beringer Blass group, a heavyweight in global wine. The wines have benefited from the new ownership. The technical team remains Italian and has the support of some of the big names in American consultant oenology. Sangiovese is king here and the style of the wines is clean and modern, without descending into over-approachable roundness.

Of the two IGTs, we preferred the Bellezza '06, a pure Sangiovese fermented and aged in a mix of medium and small casks. Coffee and clove aromas meld with lovely dark fruit notes and fresh balsamic undertones before the dense, full-bodied palate shows close-knit tannic texture and fabulous length. The excellent Chianti Classico Riserva '06 has notes of plums, blueberries and spice and a sweet, elegant palate with refined tannins and a balsamic finish. From merlot with sangiovese and cabernet sauvignon, the Alleanza '06 is less successful with too-drying tannins.

● Brunello di Montalcino '04	♟♟♟ 7
● Nobile di Montepulciano Torcalvano Fattoria di Gracciano '06	♟♟ 4
● Rosso di Montalcino '07	♟♟ 5
● Brunello di Montalcino '03	♀♀ 7
● Brunello di Montalcino '01	♀♀ 7
● Brunello di Montalcino '00	♀♀ 7
● Brunello di Montalcino La Due Sorelle Ris. '01	♀♀ 8
● Rosso di Montalcino '06	♀♀ 5
● Rosso di Montalcino '05	♀♀ 5

● Bellezza '06	♟♟ 6
● Chianti Cl. Ris. '06	♟♟ 5
● Alleanza '06	♟ 6
● Alleanza '05	♀♀ 6
● Alleanza '04	♀♀ 6
● Alleanza '01	♀♀ 7
● Bellezza '05	♀♀ 6
● Bellezza '01	♀♀ 7
● Chianti Cl. Ris. '04	♀♀ 5
● Chianti Cl. Ris. '01	♀♀ 5

Gagliole

LOC. GAGLIOLE, 42
53011 CASTELLINA IN CHIANTI [SI]
TEL. 0577740369
www.gagliole.com

CELLAR SALES
PRE-BOOKED VISITS

ANNUAL PRODUCTION **35,000 bottles**
HECTARES UNDER VINE **9.9**
VITICULTURE METHOD **Conventional**

This estate lies in one of the most beautiful and hidden pockets of the Chianti Classico in a unique setting. The only sign of man's influence is the terraced landscape, which has been here for centuries, but nature has resisted all attempts to tame it. For owners Thomas and Monika Bar, it was love at first sight and they have transformed Gagliole one step at a time into a haven of peace. This estate has great potential and stakes its bets on tradition and sangiovese. The vineyards are high at around 500 metres, ideally placed facing south south-west on a base of marl.

Thomas and Monika offered us two wines to taste this year, Chianti Classico Rubiolo '07 and Gagliole '07, a sangiovese and cabernet sauvignon blend. The first offers red fruit aromas with vegetal undertones and a palate led by excellent acidity and good progression while the Gagliole reveals its barrique-ageing and is more structured, although the tannins are a little clenched. It will open out with cellar time.

Tenuta di Ghizzano

FRAZ. GHIZZANO
VIA DELLA CHIESA, 4
56037 PECCIOLI [PI]
TEL. 0587630096
www.tenutadighizzano.com

CELLAR SALES
PRE-BOOKED VISITS
VISITOR FACILITIES

ANNUAL PRODUCTION **70,000 bottles**
HECTARES UNDER VINE **20**
VITICULTURE METHOD **Organic certified**

The Ghizzano estate extends for around 350 hectares across the gentle slopes of the splendid hinterland of Pisa. The 20 hectares planted to vine are a mix of sandy and clayey terrains full of fossilized shells, relics of the sea that once covered these valleys. With each passing harvest Ginevra Venerosi Pesciolini seems to infuse her wines with even more character and personality.

This year, Ghizzano's range surpasses itself with the Veneroso and Nambrot – both '06 – which are two absolute gems. Three Glasses went to Nambrot, a merlot-heavy blend with some cabernet sauvignon and franc, and petit verdot. The nose is generous and with complex black berry fruit, brambles and spices. The vibrant palate possesses crisp acidity and tannins of perfect extraction. Hot on its heels comes Veneroso, from mainly sangiovese with 30 per cent cabernet sauvignon. The nose is more delicate and the palate stiffer. Both will age wonderfully well. Ghizzano '08 is fruity and very pleasant.

● Chianti Cl. Rubiolo '07	🍷🍷 4
● Gagliole Rosso '07	🍷🍷 7
● Chianti Cl. Rubiolo '05	🍷🍷 4
● Gagliole Rosso '06	🍷🍷 7
● Gagliole Rosso '04	🍷🍷 6
● Gagliole Rosso '01	🍷🍷 6
● Gagliole Rosso '00	🍷🍷 6
● Gagliole Rosso '99	🍷🍷 5

● Nambrot '06	🍷🍷🍷 7
● Veneroso '06	🍷🍷 6
● il Ghizzano '08	🍷🍷 4*
● Nambrot '06	🍷🍷🍷 7
● Nambrot '05	🍷🍷🍷 7
● Nambrot '04	🍷🍷🍷 7
● Nambrot '03	🍷🍷🍷 7
● Nambrot '01	🍷🍷🍷 8
● Nambrot '00	🍷🍷🍷 8
● Veneroso '04	🍷🍷🍷 6
● Veneroso '01	🍷🍷🍷 6

I Giusti e Zanza

VIA DEI PUNTONI, 9
56043 FAUGLIA [PI]
TEL. 058544354
www.igiustiezanza.it

CELLAR SALES
PRE-BOOKED VISITO

ANNUAL PRODUCTION **84,000 bottles**
HECTARES UNDER VINE **17**
VITICULTURE METHOD **Conventional**

Paolo Giusti is a point of reference in the Pisa wine world. His vineyards of syrah, cabernet, merlot and sangiovese grow on a base of alluvial gravel which offers an ideal growing environment. Indeed, Paolo is so convinced that he has launched a project to convert I Giusti e Zanza into an organic estate. We applaud his decision to delay release of the Nemorino red and white. On retasting, previous vintages performed very well.

The wines offered for tasting were excellent as always. Belcore '07 from sangiovese and merlot shows superb structure. Black berry fruit jam and sweet spices are the prelude to a dynamic, concentrated palate that will smooth out over time. The Bordeaux blend Dulcamara '06 is good, presenting long, embracing fruity aromas on the nose followed by refreshing vegetal tones. The palate is full, linear and harmonious. PerBruno '07 from syrah only is less rewarding than usual. It could be that we tasted it at the wrong moment for it did not come across as smooth and full as in previous editions. One to keep an eye on though; it will definitely open out.

Podere Grattamacco

LOC. LUNGAGNANO
57022 CASTAGNETO CARDUCCI [LI]
TEL. 0565765069
www.collemassari.it

CELLAR SALES
PRE-BOOKED VISITS

ANNUAL PRODUCTION **80,000 bottles**
HECTARES UNDER VINE **13**
VITICULTURE METHOD **Organic certified**

Claudio Tipa is one of the most inspired entrepreneurs in today's wine world. He has succeeded in combining Podere Grattamacco's eternal allure for consumers with the business strategy required to survive by any estate. No longer a niche product for a select few, his wines comprise a solid, wide-ranging commercial line offering high quality products stamped with the unique character that this area of the Bolgheri amphitheatre zone gives to its grapes.

The '06 Grattamacco wins Three Glasses for its vibrant cornucopia of sensations. Lively aromas open out to reveal hints of red fruit jam, cinnamon and orange blossom, and the full body shows excellent continuity. In the mouth it is deep, long and evidently capable of ageing unhurriedly in bottle. L'Alberello '06 is also on top form. Currant and black cherry aromas lead into a delicious palate distinguished by silky tannins and acid linearity. The Bolgheri '07 is one of the best basic wines we tasted, although at this stage of its development it is still soft and youthful. Grattamacco Bianco '08 needs time – no news there – to reveal its full potential.

● Belcore '07	▼▼	4
● Dulcamara '06	▼▼	6
● PerBruno '07	▼	5
● Belcore '03	♀♀	4*
● Belcore '01	♀♀	4
● Dulcamara '05	♀♀	6
● Dulcamara '04	♀♀	6
● Dulcamara '03	♀♀	6
● Dulcamara '01	♀♀	6
● Dulcamara '00	♀♀	6
● PerBruno '06	♀♀	5
● PerBruno '05	♀♀	5
● PerBruno '04	♀♀	5
● PerBruno '03	♀♀	5

● Bolgheri Rosso Sup. Grattamacco '06	▼▼▼	8
● Bolgheri Sup. L'Alberello '06	▼▼	7
● Bolgheri Rosso '07	▼▼	5
○ Grattamacco '08	▼	5
● Bolgheri Rosso Sup. Grattamacco '05	♀♀♀	8
● Bolgheri Rosso Sup. Grattamacco '04	♀♀♀	8
● Bolgheri Rosso Sup. Grattamacco '03	♀♀♀	8
● Bolgheri Rosso Sup. Grattamacco '01	♀♀♀	8
● Bolgheri Rosso Sup. Grattamacco '99	♀♀♀	8
● Bolgheri Sup. L'Alberello '05	♀♀	7

Greppone Mazzi
Tenimenti Ruffino

LOC. GREPPONE
53024 MONTALCINO [SI]
TEL. 0556499717
www.ruffino.lt

PRE-BOOKED VISITS

ANNUAL PRODUCTION N.D.
HECTARES UNDER VINE 13.5
VITICULTURE METHOD Conventional

Greppone Mazzi belongs to Ruffino, one of Italy's most important wine-making groups. Situated near Montalcino, the estate is home to a beautiful 18th-century villa featuring a Leopoldo-style loggia. Its 13 hectares of Brunello are all in one block but the terrain varies in terms of soil composition and altitude. This is most obvious in the autumn when the trees lose their leaves according to where they are located. The estate's wines are aged in barrels varying in size from 30 to 60 hectolitres and undergo fairly long macerations.

The '04 Brunello di Montalcino is quite possibly the best ever produced by this estate. A lovely intense ruby announces clean, fragrant notes of wild cherry-led red berry fruit and flowery nuances of oleander and tea leaf. The concentrated palate shows elegant tannins and good acidity supporting the impressive extractive weight, lending grace to the progression, and the finale echoes the flowery notes on the nose. The Brunello di Montalcino Riserva '03 is a notch below, with tannins still to the fore.

● Brunello di Montalcino '04	▼▼▼	7
● Cortona '06	▼▼	6
● Nobile di Montepulciano Lodola Nuova '06	▼▼	6
● Nobile di Montepulciano Lodola Nuova Ris. '05	▼▼	7
● Brunello di Montalcino Ris. '03	▼	6
● Brunello di Montalcino '99	♈♈♈	8
● Brunello di Montalcino Ris. '99	♈♈♈	6
● Brunello di Montalcino '03	♈♈	7
● Brunello di Montalcino '97	♈♈	8
● Brunello di Montalcino '96	♈♈	6
● Brunello di Montalcino Ris. '01	♈♈	6
● Brunello di Montalcino Ris. '00	♈♈	8

Castelli del Grevepesa

FRAZ. MERCATALE IN VAL DI PESA
VIA GREVIGIANA, 34
50024 SAN CASCIANO IN VAL DI PESA [FI]
TEL. 055821911
www.castellidelgrevepesa.it

CELLAR SALES
PRE-BOOKED VISITS

ANNUAL PRODUCTION 5.800,000 bottles
HECTARES UNDER VINE 1000
VITICULTURE METHOD Conventional

Founded in 1965 by Gualtiero Armando Nunzi, originally with just a few members, the Castelli del Grevepesa co-operative winery today has 185 direct growers and is the largest associative group in the Chianti area. It totals 1,000 hectares of vineyards, 650 of which lie within Chianti Classico, and these have been selected and classified so as to create the highest possible standards in terms of both number of labels and quality.

This year's performance is first-rate. The Chianti Classico Castelgreve Lessenziale '07 reached our finals thanks to its crisp, complex aromatic profile. Red berry fruit aromas and citrussy notes are the prelude to a confident, rigorous palate that never threatens to dry the mouth, showing full and gratifying. The Chianti Classico Castelgreve Lessenziale Riserva '06 is even deeper. Refined spicy sensations give way to hints of red fruit and vanilla before silky tannins swathe a dense, continuous body of immense quality. The Chianti Classico 40 Vendemmie '07 is also very good, showing a long, fluent finish. All the wines from this reliable co-operative are impressive.

● Chianti Cl. Castelgreve Lessenziale '07	▼▼	4*
● Chianti Cl. Castelgreve Lessenziale Ris. '06	▼▼	5
● Chianti Cl. 40 Vendemmie '07	▼▼	5
● Chianti Cl. Clemente VII Ris. '06	▼▼	5
● Chianti Cl. Clemente VII '07	▼	4
● Chianti Cl. Clemente VII '06	♈♈	4*
● Chianti Cl. Panzano '06	♈♈	4*
● Syrah '06	♈♈	5

Grignano

FRAZ. GRIGNANO
VIA DI GRIGNANO, 22
50065 PONTASSIEVE [FI]
TEL. 0558398490
www.fattorladigrignano.com

CELLAR SALES
PRE-BOOKED VISITS

ANNUAL PRODUCTION **150,000 bottles**
HECTARES UNDER VINE **49**
VITICULTURE METHOD **Organic certified**

This was rather a disappointing performance compared to previous years from the Inghirami family estate. The Riserva Chianti Rufina '06 did best but the rest of the range failed to show the usual panache. To be fair, several of the key labels were missing from this year's line-up, including the Riserva Poggio Gualtieri and the Salicaria from sangiovese and merlot. But it was from the more territorial products that we expected to see greater things. We hope the appointment has only been postponed.

The Chianti Rufina Riserva '06 presents animal skin, plum and bell pepper on the nose. Entry on the palate is complex and balanced with a finish that is not overly long but very pleasant. The remaining products – Chianti Rufina '07 and Chardonnay '08 – are decent. The Vin Santo '02 deserves a special mention, though, presenting more convincing in its aromas of nuts, honey and spices than on the palate.

Tenuta Guado al Tasso

LOC. BELVEDERE, 140
57020 BOLGHERI [LI]
TEL. 0565749735
www.antinori.it

PRE-BOOKED VISITS

ANNUAL PRODUCTION **880,000 bottles**
HECTARES UNDER VINE **300**
VITICULTURE METHOD **Conventional**

Guado al Tasso is a major player in the Bolgheri area thanks to its immense expanse of vineyards – around 300 hectares, the largest in the territory – and the name Antinori, the noble family that owns the property and has played such a huge role in the history of Italian wine. Investments in the vineyards and cellar have enabled the estate to achieve absolute quality and maintain consistency throughout the years, adding much to the prestige of the DOCG.

The '06 edition of the flagship Guado al Tasso is without doubt one of the best in recent years. The complex nose presents ripe black fruit, blackberries, currants and cassis, with very intense vegetal and spicy sensations. The palate is rich, juicy and lingering. Excellent tannic texture showcases the naturalness of the wine and its harmony of flavour through to a liquorice-edged finish. Bolgheri Vermentino '08 also has fabulous aromatics and balance. Notes of apple-like fruit and vanilla announce a full, almost chewy body refreshed by a certain tanginess. Elegance in a glass. The Bruciato '07 is simpler with a modern slant and attractive oaky notes.

● Chianti Rufina Ris. '06	♀♀	4*
○ Chardonnay '08	♀	4
● Chianti Rufina '07	♀	3
○ Vin Santo del Chianti Rufina '02	♀	5
● Chianti Rufina '06	♀♀	3*
● Chianti Rufina Ris. '05	♀♀	4*
● Chianti Rufina Ris. '04	♀♀	4
● Salicaria '04	♀♀	6
○ Vin Santo del Chianti Capsula Oro '01	♀♀	5

● Bolgheri Rosso Sup. Guado al Tasso '06	♀♀	8
○ Bolgheri Vermentino '08	♀♀	5
● Bolgheri Rosso Bruciato '07	♀	5
● Bolgheri Rosso Sup. Guado al Tasso '01	♀♀♀	8
● Bolgheri Rosso Sup. Guado al Tasso '90	♀♀♀	8
● Bolgheri Rosso Bruciato '02	♀♀	5
● Bolgheri Rosso Sup. Guado al Tasso '05	♀♀	8
● Bolgheri Rosso Sup. Guado al Tasso '04	♀♀	8
● Bolgheri Rosso Sup. Guado al Tasso '03	♀♀	8
● Bolgheri Rosso Sup. Guado al Tasso '00	♀♀	8

Guicciardini Strozzi Fattoria Cusona

LOC. CUSONA, 5
53037 SAN GIMIGNANO [SI]
TEL. 0577950028
www.guicciardinistrozzi.it

CELLAR SALES
PRE-BOOKED VISITS

ANNUAL PRODUCTION **650,000 bottles**
HECTARES UNDER VINE **70**
VITICULTURE METHOD **Conventional**

Few wineries can boast a 1,000-year history but Cusona, which has been in the Guicciardini family since the 1500s, celebrated this anniversary some time ago. Despite its ancient roots there is no lack of enthusiasm for new ventures, witness the acquisition of the properties in Bolgheri and Maremma. This in no way diverts attention from the parent estate, however, which continues to experiment.

We were highly impressed by the second edition of the Vernaccia Cusona 1933, the '08. Golden in colour, it presents fascinating, ripe aromas with mineral tones and a rich, fruity body with a tangy, mouthwatering finish. The rest of the range is on par, although the whites show better clarity. The Vernaccia Riserva '07 has a rich palate and the fresh aromas typical of the vintage, and the pure vermentino Arabesque '08 is elegant. The reds have yet to find definition. Millanni '06, a sangiovese, cabernet sauvignon and merlot mix, is still rigid and the Sodole '06 from almost 100 per cent sangiovese is overwhelmed by the oak. The Colli Senesi '08 is well styled and drinkable.

Icario

VIA DELLE PIETROSE, 2
53045 MONTEPULCIANO [SI]
TEL. 0578758845
www.icario.it

CELLAR SALES
PRE-BOOKED VISITS

ANNUAL PRODUCTION **120,000 bottles**
HECTARES UNDER VINE **22**
VITICULTURE METHOD **Conventional**

Named after the mythological character that Dionysius tasked with spreading the culture of wine amongst men, Icario has belonged to the Cecchetti family since 1998. It is one of the newest estates within the Nobile di Montepulciano DOCG. The oenological project has seen the recent inauguration of one of the most cutting-edge cellars in the zone and aims to interpret the great Montepulciano winemaking tradition in a modern, creative fashion while seeking to imbue its wines with distinctive personality and character.

The '06 Icario Nobile di Montepulciano and the Nobile selection Vitaroccia, also '06, stand out from the range presented. The former is flavoursome and complex while the second offers captivating aromas and dense but never overwhelming structure. The Rosso Icario '07 from a blend of sangiovese, teroldego and merlot is approachable and enjoyable. Nysa '08, a white obtained from an unusual and interesting blend of pinot grigio, gewürztraminer and pinot nero, has rather oxidized tones.

○ Vernaccia di S. Gimignano Cusona 1933 '08	♥♥	4*
○ Arabesque '08	♥	4
● Chianti Colli Senesi '08	♥	3
● Millanni '06	♥	7
● Sodole '06	♥	6
○ Vernaccia di S. Gimignano Ris. '07	♥	4
○ Vernaccia di S. Gimignano Titolato Strozzi '08	♥	4
● Millanni '99	♥♥♥	7
● Bolgheri Ocra '06	♥♥	4*
● Morellino di Scansano Poggio Moreto '06	♥♥	5
● Sodole '05	♥♥	6

● Nobile di Montepulciano '06	♥♥	5
● Nobile di Montepulciano Vitaroccia '06	♥♥	6
○ Nysa '08	♥	6
● Rosso Icario '07	♥	4
● Nobile di Montepulciano '04	♥♥	5
● Nobile di Montepulciano '03	♥♥	5
● Nobile di Montepulciano Vitaroccia '05	♥♥	6
● Nobile di Montepulciano Vitaroccia '03	♥♥	5

★ Isole e Olena

LOC. ISOLE, 1
50021 BARBERINO VAL D'ELSA [FI]
TEL. 0558072763
www.isoleolena.it

CELLAR SALES
PRE-BOOKED VISITS

ANNUAL PRODUCTION 200,000 bottles
HECTARES UNDER VINE 50
VITICULTURE METHOD Conventional

Isole e Olena is one of those estates that have opened the way to a modern interpretation of Chianti Classico. Much credit goes to Paolo De Marchi and his very firm ideas about wine. With all the styles that have come and gone in Chianti Classico until just a few years ago, the wines of Isole e Olena have remained steadfastly the same and have always shown a deep sense of place. From all of the varieties in its 50 hectares of vineyards, the cellar obtains wines of crystal-clear definition on the palate that beautifully reflect their origin.

The Chianti Classico '07 was absent as it was awaiting bottling but a preliminary tasting augured well. We consoled ourselves with the all-sangiovese Cepparello '06. Initially closed, it opens into flowery notes and hints of red berry fruit followed by charming lively spice. The complex, fruity palate shows impressive continuity and a wonderfully elegant finish. Tannins are still excessive and prominent alcohol reveals the wine's youth. A magnificent wine experience signs off with a long, relaxed, lingering finish. Three Glasses.

Lanciola

LOC. POZZOLATICO
VIA IMPRUNETANA, 210
50023 IMPRUNETA [FI]
TEL. 055208324
www.lanciola.it

CELLAR SALES
PRE-BOOKED VISITS

ANNUAL PRODUCTION 250,000 bottles
HECTARES UNDER VINE 50
VITICULTURE METHOD Conventional

We applaud a fine showing by the Guarneri family estate, thanks in large part to its vineyards in Chianti Classico, which produced an excellent version from this growing year. The vineyards in Impruneta gave a lower key performance, however. These wines show scant character and their profiles on the nose are still muddled. This is no way detracts from the potential of the zone, which continues to improve. Cellaring will probably iron out the creases.

Our pick of the bunch is Chianti Classico Le Masse di Greve Riserva '06. It throws a fascinating fruity nose of ripe plums leading into layered but well-distributed structure and a captivating finish. We also liked the current version called Vigna Nuova, which debuted with the '07 vintage. It has fresh fruitiness on the nose, with hints of juicy wild berries, and an inviting palate of good length. The Vin Santo '04 is classic with citrus and nut aromas introducing a silky, soft body. Less inspiring are the Supertuscan Terricci '06 from sangiovese and the two cabernets, and Riccionero '06, obtained from pinot nero only.

● Cepparello '06	▼▼▼	8
○ Vin Santo del Chianti Classico '01	▼▼	8
● Cabernet Sauvignon '97	♀♀♀	8
● Cabernet Sauvignon '96	♀♀♀	6
● Cabernet Sauvignon '95	♀♀♀	6
● Cabernet Sauvignon '90	♀♀♀	6
● Cepparello '05	♀♀♀	8
● Cepparello '03	♀♀♀	8
● Cepparello '01	♀♀♀	7
● Cepparello '00	♀♀♀	7
● Cepparello '99	♀♀♀	6
● Cepparello '98	♀♀♀	6
● Cepparello '97	♀♀♀	5
● Syrah '99	♀♀♀	7

● Chianti Cl. Le Masse di Greve Ris. '06	▼▼	5
● Chianti Cl. V. Nuova '07	▼▼	4*
○ Vin Santo del Chianti '04	▼▼	6
● Riccionero '06	▼	6
● Terricci '06	▼	6
● Chianti Cl. Le Masse di Greve Ris. '04	♀♀	5
● Chianti Colli Fiorentini '06	♀♀	3*
● Riccionero '04	♀♀	7
● Terricci '03	♀♀	6
● Terricci '01	♀♀	6
○ Vin Santo del Chianti '03	♀♀	6
○ Vin Santo del Chianti '02	♀♀	6

Il Lebbio

LOC. SAN BENEDETTO, 11C
53037 SAN GIMIGNANO [SI]
TEL. 0577944725
www.illebbio.it

CELLAR SALES
PRE-BOOKED VISITS

ANNUAL PRODUCTION **80,000 bottles**
HECTARES UNDER VINE **21**
VITICULTURE METHOD **Conventional**

The Niccolini brothers' estate earned itself a full profile with a truly inspiring performance. The estate consists of just over 20 hectares planted mainly to red varieties but the zone planted to vernaccia is extremely wine-friendly. The brothers do meticulous work in the vineyards and cellar with the support of oenologist Luciano Bandini.

The basic Vernaccia stands out for its more vivid aromas and grip on the palate. The selection is less authoritative on the nose but has a rich, full-flavoured body with lovely length. Polito '06 from sangiovese and colorino is interesting, offering a fairly limited range of aromas but a body with well-defined structure, elegant tannins and a rising finish. Lendo '06, an unusual blend of cabernet sauvignon, montepulciano and merlot, is charming with notes of red berry fruit and faint spiciness preceding a tasty, smooth body. I Grottoni '08 is based on the same grape mix and has a pleasing palate and agreeable aromas. The Chianti '07 is simple and well styled.

Castello La Leccia

LOC. LA LECCIA
53011 CASTELLINA IN CHIANTI [SI]
TEL. 0577743148
www.castellolaleccia.com

CELLAR SALES
PRE-BOOKED VISITS

ANNUAL PRODUCTION **30,000 bottles**
HECTARES UNDER VINE **18**
VITICULTURE METHOD **Conventional**

Francesco Daddi's estate is located two kilometres from Castellina, in Chianti in an ancient village that has been producing wine since the 1500s. The vineyards lie in four different zones with different soil types, altitudes varying from 300 to 500 metres and positions facing south south-west. All varieties – sangiovese dominates with small plots of canaiolo and merlot – are harvested and vinified separately then blended by the technicians in the cellar.

Chianti Classico Riserva Bruciagna '06 is very good. It takes its name from its vineyard of origin, which enjoys fairly high average temperatures. The nose opens on ripe fruit with nuances of sweet almond but goes on to reveal more fascinating territory-derived mineral sensations intermingled with delicate, elegant flowery aromas. This is a classy, substantial wine with assertive, still rather rigid but elegant, tannins. It will come into its own with bottle time. A step below we have the Chianti Classico '07, which is less confident and uneven with a bitterish finish.

● Lendo '06	♟♟	4
● San Gimignano Rosso Polito '06	♟♟	6
○ Vernaccia di S. Gimignano '08	♟♟	4*
○ Vernaccia di S. Gimignano Tropìe '08	♟♟	4*
● Chianti '07	♟	4
● I Grottoni '08	♟	4
○ Vernaccia di S. Gimignano Tropìe '07	♟♟	4*
○ Vernaccia di S. Gimignano Tropìe '06	♟♟	4*

● Chianti Cl. Bruciagna Ris. '06	♟♟	5
● Chianti Cl. '07	♟	4
● Chianti Cl. Bruciagna Ris. '01	♟♟♟	6
● Chianti Cl. '06	♟♟	4*
● Chianti Cl. '04	♟♟	4
● Chianti Cl. Bruciagna '04	♟♟	5
● Chianti Cl. Bruciagna Ris. '05	♟♟	5

La Lecciaia

LOC. VALLAFRICO
53024 MONTALCINO [SI]
TEL. 0583928366
www.lecciaia.it

CELLAR SALES

ANNUAL PRODUCTION **300,000 bottles**
HECTARES UNDER VINE **47**
VITICULTURE METHOD **Conventional**

This estate has grown consistently and over the last few years has shown good quality across its whole range. Situated on the eastern slope of Montalcino, the vineyards have a mixed clay base with plenty of pebbles and lie at an altitude of 450 metres. The style is very traditional, although the Brunello di Montalcino selections age in large 50-hectolitre casks with ten per cent in 350-litre oak barrels. The barrel stock has recently been renovated and this has had a positive effect on the wines.

We tasted some lovely Brunello di Montalcinos this year. We particularly liked the Brunello di Montalcino Riserva '03, a rich ruby red wine with very intense, quite fruity aromas of red fruits jam, faint vegetality and juicy tannins, both of which are unusual for the growing year. There's good impetus and weight in the mouth and a laid-back, lingering finish. The two current Brunello di Montalcinos, the '04 and the Manapetra '04, have a similar style. The latter has a compact nose with lovely red fruit notes and a fruity palate with lively acidity and measured tannins.

● Brunello di Montalcino '04	♥♥	6
● Brunello di Montalcino Manapetra '04	♥♥	6
● Brunello di Montalcino Ris. '03	♥♥	8
● Rosso di Montalcino '07	♥	4
● Rosso Toscano '06	♥	4
● Sant'Antimo '05	♥	5
● Brunello di Montalcino '01	♀♀	6
● Brunello di Montalcino '00	♀♀	6
● Brunello di Montalcino Manapetra '99	♀♀	8
● Brunello di Montalcino Ris. '01	♀♀	8
● Brunello di Montalcino Ris. '98	♀♀	8

Cantine Leonardo da Vinci

VIA PROVINCIALE MERCATALE, 291
50059 VINCI [FI]
TEL. 0571902444
www.cantineleonardo.it

CELLAR SALES
PRE-BOOKED VISITS
VISITOR FACILITIES
FOOD

ANNUAL PRODUCTION **4,000,000 bottles**
HECTARES UNDER VINE **660**
VITICULTURE METHOD **Conventional**

This estate presented so many wines that we are hard pressed to do them all justice in one profile. In a few short years, Cantine Leonardo da Vinci has revamped its image and production style. Since its establishment in 1961, things have changed significantly. The headquarters has been renovated, an in-house wine bar has been set up and a wine distributor called Dalle Vigne has been created in addition to the various product lines for an ever-growing market. In the midst of all this, the wines themselves have undergone radical transformation and today's style tends to international.

Of the many wines we tasted, we were particularly impressed by Merlot degli Artisti '05. Currants and blackberries meld with notes of cinnamon and cloves, while the body is round, velvety and enjoyably, if not very long. We also liked the Sant'Ippolito '07, an equal blend of syrah and merlot with an elegant, complex bouquet that presents nice soft sensations on the palate.

● Merlot degli Artisti '05	♥♥	6
● Sant'Ippolito '07	♥♥	5
● Villa di Corsano '05	♥♥	5
○ Bianco dell'Empolese Vin Santo Tegrino '04	♥	5
● Brunello di Montalcino Cantine Leonardo '04	♥	6
● Brunello di Montalcino Da Vinci '04	♥	7
● Chianti Da Vinci Ris. '06	♥	4
● Chianti Leonardo '08	♥	4
● Chianti Leonardo Ris. '06	♥	4
● Chianti San Zio '06	♥	4
○ Ser Piero '08	♥	3
● Brunello di Montalcino Da Vinci '03	♀♀	7
● Chianti Da Vinci '07	♀♀	3
● Chianti Leonardo '07	♀♀	3
● Rosso di Montalcino Cantina di Montalcino '06	♀♀	4

Tenuta di Lilliano

LOC. LILLIANO, 8
53011 CASTELLINA IN CHIANTI [SI]
TEL. 0577743070
www.lilliano.com

CELLAR SALES
PRE-BOOKED VISITS

ANNUAL PRODUCTION **250,000 bottles**
HECTARES UNDER VINE **50**
VITICULTURE METHOD **Conventional**

Lilliano spans around 460 hectares in the municipality of Castellina in Chianti. The property dates back to medieval times and was acquired by the Ruspoli family in 1920. However, it was not until the arrival of Principessa Eleonora Ruspoli Berlingieri in 1958 that it began to sell wine. Today, Giulio and Pietro Ruspoli run the 50 hectares of vines standing mainly on alberese soil. Lilliano's wines offer a good reflection of the modern Chianti Classico character with their well-defined fruit and pleasing drinkability.

The Chianti Classico Riserva '06 has deep aromas of blackberry, cassis and liquorice. The balanced palate shows a refined tannic weave and a harmonious finish with lengthy acid backbone. The Anagallis '06 from sangiovese, colorino and merlot is also very well made. Minty notes give way to sensations of citrus fruit and spice in wonderful complexity. The palate is powerful but balanced thanks to its extremely elegant tannins and the finish is dominated by red berry fruits. Finally, the Chianti Classico '07 has an intense flowery nose and a juicy, very supple palate.

Lisini

FRAZ. SANT'ANGELO IN COLLE
POD. CASANOVA
53020 MONTALCINO [SI]
TEL. 0577844040
www.lisini.com

CELLAR SALES
PRE-BOOKED VISITS

ANNUAL PRODUCTION **81,000 bottles**
HECTARES UNDER VINE **18**
VITICULTURE METHOD **Conventional**

The Lisini farm estate lies in the south of Montalcino, just outside Sant'Angelo in Colle. Around 20 of its 154 hectares are planted to vine. The plots are very well sited at an average elevation of 350 metres and the soil is deep and loose. This is one of Montalcino's historic estates with wines, known for their traditional style, that have matured in large barrels. It is the only estate to possess a pre-phylloxera vineyard, currently being revitalized by mass selection from the plants on the plot itself.

This year, Lisini's wines are notable for their drinkability and reflect the estate's style well. The Riserva Ugolaia '03 shows the effects of its torrid growing year. The structure is impressive but the tannins are too mouth-drying and curb the finish. The Brunello di Montalcino '04 performs well, displaying delicate red berry fruit and root aromas with gamey nuances. The palate possesses more elegance than power, coming across fruity and taut with good supporting acidity. The Rosso di Montalcino '07 is less convincing, having rather too assertive tannins.

● Chianti Cl. Ris. '06	♟♟ 5
● Anagallis '06	♟♟ 6
● Chianti Cl. '07	♟♟ 4*
● Anagallis '05	♟♟ 6
● Anagallis '04	♟♟ 6
● Anagallis '99	♟♟ 6
● Chianti Cl. '06	♟♟ 4*
● Chianti Cl. '04	♟♟ 4
● Chianti Cl. Ris. '05	♟♟ 5
● Chianti Cl. Ris. '04	♟♟ 5

● Brunello di Montalcino '04	♟♟ 7
● Brunello di Montalcino Ugolaia '03	♟♟ 8
● Rosso di Montalcino '07	♟ 5
● Brunello di Montalcino Ugolaia '01	♟♟♟ 8
● Brunello di Montalcino Ugolaia '00	♟♟♟ 8
● Brunello di Montalcino '03	♟♟ 7
● Brunello di Montalcino '01	♟♟ 7
● Brunello di Montalcino '00	♟♟ 7
● Brunello di Montalcino '99	♟♟ 7
● Brunello di Montalcino Ugolaia '99	♟♟ 8

Livernano

LOC. LIVERNANO, 67A
53017 RADDA IN CHIANTI [SI]
TEL. 0577738353
www.livernano.it

CELLAR SALES
PRE-BOOKED VISITS
VISITOR FACILITIES
FOOD

ANNUAL PRODUCTION **50,000 bottles**
HECTARES UNDER VINE **20**
VITICULTURE METHOD **Naturale**

Livernano is an ancient village at Radda in Chianti. Its current owner, American producer Robert Cuillo, completely renovated the property in 1990 and it now has around 20 hectares of specialized vineyards. The soil is predominantly galestro marl, alberese and sandstone rock, perfect for cultivating vines. Livernano's innate capacity to produce a noble quality of fruit, combined with substantial investments in the cellar, make this one of the most important estates in the area.

The Chianti Classico '06 has enormous impact on the palate. The character is not territorial, but it does show continuity and balance on the palate. The nose reveals plums with hints of vanilla and chocolate, while the palate is vibrant, juicy and lingering. The finish is still redolent of sweet, balsamic caramel. The rest of the range is young as yet. The superlative Livernano '06 from cabernet sauvignon, merlot and sangiovese has ripe black berry fruit aromas with nuances of blackberry, black cherry and cinnamon. Development is checked by rather acerbic tannins that restrict its appeal on the palate.

Lunadoro

FRAZ. VALIANO DI MONTEPULCIANO
LOC. TERRAROSSA PAGLIERETO
53040 MONTEPULCIANO [SI]
TEL. 0578748154
www.lunadoro.com

CELLAR SALES
PRE-BOOKED VISITS

ANNUAL PRODUCTION **45,000 bottles**
HECTARES UNDER VINE **12**
VITICULTURE METHOD **Conventional**

This estate belonging to Dario Cappelli and Gigliola Cardinali is located in the district of Valiano. Founded in 2002, it is one of the youngest Nobile di Montepulciano producers. From the outset, its wines have combined a distinctive style and excellent quality with a reassuring level of consistency. Credit for this goes to meticulous management in the vineyards and cellar and vinification processes that eschew needlessly extreme techniques.

The Nobile di Montepulciano Quercione selection '06 is the estate's flagship product. It is also a good example of a wine that is able to reconcile well-defined execution with liveliness and character. The Rosso di Montepulciano '07 is extraordinarily drinkable. Nobile di Montepulciano '06 has aromas of earth and flowers, but its tannins show a few too many rough edges on the palate. The new red Ricordo '07, from sangiovese with small amounts of trebbiano and malvasia, is an interesting wine. Finally, Pagliareto '08, a white based on trebbiano and malvasia, is simple and coherent.

● Chianti Cl. '06	♟♟	4*
● Livernano '06	♟♟	7
● Chianti Cl. Ris. '06	♟	5
● Puro Sangue '06	♟	6
● Chianti Cl. Ris. '04	♟♟♟	5
● Livernano '05	♟♟♟	7
● Livernano '03	♟♟♟	8
● Livernano '99	♟♟♟	8
● Livernano '98	♟♟♟	8
● Livernano '97	♟♟♟	8

● Nobile di Montepulciano Quercione '06	♟♟	5
● Rosso di Montepulciano '07	♟♟	4
● Nobile di Montepulciano '06	♟	5
○ Pagliareto '08	♟	3
● Ricordo '07	♟	4
● Nobile di Montepulciano '05	♟♟	5
● Nobile di Montepulciano Quercione '05	♟♟	5
● Nobile di Montepulciano Quercione '04	♟♟	5

★ Le Macchiole

VIA BOLGHERESE, 189A
57020 BOLGHERI [LI]
TEL. 0565766092
www.lemacchiole.it

PRE-BOOKED VISITS
FOOD

ANNUAL PRODUCTION 120,000 bottles
HECTARES UNDER VINE 22
VITICULTURE METHOD Conventional

Le Macchiole has long been a star in the Italian quality wine firmament and one of the most successful cellars at communicating the essence of terroir in Bolgheri wines. Cinzia Merli's courage and determination have enabled her to implement an inspired wine project launched by her husband Eugenio, who sadly passed away before witnessing its success. From his in-depth knowledge, Eugenio set out to express the fundamental nature of the territory through wines based on single varieties.

The all-cabernet franc Paleo '06 is rather good. It has lost its previous rigidity and offers clear aromas of red fruit jam and liquorice with a varietal touch of capsicum. Entry on the palate is pervasive with clenched but elegant tannins. Overall it offers balance, length and allure. The merlot Messorio '06 is superlative and strolled off with Three Glasses. It has body and thrust on the palate and a nose of blackberry jam with youthful hints of vanilla. Even at this early stage of development, it is extraordinarily full and juicy. The syrah-only Scrio '06 is less convincing. Oaky tones dominate the fruit and cramp the taste experience.

Machiavelli

LOC. SANT'ANDREA IN PERCUSSINA
50026 SAN CASCIANO IN VAL DI PESA [FI]
TEL. 055828471
www.giv.it

CELLAR SALES
PRE-BOOKED VISITS
FOOD

ANNUAL PRODUCTION 150,000 bottles
HECTARES UNDER VINE 26
VITICULTURE METHOD Conventional

Machiavelli is one of the jewels in the Gruppo Italiano Vini's crown. The vineyards total around 26 hectares and all lie within the Chianti Classico. Overall, the estate consists of about 53 hectares. The natural bounty of the vineyards and the dependable, proven techniques employed in the cellar guarantee a high, consistent level of quality across all the typologies proposed.

This year, the wines we were offered for tasting tended to lack confidence owing, we are sure, to their youth. The Chianti Classico Solatìo dei Tani '07 is a prime example of this lack of maturity. Alcohol-rich aromas give way to chewy notes of Parma violet and the palate has lovely energy. Although clenched and hard, the tannins manage to unbend sufficiently to result in overall harmony. The Chianti Classico Vigna di Fontalle Riserva '06 marches a step ahead. Deep blackberry and vanilla aromas reveal impressive structure on the palate with well-extracted tannins and dense, fruity body.

● Messorio '06	♟♟♟	8
● Paleo Rosso '06	♟♟	8
● Scrio '06	♟	8
● Bolgheri Rosso Sup. Paleo '97	♟♟♟	8
● Bolgheri Rosso Sup. Paleo '96	♟♟♟	8
● Bolgheri Rosso Sup. Paleo '95	♟♟♟	8
● Messorio '01	♟♟♟	8
● Messorio '99	♟♟♟	8
● Messorio '98	♟♟♟	8
● Messorio '97	♟♟♟	8
● Paleo Rosso '03	♟♟♟	8
● Paleo Rosso '01	♟♟♟	8
● Scrio '01	♟♟♟	8

● Chianti Cl. V. di Fontalle Ris. '06	♟♟	6
● Chianti Cl. Solatìo del Tani '07	♟	4
● Chianti Cl. V. di Fontalle Ris. '97	♟♟♟	5
● Chianti Cl. V. di Fontalle Ris. '95	♟♟♟	5
● Il Principe '95	♟♟♟	4
● Ser Niccolò Solatìo del Tani '88	♟♟♟	4
● Chianti Cl. Solatìo del Tani '06	♟♟	5
● Chianti Cl. Solatìo del Tani '05	♟♟	6
● Chianti Cl. V. di Fontalle Ris. '05	♟♟	6
● Chianti Cl. V. di Fontalle Ris. '04	♟♟	6

La Madonnina - Triacca

LOC. STRADA IN CHIANTI
VIA PALAIA, 39
50027 GREVE IN CHIANTI [FI]
TEL. 055858003
www.triacca.com

PRE-BOOKED VISITS

ANNUAL PRODUCTION 600,000 bottles
HECTARES UNDER VINE 100
VITICULTURE METHOD Conventional

This Chianti estate belongs to the Swiss Triacca family who possess three Italian estates in Valtellina and Tuscany. Madonnina is headquartered in Strada in Chianti in the municipality of Greve. The Triaccas acquired the estate in 1969 but only finished planting the vineyards ten years later. The cellars are housed in the old Villa Franchi. Today, the estate is huge and produces around 600,000 bottles a year. Wines, all reds, are improving in quality and the varieties cultivated are sangiovese, cabernet sauvignon and merlot.

All three grape types go to make up the Chianti Classico Riserva '06. This is a truly refined red – a real thoroughbred. The nose offers nuances of cherry, medicinal herbs and spices while the palate is creamy, very savoury and deep with first-class texture. The Chianti Classico Bello Stento '07 is decent but in another class altogether. It displays faintly grassy sensations and a fairly alcoholic finish. Chianti Classico Vigna La Palaia '07 disappoints.

Fattoria di Magliano

LOC. STERPETI, 10
58051 MAGLIANO IN TOSCANA [GR]
TEL. 0564593040
www.fattoriadimagliano.it

CELLAR SALES
PRE-BOOKED VISITS

ANNUAL PRODUCTION 200,000 bottles
HECTARES UNDER VINE 47
VITICULTURE METHOD Conventional

Fattoria di Magliano is the oenological project of Agostino Lenci, a shoe manufacturer from Lucca who in 1997 decided to venture into the world of wine. In 2001, Agostino launched his first products on the market and since then this estate at Sterpeti, a representative of the new wave of Maremma winemakers, has garnered praise from connoisseurs. Its wines have an impeccable style that is anything but banal and are made with great technical skill in vineyard and cellar.

The Poggio Bestiale '07, an equal blend of cabernet sauvignon and merlot, is very interesting indeed and perhaps one of the best versions we have tasted. Rich and deep in its aromas, it is every bit as juicy and full on the palate. The pure syrah Perenzo '07 has a very intense nose but the palate is the pièce de résistance and shows very complex development. Morellino di Scansano Heba '08 is good, very tasty and flavoursome. The Sinarra '08, from sangiovese with a small addition of petit verdot, is agreeably drinkable, showing fresh with a good profile. Pagliatura '08 from vermentino is rather sweet.

● Chianti Cl. Ris. '06	♀♀ 4*
● Nobile di Montepulciano Fattoria Santa Venere '06	♀♀ 5
● Chianti Cl. Bello Stento '07	♀ 4
● Chianti Cl. V. La Palaia '07	♀ 5
● Nobile di Montepulciano Poderaccio Fattoria Santa Venere '05	♀ 5
● Chianti Cl. Ris. '04	♀♀♀ 4
● Chianti Cl. Bello Stento '03	♀♀ 4
● Chianti Cl. Ris. '05	♀♀ 4*
● Il Mandorlo '01	♀♀ 5

● Poggio Bestiale '07	♀♀ 6
● Perenzo '07	♀♀ 6
● Morellino di Scansano Heba '08	♀ 4
○ Pagliatura '08	♀ 4
● Sinarra '08	♀ 5
● Morellino di Scansano Heba '07	♀♀ 4*
● Morellino di Scansano Heba '03	♀♀ 4
● Morellino di Scansano Heba '02	♀♀ 4
● Poggio Bestiale '06	♀♀ 6
● Poggio Bestiale '05	♀♀ 6
● Poggio Bestiale '02	♀♀ 6
● Poggio Bestiale '01	♀♀ 6

Malenchini

LOC. GRASSINA
VIA LILLIANO E MEOLI, 82
50015 BAGNO A RIPOLI [FI]
TEL. 055642602
www.malenchini.it

CELLAR SALES
PRE-BOOKED VISITS

ANNUAL PRODUCTION **90,000 bottles**
HECTARES UNDER VINE **17**
VITICULTURE METHOD **Conventional**

A season in a minor key, compared to last year, for the Malenchini family. The overall level of quality is fine and the wines offer particularly good value for money. The estate is just outside Florence to the south of the city and is based in one of the most beautiful Medici villas, which still houses the old jars used to store extra virgin olive oil made at the nearby town of Impruneta, famous for its terra cotta.

The best wine of the series is the Bruzzico '06, a sangiovese and cabernet sauvignon blend displaying vegetal aromas and solid, well-structured body with smooth tannins. The rest of the range is decent. We liked the freshness of the Chianti '08, a new recruit to the ranks, the pleasantness of the Chianti Colli Fiorentini '07, and the easy-drinking palate of the Daily Quality line in both its Bianco and Rosso versions. The old-style Vin Santo '03 exhibits clear notes of nuts.

La Mannella

LOC. LA MANNELLA, 322
53024 MONTALCINO [SI]
TEL. 0577848268
http://www.lamannella.it

PRE-BOOKED VISITS

ANNUAL PRODUCTION **35,000 bottles**
HECTARES UNDER VINE **8**
VITICULTURE METHOD **Conventional**

This small winery, owned by Marco Cortonesi, continues to improve in quality. Its vineyards lie in two separate, very different sites: the northern zone of Montalcino, where the estate headquarters are also located, and the south-east slope that overlooks Val d'Orcia and Mount Amiata. The grapes from these two such diverse zones give Marco's wines a distinctive, unique style. This year's Brunello di Montalcino matures in medium-sized barrels of French oak.

Brunello di Montalcino '04 is extremely interesting and made it to our national finals. The nose is full and gratifying, revealing flowery, fruity notes with nuances of yellow peach, wild cherry and strawberry jam. The palate finds a nice balance between acidity and tannin, rounding off with a deep, long-lingering finish. This is an austere wine with backbone and will age very well. The Brunello di Montalcino I Poggiarelli, another '04, is also well made, just a little shorter in the finish. The Rosso di Montalcino '07 is a notch below, with tannins that are rather too mouth-drying.

● Bruzzico '06	♀♀ 5
● Chianti '08	♀ 3
● Chianti Colli Fiorentini '07	♀ 4
○ Daily Quality Bianco '08	♀ 3
● Daily Quality Rosso '08	♀ 3
○ Vin Santo del Chianti Colli Fiorentini '03	♀ 5
● Bruzzico '05	♀♀ 5
● Bruzzico '04	♀♀ 5
● Chianti Colli Fiorentini '06	♀♀ 4

● Brunello di Montalcino '04	♀♀ 6
● Brunello di Montalcino I Poggiarelli '04	♀♀ 6
● Brunello di Montalcino Ris. '03	♀ 7
● Rosso di Montalcino '07	♀ 4
● Brunello di Montalcino '03	♀♀ 6
● Brunello di Montalcino '02	♀♀ 6
● Rosso di Montalcino '06	♀♀ 4*

Mannucci Droandi

FRAZ. MERCATALE VALDARNO
VIA CAPOSELVI, 61
52020 MONTEVARCHI [AR]
TEL. 0559707276
www.mannuccidroandi.com

CELLAR SALES
PRE-BOOKED VISITS

ANNUAL PRODUCTION 36,000 bottles
HECTARES UNDER VINE 31
VITICULTURE METHOD Organic certified

Deprived of a profile last year, owing to one of those computer glitches that sometimes happen, Roberto Mannucci Droandi is firmly back in the Guide. This estate is a major player in Valdarno and over the years has carried out experimental vinifications with varieties on the verge of extinction. This year, Roberto presented us with the first results of what can be obtained from more unusual grape types. The estate was founded in the 19th century and for many years sold its wine in bulk. It wasn't until the early 1990s that the estate adopted a firmly quality-focused philosophy.

The Campolucci '06, a blend of cabernet sauvignon, merlot and syrah, has minty, balsamic tones on the nose, a soft body whose tannins are completely integrated with the alcohol, and a finish that builds up nicely. The two wines from experimental varieties are unusual and enjoyable. Barsaglina '07 is more vegetal on the nose but satisfyingly full on the palate while the Foglia Tonda '07 leads on fruity elements. The two Chianti Classicos are well styled.

Fattoria Mantellassi

LOC. BANDITACCIA, 26
58051 MAGLIANO IN TOSCANA [GR]
TEL. 0564592037
www.fatt-mantellassi.it

CELLAR SALES
PRE-BOOKED VISITS

ANNUAL PRODUCTION 550,000 bottles
HECTARES UNDER VINE 60
VITICULTURE METHOD Conventional

Established in 1958, Fattoria Mantellassi can be considered the oldest estate in the territory of Morellino di Scansano. Ezio Mantellassi was the pioneering spirit behind this venture and guided his winery to the forefront of Italian oenology. Today, this estate at Magliano in Tuscany is run by his sons Aleardo and Giuseppe, who go about their work with the same passion as their father, producing wines with a very distinct style.

Morellino Le Sentinelle Riserva '06 has an austere character, a fresh nose of flowery aromas and a complex palate whose decisive acid energy keeps the rather excessive oak in check. The Morellino Mentore '08 and Morellino San Giuseppe '08 are both agreeable. Mentore has refined, delicate aromas and a flavoursome palate while the San Giuseppe has nice savouriness on the palate and aromas with smoky nuances. The pure alicante Querciolaia '06 has a very supple palate but the nose has yet to open out fully. The Scalandrino '08 and Lucumone '08, both from vermentino, are uncomplicated but enjoyable.

● Campolucci '06	♟♟ 5
● Foglia Tonda '07	♟♟ 5
● Barsaglina '07	♟ 5
● Chianti Cl. Ceppeto '06	♟ 4
● Chianti Cl. Ceppeto Ris. '06	♟ 5
● Campolucci '03	♟♟ 5
● Chianti Cl. Ceppeto '04	♟♟ 4*
● Chianti Colli Aretini '05	♟♟ 3*
● Chianti Colli Aretini '04	♟♟ 3*

● Morellino di Scansano Le Sentinelle Ris. '06	♟♟ 5
● Morellino di Scansano Mentore '08	♟♟ 4
● Morellino di Scansano San Giuseppe '08	♟♟ 4
○ Lucumone '08	♟ 4
● Querciolaia '06	♟ 5
○ Vermentino Scalandrino '08	♟ 4
● Morellino di Scansano Le Sentinelle Ris. '05	♟♟ 5
● Morellino di Scansano Le Sentinelle Ris. '04	♟♟ 5
● Morellino di Scansano Le Sentinelle Ris. '01	♟♟ 5
● Morellino di Scansano San Giuseppe '06	♟♟ 4
● Morellino di Scansano San Giuseppe '05	♟♟ 4
● Morellino di Scansano San Giuseppe '04	♟♟ 4*
● Querciolaia '04	♟♟ 5
● Querciolaia '03	♟♟ 5

Cosimo Maria Masini

VIA POGGIO AL PINO, 16
56028 SAN MINIATO [PI]
TEL. 0571465032
www.cosimomariamasini.it

CELLAR SALES
PRE-BOOKED VISITS

ANNUAL PRODUCTION **40,000 bottles**
HECTARES UNDER VINE **16**
VITICULTURE METHOD **Naturale**

Cosimo Maria Masini is a rising star in Italian wine. His estate extends over 16 hectares of vineyards in the varied hilly countryside at San Miniato in the province of Pisa. Production is organic and this year the cellar surpassed itself with the results of a project focused on obtaining quality wines rooted firmly in the territory. Hats off to the two young protagonists, owner Cosimo Maria Masini and skilled oenologist Cipriano Barsanti.

The wines we tasted this year have a uniformity of style based on their fruit of origin. The Cosimo '06, almost pure sangiovese, has great energy on the palate. Closed at first, it opens out to reveal notes of red fruit and spice before the palate shows juicy and fresh. From 100 per cent trebbiano, the Daphnè '07 also shows well. It macerated on the skins in open vats for four days then aged in barriques, emerging to proffer deep grassy, minty aromas that usher in a weighty, savoury palate. We also liked the cabernet sauvignon and franc blend Nicolò '06 for its intense garnet ruby and clear red berry fruit aromas. It's a harmonious wine despite its slightly clenched tannins.

○ Annick '08	♥♥	4
● Cosimo '06	♥♥	6
○ Daphnè '07	♥♥	5
● Nicolò '06	♥♥	5
● Nicole '07	♥	4
○ Annick '07	♡♡	4*
○ Annick '06	♡♡	4
● Nicole '06	♡♡	4*

★ La Massa

VIA CASE SPARSE, 9
50020 PANZANO [FI]
TEL. 055852722
info@fattorialamassa.com

PRE-BOOKED VISITS

ANNUAL PRODUCTION **110,000 bottles**
HECTARES UNDER VINE **25**
VITICULTURE METHOD **Conventional**

This splendid estate in the western part of Panzano's Conca d'Oro is a Bordeaux enclave in Chianti territory. Its wines reflect the philosophy of their maker, Giampaolo Motta, who above all seeks balance and elegance in their tannic texture even at the expense of more typical, territorial characteristics. These wines are genuinely the products of their maker, although their current style convinces us less than in previous years.

The Giorgio Primo '06 from sangiovese and merlot is excellent as always. Smoky, mineral notes, very much in the Bordeaux mould, dominate the nose with refined, very elegant fruity nuances that hint at greater complexity to come. On the palate, the tannins are close knit but velvety and the extractive sweetness makes the sensory profile very soft and tempting. The Massa '07, from 60 per cent sangiovese with additions of merlot and cabernet sauvignon, is more approachable and drinkable, but this is also due in part to the growing year, which is tending to produce wines that are ready to drink earlier.

● Giorgio Primo '06	♥♥	8
● La Massa '07	♥♥	6
● Chianti Cl. Giorgio Primo '01	♡♡♡	8
● Chianti Cl. Giorgio Primo '00	♡♡♡	7
● Chianti Cl. Giorgio Primo '99	♡♡♡	7
● Chianti Cl. Giorgio Primo '98	♡♡♡	7
● Chianti Cl. Giorgio Primo '97	♡♡♡	7
● Chianti Cl. Giorgio Primo '96	♡♡♡	7
● Chianti Cl. Giorgio Primo '95	♡♡♡	7
● Chianti Cl. Giorgio Primo '94	♡♡♡	7
● Chianti Cl. Giorgio Primo '93	♡♡♡	7
● Giorgio Primo '03	♡♡♡	8
● La Massa '01	♡♡♡	5

Mastrojanni

FRAZ. CASTELNUOVO DELL'ABATE
POD. LORETO SAN PIO
53024 MONTALCINO [SI]
TEL. 0577835681
www.mastrojanni.com

CELLAR SALES
PRE-BOOKED VISITS

ANNUAL PRODUCTION **80,000 bottles**
HECTARES UNDER VINE **24**
VITICULTURE METHOD **Conventional**

Since its founding in the 1970s, this estate's wines have retained a classic style. It was recently acquired by new owners including the Illy group, but has maintained a strong link with tradition through the presence of Andrea Machetti, who has long played a key role on the estate. There is an ambitious new project under way to modernize the cellar and replanting of the vineyards started several years ago. They occupy an excellent position in the south-east zone of the DOCG at an altitude of 400 metres, where the soil is very loose owing to the generous fraction of pebbles.

Despite the absence of the top wine, quality was solid this year. Of the two Brunello di Montalcinos on offer, we preferred the standard '04 over the selection. A classic ruby hue announces a clear, flowery nose of oleander, medicinal herbs and not-quite-ripe black cherry. The tannins are smooth and progression on the palate is very agreeable, notable acidity making the finish very juicy. This is an elegant wine. The Schiena d'Asino '04 selection has mature notes of tobacco and leather and more evident tannins on the palate.

Maté

LOC. SANTA RESTITUTA
53024 MONTALCINO [SI]
TEL. 0577847215
www.matewine.com

CELLAR SALES

ANNUAL PRODUCTION **28,000 bottles**
HECTARES UNDER VINE **7**
VITICULTURE METHOD **Conventional**

Once upon a time, two Canadian artists, one a writer and the other a painter, came to Montalcino and fell in love with one of the most charming corners of the territory, the area around the church of Santa Restituta. They bought and restored a cottage built in the 1300s and planted high-density vineyards of sangiovese, cabernet, syrah and merlot at around 6,000 plants per hectare. The wines are matured in small and medium-sized casks.

The deep-coloured Brunello di Montalcino '04 reveals intense ripe fruit sensations on the nose with highly concentrated pyrite minerality that buttresses the spicy nuances. The palate has great impact and substance, sustained, rather dusty tannins, and confident acidity that gives length to the finish. The Sant'Antimos, all '06s, are also well made. The Cabernet has vegetal and black berry fruit aromas and a very impactful palate with persistent tannic extraction. From syrah, the Banditone is embracing, full and round. The Mantus Merlot is juicy and relaxed.

● Brunello di Montalcino '04	♟♟	7
● Brunello di Montalcino Schiena d'Asino '04	♟♟	8
● Rosso di Montalcino '07	♟	5
● Brunello di Montalcino '97	♟♟♟	7
● Brunello di Montalcino '90	♟♟♟	7
● Brunello di Montalcino Ris. '88	♟♟♟	7
● Brunello di Montalcino Schiena d'Asino '93	♟♟♟	7
● Brunello di Montalcino Schiena d'Asino '90	♟♟♟	7
● Brunello di Montalcino '01	♟♟	7
● Brunello di Montalcino '00	♟♟	7
● Brunello di Montalcino V. Schiena d'Asino '01	♟♟	8

● Brunello di Montalcino '04	♟♟	6
● Sant'Antimo Banditone Syrah '06	♟♟	7
● Sant'Antimo Cabernet '06	♟♟	7
● Sant'Antimo Mantus Merlot '06	♟♟	7

Castello di Meleto

LOC. MELETO
53013 GAIOLE IN CHIANTI [SI]
TEL. 0577749217
www.castellomeleto.it

CELLAR SALES
PRE-BOOKED VISITS
VISITOR FACILITIES
FOOD

ANNUAL PRODUCTION **480,000 bottles**
HECTARES UNDER VINE **120**
VITICULTURE METHOD **Conventional**

Meleto's history goes back to the 11th century when it was the property of Vallombrosa monks from the nearby abbey of Coltibuono. It survived the numerous conflicts that swept across the area and for many years belonged to the Ricasoli family before passing into the hands of the current owner, who has recently taken on the expert Roberto Stucchi Prinetti as director. The estate extends over an impressive 120 hectares or so, plus the 60 belonging to the property at Pieve di Spaltenna.

To our minds, the best wines were the Chianti Classico Pieve di Spaltenna '07 and in particular the Chianti Classico Riserva Vigna Casi '06. The first has wonderful fruit intensity and a good long palate that unfolds warm and flavoursome into an impressive finish. The Riserva proffers intense notes of black fruit and medicinal herbs, a full, meaty palate, and a finish that builds in intensity and sensory appeal. The Riserva Vigna Poggiarso '06 is also excellent and the Chianti Classico '07 is undemanding but agreeable.

Melini

LOC. GAGGIANO
53036 POGGIBONSI [SI]
TEL. 0577998511
www.cantinemelini.it

CELLAR SALES
PRE-BOOKED VISITS

ANNUAL PRODUCTION **4.800,000 bottles**
HECTARES UNDER VINE **145**
VITICULTURE METHOD **Conventional**

Another jewel in the crown of the Gruppo Italiano Vini, Melini's history is intertwined with that of Chianti Classico. As early as 1877, the Florence chamber of commerce and guilds awarded Melini a gold medal for its services in expanding trade in Tuscan wine abroad. Today, the estate continues this work with its sound, reliable production.

The '06 Chianti Classico Riserva La Selvanella is its usual territorial self. The vines at Radda have produced a wine with a lively nose and elegant ripe plums, liquorice and cinchona. Its vivacious character foregrounds incisive tannins framed in good breadth and progression. We gave La Selvanella Three Glasses for its huge personality and concentration. Chianti Classico Granaio '07 also shows well. It is less viscerally spontaneous than the Riserva and has rather more sensory complexity. The nose is all black fruit laced with vanilla and cinnamon spice aromas while the fruity palate has weighty extract sustained by a refreshing acid vein that enhances drinkability.

● Chianti Cl. Pieve di Spaltenna '07	♀♀ 4*
● Chianti Cl. V. Casi Ris. '06	♀♀ 6
● Chianti Cl. V. Poggiarso Ris. '06	♀♀ 6
● Chianti Cl. '07	♀ 5
● Fiore '06	♀ 6
● Chianti Cl. Ris. '03	♀♀♀ 5
● Chianti Cl. Pieve di Spaltenna '06	♀♀ 4*
● Chianti Cl. Pieve di Spaltenna '04	♀♀ 4
● Chianti Cl. V. Casi Ris. '04	♀♀ 5
● Rainero '04	♀♀ 7
● Rainero '03	♀♀ 7

● Chianti Cl. La Selvanella Ris. '06	♀♀♀ 6
● Chianti Cl. Granaio '07	♀♀ 4*
● Chianti Cl. La Selvanella Ris. '03	♀♀♀ 5
● Chianti Cl. La Selvanella Ris. '01	♀♀♀ 5
● Chianti Cl. La Selvanella Ris. '00	♀♀♀ 5
● Chianti Cl. La Selvanella Ris. '99	♀♀♀ 6
● Chianti Cl. La Selvanella Ris. '90	♀♀♀ 5
● Chianti Cl. La Selvanella Ris. '86	♀♀♀ 6

Le Miccine

LOC. LE MICCINE
S.S. TRAVERSA CHIANTIGIANA
53013 GAIOLE IN CHIANTI [SI]
TEL. 0577749526
www.lemiccine.com

CELLAR SALES
PRE-BOOKED VISITS
VISITOR FACILITIES

ANNUAL PRODUCTION 30,000 bottles
HECTARES UNDER VINE 7
VITICULTURE METHOD Conventional

Clifford and Donna Meneghetti Weaver have owned this lovely little Gaiole estate since 1996, when they slowly started to reorganize it to boost all aspects of production. There are just over seven hectares of vineyards. Remigio Bordini and Vittorio Fiore respectively provide vineyard management and oenological expertise and the team produces modern wines in a perfect marriage of oak and fruit.

We weren't 100 per cent convinced by our tastings, largely owing to toasty notes that tend to dominate the overall profile of the house reds. The Chianti Classico Don Alberto Riserva '06 is still dominated by oak on the nose, although notes of red berry fruit and cherry gradually emerge to give the palate appeal. This is an authoritative wine with good aromatic length. There were similar results from the Chianti Classico '07, which holds true to a form that seems to be a genuine production style.

Il Molino di Grace

LOC. IL VOLANO LUCARELLI
50022 PANZANO [FI]
TEL. 0558561010
www.ilmolinodigrace.com

CELLAR SALES
PRE-BOOKED VISITS

ANNUAL PRODUCTION 210,000 bottles
HECTARES UNDER VINE 44
VITICULTURE METHOD Naturale

Il Molino di Grace celebrates its tenth anniversary this year. It was in 1999 that Frank Grace and his manager Gerhard Hirmner opened the modern cellar that had been under construction since 1995. Today, the operation consists of 45 hectares planted to vine a few kilometres south of Panzano. The vines, around 25 years old, pre-date the estate and face south-west on marl-rich soil that is ideal for the cultivation of sangiovese, the main variety grown here.

The Chianti Classico Riserva '06 is a young wine that has yet to find its identity. Flowery notes of violet are enhanced by spicy sensations of cloves and vanilla. The palate is clenched with ebullient tannins and the body is buttressed by lively acidity that accompanies progression. The Chianti Classico '07 offers modern notes of black berry fruit and vanilla, and a soft, refreshing, very drinkable palate. Il Volano '07 from sangiovese and merlot is slightly detached from its extract and a bit off-balance. Le Falcole '07, another estate Supertuscan, is drinkable but too predictable.

● Chianti Cl. '07	♥♥ 4
● Chianti Cl. Don Alberto Ris. '06	♥♥ 5
● Chianti Cl. '06	♀♀ 4*
● La Pricipessa '06	♀♀ 6
○ Vin Santo del Chianti Cl. La Gloria '00	♀♀ 6

● Chianti Cl. Il Margone Ris. '06	♥♥ 7
● Chianti Cl. '07	♥ 5
○ Il Volano '07	♥ 4
● Le Falcole '07	♥ 7
● Chianti Cl. Il Margone Ris. '05	♀♀♀ 7
● Chianti Cl. Il Margone Ris. '04	♀♀♀ 7
● Chianti Cl. Ris. '01	♀♀♀ 5
● Gratius '04	♀♀♀ 7
● Gratius '00	♀♀♀ 7

Castello di Monsanto

FRAZ. MONSANTO
VIA MONSANTO, 8
50021 BARBERINO VAL D'ELSA [FI]
TEL. 0558059000
www.castellodimonsanto.it

CELLAR SALES
PRE-BOOKED VISITS
VISITOR FACILITIES

ANNUAL PRODUCTION **450,000 bottles**
HECTARES UNDER VINE **72**
VITICULTURE METHOD **Conventional**

Castello di Monsanto is a must-visit destination for all those who believe in wine as a pure expression of its territory. Fabrizio Bianchi has enhanced the unique, wine-friendly conditions of his terrain since he established his estate, and has made decisions that have broken ground in the Chianti Classico area. In 1968, he stopped using white grapes when fermenting on the skins and started bottling the Il Poggio selection separately. These moves have made Monsanto a benchmark in winemaking in Tuscany and beyond.

Embodiment of the terroir is a theme that runs through Monsanto's entire production. The Chianti Classico Riserva '06 has intense aromas, showing a flowery, chewy nose of black berry fruit, myrtle and juniper. The no-nonsense palate has impressive tannic texture that carries the intense, fruity body in a fabulous progression and the finish is all spice and black cherry. Its younger sibling, the Chianti Classico '07, shows its edgy youth. The clear, pleasant aromas of violet and red fruit are checked by rough tannins that hinder the palate's forward momentum.

Monte Bernardi

LOC. PANZANO
VIA CHIANTIGIANA KM. 33, V
50020 GREVE IN CHIANTI [FI]
TEL. 055852400
www.montebernardi.com

CELLAR SALES
PRE-BOOKED VISITS

ANNUAL PRODUCTION **12,000 bottles**
HECTARES UNDER VINE **10**
VITICULTURE METHOD **Naturale**

The Schmelzer brothers acquired Monte Bernardi in Panzano in Chianti in 2003. About ten of the estate's 54 hectares are planted to vine. The marl and alberese soil is typical of the zone and ideal for grape production. The Schmelzers' estate is organic and seeks to express the closest possible union of wines and territory via its rich vineyards, impeccable maturation processes, ambient yeasts and long macerations. We foresee a rosy future.

The Sa'etta '06 is a fabulously deep Chianti Classico. Notes of chewy red berry fruit, citrussy tangerine and cinnamon lead into a well-defined lively palate with impressive thrust and measured acidity sustaining the body. Only the finish, which is still rather cropped, holds it back. The Chianti Classico '07 is less complex but good with flowery, balsamic notes and a dynamic palate flaunting nice elegant tannins. The Tzingana '06, a merlot and cabernet sauvignon blend with some cabernet franc and petit verdot, is less harmonious than its fellows. The nose is fruity and oaky and the palate is full, but rather pedestrian. The elegant, juicy Rosé '07 is excellent.

● Chianti Cl. Ris. '06	♟♟ 5
● Chianti Cl. '07	♟ 5
● Chianti Cl. Il Poggio Ris. '88	♟♟♟ 7
● Nemo '01	♟♟♟ 7
● Chianti Cl. Il Poggio Ris. '04	♟♟ 7
○ Fabrizio Bianchi Chardonnay '06	♟♟ 5

● Chianti Cl. '07	♟♟ 5
● Chianti Cl. Sa'etta '06	♟♟ 6
⊙ Rosé '07	♟♟ 4*
● Tzingana '06	♟ 7
● Tzingana '97	♟♟♟ 6
● Chianti Cl. '03	♟♟ 5
● Chianti Cl. Sa'etta '04	♟♟ 6
● Tzingana '05	♟♟ 7
● Tzingana '04	♟♟ 7

Fattoria di Montecchio

FRAZ. SAN DONATO IN POGGIO
VIA MONTECCHIO, 4
50020 TAVARNELLE VAL DI PESA [FI]
TEL. 0558072907
www.fattoriamontecchio.it

CELLAR SALES
PRE-BOOKED VISITS
VISITOR FACILITIES

ANNUAL PRODUCTION **250,000 bottles**
HECTARES UNDER VINE **38**
VITICULTURE METHOD **Conventional**

This estate is situated on a hill overlooking San Donato in Poggio in one of the oldest zones of the Florentine Chianti Classico. The historic villa is surrounded by a park with paths that meander among ancient holm-oaks in a landscape of rare beauty. In terms of its winemaking, the vineyards planted to international varieties and sangiovese lie at an altitude of 250 to 350 metres, face south-east and south-west, and stand on typical marl and chalk-based soil. In the cellar, the wines age in new large, medium and small barrels, according to the wine type.

The Pietracupa, a sangiovese and cabernet blend, spends a minimum of 18 months in barriques. The '06 growing year has produced an extremely deep and refined wine that is as impressive as ever. The nose shows notes of blueberry and green capsicum, while the palate is fleshy and rich in flavour with wonderful continuity. The Riserva '06 possesses unusual rather grassy, balsamic notes but is very good. The Chianti Classico '06 with its fluent, supple palate is a must-try.

● Chianti Cl. '06	🍷🍷	3*
● Chianti Cl. Ris. '06	🍷🍷	5
● Pietracupa '06	🍷🍷	6
● Chianti Cl. '05	ŸŸ	4*
● Chianti Cl. Ris. '05	ŸŸ	5
● La Papessa '05	ŸŸ	6
● Pietracupa '05	ŸŸ	6

Fattoria Montellori

VIA PISTOIESE, 1
50054 FUCECCHIO [FI]
TEL. 0571260641
www.fattoriamontellori.it

CELLAR SALES
PRE-BOOKED VISITS
FOOD

ANNUAL PRODUCTION **330,000 bottles**
HECTARES UNDER VINE **55**
VITICULTURE METHOD **Conventional**

For over 100 years, the Nieri family has been making wine in a territory that remains largely undiscovered. Giuseppe Nieri set up the estate in the late 19th century when he decided to invest the profits from his leather business in the agricultural sector. It was under the guidance of the current owner's father, another Giuseppe, that the estate really took off, building its vineyards up to the current 60 hectares and completely renovating the cellar. Today, Alessandro is at the helm.

Yet again the all-syrah Tuttosole '06 gets our vote for its intensely spicy, fruity nose, soft, elegant body and sweet finish. The sangiovese-based Dicatum '06 also shows well, its classic cherry fruit notes with spicy nuances the prelude to a solid body with smooth, juicy tannins. The Vin Santo '01 offers intriguing minerally, fruity aromas and big, embracing structure. The chardonnay Montellori Pas Dosé '05 is fresh and agreeable. The rest of the range is pleasant and well styled, including Moro, from sangiovese, cabernet and merlot, and the Mandorlo '08, a blend of international white varieties.

○ Bianco dell'Empolese Vin Santo '01	🍷🍷	6
● Dicatum '06	🍷🍷	6
● Tuttosole '06	🍷🍷	5
● Chianti '08	🍷	3
● Chianti Sup. '08	🍷	4
○ Mandorlo '08	🍷	3
○ Montellori Pas Dosé '05	🍷	5
● Moro '07	🍷	4
● Chianti Fattoria Le Caselle '07	ŸŸ	3*
● Salamartano '05	ŸŸ	6
● Tuttosole '05	ŸŸ	6

Montenidoli

LOC. MONTENIDOLI
53037 SAN GIMIGNANO [SI]
TEL. 0577941565
www.montenidoli.com

★ Montevertine

LOC. MONTEVERTINE
53017 RADDA IN CHIANTI [SI]
TEL. 0577738009
www.montevertine.it

PRE-BOOKED VISITS

ANNUAL PRODUCTION **120,000 bottles**
HECTARES UNDER VINE **25**
VITICULTURE METHOD **Conventional**

ANNUAL PRODUCTION **75,000 bottles**
HECTARES UNDER VINE **15**
VITICULTURE METHOD **Conventional**

Elisabetta Fagiuoli's wines make quite an impact. They have enormous personality and even if they are not always stylistically perfect it is perhaps this that makes them so alluring. A prime example is the Vernaccia di San Gimignano Carato '05. However, while vernaccia may be Elisabetta's best-loved variety, the reds shouldn't be ignored, given the results she is also achieving in that department.

Carato '05 has complex aromas ranging from aromatic herbs to ripe fruit with faint flowery nuances. Entry on the palate is silky, the softness and initial glossiness giving way to lovely acid backbone that lends vigour. The Vernaccia Fiore '07 shows very refreshing fruit and a measured body that powers on into a lovely rising finish. The Vernaccia Tradizionale '07 hints at honey and almond on the nose and has a balanced, lip-smacking palate. The delicious Canaiuolo '08 is an inviting wine with good body. From the Chiantis, we preferred Il Garrulo '06, fuller of body and more complex in its aromas, to the Colli Senesi '06, which stiffish and more predictable.

The legendary Montevertine estate is as distinctively individual in its history as its flagship wine, Le Pergole Torte. Launched in 1971 as an sort of early Supertuscan and symbol of innovation, Le Pergole Torte then found itself representing tradition in the 1990s against the invasion of new muscular, fruity wines. Today, it "merely" occupies a place in the hall of fame of great Italian wines. The secret? It remains true to itself, quietly disdaining all fads and trends.

Le Pergole Torte '06 is no exception, even if we prefer some of the past vintages. The range of aromas is wide, lively and lingering with chewy, ripe, florality and undertones of pencil lead, cherry and iron. The palate presents a bit of an illusion. Behind its lovely drinkability lurk body and tannic structure but the extract is rather rough in texture. The Montevertine '06 has an over-evolved nose, showing notes of strawberry-tree and macerated red fruit. The palate has fabulous length and elegance, hinting at the transitional stage of the wine's evolution. We shall retaste it in a few months.

○ Vernaccia di S. Gimignano Carato '05	♈♈♈	6
⊙ Canaiuolo '08	♈♈	4*
● Chianti Colli Senesi Il Garrulo '06	♈♈	4
○ Vernaccia di S. Gimignano Fiore '07	♈♈	4*
○ Vernaccia di S. Gimignano Tradizionale '07	♈♈	4*
● Chianti Colli Senesi '06	♈	5
○ Vernaccia di S. Gimignano Carato '02	♈♈♈	6
○ Il Templare '03	♈♈	4
○ Vernaccia di S. Gimignano Carato '04	♈♈	6
○ Vernaccia di S. Gimignano Carato '03	♈♈	6
○ Vernaccia di S. Gimignano Fiore '06	♈♈	4
○ Vernaccia di S. Gimignano Tradizionale '06	♈♈	4*

● Le Pergole Torte '06	♈♈	8
● Montevertine '06	♈♈	6
● Pian del Ciampolo '07	♈	4
● Le Pergole Torte '04	♈♈♈	8
● Le Pergole Torte '03	♈♈♈	8
● Le Pergole Torte '01	♈♈♈	8
● Le Pergole Torte '99	♈♈♈	8
● Le Pergole Torte '92	♈♈♈	8
● Montevertine '04	♈♈♈	6
● Montevertine '01	♈♈♈	6

Moris Farms

LOC. CURA NUOVA
FATTORIA POGGETTI
58024 MASSA MARITTIMA [GR]
TEL. 0566918010
www.morisfarms.it

CELLAR SALES
PRE-BOOKED VISITS
VISITOR FACILITIES

ANNUAL PRODUCTION **400,000 bottles**
HECTARES UNDER VINE **71**
VITICULTURE METHOD **Conventional**

Moris Farms has reached cruising speed in terms of solid quality and has carved out a name for itself as a leader in the competitive world of Tuscan wine-making. The estate operates in two different zones, at Poggio la Mozza, in the area of Morellino, and Poggetti in Massa Marittima where the headquarters is located. Adolfo Parentini, who has headed the estate since the end of the 1970s runs it with his son, Giulio, to a philosophy that is based on sound oenology and a canny price policy.

In the absence of the estate flagship Avvoltore, the Morellino di Scansano Riserva '06 takes centre stage with its lovely, varietal character. Its nicely defined aromatics alternate between smoky nuances and gorgeous fresh flower notes. The palate shows excellent body and the sharp, confident acidity sees it unbend to reveal liveliness. The Morellino di Scansano '08 is very lively, with an extremely tasty palate although the aromatic profile is still rather closed. The Vermentino '08 has a refreshing, relaxed palate.

La Mormoraia

LOC. SANT'ANDREA, 15
53037 SAN GIMIGNANO [SI]
TEL. 0577940096
www.mormoraia.it

CELLAR SALES
PRE-BOOKED VISITS

ANNUAL PRODUCTION **170,000 bottles**
HECTARES UNDER VINE **27**
VITICULTURE METHOD **Conventional**

Mormoraia in the zone of Sant'Andrea is one of San Gimignano's most beautiful estates: 27 hectares of stunning vineyards and an avant-garde cellar. Supported by a strong team, Milan natives and Tuscany enthusiasts Pino and Franca Passoni make some truly excellent wines. Oenologist Paolo Caciornia heads production. Quality is on the up and the wines are notable for their concentration, freshness and stylistic cleanness.

The Vernaccia Riserva has always been top bottle here and the '07 is no exception. It made our finals with its intense, bright greenish straw-yellow colour and bell-clear aromas of oak-nuanced ripe fruit and medicinal herbs. The structured, succulent palate has big backbone and an elegant mineral finish. The refined Bordeaux blend Mitylus '06 is one of the best reds in the territory. An inky-dark colour announces intense black and red fruit notes over vegetality with hints of tobacco and pencil lead. Soft and structured, it finishes on long, attractive oaky, liquorice notes. The Merlot and Sangiovese Neitea, both '07s, are very decent. The rest of the range is first-rate.

● Morellino di Scansano '08	▼▼ 4
● Morellino di Scansano Ris. '06	▼▼ 5
○ Vermentino '08	▼ 4
● Avvoltore '06	▽▽▽ 6
● Avvoltore '01	▽▽▽ 6
● Avvoltore '00	▽▽▽ 6
● Avvoltore '03	▽▽ 6
● Morellino di Scansano Ris. '05	▽▽ 5
● Morellino di Scansano Ris. '00	▽▽ 5

● Mitylus '06	▼▼ 6
○ Vernaccia di S. Gimignano Ris. '07	▼▼ 5
● Chianti Colli Senesi '08	▼▼ 4*
● Neitea '07	▼▼ 5
● San Gimignano Merlot '07	▼▼ 5
○ Vernaccia di S. Gimignano '08	▼ 4
● Mitylus '05	▽▽ 6
○ Vernaccia di S. Gimignano Ris. '06	▽▽ 5
○ Vernaccia di S. Gimignano Ris. '05	▽▽ 5*

Tenute Silvio Nardi

LOC. CASALE DEL BOSCO
53024 MONTALCINO [SI]
TEL. 0577808269
www.tenutenardi.com

CELLAR SALES
PRE-BOOKED VISITS

ANNUAL PRODUCTION **250,000 bottles**
HECTARES UNDER VINE **80**
VITICULTURE METHOD **Conventional**

Silvio Nardi Estates extend across the slopes north and east of Montalcino in hills at an altitude of 140 to 480 metres. The area planted to vine is split across 36 different plots on three properties at Casale di Bosco, Manachiara and Colombaiolo. The soil is predominantly made up of clay substrates with layers of sand and silt. At Manachiara, the base is clay and silty marl with intercalations of limestone and quartz-rich sand. The main variety grown here is sangiovese and the vineyards have an average age of 20 years. Replanting was started in 1997.

This historic estate is back on stellar form. Emilia Nardi has spent years developing the estate and her wines are very solid. Sourced from an old vineyard in the territory's south-east zone, the Brunello di Montalcino Manachiara '04 reached our finals. The nose reveals clear notes of yellow peach and flowers while the palate is dense with good depth. The Rosso di Montalcino '07 is very well made, showing lovely aromas of red berry fruit and medicinal herbs followed by a taut, vibrant palate that unfolds wonderfully.

Niccolai - Palagetto

VIA MONTEOLIVETO, 46
53037 SAN GIMIGNANO [SI]
TEL. 0577943090
www.tenuteniccolai.it

CELLAR SALES
PRE-BOOKED VISITS

ANNUAL PRODUCTION **350,000 bottles**
HECTARES UNDER VINE **100**
VITICULTURE METHOD **Conventional**

Although last year's finalist, Syrah Uno dei Quattro, is missing from the line-up, the range offered by the Niccolai family's estate is still very good. The property consists of over 100 hectares planted to vine at Montalcino, San Gimignano and now also the zone of Montecucco. Sabrina Niccolai oversees them all full time and the results show just how passionate she is.

The '08 l'Niccolò, a vermentino, chardonnay and sauvignon blend, has delicious aromatic herbs, white-fleshed fruit and flowers. The palate has substance and richness of flavour in the very long finish. We also liked the '05 Sottobosco from sangiovese, syrah and cabernet sauvignon for its ripe black fruit and faint spicy pepper, a soft, concentrated body and nice succulence. Solleone '06, the Montecucco wine from the Pian de' Cerri estate made its debut. The nose has yet to find definition and the body is still rigid. The two '08 Vernaccias are most agreeable, presenting very clean and fresh in their aromas, and light and drinkable on the palate. The Colli Senesi '07 is well typed.

Wine	Rating
● Brunello di Montalcino Manachiara '04	▼▼ 8
● Rosso di Montalcino '07	▼▼ 5
● Brunello di Montalcino '04	▼ 7
● Sant'Antimo Merlot '07	▼ 4
● Brunello di Montalcino Manachiara '99	▼▼▼ 8
● Brunello di Montalcino Manachiara '97	▼▼▼ 7
● Brunello di Montalcino '01	▼▼ 7
● Brunello di Montalcino '99	▼▼ 6
● Brunello di Montalcino Manachiara '01	▼▼ 8
● Brunello di Montalcino Manachiara '00	▼▼ 8
● Brunello di Montalcino Manachiara '98	▼▼ 8

Wine	Rating
● Brunello di Montalcino La Bellarina Ris. '03	▼▼ 7
○ l'Niccolò '08	▼▼ 4*
● San Gimignano Sottobosco '05	▼▼ 5
● Brunello di Montalcino La Bellarina '04	▼ 7
● Chianti Colli Senesi '07	▼ 3
● Montecucco Rosso Solleone Pian de' Cerri '06	▼ 4
○ Vernaccia di S. Gimignano '08	▼ 3
○ Vernaccia di S. Gimignano V. Santa Chiara '08	▼ 4
● Brunello di Montalcino La Bellarina '03	▼▼ 7
○ l'Niccolò '07	▼▼ 4
● San Gimignano Syrah Uno di Quattro '05	▼▼ 7
○ Vernaccia di S. Gimignano Ris. '05	▼▼ 4

Fattoria Nittardi

LOC. NITTARDI
53011 CASTELLINA IN CHIANTI [SI]
TEL. 0577740269
www.nitardi.com

Podere Orma

VIA BOLGHERESE
57022 CASTAGNETO CARDUCCI [LI]
TEL. 0575477857
www.tenutasetteponti.it

CELLAR SALES
PRE-BOOKED VISITS

ANNUAL PRODUCTION 90,000 bottles
HECTARES UNDER VINE 27
VITICULTURE METHOD Conventional

ANNUAL PRODUCTION 9,000 bottles
HECTARES UNDER VINE 5
VITICULTURE METHOD Conventional

The Nittardi estate at Castellina in Chianti has 27 hectares under vine as part of a huge property comprising olive groves and around 120 hectares of woodland. It belongs to the Fermfert Canali family and has an important heritage of art and history as its previous owners include Michelangelo Buonarroti. Today, Nittardi produces wines of great taste density and modern character. Several years ago, the Chianti estate was expanded by the acquisition of 37 splendid hectares in Maremma.

The Chianti Classico '07 Casanuova di Nittardi's ripe black fruit is initially veiled by restrained oak. The wine is structured on the palate, which is all concentration and succulence. The Chianti Classico Riserva '06 has a long way to go. The nose remains in thrall to the oak and the rich, robust palate shows more power than elegance. From the Maremma, the '06 Nectar Dei from cabernet, merlot and syrah is very good. It reached our finals for its wonderful aromatic breadth, blackcurrant and vanilla fragrances, and long development on the palate.

This tiny estate lies in the celebrated Bolgheri wine zone. Its five hectares of vineyards face south-west and the deep soil is composed of pebbles and clay – ideal in warm areas – and a little sand. Proximity to the sea moderates the excessive temperatures of the inland areas, cooling the summers and making the winters milder. The vines have an average age of six years and are cordon-trained and spur-pruned at a density of around 7,000 plants per hectare.

It is a great shame that the estate produces only a few thousand bottles of Orma, the only wine to bear its name. Obtained from an equal blend of cabernet franc and merlot with a small amount of cabernet sauvignon, the '06 offers a full, complex nose with gorgeous notes of red and black berry fruit, and balsamic tones mingling with Mediterranean scrub. The palate is structured with confident development on the palate in true Bolgheri style. There's good acidity and clenched tannins.

● Nectar Dei '06	♟♟	7
● Chianti Cl. Casanuova di Nittardi '07	♟♟	5
● Ad Astra '06	♟	5
● Chianti Cl. Ris. '06	♟	7
● Chianti Cl. Ris. '98	♟♟♟	7
● Chianti Cl. Casanuova di Nittardi '06	♟♟	5
● Chianti Cl. Ris. '05	♟♟	7
● Chianti Cl. Ris. '04	♟♟	7
● Chianti Cl. Ris. '00	♟♟	7
● Chianti Cl. Ris. '99	♟♟	7
● Nectar Dei '05	♟♟	7
● Nectar Dei '03	♟♟	6

● Orma '06	♟♟♟	7
● Orma '05	♟♟	7

★ Tenuta dell'Ornellaia

FRAZ. BOLGHERI
VIA BOLGHERESE, 191
57022 CASTAGNETO CARDUCCI [LI]
TEL. 056571811
www.ornellaia.it

PRE-BOOKED VISITS

ANNUAL PRODUCTION 730,000 bottles
HECTARES UNDER VINE 97
VITICULTURE METHOD Conventional

The Tenuta dell'Ornellaia is a point of reference for Italian wine. From its superb soil and vineyards of the highest quality, the estate has created a perfect environment that with each passing year breathes an atmosphere of expectation and curiosity. Add to this the meticulous care dedicated to every aspect of the estate, not least the launch of the long-term Vendemmia d'Artista project led by Tenuta dell'Ornellaia, which puts the operation firmly in the front rank of the world's great wine houses.

The 2006 growing year was a bountiful one for the estate and brings us an Ornellaia and a Masseto in their best ever editions. The '06 Ornellaia already exhibits well-defined elegance with blackcurrant, aromatic herbs, liquorice and cocoa powder, and a supple body bursting with wonderful acid vigour. The prestigious seven-hectare Masseto merlot vineyard proffers a monumental, fruit-laden wine. Its mature, sumptuous nose heralds infinitely rich, enthralling raw material for another historic wine that ageing will only improve. Ornellaia's second wine, Bolgheri Serre Nuove '06, also performed very well.

Siro Pacenti

LOC. PELAGRILLI, 1
53024 MONTALCINO [SI]
TEL. 0577848662
pacentisiro@libero.it

PRE-BOOKED VISITS

ANNUAL PRODUCTION 80,000 bottles
HECTARES UNDER VINE 20
VITICULTURE METHOD Conventional

Giancarlo Pacenti has been at the helm of this family estate for years and is rightly considered the greatest innovator in the territory of Montalcino. His career, which started in the 1980s, has embraced all aspects of Brunello production, most notably the use of barriques for ageing. His experimentation with maceration has also led to the design of new fermentation vats. The vineyards lie on two very different slopes in Brunello territory: the northern and the south-eastern.

This year's top wine is the Brunello di Montalcino '04, which revealed rather stiffish tannins. It's a feature of Giancarlo's wines, especially when young, and probably derives from their great extractive weight. Further bottle-ageing, which is already lengthy, will no doubt have the desired effect. The nose is very rich, displaying notes of ripe blackberry, cherry and violet, as well as spicy nuances of cinnamon and vanilla. The well-made Rosso di Montalcino '07 has unusual grassy notes that are rather refreshing. Its youth is its only flaw.

● Masseto '06	♟♟♟	8
● Bolgheri Sup. Ornellaia '06	♟♟	8
● Bolgheri Rosso Serre Nuove '07	♟♟	7
● Le Volte '07	♟	4
● Bolgheri Sup. Ornellaia '05	♟♟♟	8
● Bolgheri Sup. Ornellaia '04	♟♟♟	8
● Bolgheri Sup. Ornellaia '02	♟♟♟	8
● Bolgheri Sup. Ornellaia '01	♟♟♟	8
● Bolgheri Sup. Ornellaia '99	♟♟♟	8
● Bolgheri Sup. Ornellaia '98	♟♟♟	8
● Masseto '04	♟♟♟	8
● Masseto '01	♟♟♟	8
● Masseto '05	♟♟	8

● Brunello di Montalcino '04	♟♟	8
● Rosso di Montalcino '07	♟	6
● Brunello di Montalcino '97	♟♟♟	8
● Brunello di Montalcino '96	♟♟♟	8
● Brunello di Montalcino '95	♟♟♟	8
● Brunello di Montalcino '88	♟♟♟	8
● Brunello di Montalcino '03	♟♟	8
● Brunello di Montalcino '01	♟♟	8
● Brunello di Montalcino '00	♟♟	8

Il Palagio

VIA CASE SPARSE, 38
50020 PANZANO [FI]
TEL. 055852933
www.palagiowineandoil.com

CELLAR SALES
PRE-BOOKED VISITS
VISITOR FACILITIES

ANNUAL PRODUCTION **N.D.**
HECTARES UNDER VINE **9.5**
VITICULTURE METHOD **Conventional**

Il Palagio belongs to the Piccini family and comprises around 13 hectares, three and a half of which are olive groves and the rest specialized vineyards. Gradual replanting has been under way for several years. The vineyards lie partly in the Conca d'Oro and partly at San Martino. The former were replanted in 2007 while the San Martino holding was replanted in 2000 and in 2004. The newly built cellar is well organized and kitted out with stainless steel vats and temperature-controlled environments. Oenologist Marco Chellini consults.

It was a great Guide debut for Il Palagio with a stunning prize-winner. Credit goes to an outstanding Chianti Classico '07 that captures the most authentic soul of the territory. On the nose, there are clear, generous aromas of fresh red berry fruit, dried flowers, faint spiciness, rain-soaked earth and roots. The palate is quite simply exquisite with all the pressure you expect from a Chianti Classico, elegant definition and immense character. This extraordinary wine fully deserves its Three Glasses.

La Palazzetta

FRAZ. CASTELNUOVO DELL'ABATE
VIA BORGO DI SOTTO
53020 MONTALCINO [SI]
TEL. 0577835631
www.palazzettafanti.com

CELLAR SALES
PRE-BOOKED VISITS
VISITOR FACILITIES

ANNUAL PRODUCTION **35,000 bottles**
HECTARES UNDER VINE **8**
VITICULTURE METHOD **Conventional**

Flavio Fanti's cellar and some of his vineyards are located in the zone south-east of Montalcino on the slopes opposite Castelnuovo dell'Abate. Here the soil is rich in quite loose marl that produces powerful wines. The other plots lie in cooler areas lower down near the abbey of Sant'Antimo and the cellar has barrel stock in various sizes. The estate also sells some rather interesting wines from another small winery, Visconti.

The Brunello di Montalcino '04 is superb. It presents a rich ruby and the classically austere nose nicely fuses its typical wild and morello cherry with the faint spiciness left by the oak. The gutsy palate shows just the right amount of acidity to accompany the progression and well-managed tannins. The finish is long and tidy. The Brunello di Montalcino '04 from Visconti also gave a very convincing performance. The Rosso di Montalcino '07 is well made if not particularly complex. The nose has good definition and freshness with lovely red berry fruit aromatics and the taut palate is eminently drinkable.

● Chianti Cl. '07	♟♟♟	5
● Chianti Cl. '06	♟	5

● Brunello di Montalcino '04	♟♟	6
● Brunello di Montalcino Visconti '04	♟♟	7
● Rosso di Montalcino '07	♟	4
● Rosso di Montalcino Visconti '07	♟	5
● Brunello di Montalcino Ris. '97	♟♟♟	8
● Brunello di Montalcino '03	♟♟	7
● Brunello di Montalcino '01	♟♟	6
● Brunello di Montalcino '00	♟♟	6

Il Palazzone

LOC. LE DUE PORTE, 245
53024 MONTALCINO [SI]
TEL. 0577846142
www.ilpalazzone.com

CELLAR SALES
PRE-BOOKED VISITS

ANNUAL PRODUCTION **12,000 bottles**
HECTARES UNDER VINE **2.6**
VITICULTURE METHOD **Conventional**

The Montalcino adventure of Richard Pearson, a well-known American executive, continues apace. Newly acquired vineyards and plans for a new cellar are among the most recent developments. The wines are austere in style, technically irreproachable and yet at the same time deeply rooted in their territory of origin. The vineyards lie in upper Montalcino on terrains with a very loose base and low clay content. This gives the wines a fairly high intrinsic level of acidity.

The '04 version of the Brunello di Montalcino is an absolute winner and went all the way to our national finals. Its lovely, rich ruby appearance is the prelude to aromas of morello cherry, blackberry and a flowery vein that meld nicely with faint wafts of tobacco. The palate presents good acid backbone and the tannic texture lends nice continuity and a long finish. At the time of our tastings, the estate's new IGTs were not available.

Marchesi Pancrazi Tenuta di Bagnolo

FRAZ. BAGNOLO
VIA MONTALESE, 156
50045 MONTEMURLO [PO]
TEL. 0574652439
www.pancrazi.it

CELLAR SALES
PRE-BOOKED VISITS

ANNUAL PRODUCTION **12,000 bottles**
HECTARES UNDER VINE **6**
VITICULTURE METHOD **Conventional**

This estate belonging to Marchese Pancrazi makes a well-deserved return thanks to the excellent level of its key wines, both obtained from pure pinot nero. Absent from the line-up were the wines produced on the San Donato farm, where more traditional varieties are cultivated, such as sangiovese and colorino. The history of the estate is an ancient one. Established in the 16th century by the Florentine Strozzi family, it was inherited by the current owners in 1965.

The '07 Vigna Baragazza selection presented this year is very convincing indeed. The initially faint aromatics go on to explode into lovely fruity sensations that recall blueberries and currants in particular. Entry on the plate is big and full with a lovely lifting mouthwatering finish. We also liked the Pinot Nero '07 for its delicate flowery notes and hints of spice, well-defined body, nice acid backbone and long tasty finish.

● Brunello di Montalcino '04	♥♥	7
● Brunello di Montalcino '01	♈♈♈	7
● Brunello di Montalcino Ris. '01	♈♈♈	7
● Brunello di Montalcino Ris. '99	♈♈♈	7
● Brunello di Montalcino '03	♈♈	7
● Brunello di Montalcino '00	♈♈	7
● Brunello di Montalcino '99	♈♈	7
● Brunello di Montalcino '98	♈♈	8
● Brunello di Montalcino '97	♈♈	8

● Pinot Nero V. Baragazza Tenuta di Bagnolo '07	♥♥	6
● Pinot Nero Villa di Bagnolo '07	♥♥	6
● Casaglia '03	♈♈	5
● Pinot Nero V. Baragazza '06	♈♈	8
● Pinot Nero V. Baragazza '04	♈♈	8
● Pinot Nero V. Baragazza '03	♈♈	8
● Pinot Nero Villa di Bagnolo '04	♈♈	7

Castello della Paneretta

LOC. MONSANTO
S.DA DELLA PANERETTA, 35
50021 BARBERINO VAL D'ELSA [FI]
TEL. 0558059003
www.paneretta.it

CELLAR SALES
PRE-BOOKED VISITS
VISITOR FACILITIES
FOOD

ANNUAL PRODUCTION 120,000 bottles
HECTARES UNDER VINE 22.5
VITICULTURE METHOD Conventional

Built around an old look-out tower after the legendary battle of Montaperti in 1260, Castello della Paneretta belongs today to the Albisetti family. It lies on the western slopes of the hills looking across Val d'Elsa towards San Gimignano. The terrain is dotted with woods and the soil is clayey Pliocene schist that varies in texture and colour. The result is a kaleidoscope of soils that give rise to as many types of wine. All are obtained from sangiovese and canaiolo nero from the estate's long-established clones.

The Chianti Classico Riserva '06 is a splendid wine. Very elegant notes of red berry fruits, citrus and minerality usher in a deliciously close-knit palate with very long flowery notes. The Riserva Torre a Destra '06 also did well, showing delicately austere in its red fruit and cocoa powder aromatics but with great flavour, sweetness and structure on the palate. The Chianti Classico '07 and the Terrine '05, from equal parts of sangiovese and canaiolo, are decent.

Giovanni Panizzi

FRAZ. SANTA MARGHERITA
LOC. RACCIANO, 34
53037 SAN GIMIGNANO [SI]
TEL. 0577941576
www.panizzi.it

CELLAR SALES
PRE-BOOKED VISITS

ANNUAL PRODUCTION 300,000 bottles
HECTARES UNDER VINE 67
VITICULTURE METHOD Conventional

Now that he has stepped down as president of the San Gimignano consortium after six eventful years that were successful and no doubt also exhausting, Giovanni now has time to dedicate himself to his estate. Not that he hasn't always done just this: look at the results he has achieved. Giovanni was one of the first to believe in the ageing potential of Vernaccia and find a new production option. This year's range lives up to expectations and there are two different vintages of the Riserva.

We were hard pressed to choose between the two but the '05 has the edge. It mingles sensations of ripe apricot and peach-led fruit with citrus. Entry on the palate is full, dense and deep and the finish is inviting. The '06 is hot on its heels with its aromatic herbs and flowers, silky but vibrant body and lip-smacking finish. The '08 Santa Margherita is refined, elegant and subtly pleasing on the palate. The Ceraso is an enjoyable wine with wild berry aromas to liven up the nose and a rich body. The '08 Vernaccia is merely good. But that's not bad.

● Chianti Cl. Ris. '06	▼▼ 5
● Chianti Cl. Torre a Destra Ris. '06	▼▼ 6
● Chianti Cl. '07	▼ 4
● Terrine '05	▼ 6
● Chianti Cl. Torre a Destra Ris. '05	♼♼ 6
● Chianti Cl. Torre a Destra Ris. '04	♼♼ 5
● Le Terrine '03	♼♼ 5
● Terrine '04	♼♼ 6
○ Vin Santo del Chianti Cl. '01	♼♼ 6

○ Vernaccia di S. Gimignano Ris. '05	▼▼▼ 6
○ Vernaccia di S. Gimignano Ris. '06	▼▼ 6
● Ceraso '08	▼▼ 4*
○ Vernaccia di San Gimignano V. Santa Margherita '08	▼▼ 4*
○ Vernaccia di S. Gimignano '08	▼ 4
○ Vernaccia di S. Gimignano Ris. '98	♼♼♼ 6
● Ceraso '07	♼♼ 4*
● Chianti Colli Senesi Vertunno Ris. '05	♼♼ 4*
● S. Gimignano Rubente '05	♼♼ 6
○ Vernaccia di S. Gimignano Ris. '03	♼♼ 6
○ Vernaccia di San Gimignano V. Santa Margherita '07	♼♼ 4*
○ Vernaccia di San Gimignano V. Santa Margherita '05	♼♼ 4

Il Paradiso

LOC. STRADA, 21A
53037 SAN GIMIGNANO [SI]
TEL. 0577941500
www.poderidelparadiso.it

CELLAR SALES
PRE-BOOKED VISITS
VISITOR FACILITIES

ANNUAL PRODUCTION **150,000 bottles**
HECTARES UNDER VINE **29**
VITICULTURE METHOD **Conventional**

This year's performance from the Cetti family production was disappointing. They presented no less than nine labels sourced from less than 30 hectares of vineyards. Each batch is bottled separately and the estate is rare for San Gimignano in that red varieties outweigh the vernaccia. The estate has produced good wine for years so we are sure this is just a momentary blip.

The best of the bunch is Silicum '06, a blend of sangiovese, merlot and syrah. It gives light fruity notes, spiciness, a balanced body, decent softness and a sweet, enjoyable finish. The '08 Vernaccia is uncomplicated yet fresh and tasty but the Saxa Calida from equal parts of merlot and cabernet sauvignon is too vegetal on the nose and unforthcoming on the palate. The merlot-only Filippo '06 flags halfway through and is very dilute but the pure sangiovese Paterno II '05 is more vibrant and fruity. The Mangiafoco '06 from cabernet sauvignon is over-extracted but the chardonnay-based Lo Cha '08 entices. The two Chianti Colli Senesis are agreeable and very drinkable.

● Silicum '06	▼▼ 5
● A Filippo '06	▼ 5
● Chianti Colli Senesi '07	▼ 3
● Chianti Colli Senesi Ris. '06	▼ 4
○ Lo Cha '08	▼ 4
● Mangiafoco '06	▼ 6
● Paterno II '05	▼ 6
● Saxa Calida '06	▼ 7
○ Vernaccia di S. Gimignano '08	▼ 4
● A Filippo '02	▼▼▼ 5
● Saxa Calida '00	▼▼▼ 6
● Saxa Calida '99	▼▼▼ 5

Petra

LOC. SAN LORENZO ALTO, 131
57028 SUVERETO [LI]
TEL. 0565845308
www.petrawine.it

CELLAR SALES
PRE-BOOKED VISITS

ANNUAL PRODUCTION **310,000 bottles**
HECTARES UNDER VINE **98**
VITICULTURE METHOD **Conventional**

Almost 100 hectares of vines and a production of about 300,000 bottles sums up Petra, one of the loveliest, most interesting estates in Suvereto. It belongs to the Terra Moretti group and is skilfully run by Francesca, daughter of Vittorio, who for years has turned out a range of high quality wines in a zone as stunning as it is challenging. It is not as easy as it looks to grow quality grapes here. The land is generous and the site climates are Mediterranean but elegance – Petra's declared aim – is hard to achieve.

The new flagship '06 Petra is a full, complex wine from 65 per cent cabernet sauvignon and the rest merlot, the fruit of a bountiful land. The wine shows the hot growing year with enveloping blackberry and plum-led fruit and even jammy notes laced with balsam and oak. The deep palate's nice acid vein curbs the sharp tannins. The pure merlot Quercegobbe '06 also showed well. Aromas of ripe black fruit, rain-soaked earth and olive paste announce a dense, mature mouthfeel with tannins that have yet to unbend. The Val di Cornia Ebo '06 has a sleek palate.

● Petra Rosso '06	▼▼ 8
● Quercegobbe '06	▼▼ 7
● Val di Cornia Ebo '06	▼▼ 4
● Zingari '07	▼ 4
● Petra Rosso '04	▼▼▼ 8
● Petra Rosso '03	▼▼ 8
● Quercegobbe '05	▼▼ 7

Fattoria Petrolo

FRAZ. MERCATALE VALDARNO
LOC. GALATRONA
VIA PETROLO, 30
52021 BUCINE [AR]
TEL. 0559911322
www.petrolo.it

PRE-BOOKED VISITS
VISITOR FACILITIES

ANNUAL PRODUCTION 60,000 bottles
HECTARES UNDER VINE 27
VITICULTURE METHOD Conventional

After this year's performance, one more Three Glass award will be enough for Luca Saintjust's estate to touch its first Star. In just a few short years, it has forged a very clear style for its products. The estate used to be part of the old medieval fief of Galatrona and was acquired by the Bazzocchi family in the 1980s. In the middle of the decade, it was Lucia, Luca's mother, who set out on the production path that has taken the cellar to today's success.

What we like about the Galatrona '07 is the complex, highly varied aromas that range from fresh greens to bell pepper and elegant spiciness. The soft, embracing palate has a lingering finish with a fabulous after-aroma of chocolate and tobacco. The '07 Torrione from pure sangiovese showed well. It has not very classic fruitiness with gamey nuances, and smooth, supple body. The intriguing Vin Santo '00 is only released in the best growing years. Its complex bouquet recalls citrus and dried fruit, the body is silky and velvety, and the finish is agreeably long.

Piaggia

LOC. POGGETTO
VIA CEGOLI, 47
59016 POGGIO A CAIANO [PO]
TEL. 0558705401
www.piaggia.com

ANNUAL PRODUCTION 65,000 bottles
HECTARES UNDER VINE 15
VITICULTURE METHOD Conventional

Silvia and Mauro Vannucci's estate romped home to another Three Glass win. Their estate has rapidly become a beacon for the Carmignano zone now they have abandoned the extremely modern style of their early years when their wines showed excessive concentration and a fullness that often felt strained. Today, the products are more relaxed, more enjoyable and therefore easier to appreciate.

This year, the top award went to the '07 Carmignano Sasso. Its dense appearance introduces a complex, concentrated nose that foregrounds aromas of wild berries and mixed spices. The body is compact and full. The Carmignano Ris. '06 also graced our finals. It offers fresher sensations on the nose with notes of aromatic herbs and balsamic tones leading to a nice entry on the palate and an enjoyable, very relaxed finish. We were less impressed by the Poggio de' Colli from cabernet franc only. It's in the cellar's former style with overripe aromatics, rich but uneven body and a rather flat finish.

● Galatrona '07	▼▼▼	8
● Torrione '07	▼▼	6
○ Vin Santo del Chianti '00	▼▼	6
● Galatrona '06	♀♀♀	8
● Galatrona '05	♀♀♀	8
● Galatrona '04	♀♀♀	7
● Galatrona '01	♀♀♀	8
● Galatrona '00	♀♀♀	8
● Galatrona '99	♀♀♀	7
● Galatrona '98	♀♀♀	7
● Galatrona '97	♀♀♀	7

● Carmignano Sasso '07	▼▼▼	5
● Carmignano Ris. '06	▼▼	6
● Poggio de' Colli '07	▼	7
● Carmignano Ris. '99	♀♀♀	6
● Carmignano Ris. '98	♀♀♀	6
● Carmignano Ris. '97	♀♀♀	5
● Il Sasso '01	♀♀♀	5
● Carmignano Ris. '05	♀♀	6
● Carmignano Ris. '04	♀♀	6
● Carmignano Ris. '03	♀♀	6
● Carmignano Sasso '06	♀♀	5
● Carmignano Sasso '05	♀♀	5

La Pieve

LOC. LA PIEVE
VIA SANTO STEFANO
50050 MONTAIONE [FI]
TEL. 0571697764
info@lapieve.net

CELLAR SALES
PRE-BOOKED VISITS
VISITOR FACILITIES

ANNUAL PRODUCTION 60,000 bottles
HECTARES UNDER VINE 18
VITICULTURE METHOD Organic certified

The Tognetti family and their estate regain a full profile in the Guide with a fine overall performance. We note with pleasure that it is possible to produce quality wines at a very competitive price. The property possesses 18 hectares planted to largely traditional varieties and vineyard management is organic. In addition to wine, the estate also produces extra virgin olive oil and offers holiday apartments to let.

The Rosso del Pievano '06 is obtained from a blend of mainly merlot with some cabernet franc and sauvignon. Its rich, wide-ranging aromas recall spices and berry fruits, leading into juicy body that displays smooth tannins and a laid-back finish. We also applauded a good showing from the all-syrah Il Gobbo Nero '07 whose nose delights with clear aromas of pepper-led spiciness. The elegant palate displays smooth, graceful tannins and a long lingering finish. Finally, the two Chiantis are very good, both showing lively on the nose followed by a taut, fresh palate with a nice finish.

Pieve Santa Restituta

LOC. CHIESA DI SANTA RESTITUTA
53024 MONTALCINO [SI]
TEL. 0173635158
pievesantarestituta@virgilio.it;
infogaijawines.com

ANNUAL PRODUCTION 45,000 bottles
HECTARES UNDER VINE 16
VITICULTURE METHOD Conventional

Angelo Gaja, one of Italy's great wine masters of world-spanning fame, bought this estate in the early 1990s. He has invested heavily in the vineyards and the replanting that finished several years ago has increased the number of plants per hectare. The largely underground cellar has also been restored. The zone is one of the best in Montalcino, located in the western part of the DOCG at an altitude of around 300 metres. Angelo produces just two Brunello di Montalcino labels, Rennina and Sugarille.

Both are excellent and we had a hard time choosing between them. Modern in style, particularly in their use of oak, they exhibit a fruity, compact nose led by blackberry and morello cherry. The Brunello di Montalcino Rennina '04 is a dense, austerely captivating wine and less rigid than its sibling, notably in its tannins, acidity guaranteeing a long, taut finish. Three effortless Glasses. The '04 Brunello di Montalcino Sugarille is so powerful and dense it probably needs more time to develop its full potential. Two different interpretations of Brunello, both with enormous personality.

● Il Gobbo Nero '07	▼▼ 4*
● Rosso del Pievano '06	▼▼ 4*
● Chianti '08	▼ 3
● Chianti Fortebraccio '07	▼ 3
● Chianti '07	♀♀ 3*
● Chianti Cl. La Pieve '06	♀♀ 3*
● Il Gobbo Nero '06	♀♀ 4
● Rosso del Pievano '05	♀♀ 4

● Brunello di Montalcino Rennina '04	▼▼▼ 8
● Brunello di Montalcino Sugarille '04	▼▼ 8
● Brunello di Montalcino Ris. '88	♀♀♀ 6
● Brunello di Montalcino Rennina '01	♀♀ 8
● Brunello di Montalcino Rennina '00	♀♀ 8
● Brunello di Montalcino Rennina '99	♀♀ 8
● Brunello di Montalcino Sugarille '01	♀♀ 8
● Brunello di Montalcino Sugarille '00	♀♀ 8
● Brunello di Montalcino Sugarille '99	♀♀ 8

Il Pinino

LOC. PODERE PININO, 327
53024 MONTALCINO [SI]
TEL. 0577849381
www.pinino.com

CELLAR SALES
PRE-BOOKED VISITS

ANNUAL PRODUCTION 85,000 bottles
HECTARES UNDER VINE 16
VITICULTURE METHOD Conventional

Il Pinino has been on the map since the 1950s but it wasn't until Max Hernandez and Andrea Gamon took over that it began to produce seriously good wine. Its 16 hectares are equally divided between Rosso and Brunello di Montalcino and lie in a zone that has a sandstone base with a clay component. The estate is small but perfectly equipped with medium-sized barrels that go up to 30 hectolitres in capacity. Despite rather lengthy macerations, the wines have a modern slant, particularly in the use of oak.

Of the two Brunello di Montalcinos presented, it was the Clandestino selection that got our vote and it won a place in our finals on its debut appearance. It possesses a lovely ruby colour that ushers in complex aromas of blueberry, cherry, blackberry and eucalyptus. The palate is concentrated and the richness of the body is sustained by lovely tannic texture that ensures the finish is anything but rigid. The '04 Brunello di Montalcino is also well made. More open on the nose of tobacco and ripe fruit, it unfolds a long, very elegantly juicy palate. The Rosso di Montalcino '07 is very pleasant, if a bit short on progression.

● Brunello di Montalcino Clandestino '04	♥♥ 7
● Brunello di Montalcino '04	♥♥ 7
● Rosso di Montalcino '07	♥ 5
● Rosso di Montalcino Clandestino '07	♥ 5
● Brunello di Montalcino '02	♥♥ 7
● Brunello di Montalcino '01	♥♥ 7
● Rosso di Montalcino '06	♥♥ 4
● Rosso di Montalcino '05	♥♥ 4
● Rosso di Montalcino '04	♥♥ 4

Podere Brizio

LOC. PODERE BRIZIO, 67
53024 MONTALCINO [SI]
TEL. 0577846004
www.poderebrizio.it

CELLAR SALES
PRE-BOOKED VISITS
VISITOR FACILITIES

ANNUAL PRODUCTION 50,000 bottles
HECTARES UNDER VINE 17
VITICULTURE METHOD Conventional

This estate is the property of Roberto Bellini, originally from Lombardy but in Montalcino for over 40 years. It lies in the western area of Montalcino on the road to the Maremma. There are around 60 hectares in all, almost one third of which are planted to vine. The soil is fairly loose and consists of marl and alberese on a limestone base, which produces wines of absolute elegance. The vineyards dedicated to Brunello are old, while the younger plots are planted to higher densities and go to make the two blends.

All the wines offered for tasting show a good level of quality. We particularly liked the Brunello di Montalcino '04, with its clean, clear, classic nose of morello cherry and tobacco. The excellently extracted tannins give the palate balance and ensure it unbends nicely to conclude a very refined sensory profile. We also had decent showings from the '06 Sant'Antimo Leonensis, based on sangiovese, merlot and cabernet sauvignon, whose tannins are a tad mouth-drying, and the fruity, very relaxed Papà Pepu '06 from cabernet and merlot.

● Brunello di Montalcino '04	♥♥ 7
● Pupà Pepu '06	♥♥ 8
● Sant'Antimo Leonensis '06	♥♥ 5
● Brunello di Montalcino Ris. '01	♥♥♥ 8
● Brunello di Montalcino '01	♥♥ 7
● Podere Brizio '03	♥♥ 5
● Pupà Pepu '03	♥♥ 8
● Rosso di Montalcino '06	♥♥ 4
● Rosso di Montalcino '04	♥♥ 4
● Sant'Antimo Leonensis '03	♥♥ 5
● Sant'Antimo Leonensis '02	♥♥ 5

Podere Fortuna

VIA SAN GIUSTO A FORTUNA, 7
50037 SAN PIERO A SIEVE [FI]
TEL. 0558487214
www.poderefortuna.com

CELLAR SALES
PRE-BOOKED VISITS
VISITOR FACILITIES

ANNUAL PRODUCTION 10,000 bottles
HECTARES UNDER VINE 6
VITICULTURE METHOD Naturale

This estate belonging to Alessandro Brogi has earned itself a full profile. This dynamic entrepreneur with a passion for wine showed great courage in opting to launch his wine-producing venture in a zone that everyone advised against. It was 2001 when Alessandro set out to produce quality wines here. To cap it all, he selected that challenging variety, pinot nero, which until then had given disappointing results in Tuscany. Throw in a good dose of stubbornness and all this has changed. Six of Alessandro's 30 hectares are planted to vine.

The Fortuni '06 from pure pinot nero went through to our finals with its alluring cornucopia of aromatics, showcasing spicy notes that meld with intense fruity sensations of blueberry and currant. Entry on the palate is authoritative and characterful, displaying balance, well-gauged pulp and a refreshing finish. The '06 Coldaia, also from pinot nero, is sourced from a single plot and offers less explosive aromas that precede a full body whose tannins tend to drain its energy, and a juicy finish.

Poggerino

LOC. POGGERINO
53017 RADDA IN CHIANTI [SI]
TEL. 0577738958
www.poggerino.com

CELLAR SALES
PRE-BOOKED VISITS
VISITOR FACILITIES
FOOD

ANNUAL PRODUCTION 60,000 bottles
HECTARES UNDER VINE 11.5
VITICULTURE METHOD Naturale

Poggerino enjoys one of the most interesting positions in the Chianti Classico area. Sitting at an altitude of around 500 metres in the upper part of Radda, the vineyards benefit from the perfect drainage offered by the largely marl-based soil. The Lanza brothers run this organic estate with great care and attention. Over the years, Poggerino wines have gradually acquired greater personality and now clearly reflect the characteristics of each growing year and their territory of origin.

Overall, we are very impressed. The Chianti Classico '06 opens on flowery, fruity notes with hints of chalk and pencil lead. The style of the palate hinges around extract and acidity that support a dense, juicy body of enormous elegance before the long finish unveils a red fruit theme. The Chianti Classico Riserva Bugialla '06 has a range of aromatics lent depth by its black berry fruit, aromatic herbs and sweet spices completing the picture. The enveloping palate develops nimbly, refreshed by acidity that enhances the body, although the finish is faintly bitterish.

● Pinot Nero Fortuni '06	♟♟ 6
● Pinot Nero Coldaia '06	♟♟ 6
● Pinot Nero Coldaia '05	♟♟ 6
● Pinot Nero Fortuni '05	♟♟ 6

● Chianti Cl. '06	♟♟ 4*
● Chianti Cl. Bugialla Ris. '06	♟♟ 6
● Chianti Cl. Ris. '90	♟♟♟ 5
● Primamateria '01	♟♟♟ 6
● Chianti Cl. '04	♟♟ 4
● Chianti Cl. '01	♟♟ 4
● Chianti Cl. Bugialla Ris. '04	♟♟ 6
● Chianti Cl. Bugialla Ris. '01	♟♟ 6
● Chianti Cl. Bugialla Ris. '00	♟♟ 6
● Primamateria '04	♟♟ 6
● Primamateria '03	♟♟ 6

Poggio al Tesoro

LOC. FELCIAINO
VIA BOLGHERESE, 189B
57020 BOLGHERI [LI]
TEL. 0565773051
info@poggioaltesoro.it

CELLAR SALES

ANNUAL PRODUCTION **80,000 bottles**
HECTARES UNDER VINE **40**
VITICULTURE METHOD **Conventional**

The Allegrini family, well-known producers in Valpolicella, and Leonardo Lo Cascio, a major wine distributor from the United States, have joined forces on the Poggio al Tesoro estate, which continues to show the growth we noted last year. The vineyards are scattered across several plots and the pebble-rich soil has a base of coarse red sand that ensures good drainage. The estate style is faithful to its territory of origin and the modern wines have impact and elegance.

The cabernet franc-only Dedicato a Walter '06 hails from the clay-rich red sands of the Via Bolgherese, which bring us a first-class wine with generous aromas of ripe red fruit, sweet spices and delicate toastiness. On the palate, the body is close-knit, balanced and fruity. Bolgheri Sondraia '06 also shows well, intense, clean vegetal, fruity aromas preceding a body that has exciting quality potential despite rather stiff-backed tannins. Syrah, merlot and cabernet sauvignon go into the very agreeable and eminently drinkable Mediterra '07 while the '08 Bolgheri Solosole, from vermentino, is its usual pleasant, relaxed self.

Poggio Antico

LOC. POGGIO ANTICO
53024 MONTALCINO [SI]
TEL. 0577848044
www.poggioantico.com

CELLAR SALES
PRE-BOOKED VISITS
FOOD

ANNUAL PRODUCTION **120,000 bottles**
HECTARES UNDER VINE **32.5**
VITICULTURE METHOD **Naturale**

Milan-born Paola Gloder has elected Montalcino as her home and has run Poggio Antico since founding it. Her stunning estate perches on a rocky spur facing south-west with a spectacular view. The vineyards fan out around the estate and are all high with the exception of Madre, a new plot lower down, while the modern cellar ensures great quality. The style of the wines varies by label: Madre and Brunello di Montalcino Alter are contemporary in their use of oak and fermentations while this year's Brunello di Montalcino and the Riserva are more traditional.

The two '04 Brunello di Montalcino are superb and Altero won Three Glasses. The nose reveals the use of new barriques, the palate is notable for its sound elegance and the tannins are perfectly extracted. The '04 Brunello di Montalcino has less spice and more fruity aromatics led by blackberry and blueberry. The palate is tannic but there is no lack of acidity and the finish is very long. The Madre '06, from equal parts of sangiovese and cabernet sauvignon, flaunts a sharp style but a tad too much oak on the nose. The drinkable Rosso di Montalcino '07 also has panache.

● Dedicato a Walter '06	▼▼ 6
○ Bolgheri Bianco Solosole '08	▼▼ 5
● Bolgheri Sondraia '06	▼▼ 6
● Mediterra '07	▼▼ 5
○ Bolgheri Bianco Solosole '07	♀♀ 5
● Dedicato a Walter '05	♀♀ 6
● Sondraia '05	♀♀ 6

● Brunello di Montalcino Altero '04	▼▼▼ 7
● Brunello di Montalcino '04	▼▼ 7
● Madre '06	▼▼ 6
● Rosso di Montalcino '07	▼▼ 5
● Brunello di Montalcino '88	♀♀♀ 7
● Brunello di Montalcino '85	♀♀♀ 7
● Brunello di Montalcino Altero '99	♀♀♀ 7
● Brunello di Montalcino Ris. '01	♀♀♀ 8
● Brunello di Montalcino Ris. '85	♀♀♀ 8
● Brunello di Montalcino Altero '03	♀♀ 7
● Madre '05	♀♀ 6
● Madre '04	♀♀ 6

Poggio Argentiera

LOC. ALBERESE
S.DA BANDITELLA, 2
58010 GROSSETO
TEL. 0564405099
www.poggioargentiera.com

CELLAR SALES
PRE-BOOKED VISITS

ANNUAL PRODUCTION **200,000 bottles**
HECTARES UNDER VINE **42**
VITICULTURE METHOD **Conventional**

Maremma agronomist Gianpaolo Paglia and his wife Justine Keeling, a British marketing manager, founded Poggio Argentiera at Banditella dell'Alberese in 1998. It immediately made a name for itself as one of the most interesting estates in the colourful patchwork of Maremma winemaking for its distinctive style. Strong character and great drinkability are the hallmarks of both the more ambitious wines and the everyday ones.

As ever, the Morellino di Scansano Capatosta '07 impressed us with the gorgeous aromatic maturity of its fruit and its complex, tasty development on the palate. The Finisterre '07, obtained from a blend of alicante and syrah, is very interesting, offering clear balsamic notes and hints of Mediterranean scrub followed by a fruity, flavoursome palate. The Morellino di Scansano Bellamarsilia '08 has rather vegetal notes and really comes into its own on the palate, where it shows full and round. The '08 Maremmante from syrah and alicante is drinking now. The two whites, both '08s, show a nice salty character. Bucce comes from ansonica and Guazza from ansonica and vermentino.

Poggio Bonelli

LOC. POGGIO BONELLI
53019 CASTELNUOVO BERARDENGA [SI]
TEL. 0577355382
www.poggiobonelli.it

CELLAR SALES
PRE-BOOKED VISITS
VISITOR FACILITIES

ANNUAL PRODUCTION **230,000 bottles**
HECTARES UNDER VINE **85**
VITICULTURE METHOD **Naturale**

Poggio Bonelli is situated at the southern-most tip of the Castelnuovo Berardenga DOCG. Its pedigree is noble and the estate has belonged to many aristocratic families, including the Piccolomini. Today, it is the property of the Monte dei Paschi di Siena bank. The estate takes in 800 hectares, 85 of which are planted to vine on clayey tufaceous soil with a high sand content. Poggio Bonelli's modern, rigorous viticultural methods produce international-style wines with great concentration and power on the palate.

This year's range is not quite up to Poggio Bonelli's usual standards. There's quality across the board but the peaks we have come to expect are missing. The Chianti Classico '07 has lovely body but is over-extracted, which curbs its development. The same goes for the '06 Riserva, which is sumptuous in its structure but rather lacks elegance. Appropriate bottle-ageing should smooth its corners. The Tramonto d'Oca '06, a blend of sangiovese and merlot, fails to match its extract with the right level of suppleness on the palate. The Chianti Villa Chigi Saracini '08 is more enjoyable.

● Finisterre '07	♀♀♀	7
● Morellino di Scansano Capatosta '07	♀♀	6
○ Bucce '08	♀	5
○ Guazza '08	♀	3
● Maremmante '08	♀	4
● Morellino di Scansano Bellamarsilia '08	♀	4
● Morellino di Scansano Capatosta '00	♀♀♀	6*
● Finisterre '05	♀♀	7
● Finisterre '04	♀♀	7
● Morellino di Scansano Capatosta '05	♀♀	6
● Morellino di Scansano Capatosta '04	♀♀	6

● Chianti Cl. Ris. '06	♀♀	6
● Chianti Cl. '07	♀	4
● Chianti Villa Chigi Saracini '08	♀	3
● Tramonto d'Oca '06	♀	6
○ Vin Santo del Chianti '00	♀	7
● Poggiassai '06	♀♀♀	6
● Chianti Cl. '04	♀♀	4
● Chianti Cl. '01	♀♀	4
● Chianti Cl. Ris. '05	♀♀	6
● Chianti Cl. Ris. '01	♀♀	6
● Poggiassai '05	♀♀	6
● Tramonto d'Oca '04	♀♀	6
● Tramonto d'Oca '03	♀♀	6
● Tramonto d'Oca '01	♀♀	6

Poggio di Sotto

FRAZ. CASTELNUOVO DELL'ABATE
LOC. POGGIO DI SOTTO
53024 MONTALCINO [SI]
TEL. 0577835502
www.poggiodisotto.com

CELLAR SALES
PRE-BOOKED VISITS
VISITOR FACILITIES

ANNUAL PRODUCTION 40,000 bottles
HECTARES UNDER VINE 12
VITICULTURE METHOD Organic certified

Piero Palmucci has become an icon for enthusiasts of classic Brunello di Montalcino. Tradition is the order of the day in the beautiful Castelnuovo dell'Abate cellar, both in terms of the fairly long macerations and the use of large barrels. The vineyards lie at varying altitudes in the zone overlooking Mount Amiata and the grapes they yield are blended to produce a range of very complex wines.

The Brunello di Montalcino '04 is back on Three Glass form. This stupendous classic possesses a compact, lingering nose that reveals wild cherry, medicinal herbs, leather and very alluring soft nuances of spice. The palate has immense structure but never oversteps the mark, its velvety tannins in perfect proportion while the acidity comes through well despite the heat of the growing zone. The unhurried finish is very long-lingering. The Rosso di Montalcino '06 is also good, perfectly reflecting Piero Palmucci's style.

Poggio Molina

LOC. POGGIO MOLINA
52021 BUCINE [AR]
TEL. 0559789402
www.poggiomolina.it

CELLAR SALES
PRE-BOOKED VISITS

ANNUAL PRODUCTION 60,000 bottles
HECTARES UNDER VINE 16
VITICULTURE METHOD Conventional

Poggio Molina is in Val d'Ambra and has 90 hectares of land, 16 of which are planted to vine. Owners Claudio and Alba Bossini dedicate themselves wholeheartedly to the estate and have achieved very impressive results in a short time. They have renovated the cellar and replanted their vineyards with international varieties, all of which has proved very successful and has stamped the wines with their own distinctive personality.

The cream of this year's crop is the '06 Lo Scopaio, a blend of sangiovese, cabernet franc and merlot. Its refreshing range of aromas include balsamic tones and hints of wild berries. Entry on the palate is soft, showing tempting substance and good acid backbone that enhances its drinkability. On the other hand, the '06 Le Caldie from merlot with some sangiovese is not as good as last year's edition. The nose is fruit-dominated but a bit muddled while the palate is fluent and full with a rising finish. Finally, the green Vinobono '07 is very lightweight on the palate and has a mid-length finish.

● Brunello di Montalcino '04	♟♟♟+	8
● Rosso di Montalcino '06	♟♟	7
● Brunello di Montalcino '99	♟♟♟	8
● Brunello di Montalcino Ris. '99	♟♟♟	8
● Brunello di Montalcino Ris. '95	♟♟♟	8
● Brunello di Montalcino '03	♟♟	8
● Brunello di Montalcino '01	♟♟	8
● Brunello di Montalcino '00	♟♟	8
● Rosso di Montalcino '05	♟♟	7
● Rosso di Montalcino '04	♟♟	6

● Le Caldie '06	♟♟	6
● Lo Scopaio '06	♟♟	5
● Vinobono '07	♟	4
● Le Caldie '05	♟♟	6
● Le Caldie '04	♟♟	6
● Lo Scopaio '05	♟♟	5
● Vinobono '05	♟♟	4*

Podere Poggio Scalette

LOC. RUFFOLI
VIA BARBIANO, 7
50022 GREVE IN CHIANTI [FI]
TEL. 0558546108
www.poggioscalette.it

PRE-BOOKED VISITS

ANNUAL PRODUCTION **35,000 bottles**
HECTARES UNDER VINE **15**
VITICULTURE METHOD **Naturale**

Podere Poggio Scalette stands on the slopes of Ruffoli in the zone of Greve in Chianti. The estate was founded in 1991 by Vittorio Fiore and he has now been joined by his son, Jurij. It enjoys a privileged position in terms of vineyard aspects and the capacity of the land for grape-growing. These terraces, in an area known as Il Carbonaione by the local farmers, were the site of the first sangiovese vines planted in the decades following the end of the First World War in the post-phylloxera era.

Il Carbonaione '06, obtained from very old sangiovese vines, shows the effects of the hot growing year. Its aromas are clear and clean but there are excessively warm, concentrated notes of brandied red fruit and sweet hints of vanilla. On the palate, the full body seems mired in its own richness and although we can't fault its texture, it lacks character. At the time of our tasting, the merlot-based Piantonaia '06 had yet to find clarity. The rather muddled nose is overwhelmed by the oak and the taste profile reveals tannins that curb its thrust on the palate.

Il Poggiolo

LOC. POGGIOLO, 259
53024 MONTALCINO [SI]
TEL. 0577848412
www.ilpoggiolomontalcino.com

CELLAR SALES
PRE-BOOKED VISITS

ANNUAL PRODUCTION **40,000 bottles**
HECTARES UNDER VINE **7**
VITICULTURE METHOD **Conventional**

Rudy Cosimi runs Il Poggiolo with a very skilled hand. His father founded the estate at the beginning of the 1970s. From around three hectares of vineyards situated in the Brunello DOCG, Rudy produces a range of wines that are very diverse in terms of the variability of their terrain, vinification style and maturation, from the least modern of the bottles, the Brunello di Montalcino, aged in barrels of around 30 hectolitres, and on to the newest arrival, the very contemporary Il mio Brunello, the Beato and the Terra Rossa.

The name Il mio Brunello '04 announces Rudy's intention to make a wine that frames his philosophy and the result is very interesting. Despite still-dominant oaky tones, the nose expresses red berry fruit, blackberry, and morello cherry and attractive spicy sensations of cinnamon, coffee and vanilla. The palate is well-structured and lively, thanks to its lovely acidity and compact, measured tannins. The '04 Brunello di Montalcino also shows well, its notes of tobacco and autumn leaf enhancing the cherry sensations, before the palate unveils tight-knit tannins and a lingering finish. The '04 Brunello di Montalcino Beato is held back by its oak.

● Il Carbonaione '06	▼▼	7
● Piantonaia '06	▼	8
● Il Carbonaione '05	▼▼▼	7
● Il Carbonaione '03	▼▼▼	8
● Il Carbonaione '00	▼▼▼	8
● Il Carbonaione '98	▼▼▼	8
● Il Carbonaione '96	▼▼▼	8

● Brunello di Montalcino Il mio Brunello '04	▼▼▼	8
● Brunello di Montalcino '04	▼▼	7
● Brunello di Montalcino Beato '04	▼▼	8
● Brunello di Montalcino Terra Rossa '04	▼	7
● Brunello di Montalcino Terra Rossa '01	▼▼▼	7
● Brunello di Montalcino Beato '03	▼▼	8
● Brunello di Montalcino Beato '01	▼▼	8
● Brunello di Montalcino Poggiolo '01	▼▼	7
● Rosso di Montalcino Quello Buono '06	▼▼	4
● Rosso di Montalcino Quello Buono '05	▼▼	4
● Rosso di Montalcino Sassello '99	▼▼	4
● Rosso di Montalcino Terra Rossa '99	▼▼	5

Tenuta Il Poggione

FRAZ. SANT'ANGELO IN COLLE
LOC. MONTEANO
53024 MONTALCINO [SI]
TEL. 0577844029
www.tenutailpoggiono.it

CELLAR SALES
PRE-BOOKED VISITS

ANNUAL PRODUCTION 500,000 bottles
HECTARES UNDER VINE 118
VITICULTURE METHOD Conventional

This historic Montalcino estate was one of the first to introduce a wider public to the drinking potential of Brunello through a keen pricing strategy it still maintains. The stunning vineyards, some of them very old, lie in the southern part of Montalcino near the village of Sant'Angelo in Colle, where the estate headquarters is located. The DOCG plots lie at altitudes of between 150 and 400 metres. Several years ago, the winery built a beautiful out-of-town basement cellar, which also has a modern olive press.

The Brunello di Montalcino Riserva '03 is truly superb, particularly in light of the challenging growing year. Thanks to the old vines, it probably withstood the torrid summer better. Notes of cherry – fruit as well as preserve – combine with delicate aromas of cocoa powder while the alcoholic richness on the palate is nicely buttressed by surprising acidity and tannins that are anything but mouth-drying. The very elegant Brunello di Montalcino '04 has rather a dark nose but a vibrant, very relaxed palate. The pleasant '07 Rosso di Montalcino is very drinkable.

Fattoria Poggiopiano

VIA DI PISIGNANO, 28/30
50026 SAN CASCIANO IN VAL DI PESA [FI]
TEL. 0558229629
www.fattoriapoggiopiano.it

CELLAR SALES
PRE-BOOKED VISITS

ANNUAL PRODUCTION 100,000 bottles
HECTARES UNDER VINE 21
VITICULTURE METHOD Conventional

Fattoria Poggiopiano is located at San Casciano Val di Pesa at an altitude of around 300 metres. The Bartoli family acquired the property in 1993 and set about living their dream of making wine. Today, they have about nine hectares of vineyards plus 12 more they rent, planted largely to sangiovese, the estate's real passion. Their decision to work small plots allows them to monitor carefully every phase of the production cycle. The wines have a modern slant and over the years have become increasingly territorial in character.

The Chianti Classico '07 shows nice aromatic verve, with citrus fruit, spring flowers and spices, notably cloves and cinnamon. The palate has yet to unbend and evolve fully but is however very well-typed, the tannins nicely sustained by acid thrust and good continuity. Our tastings revealed the extreme youth of the Chianti Classico La Tradizione '06, whose ripe fruit and macerated flowers aromatics contrast with the development of a palate marked by the rigidity of tannins that still have to relax. Greater harmony will come with time.

● Brunello di Montalcino '04	♟♟ 7
● Brunello di Montalcino Ris. '03	♟♟ 7
● Rosso di Montalcino '07	♟♟ 4*
● Brunello di Montalcino Ris. '97	♟♟♟ 8
● Brunello di Montalcino '03	♟♟ 7
● Brunello di Montalcino '02	♟♟ 6
● Brunello di Montalcino Ris. '01	♟♟ 7
● Il Poggione '06	♟♟ 4*
● Il Poggione '04	♟♟ 3*
● Il Poggione '03	♟♟ 3*
● San Leopoldo '03	♟♟ 5

● Chianti Cl. '07	♟♟ 4*
● Chianti Cl. La Tradizione '06	♟♟ 6
● Rosso di Sera '04	♟♟♟ 7
● Rosso di Sera '03	♟♟♟ 7
● Rosso di Sera '99	♟♟♟ 6
● Rosso di Sera '98	♟♟♟ 6
● Rosso di Sera '97	♟♟♟ 5
● Rosso di Sera '95	♟♟♟ 5
● Chianti Cl. La Tradizione '05	♟♟ 6
● Rosso di Sera '06	♟♟ 7

★★ Poliziano

LOC. MONTEPULCIANO STAZIONE
VIA FONTAGO, 1
53045 MONTEPULCIANO [SI]
TEL. 0578738171
www.carlettlpoliziano.com

CELLAR SALES
PRE-BOOKED VISITS
FOOD

ANNUAL PRODUCTION **600,000 bottles**
HECTARES UNDER VINE **140**
VITICULTURE METHOD **Conventional**

Federico Carletti, incumbent president of the Vino Nobile consortium, took over the reins of his family property at the end of the 1980s. In just over 20 years, he has built up a business that, not to mince words, is emblematic of the entire DOCG. Poliziano-label wine very simply always meets our every expectation thanks to a consistency of quality that is awesome to say the least and driven by meticulously managed vineyards and quite impeccable vinification.

The Nobile di Montepulciano Asinone remains the estate's undisputed standard-bearer and the '06 confidently picked up its customary Three Glass trophy. The very elegant Vin Santo '97 holds its own with the best in a territory that is historically renowned for its pre-eminence in this wine type. The rest of the range is absolutely reliable but then again we expect nothing else. Crucially, it is also very decently priced. The Le Stanze '07 and the Mandrone di Lhosa '07 will age for a further year. The latter is produced on the Maremma estate at Magliano in Toscana.

Castello di Poppiano

FRAZ. POPPIANO
VIA DI FEZZANA, 45
50025 MONTESPERTOLI [FI]
TEL. 05582315
www.conteguicciardini.it

CELLAR SALES
PRE-BOOKED VISITS

ANNUAL PRODUCTION **600,000 bottles**
HECTARES UNDER VINE **130**
VITICULTURE METHOD **Conventional**

We noted a low-key performance from Federico Guicciardini's estate, even if the wines are well-managed and offer good value for money. The castle has been in the family for 900 years but the winemaking and olive farming were developed seriously by the current owner. Federico has also risen to the challenge of the relatively new wine territory of Maremma, where he has acquired the Massi di Mandorlaia estate.

This year's out and out winner is the '07 Syrah, which also contains a small measure of sangiovese. The lovely purple colour leads into a classic nose of ripe plum and cherry-like fruit with spicy nuances of pepper. The palate is warm, juicy and inviting and the finish has a nice lift. The '06 Riserva Chianti Colli Fiorentini is also good. Aromas of jam and vanilla combine with balanced body and agreeable acid backbone. The Toscoforte '07, obtained from a blend that reverses the Syrah's assemblage, and the Tricorno '07 from sangiovese, merlot and cabernet sauvignon, both possess style and body.

● Nobile di Montepulciano Asinone '06	▼▼▼	7
● Cortona Merlot In Violas '07	▼▼	6
● Nobile di Montepulciano '06	▼▼	5
○ Vin Santo di Montepulciano '97	▼▼	7
● Morellino di Scansano '08	▼	4
● Rosso di Montepulciano '08	▼	4
● Nobile di Montepulciano Asinone '05	♈♈♈	7
● Nobile di Montepulciano Asinone '04	♈♈♈	7
● Nobile di Montepulciano Asinone '03	♈♈♈	7
● Nobile di Montepulciano Asinone '01	♈♈♈	7
● Nobile di Montepulciano Asinone '00	♈♈♈	7
● Nobile di Montepulciano Asinone '99	♈♈♈	6
● Nobile di Montepulciano Asinone '98	♈♈♈	6
● Nobile di Montepulciano Asinone '97	♈♈♈	6
● Nobile di Montepulciano Vigna dell'Asinone '95	♈♈♈	7

● Chianti Colli Fiorentini Ris. '06	▼▼	5
● Syrah '07	▼▼	5
● Chianti Colli Fiorentini Il Cortile '07	▼	4
● Morellino di Scansano Massi di Mandorlaia '07	▼	4
● Morellino di Scansano Massi di Mandorlaia Ris. '06	▼	5
● Toscoforte '07	▼	4
● Tricorno '07	▼	6
● Colpetroso Massi di Mandorlaia '05	♈♈	5
● Morellino di Scansano Massi di Mandorlaia '06	♈♈	4*
● Morellino di Scansano Massi di Mandorlaia Ris. '04	♈♈	5
● Syrah '06	♈♈	5
● Toscoforte '06	♈♈	4*

Fattoria di Presciano

LOC. PIEVE A PRESCIANO
VIA GIOVANNI XXIII, 2
52020 PERGINE VALDARNO [AR]
TEL. 0575897160
www.fattoriadipresciano.it

CELLAR SALES
PRE-BOOKED VISITS

ANNUAL PRODUCTION 100,000 bottles
HECTARES UNDER VINE 24
VITICULTURE METHOD Conventional

We have the usual array of labels from this estate belonging to the Cometti siblings. They have run the farm since 1999, when they bought it and revived the old winery. Records show that the estate has existed since the middle of the 17th century. Following modernization of the cellar, the Cornettis turned their attention to the vineyards, where they replanted long-forgotten vines like colorino del Valdarno, and international varieties. Owner and estate oenologist Pasquale Cometti is also a great proponent of the Pietraviva DOC, which features on many of the labels released.

This year's best offering is Priscus '05, a blend of sangiovese with a splash of merlot. Mature gamey aromas, austere body and lovely long length are its key attributes. The rest of the range is very well managed. The pure sangiovese I Greti '05 is a bit below par, showing too edgy, and the Pietraviva Rosso '08 is agreeable. The whites are good, particularly the Vin Santo with its hints of hazelnut and velvety mouthfeel.

★ Fattoria Le Pupille

S.DA PIAGGE DEL MAIANO
58100 GROSSETO
TEL. 0564409517
www.fattorialepupille.it

CELLAR SALES
PRE-BOOKED VISITS

ANNUAL PRODUCTION 450,000 bottles
HECTARES UNDER VINE 70
VITICULTURE METHOD Conventional

Elisabetta Geppetti is a leading light in Maremma winemaking, and particularly in the territory of Morellino di Scansano. The estate harvested its first grapes at the beginning of the 1980s but it was the release of the Saffredi in 1987 that made the name of Fattoria Le Pupille. Today, the estate is well-established as a leader and is one of the most important producers in the entire panorama of Italian wine.

The flagship wine is Saffredi '06, a blend of cabernet sauvignon, merlot and alicante, which continues to be a key product in Maremma and beyond. The nose is intriguing and well-defined while the palate is elegant, well profiled and very fruity. Our unofficial award for drinkability goes to the '08 version of Morellino di Scansano, and not for the first time. The Pelofino '08, from sangiovese, syrah, cabernet franc and cabernet sauvignon, drinks beautifully while the Rosa Mati '08 is a fresh, fragrant rosé from sangiovese and syrah. Poggio Argentato '08, from traminer and sauvignon, is uncomplicated and full flavoured.

● Priscus '05	♟♟ 5
● Chianti Sup. '06	♟ 4
○ Colli Etruria Centrale Vin Santo Passum '05	♟ 6
● I Greti '05	♟ 6
○ Pietraviva Bianco '08	♟ 4
● Pietraviva Rosso '08	♟ 4
○ Rovi '07	♟ 4
● I Greti '04	♟♟ 6
● I Greti '03	♟♟ 6
● Rosso Veleno Vigneti di Marina Mouritch '04	♟♟ 6

● Saffredi '06	♟♟ 8
● Morellino di Scansano '08	♟♟ 4
● Pelofino '08	♟♟ 3
⊙ Rosa Mati '08	♟♟ 4
○ Poggio Argentato '08	♟ 4
● Morellino di Scansano Poggio Valente '04	♟♟♟ 6
● Morellino di Scansano Poggio Valente '99	♟♟♟ 6
● Morellino di Scansano Poggio Valente '98	♟♟♟ 6
● Saffredi '05	♟♟♟ 8
● Saffredi '04	♟♟♟ 8
● Saffredi '02	♟♟♟ 8
● Saffredi '01	♟♟♟ 8
● Saffredi '00	♟♟♟ 8
● Saffredi '97	♟♟♟ 8
● Saffredi '90	♟♟♟ 8

Castello di Querceto

LOC. QUERCETO
VIA A. FRANÇOIS, 2
50020 GREVE IN CHIANTI [FI]
TEL. 05585921
www.castellodiquerceto.it

CELLAR SALES
PRE-BOOKED VISITS

ANNUAL PRODUCTION 600,000 bottles
HECTARES UNDER VINE 60
VITICULTURE METHOD Conventional

Castello di Querceto has around 190 hectares and 60 of these are given over to the cultivation of vines. The property has been in the François family since 1897. The soil is a most unusual base of schist with very high manganese and alkaline earth metal content and the vineyards are set fairly high up, rising to an altitude of 530 metres. The full potential of these distinctive characteristics is exploited during the modern, meticulous vinification process carried out in the cellar beneath the castle.

The estate's steady march towards quality over the last few years reaches cruising speed with the two Chianti Classico Riservas that made our final tastings this year. The '06 Picchio is obtained from a single vineyard and offers concentrated aromas of red berry fruit with complex sensations of leather and animal hide. The palate is full, harmonious and balanced and the long finish is very intense. The second Riserva proffers livelier, more vibrant aroma and a stiffish, tannic palate supported by acid thrust and body. The Chianti Classico '07 is fresh, balanced and harmonious.

Querceto di Castellina

LOC. QUERCETO, 9
53011 CASTELLINA IN CHIANTI [SI]
TEL. 0577733590
www.querceto.com

CELLAR SALES
PRE-BOOKED VISITS
VISITOR FACILITIES

ANNUAL PRODUCTION 40,000 bottles
HECTARES UNDER VINE 11
VITICULTURE METHOD Naturale

Querceto di Castellina is named for the village where this winery is situated. Its vineyards extend across two of the Chianti Classico's most prestigious municipalities, Radda and Castellina, and the cellar has quite a history, tracing its origins back to the 16th century when it was already on the land register of the Guelph captains. The estate is at an altitude of up to 450 metres and totals 47 hectares, 11 planted to vine and three to olive groves. The wines are modern in style, having aged in small casks, and oak conditioning often characterizes the aromatics.

The sangiovese and merlot Podalirio '07 has a deep colour with purplish highlights and attractive torrefaction-laced oak and smokiness. The palate is colossal, giving gorgeous dark fruit, enormous weight and excellent tannins. The Chianti Classico Riserva Belvedere '06 is an absolute gem, releasing cherry-like aromas, great concentration and impressive authority. The Chianti Classico L'Aura '07 is good but a little overripe, with its notes of blueberry and black cherry, and rather too oaky.

● Chianti Cl. Il Picchio Ris. '06	♥♥ 6
● Chianti Cl. Ris. '06	♥♥ 5
● Chianti Cl. '07	♥ 4
● Il Sole di Alessandro '05	♥ 8
● Querciolaia '05	♥ 7
○ Vin Santo del Chianti Cl. '05	♥ 5
● Chianti Cl. Il Picchio Ris. '05	♥♥ 6
● Chianti Cl. Il Picchio Ris. '04	♥♥ 6
● Chianti Cl. Ris. '05	♥♥ 5
● Chianti Cl. Ris. '04	♥♥ 5
● Chianti Cl. Ris. '03	♥♥ 5
● Cignale '05	♥♥ 8
● Il Sole di Alessandro '04	♥♥ 8
● La Corte '04	♥♥ 7

● Chianti Cl. Vign. Belvedere Ris. '06	♥♥ 6
● Podalirio '07	♥♥ 6
● Chianti Cl. L'Aura '07	♥ 4
● Podalirio '01	♥♥♥ 6
● Chianti Cl. L'Aura '03	♥♥ 4
● Podalirio '06	♥♥ 6
● Podalirio '05	♥♥ 6

★ Querciabella

VIA BARBIANO, 17
50022 GREVE IN CHIANTI [FI]
TEL. 05585927777
www.querciabella.com

Castello di Radda

LOC. IL BECCO
53017 RADDA IN CHIANTI [SI]
TEL. 030652382
www.castellodiradda.it

ANNUAL PRODUCTION **200,000 bottles**
HECTARES UNDER VINE **76.5**
VITICULTURE METHOD **Naturale**

We noted last year that Querciabella's wines carry an increasingly deep, fascinating territorial stamp. Its approximately 80 hectares of vineyards lie on the upper slopes of Ruffoli near Greve in Chianti and are beginning to respond to organic agriculture. In addition, the vinification techniques are now less invasive and more respectful of the fruit, particularly in the case of the Chianti Classico.

The Chianti Classico '07 has a fresh compact nose of clear dark aromatics. A spicy backdrop frames a succession of red berries, citrus, liquorice and mint sensations before the driving palate shows fruit and breadth and a lovely final hint of raspberry rounds off this complex, harmonious wine. The '06 Camartina from cabernet sauvignon and sangiovese is the usual Three Glass masterpiece. It is concentrated and supple as ever with spiky tannins that have yet to meld fully with the first-class body. The Batàr '07 also delights with its acidity and fruit verve. Finally, Mongrana '07 from Maremma has pulled off a quantum leap in quality and is now a model of drinkability.

ANNUAL PRODUCTION **100,000 bottles**
HECTARES UNDER VINE **50**
VITICULTURE METHOD **Conventional**

Castello di Radda was bought by the Beretta family in 2003. They are no strangers to winemaking, also owning Lo Sparviere in Franciacorta and Orlando Contucci Ponno in Abruzzo. The Tuscan estate is situated on the hill facing east towards the village of the same name in Chianti, almost directly beneath the castle at Volpaia. The vineyards face south-east and south-west and the moderately loose soil is composed of limestone and clay with plenty of pebbles. The wines age in oak barriques.

This year we were offered just one wine for tasting, the '06 Chianti Classico Poggio Selvale, and overall it made a positive impression. Its elegant, intriguing aromas are quite fresh and balanced, leading into a nicely textured body that presents racy, smooth and deep. Just a touch more of the vibrant acidity would have extended the length on the palate of this appealing red.

● Camartina '06	♟♟♟ 8
● Chianti Cl. '07	♟♟ 5
○ Batàr '07	♟♟ 7
● Mongrana '07	♟♟ 4*
● Camartina '05	♟♟♟ 8
● Camartina '04	♟♟♟ 8
● Camartina '03	♟♟♟ 8
● Camartina '01	♟♟♟ 8
● Camartina '00	♟♟♟ 8
● Camartina '99	♟♟♟ 8
● Camartina '97	♟♟♟ 8
● Camartina '95	♟♟♟ 8
● Camartina '94	♟♟♟ 8
● Camartina '90	♟♟♟ 8
● Chianti Cl. Ris. '95	♟♟♟ 5

● Chianti Cl. Poggio Selvale '06	♟♟ 4*
● Chianti Cl. Poggio Selvale '05	♟♟ 4*
● Chianti Cl. Poggio Selvale Ris. '04	♟♟ 5

★ Castello dei Rampolla

VIA CASE SPARSE, 22
50020 PANZANO [FI]
TEL. 055852001
castellodeirampolla.cast@tin.it

CELLAR SALES
PRE-BOOKED VISITS

ANNUAL PRODUCTION 90,000 bottles
HECTARES UNDER VINE 42
VITICULTURE METHOD Naturale

A benchmark for high-quality Italian wine, Castello dei Rampolla has a deep, ongoing link with the essence of Chianti Classico. This is not just because of its geography – the approximately 42 hectares under vine lie in the Conca d'Oro at Panzano – but also and largely because the wines produced by the Di Napoli family are sound interpretations of a country tradition that is proud, nostalgic and strong, and that only the spirit of Chianti can convey.

The d'Alceo '06 from cabernet sauvignon and petit verdot proffers aromas of blackcurrant, cherry-like red fruit, ferrous notes and spicy hints of vanilla. The palate shows a close-knit tannic texture that has yet to integrate fully with the body. Further bottle-ageing will probably serve to smooth the rough edges. The Chianti Classico '06 displays notes of dried violets, earth and aromatic herbs, an olfactory profile that beautifully mirrors the territory. The tannins are rather clenched at this point and prevent the wine from unbending into overall balance. Again, further ageing should do the trick.

La Regola

VIA A. GRAMSCI, 1
56046 RIPARBELLA [PI]
TEL. 0586698145
www.laregola.com

CELLAR SALES
PRE-BOOKED VISITS

ANNUAL PRODUCTION 80,000 bottles
HECTARES UNDER VINE 14
VITICULTURE METHOD Conventional

Last year, we noted consolidation in the quality of La Regola's production. Sitting in the Cecina river valley, the estate that belongs to the Nuti family has around 14 hectares of vineyards. The vines grow in red earth of sand and clay with some pebbles and ferrous minerals. Brothers Luca and Flavio favour modern vinification techniques using new barriques but they also fully respect the profound wine vocation that characterizes the territory of Montescudaio.

The pure sangiovese Beloro '06 is a trim and tasty wine. Earthy and lively on the nose, fragrant and lingering on the palate, it presents a harmonious overall framework and nicely layered sensory perceptions. The '07 Lauro from equal parts of chardonnay and viognier is also interesting and indeed one of the most intriguing whites on the Tuscan coast. Peach and apricot aromas with chalky nuances are the prelude to a full, vibrant body. The '06 La Regola benefits from a higher proportion of cabernet franc, offering slightly overripe red fruit notes and body with very elegant tannins. This vintage has a more dynamic, drinkable character than previous editions.

● d'Alceo '06	♟♟ 8
● Chianti Cl. '06	♟ 5
● d'Alceo '04	♟♟♟ 8
● d'Alceo '03	♟♟♟ 8
● d'Alceo '01	♟♟♟ 8
● d'Alceo '00	♟♟♟ 8
● La Vigna di Alceo '99	♟♟♟ 8
● La Vigna di Alceo '98	♟♟♟ 8
● La Vigna di Alceo '97	♟♟♟ 8
● La Vigna di Alceo '96	♟♟♟ 8
● Sammarco '05	♟♟♟ 8
● Sammarco '94	♟♟♟ 8
● Sammarco '86	♟♟♟ 8
● Sammarco '85	♟♟♟ 8

○ Lauro Bianco '07	♟♟ 5
● Montescudaio Rosso Beloro '06	♟♟ 7
● Montescudaio Rosso La Regola '06	♟♟ 7
○ Montescudaio Bianco Steccaia '07	♟♟ 4
○ Montescudaio Bianco Steccaia '01	♟♟ 4*
● Montescudaio Rosso Beloro '04	♟♟ 7
● Montescudaio Rosso La Regola '03	♟♟ 6
● Montescudaio Rosso La Regola '02	♟♟ 6
● Montescudaio Rosso La Regola '01	♟♟ 6
● Montescudaio Rosso La Regola '00	♟♟ 6*
● Montescudaio Rosso La Regola '99	♟♟ 5
● Montescudaio Rosso Vallino '05	♟♟ 5

Riecine

LOC. RIECINE
53013 GAIOLE IN CHIANTI [SI]
TEL. 0577749098
www.riecine.com

CELLAR SALES
PRE-BOOKED VISITS

ANNUAL PRODUCTION **45,000 bottles**
HECTARES UNDER VINE **11**
VITICULTURE METHOD **Organic certified**

Property of American Gary Baumann, the Riecine estate has 11 hectares of vineyards at Gaiole, which in terms of location and soil is one of the best territories in Chianti Classico. Thanks to the skills and acumen of oenologist Sean O'Callaghan, Riecine has become a model for the designation. It combines tradition and innovation in its deep, crisp, relaxed wines that also express a profound sense of territorial identity, a goal it achieves through perfect fruit and vinification based on sensitivity and in-depth technical know-how.

The Chianti Classico Riserva '05 has flowery tones enhanced by sweet fruit and spices. Entry on the palate is caressing and supple, developing fresh and tannic with full, long-lingering body. The finish is sweet and laced with balsamic sensations of wild herbs. The sangiovese-only Gioia '05 exhibits power and balance. The nose gives hints of red berry fruit, orange and spice. On the palate, the wine unfurls suppleness and structure and overall shows solidly built and harmonious. The Chianti Classico '06 also presents well, offering flowers, fruit and great drinkability.

Rignana

LOC. RIGNANA, 15
50022 GREVE IN CHIANTI [FI]
TEL. 055852065
www.rignana.it

CELLAR SALES
PRE-BOOKED VISITS
VISITOR FACILITIES
FOOD

ANNUAL PRODUCTION **40,000 bottles**
HECTARES UNDER VINE **13.9**
VITICULTURE METHOD **Conventional**

This history of Rignana is deeply rooted in the past. Some of the estate goes back to the 11th century when it was part of the property belonging to the Val di Greve league. Today, it is the property of Cosimo Gericke and Sveva Rocco di Torrepadula. Half of the hectares planted to vine are dedicated to sangiovese, the soil is limestone and clay, and the plots face south-east at an altitude of around 350 metres. Barrique conditioning gives the wines colour and intensity but this never masks the pleasing sensations of fruit.

The Chianti Classico '07 is quite simply delicious. It comes from a very good growing year and is based largely on sangiovese with a small but significant proportion of canaiolo. This captivating wine offers ferrous notes with hints of flowers and oriental spices, and an incisive palate. It is rather linear but never sacrifices any of its delicious fruit or a certain approachability of expression. Fuller but perhaps also rather more one-dimensional, the Riserva '06 immediately shows much darker fruit and comes across powerful, dense and mature with a long finish.

● Chianti Cl. Ris. '05	▼▼ 6
● La Gioia '05	▼▼ 7
● Chianti Cl. '06	▼▼ 5
● Chianti Cl. Ris. '99	▼▼▼ 8
● Chianti Cl. Ris. '88	▼▼▼ 6
● Chianti Cl. Ris. '86	▼▼▼ 5
● La Gioia '04	▼▼▼ 7
● La Gioia '01	▼▼▼ 7
● La Gioia '98	▼▼▼ 8
● La Gioia '95	▼▼▼ 8
● Chianti Cl. '05	▽▽ 5
● Chianti Cl. Ris. '04	▽▽ 6

● Chianti Cl. '07	▼▼ 4*
● Chianti Cl. Ris. '06	▼▼ 5
● Chianti Cl. '04	▽▽ 4
● Chianti Cl. Ris. '01	▽▽ 5

Rocca delle Macìe

LOC. LE MACÌE, 45
53011 CASTELLINA IN CHIANTI [SI]
TEL. 05777321
www.roccadellemacie.com

CELLAR SALES
PRE-BOOKED VISITS
VISITOR FACILITIES
FOOD

ANNUAL PRODUCTION **4.500,000 bottles**
HECTARES UNDER VINE **200**
VITICULTURE METHOD **Conventional**

Rocca delle Macìe is one of the most extensive estates in Chianti Classico. The passion and dedication of owner Sergio Zingarelli ensures that this Castellina in Chianti operation offers dependable quality across its entire production, released under a broad array of labels for a total output of several million bottles. High quality combined with a first-rate global distribution system make Rocca delle Macìe an excellent ambassador for Chianti Classico.

This year's performance is very good. The Chianti Classico Tenuta Sant'Alfonso '07 has a mature nose that melds attractive oaky notes to perfection with aromas of black fruit and spice. Full and enveloping on the palate, Tenuta Sant'Alfonso proffers a confident, pleasing sensory profile. The largely sangiovese-based Ser Gioveto '06 has character and fullness. The assertive nose reveals notes of brandied cherries and a balsamic vein of liquorice before depth on the palate is supported by elegant tannins that accompany its development. The Chianti Classico '07 is not complex but is natural and harmonious. However, the Maremma wines are not up to their usual standards.

Rocca di Castagnoli

LOC. CASTAGNOLI
53013 GAIOLE IN CHIANTI [SI]
TEL. 0577731004
www.roccadicastagnoli.com

CELLAR SALES
PRE-BOOKED VISITS
VISITOR FACILITIES
FOOD

ANNUAL PRODUCTION **300,000 bottles**
HECTARES UNDER VINE **132**
VITICULTURE METHOD **Conventional**

Two different estates under one owner. Rocca di Castagnoli lies in one of the Chianti Classico's most beautiful landscapes at Castagnoli, near Gaiole in Chianti, a village that dates back to late medieval times, and Tenuta di Capraia. Calogero Calì bought the business in 1981 and is the driving force behind the modern winemaking activities. He has invested energy and resources, his staff is top-notch and this ensures that the territory's strong points are fully expressed. The estate style perfectly mirrors the tradition of Chianti Classico.

Both estates are at their best with Chianti Classico and they both win Three Glasses. The Riserva '06 Poggio ai Frati di Rocca di Castagnoli has flowery aromas of violets and dried roses with undertones of leather and earth. The substantial body of the harmonious palate is buttressed by extract and acidity for a classy wine that will evolve excellently. The Chianti Classico Tenuta di Capraia Riserva '06 has a similar story to tell. The nose offers clear, lively notes of red fruit while the palate unveils full body and supple balance that complement a wine of complexity and length.

● Chianti Cl. Tenuta S. Alfonso '07	♟♟ 5
● Ser Gioveto '06	♟♟ 7
● Chianti Cl. '07	♟♟ 4*
● Morellino di Scansano Campomaccione '08	♟ 4
● Roccato '00	♟♟♟ 7
● Roccato '99	♟♟♟ 7
● Chianti Cl. '06	♟♟ 4
● Chianti Cl. Fizzano Ris. '05	♟♟ 6
● Chianti Cl. Tenuta S. Alfonso '06	♟♟ 5
● Roccato '05	♟♟ 7
○ Vermentino Occhio a Vento '07	♟♟ 4

● Chianti Cl. Poggio ai Frati Ris. '06	♟♟♟ 5*
● Chianti Cl. Tenuta di Capraia Ris. '06	♟♟♟ 5*
● Stielle '06	♟♟ 7
● Chianti Cl. '07	♟ 4
● Chianti Cl. Poggio ai Frati Ris. '04	♟♟♟ 5
● Chianti Cl. Tenuta di Capraia Ris. '05	♟♟♟ 5
● Stielle '00	♟♟♟ 8
● Buriano '04	♟♟ 7
● Chianti Cl. '06	♟♟ 4
● Chianti Cl. Poggio ai Frati Ris. '05	♟♟ 5
● Stielle '05	♟♟ 7

Rocca di Frassinello

LOC. GIUNCARICO
58040 GAVORRANO [GR]
TEL. 056688400
www.roccadifrassinello.it

CELLAR SALES
PRE-BOOKED VISITS

ANNUAL PRODUCTION 180,000 bottles
HECTARES UNDER VINE 70
VITICULTURE METHOD Conventional

Rocca di Frassinello's oenological project saw its first wines released to market with the 2004 vintage on the label. The masterminds are Paolo Panerai, editor, financier and owner of Castellare di Castellina, and Eric de Rothschild, who for is responsible winemaking activities within the great banking family, starting with Château Lafite. The cherry on the cake of this new, ambitious Italian wine project is the brand new cellar designed by Renzo Piano.

The Baffo Nero '07 from merlot only debuts to a Three Glass award for its fascinating aromatics and a harmonious palate. This wine is certain to join the select group of excellent Merlots that Tuscany can already boast. The Rocca di Frassinello '07 is very good, showing balance and elegance on nose and palate while Le Sughere di Frassinello '07 is a solid wine with outstanding drinkability as its strong suit. The '07 Poggio alla Guardia is fresh and lively. With the exception of the Baffo Nero, all the wines derive from a blend of sangiovese, cabernet sauvignon and merlot in varying amounts.

Rocca di Montegrossi

FRAZ. MONTI IN CHIANTI
53010 GAIOLE IN CHIANTI [SI]
TEL. 0577747977
www.roccadimontegrossi.it

CELLAR SALES
PRE-BOOKED VISITS

ANNUAL PRODUCTION 80,000 bottles
HECTARES UNDER VINE 18
VITICULTURE METHOD Conventional

This estate near Monti in Chianti belongs to Marco Ricasoli Firidolfi, a descendant of the family that has written the story of Chianti. The vineyards all lie high up at altitudes between 300 and 450 metres with splendid locations on moderately loose-packed soil of limestone origin. The cellar was renovated in 2000 and houses the oak barrels and barriques used in different proportions for the various wines.

The Chianti Classico '07 is an enjoyable, well-made wine that despite initial hesitancy on the nose has a tasty palate showing sweet fruit and expands confidently in the finish. The '06 Geremia, a Bordeaux blend of cabernet sauvignon and merlot, is not quite as harmonious. Oak notes dominate the nose, where aromas of coffee and torrefaction currently hold sway, and the palate is warm, chewy and very dense. The Vin Santo del Chianti Classico '02 is on its usual thoroughbred form. The nose hints at quince and plum jam, while the palate is caressing and concentrated.

● Baffo Nero '07	𝟏𝟏𝟏 6
● Rocca di Frassinello '07	𝟏𝟏 6
● Le Sughere di Frassinello '07	𝟏𝟏 5
● Poggio alla Guardia '07	𝟏 4
● Rocca di Frassinello '06	𝟏𝟏𝟏 6
● Rocca di Frassinello '05	𝟏𝟏𝟏 7
● Le Sughere di Frassinello '06	𝟏𝟏 5
● Le Sughere di Frassinello '05	𝟏𝟏 6
● Le Sughere di Frassinello '04	𝟏𝟏 6
● Poggio alla Guardia '06	𝟏𝟏 4*
● Poggio alla Guardia '05	𝟏𝟏 5
● Poggio alla Guardia '04	𝟏𝟏 5
● Rocca di Frassinello '04	𝟏𝟏 7

○ Vin Santo del Chianti Cl. '02	𝟏𝟏 8
● Chianti Cl. '07	𝟏𝟏 4*
● Geremia '06	𝟏 6
● Chianti Cl. Vign. S. Marcellino Ris. '99	𝟏𝟏𝟏 5
● Chianti Cl. '05	𝟏𝟏 4*
● Chianti Cl. Vign. S. Marcellino Ris. '04	𝟏𝟏 6
● Geremia '05	𝟏𝟏 6
● Geremia '04	𝟏𝟏 6
○ Vin Santo del Chianti Cl. '01	𝟏𝟏 8
○ Vin Santo del Chianti Cl. '00	𝟏𝟏 8

★ Tenimenti Ruffino

P.LE RUFFINO, 1
50065 PONTASSIEVE [FI]
TEL. 0556499717
www.ruffino.it

CELLAR SALES
PRE-BOOKED VISITS

ANNUAL PRODUCTION 14.500,000 bottles
HECTARES UNDER VINE 600
VITICULTURE METHOD Conventional

Ruffino is an enduring symbol of Italian wine. The cellar has been producing for more than 150 years and its wines are sold worldwide. In addition to this important brand, brothers Luigi and Adolfo Folonari, who own and manage the estate, also possess several other properties Tuscany's most prestigious winemaking zones, Chianti Classico, Montalcino and Montepulciano. They also have a property in Friuli, Borgo Conventi.

The Chianti Classico Riserva Santedame '06 from the Castellina in Chianti estate has an alluring nose of red berry fruit and minty, balsamic tones. The palate has a close-knit texture and good body in perfect balance with the tannins. The finish is long and relaxed. The '05 Chianti Classico Riserva Ducale Oro is a model of tradition, giving flowery notes of dried violets and a palate that shows off the wine's elegance and drinkability. Development is sustained by long acid thrust that balances the overall profile and the complex finish echoes the flowery nuances. The Chianti Classico Santedame '07 is at a delicate stage of maturation and consequently lacks balance.

Russo

LOC. PODERE LA METOCCHINA
VIA FORNI, 71
57028 SUVERETO [LI]
TEL. 0565845105
www.vinirusso.it

CELLAR SALES
PRE-BOOKED VISITS

ANNUAL PRODUCTION 80,000 bottles
HECTARES UNDER VINE 14
VITICULTURE METHOD Conventional

The Russo estate started bottling in 1998. This is an all-round agricultural property that in addition to farming grapes also raises cattle and produces vegetables, fruit and olive oil. Family-run, it is an excellent example of a well-run farm. It may be this approach to the territory that gives the Russo brothers' wines a naturalness of expression that places them in the front rank of wines made in Val di Cornia.

We applaud a fine showing from the Val di Cornia Ceppitaio '08 with its crisp black berry fruit aromas followed by good overall balance and a juicy, agreeable palate. The '06 Val di Cornia Barbicone has great depth on the palate. Despite its youth, it gives generous notes of red fruit and plain chocolate. The palate unveils close-knit, very fine-grained tannins and the sumptuous body is buttressed by acid thrust. We believe it has great potential and sent it to our final taste-offs. The Sassobucato '07 is also rather youthful and we found this edition less dynamic than usual. Pietrasca '08 from vermentino is more reliable and enjoyable.

● Chianti Cl. Ris. Ducale Oro '05	♟♟ 6
● Chianti Cl. Santedame Ris. '06	♟♟ 5
○ Libaio '08	♟♟ 3*
● Chianti Cl. Santedame '07	♟ 4
○ La Solatia Chardonnay '08	♟ 5
● Modus '06	♟ 6
● Chianti Cl. Ris. Ducale Oro '04	♟♟♟ 6
● Chianti Cl. Ris. Ducale Oro '01	♟♟♟ 6
● Chianti Cl. Ris. Ducale Oro '00	♟♟♟ 6
● Modus '04	♟♟♟ 6
● Romitorio di Santedame '00	♟♟♟ 8
● Modus '05	♟♟ 6
● Romitorio di Santedame '05	♟♟ 7

● Val di Cornia Rosso Barbicone '06	♟♟ 5
● Val di Cornia Rosso Ceppitaio '08	♟♟ 4
○ Pietrasca '08	♟ 3
● Sassobucato '07	♟ 6
● Val di Cornia Rosso Barbicone '00	♟♟♟ 5*
● Barbicone '05	♟♟ 5
● Sassobucato '06	♟♟ 6
● Sassobucato '04	♟♟ 5
● Sassobucato '03	♟♟ 5
● Sassobucato '02	♟♟ 6

La Sala

Loc. Ponterotto
via Sorripa, 34
50026 San Casciano in Val di Pesa [FI]
Tel. 055828111
www.lasala.it

CELLAR SALES
PRE-BOOKED VISITS

ANNUAL PRODUCTION 85,000 bottles
HECTARES UNDER VINE 21
VITICULTURE METHOD Conventional

Laura Baronti's estate is practically an all-female affair. Situated in the heart of a fascinating area, it has ancient origins and 11th-century chronicles document its Medicean holdings. Today, the winery has a modern fermentation cellar while the French and American barriques are housed in 19th-century underground rooms. The soil is mainly clay, with some limestone, ensuring good drainage.

We were impressed by Chianti Classico '07, an impeccably styled red with original notes. The nose is reminiscent of ripe plum-led fruit nicely accompanied by subtle, almost smoky nuances of charred oak. On the palate it shows well defined, with a pleasant balance of young, green sensations and sweeter, riper notes with a warm, full-flavoured finish that is not overly alcoholic. The Riserva '06 is one rung below, showing nicely on the palate but with a rather uncertain nose.

● Chianti Cl. '07	♟♟ 4
● Chianti Cl. Ris. '06	♟ 6
● Chianti Cl. '01	♟♟ 5
● Chianti Cl. '00	♟♟ 4*
● Chianti Cl. Ris. '05	♟♟ 6
● Chianti Cl. Ris. '04	♟♟ 6
● Chianti Cl. Ris. '99	♟♟ 5

Salcheto

Loc. Sant'Albino
via di Villa Bianca, 15
53045 Montepulciano [SI]
Tel. 0578799031
www.salcheto.it

CELLAR SALES
PRE-BOOKED VISITS

ANNUAL PRODUCTION 130,000 bottles
HECTARES UNDER VINE 33
VITICULTURE METHOD Conventional

Salcheto, founded in 1987, has decided to focus strongly on prugnolo gentile, as sangiovese is known in Montepulciano. Although this strategy may not always be the most economically viable, it makes the estate one of the most rigorous of the DOCG zone. Furthermore, the challenging Salco Evoluzione project, which releases Salcheto Nobile six years after harvest, underscores that the winery headed by Michele Manelli is uncompromising in its choices.

The flagship of the Salcheto range is Nobile di Montepulciano Salco, whose '04 vintage offers an elegant nose of red fruit lifted by flowers, autumn leaves and pipe tobacco, and a lively, juicy palate with a long, continuous finish. Nobile di Montepulciano '06 is also very good, with outstanding aromatic freshness and a nice full flavour, but it is slightly weighed down by too much oak. Rosso di Montepulciano, Chianti Colli Senesi and the Rosé, all in the '08 editions, are simple but well made.

● Nobile di Montepulciano Salco Evoluzione '04	♟♟ 7
● Nobile di Montepulciano '06	♟♟ 5
● Chianti Colli Senesi '08	♟ 4
☉ Rosato di Toscana '08	♟ 4
● Rosso di Montepulciano '08	♟ 4
● Nobile di Montepulciano '97	♟♟♟ 5
● Nobile di Montepulciano Salco Evoluzione '01	♟♟♟ 7
● Nobile di Montepulciano '05	♟♟ 5
● Nobile di Montepulciano '02	♟♟ 5
● Nobile di Montepulciano Salco '01	♟♟ 6
● Nobile di Montepulciano Salco '00	♟♟ 6
● Nobile di Montepulciano Salco Evoluzione '03	♟♟ 7

Salustri

FRAZ. POGGI DEL SASSO
LOC. LA CAVA
58040 CINIGIANO [GR]
TEL. 0564990529
www.salustri.it

CELLAR SALES
PRE-BOOKED VISITS
VISITOR FACILITIES

ANNUAL PRODUCTION 80,000 bottles
HECTARES UNDER VINE 12
VITICULTURE METHOD Organic certified

The Salustri family, who run one of Montecucco's pioneer estates, started producing their own wines in the late 1990s. They own the oldest vineyards in Poggi del Sasso, which they farm organically to make austere, sometimes slightly difficult, wines with great personality. The range brings out the full potential of sangiovese's varietal characteristics, capable of rivalling Tuscany's top interpretations of the grape.

Focusing on concentrated ripe fruit, Sangiovese Montecucco '06 Grotte Rosse has a well-defined nose and a dynamic, full palate with beautifully coordinated development and a long finish. Three Glasses went to Montecucco Sangiovese Santa Marta '06. Although its aromas are initially hazy, after breathing for a while it unleashes sensations of red fruit, flowers and rain-soaked earth. The palate is full and dynamic, with a long, sharp finish. Narà '08, a monovarietal Vermentino, is lean, drinkable and attractively fresh.

● Montecucco Santa Marta '06	▼▼▼	5
● Montecucco Grotte Rosse '06	▼▼	6
○ Narà '08	▼	4
● Montecucco Grotte Rosse '05	♀♀	6
● Montecucco Grotte Rosse '04	♀♀	6
● Montecucco Grotte Rosse '02	♀♀	6
● Montecucco Marleo '04	♀♀	4
● Montecucco Santa Marta '05	♀♀	5

Castello di San Donato in Perano

LOC. SAN DONATO IN PERANO
53013 GAIOLE IN CHIANTI [SI]
TEL. 0577744121
www.castellosandonato.it

CELLAR SALES
PRE-BOOKED VISITS

ANNUAL PRODUCTION 100,000 bottles
HECTARES UNDER VINE 75
VITICULTURE METHOD Conventional

The estate run by Mario Tribuzio boasts over 360 hectares of vineyards, olive groves and woodland around the village of Castello di San Donato in Perano, after which it is named. Located in the municipalities of Gaiole and Radda at altitudes between 300 and 500 metres, the estate is characterized by steep slopes and gravelly soil. The wines, aged in barriques and tonneaux, are very elegant and certain to improve.

Chianti Classico Vigneto Montecasi '06 is truly captivating, focusing on charming, delicate red berry fruit, with wild strawberries and raspberries. It is an elegant, extremely easy-drinking red with good grip. While not breathtakingly complex, it is a very fine example of its type. The uncomplicated, drinkable Chianti Classico '07 is also good, showing delicate and floral, with fresh fruity notes and full flavour, but we were less convinced by the over-evolved Riserva '06.

● Chianti Cl. '07	▼▼	4*
● Chianti Cl. Vign. Montecasi '06	▼▼	5
● Chianti Cl. Ris. '06	▼	6
○ Il Dolce del Castello '07	▼	6
● Chianti Cl. '06	♀♀	4*
● Chianti Cl. '05	♀♀	4*
● Chianti Cl. '04	♀♀	4*
● Chianti Cl. Ris. '05	♀♀	6

Fattoria San Fabiano Borghini Baldovinetti

LOC. SAN FABIANO, 33
52100 AREZZO
TEL. 057524566
www.fattoriasanfabiano.it

CELLAR SALES
PRE-BOOKED VISITS

ANNUAL PRODUCTION **700,000 bottles**
HECTARES UNDER VINE **120**
VITICULTURE METHOD **Naturale**

The San Fabiano estate lies outside the town walls, on the way to the Casentino valley. Although winemaking was first documented in the area in 1416, the present-day winery was founded during the post-war period and started bottling its production in the 1960s. The main estate has 80 hectares under vine but the winery also owns a further 20 hectares in Campriano and 20 in the Montepulciano area.

Armaiolo '06, from equal amounts of sangiovese and cabernet sauvignon, made it into our finals with its elegant aromas of cloves and wild berries, soft, broad body, well-calibrated tannins and an extremely satisfying finish. The rest of the list is less exciting, starting with Piocaia '06, a blend similar to Armaiolo with the addition of merlot, which displays ripe notes and a slightly dry finish. Nobile '06 is fair, with simple structure, while the two Chiantis are pleasant and drinkable, although a little lightweight.

● Armaiolo '06	TT 7
● Chianti '07	T 2
● Chianti Et. Nera '07	T 4
● Nobile di Montepulciano Poggio Uliveto '06	T 5
● Piocaia '06	T 4
● Armaiolo '05	YY 5
● Armaiolo '03	YY 5
● Nobile di Montepulciano Poggio Uliveto '05	YY 5
● Nobile di Montepulciano Poggio Uliveto '04	YY 4*
● Nobile di Montepulciano Poggio Uliveto '03	YY 4

San Fabiano Calcinaia

LOC. CELLOLE
53011 CASTELLINA IN CHIANTI [SI]
TEL. 0577979232
www.sanfabianocalcinaia.com

CELLAR SALES
PRE-BOOKED VISITS
VISITOR FACILITIES
FOOD

ANNUAL PRODUCTION **160,000 bottles**
HECTARES UNDER VINE **42**
VITICULTURE METHOD **Conventional**

San Fabiano Calcinaia's viticultural history commenced in 1983, when Guido Serio and his wife Isa decided to concentrate on the production of quality wines. Over the years the Castellina estate, which comprises over 40 hectares of vineyards, has consolidated production by gradually replanting the vineyards and renovating the winery. The style of the wines is aimed at achieving concentrated, well-defined fruit, although in recent years they appear to have acquired more Chianti-esque tones.

Despite its modernity, Chianti Classico Riserva Cellole '06 displays impressive earthy local flavour. The nose has top notes of oak, followed by full, scented black berry fruit, and the palate displays great continuity, with skilfully calibrated juiciness and extract leading to a long finish with notes of liquorice and mint. Following a good debut last year, the '07 Cabernet Sauvignon confirms its qualities, with a nose of blackcurrants and vegetal notes and a balanced, harmonious palate. Chianti Classico '07 is pleasant but a little lacking in body.

● Chianti Cl. Cellole Ris. '06	TT 6
● Cabernet Sauvignon '07	TT 5
○ Cerviolo Bianco '07	T 5
● Chianti Cl. '07	T 4
● Cerviolo Rosso '00	YYY 7
● Cerviolo Rosso '99	YYY 6
● Cerviolo Rosso '98	YYY 6
● Cerviolo Rosso '97	YYY 6
● Cerviolo Rosso '96	YYY 6
● Chianti Cl. Cellole Ris. '00	YYY 6
● Cabernet Sauvignon '06	YY 5

San Felice

LOC. SAN FELICE
53019 CASTELNUOVO BERARDENGA [SI]
TEL. 05773991
www.agricolasanfelice.it

CELLAR SALES
PRE-BOOKED VISITS
VISITOR FACILITIES
FOOD

ANNUAL PRODUCTION 1.200,000 bottles
HECTARES UNDER VINE 210
VITICULTURE METHOD Conventional

San Felice is a longstanding Chianti
Classico producer, situated at Castelnuovo
Berardenga in the southern part of the
DOCG. It is owned by the Allianz group,
which over the years has developed a
complex, wide-ranging project that has
invested in scientific research and
development of the terroir as
complementary activities to wine
production. This triple-pronged strategy
seeks to bring out the best in the native
varieties considered an integral part of
Tuscany's wine heritage.

Pugnitello '07, from the grape of the same
name, demonstrates just how effective the
group's efforts have been. It shows deep
red, with a nose of ripe plum and blackberry
fruit veined with intense chocolate and
vanilla. On the palate it has complexity, a full
body and a bright acid backbone. Chianti
Classico Riserva Il Grigio '06 is a classic.
This monovarietal sangiovese offers
lingering, deep aromas of violet, red berry
fruit and spice. The palate is enhanced by
silky, fine-grained tannins, making it a
charmingly dynamic, balanced wine.

San Filippo

LOC. SAN FILIPPO, 134
53024 MONTALCINO [SI]
TEL. 0577847176
www.sanfilippomontalcino.com

ANNUAL PRODUCTION 50,000 bottles
HECTARES UNDER VINE 10.5
VITICULTURE METHOD Conventional

San Filippo was founded in the 1970s and,
following a few years of decline, it is now
experiencing a sort of rebirth through the
single-minded efforts of Roberto Giannelli
and his faith in its potential. Large property
investments have enabled the old farm to be
renovated while a complete makeover of the
cellar, with the purchase of new barrels and
modern fermentation vats, has enabled
production of an excellent Brunello '04 in an
austere, classic style. The estate is situated
in the eastern area of the zone, in the
beautiful lower part of the Cerbaie hills.

Brunello di Montalcino Le Lucere '04 has a
slightly estery nose, with spicy hints of
medicinal herbs, followed by a light fruity
vein with white cherries and violets. In the
mouth, it reveals fine-grained but not fully
mellow tannins and excellent length. It's very
elegant with a long finish, not really suitable
for lovers of muscular wines. Rosso '07
tends to edginess since palate-stiffening
acidity tends to peek through.

● Pugnitello '07	♟♟♟ 7
● Chianti Cl. Il Grigio Ris. '06	♟♟ 5
● Chianti Cl. Poggio Rosso Ris. '03	♟♟♟ 6
● Chianti Cl. Poggio Rosso Ris. '00	♟♟♟ 6
● Chianti Cl. Poggio Rosso Ris. '95	♟♟♟ 5
● Chianti Cl. Poggio Rosso Ris. '90	♟♟♟ 6
● Pugnitello '06	♟♟♟ 7
● Vigorello '97	♟♟♟ 5
● Vigorello '88	♟♟♟ 5
● Brunello di Montalcino Campogiovanni '03	♟♟ 6
● Chianti Cl. Poggio Rosso Ris. '04	♟♟ 6
● Vigorello '04	♟♟ 7

● Brunello di Montalcino Le Lucere '04	♟♟ 7
● Rosso di Montalcino '07	♟ 4
● Brunello di Montalcino Le Coste Ris. '01	♟♟ 7

San Giorgio

FRAZ. CASTELNUOVO DELL'ABATE
LOC. SAN GIORGIO
53020 MONTALCINO [SI]
TEL. 0272094585
www.tenutasangiorgio.it

San Giuseppe

LOC. CASTELNUOVO DELL'ABATE
POD. SAN GIUSEPPE, 35
53020 MONTALCINO [SI]
TEL. 0577835754
www.stelladicampalto.it

CELLAR SALES
PRE-BOOKED VISITS

ANNUAL PRODUCTION **42,000 bottles**
HECTARES UNDER VINE **10**
VITICULTURE METHOD **Conventional**

ANNUAL PRODUCTION **9.100 bottles**
HECTARES UNDER VINE **6.3**
VITICULTURE METHOD **Organic certified**

Giorgio Folonari owns a small but handsome estate in fine wine country near Sesta, a true Montalcino cru. The vineyards are located at altitudes between 350 and 420 metres above sea level. The soil is very unusual for this area, with deep veins of limestone and yellow tufa that lighten the clay. The style of the wines tends to bring out the best of the terroir. Relatively long maceration is followed by initial ageing in partly new barriques, then in 50-hectolitre Slavonian oak barrels.

Brunello di Montalcino '04 is so memorable that it won our top accolade. Its fruity nose offers slight sensations of liquorice, typical of the zone, and chocolate. Mellow tannins and austere acidity ensure firm structure, soundness and nice development on the palate. Rosso di Montalcino '07 has a touch too much oak, with drying tannins, while the easy-drinking Cacciacone '06, from cabernet sauvignon and syrah, is spicy with an attractive nose of black berry fruit.

One of Montalcino's all-female concerns, San Giuseppe has released its first Brunello di Montalcino after having declassified both the '02 and '03 vintages. The estate employed organic methods from its purchase in 1992 until 2002, when it went over to biodynamic farming. It lies on the south-east side of the zone and its wines are characteristically austere. The soil composition is somewhat unusual, with plenty of marl, little clay and some quartz. Fermentation takes place in small wooden vats while barriques and tonneaux are used for ageing.

Always among the best of the vintage, the '07 Rosso di Montalcino has a full, fresh nose of red fruit and floral notes, and a well-defined, juicy palate with impressive grip. The first Brunello di Montalcino, a 2004 vintage, is very convincing. It shows a classic bright ruby with a fine nose dominated by wild cherry and a vibrant palate with young but well-crafted tannins. The pervasive finish echoes the nose.

● Brunello di Montalcino Ugolforte '04	♟♟♟ 7
● Cacciacone '06	♟ 6
● Rosso di Montalcino Ciampoleto '07	♟ 5
● Brunello di Montalcino '03	♟♟ 7
● Brunello di Montalcino Ugolforte '01	♟♟ 7
● Cacciacone '05	♟♟ 6

● Brunello di Montalcino '04	♟♟ 7
● Rosso di Montalcino '07	♟♟ 6
● Rosso di Montalcino '04	♟♟ 6
● Rosso di Montalcino '03	♟♟ 6
● Rosso di Montalcino '02	♟♟ 6

San Giusto a Rentennano

FRAZ. MONTI IN CHIANTI
LOC. SAN GIUSTO A RENTENNANO, 20
53013 GAIOLE IN CHIANTI [SI]
TEL. 0577747121
www.fattoriasangiusto.it

CELLAR SALES
PRE-BOOKED VISITS

ANNUAL PRODUCTION 85,000 bottles
HECTARES UNDER VINE 29
VITICULTURE METHOD Organic certified

This estate has an authentic, rustic beauty that will bewitch the careful observer. It has belonged to the Martini di Cigala family since 1957 and is situated in the southern part of the Chianti Classico zone. Although it is in the municipality of Gaiole, its distinctive features appear closer to the area around Castelnuovo Berardenga. The climate here is warm and the soil is highly variable but tends to be tufaceous. Certified organic farming methods are employed in the vineyards and the cellar uses mainly small oak casks.

Chianti Classico Riserva Le Baroncole '06, which greatly impressed us in the past, appeared reluctant to express itself this year, showing a tad too much toast. It is still a great charmer, alternating notes of attractive oak and spice with hints of ripe blood oranges and floral sensations, accompanied by a satisfying, full-flavoured palate with faintly rough tannins. Percarlo '05 is similar. It shows caressing, potent and even mineral, but very compressed by mouth-drying tannins. It seems to be seeking for an identity so we hope that it soon returns to the elegant style of the 1990s. Merlot La Ricolma '06 and Chianti Classico '07 are both good.

★★ Tenuta San Guido

LOC. BOLGHERI
LOC. CAPANNE, 27
57022 CASTAGNETO CARDUCCI [LI]
TEL. 0565762003
www.sassicaia.com

PRE-BOOKED VISITS

ANNUAL PRODUCTION 590,000 bottles
HECTARES UNDER VINE 90
VITICULTURE METHOD Conventional

Sassicaia is an awesome classic. As in literature, cinema and painting, we use the term "classic" to define something that is unchanging because it is complete, yet still keeps coming up with something new. And indeed, the finest example of Bolgheri excellence always surprises us each time we taste it. Tenuta San Guido has made this classic a legend with its simple interpretation of the best terroirs available, above all the fabulous Castiglioncello vineyard, planted with varieties formerly considered quirky but which are now cornerstones of the denomination.

Bolgheri Superiore Sassicaia '06 again took Three Glasses. It has also gone down in history as one of Italy's great wines. Concentrated blackcurrants, bergamot and elderflower and a restrained, continuous palate march in perfect step with the classy, complex mouthfeel for a wine with infinite potential. If our fantastic annual tastings have taught us anything, it is to avoid tying this masterpiece of Italian wine to a single, limiting definition. The estate's excellence is confirmed by Guidalberto '07, from cabernet sauvignon and merlot, which is simply sublime, its deep nose accompanied by extremely elegant body and juiciness.

● Chianti Cl. Le Baroncole Ris. '06	♀♀ 6
● Percarlo '05	♀♀ 8
● Chianti Cl. '07	♀♀ 5
● La Ricolma '06	♀♀ 8
● Percarlo '99	♀♀♀ 8
● Percarlo '97	♀♀♀ 8
● Percarlo '95	♀♀♀ 8
● Percarlo '88	♀♀♀ 8
● Chianti Cl. Le Baroncole Ris. '05	♀♀ 6
● Chianti Cl. Le Baroncole Ris. '02	♀♀ 6
● La Ricolma '05	♀♀ 8
● La Ricolma '04	♀♀ 7
● Percarlo '04	♀♀ 8

● Bolgheri Sassicaia '06	♀♀♀+ 8
● Guidalberto '07	♀♀ 7
● Le Difese '07	♀ 5
● Bolgheri Sassicaia '05	♀♀♀ 8
● Bolgheri Sassicaia '04	♀♀♀ 8
● Bolgheri Sassicaia '03	♀♀♀ 8
● Bolgheri Sassicaia '02	♀♀♀ 8
● Bolgheri Sassicaia '01	♀♀♀ 8
● Bolgheri Sassicaia '00	♀♀♀ 8
● Bolgheri Sassicaia '99	♀♀♀ 8
● Bolgheri Sassicaia '98	♀♀♀ 8
● Bolgheri Sassicaia '97	♀♀♀ 8
● Bolgheri Sassicaia '95	♀♀♀ 8
● Guidalberto '04	♀♀♀ 7
● Sassicaia '90	♀♀♀ 8

San Polino

LOC. CASTELNUOVO DELL'ABATE
POD. SAN POLINO, 163
53024 MONTALCINO [SI]
TEL. 0577835775
www.sanpolino.it

CELLAR SALES
PRE-BOOKED VISITS

ANNUAL PRODUCTION **10,000 bottles**
HECTARES UNDER VINE **3.6**
VITICULTURE METHOD **Organic certified**

This rapidly growing small estate is in the San Polo area, on the south-eastern side of Montalcino. Its vineyards are scrupulously tended to certified biodynamic standards but most importantly it vaunts great enthusiasm and good wines. The land under vine has mainly sandy clay soil, with plenty of gravel. Only just over a hectare is registered as Brunello so very few bottles are produced. The wines, aged in medium-sized barrels and partly in barriques, are classic in style. Katia and Luigi also craft a super selection of Brunello called Helichrysum.

We were very impressed by the '04 vintage of this Brunello. It has a complex, highly distinctive nose, with notes of pencil lead and slight nuances of coffee, followed by blackberries, blueberries and well-defined black cherries. The palate shows intriguing elegance and fine continuity, thanks to excellent mellow tannins and fair acidity before the coherent finish nicely echoes the nose. The current Brunello is also good, with a well-typed, developed nose of tobacco, leather and medicinal herbs. On the palate it is a little stiff and linear, but very pleasant.

San Polo

POD. SAN POLO DI PODERNOVI, 161
53024 MONTALCINO [SI]
TEL. 0577835101
www.poggiosanpolo.com

CELLAR SALES
PRE-BOOKED VISITS

ANNUAL PRODUCTION **70,000 bottles**
HECTARES UNDER VINE **15**
VITICULTURE METHOD **Conventional**

This stunning winery is on the eastern slope of Montalcino, on the road to Castelnuovo dell'Abate. A long dirt track leads to a magnificent terrace overlooking Val d'Orcia. Its recent takeover by Veneto producer Marilisa Allegrini has given this already decent winery a further boost. The excellent, high-density vineyards are the result of careful zoning studies to find the most suitable rootstocks and clones, while the beautiful cellar is inspired by bioarchitecture. Different sized barrels are used to age the Brunello.

Brunello di Montalcino '04 is very good. Its nose, slightly dominated by oak when young, also offers fruity notes of morello cherry and sensations of tobacco and spice. The palate displays convincingly elegant tannins and refreshing, well-calibrated acidity, topped by an attractive, deep finish. Rosso di Montalcino '06 has a touch too much oak and tannins that hinder progression, cropping the finish.

● Brunello di Montalcino Helichrysum '04	♟♟	8
● Brunello di Montalcino '04	♟♟	8
● Rosso di Montalcino '06	♟	5
● Brunello di Montalcino '01	♟♟	7
● Brunello di Montalcino Ris. '01	♟♟	7

● Brunello di Montalcino '04	♟♟	7
● Rosso di Montalcino '06	♟	5
● Brunello di Montalcino '03	♟♟	7
● Mezzopane '05	♟♟	6
● Mezzopane '00	♟♟	6
● Rosso di Montalcino '00	♟♟	5

San Quirico

LOC. PANCOLE, 39
53037 SAN GIMIGNANO [SI]
TEL. 0577955007
az.agr.sanquirico@libero.it

CELLAR SALES
PRE-BOOKED VISITS

ANNUAL PRODUCTION 200,000 bottles
HECTARES UNDER VINE 32
VITICULTURE METHOD Conventional

Andrea Veccchione's winery made it back into the Guide this year with an excellent Vernaccia Isabella Riserva '04, exemplifying the potential of a white grape that was long unexpressed. Andrea, a former triple-jump champion, shows the same dedication to his 30-hectare organically farmed estate that he did to his sporting career.

Isabella stands out for its classic fruity nose characterized by faint resinous notes, combined with almonds and hints of spice. Entry on the palate is complex and convincing, with plenty of pulp, driving nicely along with pleasing length. The full-bodied, fresh, juicy Vernaccia '08 has riper peach and apple fruit, good acid backbone and a full-flavoured, enjoyable finish. Vin Santo '02 has very typical aromas of dried fruit and nuts, including hazelnuts, figs and dates, warm alcohol and a dry finish.

Castello di San Sano

FRAZ. SAN SANO
LOC. PALAZZINO
53013 GAIOLE IN CHIANTI [SI]
TEL. 0577746056
www.castellosansano.com

CELLAR SALES
PRE-BOOKED VISITS
FOOD

ANNUAL PRODUCTION 200,000 bottles
HECTARES UNDER VINE 87
VITICULTURE METHOD Conventional

Castello di San Sano is the only farm in the little village of the same name, which is part of the municipality of Gaiole in Chianti. The estate is owned by lawyer Calogero Calli, who has long believed in the special wine vocation of this corner of Chianti. The stony soils are ideal for the vineyards, which cover an area of approximately 87 hectares on a perfectly aspected hilltop. In addition to wine, the farm also breeds Cinta Senese pigs and produces excellent olive oil.

The list of wines presented confirms the soundness of the estate's production. Chianti Classico '07 has a well-defined nose with citrus notes, combined with floral and spicy sensations. The full-bodied palate has nice progression and is marred only by rough tannins, which detract a little from its suppleness. Chianti Classico Riserva Guarnellotto '06 has a deep nose veined with salty and tertiary notes. It is accompanied by a sweet, acidity-braced palate with good complexity. Borro al Fumo '06, from sangiovese and cabernet, is a little lacking in harmony, as its concentrated fruit is not balanced by sufficient freshness.

○ Vernaccia di S. Gimignano Isabella Ris. '04	♈♈♈	5
○ San Gimignano Vin Santo '02	♈	5
○ Vernaccia di S. Gimignano '08	♈	4

● Chianti Cl. Guarnellotto Ris. '06	♈♈	5
● Chianti Cl. '07	♈♈	4*
● Borro al Fumo '06	♈	6
● Chianti Cl. '06	♈♈	4*
● Chianti Cl. Guarnellotto Ris. '05	♈♈	5

Fattoria Santa Vittoria

LOC. POZZO
VIA PIANA, 43
52045 FOIANO DELLA CHIANA [AR]
TEL. 057566807
www.fattoriasantavittoria.com

CELLAR SALES
PRE-BOOKED VISITS
VISITOR FACILITIES

ANNUAL PRODUCTION 37,000 bottles
HECTARES UNDER VINE 35
VITICULTURE METHOD Conventional

Fattoria Santa Vittoria dates back to the beginning of the 18th century and is situated in the Valdichiana hills. It belongs to the Niccolai family, whose daughter Marta has been running it since 1995. After replanting the vine stock to include several international varieties, local vines like pugnitello and foglia tonda have recently been added, giving the wines more character.

The estate's strength has always been Vin Santo, produced using traditional methods and aged in half-barriques for six years before release. The '01 version has a headily rich nose of honey, almonds and orange peel. The palate is complex, full and velvety, with good depth and a mouthwatering finish. Scannagallo '06, from sangiovese and cabernet sauvignon, also performed well, with complex aromas of fruit, flowers and animal skins, and a stylishly poised body. At its first release this year, the pugnitello Leopoldo '06 has a vegetal nose and nice weight, but a slightly short finish.

Podere Sapaio

LOC. LO SCOPAIO, 212
57022 CASTAGNETO CARDUCCI [LI]
TEL. 0565765187
www.sapaio.com

PRE-BOOKED VISITS

ANNUAL PRODUCTION 75,000 bottles
HECTARES UNDER VINE 25
VITICULTURE METHOD Conventional

Podere Sapaio has earned itself a place in the front rank of the many Bolgheri producers. Massimo Piccin, the estate's owner, uses its 25 hectares of vineyards for the production of concentrated wines with a strong international character. However, the extremely fine vineyards and Massimo's great sensibility have enriched the style with new complexity, resulting in deeper, more personal, multi-layered wines.

The Three-Glass winning Bolgheri Superiore Sapaio '06 is a fine example. Its deep nose displays vibrant morello cherry, bramble jelly and tobacco while the alcoholic palate is enlivened by fine-grained tannins and impressive thrust. It appears to have shed the lethargic opulence of the previous versions, acquiring greater lightness on the palate, which boosts complexity. Bolgheri Volpolo '07 is also good. The estate's basic wine is rather nice, even though it shows more liberal use of oak. The nice aromatic profile focuses on fruit and the palate offers depth and length.

Wine	Rating
● Scannagallo '06	♥♥ 4*
○ Valdichiana Vin Santo Ris. '01	♥♥ 6
○ Conforta '07	♥ 5
● Leopoldo '06	♥ 5
● Poggio del Tempio '07	♥ 3
○ Le Gaggiole '04	♀♀ 3*
● Poggio al Tempio '05	♀♀ 2*
● Poggio del Tempio '05	♀♀ 4*
○ Valdichiana Vin Santo '02	♀♀ 5
○ Valdichiana Vin Santo '01	♀♀ 5

Wine	Rating
● Bolgheri Sapaio Sup. '06	♥♥♥ 7
● Bolgheri Volpolo '07	♥♥ 5
● Bolgheri Sapaio Sup. '05	♀♀ 7
● Bolgheri Sapaio Sup. '04	♀♀ 7
● Bolgheri Volpolo '06	♀♀ 5

Sassotondo

PIAN DI CONATI, 52
58010 SOVANA [GR]
TEL. 0564614218
www.sassotondo.it

CELLAR SALES
PRE-BOOKED VISITS

ANNUAL PRODUCTION 50,000 bottles
HECTARES UNDER VINE 12
VITICULTURE METHOD Organic certified Naturale

In 1990, Roman documentary film-maker Edoardo Ventimiglia and his agronomist wife Carla Benini moved to Sovana, to what is now the Sassotondo estate. The first harvest of the newly renovated winery was in 1997. It was followed by the first bottling, which crowned a wine project focusing on local varieties with ancient roots, first and foremost ciliegiolo. Today, the estate is an excellent example of successful small-scale wine production that has managed to combine technology with traditional knowledge.

San Lorenzo '06, a monovarietal Ciliegiolo, has a generously intense, original nose and a deep, complex, dynamic palate with good definition and slightly over-extracted tannins. Ciliegiolo '08 captures all the potential of the variety with fresh, balsamic aromas and exceptional drinkability, thanks to a bright, flavoursome palate. The rest of Sassotondo's list is reliable, including the full-bodied Sovana Superiore '07 and the linear, zesty Bianco di Pitigliano '08.

Michele Satta

LOC. CASONE UGOLINO, 23
57022 CASTAGNETO CARDUCCI [LI]
TEL. 0565773041
www.michelesatta.com

CELLAR SALES
PRE-BOOKED VISITS

ANNUAL PRODUCTION 180,000 bottles
HECTARES UNDER VINE 28
VITICULTURE METHOD Conventional

Bolgheri is great wine country but there aren't many growers. Michele Satta is one of them. His passion for wine and the area date back 30 years, before Bolgheri appeared on wine buffs' radar. Michele's relationship with the vineyard has turned him into a benchmark for quality viticulture and all those producers who think of wine as a cultural value rather than a market commodity.

Sangiovese Cavaliere '05, which reached our finals, is a case in point. After slight reduction, it gives an earthy, sanguine nose with close-focused hints of red fruit. The palate is elegant and lingers with fine balance, preferring finesse to opulence. I Castagni '06, from cabernet sauvignon and syrah with a little teroldego, is also very pleasant. It has a concentrated, full fruity nose and a clean, vibrant palate, marred only by stiff tannins that restrain progression. The whites also showed very well, particularly Costa di Giulia '08, from vermentino and sauvignon, with its splendidly full nose and long palate.

Wine	Rating
● San Lorenzo '06	♟♟ 7
● Ciliegiolo '08	♟♟ 4
○ Bianco di Pitigliano '08	♟ 5
● Sovana Rosso Sup. '07	♟ 4
● San Lorenzo '04	♟♟ 6
● San Lorenzo '03	♟♟ 6
● San Lorenzo '02	♟♟ 6
● San Lorenzo '01	♟♟ 6
● San Lorenzo '00	♟♟ 6
● San Lorenzo '99	♟♟ 5
● San Lorenzo '98	♟♟ 5
● San Lorenzo '97	♟♟ 4
● Sassotondo Rosso '98	♟♟ 3
● Sovana Rosso Sup. Franze '99	♟♟ 4
● Sovana Rosso Sup. Franze '03	♟♟ 5
● Sovana Rosso Sup. Franze '00	♟♟ 5

Wine	Rating
● Cavaliere '05	♟♟ 8
● Bolgheri Rosso Sup. I Castagni '06	♟♟ 8
○ Costa di Giulia '08	♟♟ 5
● Diambra Rosso '07	♟♟ 4
● Bolgheri Rosso '07	♟ 5
● Bolgheri Rosso Piastraia '02	♟♟♟ 7
● Bolgheri Rosso Piastraia '01	♟♟♟ 7
○ Bolgheri Bianco '07	♟♟ 4
● Bolgheri Rosso '06	♟♟ 6
● Bolgheri Rosso Piastraia '00	♟♟ 7
● Bolgheri Rosso Sup. I Castagni '05	♟♟ 8
● Bolgheri Rosso Sup. I Castagni '03	♟♟ 8
○ Costa di Giulia '07	♟♟ 5

Savignola Paolina

VIA PETRIOLO, 58
50022 GREVE IN CHIANTI [FI]
TEL. 0558546036
www.savignolapaolina.it

CELLAR SALES
PRE-BOOKED VISITS
VISITOR FACILITIES

ANNUAL PRODUCTION **35,000 bottles**
HECTARES UNDER VINE **6**
VITICULTURE METHOD **Conventional**

This winery is named after Paolina, one of the legendary figures of Chianti Classico, a pioneering woman whose achievements are legend. Today, the winery still belongs to the same family, the Fabbris. It is situated in a rather cool area in the municipality of Greve, considered the limit for the cultivation of sangiovese, and belongs to the firmament of wineries that have achieved great success lately. Although production is low, with no more than 35,000 bottles per year, the estate is capable of impressing with the quality and land-rootedness of its wines.

Although perhaps less complex than last year, Chianti Classico Riserva '06 is captivating, with sweet aromas of ripe fruit, nuanced with saffron and attractive spicy hints. The palate also displays very evident sensations of fullness and roundness, especially on entry, which is nicely balanced by refreshing, flavoursome texture. Granaio '07, from sangiovese and merlot, is also well executed, showing taut, crisp, decidedly long and uncompromising, while Chianti Classico '07 has ripe notes and a finish that has yet to settle down.

Scopetani

VIA FIORENTINA, 33
50068 RUFINA [FI]
TEL. 0558397032
www.scopetani.it

PRE-BOOKED VISITS

ANNUAL PRODUCTION **1,000,000 bottles**
HECTARES UNDER VINE **13**
VITICULTURE METHOD **Conventional**

This estate performed well again this year. It is owned by Guido Graziano Scopetani, who manages the wine side of the business, and his sister Graziella, responsible for sales. The wines reviewed here are from the Villa Masseto property, which covers an area of 13 hectares. Other properties include Poggio Reale, below the villa of the same name that now houses the Conosorzio del Chianti Rufina.

The two best '06 Riservas stand out for their vinification style: 813 is a blend of canaiolo and sangiovese, whose name derives from the number of days that elapse from 31 October of the year of harvest to the date of bottling. It has a fresh nose of red fruit, dynamic, juicy body and a lingering finish. Stellario has vegetal and balsamic aromas, balanced body and good length. Vigna Macereto has a sweet nose of chocolate and coffee but is held back on the palate by its extract and a bitter finish.

● Chianti Cl. Ris. '06	▼▼ 5
● Granaio '07	▼▼ 5
● Chianti Cl. '07	▼ 4
● Chianti Cl. Ris. '05	♀♀ 5
● Chianti Cl. Ris. '04	♀♀ 5
● Chianti Cl. Ris. '03	♀♀ 5
● Granaio '06	♀♀ 5
● Granaio '03	♀♀ 5
● Granaio '02	♀♀ 6
● Granaio '01	♀♀ 6

● Chianti Rufina 813 Ris. '06	▼▼ 4*
● Chianti Rufina Stellario Ris. '06	▼▼ 4*
● Chianti Rufina V. Macereto Ris. '06	▼ 4
● Chianti Rufina 813 Ris. '05	♀♀ 4*
● Chianti Rufina Stellario Ris. '03	♀♀ 4*
● Chianti Rufina Vigna Macereto Ris. '01	♀♀ 5

La Selva

FRAZ. SAN DONATO - ALBINIA
LOC. FONTE BLANDA
S.P. 81, 7
58010 ORBETELLO [GR]
TEL. 0564885799
www.laselva-bio.eu

CELLAR SALES
PRE-BOOKED VISITS
VISITOR FACILITIES

ANNUAL PRODUCTION 200,000 bottles
HECTARES UNDER VINE 26
VITICULTURE METHOD Organic certified

Organic viticulture, a state-of-the-art cellar and special attention to old local varieties are the cornerstones of Karl Egger's production. These factors are flanked by a very fair pricing policy, making this Orbetello estate one of the most interesting on the Maremma wine scene, with a consistent range of balanced, pleasant wines.

Ciliegiolo '07 is characterized by fresh, clean, balsamic aromas. It is a very flavoursome wine, whose strength lies in its drinkability. Vermentino '08 is equally pleasant, with a tangy, racy palate and alluring aromas with hints of Mediterranean scrubland. Both Morellino di Scansano Colli dell'Uccellina '07 and the red Prima Causa '07, from cabernet sauvignon and merlot, have good character, although they are slightly below their usual standard.
Morellino di Scansano '08, Maremma Rosso '08, from sangiovese, and Bianco Toscano '08, a blend of vermentino and ansonica, are all reliable.

Fattoria Selvapiana

LOC. SELVAPIANA, 43
50068 RUFINA [FI]
TEL. 0558369848
www.selvapiana.it

CELLAR SALES
PRE-BOOKED VISITS

ANNUAL PRODUCTION 220,000 bottles
HECTARES UNDER VINE 59.7
VITICULTURE METHOD Conventional

We would like to borrow a term from the world of sport to describe the performance of the Giuntini family's estate this year, for it seems as though the wines have fallen prey to overtraining. This is the only explanation we can find for the significantly inferior results this year, despite the fact that tastings were repeated several times and by different panels. Nonetheless, all the wines displayed very ripe fruity aromas and a decidedly bitter finish.

The best performance was by Riserva Bucerchiale '06, named after the vineyard from which it comes, while Pomino Rosso Petrognano '07 is very drinkable. Chianti Rufina '07 is less silky while La Fornace '06, from cabernet sauvignon and merlot with a small amount of sangiovese, has overly prominent tannins for its alcohol.

● Ciliegiolo '07	⚑⚑ 5
○ Vermentino La Selva '08	⚑⚑ 4
○ Bianco Toscano '08	⚑ 3
● Maremma Rosso '08	⚑ 3
● Morellino di Scansano '08	⚑ 4
● Morellino di Scansano Colli dell'Uccellina '07	⚑ 5
● Prima Causa '07	⚑ 6
● Ciliegiolo '05	⚑⚑ 5
● Morellino di Scansano '05	⚑⚑ 3
● Morellino di Scansano Colli dell'Uccellina '05	⚑⚑ 4
● Prima Causa '06	⚑⚑ 6
● Prima Causa '05	⚑⚑ 6
● Prima Causa '04	⚑⚑ 6
● Prima Causa '01	⚑⚑ 5

● Chianti Rufina Bucerchiale Ris. '06	⚑⚑ 6
● Chianti Rufina '07	⚑ 4
● La Fornace '06	⚑ 6
● Pomino Fattoria di Petrognano '07	⚑ 4
● Chianti Rufina Bucerchiale '04	⚑⚑ 6

Serraiola

FRAZ. FRASSINE
LOC. SERRAIOLA
58025 MONTEROTONDO MARITTIMO [GR]
TEL. 0566910026
www.serraiola.it

CELLAR SALES
PRE-BOOKED VISITS

ANNUAL PRODUCTION **50,000 bottles**
HECTARES UNDER VINE **10**
VITICULTURE METHOD **Conventional**

Lying on the border between the provinces of Grosseto and Livorno, Serraiola is the last bastion of the Monteregio DOC zone. The Monterotondo Marittimo winery belongs to the Lenzi family, who planted its first vineyards in the 1970s. In 1994, the wines started to go to market but it is in recent years that they have achieved good consistent quality, putting the estate on the list of the most interesting producers in the Massa di Marittima area.

Campo di Montecristo '07, from merlot, sangiovese and syrah, is concentrated and rich, showing particularly juicy on the palate. Shiraz '07 is also good, with a nose of Mediterranean scrubland and peppery hints, accompanied by a balanced, full-bodied palate. Monteregio Lentisco '08 and Monteregio Cervone '08, with a similar nose and well-sustained, supple palates, are uncomplicated but very decent. The estate's whites are well made. Monteregio Bianco Violina '08 is fresh and upfront while Vermentino '08 has attractive tangy notes.

Sesti - Castello di Argiano

FRAZ. SANT'ANGELO IN COLLE
LOC. CASTELLO DI ARGIANO
53024 MONTALCINO [SI]
TEL. 0577843921
www.sestiwine.com

CELLAR SALES
PRE-BOOKED VISITS

ANNUAL PRODUCTION **61,000 bottles**
HECTARES UNDER VINE **9**
VITICULTURE METHOD **Conventional**

The 13th-century tower that dominates the estate formed part of the military defence system protecting the southern border of the Republic of Siena. Elisa and Giuseppe Sesti's estate offers characterful wines that reflect their terroir on the southern side of the Montalcino hill, renowned for its powerful wines. The wines are aged in barrels containing from 15 to 30 hectolitres and work in the vineyard follows the phases of the moon.

This year, we tasted a new wine, the cabernet and merlot Castello di Sesti '06. At first, the nose appears reduced before unfolding aromas of black berry fruit, vegetality and gamey notes. On the palate it shows great balance, with nicely calibrated tannins and excellent acidity. Brunello di Montalcino '04 is classic on both the nose, with notes of cherry, dried flowers and game, and the palate, where it displays more elegance than heft. Riserva Phenomena '03 is true to its vintage, with still mouth-drying tannins, while Rosso '07 is juicy, but a little insubstantial.

Wine	Rating
● Campo Montecristo '07	♟♟ 6
● Shiraz '07	♟♟ 5
○ Monteregio di Massa Marittima Bianco Violina '08	♟ 4
● Monteregio di Massa Marittima Cervone '08	♟ 4
● Monteregio di Massa Marittima Rosso Lentisco '07	♟ 4
○ Vermentino '08	♟ 4
● Campo Montecristo '06	♟♟ 6
● Campo Montecristo '05	♟♟ 6
● Campo Montecristo '04	♟♟ 6
● Campo Montecristo '01	♟♟ 6
● Monteregio di Massa Marittima Rosso Lentisco '05	♟♟ 5
● Shiraz '06	♟♟ 5
● Shiraz '05	♟♟ 5
● Shiraz '04	♟♟ 5

Wine	Rating
● Brunello di Montalcino '04	♟♟ 7
● Brunello di Montalcino Phenomena Ris. '03	♟♟ 8
● Castello Sesti '06	♟♟ 7
○ Sauvignon '08	♟♟ 4
● Rosso di Montalcino '07	♟ 5
● Brunello di Montalcino Phenomena Ris. '01	♟♟♟ 8
● Brunello di Montalcino '01	♟♟ 7
● Brunello di Montalcino Phenomena Ris. '00	♟♟ 8
● Brunello di Montalcino Phenomena Ris. '99	♟♟ 8

Tenuta Sette Ponti

LOC. VIGNA DI PALLINO
52029 CASTIGLION FIBOCCHI [AR]
TEL. 0575477857
www.tenutasetteponti.it

CELLAR SALES
PRE-BOOKED VISITS

ANNUAL PRODUCTION **230,000 bottles**
HECTARES UNDER VINE **50**
VITICULTURE METHOD **Conventional**

Fashion entrepreneur Antonio Moretti has made wine his main passion and profession. Not satisfied with owning other estates in Bolgheri, Maremma and Sicily, he has recently started overseeing the production of a Champagne that he also distributes. The estate has belonged to the family since the 1950s, when Alberto Moretti, Antonio's father, purchased it for hunting. However, it was already producing wine by 1957. In 1997, Antonio took the helm and embarked on a radical transformation.

Oreno '06, from merlot, cabernet and sangiovese, is a handsome purple colour with elegant delicate aromas ranging from chocolate to blueberry and pleasant balsamic notes with hints of roots. The palate is juicy, full and velvety with great length. Crognolo '07, from sangiovese with small amounts of merlot and cabernet, is also good, with a fruity nose and a racy, smooth, flavoursome palate. The first release of the white Anni '08, from sauvignon and viognier, is interesting, presenting a scented nose and a tight-knit, fresh, full-flavoured palate. The '08 Chianti is well made and pleasant.

Solaria - Cencioni

POD. CAPANNA, 102
53024 MONTALCINO [SI]
TEL. 0577849426
www.solariacencioni.com

CELLAR SALES
PRE-BOOKED VISITS

ANNUAL PRODUCTION **30,000 bottles**
HECTARES UNDER VINE **8.5**
VITICULTURE METHOD **Conventional**

Patrizia Cencioni is one of the few wine women who monitors every stage in the production process, from winter pruning to bottling. The results are very personal and possess that characteristic typical of great wines: they improve with ageing. All the vineyards are located at altitudes between 350 and 450 metres above sea level and cropping levels are low. Various types and sizes of barrels are used in the handsome cellar.

Again this year, Brunello di Montalcino '04 reached our finals. On the nose it proffers violet-led floral sensations in addition to classic notes of sweet tobacco, leather and thyme. The elegant, complex palate shows good attack, with attractive supporting acidity and well-integrated tannins, ending on a long, incisive, but not muscular, finish typical of the zone. Rosso di Montalcino '07 is easy drinking and one of the best of its kind, with a pleasant nose of cherries and perfect acidity, which prolongs the finish.

Wine	Rating
● Oreno '06	♟♟ 8
○ Anni '08	♟♟ 4*
● Crognolo '07	♟♟ 5
● Chianti V. di Pallino '08	♟ 3
● Morellino di Scansano Poggio al Lupo '08	♟ 4
● Poggio al Lupo '07	♟ 6
● Oreno '05	♟♟♟ 8
● Oreno '00	♟♟♟ 6
● Crognolo '06	♟♟ 5
● Crognolo '05	♟♟ 5
● Morellino di Scansano Poggio al Lupo '07	♟♟ 4
● Morellino di Scansano Poggio al Lupo '06	♟♟ 4*
● Oreno '03	♟♟ 7
● Poggio al Lupo '06	♟♟ 6
● Poggio al Lupo '05	♟♟ 6
● Poggio al Lupo '03	♟♟ 6

Wine	Rating
● Brunello di Montalcino '04	♟♟ 7
● Rosso di Montalcino '07	♟♟ 5
● Brunello di Montalcino '97	♟♟♟ 7
● Brunello di Montalcino '03	♟♟ 7
● Brunello di Montalcino '02	♟♟ 7
● Brunello di Montalcino '01	♟♟ 7
● Brunello di Montalcino '00	♟♟ 6
● Brunello di Montalcino '99	♟♟ 7
● Brunello di Montalcino Solaria 123 '01	♟♟ 6

Castello di Sonnino

VIA VOLTERRANA NORD, 6A
50025 MONTESPERTOLI [FI]
TEL. 0571609198
www.castellosonnino.it

CELLAR SALES
PRE-BOOKED VISITS

ANNUAL PRODUCTION 200,000 bottles
HECTARES UNDER VINE 45
VITICULTURE METHOD Conventional

Castello di Sonnino is a unique producer with a complex history. Once the property of the Machiavelli family, it was purchased by the Sonninos in 1830. The De Renzis family arrived here in the 19th century, when Francesco married Edith Sonnino. Today, it is one of the leading wineries in the area, where it owns approximately 30 per cent of the vineyards in the Chianti Montespertoli DOC zone. In recent years, various replantings have been made, which has introduced many international varieties.

The best wine this year was Cantinino '06, a monovarietal Sangiovese, offering a broad spectrum of aromatics, well-sustained, relaxed body and a long finish. Leone Rosso '08, an unusual blend of syrah, sangiovese, canaiolo and ancellotta, is also interesting. It has a fresh, greenish nose with a few spicy notes and supple but full body with a rising finish. The plush, velvety Vin Santo '03 is also good, with classic nut-led aromatics and a long finish.

Le Sorgenti

LOC. VALLINA
VIA DI DOCCIOLA, 8
50012 BAGNO A RIPOLI [FI]
TEL. 055696004
www.fattoria.lesorgenti.com

CELLAR SALES
PRE-BOOKED VISITS
VISITOR FACILITIES

ANNUAL PRODUCTION 40,000 bottles
HECTARES UNDER VINE 32
VITICULTURE METHOD Conventional

Le Sorgenti, owned by the Ferrari family, is one of the most promising wineries in the province of Florence, thanks to the excellent work of a winning, quality-focused team comprising the owners and staff. Work is divided up, with Gabriele in the vineyard and his son Filippo in the cellar as oenologist, a role he also performs for other estates. Elisabetta Ferrari and Cristian Giorni take care of the sales side of the business and the whole team functions smoothly.

The white Sghiras was missing but the quality of the other wines made up for this. Scirus '06, from cabernet sauvignon and merlot with a little petit verdot and malbec, again reached the finals. Its vibrant colour is accompanied by a complex, vegetal nose with notes of cloves and cinnamon. The palate is full, plush and silky, with a long, enjoyable finish. Gaiaccia '07, from sangiovese and merlot, is also good, with its delicate fruity nose, sturdy body and a nice spicy aftertaste. Chianti Colli Fiorentini Respiro '07 intrigues, combining concentrated aromas with light body, fine-grained tannins and a flavoursome finish.

● Cantinino '06	♛♛ 5
● Leone Rosso '08	♛♛ 3*
○ Vin Santo del Chianti Gold Label '03	♛ 6
● Cantinino '05	♛♛ 5
● Cantinino '04	♛♛ 5
● Leone Rosso '07	♛♛ 3*
● Lo Schiavone '05	♛♛ 6
● Sanleone '04	♛♛ 7

● Scirus '06	♛♛ 6
● Chianti Colli Fiorentini Respiro '07	♛♛ 4
● Gaiaccia '07	♛♛ 5
● Chianti Colli Fiorentini Respiro '06	♛♛ 4*
● Gaiaccia '06	♛♛ 5
● Scirus '05	♛♛ 6
● Scirus '04	♛♛ 6
● Scirus '03	♛♛ 6
● Scirus '01	♛♛ 6
○ Sghiras '06	♛♛ 5

Talenti

FRAZ. SANT'ANGELO IN COLLE
LOC. PIAN DI CONTE
53020 MONTALCINO [SI]
TEL. 0577844064
www.talentimontalcino.it

CELLAR SALES
PRE-BOOKED VISITS

ANNUAL PRODUCTION **80,000 bottles**
HECTARES UNDER VINE **21**
VITICULTURE METHOD **Conventional**

The Talenti winery was founded in the 1990s by Pierluigi, one of the founding fathers of Brunello di Montalcino, who headed Il Poggione for many years. His legacy is continued by his grandson Riccardo, who applies passion to his work in the cellar. The winery is located opposite Sant'Angelo in Colle and the vineyard extends over a single plot of about 20 hectares. It is located on a little plateau with gravelly marl soil, 450 metres above sea level, in a well-ventilated position that yields sound fruit. A new cellar, completed a few years ago, houses barrels of various sizes.

Talenti's Brunello di Montalcino again showed what it can do in great vintages, winning Three Glasses. It has a nose of balsam-veined plums and black cherries, and exceptionally well-integrated oak. On the palate the tannins are very evident but balanced by good extract and acidity. The finish is broad, concentrated and lingering. It's a fine wine from the upper southern area of the DOC zone. Both the '07 Rosso and Brunello di Montalcino Riserva '03 are held back by rather edgy tannins, as is Pian di Corte '07, from mainly sangiovese with small amounts of merlot and syrah.

Tenimenti Angelini

LOC. VAL DI CAVA
53024 MONTALCINO [SI]
TEL. 0577780411
www.tenimentiangelini.it

CELLAR SALES
PRE-BOOKED VISITS

ANNUAL PRODUCTION **900,000 bottles**
HECTARES UNDER VINE **173**
VITICULTURE METHOD **Conventional**

Tenimenti Angelini, the agricultural branch of the well-known pharmaceutical group, owns two large estates in Tuscany, Val di Suga in Montalcino and Tre Rose in Montepulciano. Restructuring work has recently been completed on the vineyards and buildings at Val di Suga. The new, high-density vineyards went into production in 2004 and the Brunello di Montalcino reflects their quality. Nor should we forget the wonderful Spuntali vineyard on the southern side of the zone, planted in the early 1980s. Although Tre Rose has little new to offer, it remains a very solid winery.

The list presented this year is topped by an elegant, refined Brunello di Montalcino '04 with classic notes of morello cherry and tobacco leaves, soft tannins and a caressing finish. Brunello di Montalcino Vigna Spuntali '03 is improving, particularly considering the difficult vintage. It has a nose of medicinal herbs and leather, with slightly edgy tannins but lots of personality. The estate presented three '06 vintages of Nobile di Montepulciano. We preferred La Villa, whose creamy tannins ensure a long finish.

● Brunello di Montalcino '04	ŸŸŸ 7
● Brunello di Montalcino Ris. '03	Ÿ 7
● Pian di Conte '07	Ÿ 6
● Rosso di Montalcino '07	Ÿ 4
● Brunello di Montalcino '88	ŸŸŸ 5
● Brunello di Montalcino Ris. '99	ŸŸŸ 7
● Brunello di Montalcino Vigna del Paretaio Ris. '01	ŸŸŸ 7
● Brunello di Montalcino '01	ŸŸ 6
● Brunello di Montalcino '00	ŸŸ 6
● Pian di Conte '06	ŸŸ 6
● Pian di Conte '05	ŸŸ 5

● Brunello di Montalcino '04	ŸŸ 7
● Brunello di Montalcino Vigna Spuntali '03	ŸŸ 8
● Nobile di Montepulciano La Villa Tenuta Tre Rose '06	ŸŸ 6
● Nobile di Montepulciano Tenuta Tre Rose '06	ŸŸ 4*
● Nobile di Montepulciano Simposio Tenuta Tre Rose '06	Ÿ 6
● Rosso di Montalcino '07	Ÿ 5
● Brunello di Montalcino V. del Lago '95	ŸŸŸ 8
● Brunello di Montalcino V. del Lago '93	ŸŸŸ 8
● Brunello di Montalcino V. del Lago '90	ŸŸŸ 8
● Brunello di Montalcino Vigna Spuntali '95	ŸŸŸ 8
● Brunello di Montalcino Vigna Spuntali '93	ŸŸŸ 8
● Brunello di Montalcino '03	ŸŸ 7

Tenimenti Luigi D'Alessandro

VIA MANZANO, 15
52042 CORTONA [AR]
TEL. 0575618667
www.tenimentidalessandro.it

PRE-BOOKED VISITS

ANNUAL PRODUCTION 150,000 bottles
HECTARES UNDER VINE 50
VITICULTURE METHOD Conventional

Two of the wines from Massimo D'Alessandro and Giuseppe Calabresi's estate reached our finals this year, and one of them, Il Bosco '06, won Three Glasses. It shows quality is not optional at a winery that has written the recent history of the Cortona DOC zone. The estate was the largest farm in Valdichiana until its purchase by Luigi Alessandro in 1967. During the 1990s, the vineyards were gradually replanted, until reaching around 50 acres of high-density plots while the successful reorganization of the cellar is a more recent development.

The estate has decided to concentrate its efforts on syrah and it thus comes as no surprise that the wines bring out the full potential of the variety. Migliara '06 unveils graceful, pleasantly spicy aromas of red fruit and dried flowers, and an elegantly sensual, velvet-smooth palate with remarkable acidity that lends tension. Il Bosco '06 is fuller and more striking, with a complex, solid palate and nice tannins. The finish is supple, long and flavoursome. Syrah '07 is also good and very moreish while Fontarca Viognier '07 has changed tack and is now juicier, fresher and crisper.

● Cortona Il Bosco '06	♀♀♀ 7
● Cortona Syrah Migliara '06	♀♀ 8
● Cortona Syrah '07	♀♀ 4*
○ Fontarca '07	♀ 6
● Cortona Il Bosco '04	♀♀♀ 7
● Cortona Il Bosco '03	♀♀♀ 7
● Cortona Il Bosco '01	♀♀♀ 7
● Podere Il Bosco '97	♀♀♀ 5
● Podere Il Bosco '95	♀♀♀ 5
● Cortona Il Bosco '05	♀♀ 7
● Cortona Il Bosco '00	♀♀ 6
● Cortona Syrah '06	♀♀ 4
● Cortona Syrah '04	♀♀ 4

Terenzi

LOC. MONTEDONICO
58054 SCANSANO [GR]
TEL. 0564599601
www.terenzi.eu

CELLAR SALES
VISITOR FACILITIES

ANNUAL PRODUCTION 180,000 bottles
HECTARES UNDER VINE 30
VITICULTURE METHOD Conventional

The Terenzi family arrived in Maremma in the early 1990s, although their estate acquired its current form only gradually, starting with a series of land purchases, construction of the modern cellar in 2004 and the release of the first wines in 2007. Today, the winery is run by Florio Terenzi, his wife Giuseppina and their son Federico, who focus firmly on quality, with lean, elegant wines offered at very interesting prices.

The Scansano-based estate has a wide range of wines and the star is Francesca Romana, from sangiovese, merlot and petit verdot, which has a generous nose and a full, attractive palate. Morellino di Scansano Riserva '06 is similar in style, with an alluring nose and a caressing palate. Bramaluce '07, from sangiovese, syrah and alicante, is interesting and Morellino di Scansano '08 is very drinkable. Balbino '08, a monovarietal Vermentino, is fresh and tangy, showing racier than Balbino '08 Etichetta Nera, which is also from vermentino but briefly aged in oak. Morellino di Scansano '07 is well executed.

● Francesca Romana '07	♀♀ 5
● Morellino di Scansano '08	♀♀ 3*
○ Balbino '08	♀♀ 4
● Bramaluce '07	♀♀ 5
● Morellino di Scansano Ris. '06	♀♀ 4
○ Balbino Etichetta Nera '08	♀ 4
● Morellino di Scansano '07	♀ 4

Terrabianca

LOC. SAN FEDELE A PATERNO
53017 RADDA IN CHIANTI [SI]
TEL. 057754029
www.terrabianca.com

CELLAR SALES
PRE-BOOKED VISITS

ANNUAL PRODUCTION 360,000 bottles
HECTARES UNDER VINE 52
VITICULTURE METHOD Conventional

Terrabianca, owned by Roberto Guidener, is located in an area with chalky – hence the name "white earth" – substrates of sand and clay dating from the Palaeozoic and Mesozoic eras. The estate covers an area of 124 hectares, including woodland and olive groves, while the south and south-east-facing vineyards are situated at altitudes between 250 and 500 metres. Each year around 360,000 bottles are produced in a wide range that embraces traditional local types as well as more international blends.

The best this year was the red Campaccio Selezione '06, from equal proportions of sangiovese and cabernet. It gives concentrated aromas of wild berries accompanied by an elegant grassy vein and notes of black pepper, showing both austere and drinkable in the mouth. Piano del Cipresso '06, a nicely aromatic Sangiovese, is also very good while Il Tesoro '06, from merlot, and the uncomplicated sangiovese and cabernet Campaccio '06, with its notes of tobacco and chocolate, are a rung below. Chianti Classico Scassino '07 is passable.

● Campaccio Sel. '06	▼▼ 6
● Piano del Cipresso '06	▼▼ 5
● Campaccio '06	▼ 6
● Ceppate '05	▼ 7
● Chianti Cl. Scassino '07	▼ 5
● Il Tesoro '06	▼ 6
● Ceppate '03	♈♈ 7
● Chianti Cl. Croce Ris. '05	♈♈ 6
● Chianti Cl. Croce Ris. '04	♈♈ 6
● Chianti Cl. Scassino '04	♈♈ 4
● Piano del Cipresso '05	♈♈ 5

Terralsole

VILLA COLLINA D'ORO
53024 MONTALCINO [SI]
TEL. 0577835678
www.terralsole.com

ANNUAL PRODUCTION 45,000 bottles
HECTARES UNDER VINE 10
VITICULTURE METHOD Conventional

Terralsole was founded by Mario Bollag in the late 1990s and has approximately ten hectares under vine: six for Brunello and four for Rosso and international varietals such as cabernet, merlot and syrah. The recently built cellar is very handsome and blends in well with its surroundings. The vineyards are located on the south-eastern side of Montalcino, at an altitude whose ventilation ensures sound fruit. All the wines are aged in tonneaux.

Following the improvement in quality we noted last year, Mario continues in style with an excellent Brunello di Montalcino '04. It shows a deep, dense ruby with a rich nose of harmonious balsamic and fruity notes reminiscent of morello cherries, blackcurrants and blackberries. The palate proffers very well-balanced tannins that fuse beautifully into the structure and nice acidity, ensuring a juicy, full finish. The supple Rosso di Montalcino '07 is also deliciously well made.

● Brunello di Montalcino '04	▼▼ 8
● Rosso di Montalcino '07	▼▼ 6
● Brunello di Montalcino '03	♈♈ 8
● Brunello di Montalcino '02	♈♈ 7
● Brunello di Montalcino '01	♈♈ 7
● Brunello di Montalcino Ris. '01	♈♈ 7
● Pasticcio '06	♈♈ 5
● Pasticcio '05	♈♈ 5
● Rosso di Montalcino '06	♈♈ 6
● Solista '06	♈♈ 4

Terre del Marchesato

FRAZ. BOLGHERI
LOC. SANT'UBERTO, 164
57020 CASTAGNETO CARDUCCI [LI]
TEL. 0565749752
www.fattoriaterredelmarchesato.it

CELLAR SALES
PRE-BOOKED VISITS

ANNUAL PRODUCTION **50,000 bottles**
HECTARES UNDER VINE **10**
VITICULTURE METHOD **Conventional**

Terre del Marchesato is situated at Sant'Uberto, not far from the Ferrugini area, where the sandy soil is darker and reddish from the presence of ferrous minerals and clay. Maurizio Fuselli continues the family tradition of farming, which commenced in the 1950s. He has chosen to specialize exclusively in viticulture and his first wines were produced in 2003. Maurizio's enthusiasm and application have enabled him to achieve excellent quality, making a name for himself as one of Bolgheri's most promising producers.

The '06 vintage did not disappoint. Marchesale '06, from syrah, has a deep, spicy nose, with notes of black pepper, ripe red fruits and medicinal herbs. Its caressing attack is underpinned by vibrant acidity, which offsets the notable extract. Tarabuso '06, from cabernet sauvignon, has elegant vegetal aromas enhanced by marked balsamic notes and sweet vanilla from new oak. Fine-grained, tight-knit tannins make it satisfying and juicy on the palate. The standard-label Emilio Primo '07, from cabernet sauvignon, merlot and syrah, is pleasantly uncomplicated, although the finish is still rather drying, which affected its score.

★ Castello del Terriccio

LOC. TERRICCIO
VIA BAGNOLI, 16
56040 CASTELLINA MARITTIMA [PI]
TEL. 050699709
www.terriccio.it

CELLAR SALES
PRE-BOOKED VISITS

ANNUAL PRODUCTION **350,000 bottles**
HECTARES UNDER VINE **62**
VITICULTURE METHOD **Conventional**

Castello del Terriccio is one of Italy's most delightful wine estates. On the hills of Castellina Marittima age-old pines give way to Australian eucalyptus trees. The estate sprawls over an area of 1,700 hectares, with more than 60 hectares under vine. The rest of the land offers idyllic rural scenes, since the main activities accompanying the production of some of Italy's greatest red wines are arable farming and horse breeding.

Lupicaia '06, from cabernet sauvignon, merlot and petit verdot, is fabulous. This magnificent version already shows impressive finesse at this early stage of maturation. Its nose of candied fruit, medicinal herbs and liquorice is underscored by the estate's hallmark balsamic hints leading into a palate that is long and opulent, with majestic tannic extraction and textbook development. As the release of Castello del Terriccio has been postponed for a year, we tasted Tassinaia '06, from cabernet sauvignon, merlot and sangiovese. Its nose of ripe fruit, vanilla and menthol notes is accompanied by an elegant, long-lingering body penalized only by a slightly bitterish finish.

● Marchesale '06	♟♟ 8
● Tarabuso '06	♟♟ 7
● Emilio Primo '07	♟ 5
○ Emilio Primo Bianco '08	♟ 6
● Syrah del Marchesato '05	♟♟ 8
● Tarabuso '05	♟♟ 6

● Lupicaia '06	♟♟♟ 8
● Tassinaia '06	♟♟ 7
● Castello del Terriccio '04	♟♟♟ 8
● Castello del Terriccio '03	♟♟♟ 8
● Castello del Terriccio '01	♟♟♟ 8
● Castello del Terriccio '00	♟♟♟ 8
● Lupicaia '05	♟♟♟ 8
● Lupicaia '04	♟♟♟ 8
● Lupicaia '01	♟♟♟ 8
● Lupicaia '00	♟♟♟ 8
● Lupicaia '99	♟♟♟ 8
● Lupicaia '98	♟♟♟ 8
● Lupicaia '97	♟♟♟ 8
● Lupicaia '95	♟♟♟ 8
● Castello del Terriccio '05	♟♟ 8
● Lupicaia '94	♟♟ 8

Teruzzi & Puthod

LOC. CASALE, 19
53037 SAN GIMIGNANO [SI]
TEL. 0577940143
www.teruzzieputhod.it

CELLAR SALES
PRE-BOOKED VISITS

ANNUAL PRODUCTION 1.200,000 bottles
HECTARES UNDER VINE 90
VITICULTURE METHOD Conventional

Our finals again saw the presence of Terre di Tufi, one of the area's most classic wines, from vernaccia, malvasia, vermentino, and chardonnay. The winery, owned by the Campari group, seems to have found the right approach to interpreting the zone, concentrating its efforts chiefly on white wines, although we would not be surprised to see some new reds in the future. The estate has around 90 hectares of vineyards, which means it can select the very best fruit.

Terre di Tufi '08 is pale straw in hue, with elegant notes of flowers and fruit. On the palate, it shows savoury and fairly light, with a medium-length finish. Vernaccia '08 is also well made, with a very invitingly fruity nose delivering notes of apricot, peach and apple, accompanied by balanced body and an enjoyably tangy finish. Carmen '07, an unusual wine from sangiovese fermented off the skins, is as singular as ever, with restrained aromatics but juicy, rich body and long flavour. Vermentino '08 is uncomplicated, with a delicate nose and a lively, fresh palate.

○ Terre di Tufi '08		▼▼ 5
○ Vernaccia di S. Gimignano '08	▼▼ 4*	
○ Carmen Puthod '07		▼ 5
○ Vermentino '08		▼ 4
● Peperino '05		♈♈ 4
○ Terre di Tufi '07		♈♈ 5
○ Vernaccia di S. Gimignano '07		♈♈ 4
○ Vernaccia di S. Gimignano V. Rondolino '07		♈♈ 4
○ Vernaccia di S. Gimignano V. Rondolino '06		♈♈ 4

Testamatta

VIA DI VINCIGLIATA, 19
50014 FIESOLE [FI]
TEL. 055597289
www.bibigraetz.com

PRE-BOOKED VISITS

ANNUAL PRODUCTION N.D.
HECTARES UNDER VINE 50
VITICULTURE METHOD Conventional

Bibi Graetz's range of wines is complete now that the second product line, Casamatta, has achieved a level of quality that offers good value for everyday consumption. The Vincigliata estate now has 50 hectares under vine, due to be joined by the ansonica vineyards on Isola del Giglio, which are currently being recovered.

We'll start with the Giglio wines. Bugia '07 has a nice mineral nose and a juicy palate while the new Cicala '08, also from ansonica but aged in steel, is refreshing and savoury with a flavoursome finish. As usual, the main estate's best wine is Testamatta '07, a Sangiovese with a complex, layered nose of concentrated fruit, attractive oak and spice preceding a rounded, full-bodied palate with a confident rising finish. Soffocone '07 and Grilli '07 are from the same blend of sangiovese, colorino and canaiolo but in different proportions. We preferred the former for its fuller nose, although both are dynamic and full-flavoured on the palate.

● Testamatta '07		▼▼ 8
○ Bugia '07		▼▼ 7
○ Cicala del Giglio '08		▼▼ 5
● Grilli del Testamatta '07		▼▼ 6
● Soffocone di Vincigliata '07		▼▼ 6
○ Casamatta Bianco '08		▼ 3
● Casamatta Rosso '07		▼ 3
○ Bugia '06		♈♈ 7
● Grilli del Testamatta '06		♈♈ 6
● Soffocone di Vincigliata '06		♈♈ 6
● Testamatta '06		♈♈ 8

Tolaini

LOC. VALLENUOVA
S. P. 9 DI PIEVASCIATA, 28
53019 CASTELNUOVO BERARDENGA [SI]
TEL. 0577356972
www.tolaini.it

CELLAR SALES
PRE-BOOKED VISITS

ANNUAL PRODUCTION **200,000 bottles**
HECTARES UNDER VINE **50**
VITICULTURE METHOD **Conventional**

Pierluigi Tolaini's winery put on a good performance, with Picconero deservedly reaching our finals. It's always a pleasure to tell the story of this Italo-Canadian entrepreneur. He left Garfagnana as a young man and subsequently founded one of Canada's leading transport companies. In 1998, he returned to Italy to make wine, purchasing an estate with over 100 hectares of woodland, vineyards and olive groves. Construction of the barrique cellar began in 2000. Today, the estate has 50 hectares under vine, planted to numerous different varieties. Expect a Chianti Classico in the future.

Picconero '06, from merlot, cabernet sauvignon and petit verdot, has a complex nose with pepper and cinnamon spice mingling with bramble jelly and vanilla. Entry on the palate is pleasant and powerful, with well-balanced tannins and alcohol taking you through to a satisfying finish. Valdisanti '06, from cabernet, franc and sauvignon with a small amount of merlot, has aromas of cocoa, good structure with nicely poised acid backbone and fine-grained tannins with a nice finish. Al Passo '06, from sangiovese and merlot, has simpler but intriguing aromas.

● Picconero '06	🍷🍷 8
● Al Passo '06	🍷🍷 5
● Valdisanti '06	🍷🍷 6
● Al Passo '04	YY 5
● Picconero '05	YY 8
● Picconero '04	YY 8
● Valdisanti '05	YY 6
● Valdisanti '04	YY 6

Fattoria Torre a Cona

LOC. SAN DONATO IN COLLINA
50010 RIGNANO SULL'ARNO [FI]
TEL. 055699000
www.villatorreacona.com

CELLAR SALES
PRE-BOOKED VISITS

ANNUAL PRODUCTION **30,000 bottles**
HECTARES UNDER VINE **14**
VITICULTURE METHOD **Conventional**

Torre a Cona, the Colli Fiorentini winery owned by the Rossi di Montelera family, confirmed its quality again this year. Work in the cellar is almost complete while the vineyards have already been entirely replanted and an old granary was converted into a handsome tasting room over a year ago. The wines tend to be traditional in style, with long maceration and ageing in tonneaux, or barriques in the case of Terre di Cino.

This year's performance showcased the estate's well-defined style and personality. The wines prefer elegance to power, faithfully reflecting the terroir. Terre di Cino '06, a monovarietal Sangiovese, has a nose of fresh red fruit with top notes of strawberry while the palate reveals the grape's more original side, giving upfront acidity and sweet tannins. Chianti dei Colli Fiorentini '07 is as delicious as ever, flaunting a juicy, full-flavoured style.

● Chianti Colli Fiorentini '07	🍷🍷 2
● Terre di Cino '06	🍷🍷 4
● Terre di Cino '05	YY 4
● Terre di Cino '04	YY 4
O Vin Santo del Chianti Merlaia '03	YY 5
O Vin Santo del Chianti Merlaia '01	YY 5

Fattoria La Traiana

LOC. TRAIANA, 16
52028 TERRANUOVA BRACCIOLINI [AR]
TEL. 0559179004
fatt.latraiana@libero.it

ANNUAL PRODUCTION **N.D.**
HECTARES UNDER VINE **60**
VITICULTURE METHOD **Organic certified**

Giandomenico Gigante's winery has earned a full profile this year. This large, complex Valdarno estate has over 60 hectares under vine, all farmed using organic methods. In addition to traditional Tuscan and international grapes, work is being carried out to recover vines that are fast disappearing, and the estate's vineyards are home to long-forgotten varieties, such as abrusco and colorino del Valdarno or mammolo.

The wine that most impressed us this year was Campo Arsiccio '05, which combines sangiovese with the lesser-known abrusco and colorino grapes. It throws a crisp, clean, confident nose with hints of medicinal herbs and a racy palate with a full-flavoured finish. The other wines are less precise. Pian del Pazzo '05, from cabernet sauvignon with a small amount of cabernet franc, displays texture and pulp but has a little trouble unbending. Chianti Superiore '07 is better, presenting more direct fruity notes and a simple, flavoursome palate while the all-chardonnay Campogialli '07 is very attractive.

Travignoli

VIA TRAVIGNOLI, 78
50060 PELAGO [FI]
TEL. 0558361098
www.travignoli.com

CELLAR SALES
PRE-BOOKED VISITS

ANNUAL PRODUCTION **250,000 bottles**
HECTARES UNDER VINE **70**
VITICULTURE METHOD **Conventional**

This was a rather low-key vintage for Giovanni Busi, president of the Chianti Rufina consortium, who has invested many years in the painstaking replanting of his vineyards. The project is now nearing completion. Overall, results are generally positive but the estate's two versions of Chianti Rufina, its great-value flagship wines, failed to impress.

This year it was Vin Santo '01, with a classic nose and a soft, sweet, caressing palate, which gave the most convincing performance. Tegolaia '06, from cabernet sauvignon and sangiovese, also did well with a complex nose of wild berries and spice followed up by a warm palate with well-distributed tannins and a long, lingering finish. The two Chianti Rufinas were more modest, with a clean nose and supple body, but lacked a little substance. We expect them to redeem themselves promptly over the next few vintages, in view of the excellent work carried out in both the vineyard and the cellar.

● Campo Arsiccio '05	♀♀ 6
○ Campogialli '07	♀ 5
● Chianti Sup. '07	♀ 4
● Pian del Pazzo '05	♀ 6
● Pian del Pazzo '04	♀♀ 6
● Pian del Pazzo '03	♀♀ 6
● Terra di Sasso Sassorlando '05	♀♀ 5

● Tegolaia '06	♀♀ 5
○ Vin Santo Chianti Rufina '01	♀♀ 5
● Chianti Rufina '07	♀ 4
● Chianti Rufina Ris. '06	♀ 5
● Calice del Conte '04	♀♀ 6
● Chianti Rufina Ris. '05	♀♀ 5
● Chianti Rufina Ris. '04	♀♀ 5
● Chianti Rufina Ris. '03	♀♀ 5
● Tegolaia '04	♀♀ 5
○ Vin Santo Chianti Rufina '00	♀♀ 5

Castello del Trebbio

VIA SANTA BRIGIDA, 9
50060 PONTASSIEVE [FI]
TEL. 0558304900
www.vinoturismo.it

ANNUAL PRODUCTION 340,000 bottles
HECTARES UNDER VINE 52
VITICULTURE METHOD Conventional

Trebbio's wines are never banal. The estate so enthusiastically and meticulously run by owner Anna Baj-Macario and her agronomist and expert grower husband Stefano Casadei manages to create very distinctive products that combine personality with pleasant drinkability. In addition to wine, Trebbio also produces olive oil and saffron, a recently revived crop that was grown in the area in ancient times.

This year, the best wine was Chianti Rufina Lastricato Riserva '06, with ripe currants and plums fruit, balsam and spice. Although the palate is not particularly broad, it is taut with a savoury finish. We also liked Merlot '06, which trades in much of its varietal character for terroir. Its gamey and tobacco notes are completed by red fruit before the taut, full palate gives well-distributed tannins and a flavoursome finish. Pazzesco '05, this year from syrah, merlot and sangiovese, is less convincing than usual. It fails to open out on the nose and development on the palate is low key. Chianti '08 is a banker, showing fresh, fruity and very pleasant.

Tenuta di Trinoro

VIA VAL D'ORCIA, 15
53047 SARTEANO [SI]
TEL. 0578267110
www.trinoro.it

ANNUAL PRODUCTION 80,000 bottles
HECTARES UNDER VINE 22
VITICULTURE METHOD Conventional

After distributing fine wines in America in the 1980s, Andrea Franchetti studied oenology in Bordeaux and subsequently moved to Val d'Orcia in the early 1990s, near Sarteano, where he launched his rigorously conceived wine project. The first experimental harvest was in 1995 and the estate's goals were already very clear: absolute excellence from concentrated, vibrant, almost chewy wines. Andrea's uncompromising work has once again been rewarded with another good performance.

Tenuta di Trinoro '07, from cabernet sauvignon, cabernet franc, merlot and petit verdot, has a complex nose and a palate featuring earthy tannins and a soft yet lively progression. Le Cupole di Trinoro '07 is more approachable. Made from the same grapes, but from the estate's younger vineyards, it has a well-rounded nose, with slightly green aromas, and a full, nicely contrasting palate.

● Chianti Rufina Lastricato Ris. '06	♀♀ 5
● Merlot '06	♀♀ 6
● Chianti '08	♀ 2*
● Pazzesco '05	♀ 6
○ Bianco della Congiura '07	♀♀ 5
● Chianti Rufina Lastricato Ris. '04	♀♀ 5
● Chianti Rufina Lastricato Ris. '03	♀♀ 5
● Pazzesco '04	♀♀ 6
● Pazzesco '03	♀♀ 6
● Rosso della Congiura '04	♀♀ 7
● Rosso della Congiura '03	♀♀ 7

● Tenuta di Trinoro '07	♀♀ 8
● Le Cupole di Trinoro '07	♀♀ 6
● Tenuta di Trinoro '04	♀♀♀ 8
● Tenuta di Trinoro '03	♀♀♀ 8
● Le Cupole di Trinoro '06	♀♀ 6
● Le Cupole di Trinoro '05	♀♀ 6
● Le Cupole di Trinoro '03	♀♀ 6
● Le Cupole di Trinoro '02	♀♀ 6
● Tenuta di Trinoro '06	♀♀ 8
● Tenuta di Trinoro '05	♀♀ 8
● Tenuta di Trinoro '01	♀♀ 8

★ Tua Rita

LOC. NOTRI, 81
57028 SUVERETO [LI]
TEL. 0565829237
www.tuarita.it

PRE-BOOKED VISITS

ANNUAL PRODUCTION **8,000 bottles**
HECTARES UNDER VINE **25**
VITICULTURE METHOD **Conventional**

Tua Rita is one of Italy's cult wineries. It made a name for itself in the mid 1990s with its flagship Redigaffi but it has become difficult to confine the estate's appeal to this wine alone. Tua Rita produces modern, structured, big-hitting wines that faithfully reflect their terroir. The vineyards cover around 25 hectares of very high-density plantings on the hillside behind the winery, from which less than 10,000 bottles are produced.

Redigaffi is Redigaffi, need we say more? The '07 vintage of this single-variety Merlot possesses the character we have come to know so well over the years. It shows clean and concentrated on the nose, where notes of ripe black fruit merge with chocolate and menthol. On the palate it is compact and caressing but with the characteristic acidity of grapes grown in the Notri area. We gave it Three Glasses. Syrah '07 has a gorgeously spicy nose and would also have won our top accolade had it not been for its slightly hard tannins. Giusto di Notri '07, from cabernet sauvignon and merlot, displayed its usual elegance.

Uccelliera

FRAZ. CASTELNUOVO DELL'ABATE
POD. UCCELLIERA, 45
53020 MONTALCINO [SI]
TEL. 0577835729
www.uccelliera-montalcino.it

CELLAR SALES
PRE-BOOKED VISITS

ANNUAL PRODUCTION **50,000 bottles**
HECTARES UNDER VINE **6**
VITICULTURE METHOD **Conventional**

Andrea Cotronesi began his adventure at Uccelliera in 1986., but his first Brunello was produced in 1993. It showed its soundness at once. However, Andrea's strong sense of self-criticism – combined with great charm – drove him to embark on a root and branch renovation of the winery, finally completed last year, to improve quality yet further. Despite their relatively low altitude, the vineyards are excellent and adjoin a former onyx quarry that imbues the wines with unique aromas. Andrea enhances these with the use of small oak, mainly tonneaux.

Brunello '04 shows a dense, almost impenetrable colour, with a nose characterized by strongly aromatic oak-derived toast, vanilla and chocolate, and a fruity vein of classic black cherry. There's a touch of over-extraction on the palate with somewhat excessive tannins that detract from its suppleness. Still, this will improve with age.

● Redigaffi '07	♟♟♟ 8
● Giusto di Notri '07	♟♟ 8
● Syrah '07	♟♟ 8
○ Perlato del Bosco Bianco '08	♟ 4
● Perlato del Bosco Rosso '07	♟ 6
● Redigaffi '06	♟♟♟ 8
● Redigaffi '04	♟♟♟ 8
● Redigaffi '03	♟♟♟ 8
● Redigaffi '02	♟♟♟ 8
● Redigaffi '01	♟♟♟ 8
● Redigaffi '00	♟♟♟ 8
● Redigaffi '99	♟♟♟ 8
● Redigaffi '98	♟♟♟ 8
● Redigaffi '96	♟♟♟ 8

● Rosso di Montalcino '07	♟♟ 5
● Brunello di Montalcino '04	♟ 8
● Rapace '06	♟ 6
● Brunello di Montalcino Ris. '97	♟♟♟ 8
● Brunello di Montalcino '01	♟♟ 7
● Brunello di Montalcino '00	♟♟ 7
● Brunello di Montalcino '99	♟♟ 7
● Brunello di Montalcino Ris. '01	♟♟ 8
● Brunello di Montalcino Ris. '99	♟♟ 8
● Rapace '01	♟♟ 6
● Rosso di Montalcino '01	♟♟ 6

Uggiano

LOC. SAN VINCENZO A TORRI
VIA EMPOLESE
50018 SCANDICCI [FI]
TEL. 055769087
www.uggiano.it

CELLAR SALES
PRE-BOOKED VISITS

ANNUAL PRODUCTION 1.200,000 bottles
HECTARES UNDER VINE 80
VITICULTURE METHOD Conventional

Giuseppe Losapio's winery, housed in the castle at Montespertoli near Florence, has once again made it into our Guide. The estate not only bottles a wide range of products from all over Italy, he also produces many wines from both local and international grape varieties. Its own wines tend to be made using traditional techniques in the quest for a style that focuses on drinkability. The estate also produces extra virgin olive oil.

Falconeri '04, from cabernet sauvignon with a splash of sangiovese, is first rate with a charming nose of spice and medicinal herbs accompanied by wafts of chocolate. The palate unveils fine-grained tannins and good acid backbone. Petraia '06, from merlot with a little cabernet sauvignon, is also very good, featuring a medley of fruit and a plush, balanced palate with a long, sweet finish. The two versions of Chianti Colli Fiorentini are more mundane. The Riserva '06 is overburdened with tannins while the '07 vintage offers attractive freshness and drinkability.

Tenuta Valdipiatta

VIA DELLA CIARLIANA, 25A
53040 MONTEPULCIANO [SI]
TEL. 0578757930
www.valdipiatta.it

CELLAR SALES
PRE-BOOKED VISITS
VISITOR FACILITIES

ANNUAL PRODUCTION 120,000 bottles
HECTARES UNDER VINE 32
VITICULTURE METHOD Conventional

Tenuta Valdipiatta was purchased by Giulio Caporali in the late 1980s and in over 20 years of production it has given its wines a well-defined style and original personality, consistently pursuing quality like few others in Montepulciano. Today, the list of wines has acquired a clear-cut style, thanks in part to Giulio's daughter Miriam, who now runs the family business.

The flagship wine is still Nobile di Montepulciano Vigna d'Alfiero, whose '06 vintage again reached our finals for its captivating nose and full-flavoured, nicely contrasting palate. Nobile di Montepulciano '06 is admirable, with a very fruity nose and punchy, well-honed tannins. Pinot Nero '06 came as a pleasant surprise. After delivering the varietal characteristics of the challenging Burgundian grape, this version also manages to offer a little complexity. Vin Santo '04 displays exceptional balance while the other wines presented are all well made.

● Falconeri '04	▼▼ 6
● Petraia '06	▼▼ 6
● Chianti Colli Fiorentini '07	▼ 4
● Chianti Colli Fiorentini Ris. '06	▼ 5
● Chianti Cl. Falco de' Neri '05	▼▼ 4*
● Petraia Merlot '05	▼▼ 6

● Nobile di Montepulciano '06	▼▼ 5
● Nobile di Montepulciano V. d'Alfiero '06	▼▼ 7
● Pinot Nero '06	▼▼ 6
○ Vin Santo di Montepulciano '04	▼▼ 7
● Nobile di Montepulciano Ris. '05	▼ 6
● Rosso di Montepulciano '07	▼ 4
● Nobile di Montepulciano Ris. '90	▼▼▼ 5
● Nobile di Montepulciano V. d'Alfiero '99	▼▼▼ 6
● Nobile di Montepulciano '05	▼▼ 5
● Nobile di Montepulciano '04	▼▼ 5
● Nobile di Montepulciano Ris. '97	▼▼ 5
● Nobile di Montepulciano V. d'Alfiero '05	▼▼ 7
● Nobile di Montepulciano V. d'Alfiero '04	▼▼ 7
● Trincerone '06	▼▼ 6

Tenuta di Valgiano

FRAZ. VALGIANO
VIA DI VALGIANO, 7
55018 LUCCA
TEL. 0583402271
www.valgiano.it

CELLAR SALES

ANNUAL PRODUCTION **70,000 bottles**
HECTARES UNDER VINE **25**
VITICULTURE METHOD **Biodynamic certified**

Valgiano continues to be a benchmark for all serious wine aficionados. Its embrace of organic agriculture, completed some ten years ago, seems to have forged the closest of bonds between its staff and their terroir. It would be hard to think of Valgiano without conjuring up the features of its owners, Moreno Petrini and Laura di Collobiano, or admiring the charisma of oenologist Saverio Petrilli. Valgiano's human faces and voices are adumbrated in its wines, which are still personal and always full of passion.

Colline Lucchesi Tenuta di Valgiano '06, with its utter elegance and finesse, again won Three Glasses. We were again persuaded not by suppleness or smooth fruit as by its energy-laden body. Earthy notes enrich dark berry fruit and spice on the nose, followed by the broadest of palates almost pulsating with acidity and lively fruit. Overall, this is a wine that has left behind the niceties of oenological parsing to make a profound, personal affirmation on its own wavelength. Colline Lucchesi Palistorti Rosso '07 combines its usual clean-edged aromas with a nervy, tannic palate. Colline Lucchesi Palistorti Bianco '08 is equally delicious.

Vecchie Terre di Montefili

VIA SAN CRESCI, 45
50022 PANZANO [FI]
TEL. 055853739
www.vecchieterredimontefili.com

CELLAR SALES
PRE-BOOKED VISITS

ANNUAL PRODUCTION **40,000 bottles**
HECTARES UNDER VINE **13.5**
VITICULTURE METHOD **Conventional**

Under the ownership of the Acuti family since 1979, Vecchie Terre di Montefili has gradually become one of the top-notch operations in Chianti Classico. The cellar considers itself held by the confines neither of Chianti Classico nor of sangiovese however, since it believes its terroir is capable of fine results with the internationals as well. Despite this modernity of approach, the wines effectively reflect their terroir. Helpful in this respect is sapient use of the barrel, which allows the local hillslopes to have their full say.

We were presented with only a single wine this year, the superb Chianti Classico '06, a wine of absolutely classic lineaments. The nose lays out a kaleidoscope of crisp, crunchy red berry fruit, dried blossoms, medicinal herbs and moist earth, followed by impressively taut tension in the mouth. Well-measured tannins are girdered by vibrant, self-confident acidity that drives through to a fruity, remarkably elegant finish of terrific length and depth. We await with bated breath for the '06 editions of the two house bluebloods, Anfiteatro and Bruno di Rocca.

● Colline Lucchesi Tenuta di Valgiano '06	ҮҮҮ+	7
○ Colline Lucchesi Palistorti Bianco '08	ҮҮ	5
● Colline Lucchesi Palistorti Rosso '07	ҮҮ	5
● Colline Lucchesi Tenuta di Valgiano '05	ҰҰҰ	7
● Colline Lucchesi Tenuta di Valgiano '04	ҰҰҰ	7
● Colline Lucchesi Tenuta di Valgiano '03	ҰҰҰ	7
● Colline Lucchesi Tenuta di Valgiano '01	ҰҰҰ	8
● Colline Lucchesi Tenuta di Valgiano '02	ҰҰ	7
● Colline Lucchesi Tenuta di Valgiano '00	ҰҰ	8

● Chianti Cl. '06	ҮҮ	5
● Anfiteatro '03	ҰҰҰ	8
● Anfiteatro '94	ҰҰҰ	8
● Anfiteatro '05	ҰҰ	8
● Anfiteatro '04	ҰҰ	8
● Anfiteatro '01	ҰҰ	8
● Bruno di Rocca '05	ҰҰ	7
● Bruno di Rocca '04	ҰҰ	8
● Bruno di Rocca '01	ҰҰ	8
● Bruno di Rocca '99	ҰҰ	8

La Velona

LOC. CASTELNUOVO DELL'ABATE
POD. PIETRANERA, 30
53024 MONTALCINO [SI]
TEL. 0577835525
www.lavolona.com

CELLAR SALES
PRE-BOOKED VISITS
VISITOR FACILITIES

ANNUAL PRODUCTION 60,000 bottles
HECTARES UNDER VINE 12
VITICULTURE METHOD Conventional

This lovely estate lies on the road from Castelnuovo dell'Abate towards Monte Amiata, its vineyards enjoying an optimal southwest-facing position. Planted to medium densities, the vines seem as classic as the oak vats used for the fermentations of both Brunello di Montalcino and Mefysto. Velona's owners, originally from Naples, craft a Brunello di Montalcino that is a magisterial synthesis of the modern and traditionalist styles. Ageing is initially in 50-hectolitre casks and then a year or so in barriques.

Brunello di Montalcino flaunts an intriguing complex of dark cherry and peach shot through with compelling notes of incense, tobacco leaf and tar. No less appealing is the compact, dense and satisfyingly long palate, with tannins already well incorporated and nervy acidity. Everything portends a lengthy, promising future. Sant'Antimo Mefysto is no less finely fashioned, showing quite ductile and approachable. Not the curviest of wines, it exhibits instead an appreciable, finely sculpted elegance.

I Veroni

VIA TIFARITI, 5
50065 PONTASSIEVE [FI]
TEL. 0558368886
www.iveroni.it

CELLAR SALES
PRE-BOOKED VISITS
VISITOR FACILITIES
FOOD

ANNUAL PRODUCTION 80,000 bottles
HECTARES UNDER VINE 15
VITICULTURE METHOD Naturale

Meriting a return to the full profiles is Laura Malesci's wine estate, which is managed with passionate verve by her son, Lorenzo Mariani. This young, wine-driven lawyer has created in just a few years a forward-looking winery, ably assisted by an equally youthful and highly motivated staff. Their modus operandi – attention to details, respect for the environment, conversion to organics in process and a weather eye out for useful innovation – has brought Veroni very satisfactory showings.

This year, too, Chianti Rufina Riserva '06 was out in front of the pack. Pungent balsam, vanilla and fresh greens are a tasty foil to richer impressions of blackberry and blackcurrant. Tannins that are just a tad drying detract nothing from a spacious palate and a toothsome, long-running finish. Vin Santo is fine, but displays an unusual piquancy, expanding beautifully, its fabric silk smooth and its finish as lengthy as one would want. Chianti Rufina '07 is soundly made, a crisp, refreshing quaffer.

● Brunello di Montalcino '04	♊♊	8
● Sant'Antimo Rosso Mefysto '06	♊♊	7
● Brunello di Montalcino '02	♈♈	8
● Brunello di Montalcino '01	♈♈	8
● Brunello di Montalcino '00	♈♈	8
● Brunello di Montalcino '99	♈♈	8
● Rosso di Montalcino '05	♈♈	6
● Rosso di Montalcino '04	♈♈	6
● Rosso di Montalcino '03	♈♈	6
● Rosso di Montalcino '01	♈♈	4
● Sant'Antimo Rosso Mefysto '03	♈♈	7
● Sant'Antimo Rosso Mefysto '01	♈♈	7

● Chianti Rufina Ris. '06	♊♊	5
○ Vin Santo del Chianti Rufina '02	♊♊	6
● Chianti Rufina '07	♊	4
● Chianti Rufina '06	♈♈	4*
● Chianti Rufina '05	♈♈	3*
● Chianti Rufina Ris. '04	♈♈	4
○ Vin Santo del Chianti Rufina '99	♈♈	5

Castello di Vicchiomaggio

LOC. LE BOLLE
VIA VICCHIOMAGGIO, 4
50022 GREVE IN CHIANTI [FI]
TEL. 055854079
www.vicchiomaggio.it

CELLAR SALES
PRE-BOOKED VISITS

ANNUAL PRODUCTION **300,000 bottles**
HECTARES UNDER VINE **33**
VITICULTURE METHOD **Conventional**

Castello di Vicchiomaggio's battlemented tower, rising proudly over the valley of river Greve, is a point of reference for the winery's vineyards as well, which amount to some 33 hectares. The Marra family acquired Vicchiomaggio in 1964, and John Matta, who currently directs the operation, took over the reins in 1982. His deep familiarity with the area and his sensitive touch have made possible the growth in quality of the wines from this property.

The wines continue to impress. Ripa delle More '06, from cabernet, sangiovese and merlot, vaunts an array of superbly defined fragrances of blackcurrant, dark cherry and vanilla, then well-fuelled progression and a palate of masterfully judicious extraction. Chianti Classico Riserva La Prima '06 is admirably terroir-driven. Fragrant blossoms linger on the nose, and a spacious palate offers luscious fruit lifted by a zippy vein of tasty acidity. We found Chianti Classico Riserva Agostino Petri da Vicchiomaggio '06 delicious, with fruit and spice introducing a perfectly crafted palate. Chianti Classico San Jacopo '07 is a reliable favourite.

Villa Cafaggio

VIA SAN MARTINO A CECIONE, 5
50020 PANZANO [FI]
TEL. 0558549094
www.villacafaggio.it

CELLAR SALES
PRE-BOOKED VISITS

ANNUAL PRODUCTION **400,000 bottles**
HECTARES UNDER VINE **40**
VITICULTURE METHOD **Conventional**

Villa Cafaggio, part of the Trentino-based Lavis group since 2005, is located in Panzano, in Chianti Classico's prestigious "Conca d'Oro". Forty of its 60 hectares are in vineyard, most of it planted to sangiovese, with some cabernet sauvignon as well. A long-term growth and marketing plan, which includes the acquisition of new vineyard properties, has given a spurt of energy to a producer always considered one of Italy's finest.

Chianti Classico Riserva '06 releases violets and black berry fruit that yield to evolved notes of moist earth. Well-extracted tannins caress a palate of fine heft and a lengthy finish is tasty and balsamic. Cortaccio '05, made from three clones of cabernet, shrugs off a difficult vintage. Remarkably well-defined aromas of blackcurrant, liquorice and herbs compel attention, as does its perfect balance in the mouth with the right degree of power, concentration and well-ripened tannins. The all-sangiovese San Martino '05 opens to generous dark berry and smooth spice, then unfurls a fine progression that an excess of tannins brings up a bit short.

● Chianti Cl. La Prima Ris. '06	♥♥ 7
● Ripa delle More '06	♥♥ 8
● Chianti Cl. Agostino Petri da Vicchiomaggio Ris. '06	♥♥ 6
● Chianti Cl. San Jacopo '07	♥ 5
● FSM '04	♥♥♥ 8
● Ripa delle More '97	♥♥♥ 6
● Ripa delle More '94	♥♥♥ 5
● FSM '05	♥♥ 8
● Ripa delle More '05	♥♥ 8

● Chianti Cl. Ris. '06	♥♥ 6
● Cortaccio '05	♥♥ 8
● San Martino '05	♥♥ 8
● Chianti Cl. '07	♥ 5
● Chianti Cl. Ris. '03	♥♥♥ 6
● Cortaccio '01	♥♥♥ 8
● Cortaccio '97	♥♥♥ 6
● Cortaccio '93	♥♥♥ 6
● San Martino '00	♥♥♥ 8
● San Martino '99	♥♥♥ 7
● San Martino '98	♥♥♥ 6
● San Martino '97	♥♥♥ 5

Villa di Geggiano

LOC. PONTE A BOZZONE
VIA DI GEGGIANO, 1
53019 CASTELNUOVO BERARDENGA [SI]
TEL. 0577356879
www.villadigeggiano.com

CELLAR SALES
PRE-BOOKED VISITS

ANNUAL PRODUCTION 35,000 bottles
HECTARES UNDER VINE 8
VITICULTURE METHOD Organic certified

Villa di Geggiano, with origins that go back to the 15th century, is located in Castelnuovo Berardenga, in the southern extremity of the Chianti Classico zone. The Bianchi Bandinelli family own the estate and manage its eight hectares of vineyard, out of the property's total of about 20. The vines are planted in galestro soils rich in silt and tufa, studded generously with cobbles, characteristics which yield refined wines with a pronounced mineral-salt tang, the hallmark of this terroir.

Chianti Classico '07 is spot on, displaying varietally faithful floral and citrus notes, with a fragrant thread of spice. Delicious and distinctive, its fine tannins and juicy fruit complement very dynamic progression. Chianti Classico Riserva '06 is along the same general lines but with a riper nose, showing dark-fleshed fruit and black liquorice interwoven with hints of earth. A lithe but luxurious progression winds down a bit too soon, though. Sangiovese, cabernet and syrah give Geggiaiolo '06 a fascinating, rich texture, following a mélange of spice, spring blossoms and balsam. Its savoury vein of acidity propels an exemplary development.

Villa Petriolo

VIA DI PETRIOLO, 7
50050 CERRETO GUIDI [FI]
TEL. 057155284
www.villapetriolo.com

PRE-BOOKED VISITS

ANNUAL PRODUCTION 55.500 bottles
HECTARES UNDER VINE 14
VITICULTURE METHOD Conventional

Since Silvia Maestrelli took over the family operation, she has been active on many fronts. In addition to launching a winery in Sicily and creating a closely watched literary prize, she brought many changes to Villa Petriolo, in particular to a house style that had been somewhat stodgy up to that point. Research in both vineyard and cellar has aimed at preserving the integrity of the fruit, which both the nose and palate of current wines amply reveals. We were unable to taste Golpaja and Vin Santo, still reposing in the cellar, but the other wines more than consoled us.

Take L'Imbrunire '08, which competed in our final round. Made exclusively of canaiolo, it boasts an ethereal blend of delicate blossoms and deliciously ripe fruit that segues into a fluid, high-register development that one appreciates immediately but wishes would last a tad longer. Rosae Mnemosis '08 is another seductress, first revealing intense purity of fruit, with dark cherry and strawberry first to emerge, then offering a thrilling succulence and well tucked-in tannins, to conclude with a self-confident, delicious finish. Chianti '08 is as tasty as you could wish.

● Chianti Cl. '07	♟♟ 4*
● Chianti Cl. Ris. '06	♟♟ 6
● Geggiaiolo '06	♟♟ 7
◉ Chianti Cl. Ris. '04	♟♟ 6

● L'Imbrunire '08	♟♟ 5
● Chianti Rosae Mnemosis '08	♟♟ 5
● Chianti Villa Petriolo '08	♟ 4
● Chianti Rosae Mnemosis '07	♟♟ 5
● Chianti Rosae Mnemosis '06	♟♟ 5
● Golpaja '06	♟♟ 5
● Golpaja '05	♟♟ 5

Villa Pillo

VIA VOLTERRANA, 24
50050 GAMBASSI TERME [FI]
TEL. 0571680212
www.villapillo.com

CELLAR SALES
PRE-BOOKED VISITS

ANNUAL PRODUCTION **300,000 bottles**
HECTARES UNDER VINE **40**
VITICULTURE METHOD **Conventional**

This year, Villa Pillo turned in performances that were less stellar than in the past. The Dyson husband and wife team have been working as growers for over 20 years now, with great dedication and passion. They have over 200 hectares on the estate, with 40 under vine. A total re-planting of what the previous owners put in has almost been completed and numerous internationals have been added to the predominant sangiovese.

The all-sangiovese Cypresses '07 is a natural standout. Emphatic notes of fresh greens quickly give way to smoother fruit, and the mouth, rich and full, exhibits splendid, savoury fruit and a tasty acidity. Syrah '07 also made a good showing. After initial hesitation, it flaunts classic black pepper and rich raw leather, then builds an energy-laden progression that has all of its tannins well in place, to end finally in full succulence. The other wines lack clarity on the nose, witness Sant'Adele '07, all merlot but too tannic, and the all-cabernet franc Vivaldaia '07, whose admirable, sturdy structure ends up hobbling it somewhat at the end.

● Cypresses '07	♟♟	4*
● Syrah '07	♟♟	6
● Borgoforte '07	♟	4
● Merlot Sant'Adele '07	♟	6
● Vivaldaia '07	♟	6
● Syrah '97	♟♟♟	5
● Borgoforte '06	♟♟	4*
● Merlot Sant'Adele '06	♟♟	6
● Syrah '06	♟♟	6
● Syrah '05	♟♟	6
○ Vin Santo del Chianti '99	♟♟	7
● Vivaldaia '06	♟♟	6

Villa Vignamaggio

VIA DI PETRIOLO, 5
50022 GREVE IN CHIANTI [FI]
TEL. 055854661
www.vignamaggio.com

CELLAR SALES
PRE-BOOKED VISITS
VISITOR FACILITIES
FOOD

ANNUAL PRODUCTION **200,000 bottles**
HECTARES UNDER VINE **42**
VITICULTURE METHOD **Conventional**

Villa Vignamaggio takes in 160 hectares in the municipality of Greve in Chianti. When owner Gianni Nunziante purchased the property in 1988, the historic residence was transformed from an architectural reliquary into the functioning headquarters of a dynamic agricultural estate. In its 42 hectares of vineyards, sangiovese reigns but cabernet franc, from very old vines, makes impressive monovarietals, in particular Vignamaggio.

Vignamaggio, always superb, effortlessly claims Three Glasses with its '06. An initial herbaceousness glides into dark berry and crisp mint while the palate betrays a beguiling elegance, with a fabric of silky tannins. With energy to spare, it drives to a long-lasting finale edged with tasty redcurrant. Spring blossoms and spice enrich the delicate fruit offered by Chianti Classico Riserva Monna Lisa '06, which turns austere in the mouth with fairly tight tannins but one still appreciates a certain depth and juiciness. The standard Chianti Classico and Chianti Classico Terre di Prenzano '07 show less complex but of magisterial construction.

● Vignamaggio '06	♟♟♟	8
● Chianti Cl. Monna Lisa Ris. '06	♟♟	6
● Chianti Cl. '07	♟	5
● Chianti Cl. Terre di Prenzano '07	♟	4
● Il Morino '07	♟	3
● Obsession '06	♟	7
● Chianti Cl. Monna Lisa Ris. '99	♟♟♟	6
● Chianti Cl. Monna Lisa Ris. '95	♟♟♟	4
● Vignamaggio '05	♟♟♟	8
● Vignamaggio '04	♟♟♟	7
● Vignamaggio '01	♟♟♟	7
● Vignamaggio '00	♟♟♟	7

Vistarenni

LOC. VISTARENNI
53013 GAIOLE IN CHIANTI [SI]
TEL. 0577738186
www.vistarenni.com

CELLAR SALES
PRE-BOOKED VISITS

ANNUAL PRODUCTION **67,000 bottles**
HECTARES UNDER VINE **77**
VITICULTURE METHOD **Conventional**

This profile covers both of the Santa Margherita group's Tuscan properties, Villa Vistarenni and Lamole di Lamole. The first, located in the municipality of Gaiole, has more than 30 hectares under vine, in addition to olive groves and woods. The latter, in Greve, has 47 hectares of vineyards in somewhat unusual conditions. The holding is divided up into many small parcels, many of them on steep, terraced hillslopes.

We immediately took a liking to Vistarenni's Chianti Classico Riserva '06, which shows lively blueberry and redcurrant accompanied by an elegant floral foil. The mouth shows plenty of delicious, full-fleshed fruit, with a creamy, luscious mid-palate, followed by fine length on the finish. Lamole's Campolungo Riserva '06 impresses immediately, with smooth spice, a dynamic progression and a spacious conclusion. Likewise superb is the more straightforward but pleasingly taut, earthy and crunchy Chianti Classico '07. Etichetta Blu '07 and Etichetta Bianca '07 are fine but offer nothing unexpected.

Tenuta Vitereta

VIA CASANUOVA, 108/1
52020 LATERINA [AR]
TEL. 057589058
www.tenutavitereta.com

CELLAR SALES
PRE-BOOKED VISITS
VISITOR FACILITIES
FOOD

ANNUAL PRODUCTION **80,000 bottles**
HECTARES UNDER VINE **45**
VITICULTURE METHOD **Organic certified**

Vitereta, owned by the Bidini and Del Tongo families, produces quite a cornucopia of wines. It also produces olive oil, raises sheep for cheesemaking plus pigs for cured meats for their own use, and grows various cereals on a large expanse of over 50 hectares. Vitereta is in fact an agricultural estate worthy of the name, with wines that display generous character and are never banal.

Vitereta's star this year is Vin Santo '04. A deep amber announces the enrapturing panoply of fragrances. Amazing profundity and length in the mouth accompany judicious and never excessive sweetness. We liked Trebbiano '07, partly made with semi-dried grapes, which gives it well-ripened fruit on the nose, nicely cut with minerally impressions. Nervy acidity makes it lithe and dynamic in the mouth and the finale brims with tangy flavours. The cabernet Villa Bernetti '05 is a first-rate effort, crisp on the nose, with solid development and excellent length. All of the other wines are soundly made.

● Chianti Cl. Campolungo Ris. '06	♟♟ 5
● Chianti Cl. Lamole di Lamole '07	♟♟ 4*
● Chianti Cl. Ris. '06	♟♟ 4*
● Chianti Cl. Lamole di Lamole Et. Bianca '07	♟ 4
● Chianti Cl. Lamole di Lamole Et. Blu '07	♟ 4
● Chianti Cl. '06	♟♟ 4*
● Chianti Cl. Lamole di Lamole '03	♟♟ 4*
● Chianti Cl. Ris. '05	♟♟ 4*

○ Trebbiano di Toscana '07	♟♟ 5
● Villa Bernetti '05	♟♟ 5
○ Vin Santo del Chianti '04	♟♟ 8
● Capitoni '07	♟ 5
○ Donna Aurora '07	♟ 5
● Ripa della Mozza '06	♟ 5
● Capitoni '06	♟♟ 4
● Capitoni '05	♟♟ 4*
● Villa Bernetti '04	♟♟ 5
○ Vin Santo '03	♟♟ 8

Viticcio

VIA SAN CRESCI, 12A
50022 GREVE IN CHIANTI [FI]
TEL. 055854210
www.fattoriaviticcio.com

CELLAR SALES
PRE-BOOKED VISITS
VISITOR FACILITIES

ANNUAL PRODUCTION 200,000 bottles
HECTARES UNDER VINE 35
VITICULTURE METHOD Naturale

Alessandro Landini's father purchased Viticcio in the 1960s, when many rural folk were heading to the cities. Improvements and changes over the years have made it a superb producer, including replanting of the vineyards and a makeover of the cellar. Its adoption of barriques, though, dates surprisingly far back, to 1985.

Chianti Classico Beatrice Riserva '06 is still in the process of digesting some oak tones but it nevertheless displays superb construction. Aromatics are nice and tight, with morello and blackberry foregrounding subtle hints of balsam, and the palate boasts smooth, tasty oak. Chianti Classico '07 is spot on, its notes of smooth vanilla and subtle herbaceousness quite pleasing, as are the succulent, juicy fruit in the mouth and its impressive volume. We were less impressed with Riserva '06, which still labours under a heavy load of oak.

Castello di Volpaia

LOC. VOLPAIA
P.ZZA DELLA CISTERNA, 1
53017 RADDA IN CHIANTI [SI]
TEL. 0577738066
www.volpaia.com

CELLAR SALES
PRE-BOOKED VISITS
VISITOR FACILITIES
FOOD

ANNUAL PRODUCTION 250,000 bottles
HECTARES UNDER VINE 46
VITICULTURE METHOD Organic certified

Volpaia is simply a magical place. For the charm of the hamlet, of course, but mostly because everything there has always revolved around wine production: the narrow lanes, the deconsecrated church and everyone living there, not to mention the fantastic underground "vinoduct". It is a terrific accomplishment for the Mascheroni Stianti family that their endeavour is so successful in a challenging area for Chianti Classico production, since vines here are at elevations reaching 500 metres. The wines are flawless, thanks to up-to-date practices and to their enchanting terroir.

Three bottlings stand out. Three Glasses right off the bat for the all-sangiovese Il Puro '06, a stunning wine, all of whose proceeds are turned over to Save the Children. Hardly less superb is Balifico '06, of sangioveto and cabernet. On the nose, aromas of spice and delicate hints of grass seem to expand forever while the palate, filled with meaty fruit, is a brilliant exercise in continuous contrasts between smoothness and acidity. On the same rung is the truly classic and utterly delicious Chianti Classico Riserva '06. Not far behind is the other Riserva '06, Coltassala, a tad riper and more rounded.

● Chianti Cl. '07	♟♟ 4*
● Chianti Cl. Beatrice Ris. '06	♟♟ 6
● Bolgheri Greppicante I Greppi '07	♟ 4
● Chianti Cl. Ris. '06	♟ 5
● Monile '06	♟ 7
● Prunaio '06	♟ 7
● Prunaio '99	♟♟♟ 7
● Chianti Cl. '06	♟♟ 4*
● Chianti Cl. Ris. '05	♟♟ 5
● Greppicaia I Greppi '05	♟♟ 6
● Prunaio '06	♟♟ 7
● Prunaio '05	♟♟ 7

● Chianti Cl. Il Puro Vign. Casanova Ris. '06	♟♟♟ 8
● Balifico '06	♟♟ 7
● Chianti Cl. Ris. '06	♟♟ 6
● Chianti Cl. Coltassala Ris. '06	♟♟ 7
○ Vin Santo del Chianti Cl. '03	♟♟ 6
● Balifico '00	♟♟♟ 7
● Chianti Cl. Coltassala Ris. '04	♟♟♟ 7
● Chianti Cl. Coltassala Ris. '01	♟♟♟ 7
○ Bianco '07	♟♟ 4*
● Chianti Cl. Ris. '05	♟♟ 6
● Prelius Morello di Prile '07	♟♟ 4*
○ Vin Santo del Chianti Cl. '98	♟♟ 6

Acquabona

LOC. ACQUABONA
57037 PORTOFERRAIO [LI]
TEL. 0565933013
www.acquabonaelba.it

There was a good performance from this estate, perhaps the oldest in Elba, which farms about 14 hectares on this lovely island in the Tuscan archipelago. Aleatico '06 is an exemplar of its type. It gives Mediterranean scrub and sour cherry followed by a mouthfilling body braced by long, bright acidity.

● Aleatico dell'Elba '06	♥♥	6
● Elba Rosso '07	♥	4
● Voltraio '07	♥	5
● Aleatico dell'Elba '05	♀♀	6

Altura

LOC. MOLINACCIO
58012 GIGLIO [GR]
TEL. 0564806106
www.arcobalena.net

Francesco Carfagna's Ansonico is different each year, thanks to the dry climate of Isola del Giglio. It is an extreme wine, made with the heart, with the heart of the territory in the bottle. The '08 is deep gold with warm aromas and notes of candied fruit. The palate is caressing and long-lingering.

○ Ansonaco '08	♥♥	6
○ Ansonico dell'Isola del Giglio '07	♀♀	5

Argiano

FRAZ. SANT'ANGELO IN COLLE
53024 MONTALCINO [SI]
TEL. 0577844037
www.argiano.net

At last, there are signs of recovery in the designation wines at this lovely, historic winery in the south-west of Montalcino. Paler than usual, the Brunello '04 is consistent in style, with a nice smoky note, ripe cherries and an unobtrusive touch of balsam. The Rosso di Montalcino '07 is good.

● Brunello di Montalcino '04	♥♥	7
● Rosso di Montalcino '07	♥♥	5
● Brunello di Montalcino Ris. '88	♀♀♀	6
● Solengo '97	♀♀♀	8

Fattoria dell'Aiola

LOC. VAGLIAGLI
53019 CASTELNUOVO BERARDENGA [SI]
TEL. 0577322615
www.aiola.net

This estate was bought in the 1930s by the family of Maria Grazia Malagodi, who runs it today, so it can justifiably be considered as one of the historic Chianti Classico wineries. The most convincing wine this year is the intensely flowery, full-bodied '07 Chianti Classico.

● Chianti Cl. '07	♥♥	4*
● Chianti Cl. Cancello Rosso Ris. '06	♥	7
● Chianti Cl. Ris. '06	♥	5
● Logaiolo '06	♥	4

Fattoria Ambra

VIA LOMBARDA, 85
59015 CARMIGNANO [PO]
TEL. 3358282552
www.fattoriaambra.it

This is a distinctly under par performance from the Rigoli family. All the wines are decent but a long way from the quality that made them stand out until very recently. There is a long list of Carmignano vineyard selections. We look forward to a swift, certain recovery.

● Carmignano Elzana Ris. '06	♥	5
● Carmignano		
Le Vigne Alte di Montalbiolo Ris. '06	♥	5
● Carmignano V. di Montefortini '07	♥	4
● Carmignano V. S. Cristina in Pilli '04	♥	4

Baroncini

LOC. CASALE, 43
53037 SAN GIMIGNANO [SI]
TEL. 0577940600
www.baroncini.it

The long-established winery founded by Jaurès Baroncini offers a huge range of San Gimignano and Tuscan wines. We picked out the generously soft and fruity San Gimignano Rosso Il Casato '05, the classic, forward Vernaccia Sovestro '08s and the barrique-aged Riserva Dometaia '07.

● S. Gimignano Rosso Il Casato '05	♥	5
○ Vernaccia di S. Gimignano Dometaia Ris. '07	♥	4
○ Vernaccia di S. Gimignano		
Poggio ai Cannici Sovestro '08	♥	4

Pietro Beconcini

FRAZ. LA SCALA
VIA MONTORZO, 13A
56020 SAN MINIATO [PI]
TEL. 0571464570
www.pietrobeconcini.com

Wines from the Beconcini winery are edgy and tight in youth, only to expand magnificently later on. The sangiovese-only '06 Reciso '06 needs a few years before it will be at its best. In the meantime, try Maurleo '07, made from sangiovese and malvasia nera grapes.

● Maurleo '07	♟♟ 4
● Reciso '06	♟♟ 6
○ Vin Santo del Chianti '01	♟♟ 6
● Ixe '07	♟ 4

Tenuta Belguardo

LOC. MONTEBOTTIGLI - VIII ZONA
58100 GROSSETO
TEL. 057773571
www.belguardo.it

As ever, Mazzeis' Maremma winery did well. Serrata di Belguardo '07 is as outstandingly drinkable as ever. From sangiovese and alicante, it gives a fresh nose with berries and medicinal herbs, then a taut, juicy palate. Tenuta '06, from the two cabernets, has yet to absorb its oak.

● Serrata di Belguardo '07	♟♟ 5
● Morellino di Scansano Bronzone '07	♟ 6
⊙ Rosé Belguardo '08	♟ 5
● Tenuta Belguardo '06	♟ 8

Borgo Scopeto

LOC. VAGLIAGLI
53010 CASTELNUOVO BERARDENGA [SI]
TEL. 0577322729
www.borgoscopeto.com

This Chianti estate is owned by Elisabetta Gnudi Angelini, proprietor of the Caparzo and Altesino wineries in Montalcino and La Doga at Magliano in Maremma. Chianti Classico Misciano Riserva '06 is a satisfying wine with aromas of flowers and blackcurrants, and a broad, nicely complex palate.

● Chianti Cl. Misciano Ris. '06	♟♟ 5
● Chianti Cl. '07	♟ 4

Tenuta Bossi

LOC. BOSSI
VIA DELLO STRACCHINO, 32
50065 PONTASSIEVE [FI]
TEL. 0558317830
www.gondi.com

The Marchesi Gondi estate is in an incipient transitional phase. A few of the most representative wines were missing but overall results were positive, with the two versions of Chianti Rufina showing well defined. The absolutely classic Vin Santo '01 is a stand-out.

○ Vin Santo del Chianti Rufina Cardinal de Retz Ris. '01	♟♟ 5
● Chianti Rufina San Giuliano '07	♟ 3
● Chianti Rufina Villa di Bossi Ris. '06	♟ 4
○ Colli dell'Etruria Centrale Sassobianco '08	♟ 3

Buccia Nera

LOC. CAMPRIANO, 10
52100 AREZZO
TEL. 0575361040
www.buccianera.it

This has been a good year for the Mancinis, who also produce honey and oil. Their range of wines is vast: Il Camprianese '07, from sangiovese and ciliegiolo, is fresh and deliciously drinkable. The rest are decent, especially the rich, tasty Amadio '07, from sangiovese with merlot and cabernet sauvignon.

● Amadio '07	♟♟ 4*
○ Chardonnay '07	♟ 4
● Chianti Sassocupo '07	♟ 4
● Il Camprianese '07	♟ 2*

Bulichella

LOC. BULICHELLA, 131
57028 SUVERETO [LI]
TEL. 0565829892
www.bulichella.it

La Bulichella is a quality benchmark for wine in Val di Cornia. Rubino '08 is a wine with a deep nose of berry fruit and a close-knit palate that tends to dry the otherwise fine body. Tuscanio '06 has a tantalizing spice and fruit nose.

● Val di Cornia Rosso Rubino '08	♟♟ 4
● Val di Cornia Col di Pietre Rosse '06	♟ 7
● Val di Cornia Rosso Tuscanio '06	♟ 6
● Val di Cornia Rosso Tuscanio '05	♟♟ 6

Caccia al Piano 1868

VIA BOLGHERESE, 279
57022 CASTAGNETO CARDUCCI [LI]
TEL. 056557022
www.berlucchi.it

It wasn't a huge performance by Guido Berlucchi's Bolgheri branch. There are around 20 hectares of vines, all at Castagneto Carducci. When we tasted, Bolgheri Levia Gravia '05 was still a little dry from the wood. Time will improve it. Ruit Hora '07 is somewhat muddled.

● Bolgheri Levia Gravia '05	♟♟ 8
● Bolgheri Ruit Hora '07	♟ 6

Camperchi

LOC. LA CORNIA
VIA DEL BURRONE, 38
52040 CIVITELLA IN VAL DI CHIANA [AR]
TEL. 0575440281
www.camperchi.com

The estate, in the Val di Chiana and Val del Casentino area, has 130 hectares, of which 24 are under vine. There were two bottles on offer. We preferred the '07 Merlot, with its marked minerality on the nose, complex fruit, juicy body and well-distributed tannins.

● Merlot '07	♟♟ 7
● Anno 0 '07	♟ 4
● Merlot '06	♟♟ 7

Campo del Monte
Eredi Benito Mantellini

VIA TRAIANA, 53A
52028 TERRANUOVA BRACCIOLINI [AR]
TEL. 0554684135
www.campodelmonte.it

Seven of Campo del Monte's 30 hectares are given over to vines. The Rodos '06, from cabernet sauvignon only, mingles scents of fruit with green notes, a full, soft body and a splendid finish. The Chianti Campo del Monte '07 is pleasantly fruity.

● Rodos '06	♟♟ 4*
○ Campo del Monte '08	♟ 3
● Chianti Campo del Monte '07	♟ 3

Camporignano

FRAZ. MONTEGUIDI
53031 CASOLE D'ELSA [SI]
TEL. 0577963915
www.camporignano.it

There's a Guide debut for this winery, which has attained serious quality in a few short years. Ten hectares out of the 40 available are under vine. The merlot and cabernet sauvignon Cerronero '06 is good, with rich vanilla and cinnamon-veined blackberry and cherry aromatics and a warm, enfolding palate.

● Cerronero '06	♟♟ 6
● Camporignano '07	♟ 4
● Mattaione '07	♟ 5

Podere Campriano

V.LE ROSA LIBRI, 36A
50022 GREVE IN CHIANTI [FI]
TEL. 055853688
www.poderecampriano.it

Podere Campriano is a small estate in Greve in Chianti, with three hectares under vine. The wines are well made and typical of the terroir. The Chianti Classico '06 is fragrant and drinkable, with floral and citrus hints also present in the deep, long-lingering Riserva Le Balze di Montefioralle '06.

● Chianti Cl. '06	♟♟ 4*
● Chianti Cl. Le Balze di Montefioralle Ris. '06	♟♟ 5

Canneto

VIA DEI CANNETI, 14
53045 MONTEPULCIANO [SI]
TEL. 0578757737
www.canneto.com

The Filippone '06, from a blend of sangiovese and merlot, is again top of the range of wines produced by Ottorino De Angelis, showing very well made, harmonious and nicely balanced. The Nobile '06 is good, solid and fruit-rich, as is the Nobile Riserva '05, despite its slightly roughish tannins.

● Filippone '06	♟♟ 6
● Nobile di Montepulciano '06	♟ 5
● Nobile di Montepulciano Ris. '05	♟ 5
● Filippone '05	♟♟ 6

Capoverso

LOC. BADELLE
VIA DI GRACCIANO NEL CORSO, 85
53045 MONTEPULCIANO [SI]
TEL. 0578757921
www.vinicapoverso.com

The Nobile '06 from Adriana Avignonesi della Lucilla's winery is well focused, with aromas that are shy at first but then opens up beautifully clean, with a palate that is approachable, well built and has a nice savoury note in the finish. The Rosso di Montepulciano '07 is uncomplicated and very lean.

● Nobile di Montepulciano '06	♟♟	5
● Rosso di Montepulciano '07	♟	4
● Cartiglio '05	♟♟	7
● Nobile di Montepulciano '05	♟♟	5

Cappella Sant'Andrea

LOC. CASALE, 26
53037 SAN GIMIGNANO [SI]
TEL. 0577940456
a.leoncini@valdelsa.net

Vernaccia Rialto '07 is the best wine from Antonella Leoncini's small winery. It has a well co-ordinated nose with scents of white-fleshed fruit and notes of vanilla followed by a full body and a tangy finish. The Vernaccia '08 is up to scratch but the reds are less focused.

○ Vernaccia di S. Gimignano Rialto '07	♟♟	4*
● Chianti Colli Senesi Arciduca '07	♟	4
● S. Gimignano Rosso Serreto '05	♟	4
○ Vernaccia di S. Gimignano '08	♟	3

Casa Dei

LOC. SAN ROCCO
57028 SUVERETO [LI]
TEL. 0558300411
info@tenutacasadei.it

Casa Dei confirms that it is doing good work in the challenging Val di Cornia territory. Filare 41 '07, from monovarietal petit verdot, is the wine that impressed us most. It has aromas of ripe fruit and vegetal notes preceding a palate still marked by wood. The Sogno Mediterraneo '07 is highly drinkable.

● Filare 41 '07	♟♟	6
● Armonia '07	♟	4
● Val di Cornia Sogno Mediterraneo '07	♟	5

Fattoria Casalbosco

FRAZ. SANTOMATO
VIA MONTALESE, 117
84020 PISTOIA
TEL. 0573479947
www.fattoriacasalbosco.com

The Becagli winery gains a Guide profile. The family has created a dynamic estate in an area little-known as yet to the general public. The most convincing wine is the Orchidea '06, an equal blend of cabernet sauvignon and merlot, with a refined, spicy bouquet, soft, velvety body and tasty finish.

● Orchidea '06	♟♟	6
● Chianti '08	♟	3
● Opus Magnum '05	♟	5

Casali in Val di Chio

VIA SANTA CRISTINA, 16
52043 CASTIGLION FIORENTINO [AR]
TEL. 0575650179
www.casaliinvaldichio.com

This is an all-female winery. The wines at the tasting were very good with the merlot Merigge '06 the stand-out. It's shy at first but then shows delightful, dynamic body with a thrilling finish. The Poventa '06 is spicy and rich; the Arrone '08 is more traditional.

● Merigge '06	♟♟	4*
● Valdichiana Arrone '08	♟	3
● Valdichiana Poventa '06	♟	4
● Merigge '05	♟♟	4*

Castelli Martinozzi

LOC. VILLA SANTA RESTITUTA
53024 MONTALCINO [SI]
TEL. 057784856

Hats off to Guide newcomer Cesare Castelli and his winery with an excellent Brunello di Montalcino '04 that gives classic peach and white cherry with floral hints of violet. The palate is elegant, thanks to well-measured tannin and vibrant acidity. A triumphantly good wine.

● Brunello di Montalcino '04	♟♟	6
● Brunello di Montalcino '97	♟♟	6
● Rosso di Montalcino '99	♟♟	4

Cennatoio Intervineas

FRAZ. PANZANO IN CHIANTI
VIA DI SAN LEOLINO, 35
50020 GREVE IN CHIANTI [FI]
TEL. 0558963230
www.cennatoio.it

The best among the wines presented by the winery of Leandro and Gabriella Alessi seems to be the Etrusco '06, from monovarietal sangiovese. Its toasty notes evoke cocoa powder and the palate has lovely sweetness and roundness. This lovely, very drinkable wine is perhaps just a little short on complexity.

● Etrusco '06	♟♟	6
● Chianti Cl. '07	♟	5
● Chianti Cl. O'Leandro Ris. '05	♟	5

Giovanni Chiappini

LOC. LE PRESELLE
POD. FELCIAINO, 189B
57020 BOLGHERI [LI]
TEL. 0565765201
www.giovannichiappini.it

Giovanni Chiappini's farm estate dates from 1978. The wines this year are again convincing. The Lienà line, which is outstanding in the cleanliness and concentration of its flavours, though it's a shame about the scant number of bottles. The Bolghero Superiore Guado de' Gemoli '06 is good.

● Bolgheri Sup. Guado de' Gemoli '06	♟♟	7
● Lienà Cabernet Franc '06	♟♟	8
● Lienà Cabernet Sauvignon '06	♟♟	8
● Lienà Petit Verdot '06	♟♟	8

La Ciarliana

FRAZ. GRACCIANO
VIA CIARLIANA, 31
53040 MONTEPULCIANO [SI]
TEL. 0578758423
www.laciarliana.it

The wines produced by Luigi Frangiosa's winery have a well-defined style. The Nobile '06 is outstanding, beautifully aromatic and gives intense fruit leading to a broad, well-structured palate. The Rosso di Montepulciano '07 is very simple and pleasing but perhaps a little too thin.

● Nobile di Montepulciano '06	♟♟	5
● Rosso di Montepulciano '07	♟	4

Cigliano

VIA CIGLIANO, 17
50026 SAN CASCIANO IN VAL DI PESA [FI]
TEL. 055820033
www.villadelcigliano.it

After last year's debut, Villa del Cigliano confirmed it is on the right track. The San Casciano winery has around 60 hectares, of which 25 are under vine. The Chianti Classico '07 is very natural in its expression and precision of flavour. It's classy, land-focused and shows the winery is on its way.

● Chianti Cl. '07	♟♟	4*
● Suganella '06	♟♟	5

Cima

FRAZ. ROMAGNANO
VIA DEL FAGIANO, 1
54100 MASSA
TEL. 0585831617
www.aziendagricolacima.it

Every year, Cima offers a wonderful range for tasting. It's an indication of love for these steep Apuan Alp slopes and the countless nuances they can impart to the various vines. The whites are nice and the best is the fruit-led, generously savoury Candia dei Colli Apuani Vigneto Alto '08.

○ Candia dei Colli Apuani Vign. Candia Alto '08	♟♟	5
○ Candia dei Colli Apuani '08	♟	4
● Massaretta '07	♟	6
○ Vermentino '08	♟	4

Fattoria Collazzi

LOC. TAVARNUZZE
VIA COLLERAMOLE, 101
50029 IMPRUNETA [FI]
TEL. 0552022528
www.collazzi.it

The winery of the Marchi siblings – Bona, Grazia and Carlo – extends over almost 400 hectares, of which 20 are under vine on clay and sandy soils. Again, the top wine is Collazzi, a blend of merlot, cabernet franc and cabernet sauvignon in variable proportions, depending on the year.

● Collazzi '07	♟♟	7
● Chianti Cl. I Bastioni '07	♟	4
● Libertà '08	♟	4

Colle di Bordocheo

LOC. SEGROMIGNO IN MONTE
VIA DI PIAGGIORI BASSO, 107
55018 CAPANNORI [LU]
TEL. 0583929821
dchelini@tin.it

Colle di Bordocheo's performance was impressive. The estate lies in the stunning natural amphitheatre of the Luccan hills and the vineyards are ideally placed to ripen the grapes. The full-bodied, dynamic Picchio Rosso '06 is seriously good and the Bianco dell'Oca '08 is fresh-tasting and juicy.

○ Colline Lucchesi Bianco dell'Oca '08	▼▼	5
● Colline Lucchesi Picchio Rosso '06	▼▼	5
○ Colline Lucchesi Bianco dell'Oca '06	♈♈	5

Fattoria Colle Verde

FRAZ. MATRAIA
LOC. CASTELLO
55010 LUCCA
TEL. 0583402310
www.colleverde.it

Colle Verde, in the Matraia hills, has always been a reliable Lucca winery. This year, the Brania delle Ghiandaie '06 is one of the best wines. From sangiovese with added syrah, it shows ruby in colour with aromas of blackberry and spice, a fruity palate and close-knit, well-gauged tannins.

● Colline Lucchesi Rosso Brania delle Ghiandaie '06	▼▼	5
● Nero della Spinosa '06	▼	6

Collelungo

LOC. COLLELUNGO
53011 CASTELLINA IN CHIANTI [SI]
TEL. 0577740489
www.collelungo.com

The Cattelan family winery has ancient roots but it is only since the 1990s that it has been developing the local potential. The Chianti Classico '07 still shows some toasty notes, with good fruit texture and assertive tannins, but overall it is a very decent wine.

● Chianti Cl. '07	▼▼	4*
● Chianti Cl. '05	♈♈	4
● Merlot '06	♈♈	5

Podere Concori

LOC. FIATTONE
VIA PROVINCIALE, 1
55027 GALLICANO [LU]
TEL. 0583766039
www.podereconcori.com

We applaud another good performance this year by the splendid Gabriele Da Prato. Melograno '07, a landmark for Garfagnana winemaking, again excelled. Biodynamics may be the explanation for the way these mountain vines manage to yield such vibrant, lively wines.

● Melograno Rosso '07	▼▼	5
● Melograno Rosso '06	♈♈	5
● Melograno Rosso '04	♈♈	5

Il Conventino

VIA DELLA CIARLIANA, 25B
53040 MONTEPULCIANO [SI]
TEL. 0578715371
www.ilconventino.it

Alberto Brini's organically farmed vines had another good year. Il Cambio '04 from savoury sangiovese is solid and distinctly agreeable. The Nobile '06 is basically elegant, though it still has some rough edges to smooth. The aromas of the Nobile Riserva '05 are not quite focused.

● Il Cambio '04	▼▼	6
● Nobile di Montepulciano '06	▼	5
● Nobile di Montepulciano Ris. '05	▼	6
● Nobile di Montepulciano Ris. '04	♈♈	6

La Cura

LOC. CURA NUOVA, 12
58024 MASSA MARITTIMA [GR]
TEL. 0566918094
www.cantinalacura.it

Enrico Corsi's estate offers consistent quality. The '07 Merlot La Cura is a wine with complex aromas and a very agreeable flavour. The rest of the range is reliable. A special mention goes to the experimental sweet passito Predicatore '08, from aleatico and merlot grapes.

● La Cura Merlot '07	▼▼	5
● Monteregio di Massa Marittima Rosso Breccerosse '08	▼	4
○ Predicatore '08	▼	6
○ Trinus '08	▼	5

Tenuta degli Dei

VIA SAN LEOLINO, 56
50020 GREVE IN CHIANTI [FI]
TEL. 055852593
www.deglidei.com

The only wine produced on Tommaso Cavalli's promising estate is made from a blend of merlot and the two cabernets, franc and sauvignon, with a little alicante, petit verdot and bouschet. It has a full, complex nose and nice fruit sprinkled with minty notes. The palate is deep with good acidity.

● Cavalli '06		🍷🍷 8
● Cavalli '05		🍷🍷 6
● Cavalli '04		🍷🍷 6

Diadema

VIA IMPRUNETANA PER TAVERNUZZE, 21
50023 IMPRUNETA [FI]
TEL. 0552311330
www.diadema-wine.com

This has been an excellent year for Alberto Giannotti, who began making wine on his estate at Impruneta in 2004. The Diadema Rosso 07, a Bordeaux blend, has a full, spicy nose with ripe forest fruits. Entry on the palate is powerful and broad, but not concentrated, and the very tasty finish lingers.

● Diadema Rosso '07		🍷🍷 8
○ Diadema Bianco '07		🍷🍷 8
● Diadema Rosso '06		🍷🍷 8

Fabrizio Dionisio

FRAZ. OSSAIA
LOC. IL CASTAGNO
52040 CORTONA [AR]
TEL. 063223541
fabdio@tin.it

Fabrizio Dionisio's Syrah reached our finals again, confirming the potential it has shown over the last few years. The wine has complex aromas that range from animal skins to spices with hints of fruit, good concentration on the palate and a soft, lingering finish. The '08 rosé is enjoyable.

● Cortona Syrah '07		🍷🍷 5
⊙ Rosa del Castagno '08		🍷 4
● Cortona Syrah '06		🍷🍷 5
● Cortona Syrah '05		🍷🍷 5

Donna Olimpia 1898

FRAZ. BOLGHERI
LOC. MIGLIARINI, 142
57020 CASTAGNETO CARDUCCI [LI]
TEL. 0272094585
www.donnaolimpia1898.it

After last year's convincing debut, Donna Olimpia 1898's wines confirmed their quality. The Bolgheri '06 is a powerful, concentrated wine, in full Bolgheri style, with a fresh, convincingly lively taste to boot. The Tageto '07 is also agreeable, just a bit tight in the finish from slightly green tannins.

● Bolgheri '06		🍷🍷 5
● Tageto '07		🍷 4
● Bolgheri '05		🍷🍷 5
● Tageto '06		🍷🍷 6

Fabbriche

VIA FABBRICHE, 2-3A
52046 LUCIGNANO [AR]
TEL. 0575836152
www.agricolafabbriche.it

The Palma family, originally from Milan, has run this winery in Val di Chiana for 50 years. Ever since Caterina moved to the area, the wine business has shifted up a gear. The Merlot '06 is very attractive, with intense fruity scents supported by vegetal notes, and a broad, well-balanced palate.

● Merlot '06		🍷🍷 6
● Camargi '06		🍷 5
○ Vin Santo del Chianti Elis '04		🍷 5

Cantine Faralli

LOC. FASCIANO, 4
52040 CORTONA [AR]
TEL. 0575613128
www.cantinefaralli.com

Cortona Merlot '06 is the wine that impressed us most from the range presented by Juri Faralli, a winemaker who owns five hectares. It has complex aromas ranging from animal skins to leather and very ripe fruit. Soft and caressing on the palate, it finishes unhurriedly.

● Cortona Merlot '06		🍷🍷 5
● Cortona Novantadieci '06		🍷 4
● Cortona Merlot '05		🍷🍷 6
● Il Sorbo '04		🍷🍷 5

Fattoi

LOC. SANTA RESTITUTA
POD. CAPANNA, 101
53024 MONTALCINO [SI]
TEL. 0577848613
www.fattoi.it

This lovely estate is in the zone below the church of Santa Restituta, where it makes traditional wines. The Brunello di Montalcino '04 is one, with classic scents of tobacco and cherry. The Brunello di Montalcino Riserva '03 is also convincing. It has a nice vein of acidity and great depth of flavour.

● Brunello di Montalcino '04	♟♟	6
● Brunello di Montalcino Ris. '03	♟♟	7
● Brunello di Montalcino '03	♀♀	6

Fertuna

LOC. GRILLI
VIA AURELIA VECCHIA KM 205
58040 GAVORRANO [GR]
TEL. 056688138
www.tertuna.it

The Gruppo Meregalli cellar produces well-made wines. The sangiovese, cabernet sauvignon and merlot Lodai '07 is terrific. Messiio '06 is a blend of sangiovese, cabernet sauvignon, merlot and syrah that shows rather tight. Plato '08, from sangiovese and cabernet sauvignon, is well proportioned.

● Lodai '07	♟♟	5
● Messiio '06	♟	6
● Plato '08	♟	5
● Lodai '05	♀♀	5
● Lodai '04	♀♀	5

Fattoria Fibbiano

VIA FIBBIANO, 2
56030 TERRICCIOLA [PI]
TEL. 0587635677
www.fattoria-fibbiano.it

It's a debut to remember for Fattoria Fibbiano. The Cantoni family winery is in Terricciola, an area ideal for wine. Aspetto '06, from sangiovese and canaiolo grapes, has an intensely fruity, clean nose and a full, lingering body. The savoury, juicy Chianti Superiore Casalini '07 is also lovely.

● L'Aspetto '06	♟♟	4
● Chianti Sup. Casalini '07	♟	3

Ficomontanino

LOC. FICOMONTANINO
53043 CHIUSI [SI]
TEL. 057821180
www.agricolaficomontanino.it

The Giannelli family estate has found its flagship wine in Lucumone. Made from cabernet sauvignon only, it is solid and well-coordinated and the '06 is testimony to its style and balance. The Chianti Colli Senesi Tutulus '07 and the Colli Senesi '07 are also well focused.

● Lucumone '06	♟♟	5
● Chianti Colli Senesi '07	♟	3
● Chianti Colli Senesi Tutulus '07	♟	5
● Lucumone '05	♀♀	6

La Fiorita

FRAZ. CASTELNUOVO DELL'ABATE
PIAGGIA DELLA PORTA, 3
53020 MONTALCINO [SI]
TEL. 0577835657
www.fattorialafiorita.it

Oenologist Roberto Cipresso established this winery with three friends at the start of the 1990s. The Brunello di Montalcino '04 is admirable with overripe wafts of blackberries and wild cherries introducing a rich, well-structured palate, with tight-knit tannins.

● Brunello di Montalcino '04	♟♟	7
● Brunello di Montalcino Ris. '03	♟	7
● Brunello di Montalcino Ris. '01	♀♀	7

Fortediga

LOC. RIBOLLA
58036 ROCCASTRADA [GR]
TEL. 3393667707
www.fortediga.it

There was a fine Guide debut for this winery at Ribolla, in the former mining area of the Maremma. The Cabernet Sauvignon-Syrah '07 is a satisfying, seriously well-made easy drinker. The cabernet sauvignon Salbro '06 is good, showing slightly evolved but with intense aromas and broad, well-structured palate.

● Cabernet Sauvignon - Syrah '07	♟♟	5
● Salebro '06	♟	5

Fossacolle

LOC. TAVERNELLE, 7
53024 MONTALCINO [SI]
TEL. 0577816013
www.fossacolle.it

Sergio Marchetti's cellar confirmed its quality. Brunello di Montalcino '04 is aged in barrels of various sizes and reflects its provenance well. There is bramble and cherry jam on the nose with a slight hint of cinnamon. The palate is big and sumptuous, with good supporting tannins.

● Brunello di Montalcino '04	🍷🍷 7
● Rosso di Montalcino '07	🍷 5

Eredi Fuligni

VIA SALONI, 33
53024 MONTALCINO [SI]
TEL. 0577848039
brunellofuligni@virgilio.it

This beautiful, influential Montalcino estate has had a somewhat disappointing year. The wines are rather muddled, showing too much wood. We look forward to a return to the more clearly defined style we so admired not so long ago.

● Brunello di Montalcino '04	🍷 7
● Rosso di Montalcino Ginestreto '07	🍷 5
● S. J. '07	🍷 4

Gattavecchi

LOC. SANTA MARIA
VIA DI COLLAZZI, 74
53045 MONTEPULCIANO [SI]
TEL. 0578757110
www.gattavecchi.it

We loved Luca Gattavecchi's dense, tangy Poggio alla Sala-label Nobile '06 with its taut, juicy, richly flavoured palate. The Gattavecchi-label Nobile '06 is also more than decent, with somewhat rustic aromas but an agreeably spirited palate. The Vin Santo Poggio alla Sala '97 is stylishly off-dry.

● Nobile di Montepulciano Poggio alla Sala '06	🍷🍷 5
● Nobile di Montepulciano '06	🍷 5
O Vin Santo di Montepulciano Poggio alla Sala '97	🍷 6

La Gerla

LOC. CANALICCHIO
POD. COLOMBAIO, 5
53024 MONTALCINO [SI]
TEL. 0577848599
www.lagerla.it

Giancarlo Rossi's winery has been in business for two years. The wines have great personality and lots of local character. The vineyards lie on two facing slopes in Montalcino. Brunello Vigna gli Angeli '04 is always good, with its acid backbone that supports beautifully stylish, lingering body.

● Brunello di Montalcino V. gli Angeli '04	🍷🍷 8
● Brunello di Montalcino '04	🍷 6
● Rosso di Montalcino '07	🍷 4

Giannoni Fabbri

LOC. SAN MARCO IN VILLA, 2
52044 CORTONA [AR]
TEL. 3475883939
www.giannonifabbri.it

Marco Giannoni Fabbri does all the work at his winery, which has confirmed its place in the Guide. Cabernet Sauvignon Vittorio '06 has cinnamon and pepper spice that melds with forest fruits. The body is well-orchestrated, with soft tannins and a tasty finish.

● Cortona Vittorio '06	🍷🍷 4*
● Cortona Cabernet '04	🍷🍷 4
O Cortona Vin Santo '02	🍷🍷 6

Azienda Agricola Godiolo

VIA DELL'ACQUAPUZZOLA, 13
53045 MONTEPULCIANO [SI]
TEL. 0578757251
www.godiolo.it

Founded just nine years ago, Franco Fiorini's winery has about six hectares under vine. The wines are seriously delicious and Nobile '06 is one of the best. It has a lovely aromatic tone and drinks tangy and well sustained. The fragrant Rosso '07 makes for great drinking with its nicely structured palate.

● Nobile di Montepulciano '06	🍷🍷 5
● Rosso di Montepulciano '07	🍷🍷 4*
● Nobile di Montepulciano '05	🍷🍷 5
● Nobile di Montepulciano Ris. '03	🍷🍷 6

OTHER WINERIES

Tenuta di Gracciano della Seta

FRAZ. GRACCIANO
VIA UMBRIA, 59
53045 MONTEPULCIANO [SI]
TEL. 0578708340
g.rigoli@agriconsulting.it

It was a good tasting for Piera Mazzucchelli's winery, founded back in 1950 and extending over 17 hectares of vine. The tasty Nobile '06 is nicely focused, with clean aromas, a supple palate and a soft finish. The Rosso '07 is simple and instantly likeable.

● Nobile di Montepulciano '06	▼▼ 5
● Rosso di Montepulciano '07	▼ 4
● Nobile di Montepulciano Ris. '04	▽▽ 5

Fattoria Il Lago

FRAZ. CAMPAGNA
50062 DICOMANO [FI]
TEL. 055838047
www.fattoriaillago.com

The Spagnoli family are constantly upping the quality of their wines and now they are in the Guide. The Vin Santo '03 is very nice, mouthfilling and delicious but all the wines are reliably made to a standard that is more than enjoyable.

○ Vin Santo del Chianti Rufina '03	▼▼ 5
● Chianti Rufina '07	▼ 4
● Chianti Rufina Ris. '06	▼ 5
● Pian de'Guardi '05	▼ 5

Lavacchio

VIA DI MONTEFIESOLE, 55
50065 PONTASSIEVE [FI]
TEL. 0558317472
www.fattorialavacchio.com

The transition period continues for the Lotteri family, who have seen their whites on top again. The Pachar '07, a blend of chardonnay, viognier and sauvignon, has refined fragrances, aromatic herbs, mineral tones and a juicy, straightforward palate.

○ Pachar '07	▼▼ 5
● Chianti Rufina Cedro Ris. '06	▼ 5
○ Oro del Cedro '07	▼ 5
○ Pachar '06	▽▽ 4*

Tenuta Lenzini

FRAZ. GRAGNANO
VIA DELLA CHIESA, 44
55010 CAPANNORI [LU]
TEL. 0583974037
www.tenutalenzini.it

Tenuta Lenzini is one of the emerging new wineries in the Lucca area. Owners Benedetta Tronci and Michele Guarino have vineyards on loose-packed, sandy soil with some lime and clay. The fruit and spice Syrah '07 and the Bordeaux blend Poggio de' Paoli '07 are both very good.

● Poggio de' Paoli '07	▼▼ 5
● Syrah '07	▼▼ 5
○ Vermentino '08	▼ 4

Fattoria Lornano

LOC. LORNANO, 11
53035 MONTERIGGIONI [SI]
TEL. 0577309059
www.fattorialornano.it

Fattoria Lornano has belonged to the Taddei family for three generations. It comprises 180 hectares in the hills to the south-west of Castellina, towards Monteriggioni with 50 hectares planted to vine. The convincing Chianti Classico '06 gives currants and hints of toastiness.

● Chianti Cl. Ris. '06	▼▼ 4
● Commendator Enrico '06	▼ 5
● Commendator Enrico '05	▽▽ 5

Tenuta della Luia

VIA TRENTO, 32
50052 CERTALDO [FI]
TEL. 3391020395
www.tenutadellaluia.it

The Syrah was missing but Luia '06 stood up well. It is a blend of merlot, cabernet sauvignon and colorino, with an enchanting swath of aromatics ranging through spices and forest fruits. It is soft on the palate and the silky mouthfeel reveals perfectly integrated tannins.

● Luia '06	▼▼ 5
● Chianti Monticello '07	▼ 2*
● Luia '05	▽▽ 6

I Luoghi

LOC. CAMPO AL CAPRIOLO, 201
57022 CASTAGNETO CARDUCCI [LI]
TEL. 0565777379
www.iluoghi.it

Stefano Granata and Paola De Fusco run the small I Luoghi estate. Their plots lie on the broad slope stretching down from Castagneto Carducci to the sea. There was a respectable debut for the '06 Bolgheri Superiore Campo al Fico, which unveils a sharp, deep nose leading into a taut, fruity palate.

● Bolgheri Sup. Campo al Fico '06	♥♥ 8
● Bolgheri Podere Ritorti '06	♥ 5

Le Macioche

S.P. 55 DI SANT'ANTIMO, KM 4,85
53024 MONTALCINO [SI]
TEL. 0577849168
lemacioche@tiscali.it

This is a solid winery on the upper part of the slope to the south-east of Montalcino. It makes a delicious Brunello di Montalcino '04 in the classic mould. The nose has very interesting evolved notes of leaf tobacco and morello cherry while the palate shows great acidity and well-sustained tannin.

● Brunello di Montalcino '04	♥♥ 7
● Rosso di Montalcino '07	♥ 5

Maremmalta

LOC. CASTEANI
58023 GAVORRANO [GR]
TEL. 0564453572
www.maremmalta.it

There was a good Guide debut for Stefano Rizzi's new project. Monteregio Poggiomaestro '08 is a wine with very fresh aromas that accompany a tasty, lively progression. Mestra Vermentino '08 and the Rosa del Salto '08 are equally enjoyable and equally salty in character.

● Monteregio di Massa Marittima Poggiomaestro '08	♥♥ 4
○ Monteregio di Massa Marittima Vermentino Lestra '08	♥ 4
⊙ Monteregio di Massa Marittima Vermentino Rosa del Salto '08	♥ 3

Il Marroneto

LOC. MADONNA DELLE GRAZIE, 307
53024 MONTALCINO [SI]
TEL. 0577849382
www.ilmarroneto.com

The tower of the Marroneto winery dominates the vines, which stand in a single plot. The Brunello di Montalcino Madonna delle Grazie '04 is very convincing. Ripe, whole cherry on the nose introduces a complex, substantial palate with great supporting acidity.

● Brunello di Montalcino Madonna delle Grazie '04	♥♥ 8
● Brunello di Montalcino '04	♥ 7
● Brunello di Montalcino '03	♥♥ 7

Fattoria Michi

VIA SAN MARTINO, 34
55015 MONTECARLO [LU]
TEL. 058322011

A further year's ageing has been most beneficial for the whites of Fattoria Michi, in Montecarlo. Vigna del Cavaliere '07 has turned into a wine with an intense, fruity nose leading into a focused, dynamic palate. The Vecchie Vigne '07 is also very pleasant and long-lingering.

○ Vecchie Vigne '07	♥♥ 4*
○ Vigna del Cavaliere '07	♥♥ 5
○ Montecarlo Bianco '08	♥ 4

Fattoria Migliarina

LOC. MIGLIARINA, 84
52021 BUCINE [AR]
TEL. 0559788243
www.migliarina.it

The farm dates back to the early 1800s and is surrounded by 500 hectares of woodland, vineyards, olive groves and wheat fields. The wines are remarkably good value for money. Vin Santo '01 is outstanding, from its scents of honey and nuts through its dense, soft body to a lovely, lingering finish.

○ Vin Santo del Chianti '01	♥♥ 5
● Cavasonno '07	♥ 4
● Chianti Sup. '07	♥ 3

OTHER WINERIES

Mocali

LOC. MOCALI
53024 MONTALCINO [SI]
TEL. 0577849485
azmocali@tiscali.it

Recently expanded by the acquisition of land in the Montecucco area, Tiziano Ciacci's winery offers a range of wines that is always reliable and always reasonably priced. The two Brunello di Montalcinos, the '04 and the Vigna delle Raunate '04, are rather nice.

● Brunello di Montalcino '04	♥♥ 7
● Brunello di Montalcino V. delle Raunate '04	♥♥ 8
● Rosso di Montalcino '07	♥ 5

Castello di Monastero

LOC. MONASTERO D'OMBRONE, 19
53019 CASTELNUOVO BERARDENGA [SI]
TEL. 0577355789
www.castellodimonastero.com

The winery belongs to Lionello Marchesi, an entrepreneur with a passion for wine who set up a series of cellars in various wine areas around Tuscany. The Chianti Classico '06 has lashings of red fruit but the palate is stiffish lacks definition while the Chardonnay '07 has pineapple-like tropical sensations.

● Brunello di Montalcino Coldisole '04	♥♥ 7
● Chianti Cl. '06	♥♥ 4*
○ Chardonnay '07	♥ 4

Podere Monastero

LOC. MONASTERO
53011 CASTELLINA IN CHIANTI [SI]
TEL. 0577740273
www.poderemonastero.com

Oenologist Alessandro Cellai's cellar releases two wines. La Pineta is from pinot nero and Campanaio is a 50-50 blend of cabernet sauvignon and merlot. The '07 versions are both well balanced and defined, the Pinot Nero giving subtler perceptions and the Bordeaux blend showing more structure.

● Campanaio '07	♥♥ 6
● La Pineta '07	♥♥ 7

Fattoria di Montechiari

VIA MONTECHIARI, 27
55015 MONTECARLO [LU]
TEL. 058322189
www.montechiari.com

Montechiari is one of the most important estates in the Montecarlo area. Moreno Panattoni and Catherine Pirmez have always believed in wines with an international style from careful selection in their best vineyards. The Cabernet '06 is lovely.

● Montechiari Cabernet '06	♥♥ 6
○ Chardonnay '08	♥ 6
● Montechiari Merlot '06	♥ 6

Tenuta di Montecucco

LOC. MONTECUCCO
58044 CINIGIANO [GR]
TEL. 0564999029
www.tenutadimontecucco.it

It was a convincing performance by Tenuta di Montecucco. The Montecucco Sangiovese Rigomoro Riserva '05 is a wine with rich character and lively progression on the palate. The Montecucco Sangiovese Le Coste '06 is in the same style while Rosso di Montecucco Passonaia '07 is eminently drinkable.

● Montecucco Le Coste '06	♥♥ 5
● Montecucco Rigomoro Ris. '05	♥♥ 6
● Montecucco Passonaia '07	♥ 4

Montepeloso

LOC. MONTEPELOSO, 82
57028 SUVERETO [LI]
TEL. 0565828180
contact@montepeloso.it

Fabio Chiarellotto's estate has seven hectares of superb vineyards. Gabbro '06 secured a place in the finals by virtue of its rich, well-balanced body, backed up by exquisitely tuned tannins.

● Gabbro '06	♥♥ 8
● Eneo '06	♥ 6

Montepepe

VIA SFORZA, 76
54038 MONTIGNOSO [MS]
TEL. 0585831042
www.montepepe.com

It was a great debut for Roberto Poggi's winery with three characterful wines. Montepepe '06, from syrah and massaretta is vegetal and spicy on the nose, with a nicely layered finish. Degeres '07, from vermentino and viognier, has complex aromatics and Montpepe Bianco '07 is pleasant and light.

● Montepepe Rosso '06	🍷🍷 5
○ Degeres '07	🍷 6
○ Montepepe Bianco '07	🍷 5

Tenuta Monteti

VIA DELLA SGRILLA, 6
58011 CAPALBIO [GR]
TEL. 0564896160
www.tenutamonteti.it

Monteti '06, a blend of cabernet sauvignon, petit verdot and cabernet franc with a little alicante and merlot, is complex and rich, though still too wood-influenced. Caburnio '06, from cabernet sauvignon, alicante and merlot, is more immediate, with subtle aromas and a nice palate.

● Caburnio '06	🍷🍷 4
● Monteti '06	🍷 6

La Mozza

LOC. MONTE CIVOLI
58051 MAGLIANO IN TOSCANA [GR]
TEL. 0432700943
www.bastiancih.com

La Mozza is the Bastianich family's Maremma estate: there are others in Friuli and Argentina. Morellino di Scansano I Perazzi '07 is very successful, with earthy and floral fragrances and a vigorous, deep palate. Also good is the soft, juicy Aragone '06, from sangiovese, alicante, syrah and carignano.

● Aragone '06	🍷🍷 5
● Morellino di Scansano I Perazzi '07	🍷🍷 4

Pagani de Marchi

LOC. LA NOCERA
VIA DELLA CAMMINATA, 2
56040 CASALE MARITTIMO [PI]
TEL. 0586653016
www.paganidemarchi.com

Pagani de Marchi was founded in 1997 with seven hectares of vineyards on south-east to south-west facing terrain of Pliocene origin. The cabernet sauvignon-only '06 Casalvecchio and the Olmata '06, from sangiovese, cabernet sauvignon and merlot, are both very good.

● Casalvecchio '06	🍷🍷 6
● Olmata '06	🍷🍷 5
● Principe Guerriero '06	🍷 5

Pagiano dei Guerrazzi

LOC. SASSOFORTINO
58036 ROCCASTRADA [GR]
TEL. 0564575512
www.pagiano.eu

We tasted two well-made wines from this Maremma estate. Pagiano Guerrazzi '07, from sangiovese, syrah and cabernet sauvignon, has charming aromas of spice, myrtle and Mediterranean shrubland, followed by a flavoursome, complex palate. The '07 Pagiano Cabernet is balsamic, tasty and bright.

● Pagiano Guerrazzi '07	🍷🍷 5
● Pagiano Cabernet '07	🍷🍷 5

Il Palagione

VIA PER CASTEL SAN GIMIGNANO, 36
53037 SAN GIMIGNANO [SI]
TEL. 0577953134
www.ilpalagione.com

There was a low-key performance from Giorgio Comotti's winery, which stands out for the Antajr '06, from sangiovese, merlot and cabernet sauvignon. Clean aromas of pepper, cinnamon and wild berries take you into a soft, succulent palate with a nice lingering finish.

● Antajr '06	🍷🍷 6
● Chianti Colli Senesi Caelum '07	🍷 4
○ Vernaccia di S. Gimignano Hydra '08	🍷 4
○ Vernaccia di S. Gimignano Ori Ris. '07	🍷 5

Panzanello

VIA CASE SPARSE, 86
50022 PANZANO [FI]
TEL. 055852470
www.panzanello.it

This estate is first mentioned in 1427 in the Florence land registry for its excellent olive oil and wine. Today, it is owned by the Sommaruga family. The Chianti Classico '07 is a fine example of its wine type, showing precise and territory-focused with complex aromas and a savoury, vertical palate.

● Chianti Cl. '07	♀♀ 5
● Chianti Cl. Panzanello '06	♀♀ 4
● Il Manuzio '03	♀♀ 7

Tenuta La Parrina

FRAZ. ALBINIA
S.DA VICINALE DELLA PARRINA
58010 ORBETELLO [GR]
TEL. 0564862636
www.parrina.it

Radaia is still the most interesting wine from Franca Spinola's estate. The '07 version of this monovarietal Merlot is nicely open and beautifully drinkable, with intensely spicy aromas. The Parrina Rosso '08 is flavoursome while the Vermentino '08 is fresh and clean but one-dimensional.

● Radaia '07	♀♀ 7
● Parrina Rosso '08	♀ 4
○ Vermentino '08	♀ 4

Paterna - Cooperativa Agricola Valdarnese

LOC. PATERNA, 96
52028 TERRANUOVA BRACCIOLINI [AR]
TEL. 055977052
www.paterna.it

Vignanova is again the best of the Paterna wines. The '05 version includes a small percentage of colorino del Valdarno with the sangiovese. Slow to open out on the nose, it then gives minerally aromas with a nice impact on the robust palate and a lingering, savoury finish.

● Vignanova '05	♀♀ 5
● Chianti Colli Aretini '07	♀ 4
○ Il Trerraio '08	♀ 3
● Rosso di Paterna '07	♀ 3

Perazzeta

LOC. MONTENERO D'ORCIA
VIA DELL'AIA, 14
58040 CASTEL DEL PIANO [GR]
TEL. 0564954158
www.perazzeta.it

The Bocci family winery produces characterful wines, although continuity is still lacking. The Montecucco Licurgo Riserva '06 is a confidently focused wine showing good characterful aromas with clearly defined hints of fruit and spice and a complex, dynamic palate.

● Montecucco Sangiovese Licurgo Ris. '06	♀♀ 6
● Montecucco Sangiovese Licurgo Ris. '01	♀♀ 5

Petreto

VIA ROSANO, 196A
50012 BAGNO A RIPOLI [FI]
TEL. 0556519021

Alessandro Fonseca is back in the Guide thanks to his leading wine. Pourriture Noble '05 is a blend of sémillon and sauvignon affected by noble rot. Amber in hue, it gives delicious aromatics from citrus fruit to honey, a full-bodied, velvety palate and a lingering, sweet finish.

○ Pourriture Noble '05	♀♀ 6
● Chianti Colli Fiorentini '07	♀ 3
○ Podere Sassaie '08	♀ 4

Piancornello

LOC. PIANCORNELLO
53024 MONTALCINO [SI]
TEL. 0577844105
piancorello@libero.it

Claudio Monaci's Brunello '04 has typically local features on the nose with blueberry jam, blackberries and nice sour cherries as well as very forward oak. Vibrant entry on the palate with warm sensations and nicely managed tannins is backed up by acidity that bolsters the weighty extract.

● Brunello di Montalcino '04	♀♀ 7
● Poggio dei Lecci '07	♀ 4

Pianirossi

LOC. PORRONA
POD. SANTA GENOVEFFA
58044 CINIGIANO [GR]
TEL. 0564990335
www.pianirossi.it

There was a good debut for the winery owned by Stefano Sincini, CEO of Tod's Shoes. The '06 Pianirossi is a blend of cabernet sauvignon, petit verdot and montepulciano with vibrant aromas and a weighty, deep palate. The more approachable Solus '07 is a blend of sangiovese, montepulciano and alicante.

● Pianirossi '06	♥♥	6
● Solus '07	♥	5

Pietrafitta

LOC. CORTENNANO, 54
53037 SAN GIMIGNANO [SI]
TEL. 0577943200
www.pietrafitta.com

We enjoyed the '07 Chianti Colli Senesi, which gives complex fruity aromas with vegetal hints, nice juicy fruit, a vibrant body and a very captivating finish. The Vigna Borghetto '08 selection has slightly unfocused aromas but a solid, mouthwatering body with refreshing acid backbone.

● Chianti Colli Senesi '07	♥♥	4*
● Campi Donne '07	♥	5
○ Vernaccia di S. Gimignano '08	♥	4
○ Vernaccia di S. Gimignano V. Borghetto '08	♥	4

Pietroso

LOC. PIETROSO
53024 MONTALCINO [SI]
TEL. 0577848573
www.pietroso.it

This four-hectare Brunello estate has a very traditional style. Long maceration and large barrels give the Brunello di Montalcino '04 a subtle, clean nose and a palate with beautiful acidity and slightly rigid tannin. The Rosso di Montalcino '07 is succulent, enjoyable and balanced.

● Brunello di Montalcino '04	♥♥	6
● Rosso di Montalcino '07	♥♥	5

Il Pino

VIA CASTIGLION UBERTINI, 78
52028 TERRANUOVA BRACCIOLINI [AR]
TEL. 0559703807
www.ilpino.com

This small winery in the heart of Tuscany is in the so-called Inferno valley where there are many organic estates. The Rubis degli Ubertini '06, a blend of merlot, cabernet sauvignon and malvasia nera, has fresh, fruity aromas, a soft, pleasant body and an intriguing finish.

● Rubis degli Ubertini '06	♥♥	4*

Podere Ciona

LOC. MONTEGROSSI
53013 GAIOLE IN CHIANTI [SI]
TEL. 0577749127
www.podereciona.com

Franco Gatteschi is doing well. His Chianti Classico Riserva is more impressive in the '06 version, beautiful fruit aromas with hints of spice and toasted coffee beans introducing a taut, sweet palate with fine-grained tannins sustaining a long finish. The merlot-based Le Diacce '06 is good but rather small.

● Chianti Cl. Ris. '06	♥♥	5
● Le Diaccie '06	♥	6

La Poderina

FRAZ. CASTELNUOVO DELL'ABATE
LOC. PODERINA
53020 MONTALCINO [SI]
TEL. 0577835737
www.saiagricola.it

This estate, part of the Saiagricola group, has recently extended the cellar and purchased more vineyards. As ever, the '07 Moscadello di Montalcino is the best of its type, showing pervasive, complex aromas of candied orange peel and flowers with an acidity-bolstered palate.

○ Moscadello di Montalcino V. T. '07	♥♥	6
● Brunello di Montalcino Poggio Banale Ris. '03	♥♥	8
● Brunello di Montalcino '04	♥	7
● Rosso di Montalcino '07	♥	5

Poggio al Sole

LOC. BADIA A PASSIGNANO
S.DA RIGNANA, 2
50028 TAVARNELLE VAL DI PESA [FI]
TEL. 0558071850
www.poggioalsole.com

This year, the '07 Chianti Classico is the most impressive of the wines presented by Poggio al Sole. Despite forward oak on the nose, the palate is full-bodied, well-structured and deep, without excessive extract. The '06 Casasilia has rather marked oakiness and the Syrah '07 is nicely drinkable.

● Chianti Cl. '07	🍷🍷 5
● Chianti Cl. Casasilia '06	🍷 7
● Syrah '07	🍷 7

Poggio dell'Aquila

LOC. POGGIOLO, 259
53024 MONTALCINO [SI]
TEL. 0577848533
www.poggiodellaquila.it

This is a new winery following the Cosimi brothers' split. Renzo's solid experience in vineyard and cellar shows in the results. The interesting, traditional Brunello '04 has aromas of tobacco, balsamic herbs, leather and a hint of cherries. Close-knit, mellow tannins balance acidity on the palate.

● Brunello di Montalcino '04	🍷🍷 4
● Rosso di Montalcino '06	🍷🍷 4

Poggio Torselli

VIA SCOPETI, 10
50026 SAN CASCIANO IN VAL DI PESA [FI]
TEL. 0558290241
www.poggiotorselli.it

Poggio Torselli is located near San Casciano on hills with a great view over the 30 hectares of vineyards and 2,700 olive trees. Tieri del Fula is a nicely made, complex monovarietal Cabernet, slightly sweet mid-palate but very flavoursome. The Chianti Classico Riserva '06 is quite good.

● Tieri del Fula '06	🍷🍷 4*
● Chianti Cl. '07	🍷 4
● Chianti Cl. Ris. '06	🍷 5

Tenuta Poggio Verrano

S.DA PROVINCIALE 9, KM 4
58051 MAGLIANO IN TOSCANA [GR]
TEL. 0564589943
www.poggioverrano.it

Francesco Bolla completes his range with the Poggio Verrano 3 '07, a delicious blend of alicante, cabernet sauvignon and merlot. Unsurprisingly, the '06 Dròmos is a very good blend of sangiovese, cabernet sauvignon, cabernet franc and alicante, as stylish on the nose as it is mouthfilling on the palate.

● Dròmos '06	🍷🍷 7
● Poggio Verrrano 3 '07	🍷 5

Tenuta Le Potazzine

LOC. LE PRATA
53024 MONTALCINO [SI]
TEL. 0577849406
www.lepotazzine.it

The very territorial Brunello di Montalcino '04 reflects upper hillslope origins, defined by sustained, crisp acidity and a long, satisfying finish. The rather raw extract is sure to mellow with time. White cherries and floral aromas come through on the nose.

● Brunello di Montalcino '04	🍷🍷 8
● Rosso di Montalcino '07	🍷 5

Prelius

LOC. PRILE
58043 CASTIGLIONE DELLA PESCAIA [GR]
TEL. 0577738066
info@volpaia.com

This is a personal adventure for Federica Mascheroni Stianti, from the family that runs Castello di Volpaia. The estate is organically farmed and is on the beautiful coastal Lake Prile. The cabernet sauvignon-heavy Morello di Prile '08 is mouthfilling, sunny and vibrant.

● Morello di Prile '08	🍷🍷 4
● Morello di Prile '07	🍷🍷 4

Querciagrossa

VIA DEL CROCIFISSO, 8
52044 CORTONA [AR]
TEL. 0575613789
www.legemelledoc.splinder.com

This seven-hectare estate produces a very impressive Cortona Merlot Le Gemelle '06. Vibrant blackberry and damson aromas with hints of spice and a soft, rounded palate with good acid backbone take you through to a sweet, flavoursome finish.

● Cortona Merlot Le Gemelle '06	♟♟ 5

La Rasina

LOC. RASINA, 132
53024 MONTALCINO [SI]
TEL. 0577848536
www.larasina.it

As ever, there was a good show from Marco Mantengoli's winery, even without the Il Divasco selection. The good Brunello di Montalcino '04 has a brooding nose and a palate that may not be huge but does have depth and sophistication. The Rosso di Montalcino '07 is dried by tannin.

● Brunello di Montalcino '04	♟♟ 7
● Rosso di Montalcino '07	♟ 5
● Brunello di Montalcino Il Divasco '03	♟♟ 8

Rigoloccio

LOC. RIGOLOCCIO
VIA PROVINCIALE, 82
58023 GAVORRANO [GR]
TEL. 056645464
www.rigoloccio.it

The Abati and Puggelli families' wines did well. Il Sorvegliante '06, from cabernet sauvignon, cabernet franc and alicante, has well-focused aromas and a soft, succulent palate. The fresh, supple Cabernet Alicante '07 is approachable. The savoury, fragrant Chardonnay Fiano '08 is good.

● Il Sorvegliante '06	♟♟ 5
● Cabernet Alicante '07	♟ 4
○ Chardonnay Fiano '08	♟ 4

Il Rio

VIA DI PADULE, 131
50039 VICCHIO [FI]
TEL. 0558407904

Back in the Guide is small Mugello winegrower Paolo Cerrini, who has created an interesting winery in an area considered unsuitable for wine production for many years. The pinot nero-led Ventisei '06 has appetizing aromas and a supple, nicely measured body with aromatic herbs in the finish.

● Ventisei '06	♟♟ 5
○ Annita '08	♟ 5

Tenuta Riseccoli

LOC. RISECCOLI
VIA CONVERTOIE, 9
50022 GREVE IN CHIANTI [FI]
TEL. 055853598
www.riseccoli.com

Tenuta di Riseccoli covers about 110 hectares in Greve in Chianti, about 22 of which are planted to vine with native and international varieties. The Petit Verdot '06 made it to the finals thanks to a spicy, meaty nose and an opulent palate nicely balanced by acidity.

● Petit Verdot '06	♟♟ 5

Le Rote

LOC. PONTE ALLE RUOTE
53037 SAN GIMIGNANO [SI]
TEL. 0577955028
www.lerote.it

Vernaccia '08 is the Scotti family's best wine. It has lovely mineral aromas, with floral and fruity hints, followed by a juicy, savoury palate with a nice lingering flavour. The pleasant Cosimo '05, a monovarietal Sangiovese, has well-defined fruit aromas and a medium body with a slightly short finish.

○ Vernaccia di S. Gimignano '08	♟♟ 4*
● Chianti Colli Senesi '07	♟ 4
● Cosimo '05	♟ 5

Italo Rubicini

San Benedetto, 17c
53037 San Gimignano [SI]
TEL. 0577944816
www.rubicini.com

The Rubicini family's best product is Vernaccia Etherea '08 with its complex, varied fruit and floral aromatics and a solid, vibrant body with a lovely tangy finish. The '08 Vernaccia is simpler but still nice. The '06 Pepe Nero from sangiovese and merlot is slightly stiff.

○ Vernaccia di S. Gimignano Etherea '08	♟♟	4*
○ Horos V.T. '06	♟	4
● San Gimignano Rosso Pepe Nero '06	♟	4
○ Vernaccia di S. Gimignano '08	♟	3

Podere Salicutti

Pod. Salicutti, 174
53024 Montalcino [SI]
TEL. 0577847003
www.poderesalicutti.it

Francesco Leanza is from Sicily but he was the first producer in Montalcino to make organic wines. Over the years, they have lost their oakiness and acquired a greater sense of place. The '04 Brunello is nicely made, with strawberry jam and sweet spice on the nose and a taut, dynamic palate.

● Brunello di Montalcino '04	♟♟	8
● Rosso di Montalcino '07	♟	5
● Brunello di Montalcino '97	♟♟♟	8

Fattoria San Pancrazio

Loc. San Pancrazio
via Certaldese, 63/65
50026 San Casciano in Val di Pesa [FI]
TEL. 0558248046
www.fattoriasanpancrazio.com

The winery is in the 14th-century village of San Pancrazio in the municipality of San Casciano in Val di Pesa, near Florence. The beautifully made '06 Chianti Classico Riserva has toasty hints on the nose, admirable texture and good tannic structure. The Chianti Classico '07 is very lively.

● Chianti Cl. Ris. '06	♟♟	5
● Chianti '07	♟	4
● Chianti Cl. '07	♟	4
● Merlot '06	♟	6

San Vincenti

Loc. San Vincenti
Pod. di Stignano, 27
53013 Gaiole in Chianti [SI]
TEL. 0577734047
www.sanvincenti.it

San Vincenti extends over about 60 hectares, with eight or so under vine in two plots. Stignano is where the sangiovese is planted and the smaller Le Corticelle farm is home to the merlot. The '06 Lo Stignano from sangiovese and merlot has a concentrated palate that combines texture and elegance.

● Stignano '06	♟♟	6
● Chianti Cl. '06	♟	5

Tenuta San Vito

via San Vito, 59
50056 Montelupo Fiorentino [FI]
TEL. 057151411
www.san-vito.com

It was a low-key year for the Drighi family, one of the pioneers of organic farming in Tuscany. The very good merlot-only Colle dei Mandorli '07 has minerally and fruity sensations on the nose and a generously soft, mouthwatering palate with a savoury finish.

● Colle dei Mandorli '07	♟♟	6
● Chianti dei Colli Fiorentini Darno '07	♟	4
● Madiere '07	♟	5

SanCarlo

via Spagni, 70
53024 Montalcino [SI]
TEL. 0577 848617
www.sancarlomontalcino.it

SanCarlo's first Brunello dates back to 1974. The cellar is on the south-west side of Montalcino, at about 400 metres above sea level. The Brunello di Montalcino '04 gives herbs, tobacco leaves and soft leather on the nose, and a well-structured palate with nicely assertive tannin.

● Brunello di Montalcino '04	♟♟	7

Podere Sanlorenzo

POD. SANLORENZO, 280
53024 MONTALCINO [SI]
TEL. 0577832965
www.poderesanlorenzo.net

This young winery, which made its first wine in 2003, is on the Maremma side of Montalcino. The style is fairly classic with long fermentation and large oak barrels. The '04 Brunello di Montalcino is lovely with cherry fruit on the nose and the balanced palate signs off with a lingering finish.

● Brunello di Montalcino Bramante '04	▼▼	7
● Rosso di Montalcino '07	▼	5

Sante Marie

LOC. VIGNONI ALTO
POD. SANTA MARIA, 95
53027 SAN QUIRICO D'ORCIA [SI]
TEL. 0577898141
studiogenerali@virgilio.it

Franco Generali makes lovely, naturally expressive wines that emphasize the features of the vintage. So there are fresh, earthy aromas in both the Curzio and the Adone from '05, which also share a thrusting palate although the Curzio has the edge, thanks to a very well-defined style.

● Orcia Rosso Curzio '05	▼▼	4
● Orcia Rosso Adone '05	▼	4
● Orcia Rosso Adone '04	▼▼	4
● Orcia Rosso Curzio '04	▼▼	4

Fattoria Sardi Giustiniani

LOC. MONTE SAN QUIRICO
VIA DELLA MAULINA, 747
55100 LUCCA
TEL. 0583341230
www.sardigiustiniani.com

Fattoria Sardi Giustiniani powers back into the Guide. The wines presented all show consistent quality and the merlot-only Sebastiano '06 made it to the finals. This is a fine quality wine with a complex nose and a full, pervasive palate. The Quinis Rosso '06 is also very good.

● Colline Lucchesi Sebastiano '06	▼▼	5
● Colline Lucchesi Quinis '06	▼▼	4
○ Colline Lucchesi Quinis Vermentino '08	▼	4

Fattoria di Sassolo

LOC. LA SERRA
VIA BUCCIANO, 59
56020 SAN MINIATO [PI]
TEL. 0571460001

We welcome the Bianco family back to the Guide. The 100-hectare estate devotes about 18 to vineyards and another ten or so to olives. The most impressive wine is the Vin Santo '00, with its attractive amber and aromas ranging from hazelnuts to honey and sweet, lingering flavour.

○ Bianco Pisano di San Torpé Vin Santo '00	▼▼	6
● Acquabona '06	▼	5
○ La Fontaccia	▼	4

Il Sassolo

VIA CITERNA, 5
59015 CARMIGNANO [PO]
TEL. 0558706488
info@ilsassolo.it

This Carmignano winery made its Guide debut thanks to the fine '06 Carmignano. A generous nose blends ripe fruit with spices and minerality before the warm, mature, mouthwatering palate takes you through to a lovely harmonious finish. The delicious Barco Reale '08 is simple but well made.

● Carmignano '06	▼▼	4
● Barco Reale '08	▼	3

Sedime

POD. SEDIME, 63
53026 PIENZA [SI]
TEL. 0578748436
capitoni.marco@libero.it

Welcome back to the Guide for Marco Capitoni's winery. The Orcia Rosso Frasi '06, from mainly sangiovese with a splash of canaiolo, is a solid wine with a supple palate. The more approachable Orcia Rosso Capitoni '07, from sangiovese and merlot, is a little mouth-drying.

● Orcia Rosso Frasi '06	▼▼	5
● Orcia Rosso Capitoni '07	▼	4

La Selva

LOC. LA SELVA, 16
53020 TREQUANDA [SI]
TEL. 057747833
www.fattorialaselvatrequanda.com

We applaud an impressive debut from this small estate near Siena, owned by the Pometti family. The stand-out is the solid, concentrated Tarchun Us '06, from cabernet sauvignon, petit verdot and sangiovese. The merlot-only Villa Boscarello '06 is well made but has less character.

● Tarchun Us '06	♥♥ 4
● Villa Boscarello '06	♀ 5

Setriolo

LOC. SETRIOLO, 61
53011 CASTELLINA IN CHIANTI [SI]
TEL. 0577743079

This small Castellina in Chianti winery has moved down, we hope temporarily, to the Other Wineries. The Chianti Classico '07 is good, if below last year's standard and masked by oak, more on the nose than the palate. Assertive acidity fleshes out the sweetness of the fruity texture.

● Chianti Cl. '07	♥♥ 5
● Memores '07	♀ 5

Signano

P.ZZA SANT'AGOSTINO, 17
53037 SAN GIMIGNANO [SI]
TEL. 0577940164

Manrico Biagini's winery makes its Guide debut. The best wine presented was the Chianti Colli Senesi Poggiarelli '06, for its lively florality-laced red berry aromas and a fresh, dynamic palate with a lovely sweet finish. The Vernaccia '08 is very clean, proffering spring flowers on the nose.

● Chianti Colli Senesi Poggiarelli '06	♥♥ 5
O Vernaccia di S. Gimignano '08	♀ 4
O Vernaccia di S. Gimignano Poggiarelli '08	♀ 4

Casale dello Sparviero

LOC. CASALE, 93
53011 CASTELLINA IN CHIANTI [SI]
TEL. 0577743228
www.casaledellosparviero.it

This 380-hectare estate in the Castellina in Chianti hills boasts a splendid 17th-century villa. The wines also impressed, above all the fleshy depth of the Riserva '06 and the juicy, dynamic Chianti Classico '07. Rosso dello Sparviero '08 is uncomplicated and youthfully alcoholic.

● Chianti Cl. '07	♥♥ 4*
● Chianti Cl. Ris. '06	♥♥ 5
● Rosso dello Sparviero '08	♀ 3

Tenuta di Sticciano

VIA DI STICCIANO, 207
50052 CERTALDO [FI]
TEL. 0571669191
www.tenutadisticciano.it

We report steady progress for the products from this estate where grapes were fermented for wine three centuries ago. The 25-hectare vineyard is mainly planted to sangiovese. Chianti Riserva della Villa '06 has vegetal aromas on the nose and a rich, juicy palate with a lingering finish.

● Chianti della Villa Ris. '06	♥♥ 4*
● Chianti Casa La Fornace '08	♀ 3
O Vin Santo del Chianti '03	♀ 5

Streda in Belvedere

VIA DI STREDA, 46
50059 VINCI [FI]
TEL. 0571729195
www.streda.it

The Lenzi family's estate of more than 80 hectares produces reliable wines. The Syrah '07 has generous spicy aromas over a base of ripe fruit while the palate is solid and nicely complex, with a mouthwatering finish. The other wines are all quite good if not particularly exciting.

● Syrah '07	♥♥ 5
● Casanova '08	♀ 4
● Chianti '08	♀ 3
● Toiano Merlot '08	♀ 5

Fattoria della Talosa

VIA PIETROSE, 15A
53045 MONTEPULCIANO [SI]
TEL. 0578758277
www.talosa.it

The Jacorossi family's winery did well again. The Nobile '06 is very impressive with light, delicate aromas and a subtle, pleasantly savoury palate. The '07 Rosso di Montepulciano is similar in style but uncertainty on the nose holds back the lovely, approachable palate.

- ● Nobile di Montepulciano '06 🍷🍷 5
- ● Rosso di Montepulciano '07 🍷 4

Podere Terenzuola

VIA VERCALDA, 14
54035 FOSDINOVO [MS]
TEL. 0187680030
www.terenzuola.com

Characterful, territory-focused wines with the tang of sea breezes. That sums up the wines of Terenzuola, a cellar that interprets vermentino with scrupulous care. The '08 Fosso di Corsano is charming if youthful while the Montesagna '08 is approachable, savoury and juicy.

- ○ Colli di Luni Vermentino Fosso di Corsano '08 🍷🍷 4
- ○ Colli di Luni Vermentino Montesagna '08 🍷🍷 4
- ● Vermentino Nero '08 🍷 4

Terreno

LOC. GRETI
VIA CITILLE, 4
50022 GREVE IN CHIANTI [FI]
TEL. 055854001
www.terreno.se

The Ruhne family's winery on the gentle Greve hills near Florence did very nicely this time. We liked the '06 Chianti Classico Riserva almost as much as last year's. The subtle wild berries on the nose introduce a sweet, flavoursome palate with texture and vitality.

- ● Chianti Cl. Ris. '06 🍷🍷 5
- ● Chianti Cl. '07 🍷 4
- ● Momento Massimo '08 🍷 7

Fattoria del Teso

VIA POLTRONIERA
55015 MONTECARLO [LU]
TEL. 0583286288
www.fattoriadelteso.it

Fattoria del Teso is one of the largest estates in Lucca with 34 hectares of vineyards on clayey, stony soil. The reds are very good, especially the sangiovese, cabernet and merlot Anfidiamante '06 with its red fruit aromas and a full, harmonious flavour. The '08 Montecarlo Rosso is forthright.

- ● Anfidiamante '06 🍷🍷 6
- ● Montecarlo Rosso '08 🍷🍷 4

Poderi Tognetti

VIA POGGIO ALLA TERRA, 18
50050 MONTAIONE [FI]
TEL. 0571698381
www.poderitognetti.it

The Tognettis make their Guide debut. Their holdings are in Chianti and Maremma and the best of the wines is the sangiovese-only Il Brigante '06 with wafts of well-defined mint-veined damsons and cherries. The palate is warm, soft and silky with an engaging finish.

- ● Il Brigante Podere Il Sapito '06 🍷🍷 5
- ● Chianti Borro ai Frati Podere Bosco Lazzeroni '07 🍷 4

Torre

LOC. VICO D'ELSA
P.ZZA TORRIGIANI, 15
50021 BARBERINO VAL D'ELSA [FI]
TEL. 0558073001
www.marchesitorrigiani.it

The winery owned by the noble Torrigianis covers over 400 hectares, 30 planted to vine. The wine we liked best was Guidacco '07, a sangiovese-heavy blend with merlot and cabernet sauvignon. Its vegetal aromas introduce a supple, relaxed palate with a nice savoury finish.

- ● Guidaccio '07 🍷🍷 5
- ● Torre di Ciardo '07 🍷 4

Fattoria La Torre

VIA PROVINCIALE DI MONTECARLO, 7
55015 MONTECARLO [LU]
TEL. 058322981
www.fattorialatorre.it

Fattoria La Torre is a reliable estate near Lucca with some of the leading vineyards at Montecarlo. The style is contemporary, aiming for wines in an international idiom that make no compromises on elegance. The syrah and cabernet Stringaio '07 and the syrah Esse '07 are outstanding.

● Esse '07	♟♟	8
● Stringaio '07	♟♟	4
○ Montecarlo La Torre '08	♟	3

Trequanda

LOC. PIAN DELLE FONTI, 100
53020 TREQUANDA [SI]
TEL. 0577662001
www.azienda-trequanda.it

There was a good guide debut for Trequanda, owned by the Cariplo bank pension fund. The '05 Orcia Invidia is savoury with a complex flavour while the '08 Vermiglio, from sangiovese, merlot, cabernet sauvignon and cabernet franc, and the sauvignon and chardonnay '08 Ghirlandaia, are both drinkable.

● Orcia Rosso Invidia '05	♟♟	4
○ Ghirlandaia '08	♟	3
● Vermiglio '08	♟	2

F.lli Vagnoni

LOC. PANCOLE, 82
53037 SAN GIMIGNANO [SI]
TEL. 0577955077
www.fratellivagnoni.com

This below par showing from the Vagnoni siblings' winery is probably just a hiccup as they have always worked carefully. The '07 Vernaccia I Mocali Riserva shows nice vanilla and fruit leading into a soft, juicy body with a slightly clenched finish. The '08 Vernaccia is simpler but flavoursome.

● Chianti Colli Senesi '07	♟	3
○ Vernaccia di S. Gimignano '08	♟	2
○ Vernaccia di S. Gimignano I Mocali Ris. '07	♟	5

Val delle Corti

LOC. LA CROCE
CASE SPARSE VAL DELLE CORTI, 144
53017 RADDA IN CHIANTI [SI]
TEL. 0577738215
www.valledellecorti.it

Val delle Corti, at Radda in Chianti, is a delightful discovery this year. The wines are textbook Radda Chiantis with kaleidoscopic aromatic and delicious fruit on the palate, embodying a lovely blend of territorial tradition and fresh flavour.

● Chianti Cl. '06	♟♟	4*
● Chianti Cl. '05	♟♟	4*
● Il Campino	♟♟	3*

Tenuta Val di Cava

LOC. VAL DI CAVA
53024 MONTALCINO [SI]
TEL. 0577848261
www.valdicava.it

We tasted Vincenzo Abbruzzese's wines before release. After a few excessive years, they now again nicely balance innovation and territorial tradition. The excellent '04 Brunello mingles sour cherries and tobacco on the nose before the full, elegant palate shows fine-grained tannin and nice acidity.

● Brunello di Montalcino '04	♟♟	7
● Brunello di Montalcino Madonna del Piano Ris. '03	♟♟	8

Valvirginio

VIA NUOVA DEL VIRGINIO, 34
50025 MONTESPERTOLI [FI]
TEL. 0571659127

The Colli Fiorentini co-operative winery, Valvirginio, debuts in the Guide with wines that offer great value for money. The '05 Baron del Nero, a blend of sangiovese, canaiolo, merlot and cabernet, impresses with lovely, fruity aromas and a supple palate. The two Chiantis are well typed.

● Baron del Nero '05	♟♟	3*
● Chianti '08	♟	1*
● Chianti Colli Fiorentini '07	♟	2*

Vescine

LOC. VESCINE
53017 RADDA IN CHIANTI [SI]
TEL. 0577741144
www.vescine.it; www.vescine.it

The village of Vèscine, after which the Paladin family's Chianti winery is named, is an enchanting corner of the municipality of Radda. The wines are excellent, from the spicy Chianti Classico '07 to the mature, concentrated Riserva Lodaiolo '06 and the accessible, well-typed Colli Senesi '07.

● Chianti Cl. '07	🍷🍷	5
● Chianti Cl. Lodolaio Ris. '06	🍷🍷	8
● Chianti Colli Senesi '07	🍷	4

Cantina Cooperativa Vignaioli del Morellino di Scansano

LOC. SARAGIOLO
58054 SCANSANO [GR]
TEL. 0564507288
www.cantinadelmorellino.it

The well-typed Morellino Roggiano '08 is again fragrant and flavoursome. The Morellino Vignabenefizio '08 is a little huskier with slightly veiled aromas and a progressive, lively palate. The evolved aromas of the Morellino Sicomoro '06 introduce nice acidity and structure on the palate.

● Morellino di Scansano Roggiano '08	🍷🍷	4
● Morellino di Scansano Sicomoro '06	🍷	5
● Morellino di Scansano Vignabenefizio '08	🍷	4

Vignavecchia

VIA SDRUCCIOLO DI PIAZZA, 7
53017 RADDA IN CHIANTI [SI]
TEL. 0577738090
www.vignavecchia.com

The Beccari family's Vignavecchia winery, one of the founders of the Consorzio del Gallo Nero, is at 500 metres near Radda in Chianti. Nineteen of the 42 hectares are planted to vine. Raddese '06, a monovarietal Sangiovese, opens with finesse and the palate is balanced, precise and dynamic.

● Raddese '06	🍷🍷	6
● Chianti Cl. Odoardo Beccari Ris. '06	🍷	5
● Chianti Cl. Ris. '06	🍷	5

Villa Corliano

LOC. BRUCIANESI
VIA DI CORLIANO, 4
50055 LASTRA A SIGNA [FI]
TEL. 0558734542
www.villacorliano.com

We welcome back to the Guide the winery owned for nearly 30 years by the Pancani family. The Ghirigoro '07 is a nice blend of cabernet sauvignon, sangiovese and foglia tonda, with spicy hints on a fresh, vegetal nose and a full, balanced palate with a long, flavoursome finish.

● Ghirigoro '07	🍷🍷	4*
● Chianti Colli Fiorentini Briccole '08	🍷	4
○ Colli dell'Etruria Centrale Vin Santo Dedicato '03	🍷	6

Villa La Ripa

LOC. ANTRIA, 38
52100 AREZZO
TEL. 0575315118
www.villalaripa.it

The enthusiastic Luzzi family runs this estate. Their '06 Psyco is a blend of equal quantities of cabernet sauvignon and sangiovese that gives fruity aromas softened by hints of vanilla and chocolate. The palate is soft and weighty with a lifting finish.

● Psyco '06	🍷🍷	3*
● Sangiovese '07	🍷	5
● Tiratari '06	🍷	5

Villa Sant'Anna

LOC. ABBADIA
VIA DELLA RESISTENZA, 143
53045 MONTEPULCIANO [SI]
TEL. 0578708017
www.villasantanna.it

The Fabroni family produces a well-made Nobile '06 with enfolding aromas and a lively hint of oriental spice before the palate shows substantial structure and good progression thanks to well-sustained acidity. The well-typed Rosso '07 is fragrant and full on the rounded palate.

● Nobile di Montepulciano '06	🍷🍷	5
● Rosso di Montepulciano '07	🍷	4
● Nobile di Montepulciano Poldo '05	🍷🍷 (white)	6
○ Vin Santo '99	🍷🍷 (white)	8

MARCHE

Two wines, showing diametrically opposed qualities, won their first Three Glasses. The first is a white, Offida Pecorino Ciprea '08, produced in the southern reaches of the Marche. This will surprise few in the region, since for some years now Simone Capecci has been putting out vintages that are among the DOC zone's finest. This award should provide further impetus for planting the variety, which increasing numbers of growers are doing, encouraged by its overwhelming success in the market. The other wine is a Sangiovese from the province of Pesaro, Valturio '07. In response to observations that this is some kind of miracle, it must be said that the wine is certainly unique, the creation of a talented visionary in a virgin territory. Adriano Galli has planted his bush-trained vines in Montefeltro, in a landscape of unblemished limestone whiteness. It should also be said that the rest of the Pesaro area could use some complexity, saddled as it is by simply well-made, easy-drinking wines that are missing the train on which other designated areas are travelling. Verdicchio is one, with a full eight awards, six to Iesi and two to Matelica. This further testifies to the power and personality of a grape that is ductile and multi-faceted, with wines that display richness of character, multi-layered fragrances and significant cellarability. Alongside the usual champions, which get more refined with each passing year, note should be taken of Montecappone, with its powerful Utopia Riserva '07, and of the return to the winner's podium of two important co-operatives, Moncaro with its Vigna Novali Riserva'06, and Belisario in Matelica with its Cambrugiano Riserva '06. A look at the reds sparks a more lively discussion. Although they garnered five awards, the one-off Valturio included, our tastings did not reveal a very widespread distribution of quality bottlings. In particular, the montepulciano-based wines may have amplitude and power but at times they lack depth and aromatic sharpness. Laurels went to wines that can point to uniqueness, such as Velenosi's austere Rosso Piceno Superiore Roggio del Filare '06, the overwhelming Regina del Bosco '06 from Dezi, the inimitable Kurni '07 from Oasi degli Angeli and Piantate Lunghe's kaleidoscopic Conero Rossini Riserva '06. It is no accident that the only real newcomer is Pelago '06 from Umani Ronchi, a wine that is elegant, natural and rich in nuances, and an object lesson, for those who have ears to hear, in what we mean by complexity and sensory refinement.

Aurora

LOC. SANTA MARIA IN CARRO
C.DA CIAFONE, 98
63035 OFFIDA [AP]
TEL. 0736810007
www.viniaurora.it

CELLAR SALES
PRE-BOOKED VISITS
VISITOR FACILITIES

ANNUAL PRODUCTION 45,000 bottles
HECTARES UNDER VINE 8.5
VITICULTURE METHOD Organic certified

Aurora is a philosophy and a lifestyle, as well as a winery. For 20 years now, the operation's five partners have lived out their respect for the earth and for the dignity of a famer's life, and a political commitment that takes an active part in reflections on the contemporary world. As to their wines, the line is always reliable. Federico Pignati, who directs winemaking, has honed his approach over the years and does an expert job with natural fermentations of Aurora's organically farmed grapes.

The classic styled Barricadiero '07, largely montepulciano with a bit of cabernet and merlot, went to our final round, impelled by its deep, crisp-edged nose and a palate displaying the noblest of tannins and a lean austerity. We liked Rosso Piceno '08 for its taut vibrancy in the mouth, and for the complexity of its bright, fragrant fruit. Fiobbo '07 is 100 per cent pecorino, part cask-fermented. It's an interesting wine but it slips out of formal categories and is best appreciated for what it does naturally in the glass. Repeated tastings of older vintages have proved its staying power and its growth into further complexity.

Belisario

VIA ARISTIDE MERLONI, 12
62024 MATELICA [MC]
TEL. 0737787247
www.belisario.it

CELLAR SALES
PRE-BOOKED VISITS

ANNUAL PRODUCTION 820,000 bottles
HECTARES UNDER VINE 300
VITICULTURE METHOD Organic certified

The upper Esino valley saw a huge influx of industry in the 1970s, and the local wine industry suffered as the farmers headed for the factories. Belisario, a co-operative in Matelica and Cerreto d'Esi founded in 1971, has ensured an income to even the smallest of producers, thus halting further abandonment of vineyards. More surprising is the fact that quite some years back it was pushing for a viticulture based more on quality than quantity. Belisario's excellent Verdicchio di Matelica bottlings earn plaudits for its expert management and the 180 members who farm 300 hectares of vines.

Cambrugiano is a single-vineyard Riserva di Verdicchio, part of which is cask aged. In '06, perfectly ripe fruit contributed to a complex, fragrant amalgam whose focus is an elegant vein of toasty oak, an eloquent expression of terroir adding to admirable complexity and length in the mouth. Vigneti del Cerro '08 shows floral, clean-edged and utterly refreshing, with a very reasonable price tag. Vigneti Belisario '08 offers good energy and savouriness in the mouth, but some fairly evolved notes on the nose. The sangiovese and merlot Rosasenzaspine is fragrant and ready to enjoy, as is the velvety Esino Bianco Ferrante.

● Barricadiero '07	♥♥ 5
○ Offida Pecorino Fiobbo '07	♥♥ 4*
● Rosso Piceno '08	♥♥ 3*
● Rosso Piceno Sup. '07	♥ 4
● Barricadiero '06	♥♥♥ 5
● Barricadiero '04	♥♥♥ 5
● Barricadiero '03	♥♥♥ 5*
● Barricadiero '02	♥♥♥ 5
● Barricadiero '01	♥♥♥ 5
○ Offida Pecorino Fiobbo '06	♥♥ 4*
● Rosso Piceno '07	♥♥ 3
● Rosso Piceno Sup. '06	♥♥ 4*

○ Verdicchio di Matelica Cambrugiano Ris. '06	♥♥♥ 4*
○ Verdicchio di Matelica Vign. Belisario '08	♥♥ 4*
○ Verdicchio di Matelica Vign. del Cerro '08	♥♥ 3*
● Aeno '08	♥ 4
○ Esino Bianco Ferrante '08	♥ 2*
⊙ Rosasenzaspine '08	♥ 2*
○ Verdicchio di Matelica Terre di Valbona '08	♥ 2*
○ Verdicchio di Matelica Cambrugiano Ris. '02	♥♥♥ 4*
● Aeno '07	♥♥ 4
○ Verdicchio di Matelica Cambrugiano Ris. '05	♥♥ 4
○ Verdicchio di Matelica Meridia '06	♥♥ 4
○ Verdicchio di Matelica Terre di Valbona '07	♥♥ 2*
○ Verdicchio di Matelica Vign. Belisario '07	♥♥ 4
○ Verdicchio di Matelica Vign. del Cerro '07	♥♥ 3*

★ Bucci

FRAZ. PONGELLI
VIA CONA, 30
60010 OSTRA VETERE [AN]
TEL. 071964179
www.villabucci.com

CELLAR SALES
PRE-BOOKED VISITS

ANNUAL PRODUCTION 120,000 bottles
HECTARES UNDER VINE 26
VITICULTURE METHOD Organic certified

Elegance, finely calibrated structure, breadth and an aromatic complexity that deepens impressively with the years are descriptors already earned by Ampelio Bucci's Verdicchios. They have recently earned one more, naturalness, this time thanks to systematic implementation of organic practices. The trick now is to find some way to maintain the wines' accustomed measured style and yet at the same time give them more territorial expressiveness while freeing vineyards and cellar from the long hand of chemistry.

Villa Bucci '07, though young, flaunts a nose of great finesse in an amalgam of hay, camomile and aniseed expressed with subtlety and self-confidence. The palate, multi-faceted but soft-contoured, is also marked by a plastic energy that ensures superb approachability. The standard Verdicchio, revealing still-tenuous evolved nuances that enrich scents of fresh greens and clean notes of dried nuts, builds distinctiveness and well-measured proportion on the palate. Rosso Piceno Pongelli '07 offers delicious drinkability, thanks to wild cherry on the palate, and velvety tannins that contribute to the overall harmony of expression.

Le Caniette

C.DA CANALI, 23
63038 RIPATRANSONE [AP]
TEL. 07359200
www.lecaniette.it

CELLAR SALES
PRE-BOOKED VISITS

ANNUAL PRODUCTION 60,000 bottles
HECTARES UNDER VINE 16
VITICULTURE METHOD Organic certified

The Vagnoni brothers pursue their own personal wine vision with admirable consistency and tenacity. For them, it is a totalizing world-view that involves not only vineyard and cellar but events off-premises as well among fellow Piceno-area producers. Making wine for the Vagnonis is a life choice that subsumes them, and quality is a crucial personal accomplishment well before it has any commercial implications. Le Caniette rises on a hill a few steps from Ripatransone, where the nearby Adriatic tempers the climate with lazy thermals and constant breezes.

The Vagnonis want their wines to exhibit a warm, mature style that presses down somewhat upon their structure. This characteristic tends to divide critics and public alike, but it is clearly visible and very deliberate. Iosonogaia '07, made from cask-fermented pecorino that is partly aged in barriques, opens very broadly over lively acidity, in spite of its warm alcohol. Sibilla Tiburtina '05, after rich zabaglione and barley, shows silky and seductive in the mouth. The reds we tasted did not shine since their considerable weight militates against the balancing out of ripeness, volume and alcoholic power.

Wine	Rating
○ Verdicchio dei Castelli di Jesi Cl. Villa Bucci Ris. '07	♛♛♛ 7
○ Verdicchio dei Castelli di Jesi Cl. Sup. '08	♛♛ 4*
● Rosso Piceno Tenuta Pongelli '07	♛♛ 4*
○ Verdicchio dei Castelli di Jesi Cl. Villa Bucci Ris. '06	♛♛♛ 7
○ Verdicchio dei Castelli di Jesi Cl. Villa Bucci Ris. '05	♛♛♛ 6
○ Verdicchio dei Castelli di Jesi Cl. Villa Bucci Ris. '04	♛♛♛ 6
○ Verdicchio dei Castelli di Jesi Cl. Villa Bucci Ris. '03	♛♛♛ 6
○ Verdicchio dei Castelli di Jesi Cl. Villa Bucci Ris. '01	♛♛♛ 6
○ Verdicchio dei Castelli di Jesi Cl. Villa Bucci Ris. '00	♛♛♛ 6
○ Verdicchio dei Castelli di Jesi Cl. Villa Bucci Ris. '99	♛♛♛ 6

Wine	Rating
○ Offida Passerina Vino Santo Sibilla Tiburtina '05	♛♛ 6
○ Offida Pecorino Iosonogaia non sono Lucrezia '07	♛♛ 5
● Rosso Piceno Morellone '05	♛ 5
● Rosso Piceno Rosso Bello '07	♛ 4
○ Offida Passerina Vino Santo Sibilla Chimica '04	♛♛ 6
○ Offida Pecorino Iosonogaia non sono Lucrezia '06	♛♛ 5
● Rosso Piceno Morellone '03	♛♛ 5
● Rosso Piceno Morellone '02	♛♛ 5
● Rosso Piceno Nero di Vite '04	♛♛ 7
● Rosso Piceno Nero di Vite '01	♛♛ 7

La Canosa

C.DA SAN PIETRO, 6
63030 ROTELLA [AP]
TEL. 0736374556
www.lacanosaagricola.it

CELLAR SALES
PRE-BOOKED VISITS

ANNUAL PRODUCTION **100,000 bottles**
HECTARES UNDER VINE **25**
VITICULTURE METHOD **Conventional**

La Canosa is an ambitious enterprise. In future, Riccardo Reina wants to make not just wines but every kind of product that this beautiful and still pristine corner of the planet can bring forth. For now, he has put in the vineyards and built his winemaking facility beneath a perfectly restructured old farm residence. Reina is much caught up by his Marche challenge, having chosen an area whose quality potential has not yet been plumbed, high in the Piceno hills and very far from the sea, where the climate exhibits great evenness.

The wines are soundly crafted and consistent, the winery's first step in understanding its terroir, an area that shows great potential for elegance. The bottlings already have plenty of finesse and growing self-confidence will bring fine surprises. The sangiovese Nullius '07 is fresh and elegant, with steady progression and a long finish. In fact, its eloquent proportions took it to the finals. The all-montepulciano Musè '07 is generously redolent of oak, then ductile and tasty in the mouth, with well-ripened tannins. Nummaria '07 is also good, with balance in the mouth following smooth fruit and spicy oak. The lithe, floral Servator '08 is from passerina.

Carminucci

VIA SAN LEONARDO, 39
63013 GROTTAMMARE [AP]
TEL. 0735735869
www.carminucci.com

CELLAR SALES

ANNUAL PRODUCTION **200,000 bottles**
HECTARES UNDER VINE **46**
VITICULTURE METHOD **Conventional**

The production of Piero and Giovanni Carminucci is actually low compared to the number of hectares they cultivate. This is not surprising, given that they have always been in the bulk trade, but in the last ten years have been concentrating on improving the line. At present, they have no one wine that is heading for the summit but the range is reliable, with a smooth, fruit-forward expression that shows the prints of talented consultant Pierluigi Lorenzetti. The operation is now certified organic, which further attests to the serious attention they give to their terroir and wines.

Litora '05, an unusual chardonnay and verdicchio blend, has a complex, taut palate and concludes with an intriguing smoky note. Falerio Naumachos '08, on the other hand, offers roasted nuts, then a supple, relaxed progression. The two natives, Pecorino and Passerina, are once again impressive, both with crisp citrus, and Belato '08 for overall tastiness. In the reds, the well-fruited Naumachos '06 opens wide to generous morello cherry, followed by notably forceful alcohol. Finally, Carminucci's Grotte sul Mare line is fragrant, reliable and reasonably priced.

● Nullius '07	⏲⏲	5
● Musè '07	⏲⏲	5
● Rosso Piceno Sup. Nummaria '07	⏲⏲	4*
● Rosso Piceno Signator '07	⏲	3
○ Servator '08	⏲	4
● Nullius '05	⏲⏲	5
● Rosso Piceno Signator '06	⏲⏲	3*
● Rosso Piceno Sup. Nummaria '06	⏲⏲	4
○ Servator '07	⏲⏲	4*

○ Falerio dei Colli Ascolani Naumachos '08	⏲⏲	3*
○ Litora '05	⏲⏲	5
○ Offida Passerina Casta '08	⏲⏲	3*
○ Offida Pecorino Belato '08	⏲⏲	4*
● Rosso Piceno Sup. Naumachos '06	⏲⏲	4*
○ Falerio dei Colli Ascolani Grotte sul Mare '08	⏲	2*
○ Falerio dei Colli Ascolani Viabore '08	⏲	2*
⊙ Rosato Grotte sul Mare '08	⏲	2*
● Rosso Piceno Grotte sul Mare '08	⏲	2*
○ Falerio dei Colli Ascolani Naumachos '07	⏲⏲	3*
○ Litora '04	⏲⏲	5
○ Offida Passerina Casta '07	⏲⏲	3*
○ Offida Pecorino Belato '07	⏲⏲	4
● Paccaosso '05	⏲⏲	8
● Rosso Piceno Sup. Naumachos '05	⏲⏲	4*

Casalfarneto

VIA FARNETO, 12
60030 SERRA DE' CONTI [AN]
TEL. 0731889001
www.casalfarneto.it

CELLAR SALES
PRE-BOOKED VISITS

ANNUAL PRODUCTION **440,000 bottles**
HECTARES UNDER VINE **13**
VITICULTURE METHOD **Conventional**

Casalfarneto was purchased a few years ago by the Togni family. With assets in mineral water and sparkling wine, plus an extensive distribution network, they thought that a perfect complement would be a high-quality viticultural concern in Marche, focusing on the distinctive verdicchio and montepulciano varieties. Considerable investment went into a new winemaking facility and the vineyards, which are planted at Serra de' Conti and Montecarotto, an area known for its fine Verdicchio. At present, the Casalfarneto whites express admirable elegance while the reds need more work.

Among the steel-fermented whites, Grancasale steals the thunder from Fontevecchia '08 for the first time. Its nose gives clean-edged almond while the palate is broad, tasty and impressively long. Fontevecchia shows unremitting energy on the palate and bright, classy citrus tones, concluding with an ultra-savoury finish. The montepulciano Merago '06 is new. Matured in 25-hectolitre casks, it offers cherry preserves and pastries and still rather noticeable tannins. Tonos '06, from montepulciano grapes grown on Mount Conero, builds a fine palate but the fruit is somewhat brooding and overripe.

○ Verdicchio dei Castelli di Jesi Cl. Sup. Fontevecchia '08		🍷🍷 4*
○ Verdicchio dei Castelli di Jesi Cl. Sup. Grancasale '08		🍷🍷 4*
● Merago '06		🍷 4
● Rosso Conero Tonos '06		🍷 4
○ Verdicchio dei Castelli di Jesi Cl. Grancasale Ris. '06		🏆🏆 4
○ Verdicchio dei Castelli di Jesi Cl. Solustro '06		🏆🏆 3*
○ Verdicchio dei Castelli di Jesi Cl. Sup. Fontevecchia '07		🏆🏆 4*
○ Verdicchio dei Castelli di Jesi Cl. Sup. Fontevecchia '06		🏆🏆 4*

Casalis Douhet

LOC. PORTO POTENZA PICENA
VIA MONTECORIOLANO,11
62018 POTENZA PICENA [MC]
TEL. 0733688121
www.coriolano.com

CELLAR SALES
PRE-BOOKED VISITS

ANNUAL PRODUCTION **30,000 bottles**
HECTARES UNDER VINE **40**
VITICULTURE METHOD **Conventional**

Casalis Douhet is a small piece of Campania in the heart of the Marche. Not for any Campanian grape varieties, but because of some rather convoluted history. The Casalis Douhet family, once viticulturalists and merchants, were without heirs and everything went to the publicly owned Colosimo institute for the blind, based in Naples, so that today the Campania regional authority owns Montecoriolano. To restore the estate's ancient splendour, the management has begun complete restructuring, beginning with the vineyards and the romantic cellar, housed in a late 19th-century structure.

Production is still modest but the wines we tasted were sure-footed. The quality leader is Giulio Douhet '07, whose montepulciano fully infuses the nose, followed by a palate that is well disciplined but supple, thanks to grippy acidity from sangiovese. Close behind is Coriolano '06, almost half and half cabernet and merlot, with a dash of montepulciano. Oak still veils the nose but ripe fruit and good spice manage to push through nicely while the palate is vibrant and dynamic. Colosimo '07 shows less complex. The all-chardonnay Oltremare '08 stands out among the whites with its emphatically fruited, ample nose.

● Coriolano '06	🍷🍷 4*
○ Oltremare Bianco '08	🍷🍷 3*
● Rosso Piceno Giulio Douhet '07	🍷🍷 4*
● Colli Maceratesi Rosso Colosimo '07	🍷 3
● Colli Maceratesi Rosso '03	🏆🏆 3*
● Merlot '03	🏆🏆 3*
● Rosso '03	🏆🏆 4*

Maria Pia Castelli

C.DA SANT'ISIDORO, 22
63015 MONTE URANO [AP]
TEL. 0734841774
www.mariapiacastelli.it

CELLAR SALES
PRE-BOOKED VISITS

ANNUAL PRODUCTION **20,000 bottles**
HECTARES UNDER VINE **8**
VITICULTURE METHOD **Natural**

Our first tastings only a few years ago revealed that the winery run by Maria Pia Castelli and Enrico Bartoletti was not going to be one of those run-of-the-mill operations. With oenological assistance from Oasi degli Angeli's Marco Casolanetti, they veer off the beaten path and aim for an alternative style that remains a judicious mix of the modern and the traditional. Castelli's wines have gone beyond expectations in their distinctiveness and character, even if the lineaments are not to everyone's taste. After all, those who brook no compromises accept such risks.

Stella Flora is the best example of this originality. A traditional blend of white trebbiano, passerina, pecorino and malvasia grapes, it ferments on the skins and is then cask-aged. The '07 is the expected kaleidoscopic array of bitter herbs, tangerines and fresh butter, complemented by a palate of stunning sapidity and length. The nose on the all-montepulciano Erasmo Castelli '07 is darker, with liquorice, untanned leather and morello cherry ushering in an equally dense, dark palate, only slightly contracted by youthful tannins that will soon mellow. Orano '08 is a Sangiovese, firm and self-confident in the mouth, and a lovely, approachable wine..

● Erasmo Castelli '07	♟♟	6
○ Stella Flora '07	♟♟	6
● Orano '08	♟♟	4*
● Erasmo Castelli '06	♟♟♟	6
● Erasmo Castelli '05	♟♟	6
● Erasmo Castelli '04	♟♟	6
○ Stella Flora '06	♟♟	6
○ Stella Flora '05	♟♟	6

Cantine di Castignano

C.DA SAN VENANZO, 31
63032 CASTIGNANO [AP]
TEL. 0736822216
www.cantinedicastignano.com

CELLAR SALES
PRE-BOOKED VISITS

ANNUAL PRODUCTION **350,000 bottles**
HECTARES UNDER VINE **520**
VITICULTURE METHOD **Conventional**

The Cantine di Castignano co-operative was launched with the mission of gathering in all of the grape growers in the larger Ascoli area, right up to the ridges of Monte dell'Ascensione. The climate here is quite different from that in the hills facing the Adriatic and nights are colder. This in turn impacts ripening, demanding careful attention by vineyard managers. The one grape that seems to thrive here is pecorino, a variety that loves the hillslopes. Castignano's wines give good quality for their reasonable prices, a policy that has always been important to its members.

The pecorino Montemisio '08 is the star, with tasty, crisp fruitiness, particularly in notes of citrus and pineapple on a palate that shows admirable proportion and length. Offida Passerina '08 is slender but well-sculpted, marching to a spirited acidity. Modern-styled Gramelot '07 is a blend of trebbiano, pecorino, passerina and verdicchio aged six months in oak. It is marked by notably succulent fruit in the mouth, plus subtle ginger, and a velvet mouthfeel. Falerio Destriero '08 unfurls a bouquet of great finesse, ending on ripe apple. Offida Gran Maestro '05 stands out for smooth, ripe blackberry and rather biting tannins.

○ Offida Pecorino Montemisio '08	♟♟	2*
○ Falerio dei Colli Ascolani Destriero '08	♟♟	2*
○ Gramelot '07	♟♟	3*
○ Offida Passerina '08	♟♟	2*
● Offida Rosso Gran Maestro '05	♟♟	4*
● Rosso Piceno Sup. Destriero '07	♟	2*
● Templaria '07	♟	3
○ Falerio dei Colli Ascolani Destriero '07	♟♟	2*
○ Gramelot '06	♟♟	3
○ Offida Passerina '07	♟♟	2*
○ Offida Pecorino Montemisio '07	♟♟	2*
● Offida Rosso Gran Maestro '04	♟♟	4
● Rosso Piceno '07	♟♟	1*
● Rosso Piceno Sup. Destriero '06	♟♟	2*
● Templaria '06	♟♟	3

Ciù Ciù

LOC. SANTA MARIA IN CARRO
C.DA CIAFONE, 106
63035 OFFIDA [AP]
TEL. 0736810001
www.ciuciu.com

CELLAR SALES
PRE-BOOKED VISITS
VISITOR FACILITIES
FOOD

ANNUAL PRODUCTION **445,000 bottles**
HECTARES UNDER VINE **98**
VITICULTURE METHOD **Organic certified**

The Bartolomei brothers already boast significant vineyard holdings in the centre of the Rosso Piceno Superiore designated area but every year sees more expansion, proof that Ciù Ciù is one of the more dynamic operations in the Piceno area. The reasons are clear. Wines display purity of fruit that is delectable without being simple or slipshod, price tags are in line with quality and winemaking that does a better job than anyone else in maintaining a traditionalist approach with modern practices. The range of dynamic, well-extracted reds and remarkably pleasurable whites is wide.

This year, we were unable to taste the star reds, Oppidum and Offida Esperanto, which were still ageing. But we had two pleasant surprises in Saggio and Rosso Piceno Superiore Gotico, both '07. The first is a Sangiovese with massive fruit laid on a crunchy, energy-laden palate. The second is equally dynamic and driving, with compelling, fleshy pulp in the mouth. Pecorino Le Merlettaie '08 is again right on the mark, with both palate and nose proffering convincing notes of honey and blossoms. Both Evoé '08, from passerina, and Falerio Oris '08 are supple and juicy, perfect for their intended place on the daily table.

● Rosso Piceno Sup. Gotico '07	🍷🍷 4*
● Saggio Sangiovese '07	🍷🍷 5
○ Evoé '08	🍷🍷 3*
○ Falerio dei Colli Ascolani Oris '08	🍷🍷 3*
○ Offida Pecorino Le Merlettaie '08	🍷🍷 4*
○ Infinito Brut	🍷 4
● Rosso Piceno Bacchus '08	🍷 3
● San Carro '08	🍷 4
○ Offida Pecorino Le Merlettaie '07	🍷🍷 4*
● Oppidum '04	🍷🍷 5
● Rosso Piceno Sup. Gotico '06	🍷🍷 4*
● Saggio Sangiovese '06	🍷🍷 5
● San Carro '07	🍷🍷 4*

Cocci Grifoni

LOC. SAN SAVINO
C.DA MESSIERI, 12
63038 RIPATRANSONE [AP]
TEL. 073590143
www.tenutaroccigrifoni.it

CELLAR SALES
PRE-BOOKED VISITS

ANNUAL PRODUCTION **360,000 bottles**
HECTARES UNDER VINE **50**
VITICULTURE METHOD **Conventional**

Guido Cocci Grifoni sums up the winemaking history of the Piceno area. This spare-charactered grower has dedicated an entire lifetime to the vine, creating among others the initial versions of Rosso Piceno Superiore in the first vintage possible after the 1968 introduction of the DOC. His too is the merit for the re-introduction of pecorino, since he recovered cuttings from ancient vineyards in Arquata del Tronto, in the Monti Sibillini. The house style here is rigorously traditional, with considerable austerity, and at times some evolution, but the wines are tasty and largely long-lived.

The '08 version of the widely acclaimed Pecorino Colle Vecchio murmurs fragrantly of aniseed, then lays out characteristically upfront savouriness. Vigna Messieri '04 is glossy and full bodied, a bit evolved rather than fresh but still offering fine sensory complexity in the mouth. Le Torri is the other Rosso Piceno Superiore whose '06 edition, the most impressive ever, missed our finals by just a hair. Its remarkable progression is powered by a broad vein of bracing acidity. Vegetal notes and still-green tannins bring Il Grifone '03 down a rung while Falerio San Basso '08 parades a traditional florality.

○ Offida Pecorino Podere Colle Vecchio '08	🍷🍷 4*
● Rosso Piceno Sup. Le Torri '06	🍷🍷 3*
● Rosso Piceno Sup. V. Messieri '04	🍷🍷 4*
○ Falerio dei Colli Ascolani Vign. San Basso '08	🍷 3
○ Offida Passerina Gaudio Magno Brut '08	🍷 4
● Offida Rosso Il Grifone '03	🍷 5
○ Falerio dei Colli Ascolani Vign. San Basso '07	🍷🍷 3
○ Offida Pecorino Podere Colle Vecchio '07	🍷🍷 4*
● Rosso Piceno Sup. Le Torri '05	🍷🍷 3*
● Rosso Piceno Sup. Le Torri '04	🍷🍷 3*
● Rosso Piceno Sup. Le Torri '03	🍷🍷 3
● Rosso Piceno Sup. V. Messieri '03	🍷🍷 4*
● Rosso Piceno Sup. V. Messieri '02	🍷🍷 4*

Collestefano

LOC. COLLE STEFANO, 3
62022 CASTELRAIMONDO [MC]
TEL. 0737640439
www.collestefano.com

CELLAR SALES
PRE-BOOKED VISITS

ANNUAL PRODUCTION **60,000 bottles**
HECTARES UNDER VINE **10**
VITICULTURE METHOD **Organic certified**

Organic viticulture and making just one white wine, the perfect reflection of its growing year and terroir, would seem to be a fairly simple affair. And yet Fabio and Silvia Marchionni have transformed it into an elegant project that shows off the distinctive character that verdicchio can achieve in this particular valley. Running north-south, it is protected by two natural barriers, isolated both from the Adriatic as well as from severity of the highest Apennine peaks. The Verdicchio di Matelica that emerges here is a subtle creature and Collestefano interprets it beautifully.

Fabio Marchionni always produces noble Verdicchios, sometimes rich and ripe, on others hard and cutting. A useful recommendation is to always hide away a few bottles in your cellar and forget them, since in a few years' time they will have acquired extraordinary complexity. Collestefano '08 is on the subtle side but displays great distinctiveness. It offers fresh citrus, then opens to a crisp but supple progression and concludes with a savoury finish. Marchionni now offers a rosé, Rosa di Elena, from sangiovese and a little cabernet. It is cleanly floral and nervy acidity leads steadily to an almost saline note at the end.

O Verdicchio di Matelica Collestefano '08	♟♟	4*
⊙ Rosa di Elena '08	♟♟	3*
O Verdicchio di Matelica Collestefano '07	♟♟♟	4*
O Verdicchio di Matelica Collestefano '06	♟♟♟	4*
O Verdicchio di Matelica Collestefano '05	♟♟	4*
O Verdicchio di Matelica Collestefano '04	♟♟	4*

Collevite - Cantine della Marca

VIA VALLE CECCHINA, 9
63030 MONSAMPOLO DEL TRONTO [AP]
TEL. 0735767050
www.collevite.com

CELLAR SALES
PRE-BOOKED VISITS

ANNUAL PRODUCTION **100,000 bottles**
HECTARES UNDER VINE **30**
VITICULTURE METHOD **Organic certified**

Collevite, launched in 2008, is an impressive, still developing project that holds terrific promise. A group of growers, many with long viticultural experience, pooled together their assets and purchased from the Ascoli Piceno consortium the premises of the Enopolio di Monsampolo del Tronto. The vineyards are scattered through Carassai, Ripatransone and Offida, areas under intense cultivation, largely to red wine grapes. And it is precisely Collevite's red wines that are yielding its most impressive initial results, in a line distinctive for its high quality and reasonable price tags.

We voted Villa Piatti Rosso '07 the line leader. Made of 60 per cent montepulciano and equal amounts of merlot and cabernet, it is both dense and smooth, brimming with succulent fruit. The alcohol and tannin extraction are considerable but they do not halt its progression. Evolved notes predominate over primary aromas on the nose of Rosso Piceno Superiore '06 and the palate offers impressive, sturdy pleasure. Rosso Piceno shows a tad rustic as well, the ripe fruit just this side of preserves. Zeroquindici '08, a sangiovese rosé, is tempting and dynamic. Among the whites, Offida Pecorino '08 parades plenty of smooth, stylish fruit.

O Offida Pecorino '08	♟♟	4*
● Rosso Piceno Sup. '06	♟♟	3*
● Villa Piatti Rosso '07	♟♟	4
O Falerio dei Colli Ascolani '08	♟	3
● Rosso Piceno '08	♟	3
O Villa Piatti Bianco '08	♟	4
⊙ Zeroquindici '08	♟	3

Colli di Serrapetrona

VIA COLLI, 7/8
62020 SERRAPETRONA [MC]
TEL. 0733908329
www.collidiserrapetrona.it

CELLAR SALES
PRE-BOOKED VISITS

ANNUAL PRODUCTION **71,000 bottles**
HECTARES UNDER VINE **23**
VITICULTURE METHOD **Conventional**

Alfiero Sabbatini , owner of Colli di Serrapetrona along with Romano De Angelis and other partners, has a clear idea of what to do with vernaccia nera grapes: leave sparkling versions aside and make dry and sweet still wines. That means a break with a well-ordered tradition and breaking brand-new ground. The first step was to bring in a winemaker from outside, the able Federico Giotto. The second was to try every road, even those that led nowhere. Now, after many ups and downs, the right balance seems to have been struck, particularly regarding oak ageing.

All of the wines are made from vernaccia nera. Robbione '06, a dry red made from grapes semi-dried for six weeks, no longer wears the oak so heavily. It now shoots out emphatic, ultra-peppery aromas, followed by a solid framework that nicely flanks a fast-flowing progression studded with a myriad tannins. No dried fruit goes into Collequanto '07 but it exhibits much the same style in a minor key. Black pepper and subtle vegetal notes animate a spacious, toothsome palate. Sommo '06, a sweet wine made from grapes dried for four months, should be tasted, to experience its unusual richness, achieved without any excessive sweetness.

La Cantina dei Colli Ripani

VIA TOSCIANO, 28
63038 RIPATRANSONE [AP]
TEL. 07359505
www.colliripani.it

CELLAR SALES
PRE-BOOKED VISITS

ANNUAL PRODUCTION **600,000 bottles**
HECTARES UNDER VINE **1100**
VITICULTURE METHOD **Organic certified**

The municipality of Ripatransone seems to be a riot of vineyards, since the historical fragmentation of fields, a legacy of the sharecropping system, results in a myriad small growers. Colli Ripani has to coordinate the activities of its 400 members who cultivate some 1,100 hectares, and direct high-quality production towards Pharus, their top line. It focuses on the local designated areas at competitive prices. Collini Ripani also has a network of direct-sales outlets throughout the Marche region that facilitate distribution of the various labels.

The reds are sturdy and spirited, the most impressive being Rosso Piceno Superiore Castellano '06. Flaunting elegant fruit, it is expansive on the palate and closes long and savoury. Offida Rosso Leo Ripanus shows less surefooted than usual, marked by burred tannins from a weak '05 growing season. The base Rosso Piceno, Rupe Nero, is soundly made. Among the whites, the '08 Falerio, Brezzolino, is a front-runner, with well-delineated ripe fruit, juicy middle and a rich-flavoured finish of some finesse. The pecorino Rugaro '08 is expansive and smooth but tangier acidity would have better balanced its heft.

● Serrapetrona Robbione '06	♟♟ 5
● Serrapetrona Collequanto '07	♟♟ 4*
● Sommo '06	♟♟ 5
● Serrapetrona Robbione '05	♟♟ 5
● Serrapetrona Robbione '04	♟♟ 5
● Sommo '05	♟♟ 5
● Sommo '04	♟♟ 5

○ Falerio dei Colli Ascolani Brezzolino '08	♟♟ 2*
● Rosso Piceno Sup. Castellano '06	♟♟ 3*
○ Offida Pecorino Rugaro '08	♟ 3
● Offida Rosso Leo Ripanus '05	♟ 4
● Rosso Piceno Rupe Nero '08	♟ 1*
○ Falerio dei Colli Ascolani Brezzolino '07	♟♟ 2*
○ Falerio dei Colli Ascolani Brezzolino '06	♟♟ 2*
● Khorakhanè '03	♟♟ 6
○ Offida Pecorino Rugaro '07	♟♟ 3*
○ Offida Pecorino Rugaro '06	♟♟ 3
● Rosso Piceno Rupe Nero '07	♟♟ 1*
● Rosso Piceno Sup. Castellano '05	♟♟ 3

Cantina Cològnola

LOC. COLÒGNOLA
62011 CINGOLI [MC]
TEL. 0733616438
www.agrarialombardi.it

CELLAR SALES
PRE-BOOKED VISITS

ANNUAL PRODUCTION **65,000 bottles**
HECTARES UNDER VINE **18**
VITICULTURE METHOD **Conventional**

Colognola, in the municipality of Cingoli and the province of Macerata, near Iesi and within the Classico zone of Verdicchio. Since the terroir is the same as Staffolo, the potential for producing great whites is quite high. It is all the more disappointing then that this fairly young operation, run by Antonietta Lombardi and Corrado Drudi, suffers from some discontinuity. We are certain that more experience will bring balance to Colognola's wines. The Verdicchios we tasted had a tangy savouriness, with well-crafted aromatics and no technical shortcomings.

San Michele della Ghiffa '07 uncorks a fine performance. Tangy mineral impressions on the nose are matched by a compelling vibrancy in the mouth, although it is a bit hot and lacks that extra length to push it up a rung. A creamy entry follows smoky nuances in Labieno Riserva '06, and it concludes with a very flavoursome, mineral-laced finale. Ghiffa '08 lays out fine, pulpy fruit to finish appealingly with dried blossoms. Passito Cingulum '07 is sweet and pleasant but somewhat under-complex. Sestiere '06, from 80 per cent merlot with the rest montepulciano, offers peppery aromas smoothed by tobacco leaf, and an evenly proportioned structure.

Colonnara

VIA MANDRIOLE, 6
60034 CUPRAMONTANA [AN]
TEL. 0731780273
www.colonnara.it

CELLAR SALES
PRE-BOOKED VISITS

ANNUAL PRODUCTION **1,000,000 bottles**
HECTARES UNDER VINE **120**
VITICULTURE METHOD **Organic certified**

Colonnara's 50th birthday fell in 2009. Those long years include successful efforts to unite the many growers spread throughout the hills on the right bank of the river Esino, owners of vineyards among the area's finest. Currently the winery boasts 110 members cultivating 120 hectares, which yield about 1,000,000 bottles. Over the years, Colonnara has gained recognition for its sparkling wines as well as for its elegant, long-lived Verdicchios, aged only in steel, some of which, like Cuprese 1992, are still sound and tasting fine.

The sparklers get the best marks. The ductility of the verdicchio grape is borne out once again by the two Metodo Classicos, both successful in amalgamating expression, sensory finesse and compelling weight. Ubaldo Rosi '04 was our favourite for its creamy palate exhibiting a crisp vein of balsam. As to the still wines, we recommend Tùfico '06, warm toned, ripe and delicious, as well as Cuprese '08, which flaunts varietally classic almond on the nose and a palate that, although not too complex, shows nicely relaxed and juicy. From the other DOCs, Offida Pecorino '08 rates well, with no-nonsense, crisp florality.

● Sestiere '06	♟♟ 5
○ Verdicchio dei Castelli di Jesi Cl. Ghiffa '08	♟♟ 4*
○ Verdicchio dei Castelli di Jesi Cl. Labieno Ris. '06	♟♟ 5
○ Verdicchio dei Castelli di Jesi Cl. Sup. San Michele della Ghiffa '07	♟♟ 4*
○ Esino Bianco Condotto '08	♟ 3
○ Verdicchio dei Castelli di Jesi Passito Cingulum '07	♟ 5
○ Esino Bianco Condotto '07	♟♟ 3*
○ Verdicchio dei Castelli di Jesi Passito Cingulum '06	♟♟ 5

○ Ubaldo Rosi Brut. Ris. '04	♟♟ 5
○ Colonnara Brut '04	♟♟ 5
○ Verdicchio dei Castelli di Jesi Cl. Sup. Cuprese '08	♟♟ 4*
○ Verdicchio dei Castelli di Jesi Cl. Sup. Tùfico '06	♟♟ 4*
○ Bianchello del Metauro '08	♟ 3
○ Colonnara Brut Charmat	♟ 3
○ Offida Pecorino '08	♟ 4
● Rosso Conero Horus '06	♟ 4
○ Verdicchio dei Castelli di Jesi Cl. Portonuovo '08	♟ 3
○ Brut Riserva Ubaldo Rosi M. Cl. '02	♟♟ 5
○ Offida Pecorino '07	♟♟ 4
● Tornamagno '03	♟♟ 4*
○ Verdicchio dei Castelli di Jesi Cl. Sup. Cuprese '07	♟♟ 4*
○ Verdicchio dei Castelli di Jesi Cl. Sup. Tùfico '05	♟♟ 4

Il Conte Villa Prandone

c.da Colle Navicchio, 28
63033 Monteprandone [AP]
tel. 073562593
www.ilcontevini.it

CELLAR SALES
PRE-BOOKED VISITS

ANNUAL PRODUCTION 130,000 bottles
HECTARES UNDER VINE 25
VITICULTURE METHOD Conventional

Monteprandone is right next to Abruzzo and just over the river Tronto are the Colline Teramane. The De Angelis family, however, pays that terroir no attention, focusing instead on varieties classic to the Marche: passerina, pecorino, sangiovese. They can hardly ignore montepulciano but it is always a blending partner. The wines display clean profiles, dense, ripe fruit and meticulous sculpting, which removes any rusticity. The other side of the coin is that they lose territorial characteristics but they do display less of the all-too-approachable softness that has marked them in the past.

Zipolo '06 remains the best bottling. A blend in which montepulciano gains a little help from sangiovese and merlot, it first suggests chocolate and morello cherry, then offers a larger dose of fruit, as well as a solid charge of well-rounded tannins. Stoked by sour black cherry, Marinus '07 is crisper but with a plush fabric as well. Conte Rosso, styled for current drinking, betrays some territoriality, thanks to morello cherry and steak tartare, which pair well with the characteristic leanness and nervy acidity of the palate. The opulent, alcohol-rich Pecorino Navicchio '08 and the citrussy Cavaceppo '08, from passerina, are both well styled.

O Offida Pecorino Navicchio '08	¶¶	4
● Rosso Piceno Conte Rosso '08	¶¶	3*
● Rosso Piceno Sup. Marinus '07	¶¶	4
● Zipolo '06	¶¶	6
O Cavaceppo Passerina '08	¶	4
O Falerio dei Colli Ascolani Aurato '08	¶	2
O Offida Passerina Spumante Emmanuel '08	¶	4
● Rosso Piceno Conte Rosso '07	¶¶	3*
● Zipolo '05	¶¶	6

Tenuta De Angelis

via San Francesco, 10
63030 Castel di Lama [AP]
tel. 073687429
www.tenutadeangelis.it

CELLAR SALES

ANNUAL PRODUCTION 500,000 bottles
HECTARES UNDER VINE 50
VITICULTURE METHOD Conventional

It has always been obvious that Quinto Fausti has a way with reds, starting with sangiovese and montepulciano. He crafts from them wines that are richly extracted, powerful and fruit-filled, wines immediately approachable but which hold up well over time. De Angelis relies on very extensive vineyards, in some of Piceno's best areas, which allows rigorous quality selection of the fruit. In addition, the winery benefits from over 50 years of accumulated winemaking experience. The good showing by their Pecorino burnish the entire line, led by the near-opaque hues of the Rosso Piceno versions.

Finely sculpted fruit, excellent balance, and a dynamic progression driven by magisterial extraction are the main reasons for the brilliant performance by Rosso Piceno Superiore '07. And the consumer will appreciate the price tag. Oro '07 is promising but still closed in and difficult. It opens to toasty impressions that contrast with massive brooding fruit while a huge block of undigested tannins still clench the mid palate, all signs of youthful growing pains. Rosso Piceno '08, though, is pleasurably fragrant and straightforward. Pecorino '08 attracts with its succulence and soft mouthfeel, then drives to a flavourful finale.

● Rosso Piceno Sup. '07	¶¶	3*
O Falerio dei Colli Ascolani '08	¶¶	2*
O Offida Pecorino '08	¶¶	3*
● Rosso Piceno '08	¶¶	2*
● Rosso Piceno Sup. Oro '07	¶¶	4
● Anghelos '01	¶¶¶	5
● Anghelos '99	¶¶¶	5
● Anghelos '06	¶¶	5
● Rosso Piceno '07	¶¶	2*
● Rosso Piceno Sup. '06	¶¶	3*
● Rosso Piceno Sup. Oro '06	¶¶	4*

Degli Azzoni
Avogadro Carradori

VIA DON MINZONI, 26
62010 MONTEFANO [MC]
TEL. 0733850219
www.degliazzoni.it

CELLAR SALES
PRE-BOOKED VISITS
VISITOR FACILITIES
FOOD

ANNUAL PRODUCTION **100,000 bottles**
HECTARES UNDER VINE **130**
VITICULTURE METHOD **Conventional**

If you happen by Montefano, a charming village in the Macerata area, you can hardly miss the Degli Azzoni brothers' estate, since it covers a full 850 hectares. They have "only" 130 hectares of vineyard, enough to make them one of the Marche's largest private wine operations. Only recently, though, did they gear up and go for high quality and their production currently hovers at only 100,000 bottles. They certainly do not lack for capital, professionalism or dynamic management but they are taking their time. Good results are beginning to trickle out from this enormous potential.

A 40-year-old montepulciano vineyard yields Passatempo '07. Still betraying a youthful rough patch or two, it offers juicy, well-ripened fruit nicely tamped down by smooth spice and subtle oak toast. Cantalupo is their mid-quality line. Its Rosso '07 is an ultra-fruited mix of montepulciano, merlot and cabernet while Bianco '08, a sauvignon blanc-assisted verdicchio, lacks interest and flashes by quickly. Grechetto '08 and Rosso Evasione '08 are lithe and approachable. Sultano '07 is an impressive partnering of overripe malvasia aromatica, chardonnay and picolit that parades candied citrus and appreciable richness in the mouth.

Fattoria Dezi

C.DA FONTEMAGGIO, 14
63029 SERVIGLIANO [AP]
TEL. 0734710090
fattoriadezi@hotmail.com

CELLAR SALES
PRE-BOOKED VISITS
VISITOR FACILITIES

ANNUAL PRODUCTION **50,000 bottles**
HECTARES UNDER VINE **16**
VITICULTURE METHOD **Natural**

The production of Stefano and Davide Dezi could almost be called artisanal, since they produce only 50,000 bottles from their 15 hectares of estate vineyards in Fontemaggio, largely planted to montepulciano and sangiovese. Their expertise and deep understanding of their vineyards are the ingredients that ensure impressive, consistently stunning results. They have not put a foot wrong in years, steadily producing elegant wines in a modern style, their barriques ageing wines from the soundest of grapes with smooth tannins slowly extracted through lengthy fermentations.

Regina del Bosco '06 is a taut, different Montepulciano that offers little at first, but then expands with increasing energy to a vigorous progression. Three Glasses with élan. The entry of Sangiovese Solo '07 is very cautious but solid tannins support and fuel its growth and intensity, as does a responsive finish scented with sour cherry. Abundant fruit marks every stage of Dezio '07, from montepulciano and a little sangiovese, including its approachable and flavoursome palate. Good marks went to Le Solagne '08, from verdicchio and 30 per cent malvasia, for its pleasurable accessibility and thrusting energy.

● Passatempo '07	▼▼ 6
● Rosso Cantalupo '07	▼▼ 4*
○ Sultano '07	▼▼ 4*
○ Bianco di Cantalupo '08	▼ 3
○ Colli Maceratesi Bianco '08	▼ 3
○ Grechetto '08	▼ 4
● Rosso Evasione '08	▼ 2*
● Rosso Piceno '08	▼ 4
○ Bianco di Cantalupo '07	▼▼ 3*
● Passatempo '06	▼▼ 5
● Rosso Cantalupo '07	▼▼ 4*
● Rosso Cantalupo '06	▼▼ 3*

● Regina del Bosco '06	▼▼▼ 7
● Solo Sangiovese '07	▼▼ 7
● Dezio Vign. Beccaccia '07	▼▼ 5
○ Le Solagne '08	▼▼ 3*
● Regina del Bosco '05	▼▼▼ 7
● Regina del Bosco '03	▼▼▼ 6
● Solo Sangiovese '05	▼▼▼ 7
● Solo Sangiovese '01	▼▼▼ 6
● Solo Sangiovese '00	▼▼▼ 6
● Dezio Vign. Beccaccia '06	▼▼ 5
○ Le Solagne '07	▼▼ 3
● Regina del Bosco '04	▼▼ 7
● Solo Sangiovese '06	▼▼ 7

Fausti

c.da Castelletta, 15
63023 Fermo [AP]
tel. 0734620492
faustivini@gmail.com

CELLAR SALES
PRE-BOOKED VISITS

ANNUAL PRODUCTION **65,000 bottles**
HECTARES UNDER VINE **11**
VITICULTURE METHOD **Natural**

Cristina Fausti and Domenico D'Angelo's winery lies to the north of Piceno's classic area but the growing conditions are similar. Soils are clay and limestone-based, the Adriatic is nearby and the vine-clad hills are just as gentle and rounded. Fausti's wines tend to the modern style, with the whites showing a soft roundedness and the reds exhibiting depth of fruit and fine spice. Syrah flourishes here and it makes an intriguing contribution, giving additional character to the aromas and a distinctive pepperiness when used without partnering varieties.

Buonissimo il Vespro '07, montepulciano e 30% di syrah, maturato 18 mesi in barrique, con ancora qualche eccesso legnoso da riassorbire nella fase aromatica ma dotato di una bocca soda e polposa, di serica potenza e sicura armonia. Poco lontano si colloca il Perdomenico '07, Syrah in purezza, dal naso dolce di lampone e tratteggi affumicati e dal un gusto pepato e progressivo, un po' contratto in chiusura. Tra i vini d'annata piace il Rosso Piceno Fausto '08 per il suo ricordo di amarena fresca ritrovata anche in un gusto succoso ed equilibrato. Ale '08 è un Pecorino avvolgente e maturo.

● Vespro '07	🍷🍷 5
○ Offida Pecorino Ale '08	🍷🍷 3*
● Perdomenico Syrah '07	🍷🍷 5
● Rosso Piceno Fausto '08	🍷🍷 2*
● Vespro '05	ΥΥΥ 5
● Vespro '03	ΥΥΥ 4*
● Perdomenico Syrah '06	ΥΥ 5
● Perdomenico Syrah '05	ΥΥ 5
● Rosso Piceno Fausto '07	ΥΥ 2*
● Vespro '06	ΥΥ 5
● Vespro '04	ΥΥ 5

Fazi Battaglia

via Roma, 117
60031 Castelplanio [AN]
tel. 073181591
www.fazibattaglia.it

CELLAR SALES
PRE-BOOKED VISITS

ANNUAL PRODUCTION **3,000,000 bottles**
HECTARES UNDER VINE **260**
VITICULTURE METHOD **Conventional**

Fazi Battaglia, Verdicchio and Anfora are an indissoluble trio and the wine in the curvaceous Titulus bottle, restyled a few years ago, is still the main focus here. Fazi Battaglia's production of 3,000,000 bottles reaches every corner of the globe. The house style is a Verdicchio that is light and smooth with a varietal, almond-edged finish. The winery strives, through various techniques, to achieve stylistic consistency in its bottlings. It succeeds in putting out self-confident, distinctive wines with a distinctive Marche stamp.

San Sisto '06 and Massaccio '06 lead the Verdicchios. The first, cask-aged, is tightly-knit and elegant, with a tangy sapidity. The second, from overripe fruit and steel aged, gives hints of botrytis and orange peel. Supple drive and impressive depth of flavour mark the standard bottlings Le Moie and Ekeos. Among the reds, the '06 is one of the best editions ever of Passo del Lupo Riserva, with a bracing progression and generous, well-meshed tannins. The refined Arkezia is a Verdicchio Passito redolent of honey and saffron, markedly sweet and seductive.

○ Verdicchio dei Castelli di Jesi Cl. San Sisto Ris. '06	🍷🍷 5
○ Verdicchio dei Castelli di Jesi Cl. Sup. Massaccio '06	🍷🍷 5
○ Arkezia Muffo di S. Sisto '06	🍷🍷 7
● Conero Passo del Lupo Ris. '06	🍷🍷 5
● Rosso Conero Ekeos '08	🍷 5
○ Verdicchio dei Castelli di Jesi Cl. Sup. Ekeos '08	🍷 5
○ Verdicchio dei Castelli di Jesi Cl. Sup. Le Moie '08	🍷 4
○ Verdicchio dei Castelli di Jesi Cl. San Sisto Ris. '05	ΥΥΥ 5
○ Verdicchio dei Castelli di Jesi Cl. Sup. Massaccio '03	ΥΥΥ 4*
○ Verdicchio dei Castelli di Jesi Cl. Sup. Massaccio '01	ΥΥΥ 4
○ Verdicchio dei Castelli di Jesi Cl. Sup. Massaccio '00	ΥΥΥ 4

Fiorano

C.DA FIORANO, 19
63030 COSSIGNANO [AP]
TEL. 073598446
www.agrifiorano.it

CELLAR SALES
PRE-BOOKED VISITS
VISITOR FACILITIES
FOOD

ANNUAL PRODUCTION **30,000 bottles**
HECTARES UNDER VINE **4.5**
VITICULTURE METHOD **Organic certified**

Paolo Beretta, originally from Milano, has laboured in the village of Cossignano for years, and lacks only a Piceno accent to be perfectly integrated into this vineyard-covered hinterland. His wines show that adaptation. Organically produced, they seem effortlessly expressive, succulent and not too managed or over-refined. Beretta's five hectares yield an almost garage-scale 33,000 bottles. An attractive agriturismo, constructed according to the canons of green building, brings additional revenue to Fiorano.

For several years now, Beretta has offered an Offida Pecorino of great originality. The '08 offers impressive hints of almond, white-fleshed fruits and sea salt, then opens dynamically to a broad vein of tangy fruit. Ser Balduzio, a Montepulciano vinified back in 2004, has been enjoying a long rest in cask and bottle. Crisp and extroverted, it is laden with dense, ripe tannins and perhaps just a touch too much sweet oak at start and finish. The delicious Terre di Giobbe '06 all but leaps out of the glass, glossy, fruited and long.

Cantine Fontezoppa

C.DA SAN DOMENICO, 24
62012 CIVITANOVA MARCHE [MC]
TEL. 0733790504
www.cantinefontezoppa.it

CELLAR SALES
PRE-BOOKED VISITS

ANNUAL PRODUCTION **150,000 bottles**
HECTARES UNDER VINE **35**
VITICULTURE METHOD **Conventional**

Fontezoppa has 35 hectares of vineyards. In Civitanova Marche, just a few kilometres from the Adriatic, their vineyards are planted to sangiovese, maceratino and the internationals while a good number of vernaccia nera vineyards are at Serrapetrona. Finally, three hectares at Matelica are in verdicchio. We were not able to taste any of the new wines made from vernaccia, since they are still ageing. The other bottlings shows fine definition and confidence, a sure sign that Giovanni Basso's efforts are proceeding in the right direction.

Verdicchio di Matelica is the best wine we tasted, compellingly varietal in its fragrant almond and aniseed, showing layered and fruity in the mid palate and savoury on the finish. And the price is right. Ribona '08 impresses with rich floral notes and a well-delineated palate. It's hardly emphatic but it is tasty and leisurely. We liked Marche Rosso '07, an equal blend of cabernet and sangiovese. Fresh and fruit-forward, it displays rounded tannins. Equally fine is the ambitious Mariné '07, a Sangiovese that received 18 months in large wood. Not overly complex, it is peppery and alcoholically warm. Piccinì '08 shines a bright florality.

● Rosso Piceno Sup. Terre di Giobbe '06	♟♟	4*
○ Offida Pecorino Donna Orgilla '08	♟♟	4*
● Ser Balduzio '04	♟♟	6
○ Donna Orgilla Pecorino '07	♟♟	4*
● Rosso Piceno Sup. Terre di Giobbe '05	♟♟	4*

○ Colli Maceratesi Ribona '08	♟♟	4*
● Marche Rosso '07	♟♟	2*
● Mariné '07	♟♟	5
○ Verdicchio di Matelica '08	♟♟	4*
● Dirosaediviola '06	♟	5
○ Marche Bianco '08	♟	4
⊙ Piccinì '08	♟	4
● Carapetto '06	♟♟	5
● Marche Rosso '06	♟♟	2*
⊙ Piccinì '05	♟♟	4*

★ Gioacchino Garofoli

P.LE G. GAROFOLI, 1
60022 CASTELFIDARDO [AN]
TEL. 0717820162
www.garofolivini.it

CELLAR SALES
PRE-BOOKED VISITS

ANNUAL PRODUCTION **2,000,000 bottles**
HECTARES UNDER VINE **42**
VITICULTURE METHOD **Conventional**

The Garofoli name enjoys wide respect, a long history and wines of the highest-quality in every important market. Its success is due to Gianfranco Garofoli's business genius and to the winemaking expertise of Carlo Garofoli, who is just as talented with sparklers as he is with reds, not to mention Verdicchio, the house specialty. It is no accident that Garofoli is Marche's most award-bedecked producer and the wines that were tasted this year provide further proof of that distinction.

Podium '07 again figures among the Three Glasses winners, with an ultra-elegant version boasting the subtlest of fragrances and the steadiest of progressions. It's a cohesive, complex masterwork. Serra Fiorese '04 is markedly different, initially revealing dense smoky impressions and then fine alcohol and a delicious sensory chiaroscuro in the mouth. The third champion is Grosso Agontano Riserva '06, which offers a rich, aromatic amalgam of tanned leather, animal fur and well-ripened fruit, then a warm, enfolding mid palate with fully mellowed tannins. Worthy of note are Garofoli Brut Metodo Classico '05 and the returning Brumato '05.

Esther Hauser

C.DA CORONCINO, 1A
60039 STAFFOLO [AN]
TEL. 0731770203
esther.hauser@virgilio.it

CELLAR SALES
PRE-BOOKED VISITS

ANNUAL PRODUCTION **6,000 bottles**
HECTARES UNDER VINE **1**
VITICULTURE METHOD **Conventional**

Esther Hauser is an intriguing character on the Marche wine stage. A kind of hermit-grower who fled civilization, in her case Switzerland, Esther holed up in an old, cramped farmhouse among oaks, olive trees and vineyards. It is hard even to communicate with her, as she ignores e-mail, and rarely answers the phone, always being out in the countryside somewhere. Nor does she evince any interest in promoting her products, among which is a fantastic extra virgin olive oil. Therefore, if you can't find her wine on the store shelves, don't give up. They are worth the sacrifice.

Both of her wines are released in miniscule quantities, barely 3,000 bottles each. Cupo '07, of all montepulciano, unleashes a fragrant attack of smooth fruit, which then broadens into pungent Mediterranean scrub and cocoa powder. In the mouth, it develops spacious and elegant, with a suite of super-refined tannins. Ceppo '07, the second label, adds small tots of cabernet and sangiovese to its montepulciano. Designed to be more open and crisp, it displays an effective contrast between energetic suppleness and dense concentration on the palate, concluding a flourish of sour cherry, thyme and other spices.

○ Verdicchio dei Castelli di Jesi Cl. Sup. Podium '07	♟♟♟ 5*
● Conero Grosso Agontano Ris. '06	♟♟ 5
○ Verdicchio dei Castelli di Jesi Cl. Serra Fiorese Ris. '06	♟♟ 5
○ Garofoli Brut '05	♟♟ 3*
☉ Kòmaros '08	♟♟ 3*
● Rosso Conero Piancarda '06	♟♟ 4*
○ Verdicchio dei Castelli di Jesi Passito Brumato '05	♟♟ 5
○ Dorato Moscato Passito '07	♟ 4
☉ Garofoli Brut Rosé '06	♟ 5
● Rosso Piceno Colle Ambro '06	♟ 3
○ Verdicchio dei Castelli di Jesi Cl. Sup. Macrina '08	♟ 4
○ Verdicchio dei Castelli di Jesi Cl. Sup. Podium '06	♟♟♟ 5*
○ Verdicchio dei Castelli di Jesi Cl. Sup. Podium '04	♟♟♟ 4*

● Il Ceppo '07	♟♟ 5
● Il Cupo '07	♟♟ 6
● Il Ceppo '06	♟♟ 5
● Il Ceppo '05	♟♟ 5
● Il Cupo '06	♟♟ 6
● Il Cupo '05	♟♟ 6
● Il Cupo '04	♟♟ 6

Fattoria Laila

VIA SAN FILIPPO SUL CESANO, 27
61040 MONDAVIO [PU]
TEL. 0721979353
www.fattorialaila.it

CELLAR SALES
PRE BOOKED VISITS

ANNUAL PRODUCTION **100,000 bottles**
HECTARES UNDER VINE **40**
VITICULTURE METHOD **Conventional**

Andrea Crocenzi hit the bull's eye. He presented five wines and all five showed well, even the standard labels. The reason is a stylistic clarity that privileges modernity, sound aromatics and freshness instead of overripeness and too-early evolution. True, the top award has not yet come his way but his iconic stars, the two Lailums, seem to have found their measure and they stand alongside the region's best wines. The prelude to this success was a sustained effort to improve the vineyards and use of technology, under the careful tutelage of Lorenzo Landi.

Lailum Riserva '07 is the leading Verdicchio, a ductile bottling with verve and drive. Its tangy, forthright sapidity fuels lengthy progression. Eklektikos '08 flaunts the same lineaments, very elegantly but in a minor key. Delicious citrus and a juicily fruited palate adorn Verdicchio '08. The Laila vineyards are in the province of Ancona so there is a Rosso Piceno, Lailum '06. Smooth tannins and ripe fruit add to its density and it ends on a fragrant note of morello cherry.

Lanari

FRAZ. VARANO
VIA POZZO, 142
60029 ANCONA
TEL. 0712861343
cantinalanari@libero.it

CELLAR SALES
PRE-BOOKED VISITS

ANNUAL PRODUCTION **50,000 bottles**
HECTARES UNDER VINE **12**
VITICULTURE METHOD **Conventional**

Grower Luca Lanari has always placed his faith in the force and generosity of the montepulciano grape, working ceaselessly to coax from it the maximum extraction and concentration possible. He utilizes ultra-ripe fruit from vineyards with perfect southeast exposures, long, slow fermentations, and sur lie maturations to produce wines that will match his conception of what Rosso Conero can be. The modest size of his operation allows him to follow every stage in both vineyard and cellar, exercising a truly artisanal approach.

All of Lanari's wines share marked concentration, particularly on the nose, where some time in glass will however reveal a very distinctive, emphatic vein of warmth. Time in the bottle will also bring into balance their imposing tannic charge, unveiling impressive character and dynamism. This is precisely the case with Fibbio Riserva '07, as dark and earthy as it is lithe and dynamic. Rosso Conero '08, on the other hand, parades unabashed minerality, forest floor and morello cherry infusing a spirited palate that may not be elegant but is quite supple. Overripe fruit precludes much aromatic forcefulness in D'Inclite Terre '07.

● Rosso Piceno Lailum '06	♟♟	5
○ Verdicchio dei Castelli di Jesi Cl. Lailum Ris. '07	♟♟	4*
● Rosso Piceno '08	♟♟	3*
○ Verdicchio dei Castelli di Jesi Cl. Sup. '08	♟♟	3*
○ Verdicchio dei Castelli di Jesi Cl. Sup. Eklektikos '08	♟♟	4*
● Rosso Piceno Lailum '05	♟♟	5
● Rosso Piceno Lailum '04	♟♟	5
○ Verdicchio dei Castelli di Jesi Cl. Lailum Ris. '05	♟♟	4
○ Verdicchio dei Castelli di Jesi Cl. Sup. Eklektikos '07	♟♟	4*
○ Verdicchio dei Castelli di Jesi Cl. Sup. Eklektikos '06	♟♟	4*

● Conero Fibbio Ris. '07	♟♟	7
● Rosso Conero '08	♟♟	4*
● Rosso Conero D'Inclite Terre '07	♟	5
● Rosso Conero Fibbio '99	♟♟♟	6
● Conero Aretè Ris. '06	♟♟	6
● Conero Fibbio Ris. '06	♟♟	6
● Rosso Conero Aretè Ris. '03	♟♟	6
● Rosso Conero Aretè Ris. '01	♟♟	6
● Rosso Conero Clivio '05	♟♟	5

Luciano Landi

VIA GAVIGLIANO, 16
60030 BELVEDERE OSTRENSE [AN]
TEL. 073162353
www.aziendalandi.it

CELLAR SALES
PRE-BOOKED VISITS

ANNUAL PRODUCTION 100,000 bottles
HECTARES UNDER VINE 18
VITICULTURE METHOD Conventional

Luciano Landi specializes in the lacrima grape, even if other varieties, such as montepulciano, merlot, syrah and verdicchio also appear in his vineyards. The wines stand out for their slightly ultra-ripe traits, which comes with the aim of maximizing the density and complexity of the fruit and ensuring that the vine achieves phenolic ripeness. This exposes the fruit to more of the risks posed by the vagaries of the weather but in the right growing year, Landi's wines can skirt the roughness and bitterness caused by the rustic tannins of this native grape in Morro d'Alba.

The base Lacrima offers a varietal nose of delicious rose petals and violets mixed with more explicit notes of fruit, and a pulpy palate displays smooth progression with no rough patches. Gavigliano '07, though more controversial, is as interesting. The overripeness emerges in candied cherry while the palate appears narrowed but with time the aromatic richness should reveal itself and accentuate the imposing framework. The '07 version of Passito seems less refined than in the past with hints of greens and a simple, dry palate. Good showings for both the imposing Goliardo '07, from 80 per cent montepulciano, and the crisp Verdicchio '08.

Conte Leopardi Dittajuti

VIA MARINA II, 24
60026 NUMANA [AN]
TEL. 0717390116
www.conteleopardi.com

CELLAR SALES
PRE-BOOKED VISITS

ANNUAL PRODUCTION 220,000 bottles
HECTARES UNDER VINE 52
VITICULTURE METHOD Conventional

After availing itself of various technical consultancies, Piervittorio Leopardi Dittajuti's operation seems to have matured its own firmly based personality, which leans towards a modern expression free of any exaggeration or extraneous influences. The reds, for example, lay on generous fruit but without resorting to overripening or invasive oak toast. The whites, with sauvignon blanc predominating, display a clean, salty tang and quite distinctive aromatics that conjure up citrus rather than the more expected vegetal impressions.

Pigmento is a Conero '06 that betrays a slight reductive note, with dark sensations of liquorice and hints of gaminess, but a few moments of air bring out broad, pulpy fruit. The palate has plenty of perhaps slightly harsh character with muscular tannins and driving alcohol. Casirano '07 is more smooth and approachable, giving well-sculpted aromas. Fructus '08 is loaded with youthful fruit, but it is tasty rather than heavy. Oakiness rather holds back Vigneti del Coppo '07. As for the two standard Sauvignons, Calcare provides more structure while Bianco del Coppo is a delicious, approachable quaffer.

● Goliardo '07	▼▼ 5
● Lacrima di Morro d'Alba '08	▼▼ 3*
● Lacrima di Morro d'Alba Sup. Gavigliano '07	▼▼ 4*
○ Verdicchio dei Castelli di Jesi Cl. '08	▼▼ 3*
● Lacrima di Morro d'Alba Passito '07	▼ 6
● Goliardo '03	♈♈ 6
● Lacrima di Morro d'Alba Passito '06	♈♈ 6
● Lacrima di Morro d'Alba Sup. Gavigliano '06	♈♈ 4*
○ Verdicchio dei Castelli di Jesi Cl. '06	♈♈ 3*

● Conero Pigmento Ris. '06	▼▼ 6
○ Bianco del Coppo Sauvignon '08	▼▼ 4*
○ Calcare Sauvignon '08	▼▼ 4
● Rosso Conero Casirano '07	▼▼ 5
● Rosso Conero Fructus '08	▼▼ 4*
⊙ Rosé del Coppo '08	▼ 3
● Rosso Conero Vign. del Coppo '07	▼ 4
○ Verdicchio dei Castelli di Jesi Cl. Castelverde '08	▼ 4
○ Bianco del Coppo Sauvignon '07	♈♈ 4*
● Conero Pigmento Ris. '04	♈♈ 6

Roberto Lucarelli

LOC. RIPALTA
VIA PIANA, 20
61030 CARTOCETO [PU]
TEL. 0721893019
www.laripo.com

CELLAR SALES
PRE-BOOKED VISITS

ANNUAL PRODUCTION **130,000 bottles**
HECTARES UNDER VINE **24**
VITICULTURE METHOD **Conventional**

The Lucarelli family has been cultivating grapes for generations. In 1998, with construction of the new cellar, Roberto launched an ambitious project to improve the stature of Bianchello and Sangiovese dei Colli Pesaresi, traditional designations that had been relegated mostly to local distribution. The 24 hectares of vineyards, planted on tufa soils, were renewed and managed with painstaking care, while careful attention was given to maturations and vinifications with more modern equipment. Encouraging results have been coming through, in particular with the reds.

Rocho '08 is an excellent, albeit rather atypical, Bianchello with fine volume in the mouth and yellow peach and tropical fruit-like aromatics. It is still very young, of course, but it seems ready to go some years with ease. La Ripe '08 is just as sound a bottling but is more approachable, with less complex fruit and a rounded, tasty mid palate. Insieme Riserva '06 shows good heft. The nose is a little evolved, followed by fine warmth and self-confidence in the mouth, although it dries out quickly. In contrast, La Ripe '08 reveals fragrant bright cherry and violets, then unfurls fluid, refined progression.

○ Bianchello del Metauro La Ripe '08	♟♟	3*
○ Bianchello del Metauro Rocho '08	♟♟	4*
● Colli Pesaresi Sangiovese Insieme Ris. '06	♟	5
● Colli Pesaresi Sangiovese La Ripe '08	♟	3
○ Bianchello del Metauro La Ripe '07	♟♟	3*
○ Bianchello del Metauro La Ripe '06	♟♟	2*
○ Bianchello del Metauro Rocho '07	♟♟	4
● Colli Pesaresi Sangiovese Goccione '06	♟♟	5
● Colli Pesaresi Sangiovese La Ripe '06	♟♟	3*

Fattoria Mancini

S.DA DEI COLLI, 35
61100 PESARO
TEL. 072151828
www.fattoriamancini.com

CELLAR SALES
PRE-BOOKED VISITS

ANNUAL PRODUCTION **75,000 bottles**
HECTARES UNDER VINE **31**
VITICULTURE METHOD **Conventional**

Writing Noir instead of Nero next to Pinot should not be seen as intellectual snobbery. Luigi Mancini has always looked on France as a model in his efforts to produce a Burgundy-style red. This sounds somewhat improbable, given his latitude, but the variety has a long history here for it arrived with the Napoleonic forces. Further, Luigi's vineyard, in the Parco del San Bartolo, was the result of meticulous clonal selection, and it is located literally over the Adriatic, a body of water that tempers the local climate. This stubborn Pesaro grower has serious arguments on his side.

Pinot Noir '07 offers a delicate, subtle nose and some complexity as well but it is somewhat evanescent. Blu '05 is an unusual blend of 85 per cent ancellota and some pinot nero that shows ripe red berry fruit and velvety vanilla on the palate, which is spacious and appealing though with little depth. Colli Pesarese Sangiovese '07 develops delicate pepperiness, then sour cherry on mid palate but it pulls up suddenly on a drying finale. Roncaglia '08, its normal fine self, is a mix of albanella and 15 per cent pinot nero fermented off the skins. It parades citrus and white peach, which continue through a smooth, tasty progression.

● Colli Pesaresi Focara Pinot Noir '07	♟♟	6
○ Colli Pesaresi Roncaglia '08	♟♟	4*
● Blu '05	♟	6
● Colli Pesaresi Sangiovese '07	♟	4
● Colli Pesaresi Focara Pinot Nero Impero Ris. '01	♟♟	6
○ Colli Pesaresi Roncaglia '07	♟♟	4*
● Colli Pesaresi Sangiovese '06	♟♟	4

Marchetti

FRAZ. PINOCCHIO
VIA DI PONTELUNGO, 166
60131 ANCONA
TEL. 071897386
www.marchettiwines.it

CELLAR SALES
PRE-BOOKED VISITS

ANNUAL PRODUCTION 60,000 bottles
HECTARES UNDER VINE 18
VITICULTURE METHOD Conventional

If you track the historical development of wines from the Conero area, you will often encounter the name Marchetti. The winery, which in the 1970s was known for its austere versions of Rosso Conero, is now guided by Maurizio Marchetti. To him goes the credit for an overall recalibration of practices: more attention in the vineyard to ripeness levels, better use of correct temperatures to preserve aromatic compounds and improved use of oak. To this end, Maurizio enlisted the forward-looking vision of Lorenzo Landi, who brings a sure hand to the difficult montepulciano.

Riserva Villa Bonomi '06 is outstanding and one of the finest Coneros around. The palate's luscious succulence comes from the union of supple tannins and emphatic alcohol, which enriches the already chewy fruit first encountered on the nose, finishing on a lengthy charge of pure energy. We found Rosso Conero '07 disappointing. It's still hard and unyielding, ascribable to its youth perhaps, although its progression left something to be desired. Among the Verdicchios, however, we were impressed by the savoury standard version, as well as by Tenuta del Cavaliere '08, which is silky and long but short on acidic grip.

● Rosso Conero Villa Bonomi Ris. '06	♟♟ 5
○ Verdicchio dei Castelli di Jesi Cl. '08	♟♟ 3*
● Rosso Conero '07	♟ 4
○ Verdicchio dei Castelli di Jesi Cl. Sup. Tenuta del Cavaliere '08	♟ 4
● Rosso Conero Villa Bonomi Ris. '02	♟♟♟ 5
● Conero Villa Bonomi Ris. '05	♟♟ 6
● Rosso Conero '06	♟♟ 4*
○ Verdicchio dei Castelli di Jesi Cl. '07	♟♟ 3*
○ Verdicchio dei Castelli di Jesi Cl. Sup. Tenuta del Cavaliere '07	♟♟ 4

Marotti Campi

VIA SANT'AMICO, 14
60030 MORRO D'ALBA [AN]
TEL. 0731618027
www.marotticampi.it

CELLAR SALES
PRE-BOOKED VISITS

ANNUAL PRODUCTION 170,000 bottles
HECTARES UNDER VINE 56
VITICULTURE METHOD Conventional

Lorenzo Marotti Campi is proud of the uniqueness of what he produces. His 56 hectares of vineyard boast two grape varieties, verdicchio and lacrima di Morro d'Alba. They are complementary, inasmuch as one is white and the other red, and both are grown practically only in Marche. But Lorenzo still has to travel since only endless tastings will spread awareness of this modest territory, one that is often misunderstood in the larger markets round the world. But Marotti Campi remains serene and ever ready to take the plane to the next tasting.

The winemaking cellar, next to the estate residence and the farmhouse, is located in a long-established cru in the Sant'Amico district, the vineyard that yields Orgiolo '07. Its nose is rather distinctive, revealing aromatic herbs and black pepper, and the palate is impressively rounded with fruit at the peak of ripeness. Bright sour cherry is the key to Rùbico '08, plus an uncomplicated but nicely supple, likeable palate. Salmariano Riserva '06 is a fine Verdicchio, from ultra-ripe fruit, which shows powerful and opulent with a long-powering finish. Luzano '08 starts with crisp citrus, then unrolls a fluid, refreshing palate veined with bright citrus.

○ Verdicchio dei Castelli di Jesi Cl. Salmariano Ris. '06	♟♟ 4*
● Lacrima di Morro d'Alba Sup. Orgiolo '07	♟♟ 4*
○ Verdicchio dei Castelli di Jesi Cl. Sup. Luzano '08	♟♟ 3*
● Lacrima di Morro d'Alba Rùbico '08	♟ 4
● Lacrima di Morro d'Alba Sup. Orgiolo '06	♟♟ 4*
○ Verdicchio dei Castelli di Jesi Cl. Albiano '07	♟♟ 2*
○ Verdicchio dei Castelli di Jesi Cl. Salmariano Ris. '05	♟♟ 4
○ Verdicchio dei Castelli di Jesi Cl. Salmariano Ris. '03	♟♟ 4*
○ Verdicchio dei Castelli di Jesi Cl. Salmariano Ris. '02	♟♟ 4*
○ Verdicchio dei Castelli di Jesi Cl. Sup. Luzano '07	♟♟ 3*

La Monacesca

C.DA MONACESCA
62024 MATELICA [MC]
TEL. 0733812602
www.monacesca.it

CELLAR SALES
PRE-BOOKED VISITS

ANNUAL PRODUCTION **170,000 bottles**
HECTARES UNDER VINE **27**
VITICULTURE METHOD **Conventional**

The exemplary way that Aldo Cifola manages his wine operation can be seen in every detail. The estate and vineyards are always in perfect order while winemaking protocols ensure that the wines will be released only when they meet the rigid requirements of Monacesca's owner. Cifola has shown his dedication to clear principles throughout his long career as a grower, privileging just a few labels, a homogeneous style over the years and terroir expressiveness. His long-lived wines flaunt distinctive personalities and a minerally profile, qualities that take some years to emerge.

Three Glasses went to a majestic Mirum Riserva '07. The nose unveils huge aromatic complexity, revealing crisp citrus, blossoms and roasted nuts, followed by a formidable palate with stunning vitality and clean-profiled, savoury fruit. The base Verdicchio is so full, long-lingering and ultra-tangy that you really should wait for a few years to enlarge its charms. The sangiovese and merlot Camerte '06 is again terrific. Initial dark impressions of blackberry preserves yield to an almost unexpected freshness on the palate, the gift of a nervy acidity well inserted into massive structure. Ecclesia '08 is an opulent, warm Chardonnay with a vibrant bouquet.

Monte Schiavo

FRAZ. MONTESCHIAVO
VIA VIVAIO
60030 MAIOLATI SPONTINI [AN]
TEL. 0731700385
www.monteschiavo.it

CELLAR SALES
PRE-BOOKED VISITS

ANNUAL PRODUCTION **1,800,000 bottles**
HECTARES UNDER VINE **115**
VITICULTURE METHOD **Conventional**

Monteschiavo, one of the largest and most prestigious wineries in the Castelli di Jesi area, began as a co-operative. The Pieralisi group purchased it and transformed it into a modern operation, with up-to-date equipment and a marketing eye fixed on exports, though not neglecting the domestic market. Cultivating 115 hectares of vineyards, Monteschiavo puts out an extensive line of wines that covers all of the local designation. Its main focus, however, is Verdicchio, produced in various selections, each with its own personal style.

The verdicchio-only Le Giuncare Riserva '07 is an ambitious wine, one quarter aged in barriques. Ample and appealing, it acquires a near-tropical impression to its ripe fruit from late-picked grapes. Pallio di San Floriano '08 shows well, hinting at sea salt and citrus, then laying out a glossy, controlled progression, while Coste del Molino '08 exudes delicious aniseed. In the reds, good marks went to Adeodato '06. It is mature and polished, yet shows some depth and character as well. Conti Cortesi '07 is less elegant but lively and effective. Gran Lasco is a lacrima-based Charmat method Brut Rosé that makes a fragrant glass for anytime.

○ Verdicchio di Matelica Mirum Ris. '07	♟♟♟ 5*
● Camerte '06	♟ 5
○ Verdicchio di Matelica La Monacesca '08	♟♟ 4*
○ Ecclesia Chardonnay '08	♟♟ 4*
● Camerte '99	♟♟♟ 5
○ Mirum '94	♟♟♟ 5
○ Mirus '91	♟♟♟ 5
○ Verdicchio di Matelica La Monacesca '94	♟♟♟ 4
○ Verdicchio di Matelica Mirum Ris. '06	♟♟♟ 5
○ Verdicchio di Matelica Mirum Ris. '04	♟♟♟ 5
○ Verdicchio di Matelica Mirum Ris. '02	♟♟♟ 5
○ Ecclesia Chardonnay '07	♟♟ 4
○ Verdicchio di Matelica La Monacesca '07	♟♟ 4*
○ Verdicchio di Matelica La Monacesca '06	♟♟ 4*

● Rosso Conero Adeodato '06	♟♟ 6
○ Verdicchio dei Castelli di Jesi Cl. Le Giuncare Ris. '07	♟♟ 4*
○ Verdicchio dei Castelli di Jesi Cl. Sup. Pallio di S. Floriano '08	♟♟♟ 4*
● Rosso Conero Conti Cortesi '07	♟♟ 4*
○ Verdicchio dei Castelli di Jesi Cl. Coste del Molino '08	♟♟ 3*
☉ Gran Lasco Brut Rosé	♟ 3
● Rosso Piceno Sup. Sassaiolo '07	♟ 3
○ Verdicchio dei Castelli di Jesi Cl. Ruviano '08	♟ 3
● Rosso Conero Adeodato '00	♟♟♟ 6
● Rosso Conero Adeodato '05	♟♟ 6
○ Verdicchio dei Castelli di Jesi Cl. Le Giuncare Ris. '06	♟♟ 4
○ Verdicchio dei Castelli di Jesi Cl. Sup. Nativo '06	♟♟ 4
○ Verdicchio dei Castelli di Jesi Cl. Sup. Pallio di S. Floriano '07	♟♟ 4

Montecappone

VIA COLLE OLIVO, 2
60035 JESI [AN]
TEL. 0731205761
www.montecappone.com

CELLAR SALES
PRE-BOOKED VISITS

ANNUAL PRODUCTION 120,000 bottles
HECTARES UNDER VINE 70
VITICULTURE METHOD Conventional

Gianluca Mirizzi's determination turned Montecappone inside out like a sock. The acquisition of the historic facility in Iesi, completed only in 1997, began a slow process of transformation and growth whose aim was to produce wines showing purity of fruit and full varietal integrity. Without pushing too fast, and correcting anything along the way that deviated from the goal, Mirizzi and oenologist Lorenzo Landi found a richly profiled, perfectly contemporary style. The solid showings of all of the bottlings are incontrovertible proof.

Three Glasses go to Utopia '07, a muscular, self-confident Verdicchio fuelled by rising tanginess that explodes at the end of the palate in a profusion of nuances, citron and almond among them. Sauvignon La Breccia '08 is luminously varietal, with scents of grapefruit and sage, plus a lunging progression. Crunchy fruit and a subtle toastiness mark the full-volumed Tabano Rosso '07 while the white version, made from verdicchio and other aromatic grapes, is long-lived and velvety. Finally, good marks went to the full and fragrant Rosso Piceno Montesecco '08 and to its Verdicchio version, taut and ultra-tasty.

○ Verdicchio dei Castelli di Jesi Cl. Utopia Ris. '07	▽▽▽ 5*
○ La Breccia Sauvignon '08	▽▽ 4*
● Colle Paradiso '08	▽▽ 3*
○ Esino Bianco Tabano '08	▽▽ 5
● Esino Rosso Tabano '07	▽▽ 5
☉ Pergolesi 1710 '08	▽▽ 4*
● Rosso Piceno Montesecco '08	▽▽ 4*
○ Verdicchio dei Castelli di Jesi Cl. Sup. Montesecco '08	▽▽ 4*
○ Verdicchio dei Castelli di Jesi Rèsio Passito '07	▽▽ 6
○ Colle Onorato Chardonnay '08	▽ 4
○ Verdicchio dei Castelli di Jesi Cl. Sup. Colle Paradiso '08	▽ 3
○ Esino Bianco Tabano '07	▽▽ 5
○ Verdicchio dei Castelli di Jesi Cl. Sup. Montesecco '07	▽▽ 4*

Alessandro Moroder

LOC. MONTACUTO
VIA MONTACUTO, 121
60029 ANCONA
TEL. 071898232
www.moroder-vini.it

PRE-BOOKED VISITS

ANNUAL PRODUCTION 140,000 bottles
HECTARES UNDER VINE 32
VITICULTURE METHOD Conventional

Alessandro and Serenella Moroder have been operating for quite some time now in the Monte Conero area. Their 32 hectares are planted largely to montepulciano, with some sangiovese and alicante nero, and a little merlot and cabernet with moscato and other white-wine grapes. Moroder has a fine reputation among wine lovers for its Conero Riserva Dorico, the first wine from its designation to win the Three Glasses, and that 1990 vintage is still drinking remarkably well. It was absent this year but we found many modern-style, fruity bottles that were quite approachable.

It was easy to predict that the '06 version would be the best of the Rosso Coneros. Rich blackberry and blueberry open and then continue to scent a linear progression, with the alcohol creating appreciable roundedness. Good fruit also marks Aiòn '07 but the wine is too ingratiating in its overly smooth nose and soft palate. Montepulciano and sangiovese make up Rosa di Montacuto '08, along with 20 per cent alicante. Raspberry scented, it flows nicely but ends quickly. Bianco Conero '08, a dessert wine, is from moscato bianco with ten per cent alicante nero. It is a low-alcohol pleaser with aromatic complexity throughout.

○ BianConero '08	▽▽ 4*
● Rosso Conero '06	▽▽ 4*
☉ Rosa di Montacuto '08	▽ 3
● Rosso Conero Aiòn '07	▽ 2*
● Rosso Conero Dorico '93	▽▽▽ 5
● Rosso Conero Dorico '90	▽▽▽ 5
● Rosso Conero Dorico '88	▽▽▽ 5
● Ankon '03	▽▽ 6
● Conero Dorico Ris. '04	▽▽ 6
● Rosso Conero Aiòn '06	▽▽ 2*
● Rosso Conero Dorico Ris. '03	▽▽ 6
● Rosso Conero Dorico Ris. '01	▽▽ 6

Oasi degli Angeli

C.DA SANT'EGIDIO, 50
63012 CUPRA MARITTIMA [AP]
TEL. 0735778569
www.kurni.it

CELLAR SALES
PRE-BOOKED VISITS

ANNUAL PRODUCTION 5,000 bottles
HECTARES UNDER VINE 7
VITICULTURE METHOD Natural

Marco Casolanetti's wines are just as unique as his outgoing, stubborn character. His passionately held convictions will not let him accept compromises that might deflect him from his personal approach to making wine. Even his very densely planted vineyards are extraordinary, requiring sensitive management and endless work-hours. The research that Marco and Eleonora carry out is intellectually rigorous, and always guided by authentic traditions. The results are certainly original, in that their wines display new facets and themes within the classic heritage of this area.

Three Glasses go to Kurni '07, a Montepulciano of stunning volume and multi-faceted refinement. Casolanetti's extreme viticulture coaxes perfect fruit from each vineyard. Every lot is then vinified and matured separately in various types of small oak. What emerges is a super-crisp wine of great depth, one that achieves impeccable balance, partly through a mass of fine tannins and in spite of a relentless density. Kupra '06 is sourced from a small grenache vineyard of great age. The grenache grape is traditional here, probably brought in by Sardinian shepherds, and the wine is elegance itself, peppery on the nose and relaxed and supple in the mouth.

Borgo Paglianetto

FRAZ. PAGLIANO
LOC. PAGLIANO, 393
62024 MATELICA [MC]
TEL. 073785465
www.borgopaglianetto.it

CELLAR SALES
PRE-BOOKED VISITS

ANNUAL PRODUCTION 100,000 bottles
HECTARES UNDER VINE 18
VITICULTURE METHOD Conventional

Borgo Paglianetto is the result of the union of two important Matelica wine operations, Terra Vignata and Del Carmine. The objective was to exploit both space and energies more rationally, resulting in a single up-to-date winery that could produce clean, intense Verdicchios whose flavours would reflect the potential of the terroir and offer more original sensory perceptions. The first results are encouraging, but this is understandable since each of the two wineries had put out good bottlings. One expects that Paglianetto will quickly climb the ladder of regional producers.

Both Verdicchios are vinified in steel but display different characteristics. Terra Vignata '08 emits youthfully exuberant fragrances of fresh greens and blossoms over a base of pear and apple before zippy acidity ensures lively energy and a citrus-edged finish. Vertis '07 exudes more complex aniseed and peach. Although the palate doesn't show particularly impressive depth, its fruit is vivacious and succulent. Matesis '07 is a large cask-aged Montepulciano. The fruit auspiciously present on the nose is soon weighed down, however, by excessive alcohol and drying tannins.

● Kurni '07	♛♛♛	8
● Kupra '06	♛♛	8
● Kurni '04	♛♛♛	8
● Kurni '03	♛♛♛	8
● Kurni '02	♛♛♛	8
● Kurni '01	♛♛♛	8
● Kurni '00	♛♛♛	8
● Kurni '98	♛♛♛	8
● Kurni '97	♛♛♛	8
● Kurni '06	♛♛	8

○ Verdicchio di Matelica Terra Vignata '08	♛♛	3*
○ Verdicchio di Matelica Vertis '07	♛♛	4*
● Mathesis '07	♛	5
● Colli Maceratesi Rosso Petrara '06	♛♛	3*
○ Verdicchio di Matelica Aja Lunga '05	♛♛	4*
○ Verdicchio di Matelica Petrara '05	♛♛	3*

Piantate Lunghe

FRAZ. CANDIA
VIA PIANTATE LUNGHE, 91
60131 ANCONA
TEL. 07136464
www.piantatelunghe.it

CELLAR SALES
PRE-BOOKED VISITS

ANNUAL PRODUCTION 30,000 bottles
HECTARES UNDER VINE 12.5
VITICULTURE METHOD Conventional

A union of mutual goals, with separately owned vineyards and a shared project. Piantate Lunghe was launched a few years ago by Amedeo Giustini and brothers Roberto and Guido Mazzoni. The few vintages so far have yielded a fine series of wines that testify to the project's sterling quality. Credit goes to the fruit from venerable montepulciano vineyards lying right on the slopes of Monte Conero, just a few metres from the Adriatic. But plaudits go of course to the owners' savvy in entrusting those vineyards to Federico Curtaz and winemaking to the talented Paolo Caciorgna.

Conero Rossini '06, largely from montepulciano with a little sangiovese, follows the excellent '05 vintage. Our Three Glasses reward its aromatic power, with a nose built on pungent herbs, white peach and juicy hints of morello cherry, a veil of delicate spice wafting about. A fine-woven fabric of tannins creates an almost creamy mouthfeel, enlivened by emphatic alcohol that contributes to dynamism and volume. The finish is a rising crescendo where fruit encountered on the nose is further enriched by dark nuances of black liquorice. Rosso Conero '07 was not ready when we tasted so we will cover it next year.

● Conero Rossini Ris. '06	♟♟♟ 6
● Conero Rossini Ris. '05	♟♟♟ 6
● Conero Ris. '04	♟♟ 6
● Rosso Conero '06	♟♟ 4*
● Rosso Conero '05	♟♟ 4*

Pievalta

VIA MONTESCHIAVO, 18
60030 MAIOLATI SPONTINI [AN]
TEL. 0731780375
www.baronepizzini.it

CELLAR SALES
PRE-BOOKED VISITS

ANNUAL PRODUCTION 66,000 bottles
HECTARES UNDER VINE 29
VITICULTURE METHOD Natural

Pievalta, Barone Pizzini's footprint in the Marche, thrives largely thanks to the fine work of Alessandro Fenino. He introduced the operation's organic philosophy, energizing it with the biodynamic teachings of Nicolas Joly. Those influences show in the indisputably original wines, thanks to natural fermentations, extraneous operations reduced to a bare minimum and the use of terracotta amphorae. The Verdicchios exemplify an unadorned character and frankness that may not please everyone, in particular those who are looking for approachability or varietal fidelity.

San Paolo Riserva '06 is rich, spacious and layered. Traits typical of overripe fruit – honey, orange peel and herbs – are on display on the nose. The palate is soft and seductive, and its savouriness infuses the finish. Dominè '08 is scented with almond, espresso bean and caramel, initially giving a sensation of sweetness in the mouth. Then grip and depth balance the progression and provide effective contrast. Pievalta '08 is more problematic, with a peppery nose and an overly soft palate. Passito Curina '07, vinified partly in amphorae, opens to briny impressions and dried fruit before developing a warm, evolved progression.

○ Verdicchio dei Castelli di Jesi Cl. San Paolo Ris. '06	♟♟ 5
○ Verdicchio dei Castelli di Jesi Cl. Sup. Dominè '08	♟♟ 4*
○ Verdicchio dei Castelli di Jesi Cl. Sup. Pievalta '08	♟ 3
○ Verdicchio dei Castelli di Jesi Passito Curina '07	♟ 5
○ Verdicchio dei Castelli di Jesi Cl. San Paolo Ris. '04	♟♟ 4*
○ Verdicchio dei Castelli di Jesi Cl. Sup. Dominè '06	♟♟ 4
○ Verdicchio dei Castelli di Jesi Cl. Sup. Pievalta '06	♟♟ 3*

Il Pollenza

VIA CASONE, 4
62029 TOLENTINO [MC]
TEL. 0733961989
www.ilpollenza.it

CELLAR SALES

ANNUAL PRODUCTION 80,000 bottles
HECTARES UNDER VINE 50
VITICULTURE METHOD Conventional

Pollenza is the result of a top-to-bottom restructuring of the farming properties owned by Aldo Brachetti Peretti, a wealthy industrialist of Marche origins. Aldo has set himself the difficult challenge of creating a Bordeaux château-like operation, right down to the varieties, bringing viticulture to an essentially virgin area. Nothing has been left to chance; no expense has been spared. And yet nature works according to its own rules. Wine needs time, particularly when starting from zero. In fact, the step backwards this year is in part ascribable to the poor 2005 growing year.

Il Pollenza '05 is made from merlot, cabernet sauvignon and cabernet franc. This is the blend used by Haut-Brion, a similarity underscored by the bottle shape. It opens to fairly prickly notes of balsam and green pepper, then presents an emotionless complexity on the palate, which falters as the progression advances. The less pretentious cabernet sauvignon Cosmino '05 follows the same style but in a humbler key and manages suppleness on the palate. The sweet Pius IX Mastai '07, produced from botrytized sauvignon blanc, shows slightly simple on the nose, hinting of pear purée, but velvet-clad forcefulness and a lengthy progression merit attention.

● Cosmino '05	♟♟	5
● Il Pollenza '05	♟♟	8
○ Pius IX Mastai '07	♟♟	6
● Cosmino '04	♟♟	5
● Cosmino '03	♟♟	5
● Il Pollenza '04	♟♟	8
● Il Pollenza '03	♟♟	8
○ Pius IX Mastai '06	♟♟	6
● Porpora '05	♟♟	4*

Saladini Pilastri

VIA SALADINI, 5
63030 SPINETOLI [AP]
TEL. 0736899534
www.saladinipilastri.it

CELLAR SALES
PRE-BOOKED VISITS

ANNUAL PRODUCTION 800,000 bottles
HECTARES UNDER VINE 150
VITICULTURE METHOD Organic certified

Saladini Pilastri, with 150 hectares of vineyard, specializes in Rosso Piceno, a denomination which allows the blending together of sangiovese and montepulciano. The versions show a common thread of generous volume, warmth and immediacy. A desire for concentration leads at times to very high ripeness levels and, consequently, to heavily extracted wines, while time in the bottle does help to tamp down some youthful excesses. The whites are resounding successes, including one of the best Pecorinos tasted, and the finest Falerios in the area, Palazzi.

The Rosso Picenos clearly show common traits but their quality levels are hierarchical. Top dog is the elegant, sustained Vigna Monteprandone '07, now back as one of the area's finest reds. Close behind is Vigna Montetinello '07, this year less sturdy but more approachable. The hefty Piediprato '07 shows reticent on the nose but recovers on the palate. Parnaso '07 is cramped on the nose although it does show gritty character. Consenso '08 is a tasty sangiovese rosé. Palazzi '08 no longer surprises with its distinctive bitter herbs and rich vegetal impressions. Finally, the dense, vibrant Pecorino '08 offers lovely broom blossoms and fruit.

○ Offida Pecorino '08	♟♟	3*
● Rosso Piceno Sup. V. Monteprandone '07	♟♟	5
○ Falerio dei Colli Ascolani V. Palazzi '08	♟♟	3*
● Pregio del Conte '07	♟♟	5
● Rosso Piceno Piediprato '07	♟♟	4*
● Rosso Piceno Sup. V. Montetinello '07	♟♟	4*
⊙ Sangiovese Consenso Rosato '08	♟♟	4*
○ Falerio dei Colli Ascolani '08	♟	1*
● Rosso Piceno '08	♟	4
● Rosso Piceno Parnaso '07	♟	4
● Pregio del Conte '02	♟♟	3*
● Rosso Piceno Parnaso '06	♟♟	4*
● Rosso Piceno Piediprato '06	♟♟	4*
● Rosso Piceno Sup. V. Monteprandone '04	♟♟	5

San Francesco

VIA SAN FRANCESCO, 4
63030 ACQUAVIVA PICENA [AP]
TEL. 0735764416
www.vinicherri.it

CELLAR SALES
PRE-BOOKED VISITS

ANNUAL PRODUCTION **100,000 bottles**
HECTARES UNDER VINE **20**
VITICULTURE METHOD **Conventional**

Paolo Cherri has carried out an extensive modernization project these past years, stripping away the incrustations of an outmoded oenology and allowing the old vineyards in the fine Acquaviva Picena terroir to express their considerable potential. San Francesco's line focuses exclusively on denomination wines, with the sole exception of a pecorino-based Brut, which gets its bubbles in another winery. Now that it has reached a certain level of consistency, another push will bring the extra dash of complexity that still seems lacking, particularly in the more ambitious wines.

The standard-label whites are all a pleasure, declined with clean, well-delineated aromas that are crisp and elegant. Both Falerio, as well as the monovarietal Pecorino and Passerina, boast a beautifully balanced approachability, avoiding the too-facile smoothness that is often the result of winemaking shortcuts. Of the Rosso Piceno Superiores, we preferred the serious approach and straightforward extractive richness of Notturno '07 to the more reticent and refined Laudi '04, which lets vegetality peek through at various points. Offida Tumbulus '05 stumbles somewhat, with veiled aromatics and burred tannins that cause some dryness on the finish.

O Falerio dei Colli Ascolani Oriente '08	♥♥	3*
O Offida Passerina Radiosa '08	♥♥	4*
O Offida Pecorino Altissimo '08	♥♥	4
● Rosso Piceno Sup. Laudi '04	♥♥	5
● Rosso Piceno Sup. Notturno '07	♥♥	4*
● Offida Tumbulus '05	♥	5

San Giovanni

C.DA CIAFONE, 41
63035 OFFIDA [AP]
TEL. 0736889032
www.vinisangiovanni.it

PRE-BOOKED VISITS

ANNUAL PRODUCTION **90,000 bottles**
HECTARES UNDER VINE **30**
VITICULTURE METHOD **Natural**

Gianni di Lorenzo owns exceptional vineyards in the heart of Ciafone, a village near Offida almost entirely covered with vines. The gently sloping hills here are perfect for a late-ripening variety such as montepulciano while the Adriatic, which is not far off, ensures cooling breezes even on the hottest days. For a few years now, San Giovanni has been putting out whites of impressive calibre, led by their star variety, pecorino, a native that is currently enjoying great success in the market. The style is unabashedly modernist, with bright aromatics, medium extractions and judicious use of the barrique.

San Giovanni's most ambitious reds, Piceno Superiore Axee and Offida Zeii, had prior engagements with maturations still in progress. So Rosso Piceno Superiore Leo Guelfus '06 stood out even better, flaunting voluminous pulp, which it handles well with measured alcohol and a smooth tannin framework. It could profit from a tad more complexity but its general level of appeal is certainly high enough. An elegant Offida Pecorino Kiara '08 presents scents of aniseed plus fine energy and savouriness. Refinement is the forte for the fairly linear Falerio Leo Guelfus '08 while Passerina Marta '08 could show more push and length

O Offida Pecorino Kiara '08	♥♥	4*
● Rosso Piceno Sup. Leo Guelfus '06	♥♥	4*
O Falerio dei Colli Ascolani Leo Guelfus '08	♥♥	3*
O Offida Passerina Marta '08	♥	3
O Offida Passerina Passito '04	♀♀	5
O Offida Pecorino Kiara '07	♀♀	4*
O Offida Pecorino Kiara '06	♀♀	4*
● Offida Rosso Zeii '04	♀♀	5
● Offida Rosso Zeii '03	♀♀	5
● Rosso Piceno Sup. Leo Guelfus '05	♀♀	4*
● Rosso Piceno Sup. Leo Guelfus '04	♀♀	4*

Poderi San Lazzaro

C.DA SAN LAZZARO, 65/67
63035 OFFIDA [AP]
TEL. 0736889189
www.poderisanlazzaro.it

CELLAR SALES
PRE-BOOKED VISITS

ANNUAL PRODUCTION **50,000 bottles**
HECTARES UNDER VINE **15**
VITICULTURE METHOD **Natural**

Paolo Capriotti's wines exude an authentic feel of their terroir. Venerable vineyards and an organic approach that coaxes out natural expressivity are two reasons for this. But above all, the secret is untiring efforts in the fields, complemented by intelligent practices in the cellar such as the idea to ferment pecorino briefly on the skins and then to mature it in mid-sized wood. San Lazzaro's reds are soundly crafted and well differentiated. Montepulciano Grifola is absent since the '07 is undergoing lengthier ageing.

Podere 72 '07, a 50-50 sangiovese and montepulciano mix, has vibrant grip, succulent fruit and minerally depth, well matched by mellow tannins and a markedly savoury finale. Still very youthful, it already shows surprising balance and glorious drinkability. Production was 15,000 bottles and it has an amazingly low price tag. Pistillo preserves its customary personality, though balance is achieved more dearly. The nose shows a bit clenched, and alcohol is high, but the fruit shines through, as does its typical "on the skins" timbre. Polesio '08 is a smooth Sangiovese easily fulfilling its role as a standard label for all seasons and pockets.

● Rosso Piceno Sup. Podere 72 '07	♟♟	4*
○ Offida Pecorino Pistillo '08	♟♟	4*
● Polesio Sangiovese '08	♟	3
● Grifola '06	♟♟	5
● Grifola '05	♟♟	5
○ Offida Pecorino Pistillo '07	♟♟	4*
● Rosso Piceno Sup. Podere 72 '06	♟♟	4*

Fattoria San Lorenzo

VIA SAN LORENZO, 6
60036 MONTECAROTTO [AN]
TEL. 073189656
az-crognaletti@libero.it

CELLAR SALES
PRE-BOOKED VISITS

ANNUAL PRODUCTION **100,000 bottles**
HECTARES UNDER VINE **36**
VITICULTURE METHOD **Natural**

Natalino Crognaletti grew up among the vines and his father Gino taught him the grower's art so that today he enjoys a deep, visceral bond with the vine and the wine cellar. Natalino works hard to make wines that will please himself first of all, in line with a philosophy that demands complexity, expressive power and ability to age. Over the years, he has radicalized his vision, having recourse to ever less invasive practices in order to craft wines with soul and distinctiveness. This works for the Verdicchios but not for the reds, which tend to overripeness and astringency.

Crognaletti's Verdicchios are not immediate communicators. It takes a while in the glass before those slightly evolved characteristics give way to layered impressions and warm fragrances. Vigna delle Oche Riserva '06 begins with aniseed but it is the palate that opens even more fully to a dynamic, deep and very natural savouriness. Riserva '07 accentuates these idiosyncratic traits, with a few shortcomings on the nose amply redeemed by an exceptionally voluminous and ultra-sapid palate. Vigna di Gino '08 expands nicely and floats out bitter almond.

○ Verdicchio dei Castelli di Jesi Cl. Sup. Vigna delle Oche '07	♟♟	4*
○ Verdicchio dei Castelli di Jesi Cl. Vigna delle Oche Ris. '06	♟♟	5
○ Verdicchio dei Castelli di Jesi Cl. Vigna di Gino '08	♟	3
○ Verdicchio dei Castelli di Jesi Cl. Vigna delle Oche Ris. '01	♟♟♟	5
○ Verdicchio dei Castelli di Jesi Cl. Sup. Vigna delle Oche '06	♟♟	4*
○ Verdicchio dei Castelli di Jesi Cl. Vigna delle Oche Ris. '04	♟♟	5
○ Verdicchio dei Castelli di Jesi Cl. Vigna delle Oche Ris. '03	♟♟	5
○ Verdicchio dei Castelli di Jesi Cl. Vigna di Gino '07	♟♟	3*

San Savino - Poderi Capecci

LOC. SAN SAVINO
VIA SANTA MARIA IN CARRO, 13
63038 RIPATRANSONE [AP]
TEL. 073590107
www.sansavino.com

CELLAR SALES
PRE-BOOKED VISITS

ANNUAL PRODUCTION **120,000 bottles**
HECTARES UNDER VINE **32**
VITICULTURE METHOD **Natural**

Simone Capecci's ideas about wine are lucidly clear. His bottles must display purity of fruit, dense but supple tannins, and a generous body that is not an end in itself but essential to superior drinkability. To achieve this, Simone gets the best out of his vineyards, which resemble immaculate gardens in the Santa Maria in Carro area between Offida and Ripatransone, and in Acquaviva Picena. His winemaking is equally meticulous and he takes advantage of modern technologies, such as refrigeration and temperature control, to obtain wines with surprisingly bright-edged aromatics.

For the first time, a Marche Pecorino, San Savino's Ciprea '08, won Three Glasses. Yellow peach and nuances of aniseed and citrus enfold a mouth of luminous aromatic complexity, gliding into a stunningly delicious finish. The sangiovese Fedus '07 presents sweet, smooth tannins that stud its broad, full-fruited density, and push relentless, dynamic progression. Quinta Regio '05 is a complex, concentrated Montepulciano, revealing morello cherry and chocolate interleaved with notes of earth and black liquorice. It builds vibrant structure on the palate, with tannins that tend to roughen towards the finish.

Santa Barbara

B.GO MAZZINI, 35
60010 BARBARA [AN]
TEL. 0719674249
www.vinisantabarbara.it

CELLAR SALES
PRE-BOOKED VISITS

ANNUAL PRODUCTION **650,000 bottles**
HECTARES UNDER VINE **40**
VITICULTURE METHOD **Conventional**

Santa Barbara is an integral part of Marche's wine history and Stefano Antonucci was an ambassador for the region's wines as well as for his winery. The open-hearted, sincere Antonucci reaches out assiduously to all of Santa Barbara's many friends outside the Marche and they know that bringing home a Santa Barbara wine really means participating in a philosophy that is cheerful and contagious. The cellar is emblematic of a convivial way of life that the world of wine is, unfortunately, turning away from.

We open with a note on Pathos '07, a red made from international varieties, which we tasted but did not give a place in the list here. Its fruit is excessively ripe and tires the wine, while the palate is weighed down by too much alcohol and extraction. Verdicchio Le Vaglie '08 is huge, and a gorgeous vein of acidity lends the progression an agile rhythm, driving into a flavourful finish. Nidastore '08 shows refreshing and fragrant while Verdicchio Stefano Antonucci '07 is impressive despite a tad too much oak. Maschio da Monte '07 is too warm and ripe to be able to soar, even though it does manage some freshness and character in the mouth.

○ Offida Pecorino Ciprea '08	▼▼▼	4*
● Fedus Sangiovese '07	▼▼	5
● Quinta Regio '05	▼▼	6
○ Offida Passerina Tufilla '08	▼▼	4*
● Rosso Piceno Sup. Picus '07	▼▼	4*
● Rosso Piceno Collemura '08	▼	3
● Fedus Sangiovese '06	♀♀♀	5
● Moggio Sangiovese '98	♀♀♀	6
● Quinta Regio '01	♀♀♀	6
● Quinta Regio '00	♀♀♀	6
○ Offida Passerina Tufilla '07	♀♀	4*
○ Offida Pecorino Ciprea '07	♀♀	4*
● Rosso Piceno Sup. Picus '06	♀♀	4*
● Ver Sacrum '06	♀♀	4

○ Verdicchio dei Castelli di Jesi Cl. Le Vaglie '08	▼▼	4*
● Rosso Piceno Il Maschio da Monte '07	▼▼	6
○ Verdicchio dei Castelli di Jesi Cl. Nidastore '08	▼▼	3*
○ Verdicchio dei Castelli di Jesi Cl. Stefano Antonucci Ris. '07	▼▼	5
○ Er +	▼	4
● Pignocco Rosso '08	▼	4
○ Verdicchio dei Castelli di Jesi Cl. Pignocco '08	▼	3
● Vigna San Bartolo	▼	4
● Pathos '01	♀♀♀	7
● Rosso Piceno Il Maschio da Monte '04	♀♀♀	5
○ Verdicchio dei Castelli di Jesi Cl. Le Vaglie '06	♀♀♀	4*
○ Verdicchio dei Castelli di Jesi Cl. Stefano Antonucci Ris. '06	♀♀♀	4*
○ Verdicchio dei Castelli di Jesi Cl. Le Vaglie '07	♀♀	4*
○ Verdicchio dei Castelli di Jesi Nidastore '07	♀♀	3*

Sartarelli

VIA COSTE DEL MOLINO, 24
60030 POGGIO SAN MARCELLO [AN]
TEL. 073189732
www.sartarelli.it

CELLAR SALES
PRE-BOOKED VISITS

ANNUAL PRODUCTION **290,000 bottles**
HECTARES UNDER VINE **60**
VITICULTURE METHOD **Conventional**

Sartarelli won fame across the world of wine for its Contrada Balciana '97, which become iconic for all late-harvest Verdicchios. A prestigious international award opened up markets then unthinkable for an almost artisanal wine operation. Since then, many things have changed at Sartarelli, including the loss of the word Contrada for its standard-bearer. Today, the 60 hectares produce almost 300,000 bottles distributed in every corner of Italy. What has remained unchanged is the dedication to verdicchio, still the only grape to enter the cellar doors.

Grapes picked considerably beyond ripeness yield in Balciana '07 a wine of massive concentration that gives sensations of honey, citrus peel and pungent herbs. The mouth is seductively glycerine-rich, with a luscious viscosity similar to that of a sweet wine. It's very much a one-off and easily recognizable. Tralivio '07, though admirable, is not up to previous editions. It shows a nice caramelled nose and appreciable energy but not much in the way of complexity. Classico '08 is stylish, vigorous and scrumptious right to the last drop. We expected more personality from Passito '07. It unveils fragrant candied fruit but the sweetness is not at all in high-relief.

Sparapani - Frati Bianchi

VIA BARCHIO, 12
60034 CUPRAMONTANA [AN]
TEL. 0731781216
www.fratibianchi.it

CELLAR SALES
PRE-BOOKED VISITS

ANNUAL PRODUCTION **35,000 bottles**
HECTARES UNDER VINE **12**
VITICULTURE METHOD **Conventional**

The Marche is an unpretentious region that has nurtured and defended the life of the small farmer. Still today it proudly preserves a close bond with its culture and traditions. It is only in this context that you can understand operations such as this, run by families who never surrender their land even when managing complex enterprises. So the Sparapanis happily multi-task, also managing a country trattoria as well as a petrol station. Yet glance behind and you'll see a modest wine cellar, and amidst the casks, an extraordinary producer.

The wines display every ounce of character that verdicchio possesses, traits that they express cleanly and with no affectations. Priore '08, made from a selection of their best grapes, competed in our finals. It starts slow off the blocks, sheltering almost timidly behind a citrussy hint of lemon rind, then bursts onto the mouth, where it unleashes a truly surprising, vibrant progression. Salerna '08 follows suit but in a calmer, more linear fashion, though it doesn't lack verve. Its almost saline finish shows a lovely bitterish almond.

O Verdicchio dei Castelli di Jesi Cl. Sup. Balciana '07	▽▽ 6
O Verdicchio dei Castelli di Jesi Cl. '08	▽▽ 3*
O Verdicchio dei Castelli di Jesi Cl. Sup. Tralivio '07	▽▽ 4*
O Verdicchio dei Castelli di Jesi Passito '07	▽ 6
O Verdicchio dei Castelli di Jesi Cl. Sup. Balciana '04	▽▽▽ 6
O Verdicchio dei Castelli di Jesi Cl. Sup. Contrada Balciana '98	▽▽▽ 6
O Verdicchio dei Castelli di Jesi Cl. Sup. Contrada Balciana '97	▽▽▽ 6
O Verdicchio dei Castelli di Jesi Cl. Sup. Contrada Balciana '95	▽▽▽ 6
O Verdicchio dei Castelli di Jesi Cl. Sup. Contrada Balciana '94	▽▽▽ 6

O Verdicchio dei Castelli di Jesi Cl. Sup. Il Priore '08	▽▽ 4*
O Verdicchio dei Castelli di Jesi Cl. Salerna '08	▽▽ 4*
O Verdicchio dei Castelli di Jesi Cl. Sup. Il Priore '06	▽▽▽ 4*
O Verdicchio dei Castelli di Jesi Cl. Salerna '07	▽▽ 4*
O Verdicchio dei Castelli di Jesi Cl. Sup. Il Priore '07	▽▽ 4*
O Verdicchio dei Castelli di Jesi Cl. Sup. Il Priore '05	▽▽ 4*

Spinsanti

VIA FONTE INFERNO, 11
60021 CAMERANO [AN]
TEL. 071731797
catiaspinsanti@alice.it

CELLAR SALES
PRE-BOOKED VISITS
VISITOR FACILITIES
FOOD

ANNUAL PRODUCTION 36,000 bottles
HECTARES UNDER VINE 7.5
VITICULTURE METHOD Natural

The building that used to house the wine facility and a country home has now been restructured into an elegant rural home, a modern, functional cellar and a jewel of a barrel room. But nothing else has changed at the Spinsanti base. In a certain sense, there is greater calm and awareness that the sturdy, montepulciano-based wines have a personality of their own, one that will emerge with the appropriate degree of maturation. This is why their iconic Sassòne is being granted another year to develop its aromatics and to temper some youthful edges.

Of the two labels presented, our preference went to Camars '07, a Montepulciano matured partly in cask and partly in cement, with a production of only 12,000 bottles. It pours out the richest scents of fruit, proffering vivacious, emphatic notes of peach and sour cherry, while the palate shows both depth and crispness, with a toothsomely fruity development. Adino is from montepulciano with some sangiovese. The nose is less clean-cut, with hints of game over morello cherry, but the mouth displays abundant pulp and crisp acidity. The finish is still contracted by sharp tannins. More ageing in the bottle will rectify this.

● Rosso Conero Adino '08	♟♟	3*
● Rosso Conero Camars '07	♟♟	4*
● Rosso Conero Adino '07	♟♟	3*
● Rosso Conero Adino '06	♟♟	3
● Rosso Conero Camars '06	♟♟	4*
● Sassòne '06	♟♟	6
● Sassòne '05	♟♟	6

Silvano Strologo

VIA OSIMANA, 89
60021 CAMERANO [AN]
TEL. 071731104
www.vinorossoconero.com

CELLAR SALES
PRE-BOOKED VISITS

ANNUAL PRODUCTION 60,000 bottles
HECTARES UNDER VINE 16
VITICULTURE METHOD Conventional

In times of economic downturn, Silvano Strologo is heading in the opposite direction. He is substantially enlarging his cellar spaces and buying new properties to plant to montepulciano and small amounts of white varieties. These will soon come onstream. Silvano has never shown any lack of courage, stubbornness or marketing savvy. His reds are quite distinctive, with lengthy macerations, saturated tonalities and complex aromatics that weave together spice and preserves with a gaminess that is sometimes excessive and at other times so fully integrated into the bouquet that it lends even more complexity and character.

Decebalo '06 unleashes a beast of a performance. The nose is almost rough-hewn, with liquorice and Mediterranean scrub, and the palate untamed, unfolding with energy and voluminous flavours that apparently scorn elegance. Here is a wine with a true character all of its own. Julius '08 lays out a massive palate that should have as its helpmate a crisper and more energetic nose. We were impressed by Muscà, a sweet wine from moscato giallo. Impressions of zabaglione and sea salt make for a fascinating palate that is sweet but never cloying.

● Conero Decebalo Ris. '06	♟♟	6
○ Muscà	♟♟	5
☉ Rosa Rosae '08	♟	3
● Rosso Conero Julius '08	♟	4
● Conero Decebalo Ris. '05	♟♟	6
● Conero Decebalo Ris. '04	♟♟	6
● Rosso Conero Caesar '07	♟♟	4*
● Rosso Conero Julius '07	♟♟	4*
● Rosso Conero Julius '06	♟♟	4*

Tenuta di Tavignano

LOC. TAVIGNANO
62011 CINGOLI [MC]
TEL. 0733617303
www.tenutaditavignano.it

CELLAR SALES
PRE-BOOKED VISITS

ANNUAL PRODUCTION **100,000 bottles**
HECTARES UNDER VINE **30**
VITICULTURE METHOD **Conventional**

Stefano Aymerich's Verdicchios display the pace and progression of the finest versions. Ever since a sensitive artist in the person of Pierluigi Lorenzetti took over the winemaking reins, this splendid winery at Tavignano di Cingoli has proved that it is a terroir like few others. The old farm residence, restructured into the production facility, main offices and tasting room, gives a striking view out over the amphitheatre of vineyards, with the hulking San Vicino massif rising in the distance. In the cellar below, various-sized casks hold just Montepulciano and Sangiovese.

Both Misco versions are masterpieces. Riserva '06 in particular offers up elegant fragrances, then a lusciously layered palate animated by driving energy that is obvious even on the finish, where it livens its considerable fruit. The standard label ably melds together mineral, citrus and almond that go on to infuse a rich, compelling palate. An expert hand is also evident in the less ambitious bottlings, which are crafted with a well-defined style combining freshness and suppleness. Tavignano '08 shows clean definition on the nose and a velvety, juicy mid palate. Vigna Verde '08 is less intense but equally delicious.

Fattoria Le Terrazze

VIA MUSONE, 4
60026 NUMANA [AN]
TEL. 0717390352
www.fattorialeterrazze.it

CELLAR SALES
PRE-BOOKED VISITS

ANNUAL PRODUCTION **90,000 bottles**
HECTARES UNDER VINE **20**
VITICULTURE METHOD **Conventional**

Antonio Terni has written some of the most thrilling pages in the history of Marche wine. From his 20 hectares with their view over Monte Conero and the Adriatic, Antonio has created Montepulcianos of elegant generosity and profundity, wines that eloquently express their terroir. Sassi Neri, Chaos and the phenomenal Vision of J, made only in exceptional years, are respected all over the globe. But international success has never influenced Antonio's style. To the contrary, in recent years his wines have yielded some of their refinement and gained a more natural, unalloyed expressivity.

Sassi Neri '06 unites the fullest of rich fruit on the nose to a lean, tannic structure that is slow to develop and contracted at the close. These traits do offer fine promise, however, for a long, satisfying life. Rosso Conero '07 is not quite as together, with overly ripe fruit and a soft but less than dynamic palate. Praeludium '08, from montepulciano and 15 per cent syrah, is berry-scented, supple and a fine quaffer, as is the more linear Le Cave '08, from chardonnay. The subtly strawberry Blanc de Noirs Donna Giulia an equal blend of montepulciano and pinot nero, is back with the '05 version.

O Verdicchio dei Castelli di Jesi Cl. Misco Ris. '06	♟♟♟ 5*
O Verdicchio dei Castelli di Jesi Cl. Sup. Misco '08	♟♟ 4
O Verdicchio dei Castelli di Jesi Cl. Sup. Tavignano '08	♟♟ 3*
O Verdicchio dei Castelli di Jesi Cl. Vigna Verde '08	♟♟ 3*
● Rosso Piceno Tavignano '07	♟ 4
O Verdicchio dei Castelli di Jesi Cl. Misco Ris. '05	♟♟♟ 5
O Verdicchio dei Castelli di Jesi Cl. Sup. Misco '06	♟♟♟ 4*
● Rosso Piceno Libenter '05	♟♟ 4
O Verdicchio dei Castelli di Jesi Cl. Misco Ris. '04	♟♟ 5

● Conero Sassi Neri Ris. '06	♟♟ 6
⊙ Donna Giulia Extra Brut '05	♟ 5
O Le Cave Chardonnay '08	♟ 4
● Rosso Conero '07	♟ 4
● Rosso Conero Praeludium '08	♟ 3
● Chaos '04	♟♟♟ 6
● Chaos '01	♟♟♟ 7
● Conero Sassi Neri Ris. '04	♟♟♟ 6
● Rosso Conero Sassi Neri '02	♟♟♟ 6
● Rosso Conero Sassi Neri '99	♟♟♟ 6
● Rosso Conero Sassi Neri '98	♟♟♟ 6
● Rosso Conero Visions of J '01	♟♟♟ 8
● Rosso Conero Visions of J '97	♟♟♟ 8

Terre Cortesi Moncaro

VIA PIANDOLE, 7A
60036 MONTECAROTTO [AN]
TEL. 073189245
www.moncaro.com

CELLAR SALES
PRE-BOOKED VISITS
FOOD

ANNUAL PRODUCTION 7.500.000 bottles
HECTARES UNDER VINE 1618
VITICULTURE METHOD Organic certified

The Terre Cortesi Moncaro co-operative at Montecarotto is massive compared to other Marche operations, most of which are minuscule in comparison. The 1,618 hectares yield 6,500,000 bottles and a very comprehensive line of wines that even includes bottles from southern Marche, thanks to the Acquaviva Picena facility. A modern vision has given the range a very high standard of quality, which translates into wines of pleasurable complexity. The star bottlings exhibit a multi-faceted richness and refined eloquence that have propelled them to leading positions in their respective designations.

The majestic Vigna Novali '06 strides into the company of Italy's finest whites. An array of fruit and blossoms pours right into an ultra-spacious palate of expressive elegance and immense depth. Tordiruta '06 is again the finest passito in the region. Intense, botrytized candied orange leads into a finely chiselled palate marked by finesse and well-calibrated sweetness. The bracing Vigneti del Parco '06 offers up super-savoury fruit, as does Campo alle Mura '06, which also unveils concentration and succulence. From the standard-label Verdicchios, we would single out Fondiglie '08 for its lovely citrus throughout and a complex palate.

O Verdicchio dei Castelli di Jesi Cl. V. Novali Ris. '06	♟♟♟	5*
● Conero Vign. del Parco Ris. '06	♟♟	5
● Rosso Piceno Sup. Campo delle Mura '06	♟♟	5
O Verdicchio dei Castelli di Jesi Passito Tordiruta '06	♟♟	7
● Conero Cimerio Ris. '06	♟♟	4*
● Conero Nerone Ris. '06	♟♟	7
O Offida Pecorino Ofithe '08	♟♟	4*
O Verdicchio dei Castelli di Jesi Cl. Le Vele '08	♟♟	4*
O Verdicchio dei Castelli di Jesi Cl. Sup. Fondiglie '08	♟♟	4*
O Verdicchio dei Castelli di Jesi Cl. Sup. Verde di Ca' Ruptae '08	♟♟	4*
● Barocco '06	♟	4
O Madreperla Brut Rosé '05	♟	7
O Verdicchio dei Castelli di Jesi Cl. Passito Tordiruta '97	♟♟♟	5

Umani Ronchi

VIA ADRIATICA, 12
60027 OSIMO [AN]
TEL. 0717108019
www.umanironchi.com

CELLAR SALES
PRE-BOOKED VISITS

ANNUAL PRODUCTION 3.300.000 bottles
HECTARES UNDER VINE 230
VITICULTURE METHOD Conventional

Since the Bernetti family enterprise combines both quality and quantity, Umani Ronchi is a valuable ambassador for the region. Its style is elegant and fruity, showing very clean-edged and easy to appreciate, never forced or off-key. The average quality of the wines is surprisingly high but that is the logical result of a partnership of experimentation, commitment, clear ideas and objectives that admit no compromise. The goal is always to grow great grapes that will make noble wines and the investments that have been made, particularly in the vineyards, are there to prove it.

A brace of Three Glass awards put Umani Ronchi into the elite of Italy's producers. The style here is a perfect example of quality, namely elegance and a distinct sense of place. Pelago '06 received the top award. A blend of cabernet, montepulciano and merlot, it shows notable finesse in its complex florality, and the palate is a paragon of savouriness, energetic progression and crispness. The ultra-fragrant Plenio '06 also picked up Three Glasses. A hint of toast complements savouriness that showcases considerable varietal fidelity. Casal di Serra Vecchie Vigne '07 is another star with a balance of near magical proportions, understated but near endless.

● Pelago '06	♟♟♟	6
O Verdicchio dei Castelli di Jesi Cl. Plenio Ris. '06	♟♟♟	5
● Conero Cùmaro Ris. '06	♟♟	5
O Verdicchio dei Castelli di Jesi Cl. Sup. Casal di Serra Vecchie Vigne '07	♟♟	5
O Maximo '06	♟♟	5
● Rosso Conero S. Lorenzo '07	♟♟	4
● Rosso Conero Serrano '08	♟♟	4*
O Verdicchio dei Castelli di Jesi Cl. Sup. Casal di Serra '08	♟♟	4
O Verdicchio dei Castelli di Jesi Cl. Villa Bianchi '08	♟♟	4*
O Verdicchio dei Castelli di Jesi Cl. Plenio Ris. '05	♟♟♟	5
O Verdicchio dei Castelli di Jesi Cl. Plenio Ris. '04	♟♟♟	5
O Verdicchio dei Castelli di Jesi Cl. Plenio Ris. '03	♟♟♟	5

Vallerosa Bonci

VIA TORRE, 13
60034 CUPRAMONTANA [AN]
TEL. 0731789129
www.vallerosa-bonci.com

CELLAR SALES
PRE-BOOKED VISITS

ANNUAL PRODUCTION **250,000 bottles**
HECTARES UNDER VINE **35**
VITICULTURE METHOD **Conventional**

Peppe Bonci, heir of a family with a 100-year-old viticultural tradition, has more than long experience with verdicchio. His is an intimate relationship with the grape. It is thus extremely easy for him to leave a personal imprint on the wines he makes. Vallerosa Bonci whites are generally alcoholic and rich, partly because the local area is warm and partly because most vineyards, like those of San Michele, face south. These ideal elevations and exposures work to ensure fine balance and ripeness in the fruit.

Two of the winery standard-bearers were not presented for tasting so this year's list is shorter. Pietrone is a Verdicchio made from overripe, almost late-picked, grapes and Le Case is a cask-aged selection of great finesse. San Michele '07, which went to the finals, is huge-volumed and forceful, showing savoury with hard-driving progression right to the end. Manciano '08 has lots of body but excessive alcohol has a drying effect on development. Viatorre '08 passes muster, although it has a bit of an odd nose of ripe fruit and dry vegetables, and the palate reveals some signs of evolution.

Valturio

VIA DEI PELASGI, 10
61023 MACERATA FELTRIA [PU]
TEL. 0722728049
www.valturio.com

CELLAR SALES
PRE-BOOKED VISITS
VISITOR FACILITIES

ANNUAL PRODUCTION **20,000 bottles**
HECTARES UNDER VINE **10**
VITICULTURE METHOD **Natural**

Montefeltro is an attractive, untouched area halfway straddling Marche and Romagna, rich in history and in fascination. Adriano Galli and his wife Isabella Santarelli reintroduced the vine here, after a hiatus of 100 years, following their instincts and putting their trust in venerable traditions that began with the dukes of Montefeltro and continued up to the early 20th century. Valturio's beautiful amphitheatre of bush-trained vines, planted at a density of 7,000 vines per hectare and meticulously managed, is beginning to testify to the success of a very original, impressive project.

The Gallis' carefully thought-out plan to produce sangiovese at high elevations of 400 to 500 metres yielded Valturio. It picked up Three Glasses, impressing with the genuineness of its dynamically clean-lined yet subtle progression and with its load of fruit presented with such austerity and elegance. The wine derives from a courageous and unusual project. The label bears a famous image of an imaginative, dragon-shaped war machine contained in the military treatise written by Roberto Valturio of Macerata Feltria for Sigismondo Malatesta in 1455. Solco, made largely from the rebo grape, also impressed, showing softer and more international in style.

○ Verdicchio dei Castelli di Jesi Cl. Sup. S. Michele '07	♈ 5*
○ Verdicchio dei Castelli di Jesi Cl. Manciano '08	♈ 4
○ Verdicchio dei Castelli di Jesi Cl. Viatorre '08	♈ 3
○ Verdicchio dei Castelli di Jesi Cl. Sup. S. Michele '06	♈♈♈ 5
○ Bonci Brut M. Cl. '04	♈♈ 5
○ Verdicchio dei Castelli di Jesi Passito Rojano '06	♈♈ 5
○ Verdicchio dei Castelli di Jesi Cl. Sup. Le Case '05	♈♈ 4*

● Valturio '07	♈♈♈ 5
● Olmo '08	♈♈ 4
● Solco '07	♈♈ 5
● Valturio '06	♈♈ 5

Velenosi

LOC. MONTICELLI
VIA DEI BIANCOSPINI, 11
63100 ASCOLI PICENO
TEL. 0736341218
www.velenosivini.com

CELLAR SALES

ANNUAL PRODUCTION **1.500.000 bottles**
HECTARES UNDER VINE **135**
VITICULTURE METHOD **Conventional**

Velenosi is characterized by terrific sparkling wines, generously complex reds, representatives of important regional denominations and wide distribution. These are the most salient traits of a project that shows serious planning and felicitous intuitions. Angela Velenosi, who represents the winery abroad, has always believed that wines should be affordable, approachable and modern in style. In a word, wines of international appeal, equally appreciated in Italy, the USA and the Far East. Sales success and the list below lend her words credence.

The duel continues between Roggio and Ludi, both from a good year. The first, more austere and complex, offers a refined expression of terroir. Ludi is more international, with a voluminous bouquet and the smoothest of tannins, but our preference goes to the natural purity of Roggio. The Rose is pinot nero, with lovely wild strawberry on the nose, plus a hint of carbonic maceration, complemented by a refined but self-confident palate. Velenosi Brut is 70 per cent chardonnay and the rest pinot nero, well rounded and emphatic, with delicious fruitiness. From the white list, Villa Angela is a tasty, full-fruited Pecorino.

Vignamato

VIA BATTINEBBIA, 4
60038 SAN PAOLO DI JESI [AN]
TEL. 0731779197
www.vignamato.com

CELLAR SALES
PRE-BOOKED VISITS

ANNUAL PRODUCTION **55,000 bottles**
HECTARES UNDER VINE **16**
VITICULTURE METHOD **Conventional**

Since 1952, Verdicchio has been Vignamato's specialty. It could hardly be otherwise, considering the historical production of San Paolo di Jesi, on the other side of the river Esino. Andrea Ceci holds the reins of the enterprise today, keeping quality high and following the lessons of parents Maurizio and Serenella, who forged Vignamato's modern identity and approach. The standard-label Verdicchios are aged in steel while Ambrosia and the passito Antares mature in barriques. Sadly, this year's reds didn't leave the bench, nailed down as they were by excessive ripeness and little energy.

We preferred Verdicchio Ambrosia Riserva '06, with its duet of bitter orange and almond, then a flowing, ductile progression with decent alcohol and complexity. Versiano '08 is a notch down in intensity, but very impressive nonetheless, centring on floral notes and crisp fruit with excellent overall balance and finesse. Both Valle delle Lame '08 and Eos '08, the latter from organic fruit, come across as appealing and straightforward, with deliciously fragrant citrus. RosAmato '08, sangiovese and montepulciano, is sound enough, showing clean-edged aromas mid palate while the passito Antares '06 lays out warm-toned candied fruit and vanilla.

● Rosso Piceno Sup. Roggio del Filare '06	♟♟♟	7
● Offida Rosso Ludi '06	♟♟	6
☉ The Rose Brut Rosé '06	♟♟	6
○ Falerio dei Colli Ascolani V. Solaria '08	♟♟	4*
○ Offida Pecorino Villa Angela '08	♟♟	4
● Rosso Piceno Sup. Brecciarolo '06	♟♟	3*
● Rosso Piceno Sup. Il Brecciarolo Gold '06	♟♟	5
○ Velenosi Brut '06	♟♟	6
● Lacrima di Morro d'Alba Querciantica '08	♟	4
○ Passerina Villa Angela '08	♟	4
○ Rêve '07	♟	5
● Rosso Piceno Sup. Roggio del Filare '05	♟♟♟	6
● Rosso Piceno Sup. Roggio del Filare '04	♟♟♟	6
● Rosso Piceno Sup. Roggio del Filare '03	♟♟♟	6
● Rosso Piceno Sup. Roggio del Filare '02	♟♟♟	5

○ Verdicchio dei Castelli di Jesi Cl. Ambrosia Ris. '06	♟♟	4*
○ Verdicchio dei Castelli di Jesi Cl. Sup. Versiano '08	♟♟	4*
○ Verdicchio dei Castelli di Jesi Cl. Eos '08	♟♟	2*
○ Verdicchio dei Castelli di Jesi Cl. Valle delle Lame '08	♟♟	3*
☉ RosAmato '08	♟	2
● Rosso Piceno Campalliano '06	♟	4
○ Verdicchio dei Castelli di Jesi Passito Antares '06	♟	5
○ Verdicchio dei Castelli di Jesi Cl. Ambrosia Ris. '05	♟♟	4
○ Verdicchio dei Castelli di Jesi Cl. Sup. Versiano '07	♟♟	4*
○ Verdicchio dei Castelli di Jesi Cl. Valle delle Lame '07	♟♟	3*

Villa Pigna

C.DA CIAFONE, 63
63035 OFFIDA [AP]
TEL. 073687525
www.villapigna.com

CELLAR SALES
PRE-BOOKED VISITS

ANNUAL PRODUCTION **600,000 bottles**
HECTARES UNDER VINE **100**
VITICULTURE METHOD **Conventional**

Villa Pigna was founded by Costantino Rozzi, the legendary chairman of the Ascoli football club. The operation is still in family hands. It's run today by Annamaria Rozzi, who not only physically resembles her father but has his straightforward, sincere character as well. The estate comprises 100 hectares of vineyard and represents most of the Piceno-area designations. A stagnant period ended some time ago and for years now the wines have shown consistency, reasonable prices and some very fine performances.

The Rozzano editions are always at the top of our preferences, including this '07. All montepulciano, it serves up concentrated morello cherry and spice, lifted by subtle nuances of balsam, well matched by a forceful, well-extracted palate that still achieves fine balance overall. Almost equally fine is the smooth Offida Cabernasco '06, showing well-ripened fruit and a palate nicely shaped by fine-grained tannins. Vergaio '07 is a tad oaky but a fluid palate makes it excellent for the price. From the whites, the pecorino Rugiasco '08 stood out with a blend of fresh greens and white peaches beautifully infusing both nose and palate.

● Rozzano '07	♥♥	5
○ Offida Pecorino Rugiasco '08	♥♥	4*
● Offida Rosso Cabernasco '06	♥♥	5
● Rosso Piceno Sup. Vergaio '07	♥♥	4
○ Offida Passerina Majia '08	♥	4
● Rosso Piceno Eliano '08	♥	3
● Vellutato '08	♥	3
● Rozzano '03	♥♥♥	5
○ Offida Passerina Majia '07	♀♀	4*
○ Offida Passerina Majia '06	♀♀	4*
○ Offida Pecorino Rugiasco '07	♀♀	4*
● Offida Rosso Cabernasco '05	♀♀	5
● Offida Rosso Cabernasco '04	♀♀	5
● Rozzano '06	♀♀	5
● Rozzano '05	♀♀	5

Zaccagnini

VIA SALMÀGINA, 9/10
60039 STAFFOLO [AN]
TEL. 0731779892
www.zaccagnini.it

CELLAR SALES
PRE-BOOKED VISITS

ANNUAL PRODUCTION **200,000 bottles**
HECTARES UNDER VINE **25**
VITICULTURE METHOD **Conventional**

The Zaccagnini family winery is back in its sturdy stride. In the 1990s, Mario Zaccagnani's wines were at the top of aficionados' lists, particularly his forceful, alcoholic Verdicchios, which were stylistic light years away from the spare, acidic bottles then in vogue. The operation comprises 25 hectares under vine, planted largely to verdicchio, in the municipality of Staffolo, where the grape yields some of the most refined and powerful versions in the designation. Completing the Zaccagnini line are some fragrant, light, easy-drinking reds.

Salmàgina '08, sourced from the vineyards surrounding the cellar, offers a sound nose redolent of anise with minerally impressions, both continuing onto a lithe, bright palate. Some further time in the bottle will bring appreciable complexity. Cima Signoria and Il Castello are supple and savoury, both delicious easy-drinkers. The more ambitious Maestro di Staffolo Riserva '07 was late-picked and it offers compelling initial richness. But the overly smooth palate lacks backbone and the development has no push. We thought the best of the reds was the Rosso Piceno '08 with clean-profiled fruit and a straightforward, rounded palate.

○ Verdicchio dei Castelli di Jesi Cl. Sup. Salmàgina '08	♥♥	4*
● Rosso Piceno '08	♥♥	3*
○ Verdicchio dei Castelli di Jesi Cl. Il Castello '08	♥♥	3
○ Verdicchio dei Castelli di Jesi Cl. Sup. Cima Signoria	♥♥	
● Lacrima di Morro d'Alba '05	♥	3
● Rosso Conero '08	♥	4
○ Verdicchio dei Castelli di Jesi Cl. Maestro di Staffolo Ris. '07	♥	5
○ Cesolano '01	♀♀	5
○ Verdicchio dei Castelli di Jesi Cl. Maestro di Staffolo Ris. '05	♀♀	5
○ Verdicchio dei Castelli di Jesi Cl. Sup. Salmàgina '07	♀♀	4*

OTHER WINERIES

Mario & Giorgio Brunori

V.LE DELLA VITTORIA, 103
60035 JESI [AN]
TEL. 0731207213
www.brunori.it

This historic Iesi winery put out an impressive San Nicolò '08, with its usual fidelity to terroir, releasing notes of almond and acacia blossoms, followed by a layered palate. Less successful is Brunori's Riserva '07, with a blurred nose, too-copious alcohol and faltering progression.

○ Verdicchio dei Castelli di Jesi Cl. Sup. San Nicolò '08	♟	4
○ Verdicchio dei Castelli di Jesi Cl. Sup. San Nicolò Ris. '07	♟	4

Capinera

VIA CROCETTE, 12
62010 MORROVALLE [MC]
TEL. 0733222444
www.capinera.com

The clean definition and personality of the Capinera brothers' Cardinal Minio '06 makes this elegant Merlot stand out from the rest of the list. From the whites, we liked the tasty, ultra-fruity Chardonnay La Capinera '08 and their crisp, floral Colli Maceratesi Ribona, Murrano '08.

● Cardinal Minio '06	♟♟	5
○ La Capinera Chardonnay '08	♟♟	4
○ Colli Maceratesi Ribona Bianco Murrano '08	♟	3

Conti di Buscareto

FRAZ. PIANELLO
VIA SAN GREGORIO, 66
60010 OSTRA [AN]
TEL. 0717913180
www.contidibuscareto.com

Ostra-based Conti di Buscareto is in a transitional year of restructuring. Meanwhile, we enjoyed the Rosso Piceno '07, which has some immature notes but shows good succulence on the palate. Verdicchio Ammazzaconte '07 and Crimà '08, from lacrima di Morro d'Alba grapes, are just fair.

● Rosso Piceno '07	♟♟	3*
● Crimà '08	♟	3
○ Verdicchio dei Castelli di Jesi Ammazzaconte '07	♟	4

Coroncino

C.DA CORONCINO, 7
60039 STAFFOLO [AN]
TEL. 0731779494
coroncino@libero.it

Lucio Canestrari was a huge influence on modern Verdicchio. Gaiospino was still maturing so we fell back on Coroncino '08. It showed well, with good varietal richness and savouriness, in spite of some evolved notes along the way.

○ Verdicchio dei Castelli di Jesi Cl. Sup. Il Coroncino '07	♟♟	4

Croce del Moro

VIA TASSANARE, 4
60030 ROSORA [AN]
TEL. 0731814158
www.tassanare.it

Croce del Moro's high-elevation vineyards in Rosora produce good flavours and complexity, embodied in the '07 Verdicchio Crocetta. Though quite measured, it boasts a full, balanced structure and a sea salt-tipped finish. Le Muse, the standard Verdicchio, shows aromatic but is quite short.

○ Verdicchio dei Castelli di Jesi Cl. Sup. Crocetta '07	♟♟	4
○ Verdicchio dei Castelli di Jesi Cl. Le Muse '08	♟	3

Pasqualino Damiani

C.DA PIANACCIOLE, 2
63038 RIPATRANSONE [AP]
TEL. 073590144

Pasqualino Damiani is a scrupulous producer of big-volumed reds that are clearly territorial, such as the massive Offida Rosso '06 and an elegant, floral Piceno Superiore '06 with dynamic progression. Offida Passerina '08 is clean and citrussy, in fact the best Passerina we tasted.

○ Offida Passerina '08	♟♟	3*
● Offida Rosso '06	♟♟	4
● Rosso Piceno Sup. '06	♟♟	3*

Castello Fageto

VIA VALDASO, 52
63016 PEDASO [AP]
TEL. 0734931784
www.castellofageto.it

Fageto has more potential to exploit, particularly in the reds, which suffer from overripe fruit. The standard label whites are best, such as the two '08s, the fresh, clean-edged Pecorino Fenèsia and the supple Falerio dei Colli Ascolani.

○ Falerio dei Colli Ascolani '08	♟♟	3*
○ Offida Pecorino Fenèsia '08	♟♟	4

Fiorini

VIA GIARDINO CAMPIOLI, 5
61040 BARCHI [PU]
TEL. 072197151
www.fioriniwines.it

Fiorini is one of the best-known producers of Bianchello del Metauro. We liked both examples, each fresh, clean and floral. The nod goes to Tenuta Campioli '08 over the more slender Sant'Ilario '08. From the reds, Bartis '07 showed well, with admirable energy, if a tad dry in the finish.

● Bartis '07	♟♟	4
○ Bianchello del Metauro Tenuta Campioli '08	♟	3
○ Bianchello del Metauro V. Sant'Ilario '08	♟	2*

Mario Lucchetti

VIA SANTA MARIA DEL FIORE, 17
60030 MORRO D'ALBA [AN]
TEL. 073163314
www.mariolucchetti.it

New developments emerged from Lucchetti, among them an excellent Verdicchio Classico Superiore, with a refined nose and terrific mid palate. The base label is fresh but too simple. The energy-laden Lacrima '08 passito exudes sweet blackberry and rose petals.

● Lacrima di Morro d'Alba '08	♟♟	3*
● Lacrima di Morro d'Alba Passito '07	♟♟	6
○ Verdicchio dei Castelli di Jesi Cl. Sup. '08	♟♟	3*
○ Verdicchio dei Castelli di Jesi Cl. '08	♟	3

Stefano Mancinelli

VIA ROMA, 62
60030 MORRO D'ALBA [AN]
TEL. 073163021
www.mancinelli-wine.com

There were few releases from Mancinelli and quality was down, a strange position for this long-standing producer at Morro d'Alba. The Sensazioni di Frutto '08 is intensely floral and a tad sweet while Verdicchio '08 shows fine flavours and evolved notes on a finish of dried fruit and nuts.

● Lacrima di Morro d'Alba Sensazioni di Frutto '08	♟	4
○ Verdicchio dei Castelli di Jesi Cl. '08	♟	2*

Clara Marcelli

VIA FONTE VECCHIA, 9
63030 CASTORANO [AP]
TEL. 073687289
info@claramarcelli.it

Clara Marcelli's wines exhibit generous character. The reds show tannic grip but the whites could be more even in quality. The imposing K'un '07, from montepulciano, is fine, as is the slightly countryish but effective Piceno Superiore '07. Pecorino Irata '08 has good savouriness but a more contentious bouquet.

● K'un '07	♟♟	4
● Piceno Rosso Sup. '07	♟♟	4
○ Offida Pecorino Irata '08	♟	4

Maurizio Marconi

VIA MELANO, 25
60030 SAN MARCELLO [AN]
TEL. 0731267223
www.cantinemarconi.it

With 120 hectares of mostly verdicchio and lacrima, Marconi makes good versions of both. Verdicchio Classico '08 offers a cleanly defined, ultra-juicy palate while Lacrima Superiore '07 is intensely fruity from first to last. We also liked the standard-version Lacrima.

● Lacrima di Morro d'Alba Sup. '07	♟♟	4
○ Verdicchio dei Castelli di Jesi Cl. '08	♟♟	3*
● Lacrima di Morro d'Alba '08	♟	4

Claudio Morelli

V.LE ROMAGNA, 47B
61032 FANO [PU]
TEL. 0721823352
www.claudiomorelli.it

We were not surprised to see some terrific versions of Bianchello del Metauro from a specialist like Claudio Morelli. La Vigna delle Terrazze '08 is outstanding: floral, elegant and utterly supple. Also fine is Borgo Torre, riper and with hints of honey, but a luscious quaffer.

○ Bianchello del Metauro Borgo Torre '08	🍷🍷 4
○ Bianchello del Metauro La Vigna delle Terrazze '08	🍷🍷 4

La Muròla

C.DA VILLAMAGNA, 9
62010 URBISAGLIA [MC]
TEL. 0733506843
www.cantinalamurola.it

Murola, with a history dating back to the 19th century, has vast lands now focused on quality production. We were surprised by a scrumptious Vin Santo-style sweet wine from trebbiano and maceratino, Priore. It lays out ultra-sweet progression and the finish radiates dried nuts and marzipan.

○ Priore	🍷🍷 5
○ Colli Maceratesi Le Jole '08	🍷🍷 4

Pontemagno

VIA BORGO SANTA MARIA, 60
60038 SAN PAOLO DI JESI [AN]
TEL. 0731703214
www.piersantivini.com

Pontemagno's Verdicchios stand out from the rest of its broad line and each is distinctive. We particularly liked the elegance and proportion of Quota 311 '08, and the citrussy fullness of Bachero '08, especially on the palate. Anfora '08, with clean, varietal aromas, is reasonably priced.

○ Verdicchio dei Castelli di Jesi Cl. Quota 311 '08	🍷🍷 2*
○ Verdicchio dei Castelli di Jesi Cl. Sup. Bachero '08	🍷🍷 2*
○ Verdicchio dei Castelli di Jesi Cl. Anfora '08	🍷 1*

Rio Maggio

C.DA VALLONE, 41
63014 MONTEGRANARO [AP]
TEL. 0734889587
www.riomaggio.it

Simone Santucci's Rio Maggio shows signs of revival. The new Pecorino '08 pleased everyone with its fruit, and with the clean edges and drive of its progression. Telusiano '08 is its usual elegant, complex self. Telusiano '08, though still very austere, is fresh and well built.

○ Colle Monteverde Offida Pecorino '08	🍷🍷 4*
○ Falerio dei Colli Ascolani Telusiano '08	🍷🍷 4*
● Rosso Piceno Rubeo '06	🍷🍷 5

Sabbionare

VIA SABBIONARE, 10
60036 MONTECAROTTO [AN]
TEL. 0731889004
sabbionare@libero.it

Donatella Paoloni's Sabbionare has made one of the finest standard-label Verdicchios for some time now. It's a white of great breeding, presenting powerful and well cadenced, with well-positioned fruit that culminates on a bright note of almond. The fragrant Passito '06 has fine, measured sweetness.

○ Verdicchio dei Castelli di Jesi Cl. Sup. Sabbionare '08	🍷🍷 4*
○ Verdicchio dei Castelli di Jesi Passito '06	🍷🍷

San Filippo

LOC. BORGO MIRIAM
C.DA CIAFONE, 17A
63035 OFFIDA [AP]
TEL. 0736889828
www.vinisanfilippo.it

Lupo del Ciafone's stars were absent and other wines seemed hesitant or even down a bit in quality. Katharsis '06 was the best, an exuberant Rosso Piceno Superiore though a little dry on the finish. The new version of Pecorino, the '08, was less complex and not so precisely profiled.

● Rosso Piceno Sup. Katharsis '06	🍷🍷 3*
○ Offida Passerina '08	🍷 2
○ Offida Pecorino '08	🍷 3
● Rosso Piceno '08	🍷 3*

Santa Cassella

C.DA SANTA CASSELLA, 7
62018 POTENZA PICENA [MC]
TEL. 0733671507
www.santacassella.it

The cabernet Conte Leopoldo '07 and Colli
Maceratesi Bianco '08 lead Santa Cassella's
offerings. The first is elegant, balsamic,
supple and harmonious, the second
fragrant, rounded and approachable. Donna
Eleonora '08 is an ultra-aromatic, smooth
chardonnay and sauvignon mix.

○ Colli Maceratesi Bianco '08	🍷🍷	3*
● Conte Leopoldo '07	🍷🍷	4
○ Donna Eleonora '08	🍷	4

Alvaro Saputi

C.DA FIASTRA, 2
62020 COLMURANO [MC]
TEL. 0733508137
www.saputi.it

Saputi presented many wines, most from
Macerata DOCs. Cantavino dei Castelli '08,
a smooth, luscious Verdicchio, stood out,
as well as Abate Pallia '06, a taut Cabernet
Sauvignon with bell pepper and dried hay
followed by a fragrant, lithe palate.

● Abate Pallia '06	🍷🍷	5
○ Verdicchio dei Castelli di Jesi Cl. Sup.		
Cantavino dei Castelli '08	🍷🍷	4*
○ Colli Maceratesi Montenereto '08	🍷	2*

Fattoria Serra San Martino

VIA SAN MARTINO, 1
60030 SERRA DE' CONTI [AN]
TEL. 0731878025
www.serrasanmartino.com

Kirsten and Thomas Weydemann's Serra
San Martino releases a tiny amount of wine
but the reds show energy and ultra-refined
tannic extraction. The finest this year are
the deep, peppery, syrah Paonazzo '06
and Lo Sconosciuto '06, a supple and
quite distinctive Sagrantino.

● Il Paonazzo Syrah '06	🍷🍷	6
● Lo Sconosciuto '06	🍷🍷	6

La Staffa

VIA CASTELLARETA, 19
60039 STAFFOLO [AN]
TEL. 0731779430

This year brings fine marks for La Staffa, a
small, dedicated Verdicchio producer.
Rincrocca '06 is excellent, showing supple
and savoury with a refined, thrusting finale
of good complexity. The standard-label
Verdicchio is crisp and tasty but the
cask-aged Ganimede Riserva '06 leaves
some doubts.

○ Verdicchio dei Castelli di Jesi Cl. Sup.		
La Rincrocca '06	🍷🍷	4*
○ Verdicchio dei Castelli di Jesi Cl. '08	🍷🍷	3
○ Verdicchio dei Castelli di Jesi Cl.		
Ganimede Ris. '06	🍷	4

Vicari

VIA POZZO BUONO, 3
60030 MORRO D'ALBA [AN]
TEL. 073163164
www.vicarivini.it

Vicari gave us the best Lacrima tasted this
year, Essenza del Pozzo Buono '08.
Carbonic maceration imparts explosive
scents of candied red berry and shows
long and harmonious in the mouth. Lacrima
del Pozzo Buono '07 is good, with some
complexity, but Rustico '08 is somewhat
overripe.

● Lacrima di Morro d'Alba		
Essenza del Pozzo Buono '08	🍷🍷	4
● Lacrima di Morro d'Alba		
Sup. del Pozzo Buono '07	🍷🍷	4

Villa Grifoni

FRAZ. SAN SAVINO DI RIPATRANSONE
C.DA MESSIERI
63038 RIPATRANSONE [AP]
TEL. 073590495
www.villa-grifoni.it

Oenologist Primo Narcisi is beginning to
put out good results from the 40 hectares
of Giuseppe Cocci Grifoni's new and
promising Villa Grifoni. Rosso Piceno
Superiore '07 is terrific, with complexity and
much fine natural energy. Offida Pecorino
'08 and the concentrated Marche Rosso
'07 are excellent.

● Rosso Piceno Sup. '07	🍷🍷	4
● Marche Rosso '07	🍷🍷	4
○ Offida Pecorino '08	🍷🍷	4
○ Bianco Natural '08	🍷	4

UMBRIA

Winemaking in Umbria seems to faces with same issues that confront Italy internationally. This small region cannot compete in numbers and so must invest in quality to earn space for itself. For several years, an area that produces less than a million hectolitres of wine a year has been punching well above its weight and production capacity.

The many ways of looking at this situation suggest that Umbria is more of a dynamic fabric than a static, well-established map. Truth to tell, the region has had more revolutions than evolution in its winemaking history. The first was during the 1960s in Torgiano when Giorgio Lungarotti quite literally invented a territory. The Caprai family accomplished the same thing on the slopes of Montefalco a few years later, but with a knock-on effect that is still producing fruit. On reflection, before these events, only Orvieto had any clear impact on the overall history of Italian wine. But those were different times. Now, a handful of brave producers are restoring the image of an area that has never had it easy, not even in the past 20 years when IGT, unconnected with classic varieties or territories, became the template for regional winemaking. Today, the trend seems to have slowed, benefiting the region's eleven DOCs and two DOCGs, Torgiano Rosso Riserva and Montefalco Sagrantino. Yet even as interesting a wine area as Trasimeno has difficulty finding a distinct identity. For now, it fails to go beyond a few individual high points. Of course, traditional varieties are experiencing a period of popularity. Grechetto for whites and sagrantino for reds are old friends by now but moving in alongside these wines are seductive interpretations of trebbiano spoletino, a pearl of a wine that seemed extinct but is still often grown on old, ungrafted vines, gamay from Trasimeno and ciliegiolo from Narni. We shall see. This year anyway seven wines took top honours. Torgiano Rosso Riserva Vigna Monticchio '05 is another great offering from the Lungarotti collection; top wines on the Sagrantino front include the amazing 25 Anni '06 from Marco Caprai, very much one-of-a-kind in the category, Gold '05 from Còlpetrone, and the 2006 from Perticaia, as well as another three wines from equally historic estates like Adanti, which delivered a great 2005, Antonelli, outstanding with the fascinating Chiusa di Pannone '04 selection, and another win for Antano with Colleallodole '06. These are reds with a relaxed profile, frequently aged in large barrels and fully capable of pointing the way to new stylistic scenarios for this territory. This year, however, there was also a white on the podium, the stupendous trebbiano spoletino Adarmando '07 from Tabarrini. Could this be the start of something new?

Adanti

LOC. ARQUATA
06031 BEVAGNA [PG]
TEL. 0742360295
www.cantineadanti.com

CELLAR SALES
PRE-BOOKED VISITS

ANNUAL PRODUCTION 150,000 bottles
HECTARES UNDER VINE 30
VITICULTURE METHOD Conventional

Adanti is one of the classic, traditional Sagrantino estates and one with a fabulous villa. The first vineyards were planted in the 1970s, not far from the village of Bevagna, where the vinification and storage cellar is housed in a classically themed structure. In the cellar, wine consultant Maurizio Castelli has recently arrived to flank the talented Daniele Palini, son of the legendary tailor-cellar worker Alvaro. There have also been various renovations to the obvious benefit of the wines.

The splendid Montefalco Sagrantino '05 aged in 30-hectolitre barrels and tonneaux, and as usual released after a year more in bottle than required by regulations. Finesse and minerality vein an aromatic profile that recalls root vegetables, pink pepper and ripe blood oranges. The wine shows great verve and earthy, dense tannins also showing long and flavourful. Montefalco Rosso '07 is also lovely, stylish and spicy, though the tannins are slightly too assertive. The Montefalco Bianco and Grechetto, both '08, are focused while Sagrantino Passito '06 is less convincing than usual.

● Montefalco Sagrantino Arquata '05	♟♟♟ 6
● Montefalco Rosso Arquata '07	♟♟ 4*
☉ Amanter '08	♟ 4
○ Colli Martani Grechetto '08	♟ 3
○ Montefalco Bianco '08	♟ 3
● Montefalco Sagrantino Passito Arquata '06	♟ 7
● Montefalco Rosso Arquata '06	♟♟ 4*
● Montefalco Sagrantino Arquata '04	♟♟ 6
● Montefalco Sagrantino Arquata '03	♟♟ 6
● Montefalco Sagrantino Arquata '02	♟♟ 6
● Montefalco Sagrantino Arquata '01	♟♟ 6
● Montefalco Sagrantino Passito Arquata '05	♟♟ 7
● Montefalco Sagrantino Passito Arquata '04	♟♟ 7

Antonelli - San Marco

LOC. SAN MARCO, 60
06036 MONTEFALCO [PG]
TEL. 0742379158
www.antonellisanmarco.it

CELLAR SALES
PRE-BOOKED VISITS
VISITOR FACILITIES

ANNUAL PRODUCTION 300,000 bottles
HECTARES UNDER VINE 45
VITICULTURE METHOD Organic certified

Filippo Antonelli's splendid estate is headquartered at San Marco, in one of the best areas of Montefalco, and has been in his family's hands since the 19th century. Numerous documents show this estate's origins go back to the Middle Ages when San Marco De Corticellis was one of the best Lombard courts for growing vines and olive. The wines reflect this very traditional feel and put the emphasis on harmony and elegance. Organic growing methods are applied and many of the wines are aged in large wood.

Montefalco Sagrantino Chiusa di Pannone is a vineyard selection from a single plot, the highest and best suited. This extraordinary red beautifully interprets the mild 2004 growing season. It shows refined and light, with leather and oriental spice aromatics while the palate is flavourful and long, with great energy and a perfect tannic weave. Three Glasses. The Sagrantino '06 is convincing, if perhaps a bit excessive in its aromatics, and the '06 Montefalco Rosso Riserva is well managed. The Montefalco Rosso '07 is excellent and the intriguing Trebbiano Spoletino '08 is rich in candied citrus and lovely notes of toast.

● Montefalco Sagrantino Chiusa di Pannone '04	♟♟♟ 7
● Montefalco Rosso '07	♟♟ 4*
● Montefalco Rosso Ris. '06	♟♟ 5
● Montefalco Sagrantino '06	♟♟ 6
○ Trebbiano Spoletino '08	♟♟ 4*
● Montefalco Sagrantino Passito '06	♟ 6
● Montefalco Rosso '06	♟♟ 4*
● Montefalco Rosso Ris. '05	♟♟ 5
● Montefalco Rosso Ris. '04	♟♟ 5
● Montefalco Sagrantino '05	♟♟ 6
● Montefalco Sagrantino '04	♟♟ 6
● Montefalco Sagrantino Chiusa di Pannone '03	♟♟ 7
● Montefalco Sagrantino Passito '05	♟♟ 6
● Montefalco Sagrantino Passito '04	♟♟ 6

Argillae

LOC. POMARRO, 45
05010 ALLERONA [TR]
TEL. 0763624604
www.argillae.it

CELLAR SALES
PRE-BOOKED VISITS

ANNUAL PRODUCTION **50,000 bottles**
HECTARES UNDER VINE **65**
VITICULTURE METHOD **Conventional**

Argillae is a joint venture by the Bonollo, Di Cosimo and Ascenzi families. The estate extends across the hills northwest of Orvieto, in the towns of Allerona and Ficulle, bordered to the east by the Rio Torto, a tributary of the Paglia. The soil is clay, sand and limestone with the characteristic gullies unique to this area. The vineyards are located at altitudes between 350 and 500 metres above sea level. The most convincing wines are the whites which, aside from the grapes used, are rather original, in addition to being technically impeccable.

Panata '08 is from only chardonnay aged in stainless steel and a few months in barrique. Intense aromas run from mango and banana tropical sensations to citrus and pleasant grassy notes. The palate has depth only slightly penalized by alcoholic hints at the back. The Grechetto '08 is splendid, stylish and deep with its attractive sensations of meadow herbs and ripe fruit. The excellent Orvieto '08 hints at yellow apples and williams pears. Finally, the Bordeaux blend Sinuoso '08 is less convincing.

○ Grechetto '08	🍷🍷	4*
○ Orvieto '08	🍷🍷	3*
○ Panata '08	🍷🍷	4*
● Sinuoso '08	🍷	3
○ Grechetto '07	ΥΥ	4*
○ Panata '07	ΥΥ	4*

Barberani - Vallesanta

LOC. CERRETO
05023 BASCHI [TR]
TEL. 0763341820
www.barberani.it

CELLAR SALES
PRE-BOOKED VISITS

ANNUAL PRODUCTION **350,000 bottles**
HECTARES UNDER VINE **55**
VITICULTURE METHOD **Organic certified**

Barberani is one of the historic Orvieto winemaking operations. The vineyards and cellar are in the hills around Lake Corbara and the quality of the wines has risen over time to above average for the area. Some traditional products like Muffa Nobile have come back into fashion, while reds from the area have been redesigned and, especially over the past few years, have started to reflect a precise style and production philosophy that has led to organic certification.

We were most impressed by the Calcaia from procanico, verdello, grechetto and sauvignon, a botrytized Orvieto Muffato which has sumptuous finesse in the '06 version. The nose reveals saffron, crème brulée, and candied orange peel while the palate is sinuous, deep and consistent. The Villa Monticelli Rosso '05, from sangiovese, merlot and cabernet, is convincing though not up to last year's level. Moscato Passito Villa Monticelli '06 is also excellent. The Pomaio '06, from procanico, grechetto and chardonnay, aged in stainless steel and large barrels, with notes of nuts and caramel, and Foresco '07, are both good.

● Lago di Corbara Rosso Villa Monticelli '05	🍷🍷	5
○ Orvieto Cl. Sup. Calcaia '06	🍷🍷	6
● Lago di Corbara Foresco '07	🍷🍷	4*
○ Moscato Passito Villa Monticelli '06	🍷🍷	6
○ Orvieto Cl. Sup. Pomaio Villa Monticelli '06	🍷🍷	5
○ Grechetto '08	🍷	4
○ Orvieto Cl. '08	🍷	4
○ Orvieto Cl. Sup. Castagnolo '08	🍷	4
● Lago di Corbara Rosso Villa Monticelli '04	ΥΥΥ	5
● Lago di Corbara Foresco '06	ΥΥ	4*
○ Orvieto Cl. Sup. Calcaia '05	ΥΥ	6
○ Orvieto Cl. Sup. Calcaia '04	ΥΥ	6
○ Orvieto Cl. Sup. Calcaia '03	ΥΥ	6

Bigi

LOC. PONTE GIULIO
05018 ORVIETO [TR]
TEL. 0763315888
www.cantinebigi.it

PRE-BOOKED VISITS

ANNUAL PRODUCTION **4.300,000 bottles**
HECTARES UNDER VINE **196**
VITICULTURE METHOD **Conventional**

This Orvieto estate owned by the Gruppo Italiano Vini has over the years achieved extraordinarily constant quality, making a major contribution to the international reputation of this cliff-top town. Founded in 1880 by Luigi Bigi, the Bigi winery at Ponte Giulio also has excellent-value labels, most of which are successful interpretations of local wine types.

Grechetto Strozza Volpe '08 is again the best from the stable. Its clear, stylish bouquet recalls white peach and verbena, and even boasts hints of sage and walnutskin. Verve and dynamism on the palate usher in a delicious finish. We also loved the Sartiano, which the '07 harvest has blessed with warmth, texture and shades of bell pepper on sweet, satisfying fruity notes. There's a touch of oak that still has to be absorbed but this wine is successful overall and we firmly recommend it. Just below this, the Orvieto Classico Torricella '08 has notes of ripe peaches and stewed apples. We thought it seemed a little forward.

★ Arnaldo Caprai

LOC. TORRE
06036 MONTEFALCO [PG]
TEL. 0742378802
www.arnaldocaprai.it

CELLAR SALES
PRE-BOOKED VISITS

ANNUAL PRODUCTION **750,000 bottles**
HECTARES UNDER VINE **136**
VITICULTURE METHOD **Conventional**

Arnaldo Caprai's estate, especially Marco, has had a revolutionary impact on the Montefalco area, creating a situation unimaginable before its arrival, reinterpreting a traditional wine and variety that few people knew, investing in research both in the vineyard and cellar, and inventing a unique, inimitable style. In other words, Caprai created the Sagrantino phenomenon and perhaps an entire territory, at least in the form we know today.

The 25 Anni is goes beyond the confines of its type. It is capable as few other wines of combining power, charm and longevity. Actually, what pulls all three elements together is time, the wine's long sojourn in the cellar. Despite its youthful exuberance, the '06 vintage from even more ruthless fruit selection, has a superb aromatic profile and a monumental palate with splendid grain and superior finesse. The second-tier wine, the Sagrantino Collepiano '06, is also terrific, as is the Montefalco Rosso Riserva from the same vintage, which arrays red berries, dark citrus, leather and tobacco. The other wines in the range are better than good.

● Sartiano '07	🍷🍷 5
○ Strozza Volpe Grechetto '08	🍷🍷 4*
○ Orvieto Cl. Torricella '08	🍷 4
○ Orvieto Cl. Vigneto Torricella '06	🍷🍷 3
● Sartiano '07	🍷🍷 5
● Sartiano '06	🍷🍷 5
● Sartiano '05	🍷🍷 4
○ Strozza Volpe Grechetto '07	🍷🍷 3*
● Tamante '06	🍷🍷 3

● Montefalco Sagrantino 25 Anni '06	🍷🍷🍷 8
● Montefalco Rosso Ris. '06	🍷🍷 7
● Montefalco Sagrantino Collepiano '06	🍷🍷 7
○ Anima Umbra Bianco '08	🍷🍷 4*
○ Colli Martani Grechetto Grecante '08	🍷🍷 4*
● Montefalco Rosso '07	🍷🍷 5
● Montefalco Sagrantino Passito '06	🍷🍷 8
● Anima Umbra Rosso '07	🍷 4
● Montefalco Sagrantino 25 Anni '05	🍷🍷🍷 8
● Montefalco Sagrantino 25 Anni '04	🍷🍷🍷 8
● Montefalco Sagrantino 25 Anni '01	🍷🍷🍷 8
● Montefalco Sagrantino 25 Anni '00	🍷🍷🍷 8
● Montefalco Sagrantino 25 Anni '99	🍷🍷🍷 8
● Montefalco Sagrantino Collepiano '03	🍷🍷🍷 7
● Montefalco Sagrantino Collepiano '02	🍷🍷🍷 7
● Rosso Outsider '03	🍷🍷🍷 8

Cardeto

FRAZ. SFERRACAVALLO
LOC. CARDETO
05018 ORVIETO [TR]
TEL. 0763340135
www.cardeto.com

CELLAR SALES
PRE-BOOKED VISITS

ANNUAL PRODUCTION 3,000,000 bottles
HECTARES UNDER VINE 880
VITICULTURE METHOD Conventional

Founded in Orvieto in 1949, Cardeto is one of the Umbrian co-operatives with the most encouraging results, at least in tasting. Almost 900 hectares belong to more than 350 member-growers around the towns of Porano, Baschi, Castiglione in Teverina, Civitella d'Agliano, Montecchio and Allerona, as well as Orvieto, of course. Many of these plots fall into the Orvieto and Orvieto Classico DOC zones, and in fact Cardeto is the top producers in the latter designation.

Starting with the reds, Nero della Greca '07 is a pure Sangiovese with rather marked balsamic and grassy sensations, showing dark in terms of fruit as well as toasty notes. We were more convinced by the Arciato '07, a Bordeaux blend with lovely complexity. The palate is juicy yet dynamic with excellent texture and flavour, cramped only by a hint of alcohol in the finish. The Rupestro '08 is simpler. From the whites, we really liked Pierleone '08, which gives a flourish of flavour and freshness veined with meadow herbs and florality. Slightly below this is the Colbadia '08 and the flabbier, more mature Febeo '08.

Carini

FRAZ. COLLE UMBERTO
S.DA DEL TEGOLARO
06070 PERUGIA
TEL. 0755829102
www.agrariacarini.it

CELLAR SALES
PRE-BOOKED VISITS

ANNUAL PRODUCTION 40,000 bottles
HECTARES UNDER VINE 10
VITICULTURE METHOD Conventional

Brothers Carlo and Marco Carini own a small gem of an estate that spreads across the rolling hills sloping down from Monte Tezio, not far from Perugia, toward the shores of Lake Trasimeno. This working farm, aside from producing wine and extra virgin olive oil, also raises cinta senese pigs. The vineyards are tended lovingly, the small winery and storage cellar are impeccable and the wines have a modern profile in their own distinctive style.

Tegolaro is the family flagship wine. This never banal blend of merlot and cabernet sauvignon is often capable of showing amazing balance, elegance and outstanding personality. However, at least at the time of our tasting, the '07 edition was a bit less convincing than usual. It tends to put the accent on dark, toasty notes and the palate is still in search of direction. The very good Poggio Canneto '08, from chardonnay and pinot bianco, shows great finesse, density and depth, just like the excellent Oscano '08, a Rhône-esque blend of sangiovese and gamay perugino, the latter related to grenache.

● Arciato '07	▼▼	5
● Nero della Greca '07	▼▼	5
○ Orvieto Cl. Pierleone '08	▼▼	3*
○ Colbadia '08	▼	4
○ Orvieto Cl. Sup. Febeo '08	▼	4
● Rupestro '08	▼	3
● Arciato '06	♀♀	5
● Arciato '05	♀♀	4
● Nero della Greca '07	♀♀	5
● Nero della Greca '06	♀♀	5
● Nero della Greca '05	♀♀	5
● Rupestro '07	♀♀	3*

● Òscano '08	▼▼	4*
○ Poggio Canneto '08	▼▼	4*
● Tegolaro '07	▼▼	6
● Tegolaro '06	♀♀	6
● Tegolaro '05	♀♀	6
● Tegolaro '04	♀♀	6
● Tegolaro '01	♀♀	6

La Carraia

LOC. TORDIMONTE, 56
05018 ORVIETO [TR]
TEL. 0763304013
www.lacarraia.it

CELLAR SALES
PRE-BOOKED VISITS

ANNUAL PRODUCTION **550,000 bottles**
HECTARES UNDER VINE **119**
VITICULTURE METHOD **Conventional**

Carraia was founded in 1988 at Tordimonte, in the heart of the Orvieto Classico DOC zone. Not far from the city of cliffs, it thrives thanks to the hard work of the Gialletti and Cotarella families, two names that are very representative of Umbria winemaking. Vineyards are varied and range from typical, central Italian varieties like grechetto, sangiovese and montepulciano to prestigious international grapes: chardonnay, merlot and cabernet sauvignon.

The estate's most famous wine is Fobiano, a merlot-heavy Bordeaux blend. Grapes come from a single vineyard, San Valentino, with volcanic soils and plenty of pebbles. The '07 has aromas of wild berries, black cherries and hints of torrefaction while the palate is meaty, yet never heavy, and has lovely depth. The splendid Sangiovese '08 shows amazing vigour and freshness, just like the Montepulciano Giro di Vite '07, albeit in a very different wine. Among the whites, there was a good showing from Le Basque '08, a powerful, floral grechetto-viogner mix, and the usual Poggio Calvelli '08, with nuances of apricot and spring flowers.

Tenuta Castelbuono

LOC. BEVAGNA
VOC. FOSSATO, 54
06031 PERUGIA
TEL. 0742362060
www.cantineferrari.it

ANNUAL PRODUCTION **74,000 bottles**
HECTARES UNDER VINE **32**
VITICULTURE METHOD **Conventional**

Famous for its designer sparklers, the Lunelli family from Trento began this impressive operation to make robust, complex Umbrian reds a few years ago. Located on the border of the municipalities of Montefalco and Bevagna, where the hills trace sinuous outlines and the land is ideal for growing sagrantino, most of the surface area under vine is planted to the variety. The wines are improving, thanks to a well thought-out approach that includes large barrels in the maturation process. The new cellar was designed by Arnaldo Pomodoro.

The splendid Montefalco Sagrantino '05 is centred on black berry fruit and fine spice. It's a rich and nicely mature wine, yet also rather elegant, showing contrast and depth. The acidity and dynamism are nice but the tannins tend to dry the mouth. The Montefalco Rosso '07 is also quite well made. It's taut with lovely toasty hints on notes of cherry and blueberry-led red and black berry fruit mingling with green and balsamic shades. The warm, caressing palate is slightly alcoholic on the finish but shows good balance overall.

● Fobiano '07	▼▼ 5
● Giro di Vite '07	▼▼ 5
○ Le Basque '08	▼▼ 4*
○ Orvieto Cl. Poggio Calvelli '08	▼▼ 3*
● Sangiovese '08	▼▼ 3*
○ Orvieto Cl. '08	▼ 2*
● Tizzonero '07	▼ 4
● Fobiano '03	♀♀♀ 5
● Fobiano '99	♀♀♀ 6
● Fobiano '98	♀♀♀ 5
● Fobiano '06	♀♀ 5
● Fobiano '05	♀♀ 5
● Giro di Vite '06	♀♀ 5
● Giro di Vite '05	♀♀ 5
○ Le Basque '07	♀♀ 4*
○ Orvieto Cl. Poggio Calvelli '07	♀♀ 3*
● Sangiovese '06	♀♀ 3*
● Tizzonero '06	♀♀ 4*
● Tizzonero '05	♀♀ 4

● Montefalco Rosso '07	▼▼ 4*
● Montefalco Sagrantino '05	▼▼ 6
● Montefalco Rosso '06	♀♀ 4*
● Montefalco Sagrantino '04	♀♀ 6

Castello delle Regine

LOC. LE REGINE
VIA DI CASTELLUCCIO
05022 AMELIA [TR]
TEL. 0744702005
www.castellodelleregine.com

CELLAR SALES
PRE-BOOKED VISITS

ANNUAL PRODUCTION **350,000 bottles**
HECTARES UNDER VINE **87**
VITICULTURE METHOD **Conventional**

Castello delle Regine's plots sprawl across more than 400 hectares in the municipalities of Narni and Amelia. Aside from vineyards, the property boasts woods, olive trees, a herd of chianina cattle and a restaurant. The project was started by the Nodaris who, at least as regards winemaking, quickly found a rather convincing style. The wines tend towards a modern profile and are obtained from classic central Italian varieties, like sangiovese, and leading international varieties, such as merlot.

The most famous wine from the estate is made from merlot but it was missing at our tasting, since the decision was made to postpone commercial release another year to allow longer bottle ageing. We shall wait. The Sangiovese Selezione del Fondatore '04 makes a good showing and, after some initial uncertainty, opens up on balsamic and ripe red berry notes. The palate is substantial and juicy with a warm, slightly tannic finish. Other wines from the range are always very reliable.

Fattoria Colle Allodole

LOC. COLLE ALLODOLE
06031 BEVAGNA [PG]
TEL. 0742361897

CELLAR SALES
PRE-BOOKED VISITS

ANNUAL PRODUCTION **30,000 bottles**
HECTARES UNDER VINE **10**
VITICULTURE METHOD **Conventional**

Francesco Antano, son of the late Milziade, one of the leading figures in the history of Sagrantino, is an energetic, authentic winemaker with great sensitivity. For a few years now, wines from his small winery near Bevagna have reached a certain stylistic maturity. They are completely personal, yet still true to the Antano history, and always capable of reflecting their land of origin, which we should mention boasts some of the area's most beautiful vineyards including the now famous Colleallodole cru.

Colleallodole, named on the label, gives us another collector's edition Montefalco Sagrantino. The '06 version, as usual aged in five-hectolitre barrels, combines power and warmth with a great attack and an extremely complex profile that recalls notes of liquorice root, bramble and black cherry. Only the tannins are a bit over the top, perhaps because of the wine's extreme youth. Kudos also goes to the Sagrantino '06, aged only in large oak, which is more austere and dynamic, while the excellent Passito '06 gives aromas of wild berry preserves and cinnamon, just like the Montefalco Rosso Riserva from the same vintage.

● Sangiovese Sel. del Fondatore '04	♟♟ 6
● Princeps '06	♟♟ 6
○ Bianco delle Regine '08	♟ 4
● Rosso di Podernovo '06	♟ 4
● Merlot '05	♟♟♟ 7
● Merlot '04	♟♟♟ 7
● Merlot '03	♟♟♟ 7
● Merlot '02	♟♟♟ 6
● Merlot '01	♟♟♟ 7

● Montefalco Sagrantino Colleallodole '06	♟♟♟ 7
● Montefalco Rosso '07	♟♟ 5
● Montefalco Rosso Ris. '06	♟♟ 6
● Montefalco Sagrantino '06	♟♟ 6
● Montefalco Sagrantino Passito '06	♟♟ 5
● Montefalco Sagrantino Colleallodole '05	♟♟♟ 7
● Montefalco Rosso '06	♟♟ 5
● Montefalco Rosso Ris. '05	♟♟ 6
● Montefalco Sagrantino '05	♟♟ 6
● Montefalco Sagrantino '04	♟♟ 6
● Montefalco Sagrantino Colle delle Allodole '04	♟♟ 7
● Montefalco Sagrantino Colle delle Allodole '03	♟♟ 7
● Montefalco Sagrantino Passito '05	♟♟ 5
● Montefalco Sagrantino Passito '04	♟♟ 5

Cantina dei Colli Amerini

LOC. FORNOLE
ZONA INDUSTRIALE
05022 AMELIA [TR]
TEL. 0744989721
www.colliamerini.it

CELLAR SALES
PRE-BOOKED VISITS

ANNUAL PRODUCTION **1,000,000 bottles**
HECTARES UNDER VINE **400**
VITICULTURE METHOD **Conventional**

Colli Amerini is a co-operative with a lot of responsibility, given its role in promoting this interesting winemaking area which vaunts a centuries-old tradition and great potential but which has also never shown any particular dynamism or spirit of initiative. Perhaps for this reason, the estate has recently released a series of new items, clear evidence of enthusiasm and a desire for renewal. Around 350 member growers represent a kaleidoscope of terrains, altitudes and microclimates.

The variety representative of this area, ciliegiolo di Narni, is featured in two major monovarietal labels. The Ciliegiolo '08 is a perfectly managed wine. The aromas are immediately pleasant, intensely floral and characterized by a red berry texture. The palate is supple, juicy, broad and flavourful, and closes out on echoes of cherry and wild strawberries. It's no monster of complexity, but it's still very nice and drinkable. On the other hand, the less convincing selection 30 Anni '07 is held back by excessive ripeness, accompanied by less than perfect extract.

● C. Amerini Rosso Sup. Carbio '07	♟♟	5
● Ciliegiolo di Narni '08	♟♟	4*
○ Grechetto Il Vignolo '08	♟♟	2*
● C. Amerini Ameroe '08	♟	2*
○ C. Amerini Greco Levante '08	♟	4
● Ciliegiolo di Narni 30 Anni '07	♟	6
● Olmeto '08	♟	4
○ Terre Auree Bianco '08	♟	3
○ Terre Auree Rosso '08	♟	3
● C. Amerini Rosso Sup. Carbio '06	♟♟	5
● C. Amerini Rosso Sup. Carbio '04	♟♟	5
● C. Amerini Rosso Sup. Carbio '01	♟♟	5
● Ciliegiolo di Narni '07	♟♟	4*

★ Còlpetrone

LOC. MARCELLANO
VIA PONTE LA MANDRIA, 8/1
06035 GUALDO CATTANEO [PG]
TEL. 074299827
www.colpetrone.it

CELLAR SALES
PRE-BOOKED VISITS

ANNUAL PRODUCTION **189,000 bottles**
HECTARES UNDER VINE **63**
VITICULTURE METHOD **Conventional**

Còlpetrone is among the greatest contributors to the history of Sagrantino. As part of the Saiagricola group, the estate shines with a special light, boasting south east-facing vineyards in the municipality of Gualdo Cattaneo where the silty soils contains some clay, the cellar is brand new and the technical and commercial staff highly efficient, all under the direction of general manager Guido Sodano.

The Montefalco Sagrantino Gold selection embodies the results of years of study and experience with this variety, and proves in form and substance to be a highly charming red, capable of playing a unique role on the local stage. The '05 vintage gives intense aromas and great energy, in a context so young that it virtually guarantees improvement in the bottle. It regales the senses with shades of wild berries and spice, a hint of oak that has yet to be absorbed and resounding flavour on a palate that finds its dimension in balance and finesse. The deep, supple Sagrantino '06 is not bad either.

● Montefalco Sagrantino Gold '05	♟♟♟	8
● Montefalco Sagrantino '06	♟♟	6
● Montefalco Sagrantino Passito '06	♟♟	6
● Montefalco Rosso '07	♟	4
● Montefalco Sagrantino '04	♟♟♟	6
● Montefalco Sagrantino '03	♟♟♟	6
● Montefalco Sagrantino '02	♟♟♟	6
● Montefalco Sagrantino '01	♟♟♟	6
● Montefalco Sagrantino '00	♟♟♟	6
● Montefalco Sagrantino '99	♟♟♟	6
● Montefalco Sagrantino '98	♟♟♟	5
● Montefalco Sagrantino '97	♟♟♟	5
● Montefalco Sagrantino '96	♟♟♟	4
● Montefalco Sagrantino Gold '04	♟♟♟	8

Duca della Corgna

VIA ROMA, 236
06061 CASTIGLIONE DEL LAGO [PG]
TEL. 0759652493
www.ducadellacorgna.it

CELLAR SALES
PRE-BOOKED VISITS

ANNUAL PRODUCTION **280,000 bottles**
HECTARES UNDER VINE **55**
VITICULTURE METHOD **Conventional**

Improvement in wines from Trasimeno, an area that could do something more compared to the current state of affairs, looks to this winery, which is farsighted when it comes to the top line, Duca della Corgna. The current president Carlo Corbacella has the task of continuing the reorganization of the estate begun a few years back, a process that involves vineyards and cellars, including the lovely ageing cellar in ancient premises at Città della Pieve.

These convincing wines are extraordinary value for money. The very good sangiovese-heavy Colli del Trasimeno Rosso Riserva Corniolo '06 is balanced, with notes of blackcurrant, just like the Divina Villa Etichetta Nera '06, from gamay del Trasimeno, a wine with a distinctly sophisticated weave. From the whites, we liked the Ascanio '08, a deep, tangily complex Grechetto that shifts nicely between sensations of sweet pineapple fruit and citrussy hints.

Goretti

LOC. PILA
S.DA DEL PINO, 4
06132 PERUGIA
TEL. 075607316
www.vinigoretti.com

CELLAR SALES
PRE-BOOKED VISITS

ANNUAL PRODUCTION **400,000 bottles**
HECTARES UNDER VINE **60**
VITICULTURE METHOD **Conventional**

In terms of history, numbers and constant quality, the Goretti winery in the Pila hills could be considered the most important winemaking operation in the Umbrian capital. Dedicated to agriculture for generations, but for years focused only on wine as the central element in their activities, the Gorettis have managed to increase, renew, and expand their prospects – lLook at the new Montefalco business: Le Mura Saracene – all still marked by a certain familial continuity.

The Colli Perugini Rosso L'Arringatore is this winery's signature bottle. This blend of sangiovese, merlot and ciliegiolo is aged for a year in barrique. The '06 has aromas of currants and red bell pepper, with toasty notes upfront, while the palate shows full with good texture, yet also rather drying tannins. The rich, compact Grechetto Il Moggio '08, with notes of summer flowers and mint leaves, and the Chardonnay '08, are both excellent. Le Mura Saracene produces a wonderful Montefalco Rosso '07, showing plums, spice and tobacco, and a less convincing Sagrantino '05.

O Ascanio '08	♥♥ 3*
● C. del Trasimeno Gamay Divina Villa Et. Bianca '08	♥♥ 4*
● C. del Trasimeno Gamay Divina Villa Et. Nera '06	♥♥ 4*
● C. del Trasimeno Rosso Corniolo Ris. '06	♥♥ 5
O C. del Trasimeno Baccio del Bianco '08	♥ 3*
● C. del Trasimeno Baccio del Rosso '08	♥ 3
O C. del Trasimeno Grechetto Nuricante '08	♥ 4
● C. del Trasimeno Rosso Corniolo '05	♀♀ 5
● C. del Trasimeno Rosso Corniolo '04	♀♀ 4
● C. del Trasimeno Rosso Corniolo '03	♀♀ 4
● C. del Trasimeno Rosso Corniolo '02	♀♀ 4

O Colli Perugini Chardonnay '08	♥♥ 3*
● Colli Perugini Rosso L'Arringatore '06	♥♥ 5
O Il Moggio '08	♥♥ 4*
● Montefalco Rosso Le Mure Saracene '07	♥♥ 4*
O Colli Perugini Grechetto '08	♥ 3
● Montefalco Sagrantino Le Mure Saracene '05	♥ 6
● Colli Perugini Rosso L'Arringatore '05	♀♀ 5
● Colli Perugini Rosso L'Arringatore '04	♀♀ 5
● Colli Perugini Rosso L'Arringatore '03	♀♀ 5
● Colli Perugini Rosso L'Arringatore '01	♀♀ 5
● Colli Perugini Rosso L'Arringatore '00	♀♀ 5

Lamborghini

LOC. SODERI, 1
06064 PANICALE [PG]
TEL. 0758350029
www.lamborghinionline.it

CELLAR SALES
PRE-BOOKED VISITS

ANNUAL PRODUCTION 132,000 bottles
HECTARES UNDER VINE 32
VITICULTURE METHOD Conventional

Conceived by Ferruccio Lamborghini in the early 1970s after he abandoned the car business, this lovely estate in Panicale is just a couple of steps from Lake Trasimeno. Aside from the vineyards, all planted to red grape varieties, there is also a splendid golf course here, as well as a lovely agriturismo. Since the mid 1990s, Ferruccio's daughter, Patrizia, has managed the estate, skilfully and energetically moving this operation forward to become one of the best in the region.

The most famous wine from Lamborghini is Campoleone, a blend of merlot and sangiovese. The wine from the '07 harvest has distinctly ripe aromas with plum and cherry notes, and hints of jam. The palate also plays a hand of intensity, fullness and richness of fruit. From the other wines, we liked the Torami '07, from cabernet, sangiovese and montepulciano, with its notes of coffee and dark fruit, and especially the new sangiovese Era '07 that brings together structure and dynamism, ripeness of fruit and notes of pencil lead. Trescone '07 from sangiovese, ciliegiolo and merlot is just below this.

Lungarotti

VIA MARIO ANGELONI, 16
06089 TORGIANO [PG]
TEL. 075988661
www.lungarotti.it

CELLAR SALES
PRE-BOOKED VISITS
VISITOR FACILITIES
FOOD

ANNUAL PRODUCTION 2.900,000 bottles
HECTARES UNDER VINE 310
VITICULTURE METHOD Conventional

Cantine Lungarotti at Torgiano has put Umbria on the world wine map, inventing a terroir and a system that have forever changed how wine is perceived in the region. Naturally, he has also created a series of extraordinarily fascinating labels, capable of evoking sensations that are more spiritual than physical, time-worn yet bang up to date and frequently exciting, with yesterday's classics and wines that will be classics tomorrow.

Torgiano Rosso Riserva Vigna Monticchio is one of the latter. This very traditional red comes from sangiovese and canaiolo sourced only from the estate's Montichhio vineyard, which has sandstone and clay in the higher part, around 300 metres above sea level, with looser sandy soils and deposits of silt and limestone increasing downhill. The '05 harvest has produced a fantastic wine with light texture, yet appealing in its light and shade of red berry to citrus and spicy hints. New items this year are Toralco '07, from cabernet, merlot and sagrantino, and Torveto '08, a blend of chardonnay and vermentino.

● Campoleone '07	♟♟	6
● Era '07	♟♟	4*
● Torami '07	♟♟	5
● Trescone '07	♟	4
● Campoleone '04	♟♟♟	7
● Campoleone '01	♟♟♟	6
● Campoleone '00	♟♟♟	6
● Campoleone '99 *	♟♟♟	6
● Campoleone '06	♟♟	6
● Campoleone '05	♟♟	6

● Torgiano Rosso Vigna Monticchio Ris. '05	♟♟♟	6*
○ Torgiano Bianco Torre di Giano V. il Pino Ris. '07	♟♟	4*
○ Aurente '07	♟♟	5
● Montefalco Rosso '07	♟♟	4*
● Montefalco Sagrantino '06	♟♟	6
● Toralco '07	♟♟	5
○ Torgiano Bianco Torre di Giano '08	♟♟	3*
● Torgiano Rosso Rubesco '06	♟♟	4*
○ Torveto '08	♟	4
● Torgiano Rosso Vigna Monticchio Ris. '04	♟♟♟	6
● Torgiano Rosso Vigna Monticchio Ris. '03	♟♟♟	6
● Torgiano Rosso Vigna Monticchio Ris. '01	♟♟♟	7
● Torgiano Rosso Vigna Monticchio Ris. '88	♟♟♟	5
● Torgiano Rosso Vigna Monticchio Ris. '78	♟♟♟	6

Madonna Alta

LOC. PIETRAVIA
VIA LUDOVICO ARIOSTO
06036 MONTEFALCO [PG]
TEL. 0742378568
www.madonnalta.it

CELLAR SALES
PRE-BOOKED VISITS

ANNUAL PRODUCTION **130,000 bottles**
HECTARES UNDER VINE **18**
VITICULTURE METHOD **Conventional**

Owned by the Ferraro family, who began buying plots in the area during the 1990s, Madonna Alta has proved over time to be a dynamic, skilful operation with one eye always on market dynamics. The estate takes its name from a 16th-century church near the first plots of land acquired and creates wines with a rounded modern profile shaped by ageing in small oak.

This year, the reds revealed clear toasty sensations. The Montefalco Rosso '07 is still the most focused and expands with nice consistency. Lovely fruit supports coffee notes on the nose while the warm palate shows assertive tannins. The Sagrantino '06 has a similar aromatic profile and, despite a polished note, shows blueberry fruit intensity and lovely stuffing. It's a pity the palate is a bit too heavy with invasive oak tannins. Just as good is the sangiovese, cabernet and merlot Falconero '08. Both whites are well managed, the Colli Martani Grechetto '08 and Falconero Bianco '08, from grechetto and chardonnay.

Castello di Magione

VIA DEI CAVALIERI DI MALTA, 31
06063 MAGIONE [PG]
TEL. 075843547
www.castellodimagione.it

CELLAR SALES
PRE-BOOKED VISITS

ANNUAL PRODUCTION **100,000 bottles**
HECTARES UNDER VINE **30**
VITICULTURE METHOD **Conventional**

The Castello di Magione has an aura of history and emotion. Owned by the Sovereign Military Order of Malta, and once a hospice for pilgrims on their way to Rome or Jerusalem, today it houses one of the up-and-coming Umbrian winemaking operations with a special talent, at least till now, for whites, especially Grechetto. Plots under vine are divided into what were once tenancies and are now crus that are still vinified separately. The new vinification cellar has only recently been opened.

Perhaps the best example of Grechetto produced in Umbria, Monterone is sourced from a single south east-facing vineyard of almost four hectares with clay loam soils and a good amount of gravel. The '08 version is really good. Notes of reduction presage positive development in bottle, then the aromas open up into generously broad, soft sensations of gunflint and pineapple-like tropical fruit. Neither does the palate disappoints. Deep, still close-knit and full-flavoured, it gives nice acidity that perfectly integrates into the body of the wine.

● Montefalco Rosso '07	♟♟ 4*
○ Colli Martani Grechetto '08	♟ 4
○ Falconero Bianco '08	♟ 3
● Montefalco Sagrantino '06	♟ 6
● Falconero Rosso '06	♟♟ 3
● Montefalco Sagrantino '05	♟♟ 6
● Montefalco Sagrantino '04	♟♟ 6
● Montefalco Sagrantino '02	♟♟ 6
● Montefalco Sagrantino Passito '04	♟♟ 6
● Montefalco Sagrantino Passito '03	♟♟ 6

○ C. del Trasimeno Grechetto Monterone '08	♟♟ 4*
● C. del Trasimeno Rosso Morcinaia '06	♟ 5
○ Grechetto '08	♟ 3
● Vino dei Cavalieri '07	♟ 4
○ C. del Trasimeno Grechetto Monterone '07	♟♟ 3*
○ C. del Trasimeno Grechetto Monterone '06	♟♟ 3*
○ C. del Trasimeno Grechetto Monterone '05	♟♟ 3*
○ C. del Trasimeno Grechetto Monterone '04	♟♟ 3*

Martinelli

LOC. VOC. SASSO
VIA MADONNA DELLA NEVE, 1
06031 BEVAGNA [PG]
TEL. 0742362124
www.cantinemartinelli.com

CELLAR SALES
PRE-BOOKED VISITS

ANNUAL PRODUCTION 155,000 bottles
HECTARES UNDER VINE 20
VITICULTURE METHOD Conventional

Bevagna is one of the towns in Sagrantino where some of the area's historic estates are located. Though Martinelli is here, it is still a rather young operation. Nevertheless, year after year it shows first-class continuity in style and quality. Vines were planted in 1999 and the cellar is also practically new. The wines are all defined, better than well managed, and in some cases really excellent. They show a style that is modern, if you like, yet not without charm and personality.

The Montefalco Sagrantino Soranna '06, a limited selection, is again the best from this battery of wines. The nose is refined, though some oak is still to be absorbed, but this is nothing to worry about given the wine's energy and texture. Aromatically, it ranges from red and black berry fruit to rhubarb root while the palate shows pressure and lovely tannins. Perhaps only the note of alcohol may be a bit excessive. The Sagrantino '06 is good with nicely handled toastiness, like the Gaite Rosso '08, from sangiovese, sagrantino, and merlot, and the excellent Gaite Bianco '08, from chardonnay, pinot bianco and grechetto.

Cantina Monrubio

FRAZ. MONTERUBIAGLIO
LOC. LE PRESE, 22
05014 CASTEL VISCARDO [TR]
TEL. 0763626064
www.monrubio.it

CELLAR SALES
PRE-BOOKED VISITS

ANNUAL PRODUCTION 900,000 bottles
HECTARES UNDER VINE 700
VITICULTURE METHOD Conventional

The Monrubio co-operative started back in 1957 when some local producers decided to combine forces to promote their own activities in a joint project that has become increasingly solid over time. The more than 300 member growers today farm around 700 hectares under vine, centrally located with respect to the Orvieto and Orvieto Classico DOC production zones. The winery has also shown skill in producing red wines, as well as in the use of international varieties.

Outstanding among the international-style wines, Palaia is a blend of cabernet, merlot and pinot nero, which in the '07 finds ripe fruit, a succulent palate and assertive tannic texture. Moving on to the traditional white, the good quality Orvieto Classico Superiore Soana '08 was still quite young at our tastings but distinguished by notes of tropical fruit and a dynamic, rich palate with decent depth. Good, but just below this, is the cabernet, merlot, sangiovese and montepulciano Monrubio '08 and the Orvieto Classico Salceto '08 has notes of peach and green shades.

● Montefalco Sagrantino Sel. Soranna '06	♀♀ 7
○ Gaite Bianco '08	♀♀ 4*
● Gaite Rosso '08	♀♀ 4*
● Montefalco Sagrantino '06	♀♀ 5
● Montefalco Rosso '07	♀ 4
● Montefalco Sagrantino '05	♀♀ 5
● Montefalco Sagrantino '04	♀♀ 5
● Montefalco Sagrantino '03	♀♀ 6
● Montefalco Sagrantino Sel. Soranna '05	♀♀ 7
● Montefalco Sagrantino Sel. Soranna '04	♀♀ 7
● Montefalco Sagrantino Sel. Soranna '03	♀♀ 7

○ Orvieto Cl. Sup. Soana '08	♀♀ 3*
● Palaia '07	♀♀ 4*
● Monrubio '08	♀ 3
○ Orvieto Cl. Salceto '08	♀ 2*
○ Orvieto Cl. Sup. Soana '07	♀♀ 3*
● Palaia '06	♀♀ 4
● Palaia '05	♀♀ 5
● Palaia '04	♀♀ 5

La Palazzola

LOC. VASCIGLIANO
05039 STRONCONE [TR]
TEL. 0744609091
www.lapalazzola.it

ANNUAL PRODUCTION 150,000 bottles
HECTARES UNDER VINE 36
VITICULTURE METHOD Conventional

Stefano Grilli is one of the great characters in Umbrian wine. He constantly comes up with surprises and has an eclectic vein, not just as a winemaker, which makes him a rather dramatic type, never boring and definitely outside the box. Palazzola, in the countryside of Vascigliano, a few steps from Terni, is a sort of palette of colours that encourage constant experimentation with great reds, sweet wines and sparklers. And it is the utterly traditional sparkling wines that provide the happiest news.

The all-pinot nero Rosé Brut '06 is truly exceptional. Introduced by a lightly veiled, pale colour, it regales the nose with notes of cereal and citrus, then swirls toward sensations of cakes, leather, and pipe tobacco, with yeastiness always to the fore. The palate is creamy, fine-grained and crunchy, with plenty of spicy hints and a slightly foxy note. The Gran Cuvée '06 is also splendid, with its oxidized notes of nuts and caramel laced with green, floral hints. The same goes for the Trebbiano Metodo Ancestrale '05, rich in notes of yeast that almost recall certain lambic beers.

Palazzone

LOC. ROCCA RIPESENA, 68
05018 ORVIETO [TR]
TEL. 0763344921
www.palazzone.com

CELLAR SALES
PRE-BOOKED VISITS

ANNUAL PRODUCTION 100,000 bottles
HECTARES UNDER VINE 24
VITICULTURE METHOD Conventional

Giovanni Dubini owns Palazzone, the lovely winery that takes its name from a large building on the property. He is also one of the leading winemakers in the Orvieto area, and among the most respected in Umbria and around the world. Giovanni makes his wines in Rocca Ripesena, near Orvieto. It's a unique spot with some strengths and differences compared with the surrounding area. These are not instantly approachable wines. At times they may be rather difficult to read, at least in their younger stages. Frequently, however, they are also capable of exciting over time, many years after the harvest.

Perhaps the estate's signature wine, Orvieto Classico Superiore Campo del Guardiano '06, is very good. From a splendid vineyard, it shows powerful and full flavoured with amazing notes of gunflint. The excellent Armaleo '06, from cabernet sauvignon with small amounts of cabernet franc, shows intense currant and blueberry fruit aromas, accompanied by elegant shades of cinnamon. The Grechetto '08 makes a great impression. A rich, powerful wine, it is also refined, with touches of melon. The Terre Vineate '08 is well crafted. Viognier L'Ultima Spiaggia '08 is simpler, yet very pleasant.

⊙ Rosé Brut '06	♈♈	5
○ Gran Cuvée Brut '06	♈♈	5
○ Trebbiano Metodo Ancestrale '05	♈♈	5
○ Vin Santo '05	♈♈	5
○ Riesling Brut M. Cl. '04	♈	5
○ Gran Cuvée Brut '05	♈♈	5
○ Gran Cuvée Brut '04	♈♈	5
● Le Petrare '06	♈♈	4*
● Merlot '05	♈♈	5
● Merlot '04	♈♈	5
○ Riesling Brut M. Cl. '03	♈♈	5
⊙ Rosé Brut '04	♈♈	5
● Rubino '05	♈♈	5
● Vin Santo Bacca Rossa '05	♈♈	5

● Armaleo '06	♈♈	8
○ Orvieto Cl. Sup. Campo del Guardiano '06	♈♈	5
○ Grechetto '08	♈♈	4*
○ Orvieto Cl. Sup. Terre Vineate '08	♈♈	4*
○ L'Ultima Spiaggia '08	♈	5
● Armaleo '00	♈♈♈	6
● Armaleo '98	♈♈♈	6
● Armaleo '97	♈♈♈	6
● Armaleo '95	♈♈♈	6
● Armaleo '05	♈♈	8
● Armaleo '99	♈♈	5
○ Orvieto Cl. Campo del Guardiano '05	♈♈	5
○ Orvieto Cl. Campo del Guardiano '04	♈♈	5

F.lli Pardi

VIA GIOVANNI PASCOLI, 7/9
06036 MONTEFALCO [PG]
TEL. 0742379023
www.cantinapardi.it

CELLAR SALES
PRE-BOOKED VISITS

ANNUAL PRODUCTION **45,000 bottles**
HECTARES UNDER VINE **11**
VITICULTURE METHOD **Conventional**

The Pardi family has an ancient history and a dual connection to the most famous activities in Montefalco: textile production, their company is one of the leaders, and wine. Winemakers since the early 20th century, they decided just a few years ago to restart this particular activity with new energy. Results are better than comforting and their wines show great balance, with fresher, more elegant tones than most that can be appreciated without too much concentration. This is no mean feat, at least around here.

Montefalco Sagrantino '06 is one product of this approach: deep and vibrant with no extractive excess, it gives lovely nuances of red berry fruit, and echoes of iron and citrus. It's a pleasant wine with splendid flavour and tannic finesse. Just as good is the Montefalco Rosso '07, which has aromatic perceptions of sandalwood and lavender, as well as classic fruity notes. We'll close with a special mention for Montefalco Bianco Colle di Giove '08, from grechetto, trebbiano, chardonnay. It's a wine type rarely made, but one that produces a fresh, zesty wine with touches of peach and sage.

Perticaia

VIA E. CATTANEO, 39
06035 GUALDO CATTANEO [PG]
TEL. 0742920328
www.perticaia.it

CELLAR SALES
PRE-BOOKED VISITS

ANNUAL PRODUCTION **90,000 bottles**
HECTARES UNDER VINE **15**
VITICULTURE METHOD **Conventional**

Guido Guardigli is an outstanding character in Italian wine. Having been at the helm of numerous estates during the rebirth of the sector, he can read events and plan the future better than almost anyone. Perticaia is his latest undertaking and takes its name from the ancient word for "plough". Guido also has an original, elegant, personal approach to interpreting wines from this area. With some exceptions, his vines are planted on medium-packed soil with a liberal content of pebbles.

Montefalco Sagrantino '06 carries the tone and style of this estate. This red has sumptuous complexity, aromatic intensity and finesse. Still quite young, it gives black berry fruits and hints of oak in a profile that will find its proper balance in time. The Montefalco Rosso '07 is also remarkable, with nuances of currants, black cherry and cloves, as well as particularly good progression on the palate. There was a good performance from the Trebbiano Spoletino '08, a white on which Guardigli, like others, seems to have wagered. Umbria Rosso '08, a sangiovese, colorino and merlot blend, is pleasant but nothing more.

● Montefalco Rosso '07	♟♟	4*
● Montefalco Sagrantino '06	♟♟	6
○ Montefalco Bianco Colle di Giove '08	♟	3
● Montefalco Rosso '06	♟♟	4*
● Montefalco Sagrantino '05	♟♟	6
● Montefalco Sagrantino '04	♟♟	6
● Montefalco Sagrantino '03	♟♟	6
● Montefalco Sagrantino Passito '03	♟♟	6

● Montefalco Sagrantino '06	♟♟♟	6
● Montefalco Rosso '07	♟♟	4*
○ Trebbiano Spoletino '08	♟♟	4*
● Umbria Rosso '08	♟	3
● Montefalco Sagrantino '05	♟♟♟	6
● Montefalco Sagrantino '04	♟♟♟	6
● Montefalco Sagrantino '03	♟♟	6
● Montefalco Sagrantino '01	♟♟	6

Pucciarella

LOC. VILLA DI MAGIONE
06063 MAGIONE [PG]
TEL. 0758409147
www.pucciarella.it

ANNUAL PRODUCTION **130,000 bottles**
HECTARES UNDER VINE **50**
VITICULTURE METHOD **Conventional**

Owned by the Cariplo bank pension fund, Pucciarella could represent a major new key to promoting the Trasimeno area if, as it seems, the strong upward curve in quality continues. Vineyards run across the municipal territories of Magione and Corciano on plots characterized by broken-up galestro limestone marl. The climate is mild and typically Mediterranean, thanks to breezes off the lake. The wines themselves have a clear, clean style that avoids seeming off-the-rack.

The splendid Empireo '07, a merlot and cabernet sauvignon with refined complexity, reaches previously unexplored levels. Black berry fruit, citron flowers and hints of cocoa powder dominate the dark, intense nose. Only a slightly alcoholic finish holds back the broad, deep palate with its high-class pulp. The Colli del Trasimeno Rosso Riserva Sant'Anna '06 is good. The chardonnay Arsiccio '07 has surprising character with aromas of grape skin and crusty bread, and a powerful palate. Also surprising is the value for money of the Colli del Trasimeno Bianco Agnolo '08.

● Empireo '07	▼▼	4*
○ Arsiccio '07	▼▼	4*
○ C. del Trasimeno Bianco Agnolo '08	▼▼	4*
● C. del Trasimeno Rosso Sant'Anna Ris. '06	▼▼	5
● C. del Trasimeno Rosso Berlingero '08	▼	4
○ C. del Trasimeno Bianco Agnolo '07	▽▽	4*
○ C. del Trasimeno Vin Santo Eletto '04	▽▽	4*
○ C. del Trasimeno Vin Santo Eletto '01	▽▽	4*
● Empireo '06	▽▽	4*

Rocca di Fabbri

LOC. FABBRI
06036 MONTEFALCO [PG]
TEL. 0742399379
www.roccadifabbri.com

CELLAR SALES
PRE-BOOKED VISITS
VISITOR FACILITIES

ANNUAL PRODUCTION **200,000 bottles**
HECTARES UNDER VINE **64**
VITICULTURE METHOD **Conventional**

This is one of the most fascinating estates in Montefalco. It takes its name from the Rocca, the imposing 14th-century fortress, rebuilt by antiquarian Pietro Vitali, which also houses the cellar. Not far from this structure are the vineyards, which stand at Fabbri, in the area that slopes down from Montefalco toward Spoleto, where the well-drained soils are mostly clayey and alkaline. Today the founder's daughters, Roberta and Simona, energetically manage this estate and maintain a fairly classic profile in their wines.

This year, we loved the Rosso di Montefalco '07. Aged for a year in large barrels, and four months in barriques, the bouquet shows coffee on nice red and black berry fruit, veined with some aromatic hints that suggest rosemary. The palate is also splendid, showing refined, energetic and lively. The excellent Montefalco Sagrantino Passito '06 opens up on the nose with sensations of blackberry accompanied by delicate balsamic and liquorice tones. The deep palate has a good finish. But the Sagrantino '06 fell short of expectations, penalized by an uncertain nose and a palate still in search of character.

● Montefalco Rosso '07	▼▼	5
● Montefalco Sagrantino Passito '06	▼▼	6
● Montefalco Sagrantino '06	▼	7
● Montefalco Rosso '06	▽▽	5
● Montefalco Sagrantino '05	▽▽	7
● Montefalco Sagrantino '04	▽▽	7
● Montefalco Sagrantino '03	▽▽	7
● Montefalco Sagrantino '02	▽▽	7
● Montefalco Sagrantino '01	▽▽	7
● Montefalco Sagrantino Passito '05	▽▽	6

Ruggeri

VIA MONTEPENNINO, 5
06036 MONTEFALCO [PG]
TEL. 0742379294

★★ Castello della Sala

LOC. SALA
05016 FICULLE [TR]
TEL. 076386051
www.antinori.it

CELLAR SALES
PRE-BOOKED VISITS

PRE-BOOKED VISITS

ANNUAL PRODUCTION **20,000 bottles**
HECTARES UNDER VINE **5**
VITICULTURE METHOD **Conventional**

ANNUAL PRODUCTION **662,000 bottles**
HECTARES UNDER VINE **160**
VITICULTURE METHOD **Conventional**

A skilled, enthusiastic grower, Giuliano Ruggeri has one of the smallest, most traditional operations in the area, with vineyards planted in the early 1970s. The estate is at Montepennino, on a hill overlooking Montefalco, deep in the Umbrian countryside. This is where you find the few hectares under vine and the new cellar with only large oak barrels for ageing the reds, rather a rare phenomenon around here, but one that contributes to the creation of a powerful identity and the expression of classic, Ruggeri-style wines.

The extraordinary Montefalco Sagrantino '06 is a powerful, dynamic red, capable of interpreting the type with in a classic mode but with originality. It's true terroir wine with an immediately complex nose that gives depth and hints of blackberry and pencil lead before the palate expands broad and flavourful, even graceful, with perfect tannic texture and an endless finish. The Montefalco Rosso '07 and Passito '06, or at least the bottles we tasted, were below par.

The Umbrian residence of Marchesi Antinori has been capable of making its own way across the Italian winemaking landscape to the very top. Purchased during the 1940s, Castello della Sala is located on a tufaceous bluff not far from Orvieto, more than 500 metres above sea level, halfway between the River Paglia and Monte Nibbio. It's clearly ideal terroir for producing great white wines, which Cervaro della Sala has been for the past two decades.

Cervaro is a great, revolutionary ageing white with few equals in Italy. Able to challenge time, it is a classic wine perfectly at home in the modern world. The '07 harvest put another champion in the history books. It's less vibrant and minerally that the last version, yet still shows impressive depth, balance, tanginess and aromatic complexity in a warm caress. Among the other excellent labels, we were struck by the Orvieto Classico Superiore San Giovanni della Sala '08, which is stylish, dense and deep, and the Pinot Nero '06, all root vegetables, raspberries and suppleness.

● Montefalco Sagrantino '06	♀♀ 6
● Montefalco Rosso '07	♀♀ 4*
● Montefalco Sagrantino Passito '06	♀♀ 6
● Montefalco Rosso '06	♀♀ 4*
● Montefalco Sagrantino '05	♀♀ 6
● Montefalco Sagrantino '04	♀♀ 6
● Montefalco Sagrantino '03	♀♀ 6
● Montefalco Sagrantino Passito '05	♀♀ 6

○ Cervaro della Sala '07	♀♀♀ 7
○ Muffato della Sala '07	♀♀ 6
○ Orvieto Cl. Sup. San Giovanni della Sala '08	♀♀ 4*
● Pinot Nero della Sala '06	♀♀ 6
○ Bramito del Cervo '08	♀ 4
○ Cervaro della Sala '06	♀♀♀ 7
○ Cervaro della Sala '05	♀♀♀ 7
○ Cervaro della Sala '04	♀♀♀ 7
○ Cervaro della Sala '03	♀♀♀ 6
○ Cervaro della Sala '02	♀♀♀ 6
○ Cervaro della Sala '01	♀♀♀ 6
○ Cervaro della Sala '00	♀♀♀ 6
○ Cervaro della Sala '99	♀♀♀ 6
○ Cervaro della Sala '98	♀♀♀ 6
○ Cervaro della Sala '96	♀♀♀ 6
○ Cervaro della Sala '95	♀♀♀ 6

Scacciadiavoli

LOC. CANTINONE, 31
06036 MONTEFALCO [PG]
TEL. 0742371210
scacciadiavoli@tin.it

CELLAR SALES
PRE-BOOKED VISITS

ANNUAL PRODUCTION **200,000 bottles**
HECTARES UNDER VINE **32**
VITICULTURE METHOD **Conventional**

The Pambuffetti family acquired Scacciadiavoli in the early 1950s when, after working there for a lifetime, the grandfather of the current owners managed to make it his own. This was quite an undertaking for this winery is spectacular. It's incredibly beautiful, rooted in local history yet surprisingly capable of anticipating the future and also significant in the size with many hectares under vine. After years of substantial anonymity, Scacciadiavoli wines have returned to centre stage, have emerged from a makeover that has focused on a modern, satisfying style.

The Montefalco Sagrantino '06, aged 16 months in barrique, has a rather intense nose where toast intersects with nicely ripe wild berries and jammy shades. The palate has a similar profile, the sweet attack continuing dense, taut and continuous. A better than convincing performance also came from the Montefalco Sagrantino Passito '06, which is spectacularly concentrated, offering notes of chocolate, liquorice and coffee with a dense yet decently supple palate. This year's new item is an enjoyable Brut from a base of sagrantino and chardonnay.

Sportoletti

LOC. CAPITAN LORETO
VIA LOMBARDIA, 1
06038 SPELLO [PG]
TEL. 0742651461
www.sportoletti.com

CELLAR SALES
PRE-BOOKED VISITS

ANNUAL PRODUCTION **233,000 bottles**
HECTARES UNDER VINE **30**
VITICULTURE METHOD **Conventional**

Owned by brothers Ernesto and Remo Sportoletti, during the 1990s this estate began a turnaround in quality and contributed more than a little to the image of Umbrian wine. True, the first bottles arrived during the 1970s and showed the area in the hills of Spello and Assisi as good wine country. But the recent modern approach has helped Sportoletti wines achieve the fame and quality we know today.

The most important wine from here is Villa Fidelia Rosso, from a blend of merlot, and cabernet sauvignon and franc, aged for a year in barrique. The '07 version has ripe aromas of red berry fruit and bell pepper while the palate has a fruity, refined texture, splendid stuffing and appealing tannins. Assisi Rosso '08, from sangiovese, merlot and cabernet, is as good as ever and great value for money. On to the whites. The excellent Grechetto '08 is powerful and nicely tangy with peaches and apricots. The less convincing Villa Fidelia '07, from chardonnay and grechetto aged four months in barrique, shows toastiness.

● Montefalco Sagrantino '06	♼ 6
● Montefalco Sagrantino Passito '06	♼ 6
● Montefalco Rosso '07	♀ 4
○ Spumante Brut	♀ 4
● Montefalco Sagrantino '05	♀♀ 6
● Montefalco Sagrantino '04	♀♀ 6
● Montefalco Sagrantino '03	♀♀ 6
● Montefalco Sagrantino '01	♀♀ 6
● Montefalco Sagrantino '00	♀♀ 6
● Montefalco Sagrantino Passito '05	♀♀ 6
● Montefalco Sagrantino Passito '04	♀♀ 6

● Villa Fidelia Rosso '07	♼ 6
● Assisi Rosso '08	♼ 4*
○ Assisi Grechetto '08	♀ 3
○ Villa Fidelia Bianco '07	♀ 4
● Villa Fidelia Rosso '98	♀♀♀ 6
● Villa Fidelia Rosso '06	♀♀ 6
● Villa Fidelia Rosso '05	♀♀ 6
● Villa Fidelia Rosso '04	♀♀ 6
● Villa Fidelia Rosso '02	♀♀ 6
● Villa Fidelia Rosso '01	♀♀ 7
● Villa Fidelia Rosso '00	♀♀ 7
● Villa Fidelia Rosso '99	♀♀ 6

Giampaolo Tabarrini

FRAZ. TURRITA
06036 MONTEFALCO [PG]
TEL. 0742379351
www.tabarrini.com

CELLAR SALES
PRE-BOOKED VISITS

ANNUAL PRODUCTION **70,000 bottles**
HECTARES UNDER VINE **11**
VITICULTURE METHOD **Conventional**

Giampaolo Tabarrini is a child prodigy on the Umbrian wine scene who has quickly carved a place for himself with ideas and projects that express, much better than talk, the restless energy that motivates this young winemaker. The vineyards at this splendid winery show such different characteristics Giampaolo has started vinifying them separately, increasing the number of labels. The wines resemble the winemaker and express their original terroir, always marked by the search for perfect ripeness and opulence.

Despite the winery's red wine identity, we review the white wines first because of the truly amazing Adarmando '07 from an old variety of trebbiano spoletino the estate has recovered. Though still young and almost reticent at first, the wine opens up continuous with intense depth on aromas ranging from mango to citrus, candied citron and floral hints. Tangy, minerally and satisfying, it's drinking splendidly now but will be magnificent in a few years. The Montefalco Sagrantino Colle alle Macchie '04 is also quite good. Rich and complex, it gives coffee, black berry fruit and pepper. The Montefalco Rosso '07 is great.

O Adarmando '07	♟♟♟	5*
● Montefalco Sagrantino Colle alle Macchie '04	♟♟	8
● Montefalco Rosso '07	♟♟	4*
● Montefalco Sagrantino Colle Grimaldesco '01	♟♟♟	6
O Adarmando '06	♟♟	4*
O Adarmando '05	♟♟	4*
● Montefalco Sagrantino Colle Grimaldesco '04	♟♟	6
● Montefalco Sagrantino Colle Grimaldesco '02	♟♟	6

Terre de La Custodia

LOC. PALOMBARA
06035 GUALDO CATTANEO [PG]
TEL. 074292951
www.terredelacustodia.it

CELLAR SALES
PRE-BOOKED VISITS

ANNUAL PRODUCTION **850,000 bottles**
HECTARES UNDER VINE **115**
VITICULTURE METHOD **Conventional**

The Farchionis are a major business family in Umbria who have built most of their success on olive oil production. However, for some years now, their principal activity has been accompanied by an important wine-producing project that has led to the creation of the Terre de La Custodia estate, including a new cellar and a serious number of hectares under vine near the towns of Gualdo Cattaneo and Montefalco, along with some vineyards in the Todi area.

The Montefalco Sagrantino '06 is a well-made wine, giving black berry fruit sensations, balsamic nuances, and touches of cocoa powder and coffee in great harmony. The palate is compact, stylistically impeccable and beautifully extracted, yet also dynamic with splendid texture and uncommon length. The Sagrantino Passito Melanto '05 is not bad, showing very intense and sweet. The Grechetto '08 is full, rich, lightly aromatic and bitterish, and the Collezione '08, from sangiovese, sagrantino and merlot, with its red berry aromas and vegetal hints, are both good though a couple of steps behind the top wine.

● Montefalco Sagrantino '06	♟♟	6
● Montefalco Sagrantino Passito Melanto '05	♟♟	6
● Collezione '08	♟	3
O Colli Martani Grechetto '08	♟	3
O Colli Martani Grechetto '07	♟♟	4*
● Montefalco Sagrantino '05	♟♟	6
● Montefalco Sagrantino '04	♟♟	8
● Montefalco Sagrantino Exubera '05	♟♟	8
● Montefalco Sagrantino Exubera '04	♟♟	7
● Montefalco Sagrantino Passito Melanto '04	♟♟	7

Todini

FRAZ. ROSCETO
VIA COLLINA, 29
06059 TODI [PG]
TEL. 075887122
www.cantinafrancotodini.com

CELLAR SALES
PRE-BOOKED VISITS
VISITOR FACILITIES
FOOD

ANNUAL PRODUCTION **280,000 bottles**
HECTARES UNDER VINE **70**
VITICULTURE METHOD **Conventional**

Todini is one of the up-and-coming estates in the region. Located in the Collevalenza area, not far from the scenic village of Todi, it's in the Colli Martani DOC production zone. Aside from typical area wines and traditional varieties, such as grechetto, the cellar makes top-quality reds with a modern character, frequently involving the use of international varieties or blends of these with local varieties.

The red Nero della Cervara created high expectations and the '07 lives up to them. Aromas from this blend of cabernet franc, merlot and petit verdot range from wild berries to pink pepper nuanced with smoky, gamey hints. Follow-though in the mouth is good by the finish is rather cropped. From the whites, the grassy, citrus Grechetto di Todi Bianco del Cavaliere '08 and the soft, weighty Eteria '08, from grechetto and chardonnay, are both excellent. Good if not very varietal, Colli Martani Sangiovese Rubro '07 shows tar and bell pepper while Tiaso '08, from sangiovese, cabernet and merlot, is pleasant.

Tudernum

PIAN DI PORTO, 146
06059 TODI [PG]
TEL. 0758989403
www.tudernum.it

CELLAR SALES
PRE-BOOKED VISITS

ANNUAL PRODUCTION **1,000,000 bottles**
HECTARES UNDER VINE **7**
VITICULTURE METHOD **Conventional**

This Todi co-operative brings together around 350 member growers and has been able to change direction in just a few years, shifting from an anonymous production to a varied range of more than convincing, often near-excellent, labels with accessible price tags. The winery easily shifts between traditional wines, above all Grechetto and Sagrantino, and products driven by enhancement of international varieties by the local terroir.

Montefalco Sagrantino plays a major role by maintaining a certain consistency in quality and style. The '06 has a relaxed, rather absorbing texture, the oak harmoniously accompanying fruity sensations without disturbing them. The refined, dynamic palate finishes long on blackberry and blueberry. The Rojano '06, from sangiovese, merlot and sagrantino, also makes a lovely impression with its leather and wild berry nose, and a flavourful, fresh palate. The Grechetto Colle Nobile '08 is very good after ageing six months in barrique and gives aromas of broom and peach. Best of the varietal wines is the Cabernet '08.

Todini	
● Nero della Cervara '07	♟♟ 6
○ Colli Martani Grechetto di Todi Bianco del Cavaliere '08	♟♟ 4*
○ Eteria '08	♟♟ 3*
● Colli Martani Sangiovese Rubro '07	♟ 5
● Tiaso '08	♟ 4
○ Colli Martani Grechetto di Todi Bianco del Cavaliere '07	♟♟ 4*
● Colli Martani Sangiovese Rubro '06	♟♟ 5
● Nero della Cervara '05	♟♟ 6
● Nero della Cervara '04	♟♟ 6
● Nero della Cervara '03	♟♟ 6

Tudernum	
● Cabernet Sauvignon '08	♟♟ 3*
○ Colli Martani Grechetto di Todi Colle Nobile '08	♟♟ 4*
● Merlot '08	♟♟ 3*
● Montefalco Sagrantino Tudernum '06	♟♟ 6
● Rojano '06	♟♟ 4*
○ Colli Martani Bianco '08	♟ 2
○ Colli Martani Grechetto di Todi '08	♟ 3
○ Le Lucrezie '08	♟ 2
● Cabernet Sauvignon '07	♟♟ 3*
○ Colli Martani Grechetto di Todi Colle Nobile '07	♟♟ 4*
● Merlot '07	♟♟ 3*
● Merlot '05	♟♟ 3*
● Montefalco Sagrantino Tudernum '05	♟♟ 6
● Montefalco Sagrantino Tudernum '04	♟♟ 6
● Montefalco Sagrantino Tudernum '03	♟♟ 6
● Montefalco Sagrantino Tudernum '01	♟♟ 5
● Rojano '05	♟♟ 4*
● Rojano '03	♟♟ 4*

Tenuta Le Velette

FRAZ. CANALE DI ORVIETO
LOC. LE VELETTE, 23
05019 ORVIETO [TR]
TEL. 076329090
www.lovelette.it

CELLAR SALES
PRE-BOOKED VISITS

ANNUAL PRODUCTION 400,000 bottles
HECTARES UNDER VINE 109
VITICULTURE METHOD Conventional

Corrado and Cecilia Bottai's estate is situated on a splendid plateau facing a cliff, a sort of natural amphitheatre dotted with vineyards in the heart of the Orvieto Classico zone. The estate is anchored to the land, jealous of its history and traditions, yet still capable of innovation in terms of shaping non-local varieties as well as interpreting wines in a modern key. Labels produced here are not only well made but also very personal, quite apart from their wine types. In other words, they stand out with distinctive character.

This year, Calanco '05 is the best, at least in our opinion. This blend of sangiovese and cabernet is intense and complex, with ripe cherry and cinnamon aromas, and some grassy hints. The palate is taut and tight-knit, yet caressing in its tannic weave, with depth as well as youth. The mature Sangiovese Accordo '06 is also good, presenting spicy and slightly gamy. From the whites, the crunchy, compact Berganorio '08 with yellow-fleshed fruit and sage, and the tangy, powerful Lunato '08, with its magnolia and rosemary sensations, are both super wines.

Villa Mongalli

LOC. CAPPUCCINI
06031 BEVAGNA [PG]
TEL. 3485110506
www.villamongalli.com

ANNUAL PRODUCTION 70,000 bottles
HECTARES UNDER VINE 15
VITICULTURE METHOD Conventional

Villa Mongalli takes its name from a historic building in a centuries-old park. Although founded fairly recently, the cellar is well known among lovers of Umbrian wine, thanks in part to one of the best interpretations of Sagrantino around. Created by the Menghini family, Villa Mongalli boasts wonderful vineyards on the hills between Bevagna and Montefalco, in excellent locations on fairly light, permeable clayey soils with plenty of pebbles.

Grapes for the Montefalco Sagrantino Della Cima '05 are sourced from a vineyard of the same name around 400 metres above sea level, near the cellar. A stupendous example of its type, this sumptuous wine is quite varietal and territorial, embracing floral and blackberry and blueberry fruit aromatics with hints of leather. The palate shows juicy, rich fruit, framed by finesse, and a superior tannic weave. The Sagrantino Pozzo del Curato '06 is also good, yet still struggles with a little too much oak that blocks the spice and forest floor sensations. Still, there's energy on the palate. The sangiovese Villa Mongalli Rosso '08 is tasty.

● Calanco '05	♟♟	5*
● Accordo '06	♟♟	4*
○ Orvieto Cl. Berganorio '08	♟♟	3*
○ Orvieto Cl. Sup. Lunato '08	♟♟	4*
● Rosso Orvietano Rosso di Spicca '08	♟	3
○ Sole Uve '08	♟	4
● Calanco '03	♟♟♟	5
● Calanco '95	♟♟♟	5
● Gaudio '03	♟♟♟	5
● Accordo '05	♟♟	4*
● Calanco '04	♟♟	5
● Gaudio '05	♟♟	5
● Gaudio '04	♟♟	5
● Rosso Orvietano Rosso di Spicca '07	♟♟	3*
● Rosso Orvietano Rosso di Spicca '06	♟♟	3*
○ Sole Uve '07	♟♟	4*

● Montefalco Sagrantino Della Cima '05	♟♟	7
● Montefalco Sagrantino Pozzo del Curato '06	♟♟	5
● Villa Mongalli Rosso '08	♟	3
● Col Cimino '06	♟♟	4*
● Montefalco Rosso Le Grazie '06	♟♟	4*
● Montefalco Rosso Le Grazie '04	♟♟	4*
● Montefalco Sagrantino Della Cima '04	♟♟	7
● Montefalco Sagrantino Pozzo del Curato '05	♟♟	5
● Montefalco Sagrantino Pozzo del Curato '04	♟♟	5

OTHER WINERIES

Cantina Altarocca

LOC. ROCCA RIPESENA, 62
05019 ORVIETO [TR]
TEL. 0763344210
www.cantinaaltarocca.com

This winery is on the spur of tufa called Rocca Ripesena, in the heart of the Orvieto Classico zone. Best wines were the merlot Rosso d'Altarocca '07, with liquorice, black berry fruit and smoke, and Albaco '08, a white from chardonnay and grechetto with brief conditioning in barrique.

O Albaco '08	♀♀ 4*
● Rosso d'Altarocca '07	♀♀ 7
O Albaco '08	♀♀ 4
● Rosso d'Altarocca '06	♀♀ 7

Tenuta Alzatura

LOC. FRATTA - ALZATURA, 108
06036 MONTEFALCO [PG]
TEL. 0742399435
www.tenuta-alzatura.it

The Cecchi family estate continues to improve. This year, we should mention an excellent version of Montefalco Sagrantino Uno di Nove '06 with berry fruit aromas, a toasty tone and a palate that is compact, precise and deep. The Montefalco Rosso '07 is just behind.

● Montefalco Sagrantino Uno di Nove '06	♀♀ 6
● Montefalco Rosso '07	♀ 4
● Montefalco Sagrantino Uno di Otto '05	♀♀ 6

Benincasa

VIA CAPRO, 23
06031 BEVAGNA [PG]
TEL. 0742361307
www.aziendabenincasa.com

Located a short distance from Bevagna, this estate was one of the first to believe in the area and grow sagrantino. The excellent Montefalco Rosso '07 is succulent, flavourful and supple with crunchy tannins. The agreeable Vincastro '07 is from a sangiovese base with a dash of merlot.

● Montefalco Rosso '07	♀♀ 4*
● Vincastro '07	♀ 2*
● Montefalco Rosso '06	♀♀ 4*
● Montefalco Sagrantino '05	♀♀ 6

Bocale

VIA FRATTA ALZATURA
06036 MONTEFALCO [PG]
TEL. 0742399233
www.bocale.it

The Bocale estate, named after the owner's family, is a small operation begun in 2002 and located at Alzatura. The great Sagrantino '06 melds blackberry notes with spice and pencil lead sensations, and shows a complex, deep and fine-grained palate.

● Montefalco Sagrantino '06	♀♀ 6
● Montefalco Rosso '07	♀ 4

Brogal Vini

LOC. BASTIA UMBRA
VIA DEGLI OLMI, 9
06083 PERUGIA
TEL. 0758001501
www.brogalvini.com

The main headquarters of this estate are in Bastia, while the most representative plots are at Torgiano and Montefalco, both the regional DOC zones. Outstanding from the first is a good Torgiano Bianco Kirnao '08; the Montefalco Rosso Ligajo '06 from Montefalco is quite pleasant.

O Torgiano Bianco Kirnao Antigniano '08	♀♀ 4
● Montefalco Rosso Ligajo Antigniano '06	♀ 5
● Torgiano Rosso Santa Caterina Antigniano Ris. '05	♀ 6

Cesarini Sartori - Signae

LOC. PURGATORIO TORRI
VIA SANTA MARIA
06035 GUALDO CATTANEO [PG]
TEL. 074299590
www.rossobastardo.it

The quality of the wines earned praise for Luciano Cesarini and Fiorella Sartori's new operation. The best this year is Rossobastardo '07, from sangiovese with merlot and cabernet sauvignon, that shows dense with taut fruit, silky tannins and a juicy finish. The other wines are less focused.

● Montefalco Rosso '07	♀ 4
● Montefalco Sagrantino '06	♀ 5
● Rossobastardo '07	♀ 4
● Montefalco Sagrantino '05	♀♀ 5

Chiorri

LOC. SANT'ENEA
VIA TODI, 100
06132 PERUGIA
TEL. 075607141
www.chiorrl.lt

Mariotti Tito, an enthusiastic, skilled winemaker, manages this operation on a hillside terrace at Perugia with help from his family, particularly daughter Monica. Best wines are the peach and magnolia Grechetto '08, the well-calibrated Sangiovese '08, and the Selezione Antonio Chiorri '07.

○ Colli Perugini Bianco '08	♥♥	2*
○ Grechetto '08	♥♥	3*
● Merlot Sel. Antonio Chiorri '07	♥♥	5
● Sangiovese '08	♥♥	3*

Castello di Corbara

LOC. CORBARA, 7
05018 ORVIETO [TR]
TEL. 0763304035
www.castellodicorbara.it

Castello di Corbara started its quality wine project in the late 1990s. Outstanding among the reds is Merlot De Coronis '06, its nose centred on cinnamon sensations and intriguing black berry fruit, followed by a precise palate. The other labels are well made but a bit under par.

● Lago di Corbara Merlot De Coronis '06	♥♥	5
● Lago di Corbara Cabernet Sauvignon '07	♥	5
● Lago di Corbara Rosso '07	♥	5
○ Orvieto Cl. Sup. Podere Il Caio '08	♥	3

Custodi

LOC. CANALE
V.LE VENERE
05018 ORVIETO [TR]
TEL. 076329053
www.cantinacustodi.com

Managed by Gian Franco Custodi and his daughters, this is one of the most dependable estates in the Orvieto area. The wines express the Canale zone, with its mainly volcanic, tufaceous and clayey soils. The mellow Austero '07 and fresh, citrussy Orvieto Classico Belloro '08 are both good.

● Austero '07	♥♥	4*
○ Orvieto Cl. Belloro '08	♥♥	2*
● Piancoleto '08	♥	3

Decugnano dei Barbi

LOC. FOSSATELLO, 50
05019 ORVIETO [TR]
TEL. 0763308255
www.decugnano.it

There are encouraging signs from Decugnano dei Barbi, a great estate with an illustrious past in Orvieto. "IL" '06 from sangiovese, montepulciano, merlot, cabernet and syrah is good, with toasty notes that accompany pepper and black berry fruit sensations. The palate is dynamic, long and rather seductive.

● "IL" Rosso '06	♥♥	6
○ Orvieto Cl. Sup. Decugnano Bianco '08	♥	4

Italo Di Filippo

VOC. CONVERSINO, 153
06033 CANNARA [PG]
TEL. 0742731242
www.vinidifilippo.com

Roberto Di Filippo and his family run this nice winemaking estate at Cannara to organic criteria. Though personal, the wines are not always flawless in their aromatic profile. The crunchy, flavourful Montefalco Sallustio '06 and the Grechetto '08 are both quite good.

○ Colli Martani Grechetto '08	♥♥	3*
● Montefalco Rosso Sallustio '06	♥♥	4*

Cantina La Spina

FRAZ. SPINA
VIA EMILIO ALESSANDRINI, 1
06055 MARSCIANO [PG]
TEL. 0758738120
www.cantinalaspina.it

The small Morena Peccia estate runs along the hills of Spina between Perugia and Marsciano. The clay soils contain a lot of gravel and authentic wines are well crafted. The mostly montepulciano Rosso Spina '07 is good, showing floral on the nose and flavourful on the palate.

● Rosso Spina '07	♥♥	5
● Merlato '08	♥	3
● Polimante '07	♥	5
● Rosso Spina '06	♥♥	5
● Rosso Spina '05	♥♥	5

OTHER WINERIES

Cantina Novelli

LOC. CASA NATICCHIA - PEDRELLE
VIA MOLINO CAPALDINI
06036 MONTEFALCO [PG]
TEL. 0744803301
www.cantinanovelli.it

The Novelli family runs an extraordinary business, although the estate wines are still in search of an identity. The good Montefalco Rosso '07 is sinuous and citrussy while the grechetto, pecorino and trebbiano spoletino-based white Cube '08 is fresh and pleasant. Other wines are less successful.

○ Bianco Cube '08	♟♟	3*
● Montefalco Rosso '07	♟♟	4*
● Montefalco Sagrantino '06	♟	6
○ Trebbiano Spoletino '08	♟	4

Peppucci

LOC. SANT'ANTIMO
FRAZ. PETRORO, 4
06059 TODI [PG]
TEL. 0758947253
www.cantinapeppucci.com

The Peppucci family's Sant'Antimo monastery stands at the centre of their estate and their stylistically flawless wines are distinctive. Petroro 4 '08, from sangiovese with merlot and cabernet, is good, crunchy and precise while the full, meaty Alter Ego '06 is a bit alcoholic at the back.

● Alter Ego '06	♟♟	6
● Petroro 4 '08	♟♟	4*
○ Montorsolo '08	♟	4
● Alter Ego '05	♟♟	5

Tenuta Poggio del Lupo

VOC. BUZZAGHETTO, 100
05011 ALLERONA [TR]
TEL. 0763628350
www.tenutapoggiodellupo.it

The Polato family decided to remodel this old farm near Orvieto. Poggio del Lupo is now a reliable brand on the Umbrian winemaking landscape. Màrneo '08, a thoroughbred grechetto and chardonnay, and Orvieto Novilunio '08, are both excellent. Silentis '07 will appear next year.

○ Colli Martani Grechetto di Todi Fiorfiore '07	♟♟	4*
○ Fiordaliso '08	♟♟	3*
○ Collina d'Oro Passito '06	♟	6

Roccafiore

LOC. COLLINA
06059 TODI [PG]
TEL. 0758942416
www.roccafiore.it

The Baccarelli family wine business was started in the beautiful hills of Todi, in a landscape of rare charm. Organic methods create authentic, personal wines but not all hit the bull's-eye. Fiordaliso '08, from grechetto and trebbiano spoletino, and Fiorfiore '07 are both good.

○ Colli Martani Grechetto di Todi Fiorfiore '07	♟♟	4*
○ Fiordaliso '08	♟♟	3*
○ Collina d'Oro Passito '06	♟	6

Tenuta di Salviano

LOC. CIVITELLA DEL LAGO
VOC. SALVIANO, 44
05020 BASCHI [TR]
TEL. 0744950459

For centuries owned by the Principi Corsini, Tenuta di Salviano with its cellar in the historic castle is located on the left bank of Lake Corbara, not far from Orvieto. Lago di Corbara Rosso Turlò '07 is good but the Orvieto Classico Superiore '08 is less convincing than usual.

● Lago di Corbara Turlò '07	♟♟	4*
○ Orvieto Cl. Sup. '08	♟	4
○ Orvieto Cl. Sup. V. T. '07	♟♟	4*

Spoletoducale - Casale Triocco

LOC. PETROGNANO, 54
06049 SPOLETO [PG]
TEL. 074356224
www.spoletoducale.it

The Petrognano co-operative winery, halfway between Montefalco and Spoleto, has lined up an array of well-made wines this year. Among the best are the Sagrantino Pagina '05, the Trebbiano Spoletino and the Grechetto '08, all from the Casale Triocco line.

○ Colli Martani Grechetto Casale Triocco '08	♟♟	3*
● Montefalco Sagrantino Pagina Casale Triocco '05	♟♟	7
○ Trebbiano Spoletino Casale Triocco '08	♟♟	3*

Terre de' Trinci

VIA FIAMENGA, 57
06034 FOLIGNO [PG]
TEL. 0742320165
www.terredetrinci.com

The Foligno co-operative is a big-numbers winery and is a major beacon for many producers in the area. Nevertheless, tastings over the past few years have not kept pace with the reputation and volumes of this long-standing operation. Montefalco Sagrantino Ugolino '06 and Luna '08 are fair.

○ Luna '08	♈ 4
● Montefalco Sagrantino Ugolino '06	♈ 7

Terre Margaritelli

LOC. MIRALDUOLO
06089 TORGIANO [PG]
TEL. 0759889032
www.terremargaritelli.com

The Margaritelli family estate is a young, dynamic operation. We liked Torgiano Rosso Mirantico '07 as relaxed and persuasive in its fruity texture as it is refined on the palate, with its great flavour and depth. Malot '07, from merlot, cabernet and a touch of sangiovese, is not bad.

● Torgiano Mirantico '07	♈♈ 4*
● Malot '07	♈ 4

Tiburzi

ZONA ARTIGIANA PIETRAUTA
06036 MONTEFALCO [PG]
TEL. 0742379864
www.tiburzicantine.com

Tiburzi wines have only been around for a few years but they did well. The good Montefalco Rosso Santambrà '07 is stylish, spicy, elegant and deep but Montefalco Sagrantino Taccalite '05 is not bad either, with its black berry fruits and crushed herbs, just a bit drying in the finish.

● Montefalco Sagrantino Taccalite '07	♈♈ 6
● Montefalco Santambrà '07	♈♈ 4*

Tenuta Vitalonga

LOC. MONTIANO
05016 FICULLE [TR]
TEL. 0763836722
www.vitalonga.it

Tenuta Vitalonga, owned by the Maravalle family, is perched on a scenic slope in the Orvieto hills at Ficulle. The wines, from both local and international varieties, have a modern profile. The very good montepulciano-merlot Terra di Confine '07 has lots of power.

● Terra di Confine '07	♈♈ 5
● Elcione '07	♈ 4
● Elcione '06	♈♈ 4*
● Terra di Confine '06	♈♈ 5

LAZIO

The current tempo of Lazio winemaking could be described as "allegro ma non troppo". Intentions are good and initiatives are under way to raise the region's profile yet by and large producers still seem to think that the most important thing is to make well-styled wines. The focus is less on the quest for premier quality or territoriality than on producing clean, defect-free wines. Now we have no objection whatsoever to tasting faultless ten-year-old wines but we do expect a bit more and very few in this region seem willing to make the quantum leap, in comparison with Campania, Abruzzo or Puglia. That being the case, we are less inclined to jump up and down over the new Cesanese del Piglio DOCG. While this is the first year we have awarded Three Glasses to a wine from this DOCG, we shouldn't let the tree conceal the wood. Lazio has won only a limited number of Three Glasses because its quality has improved at a slower rate in recent years than the rest of Italy. This is particularly true of the region's most famous and – in theory – most wine-friendly zone, Castelli Romani. Although a couple of Frascatis graced our final tasting tables, the overall level of Castelli production is at a standstill and indeed seems to have flattened off to the point of decline. Very few wines stand out and we would go so far as to say that some of the old faithfuls are losing their lustre. Add to this a challenging growing year like 2008, with all the problems of a wet spring and summer storms, and we have a quality context that depends largely on the performance of individual vineyards. All this merely reinforces the conclusion that the gap between the region's potential and its current production is still significant. However, all is not doom and gloom. The Cesanese del Piglio's first Three Glass award comes courtesy of Antonello Coletti Conti's Romanico. Both the wine and the producer have been in the running for a while but this year they were that bit more solid and reliable than in previous editions. Alongside this debut success we have two very well-known producers who also took home Three Glasses, one for his most famous wine and the other for a bottle that until now was considered a second-string wine. The first is Falesco's Montiano, a real Lazio wine given that its vines of origin are all in the region, and the second is Sergio Mottura and family, whose estate continues to be the only one in Lazio to win our top award with a white. This year, however, it is not the Latour a Civitella that took the crown but Poggio della Costa, another grechetto-based offering matured solely in stainless steel. Further proof of the estate's overall quality, and also perhaps of how tastes are starting to favour greater grip over roundness and fullness of flavour.

Marco Carpineti

LOC. CAPO LE MOLE
S.P. VELLETRI-ANZIO, KM 14,300
04010 CORI [LT]
TEL. 069679860
www.marcocarpinetl.lt

CELLAR SALES
PRE-BOOKED VISITS

ANNUAL PRODUCTION **100,000 bottles**
HECTARES UNDER VINE **41**
VITICULTURE METHOD **Organic certified**

Marco Carpineti's estate in the municipality of Cori has been in his family for generations. In 1986 he turned the production philosophy on its head and in 1994 he adopted organic agricultural methods and went on to devote himself to the study of indigenous varieties. The estate's vineyards lie at an altitude of 200-450 metres on the slopes of Mount Lepini. The soil is volcanic and the south south-west exposure guarantees a cool growing environment in summer and mild winters.

This year, Marco did not present the Moro as it is still maturing but there are plenty of other quality wines to choose from. The Cori Rosso Capolemole '07 has spicy, balsamic aromas and a palate that is close-knit yet supple with a long, pleasant finish. Collesanti '08 is just as good. From arciprete peloso, a local bellone biotype, it is still rather closed and challenging on the nose but the palate is citrussy, tangy, almost tannic and quite lovely. Tufaliccio '08 is a montepulciano and sangiovese selection. Notes of cherry and Mediterranean scrub announce a well-bodied, fruit-rich palate. The other wines are well typed.

Casale del Giglio

LOC. LE FERRIERE
S.DA CISTERNA-NETTUNO KM 13
04100 LATINA
TEL. 0692902530
www.casaledelgiglio.it

CELLAR SALES
PRE-BOOKED VISITS

ANNUAL PRODUCTION **1.200,000 bottles**
HECTARES UNDER VINE **125**
VITICULTURE METHOD **Conventional**

Antonio Santarelli's Casale del Giglio is at Le Ferriere in Borgo Montello, Agro Pontino. It was set up in 1968 and 1985 saw the launch of an experimental project in which no less than 57 varieties were planted, all international, indigenous or from neighbouring regions. The project was a huge success and has made Casale del Giglio a model for quality growth in the Pontino territory – and beyond – in recent years.

Overall, the range is high quality this year but the flagship wines lack a certain something. From syrah and 15 per cent petit verdot, Mater Matuta '06 has aromas of spice, black berry fruit and olive paste, and a fruity, well-structured palate, but its customary complexity is missing. Antinoo '07 from chardonnay and viognier is pleasant but less precise than in previous editions. The Satrico '08 from chardonnay, sauvignon and trebbiano giallo and the Cabernet Sauvignon '06 are both very good. The former has wisteria and pears and a long, supple, vigorous palate while the second is fresh and balanced with red berry fruit and rosemary.

○ Collesanti '08	▼▼ 3*
● Cori Rosso Capolemole '07	▼▼ 4*
● Tufaliccio '08	▼▼ 3*
○ Cori Bianco Capolemole '08	▼ 3
● Dithyrambus '06	▼ 5
☉ Os Rosae '08	▼ 4
○ Ludum '06	♈♈ 5
○ Moro '07	♈♈ 4*
○ Moro '06	♈♈ 4*
● Rosso Tufaliccio '07	♈♈ 3*

● Cabernet Sauvignon '06	▼▼ 5
● Mater Matuta '06	▼▼ 7
○ Satrico '08	▼▼ 3*
○ Sauvignon '08	▼▼ 4*
☉ Albiola '08	▼ 3
○ Antinoo '07	▼ 4
○ Aphrodisium V. T. '08	▼ 6
● Madreselva '06	▼ 5
○ Petit Manseng '08	▼ 4
○ Antinoo '06	♈♈ 4
○ Antinoo '05	♈♈ 4*
● Mater Matuta '05	♈♈ 7
● Mater Matuta '04	♈♈ 6
● Mater Matuta '03	♈♈ 6
● Mater Matuta '01	♈♈ 6

Castel de Paolis

VIA VAL DE PAOLIS
00046 GROTTAFERRATA [RM]
TEL. 069413648
www.casteldepaolis.it

CELLAR SALES
PRE-BOOKED VISITS

ANNUAL PRODUCTION **90,000 bottles**
HECTARES UNDER VINE **14**
VITICULTURE METHOD **Organic certified**

Set up in the late 1980s, Castel de Paolis is a point of reference in Castelli Romani. Fabrizio Santarelli uses organic methods and has taken his wines to the pinnacle of local production. Investments in new plantings and technology have made his estate one of the territory's most reliable. It's at Grottaferrata at an altitude of 270 metres and has volcanic soil. Vine stock is the result of a research project by Professor Scienza on international varieties and local ones that are almost extinct.

This historic estate gave a mixed performance. A 50 per cent viognier, 40 per cent Lazio malvasia and sauvignon blend, the Donna Adriana showed well. Citrus fruit and spring flowers lead into a fresh, flowing palate with a citrussy finish. The Frascati Cannellino '08 is very good and one of the few made. It has aromas of candied ginger and beeswax, and a simple but well-made palate hinting at honey and dried apricot. The Meno Quattro Mori, from 60 per cent syrah, 20 per cent merlot, cabernet sauvignon and petit verdot, is below par. It's simple, fruity and lacks its old complexity.

Cantina Agricola Cincinnato

VIA CORI-CISTERNA KM 2
04010 CORI [LT]
TEL. 069679380
www.cantinacincinnato.it

CELLAR SALES
PRE-BOOKED VISITS

ANNUAL PRODUCTION **300,000 bottles**
HECTARES UNDER VINE **400**
VITICULTURE METHOD **Organic certified**

The Cincinnato cooperative winery was set up at Cori in 1947. Today, it numbers no fewer than 250 members who manage to wed volume with quality while continuing to offer very competitive prices. What is also interesting is that production focuses around local varieties of the truest Lazio tradition, notably Cori's nero buono, but also cesanese, bellone, trebbiano giallo, greco and others.

This year, the Nero Buono left the biggest impression. The '06 combines black cherry and liquorice aromas with a fresh-tasting, balsamic palate that shows soft tannins and a lingering finish of blackberry and blueberry. This is a grape that still has lots of unexploited potential. A good showing also from the Cori Bianco Illirio '08, a classic blend of bellone, malvasia and trebbiano. This solid, easy-drinking wine has a citrussy, balsamic nose and a clean, well-made palate whose pleasant finish has nice acid backbone. The Bellone '07 is a step behind, lacking the elegance of the previous edition. The rest of the range is well styled.

O Donna Adriana '08	♟	5
O Campo Vecchio Bianco '08	♟	4
● Campo Vecchio Rosso '08	♟	4
O Frascati Cannellino '08	♟	4
● Quattro Mori '06	♟	6
O Muffa Nobile '07	♟♟	6
O Muffa Nobile '05	♟♟	6
● Quattro Mori '05	♟♟	6
● Quattro Mori '01	♟♟	6

● Nero Buono '06	♟♟	4*
O Cori Bianco Illirio '08	♟♟	3*
● Arcatura '07	♟	4
O Bellone '07	♟	4
O Castore '08	♟	2*
● Cori Rosso Raverosse '06	♟	3
● Arcatura '06	♟♟	4*
O Bellone '06	♟♟	4*
● Nero Buono '05	♟♟	4*

Antonello Coletti Conti

VIA VITTORIO EMANUELE, 116
03012 ANAGNI [FR]
TEL. 0775728610
www.coletticonti.it

CELLAR SALES
PRE-BOOKED VISITS

ANNUAL PRODUCTION 20,000 bottles
HECTARES UNDER VINE 20
VITICULTURE METHOD Conventional

Descended from an old Anagni house that boasts no fewer than five popes, Antonello Coletti Conti has revolutionized the family estate in the southern part of the Cesanese del Piglio production zone. He has made over the vineyards with new planting patterns and grape types, and has also built a cellar. The result is wines of character, balance and elegance.

Success comes in the best-ever Cesanese del Piglio Romanico, the '07. It took the first Three Glass trophy for a DOC zone that this year attained DOCG status. The nose reveals notes of cinchona, spice and black berry fruit while the long palate is expressive and structured yet also fresh-tasting, with a finish that echoes the wild berry aromas with a balsamic nuance. The Cosmato '07, a blend of red varieties with 70 per cent cabernet sauvignon, is good with a complex nose of cherry and cardamom followed by a long, fruity full-bodied palate. By contrast, the Cesanese del Piglio Hernicus '08 and the Arcadia '08 from incrocio Manzoni are disappointing.

Colle Picchioni Paola Di Mauro

LOC. FRATTOCCHIE
VIA COLLE PICCHIONE, 46
00040 MARINO [RM]
TEL. 0603546329
www.collepicchioni.it

CELLAR SALES
PRE-BOOKED VISITS

ANNUAL PRODUCTION 100,000 bottles
HECTARES UNDER VINE 14
VITICULTURE METHOD Naturale

Since 1974, this small Castelli Romani estate has produced some of the best wines in the region. It has always belonged to the Di Mauro family, first Paola and then her son Armando. The cellar lies on the Via Appia, less than 20 kilometres from the centre of Rome and not far from the Frattocchie hill. This is the southern part of the Marino DOC but the wines offered also include Lazio IGTs, mainly reds.

The estate gave a sterling performance this year, even without its show horse. The Vassallo '07, a classic merlot-heavy Bordeaux blend, is very good. Aromas of spice with hints of red fruit and plum are the prelude to a pleasing, well-structured palate with a long, very refreshing finish. The whole range is excellent, from the two fresh Marino '08s with their citrussy notes and fluent, lingering palates, to the Le Vignole '07, from 60 per cent malvasia 60, 25 per cent trebbiano and sauvignon. It is still oak-dominated but full with lots of yellow-fleshed fruit. The Perlaia '08 from merlot, sangiovese and cabernet sauvignon is clean and enjoyable.

● Cesanese del Piglio Romanico '07	♥♥♥ 6
● Cosmato '07	♥♥ 6
○ Arcadia '08	♥ 4
● Cesanese del Piglio Hernicus '08	♥ 4
○ Arcadia '07	♀♀ 4
● Cesanese del Piglio Hernicus '06	♀♀ 4*
● Cesanese del Piglio Hernicus '05	♀♀ 4
● Cesanese del Piglio Romanico '06	♀♀ 6
● Cesanese del Piglio Romanico '05	♀♀ 6

● Il Vassallo '07	♥♥ 6
○ Le Vignole '07	♥♥ 5
○ Marino Coste Rotonde '08	♥♥ 3*
○ Marino Donna Paola '08	♥♥ 4
● Perlaia '08	♥♥ 4
● Il Vassallo '05	♀♀♀ 6
● Vigna del Vassallo '01	♀♀♀ 6
● Vigna del Vassallo '00	♀♀♀ 6
○ Le Vignole '06	♀♀ 4*
○ Marino Donna Paola '07	♀♀ 4*

Colletonno

LOC. COLLETONNO
03012 ANAGNI [FR]
TEL. 0775769271
www.colletonno.it

CELLAR SALES
PRE-BOOKED VISITS

ANNUAL PRODUCTION **30,000 bottles**
HECTARES UNDER VINE **20**
VITICULTURE METHOD **Conventional**

Colletonno lived up to its reputation as one of the most important estates in the Cesanese del Piglio DOCG. The vineyards extend over two properties, with the red varieties, notably cesanese, in Anagni at an altitude of 300-350 metres on a volcanic base. The whites are at Ceprano and grow at 150 metres on sandy tufaceous soil. With oenologist Lorenzo Landi, the Di Cosimo family is looking to find a seat for Cesanese del Piglio on the Olympus of Italian wines.

The range did well this year. First up is the jewel in the estate's crown, Cesanese del Piglio San Magno '07. Typical and slightly rustic, it offers notes of Mediterranean scrub, red fruit and autumn leaves, good body on the palate, acid pressure, smooth tannins and a finish that echoes the notes of wild strawberry. Its younger sibling, Colle Ticchio '08, is particularly good, combining spiciness with hints of mulberry. The palate is taut, full-flavoured and oh so supple. Finally there is Colle Sape '08, a tangy, almondy blend of malvasia, chardonnay and trebbiano with nuances of pennyroyal and medlar.

Paolo e Noemia D'Amico

FRAZ. VAIANO
LOC. PALOMBARO
01024 CASTIGLIONE IN TEVERINA [VT]
TEL. 0761948034
www.paoloenoemiadamico.it

CELLAR SALES
PRE-BOOKED VISITS

ANNUAL PRODUCTION **130,000 bottles**
HECTARES UNDER VINE **25**
VITICULTURE METHOD **Conventional**

Lying in the upper Tiber valley, with its sheer ravines, Paolo and Noemia D'Amico's estate is an absolute gem. Over the last few years, it has put itself firmly on the regional wine map, building a reputation for quality and energy. The D'Amicos have concentrated their efforts on chardonnay and obtain excellent results, both with their top products, which are increasingly elegant and balanced, and their basic line, which is reliable and good value for money.

The estate's two Chardonnays are very good and again this year romped home to our final tastings. The barrique-matured Falesia '07 gives classic notes of butter and vanilla on the nose and a rich palate full of body in which the oak is much less evident than in previous years. The deep finish unveils hints of tropical fruit. The Calanchi di Vaiano '08 is aged solely in stainless steel but despite its youth shows its usual grip, with aromas of citrus fruit, white pepper and apricot, a palate full of backbone with faint mineral tones and great length. The finale is dominated by white-fleshed fruit.

● Cesanese del Piglio Colle Ticchio '08	￥￥ 4*
● Cesanese del Piglio San Magno '07	￥￥ 4
○ Colle Sape '08	￥￥ 3*
● Cesanese del Piglio Colle Ticchio '07	♀♀ 4*
● Cesanese del Piglio San Magno '06	♀♀ 4*
○ Colle Sape Corte dei Papi '07	♀♀ 3*

○ Calanchi di Vaiano '08	￥￥ 5
○ Falesia '07	￥￥ 5
○ Seiano Bianco '08	￥￥ 4*
○ Orvieto Noe '08	￥ 4
● Seiano Rosso '08	￥ 4
● Villa Tirrena '06	￥ 5
○ Calanchi di Vaiano '07	♀♀ 5*
○ Calanchi di Vaiano '06	♀♀ 4*
○ Falesia '06	♀♀ 5
○ Falesia '05	♀♀ 5

★ Falesco

LOC. SAN PIETRO
05020 MONTECCHIO [TR]
TEL. 07449556
www.falesco.it

CELLAR SALES
PRE-BOOKED VISITS
VISITOR FACILITIES

ANNUAL PRODUCTION 2.500,000 bottles
HECTARES UNDER VINE 370
VITICULTURE METHOD Conventional

This year, we move the Cotarella siblings' estate because though the winery is in Montecchio, in Umbria, most of their vineyards are located in Lazio, despite production of a Sagrantino. Created in 1979 at Montefiascone, Falesco has succeeded in the difficult undertaking of combining quantity and quality with more openly "popular" wines as well as its flagship products. We should remember this even though mostly international varieties are used for red wines, the whites are still made from native varieties like roscetto.

Merlot Montiano is one of the best wines in Italy. The 2007 has black berry fruit, pepper and Mediterranean scrub sensations and the long, tautly consistent palate shows good structure and silky tannins. The cabernet sauvignon and franc Marciliano '07 is good, showing deeper on the nose and more concentrated on the palate, with notes of black berry fruit jam, cinchona and liquorice. Another finalist was Ferentano '07, a pure Roscetto with saffron and orange flower aromas, and a powerful, minerally palate still masked by oak while the fresh, pleasant Vitiano Rosso '08 plays off fruit and sweet spice. Sagrantino R '06 made an excellent debut.

Fontana Candida

VIA FONTANA CANDIDA, 11
00040 MONTE PORZIO CATONE [RM]
TEL. 069401881
www.fontanacandida.it

CELLAR SALES
PRE-BOOKED VISITS
FOOD

ANNUAL PRODUCTION 6.500,000 bottles
HECTARES UNDER VINE 97
VITICULTURE METHOD Conventional

Monteporzio, in Castelli Romani, birthplace of Marcus Portius Cato the Elder, who as far back 200 BC noted that the vine had an ancient history in these parts. After a long, successful run as a family winery, Fontana Candida became a company in 1958 and today is one of GIV's oldest brands and a flagship estate for Castelli wines. Production is largely white, with a natural preference for Frascati in all shapes and forms from everyday drinking wines to a top product like Luna Mater.

The Luna Mater '08 is one of the best, if not the best, Frascati in production. Wonderfully crisp and complex on the nose of citrus fruit, citron and white pepper, it has a very supple palate with a rich finish full of minerally, spicy notes. We also liked the clean, fresh, citrus-dominated Malvasia '08. The Frascati Superiore Santa Teresa '08 is not quite up to our expectations, or perhaps it simply pales in comparison, but it is still pleasing and typical. The other Frascati, Terre dei Grifi '08, is good, as is Siroe '08 from 70 per cent syrah and cesanese.

● Montiano '07	♟♟♟	6
○ Ferentano '07	♟♟	5
● Marciliano '07	♟♟	7
● Sagrantino di Montefalco R² '06	♟♟	7
● Vitiano Rosso '08	♟♟	4*
○ Est Est Est di Montefiascone Poggio dei Gelsi '08	♟♟	3*
○ Passirò '07	♟♟	5
● Pesano '08	♟♟	4
● Pomele '08	♟♟	5
● Tellus '08	♟♟	4
○ Est Est Est di Montefiascone Falesco '08	♟	2*
○ Vitiano Bianco '08	♟	3
● Montiano '06	♟♟♟	6
● Montiano '05	♟♟♟	6
● Montiano '03	♟♟♟	6
● Montiano '01	♟♟♟	6
● Montiano '00	♟♟♟	6

○ Frascati Sup. Luna Mater '08	♟♟	5
○ Malvasia '08	♟♟	4
○ Frascati Sup. Santa Teresa '08	♟	4
○ Frascati Sup. Terre dei Grifi '08	♟	3
● Siroe '08	♟	4
○ Frascati Sup. Santa Teresa '07	♟♟	5
○ Frascati Sup. Santa Teresa '06	♟♟	5
○ Malvasia '07	♟♟	5

Marcella Giuliani

LOC. VICO MORICINO
VIA ANTICOLANA KM 5
03012 ANAGNI [FR]
TEL. 0644235908
www.aziendaagricolamarcellagiuliani.it

CELLAR SALES
PRE-BOOKED VISITS

ANNUAL PRODUCTION **31,000 bottles**
HECTARES UNDER VINE **10.5**
VITICULTURE METHOD **Conventional**

Marcella Giuliani continues to make great strides in her quest to bring Ciociara and its grapes, cesanese and passerina in particular, to the forefront of wine. The vineyards lie on a base of moderately loose-packed clayey soil and face south-west, enjoying an ideal cool, airy climate. Recent years have seen rigorous work in the vineyards, a move to organic systems, renovation of the cellar and the input of consultant Riccardo Cotarella, which have combined to take the wines to the front rank of regional production.

The estate did very well this year. Although the Cesanese del Piglio Dives '07 did not reach our finals, it is very good indeed. Blackberry and sweet spices announce a palate that is still rather oak-dominated but shows soft tannins, fruity aromas and good length. We found the two Alagnas better than usual. The passerina-based Bianco '08 hints at pear and quince and has a consistent, fresh palate with serious acid backbone. The Cesanese del Piglio '08 is more fluent and fresher than its elder sibling but complex and full of fruit and spice.

Wine		Rating
○ Alagna Bianco '08	🍷🍷	3*
● Cesanese del Piglio Alagna '08	🍷🍷	3*
● Cesanese del Piglio Dives '07	🍷🍷	5
● Cesanese del Piglio Dives '06	🍷🍷	5
● Cesanese del Piglio Dives '04	🍷🍷	5

Antica Cantina Leonardi

VIA DEL PINO, 12
01027 MONTEFIASCONE [VT]
TEL. 0761826028
www.cantinaleonardi.it

CELLAR SALES
PRE-BOOKED VISITS
VISITOR FACILITIES

ANNUAL PRODUCTION **100,000 bottles**
HECTARES UNDER VINE **37**
VITICULTURE METHOD **Organic certified**

Founded in the early 1900s by Domenico Leonardi, this historic Montefiascone estate is in third-generation hands. It debuts in our full profile section thanks to a very favourable growing year and a consistent level of quality. Notably, it offers the traditional whites of the zone, Grechetto and Est Est Est. The estate spans two properties, one on the slopes around the volcanic Lake Bolsena at around 450 metres, and the other in Graffignano on the Umbrian border.

The Est Est Est di Montefiascone Poggio del Cardinale '08 is one of the best of the vintage. Flowery, white pepper aromas announce a creamy, mineral palate with a long almond and citrus finish. Le Muffe '08, a botrytized trebbiano and chardonnay blend, offers candied citron and an elegant, very drinkable palate with an apricot tart finish. The Grechetto Pensiero '08 shows well with a complex nose and full, alcoholic palate but taut, fresh finish. We also liked the Don Carlo '06, from 70 per cent merlot and cabernet with tobacco aromas, and the Vivì '08, from 85 per cent vermentino and viognier, is pleasant if a tad simple.

Wine		Rating
○ Est Est Est di Montefiascone Poggio del Cardinale '08	🍷🍷	3*
○ Le Muffe '08	🍷🍷	4
○ Pensiero '08	🍷🍷	3*
● Don Carlo '06	🍷	4
○ Vivì '08	🍷	3
○ Pensiero '07	🍷🍷	3*

Sergio Mottura

LOC. POGGIO DELLA COSTA, 1
01020 CIVITELLA D'AGLIANO [VT]
TEL. 0761914533
www.motturasergio.it

CELLAR SALES
PRE-BOOKED VISITS
VISITOR FACILITIES
FOOD

ANNUAL PRODUCTION **95,000 bottles**
HECTARES UNDER VINE **37**
VITICULTURE METHOD **Organic certified**

The Mottura family estate nestles in the hills and clayey gullies of Civitella d'Agliano, east of the Tiber-fed Umbrian plain. Thanks to low yields per vine, firm respect for the typicity of the grapes and the territory, the organic methods adopted in the vineyards and the high standard of cellar work, Sergio Mottura has created a range of extremely ageworthy wines, carving a place for grechetto on the national wine map.

Yet again the house of Mottura won Three Glasses but not for the wine we might have expected. The champ is the younger sibling, Grechetto Poggio della Costa '08. Matured exclusively in stainless steel, it is clean and fragrant with wonderful minerality, acid grip, extreme length and crystal-clear aromas. A great white in the true Italian style. Latour a Civitella '07 is superb with a white pepper and citrus fruit nose and a palate mingling smoky tones with hints of white fruit. We also liked the flowery, fluent Orvieto Classico Vigna Tragugnano '08 and the soft, pleasing and well-made Civitella Rosso '08, from 80 per cent merlot and montepulciano.

Principe Pallavicini

VIA CASILINA KM 25,500
00043 COLONNA [RM]
TEL. 069438816
www.vinipallavicini.com

CELLAR SALES
PRE-BOOKED VISITS

ANNUAL PRODUCTION **480,000 bottles**
HECTARES UNDER VINE **80**
VITICULTURE METHOD **Conventional**

The Pallavicini family has been in Lazio since the 1600s and today the Principe Pallavicini Estates lie in some of the most wine-friendly zones in the territory's production areas. These include the historic zone of Colonna, home to most of the vineyards and the estate headquarters, and Cerveteri, where the cellars and maturation caves are, mainly in the zone of Maccarese the diversity of whose terrain and the grapes used distinguish the style of the house reds.

The whites remain the strong suit. The malvasia puntinata and sémillon 1670 is a very interesting project. The '07 edition gives aromas of sage and Mediterranean scrub followed by a taut, mineral palate that is tangy almost to the point of saltiness with a long finish redolent of apples and pears. Another estate classic is the Stillato '08 from part-dried malvasia puntinata, whose aromas of orange peel and dried apricot laced with chestnut and acacia blossom honey lead into a fresh-tasting palate hinting at beeswax. From the reds, we like the Soleggio '06, a Cabernet Sauvignon with warm tones and impressive depth.

O Grechetto Poggio della Costa '08	♟♟♟	4*
O Grechetto Latour a Civitella '07	♟♟	5
● Civitella Rosso '08	♟♟	4
O Orvieto Cl. V. Tragugnano '08	♟♟	4
● Magone '07	♟	5
O Orvieto '08	♟	4
O Grechetto Latour a Civitella '06	♟♟♟	5*
O Grechetto Latour a Civitella '05	♟♟♟	5*
O Grechetto Latour a Civitella '04	♟♟♟	5*
O Grechetto Latour a Civitella '01	♟♟♟	4
O Grechetto Poggio della Costa '07	♟♟	4*
O Grechetto Poggio della Costa '06	♟♟	4*

O 1670 '07	♟♟	5
● Soleggio '06	♟♟	4
O Stillato '08	♟♟	5
● Amarasco '07	♟	5
O Frascati Sup. Poggio Verde '08	♟	4
O Pagello '08	♟	4
● Syrah '08	♟	4
O 1670 '06	♟♟	5
O Stillato '07	♟♟	5

Poggio Le Volpi

VIA COLLE PISANO, 27
00040 MONTE PORZIO CATONE [RM]
TEL. 069426980
www.poggiolevolpi.it

CELLAR SALES
PRE-BOOKED VISITS

ANNUAL PRODUCTION **224,000 bottles**
HECTARES UNDER VINE **30**
VITICULTURE METHOD **Conventional**

Year after year, Felice Mergè offers us some of the best wines produced in Castelli Romani. Their consistent quality is unrivalled so all credit to the work done in the cellars, currently under renovation, and among the rows. The Monteporzio Catone vineyards lie at 400 metres on volcanic soil and are planted almost entirely to traditional grape types. They produce wines of enormous personality with a style all of their own.

The estate saw two of its wines grace our final tasting table this year, both designed to showcase local varieties. From nero buono di Cori, the Baccarossa '07 has aromas of black cherry, tar and ink, while the palate is full-bodied, tannic and long with a black fruit and liquorice finish. The Frascati Superiore Epos '08's aromatic malvasia notes are still dominated by oak but the palate is tangy, supple and well made. Felice Mergè is experimenting with vinification on the skins in the Donnaluce '08. In its absence, we were greatly consoled by the Frascati Cannellino, a clean, fresh wine with notes of apricot and candied ginger.

Sant'Andrea

LOC. BORGO VODICE
VIA RENIBBIO, 1720
04010 TERRACINA [LT]
TEL. 0773755028
www.cantinasantandrea.it

CELLAR SALES
PRE-BOOKED VISITS

ANNUAL PRODUCTION **200,000 bottles**
HECTARES UNDER VINE **70**
VITICULTURE METHOD **Conventional**

Gabriele and Andrea Pandolfo and their Sant'Andrea estate are among the greatest promoters of moscato di Terracina, a unique indigenous moscato bianco clone that grows on the hills above Terracina. They make all wine types from the variety, from dry to sweet to spumante versions. Their work was behind the establishment of the Moscato di Terracina DOC in 2007. The estate offers wines from the Pontine coastal DOCs and is also noted for the very high quality of its Circeo DOC wines.

The Moscato di Terracina Secco Oppidum '08 is one of Lazio's best whites. The varietal nose hints at sage and Mediterranean scrub, while the fresh palate is rich, deep, balanced and very pleasant. The Circeo Bianco Dune '07 also showed well. Aromas of white pepper announce a long, citrussy palate. We also liked the two Circeo '08s from the Riflessi line – the Rosso with balsamic and olive tapenade notes and the fresh, fluent Bianco – the honeyed Moscato di Terracina Passito Capitolium '07, and the aromatic Spumante Secco Oppidum '08 with its bitterish, rather aggressive finish.

● Baccarossa '07	♟♟ 5
○ Frascati Sup. Epos '08	♟♟ 4*
○ Frascati Cannellino	♟♟ 4
● Baccarossa '06	♟♟ 5
● Baccarossa '05	♟♟ 6
● Baccarossa '04	♟♟ 6
○ Donnaluce '07	♟♟ 4*
○ Frascati Sup. Epos '07	♟♟ 4*
○ Frascati Sup. Epos '06	♟♟ 5
○ Passito Odôs '06	♟♟ 5

○ Moscato di Terracina Secco Oppidum '08	♟♟ 3*
○ Circeo Bianco Dune '07	♟♟ 4*
○ Circeo Bianco Riflessi '08	♟ 2*
● Circeo Rosso Riflessi '08	♟ 2*
○ Moscato di Terracina Passito Capitolium '07	♟ 4
○ Moscato di Terracina Secco Oppidum Spumante '08	♟ 3
○ Moscato di Terracina Passito Capitolium '06	♟♟ 4*
○ Moscato di Terracina Secco Oppidum '07	♟♟ 3*

Sant'Isidoro

loc. Portaccia
01016 Tarquinia [VT]
tel. 0766869716
www.santisidoro.net

CELLAR SALES
PRE-BOOKED VISITS

ANNUAL PRODUCTION 120,000 bottles
HECTARES UNDER VINE 57
VITICULTURE METHOD Conventional

Sant'Isidoro was founded in the late 1930s. Its over 800 hectares host orchards, cereals and herds of field-raised cows and sheep while the vineyards lie ten kilometres from the coast between Tarquinia and Montalto di Castro. The third generation of Palombis now runs the estate and in the late 1990s their quest for quality saw the planting of several new plots to local varieties, such as montepulciano and sangiovese, and international grapes like merlot, cabernet sauvignon and petit verdot.

Soremidio starred in our finals again as one of the best reds from Lazio. In the '07, this monovarietal Montepulciano gives leather, spice and black plums and then a full, intense palate with coffee, black fruit and Mediterranean scrubland. The Corithus '08, from cabernet sauvignon, montepulciano and sangiovese, also showed well, with a medley of smokiness and red berry and pepper notes. The palate has good texture but the tannins are rather aggressive. The very fruity Forca di Palma '08, from 70 per cent chardonnay and trebbiano, and the simple, fruity Terzolo '08 from 90 per cent cabernet sauvignon and merlot, are both well typed.

● Soremidio '07	🍷🍷	5
● Corithus '08	🍷🍷	4*
○ Forca di Palma '08	🍷	3
● Terzolo '08	🍷	3
● Corithus '07	🍸🍸	4*
● Soremidio '06	🍸🍸	5
● Soremidio '05	🍸🍸	6

Giovanni Terenzi

loc. La Forma
via Forese, 13
03010 Serrone [FR]
tel. 0775594286
www.viniterenzi.com

CELLAR SALES
PRE-BOOKED VISITS

ANNUAL PRODUCTION 80,000 bottles
HECTARES UNDER VINE 12
VITICULTURE METHOD Conventional

Established at the end of the 1960s, Giovanni Terenzi's estate is a family affair involving his wife and children. Thirty years ago, he decided to focus on the potential of the territory and the local varieties, long before he started to enjoy the success of recent years. Back then, everyone was putting their bets on international grape types. Giovanni's vines grow at an average elevation of 450 metres on chalk-based soil and face south, south-east and south-west. Breezes and temperature fluctuations ripen the grapes to perfection.

Giovanni had no finalists this year but his wines are very reliable. The Cesanese del Piglio Vajoscuro '06 has intense notes of tar with toasty nuances and a soft, well-made palate flaunting well-integrated tannins and a long wild berry finish. His Passerina del Frusinate, the Villa Santa '08 is also excellent, with notes of white-fleshed fruits and a very fresh, varietal palate with good acid grip. Velobra '07 is in a lower key than last year. Its currant aromas are fresh but the palate is rather lean. The "non-local" San Quirico '07 Cesanese is good with nice fruit.

● Cesanese del Piglio Vajoscuro '06	🍷🍷	5
○ Passerina Villa Santa '08	🍷🍷	4*
● Cesanese del Piglio Velobra '07	🍷	4
● Cesanese di Olevano Romano Colle S. Quirico '07	🍷	4
● Cesanese del Piglio Colle Forma '06	🍸🍸	5
● Cesanese del Piglio Colle Forma '05	🍸🍸	5
● Cesanese del Piglio Vajoscuro '05	🍸🍸	5
● Cesanese del Piglio Velobra '06	🍸🍸	4*

Trappolini

VIA DEL RIVELLINO, 65
01024 CASTIGLIONE IN TEVERINA [VT]
TEL. 0761948381
www.trappolini.com

CELLAR SALES
PRE-BOOKED VISITS

ANNUAL PRODUCTION 150,000 bottles
HECTARES UNDER VINE 25
VITICULTURE METHOD Conventional

The Trappolini family continues to produce an excellent range based on the zone's major varieties, from sangiovese to grechetto to aleatico. Their estate has long been a point of reference for Viterbo wine and has gained a reputation for the quality of its products and its tireless efforts to promote the overall growth of the upper Tiber valley. Without doubt its flagship wine is Paterno, a pure Sangiovese, but it is also working to relaunch aleatico with Idea, a sweet wine.

The '07 version of Paterno is very good. A balsamic, spicy nose is the prelude to a concentrated palate revealing notes of red berry fruit and liquorice. The finish is supple, gutsy and long. Brecceto '08, from grechetto and chardonnay in equal parts, is rich and rather closed as yet but already pleasant on the palate. The Cenereto '08 from sangiovese and montepulciano has fruity aromas and a fresh, tangy, no-nonsense palate. From trebbiano and malvasia, the flowery Sartei '08 has backbone and energy. Idea '08, a sweet Aleatico, offers black cherry and cinnamon sensations and a fresh finish.

Villa Gianna

LOC. B.GO SAN DONATO
S.DA MAREMMANA
04010 SABAUDIA [LT]
TEL. 0773250034
www.villagianna.it

CELLAR SALES
PRE-BOOKED VISITS

ANNUAL PRODUCTION 830,000 bottles
HECTARES UNDER VINE 50
VITICULTURE METHOD Organic certified

In just a few short years, the Giannini family has transformed Villa Gianna into one of the region's most interesting estates, yet it still manages to maintain high-volume production. We take our hats off to the excellent levels of quality achieved across the wide selection of labels in a range that, particularly in recent years, has obtained its most prestigious wines and major successes from the Circeo DOC territory.

We applaud Gianluca Giannini, who this year offered us one of the best ranges of wines in Lazio, proving that he knows how to get the best out of the Circeo DOC. Circeo Bianco Innato '08 has an aromatic nose and a harmonious, tangy palate with peach and almond sensations while the Circeo Rosso Nobilvite '08 offers red fruits aromas and a fresh, fruity, pleasant palate. The Vigne del Borgo line from international varieties is also good. Its Chardonnay '08 is flowery with unusual notes of prickly pear. The '07 Cabernet Sauvignon offers cherry and Mediterranean scrubland and the Sauvignon '08 is varietal and well structured.

Wine	Rating
● Paterno '07	♟♟ 4*
○ Brecceto '08	♟♟ 4*
● Cenereto '08	♟♟ 3*
● Idea '08	♟♟ 4
○ Sartei '08	♟♟ 2*
○ Est Est Est di Montefiascone '08	♟ 2
○ Brecceto '07	♟♟ 4*
● Cenereto '07	♟♟ 3*
● Paterno '06	♟♟ 4*
● Paterno '04	♟♟ 4
● Paterno '99	♟♟ 3*

Wine	Rating
○ Circeo Bianco Innato '08	♟♟ 4*
● Circeo Rosso Nobilvite '08	♟♟ 3*
● Vigne del Borgo Cabernet Sauvignon '07	♟♟ 4*
○ Vigne del Borgo Chardonnay '08	♟♟ 3*
○ Vigne del Borgo Sauvignon '08	♟♟ 3*
● Barriano '06	♟ 4
○ Bianco di Caprolace Chardonnay '08	♟ 3
○ Elogio Mediterraneo '07	♟ 5
● Rudèstro '07	♟ 3

Casale Cento Corvi

VIA AURELIA KM 45,500
00052 CERVETERI [RM]
TEL. 069903902
www.casalecentocorvi.com

Casale Cento Corvi showed well but it hasn't made the hoped-for leap in quality. Giacché '07 from the same variety is good, with tobacco, plum and black cherry notes and a clean, fresh, fruity palate. The whites are decent, notably the '08 Zilath from malvasia and trebbiano. The reds are a notch below.

● Giacché '07	🍷🍷	7
○ Kantharos Bianco '08	🍷	4
○ Kottabos Bianco '08	🍷	4
○ Zilath Bianco '08	🍷	2*

Casale della Ioria

P.ZZA REGINA MARGHERITA, 1
03010 ACUTO [FR]
TEL. 0775744282
www.casaledellaioria.com

Paolo Perinelli's Cesaneses are back, notably the Torre del Piano '07 with aromas of Mediterranean scrub and blackberry. The palate has body and rather rough tannins with a fresh, currant finish. The Cesanese del Piglio Casale della Ioria '07 and the Passerina Colle Bianco '08 are only decent.

● Cesanese del Piglio Torre del Piano '07	🍷🍷	5
● Cesanese del Piglio Casale della Ioria '07	🍷	4
○ Colle Bianco '08	🍷	3

Casale Marchese

VIA DI VERMICINO, 68
00044 FRASCATI [RM]
TEL. 069408932
www.casalemarchese.it

At the time of our tasting, the Clemens had not yet been bottled so the Frascati Superiore '08 stepped into the limelight. The nose is pervasive, clean, citrussy and flowery with hints of kiwi and spice. The palate is consistent and well made, if a bit simple, and the finish has good length and pressure.

○ Frascati Sup. '08	🍷🍷	3*
● Rosso di Casale Marchese '08	🍷	4

Casale Mattia

LOC. COLLE MATTIA
VIA MONTE MELLONE, 19
00040 MONTECOMPATRI [RM]
TEL. 069426249
www.casalemattia.it

Roberto Rotelli's estate is responsible for one of the best '08 Frascatis. Terre Laviche has a delicate nose of spring flowers and a fresh, citrussy palate with typical almond notes. The rest of the wines on offer are good, in particular the varietal Malvasia Nemesis '08.

○ Frascati Sup. Terre Laviche '08	🍷🍷	4*
● Merlot Costamagna '08	🍷🍷	4
○ Malvasia Nemesis '08	🍷	3

Cavalieri

VIA MONTECAGNOLO, 16
00045 GENZANO DI ROMA [RM]
TEL. 069375807
www.cavalieri.it

A low-key year for Fabrizio Cavalieri, who is still one of the few points of reference for Colli Lanuvini DOC. His Superiore '08 has citrus aromas and a simple, refreshing palate with a typical almond finish. We also liked the Facesole '07 from cesanese, merlot, sangiovese and cabernet.

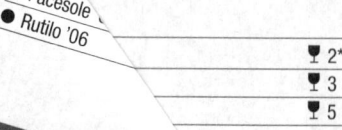

○ Colli Lanuvini Sup. '08	🍷	2*
● Facesole '07	🍷	3
● Rutilo '06	🍷	5

Cantina Cerveteri

VIA AURELIA KM 42,700
00052 CERVETERI [RM]
TEL. 06994441
www.cantinacerveteri.it

The Cerveteri co-operative winery continues to juggle volume and consistent quality. The cream of this year's crop is the Malvasia Novae '08, which gives citrus and ginger sensations and a well-structured palate with length and nice mineral tones. The other wines are well made.

○ Novae '08	🍷🍷	3*
○ Cerveteri Bianco Viniae Grande '08	🍷	4
● Menade '07	🍷	3

OTHER WINERIES

Damiano Ciolli
VIA DEL CORSO
00035 OLEVANO ROMANO [RM]
TEL. 069564547
www.damianociolli.it

Damiano Ciolli is indisputably the number one producer in Olevano and of its Cesanese, even if a certain inconsistency leaves us puzzled. His Cirsium '06 has notes of tapenade and Mediterranean scrub with a rich palate hinting at black olives and red fruit. Silene '07 is spicy, tangy and supple.

● Cesanese di Olevano Cirsium '06	🍷🍷 5
● Cesanese di Olevano Silene '07	🍷🍷 4*

Colacicchi
VIA ROMAGNANO, 2
03012 ANAGNI [FR]
TEL. 064469661
info@trimani.com

The jury is out on the Trimani family estate, as the reds were held back for a year to allow them to mature. The only wine on offer was Romagnano Bianco '08, a blend of malvasia puntinata, passerina, chardonnay and other local varieties. It is fresh, well-structured, aromatic and mineral.

○ Romagnano Bianco '08	🍷🍷 5
● Torre Ercolana '05	🍷🍷 7
● Torre Ercolana '04	🍷🍷 7
● Torre Ercolana '01	🍷🍷 6

Colle di Maggio
VIA PASSO DEI CORESI, 25
00049 VELLETRI [RM]
TEL. 0696453072
www.colledimaggio.com

Pleasant, well-made wines, but that's about it. Such are the tasting notes for Colle di Maggio. Derived from a blend of merlot and syrah, Cesare Ottaviano Augusto is an interesting wine with a spicy nose and black fruit notes on the palate. The three whites on offer are fresh and agreeable.

● Cesare Ottaviano Augusto '07	🍷 6
○ Don Mimì '08	🍷 3
○ Porticato Bianco '08	🍷 4
○ Tulino Chardonnay '08	🍷 4

La Ferriera
LOC. ROSAMISCO
03042 ATINA [FR]
TEL. 0776610413
www.laferriera.it

Lucio Mancini's young estate showed well. We liked Ferrato '08, from equal parts syrah, petit verdot and cabernet, to the Atina Cabernet Forgiato '07. The first has ripe black fruit aromas rather dominated by the oak and a clean, medium-bodied palate whereas the second has varietal bell pepper notes.

● Ferrato '08	🍷🍷 4*
● Atina Cabernet Forgiato '07	🍷 5

Fontana di Papa
VIA NETTUNENSE KM 10,800
00040 ARICCIA [RM]
TEL. 06934781
www.fontanadipapa.com

Fontana di Papa maintains its place in the Guide but failed to thrill. All the wines are solid and well crafted. The Malvasia '08 offers a flowery nose and nice notes of pear and annurca apple on the palate. Castelli Romani Rosso Calathus '07 is youthfully alcoholic with fresh hints of blueberry.

● Castelli Romani Calathus '07	🍷 3
● Cesanese del Lazio Grotte '08	🍷 2*
○ Malvasia del Lazio Grotte '08	🍷 2*

Giangirolami
LOC. BORGO MONTELLO
VIA DEL CAVALIERE, 1414
04100 LATINA
TEL. 3358394890
www.donatogiangirolami.it

A fine showing from Donato Giangirolami's organic estate. Sauvignon Regius '08 is perfectly aromatic and flowery with a pleasant palate of apple-like and peachy fruit. The Pietraliscia '07 from petit verdot and syrah has notes of cherry and cocoa powder, good texture and soft, well-managed tannins.

○ Sauvignon Regius '08	🍷🍷 4*
○ Colle Alto '08	🍷 4
● Pietraliscia '07	🍷 4

Gotto d'Oro

LOC. FRATTOCCHIE
VIA DEL DIVINO AMORE, 115
00040 MARINO [RM]
TEL. 0693022211
www.gottodoro.lt

Gotto d'Oro is on the road to quality with a series of pleasing, well-made wines. Our pick is the Malvasia '08 with its aromas of citron and mint and palate hinting at apple and citrus fruit. The Mitreo line featuring the Marino Taurus '07 and the merlot-based Korex '07 also showed well.

○ Malvasia del Lazio '08	♙♙	3*
○ Marino Mitreo Taurus '07	♙	4
● Mitreo Korex '07	♙	4

Le Lase

LOC. RESANO
01028 ORTE [VT]
TEL. 0761281460
www.lelase.com

This young Viterbo estate debuts in the Guide thanks to a couple of very well-made wines. Cautha '07 from cabernet sauvignon and petit verdot is fresh and fruity with aromas of fresh-cut grass and black cherry. The Zefiro '08 from incrocio Manzoni is citrussy and very pleasing.

● Cautha '07	♙♙	5
○ Zefiro '08	♙♙	4
○ Goccia '08	♙	4
● Terra '07	♙	4

Isabella Mottura

LOC. RIO CHIARO, 1
01020 CIVITELLA D'AGLIANO [VT]
TEL. 3357077931
www.isabellamottura.com

A leading light in the Tuscia wine world, Isabella Mottura produces well-made, characterful wines. This year, we particularly liked her Colli Etruschi Viterbesi Merlot Akemi '08 for its notes of cherry and cut grass. The palate is rather rustic but it has good body and a black fruit and tobacco finish.

● Colli Etruschi Viterbesi Akemi '08	♙♙	4*
● Colli Etruschi Viterbesi Amadis '07	♙	6
○ Tregoniano '08	♙	3

L'Olivella

VIA DI COLLE PISANO, 5
00044 FRASCATI [RM]
TEL. 069424527
www.racemo.it

A low-key year for the Notarnicola family estate. Racemo Rosso '06, a blend of mainly cesanese, is good with nice body and lots of fruit. The Frascati Superiore Racemo '08 is rather vegetal with citron and lemon aromas. Cesanese Maggiore '07 is balsamic but simpler than the last edition.

● Racemo Rosso '06	♙♙	5
○ Frascati Sup. Racemo '08	♙	4
● Maggiore '07	♙	5

I Pampini

LOC. ACCIARELLA
S.DA FOGLINO, 1126
04010 LATINA
TEL. 0773643144
www.ipampini.it

Pampini is one of the best-known organic estates in Lazio. We still prefer the reds, such as Kubizzo '06, a Mediterranean Merlot with nuances of rosemary and cherry, the fresh, balsamic Syrah '07, and the other Merlot, Coboldo '06, with its darker sensations of plum and liquorice.

● Coboldo '06	♙♙	3*
● Kubizzo '06	♙♙	4*
○ Maroso '08	♙	4
● Syrah '07	♙	4

La Pazzaglia

S.DA DI BAGNOREGIO, 4
01024 CASTIGLIONE IN TEVERINA [VT]
TEL. 0761947114
www.tenutalapazzaglia.com

The Verdecchia family estate is one of the best in the territory, although quality-wise it seems to be stuck. The Merlot Montijone '08 is fresh with pleasant varietal notes and nice length. Aurelius '08, from merlot and sangiovese, and Corno '08, a grechetto-based blend, are simple and well made.

● Montijone '08	♙♙	5
● Aurelius '08	♙	4
○ Il Corno '08	♙	4

OTHER WINERIES

Pietra Pinta

S.P. PASTINE KM 20,200
04010 CORI [LT]
TEL. 069678001-9677151
www.pietrapinta.com

Pietra Pinta only offered us whites to taste. The well-made Chardonnay '08 has notes of ginger and jasmine and a tangy, refreshing palate with a bitterish almondy finish. The flowery Falanghina '08 with tropical fruit aromas and the varietal Malvasia Puntinata '08 are pleasant but a tad simple.

○ Chardonnay '08	♟♟	3*
○ Falanghina '08	♟	3
○ Malvasia Puntinata '08	♟	3

Il Quadrifoglio

LOC. DOGANELLA DI NINFA
VIA ALESSANDRO III, 5
04012 CISTERNA DI LATINA [LT]
TEL. 069601530
ilquadrifoglio.ss@libero.it

The De Gregorios' estate re-entered the Guide with a good Perazzeto '07, a syrah and merlot blend in which earthy, wild berry sensations are the prelude to a long, agreeable palate. From montepulciano and cabernet sauvignon, the correct Muro Pecoraro '07 gives aromatic herbs but is rather uninteresting.

● Muro Pecoraro '07	♟	4
● Perazzeto '07	♟	3

Riserva della Cascina

LOC. FIORANO
VIA APPIA ANTICA, 560
00134 ROMA
TEL. 067917221
riservadellacascina@inwind.it

The Brannettis' estate made its Guide comeback with its well-typed, organic wines. We liked the Castelli Romani Rosso '08 for its flowery nose and agreeable, refreshing palate with a red berry fruit finish. There was also a good showing from the taut and fruity if rather simple Marino Superiore '08.

● Castelli Romani Rosso '08	♟♟	3*
○ Marino Sup. '08	♟	3

Tenuta Ronci di Nepi

LOC. VALLE RONCI
01036 NEPI [VT]
TEL. 0761555125
www.roncidinepi.com

Top pick this year is Vigna Ronci, a pure Cabernet Sauvignon. The 2005 has notes of spice, leather and cinchona and a palate that is still oak-dominated but shows decent freshness. The Chardonnay Villa Manti '07 and the Veste Porpora '06 from cabernet sauvignon and sangiovese are well typed.

● Vigna Ronci '05	♟♟	6
● Veste Porpora '06	♟	4
○ Vigna Manti '07	♟	5

Cantine San Marco

LOC. VERMICINO
VIA DI MOLA CAVONA, 26/28
00044 FRASCATI [RM]
TEL. 069409403
www.sanmarcofrascati.it

It has been years since a Frascati came out top at this historic estate but Solofrascati '08 is one of the best of the vintage, offering grassy, citrussy aromas and a dynamic palate with good texture and acid pressure. The Solomerlot '07 is also well made with black fruit sensations.

○ Solofrascati '08	♟♟	4*
○ Solomalvasia '08	♟	4
● Solomerlot '07	♟	4

Tenuta Santa Lucia

LOC. SANTA LUCIA
02047 POGGIO MIRTETO [RI]
TEL. 076524616
www.tenutasantalucia.com

The only Reatino estate in the Guide showed its mettle with a good range of wines. Top is the Morrone Riserva '05, a pure Syrah with lovely complexity, aromas of cigar tobacco, red fruit and pepper, and a full, long, relaxed palate with a finish redolent of plum and sweet spices.

● Morrone Ris. '05	♟♟	6
● Colli della Sabina Collis Pollionis Rosso '08	♟	4
● Otio '07	♟	5

Stefanoni

LOC. ZEPPONAMI
VIA STEFANONI, 48
01027 MONTEFIASCONE [VT]
TEL. 0761827031
www.cantinastefanoni.it

Established in the 1950s, Stefanoni made progress and now releases one of the top Est Est Ests. The Foltone '08 has jasmine and peach aromas and a clean palate with a citrus finish. Roscetto Colle de Poggeri '08 is full but still oak-dominated. The aleatico-only L'Eatico '08 is good.

○ Est Est Est di Montefiascone Foltone '08	♟♟	3*
○ Roscetto Colle de Poggeri '08	♟♟	3*
● L'Eatico '08	♟	3

Terra delle Ginestre

VIA FORNELLO, 94
04020 SPIGNO SATURNIA [LT]
TEL. 0771700297
www.terradelleginestre.it

This small six-member co-operative impressed us with its dry Moscato di Terracina Invito '08. Citrus and vanilla load into a more vegetal, fresh, long palate with a pleasant fruity finish. Il Generale is an interestingly full, intense red made from the all-but-forgotten abbuoto and uva vipera.

○ Moscato di Terracina Invito '08	♟♟	3*
● Il Generale '07	♟	4

Castello Torre in Pietra

VIA DI TORRIMPIETRA, 247
00050 FIUMICINO [RM]
TEL. 0661697070
www.castelloditorreinpietra.it

This major organic estate secured its place in the Guide, and also a Guide presence for the Tarquinia DOC, but it did not really impress this year. The Tarquinia Bianco '08 is good, showing notes of pennyroyal and apple and a fresh, fluent palate while the fragrant Chardonnay '08 is decent.

○ Chardonnay '08	♟	3
○ Tarquinia Bianco '08	♟	2*

Tre Botti

S.DA DELLA POGGETTA, 10
01024 CASTIGLIONE IN TEVERINA [VT]
TEL. 0761948930
www.trebotti.it

The Botti family estate debuts in the Guide in its fourth bottling year with some extremely well-made wines, notably the Aleatico Bludom '08. The result of an in-depth study of the variety, it has notes of cinnamon, cherry and black olive and a palate that balances residual sugar, tannins and acidity.

● Bludom '08	♟♟	5
○ Orvieto Canthus '08	♟♟	3*
● Tusco '07	♟	3

Villa Simone

VIA FRASCATI COLONNA, 29
00040 MONTE PORZIO CATONE [RM]
TEL. 069449717
www.pierocostantini.it

This year, Piero Costantini's estate offered a range of well-made but not very inspiring wines. The most interesting is the Frascati Superiore '08 with lemon notes and a fresh, consistent palate. The Vigneto Filonardi '08 is good but Ferro e Seta '06 from cesanese and sangiovese is way too simple.

○ Frascati Sup. Villa Simone '08	♟♟	3*
● Ferro e Seta '06	♟	6
○ Frascati Sup. Vign. Filonardi '08	♟	4

Cantine Volpetti

VIA NETTUNENSE, 21
00040 ARICCIA [RM]
TEL. 069342000
www.cantinevolpetti.it

This Ariccia estate has an interesting Cesanese del Piglio, Campo alle Rose '05, which shows fresh and supple with spice, black cherry and verbena. The Elegie Romane line classics are also good. The Colli Albani Superiore '08 is flowery with an almond finish and the Frascati Superiore '08 is nicely aromatic.

● Cesanese del Piglio Campo alle Rose '05	♟♟	3*
○ Colli Albani Sup. Elegie Romane '08	♟	1*
○ Frascati Sup. Elegie Romane '08	♟	2*

ABRUZZO

The sheer numbers from Abruzzo this year are impressive. Somehow they offer a proud response to the problems that many regional wineries encountered after the terrible earthquake of April 2009 which hit the city and hinterland of L'Aquila so badly, also affecting business overall. In comparison to the situation of just five or six years ago, we are now looking at a completely different picture. We tasted no less than 550 wines, which produced almost 50 finalists and 13 Three Glass winners. There are many new wineries, some consolidated old-timers, quite a few newcomers and, sadly, some which had to be excluded from the Guide this time around. For the first time, several producers saw their wines make the finals even though they didn't actually get a full profile. As far as Montepulciano d'Abruzzo is concerned, it's no longer the cheap, approachable big wine that many remember. Nowadays, it's powerful and rich in the Teramo Hills, including the Colline Teramane DOCG, much leaner at Popoli and Capestrano, and big-bodied and cellarable at San Martino sulla Marrucina and Loreto Aprutino. The same goes for Trebbiano d'Abruzzo, no longer a workhorse white, and for Pecorino, perhaps Abruzzo wine's new frontier although it still lacks proper designations and safeguards. Recent vintages have been admirable, especially the warm, consistent 2007, and a more variegated, sometimes challenging 2006, which produced a few quite alcoholic wines. The last 2005s were leaner as the cool growing year produced elegant wines, although without the backbone of other vintages. One of the most impressive producers was Masciarelli, whose entire range seems to rebel against the premature death of its creator, Gianni Masciarelli. His widow Marina, daughter Miriam and trusted oenologist Romeo Taraborrelli applied their hearts and minds to the job and the '07 Trebbiano Castello di Semivicoli actually earned itself the editor's Three Glass Plus award. Luigi Cataldi Madonna confirmed his status and this year's real outsider, the Barba family, came up with a range of noteworthy labels. Lastly, we want to mention another Three Glass Plus wine, Valle Reale's Montepulciano d'Abruzzo San Calisto '06.

Agriverde

LOC. CALDARI
VIA STORTINI, 32A
66020 ORTONA [CH]
TEL. 0859032101
www.agriverde.it

CELLAR SALES
PRE-BOOKED VISITS
VISITOR FACILITIES
FOOD

ANNUAL PRODUCTION **700,000 bottles**
HECTARES UNDER VINE **65**
VITICULTURE METHOD **Organic certified**

It hasn't been easy but Giannicola Di Carlo
has battled on doggedly with his ambitious
idea of creating a smart, modern winery
based on old-style attention to organic
agriculture and bio-architecture. The results
are there for everyone to see. His Agriverde
project has a hi-tech cellar, lovely
vineyards, a spa that has made wine
therapy its specialty and elegant farmhouse
accommodation with its own restaurant
serving local cuisine. Not to mention his
range of commendable wines.

Best of all was the '04 vintage
Montepulciano d'Abruzzo Plateo, a very
typical, complex, forceful red. It came
across with its usual strength but the great
growing year has enhanced its finesse.
We'd also mention the other Montepulciano
d'Abruzzos, which include a well-made
young Riseis '07,a Piane di Maggio '08 and
a budget-friendly Natum '08. The fragrant
Cerasuolo is appealing, as are several
whites, like the feisty, aromatic Pecorino
Riseis '08 and two honest, pleasant
Trebbiano d'Abruzzos, Piane di Maggio and
Riseis, both 2008. We weren't keen on the
over-heavy Trebbiano d'Abruzzo Solàrea
'07, which has too much oak.

Anfra

VIA COLLE MORINO, 8
64025 PINETO [TE]
TEL. 3471154504
www.anfra.it

CELLAR SALES
PRE-BOOKED VISITS
FOOD

ANNUAL PRODUCTION **30,000 bottles**
HECTARES UNDER VINE **10**
VITICULTURE METHOD **Conventional**

Every year, our tastings bring to light
striking newcomers, a clear indication of
the energy Abruzzo puts into winemaking.
This time, we discovered Anfra, a young
winery located on the Cerrano hillside in
the province of Teramo, with views of the
Adriatic Sea and Mount Gran Sasso. Anfra
has just four labels and its well-rounded
wines are modern in style but respect
traditional methods and typicity. A
successful exercise in blending the past
with the present.

An ambitious Montepulciano Nero dei due
Mori '06, with its layers of fruit-rich aromas,
had no trouble getting to the national
finals. We tasted a juicy, crisp red that
finished on a nice, tangy note. The less
complex Montepulciano d'Abruzzo '08 has
brisk hints of black cherry and is enfolding,
feisty and savoury, exactly what a basic
red ought to be. The very drinkable
Cerasuolo '08 is uncomplicated, as these
rosés are, but also vibrant and firm. The
last label was a Trebbiano d'Abruzzo '08.
It's not terribly varietal but it is well made
with intense white-fleshed fruit aromas and
a fresh, spirited palate.

● Montepulciano d'Abruzzo Plateo '04	▼▼▼	7
● Montepulciano d'Abruzzo Riseis '07	▼▼	4*
⊙ Montepulciano d'Abruzzo Cerasuolo Solàrea '08	▼▼	4*
● Montepulciano d'Abruzzo Natum '08	▼▼	4*
● Montepulciano d'Abruzzo Piane di Maggio '08	▼▼	3*
○ Pecorino Riseis '08	▼▼	4*
○ Trebbiano d'Abruzzo Piane di Maggio '08	▼▼	3*
○ Trebbiano d'Abruzzo Riseis '08	▼▼	4*
○ Trebbiano d'Abruzzo Solarea '07	▼	5
● Montepulciano d'Abruzzo Plateo '01	▼▼▼	7
● Montepulciano d'Abruzzo Plateo '00	▼▼▼	7
● Montepulciano d'Abruzzo Plateo '98	▼▼▼	6
● Montepulciano d'Abruzzo Solàrea '03	▼▼▼	5
● Montepulciano d'Abruzzo Plateo '03	▼▼	7
○ Trebbiano d'Abruzzo Solarea '04	▼▼	4

● Montepulciano d'Abruzzo Nero dei due Mori '06	▼▼	5
● Montepulciano d'Abruzzo '08	▼▼	5
⊙ Montepulciano d'Abruzzo Cerasuolo '08	▼▼	4*
○ Trebbiano d'Abruzzo '08	▼▼	4*

F.lli Barba

LOC. SCERNE DI PINETO
S.DA ROTABILE PER CASOLI
64020 PINETO [TE]
TEL. 0859461020
www.fratellibarba.it

CELLAR SALES
PRE-BOOKED VISITS

ANNUAL PRODUCTION **350,000 bottles**
HECTARES UNDER VINE **68**
VITICULTURE METHOD **Conventional**

This established Colline Teramane operation is a full-scale farm, producing not just wine but also grain, fruit, vegetables, grapes and olives. Giovanni Barba's passion for traditional Abruzzo wines led him to set up a small laboratory to develop a superior product. In recent years, Giovanni has worked hard to upgrade his wines and they are now some of the best in the region. This year, he sent us an astonishing selection and won not one but two top awards.

The refined, fruity Trebbiano d'Abruzzo '06 has well-handled body and subtle, elegant aromas, nuanced with fermentation oak. It's balanced and will improve with age. The Montepulciano Vignafranca '06, an ambitious red with exuberant black cherry and cocoa powder aromas, is nice and juicy, despite major structure. A new selection, the traditional Montepulciano I Vasari, made the national finals with its first shot. This is a thoroughbred in the making. We weren't sure about Vignafranca '07, a Trebbiano d'Abruzzo that shows rather over-evolved on the nose. The Colle Morino Montepulciano '08 is a surprise and may even be too pulpy for the wine type.

Barone Cornacchia

VILLA TORRI, 20
64010 TORANO NUOVO [TE]
TEL. 0861887412
www.baronecornacchia.it

CELLAR SALES
PRE-BOOKED VISITS
VISITOR FACILITIES

ANNUAL PRODUCTION **300,000 bottles**
HECTARES UNDER VINE **42**
VITICULTURE METHOD **Organic certified**

Baroni Cornacchia is in one of Abruzzo's prime wine spots for sunlight and terrain, the municipality of Torano Nuovo, one of the territories that helped earn the Colline Teramane DOCG status. The noble Cornacchias have been producing traditional, varietal wines for over a century. Piero, the current owner, continues the tradition, offering a very acceptable range in which we thought the younger, more straightforward wines were the most interesting.

The opulent Colline Teramane Vizzarro '05 is a fragrant, intense Montepulciano with varietal balsamic notes, smooth, fruity progression and a slightly tart finish. The modern, coherent Montepulciano '07, its fresh, fruity hints slightly masked by the oak, has a spirited palate with lively, complex tannins. The Trebbiano '08, a dynamic white with typical aromas, developed easily on a husky palate. We're not keen on the winery's ambitious Montepulciano selections. Poggio Varano '06 has oxidative, gamey aromas, and tricky follow-through hindered by a weighty body, and the well-typed, varietal Vigna Le Coste '06 is husky with acidity slightly out of kilter.

Wine	Rating
● Montepulciano d'Abruzzo Vignafranca '06	▼▼▼ 4*
○ Trebbiano d'Abruzzo '06	▼▼▼ 5*
● Montepulciano d'Abruzzo I Vasari '06	▼▼ 5
● Montepulciano d'Abruzzo Colle Morino '08	▼▼ 3*
○ Trebbiano d'Abruzzo Colle Morino '08	▼ 2*
○ Vignafranca Bianco '07	▼ 4
● Montepulciano d'Abruzzo Vignafranca '05	♈♈ 4*
● Montepulciano d'Abruzzo Vignafranca '04	♈♈ 4
● Montepulciano d'Abruzzo Vignafranca '03	♈♈ 4*
● Montepulciano d'Abruzzo Vignafranca '01	♈♈ 4*
● Montepulciano d'Abruzzo Vignafranca '00	♈♈ 4
○ Trebbiano d'Abruzzo '05	♈♈ 5

Wine	Rating
● Montepulciano d'Abruzzo '07	▼▼ 3*
● Montepulciano d'Abruzzo Colline Teramane Vizzarro '05	▼▼ 6
○ Trebbiano d'Abruzzo '08	▼▼ 3*
● Montepulciano d'Abruzzo Poggio Varano '06	▼ 4
● Montepulciano d'Abruzzo V. Le Coste '06	▼ 4
● Montepulciano d'Abruzzo '06	♈♈ 3*
● Montepulciano d'Abruzzo Poggio Varano '04	♈♈ 4
● Montepulciano d'Abruzzo V. Le Coste '05	♈♈ 4*
○ Trebbiano d'Abruzzo '07	♈♈ 3*

Podere Castorani

VIA CASTORANI, 5
65020 ALANNO [PE]
TEL. 0852012513
www.poderecastorani.it

CELLAR SALES
PRE-BOOKED VISITS

ANNUAL PRODUCTION 965,000 bottles
HECTARES UNDER VINE 70
VITICULTURE METHOD Organic certified

One racing driver Jarno Trulli's family opened this winery in 2002. They manage their Pescara hill estate with care and passion, producing idiosyncratic, enterprising and totally unique wines. The range of labels and types may be a little too extensive and while we're in no doubt the wines are all well made, there seem to be rather a lot of them for a mid-sized winery like this.

Cadetto '08 is a new, unfussy Montepulciano and the only small thing about it is the price. Fruit-rich, varietal aromas complement an elegant, uncluttered palate. We liked the refined aromas of the Montepulciano Amorino '06. It's not entirely true to type but is nicely layered. The muscular palate has flair but finishes on a bitterish note. The more authoritative Montepulciano, Costa delle Plaie '06, has a lovely mouthfeel and evolved aromas. The Pecorino Amorino '08, a well-typed, varietal white, has a fresh, appealing follow-through, finishing with the grape's signature bitterish note. The Trebbiano Costa delle Plaie '08 is varietal and bright.

Luigi Cataldi Madonna

LOC. PIANO
67025 OFENA [AQ]
TEL. 0862954252
cataldimadonna@virgilio.it

CELLAR SALES
PRE-BOOKED VISITS

ANNUAL PRODUCTION 260,000 bottles
HECTARES UNDER VINE 27.5
VITICULTURE METHOD Conventional

Abruzzo's furnace' is the traditional name for the mountain-girt Ofena tableland. With the Gran Sasso massif looming behind and Majella in front, it has a wide range of temperatures that make the territory the new frontier of Abruzzo winemaking. Luigi Cataldi Madonna, who teaches philosophy, has for many years brought his intuition to this area, making time-honoured regional wines. The professor exploits the Ofena site climates to craft wines that combine modernity with tradition, very much in the spirit of our times.

This year confirmed the usual pair of aces, Pecorino '07 and Montepulciano Tonì '06. The former is an awesome white. Luigi was the first to invest in this native grape and has changed its profile in the decade since he first planted it. He doesn't appreciate comparisons to a great Sauvignon. For us the '06 Tonì is the best ever thanks to its elegant aromas and juicy, smooth follow-through. Cerasuolo Piä delle Vigne '07 is a great rosé, a remarkable blend of drinkability and style. The winery's second-label Montepulciano, Malandrino '07, puts the accent on fruit as always, but seems to suffer from too much oak.

Wine	Rating
○ Amorino '08	♀♀ 4*
● Montepulciano d'Abruzzo Amorino '06	♀♀ 4*
● Montepulciano d'Abruzzo Cadetto '08	♀♀ 2*
● Montepulciano d'Abruzzo Costa delle Plaie '06	♀♀ 4
○ Trebbiano d'Abruzzo Costa delle Plaie '08	♀♀ 4*
● Amorino Rosso '05	♀♀ 4
● Montepulciano d'Abruzzo Costa delle Plaie '04	♀♀ 4*
● Montepulciano d'Abruzzo Podere Castorani '03	♀♀ 6
● Montepulciano d'Abruzzo Podere Castorani '01	♀♀ 5

Wine	Rating
● Montepulciano d'Abruzzo Tonì '06	♀♀♀ 6
○ Pecorino '07	♀♀♀ 6
☉ Montepulciano d'Abruzzo Cerasuolo Piè delle Vigne '07	♀♀ 5
● Montepulciano d'Abruzzo Malandrino '07	♀♀ 5
● Montepulciano d'Abruzzo '07	♀♀ 4*
☉ Montepulciano d'Abruzzo Cerasuolo '08	♀♀ 3*
○ Trebbiano d'Abruzzo '08	♀♀ 3*
● Montepulciano d'Abruzzo Malandrino '06	♀♀♀ 5
● Montepulciano d'Abruzzo Malandrino '04	♀♀♀ 5*
● Montepulciano d'Abruzzo Malandrino '03	♀♀♀ 5
● Montepulciano d'Abruzzo Tonì '04	♀♀♀ 6
● Montepulciano d'Abruzzo Tonì '03	♀♀♀ 6
○ Pecorino '06	♀♀♀ 6
○ Pecorino '05	♀♀♀ 6

Centorame

LOC. CASOLI DI ATRI
VIA DELLE FORNACI, 15
64030 ATRI [TE]
TEL. 0858709115
www.centorame.it

CELLAR SALES
PRE-BOOKED VISITS

ANNUAL PRODUCTION **82,000 bottles**
HECTARES UNDER VINE **8**
VITICULTURE METHOD **Conventional**

In just a few years, this small winery has managed to carve itself a nice little niche in the complex, competitive Colline Teramane territory. Casoli d'Atri, Gran Sasso on one side and the Adriatic on the other, lies on clay terrain that enjoys some very hot sunshine. Lorenzo Vannucci, the determined owner and soul of the business, coaxes the maximum from this special terroir to forge rich, old-style wines.

The winery top label Castellum Vetus, a Montepulciano Colline Teramane as ambitious as its name, was absent. Still, San Michele, a less challenging Montepulciano, is a worthy substitute, with the '07 reaching national finals thanks to its brisk, fruit-rich nose and progression that is sprightly, despite the weighty, savoury body. We liked the classic '07 Trebbiano Castellum Vetus, whose rich varietal aromas herald a palate with great body and backbone, veiled by excessive oak. The easy-drinking Trebbiano San Michele flows nicely across the palate. Tuapina, the new white, is a fresh, crisp sauvignon and pecorino blend, but disappoints in the mouth.

● Montepulciano d'Abruzzo San Michele '07	🍷🍷 4*
○ Trebbiano d'Abruzzo Castellum Vetus '07	🍷🍷 4*
○ Trebbiano d'Abruzzo San Michele '08	🍷🍷 3*
○ Tuapina '08	🍷 4
● Montepulciano d'Abruzzo Colline Teramane Castellum Vetus '06	🍷🍷 5
● Montepulciano d'Abruzzo Colline Teramane Castellum Vetus '05	🍷🍷 5
● Montepulciano d'Abruzzo Colline Teramane Castellum Vetus '04	🍷🍷 5
● Montepulciano d'Abruzzo San Michele '06	🍷🍷 3*
● Montepulciano d'Abruzzo San Michele '05	🍷🍷 3*
● Montepulciano d'Abruzzo San Michele '04	🍷🍷 3*
○ Trebbiano d'Abruzzo Castellum Vetus '06	🍷🍷 4*
○ Trebbiano d'Abruzzo Castellum Vetus '04	🍷🍷 4

Cerulli Irelli Spinozzi

LOC. CASALE 26
S.S. 150 DEL VOMANO KM 17,600
64020 CANZANO [TE]
TEL. 086157193
www.cerullispinozzi.it

PRE-BOOKED VISITS
VISITOR FACILITIES
FOOD

ANNUAL PRODUCTION **180,000 bottles**
HECTARES UNDER VINE **32**
VITICULTURE METHOD **Organic certified**

This Teramo winery located on the outermost edge of Abruzzo works hard to achieve quality and protect the territory. And it's no longer just a promise. Now it's a solid maker of ambitious, well-typed regional wines. Enrico Cerulli has very clear ideas for his Canzano estate, including the development of traditional varieties native to this region, production of modern, but land-rooted wines, and intermittent attention to the Colline Teramane DOCG.

We gave the Torre Migliori '04, a Montepulciano Colline Teramane Riserva, another go this year and liked the lively fruit aromas with balsamic notes and full, savoury, complex palate. It can only improve with time. The modern, forceful Torre Migliori Riserva '05 is another Montepulciano Colline Teramane, still veiled with new oak aromas and slightly cropped on the palate. The Montepulciano '07 had evolved aromas and a full palate but was let down by a tart finish. We've got used to Cortalto being a very interesting Pecorino and this fragrant '08 is nicely rustic and really drinkable. The uncomplicated, drinkable Trebbiano '08 is well made.

● Montepulciano d'Abruzzo Colline Teramane Torre Migliori Ris. '05	🍷🍷 6
○ Pecorino Cortalto '08	🍷🍷 4*
● Montepulciano d'Abruzzo '07	🍷 3
○ Trebbiano d'Abruzzo '08	🍷 3
○ Cortalto '06	🍷🍷 3*
● Montepulciano d'Abruzzo '05	🍷🍷 4*
● Montepulciano d'Abruzzo Colline Teramane Torre Migliori Ris. '04	🍷🍷 6
○ Pecorino Cortalto '07	🍷🍷 3*

Collefrisio

loc. Piane di Maggio
66030 Frisa [CH]
tel. 0859039074
www.collefrisio.it

PRE-BOOKED VISITS

ANNUAL PRODUCTION **205,000 bottles**
HECTARES UNDER VINE **35**
VITICULTURE METHOD **Organic certified**

"This young winery is groomed with loving care. It has two estates on two different, fascinating territories. One is on the Ortona hills, looking out over the Adriatic; the other on the Chieti hillside, cooled by the nearby Majella massif. All this has allowed Collefrisio to work its way up the Guide's classifications and place two wines in the national finals."

The Zero '07 is a fresh, well-typed, well-priced Montepulciano that hits the spot with a vibrant nose and elegant, structured progression revealing fresh acidity. The new jewel is a high-flying Montepulciano '05, with dark quinine and pencil lead aromas, and good thrust still veiled with some strong oak. The Uno '06, a well-made, crisp Montepulciano is a success, as is the Trebbiano Zero '08, a nicely edgy, husky white. The excellent Trebbiano Uno is more ambitious and the '08 has varietal aromas and toastiness, with a savoury, vibrant palate. The Pecorino '08 is as pleasing and fresh as we expect it to be, with a hint of bitterness at the back.

● Montepulciano d'Abruzzo '05	🍷🍷	4
● Montepulciano d'Abruzzo Zero '07	🍷🍷	4*
● Montepulciano d'Abruzzo Uno '06	🍷🍷	4
○ Pecorino '08	🍷🍷	4
○ Trebbiano d'Abruzzo Uno '08	🍷🍷	4
○ Trebbiano d'Abruzzo Zero '08	🍷🍷	3*
⊙ Montepulciano d'Abruzzo Cerasuolo '08	🍷	4
⊙ Montepulciano d'Abruzzo Cerasuolo '07	🍷🍷 (white)	4*
● Montepulciano d'Abruzzo Uno '05	🍷🍷 (white)	4*
● Montepulciano d'Abruzzo Zero '06	🍷🍷 (white)	4*
● Montepulciano d'Abruzzo Zero '05	🍷🍷 (white)	3*
○ Pecorino '07	🍷🍷 (white)	4*
○ Trebbiano d'Abruzzo Uno '07	🍷🍷 (white)	4*

Contesa

c.da Caparrone, 4
65010 Collecorvino [PE]
tel. 0858205078
www.contesa.it

CELLAR SALES
PRE-BOOKED VISITS

ANNUAL PRODUCTION **200,000 bottles**
HECTARES UNDER VINE **39**
VITICULTURE METHOD **Conventional**

Contesa is a modern, hi-tech winery and something of a dream come true for its owner and winemaker Rocco Pasetti, who is a leading player on the Abruzzo wine scene. The location is Collecorvino, in the sun-kissed Pescara hills, in countryside that is ideal for grow grapes.

We open with Sorab, a new, ambitious Pecorino '07, steel-fermented then bottle aged for a year. The nose is terpenic and the fruity palate tantalizes. The basic Pecorino '08 has a fresh, fruity nose, relaxed progression and an enticing style, despite its heavy structure for this wine type. Crisp, fruit-rich Cerasuolo '08 Vigna Corvino is a good, modern, strawberry and almonds rosÉ made by fermenting montepulciano off the skins. The forceful Montepulciano Amir '06 has striking body and pervasive aromas, clinging to oaky notes that fade with time. The brisk, rounded palate has a great savoury finish supporting progression.

● Montepulciano d'Abruzzo Amir '06	🍷🍷	5
⊙ Montepulciano d'Abruzzo Cerasuolo V. Corvino '08	🍷🍷	3*
○ Pecorino '08	🍷🍷	4*
○ Pecorino Sorab '07	🍷🍷	5
● Montepulciano d'Abruzzo V. Corvino '07	🍷	3
○ Chardonnay '07	🍷🍷 (white)	4*
● Montepulciano d'Abruzzo '05	🍷🍷 (white)	5
● Montepulciano d'Abruzzo '03	🍷🍷 (white)	5
● Montepulciano d'Abruzzo Nerone '04	🍷🍷 (white)	5
○ Pecorino '07	🍷🍷 (white)	4*
○ Pecorino '06	🍷🍷 (white)	4
○ Trebbiano d'Abruzzo '04	🍷🍷 (white)	4

Cantina Frentana

VIA PERAZZA, 32
66020 ROCCA SAN GIOVANNI [CH]
TEL. 087260152
www.cantinafrentana.it

CELLAR SALES
PRE-BOOKED VISITS

ANNUAL PRODUCTION 480,000 bottles
HECTARES UNDER VINE N.D.
VITICULTURE METHOD Conventional

Cantina Frentana reconfirms its status this year as a leading co-operative in the regional winemaking system, all thanks to the reliable quality of the wines it offers. It's a medium-sized winery and most of its produce is sold unbottled but the range of labels on offer includes some very valid selections.

The finalist is a fragrant, varietal Montepulciano d'Abruzzo Panarda '06. It's unfussy, with delicious fruity and mineral aromas, and a crisp, rounded, full palate. The feisty, savoury Montepulciano Rubesto '07 is also pleasant and well-made, as befits a wine of this level, tripping only on a slightly bitterish conclusion. Terre Valse '08 is less successful, with evolved, fruit-driven aromas and full, overripe progression. We liked the simple Pecorino '08, with its juicy, spirited palate, and the fragrant, very drinkable Trebbiano Terre Valse '08. The ambitious Chardonnay Donna Greta '07 is a little ordinary in the end, despite its mineral aromas.

Dino Illuminati

C.DA SAN BIAGIO, 18
64010 CONTROGUERRA [TE]
TEL. 0861808008
www.illuminatilvini.it

CELLAR SALES
PRE-BOOKED VISITS

ANNUAL PRODUCTION 1.200,000 bottles
HECTARES UNDER VINE 120
VITICULTURE METHOD Conventional

Cavalier Dino Illuminati is the most iconic of the Colline Teramane winemakers. For years, he's been active in the Controguerra zone, some of Abruzzo's most typical vineyard country, where he runs his family winery founded back in 1890. His wines are larger than life, often very territorial, and are stalwarts on the region's winemaking scenario.

Lumen is a modern, full-bodied montepulciano and cabernet Controguerra, with the '06 vintage showing in a muscular body and pervasive black cherry and cocoa powder. As ever, the well-typed, varietal Montepulciano Colline Teramane Zanna '06 has husky aromas and pleasing, juicy progression. Montepulciano Riparosso '08 is an easy drinker and a reliable buy, released in hundreds of thousands of units. The Spiano '08 shares the fragrance and drinkability of Riparosso. Whites worth uncorking include two Controguerras: a simple, juicy Ciafré '08 and the slightly passé, new oak-dominated Daniele '06 from trebbiano, chardonnay and passerina.

● Montepulciano d'Abruzzo Panarda '06	❷❷ 5
● Montepulciano d'Abruzzo Rubesto '07	❷❷ 3*
○ Pecorino '08	❷❷ 3*
○ Trebbiano d'Abruzzo Terre Valse '08	❷❷ 2*
○ Donna Greta '07	❷ 5
● Montepulciano d'Abruzzo Terre Valse '08	❷ 2*
● Montepulciano d'Abruzzo Panarda '05	❷❷ 5*
● Montepulciano d'Abruzzo Panarda '04	❷❷ 4
● Montepulciano d'Abruzzo Panarda '03	❷❷ 4
● Montepulciano d'Abruzzo Panarda '01	❷❷ 4
● Montepulciano d'Abruzzo Rubesto '06	❷❷ 4*
● Montepulciano d'Abruzzo Terre Valse '07	❷ 2*

● Montepulciano d'Abruzzo Colline Teramane Zanna Ris. '06	❷❷❷ 6
○ Controguerra Bianco Ciafré '08	❷❷ 4
○ Controguerra Bianco Daniele '06	❷❷ 5
● Controguerra Rosso Lumen '06	❷❷ 6
● Montepulciano d'Abruzzo Riparosso '08	❷❷ 3*
● Montepulciano d'Abruzzo Spiano '08	❷❷ 3*
○ Pecorino '08	❷ 4
● Controguerra Rosso Lumen '97	❷❷❷ 6
● Montepulciano d'Abruzzo Colline Teramane Pieluni Ris. '01	❷❷❷ 7
● Montepulciano d'Abruzzo Colline Teramane Pieluni Ris. '00	❷❷❷ 7
● Montepulciano d'Abruzzo Colline Teramane Zanna Ris. '05	❷❷❷ 6
● Montepulciano d'Abruzzo Colline Teramane Zanna Ris. '03	❷❷❷ 6
● Montepulciano d'Abruzzo Colline Teramane Zanna Ris. '01	❷❷❷ 5

Lepore

C.DA CIVITA, 29
64010 COLONNELLA [TE]
TEL. 086170860
www.vinilepore.it

CELLAR SALES
PRE-BOOKED VISITS

ANNUAL PRODUCTION **420,000 bottles**
HECTARES UNDER VINE **43**
VITICULTURE METHOD **Conventional**

How happy we are to give a full profile again to this renowned Colonnella winery in the heartlands of the Teramo hills. Gaspare Lepore owns a 40-hectare estate overlooking the Adriatic coast and manages his vineyards in a traditional, non-intrusive manner, which means the cellar receives carefully selected, intact fruit, perfect for making typical wines made in a traditional style.

The simple Montepulciano d'Abruzzo '07 strolled into the finals with pervasive varietal aromas nuanced with black cherry, a juicy palate, and powerful body braced by poised acidity. The ambitious Montepulciano Colline Teramane Re '07 has a traditional nose and a fruity, savoury progression of surprising agility. Riserva del Fondatore Luigi Lepore is an imposing Montepulciano Colline Teramane with lactic hints and full, rich palate, finishing tart and tannic. The upfront Montepulciano Tramonto '08 gives fragrant, fruity notes and a richly extracted palate that has good momentum despite a sturdy body. The very simple, rustic whites were less convincing.

Lidia e Amato

C.DA SAN BIAGIO
64010 CONTROGUERRA [TE]
TEL. 0861817041
www.lidiaeamatoviticoltori.com

CELLAR SALES
PRE-BOOKED VISITS

ANNUAL PRODUCTION **25,000 bottles**
HECTARES UNDER VINE **12**
VITICULTURE METHOD **Conventional**

This tiny Controguerra winery is opposite the illustrious Illuminati estate. Lidia Tavoletti and her husband Amato apply traditional, farm-style management to their limited number of hectares as well as lots of passion and family commitment. Over the past few years, the Tavolettis have been amazing us with pleasant, well-typed wines that they name after their grandchildren.

The '06 Controguerra Sebastian gives subtle, elegant black cherry and blackberry, with a refined concentrated palate and a unique salty vein. There is too much oak for us in the ambitious Colline Teramane Riccardo '06, even with the interesting texture. A lively, appealing Controguerra Lidia '08, with attractive yellow damson aromas, has a pleasant, lively progression, despite the structure. The fresh, crisp Pecorino Greta '08 has clean aromas and a round palate following through nicely. The coherent Trebbiano Palù '08 is well made and good value. Passerina Elena '08 is a fun white with a quirky individuality, despite the rustic grape.

Wine	Rating
● Montepulciano d'Abruzzo '07	▼▼ 4*
● Montepulciano d'Abruzzo Colline Teramane Luigi Lepore Ris. '03	▼▼ 5
● Montepulciano d'Abruzzo Colline Teramane Re '07	▼▼ 5
● Montepulciano d'Abruzzo Tramonto '08	▼▼ 3*
⊙ Montepulciano d'Abruzzo Cerasuolo '08	▼ 4
○ Passera delle Vigne '08	▼ 4
○ Passerina Do '07	▼ 4
○ Trebbiano d'Abruzzo '08	▼ 3
○ Controguerra Passerina Sol '00	▼▼ 4
⊙ Montepulciano d'Abruzzo Cerasuolo '07	▼▼ 4*
⊙ Montepulciano d'Abruzzo Cerasuolo '03	▼▼ 3*
● Montepulciano d'Abruzzo Colline Teramane Re '05	▼▼ 5
● Montepulciano d'Abruzzo Colline Teramane Re '03	▼▼ 5
● Montepulciano d'Abruzzo Colline Teramane Re '01	▼▼ 5

Wine	Rating
● Controguerra Sebastian '06	▼▼ 4*
○ Controguerra Lidia '08	▼▼ 3*
○ Greta '08	▼▼ 4*
● Montepulciano d'Abruzzo Colline Teramane Riccardo '06	▼▼ 4*
○ Controguerra Elena '08	▼ 3
○ Trebbiano d'Abruzzo Palù '08	▼ 2*
● Montepulciano d'Abruzzo Colline Teramane Riccardo '05	▼▼ 4*
● Montepulciano d'Abruzzo Forty '07	▼▼ 3*

★★ Masciarelli

VIA GAMBERALE, 1
66010 SAN MARTINO SULLA MARRUCINA [CH]
TEL. 087185241
www.masciarelli.it

CELLAR SALES
PRE-BOOKED VISITS

ANNUAL PRODUCTION **2,000,000 bottles**
HECTARES UNDER VINE **195**
VITICULTURE METHOD **Conventional**

Gianni Masciarelli died last year. He was far too young but his wines and winery survive as a monument to his work and the two decades of passion that took him to the heights of Abruzzo and Italian winemaking. The business is now in the hands of his wife Marina Cvetic and daughter Miriam, assisted by oenologist Romeo Taraborelli, Gianni's close friend. The range is every bit as excellent as it ever was. The great wines come from meticulous viticulture that respects the territory, paired with winemaking technique that has few peers.

Trebbiano Castello di Semivicoli '07, made without wood, is amazing. The intense, almost aromatic nose leans heavily to minerality and the solid palate shows rich, elegant and warm. A superlative white. The '06 Montepulciano Villa Gemma may well be the best from the last few years, giving spice on the nose and managing to combine subtlety and muscle as only a great wine can. But the whole range is fantastic, from the charming Cerasuolo Villa Gemma '08 to the Chardonnay Marina Cvetic '07, the Montepulciano Marina Cvetic '06 and the winery's classic standards, '07 and Trebbiano '08. A faultless performance.

Camillo Montori

LOC. PIANE TRONTO, 82
64010 CONTROGUERRA [TE]
TEL. 0861809900
www.montorivini.it

CELLAR SALES
PRE-BOOKED VISITS
VISITOR FACILITIES
FOOD

ANNUAL PRODUCTION **600,000 bottles**
HECTARES UNDER VINE **50**
VITICULTURE METHOD **Conventional**

Montori is synonymous with the Teramo hills and was one of the main players in the campaign for the Colline Teramane DOCG. It's almost a legend around Controguerra, with wines typified by the nicely husky, traditional style that makes them so easy to recognize and always interesting. This year, the leading labels were missing but the four samples we tasted made a good showing.

Montepulciano d'Abruzzo '07 is a traditional, typical expression of the grape, with mineral aromas and an agile, fruity progression. It's a red with lots of character and all the charm of an old-school wine. The Pecorino '08 is simply one of the best in Abruzzo. Of course, Camillo Montori was the first in the area to believe in this native vine and it shows. The aromatics are true to type and on the palate it's pleasant and far from mundane. The varietal, rustic Trebbiano Fonte Cupa '08 has heady, fresh aromas and an assertive palate. Lastly, Cerasuolo '08 is a typical fruit-rich, pervasive rosé, with a round, savoury palate.

Masciarelli		
● Montepulciano d'Abruzzo Villa Gemma '06	▼▼▼	8
○ Trebbiano d'Abruzzo Castello di Semivicoli '07	▼▼▼+	6
○ Chardonnay Marina Cvetic '07	▼	6
☉ Montepulciano d'Abruzzo Cerasuolo Villa Gemma '08	▼▼	4*
● Montepulciano d'Abruzzo Marina Cvetic '06	▼▼	5
● Montepulciano d'Abruzzo '07	▼▼	3*
○ Trebbiano d'Abruzzo '08	▼▼	3*
○ Trebbiano d'Abruzzo Marina Cvetic '07	▼▼	6
● Montepulciano d'Abruzzo Marina Cvetic '05	♀♀♀	5
● Montepulciano d'Abruzzo Marina Cvetic '03	♀♀♀	5*
● Montepulciano d'Abruzzo Villa Gemma '05	♀♀♀	8
● Montepulciano d'Abruzzo Villa Gemma '04	♀♀♀	8
● Montepulciano d'Abruzzo Villa Gemma '03	♀♀♀	8
● Montepulciano d'Abruzzo Villa Gemma '01	♀♀♀	8
● Montepulciano d'Abruzzo Villa Gemma '00	♀♀♀	8
○ Trebbiano d'Abruzzo Castello di Semivicoli '05	♀♀♀	6

Camillo Montori		
● Montepulciano d'Abruzzo '07	▼▼	3*
☉ Montepulciano d'Abruzzo Cerasuolo '08	▼▼	3*
○ Pecorino '08	▼▼	4*
○ Trebbiano d'Abruzzo Fonte Cupa '08	▼▼	4
● Controguerra Leneo Moro '00	♀♀	5
● Montepulciano d'Abruzzo '06	♀♀	3*
● Montepulciano d'Abruzzo Colline Teramane Fonte Cupa '05	♀♀	6
○ Pecorino '07	♀♀	4*
○ Trebbiano d'Abruzzo Fonte Cupa '07	♀♀	4*

Bruno Nicodemi

C.DA VENIGLIO
64024 NOTARESCO [TE]
TEL. 085895493
www.nicodemi.com

CELLAR SALES
PRE-BOOKED VISITS

ANNUAL PRODUCTION 200,000 bottles
HECTARES UNDER VINE 30
VITICULTURE METHOD Conventional

The Notaresco tableland is one of the loveliest such areas in the Teramo hills and Cantina Nicodemi has always been the top producer in these parts. The winery is small and is managed by a committed, enthusiastic sister and brother team, Elena and Alessandro, who have a very distinctive personal style. To understand, just take a look at the lovely, meticulously groomed vines and clean, unfussy cellars, but most of all, just sample the wines they are making here.

The winery's flagship Montepulciano d'Abruzzo Neromoro '05 wasn't around this year but the 2006 Notàri, the best we've tasted, almost got the top award. It's a lusty Montepulciano Colline Teramane, with intense aromas, firm structure and rich flavour. The Montepulciano d'Abruzzo '07 isn't so convincing, less brisk and crisp on the nose than usual and with a clenched, slightly tannic palate. The Trebbiano d'Abruzzo '08 is excellent showing a varietal nose and spirited, fresh-tasting palate. The ambitious Trebbiano d'Abruzzo Notàri '08 has well-typed varietal aromas but the heavy palate fails to hold up. The Cerasuolo '08 is fresh and pleasing, as a rosé should be.

Franco Pasetti

LOC. C.DA PRETARO
VIA SAN PAOLO, 21
66023 FRANCAVILLA AL MARE [CH]
TEL. 08561875
www.pasettivini.lt

CELLAR SALES
PRE-BOOKED VISITS
VISITOR FACILITIES

ANNUAL PRODUCTION 500,000 bottles
HECTARES UNDER VINE 40
VITICULTURE METHOD Conventional

In recent years, this winery has significantly upped its sales both locally and elsewhere, thanks to the hard work and sheer passion of Mimmo Pasetti, the tireless, dynamic owner. Fruit from a series of estates scattered all over Abruzzo is delivered to the Francavilla al Mare cellars where some very interesting wines are made.

Testarossa '05 is a varietal Montepulciano with fruity aromas that still have some unfolding to do. This traditional, rugged red has vigorous structure and tangy acidity. Montepulciano Harimann '04 is an old-fashioned wine, richly extracted but balanced overall despite oak and pulp. The fruity, intense Cerasuolo '08 is one of the region's best. But the Pasetti ace is its absolutely reliable Pecorino '08, produced in serious numbers. The Zarachä Trebbiano has structure and spirited, true-to-type drinkability. The biggest surprise is a new Colle Civetta '08, a high-flying Pecorino with typical, elegant aromas and round, juicy progression, which will evolve nicely.

● Montepulciano d'Abruzzo Colline Teramane Notàri '06	🍷🍷 5
☉ Montepulciano d'Abruzzo Cerasuolo '08	🍷🍷 3*
○ Trebbiano d'Abruzzo '08	🍷🍷 3*
● Montepulciano d'Abruzzo '07	🍷 4
○ Trebbiano d'Abruzzo Notàri '08	🍷 4
● Montepulciano d'Abruzzo Colline Teramane Neromoro Ris. '03	🍷🍷🍷 6
● Montepulciano d'Abruzzo '06	🍷🍷 4*
● Montepulciano d'Abruzzo '05	🍷🍷 4*
● Montepulciano d'Abruzzo Colline Teramane Neromoro Ris. '04	🍷🍷 6
○ Trebbiano d'Abruzzo '07	🍷🍷 3*
○ Trebbiano d'Abruzzo '06	🍷🍷 3*
○ Trebbiano d'Abruzzo Notàri '07	🍷🍷 4

● Montepulciano d'Abruzzo Tenuta di Testarossa '05	🍷🍷 5
☉ Montepulciano d'Abruzzo Cerasuolo Pasetti '08	🍷🍷 3*
● Montepulciano d'Abruzzo Harimann '04	🍷🍷 7
○ Pecorino Pasetti Colle Civita '08	🍷🍷 5
○ Trebbiano d'Abruzzo Zarachè '08	🍷🍷 4*
○ Pecorino Pasetti '08	🍷 4
● Montepulciano d'Abruzzo Fattoria Pasetti '06	🍷🍷 4*
● Montepulciano d'Abruzzo Fattoria Pasetti '05	🍷🍷 4*
● Montepulciano d'Abruzzo Fattoria Pasetti '04	🍷🍷 4*
● Montepulciano d'Abruzzo Harimann '02	🍷🍷 7
● Montepulciano d'Abruzzo Tenuta di Testarossa '04	🍷🍷 5
● Montepulciano d'Abruzzo Tenuta di Testarossa '03	🍷🍷 5
● Montepulciano d'Abruzzo Tenuta di Testarossa '02	🍷🍷 5

Emidio Pepe

VIA CHIESI, 10
64010 TORANO NUOVO [TE]
TEL. 0861856493
www.emidiopepe.com

CELLAR SALES
PRE-BOOKED VISITS
VISITOR FACILITIES

ANNUAL PRODUCTION **80,000 bottles**
HECTARES UNDER VINE **12.5**
VITICULTURE METHOD **Natural**

The Torano Nuova winery is one of the most traditional in Abruzzo. From the time of Mario Soldati, the renowned author who wrote about it in the 1960s, vinification and cultivation techniques have not changed very much. Only cement vats are used for fermentation and maturing, bottle ageing is lengthy, vines are tended with traditional peasant skills, the idiosyncrasies of each vintage are respected and recently, attention has focused on organic farming, the only innovation from the new management, Sofia Pepe, daughter of founder Emidio.

This year, the winery sent us a limited selection but it was very convincing. There was no sign of a champion that everyone agrees on, as there was last year with the monumental Montepulciano '98. The very well-balanced Montepulciano Colline Teramane '06 is still young and undeveloped but will open up given time. It has varietal aromas and a compact, layered body. The Trebbiano '07 is delightful, with subtle, floral aromas and a characteristic layered progression that is nicely acidic.

● Montepulciano d'Abruzzo Colline Teramane '06	**ΨΨ**	8
○ Trebbiano d'Abruzzo '07	**ΨΨ**	6
● Montepulciano d'Abruzzo '98	ΨΨΨ	8
● Montepulciano d'Abruzzo '04	ΨΨ	5
● Montepulciano d'Abruzzo '03	ΨΨ	5
● Montepulciano d'Abruzzo '01	ΨΨ	6
● Montepulciano d'Abruzzo Bio '05	ΨΨ	8
⊙ Montepulciano d'Abruzzo Cerasuolo '07	ΨΨ	5
● Montepulciano d'Abruzzo Colline Teramane '03	ΨΨ	8
○ Trebbiano d'Abruzzo '06	ΨΨ	6
○ Trebbiano d'Abruzzo '03	ΨΨ	6
○ Trebbiano d'Abruzzo '02	ΨΨ	5
○ Trebbiano d'Abruzzo '01	ΨΨ	6

La Quercia

C.DA COLLE CROCE
64020 MORRO D'ORO [TE]
TEL. 0858959110
www.vinilaquercia.it

CELLAR SALES
PRE-BOOKED VISITS

ANNUAL PRODUCTION **110,000 bottles**
HECTARES UNDER VINE **12.5**
VITICULTURE METHOD **Natural**

We're very fond of the authentic, slightly rustic style of this estate's wines. Its 12 hectares or so of vineyards are in Morro d'Oro territory, in the heart of the Colline Teramane hills, overlooking the sea. They are tended with precision and passion, and a non-intrusive style of cultivation. The wines produced are territory-focused and very rooted in traditional viticultural practices.

The well-typed, inexpensive Montepulciano d'Abruzzo '07 reached the national finals. Brisk black cherry and fine liquorice aromas precede a round, intact palate with fresh, savoury progression. The fresh, fruit-rich Montepulciano Peladi '08 has varietal nuances. The ambitious Mastrobono '03, a Montepulciano Colline Teramane Riserva, suffered a difficult year. It gives blurred stewed fruit aromas, a muscular body and spiky tannins. The Trebbiano d'Abruzzo '08 has white-fleshed fruit on the nose and a crisp, very drinkable palate, which is true to type. The modern Trebbiano Peladi '08 is less persuasive with its flattish progression. The two '08 Cerasuolos are good.

● Montepulciano d'Abruzzo '07	**ΨΨ**	4*
⊙ Montepulciano d'Abruzzo Cerasuolo Peladi '08	**ΨΨ**	2
⊙ Montepulciano d'Abruzzo Cerasuolo Primamadre '08	**ΨΨ**	4*
● Montepulciano d'Abruzzo Peladi '08	**ΨΨ**	4
○ Trebbiano d'Abruzzo '08	**ΨΨ**	3*
● Montepulciano d'Abruzzo Colline Teramane Mastrobono Ris. '03	**Ψ**	6
○ Trebbiano d'Abruzzo Peladi '08	**Ψ**	4
● Montepulciano d'Abruzzo Colline Teramane La Quercia Ris. '02	ΨΨ	5
● Montepulciano d'Abruzzo Colline Teramane Primamadre '04	ΨΨ	5
● Montepulciano d'Abruzzo Primamadre '05	ΨΨ	4*

San Lorenzo

C.DA PLAVIGNANO, 2
64035 CASTILENTI [TE]
TEL. 0861999325
www.sanlorenzovini.com

CELLAR SALES
PRE-BOOKED VISITS

ANNUAL PRODUCTION N.D.
HECTARES UNDER VINE 150
VITICULTURE METHOD Conventional

With each passing year, this large Colline Teramane winery, under the eager, dynamic management of Guido and Giuseppina Barbone, and Gianluca Galasso, confirms its many merits and the odd flaw. The former include an impressive territory in the provinces of Pescara and Teramo, with obvious potential. By flaws we mean mainly too many labels, which risks diluting interest with too many lines of production.

"Wines here range from high-profile Montepulciano d'Abruzzos to international varieties. We were happy with the Montepulciano Antares '07, which we sent to the finals for its subtle, typical aromas and round, savoury progression. The bold Montepulciano Colline Teramane Oinos '06 is muscular and concentrated, with balsam and oak, and a smooth, full-flavoured palate, despite hefty texture. We liked the effective Montepulciano Sirio '07 for its typicity and drinkability. We enjoyed two whites: an ambitious Chardonnay '05 with tropical fruit and vanilla on the nose, and a rich, enfolding palate; and Biancoluce '07, a pleasant, trebbiano and monsonico blend that hit the spot."

Nicola Santoleri

VIA DEI CAVALIERI, 20
66016 GUARDIAGRELE [CH]
TEL. 0871893301
www.nicolasantoleri.it

ANNUAL PRODUCTION 40,000 bottles
HECTARES UNDER VINE 30
VITICULTURE METHOD Conventional

We welcome Santoleri's wines back, our joy tinged with sorrow at Nicola, a friend and true gentleman of the Abruzzo wine world, who left us one sad dawn last year. His heirs have taken up the challenge with great spirit, wisely changing virtually nothing of the house style. The wines are always traditional, with a proud farmhouse style, worthy offspring of the Guardiagrele vineyards in the Chieti hills.

We were sent only three wines but they did well. First, a Crognaleto Riserva, a varietal, rustic 2000 Montepulciano with perfect development and a layered nose. Despite a demanding vintage, the wine is supported by a fine, surprisingly fresh palate. The less complex Montepulciano Crognaleto '04 is exceptionally fresh and typical. Intense, fruit-rich aromas are a prelude to a feisty palate, tamed by an almost salty finish. The Trebbiano '07 is upfront but not ordinary, with husky, varietal aromas, well-settled oak and a round, succulent palate.

● Montepulciano d'Abruzzo Antares '07	▼▼	3*
○ Biancoluce '07	▼▼	5
○ Chardonnay '05	▼▼	5
● Montepulciano d'Abruzzo Colline Teramane Oinos '06	▼▼	5
● Montepulciano d'Abruzzo Sirio '07	▼▼	2*
● Montepulciano d'Abruzzo Colline Teramane Escol Ris. '05	♈♈	5
● Montepulciano d'Abruzzo Colline Teramane Escol Ris. '04	♈♈	5
● Montepulciano d'Abruzzo Colline Teramane Escol Ris. '03	♈♈	5
● Montepulciano d'Abruzzo Colline Teramane Escol Ris. '02	♈♈	5
● Montepulciano d'Abruzzo Colline Teramane Escol Ris. '01	♈♈	6

● Montepulciano d'Abruzzo Crognaleto '04	▼▼	6
● Montepulciano d'Abruzzo Crognaleto Ris. '00	▼▼	6
○ Trebbiano d'Abruzzo Crognaleto '07	▼▼	5
○ Trebbiano d'Abruzzo '03	♈♈	4*

Cantine Talamonti

C.DA PALAZZO
65014 LORETO APRUTINO [PE]
TEL. 0858289039
www.cantinetalamonti.it

CELLAR SALES
PRE-BOOKED VISITS

ANNUAL PRODUCTION 450,000 bottles
HECTARES UNDER VINE 25
VITICULTURE METHOD Conventional

Year after year, this young winery in the Loreto Aprutino area brings us up-to-date wines with striking overall quality. The keen young winery staff has been in charge since 2001, dedicatedly supervising an extensive but not endless range of labels. We tasted five wines and all easily attained Two Glasses, bearing witness to the standards achieved.

The muscular, striving Montepulciano Tre Saggi '07 seems to have found its style. Intense, pervasive black cherry and spicy oak aromas precede a round, concentrated, fruit-rich palate. The simpler Modà '08 reveals gamey and varietal notes and an intense, traditional palate, supported by crisp, fresh acidity. The Kudos '06 montepulciano and merlot blend is a punchy red with layered, balsamic aromas and a generous palate. The Trebbiano d'Abruzzo Trebì '08 is as fresh and drinkable as its chirpy name suggests. The more ambitious Aeternum '07 is a traditional Trebbiano, aged to develop pleasant toasty layered notes.

Tiberio

C.DA LA VOTA
65020 CUGNOLI [PE]
TEL. 0858576744
www.tiberio.it

CELLAR SALES
PRE-BOOKED VISITS

ANNUAL PRODUCTION 60,000 bottles
HECTARES UNDER VINE 27
VITICULTURE METHOD Conventional

The results from this winery in the interior of the Colli Pescaresi are no surprise. It's managed with passion by the keen Tiberio family and their prestigious advisor, Riccardo Cotarella. The Cugnoli vineyards are set between the Majella and Gran Sasso massifs, and yield excellent grapes that are vinified in a personal style, respectful of local characteristics. The wines have the pronounced acidity and intense fruit aromas typical of the local soil, weather and range of temperatures

The Montepulciano '07 has pervasive ripe fruit aromas, a palate with a compact, richly extracted body and an enticing savoury finish. It's an interesting red, bridging past and present. The modern Cerasuolo '08 is pleasing, spirited and easy-drinking. The Pecorino '08 shows a simple but effective interpretation of this currently fashionable grape, achieving varietal aromas and fresh, lively drinkability. The plush Trebbiano '08 has white peach notes on the nose but the palate is slightly heavy. The ambitious and over-technical Althea is a modern, fragrant white with sophisticated oak and banana aromatics.

● Kudos '06	♀♀ 5
● Montepulciano d'Abruzzo Modà '08	♀♀ 3*
● Montepulciano d'Abruzzo Tre Saggi '07	♀♀ 4*
○ Trebbiano d'Abruzzo Aternum '07	♀♀ 4*
○ Trebbiano d'Abruzzo Trebì '08	♀♀ 3*
● Montepulciano d'Abruzzo Modà '07	♀♀ 3*
○ Trebbiano d'Abruzzo Aternum '06	♀♀ 4*

● Montepulciano d'Abruzzo '07	♀♀ 4*
○ Althea '07	♀♀ 4
⊙ Montepulciano d'Abruzzo Cerasuolo '08	♀♀ 4*
○ Pecorino '08	♀♀ 4
○ Trebbiano d'Abruzzo '08	♀ 4
● Montepulciano d'Abruzzo '06	♀♀ 3*
● Montepulciano d'Abruzzo Althea '05	♀♀ 5
○ Pecorino '07	♀♀ 4*

Cantina Tollo

VIA GARIBALDI, 68
66010 TOLLO [CH]
TEL. 087196251
www.cantinatollo.it

CELLAR SALES
PRE-BOOKED VISITS

ANNUAL PRODUCTION **12.500,000 bottles**
HECTARES UNDER VINE **3500**
VITICULTURE METHOD **Conventional**

This great co-operative winery was one of the first to work on quality, having realized the massive potential of Abruzzo's countless small and medium-sized growers. Winery staff, coordinated by oenologist Riccardo Brighigna, work with this raw material each year to offer a vast, reliable range of wines in various lines and types, all faultlessly made and excellent value for money.

Our favourite was the Cagiòlo, a Montepulciano d'Abruzzo fast becoming a classic and the top of Tollo's range, produced only from the best harvests. The '06 has pervasive, layered aromas, just veiled by the oak, and a nicely savoury, salty palate, with a hint of bitterish roughness at the back. Aldiano Montepulciano '07, a varietal, fragrant red, has crisp, balsamic notes on the nose and a layered, savoury palate. From the whites, the '08 Trebbiano was its typical, spirited self, with fruit-rich progression and considerable texture. The new Duecuori line appealed to us mainly for the fresh, spirited Trebbiano '08.

Torre dei Beati

C.DA POGGIORAGONE, 56
65014 LORETO APRUTINO [PE]
TEL. 3333832344
www.torredeibeati.it

CELLAR SALES
PRE-BOOKED VISITS

ANNUAL PRODUCTION **60,000 bottles**
HECTARES UNDER VINE **17**
VITICULTURE METHOD **Organic certified**

Torre dei Beati is the life project of a young, dedicated couple, Fausto Albanesi and Adriana Galasso. A few years ago, they decided to give up the security of their steady jobs to concentrate on their passion for wine. The location is their lovely Loreto Aprutino estate where there were already some old, well-established vineyards.

We were surprised that the Montepulciano d'Abruzzo '07 took first place, bewitching us with its layered aromas, intact, lively fruit and concentrated continuity on the palate. Our favourite was the traditional Montepulciano Cocciapazza '06, with its fruit-rich nose just misted with oak, and a complex, potent palate. The second selection, Mazzamurello, is less successful, giving quinine and some over-evolution, then a salty palate still trying to settle. The Rosa-ae is one of the region's three top Cerasuolos, a quirky wine with elegant, brooding sensations. This year's newcomer, a pecorino-heavy Primo Bianco '08 is a simple, fresh wine from younger vines.

● Montepulciano d'Abruzzo Cagiòlo '06	♔♔	5
○ Chardonnay Cretico '07	♔♔	5
● Montepulciano d'Abruzzo Aldiano '07	♔♔	4*
● Montepulciano d'Abruzzo Colle Secco Rubino '06	♔♔	4*
● Montepulciano d'Abruzzo Duecuori '07	♔♔	3*
○ Trebbiano d'Abruzzo Aldiano '08	♔♔	4*
○ Trebbiano d'Abruzzo Duecuori '08	♔♔	3*
○ Trebbiano d'Abruzzo Menir '07	♔♔	5
○ Pecorino '08	♔	4
● Montepulciano d'Abruzzo Aldiano '06	♔♔	4*
● Montepulciano d'Abruzzo Cagiòlo '05	♔♔	5
● Montepulciano d'Abruzzo Cagiòlo '04	♔♔	5
● Montepulciano d'Abruzzo Colle Secco '05	♔♔	4*
● Montepulciano d'Abruzzo Colle Secco Rubino '05	♔♔	4*

● Montepulciano d'Abruzzo '07	♔♔♔	4*
☉ Montepulciano d'Abruzzo Cerasuolo Rosa-ae '08	♔♔	3*
● Montepulciano d'Abruzzo Cocciapazza '06	♔♔	5
○ Primo Bianco '08	♔♔	4*
● Montepulciano d'Abruzzo Mazzamurello '06	♔	6
● Montepulciano d'Abruzzo '05	♔♔	4*
● Montepulciano d'Abruzzo Cocciapazza '04	♔♔	5
● Montepulciano d'Abruzzo Cocciapazza '03	♔♔	5
● Montepulciano d'Abruzzo Mazzamurello '05	♔♔	5
● Montepulciano d'Abruzzo Mazzamurello '04	♔♔	5

La Valentina

VIA TORRETTA, 52
65010 SPOLTORE [PE]
TEL. 0854478158
www.fattorialavalentina.it

CELLAR SALES
PRE-BOOKED VISITS

ANNUAL PRODUCTION 350,000 bottles
HECTARES UNDER VINE 40
VITICULTURE METHOD Conventional

There was a good performance from this ambitious Pescara hills winery. The recipe is one of dependability and dedication, attention to sustainable viticulture and oenology, an up-to-date cellar, respect for Abruzzo traditions, and the sheer passion that the Di Properzios pour into every aspect of their business, now approaching its 20th birthday.

The best wine this year was the '05 Spelt, an elegant Montepulciano with still slightly closed balsamic notes and a fruity palate, with well-handled extract. Last year's leader, Bellovedere, had a difficult vintage this year. The nose is gently spiced with oak and the palate is round and savoury, but trips up on a clenched, bitterish finish. The third label, a Montepulciano Binomio, is sourced from vines at the foot of the Majella massif. It's still very young and oaky. The palate is cropped but the generous pulp should point it in the right direction. From the whites, we liked the simple, clean Trebbiano '08 and the Pecorino '08, a well-typed version of this trendy wine.

★★ Valentini

VIA DEL BAIO, 2
65014 LORETO APRUTINO [PE]
TEL. 0858291138

ANNUAL PRODUCTION 40,000 bottles
HECTARES UNDER VINE 64
VITICULTURE METHOD Natural

Francesco Paolo Valentini is a worthy successor to his father Edoardo, having inherited the latter's professional approach to winemaking. In fact, if something isn't perfect, the wine doesn't even go on sale. It's sent to the local co-operative winery, which then surprises with an unexpected riserva or two. What's more, the Valentini style never changes. The Montepulciano and Trebbiano wines are long-lived, and even the Cerasuolo can age for ten years and more.

Cerasuolo is in the spotlight this year, since there's no Montepulciano '04 and or Trebbiano '06. They were judged not to be up to scratch and won't be marketed. But there are two rosés, the '07 and the '08. The former is poised and complex, with fragrant yeast and cherry on the nose, and a muscular palate with softer extract. The '08 is feistier, with more distinctive aromas of intense fruit, but also some smoky hints that make us optimistic for its evolution. The palate is rounder but more spirited and elegant. We preferred the '08 but both are worth uncorking.

● Montepulciano d'Abruzzo Spelt '05	♙♙♙ 5
● Montepulciano d'Abruzzo Bellovedere '06	♙♙ 7
● Montepulciano d'Abruzzo Binomio '06	♙♙ 6
O Pecorino '08	♙♙ 4*
O Trebbiano d'Abruzzo '08	♙♙ 3*
● Montepulciano d'Abruzzo Bellovedere '05	♛♛♛ 7
● Montepulciano d'Abruzzo '05	♛♛ 3*
● Montepulciano d'Abruzzo '04	♛♛ 3*
● Montepulciano d'Abruzzo Bellovedere '04	♛♛ 7
● Montepulciano d'Abruzzo Binomio '05	♛♛ 6
O Trebbiano d'Abruzzo '05	♛♛ 3

☉ Montepulciano d'Abruzzo Cerasuolo '08	♙♙♙ 7
☉ Montepulciano d'Abruzzo Cerasuolo '07	♙♙♙ 7
● Montepulciano d'Abruzzo '02	♛♛♛ 8
● Montepulciano d'Abruzzo '01	♛♛♛ 8
● Montepulciano d'Abruzzo '00	♛♛♛ 8
● Montepulciano d'Abruzzo '97	♛♛♛ 7
● Montepulciano d'Abruzzo '95	♛♛♛ 6
● Montepulciano d'Abruzzo '92	♛♛♛ 6
● Montepulciano d'Abruzzo '90	♛♛♛ 6
● Montepulciano d'Abruzzo '85	♛♛♛ 6
☉ Montepulciano d'Abruzzo Cerasuolo '06	♛♛♛ 7
O Trebbiano d'Abruzzo '05	♛♛♛ 7
O Trebbiano d'Abruzzo '04	♛♛♛ 7
O Trebbiano d'Abruzzo '02	♛♛♛ 7
O Trebbiano d'Abruzzo '01	♛♛♛ 6
O Trebbiano d'Abruzzo '00	♛♛♛ 6
O Trebbiano d'Abruzzo '99	♛♛♛ 8

Valle Reale

LOC. SAN CALISTO
65026 POPOLI [PE]
TEL. 0859871039
www.vallereale.it

CELLAR SALES
PRE-BOOKED VISITS

ANNUAL PRODUCTION 565,000 bottles
HECTARES UNDER VINE 60
VITICULTURE METHOD Conventional

The stunning Capestrano and Popoli estates guarantee distinctive wines whose key trait is elegance. These are two mountain vineyards: Popoli on the slopes of the Majella massif and Capestrano in the Gran Sasso foothills. Extreme altitudes, cool climate and extensive temperature ranges create wines shaped by the cold and the rock.

The Montepulciano San Calisto '06 was the year's top scorer in its class for its refined elegance and stylish aromatics. The palate is well-managed and full, with savouriness sustaining progression. The real surprise was the new Trebbiano Vigna di Capestrano '07, ambitiously executed with spontaneous fermentation and no filtration for a natural yet crisp, modern wine. The wager has been won. The typical toasty aromas are those of a great Trebbiano, with some initial citrus that then makes way for smoother, layered flavours at the back. Valle Reale '07 is a classic, elegant Montepulciano with a fresh, appealing progression. The basic Vigne Nuove line is well typed and well priced.

Valori

VIA TORQUATO AL SALINELLO, 8
64027 SANT'OMERO [TE]
TEL. 086188461
vinivalori@tin.it

PRE-BOOKED VISITS

ANNUAL PRODUCTION 30,000 bottles
HECTARES UNDER VINE 16
VITICULTURE METHOD Conventional

To understand the Valori winery, you have to see the obsessively well-tended Sant_Omero vines. The estates are over in the heartland of the Colline Teramane, almost in the Marches. This area gives grapes of excellent quality that make assertive, complex reds, which Valori produces with the assistance of the technical facilities of Marina Cvetic Masciarelli, who is a partner in the winery.

The wines are few but crafted with care and passion. Montepulciano Vigna Sant'Angelo, a wine we have praised recently, was not presented. Its place was taken by a newcomer, a pure Merlot as original as its name: Inkiostro. The inky hue introduces complex layers of blackberry and tobacco and the powerful, concentrated palate is delicate yet full flavoured. It's an excellent, full-bodied, compact Mediterranean Merlot. The simple, big-numbers Montepulciano d'Abruzzo '08 maintained its usual quality. The Trebbiano '08 is a crisp, consistent expression of the grape, a modern, drinkable white with persuasive progression.

● Montepulciano d'Abruzzo San Calisto '06	♀♀♀+ 6
● Montepulciano d'Abruzzo Valle Reale '07	♀♀ 4*
○ Trebbiano d'Abruzzo V. di Capestrano '07	♀♀ 5
☉ Montepulciano d'Abruzzo Cerasuolo Vigne Nuove '08	♀ 3*
○ Trebbiano d'Abruzzo Vigne Nuove '08	♀♀ 3*
● Montepulciano d'Abruzzo Vigne Nuove '08	♀ 3
● Montepulciano d'Abruzzo San Calisto '05	♀♀♀ 6
● Montepulciano d'Abruzzo San Calisto '04	♀♀♀ 6
● Montepulciano d'Abruzzo Valle Reale '06	♀♀♀ 4*
● Montepulciano d'Abruzzo San Calisto '03	♀♀ 5
● Montepulciano d'Abruzzo Valle Reale '04	♀♀ 4
● Montepulciano d'Abruzzo Vigne Nuove '06	♀♀ 2*
○ Trebbiano d'Abruzzo Vigne Nuove '07	♀♀ 4*

● Inkiostro '05	♀♀ 5
● Montepulciano d'Abruzzo '08	♀♀ 3*
○ Trebbiano d'Abruzzo '08	♀♀ 3*
● Montepulciano d'Abruzzo V. Sant' Angelo '03	♀♀♀ 5
● Montepulciano d'Abruzzo '07	♀♀ 3*
● Montepulciano d'Abruzzo V. Sant' Angelo '05	♀♀ 5
● Montepulciano d'Abruzzo V. Sant' Angelo '04	♀♀ 5
● Montepulciano d'Abruzzo V. Sant'Angelo '06	♀♀ 5

Villa Medoro

FRAZ. FONTANELLE
64030 ATRI [TE]
TEL. 0858708142
www.villamedoro.it

CELLAR SALES
PRE-BOOKED VISITS

ANNUAL PRODUCTION **300,000 bottles**
HECTARES UNDER VINE **N.D.**
VITICULTURE METHOD **Conventional**

This admirable Atri winery on the Colline Teramane comprises almost 100 hectares of vines tended like a garden by the enthusiastic staff and, above all, by a thoroughly charming owner, Federica Morricone, whose commitment to wine is quite contagious. These are the secrets of Villa Medoro, which has taken less than a decade to carve itself a niche in the forefront of Abruzzo winemaking.

We again tasted some valid wines and Three Glasses went to the famous Adrano in an impressive '06 version. This Montepulciano Colline Teramane has elegant, varietal notes, a fine, intense nose, and a well-handled mouthfeel with a round, savoury structure. The Montepulciano '07 is very convincing. It's not easy to find a wine of this quality at such a low price. The Rosso del Duca '07 is a modern, full-bodied Montepulciano. The whites included two '08s, a Chimera trebbiano and falanghina blend, and a simple, effective Trebbiano. The new Vigna San Martino '07 is an ambitious Trebbiano but still marked by the oak. The Cerasuolo '08 is excellent.

Ciccio Zaccagnini

C.DA POZZO
65020 BOLOGNANO [PE]
TEL. 0858880195
www.cantinazaccagnini.it

CELLAR SALES
PRE-BOOKED VISITS

ANNUAL PRODUCTION **1.200,000 bottles**
HECTARES UNDER VINE **150**
VITICULTURE METHOD **Conventional**

Zaccagnini of Bolognano has played a significant role in Abruzzo winemaking for over 30 years. The up-to-date cellars process grapes from various parts of the region, in particular the hills on the Pescara side of the Majella massif. There are wines for all purposes, ranging from fresh rosés to more high-profile, modern Montepulcianos, but the laudable aim is always to reconcile quality and quantity.

There were quite a few wines but there was no sign of the new version of the top-of-the-range Trebbiano San Clemente. The masterly Montepulciano d'Abruzzo Terre di Casauria San Clemente Riserva '06 made its debut with a new subzone designation. The beefy Montepulciano Castello di Salle '06 is marred by a hint of bitterness in the finish. Montepulciano Cuvée dell'Abate '07, however, has very varietal pervasive aromas, and a round, savoury palate. The Montepulciano Tralcetto '07, as usual, is charming and well made. The white Pecorino Yamada '08 has layered aromas and an intense palate. The others are all at least well typed.

● Montepulciano d'Abruzzo Colline Teramane Adrano '06	♟♟♟ 6
● Montepulciano d'Abruzzo '07	♟♟ 3*
○ Chimera Bianco '08	♟♟ 4*
⊙ Montepulciano d'Abruzzo Cerasuolo '08	♟♟ 3*
● Montepulciano d'Abruzzo Rosso del Duca '07	♟♟ 4
○ Trebbiano d'Abruzzo '08	♟♟ 3*
○ Trebbiano d'Abruzzo V. San Martino '07	♟♟ 5
● Montepulciano d'Abruzzo '06	♟♟♟ 3*
● Montepulciano d'Abruzzo Colline Teramane Adrano '05	♟♟♟ 6
● Montepulciano d'Abruzzo Colline Teramane Adrano '04	♟♟♟ 6
● Montepulciano d'Abruzzo Colline Teramane Adrano '03	♟♟♟ 6
● Montepulciano d'Abruzzo Rosso del Duca '06	♟♟ 4*
● Montepulciano d'Abruzzo Rosso del Duca '05	♟♟ 4*
● Montepulciano d'Abruzzo Rosso del Duca '04	♟♟ 4*

● Montepulciano d'Abruzzo Castello di Salle '06	♟♟ 4*
● Montepulciano d'Abruzzo Terre di Casauria S. Clemente Ris. '06	♟♟ 7
● Montepulciano d'Abruzzo Cuvée dell'Abate '07	♟♟ 3*
● Montepulciano d'Abruzzo Tralcetto '07	♟♟ 3*
○ Plaisir Bianco '08	♟♟ 5
○ Yamada '08	♟♟ 4*
● Montepulciano d'Abruzzo Chronicon '06	♟ 4
● Capsico Rosso '00	♟♟ 5
○ Chardonnay Abbazia S. Clemente '03	♟♟ 5
● Montepulciano d'Abruzzo Abbazia S. Clemente '02	♟♟ 6
● Montepulciano d'Abruzzo Abbazia S. Clemente '00	♟♟ 5
● Montepulciano d'Abruzzo S. Clemente '06	♟♟ 6
● Montepulciano d'Abruzzo S. Clemente '05	♟♟ 6
● Montepulciano d'Abruzzo S. Clemente '04	♟♟ 6
● Montepulciano d'Abruzzo S. Clemente '03	♟♟ 6

Tenute Barone di Valforte

C.DA PIOMBA, 11
64029 SILVI MARINA [TE]
TEL. 0859353432
www.baronedivalforte.it

Guido Sorricchio runs his Pescara hills winery with passion, improving each year. The big house wines were missing but all the '08s did well. The Montepulciano has fine-woven tannins and an elegant, fruit-rich body. The fresh Pecorino is one of the best. The Trebbiano and the Cerasuolo are well typed.

● Montepulciano d'Abruzzo '08	♟♟	3*
○ Pecorino '08	♟♟	4*
⊙ Montepulciano d'Abruzzo Cerasuolo '08	♟	3*
○ Trebbiano d'Abruzzo '08	♟	3*

Nestore Bosco

C.DA CASALI, 147
65010 NOCCIANO [PE]
TEL. 085847345
www.nestorebosco.com

As usual, Bosco presented two lines. We weren't so sure about the richly extracted modern wines with high-flown names but the more traditional line is persuasive enough. The best of the bunch is the Trebbiano d'Abruzzo '08, an appealing varietal white that relies on acidity and freshness.

○ Trebbiano d'Abruzzo '08	♟♟	4*
● Montepulciano d'Abruzzo Don Bosco '05	♟	5
○ Pecorino '08	♟	4
● Montepulciano d'Abruzzo Don Bosco '04	♟♟	5

Chiarieri

C.DA GRANARO, 18
65019 PIANELLA [PE]
TEL. 085973313
www.chiarieri.it

We quite liked the wines we tasted, which were all typical and hit the mark. Some are a little too naive, or tend to be over-concentrated. In general, the simpler, huskier whites are better with the Montepulcianos suffering from an old-school tendency to favour overripe fruit.

○ Trebbiano d'Abruzzo Invidia '08	♟♟	3*
○ Trebbiano d'Abruzzo Senso '06	♟♟	4
● Montepulciano d'Abruzzo Hannibal '04	♟	5
○ Trebbiano d'Abruzzo Granaro '07	♟♟	3*

Giuseppe Ciavolich

LOC. QUATTRO STRADE
C.DA CERRETO, 37
66010 MIGLIANICO [CH]
TEL. 0871958797
www.ciavolich.com

This traditional winery in the Chieti hills has a century of winemaking under its belt. The mature Antrum '03 is an ambitious, minerally Montepulciano. Ancilla '08 has evolved, husky notes. The full-bodied Pecorino Aries '08 with its attractive palate is good. Trebbiano Divus '08 isn't bad.

● Montepulciano d'Abruzzo Ancilla '08	♟	4
● Montepulciano d'Abruzzo Antrum '03	♟	6
○ Pecorino Aries '08	♟	4
○ Trebbiano d'Abruzzo Divus '08	♟	3

Citra

C.DA CUCULLO
66026 ORTONA [CH]
TEL. 0859031342
www.citra.it

Each year, Citra sends a huge range of wines, from supermarket whites to high-flying Montepulcianos. All are modern and winemaking is impeccable. As usual, we enjoyed the crisp, eminently drinkable Trebbiano, Pecorino and Montepulciano from the Sistina line.

○ Trebbiano d'Abruzzo Sistina '08	♟♟	3*
○ Pecorino Sistina '08	♟	3
● Montepulciano d'Abruzzo Sistina '06	♟♟	4*

Col del Mondo

C.DA CAMPOTINO, 35c
65010 COLLECORVINO [PE]
TEL. 0858207831
www.coldelmondo.com

This Collecorvino winery in the Chieti hills offers a value-for-money range that includes an excellent Montepulciano d'Abruzzo '06. Elegant aromas combine with a tannic palate the slightly bitter finish marked it down. The simple, true-to-type Trebbiano and Montepulciano Sunnae aren't bad.

● Montepulciano d'Abruzzo '06	♟♟	4*
● Montepulciano d'Abruzzo Sunnae '07	♟	3
○ Trebbiano d'Abruzzo Sunnae '08	♟	3
● Montepulciano d'Abruzzo '05	♟♟	4*

OTHER WINERIES

De Angelis Corvi

C.DA PIGNOTTO
64010 CONTROGUERRA [TE]
TEL. 086189475
www.deangeliscorvi.it

This interesting new Colline Teramane winery didn't offer much for tasting this year and its high-profile labels were missing. The succulent Montepulciano d'Abruzzo '07 is true to type but sadly closes on very bitter tannins. The uncomplicated Trebbiano '08 is a good example of its genre.

○ Trebbiano d'Abruzzo Fonte Raviliano '08	♟♟	3*
● Montepulciano d'Abruzzo Fonte Raviliano '07	♟	4

Tenuta I Fauri

S.DA CORTA, 9
66100 CHIETI
TEL. 0871332627
www.tenutaifauri.it

This renowned Chieti hills winery can't reap the rewards it deserves. The wines are well managed but just don't take off. The Pecorino '08 has typical, layered aromas with aromatic hints. The simple Montepulciano Ottobre Rosso '08 is husky. The Baldovino line Trebbiano and Montepulciano aren't bad.

○ Pecorino dei Fauri '08	♟♟	4
● Montepulciano d'Abruzzo Baldovino '08	♟	3
● Montepulciano d'Abruzzo Ottobre Rosso '08	♟	4
○ Trebbiano d'Abruzzo Baldovino '08	♟	3

Il Feuduccio di Santa Maria d'Orni

VIA FEUDUCCIO, 1A
66036 ORSOGNA [CH]
TEL. 0871891646
www.ilfeuduccio.it

We_re pleased to see this Pescara hills winery back, although the ace was missing. In the past, we picked out Montepulciano Margae but we liked the simple Fonte Venna '07 we tried this year. This rounded, savoury Montepulciano is still veiled by oak. Yare '07 is a varietal, fruit-rich Pecorino.

● Montepulciano d'Abruzzo Fonte Venna '07	♟♟	4*
○ Yare '07	♟♟	4*

Filomusi Guelfi

VIA F. FILOMUSI GUELFI, 11
65028 TOCCO DA CASAURIA [PE]
TEL. 085986908
elleffegi@tiscali.it

Lorenzo Filomusi's has a passion for Abruzzo wine and a traditional way of making wine. Sadly, the wines sometimes disappoint as they are just too rustic. The best we tried is the Fonte Dei '04, which already came up last year. The others are simpler. They_re generally well managed but that's it.

● Montepulciano d'Abruzzo '06	♟	4
⊙ Montepulciano d'Abruzzo Cerasuolo '08	♟	3
● Montepulciano d'Abruzzo Fonte Dei '01	♟♟	6

Gentile

VIA DEL GIARDINO, 7
67025 OFENA [AQ]
TEL. 0862956618
www.gentilevini.it

This Alto Tirino winery sent just three labels for tasting. The Zeus won a place in the finals again for its '06 vintage. It's a varietal Montepulciano with nicely subtle fruit-rich aromas and a pleasant palate that shows vibrant and fresh. We also liked the more muscular Zefiro '05.

● Montepulciano d'Abruzzo Zeus '06	♟♟	6
● Montepulciano d'Abruzzo Zefiro '05	♟♟	5
○ Trebbiano d'Abruzzo Ares '08	♟	3
● Montepulciano d'Abruzzo Zeus '05	♟♟	6

Antonio e Elio Monti

VIA PIGNOTTO, 62
64010 CONTROGUERRA [TE]
TEL. 086189042
www.vinimonti.it

We were taken with just two of the wines tasted, which is not enough to award a full profile to this well-established winery. Senior '04 is a traditional, varietal Colline Teramane with balsamic aromas and a pleasantly husky, full body. Raggio di Luna '08 is a well-typed Chardonnay with a fruit-rich palate.

○ Controguerra Bianco Raggio di Luna '08	♟♟	4*
● Montepulciano d'Abruzzo Colline Teramane Senior '04	♟♟	4

OTHER WINERIES

Pietrantonj

VIA SAN SEBASTIANO, 38
67030 VITTORITO [AQ]
TEL. 0864727102
www.vinipietrantonj.it

These are mountain wines with a traditional style and sharp acidity but they can be a bit too rustic. We liked the fresh Trebbiano Arboreo '08 best for its varietal aromas and relaxed progression. The edgy, rustic Montepulciano from the same range is rather too lean in this 2006 version and not so appealing.

○ Trebbiano d'Abruzzo Arboreo '08	♥♥	4
● Montepulciano d'Abruzzo Arboreo '06	♥	5
● Montepulciano d'Abruzzo Cerano '05	♥♥	3*

Tenuta del Priore

C.DA CAMPOTINO, 35C
65010 COLLECORVINO [PE]
TEL. 0858207162
www.priore.it

This winery at Collecorvino, in the Pescara hills, presented a nice range of wines. Montepulciano Il Vecchio Priore '06 got through to national finals with its typical, pervasive aromas and a savoury palato that unfolds elegantly. The appealing '08 Trebbiano and Montepulciano Campotino are both well typed.

● Montepulciano d'Abruzzo Il Vecchio Priore '06	♥♥	5
● Montepulciano d'Abruzzo Campotino '08	♥	2
○ Trebbiano d'Abruzzo Campotino '08	♥	2

Strappelli

LOC. TORRI
VIA TORRI, 15
64010 TORANO NUOVO [TE]
TEL. 0861887402
www.cantinastrappelli.it

We_re very fond of this country winery. The wines have a traditional, typical style but only two labels were sent for tasting this year. We preferred the Montepulciano '06, which strolled through to national finals thanks to complex aromas with lively fruit to the fore and a full, nicely savoury palate.

● Montepulciano d'Abruzzo '06	♥♥	4*
○ Pecorino Soprano '08	♥	4
● Montepulciano d'Abruzzo '05	♥♥	4*
◉ Montepulciano d'Abruzzo Cerasuolo '07	♥♥	4*

Tenimenti del Grifone

VIA ISTONIA, 81 2E
66054 VASTO [CH]
TEL. 3358390720
www.vinimastrangelo.com

These wines are quite persuasive. Oro del Cardinale '05 is a true-to-type Trebbiano, evolved with subtle, complex aromas and a refined progression. The varietal, pervasive Montepulciano La Riserva del Vicario '04 has a refined palate, even if the tannins are somewhat rough

● Montepulciano d'Abruzzo		
La Riserva del Vicario '04	♥♥	5
○ Trebbiano d'Abruzzo L'Oro del Cardinale '05	♥♥	5

Terra d'Aligi

LOC. PIAZZANO
VIA PIANA LA FARA, 90
66041 ATESSA [CH]
TEL. 0872897916
www.terradaligi.it

It wasn't such a good performance from Terra d'Aligi. We liked the 2006 Tatone, a potent, noble Montepulciano, but the overripe aromas were too evolved despite a generous palate with good extract. Tolos is a quintessentially husky Montepulciano the tannins are a little rough.

● Montepulciano d'Abruzzo Tatone '06	♥♥	4
● Montepulciano d'Abruzzo '07	♥	3
● Montepulciano d'Abruzzo Tolos '06	♥	6
● Montepulciano d'Abruzzo Tolos '05	♥♥	6

Valle Martello

C.DA VALLE MARTELLO, 10
66010 VILLAMAGNA [CH]
TEL. 0871300330
katmasci@vallemartello.net

The wines that the Masci family's country winery turns out are never a let-down. The seamless Montepulciano d'Abruzzo '08 is spot on with a fresh, varietal palate. The drinkable Trebbiano '08 has varietal, toasty notes and a crisp palate. The other Montepulcianos aren't bad.

● Montepulciano d'Abruzzo '08	♥♥	3*
○ Trebbiano d'Abruzzo '08	♥♥	3*
● Montepulciano d'Abruzzo Brado '08	♥	4
● Montepulciano d'Abruzzo Prima Terra '06	♥	5

MOLISE

Molise is one of Italy's smallest regions, comprising mainly mountains and tableland. The climate, at least inland, tends to be more similar to the north than to the Mediterranean area where Molise is actually located. Nonetheless, the region enjoys an excellent standard of viticulture that continues to improve with each passing season. The vine heritage is typical of crossroads regions where various traditions meet and the most widely planted grape is montepulciano. It came from neighbouring Abruzzo, a very different region altogether but which was administratively united with Molise for decades. Then we have trebbiano, also from Abruzzo, while falanghina comes from Sannio, a subregion Molise shares with Campania. Other varieties include greco from Irpinia and, above all, aglianico, whose domain starts shyly here extending confidently into Puglia's centre-north, Campania, Basilicata and even small areas of Calabria. The only wine we picked out this year was in fact a Molise Aglianico, Alessio Di Majo Norante's '07 Contado Riserva, which not only picked up Three Glasses but also received a prestigious pat on the back for being the best-value wine of the year. But the grape now making its mark on the Molise wine scene is tintilia, a native variety back in the limelight after years of neglect. This is excellent news and it shows the region is now truly independent in its wine production. No longer does Molise have to rely on varieties that may be traditional but are better known and more popular in other areas. An admirable wine from this grape made our finals, the Molise Tintilia Rutilia '07 by Pasquale Salvatore, a winemaker who bodes well for the future of quality wines in this region. Of course, there are still very few wineries around but the results in this edition of the Guide are clear signals of very encouraging overall improvement. Which is also great news.

Borgo di Colloredo

LOC. NUOVA CLITERNIA
C.DA ZEZZA, 8
86042 CAMPOMARINO [CB]
TEL. 087557453
www.borgodicolloredo.com

CELLAR SALES
PRE-BOOKED VISITS
VISITOR FACILITIES
FOOD

ANNUAL PRODUCTION 300,000 bottles
HECTARES UNDER VINE 60
VITICULTURE METHOD Conventional

Once again, Cantina Borgo di Colloredo wines came up with the goods. For years, the Di Giulio family has been enthusiastically managing a winery whose vineyards are located in the municipality of Campomarino, a stone's throw from the Molise coast. For this year's Guide, the winery proved its solid ongoing commitment with a range of appealing, excellent-value wines. In the past, the whites have prevailed but this year the reds earned some well-justified praise.

The usual vibrant Greco '08, with varietal aromas and a firm, confident palate, was flanked by a persuasive Biferno Bianco Gironia '08 that shows nice aromatics on a tropical nose and full, fresh flavour. The reds were also surprising. The '06 Molise Rosso Montepulciano, whose subtle nose had ripe notes and a modern-style palate, despite rather raw tannins, finished confidently long. The '04 Biferno Rosso Gironia has slightly over-evolved aromas but a full-bodied, concentrated palate. Over-assertive extract in the '06 Aglianico made it less appealing. Lastly, Falanghina del Molise '08 and Biferno Rosato Gironia '08 are both uncomplicated and drinkable.

Di Majo Norante

FRAZ. NUOVA CLITERNIA
C.DA RAMITELLI, 4
86042 CAMPOMARINO [CB]
TEL. 087557208
www.dimajonorante.com

CELLAR SALES
PRE-BOOKED VISITS

ANNUAL PRODUCTION 800,000 bottles
HECTARES UNDER VINE 85
VITICULTURE METHOD Organic certified

We applaud an excellent performance from the Di Majo Norante winery, which has to deliver as it's the leader in a region that still lags behind on Italy's wine scene. Owner Alessio Di Majo has strong bonds with this territory and has recently been achieving some great results with his wines thanks to hard work in the vineyard and investment in the cellar. It's example to be imitated but also proof that despite its modest size, Molise has potential.

Three Glasses went to a plush Aglianico del Molise Contado Riserva '07 for its layered, balsamic aromas. This mouthfilling red has great structure but also depth, with a long finish hinting it will improve with age. The top of the range Molise Rosso Don Luigi Riserva '07, a montepulciano and aglianico blend, gives intense, complex aromas and a forceful palate with plenty of backbone, although it's slightly masked by the oak. The winery's emblematic Biferno Rosso Ramitello Riserva '07, from montepulciano and aglianico, was on its best-ever form. We loved its aromas of mountain herbs and liquorice, and the soft-textured, balanced finish.

○ Biferno Bianco Gironia '08	♥♥	4*
● Biferno Rosso Gironia '04	♥♥	4*
○ Greco '08	♥♥	3*
● Molise Montepulciano '06	♥♥	4*
● Aglianico '06	♥	4
⊙ Biferno Rosato Gironia '08	♥	4
○ Molise Falanghina '08	♥	4
● Aglianico '05	♀♀	4*
● Biferno Rosso Gironia '00	♀♀	4
● Biferno Rosso Gironia '98	♀♀	4
○ Greco '07	♀♀	3*

● Molise Aglianico Contado Ris. '07	♥♥♥	4*
● Biferno Rosso Ramitello Ris. '07	♥♥	4*
● Molise Don Luigi Ris. '07	♥♥	6
○ Molise Apianae '07	♥♥	5
● Molise Tintilia '06	♥♥	5
○ Molì Bianco '08	♥	2
⊙ Molì Rosato '08	♥	3
● Molì Rosso '08	♥	3
○ Molise Falanghina '08	♥	4
○ Molise Greco '08	♥	4
● Sangiovese '08	♥	3
● Molise Aglianico Contado '03	♀♀♀	4*
● Molise Aglianico Contado '99	♀♀♀	4*
● Molise Don Luigi '05	♀♀♀	6
● Molise Don Luigi '99	♀♀♀	5
● Molise Don Luigi Ris. '06	♀♀♀	6

I.A.C. - Catabbo

c.da Petriera
86046 San Martino in Pensilis [CB]
tel. 0875604945
www.catabbo.it

CELLAR SALES

ANNUAL PRODUCTION 160,000 bottles
HECTARES UNDER VINE 40
VITICULTURE METHOD Conventional

We're pleased to give the Catabbo winery space among the main profiles, rewarding the family's commitment over recent years. Vincenzo is at the helm of this family business whose splendid vineyards surround the San Martino in Pensilis winery, where everyone has been working hard to improve standards overall. The Catabbos are leaders in the revival of tintilia, a vine they have invested in heavily and which they hope will soon repay their faith.

The '05 Molise Rosso Vincè was a worthy finalist. This montepulciano, merlot and syrah blend has layered aromas and a powerful yet balanced and restrained palate that closes in lingering harmony. Both tintilia wines were admirable. Molise Tintilia '06 has a fruit-rich nose and an enfolding palate while the more rustic Riserva '05 is evolved on the nose. Rosso Petriera '08, a Montepulciano with secondary aromas, has good structure. Bianco Petriera '08, a trebbiano and chardonnay blend, is peach-themed and offers a tangy, juicy palate. Standards are impressive throughout the range, which we trust will stay true to form in the future.

● Molise Rosso Vincè '05	🍷🍷 6
● Molise Tintilia '06	🍷🍷 5
● Molise Tintilia Ris. '05	🍷🍷 6
○ Petriera Bianco '08	🍷🍷 3
● Petriera Rosso '08	🍷🍷 3
● Molise Tintilia Ris. '04	🍷🍷 6

Cantine Salvatore

c.da Vigne
86049 Ururi [CB]
tel. 0874830656
www.cantinesalvatore.it

CELLAR SALES
PRE-BOOKED VISITS

ANNUAL PRODUCTION 40,000 bottles
HECTARES UNDER VINE 15
VITICULTURE METHOD Conventional

Pasquale Salvatore is Molise's youngest winemaker. His enthusiasm and his love of this territory are helping him develop a first-rate business in the village of Ururi, where he has recently invested in the family estate. Pasquale is determined to upgrade his vines and refurbish his cellar. He has support from a talented oenologist, Carmine De Iure, in a project to re-establish the quintessential Molise grape, tintilia. It was our favourite from the range we tasted.

The '07 Molise Tintilia Rutilia is a fine wine and made this year's finals. The nose is well-developed and intense, with a nice balsamic note and varietal aromatics introducing a juicy, full-bodied palate with an appealing long finish that bodes well for future vintages. Falanghina del Molise Nysias '08 has improved significantly over last year, with an intense, slightly evolved nose and a full, pervasive palate that shows the wine to best advantage. The montepulciano-only Molise Rosso Biberius '08 is stiff and cropped, with over-evolved aromas, although it impresses rather more on the palate.

● Molise Tintilia Rutilia '07	🍷🍷 5
○ Molise Falanghina Nysias '08	🍷🍷 4*
● Molise Rosso Biberius '08	🍷 4

Cianfagna

C.DA BOSCO PAMPINI, 3
86030 ACQUAVIVA COLLECROCE [CB]
TEL. 0875970253
www.cianfagna.com

Vincenzo Cianfagna is a tintilia specialist, as his Molise Tintilia Sator '07 proves with its varietal aromas of spice and wild herbs and soft palate with slightly aggressive tannins. Vincenzo's top wine is Aglianico del Molise Riserva '04, a mighty, concentrated red with lovely weight and texture.

● Molise Aglianico Militum Christi Ris. '04	▼▼	5
● Molise Tintilia Sator '07	▼▼	6
● Pietrafitta '07	▼	5

Cantine Cipressi

C.DA MONTAGNA
86030 SAN FELICE DEL MOLISE [CB]
TEL. 0874874535
www.cantinecipressi.it

Sadly, for editorial reasons, we had to relegate the Cipressi winery to the Other Wineries, despite the overall quality of the entire range. Molise Tintilia Macchiarossa '07 gives characteristic spicy aromas and the powerful Montepulciano Molise Rosso Mekan '07 is nice. The future is bright.

● Molise Rosso Mekan '07	▼▼	4*
● Molise Tintilia Macchiarossa '07	▼▼	5
● Molise Aglianico Elkon '07	▼	4
● Molise Rosso Rumen '07	▼	3

D'Uva

C.DA RICUPO, 13
86035 LARINO [CB]
TEL. 0874822320
www.cantineduva.com

Again this year, the D'Uva winery, deep in the Larino countryside, presented a limited range. The Molise Kantharos '08 and Keres '08 are both trebbiano-based whites, which we found to be uncomplicated, well-made wines with hints of citrus Kantharos is nicely tangy and Keres is riper and more aromatic.

○ Keres '08	▼	3
○ Molise Trebbiano Kantharos '08	▼	4

Masserie Flocco

C.DA DIFENSOLA
86045 PORTOCANNONE [CB]
TEL. 0875590032
www.masserieflocco.com

The wines from the Portocannone winery were not quite up to previous standards. Overall the range was decent, with the Falanghina '08 and chardonnay-based Podere del Canneto '08 a notch better than the rest. We hope to see the winery back on form soon.

○ Falanghina '08	▼▼	3
○ Podere del Canneto '08	▼▼	3

Terresacre

C.DA MONTEBELLO
86036 MONTENERO DI BISACCIA [CB]
TEL. 0875960191
www.terresacre.net

Terresacre at Montenero di Bisaccia, on the Abruzzo border, is a Guide newcomer. The wines are good. Molise Trebbiano Orovite '08 has pleasing aromas and a tangy, concentrated palate. The simpler Molise Rosso Neravite '07 gives blackberries. The winery's flagship, Molise Rosso Tempora '06, is richly extracted but shows too much oak.

● Molise Rosso Tempora '06	▼▼	5
○ Molise Trebbiano Orovite '08	▼▼	3
● Molise Rosso Neravite '07	▼	3

CAMPANIA

No offence to Pliny and Livy, but we think that the present of Campanian wine is just as fascinating as the glorious past they chronicled. The ancient historians tell of Greek colonists and emperors, legendary Falerno wines and vines that came from the sea. Our rather more modest task is to describe what is currently making Campania one of the most stimulating areas for wine enthusiasts. Everything here seems to be celebrating diversity: an unusually rich ampelographic heritage, numerous zones and subzones with very different soil and climate conditions that yield wines all sorts of temperaments, and a firmament of wineries with their own histories, sensibilities, numbers and stylistic identities. The region is certainly no stranger to contradictions and delays but it seems to have room for both huge producers turning out millions of bottles and small producers with long-standing estates joined by dozens of newcomers each year. In this situation, our task of screening is increasingly difficult but also very exciting. The Guide lists just under half the estates that took part at our tastings and of the almost 1,000 wines that we assessed, readers will find around 60 selected for the finals. We awarded Three Glasses to 16 wines. In an imaginary journey from north to south, we first encounter a fantastic trio by consultant Riccardo Cotarella, who knows how to bring out the different temperaments of aglianico in the area north of Caserta: Galardi's Terra di Lavoro '07, Adolfo Spada's Gladius '07 and Villa Matilde's Falerno del Massico Camarato '05. A few kilometres further south, Terre del Principe completes a winning brace, bringing casavecchia back into the limelight after pallagrello with the explosive Centomoggia '07. While the province of Naples shows a few hesitant signs of recovery, particularly in Ischia and Campi Flegrei, the situation appears more alarming in Sannio, where the best performers are from Fattoria La Rivolta. Costa d'Amalfi continues to come on, with the new star of Fiorduva shining in the '08 vintage, while the memorable '07 version of Montevetrano rules supreme in the Salerno hills. Cilento does not look to be particularly dynamic but can always count on Luigi Maffini and his Pietraincatenata '07. In Irpinia, the surprising '05 vintage for Taurasi finally allowed Di Prisco and Urciuolo to achieve their first, well-deserved Three Glass award, alongside Mastroberardino's Radici and Molettieri's Cinque Querce, which encored with the Riserva '04. Turning to the whites, Pietracupa and Vadiaperti col Tornante are the best representatives of Greco di Tufo '08. Lapio chimed in with another fantastic pair, formed by the '08 Fiano di Avellinos by Rocca del Principe and Colli di Lapio, which took the White of the Year award in this year's Guide.

A Casa

LOC. PIANODARDINE
FILANDE, 6
83100 AVELLINO
TEL. 0825626406
www.cantineacasa.it

CELLAR SALES

ANNUAL PRODUCTION 200,000 bottles
HECTARES UNDER VINE 64
VITICULTURE METHOD Conventional

Behind A Casa's adventure lies one of the most important and ambitious projects launched in Campania in recent years. The newly founded Avellino winery sees the return to action of Enzo Ercolino, former chairman of Feudi di San Gregorio, aided by other prominent figures, such as Tommaso Iavarone, Claudio Velardi, Antonio Napoli and Paolo Vasquez. From the very outset, priority was given to the purchase of vineyards and strategically located land, and in the long term we look forward to a well-established medium-sized winery that concentrates on Irpinia and Sannio's main varieties.

The very satisfactory quality quickly achieved by the cellar's wines does not prevent us from expressing a few reservations, particularly with regard to our high expectations. Accentuation of the fruity and fermentative characteristics of the whites seems to limit varietal and territorial expression. The factors that impress in terms of technical precision and substance in the glass tend to detract from the wines' personality. But Greco di Tufo Bussi '08 is excellent. The reds, too, focus on softness rather than grip, ultimately making Piedirosso Fiore dell'Isca '07 the most articulate wine on the list.

Antonio Caggiano

C.DA SALA
83030 TAURASI [AV]
TEL. 082774723
www.cantinecaggiano.it

CELLAR SALES
PRE-BOOKED VISITS
VISITOR FACILITIES
FOOD

ANNUAL PRODUCTION 150,000 bottles
HECTARES UNDER VINE 20
VITICULTURE METHOD Conventional

Regardless of what you think of his wines, Antonio Caggiano is one of those figures who has done, and continues to do, much good for the Irpinia wine world. From the very outset, the globetrotting photographer with a love of wine brought a breath of fresh air to the area and an approach driven by curiosity and gambles rather than certainties. Together with his friend and advisor Luigi Moio, Antonio is responsible for the first modern Taurasi, as well as one of Irpinia's first real crus, the much lauded Vigna Macchia dei Goti.

This was one of the estate's best performances ever, with three wines in the finals and, above all, the emergence of an easily recognisable style, far removed from exaggeration and corner-cutting. Both the reds and the whites show well-calibrated use of small oak casks that enhances their fruity notes without affecting grip or drinkability. Greco di Tufo Devon '08 and Fiano di Avellino Béchar '08 both tempt with invigorating, flavoursome progression on the palate while Taurasi Vigna Macchia dei Goti '05 is appealingly elegant, with earthy notes and hints of spicy oak, faltering slightly only on the finish.

○ Fiano di Avellino Oro del Passo '08	♀♀	4
○ Greco di Tufo Bussi '08	♀♀	4
● Sannio Piedirosso Fiore dell'Isca '07	♀♀	4
● Irpinia Aglianico Vecchio Postale '07	♀	4
○ Sannio Coda di Volpe Bebiana '08	♀	4
○ Sannio Falanghina Cortenuda '08	♀	4
○ Fiano di Avellino '07	♀♀	4*
○ Greco di Tufo '07	♀♀	4*

○ Fiano di Avellino Béchar '08	♀♀	5
○ Greco di Tufo Devon '08	♀♀	5
● Taurasi V. Macchia dei Goti '05	♀♀	6
○ Fiagre '08	♀	4
● Irpinia Aglianico Taurì '07	♀	4
● Taurasi V. Macchia dei Goti '04	♀♀♀	6
● Taurasi V. Macchia dei Goti '99	♀♀♀	7
○ Fiano di Avellino Béchar '06	♀♀	4*
○ Greco di Tufo Devon '06	♀♀	4*
● Taurasi V. Macchia dei Goti '03	♀♀	6
● Taurasi V. Macchia dei Goti '01	♀♀	7
● Taurasi V. Macchia dei Goti '00	♀♀	7
● Taurasi V. Macchia dei Goti '98	♀♀	7

Viticoltori del Casavecchia

VIA MADONNA DELLE GRAZIE, 28
81040 PONTELATONE [CE]
TEL. 0823659198
www.viticoltoridelcasavecchia.it

CELLAR SALES
PRE-BOOKED VISITS

ANNUAL PRODUCTION **35,000 bottles**
HECTARES UNDER VINE **20**
VITICULTURE METHOD **Conventional**

The great little Pontelatone co-operative winery deserves far more attention than it has received so far. With 20 hectares of vineyards owned by 40 members, it is an important concern that is earning admiration for the special mix of humility and dedication shown by the successful, close-knit team of Alfonso Cutillo, Battista Perrone and Maurizio Alongi. Skilfully gauged oak is a feature of the three versions of casavecchia, used for a red wine, a rosé and a sweet wine. Pallagrello Bianco is the only white produced.

Vigna Prea, from casavecchia, reached our finals for the second year running. The '06 vintage has strikingly complex notes of rain-soaked earth and liquorice with impressively tight, flavoursome structure, avoiding the easy route of primary fruit aromatics. Futo '07 is one of Campania's best dried-grape wines and Sfizio Rosa '08 again reveals the potential of this local variety for scented, appetizing rosés. Pallagrello Bianco '08 is firm and crisp, while Casavecchia Corte Rosa '07 and Erta dei Ciliegi '08 are currently held back by a tad too much stiffness.

Colli di Castelfranci

C.DA BRAUDIANO
83040 CASTELFRANCI [AV]
TEL. 082772392
www.collidicastelfranci.com

CELLAR SALES
PRE-BOOKED VISITS
VISITOR FACILITIES
FOOD

ANNUAL PRODUCTION **160,000 bottles**
HECTARES UNDER VINE **25**
VITICULTURE METHOD **Natural**

With a 25-hectare estate and an annual production of around 160,000 bottles, Colli di Castelfranci is a mid-sized Irpinia winery run by brothers-in-law Gerardo Colucci and Mario Gregorio, with the aid of Carmine Valentino in the cellar. Ever since the first vintage in 2002, the estate's whites, all aged in steel, have impressed us with their definition and fragrance. We would like to see a little more acidity in the top reds, whose austere oak is very commendable.

Again, it was the whites that gave the best performance. The most notable is Greco di Tufo Grotte '08, with an original nose juxtaposing red fruit and musky notes, and a decidedly sharp palate enlivened by an attractive salty vein. Fiano di Avellino Pendino '08 drinks more extracted and glycerine-rich, showing less thrust but good weight. Taurasi Gagliardo '04 has a very pleasantly fresh, variegated nose but its tannins are a little too austere and it is somewhat short on finish. Paladino '08, from late-harvest fiano grapes, falls between two stools in some respects.

● Vigna Prea '06	♈	5
● Futo '07	♈	5
○ Pallagrello Bianco '08	♈	4*
☉ Sfizio Rosa '08	♈	3*
● Corte Rosa '07	♈	4
● Erta dei Ciliegi '08	♈	3
● Corte Rosa '06	♈♈	4*
● Erta dei Ciliegi '07	♈♈	3*
● Erta dei Ciliegi '06	♈♈	3*
☉ Sfizio Rosa '06	♈♈	3*
● Vigna Prea '05	♈♈	5

○ Greco di Tufo Grotte '08	♈	4*
○ Fiano di Avellino Pendino '08	♈	4*
● Taurasi Gagliardo '04	♈	6
☉ Irpinia Aglianico Rosato Crote '08	♈	4
○ Irpinia Paladino V. T. '08	♈	4
○ Fiano di Avellino Pendino '07	♈♈	4*
○ Fiano di Avellino Pendino '05	♈♈	4*
○ Greco di Tufo Grotte '07	♈♈	4*
☉ Irpinia Aglianico Rosato Crote '07	♈♈	4*
☉ Irpinia Aglianico Rosato Crote '07	♈♈	4*
○ Irpinia Paladino V. T. '07	♈♈	4*
○ Paladino '03	♈♈	5
○ Paladino V.T. '04	♈♈	4

Colli di Lapio

VIA ARIANIELLO, 47
83030 LAPIO [AV]
TEL. 0825982184
collidilapio@libero.it

CELLAR SALES
PRE-BOOKED VISITS

ANNUAL PRODUCTION **50,000 bottles**
HECTARES UNDER VINE **6**
VITICULTURE METHOD **Conventional**

Vineyard, terroir, winemaker and minerality. Take all these overused wine terms and for once have no fear of abusing them. We are talking about a genuine wine family, Angelo and Clelia Romano and their children, an incredible terroir for Fiano di Avellino, vineyards at Stazzone, Scarpone and Arianiello di Lapio, and a wine that is still far too little known but which has long deserved to belong to the elite of great Italian whites.

By the time you read this profile, approximately 80 per cent of the 30,000-bottle production will already have been drunk, as usual. This is understandable, because Fiano di Avellino '08 from Colli di Lapio is not a wine you have to wait for. It casts a spell that has you draining the glass to explore its overwhelming flavour and genuinely minerally, almost salty verve. This could cause some regret because like all top-notchers, it is good now but it will be even better in ten years' time, when a fantastic vintage for this wine will be at its peak. Wait to see why we chose it as our White of the Year this time.

Contrade di Taurasi

VIA MUNICIPIO, 39
83030 TAURASI [AV]
TEL. 0815442457
www.contradeditaurasi.it

CELLAR SALES
PRE-BOOKED VISITS

ANNUAL PRODUCTION **20,000 bottles**
HECTARES UNDER VINE **5**
VITICULTURE METHOD **Conventional**

Without detracting from Campania's many other important estates, the Lonardo family's operation really is what we'd call a serious winery. Loyal to its old peasant roots, it adopts a rigorous approach in both the vineyard and the cellar, rising to challenges and seeking a personal style that reflects years of experience. The way the Taurasi has gone is emblematic in this respect, for it refuses to fit into the tired two-category model of traditional and modern, faithfully expressing the volcanic terroirs of Case d'Alto, San Martino and Costa Morante.

While the '04 Taurasi was obviously the most complete and elegant interpretation of the vintage, the '05 version gave more contradictory results, with some bottles displaying an airy, dynamic profile and others with more sombre, clenched sensations. Its aromatics are probably still developing and we wouldn't be surprised to find it showing very well in a few years' time. Nonetheless, we thought that it lacked a little in pulp to accompany the fine but slightly dry tannins, in comparison with the best versions from a difficult vintage. The Irpinia Aglianico is also improving and the '07 version is excellent.

○ Fiano di Avellino '08	♟♟♟+ 5*
● Taurasi V. Andrea '05	♟ 6
● Campi Taurasini Irpinia Donna Chiara '07	♟♟ 5
○ Fiano di Avellino '07	♟♟♟ 5
○ Fiano di Avellino '05	♟♟♟ 5
○ Fiano di Avellino '04	♟♟♟ 5
● Campi Taurasini Irpinia Donna Chiara '06	♟♟ 5
● Campi Taurasini Irpinia Donna Chiara '06	♟♟ 5
○ Fiano di Avellino '03	♟♟ 5
○ Fiano di Avellino '02	♟♟ 5
○ Fiano di Avellino '01	♟♟ 5
● Taurasi Vigna Andrea '04	♟♟ 6
● Taurasi Vigna Andrea '03	♟♟ 6
● Taurasi Vigna Andrea '01	♟♟ 6

● Taurasi '05	♟♟ 7
● Irpinia Aglianico '07	♟♟ 4*
● Taurasi '04	♟♟♟ 7
● Aglianico '05	♟♟ 4
● Taurasi '03	♟♟ 6
● Taurasi '01	♟♟ 6
● Taurasi '00	♟♟ 6
● Taurasi '99	♟♟ 7
● Taurasi Ris. '01	♟♟ 7

Marisa Cuomo

VIA G. B. LAMA, 16/18
84010 FURORE [SA]
TEL. 089830348
www.granfuror.it

CELLAR SALES
PRE-BOOKED VISITS

ANNUAL PRODUCTION **97,000 bottles**
HECTARES UNDER VINE **14.5**
VITICULTURE METHOD **Natural**

Ripoli, Fenile and Ginestra form a sort of viticultural mantra underpinning the success of one of Italy's best-loved and most sought-after wines, and with it an entire zone that will be increasingly difficult not to consider among the great up-and-coming terroirs. Fiorduva is the symbol of Costa d'Amalfi and Marisa Cuomo is the leading winery in the exciting story that starts with the recovery of the vineyards in one of the most impervious and rugged areas of southern Italy.

Fiorduva won its fifth consecutive Three Glass award with the '08 vintage. As always, it did so very confidently, albeit with a more controversial profile than usual. The customary orange blossom mingles with nuances of almond and peat, echoed on a concentrated, dry palate that is still developing. Furore Bianco '08 is an entirely different kettle of fish. It's no base wine: this is a fantastic bottle from the coast, imbued with iodine and citrus notes and almost salty on the palate. A hint of alcohol and less than perfect tannins detract somewhat from the very good aglianico and piedirosso Furore Rosso Riserva '06.

D'Ambra Vini d'Ischia

FRAZ. PANZA
VIA MARIO D'AMBRA, 16
80077 FORIO [NA]
TEL. 081907210
www.dambravini.com

CELLAR SALES
PRE-BOOKED VISITS

ANNUAL PRODUCTION **500,000 bottles**
HECTARES UNDER VINE **18**
VITICULTURE METHOD **Conventional**

Founded in 1888, Casa D'Ambra is one of Campania's oldest wineries and the most important on Ischia, the largest of the islands in the Bay of Naples. It is run by Andrea D'Ambra, whose chief merit is to have combined the winery's image as an icon of island tradition with that of a highly innovative producer. On one hand, there are wines from biancolella, forastera, piedirosso and guarnaccia, and on the other we note several successful experiments with minor Aegean varieties and, more recently, other Campanian varieties such as fiano and greco.

While awaiting further new developments at the Calitto estate, we again noted the high quality of the classic wines. Ischia Biancolella Tenuta Frassitelli '08, aged in steel, completes a fabulous trio of vintages inaugurated by the '06. Like the most successful versions, it is initially bashful, its special touch lying in its delicacy and the fusion of its acidity. Ischia Biancolella '08 is not as deep but just as forthright and recognizable, while Ischia Bianco '08, from equal parts of biancolella and forastera, is very convincing on palate and pocketbook.

○ Costa d'Amalfi Fiorduva '08	♟♟♟	7
○ Costa d'Amalfi Bianco Furore '08	♟♟	5
● Costa d'Amalfi Rosso Furore Ris. '06	♟♟	7
○ Costa d'Amalfi Bianco Ravello '08	♟♟	5
⊙ Costa d'Amalfi Rosato '08	♟♟	5
● Costa d'Amalfi Rosso Ravello Ris. '06	♟♟	6
● Costa d'Amalfi Rosso Furore '08	♟	5
○ Costa d'Amalfi Fiorduva '07	♟♟♟	7
○ Costa d'Amalfi Fiorduva '06	♟♟♟	7
○ Costa d'Amalfi Fiorduva '05	♟♟♟	7
○ Costa d'Amalfi Fiorduva '04	♟♟♟	7
● Costa d'Amalfi Rosso Furore Ris. '04	♟♟	7
● Costa d'Amalfi Rosso Furore Ris. '03	♟♟	7
● Costa d'Amalfi Rosso Furore Ris. '02	♟♟	7
● Costa d'Amalfi Rosso Ravello Ris. '05	♟♟	6

○ Ischia Biancolella Tenuta Frassitelli '08	♟♟	5
○ Ischia Bianco '08	♟♟	3*
○ Ischia Biancolella '08	♟♟	4
○ Ischia Biancolella Calitto '08	♟	4
○ Ischia Forastera Euposia '08	♟	4
● Ischia Per''e Palummo '08	♟	4
● Ischia Rosso Dedicato a Mario d'Ambra '05	♟	6
○ Passito Gocce d'Ambra	♟	6
○ Ischia Biancolella Tenuta Frassitelli '90	♟♟♟	4
○ Ischia Bianco Kyme '05	♟♟	5
○ Ischia Biancolella Tenuta Frassitelli '07	♟♟	5
○ Ischia Biancolella Tenuta Frassitelli '06	♟♟	5
○ Ischia Forastera Euposia '07	♟♟	5

Viticoltori De Conciliis

LOC. QUERCE
84060 PRIGNANO CILENTO [SA]
TEL. 0974831090
www.viticoltorideconciliis.it

CELLAR SALES
PRE-BOOKED VISITS

ANNUAL PRODUCTION 150,000 bottles
HECTARES UNDER VINE 28
VITICULTURE METHOD Conventional

It is practically impossible to describe this great little Prignano winery without constant reference to the story and ideas of Bruno De Conciliis, oenologist, artist, "maître à penser" and leader of a movement that continues to play a fundamental impact in reviving Campanian wine production. Unlike a traditional consultant oenologist, all the projects Bruno oversees are born of elective affinities and many young growers have trained with him. However, his most important laboratory remains the family estate.

This year's new wine is Bacioilcielo '08, a blend of aglianico, barbera and primitivo harvested from young vineyards with the aim of beefing up Donnaluna Aglianico, destined for longer ageing. Naima, a monovarietal Aglianico, remains the benchmark. The '05 vintage is lighter and more restrained, in terms of both oak and tannic extraction, but perhaps also a little sedate in its development. Just one rung below is the beautifully poised Zero '05, from 40 per cent partially dried aglianico grapes. Ka! '06, from dried moscato and malvasia grapes, is simply the best Campanian sweet wine.

Di Prisco

C.DA ROTOLE, 27
83040 FONTANAROSA [AV]
TEL. 0825475738
www.cantinadiprisco.it

CELLAR SALES
PRE-BOOKED VISITS

ANNUAL PRODUCTION 100,000 bottles
HECTARES UNDER VINE 10
VITICULTURE METHOD Conventional

Pasqualino Di Prisco is emblematic of Irpinian wine men. He's a tireless grower, with strong emotional ties to his land, who is not really comfortable among tasting stands and wine buffs. He also possesses the true countryman's somewhat pessimistic streak of fatalism. This sensibility is can clash with the awareness that, together with his friend Carmine Valentino, he runs one of the province's finest estates for mid-level wines. There are several peaks of excellence and Pasqualino can count on an ideal subzone for the production of sinuously elegant Taurasis that have real substance.

We were convinced that it was merely a matter of time, and in fact Taurasi '05 has earned Pasqualino his first Three Glasses. It is a reward for his constancy but above all for a splendid wine, aged in barrels of different sizes and ages, that is illuminated by citrus and floral hints and veined with earthy, austere minerality. It is a young wine but one with juiciness and flavour already make the difference. The whites, all aged in steel and released about two years after harvest, also did very well. Greco di Tufo Pietrarosa '07 is the best, showing dense and harmonious with very sound aromatics.

Wine	Rating
O Ka! '06	🍷🍷 6
● Naima '05	🍷🍷 7
● Zero '05	🍷🍷 8
● Bacioilcielo '08	🍷 4
O Donnaluna Fiano '08	🍷 4
● Naima '01	🍷🍷🍷 6
● Decimo Anno Aglianico '06	🍷🍷 4
● Donnaluna Aglianico '07	🍷🍷 4*
● Donnaluna Aglianico '05	🍷🍷 4
O Donnaluna Fiano '07	🍷🍷 4*
O Donnaluna Fiano '05	🍷🍷 4
● Naima '04	🍷🍷 7
● Rà!	🍷🍷 7
● Zero '04	🍷🍷 8

Wine	Rating
● Taurasi '05	🍷🍷🍷 6*
O Fiano di Avellino '07	🍷🍷 4*
O Greco di Tufo '07	🍷🍷 4*
O Greco di Tufo Pietrarosa '07	🍷🍷 4
O Irpinia Coda di Volpe '08	🍷 3
● Aglianico '03	🍷🍷 4
O Fiano di Avellino '05	🍷🍷 4
O Greco di Tufo '06	🍷🍷 4*
O Greco di Tufo Pietrarosa '05	🍷🍷 4*
● Taurasi '04	🍷🍷 6
● Taurasi '03	🍷🍷 6
● Taurasi '02	🍷🍷 6
● Taurasi '01	🍷🍷 6

DonnaChiara

LOC. PIETRACUPA
VIA STAZIONE
83030 MONTEFALCIONE [AV]
TEL. 0825977135
www.donnachiara.it

CELLAR SALES
PRE-BOOKED VISITS
FOOD

ANNUAL PRODUCTION 100,000 bottles
HECTARES UNDER VINE 15
VITICULTURE METHOD Conventional

Don't let the figures fool you. Donnachiara may be a small, young winery but it has the long entrepreneurial history of Umberto Pettito and his group behind it. The project, headed by Umberto's wife Chiara and his daughter Ilaria, revolves around the family's vineyards and a complete range of Irpinian wines crafted by Angelo Valentino. The whites are aged in steel and are big and fruity while the aglianico-based reds, from the Venticano zone, combine weight and definition.

With the cellar's first Taurasi upcoming, a flagship wine was missing from the selection that we tasted. However, the wines confirm the impression of confidence and reliability that we pointed out in the last Guide. Fiano di Avellino '08 was the top performer, with very open notes of tropical fruit and soft, relaxed development. It still has a yeasty fermentative vein, which we thought detracted a little from its complexity, but it is solid and balanced on the palate. Greco di Tufo '08 has a more controversial nose but it is full and meaty, while Irpinia Aglianico Preludio '07 is earthy and balsamic with a slightly closed finish.

○ Fiano di Avellino '08	🍷🍷	4*
○ Greco di Tufo '08	🍷🍷	4*
● Irpinia Aglianico Preludio '07	🍷🍷	4
○ Falanghina '08	🍷	4
○ Fiano di Avellino '07	🍷🍷	4*
● Irpinia Aglianico Preludio '06	🍷🍷	4*

I Favati

P.ZZA DI DONATO
83020 CESINALI [AV]
TEL. 0825666898
www.cantineifavati.it

CELLAR SALES
PRE-BOOKED VISITS

ANNUAL PRODUCTION 50,000 bottles
HECTARES UNDER VINE 10
VITICULTURE METHOD Conventional

With ten hectares of vineyards and an annual production of about 50,000 bottles, I Favati is a small winery that has carved out a niche for itself since the very first harvest. The consistent, comprehensive range of Irpinian wines hinges on Pietramara, a fiano vineyard situated in the cooler, wooded zone of Atripalda with loose soils. Vincenzo Mercurio's technical expertise is exploring new directions, experimenting in particular with the fermentation of whites, but the estate's genius loci has a decidedly classic air.

Again this year, I Favati's wines expressed their potential to the full. Fiano di Avellino Pietramara '08 displays attractive contrasts, flanking almost cereal-like notes of husks with greener hints of moss and bitter herbs. On the palate, it vaunts flawlessly balanced fullness and backbone, although the finish is slightly lacking in depth. Greco di Tufo Terrantica '08 is similar, but with more tropical aromas, while Taurasi Terzo Tratto '05 is very pleasant, despite oak that has still to be absorbed..

○ Fiano di Avellino Pietramara '08	🍷🍷	4*
○ Greco di Tufo Terrantica '08	🍷🍷	4
● Irpinia Campi Taurasini Cretarossa '07	🍷🍷	4
● Taurasi Terzo Tratto '05	🍷🍷	5
○ Fiano di Avellino Pietramara '07	🍷🍷	4*
○ Fiano di Avellino Pietramara '06	🍷🍷	4
○ Fiano di Avellino Pietramara Et. Bianca '07	🍷🍷	4*
○ Greco di Tufo Terrantica '07	🍷🍷	4*
● Irpinia Campi Taurasini Cretarossa '06	🍷🍷	4*
● Taurasi Terzo Tratto '04	🍷🍷	5

Benito Ferrara

FRAZ. SAN PAOLO, 14A
83010 TUFO [AV]
TEL. 0825998194
www.benitoferrara.it

CELLAR SALES
PRE-BOOKED VISITS

ANNUAL PRODUCTION **45,000 bottles**
HECTARES UNDER VINE **8.5**
VITICULTURE METHOD **Conventional**

You have to leave the little village of Tufo and climb up to the hamlet of San Paolo, 500 metres above sea level, to meet Gabriella Ferrara and her husband Sergio, who own one of the cult wineries in this small Irpinian DOC zone. Their best-known wine is Vigna Cicogna, one of the province's first Greco di Tufo vineyard selections, which comes from a splendid south-facing plot of approximately two hectares. The depths of its mineral-rich soil yield the sulphur that supported the area's economy for almost a century.

This year, our tastings seem to turn the estate's hierarchy on its head, highlighting the fabulous Greco di Tufo '08. We're not talking about a straightforward basic wine. This one has remarkable personality that, compared to its elder brother, manages to express the abundant freshness and energy that you always expect from the grape in these areas. Vigna Cicogna '08 is absolutely true to itself, with rich glycerine and extract, but it also has a rather oxidized aromatic framework that we thought was somewhat limiting for a vineyard selection of this standard. The excellent Fiano di Avellino '08 is in the same style.

★★ Feudi di San Gregorio

LOC. CERZA GROSSA
83050 SORBO SERPICO [AV]
TEL. 0825986683
www.feudi.it

CELLAR SALES
PRE-BOOKED VISITS

ANNUAL PRODUCTION **3.900,000 bottles**
HECTARES UNDER VINE **216**
VITICULTURE METHOD **Conventional**

This label has contributed more than any other to revolutionizing the image of Campanian wine over the past 20 years. It is impossible to reduce Feudi di San Gregorio's history to a few lines, but it leads up to an estate that is currently undergoing great changes in terms of strategy and management, which is inevitably reflected in the wines. The new chairman is the energetic young Antonio Capaldo, while Pierpaolo Sirch holds the dual position of managing director and production manager, flanked by Marco Simonit.

This year, the overall performance was very good, reflecting a stylistic journey that is not yet over. The whites have a yeasty, primary character that holds them back slightly and contrasts with their rather dry, phenolic development on the palate. Exceptions to this are the two Fiano di Avellinos '08. The basic wine has a stylishly outgoing, racy acidity the Pietracalda focuses on richness and extraction, losing a touch of its elegance on the finish, which is more closed and alcoholic than expected. Rubrato '07, a consistently reliable Aglianico, and Pàtrimo '06, a Merlot, are the only reds that we tasted.

○ Greco di Tufo '08	♟♟	4
○ Fiano di Avellino '08	♟	5
○ Greco di Tufo V. Cicogna '08	♟	5
○ Fiano di Avellino '06	♟♟	5
○ Greco di Tufo '06	♟♟	4*
○ Greco di Tufo V. Cicogna '07	♟♟	5
○ Greco di Tufo V. Cicogna '06	♟♟	5

○ Fiano di Avellino '08	♟♟	4
○ Fiano di Avellino Pietracalda '08	♟♟	5
○ Dubl Greco Brut '05	♟♟	7
○ Greco di Tufo Cutizzi '08	♟♟	5
○ Irpinia Campanaro '08	♟♟	6
● Pàtrimo '06	♟♟	8
● Rubrato '07	♟♟	4*
○ Sannio Falanghina Serrocielo '08	♟♟	5
○ Dubl Falanghina Brut '06	♟	5
☉ Dubl Rosato Brut '06	♟	6
○ Greco di Tufo '08	♟	4
☉ Irpinia Ros'Aura '08	♟	4
○ Privilegio '07	♟	6
○ Sannio Falanghina '08	♟	4
○ Greco di Tufo Cutizzi '07	♟♟♟	4*
○ Greco di Tufo Cutizzi '06	♟♟♟	4*
● Irpinia Serpico '05	♟♟♟	8
● Pàtrimo '04	♟♟♟	8
● Serpico '04	♟♟♟	8
● Serpico '03	♟♟♟	8

Galardi

FRAZ. SAN CARLO
S.P. SESSA-MIGNANO
81037 SESSA AURUNCA [CE]
TEL. 0823708900
www.terradilavoro.com

PRE-BOOKED VISITS

ANNUAL PRODUCTION **25,000 bottles**
HECTARES UNDER VINE **10**
VITICULTURE METHOD **Organic certified**

Fontana Galardi is a small estate situated in the hamlet of San Carlo di Sessa Aurunca, about 400 metres above sea level, on top of a cool hill surrounded by olive groves and chestnut and oak woods. The very deep soils are alluvial and volcanic, with significant proportions of limestone and schist. It is the home of Campania's most famous blend of aglianico and piedirosso, and this legendary wine is the fruit of the toil of Luisa Murena, Arturo Celentano, Francesco and Dora Catello and their friend and advisor Riccardo Cotarella.

In the case of Terra di Lavoro we are forced to admit the limits of blindfolded tasting. Its personality is so distinctive, and it is so easily to recognize, that you inevitably end up comparing it with itself and its most successful vintages instead of the other wines on the list. It was clear at once that the '07 is a great vintage. Generous, but not over-extracted, it is powerful but never heavy and so lifted by aromatic freshness that it soars on the finish, which is dominated by classy tannins. It's already ahead of the pack in terms of continuity and flavour, and in a decade it will probably go into overdrive.

Cantina Giardino

VIA PETRARA, 21B
83031 ARIANO IRPINO [AV]
TEL. 0825873084
www.cantinagiardino.com

CELLAR SALES
PRE-BOOKED VISITS

ANNUAL PRODUCTION **13,000 bottles**
HECTARES UNDER VINE **4**
VITICULTURE METHOD **Natural**

Cantina Giardino is not merely a winery. First and foremost, it's a wine culture project, as Antonio Di Gruttola, his friends and partners define it. While it is regularly taken as a benchmark for the so-called natural trend, we think it is more interesting to emphasize the work it has carried out in recent years on old vineyards and clones that had almost died out. The wines are not fined or filtered, and the whites are produced with skin contact. During the past few vintages, experiments with ageing in terracotta jars and amphorae have been launched.

Nude, an Aglianico from the grapes of an 80-year-old vineyard, is again the top scorer. The '05 vintage has an initial esteriness and austere, astringent tannins on the finish. In the middle is the usual rich glycerine and extract, which could make it more harmonious in time. The other two Aglianicos, Le Fole '07 and Drogone '06, are still evolving. From the macerated whites, we preferred Adam '06, from greco, with a variegated, delicately toasted nose of hops and aniseed, and a supple palate with almost red-like warmth. T'Ara Rà '07, also from greco, is firm but more oxidized.

● Terra di Lavoro '07	♟♟♟ 8
● Terra di Lavoro '06	♟♟♟ 8
● Terra di Lavoro '05	♟♟♟ 8
● Terra di Lavoro '04	♟♟♟ 8
● Terra di Lavoro '03	♟♟♟ 7
● Terra di Lavoro '02	♟♟♟ 7
● Terra di Lavoro '99	♟♟♟ 7

○ Adam '06	♟♟ 6
● Drogone '06	♟♟ 6
● Le Fole '07	♟♟ 4*
● Nude '05	♟♟ 7
○ T'Ara Rà '07	♟ 6
● Drogone '05	♟♟ 6
● Nude '04	♟♟ 7
○ T'Ara Rà '06	♟♟ 6

Cantine Grotta del Sole

VIA SPINELLI, 2
80010 QUARTO [NA]
TEL. 0818762566
www.grottadelsole.it

CELLAR SALES
PRE-BOOKED VISITS

ANNUAL PRODUCTION 850,000 bottles
HECTARES UNDER VINE 42
VITICULTURE METHOD Natural

Grotta del Sole is far more than the benchmark winery for the Campi Flegrei area south of Naples. In the space of little over 20 years, the Martusciello family has created a veritable bastion for the region, with a list ranging from the Sorrento peninsula to Vesuvius, Benevento, Irpinia and Asprinio d'Aversa, offering both still and sparkling wines. Technical management is in the hands of Attilio Pagli and Francesco Martusciello Jr.

Grotta del Sole's strength has always been its very wide range. However, this year its overall performance was less impressive than in the past. On the one hand, we missed the flagship Quarto di Sole and on the other we tasted a series of wines that are technically impeccable, but a little too closed and linear, sometimes even bitterish. The excellent Greco di Tufo Quarto di Luna '07, aged in oak and steel for 12 months, stands out from the group, with hints of aniseed and musk and imposing structural soundness.

La Guardiense

LOC. SANTA LUCIA, 104-105
82034 GUARDIA SANFRAMONDI [BN]
TEL. 0824864034
www.laguardiense.it

CELLAR SALES
PRE-BOOKED VISITS

ANNUAL PRODUCTION 4,000,000 bottles
HECTARES UNDER VINE 2000
VITICULTURE METHOD Conventional

Fifty years of history, 990 member growers, 4,000,000 bottles a year and 2,000 hectares under vine. These figures make La Guardiense one of the most important co-operative wineries in southern Italy. After years of relative anonymity, the Guardia Sanframondi colossus is raising its sights under manager Domizio Pigna and consultant oenologist Riccardo Cotarella. The range of basic wines, offered at fantastic prices, appears to have benefited immediately.

Guardiolo Aglianico '08 was the only red presented for our tastings but it is a captivating wine and one of the best-value finalists in this edition of the Guide. Aged for six months in barrels and steel tanks, it has an attractive soft oak character, carried by a dense, caressing palate. The dynamic, racy Sannio Fiano Colle di Tilio '08 from the Janare range gives white-fleshed fruits and candied peel. Sannio Greco Pietralata Janare '08 is very similar but even tauter, despite its alcoholic finish. The three whites from the Selezione range are decent.

Wine	Rating
○ Greco di Tufo Quarto di Luna '07	♟♟ 5
○ Asprinio d'Aversa Brut	♟ 4
○ Campi Flegrei Falanghina '08	♟ 4
● Campi Flegrei Piedirosso '08	♟ 4
○ Coda di Volpe '08	♟ 3
○ Fiano di Avellino '08	♟ 4
● Penisola Sorrentina Gragnano '08	♟ 4
● Penisola Sorrentina Lettere '08	♟ 4
○ Vesuvio Lacryma Christi Bianco '08	♟ 4
○ Vesuvio Lacryma Christi Dolce	♟ 4
● Vesuvio Lacryma Christi Rosso '08	♟ 4
○ Campi Flegrei Falanghina Coste di Cuma '06	♟♟ 5
○ Fiano di Avellino '07	♟♟ 4*
○ Greco di Tufo Quarto di Luna '06	♟♟ 5
● Quarto di Sole '05	♟♟ 5

Wine	Rating
● Guardiolo Aglianico Sel. '08	♟♟ 3*
○ Sannio Fiano Colle di Tilio Janare '08	♟♟ 4
○ Sannio Greco Pietralata Janare '08	♟♟ 4*
○ Guardiolo Falanghina Sel. '08	♟ 3
○ Guardiolo Falanghina Senete Janare '08	♟ 4
○ Sannio Fiano Sel. '08	♟ 3
○ Sannio Greco Sel. '08	♟ 3
● Guardiolo Aglianico Cantari Ris. '06	♟♟ 5
● Guardiolo Aglianico Lucchero '05	♟♟ 4*
● Guardiolo Aglianico Sel. '06	♟♟ 3*
● Guardiolo Rosso Ris. '06	♟♟ 3*
○ Sannio Fiano Sel. '07	♟♟ 3*
○ Sannio Greco Pietralata '06	♟♟ 4*
○ Sannio Greco Sel. '07	♟♟ 3*
○ Sannio Greco Sel. '06	♟♟ 3

Luigi Maffini

FRAZ. SAN MARCO
LOC. CENITO
84048 CASTELLABATE [SA]
TEL. 0974966345
www.maffini-vini.com

CELLAR SALES
PRE-BOOKED VISITS

ANNUAL PRODUCTION **100,000 bottles**
HECTARES UNDER VINE **18**
VITICULTURE METHOD **Conventional**

It is certainly no coincidence that Luigi Maffini has become a beacon for Salerno winemaking. The Castellabate agronomist's painstaking work on aglianico and fiano with Luigi Molo has yielded the key to combining the innate firepower of the Cilento terroir with drinkability and suppleness. His wines are technical, with prominent but never overwhelming oak derived from the use of small casks. The most successful ones offer body and depth to compensate the sensation of aloofness for which we sometimes reproach him.

This is certainly not the case with Pietraincatenata '07, a fiano vineyard selection aged for eight months in barrique and sourced from a plot in Giungano, a stone's throw from the Tyrrhenian Sea. Oak merges with hints of saffron, deepening with a balsamic energy that supports and lingers on the fruity, glycerine-rich palate. We gave it Three Glasses. The opulent Cilento Aglianico Cenito '06 almost repeated the feat, held back only by its more banal aromatic development of coffee and cocoa powder. Denazzano '08, a rosé Aglianico, is salty with perfectly calibrated weight but the '08 vintage of Kratos is not the best we've tasted.

★ Mastroberardino

VIA MANFREDI, 75/81
83042 ATRIPALDA [AV]
TEL. 0825614111
www.mastroberardino.com

CELLAR SALES
PRE-BOOKED VISITS
VISITOR FACILITIES
FOOD

ANNUAL PRODUCTION **2.500.000 bottles**
HECTARES UNDER VINE **340**
VITICULTURE METHOD **Conventional**

Ne abbiamo per molto tempo celebrato la storia e il contributo decisivo nel recupero e nella valorizzazione dei più antichi e prestigiosi vitigni campani. Ma la cantina di Atripalda è tutt'altro che un'azienda incatenata a nostalgie del passato e oggi ne raccontiamo soprattutto il piglio deciso e moderno con cui Piero Mastroberardino l'ha lanciata nel terzo millennio. Il nucleo di tutto il lavoro è concentrato nella tenuta di Mirabella, la più grande collina vitata irpina, luogo privilegiato di ricerca e sperimentazione.

We have long praised the decisive contribution that this Atripalda winery has made to the revival and improvement of the oldest and finest of Campania's grape varieties. However, this is by no means an estate that looks to the past and this year we'd like to mention the determined, modern approach with which Piero Mastroberardino has led it into the third millennium. The nucleus of all the work is concentrated in the Mirabella estate, the largest hill under vine in Irpinia, where much research and experimentation is under way.

○ Pietraincatenata '07	♟♟♟	5
● Cilento Aglianico Cenito '06	♟♟	6
☉ Denazzano Rosato '08	♟♟	4*
○ Kràtos '08	♟	4
● Cilento Aglianico Cenito '03	♟♟♟	6
○ Pietraincatenata '04	♟♟♟	5
● Cilento Aglianico Cenito '05	♟♟	6
● Cilento Aglianico Cenito '04	♟♟	6
● Klèos '06	♟♟	4*
○ Kràtos '07	♟♟	4*
○ Pietraincatenata '06	♟♟	5

● Taurasi Radici '05	♟♟♟	6
○ Fiano di Avellino Radici '08	♟♟	4*
○ Greco di Tufo Novaserra '08	♟♟	4*
● Taurasi Naturalis Historia '05	♟♟	7
● Aglianico '07	♟♟	4*
○ Fiano di Avellino '08	♟♟	4*
○ Fiano di Avellino More Maiorum '07	♟♟	5
○ Greco di Tufo '08	♟	4
○ Irpinia Falanghina Morabianca '08	♟	4
○ Irpinia Fiano Passito Melizie '08	♟	5
☉ Lacrimarosa '08	♟	4
○ Vesuvio Lacryma Christi Bianco '08	♟	4
● Vesuvio Lacryma Christi Rosso '08	♟	4
○ Greco di Tufo Novaserra '07	♟♟♟	4*
○ Greco di Tufo Novaserra '06	♟♟♟	4*
● Taurasi Naturalis Historia '04	♟♟♟	7
● Taurasi Radici Ris. '01	♟♟♟	6

Salvatore Molettieri

C.DA MUSANNI, 19B
83040 MONTEMARANO [AV]
TEL. 082763424
www.salvatoremolettieri.it

CELLAR SALES
PRE-BOOKED VISITS

ANNUAL PRODUCTION **66,000 bottles**
HECTARES UNDER VINE **13**
VITICULTURE METHOD **Conventional**

Cinque Querce – "five oaks" – looks to be an understatement! Seeing Salvatore Molettieri and his four sons at work reminds us of an entire redwood forest. The simple secret of one of Italy's finest wineries lies in those huge hands and almost 30 years of sacrifice. All the essence of the Taurasis of the Montemarano subzone can be found in the seven hectares of vineyards with clay and limestone soils located almost 600 metres above sea level: weight, alcohol, explosive acidity and tannic vigour, tamed by the combined use of small and large oak barrels and, above all, ridiculously low cropping levels.

The combination of style, soil and climate ensures that Taurasi Cinque Querce is always skating on thin ice. In some vintages, the power of the glycerine and extract is so overwhelming that it pushes the fruit to levels bordering on superripeness and over-extraction. But in the right year, it is unrivalled, as we saw at our latest tastings. The tannic grain of the '05 is practically perfect while the Riserva '04 has a more austere profile but amazing minerality. It is no coincidence that two basically cool vintages have produced such fabulous wines.

★ Montevetrano

LOC. NIDO
VIA MONTEVETRANO, 3
84099 SAN CIPRIANO PICENTINO [SA]
TEL. 089882285
www.montevetrano.it

PRE-BOOKED VISITS

ANNUAL PRODUCTION **30,000 bottles**
HECTARES UNDER VINE **5**
VITICULTURE METHOD **Conventional**

This is the Campanian winery with the highest number of Three Glass awards, which it has won every time with the exception of '94 and the first two vintages, '91 and '92, which were almost experimental in terms of numbers of bottles and fermentation procedures. The estate has revolutionized the image of an entire region and now has the presence of an enduring classic rather than an avant-garde daub. It is the dream of Silvia Imparato, who has transformed the unusual Picentino blend of cabernet sauvignon, merlot and aglianico into a splendid territory wine with Riccardo Cotarella's help.

It took only a moment to realize that the spectacular blend of pencil lead, talcum powder and red berry fruit had us all thinking the same thing: the '07 version of Montevetrano bears an uncanny resemblance to the '01, which puts it on the podium of the best ever versions of this stunning wine. All our preconceived ideas about a vintage that we had imagined to be warm and concentrated were swept away by an elegant, silky weave that seems to spread its wings on the palate, aided by utterly impeccable oak.

● Taurasi Vigna Cinque Querce '05	♥♥♥+ 7
● Taurasi Vigna Cinque Querce Ris. '04	♥♥♥ 8
● Irpinia Campi Taurasini Cinque Quercie '06	♥♥ 5
● Irpinia Aglianico Cinque Querce '07	♥ 6
● Irpinia Rosso Ischia Piana '07	♥ 4
● Taurasi Vigna Cinque Querce '04	♥♥♥ 7
● Taurasi Vigna Cinque Querce '01	♥♥♥ 6
● Taurasi Vigna Cinque Querce Ris. '01	♥♥♥ 8
● Aglianico Cinque Querce '03	♥♥ 5
● Aglianico Cinque Querce '02	♥♥ 5
● Taurasi Vigna Cinque Querce '03	♥♥ 8
● Taurasi Vigna Cinque Querce '00	♥♥ 6
● Taurasi Vigna Cinque Querce Ris. '03	♥♥ 8
● Taurasi Vigna Cinque Querce Ris. '00	♥♥ 7

● Montevetrano '07	♥♥♥+ 8
● Montevetrano '06	♥♥♥ 8
● Montevetrano '05	♥♥♥ 8
● Montevetrano '04	♥♥♥ 8
● Montevetrano '03	♥♥♥ 8
● Montevetrano '02	♥♥♥ 8
● Montevetrano '01	♥♥♥ 8
● Montevetrano '00	♥♥♥ 8
● Montevetrano '99	♥♥♥ 8
● Montevetrano '98	♥♥♥ 8
● Montevetrano '97	♥♥♥ 8
● Montevetrano '96	♥♥♥ 8
● Montevetrano '95	♥♥♥ 8
● Montevetrano '93	♥♥♥ 8

Perillo

C.DA VALLE, 19
83040 CASTELFRANCI [AV]
TEL. 082772252
cantinaperillo@libero.it

CELLAR SALES

ANNUAL PRODUCTION **20,000 bottles**
HECTARES UNDER VINE **4**
VITICULTURE METHOD **Conventional**

An ideal list of Irpinian garage wines would certainly be topped by Michele Perillo and Anna Maria Romano's Taurasi. The winery is inextricably tied to a unique subzone, with the highest altitudes in the DOC and many old raggiera-trained vines, where the aglianico clone locally known as "coda di cavallo" is often found. Such conditions naturally combine to create very glycerine-rich wines with powerful tannins, which demand careful attention and lots of patience.

Last year, Michele decided to delay release of his Taurasi '04 by a year. We feel that this was the right decision. The wine still appears extremely young and very consistent with the classic, austere character that we associate with the vintage. Although the nose is still developing, it reveals top notes of resin and chocolate, with a touch of oak that has not yet been absorbed. On the palate, there is big texture, which may be better integrated in time but is currently held back by slightly uneven tannins and more breadth than length. We are once again very close to the top but we are sure that the best is yet to come.

● Taurasi '04	🍷🍷 5*
● Taurasi '03	YY 6
● Taurasi '02	YY 6
● Taurasi '01	YY 6
● Taurasi '00	YY 6
● Taurasi '99	YY 6
● Taurasi Ris. '01	YY 6
● Taurasi Ris. '00	YY 6

Pietracupa

C.DA VADIAPERTI, 17
83030 MONTEFREDANE [AV]
TEL. 0825607418
pietracupa@email.it

CELLAR SALES
PRE-BOOKED VISITS

ANNUAL PRODUCTION **35,000 bottles**
HECTARES UNDER VINE **3.5**
VITICULTURE METHOD **Conventional**

It's been a long time since words like "surprise" or "outsider" could be used to refer to Pietracupa, the small estate founded by Peppino Loffredo in 1989 and now headed by his son Sabino. Today, his wines reveal an authority and maturity that will surprise only those not acquainted with the less exuberant, more stubborn side of the former sports instructor from Montefredane. The steel-aged whites intensify the linearity and mineral notes of the Irpinian varieties while the reds improve exponentially from year to year, focusing on elegance and richness of flavour.

We don't think it's an exaggeration to say that Pietracupa's Greco di Tufo '08, from a Santa Paolina vineyard, seems destined to become a milestone in the history of the DOC zone. It is an extraordinary, unrivalled wine, with almost Mosel-like rocky minerality and simply devastatingly lustrous length. It could overturn convictions regarding the varietal's evolutionary and aromatic potential. In the presence of such a world-class wine, there is a risk of overlooking the rest of the excellent list, commencing with the barrel-aged Taurasi '05, which is compact, sound and very smoky.

○ Greco di Tufo '08	🍷🍷🍷+ 4*
○ Fiano di Avellino '08	🍷🍷 4*
● Taurasi '05	🍷🍷 6
● Quirico '07	🍷🍷 5
○ Cupo '05	YYY 5
○ Cupo '03	YYY 4*
○ Greco di Tufo '07	YYY 4*
○ Greco di Tufo '06	YYY 4*
○ Fiano di Avellino '07	YY 4*
○ Fiano di Avellino '06	YY 4*
○ Fiano di Avellino '05	YY 4*
○ Fiano di Avellino '04	YY 4
○ Greco di Tufo '05	YY 4*
○ Greco di Tufo '04	YY 4
○ Greco di Tufo "G" '03	YY 4
● Taurasi '04	YY 6

Tenuta Ponte

VIA CARAZITA, 1
83040 LUOGOSANO [AV]
TEL. 082773564
www.tenutaponte.it

CELLAR SALES
PRE-BOOKED VISITS

ANNUAL PRODUCTION **180,000 bottles**
HECTARES UNDER VINE **35**
VITICULTURE METHOD **Conventional**

Founded in 1995, Tenuta Ponte is a project involving five partners from Luogosano, with the technical expertise of cellarman Carmine Valentino. We have long been amazed by the average standard of the range covering the entire spectrum of Irpinian wines, which are offered at very budget-friendly prices. All the whites are aged in steel alone while the top reds are aged partly in new barriques for 12 months and for a further 12 in larger barrels.

While overall performance was excellent, as always, we were slightly disappointed by the latest releases of Taurasi, particularly in view of the potential of the Pesco, Pesano and Carazita vineyards. The '05 vintage has character and flesh but the aromatic profile is overly sombre and earthy while the palate is a little short on openness and suppleness. However, Fiano di Avellino '08 is very successful, with a rather mountain-style profile of thyme and lemon peel, the distinctive mark of an east-facing vineyard in Lapio. The elegant palate shows a well-integrated, acidulous, almost salty verve and a finish that tapers off slightly.

Quintodecimo

VIA SAN LEONARDO, 27
83036 MIRABELLA ECLANO [AV]
TEL. 0825449321
www.quintodecimo.it

CELLAR SALES
PRE-BOOKED VISITS
VISITOR FACILITIES

ANNUAL PRODUCTION **30,000 bottles**
HECTARES UNDER VINE **12**
VITICULTURE METHOD **Natural**

Quintodecimo is the name of the Mirabella estate and the vineyard that Luigi Moio, together with his partner Laura Di Marzio, chose for his adventure as grower-cum-professor. Moio decided to test his skill with the main varieties of the inland areas – aglianico, fiano, greco and falanghina – interpreting them in his own way in the vineyard and the cellar by bringing out the soundness of the fruit and potential to evolve over time. These are wines with prominent notes of oak, to be purchased chiefly with one eye on the future.

It was one of the most eagerly awaited tastings, not least because of the price bracket, but the first release of Taurasi Vigna Quintodecimo Riserva lived up to our expectations. The '04 has a modern aromatic framework, with top notes of toast and spice, and a powerful, meaty palate that tapers off slightly on the finish. It is an evolving wine, which we look forward to monitoring over the coming months. Among the whites, Falanghina Via del Campo '07 is top rate, with greater harmony and better integrated oak than the nonetheless excellent Fiano di Avellino Exultet and Greco di Tufo Giallo d'Arles from the same vintage.

○ Fiano di Avellino '08	♟♟ 4*
○ Greco di Tufo '08	♟♟ 4*
● Taurasi '05	♟♟ 4
● Irpinia Aglianico La Loggia '07	♟ 2
○ Greco di Tufo '07	♟♟ 4*

● Taurasi V. Quintodecimo Ris. '04	♟♟ 8
○ Via Del Campo Falanghina '07	♟♟ 6
○ Fiano di Avellino Exultet '07	♟♟ 7
○ Greco di Tufo Giallo D'Arles '07	♟♟ 7
● Irpinia Aglianico Terra D'Eclano '06	♟♟ 7
○ Fiano di Avellino Exultet '06	♟♟ 7
● Terra d'Eclano '05	♟♟ 7
● Terra d'Eclano '04	♟♟ 6
○ Via Del Campo Falanghina '06	♟♟ 6

Fattoria La Rivolta

C.DA RIVOLTA
82030 TORRECUSO [BN]
TEL. 0824872921
www.fattorialarivolta.com

CELLAR SALES
PRE-BOOKED VISITS
VISITOR FACILITIES

ANNUAL PRODUCTION **160,000 bottles**
HECTARES UNDER VINE **29**
VITICULTURE METHOD **Organic certified**

Without beating about the bush, we can say that Fattoria La Rivolta is currently the best winery in Sannio, an area with great potential that is has yet to realize its full potential. The cellar acquired this leadership chiefly through its top-rate list focusing on Campania's main grape varieties. The whites are fermented in steel, and consistently stand out for their weight and aromatic definition, while the barrique-aged top reds and are concise and austere.

Despite this year's brilliant overall performance, a high note seemed to be missing. Aglianico Terra di Rivolta Riserva was again the best of the list. The '06 vintage has the structure and stuffing of a big wine but seems to lack that extra something required from a world-beater, largely because of still pervasive oak notes. Sogno di Rivolta '08, an original blend of falanghina, fiano and greco, made it through to our finals for the first time with its almost marine tertiary aromas while the delicious Taburno Piedirosso '08 shows exemplary cleanliness and verve with almost piquant fruit.

Rocca del Principe

LOC. ARIANIELLO
VIA ARIANIELLO, 9
83030 LAPIO [AV]
TEL. 0825982435
roccadelprincipe@libero.it

CELLAR SALES
PRE-BOOKED VISITS

ANNUAL PRODUCTION **17,000 bottles**
HECTARES UNDER VINE **4.5**
VITICULTURE METHOD **Conventional**

With the help of Carmine Valentino, Ercole Zarrella and his wife Aurelia Fabrizio manage a tiny four-hectare estate that produces just one wine. In the space of a very short time, the winery has become a benchmark for lovers of Fiano di Avellino. Despite its small size, the keenness of the husband-and-wife team allows the Arianiello vineyards to express themselves coherently, reinforcing our opinion that the little village of Lapio really is one of the DOC zone's grands crus.

After last year's fantastic performance, which won Rocca del Principe the title of Up-and-Coming Winery, we were expecting the promise to be maintained. It was. Fiano di Avellino '08 is probably an even more successful version. Harvested during the first half of October and aged in steel for six months, it has a gutsy, earthy character with which we were not fully acquainted. Typical citrus sensations are accompanied by almost black fruit that permeates the very young, assertive, clenched palate. In some respects, it combines the graceful aromatics of a Fiano di Lapio with the mineral power of a Fiano di Monfredane.

● Aglianico del Taburno Terra di Rivolta Ris. '06	♟♟	6
○ Sogno di Rivolta '08	♟♟	4
○ Taburno Greco '08	♟♟	4*
● Taburno Piedirosso '08	♟♟	4*
○ Sannio Fiano '08	♟	4
○ Taburno Coda di Volpe '08	♟	4
○ Taburno Falanghina '08	♟	4
● Aglianico del Taburno '05	♀♀	4*
● Aglianico del Taburno Terra di Rivolta Ris. '04	♀♀	6
● Aglianico del Taburno Terra di Rivolta Ris. '03	♀♀	6
○ Sogno di Rivolta '07	♀♀	4*
○ Sogno di Rivolta '06	♀♀	4*

○ Fiano di Avellino '08	♟♟♟	4*
○ Fiano di Avellino '07	♀♀♀	4*
○ Fiano di Avellino '06	♀♀	4*

Ettore Sammarco

VIA CIVITA, 9
84010 RAVELLO [SA]
TEL. 089872774
www.ettoresammarco.it

CELLAR SALES
PRE-BOOKED VISITS

ANNUAL PRODUCTION **72,000 bottles**
HECTARES UNDER VINE **10**
VITICULTURE METHOD **Conventional**

With almost 50 harvests under its belt, Bartolo Sammarco's winery is one of Costa d'Amalfi's veterans. That said, the progress that we have witnessed over the past few years actually makes it a very pleasant kind of recent discovery. What were previously acceptable wines now form an exceptionally elegant, genuine range, which brings out the best of the dozens of varieties grown in the Ravello subzone, whose fruit is often purchased from long-standing growers.

Sammarco's list is as long and varied as ever, particularly in whites, almost all aged in steel. Vigna Grotta Piana '08, from ginestrella, falanghina and biancolella, is an exception and shows hints of walnutskin that hint at a brief acquaintance with new wood. We just preferred Terre Saracene Bianco '08, a blend of biancatenera and pepella with clear hints of basil and iodine. But again the best performance came from Selva delle Monache Riserva, from aglianico and piedirosso, whose '05 vintage is an emblematic coastal red, with a dynamic, multi-faceted nose and a complex, salty palate.

Tenuta Adolfo Spada

FRAZ. VAGLIE
S.P. 14 SESSA MIGNANO
81044 GALLUCCIO [CE]
TEL. 0823925709
www.tenutaspada.it

ANNUAL PRODUCTION **80,000 bottles**
HECTARES UNDER VINE **21**
VITICULTURE METHOD **Conventional**

Ernesto and Vincenzo Spada are the owners of this estate, founded in 1973 by their father Adolfo and relaunched in 2000 following the replanting of over 20 hectares of vineyards. It is situated in Galluccio, in the heart of the Roccomonfina regional park, an area with deep volcanic soils and considerable temperature fluctuations. Montepulciano, aglianico, piedirosso, falanghina and fiano are the grape varieties used for the estate's five wines, crafted by Riccardo Cotarella in his usual effective, reassuring style.

Gladius is the estate's flagship wine. This aglianico and piedirosso blend, aged in barriques for approximately 18 months, took its second consecutive Three Glass award. The '07 vintage won us over with a modern, open character that does not conceal a strongly territorial streak of dark charcoal, black pepper and crushed berries, echoed on the generous, caressing palate with clenched but never dry tannins. Oak plays a supporting role rather than amplifying. Flores '08, from falanghina with a small amount of fiano, is also good, showing delicate and drinkable.

● Costa d'Amalfi Ravello Rosso Selva delle Monache Ris. '05	▼▼ 5
○ Costa d'Amalfi Bianco Terre Saracene '08	▼▼ 4*
○ Costa d'Amalfi Ravello Bianco Selva delle Monache '08	▼▼ 4*
○ Costa d'Amalfi Ravello Bianco V. Grotta Piana '08	▼▼ 5
⊙ Costa d'Amalfi Ravello Rosato Selva delle Monache '08	▼▼ 4*
○ Costa d'Amalfi Ravello Bianco Selva delle Monache '07	♀♀ 4*
● Costa d'Amalfi Ravello Rosso Selva delle Monache Ris. '04	♀♀ 5
● Costa d'Amalfi Ravello Rosso Selva delle Monache Ris. '03	♀♀ 5
○ Costa d'Amalfi Terre Sarecene Bianco '07	♀♀ 4*
● Costa d'Amalfi Terre Sarecene Rosso '07	♀♀ 4*

● Gladius '07	▼▼▼ 5*
○ Flores '08	▼▼ 4*
● Sabus '08	▼ 4
● Gladius '06	♀♀♀ 5
● Gladius '05	♀♀ 5
● Gladius '04	♀♀ 5
● Gladius '03	♀♀ 5
● Gladius '02	♀♀ 4*
● Sabus '07	♀♀ 4*

Terre del Principe

FRAZ. SQUILLE
VIA SS. GIOVANNI E PAOLO, 30
81010 CASTEL CAMPAGNANO [CE]
TEL. 0823867126
www.terredelprincipe.com

CELLAR SALES
PRE-BOOKED VISITS

ANNUAL PRODUCTION 55,000 bottles
HECTARES UNDER VINE 11
VITICULTURE METHOD Conventional

The world of wine is full of splendid adventures that follow painful events. Manuela Piancastelli and Peppe Mancini's story is a good example. After splitting up with their partners in Vestini Campagnano, they founded Terre del Principe in 2003, embarking on the tiring but exciting task of vine recovery that has made it possible for us to talk knowledgeably about pallagrello and casavecchia today. Their interpretation is a modern one, which accentuates the natural concentration of the native varieties of the Caiatine hills by thorough ripening and ageing in small oak casks.

The fairytale of the little Castel Campagnano winery could not have a happier ending. Following the award won by Pallagrello Nero Ambruco, this year Casavecchia Centomoggia '07 took our highest accolade. Its aromatic spectrum features autumn leaves, plums and liquorice, evoking pulp and fullness, but also complex earthy, smoky notes. The variety's generally rustic tannins are treated with great precision, allowing the wine to benefit in length. We were also impressed by the rest of the range, from the round Pallagrello Bianco Le Serole '08 to the racy Castello delle Femmine '07.

Terredora

VIA SERRA
83030 MONTEFUSCO [AV]
TEL. 0825968215
www.terredora.com

CELLAR SALES
PRE-BOOKED VISITS

ANNUAL PRODUCTION 1.200,000 bottles
HECTARES UNDER VINE 180
VITICULTURE METHOD Conventional

Any annual screening of the state of health of Irpinian wine must take in Terredora's extensive, solid range. Serra di Montefusco, Campore di Lapio and Santa Lucia di Santa Paolina: Walter Mastroberardino and his children own some of the finest vineyards in the province. This is why we would like the territorial personality to emerge with greater clarity, fusing with the modern, extrovert style that is the hallmark of the influential Montefusco winery.

The results of this year's tastings were very similar to those of the last editions, with many wines above Two Glasses. The two Taurasi '04 crus still feel the effects of ageing and are a little short on length, while a series of whites offers notable drinkability and density despite sometimes lingering slightly too long on faintly fermentative, yeasty notes. Greco di Tufo Loggia della Serra '08 has more character, juxtaposing fine smoky, spicy notes with sweet, open fruit that is echoed nicely on the palate. Greco di Tufo Terre degli Angeli '08 is equally potent, but a touch dry on the finish.

Wine	Rating
● Centomoggia '07	▼▼▼ 6
● Ambruco '07	▼▼ 6
○ Le Serole Pallagrello Bianco '08	▼▼ 5
● V. Piancastelli '05	▼▼ 7
● Castello delle Femmine '07	▼ 4
○ Fontanavigna Pallagrello Bianco '08	▼ 5
● Ambruco '06	♀♀♀ 6
● Castello delle Femmine '05	♀♀ 4
● Centomoggia '06	♀♀ 6
● Centomoggia '05	♀♀ 6
○ Fontanavigna Pallagrello Bianco '07	♀♀ 5
○ Fontanavigna Pallagrello Bianco '06	♀♀ 5
○ Le Serole Pallagrello Bianco '07	♀♀ 5
● V. Piancastelli '04	♀♀ 7

Wine	Rating
○ Greco di Tufo Loggia della Serra '08	▼▼ 4*
○ Falanghina '08	▼▼ 4*
○ Fiano di Avellino Terre di Dora '08	▼▼ 4*
○ Greco di Tufo Terre degli Angeli '08	▼▼ 4
● Taurasi Fatica Contadina '04	▼▼ 6
● Taurasi Pago dei Fusi '04	▼▼ 6
○ Irpinia Falanghina '08	▼ 4
⊙ Irpinia Rosato Rosaenovae '08	▼ 4
○ Fiano di Avellino Terre di Dora '06	♀♀ 4*
○ Fiano di Avellino Terre di Dora '04	♀♀ 4*
○ Greco di Tufo Loggia della Serra '05	♀♀ 4*
○ Greco di Tufo Terra degli Angeli '05	♀♀ 4*
○ Greco di Tufo Terre degli Angeli '07	♀♀ 4*

Torricino

LOC. TORRICINO
VIA NAZIONALE
83010 TUFO [AV]
TEL. 0825990119
www.torricino.com

CELLAR SALES
PRE-BOOKED VISITS

ANNUAL PRODUCTION **40,000 bottles**
HECTARES UNDER VINE **10**
VITICULTURE METHOD **Organic certified**

We had absolutely no doubt that Torricino would rapidly recover the place that we believe it deserves among the region's best producers. This is because Stefano Di Marzo is a competent, intelligent grower who is able to count on some of the finest vineyards in the area west of Tufo, which was home to sulphur mines until the early 1980s. Fiano di Avellino and the standard Greco di Tufo are aged in steel only and the Raone is barrel-aged for six months. The Aglianico, on the other hand, comes from vineyards in Montemarano.

This year, Stefano Di Marzo's Greco di Tufo was very different to how we remembered it. Indeed, the '08 vintage is a far cry from the big, opulent, and in many respects oxidized, versions to which Torricino's style had accustomed us. This new approach seems far more interesting because it pays tribute to the mineral identity of the vineyards and unleashes the variety's acid backbone, despite the slightly closed, grassy finish. The approach also enhances the original character of the Raone; its '07 vintage is sweet and extracted as usual, but also dynamic and complex with notes of beeswax and roast chestnuts.

Urciuolo

FRAZ. CELZI
VIA DUE PRINCIPATI, 9
83020 FORINO [AV]
TEL. 0825761649
www.fratelliurciuolo.it

CELLAR SALES
PRE-BOOKED VISITS

ANNUAL PRODUCTION **100,000 bottles**
HECTARES UNDER VINE **25**
VITICULTURE METHOD **Conventional**

Ciro and Antonello Urciuolo from Forino have dedicated their lives to the family business that their father Nicola founded for the sale of wines and chestnut stakes. It is one of the few regional wineries able to combine aspirations to quality with quantities on a scale larger than garage production. The whites, aged in steel with extended contact with the fine lees, have an international character, focusing on extract and fullness, while the reds, aged in barrels of varying sizes, are a tribute to the austerity of aglianico and make no concessions to approachability.

Again this year, the Urciuolos presented us with a solid, reliable range, in which the '07 Aglianico is much more than a mere best buy and all the whites are truly convincing. Broader and harder-hitting than it is deep, Fiano di Avellino Faliesi '08 is a perfect example. We have long been convinced that the winery's true soul is fundamentally red and the '05 Taurasi removes any lingering doubts. The Mirabella, Castelfranci and Montemarano vineyards are the sources of a thoroughly austere wine with spicy, smoky base notes, which is hard and tannic but destined for a great future.

Torricino		Urciuolo	
O Greco di Tufo '08	♟♟ 4*	● Taurasi '05	♟♟♟ 6
O Greco di Tufo Raone '07	♟♟ 4*	● Aglianico '07	♟♟ 3*
O Fiano di Avellino '08	♟♟ 4	O Fiano di Avellino '08	♟♟ 4
● Irpinia Campi Taurasini Rosso '07	♟ 4	O Fiano di Avellino Faliesi '08	♟♟ 4
● Aglianico '05	♟♟ 4*	O Greco di Tufo '08	♟♟ 4*
O Fiano di Avellino '07	♟♟ 4*	● Taurasi '04	♟♟ 6
O Fiano di Avellino '06	♟♟ 4*	● Aglianico '06	♟♟ 3*
O Greco di Tufo '07	♟♟ 4*	● Aglianico '05	♟♟ 3*
O Greco di Tufo '06	♟♟ 4*	O Fiano di Avellino '07	♟♟ 4*
O Greco di Tufo Raone '05	♟♟ 4*	O Fiano di Avellino '06	♟♟ 4*
		O Fiano di Avellino Faliesi '06	♟♟ 4*
		O Fiano di Avellino Faliesi '05	♟♟ 4*
		O Greco di Tufo '07	♟♟ 4*
		O Greco di Tufo '06	♟♟ 4*
		● Taurasi '03	♟♟ 6
		● Taurasi '02	♟♟ 6
		● Taurasi '01	♟♟ 5

Vadiaperti

C.DA VADIAPERTI
83030 MONTEFREDANE [AV]
TEL. 0825607270
www.vadiaperti.it

CELLAR SALES
PRE-BOOKED VISITS

ANNUAL PRODUCTION **50,000 bottles**
HECTARES UNDER VINE **8**
VITICULTURE METHOD **Conventional**

If you're looking for docility, constancy and approachability, look elsewhere. This is because we are talking about Raffaele Troisi and his unique, extreme manner of interpreting Irpinian whites. The strongly reductive style and a decision to carry out only partial malolactic fermentation mean that Vadiaperti's wines are particularly difficult to decipher during their early months, and sometimes during their early years. They require patience and attention, but the investment often pays off over time with wines that eventually achieve heights of absolute emotion.

As happens every year, we find ourselves physically struggling with a series of confusing wines, especially in terms of aromas, where the clear-cut finish and lack of definition can be misleading because the palate is completely different, eager and well sustained. However, this is not the case of Greco di Tufo Tornante '08, from a Montefusco vineyard, which earned Vadiaperti the first Three Glasses in its long, fascinating history. It is an old-style wine, sharp but never grassy, with spectacular saline and mineral stratification that is simply oozing with character.

Vestini - Campagnano

FRAZ. SS. GIOVANNI E PAOLO
VIA BARRACCONE, 5
81013 CAIAZZO [CE]
TEL. 0823679087
www.vestinicampagnano.it

CELLAR SALES
PRE-BOOKED VISITS

ANNUAL PRODUCTION **38,000 bottles**
HECTARES UNDER VINE **6**
VITICULTURE METHOD **Organic certified**

Vestini Campagnano is synonymous with pallagrello and casavecchia, two native varieties of which Luigi Veronelli talked in glowing terms, and which were literally disappearing from the Caserta countryside. Manuela Piancastelli, Peppe Mancini and Luigi Moio have left the original team, which is now headed by the Barletta and Quaranta families, with the aid of Paolo Caciorgna in the cellar. The profile also reviews the wines produced by Poderi Foglia, founded by the same owners in 2003 at Conca della Campania.

Vestini Campagnano is a one-off on the competitive Campanian wine scene. Its reds have substantial oak but a classic, pleasantly retro character can be sensed deep down. Poderi Foglia's Concarosso R. '06, from aglianico and pallagrello nero, is the best example of this. Pallagrello Bianco '08 came very close to its former splendour and we thought it was the most successful interpretation of the grape this year. Well-defined notes of pear merge with balsamic vegetal nuances while the palate is full but with nice acidity. Casa Vecchia '06 is still very immature but has great body.

O Greco di Tufo Tornante '08	♟♟♟ 4*
O Fiano di Avellino Aipierti '07	♟♟ 4*
O Fiano di Avellino '08	♟♟ 4
O Greco di Tufo '08	♟♟ 4
O Irpinia Coda di Volpe '08	♟♟ 4*
● Aglianico '05	♟ 4
O Irpinia Coda di Volpe '07	♟♟ 4*

● Casa Vecchia '06	♟♟ 6
● Concarosso R. Poderi Foglia '06	♟♟ 5
O Galluccio Falanghina Concabianco Poderi Foglia '08	♟♟ 4
● Kajanero '06	♟♟ 3*
O Pallagrello Bianco '08	♟♟ 5
● Pallagrello Nero '06	♟ 6
● Casa Vecchia '05	♟♟ 6
O Concabianco '04	♟♟ 5
● Concarosso '04	♟♟ 5
● Connubio '03	♟♟ 8
● Kajanero '05	♟♟ 3*
O Pallagrello Bianco '06	♟♟ 5
● Pallagrello Nero '02	♟♟ 7

Villa Diamante

VIA TOPPOLE, 16
83030 MONTEFREDANE [AV]
TEL. 0825670014
www.villadiamante.eu

CELLAR SALES
PRE-BOOKED VISITS

ANNUAL PRODUCTION **10,000 bottles**
HECTARES UNDER VINE **2.8**
VITICULTURE METHOD **Organic certified**

Vigna della Congregazione is a vineyard covering about four hectares on a hill facing north-east and south-west, just over 400 metres above sea level, with marly clay and limestone soils. It is one of the sites that most closely reflects the distinctive characteristics of Fiano di Montefredane, which can be recognized by its prominent smoky mineral notes and firm, sharp structure. Antoine Gaita and Diamante Renna interpret the grape using non-invasive techniques, avoiding fining and filtration, and ageing for extended periods in steel only.

After the vibrant, youthful '06 vintage, this is a very different wine, with clearly defined tertiary and phenolic notes of honey, barley and peat. It is almost extractive, with poorly integrated alcohol on a mid palate that is less dynamic than usual. We could pass it off as the curse of the odd-numbered vintage but more realistically we accept this stylistic variability as the price for enjoying a hand-crafted wine in the true sense of the word. This philosophy has allowed Antoine to present Cuvée Enrico '00, a new wine from fiano, aged for six years in partially filled barrels like the Jura speciality vin jaune.

Villa Matilde

S.S. DOMITIANA, 18
81030 CELLOLE [CE]
TEL. 0823932088
www.villamatilde.it

CELLAR SALES
PRE-BOOKED VISITS
VISITOR FACILITIES
FOOD

ANNUAL PRODUCTION **700,000 bottles**
HECTARES UNDER VINE **120**
VITICULTURE METHOD **Conventional**

The estate is a veteran of the Caserta wine scene and its strong, unremitting drive for renewal has attracted the attention of enthusiasts back to the area where the legendary Falerno was produced in ancient times. Villa Matilde is run by Salvatore and Maria Ida Avallone, with the aid of Riccardo Cotarella, who crafts a series of wines from falanghina, aglianico, piedirosso and primitivo that can be defined as discerningly modern. Following the acquisition of Tenute di Altavilla in Irpinia, the range has been extended with Greco di Tufo, Fiano di Avellino and Taurasi.

We realize that we've said this before but Villa Matilde's performance this year really is its best ever. The fact is that each time we get the impression that the list has improved in both substance and stylistic identity. Falanghina Rocca dei Leoni '08 must be tasted to be believed, as it is far more than just a good-value wine. Cecubo, a blend of primitivo, piedirosso and aglianico, is increasingly on the ball, showing full-bodied and balanced in the '07 version. Falerno Bianco Caracci '07 has just a tad too much oak while Falerno Rosso Camarato '05 is flawless, showing more Mediterranean and terroir-true than ever.

○ Fiano di Avellino Cuvée Enrico '00	♟♟ 7
○ Fiano di Avellino Vigna della Congregazione '07	♟♟ 5
⊙ Serena Rosé '07	♟ 5
○ Fiano di Avellino Vigna della Congregazione '06	♟♟♟ 5
○ Fiano di Avellino Vigna della Congregazione '04	♟♟♟ 5
○ Fiano di Avellino Vigna della Congregazione '05	♟♟ 5
○ Fiano di Avellino Vigna della Congregazione '02	♟♟ 5

● Falerno del Massico Camarato '05	♟♟♟ 7
● Cecubo '07	♟♟ 5
○ Falanghina Rocca dei Leoni '08	♟♟ 3*
○ Falerno del Massico Bianco Vigna Caracci '07	♟♟ 5
○ Falerno del Massico Bianco '08	♟♟ 4*
○ Greco di Tufo Tenute di Altavilla '08	♟♟ 4
● Taurasi Tenute di Altavilla '05	♟♟ 6
● Aglianico Rocca dei Leoni '08	♟ 3
○ Falanghina di Roccamonfina '08	♟ 4
○ Fiano di Avellino Tenute di Altavilla '08	♟ 4
⊙ Terre Cerase '08	♟ 3
○ Falerno del Massico Bianco Vigna Caracci '05	♟♟♟ 5
○ Falerno del Massico Bianco Vigna Caracci '04	♟♟♟ 4*
● Falerno del Massico Camarato '04	♟♟♟ 6
● Falerno del Massico Camarato '01	♟♟♟ 6
● Falerno del Massico Rosso Vigna Camarato '00	♟♟♟ 6
● Falerno del Massico Rosso Vigna Camarato '98	♟♟♟ 6
● Falerno del Massico Rosso Vigna Camarato '97	♟♟♟ 6
● Vigna Camarato '95	♟♟♟ 5
● Cecubo '06	♟♟ 5

Aia dei Colombi

C.DA SAPENZE
82034 GUARDIA SANFRAMONDI [BN]
TEL. 0824817384
www.aiadeicolombi.it

The Pascale brothers' small estate is one of the most authentic voices in the Guardia Sanframondi area. As often before, we were impressed chiefly by the whites, which have clarity, flesh and tension. Sannio Fiano '08 is reminiscent of the splendid '06 while Guardiolo Falanghina '08 is one rung below.

O Sannio Fiano '08	💬💬 4*
O Guardiolo Falanghina '08	💬 3

Alois

LOC. AUDELINO
VIA RAGAZZANO
81040 PONTELATONE [CE]
TEL. 0823876710
www.vinialois.it

This year, we gave a short profile to Alois, the old Caserta family famous for its silks, which entered the world of wine in 1992. The list is currently being redefined and the top performer was Settimo '07, from equal parts of pallagrello nero and casavecchia.

● Settimo '07	💬💬 4*
O Caulino '08	💬 4

Aminea

VIA SANTA LUCIA
83040 CASTELVETERE SUL CALORE [AV]
TEL. 082765787
www.aminea.com

With an annual production of over 600,000 bottles, Aminea is one of the largest wineries in the fragmented Irpinia district. It is a joint project involving Michele Fede, Mimì Mongiello, Antonio D'Aliasi and Michele Morza, and stands out for its reliable production offered at reasonable prices.

● Irpinia Aglianico Monsignore '07	💬 5
O Sannio Falanghina Tre Rupi '08	💬 4

Angelarosa

VIA ARIELLA, 1
83030 SANTA PAOLINA [AV]
TEL. 0825964431
www.angelarosa.it

Almost 40 years of hands-on experience accumulated by Nunzio Aurisicchio lie behind this young winery. The vineyards are situated in some of the finest wine country in the Greco di Tufo area, between Sanata Paolina and Montefusco, so it is no surprise that the Greco di Tufo '08 is excellent.

O Greco di Tufo '08	💬💬 4*
● Irpinia Campi Taurasini '07	💬💬 4

Giuseppe Apicella

FRAZ. CAPITIGNANO
VIA CASTELLO SANTA MARIA, 1
84010 TRAMONTI [SA]
TEL. 089856209
www.giuseppeapicella.it

Giuseppe Apicella's wines are among the best that the Costa d'Amalfi can muster to show off its qualities as a superb terroir. An original crafter of reds, Apicella won us over with Colle Santa Marina '08, a racy, appetizing white. 'A Scippata Riserva '05 still has a way to go.

O Costa d'Amalfi Tramonti Bianco Colle Santa Marina '08	💬💬 4*
● Costa d'Amalfi Tramonti Rosso '07	💬💬 4*
● Costa d'Amalfi Tramonti Rosso A' Scippata Ris. '05	💬💬 6

Cantine degli Astroni

FRAZ. ASTRONI
VIA SARTANIA, 48
80126 NAPOLI
TEL. 0815884182
www.cantineastroni.com

The Astroni hill, between Agnano and Pozzuoli, is part of the splendid Campi Flegrei zone, where piedirosso and falanghina have traditionally been grown. The winery run by Gerardo Vernazzaro, a leading figure on the Neapolitan wine scene, offers a wide, diversified range.

O Fiano di Avellino Vitis Apianus '08	💬💬 4*
O Astro Falanghina Extra Dry	💬 4
O Campi Flegrei Falanghina Colle Imperatrice '08	💬 4
O Campi Flegrei Falanghina Strione '07	💬 5

Bambinuto

via Cerro
83030 Santa Paolina [AV]
tel. 0825964634
info@cantinabambinuto.com

Bambinuto is one of the many small wineries established by long-time growers in Irpinia in the last 20 years in response to the fall in grape prices. However, Raffaele Aufiero and his family have set their sights high, as testified by the excellent Greco di Tufo Picoli '08.

○ Greco di Tufo Picoli '08	🍷🍷	5

Barone

via Giardino, 2
84070 Rutino [SA]
tel. 0974830463
www.cantinebarone.it

Barone's wines are very important in an area like Cilento, which has great but often unexpressed potential. Giuseppe Di Fiore, aided by Vincenzo Mercurio, has put together an effective list with a recognizable style, in which the ready-to drink wines are currently the best.

● Pietralena Aglianico '08	🍷🍷	4*
● Cilento Aglianico '07	🍷	4
● Miles '07	🍷	6

Boccella

via Sant'Eustachio
83040 Castelfranci [AV]
tel. 082772574
giuseppebocella@hotmail.it

This tiny Castelfranci winery, run by Raffaele Boccella with the help of Fortunato Sebastiano, is ready to join the big names. Its first release of Taurasi, the '05, strolled straight into our finals, where it impressed us with a powerful, forthright character, despite aggressive extract.

● Taurasi '05	🍷🍷	6
● Irpinia Campi Taurasini Rasott '07	🍷🍷	4
○ Irpinia Fiano '06	ΥΥ	4*

Ca' Stelle

via Nazionale Sannitica, 48
82030 Castelvenere [BN]
tel. 0824940232
www.castelle.it

The Assini brothers are quietly consolidating the family winery, which is one of the most reliable in the municipality with the greatest area under vine in Campania. Their range is wide and varied in terms of varieties and wine types. We found Sannio Falanghina '08 very convincing.

○ Sannio Falanghina '08	🍷🍷	3*
● Sannio Barbera '08	🍷	4
⊙ Sannio Rosato '08	🍷	4

Calafè

loc. Vigna
83030 Prata di Principato Ultra [AV]
tel. 0825781010
calafe@alice.it

Calafè is a conflation of Camilla, Laura and Federica, the granddaughters of Benito Petrillo, who is behind an ambitious project that focuses strongly on Greco di Tufo. It immediately set out to release a selection, Ariavecchia, and market it at least a year after harvest.

○ Greco di Tufo Ariavecchia '07	🍷🍷	6
● Irpinia Campi Taurasini '07	🍷🍷	4
○ Greco di Tufo '07	🍷	4

Il Cancelliere

c.da Iampenne, 45
Montemarano [AV]
tel. 082763557
www.ilcancelliere.it

"Il Cancelliere" (The Chancellor) is the nickname of Soccorso Romano, the founder of this Montemarano winery. Plots in the best areas, careful use of oak and Antionio Di Gruttola in the cellar make the memorable Taurasi Nero Nè '05 the natural outcome of what looks set to be glorious future.

● Taurasi Nero Nè '05	🍷🍷	4

OTHER WINERIES

Alexia Capolino Perlingieri

VIA MARRAIOLI, 58
82037 CASTELVENERE [BN]
TEL. 0824971541
www.capolinoperlingieri.com

Alexia Capolino Perlingieri carries on the adventure started by the Volla winery and relaunched 15 years later with the expansion of the cellar and the vineyards. The reds and rosés are from sciascinoso, aglianico and sangiovese while Sannio Greco Vento '08, the only white currently produced, is from greco.

○ Sannio Greco Vento '08		♔♔ 4*
● Sannio Sciascì '07		♔ 4

Caputo

VIA CONSORTILE
81032 CARINARO [CE]
TEL. 0818119337
www.caputo1890.it

Caputo's wines had been absent from our tastings for several years but this time they returned better than ever. The stars of the wide array of varietal and Campanian DOC wines are the powerful Greco di Tufo Vigne dei Lupo '08 and Asprinio d'Aversa Fescine '08, which offers impressive density and balance.

○ Asprinio d'Aversa Fescine '08		♔♔ 4*
○ Greco di Tufo V. dei Lupi '08		♔♔ 4*
● Casavecchia V. Reali '06		♔ 5
● Sannio Aglianico Clanius '08		♔ 4

La Casa dell'Orco

FRAZ. SAN MICHELE
VIA LIMATURO, 52
83039 PRATOLA SERRA [AV]
TEL. 0825967038
www.lacasadellorco.it

We are very pleased to welcome this Irpinia winery back to the Guide. The Musto family's estate produces a series of wines in a highly distinctive, soft-textured style, which works particularly well with the '08 vintage of Irpinia Coda di Volpe and Sannio Falanghina.

○ Irpinia Coda di Volpe '08		♔♔ 4*
○ Sannio Falanghina '08		♔♔ 4
○ Fiano di Avellino '08		♔ 4
○ Greco di Tufo '08		♔ 4

Tenuta del Cavalier Pepe

VIA SANTA VARA
83040 LUOGOSANO [AV]
TEL. 082773766
www.tenutacavalierpepe.it

Tenuta del Cavalier Pepe, an ambitious winery headed by the enthusiastic half-Belgian Milena Pepe, continues its rise. As we awaited its Taurasi, we were impressed by the brilliant performance of the three Aglianicos, particularly the excellent Terra del Varo '07.

● Irpinia Aglianico Terra del Varo '07		♔♔ 4*
● Irpinia Campi Taurasini Santo Stefano '07		♔♔ 5
⊙ Irpinia Aglianico Rosato del Varo '08		♔ 4
○ Irpinia Coda di Volpe Bianco di Bellona '08		♔ 4

Colle di San Domenico

S.S. OFANTINA KM 7,500
83040 CHIUSANO DI SAN DOMENICO [AV]
TEL. 0825985423
www.cantinecolledisandomenico.it

Colle di San Domenico is owned by the Violano family and has an annual production of 300,000 bottles. Its progress over the past few years has been slow but steady. While its wide range of Irpinian wines may not be electrifying, it continues to shine for above-average consistency and precision.

● Aglianico '07		♔♔ 3*
○ Falanghina del Beneventano '08		♔♔ 4
○ Greco di Tufo '08		♔ 5
● Irpinia Aglianico '07		♔ 4

D'Antiche Terre - Vega

C.DA LO PIANO - S.S. 7 BIS
83030 MANOCALZATI [AV]
TEL. 0825675358
www.danticheterre.it

The fact that we've assigned a short profile to one of Irpinia's veteran wineries is merely a matter of turnover. D'Antiche Terre's wines are as good as ever, commencing with Fiano di Avellino '08, which gives well-expressed, almost salty notes and even red fruits.

○ Fiano di Avellino '08		♔♔ 4*
○ Greco di Tufo '08		♔♔ 4*
○ Irpinia Coda di Volpe '08		♔♔ 3*
○ Eliseo di Serra '08		♔ 3

De Falco

VIA FIGLIOLA
80040 SAN SEBASTIANO AL VESUVIO [NA]
TEL. 0817713755
www.defalco.it

Sooner or later, we would like to see this important Vesuvian winery with almost 20 harvests behind it among the big names. De Falco consistently offers top quality in its rich, precisely crafted range, led this year by the memorable Vesuvio Lacryma Christi '08, in both red and white versions.

○ Vesuvio Lacryma Christi Bianco '08	▼▼	4*
● Vesuvio Lacryma Christi Rosso '08	▼▼	4*
○ Falanghina del Beneventano '08	▼	4
● Penisola Sorrentina Gragnano '08	▼	4

Di Meo

C.DA COCCOVONI, 1
83050 SALZA IRPINA [AV]
TEL. 0825981419
www.dimeo.it

In such a lively wine region as Campania, it is even possible that an estate like De Meo has to make do with a short profile. Although the quality of its wines remains as high as ever, we feel that the time has come for a change.

● Irpinia Rosso Don Generoso '04	▼▼	4*
○ Sannio Falanghina '08	▼▼	4*
○ Coda di Volpe '08	▼	4
○ Fiano di Avellino '08	▼	4

Donna Carmela

V.LE KENNEDY, 41
83030 MONTEFUSCO [AV]
TEL. 0825628030
aziendadonnacarmela@alice.it

Donna Carmela is run by its founder Pasquale Manganello, aided by Fortunato Sebastiano in the cellar. Following its stunning debut, the '08 vintage of Fiano di Avellino confirmed its quality with a distinctive interpretation of this Irpinian grape. Irpinia Aglianico '08 is very approachable.

○ Fiano di Avellino '08	▼▼	4*
○ Greco di Tufo '08	▼	4
● Irpinia Aglianico '08	▼	3
○ Fiano di Avellino Borgalanti '07	▼▼	4*

Castello Ducale

VIA CHIESA, 35
81010 CASTEL CAMPAGNANO [CE]
TEL. 0824972460
www.castelloducale.com

Castello Ducale, the Caserta winery owned by the Donato family, has an annual production of 100,000 bottles and performed very well in this year's tastings. The charming, heady Pallagrello Nero '06 is one of the very best of its kind while Sannio Falanghina '08 combines weight and varietal typicity.

● Pallagrello Nero '06	▼▼	5
○ Sannio Falanghina '08	▼▼	4
● Aglianico Contessa Ferrara '05	▼	5
○ Pallagrello Bianco del Ventaglio '08	▼	4

Cantine Elmi

C.DA CHIANZANO
83040 MONTEMARANO [AV]
TEL. 082765354
www.cantineelmi.it

Best known for its Avi di Chianzano brand, Elmi today is very different from the estate that took its first steps in the world of Irpinian wine. Orazio Delisio and Carmine Valentino are remodelling the range, which already features the juicy Irpinia Campi Taurasini '05.

● Irpinia Campi Taurasini '05	▼▼	5

Cantina Farro

FRAZ. BACOLI - LOC. FUSARO
VIA VIRGILIO, 16/24
80070 NAPOLI
TEL. 0818545555
www.cantinefarro.it

Michele Farro is one of the touchstones of the Campi Flegrei area. In addition to owning one of its long-established wineries, he is president of the consortium and the leading figure of a booming movement. His wines are reliably well typed, as demonstrated by Depié Rosé '08, from piedirosso.

⊙ Depié Rosé '08	▼▼	4*
○ Campi Flegrei Falanghina '08	▼	4
● Campi Flegrei Piedirosso '08	▼	4

Cantine Federiciane Monteleone

FRAZ. SAN ROCCO
VIA ANTICA CONSOLARE CAMPANA, 34
80016 MARANO DI NAPOLI [NA]
TEL. 0815764153
www.cantinefedericiane.com

This winery is one of the most consistent on the crowded Neapolitan wine scene. Production covers a wide area, from Irpinia to Sannio, the Sorrento peninsula and Campi Flegrei. Falanghina dei Campi Flegrei '08 is excellent.

○ Campi Flegrei Falanghina '08	🍷🍷 4*
● Penisola Sorrentina Gragnano '08	🍷 4
● Penisola Sorrentina Lettere '08	🍷 4
● Sannio Aglianico '07	🍷 4

Fontanavecchia

VIA FONTANAVECCHIA
82030 TORRECUSO [BN]
TEL. 0824876275
www.fontanavecchia.info

The passion with which Libero Rilla has built up the success of Fontanavecchia, a benchmark for connoisseurs of Taburno wines, is a given. We nonetheless feel that the estate's wines could express more verve and personality, particularly the big oak-aged reds.

● Aglianico del Taburno '06	🍷🍷 4*
○ Aglianico del Taburno Rosato '08	🍷 4
⊙ Principe Lotario Brut '06	🍷 5
○ Taburno Falanghina '08	🍷 3

Iannella

VIA TORA
82030 TORRECUSO [BN]
TEL. 0824872392
www.cantineiannellainterfree.it

There is always a chance of being profiled in our Guide, particularly if the producer can point to the precision and solidity of the wines crafted by Iannella, a Torrecusana estate that frequently combines quality with quantity and very reasonable prices. For proof, try the Taburno Falanghina '08.

○ Taburno Coda di Volpe '08	🍷🍷 4
○ Taburno Falanghina '08	🍷🍷 4
● Taburno Aglianico '06	🍷 4
● Taburno Aglianico 1920 '04	🍷 4

Macchialupa

FRAZ. SAN PIETRO IRPINO
VIA FONTANA
83020 CHIANCHE [AV]
TEL. 0825996396
www.macchialupa.it

Cleanliness, clarity and sound fruit sum up the style that we have come to expect from Angelo Valentino at the many wineries with which he works, but above all in the wines from his own estate. Macchialupa's list is topped by the splendid Taurasi '05 and Greco di Tufo '08.

○ Greco di Tufo '08	🍷🍷 4*
● Taurasi '05	🍷🍷 6
● Aglianico '07	🍷 4
○ Fiano di Avellino '08	🍷 4

Marianna

VIA DEI VIGNETI, 5
83010 GROTTOLELLA [AV]
TEL. 0825671252
www.vinimarianna.it

This year's Guide sees the return in grand style of the wines produced by Marianna, the longstanding Irpinia estate founded by Ciriaco Coscia and headed by Raffaele Panarella. The entire list is good, displaying precision and presence. Fiano di Avellino Ghirlandaio '07 is the stand-out.

○ Fiano di Avellino Ghirlandaio '07	🍷🍷 5
● Irpinia Aglianico Moro di Pietra '07	🍷🍷 4
○ Irpinia Coda di Volpe '08	🍷🍷 4
● Taurasi Ris. '04	🍷🍷 6

Guido Marsella

VIA MARONE, 2
83010 SUMMONTE [AV]
TEL. 0825626555

Although the charming, determined Guido Marsella has not sent any samples for our Guide for several years now, we feel it our duty to taste his Fiano di Avellino, which is a mainstay of the DOC zone. The '07 is as rich and opulent as ever but slightly lacking in depth.

○ Fiano di Avellino '07	🍷🍷 4*
○ Fiano di Avellino '05	🍷🍷 4*
○ Fiano di Avellino '04	🍷🍷 4

Masseria Felicia

FRAZ. CARANO
LOC. SAN TERENZANO
81030 SESSA AURUNCA [CE]
TEL. 0823935095
www.masseriafelicia.it

Masseria Felicia is a solid, serious winery whose chief aim is to bring out the very best in the unique features of the volcanic vineyards of Sessa Aurunca. This is ideal country for making concentrated, minerally Falernos like Etichetta Bronzo, whose '06 version missed our finals by a hair's breadth.

○ Falerno del Massico Bianco Anthologia '08	🍷🍷	4*
● Falerno del Massico Rosso Etichetta Bronzo '06	🍷🍷	6
● Falerno del Massico Rosso '07	🍷	4
○ Sinopea '08	🍷	4

Masseria Frattasi

VIA TORRE VARONI, 15
82016 MONTESARCHIO [BN]
TEL. 0823351740
www.masseriafrattasi.it

One of the finest growing areas for falanghina is the side of the Taburno that slopes down towards Montesarchio, where the mineral characteristics of this Sannio grape are enhanced to the full. Masseria Frattasi's Falanghina di Bonea '08 is exemplary in this respect and is the best wine on a reliable list.

○ Fiano Acquafredda '08	🍷🍷	4*
○ Taburno Falanghina di Bonea '08	🍷🍷	4*
● Taburno Iovi Tonant '05	🍷	7

Migliozzi

FRAZ. CASALE DI CARINOLA
VIA APPIA KM 179
CARINOLA [CE]
TEL. 0823704275
www.rampaniuci.it

The Falerno area, once mentioned almost solely in association with its glorious but very distant past, is taking on an increasingly important role in the present. This is due in particular to new wineries, such as Viticoltori Migliozzi, whose Falerno del Massico Rosso Rampaniuci '07 is very convincing..

● Falerno del Massico Rampaniuci '07	🍷🍷	5

La Molara

C.DA PESCO
83040 LUOGOSANO [AV]
TEL. 082778017
www.lamolara.com

Although Taurasi '05 did not repeat the splendid performances of the past two vintages, it remains the most representative wine from Luogosano estate La Molara, owned by seven partners. Aged exclusively in large barrels, it focuses on acidity rather than extract, displaying a slightly grassy finish.

● Taurasi Santa Vara '05	🍷🍷	6
○ Fiano di Avellino Jovis '08	🍷	4

Cantina dei Monaci

FRAZ. SANTA LUCIA, 206
83030 SANTA PAOLINA [AV]
TEL. 0825964350
www.cantinadeimonaci.it

Angelo Carpenito and Maria Coppola own one of Irpinia's best wineries in terms of average quality and peaks of excellence. For several years now, it has given us an excellent duo of Fiano di Avellino and Greco di Tufo. Fiano di Avellino is superior in the '08 version, showing minerality and great flavour.

○ Fiano di Avellino '08	🍷🍷	4
○ Greco di Tufo '08	🍷🍷	4
○ Greco di Tufo '06	🍷🍷	4*

Abbazia di Montevergine

FRAZ. MERCOGLIANO
VIA LORETO, 1
83013 AVELLINO
www.vinidimontevergine.it

Montevergine is one of the best-known shrines to the Virgin in southern Italy. Its traditions are safeguarded Benedictine monks, some in the form of products and recipes like the famous Anthemis herb liqueur. Now there is also a range of Irpinian wines, crafted by Riccardo Cotarella.

○ Fiano di Avellino San Guglielmo '08	🍷🍷	4*
○ Greco di Tufo San Guglielmo '08	🍷	4
● Irpinia Aglianico San Guglielmo '07	🍷	4

Mustilli

VIA CAUDINA, 10
82019 SANT'AGATA DE' GOTI [BN]
TEL. 0823718142
www.mustilli.com

Is it possible for one of the region's oldest wineries to present itself as an intriguing newcomer? The answer is yes, if it gives itself the kind of makeover Mustilli appears to have had in the past few years. Four of its wines won Two Glasses with their simple, forthright style.

O Falanghina Spumante Brut	♥♥	5
● S. Agata dei Goti Aglianico Cesco di Nece '06	♥♥	5
O S. Agata dei Goti Falanghina '08	♥♥	4*
O S. Agata dei Goti Falanghina V. Segreta '08	♥♥	4

Ocone

LOC. LA MADONNELLA
VIA DEL MONTE, 56
82030 PONTE [BN]
TEL. 0824874040
www.oconevini.it

We admit that we have a weakness for Ocone's wines. Although not flawless, they reveal genuine soul. Taburno Aglianico Diomede '04 is a great classic, with notes of roots and spices, while the '08 vintage of Fiano Oca Bianca is the best ever.

● Aglianico del Taburno Diomede '04	♥♥	5
O Oca Bianca '08	♥♥	4
O Taburno Falanghina '08	♥	4
O Taburno Falanghina V. del Monaco '08	♥	4

Oppida Aminea - Muratori

LOC. EREMITA
82100 BENEVENTO
TEL. 0824334061
www.fratellimuratori.com

Brescian producer Muratori has been present in Campania for a few years with a dual-location project based in Sannio with Oppida Aminea, focusing on supple, weighty whites, and on Ischia with Giardini Arimei, known for its wine made from overripe native grapes.

O Sannio Caucino '08	♥♥	4*
O Giardini Arimei	♥	6
O Sannio Fiano Pelike '08	♥	4

Gennaro Papa

P.ZZA LIMATA, 2
81030 FALCIANO DEL MASSICO [CE]
TEL. 0823931267
www.cantinapapa.it

Antonio Papa is becoming the prince of primitivo-based Falerno, a variety that has been grown in Terra di Lavoro for around 200 years. His best-known wine is Falerno del Massico Campantuono, whose '07 vintage confirms its big, powerful style, nicely supported by acid backbone and an elegant tannic weave.

● Falerno del Massico Primitivo Campantuono '07	♥♥	6
● Falerno del Massico Primitivo Campantuono '06	♀♀	6
● Falerno del Massico Primitivo Campantuono '05	♀♀	6

Petilia

LOC. CAMPO FIORITO
C.DA PINCERA
83011 ALTAVILLA IRPINA [AV]
TEL. 0825991696
petilia@interfree.it

We have to admit we are a little disappointed. After two spectacular versions, we were hoping that Greco di Tufo di Petilia '08 would take our highest accolade. Instead, we have to make do with a wine that is merely excellent. This year, we preferred the firm, dynamic Fiano di Avellino '08.

O Fiano di Avellino '08	♥♥	4*
O Greco di Tufo '08	♥♥	4*
☉ Irpinia Aglianico Campo Fiorito '08	♥	4

Ciro Picariello

VIA MARRONI
83010 SUMMONTE [AV]
TEL. 0825702516
www.ciropicariello.com

The special combination of Summonte and Monfredane vineyards has allowed Ciro Picariello and his wife Rita's Fiano di Avellino to become a touchstone for the DOC zone. This is confirmed by the '07 edition, which is the best from the vintage tasted this year.

O Fiano di Avellino '07	♥♥	4*
O Fiano di Avellino '06	♀♀	4*
O Fiano di Avellino '05	♀♀	4*

La Pietra di Tommasone

VIA PROVINCIALE FANGO, 98
80076 LACCO AMENO [NA]
TEL. 0813330330
www.tommasonevini.it

This winery has long been a banker at our Campanian tastings. Credit goes to Antonio Monti and his ability to interpret Ischia's varied ampelographic heritage without distorting the true nature of the grapes. In this edition, the whites performed best, starting with Ischia Biancolella '08.

○ Ischia Biancolella '08	🍷🍷 4*
○ Terradei '08	🍷🍷 4*
○ Pithecusa Bianco '08	🍷 4
● Pithecusa Rosso '07	🍷 5

Il Poggio

VIA DEFENZE, 4
82030 TORRECUSO [BN]
TEL. 0824874068
www.ilpoggiovini.it

Vintage after vintage, Carmine Fusco's wines confirm their place among the best buys from the Torrecusa area. Falanghina del Taburno '08 echoes the harmonious, carefree style of the previous versions while Aglianico del Taburno '05 is subtle yet lively.

● Taburno Aglianico '05	🍷🍷 4*
○ Taburno Falanghina '08	🍷🍷 4*
○ Falanghina Extra Dry	🍷 4
● Mirabilis '06	🍷 4

Andrea Reale

LOC. BORGO DI GETE
VIA CARDAMONE, 75
84010 TRAMONTI [SA]
TEL. 089856144
www.aziendaagricolareale.it

Although not technically DOC wines, Luigi Reale's production is to all intents and purposes the offspring of Costa d'Amalfi. The whites are made from biancazita and biancolella, and the reds from piedirosso, the typical varieties of the Tramonti area, which Luigi interprets in a dry, flavoursome style.

● Borgo di Gete '07	🍷🍷 7
● Cardamone '08	🍷🍷 5
○ Aliseo '08	🍷 4
⊙ Getis '08	🍷 4

Russo

LOC. CARAZITA
VIA FONTANA DELLO SPALATRONE
83030 TAURASI [AV]
TEL. 063240964
www.cantinerussotaurasi.com

This young Taurasi winery, run by Ermanno Russo and his daughter Marcella, will certainly not settle for anything less than a starring role. Its vocation as a red-producing estate is testified by the beefy, palate-caressing Taurasi Spalatrone '05. Irpinia Campi Taurasini Macrì '06 is also decent.

● Taurasi Spalatrone '05	🍷🍷 6
● Irpinia Campi Taurasini Macri '06	🍷 4

San Francesco

FRAZ. CORSANO
VIA SOFILCIANO, 18
84010 TRAMONTI [SA]
TEL. 089876748
www.vinitenutasanfrancesco.it

This year saw the best-ever performance by the delightful winery owned by Chiara Di Palma and Gaetano Bove, stars of the Costa d'Amalfi Tramonti subzone. We've noted the delicate poise of its whites several times in the past but this year we admired a vigorous Tramonti Rosso Quattro Spine Riserva '06.

○ Costa d'Amalfi Bianco Per Eva '08	🍷🍷 4*
⊙ Costa d'Amalfi Tramonti Rosato '08	🍷🍷 4*
● Costa d'Amalfi Tramonti Rosso Quattrospine Ris. '06	🍷🍷 6
○ Costa d'Amalfi Tramonti Bianco '08	🍷 4

Sanpaolo - Magistra Vini

C.DA SAN PAOLO
83042 ATRIPALDA [AV]
TEL. 0825610307
info@cantineemera.com

Torrioni's biggest winery is even larger. Although located in the heart of Greco di Tufo country, this year's best scores came from the '08 Falanghinas. Aria, Acqua, Terra and Fuoco are four separately fermented selections that mark the first stage of a plan involving consultant oenologist Vincenzo Mercurio.

○ Falanghina Aria '08	🍷🍷 4
○ Falanghina del Beneventano '08	🍷🍷 4
○ Falanghina Fuoco '08	🍷🍷 4
○ Falanghina Terra '08	🍷 4

OTHER WINERIES

Santiquaranta

C.DA TORREPALAZZO
82030 TORRECUSO [BN]
TEL. 0824876128
www.santiquaranta.it

Santiquaranta is the fruit of a joint venture between Fortore cider producer Luca Baldino and Enrico De Lucia, owner of a long-established Benevento winery. The list is very interesting and its highlights this year are the firm Aglianico del Beneventano '06 and the balanced Moscato Passito '07.

● Aglianico del Beneventano '06	🍷🍷 5
○ Moscato Passito '07	🍷🍷 6
● Sannio Aglianico '07	🍷 4

Fattoria Selvanova

VIA SELVANOVA
81010 CASTEL CAMPAGNANO [CE]
TEL. 0823867261
www.fattoriaselvanova.com

Antonio Buono's delightful winery never puts a foot wrong. The decision to focus on aglianico in the Caiazzo area has produced a trio of impressive wines with aromatic integrity and well-defined tannins. A tad more complexity would have brought the leap forward we have been expecting for a few vintages.

● Aglianico Selvanova '05	🍷🍷 6
○ Pallagrello Bianco Acquavigna '07	🍷🍷 5
● Silicata '05	🍷🍷 6
● Vignantica '07	🍷 4

La Sibilla

FRAZ. BAIA
VIA OTTAVIANO AUGUSTO, 19
80070 BACOLI [NA]
TEL. 0818688778
www.sibillavini.it

You can't talk about surprises when it comes to one of the best-equipped wineries in the province of Naples. But we get the distinct impression that the Di Meo family's cellar has upped its pace, for Falanghina dei Campi Flegrei Cruna Delago '07 is a little gem of complexity and flavour.

○ Campi Flegrei Falanghina Cruna Delago '07	🍷🍷 5
● Marsiliano '07	🍷🍷 6

Sorrentino

VIA CASCIELLO, 5
80042 BOSCOTRECASE [NA]
TEL. 0818584963
www.vinivesuvio.com

It is thanks to cellars like this, owned by the Sorrentino family, that Vesuvian wines are more than just a name evoking a unique area. Fragrance, lightness and minerality are the shared characteristics of an excellent list, topped by the surprising Natì '07, from coda di volpe.

● Don Paolo '07	🍷🍷 4*
○ Natì '07	🍷🍷 4*
☉ Vesuvio Lacryma Christi Rosato '08	🍷🍷 3
○ Vesuvio Lacryma Christi Bianco V. Lapillo '08	🍷 4

Cantina del Taburno

VIA SALA, 16
82030 FOGLIANISE [BN]
TEL. 0824871338
www.cantinadeltaburno.it

Cantina del Taburno is one of the most important co-operative wineries in central and southern Italy. This year, its range has been drastically remodelled. Without Bue Apis and Delius, Serra Docile '06, from coda di volpe, leads a list that is decent but without any particular highlights.

○ Coda di Volpe Serra Docile '06	🍷🍷 4
○ Fiano '08	🍷 4
● Piedirosso '06	🍷 5
○ Taburno Falanghina '08	🍷 4

Luigi Tecce

C.DA TRINITÀ
83052 PATERNOPOLI [AV]
TEL. 082771375
ltecce@libero.it

The winery patiently established by Luigi Tecce is first and foremost a workshop. Chestnut tuns, barrels, barriques and native yeasts are among the ingredients in an original winemaking process that is still being refined. There's great potential in the complex, tight-knit Taurasi Poliphemo '05.

● Taurasi Poliphemo '05	🍷🍷 7

Telaro

LOC. CALABRITTO
VIA CINQUE PIETRE, 2
81045 GALLUCCIO [CE]
TEL. 0823925841
www.vinitelaro.lt

The years go by but Telaro's wines are always there to recount the distinctive features of the Galluccio and Roccamonfina areas. As usual, this profile does not have enough space to list all the wines worthy of mention, which are headed by Galluccio Rosso Ara Mundi Riserva '06.

● Calivierno '07	♛♛ 5
● Galluccio Ara Mundi Ris. '06	♛♛ 5
○ Fiano Le Cinque Pietre '08	♛ 4
○ Greco di Roccamonfina Le Cinque Pietre '08	♛ 4

Terre Irpine

P.ZZA MUNICIPIO, 6
83055 STURNO [AV]
TEL. 0825448774
WWW.terreirpine.it

This Campanian winery is a new entry that looks set to stay. It is situated in Sturno, a little mountain town in the Ufita and Miscano valleys. In the cellar Fortunato Sebastiano's hand is discernible in the Taurasi '05, which expresses warm vigour despite its slightly rustic tannins.

● Taurasi '05	♛♛ 6

Torre Varano

LOC. TORREVONO, 2
82030 TORRECUSO [BN]
TEL. 0824876372
www.torrevarano.it

The winery founded in 2003 in the Torrecusa area by Nicola D'Occhio is a very pleasant surprise. Its highly consistent list is made even more interesting by its extremely fair prices. The flagship wine is Taburno Aglianico Trentasei+Sei, whose '05 version is excellent.

● Taburno Aglianico Trentasei+Sei '05	♛♛ 5
● Taburno Aglianico '06	♛ 4
⊙ Taburno Aglianico Rosato '08	♛ 3
○ Taburno Falanghina '08	♛ 3

Antica Masseria Venditti

VIA SANNITICA, 120/122
82037 CASTELVENERE [BN]
TEL. 0824940306
www.venditti.it

Nicola Venditti, one of the first Campanian producers to focus on sustainable viticulture, is making excellent progress. His wines may sometimes surprise but they have a deep, earthy energy that becomes even more evident with bottle ageing.

● Sannio Aglianico Marraioli '06	♛♛ 4
○ Sannio Falanghina Vàndari '08	♛ 4
○ Solopaca Bianco Vigna Bacalàt '08	♛ 4

Villa Raiano

LOC. SAN MICHELE DI SERINO
VIA CERRETO S.N.
83020 SERINO [AV]
TEL. 0825595663
www.villaraiano.it

This is not a dismissal but simply an invitation to return to its role as a gifted outsider that has made Villa Raiano one of Campania's best wineries. All the wines are decent but they could be better still, particularly considering the estate's great viticultural and technical resources.

○ Fiano di Avellino '08	♛♛ 4
○ Fiano di Avellino Ripa Alta '07	♛♛ 5
○ Greco di Tufo '08	♛♛ 4
○ Falanghina Beneventano '08	♛ 4

Volpara

FRAZ. TUORO
VIA PODESTI, 23
81037 SESSA AURUNCA [CE]
TEL. 0823938051

We will be keeping an eye on this new Sessa Aurunca winery. At its debut this year, it strolled straight into our finals with Falerno del Massico Tuoro Riserva '06, which is elegant, earthy and spice-veined. The other wines are a fair way behind, the best being Falerno Bianco Donna Jolanda '08.

● Falerno del Massico Rosso Tuoro Ris. '06	♛♛ 5
○ Falerno del Massico Bianco Donna Jolanda '08	♛ 4
● Falerno del Massico Rosso Tuoro '04	♛ 4

BASILICATA

Step by step and harvest by harvest, Basilicata's wine sector is consolidating its status as a wine region. For us, that means average production standards are getting more reliable, it is easier to read the various traits of each zone and some of the more mature, reflective style decisions will be reinforced. As always, the heart of this evolution is in the Vulture area, with its well-established wineries and several newcomers to the scene. Some of the producers are natives while others have come from further afield to make major investments. For some time, this wide range of perspectives and wine cultures was seen by the territory as a limitation, allowing individuals to emerge but not an integrated system. One consequence of the environment was that a lot of energy was wasted. A certain anarchy in wine production generated confusion among critics and aficionados. It still does. Dealing with the Aglianico del Vulture designation means sorting through at least four different vintages each year, as well as struggling with early-drinking wines, selections, crus and riserva wine. Alongside powerful, concentrated Aglianicos, possibly even with a generous helping of new oak, we find more elegant, nuanced interpretations that play on completely different registers. In this respect, it is crucial to know the players in the field beforehand. We feel that at this moment in time the mood is decidedly less oppressive and we perceive that producers are working better together, with more chances for discussion and the area's image becoming more distinct. Of course old habits die hard. We mean those wineries who decided not to send their samples this time because they didn't like what we said about them in the past. We're sorry about that but luckily there are plenty of new recruits who deserve attention, especially Carbone and Eleano, but also Cardinale and Lucania. We can't really say those on the list of award winners are newcomers but they do reveal the underlying sea change. A vintage as generous yet classic as 2006 ensured Three Glasses again went to Basilisco's Aglianico del Vulture. We were delighted that Paternoster's fantastic Don Anselmo Riserva '05 strode back into the big league. The '07 version of Elena Fucci's usual potent Titolo completes a formidable trio, where Bisceglia and Terre degli Svevi have slipped back but are nonetheless excellent. Just pipped at the post were Macarico, D'Angelo and Cantine del Notaio, and we also hail Cantina di Venosa's best performance ever. Things were a little more complicated around Matera, an area still looking for a solid identity for its vineyards and production. That said, we see excellent potential in wineries like Battifarano, Dragone, Masseria Cardillo, Taverna and Guide newcomer Crocco.

Basilisco

VIA PIAVE, 35
85022 BARILE [PZ]
TEL. 0972725477
basilisco@interfree.it

CELLAR SALES
PRE-BOOKED VISITS

ANNUAL PRODUCTION **31,000 bottles**
HECTARES UNDER VINE **10**
VITICULTURE METHOD **Conventional**

Michele Cutolo's passion, Nunzia Calabrese's clear-headed pragmatism and Lorenzo Landi's calm precision all make for a great team that has quickly turned the Agricola Basilisco business into a leader in Vulture. The winery also has its own very distinct style, focusing on flavour and smoothness, with elegant use of oak. The vineyards are in the Barile countryside, at Macarico and Gelosia.

We know that historically Aglianico del Vulture Basilisco is a classic wine that prefers a classic vintage. When we tasted the '06, we couldn't help recalling the splendid '01. It has the same capacity to interweave heat and vigour, allowing graceful, close-knit tannins to emerge. The profile on the nose is still evolving, with brooding hints of burnt embers and coffee beans, but we gave it Three Glasses straight away. It's a great red with a long life ahead of it. The Aglianico del Vulture Teodosio '07 was also good news, a second wine with a firm, incisive weave and a hint of piquancy in the finish.

● Aglianico del Vulture Basilisco '06	♟♟♟	6
● Aglianico del Vulture Teodosio '07	♟♟	4
● Aglianico del Vulture Basilisco '04	♟♟♟	6
● Aglianico del Vulture Basilisco '01	♟♟♟	6
● Aglianico del Vulture Basilisco '05	♟♟	6

Bisceglia

C.DA FINOCCHIARO
85024 LAVELLO [PZ]
TEL. 097288409
www.agricolabisceglia.com

CELLAR SALES
PRE-BOOKED VISITS

ANNUAL PRODUCTION **400,000 bottles**
HECTARES UNDER VINE **55**
VITICULTURE METHOD **Organic certified**

The Bisceglia phenomenon swept across the Vulture district like a hurricane. This Lavello winery, with Maurizio Angeletti managing the cellars, became the local leader in no time at all. Bisceglia has put together a fantastic vineyard holding and consolidated production to something like 500,000 bottles. The winery's core grape is aglianico, used for both current and riserva versions of Gudarrà. The rest of the range features syrah and chardonnay.

Bisceglia didn't get its third consecutive accolade this year but that's not to say the performance was disappointing. It just missed a top prize but the '03 Aglianico del Vulture Gudarrà Riserva was one of the year's best in Italy. There were virtually no signs of the scorchingly hot growing year and we found intact, juicy black berry fruits over hints of blossom and, above all, a smattering of quite fiery black pepper on the nose. Nor did the palate seem very much like a typical 2003, showing fresh, dynamic and with slightly over-evolved but very fine-grained tannins. The Armille Syrah '08 is full-bodied and earthy.

● Aglianico del Vulture Gudarrà Ris. '03	♟♟	6
● Armille '08	♟♟	4
● Aglianico del Vulture Gudarrà '05	♟♟♟	5
● Aglianico del Vulture Gudarrà '04	♟♟♟	5*

Cantine del Notaio

VIA ROMA, 159
85028 RIONERO IN VULTURE [PZ]
TEL. 0972723689
www.cantinedelnotaio.com

CELLAR SALES
PRE-BOOKED VISITS

ANNUAL PRODUCTION 170,000 bottles
HECTARES UNDER VINE 27
VITICULTURE METHOD Biodinamico certificato

The Cantine del Notaio saga marked the start of a new era in the history of Basilicata wine. Tenacious Gerardo Giuratrabocchetti, with Luigi Moio at his side, was one of the first to show what could be achieved by careful vine management, limited yields and new cellar techniques like ageing in small casks. Currently, the Rionero in Vulture winery has 27 biodynamically managed hectares planted vine and produces a series of aglianico wines. The labels are differentiated by ageing and labelled with notarial terms in tribute to the winery's name.

Aglianico del Vulture La Firma '06 just about sums up Cantine del Notaio's innovative, pioneering spirit. It's a very modern wine whose concentration and rich extraction are its most evident traits. But they're traits we'd now like to see combined with enhanced layering and better integration of the oak. An excellent Aglianico del Vulture Il Repertorio '07, considered a sort of younger sibling, confirmed its highly respectable standing. The biggest surprise, however, came from Il Preliminare and La Raccolta, two '08 Aglianicos fermented off the skins.

Carbone

VIA NITTI, 48
85025 MELFI [PZ]
TEL. 0972237866
www.carbonevini.it

CELLAR SALES
PRE-BOOKED VISITS

ANNUAL PRODUCTION 45,000 bottles
HECTARES UNDER VINE 18
VITICULTURE METHOD Conventional

Luca and Sara Carbone's small winery has changed its line-up slightly but is still one of the most interesting new businesses in the Vulture district. Despite the fact it is still finding its feet to some extent – the new cellar is still being built – the winery manages to make its mark. Credit goes to the owners and a serious holding of old vines in the Melfi area, at an elevation of about 550 metres, which are managed with a pared-down, minimalist approach. Technical support is provided by Sergio Paternoster.

Carbone's flagship label was missing this year. Sara and Luca decided to leave their Aglianico del Vulture Stupor Mundi in the cellar for some extra ageing. It's a decision we approve and it allows us to focus on their second and third-label wines. The Aglianico del Vulture 400 Some '07, after 12 months in barrique, is broad and complex but held back slightly by the oak and slightly dusty tannins. We thought Aglianico del Vulture Terra dei Fuochi '07, aged partly in steel and partly in pre-used barriques, was more straightforward but also suppler and racier.

● Aglianico del Vulture La Firma '06	▼▼ 7
● Aglianico del Vulture Il Repertorio '07	▼▼ 5
○ Il Preliminare '08	▼▼ 4
○ La Raccolta '08	▼▼ 6
◉ Il Rogito '07	▼ 5
● L'Atto '07	▼ 4
○ La Stipula Brut '06	▼ 5
● Aglianico del Vulture La Firma '00	♀♀♀ 6
● Aglianico del Vulture Il Sigillo '03	♀♀ 7
● Aglianico del Vulture La Firma '05	♀♀ 7
○ L'Autentica '06	♀♀ 6

● Aglianico del Vulture 400 Some '07	▼▼ 5
● Aglianico del Vulture Terra dei Fuochi '07	▼▼ 4*
● Aglianico del Vulture 400 Some '06	♀♀ 5
● Aglianico del Vulture Stupor Mundi '06	♀♀ 6
● Aglianico del Vulture Terra dei Fuochi '06	♀♀ 4*

D'Angelo

VIA PROVINCIALE, 8
85028 RIONERO IN VULTURE [PZ]
TEL. 0972721517
www.dangelowine.com

CELLAR SALES
PRE-BOOKED VISITS

ANNUAL PRODUCTION **380,000 bottles**
HECTARES UNDER VINE **50**
VITICULTURE METHOD **Conventional**

With all due respect to the other prestigious local wineries, D'Angelo is an icon on the Vulture panorama. The approach to winemaking is consistent and rigorous, based on long maceration and extended cask time, which results in wines that are not always easy to read but are absolutely intriguing. The evergreens have gradually been flanked with a series of wines with a rather more modern attitude and greater focus on fruit definition. Donato D'Angelo can now line up a more cohesive, dependable array.

We missed the elegance and depth in the better vintages of the first-rate Vigna Casellera this year. Nevertheless, the winery performed well and the Aglianico del Vulture Donato D'Angelo '07 was enough banish our regrets for the missing label. The nose has a tertiary style, with nuances of leather and sandalwood enhancing jammy notes. Lean and rakish on the palate, it has a no-nonsense feel about it. Light years away are the Serra delle Querce '07, an aglianico and merlot blend, and the nicely oaky Aglianico del Vulture Valle del Noce '07.

Cantine Di Palma

C.DA SCAVONI
85028 RIONERO IN VULTURE [PZ]
TEL. 0972722891
www.cantinedipalma.com

CELLAR SALES
PRE-BOOKED VISITS

ANNUAL PRODUCTION **130,000 bottles**
HECTARES UNDER VINE **15.5**
VITICULTURE METHOD **Conventional**

Antonio Di Palma and his family run a tight ship on their 15 or so hectares of vines in the Rionero and Barile areas. The winery produces only Aglianico del Vulture, presented as first and second labels. Nibbio Grigio is matured almost totally in new wood whereas Tenuta Piano Regio ages in small once and twice-used casks. The wines are generally rich and concentrated, acquiring complexity and unfolding with the passage of time.

The line-up this year was only at half strength. Aglianico del Vulture Il Nibbio Grigio '07 was available for tasting only from the cask. We were impressed by what we tasted but we're reserving judgment until next time around. In the meantime, we can compliment Di Palma on another fine version of the Aglianico del Vulture Tenuta Piano Regio. The 2007 is outstanding for its fruit-rich pulp and minerally depth, with smoky, spicy nuances never too far away. The palate lacks the fullness and the final acid kick of a real champion but it does expand purposefully with nice tannic grip.

● Aglianico del Vulture Donato D'Angelo '07	▼▼	5
● Aglianico del Vulture Valle del Noce '07	▼▼	6
● Serra delle Querce '07	▼▼	6
● Canneto '07	▼	5
● Aglianico del Vulture V. Caselle Ris. '01	♀♀♀	4*
● Aglianico del Vulture Donato D'Angelo '06	♀♀	5
● Aglianico del Vulture V. Caselle Ris. '04	♀♀	5
● Aglianico del Vulture V. Caselle Ris. '03	♀♀	5
● Aglianico del Vulture Valle del Noce '05	♀♀	6
● Serra delle Querce '06	♀♀	6

● Aglianico del Vulture Tenuta Piano Regio '07	▼▼	4*
● Aglianico del Vulture Il Nibbio Grigio Et. Nera '03	♀♀♀	6
● Aglianico del Vulture Il Nibbio Grigio Et. Nera '05	♀♀	6
● Aglianico del Vulture Il Nibbio Grigio Et. Nera '04	♀♀	6
● Aglianico del Vulture Tenuta Piano Regio '05	♀♀	4*
● Aglianico del Vulture Tenuta Piano Regio '04	♀♀	4*

Eleano

C.DA PIAZZOLLA, 10
85028 RIONERO IN VULTURE [PZ]
TEL. 0972722273
www.eleano.it

CELLAR SALES
PRE-BOOKED VISITS

ANNUAL PRODUCTION **26,000 bottles**
HECTARES UNDER VINE **5**
VITICULTURE METHOD **Conventional**

The Vulture area also has its garage wineries. One is Alfredo Cordisco and Francesca Grieco's tiny Rionero operation, set up in 2002 and now working with Cristoforo Pastore. Production doesn't reach 30,000 bottles but that's already enough to reveal the enormous potential of a fast-growing business. Eleano is making its mark thanks mainly to a style that is distinctive and quite personal, based on understatement and evolution rather than on muscle, with astute use of oak. We'll be keeping an eye out.

Although the winery lists Aglianico del Vulture Dionysus as the second label, we were thought it was the top product this time and sent the '06 vintage to the finals, where it was just a whisper away from the top award. The wine is aged in steel and barrique, and its allure lies in a substantial, breezy nose laden with balsam and spice, as well as pencil lead and orange peel. Compact and well sustained, it is even more succulent and crisp in the mouth, braced by a solid, ripe extract. The Eleano '05 suffers from slight reduction and a bitter note in the finish but we enjoyed its graceful, salty temperament.

Elena Fucci

C.DA SOLAGNA DEL TITOLO
85022 BARILE [PZ]
TEL. 0972770736
az.elenafucci@tiscall.lt

CELLAR SALES
PRE-BOOKED VISITS

ANNUAL PRODUCTION **18,000 bottles**
HECTARES UNDER VINE **6.15**
VITICULTURE METHOD **Natural**

In 2000, Elena decided to tackle just one label, approximately three and a half – six with the new plantings – hectares under vine at Contrada Solagna near Barile, at an altitude of over 600 metres. Titolo is concentrated but never over the top and we see it as today's concept of a modern Aglianico in the strictest sense of the term: innovative in structure but very classic in essence.

It wasn't an easy task to repeat the success of the stunning '06 but Elena and family managed to raise our surprise and admiration another notch. We expected even more fruitiness from the '07 harvest but perhaps at the risk of overdoing aromas and structure. Instead we found a luscious, incisive wine with enticing nuances of incense and oak that adds layers without being aggressive. Above all, the caressing, creamy palate has plenty of backbone, holding its own right through to the finish. A worthy Three Glass encore.

- Aglianico del Vulture Dioniso '06   4*
- Aglianico del Vulture Eleano '05   6
- Aglianico del Vulture Dioniso '05   4
- Aglianico del Vulture Pian dell'Altare '03   6

- Aglianico del Vulture Titolo '07   + 7
- Aglianico del Vulture Titolo '06   6
- Aglianico del Vulture Titolo '05   6
- Aglianico del Vulture Titolo '02   6

Macarico

P.ZZA CARACCIOLO, 7
85022 BARILE [PZ]
TEL. 0972771051
www.macaricovini.it

CELLAR SALES
PRE-BOOKED VISITS
FOOD

ANNUAL PRODUCTION 22,000 bottles
HECTARES UNDER VINE 5
VITICULTURE METHOD Natural

We're sure it won't be long before Rino Botte and Renato Abrami's excellent winery gets its first Three Glass prize. It's a small business, established in 2001, and now makes just over 20,000 bottles. Its mission is to imbue their wines with the best of the powerful, austere fruit from their splendid Contrada Macarico vines. The two Aglianico del Vulture labels in the range are barrique aged, with perceptibly more new oak in the Macarico. Both wines are richly extracted but also very edgy and difficult to evaluate in the first few months but we think they should age well.

For the second year in a row, Rino Botte managed to get both family treasures into the finals. The Aglianico del Vulture Macarç '07 has intriguing oriental spices on the nose, interwoven with intact juicy red berries. It's vibrant in the mouth but the finish lacks a little complexity. The Aglianico del Vulture '06 is more massive but also more unsettled. Elegant juniper, cocoa powder, pencil lead and coffee chiaroscuros greet the nose to return on a creamy palate only just dried by tannins from the oak. We'll be interested to see how it evolves over the next few years. For the moment, we'll err on the side of caution.

● Aglianico del Vulture '06	♟♟	6
● Aglianico del Vulture Macarì '07	♟♟	5*
● Aglianico del Vulture '05	♟♟	6
● Aglianico del Vulture '04	♟♟	6
● Aglianico del Vulture '03	♟♟	6
● Aglianico del Vulture Macarì '06	♟♟	5

Paternoster

C.DA VALLE DEL TITOLO
85022 BARILE [PZ]
TEL. 0972770224
www.paternostervini.it

CELLAR SALES
PRE-BOOKED VISITS

ANNUAL PRODUCTION 150,000 bottles
HECTARES UNDER VINE 20
VITICULTURE METHOD Organic certified

The story of the Paternoster family is stamped with all the stubborn pride so typical of people from Basilicata. They can boast 80 harvests, a world-famous label, and a production strategy that has dealt with today's challenges by building new cellars in Contrada Valle del Titolo and creating a second label, Villa Rotondo. The dialogue between past and future is reflected in the wines, which can be decidedly innovative or equally successful classics. The range includes a sparkling Moscato called Clivus and Barigliott, a semi-sparkling Aglianico.

We'll get straight to the point and say how pleased we are to see Paternoster back on the Three Glass list. What a comeback it is. Aglianico del Vulture Don Anselmo Riserva '05 is just fantastic, with enticing smoky notes of cigar and quinine, but above all able it has an ability to change pace on the palate in a succession of shock waves that reminded us of some superb versions from the early 1990s. The finishing touch came from the Aglianico del Vulture Rotondo '06. It's opulent but with a more predictable evolution and the oak seems to curb the fruit to some extent.

● Aglianico del Vulture Don Anselmo Ris. '05	♟♟♟+	7
● Aglianico del Vulture Rotondo '06	♟♟	6
● Barigliòtt '08	♟♟	4*
○ Moscato della Basilicata Clivus '08	♟♟	4*
● Aglianico del Vulture Synthesi '06	♟	4
● Aglianico del Vulture Don Anselmo '94	♟♟♟	5
● Aglianico del Vulture Rotondo '01	♟♟♟	6
● Aglianico del Vulture Rotondo '00	♟♟♟	6
● Aglianico del Vulture Rotondo '98	♟♟♟	5*
● Aglianico del Vulture Don Anselmo '04	♟♟	7
● Aglianico del Vulture Rotondo '05	♟♟	6

Terre degli Svevi

LOC. PIAN DI CAMERA
85029 VENOSA [PZ]
TEL. 097231263
www.giv.it

CELLAR SALES
PRE-BOOKED VISITS
FOOD

ANNUAL PRODUCTION **300,000 bottles**
HECTARES UNDER VINE **120**
VITICULTURE METHOD **Conventional**

This is the Basilicata branch of Gruppo Italiano Vini, one of the first large-scale investments the group has made in this region. Terre degli Svevi was set up in 1998 and now has 120 hectares under vine in the Venosa, Barile and Maschito areas. The vineyards are mainly aglianico, with a little müller thurgau and gewårztraminer. Technical management is in the hands of Nunzio Capurso, whose style can be seen in the solid, up-to-date yet never over-blown style of the wines. The flagship reds are aged in barriques, only some of which are new.

Despite just missing Three Glasses, this year's tastings were well up to other recent vintages. Above all, we're pleased to note that the most representative wines have lightened further, beginning with the lovely Aglianico del Vulture Re Manfredi '06, whose earth and sea notes tickle a laid-back, subtly salty, palate. It's held back by being slightly over-evolved but we're on what seems to be the right track. Lagging not far behind was the Aglianico del Vulture Serpara '05. The pure aglianico Re Manfredi Rosato '08 is impressive.

● Aglianico del Vulture Re Manfredi '06	🍷🍷	5
● Aglianico del Vulture Vign. Serpara '05	🍷🍷	7
⊙ Re Manfredi Rosato '08	🍷🍷	4
○ Re Manfredi Bianco '08	🍷	5
● Aglianico del Vulture Re Manfredi '05	YYY	5
● Aglianico del Vulture Re Manfredi '99	YYY	5*
● Aglianico del Vulture Vign. Serpara '03	YYY	5*

Cantina di Venosa

LOC. VIGNALI
VIA APPIA
85029 VENOSA [PZ]
TEL. 097236702
www.cantinadivenosa.it

CELLAR SALES
PRE-BOOKED VISITS

ANNUAL PRODUCTION **700,000 bottles**
HECTARES UNDER VINE **800**
VITICULTURE METHOD **Conventional**

The determination of 450 member growers was the motor that drove Cantina di Venosa back to its rightful place amongst Basilicata's leading winemakers. It may be a surprise but the distinction is well deserved because the Cantina di Venosa is one of Southern Italy's top co-operatives. Since 1957, it has been contributing significantly to the development of this great little wine district. The outright star of a range focusing keenly on the price factor is the Aglianico, presented in various vintages and with various degrees of oak maturation.

Three wines in the finals speak louder than words for the state of health of the selection sent to us by Cantina di Venosa. The list leader performed over and above the call of duty as the '06 Aglianico del Vulture Carato Venusio emerged with an almost aristocratic profile, comprising notes of leather and tobacco, and a distinctly tempting style. Aglianico del Vulture Vignali '07 is on the same wavelength, showing barely overripe but subtle and salty. The Aglianico del Vulture Terre di Orazio '07 is austere with maturation-derived aromatics that come through in truffle and humus nuances.

● Aglianico del Vulture Carato Venusio '06	🍷🍷	6
● Aglianico del Vulture Terre di Orazio '07	🍷🍷	4*
● Aglianico del Vulture Vignali '07	🍷🍷	4*
● Aglianico del Vulture Gesualdo da Venosa '06	🍷🍷	5
● Aglianico del Vulture Bali'Aggio '07	🍷	3
○ Dry Muscat Terre di Orazio '08	🍷	3
⊙ Terre di Orazio Rosé '08	🍷	4
● Aglianico del Vulture Carato Venusio '03	YY	5
● Aglianico del Vulture Carato Venusio '01	YY	5

Alovini

VIA GRAMSCI, 30
85013 GENZANO DI LUCANIA [PZ]
TEL. 0971776372
www.alovini.it

Oronzo Alò's lovely winery continues to grow, producing Aglianico del Vulture in the Genzano di Lucania area. Despite a decidedly difficult vintage, the best impression was made by the close-woven, intact Aglianico del Vulture Al Volo '03, with its lively nuance of dried roses

● Aglianico del Vulture Al Volo '03	♟♟	5
● Le Ralle Rosso '08	♟	3

Francesco Bonifacio

C.DA PIANI DI CAMERA
85029 VENOSA [PZ]
TEL. 097231436
www.cantinebonifacio.it

Francesco Bonifacio is the brains behind this interesting Venosa winery, founded in 2002 and now producing more than 100,000 bottles a year. Watch out for the prices and for the Aglianico del Vulture La Sfida '05. It's slightly reined in by oak, but very dense.

● Aglianico del Vulture La Sfida '05	♟♟	4
● La Sfida '08	♟	2
○ Miky Bì '08	♟	3

Masseria Cardillo

S.S. 407 BASENTANA KM. 97,5
75012 BERNALDA [MT]
TEL. 0835748992
www.masseriacardillo.it

Rocco and Giovanni Graziadei were determined to develop a dynamic winery with partner Oronzo Alò. It is one of the healthiest wineries in the Matera area. This year, we liked the Matera Moro Malandrina '06, a blend of primitivo, cabernet and merlot, with opulent fruit and well-gauged oak.

● Matera Moro Malandrina '06	♟♟	5
⊙ Bacche Rosa '08	♟	3
○ Ovo Di Elena '08	♟	3
● Vigna Giadi '07	♟	3

Tenuta Cardinale

C.DA GELOSIA
85022 BARILE [PZ]
TEL. 0804316340
www.tenutecardinale.com

Contrada Gelosia di Barile is one of the most typical subzones in the Aglianico del Vulture area. It's also the home of the Tenuta Cardinale, a small, young winery that has already caught our eye, above all for Priore '06. It combines spice and oak with a supple, edgy palate.

● Aglianico del Vulture Priore '06	♟♟	5
○ Donna Giulia '08	♟	4

Cantine Cerrolongo

C.DA CERROLONGO, 1
75020 NOVA SIRI [MT]
TEL. 0835536174
www.cerrolongo.it

The wide range of varieties may well be the most striking aspect of the fast-developing Matera district, which is home to the Battifarano family's long-standing winery. We were happy with Cerrolongo Rosato '08, a sangiovese and syrah blend, and the all-chardonnay Toccacielo Bianco '08.

⊙ Cerrolongo Rosato '08	♟	3
○ Chardonnay Toccacielo '08	♟	4

Crocco

VIA KENNEDY, 36
75023 MONTALBANO JONICO [MT]
TEL. 3391933941
masseriacrocco@tiscali.it

If they've started as they mean to go on, there should be a rosy future ahead for this small new winery named for the most famous of local brigands. For its Guide debut, Crocco gave us a Merlot, Il Brigante and a Primitivo, Matinone, both '08. Both are drinkable and anything but dull.

● Il Brigante '08	♟♟	4
● Mantinone '08	♟	4

OTHER WINERIES

Dragone

LOC. PIETRAPENTA
PIAZZA DEGLI OLMI, 66
75100 MATERATEL. 0835261740
www.dragonevini.it

The doyen of Matera wineries, now run by Michele Dragone, has tradition and experience in spades. In the past, we pointed out its potential on the sparkling wine front but this year we're going to highlight a soft, creamy Matera Primitivo Pietrapenta '06.

● Matera Primitivo Pietrapenta '06	♈♈	4*

Eubea

S.DA PROVINCIALE, 8
85020 RIPACANDIDA [PZ]
TEL. 0972723574
www.agricolaeubea.com

The Sasso family winery is still one of the most original in the Vulture district. This year, we only managed to taste a cask sample of the two leading labels, Roinos and Covo dei Briganti '07. We're reserving judgement until next time around.

● Aglianico del Vulture Il Covo dei Briganti '06	♈	6
● Aglianico del Vulture Ròinos '06	♈	8

Giannattasio

P.ZZA ANGELO BOZZA, 5
85022 BARILE [PZ]
TEL. 0972770571
www.giannattasio.net

Once again, Giannattasio gave us a couple of striking wines. The Aglianico del Vulture Arcà '06 is one of the best wines from the region, with a fleshy, minerally profile that reveals nuances of talc and forest floor. Bramea '07 successfully tempers softness with vigour.

● Aglianico del Vulture Arcà '06	♈♈	5
● Aglianico del Vulture Bramea '07	♈♈	4*
● Aglianico del Vulture Arcà '05	♈♈	5

Grifalco della Lucania

LOC. PIAN DI CAMERA
85029 VENOSA [PZ]
TEL. 097231002
grifaicodellalucania@email.it

Fabrizio and Cecilia Piccin's wines again gave a noteworthy performance and again it was thanks to the Aglianico del Vulture Grifalco. The '07 resembles the preceding vintage but with slightly more oak, which the wine has more than enough body to absorb over time. We also liked the Gricos '07.

● Aglianico del Vulture Gricos '07	♈♈	3*
● Aglianico del Vulture Grifalco '07	♈♈	4

Viticoltori in Vulture Lagala

C.DA LA MADDALENA
85029 VENOSA [PZ]
TEL. 0972375007
www.lagala.it

Here's another promising newcomer from the Venosa area, this time from Contrada Maddalena. The Antonio Lagala winery has chosen to celebrate two famous local figures on its labels: Major Mario De Bernardi, known as the "Eagle of Vulture", and Pirro del Balzo, Prince of Altamura

● Aglianico del Vulture Aquila del Vulture '05	♈♈	6
● Rosso del Balzo '06	♈	3

Lelusi Viticoltori

VIA CROCE, 3
85022 BARILE [PZ]
TEL. 024043805
www.lelusivini.com

Simona and Luca Labarbuta, aided by Sergio Paternoster, are the couple behind one of Barile's emerging wineries. We believe there is plenty of room for improvement, especially as regards fine-tuning the aromatics, but overall we were happy, particularly with Aglianico del Vulture Shesh '07.

● Aglianico del Vulture Lelusi '06	♈	6
● Aglianico del Vulture Shesh '07	♈	4

Cantine Madonna delle Grazie

LOC. VIGNALI
VIA APPIA
85029 VENOSA [PZ]
TEL. 097235704
www.cantinemadonnadellegrazie.it

The wines we get each year from the Latorraon family's well-established Vignali di Venosa winery are anything but standardized. Try the Aglianico del Vulture Liscone '06, which may kick off with a slightly confused nose of mushrooms and leaves but then unfurls hefty extract.

● Aglianico del Vulture Liscone '06	♥♥	4

Armando Martino

VIA LUIGI LAVISTA, 2A
85028 RIONERO IN VULTURE [PZ]
TEL. 0972721422
www.martinovini.com

Aglianico del Vulture wouldn't be the same without the far-sighted passion of Armando Martino, who owns one of the best-known local wineries. He isn't resting on his laurels, if this year's samples are anything to go by. Pretoriano '05 almost made the finals with its classic tobacco and rose.

● Aglianico del Vulture Bel Poggio '05	♥♥	5
● Aglianico del Vulture Oraziano '05	♥♥	6
● Aglianico del Vulture Pretoriano '05	♥♥	6

Tenuta del Portale

LOC. LE QUERCE
85022 BARILE [PZ]
TEL. 0972724691
tenutadelportale@tiscali.it

Le Querce di Barile. The name – The Oaks of Barile – tells you that you are right in the heart of Vulture and aglianico country. This is where Filomena Ruppi's small winery currently produces two wines, a basic Aglianico del Vulture and the Le Vigne a Capanno selection.

● Aglianico del Vulture '07	♥	4
● Aglianico del Vulture Le Vigne a Capanno '07	♥	5

Regio Cantina

LOC. PIANO REGIO
85029 VENOSA [PZ]
TEL. 3346966263
www.regiocantina.it

If Paolo Zamparelli's appealing winery can find a complete style, it will start to shoot up the regional wine hit parade. Paolo's range is already dependable and Aglianico del Vulture Donpà '06 has what it takes to be the winery's flagship.

● Aglianico del Vulture Donpà '06	♥♥	5
● Aglianico del Vulture Solagna '07	♥	3
O Brinato '08	♥	3

Taverna

C.DA TAVERNA, 15
75020 NOVA SIRI [MT]
TEL. 0835877083
www.aataverna.com

This long-established Matera winery only presented two labels this year, but that was enough to show how that Taverna is forging ahead in fine style. The Lagarino di Dioniso '06 merlot, cabernet and aglianico blend is simply one of Basilicata's best IGTs.

● Lagarino di Dioniso '06	♥♥	4
● Syrah '07	♥	3

Terra dei Re

VIA MONTICCHIO S. S. 167 KM 2,700
85028 RIONERO IN VULTURE [PZ]
TEL. 0972725116
www.terradeire.com

There's no denying that this is one of the most professional, ambitious wineries to have emerged in Basilicata wine in recent years. The bottles we tried this year revealed the usual appreciable fruit-rich pulp, blunted by some uncertainty on the nose that wasn't there in the past.

● Aglianico del Vulture Divinus '06	♥	5
● Aglianico del Vulture Vultur '07	♥	4
● Pacus '07	♥	4

PUGLIA

This excellent vintage year has shown exceptional results. No other words can describe the outcome of this year's tastings. For years, we have been writing about Puglia's as yet unexpressed potential and progressive growth in quality, but we never really expected such a significant leap forward, furthermore with the (re)discovery of an area like Gioia del Colle that seemed completely forgotten and almost destined to obscurity. Puglia has now actually moved into double digits, from seven to twelve Three Glass awards, with truly extraordinary growth. Two estates (both with a Primitivo di Gioia del Colle) won Three Glasses the same year they entered the Guide (another two reached our finals). These are not estates that were "forgotten" in previous editions, but rather young producers in their early years of production. This was a year for primitivo with twice the number of prizewinning wines. Generally speaking, wines from this variety have excited us like never before. More and more attention is also being paid to bush-trained vines, protecting old vineyards, and low yields per hectare; as if awareness had been silently growing over the past few years of the unique quality and importance for Puglia of this type planting system and the age of the vines. Although up till a few years ago only two or three growers spoke out in defence of this sort of viticulture, today more than a few are convinced this is a real asset for wine in Puglia. We mention all this without forgetting that even now hectares and hectares of bush-trained vines are being uprooted to obtain European financing for reducing surface area under vine, without realizing those are precisely the vineyards that should not be eradicated, considering they produce low yields and naturally tend toward quality. Returning to our results, four estates received Three Glasses for the first time: Chiaromonte with the Gioia del Colle Primitivo Ris. '06, Pietraventosa with the Gioia del Colle Primitivo Riserva '06, Morella with the Primitivo Old Vines '07, and Rasciatano with the Rasciatano Nero di Troia '07. Three greats have returned: Conti Zecca with the Nero '06, Leone de Castris with the Salice Salentino Rosso Donna Lisa Riserva '05, and Cantele with the Amativo '07. Finally, five wines from last year have proven themselves once again, furthermore with the same label: Torrevento with the Castel del Monte Rosso Vigna Pedale Riserva '06, Due Palme with the Salice Salentino Rosso Selvarossa Riserva '06, Fino with the Primitivo di Manduria Es '07, Castello Monaci with the Artas '07, and Tormaresca with the Masseria Maime '07. Last but not least, Gianfranco Fino won the award as Grower of the Year, also a first for Puglia.

A Mano

5° TRAV. PROV. CASAMASSIMA, 8
70023 GIOIA DEL COLLE [BA]
TEL. 0803434872
www.amanowine.com

PRE-BOOKED VISITS

ANNUAL PRODUCTION **235,000 bottles**
HECTARES UNDER VINE **N.D.**
VITICULTURE METHOD **Conventional**

Elvezia Sbalchiero, from Friuli, and Californian oenologist Mark Shannon have created a winery that produces quality wines with no vineyards of its own. In 1999, they started looking for old, bush-trained vineyards and contacting growers and small winemakers with a view to creating high-quality products. Since then, business has developed further, so much so that today they follow the progress of vineyards across Puglia, constantly assisting growers with their vines and, thanks to exceptional efforts in the cellar, making some of Puglia's most interesting wines.

Let's start with a correction. The Prima Mano and Negroamaro reviewed last year were respectively from 2005 and 2006. Having said this, the Sbalchiero-Shannon duo continues to improve so much that they reached our finals with two wines, both from primitivo. Prima Mano '06 has great aromatic precision, giving iodine and hints of Mediterranean scrub, blackberry and ink, and a full palate, rich in fruit, and good length. Also excellent is the suppler and fresher Primitivo '07, which is always focused and taut, completely drinkable. The pleasant, fruity Negroamaro '07 and citrussy, full-flavoured Fiano Greco '08 are both very good.

● Prima Mano '06	♀♀	5
● Primitivo '07	♀♀	3*
○ Fiano - Greco '08	♀♀	3*
● Negroamaro '07	♀♀	3*
○ Fiano - Greco '07	♀♀	3*
● Prima Mano '05	♀♀	5

Cantina Albea

VIA DUE MACELLI, 8
70011 ALBEROBELLO [BA]
TEL. 0804323548
www.albeavini.com

CELLAR SALES
PRE-BOOKED VISITS

ANNUAL PRODUCTION **300,000 bottles**
HECTARES UNDER VINE **40**
VITICULTURE METHOD **Conventional**

Started in the early 20th century, Cantina Albea – from the old name of Alberobello – has over the past few years become a benchmark in the area for making the most of native grape varieties and one of Puglia's top winemakers. But there is more to the range here than just nero di Troia, primitivo and negroamaro; chardonnay, sauvignon and montepulciano complete the significant production thanks to the efforts of the staff led by Claudio Sisto with consultancy from Riccardo Cotarella.

No Three Glass awards this year but the monovarietal Nero di Troia Lui '07 is high quality. A complex nose of black and sour cherry with sweet tobacco ushers in a long, vibrantly substantial if still young palate with nice stuffing and fresh fruit. Worth waiting for. Also good is the clean, fresh Petranera '07, a Primitivo with intense black berry fruit aromas, which is simpler but pleasing and an easy drinker. The Locorotondo Il Selva '08 is floral and well crafted, yet shows a slightly sweet finish that fails to deliver the right freshness while the supple Raro '07 from negroamaro and primitivo has notes of olive paste. Both are well typed.

● Lui '07	♀♀	6
● Petranera '07	♀♀	4
○ Locorotondo Il Selva '08	♀	3
● Raro '07	♀	5
● Lui '06	♀♀♀	6
● Lui '05	♀♀♀	6
● Lui '04	♀♀	6

Giuseppe Attanasio

via per Oria, 13
74024 Manduria [TA]
tel. 0999737121
www.primitivo-attanasio.com

ANNUAL PRODUCTION 11,000 bottles
HECTARES UNDER VINE 6
VITICULTURE METHOD Conventional

This estate has just a few hectares of vineyards in the area around Manduria and produces exclusively Primitivo di Manduria DOC. The bush-trained vines are low-yielding and grow on tufaceous-limestone soils. Since 2000, grapes have been fermented in a modern cellar built inside a skilfully restored 19th-century structure and Luca Attanasio, with the collaboration of oenologist Bruno Garofano, has been progressively converting vineyard management from conventional to biodynamic.

Luca Attanasio's estate goes straight into the Guide's main section thanks to some really exciting wines. Two reached our finals. Primitivo di Manduria '07 gives caressing aromas of cocoa powder, red berry fruits, rhubarb and Mediterranean scrub, and an intense, round palate with good fruit and a slight sweet note in the finish. Primitivo di Manduria Dolce Naturale 15,5° '06 is a wine Attanasio produces only in the best years. It offers elegant red berry fruit and spice with great length. The Dolce Naturale 15° '07 is also good, showing balsamic and fruity with notes of cakes and dried figs but with a bit less length.

● Primitivo di Manduria '07	🍷🍷	5
● Primitivo di Manduria Dolce Naturale 15,5° '06	🍷🍷	6
● Primitivo di Manduria Dolce Naturale 15° '07	🍷🍷	6

Cantele

s.p. Salice Salentino San Donaci
km 35,600
73010 Guagnano [LE]
tel. 0832705010
www.cantele.it

CELLAR SALES
PRE-BOOKED VISITS

ANNUAL PRODUCTION 1.800,000 bottles
HECTARES UNDER VINE 150
VITICULTURE METHOD Conventional

The Cantele family still expertly manages this large, reliable estate in Salento, which started out in the mid 20th century. The family has learned how to combine quantity with quality, producing a broad range of wines from native as well as international varieties, some harvested from their own vineyards and some purchased from the many local growers they have been working with for decades. We should mention the consistent quality that characterizes both the niche products as well as wines produced in bigger quantities.

The 60-40 primitivo and negroamaro blend Amativo has won Three Glasses again. The 2007 version has a deep, balsamic nose with hints of liquorice and black berry fruit before the nice, taut palate shows fruity and balanced. Another great wine is Teresa Manara Negroamaro '07. It has floral aromas and an elegant, fruit-rich palate with lovely length and easy drinkability. Varius '07, a blend of half negroamaro with cabernet sauvignon and merlot is good, as is Teresa Manara Chardonnay '08, one of the best Puglian whites with citrussy aromas and a rich, fresh palate. But this estate's entire range is very dependable.

● Amativo '07	🍷🍷🍷	5*
● Teresa Manara Negroamaro '07	🍷🍷	4
○ Teresa Manara Chardonnay '08	🍷🍷	4*
● Varius '07	🍷🍷	4*
⊙ Negroamaro '08	🍷	3
● Primitivo '07	🍷	3
● Salice Salentino Rosso Ris. '06	🍷	3
● Amativo '03	🍷🍷🍷 (outline)	5*
● Amativo '05	🍷🍷 (outline)	5*
● Amativo '04	🍷🍷 (outline)	5*
● Varius '05	🍷🍷 (outline)	4*

Giancarlo Ceci

C.DA SANT'AGOSTINO
70031 ANDRIA [BA]
TEL. 0883564938
www.agrinatura.net

Chiaromonte

VIA PER SAMMICHELE Z.I.
70021 ACQUAVIVA DELLE FONTI [BA]
TEL. 080768575
nicola.chiaromonte@tin.it

ANNUAL PRODUCTION **500,000 bottles**
HECTARES UNDER VINE **70**
VITICULTURE METHOD **Organic certified**

Giancarlo Ceci's historic estate, located in the Andria countryside, produces organic wine, olive oil, fruit and vegetables and is one of the most reliable, promising wine operations around Castel del Monte. Giancarlo's philosophy involves respect for the land and biodiversity, and his wines – made mostly from native varieties – manage to express the best characteristics of this terroir.

All Ceci's wines are labelled Castel del Monte DOC. There are two Nero di Troia reds, the exciting Parco Marano '06 shows blackcurrant and smoky aromas leading to a structured palate with fine-grained tannins and an elegant finish themed with cinchona and liquorice. The less interesting Parco Grande '08 is simple, alcoholic and floral. The nice no Bianco '08 is poised and pleasant with peach and apricot notes. Ferula '08, a rosé from bombino nero, has rosewood aromas and a fresh palate and Pozzo Sorgente '08, a Chardonnay, shows camomile and citrus. Both are well made.

ANNUAL PRODUCTION **30,000 bottles**
HECTARES UNDER VINE **30**
VITICULTURE METHOD **Organic certified**

Founded in 1826, the historic Chiaromonte estate has worked hard at expanding and improving quality over the past few years. Nicola Chiaromonte represents the latest generation of this winemaking family and is the owner of the winery as well as the house oenologist. Alongside old, bush-trained vineyards, we now find several new, high-trained plantings, all organically grown. Only one variety – primitivo – is produced and used to create the three labels from the estate.

Almost no one has ever won Three Glasses on a Guide debut. But Nicola Chiaromonte did just that, totally charming us with his Gioia del Colle Primitivo Riserva '06. The dark ruby red wine has depth on the nose, which runs from ripe black berry fruit to spices and Mediterranean scrubland. The palate is elegant, yet at the same time shows great texture, density and fullness, driving on long and savoury with iodine notes with complexity and balance, despite 18% alcohol. A great Mediterranean wine. The estate also submitted the 2005 and there was little difference between the two vintages. The latter is fresher on the palate and slightly less full.

● Castel del Monte Rosso Parco Marano '06	♟♟	4
○ Castel del Monte Bianco '08	♟♟	3*
○ Castel del Monte Chardonnay Pozzo Sorgente '08	♟	3
☉ Castel del Monte Rosato Ferula '08	♟	3
● Castel del Monte Rosso Parco Grande '08	♟	3
● Castel del Monte Rosso Parco Grande '07	♟♟	3*
● Castel del Monte Rosso Parco Marano '05	♟♟	4*

● Gioia del Colle Primitivo Ris. '06	♟♟♟	8
● Gioia del Colle Primitivo Ris. '05	♟♟	7

D'Alfonso del Sordo

c.da Sant'Antonino
71016 San Severo [FG]
tel. 0882221444
www.dalfonsodelsordo.it

CELLAR SALES
PRE-BOOKED VISITS

ANNUAL PRODUCTION **390,000 bottles**
HECTARES UNDER VINE **90**
VITICULTURE METHOD **Conventional**

In 2001, the historic D'Alfonso del Sordo estate in the province of Foggia began collaborating with the agriculture department at the university of Foggia on various research projects, including one co-ordinated by Professor Luigi Moio to promote the nero di Troia variety. The vineyards near San Severo, standing at between 80 and 120 metres in altitude, are divided into three plots: Cotinone, Cappuccini and Coppanetta, where vinification and bottling are carried out. All the vineyards have north to north-west exposure and mainly limestone and clay soil.

In the absence of Doganera and Montero, the estate's top line was represented only the Guado San Leo '07 and Cava del Re '06. The first is a monovarietal Nero di Troia, introduced as usual with oak-veined aromas and hints of chocolate and cherry followed by a consistent palate that gives red berry fruit. Cava del Re is a single-varietal Cabernet Sauvignon with black berry fruit, nice body, close-knit tannins and great texture still masked by oak and hard to assess. The '08 San Severos from the Posta Arignano line are fresh and pleasant with good fruit.

● Cava del Re Cabernet Sauvignon '06	▼▼	6
● Guado San Leo '07	▼▼	5
○ San Severo Bianco Posta Arignano '08	▼	3
● San Severo Rosso Posta Arignano '08	▼	3
● Cava del Re Cabernet Sauvignon '05	▽▽	6
● Doganera '06	▽▽	6
● Doganera Merlot '05	▽▽	6
● Guado San Leo '06	▽▽	6
● Guado San Leo '05	▽▽	6
● Montero '07	▽▽	4*
● Montero '06	▽▽	4*

Cantine Due Palme

via San Marco, 130
72020 Cellino San Marco [BR]
tel. 0831617909
www.cantineduepalme.it

PRE-BOOKED VISITS

ANNUAL PRODUCTION **5,000,000 bottles**
HECTARES UNDER VINE **2000**
VITICULTURE METHOD **Conventional**

Due Palme is a growing, co-operative operation founded in 1989 that now includes around 850 member-growers. A major enterprise, over the past few years the winery has been outstanding for the remarkable quality of its products. The talented Angelo Maci, the co-operative's oenologist and president, has worked hard to protect the land and legacy of bush-trained vines that characterize this region, focusing particularly on the traditional varieties that best express the features of this terroir.

This makes three. Salice Salentino Rosso Selvarossa Riserva won Three Glasses for the third year running. The 2006 version has a spicy, balsamic nose with intense notes of black berry fruit. The palate is rich with good, dense texture, softness and length perked up by vibrant tension and nice balance. The rest of the range is also good. Bagnara '08 is a savoury, pleasant Fiano with nice freshness. Brindisi Rosso '07 has aromas of black berry fruit and liquorice, and a fresh, supple palate with a balsamic finish. Serre '08, a Susumaniello, shows upfront notes of plums and coffee, thrust and a pleasingly long finish.

● Salice Salentino Rosso Selvarossa Ris. '06	▼▼▼	5*
○ Bagnara '08	▼▼	4
● Brindisi Rosso '07	▼▼	4
● Serre '08	▼▼	4
● Squinzano Rosso '07	▼	4
● Salice Salentino Rosso Selvarossa Ris. '05	▽▽▽	5*
● Salice Salentino Rosso Selvarossa Ris. '04	▽▽▽	4*

Felline - Pervini

VIA SANTO STASI PRIMO - Z. I.
74024 MANDURIA [TA]
TEL. 0999711660
www.accademiadeiracemi.it

CELLAR SALES
PRE-BOOKED VISITS

ANNUAL PRODUCTION **180,000 bottles**
HECTARES UNDER VINE **23**
VITICULTURE METHOD **Conventional**

More than 15 years ago, Gregory Perrucci realized that the quality of Primitivo di Manduria, and wine from Puglia in general, would have to involve utilizing and restoring old bush-trained vineyards planted on red, limestone soil. Since then, he has ceaselessly promoted bush-training, striving to obtain the utmost from his vines in terms of typicity and drinkability, both in the good-quality, competitively priced Pervini line as well as Felline, where his oldest vineyards are located.

Gregory Perrucci's estate put on a solid performance, starting with the Primitivo di Manduria Felline '07, a pleasant, supple wine with aromas of cherry, spice and tobacco, and a fresh, fruity finish. Also very good is the Alberello '08, a blend of primitivo and negroamaro with black berry fruit and cherry tones, good body and balance. Vigna del Feudo '07, from primitivo, malvasia nera and ottavianello, is rich, full and spicy with good fruit. The simple, yet fresh Primitivo di Manduria Segnavento '08 with its good length, and the Primitivo di Manduria Archidamo '07, which offers clean floral and red berry aromas, are both well-crafted.

Gianfranco Fino

LOC. LAMA
VIA FIOR DI SALVIA, 8
74100 TARANTO
TEL. 0997773970
www.gianfrancofino.it

PRE-BOOKED VISITS

ANNUAL PRODUCTION **12,000 bottles**
HECTARES UNDER VINE **8**
VITICULTURE METHOD **Natural**

Gianfranco Fino set up this young estate in 2004 when he bought a 50-year-old, bush-trained vineyard of primitivo. Two years later, he acquired another bush-trained vineyard of negroamaro. Stringent bunch thinning and careful work in vineyard and cellar reflect his desire to produce unique wines while taking advantage of typical techniques and varieties from the local area. Despite its recent start, the estate has become a reference point for many young winemakers in the region. Gianfranco's wines have something of a cult following among reviewers and aficionados.

Again this year, Primitivo di Manduria Es won Three Glasses, maintaining high quality in the 2007 edition. The nose proffers a broad, intense, spice-and-balsam bouquet with notes of tobacco and wild berries to the fore. The palate is rich, full, deep, elegant and fresh despite rich alcohol and sweet fruit notes with a long, expansive finish. The monovarietal Negroamaro, Jo '07, is just as deep with dried fig and sweet almond aromas but the palate lacks a little savouriness and freshness, leaving it a bit too sweet with a finish of overripe black berry fruit.

● Alberello '08	♀♀ 3*
● Primitivo di Manduria Felline '07	♀♀ 4
● Vigna del Feudo '07	♀♀ 5
● Primitivo di Manduria Archidamo '07	♀ 3
● Primitivo di Manduria Segnavento '08	♀ 3
● Primitivo di Manduria Archidamo '06	♀♀ 3*
● Vigna del Feudo '06	♀♀ 5
● Vigna del Feudo '05	♀♀ 5
● Vigna del Feudo '04	♀♀ 5

● Primitivo di Manduria Es '07	♀♀♀+ 7
● Jo '07	♀♀ 7
● Primitivo di Manduria Es '06	♀♀ 6
● Jo '06	♀♀ 6
● Primitivo di Manduria Es '05	♀♀ 6
● Primitivo di Manduria Es '04	♀♀ 6

Masseria L'Astore

LOC. L'ASTORE
VIA G. DI VITTORIO, 1
73020 CUTROFIANO [LE]
TEL. 0836542020
www.lastoremasseria.it

CELLAR SALES
PRE-BOOKED VISITS

ANNUAL PRODUCTION **80,000 bottles**
HECTARES UNDER VINE **18**
VITICULTURE METHOD **Organic certified**

Astore Masseria has been the property of the Benegiamo-Di Summa family since the 1930s. At the end of the 1990s, Achille and his sons Paolo, Stefano and Luca Benegiamo decided to restart production, focusing on quality with a careful vineyard replanting programme. The vines are located in the area of Cutrofiano, 20 kilometres from the Ionian and Adriatic seas. Alongside classic native Salento varieties, there is also room for international varieties that help to express the rich, unique qualities of the Salento terroir.

The Benegiamo estate won a full profile thanks to Astore '06, a blend of aglianico and petit verdot with great structure and aromas of plum, spice, and black olive tapenade. The palate is still closed yet deep and intense. Primitivo Jema '07 is good, perhaps less rich, yet pleasant and balanced with floral notes of hyacinth and black berry fruit, well-integrated tannins and a long, fresh, fruity finish. Other wines are more than well-managed, particularly Massaro Rosa '08, a negroamaro rosé with a fruity nose running from cherry to blackberry and lychees, and a pleasant palate lacking only a hint of verve and tension to move to the next level.

Leone de Castris

VIA SENATORE DE CASTRIS, 26
73015 SALICE SALENTINO [LE]
TEL. 0832731112
www.leonedecastris.com

CELLAR SALES
PRE-BOOKED VISITS
FOOD

ANNUAL PRODUCTION **2.500,000 bottles**
HECTARES UNDER VINE **250**
VITICULTURE METHOD **Conventional**

Founded in 1665, the Leone De Castris estate could be defined as one of the symbols of wine and grape production in Puglia. The broad range has shown remarkably consistent quality over the years, thanks to the considerable effort expended in the vineyards and cellar. Though great attention is paid to the international market, the cellar works in full respect of the local area and strives to promote it.

Three Glasses return to Leone De Castris with Salice Salentino Rosso Donna Lisa Riserva '05. Rich, caressing aromas of ripe black cherries and Mediterranean scrub usher in a fresh palate with good texture and great depth. Five Roses Anniversario 65° Anno '08, from negroamaro and malvasia nera, is one of the best Italian rosés. On the nose, there are aromas of red berry fruit, wild roses and pomegranate, and then the palate shows fruit, length and acidity. Excellent scores also went to the Vigne Case Alte '08, a clean Sauvignon with notes of honey, dried spring flowers and almonds, and a crisp, fresh finish.

● L'Astore '06	♟♟ 5
● Jema '07	♟♟ 4*
● Filimei '08	♟ 4
⊙ Il Massaro Rosa '08	♟ 4
○ Krita '08	♟ 4
● Filimei '07	♟♟ 4
● L'Astore '05	♟♟ 5*

● Salice Salentino Rosso Donna Lisa Ris. '05	♟♟♟ 6
⊙ Five Roses Anniversario 65° Anno '08	♟♟ 4*
○ Vigna Case Alte '08	♟♟ 3*
● Elo Veni '08	♟ 4
⊙ Five Roses '08	♟ 4
○ Imago '08	♟ 3
○ Messapia '08	♟ 3
● Salice Salentino Rosso 50° Vendemmia Ris. '06	♟ 4
● Salice Salentino Rosso Maiana '08	♟ 3
● Salice Salentino Rosso Donna Lisa Ris. '01	♟♟♟ 6
● Salice Salentino Rosso Donna Lisa Ris. '00	♟♟♟ 6
● Salice Salentino Rosso Donna Lisa Ris. '99	♟♟♟ 6
● Salice Salentino Rosso Donna Lisa Ris. '95	♟♟♟ 5
⊙ Five Roses Anniversario 64° Anno '07	♟♟ 4*

Lomazzi & Sarli

C.DA PARTEMIO, S.S. 7
72022 LATIANO [BR]
TEL. 0831725898
www.vinilomazzi.it

CELLAR SALES
PRE-BOOKED VISITS
VISITOR FACILITIES
FOOD

ANNUAL PRODUCTION 1,000,000 bottles
HECTARES UNDER VINE 150
VITICULTURE METHOD Conventional

Structural renovations on the cellar and consultancy from Franco and Marco Bernabei have given new life to Lomazzi & Sarli over the past few years. This large estate, owned by the Dimastrodonato family and located near the Brindisi plain, has 30 per cent bush-trained vines – on plots with alluvial soil at a density of between 5,000 and 6,000 plants per hectare – and produces reliable wines sold mainly on foreign markets.

In spite of the low-key year, the Dimastrodonato quality is still dependable. Latias '07 is nice. It's a Primitivo with spicy, ripe fruit tones, and good grip and mouthfeel. Equally attractive is the fresher, more vibrant Salice Salentino Tenuta Partemio '07, with floral and black berry fruit sensations accompanied by oriental spice and cocoa powder. The other wines are well typed and well crafted, starting with the Brindisis, the fresh, floral Tenuta Partemio '06 and Solise Riserva '06. From sussumaniello, the Nomas '06 is below par, with fruit covered by oak on the nose and a note of over-extraction on the palate.

Alberto Longo

C.DA PADULECCHIA, S.P. 5
LUCERA-PIETRAMONTECORVINO KM 4
71036 LUCERA [FG]
TEL. 0881539057
www.albortolongo.it

CELLAR SALES
PRE-BOOKED VISITS

ANNUAL PRODUCTION 250,000 bottles
HECTARES UNDER VINE 35
VITICULTURE METHOD Conventional

This estate came from Alberto Longo's desire to create an estate that would take advantage of the terroir in Daunia. The cellar is housed in a lovely 19th-century farmhouse and the 35 hectares of vineyards are at Fattoria Cavalli and Masseria Celentano. Low yields and dense planting at from 6,000 to 12,000 plants per hectare show the commitment to producing top-quality wines from native as well as international varieties.

Alberto Longo's project continues to grow and develop, bearing fruit as it were. He made our finals for the first time with Le Cruste '07, a rich, intense Nero di Troia with touches of violet, black berry fruit and tobacco, and a fresh, dynamic palate with soft tannins. The new entry is also good. Griccio '08 is a single-variety Syrah with pleasant spice and outstanding fruity notes of cherry and red wild berries. Also nice is the classic Donnadele '08, a very pale pink "vin gris" with its own fan base, which shows floral aromas and a subtle, fascinating palate. The rest of the production is well made.

● Latias '07	♈♈ 4
● Salice Salentino Tenuta Partemio '06	♈♈ 3*
● Brindisi Rosso Solise Ris. '06	♈ 5
● Brindisi Rosso Tenuta Partemio '07	♈ 3
● Nomas '06	♈ 6
● Salice Salentino Rosso Irenico Ris. '06	♈ 5
● Tenuta Partemio Negroamaro '07	♈ 3
● Tenuta Partemio Primitivo '07	♈ 3
☉ Tenuta Partemio Rosato '08	♈ 3
● Nomas '05	♈♈ 6
● Nomas '04	♈♈ 5

● Le Cruste '07	♈♈ 5
☉ Donnadele '08	♈♈ 4
● Il Griccio '08	♈♈ 5
● Cacc'e Mmitte di Lucera '08	♈ 4
● Capoposto '08	♈ 4
○ Le Fossette '08	♈ 4
● Cacc'e Mmitte di Lucera '06	♈♈ 4
● Calcara Vecchia '06	♈♈ 4
● Le Cruste '06	♈♈ 5
● Le Cruste '05	♈♈ 5
● Le Cruste '04	♈♈ 5

Tenute Mater Domini

VIA DEI MARTIRI, 17/19
73012 CAMPI SALENTINA [LE]
TEL. 0832792442
www.tenutematerdomini.it

PRE-BOOKED VISITS

ANNUAL PRODUCTION **50,000 bottles**
HECTARES UNDER VINE **40**
VITICULTURE METHOD **Conventional**

Founded in 2003, Tenute Mater Domini is part of the revitalization of the Salice Salentino DOC. The Semeraro family, who manage the estate, has decided to wager everything on the main Salento variety, negroamaro, in many different planting patterns, from Guyot to cordon trained, but crucially half the estate is planted to traditional bush-trained vines that bring out the best in the variety.

The first '06 version of Salice Salentino Casili Riserva is almost negroamaro with just five per cent malvasia nera. The Semeraro family sent it to our finals thanks to a broad nose with good complexity and outstanding notes of wild red berries and leather. The substantial palate is rich in fruit and finishes supple, well sustained by acid backbone that favours easy drinking. The well-typed Marangi Negroamaro '06 is also good, with notes of plums and black damsons before the full, expansive palate reveals a pleasant soft finish that is a touch forward.

Mille Una

L.GO CHIESA, 11
74020 LIZZANO [TA]
TEL. 0999552638
www.milleuna.it

CELLAR SALES
PRE-BOOKED VISITS
VISITOR FACILITIES

ANNUAL PRODUCTION **70,000 bottles**
HECTARES UNDER VINE **33**
VITICULTURE METHOD **Natural**

This estate in the province of Taranto confirmed last year's good reviews. The vineyards – for the most part bush-trained and about 30 years old – are located on mineral-rich red earth near the sea around the towns of Sava, Lizzano and Maruggio, in one of the best areas for primitivo. Mille Una releases many labels principally from native varieties, first and foremost primitivo.

Outstanding wines this year are: Majara '07, a pure Negroamaro with a heady nose of fresh black berry fruit and a pleasant palate with good structure; Genius '06, a sweet Primitivo giving aniseed and liquorice sensations, and a balanced palate with a long, taut finish; and the more classic Tre Tarante '06, again from primitivo, with slightly too pronounced sweet chocolate, cinnamon and fruit preserves. Ori di Taranto '08 is a Chardonnay with frank notes of apples, pears and bananas, and good texture. It's well crafted but lacks a bit of acid thrust in the finish. Finally, the supple Primitivo Ori di Taranto '06 is also well made and gives cherry-like perceptions.

● Salice Salentino Casili Ris. '06	♟♟ 6
● Marangi Negroamaro '06	♟♟ 4

● Genius '06	♟♟ 8
● Majara '07	♟♟ 5
● Tre Tarante '06	♟♟ 8
○ Ori di Taranto Chardonnay '08	♟ 4
● Ori di Taranto Primitivo '06	♟ 5
● Tre Tarante '05	♟♟ 8

Castello Monaci

C.DA MONACI
73015 SALICE SALENTINO [LE]
TEL. 0831665700
www.castellomonaci.it

CELLAR SALES
PRE-BOOKED VISITS

ANNUAL PRODUCTION 2.200,000 bottles
HECTARES UNDER VINE 150
VITICULTURE METHOD Conventional

A large estate owned by Gruppo Italiano
Vini, Castello Monaci has vineyards
between Lecce and Taranto on the site
of the beautiful, Norman structure that
also serves as the estate headquarters.
The broad range from this major Puglian
operation has stood out over the past few
years for its remarkable consistency. The
wines are the result of major efforts in the
vineyard, with careful selection of clones
and rootstocks, and the cellar, which give
them a clear sense of place.

This makes four. The balanced, fluent
Primitivo Artas has won Three Glasses
for four years now. It's a wine that may
run counter to the growing trend in Puglia
for fullness and alcoholic richness, but it
is very easy drinking and the bottle soon
empties. The 2007 version has black berry
fruit and printer's ink aromas, and a taut,
full flavoured palate with nice acid tension
and a long, well-sustained finish. Another
well-crafted wine, the Negroamaro Maru
'08, has floral, earthy and black berry fruit
sensations introducing a palate that is
nicely textured yet also fresh, balanced and
pleasant. The other wines are well made.

Morella

VIA PER UGGIANO, 147
74024 MANDURIA [TA]
TEL. 0999791482
www.morellavini.com

CELLAR SALES
PRE-BOOKED VISITS

ANNUAL PRODUCTION 15,000 bottles
HECTARES UNDER VINE 7
VITICULTURE METHOD Conventional

This small estate owned by Lisa Gilbee,
an Australian oenologist transplanted to
Puglia, celebrates its tenth anniversary,
a decade of efforts to bring out the best
of primitivo grown in one of the most
favourable areas. The old bush-trained
vines, between 40 and 75 years old,
produce a small range of wines, created
in a modern style, with great attention to
yields, yet also without stress. In fact, the
aim is to recover the best characteristics of
variety and territory.

For the past few years, we have enjoyed
Lisa Gilbee's wines. This time, she finally
managed went the extra mile and picked
up Three well-deserved Glasses for
Primitivo Old Vines '07. The complex,
stylish nose has hints of spice, ripe black
berry fruit, figs and tobacco and the
focused palate is fresh and fruity with good
backbone and a remarkably deep finish.
The '07 Primitivo Negroamaro is also great
with a balsamic bouquet showing touches
of spice, black cherry and forest floor and a
pleasantly long, dynamic palate veined with
blackberries and blueberries. The classic
Primitivo Malbek '07 is good but a overripe
and slightly drying.

● Artas '07	♟♟♟	6
● Maru '08	♟♟	4
● Medos '08	♟	4
● Pilùna '08	♟	4
● Salice Salentino Aiace Ris. '06	♟	4
● Salice Salentino Liante '08	♟	4
○ Simera '08	♟	4
● Artas '06	♟♟♟	5
● Artas '05	♟♟♟	5*
● Artas '04	♟♟♟	5*
● Medos '07	♟♟	4
● Salice Salentino Aiace Ris. '05	♟♟	4

● Primitivo Old Vines '07	♟♟♟	6
● Primitivo Negroamaro '07	♟♟	5*
● Primitivo Malbek '07	♟	5
● Primitivo La Signora '05	♟♟	6
● Primitivo Negroamaro '06	♟♟	5
● Primitivo Old Vines '06	♟♟	6
● Primitivo Old Vines '05	♟♟	6
● Primitivo Old Vines '04	♟♟	6

Cosimo Palamà

VIA A. DIAZ, 6
73020 CUTROFIANO [LE]
TEL. 0836542865
www.vinicolapalama.com

CELLAR SALES
PRE-BOOKED VISITS

ANNUAL PRODUCTION 230,000 bottles
HECTARES UNDER VINE 15
VITICULTURE METHOD Conventional

Founded in 1936 and passed down from father to son, this Salento estate has grown so much over the past few years that it has earned a full Guide profile. The work of upgrading production during the 1990s has given greater definition to the wines while maintaining the strong ties to the local area that distinguish the range. Vines on the property are part Guyot and part bush-trained. The cellar releases four different lines, all from native grape varieties.

This year, we sent Mavro '07 to the finals. From 80 per cent negroamaro and malvasia nera di Lecce, it shows spice, cinchona and black berry fruit, and a rich, caressing palate with great structure. But the entire range impressed us, from the clean, long, leather and black cherry Salice Salentino Albarossa '07 to the Metiusco line. Rosso '08, a blend of negroamaro, malvasia, montepulciano and primitivo, shows notes of plum and black pepper and the fresh, floral Bianco '08, from verdeca and malvasia, has a spirited finish. The nice, lingering negroamaro Rosato '08, one of Puglia's best rosés, is floral with red berries.

Pietraventosa

C.DA PARCO LARGO
70023 GIOIA DEL COLLE [BA]
TEL. 0805034436
www.pietraventosa.it

CELLAR SALES
PRE-BOOKED VISITS

ANNUAL PRODUCTION 14,000 bottles
HECTARES UNDER VINE 5.4
VITICULTURE METHOD Organic certified

This young estate in Gioia del Colle is already earning a place on the complex Puglian winemaking scene. The owner, Marianna Annio, assisted by oenologist Oronzo Alò, has worked hard to bring out the territorial characteristics, creating a few organic wines from native varieties. The vines grow on rocky soil in the area west of Gioia del Colle at an altitude of around 380 metres, and vine density is between 7,000 and 8,000 plants per hectare.

An entry to remember. The only wine submitted, Gioia del Colle Primitivo Riserva '06, swept up Three Glasses. Aged three months in stainless steel and 18 months in tonneaux, it throws a nose of Mediterranean scrub, printer's ink, black damson, plum, and black cherry-like fruit and spice. The palate has lashings of fruit, a full, juicy body, good texture and upfront, yet soft and fragrant tannins. This exciting wine authentically expresses its terroir and reflects hard work in the cellar. Pietravento, along with other young producers, is giving a new dimension to Primitivo di Gioia del Colle.

● Mavro '07	♟♟	4*
○ Metiusco Bianco '08	♟♟	3*
⊙ Metiusco Rosato '08	♟♟	3*
● Metiusco Rosso '08	♟♟	4*
● Salice Salentino Rosso Albarossa '07	♟♟	1*
● Albarossa Primitivo '07	♟	2*
● Mavro '06	♟♟	4
● Mavro '05	♟♟	4*
● Mavro '04	♟♟	3*

● Gioia del Colle Primitivo Ris. '06	♟♟♟	5

Polvanera

S.DA VICINALE LAMIE MARCHESANA, 601
70023 GIOIA DEL COLLE [BA]
TEL. 080758900
www.cantinepolvanera.com

Racemi

VIA SANTO STASI PRIMO - Z. I.
74024 MANDURIA [TA]
TEL. 0999711660
www.racemi.it

CELLAR SALES
PRE-BOOKED VISITS

ANNUAL PRODUCTION 150,000 bottles
HECTARES UNDER VINE 30
VITICULTURE METHOD Organic certified

Launched in 2003 with the idea of reviving the Gioia del Colle DOC, this estate is headquartered in an old farmhouse surrounded by dark brown plots of land, hence the name Polvanera (Black Dust). The strong point for Filippo Cassano and his partners is to have maintained five hectares of bush-trained 60-year-old primitivo vines at between 6,000 and 8,000 plants per hectare. The rest of the vineyards are cordon-trained. Aside from primitivo grapes, aglianico, aleatico, fiano minutolo, falanghina and moscato bianco are also grown and contribute to a broad selection of wines.

Polvanera's admirable Giude debut immediately sent Gioia del Colle Primitivo 17 '06 to the finals. The aromas of aromatic herbs and black berry fruit are intense and nuanced with balsam. The palate is fresh, elegant and balanced with a unique, yet pleasant minerally iron note and good length. The interesting Gioia del Colle Primitivo 16 '06 shows spicy aromas and rich fruit, and is more closed and tannic than its big brother. Finally, the well-executed primitivo Zaniah '06 gives incense, thyme and capers, and a ripe palate with distinct notes of strawberry jam.

ANNUAL PRODUCTION 1.200,000 bottles
HECTARES UNDER VINE 150
VITICULTURE METHOD Organic certified

Gregory Perrucci's project to combine several small farms under the Racemi umbrella has proved decisive for the survival of the area's winemaking and growing traditions. The farms are: Masseria Pepe, with primitivo vineyards growing on sand near the sea; Sinfarosa, with deep, black soils; Tenuta Pozzopalo, a small, well-ventilated hill with black, tufaceous soil; Torre Guaceto, with replanted ottavianello and sussumaniello vines; Torre Guaceto, site of the nature reserve of the same name; and Casale Bevagna, with medium-textured red earth soils at Guagnano.

Racemi had a great year even without Three Glasses. Primitivo di Manduria Dunico Masseria Pepe '07 went to the finals with its broad nose of cherry and Mediterranean scrub, and complex, iodine palate, as did Primitivo di Manduria Giravolta Tenuta Pozzopalo '07 with salt and balsam aromas, spice, camomile, good fruit and soft tannins. Other good wines include the pleasant, balanced Anarkos '08, from malvasia nera, primitivo and negroamaro, the fresh, fruity Zinfandel Sinfarosa '07, the floral Ottavianello Dedalo Torre Guaceto '07 with its black berry fruit jam, and the deep, concentrated Susumaniello Sum Torre Guaceto '07.

● Gioia del Colle Primitivo 17 '06	♟♟	4*
● Gioia del Colle Primitivo 16 '06	♟♟	4
● Zaniah '06	♟	2*

● Primitivo di Manduria Dunico Masseria Pepe '07	♟♟	6
● Primitivo di Manduria Giravolta Tenuta Pozzopalo '07	♟♟	5
● Anarkos '08	♟♟	3*
● Ottavianello Dedalo Torre Guaceto '07	♟♟	4
● Primitivo di Manduria Zinfandel Sinfarosa '07	♟♟	5
● Susumaniello Sum Torre Guaceto '07	♟♟	5
● Primitivo di Manduria Dunico Masseria Pepe '05	♟♟♟	6*
● Primitivo di Manduria Zinfandel Sinfarosa '06	♟♟♟	5*
● Primitivo di Manduria Giravolta Tenuta Pozzopalo '04	♟♟	4*
● Primitivo di Manduria Zinfandel Sinfarosa '05	♟♟	5
● Susumaniello Sum Torre Guaceto '06	♟♟	5

Rasciatano

C.DA RASCIATANO
70051 BARLETTA [BA]
TEL. 0883510999
www.rasciatano.com

CELLAR SALES
PRE-BOOKED VISITS

ANNUAL PRODUCTION 19,000 bottles
HECTARES UNDER VINE 18
VITICULTURE METHOD Conventional

Until a few years ago, Rasciatano was known almost exclusively for its great extra virgin olive oil but thanks in part to collaboration with Professor Luigi Moio, the estate is earning a place on the wine scene in Puglia and beyond. The vineyards were planted mostly to native varieties between 1992 and 2002, and stand at between 120 and 180 metres above sea level on sandy soils over strata of chalky stone, facing north and north-west.

In its second year of production, the Porro family estate won Three Glasses with its new Rasciatano Nero di Troia '07 after reaching the finals last year. The nose unveils aromas of violet and Mediterranean scrub with a balsamic shade contributed by a judicious use of oak. The palate pairs dense tannins and solid structure with lovely freshness and acid tension, finishing on black berry fruit and tobacco. Rasciatano Rosé '08, a monovarietal Montepulciano, shows aromas of wild roses and green olives, and is slightly alcoholic and sweet on the palate. It's well enough made but we were expecting more.

Rivera

C.DA RIVERA, S.P. 231 KM 60,500
70031 ANDRIA [BA]
TEL. 0883560501
www.rivera.it

CELLAR SALES
PRE-BOOKED VISITS

ANNUAL PRODUCTION 1.500,000 bottles
HECTARES UNDER VINE 95
VITICULTURE METHOD Conventional

The large Rivera estate near Andria was founded in 1950 by Sebastiano De Corato and is currently managed by his son Carlo. The desire to promote native varieties, without neglecting international varieties planted during the 1980s, has given rise to a broad range of high quality, extremely dependable wines, with special attention focused on the Castel del Monte DOC. The vineyards are spurred cordon-trained and planted on limestone-tufaceous soils between 200 and 220 metres above sea level, and on the rocky hills of Murgia at 300 to 350 metres.

We felt the absence of Puer Apuliae but as usual there is a series of high quality wines, beginning with the historic Castel del Monte Il Falcone Riserva '06, a 70-30 mix of nero di Troia and montepulciano, with its balsamic, fruity nose laced with cherry and tar, and nice texture on the palate. Two well-managed wines are the Moscato di Trani Piani di Tufara '08, with varietal aromas of candied citrus peel and a long, complex palate, and the Castel del Monte Preludio n°1, a Chardonnay with touches of pepper, citrus and white-fleshed fruit, and a clean, consistent, well-crafted palate.

● Rasciatano Nero di Troia '07	▾▾▾	7
⊙ Rasciatano Rosé '08	▾	5
● Rasciatano Rosso '06	♀♀	7

○ Castel del Monte Chardonnay Preludio n° 1 '08	▾▾	4*
● Castel del Monte Rosso Il Falcone Ris. '06	▾▾	5
○ Moscato di Trani Piani di Tufara '08	▾▾	4*
○ Castel del Monte Bianco Fedora '08	▾	2*
○ Castel del Monte Chardonnay Lama di Corvo '08	▾	5
○ Castel del Monte Sauvignon Terre al Monte '08	▾	4
○ Locorotondo '08	▾	2*
● Castel del Monte Nero di Troia Puer Apuliae '04	♀♀♀	7
● Castel del Monte Nero di Troia Puer Apuliae '03	♀♀♀	7
● Castel del Monte Nero di Troia Puer Apuliae '06	♀♀	7
● Castel del Monte Nero di Troia Puer Apuliae '05	♀♀	7
○ Moscato di Trani Piani di Tufara '06	♀♀	4*

Tenute Rubino

VIA E. FERMI, 50
72100 BRINDISI
TEL. 0831571955
www.tenuterubino.it

CELLAR SALES
PRE-BOOKED VISITS

ANNUAL PRODUCTION **800,000 bottles**
HECTARES UNDER VINE **200**
VITICULTURE METHOD **Conventional**

This large estate, founded in the 1980s, quickly became so well-known for is the average production standards – and some excellent peaks – it is one of the most important in the region. The vineyards, most spurred cordon-trained and a small percentage bush-trained, spread inland from the Adriatic ridge at a density of between 4,000 and 6,000 plants per hectare. Cropping levels are low. Tenute Rubino exports around 70 per cent of its production but never forgets the importance of varietal typicity and the local terroir in its wines.

The two outstanding wines are again Brindisi Rosso Jaddico and Visellio, both from 2007. The first has aromas of plums, tobacco, wood and cherry, and a rich, modern, palate with good length, but it's weighed down by sweetness. Visellio, from primitivo, shows smoky and toasty on the nose followed by a fresher, more fruity palate with remarkable density and intensity. Torre Testa, a pure Sussumaniello, is good with wild black berry notes, and as always the two '08 Marmorelles are pleasant and well crafted. The Bianco is from chardonnay and malvasia, and the Rosso from negroamaro and malvasia nera. Everything else is better than just well made.

● Brindisi Rosso Jaddico '07	⟡⟡	5
● Visellio '07	⟡⟡	5
● Torre Testa '07	⟡⟡	7
○ Giancola '08	⟡	4
○ Marmorelle Bianco '08	⟡	3
● Marmorelle Rosso '08	⟡	3
● Negroamaro '07	⟡	4
● Primitivo Punta Aquila '08	⟡	4
⊙ Saturnino '08	⟡	3
● Torre Testa '02	⟡⟡⟡	6
● Torre Testa '01	⟡⟡⟡	6
● Brindisi Rosso Jaddico '06	⟡⟡	5
● Visellio '06	⟡⟡	5

Cosimo Taurino

S.S. 605
73010 GUAGNANO [LE]
TEL. 0832706490
www.taurinovini.it

CELLAR SALES
PRE-BOOKED VISITS

ANNUAL PRODUCTION **800,000 bottles**
HECTARES UNDER VINE **111**
VITICULTURE METHOD **Conventional**

Founded in 1970, this estate was one of the benchmarks in Puglia winemaking and a beacon for production in Salento. Today, it is managed by Francesco and Rosanna Taurino, children of the founder Cosimo, who after a few difficult years seem to have got everything back on track and are producing a range of excellent wines, basing their strategy on the area's typical grape varieties from mostly bush-trained vineyards in the Puglian tradition.

The 2003 version of the Patriglione, a monovarietal Negroamaro, is charming but still short of those landmark wines from a few years back. Nicely complex, it reveals notes of coffee and slightly jammy black berry fruit, finishing slightly sweet as it flows over the palate. The dependable negroamaro-based Notarpanaro '06 has spicy aromas tinged with chocolate and black cherry, leading to a warm, substantial palate with red and black berry fruits and a peppery finish. The Salice Salentino Rosso Riserva '06 is a pleaser with plenty of red berry fruit. It's perhaps a bit small but pleasantly drinkable and very fresh.

● Notarpanaro '06	⟡⟡	4
● Patriglione '03	⟡⟡	7
● Salice Salentino Rosso Ris. '06	⟡⟡	5
● Patriglione '94	⟡⟡⟡	8
● Patriglione '88	⟡⟡⟡	5
● Patriglione '85	⟡⟡⟡	5
● Notarpanaro '04	⟡⟡	4
● Patriglione '99	⟡⟡	8
● Patriglione '95	⟡⟡	8

Tormaresca

LOC. TOFANO
C.DA TORRE D'ISOLA
70055 BARI
TEL. 0883692631
www.tormaresca.it

PRE-BOOKED VISITS

ANNUAL PRODUCTION 2,000,000 bottles
HECTARES UNDER VINE 350
VITICULTURE METHOD Organic certified

Faith in Puglia's potential led the Antinoris to invest in the production of great wines, particularly from native varieties. This lovely estate was created from two farms, Bocca di Lupo in Minervino Murge, and Masseria Maime in San Pietro Vernotico. The former is located around 250 metres above sea level and characterized by significant day-night temperature fluctuations while the latter is in the Salentino area, near the Adriatic coast, halfway between Lecce and Brindisi.

Tormaresca submitted an impeccable array of wines again. Three Glasses went to Masseria Maime '07, a single-variety Negroamaro with a balsamic nose showing hints of black berry fruit, and a palate with great texture and lots of fruit. It's still a bit woody but time should sort that out. Aglianico Castel del Monte Bocca di Lupo '06 gives spice and figs, drinking fresh, stylish and pleasant with good length. These two champions lead a pack of particularly successful wines, from the taut, elegant Chardonnay Castel del Monte Pietrabianca '08, with floral, citrussy notes, and Torcicoda '07, a full-bodied, caressing Primitivo.

Torre Quarto

C.DA QUARTO, 5
71042 CERIGNOLA [FG]
TEL. 0885418453
www.torrequartocantine.it

CELLAR SALES
PRE-BOOKED VISITS
VISITOR FACILITIES
FOOD

ANNUAL PRODUCTION 500,000 bottles
HECTARES UNDER VINE 45
VITICULTURE METHOD Conventional

After two not exactly brilliant years, Stefano Cirillo Farrusi's winery is back with a full profile. Founded in 1847 and owned by his family since the 1930s, Stefano's estate has a long, important history. Over the past few years, major work has been done replanting vines and modernizing the cellar, which has given new life to a wine production that also uses some leased vineyards.

Torre Quarto went back to the finals with the first release of Primitivo di Manduria Tarabuso '06, an intense wine, smoky on the nose with hints of damson, spice and coffee, and fresh and elegant on the taut, long palate with nice black berry fruit. Other good wines are: the classic Tarabuso '08, a balsamic Primitivo still slightly marked by oak but with good length and a black berry fruit finish; Hirondelle '08, from greco, which is clean with citrussy aromas, not complex but supple and pleasant; and Don Marcello '08, from negroamaro and sangiovese, with dark toast and spice aromas, and a palate of blackberry and red berry fruit.

Wine	Rating
● Masseria Maime '07	♟♟♟ 5
● Castel del Monte Rosso Bocca di Lupo '06	♟♟ 6
○ Castel del Monte Chardonnay Pietrabianca '08	♟♟ 5
○ Moscato di Trani Kaloro '07	♟♟ 6
● Neprica Rosso '08	♟♟ 3*
● Torcicoda '07	♟♟ 5
● Fichimori '08	♟ 4
○ Tormaresca Chardonnay '08	♟ 3
● Masseria Maime '06	♟♟♟ 5
● Masseria Maime '05	♟♟♟ 5*
● Masseria Maime '04	♟♟♟ 5*
● Masseria Maime '02	♟♟♟ 5
● Masseria Maime '00	♟♟♟ 5*
● Torcicoda '01	♟♟♟ 5*

Wine	Rating
● Primitivo di Manduria Tarabuso '06	♟♟ 4*
● Don Marcello '08	♟♟ 3*
○ Hirondelle '08	♟♟ 3*
● Tarabuso '08	♟♟ 4*
● Bottaccia '08	♟ 4
○ Nina '08	♟ 3
● Sangue Blu '08	♟ 4
● Bottaccia '07	♟♟ 4*
● Tarabuso '07	♟♟ 4*

Torrevento

LOC. CASTEL DEL MONTE
S.P. 234 KM 10,600
70033 CORATO [BA]
TEL. 0808980923
www.torrevento.it

CELLAR SALES
PRE-BOOKED VISITS
VISITOR FACILITIES
FOOD

ANNUAL PRODUCTION 2.500,000 bottles
HECTARES UNDER VINE 400
VITICULTURE METHOD Organic certified

Located in the north-west Murgia, this large estate includes 400 hectares of vineyards, about half the total property. At Torrevento, breadth of production goes hand in hand with the search for quality and protecting the local environment. The estate is in fact certified ISO 14001 for environmental quality and wine production is certified organic. The range reflects this approach and a territory particularly well suited for viticulture.

Castel del Monte Rosso Vigna Pedale '06, from nero di Troia, confirmed its status with Three well-deserved Glasses. This elegant wine has a spice and black berry fruit bouquet, and the stylish palate is taut, supple and long. Moscato di Trani Dulcis in Fundo '07 is also well crafted. Its notes of cakes and star anise never weigh down the nicely sweet, aromatic palate. The other wines are all well made, in particular the well-typed and technically clean Castel del Montes, as well as the floral, fresh Rosato Primaronda '08 and fruit-forward Rosso Bolonero '07.

Agricole Vallone

VIA XXV LUGLIO, 5
73100 LECCE
TEL. 0832308041
www.agricolevallone.it

PRE-BOOKED VISITS

ANNUAL PRODUCTION 527,000 bottles
HECTARES UNDER VINE 170
VITICULTURE METHOD Organic certified

Founded in 1934, the Vallone sisters' estate is a major operation, founded on a faithful interpretation of winemaking traditions in Puglia, and divided into three holdings: Flaminio, near Brindisi, Iore, near San Pancrazio Salentino, and Castelserranova, near Carovigno. The vine stock was planted in various stages, some about 50 years ago, on limestone and clay soils. International varieties like sauvignon grow alongside typical varieties from Puglia.

We felt Graticciaia was not its best. As always, the 2005 version of this historic Negroamaro is expansive and evolved, with chocolate, cinnamon and liquorice, but it's a bit too sweet, lacks depth and finishes bitter. The sweet, 80-20 sauvignon and malvasia Passo delle Viscarde '05 is good, showing dried figs and almonds, and a long finish. Other good wines are: Corte Valesio '08, a fresh Sauvignon with flower and citrus notes; the supple, spicy Versante Negramaro '07; and Brindisi Rosato Vigna Flaminio '08, from 70-20-10 negroamaro, montepulciano and malvasia nera, which gives florality and pomegranates.

● Castel del Monte Rosso V. Pedale Ris. '06	♟♟♟ 4*
○ Moscato di Trani Dulcis in Fundo '07	♟♟ 4*
◉ Castel del Monte Bianco Pezzapiana '08	♟ 3
◉ Castel del Monte Rosato Primaronda '08	♟ 3
● Castel del Monte Rosso Bolonero '07	♟ 3
○ Matervitae Bombino Bianco '08	♟ 4
◉ Matervitae Bombino Nero '08	♟ 4
● Castel del Monte Rosso V. Pedale Ris. '05	♟♟♟ 4*
● Castel del Monte Rosso V. Pedale Ris. '04	♟♟♟ 4*

● Graticciaia '05	♟♟ 7
○ Passo delle Viscarde '05	♟♟ 5
◉ Brindisi Rosato V. Flaminio '08	♟ 3
○ Corte Valesio Sauvignon '08	♟ 3
● Versante Negramaro '07	♟ 2
● Vigna Castello '07	♟ 5
● Graticciaia '03	♟♟♟ 7
● Graticciaia '01	♟♟♟ 7
● Graticciaia '00	♟♟ 7
● Graticciaia '98	♟♟ 7

Vetrere

FRAZ. VETRERE
S.P. MONTEIASI-MONTEMESOLA KM 16
74100 TARANTO
TEL. 0995661054
www.vetrere.it

CELLAR SALES
PRE-BOOKED VISITS

ANNUAL PRODUCTION 170,000 bottles
HECTARES UNDER VINE 37
VITICULTURE METHOD Conventional

Sisters Annamaria and Francesca Bruni's historic estate in Salento, founded in 1900, is famous not only for production of an excellent extra virgin olive oil but also for the quality of its wines. The broad range of bottles is respected for its solidity and reliability. Spurred cordon and bush-trained vineyards surround the main villa, where the old cellar carved from the tufaceous rock has been remodelled to accommodate modern winemaking kit.

Again this year, the Bruni sisters' winery can be defined by two words, consistent quality. All the estate's wines are well made, focused and stylistically precise. Laureato '08 from chardonnay, malvasia bianca and fiano has damson and white pepper aromas, depth, nice texture and length, although it is a tad sweet. The same goes for Negroamaro Tempio di Giano '08 with its touches of plums and Mediterranean herbs, and elegantly fresh, fruity palate. Also nice is the rosé from negroamaro and malvasia nera, Taranta '08 with its fragrant jasmine aromatics, good texture and nice acidity.

Conti Zecca

VIA CESAREA
73045 LEVERANO [LE]
TEL. 0832925613
www.contizecca.it

CELLAR SALES
PRE-BOOKED VISITS

ANNUAL PRODUCTION 2,000,000 bottles
HECTARES UNDER VINE 320
VITICULTURE METHOD Conventional

The Zecca brother's estate has a centuries-old history of grape growing and winemaking in Salento, skilfully combining quality, big numbers and honest prices. The estate is split into four holdings – Cantalupi, Saraceno, Donna Marzia and Santo Stefano – where mostly native varieties are grown, alongside some chardonnay, cabernet sauvignon and other non-local varieties. In other words, this is an estate that hews to Puglia's winemaking traditions while striving to renovate it.

The Nero was not submitted last time. Letting it age for another year evidently helped to secure another Three Glasses. From 70 per cent negroamaro and cabernet sauvignon, it regales the nostrils with coffee, tobacco and Mediterranean scrub before the taut, pleasant palate shows good texture and a long, deep finish. But there is impressive quality across the range, from the fruity Leverano Terra Riserva '05, with its notes of tobacco and chocolate, to the smoky Salice Salentino Cantalupi Riserva '06, which gives black berry fruit, and the various single-variety wines, Negramaro '06, Primitivo '07 and Fiano '08. All are extremely good.

○ Laureato '08	♟	4
☉ Taranta '08	♟	3*
● Tempio di Giano '08	♟	3*
● Barone Pazzo '07	♟	4
○ Crè '08	♟	4
○ Finis Terrae '08	♟	3
● Lago della Pergola '07	♟	4
● Livruni '08	♟	3
● Barone Pazzo '06	♟♟	4
● Livruni '06	♟♟	3*
● Tempio di Giano '07	♟♟	3*

● Nero '06	♟♟♟	6
● Cantalupi Negramaro '07	♟♟	3*
○ Fiano '08	♟♟	4
● Leverano Rosso Terra Ris. '05	♟♟	5
● Negramaro '06	♟♟	4
● Primitivo '07	♟♟	4
● Salice Salentino Rosso Cantalupi Ris. '06	♟♟	4
● Nero '03	♟♟♟	6
● Nero '02	♟♟♟	6
● Nero '01	♟♟♟	6

OTHER WINERIES

Agrialp

S.P. BURGO COCCARO
72015 FASANO [BR]
TEL. 0804827830
www.agrialp.it

This small estate produces extra virgin olive oil and wine. Outstanding among the many labels produced from the 80 per cent bush-trained vines are the monovarietal Primitivo Sarzano '07, with wild berry touches and a full, aromatic palate, and the floral, citrussy Martina Franca Monte Pizzuto '08.

○ Martina Franca Monte Pizzuto '08	♈♈	4*
● Sarzano '07	♈♈	4*
● Fiero '07	♈	4

Masseria Altemura

C.DA PALOMBARA - SP 69
72028 TORRE SANTA SUSANNA [BR]
TEL. 0831740485
www.masseriaaltemura.it

This Puglia estate owned by the Zonin family has had a positive, if not extraordinary, year. An excellent score went to the negroamaro Rosato '08, which flaunts red berry fruit, pomegranate and Mediterranean herbs, and good length on the palate. The well-typed Aglianico '07 has notes of ripe fruit.

● Aglianico '07	♈♈	4
☉ Rosato '08	♈♈	4

Antica Enotria

S.P. 65 C.DA RISICATA
71042 CERIGNOLA [FG]
TEL. 0885418462
www.anticaenotria.it

A well-known organically farmed estate, Antica Enotria returns to the Guide with several well-made wines, from the fruity, pleasantly fresh montepulciano Falù '07, to the dense, rich Aglianico '07, with blackberry notes, and the sulphite-free Montepulciano Senzazolfo '08.

● Aglianico '07	♈	4
● Falù '07	♈	3
● Senzazolfo '08	♈	4

Apollonio

VIA SAN PIETRO IN LAMA, 7
73047 MONTERONI DI LECCE [LE]
TEL. 0832327182
www.apolloniovini.it

We expected great things from this historic estate but sadly they didn't arrive. We found two well-made labels this year, the pleasant, fruity Elfo Rosato '08, from 80-20 negroamaro and malvasia, and the simple, slightly too oaky Salice Salentino Bianco '08, with its apple-like notes.

☉ Elfo Rosato '08	♈	3
○ Salice Salentino Bianco '08	♈	4
● Terragnolo Negroamaro '03	♈	5

Cantine Botromagno

LOC. ZONA PIP
VIA ARCHIMEDE, 22
70024 GRAVINA IN PUGLIA [BA]
TEL. 0803265865
www.botromagno.it

Management changes and cellar improvements have started to bring the first results. As we wait for Gravisano, we felt the Gravina Poggio al Bosco '08 was interesting. A genuine vineyard selection, it's still closed on the nose but has an intense, mineral palate and a savoury flavour. A wine to watch.

○ Gravina Poggio al Bosco '08	♈♈	5
● Primitivo '08	♈	4
☉ Silvium '08	♈	3

Michele Calò & Figli

VIA MASSERIA VECCHIA, 1
73058 TUGLIE [LE]
TEL. 0833596242
www.michelecalo.it

This long-standing estate returns to the Guide with a brace of well-managed wines. From negroamaro, the Mjère Rosso '07 has balsamic, fruity aromas and a long, balanced palate. Moscato Stella Tulliae '07 has florality, honey and peaches in syrup with a sweet but not cloying flavour.

● Mjère Rosso '07	♈♈	4
○ Stella Tulliae Bianco '07	♈♈	5

Francesco Candido

VIA A. DIAZ, 46
72025 SAN DONACI [BR]
TEL. 0831635674
www.candidowines.il

This year has not been good for Alessandro Candido's estate. The best wines are Paule Calle '06, a dried-grape passito from chardonnay and malvasia bianca with nutty aromas and a pleasant, balanced palate, and the rose-led Salice Salentino Bianco Porta Falsa '08 with good body and acidity.

○ Paule Calle '06	♥♥ 5
○ Salice Salentino Bianco Porta Falsa '08	♥♥ 3*

Cantolio Manduria

VIA PER LECCE KM 25
74024 MANDURIA [TA]
TEL. 0999796045
www.cantolio.it

This co-operative winery has had a less than brilliant year but still managed to present good wines. From its Primitivo di Manduria line, we preferred the 15° '06, with sumptuous toastiness and ripe fruit well supported by acidity, and the simpler, more agile 14,5° '06.

● Primitivo di Manduria 14.5° '06	♥ 4
● Primitivo di Manduria 15° '06	♥ 4

Vini Classici Cardone

VIA MARTIRI DELLA LIBERTÀ, 32
70010 LOCOROTONDO [BA]
TEL. 0804312561
www.cardonevini.com

This influential Valle d'Itria winery is back after two years. Vigna del Fragno '07, from cabernet, malbec and merlot, gives black olives and a focused, expansive palate, while the classic Locorotondo Il Castillo '08 is slightly aromatic and balanced with citrus and white damson fruit. Both are very good.

○ Locorotondo Il Castillo '08	♥♥ 4*
● Vigna del Fragno '07	♥♥ 5
○ Falera Fiano '08	♥ 4
○ Placeo '08	♥ 4

Cefalicchio

C.SO SAN SABINO, 6
70053 CANOSA DI PUGLIA [BA]
TEL. 0833617601
www.cefalicchio.it

The Rossi brothers' biodynamic wines continue to convince us. We especially like the simplest wine, the floral Rosato di Puglia '08, from montepulciano, with red berry fruit and a pleasant, full-flavoured palate. The Moscato di Jalal '08 and Chardonnay La Pietraia '08 are both good.

⊙ Rosato di Puglia '08	♥♥ 2*
○ La Pietraia '08	♥ 4
○ Moscato di Jalal '08	♥ 5

Tenuta Coppadoro

VIA TIBERIO SOLIS, 128
71016 SAN SEVERO [FG]
TEL. 0882242301
www.tenutacoppadoro.it

Coppadoro has fallen off a bit. Cotinone '08, from aglianico, montepulciano and cabernet sauvignon, has fruit and concentration but lacks some length. The monovarietal Nero di Troia Brando '07 has sweet fruit and spice. But Montepulciano Radicosa '07 is marked by oak.

● Brando '07	♥♥ 4
● Cotinone '08	♥♥ 5
● Radicosa '07	♥ 6

Coppi

CIR.NE SUD - Il TRATTO
70010 TURI [BA]
TEL. 0808915049
www.vinicoppi.it

This historic Puglia estate returns to the Guide after a few years' absence. Two wines stand out. Malvasia Bianca '08 offers an aromatic, floral nose and unusual depth on its fresh palate whereas Gioia del Colle Primitivo Siniscalco '06 is fruity and elegant with notes of red berries.

● Gioia del Colle Primitivo Siniscalco '06	♥♥ 4
○ Malvasia Bianca '08	♥♥ 2*
○ Torre Bianca '08	♥ 3

Cantina Crifo

VIA MADONNA DELLE GRAZIE, 8A
70037 RUVO DI PUGLIA [BA]
TEL. 0803601611
www.cantinacrifo.it

A lovely array of wines has brought this major co-operative winery back into the Guide. Augustale Oro '06, from moscatello, is fresh with almond and citrus notes. The uva di Troia and montepulciano Castel del Monte Rosso Due Carri '06 is nice, giving red berry fruit and good length.

○ Augustale Oro '06	♟♟	4*
● Castel del Monte Rosso Due Carri '06	♟♟	1*
○ I Pavoni Le Mattine '08	♟♟	4*

d'Aprì

VIA ZANNOTTI, 30
71016 SAN SEVERO [FG]
TEL. 0882227643
www.darapri.it

D'Aprì is the only winery in central-southern Italy specializing in classic method sparklers. From pinot nero and montepulciano, the new cuvée La Dama Forestiera '03, although not exactly inexpensive, is very pleasing with wafts of toasted almonds and baking. The Brut and Pas Dosé are good.

○ La Dama Forestiera di d'Aprì '03	♟♟	8
○ d'Aprì Brut	♟	5
○ d'Aprì Pas Dosé	♟	5

Emèra

VIA PROVINCIALE, 222
73010 GUAGNANO [LE]
TEL. 0825998977
www.cantineemera.com

Claudio Quarta's estate is back in the Guide with a fine Anima di Primitivo '07 with balsamic and black berry fruit notes. It's still a bit oaky but has good consistency and mouthfeel. The cherry-toned Salice Salentino '07 and floral, citrussy Amure '08, from malvasia bianca and chardonnay, are nice.

● Anima di Primitivo '07	♟♟	4*
○ Amure '08	♟	3
● Salice Salentino '07	♟	4

Ferri

VIA BARI, 347
70010 VALENZANO [BA]
TEL. 0804671753
www.cantineferri.it

This tiny estate – only one and a half hectares – enters the Guide with Ebrius '08 and Duo '07. The former is a fruity, rich blend of cabernet sauvignon and primitivo while Duo, from cabernet sauvignon and uva di Troia, is spicy with pomegranate notes but a bit marked by oak.

● Duo '07	♟♟	4
● Ebrius '08	♟♟	4*

Feudi di Terra D'Otranto

VIA ARNEO MARE
73010 VEGLIE [LE]
TEL. 066832448
www.feudidotranto.com

There was a great performance from this collaboration between Conti del Balzo and Vignamaggio. Aglianico '08 from the Le Maschere line proffers remarkable density, yet is still fresh and supple with pleasant red berry notes. Le Maschere Syrah '08 is well made but too edgy and one-dimensional.

● Le Maschere Aglianico '08	♟♟	3*
● Le Maschere Syrah '08	♟	3

Tenuta Fujanera

C.DA QUADRONE DELLE VIGNE, KM 2,500
VIA BARI
71100 FOGGIA
TEL. 0881630003
www.fujanera.it

Giusy Albano's estate enters the Guide in its first year of production thanks to technically well-made wines with great aromatic precision, like the fruit and violets Nero di Troia Arrocco '08 and the savoury, well-structured Falanghina Bellalma '08.

● Arrocco '08	♟♟	4
○ Bellalma '08	♟♟	3*
● Lamadàli '07	♟	4

Cantina Locorotondo

VIA MADONNA DELLA CATENA, 99
70010 LOCOROTONDO [BA]
TEL. 0804311644
www.locorotondodoc.com

This historic winery continues to produce good quality wines but the reds and rosés really shine, particularly from the Cummerse line. The pinot nero Rosato '08 has red berries and citrus. Rosso '06, a blend of aglianico, nero di Troia and cabernet sauvignon, is toasty with cherry and blackberry notes.

☉ Casale San Giorgio Rosato '08	♀ 4
☉ Cummerse Rosato '08	♀ 4
● Cummerse Rosso '06	♀ 4

Masseria Li Veli

S.P. CELLINO-CAMPI, KM 1
72020 CELLINO SAN MARCO [BR]
TEL. 0831617906
www.liveli.it

The Falvo family is concentrating on Puglia. The Salice Salentino Rosso Pezzo Morgana '07 has balsamic aromas with black berry fruit notes. The palate shows body, well-integrated tannins and good acid backbone. Less successful is the dense Negroamaro Passamante '08, which lacks balance.

● Salice Salentino Rosso Pezzo Morgana '07	♀♀ 5
● Passamante '08	♀ 3

Menhir

VIA SCARCIGLIA, 18
73027 MINERVINO DI LECCE [LE]
TEL. 0836818191
www.cantinemenhir.com

Gaetano Marangelli's five-year old estate skilfully crafts a broad, dependable range of wines. The most interesting this year is the complex, fruit-led Primitivo di Manduria '07, which is nicely balanced. The pleasant Salice Salentino Rosso '07 has good fruit and Novementi Bianco '08 is fresh and floral.

● Primitivo di Manduria '07	♀♀ 4
○ Novementi Bianco '08	♀ 3
● Salice Salentino Rosso '07	♀ 4

Mocavero

VIA MALLACCA ZUMMARI
73010 ARNESANO [LE]
TEL. 0832327194
www.mocaverovini.it

It was a good year for Mocavero but not as brilliant as last year. We liked Pietrafitta '08, a single-variety Primitivo with dried figs and spice, and a long palate. The floral Santufili '05, again from primitivo, has good pulp. Salice Salentino Rosso Puteus Riserva '05 is rustic and fruity.

● Pietrafitta '08	♀♀ 2*
● Salice Salentino Rosso Puteus Ris. '05	♀ 4
● Santufili '05	♀ 5

Azienda Monaci

LOC. TENUTA MONACI
73043 COPERTINO [LE]
TEL. 0832947512
www.aziendamonaci.com

This year has been unfortunate for the Garofano family's wines, not least because there is no Le Braci. Girofle '08, a rosé from negroamaro, shows cherry notes and nice freshness. Copertino Rosso Eloquenzia '06, again from negroamaro, has notes of black berry fruit but is husky and a bit simple.

● Copertino Rosso Eloquenzia '06	♀ 4
☉ Girofle '08	♀ 4

Villa Mottura

P.ZZA MELICA, 4
73058 TUGLIE [LE]
TEL. 0833596601
www.motturavini.it

This Salento estate is back in the Guide, thanks especially to the fresh Salice Salentino Rosso '06 with its plum and cherry notes, and good body. The Rosé '08, with its distinctive floral-shaded oriental spices, and the fruity Negroamaro '07, which lacks a little acid grip, are both well-made wines.

● Salice Salentino Rosso '06	♀♀ 4
● Negroamaro '07	♀ 4
☉ Rosé '08	♀ 4

Podere Belmantello

VIA RAFFAELE TAMMA
71042 CERIGNOLA [FG]
TEL. 0885896179
www.belmantello.it

Angelo Paradiso's wine adventure starts again at Podere Belmantello. These nice wines still need to find a length. The primitivo Darione '08 is fluent and fruity, the nero di Troia Secondopasso '08 is fairly complex with strawberry aromas, and the Salàpia '08, from bombino bianco, shows fresh and floral.

● Darione '08	♀	4
○ Salàpia '08	♀	4
● Secondopasso '08	♀	4

Primis

VIA C. COLOMBO, 44
71048 STORNARELLA [FG]
TEL. 0885433333
www.primisvini.com

This young estate has already shown it can make good wines. Among the many labels this year, the '08 Chardonnay tops the list with citrus touches, a rich palate of grapefruit-veined florality and a nice finish. Nero di Troia '07 has good fruit and the Negroamaro '07 is slightly rustic. Both are well typed.

○ Chardonnay '08	♀♀	4*
● Negroamaro '07	♀	4
● Nero di Troia '07	♀	4

Rosa del Golfo

VIA GARIBALDI, 56
73011 ALEZIO [LE]
TEL. 0833281045
www.rosadelgolfo.com

Wines from Rosa del Golfo are well made yet lack verve. Vigna Mazzì '08, a rosé from negroamaro and ten per cent malvasia nera is as rich as ever but falls short on backbone and acidity. Scaliere '08, again from negroamaro with ten per cent aglianico, is pleasant and fruity.

● Quarantale '07	♀	6
● Scaliere '08	♀	3
☉ Vigna Mazzì '08	♀	4

Cantina Cooperativa di San Donaci

VIA MESAGNE, 62
72025 SAN DONACI [BR]
TEL. 0831681085
www.cantinasandonaci.it

San Donaci held onto its profile in the Guide, even in a less successful vintage. The well-crafted Chardonnay Anticaia '08 is grassy, citrussy and fresh. The two Salice Salentino Anticaias are well made, the Riserva '05 gives tanned leather and cinchona but the pleasant, fruity '07 is a tad simple.

○ Chardonnay Anticaia '08	♀	3
● Salice Salentino Anticaia '07	♀	3
● Salice Salentino Anticaia Ris. '05	♀	4

Feudo di Santa Croce

LOC. CUREZZA
74021 CAROSINO [TA]
TEL. 0456470697
www.tinazzi.it

Scores were quite interesting from the Taranto branch of the Tinazzi family. Malvasia Bianca Monteiasi '08 has aromas of grapefruit and bergamot, and a very nice taut, mineral palate. Primitivo di Manduria Bisanzio '07 is pleasant and fruity, and the Salice Salentino Rosso '07 is typical and well crafted.

○ Monteiasi '08	♀♀	4*
● Primitivo di Manduria Bisanzio '07	♀♀	4
● Salice Salentino Rosso '07	♀	4

Santa Lucia

S. C. SAN VITTORE, 1
70033 CORATO [BA]
TEL. 0817642888
www.vinisantalucia.com

This year, the top wine from this small estate is Castel del Monte Rosso Vigna del Melograno '07, whose elegant ripe fruit-themed aromas lead to a velvety, deep, substantial palate with stylish tannins. Gazza Nera '08, from negroamaro, is pleasant and fruity, and Fiano Gazza Ladra '08 is well crafted.

● Castel del Monte Rosso V. del Melograno '07	♀♀	4
○ Gazza Ladra '08	♀	4
● Gazza Nera '08	♀	4

Santa Maria del Morige

FRAZ. CARPIGNANA
VIA DEL MARE, KM 2
73044 GALATONE [LE]
TEL. 3458592276
www.santamariadelmorige.com

Annalisa Conserva's small, young estate repeats the successes of the past with an excellent Cinabro '06, a monovarietal Negroamaro that shows notes of cherry and chocolate. The palate has good body brushed with violets and dried roses. The Asteri '08 is also better than just pleasant.

● Cinabro '06	♟♟	4
○ Asteri '08	♟	4

Schola Sarmenti

VIA AVV. P. INGUSCI, 45
73048 NARDÒ [LE]
TEL. 0833567247
www.scholasarmenti.it

With 20 hectares under vine, Luigi Carlo Marra's Salento estate rounded off another good year with the excellent Critèra '06, a Primitivo with ripe black berry fruit and spice on the nose, and a sweet, caressing palate. The aromas of the decent Nardò Roccamora '06 lack focus but the palate is long and taut.

● Critèra '06	♟♟	4*
☉ Masserei '08	♟	4
● Nardò Nerìo Ris. '04	♟	4
● Nardò Rosso Roccamora '06	♟	4

Setteterre

VIA PER FAGGIANO, 228
74100 MARUGGIO [TA]
TEL. 0994527396
setteterre@hotmail.it

In its second year in the Guide, Setteterre repeats last year's excellent results but with a different label that stopped just short of the finals. We refer to Uva Prigioniera '07, a monovarietal Negroamaro redolent of black berry fruit with a deep, fruity palate bolstered by remarkable structure.

● Uva Prigioniera '07	♟♟	5

Cantine Soloperto

S.S. 7 TER
74024 MANDURIA [TA]
TEL. 0999794286
www.soloperto.it

Hard work in vineyard and cellar are producing good fruit. This year, Soloperto submitted two excellent versions of Primitivo di Manduria. Centofuochi '07 – still young and inexpressive on the nose, yet with good texture and red berry fruit on the palate – and the rich, fruity Mono '06.

● Primitivo di Manduria Centofuochi Tenuta Bagnolo '07	♟♟	5
● Primitivo di Manduria Mono '06	♟♟	5

Conte Spagnoletti Zeuli

FRAZ. MONTEGROSSO
C.DA SAN DOMENICO, S.P. 231 KM 60,000
70031 ANDRIA [BA]
TEL. 0883569511
www.contespagnolettizeuli.it

Historic Spagnoletti Zeuli produced only fair results this year. We particularly like Castel del Monte Rosato Mezzana '08, with its austere nose veined with wild berry notes, and taut, minerally palate. The well-managed Castel del Monte Rosso Vigna Grande '06 is fruity and mid-bodied.

☉ Castel del Monte Rosato Mezzana '08	♟♟	4*
○ Castel del Monte Bianco La Piana '08	♟	4
● Castel del Monte Rosso V. Grande '06	♟	4

Teanum

VIA SALVEMINI, 1
71010 SAN PAOLO DI CIVITATE [FG]
TEL. 0882551056
www.teanum.it

This large Capitanata estate embraces 120 hectares under vine and has recently finished work on the cellar. The Alta line has good wines, including a full-bodied, fruity Cabernet Sauvignon '07, a long, currant-veined Merlot '07 and the elegant Otre Aglianico '07 with its forest floor aromas.

● Alta Cabernet Sauvignon '07	♟♟	4
● Alta Merlot '07	♟♟	4
● Otre Aglianico '07	♟♟	3*

Terranostra

VIA CASTEL DEL MONTE, 190
70010 CORATO [BA]
TEL. 0808722572
info@terranostra-corato.it

This small organic estate enters the Guide with an excellent performance. Castel del Monte Rosso Piano Mangieri '07 is complex with hints of red berries and spice. Castel del Monte Bianco Piano Mangieri '08 is quite pleasant, especially on the palate, with notes of apple and citrus.

○ Castel del Monte Bianco Piano Mangieri '08	🍷🍷 3*
● Castel del Monte Rosso Piano Mangieri '07	🍷🍷 4
⊙ Castel del Monte Rosato Piano Mangieri '08	🍷 3

Valle dell'Asso

VIA GUIDANO, 18
73024 GALATINA [LE]
TEL. 0836561470
www.valleasso.it

Gino Vallone's wines did well, starting with the classic Piromàfo '05, a Negroamaro with chocolate and coffee tones, smoky sensations and rich black berry fruit. Macàro, a blend of part-dried aleatico and malvasia nera aged for six years in large barrels in an oxidized style, has rich, nutty notes.

● Piromàfo '05	🍷🍷 5
● Macàro	🍷 6

Cantina Sociale Cooperativa Vecchia Torre

VIA MARCHE, 1
73045 LEVERANO [LE]
TEL. 0832925053
www.cantinavecchiatorre.it

With more than 1,300 hectares under vine, this co-operative returns to the Guide thanks to its traditional wines, particularly the Leverano Rosso '07 with spice, plum and red berry fruit aromas, and a fresh palate with nice fullness and a long finish.

● Leverano Rosso '07	🍷🍷 2*
⊙ Leverano Rosato '08	🍷 2*
● Leverano Rosso Ris. '05	🍷 3

Vigne & Vini

VIA AMENDOLA, 36
74020 LEPORANO [TA]
TEL. 0995332254
www.vigneevini.it

This reliable operation made a good showing. The best wines are: Primitivo di Manduria Moi '07, with vegetal aromas of carob and ripe fruit, and a full, lingering palate; Papale Highest Quality '03, from 85 per cent negroamaro and malvasia nera, with aromatic herbs and spices, and nice grip in the finish.

● Papale Highest Quality '03	🍷🍷 5
● Primitivo di Manduria Moi '07	🍷🍷 4
● Primitivo di Manduria Papale '07	🍷 5

Consorzio Produttori Vini e Mosti Rossi

VIA FABIO MASSIMO, 19
74024 MANDURIA [TA]
TEL. 0999735332
www.cpvini.com

After two years' absence, this historic co-operative founded in 1932 returns to the Guide. We liked both the Primitivo di Manduria Elegia '06, characterized by touches of cherries, plums and dried figs, and the simple yet elegant Primitivo di Manduria Lirica '06 with its strong spicy notes.

● Primitivo di Manduria Elegia '06	🍷🍷 5
● Primitivo di Manduria Lirica '06	🍷🍷 3*

Vinicola Mediterranea

VIA MATERNITÀ INFANZIA, 22
72027 SAN PIETRO VERNOTICO [BR]
TEL. 0831676323
www.vinicolamediterranea.it

Scores were a bit uneven from this winery, which failed to convince us this year. The well-made Primitivo Dolce Naturale Oblio '07 shows black berry fruit and a soft, nicely full palate. The nicely crafted Don Vito '08, from 60-40 primitivo and negroamaro, is rich and fruity yet lacks freshness.

● Primitivo Dolce Naturale Oblio '07	🍷🍷 4
● Don Vito '08	🍷 3

CALABRIA

Over the last five years Calabrian wine production has amounted to roughly 500,000 hectolitres, around one per cent of national production, which is not really that much for one the largest regions in southern Italy. At the same time, the area of land under vine has increased and now stands at around 15,000 hectares while yield per hectare has noticeably dropped, a sure sign that producers are focusing on quality. This is also confirmed by the rise in the proportion of IGT, DOC and DOCG bottled wines, which over the same period have practically doubled and now account for well over 30 per cent of the region's production. Although obviously much lower than the national average, which hovers around 60 per cent, this is nevertheless a promising trend. The statistics, then, inspire optimism about the intentions of Calabrian producers and everything suggests that they have latched onto quality as their guiding principle. We are glad to say that this year's tastings led us to the same conclusions. We received samples from a large number of new wineries and only lack of space, regretfully, forces us to leave some out. The wines of Cirò were in fine fettle. Over recent years, they have established themselves as leading players on the regional wine scene. In addition to those from the wineries listed, we also liked Ciròs from estates such as Vulcano, Parilla, Luigi Scala, Enotria and Zito. The upper part of the province of Cosenza also boasts some interesting producers, and is home to a group of newcomers to the Guide who bode well for the future of this important Calabrian winemaking area. We should save a special mention for the enclave of Saracena, where the brilliant performance of Luigi Viola has spawned a number of successful emulators. Worthy of note, even though you won't find them in the following pages, are the Moscato Passito di Saracena produced by Pandolfi, and the wines from Feudo dei Sanseverino. Meanwhile, there was not much to report from the south of the region, except for some activity around Reggio Calabria, mainly thanks to renewed interest in the historic Greco di Bianco.

Roberto Ceraudo

LOC. MARINA DI STRONGOLI
C.DA DATTILO
88815 CROTONE
TEL. 0962865613
www.dattilo.it

CELLAR SALES
PRE-BOOKED VISITS
VISITOR FACILITIES
FOOD

ANNUAL PRODUCTION **70,000 bottles**
HECTARES UNDER VINE **20**
VITICULTURE METHOD **Organic certified**

Roberto Ceraudo is not just a skilled, passionate grower. He is one of a dying breed, a real country gent of the old school. This is another reason why we are so glad to see his winery once more up there with Calabria's best. The Dattilo estate, one of the first in the region to go organic, is situated in a hilly area overlooking the sea and is ideal territory for growing grapes. Roberto is helped out by his children, Susy and Giuseppe, who work respectively in the estate office and the cellar.

Petraro '06, an elegant blend of cabernet sauvignon and gaglioppo, earned a well-deserved place in the finals. Its balsamic aromas open onto a fresh, concentrated palate with a velvety mouthfeel where silky tannins combine well with succulent fruit. The Gaglioppo Rosato Grayasusi Etichetta Argento '08, with its spice and citrus aromas, provides highly enjoyable drinking. Grisara '08, an interesting white from pecorello, has fresh eucalyptus and mint leading into a tangy, well-structured palate. The Chardonnay Imyr '08 has good potential but is still a touch too oaky.

iGreco

C.DA GUARDAPIEDI
87062 CARIATI [CS]
TEL. 0983969441
www.igreco.it

CELLAR SALES
PRE-BOOKED VISITS
VISITOR FACILITIES
FOOD

ANNUAL PRODUCTION **308,000 bottles**
HECTARES UNDER VINE **80**
VITICULTURE METHOD **Organic certified**

The Greco brothers' fine estate covers over 1,000 hectares of land farmed using organic methods. Already one of Italy's best known olive oil producers, with a host of awards, Greco recently decided to embark on an exciting new adventure: the production of quality wines that could confidently hold their own on the market. The aim is to make modern wines that fulfil Calabria's still underdeveloped potential while remaining firmly anchored to territory and tradition.

We liked the selection presented this year, especially the monovarietal calabrese Masino '08 with its full nose and a vein of spice, followed by a succulent, well-structured palate. The fresh, easy-drinking Gaglioppo Catà '07 is exceptional value for money, and shows typical aromas shot through with elegant hints of tobacco. Riticella '08 stands out from the other whites. This blend of greco with 30 per cent late-harvest malvasia won us over with its sweet floral aromas and mineral undertones. On the palate, it shows fresh, attractively citrussy and long-lingering.

● Petraro '06	♟♟	6
☉ Grayasusi Etichetta Argento '08	♟♟	5
○ Grisara '08	♟♟	5
○ Ymyr '08	♟♟	5
● Dattilo '06	♟	4
☉ Grayasusi Etichetta Rame '08	♟	5
○ Petelia '08	♟	4
● DoroBe '01	♟♟	8
○ Grisara '07	♟♟	5

● Masino '08	♟♟	4
● Gaglioppo Catà '07	♟♟	3*
○ Riticella '08	♟♟	5
☉ Gaglioppo Savù '08	♟	3
○ Greco Filù '08	♟	3
● Sette Fratelli '06	♟	8
○ Greco Filù '06	♟♟	3*
● Tumà '06	♟♟	4

Cantine Lento

VIA DEL PROGRESSO, 1
88046 LAMEZIA TERME [CZ]
TEL. 096828028
www.cantinelento.it

CELLAR SALES
PRE-BOOKED VISITS

ANNUAL PRODUCTION **650,000 bottles**
HECTARES UNDER VINE **70**
VITICULTURE METHOD **Conventional**

In just a few years, the Lento family has managed to transform a small winery into a modern winemaking facility capable of keeping pace with the times and the complex demands of the global wine market. To their credit, the Lentos have taken these changes in their stride, even when results were slow in coming. Not only have they maintained their local roots; their family identity is still solid. Now that the Amato estate is running at full steam, the Lentos have also finally achieved full autonomy of production, all to the benefit of quality.

The delicious Federico II '06, from gaglioppo and cabernet sauvignon, has a fruity, elegant nose and silky tannins that very nearly won it top honours. Lamezia Riserva '04 has a more austere character, offering jammy red berry fruit over a harmonious, rounded palate. The Tisaloro '07, from magliocco and merlot, also made a good debut, regaling the nostrils with aromas of fruit and Mediterranean herbs, followed by a fresh, tasty, succulent palate. The intense, varietal Sauvignon Blanc Contessa Emburga '08 proffers peaches, apricots and aromatic herbs, and then a supple palate with a lovely fresh aniseed finish. The other wines are all good.

● Federico II '06	🍷🍷	5
○ Contessa Emburga '08	🍷🍷	4*
● Lamezia Ris. '04	🍷🍷	5
● Tisaloro '07	🍷🍷	6
○ Lamezia Bianco Dragone '08	🍷	4
○ Lamezia Greco '08	🍷	4
⊙ Lamezia Rosato Dragone '08	🍷	4
● Lamezia Rosso Dragone '07	🍷	4
● Federico II '05	YY	5
● Federico II '04	YY	5
● Lamezia Rosso Ris. '03	YY	5

Librandi

LOC. SAN GENNARO
S.S. JONICA 106
88811 CIRÒ MARINA [KR]
TEL. 096231518
www.librandi.it

CELLAR SALES
PRE-BOOKED VISITS

ANNUAL PRODUCTION **2.200,000 bottles**
HECTARES UNDER VINE **232**
VITICULTURE METHOD **Conventional**

In the space of just a few years, the Librandi brothers' winery has become a benchmark for the whole region, mainly thanks to Nicodemo and Tonino's experience and unbounded passion for their land and work. Passion alone, however, does not explain the exceptional leap in quality we have witnessed over the last five years. We also need to consider the extraordinary commitment, and money, that the Librandis have invested in research, clonal selection and safeguarding native Calabrian grape varieties.

It is no surprise that Cirò Riserva Duca Sanfelice '07's innate elegance and beautifully complex palate once again earned it Three Glasses. A complex nose of fruit, balsam, flowers and soft chocolate, is followed by masterful balance on the palate, with structure and fruit nicely offset by forthright tannins. Also in the finals were the stylish, harmonious Gravello '07, from gaglioppo and cabernet, with good flesh and elegant tannins, and the Efeso '08, a lingering, flavoursome Mantonico, with rich fruit and fresh acidity. We liked the other wines, especially the concentrated, finely balanced Magliocco Magno Megonio '07.

● Cirò Rosso Duca Sanfelice Ris. '07	🍷🍷🍷	4*
○ Efeso '08	🍷🍷	5
● Gravello '07	🍷🍷	6
○ Critone '08	🍷🍷	4
● Magno Megonio '07	🍷🍷	5
○ Melissa Asylia Bianco '08	🍷🍷	4
⊙ Cirò Rosato '08	🍷	3
● Melissa Asylia Rosso '08	🍷	4
⊙ Terre Lontane '08	🍷	4
● Cirò Rosso Cl. Duca Sanfelice Ris. '05	YYY	4*
● Gravello '05	YYY	5

G.B. Odoardi

C.DA CAMPODORATO
88047 NOCERA TERINESE [CZ]
TEL. 098429961
odoardi@tin.it

PRE-BOOKED VISITS

ANNUAL PRODUCTION **300,000 bottles**
HECTARES UNDER VINE **95**
VITICULTURE METHOD **Conventional**

Gregorio Odoardi manages to excel as both a doctor and a grower. He had no hesitation in taking on single-handed the estate in Nocera Terinese that has been in the family for five centuries. Always on the cutting edge, Gregorio was one of the first to adopt high-density planting, with around 11,000 vines per hectare, and to install a modern, technologically advanced winery.

This year's wines are decidedly modern in style, showing rich in extract and full of character. One example is Vigna Garrone '07, from gaglioffo with small amounts of other varieties, which made our finals. Austere, fruit-driven and faintly grassy, it attacks the palate with refreshing acidity and elegant tannins, opening up to fill the mouth before signing off with a lingering finish. The full-bodied Polpicello '06, from gaglioffo, magliocco and nocera, almost made the finals but was a tad less concentrated than usual. We liked the other wines, such as the fresh, fruity Scavigna Rosato '08, with its attractive fruit and minerality.

Senatore Vini

LOC. SAN LORENZO
88811 CIRÒ MARINA [KR]
TEL. 096232350
www.senatorevini.com

CELLAR SALES
PRE-BOOKED VISITS

ANNUAL PRODUCTION **250,000 bottles**
HECTARES UNDER VINE **27**
VITICULTURE METHOD **Organic certified**

After a fine debut last year, this edition's tastings confirmed the level achieved by the Senatore family. The new generations have changed the face of this historic winery, which in a few years has been completely transformed both in terms of vineyard management and winemaking. Planting patterns in the vineyards have been reviewed and a large, modern winery built. These changes were necessary if the Senatore family were to make the most of the layout of their vineyards, currently divided into four different plots, all falling within the Cirò DOC zone.

We applauded a fine performance from Cirò Arcano Riserva '06, which opens with wild berries, progressing to balsamic and mineral notes. It is equally attractive on the palate, where the mouthfilling warmth is backed up by juicy tannins. The Gaglioppo Merlot '08 blend also impressed. After aerating briefly. It presents red berry fruits mingling with candied peel and tobacco on the nose introducing an intense, harmonious palate. The pleasingly drinkable Cirò Arcano '07 shows clear veins of cherry and balsam, and then a fresh, invigorating palate brimming with silky tannins.

● Scavigna Vigna Garrone '07	▼▼ 6
● Scavigna Polpicello '06	▼▼ 7
● Savuto '07	▼ 4
○ Scavigna Bianco '08	▼ 4
○ Scavigna Pian della Corte '08	▼ 4
◉ Scavigna Rosato '08	▼ 3
● Scavigna Vigna Garrone '04	▼▼▼ 6
● Scavigna Vigna Garrone '03	▼▼▼ 6
● Savuto Sup. V. Mortilla '05	▽▽ 5
● Scavigna Vigna Garrone '05	▽▽ 6

● Cirò Rosso Cl. Arcano '07	▼▼ 4*
● Cirò Rosso Cl. Arcano Ris. '06	▼▼ 5
● Gaglioppo Merlot '08	▼▼ 4
○ Cirò Bianco Alaei '08	▼ 4
◉ Cirò Rosato Puntalice '08	▼ 4
● Ehos '07	▼ 4
● Nerello '07	▼ 5
○ Silò '08	▼ 4
● Cirò Rosso Cl. Arcano '06	▽▽ 4*
● Ehos '06	▽▽ 4*

Statti

C.DA LENTI
88046 LAMEZIA TERME [CZ]
TEL. 0968456138
www.statti.com

CELLAR SALES
PRE-BOOKED VISITS
FOOD

ANNUAL PRODUCTION **300,000 bottles**
HECTARES UNDER VINE **55**
VITICULTURE METHOD **Conventional**

Year after year, the Statti siblings' winery gives us increasingly impressive wines. Known above all for their olive oil, citrus fruits and pedigree cattle breeding, the Stattis decided to add a wine string to their bow. The first goal was to produce modern wines of outstanding quality while remaining true to the territory and local varieties. This was an ambitious goal, involving significant investment in both vineyard and winery, long, hard work on clonal selections and hundreds of small-batch trial fermentations.

The fact that Arvino '07 missed Three Glasses this year by a whisker bodes well for the future, and is a sign that the Stattis are on the right track. Balsam and wild berries on the nose mark out this gaglioppo and cabernet sauvignon blend, which follows up with powerful, succulent fruit on the palate and beautifully smooth tannins. The attractive Gaglioppo '08 shows appealing wild strawberry and raspberry aromas, with whole fruit and good length on the palate. Lamezia Bianco '08 passed muster, with apple-like fruit and mint aromas. The palate has a nice balance of fruit and acidity, signing off long and savoury.

Luigi Viola

VIA ROMA, 18
87010 SARACENA [CS]
TEL. 0981349495
www.cantineviola.it

CELLAR SALES
PRE-BOOKED VISITS

ANNUAL PRODUCTION **7,000 bottles**
HECTARES UNDER VINE **3**
VITICULTURE METHOD **Organic certified**

After his sudden rise to fame last year after securing our Best Sweet Wine title, we could have forgiven Luigi Viola for resting on his laurels, but he clearly has no intention of doing so. This year, his splendid Moscato was on mid-season form, romping off with Three Glasses. The few hectares of Viola family vineyards are situated in the Pollino national park while the winery and offices are housed in an old converted cinema in the centre of Saracena. Luckily, the fame achieved by the Viola family is anything but a flash in the pan.

Over the years, the experience of Luigi and his children has shown the way for a number of Saracena wineries producing Moscato. This year, no fewer than five were presented. That might not seem many but only five years ago, this ancient wine was on the verge of extinction. The Moscato Passito '08 is a concerto of elegance and complexity, with balsam, dates, aromas of lavender, Mediterranean herbs and camomile. The palate shows exceptional finesse, extraordinarily well-judged balance and great length.

● Arvino '07	♟♟	4*
● Gaglioppo Rosso '08	♟♟	3*
○ Greco '08	♟♟	4*
○ Gaglioppo Bianco '08	♟	3
○ I Gelsi Bianco '08	♟	2
● I Gelsi Rosso '08	♟	2
○ Lamezia Bianco '08	♟	3
● Lamezia Rosso '08	♟	3
○ Mantonico '08	♟	4
● Cauro '06	♟♟	5
○ Nosside '07	♟♟	5
○ Nosside '05	♟♟	5

○ Moscato Passito '08	♟♟♟	7
○ Moscato Passito '07	♟♟♟	7
○ Moscato di Saracena '05	♟♟	7
○ Moscato di Saracena '04	♟♟	7
○ Moscato di Saracena '03	♟♟	6
○ Moscato di Saracena '01	♟♟	4
○ Moscato di Saracena '00	♟♟	4
○ Moscato Passito '06	♟♟	7

L'Acino

VIA XX SETTEMBRE, 98
87018 SAN MARCO ARGENTANO [CS]
TEL. 0984512095
info@acinovini.com

There was a fine debut from this new, dynamic winery near Cosenza. The interesting Tocco Magliocco '07 has red berries with fresh vegetal notes against a balsamic backdrop, and is nicely long on the palate. The goodish white Oz '08, a monovarietal Mantonico Pinto, is a savoury, nicely structured and long.

○ Oz '08	♟♟	5
● Tocco Magliocco '07	♟♟	5
● Tocco Cabernet Sauvignon '07	♟	5

Capo Zefirio

VIA LUNGOFERROVIA, 20
89032 BIANCO [RC]
TEL. 0964911446
www.capozefirio.com

This winery is a passionate producer of Greco di Bianco, whose history dates back to the Greek colonization of Calabria but which has risked extinction in the past ten years. The '06 edition offers figs, pineapple and citrus fruit, backed up by a fresh, well-balanced palate and a nice bitterish finish.

○ Greco di Bianco '06	♟♟	7
○ Greco di Bianco '02	♟♟	7

Umberto Ceratti

VIA DEGLI UFFIZI, 5
89030 CARAFFA DEL BIANCO [RC]
TEL. 0964956008

There are no Superiore and Riserva categories for Greco di Bianco DOC so Umberto Ceratti simply changed the label colour on his barrique-aged wines. The intriguing Mantonico '05 is oxidative, with tropical fruit aromas and a mineral, fresh lingering palate. Greco di Bianco '05 is more straightforward.

○ Mantonico Et. Bianca '05	♟♟	5
○ Greco di Bianco Et. Nera '05	♟	5

Colacino

VIA A. GUARASCI, 5
87054 ROGLIANO [CS]
TEL. 0984961034
www.colacino.it

This relative newcomer from Cosenza is one of the rising stars on Calabria's wine scene. Britto '06 performed excellently with an intense complex nose, and a pleasantly smooth, lingering palate. The appealing Vigna Colle Barabba '08 shows balsamic with red berry fruit and florality, and fine structure.

● Amazio '08	♟♟	4*
● Savuto Sup. Britto '06	♟♟	5
● Savuto V. Colle Barabba '08	♟♟	4
○ Quarto '08	♟	4

Donnici 99

C.DA VERZANO
87100 COSENZA
TEL. 0984781842
www.donnici99.com

The wines from this new Donnici-based winery did well. Audace Diverzano '06, from barbera and merlot, proffers a complex, variegated nose and tight-knit, rounded tannins. The well-structured Antico Diverzano '06, an elegant blend of magliocco and greco nero, displays balsamic notes.

● Audace Diverzano '06	♟♟	4
● Donnici Antico Diverzano '06	♟♟	5
● Ardente Diverzano '06	♟	5
☉ Fugace Diverzano '08	♟	3

Du Cropio

VIA SELE, 5
88811 CIRÒ MARINA [KR]
TEL. 096235515
www.viniducropio.it

Cirò Don Giuvà '05 opens on aromatic herbs and topsoil, and a stylishly austere palate. The crisp '06 shows edgy tannins and fair length. Serra Sanguigna '05, from gaglioppo with 30 per cent malvasia nera and greco nero, offers sour and black cherries over a tannic palate with a fruity finish. The '06 is less intense.

● Cirò Don Giuvà '05	♟♟	5
● Serra Sanguigna '05	♟♟	5
● Cirò Don Giuvà '06	♟	5
● Serra Sanguigna '06	♟	5

Ippolito 1845

VIA TIRONE, 118
88811 CIRÒ MARINA [KR]
TEL. 096231106
www.ippolito1845.it

Ippolito, a long-standing Cirò producer, has a reputation for reliability. The interesting Calabrise '08 shows violets, fruit and minerality, with fresh acidity and vibrant tannins. We also liked the fresh, citrussy Cirò Rosato Mabilia '08. Juicy fruit and lively tannins mark out the Liber Pater '07.

● Calabrise '08	⬤⬤	4
◉ Cirò Rosato Mabilia '08	⬤	3
● Cirò Rosso Cl. '07	⬤	3
● Cirò Rosso Cl. Sup. Liber Pater '07	⬤	3

Iuzzolini

LOC. FRASSÀ
88811 CIRÒ MARINA [KR]
TEL. 0962371326
www.tenutaiuzzolini.it

This is a winery to watch, and presented a range of well-made, modern wines. The well-structured Cirò Classico '07 brims with raspberry and cola aromas, and lingers on the palate. Bristace '08 is a fine Greco Passito with lavender and quince aromas leading to a fresh, well-balanced palate.

○ Bristace '08	⬤⬤	7
● Cirò Rosso Cl. '07	⬤⬤	3*
● Artino '08	⬤	5
◉ Lumare '08	⬤	5

Azienda Vinicola Malaspina

VIA PALLICA, 67
89063 MELITO DI PORTO SALVO [RC]
TEL. 0965781632
www.aziendavinicolamalaspina.com

Malaspina's star is Patros Pietro '06, a blend of magliocco and cabernet, with fruit, tobacco and chocolate on the nose and a tannic, lingering palate. The elegant Palikos '07, from gaglioppo and nerello cappuccio, boasts red berry fruit and spice, a balanced palate and a long, well-orchestrated finish.

● Palikos '07	⬤⬤	3*
● Patros Pietro '06	⬤⬤	5
○ Palika '08	⬤	3
● Pellaro '06	⬤	4

Malena

LOC. PETRARO
S.S. JONICA 106
88811 CIRÒ MARINA [KR]
TEL. 096231758
www.malena.it

The Malena family's rosés were particularly good this year. Bacco '08 has small red berry fruit and fresh mint aromas introducing a substantial palate, nicely offset by fresh acidity. The deep pink Cirò Rosato '08 is less complex and almost tannic but has a longish, fruity finish.

◉ Bacco Rosato '08	⬤⬤	4
◉ Cirò Rosato '08	⬤⬤	3*
○ Cirò Bianco '08	⬤	3
● Cirò Rosso Cl. '07	⬤	3

Fattoria San Francesco

LOC. QUATTROMANI
88813 CIRÒ [KR]
TEL. 096232228
www.fattoriasanfrancesco.it

The best wine from this Cirò estate was Cirò Rosso Classico '08. It's varietal on the nose, fresh and vibrant on the palate. We enjoyed the Cirò Rosato '08 Ronco dei Quattroventi with its fresh fruit and good backbone, shot through with green notes. The flowery Greco Fata Morgana '08 is fresh and savoury.

● Cirò Rosso Cl. '08	⬤⬤	3*
◉ Cirò Rosato Cl. Ronco dei Quattroventi '08	⬤	5
● Donna Madda '07	⬤	5
○ Fata Morgana '08	⬤	5

Santa Venere

LOC. TENUTA VOLTAGRANDE
S.P. 04 KM 10,00
88813 CIRÒ [KR]
TEL. 096238519
www.santavenere.com

The Scala family estate in Cirò farms organically. Top of the range is Cirò Bianco '08, with aromas of peach and lime preceding a succulent, zippy palate. From the reds, we liked Vurgadà '08, a blend of nerello, merlot and gaglioppo, with a fresh, juicy palate following sumptuous fruit and spice.

○ Cirò Bianco '08	⬤⬤	4
● Vurgadà '08	⬤⬤	4
● Cirò Rosso Cl. '08	⬤	4
○ Vescovado '08	⬤	4

Serracavallo

C.DA SERRACAVALLO
87043 BISIGNANO [CS]
TEL. 098421144
www.viniserracavallo.it

The fleshy, concentrated Terraccia '07 from magliocco and cabernet gives ripe fruit and florality that took it to our finals. Sette Chiese '08, from the same grapes, shows wild berries and flowers, and then glossy tannins. The stylish Besiadiae '08, from chardonnay, pecorello and riesling, is fresh and savoury.

● Terraccia '07	���♟	5
● Sette Chiese '08	♟♟	4
○ Besiadiae '08	♟	3
● Terraccia '06	♟♟	5

Terre del Gufo - Muzzillo

FRAZ. DONNICI INFERIORE
C.DA ALBO SAN MARTINO
87100 COSENZA
TEL. 3357725614
www.terredelgufo.com

Eugenio Mozzillo makes an excellent debut in the Guide this year. His Timpamara '08, a blend of international varieties and magliocco, is first-rate, with cherry, balsam and oak followed by a tight-knit, sumptuous, lingering palate. The elegant Portapiana '08 was spicy, wrapped in silky smooth tannins.

● Portapiana Donnici '08	♟♟	5
● Timpamara '08	♟♟	7

Tenuta Terre Nobili

LOC. MONTALTO UFFUGO
VIA CARIGLIALTO
87046 MONTALTO UFFUGO [CS]
TEL. 0984934005
lidia.matera@libero.it

This was another good year for Lidia Matera's wines. The Alarico '08, from nerello and aglianico, confirmed its worth, with fruit and balsam on the nose and a well-profiled palate. We were also impressed with the Santa Chiara '08, from greco and a touch of chardonnay, with floral scents and a fresh, zesty palate.

● Alarico '08	♟♟	4
○ Santa Chiara '08	♟♟	4
● Cariglio '08	♟	4
⊙ Donn'Eleonò '08	♟	4

Tramontana

LOC. GALLICO MARINA
VIA CASA SAVOIA, 156
89139 REGGIO CALABRIA
TEL. 0965370067
www.vinitramontana.it

Once again, we appreciated the quality of Tramontana wines, especially the two from nerello. The complex aromas of the 1890 '06 pave the way for a close-knit, succulent palate. We also liked Vorea '08, which gives an intense variegated nose and a fresh, supple palate.

● 1890 '06	♟♟	6
● Vorea '08	♟♟	5
○ Calabria Bianco '08	♟	4
● To Crasì '06	♟	4

Val di Neto

C.DA MARGHERITA
VIA DELLE MAGNOLIE
88900 SCANDALE [KR]
TEL. 096254079
www.cantinavaldineto.com

The Cappa family celebrates its tenth harvest this year with another range of reliable wines. The attractively complex nose of the '07 Mutrò introduces a well-structured tannic palate. The Arkè '07, a blend of aglianico and gaglioppo with a splash of greco nero, is elegant and well balanced.

● Arkè '07	♟♟	4
● Melissa Rosso Sup. Mutrò '07	♟♟	5
⊙ Amistà '08	♟	4
● Melissa Don Armando '08	♟	4

F.lli Zagarella

VIA ROMA, 2
89121 REGGIO CALABRIA
TEL. 0965679521
www.aziendazagarella.it

The Zagarella family winery is back in the Guide. Alfieri '08, a monovarietal Malvasia Nera brimming with cherry fruit, offers approachable, easy drinking. Alfieri Bianco '08 is a fresh, supple blend of malvasia, sauvignon and inzolia with complex grassy, citrus-like aromas.

○ Alfieri Bianco '08	♟	4
⊙ Alfieri Rosato '08	♟	4
● Alfieri Rosso '08	♟	4
● Terragrande '08	♟	4

SICILY

With annual production amounting to over 6,000,000 hectolitres, this large Mediterranean island accounts for between 13 and 14 per cent of Italian wine production as a whole, and is Italy's fourth largest regional producer. Statistics aside, the success of Sicilian wines on domestic and international markets is indisputable. In just over 20 years, the image of the region's bottles has radically changed, and wine tankers sailing to other countries are a thing of the past. Although, until quite recently, most of the wine produced here was sold in bulk, 24 per cent of the island's production is now bottled. But this is not the place to get bogged down in numbers. We just wanted to provide a few figures to show the efforts that producers have made to modernize and pursue quality in such a short time. Today, Nero d'Avola has become a well-known, household name, evoking Sicily, the Mediterranean, and quality. Even though the average consumer's knowledge of Sicilian wine goes no further than the name of the variety or producer – there are very few people who distinguish between wines from eastern and western Sicily – there is one area that has quickly made an impressive name for itself: Etna, the promised land of a new generation of producers. In spite of the limited area under vine, with the whole province of Catania accounting for little more than two and a half per cent of the island's total vineyard area, the name Etna now seems to be surrounded by an aura of prestige comparable to those of classic prestige wines, such as Barolo, Brunello di Montalcino and Amarone, despite Etna's very low production. Ah, but what wines they are! This year, no fewer than seven Etnas won top honours, and two of those were making their debut in the Guide, while another was only here for the second time. This gives an idea of an extraordinarily fine territory, that today is attracting significant investment not only from the island itself and the rest of Italy, but also from abroad. Moreover, with 18 wines taking Three Glasses, this is Sicily's best-ever performance, confirming the excellence and enthusiasm of its producers, both small growers, often using natural methods, and the large internationally renowned wineries. Even though catarratto is still the most widely grown variety, accounting for over 30 per cent of the total, nero d'Avola, insolia, grillo, frappato and nerello mascalese are rapidly making ground, confirming that the future of Sicilian winemaking lies in its native varieties, natural methods and terroir. Keep up the good work!

Abbazia Santa Anastasia

C.DA SANTA ANASTASIA
90013 CASTELBUONO [PA]
TEL. 091671959
www.abbaziasantanastasia.it

CELLAR SALES
PRE-BOOKED VISITS

ANNUAL PRODUCTION 650,000 bottles
HECTARES UNDER VINE 62
VITICULTURE METHOD Organic certified

Francesco Lena's commitment to biodynamic viticulture continues. His concept is based on a holistic approach, which will make the winery completely self-sufficient both in terms of energy – almost 800 square metres of solar panels have been installed – and in terms of the dictates of Steiner's philosophy. With the integration of livestock farming for meat, milk and eggs with agriculture, a virtuous process has been set in motion, around which the production of biodynamic wines rotates.

Whilst awaiting Litra, held back for further ageing, we saw a brilliant performance by the biodynamic Nero d'Avola, Sens(i)nverso '07, into the finals with its intensity, vibrant mineral elegance, weighty palate, fine-grained tannins and a long finish. The new biodynamic Cabernet Sauvignon Sens(i)nverso '07, is big on verve and concentration, although still slightly rough. A fresh, lingering, focused Sauvignon Blanc Sinestesìa '08 is spot-on, releasing intense varietal aromas. The other wines are consistently good, in particular the Contempo Nerello Mascalese '08 and the deliciously drinkable Contempo Nero d'Avola '08.

Baglio del Cristo

C.DA FAVAROTTA, S.S. 123 KM 19,200
92023 CAMPOBELLO DI LICATA [AG]
TEL. 0922 877709
www.cristodicampobello.it

CELLAR SALES
PRE-BOOKED VISITS

ANNUAL PRODUCTION 300,000 bottles
HECTARES UNDER VINE 32
VITICULTURE METHOD Conventional

The estate of Angelo Bonetta and his sons Carmelo and Riccardo covers 50 hectares of lime and chalk-based soil, 32 under vine, spread over low hills close to the sea. The special site climate is characterized by a day-night temperature swing of as much as 20 degrees Celsius, thanks to the sea breezes. For over 200 years, a much-venerated statue of Christ has been standing in the middle of the vineyards, and it is to him that the winery, housed in a converted late-17th century fortified farm, has been dedicated.

Lu Patri '07, a classic-style Nero d'Avola, from a five-hectare plot, steamed into the finals. This intense, varietal, concentrated, mouthfilling red opens on notes of bitter cherry, nutmeg and aromatic herbs, leading to a warm, spicy palate with already polished tannins. Another finalist was the stylish, citrussy Chardonnay Laudàri '07, which ages on the lees for six months. Its charming floral and mineral hints usher in a well-balanced, supple, zesty palate. The fresh Adènzia '08, from grillo and chardonnay, also performed well, with pleasing, lingering overtones of almond, lime and white peach.

● Sens(i)nverso Nero d'Avola '07	♟♟	6
● Sens(i)nverso Cabernet Sauvignon '07	♟♟	6
○ Sinestesìa '08	♟♟	4*
○ Baccante '08	♟	5
○ Contempo Grillo '08	♟	3
○ Contempo Insolia '08	♟	3
● Contempo Nerello Mascalese '08	♟	3
● Contempo Nero d'Avola '08	♟	3
○ Gemelli '08	♟	5
● Passomaggio '07	♟	4
○ Zurrica '08	♟	4
● Litra '04	♟♟♟	7
● Litra '01	♟♟♟	8
● Montenero '04	♟♟♟	5

○ Laudàri '07	♟♟	6
● Lu Patri '07	♟♟	6
○ Adènzia '08	♟♟	4*
● Lusirà '07	♟	6

Baglio di Pianetto

VIA FRANCIA
90030 SANTA CRISTINA GELA [PA]
TEL. 0918570002
www.bagliodipianetto.com

CELLAR SALES
PRE-BOOKED VISITS

ANNUAL PRODUCTION 400,000 bottles
HECTARES UNDER VINE 95
VITICULTURE METHOD Conventional

Paolo Marzotto's winery has two separate production facilities: in Noto, at Contrada Baroni, and in Pianetto, 20 kilometres from Palermo, areas which have always been wine country. They are geologically different but both have fairly mild, uniform site climate, regulated respectively by the nearness of the sea and the elevation, at around 600 metres. The care taken in production is such that at Baroni they have a special winery for the vinification of the estate's grapes before transfer to the main facility in Pianetto for maturation.

No wine really stood out, but all the labels presented lived up to the winery's reputation. The deep ruby Shymer '07, a blend of syrah and merlot, shows fragrant red berry fruit and spice, followed on the palate by supple tannins and a long, leisurely finish. Nero d'Avola and merlot come together in the deep ruby Ramione '05, brimming with red berry preserve and taut, tight-knit tannins. The stylish Viognier Piana del Ginolfo '08 opens with mineral, smoky and aniseed aromas, leading to a well-balanced palate with a gratifying finish. The Nero d'Avola '06 is intense, velvety and varietal.

★ Benanti

VIA G. GARIBALDI, 475
95029 VIAGRANDE [CT]
TEL. 0957893438
www.vinicolabenanti.it

CELLAR SALES
PRE-BOOKED VISITS

ANNUAL PRODUCTION 180,000 bottles
HECTARES UNDER VINE 50
VITICULTURE METHOD Conventional

The prestigious winery of Cavaliere del Lavoro Giuseppe Benanti is credited with being the first to put Etna winemaking in the international limelight, with the invaluable help of oenologist Salvo Foti. Today, the winery adopts traditional methods, with the reintroduction of bush training and the use of natural yeasts. The business has also found renewed verve thanks to the help of Giuseppe's sons, Antonio and Salvino, and has recently acquired an estate at Pachino, the homeland of nero d'Avola, which is producing excellent results.

The Etna Rosso Serra della Contessa '06, from nerello mascalese and nerello cappuccio, one of the estate's thoroughbreds, confidently took top honours. Its enchanting, well-coordinated blackcurrant and spice aromas interweave with an attractive minty vein. The potent, austerely vigorous palate perfectly evokes the great volcano's energy and marvellous minerality. Equally attractive is the famous Etna Bianco Superiore Pietramarina '05, from carricante, which shows vibrant, stylish and zesty, with seductive flinty notes. All the other wines are terroir-driven and evocative, especially Il Drappo '06, a deep, varietal Nero d'Avola from Pachino.

● Nero d'Avola '06	🍷🍷	4*
○ Piana del Ginolfo '08	🍷🍷	4*
● Ramione '05	🍷🍷	4*
● Shymer '07	🍷🍷	4*
○ Ficiligno '08	🍷	4
● Ramione '04	🍷🍷🍷	4*
● Chianu Carduni '05	🍷🍷	7
● Nero d'Avola '04	🍷🍷	4
○ Ra'is '05	🍷🍷	5
● Shymer '06	🍷🍷	4*
● Shymer '05	🍷🍷	4

● Etna Rosso Serra della Contessa '06	🍷🍷🍷	8
○ Etna Bianco Sup. Pietramarina '05	🍷🍷	7
○ Edelmio '07	🍷🍷	5
○ Etna Bianco di Caselle '08	🍷🍷	4*
● Etna Rosso Rosso di Verzella '06	🍷🍷	4*
● Etna Rosso Rovittello '05	🍷🍷	6
● Il Drappo '06	🍷🍷	7*
● Lamorèmio '05	🍷🍷	6
● Majora '06	🍷🍷	8
● Nerello Cappuccio Il Monovitigno '06	🍷🍷	6
● Nerello Mascalese Il Monovitigno '06	🍷🍷	6
○ Il Musico Passito '08	🍷	5
○ Etna Bianco Sup. Pietramarina '04	🍷🍷🍷	7
○ Etna Bianco Sup. Pietramarina '02	🍷🍷🍷	6
● Etna Rosso Serra della Contessa '04	🍷🍷🍷	8
● Il Drappo '04	🍷🍷🍷	6

Vini Biondi

c.so SICILIA, 20
95039 TRECASTAGNI [CT]
TEL. 0957633933
www.vinibiondi.it

CELLAR SALES
PRE-BOOKED VISITS

ANNUAL PRODUCTION **20,000 bottles**
HECTARES UNDER VINE **14**
VITICULTURE METHOD **Naturale**

The Biondis' passion for Etna wine is in the blood and Ciro deserves full credit for reviving the family business. The grapes come from vineyards on the eastern slopes of the volcano, all at altitude and bush-trained, with an average age of over 40 years. A real gem of Etna winemaking is the vineyard on Monte Ilice, which climbs to an altitude of 900 metres on a 50 per cent incline without terracing, literally clinging to an ancient satellite cone of the volcano.

Ciro Biondi thrilled us with his Etna Rosso M.I. '07, vinified from the Monte Ilice cru, which flaunts a splendidly focused bouquet of breathtaking complexity, showing beautifully elegant notes of liqueur cherries, tobacco and chocolate. On the palate, there's exceptional power, freshness and energy, and incredible aromatic length. This masterpiece received our highest honour, Three Glasses. The '06 version of the Etna Rosso Outis is almost as good as the previous edition, with mature finesse, well-expressed typical minerality, authoritative, austere tannins and a beautifully clean, long finish.

● Etna Rosso M.I. '07	♈♈♈	6
● Etna Rosso Outis '06	♈♈	6
● Etna Rosso Outis '05	♈♈♈	6
○ Etna Bianco Outis '06	♈♈	5
● Etna Rosso Outis '04	♈♈	6
○ Gurna Bianco '05	♈♈	5
● Outis '03	♈♈	5

Calatrasi

c.DA PIANO PIRAINO
90040 SAN CIPIRELLO [PA]
TEL. 0918576767
www.calatrasi.it

CELLAR SALES
PRE-BOOKED VISITS

ANNUAL PRODUCTION **4.723,000 bottles**
HECTARES UNDER VINE **700**
VITICULTURE METHOD **Organic certified**

Calatrasi was established in 1980 by brothers Giuseppe and Maurizio Miccichè, the latter a doctor with a bent for viticulture. They were inspired by their father Vincenzo, another doctor with a passion for winegrowing. Wine has now become an impressive business, with over 1,750 hectares of land distributed over three production facilities, each with a vinification plant, in Sicily, Puglia and Tunisia. The aim is to offer wines of quality with local typing at tempting prices.

The dark violet Terre di Ginestra '07, from nero d'Avola and syrah, waltzed into the finals. Stylish, focused aromas of cherry and chocolate lead to a close-knit, fresh, gutsy, rich palate with caressing tannins. The warm, varietal Terre di Ginestra Nero d'Avola '06 shows seductive sweet spice, mint and red berry liqueur fruit, followed by a well-structured palate underpinned by nice acidity. The attractive new Terre di Ginestra FranQ '08, a blend of various red grape varieties led by cabernet franc, was juicy, flavourful, rounded and long. 'A Naca Rosso '06, a soft, appealing monovarietal nero d'Avola, is intense, and slightly overripe.

● Terre di Ginestra 651 '07	♈	5
● 'A Naca '06	♈♈	6
● Terre di Ginestra FrancQ '08	♈♈	4
● Terre di Ginestra Magnifico '07	♈♈	5
● Terre di Ginestra Nero d'Avola '06	♈♈	4*
○ Terre di Ginestra BlanQ '08	♈	4
○ Terre di Ginestra Catarratto '08	♈	4
○ Terre di Ginestra Viognier '08	♈	4
● Terre di Ginestra 651 '06	♈♈	5
● Terre di Ginestra 651 Nero d'Avola '07	♈♈	5

Cantina Viticoltori Associati Canicattì

C.DA AQUILATA
92024 CANICATTÌ [AG]
TEL. 0922829371
www.viticultoriassociati.it

CELLAR SALES
PRE-BOOKED VISITS

ANNUAL PRODUCTION 700,000 bottles
HECTARES UNDER VINE 1000
VITICULTURE METHOD Conventional

Viticoltori Associati di Canicattì, one of the oldest Sicilian co-operative wineries, was established more than 40 years ago, and has almost 500 members. They farm over 1,000 hectares under vine, and the co-operative is without doubt one of the most dynamic businesses in the island's winemaking sector. Over recent years, there have been significant investments in technology, which have made it possible to equip the large winery with the latest vinification systems, including temperature control and the recent reintroduction of concrete vats, for the reds.

The excellent Scialo '07, a blend of nero d'Avola and syrah, boasts intense notes of red berry fruit and spice, leading to a tannic, well-structured palate. Among the monovarietals, the dark, concentrated Aquilae Cabernet Sauvignon '08 stood out, with subtle grassy aromas backed up by a juicy, complex palate, and a long, gratifying finish. We were also impressed by the deep ruby Aquilae Syrah '08, which gives a pervasive nose of blueberries and cherries alongside balsamic nuances, over a well-rounded, nicely calibrated palate. We also liked the spicy Aquilae Merlot '08, with grassy aromas leading to a fruity, well-orchestrated, rounded palate.

COS

S.P. 3 AGATE-CHIARAMONTE KM 14,300
97019 VITTORIA [RG]
TEL. 0932876145
www.cosvittoria.it

CELLAR SALES
PRE-BOOKED VISITS

ANNUAL PRODUCTION 160,000 bottles
HECTARES UNDER VINE 25
VITICULTURE METHOD Naturale

The adventure of Giusto Occhipinti and "Titta" Cilia, school friends and colleagues at university, both successful architects, almost began as a game back in 1980. Now, with the inauguration of their beautiful new winery, they are enjoying real success. Shunning fashion and eschewing easy options, at Cos they consistently pursue an approach based on giving priority to the terroir, the vineyard and natural methods. As if to emphasize their relationship with the land, they have also purchased 140 Spanish 400-litre amphorae for fermentation.

Normal business considerations have no effect on release dates here. Among those ready for our tastings, we particularly liked the stylish, mature, terroir-driven Cerasuolo di Vittoria Classico '07, from nero d'Avola and frappato, with lovely tones of ripe plum and black pepper, which is fresh, dynamic and wonderfully drinkable. The varietal, well-typed Syre '05, from nero d'Avola, is slightly overripe, but charmed us with its nicely rounded, lively tannins. The intense cerasuolo-hued Frappato '08, with clear violet and citrus notes, is to be a subtle, intriguing wine, a perfect expression of the terroir of eastern Sicily.

● Aquilae Cabernet Sauvignon '08	♟♟ 3*
● Aquilae Merlot '08	♟♟ 3*
● Aquilae Syrah '08	♟♟ 3*
● Scialo '07	♟♟ 4*
○ Aquilae Catarratto Inzolia '08	♟ 3
○ Aquilae Chardonnay '08	♟ 3
○ Aquilae Grillo '08	♟ 3
● Aquilae Nero d'Avola '08	♟ 3
● Calìo '08	♟ 4
● Aquilae Cabernet Sauvignon '05	♟♟ 3*
● Aquilae Syrah '07	♟♟ 3*
● Aynat '06	♟♟ 5
● Aynat '05	♟♟ 5*
● Aynat '04	♟♟ 4*
● Scialo '06	♟♟ 4*

● Cerasuolo di Vittoria Classico '07	♟♟ 5
● Frappato '08	♟♟ 4*
● Syre '05	♟♟ 6
○ Ramì '08	♟ 4
● Cerasuolo di Vittoria '05	♟♟ 4
● Cerasuolo di Vittoria Classico '06	♟♟ 5
● Contrade Labirinto '04	♟♟ 8
● Contrade Labirinto '01	♟♟ 8
● Frappato '07	♟♟ 4*
○ Ramì '07	♟♟ 4*

Cottanera

LOC. IANNAZZO
S.P. 89
95030 CASTIGLIONE DI SICILIA [CT]
TEL. 0942963601
www.cottanera.lt

CELLAR SALES
PRE-BOOKED VISITS

ANNUAL PRODUCTION **300,000 bottles**
HECTARES UNDER VINE **55**
VITICULTURE METHOD **Conventional**

Unfortunately, Gugliemo Cambria, the founder of this fine winery, has left us. Now it is managed, with the same indefatigable passion, by his children Mariangela and Francesco, and his brother Enzo. Among the first to sense the potential of the Etna terroir, inexplicably neglected for years, the Cambrias about a decade ago reorganized the family business, intent on producing elegant, modern wines with a strong sense of place.

Three Glasses went to the Etna Rosso '06, a stylish wine with great personality and typicity that unfurls a well-developed, lingering palate behind a fruity, mineral nose. The fruit-driven, spicy L'Ardenza '07, from mondeuse grapes, shows great, complex structure and also made the finals, where it was joined by the highly age-worthy Cabernet Sauvignon, Nume '06. We were also impressed by the dense ruby-garnet Fatagione '07, a Nerello Mascalese, boasting red berry fruit and well-integrated oak, accompanied by a long, well-balanced palate, and the attractive Merlot Grammonte '07, which is a little less mature than the others.

★ Cusumano

C.DA SAN CARLO S.S. 113
90047 PARTINICO [PA]
TEL. 0918903456
www.cusumano.it

PRE-BOOKED VISITS

ANNUAL PRODUCTION **2.500,000 bottles**
HECTARES UNDER VINE **450**
VITICULTURE METHOD **Conventional**

Alberto and Diego Cusumano's winery is one of the most important in Sicily, with estates at Salemi, Pachino, Piana degli Albanesi and Butera. Without doubt, theirs is a modern, dynamic part of the Sicilian wine scene, both in terms of the individual wines, which are technically impeccable, terroir-driven and reasonably priced, and because of the diversified approach to the international market and its constantly changing moods, which Cusumano manages to interpret, and at times anticipate, with great shrewdness.

The Sàgana '07 again did well and deservedly won Three Glasses. This intense, deep, characterful Nero d'Avola from Butera is stylish, meaty and lingering. Three other wines also made our finals, a perfect example of the estate's style: the seductive, elegant Noà '07, from nero d'Avola, cabernet sauvignon and merlot, with complex, balsamic aromas and silky tannins; the equally good Benuara '08, a soft, spicy, convincing blend of nero d'Avola and syrah; and the Cubìa '08, a citrussy, grassy, zesty Inzolia. The rest of the wines are extremely good.

Wine	Rating
● Etna Rosso '06	▼▼▼ 6
● L'Ardenza '07	▼▼ 5
● Nume '06	▼▼ 5
● Fatagione '07	▼▼ 5
● Grammonte '07	▼▼ 5
○ Barbazzale Bianco '08	▼ 3
● Barbazzale Rosso '08	▼ 3
● Etna Rosso '05	♀♀♀ 6
● Fatagione '06	♀♀ 5
● Fatagione '05	♀♀ 5
● Grammonte '06	♀♀ 5
● Grammonte '05	♀♀ 5
● L'Ardenza '06	♀♀ 5
● L'Ardenza '05	♀♀ 5
● Sole di Sesta '06	♀♀ 5

Wine	Rating
● Sàgana '07	▼▼▼ 5
● Benuara '08	▼▼ 4*
○ Cubìa '08	▼▼ 4*
● Noà '07	▼▼ 5
○ Angimbé '08	▼▼ 4*
○ Jalé '08	▼▼ 5
● Merlot '08	▼▼ 5
● Nero d'Avola '08	▼▼ 3*
● Pinot Nero '07	▼▼ 5
☉ Rosato '08	▼▼ 3*
● Syrah '08	▼▼ 3*
○ Alcamo Bianco '08	▼ 3*
○ Inzolia '08	▼ 3*
● Noà '05	♀♀♀ 5
● Sàgana '06	♀♀♀ 5

★ Donnafugata

VIA SEBASTIANO LIPARI, 18
91025 MARSALA [TP]
TEL. 0923724200
www.donnafugata.it

CELLAR SALES
PRE-BOOKED VISITS

ANNUAL PRODUCTION 2.700.000 bottles
HECTARES UNDER VINE 328
VITICULTURE METHOD Conventional

Right since the beginning back in 1983, Giacomo Rallo's winery has had a reputation for modern, technically perfect wines. His dramatic entrance into what had been a static market, basically dominated by a single brand, helped give a much-needed wake-up call to winemaking on the island. Today, Giacomo is helped out by his sons, Josè and Antonio, who respectively deal with marketing and production. Recent news includes the inauguration of the large air-conditioned barrique cellar at Marsala and the new winery on Pantelleria.

The '06 version of Mille e una Notte is nothing short of masterly, and easily took Three Glasses. This Nero d'Avola vaunts intriguing aromas, well-integrated with complex balsamic and spicy notes, and piquant hints of the sea that come back to haunt the palate, where the fruit is underpinned by fresh acidity and well-honed tannins. The intense Ben Ryé '08, from moscato d'Alessandria, also made the finals and brims with minerality, apricots and citrus fruits over a fresh, beautifully sweet, lingering palate. From the whites, the stand-out is the zesty Lighea '08, from zibibbo, inzolia and catarratto, with its mint and peach nuances.

Duca di Salaparuta - Vini Corvo

VIA NAZIONALE, S.S. 113
90014 CASTELDACCIA [PA]
TEL. 091945201
www.duca.it

CELLAR SALES
PRE-BOOKED VISITS

ANNUAL PRODUCTION 10,000,000 bottles
HECTARES UNDER VINE 155
VITICULTURE METHOD Conventional

The union of the three historic brands, Duca di Salaparuta, Corvo and Florio, under ILLVA from Saronno is complete, and we can now talk of a single company with an enviable 180 years of history. The modern headquarters at Casteldaccia and the splendid wineries in Marsala built by Vincenzo Florio in 1832 are the pride of the group, which can count on excellent raw materials from its own vineyards in ideal wine country at Butera, Salemi and Castiglione di Sicilia.

Elegant aromas, subtle balsam and a silky-soft palate are what took the Nero d'Avola Duca Enrico '05 into the finals. We will have to wait for the Inzolia Bianca di Valguarnera '07, which needs further ageing. Meanwhile, we were impressed by Nero d'Avola Passo delle Mule '07, the Calanìca Rosso '07, a new blend of nero d'Avola and merlot and the corresponding Bianco '08, from inzolia and chardonnay, a deliciously clean wine. The Corvo line has two well-made newcomers, the Terrae Dei '07 and '08, respectively a Nero d'Avola and a Grillo. At the top of the Florio range is the sunny, lingering Malvasia delle Lipari Passito '08, which flaunts sweet notes of candied peel.

Wine	Rating	Score
● Contessa Entellina Milleunanotte '06	♙♙♙	8
○ Passito di Pantelleria Ben Ryé '08	♙♙	8
● Angheli '07	♙♙	5
○ Contessa Entellina Chiarandà del Merlo '07	♙♙	6
○ Lighea '08	♙♙	4*
○ Contessa Entellina Chardonnay La Fuga '08	♙	4
○ Contessa Entellina Vigna di Gabri '08	♙	4
● Sedàra '08	♙	4
○ Contessa Entellina Chiarandà del Merlo '99	♙♙♙	5
● Contessa Entellina Milleunanotte '05	♙♙♙	8
● Contessa Entellina Milleunanotte '04	♙♙♙	7
● Contessa Entellina Milleunanotte '03	♙♙♙	7
● Contessa Entellina Milleunanotte '02	♙♙♙	7
● Contessa Entellina Milleunanotte '01	♙♙♙	7
● Contessa Entellina Milleunanotte '00	♙♙♙	7
○ Passito di Pantelleria Ben Ryé '06	♙♙♙	7

Wine	Rating	Score
● Duca Enrico '05	♙♙	8
● Calanìca Rosso '07	♙♙	4*
○ Florio Malvasia delle Lipari Passito '08	♙♙	6
○ Florio Passito di Pantelleria '07	♙♙	6
● Lavico Tenuta Vajasindi '06	♙♙	4
● Passo delle Mule '07	♙♙	6
○ Calanìca Bianco '08	♙	4
○ Colomba Platino '08	♙	4
● Corvo Rosso '07	♙	4
● Corvo Sciaranera '08	♙	4
○ Corvo Terrae Dei Bianco '08	♙	3
● Corvo Terrae Dei Rosso '07	♙	3
○ Florio Zibibbo Liquoroso Annur	♙	3
● Triskelè '06	♙	5
● Duca Enrico '03	♙♙♙	7

Fatascià

VIA MAZZINI, 40
90139 PALERMO
TEL. 091332505
www.fatascia.it

PRE-BOOKED VISITS

ANNUAL PRODUCTION **390,000 bottles**
HECTARES UNDER VINE **30**
VITICULTURE METHOD **Conventional**

In 2001, after ten years of crucial experience in her father's winery at Abbazia Santa Anastasia, the talented oenologist Stefania Lena decided to break away and fend for herself, in search of her own identity and original ideas, focusing on typicity and innovation. She had considerable market success, and together with her husband Giuseppe Natoli, farms 30 hectares in Palermo's hinterland. Vinification is carried out at the historic Baglio Abate in Balestrate.

Pride of place this year goes to Rosso del Presidente '07, from cabernet franc and nero d'Avola, with intense fruit on the nose, and a concentrated, supple palate with caressing tannins. We also liked the dense, solid L'Insolente '07, from merlot and cabernet sauvignon, with pleasing its ripe fruit and well-dosed vanilla. This extremely long wine shows marvellous harmony between the impressive structure and the vibrant supporting acidity. Almanera '07, a slightly overripe monovarietal Nero d'Avola, boasts varietal notes of topsoil and spices, shot through with faint iodine nuances. The rest of the range is good and well priced.

● Almanera '07	♟♟ 4*
● L'Insolente '07	♟♟ 7
● Rosso del Presidente '07	♟♟ 5
● Aliré '07	♟ 4*
○ Inzolia & Grillo '08	♟ 4
● Nero d'Avola '08	♟ 4
● Syrah '08	♟ 4
● Almanera '06	♟♟ 4*
● L'Insolente '06	♟♟ 7
● Rosso del Presidente '06	♟♟ 5

Tenuta di Fessina

LOC. CONTRADA ROVITTELLO
VIA NAZIONALE 120, 22
95012 CASTIGLIONE DI SICILIA [CT]
TEL. 057155284

PRE-BOOKED VISITS

ANNUAL PRODUCTION **30,000 bottles**
HECTARES UNDER VINE **9**
VITICULTURE METHOD **Naturale**

Fessina expresses the love for Sicily of Silvia Maestrelli, a Tuscan producer, her husband Roberto Silva and the agronomist-oenologist Federico Curtaz. The three properties, each covering a few hectares, are in Segesta, in the province of Trapani; Noto, in the province of Siracusa; and on the northern slopes of Etna, in Contrada Rovittello, near Castiglione di Sicilia. The last was their first and most important acquisition, and boasts densely planted bush-trained vines, aged between 60 and 90 years, with some plants over 100 years old.

On its debut, Etna Rosso Musmeci '07 authoritatively claimed Three Glasses. This magnificent union of nerello mascalese and nerello cappuccio from the oldest, high-altitude vineyards, enchanted the tasting panel with its great class, focused, ripe fruit notes, marked minerality and incomparable vitality. The very good Etna Rosso Erse '08, from the same grapes, provides fresh, stylish and extremely pleasurable drinking. Also interesting are the Chardonnay di Segesta Nakone '07 and Ero '08, a dark, concentrated Nero d'Avola from Val di Noto, which is richly varietal, fragrant and spicy, with boisterous tannins.

● Etna Rosso Musmeci '07	♟♟♟ 7
● Etna Rosso Erse '08	♟♟ 5
● Ero '08	♟ 4
○ Nakone '07	♟ 4

Feudi del Pisciotto

LOC. PISCIOTTO
93015 NISCEMI [CL]
TEL. 0577742903
www.castellare.it

PRE-BOOKED VISITS

ANNUAL PRODUCTION **220,000 bottles**
HECTARES UNDER VINE **50**
VITICULTURE METHOD **Naturale**

Wine has always been important here, as testified by the splendid, perfectly restored 18th-century wine press, symbolically attached to the large, ultra-modern winery. Situated in the hills between Piazza Armerina and Caltagirone, the altitude, but above all the closeness to the sea, gives this attractive winery a particularly temperate site climate. We should also mention that thanks to an agreement with a group of famous Italian fashions designers, all of the Feudo's crus will boast designer labels, and some of the proceeds each year will be used to restore a Sicilian work of art.

The complex, balsamic Nero d'Avola Versace '07 took Three Glasses. Following plum and blackberry sweetness on the nose, the palate is concentrated yet not oppressive, with fruit balanced by close-knit, elegant tannins and a lovely, gratifying finish. Mineral notes are to the fore in the stylish, fresh, fleshy Chardonnay Alberta Ferretti '07. The well-managed Merlot Valentino '07 shows hints of cherry and red berry fruit, leading to a full palate, well underpinned by the tannins. The austere Cabernet Sauvignon Missoni '07 shows elegant notes of raspberries, blackcurrants and fines herbes, accompanied by a nicely developed, lingering palate.

Feudo Maccari

C.DA MACCARI, S.P. PACHINO-NOTO, KM 13,500
96017 NOTO [SR]
TEL. 0931596894
www.feudomaccari.it

CELLAR SALES
PRE-BOOKED VISITS

ANNUAL PRODUCTION **186,000 bottles**
HECTARES UNDER VINE **100**
VITICULTURE METHOD **Naturale**

The great reliability displayed by all the wines from Feudo Maccari has earned Antonio Moretti's winery a place in the Sicilian winemaking elite. This estate, with almost 100 hectares under vine, and a large, new, air-conditioned winery, is located between Noto and Pachino, a territory that has always been considered the heartland of nero d'Avola at its most typical. Moretti has recovered all the old bush-trained vineyards, some over 40 years old, but above all has decided to use this traditional system for all the new plantings.

The extraordinary elegance and personality of the Nero d'Avola Saia '07 not only validates Antonio's technical choices but also brings him Three Glasses. An intriguing nose of black berry fruit, combined with tobacco, spice, chocolate and balsamic and mineral notes, ushers in a consistent palate, where the impressive weight is balanced by its elegant tannic architecture. The finals were also graced by the characterful Mahâris '07, a blend of nero d'Avola, cabernet and syrah, showing pervasive aromas, and a concentrated, well-coordinated palate. The varietal Nero d'Avola '08 is simply delicious, with soft tannins and lively, fragrant fruit.

● Nero d'Avola Versace '07	♟♟♟	5*
○ Chardonnay Alberta Ferretti '07	♟	5
● Baglio del Sole Nero d'Avola '07	♟	4*
● Cabernet Sauvignon Missoni '07	♟	5
● Frappato Carolina Marengo '07	♟	5
○ Grillo Carolina Marengo '07	♟	5
● Merlot Valentino '07	♟	5
○ Baglio del Sole Inzolia '08	♟	3
○ Baglio del Sole Inzolia Catarratto '08	♟	3
● Baglio del Sole Nero d'Avola '06	♟♟	4*
● Baglio del Sole Nero d'Avola '05	♟♟	4*

● Saia '07	♟♟♟	5*
● Mahâris '07	♟	7
● ReNoto Nero d'Avola '08	♟	4*
⊙ ReNoto Rosè '08	♟	3*
● Saia '06	♟♟♟	5
● Mahâris '06	♟♟	7
● Mahâris '05	♟♟	6
● ReNoto '07	♟♟	4*
● Saia '05	♟♟	5
● Saia '04	♟♟	5

Feudo Principi di Butera

C.DA DELIELLA
93011 BUTERA [CL]
TEL. 0934347726
www.feudobutera.it

ANNUAL PRODUCTION **800,000 bottles**
HECTARES UNDER VINE **180**
VITICULTURE METHOD **Conventional**

Feudo Principi di Butera is set in rolling hills between Butera and Riesi, close to the sea, in an area of limestone-based soil with a characteristic whitish colour. The estate used to belong to the noble Deliella family, and is still dominated by the tower in the historic village. The whole estate spreads out before your eyes, and the immense vineyard is kept like a garden, unfurling in the sunlight like a handkerchief fluttering gently in the breeze. The estate also has a modern winery, built entirely underground, where all the vinification and maturation procedures take place.

The Deliella '06 almost achieved top honours. This Nero d'Avola shows intense, varied aromas, in which wild berries, leather and tobacco alternate against a lovely balsamic backdrop. The warm, well-structured palate shows full, silky, nicely ripe tannins and great length. The other wines are all good, starting with the attractive Nero d'Avola '07, with generous, varietal aromas and a balanced palate. The Cabernet Sauvignon '07 unveils red berry fruit and Mediterranean scrub, and goodish structure. The dry, well-rounded, long Syrah '07 has a solid palate, brimming with fruit and spice.

Firriato

VIA TRAPANI, 4
91027 PACECO [TP]
TEL. 0923882755
www.firriato.it

ANNUAL PRODUCTION **4.700,000 bottles**
HECTARES UNDER VINE **200**
VITICULTURE METHOD **Conventional**

This impressive operation, in terms of turnover and image, is the result of Vinzia and Salvatore Di Gaetano's unremitting commitment and vision over the last ten years. They have given priority to the quality of the wines, and emphasized the importance of the vineyards of origin. The latest news is the purchase of a fine estate on Etna, at Castiglione di Sicilia, and of five hectares on Favignana, a holding farmed using organic methods which is the only vineyard on the Egadi islands.

Harmonium '07, a Nero d'Avola from the Borgo Guarini winery, confidently claimed Three Glasses. This extraordinarily intense, varietal wine shows layered plum, topsoil and sweet spices, over a vital, throbbing palate with nicely rounded tannins. The other finalists were almost as good: a vigorous Ribeca '07, now a monovarietal perricone, and the lovely, juicy, fruit-rich Quater Rosso '07, from nero d'Avola, perricone, frappato and nerello cappuccio. The elegant, well-focused Etna Rosso Cavanera '07, from 22-year-old vines of nerello mascalese and cappuccio, debuted well, as did the smooth Passito L'Ecrù, from zibibbo with a dash of malvasia.

● Deliella '06	♟♟	7
● Nero d'Avola '07	♟♟	4*
● Cabernet Sauvignon '07	♟	4
● Merlot '07	♟	4
● Riesi '07	♟	4
○ Surya Bianco '08	♟	4
● Surya Rosso '07	♟	3
● Syrah '07	♟	4
● Deliella '05	♟♟♟	7
● Deliella '02	♟♟♟	8
● Deliella '00	♟♟♟	6
● Nero d'Avola '06	♟♟	4
● Nero d'Avola '05	♟♟	4
● Riesi '06	♟♟	4
● Syrah '06	♟♟	4

● Harmonium '07	♟♟♟	5*
● Quater Rosso '07	♟♟	5*
● Ribeca '07	♟♟	6
○ Altavilla della Corte Grillo '08	♟♟	3*
● Altavilla della Corte Rosso '07	♟♟	4*
● Camelot '07	♟♟	7
○ Chiaramonte Ansonica '08	♟♟	4*
● Chiaramonte Rosso Nero d'Avola '07	♟♟	4*
● Etna Rosso Cavanera '07	♟♟	6
○ Passito L'Ecrù '07	♟♟	6
○ Quater Bianco '08	♟♟	5
○ Santagostino Bianco Baglio Soria '08	♟♟	5
● Santagostino Rosso Baglio Soria '07	♟♟	5
● Harmonium '06	♟♟♟	5*
● Quater Rosso '05	♟♟♟	5
● Ribeca '04	♟♟♟	6

Guccione

C.DA CERASA
S.P. 102 BIS
90046 MONREALE [PA]
TEL. 0916116686
www.guccione.eu

CELLAR SALES
PRE-BOOKED VISITS

ANNUAL PRODUCTION 35,000 bottles
HECTARES UNDER VINE 6
VITICULTURE METHOD Natural

Given old vineyards of trebbiano, catarratto, perricone and nerello in a zone famous for the quality of its grapes, others would have started again from scratch, and planted international varieties, but Manfredi and Francesco Guccione resisted. They embraced the organic credo, giving priority to the relationship that bonds soil, plants and climate. In 2005, they began vinifying using natural yeasts and no temperature control. The results immediately proved to be excellent, and their success, like the quality of their wines, continued to grow.

The work of these two enthusiastic brothers has always impressed us, so we knew that an award was near. This year, Lolik '07, a natural cask-conditioned Trebbiano took home Three Glasses. Its captivating notes of summer flowers against a clayey mineral backdrop lead to a fresh, zesty, lingering palate. The Catarratto Girgis '07, taut on nose and palate, also made the finals. The minerally, fresh, elegantly fruited Trebbiano, Veruzza '07, matured in steel tanks, was good again. Another Trebbiano, the Vendemmia Tardiva '08, shows intensity and caressing softness. Equally appealing is the warm, dry Perpetuo di Cerasa, with elegant walnutskin notes.

Gulfi

C.DA PATRIA
97012 CHIARAMONTE GULFI [RG]
TEL. 0932921654
www.gulfi.it

PRE-BOOKED VISITS
VISITOR FACILITIES
FOOD

ANNUAL PRODUCTION 180,000 bottles
HECTARES UNDER VINE 75
VITICULTURE METHOD Organic certified

Starting with a vineyard inherited from his father, in just a few years Vito Catania has created a model winery. Without making any concessions to fashion, from his very first harvest all his wines have displayed absolute respect for the territory, and the bush-training system is still used in the rows, as it was 2,000 years ago. The soils and aspects change radically from district to district, meaning that each of his vineyards gives a unique sensory profile. The logical consequence was the decision to bottle all of the winery's nero d'Avola crus separately.

Nerobaronj '06 has great personality, combining an elegant, mineral nose with a substantial palate underpinned by close-knit, silky tannins. The varietal Neromàccarj '06 displays fruit aromas faintly veined with attractive marine notes, and a soft, well-distributed palate. The other two Nero d'Avola crus are also well typed and terroir-driven. The ripe, minerally Nerosanlorè '06 is long and the Nerobufaleffj '06 reveals good structure and well-integrated oak. The elegant, austere Reseca '05, a blend of local grapes, is produced at the new estate on Etna and the minerally Carjcanti '07 is from carricante.

○ Lolik '07	♟♟♟	4*
○ Girgis '07	♟♟	4*
☉ Bonè '08	♟♟	4
● Cerasa V.T. '08	♟♟	5
○ Monreale Girgis Extra '07	♟♟	4
○ Perpetuo di Cerasa	♟♟	5
○ Veruzza '07	♟♟	4*
● Arturo di Lanzeria '06	♟♟	5
○ Girgis '05	♟♟	4*
○ Lolik '06	♟♟	4*
○ Veruzza '06	♟♟	4*
○ Veruzza '05	♟	3*

● Nerobaronj '06	♟♟	6
○ Carjcanti '07	♟♟	5
● Cerasuolo di Vittoria '08	♟♟	4*
● Nerobufaleffj '06	♟♟	6
● Neromàccarj '06	♟♟	6
● Nerosanlorè '06	♟♟	6
● Reseca '05	♟♟	6
● Nerojbleo '07	♟	4
● Rossojbleo '08	♟	4
○ Valcanzjria '08	♟	4
● Neromàccarj '04	♟♟♟	6
● Nerosanlorè '05	♟♟♟	6
● Nerobufaleffj '05	♟♟	6
● Nerobufaleffj '04	♟♟	6
● Neromàccarj '05	♟♟	6

Marabino

C.DA BUONIVINI
S.P. ROSOLINI
PACHINO KM 8,5
97017 NOTO [SR]
TEL. 3355284101
www.marabino.it

CELLAR SALES
PRE-BOOKED VISITS
VISITOR FACILITIES
FOOD

ANNUAL PRODUCTION **150,000 bottles**
HECTARES UNDER VINE **26**
VITICULTURE METHOD **Conventional**

The philosophy adopted by Nello Messina since 2002, when he established the company that today is managed by his young son Pierpaolo, involves getting the most out of the territory without compromising or taking shortcuts. Marabino's secret is the use of organic farming methods and modern winemaking techniques while retaining the best of what tradition has to offer, and the strategy has become a model of development for other nearby estates. The vineyards fall within the Eloro and Noto DOC zones. A real gem is their three-hectare plot of old bush-trained nero d'Avola in the Vigna di Archimede cru.

Moscato della Torre '08 achieved another great result, with its rich, sensual nose showing notes of iodine, and rich aromas of peach and damson leading into a fresh, velvety, lingering palate, which is sweet yet not cloying. It was joined in the finals by the Eloro Nero d'Avola Archimede '07, the best version yet. Dense, intense and deep, it gives elegant varietal notes. On the palate, aristocratic self-assuredness meets pliant tannins and a minerally after-aroma, with a long, clean finish. The Nero d'Avola Carmen '08, with attractive Mediterranean notes, and the fresh, zesty Violetta '08, a markedly mineral Inzolia, are attractively spontaneous.

● Eloro Archimede '07	🍷🍷	5
○ Moscato di Noto Moscato della Torre '08	🍷🍷	6
● Carmen '08	🍷	3
○ Violetta '08	🍷	3
● Eloro Don Pasquale '07	🍷🍷	4*
○ Moscato di Noto Moscato della Torre '07	🍷🍷	6
○ Moscato di Noto Moscato della Torre '06	🍷🍷	6
○ Moscato di Noto Moscato della Torre '05	🍷🍷	6

Morgante

C.DA RACALMARE
92020 GROTTE [AG]
TEL. 0922945579
www.morgantevini.it

CELLAR SALES
PRE-BOOKED VISITS

ANNUAL PRODUCTION **335,000 bottles**
HECTARES UNDER VINE **60**
VITICULTURE METHOD **Conventional**

The Morgante family has practised the noble craft of farming for generations in a land of wild beauty, the countryside of Grotte, among abandoned sulphur mines, fields of wheat, almond groves and vineyards. On these hillsides, nero d'Avola develops a unique character, and Antonio and his sons Carmelo and Giovanni have nurtured and interpreted this raw material with stunning results for over 15 years, helped by a big name in international winemaking, Riccardo Cotarella.

Once again, and this is the eighth time, top marks went to Don Antonio, the best selection from the Morgante vineyards, a Nero d'Avola that every year seems to become more distinct and focused. The '07 displays deep, austere elegance, with intense, sunny, ripe bitter cherry and plum fruit. The characterful, generous palate reveals well-crafted tannins, a lively, supple structure and a long, extremely clean finish. The mature, reliable, varietal Nero d'Avola '08 is well rounded and fruity. There is also a new arrival, the attractively fruit-led, fragrant Scinthilì '08, a Nero d'Avola designed to be drunk chilled.

● Don Antonio '07	🍷🍷🍷	5
● Nero d'Avola '08	🍷🍷	3
● Schinthilì '08	🍷	3
● Don Antonio '06	🍷🍷🍷	5
● Don Antonio '03	🍷🍷🍷	5
● Don Antonio '02	🍷🍷🍷	5
● Don Antonio '01	🍷🍷🍷	5
● Don Antonio '00	🍷🍷🍷	6
● Don Antonio '99	🍷🍷🍷	5
● Don Antonio '98	🍷🍷🍷	5

★ Palari

LOC. SANTO STEFANO BRIGA
C.DA BARNA
98137 MESSINA
TEL. 090630194
www.palari.it

PRE-BOOKED VISITS

ANNUAL PRODUCTION **50,000 bottles**
HECTARES UNDER VINE **7**
VITICULTURE METHOD **Conventional**

Salvatore Geraci is a man of many talents. A renowned architect with significant political experience, he is also a university lecturer and antiques expert. But for wine lovers, Turi is simply the man who, with the help of his irreplaceable brother Giampiero and the brilliant consultant Donato Lanati, has saved from oblivion that unique, precious wine, Faro, a gem of international, and not only Sicilian wine. Despite such a reputation, this small cellar still works on a human, artisanal scale, making it genuinely unique.

Yet again, unbelievably, we were surprised by the final tasting of Faro Palari '07, from 50 per cent nerello mascalese with small amounts of other varieties, some extremely rare, including acitana, galatena, core 'e palumba and nocera. Dark ruby with faint garnet hints, it shows a balsamic nose, with red and black berry fruit and pencil lead of extraordinary finesse, over a breathtaking palate. In a stunning double, it took home the umpteenth Three Glass award of its career, alongside the fantastic Rosso del Soprano '07, from the same grapes, with intense notes of sorb apple, wild berries, cherries, ferns and nettles.

Passopisciaro

LOC. PASSOPISCIARO
VIA SANTO SPIRITO
95030 CASTIGLIONE DI SICILIA [CT]
TEL. 057826110
www.passopisciaro.com

ANNUAL PRODUCTION **39,000 bottles**
HECTARES UNDER VINE **29**
VITICULTURE METHOD **Conventional**

The exuberance of the restless volcano seems to perfectly reflect the energy and dynamism of Andrea Franchetti, the brilliant owner of Tenuta di Trinoro in Tuscany. Here, at his estate on the northern slopes of Etna, in Contrada Guardiola, between Randazzo and Castiglione, Andrea shows all his talent as an unconventional producer, oenologist and agronomist. He is equally unconventional in choosing non-native varieties and effectively promoting the territory, as in the case of the extremely successful Contrade event, which he organized.

The stylish, delicate monovarietal Nerello Mascalese Passopisciaro '07 shows garnet tinges and an old-fashioned touch which makes it even more charming. It has aromatic intensity, focused, well-defined fruit, marked minerality and extraordinary drinkability. We were also intrigued by the high-altitude Chardonnay, Passopisciaro Bianco '08, which presents an inviting gold proffering delicious ripe fruit and floral aromas ranging from mango to broom. The Vino da Tavola Bianco Dolce, from native white grape varieties grown around the volcano, also displays a certain originality.

● Faro Palari '07	♟♟♟+	7
● Rosso del Soprano '07	♟♟♟	5
● Faro Palari '06	♟♟♟	7
● Faro Palari '05	♟♟♟	7*
● Faro Palari '04	♟♟♟	8
● Faro Palari '03	♟♟♟	7
● Faro Palari '02	♟♟♟	7
● Faro Palari '01	♟♟♟	7
● Faro Palari '00	♟♟♟	7
● Faro Palari '98	♟♟♟	7
● Faro Palari '96	♟♟♟	7
● Faro Palari '99	♟♟	7

● Passopisciaro '07	♟♟	6
○ Passopisciaro Bianco '08	♟♟	6
○ Vino da Tavola Bianco Dolce	♟	5
● Passopisciaro '04	♟♟♟	6
● Franchetti '06	♟♟	8
○ Guardiola '07	♟♟	6
● Passopisciaro '06	♟♟	6
● Passopisciaro '05	♟♟	6

Carlo Pellegrino

VIA DEL FANTE, 39
91025 MARSALA [TP]
TEL. 0923719911
www.carlopellegrino.it

CELLAR SALES
PRE-BOOKED VISITS

ANNUAL PRODUCTION 7.500,000 bottles
HECTARES UNDER VINE 150
VITICULTURE METHOD Conventional

The year 2010 marks the 130th birthday of Pellegrino, a monument to Sicilian winemaking, with three production facilities: the historic wineries in Marsala; the modern facility of Duca di Castelmonte; and the winery on Pantelleria, in contrada Cuddìe Rosse. The business is run by the direct descendants of the family: chairman Pietro Alagna and CEO Benedetto Renda, alongside Massimo Bellina, Emilio Ridolfi, Paola Alagna and Caterina Tumbarello. The big news is the recent agreement for the distribution of Hauner wines from Salina.

The '97 Marsala Vergine Riserva is breathtaking, and joins the historic '62 and '80 vintages. Evocative marine notes and Mediterranean scrub frame a rich, seductive bouquet while the supple, if over-edgy and austere, palate has wonderful finesse in its savoury, lingering finish. From the Duca di Castelmonte line, we were impressed by the aromatic, zestily full Zibibbo Secco Gibelè '08 and Tripudium '06, from nero d'Avola, syrah and cabernet sauvignon, which gives slightly overripe yet solid fruit on the palate. The pervasive Passito di Pantelleria Nes '07 is warm and we liked the Dinari del Duca Grillo '08.

○ Marsala Vergine Ris. '97	🍷🍷	6
○ Dinari del Duca Grillo Duca di Castelmonte '08	🍷🍷	4*
○ Gibelè Duca di Castelmonte '08	🍷🍷	4*
○ Marsala Sup. Oro Dolce Ris.	🍷🍷	5
○ Passito di Pantelleria Nes Duca di Castelmonte '07	🍷🍷	6
● Tripudium Rosso Duca di Castelmonte '06	🍷🍷	5
○ Passito di Pantelleria Liquoroso '08	🍷	3
○ Passito di Pantelleria Liquoroso Duca di Castelmonte '08	🍷	5
○ Duca di Castelmonte Dinari del Duca Grillo '07	🍷🍷 (white)	4*
● Duca di Castelmonte Dinari del Duca Syrah '06	🍷🍷 (white)	4*
○ Duca di Castelmonte Passito di Pantelleria Nes '06	🍷🍷 (white)	6
● Duca di Castelmonte Tripudium Rosso '05	🍷🍷 (white)	5

Pietradolce

FRAZ. SOLICCHIATA
C.DA MONAGAZZI
95012 CASTIGLIONE DI SICILIA [CT]
TEL. 3484037792
www.pietradolce.it

CELLAR SALES
PRE-BOOKED VISITS
VISITOR FACILITIES
FOOD

ANNUAL PRODUCTION 5,000 bottles
HECTARES UNDER VINE 8
VITICULTURE METHOD Conventional

The vineyards of the Pietradolce winery, established in 2005 by Michele Faro, one of the best-known nurserymen in Italy, are located in Solicchiata and Passopisciaro near Castiglione di Sicilia, some of the best wine country in the whole of the Etna area. For the most part, the plants are bush-trained vines of 50 years or older, situated at around 700 metres above sea level on the northern slopes of the volcano. The small but extremely well-equipped winery is nearby, at Riposto, but work should soon begin on the new, larger facility right next to the vineyards.

Three well-deserved Glasses went to Etna Rosso Archineri '07, the result of Michele's painstaking work in the vineyard and cellar. Wisely, he left the wine to age in glass for a couple of years, so that he could debut with the product he had in mind. Elegant, and complex, the Archineri is pervasive and wide-ranging on the nose, where intriguing aromas of forest fruits, dried flowers, leather, tobacco and chocolate mingle with fresh iodine notes. The big, stylishly well-developed palate shows nice balance between the savoury mineral attack and fruit sweetness, and abounds in fine-grained tannins. The finish lingers beautifully.

● Etna Rosso Archineri '07	🍷🍷🍷	5*

★★ Planeta

C.DA DISPENSA
92013 MENFI [AG]
TEL. 091327965
www.planeta.it

PRE-BOOKED VISITS

ANNUAL PRODUCTION **2.200,000 bottles**
HECTARES UNDER VINE **390**
VITICULTURE METHOD **Conventional**

Since the mid 1990s, dynamic cousins Alessio, Francesca and Santi Planeta have played a leading role in the renaissance and consolidation of Sicilian winemaking. Their estates are well distributed over the region, from Noto to Sambuca, not to mention Vittoria and Menfi. In 2006, they also acquired around 20 hectares at Castiglione di Sicilia, on the northern slopes of Etna, where, as in their other facilities, a new cellar is being built. Knowing the Planetas, we reckon it will soon be producing its own gems.

Cometa '08 showed its great class and easily took Three Glasses. This white Fiano, whose beauty is already clear in its deep, straw-yellow, flaunts elegant hints of peach, tropical fruit and camomile. On the palate, it is engaging, mineral, fleshy, full-flavoured, and wonderfully long. But there are plenty of thoroughbreds in this young winery's stables, from the deep, varietal Santa Cecilia '07, a single-varietal, summery Nero d'Avola of great finesse, to the excellent Merlot and Syrah, both '07s, with pervasive aromas and lashings of fruit. The fresh, fragrant Cerasuolo di Vittoria '08, from nero d'Avola and frappato, is extremely good.

Tenute Rapitalà

C.DA RAPITALÀ
90043 CAMPOREALE [PA]
TEL. 092437233
www.rapitala.it

CELLAR SALES
PRE-BOOKED VISITS

ANNUAL PRODUCTION **3.200,000 bottles**
HECTARES UNDER VINE **175**
VITICULTURE METHOD **Conventional**

Gigi and Hugues de la Gatinais have been at the heart of the movement to boost the profile of Sicilian wine for over 40 years. Theirs is a heart-warming story of love and wine, and they have passed on their passion and commitment to their son Laurent, who runs the operation in collaboration with GIV. The vineyards are situated in some of the best wine country in western Sicily in the hills rolling down from Camporeale towards Alcamo and the sea, at an altitude of between 300 and 600 metres.

Hugonis '07, a blend of cabernet sauvignon and nero d'Avola, easily made our finals, with its great finesse and intense aromas backed up by vibrant weight on the palate. The Chardonnay Conte Hugues Bernard de la Gatinais '07 regales elegantly floral, fruity aromas, and well-integrated, never too dominant, oak followed by a lovely, fresh palate and a lingering finish. The generous, slightly overripe Syrah Solinero '07 has great raw material, with generously opulent, solid fruit. Nuhar '07, from nero d'Avola and pinot nero, is extremely good, boasting delicate aromas and real Mediterranean character. The other wines are excellent.

○ Cometa '08	🍷🍷🍷 6
● Merlot '07	🍷🍷 5
● Santa Cecilia '07	🍷🍷 5
● Syrah '07	🍷🍷 5
○ Alastro '08	🍷🍷 4
● Burdese '07	🍷🍷 5
● Cerasuolo di Vittoria '08	🍷🍷 4*
○ La Segreta Bianco '08	🍷🍷 3*
● La Segreta Rosso '08	🍷🍷 3*
○ Passito di Noto '08	🍷🍷 6
● Burdese '05	🍷🍷🍷 5*
○ Cometa '05	🍷🍷🍷 5
● Merlot '04	🍷🍷🍷 5
● Santa Cecilia '06	🍷🍷🍷 5

● Hugonis '07	🍷🍷 6
○ Campo Reale '08	🍷🍷 3*
○ Casalj '08	🍷🍷 4
○ Conte Hugues Bernard de la Gatinais '07	🍷🍷 5
● Nuhar '07	🍷🍷 4
● Solinero '07	🍷🍷 6
○ Bouquet '08	🍷 4
○ Cielo d'Alcamo '07	🍷 6
○ Piano Maltese Bianco '08	🍷 4
● Solinero '03	🍷🍷🍷 6
● Hugonis '06	🍷🍷 6
● Hugonis '05	🍷🍷 6
● Solinero '06	🍷🍷 6
● Solinero '04	🍷🍷 6

Girolamo Russo

LOC. PASSOPISCIARO
VIA REGINA MARGHERITA, 78
95012 CASTIGLIONE DI SICILIA [CT]
TEL. 3283840247
www.girolamorusso.lt

CELLAR SALES
PRE-BOOKED VISITS

ANNUAL PRODUCTION **12.500 bottles**
HECTARES UNDER VINE **16**
VITICULTURE METHOD **Organic certified**

The turnaround for this small winery, which opened in 1940, arrived in 2003 when Giuseppe Russo, with his artistic sensitivity as a literature graduate and qualified pianist, decided to take over the reins of the family estate. The property has plots in Castiglione di Sicilia and Randazzo, with vines aged between 50 and 100 years old, and Giuseppe bottles the wines himself. His guiding principle is to create elegant, recognizable wines with a real sense of place.

The Etna Rosso Feudo '07, from old vineyards planted to nerello mascalese and cappuccio, romped off with Three Glasses. We loved its elegant notes of red berry fruit, quinine and rhubarb, and it proved to be extraordinarily rich, well-managed and stylish in the mouth, with perfectly resolved tannins. The Etna Rosso San Lorenzo '07, from nerello mascalese with a splash of cappuccio, put on a good show, easily making the finals with its aromatic intensity, enviable complexity and impressive structure. The hat-trick was completed by the fleshy, ripe, mineral-rich Etna Rosso 'A Rina' '07, from the same grapes, which has a delightfully long, leisurely finish.

● Etna Rosso Feudo '07	♟♟♟	6
● Etna Rosso San Lorenzo '07	♟♟	6
● Etna Rosso 'A Rina' '07	♟♟	5
● Etna Rosso Feudo '06	♟♟	6
● Etna Rosso 'A Rina' '06	♟♟	5
● Etna Rosso San Lorenzo '06	♟♟	6

Settesoli

S.S. 115
92013 MENFI [AG]
TEL. 092577111
www.mandrarossa.it

CELLAR SALES
PRE-BOOKED VISITS

ANNUAL PRODUCTION **1.750,000 bottles**
HECTARES UNDER VINE **6500**
VITICULTURE METHOD **Conventional**

Settesoli recently celebrated its 50th birthday but the turnaround in the company dates back to 1973, when the far-sighted manager, Diego Planeta, became chairman. It is in fact thanks to his vision that the winery became the solid, dynamic producer that it is today. Settesoli is one of the largest co-operative wineries in Europe, with over 2,300 members, 6,500 hectares under vine, around 3,000 people involved in the production cycle in one way or another and a turnover of over 40,000,000 euros per year.

All the many wines presented this year are great value for money. The dark Nero d'Avola Mandrarossa Chartago '07, combining a balsamic, elegantly complex, nose with an austere, well-distributed palate, reached the finals. The Bendicò '07, from nero d'Avola, merlot and syrah, is complex, fruit-heavy and perfectly ripe. The deliciously drinkable Furetta '08, a blend of fiano and chardonnay, boasts white peaches and spice. We also liked the fresh, focused Chardonnay '08, and the fruit-driven, fragrant Viognier '08 with its hints of fresh greens. The other wines, which are enjoyable and impeccably well made, show great respect for their raw materials.

● Cartagho Mandrarossa '07	♟	5
● Bendicò Mandrarossa '07	♟♟	5
○ Chardonnay Mandrarossa '08	♟♟	4*
○ Furetta Mandrarossa '08	♟♟	5
○ Viognier Mandrarossa '08	♟♟	4*
● Bonera Mandrarossa '07	♟	4
○ Fiano Mandrarossa '08	♟	4
● Nero d'Avola Mandrarossa '08	♟	4
● Cartagho Mandrarossa '06	♟♟♟	5
● Bendicò Mandrarossa '06	♟♟	5
● Bendicò Mandrarossa '05	♟♟	4
● Bonera Mandrarossa '06	♟♟	4*
● Bonera Mandrarossa '04	♟♟	4*
● Cabernet Sauvignon Mandrarossa '07	♟♟	4*
● Merlot Mandrarossa '07	♟♟	4*

Spadafora

VIA AUSONIA, 90
90144 PALERMO
TEL. 091514952
www.spadafora.com

CELLAR SALES
PRE-BOOKED VISITS
VISITOR FACILITIES
FOOD

ANNUAL PRODUCTION **260,000 bottles**
HECTARES UNDER VINE **100**
VITICULTURE METHOD **Conventional**

Francesco Spadafora is one of the pioneers of Sicily's winemaking renaissance, and in just a few years, he has completely revolutionized his fine estate at Virzì, and rethought the winery's philosophy. Francesco has replanted much of the old vine stock to modern planting patterns, brought the winery up to date and introduced the use of temperature-controlled fermentation and small oak barrels for maturation. Lastly, Francesco has flanked traditional native grapes with international varieties, particularly syrah, of which he is considered one of the finest growers in the whole of Sicily.

The impenetrable ruby Syrah Sole dei Padri '06 made our finals, showing intense red berry fruit, spice, and tobacco aromas, perfectly integrated oak, and a long, focused finish. Equally good is the Schietto Syrah '05, with well-dosed tannins and seductive perceptions of cassis, spice and chocolate, leading to an elegant, beautifully well-orchestrated palate. The stylish, well-rounded Don Pietro '06, from nero d'Avola and cabernet sauvignon, gives delicious notes of wild berry preserve and is graced with an intense, fruit-fuelled palate. The rest of the wines are good.

★ Tasca d'Almerita

C.DA REGALEALI
90020 SCLAFANI BAGNI [PA]
TEL. 0916459711
www.tascadalmerita.it

CELLAR SALES
PRE-BOOKED VISITS
VISITOR FACILITIES
FOOD

ANNUAL PRODUCTION **3,000,000 bottles**
HECTARES UNDER VINE **460**
VITICULTURE METHOD **Conventional**

It is hard to summarize in a few words the story of the passions behind this splendid estate, the heart and soul of this famous wine house since its foundation in 1830. At Regaleali, tradition has always lived alongside innovation. It was here that the Tasca family made its first mass and clonal selections, working on international varieties before it became fashionable. If we had to make a comparison, we could say that this is the only Sicilian winery that, in terms of history and tradition, can look the great Bordeaux châteaux square in the eye.

The sumptuous Cabernet Sauvignon '07 won Three Glasses. This impenetrably dark ruby wine gives aromas of red berry fruit, blackberries, cherries and spice, laced with perfectly integrated oak. The vibrant palate shows close-knit, elegant tannins, and a beautifully lingering, juicy finish. Elegant and finely-crafted, Rosso del Conte '06 is from a blend dominated by nero d'Avola that presents varietal on the nose with a palate lifted by a sweet tannic weave and fruit-fuelled length. Peach, apricots and hints of Mediterranean scrub distinguish the complex nose of the elegant, nicely oaky Chardonnay '07. The rest of the wines are excellent.

● Schietto Syrah '05	♟♟ 5
● Sole dei Padri '06	♟♟ 7
● Don Pietro Rosso '06	♟♟ 4*
○ Don Pietro Bianco '08	♟ 4
○ Monreale Bianco Alhambra '08	♟ 3
○ Schietto Chardonnay '08	♟ 5
○ Schietto Grillo '08	♟ 4
● Schietto Cabernet Sauvignon '05	♟♟ 6
● Schietto Cabernet Sauvignon '04	♟♟ 6
● Schietto Syrah '04	♟♟ 5
● Sole dei Padri '05	♟♟ 7
● Sole dei Padri '04	♟♟ 7
● Sole dei Padri '03	♟♟ 8
● Sole dei Padri '02	♟♟ 8
● Sole dei Padri '01	♟♟ 8

● Cabernet Sauvignon '07	♟♟♟ 6
○ Chardonnay '07	♟♟ 6
● Contea di Sclafani Rosso del Conte '06	♟♟ 7
○ Contea di Sclafani Almerita Brut '06	♟♟ 6
○ Contea di Sclafani Nozze d'Oro '08	♟♟ 5
● Cygnus '07	♟♟ 5
○ Diamante d'Almerita '08	♟♟ 6
○ Regaleali Bianco '08	♟♟ 4
⊙ Regaleali Le Rose '08	♟♟ 4*
● Regaleali Rosso '08	♟♟ 3*
○ Tasca d'Almerita Whitaker Grillo '08	♟♟ 4
○ Tenuta Capofaro Malvasia '08	♟♟ 6
○ Chardonnay '06	♟♟♟ 6
● Contea di Sclafani Rosso del Conte '05	♟♟♟ 7
● Contea di Sclafani Rosso del Conte '04	♟♟♟ 7

Tenuta delle Terre Nere

C.DA CALDERARA
95036 RANDAZZO [CT]
TEL. 095924002
tenutaterrenere@tiscali.it

CELLAR SALES
PRE-BOOKED VISITS

ANNUAL PRODUCTION **100,000 bottles**
HECTARES UNDER VINE **22**
VITICULTURE METHOD **Organic certified**

Marc De Grazia's love for the Etna terroir continues to bear fruit, as the list of vineyards he has rediscovered grows. He vinifies their grapes separately in order to bring the best out of each cru. The Santo Spirito vineyard, covering just under one hectare almost all planted to nerello mascalese in the 1950s and 1960s, now joins the others: Calderara Sottana, Guardiola, Feudo di Mezzo and Vigna di Don Peppino, a winemaking marvel, whose ungrafted vines date back to before 1870.

The spellbinding Etna Rosso Prephylloxera '07 surprised us with its rousing, lingering nose of spicy and mineral finesse, backed up by an enthralling, achingly beautiful, unbelievably long palate. Three Glasses were never in doubt. But there's more good news: the wonderfully terroir-driven Calderara Sottana '07 was the best ever, with exceptionally subtle notes of Virginia tobacco and peach preserve. Another finalist was the new Santo Spirito '07, with its rarefied elegance of ferrous notes and ripe, generous fruit. The Guardiola '07 was almost masculine and sanguine, the Feudo di Mezzo '07 somewhat austere, and the Rosato '08 delicious.

Valle dell'Acate

C.DA BIDINI
97011 ACATE [RG]
TEL. 0932874166
www.vallodellacate.it

CELLAR SALES
PRE-BOOKED VISITS

ANNUAL PRODUCTION **453,000 bottles**
HECTARES UNDER VINE **100**
VITICULTURE METHOD **Natural**

On the attractive Bidini estate in the countryside at Acate, near the river Dirillo, the Jacono family have been growing wine grapes for almost two centuries. In recent years, the winery has undergone a radical metamorphosis with the arrival of the effervescent Gaetana, who has a pharmacy degree and an inborn, almost genetic passion for oenology. The fine production facility has been brought up to date technologically, and the original buildings have been attractively converted, while the wines have changed, too. The range is becoming more reliable and easier to drink.

Our finals were graced by Cerasuolo di Vittoria '07, from nero d'Avola and frappato, which impressed us with its intense, elegant notes of red berry fruit veined with fresh Mediterranean herbs, leading into a juicy, vibrantly lingering palate. The utterly delicious Frappato '08 has a pervasively fragrant, aromatic nose, followed by a fresh, lively palate. The varietal Nero d'Avola Il Moro '07, brims with spice and flowers over a fleshy, lingering palate. Finally, the clean and concentrated Tanè '06, is a fruit-fuelled, well-rounded blend of nero d'Avola and syrah with boisterous tannins.

● Etna Rosso Prephilloxera La V. di Don Peppino '07	♆♆♆ 8
● Etna Rosso Calderara Sottana '07	♆♆ 7
● Etna Rosso Santo Spirito '07	♆♆ 7
○ Etna Bianco '08	♆♆ 4*
⊙ Etna Rosato '08	♆♆ 4*
● Etna Rosso Feudo di Mezzo Quadro delle Rose '07	♆♆ 7
● Etna Rosso Guardiola '07	♆♆ 7
○ Etna Bianco Le Vigne Niche '07	♆ 6
● Etna Rosso Feudo di Mezzo Quadro delle Rose '05	♕♕♕ 7
● Etna Rosso Feudo di Mezzo Quadro delle Rose '04	♕♕♕ 6
● Etna Rosso Prephilloxera La V. di Don Peppino '06	♕♕♕ 7

● Cerasuolo di Vittoria '07	♆ 4
● Il Moro '07	♆♆ 4
● Tanè '06	♆♆ 6
○ Vittoria Il Frappato '08	♆♆ 4*
○ Vittoria Insolia '08	♆ 3
○ Zagra '08	♆ 4
○ Bidis '06	♕♕ 5
● Cerasuolo di Vittoria '06	♕♕ 4
● Tanè '04	♕♕ 6
● Tanè '03	♕♕ 6
● Vittoria Il Frappato '07	♕♕ 4*
○ Zagra '07	♕♕ 4

OTHER WINERIES

Tenuta dell' Abate

VIA KENNEDY, 46
93100 CALTANISSETTA
TEL. 0934584188
tenutadellabate@hotmail.com

The whites did well. The zesty Terre del Palco Grillo Viognier '08 blend has intense damson and citrus while Inzolia Lissandrello '08 gives lovely, elegant marine notes and whole fruit. Terre del Palco Nero d'Avola '08 is coherent and varietal while the Cabernet-Syrah blend, Giffarrò '06, is overripe.

○ Lissandrello '08	🍷🍷	3*
○ Terre del Palco Grillo Viognier '08	🍷🍷	4
● Giffarrò '06	🍷	4
● Terre del Palco Nero d'Avola '08	🍷	4

Goffredo Adragna

VIA REGINA ELENA, 4
91100 TRAPANI
TEL. 092326401
www.tenuteadragna.it

The complex Roccagiglio '06, from cabernet sauvignon and merlot, reached the finals, with its hints of red berry fruit, quinine and a fresh balsamic vein returning in the mouth and on the lingering finish. The estery, varietal Corallovecchio '06 is an austere, stylish Nero d'Avola.

● Roccagiglio '06	🍷🍷	5
● Corallovecchio '06	🍷🍷	5
○ Inzolia '08	🍷	4
● Nero d'Avola '08	🍷	4

AgroGento

C.DA ANGUILLA
92017 SAMBUCA DI SICILIA [AG]
TEL. 0423860930
www.agroargento.it

A new brand for the Moretti Polegato and Maggio families' Sambuca operation, and another excellent performance from Timoleonte '06. This blend of nero d'Avola and international varieties offers balsamic notes in a ripe framework with serious structure. Grillo Calancùni '08 has attractive grassy notes.

● Timoleonte '06	🍷🍷	4
○ Calancùni '08	🍷	4
● Carrivàli '07	🍷	4

Ajello

C.DA GIUDEO
91025 MAZARA DEL VALLO [TP]
TEL. 091309107
www.ajello.info

Salvatore Ajello was spot-on with his Rosato '08, a charmingly tasty, drinkable Syrah with fragrant, estery notes of sweet and bitter cherry. The spicy, fruit-driven Nero d'Avola '08 and the smooth, inviting Syrah '08 are both varietal. We also liked Shams '08, from moscato, grillo, inzolia and catarratto.

⊙ Rosato '08	🍷🍷	4*
● Nero d'Avola '08	🍷	4
○ Shams '08	🍷	5
● Syrah '08	🍷	4

Al Cantàra

VIA ANTONIO CECCHI, 23
95100 CATANIA
TEL. 095222644
www.al-cantara.it

There was a good debut from this winery whose wines come from vineyards near Randazzo, crossed by the river Alcantara. Etna Rosso O' Scuru O' Scuru '06, from nerello mascalese and cappuccio, is intense, fine, minerally, slightly overripe and has a nicely balanced palate. The rest are good.

● Etna Rosso O' Scuru O' Scuru '06	🍷🍷	7
○ 'A Notturna '07	🍷	5
⊙ Amuri di Fimmina e Amuri di Matri '08	🍷	5
● Cappidazzu Paga Tuttu '06	🍷	6

Alessandro di Camporeale

C.DA MANDRANOVA
90043 CAMPOREALE [PA]
TEL. 092437038
www.alessandrodicamporeale.it

Kaid made the finals again. The '07 stylishly flaunts varietal notes of syrah and its solid, silky palate boasts great length. The stylish, pleasing Catarratto Benedè '08 gives attractive grassiness and peach aromas followed by a fresh, fleshy palate. The Nero d'Avola DonnaTà '08 is varietal on the nose.

● Kaid '07	🍷🍷	5
○ Benedè '08	🍷🍷	4*
● DonnaTà '08	🍷	4

Avide

C.DA MASTRELLA, 346
97013 COMISO [RG]
TEL. 0932967456
www.avide.it

No Cerasuolo Barocco this year so we tasted the other top reds: the evolved nicely varietal Nero d'Avola 3 Carati '05; and Sigillo '04, from nero d'Avola and cabernet sauvignon, with texture and finesse to spare framing assertive but well-integrated oak. The rest of the wines are first-rate.

● 3 Carati '05	♟♟	5
● Sigillo '04	♟♟	6
● Herea Frappato '08	♟	3
● Herea Nero d'Avola '08	♟	3

Barbera

C.DA TORRENOVA, S.P. 79
92013 MENFI [AG]
TEL. 0925570442
www.cantinebarbera.it

Barbera's appealing basic Inzolia '08 surprised us with its clean balance and fresh, solid fruit. The ripe Menfi Merlot Azimut '07 is well typed while the fresh, tangy Menfi Inzolia Dietro le Case '08 proffers elegant, subtle hints of aniseed. The rest of the wines did well as a whole.

○ Inzolia '08	♟♟	4*
● Menfi Azimut '07	♟♟	4
○ Inzolia Dietro le Case '08	♟	4
● Menfi Cabernet Sauvignon La Vota '07	♟	5

Alice Bonaccorsi

LOC. PASSOPISCIARO
C.DA CROCE MONACI
95036 RANDAZZO [CT]
TEL. 095337134
www.valcerasa.com

Only the Etna Rosso Valcerasa '06, from nerello mascalese and nerello cappuccio, was ready in time for our tastings. It shows all the qualities we have appreciated in the past: garnet colour, elegant, estery notes of great charm, stylish, rounded tannins, generous fruit and a satisfying finish.

● Etna Rosso Valcerasa '06	♟♟	5
○ Etna Bianco Valcerasa '05	♟♟	4*
● Etna Rosso Valcerasa '05	♟♟	4

Bonavita

LOC. FARO SUPERIORE
C.DA CORSO
98158 MESSINA
TEL. 0902932106
www.bonavitafaro.it

The Scarfone family's vineyards lie at Faro Superiore and Curcuraci, in the rolling hills overlooking the Strait of Messina. The good Faro '07, from nerello mascalese, cappuccio and nocera, shows generous fruit and florality, and a palate playing on balance between its chewiness and its tannins.

● Faro '07	♟♟	6
● Faro '06	♟♟	5

Brugnano

C.DA SAN CARLO, S.S. 113, KM 307
90047 PARTINICO [PA]
TEL. 0918783360
www.brugnano.it

The wine from Antonella Brugnano that most impressed our tasters was Honoris Causa '06, a spicy blend of nero d'Avola and syrah, which regales intense, ripe fruit that develops confidently on a palate caressed by graceful, well-balanced tannins. The varietal Nero d'Avola Lunario '07 is also very good.

● Honoris Causa '06	♟♟	4*
● Lunario '07	♟♟	4*
○ Kue '08	♟	4
● V90 Rosso '07	♟	3

Buceci

VIA UNITÀ D'ITALIA, 3
90035 MARINEO [PA]
TEL. 0918726367
www.bucecivini.it

Francesco Calderone's organic winery, just outside Palermo, performed convincingly. We loved the deep, intense Doncarmè Rosso '07, from pinot nero and cabernet sauvignon, with its fine-grained, well-calibrated tannins. The complex, appealing Pinot Nero Millemetri '06 captivates.

● Doncarmè Rosso '07	♟♟	4
● Millemetri '06	♟♟	6
○ Buceci Bianco '08	♟	4
● Buceci Rosso '07	♟	4

Capo Croce - Vini Gancia

C.DA CASTELLAZZO
91027 TRAPANI
TEL. 03489999382
www.gancia.it

We will have to wait for the Addumari, but the intense '07 Nero d'Avola Pulpito is the best ever, with focused varietal morello cherry notes, chewy consistency, soft extract and a long finish. The Nero d'Avola Nartece '08 was very enjoyable, as were the Grillo Pulvino '08 and Catarratto-Inzolia Sapiri '08.

● Pulpito '07	🍷🍷 5
● Nartece '08	🍷🍷 4
○ Pulvino '08	🍷 4
○ Sapiri '08	🍷 4

Caruso & Minini

VIA SALEMI, 3
91025 MARSALA [TP]
TEL. 0923982356
www.carusoeminini.it

The basic wines of this winery from Marsala, with vineyards at Salemi and Mazara del Vallo, were in very good form with a well-typed, but still raw, Nero d'Avola '07 and a simple, coherent Grecanico '08. From the top-range wines, Catarratto Isula '08 passes muster but shows a touch too much oak.

○ Terre di Giumara Grecanico '08	🍷 3
○ Terre di Giumara Isula '08	🍷 4
● Terre di Giumara Nero d'Avola '07	🍷 3
○ Timpune '08	🍷 4

Castellucci Miano

VIA SICILIA, 1
90029 VALLEDOLMO [PA]
TEL. 0921542385
www.castelluccimiano.it

The high-altitude selections of catarratto from the Valledolmo co-operative winery are well known but this year we preferred the no-nonsense Miano '08, with wafts of green apple and mint, and fresh, weighty fruit. The attractively subtle, close-knit, Nero d'Avola '07 is soft and lingers on the palate.

○ Catarratto Miano '08	🍷🍷 4*
● Nero d'Avola '07	🍷🍷 4*
○ Shiarà '08	🍷 4
● Syrah '07	🍷 4

Centopassi

VIA PORTA PALERMO, 132
90048 SAN GIUSEPPE JATO [PA]
TEL. 0918577655
www.cantinacentopassi.it

Commitment and organic viticulture meet at this co-operative, whose vineyards were confiscated from the Mafia. We liked the new line of monovarietals, including the Catarratto Terre Rosse di Giabbascio '08, dedicated to Pio La Torre, and the Grillo Rocce di Pietra Longa '08, dedicated to Nicolò Azoti.

○ Centopassi Placido Rizzotto Bianco '08	🍷🍷 3*
○ Rocce di Pietra Longa '08	🍷🍷 4*
○ Terre Rosse di Giabbascio '08	🍷🍷 4*
● Argille di Tagghia Via '08	🍷 4

Ceuso

LOC. SEGESTA
C.DA VIVIGNATO
91013 CALATAFIMI [TP]
TEL. 092422836
www.ceuso.it

The Fastaia '07 is a wonderfully meaty, intensely exuberant Bordeaux blend, with supple, weighty tannins on the palate. The ripe, concentrated Ceuso '06, from nero d'Avola, cabernet and merlot, has dense, still untamed body and fairly intrusive oak.

● Ceuso '06	🍷🍷 6
● Fastaia '07	🍷🍷 4
○ Scurati Bianco '08	🍷 4
● Scurati Rosso '08	🍷 4

Tenuta Chiuse del Signore

C.DA CHIUSE DEL SIGNORE
S.P. LINGUAGLOSSA-ZAFFERANA KM 2
95015 LINGUAGLOSSA [CT]
TEL. 0942611340
www.gaishotels.com

Every year, Sergio De Luca's dynamic winery produces reliable wines. The nicely structured, elegant Serrantico '07, from merlot and syrah, easily made the finals. The intense, stylish Rasule Alte Rosso '08, from nerello mascalese and merlot, is excellent value for money.

● Serrantico '07	🍷🍷 6
● Pinot Nero '06	🍷🍷 7
● Rasule Alte Rosso '08	🍷🍷 4*
○ Rasule Alte Bianco '08	🍷 4

Curto

S.S. 115 ISPICA - ROSOLINI KM 358
97014 ISPICA [RG]
TEL. 0932950161
www.curto.it

Francesca Curto's wines are always convincing. Eloro Nero d'Avola '06 is varietal, nicely balanced and opens ripe and sunny on the palate. We also love Ikano '07, from nero d'Avola and merlot, with its spicy aromas and silky tannins. We enjoyed the delicious, fragrant rosé Eloro Nero d'Avola Eos '08.

● Curto Ikano '07	♟♟ 4*
● Eloro Nero d'Avola '06	♟♟ 3*
⊙ Eloro Nero d'Avola Eos '08	♟♟ 3*
○ Curto Poiano '08	♟ 3

Marco De Bartoli

C.DA FORNARA SAMPERI, 292
91025 MARSALA [TP]
TEL. 0923962093
www.marcodebartoli.com

Marco De Bartoli is a big name in Sicilian wine. His Baglio Samperi has revitalized the image of Marsala by producing outstanding wines. On Pantelleria, he creates stylish Zibibbos, such as the Pietranera '08. The excellent Grecanico Dorato '07 is rigorously vinified with skin contact and no filtration.

○ Integer Grecanico Dorato '07	♟♟ 5
○ Pietranera '08	♟♟ 5
○ Marsala Sup. 10 Anni	♟♟♟ 7

Gaspare Di Prima

VIA G. GUASTO, 27
92017 SAMBUCA DI SICILIA [AG]
TEL. 0925941201
www.diprimavini.it

Syrah Villamaura '06 went to the finals with its subtle balsam and sweet spice, ushering in a juicy fruit palate with prominent but polished tannins and an admirably clean finish. The pleasing, fragrant Pepita '08, a nero d'Avola and syrah blend, and the velvety Merlot Gibilmoro '07, were also good.

● Villamaura Syrah '06	♟♟ 6
● Pepita Rosso '08	♟♟ 4*
● Gibilmoro Merlot '07	♟ 4
○ Pepita Bianco '08	♟ 4

Disisa

VIA ROMA, 392
90139 PALERMO
TEL. 091588557
www.vinidisisa.it

The dark, deep, intense Tornamira '06, from cabernet sauvignon, merlot and syrah, is the Di Lorenzo winery's thoroughbred, with a pervasive nose of red berries, cinnamon and black pepper, and long development on the palate. Chara '08, from catarratto and inzolia, is grassy, fresh and tangy.

● Tornamira '06	♟♟ 5
○ Chara '08	♟ 3*
● Monreale Vuaria '07	♟ 5
○ Piana delle Fate '08	♟ 5

Francesco Fenech

VIA F.LLI MIRABITO, 41
98050 MALFA [ME]
TEL. 0909844041
www.eolienet.it

In only a few years, Francesco Fenech has brought new prestige to the family's seven-hectare estate, which dates from the 19th century. The classy, deep gold Malvasia delle Lipari Passito '06, from malvasia and corinto nero, has elegant notes of citrus and herbs with good sugar-acidity balance.

○ Malvasia delle Lipari Passito '06	♟♟ 7
○ Perciato Bianco '07	♟ 4

Feotto dello Jato

C.DA FEOTTO
90048 SAN GIUSEPPE JATO [PA]
TEL. 0918572650
www.feottodellojato.it

The wines from this dynamic estate in the Palermo hinterland showed well. The intense, long Monreale Rosso Sirae '06, a monovarietal Syrah, scored well. The big, deep Terre di Giulia '06, from nero d'Avola, merlot and syrah, has soft, complex aromas.

● Monreale Rosso Sirae '06	♟♟ 5
● Terre di Giulia '06	♟♟ 5
○ Iris '08	♟ 4

Ferreri

C.DA SALINELLA
91029 SANTA NINFA [TP]
TEL. 092461871
www.ferrerivini.it

The wine we liked most this year from the Ferreri winery in Trapani was the Nero d'Avola Al Merat '06. Varietal, intense, with well-defined topsoil, plum and spice aromas, it impressed us with its great texture, exemplary freshness and length. The other wines are also first-rate.

● Al Merat '06	▼▼	5
● Karren '06	▼▼	5
● Nero d'Avola '07	▼▼	4
● Cabernet Sauvignon '07	▼	5

Feudo Arancio

C.DA PORTELLA MISILBESI
92017 SAMBUCA DI SICILIA [AG]
TEL. 0925579000
www.feudoarancio.it

The wines from the Mezzacorona Group's Sicilian estate get better and better, and offer fantastic value for money. The deep, intense, complex Hedonis '06, from nero d'Avola and syrah, shows ripe, well-focused notes of black berry fruit and spice. The rest are good.

● Hedonis '06	▼▼	4*
○ Grillo '08	▼	4
○ Inzolia '08	▼	4
● Nero d'Avola '07	▼	4

Feudo di Santa Tresa

S.DA COMUNALE MARANGIO, 35
97019 VITTORIA [RG]
TEL. 0932513126
www.santatresa.it

The deep ruby Nivuro '07, a spot-on blend of nero d'Avola and cabernet sauvignon, shows pervasive blackberry, cherry, black pepper and tobacco, with powerful structure and softness, well balanced by fresh, lively supporting acidity. The well-styled Avulisi '07 is a concentrated, varietal Nero d'Avola.

● Nivuro '07	▼▼	4
● Avulisi '07	▼	4
○ Rina Ianca '08	▼	3

Feudo Montoni

C.DA MONTONI VECCHI
90144 CAMMARATA [AG]
TEL. 091513106
www.feudomontoni.it

The wines from the dynamic Fabio Sireci are always reliable. Vrucara '06, an austere Nero d'Avola, is warm and mouthfilling. We loved the vibrant, early drinking Nero d'Avola '07. The whites are nice too, especially the Grillo '08, with orange blossom, Mediterranean herbs and a lovely palate.

○ Grillo '08	▼▼	3*
● Nero d'Avola '07	▼▼	4*
● Nero d'Avola Sel. Speciale Vrucara '06	▼▼	6
○ Catarratto '08	▼	3

Fondo Antico

FRAZ. RILIEVO
VIA FIORAME, 54A
91020 TRAPANI
TEL. 0923864339
www.fondoantico.it

This dynamic Trapani estate gave us lots of wines this year. The appealing Grillo Parlante '08 flaunts lovely florality and candied peel, backed up by a zesty, fragrant palate. From the reds, we liked the fresh, drinkable Syrah '08, with cherry and spice on the nose and a well-rounded, velvety palate.

○ Grillo Parlante '08	▼▼	4*
● Syrah '08	▼▼	4*
● Nero d'Avola '08	▼	4
● Versi Rosso '08	▼	3*

Cantine Foraci

C.DA SERRONI
91026 MAZARA DEL VALLO [TP]
TEL. 0923934286
www.foraci.it

Once again, Cantine Foraci sent a good range of reliable wines, such as O'Feo Nero d'Avola '07, from organic grapes, with a fresh palate following an intensely fruity nose. The Grillo '08, also from organic grapes, shows subtle notes of camomile and peaches over a zesty, vibrant palate.

○ Grillo '08	▼	3
○ O' Feo Inzolia '08	▼	3
● O' Feo Nero d'Avola '07	▼	3
● Satiro Danzante Nero d'Avola '07	▼	4

Tenuta Gorghi Tondi

C.DA SAN NICOLA
91026 MARSALA [TP]
TEL. 0923719741
www.gorghitondi.com

Clara and Annamaria Sala's attractive modern winery is clearly on the up. The intense, flowor and fruit Chardonnay '08 provides fresh, pleasurable drinking. The grillo-chardonnay Coste a Preola Bianco '08, and the Nero d'Avola '07, with marked fruitiness, are first-rate, elegant and varietal.

○ Chardonnay '08	♟♟	5
○ Coste a Preola Bianco '08	♟♟	3*
● Nero d'Avola '07	♟♟	5
○ Kheirè '08	♟	4

Graci

LOC. PASSOPISCIARO
C.DA ARCURIA
95012 CASTIGLIONE DI SICILIA [CT]
TEL. 3487016773
www.graci.eu

Alberto Aiello Graci's wines live up to expectations. The Etna Rosso Quota 600 '07, from nerello mascalese, shows a complex, rounded nose, and a vibrant, stylish palate. The varietal Etna Rosso '07, from a selection of nerello mascalese, shows a strong sense of place.

● Etna Rosso '07	♟♟	4
● Etna Rosso Quota 600 '07	♟♟	6

Hauner

LOC. SANTA MARIA
VIA UMBERTO I
98050 LIPARI [ME]
TEL. 0909843141
www.hauner.it

The complex, lingering Malvasia Passito Carlo Hauner '06 shows admirably balanced sweetness and acidity, and deservedly reached our finals. The appealingly intense, minerally Hierà '07, from nero d'Avola, alicante and nocera, shows delicate, focused ripe cherry and plum aromas.

○ Malvasia Passito Carlo Hauner '06	♟♟	7
● Hierà '07	♟♟	4
○ Malvasia delle Lipari '08	♟	5
○ Malvasia delle Lipari Passito '08	♟	6

La 3 D - Destro Vini

LOC. MONTELAGUARDIA
95036 RANDAZZO [CT]
TEL. 095937060
www.destrovini.com

The Destro Pastizzaro family estate, with its warehouses and renovated country cottages, lies just outside Randazzo, to the north of Etna in the village of Montelaguardia. The stylish Etna Rosso Sciarakè '07, from nerello mascalese, shows ripe, spicy, fruity and fantastically long.

● Etna Rosso Sciarakè '07	♟♟	5
⊙ Etna Rosato Zàhra '08	♟	4
● Zerilò '07	♟	5

Martorana

LOC. GIARDINA GALLOTTI
VIA SALERNO, 7
92100 AGRIGENTO
TEL. 0922410407
vinimartorana@sicilia.it

The Syrah '06, the leading wine from Giuseppe and Maria Giovanna Martorana's winery near to the Valley of the Temples, impressed our panel with its concentration, hints of plum, pepper, incense, juniper and quinine, and its composed, austere elegance. The other wines are good.

● Syrah '06	♟♟	4
● Contrada Ragabo '07	♟	4
● Nero d'Avola '06	♟	3

Masseria Feudo

C.DA GROTTAROSSA
93100 CALTANISSETTA
TEL. 0934856575
www.masseriadelfeudo.it

Hermosa '07, from selected chardonnay grapes, is on great form, giving subtle, elegant notes of aromatic herbs, summer flowers and aniseed. But Carolina and Francesco Cucurullo can also be satisfied with their other wines, especially the fresh, drinkable Syrah '08 with its balance and spiciness.

○ Haermosa '07	♟♟	5
● Syrah '08	♟♟	4*
○ Il Giglio Bianco '08	♟	3
○ Vino da Tavola '07	♟	3

Miceli

C.DA PIANA SCUNCHIPANI, 190
92019 SCIACCA [AG]
TEL. 092580188
www.miceli.net

Once again, the best Miceli wines are from Pantelleria. The intensely aromatic Yrnm '07 opens with Mediterranean scrubland, leading to a velvety, fresh, aromatic palate. We also liked the Passito Nun '07, with subtle mineral notes and balanced sweetness. The Syrah Smodato '06 has serious extract.

○ Passito di Pantelleria Nun '07	♟♟	6*
○ Yrnm '07	♟♟	4*
○ Jardini di Baarìa '08	♟	3
● Smodato '06	♟	6

Cantina Modica di San Giovanni

C.DA BUFALEFI
96017 NOTO [SR]
TEL. 0931573576
www.olioevinobufalefi.it

This estate has 300 hectares, 40 under vine, in the heart of the Eloro DOC and was taken over by Alessandro from his father Felice in 2007. Eloro Nero d'Avola Filinona '06 is well typed, the dried-grape Nero d'Avola Dolcenero has depth and Inzolia Lupara '08 has upfront vegetality.

● Dolcenero	♟♟	5
● Eloro Nero d' Avola Filinona '06	♟♟	4
○ Lupara '08	♟	4

Tenute Moganazzi

VIA MONSIGNOR BIRELLI, 6
RANDAZZO [CT]
TEL. 0957463571
www.moganazzi.com

This small winery at Castiglione di Sicilia, in the Etna foothills, had a good debut. The fresh, fruit-rich Etna Rosso Don Michele '07, from nerello cappuccio and mascalese, has blackberries and spice on the nose while the intense, mineral Etna Rosato '08, from the same grapes, is vibrant and structured.

⊙ Etna Rosato Don Michele '08	♟♟	5
● Etna Rosso Don Michele '07	♟♟	6

Salvatore Murana

C.DA KHAMMA, 276
91017 PANTELLERIA [TP]
TEL. 0923915231
www.salvatoremurana.com

The opulent, lingeringly sweet Passito di Pantelleria Martingana '03 has minerality and finesse, despite its extreme concentration, and blazed into the finals. The delightful, velvety Passito Khamma '04 charmed us with its elegance and intense notes of dates, apricots and tropical fruit.

○ Moscato Passito di Pantelleria Martingana '03	♟♟	8
○ Moscato Passito di Pantelleria Khamma '04	♟♟	7
○ Gadì '08	♟	4
○ Moscato Passito di Pantelleria Mueggen '07	♟	7

Occhipinti

C.DA FOSSA DI LUPO
VIA DEI MILLE, 55
97019 VITTORIA [RG]
TEL. 0932868222
www.agricolaocchipinti.it

We were won over by the wines from the talented Arianna Occhipinti, an experienced grower and pioneer of natural farming methods in Sicily. The fruit, mineral and spice Frappato '07 is ripe and long on the palate. The '08 SP 68, an intriguing mix of nero d'Avola and frappato, is fresh and stylish.

● Frappato '07	♟♟	6
● Vittoria Rosso SP 68 '08	♟♟	4*

Piana dei Cieli

C.DA BERTOLINO - SCIFITELLI
92013 MENFI [AG]
TEL. 092572060
www.pianadeicieli.com

Among Giambalvo's '07 reds, pride of place goes to the Nero d'Avola, whose lovely ripe fruit with elegant vegetal hints, and supple palate make for highly enjoyable drinking. The Syrah '07, although slightly overripe, is solid and chewy. The appealing Chardonnay Grecanico '08 has a fragrant nose.

● Nero d'Avola '07	♟♟	4
○ Chardonnay-Grecanico '08	♟	4
● Mascarò '07	♟	4
● Syrah '07	♟	4

Poggio di Bortolone

FRAZ. ROCCAZZO
VIA BORTOLONE, 19
97010 CHIARAMONTE GULFI [RG]
TEL. 0932921161
www.poggiodibortolone.it

Vigna Para Para requires further ageing, and was not available, so Cerasuolo di Vittoria Poggio Bortolone '07 played top wine for this fine, family-run estate, presenting ripe, terroir-driven, focused and well-developed. We also liked the well-typed, characterful Cerasuolo Contessa Costanza '07.

● Cerasuolo di Vittoria Contessa Costanza '07	♀♀ 4
● Cerasuolo di Vittoria Poggio di Bortolone '07	♀♀ 4
● Cerasuolo di Vittoria V. Para Para '05	♀♀♀ 5

Porta del Vento

C.DA VALDIBELLA
90043 CAMPOREALE [PA]
TEL. 0916116531
www.portadelvento.it

Marco Sferlazzo uses exclusively organic methods. He hardly intervenes in the winery, using natural yeasts and virtually no sulphites. We were surprised by Catarratto Saharay '08, fermented on the skins in open vats, which shows appealing floral and quince aromas, backed up by a rich, lingering palate.

○ Porta del Vento Catarratto '07	♀♀ 5
○ Saharay '08	♀♀ 5
● Ishac '07	♀ 5
○ Porta del Vento Catarratto '08	♀ 4

Pupillo

C.DA LA TARGIA
96100 SIRACUSA
TEL. 0931494029
www.solacium.it

Nino Pupillo's top wine, Moscato di Siracusa Solacium '08, flew into the finals, seducing us with its brilliant gold colour, its delicious citrus fruit, apricots and acacia honey, and its enviable balance of intense sweetness and acid grip. The Cyane '08, also from moscato, is delicate and aromatic.

○ Moscato di Siracusa Solacium '08	♀ 5
○ Cyane '08	♀♀ 4*
● Re Federico '08	♀ 4

Cantine Rallo

VIA VINCENZO FLORIO, 2
91025 MARSALA [TP]
TEL. 0923721633
www.cantinerallo.it

Some time ago, Andrea Vesco went organic at his fine winery in Marsala. This year, he again presented a quality range, including the austere Alaò '06, a stylish single-varietal Nero d'Avola. The attractive Grillo '08 and Alcamo Carta d'Oro '08, from catarratto, were fresh and tasty.

● Alaò '06	♀♀ 5
○ Alcamo Carta d'Oro '08	♀ 3*
○ Grillo '08	♀ 4
○ Marsala Vergine Soleras Ris. Venti Anni	♀ 6

Riofavara

C.DA FAVARA S.P. 49 ISPICA - PACHINO
97014 ISPICA [RG]
TEL. 0932705130
www.riofavara.it

This lovely estate in eastern Sicily performed very well, reaching our finals. The outstanding, highly drinkable Eloro Sciavé '07, from nero d'Avola, shows great structure and is vibrant and hangs well together. The fresh, zesty Moscato di Noto Notissimo '08 gives elegant citrus and Mediterranean scrub.

● Eloro Nero d'Avola Sciavé '07	♀♀ 5
○ Marzaiolo '08	♀♀ 4*
○ Moscato di Nota Notissimo '08	♀♀ 4*
● San Basilio '06	♀ 4

Rizzuto

C.DA PICONELLO
92011 CATTOLICA ERACLEA [AG]
TEL. 091333081
www.rizzutoguccione.com

The deep ruby Piconello Cabernet Sauvignon '06, from the talented Ruggero Rizzuto, lived up to expectations, proffering forest fruits, tobacco and incense over a weighty, juicy palate underpinned by elegant tannins. The fragrant, drinkable Syrah Riz '08 is more straightforward.

● Piconello Cabernet Sauvignon '06	♀♀ 4*
● Riz '08	♀ 4

OTHER WINERIES

Rocca d'Api

VIA ROCCA D'API, 72
95019 ZAFFERANA ETNEA [CT]
TEL. 0957082594

The Castorina family's certified organic winery owns 25 hectares at Zafferana Etnea, Castiglione di Sicilia and Biancavilla. We very much liked the sweet, succulent Etna Rosso Le Moire '07, from nerello mascalese and cappuccio, and the deliciously smooth Moscato, Pietra Focaia Passito '08.

● Etna Rosso Le Moire '07	♟♟ 4*
○ Pietra Focaia Passito '08	♟♟ 6
○ Etna Bianco Le Moire '08	♟ 4

Sallier de la Tour

C.DA PERNICE
90144 MONREALE [PA]
TEL. 0916459711
www.sallierdelatour.it

The wines from Principe Filiberto's estate are consistent and reliable. The lovely, intense ruby Syrah '07 seduces with appealing mulberry and liquorice laced with mint, followed by a balanced palate and ripe tannins. The Cabernet '07 is broad and lingering.

● Cabernet '07	♟♟ 3*
● Syrah '07	♟♟ 3*
● Merlot '07	♟ 4
● Sallier de la Tour Rosso '05	♟ 5

Emanuele Scammacca del Murgo

VIA ZAFFERANA, 13
95010 SANTA VENERINA [CT]
TEL. 095950520
www.murgo.it

This historic Etna winery increasingly specializes in sparklers but has not neglected traditional wines. The lovely Murgo Brut '06, a Nerello Mascalese with apple-like fruit on the nose, has a fresh, vibrant palate. Elegant floral and mineral aromas mark out the zesty carricante-only Etna Bianco '08.

○ Etna Bianco '08	♟♟ 4*
○ Murgo Brut '06	♟♟ 4
⊙ Murgo Rosé Brut '06	♟♟ 5
⊙ Etna Rosato '08	♟ 4

Tenuta Scilio di Valle Galfina

C.DA ARRIGO
95015 LINGUAGLOSSA [CT]
TEL. 095932822
www.scilio.com

Stylish, minerally and seriously drinkable, the '06 Etna Rosso swaggered into our finals. The excellent, ripe Etna Rosso Orphéus '02 shows evocative tertiary aromas, and charmed us with its finesse, length and elegant notes of well-dosed new oak.

● Etna Rosso '06	♟♟ 4*
● Etna Rosso Orphéus '02	♟♟ 5
○ Etna Bianco '08	♟ 4
⊙ Etna Rosato '08	♟ 4

Barone di Serramarrocco

FRAZ. FULGATORE
VIA ALCIDE DE GASPERI, 15
91100 TRAPANI
TEL. 063220973
www.serramarrocco.com

Marco and Massimiliano Marrocco Trischitta's wines were on great form. The Serramarrocco '07, from cabernet sauvignon and merlot, shows undisputed class, unveiling intensity and finesse, with focused notes of plum and sweet spices. The Barone di Serramarrocco '06, from pignatello and nero d'Avola, has style.

● Barone di Serramarrocco '06	♟♟ 7
● Nero di Serramarrocco '07	♟♟ 5
● Serramarrocco '07	♟♟ 6
○ Grillo del Barone '08	♟ 3

Solidea

C.DA KADDIUGGIA
91017 PANTELLERIA [TP]
TEL. 0923913016
www.solideavini.it

Reliability and consistent quality have always distinguished the wines of the small winery of Solidea and Giacomo D'Ancona. The Passito di Pantelleria '08 suggests bewitching citrus leading to a velvety sweet palate bolstered by lively acidity. Ilios '08, also from moscato, is generous, fresh and classy.

○ Ilios '08	♟♟ 4*
○ Passito di Pantelleria '08	♟♟ 6
○ Moscato di Pantelleria '08	♟ 5

Stoccatello

VIA IMBORNONE, 5
92013 MENFI [AG]
TEL. 3495822217
www.stoccatello.it

Renzo Barbera's Agrigento winery debuted well with an original interpretation of the territory. The elegant, balsamic Nero d'Avola '06 is mellowed by spicy oak. Ignis '07, from nero d'Avola and cabernet sauvignon, has less structure but complexity on the nose and a fresh, supple palate.

● Ignis '07	¶¶	4
● Nero d'Avola '06	¶¶	6
○ Animi '08	¶	4
○ Chardonnay '07	¶	5

Tamburello

C.DA PIETRAGNELLA
90144 MONREALE [PA]
TEL. 0918465272
www.aziendetamburello.it

The new edition of Monreale Pietragavina Perricone, which has given the dynamic Mirella Tamburello such satisfaction, was not ready so the estate's two basic wines were on show this year. We liked the Dagala Rosso '07, a fruit-driven, spicy Nero d'Avola, and the lively, drinkable Inzolia Dagala Bianco '08.

○ Dagala Bianco '08	¶	2*
● Dagala Rosso '07	¶	3
● Monreale Pietragavina Perricone '03	¶¶	4*

Terre di Giurfo

VIA PALESTRO, 536
97019 VITTORIA [RG]
TEL. 0957221551
www.terredigiurfo.it

The deep, minerally, intensely fruit-driven Kudyah '07, a monovarietal Nero d'Avola, was the best wine this year from this reliable estate in eastern Sicily. We also loved the attractive Ronna '07, an extremely elegant, drinkable Syrah, with subtle pepper and cinnamon. The other wines are good.

● Belsito '08	¶¶	5
● Kudyah '07	¶¶	5
● Ronna '07	¶¶	5
● Maskaria '06	¶	5

Terrelíade

LOC. SILENE
C.DA PORTELLA MISILBESI
92017 SAMBUCA DI SICILIA [AG]
TEL. 0421246281
www.terreliade.com

More good results this year for the wines from the Sambuca estate of the Santa Margherita Group. The savoury, fragrantly zesty Timpa Giadda '08 is a well-focused, textbook Grillo with great length. Equally good is Nirà '07, a deep, intense Nero d'Avola that gives captivating fragrances of plum and spice.

● Nirà '07	¶¶	4*
○ Timpa Giadda '08	¶¶	4*
● (Utti) Majuri '07	¶	5
● Musia '07	¶	4

Barone di Villagrande

VIA DEL BOSCO, 25
95025 MILO [CT]
TEL. 0957082175
www.villagrande.it

We were delighted with the Etna Bianco Superiore '08, from carricante, which has subtle minerality, focused fruit and appealing length. Equally good is the ripe, textured Sciara '05, from mainly merlot and nerello mascalese, which shows strong, well-managed character. The other wines pass muster.

○ Etna Bianco Sup. '08	¶¶	4*
● Sciara '05	¶¶	5
● Etna Rosso di Villagrande '07	¶	4
○ Fiore '07	¶	5

Zisola

C.DA ZISOLA
96017 NOTO [SR]
TEL. 057773571
www.zisola.it

The new wine from the Mazzei family's Sicilian estate, Doppiozeta '06, from nero d'Avola, syrah and cabernet franc, made a great debut. It flew into the finals with its intensity, focused, well-coordinated fruit and alluring tannins. Zisola '07, an excellent Nero d'Avola, has class.

● Doppiozeta '06	¶¶	8
● Zisola '07	¶¶	6

SARDINIA

Winemaking in Sardinia is still on the rise in numbers – of wines produced and wineries – and in quality. We mentioned these facts last year, stressing improvements in quality reflected the tripling of Three Glass prizes awarded. This year there are 11, one fewer than last time, but average quality has again risen. This is simply because the region' growers and producers have been making serious efforts for years now. The days are long gone when only the usual names were worth mentioning, frequently for IGT wines that failed to take advantage of Sardinia's great heritage of native grape varieties. Now, however, many growers now positively and actively flaunt their island pride to the benefit of local varieties, territories and designated zones. No one speaks anymore merely of Cannonau or Sardinia Cannonau. You're much more likely to hear talk of Cannonau from Mamoiada, Jerzu, or Capo Ferrato, and those venerable bush-trained vines. We only have to point to Carignano, which has brought visibility to the still underrated Sulcis zone with its legacy of ancient, ungrafted vines and perfect marine site climates. Not to mention Vermentino, which is softer and more Mediterranean in southern areas, fresher, more minerally and tangier on the granite-based soils of Gallura. We could go on for hours but we'll restrict ourselves to mentioning a few special treats from those native varieties, a wager that has been won by many producers: nasco in the south of the island; nuragus in the province of Cagliari; or Vernaccia di Oristano and Malvasia di Bosa, two great sipping wines envied by many. Among the wineries, we were most impressed by Argiolas and Sella & Mosca, which confirmed their status as the most prestigious estates on the island. But this is no surprise when you remember their work in the early 1990s. Results were also excellent from the co-operative wineries that in Sardinia are so vibrantly active. This year, they took four top prizes. We applaud Giuseppe Gabbas, a genuine wine man from Nuoro, who won his second consecutive Three Glass prize with Dule. And with its first Three Glasses, Feudi della Medusa reaped a well-deserved dividend for the investment made by the owners since they set up this winery. But fortunately Sardinia also manages to produce idiosyncratic country-style wines, fascinating tributes to a winemaking tradition that goes back thousands of years. One lovely example of this is Perda Pintà di Sedilesu, a white based on granazza di Mamoiada from an ancient viticultural tradition that has never looked so modern.

Agricola Punica

LOC. BARRUA
09010 SANTADI [CI]
TEL. 0781950127
www.agripunica.it

PRE-BOOKED VISITS

ANNUAL PRODUCTION 150,000 bottles
HECTARES UNDER VINE 50
VITICULTURE METHOD Conventional

Sebastiano Rosa, formerly director of Tenuta San Guido, manages the Agricola Punica winery. This joint venture with Cantina di Santadi continues to focus everything on the area where it operates, Sulcis, and a great local variety, carignano. The soul of the estate is still Giacomo Tachis, who has always believed in this territory. Two wines are produced, both from mostly carignano, though in different proportions, with a small amount of international varieties. All the grapes are sourced from vineyards, some still ungrafted, on sandy, clayey soil.

Barrua '06, from carignano with a splash of cabernet and merlot, is a structured Mediterranean wine. The profile on the nose plays off black pepper spice with blackberry and plum-led fruit. The palate is elegant on entry, the tannic weave integrating perfectly into the body. The only thing missing is that pinch of length that would make it deeper and gutsier. The Montessu '07, the estate's second wine from 60 per cent carignano, is an unpretentious, well-made wine with alcohol-rich aromas and a well-tuned palate.

★ Argiolas

VIA ROMA, 28
09040 SERDIANA [CA]
TEL. 070740606
www.argiolas.it

CELLAR SALES
PRE-BOOKED VISITS
VISITOR FACILITIES

ANNUAL PRODUCTION 2,000,000 bottles
HECTARES UNDER VINE 230
VITICULTURE METHOD Conventional

If Argiolas is synonymous worldwide with prestige and quality in winemaking, we are convinced credit goes above all to Antonio Argiolas, the estate's founder, who passed away last June at the age of 102. Our thoughts go out to him and his extraordinary winemaking family. Much has happened since the estate was founded in 1938. Now there are 230 hectares of vineyards, mostly bush-trained with lots of old vines, especially at Sulcis, an area that is very important for the estate.

This exceptional range of wines produced four finalists at our tastings. Once again in centre stage was the Turriga, the '05 vintage, which shows great complexity on the nose with fruity sensations accompanying special balsam and vegetality. The palate is powerful and structured, yet never lacks a touch of acidity that refreshes the mouthfeel. Three Glasses also went to the '06 Angialis, a sweet wine from a base of nasco, which gives captivating wafts of nuts, orange blossom and chestnut honey. Our final comments are for two other reds: Korem '07, from bovale, carignano and cannonau, and Is Solinas '07, a splendidly Mediterranean Carignano.

● Barrua '06	▼▼ 6
● Montessu '07	▼ 4
● Barrua '05	♀♀♀ 6
● Barrua '04	♀♀ 6
● Barrua '03	♀♀ 8

○ Angialis '06	▼▼▼ 5
● Turriga '05	▼▼▼ 7
● Is Solinas '07	▼▼ 4*
● Korem '07	▼▼ 6
● Cannonau di Sardegna Costera '08	▼▼ 4
○ Cerdeña '07	▼▼ 6
● Monica di Sardegna Perdera '08	▼▼ 3*
○ Vermentino di Sardegna Costamolino '08	▼▼ 3*
○ Vermentino di Sardegna Is Argiolas '08	▼▼ 4*
○ Nuragus di Cagliari S'Elegas '08	▼ 2*
○ Angialis '01	♀♀♀ 6
● Turriga '04	♀♀♀ 8
● Turriga '02	♀♀♀ 8
● Turriga '01	♀♀♀ 8
● Turriga '00	♀♀♀ 8
● Turriga '99	♀♀♀ 8
● Turriga '98	♀♀♀ 8
● Turriga '97	♀♀♀ 7

Carpante

VIA GARIBALDI, 151
07049 USINI [SS]
TEL. 079380614
www.carpante.it

CELLAR SALES
PRE-BOOKED VISITS

ANNUAL PRODUCTION **30,000 bottles**
HECTARES UNDER VINE **8**
VITICULTURE METHOD **Conventional**

Created six years ago by three friends who became partners, Carpante immediately showed clear ideas about estate strategies. The trio decided to concentrate their attention on native varieties, especially cagnulari, and low yields. Add to this a terroir with clayey soils and ideal site climates for vines, and results were not long in coming. Now the estate plays a major role in Sardinian winemaking and we are sure that, given this track record, winemaking excellence will not be far behind.

The two wines we consider the estate's most important were not ready at the time of our tastings so they will be reviewed next year. However, there is plenty to say about the wines we did taste in view of their evident quality and above all stylistic precision. The citrussy Vermentino di Sardegna Frinas '08 shows a pleasant grassy note, and a fresh, savoury palate with good depth. The excellent Cannonau di Sardegna '07 has a soft palate and fruity nose with a light spicy vein. The other white, Vermentino di Sardegna Longhera '08, is simpler but excellently crafted, just like Lizzos '07, from cagnulari with a touch of cannonau and muristellu.

Giovanni Cherchi

LOC. SA PALA E SA CHESSA
07049 USINI [SS]
TEL. 079380273
www.vinicolacherchi.it

CELLAR SALES
PRE-BOOKED VISITS

ANNUAL PRODUCTION **170,000 bottles**
HECTARES UNDER VINE **30**
VITICULTURE METHOD **Conventional**

The work done by Giovanni Cherchi over the years deserves a round of applause. Not only has he produced excellent wines, he has also put his money on cagnulari, a variety that might have been lost without him. Giovanni also had an effect on the entire area, encouraging other producers to make the same choices. Everyone can see the results. A special mention also goes to Giovanni's skill in communicating his enthusiasm to his children, who now carry on what their father built with equally positive results.

Wines from the Cherchi estate give an excellent performance this year and two reached our finals. From equal parts cannonau and cagnulari, the pleasant Luzzana '07 shows vegetal and balsamic notes, and an elegant, fresh and tannic palate. The Vermentino di Sardegna Tuvaoes '08 is one-of-a-kind in its category with a minerally, fruity and floral nose introducing a savoury palate with excellent thrust. Despite being a simpler wine, the Vermentino di Sardegna Pigalva '08 is never disappointing, just like the other Cerchi house red, the Soberanu '06, a spicy, deep Cagnulari released only in magnums.

● Cannonau di Sardegna '07	♀♀ 4*
○ Vermentino di Sardegna Frinas '08	♀♀ 5
● Lizzos '07	♀ 5
○ Vermentino di Sardegna Longhera '08	♀ 4
● Cagnulari '06	♀♀ 4
● Cagnulari '05	♀♀ 4
● Cannonau di Sardegna '05	♀♀ 4
● Carpante '06	♀♀ 5
● Carpante '03	♀♀ 5
● Lizzos '05	♀♀ 5
○ Vermentino di Sardegna Frinas '07	♀♀ 5
○ Vermentino di Sardegna Longhera '07	♀♀ 4*

● Luzzana '07	♀♀ 5
○ Vermentino di Sardegna Tuvaoes '08	♀♀ 4*
● Cagnulari '08	♀♀ 4*
● Cannonau di Sardegna '07	♀♀ 4*
● Soberanu '06	♀♀ 8
○ Vermentino di Sardegna Pigalva '08	♀♀ 4*
○ Boghes '07	♀ 5
○ Boghes '06	♀♀ 6
● Cagnulari '06	♀♀ 5
● Cagnulari '05	♀♀ 5
● Cannonau di Sardegna '06	♀♀ 5
● Luzzana '06	♀♀ 5
● Luzzana '05	♀♀ 6
● Luzzana '04	♀♀ 6
● Soberanu '03	♀♀ 8

Attilio Contini

VIA GENOVA, 48/50
09072 CABRAS [OR]
TEL. 0783290806
www.vinicontini.it

CELLAR SALES
PRE-BOOKED VISITS

ANNUAL PRODUCTION 600,000 bottles
HECTARES UNDER VINE 70
VITICULTURE METHOD Conventional

The undisputed leader in the Oristano area, Contini could also be considered among the top wineries in its class on the entire island. The winery warhorse remains the Vernaccia di Oristano made using both the solera system and in a long-aged version that spends 15 to 20 years in large chestnut and oak barrels. There are also the fragrant, fresh standard versions. The rest of the range is just as good, with the addition this year of the Terre di Ossidiana line, an excellently crafted range of white and red wines.

We love Contini wines. They're well-made, varietal and closely tied to their terroir. The Vernaccia di Oristano Antico Gregori cuvée, made with the solera process, is a classic savoury sipping wine with marine tones and attractively nutty oxidative tones, chestnut honey and Mediterranean herbs. The surprising Karmis '08 is a fragrant, fresh wine from mostly vernaccia. The other great white, the Tyrsos '08, is a floral, flavoursome Vermentino di Sardegna. We close with two wines from the Terre di Ossidiana line: the long, harmonious Cannonau di Sardegna Florissa Riserva '05; and the fruity, soft Vermentino di Sardegna Salmastro '08.

Ferruccio Deiana

LOC. SU LEUNAXI
VIA GIALETO, 7
09040 SETTIMO SAN PIETRO [CA]
TEL. 070749117
www.ferrucciodeiana.it

CELLAR SALES
PRE-BOOKED VISITS

ANNUAL PRODUCTION 458,000 bottles
HECTARES UNDER VINE 74
VITICULTURE METHOD Organic certified

All the experience Ferruccio Deiana has acquired over the years in the wine sector now goes into his estate at Settimo San Pietro, not far from the town centre. This is really a lovely operation. The modern, well-equipped facilities are set among the estate vineyards, which Ferruccio diligently looks after. As a skilled winemaker, he also follows all stages of vinification. These traditional varieties are produced in many versions, from the simplest, which sees only steel, to more sophisticated wines that spend time in French oak barriques.

While waiting for the release of the new vintage of Ajana, the estate's showcase red, it was the Cannonaus that convinced us most this time. In aromatic profile as well as depth on the palate, the Cannonau di Sardegna Sileno Riserva '06 is the most complex, showing spicy and slightly smoky with a perfect balance of tannins and acidity. The current version Cannonau di Sardegna Sileno '08 is warm with rose and wild berry aromas. Among the whites, the Pluminus '08, from vermentino and nasco, shows outstanding structure and complexity, though at this early stage it is still rather dominated by oak-derived aromatics.

○ Karmis '08	♈♈ 4*
○ Vernaccia di Oristano Antico Gregori	♈♈ 7
● Cannonau di Sardegna Florissa Ris. Terre di Ossidiana '05	♈♈ 4*
○ Vermentino di Sardegna Salmastro Terre di Ossidiana '08	♈♈ 4*
○ Vermentino di Sardegna Tyrsos '08	♈♈ 3*
● Cannonau di Sardegna Tonaghe '07	♈ 4
● Nieddera Terre di Ossidiana '06	♈ 4
● Rosso di Contini '08	♈ 3
○ Vermentino di Sardegna Arethusa Terre di Ossidiana '08	♈ 4
○ Vernaccia di Oristano Flor '98	♈ 4
○ Pontis '00	♈♈♈ 5
● Cannonau di Sardegna Inu Ris. '05	♈♈ 5
● Cannonau di Sardegna Inu Ris. '04	♈♈ 5
● Cannonau di Sardegna Tonaghe '06	♈♈ 4*
● Nieddera Rosso '06	♈♈ 4*
○ Vernaccia di Oristano Ris. '88	♈♈ 5

● Cannonau di Sardegna Sanremy '08	♈♈ 4*
● Cannonau di Sardegna Sileno '08	♈♈ 4*
● Cannonau di Sardegna Sileno Ris. '06	♈♈ 5
○ Pluminus '08	♈♈ 7
● Monica di Sardegna Karel '08	♈ 4
● Monica di Sardegna Sanremy '08	♈ 3
○ Oirad '08	♈ 6
○ Vermentino di Sardegna Donnikalia '08	♈ 4
● Ajana '02	♈♈♈ 7
● Ajana '05	♈♈ 7
● Ajana '04	♈♈ 7
○ Pluminus '07	♈♈ 7

Tenute Dettori

LOC. BADDE NIGOLOSU
07036 SENNORI [SS]
TEL. 079514711
www.tenutedettori.it

PRE-BOOKED VISITS

ANNUAL PRODUCTION 55,000 bottles
HECTARES UNDER VINE 18
VITICULTURE METHOD Naturale

When you talk about Dettori wines, you're talking about products that, quality aside, are outside the norm. Alessandro's aim is to let the land speak for itself while he continues to make wine the way his family has always done. As a result, a few wines may have some defects or muzziness. But that might be the secret of the bottles from his winery at Badde Nigolosu. These are wines that take us back centuries, wines that spark debate or discussion. From this standpoint, wines from Tenute Dettori are pure pleasure.

We are unable to make our usual entry for Tenute Dettori. This year, Alessandro decided to bottle almost all his wines later, after the summer. So we could only do our tastings in the cellar, directly from the glass-lined cement tanks used for ageing. We can only predict that, as always, something really interesting is on the way. In addition, the table shows wines reviewed in past years, the best, but also the bottles that have stood the test of time.

Cantine Dolianova

LOC. SAN'ESU
S.S. 387 KM 17,150
09041 DOLIANOVA [CA]
TEL. 070744101
www.cantinedidolianova.it

CELLAR SALES
PRE-BOOKED VISITS

ANNUAL PRODUCTION 4,000,000 bottles
HECTARES UNDER VINE 1200
VITICULTURE METHOD Conventional

Cantine Dolianova is a big-numbers winery. Production runs to 4,000,000 bottles, there are more than 630 member growers and 1,200 hectares under vine. Add to this very respectable quality levels that are above all dependable over the years, along with commercial management adept at tackling international markets, and we are dealing with a co-operative operation that has few rivals on the island. Priority is given to native varieties – they're doing excellent work with the now forgotten nuragus grape – although there is no lack of international varieties, especially in the IGT wines.

It was the reds submitted by this co-operative winery that most convinced us this year. The Falconaro '06, a blend of cannonau, carignano and montepulciano, is a powerful, structured wine that never loses its finesse or elegance. The wines from the San Pantaleo line are also good. The Cannonau di Sardegna Anzenas '07 is pleasantly full-flavoured, juicy and fragrant while the Monica di Sardegna Arenada '07 is softer and simpler, yet always gutsy. Finally, the Nuragus di Cagliari Perlas '08 is pleasant and minerally with touches of rennet apple.

○ Dettori Bianco Un anno dopo '06	♟♟♟ 6
● Dettori Rosso '04	♟♟♟ 8
● Tenores '03	♟♟♟ 8
● Chimbanta '04	♟♟ 6
○ Dettori Bianco '06	♟♟ 6
○ Dettori Bianco '04	♟♟ 5
● Dettori Rosso '05	♟♟ 8
○ Moscadeddu '06	♟♟ 6
○ Moscadeddu '05	♟♟ 6
● Tenores '05	♟♟ 8
● Tuderi '05	♟♟ 6
● Tuderi '04	♟♟ 6
● Tuderi '03	♟♟ 6

● Cannonau di Sardegna Anzenas San Pantaleo '07	♟♟ 3*
● Falconaro '06	♟♟ 5
● Monica di Sardegna Arenada San Pantaleo '07	♟♟ 3*
○ Nuragus di Cagliari Perlas San Pantaleo '08	♟ 2*
○ Vermentino di Sardegna Naeli '08	♟ 4
● Cannonau di Sardegna Anzenas '05	♟♟ 3*
● Falconaro '04	♟♟ 5
○ Montesicci '07	♟♟ 4*
○ Montesicci '06	♟♟ 4
● Terresicci '05	♟♟ 6
● Terresicci '04	♟♟ 6

Cantina Sociale Dorgali

VIA PIEMONTE, 11
08022 DORGALI [NU]
TEL. 078496143
www.csdorgali.com

CELLAR SALES
PRE-BOOKED VISITS

ANNUAL PRODUCTION **1.600,000 bottles**
HECTARES UNDER VINE **750**
VITICULTURE METHOD **Conventional**

An excellent Cannonau from the Dorgali winery is no longer a surprise. What is surprising is that this co-operative has made such great investments over the past few years it is becoming difficult to find wines from this range that are anything but excellent. It is a pleasure to see results of this calibre from this winery more than 50 years after its founding. As we said, cannonau is the boss here and is also used in blends with small amounts of international varieties.

Awarding Three Glasses to a Cannonau from the Dorgali winery gives us great satisfaction. It is fitting recognition of this most traditional of the island's varieties, cultivated since time immemorial by so many committed growers. The Cannonau di Sardegna Vinìola Riserva '06 shows delicious ripe fruit notes led by clear peach and the stylish, elegant palate has a long, balsamic finish that swept up Three Glasses. From the other Cannonaus, all of which are convincing in their stylistic precision and pleasant drinkability, special mention goes to the Cannonau di Sardegna Vigna di Isalle '08, a fragrant, juicy wine with good development.

● Cannonau di Sardegna Vinìola Ris. '06	▽▽▽	5*
● Cannonau di Sardegna Filieri '08	▽▽	4*
● Cannonau di Sardegna V. di Isalle '08	▽▽	4*
● Fùili '07	▽▽	5
● Noriolo '07	▽▽	4*
● Cannonau di Sardegna Tunila '08	▽	3
○ Vermentino di Sardegna Isalle '08	▽	3
● Cannonau di Sardegna V. di Isalle '07	♈♈	4*
● Cannonau di Sardegna V. di Isalle '06	♈♈	4*
● Cannonau di Sardegna Vinìola Ris. '04	♈♈	5
● Filieri Rosso '07	♈♈	2*
● Filieri Rosso '06	♈♈	2*

Feudi della Medusa

LOC. SANTA MARGHERITA
PODERE SAN LEONARDO, 15
09010 PULA [CA]
TEL. 0709259019
www.feudidellamedusa.it

CELLAR SALES
PRE-BOOKED VISITS

ANNUAL PRODUCTION **N.D.**
HECTARES UNDER VINE **70**
VITICULTURE METHOD **Conventional**

The Siclaris' love for Sardinia – he's from Sicily and she is from Germany – can be seen in the structure they have built. Both the winery and the reception area are superb and perfectly reflect the production philosophy applied to the wines and vineyards since the early years. Attention and encouragement are focused on native varieties, and efforts are made to take full advantage of the various terroirs. All this is done with constant investment and input from internationally famous consultants.

Gerione moves up in the ranks, thanks to a convincing '06 version mainly from cagnulari, with touches of cabernet franc and syrah. As the wine pours into the glass, the nose hesitates slightly before opening up on sensations of Mediterranean scrub, with myrtle upfront, medicinal herbs and tobacco. The delightful palate is long and tannins are elegant and well tapered. Although still youthful, the wine is already enjoyable and will show its best in a few years. Another winner is the Crisaore '06 from cagnulari with a small amount of bovale sardo. The slightly estery, balsamic nose leads into a fresh, pleasantly tannic palate.

● Gerione '06	▽▽▽	8
● Crisaore '06	▽▽	6
○ Alba Nora '07	▽▽	5
● Cannonau di Sardegna '07	▽▽	5
○ Albachia '08	▽	4
○ Vermentino di Sardegna Albithia '08	▽	4
● Arrubias '06	♈♈	6
● Arrubias '05	♈♈	7
● Biddas '05	♈♈	4*
● Cannonau di Sardegna '06	♈♈	5
● Cannonau di Sardegna '05	♈♈	5
● Gerione '04	♈♈	8
● Norace '06	♈♈	6
● Norace '05	♈♈	7
○ Sa Perda Bianca '05	♈♈	5

Giuseppe Gabbas

VIA TRIESTE, 65
08100 NUORO
TEL. 078433745
ggabbas@tiscali.it

PRE-BOOKED VISITS

ANNUAL PRODUCTION **70,000 bottles**
HECTARES UNDER VINE **13**
VITICULTURE METHOD **Conventional**

In the heart of Barbagia, in an area bounded by Orgosolo, Oliena and Nuoro, Giuseppe Gabbas diligently tends his 13 hectares under vine. His affection for cannonau is clear, though his vineyards make room for other varieties, international as well as native. Knowledge of variety and terroir, ideal site climates and several bush-trained vineyards grown at high altitudes, but above all constant experimentation, all combine to make this Nuoro winery one of the most important on the island.

All the wines produced have cannonau in common. For the second consecutive year, we gave the Cannonau di Sardegna Dule Riserva – the '06 this time – Three Glasses. We feel this is a perfect example of an elegance-driven Cannonau. Freshness on the palate makes the difference, softening the texture, and the tannic impact is agreeable and caressing. Wild berries and dried roses triumph on a nose that ushers in a stupendously clean, dynamic finish. The lean, juicy Cannonau di Sardegna Lillové '08 is ready to drink. Finally, the special cabernet-cannonau blend distinguishes the Arbeskia '06, a well-made wine with classic vegetal sensations.

Cantina Gallura

VIA VAL DI COSSU, 9
07029 TEMPIO PAUSANIA [OT]
TEL. 079631241
www.cantinagallura.com

CELLAR SALES
PRE-BOOKED VISITS

ANNUAL PRODUCTION **1.300,000 bottles**
HECTARES UNDER VINE **350**
VITICULTURE METHOD **Conventional**

This co-operative operation has 135 member growers who work 350 hectares under vine. Statistics may be important but a round of applause goes to winery manager Dino Addis who, especially in the last few years, has created a range of excellent wines, focusing on the dominant variety in Gallura, vermentino, without of course neglecting other varieties, especially moscato that has DOC status here. Stylistic precision is the house style in showcase products as well as in the base line, which is always released at very honest prices.

Over the past two years, we have become accustomed to versions of Vermentino di Gallura Superiore Genesi that were great but always seemed missing something that would have secured our highest prize. Because of the favourable 2008 growing season and Cantina Gallura's constant efforts, this year we happily award Three Glasses to this Mediterranean white with an incredibly intense nose and complex palate. Aromatic herbs mingle with touches of scrub and spring flowers before the savoury, almost salty palate shows fresh and long. Almost as good is another version of Vermentino di Gallura Superiore, Canayli '08, on sale at a stunningly good price.

Wine	Rating
● Cannonau di Sardegna Dule Ris. '06	♟♟♟ 5*
● Arbeskia '06	♟♟ 5
● Cannonau di Sardegna Lillové '08	♟♟ 4*
● Cannonau di Sardegna Dule Ris. '05	♟♟♟ 4*
● Arbeskia '05	♟♟ 5
● Arbeskia '04	♟♟ 5
● Arbeskia '03	♟♟ 5
● Cannonau di Sardegna Dule Ris. '04	♟♟ 4*
● Cannonau di Sardegna Lillové '07	♟♟ 4*
● Cannonau di Sardegna Lillové '06	♟♟ 4*

Wine	Rating
○ Vermentino di Gallura Sup. Genesi '08	♟♟♟ 6
○ Vermentino di Gallura Sup. Canayli '08	♟♟ 4*
○ Vermentino di Gallura Gemellae '08	♟♟ 3*
○ Vermentino di Gallura Piras '08	♟♟ 3*
● Karana Nebbiolo '08	♟ 3
○ Moscato di Tempio Pausania	♟ 4
○ Vermentino di Gallura Mavriana '08	♟ 3
○ Zivula	♟ 5
○ Vermentino di Gallura Gemellae '07	♟♟ 3*
○ Vermentino di Gallura Mavriana '07	♟♟ 3*
○ Vermentino di Gallura Piras '07	♟♟ 3*
○ Vermentino di Gallura Sup. Canayli '07	♟♟ 4*
○ Vermentino di Gallura Sup. Genesi '07	♟♟ 6
○ Vermentino di Gallura Sup. Genesi '06	♟♟ 6

Cantina del Giogantinu

VIA MILANO, 30
07022 BERCHIDDA [OT]
TEL. 079704163
www.giogantinu.it

CELLAR SALES
PRE-BOOKED VISITS

ANNUAL PRODUCTION **1.568,000 bottles**
HECTARES UNDER VINE **320**
VITICULTURE METHOD **Conventional**

Despite fewer hectares under vine and bottles produced compared to other co-operatives on the island, Giogantinu can still boast around 320 hectares of vineyards, all on sandy, granite-based soils. Many vines are still bush-trained and ungrafted. The winery has focused on these features, especially in the last few years, and in so doing has achieved truly high quality. Here in Gallura, specifically at Berchidda, the main variety could only be vermentino, though some reds are also produced.

Most of the many wines produced here are Vermentino di Gallura. We felt the most convincing was the Aldia Superiore, which in the '08 vintage shows an extremely complex nose and a long, continuous palate with outstanding tones of fruit, flowers and Mediterranean scrub. The palate is soft, yet fresh and savoury with a pleasantly almond finish. From the reds, Terra Saliosa '08, a blend of merlot, muristellu and carignano, gives caressing plum and cherry aromas that return on the fresh, inviting palate.

Antichi Poderi Jerzu

VIA UMBERTO I, 1
08044 JERZU [OG]
TEL. 078270028
www.jerzuantichipoderi.it

CELLAR SALES
PRE-BOOKED VISITS

ANNUAL PRODUCTION **2.500,000 bottles**
HECTARES UNDER VINE **750**
VITICULTURE METHOD **Conventional**

This winery was founded in 1950. Jerzu, a town in the province of Ogliastra that has always been a centre of winemaking, is also a subzone of the Cannonau di Sardegna DOC so it is no coincidence that the historic native variety reigns supreme among the various wines produced here. Some years ago, the estate rethought its production philosophy with immediate results, confirming there is no lack of terrain or site climates here for excellent vineyards.

The quality of the Cannonaus produced by Antichi Poderi di Jerzu continues to impress. The most convincing is still the Cannonau di Sardegna Josto Miglior Riserva '06, with dried roses and jam introducing a slightly astringent, tannic palate that has good depth. There was a welcome surprise from the Cannonau di Sardegna Bantu '08, a very drinkable standard-label wine with extremely pleasant youthfully heady aromas. Another excellently made wine is Cannonau di Sardegna Marghìa '07, whose silky tannins integrate well with the texture. We'll close with an excellent white, the Vermentino di Sardegna Telavè '08, which shows warm, Mediterranean aromas.

● Terra Saliosa '08	▼▼ 4*
○ Vermentino di Gallura Sup. Aldia '08	▼▼ 4*
● Nastarrè '08	▼ 3
○ Vermentino di Gallura 12° '08	▼ 3
○ Vermentino di Gallura Lunghente '08	▼ 4
○ Vermentino di Gallura Sup. Karenzia '07	▼ 5
● Cannonau di Sardegna Eja '06	♀♀ 4*
● Terra Mala '05	♀♀ 6
● Terra Saliosa '07	♀♀ 4*
○ Vermentino di Gallura 12° '07	♀♀ 3*
○ Vermentino di Gallura Sup. 13° '07	♀♀ 3*

● Cannonau di Sardegna Josto Miglior Ris. '06	▼▼ 5
● Cannonau di Sardegna Bantu '08	▼▼ 3*
● Cannonau di Sardegna Chuerra Ris. '06	▼▼ 5
● Cannonau di Sardegna Marghìa '07	▼▼ 4*
○ Vermentino di Sardegna Telavè '08	▼▼ 3*
● Cannonau di Sardegna Josto Miglior Ris. '05	♀♀♀ 5
● Radames '01	♀♀♀ 6
● Cannonau di Sardegna Marghìa '06	♀♀ 4*
● Cannonau di Sardegna Marghìa '05	♀♀ 4*
● Cannonau di Sardegna Marghìa '04	♀♀ 4

Alberto Loi

SS 125 km. 124,200
08040 Cardedu [OG]
TEL. 070240866
www.cantina.it/albertoloi

CELLAR SALES
PRE-BOOKED VISITS
VISITOR FACILITIES

ANNUAL PRODUCTION **240,000 bottles**
HECTARES UNDER VINE **51**
VITICULTURE METHOD **Conventional**

The Alberto Loi estate continues to produce quality wines thanks to the third generation of growers. The reins of the winery are now in the hands of Alberto's children, who have made the necessary moves to innovate and remain competitive while never forgetting the traditions they have inherited. Cannonau is the star for 75 per cent of the cellar's production is Sardinia's, and especially Ogliastra's, most widely grown red variety. But the range of wines still features a few whites, especially from vermentino.

This year, the biggest surprise came from the '06 Astangia, from cannonau with small amounts of other traditional varieties. It reveals typical fruity and balsamic notes with pleasant eucalyptus to the fore. The palate is full flavoured, fairly soft and shot through with an acid vein that refreshes the palate. The Cannonau di Sardegna Jerzu Sa Mola '07 is not bad either. It's a juicy, flavourful, harmonious wine with good balance. A bit under par with respect to other years are the Tuvara and Loi Corona, both from the '05 vintage. They're good, but cramped by faint notes of oxidation, especially on the nose.

Masone Mannu

LOC. Su Canale
SS 199 km 48
07020 Olbia
TEL. 078947140
www.masonemannu.com

CELLAR SALES
PRE-BOOKED VISITS

ANNUAL PRODUCTION **100,000 bottles**
HECTARES UNDER VINE **18**
VITICULTURE METHOD **Conventional**

This estate has everything it takes to become one of the best wineries on the island. Almost 20 hectares yield around 100,000 bottles of wines from native as well as international varieties. Vineyards are almost all planted on granite-based soils and imbue the wines with the minerality and freshness you expect here in Gallura when you're looking for authentic wines from the territory.

The most convincing of Masone Mannu's exceptional wines this year is Vermentino di Gallura Superiore Costarenas '08, varietal and savoury with charming notes of aromatic and Mediterranean herbs. Simpler, yet still a great wine, is the Vermentino di Gallura Petrizza '08, which has a citrussy, mineral-veined nose and a long, balanced palate. On the red wine front, there is a good Cannonau di Sardegna '07, but above all a delicious Entu '07, from a base of cannonau and carignano, with distinct notes of spice and pencil lead, and a deep, austerely tannic palate.

● Astangia '06	♀♀ 5
● Cannonau di Sardegna Jerzu Sa Mola '07	♀♀ 4*
● Cannonau di Sardegna Jerzu Cardedo Ris. '06	♀ 4
● Loi Corona '05	♀ 7
● Tuvara '05	♀ 6
○ Vermentino di Sardegna Theria '08	♀ 4
● Cannonau di Sardegna Jerzu Alberto Loi Ris. '03	♀♀ 5
● Cannonau di Sardegna Jerzu Cardedo Ris. '05	♀♀ 4*
● Cannonau di Sardegna Jerzu Cardedo Ris. '04	♀♀ 4
● Cannonau di Sardegna Ris. '04	♀♀ 4*

○ Vermentino di Gallura Sup. Costarenas '08	♀♀ 5
○ Ammentu '07	♀♀ 6
● Entu '07	♀♀ 5
○ Vermentino di Gallura Petrizza '08	♀♀ 4*
● Cannonau di Sardegna '07	♀ 5
○ Ammentu '05	♀♀ 6
● Entu '06	♀♀ 5
● Entu '05	♀♀ 5
● Mannu '06	♀♀ 8
● Mannu '05	♀♀ 8
○ Vermentino di Gallura Petrizza '07	♀♀ 4*
○ Vermentino di Gallura Sup. Costarenas '06	♀♀ 5

Mesa

LOC. SU BARONI
09010 SANT'ANNA ARRESI [CI]
TEL. 0781965057
www.cantinamesa.it

CELLAR SALES
PRE-BOOKED VISITS

ANNUAL PRODUCTION **500,000 bottles**
HECTARES UNDER VINE **70**
VITICULTURE METHOD **Conventional**

Run by advertising guru Gavino Sanna, the Mesa estate has shown clear ideas right from the start about quality wines. Clearly not all the vintages are excellent, but with commitment, investment and the right choices, it is not difficult to produce a range of wines worthy of the varieties used and the original terroir. We refer to Sulcis and to carignano, the variety on which this winery has concentrated from the beginning. But production does not stop there. Other wines come from cannonau and vermentino, as well as international varieties.

After a transitional year, Mesa estate wines have returned to high quality. This is no surprise given the estate's potential and declared strategy. The best of the wines is the Buio Buio '07, from only carignano. Aromas of Mediterranean scrub, spice and tobacco give way to a palate with structure, a good tannic weave and a lean, clean finish. Well crafted, though deliberately made in a simpler style, is the '07 Buio, again from carignano, but fermented only in stainless steel. The whites are also interesting. The barrique-aged Vermentino di Sardegna Opale '08 and the fresh, floral Vermentino di Sardegna Giunco '08 are both excellent.

Pala

VIA VERDI, 7
09040 SERDIANA [CA]
TEL. 070740284
www.pala.it

CELLAR SALES
PRE-BOOKED VISITS

ANNUAL PRODUCTION **450,000 bottles**
HECTARES UNDER VINE **98**
VITICULTURE METHOD **Conventional**

Fifteen years have passed since the Pala brothers took over this operation in the south of the island, following in the footsteps of their father Salvatore, who founded it in 1950. The vineyards are divided into five plots located in the hills at Parteolla. The plots, both sandy and clayey, have excellent locations and sunshine for growing vines. Traditional island varieties are grown, and there is a special commitment to nuragus, nasco and bovale, major native varieties which the estate has always wagered promoted.

The Palas submitted some surprising wines this year. The whites are the best so we'll begin with these. A star if only for its honest price-tag, Nuragus di Cagliari Sàlnico '08 is minerally, citrus-brushed and slightly grassy on the nose and the long, progressive palate has a pleasant mouthfeel. Just as good is the Entemari '08, a blend of vermentino, chardonnay and malvasia. The palate is more savoury and nose leads with apricot and aromatic herb tones. The two Vermentino di Sardegnas, Stellato and Crabilis, are both from the '08 vintage and both convince. A special mention goes to the S'Arai '06, from cannonau, carignano and bovale.

● Buio '07	♛♛	4*
● Buio Buio '07	♛♛	5
○ Vermentino di Sardegna Giunco '08	♛♛	4*
○ Vermentino di Sardegna Opale '08	♛♛	5
● Cannonau di Sardegna Moro '08	♛	5
● Buio Buio '05	♕♕	5
● Buio Buio '04	♕♕	5
● Cannonau di Sardegna Moro '06	♕♕	5
● Malombra '05	♕♕	7
● Malombra '04	♕♕	7

○ Entemari '08	♛♛	5
○ Nuragus di Cagliari Sàlnico '08	♛♛	3*
● S'Arai '06	♛♛	6
○ Vermentino di Sardegna Crabilis '08	♛♛	3*
○ Vermentino di Sardegna Stellato '08	♛♛	4*
○ Assoluto '07	♛	5
● Cannonau di Sardegna Triente '08	♛	4
● Monica di Sardegna Elima '08	♛	3
○ Silenzi Bianco '08	♛	2*
● Silenzi Rosso '08	♛	2*
● Essentija '06	♕♕	4*
○ Nuragus di Cagliari Sàlnico '07	♕♕	3*
● S'Arai '05	♕♕	6
● S'Arai '04	♕♕	6
○ Silenzi Bianco '07	♕♕	2*

Pedres

Z. I. Settore 7
07026 Olbia
tel. 0789595075
www.cantinapedres.it

CELLAR SALES
PRE-BOOKED VISITS

ANNUAL PRODUCTION **300,000 bottles**
HECTARES UNDER VINE **40**
VITICULTURE METHOD **Conventional**

The Mancini family winemaking tradition began at the end of the 19th century but Giovanni Mancini started the Pedres winery in 2002. Since this is Gallura, priority goes to white varieties, first of all vermentino, but great attention is also paid to moscato, vinified in this area in a sparkling version. The vineyards are grown on the classic sandy, granite soils of northeast Sardinia. Thanks to the qualities imparted by these soils, the clean, elegant Pedres wines are well-typed, refined and of course minerally.

Again this year, the leading labels from Pedres are the two versions of Vermentino di Gallura. The Superiore Thilibas '08 is complex on the nose with touches of almonds and rosemary while the palate is intense, fresh, pleasant and elegant. The Jaldini '08 feels smaller, yet shows great finesse and harmony, and proffers distinctive minerality and citrus notes. From the reds, it was the Cannonau di Sardegna Cerasio '06 that showed best with pepper and red berry fruit, and a nice tannic weave on the palate. Finally, the good sparkling Moscato di Sardegna Assolo is aromatic with sage sensations.

Cantina Sociale Santa Maria La Palma

loc. Santa Maria La Palma
07041 Alghero [SS]
tel. 079999008
www.santamarialapalma.it

CELLAR SALES
PRE-BOOKED VISITS

ANNUAL PRODUCTION **3.600,000 bottles**
HECTARES UNDER VINE **700**
VITICULTURE METHOD **Organic certified**

More than 300 members, with a total of around 700 hectares under vine, produce 3,600,000 bottles, big numbers that accompany an incredible range of fantastic value for money wines. This all has to be said in a profile of this fine co-operative, headquartered in Alghero and operating since 1959. The many labels are split across various lines with native varieties prominent, but there is no lack of the internationals that have always been used in vineyards in the northwest of the island.

As always, the broad range of products from Santa Maria La Palma is very high quality. Three reds are notable, all from native varieties. The Cagnulari '07 is seductively rustic in its aromatics of leather, tobacco and spice while the tannins on the supple palate are well integrated into the texture. There was another great performance from the '08 Cannonau di Sardegna Le Bombarde, which that won us over with green eucalyptus sensations and a fresh, vibrant palate. Finally come the reds. Monica di Sardegna '08 is fruity on the nose, and soft and caressing on the palate. We would also mention the focused, well-made Vermentino di Sardegna '08 I Papiri.

● Cannonau di Sardegna Cerasio '06	♟♟ 4*
○ Vermentino di Gallura Jaldinu '08	♟♟ 4*
○ Vermentino di Gallura Sup. Thilibas '08	♟♟ 4*
● Cannonau di Sardegna Sulitài '06	♟ 4
● Maranto '06	♟ 4
○ Moscato di Sardegna Assolo	♟ 4
○ Moscato di Sardegna	♟♟ 4*
○ Vermentino di Gallura Jaldinu '07	♟♟ 4*
○ Vermentino di Gallura Plebi '07	♟♟ 4*
○ Vermentino di Gallura Sup. Thilibas '07	♟♟ 4*

● Alghero Cagnulari '07	♟♟ 5
● Cannonau di Sardegna Le Bombarde '08	♟♟ 4*
● Monica di Sardegna '08	♟♟ 3*
● Alghero Cabirol '07	♟ 4
● Cannonau di Sardegna '04	♟ 4
○ Vermentino di Sardegna I Papiri '08	♟ 4
● Alghero Cabirol '06	♟♟ 4*
● Alghero Cagnulari '06	♟♟ 5
● Alghero Cagnulari '05	♟♟ 5
● Cannonau di Sardegna Le Bombarde '07	♟♟ 4*
● Cannonau di Sardegna Le Bombarde '06	♟♟ 4*

SARDINIA

★ Cantina Sociale di Santadi

VIA CAGLIARI, 78
09010 SANTADI [CI]
TEL. 0781950127
www.cantinadisantadi.it

Sardus Pater

VIA RINASCITA, 46
09017 SANT'ANTIOCO [CI]
TEL. 0781800274
www.cantinesarduspater.com

CELLAR SALES
PRE-BOOKED VISITS

CELLAR SALES
PRE-BOOKED VISITS

ANNUAL PRODUCTION 1.700,000 bottles
HECTARES UNDER VINE 000
VITICULTURE METHOD Conventional

ANNUAL PRODUCTION 500,000 bottles
HECTARES UNDER VINE 300
VITICULTURE METHOD Conventional

We can say without fear of contradiction that the Santadi co-operative has been responsible for Carignano and Sulcis becoming so well known and important. Carignano is produced in various versions, from the standard label, fermented only in stainless steel, all the way up to the Superiore and Riserva, for which French oak barriques are preferred. Further credit should also be given Santadi for bringing back another important native variety, nasco, which can yield fantastic sipping wines.

Once again, the Carignano del Sulcis Superiore Terre Brune won Three Glasses. The '05 version is simply extraordinary. The nose shows great complexity and alternating notes of spice, tobacco, leather and plum jam. The palate is fresh, full-flavoured and tannic, boding well for its future in the cellar. Its little brother, the Carignano del Sulcis Rocca Rubia Riserva '06, gives caressingly soft, close-knit tannins after ripe fruit and spice on the nose. From the whites, we would point out the Vermentino di Sardegna Cala Silente '08, a fresh, thoroughly drinkable tipple with citrus-led aromatics.

Co-operative wineries in Sardinia have at least two things in common: the period when they were founded, around the mid 1950s, and their average quality, which is very high. Sardus Pater is no exception. Over the past few years, it has made further progress in quality, becoming a leader in Sardinian wine production. Here in Sulcis, at Sant'Antioco, carignano reigns unchallenged. The sandy vineyards are near the sea, the vines are bush-trained and there is no lack of ungrafted vines, especially the longer-established plants, which may be up to 80 years old.

We can safely say the entire range of Carignanos submitted is top quality. And there are even some excellent wines, such as the Carignano del Sulcis Is Arenas Riserva '06, whose fantastic great nose is marked by spice and ripe blackberry and blueberry fruit. The palate is tempting and caressing, thanks to ripe tannins and the acid backbone that takes you through to the lovely finish. Also quite good is the current Carignano del Sulcis Nur '08, a very pleasant easy-drinker. Another really interesting Carignano is the Kanai Riserva '07, which is fragrant and intense with a deep finish and a hint of youthful astringency.

Wine	Rating
● Carignano del Sulcis Sup. Terre Brune '05	♟♟♟ 8
● Carignano del Sulcis Rocca Rubia Ris. '06	♟♟ 5
● Shardana '05	♟♟ 6
○ Vermentino di Sardegna Cala Silente '08	♟♟ 4*
● Monica di Sardegna Antigua '08	♟ 4
○ Nuragus di Cagliari Pedraia '08	♟ 4
○ Vermentino di Sardegna Villa Solais '08	♟ 3
○ Villa di Chiesa '07	♟ 6
● Carignano del Sulcis Sup. Terre Brune '04	♟♟♟ 8
● Carignano del Sulcis Sup. Terre Brune '03	♟♟♟ 7
● Carignano del Sulcis Sup. Terre Brune '01	♟♟♟ 7
● Carignano del Sulcis Sup. Terre Brune '00	♟♟♟ 7
● Carignano del Sulcis Sup. Terre Brune '98	♟♟♟ 6
○ Latinia '01	♟♟♟ 5
○ Latinia '99	♟♟♟ 4*
○ Villa di Chiesa '99	♟♟♟ 4

Wine	Rating
● Carignano del Sulcis Is Arenas Ris. '06	♟♟♟ 5*
● Carignano del Sulcis Nur '08	♟♟ 4*
● Carignano del Sulcis Is Solus '08	♟♟ 4*
● Carignano del Sulcis Kanai Ris. '07	♟♟ 5
○ Vermentino di Sardegna Lugore '08	♟ 4
○ Vermentino di Sardegna Terre Fenicie '08	♟ 3
● Carignano del Sulcis Is Solus '07	♟♟ 4*
● Carignano del Sulcis Is Solus '06	♟♟ 4*
● Carignano del Sulcis Kanai Ris. '06	♟♟ 5
● Carignano del Sulcis Nur '07	♟♟ 4*
● Carignano del Sulcis Nur '06	♟♟ 4*
○ Moscato di Cagliari Amentos '07	♟♟ 5

Giuseppe Sedilesu

VIA ADUA, 2
08024 MAMOIADA [NU]
TEL. 078456333
www.giuseppesedilesu.com

CELLAR SALES
PRE-BOOKED VISITS

ANNUAL PRODUCTION 60,000 bottles
HECTARES UNDER VINE 15
VITICULTURE METHOD Naturale

Everyone knows cannonau is grown throughout Sardinia but there are as many different versions of the variety as there are places on the island where thrives. The cannonau from here is less generically Sardinian than typical of Mamoiada, a town in Barbagia that has Sedilesu to thank for creating a wine that stands apart from the rest of the island. These wines are structured yet elegant, properly tannic, yet always caressed by a fresh vein. In other words, these fascinating, traditional, authentic wines reflect in exemplary fashion the philosophy of the estate and the land they come from.

Despite the unique dedication of Sedilesu to Cannonau, this year we were pleasantly surprised by the only white produced, the Perda Pintà. This delightful wine is obtained from guarnaccia di Mamoiada. The '07 shows intriguing aromas that run from nuts to iodine, orange peel and strawberry tree honey. The soft, dry palate shows good acidity and is lifted by faint hints of oxidation. From the reds, we picked out the estery, alcoholic Cannonau di Sardegna Mamuthone '07, an easy drinker if a little too soft in texture because of its substantial alcohol.

○ Perda Pintà '07	♔♔♔	6
● Cannonau di Sardegna Mamuthone '07	♔♔	4*
● Cannonau di Sardegna Ballutundu Ris. '06	♔♔	7
● Cannonau di Sardegna Ballutundu Ris. '05	♕♕	7
● Cannonau di Sardegna Carnevale '06	♕♕	6
● Cannonau di Sardegna Carnevale '03	♕♕	6
● Cannonau di Sardegna Mamuthone '06	♕♕	4*
● Cannonau di Sardegna Mamuthone '04	♕♕	4
○ Perda Pintà '06	♕♕	6

★ Tenute Sella & Mosca

LOC. I PIANI
07041 ALGHERO [SS]
TEL. 079997700
www.sellaemosca.com

CELLAR SALES
PRE-BOOKED VISITS

ANNUAL PRODUCTION 7,000,000 bottles
HECTARES UNDER VINE 550
VITICULTURE METHOD Conventional

It is not always true that you can't combine serious numbers with high quality and excellent results. Look at the work of Sella & Mosca, the long-standing Alghero estate that is now part of the Campari empire. Seven million bottles come from the 550 hectares under vine, located mostly in the northwest of the island, although some vineyards are in Gallura. The broad range of wines starts from a basic line, which always offers excellent value for money, and moves up to slightly sparkling and liqueur wines, reaching peaks of excellence in both whites and reds.

We begin with a spectacular '04 version of Alghero Marchese di Villamarina. We feel it's one of the best ever made. Sella & Mosca's house Cabernet Sauvignon unveils an extremely complex nose before the elegant extract and taut acid backbone give the palate balance and harmony. Hearty congratulations. Just as good is the '08 Vermentino di Gallura Monteoro from estate vineyards in the northeast of the island. This wine has typical notes of minerals and scrub, as well as strawflower aromatics, and the fresh, pleasing palate shows great depth. A final mention goes to Alghero Tanca Farrà '05, a beautifully typed floral mix of cannonau and cabernet.

● Alghero Marchese di Villamarina '04	♔♔♔	7
○ Vermentino di Gallura Monteoro '08	♔♔♔	4*
● Alghero Tanca Farrà '05	♔♔	5
○ Alghero Torbato Terre Bianche Cuvée 161 '08	♔♔	4*
● Cannonau di Sardegna Ris. '06	♔♔	4*
○ Alghero Torbato Terre Bianche '08	♔	4
● Raim '06	♔	4
○ Vermentino di Sardegna Cala Reale '08	♔	4
○ Vermentino di Sardegna La Cala '08	♔	4
● Alghero Marchese di Villamarina '03	♕♕♕	7
● Alghero Marchese di Villamarina '01	♕♕♕	7
● Alghero Marchese di Villamarina '00	♕♕♕	7
● Alghero Marchese di Villamarina '99	♕♕♕	6
● Alghero Marchese di Villamarina '97	♕♕♕	6
● Alghero Marchese di Villamarina '95	♕♕♕	7
○ Alghero Torbato Terre Bianche Cuvée 161 '07	♕♕♕	4*

Tenute Soletta

LOC. SIGNOR'ANNA
07040 CODRONGIANOS [SS]
TEL. 079435067
www.tenutesoletta.it

CELLAR SALES
PRE-BOOKED VISITS

ANNUAL PRODUCTION **100,000 bottles**
HECTARES UNDER VINE **15**
VITICULTURE METHOD **Conventional**

It is always a pleasure to talk about estates that have built great winemaking reputations based on quality not size in just a few years. One such estate is Soletta. The main actors are three siblings: Umberto in the cellar, Pina in sales, and Francesco, who manages exports to the United States. There are now 15 hectares under vine, planted mostly to cannonau, vermentino and moscato, although there are also internationals and less common varieties like incrocio Manzoni.

One of the showcase products, Riserva di Cannonau Keramos, won Three Glasses last year but was not ready for our tastings this time. We had to make do with the rest of the wines, which were far from disappointing. The white Kianos '08, from incrocio Manzoni and vermentino, was an eye-opener. This tangy, almost salty Mediterranean wine charms the nose with minerals and medicinal herbs. The always gutsy Cannonau di Sardegna Corona Majore Riserva '06 is fragrant with ripe fruit and bottled cherries, followed by a fresh, vibrant palate. Perhaps not as good as previous versions but still a fine bottle, the '06 Hermes is from part-dried moscato.

Cantina Trexenta

V.LE PIEMONTE, 40
09040 SENORBÌ [CA]
TEL. 0709808863
www.cantina-trexenta.it

CELLAR SALES
PRE-BOOKED VISITS

ANNUAL PRODUCTION **1,000,000 bottles**
HECTARES UNDER VINE **350**
VITICULTURE METHOD **Conventional**

After some uneven results in the past, we confirm the respectable results from Trexenta, a co-operative that farms around 350 hectares under vine. The project began by recovering traditional training systems, including bush trained vines, and focusing on native varieties instead of international and standardized clones. All this has been done while keeping an eye on prices.

Despite some well-made whites, the reds were in fine fettle this year with cannonau the undisputed leader. The Cannonau di Sardegna Corte Adua '06 has a stunning price, amazing aromatic and structural complexity, well-honed tannins and good acid backbone. The Cannonau di Sardegna Baione '06 has pleasant fruity notes, with blackberry and yellow peach to the fore, and a juicy, caressing palate. Finally, we point out another Cannonau di Sardegna, the Bingias '06, with floral aromas and a lean, clean palate.

● Cannonau di Sardegna Corona Majore Ris. '06	⚇ 5
○ Kianos '08	⚇ 5
○ Hermes '06	⚇ 5
○ Vermentino di Sardegna Chimera '08	⚇ 4
● Cannonau di Sardegna Keramos Ris. '04	⚇⚇⚇ 5
● Cannonau di Sardegna Corona Majore Ris. '05	⚇⚇ 5
● Cannonau di Sardegna Firmadu '05	⚇⚇ 4*
● Cannonau di Sardegna Ris. '04	⚇⚇ 4
○ Dolce Valle Moscato Passito '04	⚇⚇ 4*
○ Hermes '05	⚇⚇ 5
○ Kianos '05	⚇⚇ 5

● Cannonau di Sardegna Baione '06	⚇⚇ 3*
● Cannonau di Sardegna Bingias '06	⚇⚇ 3*
● Cannonau di Sardegna Corte Adua '06	⚇⚇ 2*
● Monica di Sardegna Bingias '06	⚇ 3
○ Nuragus di Cagliari Tenute San Mauro '08	⚇ 1*
○ Vermentino di Sardegna Contissa '08	⚇ 2*
○ Vermentino di Sardegna Donna Leonora '08	⚇ 1*
● Cannonau di Sardegna Baione '05	⚇⚇ 3*
● Cannonau di Sardegna Baione '04	⚇⚇ 3
● Monica di Sardegna Duca di Mandas '06	⚇⚇ 2*
○ Moscato di Cagliari Simieri '05	⚇⚇ 4*

6 Mura

Is Pascais, 18
09010 Giba [CI]
TEL. 0781964370
www.6mura.com

Last year, we were surprised by the Carignano produced by 6 Mura but this year we are even more amazed when the wine landed in our finals. The 6 Mura Rosso '06 shows complex on the nose with spicy notes, and elegance reigns on the palate, thanks to silky tannins and lovely acidity.

● 6 Mura Rosso '06	¶¶	5
● 6 Mura Rosso '05	¶¶	5

Cantina del Bovale

LOC. S'Isca
09098 Terralba [OR]
TEL. 078383462
www.cantinadelbovale.it

This estate in the Terralba DOC zone deserves its first Guide profile. The two best wines are a fragrant, fresh Vermentino di Sardegna Sabbie d'Oro '08 and Terralba Majorale '07 from bovale. Other wines are well made, particularly Monica di Sardegna Sustanzia '07 and Sinnos '07, a blend of traditional varieties.

O Vermentino di Sardegna Sabbie d'Oro '08	¶¶	4*
● Monica di Sardegna Sustanzia '07	¶	4
● Sinnos '07	¶	4
● Terralba Majorale '07	¶	6

Cantina di Calasetta

VIA Roma, 134
09011 Calasetta [CI]
TEL. 078188413
www.cantinacalasetta.com

Efforts by Cantina di Calasetta to promote Carignano and Sulcis can be seen in all the wines presented. Carignano del Sulcis Piede Franco '07 is spicy on the nose and unswervingly elegant on the fresh, firmly structured palate. Tupei '07 shows good fruit and depth.

● Carignano del Sulcis Piede Franco '07	¶¶	4*
● Carignano del Sulcis Tupei '07	¶¶	4*
● Maccòri '06	¶¶	3*

Cantina Sociale di Castiadas

LOC. Olia Speciosa
09040 Castiadas [CA]
TEL. 0709949004
www.cantinacastiadas.com

The Cannonau di Sardegna DOC includes the Capo Ferrato subzone, with the Castiadas winery as its flag-bearer. The excellent Cannonau di Sardegna Rei '05 is structured but not heavy. Good scores also went to the whites, including a deliciously fresh, citrus-veined Vermentino di Sardegna Praidis '08.

● Cannonau di Sardegna Capo Ferrato Rei '05	¶¶	3*
O Vermentino di Sardegna Praidis '08	¶¶	3*
● Monica di Sardegna Genis '08	¶	3

Chessa

VIA San Giorgio
07049 Usini [SS]
TEL. 3283747069
www.cantinechessa.it

Winemaker Giovanna Chessa did well again this year with the '07 Lugherra, from cagnulari, which shows a dense, complex nose and a well-sustained, tannic palate. The equally well-made Vermentino di Sardegna Mattariga '08 has pleasant florality, as has Kentàles, a sweet wine from moscato.

● Lugherra '07	¶¶	6
O Kentàles	¶	6
O Vermentino di Sardegna Mattariga '08	¶	5

Deidda

s.s. 388, KM 7.200
09088 Simaxis [OR]
TEL. 0783406142
www.cantinadeidda.it

Giampiero Deidda's zeal for classic method sparklers is obvious in his Marzani Brut Riserva with notes of cake on the nose and a rich, deep palate. The two '07 Cannonau di Sardegnas, Arcais and Mariano IV, are excellent, like the '05 Simmaco from cannonau, carignano and cabernet.

● Cannonau di Sardegna Arcais '07	¶¶	4*
O Marzani Brut Ris.	¶¶	5
● Cannonau di Sardegna Mariano IV '07	¶	5
● Simmaco '05	¶	5

Paolo Depperu

LOC. SAS RUINAS
07025 LURAS [OT]
TEL. 079647314
azienda.depperu@tiscali.it

The Depperu brothers have done an excellent job promoting vermentino in an excellent zone for the variety. The result of these efforts is Ruinas in an especially good '08 version. The citrussy nose has faint hints of almonds and a palate that has depth but is shot through with well-gauged freshness.

○ Ruinas '08	♟♟	5
● Kabaradis '05	♟	5
○ Ruinas '07	♟♟	5

Vigne Deriu

LOC. SIGNORANNA
07040 CODRONGIANOS [SS]
TEL. 079435101
www.vignederiu.it

After a sound debut last year, wines from the Derlu family have improved even further. The dried rose Cannonau di Sardegna '07 is so good it made the finals. The Vermentino di Sardegna '08, the Tiu Filippu '07, from cannonau and cabernet, and the Moscato Oro Ere '07 are all convincing.

● Cannonau di Sardegna '07	♟♟	4*
○ Oro Ere '07	♟♟	6
● Tiu Filippu '07	♟♟	6
○ Vermentino di Sardegna '08	♟♟	4*

Fradiles

VIA SANDRO PERTINI, 2
08030 ATZARA [NU]
TEL. 3331761683
www.fradiles.it

This small operation in the heart of Mandrolisai shows off all the characteristics of wines from the DOC. Both Mandrolisai labels submitted are good. Antiogu '06 has a broad nose and a fresh, tannic palate. Fradiles '07 shows touches of pepper and cocoa powder, and a deep, soft palate.

● Mandrolisai Antiogu '06	♟♟	5
● Mandrolisai Fradiles '07	♟♟	4*
● Mandrolisai Antiogu '05	♟♟	5
● Mandrolisai Fradiles '06	♟♟	4*

Antonella Ledà d'Ittiri

LOC. ARENOSLI, 29
07100 ALGHERO [SS]
TEL. 3292528891
www.margallo.it

This small operation in northwest Sardinia makes nice authentic wines. Margallò '07, from cabernet franc, merlot and sangiovese, is dense and deep while Ginjol '07, although simple, is pleasant and well-made. The other two wines, the cagnulari Cigala '08 and the Vermentino di Sardegna Vi Marì '08, are decent.

● Margallò '07	♟♟	4*
● Cigala '08	♟	4
● Ginjol '07	♟	4
○ Vermentino di Sardegna Vi Marì '08	♟	4

Li Seddi

VIA MARE, 29
07030 BADESI [SS]
TEL. 079683052
www.cantinaliseddi.it

This interesting little operation at Badesi has lovely vineyards along the island's northern coast and sent us well-crafted wines this year. The most convincing was Petra Ruja '07, a blend of cannonau, bovale, monica and girò, which has a complex aromatic profile and a stylish palate with good depth.

● Petra Ruja '07	♟♟	4*
● Lu Ghiali '07	♟	5

Sebastiano Ligios

C.SO EUROPA, 111
07039 VALLEDORIA [SS]
TEL. 3296724241
www.cantinaligios.it

Sebastiano Ligios makes excellent wines. The most convincing this year is Campamara '06, from cabernet with some traditional varieties. The nose offers subtle plums, geraniums and green bell peppers, and palate is full-flavoured and deep. Cannonau di Sardegna Carammare '06 is well-made.

● Campanara '06	♟♟	5
● Cannonau di Sardegna Carammare '06	♟♟	4*

Piero Mancini

LOC. CALA SACCAIA
07026 OLBIA
TEL. 078950717
www.pieromancini.it

This Gallura winery has always focused on Vermentino but also uses other varieties. Vermentino di Gallura Primo '08 is savoury and fresh with a citrus nose that ends on almonds. The other '08 Vermentino di Gallura, Cucaione, is simpler but well made. Finally, the Cannonau di Sardegna Falcale '06 is decent.

● Cannonau di Sardegna Falcale '06	♥ 4
○ Vermentino di Gallura Cucaione '08	♥ 4
○ Vermentino di Gallura Primo '08	♥ 5

Tenute Massidda

LOC. GIUANNI PORCU
09040 DONORI [CA]
TEL. 3478088683

This Guide entry could not have gone better for Tenute Massidda. The biggest surprise from the labels submitted was Cannonau di Sardegna Arenargiu '07, a wine that shows structure, elegance, flavour and balance. The Monica di Sardegna Bainosa '07 is well made, pleasant and warm.

● Cannonau di Sardegna Arenargiu '07	♥♥ 4*
● Monica di Sardegna Bainosa '07	♥ 4
○ Vermentino di Sardegna Cannisonis '07	♥ 4

Abele Melis

VIA SANTA SUINA, 3
09098 TERRALBA [OR]
TEL. 0783851090
melis.vini@tiscali.it

Abele Melis still focuses on the bovale sardo variety with great results, though the whites are far from disappointing. The single-variety Bovale, Terralba Dominariu '06, has a rustic but delightful nose and a savoury, tannic palate. The Vermentino di Sardegna localia '08 is fresh, citrussy and stylish.

● Terralba Dominariu '06	♥♥ 5
○ Vermentino di Sardegna localia '08	♥♥ 4*

Meloni Vini

VIA GALLUS, 79
09047 SELARGIUS [CA]
TEL. 070852822
www.melonivini.com

Some wines from Meloni's wide range are always good. The '06 Cannonau di Sardegna Terreforru is good, soft and savoury. The Vermentino di Sardegna Salike '08 is fresh and balanced, and the sweet Girò di Cagliari Donna Jolanda '04 is harmonious, thanks to good tannins that perk up the sugar.

● Cannonau di Sardegna Terreforru '06	♥ 3
● Girò di Cagliari Donna Jolanda '04	♥ 5
○ Vermentino di Sardegna Le Sabbie '08	♥ 4
○ Vermentino di Sardegna Salike '08	♥ 3

Giovanni Montisci

VIA ASIAGO, 7B
08024 MAMOIADA [NU]
TEL. 0784569021
www.barrosu.it

Giovanni Montisci feels Cannonau should be made in the vineyard, not the cellar, where technique is based only on experience. He debuts in the Guide with two Cannonau di Sardegnas. Barrosu '07 is powerful, yet fresh with caressing tannins. Barrosu Riserva '07 is slightly more structured and husky.

● Cannonau di Sardegna Barrosu '07	♥♥ 6
● Cannonau di Sardegna Barrosu Ris. '07	♥ 7

Mura

LOC. AZZANIDÒ, 1
07020 LOIRI PORTO SAN PAOLO [OT]
TEL. 078941070
www.vinimura.it

Wines from the Mura family are always well made and some are really excellent. Two good examples are the Vermentino di Galluras from the 2008 vintage. The Superiore Sienda is fresh, zesty and pleasantly bitterish in the finish. The Cheremi is also very good, though simpler.

○ Vermentino di Gallura Cheremi '08	♥♥ 4*
○ Vermentino di Gallura Sup. Sienda '08	♥♥ 4*
● Baja '05	♀♀ 6
○ Vermentino di Gallura Sup. Sienda '07	♀♀ 4*

Cantina Sociale di Ogliastra

VIA BACCASERA, 36
08048 TORTOLÌ [NU]
TEL. 0782623228
cantina.ogliastra@live.it

This co-operative winery headquartered at Tortolì presented a lovely range of land-rooted wines this year. From cannonau with added amounts of monica and bovale sardo, the Nou '08 is warm and highly pleasing. The Cannonau di Sardegna Frailis '06 is typical and savoury.

● Cannonau di Sardegna Frailis '06	🍷🍷	3*
● Nou '08	🍷🍷	4*
● Cannonau di Sardegna Violante de Carroz '06	🍷	3

Tenute Olbios

LOC. VENAFIORITA
VIA LOIRI, 83
07026 OLBIA
TEL. 0789641003
info@tenuteolbios.com

Especially in the best vintages, wines from Olbios stand out for that added value that sets them apart from the crowd. Vermentino di Sardegna In Vino Veritas '06 introduces fresh almonds and evolved tones. Nessuno '07 is an interesting blend of cannonau and bovale.

● Nessuno '07	🍷	6
○ Vermentino di Sardegna In Vino Veritas '06	🍷	6
○ Vermentino di Sardegna Lupus in Fabula '06	🥂🥂	5

Olianas

LOC. PORRUDDU
08030 GERGEI [CA]
TEL. 0558300411
www.sardegnavini.eu

This young Gergei estate makes excellent wines from 12 hectares under vine. The fine Cannonau di Sardegna '08 has notes of blackberry and lemon marmalade. Perdixi '07, from cannonau with splashes of bovale, alicante and cabernet, is nice. The Vermentino '08 is uncomplicated but pleasant.

● Cannonau di Sardegna '08	🍷🍷	4*
● Perdixi '07	🍷🍷	5
○ Vermentino di Sardegna '08	🍷	4
● Cannonau di Sardegna '06	🥂🥂	4*

Cantina Cooperativa di Oliena

VIA NUORO, 112
08025 OLIENA [NU]
TEL. 0784287509
www.cantinasocialeoliena.it

This co-operative winery's strong point has always been the Nepente di Oliena, a subzone of the Cannonau di Sardegna DOC. The base version was not yet ready at our tastings but the Riserva '05 Corrasi convinced us with forest floor and ripe fruit on the nose, and a palate with structure, balance and depth.

● Cannonau di Sardegna Corrasi Nepente di Oliena Ris. '05	🍷🍷	5

Cantine di Orgosolo

VIA SANTA LUCIA
08027 ORGOSOLO [NU]
TEL. 0784403096
www.cantinediorgosolo.it

Cantine di Orgosolo, a group of 19 small local producers, made a promising Guide debut. The main variety could only be cannonau, though others are present. Both the '07 and '08 vintages of Cannonau di Sardegna Urulu are good. The younger edition in particular is fresh and attractive.

● Cannonau di Sardegna Urulu '08	🍷🍷	5
● Cannonau di Sardegna Urulu '07	🍷🍷	5
● Locoe '07	🍷	4

Pedra Majore

VIA ROMA, 106
07020 MONTI [OT]
TEL. 078943185
www.pedramajore.it

You won't go wrong buying wines from Pedra Majore, a mid- sized estate at Monti. Vermentino di Gallura Superiore Hysonj '08 is savoury with a typical almondy finish. The Vermentino di Gallura I Graniti '08 is simpler. Finally, the Mirju, a dried-grape Moscato, has well-balanced sweetness and acidity.

○ Mirju	🍷🍷	6
○ Vermentino di Gallura Sup. Hysonj '08	🍷🍷	5
○ Majore ad Maiora '07	🍷	6
○ Vermentino di Gallura I Graniti '08	🍷	4

OTHER WINERIES

F.lli Porcu

LOC. SU E GIAGU
08019 MODOLO [NU]
TEL. 078535420
fratelliporcu@tiscali.it

Young Carlo manages the Porcu estate with four hectares under vine. Unfussy vinification includes brief maceration on the skins and ageing is only in stainless steel. Terroir makes the difference and the Malvasia di Bosa '06 reflects this showing savoury and fresh with wafts of Mediterranean scrub.

○ Malvasia di Bosa '06	♥♥	5
○ Malvasia di Bosa '05	♥♥♥	5
○ Malvasia di Bosa '02	♥♥	5

Cantine Marcello Puddu

VIA MARZABOTTO, 3A
08025 OLIENA [NU]
TEL. 3498115090
cantine.puddu@tiscali.it

Marcello Puddu made a grand debut. For some years, he has been making a Cannonau di Sardegna Nepente at Oliena that convinced us in the '07 vintage. The complex nose has tones of ripe fruit and dried roses while the deep palate shows good acidity and a long, clean finish.

● Cannonau di Sardegna Nepente di Oliena Mandras '07	♥♥	4*

F.lli Puddu

LOC. ORBUDDAI
08025 OLIENA [NU]
TEL. 0784288457
azienda.puddu@tiscali.it

There are only two or three producers in the Oliena subzone of Cannonau di Sardegna Nepente but they make interesting wines. One is Puddu, which releases two superlative Nepentes: the elegant, full-flavoured Nepente di Oliena '07 and the more powerful, structured Nepente di Oliena Pro Vois Riserva '06.

● Cannonau di Sardegna Nepente di Oliena '07	♥♥	4*
● Cannonau di Sardegna Nepente di Oliena Pro Vois Ris. '06	♥♥	6

Giampietro Puggioni

VIA NUORO, 11
08024 MAMOIADA [NU]
TEL. 0784203516
www.cantinagiampietropuggioni.it

At his Mamoiada estate, Giampietro Puggioni makes typically concentrated Cannonaus. Both labels submitted are convincing. The Cannonau di Sardegna Lakana '06 is more harmonious, with a nose of plums and wild berries, and a fresh, powerful palate with good flavour and excellent development.

● Cannonau di Sardegna Ilisi '06	♥♥	6
● Cannonau di Sardegna Lakana '06	♥♥	4*
● Cannonau di Sardegna Mamuthone '05	♥♥	4*

Cooperativa Romangia

VIA MARINA, 5
07037 SORSO [SS]
TEL. 079351666
www.vinidellaromangia.it

After some up and down results, Cantina Cooperativa Romangia presented a very decent range. Two reds are outstanding. Cannonau di Sardegna Lamarina Riserva '05 has focused aromas and a balanced palate, while the Cannonau di Sardegna Jennos '06 is simpler, yet warm and easy to enjoy.

● Cannonau di Sardegna Lamarina Ris. '05	♥♥	5
● Cannonau di Sardegna Jennos '06	♥	4

Cantine Surrau

S.P. ARZACHENA - PORTO CERVO
07021 ARZACHENA [OT]
TEL. 078982933
www.vignesurrau.it

This young, promising estate in Gallura continues its rise. This year, the two reds presented have shifted into high gear. The Surrau '07, from cannonau, carignano, cabernet and muristellu, is soft and fresh with good length. The deep, balanced Cannonau di Sardegna Sincaru '07 is also good.

● Cannonau di Sardegna Sincaru '07	♥♥	6
● Surrau '07	♥♥	5
○ Vermentino di Gallura Branu '08	♥	5

Tanca Gioia Carloforte

LOC. GIOIA
09014 CARLOFORTE [CI]
TEL. 3356359329
www.u-tabarka.com

Though a newcomer, this Carloforte estate produces a fine range of wines. The whites are the most convincing. The vermentino-based U Tabarka Giancu '08 is savoury, almost salty, fresh-tasting and subtle. U Tabarka Quae '08, from mostly moscato di Calasetta, is sweet and fragrant.

○ U Tabarka Giancu '08	♼♼	5
○ U Tabarka Quae '08	♼♼	6
● U Tabarka Ciù Roussou '07	♼	5

Cantina Tondini

LOC. SAN LEONARDO
07023 CALANGIANUS [OT]
TEL. 079661359
cantinatondini@tiscali.it

The Tondini winery knows how to make wine and rightly takes advantage of varieties and terroir. The best in the range is the structured, elegant Siddaju '06. The savoury, almond-edged Vermentino di Gallura Karagnanj '08 is also excellent and the '06 Lajcheddu is a deep, aromatic sweet wine.

○ Lajcheddu '06	♼♼	7
● Siddaju '06	♼♼	7
○ Vermentino di Gallura Karagnanj '08	♼♼	5
● Cannonau di Sardegna Taronj '08	♼	4

Carlo Tramaloni

VIA GIOVANNI XXIII, 37
08024 MAMOIADA [NU]
TEL. 079277827
www.cantinatramaloni.it

Estates at Mamoiada are on the way up. The Barbagia town makes great Cannonaus and in his Guide debut, Carlo Tramaloni impressed with both his Cannonau di Sardegnas. Issohadore '06 has something special, with spices and dried flowers, and a warm, powerful palate lifted by good acidity.

● Cannonau di Sardegna Issohadore '06	♼♼	4*
● Cannonau di Sardegna Orturù '07	♼	4

Cantina del Vermentino

VIA SAN PAOLO, 1
07020 MONTI [OT]
TEL. 078944012
www.vermentinomonti.it

Cantina del Vermentino makes excellent, great-value wines. Vermentino di Gallura Funtanaliras '08 is very good, showing fresh and savoury with an almond finish. Cannonau di Sardegna Tamara '07 is also interesting with good depth and an easy-drinking nature.

○ Vermentino di Gallura Funtanaliras '08	♼♼	5
● Abbaìa '08	♼	3
● Cannonau di Sardegna Tamara '07	♼	4
○ Vermentino di Gallura S'Eleme '08	♼	3

Cantina Sociale Cooperativa di Vernaccia

LOC. RIMEDIO
VIA ORISTANO, 6A
09170 ORISTANO
TEL. 078333155
www.vinovernaccia.com

This co-operative operation makes good wines apart from Vernaccia. The excellently crafted Cannonau di Sardegna Ambito '07 is long, warm and fragrant. Vermentino di Sardegna Benas '08 shows amazing balance and complexity. Finally, Terresinis '08 is a simple, easy-drinking, current Vernaccia.

● Cannonau di Sardegna Ambito '07	♼♼	3*
○ Vermentino di Sardegna Benas '08	♼♼	2*
● Nieddera '07	♼	2*
○ Terresinis '08	♼	3

Villa di Quartu

LOC. CEPOLA
VIA G. GARIBALDI, 90
09045 QUARTU SANT'ELENA [CA]
TEL. 070820947
www.villadiquartu.com

Wines from Villa di Quartu rarely disappoint us. The house trademarks are its clean style and clarity of definition. Cepola Rosso '07, from monica, barbera, cannonau and bovale, is the best on the list, with ripe fruit aromas and a note of spice, followed by a dynamic palate with good tannic weave.

● Cepola Rosso '07	♼♼	4*
● Cannonau di Sardegna Parillas '07	♼	5
○ Vermentino di Sardegna Poetho '08	♼	4

PRODUCERS IN ALPHABETICAL ORDER

PRODUCERS BY REGION

PRODUCERS IN ALPHABETICAL ORDER

PRODUCERS IN ALPHABETICAL ORDER

PRODUCERS IN ALPHABETICAL ORDER

PRODUCERS IN ALPHABETICAL ORDER

PRODUCERS IN ALPHABETICAL ORDER

PRODUCERS IN ALPHABETICAL ORDER

PRODUCERS IN ALPHABETICAL ORDER

PRODUCERS IN ALPHABETICAL ORDER

PRODUCERS IN ALPHABETICAL ORDER

PRODUCERS IN ALPHABETICAL ORDER

PRODUCERS IN ALPHABETICAL ORDER

PRODUCERS IN ALPHABETICAL ORDER

PRODUCERS IN ALPHABETICAL ORDER

PRODUCERS IN ALPHABETICAL ORDER

PRODUCERS IN ALPHABETICAL ORDER

PRODUCERS IN ALPHABETICAL ORDER

PRODUCERS BY REGION

PRODUCERS BY REGION

PRODUCERS BY REGION

PRODUCERS BY REGION

PRODUCERS BY REGION

PRODUCERS BY REGION

PRODUCERS BY REGION

PRODUCERS BY REGION

PRODUCERS BY REGION

PRODUCERS BY REGION

PRODUCERS BY REGION

PRODUCERS BY REGION

PRODUCERS BY REGION

PRODUCERS BY REGION

PRODUCERS BY REGION

PRODUCERS BY REGION

PRODUCERS BY REGION